The Encyclopedia of Philosophy

Volumes *7* and *8*

Index

Complete and Unabridged

The
ENCYCLOPEDIA
of
PHILOSOPHY

PAUL EDWARDS, *Editor in Chief*

VOLUME SEVEN

Macmillan Publishing Co., Inc. & The Free Press
NEW YORK
COLLIER MACMILLAN PUBLISHERS
LONDON

MACMILLAN PUBLISHING CO., INC.
COLLIER-MACMILLAN CANADA LTD.

MANUFACTURED IN THE UNITED STATES OF AMERICA

REPRINT EDITION 1972

The Encyclopedia of Philosophy

P

[CONTINUED]

PSYCHOLOGY. In the development of psychology, the study of the mental life and activities of animals and men, three phases can be conveniently distinguished—the presystematic, the systematic but prescientific, and the scientific. The presystematic, by far the longest of the three phases, is that in which men observed and reflected on human ways and embodied their reflections in aphorisms, anecdotes, and fables. Presystematic thinking is important since it has been passed down through the ages and is continually augmented by that amalgam of wisdom, superstition, and dogma which those who claim no professional competence like to describe as the fruits of their experience. The presystematic psychology of contemporary primitive groups has been recorded by anthropologists, but little is known of the corresponding ideas of the precursors of the systematic psychology of the European tradition. The doctrines of the pre-Socratic philosophers are transitional.

SYSTEMATIC PHILOSOPHY OF MIND

Mind, body, and nature. Systematic psychology began with Aristotle's *De Anima,* which was of outstanding importance at an early stage because it provided a solid, biologically based conceptual scheme. This involved, first, an elucidation of the concept of soul ($\psi\acute{v}\chi\eta$) and such related concepts as mind ($vo\hat{v}s$), which were regarded as the differentiating properties of the phenomena to be studied. Aristotle's scheme laid down the lines along which the relationship between various manifestations of soul and mind were conceived until the seventeenth century.

Second, life and mind, being closely connected with the functioning of the body, must be conceived of in a way that does justice to the peculiar intimacy of this relationship. Aristotle paid close attention to this relationship.

Third, there is the problem of how the relationship between psychological phenomena and other phenomena of the natural world is to be conceived. Are psychological concepts and categories of explanation reducible to others? Aristotle, again, was particularly interested in this question because of the attempts of some of his contemporaries and predecessors to show that human behavior fell under the concept of motion, which had a wide applicability in the natural world.

In the exposition of the systematic period of psychology these problems will be employed not simply as a framework for expounding the main lines of Aristotle's system of psychology but also as a framework for picking out the main features of the most important theoretical systems since Aristotle laid the foundation of psychology.

Plato and Aristotle. Aristotle (384–322 B.C.) insisted on the widest possible definition of soul, thus returning to the pre-Platonic view that soul is virtually the principal of all life. The natural expression for a living thing was $\check{\epsilon}\mu\psi\nu\chi\sigma\nu$ $\sigma\hat{\omega}\mu\alpha$—"body with a soul." Aristotle started from the linguistic point that some bodies are so described whereas others are not and asked by what criterion this distinction was made. His answer was that it is life but that there are different levels of life. Intellect, sensation, nutrition, motion, are all forms of being alive. What they have in common, however, is a self-originating tendency to persist toward an end.

This marked both a return to and a great improvement on pre-Platonic views of soul. In early Greek thought soul was thought of simply as that which keeps a man alive and which leaves his body when he dies. It was connected with breathing. Spirit ($\theta\acute{v}\mu\sigma s$), on the other hand, was thought of as the generator of movement; it was connected with the movement of the limbs and with emotional states. It was thought of as quite distinct both from soul and from mind, which was regarded as the source of images and ideas. The notion of the soul as a whole of which spirit and mind were attributes emerged only gradually.

Plato (427?–347) tried to combine the concept of the soul as a whole with a stress on the pre-eminence of mind, which he inherited from Anaxagoras. His account, therefore, of the soul as a whole was constantly confused by the special status which he accorded to mind. In the *Republic* he spoke of the soul as having three parts—reason or mind, spirit, and desire ($\acute{\epsilon}\pi\iota\theta\nu\mu\acute{\iota}\alpha$). But he also thought that reason was the defining property of an immaterial substance which survived bodily death whereas spirit and desire passed away with the body. Similarly, in the cognitive sphere he regarded sensation and imagination as inferior to reason and as intimately connected with the body. This represented a fusion of the Orphic belief in the survival of the soul with an exaltation of mathematical reasoning as the only way of obtaining certain knowledge, which Plato took from the Pythagoreans. He thought that in mathematics the soul grasps forms that are eternal and nondeceptive. As like can be known only by like, the soul, in its rational aspect, must also be eternal. Plato's conviction was reinforced by such considerations as those that he adduced in the *Meno,* in which the grasp of mathematical truths was exhibited in an untutored slave. According to Plato, this indicated that the slave was being made to remember what he had known previous to his embodiment. Thus, Plato's preoccupation with epistemology led him to make a sharp cleavage between the rational and irrational parts of the soul.

Aristotle approached the matter from a biological rather than an epistemological standpoint. Reason, spirit, and desire represented different levels of being alive. To be alive is to possess a self-originating tendency toward an end. This is exhibited at the lowest level in nutrition and reproduction. Thus, plants have a low-grade soul. Animals have sensation, locomotion, and desire superimposed upon nutrition and reproduction. Men, in addition, have reason, or mind, by means of which a rule or plan is imposed upon desire. By mind is meant self-direction in accordance with a rational formula.

Aristotle maintained that the lower level of soul is a necessary condition for the higher and that the possession of a higher type of soul also changes the way in which the lower functions. Because men are rational, they feed, reproduce, perceive, and act in a manner which differs from that of animals.

Soul and body. Plato's view of the special status of reason was plausible at a time when almost nothing was known about the functioning of the brain and nervous system, for abstract thought seems to proceed with little dependence on bodily organs. Furthermore, the identity of a subject of experience through time does not seem to depend entirely on bodily continuity. There is thus a case for Plato's concept of the rational soul as some kind of active agency which inhabits the body for a brief period.

Plato thought that the rational soul inhabits the head because the head is round (the most perfect shape and, hence, an appropriate place for the seat of reason) and the part of the body nearest the heavens. It makes contact with the brain, which was conceived of as a kind of marrow encased in the skull. The irrational soul makes contact with the marrow of the spinal cord in its bony sheath. The better part of the irrational soul, spirit, inhabits the heart and functions in such manifestations of life as energy, courage, and ambition; the worse part, desire, functions below the diaphragm, in appetite, nutrition, and reproduction. The rational and irrational parts affect each other through the liver, which acts as a sort of mirror of thought.

In sleep the soul is shut up, and its motions subside. A few agitations remain, however, and produce dreams. Usually dreams are the expressions of desires which are suppressed—an interesting anticipation of Freud's theory of dreams. The good man controls his desires sensibly and so is not unduly disturbed by them in sleep. In the *Republic* Plato also suggested that in sleep the rational soul, if not troubled by irrational desires, can attain truths not otherwise revealed.

Plato thought of sensation as a transmission of motions.

The human body receives an impression from without and responds with an inner motion. Some parts of the body—for instance, the hair and the nails—are subject to shock but do not respond with inner movements. Sense organs, however, are good conductors of motion. Thus, hearing, for instance, is the end product of a kind of shock. By means of air in the cavities of the body a blow is transmitted through the ears to the blood and brain and then to the soul. Knowledge does not consist just in sensation but in the activity of the soul in relation to what is thus transmitted. This transmission is complicated by the intervention of memory, imagination, feeling, and association, all of which act as intermediaries between reason and sensation.

Aristotle believed that there was a very intimate connection between soul and body which was a particular case of the more general relationship between form and matter. The soul is "the first actuality of a natural body furnished with organs." He used other examples to illustrate this relationship. If the eye were an animal, he said, eyesight would be its soul, this being the form or capacity of the eye. To speak of soul is to speak of a capacity or propensity to function in a certain way which depends on a certain bodily structure, or it is to speak of the actual exercise of such a capacity or propensity, which is the second kind of actuality. Thus, anger, for instance, can be the appetite of returning pain for pain or the boiling of the blood around the heart, depending on whether the dialectician or the physical scientist is considering it; there is always a biological and a psychological account to be given.

The soul, Aristotle argued, is the cause of the body in three ways. It is its efficient cause in that reference to some concept, such as desire, is required to explain movement. It is the formal cause in that behavior is explained as the exercise of a capacity or tendency. It is the final cause in that reference must be made to "the reason for the sake of which" movements of the body take place. If the behavior is explained by recourse to the rational soul, then plans and rules are imposed on desire. In choice, for instance, means are worked out and adapted to attain an end.

Generally speaking, Aristotle held that soul and body are a particular case of the more general correlatives, form and matter. When he spoke of theoretical reason rather than practical reason, he suggested that the distinction between matter and form is again exemplified in that reason is both passive and active. But he hinted at another sort of doctrine when he also claimed that active reason comes from without and is divine. It is like a helmsman in a ship. This looks like a concession to the Platonic view of mind.

The details of Aristotle's physiology were carefully related to his idea of the levels of soul. The primary function of the nutritive soul is the absorption of nourishment, but its end is to generate another being like itself. The unity of the species is thus preserved though individual members perish. The stomach was thought of as an oven where animal heat cooks the food and blood in the heart. The heart is the seat of life, sensation, motion, and heat.

Sensation is a discriminative power from which the higher cognitive functions develop. There is the organ, the power to receive sensible forms, and the sense, regarded as constituted of both matter and form. In sensation the sense organ is assimilated to its object—for example, the eye becomes colored. But whereas in nutrition both matter and form of external objects are absorbed, in sensation only form without matter is taken in, like wax taking the imprint of a seal ring. Each sense is sensitive to one or more qualities ranging between extremes. Too little would not register; too much would destroy the organ. This was an application of Aristotle's doctrine of the mean which he developed in relation to moral conduct.

The particular senses are all developments of touch, depending on the intervention of a more refined medium. Taste, for instance, apprehends the savory properties of bodies through the intermediary of moisture; smell, the odorous properties conveyed through the air. In the transmission of sensations to the heart and in the vitality which flows from the heart, the "connatural spirits" play an important role. They were thought of as a kind of inner air quite distinct from the outer air which we breathe. Closely associated with the blood, they acted as a universal internal medium for the transmission of sensation. Besides the specific senses there is *sensus communis,* which is not a sixth sense but a generic power of sensation as such which provides unity for the sensitive soul in its particular manifestations. The ear does not see; however, the man who hears also sees, and some qualities are presented through more than one sense—for example, roundness by sight and touch. By *sensus communis* we also perceive the common sensibles of figure, motion, rest, magnitude, and also what Aristotle called the accidental sensibles, which are the principles of association of ideas—similarity, contiguity, and the like. We also perceive that we perceive through *sensus communis.*

Imagination is a by-product of sensation. Forms provided by sensation are manipulated in the absence of physical objects. Memory is a combination of imagination and *sensus communis.* There is an image of something plus an awareness of its pastness. Recollection is rather different, for it involves the exciting of an image and the release of a whole chain of images joined by habit according to the principles of association. Imagination also provides a link between knowledge and action, for desire presupposes the imagination of an end to be attained. It may be deliberative, if influenced by reason, or merely sensitive. Desire is thus dependent on sensation and thought. In this way Aristotle was able to maintain his three levels of soul by making desire appear at two levels, depending on whether it is rational or irrational.

Psychological and mechanical concepts. Aristotle believed not only that there were certain very general concepts, such as form, matter, and change, which could be applied to everything; he also extended teleological categories of explanation—his ill-fated final causes—to all nature. Nature, he thought, was composed of natural kinds which could be classified by genus and differentia, which all had a natural place, and which all tended toward the realization of their essence. "Nature, like mind, always does whatever it does for the sake of something, which something is its end." Such modes of explanation proved singularly unfruitful when extended to the physical world. But because they were taken from the realm of life, where Aristotle, a marine biologist and the son of a doctor, was particularly acute, they fitted very well, in a general sort

of way, that realm of phenomena in which they had their natural home. Aristotle was often accused by later mechanists of being anthropomorphic, but there is not much wrong with being anthropomorphic about men. Indeed, those who later attempted to explain human behavior in mechanical terms applicable to the physical world may well have made the obverse mistake to Aristotle's.

Aristotle himself, in criticizing the mechanists of his day, gave some very interesting arguments to show why the soul, which is the source of movement, cannot itself be moved. Plato had steadfastly claimed that the soul was the source of motion. In a famous passage in the *Phaedo* (98B–99D) he made clear his objection to extending mechanical explanations to cover human conduct. Plato admitted that some kind of physical account could be given of the movements which led up to Socrates' sitting in his prison cell, awaiting his death. But he scorned the suggestion that this account would be a satisfactory explanation of the situation, for an explanation must include some reference to Socrates' reasons for being there. Plato did not, however, develop elaborate arguments against mechanical theories.

Aristotle, on the other hand, wrote his *De Anima* as part of his systematic attempt to classify the different sciences on the basis of the subject matter with which they were concerned. He was therefore very much concerned both with demarcating the field of application of various families of concepts and with sketching the ways in which they were related to each other. Movement (κίνησις) was only a particular type of change. He was most anxious to deny that it was either the only or the fundamental type.

Aristotle argued, first, that a logical mistake is made if the soul as a formal cause is thought of as moved in the physical sense. How can a capacity or tendency be conceived of as moving or being moved? Nor can the actualizations of soul in particular cases be properly conceived of as movements, for in practical thought the processes have unity because they go on for the sake of some end. Their particular type of unity cannot be assimilated to such physical unities as the parts of a spatial magnitude; it is more like the unity of a series of numbers. Reference to an end is a conceptual device for picking out how a series of movements are to be thought of as constituting one action; such an end is not itself an extra movement. In the case, too, of some processes of theoretical thought, such as inferring, "thinking has more resemblance to a coming to rest or arrest than to a movement." The end is, as it were, built into the meaning of the term. "Inferring," "concluding," and even "perceiving" are terms which intimate the attainment of ends or standards which are intrinsic to the processes themselves.

Concept of consciousness. Arguments of the Aristotelian type have been revived in recent times by such philosophers as Gilbert Ryle, who have defended a predominantly Aristotelian concept of mind in opposition to a Platonic or mechanical concept. Such a concept of mind is in keeping with the biological orientation of psychology which followed the impact of Darwin. However, it sprang out of the post-Wittgenstein reaction against privacy as the hallmark of the mental, which had characterized most psychological theories since the time of Descartes.

It is difficult for modern Western man to grasp that the Greeks really had no concept of consciousness in that they did not class together phenomena as varied as problem solving, remembering, imagining, perceiving, feeling pain, dreaming, and acting on the grounds that all these are manifestations of being aware or being conscious. Historically, this emphasis on private experience presupposed the development of individualism as a social movement. The Greeks of the city-states lived in a public world of public feats and public concerns. Their word ἰδιώτης, from which we derive the word "idiot," was a term of disdain for a man who concerned himself only with private matters. Socrates, with his stress on individual self-knowledge and the care of the individual soul, was a moral innovator. With the conquests of Philip and Alexander the Great and the breakup of the small autonomous Greek states, this moral innovation became systematized in the codes of the Stoics and Epicureans. The ideal of individual self-sufficiency developed as a substitute for the much-lauded self-sufficiency of the city-states. Man, it was claimed, was a citizen of the world who should either discipline himself and purify his individual soul (Stoics) or slip through life unobtrusively by cutting down the possible sources of misery (Epicureans). This led to an increase of interest in the will and the emotions and to an emphasis on individual experience.

This turning inward was institutionalized by Christianity, with its stress on personal salvation and the purity of soul. Introspection vied with revelation as a source of knowledge. St. Augustine paved the way for Descartes's first certainty, *cogito ergo sum*. With Descartes the Platonic view of the soul and of knowledge was reinterpreted in the light of the rise of the mathematical sciences, but there was a difference—the stress on the certainty of our knowledge of our own mental states. Mind was no longer simply associated with reason; it was something to which we have private access and whose rational activity it is self-contradictory to doubt. This stress on privacy as a hallmark of the mental was a far cry from Aristotle's view of soul as characterized by a self-originating tendency to pursue an end. A brief mention, however, should be made of some of the intervening systems, though from the point of view of psychological theory, nothing of any great importance happened after the death of Aristotle in 322 B.C. until the seventeenth century, when new systems were inspired by the rise of the physical sciences.

Stoics and Epicureans. The Stoics and Epicureans provided an interesting contrast in respect to their views about the relation between soul and the rest of nature. Both attempted a monistic view, but whereas the Stoics reverted to Plato and tried to extend the concept of soul so that it permeated all nature, the Epicureans reverted to Democritus and extended a mechanical atomistic account of nature to include life and mind.

Stoics. The Stoics thought of everything in the universe as being either active or passive; hence, there was no opposition between dead matter and soul. The ultimate substance is fire, which has different forms at different levels of being, ranging from cohesion at the inorganic level, through growth at the plant level, to life of a rational or irrational type at the animal and human level. Fire is thus the all-pervading principle of activity as well as the reason or regulator of change in the universe. Mental activity as found in men is a concentrated form of the universal reason, creatures being vehicles for the operation of this universal regulation. Hence the Stoic injunction to live according to nature, for in simple instinctive tendencies reason is often manifest in an incorrupted form.

The Stoics believed that the soul of man is a very subtle form of the all-pervasive fire, for the corporeal can be affected only by what is corporeal. The soul is affected by the body; therefore, the soul, too, must be corporeal. It combines heat, mobility, and a high degree of rarefaction. Indeed, it was more or less identified with the "connatural spirits" of Aristotle which course through the body closely associated with the blood, which are transmitted in generation, and which are similar in nature to the warm outer air, which is also essential to life. The breast is the seat of the soul.

Perhaps the most interesting and important contribution of the Stoics to psychology was their application of the Aristotelian categories of activity and passivity, which they thought to be the defining attributes of what is real, to the mind. Mental activity, they held, is characterized by assent (συγκατάθεσις), which can be exhibited in perception and memory, as well as in practical and intellectual judgment. This may be justified or erroneous, but truth is natural and error unnatural. When error of a perceptual, intellectual, or practical kind occurs, the explanation is to be sought in the theory of emotions or mental disturbances. Basic to this Stoic account was the notion of impulse, which covered both appetite and aversion and which operates obscurely at the level of sensation as well as at the rational level, when it is transformed into the adoption of ends for action. Emotions are thus unsuccessful attempts at full rational choice. The early Stoics left such failures unexplained; the later Stoics assigned the cause to circumstances and, therefore, to things that are beyond our power. From this came their characteristic emphasis on the assertion of will over adversity, of rational choice over irrational promptings.

Epicureans. The main interest of Epicurean psychology was its anticipation of mechanical theories of the seventeenth and subsequent centuries. Everything, Epicurus (341–270) believed, was constructed from atoms and, therefore, everything, including minds, could be explained in terms of the mechanical laws governing atoms. The soul differs from other atoms in that it is lighter and more mobile; heat is fundamental to its nature, but it is not identical with fire. It permeates the body like a subtle air and gives it life.

Sensations are effects produced in sense organs by effluxes from objects, differences in sensations being explained in terms of differences in external movements and in the configurations of the underlying atoms. Similarly, ideas are caused by atoms striking the subtle matter of the thinking soul. Incoming impressions set up other motions in the mind, making possible judgment, which is a motion of the mind superimposed upon an impression. Error occurs when impressions are accompanied by irrelevant motions of the mind. The motions of the mind can be linked together to form complex ideas by principles of association. Reason is simply the use of general ideas brought about by the fusion of images into composite pictures.

It is difficult to see how notions like error and truth could be generated by such descriptions of mere movements of atoms. Indeed, Epicurus did nothing to meet Aristotle's acute criticisms of mechanical descriptions of thought. He did something, however, to meet the charge of fatalism in his notorious doctrine of the swerve of the atom, which was a consequence of the self-motion postulated for all atoms. The power of the mind to incline this way or that constitutes its freedom. Man is poised between pain, which is one sort of motion, and pleasure, which is an excessive reaction to pain. Between these two extremes there is an equilibrium, which is more permanently satisfying and which reason can guide men to attain. This he called freedom from disturbance (ἀταράξια), which is inseparable from the use of reason.

Theological psychology. The psychology of the Greeks had always been, in varying degrees, subservient to epistemological and ethical concerns. The account of reason, for instance, or the role ascribed to the passions was a graphic way of presenting solutions to problems about knowledge and conduct. But there was also the Greek passion for speculation about the ultimate nature of things, about the One in the many, and about the status of mind in the universe and its relation to the body. With the coming of Christianity, which brought with it the Biblical account of the creation of the world, this radical metaphysical speculation abated, and the body was seen largely as something that had to be considered as a potent source of temptation. Psychological theory became almost entirely an offshoot of epistemology and ethics, for the supreme purpose of life for thinking men became the knowledge of God and the quest for salvation.

The religious preoccupations of such writers as Plotinus, Clement, and St. Augustine introduced, of course, a different emphasis into epistemology and ethics. This was manifest before the coming of Christianity in the work of Philo Judaeus (c. 20 B.C.–c. A.D. 40), who thought that real knowledge was a possession only of minds which had been so purified that they received divine illumination. Philo was the first systematic thinker to fuse the religious fervor of the Hebrew tradition with a selection from the conceptual schemes of Plato, Aristotle, and the Stoics. Knowledge of God and a divinely sanctioned code of conduct had somehow to be fitted into the speculative schemes of the Greeks. Because neither God nor his purposes are manifest to the senses, increasing importance was attached to inner experience as a way of knowing. Philo even wrote a treatise entitled *On Dreams Sent From God.*

This shift of emphasis from the outer world to the inner world is clearly seen in the Neoplatonism of Plotinus (205–270). Plato, like all the Greeks, was supremely interested in action, politics, and the external world. His theory of Forms was, in the main, explanatory—his version of the search of the Greek cosmologists for the One in the many. Even the supreme Form, the Form of the Good, was both the source of the intelligibility of the world and the supreme ideal of action. Plotinus, on the other hand, saw mystical contemplation and absorption in the One as an end in itself. Psychology therefore became harnessed to the exploration and mapping of inner experience. As G. S. Brett remarks in his *History of Psychology:* "In Plotinus, for the first time in its history, psychology becomes the science of the phenomena of consciousness, conceived as self-consciousness" (R. S. Peters, ed., rev. ed., p. 206).

With the adoption of Christianity as the official religion of the Roman Empire a place had to be found for revelation as well as for knowledge found in inner experience. St. Augustine (354–430) managed to combine these two sources of knowledge. Insofar as there was no revealed doctrine on a matter, he dealt with it within the framework of Platonism penetrated by Christian mysticism. For instance, the growing knowledge of the self and of God was fitted into a Christianized version of Plato's doctrine of reminiscence. Questions about the body, on the other hand, were dealt with by an appeal to the Scriptures. So, too, was the origin of the soul, for it was transmitted into the body when God breathed upon Adam. The lasting influence, however, of Augustine's *Confessions* was the importance attached to introspection and private experience. No man can escape from his own experience; he can obtain knowledge, insofar as he does not rely on revelation, only by working backward to the presuppositions of his experience as a thinking being. In this approach to the mind Augustine anticipated Descartes.

A corrective to this extreme subjectivity was provided by the rediscovery of Aristotle and the meticulous transmission of his texts by Islamic theologians. The adaptation of Aristotle in the service of Christian theology reached its climax in the work of St. Thomas Aquinas (1225–1274). But using Aristotle as a substructure to support Christian theology was not entirely straightforward. To start with, there was the problem about the status of reason, one of the most debated topics during the Middle Ages. Aristotle's account of the Active Intellect suffered from notorious obscurities, and there was the worry about its relation to revelation as well. Furthermore, the Islamic school, culminating in Averroës, had tended to favor a mildly pantheistic interpretation of Aristotle's doctrine of Active Intellect. Averroës held that the reasons of individual men are but fleeting manifestations of universal reason. Aquinas rejected this interpretation, completely following his teacher Albert the Great (1193/1206–1280).

Aquinas defined intellect as the faculty of comprehension which each individual possesses as an intelligent being. Nevertheless, reason was still regarded, as by Plato and Aristotle, as the mark of man's difference from animals and as, in some sense, superhuman. It is qualitatively distinct from sensation and any other processes which are intimately connected with the body.

Apart from this query about the status of reason, which was itself a legacy from Aristotle, Aquinas tried to stick to the Aristotelian view of the soul as the form of the body. He deliberately rejected the more Platonic theory that a man is a soul using a body. It was not just respect for the authority of Aristotle that influenced Aquinas. The fact was that Christianity was committed to the belief in the resurrection of the body. The intimacy of the connection between soul and body postulated by Aristotle was a better foundation for this doctrine than the more Platonic view occasioning that contempt for the body which culminated in the Albigensian heresy that the body had been created by the devil. Aquinas followed Aristotle closely in his account of sensation, *sensus communis,* memory, and imagination. What was lacking was Aristotle's stress on striving toward an end as the defining characteristic of soul. The intuitive certainties of self-consciousness explored by St. Augustine remained the foundation both of psychology and of epistemology.

Scholasticism has now become a byword for sustained attention to minor questions within a system whose foundations in revelation were not questioned. There is point in such criticisms. Nevertheless, the Schoolmen preserved and spread a tradition of disciplined discussion which is the lifeblood of science and philosophy. Furthermore, in psychology they handed down not only the general outlines of Aristotle's conceptual scheme but also the details of his psychological system.

The great natural philosophers were nurtured in this Aristotelian tradition even though they eventually overthrew it. At Padua, for instance, where Galileo was trained, there was a flourishing branch of the Averroistic type of Aristotelianism. Descartes was trained by the Schoolmen at La Flèche, and his *Passions of the Soul* bears witness to these early influences. Even Thomas Hobbes, one of the archenemies of Aristotelian essences, relied on Aristotle's *Rhetoric* for the details of his psychology. He merely poured a traditional content into a mechanical mold which he adapted from Galileo, Gassendi, and the ancient atomists. The Schoolmen provided the thinkers of the seventeenth century with something solid and disciplined to revolt against. And, as with most rebels, these thinkers were really revolting against a mass of assumptions that were deeply embedded in their own consciousness. Indeed, in a certain sense their revolt was only a return to other elements in their intellectual heritage—the precipitates left by the Pythagoreans, Plato, and the atomists.

Descartes. Descartes's view of the mind was a return to Plato, enriched by the introspective musings of St. Augustine and made more precise by developments in the natural sciences.

Nature and mind. The natural sciences had made leaps forward not because of a vast accumulation of new facts, though one of the features of the Renaissance had been man's turning his gaze out toward the natural world; it was, rather, because of the amazing success that had attended the application of geometry to the phenomena of the natural world.

The success of geometric thinking about nature tended to corroborate what Plato had said about the status of reason as contrasted with the senses; it also convinced the new natural philosophers like Kepler, Galileo, and Descartes (1596–1650) that the real qualities of the natural world were those which could be treated geometrically. Matter was homogeneous, as the atomists had said. Qualitative distinctions, which had been exalted by Aristotle into irreducible natural kinds, were appearances of the varying motions and configurations of the underlying bodies. The Aristotelian doctrine of form and matter was banished; so were the final causes which he had postulated in nature.

How, then, was mind to be conceived, once the Aristotelian doctrine of form and matter had been discredited? There were two obvious possibilities. One was to adopt Epicurus' view that soul and mind were configurations of light and mobile atoms. The other was to revert to the Platonic view that mind is an altogether different type of substance that inhabits the body. Descartes adopted the second course, partly because he shared Plato's view about the wonder of reason and its difference from sensation and bodily processes and partly, no doubt, because of his Christian convictions about God, freedom, and immortality.

Mind. Descartes's departure from Aristotle was much more radical in his account of the soul than in his account of the mind. Whereas Aristotle had described the soul, even in its most primitive manifestations, in teleological terms, Descartes attempted to describe all its lower functions, which were connected with the body, mechanically. His account of mind was not dissimilar in its main outlines from Aristotle's account of reason, which was the most Platonic part of his doctrine, for both accounts held that mind comes from without, furnishes the ultimate principles of thought, and may be considered apart from the body. Indeed, Descartes stated emphatically that the mind can think without a body.

For his account of mind Descartes looked into himself in the manner of St. Augustine, but he rejected that reliance on faith which was epitomized by the protestation *Credo quia absurdum* ("I believe because it is absurd"). Nothing that was not clearly and distinctly present to the mind was to be included in a judgment. Everything must be doubted—even mathematical truths—until a belief can be found that applies to what exists and that it would be self-contradictory to deny. Descartes's *cogito ergo sum*—his more precise rendering of St. Augustine's intuitive certainty about his existence as a thinking being—was the result.

Descartes explored the rest of what was intimated in this first certainty and tried to spin out of it all sorts of other truths—for example, the existence of God and of an external world. The details of his attempted demonstration do not concern us here. They effectively established, in Descartes's view, the existence of thinking substances which were innately so constituted that they would come to form clear and distinct ideas of extension, figure, motion, and other simple natures. Ideas are all mental; as images they are presented through bodily processes, images being apparently corporeal.

Minds were thought to be passive in cognition. When a mind is thinking clearly and distinctly, its ideas correspond to the real qualities of objects. But minds are also active in volition. At the intellectual level their activity consists only in assent to the necessary connection between ideas, and volition is one of the most potent sources of error, for there is often assent when ideas are not clear and distinct. Volition is also the cause of action and is operative in attention, recollection, and fantasy.

Body–mind relation. Descartes's account of the body–mind relation was not dictated solely by Platonized Christian piety. It was equally the product of his knowledge of science and his convictions about scientific method. First, Descartes was convinced that the body is a machine and that animals' behavior could be explained mechanically, animals having no souls. He was acquainted with the discoveries of William Harvey which showed the circulation of the blood to be a mechanical process. Furthermore, mechanical models were a feature of the age. Decorative fountains were constructed with model men that were moved hydraulically and even uttered sounds like words. Descartes thought that the body contained tubes like water pipes along which the animal spirits (the up-to-date rendering of Aristotle's "connatural spirits") coursed. Because many movements of the body can be executed without conscious intentions, Descartes assumed that these could be explained in the same way as the movements of the hydraulic men. He has thus been credited with the discovery of reflex actions. He thought that all animal behavior could be explained in this way.

Second, Descartes believed in the principle of conservation of energy. The quantity of motion imparted to and conserved in a system being constant, there could be no extra source of energy deriving from volition. Thus, the relationship between body and mind had to be conceived in a way which was consistent with this principle.

Third, Descartes held that scientific explanation consisted of making deductions from relations grasped between clear and distinct ideas. Clear and distinct ideas were available of the simple natures of body (for example, extension, figure, motion) and of mind (thinking, willing) but not of the relation between them. Descartes held fast to the obvious fact that body and mind interact (for when I will, it is my arm that moves; I feel pain when my body falls and not when a stone falls). But we have only a confused idea of this interaction. His account of the relationship between them was therefore only a likely story with which he was not really satisfied. It only narrowed down the point at which the crucial philosophical difficulties occurred.

Descartes knew that muscles operate in opposing pairs and that nerves are necessary for sensation and movement. He pictured nerves as tubes along which animal spirits flow. Changes in the motion of these animal spirits cause them to open some pores in the brain rather than others. When this happens, the spirits are deflected into muscles which move the body by being distended laterally and, thus, shortened. At the level of instinct and habit this process is purely mechanical. At the level of conscious intention, however, something more had to be postulated, the impact of mind on body at the crucial switching point of the spirits, the pineal gland.

Descartes supposed that in sensation motion was transmitted from the stimulus object through a medium to the sense organ and thence along the spirits in the nerves to the pineal gland in the center of the brain, where an impression was made like that of a seal on wax. This was a material image which stimulated the soul to produce a corresponding idea. Descartes gave a similar account of passions in the narrow sense of emotions and organically initiated disturbances, which have their source in the agitation of the spirits. By passions in a general sense, Descartes meant all things that *happen* to minds, including sensations, lower forms of memory, feelings, emotions, and other disturbances of reason. These he contrasted with the mind's activity. All such incoming stimuli generally give rise to an act of will. Willing again makes contact with the body at the pineal gland, and a chain of events is started in the body terminating with the movement of the muscles, which produces voluntary action. The soul is like a pilot in a ship in that it can effect the direction but not the amount of bodily movement. Thus, Aristotle's image of active reason could be reconciled with the principle of the conservation of energy. Descartes's hypothesis that interaction between body and mind occurred at the pineal gland did nothing to dispel the philosophical perplexity about how this interaction could be conceived, and then the pineal gland later was shown to be nothing more than an obsolescent eye. Descartes was attached to this idea because the pineal gland was the only part of the brain which was not duplicated in both halves of the brain. He was convinced that the soul, being unitary, could not affect the body at two points. His hypothesis enabled him to keep his mechanistic account of the body intact.

For a long time it has been fashionable to deride Descartes's rather disastrous form of dualism and even to suggest that he created the body–mind problem. This is a piece of intellectual insularity. Descartes was perhaps the first thinker to formulate the problem at all clearly. It would be possible to deny his basic assumption that body and mind are qualitatively distinct substances and still to claim that apart from this metaphysical extravagance his statement of the problem brought out at least two cardinal points which are involved in it. First, he obviously saw the logical incongruity of explaining mental processes, such as geometric reasoning and deliberating before action, in mechanical terms. There is a logical gap between the types of explanation used, as Aristotle had pointed out in his criticisms of the mechanists who held that the soul was moved. Descartes, in his account of the transactions which were alleged to take place at the pineal gland, must have thought that motion at this point is somehow identical or correlated with the mental activity involved in producing an idea or making an act of will. His hypothesis did much to draw attention to this logical disparity between the two types of description.

Second, Descartes's account did much to establish privacy, rather than Aristotle's criterion of purpose with plans and rules superimposed at the level of the rational soul, as the main hallmark of the mental. As has been indicated, Descartes's theory in this respect marked the culmination of a trend that can be traced back through St. Augustine and Plotinus to Philo. To attribute mind to something is not just to say that men act in accordance with rules and that their movements persist toward ends. It is to say that they act like this because of their knowledge of rules and because they are conscious of ends. Consciousness is crucial for picking out the obvious respect in which men differ from cunningly contrived machines. Descartes must be credited with the clearheadedness to have stood firm on this cardinal point.

Spinoza. Spinoza's system was a consequence of pushing Descartes's assumptions to their logical conclusions.

Nature and mind. Descartes had accepted the traditional notion of substance as that which is a cause of itself, can be conceived through itself, and needs only itself in order to exist. Spinoza (1632–1677) argued that if this is the definition of substance and if there is such a substance, there can be only one such substance, which can be called either nature or God. Nature, so conceived, must have infinite attributes, but we know only two of them, thought and extension. God is therefore "the place of the world and the whole system of thinking." Everything is a mode or modification of God. Thus, nothing can be adequately explained unless its occurrence can be deduced from principles applying to the system as a whole.

Explanation is deductive in character and accords with mechanical principles. Unlike Descartes, Spinoza envisaged a science of psychology in which mental as well as physical phenomena could be deduced from quantitatively expressed laws. Emotions, he argued, must obey laws just as lines, planes, and bodies do. Human beings, as part of nature, must exhibit the general characteristics of all modifications of God or nature. They must be determined within a system; they must have a mental and a physical aspect; and they must exhibit conatus, or the striving to persist within their own being. These characteristics must now be considered in turn.

In stating that human behavior was determined within a system, Spinoza wished to oppose what he considered to be two basic illusions which men had with respect to themselves. The first of these was the illusion of free will. Men are convinced that they have free will, he argued, because they are conscious of their actions but ignorant of their causes; thus, they conclude that they are uncaused. If stones were conscious, they, too, would believe in free will. Yet human behavior can be explained just as can the movements of stones. In both cases the explanation will consist in deducing what occurs from the laws of the system of which they both are part, ultimately the system of nature as a whole. The human body is a system of simpler elements maintained in an equilibrium, but this system is part of a broader system, not a self-contained isolable system. Adequate explanation is seeing events as part of the whole system of nature; in this system there are no final causes. Nature just is, like a vast, timeless machine.

Body and mind. How then was the body–mind relation to be conceived? Spinoza was one of the first to point to the difficulties in Descartes's pineal gland hypothesis. Spinoza's solution was to suggest that interaction does not take place for the very good reason that body and mind are correlated attributes of the same underlying substance, not distinct substances. Indeed, Spinoza says that the mind is the idea of the body. This is obvious enough at the level of immediate confused ideas which are of bodily states. But the changes in a man's body are part of a larger system, which includes the properties of the food absorbed in nutrition. A wider knowledge of the events in a man's stomach is possible for a physiologist who can understand the laws governing them. He would see these events as part of an ever widening network of events which constitute nature. The man's feeling of stomach-ache, on the other hand, would be confused, fragmentary, and inadequate, an idea of an effect cut loose from its causes.

This illustrates the difference between what Spinoza called the first and second grades of knowledge. The materials of the first grade are the confused ideas of bodily states which we call feelings and sensations. These ideas are connected only by principles of association. This is the level of sense perception and imagery, of uncritical beliefs founded on animal instinct, association, and hearsay. The second grade of knowledge is rational insight. At this level rational connections are grasped as general notions develop which connect an ever widening system of events. The more abstract and general thought becomes, the nearer it approaches the thought of the Cartesian physicist and, ultimately, God's thought. There is also a third grade of knowledge, called *scientia intuitiva* by Spinoza, which is more mystical. It is a return from the abstract laws of the scientist to a grasp of the particular as illuminated by such laws. The role of the body, as that which is correlated with mind and of which mind is an idea, seemed to recede when Spinoza passed to reason, or the second grade of knowledge. Mind as the idea of the body becomes at this point almost as difficult a notion as Descartes's notion of mental activity somehow mirroring movement in the brain, for thinking is not of or about body or brain states any more than it is a form of movement which is similar to or identical with brain states.

Conative aspect of mind. Spinoza's account of mental phenomena was much less intellectualistic than that of Descartes. Indeed, in certain respects he reverted to Aristotle's emphasis on teleology and self-maintenance. Spinoza held that the most important characteristic of every modification of nature was its conatus, its striving to persist in its own essence. In man, as in every other natural modification, there is an inherent tendency to react to all changes in a way that maintains its characteristic unity and equilibrium. A man differs from animals in being self-conscious in this endeavor.

Spinoza employed this homeostatic postulate to rewrite Descartes's account of the passions as presented in *Les Passions de l'âme.* Descartes had paid particular attention to the causal influence of animal spirits and had left rather vague the part played by the cognitive grasp of the situation, though he generally put forward an ideomotor theory. Spinoza evinced little interest in the physiology of the matter. Instead, he developed a theory of motivation by harnessing Descartes's passions to his own homeostatic principle. He postulated that whenever a body is acted on by another body, its vitality may be increased, may be diminished, or may remain constant. The awareness of these occurrences is the mental aspect of the psychophysical states which are called emotions. There are thus three primary emotions corresponding to increase, diminution, or maintenance of bodily vitality. These are joy (*laetitia*), grief (*tristitia*), and desire (*cupiditas*). As a result of experience men tend to keep before them what will increase their vitality and remove what will decrease it. "Love" is thus defined as "joy accompanied by the idea of an external cause."

Spinoza drew a sharp distinction between the passive emotions which characterize the first grade of knowledge and the active ones which mark the second and third grades. Men are passive when the cause of changes in them lies outside them. In this state of human bondage the emotions which accompany confused, fragmentary ideas are thrust on people; they tend to be sporadic, inordinate, unpredictable, and obsessive. Men are subject to panic, jealousy, and overmastering loves and hates. When a man passes to the second grade of knowledge, however, his vitality is increased, and there is a distinctive form of joy which goes with the use of reason. The explanation of man's conduct is now to be sought within him, in his clear understanding of the world and of his relation to it. By understanding himself, including his own emotions and history, as part of the system of nature, a man can attain a kind of freedom, which depends upon his acceptance of his own nature. He is then capable of rational self-love and rational benevolence and can attain glimmerings of the greatest good which he can possess—"the knowledge of the union which the mind has with the rest of nature." The attainment of this state brings its own delight.

In making suggestions for attaining this state of blessedness, Spinoza in many respects anticipated later psychoanalytic techniques, as well as the general psychoanalytic aim of replacing subservience to irrational promptings by rational control based on self-knowledge. He thought, for instance, that many irrational reactions could be traced back to an early reaction to an object to which the present object had become associated by irrelevant similarities. Scientific understanding of this might help to dissociate the emotion from the irrelevant stimulus. He was not so naive, however, as to suppose that mere intellectual understanding could free a man from the obsessiveness of emotion. It takes an emotion to master an emotion. And Spinoza thought that seeing things "under the aspect of eternity" had a specific emotional accompaniment. Hence, the psychological shrewdness as well as the ethical profundity of his remark, "Blessedness is not the reward of right living; it is the right living itself. Nor do we delight in blessedness because we restrain our desires. On the contrary it is because we delight in it that we restrain them."

Hobbes. Hobbes (1588–1679) already subscribed to the deductive model of geometry when he visited Galileo in 1636. He returned replete with concepts and laws which were to form the foundation of his psychology. For the idea had dawned on him, perhaps suggested by Galileo, of applying the new natural philosophy to human behavior. Of course, Epicurus had long ago sketched a mechanical theory of mind, but it was very general. Galileo had worked out the details of a new theory of motion. Could not still further consequences be deduced from the law of inertia? Harvey had deduced the theory of the circulation of the blood from mechanical postulates. Could not Hobbes apply the details of this new theory of motion to psychology and politics?

Body and mind. Hobbes did not really see any particular problem about the relationship between body and mind because for him everything was body. Even God must have a body if he exists, for "substance incorporeal" is a contradiction in terms.

Thus, "conceptions and apparitions are nothing really but motions in some internal substance of the head." Sensation is "some internal motion in the sentient," and pleasure is "nothing really but motion about the heart."

In truth, Hobbes was not much worried by such philosophical niceties as whether, according to his theory, mental phenomena like thinking were being postulated as identical with or merely causally dependent on motions in the head. He was much more interested in working out a mechanical explanation of these phenomena. This is what makes his psychology of absorbing interest. It represents just about the first attempt in the history of psychology to put forward in any detail something that begins to look like a scientific theory.

Mechanical theory of mind. According to Hobbes, in sensation the sense organs were agitated by external motions without which there could be no discrimination and, hence, no sensation. The selectivity of perception was explained by suggesting that while a sense organ retains motion from one object it cannot react to another; similarly, in attention the motion from the root of the nerves persists "contumaciously" and makes the sense organ impervious to the registering of other motions. Imagination was explained by a strict deduction from the law of inertia: "When a body is once in motion, it moveth, unless something else hinder it, eternally; . . . so also it happeneth in that motion, which is made in the internal parts of man, then, when he sees, dreams, etc. . . . Imagination therefore is nothing but decaying sense." This decay is not a decay in motion, which would be contrary to the law of inertia. It comes about because the sense organs are moved by other objects. This explains why dreams are so vivid, for in sleep there are no competing motions from the outside world. Thus, the longer the time that elapses after sensing an object, the weaker the imagination. Memory is imagination with a sense of pastness added to it.

This was an exciting and an ingenious theory. The difficulty about it is that the type of distinction implied in the explicanda cannot really be deduced from the mechanical postulates of the theory, for the differences between perceiving, imagining, and remembering are basically epistemological ones implying standards and criteria different from those that might be attributed to mere movements. Hobbes never faced the basic difficulties which Aristotle first formulated in his opposition to the theory that the soul was itself moved. Nevertheless, Hobbes did produce something that looked like a scientific theory. Its conceptual difficulties attend all psychological theories that attempt to translate epistemological distinctions into differences of process.

Mechanical theory of action. In the theory of action Hobbes attempted to get rid of final causes and to substitute efficient causes for them. To do this, he had to introduce the concept of endeavor, which was very different from Spinoza's conatus. He used the term "endeavor" to designate infinitely small motions, which he postulated as occurring in the medium between the object and the sense organ, between the sense organ and the brain, and heart. His theory of motivation was that external objects transmit motions by a medium to the sense organs and from there to the brain and to the heart; this results not only in the production of images but also in some alteration or diversion of vital motions round the heart. When these incoming motions help the circulation of vital motions, it appears to us as pleasure, and the body is guided to preserve the motions by staying in the presence of the stimulating object; and conversely with pain. Appetite and aversion are thus the first endeavors of animal motion. They are succeeded by the flow of animal spirits into some receptacle near the "original" of the nerves which brings about a swelling and relaxation of the muscles causing contraction and extension of the limbs, which is animal motion.

Hobbes thought this mechanical account of action was quite consistent with ascribing a central role to consciousness, for in Hobbes's view all action was voluntary in the very strong sense that it is preceded by the thought of an end to be attained. He also claimed that the only way to develop a science of human nature was to look into ourselves and analyze what we find there. Hobbes found two basic motions of the mind, "the one arising from the concupiscible part, which desires to appropriate to itself the use of those things in which all others have a joint interest; the other proceeding from the rational which teaches every man to fly a contra-natural dissolution, as the greatest mischief that can arrive to nature." Everything we do is derived from the desire for power or the fear of death. Conflict between manifestations of these basic motions of the mind leads to deliberation. In this "alternate succession of appetite and fear" the one that emerges triumphant is called "will." "Will therefore is the last appetite in deliberation." Free will is an illusion, for the outcome of such conflicts can be explained mechanically.

Theory of passions. On top of this mechanical ground plan Hobbes superimposed an account of the passions taken largely from Aristotle's *Rhetoric.* They are to be distinguished by reference to the objects of appetite and aversion as well as by our opinion of attaining such objects. Ambition, for instance, is desire for office; hope is appetite with an opinion of attaining. Individual differences are due, in the main, to differences in the mobility and agility of the animal spirits. Dullness, for instance, derives from "a grossness and difficulty of the motion of the spirits about the heart." Hobbes even had a theory of laughter, which he thought to be the expression of sudden glory caused by something new and unexpected in which we somehow discover ourselves superior to others.

Hobbes assigned a special place in his theory of the passions to curiosity, which, together with the ability to name things and hence to reason deductively, distinguishes men from animals.

Hobbes's account of the passions was unusual in that it was so positive. For him passions were not, as for the Stoics, imperfect reasonings; they were a particular case of motion in the natural world on which his account of human nature was erected. Nevertheless, when he dealt with what was distinctive of man, his reason, Hobbes parted company with both naturalism and mechanical theory. The type of reason, called prudence, which enables man to satisfy his desires more efficiently, on the basis of experience, must be sharply distinguished from the reason by means of which men are able to arrive at the universal truths of geometry and philosophy.

Scope of mechanical theory. This is not the place to enter into the tortuous details of Hobbes's nominalist theory of meaning or his conventionist theory of truth. It is important to note, however, that in dealing with these specifically human facets of behavior, just as in his treatment of the foundations of civil society, Hobbes defended a position which stressed above all the role of artifice and

convention. He even put forward a kind of contract theory of definition to parallel his social contract theory of government. These accounts were underpinned by a very crude causal theory of signs as well as by a mechanical theory of human nature. But no clear connection was ever made between the conventionist and naturalistic elements. Hume later tried to make such a connection by suggesting that reason was a wonderful and unintelligible instinct in human nature. Hobbes, however, more or less ignored his own mechanical theory when he dealt with geometry, law, logic, and other such artificial creations of human reason.

Thus, although Hobbes was the first thinker to develop in any detail a mechanical theory of mind, he also, more or less unwittingly, exhibited the glaring difficulties in such an undertaking. Indeed, the things in which he was most interested, apart from politics, were precisely those things which it is very difficult to accommodate within a mechanical theory.

Leibniz. Leibniz (1646–1716) understood much better than Hobbes the new natural philosophy; indeed, his discovery of the infinitesimal calculus contributed considerably to it. However, he resisted its mechanistic implications. Descartes had viewed nature, the animal world, and bodies as machines but had stopped short at mind; Hobbes had mechanized mind as well. Leibniz went to the other extreme and mentalized nature. In many respects he reverted to Aristotle.

Nature and mind. The *Monadology* was a brilliant synthesis of Aristotelian logic taken seriously and a variety of trends in the natural sciences. The whole Cartesian philosophy presupposed the subject–predicate view of judgment in which every proposition, when reduced to logical form, has a subject and a predicate. Moreover, the predicate was thought to be contained in the subject. The Aristotelians thought that this common structure of language mirrored a world of substances composed of various attributes. Leibniz, like Spinoza, took the definition of substance seriously; he thought that it was the cause of itself, could be conceived by itself, and needed only itself in order to exist. But where Spinoza concluded that if this was the definition of substance, there could be only one— namely, God or nature—Leibniz concluded that the world must be composed of countless substances all exhibiting the features picked out in their definition. These monads develop according to an immanent principle which is their force or essence. Everything that will ever happen to them, their predicates, is included in their original notion. The principle of sufficient reason explains the succession of these states in time, the identity of a substance at different times being recognized by "the persistence of the same law of the series." Now I am a substance and know by introspection that I am characterized by appetition and perception. What I know about myself must in general be a paradigm for the basic structure of all substances. But no two substances are alike. In perception they all mirror the universe from a particular point of view. There is no interaction, however. Each monad is windowless and develops because of its own immanent principle, not because of external causal influences. The monads seem to influence one another only because of the pre-established harmony of their immanent development.

This bizarre application of an ancient logical doctrine to the world accorded nicely with various new developments in the sciences. Leibniz naturally regarded it as consistent with his discovery of the infinitesimal calculus, the guiding idea of which was that a succession of states develops according to a law governing the series. The successive states of a monad flow into one another like a series of terms differing infinitesimally, their development being defined by the law of the series. This fitted well with the law of continuity, which held that *natura non facit saltus* ("nature makes no leaps"). Change is a summation of infinitesimal degrees of change. Furthermore, the recent discovery of the microscope revealed that if a piece of cheese or a seemingly empty pool is examined, each will be found to be teeming with life. Could not all nature, therefore, be alive—a vast system of monads at varying levels of development? In embryology, too, the doctrine of preformation was in vogue. The assumption that all the characteristics of an adult animal exist in embryonic form from the moment of generation supported Leibniz' view that from the original notion of the monad all its later states and characteristics could be deduced. His conception of the essence of monads being force or activity was connected, too, with his contribution to the dispute in dynamics about the relationship between force and mass. Leibniz held that his concept of *vis viva* or activity directed toward the future states of the monad was required by his discovery of the conservation of momentum.

The synthesis of Aristotelian logic and these trends in science made Leibniz utterly opposed to the mechanistic picture of nature and of man in which the real world was a world of bodies in motion having only primary qualities whose changes were to be explained only by reference to efficient causes. What is real, he claimed, is not what is mathematically measurable but our experience of activity and perceiving. Nature, as well as man, is characterized by appetition and perception. Final causes are reconciled with the laws of motion by the principle of sufficient reason, which governs the unfolding of the immanent nature of the monads. The difference between substances is only one of degree of clarity in perception and of self-consciousness in appetition. Bare monads have a minimum of perception and appetition. Their perception is confused, and their appetition is blind. Souls, or conscious monads, have memory, feeling, and attention. Animals, or, rather, the dominant monads of animals, are examples. Rational souls, or spirits, are self-conscious; unlike brutes, which are "empirics" and are aware only of particulars, they can reason and understand necessary truths. Extension is only an appearance, the way in which low-grade monads appear to us; the laws of motion are just appearances of the laws of appetition which depend ultimately on God's choice of what is best. Aristotle and Galileo are reconciled, but Galileo's and Newton's laws are, at best, laws of appearances.

Concept of mind. Leibniz' concept of mind or soul was articulated in what he said about perception and appetition. He regarded perception as marvelous because it cannot be conceived of as an action of the object on the percipient, for the monads are windowless. Perception is better regarded as the expression of a plurality in a unity. One thing may be said to express another when there is a constant and regular relation between what can be said about the one and about the other. It is thus that a projection in perspective expresses its original. The monads are perspectives of the universe from different points of view. Expression is thus the genus of which perception, animal feeling, and intellectual knowledge are species.

Leibniz combined this highly metaphysical account of perception with some shrewd objections to Locke's *tabula rasa* theory of the mind. He held that the senses provide us only with instances and by themselves cannot provide the sort of universal knowledge which we have in science. The mind is active and categorizes experience by means of which it interprets the testimony of the senses. The proper analogy for the mind is not a *tabula rasa* but a block of veined marble. In this doctrine Leibniz harked back to Aristotle's active reason and laid the foundation for Kant's categories. Locke, he argued, had in fact tacitly admitted this in postulating mental operations that are known by reflection.

Leibniz maintained that Locke was wrong in saying that the mind does not always think. We have an infinite number of perceptions of which we are not aware. Habituation and wandering attention, as well as the smallness of the perceptions, explain our failure to notice them. Our attention is often drawn to a sound that has just occurred and that we would not otherwise have consciously noticed, although we registered it. "These insensible perceptions are also the signs of personal identity and its constituents; the individual is characterized by traces of his previous states which these perceptions preserve by connecting them with his present state." They are also the means of recollection. They explain decisions which seem arbitrary to us, like turning to the left rather than to the right; they explain frequent feelings of uneasiness which are not intense enough to be felt as pain. These insensible perceptions, he argued, are "as much use in pneumatics as is the insensible corpuscle in physics." Both are beyond the reach of our senses, and there are as good grounds for believing in one as in the other. Since "nature makes no leaps," these insensible perceptions must accord with the law of continuity. "All this brings us to the conclusion that observable perceptions come by degrees from those which are too small to be observed."

Although Leibniz confused some rather different things in this doctrine—for example, unconscious perceptions, minute perceptions which summate like the noise of waves in the roar of the sea, and confused perceptions—he prepared the ground for the concept of unconscious mental processes which was to prove so important in nineteenth-century thought, and he anticipated later investigations of subliminal perception and "determining tendencies." This shows how a highly speculative theory can lead to the emphasis on facets of experience which may be very important but which have previously been disregarded.

Leibniz' emphasis on appetition as the other main characteristic of monads was a welcome change from the intellectualism of Descartes and Locke. However, Leibniz made no detailed empirical derivations from this notion to match the derivations made from his concept of perception. It had more affinities with Spinoza's "conatus" than with Hobbes's "endeavor," although it was really the Aristotelian conception of the formal and final cause brought up to date and made compatible with dynamic theory. His concept can best be elucidated by quoting him; he calls his concept by the Aristotelian term "entelechy," which is "a power mediating between the simple faculty of acting and the definite or effected act. It contains and includes effort. It is self-determined to action, not requiring to be aided, but only requiring not to be inhibited. The illustration of a weight which stretches the cord it is attached to, or of a bent bow, may elucidate the notion."

Soul and body. Leibniz believed that every living creature is composed of a vast number of special organic structures each developing in its own characteristic way; they are all so coordinated and mutually complementary, however, that together they act as an individual. The unity is the soul or the dominant monad; the multiplicity is the body or assemblage of bare monads. The monads of the body all have their own activity, and they are represented or mirrored in the perceptions of the dominant monad or mind. The mind has no power to interfere with or penetrate the forces which it seems to direct. The activities of the monads of the body subserve the dominant activity of the mind as the players of an orchestra, each playing independent parts, subserve the performance of the symphony, and the symphony is the resultant harmony, which has been pre-established. The manifold activities of the bare monads thus combine to bring about the end of the dominant monad. Thus, the body depends on the mind in the sense that the reason of what happens in the body is to be found in the mind (compare to Aristotle's view of soul and body).

Thus, Leibniz reverted to a view of mind and nature which was basically Aristotelian, but he transformed the Aristotelian entelechy by giving it the basic hallmarks of Cartesian mind—thinking and willing as experienced from within. Furthermore, he pressed the emphasis on privacy much further than Descartes by claiming that the monads are windowless and that everything that will ever happen to them is contained in their original notion.

There was, however, another radically different concept of mind which developed out of Descartes's stress on privacy and incorrigibility as the hallmarks of mental states. This was that of British empiricism, which culminated in Hume and the associationists.

Hume. The contribution of Hume (1711–1776) to psychology was not very extensive in its details because his theorizing about the mind, like that of Berkeley and Locke, was mainly a way of doing epistemology. And there were special reasons, deriving from his epistemological position, for his eschewing speculation about the relationship between mind and body and the general status of mind in nature. Nevertheless, his general concept of mind was of considerable historical importance. It was the first thoroughgoing attempt to eliminate spiritual substance altogether, and it was the first theory to make reason subservient to the passions and to extol the importance of instinct and habit. It was also the first attempt to develop a Newtonian theory of mind and to erect the principles of the association of ideas into scientific postulates—an undertaking which considerably influenced Hartley and hence the course of associationist psychology.

Hume's predecessors. John Locke (1632–1704) took from Descartes the assumption that we are confronted with our own ideas, not with things, and that some kind of certainty is both desirable and attainable. He rejected, however, Descartes's doctrine of innate ideas and adopted a Baconian version of empiricism. He postulated simple ideas of sense that made their imprint on the passive *tabula rasa* of the mind. Once ideas got into the mind, Locke's theory more or less followed Descartes's, for he believed that the active spiritual substance within intuits relations between ideas, the relations which form the foundations of knowledge. Locke, however, did not stick consistently to his "way of ideas." For example, he asserted, like Descartes, that we have intuitive knowledge about our own existence as selves and "sensitive" knowledge of things existing independently of our perceptions of them. They are material substances which support "powers" to produce in us ideas of primary qualities, which are real properties of the things in question, and secondary qualities which are not real.

George Berkeley (1685–1753) stuck more consistently to the way of ideas and eliminated material substance, of which we have and could have no idea because it is a logical absurdity; the representative theory of perception; and the distinction between primary and secondary qualities. He claimed, however, that we have "notions," rather than ideas, of ourselves as active agents and of other minds, including God. We also have a notion of our own causal activity. Berkeley relied on this notion to distinguish ideas of sense from ideas of imagination, for having eliminated the concept of a thing independent of our perceptions, Berkeley had to have a criterion for distinguishing what are commonly called things from the mere coexistence of qualities; imaginary objects, for instance, appear to us as clusters of coexisting qualities. Thus, he claimed that when we see objects, it is God talking the divine sense language and producing ideas in our minds; when we imagine objects, we are doing the producing ourselves and have a notion of our own agency in so doing. Berkeley's stress on the activity of the mind contrasted strongly with Locke's *tabula rasa*.

Hume simply stuck rigorously to the way of ideas and eliminated Berkeley's "notions." There was no simple idea of material substance, of ourselves and others as spiritual substances, of God, or of causal agency. All that was left, therefore, as genuine components of the mind were ideas themselves and certain links between them. Hume likened the mind to a theater "where several perceptions successively make their appearances, pass, repass, glide away," and to a political organization in which the members come and go but the principles of organization—the principles of the association of ideas—persist.

Hume's contributions. Hume was the first to attempt an explicit distinction between images, which he called impressions, and what we would now call sensations—he called them ideas. He regarded them as two sorts of perceptions. Impressions could not be distinguished from ideas in a Lockian way by their relation to an external object. For Hume, following the way of ideas, disclaimed any possibility of knowledge of a world of objects existing independently of our perceptions. And, because he ruled out notions, Berkeley's appeal to awareness of our causal agency in producing ideas of imagination was not open to him. Of course, like Berkeley, Hume agreed that what we call things exhibit a certain constancy and coherence; they resemble past clusters of qualities. We assume independent existence in order to connect past with present perceptions. But, he argued, we can no more demonstrate the existence of a world independent of us than we can demonstrate that pleasure is preferable to pain.

There are, however, subjective criteria for making the distinction between images and sensations, which is all that remains once belief in a world of independent objects has been ruled out. These are the criteria of vividness and order. Hume suggested that ideas could be picked out because they were faint copies of previous impressions. In other words, impressions are both more vivid than ideas and prior to them. But he gave counterexamples to both these criteria—those of vivid ideas in fever or madness and of forming an idea of a color that had never previously been presented as an impression. In the case of fever or madness Hume suggested that the imagination transfers the vividness of an impression to an idea. Similarly, our belief in an external world is a work of the imagination.

Hume's recourse to the imagination was of cardinal importance in his account of the mind because it linked his theory of knowledge with his rehabilitation of feeling. It has often been remarked that one of the main features of Hume's philosophy was a reversal of the roles hitherto ascribed to reason and feeling. He brought over into epistemology his ethical theory, which he adapted from Francis Hutcheson's theory of moral sense, that moral judgments are based on feeling. "Reason is, and ought always to be, the slave of the passions." This moral sense was the product of biological properties inherent in the species; it had its counterpart in our judgments of matters of fact and existence. Reasoning is "nothing but a wonderful and unintelligible instinct in our souls." Our belief in the reality of causal connections or in the existence of an external world or that the future will resemble the past are instinctive and indemonstrable. "Nature, by an absolute and uncontrollable necessity, has determined us to judge as well as to breathe and feel." The categories used by scientists in their theories, such as continuity and causality, are largely products of the imagination.

Hume stressed facets of human nature that had been largely neglected since Aristotle. He postulated an original fabric of human nature consisting of various propensities not unlike that of later instinct theorists. He also extolled the place of habit in conduct, not simply in explaining such developed forms of behavior as obedience to government but also in explaining the origin of some indemonstrable beliefs. For instance, he held that the idea of causal connection could be analyzed into the elements of priority in time of event *A* to event *B* and constant conjunction of event *A* with event *B*, together with a conviction of the necessity that *B* must follow *A*. As there was no impression of this necessity given in experience, Hume attributed our belief in it to habit or a "determination of the mind" brought about by experience of such constant conjunction and the force of the imagination.

The passions. Appropriately enough, the details of

Hume's psychology consisted mainly of an elaborate and highly complex theory of the passions, stated in Book 2 of his *Treatise of Human Nature.* One of Hume's tasks was to rehabilitate the passions, the natural feelings of decent people, from the Puritans' distrust and the rationalists' disregard. He also had to demolish sophisticated theories, deriving from Hobbes, in which all passions were regarded as forms of self-love. Whereas Bishop Butler attacked psychological hedonism in order to establish the supremacy of conscience, Hume refuted the hypothesis of self-love in order to make way for his rival hypothesis of innate benevolence and sympathy.

He also regarded the sensations of pleasure and pain as part of the original fabric. In a passion one of these sensations is accompanied by an affection. The direct affections include desire and aversion, joy and grief, hope and fear. The difference between these depends on the character of the expectation of good or evil. Desire is for present good, joy for assured good in the future, and hope for probable though remote good in the future. Hume thought that through experience these affections, together with the sensation of pleasure or pain associated with them, can become associated with an object. This generates such indirect passions as pride and humility, when the object is ourselves, or love and hate, when the object is other people. Benevolence and malevolence, however, are not derived from love and hate. Hume classed them as direct and instinctive.

Sympathy occupied a role in Hume's theory of passions somewhat similar to imagination in his theory of belief. The idea of another person's feeling is said to be associated with the idea of oneself, and the required liveliness is thus imparted to the otherwise neutral conception of another person's joy or sorrow.

The idea of the self played an important part in Hume's intricate account of the passions. Like the idea of causality, it presented a serious problem for analysis, for we believe strongly in the reality of both of them. Yet, Hume argued, there was no simple impression of sense from which these ideas derived. Introspection revealed only "some particular perception or other, of heat or cold, light or shade, love or hatred, pain or pleasure." What we call self must therefore be "a bundle of perceptions." Like Locke, Hume then went on to compare the self to an oak, a vegetable, or any type of organism which maintains itself through change by virtue of its relations. Another apt analogy is the self-maintained unity of a political association. But Hume maintained that the unity of this bundle, which makes it a "connected heap," is associative, not real; there are no grounds for ascribing to it the simplicity and permanence which are required for real unity. Perceptions are loose, separate, perishing existences. There can be no real links between them. The problem is to explain how we come to believe that there are.

Hume made the same type of move in relation to the idea of self that he made in the case of causality. He demonstrated that if the way of ideas is followed, there is no ground in experience for believing in the reality of the self; he then embarked upon some speculative psychology to explain how we come to have this belief. He suggested that members of the bundle are related to one another in a specific way in time, the order being preserved by memory. The members have the relations of resemblance and cause and effect between them. But cause and effect is not a real relation; thus, no real unity characterizes the self. We come to believe in it because of the "felt smoothness" with which we pass from one idea to another once the associative links have been established.

Nature and mind. Although Hume's adherence to the way of ideas ruled out wide speculations about the place of mind in nature, there was a highly imaginative idea behind his positivistic system. Hume regarded himself as the Newton of the sciences of man. He made frequent references to his pursuit of the experimental method and thought his rigorous interpretation of the way of ideas to be thoroughly consistent with Newton's methodological canons of economy and simplicity in explanation, testability of hypotheses, and refusal to postulate occult causes. Hume stressed that once we have arrived at the original fabric of human nature, it is futile to attempt to satisfy any further our intemperate desire to search for other causes.

But Hume did not emulate Newton merely in his methodology. He also regarded his concepts in the psychological sphere as parallel to Newton's concepts in the physical. His simple impressions were the equivalent of Newtonian atoms, and his principles of association were likened to the "gentle force" of Newton's principles of gravitational attraction. Indeed, Hume regarded imagination and, perhaps, sympathy as cohesive forces. When imagination works according to the associative principles of resemblance, contiguity, and cause and effect, the result is what Hume called the understanding. When it works capriciously, the result is fancy. Of course, the principles of association were as old as Aristotle, though Aristotle's principles were not the same as Hume's. Hobbes, too, had made use of them, though he believed that thought which was guided by desire or which exhibited a plan was more important. However, in Hume's system for the first time they were looked upon as important *scientific* principles governing the working of the mind. This conception was taken up by Hartley in his theory of vibrations and developed into the associationist school of psychology.

Hume's theory was also important in the history of psychology because it firmly established psychology as the science of the contents of consciousness. Although Descartes's first certainty was rejected in relation to its content, what persisted was the assumption that a man has some incorrigible sort of knowledge about his own mental states. Hume rejected Descartes's search for simple natures, which appear to the mind as clear and distinct ideas, as the foundations of science. Instead, he postulated simple impressions of sense, perishing existences about which we can be certain provided that we make no inferences beyond them. Because Hume, like Locke, consistently confused psychology with epistemology, two parallel traditions developed from his work. On one hand, there was the search in epistemology for sense data which could provide an incorrigible basis for a system of knowledge; on the other hand, there was the development of introspective psychology whose task was envisaged as cataloguing the contents of the mind, analyzing them into simple units,

and attempting generalizations about the links between these units which explained the generation of complex ideas and states.

Body and mind. Hume, understandably enough, had little to say about the relationship between mind and body. Body, according to his theory, stood for another bundle of impressions. He did not even connect the idea of self with impressions of bodily states, which might have been an obvious move if he had looked seriously for specific impressions, from which the idea of self is derived. In the Humean tradition William James, for instance, later suggested that the idea of self was intimately connected with impressions of breathing, cephalic movements, and the like. But Hume made no such suggestion. He noted the inexplicability of the fact that "the motion of our body follows upon the command of our will." "Will," he suggested, was another name for the strongest motive (compare to Hobbes's account). But we simply have to accept these de facto connections between events. To speculate further would be to postulate occult causes and thus to sin against both Newtonian methodology and the way of ideas.

Kant. It would be very difficult to sketch the contribution of Kant (1724–1804) to psychology within the framework previously used, partly because he made very little direct and explicit contribution to psychology and partly because his Copernican revolution in philosophy involved a radical reformulation of questions asked under such a framework. Furthermore, though Kant's concept of mind may, in fact, be extremely important insofar as it delimits the sphere of empirical psychology, those who developed empirical psychology in fact paid little heed to the implications of Kant's position. Perhaps that was a pity, for Kant made a sustained effort to separate epistemology from empirical psychology, and until these two are clearly distinguished, there will continue to be confusion in this area, as is demonstrated in the genetic psychology of Piaget. Nevertheless, Kant's influence on psychology was largely negative and indirect; thus, only a short exposition will be given of those parts of his critical philosophy which seem relevant to psychology.

First and foremost, Kant rejected the notion of the empiricists that what is called mind could be explained as the product of ideas arising from experience and systematizing themselves according to laws of association. Kant maintained that the mind must be regarded as a structure regulated by principles of its own activity. These principles could not be arrived at empirically, for they were presupposed by any empirical investigation, including psychology. They could be arrived at only by critical philosophy, which asked the question "What must be presupposed for our experience to be possible?"

Kant was particularly interested in two realms of experience—Newtonian science and the autonomous morality of thinkers of the French Revolution. Kant attempted to reconcile the rationalism of Wolff and Leibniz with the empiricist position of Hume by postulating an active mind whose nature was to impose a structure on experience to make it intelligible. This structure was composed of the categories used by scientists, such as substance, cause and effect, and continuity, which Hume had assigned to the imagination; Kant attributed the structure to reason, which synthesizes the data of sense. The content is provided by the senses, but the form is provided by reason. Thus, what we call nature is in part the work of mind. It is composed ultimately of things-in-themselves, whose real nature must be forever unknowable. We, too, must exist as noumenal selves, as things-in-ourselves. Of course, Hume was right in maintaining that we have no impressions of such selves. At best, we have intimations of such selves behind the appearances in our moral experience as active rational beings.

Men have empirical selves insofar as they have bodies and psychic functions—for example, sensation, imagery, feeling, purposes—which depend on embodiment. Such selves can be known by inner sense, and their manifestations can be investigated empirically; Kant called such a study anthropology. Kant made his mark on the history of introspective psychology by imposing on these phenomena the tripartite division—knowing, feeling, and willing—worked out in his *Critique of Judgment*. But he did not note anything particularly novel about the phenomena thus investigated, although he did declare that such investigations could never be properly scientific. He was convinced that science involved quantification and that since the phenomena studied by anthropology could not be subsumed under mathematically expressed laws, psychology could at best be a collection of descriptive material classified under the headings which he suggested. Thus, Kant's extrapolation of Newtonian physics as the paradigm of all sciences had the negative effect of making it incumbent on those who wanted to develop psychology as a science to attempt the quantification of the phenomena to be studied. The result was Fechner's psychophysics, Herbart's attempt at mathematical laws of consciousness, and countless other premature attempts at quantification.

Another result of Kant's analysis was an increase of interest in the problems connected with the self. The controversy about the existence of a pure self and whether it was a proper object of study occupied most thinkers during the nineteenth century. Of much more importance for psychology, however, was Kant's doctrine that there can be no science of human actions, though its importance has seldom been recognized by those who are committed to empirical psychology. Human actions are the product of human reason, deliberation, and choice, and Kant held that insofar as a man's reason is involved, his behavior is not explicable in terms of the mechanical laws of nature. He acts freely and is determined only by rational laws of his own creation. This was similar to Spinoza's doctrine of freedom and activity. It raises all sorts of problems about the relationship between reason and emotion and between mind and body, problems which Kant did not seriously tackle. His concept of a rational being as a noumenon which was somehow related to a phenomenal embodied self was a metaphysical model that dramatized difficulties connected with the mechanical explanation of thought and rational action which Descartes had used a different model to depict. Kant laid more stress on the concept of will and rational action than did Descartes, but both men picked

out a crucial problem for the development of psychology to which no satisfactory answer has yet been given.

TRANSITION FROM PHILOSOPHY TO SCIENCE

The history of psychology as thus far reviewed is in the main a history of the philosophy of mind, and the issues discussed have been mainly philosophical issues. The rest of the history, however, will be concerned with the slow but progressive disentanglement of psychology as an empirical science from philosophical speculation.

Although it is possible to consider Aristotle's *De Anima* as the transition from presystematic to systematic psychology, the transition from philosophy to empirical science cannot be pinpointed so precisely. This was not so much a transition as a process of differentiation. Indeed, it began with Aristotle, but it becomes unmistakable in the psychologies of Descartes and Hobbes, both of whom were affected by the impact of Galileo's physics. Both framed hypotheses about the physical and physiological mechanisms of consciousness and behavior which were in principle testable by observation and experiment. From Descartes and Hobbes the main line of development in empirical psychology was through the British empiricists Locke, Berkeley, and Hume.

Eighteenth-century British psychology. Locke's new way of ideas laid the foundations for the twin doctrines of sensationism and associationism. The theory was that the mind is composed only of sensations and mental images (mental images being faint copies of sensations), that all complex percepts or ideas are formed through association, and that all trains of thought arise through association. Locke's analysis of mind was not so simple as that. He included ideas of reflection, abstract ideas, and the self, or possessor of sensations and ideas. Berkeley contested the existence of abstract ideas and furthered the development of associationism by giving an associationist explanation of the perception of the third dimension of space—another hypothesis which was to become the subject of experimental study. Hume further refined sensationism by eliminating the self on the basis of the negative result of his attempt to observe it by introspection. The next important step was taken by David Hartley, who proposed a neural basis of conscious processes. His hypotheses, too, could in principle be tested by observation and experiment. Further refinements and elaborations of associationism are to be found in the works of James Mill, J. S. Mill, Thomas Brown, and Alexander Bain. The associationist doctrines spread to the Continent and as experimental psychology later returned to England and went to the United States.

A second major influence on the advance of psychology toward the status of an empirical science was provided by the biological sciences, notably in the evolutionary doctrine of Charles Darwin. This influence was later to prove one of the causes of the disruption of associationist psychology.

Hartley. While David Hartley (1705–1757) was practicing medicine, he made many observations of psychological interest and wrote his major opus, *Observations on Man, His Frame, His Duty, and His Expectations* (1749). It was a thoroughgoing attempt to provide a neurophysiological basis for the mental processes of sensation, imagery, and association. Influenced by Newton's *Opticks,* he proposed an explanation of conscious experience and association in terms of vibrations transmitted through nerves, which were conceived of as solid fibers, thus breaking from the earlier conception of nerves as hollow tubes for the conduction of the animal spirits. For every kind of sensation there are different kinds of vibrations or vibrations differently located; corresponding to images or memories, there are vibratiuncles, miniature vibrations which can persist after the larger vibrations have subsided and which form the physical substratum of memory. The associative processes occur by virtue of the fact that if two stimuli occur simultaneously and produce two corresponding vibrations in two regions of the brain—say, vibration A arising from a visual stimulus and vibration B arising from an auditory stimulus—the repetition of only the visual stimulus producing vibration A will arouse vibration B in the absence of the original stimulus which produced B. This is a simple translation into neurophysiological terms of the traditional principle of association of ideas, explaining, for example, the association of thunder with lightning. Hartley further advanced associationist theory by suggesting ways in which some of the several special laws of association—contiguity in space, contiguity in time, contrast, and similarity—could be reduced to the single law of association by temporal contiguity. He also offered a more detailed account than had yet been given, in terms of association, of the formation of general ideas.

Brown. As professor of moral philosophy in Edinburgh, Thomas Brown (1778–1820) delivered a series of lectures subsequently published under the title *Lectures on the Philosophy of the Human Mind.* Though not himself an associationist, he made very important contributions to the theory of association, which he preferred to describe as suggestion. Two of his ideas were of especial importance. First, he distinguished between simple suggestion, which is association in the commonly accepted sense, and relative suggestion, which is not in any sense an associative process but is a process which was later to be described by Charles Spearman as the "eduction of relations." Second, Brown formulated the secondary laws of association—the principles of recency, frequency, duration, liveliness, and so on. These were later to become the subject of innumerable experimental studies.

Nineteenth-century British psychology. Brown's philosophy was severely criticized by Sir William Hamilton (1788–1856) in his *Discussions on Philosophy and Literature* (1852) and his *Lectures on Metaphysics and Logic* (posthumously published in 1859–1860), but Brown was defended with no less force by J. S. Mill in *An Examination of Sir William Hamilton's Philosophy* (1865). Hamilton, who was professor of logic and metaphysics at Edinburgh from 1836 until his death, had been greatly attracted by German philosophy and contributed to the rise of the British idealistic school of philosophy later to be represented by T. H. Green and F. H. Bradley. This school, deriving its inspiration from the intellectualist and idealist thought of Hegel and other Continental philosophers, had no common ground with the mechanistic empiricist and

physiological approach of the British psychologists, but in its criticism contributed to the refinement, as well as the demise, of associationism. It was Bradley who, in attacking the atomistic features in associationism, phrased the dictum "Association marries only Universals." This theme was to be developed in an original way in G. F. Stout's doctrines of noetic synthesis and relative suggestion.

James Mill and John Stuart Mill. Associationism reached its zenith in the work of James Mill (1773–1836). An economist and historian rather than a philosopher or psychologist, he learned his philosophy—hedonistic utilitarianism—from Hartley. His psychology, however, was a refinement of Hartley's and his analysis of mind was much more acute. *The Analysis of the Human Mind* appeared in 1829. Mental life was reduced to sensory elements, and the development of complex ideas was explained by the principle of association. Mill gave a clearer account than had Hartley of the way in which the several laws of association could be reduced to the single law of contiguity. He refined previous accounts of emotional experience in terms of sensations. Like Hartley, he attempted to apply the principles of associationism to the explanation of the complex phenomena of conscience and religion.

John Stuart Mill (1806–1873), his son, was a more subtle and acute philosopher than his father. He was certainly more disposed to take seriously any objection to a theory he wished to defend. In his rational and reasonable way he was inclined to make concessions which resulted in his rejecting the original theory. He sacrificed simple hedonism by conceding that pleasures might differ in quality. He gave up associationism by introducing the concept of mental chemistry—the idea that mental compounds, like chemical compounds, might exhibit properties not deducible from the properties of the elements. This breach in the associationist defenses was to be widened later by doctrines of creative synthesis and Gestalt qualities and the biological concept of emergent evolution—ideas all at variance with pure associationist doctrines. J. S. Mill was less concerned with sensationism as a psychological doctrine than with its philosophical counterpart, phenomenalism—the description of material things and the physical world in terms of sense data or "permanent possibilities of sensation."

Bain. Though in the associationist tradition, Alexander Bain (1818–1903) was less interested in the philosophy of mind than in psychology as an empirical science. He was emphatic in his demand that psychology should be cleared of metaphysics. His *Manual of Mental and Moral Science* (1868) was virtually a textbook of empirical psychology. It was a condensation of his two major works, *The Senses and the Intellect* (1855; rev. ed., 1894) and *The Emotions and the Will* (1859). He was thoroughgoing in his insistence on the need for a physiological basis for psychology not merely in general terms but in terms of known physiological facts, about which he made it his business to be well informed. As far as this implied a philosophy of mind, it found expression in his formulation of the principle of psychophysical parallelism. Especially important were his accounts of habit formation and learning. His treatment of habit was in large measure the inspiration behind the eloquent chapter on this topic in William James's *Principles* of *Psychology*. E. L. Thorndike and other "learning theorists" owe to Bain the first clear formulation of the law of effect, the principle that responses are ingrained by the reward of pleasure. Even his sillier theories contributed to enlightenment. One of the silliest theories in the history of psychology—that maternal love is based on the pleasurable tactile sensations experienced from contact with a baby—foreshadows the subtler theories of Freud concerning erogenous zones in the body and, more remotely, the "releaser mechanisms" of the ethologists. Bain's associationism was not an ideology. It was merely that he had assimilated the dominant features of the current psychological climate of opinion.

Two other developments were to complete the transformation of psychology from a branch of philosophy into an empirical science: (1) the impact of the theory of evolution and (2) the establishment of laboratories for experimental psychology. The theory of evolution had its origin in England in the work of Charles Darwin; the idea of laboratories for experimental psychology came chiefly from the Continent.

Evolutionary psychology. Darwin's theory of evolution as set out in his *Origin of Species* (1859) was a very large theory, but it was a scientific, not a philosophical, theory. It was supported by an enormous body of empirical observations. Theories of evolution date back to antiquity. Charles Darwin's grandfather Erasmus Darwin had adumbrated a Lamarckian theory of evolution. Alfred Russel Wallace anticipated Darwin's theory by a few months. Herbert Spencer (1820–1903), who had propounded philosophical and psychological theories of evolution for some years before the appearance of the *Origin of Species,* was accordingly well placed to capitalize on Darwinism in the development of his own ambitious "synthetic philosophy."

Darwin (1809–1882) himself wrote on distinctively psychological topics. His *Descent of Man* (1871) discusses the similarities between the mental processes of man and of animals. His work *Expression of Emotions in Man and Animals* gives an evolutionary interpretation of changes in features and postures and assigns biological utility to these changes. The evolutionary approach stimulated many studies by amateur and professional naturalists. G. J. Romanes (1848–1894) collected evidence for the continuity of development from the animal to the human mind, and Sir John Lubbock (1834–1913) was among the first to use laboratory techniques in the study of insects. Laboratory studies like these were to be developed later on a grand scale by such American comparative psychologists as E. L. Thorndike and R. M. Yerkes.

Galton. Sir Francis Galton (1822–1911), the versatile cousin of Charles Darwin, contributed to meteorology, anthropology, anthropometry, and psychology and to the development of statistical and other metric methods in psychology. Among his major interests was the inheritance of mental characteristics, for the study of which he devised ingenious methods. He stressed heredity as a determinant of mental life and behavior. His records of the behavior of twins are reminiscent of the Leibnizian concept of a preestablished harmony. According to his records, twins can behave exactly like two clocks each causally insulated from environmental influences and from each other, behaving

similarly and thinking in unison almost entirely in consequence of the similarities of their innate constitution. His major psychological works were *Hereditary Genius* (1869) and *Inquiries Into Human Faculty* (1883). He set up the first two English psychological laboratories—the first at the International Health Exhibition of 1884 and the second in the South Kensington Museum. He pioneered the application of physical and psychometric tests in schools.

Ward and Stout. Philosophical psychology was to feel the impact of the new biological approach. James Ward's revolutionary article on psychology in the ninth edition of the *Encyclopaedia Britannica* (1886) mounted a devastating attack upon associationism, recasting psychology in terms of a "psychoplasm," or "presentational continuum," which, like bodily tissues, undergoes progressive differentiation and integration. Ward's distinguished pupil G. F. Stout wrote *Manual of Psychology,* a standard text for some three decades, in 1898. This was described as being written from a genetic point of view; thereafter, almost every textbook of psychology had a biological orientation.

Empiricism in Europe. The empiricist philosophy was introduced into France by littérateurs and essayists like Voltaire and Diderot, not by philosophers or psychologists.

Voltaire had lived in England from 1726 to 1729, and so was in a position to introduce British ways of thought in philosophy into the intellectual life of France. Diderot had a clearer understanding of British empirical psychology. He particularly interested himself in the mental life of persons deprived of one sense—for example, sight.

The first of the French empiricist philosophers to contribute to sensationism was Étienne Bonnot de Condillac (1715–1780). Diderot had been concerned with the mental life of persons deprived of one sense; Condillac started from the imaginary case of a person deprived of all senses except one. He took the case of a statue endowed only with the sense of smell, selecting smell because of its relative simplicity. From this he proceeded to add other senses and to explain in sensationist terms attention, memory, imagination, and reason. He attached no importance to association. He believed that the experience of one sensation after another is *ipso facto* a comparison of the two and that the occurrence of the unpleasant sensation constitutes the will to terminate the sensation. Condillac's sensationism was perhaps the simplest and most elegant form of the doctrine in the history of psychology. His views are set out in the *Traité des sensations* (1754).

Claude-Adrien Helvétius (1715–1771), author of a volume of essays entitled *De l'Esprit* (1758), was a minor social and political philosopher who seized upon Locke's empiricism and concept of the *tabula rasa* to defend an extreme doctrine concerning the equality and perfectibility of men. His basic thesis was that all differences between men are due to differences in experience and education. All error was due to passion or ignorance.

The doctrines that Helvétius derived from Locke were to return to England in the works of William Godwin, especially in his *Political Justice* (1793). Like Helvétius, Godwin taught that all men are equal at birth and that their subsequent differences were due to experience and education. Voluntary actions originate in opinions, which can be changed by rational persuasion. Vice is error, which can be corrected. In Helvétius and in Godwin the association of empirical philosophy with an intellectualist hedonism is displayed in its most extreme form.

Through Condillac the influence of Locke spread to Italy and Switzerland. In Italy this influence is to be seen in the teachings of several all-but-forgotten writers. In Switzerland, Charles Bonnet (1720–1790) of Geneva was the outstanding figure in empirical philosophy. His chief work in psychology was the *Essai analytique sur les facultés de l'âme* (1760). Although he followed Condillac for the most part, Bonnet differed chiefly in the importance he attached to physiological explanations.

German psychology and experimentation. Throughout the seventeenth, eighteenth, and early nineteenth centuries German psychology was dominated by the philosophical doctrines of Leibniz, Kant, and Hegel, each of whom contributed to a rationalist idealism very unfavorable to the development of psychology as a science.

Hegel. Georg Wilhelm Friedrich Hegel (1770–1831) has received scant attention in the histories of psychology, understandably so since his form of rationalism is the most extreme antithesis to the empiricist philosophy that had favored the development of psychology as an empirical science. He is, however, not without importance in the history of psychology.

One of Hegel's theses was that it is a mistake to suppose that complex phenomena are explained only by reference to simpler phenomena, that we can, for example, understand religion in its developed form by the study of cults of primitive people or that we can understand man only through the study of lower forms of animal life. In this he challenged what had long been and still is a basic principle of comparative psychology, but Hegel's thesis survives in the view of psychologists who hold that the proper study of mankind is man and that we should begin with civilized man in advanced societies. It lives on in the contention of Freudian psychologists that the evidence for infantile sexuality can be appreciated only in the light of adult sexual behavior.

Equally important for psychology is the Hegelian dialectical progression—thesis, antithesis, synthesis. When this progression is stated as an empirical observation of movements of thought and action, not as a metaphysical principle or a principle of logic, it illuminates many sequences in the history of politics, philosophy, and science. A dialectical progression is illustrated in the fate of Hegel's own philosophy. Its influence in Germany was short-lived. His rationalistic thesis issued in an empiricist antithesis, Wundtian experimental psychology. The dialectical progression is illustrated by the British vogue for Hegelianism among philosophers who found in it an antithesis with which to confront the prevailing empiricist philosophy and psychology. The progression is illustrated by the sequence from Hegel's idealist thesis to the antithesis of dialectical materialism which was to become a central tenet of communist philosophy. Although it provides no comprehensive philosophy of history, the concept of dialectical progression affords a rather more subtle and articulate account of historical movements than conventional, common-sense accounts in terms of "the swing of the pendulum."

Hegel's doctrines were associated with, and conferred philosophical status upon, a widespread romantic and mystical philosophy of nature according to which everything in nature had some spiritual and symbolical significance. The influence of this philosophy of nature persisted far into the nineteenth century and in the biological sciences favored vitalistic, as opposed to mechanistic, accounts of mind, body, and nature. Psychologists divided progressively into two groups. The first comprised the philosophers—that is, those who primarily taught philosophy and whose philosophy of mind contained much metaphysics. The second group consisted of natural scientists whose approach was from mathematics, physics, and the biological sciences. The distinction is not sharp, since romanticism and metaphysics were in the air which every German student, even students of the natural sciences, breathed.

The first steps in the transition from the philosophy of mind to scientific psychology were taken when Kant challenged psychologists to show that their subject could claim scientific status. This challenge was taken up by Herbart, Weber, and Fechner. That it could be an experimental science was argued by Weber, Fechner, Müller, Helmholtz, and others. Wundt finally established it as a science which required a distinctive kind of laboratory.

Herbart. Johann Friedrich Herbart (1776–1841) set out to establish a basis for psychology other than that of the prevailing "faculty" psychology associated with Christian Wolff (1679–1754), a disciple of Leibniz and precursor of Kant who was much less distinguished than either. Herbart tried to show that the laws describing mental process could be put into precise mathematical form. Herbart's first achievement was the grafting of associationism onto a rationalist metaphysical root. The soul was retained, serving the traditional function of giving unity to the mind, but the data of empirical psychology were, as in associationism, sensations and ideas. In Herbart's system ideas were not just passively associated. They interacted by attractions and repulsions in accordance with which they were drawn into or forced out of consciousness. The behavior of ideas in Herbart's psychology resembles that of the "reals" in his pluralistic metaphysics. Two "reals"—for instance, *A* and *B*—differing in quality, tend to disturb each other because of their difference, but each also tends to preserve itself by resisting the disturbing effect of the other. This principle of self-preservation is reminiscent of the Spinozistic doctrine that "everything that is in itself endeavors to persist in its own being" and, when applied in Herbart's psychology, foreshadows the concept of homeostasis which was to be current in psychology a century later.

Herbart's account of the way in which ideas enter consciousness and are expelled from it represents a phase in the history of the theory of the unconscious midway between Leibniz and Freud; his concept of the apperceptive mass, a system of ideas bound together by mutual attraction, was still current when psychoanalytic writers were developing the concept of a mental complex. Herbart's metaphysics and mathematics were to be forgotten, and he did not contribute directly to the development of psychology as an experimental science. His most lasting influence was in the field of educational psychology, chiefly in the application of his theory of apperception to the process of learning.

Lotze. Rudolf Hermann Lotze (1817–1881) succeeded Herbart in the chair of philosophy at Göttingen. His most influential work was his *Medizinische Psychologie* (1852), the first systematic work on physiological psychology and one of the very few written by an author qualified in both physiology and philosophy. Against the then prevailing view he defended the thesis that every mental phenomenon has its physiological counterpart and that the laws which apply to inorganic matter also apply to organic matter. Final causes, vital and mental forces, and the soul itself can act only through mechanical causation. He insisted, however, that physiology alone cannot explain mental phenomena. Lotze is best known in psychology for his doctrine of local signs, a contribution to the theory of space perception.

Weber and Fechner. Experimentation and the use of quantitative methods in psychology were greatly advanced by Ernst Heinrich Weber (1795–1878) and Gustav Theodor Fechner (1801–1887), who were colleagues in the University of Leipzig and who both taught Lotze.

Weber taught anatomy and physiology. His early work *De Tactu* (1834) reported studies demonstrating the difference between muscle sense and touch. These studies were extended to pain, pressure, and temperature, through which emerged the concept of thresholds and the famous law which has come to be called Weber's law. This states that the smallest increment in a stimulus required to produce a difference in the sensation experienced is not an absolute amount but is relative to the magnitude of the stimulus in question. Like most German scientists of his time, Weber was to some degree under the spell of the current metaphysics and the romantic philosophy of nature, but neither of these influenced his experimental studies. His metaphysics and his science were kept apart.

With Fechner the case was different. Fechner's intellectual life was a pilgrimage from physics and chemistry, through physiology and medicine, to metaphysics and mysticism. From an early age he had been preoccupied with the problem of the relation between matter and spirit. He was attracted to a form of panpsychism according to which not only man and the lower animals have consciousness but also the earth and the other planets—indeed, all material things. In this view all souls are parts of the soul of the universe.

Fechner concluded, on the obscurest of grounds, that the mystery of the relation between mind and body would be resolved by ascertaining the quantitative relations between stimuli and sensations. He suggested that Weber's law could be put into a quantitative form. Weber's law thus became the Weber-Fechner law, according to which the relation between stimulus and sensation is expressed in the formula $S = k \log R$ where S is the experienced intensity, R is the physical intensity, and k is a constant for the particular sense in question. For the verification of this law Fechner designed what are known as the psychophysical methods. These methods have been used in the most tedious of laboratory exercises to which many generations of students of experimental psychology have since been subjected, and the published results of these exercises are among the most tedious controversies in the history of science. But the possibility of experiment and measurement in psychology was established—paradoxically, by a metaphysical mystic. The metaphysics and the mysticism were soon forgotten, but the exercises live on.

Beneke. Friedrich Eduard Beneke (1798–1854), a contemporary of Herbart, was another philosopher who contributed to the foundation of a science of empirical psychology, which, he claimed, was the basis of all philosophy. Like Herbart, he set out to provide a basis for psychology other than that of a doctrine of faculties, and like Herbart, he stressed the activity of the mind. Among his works on psychology are *Lehrbuch der Psychologie* (1832) and *Die neue Psychologie* (1845). Because of his rejection of the prevailing Hegelian philosophy of the Absolute, Beneke was dismissed from his post in the University of Berlin, but after Hegel's death he was reinstated. His best-known contribution to psychological theory was his doctrine of mental, as contrasted with physiological, traces for the explanation of the facts of memory. This doctrine was later to be developed in Great Britain by G. F. Stout.

Müller. Johannes Müller (1801–1858) was a contemporary of Beneke at Berlin. He was the first to hold the title of professor of physiology. (Hitherto, the subject had been taught as a branch of medicine.) He had been under the influence of the prevailing philosophy of nature but contributed to the clarification of the concepts of mind, body, and nature by distinguishing the mental principle, which is restricted in its operation to the nervous system, from the vital principle, which is diffused throughout the organism. He was also preoccupied with the opposition between nativistic and empiricist explanations of space perception as represented, respectively, in the doctrines of Kant and Herbart. Müller reformulated the issue in terms which made it possible to submit the question to experimental tests. He also formulated the theory of specific energies in the nervous system—the hypothesis that the sensory qualities are generated by specific activities of the organs of sense or by specific differentiation in corresponding realities in the brain.

Helmholtz. Hermann von Helmholtz (1821–1894), Müller's distinguished pupil, is acknowledged to be the most outstanding of the physicist-physiologists who have contributed to the development of experimental psychology. In the range of his pioneering studies he has been compared with Francis Galton. His publications were more numerous than Galton's, and his investigations were carried further. He was the first to make a realistic calculation of the speed of nervous impulses, which are important, among other things, in the study of reaction times. He developed Müller's doctrine of specific energies and Young's three-color theory of vision.

Helmholtz' *Handbuch der physiologischen Optik*, published in three volumes (1856–1866), remained an authoritative text for many decades, although it was not translated into English until 1924–1925. No less outstanding were his contributions to the theory of hearing and the related subjects of phonetics and music. He was essentially a scientist with little interest in philosophy and still less patience with transcendentalism. There is, however, much in his writings of philosophical interest—for example, his puzzling concept of unconscious inference in perceptual judgments. His discussions of the principle of the conservation of energy are important in the history and philosophy of science.

Wundt. The last phase in the transition of psychology from a branch of philosophy to psychology as an independent empirical science is conveniently dated as beginning in 1879, when Wilhelm Wundt (1832–1920) established the first psychological laboratory. Wundt's chief claim to a place in the history of philosophy arises from the conceptual system in terms of which he interpreted the experimental data from his own and other laboratories. His philosophy of mind deviated from the simpler forms of atomistic sensationism in that the ultimate elements of mind were, according to him, of two kinds, sensations and feelings. He and his disciples devoted much energy and skill to defining the differences between sensations and feelings and to elucidating his curious tridimensional theory of feeling, but the general program was to analyze experience into its elements, to define the fundamental attributes of these elements, and to formulate the laws in accordance with which these elements are combined. The account leaned heavily on the principle of association but deviated from traditional associationist doctrines in introducing a concept of creative synthesis. This concept was a variant of the concept of apperception and embodied a theory of attention. It had some points in common with J. S. Mill's conception of mental chemistry and in some degree foreshadowed later theories of emergent properties and the doctrine of the Gestalt psychologists that a complex experience is more than the sum of its parts. His most influential work was *Grundzüge der physiologischen Psychologie* (1873). In later years he published two works which contributed to the incursion of psychology into sociology and anthropology.

Ebbinghaus and Külpe. Among other outstanding experimental psychologists were two of Wundt's pupils, Hermann Ebbinghaus (1850–1909) and Oswald Külpe (1862–1915). Wundt's laboratory research had been chiefly concerned with sensation and perception and with relatively simple processes of reaction and association. Ebbinghaus and Külpe extended the experimental method into the study of the higher and more complex functions of memory and the processes of thinking.

In a monumental work, *Über das Gedächtnis* (1885), Ebbinghaus published the results of what has been described by J. C. Flügel in his *A Hundred Years of Psychology* as "the most brilliant single investigation that has ever been made in experimental psychology." Ebbinghaus' outstanding achievement was to extend the experimental method to the "higher thought processes." He was the first to establish quantitative laws concerning the process of memorization. In 1894 he succeeded Theodor Lipps, a pupil of Wundt's most widely known for his studies in psychological aesthetics, in the chair of psychology at Breslau. There Ebbinghaus pioneered in the study of intelligence and devised the completion test, which remains an important component of intelligence tests.

Külpe directed the laboratory at Würzburg, which achieved great fame through its investigations of willing and judging. Through the discovery of imageless thoughts these studies contributed both to the breakdown of sensationism and, in consequence of the inconclusive disputes this discovery provoked, to the behaviorist revolt against introspective methods. At Würzburg as at Leipzig confusion arose through the interpretation of experimental data in terms of implicit philosophical concepts and assumptions, and the conclusions drawn have had to wait for review in the light of further clarification of the distinction between empirical psychology and the philosophy of mind.

The shift to the United States. In the age of Wundt, psychology was a Germanic science, and Germany was the heart of the empire. Mainly through Wundt's influence upon those who came to Leipzig from the United States, psychology became an American science with the United States as the new seat of dominance. Among those who studied abroad and then returned to America were Stanley Hall, who established the first American psychological laboratory at Johns Hopkins in 1888; J. McKeen Cattell, who after several years as assistant to Wundt founded the laboratory at Pennsylvania; and Hugo Münsterberg, who, having established a laboratory at Freiburg, was invited by William James to Harvard in 1892. In the same year E. W. Scripture took charge of the laboratory at Yale. By 1897 there were 15 psychological laboratories in the United States, and by the end of the century there were 26, all based, to begin with, on the laboratory in Leipzig. Most of Wundt's American pupils, however, were soon to deviate from the German pattern and to open up approaches characteristically American—allergic to philosophical speculation, distrustful of introspective methods, and much concerned with the practical applications of their science. Hall became famous for his studies of adolescence. Cattell, more influenced by Galton than by Wundt, concentrated on the measurement of individual differences. Münsterberg's interest turned to applications of psychology to industry and criminology. The mantle of Wundt fell upon E. B. Titchener, an Englishman from Oxford who after his studies at Leipzig went to the United States to develop experimental psychology at Cornell.

The established order of 1900. Wundtian psychology was one important form of and ingredient in what has been called the established order of 1900, against which many revolts were to be mounted. There were, in fact, at least two established orders, one in Britain, represented by James Ward and G. F. Stout, and the other in the United States, represented by E. B. Titchener. These were very different establishments, but they had in common a foundation in some form of body–mind dualism and the acceptance of the facts of consciousness, observed by introspection, as defining the subject matter of psychology.

Ward. James Ward (1843–1925) presented his own system as a sort of synthesis of the too objective thesis of Aristotle's psychology and the too subjective antithesis of Descartes's psychology. His basic conceptual framework was doubly tripartite. In his analysis of experience he distinguished the three modes of consciousness—cognition, feeling, and conation; his analysis of each kind of experience referred to a self or ego, an act or mental attitude, and a presentation (a mental object, sensation, or idea). The most interesting features of his system are contained in his detailed analysis of the phases of development from simple sensation to perception and from perception to the construction of a memory thread and an ideational tissue. Though qua psychologist Ward can be treated as a dualist, his background metaphysics was a variant of an idealistic monadology of the Leibnizian type.

Stout. G. F. Stout (1860–1944) developed Ward's psychology in an individual way, creating an original and independent system. As a psychologist Stout, like Ward, developed a dualistic psychology, but as a philosopher he developed an original theory of mind, body, and nature.

Titchener. Titchener's laboratory at Cornell was the temple of the Wundtian form of the established order, and Titchener (1867–1927) was its high priest. Here as elsewhere, however, empirical psychology continued to be inextricably entangled with philosophy. Titchener's deviations from sensationist and associationist psychology were less fundamental than he himself believed. He was a dualist, and he confessed to a bias in favor of sensationism. He was reductionist in his treatment of conation. He differed from the classical sensationists in accepting feelings as basic elements; he also differed from them in the treatment of the elements as existences, as contrasted with meanings. He sought to explain complex mental states as arising from the synthesis of elements and thus to display the structure of the mind. Accordingly, he is described as a structural, as opposed to a functional, psychologist. His cardinal tenet, which was to become the major object of attack, was his thoroughgoing proclamation of introspection as *the* distinctive method of psychology. His two most important works were his *Lectures on the Psychology of Feeling and Attention* (1908), a detailed exposition of the thesis that "the system of psychology rests upon a threefold foundation: the doctrine of sensation and image, the elementary doctrine of feeling and the doctrine of attention," and the *Lectures on the Experimental Psychology of the Thought* (1909), an equally thoroughgoing examination of the claims for the discovery of an imageless thought element and a polemic against the doctrine of Brentano and Stout that references to object is the criterion of mind.

Revolts and the era of the schools. The established order of the United States and the established order of Britain were to become the objects of attack from four directions: (1) The behaviorist attack directed in the main against dualism, the concept of consciousness, and the reliance upon introspection; (2) the attack of the Gestalt psychologists against all forms of psychological atomism; (3) the psychoanalytic attack against the overemphasis on conscious processes and inadequate recognition of the unconscious mind; and (4) the attack of the hormic psychologists, which was directed against the intellectualism of traditional psychology—that is, the overemphasis on cognitive processes and the relative disregard for conation or purposiveness in the explanation of conscious experience and behavior.

In the four revolts the schools were all fighting on more than one front. Each was attacking traditional psychology, and each engaged in polemics with the other revolting schools. Confusion was increased by the fact that within each school there were conflicting factions and by the general failure to distinguish straight empirical issues from issues of philosophy and of linguistic usage.

Behaviorism. The conception of psychology as the study of behavior and as an essentially biological science dates back to Aristotle, but behaviorism as an ideology can be dated precisely. It began in 1914, when J. B. Watson (1878–1958) published *Behavior* while a professor at Johns Hopkins University.

This book was a protest and a revolt against dualism, the concept of consciousness, and *any* use of the introspective method in psychology. Psychology is to be the study of behavior by objective methods. It was a protest in defense of animal psychology, in which statements about the animal mind and the consciousness of animals must be pure guesswork, and it was a protest against the interminable and inconclusive disputes between introspective psychologists about the differentiation of sensations and feelings, the James–Lange theory of emotion, and imageless thought. It was also an attack on the traditional theory of consciousness in which some sort of mental stuff was thought to be the subject matter of psychology.

In *Behavior* and two other important books, *Psychology From the Standpoint of a Behaviorist* (1919) and *Behaviorism* (1924), Watson developed his distinctive account of all the major topics which constitute psychology. Like the structuralists he set out to exhibit complexes in terms of simple elements, complex responses to situations as derived from simple responses, native and acquired. The analysis of behavior was in terms of stimulus and response (an analysis to be elaborated later by Tolman in terms of intervening variables). Sensation and perception were described as responses to present stimuli and constellations of stimuli, memory and learning as responses to past stimuli and neural traces, feelings and emotions as types of sensorimotor responses, and thinking as subvocal verbal behavior. Introspection itself was redescribed as verbal behavior. In his system Watson included much that was irrelevant to the major principle—for example, a bias toward explanations in terms of environmental influence and a bias against explanations in terms of heredity. He had a special bias against the concept of purpose, though later behaviorists found no difficulty in assimilating purposive behavior as goal-directedness. His laws of conditioning were the old laws of association transformed into generalizations about bonds between simple reflexes instead of between simple ideas.

Watson's writings were naive and often confused, but his behaviorism sailed on the tides of the time. Behaviorism was inevitable. Watson's behaviorism was fortunate in that it was reinforced by the most important philosophical movements of the period, positivism and physicalism. It was also reinforced by the logicians and the methodologists of the inductive school, who maintained that scientific laws state correlations between observables. Watson accordingly assumed that because mind was unobservable, it could not be discussed or referred to in science. When logicians later began to proclaim that scientific systems were hypothetico-deductive, such behaviorists as Tolman and C. L. Hull conceded the importance of unobservables in the form of intervening variables and hypothetical constructs. This return to the methodology of Galileo made any simple form of behaviorism difficult to maintain. Nevertheless, B. F. Skinner stuck to the old inductive concept of scientific method and proclaimed that his findings involved no theory. Behaviorism was further supported by a number of outstanding experimental psychologists—for example, K. S. Lashley and W. S. Hunter—sympathetic to Watson's approach.

Lashley was primarily a neurophysiologist who as a behaviorist was more sympathetic to the views of the Gestalt psychologists than to those of Watson. He contributed in an important way to the advance of knowledge concerning the localization of the higher functions in the cortex.

Hunter, a distinguished experimental psychologist, rallied to the support of behaviorism through an odd philosophical argument, based on a very naive form of realism, that consciousness or experience is merely a name applied to what other people call the environment. This argument is reminiscent of a characteristic doctrine of Ward and Stout that the subject matter of psychology comprises "the whole choir of heaven and earth" as it appears to the observer, a view later to be defended by the Gestalt psychologists in terms of the behavioral, as contrasted with the geographical, environment—another variant of the view that things as they appear are appropriate objects of psychological science.

As professor of psychology at the University of California, E. C. Tolman (1886–1959) developed an original system of purposive behaviorism which had perhaps much more in common with the psychology of McDougall than it had with the psychology of Watson. Watson was preoccupied with responses to stimuli. Tolman described Watson's behaviorism as molecular, for it was concerned mostly with physiological details; his own he described as molar, for it was concerned with external and integrated behavior and with emergent properties.

Clark L. Hull (1884–1952), professor at Yale, is known for his inventiveness and originality. His contribution to behaviorism reflects his own interest in methodological studies and the concept of hypothetico-deductive systems. He constructed a miniature system of this type aimed at a rigorous ordering of some of the basic laws of behavior. His deductive dream and his attempt to develop a Galileo-like resolution of behavior into simple externally initiated movements bore a marked similarity to the mechanistic system of Hobbes.

Behaviorism is not strictly an arguable thesis; it is a pronunciamento, a policy statement. The traditional psychologist declares, "I propose to study consciousness by introspection"; the behaviorist says, "I do not; I propose to study behavior by objective methods." The issue is almost as simple as that. There are, however, many arguable issues in particular systems of behaviorism. Reasons can be given for and against policy decisions. There are larger philosophical issues which cannot be evaded. Roughly three types of behaviorism have emerged: a metaphysical type which says that consciousness does not exist; a methodological type which says that consciousness is not amenable to scientific procedures of investigation; and a radical analytic type, defended chiefly by philosophers, according to which mental facts can all be analyzed in terms of behavior and dispositions to behavior. In Wat-

son's behaviorism and in many others these issues are confused. The behaviorists, no less than Titchener, confused questions of empirical fact with questions of philosophical analysis. It is not possible to know what an emotion is by the introspective observation of emotional states. A prior decision has to be made concerning what to observe, what is to count as an emotion. In the same way it is not possible to know what behavior is by the objective observation of behavior. A prior decision has to be taken about what to observe and about what is to count and what is not to count as an example of behavior. For example, before describing a movement of the body like raising an arm as signaling to a friend or testing the direction of the wind, a person must know what the agent had in mind. This inadequate attention to the question of what constitutes behavior was one of the major weaknesses of behaviorism. Behaviorism is no less riddled by interminable and inconclusive disputes than is introspective psychology. Nevertheless, it has contributed very effectively to the advance of psychology as a biological and an experimental science.

Gestalt psychology. The term "Gestalt psychology" applies primarily to a school of psychology pioneered by Max Wertheimer (1880–1943), Kurt Koffka (1886–1941), and Wolfgang Köhler (born 1887). Their polemic was directed chiefly against the atomism of traditional psychology and of the established order. They opposed the thesis that perceptual experience is to be explained by a bricks and mortar account of the combining of simple sensations. Their positive thesis was that what is experienced is always organized and consists of wholes which are greater than the sum of their parts. Like all revolutionaries, they exaggerated the difference between their own ideology and traditional doctrine. The fact with which they were concerned had preoccupied philosophers and psychologists from the beginnings of systematic thought. Aristotle's formal cause was a Gestalt concept, and Kant had grappled with the problem in his treatment of the categories; Ward and Stout had grappled with it in their accounts of the development of the perception of space, time, thinghood, and causality, and Mill had seen the problem when he wrote about mental chemistry. Christian von Ehrenfels (1859–1932), an Austrian philosophical psychologist, introduced the concept of form qualities. There were also contemporary psychologists—for example, Charles Spearman and Henry J. Watt—who were concerned with the concepts of Gestalt psychology in their own ways.

The outstanding contribution of the Gestalt psychologists was in the number, the variety, and the ingenuity of their experiments. Wertheimer's elegant experiments on the perception of movement were followed by no less elegant experiments by himself, his colleagues, and his disciples on the principles of organization in perceptual experience. In the earlier phases Gestalt psychology was as intellectualist as traditional psychology in its preoccupation with the cognitive experience of the normal adult human mind. Its interest extended, however, to child psychology in the studies by Koffka and to animal psychology in Köhler's studies of insight and learning in apes. Kurt Lewin (1890–1947) used Gestalt concepts in the study of problems of personality and of human motivation. The Gestalt psychologists were distinguished chiefly by their experimental inquiries, but in their writings there are many pronouncements relevant to the philosophy of mind.

The slogan "The whole is more than the sum of its parts" is a near tautology but a useful tautology. The increasing emphasis placed by Köhler and Lewin on field theory (the theory concerning properties of total fields of activity as contrasted to the properties of isolated units) has also contributed to the philosophy of science in its application to psychology.

The concept of isomorphism (the parallelism between phenomenal experience and neural processes) has given a new slant to the discussion of classical theories concerning the relations of body and mind.

The experimental findings of the Gestalt psychologists have been assimilated into empirical psychology. Its evaluation as a philosophy of nature, life, and mind must take into account not only its historical antecedents but also some less well known but important contemporary theories, such as those, for example, of Spearman and Watt.

Alternatives to Gestalt psychology. Charles Spearman (1863–1945) made two significant contributions to the development of psychology in the early decades of the twentieth century. The first was through the development of statistical methods in psychology. Building on the studies of Galton and Karl Pearson, he elaborated his two-factor theory for the analysis of human abilities. His second notable contribution was an attempt to formulate principles of cognition, which he believed to be as basic to psychology as Newton's laws had been basic to physics. It was an ambitious plan in which three noegenetic principles—the apprehension of experience, the eduction of relations, and the eduction of correlates—were set out as necessary and sufficient for the explanation of all the cognitive operations of the human mind. The principles of the eduction of relations had been anticipated by Brown's concept of relative suggestion, but in its detailed elaboration it covered most of the facts of cognitive experience studied by the Gestalt psychologists.

Henry J. Watt (1879–1925) enters the history of psychology through his experimental studies of judgment and the higher thought process at the Würzburg laboratory. After his return to Britain he spent the rest of his life at the University of Glasgow elaborating a comprehensive theory which was finally presented in his *Sensory Basis and Structure of Knowledge* (1925). It is a paradoxical fact that atomism, against which Gestalt psychology was directed, should have received its most precise and systematic formulation by a psychologist preoccupied with precisely the facts that Gestalt psychologists were concerned with. Watt offered an ingenious alternative to Gestalt theory made possible by the sharp distinction he drew between sensationism and associationism, whereas Titchener had treated them as equivalent doctrines. Watt agreed that traditional psychology rested upon two postulates—(1) that the elements of mind are sensations and (2) that the compounds are produced by association. He not only accepted the first postulate, but he also refined it with great subtlety. He rejected the second postulate, replacing it with the doctrine that complex cognitive experiences arise through a distinct process of integration—a concept to which he gave a new definition and which he illustrated in great detail. Watt produced an original account of the facts which had previously been interpreted in terms of Mill's mental chemistry, Wundt's creative synthesis, Spearman's noetic principles of eduction, and the principles of Gestalt psychology.

The Gestalt psychologists captured the headlines in the journals of psychology. For a time Spearman had a band of disciples, although Watt's book did not have a second edition. Spearman and Watt had the misfortune of attracting disciples who could neither advance their theory nor excite impassioned critics. Thus, both have been forgotten. Both, however, may be classed among the mute inglorious Miltons of psychology whose works may yet attract the attention of future historians of science.

The philosophy of nature, life, and mind of both Spearman and Watt were, though different from each other, both in the tradition of dualism. That of the Gestalt psychologists was rather different—a dualism of physics and phenomenology. A residual doubt remains. There would appear to be no empirical procedure for deciding between the doctrines of the Gestalt psychologists, of Spearman, and of Watt. The case may again be one in which a choice must be made on grounds of terminological convenience.

Psychoanalysis and derivative schools. The most important revolt against traditional psychology at the turn of the century was that of Freud and his disciples.

Sigmund Freud created an entirely new psychology—psychoanalysis. This is both a technique of psychotherapy and a body of theory providing a rationale for the technique. The theory developed into an over-all account of nature, life, and mind. Freud's philosophy of nature was a conventional nineteenth-century mechanistic materialism predisposing him to an equally conventional preference for physiological explanations of the mind. Thus, it is even more remarkable that his most distinctive and revolutionary doctrines assumed the form of hypotheses to which mechanism and physiology are completely irrelevant. Central in his system of psychology is the concept of the unconscious. Mind is divided into the conscious, the preconscious, and the unconscious. The conscious is the traditional, familiar, introspectable part of the mind—introspectable thoughts, feelings, and desires. The preconscious consists of all that is out of mind but which can be brought to mind at will or which readily returns to mind in accordance with the accepted laws of association. The unconscious, on the other hand, consists of ideas and wishes, especially wishes, which can be brought into consciousness only by special techniques, of which psychoanalysis is said to be the most fundamental. Freud's originality did not consist in the discovery of the unconscious, for others before him had hit on this notion, but in postulating that the mind worked in accordance with two different types of laws—those of the primary processes, which included unconscious processes, and those of the secondary processes of thought. The first were ruled by the pleasure principle, the second by the reality principle. The laws of the primary processes were principles of emotive congruence appropriate to wishes. Freud's great contribution to psychological theory lay in postulating these laws of primary processes to explain such phenomena as hysteria, dreams, parapraxes, and so on which were previously unexplained and among which no one had previously seen any connection.

There are some superficial resemblances between Freud's and Herbart's psychology, but these are only superficial. In Herbart's system the contents of the unconscious were ideas; in Freud's system they were mainly wishes. Herbart was concerned with the movement of ideas between consciousness and Freud's preconscious. He had no clear conception of the unconscious mind in Freud's sense. Herbart's explanation of the movements of ideas were formulated in terms of quasi-mechanical forces, efficient causes, whereas Freud's explanatory principles were, in effect, formulated in terms of a truncated type of teleological concept, the Freudian wish. Similarly, Freud's defense mechanisms—sublimation, projection, reaction formation, and the like—were quite unmechanical mechanisms. They were goal-directed procedures for protecting the conscious mind against the unwelcome wishes and ideas which had been repressed.

From first to last Freud was concerned with mental conflict, the conflict between opposing motives. At the beginning he emphasized the conflict between primitive instinctive impulses, mainly sexual, and the need to conform to the rules and norms of society. The emphasis later shifted to the conflict between the life and death wishes. At first the world was astounded and shocked by Freud's theories about sex, especially by his account of infantile sexuality. So prominent was sex in his system that a Freudian explanation of any form of behavior came to be generally thought of as an explanation by reference to unconscious sexual desires. His generalized concept of sex was that all pleasure is essentially the pleasure of sexual experience, including the satisfaction of defecation (anal eroticism) and the satisfaction of sucking and feeding (oral eroticism), as well as the satisfaction derived from the genital organs (genital eroticism). This general theory of affective experience makes the thesis of infantile sexuality almost tautological. More significant empirically was the thesis of the universality of the Oedipus complex—the thesis that every male child unconsciously wishes to kill his father and have sexual relations with his mother (female children have an Electra complex—the unconscious wish to replace the mother in her relation to the father). These unconscious desires are obvious sources of the conflicts which issue in neuroses and other forms of aberrant behavior.

In Freud's later writings the emphasis was transferred to the conflict between the life-promoting instincts and the desire for death—Eros and Thanatos. When directed outward, the death wish is a source of violence and destruction; when directed inward, it results in suicidal behavior. The concept of the death wish was, however, further generalized. It covered not only the desire to kill and to be destroyed but also the desire to inflict pain and to suffer pain. Thus the odd phenomena of sadism and masochism are explained. As he often did, Freud attempted to reinforce limited hypotheses by highly general theories. The hypothesis of the death wish was based upon the general

theory that in all the processes of nature there is a tendency for animated matter to revert to an inorganic state. Slightly less generalized was the theory that all responses to stimuli by an organism were directed to the removal of the stimulus and are thus consummated in unconsciousness, in sleep or death. These speculations were disturbing to his disciples, who felt an obligation to defend them, since these ideas were all but demonstrably mistaken and on the face of it inconsistent with Freud's more basic hedonistic account of human motivation. They were not at all essential to his general theory.

To this phase of Freud's speculations belongs the doctrine that the total personality is organized on three levels—the id, the ego, and the superego. The id consists of the totality of primitive instinctive impulses, and the ego contains the conscious motives. The concept of the superego is the most interesting and original feature of this hierarchy. Although it was often described as the primitive unconscious conscience, Freud explained it as an introjected image of the parent which continued to issue commands and to administer punishment when those commands were disobeyed. Not a few of Freud's disciples have treated the superego as the source of conscience as traditionally conceived and believe it is the explanation of action that accords with moral principles. This, however, was not Freud's view. He was himself a man of great integrity with very definite ethical principles. These principles were not derived from his own superego but are to be explained in terms of the distinction between the pleasure principle and the reality principle. Action in accordance with the pleasure principle is directed to immediate pleasure regardless of consequences; action in accordance with the reality principle is directed to maximizing pleasure in the long run. This may be little more than a terminological variation on traditional hedonism, but as is often the case, terminological innovation can contribute to enlightenment.

By 1950 Freudian theory was the dominating influence in psychology. Neither the technique of psychoanalysis nor the supporting theory has received scientific validation, but no theory of human motivation and no form of psychotherapy can ignore the theories and practice of Freud. Freud himself protested that psychoanalysis does not attempt to explain everything, but in the human and social sciences there is hardly a question to which Freudian theory is quite irrelevant. The theory of the unconscious has been advanced and the techniques of analysis developed by such distinguished disciples as his daughter Anna Freud, Melanie Klein (a specialist in the analysis of children), and many others in Europe and the United States. Theory and techniques have also been developed by many disciples and eclectics. Two of Freud's disciples who deviated from his theories—Alfred Adler and Carl Jung—have had very considerable influence.

Alfred Adler (1870–1937) distinguished his system from psychoanalysis by labeling it individual psychology. Before meeting Freud, he had made a special study of the biological phenomena of compensation for defective bodily organs. After his association with Freud he extended his principles to account for all forms of compensation for inferiority, the "inferiority complex." In deviating from Freud, he assigned less importance to unconscious motivation and to sexuality.

Carl Gustav Jung (1875–1961) labeled his system analytical psychology. He differed from Freud in assigning a less important place to sexual motives and in his account of the unconscious. Jung regarded the libido as an undifferentiated "life force" which became differentiated into a number of instincts or drives. In his long life Jung developed a number of important but highly controversial theories. He elaborated the controversial and obscure concept of the collective unconscious and a theory of archetypal ideas (which has been confused by some with the Platonic concept of archetypes). Less controversial were the results of his experimental studies of word association and his suggestions regarding personality types. His wide-ranging speculations covered alchemy, mythology, and the psychology of religion. Students of religion have found in Jung much of what they found absent or uncongenial in the writings of Freud. The opposition between Freudian and Jungian psychology has provided a modern parallel to the classical distinction between the Aristotelians and the Platonists.

Hormic psychology. In the Wundtian system as interpreted by Titchener the elements of mind were sensations and feelings. Conative experience had been eliminated by reductive analysis. Similarly, the concept of conative behavior had no place in Watsonian behaviorism. The concept of conation was not prominent in early Gestalt theory. Before 1950, however, the concept of conative or goal-directed behavior had been restored as a key concept in most systems of psychology. Tolman, the most sophisticated of the self-proclaimed behaviorists, established a new purposive behaviorism, and Lewin steered Gestalt psychology into the study of volitional processes. Throughout, Freudian theory is permeated by the facts of goal-directedness. The most thoroughgoing exponent of a conative psychology was William McDougall.

McDougall (1871–1938) had a medical education but devoted himself to research in physiology, making several significant discoveries. An important early publication was his brief *Physiological Psychology* (1905), which contains the germs of his later theories. His most important publication was his *Introduction to Social Psychology* (1908). This title was unfortunate since the book contains the essentials of his general theory of motivation. Central to this theory was the thesis that there is a limited number of prime movers by whose conative force every train of thought and every bodily activity is initiated and sustained. These prime movers were first described as instincts, but the objections that were raised to its extreme deviation from the traditional biological conception of an instinct led McDougall to redescribe them as propensities. In his detailed elaboration of these "propensities" McDougall developed an account of instinctive behavior originally suggested by William James. Prior to James instinct had been regarded as a biological mechanism producing rigid and stereotyped forms of behavior which were neither learned nor modified by experience. James drew attention to the cognitive emotional and impulsive components in instinctive

action. McDougall developed this idea within the framework of the tripartite analysis of conscious experience which he had learned from Stout. Stressing the extent to which instinctive dispositions are modified both on the cognitive (receptive) side and on the conative (responsive) side, he suggested that the primary instincts are to be defined by reference to the central or affective components, the "primary emotions." He went on to describe the ways in which instinctive dispositions are modified and the ways in which they are organized into more complex motivating dispositions, the sentiments. A sentiment was conceived of as a system of instinctive disposition organized around an idea. Patriotism, for example, is a complex organization of instincts directed to promoting the welfare of a national group. McDougall's account of the structure of human personality was similar to that first set out in the famous sermons of Bishop Butler on human nature (1726). With McDougall, as with Butler, the motivating forces in man are organized in a three-tiered hierarchy. At the base are the primary instincts or propensities. At the second level in Butler's system were certain regulating and controlling principles, such as benevolence and cool self-love, and at the summit was the ultimate controlling principle, which was identified with conscience.

In McDougall's system the basic instincts are organized into and controlled by the sentiments, which function in a similar way to Butler's principles of benevolence and cool self-love. Thus, the parental sentiment is an organization of the maternal instinct together with other instincts, and in McDougall's view it explains all disinterested altruism. The self-regarding sentiment is an organization of the instincts of self-assertion together with others which exercise a similar control over primitive aggressive instincts. It functions in McDougall's theory in a way similar to Butler's cool self-love and Freud's reality principle. At the head of the hierarchy in McDougall's system as the supreme controlling force is a master sentiment which is an elaborated form of the sentiment of self-regard.

Both Butler's and McDougall's accounts of the structure of human personality, of human motivation, and of the basis of volition or self-control have important similarities with, but also important differences from, Freud's hierarchy of id, ego, and superego. Butler's analysis had greater philosophical subtlety than McDougall's, but McDougall's was developed in much greater detail. The central theses were contained in *Social Psychology*. The details were further elaborated in his later works, such as the *Outline of Psychology* (1923) and the *Outline of Abnormal Psychology* (1926). McDougall was himself surprised, as well as gratified, by the outstanding success of his *Introduction to Social Psychology*. He was to be surprised and disappointed by the reception of what he intended to be his magnum opus, *Body and Mind: A History and Defense of Animism* (1911). This contained a critical review of the traditional theories of the relations of body and mind in which he eventually decided in favor of interactionism. His general philosophy of nature, life, and mind was that of an orthodox dualist and interactionist. This was later developed into a Leibnizian monadology. The personality of man was conceived as a hierarchy of monads. Every monad is potentially a thinking, striving self, but each differs in degrees of development. At the head of the hierarchy is the supreme monad—the self, which is in command of, and directly or indirectly in communication with, all subordinate monads. The mode of communication was conceived to be telepathic.

McDougall was one of the last of the academic psychologists to attempt a comprehensive system covering all the facts of cognition, feeling, and conation as well as the facts of unconscious motivation. His theories, however, fell out of favor, though not entirely because of specific objections to them. They were outmoded by current trends in both psychology and philosophy. Nevertheless, he exercised a considerable influence on thought and research in motivation theory, not least upon those who differed from him, and he contributed to the reunification of psychology and the biological sciences, which had been separated since Aristotle's day. Indeed, it could be argued that McDougall, like Aristotle, saw that the concept of purpose was both logically irreducible to mechanistic concepts and fundamental for the explanation of human behavior. His mistake was to translate this eminently defensible conceptual doctrine into a genetic doctrine about the origins of behavior. The two do not necessarily go together, for the doctrine that human behavior cannot be explained without recourse to a concept like purpose does not entail the genetic doctrine that men must come into the world equipped with a myriad of built-in purposes.

Reaction against reactions. The proliferation of schools continued into the 1930s. Carl Murchison's *Psychologies of 1925* was followed by his *Psychologies of 1930,* and at the time no end to such quinquennial volumes could be foreseen. Psychologists, however, began to tire of these battles among the schools, each of which was in revolt against the established order and at war with the others in revolt. There came a revolt against revolt, a reaction against reactions. Robert S. Woodworth (1869–1962), who had written the most influential critical commentary on the schools, *Contemporary Schools of Psychology* (1931), was a leading advocate of a middle-of-the-road psychology. Teaching and practicing psychologists tended to be eclectic; many leaned heavily on one or another of the schools, and only a few remained uncommitted.

Schools were then replaced by "approaches," a term which suggests convergence rather than divergence. Approaches, like viewpoints, are complementary. The new situation favored the emergence of groups of psychologists united in discipleship to a single dominating personality. These groups differed from the schools in that a school was created by several outstanding personalities who, though agreeing on certain basic theses, made individual contributions to the system of psychology defended by the school. There have always been groups of the simpler leader-and-disciples type. Before the age of the schools there were philosophical psychologists with their disciples—for example, Brentano and Meinong on the Continent, Ward and Stout in Great Britain, James in the United States. In the schools themselves there were subgroups composed of a man and his disciples—the Freudians, the Jungians, the Pavlovians, and so on. After the dissolution of the schools new personalities emerged, each with an individual approach or field of specialization; there were psychologists like Jean Piaget at Geneva, Albert Michotte at Louvain, and E. C. Tolman and many others in the United States.

Relation to philosophy. The history of psychology in the twentieth century is a story of the divorce and remarriage of psychology and philosophy. The trouble began when psychologists claimed the status of empirical scientists. At first the philosophers were the more aggressive, deriding the young science as a bogus discipline. The psychologists hit back and made contemptuous remarks about philosophical logic-chopping and armchair psychology. The arguments were charged with emotion, and neither side emerged with great credit. Slowly, some progress was made toward a diagnosis of the situation, a diagnosis which may well provide the basis for a happy reconciliation.

Psychology has always been, and may well always remain, a parasitic discipline. For twenty centuries it was just a branch of philosophy. To gain emancipation, it entered into willing bondage to the established natural sciences. Increasingly it has claimed to be, and has been increasingly accepted as, a biological science. Aristotle's psychology had a biological orientation, and theories of the temperaments have always had a physiological slant. Since Darwin psychologists have attempted to work down to the biological foundations of mental life, and biologists have extended their field of interest upward to include the more complex functions of organisms traditionally described as mental—perception, learning, problem solving. In the twentieth century psychologists and biologists have found a common approach, frame of reference, and interest in such new special studies as ethology, cybernetics, and information theory and a common lack of interest or only a peripheral interest in problems of the philosophy of mind. There have, however, been other developments which have helped to resolve the conflicts between philosophers and psychologists and to clarify the lines of demarcation between work that can properly be done in an armchair and work that must be done on a laboratory stool, in a bird watcher's blind, or behind a one-way screen.

The behaviorists, in their revolt against Titchener's introspectionism, had taken over quite uncritically Titchener's greatest error. Hegel had attempted to answer questions of empirical fact by a priori reasoning. Titchener made the opposite mistake, supposing that questions of philosophical analysis could be settled by observations made in a laboratory. His mistake is on record; he recalled that in 1888, when first reading James Mill's *Analysis of the Human Mind,* the conviction flashed upon him, "You can test all this for yourself." He thought he could test it by introspection. The *Analysis* of James Mill was an exercise in philosophical analysis which can be carried out in a soft armchair, perhaps more efficiently there than on a hard laboratory stool. The behaviorists also fell victim to the same error in confusing introspection and philosophical analysis, in failing to see that questions of analysis arise not only in regard to introspective reports but also in regard to behavioral concepts—stimulus, response, and behavior itself.

However, behaviorists and other biologically minded psychologists were little disposed to either philosophical speculation or philosophical analysis. They were content, like most biologists, to think of the world, regardless of consistency, *both* in terms of common-sense realism and in terms of the billiard-ball atomism of nineteenth-century physics, thereby following the physicists whenever they revised their theories. Those who had some interest in philosophy followed the prevailing trend in philosophy to some form of phenomenalism.

Reduction of mental concepts. There had been three centuries of philosophical thinking devoted to the elimination of superfluous psychological concepts. At first a mind was thought of as an immaterial substance which, like a material substance, persists through changing states. As a rod of iron passes through states of being hard and soft or black, red, and white in accordance with changes of temperature, so a mind passes through states of joy, sorrow, and so on in accordance with the success and failure of its endeavors. Descartes had described all modes of consciousness as states of the soul, some of which appear to be states of external bodies, others of which appear to be states of the body in which the soul is embodied, and others which really are, as they appear to be, states of the soul itself. In his new way of ideas Locke redescribed experience in terms of the soul, self, or ego being presented with and attending to objects in the mind which chiefly represent things in the external world. Berkeley pointed out, cogently, that there is no way of comparing these representative ideas with the things they are supposed to represent. There were, he suggested, no reasons for, and there were reasons against, supposing that there are material things to be represented. Exit the material world. Then came Hume, who gave an important negative introspective report. He could not observe this soul, self, or ego to which presentations were said to be presented. Exit the soul.

For a long time attempts were made to defend what Titchener described as an act and content psychology—the doctrine that mind consists in mental contents and acts of willing and attending concerned with these contents (without, however, anyone to perform these acts). Late in the nineteenth century Brentano argued that these acts or attitudes are what is distinctive of mind. G. E. Moore based his refutation of idealism on this thesis by distinguishing in sensation the sensing, which alone is distinctively mental, from the sense datum sensed. But, like Hume, he made another negative introspective report—that the act is diaphanous, unintrospectable. Exit the act, the last claimant to mentality.

This reduction and elimination acquired a temporary finality in Russell's neutral monism. Influenced by Moore, Mach, and William James, he proposed the over-all theory that the stuff of which the universe is composed is neutral, not mental or physical. Organized in one way, it issues in the laws of physics; organized in another way, it results in the laws of psychology. Combining these, we have an account of nature. In this long reductive process man first had lost his soul, then his mind, then his consciousness, and finally even his body, which was reduced to a permanent possibility of neutralized sensations.

Linguistic approach. The finality of this form of phenomenalism was short-lived. The conception of philosophy

as an inquiry into the ultimate nature of reality was supplanted by the idea that philosophy is the critical analysis of the concepts of science and of common sense. This was in turn replaced by the idea of philosophy as the study of linguistic usages. Instead of asking what mind is, philosophers set out to disentangle the various uses of the word "mental," and they became interested in the depth psychologists' uses of new words and of old words in new senses. Philosophers and psychologists began to find a new basis for collaboration. The philosophers clarified concepts; the psychologists attempted to verify by laboratory procedures the hypotheses stated in these concepts.

Not all issues between philosophers and psychologists have been resolved, but there has been notable progress toward a policy of coexistence, and here and there some progress toward cooperation has been made.

(See also ANIMAL SOUL; APPERCEPTION; BEHAVIORISM; CONSCIOUSNESS; CYBERNETICS; DREAMS; EMOTION AND FEELING; EXISTENTIAL PSYCHOANALYSIS; EXPERIENCE; GESTALT THEORY; GUILT; HAPPINESS; HEAT, SENSATIONS OF; HUMOR; IMAGES; IMAGINATION; INTENTION; INTUITION; MEMORY; MIND–BODY PROBLEM; MOTIVES AND MOTIVATION; PERCEPTION; PHILOSOPHY OF EDUCATION, INFLUENCE OF MODERN PSYCHOLOGY ON; PLEASURE; PSYCHOANALYTIC THEORIES, LOGICAL STATUS OF; PSYCHOLOGICAL BEHAVIORISM; RELIGION, PSYCHOLOGICAL EXPLANATIONS OF; SOUND; THINKING; TIME, CONSCIOUSNESS OF; TOUCH; UNCONSCIOUS; UNCONSCIOUS, PSYCHOANALYTIC THEORIES OF THE; VISION; and VOLITION. See Psychology in Index for articles on psychologists.)

Bibliography

Boring, E. G., *Sensation and Perception in the History of Experimental Psychology.* New York, 1942.

Boring, E. G., *A History of Experimental Psychology*, 2d ed. New York, 1950.

Boring, E. G., et al., *History, Psychology, and Science: Selected Papers.* New York, 1963.

Flügel, J. C., *A Hundred Years of Psychology, 1833–1963.* London, 1933; enl. ed., New York, 1964. The enlarged edition has an additional part, by Donald J. West, on the period from 1933 to 1963.

Hamlyn, D. W., *Sensation and Perception.* London, 1962.

Hearnshaw, L. S., *Short History of British Psychology, 1840–1940.* London and New York, 1964.

Murphy, Gardner, *Historical Introduction to Modern Psychology,* rev. ed. New York, 1949.

Peters, R. S., ed., *Brett's History of Psychology*, rev. ed. London and New York, 1962. Consult pp. 769–772 for a bibliography of all major texts in the history of psychology. This work is an abridgment and updating of G. S. Brett's three-volume *History of Psychology* (London, 1912) and is the only complete history of psychology.

R. S. PETERS
C. A. MACE

PSYCHOLOGY, GESTALT. See GESTALT THEORY.

PSYCHOLOGY AND EDUCATION. See PHILOSOPHY OF EDUCATION, INFLUENCE OF MODERN PSYCHOLOGY ON.

PUFENDORF, SAMUEL VON (1632–1694), German political and legal philosopher and historian, was born in Dorfchemnitz, in Meissen, Saxony, the son of a poor Lutheran pastor. A scholarship enabled Pufendorf to attend the famous Prince's School at Grimma. From 1650 to 1656 he attended lectures on Lutheran theology and Aristotelian philosophy at Leipzig. Somewhat later he studied contemporary philosophy at Jena, where he also read newly published books on mathematics and discovered the works of Hugo Grotius and Thomas Hobbes. At Jena he came in contact with Erhard Weigel, a former teacher of Leibniz, whose strange but original method of teaching ethics "mathematically" made a lasting impression upon Pufendorf. To Weigel, Pufendorf owed the inspiration for his first work on the general principles of law, *Elementorum Jurisprudentiae Universalis*. In 1658 Pufendorf became a tutor in the house of the Swedish ambassador to Denmark. When war broke out between Sweden and Denmark, Pufendorf was imprisoned for eight months, and it was during this imprisonment that he composed the booklet inspired by Weigel. Upon his release Pufendorf migrated in 1659 to the Netherlands, where the work was published in 1660.

On the recommendation of Grotius' elder son, Pufendorf was offered the chair of natural and international law at Heidelberg, the first such chair at a German university. He was soon appointed also as instructor of the heir to the crown of the Palatinate, and thus he began to mix with the electoral court, where he avidly studied the burning contemporary political problems. Out of this study came a pseudonymous work on the condition of the Holy Roman Empire, *De Statu Imperii Germanici* (1667), a work later famous for its statement that the constitution of the Empire resembles a monster, being neither a monarchy nor an aristocracy nor a democracy.

After his appointment as professor of natural law at the University of Lund in Sweden, Pufendorf wrote his fundamental work on national and international law, *De Jure Naturae et Gentium* (1672). The eight volumes of this compendium, which contains a veritable encyclopedia of the social sciences, are rather difficult reading. Pufendorf therefore produced an abstract of this work, entitled *De Officio Hominis et Civis* (1673), which was soon translated into English, French, and German and thus found many readers abroad. By 1684 a Swiss Calvinist theologian was lecturing on the *De Officio Hominis* at Lausanne, but Lutheran theologians in both Sweden and Germany criticized Pufendorf's ideas vehemently. The king of Sweden himself had to protect his professor of law and induce the authorities of the university to defend Pufendorf against the charge of heresy. Pufendorf replied bitterly to the charge, and a long paper war ensued. Finally, Pufendorf published a "sanguinary" (his own description) polemical treatise entitled *Eris Scandica* (Frankfurt, 1686), containing all his essays and letters relating to the controversy.

In 1677 Pufendorf was appointed by the king as court historian in Stockholm, where he spent ten years working on his extensive, 33-volume history of Sweden, a work of no importance today except as an example of careful work and precise reporting. His shorter *Einleitung zu der Historie der vornehmster Reiche und Staaten* (2 vols., Frankfurt, 1682–1685) is more highly esteemed.

From 1688 until his death shortly after having been knighted by his former sovereign, the king of Sweden,

Pufendorf lived in Berlin, where he had been called as court historian by the elector of Brandenburg.

A noted representative of the Baroque era, Pufendorf was a man of great self-confidence and stolid self-reliance. He had unshakable faith in the power of scientific reason and wished to establish it in the fields of jurisprudence and politics. He believed in the certainty of mathematics and rejoiced in the reunion of philosophy and mathematics then taking place. Although he wished to treat the problematic questions of jurisprudence and politics "mathematically," he was a true empiricist who sought to introduce a "scientific" method into the study of history. He was therefore eager to undertake the thoroughly planned research into public archives that resulted in his history of Sweden.

Pufendorf thus united the two major trends of his age, Baconian empiricism and Cartesian logicism. One of the last polyhistors, he united in his work all the methods of historical, sociological, and juridical thinking. A political figure rather than simply a lawyer, Pufendorf profoundly criticized the constitution of the Holy Roman Empire and its political conception. He argued for the founding of a European federation of sovereign states. He did not defend national or regional absolutism, however popular they were at the time; instead, he tried to unite the Hobbesian doctrine that the state should be governed by the rule of law and based on natural law in the empirical sense of the term (the war of all against all, *status necessitatis*) with the Grotian doctrine that the rule of international law should be based on natural law in an emotional sense (an inclination for society, *ordo amoris*). On this account Pufendorf has often been called a predecessor of eighteenth-century rationalism. Such a view is supported by his letter to his younger friend Christian Thomasius, in which he claimed that he "never had boldness enough to draw the utmost conclusions" from his philosophical rationalism and voluntarism.

Despite Leibniz' opinion that Pufendorf was "a man of no great judgment," his legal thought was of considerable importance and great philosophical interest. He was undoubtedly one of the most outstanding social philosophers on the European continent in the seventeenth century. It may be an exaggeration to call Pufendorf the first "philosopher of culture" (*Kulturphilosoph*) in Germany, but he was the first to grasp the fundamental concept of the sociological theory of law and politics. He saw the social realities of human life as a whole. His structural distinction between physical facts and moral institutions inspired a new way of studying social facts in their independence and uniqueness. Following Erhard Weigel, Pufendorf distinguished four elements of social being: personality (*persona*), rank or profession (*status*), quality, and quantity. Every pattern of social order should be examined on the basis of these fundamental structures; for example, a state may be described in terms of its sovereignty, type of government, power, and population.

These elements, the ontological foundations of every community, have simultaneously to be interpreted as fundamental ethical principles of social life. Pufendorf designated three patterns of well-formed communities: humanity, ordered by the law of reason; Christianity, ordered by the law of God; and citizenship, ordered by the law of the state. Natural law, including religious and rational principles, therefore limits both civic and moral duties. Philosophy of law comprises both sociology and political science on the one hand, and jurisprudence and ethics on the other. This new discipline, which Pufendorf called simply natural law, was intended to unite all the tasks of interpreting social order and to combine the scholastic methods of the sixteenth-century Spanish thinkers with the newer ideas of Grotius and Hobbes.

In apparent contradiction to these sources of his thought on social order was Pufendorf's strong belief in reason of state (*ratio status*). Although he often emphasized the self-determination and self-sufficiency of the state, he did not mean by this a totalitarian absolutism. And although he proclaimed the independence of political power against every ecclesiastical claim, he never taught the modern ideology of unlimited government, and his views were therefore not contradictory to the rule of law. What Pufendorf said about the relation of church and state must be interpreted dialectically. He conceded neither decisive authority to reason of state nor the right of moral constraint to the church.

Pufendorf may be called the initiator of the seventeenth-century movement of "scientific" natural law in Germany. By introducing the ideas of Grotius and Hobbes into German thought he made their ideas really effective for the first time. He liberated the natural-law theory from the domination of scholasticism and humanism. In so doing he built up an independent political science that always took into account contemporary history and reason of state. A clever and level-headed politician, he predicted the decline of the Hapsburg monarchy after the Treaty of Westphalia. In criticizing the "monstrous" constitution of the empire he sought to advance a European commonwealth based on the natural and rational principles of international law. As a historian, Pufendorf introduced the empirical study of archives and gave an effective example of a new method of historical insight, and he may be regarded as an important predecessor of nineteenth-century historicism.

Works by Pufendorf

Elementorum Jurisprudentiae Universalis Libri Duo. The Hague, 1660.
De Statu Imperii Germanici ad Laelium Fratrem, Dominum Trezolani, Liber Unus. Geneva, 1667.
De Jure Naturae et Gentium Libri Octo. Lund, Sweden, 1672. Translated by Basil Kennett as *Of the Law of Nature and Nations.* London, 1710.
De Officio Hominis et Civis Prout Ipsi Praescribuntur Lege Naturali. Libri Duo. Lund, Sweden, 1673. Reprinted with translation by F. G. Moore, 2 vols. Oxford, 1927.
De Habitu Religionis Christianae ad Vitam Civilem. Bremen, 1687. Translated as *Of the relation between Church and State.* London, 1719.

Works on Pufendorf

Krieger, Leonard, *The Politics of Discretion: Pufendorf and the Acceptance of Natural Law.* Chicago, 1965.
Scheuner, Ulrich, "Samuel Freiherr von Pufendorf," in *Die Grossen Deutschen,* Vol. V. Berlin, 1957. Pp. 126 ff.
Welzel, Hans, *Die Naturrechtslehre Samuel Pufendorfs.* Berlin, 1958.

Wolf, Erik, *Grosse Rechtsdenker der deutschen Geistesgeschichte,* 4th ed. Tübingen, 1963. Pp. 311–366. Bibliography on pp. 367–370.

ERIK WOLF

PUNISHMENT. The word "punishment" is used in varying contexts. The punishment meted out by the state to a criminal or by a parent to his children is not the same as the punishment boxers give or receive. The latter, however, is punishment only in a metaphorical sense, for it lacks several of the features necessary to a standard case of punishment. Characteristically, punishment is unpleasant. It is inflicted on an offender because of an offense he has committed; it is deliberately imposed, not just the natural consequence of a person's action (like a hang-over), and the unpleasantness is essential to it, not an accidental accompaniment to some other treatment (like the pain of the dentist's drill). It is imposed by an agent authorized by the system of rules against which an offense has been committed; a lynching is not a standard case of punishment. Philosophers who have written on punishment have usually had in mind punishment in the standard sense rather than in any extended or metaphorical sense.

The philosopher's interest in punishment is mainly connected with questions of justification. It is, prima facie, wrong to deliberately inflict suffering or deprivation on another person, yet punishment consists in doing precisely this. What conditions, the philosopher asks, would justify it? Or, more generally, what kind of consideration would count toward a justification? For instance, if a person had already committed a crime, that would clearly be relevant to the question of whether he ought to be punished (although it might not be conclusive). What if he were only expected to commit a crime in the future? Or, again, is it relevant to the question of whether this man should be punished to say that punishing him would deter others? And assuming that criminals ought to be punished, how should we set about deciding appropriate penalties?

It is not, of course, the business of the moral or social philosopher to provide a justification for any particular act or system of punishment or even of the institution of punishment in general. Philosophers are not necessarily apologists for their society and age. They are interested in the procedures and modes of argument that we are committed to by our fundamental conceptions of morality and in criteria of criticism and justification rather than in inquiries into whether actual institutions satisfy them.

Philosophers, it is true, have not always made this distinction; they have often worked on the understanding that a philosophical argument could be seriously shaken by showing that it leads to conclusions inconsistent with some widely approved institution or moral rule. Moreover, for many philosophers, if such a rule or institution seemed to imply a principle inconsistent with other moral principles accepted by the society, there must necessarily be some broader principle, which a philosopher could discover and by which the conflict could be resolved. Applied to the case of punishment, this would mean that a philosopher must reconcile the apparently conflicting principles that wrongdoers should be punished and that it is wrong to deliberately make another man suffer. But this is surely a misconception of the nature of philosophy. There is no point, after all, in asking whether and and how punishment can be justified if one assumed in advance that it can. For justification a number of contingent facts are required that the philosopher as such is not qualified to provide. His task is to analyze what is being asked for and so to point out what kinds of facts and arguments are admissible to the discussion.

JUSTIFICATION OF PUNISHMENT

The question of justification arises at two levels. One can take for granted the principle that wrongdoers should be punished and ask whether a particular case of punishment was justified. At this level the philosopher is concerned with the criteria in a general system which any particular act of punishment must satisfy. One can, however, question the very idea of punishment as an institution which involves deliberately inflicting pain or deprivation. This raises the philosophical question of how one justifies a set of rules or an institution like a penal system. Corresponding to these two levels of justification are two broadly opposed approaches to punishment, the retributivist and the utilitarian. Each, in fact, has been taken to offer an answer to the problems at both levels, but the persuasive force of retributivism is mainly in its answers to problems of the first type, and of utilitarianism to questions of the second type. Characteristically, the retributivist stresses guilt and desert, looking back to the crime to justify punishment and denying that the consequences of punishment, beneficial or otherwise, have any relevance to justification. The utilitarian, on the other hand, insists that punishment can be justified only if it has beneficent consequences that outweigh the intrinsic evil of inflicting suffering on human beings.

Retributivist theories. The most thoroughgoing retributivists, exemplified by Kant, maintain that the punishment of crime is right in itself, that it is fitting that the guilty should suffer, and that justice, or the moral order, requires the institution of punishment. This, however, is not to justify punishment but, rather, to deny that it needs any justification. To say that something is right or good in itself means that it does not need to be justified in terms of the value or rightness of anything else. Its intrinsic value is appreciated immediately or intuitively. But since at least some people do doubt that punishment is right, an appeal to intuition is necessarily unsatisfactory. Again, to say "it is fitting" or "justice demands" that the guilty should suffer is only to reaffirm that punishment is right, not to give grounds for thinking so.

Some retributivists, while admitting that punishment is, prima facie, evil, maintain that it is nevertheless better that the wicked should be punished than that they should prosper more than the virtuous and, perhaps, at their expense. In this view, the function of criminal law is to punish wickedness or immorality in order to maintain a kind of cosmic distributive justice. However, it is not self-evident that wickedness should be punished any more than it is self-evident that legal guilt should be. Archbishop Temple, himself a retributivist, declared that he had no "intuition that it is good that the wicked should suffer." Nor is it clear that virtue must be rewarded or that universal justice re-

quires the kind of human rectification that this sort of retributivism envisages. Of course, in a universe in which the wicked prospered, there might be no incentive to virtue, but this is essentially a utilitarian mode of argument. Again, evil motives and a bad character are necessary conditions of wickedness but not of legal guilt and criminal liability. The state's function is to punish breaches of those rules which in the public interest ought to be upheld; it is a matter of indifference in law (but not in morals) that some men who observe the rules do so from the unworthy motive of fear and others break them from laudable motives of principle. Conversely, it is at least doubtful whether the criminal law should provide penalties for offenses against morality except where the public interest is at stake—e.g., whether it should extend to cases of lying other than, say, false pretenses and perjury.

Though immorality is neither a necessary nor a sufficient condition for punishment, the relation between law and morals is nevertheless a close one, and what punishment is to the one, blame is to the other. Both regulate social intercourse, and in any given society the aims and ideals upheld by the law will usually correspond, more or less, with those upheld by the dominant morality. Moreover, in the family and the school punishment is often used to reinforce moral condemnation as part of the process of moral education. Some writers who regard punishment as moral retribution couple this idea with the argument that the point of punishment is to be found in what Lord Justice Denning has called "the emphatic denunciation by the community of a crime." In this view, punishment reinforces the community's respect for its legal and moral standards, which criminal acts would tend to undermine if they were not solemnly denounced. There is, however, no intrinsic reason why denunciation should take precisely the form of inflicting suffering on criminals, unless, perhaps, one accepts Ewing's view that punishment has the advantage of impressing both on the criminal and on everyone else that a breach of law and morals is so serious that society must do something to prevent it. That, however, is surely to justify punishment by its utility in maintaining respect for the law. Rashdall refers to "the enormous importance of the criminal law in promoting the moral education of the public mind," but Rashdall was a utilitarian who justified punishment by reference to "the production of good effects on conscious beings."

For Hegel punishment is necessary to annul the wrong done by the criminal. By this he means something more than restitution or compensation, neither of which is, strictly speaking, punishment. It is, rather, that the criminal has upset the balance of the moral order, which can be restored only by his being made to suffer. Or, in terms of the dialectic, crime is a negation of right and as such a nullity; punishment negates the negation, thus reaffirming the right. But in what sense can punishment be said to restore the balance or annul the wrong, unless it is taken for granted that criminals deserve to be punished? This is precisely the point in question.

Utilitarian theories. The utilitarian position is exemplified in Bentham's remark that "all punishment is a mischief. . . . If it ought at all to be admitted, it ought only to be admitted in as far as it promises to exclude some greater evil." By reforming the criminal, by deterring him or others from similar offenses in the future, or by directly preventing further offenses by imprisonment, deportation, or execution, the good that comes out of punishment may outweigh (so the utilitarian argues) the intrinsic evil of suffering deliberately inflicted. Without such effects, or if the suffering inflicted exceeded the suffering avoided, the institution would be unjustified.

The critics of utilitarianism claim that if people generally could be persuaded that an innocent man was guilty, utilitarianism would justify punishing him since as a warning to others he would be just as useful as a genuine offender. Again, offenders might be deterred by threatening to punish their wives and children, particularly, if as is so often the case with political terrorists and resistance fighters, it were difficult to catch the offenders themselves. Or, again, if punishment could be justified as a way of reforming criminals, it would seem better to punish them before, rather than after, they committed their crimes. Retributivists claim that utilitarians are in danger of losing sight of two conditions which are necessary to the very idea of punishment—namely, that an offense should have been committed and that punishment shall be of the offender himself, who alone can be said to deserve it. "Punishment is punishment," wrote F. H. Bradley, "only when it is deserved"; punishment for any other reason is "a crying injustice."

The dilemma of utilitarianism, then, at least in its crude form, is that it justifies punishing innocent people provided that such punishment causes less suffering than might otherwise be caused by the would-be criminals it deters. Some utilitarians argue that in the end the deception would break down, that it could not be used systematically, or that the long-term consequences would be bad for society. But these answers are unsatisfactory because they depend on assumptions of purely contingent consequences. Our revulsion against punishing innocent men seems to go deeper than that. In any case, these answers will not meet the case for punishing hostages, which can certainly be done systematically and requires no deception or secrecy.

Punishment and principles of justice. To meet the above criticisms, a crude utilitarianism would have to be supplemented by other moral principles—namely, that differences in treatment must be justified by relevant differences in circumstance or condition, where "relevance" is defined in the light of general rules, and that every human being should be treated with at least a minimum of respect as a source of claims and not as a mere instrument for the promotion of the interests of others. It can be argued that punishment of the innocent or of hostages is an abuse not because it necessarily makes for more unhappiness than it prevents but because it treats innocent men in a way that is appropriate only for the guilty and makes an arbitrary difference in treatment between them and other innocent men. Moreover, a legal system is designed to guide conduct by laying down rules and attaching penalties to those who choose to break them. It is acceptable, in the words of J. D. Mabbott, only because "the criminal makes the essential choice; he 'brings it on himself.'" Otherwise, punishment would not be consistent with the principle of respect for persons. The hostage, on the other hand, has no chance to settle his own fate; he is used as a mere lever for manipulating other people's conduct, and his own interest is subordinate to that of the other members of society. Punishment of the innocent ignores, in short, fundamental procedural rules of justice and morality without which utilitarianism would make little sense, for unless everyone is worthy of equal consideration as a source of claims, whose interest is to count in assessing the utility of a course of action? Whom are we entitled to treat as simply a tool for advancing other men's interests—as Aristotle's "slave by nature"—and what would count as a reason for considering other men before him?

This has bearing, too, on the reasons for accepting as excuses such defenses as duress, unavoidable accident, or ignorance of fact—conditions under which an offender can claim that he could not help doing what he did. Bentham argued that to punish anyone under such conditions would be pointless and, therefore, mischievous, because the threat of penalties could not possibly deter anyone in the future who was similarly placed. Now, it is true that nothing would be lost if such people escaped punishment, provided they could be distinguished from cheats trying to take advantage of such excuses and provided enough offenders without such excuses could be detected to furnish examples for others. The principle of "strict liability," which exists in some legal systems for certain offenses, has been defended on the utilitarian ground that it is impossible to tell a genuine excuse from a pretense. It is questionable, however, whether a person who would otherwise be treated as innocent ought to be treated as guilty because someone else might otherwise escape a merited penalty. Punishing the man who commits an offense through ignorance or accident, because it is too difficult to tell whether he really did it on purpose or because we have to make an example of *someone,* is very like punishing the innocent as a warning to the guilty. The utilitarian case for these excuses is unsatisfactory inasmuch as it makes them subject to such qualifications.

A better ground for such excuses is that punishment is morally acceptable only if it is the consequence of an act freely chosen by the criminal, which it would not be under these conditions. A man acting in ignorance or by accident cannot be said to bring his punishment on himself. Punishment, seen as a way of influencing conduct, cannot be justified if there has been no real possibility of choice. Moreover, the punishment of involuntary offenses introduces into men's lives the possibility of disasters which they can neither foresee nor avert.

Utilitarianism, then, must be supplemented by principles of justice if it is not to clash with other moral principles that are usually considered fundamental. It has, however, the merit, as an approach to the justification of punishment, that it provides a clear procedure for determining whether the institution is acceptable in general terms. This the retributivist approach cannot do because it denies the relevance of weighing advantages and disadvantages, which is what we ultimately must do in moral criticism of rules and institutions. Consequently, a retributivist justification of punishment as an institution usually turns out to be a denial of the necessity for justification, a veiled reference to the beneficial results of punishment (a utilitarianism in disguise), or an appeal to religious authority.

When it is a question of justifying a particular case of

punishment, however, the retributivist is in a far stronger position. There would be no point in having a general rule if on every occasion that it had to be applied one had to consider whether the advantages in this particular case warranted acting in accordance with it. Moreover, the point of punishment as deterrent would be quite lost were there no general expectation, based on the general operation of the rule, that guilty men would be punished. Assuming, then, that a penal system can be justified in utilitarian terms, any offense is at least prima facie an occasion for a penalty. Equally, without an offense there is no question of a penalty. The retributivist contention that punishment is justified if, and only if, it is deserved is really applicable, therefore, to the justification of particular instances of punishment, the institution as such being taken for granted.

SEVERITY OF PUNISHMENT

The clash between the utilitarian and retributivist approaches to punishment also arises in considering the criteria by which appropriate punishments are assessed. The retributivist insists that the punishment must fit the crime; the utilitarian relates the penalty to the general aims of the system, to the prevention of further crime, and, perhaps, to the reform of the criminal.

The most extreme form of retributivism is the law of retaliation: "an eye for an eye." This alone, Kant claimed, could provide a just measure of the penalty, since it was the crime itself and nothing else that settled it. However, to try to apply it literally might be monstrously cruel, or, as Kant recognized, it might be absurd. Thieves can be deprived of their property and murderers hanged, but what penalty is appropriate to the dope-peddler, the black-mailer, and the smuggler?

There is not much sense, either, in trying to construct a table of equivalents so that the amount of suffering inflicted by the criminal could be meted out to him in some other form. How can such a table be drawn up? How many years must a blackmailer spend in jail to experience suffering equal to his victim's? Is it possible, in any case, to make comparisons of suffering between persons? Of course, we do assess the gravity of an offense and try to ensure that the punishment for a trivial offense is less severe than for a serious one. But this is possible only because we take for granted an existing scale of penalties and grade new offenses accordingly. Such grading does not imply an intrinsic relation between the crime and the penalty apart from that established by the scale. Some retributivists admit this but claim nevertheless that the penalties prescribed by the law ought to reflect the moral heinousness of the offense. The most serious offenses against morals deserve the most severe penalties. This, however, only shifts the question a step back, for what makes one moral offense more serious than another?

Utilitarians have tended to concentrate on deterrence, turning away from the actual criminal act except as one of a class of actions that might be prevented by punishing the particular instance severely enough (but only just enough) to make the action unattractive to the offender and to possible future offenders. Unfortunately, there are always people who cannot be deterred or reformed. Beyond a

certain point the additional suffering one would have to inflict on all offenders to reduce their number might be so great as to exceed the amount of suffering thereby averted. The aim of the utilitarian, then, would presumably be to select the penalty at which the aggregate of suffering caused by crimes actually committed and punishments actually inflicted would be the smallest possible.

The utilitarian approach has often been criticized as justifying severe penalties for trivial offenses and vice versa. To eliminate parking offenses might need heavier penalties then to eliminate blackmail, which would be monstrous. But this criticism misses the point of the utilitarian case. There would, indeed, be no objection to threatening the severest penalty for any offense providing the threat never had to be carried out. Punishment is only an unfortunate consequence of the fact that the threats, which are the true operative elements in the system, are partially ineffective and would be wholly ineffective if they were not carried out when they failed to deter. In fixing penalties, the utilitarian's problem is not, therefore, to minimize the number of offenses, irrespective of the punishment inflicted, but to minimize the total amount of suffering from both sources. If we call parking offenses trivial, we mean that each one causes relatively little suffering; therefore, we are prepared to put up with a large number of them rather than incur the cost of making offenders suffer heavy penalties. Blackmail, on the other hand, causes so much suffering that if heavier penalties would yield even a small reduction in the number of offenses, there might be a net gain even though offenders would suffer more than they did before. In this way a utilitarian might agree with the retributivist that severe penalties ought to be restricted to serious offenses, but he would argue that we call an offense serious precisely because it causes a great deal of suffering. For the retributivist only serious crimes *deserve* severe penalties; for the utilitarian only serious crimes are worth averting at the cost of severe penalties.

The utilitarian approach to this matter does not supply a procedure for sentencing particular criminals (any more than a justification for punishment as an institution would be a case for any particular application of it). Arguing from expected consequences, one might establish a kind of standard penalty for each class of offense. Officials drafting new rules might consider whether a proposed maximum penalty would keep offenses down to manageable proportions, or people concerned about road accidents might argue that heavier penalties for motoring offenses would make drivers more careful. Deciding the sentence in a particular case, however, is clearly a different matter. The maximum penalty is a limiting factor, but questions like the degree of responsibility, provocation, and the offender's previous record are all relevant. However, one might reasonably ask why, as a matter of principle, they should be relevant.

PUNISHMENT AND RESPONSIBILITY

The problem of responsibility arises in relation to punishment as it does in relation to blame in moral theory. The principle, discussed already, that a man ought not to be punished for doing what he cannot help creates difficulties when extended to actions which a man could not help doing because of his own state of mind instead of external or contingent factors, like duress or ignorance of fact. An insane man, as defined, say, by the M'Naghten rules (that is, one who did not know what he was doing or did not know that what he was doing was wrong), cannot be said to choose his act because he cannot know it for what it is. But sometimes a man may know that what he is doing is wrong yet still be unable to stop himself from doing it. He may be subject, for instance, to an irresistible temptation or provocation. But how is that to be understood? A temptation is not irresistible merely because a particular man has yielded to it or even because he might have been expected to yield to it. However, a temptation may be so strong that we might expect any ordinary person to yield to it (even though a few people may in fact resist it), or, as one might say, it might be "more than human nature can stand." In that sense it may be "irresistible."

Some people, of course, find it much more difficult than others to resist temptation. Some, like kleptomaniacs, are "impelled" to act in the sense that deliberation neither plays, nor could play, any part in what they do. Such people might be distinguished from plain wrongdoers by the fact that nothing—not blame, punishment, praise, or rational argument—seems to affect their disposition to break the rules. Or, again, their actions may lack any point, or if they can be said to have any point, it is only in relation to a set of aims and standards of achievment so distorted and eccentric that they are intelligible only to a psychiatrist. The kleptomaniac who steals nylon stockings for which he has no possible use (according to ordinary standards of utility) might properly be said to be unable to help stealing them. Far more difficult is the case of the psychopath, who seems to have no wish to resist temptation or, rather, who knows that some of the things he wants to do are wrong in the sense that other people disapprove of them but on whom this knowledge enforces no internal restraint beyond prompting a degree of caution. Criminals of this type would once have been described as "wicked" but are now often described as incapable of self-control. To say, however, that they are not responsible for their acts creates the odd situation that anyone is liable to punishment who usually resists temptation but sometimes fails, whereas the man who never resists is not liable at all.

The determinist has a short way with these difficulties. Since everyone's actions are the response of his character to a given set of circumstances, how can anyone ever be held responsible for his actions? We do what we must, given what we are, and what we are is the end of a causal chain going back to before we were born. If one knew a person well enough, one might predict that under given conditions he would commit a crime. Is this compatible with saying that he can choose whether to do so, or is his belief in his freedom to choose simply an illusion? Can the result of a genuine choice be predicted?

To say that something is predictable is not, however, the same as saying it is unavoidable. We can forecast a man's actions just because we know the kind of choices that he regularly makes. The more we know of his dispositions and his preferences, the more likely we are to be right. But that does not mean that he never acts voluntarily or that he never makes a real choice but only thinks he does. If all choices are illusions, what would a real choice be like? A man's behavior may be predictable because he can be relied upon to do what is reasonable, but to act with good reason is the very reverse of being subject to an inner compulsion. An essential difference between voluntary and involuntary action is that it makes sense to speak of the motives, aims, and reasons for the former but only of the causes of the latter. It is only when a person's behavior seems pointless or when explanations in terms of aims do not seem sufficient that we look for the kind of cause which would justify saying that he could not help himself. Of course, a complete account of voluntary and rational behavior must refer to causes as necessary conditions for action, but such causes would not constitute a sufficient explanation. An account of the electronic activity in the brain would not provide a sufficient explanation of a move in a game of chess unless the move was so completely and absurdly irrelevant that it had to be accounted for simply as the result of a nervous twitch. In that case, however, it would not really be a move in the game at all, not an action, indeed, but something that happens to the player. The weakness of the determinist position, insofar as it purports to undermine the notion of responsibility, is that it treats such abnormalities as the explanatory model for the normal.

It is arguable, in any case, that the concept of responsibility *requires* that human behavior be causally accountable rather than the reverse. As Hume pointed out in *An Enquiry Concerning Human Understanding,*

[Where actions] . . . proceed not from some *cause* in the character and disposition of the person who performed them, they can neither redound to his honour, if good; nor infamy, if evil. . . . The person is not answerable for them; and as they proceeded from nothing in him that is durable and constant, and leave nothing of that nature behind them, it is impossible [that] he can, upon their account, become the object of punishment or vengeance.

In Hume's view universal causality is consistent with the concept of choice and is a necessary condition for responsibility and, therefore, for blame and punishment.

Strictly speaking, all that is necessary for a theory of punishment is that human conduct should be capable of being modified by threats. For some people—for instance, compulsive lawbreakers like kleptomaniacs—that is not the case. Others, however, commit crimes believing they can escape punishment; still others, in a spirit of rebellion, indifference, or, more rarely, of martyrdom, prefer to do what they want and risk the consequences rather than conform. Why they prefer it—what conditions account for their being the men they are—is irrelevant. To say "they prefer it" is to say they might have chosen to do otherwise but did not, and that is all that is necessary for the concept "responsibility." To ask whether they were free to prefer otherwise, being what they were, is to ask whether they could choose to choose, and it is not clear that this really means anything. The experience of punishment may provide a reason for choosing differently next time, but to have a reason for choosing is not to be without a choice and, therefore, without responsibility.

Extenuation. Though a criminal may be held responsible for his actions, there may nevertheless be circumstances which, so it is said, diminish responsibility or extenuate guilt. Temptation or provocation, though not irresistible may have been very great. The offender may have had a good character, and there may be no reason to expect any future lapse.

In some cases mitigation of sentence on such grounds can be readily justified in utilitarian terms. Little is to be gained by punishing the obviously exceptional lapse; a very small penalty might be enough to dissuade other respectable people who might otherwise be tempted to imitate it and for whom the shame of being treated as a criminal, whatever the penalty, is usually deterrent enough.

However, it is not easy to show, at least in utilitarian terms, that mitigation is reasonable in all the instances in which it is commonly thought appropriate. Nor does everyone agree on what are extenuating circumstances. It is not self-evident that whoever is sorely (but not irresistibly) tempted should be treated more leniently than people who have done the same thing but under less temptation. A strong temptation might be withstood if there were sufficient counterinducement. Leniency might weaken the resolve of others in the future. Some people treat crimes of passion leniently; others would say that the temptation is so commonly felt that if people were not discouraged from taking the law into their own hands by treating offenses of this kind severely, such offenses would rapidly multiply. Again, some people would accept a plea of drunkenness as an extenuation of an offense, whereas others would consider it an aggravation.

It is doubtful whether our ideas on this aspect of punishment depend on utilitarian considerations. Nor is there any reason to suppose that any system of utilitarian argument could show them to be consistent and rational. It was suggested earlier that though the criteria of morality and law, of blame and punishment, are not identical, they influence one another. If we blame people less for yielding to strong temptation, we also feel they deserve a less severe punishment. But this only shifts the question a step back. Why should temptation mitigate blame?

A possible answer might be that at least some temptations can be pleaded as partial justifications. Thus, a man who pleads that he killed someone to shorten his sufferings or a woman who kills her deformed baby is appealing to another moral principle to excuse the act. Similarly, a man who kills his wife's lover might claim that his victim was violating his rights. These are not complete justifications, as a plea of self-defense would be, but they are excuses which count, as it were, against the initial presumption of guilt and so incline us to look at the offense more sympathetically and more leniently, whatever the advantages of severity in terms of deterrence, prevention, or reform. There is nothing irrational in striking a balance of desert.

But differences of opinion about a criminal's deserts often turn not on the way such a balance is struck but on the extent to which his judges (or their critics) are able to comprehend his action. Anyone who could imagine himself tempted in similar circumstances would probably be more sympathetic than someone who could not and who would therefore see no reason for being indulgent. On the other hand, anyone who suspected that he himself might yield to such a temptation and who flinched from the possibility might react to it with very great severity indeed.

PUNISHMENT AND REFORM

There is no reason to suppose, then, that the sentencing practice of the courts will display rational and consistent principles; furthermore, any attempt to set up criteria of rational judgment on strictly utilitarian principles is likely to cut across deeply rooted moral convictions. Accordingly, some criminologists and psychiatrists, like Eliot Slater and Bernard Glueck, and some penal reformers, like Barbara Wootton, have swung away from the general conceptions of punishment and desert. Instead of asking what penalty is warranted by the crime, whether the agent was fully responsible for his action, whether circumstances exonerate him wholly or in part, they prefer to ask what kind of treatment is most likely to rehabilitate him, subject, of course, to the example it might set for others.

This comes very close to repudiating altogether the concept of punishment as a deliberate infliction of suffering, which the criminal deserves, consequent to a voluntary breach of the law. First, the treatment most likely to rehabilitate him need not be unpleasant (though if it is to instill a measure of discipline, it very well may be). And, second, avoiding the question of moral responsibility, the reformer also avoids the question of what the criminal deserves, because the reformer's prime concern is with the treatment he needs. Criminals would no more deserve punishment than the sick deserve medicine. Indeed, for such writers as Samuel Butler and the American lawyer Clarence Darrow, criminality is a kind of sickness to be treated rather than a wrong to be punished.

Attractive as this approach may seem on humanitarian grounds, it has at least one serious consequence. The concepts of responsibility and desert cannot be discarded without some loss. For it is not a necessary condition of medical treatment that a patient must have shown symptoms of a disease; those exposed to smallpox are vaccinated before they develop a fever. Without the principle that punishment must be deserved, there would be no obstacle to subjecting people likely to become criminals to corresponding forms of penal prophylaxis. Moreover, if we substitute for punishment the idea of rehabilitative treatment, there is nothing against sentencing a person of bad character to a severe course of treatment for the most trivial offense if his character would be better for it in the end. This would clearly be incompatible with the usually accepted principle that trivial offenses should not carry severe penalties.

Reformism of this kind is open to attack from another quarter. The point has been made by Hegel and Bosanquet, among others, that retributive punishment is a kind of tribute to the moral personality of the criminal. It is precisely as a morally responsible agent, recognized as capable of making reasoned choices and accepting the consequences, that the criminal is punishable. Bosanquet goes so far as to say that punishment is "his right, of which he must not be defrauded." It is to be distinguished, argued Bradley, from the discipline or correction appropriately administered to animals and children. Punishment "is inflicted because of wrong-doing, as desert, the latter is applied as means of improvement." Since rational adults are neither animals nor children, no one has the right to treat them as if they were. It might be similarly argued that lunatics are under tutelage because they are incapable of looking after their own interests and cannot be expected to respect those of other people. The sane criminal, on the contrary, can be made to pay for his antisocial choices in order to demonstrate to him and, through him, to others that crime does not pay, but it diminishes his stature as a rational adult to deny that he is responsible for ordering his own life and to impose upon him ends of another person's choosing.

Nevertheless, retributivists have often been much concerned with moral reformation. They have insisted, however, that this was something the criminal must do for himself. Because it was associated with shame and rejection, punishment could bring the criminal up short and force him to reconsider his life in the light of society's condemnation of his actions. But the remorse which was a necessary condition for self-reformation was entirely dependent on the criminal's recognition that his punishment was deserved. Without that there could be no inward reformation, no reassertion of moral standards, but only a sense of resentment and injustice. Accordingly, punishment can yield the benefits of reform only if it is thought of, above everything else, as retributive—as the appropriate desert of a responsible guilty agent. It is this which distinguishes the retributive approach to moral reformation from the kind of utilitarianism which turns its back on desert and responsibility and is concerned only with the needs of rehabilitation.

It is, of course, an open question whether punishment ever does produce the kind of self-reformation the Hegelians had in mind or whether it does so more often than it produces a moral decay. Indeed, our knowledge of the facts of criminal behavior is probably far too scanty and uncertain for us to know how relevant much of the philosophical discussion of punishment really is. We cannot say for sure that a penal system is justified because it tends to reform criminals. Nor do we know, for that matter, whether the deterrent view of punishment is applicable to all kinds of crime. Many people commit offenses without seeming to take any account of consequences before they act, and they repeat the same offenses again and again in spite of punishment. Perhaps those who do not, would not repeat them even without punishment. Perhaps there would be no more cases of certain classes of crime than there are already; perhaps the only people to commit them are those who also do not take account of consequences before they act. It seems likely that some potential offenders are deterred from evading taxes or from smuggling by the threat of punishment, but is there any certain evidence that the threat of punishment deters anyone who would otherwise commit rape or arson? Utilitarians tend to assume that punishment as an institution can be justified by its beneficial consequences, but the argument depends on

certain a priori assumptions about criminal (or would-be criminal) behavior that may be greatly overintellectualized. However, even though research should prove the usual utilitarian justifications for punishment groundless, that does not mean that some other, nonutilitarian justification is better. The proper procedure may well be to ask, with the utilitarian, whether the consequences are by and large beneficial; it is equally possible that punishment as an institution might fail that test. A theory of punishment that led to the conclusion that all punishment was wrong need be no more necessarily mistaken than a theory that led to a similar conclusion as regards, say, slavery, which, after all, was accepted as uncritically in Aristotle's day as punishment is today.

Bibliography

For a broad treatment of the subject, see A. C. Ewing, *The Morality of Punishment* (London, 1929). For classic expositions of retributive positions, see Immanuel Kant, "Metaphysische Anfangsgründe der Rechtslehre," in *Die Metaphysik der Sitten* (1797), in *Werke*, Vol. VII (Berlin, 1922), translated by W. Hastie as *Kant's Philosophy of Law* (Edinburgh, 1887); G. W. F. Hegel, *Philosophie des Rechts* (1821), in *Werke*, Vol. VIII (Berlin, 1833), translated by T. M. Knox as *Hegel's Philosophy of Right* (Oxford, 1942). See also Ch. 8 of Bernard Bosanquet, *Philosophical Theory of the State* (London, 1899; 4th ed., 1923), and Essay 1 of F. H. Bradley, *Ethical Studies* (London, 1876; 2d ed., rev., Oxford, 1927). Extensive bibliographic notes can be found in Giorgio Del Vecchio, *La giustizia*, which was originally published in *Annuario dell'Università di Roma* (1922–1923), 4th ed. (Rome, 1951), translated by Lady Guthrie as *Justice*, A. H. Campbell, ed. (Edinburgh, 1952).

Recent analyses, mainly in retributive terms, can be found in J. D. Mabbott, "Punishment," in *Mind*, Vol. 48 (1939), 152–167; C. W. K. Mundle, "Punishment and Desert," in *Philosophical Quarterly*, Vol. 4, No. 16 (1954), 216–228; D. C. Hodges, "Punishment," in *Philosophy and Phenomenological Research*, Vol. 18, No. 2 (1957–1958), 209 (a case for viewing punishment as reparation). K. Baier, "Is Punishment Retributive?," in *Analysis*, Vol. 16, No. 2 (1955), 25–32, argues that the concept of punishment entails retribution but does not deal with problems of justification. See also A. R. Manser, "It Serves You Right," in *Philosophy*, Vol. 37, No. 142 (1962), 293–306. H. J. McCloskey, "The Complexity of the Concepts of Punishment," *ibid.*, 307–326, draws attention to variety of contexts in which "punishment" is used and argues against analysis in terms of a standard case.

For classic statements of utilitarian positions, see C. B. Beccaria, *Dei delitti e delle pene* (1764); *An Essay on Crimes and Punishment, Translated from the Italian*, 4th ed. (London, 1785); Jeremy Bentham, *Introduction to the Principles of Morals and Legislation* (1789), Wilfrid Harrison, ed. (Oxford, 1948), and *Traités de législation, civile et pénale*, E. Dumont, ed. (Paris, 1802), translated by R. Hildreth as *Theory of Legislation*, C. K. Ogden, ed. (London, 1931). See T. H. Green, *Lectures on the Principles of Political Obligation*, in R. L. Nettleship, ed., *Works*, Vol. II (London, 1885), or in a separate edition, with an introduction by A. D. Lindsay (London, 1941); Green repudiates retributivism but stresses moral reformation as a function of punishment and, therefore, the importance of the concept of desert (cf. Bosanquet, *op. cit.*). See also Vol. I of Hastings Rashdall, *Theory of Good and Evil*, 2 vols. (Oxford, 1907; 2d ed., 1924).

The following examples of recent analyses of the problems of punishment are mainly utilitarian in emphasis but try to allow some place for retributivism in a general theory. In W. D. Ross, *The Right and the Good* (Oxford, 1930), especially Appendix II, Ross argues that the state is entitled to punish offenders in the public interest because by invading the rights of others, they forfeit their own claim to protection. On this subject see also A. G. N. Flew, "The Justification of Punishment," in *Philosophy*, Vol. 29, No. 3 (1954), 291–307; H. L. A. Hart, "Prolegomenon to the

Principles of Punishment," in *PAS*, Vol. 60 (1959–1960), 1, and "Murder and the Principles of Punishment: England and the United States," in *Northwestern University Law Review*, Vol. 52, No. 4 (1957), 433. Also, see A. Quinton, "On Punishment," and Stanley I. Benn, "An Approach to the Problems of Punishment," in Herbert Morris, ed., *Freedom and Responsibility* (Stanford, Calif., 1961); J. Rawls, "Two Concepts of Rules," in F. A. Olafson, ed., *Society, Law, and Morality* (Englewood Cliffs, N.J., 1961); Stanley I. Benn and R. S. Peters, *Social Principles and the Democratic State* (London, 1959), especially Chs. 8–9. Patrick J. Fitzgerald, *Criminal Law and Punishment* (Oxford, 1962), deals with the philosophical problems in the broad context of English criminal law. For a discussion of the relations of law, morality, and punishment, see Patrick Devlin, *The Enforcement of Morals* (London, 1965), and H. L. A. Hart, *Law, Liberty and Morality* (London, 1963).

For discussions of free will, determinism, and responsibility in relation to punishment, see H. L. A. Hart, Paul Edwards, and John Hospers, symposium on "Determinism and Freedom in Law and Ethics," in Sidney Hook, ed., *Determinism and Freedom* (New York, 1958); J. D. Mabbott, "Freewill and Punishment," in H. D. Lewis, ed., *Contemporary British Philosophy*, 3d series (London, 1956). In Barbara Wootton, *Social Science and Social Pathology* (London, 1959), there is a survey of recent trends in psychiatric and criminological studies critical of the concept "responsibility"; see especially Ch. 8. For a criticism of these trends, see H. L. A. Hart, *Punishment and the Elimination of Responsibility* (London, 1962). *Freedom and Responsibility* (see above) is a useful collection of readings on various aspects of the problem of responsibility, including its relation to punishment, extenuation, and so on; it includes an extensive bibliography.

STANLEY I. BENN

PYRRHO (c. 360–c. 270 B.C.), the first great "skeptic," or "inquirer" (which was the original meaning of the Greek word *skeptikos*), was born and died in the city of Elis on the Greek Peloponnesus. For a while he made a very modest living as a painter, but in 334 B.C., one year after Aristotle had founded the Lyceum, he joined Alexander the Great as a court philosopher and traveled with Alexander and his armies into India, where he is said to have met and been influenced by the ascetic, morally exemplary Gymnosophists and Magi. In that same court was Anaxarchus, the eudaemonist, the "happy man," who was Pyrrho's teacher. Anaxarchus, a follower of Democritus, shared with the great atomist the doctrine that sense perceptions contradict each other and are therefore not trustworthy, but he emphasized more than Democritus had done the eudaemonistic function of philosophy. Upon Alexander's death in 323 B.C. Pyrrho returned to Elis in poverty and spent the rest of his life there, living with his sister Philistia, who was a midwife. In Elis he apparently lectured to some large groups, as well as discussing philosophy with a few students as they wandered across the countryside. The city of Elis made him a high priest and exempted philosophers from paying taxes because of his services to the community.

Pyrrhonism as a way of life. Pyrrho did not leave any philosophical writings, but his most distinguished student, Timon of Phlius, insisted, as did all philosophers of antiquity interested in Pyrrho, that what he contributed was not so much a body of doctrine or a dialectical method as an *agoge*, a way of living. To be a Pyrrhonian was to imitate Pyrrho himself. But because only a few fragments of Timon's writings and a paucity of first-hand accounts of Pyrrho's life have come down to us, that *agoge* is rather difficult to ascertain. None of the accounts reveal a logi-

cally agile philosopher; and all of them reveal a man primarily interested in living a happy, peaceful, independent life within the limits set by the customs and laws of his country. But beyond these facts discrepancies arise among the various biographical accounts now available to us. According to one tradition, his was a life that emphasized heroic indifference, apathy toward phenomena and external objects, to such a great extent that his health was always in danger. Diogenes Laërtius in his life of Pyrrho tells us that he would not look where he was going and that only his more commonsensical friends preserved him from death or maiming from "carts, precipices, dogs or what not." Diogenes also tells us that once, when his teacher Anaxarchus was stuck in a slough, Pyrrho walked right by him without offering any help. In this same tradition of heroic skepticism is the story of Pyrrho and the wild dog. Pyrrho was suddenly attacked by a dog and became terrified; but shortly thereafter he apologized for his terror, saying that it was not easy to strip oneself of human weakness, even though one should try with all one's might to do so.

However, there is another tradition, subscribed to by Aenesidemus and others, that claims such stories to be alien to the *agoge* of Pyrrho. This tradition, followed by Montaigne, saw Pyrrho as a man of common sense and good judgment in everyday matters, who would not endanger his health or life out of a doctrinaire indifference to the senses, who avoided carts, precipices, and dogs in everyday life, who was indifferent only to the dogmatic opinions of philosophers, and who moderated his feelings when faced with the brutal, inevitable forces of nature (*metriopathie*). In this second tradition belongs another story, this one told by Posidonius. Once Pyrrho was on a ship whose passengers were unnerved by a storm while Pyrrho himself remained calm and confident. At the height of the storm he pointed out to them a little pig standing on the deck calmly eating its food, and he told them that such was the unperturbed way a wise man should live in all situations. This tradition emphasizes similarities between men and other animals, at least when men are wisest, and makes indifference not an end in itself, but an instrument that the commonsensical man uses only in order to preserve his peace of mind and health of body. It reveals a Pyrrho willing to accept and live in a world of phenomena, not an ascetic trying to act as if he had no body.

Philosophical grounds. We do have one quite fragmentary account of the teachings of Pyrrho that gives us some idea of the philosophical grounds of his *agoge*, whatever it was in detail. Timon tells us that according to Pyrrho, a philosopher—if he would be happy—should ask himself three questions and answer them honestly. The first question is: How are things constituted? Pyrrho answered that our mutually contradictory sensations of things reveal that all we know are phenomena, not the inner constitution of things—phenomena that cannot be classified as either true or false, since we do not know the things in themselves beyond them. If we knew the hidden things (*adela*), we could compare the phenomena to them.

Pyrrho may have learned from Democritus by way of Anaxarchus the notion of *isosthenia*, the balancing of opposing evidence or arguments against each other so that they cancel each other out. But whatever its origin, the concept of equally probable, mutually contradictory claims became the main stratagem of Pyrrhonism. It was symbolized by a pair of scales whose two plates are in perfect equilibrium, neither containing matter more weighty than the other.

The second question is: In what relation do we stand to things around us? Pyrrho's answer to this question was a direct consequence of his answer to the first. We must suspend judgment, must neither accept nor reject these things, since all we know of them are our own sensations. We must, through our *epoche*, or suspension of judgment (there is some dispute as to whether Pyrrho or Arcesilaus first used this crucial term), acknowledge our *akatalepsia*, or lack of comprehension of these things, and we must embody this awareness of our lack of comprehension in *aphasia*, or silence concerning them.

The last question Timon mentions is: What will result from the relationship of our *epoche*, *akatalepsia*, and *aphasia*? And the answer Pyrrho gave was tranquillity of mind, *ataraxia*. We shall be content to live a peaceful life with phenomena, without yearning to possess or know things themselves and without dogmatically and zealously defending any set of conclusions about those things. Again, the upshot of wisdom or philosophy for Pyrrho, as for Anaxarchus, was happiness.

Pyrrho and other Skeptics. The differences between later Academic Skepticism and what we know of Pyrrho's philosophy are great. Apparently Pyrrho felt that philosophy should teach men to dispense with elaborate dialectic and should cause them to seek, above all, to make themselves morally and psychologically independent of both philosophical methods and external things. But Arcesilaus and Carneades, like Aenesidemus and Sextus Empiricus, were masters of dialectic, used it as an important philosophical tool, and felt that the philosopher should acquire both philosophical skills and goods of a worldly sort. The indifference to strict methods and external things that Pyrrho had taught, whether it was in fact heroic indifference or commonsensical poise, was considerably mitigated by the Skeptics who succeeded him.

Bibliography

Our main source concerning Pyrrho's life and thought is Diogenes Laërtius, "Pyrrho," in his *Lives of Eminent Philosophers*, translated by R. D. Hicks (New York, 1925), Vol. I, Bk. 9, but this account was written from a distance of about six centuries, using legends as well as a few more or less second-hand documents as primary sources.

A clear statement of differing interpretations of Pyrrho's life and works may be found in Victor Brochard, *Les Sceptiques grecs* (Paris, 1923). Norman MacColl, *The Greek Sceptics From Pyrrho to Sextus* (London, 1869), builds up a picture of Pyrrhonism as against the Middle and New Academy, but it begs too many questions to be conclusive. Léon Robin, *Pyrrhon et le scepticisme grec* (Paris, 1944), contains a careful, lucid, illuminating account of the sources of our knowledge of Pyrrho.

PHILIP P. HALLIE

PYTHAGORAS AND PYTHAGOREANISM. Pythagoras was an Ionian Greek born on the island of Samos, probably about 570 B.C. His dislike of the policies of the Samian tyrant Polycrates caused him to immigrate to Crotona in southern Italy. There he founded a society with religious and political, as well as philosophical, aims which gained

power in the city and considerably extended its influence over the surrounding area. A certain Cylon, however, stirred up a revolt against the society in which a number of its leading members were killed, and Pythagoras retired to Metapontum. The community recovered its influence until a more serious persecution took place in the middle of the fifth century, from which the survivors scattered to various parts of the Greek world—notably Thebes, Phleius, and Tarentum. In these places "they preserved their original ways and their science, although the sect was dwindling, until, not ignobly, they died out" (in the late fourth century), to quote the epitaph written by a contemporary.

Nature of the evidence. The obstacles to an appraisal of classical Pythagoreanism are formidable. There exists no Pythagorean literature before Plato, and it was said that little had been written, owing to a rule of secrecy. Information from the Christian era is abundant but highly suspect. Pythagoras himself, though a fully historical figure, underwent a kind of canonization. His life was quickly obscured by legend, and piety attributed all the school's teaching to him personally. Moreover, the dispersion of the school inevitably led to divergences of doctrine in the various groups. Aristotle makes it clear that by the late fifth century some Pythagoreans were teaching one thing and some another. A further reason for division was that the universal genius of Pythagoras, for whom religion and science were two aspects of the same integrated world view, was beyond the scope of lesser men. Some naturally inclined more to the religious and superstitious; others, to the intellectual and scientific side, as is confirmed by later references to the division between *acusmatici* and *mathematici*.

As early evidence there are several references to Pythagoras in works of his contemporaries or near contemporaries (for instance, Xenophanes satirized his belief in the transmigration of souls), a valuable reference in Plato to the relationship between astronomy and harmonics in the Pythagorean system, a quantity of information from Aristotle (who at least would not confuse the Pythagoreans with Plato, as later writers excusably did), and some quotations from pupils of Aristotle who were personally acquainted with the last generation of the school.

Given the nature of the sources, the following is a fairly conservative summary of Pythagoreanism before Plato.

Man and the cosmos. In contrast with the Milesians, the Pythagoreans were not motivated by disinterested scientific curiosity. For Pythagoras, philosophy was the basis of a way of life, leading to salvation of the soul. "Their whole life," said a fourth-century writer, "is ordered with a view to following God, and it is the governing principle of their philosophy." At philosophy's center, therefore, were man and his relation to other forms of life and to the cosmos. Purity was to be sought by silence, self-examination, abstention from flesh and beans, and the observance of other primitive taboos which the Pythagoreans interpreted symbolically. Of the recognized gods they worshiped Apollo, guardian of the typically Greek ideal of moderation ("nothing too much"), of whom Pythagoras was believed to be an incarnation.

Behind both the superstition and the science was the notion of kinship or sympathy. The kinship and essential unity of all life made possible the belief in the transmigration of souls and accounted for the prohibition of meat: a sheep might house the soul of an ancestor. Not only animate nature in our sense but the whole world was akin, for the cosmos itself was a living, breathing creature. The cosmos was one, eternal, and divine; men were divided and mortal. But the essential part of man, his soul, was not mortal; it was a fragment of the divine, universal soul that was cut off and imprisoned in a mortal body. Men should therefore cultivate and purify the soul, preparing it for a return to the universal soul of which it was a part. Until then, since it was still contaminated by the body, it must tread the wheel of reincarnation, entering a new body of man or animal after the death of its previous tenement.

These tenets were also taught by the religious movement known as Orphism, from which the religious side of Pythagoreanism can hardly be separated. (Pythagoras himself was said in the fifth century to have written books under the name of Orpheus.) But whereas the Orphics sought salvation by purely religious means—sacramental ceremonies and the observance of ritual prohibitions—Pythagoras added a new way, the way of philosophy.

Philosophy, for Pythagoras as for others, meant the use of reason and observation to gain understanding of the universe. The link between this procedure and his overriding aim of salvation seems to have been the principle that like is known by like, a widespread tenet of pre-Socratic thought, common to such diverse systems as the philosophicoreligious synthesis of Empedocles and the scientific atomism of Democritus. Hence, an understanding of the divine universe would bring man's nature closer to its own. In this conception we meet the typically Pythagorean conception of *kosmos*, a word which combines in an untranslatable way the notion of orderly arrangement or structural perfection with that of beauty. Closely linked with it is *peras*, meaning limit. An organic whole, particularly one that, like the universe, lives forever, must of necessity exhibit limit and order in the highest degree. What is unlimited has no *telos* (end) and is *a-teles*, which means both "endless" and "incomplete." But the world is a perfect whole, a model of order and regularity, supremely exemplified in Greek eyes by the ceaseless wheeling of the heavenly bodies in (as they believed) perfect circles, bringing about the unvarying succession of day and night and seasons. It was said of Pythagoras that he was the first to call the world *kosmos*, "from its inherent order." By studying this order, we reproduce it in our own souls, and philosophy becomes an assimilation to the divine, as far as that is possible within the limitations imposed by our mortal bodies.

The doctrine that things are numbers. The Pythagoreans studied mathematics in a cosmic context, and for them numbers always retained a mystical significance as the key to the divine cosmos. "They supposed the whole heaven to be a *harmonia* and a number," said Aristotle. *Harmonia*, though specially applied to music, could signify any well-organized structure of parts fitted together in due proportion. Its effect in music seems to have burst on Pythagoras as a revelation of the whole cosmic system. We may accept the many later statements that he discovered the numerical ratios underlying the intervals which the Greeks called consonant and used as the basis of their scale. They involve only the numbers 1 to 4—1:2, octave; 3:2, fifth; 4:3, fourth. These numbers add up to 10, a sacred number for the Pythagoreans, which was symbolized by the dotted triangle (*tetractys*), "source and root of everlasting nature." From the discovery that the sounds they recognized as beautiful depended on inherent, objective, mathematical order, they leaped to the conclusion that number was the key to the element of order in nature as a whole.

With this innovation the Pythagoreans would seem to have taken the momentous step from explanation in terms of matter (as the Milesians had sought it) to explanation in terms of form. Yet philosophy was not quite ready for that step, nor could the distinction between matter and form be clearly grasped. They saw simply the ultimate, single nature (*physis*) of things in their mathematical structure. There seems little doubt that probably until well on in the fifth century they thought it possible to speak of things as actually made up of "numbers" that were regarded simultaneously as units, geometrical points, and physical atoms. Lines are made of points; surfaces, of lines; solids, of surfaces; and physical bodies, of solids. In this scheme two points made a line; three, the minimum surface (triangle); four, the minimum solid (tetrahedron). A later theory spoke of the "fluxion" of point into line, line into surface, and so on, which gave a geometrical progression (1, 2, 4, 8) instead of the arithmetical (1, 2, 3, 4), and the sequence of point, line, square, cube. Based on continuity, it seems designed to avoid the problem of incommensurable magnitudes or irrational numbers.

Whenever they were discovered (probably not much later than 450), incommensurables had dealt a blow to the original "things are numbers" doctrine, the idea that geometrical figures—and thus ultimately the physical world—are based on a series of integers. No ratio between integers can either describe the relation between the diagonal of a square and its side or serve as the basis of construction of a right triangle. If, however, magnitudes are regarded as continuous and hence infinitely divisible, the existence of incommensurable or irrational magnitudes (those which cannot be expressed as a ratio of natural numbers) could be explained and the difficulty overcome.

The ultimate principles. The analysis went further than that outlined above, for numbers themselves have their elements. The ultimate principles were limit and the unlimited, which were equated with good and bad respectively; moral concepts went side by side with physical concepts in this extraordinary system. Abstractions as well as physical phenomena were equated with numbers; for instance, justice was 4, the first square number, symbolizing equality or requital. After limit and the unlimited came odd and even, instances respectively of these two. They generated the unit (considered to be outside the number series, and both odd and even), from the unit sprang numbers, and from numbers came the world. There seems no doubt that the scheme goes back to an ultimate duality that corresponds to the moral dualism of Pythagoreanism, but one can also see how monistically minded Neoplatonic commentators could speak of the cosmos as originating from the One. In general terms, *kosmos* was achieved by the imposition of limit on the unlimited in order to make the limited, just as the imposition of definite ratios on the indefinite range of musical pitch produced the *harmonia* of the scale.

Cosmogony and cosmology. Cosmogony starts with the planting of a unit in the infinite. Aristotle called it, among other things, a seed; and since limit was associated with male and unlimited with female, the Pythagoreans probably thought of the generation of the living cosmos as taking place as did that of other animals. It grows by drawing in and assimilating the unlimited outside, that is, by conforming it to limit and giving it numerical structure. Physically the process resembles inspiration, and the unlimited is also called breath.

The unit seed had the nature of fire and in the completed cosmos (which evidently grew from the center outward) became a fire at its center. There are traces of two different cosmological schemes, a geocentric one which spoke of a fire at the center of the earth, and a more remarkable one attributed, in later sources at least, to the fifth-century Pythagorean Philolaus, which made the earth a planet. (Copernicus in *De Revolutionibus* says that reading of this Pythagorean doctrine gave him courage to consider explaining the heavenly motions on the basis of a moving earth.) According to this latter scheme, earth, planets, sun, and moon—and an extra body called the counterearth—all revolved about the center of the universe, which was occupied by a fire invisible to man because he lived on the opposite side of the earth. It was known that the moon's light is borrowed, and the idea was extended to the sun, whose heat and light were said to be reflected from the central fire. The moon was eclipsed by the interposition of both the earth and the counterearth and, according to some, of further, otherwise unknown, planetary bodies. These caused the comparatively frequent lunar eclipses.

In this system, the mixture of religion and science in Pythagoreanism is well brought out. Fire was given the central position, not for any scientific reason but because it was regarded with religious awe—and the center is the most "honorable" place. It was lauded with such titles as Hearth of the Universe, Tower of Zeus, and Throne of Zeus. Yet the same thinkers were aware that with the earth in orbit "the phenomena would not be the same" as in a geocentric scheme (presumably they were thinking of the lack of stellar parallax and variations in the apparent size of the sun and moon). They pointed out that even with a central earth, an observer would be separated from the center by the distance of its radius, and they argued that the visible effect would be as negligible in one case as in the other. This assumes that the heavenly bodies are at vast distances from the earth; and it is not known how, if at all, this system was related to the theory later known as the harmony of the spheres.

In any case, there are many divergent versions of this doctrine. In outline, the idea was that large bodies in motion must inevitably produce a sound; that the speeds of the heavenly bodies, judged by their distances, are in the ratios of the musical consonances; and that therefore the sound made by their simultaneous revolution is concordant. We do not hear it because it has been with us from birth, and sound is perceptible only by contrast with silence. It has been plausibly argued that in the original version Pythagoras, like Anaximander, took only three

orbits into account (sun, moon, and all the stars); this would relate it to his original musical discovery about the fourth, fifth, and octave. Later versions speak of seven, eight (Plato), and ten orbits. In any form, the doctrine emphasizes the universal importance, in Pythagorean eyes, of mathematical and musical laws and their intimate relation to astronomy.

Neo-Pythagoreanism. The influence of Pythagorean thought on the history of philosophy and religion has been exercised largely through the medium of Plato, who enthusiastically adopted its main doctrines of the immortality of the soul, philosophy as an assimilation to the divine, and the mathematical basis of the cosmos. Later antiquity regarded him as a Pythagorean source, so that post-Platonic writings are of little help in distinguishing Pythagorean from original Platonic material in the dialogues. The Neo-Pythagorean movement, which started in the first century B.C., was an amalgam of early Pythagorean material with the teachings of Plato, the Peripatetics, and the Stoics. All of this material was credited to Pythagoras, who was revered as the revealer of esoteric religious truths. The interests of Neo-Pythagoreanism were religious and, in accordance with the prevailing tendencies of the time, it emphasized the mystical and superstitious sides of the earlier doctrine, its astral theology and number-mysticism, to the detriment of philosophical thinking. It cannot be called a system, but rather is a trend which in different forms continued until the rise of Neoplatonism in the third century A.D., when it lost its identity in that broader and more powerful current. Besides contributing to Neoplatonism, it influenced Jewish thought through Philo of Alexandria and Christian thought through Clement of Alexandria. Prominent Neo-Pythagoreans were Cicero's acquaintance, Nigidius Figulus, and Apollonius of Tyana, a wandering mystic and ascetic of the first century A.D., credited with miraculous and prophetic powers. Numenius of Apamea in the late second century was called both Pythagorean and Platonist, and was the immediate precursor of Neoplatonism.

Bibliography

Delatte, A., *Études sur la littérature pythagoricienne.* Paris, 1915. For specialists.

Fritz, K. von, *Pythagorean Politics in South Italy: An Analysis of the Sources.* New York, 1940.

Guthrie, W. K. C., "Pythagoras and the Pythagoreans," in his *History of Greek Philosophy,* Vol. I. Cambridge, 1962. Pp. 146–340. References to much of the literature of the subject will be found in this general account.

Minar, E. L., Jr., *Early Pythagorean Politics.* Baltimore, 1942.

Morrison, J. S., "Pythagoras of Samos." *Classical Quarterly,* N. S. Vol. 6 (1956), 135–156.

Thesleff, H., *An Introduction to the Pythagorean Writings of the Hellenistic Period.* Turku, Finland, 1961. For specialists.

Timpanaro-Cardini, Maria, *Pitagorici: testimonianze e frammenti,* 2 vols. Florence, 1958 and 1962. Texts from H. Diels and W. Kranz, eds., *Fragmente der Vorsokratiker,* translated into Italian, with introduction and commentary.

Van der Waerden, B. L., "Die Arithmetik der Pythagoreer." *Mathematische Annalen,* Vol. 120 (1948), 127–153 and 676–700. For specialists.

Van der Waerden, B. L., *Die Astronomie der Pythagoreer.* Amsterdam, 1951. For specialists. Both this and the other van der Waerden work do not require a knowledge of Greek; texts are given in German.

W. K. C. GUTHRIE

Q

QUALITIES, PRIMARY AND SECONDARY. See
PRIMARY AND SECONDARY QUALITIES.

QUALITY AND QUANTITY. See CATEGORIES; DIA-
LECTICAL MATERIALISM; PRIMARY AND SECONDARY
QUALITIES.

QUANTITY. See MEASUREMENT.

**QUANTUM MECHANICS, PHILOSOPHICAL IM-
PLICATIONS OF.** It has often been claimed that
quantum mechanics in general, and the quantum concepts
in particular, have important philosophical implications.
But how can a factual discipline, one constituted by synthetic observation claims, have philosophical implications
if such implications are never merely factual or simply synthetic? Popular pronouncements crediting empirical sciences with philosophical consequences might seem to be
type confusions to anyone unsympathetic to the view that
factual disciplines are structured by conceptual frameworks whose function is not to provide any new information but rather to organize and interrelate the lower-order
factual information within higher-order clusters of theory
and patterns of inference. The principles of organization
and interrelationship which inform the data and ideas of
quantum mechanics, since they are so different from those
which structure every other empirical science, generate
philosophical perplexities concerning (1) the significance
of scientific knowledge; (2) the possibility of gaining objective information about the world—a question for all science, but particularly pertinent to quantum mechanics;
(3) the real nature of physical interactions between phenomena—for example, is causality everywhere ontologically
operative?; (4) the proper function of scientific theories—
for example, do they just describe phenomena or just predict them, or do they explain them? do they provide
representations of them?

The fundamental concepts of matter, energy, and cause
and effect, and even that of "the external world" itself,
have been affected and disturbed by the advent of quantum mechanics, and therefore re-examined. Philosophers
should be equally concerned with these notions within
classical physics or everyday experience. But the unfa-

miliar conceptual framework within which the data of quantum physics are placed has given new energy and direction to discussions of these ancient philosophical issues.
Indeed, this very unfamiliarity is largely responsible for
focusing the attention of philosophers on the conceptual
frameworks themselves; it is now clear that discussions
of frameworks must be managed differently from discussions of the facts structured by those frameworks. It is the
belated recognition of this point by philosophers that
creates the impression that quantum mechanics is philosophically more consequential than the other sciences.

This article will survey some historical antecedents of
quantum theory, give an exposition of the "Copenhagen
interpretation" and discuss the philosophical criticisms of
it, reply to some of these criticisms, and present some
concluding remarks concerning the nature of quantum
mechanics, the philosophy of physics, and the changes
wrought in philosophy of science by the development of
quantum mechanics.

HISTORICAL REMARKS

Quantum theory did not originate with the ideas of Niels
Bohr alone. His conceptions had historical antecedents.
Seventeenth-century, eighteenth-century and nineteenth-
century controversy concerning the nature of light is remarkably analogous to contemporary concern with the
interpretation of the square of the modulus of the ψ-func-
tion. Does $|\psi(p)|^2$ represent a wavelike microphenomenal
substratum which manifests itself as point-masses at the
molar level? Or is this substratum basically granular and
particulate with undulatory distributions occurring within
our macrophysical observations? Or is it both wavelike and
particulate at a fundamental ontological level? Or is it
neither? Francesco Maria Grimaldi's undulatory theory of
light, as developed by Christian Huygens, speculated
about by Robert Hooke, and ultimately confirmed by
Thomas Young, A. H. Fizeau, and J. B. Foucault, encountered the energetic opposition of "corpuscularians" like
Isaac Newton, M. A. Biot, Roger Boscovich, and Pierre
Simon de Laplace. The conceptual interplay between these
two groups of natural philosophies is quite intricate. But in
the nineteenth century the controversy was seemingly
resolved through the work of Young and Foucault, which

apparently showed decisively that the particulate theory of light was false.

We now realize that Young, Fizeau, and Foucault proved conclusively only that light is wavelike but did not establish that light is therefore in no way corpuscular. Newton's theory of fits—a theory which associated corpuscles of light with waves or "pressions" within the ether through which those corpuscles traveled—would have allowed light to have been simultaneously both undulatory and particulate. But in the nineteenth century the very ideas of particle and wave came to be fashioned in logical opposition to each other. Particle dynamics and electromagnetic field theory matured as mutually exclusive and incompatible theories. Thus, a particle seemed to be an entity with ideally sharp coordinates—that is, in one place at one time, and exclusively so. This is part of the conceptual structure of punctiform mass theory in Newton's *Principia*. Particles collide and rebound, with a precisely calculable energy exchange. On the other hand, a wave disturbance essentially lacks sharp coordinates. It spreads boundlessly throughout the undulating medium; it *is* the undulation of that medium. The expression "a wave motion at one geometrical point" would have been, for Newton and James Clerk Maxwell alike, completely unintelligible. Moreover, waves are never exclusively in any one place, and two waves can be in the same place at the same time, as when surf waves cross at a point. Nothing in wave motion corresponds strictly to particulate collision, impact, and recoil; billiard balls and pond ripples are entities different in kind. All this came to seem conceptually binding within nineteenth-century physics and so precisely expressed by the algebra of Maxwell and H. A. Lorentz that one could virtually treat any class of wave properties a, b, and c as the obverse of some comparable class of particulate properties $\sim a$, $\sim b$, and $\sim c$. Ideally, a wave extends to infinity; ideally, a particle collapses onto a dimensionless point. Ideally, a coordinate intersection can locate an infinite number of waves but only one particle. Ideally, a particle is indivisible; a wave must be divisible if its essential periodicity (in space) is ever to be in evidence. It became unthinkable that any event could be describable in both these ways at once. "Unthinkable" here means not simply "unimaginable" but also "notationally impossible." For in the only languages then available for describing particle and wave dynamics, such a joint description of phenomena would have constituted a virtual contradiction. Wave and particle ideas had become conceptual opposites within the structural framework of physical thinking: like "figure" and "ground," these notions were each made intelligible only in their contrast with and dependence upon the other. Every conceivable energy transfer could be expressed either in wave or in particulate terms, never in both ways at once. This constitutes the major conceptual consequence of post-Newtonian optical theory. As with every great theoretical advance, this way of thinking allowed a codification and classification of all known dynamic interactions while at the same time rendering alternative ways of thinking almost conceptually impossible ("almost," because the Cartesian notion of a vortex—a persisting pattern, within a substratum, that behaves like a physical entity—was not wholly dead,

even though it had little noticeable effect on eighteenth-century and nineteenth-century physical thought). The notion of "wave–particle duality," which, as we shall see, constituted the most startling innovation ever encountered in scientific theory, was the inevitable product of classical natural philosophers' having insisted on a rigorous wave-or-particle singularity—a mutually exclusive shaping of these ideas. Had Newton's doctrine of fits prevailed, the choice between waves and particles might not have been made exclusive; we might have been conceptually comfortable with entities possessing both undulatory and granular characteristics.

Various examples of phenomena which were incapable of being described exclusively in either purely wave or purely particulate terms were discovered between 1887 and 1927. These phenomena required using a descriptive apparatus which was simultaneously appropriate to the wavelike and to the particulate properties of single objects.

This larger history contains several smaller histories of successive shocks to other structural features of classical physical theory. The discovery that cathode rays were made up of particulate components and that, therefore, not all radiation was indissolubly undulatory; the discovery by Max Planck of the discontinuous emission of energy from radiant black bodies, the detection of the fact that photoelectron energy rises with the frequency of the incidence of light, quite independently of the intensity; Einstein's photon theory of 1905—an attempt to resolve Planck's perplexities by references to "particles of light" and "quanta of action"; the well-known "effects" discovered by A. H. Compton and C. V. Raman; and the first confirmations of the de Broglie–Schrödinger wave theory of matter by C. J. Davisson, L. H. Germer, and G. P. Thomson—all these helped establish that radiation had a granular texture and that matter possessed a wavelike fine-structure. Thus, microparticles could be described only in particulate and wave terms simultaneously. Yet the only terms available for such description were stamped with the inflexibly bipartite logic of Maxwell's successors.

In the middle of this dramatic history came the epoch-making research of Ernest Rutherford, Bohr, and Arnold Sommerfeld. By bombarding matter with alpha rays and then carefully noting the distributions of the scattered alpha particles, Rutherford was able to give experimental support to Hantaro Nagaoka's conjecture of 1903—sometimes called the Saturnian hypothesis—to the effect that an atom is only a tiny but massy point around which revolve clouds of much lighter particles. Of course, this simple particulate picture becomes more complex when one wishes to learn something about the distances from the nucleus of these lighter particles, as well as about their energies and other properties. Indeed, it was in determining these further attributes of the lighter particles that wave-theoretical considerations had later to be introduced.

However, the work of Rutherford, as developed into Bohr's monumental "old" quantum theory of 1913, was fundamentally a microphysics of particles plus mysterious "quantum jumps." Bohr took these jumps as basic, not to be explained in terms of other processes (for example, waves or fields) but to serve as the ultimate explanations of the things observed in the laboratory. The nineteenth century took it as a principle that a moving charge radiates. In Bohr's theory, within the microphysical domain it does not. But Bohr succeeded in bringing together an immense amount of previously unorganized data, structuring and relating all of it in terms of "energy levels," the particle-theoretic analogue of Planck's discovery that emissions from radiant bodies do not take place beneath certain energy outputs. Microphysical nature was found to be more like the keyboard of a piano than like the strings of a violin; action proceeds discontinuously from one discrete stage to another, not in terms of glissandi.

Sommerfeld imparted considerable algebraic sophistication to the Bohr scheme. The orbits assigned to the circling electrons were described with the techniques of differential geometry and higher analysis, but the field-theoretic aspect of microphenomena remained unexamined. Microparticles seemed to travel only at certain definite speeds, along certain definite paths; they moved to other paths only by disappearing and then reappearing at a new location. Before the early 1920s no one perceived in all this any analogue to the behavior of ensembles of particles, such as had been studied by Willard Gibbs in the nineteenth century. It was left to Louis de Broglie (1924) and Erwin Schrödinger (1925) to comprehend the distributional features in the particle domain. But in bringing together the concepts of wave and particle in the "wave–particle duality" they were seeking to unite notions which the nineteenth century had analytically sundered.

THE COPENHAGEN INTERPRETATION

All the philosophical problems and the conceptual difficulties of quantum theory, including the Copenhagen interpretation, arise from the practical necessity of describing micronature in terms of both waves and particles. The Copenhagen interpretation of quantum mechanics is the view that fundamental micronature is indivisibly bipartite—the wave–particle duality. If in our scientific analyses one of these aspects were subordinated to the other, the result would be not only an unbalanced picture of elementary particles but also a factually false one. The numbers used in experimentation and prediction in quantum mechanics must be generated by calculational techniques that are dependent on both field-theoretic and particle-theoretic considerations. According to the Copenhagen interpretation, there will never be any turning back from this state of affairs. It is idle to hope to discover some analytical error within past calculations or some new datum within future experiments that will restore our microphysical thinking to the level of classical determinism. Why "determinism"? Because the only theory that *works* in accounting for microphysical phenomena is *essentially* structured along conceptual lines which run through both the wave and the particle idea-frameworks—through both field theory and the notion of a singularity. This forces a compromise upon both conceptions; it "spreads" singularities indeterminately in the direction of becoming tiny fields ("electron clouds") and "restricts" fields in the direction of becoming small signal-centers ("wave packets"). The expression of all this in the operator calculus of Dirac consists in the noncommutative relationship between

particulate parameters like position and momentum or time and energy. This entails that the *most* we can know of a microparticle is its *partially* defined state—that is, its "contribution" to an irresolvable ensemble. This must be sharply contrasted with the classical idea wherein a particle state can be completely defined when its place at x, y, z (at time t) is determined. Classical determinism, however, requires just such a location of "causal events" in terms of their complete state specifications in order that a totally deterministic account of the "effect event" should be forthcoming. It is this which quantum mechanics in principle cannot supply.

Moreover, a host of conceptual limitations results at once from this forced combination of antithetical ideas. We must learn to live in thought with the uncertainty relations, the correspondence principle, and related notions because modern physics has disclosed that we have always been living with them in *fact*. Thus, the Copenhagen interpretation is threefold: it identifies a disturbing union of ideas as fundamental in nature, it urges that this union will not be overthrown in any future science, and it identifies the conceptual restraints of quantum mechanics as being nothing but the logical reflection of this basic commitment.

References to this philosophy of quantum physics, as it has been espoused by Bohr, Werner Heisenberg, L. Rosenfeld, and others, are usually met unsympathetically by professional philosophers, for most of whom the words "Copenhagen interpretation" signal a narrow restriction of thought in the older positivistic tradition. This response is elicited not so much, perhaps, by the conceptual content of the Copenhagen argument as by the often polemical and inflexible nature of these scientists' popular presentations of the theory. Although it has been criticized as unrealistic, unreflective, and unnecessary by philosophers of science, the intellectual content of the Copenhagen interpretation has virtually shaped the outlook of practicing physicists. Moreover, this interpretation is philosophically defensible and deserves more dispassionate delineation than it usually receives.

In contemporary microphysics it is arbitrary whether one uses a wave or a particle notation and language for one's observational descriptions—so long as it is realized that both are jointly valid. (There is doubt about this equivalence: For instance, P. A. M. Dirac, the principal spokesman for the view that microprocesses can be viewed indifferently either wave-theoretically or matrix-theoretically—i.e., in terms of singularity sets, or particle ensembles—has recently (1964) denied the equivalence of these two outlooks. But this article will treat Dirac's operator calculus of 1931 as the formal instrument by the use of which any wave-mechanical description can be transformed into an equivalent matrix-mechanical one, and vice versa.) Since neither the wave nor the particle approach to elementary processes is more fundamental than the other, a near-perfect symmetry has been maintained in the most successful formal treatments of fundamental particles. (Sometimes this sort of symmetry is taken too much for granted. Fourier transformations are done mechanically as if the two representations—wave-theoretic and matrix-theoretic—were absolutely equivalent. Perhaps there has been a conventional "philosophy" at work within quantum mechanics since Dirac's great work of the early 1930s—a philosophy that blinds scientists to a possibly more complex physical truth.)

THE UNCERTAINTY RELATIONS

Concepts which the nineteenth century had sundered had, as a matter of scientific logic, to be recombined in our time. It has been the triumph of quantum mechanics to have achieved a largely satisfactory recombination. The recognition of the nature of this triumph, however, leads directly to a qualitative appreciation of the uncertainty relations.

Heisenberg discovered this fundamental structural feature of quantum mechanics in something like the following manner: suppose a microphenomenon—for example, an orbiting electron—is provisionally described, in the manner of Schrödinger, as a cluster of the interference maxima of an otherwise undefined wave group. To *locate* that electron, as a classical "punctiform mass," precisely at the intersection of four coordinates would require the introduction of an infinite number of further waves, of infinitely varying amplitudes and frequencies, so as to increase destructive interference along the line of orbital propagation, thus "squeezing" the wave packet to a "vertical" line (in abstract, calculation space). This formal move, necessary to the narrowing of any wave cluster, will coagulate the electronic entity very closely around the coordinate intersection: it is as if the increasing number of associated waves press the "particle" to a point. But it will render unknowable the electron's energy, which is conceptually linked with the amplitude and the frequency of all the component phase waves in the configuration space (that is, the abstract, computation space). In short, one narrows the range of the particle's possible positions by chopping off its fuzzy "edges" with sharply differentiated component waves. This makes it impossible to determine *which* of all the different phase waves is to be identified with the electron's energy.

If, on the other hand, one seeks to determine the particle's energy, then these different phase waves must be decreased in number, allowing the "wavicle" ultimately to spread monochromatically through the entire configuration space. That is, one decreases the uncertainty concerning the particle's energy by decreasing the number of component phase waves having different energies. This decrease, however, permits the electronic entity to occupy any one of an infinite number of possible positions, since the particle is no longer "clustered onto" a geometrical point. It now spreads throughout all the configuration space. Again, in still other words, one "zeroes in" on a particulate position by completely diversifying the component wave structure of the particle. One "zeroes in" on the energy by simplifying its phase-wave structure.

This is not simply an elaborate way of translating into quantum physics pronouncements one might expect within classical statistical mechanics. Treating statistically the molecules of a thermally excited volume of gas is something forced upon us by experimental complexity alone. Our knowledge of the properties of gas molecules per se is not destroyed by such laboratory limitations; we do not deny that such molecules have positions and velocities simultaneously just because when we undertake to learn their positions precisely we make it increasingly difficult to learn anything of their energies, and vice versa. (This, it seems, is all that Max Born's "demonstration of the uncertainty of classical mechanics" really comes to.) In classical thermodynamics we have a kinetic theory that provides an understanding of the microstructure of gases and a statistical thermodynamics that provides an algorithm for managing the gross macrophysical observations of familiar gases—such things as the relationships between pressure, volume, temperature, and time. But these two approaches to gas theory fit together with consummate elegance and with a corresponding success in explanation and prediction. This is because the statistics used in classical thermodynamics have to do not with our basic understanding of the constituent microparticles of gases but rather with our abilities to formulate reliable predictions of the observed macrobehavior of gases. The "statistical waves" of gas theory are thus a feature of our inferential techniques, not of our understanding of how gases are made. The situation appears to be different in quantum mechanics in general and in quantum statistics in particular.

The fact that nature presents elementary particles to us as irresolvable combinations of wave and particle properties does not permit us to regard the waves just as ensembles, whose singularities are all classical point masses as the singularities within a gas are all classical point molecules. The philosopher's question "But surely the uncertainty relations do not entail that electrons *lack* a simultaneous position and energy?" reflects this older view that electrons are in precisely defined states but that we (because of our crude techniques of investigation) cannot know what those states are; *we* cannot define them precisely although they *are* precisely defined. But this older view seeks what no physical theory can hope for—a knowledge of nature that transcends what our best hypotheses and experiments suggest.

Quantum mechanics is a single, unified theory within which wave conceptions (or field or distribution or probabilistic conceptions) and particle conceptions (or point mass or singularity or granular conceptions) are equally fundamental in explaining and predicting the associated phenomena. Microphenomena show themselves to us as dual in nature. It is science's task to describe them intelligibly. Our basic knowledge of electrons does not remain wholly unaffected by limitations of laboratory technique. Rather, our very understanding of the subject matter of microphysics is part of what constitutes laboratory techniques in that the uncertainty relations constitute a major structural feature of both the techniques and our understanding. Classical statistical mechanics requires that it always make sense that one could, in principle, discuss the molecular elements of an ensemble as discrete, classically propertied entities. Quantum statistical mechanics requires that nothing be said of the microconstituents of an ensemble beyond what can be said of the macrobehavior of the ensemble itself. It is wrong, then, to treat quantum mechanics as but a special application of classical statistical mechanics, as do many physicists and philosophers who yearn for the conceptual tidiness of nineteenth-century gas theory, even when facing the comparatively untidy subject matter of twentieth-century quantum theory. But it is essential that philosophers attend to the marked differences between the two theories as statistical disciplines. We know what gas molecules are like, but we cannot deal with them separately. We cannot deal with electrons separately, and therefore we cannot know what they are like—or, rather, it would be epistemologically irresponsible of us to describe electrons in terms that transcend our capacities to observe them. (This point is supported by the existence of real differences within the mathematics of quantum theory. "Interference terms" appear in the theory as dependent upon products of ψ functions, not just as products of probabilities.)

A familiar response is to claim that quantum statistical mechanics must therefore be false or inadequate. But it is never accompanied by any alternative calculational technique that can achieve anything approaching what orthodox quantum mechanics has accomplished. Philosophers of science are so preoccupied with the limitations of contemporary microphysical theory that they sometimes fail to realize that there is no other known scientific theory that can begin to accomplish simultaneously the following ten points (abstracted from a similar list in J. H. Van Vleck, "Quantum Mechanics," in *Encyclopaedia Britannica*, Vol. XVIII, Chicago, 1962, pp. 827–828):

(1) Embrace the older Bohr theory, with all its advantages. This original version of quantum theory explained the spectral frequencies of such atoms as hydrogen and ionized helium.

(2) Give procedures for calculating the intensities, as well as the frequencies, of spectral lines.

(3) Supply an understanding (at least in principle) of the spectra of nonhydrogenic atoms. Atoms possessing more than one electron require solutions to the wave equations which are mathematically too complex for any exact determination; quantitative precision is therefore unobtainable. But through quantum mechanics it is possible to calculate the energy levels of the helium atom very accurately. The computations agree with the observations to within 1 part in 10,000.

(4) Generate some understanding of the phenomena of magnetism—largely by means of the concept of electron spin; this is a fundamental component within Dirac's formulation of relativistic quantum mechanics.

(5) Construct a quantum theory of the chemical bond. Chemical processes are so complex that one cannot calculate (from any theory) the heats of reactions or other macro-observables. But quantum mechanics provides an understanding of most salient features: it suggests reasons for the valence rules and for the existence of saturated bonds, etc. The spin quantum number of an atom is conceptually connected with its valence. (Atoms with nonzero spins are treated as having unsaturated valences.) A qualitative explanation of the directional valence within stereochemistry is also offered by quantum mechanics. The concept of "resonance energy" in chemical bonds is strictly a development of quantum mechanics. Pre-

viously, a molecule had been thought of as having a fixed structure; quantum mechanics reveals that it can conceivably and consistently exist in several states at once—which shakes the sensibilities of aprioristic students of science.

(6) Lead to a theory of the solid state of matter. Why and how atoms hold together in solid bodies is made intelligible by quantum mechanics. Such properties of objects as compressibility, thermal and electrical conductivity, superconductivity, and specific heat, as well as the properties of liquid helium, can also be understood through quantum theory.

(7) Provide a rational basis for the interpretation of ionization potentials, capture phenomena, and the scattering of electrons, neutrons, and protons when these particles come close to atoms or to molecules.

(8) Explain many perplexing phenomena associated with the interaction of radiation and matter, such as the Compton effect, the photoelectric effect, and several varieties of absorption and emission. H. A. Kramers' formula provides a much better description of dispersion than anything ever provided in classical theory.

(9) Give a coherent, intelligible pattern of concepts for understanding the existence of antiparticles, such as the positron and the antiproton.

(10) Make available at least the rudiments of a quantum electrodynamics, dealing with many mystifying radiation processes and with the coupling of electrons. (Successes have been most limited in this area, and some profound shortcomings of the algorithm of quantum theory have here been disclosed—those, for example, within the technique of "renormalization.")

Some may feel that this listing of factual achievements of quantum mechanics is out of place in any discussion of the philosophical aspects of that discipline and that it is an evasion of conceptual perplexities. But this is too easy a judgment. None of the many philosophically motivated alternatives to orthodox quantum mechanics has achieved even a fraction of what has just been set out seriatim. Presenting this list is not merely a way of replying "If you don't like my theory, then you do better." If the philosophical critics of orthodox quantum mechanics cannot even specify what it would be like to "do better" (in some calculational detail), then there is a philosophical point to this rhetorical reply. And the achievements listed above have been made by a theory within which the uncertainty relations are not simply an annoying indication of some incompleteness—the Einstein–de Broglie–Jeffreys suggestion—but rather constitute the fundamental structural feature of the theory. (John von Neumann generated all of quantum mechanics from an operationally suitable statement of the uncertainty relations *alone;* that is how fundamental to the theory's structure those relations are. One might risk arguing that the uncertainty relations *are* the conceptual structure of quantum theory. The theory essentially requires the interdependence of continuities and discontinuities; the uncertainty relations are little more than an expression of that strained interdependence.) Thus, the philosophical critic who desires a deterministic microphysical theory within which causality is classical, state descriptions are complete, and theoretical terms can be completely defined in terms of molar operations and observations has only to provide such an algebraically articulated theory that can claim a list of successes like those above in order to earn the gratitude and admiration of philosophers and scientists alike.

The uncertainty relations thus constitute a profound philosophical legacy of quantum mechanics. Were the theory markedly unsuccessful in observation and experiment, there would be no reason whatsoever to ponder over this particular structural feature, which is so strange and unsettling. But the theory has no serious rival at all, and it has achieved very much in a short time. Therefore, philosophers are rightly concerned at being confronted with a variety of scientific explanation that depends on there being a lower limit to the degree to which the state of the microparticle can be precisely described. In quantum mechanics there exists no concept of "the exact state of the microparticle." Indeed, the algebraic analogue of "electron e is exactly at position x, y, z at time t with precisely the energy v" is virtually ungrammatical in quantum mechanics, whose rules of construction and transformation could attach no meaning to such a symbol cluster. Not only does this make the character of our knowledge of microparticles different in kind from our (apparent) knowledge of classical microparticles, it immediately renders all laws within quantum mechanics irreducibly probabilistic. Answers to many well-made questions within quantum mechanics do not come as discrete quantitative values for general algebraic variables. They come rather as ribbons or belts or brackets or packets of possible values for the variables which figure in one's questions about nature. (The notions "good quantum numbers," "spin," "classifications schema," etc., all of which *can* be specified in terms of sharp numerical designations, are exceptions. But state descriptions are profoundly different conceptually.)

The problem immediately arises whether one's a priori expectations concerning what micronature must be like (punctiform and deterministic or fieldlike and precisely calculable) can establish that micro-objects in nature must be in distinct states at specifiable times, quantum mechanics to the contrary notwithstanding. The difficulties and errors in thus allowing one's expectations to dictate the results that one will accept will be obvious to every student of the history of thought. (Quantum theory, it should be observed, is built upon uncertainties even more comprehensive than that concerning position and momentum; energy and time and number and phase constitute equally pervasive structural features of quantum mechanics, each involving analogous uncertainties. The position–momentum uncertainty, although the easiest to articulate, should not be overemphasized lest it be thought that refinements in experimental technique would be sufficient to overhaul what is in fact the logical backbone of *all* of quantum theory.)

What alternative is there but to concede that the physical theory which tells us the truth, or a good part of the truth, about micronature can do so only if we accept *its* rules? Such rules as do structure quantum mechanics run clearly counter to any metaphysical preconceptions familiar to

philosophers with a nineteenth-century outlook. Therefore, it becomes a reasonable metaphysical possibility that nature is fundamentally indeterministic; that elementary particles are, ontologically, always in partially defined states; that they do not in any sense that is scientifically respectable and philosophically intelligible have both a precise position and an exact energy. This position lacks the aura of familiarity and intellectual comfort that Newtonian determinism had come to possess by the nineteenth century, but it has what determinism in micromechanics completely lacks—an extensive observational support structured by an inferentially well-made theory.

The philosopher's perplexity may become profound when it is further noted that "the constituents of the atom, being smaller than a wave-length of light, cannot be carriers of color; being subject to the Uncertainty Principle, they cannot always possess determinate positions or sizes; in short, . . . they may not be endowed with sensory qualities at all" (Henry Margenau, "Objectivity in Quantum Mechanics," in W. Reece, ed., The Delaware Series in Philosophy of Science, III). A subject matter like this must be puzzling to anyone at any time. But when it is articulated by so unprecedented and strange a theory and is then characterized as "elementary," "fundamental," and "basic," the philosopher will inevitably reappraise his own theoretical views. If Kant was "awakened from his dogmatic slumbers" by Hume's characterization of the subject matter of Newtonian physics, how much more must we today reconsider our preconceptions in light of the contemporary quantum physicist's characterization of ultimate microphysical matter?

PHILOSOPHICAL CRITICS OF THE COPENHAGEN INTERPRETATION

Undoubtedly the polemical tone of many of the writings of Bohr, Heisenberg, and Rosenfeld upset physicists and philosophers as much as their revelations of new data and new theoretical constructions did. Karl Popper could not admit that it had been established what could or could not be said meaningfully throughout all future scientific discourse. David Bohm undertook to determine precisely what von Neumann's vaunted "proof of the impossibility of hidden parameters within quantum mechanics" really did entail. He perceived, as did Popper, that the von Neumann proof simply made it clear that *if* one accepted the fundamental premises of orthodox quantum theory, then one could not also accept the possibility of there being microprocesses that were at once deterministic yet hidden beneath the surface of what is at present observable. (One cannot both play chess, as it is universally known, and also opt for the possibility that in some future game of chess, bishops might legitimately move parallel to the edge of the board.) This "proof" does not rule out the possibility of the formulation, at some time in the future, of entirely new rules whose consequences might be entirely distinct from what are now considered the restrictions of contemporary quantum theory.

Paul Feyerabend distinguishes the metaphysical content of orthodox quantum mechanics as enunciated in Copenhagen from the minimal algebraic transformations and factual data upon which any future microphysics must be built (for example, scattering of particles and noncommutativity of operators). He urges that the metaphysics be abandoned as being philosophically indefensible—or, at least, as not having been philosophically defended by the Copenhagen theorists. He holds that the minimal scientific content is quite compatible with some interpretation markedly different from the Copenhagen one. Jean Pierre Vigier has actually undertaken some impressive algebraic studies aimed at achieving all the predictions of quantum mechanics without being committed to the standard assumptions from which most microphysicists begin their calculations. And surely to accept another's conclusions does not oblige one to accept also the entire argument leading up to those conclusions.

Any scientific theory which is as philosophically fruitful as quantum mechanics has been must inevitably encounter serious examination, scrutiny, and criticism. Many of its critics are well trained in modern physics, some being professional physicists, and are philosophically quite sophisticated. It is reasonable, therefore, to suppose that their dissatisfactions with orthodox quantum theory and with the Copenhagen interpretation of it may reveal weaknesses in the standard position. And it is true that the popular pronouncements of the Copenhagen theorists have often seemed calculated to stifle all opposition as uninformed or archaic, or worse. A "minimal" exposition of quantum mechanics, stripped of metaphysics, may provide an adequate basis for a discipline that is quite neutral with respect to one's philosophy of science, although no less true to the facts than is quantum theory as it now stands. All this would seem to constitute a philosophically legitimate area of reflection and speculation. But speculation is not the same thing as "alternative scientific theory."

This is not to say that there *could not* be alternative theories—although any return to something like classical determinism is almost inconceivable. Nonetheless, since scientific disciplines are fundamentally empirical, informative, and constituted by synthetic claims, there must be consistent alternatives to them, however improbable. The philosophical critics of orthodox quantum theory have shown ingenuity and industry in noting many features of microphysics to which there are consistent alternatives. However, they have not yet provided anything resembling a workable alternative theory, nor have they provided workable alternatives to parts of the orthodox theory. Someone might do so, and since this possibility remains open it is hardly legitimate to regard the philosophy of microphysics as the exclusive property of the Copenhagen theorists. Let us all speculate, for that is how science changes and improves, but let us never confuse the speculations with the changes and the improvements themselves. Philosophers of science are particularly prone to this confusion—a fact which professional physicists are not slow to point out. In discussing the philosophical implications of quantum mechanics *as it is*, such a confusion is intolerable.

Given that the ultimate "stuff" of microphysics lacks sensory qualities, its relationship to actual observations must be intricate and tenuous. Yet "explanations" in quantum mechanics often consist in references to the properties of just this ultimate stuff. Tough positivists, from Ernst Mach on, would treat such references as heuristic shorthand merely, ultimately to be cashed in terms of laboratory observations or else dismissed as unwarranted metaphysics, operationally vacuous speculation. A streak of this positivism can be found in Heisenberg's early expositions of matrix mechanics. But this should cause no anxiety. Such a tough-minded attitude would have scored early references to positive electrons as being themselves metaphysical constructions invoked only to make observations of "wrongly" curving electronic particle paths intelligible and comfortable—but the positron has now been discovered; all the evidence indicates conclusively the existence of a particle one of whose many manifestations consists in "wrongly" curving electronic paths. Similarly, after Mach the atom was actually discovered. A Machian positivist *could* continue to deny the existence of atoms and positrons—but this would be doubt transformed into dogma. In Mach's day the evidence was partial and circumstantial. Today it is much more complete and direct, so much so that a denial of the existence of microentities now could hardly be expected of an empiricist. The ingenious clustering of properties that theoreticians pack into references concerning elementary particles often "explain" perplexing macrophysical phenomena. These theoretical cluster concepts are not just another way of referring to the macrophysical perplexities themselves—they do more. They connect, dovetail, splice, and structure the observations within conceptual frameworks that shape our theories of the microphenomenal substratum; the quantum physical properties of this substratum are responsible for what is observed in the laboratory. To paraphrase Wilfrid Sellars, quantum theory explains why laboratory observations fall under the empirical laws they do fall under ("The Language of Theories," in Herbert Feigl and Grover Maxwell, eds., *Current Issues in the Philosophy of Science,* New York, 1961). And "explaining why" in this sense is doing considerably more than simply reiterating references (in abstruse algebra) to the laboratory encounters themselves.

Thus, the theoretical terms of quantum theory cannot be exhaustively defined by means of the experiential encounters which triggered modern microphysics to begin with. Today Mach would hardly deny the *de facto* existence of atoms; he was too good an empiricist. But he might try to correlate exactly such terms as "electron," "positron," and "proton" with, and only with, the macrophysical laboratory observations in connection with which such particle names seem to have designatory value today. And this would be an unnecessarily narrow correlation. Terms like "electron," "neutrino," "psi," and "delta" are *pattern providers.* They theoretically position phenomena that can provide no conceptual pattern for themselves. Views on this matter differ, certainly among philosophers and even among physicists. But a "Craig-theoretic" reconstruction of quantum mechanics, whereby all of its theoretical entities are decomposed into corresponding lists of observation claims (the Machian ideal), seems implausible to the majority of physicists and philosophers of science (see CRAIG'S THEOREM). For any given list of observation claims will be compatible with a variety of microphysical theories, the differences between which will be clear from their different choices of theoretical terms (pattern providers) and the functions assigned to them in calculation and inference.

Microphenomena, as discovered in this century, have required the combination of two descriptive vocabularies which our predecessors had so defined that they were incompatible with each other. Thus, a host of conceptual perplexities has resulted from the perceptual complexities of the laboratory. Philosophers have been forced to reassess traditional analyses of causality and determinism, of explanation and prediction, of objectivity and subjectivity, of theoretical terms and observational descriptions. Every scientific revolution requires some such philosophical reassessment of the categories of conceptual analysis, but the advent of quantum mechanics seems, in a special and pointed way, to have gone to the heart of the corpus of philosophical commitments concerning the presuppositions within our knowledge of matter and of our understanding of the world in which we live. The great physicists who spearheaded the spectacular advances of quantum mechanics reached philosophical conclusions concerning their own work far too hastily and without the care they lavished on the strictly scientific components of their research. Some statements of the Copenhagen interpretation have struck responsible philosophers as being a mixture of crude positivism (for example, that of Heisenberg) and naive metaphysics (for example, that of Bohr). But this should not blind us to the fundamental fact that quantum mechanics has changed the shape of the philosophical world for all of us. We can no longer view it as an uncomfortable and annoying phase through which science is progressing, later surely to settle down as "philosophically more respectable." The "awkward" features of the conceptual structure of the new quantum mechanics (of Schrödinger, Heisenberg, Dirac, etc.) seem likely to be with us through an indefinite future. It was perhaps the perceptive recognition of this fact that generated the enthusiastic statements of the early Bohr and the later Heisenberg. But the initial skepticism natural in professional philosophers should not obscure the deep departure from philosophical tradition that is built into the very heart of quantum mechanics.

Bibliography

CLASSICAL PAPERS

Bohr, Niels, "On the Constitution of Atoms and Molecules." *Philosophical Magazine*, Vol. 26 (1913), 1–25, 476–502, 857–875.

Bohr, Niels, "On the Quantum Theory of Line Spectra." *Det kongelige danske Videnskabernes Selskab. Skrifter Naturvidenskabelig og mathematisk Afdeling.* Series 8, Vol. 4 (1918) 108–118.

Bohr, Niels, "Atomic Structure." *Nature*, Vol. 107 (1921), 104–107.

Bohr, Niels, "Über die Anwendung der Quantentheorie auf den Atombau. I. Die Grundpostulate der Quantentheorie." *Zeitschrift für Physik*, Vol. 13 (1923), 117–165.

Bohr, Niels, "The Quantum Postulate and the Recent Development of Atomic Theory." *Nature*, Vol. 121 (1928), 580–590.

Bohr, Niels; Kramers, H. A.; and Slater, J. C., "The Quantum Theory of Radiation." *Philosophical Magazine*, Vol. 47 (1924), 785–802.

Born, Max, "Quantenmechanik der Stossvorgänge." *Zeitschrift für Physik*, Vol. 38 (1926), 803–827.

Born, Max; Heisenberg, Werner; and Jordan, Pascual, "Zur Quantenmechanik. II." *Zeitschrift für Physik*, Vol. 35 (1926), 557–615.

Born, Max, and Jordan, Pascual, "Zur Quantenmechanik." *Zeitschrift für Physik*, Vol. 34 (1925), 858–888.

Broglie, Louis de, "A Tentative Theory of Light Quanta." *Philosophical Magazine*, Vol. 47 (1924), 446–458.

Debye, Peter, "Quantenhypothese und Zeeman-Effekt." *Physikalische Zeitschrift*, Vol. 17 (1916), 507–512.

Dirac, P. A. M., "On the Theory of Quantum Mechanics." *Proceedings of the Royal Society A*, Vol. 112 (1926), 661–677.

Dirac, P. A. M., "The Physical Interpretation of the Quantum Dynamics." *Proceedings of the Royal Society A*, Vol. 113 (1926), 621–641.

Dirac, P. A. M., "The Quantum Theory of the Electron." *Proceedings of the Royal Society A*, Vol. 117 (1928), 610–624.

Dirac, P. A. M., "The Quantum Theory of the Electron. Part II." *Proceedings of the Royal Society A*, Vol. 118 (1928), 351–361.

Einstein, Albert, "Über einen die Erzeugung und Verwandlung des Lichtes betreffenden heuristischen Gesichtspunkt." *Annalen der Physik*, Vol. 17 (1905), 132–148.

Einstein, Albert, "Die Plancksche Theorie der Strahlung und die Theorie der spezifischen Wärme." *Annalen der Physik*, Vol. 22 (1907), 180–190.

Goudsmit, S. A., and Uhlenbeck, G. E., "Opmerking over de Spectra van Waterstof en Helium." *Physica*, Vol. 5 (1925), 266–270.

Goudsmit, S. A., and Uhlenbeck, G. E., "Spinning Electrons and the Structure of Spectra." *Nature*, Vol. 117 (1926), 264–265.

Goudsmit, S. A., and Uhlenbeck, G. E., "Die Kopplungsmöglichkeiten der Quantenvektoren." *Zeitschrift für Physik*, Vol. 35 (1926), 618–625.

Heisenberg, Werner, "Zur Quantentheorie der Linienstruktur und der anomalen Zeemaneffekte." *Zeitschrift für Physik*, Vol. 8 (1921), 273–297.

Heisenberg, Werner, "Über Quantentheoretische Umdeutung kinematischer und mechanischer Beziehungen." *Zeitschrift für Physik*, Vol. 33 (1925), 879–893.

Heisenberg, Werner, "Über quantentheoretische Kinematik und Mechanik." *Mathematische Annalen*, Vol. 95 (1926), 683–705.

Heisenberg, Werner, "Über den anschaulichen Inhalt der quantentheoretischen Kinematik und Mechanik." *Zeitschrift für Physik*, Vol. 43 (1927), 172–198.

Kramers, H. A., "The Quantum Theory of Dispersion." *Nature*, Vol. 114 (1924), 310.

Planck, Max, "Zur Theorie des Gesetzes der Energieverteilung im Normal-spectrum." *Verhandlungen des Deutschen Physikalischen Gesellschaft*, Vol. 2 (1900), 237–245.

Planck, Max, "Über die Elementarquanta der Materie und der Elektrizität." *Annalen der Physik*, Vol. 4 (1901), 564–568.

Schrödinger, Erwin, "Quantisierung als Eigenwertproblem." *Annalen der Physik*, Vol. 79 (1926), 361–376, 489–527, 734–756; Vol. 80 (1926), 437–490; Vol. 81 (1926), 109–139.

Sommerfeld, Arnold, "Zur Quantentheorie der Spektrallinien. I und II." *Annalen der Physik*, Vol. 51 (1916), 1–94.

Sommerfeld, Arnold, "Zur Quantentheorie der Spektrallinien. III. Theorie der Röntgenspektren." *Annalen der Physik*, Vol. 51 (1916).

Wilson, William, "The Quantum of Action." *Philosophical Magazine*, Vol. 31 (1916), 156–162.

MODERN EXPOSITIONS

Bohm, David, *Quantum Theory.* Englewood Cliffs, N.J., 1951. Advanced.

Dirac, P. A. M., *The Principles of Quantum Mechanics,* 3d ed. Oxford and New York, 1947.

Houston, W. V., *Principles of Quantum Mechanics.* New York, 1951.

Kemble, E. C., *The Fundamental Principles of Quantum Mechanics.* New York, 1937.

Neumann, John von, *The Mathematical Foundations of Quantum Mechanics.* Princeton, N.J., 1955.

Rojansky, V. B., *Introductory Quantum Mechanics.* Englewood Cliffs, N.J., 1938.

Schiff, Leonard I., *Quantum Mechanics,* 2d ed. New York, 1955.

PHILOSOPHICAL WORKS ON QUANTUM MECHANICS

Bohm, David, *Causality and Chance in Modern Physics.* Princeton, N.J., 1957.

Bohr, Niels, "Discussions with Einstein on Epistemological Problems in Atomic Physics," in P. A. Schilpp, ed., *Albert Einstein, Philosopher-scientist.* New York, 1951. See also Einstein's "A Reply to Criticisms" in the same volume.

Bunge, Mario, *Causality.* Cambridge, Mass., 1959.

Čapek, Milič, *Philosophical Impact of Contemporary Physics.* Princeton, N.J., 1961.

Feyerabend, P. K., "The Quantum Theory of Measurement," in Stephan Körner, ed., *Observation and Interpretation.* London, 1957.

Feyerabend, P. K., "Explanation, Reduction, and Empiricism," in *Minnesota Studies in the Philosophy of Science,* Vol. III, Herbert Feigl and Grover Maxwell, eds. Minneapolis, 1962.

Feyerabend, P. K., "Problems of Microphysics," in R. G. Colodny, ed., *Frontiers of Science and Philosophy.* Pittsburgh, 1962.

Hanson, N. R., *Patterns of Discovery.* Cambridge, 1958.

Hanson, N. R., *The Concept of the Positron.* Cambridge, 1963.

Hook, Sidney, ed., *Determinism and Freedom in the Age of Modern Science.* New York, 1958. See articles by P. W. Bridgman, Alfred Landé, and M. K. Munitz.

Landé, Alfred, "From Duality to Unity in Quantum Mechanics," in *Current Issues in the Philosophy of Science.* New York, 1961.

Lenzen, Victor, *Physical Theory.* New York, 1931.

Lindsay, R. B., and Margenau, Henry, *The Foundations of Physics.* New York, 1936.

Margenau, Henry, *The Nature of Physical Reality.* New York, 1950.

Mehlberg, Henry, "The Observational Problem of Quantum Theory." Read at the May 1958 meeting of the American Philosophical Association, Western Division.

Nagel, Ernest, *The Structure of Science.* New York, 1961. Ch. 10.

Popper, Karl, *Logik der Forschung.* Vienna, 1935. Translated by Popper, with the assistance of Julius Freed and Lan Freed, as *The Logic of Scientific Discovery.* London, New York, and Toronto, 1959.

Popper, Karl, "Indeterminism in Quantum Physics and in Classical Physics." *British Journal for the Philosophy of Science,* Vol. 1 (1950) 117–133; 173–195.

Planck, Max, *Where Is Science Going?* New York, 1932.

Reichenbach, Hans, *Philosophic Foundations of Quantum Mechanics.* Berkeley and Los Angeles, 1945.

Schlick, Moritz, "Die Kausalität in der gegenwärtigen Physik." *Naturwissenschaften* (1931). Translated by David Rynin as "Causality in Contemporary Physics." *British Journal for the Philosophy of Science,* Vol. 12 (1961–1962), 177–193; 281–298.

Waismann, Friedrich, "The Decline and Fall of Causality," in A. C. Crombie, ed., *Turning Points in Physics.* New York, 1961.

NORWOOD RUSSELL HANSON

QUESTIONS. The study of questions as distinct logical entities is quite ancient, having been initiated by Aristotle and pursued in the Middle Ages by Adam of Balsham. M. L. Prior and A. N. Prior have discussed the important contributions of Richard Whately early in the nineteenth century. Most of the appreciable work on the subject, however, is very recent.

Questions are not to be distinguished on grammatical criteria alone from locutions of other kinds. On occasion we wish to classify such an indicative sentence as "I wonder whether you agree" as "really a question," or such an interrogative sentence as "Are we downhearted?" as "really not a question at all." In any case, even the linguist ultimately needs an extragrammatical test of what is or is not the interrogative mood. Questioning is an activity which can have various kinds of linguistic expression and can even be carried on without language. However, provided there exists a well-defined interrogative idiom—which appears to be the case in virtually all natural languages—a reasonably satisfactory criterion of being a question must involve "appropriate" expressibility in that idiom.

Kinds of question. The word "question" is often used to mean simply "subject" or "topic," and questions are loosely classified according to their subject matter as historical, literary, agricultural, architectural, and so on. This classification, however, merges with one based on the form of the required answer. Thus, a "moral" question is not merely a question on the subject of morals but also one that requires a moral judgment as answer; and since statements that express moral judgments are distinct from other kinds of statement, the corresponding questions are similarly different in kind. In general, theories of meaning, insofar as they make distinctions between kinds of statement, will normally lead to parallel distinctions between kinds of question. Such theories have sometimes been stated primarily in terms of questions rather than statements. Thus Moritz Schlick distinguished metaphysical questions from others and categorized them as "unanswerable," on the same grounds that he would have used to castigate proposed answers to them as "unverifiable." This terminology suggests that there may exist meaningful questions that have no meaningful answers. It is possible, however, to treat both questions and their answers as equally and in the same manner involved in issues of meaning, wherever they arise; hence "unanswerable" questions could equally be termed "unaskable."

A rather different distinction was made by D. A. T. Gasking, who showed that one and the same question may be variously classified, depending on details of the situation in which it is asked. Thus, "Is Smith a trustee of the estate?" may be a factual or "scientific" question if no issue of interpretation arises, or a "logical" question if the facts concerning Smith are known but it remains to be determined whether they satisfy the definition of "trustee." Again, it may be what Gasking termed a "philosophical" question, in that what is called for is not information but rather some kind of new decision. Thus, the facts may be such that there is no clear precedent for whether Smith is or is not a trustee; or, for whatever reason, the question may arise of a variant redecision even in a case that would normally be regarded as closed.

J. M. O. Wheatley and Bernard Mayo make a similar point about such questions as "What shall I do now?" which, asked of oneself, call for decision on a course of action rather than determination of an unknown fact.

Do questions have a logic? It is sometimes held that the activities of statement-making and question-asking (and others), although pragmatically different, are built on a basic logic that is the same for all the activities.

This attitude may arise from the belief that all questions

are "yes–no" questions and thus may be put in the form "Is *P* true?," where *P* is a proposition. Questions may, however, involve three or more explicit alternatives, as in "Is it animal, vegetable, or mineral?" or an undefined number of unlisted alternatives, as in the case of Rudolf Carnap's "W-questions," which are questions introduced by "who," "what," "where," "which," "why," or (in English, unalphabetically) "how." Consequently there is no one-to-one correspondence between statements and questions, and questions cannot be analyzed in purely propositional terms.

A similar attitude, however, is taken by others, who conceive logic, however broadly, as a formal study transcending linguistic practice.

Those who want a common fundamental logic do not always want to reduce questions to statements. Questions have sometimes been conceived as more fundamental than statements from the point of view of meaning; for example, by R. G. Collingwood, who claimed that to understand a statement it is necessary to know to what question the statement is intended to be an answer. This attitude, however, is inimical to the development of a formal analysis of questions; mainly because, as indicated by the Priors, it is inimical to the development of any formal logic at all.

Questions and statements. Even yes–no questions of the form "Is *P* true?" do not correspond one to one with statements unless it is stipulated that "Is *S* true?" and "Is not-*S* true?" are to count as different questions; and this is less than reasonable, since the second question presents the same pair of alternative possible answers as the first. H. S. Leonard, who distinguished between the "concern" of a statement and its "topic of concern," achieved a one-to-one correspondence by taking the topic of concern of a question to be that of its correct answer. In so doing, however, he went beyond a purely logical analysis, since it should be possible to know how to analyze a question without knowing the answer to it. When W-questions are considered, the one-to-one correspondence in any case vanishes again, since "Caesar invaded Britain in 55 B.C." is the answer not only to "Did Caesar invade Britain in 55 B.C.?" but also to "When did Caesar invade Britain?" and others.

Another kind of identification of questions with statements was made by David Harrah and N. D. Belnap, Jr., who classified questions as "true" or "false" according to whether they involve true or false presuppositions. A yes–no question, Harrah claimed, is equivalent to the exclusive disjunction of its possible answers; and a W-question is equivalent to a corresponding existential statement. Thus, "Is it raining?" would be said to be equivalent to "Either it is raining or it isn't (but not both)," and "What is the square root of 16?" to "16 has one and only one square root." Most questions would be, as in the former case, equivalent to tautologies; but in the latter case the statement is, of course, false if we allow negative numbers, and hence the question involves a false presupposition. The classic "Have you stopped beating your wife?" would be equivalent to some such statement as "Either you used to beat your wife and still do, or you used to beat her and do so no longer (but not both)," that is, to "You used to beat your wife." A "false" question has no correct answer.

The terminology is misleading, however, if it suggests that what is proposed is a reductive account of the logic of questions in terms of statements: what is given is an account, within a logic of questions, of a particular feature of that logic.

Questions, then, stand in relation to certain statements as answers and to certain others as presuppositions. The answer to a question, however, is not always a statement. When a question such as "Shall I open the window?" is answered with "Yes" or "No," these answers are abbreviations not of statements, since they cannot be classified as true or false, but of the imperative locution "Open the window" or "Do not open the window." Commands, requests, advice, recipes, suggestions, imprecations, or any other of the various kinds of imperatives may be given in answer to questions. There are also W-questions requiring imperative answers, such as "When shall I come?" Little work has been done in this area, although the "deliberative questions" of Wheatley and Mayo might be considered to be of this kind.

Otto Jespersen described what he called a question raised to the second power, a question that is itself questioned. If *A* asks *B*, "How are you feeling today?," and *B* replies, "How am I feeling? Do I look ill?," *B*'s reply is of this kind, since if *A* were to reply "Yes"—meaning, that is, "Yes, how are you feeling?"—his reply would be equivalent to his original question. Hence, questions may even have questions as answers.

Questions as propositional functions. F. S. Cohen suggested identifying questions with propositional functions. Any W-question can be resolved into a "what" question: "at what time" for "when," "at what place" for "where," and so on. Sometimes less direct translation seems appropriate: "Why do the planets move in ellipses?" becomes "What facts explain the planets' elliptical motion?" Further, some "what" questions—those which ask for definitions—in turn seem to require lengthy translation, as when "What is a palimpsest?" becomes, say, "What true statement *S* is such that every true statement containing the word 'palimpsest' is inferable from *S* (taken together with certain acceptable presuppositions not containing the word)?" With these exceptions, however, "what" questions, and hence all W-questions, can normally be interpreted as asking for the allocation of a suitable value to a variable or variables in some propositional function containing them. Carnap suggested a symbolic notation in which the variable or variables are prefixed to the propositional function as they are in quantification. Thus "When was Karl in Berlin?" is symbolized $(?t)$(Karl was in Berlin at time t). The prefix $(?t)$ might be called an erotetic quantifier. (The adjective "erotetic," from the Greek $\epsilon\rho\omega\tau\eta\mu\alpha$, "question," was coined by the Priors in a different connection.)

It is tempting to try to use a similar notation in the case of yes–no questions and questions with listed-alternative answers. Yes–no questions can be fitted without undue strain into the form $(?X)$(The truth-value of *S* is *X*), or, if *X* is allowed to be a variable operator with two values that make *XS* equivalent to *S* and not-*S* respectively, in the form, due to J. L. Mackie, $(?X)(XS)$. Listed-alternative questions are more recalcitrant: "Did she wear the red hat or the blue or the white?" cannot be translated "What was the color of her hat?" since the category word "color" permits alternatives other than "red," "white," and "blue." Unless we are prepared to accept *ad hoc* definition of category words virtually without limit, we must recognize listed-alternative questions as in principle different from W-questions and not, like the latter, normally assimilable to propositional functions at all. But yes – no questions are easily assimilable to listed-alternative questions, and there thus seems to be no reason to invent an *ad hoc* category to accommodate them.

The concept of category has been connected with the subject of questions since Aristotle's *Categories*. This leads to further doubt concerning the possibility or the utility of reducing even W-questions to propositional functions. The function must have coupled to it an indication of the category of the variable for which substitution is to be made. Thus "Who discovered **America**?" requires in its answer the specification of a historical person, whereas "What is the smallest prime?" requires the specification of a number; but in the proposed representation there is nothing to indicate this. "Seventeen discovered America" and "Peter the Great is the smallest prime" are incorrect but, so far as the symbolism shows, permissible answers. Conjoining a category specification, as in "What is such that it is a historical person and discovered America?" does not help. Possibly the problem is a general one for quantification theory. However, English idiom provides routinely for a category word in questions, as in "What HISTORICAL PERSON discovered America?" and "What NUMBER is the smallest prime?" The differentiation in form of the W-words also helps to distinguish categories. A symbolism incorporating category specification has been given by Belnap.

The theory of W-questions as propositional functions naturally does not apply at all to those W-questions whose answers are imperatives, although an analogous account in terms of functions taking imperatives as values could be given.

Kinds of erotetic quantifiers. The question "When was Karl in Berlin?" is ambiguous in that it does not make clear whether it presumes that Karl's visit was a unique event or allows the possibility of many visits or none at all; and, if the latter, whether it asks for a complete list of the visits or is to be satisfied with a specimen one or a representative selection. Belnap was the first to codify the richness of these alternatives. His analysis is not confined to W-questions but extends to the case of listed alternatives. Given a set of alternatives in some form, Belnap distinguished, in particular (without claiming that they are exhaustive), three kinds of question that can be asked: (*a*) A "unique-alternative" question, which asks for a single choice among the alternatives, on the assumption that there is only one correct one, as in "What is the sum of 5 and 7?" or "Did she wear the red hat or the blue or the white?" The assumption may be false, as in "Which number less than 10 is prime?" (*b*) A "complete-list" question, which asks for all true alternatives, as in "Which of Ghana, India, Canada, and Australia are republics?" or "What numbers less than 10 are primes?" Complete-list questions may be construed as assuming the existence of at

least one true alternative, or not. (*c*) A "nonexclusive" question, which asks for some of an indeterminate number of true alternatives, as "What is an example of a prime?" or "What's good on the menu today?" In the absence of special qualification (as in "What, if anything, is good on the menu today?") these normally assume the existence of at least one true alternative, but again this is not formally essential.

There are two kinds of conditions in Belnap's classification: conditions as to the number of alternatives the answer is to contain, and conditions as to the number of alternatives that are assumed to be true ones and hence available for inclusion in the correct answer. A common assumption concerning the possible answers to a question is that they are mutually exclusive and that there is, therefore, only one true alternative. This does not exclude the possibility of complete-list questions, since—for example, in the case of "What numbers less than 10 are primes?"—the set of alternatives may be considered to be not the statements affirming primehood of individual numbers less than 10 but, instead, the possible conjunctions of such statements. It does, however, rule out questions of the nonexclusive variety. Belnap introduced a notation to differentiate the three kinds of question: in the case of W-questions there are, in effect, three kinds of erotetic quantifier. That the classification is not exhaustive is illustrated by the existence of other possible conditions on the number of alternatives in the answer or of assumptions concerning the number of alternatives. Simple examples are "What are at least two of the primes?," "Which four numbers between 10 and 20 are prime?," and "Who are at least four of the presidents of the United States?" In the case of more complicated examples it is usual in ordinary speech to employ circumlocutions avoiding the interrogative mood, as in "Name at least three, and preferably all, of the countries of the Common Market," but this is not due to any formal limitation. On the other hand, "how" and "why" questions such as "How did Hitler die?" and "Why doesn't gold dissolve in nitric acid?" commonly have considerably more complicated, but less easily specifiable, criteria of what counts as an answer.

Questions with multiple quantifiers provide another case in which answers are not necessarily mutually exclusive. Presumably "Who did what when?" could be considered satisfied by a description of any event of human history. It is not uncommon, however, to find that such questions are resoluble into separate components with single operators. Thus "Which Roman generals courted which Egyptian queen?" becomes "Which Roman generals courted a certain Egyptian queen?," together with "Who was she?"

Presuppositions of questions. The kind of presupposition that occurs in the questions "Have you stopped beating your wife?" and "Is the present king of France hairy?" is due to the fact that the indicated alternative answers are not exhaustive. Thus neither the answer "Yes, the present king of France is hairy" nor the apparent contradictory "No, the present king of France is not hairy" is true, since they both make a false existential presupposition. Questions very commonly predispose the answerer toward an existential presupposition and may, in consequence, be regarded as having existential (or other) presuppositions themselves. To those who reject the thesis of Harrah and Belnap that questions may have propositional components, the fact that questions, like statements, have presuppositions might, on the other hand, be one of the strongest arguments for P. F. Strawson's account of presupposition, as opposed to Russell's conflation of it with implication (see PRESUPPOSING).

A concept resembling that of presupposition seems called for by a different class of cases. Some of those who have attempted to analyze questions have identified them with descriptions of attitudes of the questioner. Thus, Jeffreys wrote that "Is Mr. Smith at home?" is equivalent to the trio of statements "I do not know whether Mr. Smith is at home: I want to know whether Mr. Smith is at home: I think you know whether Mr. Smith is at home." As a reductive analysis this is unsatisfactory. In the first place, it does not translate the question away but only throws it into an interrogative subordinate clause "whether Mr. Smith is at home," and in general treats any question Q as translatable into "I do not know the answer to Q: (etc.)," where the definiendum appears as part of the definiens. J. L. Mackie pointed out that in the present context the interrogative clause can be replaced throughout by the disjunction of noninterrogative clauses "either that Mr. Smith is at home or that Mr. Smith is not at home," but there would be some difficulty in effecting this replacement if the original question had been a W-question. Second, Jeffreys' analysis gives an account not of the content of the question itself but rather of the situation in which the question is asked: a similar comparison could be made between any statement S and some other group of statements, such as "I believe that S: I think you do not believe that S: I want you to believe that S." Yet it has often been recognized that in a pragmatic sense the making of a statement S implies certain attitudes in the speaker toward S and related statements. Thus, Jeffreys' analysis, and those like it, may remind us that, if we enlarge the domain of formal logic to include questions as well as statements (and locutions of other moods), we create the need for some kind of differential pragmatics of mood. Just as we may want to say that to make a statement S is (pragmatically) to imply a belief in S, we may also want to say that asking a question Q pragmatically implies lack of knowledge of, and desire to know, the answer to Q, and belief that the person addressed knows the answer. These "implications" of a question are not all present in all contexts. A special case is that of questions asked to test the addressee's knowledge. Bernard Bosanquet and Christoph Sigwart argued that these are really not questions but imperatives. Nevertheless, it is clear that the pragmatic considerations surrounding the asking of questions are typically quite different from those surrounding the making of statements. It is in this territory, which is also largely unexplored, that the answer to the opening question concerning what is "appropriately" expressed in the interrogative mood is to be found.

Whether presuppositions of questions are all to be treated as cases of pragmatic implication is not important here. It should be said, however, that they are frequently themselves matters of context. Thus "Have you stopped beating your wife?" is a perfectly proper question if it has been preceded by the question "Did you use to beat your wife?" and if this has been answered in the affirmative.

A not inconsiderable superstructure has been built on the logic of questions, which is basic to the construction of formal accounts of topic and relevance, and to the concepts required in the theory of communication.

Bibliography

Adam of Balsham, *Ars Disserendi*, in L. Minio-Paluello, ed., *Twelfth Century Logic, Texts and Studies*, Vol I. Rome, 1956.
Aristotle, *Interpretation.* 20b27–31.
Aristotle, *Sophistical Refutations.* 167b39–168a12.
Belnap, N. D., Jr., *An Analysis of Questions: Preliminary Report.* Santa Monica, Calif., 1963.
Bosanquet, Bernard, *Logic*, 2 vols. Oxford, 1888.
Carnap, Rudolf, *Logische Syntax der Sprache.* Vienna, 1934. Translated by Amethe Smeaton as *Logical Syntax of Language.* London, 1937. P. 296.
Cohen, F. S., "What Is a Question?" *Monist,* Vol. 39 (1929), 350–364.
Collingwood, R. G., *Autobiography.* Oxford, 1939. Ch. 5.
Cresswell, M. J., "The Logic of Interrogatives," in J. N. Crossley and M. A. E. Dummett, eds., *Formal Systems and Recursive Functions.* Amsterdam, 1965.
Gasking, D. A. T., "Types of Questions." *Melbourne University Magazine* (1946), 4–6.
Hamblin, C. L., "Questions." *Australasian Journal of Philosophy,* Vol. 36 (1958), 159–168.
Hamblin, C. L., "Questions Aren't Statements." *Philosophy of Science,* Vol. 30 (1963), 62–63.
Harrah, David, "A Logic of Questions and Answers." *Philosophy of Science,* Vol. 28 (1961), 40–46.
Harrah, David, *Communication: A Logical Model.* Cambridge, Mass., 1963.
Harrah, David, "A Model for Applying Information and Utility Functions." *Philosophy of Science,* Vol. 30 (1963), 267–273.
Hiż, Henry, "Questions and Answers." *Journal of Philosophy,* Vol. 59 (1962), 253–265.
Jeffreys, Harold, *Theory of Probability,* 2d ed. Oxford, 1948. P. 378
Jespersen, J. O. H., *Modern English Grammar.* Heidelberg, 1931. Vol. V, Para. 25.34, pp. 495–496.
Kubinski, Tadeusz, "Essay in the Logic of Questions," in *Atti del XII congresso internazionale di filosofia, Venezia 1958.* Florence, 1960. Pp. 315–322.
Leonard, H. S., *Principles of Right Reason.* New York, 1957.
Leonard, H. S., "Interrogatives, Imperatives, Truth, Falsity and Lies." *Philosophy of Science,* Vol. 26 (1959), 172–186.
Leonard, H. S., "A Reply to Professor Wheatley." *Philosophy of Science,* Vol. 28 (1961), 55–64.
Lewis, C. I., and Langford, C. H., *Symbolic Logic.* New York, 1932. Pp. 332–334.
Llewelyn, J. E., "What Is a Question?" *Australasian Journal of Philosophy,* Vol. 42 (1964), 69–85.
Mayo, Bernard, "Deliberative Questions: A Criticism." *Analysis,* Vol. 16 (1955), 58–63.
Presley, C. F., "A Note on Questions." *Australasian Journal of Philosophy,* Vol. 37 (1959), 64–66.
Prior, M. L., and Prior, A. N., "Erotetic Logic." *Philosophical Review,* Vol. 64 (1955), 43–59.
Reichenbach, Hans, *Elements of Symbolic Logic.* New York, 1947. Pp. 339–342.
Ryle, Gilbert, "Categories." *PAS,* Vol. 38 (1937), 189–206. Reprinted in A. G. N. Flew, ed., *Logic and Language,* 2d series. Oxford, 1953.
Schlick, Moritz, "A New Philosophy of Experience." Publications in Philosophy of the College of the Pacific. Stockton, Calif., 1932. Reprinted in Schlick's *Gesammelte Aufsätze.* Vienna, 1938.
Sigwart, Christoph, *Logik.* Tübingen, 1873. Translated by Helen Dendy. London, 1895. P. 177.
Stahl, Gerold, "La lógica de las preguntas." *Anales de la universidad de Chile,* Vol. 102 (1956), 71–75.

Stahl, Gerold, "Fragenfolgen," in M. U. Kaesbauer and F. Kutschen, eds., *Logik und Logikkalkul.* Freiburg and Munich, 1962. Pp. 149–157.

Whately, Richard, *Elements of Logic.* London, 1826.

Wheatley, J. M. O., "Deliberative Questions." *Analysis,* Vol. 15 (1954), 49–60.

Wheatley, J. M. O., "Note on Professor Leonard's Analysis of Interrogatives etc." *Philosophy of Science,* Vol. 29 (1961), 52–54.

Wittgenstein, Ludwig, *Philosophical Investigations.* Oxford, 1953. Secs. 23–24.

C. L. HAMBLIN

QUINE, WILLARD VAN ORMAN, Edgar Pierce professor of philosophy at Harvard, was born in Akron, Ohio, in 1908. In 1930 he was graduated from Oberlin, where he majored in mathematics, and he wrote a doctoral dissertation in logic under Alfred North Whitehead at Harvard. He visited Vienna, studied mathematical logic at Warsaw, and at Prague met Rudolf Carnap, whose work was to inspire and influence him.

Some of Quine's publications are in philosophy, some in symbolic logic, and others are concerned with the logical regimentation of ordinary language. It is his philosophy and related aspects of his advocated regimentation of language that concern us here, his contributions to logic being dealt with elsewhere (see LOGIC, HISTORY OF, section on Quine).

Analytic–synthetic distinction. Some philosophers have attempted to distinguish between such statements as "A river flows through Brisbane," which, they contend, are true as a matter of fact, and statements like "No bachelor is married," the truth of which is said to be independent of matters of fact. The former have been described as synthetic, the latter as analytic. Quine maintains, first, that the analytic–synthetic distinction has never satisfactorily been made and, second, that there is no good reason for believing that it can be made.

Logical truth. Given a list of logical particles and the notion of truth, with which Quine is comparatively satisfied, we may, he contends, derive the notion of logical truth. "All birds are birds" is logically true because it is both true and such that if we leave its logical parts alone and replace "birds" with some other word, then if we get a statement at all, we get a true one—for example, "All snakes are snakes." But even though this analytic statement is logically true, there are analytic statements like "No bachelor is married" which are not, and thus analyticity remains to be explained. If we replace "bachelor" with the synonymous "unmarried man," we have a logical truth, and it would thus appear that an analytic statement either is a logical truth or is reducible to one by interchange of synonyms.

Synonymy. However, according to Quine, an account of analyticity that depends on the notion of synonymy is unsatisfactory. Suppose that all and only Guards officers are very tall soldiers with long hair. Since "Guards officers" and "very tall soldiers with long hair" are coextensive expressions, there are statements whose truth or falsity cannot be affected by interchanging these expressions. But because they are not synonymous expressions, there are also statements like "Necessarily, all and only Guards officers are Guards officers" which can be so affected. In contrast, the truth of the statement "Necessarily, all and only bachelors are bachelors" cannot be affected by interchanging "bachelors" and "unmarried men" because these expressions are synonymous. But to make the last statement is to say that "All and only bachelors are bachelors" is analytic. Thus, we give an account of synonymy in terms of the effects of interchanging expressions in certain contexts. But because these contexts cannot be specified without reference to analyticity or some equivalent notion, we cannot, without circularity, use the notion of synonymy in giving an account of analyticity. Similar difficulties frustrate the derivation of self-contradictoriness from logical falsity.

Quine also discusses the possibility of giving an account of the analyticity of statements in artificial languages, but here, as in natural languages, the difficulty is, he contends, that each of the key notions in the theory of meaning is definable only in terms of the others.

Anyone who produced an account of these notions acceptable to Quine would thereby refute him, but what sort of account this would be remains to be seen. In the meantime the strongest argument against him is *ad hominem.* "All the illuminated manuscripts are illuminated" is logically true only if "illuminated" has the same meaning in each of its occurrences. Thus, the notion of logical truth, which Quine accepts, is dependent upon the notion of synonymy, which he rejects.

Radical translations. Quine's theory of meaning is further developed in his discussion of the difficulties that would arise if we were to attempt to translate the language of a hitherto isolated tribe. Radical translation, as he calls it, would have to begin not with words but with those sentences which have a comparatively direct relation to stimulus conditions. The stimulus meaning of a sentence for a person is defined in terms of the class which has as its members the kinds of stimulation which would prompt the person's assent to the sentence. Intrasubjective stimulus synonymy is sameness of stimulus meaning for one speaker, and two sentences are socially stimulus-synonymous if they are intrasubjectively stimulus-synonymous for nearly everyone who speaks the language. A sentence is stimulus-analytic for a person if he would assent to it, if to anything, after every stimulation, and a socially stimulus-analytic sentence is stimulus-analytic for nearly every speaker of the language.

In order to see that these are not our intuitive notions of synonymy and analyticity, we need to distinguish occasion sentences and standing sentences. If every minute or so we are asked to assent to "John has hiccups," we cannot do so without having another look at John on each occasion. In contrast, having once assented to the standing sentence "Salt is soluble in water," we may assent again without observing salt or anything else again. Applied to occasion sentences, intrasubjective stimulus synonymy approximates sameness of meaning; standing sentences, however, are related to experience indirectly, and the kinds of stimulus that would prompt assent to a standing sentence vary from speaker to speaker. Thus, the stimulus meaning of a standing sentence falls short of our intuitive notion of meaning; stimulus synonymy is correspondingly inadequate, and some socially stimulus-analytic sentences would normally be described not as analytic but as conveying information common to the whole community.

Quine demands of those who talk of analyticity and synonymy that they give of their concepts the sort of account in terms of dispositions to verbal behavior that he has given of his.

By observing and testing native speech behavior dispositions, the linguist can come to translate some occasion sentences and to recognize stimulus analyticity and synonymy. But in order to complete the radical translation of a language, he must frame analytical hypotheses. This consists of segmenting what he hears into native words and hypothetically equating these to English expressions. Quine contends that there will be many sets of analytical hypotheses that fit all native dispositions to speech behavior and yet lead to incompatible translations of countless sentences in their language. Suppose that, observing the circumstances in which a native utters "Gavagai," we translate this sentence as "Rabbit!" Whether the word "gavagai" is to be taken to apply to rabbits, temporal stages of rabbits, or something even stranger to us can be settled only when we can ask questions like "Is this the same rabbit as that?" This cannot be done until we have translated the parts of speech that make up the native system of reference, and since this is part of what we do when we adopt a set of analytical hypotheses, there is more than one way of doing it. For example, the sentence translated as "Is this (the same) (rabbit) as that?" might, on another set of empirically satisfactory hypotheses, be translated as "Is this (a rabbit stage) (of the same series) as that?"

In this way Quine arrives at the principle of the indeterminacy of translation, which says that it is possible to compile incompatible manuals for translating one language into another, all of which fit all observable speech dispositions, and that there is no sense in asking which is the right manual. It is only in exceptional cases that we can talk of the meaning of a single sentence, and when our statements about the world conflict with experience, they do so not individually but as a system. Thus, we have what might be called the Quine–Duhem conventionalist thesis that any statement can be held to be true no matter what is observed, provided that adjustments are made elsewhere in the system; it is from this thesis that Quine infers that it is impossible to make the analytic–synthetic distinction.

Quine believes that his discussion of radical translation reveals the possiblity of differences between the conceptual schemes of people that are not empirically conditioned. In the case of two compatriot linguists working independently on the radical translation of a language, one linguist might conclude that he and the native see the world in the same way, as consisting of tables, chairs, ducks, and rabbits, while the other finds that the native speaks of rabbit stages, not of rabbits, and concludes that the native's outlook is different from his own. Now, in order to determine what the native's outlook really is, it is necessary to discover which is the correct way of translating the native's language. But according to the principle of the indeterminacy of translation, it does not make sense even to ask this, and consequently it cannot make sense to ask what the native's outlook is. It can be shown that the native is in no better position than the linguist here, and it

then becomes hard to see the sense of talking about an outlook when there is no conceivable way of discovering what this outlook is. Quine's position here is not clear. He admits that these differences of outlook are in principle undetectable and grants that such cultural contrasts are threatened with meaninglessness, but he continues to speak of them.

As radical translation is not known ever to have been undertaken, the absence of incompatible manuals of translation does not count against the principle of indeterminacy. Nevertheless, it might well be contended that until there are more conclusive arguments for it, the principle is to be taken as the incredible consequence of unsound premises. Quine, in discussing meaning, does concentrate on the statement-making function of language, and it has, in fact, been argued that by neglecting the countless other uses of language, he arrives at a concept of synonymy the inadequacy of which is revealed by the fact that it makes translation indeterminate.

Ontology. Philosophers have disagreed as to what there is; some have held, for example, that there are only material things, and others have denied this. Quine calls such theories "ontic theories" and maintains that they are a part of the sciences distinguished only by extreme generality. Given that there are physical objects, it is the natural scientist who discovers whether there are wombats; and given classes, it is the mathematician who finds out whether there are even prime numbers. Whether there are physical objects and classes, however, is the concern of the philosopher. The integration of established theories, which is one of the aims of scientific work, may lead to any one of many equally satisfactory accounts of the world, each with its ontic theory, and there is no sense in asking which of these accounts is the true one. Thus, Quine takes a conventionalist view even of the theses of ontologists.

Today it is commonly maintained that since there is no way of settling an ontic dispute, ontologists have unwittingly concerned themselves with pseudo questions. Quine, in proposing a method of determining the ontic import of a theory, attempts to make such questions decidable and thus real. His method is, in outline, as follows: "$(\exists x)(x$ is a cat)" may be read as "There is an x such that x is a cat" or as "There is something such that it is a cat." According to Quine, anyone who makes this statement is thereby committed to the existence of cats. The statement consists of the existential quantifier "$(\exists x)$," the predicate "——— is a cat," and an "x" which works like a pronoun and is needed in any but the simplest cases to show under which quantifier a predicate comes. If we add to this equipment such truth-functional words as "and" and "not," we can make statements like "$(\exists x)(x$ is a book, and x is boring), and $(\exists x)(x$ is a book, and x is not boring)." This is a paraphrase of "Some but not all books are boring," which, it is alleged, reveals the ontic import of this statement. Russell, Quine, and others have suggested similarly revealing paraphrases of general hypotheticals, of statements containing proper names, and of statements containing such descriptive phrases as "the prime number between 5 and 11." Quine contends that in adopting any theory, we commit ourselves to the existence of certain entities and that by translating the theory into a language in which the only formal devices are predication, quantification, and truth-functional composition, we make these commitments explicit.

Ontic commitments. The commitments revealed in the above manner are incurred when certain words are used in certain ways. We are, according to Quine, committed to the existence of physical objects because of the ways in which physical object terms function in our language. In contrast, we are not committed to such objects as "sakes," because even though we do some things for the sake of others, "sake" functions in only a few of the ways in which a term does. When constructing theories, we are, within limits, free to decide what expressions will function as terms, and by such decisions we might commit ourselves to the existence of atoms, for example, but not to that of meters. We accept the reality of physical objects more readily than we do that of atoms because typical sentences about physical objects are more closely associated with sensory stimulation than are typical sentences about atoms. By this criterion sense data are even more acceptable than physical objects, but this is counteracted by the fact that sense data are a less satisfactory basis for an account of the world. On the grounds of utility for theory, classes are to be preferred to attributes and sentences to propositions.

Many would maintain that it is only when Quine is discussing the considerations which influence ontic decisions that he tackles philosophical problems and that he does this in a way which he himself admits to be sketchy. He does this sketchily because it has been done in detail by others to whom he refers, and believing that ontologists must take account of scientific theories, he is especially interested in working out how this is to be done. Perhaps the major philosophical problem raised by Quine's proposed criterion of ontic commitment is that of the nature of this commitment: I may know what it is like for a nation to be, or not to be, committed to an isolationist foreign policy, but what is it like to be, or not to be, committed to the existence of physical objects?

Regimentation of ordinary language. The regimentation of language serves purposes other than that of revealing ontic commitments. The logic of ordinary language is difficult to formulate, and consequently it is more economical to theorize in a language which is ordinary except in its logical parts, which are designed to facilitate deduction. And if there are fewer kinds of construction and less obscurity in a regimented language, then in moving into it we simplify and clarify our conceptual scheme.

Because of misgivings about synonymy Quine cannot maintain that for an ordinary-language sentence to be replaced by a regimented one, the two must be synonymous. Indeed, we may be making the replacement just because one sentence is ambiguous and the other is not. Paraphrase into a regimented language consists, he maintains, of replacements which, in certain contexts, forward certain programs. Against this it has been argued that for any two sentences there will be a program which is forwarded by replacing one with the other, and consequently Quine's notion of paraphrase is vacuous unless contexts and programs can be specified. If this can be done, however, the notion of sentence synonymy can be derived. This notion is no less satisfactory, and no more difficult to make adequate sense of, than the notion of paraphrase, without which Quine cannot talk of putting theories into a regimented language.

The bulk of Quine's philosophical work has been published since 1947. By 1960 he had combined into a coherent position theses some of which were first put forward ten years earlier. Between 1947 and 1960 certain changes in his views occurred. From declaring, in 1947, that he did not believe in abstract entities, he has come not only to accept such entities but also to claim that he has always done so; from counting phenomenalism, in 1948, as a conceptual scheme suitable for certain purposes, he has come to reject it; and from maintaining, in 1951, that in the face of recalcitrant experience we could change our logical laws, he has apparently come to hold that there is nothing that would count as changing our logical laws.

Quine's status as a philosopher has never depended upon the number of people who have agreed with him. On the contrary, the sign of his achievement is the valuable discussion he has provoked by his persistent and penetrating attacks on analyticity and related notions and by his unfashionable conviction that philosophers want to discover what reality is like.

Bibliography

The topics of the two main sections above were first treated in detail in "Two Dogmas of Empiricism" (1951) and "On What There Is" (1948), reprinted in Quine's *From a Logical Point of View* (Cambridge, Mass., 1953). A definitive statement of Quine's position, including an exposition of the indeterminacy thesis, is in his *Word and Object* (New York and London, 1960), in which a list of Quine's many other philosophical publications will be found. His views on analyticity and logical truth are briefly stated in his "Mr. Strawson on Logical Theory," in *Mind,* Vol. 62 (1953), 433–451. Important earlier articles are his "Truth by Convention," in *Philosophical Essays for Alfred North Whitehead* (New York, 1936), reprinted in Herbert Feigl and Wilfrid Sellars, eds., *Readings in Philosophical Analysis* (New York, 1949), and "Steps Toward a Constructive Nominalism," in *Journal of Symbolic Logic,* Vol. 12 (1947), 105–122, which he wrote with Nelson Goodman.

Among the many discussions of Quine's views are the following, which are the sources of critical points made in this article. H. P. Grice and P. F. Strawson, "In Defence of a Dogma," in *Philosophical Review,* Vol. 65 (1956), 141–158, defend the analytic–synthetic distinction. P. F. Strawson, "Propositions, Concepts and Logical Truths," in *Philosophical Quarterly,* Vol. 7 (1957), 15–25, is an attack on Quine's notion of logical truth. Comments on indeterminacy are made in L. J. Cohen, *The Diversity of Meaning* (London, 1962), pp. 67–74. Quine's views on ontology are criticized by G. J. Warnock in "Metaphysics in Logic," in A. G. N. Flew, ed., *Essays in Conceptual Analysis* (London, 1956), pp. 75–93, and from a different standpoint in Rudolf Carnap, *Meaning and Necessity* (Chicago, 1947). The relation between conventionalism and the analytic–synthetic distinction is discussed in G. H. Herburt, "The Analytic and the Synthetic," in *Philosophy of Science,* Vol. 26 (1959), 104–113. Some points made above are also developed in C. F. Presley, "Quine's *Word and Object,*" in *Australasian Journal of Philosophy,* Vol. 39 (1961), 175–190.

C. F. PRESLEY

R

RABELAIS, FRANÇOIS (c. 1494–1553), French Renaissance author, was born at Chinon, in Touraine, the son of a prosperous lawyer. By 1520 he was a priest in the strict Observant branch of the Franciscans, was learning Greek, and was in contact with leading humanists. He then transferred to the Benedictines and took up medical studies, which he seems to have pursued in Paris for a year or two about 1527. (In Paris he also fathered at least two illegitimate children.) In 1530 he matriculated at Montpellier University, soon becoming bachelor of medicine (doctor in 1537), then taking a post in the city hospital at Lyon. His growing reputation as a scholar was enhanced by publication in 1532 of two learned works, editions of Hippocrates' *Aphorisms* and of the (spurious) *Testament* of Cuspidius. Almost certainly to earn money he anonymously published *Pantagruel* (1532), as a sequel to an anonymous popular work about another giant, Gargantua, of which he then published his own, much superior, version as *Gargantua* (1534). From 1534 he was in the service of the brothers Jean and Guillaume du Bellay, France's leading diplomats. He accompanied Jean, cardinal and bishop of Paris, to Rome several times and through his influence legally exchanged his Benedictine habit for that of a secular priest. He also spent some four years with Guillaume, French viceroy at Turin.

In 1546 a third book (*Tiers Livre*) appeared under his own name, followed by a fourth (*Quart Livre*) in 1552 (partial edition 1548). Both were condemned by the Sorbonne despite the eminence of Rabelais's protectors, who included Marguerite de Navarre. He lived precariously, often in flight, but seems to have died in danger rather than in prison. The authorship of a fifth book, part of which was posthumously published in 1562, on the eve of the Religious Wars, followed by the whole in 1564, is problematic. However, much of the material is certainly by Rabelais, probably left by him as a rough draft. A few letters and some occasional pieces in Latin and French constitute the rest of his work.

Rabelais's scholastic training as a friar, together with his subsequently acquired professional competence in medicine and his wide classical erudition, give his thought great richness and complexity. The most obvious message of these books designed ostensibly for entertainment is the exhortation to practice Pantagruelism. This is a way of life not so much expounded as illustrated and embodied in the words, deeds, and character of the eponymous hero. The three giants, Grandgousier, Gargantua, and Pantagruel, enjoy the special prestige of heroes from the first; but with the *Tiers Livre* Pantagruel (whose gigantic stature is now forgotten) becomes Rabelais's accredited spokesman and the surest guide to intentions obscured by comic tone and dialogue form, let alone prudential considerations. The simple injunctions to good cheer of the first books evolve into a pattern whose main features are plainly Stoic, the virtues of self-mastery, indifference to fortuitous events, and generosity to others are exalted. To these must be added gaiety and, above all, positive Christianity. At every crisis Pantagruel prays, and then exerts himself strenuously, showing active, not passive, faith. New Testament, especially Pauline, quotations stress the religious basis for Pantagruelism.

Rabelais's religion remains highly controversial. His early reverence for Erasmus persisted to the end, and he is perhaps best described as an anachronistic Erasmian, holding to an evangelical Christianity bypassed by events. His initial sympathy for Protestantism did not extend to Calvinism as developed in Geneva. In the *Quart Livre* Rabelais satirized both papacy and Protestants, but also affirmed his personal belief in Christ as the Redeemer. Religion in all the books is a personal, not an institutional, affair, consisting in private devotion and active charity, not mechanical piety or superstitious practices.

This dislike of institutional authority is systematized in the ideal community of Thélème, described in the concluding chapters of *Gargantua*. The only rule of this anti-abbey is "Do as you will," and it has often been interpreted as a secular utopia that possessed the elegance of Italian Renaissance courts and displayed boundless optimism about human nature. Such claims for Rabelais's secularism ignore the solidly religious program of education that had been outlined earlier in the book and was clearly intended as preparation for the self-reliant virtue of those who, like the Thelemites, need no externally imposed rules.

The educational chapters in *Gargantua* stress oral learning, accompanied by vigorous physical and spiritual exercise, and they must be read in conjunction with the detailed syllabus of *Pantagruel* (Ch. 8). Classical culture, civil law, and science are indispensable equipment for the educated man, but Bible study is the ultimate aim, bringing the highest wisdom. Thus, Hebrew, Arabic, and Chaldaic, in addition to Latin and Greek, are chosen as the basis of learning. The later books show that Rabelais's metaphysics are largely Platonic, derived principally through Plutarch; and while this was in line with prevailing humanist fashion, it also continued the strongly Platonizing tendency of Franciscan teaching. Thus, Rabelais showed keen interest in the spirit world and in theories of dreams and of knowledge. His usual treatment of all such questions was syncretic, and no Platonic theory was rejected that could possibly be reconciled with Christianity.

In politics Rabelais was a typical humanist, although influenced by personal experience in diplomacy. His pacifism did not extend to the condemnation of defensive war; no considerations of statecraft outweighed humanitarian principles; he advocated justice insured by a judiciary free of both royal and ecclesiastical interference. However, he also approved of a patriarchal and idealized feudalism.

Rabelais was a truly universal genius. Drawing on unrivaled literary resources, he integrated all human activity, base and lofty alike, into a positive and balanced harmony. His Pantagruelism represents a joyful sanity of body, mind, and spirit.

Works by Rabelais

Oeuvres, A. Lefranc and others, eds., 6 vols. Paris, 1912—.
Oeuvres, 2d ed. Bibliothèque de la Pléiade. Paris, 1955.
Gargantua and Pantagruel, translated by J. M. Cohen. London, 1955.
Countless other editions, of collected or individual works, and translations exist.

Works on Rabelais

Febvre, L., *Le Problème de l'incroyance au XVIe siècle. La Religion de Rabelais*, 2d ed. Paris, 1947.
Grève, M. de, *L'Interprétation de Rabelais au XVIe siècle*. Geneva, 1961.
Krailsheimer, A. J., *Rabelais and the Franciscans*. Oxford, 1963.
Plattard, J., *Rabelais, l'homme et l'oeuvre*. Paris, 1939.
Screech, M. A., *L'Évangélisme de Rabelais*. Geneva, 1959.
These are only the latest items in the vast bibliography on Rabelais. Progress in this field can be followed in the periodical *Bibliothèque d'humanisme et Renaissance*.

A. J. KRAILSHEIMER

RACISM is the doctrine that one group of men is morally or mentally superior to another and that this superiority arises out of inherited biological differences. Of the modern theories aimed at dividing one portion of humanity from another, it is the most morally reprehensible and the least substantially based. Nationalism has a certain rationale in the existence of nation-states, and it does not, at least not necessarily, imply the inferiority of one nation to another. The various doctrines of the struggle between economic classes can point to a wide assortment of empirical evidence in support of their claims; in the Marxist version the exploiting capitalist is as much a victim of the capitalist system as is the exploited proletarian, and the eventual overcoming of all class distinctions is a moral aim as well as a prophesied event. The tenets of racism, however, lead to moral conclusions that contradict many of the most generally accepted civilized standards and have notoriously led to what on ordinary grounds are inconceivable crimes. It might be claimed that ordinary standards are mistaken and that, for example, it was morally imperative that the Nazis exterminate the Jews—if racist claims had a substantial factual basis. Fortunately for ordinary moral standards, if not for the exterminated Jews and other victims of racial persecution, the tenets of racism are not merely unsubstantiated by the facts but in large measure contradicted by the facts.

Nor have the most important racist theorists been equipped to judge the alleged facts on which they based their claims. The question of race is an enormously complex one, and a judgment on it requires a synthesis of materials from history and prehistory and from a wide variety of biological, anthropological, and psychological disciplines, but primarily from genetics. Many of the necessary facts have only recently become available, and major questions remain unanswered. Yet most racist theories were put forth prior to the accumulation of this evidence, and even most contemporary racist theories are based on outdated biology. Furthermore, most racists—Houston Stewart Chamberlain, with his varied but erratic education, is a possible exception—have lacked the scientific training required to judge whatever evidence was available at the time they wrote. And until a racist theory can be substantiated to a very high degree of probability, the unsavoriness of the conclusion that there are inequalities in the capacities of groups of men requires that the theory be rejected.

Outline of the theory. Although there are many variations on the racist theme (the number of contradictions among racist claims, notably about which are the privileged races, is enough in itself to cast doubt on the tenability of the whole racist enterprise), a model set of racist tenets, divisible into three groups of claims, can be isolated.

The first group starts with the premise that mankind is now, has been in the past, or ought to be in the future divided up into biologically distinct groups. The different tenses must be distinguished because in some instances the claim is made that the superior race is not now in existence but should be bred from the "best blood" among various existing groups. This claim is the link between racism and eugenics, but although eugenicists often fall into racist language or hold racist beliefs (Sir Francis Galton, the founder of eugenics, rated Negroes as about two grades below the Anglo-Saxon "race," and the British pragmatist philosopher F. C. S. Schiller supported both eugenics and the English fascist Sir Oswald Mosley), the connection between the two theories is not inevitable.

The distinction between groups of mankind is held to be based on the common biological heredity of the members of each group. Among the biological distinctions between groups are inherited capacities for certain cultural activities—some races, it is claimed, are more warlike than others, some more musical, others predestined to be dominated. These are factual claims, seemingly open to confirmation or refutation by a scientific examination of the evidence, and the evidence seems overwhelmingly against every one of them. Someone who upheld these views would not necessarily be a racist, but they are essential to the racist position.

In a class by itself is the claim that the mechanism of transmission of group characteristics is the blood. Of all racist claims this is the one most surely refuted, and it would seem to be inessential to the doctrine. Yet the insistent stress on this claim even in the face of overwhelming evidence of its falsity is an index of the nonrational sources of racist thinking. Theories of inheritance through the blood, of blood kinship, of bluebloods, and of good and bad blood are survivals of age-old prescientific thought, on the same order as the view that the soul is the breath.

The final set of doctrines are essential to racism and distinctive of it. Not only are human groups different from one another but some are "better," "stronger," "higher," or "more creative" than others—physically, intellectually, or morally. (The proponent of a particular racist doctrine quite naturally almost always identifies himself with the race he judges superior. Thus, Count Joseph Arthur de Gobineau, who was born in the south of France and who placed the "Nordic race" at the pinnacle of humanity, devoted considerable research to proving his own descent from the Viking Otto Jarl; the British-born, French and Swiss-educated Chamberlain, who espoused Aryan or Teutonic superiority, included the contemporary English—and the Slavs and Celts—among the Teutons.) The higher race or races, it is claimed, have a moral right to dominate, to enslave, or even to eradicate the lower races. Finally, higher and lower races should not intermarry. Race mixture, or "mongrelization," is against nature. For the superior race it can lead only to the lowering of standards and to racial degeneration. It would seem that race mixture would improve the "lower" race, but this is generally denied either on biological or on historical grounds. Thus, Chamberlain held that the "lower" Jewish race was not improved by an alleged ancient admixture of Aryan blood, which came too little and too late.

Criticism. No complete examination of the fallacies of racist doctrines can be presented here. What seems most important is that there are not now and, so far as anthropological evidence shows, there never have been any pure races of men and that the very concept of race as applied to groups of human beings is suspect. In the vast number of its traits mankind is one, and there has been constant intermarriage and a consequent diffusion of genetic traits throughout the species. There are obvious dissimilarities among groups of people, but these differences more or less gradually shade off into one another; it is a question of statistical predominance of certain physical or physiological traits in a population rather than of sharply defined group differences.

Estimates of the number of genes in man range from 10,000 to 100,000, whereas the number of genes that control skin color, shape of lips and nose, and hair form are few. Racists want to correlate these obvious differences —which in themselves are purely statistical and thus no certain guide to the ancestry of a particular person—with differences in innate inheritable mental characteristics. Yet the evidence is against any such correlation. Each gene or gene cluster, except for certain linked genes, is inherited individually; on the average, half comes from the father and half from the mother. The number of possible combinations of ancestral genes is astronomical, and the question whether specific mental characteristics are linked with a particular genetic heritage can almost certainly be answered in the negative for human beings, if not, perhaps, for certain domestic animals.

In any case, mankind has apparently been faced with an environment that puts a premium on intelligence, and there seem to be no detectable group differences in intelligence. It is practically impossible to devise a satisfactory test to determine whether there are biological differences in intelligence. In most cases the available methods of classifying by ancestry those to be tested are quite fallible. It is equally difficult to find two groups genetically distinct and culturally alike, and intelligence tests are quite generally distorted by cultural factors and place a premium on particular cultural achievements that obscures any possible genetic factors in the results.

Finally, if there were any evolutionary reasons for thinking that some race was at one time constitutionally better fitted to one environment than another, the rate of human cultural change is such that this supposed superiority would have been insignificant for many centuries. There is no reason to think that one group of mankind is mentally or physically better fitted than another to cope with the complexities of modern urban civilization and an internationally dispersed technology.

To the above summary and inadequate account of the biological claims that contradict racism should be added the overwhelming historical evidence of constant migrations and intermarriages of human groups and the highly probable inference that movement and mixture was also the rule during the prehistory of the human species. This has been especially true of the two alleged races most notoriously prominent in racist literature, Aryans and Jews. The Aryan is generally presented as a pure and superior race and the Jewish "race" as inferior, contradictorily characterized as both pure and bastardized, often by the same author. However, there neither is nor could be evidence that either race is more or less "pure" than the other. Each group is an amalgam of people of varied ancestry, and mixture has produced no apparent genetic debilitation of the sort that racists inveigh against when they deplore the "mongrelization of the race." Cultural differences exist between Germans and Jews, but there are likewise cultural differences between different groups of Germans and between groups of Jews, as well as cultural similarities between German and Jewish groups. To assign these likenesses and similarities to race rather than to a vast complex of recognized sociocultural factors is to ignore a great bulk of historical evidence.

The irrationalism of racists. Arguing with a proponent of racism is like arguing with someone who would today claim that the earth is flat and at the center of the universe. The evidence that the earth is round is so overwhelming, and so bound up with our very conception of what physical science is, that in the face of someone who claims that the earth is flat we can only point helplessly at the great body of scientific factual claims and scientific laws and ask, "But don't you see?" Similarly, when we are faced with the claims of a racist who persists in his doctrine in the face of our very notions of what constitutes biology and what constitutes historical research, we have no common ground for argument with him. An extreme but typical racist statement can be used as an example:

It is established for all time: "alien albumen" is the sperm of a man of alien race. The male sperm is partially or completely absorbed by the female and thus enters her bloodstream. One single cohabitation of a Jew with an Aryan woman is sufficient to poison her blood forever. Together with the "alien albumen" she has absorbed the alien soul. Never again will she be able to bear purely Aryan children . . . they will all be bastards. (Julius Streicher, quoted in Quentin Reynolds, Ephraim Katz, and Zwy Aldouby, *Minister of Death*, New York, 1960, p. 150)

To someone with the most elementary acquaintance with contemporary biology it is unnecessary to point out the false assumptions and false statements in this quotation. But to refute the argument in a way that would satisfy its maker is impossible, because he denies the very grounds on which a scientific refutation as we understand it could be based.

The racist views in Hitler's *Mein Kampf* likewise seem based on a different biology from the one we know, but in Hitler's thought there is an added historical dimension. The picture Hitler draws of the sociopolitical situation in Germany and Austria during his own lifetime is often shrewd, but it is open to rational criticism: he makes factual claims that can be shown to be historically untrue and historical interpretations that can be challenged by an appeal to evidence and probability. His picture of the Aryans as the only culture-creating people, whose presence in a certain area at a certain time can be demonstrated simply because cultural innovation must have taken place then and there, bears no relation to what we know of the movements of peoples or to our notions of probability. In the chapter "Nation and Race," Hitler uses few examples, and when examples are given they are used tendentiously to show what they could not prove. Thus, the culture of contemporary Japan, he claims, is the product of European stimulation: it is Western culture and technology with Japanese trimmings. Without continued infusions of Western culture, the culture of contemporary Japan is doomed to decay, and the culture found in Japan by Western explorers must itself have been the ossified remnants of some earlier, but forgotten, Aryan invasion. Hitler's arguments do not generally reach even the level of this one, circular as it is. Yet to show that no such invasion took place in historical times, and probably could not have taken place in prehistoric times, seems no answer to Hitler's claims. The picture he presents of the past is a deliberately mythical one, on a deliberately mythical time scale that bears no apparent relation to the known events and temporal ordering of history. In the absence of such relationships, all appeals to facts become irrelevant, and facts are notably absent from the argument.

Racism outside Germany. Although racism as a fully articulated doctrine and the central feature of official policy is notoriously associated with Germany, it has been powerful elsewhere. It was among thinkers of the French Enlightenment—Boulainvilliers, Buffon, and Montesquieu—that the concept of race was first made explicit and the germs of racism were implanted. Gobineau, in the mid-nineteenth century, was the true originator of the doctrine of racism, and throughout the nineteenth century and later, French thinkers vied with one another to show their descent from Gauls, Romans, Gallo-Romans, Celts, or Teutons and the superior Frenchness of one of these purported races over another.

In the United States and England also racism has flourished, and in these countries the complex interconnection of racist doctrines with social and economic factors is most apparent. In English thought racism has been mainly a concomitant of imperialism. The recent influx of darker-skinned peoples from the Commonwealth has led both to widespread resentment and to the expression of racist sentiments, but not as yet to any new fully developed racist theories. In the United States racism first arose in the South as a defense of slavery, was invoked as a justification of American imperialist expansion into the western Pacific and the Caribbean and for the restriction of the immigration of "undesirable" stock into the United States, and has arisen again as a defense of segregation.

Recent arguments that the Negro is biologically inferior are not essentially different from earlier ones, of which Samuel Cartwright's "The Prognathous Species of Mankind" (1857) is an example. The argument moves from stressed and exaggerated physiological differences between Negroes and whites to the claim of broad mental differences. Features of the "typical negro" are closer to "the simiadiae and the brute creation" than to whites. The standard Negro color is a shiny, oily black, and lighter colors are the result not of intermixture with whites but of sickness or degeneration. In "the bleaching process of bad health or degeneration" even the pigment of the iris is lost, and the degenerate Negro is clairvoyant at night. The Negro does not have real hair: ". . . the shaft of each hair is surrounded with a scaly covering like sheep's wool, and, like wool, is capable of being felted. True hair does not possess this property. . . . the negro approximates the lower animals in his sense of smell, and can detect snakes by that sense alone. All the senses are more acute, but less delicate and discriminating than the white man's." Natural history, like the Bible, "proves the existence of at least three distinct species of the genus man, differing in their instincts, form, habit, and color. The white species having qualities denied to the black—one with a free and the other with a servile mind—one a thinking and reflective being, the other a creature of feeling and imitation, almost void of reflective faculties, and consequently unable to provide for and take care of himself."

Several racial theories, notably those of Madison Grant and Lothrop Stoddard, reflected the growing awareness among the descendants of earlier groups of immigrants to the United States of the changing national origins of later groups. The works of these men both promoted the fear of the ultimate extinction of the "white race" (which was often meant to exclude southern and eastern Europeans) by rising birth rates among Asians and Africans and influenced the restrictive immigration laws of the 1920s. But it is doubtful whether these or later writers have added anything substantially new to the racist theses.

Bibliography

RACIST WRITINGS

The fountainhead of racist doctrines is Count Joseph Arthur de Gobineau's four-volume *Essai sur l'inégalité des races humaines* (Paris, 1853–1855); Vol. I has been translated by Adrian Collins as *Essay on the Inequality of Races* (London and New York, 1915). The first two volumes were also published at Philadelphia as early as 1856 in a translation by H. Hotz and with an introduction by Josiah C. Nott, both of whom were propagandists for slavery. For an early refutation of Gobineau's views based on moral grounds, see Alexis de Tocqueville's correspondence in his *"The European Revolution" & Correspondence with Gobineau*, edited by John Lukacs (Garden City, N.Y., 1959).

Richard Wagner published his anti-Semitic essay, "The Jews in Music," in 1850. Wagner later became an enthusiastic supporter of Gobineau, and Gobineau of Wagnerism. Representative writings of Wagner on race are available in *Wagner on Music and Drama*, compiled by Albert Goldman and Evert Sprinchorn (New York, 1964). Also important in disseminating Gobineau's views in Germay was Ludwig Schemann, founder of the Gobineau-Verein, translator, editor, and biographer of Gobineau, and author of such racist works as *Die Rassenfrage im Schrifttum der Neuzeit* (Munich, 1931).

Houston Stewart Chamberlain, Wagner's son-in-law, ranks with Gobineau as a race theorist; the two-volume *Die Grundlagen des neunzehnten Jahrhunderts* (Munich, 1899), his major work, was translated by John Lees as *The Foundations of the Nineteenth Century*, 2 vols. (London and New York, 1910). Chamberlain influenced both Adolf Hitler's *Mein Kampf* (2 vols., Munich, 1925–1927) and Alfred Rosenberg's *Der Mythus des 20. Jahrhunderts* (Munich, 1930).

The term "Aryan" was popularized by Friedrich Max Müller as a label for the speakers of the hypothetical language from which Indo-European languages were allegedly descended. Although Müller later denied that the term had any racial significance, the romantic claim that language expresses the soul of the race made the identification of Aryan speakers with an Aryan race almost inevitable, and Müller's own writings abound in such identifications. See, for example, *Lectures on the Science of Language*, 2 vols. (London, 1861–1864).

In defense of slavery on racial grounds, see, in addition to Cartwright's essay, Josiah Nott's *Types of Mankind* (Philadelphia, 1854), parts of which are reprinted with Cartwright's essay and other writings in Eric L. McKitrick, ed., *Slavery Defended: The Views of the Old South* (Englewood Cliffs, N.J., 1963). Other American works are Madison Grant, *The Passing of the Great Race* (New York, 1916), and Lothrop Stoddard, *The Rising Tide of Color Against White Supremacy* (New York, 1920).

WORKS ON RACE AND RACISM

Jacques Barzun, *Race: A Study in Superstition*, 2d ed. (New York, 1965), is a historical survey. See also Ernst Cassirer, *The Myth of the State* (New Haven, 1946), Ch. 16, and Hannah Arendt, *The Origins of Totalitarianism*, 2d ed. (New York, 1958), especially Ch. 6.

Ashley Montague, *Man's Most Dangerous Myth*, 4th ed. (New York, 1964), and Ashley Montague, ed., *The Concept of Race* (New York, 1964), together survey much of the present relevant biological knowledge and opinion. L. C. Dunn and Theodosius Dobzhansky, *Heredity, Race, and Society*, 2d ed. (New York, 1952), is a clear and useful account of the genetic aspects. Carlton S. Coon, *The Origin of Races* (New York, 1962), is a recent work by a physical anthropologist who believes in the existence of biological differences between human groups that are associated with intellectual differences. Henry E. Garrett, "The Equalitarian Dogma," in *Perspectives in Biology and Medicine*, Vol. 4 (1961), 480–484, presents a minority view by a former head of the American Psychological Association.

PHILIP W. CUMMINGS

RADBRUCH, GUSTAV (1878–1949), German legal philosopher whose name and work have become widely known outside Germany only since the end of World War II. During his lifetime, the interests and activities of scholar, politician, and reformer of law were closely intermingled. After World War I, Radbruch became active in the Social Democratic party and twice served as minister of justice of the Weimar Republic. His principal work was the draft of a new criminal code. Later he held a chair of law at the University of Heidelberg, from which he was dismissed by the Nazi regime. After World War II he was recalled and exercised a predominant influence in the reorientation of German legal education and philosophy until his death.

Radbruch's legal philosophy, generally known as "relativism," is closely akin to the position of his friend and teacher Max Weber. Radbruch believed, like Weber, that values could not be scientifically proved and that they were "a matter of conscience (*Gewissen*), not of science (*Wissenschaft*)," This in no way implied indifference to values. Radbruch differed both from Rudolf Stammler, who sought to formulate a theoretically valid concept of justice, and from Hans Kelsen, who detached legal science altogether from a philosophy of values. Radbruch, while starting from the Kantian distinction of "is" (*Sein*) and "ought" (*Sollen*), was guided mainly by the teachings of Heinrich Rickert and Emil Lask in treating law as a *Kulturwissenschaft*, a science directed to the realization of values. He therefore considered that the task of legal philosophy was to relate legal reality to basic ideas. But the truth of specific ideas and values cannot be scientifically proved. Radbruch instead developed—and applied to numerous specific problems of law—a series of antinomies of legal values. Thus, the Aristotelian idea of distributive justice, which directs equals to be treated equally, says nothing about the perspective from which they are to be characterized as equals or unequals. Justice, which cannot yield objective criteria of equality, must be supplemented by a second value, "utility," and a third, "security." Between these three values there is constant tension. In another perspective, law can be directed to individual values, collective values, or work values. Accordingly, a legal system emphasizes either individualism, collectivism, or transpersonalism. For the first, the ultimate idea is liberty; for the second, the nation; and for the third, civilization.

After the war, Radbruch recoiled from the extremes of tolerance—as practiced by the Weimar Republic during the rise of the Nazi movement—having witnessed the unprecedented barbarism of the Third Reich, which was largely covered by a formal notion of law. He tentatively turned to a moderate natural-law philosophy, holding that in certain extreme cases a contradiction between positive law and justice might reach such an intolerable degree that the law as unjust law (unlawful law, *unrechtiges*

Recht) must cede to the higher demands of justice. Radbruch died before he could elaborate his thesis beyond the postulate that special courts should be empowered to adjudge the validity of laws.

Works by Radbruch

Einführung in die Rechtswissenschaft. Leipzig, 1907. K. Zweigert, ed., 1961.

Rechtsphilosophie. Leipzig, 1914. 3d ed. revised and enlarged, Leipzig, 1932. 5th ed., completed with a preface by Erik Wolf, Stuttgart, 1956. Translated from the German edition by Kurt Wilk with introduction by E. W. Patterson in *The Legal Philosophies of Lask, Radbruch and Dabin.* Cambridge, Mass., 1950.

"Gesetzliches Unrecht und übergesetzliches Recht." *Süddeutsche Juristenzeitung,* Vol. 5 (1946), 107 ff.

Der Geist des englischen Rechts. 2d ed., Heidelberg, 1947.

Vorschule der Rechtsphilosophie. Willsbach, 1947.

Works on Radbruch

Campbell, A. H., *Gustav Radbruchs Rechtsphilosophie.* Hanover, 1949.

Cattaneo, M. A., "Il Positivismo giuridico e la separazione tra il Diritto e la Morale." *Rendiconti* of the Istituto Lombardo, Vol. 94 (1960), 701–742.

Friedmann, Wolfgang, "Gustav Radbruch." *Vanderbilt Law Review,* Vol. 14 (1960), 191–209.

Wolf, Erik, *Rechtsgedanke und biblische Weisung.* Tübingen, 1948.

Wolf, Erik, *Griechisches Rechtsdenken,* 3 vols. Tübingen, 1950–1954.

Wolf, Erik, *Grosse Rechtsdenker der deutschen Geistesgeschichte.* 3d ed., Tübingen, 1951.

Wolf, Erik, *Das Problem der Naturrechtslehre: Versuch einer Orientierung.* Tübingen, 1955. 2d ed., Tübingen, 1959.

WOLFGANG FRIEDMANN

RADHAKRISHNAN, SARVEPALLI, philosopher and Hindu apologist, was born in 1888 in south India. He has held chairs of philosophy at the universities of Mysore and Calcutta and at Banaras (Benares) Hindu University, of which he was also vice-chancellor. Since India gained independence in 1947 he has been ambassador to the Soviet Union, Spalding professor of Eastern religions and ethics at Oxford, and vice-president and president of India.

Radhakrishnan's philosophical interests have centered on religion, and he has been the foremost exponent of a modern Hinduism based upon a version of the Vedānta, in which he modifies and reinterprets the teachings of Śankara. His influential *Indian Philosophy* gives a historical account of the Indian tradition in which an absolute idealism emerges as the central expression of Indian thought. His Neo-Hinduism also forms the basis of an attempt to reconcile the teachings of the different world religions. He interprets these as essentially affirming, or reaching toward, what is to be found in Vedānta, and is critical of dogmatic, and therefore divisive, attitudes in religion: they are a main cause of conflict between faiths.

Radhakrishnan's claim that religious teachings are a proper concern of philosophy rather than of theology rests on his view of knowledge. He holds that intuition, as well as perception and inference, is a valid means of discovering truths. By intuition he means, among other things, contemplative experience (scientific insight and ethical insight are other forms). Thus, he is not committed to treating Indian scriptures as authoritative in themselves; their importance derives from the way in which they witness to, and express, mystical experience. Although Radhakrishnan, following much of the Indian tradition, places great emphasis on such intuitions, he also interprets them as having to do with a relationship to God conceived as a personal object of worship. Consequently, he holds that naturalistic accounts of the world are inadequate.

His criticisms of naturalism are as follows. First, it neglects or denies spiritual intuitions. Second, naturalism is an attempt to explain the universe on mechanistic principles, and this is "to confuse a descriptive method for the creative cause" (*The Philosophy of Sarvepalli Radhakrishnan,* p. 32). Third, and connectedly, we are obliged to assume a controlling or directing intelligence in the cosmic process. Further, Radhakrishnan argues for the doctrine of reincarnation, which is incompatible (at least seemingly) with materialism.

Although Radhakrishnan relies heavily on nondualistic Vedānta, he introduces modifications into earlier interpretations of it. Thus he treats the personal God as an aspect of the Absolute, rather than as a lower, illusory manifestation of it. Or, to put his position more correctly, the divine Being in its nonrelational aspect is the Absolute, and in its relational aspect it is the Lord and Creator. Radhakrishnan holds that the distinction is logical, rather than ontological. Further, he modifies the usual interpretation of Śankara's doctrine of *māyā* or the cosmic "illusion." He argues that the essential purport of the doctrine is not that the world which we experience is unreal but that it is temporal and dependent, in contrast with the supreme Being, which is uncreated and eternal.

These aspects of Radhakrishnan's theology help to explain his influence as an exponent of Neo-Hinduism. He is able to represent the thesis of the essential unity of religions in a way which does not imply that the concept of a personal God is demoted to a subsidiary role (an implication found in much contemporary Hindu apologetic); at the same time, he is able to represent Hinduism as concerned with technological, social, and political progress and not, as some critics have urged, committed to an illusionist, world-negating view.

A further diplomatic aspect of Radhakrishnan's theology is his doctrine of salvation. He believes that salvation will be universal, for freedom means harmony not only within the self but also with the environment. Consequently, those who have attained realization of the Eternal will continue to work for the redemption of other beings, until there is a final consummation in which all are released.

Since Radhakrishnan's position involves a view concerning the Indian tradition, as well as concerning other religions, he is committed to certain historical interpretations, some of which are questionable. For instance, he sees the Buddha's denial of the self as implying, rather than denying, the doctrine of an eternal self or soul; he thinks that it is a denial of the *empirical* self. This interpretation runs deeply contrary to virtually the whole of the Buddhist tradition and makes the Buddha less original than he seems to have been. His interpretation of Christianity assimilates Jesus' teaching to that of Hinduism while he glosses over claims about Jesus' divinity, which, rightly or wrongly, have formed a central part of Christian faith since quite early times. In both cases he reconstructs a religion, rather than describing it.

Radhakrishnan has not made any serious attempt to relate his way of philosophizing to recent developments in analytic philosophy, nor has he greatly interested himself in the relation between science and religion, except insofar as he rejects naturalism. Thus, his writings have been more influential among those who already accept some sort of theological position than among those engaged in the critical philosophy of religion. His strictures on religious dogmatism and his reinterpretation of the Hindu tradition, however, have been useful stimulants to interreligious discussion.

Bibliography

Radhakrishnan's most important writings are *Indian Philosophy*, 2 vols. (London, 1923–1927); *The Hindu View of Life* (London, 1926); and *Eastern Religions and Western Thought* (London, 1939; 2d ed., rev., 1940). Translations and commentaries are *The Bhagavadgītā* (2d ed., London, 1949); *The Principal Upaniṣads* (London, 1958); and *The Brahma Sūtra* (London, 1959).

A work on Radhakrishnan is P. A. Schilpp, ed., *The Philosophy of Sarvepalli Radhakrishnan* (New York, 1952).

NINIAN SMART

RADISHCHEV, ALEXANDER NIKOLAYEVICH

(1749–1802), was the leading social critic and philosopher of the Russian Enlightenment. He was born in Moscow, the son of a prosperous landowner, and was educated in Moscow, in St. Petersburg, and, from 1766 to 1771, at the University of Leipzig. At Leipzig he studied under the Leibnizian Ernst Platner and read widely in current French philosophy. Upon his return to Russia he pursued a successful career in the civil and military service until 1790, when his radical work *Puteshestviye iz Peterburga v Moskvu* (St. Petersburg, 1790; translated as *A Journey From St. Petersburg to Moscow*) aroused the ire of Catherine the Great and he was exiled to Siberia. Paul I permitted him to return to European Russia in 1796. After the accession of Alexander I, in 1801, Radishchev was appointed to a special legislative commission, but his egalitarian, libertarian proposals went unheeded, and in September 1802 he took his own life in St. Petersburg.

In the *Journey*, Radishchev employed the principles of natural law and the social contract to support a severe critique of Russian social institutions, serfdom in particular. Under the inspiration of Rousseau, Voltaire, Raynal, and other French thinkers, he condemned serfdom as morally wrong and economically inefficient, criticized autocracy, and attacked censorship and other practices that violate men's natural rights to freedom and equality. He advocated immediate reforms to avert revolution and called generally for enlightenment and "naturalness" in social arrangements, manners, and morals.

In Siberia, Radishchev wrote his principal philosophic work, *O Cheloveke, o Yevo Smertnosti i Bessmertii* ("On Man, His Mortality and Immortality," published posthumously, St. Petersburg, 1809), a close examination of the cases for and against personal immortality. In the end he rejected materialistic denials of immortality in favor of

various arguments—from personal identity and the conservation of force, among others—that suggest the existence of an incorporeal soul that survives the body and passes into a more perfect state. In epistemology Radishchev adopted a realistic position and accepted experience as the only basis for knowledge but maintained that in addition to sensory experience there is "rational experience" of the relationships of things and that man "feels" the existence of a Supreme Being. He also maintained that things in themselves are unknowable, asserting that thought, like the verbal expression it employs, is merely symbolic of reality.

Radishchev's treatise "On Man" was one of the first original philosophic works in the Russian language, and the influence his pioneering social criticism had on Pushkin, the Decembrists, and subsequent generations of Russian reformers and revolutionaries has led to his being regarded as the father of social radicalism in Russia. He was also a poet of considerable talent.

Works by Radishchev

Polnoye Sobraniye Sochineni ("Complete Works"), 3 vols. Moscow and Leningrad, 1938–1952.

A Journey From St. Petersburg to Moscow, translated by Leo Wiener. Cambridge, Mass., 1958.

"On Man, His Mortality and Immortality," selections translated by Frank Y. Gladney and George L. Kline, in J. M. Edie, J. P. Scanlan, and M.-B. Zeldin, eds., *Russian Philosophy*. Chicago, 1965.

Works on Radishchev

Dynnik, M. A., et al., eds., *Istoriya Filosofii*, 6 vols. Moscow, 1957—.

Lapshin, I. I., *Filosofskiye Vzglyady A. N. Radishcheva* ("Philosophical Views of A. N. Radishchev"). Petrograd, 1922.

Zenkovsky, V. V., *Istoriya Russkoy Filosofii*, 2 vols. Paris, 1948–1950. Translated by George L. Kline as *A History of Russian Philosophy*, 2 vols. New York and London, 1953.

JAMES P. SCANLAN

RĂDULESCU-MOTRU, CONSTANTIN (1868–1954),

Rumanian philosopher of energetic personalism, studied at the universities of Bucharest, Paris, Munich, and Leipzig. He obtained his doctorate from Leipzig in 1893 with a thesis on the development of Kant's theory of causality in nature, published in Wilhelm Wundt's *Philosophische Studien*. In 1904 he became professor of psychology and logic at the University of Bucharest. He founded the journals *Noua Revista Română* (1900), *Studii Filosofice* (1905, after 1920 called *Revista de Filosofie*), *Anale de Psihologie* (1935), and *Jurnal de Psihotehnică* (1937), as well as the Rumanian Society of Philosophy.

Rădulescu-Motru was the dominant figure in Rumanian philosophy from 1905 to 1930. The most articulate expression of his philosophical system is to be found in his *Personalismul Energetic* (1927). Influenced by the work of Wilhelm Ostwald and William Stern, it was an impressive effort to unify the results of natural science, biology, and psychology. Rădulescu-Motru called his system personalistic because the human personality plays the central role within it, and energetic because he considered personality to be the highest form of cosmic energy. The universe is in continuous evolution, and its goal is the creation of energetic personality. Rādulescu-Motru distinguished six stages of the evolutionary process: cosmic energy, adaptation, organic individuality, consciousness, ego, and personality. Personality is both modified and enriched through evolution from the primitive *homo divinans* to *homo faber*. Finally, through Stoicism, Christianity, and science, the energetic personality, the vocational or professional man, emerges. With the achievement of a personality having a total comprehension of the universe, the evolutionary process will come to an end; Nature will have reached its ultimate goal.

Works by Rādulescu-Motru

Puterea Sufleteasca. Bucharest, 1907.
Elemente de Metafizică (1912). Definitive edition Bucharest, 1928.
Curs de Psihologie. Bucharest, 1924.
Personalismul Energetic. Bucharest, 1927.
Vocaţia. Bucharest, 1932.
Românismul. Bucharest, 1936.

Works on Rādulescu-Motru

Omagiu profesorului C. Rādulescu-Motru. Bucharest, 1932.
Rus, G., "Il personalismo energetico di C. Rādulescu-Motru." *Acta Philosophica et Theologica,* Vol. 2 (1964), 411–438.

MIRCEA ELIADE

RĀMĀNUJA, a south Indian Brahmin, was born in Bhūtapurī and studied with the teacher Yāmuna (tenth–eleventh centuries). His dates are traditionally given as 1017–1137; but most probably his birth occurred several decades later, and the date of his death may also be somewhat later. Rāmānuja owed something to the Bhedābheda ("Identity-in-Difference") school of Indian philosophy and to the fervently devotional poetry of the Tamil religious poets known as the Ālvārs. His chief work was his commentary on the *Brahma-Sūtra;* other important works were the *Vedārthsamgraha* ("Compendium of the Sense of the Veda") and the *Vedāntasāra* ("Essence of Vedānta").

Rāmānuja became the chief exponent and virtual founder of the Vedānta school of Hinduism known as Viśiṣṭādvaita, or Qualified Nondualism, which expressed a religious reaction against Śankara's Nondualism. Rāmānuja wished to show that there exists a distinction between the self (*ātman*) or eternal soul and ultimate reality, that is, between *ātman* and *Brahman*. This distinction makes sense of the religion of worship and devotion to which Rāmānuja was committed, for the devotee cannot think of the Person whom he worships as identical with himself—a sense of separation and distinction is phenomenologically central to this form of religion. Furthermore, Śankara's monism contained philosophical difficulties which Rāmānuja sought to expose. On the other hand, he recognized the monistic character of certain key passages in revelation (*śruti*), which implied that the self and *Brahman* are in some sense one. Thus, his system was conceived as one in which it was possible to show that distinctions between selves, the world, and God were maintained and yet at the same time the three categories were in some sense a unity.

He achieved this goal in an ingenious way, replacing Śankara's idealism with a form of realism. His system was further elaborated by his successors, notably Veṅkatanātha (1268–c. 1369).

Given that the world and a plurality of selves are real and yet also that they are in some way identical with, or united with, God, Rāmānuja was not content, as the Bhedābheda school tended to be, to affirm both sides of an apparent contradiction. He wished to show that a sensible account can be given of how the Absolute embraces both what changes and what is changeless. He approached this problem through an analysis of the relation between body and soul (self). There is an extensive discussion in Qualified Nondualistic literature of the correct definition of "body." The definition arrived at has two facets. One refers to the causal relation between soul and body and the other to the conceptual relation.

First, when a person is said to possess a body, it is implied that the body subserves the soul—that the movements of the body are controlled by the soul. Certain modifications of this aspect of the definition are needed—for example, a servant is controlled by his master; but he is not the latter's body, since some of his acts are not controlled by the master. By analogy, the material cosmos and souls are the body of God, since they are governed by him, and a teleological account of material changes in his "body" is given. Rāmānuja conceived of matter as possessing a fine, or subtle, form and a gross form. The Lord, in his creative activity, brings the subtle form into a state of actualization. Likewise, he controls souls and brings about their release. Thus, from the causal point of view, the body is defined as instrumental to a soul; and the world likewise is an instrument of God.

From the conceptual point of view, Rāmānuja held that body and soul are inseparable. That is, not merely is there a continuous association between body and soul so that they are never in fact separated, but also they are mutually definable. By definition, a body is *of* some self; and by definition, a self is something having a body. This relation is one–many, in that selves transmigrate, but because of Rāmānuja's doctrine of inseparability (*apṛthaksiddhi*) it is held that even in *mokṣa* (release) a liberated self has a (suitably refined) body. At any given time there is a one–one correlation between a body and its soul.

However, both aspects of the definition so far fail to show properly the difference in character between the self and its body. It is therefore necessary to add the further proviso that the self has experiences, while the body does not—although it conditions the experiences of the self. A self always has experiences from a certain point of view, and it is by the body that this point of view is determined. Finally, it may be noted that the term used here for "body" (*śarīra*) means primarily an organic body rather than simply a material object.

As a person is indivisible, in Rāmānuja's account, and yet has two aspects—his consciousness and bodily state—so the Absolute is, by this *analogia personae*, both supreme Self (God as Lord) and cosmos. Yet he is supposedly changeless, while the cosmos clearly includes changes within it. It is argued that locutions like "I know such and such" presuppose a self as knower. Personal identity cannot rest on memory states, however, since these themselves presuppose a continuity in personal identity. It follows that something changeless underlies such psychical changes. By analogy, God is the pure, changeless supreme Self. Although in this respect he is unchanging, changes occur in the Lord's "body," the cosmos. Thus he can, without contradiction, be conceived of as both changing and changeless. Rāmānuja and his successors also used the notion of substance and its attributes to illustrate the relation between God and the cosmos. A substance can, for the purposes of analysis, be distinguished from its changing qualities. The distinction, although conceptually possible—and, indeed, necessary—does not entail that there can be qualityless substances or substanceless qualities.

Rāmānuja also wished to show, in opposition to Śankara, that there are many finite selves distinguished from each other and from God. This induced a complication in his body–self analogy. Thus, he evolved a dual theory: not only is the material cosmos God's body, but so also are individual selves; and God acts from within souls as their *antaryāmin*, or inner controller. This tied in with Rāmānuja's insistence on God's grace as operative toward salvation. His successors were divided between a strong interpretation of this notion (salvation is due solely to God's activity) and a weak interpretation (salvation requires cooperation on the part of the individual with God's grace).

Rāmānuja's cosmology made use of Sāṃkhya concepts. Nature (*prakṛti*) was given a theistic interpretation, as the body of God. In Sāṃkhya, atomism, as a cosmological hypothesis, was rejected in favor of the doctrine of a unitary material substrate which evolves into the gross forms of substance encountered in perceptual experience. However, Rāmānuja did hold that selves are atomic (Indian thought tended to vacillate between treating selves as all-pervasive and as atomic) on two grounds: first, noninfinitesimal finite entities were considered to be perishable; second, the self is not easily given the attributes of extension. However, it was then necessary for Rāmānuja to show how the infinitesimal self (having no extension, but location) is connected with the body, for sensations are felt in different parts of the body. The Qualified Nondualists introduced a bridge entity to close this gap, the attributive intelligence (*dharma-bhūtajñāna*), which is capable of extension. This also served a theological purpose. The Lord's attributive intelligence pervades the whole cosmos. In the state of liberation, moreover, the self puts off its limitations and becomes all-pervasive through its attributive intelligence. It is thus godlike in the state of salvation. Thus, Rāmānuja was able to interpret the so-called identity texts in revelation, such as *tat tvam asi* ("That thou art"), as meaning that the self and God are intrinsically similar. But the self, although godlike, remains dependent on God. However, with a certain magnanimity, Rāmānuja allowed a lower form of release for those who seek identity with *Brahman*. Their souls stay in a state of painless isolation but do not realize the highest happiness, communion with the Lord.

In such ways, Rāmānuja combined a realistic metaphysics with a theology which depended upon revelation.

Bibliography

TRANSLATIONS

Radhakrishnan, S., and Moore, C., eds., *A Source Book in Indian Philosophy*. Princeton, N. J., 1957.
The Vedānta Sutras With the Commentary of Rāmānuja, translated by G. Thibaut. Sacred Books of the East, Vol. XLVIII. Oxford, 1904.
The Vedāntatattvasāra Ascribed to Rāmānujācārya, translated by J. Johnson. Banaras, 1898.
Vedārthasaṃgraha of Śrī Rāmānujācārya, edited and translated by S. S. Raghavachar. Mysore, 1956. Also translated by J. A. B. van Buitenen. Poona, 1956.

GENERAL ACCOUNTS

Bhattacharyya, H., ed., *The Cultural Heritage of India*. Calcutta, 1953. Ch. 16.
Dasgupta, S. N., *A History of Indian Philosophy*. Cambridge, 1940. Vol. III.
Lacombe, O., *L'Absolu selon le Védânta*. Paris, 1937.
Srinivasachari, P. N., *The Philosophy of Viśiṣṭādvaita*. Adyar, 1943.
Srinivasachari, P. N., *The Philosophy of Bhedābheda*, 2d ed. Adyar, 1950.
Srinivasachari, S. M., *Advaita and Viśiṣṭādvaita*. London, 1961.
Varadachari, K. C., *Śrī Rāmānuja's Theory of Knowledge*. Tirupati, 1943.

NINIAN SMART

RAMSEY, FRANK PLUMPTON (1903–1930), Cambridge mathematician and philosopher, was one of the most brilliant men of his generation; his highly original papers on the foundations of mathematics, the nature of scientific theory, probability, and epistemology are still widely studied. He also wrote two studies in economics, the second of which was described by J. M. Keynes as "one of the most remarkable contributions to mathematical economics ever made." Ramsey's earlier work led to radical criticisms of A. N. Whitehead and Bertrand Russell's *Principia Mathematica*, some of which were incorporated in the second edition of the *Principia*. Ramsey was one of the first to expound the early teachings of Wittgenstein, by whom he was greatly influenced. In his last papers he was moving toward a modified and sophisticated pragmatism.

The foundations of mathematics. A stumbling block in the reduction of mathematics to logic attempted in *Principia Mathematica* has long been its appeal to the so-called ramified theory of types, introduced in order to cope with the paradoxes discovered by Russell and others. The excessive restrictions demanded by the theory of types were mitigated by introducing an *ad hoc* axiom of reducibility, which Ramsey, following Wittgenstein, held to be at best contingently true. Ramsey was one of the first to argue, following Giuseppe Peano, that many of the notorious paradoxes depended on the use of equivocal semantic notions having no place in mathematics. By introducing the notion of "predicative functions"—roughly speaking, truth-functions permitting infinitely many arguments—Ramsey was able to show that the paradoxes could be avoided without appeal to an axiom of reducibility. In order to improve what he regarded as an unsatisfactory conception of identity in *Principia Mathematica*, Ramsey proposed the wider concept of "propositional functions in extension," considered as correlations, not necessarily definable, between individuals and associated propositions. Fully elaborated, this view would seem to lead to a markedly nonconstructivistic set theory, which most contemporaries would find unacceptable. Ramsey's distinction between semantic and logical paradoxes and his rejection of that part of the theory of types that subdivides types into "orders" has been almost universally accepted by his successors.

Philosophy of science. In a striking paper, "Theories," Ramsey developed a novel method for eliminating overt reference to theoretical entities in the formal statement of scientific theory. The method consists of replacing, in the axioms of the formal system expressing the scientific theory in question, every constant designating a theoretical entity with an appropriate variable and then applying universal quantification over the propositional matrices thus obtained. Ramsey was able to show that the conjunction of the universally quantified statements thus derived from the original axioms would have the same observational consequences as the original axiom system. This technique is of interest to philosophers concerned with the ontological implications or commitments of scientific theory.

Probability. Ramsey sketched a theory of probability considered as measuring a degree of "partial belief," thereby providing a stimulus to what are sometimes called "subjective" or "personalistic" analyses of probability. His most important idea was an operational test for degree of belief. Suppose somebody, P, has no preference between the following options: (1) to receive m_1 for certain, and (2) to receive m_2 if p is true but m_3 if p is false, where p is some definite proposition and m_1, m_2, and m_3 are monetary or other suitable measures of utility for P. Then P's degree of belief in p is proposed to be measured by the ratio $(m_1 - m_3)/(m_2 - m_3)$—roughly speaking, therefore, by the betting odds that P will accept in favor of p's being true, given the relative values to him of the possible outcomes.

General philosophy. Ramsey's most suggestive idea in general philosophy was that of treating a general proposition, say of the form "all A's are B," as a "variable hypothetical," considered not as a truth-function (as it had been in his earlier papers) but rather as a *rule* for judging that if something is found to be an A it will be judged to be a B—that is, as a formula for deriving propositions in certain ways rather than as an authentic proposition having truth-value. This idea is connected with Ramsey's unfortunately fragmentary explorations into the connections between belief, habit, and behavior. Ramsey's papers on facts, propositions, and universals also have not outlived their usefulness.

Bibliography

A collection of Ramsey's work, including previously unpublished papers, was published posthumously as *The Foundations of Mathematics and Other Logical Essays,* edited by Richard B. Braithwaite (London, 1931). This collection has a preface by G. E. Moore, a useful editor's introduction, and a complete bibliography. For the definitions of "predicative functions" and "functions in extension," see especially pp. 39–42, 52–53; Ramsey's discussion of theories is mainly on pp. 212–236; the generalized betting definition of degree of belief occurs on p. 179.

For discussions of Ramsey's work, see Israel Scheffler, *The Anatomy of Inquiry* (New York, 1963), pp. 203–222, which contains a critical exposition of Ramsey's procedure for eliminating theoretical terms; Herbert Gaylord Bohnert, *The Interpretation of Theory* (Ph.D. thesis, University of Pennsylvania, 1961), further elaboration of Ramsey's work on the nature of scientific theory; Leonard J. Savage, *The Foundations of Statistics* (New York, 1954), which acknowledges indebtedness to Ramsey's definition of partial belief; and Gilbert Ryle, "'If,' 'So,' and 'Because,'" in Max Black, ed., *Philosophical Analysis* (Ithaca, N.Y., 1950; reprinted, New York, 1963), which is a discussion of hypothetical statements as "inference licenses."

MAX BLACK

RAMUS, PETER (1515–1572), logician, educational reformer, and author of many widely used works on philosophy and letters. He was born Pierre de la Ramée in Cuts (Oise), in northern France, the son of an impoverished descendant of a noble family from Liége. After beginning Latin at Cuts, he went to study at Paris, probably between the ages of eight and twelve, and despite grave financial difficulties received his master of arts degree there at the age of 21. His master's inaugural thesis, according to one still widely circulated but questionable report, was *Quaecumque ab Aristotele Dicta Essent, Commentitia Esse* ("Whatever Aristotle Has Said Is a Fabrication"; the common translation of *commentitia* as "false" is oversimplified).

In 1543, Ramus (he had adopted Petrus Ramus as the Latin form of his name) published two works growing out of his teaching, *Dialecticae Partitiones* ("The Structure of Dialectic," also entitled *Institutiones Dialecticae* or "Training in Dialectic") and *Aristotelicae Animadversiones* ("Remarks on Aristotle"), which violently attacked Aristotle and the university curriculum as confused and disorganized. The university faculty, led largely by doctors of medicine, secured from Francis I a decree forbidding the sale of these books and prohibiting their author from teaching publicly and from writing on philosophy (which included all academic subjects other than grammar, rhetoric, medicine, law, and theology). Ramus, however, quietly continued to teach and write and in 1545 moved to the Collège de Presles in Paris, where he was joined by his earlier associate, Omer Talon (Audomarus Talaeus). Ramus soon became principal and dedicated himself, with great success, to promoting more purposeful and effective teaching. In 1547, Henry II lifted the ban against Ramus and in 1551 appointed him professor of eloquence and philosophy in the body of professors supported by the king, which was later known as the Collège de France; Ramus became its first dean. Earlier an observant Catholic, he embraced the Protestant reform around 1562, withdrawing to Fontainebleau in 1562–1563 during the religious wars and to Rhenish Germany and Switzerland from 1568–1570. He returned, however, and was murdered on the third day of the Massacre of St. Bartholomew. C. Waddington's assignment of his murder to an academic opponent, the physician Jacques Charpentier, is repeated in many encyclopedia articles but is without demonstrable foundation.

Works. Ramus' published works run to some sixty-odd titles, supplemented by 13 additional works of Talon, his frequent collaborator. The works of the two men appeared mostly between 1543 and 1650, in nearly eight hundred (at present) known editions and adaptations (some eleven hundred if works published in collected editions are separately enumerated). Besides the pivotal writings on dialectic, or logic, and on rhetoric, Ramus' works include classical editions and commentaries; lectures on physics, metaphysics, and mathematics; textbooks for grammar, arithmetic, algebra, and geometry; miscellaneous orations and open letters; and the posthumously published *Commentariorum de Religione Christiana Libri Quatuor* (1576), a basically Zwinglian theological work, unoriginal and apparently of little influence. Other works, notably Latin translations from the Greek, remained unpublished at his death. Although most of his writing was in academic Latin, he published a few works in French, including a *Gramere* of the French language (1562) in a reformed spelling that was developed from that of Louis Meigret.

Philosophy. The striking orderliness of Ramus' philosophy is superficial and is determined by pedagogical serviceability rather than by insight. His *Dialectica* (French, 1555; Latin, 1556, with subsequent revisions), later called also *Logica*, is the key work in the Ramist canon and appeared in nearly 250 extant editions or adaptations, chiefly Latin. The *Dialectica* grew out of his 1543 works and proposed to supplant the highly complex quantified logic of the Middle Ages, so objectionable to humanists. Actually, it exaggerates—at times grotesquely—the quantifying drives built up in medieval Scholasticism. Following the *De Inventione Dialectica* of Rudolph Agricola, Ramus reduced all argumentation to one "art of discourse" (*ars disserendi*, a Ciceronian definition common during the Middle Ages), which he called indifferently dialectic or logic. He thus did away with dialectic as a separate art that argues from probabilities and is thereby distinct from a scientific logic, which argues from certainties or necessity.

Rhetoric. By the same token, he also dispensed with rhetoric as a separate argumentative art persuading to action. The Ramist *Rhetorica* (1548), published under Talon's name but with Ramus' close collaboration (in some 175 known extant editions or adaptations), reduced rhetoric explicitly to mere "ornamentation," or the application of tropes and figures, conforming to what had been, in fact, a strong trend in medieval thinking about rhetoric. Like Agricola, Ramus treated logic or dialectic as made up of *inventio* (discovery of arguments for any kind of discourse, from mathematics to poetry) and *iudicium* or *dispositio* (the arrangement of arguments, including for Ramus not only syllogism but also method, likewise referable to any and all discourse). Ramus' treatment of syllogism varied somewhat from some previous treatments but in no original or insightful way, and he did nothing to advance formal logic. Still, his influence was vast and symptomatic.

Logic. In the wake of Scholasticism, logic had a high prestige value even among humanists. Ramus made it accessible to all by withdrawing it, more than even medieval Scholasticism had done, from the scientifically elusive world of sound and word and by associating it more with the sense of vision through overt or covert resort to spatial constructs or models in his teaching. Most notable among these models were the dichotomized divisions, often ar-

ranged in bracketed tabular form, for analysis of everything under the sun. One divided a subject into two parts, subdivided each of these into two, then again dichotomized each subdivision, and so on. The resulting structure somehow corresponded both to extramental actuality and to the contents of the mind. The intensified passion for this far-from-new procedure was associated with the new medium of typography, which reproduced these and other spatial constructs with an ease and conviction unknown in a manuscript-oriented civilization.

Method. In this climate Ramists gave the term "logical analysis" its first extensive currency and developed concern with method. Between 1543 and 1547 the treatment of method earlier found largely in rhetoric manuals had been transplanted into logic manuals published separately by Johannes Sturm and Philipp Melanchthon. During this period Ramus effected the same transplantation in a pseudonymous 1546 revision of his *Dialecticae Partitiones*, from which method made its way into the *Dialectica* from 1555 on. For Ramus, method prescribed treating any subject by going from the general to the particular, although for special reasons one could use cryptic method, proceeding from the particular to the general. Dichotomization implemented method.

Metaphysics was absorbed or displaced by logic, which Ramus passionately but unconvincingly identified with Plato's dialectic. Ethics was to be taught by methodized analysis of biography and history, and the physics that had formed so great a part of Scholastic philosophy was replaced, in principle at least, by analytic study of works on natural history such as Vergil's *Georgics*.

Influence. Ramus' realignments involved him in disputes with Antonio de Gouveia, Joachim de Perion, Pierre Galland, Jacques Charpentier, Adrien Turnèbe, Jean Riolan the elder, and Jakob Schegk, disputes protracted after Ramus' death by hundreds of litigants. Ramist-inspired agitation over method set the stage for Descartes (who at La Flèche studied a post-Ramist logic textbook with a section on method) and helped make meaningful the application of the nickname "Methodists" to John Wesley's followers. The modern encyclopedia owes a good deal of its organization to the Ramist and semi-Ramist tradition as represented by polymath organizers of knowledge such as Johann Heinrich Alsted. Ramus' followers, numbered by the thousands in the sixteenth and seventeenth centuries, were distributed, in descending abundance, through Germany, the British Isles and their American colonies, France, Switzerland, the Low Countries, and Scandinavia. Anti-Ramists such as Nicolas de Grouchy, Everard Digby, and Francis Bacon and Ramists such as Johann Thomas Freige (Freigius), Gabriel Harvey, and John Milton crossbred to produce various syncretists, such as Bartholomew Keckermann, Andreas Libavius, Alsted, and Robert Sanderson. Ramism and its derivatives were particularly popular in Calvinist "middle" or secondary schools for cultural and psychological rather than directly religious reasons: the Ramist account-book interpretation of knowledge and actuality appealed strongly to the bourgeois mind. Influence in strictly university circles and on speculative thought was more intermittent or indirect, but extraordinarily pervasive.

Bibliography

Ong, Walter J., S.J., *Ramus, Method, and the Decay of Dialogue.* Cambridge, Mass., 1958. Includes an exhaustive bibliography.

Ong, Walter J., S.J., *Ramus and Talon Inventory.* Cambridge, Mass., 1958.

Ong, Walter J., S.J., "Ramist Method and the Commercial Mind." *Studies in the Renaissance,* Vol. 8 (1961), pp. 155–172.

Risse, Wilhelm, *Die Logik der Neuzeit.* Stuttgart, 1963. Vol. I.

Waddington, Charles, *Ramus.* Paris, 1855.

WALTER J. ONG, S.J.

RASHDALL, HASTINGS (1858–1924), English theologian, philosopher, and historian, was born in London, the son of an evangelical clergyman. He was educated at Harrow and at New College, Oxford, where he read Classical Moderations and "Greats." He remained at Oxford two years after graduation, reading philosophy and theology and working on an essay on the history of medieval universities, for which he won the chancellor's prize in 1883. Much of his next 12 years was taken up with expanding this essay for publication in 1895 as a work in three volumes.

In 1883 he left Oxford to become a lecturer at St. David's College, a college for the education of the clergy in Lampeter, Wales, and in December of that year he was appointed a tutor in theology at University College, Durham. In 1889 he returned to Oxford as a fellow of Hertford College and in 1894 was appointed for a year as chaplain and divinity tutor at Balliol, without relinquishing his Hertford fellowship. He returned in 1895 to New College as fellow and tutor and dean of divinity. He retained his New College fellowship but not his tutorship on his appointment in 1910 as a canon of Hereford Cathedral. He remained in Hereford until 1917, when he became dean of Carlisle, an office he retained until his death.

Rashdall was primarily a theologian and secondarily a philosopher, although he would have been unwilling to draw a clear distinction between the two. His aim was to keep philosophy religious and religion philosophical. Even his history of medieval universities aimed at establishing the rational foundations of religion and ethics, the close connection between the intellectual and spiritual life, and the place of mind in the constitution of the world.

Rashdall justly described himself as "on the left wing of the Church and the right wing of the philosophers." His liberalism in religion and forthright opposition to bigotry kept getting him into trouble with the defenders of orthodoxy. The last years of his life were clouded by the false charge that he denied the divinity of Christ—a charge based on a newspaper misrepresentation of his observation that Jesus never claimed divinity for himself.

Philosophically Rashdall was a personal idealist. Although he held that there is no matter apart from mind—a personal Mind, "in which and for which everything that is not mind has its being"—he rejected monism. Minds are substantial, and every consciousness is exclusive of every other. Individual minds are produced by the eternal Mind, which is God, but are neither included in it nor adjectives of it. In line both with this metaphysical position and with his general distrust of mysticism, Rashdall held our knowledge of God to be inferential.

Rashdall's most important philosophical work is his two-volume *The Theory of Good and Evil.* Although it made no distinctively original contribution to ethics, it is perhaps the best general introduction to the subject written from an objectivist point of view, before the advent of metaethics and the application of philosophical analysis. Rashdall's treatment is thorough and comprehensive, and the book leaves no doubt about the importance for theory and practice of the issues discussed. Although it is not a history of ethics, it includes illuminating expositions and criticisms of theories of classical moral philosophers where these are relevant to the development of his own theme.

Rashdall's emphasis on the value of human personality found expression in his moral theory. Intuitionism, in the sense of acceptance of impersonal moral laws binding independently of their consequences, was wholly alien to his thought. He was an uncompromising utilitarian, for whom actions are to be judged by their tendency to produce the greatest good or well-being for human beings. There are, indeed, moral intuitions, but they are about the relative value of ends, not about the rightness of rules of conduct. The good that it is the duty of each to produce for all is a personal good but is not confined to pleasure or happiness. Pleasure is only one element which, in interrelation with other mutually modifying elements, including morality, contributes to form an ideally good pattern of life. It was Rashdall who coined the term "ideal utilitarianism" to distinguish this form of the theory from the traditional hedonistic utilitarianism which it has generally replaced, partly through his own influence. One advantage of the abandonment of hedonism claimed by Rashdall is that it enables the utilitarian to include in moral judgment the quality of the act itself as well as of its consequences. Thus, the disposition to promote the general good can be taken as itself part of the good to be promoted.

Much of the second volume of *The Theory of Good and Evil* deals with the metaphysical and theological presuppositions of an absolute objective morality. Rashdall held that only in metaphysics can we find an ultimate defense of the validity of moral judgments and that personal idealism has the best chance of supplying it. One postulate of morality is the existence of individual selves to which actions may be attributed; another is the existence of God, as possessing and willing the absolute moral ideal; and a third is immortality. Although he was a determinist, Rashdall escaped having to hold God responsible for evil in human willing because he regarded God not as strictly omnipotent but as limited by those eternal necessities which are part of his own nature.

Bibliography

Rashdall's works include *The Universities of Europe in the Middle Ages,* 3 vols. (Oxford, 1895); "Personality Human and Divine," in Henry Sturt, ed., *Personal Idealism* (London and New York, 1902); *The Theory of Good and Evil,* 2 vols. (London, 1907; 2d ed., 1924); *Philosophy and Religion* (London, 1909); *The Problem of Evil* (Manchester, 1912); *Is Conscience an Emotion?* (London, 1914); and *The Moral Argument for Personal Immortality* (London, 1920).

For a discussion of Rashdall, see P. E. Matheson, *The Life of Hastings Rashdall* (London, 1928).

A. K. STOUT

RATIONALISM. The term "rationalism" (from the Latin *ratio,* "reason") has been used to refer to several different outlooks and movements of ideas. By far the most important of these is the philosophical outlook or program which stresses the power of a priori reason to grasp substantial truths about the world and correspondingly tends to regard natural science as a basically a priori enterprise. Although philosophies which fall under this general description have appeared at various times, the spirit of rationalism in this sense is particularly associated with certain philosophers of the seventeenth and early eighteenth centuries, the most important being Descartes, Spinoza, and Leibniz. It is rationalism of this type that will be the subject of this article.

Two other applications of the term should, however, be distinguished.

Rationalism in the Enlightenment. The term "rationalism" is often loosely used to describe an outlook allegedly characteristic of some eighteenth-century thinkers of the Enlightenment, particularly in France, who held an optimistic view of the power of scientific inquiry and of education to increase the happiness of mankind and to provide the foundations of a free but harmonious social order. In this connection "rationalistic" is often used as a term of criticism, to suggest a naive or superficial view of human nature which overestimates the influence of benevolence and of utilitarian calculation and underestimates both the force of destructive impulses in motivation and the importance of such nonrational factors as tradition and faith in the human economy. D'Alembert, Voltaire, and Condorcet, among others, are often cited in this connection. Although there is some truth in these criticisms, the naïvete of these and other Enlightenment writers has often been grossly exaggerated. Also, insofar as "reason" is contrasted with "feeling" or "sentiment," it is somewhat misleading to describe the Enlightenment writers as rationalistic, for many of them (Diderot, for example) characteristically emphasized the role of sentiment. Reason was praised in contrast with faith, traditional authority, fanaticism, and superstition. It chiefly represented, therefore, an opposition to traditional Christianity.

Here there are two contrasts with the seventeenth-century rationalism of Descartes and others. First, this rationalism is not characteristically antireligious or nonreligious; on the contrary, God in some sense, often in a traditional sense, plays a large role in rationalist systems (although Spinoza's notion of God was extremely unorthodox, and it is notable that the opposition of reason and faith is important in his *Tractatus Theologico–politicus*). Second, the view of science held by such Enlightenment thinkers as Voltaire was different from that of rationalism, being much more empiricist. The central contrast embodied in the term "rationalism" as applied to the earlier systems is that of reason versus experience, a contrast which is certainly not present in the Enlightenment praise of the "rational." Parallel to this difference, there is a difference between the characteristic seventeenth- and eighteenth-century views on the nature and importance of system; the eighteenth century declared itself against the *esprit de système* of the seventeenth century, with its elaborate metaphysical systems, and in favor of an *esprit systématique,* which could be orderly without being speculatively ambitious. (See d'Alembert, *Preliminary Discourse* to the *Encyclopédie* and Condillac, *Traité des systèmes.*)

Rationalism in theology. The Enlightenment spirit of rational criticism directed against the supposed revealed truth of the Scriptures also had effects within Christianity itself. In this connection the term "rationalism" is used in a specific theological sense to refer to the doctrines of a school of German theologians which was prominent roughly between 1740 and 1840, and which had great influence on the development of Biblical criticism. With their spirit of antisupernaturalism can be associated Kant's *Die Religion innerhalb der Grenzen der blossen Vernunft* (1793), in which rational morality is the basis of religious belief.

However, the best-known use of "rationalism" in a religious connection is an entirely negative one, in which it stands for an antireligious and anticlerical movement of generally utilitarian outlook, laying great weight on historical and scientific arguments against theism. This use of the term, a popular rather than a technical one, seems now to be obsolescent, its place being taken by "humanism."

Rationalism versus empiricism. Rationalism as it will be discussed here is standardly contrasted with empiricism. This contrast (which rests on that contrast between reason and experience which has already been mentioned) is now so basic to the use of the terms that no account can afford to ignore it, and a number of comparisons between views associated with these two outlooks will be made in the course of this article. It is of course impossible to give a detailed comparison of the two outlooks, and in general comparisons will be introduced incidentally to the account of rationalist ideas. There is, however, one issue, that of innate ideas, which embodies a central disagreement between the two, and regarding which an account merely from the rationalist side would be particularly unilluminating. On this issue the disagreements will be considered in rather greater detail than elsewhere. At the same time, it is hoped that the treatment of this issue will give slightly more insight into the rationalist outlook than can be achieved by what is at other points inevitably a very selective summary of rationalist opinions.

INNATE IDEAS

Descartes distinguished three classes of "ideas" (by which he meant merely whatever it is in a man's mind in virtue of which he can be said to be thinking of a given thing): adventitious, factitious, and innate. The first type came to the mind from experience, the second were constructed by the mind's own activity, and the third were created by God together with the mind or soul itself. The last included what were for Descartes the three fundamental ideas of the basic types of substance: God, mind, and matter (or extension). For the most part Descartes argued negatively for the view that these ideas are innate, trying to show that they could not be derived from experience (where this means, fundamentally, sensation). His argument had two main points. First, the ideas are pure, containing no sensory material; these ideas are not images, reproductions, or copies of sensory experience. Descartes regarded this as fairly obvious in the cases of God and of mind; and he made a particular effort (as in the argument of the wax in *Meditations* II) to establish the same claim for matter. Second, the fundamental ideas implicitly contain, in different ways, some idea of infinity, and in grasping the idea one thereby grasps the possibility of infinitely many and various modifications to which mind and matter can be subject. In the case of God this argument goes further, for here we grasp an *actual* infinity of perfections implicit in the idea. The same point, however, holds for all these ideas: the grasp of infinitely many possibilities must transcend what has been given to us in experience, since experience could have given us at best only a limited set of such conceptions, corresponding to what had actually been experienced.

Even if both points of the argument are granted as showing that these ideas are not totally derived from experience, it might be doubted whether they are enough to show that the ideas are innate. For might they not be grasped in some nonempirical manner at a later stage of life—for example, when (or if) someone comes to think in these very general terms? In Descartes's philosophy there is at least an implicit answer to this objection. Descartes thought that the pure ideas of mind and matter are used in the comprehension of experience even before they become conscious in reflection. It is by reference to these ideas that one forms the ordinary unreflective conceptions of oneself as having a series of thoughts or of a material object as enduring, occupying space, and having various characteristics, even though, before reflection, one's conceptions of these things will be confused. Thus, the operation of the pure idea is implicit in ordinary prereflective experience, and such experience begins to be acquired from the moment of birth; therefore, there is ground for calling the pure ideas innate.

In the case of God the argument is slightly different, since it is less clear that this idea is "put to use" in any prereflective way. Here Descartes may have meant to claim merely that it would be natural to the power and economy of God's operations that he should implant the idea of himself in the soul at its creation, "the mark," as Descartes put it, "of the workman on his work." There is indeed a difficulty in seeing how, for Descartes, there could be an idea in the mind of which the mind is not fully conscious (as this account implies), since for Descartes "mind" and "consciousness" were virtually equivalent. And this difficulty also arises for the ideas of mind and matter, since Descartes explicitly denied (presumably there was no alternative) that the infant or young person is fully conscious of his innate ideas; they are latent and emerge only later—in the process of learning language, for instance. Nevertheless, Descartes's claims for the operation of fundamental ideas in prereflective consciousness, although not quite consistent with his metaphysics of the mind, became an important element in later theories of innate ideas, especially in the debate with empiricism.

Innate principles. Descartes appealed only to innate ideas, or concepts, the materials of judgments and beliefs. He did not invoke innate principles, or propositions, his view apparently being that granted innate ideas, we have

only to grant in addition a certain power of the mind to elicit features implicit in these ideas in order to explain how necessary knowledge could be derived from innate ideas (as he supposed it could).

Leibniz, however, who continued the Cartesian insistence on innate ideas, added a requirement for innate principles. His argument was of the same general type as that ascribed to Descartes with respect to the ideas of mind and matter: if there were no innate and unlearned propositions, we could learn no propositions at all—at least not by way of logical deduction. For, he argued, confronted with any valid inference of the form "*P*, so *Q*," we could not see that *Q* followed from *P* except by having already grasped the necessary truth of the proposition "if *P* then *Q*." Thus, in order to follow any inference and to learn anything by deduction, first premises are required which must themselves be unlearned. An objection to this argument can be seen from the famous difficulty raised by Charles L. Dodgson (Lewis Carroll) that if there is necessarily a difficulty in seeing the validity of the original inference as it stands, the same difficulty will recur with the inference obtained by the addition of the "innate" major premise; to grasp the validity of this inference, another major premise would seem to be required, and so on, thus starting a vicious regress. Dodgson's point makes it clear that no multiplication of premises can be adequate to extricate the validity of an inference; what is needed is something of a different category, a rule. At this point a characteristic empiricist rejoinder to Leibniz' puzzle is to claim that the rules of inference are not unlearned but are learned in the course of learning a language (they are the rules implicit in the correct use of "if," "then," "not," and so on). This illustrates the natural and perhaps inevitable tendency of empiricism, in contrast with rationalism, to turn to a linguistic account of logical necessity. (Such an account, however, even if adequate in itself, may not dispose of the issues as thoroughly as empiricism has tended to believe; the question remains of what is involved in learning a language.)

Leibniz, in introducing the argument just considered, explicitly stated that he was of the "Platonic" opinion that a priori knowledge (at least) is innate and "recollected" (*New Essays*, Book I). There is a difficulty, however, in knowing how far the doctrine is supposed to range: Leibniz' doctrine that the soul is a monad and that every monad only develops its own inner potentialities, being unaffected by anything outside, implies that in one sense all thoughts, of whatever kind, are innate. This problem involves major questions in the interpretation of Leibniz—in particular, of his views on sense perception. However, it seems reasonable to say that at least in his remarks on innateness in the *New Essays* Leibniz was distinguishing between kinds of knowledge and ideas, such that some (the pure and a priori) can be said to be innate and others cannot.

Leibniz' remarks were in criticism of the First Book of Locke's *Essay Concerning Human Understanding*, and they constitute a subtle consideration of the issues lying between rationalism and empiricism at this point. Locke's First Book, although called "Of Innate Ideas," is in fact chiefly concerned with innate principles (and in some part with the alleged innate principles of morality that had been advanced by his adversary, Lord Herbert of Cherbury). Locke considered various characteristics supposed to show that a given proposition is innate (that it is universally believed, that it is assented to as soon as understood, and so forth), and had little difficulty in showing that these are inadequate. He then turned to the consideration that tiny children do not display elaborate conceptions of logic and mathematics such as are alleged by rationalists to be innate. His principle in this instance was "There is nothing in the mind of which the mind is not conscious"; if these conceptions were innate, they would be in the infant's mind, hence it would be conscious of them and (presumably) could display this consciousness. Leibniz, in reply, claimed that this so patently follows that Locke, in insisting on the principle about consciousness, was in effect begging the question: this principle is what the issue turns on. But, as has been seen, this was not how Descartes put the matter. Leibniz here made the cardinal point of the discussion his own non-Cartesian doctrine of subconscious perceptions (connected with his general doctrine of continuity).

Debate with empiricism. Once the obvious fact is granted that the allegedly innate ideas do not manifest themselves temporally before other experience, it may be wondered whether any point remains to calling them innate. It has sometimes been suggested that the doctrine of innate ideas merely depends on a confusion between a logical and a temporal sense of "prior." However, this is to underestimate the force of the rationalist claims that the allegedly innate material is such that its operation is a precondition of our learning anything else. It is not easy to decide how to evaluate these claims, as against the central empiricist claim that no such pre-existing material need be postulated (the so-called *tabula rasa* theory of the mind). For one thing, empiricism in its first developments tended to make up for the lack of original raw material by crediting the mind with a very elaborate set of operations. This was evidently the case with Locke, who used such notions as "abstraction," "reflection," and "intuition"; who spoke of "ideas" which are not evidently mere copies from sense perception; and who admitted a nonempirical notion of "substance" and its powers. His position retained a number of rationalist elements. The much more economical apparatus of Hume, which in effect admits nothing but sensations, their copies, and the operations of association, defines a quite distinctive empiricist theory.

If the debate about innate ideas is cast in terms of a Humean empiricism, there remain principally two issues, one logical and one psychological. The logical issue concerns the question whether highly general concepts, such as those used in mathematics and the sciences, are reducible to or analyzable into those sorts of empirical concepts which can plausibly be said to be derived from sense experience. It would be widely agreed that the answer to this question would be "no." The second, psychological issue is whether the acquisition of concepts, such as occurs in language learning—and this would include even the supposedly straightforward empirical concepts—can be adequately explained by a psychological model postulating

only the minimum empiricist requirements of sense perception, retention, association, and so forth. There is influential opinion (held by Noam Chomsky and others) that the answer to this, too, must be "no"; any adequate model may well require stringent innate constraints on the direction and nature of generalization from learning situations. How far these restraints might be supposed to approximate to the rationalists' conceptions of innate ideas—or, in other words, whether the model demands an innate analogue to the possession of concepts—remains to be seen. If this is indeed an open question, then there is an explicitly psychological version of the rationalist view which is still worth serious consideration. This is not, of course, to say that the innate elements in an adequate model would be likely to correspond to the particular sorts of "ideas" that the rationalists selected for this status— such as the metaphysical notions of God, matter, and mind. Also, there was certainly an endemic confusion, in both the rationalist and the empiricist position on this issue, between psychological and logical issues. Nevertheless, there is still some life in the question, in both its logical and its psychological aspects, the occurrence of the psychological term "innate" in the original debate not being merely the result of confusion.

KNOWLEDGE

It was remarked above that there would now be wide agreement that many general theoretical concepts of mathematics and the sciences do not admit of total reduction to empirical concepts. In contrast with positivist or operationalist views it would be agreed by many that such concepts as "mass," for instance, are not a mere shorthand for sets of possible observation data. Such agreement, however, although it would constitute a rejection of strict empiricism, would not in itself constitute an acceptance of rationalist views about such concepts. It is possible to think that these concepts "transcend," or "go beyond," the empirical merely in virtue of conventional elements—that they are parts of humanly constructed models of reality which relate the observable by imposing a structure on it. Essential to rationalism, however, is a realistic view (incompatible with even a modified empiricism) about the relation of these concepts to reality and about the necessary relations obtaining between these concepts themselves. The intellectual grasp of these concepts and the truths involved in them is seen as an insight into an existing and unique structure of the world. It is not easy to express this picture (which in varying degrees dominated the rationalists) in less figurative language, but the picture has at least two consequences: that there is a unique set of concepts and a unique set of propositions employing these concepts that adequately express the nature of the world, and that these propositions form a system and could ideally be recognized as a set of necessary truths. There are, admittedly, difficulties about the last point, particularly with reference to Leibniz (these will be considered in the next section). However, something like this general picture is central to rationalism and leads immediately to the question of how anyone can come to know this uniquely correct representation of the world. This invites two more specific questions: what, in general, is the guarantee that knowledge of the world is possible? how can any individual tell in a particular case whether he has hit on some genuine piece of knowledge?

Descartes's epistemology. Most rationalists tended to answer the first of the above questions by referring to God; some, but not all, did the same for the second; and they varied in the priority that they assigned to the two questions. Descartes started famously with the second question and found the answer in the "clear and distinct perceptions" of the intellect. Proving, as he supposed, the existence of God via clear and distinct perception, he then employed God's perfection of "being no deceiver" to establish in general terms the reliability of beliefs that went beyond clear and distinct perception. He was, however, so impressed by the thought that it was only in virtue of man's being created and sustained by God that he could know anything at all, that he was constantly tempted to double back and use the divine perfection to guarantee even the basic clear and distinct perceptions, thus laying himself open to the charge of arguing in a circle.

However this may be, it is notable that in Descartes "clear and distinct perception" is a thoroughly epistemological category. The truths that can be clearly and distinctly perceived do not constitute one homogeneous logical or metaphysical class of truths; the class includes at least statements of contingent existence (his own, in the *cogito*) and of necessary existence (that of God), contingent statements about immediate psychological experience, and necessary truths about the relations of ideas. The status of these last, which Descartes called eternal truths, is somewhat obscure. Descartes held, in the Augustinian–Scotist tradition, that they were the products of God's will; but it is left unclear what it is that God has brought about in creating eternal truths, and hence what it is that one knows in knowing them.

The Cartesian tradition. The development of the Cartesian tradition within rationalism tended to emphasize to an even greater extent the theological elements in Descartes's theory of knowledge. Thus Nicolas Malebranche retained for the individual case the test of "clear and distinct perception" in a style which seems to assimilate it to moral perception and the promptings of conscience: "One should never give one's complete assent except to propositions which seem so evidently true that one could not reject them without feeling an interior pain, and secret reproaches of the reason" (*De la Recherche de la vérité*, I, Ch. 2; for the moral analogue, see Bossuet, *Traité de la connaissance de Dieu et de soi-même*, Ch. 1, Sec. 7).

Malebranch gives a strongly Augustinian and indeed Neoplatonist turn to the general account of God's guarantee of the possibility of knowledge. His doctrine was that all our knowledge of the external world is mediated by God; the mind of God contains paradigm ideas in whose form he created the world, and it is these same ideas of which we are conscious when thinking about the world. This is the meaning of Malebranche's saying that we see all things in God. This doctrine, apart from serving religious purposes, was also an attempt to get around the difficulties inherent in Descartes's own causal account of

relations between matter and mind (which will be considered more generally later in this article).

The role of God in the foundations of knowledge takes different and less extreme forms in other areas of the rationalist tradition. The greatest contrast to the Malebranche development of Cartesianism might plausibly be said to be Spinoza's system. It is true that Spinoza did assert that it is the nature of God that guarantees the correspondence of our thoughts to the world, but he so transmuted the notion of God that the doctrine is only verbally similar to Cartesianism. "God" is one name ("Nature" is another) for the one substance, that is, everything that there is. This substance has infinitely many attributes, of which we can comprehend only two, mind and matter. These two attributes are necessarily parallel to one another, and corresponding to any mode of the one attribute there must be a mode of the other. Hence, thought and the material world are inherently adjusted to one another, and the development of knowledge consists in the project of rendering the thought component of this relation as clear (in Spinoza's term, as "active") as possible. It admittedly remains obscure how, within the constraints of Spinoza's determinism, this can be regarded as a "project" at all. Despite this and the other notorious difficulties, Spinoza's system is particularly interesting in the present connection as a thoroughgoing attempt to answer the crucial question which was left very much in the air in Descartes's thought, namely, how any knowledge of a necessary truth, regarded as knowledge of the relations of ideas, could also constitute knowledge of the world.

Leibniz' system, for all its radical differences from Spinoza's, resembles it in one respect having to do with the foundation of knowledge: the general possibility of the correspondence of thought to the world is guaranteed metaphysically by the existence of a correlation between the two. The monads are not affected by anything outside and each develops its own activity from within, but a correspondence between the activities of the monads is given by the "Pre-established Harmony"; and knowledge, the correspondence between "conscious" states of certain monads and other monads, is a special case of this. The Pre-established Harmony, however, depends on God's optimal choice, that is, on God's benevolence. Thus, in a less explicitly epistemological form, Leibniz (in contrast with Spinoza) reverted to the original Cartesian standpoint, in that there is a transcendent and personal God who has a will, and it is a result of his will that there is an ultimate guarantee of the possibility of knowledge.

In general, however, Leibniz was not much concerned with epistemological problems; in particular, he was uninterested in the question that was the starting point for Descartes: how can the individual be certain of the truth of anything? Spinoza *was* concerned with this question, and tried to develop a theory of knowledge which would avoid the regress latent in Descartes's method, arising from the question of how one knows that one knows. In Spinoza's "degrees of knowledge" it is an essential property of the highest, or intuitive, degree that it is self-guaranteeing. Even so, there is an evident shift in the Spinozan outlook away from the Cartesian question "What do I know, and how do I know it?" Spinoza, like Leibniz and many other rationalists, gave the metaphysical description of the world from "outside," from a "God's-eye" standpoint rather than from the subjective epistemological standpoint from which Descartes (although unsuccessfully) tried to work. It is, perhaps, a mild irony of the history of philosophy that Descartes's attempt to start with subjective questions of epistemology and to "work out" from there had more influence on the development of empiricism than on later rationalism.

SCIENCE AND SCIENTIFIC METHOD

No attempt will be made here to give an account of the detailed developments of the philosophy of science within rationalist thought, or of the actual scientific conceptions held by or associated with rationalists, although these are of course of great importance, most notably in Leibniz' critique of Cartesian physics and in the development of his concept of force. We shall consider only one or two general points about the rationalists' conception of a completed science and associated notions of scientific method.

Rationalist developments in these matters can usefully be seen in the light of an unresolved conflict within Descartes's system between the method of approaching scientific inquiry and the expected shape of the final product. Descartes favored in principle an approach to inquiry which might be called systematically exploratory. This he called the analytic method; and the straightforward exposition of the results of such an inquiry would be heuristic in style, explaining the resolution of difficulties as they were encountered in the systematic progress. He seems, however, also to have had a picture of a completed science as a complete deductive system, ideally expressed in a unique system of theorems with necessary truths (of a metaphysical character) as its axioms; this he termed the synthetic method of exposition. There is, perhaps, no essential clash between these two ideas of method and result; but Descartes seems not to have been clear about the relation between the two or how this specific method, fully pursued, would yield this specific result. Ambiguities about this question emerge in Descartes's accounts of the role of experiment, in which he sometimes gives the incoherent impression that he is both engaged in logical deduction of scientific laws from self-evident metaphysical premises and doing experiments to assist him in this deduction. On the whole, it is probably better to regard the idea of a complete formally deductive metaphysico-scientific system as less important in Descartes's thought than is sometimes supposed, and to see him as using certain limiting principles of scientific explanation, within which he constructs models to explain particular phenomena.

The idea of the total deductive system, however, had a powerful effect on rationalism and reached its most extreme expression in the work of Spinoza, where the "synthetic" method of Euclidean demonstration is explicitly regarded as necessary to the highest form of understanding. This was not just an expository preference; it was an expression of the basic Spinozist outlook, which regarded the relation of cause to effect as that of logical ground to consequence—for Spinoza all explanatory relations were logical and timeless. The parallel orders of thought and

matter, remarked on earlier, supposedly guarantee that the logical relations of ideas will constitute a totally adequate expression of the nature of the world. (A singular application of this notion of total parallelism is to be found in Ehrenfried Walter von Tschirnhaus, who in *Medicina Mentis* (1687) argued that an adequate definition of laughter should be able to produce laughter.

Leibniz, partly under the influence of Erhard Weigel, was also attracted to the "geometrical method." He devoted a good deal of effort to the project of a universal calculus, which would enable arguments on any subject matter to be cast into a rigorous demonstrative form. However, the idea of such a calculus in no way presupposes an ideal of being able to demonstrate scientific truths from metaphysical or other supposedly self-evident axioms, which was the Spinozan and, on occasion, the Cartesian ideal. Even if Leibniz started with the notion that it should be possible to settle any argument by appeal to the self-evident, he abandoned it in his mature philosophy, in which he made fundamental the distinction between "truths of reason," which can be established by logical insight on the basis of the law of noncontradiction, and "truths of fact," which depend on the principle of sufficient reason and cannot be established on logical grounds alone. There are some notorious difficulties about this distinction, especially concerning the question of the nature of the contingency of "truths of fact," since Leibniz also held the further general principle that in all true propositions the predicate is contained in the subject. It does seem clear, however, that there is an ineliminable contingency about "truths of fact," and hence that the aspiration of reducing all knowledge to a system of deductions from self-evident premises must be impossible in the Leibnizian system.

Francis Bacon said in his *Cogitata et Visa* (1607), "Empiricists are like ants, they collect and put to use; but rationalists, like spiders, spin threads out of themselves." Bacon, of course, preferred the ants. Although there is some element of truth in the image of the spider, as applied to some rationalist thinkers, it does less than justice to the substantial empirical work done under rationalist inspiration. This is all the more so if one counts Galileo's view of science as fundamentally rationalist. He certainly rejected any kind of Baconian empiricism and shared the rationalist vision of a mathematical structure of reality which intellectual insight could grasp; but he perhaps had a more sophisticated feeling than any of the philosophers for the balance of imagination and experiment in physics. The rationalist tradition certainly embodied fundamental insights (lacking in empiricism) about the nature of science; above all, it saw the importance of mathematical structures in physical explanation and the vital possibility of a theory's making a conceptual jump beyond the observations and not merely (as in empiricism) an advance in generality. Its sense of the activity of the scientific mind, of its restructuring of observations through concepts and models, was very significant. On the other hand, empiricism rightly fought for a clearer distinction between pure mathematics and natural science, undermined the aspirations to final certainty that dogged the rationalists, and emphasized the role of laborious observation and experiment in contrast with the rather dreamlike quality of rationalist visions of the universe. No clearer case exists in the history of philosophy of the need for, and eventual occurrence of, a synthesis; one aspect of that synthesis is neatly summed up in a remark of Giorgio de Santillana that "the true scientist has an empiricist conscience and a rationalist imagination."

SUBSTANCE AND CAUSALITY

In the history of classical empiricism the concepts of substance and of active causal power together became progressively weaker and were finally abandoned. Thus Locke employed the full Cartesian array of both material and mental substances, both possessing causal power; Berkeley banished material substance, partly on the ground that it could not be conceived of as possessing causal activity, which belongs only to mental substance; Hume maintained that the notions of substance and of causal activity are unintelligible. By contrast, in the rationalist tradition the notion of substance has not declined; developments in the idea of causal activity, although partly parallel to the idea of substance, are very different; in general the fortunes of "substance" and of "causal activity" have not been directly linked, as they have proved to be in empiricism—both have undergone considerable and partly independent variations. In the case of substance (which will be very briefly considered here) the concept has not so much been criticized as used in differing ways to express differing metaphysical views of the world. On one measure, at least, the extremes in this respect are represented by the philosophies of Spinoza and Leibniz. Spinoza gave what he claimed was an a priori demonstration that there could be only one substance (*Deus sive Natura*, God or Nature); this was intrinsically neither material nor mental, these distinctions arising (as noted above) only at the level of the different attributes of this same substance. Essential to Leibniz' outlook, on the other hand, was an infinite set of substances, the monads, each of them different from all the others. In their character, although there are difficulties of interpretation on this point, they are more of a mental than of a material kind.

On the question of causality an important stream in the history of rationalism stems from the problem left by Descartes, concerning the causal interaction of mind and matter. Descartes's own view, which postulated simple efficient causation as holding between the two types of substance, failed to appeal to even the most ardent Cartesians, and their attention was particularly directed to this question, although difficulties about the meaning of causation even between material bodies also were considered. The natural tendency in the Cartesian tradition was to move toward attributing all causal power to God, and this movement of thought culminated in the doctrine of occasionalism—that both physical and mental events in the world are occasions for the application of God's power, which itself directly produces what would normally be called the effects of those events. This doctrine is most thoroughly expressed in the writings of Malebranche. Similar views, however, are to be found in Louis de la Forge (*Le Traité de l'esprit et de l'homme*, 1666) and Geraud de Cordemoy (*Le Discernement du corps et de l'âme*, 1666), whose work was known to Malebranche.

The theory of occasionalism can be usefully contrasted with Berkeley's empiricist account of causation. For both the only genuine activity was spiritual. For Berkeley the effects of such activity were also spiritual (mind can affect only mind), and indeed there was no other type of substance. The occasionalists retained material substance and did not find it unintelligible that mind can act upon matter; however, they held that the only mind for which such action is intelligible is the infinite mind of God. Here, as elsewhere, the questions of the gulf between mind and matter and of causation as activity emerge as of common concern to both rationalist and empiricist metaphysics, the influence of Descartes being clearly discernible in both.

Another writer who inclined to occasionalism was Arnold Geulincx (*Ethics*, 1665; 2d ed., 1675); however, he also suggested a different model for causality, in which God did not, as in occasionalism, make a constant series of miraculous interventions into the natural order but had established *ab initio* a series of coordinated developments, the relations between which are what is taken for causal interaction. In this connection Geulincx introduced the example of the two clocks, perfectly adjusted to keep the same time, one of which strikes when the other shows the hour; the appearance of causal connection between them is only a result of precise prearrangement. This same analogy was frequently employed by Leibniz in explaining his own very thoroughgoing version of this thesis, in which all appearance of causal interaction is an instance of the preestablished harmony between the several developments of the monads. Here again there is a notable contrast with and a similarity to empiricism: both Leibniz and Hume, each representing the culmination of one of the two traditions in its classical form, deny the existence of "transeunt action" between different things and see what is called causation as a correlation between phenomena. Leibniz, however, emphasized some kind of spontaneous activity within the monad, while for Hume neither such activity, nor any notion of a substance, such as a monad, was acceptable. The views of these two philosophers are also worthy of comparison on other subjects, such as space and time; and the points of contact between them are the more significant in the light of the radical and very obvious differences in the spirit, method, and presuppositions of their two philosophies. These differences in the two culminating figures constitute a paradigm, almost a caricature, of the divergent styles of thought associated with rationalism and empiricism, while at the same time similar pressures in the history of thought produced partly parallel developments in each.

Bibliography

For an understanding of rationalism, writings by and about particular rationalist philosophers should be read; references to these will be found in the bibliographies of the appropriate articles.

GENERAL WORKS

Bouillier, Francisque, *Histoire de la philosophie cartésienne*, 3d ed. Paris, 1868.

Cassirer, Ernst, *The Philosophy of the Enlightenment*, translated by Fritz Koelln and James Pettegrove. Princeton, N.J., 1951. As the title indicates, this is not directly on seventeenth-century rationalism but relates to it.

Lecky, W. E. H., *History of the Rise and Influence of the Spirit of Rationalism in Europe.*London, 1865; rev. ed., London, 1910.

Santillana, Giorgio de, and Zilsel, Edgar, "The Development of Rationalism and Empiricism," in *International Encyclopedia of Unified Science.* Chicago, 1941. Vol. II.

Windelband, Wilhelm, *A History of Philosophy,* translated by J. H. Tufts. New York, 1901. Part IV, Ch. 2; Part V, Ch. 1. Cites the works and—summarily—the views of many philosophers, including minor ones.

PHILOSOPHY OF SCIENCE

Burtt, E. A., *The Metaphysical Foundations of Modern Physical Science.* Rev. ed., New York, 1952; paperback reprint, Garden City, N.Y., 1954.

Dijksterhuis, E. J., *The Mechanization of the World Picture,* translated by C. Dikshoorn. Oxford, 1961.

Gillispie, C. C., *The Edge of Objectivity.* Princeton, N.J., 1960.

INNATE ELEMENTS IN LANGUAGE ACQUISITION

Fodor, J. A., and Katz, J. J., eds., *The Structure of Language.* Englewood Cliffs, N.J., 1964. Chs. 21 and 22. Papers by Noam Chomsky and E. H. Lenneberg, respectively.

BERNARD WILLIAMS

RAVAISSON-MOLLIEN, JEAN GASPARD FÉLIX

(1813–1900), French spiritualist philosopher and art historian. Ravaisson was born in Namur; he received his philosophical training in Munich under Schelling and took a degree in Paris in 1838 under Victor Cousin. His philosophical work began with his prize essay, *Essai sur la métaphysique d'Aristote,* and a short teaching career at Rennes in 1838. In 1840 he was appointed inspector general of libraries, a post which he held until 1860, when he became inspector general in the department of higher education. Meanwhile, as a semiprofessional painter he had become interested in classical antiquities, and in 1870 he was made curator in the department of antiquities in the Louvre. The fruit of this was his well-known set of reconstructions of the Venus de Milo.

The most influential of Ravaisson's publications was his *Rapport sur la philosophie en France au XIX*ᵉ *siècle,* made at the request of the imperial government in 1867. At this time the school of Cousin was in the ascendancy in France, and it was difficult, indeed practically impossible, for a man who was not an eclectic to get an appointment in the university system. Ravaisson's purpose in his report was to show that there was a continuity in the French philosophical tradition and that French philosophers had always presupposed metaphysical principles that implied what he called spiritualism. This tradition, he maintained, always swung between sensationalism, phenomenalism, and materialism, on the one hand, and idealism, on the other. But spiritualism really began in the nineteenth century with Maine de Biran, who used as his starting point the human will and who held that the will is independent both of sensations and of ideas. This viewpoint, Ravaisson argued, was not only the proper beginning of a philosophy but also the only one which could unify the opposing tendencies of empiricism and idealism.

Such a conclusion was in clear contradiction to the tenets of Cousin's eclecticism, which aspired to fuse "the best in each philosopher." Ravaisson tried to show that such a fusion in reality consists in refuting those philosophies which displease the eclectic and retaining those which

please him. In classifying all philosophies under the headings of sensualism, idealism, mysticism, and skepticism, Cousin accepted only that philosophy which he called idealism but which, said Ravaisson, was really a simple mixture of the Scottish philosophy of common sense with a few ideas from Maine de Biran. The eclectics, moreover, failed to understand these ideas. Ravaisson claimed for himself the credit of introducing the true thought of Maine de Biran to his contemporaries. Readers of this report were thus informed that the *de facto* official philosophy of the French universities was not only a foreign importation but also untrue.

Ravaisson was not satisfied with undermining eclecticism. He also felt it important to point out the weaknesses of positivism. These weaknesses, he claimed, arose from the identification of philosophical method with the methods of science. Science, which admittedly studies the external world, can never tell us anything about the internal world of thoughts, aspirations, desires, and dreams; and when it attempts to do so, it transforms them into quasi-external objects. This inevitably leads to materialism, for the laws of matter are the only laws which science can formulate. Science's basic categories are space and quantity, and its basic method is analysis. But the phenomena of consciousness are never spatial or quantitative, and to attempt to categorize them in these terms is to change their essential nature.

Ravaisson's report reviewed all the contemporary schools of thought and all the contemporary philosophers. It was a model of patience and thorough investigation and has become the primary source of information about individuals who are obscure and in some cases forgotten. It did not stop at professional philosophers but looked into the presuppositions of scientists, such as the physiologist Claude Bernard and the psychiatrist Albert Lemoine. In every case, Ravaisson found either too strong an emphasis on the dependence of the "spirit" upon material causes or an identification of ideas with strictly logical, hence analytical, reason. Whereas one set of philosophers tried to explain the mind in terms which were inappropriate, the other failed to ask the central question of why the mind operated as it did. Neither group could explain our undeniable feeling of being active causes; neither could see why the spirit needs both analysis and synthesis.

Whether the object of our thinking is the external or the internal world, it will be found that we have to utilize two absolutely general metaphysical principles, that of an infinite reality and that of limitation. The dialectical reason for this is that every analytical sentence distinguishes between parts of a whole and no whole can be discussed except by reference to its constituent parts. But Ravaisson did not rest his doctrine on this dialectical argument. On the contrary, he believed that history had shown that every philosopher presupposes these principles, whether he knows it or not. The tendency of the history of philosophy is toward the progressive realization of this truth. It is implicit in all philosophy and is steadily becoming explicit. Ravaisson's report thus presented not only an exposition of contemporary French philosophies but also a theory about the history of philosophy.

In a shorter study, *De l'Habitude,* written as a thesis at the Sorbonne in 1838, Ravaisson returned to the problem raised in Maine de Biran's prize-winning essay on the influence of habit on thinking. Ravaisson's study is of special historical interest since it forms the nucleus of the philosophy of Henri Bergson.

At the beginning of his argument Ravaisson laid down a fundamental distinction between the roles played by space and time in our lives. "Space," he said, "is the most obvious and elementary condition and form of stability or permanence; time the universal condition of change." Corresponding to these two basic principles are matter and life respectively. In matter there is no individuality and no possibility of habit, a point which Ravaisson probably encountered in his study of Aristotle. Life, on the contrary, forms a world of its own, a world which is internal to the living being. A set of oppositions follows, that of necessity (matter) versus that of "nature" (life), a set which echoes the two realms of necessity and freedom elaborated by Schelling. The repetition of a change modifies "nature," and the living being swings between the limitations of its material conditions and its own inner freedom. As the forms of life develop, their power of spontaneous action becomes greater, so that although the inorganic is timeless, life implies a "definite continuous *durée*." As we move up from vegetable to animal to human life, we find that whereas sensory impressions become weaker when repeated, our powers of movement become stronger and stronger.

Corresponding to these dualities is another. Within the human soul are the two powers of understanding and of activity. The understanding sees everything under the aspects of diversity, quantity, and space; the power of activity appears primarily in our feeling of effort, which is gradually reduced by habit. Habit transforms voluntary movements into instinctive movements. Voluntary movements could not be made if there were no resistance from without, but for them to be made at all requires that somewhere there be an undetermined center of activity, which is the will. And when one asks what the will is seeking, the answer is that it seeks the good, or God. It is not difficult to see in these views both the influence of Schelling and the anticipation of Bergson.

Works by Ravaisson

Essai sur la métaphysique d'Aristote, 2 vols. Paris, 1837–1846.
De L'Habitude. Paris, 1838. Reprinted in *Revue de métaphysique et de morale*, Vol. 2 (1894), 1–35.
Rapport sur la philosophie en France au XIXe siècle. Paris, 1867.
Testament philosophique et fragments. Paris, n.d. Published posthumously, with bibliography.

Works on Ravaisson

Bergson, Henri, "Notice sur la vie et les oeuvres de M. Félix Ravaisson-Mollien." *Comptes-rendus de l'Académie des sciences morales et politiques* (1904). Reprinted in Bergson's *La Pensée et le mouvant* (Paris, 1934) as well as in the *Testament philosophique* of Ravaisson.
Dopp, Joseph, *Félix Ravaisson, la formation de sa pensée d'après des documents inédits*. Louvain, 1933.
Gunn, J. Alexander, *Modern French Philosophy*. London, 1922. Pp. 73–75 and *passim*.

GEORGE BOAS

REALE, MIGUEL, Brazilian philosopher of law, historian of ideas, and politician, was born in 1910. He is professor of law and a former rector at the University of São Paulo, where he founded the Instituto Brasileiro de Filosofia and its journal, *Revista brasileira de filosofia*. Reale is a prolific author, and his books embrace the full range of his concerns, although his greatest contribution lies in the philosophy of law.

Reale has developed an analytical method (derived from German phenomenology and Italian historicism) that he calls "critical ontognoseological historicism." Rejecting both traditional realism and idealism, he locates the transcendental conditions of human experience and knowledge in a fundamental and inseparable correlation of subject and object. These conditions are mutually implicit and reciprocally necessary and are comprehensible only as moments in a polar dialectical process. Man's being emerges only through his own historicity, as values are realized in time through his conduct. The person finds his essence (*ser*) in what he ought to be (*dever-ser*), and he is the source of all values. Values are possible only where there are persons, and personality consists in conduct that is comprehensible only with reference to ends and values. A phenomenological description of human action reveals its essential orientation toward ends that represent values determining action and serving as the foundation of the "ought-to-be" in which man finds his essence. Reale interprets human history as a process through which values are converted into ends, accompanied by cultural crises whenever a new generation refuses to recognize the value of traditional ends.

Legal phenomena are basic to the realization of values in common. In law, two persons are joined in a polar nexus of common needs. Reale distinguishes three traditional approaches to the understanding of the nature of law. Sociologism interprets law as a positive fact and explains it in sociological and historical terms. Neopositivism interprets law as the expression of the operative norms of a given society and analyzes its function therein. Culturalism interprets law as axiological in nature and investigates the transcendental conditions that make it possible. Reale rejects all three as merely partial interpretations. Fact, norm, and value, in his view, are dialectically unified and not merely juxtaposed. Law is a fact through which values are made concrete in history and through which intersubjective relations are normatively ordered.

Works by Reale

Teoria do direito e do estado ("Theory of Law and the State"). São Paulo, 1960.
Filosofia do direito ("Philosophy of Law"). São Paulo, 1962.
Pluralismo e liberdade ("Pluralism and Liberty"). São Paulo, 1963.

Works on Reale

Revista brasileira de filosofia, Vol. 11, Fasc. 42 (April–June 1961). Dedicated to Reale on the occasion of his fiftieth birthday, this issue contains five expository articles as well as other material about him, his thought, and activity.

FRED GILLETTE STURM

REALISM. In the early history of philosophy, particularly in medieval thought, the term "realism" was used, in opposition to nominalism, for the doctrine that universals have a real, objective existence. In modern philosophy, however, it is used for the view that material objects exist externally to us and independently of our sense experience. Realism is thus opposed to idealism, which holds that no such material objects or external realities exist apart from our knowledge or consciousness of them, the whole universe thus being dependent on the mind or in some sense mental. It also clashes with phenomenalism, which, while avoiding much idealist metaphysics, would deny that material objects exist except as groups or sequences of sensa, actual and possible.

THE POLEMIC AGAINST IDEALISM

At the close of the nineteenth century, idealism was the dominant Western philosophy, but with the opening of the twentieth century, there was an upsurge of realism in Britain and North America, associated in the former with G. E. Moore, Bertrand Russell, and Samuel Alexander and in the latter with William James (despite his pragmatism), the new realists, and later the critical realists. Before a discussion of realist doctrine, a brief survey may be given of its attack on idealism. The claim that material objects cannot exist independently of mind had been made on various grounds. First, the analysis of perception, especially of illusions, was held to show that our knowledge was limited to groups of sensations "in the mind" or to products of the synthesis or interpretation of sensory data. Later idealists, under the slogan "all cognition is judgment," stressed the role of judgment and interpretation in perception, concluding that objects as we know them must be largely or even wholly the work of the mind. Second, physical objects cannot exist independently of the mind, for whatever is known is relative to the mind that knows it. This is the "egocentric predicament"—that one can never eliminate the "human mind" from knowledge and discover what things are like apart from one's consciousness or, indeed, whether they exist when they are not known, for the discovery itself involves consciousness and thus would be knowing. This may also be stated in terms of the doctrine of internal relations—that the nature of anything is grounded in and constituted by the relations it has with other things; no two related things could be what they are if the relation between them did not exist, and so, as a special case of this, physical objects could not be as they are apart from their relation to the mind that knows them.

Status of the objects of perception. Concerning the analysis of perception, realist philosophers have devoted considerable attention to showing that in perception we obtain knowledge of external physical objects either directly or by means of sensa. Their accounts of perceiving and their solutions to the problems raised by illusions and other facts of perception differ greatly, but they agree in rejecting the view that things cannot exist unperceived. G. E. Moore's influential "Refutation of Idealism" consisted in an attack on this thesis, which, following Berkeley, he stated as "*esse* is *percipi*" ("to be is to be perceived"). He claimed that in maintaining this the idealists had failed to distinguish between the act and the object in sensation. They had confused the sensation of blue with its object blue or, when claiming to distinguish them, inconsistently treated them as identical. Sensations are alike in being acts of awareness but differ in what they are awareness of. Once the object is distinguished from the awareness of it, there is no reason to deny its existence unperceived. Further, in no other situation have we a better claim to be aware of something distinct, so that if sensations are not cases of awareness of objects, no awareness is ever awareness of anything, and we cannot be aware of other persons or even of ourselves and our own sensations. Fundamentally, Moore's thesis concerning sensations rested on introspection; it has been denied on a similar introspective appeal by upholders of the adverbial analysis of sensing, and Moore himself later had grave doubts about it. Common-sense realists would say that he conceded too much in talking of sensations and interpreting "being perceived" (*percipi*) as "being sensed" (*sentiri*); the proper starting point is our awareness of material objects. But Moore was no doubt accepting the usual conclusions from the argument from illusion. From his analysis arises the question: "What is the object of sensation?" The answer, "A sense datum," posed the problem, which he never solved, of the relation between sense data and material objects. It was met by others with some form of representative realism or, more usually, phenomenalism. Phenomenalism, however, particularly if coupled with the adverbial analysis of sensing, means the abandonment of realism. The idealist stress on judgment in perception was at first little discussed, but critical realism and the sense-datum theory later offered more plausible alternatives.

The egocentric predicament. The realist attack on the egocentric predicament involved considerable discussion, particularly in the United States, and led to some close argument—for example, in attempts to show that the idealist principle led to self-contradiction or circularity when developed. The egocentric predicament was claimed to have no idealist implications. To infer from it that nothing exists outside consciousness is simply fallacious—that one cannot discover X does not mean that X does not exist or even that it is unreasonable to suppose that X exists. Indeed, if it were true that things could not exist apart from a person's consciousness of them, neither, presumably, could other persons; the predicament would imply an incredible solipsism. Nor is there any evidence of the lesser conclusion that objects outside consciousness would be quite different. No conclusion about the degree of distortion introduced by our consciousness follows from its ubiquity, and it may be negligible; one can only try to discover the degree by comparing various methods of knowing. (Distortion by the method of observation may be serious in atomic physics, but the same argument which establishes distortion there shows it to be negligible for objects larger than atoms.) The predicament is sometimes stated in terms of the privacy of experience—a person can never know anything which is not a content of his private experience. This, however, is question-begging in that it simply denies the ordinary assumptions that we are aware of other persons and external public objects. There may be grounds for denying these assumptions in certain cases, but such grounds rest on evidence of causal processes and of illusions, evidence which is largely obtained from other persons, or with the aid of public objects, or from comparisons with perceptions of public objects. Further, though more dubiously, Wittgenstein has argued that if we had only private experiences, not only would they be incommunicable, but also we could not describe or speak about them even to ourselves, for the use of language implies rules which are communal and have to be established and checked with respect to public objects.

Against the doctrine of internal relations it was claimed that relatedness is compatible with independence, that the same thing can enter into a variety of relations without losing its identity. This seemed so obvious that James confessed to finding it "weird" to have to argue for it. (Anticipating a contemporary approach, he accused the idealists of confusing linguistic or conceptual differences with factual ones; in referring to two relations of an object, our phrases and thoughts differ, but there is no corresponding difference in the object itself.) As the realists were defending what in their eyes was obvious, they were forced into detailed criticism rather than into the kind of positive thesis that can be readily summarized.

This battle was certainly won by the realists in that few English-speaking philosophers in the twentieth century would espouse idealism. Indeed, to anyone coming from contemporary discussions, the controversy has an air of unreality. Partly this is because in a climate of thought that respects common sense and science, realism seems so obvious a starting point that it is difficult to explain how the idealist view ever seemed plausible; partly it is because current idioms, issues, and logical presuppositions are so different from earlier ones. Granted, however, that material objects exist independently of our perception, the difficulties facing a realist account of this perception still remain and cause serious divisions among realists.

DIRECT REALISM

Direct realism is the general view that perception is a direct awareness, a straightforward confrontation (or in touch, contact) with the external object. It may be further subdivided according to the various attitudes then taken toward illusions and hallucinations. In contrast, there are the various types of indirect or dualist realism, which claim that perception is primarily of mental representations of the external object, as in traditional representative realism, or that our perception of the external object is by means of private, mental sensa.

Naive realism. Naive realism is the simplest form of direct realism and is usually alleged by philosophers to be an innocent prejudice of the plain man that has to be overcome if philosophical progress is to be made. It is normally stated in terms of sensible qualities or sensa. When we look around us, we can distinguish various colored, shaped expanses that we suppose to be the surfaces of material objects, we may hear various sounds that we suppose to come from such objects, we may feel something smooth and hard that we suppose to be a table top, and so on. Naive realism claims that these suppositions are all correct—that the shapes, colors, sounds, and smooth, hard

expanses (the sensible qualities) are always the intrinsic properties of material objects and in sight and touch are their surfaces. Such a claim can easily be shown to be erroneous by the argument from illusion. When *A* looks at the table from above, he sees a round expanse; when *B* looks at it from a distance, he sees an elliptical one. Without self-contradiction, however, the round and elliptical shapes cannot both be the surface of the table—that is, an intrinsic property. Similarly, when *C*, who is color-blind, looks at a red book, he sees a black shape which, again, cannot be the surface of that red book; when *D*, a drunkard, sees snakelike shapes on the bed, they are not real snakes. Such examples may be multiplied indefinitely and dispose of naive realism as thus stated, but common-sense realists would say that the doctrine misrepresents the views of the plain man and that philosophical discussions of it beg the question in favor of dualism by speaking of sensible qualities or sensa as distinct from physical objects.

New realism and the selective theory. The new realists—E. B. Holt, W. T. Marvin, W. P. Montague, R. B. Perry, W. B. Pitkin, and E. G. Spaulding—are notable chiefly for a common realist platform published in 1910 and expanded in 1912 and for their polemic against idealism. Their realism was carried to the Platonic extreme of claiming real existence for logical and mathematical entities, and they had difficult and conflicting views about consciousness. Without, however, pursuing these, we may note their main attempt (by Holt) to deal with illusions, which is a version of what is often called the selective theory. The essential points of this theory are, first, all the various appearances of an object are its intrinsic, objective properties and are directly apprehended by the percipient. For example, the table which looks round to *A* and elliptical to *B* is intrinsically both round and elliptical; the mountain which looks green close up and blue in the distance is both green and blue. There is nothing private or mental about such appearances, for they can be photographed, as can mirror images and various optical illusions. Second, the function of the nervous system and of the causal processes in perception is to select and reveal to the percipient one property from each set of properties, for example either the elliptical or the round shape of the table.

One difficulty in this is that it does not really account for error. If we are always directly aware of actual characteristics of objects, what sense does it make to talk, as we do, of illusions, mistakes, or misperceptions? Another lies in the weakness of the selective theory compared with the generative theory, adopted by dualist realism, which states that the sensible qualities, or sensa, are "generated," by the action of the object on the sense organs and nervous system and thus are not intrinsic properties of external objects. The usual reasons for preferring the generative theory are, on the one hand, that it is self-contradictory to say the table is intrinsically both round and elliptical or the mountain is intrinsically both green and blue. Furthermore, objects must be incredibly complex if they are to possess all these shapes and colors, plus, presumably, qualities corresponding to the queer appearance of objects when one has taken mescaline or suffers from giddiness or double vision. On the other hand, it is not clear how the nervous system specifically responds to or selects one of the various shapes, colors, and so on. This is particularly so in such cases as color blindness, drugs, and double vision, where the different appearances are the result of differences in the percipient and where the pattern of light waves can be detected as already differentiated for the shape and color normally perceived.

The generative theory, however, fits the facts of the causal processes quite well; it is natural to suppose that the generation of the sensory experience and its sensum occurs at the end of the causal chain which extends from object to brain by way of sense organ and nerves. This is confirmed by the reproduction of such experiences in mental imagery (presumably because the appropriate brain activity recurs), by the sensations resulting from electrical stimulation of the brain, and by the time lag which may occur between an event and our perception of it—all things which the selective theory cannot explain. Also, the generative theory can explain how voluntary selection occurs. When we turn our head to look at X rather than Y, we are allowing light from X rather than Y to strike our eyes and thus bring into being the sensa appropriate to X. As to photographing appearances, the photograph corresponds to the retinal image, not the sensum—that is, it reproduces not the perceived appearance but an intermediate cause of it; to enter into human experience, it must, in turn, be perceived by generating sensa.

Perspective realism and theories of appearing. The first objection to the selective theory—that it makes objects possess contradictory qualities—might be met by stressing that shapes, colors, and other qualities are not intrinsic but relative properties. The table is round from here, elliptical from there; the mountains are green in this light, blue in that light, and so on. This idea has been coupled with direct realism in a number of similar theories: perspective realism (E. B. McGilvary), objective relativism (A. E. Murphy), or the theory of appearing. (This last name was given by H. H. Price to a view put forward by H. A. Prichard. Roderick M. Chisholm, however, uses it more widely, and it is convenient to class all these views as theories of appearing.) Their central point is that direct realism can deal with illusions, or at least perceptual relativity, by saying that sensible qualities are not possessed by the object *simpliciter* but are always relative to some point of view or standing conditions. We always perceive sensible qualities in some perspective—spatial, even temporal (we see the distant star as it is from here and now), or illuminative (the object as it is in this light). (In such theories the shape, color, and so on are possessed by the object at its own location but are perceived subject to perspective, meaning from a viewpoint. In contrast, Bertrand Russell had a phenomenalistic theory of "perspectives" that were spread through space as possible sensa and actualized by or in the percipient.)

Such perspective-realist statements as "The table is round from here" sound forced, for the natural word to use is "looks," not "is," and it is possible to express this kind of direct realism in terms of looking or appearing. Physical objects simply are such that they appear different from different positions, and we see them as they appear from a viewpoint or in certain conditions. Thus, we may see the round table looking elliptical from here, but even so it is still the table that we see. Thus far the theory is trite and does little more than state the situation in a way which dualists could accept and then claim to analyze. To be distinctive, it must, as its essential characteristic, separate directness and incorrigibility. Sense-datum theory links the two, assuming that if we see an object directly, we must see it as it actually is. Thus, when the round table looks elliptical, we do not see it directly; what we see directly is an elliptical datum belonging to it. In contrast, theories of appearing must simply claim that seeing an object directly is compatible with variation or even error in perception, so that we still see it directly when according to viewpoint, lighting, and similar factors, it appears really different from what it is. (Some might object that the theory cannot admit that perceiving is ever erroneous. Perspective realism treats all properties as relative and all perspectives as equal—the table is round from here, elliptical from there, but not round in itself; similarly all appearances should be treated as equally valid. Nevertheless, it seems more plausible to treat some appearances as privileged; in some conditions we see the real shape, the round object appearing as it is—that is, round. It may be considered a weakness of the perspective theory that it does not take into account the fact that objects do seem to have real [measured] shapes and volumes absolutely, not relative to a viewpoint.)

The approach of theories of appearing may deal plausibly with perspectival and similar variations, but it has two main defects. First, not all variations are of this nature. In double vision or mescaline illusions there seems to be existential appearing—there may appear to be two or even many tables when we look at one table. Price has argued that this cannot really be a case of directly seeing one table, for it differs significantly from seeing something merely with different properties, such as seeing a brown table instead of a black one. Also, many illusions are the result of subjective factors, so that it is difficult to say that one has a genuine perspective. Talk of physiological perspectives is little help. "The bottle from here" is not on a par with "the bottle as it is to someone who has taken mescaline," for mescaline may cause a range of different experiences. Similarly, when a sentry at night is convinced he sees the enemy approaching but only a shadow is there, is he directly seeing the shadow in some special perspective, such as "the way it is to an anxious sentry" or "looking like a man"? Another anxious sentry might see it as a shadow and say it does not look like a man. And in a full hallucination there is no object at all. Second, theories of appearing cannot deal plausibly with the causal processes in perception since they have to adopt the selective theory. Further, we do know with varying degrees of completeness why things suffer perspectival distortion or how they cause illusion. The explanations concerned are often in terms of the causal processes (see ILLUSIONS) and so seem to call for the generative theory and the abandonment of direct realism.

Common-sense realism. In the tradition of Thomas Reid, revived by G. E. Moore, many twentieth-century British philosophers have defended what they take to be a common-sense view of perception. Moore's defense was primarily of the certainty of such simple perceptual statements as "This is a hand"; he argued that denial of these statements leads to inconsistency in beliefs and behavior and that the grounds for their denial involve propositions less certain than they are. However, his analysis of such statements in terms of sense data led away from direct realism and the common-sense view of the nature (as opposed to the reliability) of perception. Defense of common sense became particularly associated with the Oxford linguistic analysts. Strong critics of the sense-datum theory (unlike Moore), they also reject the traditional naive realism as unfair to common sense—after all, we do not think that everything we see is the surface of a physical object (certainly not lightning flashes or rainbows) and are quite ready to admit that we often see things looking different from what they are. Although quarreling with the common philosophical uses of "appear," "direct," and "real," they maintain a direct realism not unlike the theories of appearing and attempt to show in detail that in so-called illusions, including reflection and refraction, we do actually see the physical object concerned. Criticism has been made of the view that hallucinations are indistinguishable from normal perception, and more positively it may be claimed that hallucinations are mental images confused with perceptions owing to such special circumstances as drugs or fever. It is doubtful whether this can explain all the cases, and the role of the psychological processes—for example, in attention or in the influence of expectation and past experience—throws doubt on the directness of perceiving.

Some attempt has also been made to deal with the causal processes, but not very convincingly. Attacks have been made on the dualist interpretation for making it seem that we perceive something in our heads and not external objects and for the view that perceiving involves awareness of sensations. But linguistic analysts have said little of a positive nature; their main attitude is that the causal processes are at most only the conditions of perception and are the concern of the scientist but that the philosopher is concerned with perception itself, which is a skill or instantaneous achievement, not a physical process or the final stage of one. Unfortunately, scientists generally claim that the study of the causal processes requires representative realism, and even if the plain man does not bother about them, an adequate philosophical theory cannot ignore the causes and conditions of perceiving, particularly since the explanation of illusions depends on them.

INDIRECT OR DUALIST REALISM

Many realists are persuaded by the argument from illusion and by their study of the causal and psychological processes in perception to reject direct realism and to distinguish between external material objects as the causes and ultimate objects of perceiving and private sensa which are the mental effects of brain processes due to the action of those objects on the sense organs. The classic form of this general view was the representative realism (also called the representative or causal theory) of Descartes and Locke, which is still maintained in principle by many scientists.

From Berkeley on it suffered much criticism, and its defects led to its being unpopular among philosophers. Modern attempts have been made, however, to remedy these defects and to propose an acceptable theory. The resultant position we shall discuss as critical realism. Although they start from an analysis of perceptual experience and do not argue from the causal processes underlying it, supporters of the sense-datum analysis who are not phenomenalists are forced into one of these kinds of dualist realism.

Representative realism. In what is loosely called "seeing a table," light rays reflected from the table strike the eye, cause chemical changes in the retina, and send a train of impulses along the optic nerve to the brain. The resultant brain activity is then said to cause the mind of the percipient to be directly aware of private sensa (Locke called them "ideas") which represent the shape, color, and other visual properties of the table. A similar account is given for the other senses. The essential point is that perceiving proper is the direct awareness of sensa; perceiving external objects is redefined as perceiving sensa caused by them, and so all our awareness is strictly limited to sensa. "Represent" is usually interpreted in accordance with the doctrine of primary and secondary qualities—that is, the sensa resemble the object in spatiotemporal properties but not insofar as colors, sounds, smells, and other secondary qualities are concerned. Modern analogies of "representing" are the relation between a map or radar screen and the region they cover or between television or movies and the studio events reproduced.

Merits of representative realism. Representative realism has important merits. It is the easiest inference from the scientific account of the causal processes up to the brain in all perceiving and fits other scientific evidence. Thus, color blindness and deafness are the result of defects in the sense organs which so affect all subsequent stages in the causal transmission that the resultant sensa are different from normal. That electrical stimulation of the brain causes sensations of color, smell, and so on, according to location, seems to confirm the theory, and it can easily accommodate the time lag in perception. Further, by holding that representation does not amount to resemblance in the case of secondary qualities, it can be made to fit the distinction between the world as we see it (that is, the sensa grouped as ostensible objects) and the scientific account of material objects, which is in terms of colorless, tasteless, and smell-less elementary particles.

Representative realism also accounts for illusions, dreams, images, hallucinations, and the relativity of perception. Relativity and many illusions result from changes in the stimulation of the sense organs because of distance, medium, angle of sight, and other relevant factors; such changes affect all that follows and so vary the sensa caused. Other illusions are the result of misinterpretation of sensa. In imagery and dreams the brain activity that occurred in corresponding perceptions is reactivated as the result of internal causes and so brings about the recurrence of similar sensa. (The reactivation may be only partial, and the resultant data may be consciously or unconsciously altered by the mind.) Hallucinations are also imagery. Since the images are of a similar character to normally perceived data and are the result of a similar immediate cause in the brain, it is easy to see how they may merge in integrated or triggered hallucinations or how perception may be imaginatively supplemented. The standard explanation of phantom limbs—that they are sensations caused by irritation at the stump of nerves normally coming from the amputated limb—is also accommodated. As perception is confined strictly to the effects of the causal chain, interference with it en route may readily deceive us.

Finally, representative realism has also traditionally been part of the widely accepted interactionist or dualist account of the relation of mind and body: The body affects mind in perception, mind affects the body in voluntary action. Not all who accept that theory realize that they are saddled with representative realism.

Defects of representative realism. Despite its merits, representative realism has some serious defects.

If, as it claims, our perceiving is strictly awareness of the mental ideas or sensa, it is difficult to see how we can break out of the circle of sensa and observe external objects. How can we tell what these objects are like; indeed, how do we know that there are such objects? If we try to verify the existence of the table by touching it, we simply obtain more sensa—tactile ones—and if we see our hands touching the table, we are just having visual sensa. Whenever we try to peer over the barrier of sensa, we just get more sensa. This difficulty undermines the analogies used in the theory. Representation is conceived of as something like mapping or photographing, but we know a map represents or a photograph resembles an object because we can observe both and compare them; *ex hypothesi*, however, we can never strictly observe both objects and sensa to compare them. Observing objects is just observing sensa, so we do not know that objects and sensa resemble each other in primary but not in secondary qualities.

It is often said that representative realism not only leads to skepticism but is also self-refuting, cutting off the branch on which it sits. Its premises and evidence assume that we discover the action of the objects on the sense organs by observing them. Its conclusion—all our perception is of sensa—denies that we can do this. However, there would be self-refutation only if the conclusion contradicted the premises, which it need not do if carefully stated. The theory may be regarded as really distinguishing two types of perceiving: perception in its everyday meaning, which is discovering about external objects by means of the senses, and perception proper—direct awareness of sensa. It is saying that the first type really amounts to or, better, is really effected by the second type. Thus, granted that by perceiving sensa we do discover the nature of objects (at least insofar as their primary qualities are concerned) and their interaction, the first type of perception and the evidence it gives still hold good, and there is no self-refutation. Nevertheless, the skepticism remains, for since our direct awareness is limited to sensa, we do not *know* that there are objects or what they are like; we only suppose or guess that and what they are.

Even though representative realism need not be self-refuting, it is open to the charge of circularity if considered as an attempt to explain perceiving. It appears simply to transfer perceiving as ordinarily conceived (a face-to-face confrontation) from outside to inside the person; perceiving external objects is now put forward as perceiving private replicas of them, for we look at maps and television pictures in the same way that we look at the countryside. Even if we say perceiving objects is achieved by perceiving sensa, there is the same duplication of perceiving, which is thus explained in terms of itself.

Representative realism's view of the mind is rather crude, for it tends to speak almost as if the self or mind were a little person in the head looking at pictures of the outside world. It is not clear how sensa can exist in an unextended mind, since they apparently possess shape and size; nor is any serious attempt made to fit the psychological processes of perception into the general scheme.

There are special difficulties for those versions of the theory which claim that in perceiving objects we infer the existence or nature of external objects from our sensa. Apart from the inevitable dubiety of such inference, the main objection is that we are never conscious of these inferences nor are we aware of sensa as such—that is, as private mental data. If we were, it is difficult to see how the notion of publicly observable causes would occur to us. But the representative theory may simply say that the sensa seem to be external (or externally caused) from the start and that any inference is justificatory to deal with skeptics. (This seems to have been Locke's view in his *Essay Concerning Human Understanding,* Bk. IV, Ch. xi, Sec. 2.)

Critical realism. Critical realism is the name primarily given to the views expressed by the American authors of *Essays in Critical Realism*—namely, that the data in perception (that is, what is intuited, what we are directly aware of) are not actually part of external objects but are "character-complexes . . . irresistibly *taken,* in the moment of perception, to be the characters of existing outer objects" (p. 20). In veridical perception these characters are the characters of external objects; in illusions they are not. The authors were unfortunately divided over the nature of this datum or character complex, Durant Drake, A. K. Rogers, George Santayana, and C. A. Strong claiming that it was not a mental existent or any kind of existent, but only an essence, a mere logical entity or universal, whereas A. O. Lovejoy, J. B. Pratt, and R. W. Sellars held that it was a mental existent, a content of sensory experience. It is difficult to grasp what the datum can be if it is not a mental content or existent, and so the second version is the more plausible and is adopted here. Although clearly dualist, it should not be confused with representative realism; in fact, it provides remedies for representative realism's main faults.

The critical realists held that the root of the troubles of representative realism lay in its failure to analyze perceiving or perceptual knowledge. Accepting the ordinary notion of perceiving as intuiting, which means a direct awareness or confrontation, and finding that because of the causal processes and of illusions such awareness was not of external objects, Locke concluded that it must be of intra-mental ideas and so imprisoned us in the circle of such ideas. The more reasonable conclusion, however, would be that this ordinary notion of perceiving is wrong and that a more careful analysis is needed. This will show that an essential feature of perceiving, even as ordinarily understood, is that it is the way we discover the existence and nature of external objects—that it is, in fact, a claim, often justified, to knowledge. If we appreciate this from the start, we shall not be tempted by the apparently intuitive character of perceiving into an analysis which limits it to ideas, and if we remember that this knowledge claim is not always justified—that is, that there are illusions and errors—we shall avoid the other pitfall of direct realism, in which error becomes inexplicable. The next step is to realize that though it involves an intuition or direct awareness, perceiving is much more than this. It also involves an active external reference, as is implied by the knowledge claim; we refer this intuited mental content or character complex to an external object—that is, we explicitly judge that it is, or is the character of, an external object or we unreflectingly take it to be this or we immediately react to it as if it were an external object. These modes of reference are differently stressed by different writers, but the point seems to be that they occur in varying degrees according to circumstances. Our perception is sometimes an explicit identification or judgment, or at least it immediately issues in one—for example, we say, "Here's our bus" or "There's Tommy"; more often we just see that it is Tommy without formulating any judgment, or our perception that it is our bus and our starting to go and catch it seem indistinguishable, for the reference to the external object is manifest in an immediate physical response.

All the same, in contrast to the behaviorists, the critical realists stressed that there was an intuited mental content, the character complex of which we were directly aware. Attempts were made to fit the analysis in with current psychology by explaining how this external reference arose in childhood—the apparent externality of the content was with us from the beginning of perceptual discrimination, largely because the external reference was founded in physical response to the object.

There is some similarity between this "reference of an intuited datum to an external object" and the "taking for granted that a sense datum belongs to a material object" of Price's sense-datum theory, especially since both stress that no distinction between datum and object is drawn by the percipient at the time. But there is a difference in starting point and emphasis. Price began with sense data, treating them as distinct existents and willing to allow that material objects consisted of them. This branch of critical realism began with knowledge of external objects, but, being mental, the content or datum distinguished within it was not regarded as capable of distinct existence and was very difficult—much more so than Price thought—to isolate even subsequently from the associated reference. Also, reference covered a wider set of activities than taking for granted, for it also involved the bodily reactions. In order to stress the relative subordination of the datum, some critical realists spoke of perceiving external objects by means of, guided by, or mediated by, the datum.

Since critical realism can agree that the datum is generated, it is free from the difficulties of the selective theory and can share in the advantages of representative realism. In this version it seems able to avoid the latter's worst faults. There is no self-refutation, for from the start perceiving is always perception of external objects by means

of the intuited data, an analysis which does not deny that we perceive such objects. There is no duplication or circularity, for the direct awareness of the datum is not a replica of perceiving; insofar as it can be distinguished at all, it is much less complex than perceiving, for it involves no identification with external objects and is not in itself directed on them—hence, the map and movie analogies are essentially faulty. Common sense is not being offered an explanation of perceiving in terms of perceiving; it is being shown that perceiving is far more complex than common sense supposes, involving not only causal processes which bring about the datum or mental content but also the psychological processes of reference or response.

Moreover, there need be no skepticism. True, in perceiving we only take the datum to be an external object or its properties, and this may, of course, be erroneous. In a sense it is always erroneous in that the datum or content is never the object, but normally the taking or reference is correct to the extent that we are perceiving an external object and that the intuited characters also do characterize the external object insofar as primary qualities are concerned; to that extent we are perceiving actual properties or at least projections of them. In general, the claim that perceiving is thus far veridical and amounts to knowledge is said to be the best hypothesis to explain the order and nature of our sense experiences. The realist claim is simply that once ordinary errors and illusions are ruled out by comparing the evidence of different senses or of different persons, the simplest explanation of the situation is that there are external objects causing the sense data or contents and corresponding to them in primary qualities. And this is plausible because if we dismiss as incredible solipsism the view that only oneself and one's own sense experiences exist, then the only real alternative is phenomenalism, a view which has fatal weaknesses and really amounts to proposing a series of deceptive coincidences.

Critical realism is not fully satisfactory, however, particularly if regarded as a theory of perceptual consciousness—that is, as an account of the mental activity that goes on in perception. Thus, the alleged datum or character complex suggests a group of sense data and invites the objections discussed under SENSA. A closer examination is required not only of the concepts of datum and reference but also of the general relation of mind and body presupposed in perception and of the nature of mental contents; above all, the theory must take full account of the numerous quasi-interpretative activities which modern psychology has found to be involved in perception.

Bibliography

GENERAL

A clear, simple introduction to the philosophical problems of perception is Bertrand Russell, *Problems of Philosophy* (London, 1912), and a fuller one is W. P. Montague, *The Ways of Knowing* (London and New York, 1925). A good account of modern positions on perception is given by T. E. Hill, *Contemporary Theories of Knowledge* (New York, 1961). Detailed summaries of many realist works are given by W. H. Werkmeister, *A History of Philosophical Ideas in America* (New York, 1949). Less detailed but more intelligible is John Passmore, *A Hundred Years of Philosophy* (London, 1957); also see Rudolf Metz, *A Hundred Years of British Philosophy* (London and New York, 1938). Many of the works listed below deal with the topics of more than one section.

THE REALIST POLEMIC AND NEW REALISM

The main source for new realism is E. B. Holt and others, *The New Realism* (New York, 1912), but new realism owed much to William James; see the papers (dating from 1904) collected in his *Essays in Radical Empiricism* (London and New York, 1912). For a useful collection of articles from this early period see Roderick M. Chisholm, *Realism and the Background of Phenomenology* (Glencoe, Ill., 1960; London, 1962). Among other important and often closely reasoned articles are R. B. Perry, "The Ego-centric Predicament," *Journal of Philosophy*, Vol. 7, No. 1 (1910), 5–14; Bertrand Russell, "On the Nature of Truth," *PAS*, Vol. 7 (1906–1907), 28–49; and G. E. Moore, "The Refutation of Idealism," in his *Philosophical Studies* (London, 1922), to which compare W. T. Stace's counterattack, "The Refutation of Realism," *Mind*, Vol. 43, No. 170 (1934), 145–155. For a general summing up in favor of realism, see D. C. Williams, "The A Priori Argument for Subjectivism," *The Monist*, Vol. 43 (1933), 173–202, "The Inductive Argument for Subjectivism" and "The Inductive Argument for Realism," *The Monist*, Vol. 44 (1934), 80–107, 186–209. For a once influential direct-realism treatment of perceptual problems, see T. P. Nunn, "Are Secondary Qualities Independent of Perception?," *PAS*, Vol. 10 (1909–1910), 191–218. Ludwig Wittgenstein's language arguments are in his *Philosophical Investigations* (Oxford, 1958), Secs. 256 ff.; for criticisms see Carl Wellman, "Wittgenstein and the Ego-centric Predicament," *Mind*, Vol. 68, No. 270 (1959), 223–233, or the symposium "Can There Be a Private Language?," *PAS*, Supp. Vol. 28 (1954).

PERSPECTIVE REALISM AND ALLIED THEORIES

Perspective realism and allied theories are stated by Evander Bradley McGilvary in *Toward a Perspective Realism* (La Salle, Ill., 1956) and in "Perceptual and Memory Perspectives," *Journal of Philosophy*, Vol. 30 (1933), 310 ff. Older versions are by Samuel Alexander, "On Sensations and Images," *PAS*, Vol. 10 (1909–1910), 1–35, and H. A. Prichard, *Kant's Theory of Knowledge* (Oxford, 1909), Ch. 4. Despite its title, G. Dawes Hicks, *Critical Realism* (London, 1938), gives a theory of appearing. Such theories are lucidly discussed by Roderick M. Chisholm, "The Theory of Appearing," in Max Black, ed., *Philosophical Analysis* (Ithaca, N.Y., 1950). C. D. Broad, *The Mind and its Place in Nature* (London, 1925), and H. H. Price, *Perception* (London, 1932), criticize these theories carefully from a sense-datum standpoint, though Price's article "Illusions," in H. D. Lewis, ed., *Contemporary British Philosophy* (London, 1956), Vol. 3, defends a limited perspective realism.

COMMON-SENSE REALISM

For common-sense realism see G. E. Moore's "A Defense of Common Sense" and "Proof of an External World," which are in his *Philosophical Papers* (London, 1959), but also see his *Some Main Problems of Philosophy* (London, 1953). The stanchest recent defender of common sense against the argument from illusion is J. L. Austin in his lucid and lively *Sense and Sensibilia* (London, 1962), and somewhat similar views are clearly and concisely expressed by Anthony M. Quinton, "The Problem of Perception," *Mind*, Vol. 64, No. 253 (1955), 28–51. Gilbert Ryle's "Sensations," in H. D. Lewis, ed., *Contemporary British Philosophy* (London, 1956), Vol. III, and Ryle's *Dilemmas* (Cambridge, 1954) try to deal also with the causal argument in a nontechnical manner. D. M. Armstrong, *Perception and the Physical World* (London, 1961), defends direct realism but in so doing is driven toward behaviorism.

REPRESENTATIVE REALISM (OR THE CAUSAL THEORY)

For early statements of representative realism, see René Descartes, *Principles of Philosophy*, Pt. IV, and John Locke, *Essay Concerning Human Understanding*, Bk. 2, Ch. 8.

Representative realism is assumed by many modern neurologists, though often not under its philosophical title. Walter Russell Brain states and discusses it as "physiological idealism" in "The Neurological Approach to the Problem of Perception," *Philosophy*, Vol. 21, No. 79 (1946), 133–146, reprinted with further con-

sideration of perception in his *Mind, Perception and Science* (Oxford, 1951); he gives a further defense of his position in his *The Nature of Experience* (London, 1959). J. C. Eccles, *The Neurophysiological Basis of Mind* (Oxford, 1953), pp. 279–281, outlines the theory as if it were fact. J. R. Smythies, *Analysis of Perception* (London, 1956), puts forward an improved form of it closer to critical realism.

CRITICAL REALISM

The main source for critical realism is Durant Drake and others, *Essays in Critical Realism* (New York and London, 1920), which reveals the differences as well as agreements; see also other works by the essayists, especially R. W. Sellars' comprehensive *The Philosophy of Physical Realism* (New York, 1932), his general apologia, "A Statement of Critical Realism," *Revue internationale de philosophie*, Vol. I (1938–1939), 472–498, and A. O. Lovejoy's impressive general defense, *The Revolt Against Dualism* (New York, 1930). R. J. Hirst, *The Problems of Perception* (London, 1959), also discusses common-sense and representative realism and reaches a somewhat similar position. A primarily pragmatist view which has affinities to and criticism of critical realism is C. I. Lewis, *Mind and the World Order* (New York, 1929).

R. J. HIRST

REALISM, LEGAL. See LEGAL REALISM.

REALISM AND NOMINALISM. See UNIVERSALS.

REALITY. See APPEARANCE AND REALITY; BEING.

REALITY, PHYSICAL. See LAWS AND THEORIES; PHILOSOPHY OF SCIENCE, HISTORY OF; PHILOSOPHY OF SCIENCE, PROBLEMS OF.

REASON. In English the word "reason" has long had, and still has, a large number and a wide variety of senses and uses, related to one another in ways that are often complicated and often not clear. However, there is one particular sense of the word in which it, with its synonyms or analogues in other languages, has figured prominently in philosophical controversy. This is the sense, sometimes distinguished typographically by an initial capital, in which the term is taken to designate a mental faculty or capacity—in which reason might, for example, be regarded as coordinate with, but distinguishable from, sensation, emotion, or will.

Questions to be examined. The question which has been chiefly debated by philosophers might be expressed succinctly, but far from clearly, as "What can reason do?" However, there has also been discussion of the question whether the faculty of reason is peculiar to humanity (and presumably to "higher" beings, if there are any), or whether its possession and exercise in some degree can also be ascribed to "lower" animals. It should perhaps be added that in recent years there has been much debate as to whether machines can, or in principle ever could, properly be said to think; for if an affirmative answer were to be given to this question, then there is a quite common sense of "reason" in which it would follow that that faculty could be exercised by a machine. Only the first of these questions is dealt with here.

The short but unclear question "What can reason do?" is peculiarly liable to give rise to theoretical dissension. The question may, however, be transformed with advantage into a question not directly about the "faculty" of reason itself but about those beings to whom this faculty is attributed. What, we may ask, are human beings in a position to do, in virtue of their possession of the faculty of reason? What, by means of reasoning, are we in a position to achieve? In this form it becomes very clear that the question raises at least two highly disputable issues. First, it is far from immediately clear what reasoning is—on what occasions, in what activities or processes, reason is exercised. And second, if we determine—probably with some degree of arbitrariness—what reasoning is, it may very well remain highly disputable whether this or that can or cannot be achieved by reasoning. One should, indeed, distinguish further at this point between two radically different kinds of dispute that may arise; if it were held that, for instance, knowledge of God cannot be attained by reasoning, there would plainly be an important further distinction between holding this to be true in fact and true in principle. It might be maintained that the reasoning necessary for knowledge of God is, as a matter of fact, too difficult for frail and mortal human beings to manage; or it might be maintained, quite differently, that the kind of conclusion capable of being established by reasoning excludes in principle that kind, if there is any such, to which knowledge of God must belong. This sort of distinction can be seen as differentiating the positivism preached by Comte in the nineteenth century from the logical positivism of recent philosophy.

Many senses of "reason." What, then, is reason? Alternatively, what is reasoning? It seems scarcely possible to maintain that these questions can be given definite answers. The definitions, implicit or explicit, of the relevant terms that have been employed by philosophers and other writers vary widely and significantly; and while some may be judged preferable to others, or may adhere more closely than others to senses which the terms may bear in ordinary discourse, there seems to be no basis secure enough to support a pronouncement that a particular meaning, and hence a particular answer to the question, is exclusively correct. In any case, what is important to the understanding of philosophical writing on this topic is not that one should know what "reason" means but, rather, that one should discern, so far as possible, what meaning is attached to "reason" by an author.

Contrasts with other terms. Here it seems particularly important and helpful to consider with what reason is contrasted, or from what it is distinguished. There is, for example, a large body of literature in which reason stands essentially in contrast with faith. In this context, what we can achieve by reason is taken to embrace the entire field of knowledge and inquiry in which, with varying degrees of skill and success, we produce or seek reasons for our views, proofs of or evidence for our conclusions, and grounds for our opinions. This whole field is set in contrast with another, in which supposedly we may—or should or must—accept certain propositions or doctrines without any grounds but rather on authority or perhaps on unreasoned conviction.

There is another large body of literature in which reason stands in contrast with experience. In this context, what we can achieve by reason is much more narrowly circumscribed; here a distinction is being made between, roughly, what we can discover or establish by merely sitting and thinking, and what we can discover or establish only by the use of our senses, by observation or by experiment. It will be observed that there are, corresponding to these wider and narrower senses of "reason," also wider and narrower senses of the term "rationalist"; a rationalist in the one sense is concerned with denying or belittling the claims or the role of faith, and in the other with denying or belittling the role, in the acquisition of knowledge, of experience. There is no particular reason why one who is a rationalist in either one of these senses should be expected to be a rationalist in the other sense also; the two positions are quite independent of one another.

The objects of reason. There is, then, no universally agreed or uniquely correct sense of "reason." This is obvious enough, perhaps; but it is not unimportant. Clearly, even though philosophers may use this term in diverse senses without being wrong, the fact that they do so must, if unobserved by them or their readers, generate confusion and argument at cross purposes. Further, as was noted above, even if we avoid confusion at this point, many problems as to the "scope" or the "powers" of reason remain. They are, in fact, some of the major and central problems of philosophy.

Suppose that, following Brand Blanshard in his *Reason and Analysis,* we define "reason" as "the faculty and function of grasping necessary connections." We may feel that this is not a very good definition, since it seems excessively restrictive. For example, a judge arguing his way to a decision, or a meteorologist setting forth his grounds for a weather forecast, would in this sense not be exercising the faculty of reason; the argument in each case is nondemonstrative—that is, it does not set out or rely on strictly necessary connections. However, waiving that point, the definition is at least a clear one. But notwithstanding its possession of the important virtue of clarity, the question of what reason can do is not thereby settled. In order to settle this question, we must decide what necessary connections there are and in what cases or what fields there are necessary connections to be grasped; and the determination of this question raises, or might very well raise, almost every problem of philosophy. Are we to hold, with Plato, that no necessary connections are to be discerned in the everyday world, but only in an intelligible world of Forms? Or are we to hold, with Hume and many others, that strictly necessary connections are to be found only in the formal, abstract relations between our concepts or ideas? Was Kant right in supposing that the moral law can be demonstrated a priori, and is therefore necessary? Or, on the contrary, was Hume correct in holding that in the field of moral judgment "reason is the slave of the passions"? Are causal relationships cases of necessary connection? Are they perhaps, as Locke seems to have held, really cases of necessary connection which in practice, however, we are inveterately unable to grasp as such? And so on.

Basic questions. The point that emerges here is simply this: whatever particular definition of the faculty of reason we may, implicitly or explicitly, adopt, it seems unavoidable that it will be attempted thereby to distinguish this faculty from others as being that by the exercise of which we can perceive, or arrive at, truths of some particular kind or kinds; and this kind of truth, or these kinds of truths, will in turn be distinguished from other kinds on logical or epistemological grounds. If so, then the question of what we can actually achieve or come to know by reason unavoidably becomes the question of what propositions are of that kind or those kinds; and this is precisely the question about which, in any field, philosophical controversy may, and characteristically does, arise. Thus the apparently simple question "What can reason do?" is not a neutral question on which otherwise dissentient philosophers may expect to be in agreement. On the contrary, it is very likely that their disagreement consists precisely in their diverse answers to this question. It may further be felt, with justice, that if this innocent-looking question unavoidably raises major philosophical issues concerning the logical and epistemological analysis and classification of propositions, it would probably be advantageous to raise those questions directly and overtly rather than as an only half-acknowledged corollary of a discussion that is ostensibly concerned with a faculty of the mind. There are few modern philosophers who would naturally cast their discussions in this latter idiom.

One final risk of confusion is worth pointing out. It is probably true that in recent philosophy there has been a persistent tendency to narrow the field in which necessities, strictly speaking, are admitted to be found; and also, perhaps more significantly, a persistent tendency to take the awesomeness out of necessity by attempts, more or less successful in various fields, to exhibit necessity as fundamentally derived from the unpuzzling, and perhaps unimposing, phenomenon of tautology. In this sense, then, it can be said that there has been some tendency both to narrow the scope conceded to reason and perhaps also to make reason itself seem less mysterious and grand. In some, this tendency has occasioned considerable distress: as Bertrand Russell has expressed it, "My intellectual journeys have been, in some respects, disappointing. . . . I thought of mathematics with reverence, and suffered when Wittgenstein led me to regard it as nothing but tautologies" (*The Philosophy of Bertrand Russell*, P. A. Schilpp, ed., Evanston, Ill., 1946, p. 19).

Examination of reason's powers. There are several instances in which Russell's sense of distress has been expressed in curiously bellicose terms. Books have been written in defense of reason, and exponents of the contemporary trend have been castigated as reason's enemies. But this latter charge, even if there is some sense in which it might be well founded, is peculiarly liable to mislead, and very commonly has misled, those who urge it. One thinks, naturally and rightly, of an enemy of reason as one who is opposed or hostile to the exercise of reason. Such a person might be, for instance, a religious bigot, fearful that reason might shake the obscure foundations of his bigotry; he might be a political or racial fanatic, hostile to the careful weighing of arguments and evidence because he is half conscious that his program or doctrine lacks reasonable grounds; or he might, less malignantly, hold some doctrine about the merits of unreflecting spontaneity, disliking the slow pace, the qualifications and hedging, of rational

thought. It is obvious, however, that scarcely any philosopher is, or ever has been, an enemy of reason in this sense.

Nor, to mention a group not uncommonly arraigned on the same charge, is the psychoanalyst. It is a tenet of psychoanalytic theory that reason, the dispassionate consideration of arguments and evidence, is a less conspicuous and influential determinant of the beliefs and the conduct of men than has often been supposed, or than most people might like to admit; but the psychoanalyst does not, as would an enemy of reason, rejoice in this circumstance or seek to aggravate it. Quite the contrary: recognizing the state of the case as being what, in the light of his evidence, he takes it to be, he deploys his art in the attempt to enable people to become more rational than they would otherwise be. He may be mistaken in his theory and unsuccessful in his practice, but in any case neither in theory nor in practice does he display the least enmity toward reason.

Somewhat similarly, the philosopher who produces an argument against high traditional claims for, or traditional characterizations of, reason is, in so doing, exercising reason to the best of his ability; nor does it occur to him to question the desirability of doing so. Thus, to dissent from rationalism as a philosophical doctrine is certainly not to disparage reason; the man who values, and shows that he values, reason is not he who merely pitches reason's claims exceptionally high but, rather, he who attempts, by painstaking reasoning, to determine how high those claims may justifiably be pitched. Philosophers, whose work consists mostly in sitting and thinking, have often enough and naturally enough been prone to estimate very highly the range and significance of the results that can thereby be achieved. However, this propensity is scarcely an indication of devotion to reason; rather, it is an indication, if of anything, of pardonable self-importance.

Bibliography

Blanshard, Brand, *Reason and Analysis*. London, 1962.
Ewing, A. C., *Reason and Intuition*. Oxford, 1942.
Freud, Sigmund, *The Future of an Illusion*, translated by W. D. Robson-Scott. London, 1928.
Murphy, Arthur E., *The Uses of Reason*. New York, 1943.
Nagel, Ernest, *Sovereign Reason*. Glencoe, Ill., 1954.
Russell, Bertrand, *Skeptical Essays*. New York, 1928.
Santayana, George, *The Life of Reason*, rev. ed. New York, 1954.
Walsh, W. H., *Reason and Experience*. Oxford, 1947.
Whitehead, A. N., *The Function of Reason*. Princeton, N.J., 1929.

G. J. WARNOCK

REASONING. See THINKING.

REASONS AND CAUSES. In recent philosophy a distinction between reasons and causes has been urged by a number of philosophers. In particular, they say that to cite a man's reasons for his intentional acts is not to give their causes. (A similar distinction may hold in other cases as well, for example, between the reasons for a man's anger and the causes of the anger. In this article only intentional acts will be discussed.) If there is such a distinction, many philosophers seem to have ignored it. For example, the classical reconciliation of causal determinism with freedom of the will depends on the claim that acts of will cause intentional actions and are in turn caused by one's motives, desires, and beliefs; and motives, desires, and beliefs are mentioned in giving a man's reasons for acting.

Reasons treated as causes. There are some facts about explanations of actions in terms of reasons which lend support to the belief that these explanations are causal. First, ordinary language sometimes employs the word "caused" and frequently the word "because" where motives and reasons are involved. One might say "The boring conversation caused me to leave early." The same thought can be expressed by "I left early because the conversation was so boring" or by "My reason for leaving early was that the conversation was so boring." While appeal to such facts about ordinary usage may shift the burden of proof to the other side, it does little to establish that reason explanations are straightforward causal explanations. The word "cause" may have a different use in these circumstances, or it may only be a way of emphasizing, somewhat metaphorically, the "compelling" nature of the reason. And it is clear that the word "because" cannot be counted on to indicate causal connection—it can be used, for example, to indicate the relation between premises and conclusion of a valid argument, which is surely not a causal relation.

Second, reasons for acting are similar to causes in that we refer to them in explanations. Again, this does not preclude a radical difference; they may enter into radically different sorts of explanations.

Third, as Hume pointed out, there are apparent regularities between motives and reasons on the one hand and actions on the other. We expect a man bent on revenge to behave in a certain way and a man who wants a loaf of bread to do certain things. On Hume's view, at any rate, regularity is the essence of causal connections. Even if Hume is right, however, the existence of such regularities is not conclusive. For one thing, we must distinguish two questions: (1) Are reasons ever causes of intentional actions? and (2) Are explanations in terms of reasons causal explanations? Even if we answer the first of these questions affirmatively, we are not compelled thereby to answer to the second affirmatively. Also, while regularity is the core of the causal relation for Hume, it must be a regularity of a certain kind: an empirical regularity. Whether the connection between reasons and actions is merely empirical has been strongly questioned.

The considerations so far mentioned are inconclusive, so there is good reason to see whether the treatment of reasons as causes can be sustained against objections. When we explain action by reference to a person's reasons, the explanatory force is not exhausted by the mere conjunction of the action with the agent's possession of reasons for acting. It is possible for a man to do something, to have reasons for doing it, and yet not to have done it *because* he had those reasons. Hence, any final account of explanations in terms of reasons for acting must take into consideration the additional force of "because." And, of course, this would be accomplished if "because" can be taken as indicating causal connection.

In the recent literature on the topic, the tide first ran strongly in favor of making a clear-cut distinction between reason explanations and causal explanations. More recently, however, doubts have been expressed about several of the methods used to mark off the two modes of explanations. The state of things is therefore somewhat unclear, and here we can only review some of the arguments and counterarguments.

"Intentionality." Statements assigning reasons to actions can take several forms. One of these cites the intention with which the act was performed, for example, "Smith went to the store in order to get bread." If by "Smith's reason for going to the store" we mean in such a case what is expressed by the words "to get some bread," an immediate difficulty stands in the way of taking this reason as a cause. It is generally accepted that causes cannot follow their effects. But getting bread, in this example, will occur after going to the store. Moreover, a causal statement about particular events can be true only if the cause did actually occur or exist. But it may well be true that Smith went to the store in order to get bread even though he never got bread.

These difficulties arise, however, only if we try to take as the cause of a man's action the *object* of his desire rather than the desire itself. Smith's *desire* to get bread, if the statement of his reason for going to the store is true, existed prior to his going, and it existed whether or not he finally gets bread. Those philosophers who have argued or assumed that reason explanations are causal would presumably point to the desire, not its object, as the cause.

Other reason-assigning statements imply the existence of beliefs on the part of the agent. For example, "Smith went to the store because he was out of bread" implies "Smith believed he was out of bread." Still others seem to imply the existence of feelings, for example, "He helped the old man out of pity." The crucial questions, then, are whether or not desires, beliefs, and feelings can act as causes of action, and, if so, whether or not reason explanations of actions simply assign these desires, beliefs, and feelings as causes.

The "logical connection" argument. Perhaps the most discussed of the arguments for distinguishing reason explanations from causal explanations is the one that depends upon the empirical and contingent nature of the causal connection. There is not, it is said, the required logical independence of desires, beliefs, and feelings on the one hand and of human action on the other. But this argument, persuasive as it has seemed, is not easy to formulate in precise detail.

There must, of course, be two things or events in a causal relation. Desires and actions, however, seem to meet this simple condition. The one may occur without the other. (This does not damage the case for a causal connection; consider the natural locution "A sometimes causes B.") Nevertheless, it has been argued that there is a more than contingent relation between desires, beliefs, and feelings on the one hand and action on the other; for desires, beliefs, and feelings could not exist without actions. We cannot imagine, that is, a world in which there are beings who have desires, beliefs, and feelings but never act on them. Without actions, there would be no reason to ascribe such states of mind to them.

It is perhaps possible to question the premises of this argument as well as the validity of moving from the impossibility of knowledge about desires to their nonexistence in such a world. Perhaps more importantly, the argument assumes a fairly strong condition on causal connections. If a causal connection exists, there must be two distinct terms to the causal relation, and independence must be maintained between broader classes to which the cause and the effect respectively belong.

We move from considering particular desires to desiring in general and from particular acts to acting in general. Clearly some limit has to be put on the condition of causal explanation, since in general both causes and effects will belong to some common—and therefore not logically independent—classes, for example, the class of events. We also can find examples of causal relations which seem to exhibit a lack of logical independence between the general classes to which cause and effect belong. This lack is quite similar to that pointed out concerning desires and actions. Hypnotic suggestion can apparently cause later actions. Yet, could we imagine a world in which there is hypnotic suggestion but no human action? How, in such a world, could one suggest to another that he act in a certain way? In such a world it would seem impossible for any being to have the concept of acting in this way or that. Again, lack of confidence in the value of currency can cause it to lose value. Can we imagine, say, a world in which there is no currency to lose value, and yet still imagine there to be a lack of confidence in the value of currency?

These examples serve to illustrate the general problem. It is not enough merely to point out *some* logical connection between the concepts of desire, belief, and feeling and that of action; the connection must be one which is clearly absent in undisputed cases of causal connections. Thus, merely to exhibit the obvious internal connection between "desiring to do X" and "doing X" is not sufficient because of the equally obvious internal connection between, for example, exposure to the sun and sunburn, which are the terms of a well-known causal connection.

Wanting as a tendency to act. One attempt to specify the logical connection between reasons and actions (if there is one) deserves special mention. As we have seen, many reason explanations have to do with a person's desires or wants, even those explanations which do not imply something about what the agent wanted. That Smith went to the store because he believed he was out of bread is accepted as an explanation only on the assumption that Smith wanted bread.

It has been argued that if we examine the concept of wanting something, it becomes clear that to want something is to be prepared in certain circumstances to take the steps necessary to getting it. Can we continue to credit a man with a desire for something if he refuses to seize the opportunity when he is put in a position to get it without thwarting other desires? It thus may appear that wanting to do something is, at least in part, to have a tendency to do it. The fact that we might be hard pressed to specify in any detail the circumstances in which, if the want is genuine, action would necessarily result, does not destroy the thesis; nor does the fact that in any particular circumstances we might not be forced to deny the existence of the want not acted upon. Brittleness is a tendency to break or shatter, even though it seems impossible to specify the circumstances in which a brittle object *must* break (unless we use some such expression as "with a blow of *sufficient* strength").

If wanting and desiring are tendencies to action, then it may seem odd to count them as causes of action and to construe their relation to action as contingent. To be sure, it can be an explanation of a person's doing X that he wanted Y, where X and Y are different. And no one would say that the wanting of Y is a tendency to do X. The connection between the want and the action seems contingent in such a case. However, we would count the fact that Smith wanted bread as an explanation of his going to the store only on the assumption that he believed that going to the store was a reasonable means of getting bread in the circumstances. So here it might be said that the wanting of Y and the belief that X is a reasonable means of getting Y together imply a tendency to do X.

It might be said that there are some things a man may want to do which he would in *no* circumstances actually do. He may want to kill his mother-in-law but still not be prepared to do this in any circumstances, perhaps because of his belief in the moral wrongness of such an act. Still, if this is a genuine desire and not an idle wish, we should suppose that the action is to some degree tempting to him. And hence we may take a weakening of his moral inhibitions as part of the possible circumstances in which he would do the act.

Does this argument, if its premises are correct, destroy the causal thesis? Unfortunately, it does not. There is an ambiguity in the notion of having a tendency to do something. Let it be granted that if a man wants to do something, then there are conceivable circumstances in which he would choose to do it. It will not follow that even in those circumstances he *will* do it, for he may be unable to do it. That is to say, it must be borne in mind that the causal connection in question is supposed to hold between wanting and *doing*—whether there is a causal connection between wanting and *choosing* to do is another question. And so far this argument at best establishes a logical connection between wanting and choosing. If, at this juncture, we were to pack into the circumstances the *ability* to perform the act, we might, to be sure, obtain a logical connection between wanting to do something and doing it. But the trouble now is that the ability to do something may be analyzed by one holding the causal thesis as being, in part, the existence of a causal connection between a person's wants and his actions. Suppose, to take an example, a man wants to wiggle his ears. It may follow from this that in certain circumstances (when he believes that he can do it, has the opportunity, does not believe there will be embarrassing consequences, etc.) he will form the intention to wiggle his ears. Unless we add the ability to wiggle his ears, however, it will not follow that he will wiggle his ears. But should we add that, the holder of the causal thesis can claim that we are now begging the question, for the ability to wiggle one's ears, on his view, amounts to the existence of a causal connection between wanting to wiggle one's ears and their being wiggled. And it is no surprise that from A, together with the assertion of a causal connection between A and B, we obtain a tendency for B to happen.

A final argument. The considerations of the previous

section ran into trouble because they depended upon finding a logical connection between wants and actions. Whether or not an airtight argument of this form can be constructed to show that wants are not causes of actions remains controversial at this time. But if the program is the more modest one of showing that reason explanations are not causal explanations, then the prognosis seems more hopeful.

Two apparent facts about reason explanations which have not so far been mentioned are sometimes cited in support of the contention that reason explanations are not causal explanations. First, the agent seems to have a privileged position concerning the reasons for his actions, although the possibility of unconscious reasons casts doubt upon whether this amounts to incorrigible knowledge. He does not, at any rate, utilize evidence and empirical investigation in the normal case to establish what his reasons are. Second, we seem to accept reason explanations, without supposing the necessity for some generalization to a larger class of cases, of the relationship between the reason and the action. If a man acts from certain reasons in this instance, we may, but do not have to, suppose that either he or others will act in this way when they have these reasons in other cases. These two facts, if such they be, seem foreign to causal explanations—or at any rate such causal explanations as those given about the physical world.

These facts also appear strange, however, when we reflect that we are dealing with what appear to be explanations of actions, events that are, after all, observable happenings and that can in turn be cited in explanation of physical happenings.

Although a request for a reason explanation is often couched in terms of the action, for example, "Why did Smith go to the store?," it is also frequently put as a question about his decision or choice, for example, "Why did he decide to go to the store?" Even when we ask for an explanation of the action, it would seem that what is explained is, to put it generally, the formation of the intention, for we assume in asking for reasons that the action was intentional. If this is so, if reason explanations are direct explanations of why a certain intention was formed and only together with certain other assumptions are explanations of observable actions, it seems easier to argue that they are not causal. The defense of the causal thesis given in the previous section, for example, would not have application and the "tendency" argument would regain its force.

Moreover, this observation, together with certain other facts about reason explanations, tends both to explain the two characteristics which philosophers have ascribed to these explanations and to support the view that they are not causal. That Smith wanted bread explains the formation of his intention to go to the store only on an assumption about his beliefs, that is, that he believed that in the circumstances this was a reasonable means of getting bread. If this is so, the linkage between his intention to go to the store and his desire for bread is contained in a particular fact about him (his belief), rather than in a law or generalization. Second, given that Smith formed the intention to go to the store, the two particular facts about him

(that he had this desire and that he had this belief), constitute at least a prima-facie explanation. (They will fail to explain if, for example, it is known that Smith has other desires, stronger than that for bread, which would be thwarted by going to the store.) That two particular facts should constitute a prima-facie explanation seems antithetical to the usual notion of a causal explanation. This perhaps also shows why the agent is in a privileged position concerning such explanations: he can at least construct a prima-facie explanation simply by knowing his own desires and beliefs. Finally, in the case of many intentions (such as the present example), it seems necessary for a person to have some want and belief connected in the pattern pointed out if he is to have formed the intention. That is, while some things may be desired for their own sake when a person forms the intention to get them (in which case no further want is involved), it does not seem possible for a person to form the intention to go to the store without some further want which he thinks will possibly be satisfied by going. And this, in turn, will necessitate a belief connecting the want with the intention. If this is so, we have found a further difference between reason explanations and causal explanations as usually conceived.

What seemed to be a fairly simple and clear-cut distinction between reasons and causes has proved to be a difficult one to draw. It is a much more complex matter than it seemed at first sight. The extraordinary interest taken by recent philosophy in the concept of human action will undoubtedly generate further arguments on both sides.

Bibliography

HISTORICAL WORKS

Hume, David, *A Treatise of Human Nature.*
Mill, John Stuart, *A System of Logic.* Book VI, Ch. 2.

WORKS FAVORABLE TO THE DISTINCTION

Anscombe, G. E. M., *Intention,* 2d ed. Ithaca, N.Y., 1963.
Foot, Philippa, "Free Will as Involving Determinism." *The Philosophical Review,* Vol. 66 (1957), 439–450.
Hart, H. L. A., and Honoré, A. M., *Causation in the Law.* Oxford, 1959.
Melden, A. I., *Free Action.* London, 1961.
Peters, R. S., *The Concept of Motivation.* London, 1958.
Wittgenstein, Ludwig, "The Blue Book," in his *The Blue and Brown Books.* New York, 1958.

WORKS CRITICAL OF THE DISTINCTION

Berofsky, B., "Determinism and the Concept of a Person." *The Journal of Philosophy,* Vol. 60 (1963), 685–700.
Brandt, R., and Kim, J., "Wants as Explanations of Actions." *The Journal of Philosophy,* Vol. 61 (1964), 461–475.
Davidson, Donald, "Actions, Reasons, and Causes." *The Journal of Philosophy,* Vol. 60 (1963), 425–435.

OTHER RELEVANT DISCUSSIONS

Bennett, Daniel, "Action, Reason, and Purpose." *The Journal of Philosophy,* Vol. 62 (1965), 85–96.
Pears, David, "Causes and Objects of Some Feelings and Psychological Reactions." *Ratio,* Vol. 4 (1962), 91–111.

KEITH S. DONNELLAN

REBIRTH. See REINCARNATION.

RECURSIVE FUNCTION THEORY, also known as computability theory and as the theory of algorithms, is a branch of mathematics which classifies certain functions (or correspondences, mappings, operations) from the point of view of the existence of computing algorithms (finite purely combinatorial procedures, effective procedures) by means of which values of the functions can be obtained. The subject, then, may be viewed in two ways. On the one hand, it is a branch of mathematics dealing with a certain well-defined class of functions (the class of recursive functions, defined below), and its results are rigorously demonstrated theorems of pure mathematics. On the other hand, if one asserts that this class consists of just those functions for which it is *in principle* possible to give a procedure for computing values—that is to say, if one chooses to explicate the notion "mechanically calculable function" by equating it (at least in extension) with the notion of recursive function—then the subject assumes foundational, even philosophical, significance. Of course, the cogency of philosophical conclusions so derived will depend on the correctness of the original explication. In fact, a number of very different (at least in formulation) explications of the notion of mechanically computable function were suggested by various logicians (some of them independently of one another). However, all have turned out to be equivalent, and the very equivalence of these explications has been taken as confirming to a certain extent the legitimacy of each of them.

BASIC RESULTS OF THE THEORY

Proofs of the important theorems of recursive function theory are quite insensitive to the particular formulation (that is, explication) employed and depend only on the existence of an explication possessing a few desirable properties. We begin here by listing a few of these properties and showing how to obtain some of the key theorems of recursive function theory. Later we shall discuss various formulations which were important in the development of the subject.

Let a certain finite list of symbols be given as alphabet. (This list could, for example, consist of the letters and punctuation marks used in English.) We shall speak of expressions (or words) on the given alphabet, meaning any finite string (sequence) of the symbols of the alphabet (repetitions permitted). Among the infinite number of possible expressions, two classes of expressions are to be singled out and referred to as inputs and instructions.

To make matters explicit we may consider the following example in which the alphabet consists of the six symbols $B, E, |, X, Y, —$. We take the inputs to consist of those expressions consisting of a B followed by zero or more occurrences of $|$ followed by another B. The instructions are to be expressions made up of three parts: a string of $|$'s, B's, X's and Y's, a dash $—$, and a concluding string of $|$'s, E's, X's and Y's. For example, "$X|X—E|X|$" is an instruction; we speak of "$X|X$" as its left half and "$E|X|$" as its right half.

We assume also that there are rules given for interpreting the inputs and instructions. Each input is to be interpreted as a notation for a unique nonnegative integer, and each integer is to have just one input as its interpretation. In our example BB is the intended interpretation of the number $0, B|B$ of $1, B||B$ of 2, and so on. Each instruction is to be interpreted as a computational rule for proceeding from certain given expressions to another expression. In the example above, the instruction is to permit the replacement of the instruction's left half, in any expression of which the left half is a part, by its right half; for example, the instruction $X|X—E|X|$ permits proceeding from $B|X|X|$ to $B|E|X||$. Finally, certain of the expressions are to be regarded as outputs from which a numerical answer can be read off. Continuing our example, the possible outputs will be $EE, E|E, E||E, E|||E$, and so on, which correspond, respectively, to the answers 0, 1, 2, 3, and so on.

Now, let I be some *finite* list of instructions. A sequence of expressions $P_1, P_2, \cdots, P_n$ is called a computation by I if P_1 is an input, P_n is an output, and each expression P_i (called a step of the computation) can be obtained from preceding expressions in the sequence by using one of the instructions from I. In our example we may take I_1 to consist of the instructions $BB—EE, B|—EX|, X|—||X, XB—E$. Then, beginning with the input $B||B$ (representing 2), we obtain the computation $B||B, EX||B, E||X|B, E||||XB, E||||E$. The output corresponds to 4. In fact, these instructions have the effect of doubling a given input. Again, let I_2 consist of $BB—EE, B|—EX|, X||—X, XB—E, X|B—|E$. These instructions have the same effect of mapping an even input into 0 and an odd input into 1. (For example, consider the computation $B|||||B, EX|||||B, EX|||B, EX|B, E|E$.) In general, let I be a set of instructions with the property that each given input begins a computation terminating in some output and that for a given input exactly one numerical value can be read from a corresponding output. Then we may define a function g_I as follows: If P_1 is the input expression whose interpretation is n and $P_1, P_2, \cdots, P_k$ is a computation by I terminating in the output P_k, then $g_I(n)$ is the numerical value of P_k. (In the above examples $g_{I_1}(n) = 2n$, and $g_{I_2}(n) = 0$ if n is even and $g_{I_2}(n) = 1$ if n is odd.) Finally, a given function f is to be called computable (or recursive) if there is a set of instructions I such that for all $n, f(n) = g_I(n)$. In particular, if a function f is computable by a set of instructions of the kind specified in our example, we shall say that it is computable (X). Now, according to this development, for each choice of alphabet and specification of what constitutes an instruction, an input, and an output, we will obtain a notion of computability (recursiveness). And we certainly have no right to expect that the class of computable functions so obtained will be the same regardless of how this specification is made. Nevertheless, it does turn out that for a wide class of such specifications it is actually the case that the class of functions is the same.

It is also desirable to speak of functions of more than one argument ($x + y$, for example, is a function of two arguments) as being computable (recursive). So we enlarge the class of inputs to permit inputs whose interpretations are ordered pairs, triples, etc., of natural numbers. (In our example we can represent the triple (2,3,5) by $B|X||X|||||B$; (1,0,2) would then be represented by $B|XX||B$. We are using the X as a punctuation mark.) This enables us, simply by rereading our previous definition, to call a function of several arguments computable or recursive (or, using our example, computable (X); $x + y$ is computable (X) by the instructions $B\,|{-}EX\,|$, $BX{-}EX$, $X\,|{-}|X$, $XX{-}X$, $XB{-}E$). We may also speak of predicates (such as $x + y = z$, $x < y$, x is a prime) as computable or recursive (or computable (X)) by using the standard device of identifying the computability (or computability (X)) of a predicate with that of its characteristic function, which equals 1 where the predicate is true and equals 0 where it is false. A set S of natural numbers is computable or recursive if the predicate $x \in S$ is.

Although each computable function is associated with a list of instructions (in general, with more than one list of instructions), not every list determines a computable function. For a given input, a list of instructions may lead (1) to no computation, (2) to computations terminating in outputs having different numerical values, or (3) to computations all terminating in outputs of the same numerical value. Now, a list of instructions determines a computable function (of, say, one argument) just in case possibility (3) holds for each input (whose interpretation is a single number). We shall first insist that the ambiguity resulting from the occurrence of possibility (2) be eliminated by rules of choice which force the next step in a computation where several possibilities exist. In our example we can accomplish this by ruling that (a) the first applicable instruction should be used (b) on the leftmost applicable part of the previous step of the computation. Thus, for each input we get a unique output or no output at all. We may therefore associate with any list of instructions I a "partial" function g_I defined for those numbers n for which possibility (1) does not hold. And a given partial function f is partially computable or partial recursive if there is a list of instructions I such that $f = g_I$ (meaning that f and g_I are defined for the same values of n and have the same values where defined). In our example, we speak of f being partially computable (X). The function $f(n)$, which equals 0 when n is even and is undefined when n is odd, is partially computable (X); to produce a list of instructions for $f(n)$, simply remove the last instruction from I_2.

Now let us in some definite way associate with each finite sequence of expressions a natural number in such a way that no two sequences of expressions are associated with the same number. This can be done by Kurt Gödel's technique (see GÖDEL'S THEOREM) or by many other methods. In our example we may agree to write a finite sequence of expressions by writing them consecutively and inserting commas between expressions; then we may replace symbols by digits according to the following scheme: B is replaced by 1, E by 2, $|$ by 3, X by 4, Y by 5, $-$ by 6, , by 7. So the number corresponding to the list of instructions I_1 is 116227136243743633474162. Assuming this assignment of numbers to sequences of expressions to be accomplished, let us say that the function $\Phi(i,n)$ is undefined unless i is the number of a list of instructions I for which $g_I(n)$ is defined, and when i satisfies this condition we set $\Phi(i,n) = g_I(n)$. We also make the key assumption that Φ is partially computable. (In our example—as in any specific formulation—this assumption becomes a mathematical theorem to be proved; that is, we would prove that

Φ is partially computable (X). Later we will indicate how such a proof can be carried out.) If our decision to use a particular formulation of computability as an explication of mechanical calculability is right, then Φ must be partially computable, since its values can be calculated. The calculation can be carried out as follows: From i obtain the list I (if any) whose number is i. Then to compute $\Phi(i,n)$ apply the instructions of I to the input corresponding to n.

If f is some definite partially computable function, the set S of all n for which $f(n)$ is defined is called a recursively enumerable (abbreviated r.e.) set. For each i, let ω_i be the set of n for which the function $\Phi(i,n)$ is defined. If f is partially computable, using instruction I with associated number i, then the set S as just defined will be ω_i. So we have proved the enumeration theorem.

Enumeration theorem. S is r.e. if and only if for some i, $S = \omega_i$.

We also have:

S is recursive if and only if S and $\bar{S}$ ($\bar{S}$ is the set of natural numbers not in S) are r.e.

To prove the last statement, note that if S is recursive, there is a list of instructions by which the function f is computed, where $f(x) = 1$ for $x \in S$ and $f(x) = 0$ for $x \notin S$. But these instructions can be modified to compute the partial functions $f^+(x)$, which equals 1 for $x \in S$ and is undefined for $x \notin S$, and $f^-(x)$, which equals 0 for $x \notin S$ and is undefined for $x \in S$. Therefore S and $\bar{S}$ are r.e.

Conversely, if S and $\bar{S}$ are both r.e., we have lists of instructions I^+, I^- which yield outputs for a given input n, if $n \in S$ (in which case I^+ will yield an output) or $n \notin S$ (in which case I^- will yield an output). We construct a set of instructions I whose effect on a given input is to construct longer and longer computations, alternately using I^+ and I^- until an output is obtained. (This must happen eventually because each n belongs either to S or to $\bar{S}$.) Furthermore, our new instructions modify such an output in such a way that it becomes an output whose value is 1 if I^+ was last used and 0 if I^- was last used. The characteristic function of $n \in S$ is thus computable by I, and therefore S is recursive. This completes the proof.

For the next result we let K be the set of i's which belong to ω_i; that is, $n \in K \leftrightarrow n \in \omega_n$. (We will use "$\leftrightarrow$" for material equivalence and "$\rightarrow$" for material implication.)

Unsolvability theorem. K is r.e. but not recursive.

Proof: K is r.e. because it is the set of values where the partially computable function $\Phi(n,n)$ is defined. If K were recursive, $\bar{K}$ would be r.e. by what has just been proved; then, using the enumeration theorem, $\bar{K} = \omega_i$ for some fixed i. Now, does i itself belong to K or to $\bar{K}$? We have:

$$i \in K \leftrightarrow i \in \omega_i \leftrightarrow i \in \bar{K}.$$

But this is a contradiction, so there is no such i and $\bar{K}$ is not r.e. This proves the theorem.

Accepting the correctness of our basic explication, the unsolvability theorem is a remarkable result. Although the set K is perfectly explicit (at least for any definite formulation—for example, computability (X)), it is in a precise sense forever unknowable. No computing procedure will ever be devised for sorting the numbers which belong to K from those which do not!

We have shown that we never have $\omega_i = \bar{K}$. Suppose, however, that $\omega_i \subset \bar{K}$; that is,

$$n \in \omega_i \rightarrow n \in \bar{K}.$$

Then

$$n \in \omega_i \rightarrow n \notin \omega_n,$$

so that

$$i \in \omega_i \rightarrow i \notin \omega_i.$$

We conclude that $i \notin \omega_i$ (since $(p \rightarrow \sim p) \rightarrow \sim p$ is a tautology). Thus, i belongs to $\bar{K}$ but not to ω_i. We have just proved the creativity theorem.

Creativity theorem. There is a computable function f such that whenever $\omega_i \subset \bar{K}$, $f(i) \in \bar{K}$ but $f(i) \notin \omega_i$.

In fact, we proved the theorem using the simple function $f(x) = x$. Any r.e. set having the property asserted of K in the creativity theorem is called a creative set. The creativity of a set S certainly implies that it is not recursive (otherwise $\bar{S} = \omega_i$ for some i so that $\bar{S} - \omega_i$ is empty). Moreover, not only must S be forever "unknowable," but any effort to "know" S by providing a computing procedure that will detect some of the elements of $\bar{S}$ (for example, $\omega_i \subset \bar{S}$) will enable one to produce mechanically a "token"—namely, $f(i)$—of the partial failure of our effort.

RECURSIVE FUNCTIONS AND GÖDEL'S THEOREM

The effort to formalize mathematics leads to associating with various propositions of mathematics corresponding expressions on an appropriate alphabet; these expressions are called sentences. Rules of proof are given by means of which certain of these sentences may be "proved." Let us fix our attention on the proposition "$n \notin R$," where R is a given r.e. set. Suppose that we are considering a proposed formalization intended to be adequate (in a suitable sense) for R. Let S_n be the sentence in the formalization which corresponds to the proposition that $n \notin R$. Let some method of associating numbers with proofs in the formalization be given (for example, the method of Gödel numbering or a digital method like that mentioned above), and consider the "proof predicate" $P(m,n)$ which states that m is the number of a proof of S_n. We stipulate that $P(m,n)$ is recursive. This stipulation amounts (via the basic explication) to a demand that there be a mechanical procedure by which an alleged proof of a sentence may be tested to see whether or not it really is one. For actual proposed formalizations it is in any case possible to demonstrate explicitly that $P(m,n)$ is recursive (even primitive recursive—see below). It follows that:

The set of n for which S_n is provable is r.e.

Proof: The instructions for testing $P(m,n)$ may (for given n) be used to successively test $P(0,n)$, $P(1,n)$, $P(2,n)$, and so on, until a case where $P(m,n)$ is true is obtained, at which point the computation terminates; if $P(m,n)$ is always false (that is, if S_n is not provable), the computation never halts. This new set of instructions computes the partial recursive function which comes out 1 when S_n is provable and is undefined otherwise. So the set of such n is r.e.

Let us call a formalization of the kind being considered sound if for each n for which S_n is provable, $n \notin R$ (that is, if the proposition "expressed" by a provable sentence is true), and complete if it is sound and if $n \notin R$ also implies that S_n is provable (that is, if each true proposition $n \notin R$ is expressed by a provable sentence). Then we have:

If a formalization (of the kind stipulated) is both sound and complete, then R is recursive.

For if the formalization is both sound and complete, then $\bar{R}$ is identical to the set of n for which S_n is provable, and hence $\bar{R}$ is r.e. But then R is recursive (since both it and $\bar{R}$ are r.e.). This result is a form of Gödel's theorem, as may be seen by writing its contrapositive.

Gödel's theorem (Kleene–Post form). If R is not recursive, then no formalization (of the stipulated kind) can be both sound and complete; if sound, it must be incomplete.

So there will be a proposition $n \notin R$ which is true but for which the corresponding sentence S_n is not provable. If we take $R = K$ (K is, as we have noted, creative), we can say even more. Let Q be the set of n for which S_n is provable in some sound formalization. Then Q is r.e., so $Q = \omega_i$, and $\omega_i \subset \bar{K}$. It can be shown (using a technical device known as the iteration theorem) that the number i can be calculated purely mechanically from a description of the formalization. But as we have seen, $i \in \bar{K}$ and $i \notin \omega_i$; that is, the proposition $i \notin K$ is true, but the sentence S_i is unprovable. So we have (and this fact explains Post's use of the word creative):

There is a fixed mechanical procedure for associating with each sound formalization (for the set K), a proposition which is true but for which the corresponding sentence is unprovable in the formalization.

PRIMITIVE AND GENERAL RECURSIVE FUNCTIONS

The importance of recursion in defining functions of natural numbers was noted by Richard Dedekind and Giuseppe Peano. Later, Thoralf Skolem and David Hilbert each emphasized the foundational importance of this mode of definition. Finally, Gödel used the class of primitive recursive functions as the cornerstone of his rigorous proof of his incompleteness theorem. The numerical function $\phi(x_1, \cdots, x_n)$ is said to be defined by primitive recursion from the numerical functions $\psi(x_1, x_2, \cdots, x_{n-1})$ and $\mu(x_1, x_2, \cdots, x_{n+1})$ if

$$\phi(0, x_1, \cdots, x_{n-1}) = \psi(x_1, \cdots, x_{n-1}),$$
$$\phi(k+1, x_1, \cdots, x_{n-1}) = \mu(k, \phi(k, x_1, \cdots, x_{n-1}), x_1, \cdots, x_{n-1}).$$

For example, if we set $\psi(x) = 0$ for all x and we set $\mu(t,u,v) = t + u$, then $x \cdot y$ is defined by primitive recursion from ψ and μ, since

$$0 \cdot x = \psi(x)$$
$$(k+1) \cdot x = \mu(k, (k \cdot x), x).$$

A numerical function σ is called primitive recursive if there is a finite sequence $\sigma_1, \cdots, \sigma_n$ which ends with σ and is such that each function in the sequence is a constant or the successor function $x + 1$ or results from previous functions in the sequence by substitution of functions for variables or is defined by primitive recursion from a previous pair of functions in the sequence. A predicate or set is primitive recursive if its characteristic function is. All of the usual numerical functions (and many complicated and unusual ones as well) turn out to be primitive recursive. However, it is easy to construct deliberately a function which is not primitive recursive. We shall do so, employing a simple characterization, due to R. M. Robinson, of primitive recursive functions of one argument. Robinson showed that each such function can be obtained from the successor function $x+1$ and the special function $E(x)$, the difference between x and the largest perfect square which does not exceed x (for example, $E(5)=5-4=1$, $E(24)=24-16=8$, $E(25)=25-25=0$), by applying three operations: (1) going from $F(x)$ and $G(x)$ to $F(x)+G(x)$; (2) going from $F(x)$ and $G(x)$ to $F(G(x))$; and (3) going from $F(x)$ to $F^x(0)$, where $F^0(0)=0$, $F^{x+1}(0)=F(F^x(0))$. Then we may define the enumerating function $W(x,n)=W_n(x)$ by the following equations:

$$W_0(x) = x+1.$$
$$W_1(x) = E(x).$$
$$W_m(x) = W_q(W_r(x)), \qquad \text{if } 1 < m = 2^q(4r+5).$$
$$W_m(x) = W_q(x) + W_r(x), \qquad \text{if } 1 < m = 2^q(4r+3).$$
$$W_m(x) = W_q^{\ x}(0), \qquad \text{if } 1 < m = 2^q.$$

By Robinson's quoted result, $f(x)$ is primitive recursive if and only if there is some value of n such that $f(x)=W_n(x)$. Let $d(n)=W_n(n)+1$. Then $d(n)$ is not primitive recursive. (If it were, then since $d(n)=W_i(n)$, setting $n=i$ would yield $W_i(i)=W_i(i)+1$.) Hence, $W(x,n)$ is not primitive recursive. Yet its mode of definition is recursive in the sense that its values are determined from prior values, and it is certainly mechanically calculable in the intuitive sense. Such considerations led Gödel, in his lectures at the Institute for Advanced Study at Princeton in 1934, to propose a general definition of recursive function (using a suggestion of Jacques Herbrand's). Gödel's definition and various (as it turned out) equivalent, closely related definitions were studied by S. C. Kleene. This Herbrand–Gödel–Kleene notion of general recursive function can be put in the context of instructions and computations discussed above.

As alphabet we use the symbols

$$0 \quad S \quad (\quad) \quad , \quad =$$

an infinite list of number variables

$$\xi_1, \xi_2, \xi_3, \cdots,$$

and an infinite list of function variables

$$F_1, F_2, F_3, F_4, \cdots$$

(Technically we require a finite alphabet; we may, if we wish, satisfy this requirement by regarding, say, ξ_{79} as consisting of the three symbols ξ, $_7$, $_9$.) Instructions are equations (beginning with function variables) that can be constructed in terms of the given symbolism (precise formation rules are readily supplied); for example,

$$F_1(\xi_1, 0) = \xi_1.$$
$$F_1(\xi_1, S\xi_2) = SF_1(\xi_1, \xi_2).$$
$$F_2(\xi_1, 0) = 0.$$
$$F_2(\xi_1, S\xi_2) = F_1(F_2(\xi_1, \xi_2), \xi_1).$$

Numerals are expressions consisting of "0" preceded by zero or more occurrences of "S" and denoting the number n of S's it contains; for example, "$SSS0$" denotes 3. The inputs are expressions $(\alpha_1, \alpha_2, \cdots, \alpha_k)$ where the α's are numerals. In a list of instructions the initial function symbol F_j of the final equation is called the principal function symbol (*PFS*). A computation, or derivation, from a list of initial equations, or instructions, is a set of equations derived according to both of the following procedures: (1) an equation may be derived from one of the instructions by replacing all variables by numerals; (2) from a pair of derived equations one of which is $F_i(\alpha_1, \cdots, \alpha_k)=\alpha$, where $\alpha_1, \cdots, \alpha_k, \alpha$ are numerals, and the other of which contains an occurrence of $F_i(\alpha_1, \cdots, \alpha_k)$, the equation obtained by replacing that occurrence of $F_i(\alpha_1, \cdots, \alpha_k)$ by α may be derived. Corresponding to an input $(\beta_1, \cdots, \beta_k)$ an output will be a derived equation $F_j(\beta_1, \cdots, \beta_k)=\beta$, where β is a numeral; the numerical value to be read off is that denoted by β. The functions that are computable according to this formulation were called general recursive by Kleene. The list of four equations given above serves to compute the product function $x \cdot y$. Consider, for example, the computation

$$F_1(0,0) = 0,$$
$$F_2(0,0) = 0,$$
$$F_2(0,S0) = F_1(F_2(0,0),0),$$
$$F_2(0,S0) = F_2(0,0),$$
$$F_2(0,S0) = 0,$$

which leads from the input $(0,S0)$ to the output $F_2(0,S0)=0$ (corresponding to the fact that $0 \cdot 1 = 0$). To define the notion of partial recursive function we must specify some order in which the derived equations are to be generated. (The details are omitted here.)

Let a numbering scheme be adopted (it is desirable for technical reasons that computations generated first have smaller numbers), and let us define the predicate $T(z,x,y)$ which states that z is the number of a list of equations (with F_j as *PFS*) and y is the number of a computation of an equation $F_j(\alpha)=\beta$ from that list, where α denotes the number x and β is a numeral. Furthermore, let $U(y)$ be the function which is equal to 0 except when y is the number of a computation terminating with an equation where the right-hand side is a numeral β, in which case $U(y)$ is equal to the number denoted by β. Then we have Kleene's equation

$$\Phi(i,n) = U(\min_y T(i,n,y)),$$

where $\Phi(i,n)$ is defined as above—but of course in terms of the present formulation instead of computability (X). Here "$\min_y$" is to be read "the least y such that," and the equation follows from the meaning of "U" and "T". Thus, each partial recursive function can be written $U(\min_y T(i,n,y))$ for suitable i. Generalizing the "T" predicate to arbitrary inputs $T_n(z,x_1,\cdots,x_n,y)$, we obtain a result of Kleene's, the normal form theorem.

Normal form theorem. For every partial recursive function $f(x_1,\cdots,x_n)$ there is a number e such that

$$f(x_1,\cdots,x_n)=U(\min_y T_n(e,x_1,\cdots,x_n,y)).$$

Thus, all partial recursive functions can be obtained from primitive recursive functions using the one new operation, minimalization. Conversely, if $f(x_1,\cdots,x_n,y)$ is a recursive function, then $g(x_1,\cdots,x_n)$ is partial recursive where

$$g(x_1,\cdots,x_n)=\min_y[f(x_1,\cdots,x_n,y)=0].$$

This can be seen by adjoining to the list of equations computing f (with F^N as PFS and no function variables F^i with $i>N$) the following equations:

$$F^{N+1}(0,\xi_1,\cdots,\xi_n,\xi_{n+1})=\xi_{n+1}.$$
$$F^{N+1}(S\xi_{n+2},\xi_1,\cdots,\xi_n,\xi_{n+1})=$$
$$F^{N+1}(F^N(\xi_1,\cdots,\xi_n,S\xi_{n+1}),\xi_1,\cdots,\xi_n,S\xi_{n+1}).$$
$$F^{N+2}(\xi_1,\cdots,\xi_n)=F^{N+1}(F^N(\xi_1,\cdots,\xi_n,0),\xi_1,\cdots,\xi_n,0).$$

We also have, using Kleene's equation that ω_i is the set of n for which $(\exists y)T(i,n,y)$, the following:

Every r.e. set is defined by a predicate of the form $(\exists y)R(x,y)$, where R is primitive recursive.

The converse is likewise true (even omitting the word "primitive"), as can be seen by considering the partial recursive function $\min_y R(x,y)$.

We also have:

A nonempty set is r.e. if and only if there is a (primitive) recursive function f such that the set consists of the values $f(0),f(1),f(2),\cdots$ enumerated by f. (The term "recursively enumerable" stems from this characterization.)

If there is such an f, then the set S is given by

$$x\in S\leftrightarrow(\exists y)[x=f(y)],$$

where "$x=f(y)$" is a recursive predicate. Conversely, if S satisfies the condition

$$x\in S\leftrightarrow(\exists y)R(x,y),$$

where R is primitive recursive, and if m is the least member of the nonempty set S, then we set

$$g(x,y)=\begin{cases}x & \text{if } R(x,y) \text{ is true,}\\ m & \text{if } R(x,y) \text{ is false.}\end{cases}$$

Now, g is easily seen to be primitive recursive and assumes the same values as the primitive recursive function f for which

$$f(2^x(2y+1))=g(x,y)$$

The suggestion that mechanical calculability might be identified with definability by a sufficiently general form of recursion occurred in Gödel's 1934 lectures. However, the proposal to identify mechanical calculability with general recursiveness was first made by Alonzo Church in "An Unsolvable Problem of Elementary Number Theory" and is therefore called Church's thesis.

OTHER FORMULATIONS

Turing machines. Independently of Church, A. M. Turing proposed a superficially quite different explication of mechanical calculability. Turing was led from "mechanical" to machines. He proposed consideration of a simple class of automatic computing machines. These were to operate on a linear array of symbols (thought of as arranged on a "tape"), to be sensitive to one symbol at a time, and to operate by changing this symbol or by moving one square to the left or right. Turing argued that a human computer's steps may all be regarded as being of this simple form. The use of two-dimensional paper is inessential, and whatever expressions a human being can take in "at a glance" are to be thought of as the symbols. We may place Turing's machines (modified in a quite inessential manner) in the context of our general formulation as follows: We choose for our alphabet the symbols $q_1, q_2, \cdots, S_0, S_1, S_2, \cdots, R, L$. The q's are thought of as internal "states" or "configurations" of a machine; the S's are symbols "on the machine's tape." We write B for S_0 (B is to mean blank) and $|$ for S_1. Instructions are "quadruples" of one of the following three kinds, $q_iS_jS_kq_l$, $q_iS_jRq_l$, or $q_iS_jLq_l$. The inputs are of the form $q_11^{m_1+1}B1^{m_2+1}B\cdots B1^{m_k+1}$ (where the exponents on the 1 indicate repetition—for example, $1^3=111$), representing the k-tuple $(m_1,m_2,\cdots,m_k)$. A Turing machine is taken to be a finite list of instructions (quadruples); the instructions are to be read as follows: "$q_iS_jS_kq_l$" as "replace q_iS_j by q_lS_k"; "$q_iS_jRq_l$" as "replace $q_iS_jS_k$ by $S_jq_lS_k$ and q_iS_j at the right-hand end of an expression by $S_jq_lS_0$"; "$q_iS_jLq_l$" as "replace $S_kq_iS_j$ by $q_lS_kS_j$ and q_iS_j at the left-hand end of an expression by $q_lS_0S_j$." The instructions thus correspond to overprinting, motion to the right, and motion to the left, respectively. When more than one instruction is applicable, the one occurring first is to be used. Any expression is an output with respect to a given Turing machine if none of the quadruples are applicable to the expression. An output is also called terminal. Its numerical value is simply the number of $|$'s present. For example, consider the Turing machine

$$\begin{aligned}
q_1&\,|\,R\,q_1\\
q_1&\,B\,|\,q_2\\
q_2&\,|\,R\,q_3\\
q_3&\,B\,|\,q_3
\end{aligned}$$

It computes the function $x+3$. (Consider the following computation beginning with the input corresponding to 2: $q_1|||, |q_1||, ||q_1|, |||q_1B, |||q_2|, ||||q_3B, ||||q_3|$.)

The Turing machine that computes the partially computable function $\Phi(i,n)$ is called universal. This is because each partially computable function can be computed by this machine by placing the appropriate "code" for i on its tape. The existence of a universal Turing machine is the theoretical justification for the empirical view that existing electronic digital computers are all-purpose machines which can accomplish any computation whatever, given enough time and storage capacity.

A slight variant of Turing's notion was Emil Post's notion of a finite combinatory process; Post's work was independent of Turing's.

Reckonability. Let L be a system of logic formulated in the first-order functional calculus (quantification theory). Let certain terms containing no variables be regarded as numerals having unique natural numbers as their denotation. For each n, let t_n be the unique numeral denoting n. Then a function $g(x)$ is called reckonable in L if there is a formula $\alpha(x,y)$ containing two free variables such that

$$g(m) = n \text{ if and only if } \vdash_L \alpha(t_m, t_n).$$

This notion, or, rather, a closely related one, was first introduced by Gödel in his paper "Über formal unentscheidbare Sätze der Principia Mathematica und verwandter Systeme I" (1931). Later, in "Über die Länge von Beweisen" (1936), he observed that it has an absolute character in the sense that the same class is obtained for "weak" and for "strong" systems of logic. Actually, the reckonable functions (in a wide class of systems of logic) are the same as the recursive functions, as was remarked by Rosser in a review of the 1936 paper.

Lambda-definability. The λ-notation was introduced to express the operation of proceeding from an expression containing variables to the function defined by that expression. For example, "$\lambda x \cdot x^2$" is intended to denote the function which maps each natural number onto its square. In this expression "x" is a bound variable, so

$$\lambda x \cdot x^2 = \lambda y \cdot y^2.$$

Church systematically developed the formal rules appropriate for manipulating expressions involving this λ-notation. Kleene showed how a theory of positive integers could be developed in this theory, and Church capitalized on Kleene's work in introducing his notion of λ-definability of a function as a proposed explication of mechanical calculability. Details are omitted here (see LOGIC, COMBINATORY).

Canonical and normal systems. Some of the ideas discussed in this article were anticipated by Post in the years 1921 to 1924. His basic formulation permits an arbitrary alphabet and instructions permitting simultaneous amalgamation of parts of previous words in a computation with certain constant words. Post's main theorem indicates that such instructions may be replaced by instructions of the "normal" form $gP \to P\bar{g}$, which permit one to go from any word beginning with g to the word obtained by crossing out g and placing $\bar{g}$ at the end of the terminated word.

Still another formulation is A. A. Markov's notion of normal algorithm. The alphabet is arbitrary and the instructions permit specified substitutions of certain fixed words for others (as in our development of computability (X)). Again, the details are omitted.

Equivalence of the formulations. The equivalence of recursiveness and λ-definability was proved by Kleene in 1936 and that of λ-definability and Turing computability by Turing in 1937. It is perhaps easiest to see these results for a given formulation F by first showing that constant functions and $x+1$ are computable by F and that the class of functions computable by F is closed under primitive recursion, minimalization, and substitution, so that every recursive function is computable by F. Then one defines

T_n predicates and a U function for formulation F which one shows to be primitive recursive, so every function computable by F has the form $U(\min_y T_n(e,x_1,\cdots,x_n,y))$ and is therefore recursive. This is done for Turing computability by Martin Davis in *Computability and Unsolvability*, where there is also a discussion of normal systems. Computability (X) as discussed above can easily be seen via direct reasoning to be equivalent to Turing computability. An equivalence proof for normal algorithms is given in Elliott Mendelson's *Introduction to Mathematical Logic*.

PROBLEMS AND APPLICATIONS

Unsolvable problems. The unsolvability theorem can be used to demonstrate the unsolvability of various problems in mathematics for which solutions were actually sought. The most important of these remains the Church–Turing result that Hilbert's *Entscheidungsproblem,* the decision problem for the first-order functional calculus, is unsolvable. For a survey of other unsolvability results, see Martin Davis, "Unsolvable Problems—A Review."

Turing reducibility and Post's problem. Turing proposed that his definition of computability be extended to permit the machine access to an "oracle" which has at its disposal ("on tape") all information about membership in some set (possibly nonrecursive). Set R is called Turing reducible to S if R can be computed using S as an oracle. Post proved that there is an r.e. set C to which every r.e. set is Turing reducible and raised the question (subsequently known as Post's problem) "Is there an r.e. nonrecursive set R to which C is not Turing reducible?" The existence of such a set was proved (independently) by Richard M. Friedberg in 1957 and by A. A. Mucnik in 1956.

Philosophical and foundational issues. The philosophical issues raised by recursive function theory center about Church's thesis—that is, the proposal to identify the intuitive notion of calculability by an algorithm with the precise notion of recursive function. Is Church's thesis (so named by Kleene) to be regarded as a mathematical definition, replacing a vague notion by a precise one? Or is it a synthetic proposition for which evidence pro and con should be sought and which, like the propositions of empirical science, can only be rendered more plausible but never made absolutely certain? Church's writings favor the first view, whereas Post's and Turing's favor the second.

If we do accept Church's thesis, we are led (as we have seen) to the existence of absolutely unsolvable problems, a result strikingly opposed to the tenor of twentieth-century antiabsolutism in philosophy. One might even go so far as to assert that the recursively enumerable but not recursive set K embodies an object which is forever unknowable but is such that we know it to be unknowable.

Continuing to accept Church's thesis, the Kleene–Post form of Gödel's theorem shows that Gödel's discovery of the necessary incompleteness of arithmetic cannot be vitiated by even the most radical alteration in the accepted rules of proof; so long as we insist on the existence of an algorithm for checking the credentials of an alleged proof, there will be a true sentence of arithmetic undecidable by the rules of proof.

Finally, the success of recursive function theory encourages one to hope that precise characterizations will be found of other, hitherto vague notions occurring in the foundations of mathematics.

Bibliography

Church, Alonzo, "An Unsolvable Problem of Elementary Number Theory." *American Journal of Mathematics,* Vol. 58 (1936), 345–363. Reprinted in Martin Davis, ed., *The Undecidable.*

Church, Alonzo, "A Note on the Entscheidungsproblem." *Journal of Symbolic Logic,* Vol. 1 (1936), 40–41. Correction, *ibid.,* 101–102. Reprinted in Martin Davis, ed., *The Undecidable.*

Church, Alonzo, "The Calculi of Lambda-conversion." *Annals of Mathematics Studies,* No. 6. Princeton, N.J., 1941; reprinted, 1951.

Davis, Martin, *Computability and Unsolvability.* New York, 1958.

Davis, Martin, "Unsolvable Problems—A Review," in *Proceedings of the Symposium on Mathematical Theory of Automata,* Polytechnic Institute of Brooklyn. New York, 1962. Pp. 15–22.

Davis, Martin, ed., *The Undecidable.* Hewlett, N.Y., 1965.

Friedberg, Richard M., "Two Recursively Enumerable Sets of Incomparable Degrees of Unsolvability (Solution of Post's Problem, 1944)." *Proceedings of the National Academy of Sciences,* Vol. 43 (1957), 236–238.

Gödel, Kurt, "Über formal unentscheidbare Sätze der Principia Mathematica und verwandter Systeme I." *Monatshefte für Mathematik und Physik,* Vol. 38 (1931), 173–198. Translated by Elliott Mendelson as "On Formally Undecidable Propositions of Principia Mathematica and Related Systems I," in Martin Davis, ed., *The Undecidable.*

Gödel, Kurt, *On Undecidable Propositions of Formal Mathematical Systems.* Princeton, N.J., 1934. Mimeographed lecture notes, Institute for Advanced Study. Reprinted in Martin Davis, ed., *The Undecidable.*

Gödel, Kurt, "Über die Länge von Beweisen." *Ergebnisse eines mathematischen Kolloquium,* Vol. 4 (1936), 34–38. Translated by Martin Davis as "On the Length of Proofs," in *The Undecidable.*

Hermes, Hans, *Aufzählbarkeit, Entscheidbarkeit, Berechenbarkeit.* Berlin, Göttingen, and Heidelberg, 1961.

Kleene, S. C., "General Recursive Functions of Natural Numbers." *Mathematische Annalen,* Vol. 112 (1936), 727–742. Reprinted in Martin Davis, ed., *The Undecidable.*

Kleene, S. C., "λ-Definability and Recursiveness." *Duke Mathematical Journal,* Vol. 2 (1936), 340–353.

Kleene, S. C., "Recursive Predicates and Quantifiers." *Transactions of the American Mathematical Society,* Vol. 53 (1943), 41–73. Reprinted in Martin Davis, ed., *The Undecidable.*

Kleene, S. C., *Introduction to Metamathematics.* Princeton, N.J., 1952.

Markov, A. A., *Theory of Algorithms,* translated from the Russian. U.S. Department of Commerce, Washington, 1962.

Mendelson, Elliott, *Introduction to Mathematical Logic.* Princeton, N.J., 1964.

Mostowski, Andrzej, "On Definable Sets of Positive Integers." *Fundamenta Mathematicae,* Vol. 34 (1947), 81–112.

Mucnik, A. A., "Negative Answer to the Problem of Reducibility of the Theory of Algorithms" (Russian). *Doklady Akademii Nauk S.S.S.R.,* N.S. Vol. 108 (1956), 194–197.

Péter, Rózsa, *Rekursive Funktionen.* Budapest, 1951; 2d ed., 1957.

Post, Emil L., "Finite Combinatory Processes—Formulation I." *Journal of Symbolic Logic,* Vol. 1 (1936), 103–105. Reprinted in Martin Davis, ed., *The Undecidable.*

Post, Emil L., "Formal Reductions of the General Combinatorial Decision Problem." *American Journal of Mathematics,* Vol. 65 (1943), 197–215.

Post, Emil L., "Recursively Enumerable Sets of Positive Integers and Their Decision Problems." *Bulletin of the American Mathematical Society,* Vol. 50 (1944), 284–316.

Post, Emil L., "Absolutely Unsolvable Problems and Relatively Undecidable Propositions—Account of an Anticipation," in Martin Davis, ed., *The Undecidable.*

Robinson, Raphael M., "Primitive Recursive Functions." *Bulletin of the American Mathematical Society,* Vol. 53 (1947), 925–942.

Rosser, J. B., review of "Über die Länge von Beweisen." *Journal of Symbolic Logic,* Vol. 1 (1936), 116.

Skolem, Thoralf, *Begrundung der elementaren Arithmetik durch die rekurrierende Denkweise ohne Anwendung scheinbarer Veränderlichen mit unendlichem Ausdehnungsbereich.* Oslo, 1923.

Smullyan, Raymond, *Theory of Formal Systems.* Princeton, N.J., 1961.

Tarski, Alfred; Mostowski, Andrzej; and Robinson, Raphael M., *Undecidable Theories.* Amsterdam, 1953.

Turing, A. M., "On Computable Numbers, With an Application to the Entscheidungsproblem." *Proceedings of the London Mathematical Society,* Series 2, Vol. 42 (1936–1937), 230–265. Correction, *ibid.,* Vol. 43 (1937), 544–546. Reprinted in Martin Davis, ed., *The Undecidable.*

Turing, A. M., "Computability and λ-Definability." *The Journal of Symbolic Logic,* Vol. 2 (1937), 153–163.

Turing, A. M., "Systems of Logic Based on Ordinals." *Proceedings of the London Mathematical Society,* Series 2, Vol. 45 (1939), 161–228. Reprinted in Martin Davis, ed., *The Undecidable.*

MARTIN DAVIS

REDUCIBILITY, AXIOM OF. See RUSSELL, BERTRAND, section on logic and mathematics.

REDUCTIONISM. See LAWS AND THEORIES; PHILOSOPHY OF SCIENCE, HISTORY OF.

REFERRING has had a central position in philosophical discussion from the very beginning of the twentieth century. It has been a focal point of controversy because, apart from its intrinsic interest, it has served as a test case in the conflict of opposing schools of philosophical analysis. The principle contending views are Frege's theory of sense and reference, Russell's theory of descriptions, and Strawson's theory of referring.

GOTTLOB FREGE

Initially Frege introduced his distinction between the sense and the reference of a name in order to be able to deal with a puzzle about identity ("="). He opens his "On Sense and Reference" with this question about it: "Is it a relation? A relation between objects, or between names or signs of objects?" If we take the first of these alternatives and regard identity as a relation between objects, Frege reasons, then the statement "$a=b$" should mean the same thing as "$a=a$," if "$a=b$" is true. For if "$a=b$" is true, then "a" and "b" are two names for the *same* object, and "$a=b$" can tell us no more than that $a=a$. Identity is a relation in which a thing can stand only to itself, not to another thing. Thus, this interpretation of identity statements must be false, because statements of the form "$a=b$" are sometimes highly informative, and "$a=a$" is never informative. For example, it was an astronomical discovery of some importance that the morning star and the evening star are one and the same planet.

Nor is Frege able to accept the other of the two alternatives, that identity is a relation between names or signs of objects. In such a case "$a=b$" would say that the name "a" and the name "b" were names for the same thing. This analysis cannot be correct, Frege argues, because the fact that "*a*" is a name for *a* and that "*b*" is also a name for *a* results from a purely arbitrary agreement concerning the use of these marks (or sounds). But here again, when I say that Venus is the morning star, I am conveying information about the heavens, not about the arbitrary use of names.

Frege now proceeds to his distinction between the sense (*Sinn*) and the reference (*Bedeutung*) of signs. The reference of an expression is the object named or denoted by it. We must distinguish this object from the sense of the expression, which is "grasped by everybody who is sufficiently familiar with the language." The sense of a sign, Frege says, contains the "mode of presentation" whereby the sign gives us its reference. Perhaps the following example, from "Sense and Reference," will help to clarify the distinction. "Let *a, b, c,* be the lines connecting the vertices of a triangle with the mid points of the opposite sides. The point of intersection of *a* and *b* is then the same as the point of intersection of *b* and *c*. So we have different designations for the same point, and these names ('point of intersection of *a* and *b*,' 'point of intersection of *b* and *c*') likewise indicate the mode of presentation; and hence the statement contains actual knowledge." Thus, we can say here that the two expressions "the point of intersection of *a* and *b*" and "the point of intersection of *b* and *c*" have the same reference but differ in sense. Similarly, "the morning star" and "Venus" have the same reference but differ in sense. Because of this difference the statement "Venus is the morning star" conveys actual knowledge, and "Venus is Venus" does not.

"If words are used in their ordinary way," says Frege, "what one intends to speak of is their reference. It can also happen, however, that one wishes to talk about the words themselves or their sense." An example of this occurs when one reports the words of another in *oratio recta* (direct quotation). Thus, if I say, "He said 'the cat is on the mat,'" my words have as their reference the words of the person whose speech is reported; and for this reason, words standing between quotation marks in *oratio recta* must not be taken as having their ordinary (customary) sense and reference.

In other special constructions Frege holds the reference of our words to be their customary sense rather than their customary reference. For example, in the statement "Smith knows that Venus is the morning star," the names "Venus" and "the morning star" have their indirect reference rather than their customary reference. Frege's reason for maintaining this is as follows: If we suppose that in the statement "Smith knows that Venus is the morning star," the expression "the morning star" has its customary reference (Venus), we ought to be able to replace that expression by any other expression referring to Venus. But if we replace the expression "the morning star" by "the evening star," our statement may well become false, for it is perfectly possible that Smith should know that Venus is the morning star and yet not know that Venus is the evening star. If, on the other hand, we replace the expression "the morning star" in our statement with another expression having the same customary sense, our statement could not possibly become false.

Frege concludes that this customary sense is the reference (the indirect reference) of the words "the morning star" in our statement. "We distinguish accordingly the *customary* from the *indirect* reference of a word; and its *customary* sense from its *indirect* sense. The indirect reference of a word is accordingly its customary sense."

It should be noted that Frege's argument here rests upon the principle that if two expressions have the same reference, then the one expression may replace the other in any statement in which it occurs, *salva veritate* (without altering the truth of the statement). Frege explicitly embraces this principle and quotes Leibniz' famous definition in support of it: *Eadem sunt, quae sibi mutuo substitui possunt, salva veritate* ("Things are identical which can be substituted for one another without change in the truth.") The distinction between the customary and indirect senses and references of expressions would seem to be imposed on Frege by his adherence to Leibniz' law, for without some such distinction as Frege makes, the law admits counterexamples. Expressions occupying positions within clauses governed by such words as "knows," "believes," "thinks," and "supposes" (the so-called verbs of propositional attitude) cannot be replaced in those positions by other expressions standing for the same customary reference, *salva veritate*. The morning star – evening star example above is a case in point. Leibniz' law is saved, however, once it is pointed out that an expression occupying these positions does not stand for its customary reference but for its customary sense (its indirect reference).

Frege also maintains the distinction between sense and reference for the whole declarative sentence containing proper names and definite descriptions. A declarative sentence spoken in the making of a statement—not, for instance, in fiction or on the stage—has both sense and reference. The customary reference of such a declarative sentence is its truth-value, "the True" or "the False." The sense of the sentence is the thought which it expresses. Frege is most anxious to cancel the psychological connotations of the word "thought" from his concept of sense, and it is clear that by the thought expressed by a declarative sentence he means what other philosophers call a proposition.

Once again, in view of Frege's adherence to the principle of substitutivity stated above (Leibniz' law), it will be seen that it is necessary for Frege to extend the distinction between the customary and indirect senses and references to the case of whole declarative sentences. Taking the reference of such a sentence to be always a truth-value, it can be shown that the principle of substitutivity permits counterexamples. Consider the sentence "Copernicus believed that the planetary orbits are circles." Here the words following "that" are a full declarative sentence whose customary reference is "the False." But one cannot replace this false statement by *any* false statement *salva veritate*, for that would be to make the absurd claim that Copernicus believed all false statements, since he did believe that the planetary orbits are circles.

This conclusion is avoided when it is realized that the statement "The planetary orbits are circles" does not have its customary reference when it occurs in the larger statement about Copernicus. Here it has its indirect reference—according to Frege's rule, its customary sense—the proposition that the planetary orbits are circles. The principle of substitutivity requires not that the statement "The planetary orbits are circles" be replaceable in the statement about Copernicus by any other sentence standing for the same truth-value but by any other sentence expressing the same proposition. Hence, once the distinction between the customary and the indirect senses and references is recognized for whole declarative sentences, these paradoxes of substitutivity can be avoided.

BERTRAND RUSSELL

Russell's theory of descriptions is designed to deal with the same perplexities which exercised Frege, but his attack on these problems is radically different. The theory appeared in full, for the first time, in "On Denoting," in which Russell presents his theory of "denoting phrases" (he later divided these expressions into "indefinite descriptions" and "definite descriptions"). "This is the principle of the theory of denoting I wish to advocate: that denoting phrases never have any meaning in themselves, but that every proposition in whose verbal expression they occur has a meaning." By way of explaining what a denoting phrase is, Russell offers a list: "a man, some man, any man, every man, all men, the present King of England, the present King of France, the center of mass of the solar system at the first instant of the twentieth century . . . ." These phrases, in Russell's view, have no meaning in themselves. In this respect they are contrasted with proper names. In his *Introduction to Mathematical Philosophy* (Ch. 16) the following definition is given of a proper name: "A name is a simple symbol, directly designating an individual, which is its meaning, and having this meaning in its own right, independently of the meanings of all other words."

The contrast between "denoting phrases" and "proper names" is the contrast between expressions which have no meaning in themselves and expressions which have meaning in their own right. Russell makes the distinction in this way because he is attempting to avoid certain paradoxes which seem to him to arise through the neglect of this difference. If I say, "Socrates was the teacher of Plato," then I state some fact about both Socrates and Plato (the men themselves, not their names). But suppose I say, "The round square does not exist." Surely, Russell argues, this is true, yet my words cannot be taken as asserting of a certain object that it does not exist. For if there were such an object, then it would exist and the assertion that it does not exist would not be true but false. Thus, there is a general problem as to how one can ever assert truly that something does not exist.

Since such assertions can be made, it follows that "the round square" is not a proper name. Russell assumes that the meaning of a proper name is the object it names. Since the round square does not exist, there is *no* object to be named, and if it were taken as a proper name, "the round square" would necessarily be meaningless. But if it were meaningless, the assertion "The round square does not exist" would also be meaningless. Since it is not meaningless but true, it follows that "the round square" is not a proper name; it has no meaning in itself. Every statement whose grammatical subject seems to name a nonexistent object must be so analyzed that that grammatical subject does not appear in the correctly analyzed proposition.

Let us consider, for example, "The round square does not exist." According to Russell's analysis, this becomes "It is false that there is one and only one object which is both round and square." Here the descriptive phrase "the round square" does not appear at all.

Russell argues that no definite description is a proper name. Consider the statement "Scott is the author of *Waverley*." If "the author of *Waverley*" were a proper name, there would be some object, call it *c*, which this name directly designates and which would be the meaning of "the author of *Waverley*." The statement "Scott is the author of *Waverley*" would then mean the same as "Scott is *c*." There are only two possibilities: either Scott is not *c*, in which case "Scott is *c*" is false, or Scott is *c*, in which case "Scott is *c*" means "Scott is Scott." Thus, if "the author of *Waverley*" is a name, "Scott is the author of *Waverley*" is either false or trivial, meaning just "Scott is Scott." But since it is neither false nor trivial in this way, it follows that "the author of *Waverley*" is not a proper name; and since the same reasoning applies to every definite description, it follows that no definite description is a name.

Essentially, Russell's theory provides a way of restating statements containing definite descriptions in such a way that the same thing is said without their use. There are two kinds of statements, then, for which such an elimination rule must be supplied. The first kind is that of statements of the form "The so-and-so exists." Such statements are analyzed as asserting the conjunction of the following two propositions: "At least one thing has the property so-and-so" and "At most one thing has the property so-and-so." In other words, exactly one thing has the property so-and-so. For example, "The present king of France exists" is analyzed as saying "Exactly one thing is a king of France."

The other kind of statement from which definite descriptions must be eliminated is that in which some characteristic is asserted of the so-and-so; statements of the form "The so-and-so is such-and-such." Take as an example "The author of *Waverley* was a poet." This means the same as the conjunction of the following three propositions: "Someone wrote *Waverley*"; "Only one man wrote *Waverley*"; "Whoever wrote *Waverley* was a poet." Thus, the statement "The author of *Waverley* was a poet" can be analyzed into "One and only one person wrote *Waverley* and he was a poet." In this latter statement "the author of *Waverley*" does not appear. One important consequence of this analysis, later criticized by Strawson, is that every statement of the form "The so-and-so is such-and-such" is false when the so-and-so does not exist.

Russell claims in support of his theory that it is the only theory of denoting which can satisfactorily solve certain puzzles which troubled both Frege and Meinong. He answers the problem of how statements of identity ($a=b$) can be informative by claiming that this is possible only when at least one of the terms of the identity statement is a definite description. The statement will then have the meaning his theory gives it. There is also the puzzle of why it does not follow from the true premises (1) "George IV wished to know whether Scott was the author of *Waverley*" and (2) "Scott was the author of *Waverley*" that (3) "George IV wished to know whether Scott was Scott."

Russell's solution goes as follows. If one is inclined to accept the inference from (1) and (2) to the false statement (3), it is because he regards the inference as warranted by

Leibniz' law—as arising from the replacement of "the author of *Waverley*" by "Scott" in (1) on the basis of the true identity statement (2). But on Russell's analysis this would be a mistake, for when (1) and (2) are properly analyzed, the phrase "the author of *Waverley*" disappears from them. Russell is also able to explain how it is possible to deny the existence of something. If I say, "The round square does not exist," I am not naming some object whose existence I am denying, for "the round square" is not a name. When the statement is properly analyzed, the description disappears; and one is no longer tempted to think of it as naming an object whose existence it is denying.

One important consequence of Russell's theory is that every statement of the form "The so-and-so is such-and-such" implies that the so-and-so exists. For example, "The author of *Waverley* was a poet" implies that someone wrote *Waverley* and that only one person wrote *Waverley*. But according to Russell's theory these two mean only that the author of *Waverley* exists. This enables Russell to deal with the Ontological Argument for the existence of God. The first premise of this argument says that God is the most perfect being. "The most perfect being" is a definite description, and therefore this premise implies that the most perfect being exists. But this is what the argument is supposed to prove, and to assume it in the premises is to beg the question.

P. F. STRAWSON

Strawson's views are presented in his article "On Referring," which is in large part an attack on Russell's theory. Consider the sentence "The king of France is wise." According to Strawson, there are two false things which Russell would say about this sentence: that anyone now uttering the sentence would be making an assertion which would be either true or false, and that part of what was being said in saying these words is that at present one and only one king of France exists.

Strawson claims that these contentions of Russell are not in accord with our ordinary ways of talking about these matters. His contention is that Russell's theory fails as an account of our use of referring expressions in ordinary language, however adequate it may be for formal logic and mathematics. Consider the first of Russell's views mentioned above. Suppose someone were to say to us in a perfectly serious way, "The present king of France is wise." Would we say, "That's false"? Strawson contends that we would not. Rather, we would say that the speaker is under some misapprehension, that France is no longer a monarchy, or something of the kind. And if someone insisted that we make up our mind whether it is true or false, we would say that that question simply *does not arise* because there is no king of France. This, of course, is directly opposed to Russell's account, for according to his view every assertion of the form "The so-and-so is such-and-such" implies that the so-and-so exists. Hence, if the so-and-so does not exist, the assertion is false.

Strawson's view is that when we say, "The king of France is wise," we are *implying* (although not in the sense of logical entailment) that there is a king of France. That this sense of "implies" is not (as Russell maintains)

logical entailment can be seen as follows. When in response to the statement "The present king of France is wise" we say, "There is no king of France," ". . . we should certainly *not* say we were *contradicting* the statement that the king of France is wise. We are certainly not saying that it is false. We are, rather, giving a reason for saying that the question of whether it is true or false simply does not arise."

Strawson's views were later elaborated in his *Introduction to Logical Theory* (1952), where he introduces the word "presupposition" to explain his sense of "implies." The statement "The present king of France is wise" *presupposes* that there is one and only one king of France. This is explained as follows: If S is the presupposing statement and S' the statement presupposed, then "S presupposes S'" means "The truth of S' is a necessary condition of the truth or falsity of S." In other words, if there is no such thing as "the so-and-so," then the assertion "The so-and-so is such-and-such" is neither true nor false.

Russell's mistake was due, Strawson believes, to his failure to distinguish between sentences and the statements which are made by the use of these sentences on particular occasions and in particular circumstances. Thus, we must distinguish between the case when a man utters the sentence "The king of France is wise" when France is a monarchy, and the case of the man who says these same words today, when France is not a monarchy. Assuming that both men mean to make an assertion (are not play-acting or practicing elocution), the first man succeeds in making a true or false statement (depending upon whether the monarch is or is not wise), but the second man says nothing true or false at all, since the statement presupposed by his words is false. Yet both men have uttered exactly the same sentence.

Russell, Strawson supposes, concluded that because the sentence "The present king of France is wise" was not meaningless, any utterance of it must be either true or false. Again Russell's confusion of sentence and statement is at fault. Sentences have meaning, but they cannot be true or false. Rather, a sentence which is not meaningless can be used to make statements, some true and some false. Truth and falsity characterize statements, not sentences. And if the statement presupposed by a given statement is not true, then nothing true or false has been stated, although a significant sentence has been uttered.

Another point of criticism of Russell's theory which is common to many contemporary philosophers perhaps originates with Wittgenstein rather than with Strawson. This concerns Wittgenstein's dictum "Don't confuse the meaning of a name with the bearer of the name." Russell argued that if "the author of *Waverley*" was a name, then it would name something c, and hence "Scott is the author of *Waverley*" would mean "Scott is c." But this would follow only if it somehow followed that if "the author of *Waverley*" were a name for c, then it would mean the same thing as any other name for c, say "c." Russell of course did assume this latter because he thought that the meaning of a name was the bearer of that name. In that case, two names having the same bearer would have the same meaning, and Russell's argument would be valid.

Both Wittgenstein and Strawson have objected to this

identification of the meaning of a name with its bearer. Strawson has also objected to Wittgenstein's dictum because it seems to assume that although the bearer of a name is not its meaning, something else is. But, in fact, names do not in general have meanings at all. Strawson observes that if you do not know who George Washington is, you do not ask what the name "George Washington" means.

Bibliography

FREGE'S THEORY

Frege, Gottlob, "Über Sinn und Bedeutung." *Zeitschrift für Philosophie und philosophische Kritik,* Vol. 100 (1892). Translated by Max Black as "On Sense and Reference," in Peter Geach and Max Black, eds., *Translations from the Philosophical Writings of Gottlob Frege.* Oxford and New York, 1952.

RUSSELL'S THEORY

Russell, Bertrand, "On Denoting." *Mind* (1905). Reprinted in his *Logic and Knowledge.* London, 1956.
Russell, Bertrand, "The Philosophy of Logical Atomism." *Monist* (1918), especially Lecture 6. Reprinted in his *Logic and Knowledge,* Robert C. Marsh, ed. London, 1956.
Russell, Bertrand, "Descriptions," in *Introduction to Mathematical Philosophy.* London, 1919. Reprinted in Leonard Linsky, ed., *Semantics and the Philosophy of Language.* Urbana, Ill., 1952.
Russell, Bertrand, "Mr. Strawson on Referring." *Mind* (1957). Reprinted in his *My Philosophical Development.* London, 1959. Pp. 238–245.

STRAWSON'S THEORY

Sellars, W. F., "Presupposing." *Philosophical Review* (1954).
Strawson, P. F., "On Referring." *Mind* (1950). Reprinted in A. G. N. Flew, ed., *Essays in Conceptual Analysis.* London, 1956.
Strawson, P. F., *Introduction to Logical Theory.* London, 1952. Especially Ch. 6.
Strawson, P. F., "A Reply to Mr. Sellars." *Philosophical Review* (1954).

GENERAL DISCUSSIONS

Cartwright, R. L., "Negative Existentials." *Journal of Philosophy* (1960), Reprinted in C. E. Caton, ed., *Philosophy and Ordinary Language.* Urbana, Ill., 1963.
Fitch, F. B., "Some Logical Aspects of Reference and Existence." *Journal of Philosophy* (1960).
Linsky, Leonard, "Hesperus and Phosphorus." *Philosophical Review* (1959).
Linsky, Leonard, "Reference and Referents," in C. E. Caton, ed., *Philosophy and Ordinary Language.* Urbana, Ill., 1963.
Ryle, Gilbert, "Systematically Misleading Expressions," in A. G. N. Flew, ed., *Essays in Logic and Language,* 1st series. Oxford, 1950.
Ryle, Gilbert, "The Theory of Meaning," in C. A. Mace, ed., *British Philosophy in the Mid-Century.* London, 1957.
Wittgenstein, Ludwig, *Philosophical Investigations.* Oxford, 1953.

LEONARD LINSKY

REFORMATION. In the narrower and probably most common sense, Reformation is the name given to the spiritual crisis of the sixteenth century which resulted in the permanent division of the Western church. The birthdate of the Reformation is traditionally given as 1517, the year in which Luther posted his 95 Theses on the door of the Castle Church in Wittenberg; the termination of the period may be assigned to the 1550s, by which time an ecclesiastical stalemate between the Protestants and the Roman Catholics appeared unavoidable. Sometimes the Reformation is extended backward to include such early reform movements as Lollardy or forward to include the religious conflicts, lasting into the seventeenth century, that sought to resolve the Catholic–Protestant stalemate forcibly or to readjust the divisions between the various Protestant groups. Reformation describes the aspirations of the age rather than its achievements. The Protestants did not succeed in reforming the church but only in splitting it into rival groups, each of which claimed for itself the fulfillment of the old dream of reformation in head and members.

The age of reformation. The Protestant movement was not the only attempt to bring the dream into reality. It can, indeed, be correctly interpreted only in relation to other reform movements even if we determine not to include these under the same general descriptive label. The sixteenth century was the age of reformation (or of reformations, in the plural), not just of the Reformation, and this is a fact of some importance in assessing the impact of the spiritual crisis on Western intellectual history. We should distinguish four reform groups in the sixteenth century, each of which left its own distinctive mark on Western culture.

Humanistic reformers. The humanists were not merely (as Luther himself thought) forerunners who prepared the way for the Protestants. They developed a reform program of their own which did not lead to the formation of independent institutions but continued, even after the appearance of Luther, to exercise influence from within both of the two main confessional groups. The foremost humanistic reformer in northern Europe was Erasmus, who wished to purify the church by returning to its primitive sources—the New Testament and the writings of the Fathers. His "philosophy of Christ" minimized the dogmatic and the institutional and treated Christ mainly as a teacher of virtue and Christianity as an ethical affair not essentially different from the pagan philosophies. Although not less critical of ecclesiastical abuses than was Luther, Erasmus deplored any action which might disrupt the unity and peace of Christendom, and this was one of the reasons that he remained aloof from the Protestant Reformation.

Radical reformers. "Radical reformers" is a general term for a variety of groups and individuals who felt that the Protestant leaders had not gone far enough and that reform could not be brought about without abandoning the old idea of the state church (the *corpus Christianum*). Of these radical or left-wing reformers, the Anabaptists (Swiss Brethren, Hutterites, and Mennonites) were Biblical literalists who sought to establish voluntary associations of the regenerate on the New Testament pattern. The spiritualists (Andreas Carlstadt, Thomas Münzer, Sebastian Franck, Caspar Schwenckfeld), appealing to the Spirit who caused the Scriptures to be written, laid claim to immediate converse with God. The rationalists (notably the two Sozzini) read the Bible in the light of reason even when reason led them to deny Christ's full deity and atoning sacrifice. A few of the radicals (for example, the leaders of the Münster uprising in 1534) were revolutionaries who brought total destruction upon themselves; many, like Michael Servetus, were free spirits who founded no school, but the influence of others, despite brutal persecution by Roman Catholics and Protestants alike, still survives in some present-day denominations and sects.

Catholic reformers. The Roman Catholics rejected the Protestant reform as essentially a revolt against the church, and they sought renewal of the church by the twofold means of fostering a churchly piety and taking an official stand on the administrative and dogmatic demands of the "heretics." Two of the greatest landmarks of the Catholic reformation were the establishment of the Jesuit order under the leadership of Ignatius Loyola and the work of the Council of Trent (1545–1563). The council, not without political and theological difficulties, sought to repudiate Protestant errors on authority, justification, and the sacraments. Yet the Tridentine fathers opposed many of the practical abuses and even theological inadequacies which had first provoked the Protestant movement. Preoccupation with Protestant errors, together with the militant campaign of suppression which followed the council, make it not inappropriate to speak of the Catholic reformation as the Counter Reformation, though it was not merely this and had its roots in pre-Lutheran piety.

The Protestant Reformation. The Protestant leaders (the reformers in the narrower sense) were themselves not strictly a single group. Protestantism took three distinctive, though fundamentally related, forms.

Lutheranism, rooted in the religious struggles of Martin Luther and his revolt against the papacy, prevailed in most of Germany and was wholly victorious in the Scandinavian countries. It was the Lutheran princes and cities represented at the Imperial Diet of Speyer in 1529 who, by making their historic protest, gave the Lutheran movement its nickname Protestantism. The classic formulation of Lutheran belief is the Augsburg Confession of 1530.

The so-called Reformed churches grew up first in Switzerland (under Zwingli and Calvin); won majorities in Scotland, Holland, and parts of Germany; and maintained strong pockets of influence in France, England (where they were called Presbyterians), and eastern Europe. From their beginning they were a less homogeneous group than the Lutherans and produced a variety of national confessions rather than a single statement comparable to the Lutheran Augsburg Confession. Nevertheless, the Lutheran interpretation of the Gospel exercised a decisive influence over the Reformed confessions, and though Zwingli sought to affirm his relative independence from the Germans, Calvin was one of Luther's stanchest admirers.

The Anglican reformation proceeded slowly, largely for political reasons. The repudiation of papal authority by Henry VIII, though not intended to alter Catholic doctrine, left the door open to Protestant reform in the reign of his son Edward VI, and the Romanizing reaction under Mary only temporarily reversed the trend. The 39 Articles of Religion (Latin 1563, English 1571), adopted under Elizabeth I as the official doctrinal standard of the reformed Church of England, are largely a compilation of Continental Protestant ideas. Parts of the Lutheran confessions of Augsburg and Württemberg are reproduced verbatim, and the articles on predestination and the Eucharist are clearly indebted to Reformed (Calvinistic) theology.

Essential Protestant doctrines. In all three of its branches the Protestant Reformation was inextricably bound up with social and political factors, so that its triumph was always, in the final analysis, contingent on governmental support. Nevertheless, it was essentially a religious movement and its theological ideas have left their mark on European intellectual history—sometimes, however, because they have been misinterpreted or interpreted too one-sidedly. Three beliefs are particularly associated with the Protestant movement: the authority of the Word, justification by faith alone, and the priesthood of all believers. These beliefs have frequently been explained as the advent of individualism in the religious sphere, as though the intention were to regard the individual as his own priest with immediate access to God, to leave him in solitude with his conscience and his Bible, or to make each man his own pope in the interpretation of Scripture. Fundamentally, however, the original Protestant reformers were suspicious of "immediate access to God," which they associated with the spiritualists, and they sought, rather, to replace the medieval notion of institutional means with a concept of the Christian fellowship as the locus of God's Word. The Word of God was understood chiefly as an effective proclamation of the Gospel, based on the Scriptures, which evokes faith and sustains a fellowship of believers each of whom is priest to his brothers. The heart of this proclamation is the promise of free forgiveness (justification) through Christ, which needs only to be accepted by the faith that is awakened through the proclamation itself. We may perhaps add a fourth idea of great religious and even social consequence: vocation—that the good works required of the justified man are not so much special religious acts as the thankful performance of his calling for the good of his neighbor. These four ideas were held in common by all three Protestant groups, and their formulation may be traced to Luther himself. Characteristic differences among the groups also developed; for example, the Reformed differed from the Lutherans, as is well known, on the manner in which the benefits of Christ's Passion are received in the Eucharist.

The Reformation and Western thought. The Reformation's role in the making of the modern mind is a complex question which has ramifications in areas as diverse as social, economic, political, and artistic history as well as in the history of philosophy and science. Sometimes the Reformation has been represented as the great watershed between the medieval and modern worlds. This is, perhaps, partly because the individualism of Reformation thought has been overestimated and partly because certain isolated events in Luther's life—the burning of the papal bull, the defiant stand before the Diet at Worms—have deeply impressed themselves on the German imagination. In some respects, however, the Reformation can be better understood as a late phase of medieval history than as an early stirring of the modern mind. The fundamental concerns of Luther were medieval, and it may be argued that in giving fresh vitality to religious questions he merely postponed for a while the triumph of Renaissance secularism. Moreover, though the Protestant reformers spoke ideally of a communion of saints (believers), in practice they refused to abandon the medieval concept of a Christian society (that is, an authoritarian, church-dominated society). Unquestionably, the very existence of the Protestant churches alongside the Roman Catholic church weakened the authoritarian ideal. But this was an accidental product of the Reformation—a consequence, indeed, of its failure rather than of its cherished principles. It was the humanistic reformers, not the Protestants, who undermined the dogmatic conception of religion, and it was the radicals who broke with the old alliance between the spiritual and secular arms of the *corpus Christianum*. Similarly, if, as has been argued, Calvinistic ideas had revolutionary economic and political consequences, this was hardly the reformer's intention. On the other hand, the Reformation did, by its very nature, make a powerful impact on literature and music, education and scholarship; even its influence on the visual arts was not always uncreative.

Reformation and science. The chief contribution of the Reformation to the history of Western philosophy was no doubt the accidental one of helping philosophy toward autonomy by weakening ecclesiastical domination. Attempts to establish the influence of Lutheran ideas on some of the German philosophers are often interesting but seldom of very great importance and sometimes farfetched. It might have been a service for philosophy, as it was for theology, that Luther shattered the medieval synthesis of Christianity and Aristotelianism, but the reformer's immediate successors reinstated the Greek philosopher, and the Christian faith was perilously entangled in an obsolete cosmology. (Ironically, Melanchthon repudiated Copernican astronomy on the ground that it represented merely a revival of outmoded theories which had already been rejected in the ancient world.)

Luther himself prepared the way for the conflict of theology and the modern world view by refuting a scientific theory on theological grounds—if, indeed, the notorious passage from the *Table Talk*, "Joshua commanded the sun, not the earth, to stand still," is authentic. Yet an open clash of science and religion was not unavoidable until post-Reformation theologians in the age of Protestant scholasticism had reaffirmed the old partnership with Aristotelianism and had come to think of the Scriptures as containing a "Biblical science" which could compete with Copernican science. Luther and Calvin themselves did not accept the Ptolemaic cosmology in defiance of scientific evidence since the weight of the evidence during their lifetimes was still against Copernicus. In principle, they were not suspicious of scientific progress. On the contrary, Luther welcomed the stirring of the new science, in which he saw a partial recovery of Adam's lost dominion over nature, and Calvin envied the astronomer's closeness to the mind of the Maker. They were both interested in the Bible not as an encyclopedia of supernaturally communicated information but as the vehicle of Christ's presence to his church in the Gospel proclamation.

Luther had grasped clearly that theological and scientific interest in nature are two distinct things. For example, from the religious viewpoint the light of the moon was for

him a symbol of divine care, but he recognized that the astronomer's concern was to show how the moon's light was borrowed from the sun. Similarly, Calvin argued that Biblical observations on the heavenly bodies, such as those in Genesis and the Nineteenth Psalm, are not scientific statements but homely forms of speech accommodated to the unlearned. Luther understood even better than Calvin that theology's heaven is not the same as the astronomical heavens; hence, the celebrated *Dextera Dei est ubique* ("God's right hand is everywhere"). Elementary though they may seem today, such concessions and insights, had they not been neglected or expressly repudiated by Protestant orthodoxy, could have saved the Reformation churches from their warfare with science. Conversely, they might have prevented skeptics from drawing overhasty theological conclusions from natural science.

(See Reformation in Index for articles on Reformation figures and movements.)

Bibliography

Recent studies of the Reformation include Roland H. Bainton, *The Reformation of the Sixteenth Century* (Boston, 1952); Harold J. Grimm, *The Reformation Era* (New York, 1954); G. R. Elton, ed., *The New Cambridge Modern History*, Vol. II, *The Reformation 1520–1559* (Cambridge, 1958); Émile G. Léonard, *Histoire générale du protestantisme*, Vol. I, *La Réformation* (Paris, 1961); H. A. Enno van Gelder, *The Two Reformations in the 16th Century: A Study of the Religious Aspects and Consequences of Renaissance and Humanism* (The Hague, 1961); George Huntston Williams, *The Radical Reformation* (Philadelphia, 1962); and H. Daniel-Rops, *The Catholic Reformation*, translated by John Warrington (London and New York, 1962).

The Augsburg Confession, the 39 Articles, and a representative Reformed confession will be found in B. A. Gerrish, ed., *The Faith of Christendom: A Source Book of Creeds and Confessions* (New York, 1963). For the religious ideas of the reformers there are excellent bibliographies in the studies by Grimm and Léonard.

On the special question of the Reformation in relation to Western culture and thought, see Heinrich Bornkamm, *Luther's World of Thought*, translated by Martin H. Bertram (St. Louis, 1958); John Dillenberger, *Protestant Thought and Natural Science: An Historical Interpretation* (New York, 1960); Karl Holl, *The Cultural Significance of the Reformation*, translated by Karl Hertz and Barbara Hertz and John H. Lichtblau (New York, 1959); Jaroslav Pelikan, *From Luther to Kierkegaard: A Study in the History of Theology* (St. Louis, Mo., 1950); and Ernst Troeltsch, *Protestantism and Progress: A Historical Study of the Relation of Protestantism to the Modern World*, translated by W. Montgomery (London 1912).

B. A. GERRISH

RÉGIS, PIERRE-SYLVAIN (1632–1707), French Cartesian philosopher and scientist, was a student of the physicist Jacques Rohault. Like Rohault, Régis expounded Cartesianism in lectures and in the *Journal des savants*. In 1680 Harlay, the archbishop of Paris, conveyed to Régis the desire of Louis XIV that no more public lectures be given; the monarch feared that the uproar over the Cartesian explanation of transubstantiation would get out of hand. Régis continued to give private lessons, and by 1699 the conflict over Cartesianism had subsided enough for him to be admitted to the Académie des Sciences, along with Malebranche.

Régis's system is based upon 14 self-evident metaphysical principles derived from the *cogito*. Ontologically, these principles state that whatever exists is either a substance or a modification of a substance and that modifications cannot belong to nothing. Epistemologically, they state that external things are known only by way of ideas. The central principle is a causal one which asserts that all effects presuppose causes which must have as much or more perfection than do the effects. Modifications seen as effects are thus ultimately caused by a substance, and ideas which are effects can be asserted to represent all the perfections of their causes. Régis's answer to the traditional question "How can Cartesian mind know or causally interact with Cartesian matter, which is essentially unlike it?" was to insist that God can make such things be, even though man does not understand how.

Régis said his metaphysics, logic (which follows Arnauld's), and ethics (based on self-interest) are certain and complete. Physical explanations are also based on self-evident principles but are only probable, because within his physics several are deducible for each event; the simplest is the most probable. Complete knowledge of the deductive system would give certainty in physics. Régis opposed "arbitrary hypotheses," explanations not deducible from self-evident principles within a system.

The most distinctive feature of Régis's Cartesianism is his doctrine concerning man as compound substance. Man, he explained, is an accidental union of spirit and body; only in union is a spirit a soul. Although operations of the body can be understood by reason, consequences of union can be accepted only on faith. Because of the union, the soul always has the idea of extension. Particular brain movements always give rise to particular sensations and ideas of objects affecting the brain. All the soul's ideas, even of God, depend upon brain movements. Pleasure and pain lead men to love and pursue, or to hate and flee, objects of ideas for self-preservation. But after the separation of spirit and body in death, spirit no longer has the idea of extension, no imagination or memory of, or power over, the material world. Spirit not united with body can know and love only itself and God.

Régis was known as a polemicist, and his criticisms are acute. He pointed out that Pierre-Daniel Huet does not distinguish methodological doubt from real doubt. Malebranche's theory of seeing all things in God was shown to require an impossible union of man with God. Jean Du Hamel was accused of failing to see that nonresembling ideas make their objects known. Against Spinoza, Régis insisted that the "great atheist" fails to distinguish existing in itself from existing by itself and fails to see that God is not just an ordinary substance.

Reason and faith, Régis insisted in his final work, do not conflict. Reason is infallible in the order of nature; faith, in the order of grace. Events in one order cannot be explained with principles of the other. Thus Régis himself offered no physical explanation of transubstantiation—as did other Cartesians and the scholastic physicists—for he thought it was an event not in the order of nature but in the order of grace.

Works by Régis

Système de philosophie, contenant la logique, la métaphysique, la physique, et la morale. Paris, 1690.

Réponse au livre qui a pour titre P. Danielis Huetii, . . . Censure Philosophiae Cartesianae. . . . Paris, 1691.

Réponse aux réflexiones critiques de M. Du Hamel . . . . Paris, 1692.

L'Usage de la raison et de la foy, ou l'accord de la foy et de la raison. Paris, 1704.

Works on Régis

Bouillier, F., *Histoire de la philosophie cartésienne.* Paris, 1854.
Damiron, J. P., *Essai sur l'histoire de la philosophie en France au XVIIe siècle.* Paris, 1846.
Mouy, P., *Le Développement de la physique cartésienne 1646–1712.* Paris, 1934.
Watson, R. A., *The Downfall of Cartesianism, 1673–1712.* The Hague, 1966.

RICHARD A. WATSON

REHMKE, JOHANNES (1848–1930), German epistemologist, ontologist, and ethical philosopher. He was born at Elmshorn in Schleswig-Holstein. Rehmke studied evangelical theology and philosophy at Kiel and Zurich from 1867 to 1871, receiving his doctorate in philosophy at Zurich in 1873. After some years as a high school teacher at St. Gallen, he was appointed unsalaried lecturer in philosophy at the University of Berlin in 1884. The following year he became professor of philosophy at the University of Greifswald, where he taught until 1921.

Theory of knowledge. Rehmke did not assume the existence of two worlds: a world, only indirectly knowable, of transsubjective objects, and an immediately knowable world, with intrasubjective perceptions and the like as contents. Rather, he asserted the existence of directly knowable real objects. This epistemological monism was a consequence of his ontological dualism of two essentially different kinds of being. Physical (material) beings are spatially extended and occupy a place; mental (immaterial) beings are not extended and have no place.

The nonspatial, placeless character of consciousness conflicts with the uncritical application to the subject of such concepts as "in" and "external," as exemplified in such terms as "intrasubjective" and "transsubjective" —in other words, "immanent" and "transcendent," or "content of consciousness" and "external object." Not only does consciousness not involve the having of a content; it does not involve any kind of having by means of a relation, in any event one that presupposes the existence of at least two realities separated from one another. On the contrary, knowing without any relation between diverse things is possible from the outset, as can be seen in self-consciousness. In self-consciousness only one thing is given, the particular knowing consciousness as knowing itself and as being known by itself. Thus, Rehmke's proposition "Knowing is having without a relation" expresses the immediacy of all knowledge, including knowledge of the so-called external world, the world of objects outside the body.

In his *Logik oder Philosophie als Wissenslehre* (Leipzig, 1918), Rehmke sought to demonstrate the importance of the general or universal for the movement of knowledge toward clarity. In accord with his proof of the immediacy of cognition, he rejected as false the notion that thinking is an internal, that is, intramental, activity and even rejected the notion of thought activity because the purported activity never produces a change in objects. Thinking is not a "doing" but a "finding." If, for example, someone makes the judgment "A boiled crayfish is red," this observation signifies that he as thinker finds anew in the object the red known before. What is thus discovered in the object is never something single, an individual being, but something repeated, a universal.

Because the universal forms part of each particular object, it is something objective. If red is found in the crayfish, the logical subject of the judgment is not simply "(boiled) crayfish," but "red boiled crayfish." Consequently, every judgment, with respect to the universal discovered in the particular object, is logically analytic. Grammatically, with regard to the joining of the linguistic signs into a sentence, it is synthetic.

In its function as predicate of a judgment, an objective universal is called a concept. Every concept is thus a universal. Because of its objectivity, the universal as concept, despite its relation to the thinking subject, cannot be merely subjective. It is equally erroneous to confuse or to equate the concept, which is always bound up with a particular word, with that word, that is, with the phonic structure as linguistic sign.

The objectivity of the universal as a possible concept reveals the error in the phrase "concept formation." A concept (for example, "tree") is not first constructed by comparing several objects (for example, pines, beeches, and alders) by means of an "internal activity" of thought. The concept is presupposed in the very selection of objects of the same kind. Concept formation is really conceptual clarification, the determination of which characteristics in union constitute a concept already given. Clarity is the guiding notion in Rehmke's logic. He claimed that, in any deepening of knowledge, the universal as logical predicate helps consciousness to obtain clarity, and ultimately unquestionable clarity.

Rehmke's conception of logic, that is, philosophy as theory of knowledge, is linked with his notion of philosophy as fundamental science, expressed in his *Philosophie als Grundwissenschaft* (Frankfurt, 1910). Both theory of knowledge and fundamental science are genuine sciences, directed toward that which is simply given, that is, toward objects regardless of their being real or unreal. They are also in equal measure philosophy because they deal with the totality of the given, in contrast with the particular sciences, each of which deals with only a particular section of the world. Theory of knowledge deals with the given as that which is thought (known); fundamental science deals with it in regard to its most universal character. But while logic presupposes the concept "universal," and each special science presupposes its own fundamental concepts, the task of philosophy as fundamental science is to elucidate without prejudice precisely the basic "that which is most universal."

The traditional ontology. Theory of knowledge is not a fundamental science. Historically, it arose from an epistemological dualism, and as a consequence its form is faulty. In any case, it must presuppose the basic distinction between knower and other. Rehmke's painstaking ontological studies in *Philosophie als Grundwissenschaft* of the manifold "most universal" embrace five paired notions: (1) matter and consciousness, (2) the universal and the unique, (3) unity and simplicity, (4) the changeable and the unchangeable, (5) the real and the unreal. For Rehmke, of

course, the first pair was primary. Beyond the merely negative description—immaterial, nonspatial, and placeless—the essence of the mental is completely determined by the concept of consciousness, or knowledge. Rehmke therefore opposed both materialism and idealism (spiritualism), as well as Spinozism.

Everything without exception proves to be either a unique thing (something that occurs only once, such as a unique tree) or a universal (something that is repeated, such as green or "treeness"). It follows that the unique and the universal do not exist without each other; indeed, objectively the universal belongs to the unique. Rehmke classified the unique into individuals (for example, individual trees) and units of individuals. He divided the latter into operational units (for example, an auto with a trailer) and living units (for example, a state). The universal is either a determination (such as angularity) or a relation (such as similarity). Rehmke attached great value to his recognition that many seemingly ontological concepts, such as space, time, being, and value, are merely relational ones.

In connection with the third of his five pairs, unity and simplicity, Rehmke distinguished between individuals that are composed of individuals (and hence are ephemeral, passing) and individuals that are absolutely simple (and hence are everlasting). Examples of the latter are elementary particles and consciousness. Denying the theory of substance, he held that the individual is a union of its determinations (a body, for instance, is a union of size, shape, and location). He also analyzed each specific determination into determination as such (for instance, shape as such) and particularity.

Rehmke equated the fourth relationship, the changeable and the unchangeable, with the distinction between individual and universal. In this context he pointed out that the concept of change refers only to exchange of individual characteristics, with the determination as such (for instance, the shape as such) remaining the same.

Rehmke treated in detail the relationship between the real and the unreal. He defined the real as consisting in relationship of action. This enabled him to do justice to such properties of things as sweetness, which are often dismissed as merely subjective.

Psychology and ethics. In his *Lehrbuch der Allgemeinen Psychologie* (Frankfurt, 1894), Rehmke stressed that human consciousness (mind) is a simple, immaterial individual being, in a constant unity of action with an essentially different body. Thus, man is not a "double-beinged" individual. There are four general characteristics of consciousness: (1) determination of objects, each one directly perceived or imagined, even though the perception is mediated by the sense organs; (2) states (conditions), for example, delight or listlessness; (3) thought—either distinguishing (being aware of the distinct) or uniting (awareness of unity); (4) the subject, the determination of which establishes at the same time the unity of the ego. These determinations are not to be construed as mental activities.

Because of its intermittent character, volition, despite its relations with the above determinations, is not one of them. Rehmke's analysis of volition aided him in his solution of the problem of free will. He separated the problem into four parts, each of which is answerable: (1) Is an act of the will prevented or not? (2) Is the volition random or conditioned? (3) Is there a genuine possibility of choice, or is the will constrained? (4) Is the volition freely self-determined or not?

Rehmke's theory of the will constitutes the background for his ethics. He distinguished five forms of ethics—four false and one genuine. The ethics of shrewdness has to do with men "for themselves." The ethics of the unity of control expresses duty as an "ought." The ethics of the unity of life expresses duty as a "must" and comprises the ethics of society (in which unity as "being with one another" is a means to a selfish end) and the ethics of community (in which unity as "being for one another" is an end in itself). Finally, separating the merely social from the moral proper is the ethics of selfless love of one person as such "for another," arising from his knowledge of himself as at one with the other.

Additional Works by Rehmke

Unsere Gewissheit von der Aussenwelt ("Our Certainty About the External World"). Heilbronn, 1892.
Grundlegung der Ethik als Wissenschaft ("Foundations of Ethics as a Science"). Leipzig, 1925.
Die Willensfreiheit ("The Freedom of the Will"). Leipzig, 1925.
Gesammelte philosophische Aufsätze ("Collected Philosophical Essays"), K. Gassen, ed. Erfurt, 1928.
"Selbstdarstellung," in Raymund Schmidt, ed., *Die Philosophie der Gegenwart in Selbstdarstellung*, 7 vols. Leipzig, 1921–1929. Vol. I, pp. 177–200.
For a full bibliography see *Grundwissenschaft. Philosophische Zeitschrift der Johannes-Rehmke-Gesellschaft*, Vol. 1 (1919), 72–88, and Vol. 10 (1931), 36–44.

Works on Rehmke

Heyde, J. E., *Grundwissenschaftliche Philosophie*. Leipzig, 1924.
Heyde, J. E., "Johannes Rehmke." *Grundwissenschaft. Philosophische Zeitschrift der Johannes-Rehmke-Gesellschaft*, Vol. 10 (1931), 1–35.
Heyde, J. E., "Johannes Rehmke." *Zeitschrift für philosophische Forschung*, Vol. 2 (1947), 603–606.
Heyde, J. E., "Johannes Rehmke 1848–1930." *Philosophische Studien*, Vol. 2 (1951), 260–271.
"Johannes Rehmke," in F. Schneider, ed., *Grundriss der Geschichte der Philosophie*. Bonn. 1959. Pp. 319–329.

JOH'S ERICH HEYDE
Translated by *Albert E. Blumberg*

REICH, WILHELM (1897–1957), Austrian psychiatrist and social critic. After serving in the Austrian army during World War I, Reich became a medical student. He obtained his M.D. from the University of Vienna in 1922 and worked for some time as assistant to Julius Wagner-Jauregg at the latter's psychiatric clinic. Even before his graduation Reich began practice as a psychoanalyst and soon came to occupy an influential position in the psychoanalytic movement. From 1924 to 1930 he conducted what came to be known as the Vienna Seminar for Psychoanalytic Therapy, the first organized attempt to devise a systematic and effective analytic technique.

Reich also founded and directed sex hygiene clinics among the industrial workers of Vienna and later, on a much larger scale, in Berlin and other German cities. During his years in Germany, Reich was a member of the

Communist party, and he attempted to integrate his work as a sex counselor within the broader revolutionary movement. Hitler's assumption of power forced Reich to flee to Denmark. His activities had always been viewed with suspicion by the leaders of the Communist party, and Reich was finally expelled from the party after the publication of *Die Massenpsychologie des Faschismus* (Copenhagen, 1933), in which he repudiated the official communist theory about the nature of fascism and the factors leading to its victory in Germany. Also, by 1933 Reich's psychiatric views were so far removed from those of orthodox psychoanalysis that the Internationaler Psychoanalytischer Verlag handled and printed but did not "publish" (that is, refused its imprint to) the first edition of Reich's *Charakteranalyse*. The break with the psychoanalytic organization became official at the Lucerne conference of the International Psychoanalytic Association in 1934.

Attacks by orthodox psychiatrists made it necessary for Reich to leave Denmark for Sweden, but in Sweden too there was official hostility and suspicion. Reich therefore gladly accepted an invitation by the Norwegian psychologist and philosopher Harald Schjelderup to teach at the University of Oslo, where he also hoped to undertake various physiological experiments. Reich worked in Norway from 1934 to 1939. Among his students and patients at that time were the English educational reformer A. S. Neill, the American psychiatrist and pioneer in psychosomatic research T. B. Wolfe, and leading figures in Norwegian psychiatry, including Nic Hoel (Waal), Ola Raknes, and Odd Havrevold. The distinguished Norwegian novelist Sigurd Hoel was also closely associated with Reich at this time—in fact, he succeeded Reich as editor of the journal *Zeitschrift für politische Psychologie und Sexualökonomie*. In 1937 Reich became the victim of a campaign in sections of the Norwegian press. Although he had a number of influential defenders and the government renewed his permit to stay in the country, he decided to move to New York City, where he resumed his psychiatric practice and trained numerous psychiatrists in the new technique which he had worked out during his stay in Scandinavia. Reich also lectured at the New School for Social Research from 1939 to 1941.

In the last years of his life Reich showed little interest in psychiatry, devoting all his energies to what he took to be his great discoveries in physics. In 1956 he was sentenced to two years' imprisonment for disobeying a government injunction. He died in Lewisburg Penitentiary in 1957. A brief account of the main events leading to Reich's imprisonment will be found in the last section of the present article.

It will be convenient to distinguish three phases in Reich's career: (1) his work within the psychoanalytic movement, marked, however, by some significant departures from orthodox psychoanalysis—the rejection of symptom analysis in favor of what Reich called "character analysis," the orgasm theory, and the attempt to understand the social function of sexual repression and neurosis: (2) Reich's efforts to relate neurotic attitudes to their somatic foundation and the development of what he called "character-analytic vegetotherapy"—a technique which constituted a drastic departure from all that preceded it;

and (3) his theories about orgone energy—Reich's claim to have discovered a form of energy which is found in the atmosphere and also in the living organism and which can be concentrated in various ways, including the "orgone accumulator." What Reich claimed during the third period is of no philosophical interest. If any of the assertions in question were true, they would be of great scientific interest; but, in fact, most professional physicists who have heard of the orgone theory have dismissed it as nonsense. In fairness to Reich it should be added that a really unbiased investigation of his physical theories remains to be undertaken.

We shall here be exclusively concerned with certain of the ideas advanced by Reich during the first two periods. Of interest to philosophers are Reich's views concerning the origin of religious and metaphysical needs, the relation between the individual and society and the possibility of social progress, and, above all, the implications of his psychiatry for certain aspects of the mind–body problem. It is regrettable that, partly because Reich's books and articles were not easily accessible and partly because the wild claims of his last years created widespread distrust of his entire work, the remarkable achievements of his second phase are relatively little-known. To those who are put off by the recent metaphysical and pro-religious trends in psychiatry, as exhibited in the vogue of existentialist psychoanalysis and in the metapsychological speculations of Jung and various Freudian analysts, Reich's concentration on the somatic basis of neurotic disturbances and the sexual problems and longings of human beings will come as a pleasant and refreshing change.

THERAPEUTIC INNOVATIONS

The philosophically most interesting part of Reich's work is unquestionably what he called "the breakthrough into the vegetative realm," that is, his attempt to determine the physiological basis of neurotic phenomena. However, first we should briefly describe Reich's earlier psychiatric work. In the early 1920s Freudian psychiatrists practiced what in retrospect came to be known as "symptom analysis." Neurotic symptoms were regarded as foreign bodies in an otherwise psychologically healthy organism; they are expressions of a repressed infantile drive that has reappeared in a disguised form. The task of therapy is to eliminate the repression: the symptom is removed by bringing the repressed part of the personality into harmony with the rest of the ego. By his own account, Reich soon became dissatisfied with this approach. The traumatic experiences leading to repression and the repressed drives were to be elucidated by means of free association and dream interpretation, but in fact only very few patients were capable of giving their associations free rein. Furthermore, Reich was critical of the superficial criteria of "cure" current at that time. Patients were considered "cured" upon the disappearance or alleviation of the symptom of which they had complained. However, Reich believed that the elimination of symptoms is quite compatible with the continuation of a character disturbance. Also, he questioned the existence of "monosymptomatic neuroses"—neuroses with only one serious symptom. "There are no neurotic symptoms," he later observed, "without a disturbance of the

total character. Neurotic symptoms are, as it were, nothing but peaks of a mountain chain representing the neurotic character" (*The Function of the Orgasm*, p. 16). It was Reich's contention that, unless the characterological basis of a symptom has been eliminated, it or some equally troublesome symptom is likely to reappear.

On the few occasions on which either Reich or his associates at the Vienna Seminar appeared to achieve impressive and lasting improvements, this was invariably the result of the release of powerful dammed-up emotions like rage and hatred. Some years earlier, while working in Wagner-Jauregg's clinic, Reich had been struck by a catatonic who suddenly abandoned his stupor. "It was one great discharge of rage and aggression," Reich writes. "After the seizure had subsided he was clear and accessible. He assured me that his explosion had been a pleasurable experience, a state of happiness. He did not remember the previous stuporous phase. . . . It was very impressive, and could not be explained on the basis of the psychoanalytic theory of catatonia" (*ibid.*, pp. 43–44). Neurotics, too, showed noticeable improvement only when, instead of merely achieving an intellectual recognition of a repression, the impulse or emotion in question could actually be experienced. Such "liberations" were, however, infrequent and, what is more, they occurred more or less accidentally. An effective therapy would have to bring them about in a controlled fashion.

The "character armor." Something should be said at this stage about Reich's concept of the "character armor" that came to play a central role in the technique of character analysis with which he gradually replaced the technique of symptom analysis. This concept was originally introduced in connection with certain cases of compulsion neurosis. Freud had shown that compulsion symptoms always bind anxiety. If such a symptom is disturbed, the anxiety frequently appears. It does not, however, always appear—anxiety cannot usually be released in this way either in compulsion neuroses of long standing or in cases of chronic depression. Such patients appeared quite inaccessible. "Emotionally blocked compulsive characters gave associations in great numbers freely, but there never was a trace of affect. All therapeutic efforts bounced back, as it were, from a thick, hard wall" (*ibid.*, p. 114). These patients were "armored" against any attack. Over the years they had developed a set of attitudes whose function was to protect the individual against external injury (such as being hurt or rejected by other human beings) and to protect him against feeling his own repressed emotions, especially (though not exclusively) various kinds of destructiveness. Reich introduced the term "character armor" to refer to the totality of the typical or chronic attitudes of this kind characterizing a given individual. It is, writes Reich, "as if the affective personality put on an armor, a rigid shell on which the knocks from the outer world as well as the inner demands rebound. This armor makes the individual less sensitive to unpleasure, but it also reduces his libidinal and aggressive motility and, with that, his capacity for pleasure and achievement" (*Character Analysis*, p. 310). Patients who do not suffer from a severe compulsion neurosis (and indeed most people growing up in a repressive environment) also have a character armor, but in their cases it can usually be attacked or broken down more easily.

The technique used to attack the character armor emphasizes the so-called "negative transference." According to Reich, every patient has a deep mistrust of the treatment and feels strong hostility to the psychiatrist. Although patients wish to be cured, they *also* resent any attempt to disturb their "neurotic equilibrium." It is tempting for the analyst to shy away from these negative reactions, since it takes a great deal of strength and composure to bear the often furious hatred that is released when the armor begins to "crack." Nevertheless, it is precisely this negative reaction which can and must be used as the foundation of the treatment. The patient must feel free to criticize the analyst, and any attitudes which mask his hostility have to be broken down. Reference to the case of a "passive-feminine young man with hysterical symptoms" may give some idea of what this technique is like. The patient was excessively polite and, because of his fears, extremely sly. He always yielded and produced abundant material, but without any inner conviction. "Instead of discussing this material," Reich reports,

I only kept pointing out his politeness as a defense against me and any really affective insight. As time went on, his hidden aggression appeared increasingly in his dreams. As the politeness decreased, he became offensive. In other words, *the politeness had been warding off the hatred.* I let the hatred come out fully by destroying every defense mechanism against it. The hatred up to that time had been unconscious. Hatred and politeness were antitheses, and at the same time the over-politeness was a disguised manifestation of hatred. (*The Function of the Orgasm,* p. 117)

If in this way repressed emotions are released and the patient actually experiences them, it is unnecessary to persuade him that he "really," "unconsciously" feels this or that. "The patient no longer talked about his hatred, he felt it; he could not escape it as long as his armor was being correctly taken apart" (*ibid.,* p. 146).

The armor, according to Reich, varies from patient to patient, depending on his individual history, and the technique of destroying it has to be fitted to the individual case. The armor may be viewed as consisting of several layers. These layers, in Reich's words, "may be compared to geological or archaeological strata which, similarly, are solidified history. A conflict which has been active at a certain period of life always leaves its trace in the character, in the form of a rigidity" (*ibid.,* pp. 121–122). The neurosis of each patient has a specific structure which corresponds to its historical development, but in reverse order: "that which had been repressed latest in childhood was found to lie nearest the surface" (*ibid.,* p. 121).

Anger and hate are not the only emotions bound by the character armor. Although destructiveness has to be emphasized and liberated in the early stages of the treatment, eventually genuine love and tenderness which had to be suppressed will also be released. The destructiveness, in the last resort, is "nothing but anger about frustration in general and denial of sexual gratification in particular"

(*ibid.,* p. 124). Destructive tendencies are most frequently "reactions to disappointment in love or to loss of love" (*ibid.*). An organism which has been freed of its dammed-up destructiveness becomes once again capable of love. Reich referred to persons who are unarmored and who possess the capacity for love in the fullest sense as "genital characters"; and the goal of therapy is to change the patient's neurotic character into a genital structure. According to Reich, the "energy" which nourishes neurotic symptoms and various destructive attitudes can be adequately discharged only in fully satisfactory sexual intercourse. A person with a genital character, unlike the neurotic, possesses "orgastic potency." This Reich defined as "the capacity for surrender to the flow of energy in the orgasm without any inhibitions; the capacity for complete discharge of all dammed-up sexual excitation through involuntary pleasurable contractions . . . free of anxiety and unpleasure and unaccompanied by phantasies. . ." (*The Function of the Orgasm,* p. 79).

An individual with a genital character has undisturbed contact with his own drives and with his environment and, as a consequence, he has no need for any of the endless variety of substitute contacts and substitute gratifications of the neurotic individual. He, too, may not succeed in achieving a happy existence, since this depends on a great many factors, not all of which are within his control, but he will at least not be hampered in his struggle for happiness by irrational and destructive emotions or by excessive respect for the institutions of a life-denying society. Reich vigorously repudiated the suggestion that, either in his therapy or in his social philosophy, his goal was a world "containing nothing but pleasure." The function of the armor, he observed, is to protect against pain, and in breaking it down, Reich's therapy aimed at re-establishing the capacity to feel pain as well as pleasure. "Pleasure and *joie de vivre* are inconceivable without fight, without painful experiences and without unpleasurable struggling with oneself" (*ibid.,* p. 173). The goal is not a positive "hedonic balance" which, for all one can prove to the contrary, might be more effectively achieved by a life of monasticism but "full vitality in all possible situations of life." The capacity to take happiness and to give love goes hand in hand with "the capacity of tolerating unpleasure and pain without fleeing disillusioned into a state of rigidity" (*ibid.*).

Repressions and chronic muscular rigidities. Reich was led to his study of what he calls the "physiological anchoring" of neurotic conflicts and traumatic experiences partly as a result of his fundamentally materialistic orientation and partly because of the special attention paid in his technique of character analysis to the *manner* in which patients talked and acted. It is a mistake, he said, to regard rage and love (or any other emotion) as events "in the mind." They *are* physiological processes, and if an emotion is repressed, there must be some physiological mechanism by whose means the energy in question is "bound." Furthermore, Reich was convinced that if an adult's neurotic character attitude is the result of childhood experiences, this can be so only if the person's organism has in some way been chronically altered. The employment of "theoretical" terms like "Id" and "unconscious" can easily lead to pseudo-explanations in this context. To say, for example, that a repressed childhood conflict exerts its influence "from the unconscious" may call attention to a suspected causal relation between the childhood experience and the present difficulties of the individual, but beyond that it simply amounts to admitting that one does not know how the influence in question is exerted. On occasions, it is true, Freud himself said as much and expressed his hope that some day explanations in terms of unconscious conflicts would be given a physiological meaning. At other times, however, Freud treated his theoretical terms as if they designated real and eternally inaccessible entities; and many of Freud's followers, according to Reich, became metaphysicians whose theorizing was euphemistically labeled "metapsychology."

Perhaps of greater influence than these general reflections was Reich's interest in the "how" of the patient's communications. The infantile structure, Reich observes in one place, is "conserved" in *what* an individual does as well as in the *way* in which he acts, talks, and thinks (*Character Analysis*, p. 188). Elsewhere Reich explains that he made himself independent of the so-called fundamental psychoanalytic rule ("to say everything that comes to mind"), since it was impracticable with most patients, and that instead he took as "point of attack not only what the patient said, but *everything* he presented, particularly the *manner* of his communications or of his silence. Patients who kept silent were also communicating, were expressing something that gradually could be understood and handled" (*The Function of the Orgasm*, p. 145). It became increasingly evident to him, Reich adds, that "the *form* of behavior and communications, was much more essential than what the patient related. Words can lie. *The mode of expression never lies*" (*ibid.*).

Special attention to the "how" of a patient's behavior very naturally led to close observation of the changes in his organism during and after the release of repressed emotions. Reich's earlier clinical reports already contained remarks about the awkwardness and the rigid movements of certain types of patients. However, it was not until the early 1930s that he began to elucidate the precise role played by muscular rigidities in the binding of impulses and emotions that had to be suppressed. The following extracts describing the beginning of a treatment in 1933 will perhaps convey better than any definition what Reich meant by the "physiological anchoring" of affects:

In Copenhagen in 1933, I treated a man who put up especially strong resistances against the uncovering of his passive-homosexual phantasies. This resistance was manifested in an extreme attitude of stiffness of the neck. . . . After an energetic attack upon his resistance he suddenly gave in, but in a rather alarming manner. For three days, he presented severe manifestations of vegetative shock. The color of his face kept changing rapidly from white to yellow or blue; the skin was mottled and of various tints; he had severe pains in the neck and the occiput; the heartbeat was rapid; he had diarrhea, felt worn out, and seemed to have lost hold. . . . *Affects had broken through somatically after the patient had yielded in a psychic defense attitude*. The stiff neck, expressing an attitude of

tense masculinity, apparently had bound vegetative energies which now broke loose in an uncontrolled and disordered fashion. . . . It was the musculature that served this inhibitory function. When the muscles of the neck relaxed, powerful impulses broke through, as if propelled by a spring. (*The Function of the Orgasm*, pp. 239–240)

This and other cases led Reich to a systematic study of chronic muscular rigidities and their relation to neurotic character attitudes. He reached the conclusion that "every neurotic is muscularly dystonic and every cure is directly reflected in a change of muscular habitus" (*Character Analysis*, pp. 311–312). Chronic muscular rigidities or spasms are found all over the bodies of the patients: in the forehead, around the mouth and in the chin, in the throat, the shoulders, the chest, the abdomen, the pelvis and thighs, and many other places. The rigid expression in the eyes of many patients, their chronic "stare," is the result of a chronic rigidity in the lid muscles. The breathing of neurotic individuals is disturbed in comparison with the natural and free respiration of emotionally healthy people. Reich referred to the totality of these chronic muscular rigidities which an individual develops as the "muscular armor."

Reich emphasized that it is muscle groups rather than individual muscles that become spastic—muscle groups which jointly serve a certain function, for example, to suppress the impulse to cry. Not only do the lower lips become tense in this event but also "the whole musculature of the mouth, the jaw and the throat; that is, all the muscles which, as a functional unit, become active in the process of crying" (*The Function of the Orgasm*, p. 269). In discussing the spasms frequently found in the mouth, chin, and neck, Reich enlarges on the tensions set up by the stifling of impulses to cry:

Many people have a mask-like facial expression. The chin is pushed forward and looks broad; the neck below the chin is 'lifeless.' The lateral neck muscles which go to the breastbone stand out as thick cords; the muscles under the chin are tense. Such patients often suffer from nausea. Their voice is usually low, monotonous, 'thin.'. . . (*Ibid.*, p. 271)

This is not the place to discuss in detail other of the typical rigidities which make up the muscular armor. The interested reader will find these described in various of the publications devoted to the new technique.

Upon discovering the muscular spasms and their relation to suppressed impulses and emotions, Reich devised various ways of attacking or "dissolving" them directly. In working on tensions in and around the eyes, for example, it is frequently possible to release a great deal of anxiety; in loosening up and encouraging the movement of certain muscles around the mouth, suppressed feelings of disgust can be liberated; by suitable work on the chin, it is possible, in Reich's words, "to set free an unbelievable amount of anger." Reich writes that he had previously been able to bring about the release of repressed impulses and emotions by way of dissolving purely characterological inhibitions and attitudes. Now, however, "the break-through of biological energy was more complete, more forceful, more thoroughly experienced, and it occurred more *rapidly*. Also, it was accompanied in many patients by a spontaneous dissolution of the characterological inhibitions" (*ibid.*, p. 241). Reich warns, however, that it is not possible to dispense with work on character attitudes. "Everyday practise soon teaches one," he writes, "that it is not permissible to exclude one form of work at the expense of the other" (*ibid.*, p. 293). With some patients work on the muscular rigidities will predominate from the beginning; with others, work on the character attitudes; but in all cases work on the muscular armor becomes more important in the later stages of the treatment.

Mind–body problem. The facts he discovered about chronic muscular rigidities and their relation to character attitudes and repressed emotions, Reich maintained, required the abandonment of the dualistic theories about body and mind tacitly or explicitly accepted by many psychologists and most psychoanalysts. It is a mistake to regard the muscular rigidity as a mere accompaniment or as an effect of the corresponding character attitude: it is "its somatic side and the basis for its continued existence" (*The Function of the Orgasm*, p. 269). The rigidity of a muscle group and the corresponding attitude serve the same function, namely, that of holding back a repressed emotion. The muscular armor and the character armor may therefore be said to be "functionally" identical. The only tenable answer to the body–mind problem, according to Reich (who quotes La Mettrie as anticipating his position), is a materialistic form of the identity theory. Reich's identity theory is materialistic, not in the sense that introspection is regarded as illusory or as devoid of scientific value but in holding that a change in a person's character, or indeed any change in a human being, cannot come about without appropriate physiological changes. The notion, writes Reich, that "the psychic apparatus functions by itself and influences the somatic apparatus is not in keeping with the facts" (*ibid.*, p. 313). Even an idea such as that of going to sleep will not "exert a somatic influence unless it is already the expression of a vegetative impulse" (*ibid.*). This conclusion, Reich insists, is not contradicted by the observation that a patient (or anybody) feels relieved when a previously repressed idea or impulse is allowed to become conscious. "We used to say," writes Reich, "that it is a matter of a discharge of psychic energy which previously was bound" (*Character Analysis*, p. 311). Closer examination will show in such a case that both the tension and the relaxation are clearly observable somatic processes. What is introspectively felt as tension and as relief are in fact certain fairly typical rigidities and relaxations of muscles—in the forehead, in the eyes, and elsewhere in the body. Both Reich and his translator, T. P. Wolfe, insist that the issue between dualism and the identity theory is not merely a question of alternative languages but makes a difference to therapeutic practice and further research. Wolfe in particular claims that only a theory of "psychosomatic identity" makes sense of the vast array of facts that had accumulated in psychosomatic studies by 1940 and that only such a theory can provide a fruitful method of research (*The Function of the Orgasm*, pp. x and xiii).

There are two very different questions which may be raised about all of this. One may ask whether, granting that Reich has hit upon something interesting and important in connection with muscular rigidities, their origin, and their possible dissolution, an identity theory is the only philosophical position which can accommodate these facts. More fundamentally, one may raise the question of whether Reich's empirical claims about the muscular armor are true in the first place.

As to the first of these questions, it should be pointed out that when Reich speaks of the "*functional* identity" of the character and the muscular armor, he does not seem to mean by "identity" anything as strong as has been claimed by philosophical defenders of the identity theory. To say that a certain character attitude and a certain muscular rigidity have the same function, for example, that of binding anxiety or anger, is not anything that a dualist is required to deny. It is certainly compatible with, but it does not by itself imply, the claim that the character attitude and the muscular rigidity are two aspects of the same phenomenon. It might be argued that Reich's work on the connection between muscular rigidities and character attitudes, rather than proving any traditional version of the identity theory, shows the inadequacy of *interactionistic* forms of dualism. Interactionism, in allowing only for *causal* relations between physical and psychological phenomena, could not do justice to the intimate relations between muscular rigidities and character attitudes to which Reich has called attention. There is no reason to suppose, however, that a more open-minded form of dualism, which would not restrict the relations between body and mind to one simple type, could not accommodate the facts in question.

In the present article we cannot attempt to answer the second of our two questions—whether Reich's empirical claims about the muscular armor can in fact be sustained. Perhaps, however, it is permissible to remark, especially since this part of Reich's work has received so much less publicity than his orgone theory, that psychiatrists and others who have some first-hand knowledge of it have generally been enthusiastic. This includes persons who have observed and treated children in the light of Reich's account of the muscular armor. Since the process of repression as well as the process of cure would, on almost any theory, be most readily observable in children, confirmations (or disconfirmations) here would seem to be of special significance.

CULTURE, SOCIETY, AND CHARACTER STRUCTURE

Culture, morality, and the death instinct. On the basis of both his clinical observations and his very extensive social work, Reich maintained that there is nothing more deadly than to be subjected to the moralistic and authoritarian upbringing which is or which was until very recently the lot of the great majority of children all over the world. The preaching and the antisexual moralism of the religious home and the authoritarian character of the conventional school stifle every vital impulse in the child. Insofar as traditional education is successful, it produces human beings with a craving for authority, a fear of responsibility, mystical longings, impotent rebelliousness, and pathological drives of all kinds. The "morals" fostered by religious mysticism and slavishly followed by many who no longer believe in religion "create the very perverted sexual life which it presumes to regulate moralistically; and the elimination of these 'morals' is the prerequisite for an elimination of that immorality which it tries in vain to fight" (*The Mass Psychology of Fascism*, p. 156).

There is nevertheless an important element of truth in the contention of conservative ideology that if one were to "eliminate morals," the "animal instincts" would gain the upper hand, and that this would lead to social chaos. What is true in this contention is that the average person in our culture carries within himself an "unconscious inferno," and while his perverse and destructive impulses are not in most cases adequately controlled by moral inhibitions, they would presumably dominate personal and social life to an even greater extent in the absence of moral regulations. This fact makes it clear that any transition from an authoritarian to a rational self-governing society must be gradual and cannot be accomplished by simply telling people, *as they now are*, to live according to their impulses. It does not, however, provide a justification for an ascetic morality or for the usual conservative theory which maintains that culture is based on sexual repression.

The conservative theorist errs in assuming that the antisocial impulses are "absolute and biologically given" (*The Sexual Revolution*, p. 20). This view is advocated not only in the writings of religious moralists and others to whom Reich contemptuously referred as "uplifters" or "guardians of the higher values" but also in many of the later writings of Freud and those of Freud's followers who accepted the theory of the death instinct. Accordingly, Reich devoted much effort to a very detailed attack on the theory of the death instinct, especially as it is applied to human society and culture in Freud's *Civilization and Its Discontents*.

On Freud's view, Thanatos, or the striving for peace and extinction, is just as much biologically given as Eros, or the sexual strivings. Although the death instinct itself cannot be perceived, it manifests itself in a great many ways—in various forms of aggression, in self-destructiveness, and in the masochistic "need for punishment." It also accounts for the resistances put up by patients against getting well. According to Reich, however, both clinical experience and observation of children show that the phenomena which supposedly prove the death instinct are "secondary formations," the products of the neurosis, and not "primary" and "biological" like the sexual instinct or the need for food. Investigation reveals that suicide is either an unconscious revenge upon another person or a way of escaping the pressure of a situation that has become overwhelming. The neurotic fear of and concern with death which is frequently found in quite young people can in every case be reduced to a fear of catastrophe, and this, in turn, to genital anxiety. As for aggressiveness, Reich claimed that the proponents of the death instinct did not sufficiently distinguish between perfectly healthy forms and those which are sadistic and destructive. The former are intimately connected with life-affirming tendencies, and the latter are always reactions of the organism to the denial of the gratification of a vital need. Reich equally denied that

there is any evidence whatsoever for the theory of "primary masochism." All clinical observations support Freud's *earlier* theory that patients "had come to grief as a result of their *fear* of punishment for sexual behavior and not as a result of any *desire* to be punished for it" (*The Function of the Orgasm*, pp. 103–104). The theory of the death instinct, furthermore, is therapeutically sterile and offers an excellent excuse for one's inability to handle a difficult resistance. In addition to providing an alibi for therapeutic failures, it serves the same function as the discredited biologistic theory of congenital criminality or the view of Magnus Hirschfeld that exhibitionism is due to special "exhibitionistic hormones": all such views shift problems from the social to the biological realm, where nothing can—and need—be done about them.

Conservative theorists who maintain that there is an antithesis between sexuality and work fail to distinguish between "compulsive-unpleasurable" work, which is indeed regarded as a burdensome duty, and "natural joyful work," which frequently requires discipline but which is nevertheless a pleasurable gratification of a need. Reich regards as especially significant his observations on patients who achieved sexual happiness. He reports that those who, because of neurotic disturbances, had not been working, began to feel a strong need for some vital work. Those who had been engaged in work which was intrinsically interesting now blossomed and gave full rein to their talents. In some cases, however, there was a complete breakdown of work. This at first seemed to confirm the view of the antisexual moralists, but closer inspection showed that these people had previously been driven by a compulsive sense of duty and that what they rebelled against was empty and mechanical work, and not work as such. Their aversion was to *pleasureless* work, and their impulses were by no means antisocial. Just as society rewards some highly antisocial activities with fame and honor, Reich remarks, so "there are highly valuable, even culturally important traits and impulses which have to be repressed for considerations of material survival" (*ibid.*, p. 150). If there were more human beings with a genital character, this would not result in the end of "civilization," but it would in all probability lead to radical changes in the ways in which the world's work is done.

Reich concluded that civilization and culture do not depend on instinctual repression. If authoritarian education were abolished and if children grew up in a sex-affirmative environment, people would be more, and not less, peaceful and cooperative. Some types of work, namely, those in which only a person with a compulsive character can take any interest, would indeed suffer, but the arts and sciences would in all likelihood flourish as never before. Reich was not an irrationalist in any sense of the word, and like Freud he favored "the primacy of the intellect," adding, however, that the full utilization of a person's intellectual capacities presupposes "an orderly libido economy." "Genital and intellectual primacy have the same mutual relationship as have sexual stasis and neurosis, guilt feelings and religion, hysteria and superstition" (*Character Analysis*, p. 170).

Society and character structure. Freudian social theory, insofar as it existed at all when Reich began his elaborate critique of what he called "authoritarian" society, was vitiated by its "biologism" as well as its "psychological atomism," or, as Reich also called it, a "feudal individualistic psychology." By "biologism" Reich meant the tendency to treat as universal and biologically inevitable attitudes and impulses which were determined by cultural conditions. When he spoke of Freud's "psychological atomism," Reich referred to the tendency to treat individual patients and their families in isolation from the social environment which had in fact a great deal to do with their tribulations. Rejecting Freud's biologism and accepting the early Freudian view that neurosis is basically the result of the conflict between instinctual needs and the reality which frustrates them, Reich naturally asked whether and how this frustrating reality could be significantly altered. His work at the sex hygiene clinics, furthermore, had convinced him that neuroses were by no means the fads of middle-class women who did not know what to do with their time but were emotionally crippling illnesses of almost epidemic proportions. Contrary to the assertions of the more doctrinaire and narrow-minded Marxists, there could be no doubt in Reich's view that "sexual repression, biological rigidity, moralism and puritanism are ubiquitous" and not confined to certain classes or groups of the population (*The Function of the Orgasm*, p. xxiii). The vast majority of people suffering from psychological disturbances cannot, however, be reached by individual therapy, disregarding here all the difficulties and limitations of such therapy when it is available.

If one is to do anything about this deplorable state of affairs, one must first achieve an understanding of the precise relations between society and the individual and, more specifically, between social institutions and neurotic disturbances. "Society," Reich writes, "is not the result of a certain psychic structure, but the reverse is true: character structure is the result of a certain society" ("Character and Society," p. 254). The ideology of a given society can anchor itself only in a certain character structure, and the institutions of the society serve the function of producing this character structure. If, as in all authoritarian societies, a minority holds economic and political power, it also has the power to form ideology and structure. As a consequence, in authoritarian society, the thinking and the structure of the majority of people "corresponds to the interests of the political and economic rulers" (*The Sexual Revolution*, p. xx). The majority of human beings (Reich is writing in 1936) are "suppressed and exploited and spend most of their working hours doing monotonous and mechanical labor which they cannot help regarding as a loathsome duty." How is it possible that "people can bear it, that they are unable to change it, that they seem to endure in silence the suffering it imposes on them?" ("Character and Society," p. 252). They can bear their fate because the ruling economic system is "anchored in the psychic structure of the very people who are suppressed" (*People in Trouble*, p. 100). The most important structure-forming institutions in authoritarian society are the authoritarian family, the authoritarian school, and religion. "From infancy on," writes Reich, "people are trained to be falsely modest, self-effacing and mechanically obedient, trained to suppress their natural instinctual energies"

("Character and Society," p. 252). In this way children become subservient to their parents and people in general "subservient to the authoritarian state power and capitalistic exploitation" (*People in Trouble*, p. 99). The most powerful instrument in achieving this mass structure is sexual repression, which is fostered in the home, in the school, and above all through the influence of religious moralism. The major mechanisms of sexual suppression in Christian countries are the prohibition of infantile masturbation, the prevention of sexual gratification in adolescence, and the institution of compulsorily lifelong monogamy, accompanied by the belief that the function of sexuality is procreation rather than pleasure. The parents who punish children for masturbating and who do their best to prevent adolescents from having a full sex life are unwittingly carrying out the purpose of the ruling powers.

There is something plausible about Reich's contention that an atomistic psychology, no matter how correctly it may determine the causes of mental health and illness, will not by itself explain why various institutions which are plainly inimical to life and happiness nevertheless flourish and receive the support of all the major official and unofficial agencies of society. However, it is not entirely clear what he means by his claim that character structure is the result of social structure and, more specifically, that the "function" of sex-denying institutions is to make the masses helpless and dependent. Although he occasionally uses the word "purpose," Reich is presumably asserting the existence of a "latent" rather than a "manifest" function, to use the terminology introduced by R. K. Merton (see FUNCTIONALISM IN SOCIOLOGY). While it may be plausibly argued that *some* rulers, like Stalin and certain church figures, have been aware of the connection between sexual suppression and such "desirable" traits as obedience and uncritical acceptance of the *status quo*, it would be far-fetched to hold that either in capitalistic or in other societies the ruling circles *deliberately* support sex-denying institutions in order to perpetuate their power and privileges. But if the rulers are not conscious of the causal connection between sexual suppression and the submissive traits it produces, in what sense is a reference to their interest an explanation of the institutions in question? It is tempting to speak here of an "unconscious knowledge" or "unconscious realization" that sexual suppression produces submissiveness, but it is far from clear what these expressions would mean.

Reich's views about the relation between the ideology that prevails in a society and the interests of the holders of power has obvious affinities with Marxism, and in fact a number of Marxist writers of the late 1920s and early 1930s hailed his account of the social function of sexual repression as a valuable supplement to historical materialism. However, the most influential Marxist ideologists, socialist as well as communist, rejected Reich's account and also strongly opposed his work in his sex hygiene clinics. In his turn, Reich repudiated what he called the "economism" of Marxist theory as emphatically as he attacked the atomism of psychoanalysis. "Marxists again and again argued," he recalls, "that the sexual etiology of the neuroses was a bourgeois fancy idea, that only 'material want' caused neuroses . . . as if the sexual want were not a 'material' one: It was not the 'material want' in the sense of the

Marxian theorists that caused the neuroses, but the neuroses of these people robbed them of their ability to do anything sensible about their needs, actually to do something constructive about their situation, to stand the competition on the labor market, to get together with others in similar social circumstances, to keep a cool head to think things out. . . ." (*The Function of the Orgasm,* pp. 56–57). Moreover, just as it is wrong to think that neuroses are (except very indirectly) caused by economic hardships, so it is a mistake to suppose that the social and political actions of the working classes can be predicted on the basis of their economic interests alone. Factors such as mystical and sexual longings and perverse sadistic fantasies may exert very powerful influences, as Hitler, unlike the communist, socialist, and liberal politicians, understood only too well. Fascism, to take but one example, is very incompletely characterized as a movement engineered by capitalists to prevent the establishment of socialism. At least the German variety of fascism differed from other reactionary movements in that it was "supported and championed by masses of people" (*The Mass Psychology of Fascism,* p. ix). Marxist theory, which assumes that with few exceptions the underprivileged will be guided by their rational economic interests, is incapable of accounting for such a phenomenon.

THE STRUGGLE AGAINST RELIGION

Mystical feelings and sexual inhibitions. According to Reich, both Marx and Freud made significant contributions to our understanding of religion. Patriarchal religions are always politically reactionary, and Marxists are perfectly right in pointing out that "in every class society they are in the service of the powers that be" (*ibid.,* p. 124). Freud, too, was correct in his view that the idea of God derives from the idea of the father and, more generally, that "the psychic contents of religion stem from the infantile family situation" (*ibid.*). Granting all of this, there remains a question which is not answered by the Marxist or the Freudian account, or by any of the great eighteenth-century critics of religion. Indeed, it is a question which most of these writers did not even raise but which must be asked and answered if one is to have an adequate comprehension of religion. How are we to account for the fact that "religious ideas are invested with such intense feelings"? What explains the "enormous emotional power of mysticism" (*ibid.,* p. 122)? Or, using Reich's favorite terminology, what is the "energy" which enables religions to gain such a firm hold on people? What is it that compels human beings not only to accept the idea of a pleasure-prohibiting, all-seeing God and the ideologies of sin and punishment, and "not to feel them as a burden but, on the contrary, to uphold and fervently defend them, at the sacrifice of their most primitive life interests?" (*ibid.,* p. 124).

Reich is strongly opposed to the tendency of "emancipated" unbelievers to dismiss religions as nothing more than the fancies of silly and ignorant people. He insists that a study of religious people—of the content of their emotions and beliefs, of the ways in which these are implanted, and of the function which they fulfill in their psychological economy—is highly rewarding. It sheds light on many other phenomena, including, for example, the psychological basis of fascism and of reactionary political movements. Such a study also explains why, by and large, free-thought propaganda is so unsuccessful in spite of the fact that from a purely rational point of view the positions defended by freethinkers are vastly superior to the religious claims—something that is not altogether unknown among believers. Above all, a happy life for the majority of mankind is impossible unless the power of religion is broken, unless one can prevent "the mystical infestation of the masses" (*ibid.,* p. 161). However, in order to be effective in "the relentless fight against mysticism," one must have a full comprehension of its origin and its psychological sources of strength so that one can meet its "artful apparatus . . . with adequate counter-measures" (*ibid.,* p. 152). To suppose that mystical attitudes become anchored in human beings simply as a result of intellectual indoctrination is a naive and dangerous mistake. It should be noted that Reich sharply distinguishes mysticism from primitive animism. The latter is best regarded as bad science. Reich does not offer an explicit definition of "mysticism," but it seems clear from his various writings on the subject that mysticism in the "strict and wider sense" is characterized by the belief (or feeling) that the ordinary world of physical objects and human emotions is *not enough* and the related view that there are some grand truths which human beings can come to know by nonscientific or superscientific means. Various nontheological systems of metaphysics and ontology, as well as the standpoint of those who deny that psychology can properly be a natural science (Reich is specially scathing in his comments about Klages and Jaspers), are treated by him as forms of mysticism.

The most basic feature of what Reich variously calls "religious excitations" or "mystical feelings" is that they are "at one and the same time *anti*-sexual and a *substitute* for sexuality" (*ibid.,* p. 125). Reich claims that this conclusion is borne out by the close observation of genuinely religious people (as contrasted with those who merely pretend belief for purposes of personal gain and advancement); by character-analytic treatment of religious individuals and patients having mystical feelings of any kind; by observation of children, especially those suffering from prayer compulsions; by the writings of the mystics themselves; and also by what is known about the changes that occurred when social organization passed from matriarchy to patriarchy and class society. Biologically, the religious individual is subject to states of sexual tension like any other living being. However, as a consequence of his sex-negating upbringing and especially his fear of punishment, he has lost the capacity for normal sexual stimulation and gratification. The result of this is that he suffers from a chronic state of *excessive* somatic excitation. The more thorough his religious education has been, the more it appears to him that happiness is not attainable for him in this world and, in the long run, it does not even seem desirable any more. However, he remains a biological organism and hence cannot completely renounce the goals of "happiness, relaxation and satisfaction." In these circumstances all he can do is seek "the *illusory* happiness provided by the religious *forepleasure* excitations" (*ibid.,* p. 126).

The "somatic suffering" of the religious person creates in him the need for consolation and help from outside himself, particularly in his fight against what he terms the "evil instincts," which in turn are identified with the "evils of the flesh." His religious ideas enable him to attain a state of "vegetative excitation which resembles gratification but does not, in reality, bring about somatic relaxation" (*ibid.*, p. 127). Not even religious ecstasies bring about anything comparable to the orgastic relief of a satisfying sexual experience. What the religious person calls his longing for "delivery from sin" is in fact a longing for relief from sexual tension. To people who cannot achieve sexual gratification, sexual excitation gradually and inevitably becomes something "torturing and destructive." In this way the religious conception of sex as evil and debasing has its foundation in real somatic processes. People who feel a disgust for their body quite naturally develop obsessive concepts of "purity" and "perfection" (*ibid.*, p. 144).

It would lead too far afield to discuss here the various ways in which, according to Reich, the "mystical idea of God" becomes anchored in people. These mechanisms may vary in detail, but they all involve the implanting of sexual anxieties; and Reich concludes that from the point of view of energy, mystical feelings *are* "sexual excitations which have changed their content and goal." The energy of these emotions is the energy of natural sexuality which has become transformed and attached to mystical, psychic contents. Religious patients, upon establishing a fully satisfying sex life, invariably lose their God-fixation.

Once one comprehends the nature of "religious excitations," it becomes clear why the free-thought movement "cannot make itself felt as a counter-force" (*ibid.*, p. 147). Aside from the fact that in many countries the churches enjoy the support of the state and that generally the mass information media are grossly biased in favor of religion and religious morality, the impact of free-thought propaganda is limited because it relies almost exclusively on intellectual arguments. These are not, indeed, a negligible factor, but they are no match for the "most powerful emotion" on which the mass-psychological influence of religious institutions is based: sexual anxiety and sexual repression. People with a religious upbringing who, as a result of the study of science and philosophy, have turned into unbelievers very frequently retain religious longings and emotions. Some of them even continue to pray compulsively. This does not prove, as some advocates of religion argue, that religious needs are "eternal and ineradicable." It does, however, show that "while the religious feeling is opposed by the power of the intellect, its sources have not been touched" (*ibid.*, p. 152).

The fight against religion is nevertheless far from hopeless. Mysticism can be eradicated if, in addition to depriving the churches of their "evil right of preparing the children's minds for the reception of reactionary ideologies" (*ibid.*, p. 148), one is guided in the struggle by one's knowledge that mysticism stems from inhibited sexuality. From this insight it follows incontrovertibly that "full sexual consciousness and a natural regulation of sexual life mean the end of mystical feelings of any kind, that, in other words, natural sexuality is the deadly enemy of mystical religion" (*ibid.*, p. 152). Any social efforts which are directed toward making people affirm their sexual rights will *ipso facto* weaken the forces of mysticism. The most

good can be done with children and adolescents. Reich gives numerous instances from his experience in Germany of the "burning interest" of children in sexual questions which made even the most enlightened adults ashamed of their prudishness and hesitation. "Once children and adolescents are reached on a mass basis through their sexual interests," there will be a "powerful counterweight against the reactionary forces" (*ibid.*, p. 169). As for those people who are too old to have their structure basically altered, it is still all to the good to bring "silent suffering to the surface." They might then be less likely to become instruments in the process of maiming their own children, and they will not continue to support sex-repressive laws.

The great cultural revolution. Reich never abandoned the conviction he had reached during his Marxist phase that individual therapy is socially insignificant and that "alteration of the social structure is a prerequisite for an alteration of the psychic structure on a mass scale" ("Character and Society," p. 255). However, after his separation from organized Marxism, he gradually came to the conclusion that *political* action was of little consequence and that it was a grave error to judge social developments primarily in terms of a rigid, clear-cut class war. If one is not blinded by the political slogans of an earlier age, one cannot help noticing that we are in the midst of a "deep-reaching revolution of cultural living" (*The Sexual Revolution*, p. xiv). It is a revolution "without parades, uniforms, drum or cannon salutes," but, unlike the Russian Revolution of 1917, which was merely "politico-ideological," it is a "genuine social revolution" (*The Mass Psychology of Fascism*, p. 201). It is not a revolution by the proletariat against the bourgeoisie, and it remains to be seen what major economic changes will accompany it. What *is* happening is that "the senses of the animal, man, for his natural life functions are awakening from a sleep of thousands of years" (*ibid.*, p. xiv). Ever since the beginning of the century, numerous social factors have been operating in the direction of freedom and health. These factors include the creation of huge industrial plants with vast armies of workers of both sexes and the gradual undermining of the authoritarian parental home. There has been a "thorough disintegration of the moralistic ascetic forms of living," and this "objective loosening of the reactionary fetters on sexuality cannot be undone" (*ibid.*, p. 164), regardless of how vociferously the churches and their conscious or unconscious allies continue to preach the old morality.

This "great cultural revolution" is bound to be chaotic and to give rise to all kinds of grotesque developments. The disintegration of the old moralistic institutions and customs expresses itself at first as a rebellion which takes pathological forms, but it is not difficult to see that healthy forces are trying to break through in these pathological manifestations. At one time Reich envisaged a "powerful international organization" which would create an atmosphere of sex-affirmation and thus help to "guide the rebellion into rational channels" (*The Mass Psychology of Fascism*, p. 121). However, regardless of whether any organizations are brought into being which could accelerate the process and make it less painful, there is no reason to "fear for the final outcome." As yet, human beings, "moved by obscure, 'oceanic' feelings, dream instead of mastering their existence; and they perish from these dreams" (*Character Analysis,* p. 324). But when once they master their existence, when they become capable of giving and receiving love and when work will be a source of pleasure and not a burden, this will mean "the death-knell of all transcendental mysticism, of the 'absolute objective spirit,' " and of all the metaphysical and irrationalist philosophies that are "subsumed under mysticism in the . . . wider sense" (*ibid.*). An individual "who is sexually happy does not need an inhibiting 'morality' or a supernatural 'religious experience.' Basically, life is as simple as that. It becomes complicated only by the human structure which is characterized by the fear of life" (*The Sexual Revolution,* p. 269).

REICH'S LAST YEARS

It is not surprising that the ideas sketched in the preceding sections of this article should have appealed to many who were dissatisfied with the conservative developments of psychoanalysis as well as to those who, disillusioned with the results of communism in Russia, nevertheless strongly believed in social progress. During his early years in the United States, Reich did in fact count among his followers or sympathizers a number of remarkably talented men, from the most varied walks of life, who saw the dawn of a new enlightenment in his psychiatry and in the implications of his theories for education and for the proper direction of social reform. It would be difficult to convey to anybody who was not actually living in New York at that time the enthusiasm that was felt for Reich personally and for what were regarded as his liberating insights. As was to be expected, communists and psychiatrists of other schools were violently hostile, but this only served to heighten people's admiration for Reich's independence and for his uncompromising integrity.

It was mentioned previously that Reich himself became less and less interested in psychiatry. He also gradually lost most of his concern to guide into rational channels the "great cultural revolution" which he had diagnosed in his writings. The publications of his last years do indeed contain numerous discussions of social topics, but, at least in the opinion of the present writer, most of what Reich now had to say was flat and trivial. He became increasingly obsessed with the evil conspiracies of "red fascism" (some of Reich's remarks during this period could be quoted with approval by members of the John Birch Society) and with the menace of the "emotional plague." This term was originally introduced to refer to the harmful activities of individuals who take out their sexual sickness and frustrations on the rest of mankind, usually under the pretense of promoting some worthy cause. Reich's earlier description of emotional plague reactions and motives had been extremely perceptive, but now anybody who was in any way opposed to any of his ideas became automatically classified as an agent of the emotional plague. The writings of the last years are also filled, in a manner reminiscent of Nietzsche's *Ecce Homo,* with hymns of self-praise (sometimes in the third person), and there is much evidence of extreme bitterness toward a world which did not accept or

even pay attention to his theories. From the available accounts it appears that Reich had always been impatient and somewhat autocratic, but he had also been singularly compassionate and generous. Dr. Nic Waal, in her sketch of Reich, describes him as "enormously stimulating and lovable" but adds that in his last years he "became less and less patient, less loving . . . and finally pathologically suspicious" (*Wilhelm Reich—A Memorial Volume,* p. 37).

If Reich became increasingly bitter, this was not without a good deal of justification. Right from the beginning, even while he was a psychoanalyst "in good standing," Reich was the victim of an extraordinary amount of spite and slander. Any study of the records will make it clear that he was treated outrageously by the officials of the Psychoanalytic Association both before and at the Lucerne Conference. We have already mentioned Reich's troubles in Scandinavia. In New York, he was arrested by the F.B.I. in December 1941 and held at Ellis Island for three weeks. The reasons for the arrest were never divulged. In 1947 an exceptionally vicious campaign was initiated in *The New Republic,* by the journalist Mildred E. Brady. There was not a paragraph in her article that did not contain a major distortion, but it was nevertheless quoted and reprinted all over America.

In an article ten years earlier, the German poet Stephan Lackner had expressed his indignation at the treatment which Reich had received and continued to receive from leading figures among the psychoanalysts and the left-wing parties. "It was not enough," wrote Lackner, "to expel Reich from their organizations"; in the struggle against this man and his disturbing ideas, "every kind of slander and distortion is a permissible weapon" (*Das neue Tagebuch,* February 1937, p. 140). This last remark applies, word for word, to the campaign instigated by Mrs. Brady and her associates. In March 1954, the Food and Drug Administration obtained an injunction against Reich and his foundation, ordering the destruction of all orgone accumulators, all of Reich's journals, and some of his books; the books that were not destroyed were to be impounded. Among the works proscribed on the ground that they constituted "labeling" of the orgone accumulator were books like *The Function of the Orgasm* and *Character Analysis,* in which the accumulator is not so much as mentioned.

Nobody except fanatical partisans of Reich can dispute the right of the Food and Drug Administration to intervene. When on the defensive, Reich denied that he had ever claimed any curative powers for the orgone accumulator, but the truth is that the literature is full of such claims. However, granting that the Food and Drug Administration had evidence to show the accumulator medically worthless (no such evidence has ever been published), the injunction is nevertheless a startling document constituting a blanket attack on Reich's character and his entire work.

Reich had two weeks in which to appeal, but to everybody's consternation he refused to appear in court. Instead, he wrote a letter to the judge in the case, declaring that a court of law was not the appropriate place for adjudicating scientific questions. For some months Reich obeyed the injunction, but in October 1954 he notified the authorities that he was about to resume all the activities of his institute, including the sale of books and periodicals. This led to a trial in 1956, at which Reich was given the maximum sentence of two years in a federal penitentiary. Reich died of a heart attack eight months after he had started serving his sentence. All journals published by Reich's institute that were seized by government agents were burned in two separate actions in 1956 and 1960, and his books were impounded until they began to be republished by a commercial house in 1960.

There is no doubt in the mind of the present writer that during his last years Reich was mentally ill. Some of those who were close to him deny this, and the prison psychiatrist who examined Reich certified him as sane. Nevertheless, if one reads the records of the trial or the brief which Reich filed in his appeal, one can hardly resist drawing the conclusion that a great man had broken down. Reich finally "went to pieces," observed Dr. Waal, "partly on his own—but mostly due to other people," adding that "a human being cannot bear cruelty and loneliness in the long run" (*op. cit.*, pp. 38–39). It is worth recalling the words of Popper-Lynkeus, whose ideas bear little resemblance to Reich's but who was also described as "mad" during the better part of his life. "I assure you," he told his biographer, "[that] of all experiences none is more painful than that of finding oneself described as mad as a consequence of having discovered something that is good and true: of all martyrdoms, this is perhaps the most terrible" (A. Gelber, *Josef Popper-Lynkeus*, p. 101).

Bibliography

The following abbreviations are used throughout; ZPS for *Zeitschrift für politische Psychologie und Sexualökonomie* and *IJSO* for *International Journal for Sex-Economy and Orgone Research*. Several biographies of Reich have been announced, but none had been published by the time this article went to press. The only published sketches of Reich are A. S. Neill's "The Man Reich" and Nic Waal's "On Wilhelm Reich," both in Paul Ritter, ed., *Wilhelm Reich—A Memorial Volume* (London, 1958). There is a good deal of autobiographical material, especially on his relations with Freud, in Reich's *The Function of the Orgasm*, translated from the German manuscript by T. P. Wolfe (New York, 1942; paperback reprint, 1961). This book is a good introduction to all of Reich's theories discussed in the present article. The reader should be warned, however, that in the 1961 reprint the very valuable introduction by Dr. Wolfe has been deleted. *People in Trouble* (Rangeley, Me., 1953) contains an account of Reich's work at his sex hygiene clinics and of his difficulties with communist functionaries in Germany and Denmark. Reich's attempt to organize an international movement in support of a sex-affirmative culture is described by him in two articles: "Zur Geschichte der Sexpol Bewegung," in *ZPS*, Vol. 1 (1934), 259–269, and "Geschichte der deutschen Sexpol-Bewegung," in *ZPS*, Vol. 2 (1935), 64–70. The only published account of Reich's troubles in Norway is Gunnar Leistikow, "The Fascist Newspaper Campaign in Norway," in *IJSO*, Vol. 1 (1942), 266–273. This article also discusses Reich's troubles in Denmark. Its title is misleading in that many of Reich's opponents were not fascists. Reich's *Listen Little Man*, translated from the German manuscript by T. P. Wolfe, with illustrations by William Steig (New York, 1948), is a moving outburst against the various people who harassed and defamed him.

The fullest published account of Reich's technique of vegetotherapy is *Orgasmusreflex, Muskelhaltung und Körperausdruck* (Copenhagen, 1937), parts of which are translated in Chapter 8 of *The Function of the Orgasm* and Chapter 15 of the third edition of *Character Analysis* (New York, 1949). Various aspects of Reich's new technique are also discussed in the following articles: Odd Havrevold, "Vegetotherapy," in *IJSO*, Vol. 1 (1942), 65–87, writ-

ten under the pseudonym Walter Frank; Ola Raknes, "The Treatment of a Depression," in *IJSO*, Vol. 1 (1942), 163–170, and "Sex-Economy," in *IJSO*, Vol. 3 (1944), 17–37, written under the pseudonym Carl Arnold. (These pseudonyms were necessary during the Nazi occupation of Norway.)

Child therapy is discussed in Felicia Saxe, "A Case History," in *IJSO*, Vol. 4 (1945), 59–71, and "Armored Human Beings Versus the Healthy Child," in *Annals of the Orgone Institute*, Vol. 1 (1947), 35–72; and in Nic Waal, "A Case of Anxiety Neurosis in a Small Child," in *Bulletin of the Menninger Clinic*, Vol. 12 (1948), and "A Special Technique of Psychotherapy With an Autistic Child," in G. Caplan, ed., *Emotional Problems of Early Childhood* (London, 1955).

The fullest statement of Reich's views on religion is found in Chapters 6 and 7 of *Massenpsychologie des Faschismus* (Copenhagen, 1933), third edition translated by T. P. Wolfe as *The Mass Psychology of Fascism* (New York, 1946). Discussions of religion strongly influenced by Reich are J. H. Leunbach, "Religion und Sexualität," in *ZPS*, Vol. 1 (1934), 70–72; Karl Teschitz, "Grundlagen der Religion," in *ZPS*, Vol. 2 (1935), 103–129, and "Religiöse Ekstase als Ersatz der sexuellen Auslösung," in *ZPS*, Vol. 4 (1937), 23–34; and Theodor Hartwig, "Religion und Sexualität," in *Der Freidenker* (Bern, April 1936), and "Der Sinn der 'religiös-sittlichen Erziehung,'" in *ZPS*, Vol. 4 (1937), 203–205. Of philosophical interest are Reich's articles "Zur Anwendung der Psychoanalyse in der Geschichtsforschung," in *ZPS*, Vol. 1 (1934), 4–16, and "Die Funktion der 'objektiven Wertwelt,'" in *ZPS*, Vol. 2 (1935), 32–43. For some years Reich considered himself a dialectical materialist. His attempt to give empirical meaning to the so-called "dialectical laws" can be found in *Dialektischer Materialismus und Psychoanalyse* (Berlin, 1929; 2d ed., Copenhagen, 1934).

Reich's views concerning the relation between society and character structure are stated succinctly in "Charakter und Gesellschaft," in *ZPS*, Vol. 3 (1936), translated by T. P. Wolfe as "Character and Society," in *IJSO*, Vol. 1 (1942), 247–256, and much more fully in *The Mass Psychology of Fascism* and in *Die Sexualität im Kulturkampf* (Copenhagen, 1936), translated by T. P. Wolfe as *The Sexual Revolution* (New York, 1945). Reich's claims about the "function" of sexual suppression are partly based on his anthropological theories, which are an extension of the work of Malinowski. The fullest statement of these theories is found in *Der Einbuch der Sexualmoral* (Berlin, 1932). There is a critical discussion of Reich's anthropology in a review of this book by Erich Fromm, in *Zeitschrift für Sozialforschung*, Vol. 2 (1933), 119–122.

Critical discussions of Reich's character-analytic technique are found in Carl M. Herold, "A Controversy About Technique," in *The Psychoanalytic Quarterly*, Vol. 8 (1939), 219–243; and in Richard Sterba, "Clinical and Therapeutic Aspects of Character Resistance," in *The Psychoanalytic Quarterly*, Vol. 22 (1953), 1–20. The dispute over the existence of "primary masochism" is surveyed in C. G. Flugel, *Man, Morals and Society* (London, 1945). Flugel, after some hesitation, sides with Theodor Reik and Franz Alexander against Reich. Even sympathetic commentators have frequently expressed doubts about what they take to be the excessively simple and "Rousseauist" view concerning the "natural" man that is implicit in many of Reich's discussions. Reich's view on this subject is condemned as "a stale left-over of the eighteenth-century imagination" in Philip Rieff, "The World of Wilhelm Reich," in *Commentary*, Vol. 38 (September 1964), 50–58. There are replies to Rieff in *Commentary*, Vol. 39 (February 1965), 19–22. Perhaps the best-known attack on Reich is found in Chapter 21 of Martin Gardner, *Fads and Fallacies in the Name of Science* (New York, 1952; 2d ed., 1957). In the opinion of the present writer, Gardner gives an extremely distorted picture of Reich's significance, concentrating on the wild claims of his last years and doing scant justice to the ideas discussed in the present article.

Various of Reich's theories are sympathetically discussed in Max Hodann, *A History of Modern Morals* (London, 1937); Stephan Lackner, "Ein moderner Ketzer," in *Das neue Tagebuch* (Paris), Vol. 5 (1937), 140–141; Harald K. Schjelderup, *Nervose Og Opdragelse* (Oslo, 1937); Neil McInnes, "An Examination of the

Work of Wilhelm Reich," in *Hermes*, Vol. 48 (1946), 26–29; Paul Goodman, "The Political Meaning of Some Recent Revisions of Freud," in *Politics*, Vol. 2 (1945), 197–203, and "Dr. Reich's Banned Books," in *Kulchur* (1960), reprinted in Goodman's *Utopian Essays and Practical Proposals* (New York, 1964), C. Berg, *Psychotherapy* (New York, 1948); Rudolf Brun, *General Theory of Neuroses*, translated by B. Miall (New York, 1951); and R. A. Wilson, "Wilhelm Reich and the Book Burners," in *The Minority of One*, Vol. 3 (February 1961), 6–7. There are constant references to Reich's therapy and to his social theories in the books written by A. S. Neill from 1939 on, such as *The Problem Teacher* (London, 1939), *Hearts Not Heads in the School* (London, 1945), and *The Problem Family* (London, 1949).

The *Orgone Energy Bulletin*, Vol. 5 (1953), 1–137, contains a very extensive bibliography of writings by and about Reich up to 1952. Unfortunately all issues of this periodical, as well as all issues of *IJSO*, are among the publications that were burned by the United States government.

Paul Edwards

REICHENBACH, HANS (1891–1953), German-American philosopher of science, was born in Hamburg. He attended the Technische Hochschule at Stuttgart and the universities of Berlin, Munich, and Göttingen and in 1915 obtained his doctorate in philosophy at the University of Erlangen with a dissertation on probability. From 1920 to 1926 he taught at the Technische Hochschule in Stuttgart, from 1926 to 1933 at the University of Berlin, from 1933 to 1938 at the University of Istanbul, and from 1938 to 1953 at the University of California. In 1947 he lectured at Columbia University and in 1952 at the Sorbonne. He was to have given the William James lectures at Harvard in the fall of 1953 but was prevented from doing so by his untimely death.

Reichenbach made important contributions to the study of probability and induction, space, time, geometry, relativity, the foundations of quantum mechanics, scientific laws, and meaning and verifiability. He was closely associated with the development of logical positivism in the 1920s and 1930s, although, since he was in Berlin during most of this period, he was not a member of the Vienna circle. With Rudolf Carnap he edited *Erkenntnis* (later called the *Journal of Unified Science*), the official journal of logical positivism; however, Reichenbach stressed his differences with the positivists and preferred to speak of himself as a logical empiricist. He published numerous books and articles on technical philosophical issues in science and also a number of more popular works.

Theory of knowledge. Reichenbach's theory of knowledge differs from the related verifiability theory of logical positivism in several respects. One version of the verifiability theory asserts that a proposition has meaning if and only if it is verifiable as true or false and that two propositions have the same meaning if every observation that verifies the one verifies the other, and vice versa. If we now distinguish direct observational propositions (such as "This is warm") from indirect ones (such as "The entropy of this system is increasing"), the positivist claim implies that an indirect proposition is logically equivalent to a set of direct propositions, a conclusion that Reichenbach rejected. First, there are an infinite number of observational consequences of an indirect proposition. Second, such propositions have a "surplus meaning," a meaning in addition to that given by their observational consequences.

Finally, the relationship between direct and indirect propositions must not be construed as deductive, as some positivists suggest, but rather as probabilistic. For these reasons Reichenbach rejected a truth theory of meaning and advocated instead a probability theory of meaning: A proposition is meaningful if it is possible to determine a degree of probability for it, and two propositions have the same meaning if they obtain the same degree of probability by every possible observation.

Reichenbach thought that this theory had an important bearing on the traditional problem of the existence of the external world. Suppose that we distinguish our sense impressions, reports of which are taken to be certain, from physical states of affairs, which are described by statements much less certain. What justification do we have for believing statements about physical states of affairs on the basis of sense impressions? According to one version of positivism, this problem can be solved by reducing statements about physical states of affairs to those reporting impressions. This view Reichenbach rejected since statements about physical states of affairs, like indirect propositions in science, have "surplus meaning." Physical statements and sense-impression statements are not equivalent in meaning but are related probabilistically. Given various sense impressions, we infer with a certain probability the existence of physical states which are independent of these impressions and, in certain cases, causally responsible for them. Moreover, even though human beings "observe" only their own impressions and never the physical states producing them, propositions asserting the existence of those states could, under appropriate conditions, receive a high degree of probability, thus justifying our belief in external objects.

In developing this theory Reichenbach began by treating statements describing sense impressions as if they were absolutely certain. But this assumption, he decided, needs to be rejected. All propositions are probable and must be given weights in accordance with their degree of probability. If we wish to provide a rational reconstruction of our knowledge of the world, we must recognize the logical arbitrariness of the epistemological base. The question whether we should start with a "concreta" base (physical objects accessible to direct observation), an impression base (previously mentioned), or an atomic base (elementary particles of physics)—each of which is possible—cannot be decided on theoretical grounds. Rather, we must recognize the importance of convention and decision based upon pragmatic and historical considerations. Reichenbach chose to start with concreta and then to consider the inferences to scientific items (*illata*) that are neither concrete nor abstract entities (for example, electricity, atoms). These inferences are not equivalences but probability inferences to independently existing items which we never observe. Yet Reichenbach did not hesitate to draw a conclusion that would be rejected by many contemporary empiricists: Strictly speaking, he asserted, we do not observe even the concreta "as they objectively are but in a distorted form ['from the standpoint of our middle-sized dimensions']; we see a *substitute world*—not the world as it is, objectively speaking" (*Experience and Prediction*, p. 220). Nevertheless, we can assign probability weights to statements about concrete objects. In Reichenbach's reconstruction these weights will be the highest and will form a basis upon which lesser weights can be assigned to inferred propositions describing the objects postulated by the scientist.

Probability and induction. Much of Reichenbach's theory of knowledge turns on the concept of probability, to which he devoted considerable attention in his writings. A statement such as "The probability of getting a face showing 1 when tossing this die is 1/6," when correctly analyzed, assumes the character of a "probability implication." The event and outcome are considered as belonging to certain ordered classes whose members x_i and y_i are correlated. We consider the class of tosses of this die and the corresponding class of faces shown. The probability implication is as follows: For every correlated pair x_i, y_i, "x_i is a toss of this die" implies with degree of probability 1/6 that "y_i is a face showing 1." Reichenbach developed formal rules governing such implications, and on the basis of these rules he generated customary theorems of the probability calculus. The formal notion of probability that is involved must be interpreted, and this can be done in several ways. Reichenbach chose a frequency interpretation, according to which the probability of an event is defined as the limit of the relative frequency of that type of event within a given infinite sequence. Thus, in the previous example the probability statement would receive the following interpretation: In an infinite sequence of tosses with this die, the relative frequency of a face showing 1 converges to 1/6 as a limit. Moreover, Reichenbach contended, a frequency interpretation can be given for all uses of the term "probability." He called this thesis the identity conception of probability to distinguish it from a view (held, for example, by Rudolf Carnap) according to which the term "probability" must be given two separate interpretations, one as a frequency, the other as a logical relationship between evidence and hypothesis.

The most difficult objection to the identity conception concerns the probability attributed to single events—for example, the probability that Napoleon was ill during the Battle of Leipzig. According to Reichenbach we must treat statements about particular events as neither true nor false but rather as "posits," or wagers (just as the gambler lays a wager on an event without ascribing a determinate truth-value to it). A weight can be assigned to such a statement by placing the event in question in the narrowest class of events of that type for which we have reliable statistics and then determining the relative frequency of relevant outcomes within this class. A weight assigned to a posit is what a degree of probability becomes if it is applied to a single case.

In determining weights for individual posits, as well as probability values generally, use must be made of a rule of induction which, since we have no direct knowledge of the limits of relative frequencies, allows us to infer the existence of such limits from finite observations. According to this rule, if an initial section of elements of a sequence is given, resulting in a relative frequency f of a certain property, and if no second-level information is known concerning the limit of that sequence, then we posit that the relative frequency will approach a limit approximating f as the sequence is continued. This rule is used to justify all probability statements. But what justification does the rule itself have? This question Reichenbach considered to be a generalized formulation of the traditional problem of justifying inductive inference. He proposed a solution that has had considerable influence in the philosophy of induction and has given rise to much controversy. According to Reichenbach's solution, although we do not, and in principle cannot, know whether sequences in nature actually have limits (with respect to the relative frequencies of various properties), nevertheless, *if* they do, then by continued use of the rule of induction it can be demonstrated that we shall approach these limits to within any desired degree of approximation. In short, if the universe is orderly (in the sense of containing limits of frequencies), then by continuing to employ the rule of induction we shall discover the order. This suffices to justify our use of the rule, just as, by analogy, a surgeon is justified in operating on a dying patient even if he does not know whether the operation will cure the patient but knows only that if a cure is possible an operation will achieve it.

Principles constituting a scientific system can be shown to be justified, if at all, by the use of the rule of induction. In science we must recognize the existence of a concatenation of inductive inferences which allows the correction of initial posits. Thus, if all observed instances of carbon have not melted at various high temperatures, the rule of induction would lead us to a first-level posit that carbon is infusible. But observation of other substances that do melt at sufficiently high temperatures allows us to assign a weight of zero to the initial posit and thus to adopt a second-level posit to the effect that carbon will melt if the temperature gets sufficiently high. In this manner scientific hypotheses are constructed in such a way as to continually modify existing ones.

Reichenbach also proposed that a probability logic be substituted for the usual two-valued (true–false) logic. A probability logic replaces single propositions with sequences of propositions to which probability values are assigned ranging over all real numbers from 0 to 1.

Space and time. The existence of internally consistent alternative geometries (for example, Euclidean and Riemannian geometries) suggests the question of which of these, if any, applies to the actual physical world. To answer this question Reichenbach emphasized the importance of conventional as well as empirical considerations. The conventional aspect involves providing so-called coordinative definitions for certain concepts. (These are definitions that relate a given concept to an observable object, property, or phenomenon.) Thus, the concept *unit of length* can be coordinated to the standard meter in Paris. Consider now the notion of congruence, or equality of length, a concept basic to any geometry. It is an empirical (and hence nonconventional) fact that two measuring rods found to be equal in length when brought together and compared at one point in space will also be found to be equal in length when brought together and compared at another place. But it cannot be empirically determined whether on the way the rods expand, contract, or stay the same. We might imagine the presence of universal forces which affect all bodies in the same way and against which there are no insulating walls. Such forces (which might, for example, cause everything in the universe, including measuring rods, to double in length overnight) could not be detected by empirical means. Thus, a convention must be adopted according to which congruence is defined for rods (or any objects) at different places. If rods which are equal in length when brought together are defined as congruent under transport, then by definition universal forces are set equal to zero. If universal forces are assumed, there will be a different definition of congruence. It is only when congruence between objects at different places is determined by convention that the question of which geometry is applicable to physical space becomes an empirical issue. Which definition of congruence is chosen will depend upon considerations of simplicity and of the least possible change in the results of science. Using such criteria, Reichenbach advocated that definition of congruence according to which universal forces are set equal to zero. This means adopting a non-Euclidean geometry for the neighborhood of heavenly bodies, since Euclidean geometry would require the postulation of universal forces that cause light to bend in the vicinity of such bodies.

Analogous considerations apply to the study of physical time. Coordinative definitions are required, not only for a unit of time but also for simultaneity. "As in geometry, the equality of successive time intervals is not a matter of *knowledge,* but a matter of *definition*" (*Space and Time,* p. 116). According to Reichenbach, Einstein's special theory of relativity is based in large measure on the realization that the simultaneity of events occurring at distant places is a matter of definition. The "relativity" involved in this theory means "relative to a certain definitional system." Thus, depending upon definitions, different, though equivalent, descriptions of physical motion become possible (in somewhat the same manner, Reichenbach claimed, that "This room is 21 feet long" and "This room is 7 yards long" are equivalent descriptions based upon different definitions of a unit of length). Reichenbach developed an axiomatic system for relativistic mechanics in which he carefully distinguished the physical, or empirical, assertions of this theory from the coordinative definitions which provide an epistemological foundation for the theory.

Two other temporal notions that require definitions are temporal order and direction, which must be defined by reference to physics. Consider the analogy between events in time and points on a line. Points can be ordered by considering which points are between which others, without regard for whether the direction taken is right or left. In an analogous manner physical events can be conceived of as ordered in time, without specifying what is to be taken as the direction from earlier to later. A temporal ordering of events is provided by laws of physics that describe mechanical processes. For example, differential equations of mechanics allow one to describe the various states in the parabolic flight of a ball. Yet it is perfectly consistent with these laws to describe the same process by reversing the temporal direction and imagining that these processes occur "backward" in time, just as we could reverse a film depicting the flight of the ball, where the reverse sequence shown does not violate physical princi-

ples. The laws of mechanics, therefore, define a temporal order of events but not a temporal direction. The latter must be defined by reference to those processes in nature that are irreversible, such as the passage of heat from bodies of higher to bodies of lower temperature, processes which, according to the second law of thermodynamics, involve an increase in entropy. The direction of positive time can be defined as that in which most thermodynamic processes occur ("most" being required because of the statistical nature of the second law of thermodynamics). We cannot, however, speak of a direction for time as a whole but only for certain segments in which relatively isolated ("branch") systems undergo thermodynamic changes. For some segments (those in which processes may occur in such a way that entropy decreases), we shall have to recognize the peculiar possibility of a reversal in time direction.

Quantum theory. Reichenbach proposed a novel interpretation of quantum mechanics. He began by distinguishing what he called phenomena (for example, collisions between elementary particles observed in the cloud chamber) from interphenomena (for example, the unobservable behavior of particles between collisions). The physicist determines the phenomena by experiment and attempts to construct a theory describing both the observed phenomena and the unobservable interphenomena. Two types of descriptive systems are possible—those in which the laws of nature are the same irrespective of whether the objects are observed and those in which they are not. Systems of the former sort Reichenbach called normal. For example, when we look at a tree we observe certain phenomena; when we are not observing the tree we postulate interphenomena involving the tree remaining the same. As an alternative we could imagine that the tree disappears when we do not look at it and that it suddenly reappears when we do. The latter description, as opposed to the former, would be nonnormal, since it would make the tree's characteristics depend upon our observations. Although a nonnormal description will introduce "causal anomalies," nevertheless, since both normal and nonnormal systems provide equivalent descriptions of observable phenomena, they are equally usable; which one is chosen is a matter of convention.

In quantum mechanics both the wave and the particle interpretations involve systems describing interphenomena, but neither description can be carried through without introducing causal anomalies. (For example, the individual flashes observed in an electron diffraction experiment introduce a causal anomaly into the wave description, whereas the diffraction pattern introduces a causal anomaly into the particle interpretation.) Moreover, Reichenbach showed, neither interpretation provides a normal description. How, then, shall we interpret the principles of quantum mechanics? We might want to adopt either the wave or the particle description, each of which, because it completely describes interphenomena, is called an exhaustive interpretation. If we follow this procedure we will have to recognize the impossibility of characterizing interphenomena in such a way that the postulates of causality are satisfied. There is, however, an alternative procedure involving a so-called restrictive interpretation:

we agree to renounce any description of interphenomena and restrict quantum mechanics to statements describing phenomena. According to one rule of restriction, attributed to Niels Bohr and Werner Heisenberg, statements about interphenomena will be treated as meaningless. (Thus, in an interference experiment in which electrons pass through two slits forming an interference pattern on a screen, the statement "The electron went through the upper slit rather than the lower one" would be considered lacking in cognitive meaning.) According to another interpretation, which Reichenbach himself advocated, statements describing interphenomena will be considered meaningful but indeterminate in truth-value. With this way of reconstructing quantum mechanics, use must be made of a three-valued logic, in which sentences receive the values T (true), F (false), or I (indeterminate). Causal anomalies will thus be eliminated from the descriptive system in the sense that statements describing them will be considered to be neither true nor false. Which interpretation is chosen, however, will reflect a volitional decision and is not something that can be proved or disproved. Reichenbach claimed that the advantage of his interpretation is that it contains a system of rules allowing statements about observables to be derived from statements about unobservables, without requiring the latter to be considered devoid of sense.

Scientific laws and logical operations. Logicians define operators such as "or," "and," "if–then," and "not" in a way that allows them to express postulates of classical mathematics and set theory in symbolic notation and to derive appropriate theorems. However, when so defined and employed without restriction in empirical science, these operators produce unreasonable results. (For example, given the logician's definition of "if–then," the sentence "If snow is not white, then sugar is sour" counts as true because of the falsity of the antecedent.) Scientific laws expressed in the if–then form ("If a metal is heated, then it expands") Reichenbach called nomological implications. He sought to define the notion of a nomological statement or law, using the operators supplied by the logician but devising requirements that sentences expressed in such a notation must satisfy if they are to count as laws.

First, Reichenbach defined the notion of an original (or basic) nomological statement P by specifying a set of conditions that P must satisfy: P must be verifiably true (verified as highly probable at some time in the past or future); P must be universal in the sense that it must not contain essential references to particular space-time regions; P must be an "all" statement—that is, one capable of being written with an "all" operator in front; P must satisfy a generalization of the requirement that the antecedent of an if–then statement cannot always be false (otherwise the entire statement would be trivially true); and so forth. He then defined a derived nomological statement as one deductively implied by a set of original nomological statements and the set of nomological statements as comprising the original and derived ones. This set can be used to define modal operators, such as "necessary," "possible," and "impossible." Thus, "P is necessary" means "'P' is a nomological statement"; "P is impossible" means "the negation of 'P' is a nomological statement"; and "P is pos-

sible" means "neither 'P' nor its negation is a nomological statement." All original, but not all derived, nomological statements can be shown to be admissible in science. Accordingly, within the set of nomological statements Reichenbach defined a class of admissible statements that he regarded as supplying reasonable logical operations.

Works by Reichenbach

Axiomatik der relativistichen Raum-Zeit-Lehre. Braunschweig, Germany, 1924.
Philosophie der Raum-Zeit-Lehre. Berlin and Leipzig, 1928. Translated by Maria Reichenbach and John Freund as *The Philosophy of Space and Time.* New York, 1958.
Wahrscheinlichkeitslehre. Leiden, 1935. Translated by Ernest H. Hutten and Maria Reichenbach as *The Theory of Probability,* 2d ed. Berkeley and Los Angeles, 1949.
Experience and Prediction. Chicago, 1938.
"On the Justification of Induction." *Journal of Philosophy,* Vol. 37 (1940), 97–103.
"On Meaning." *Journal of Unified Science,* Vol. 9 (1940), 134–135.
Philosophical Foundations of Quantum Mechanics. Berkeley and Los Angeles, 1944.
Elements of Symbolic Logic. New York, 1947.
"Rationalism and Empiricism." *Philosophical Review,* Vol. 57 (1948), 330–346.
"The Philosophical Significance of the Theory of Relativity," in P. A. Schilpp, ed., *Albert Einstein: Philosopher-scientist.* Evanston, Ill., 1949.
The Rise of Scientific Philosophy. Berkeley and Los Angeles, 1951.
"Are Phenomenal Reports Absolutely Certain?" *Philosophical Review,* Vol. 61 (1952), 147–159.
"The Syllogism Revised." *Philosophy of Science,* Vol. 19 (1952), 1–16.
Nomological Statements and Admissible Operations. Amsterdam, 1954.
The Direction of Time. Berkeley and Los Angeles, 1956.
Modern Philosophy of Science. London, 1958.

Works on Reichenbach

Grünbaum, Adolf, *Philosophical Problems of Space and Time.* New York, 1963. Ch. 3 discusses Reichenbach's philosophy of geometry.
Nagel, Ernest, review of *Philosophical Foundations of Quantum Mechanics. Journal of Philosophy,* Vol. 42 (1945), 437–444.
Nagel, Ernest, "Probability and the Theory of Knowledge," in his *Sovereign Reason.* Glencoe, Ill., 1954.
Putnam, Hilary, review of *The Direction of Time. Journal of Philosophy,* Vol. 59 (1962), 213–216.
Quine, W. V., review of *Elements of Symbolic Logic. Journal of Philosophy,* Vol. 45 (1948), 161–166.
Salmon, Wesley, "Should We Attempt to Justify Induction?" *Philosophical Studies,* Vol. 8 (1957), 33–48.
Symposium on Probability in *Philosophy and Phenomenological Research,* Vols. 5–6 (1945). Papers by Reichenbach, D. C. Williams, Ernest Nagel, Rudolf Carnap, Henry Margenau, and others.

PETER ACHINSTEIN

REID, THOMAS (1710–1796), originator of the Scottish philosophy of common sense, was born near Aberdeen. At Marischal College, Aberdeen, he was taught by George Turnbull and probably learned from him to regard common language as, in Turnbull's words, "built on fact" and as manifesting common convictions of mankind. While Presbyterian minister at New Machar he studied Hume's *Treatise of Human Nature* (1739). He renounced both his Berkeleian views and the theory that had led him to them after seeing in Hume what he took to be the theory's unrestricted consequences. In 1751 he was appointed to a regentship at King's College, Aberdeen. His *An Inquiry into the Human Mind on the Principles of Common Sense* was published in 1764, and in the same year he went to Glasgow as professor of moral philosophy. Besides several small pieces he wrote two other books—the *Essays on the Intellectual Powers of Man* (1785) and the *Essays on the Active Powers of Man* (1788).

Theory of ideas. In Hume's philosophy Reid saw the dissolution of the world—persons and things alike—into fugitive atoms of experience occurring associatively in clusters; between items in a cluster or between clusters themselves there existed no real connection but only bare "conjunction." For Reid anything in the *Treatise* inconsistent with these conclusions, any mitigating gloss upon them, was inconsistent with Hume's presuppositions. What gave these presuppositions their great importance was their inclusion of a principle that was in no way peculiar to Hume; it could claim, Reid thought, the very general, if not the universal, sanction of philosophers. This principle asserts that we can know nothing of anything outside the mind except by means of some representative substitute for it within the privacy of the mind. "Ideas" had become the most familiar of the many names given to these entities, and what Reid called the theory of ideas was a theory of perception, memory, and thought structured in conformity with this principle. According to the theory, everything external to us that is perceived or thought of, everything remembered, is represented to us by ideas, which are immediately present to the mind as the things themselves cannot be.

The theory fails completely, Reid argued, as an explanation of the possibility of perception, thought, and memory. Before we can know that ideas do inform us representatively of their objects, we should have to do what the theory declares impossible, that is, cross the chasms of externality and temporal remoteness that supposedly made ideas necessary, in order to compare them with their objects. In particular, Reid rejected the theory's account of memory and thought as quite unintelligible. If we remember or think of something, we remember or think of the object itself. It is the object that is before the mind and as immediately as its idea could have been; the distinction between mediate and immediate is here meaninglessly out of place. But the theory, in Reid's opinion, does not simply fail: "Ideas seem to have something in their nature unfriendly to other existences," and unable to fulfill the representative function assigned to them, they take on an absolute character, supplanting the things they were supposed to represent. Originally the mind's immediate objects, they became its only objects.

Critique of Berkeley. It was not until Berkeley's criticism of Locke, Reid thought, that the latent paradox and skepticism in the theory began to reveal themselves unmistakably. Berkeley realized that nothing could be like an idea but another idea and that it was absurd to imagine, as Locke had done, that any of the ideas we were supposed to receive in perception from the qualities of physical objects could be like any of these qualities. Proceeding on the assumption he shared with Locke, that we

could have no conception of such qualities except through ideas resembling them, Berkeley discarded as an empty fiction the notion that physical objects exist independently of our perception and allowed existence only to minds and their ideas. He did not realize, Reid said, that by disembodying us in obedience to the logic of the theory of ideas, he condemned each of us to a solitary existence. My dealings with other men have become transactions with ideas "in my own mind." Hume finished the work; with him the mind collapses into its ideas.

Reid was unconscious of the extent to which he was inferring Hume's and Berkeley's "principles" from their "conclusions," and he was, in fact, unable to exhibit this collapse purely as a consequence of the supposition of representative ideas. These ideas were to mediate the mind's awareness of everything external to itself, and at issue here is the mind's knowledge of itself. What Reid did at this point was to word the theory of ideas in such a way as to have it state, in effect, the conclusions to be derived from it: "It is a fundamental principle of the ideal system, that every object of thought must be an impression or an idea—that is, a faint copy of some preceding impression" (*Inquiry into the Human Mind,* Ch. II, Sec. vi). Impressions and ideas in Hume's terminology are two different sorts of ideas in Reid's. To find the preparation for Hume's conclusions with regard to the mind in earlier opinions, it is necessary to go outside a theory of knowledge through the mediation of ideas to the conceptual empiricism Reid associated with the theory. Locke had allowed no conceptions not ultimately derived either from sense experience or from the mind's awareness of its actions and passions. For Hume these notions have to copy what they are derived from. Otherwise, he spoke with Locke when he said that we have no ideas without preceding impressions. When Hume added that we look in vain for any impression, any experience, of a substantival self holding together our experience, he was close to his fragmentation of the mind.

Many of the characteristic features of Reid's philosophy are related to his attack on the theory of ideas. Thus, it incorporates his demand for an experiential approach to all philosophical inquiry. Only the negative side of this method is visible when Reid uses it against the theory of ideas. Reid wanted matter-of-fact evidence that ideas, in the theory sense of the word, existed and that they were not philosophers' inventions. Searching his own mind, he was unable to discover their presence. He could, of course, find sensations and conceptions, and these had been treated by philosophers as varieties of ideas. But as far as he could discover, they showed no sign of the office assigned to them by the theory. They did not present themselves as objects, let alone as objects mediating remote objects.

Reid thought that the philosophy of the mind was full of more or less plausible and groundless hypotheses and that its reformation must begin with their thorough proscription. It had to be purged especially of attempts to assimilate by analogy the mind's operations to the behavior of bodies. One of these analogies in particular, Reid considered, had carried philosophers a long way toward the theory of ideas—through the subterranean influence of physical imagery, the mind and its objects in perception, thought, and memory were treated as if they were remote interacting bodies needing a medium to connect them. From the positive application of empirical procedures Reid hoped for, and set little account by his progress toward, a philosophy of the mind that might eventually arrive at a knowledge of "the original powers and laws of our constitution" and thus make possible unifying explanations of the "phenomena of human nature."

The theory of ideas resulted, Reid argued, in conclusions "shocking to common sense." But quite apart from its consequences, he condemned it in its very principle as rejecting what we all ordinarily take for granted as a matter of fundamental conviction: the immediacy of perception, memory, and thought. Reid was a damaging critic of Locke's and Hume's opinions on the nature of memory. He himself had nothing that could properly be called a theory of memory: "The knowledge which I have of things past, by my memory, seems to me as unaccountable as an immediate knowledge would be of things to come" (*Intellectual Powers*, Essay III, Ch. ii). Thought about things distant from us in place or time does not seem to have occasioned any philosophical perplexity in Reid. Thought about what does not exist involved him in a great deal of trouble, and his only sustained obscurity comes with his attempt to avoid having ideas for its objects. He had a fairly elaborate theory of perception, though "theory" was not his word for what he regarded as a plain description of the facts of perception with the gaps where knowledge is necessarily unobtainable left unbridged by conjecture.

Perception. Reid regarded perception as a complex of sensation, conception, and belief. We perceive the smoothness, hardness, and roundness of something we are holding in our hands. Apart from sight, what means of information are at our disposal in this perception? The sensations in our fingers and the palms of our hands, Reid answered; there is nothing else. The perception is not made possible by any resemblance between the sensations and the qualities; the roundness of a ball and the feelings in bent fingers, for example, could not be more unlike each other. There are no discoverable connections between them that would justify inference, but we attempt no inference. Inexplicably and immediately, we pass from the sensations to a conception of the nature of the qualities and to the belief that they exist, and do so independently of our perception. According to Reid, sensations that result in perception are "natural signs"; they do something analogous to the work done by words. But words are "conventional signs," and their meaning has to be learned. We do not have to, nor could we, learn what these sensations of touch primitively signify; we are so constituted that we are able to interpret them intuitively. They function, moreover, not only like words but like familiar words. A familiar word takes us straight to its meaning without obtruding itself on our attention. Similarly, the sensations of touch normally work unnoticed when they effect our perception of the primary qualities of a body; our attention, wholly outer-directed, slides over them to what they signify. All perception that resembles this in being quite untutored Reid called original perception. As there is a natural language of sensation, so there is also analogously, Reid thought, an untaught language of gesture, facial expression, and intonation which for each of us lies at the foundation of our knowledge of other men's minds.

When we perceive the secondary qualities of a body—its color, sound, taste, and so forth—we do so again, Reid argued, by means of the significatory powers of sensations. Unlike the sensations related to the primary qualities, which "give us a direct and a distinct notion of the primary qualities, and inform us what they are in themselves" (*Intellectual Powers*, Essay II, Ch. xvi), these sensations signify originally no more than their unknown causes. It is for science to discover the nature of taste, for example, or of smell as a property of a physical object. The sensations of this class therefore do not go unnoticed; on the contrary, they are essential to our distinctions between the various secondary qualities. In contrast with perception by touch, Reid held that the perception by sight of a thing's shape or size from its visible appearance is not original but acquired perception; we have learned by experience the meaning of the signs involved. Most of our perception, he thought, is acquired. It is in this way that, for example, we perceive a rose by its smell and the passing of a coach by its sound. It is a nice question how far Reid's theory of perception is of a type embraced by the theory of ideas.

Common sense. In the grip of theory, Reid said, philosophers have promulgated opinions contrary to common sense. For Reid the task of a philosopher defending common sense was unavoidably restricted; he can argue against such theories, against particular objections to any of the beliefs of common sense and against proposed alternatives to them, but he is not in a position to argue for them if this means providing them with proofs from more evident premises. When their truth is brought into dispute, they are both well and badly placed. They suffer the disability of being first principles; there are no more ultimate truths from which they can be derived. But they have the authority of first principles; they carry their evidence with them, or, in Reid's alternative way of putting it, they are imposed upon us by "the constitution of our nature." Their positive defense thus becomes a matter of drawing attention to their authority. It has a manifold command over us. The principles of common sense are obviously true, although their evidence can be dimmed by "the enchantment of words." There is more than obvious falsity in their denial. To deny or even to doubt any of them is to involve oneself in absurdity. Anyone doubting or denying, for example, the existence of things outside his perception, his own identity of being through time, or the existence of other minds besides his own can depend on derisive incredulity if his words are plain enough to be understood. These principles are implicit in our conduct, so much so that we have no choice but to act in accordance with them whether or not we acknowledge them. Many of them have helped to mold the structure of common language everywhere. They have been bedrock convictions of the vast generality of mankind, learned and unlearned alike.

In Reid's doctrine the existence of common sense has theistic presuppositions; its truths are "the inspiration of the Almighty." Reid did not maintain that belief in them depends upon belief in God; they are imposed upon us by the constitution of our nature, whatever our other beliefs. His implication is that we have to go behind common sense, if we are to explain its competence, to the fact that our nature has been constituted by God. We have the same sort of evidence for the existence of God that we have for intelligence and will in our fellow men: self-identifying marks of intelligence and will. The man who can see no grounds for a belief in God ought in consistency, Reid thought, to see no grounds for a belief in any mind besides his own.

It was a standing charge against Reid that in setting up common sense as an authority in philosophical matters, he was canonizing "the judgment of the crowd." He was certainly not doing anything so simple and disreputable. In appealing to common sense against philosophical paradox and skepticism, he believed he was appealing to principles with an array of characteristics that no vulgar prejudice—however extensive—possessed. What he failed to do was to produce the undeniable warrant of common sense for the metaphysical content that he discerned in many of its dictates. Nor did he often attempt to show that opinions he rejected as contrary to common sense have to be given up in practice. Thus, to take a simple example, the phenomenalist opinion that physical objects are to be resolved into sense impressions contradicts common sense, Reid thought. But he did not explain how the phenomenalist was committed by his opinion to behaving differently from other men.

Morality. Reid's moral theory was developed largely in recoil from the theory of ideas. The same drive toward subjectivity that turned the world into sense impressions, he thought, turned the distinction between right and wrong into mere feelings of approval and disapproval and met the same unyielding resistance from common sense. The language in which our moral assertions are cast shows them to be real judgments and not merely expressions of certain feelings, and it embodies original concepts that differ in kind from all other concepts. Moral truths therefore have both thorough objectivity and unique content. They are intuitively discerned, or if they are reached by reasoning, it is from premises that must include a self-evident moral premise. In his argument for the objectivity of right and wrong, Reid had Hume particularly in mind; he again concerned himself with Hume in dealing with the principles of action. Reason, Reid maintained, has always had ascribed to it the double office of regulating our belief and our conduct. And reason prescribes two great ends, different but unopposed, to our conduct: our happiness and our duty. It is therefore evident that the passions should be governed by reason. According to Hume, "Reason is, and ought only to be the slave of the passions." This at first sight appears "a shocking paradox," Reid said, "repugnant to good morals and to common sense," but when its meaning is elicited, it turns out, "like other paradoxes," to be "nothing but an abuse of words." "For if we give the name of *passion* to every principle of action, in every degree, and give the name of *reason* solely to the power of discerning the fitness of means to ends, it will be true that the use of reason is to be subservient to the passions" (*Active Powers*, Essay III, Part II, Ch. vi). In defending our free agency against various forms of determinism, Reid effectively calls attention to the distorting analogies that hurry into the mind when the notion of human agency is considered; the agent is easily regarded as the subject of impressed forces and his action as their result. In Reid's opinion, we do not have to be brought to the belief that we are capable of genuinely originating action, of making choices which are not the necessary issue of a combination of character and circumstances. But the consistency of this belief with other things that we take for granted has to be shown, and arguments in favor of determinism have to be dealt with. Both are substantial topics in Reid's discussion of free will.

Influence. The school of common sense, which derived from Reid, acquired with Dugald Stewart the stability of an institution. Its teachings—specifically those of Reid—made a deep impression on Thomas Brown, who revolted against them, and on Sir William Hamilton, who attempted to combine them with notions obtained from Kant. Its influence spread far beyond philosophers to permeate Scottish intellectual life for several generations. During the first half of the nineteenth century it had a similar influence in America. In both countries it did more than supply a set of opinions; it established a way of thinking. Reid's ideas were introduced into France early in the nineteenth century by Pierre-Paul Royer-Collard; they were taken up by Victor Cousin and were used as weapons against the ascendancy of an extreme and doctrinaire empiricism. Reid was carefully studied in Italy and Belgium. Although the school of common sense had lost its authority well before the end of the nineteenth century, Reid continued to influence individual thinkers (a notable example in America being C. S. Peirce), and when G. E. Moore made common sense a topic of great importance in recent philosophy, interest in Reid revived. He has more than a historical claim on contemporary attention.

Works by Reid

Works, Sir William Hamilton, ed., 2 vols. Edinburgh, 1846–1863. Contains Stewart's *Life* of Reid and a long dissertation on common sense by Hamilton.

Philosophical Orations, W. R. Humphries, ed. Aberdeen, 1937. Addresses delivered at graduation ceremonies at King's College, Aberdeen.

Essays on the Intellectual Powers of Man (abridged), A. D. Woozley, ed. London, 1941.

Works on Reid

Chastaing, M., "Reid, la philosophie du sens commun." *Revue philosophique de la France et de l'étranger,* Vol. 144 (1954), 352–399.

Cousin, Victor, *Philosophie écossaise,* 3d ed. Paris, 1857.

Fraser, A. C., *Thomas Reid.* Edinburgh, 1898.

Grave, S. A., *The Scottish Philosophy of Common Sense.* Oxford, 1960.

Jones, O. M., *Empiricism and Intuitionism in Reid's Common Sense Philosophy.* Princeton, N.J., 1927.

McCosh, J., *The Scottish Philosophy.* London, 1875. Pp. 192–227, 473–476.

Martin, T., *The Instructed Vision.* Bloomington, Ind., 1961. Shows the influence of the common-sense school on the American mind.

Priestley, Joseph, *An Examination of Dr. Reid's Inquiry, etc.* London, 1774. Unsparing criticism of the early common-sense school.

Sciacca, M. F., *La filosofia di Tommaso Reid,* 3d ed. Milan, 1963.

Seth (Pringle-Pattison), Andrew, *Scottish Philosophy.* Edinburgh, 1885.

S. A. GRAVE

REIMARUS, HERMANN SAMUEL (1694–1768), German philosopher and theologian, was born in Hamburg and studied theology at Jena. After serving as a lecturer in Wittenberg and as director of a high school in Wismar, he became a teacher of oriental languages at the Johannes-gymnasium in Hamburg. He began writing very late in life, when he was about 60. One of his most important works, *Apologie oder Schutzschrift für die vernünftigen Verehrer Gottes* ("Apology for or Defense of the Rational Worshiper of God"), was first published by Lessing—posthumously and only in part—as fragments of an allegedly anonymous manuscript found in the Wolfenbüttel Library, where Lessing was librarian ("Wolfenbüttler Fragmente eines Ungenannten," in *Beiträge zur Geschichte und Literatur*, 1774–1777).

Reimarus was originally a Wolffian, and Wolffianism was a lasting foundation for his thought; but he developed individual doctrines in both philosophy and theology as one of the "popular philosophers." He stressed the moral aim of philosophy, that is, the happiness and moral perfectibility of man. He dissented from Wolff chiefly in his views of philosophical methodology. He wrote in a "popular," or nonscholastic, style; he asserted that philosophy can be neither as certain as mathematics nor mathematically demonstrated; he stressed the function of common sense in knowledge; and he tried to simplify logic. In metaphysics, his main points of divergence from Wolff were his admission of a real interaction of soul and body and his view that life cannot be mechanically explained, but that it is an effect of the soul.

Reimarus' most important work was in the field of animal psychology and in his classification of the instincts of animals. Man, unlike animals, has only a very few instincts. This lack may be a disadvantage for material life, but it is the basis for morality.

Reimarus appeared in his lifetime to be a moderate advocate of natural religion who did not openly oppose Christian revelation. But in the posthumous *Apologie* he submitted Christian revelation to a radical criticism in the spirit of English deism. In this work, for the first time in Germany the traditional view of Christianity was attacked neither on a speculative plan nor through superficial historical arguments, but on the basis of sound historical scholarship. Reimarus pointed out discordances between the Old and the New Testaments and between the different sections of each. He refused to accept the Gospels as the word of God, but described them as being an exposition of theological views elaborated by Jesus' successors in the leadership of Christianity. He considered the accounts of miracles, and in particular the account of the resurrection of Jesus, to relate events that never happened and to be forgeries of the Apostles. This purely rationalistic criticism made a tremendous impression on late eighteenth-century Germany, and deeply influenced the subsequent evolution of German theology.

Additional Works by Reimarus

Abhandlungen von den vornehmsten Wahrheiten der natürlichen Religion. Hamburg, 1754.

Vernunftlehre. Hamburg and Kiel, 1756.

Allgemeine Betrachtungen über die Triebe der Tiere. Hamburg, 1760.

Uebrigen noch ungedruckte Werke des Wolfenbüttelschen Fragmentisten, C. A. E. Schmidt, ed. Berlin, 1786. Contains further portions of the *Apologie.*

Works on Reimarus

Aner, Karl, *Die Theologie der Lessingzeit.* Halle, 1929; reprinted Hildesheim, 1964.

Büttner, W., *H. S. Reimarus als Metaphysiker.* Würzburg, 1909.

Engert, Joseph, *H. S. Reimarus als Metaphysiker.* Paderborn, 1909.

Engert, Joseph, *Der Deismus und die Religions- und Offenbarungskritik des H. S. Reimarus.* Vienna, 1915.

Fittbogen, G., "Lessings Entwicklung bis zur Begegnung mit Reimarus Werk." *Preussischer Jahrbücher,* Vol. 73 (1918).

Richardt, H., *Darstellung der moralphilosophischen Anschauungen H. S. Reimarus.* Leipzig, 1906.

Schettler, R., *Die Stellung des Philosophen H. S. Reimarus zur Religion.* Leipzig, 1904.

Strauss, D. F., *H. S. Reimarus und seine Schutzschrift für die vernünftigen Verehrer Gottes.* Leipzig, 1862.

GIORGIO TONELLI

REINCARNATION. The doctrine variously called transmigration of souls, metempsychosis, palingenesis, rebirth, and reincarnation has been and continues to be widely believed. Although some of these terms imply belief in an immortal soul that transmigrates or reincarnates, Buddhism, while teaching rebirth, denies the eternity of the soul. The word "rebirth" is therefore the most comprehensive for referring to this range of beliefs.

In one form or another the doctrine of rebirth has been held in various cultures. It was expressed in ancient Greece (Pythagoras, Empedocles, Orphism, Plato, and later, Plotinus); among some Gnostics and in some Christian heresies such as the medieval Cathari; in some phases of Jewish Cabalism; in some cultures of tropical Africa; and most notably in such Eastern religions as Jainism, Buddhism, Hinduism, and Sikhism. Some European philosophers, notably Schopenhauer and J. M. E. McTaggart, have incorporated the doctrine into their metaphysics. The origin of the doctrine of rebirth as a religious belief is obscure. There is evidence, both in Greece and India, that it was not characteristic of early Aryan cultures. It is virtually certain that in India it goes back to prehistoric times; it was then taken up by Brahmanic religion and appears as a new doctrine in the Upanisads.

Views vary about the scope and mechanism of rebirth. It is part of Indian thought, for instance—but not of African beliefs—that men can be reborn as animals and even as plants (not to mention as gods and spirits). Rebirth can take place not merely on earth but also in a multiplicity of heavens and purgatories. Thus, although the prevalent belief is that rebirth occurs immediately upon death, this does not entail immediate earthly reincarnation, a feature that helps to make rebirth theory incapable of empirical disproof. In the Buddhist *Tibetan Book of the Dead,* however, a transitional period (*bardo*) of 49 days between death and rebirth is postulated. During this state the individual is translated to a realm where he perceives the divine secrets; for the impure, these are so frightening that they flee back to earth and are reborn.

In Indian thought, there is a fairly large amount of speculation about the embryological mechanics of rebirth.

Thus the Sāṃkhya school of Indian philosophy holds that the mental aspect of a person bears the impression of previous deeds (karma) and that it accordingly becomes associated with a particular fetus. But since during the period of fetal development the growing body is not capable of supporting the mental aspect, a "subtle" (unobservably refined) body is postulated. Thus the continuous element throughout rebirth and until liberation is the mental aspect associated with the subtle body.

In Buddhism it is held that the fetus results from the interaction of the sperm and material in the mother. These combine in a suitable way when associated with conscious states, as a further element in the process, to produce the right sort of individual to fit previous karma. Broadly speaking, then, rebirth theory implies that the genetic endowment of a person does not fully determine his early development but that a mental or spiritual factor associates itself with a suitable organism at conception. Thus karma is often taken to function through the homing of a soul upon a morally and physically appropriate fetus. McTaggart, in urging this, uses the analogy of chemical affinities.

A number of arguments in favor of the theory have been propounded; they can be classified as metaphysical, empirical, and theological. It is convenient to record here those arguments that do not depend too closely on metaphysical conclusions peculiar to particular philosophers, such as the argument for rebirth as accounting for knowledge of the Forms, as in Plato, and the complex metaphysical argument in McTaggart that depends in part on his theory of causation.

In Indian sources, two main metaphysical arguments have been employed. It may be noted that there has been relatively little explicit discussion of the issue in Indian philosophy, since no school was concerned with denying the doctrine, except the Materialist school, which was extinct by medieval times. (1) A Buddhist argument can be expressed as follows. All states have prior causes; some conscious states are not caused by bodily states; therefore the first physically uncaused state of an individual must have a prior nonphysical cause. But the existence of God is not admitted; hence there must be an empirical conscious state prior to conception and birth. This argument applies indefinitely in a backward direction through previous births. (It may be noted that the argument is consistent with the Buddhist denial of an eternal soul, since the mental states of an organism are no more permanent than the physical ones.) (2) There is a Hindu argument from the eternity of the soul, which has been used in modern times by Radhakrishnan. Souls are eternal, but the normal condition for a soul is to be associated with a body. Hence it is likely that the soul in the past and future has a virtually everlasting succession of bodies. Thus metaphysical arguments attempting to establish the eternity of the soul have been taken to imply pre-existence as well as postexistence.

Empirical arguments are as follows. (3) Children have instinctive capacities, which suggests that there must be learning prior to birth. Similarly, it is sometimes argued that child geniuses, such as Mozart, indicate prenatal training. (4) Some people claim to remember past births, as in the case of Bridey Murphy. This claim is commonly made in the East for yogis and persons of deep spiritual insight, such as the Buddha and Buddhist saints. (5) The *déjà vu* experience and claims to knowledge of people and places that are not based on previous experience in this life have been cited as indicating rebirth. A counterargument is used against the objection that most people have no memories of such previous lives: death is a traumatic experience (and so is birth), likely to cause amnesia. (6) The soul is indivisible and thus cannot derive from the parents, since it would then have to be a combination of parts.

The three important forms of theological argument are as follows. (7) Hindu and other scriptures and theologians are reliable in other matters and so ought to be reliable with respect to the teaching of rebirth. (8) Rebirth, associated with karma, provides a solution to part of the problem of evil, since inequalities and sufferings are the result of people's past deeds. (9) The doctrine of rebirth provides the possibility of a long process of self-perfection, which harmonizes well with the religious vision of the world as a theater for moral striving.

The following are the objections that have been or can be brought against the arguments for reincarnation. Three objections to argument (1) are, first, the concept of emergent characteristics obviates the difficulty in explaining the cause of psychical states, although perhaps at the expense of being obscure. Second, the first premise (that all states have prior causes) is arguable, and it might be that nonphysically-caused mental states are simply not caused. Third, the existence of God cannot be ruled out. (2) The plausibility of the argument depends on the plausibility of arguments for the eternity of the soul. Further, in Indian religious thought there is the possibility of *mokṣa*, or nirvana, a state of liberation in which there is no more rebirth. Consequently, it is inconsistent to hold that embodiment is necessary to souls. The Buddhist denial of a permanent self occasioned the criticism that there is nothing carried over to another life that would ensure individual continuity—the reply being that, on the Buddhist analysis, the individual in his present life is only a series of events, so that there is no essential difference in considering a succession of lives as constituting an individual series.

The following are objections to the empirical arguments. (3) Modern biology can sketch alternative explanations of instinct and genius in children. (4) Although some people seem to remember past lives, the evidence is not so unambiguous as to be conclusive; and if saintliness is a condition for remembering previous births, it would be difficult to verify such a memory—it would be hard to conduct an "experiment" in becoming a saint. (5) Similar problems arise with the evidence of *déjà vu* experiences. As to whether death is a traumatic experience, there is no evidence. (6) The creation of souls by God is compatible with the argument concerning the indivisibility of the soul; but in any case the argument depends on a soul–body distinction that may not be acceptable.

The objections to theological arguments are the following. (7) The validity of particular scriptures and theologies on matters of detail is especially suspect. (8) The argument that rebirth explains the existence of evil could not by itself be conclusive, since the problem of evil exists only for those who believe in a good God. (9) A similar consideration applies to the argument that rebirth allows the possibility of self-perfection.

Although believers in rebirth have scarcely touched on the matter, the theory of evolution also presents considerable difficulties to the traditional doctrine of a virtually infinite series stretching back into the past. In Indian mythological cosmology, however, there are periodic destructions of the cosmos, and during these periods embodied souls continue to exist latently; no doubt a similar assumption may deal with the above biological difficulties by arguing that before the emergence of life, souls existed latently, or in other parts of the cosmos. The problem remains, however, that this account would not be easily, if at all, checked by empirical evidence.

The hypothesis of reincarnation presents interesting problems about personal identity. If personal identity is analyzed in terms of memory, there would seem to be only a vacuous distinction between saying that *A* is reborn as *B* and that *A* and *B* are separate persons. C. J. Ducasse, however, has argued (*The Belief in a Life After Death*, p. 225) that memory of any given life may be regained at some time or other in the series, and this would hold the series together. If bodily identity were held to be necessary to personal identity, rebirth could scarcely be meaningful, as it involves causal action at a distance in the transition from *A*'s death to *B*'s birth or conception.

Bibliography

Brandon, S. F. G., *Man and His Destiny in the World's Religions.* Manchester, 1962.

Dasgupta, S. N., *History of Indian Philosophy*, 5 vols. Cambridge, 1922–1955.

Ducasse, C. J., *The Belief in a Life After Death.* New York, 1961.

McTaggart, J. M. E., *Some Dogmas of Religion.* London, 1906.

Radhakrishnan, S., *The Brahma Sūtra.* London, 1959. Translation with commentary plus a lengthy introduction to Vedānta.

Smart, N., *Doctrine and Argument in Indian Philosophy.* London, 1964. Ch. 12.

Stevenson, Ian, *The Evidence for Survival from Claimed Memories of Former Incarnations.* New York, 1961.

NINIAN SMART

REINHOLD, KARL LEONHARD (1758–1823), Austrian philosopher. Reinhold was educated by Jesuits until the dissolution of their order in 1773, when he entered the Catholic college of the Barnabites, where he also taught, from 1778 to 1783. In 1783 Reinhold left Vienna for Leipzig and in the same year abandoned Catholicism in favor of Protestantism. A year later he moved to Weimar, where he was invited by Wieland to contribute to his *Teutscher Merkur.* Soon he was not only Wieland's closest friend but also his son-in-law. Reinhold's first article, "Gedanken über Aufklärung," in which he traced the emergence of Enlightenment thought, appeared in July 1784, just a few months before the publication of Kant's famous essay "What Is Enlightenment?" In his article Reinhold pleaded for the fuller realization of such. Enlightenment aims as greater tolerance toward religious minorities, more widespread secularization of knowledge and its greater accessibility to all sections of the population, and, above all, for the right of the individual to seek and assert truth free from fear, according to his critical reason and moral convictions.

Although two years later (1786) he was to publish a series of articles in support of Kant's critical philosophy, his second article in the *Merkur* (1785) was directed against Kant's unfavorable review of Herder's *Ideen.* The article appeared anonymously, but Reinhold later admitted his authorship to Kant. The articles dealing with Kant's *Critique of Pure Reason*, published under the title "Briefe über die Kantische Philosophie" from 1786 to 1787, established Reinhold's reputation as the most skillful exponent of Kant's philosophy and resulted in his being offered the chair of philosophy at the University of Jena in 1787. Reinhold was no less successful as a university teacher, and soon after his arrival Jena became one of the chief centers of Kantian studies. He attracted many students to Jena, and so great was his popularity that he was repeatedly urged to refuse the appointment offered him at the University of Kiel. Reinhold hesitated at first but eventually decided to move to Kiel in 1794, where he remained until his death. One of the reasons for his departure, perhaps the most decisive, is revealed in a letter to Wieland which Reinhold later published in a selection of essays (*Auswahl vermischter Schriften*, Jena, 1796), under the title "Ueber die teutschen Beurtheilungen der französischen Revolution." Reinhold became increasingly worried over his countrymen's reactions to the excesses of the French revolutionary tribunals. In Kiel, which was then under Danish rule, he hoped to find a calmer political climate. Without condoning the terror of the revolutionaries, he nevertheless deplored the inferences that were drawn from it by leading public figures in Germany. In particular he viewed with anxiety the introduction of repressive measures and the tendency to regard the French Revolution as a conspiracy of the philosophers. The French revolutionaries, he argued, may have been mistaken in attempting to deduce political rules from abstract principles which were often inadequately understood, but they were correct in their assessment of the desperate plight of their compatriots. If inferences were to be drawn, these would not suggest that philosophy presented a danger to orderly government but rather that disorderly government encouraged men to invoke philosophy in a manner unwarranted by its inherent limitations. Practical considerations such as these, no less than more strictly theoretical ones, prompted Reinhold to inquire more closely into the nature and scope of philosophical speculation.

Most of the works that he wrote at Kiel advanced a "fundamental philosophy" concerned with the basic presuppositions of scientifically valid thought. As the basic axiom of his "fundamental philosophy" Reinhold postulated the principle of consciousness, which he formulated in this way: By virtue of consciousness the perceiving (*erkennende*) subject is capable of distinguishing himself as something distinct from, while at the same time related to, the object of his consciousness, which, however, is not the object itself but rather the idea or notion (*Vorstellung*) of it. The consciousness itself constitutes a basic and irreducible fact, capable of neither proof nor further definition. It can only verify itself by reflecting upon itself. Reinhold was anxious to demonstrate that every thought process involves both a priori and a posteriori elements. The relation of the *Vorstellung* to the external object embodies its a posteriori material content (*Stoff*), whereas the subjective activity involved (*Vorstellungsvermögen*) in shaping the material content into a clear *Vorstellung* constitutes its a priori form (*Form*).

Reinhold stipulated three interconnected stages in the operation of consciousness: sense perception (*Anschauung*), which he classified as a receptive activity, and cognitive understanding (*Verstand*) and reflective reasoning (*Vernunft*), both of which he described as spontaneous activities. The product of these combined activities is the *Vorstellung*, which, Reinhold warned, must not be confused with an "image" or an "impression," for both terms suggest mere receptivity. Nor must it be identified with a "representation" of the object, since there is no way of either proving the identity of the *Vorstellung* with the object or even of comparing its similarity to the object. It follows that the object as such, no less than the subject as such, remains not only unknowable (as Kant realized) but also inconceivable. Both subject and object, therefore, as things-in-themselves are pure abstractions. They are the residue of a *Vorstellung*, the thing minus the notion or conception of it. Without denying the existence of things-in-themselves, Reinhold refused to commit himself as to the nature of their existence. He explicitly stated that he was merely anxious to determine the possibility and the limitations of cognition, not to inquire into its psychological origins or into the ontological nature of the objects of cognition. His declared aim was to provide a descriptive account, a phenomenology, rather than a theory of cognition, together with an analysis of the terminology commonly employed in this field. In spite of, or perhaps because of, Reinhold's deliberate delimitation of his theoretical undertaking, his works provided suggestively fertile starting points for subsequent Kantian research from Fichte to Schopenhauer.

Additional Works by Reinhold

Versuch einer neuen Theorie des menschlichen Vorstellungsvermögens. Prague and Jena, 1789.

Beyträge zur Berichtigung bisheriger Missverständnisse der Philosophen, 2 vols. Jena, 1790 and 1794.

Ueber das Fundament des philosophischen Wissens. Jena, 1791.

Versuch einer Kritik der Logik aus dem Gesichtspunkt der Sprache. Kiel, 1806.

Grundlegung einer Synonymik für den allgemeinen Sprachgebrauch in den philosophischen Wissenschaften. Kiel, 1812.

Das menschliche Erkenntnisvermögen aus dem Gesichtspunkt der durch die Wortsprache vermittelten Zusammenhänge zwischen Sinnlichkeit und dem Denkvermögen. Kiel, 1816.

Works on Reinhold

Adam, Herbert, *Carl Leonhard Reinholds philosophischer Systemwechsel*. Heidelberg, 1930.

Cassirer, Ernst, *Das Erkenntnisproblem*. Berlin, 1923. Vol. III, pp. 33–57.

Klemmt, Alfred, *Karl Leonhard Reinholds Elementarphilosophie*. Hamburg, 1958.

Kroner, Richard, *Von Kant bis Hegel*. Tübingen, 1921. Vol. I, pp. 315–326.

Reinhold, Ernst, *Karl Leonhard Reinholds Leben und literarisches Wirken*. Jena, 1825.

Selling, Magnus, *Karl Leonhard Reinholds Elementarphilosophie in ihrem philosophischen Zusammenhang*. Lund, 1938.

FREDERICK M. BARNARD

RELATIONS, INTERNAL AND EXTERNAL. Common sense would seem to hold that if some properties of a thing were taken away from it, it would no longer be the same thing. Further, it seems to hold that this is not the case for *all* properties of the thing. This intuition is the basis of the distinction between essential and accidental properties of a thing. It is also the basis of the distinction between the internal and the external relations which that thing bears to other things. For if among the properties which are essential to a thing (for example, the state of Maine) are relational properties, properties whose characterization essentially involves reference to some other thing (for example, the property of being north of Boston), then we say that the relations in question (for example, the relation between Maine and Boston) are *internal* to that thing (Maine). If we think that the thing would be the same were it (for example) not north of Boston—as in the case of a railroad car traveling through Maine—then we say that the relation in question is merely *external* to that thing.

The most familiar sort of relations considered when the topic of internal relations is discussed are relations between two or more particulars. However, the same internal–external distinction may be drawn in the case of relations between universals and particulars and also in the case of relations between two or more universals. If one holds that for every property P which a particular X displays, there is a universal, P-hood, to which X stands in the relation of "exemplification," then *all* of X's properties may be construed as relational properties. Some of these relations of exemplification may be regarded as internal to X and others as external. Again, one may say that a universal such as "manhood" stands in an internal relation to certain other universals (for example, "rationality") and in an external relation to other universals (for example, "philosopherhood"). Here the internal relation in question will be entailment, in the sense of "entails" in which we say that a given property ("being a man") entails another property ("being rational"). In what follows, however, we shall confine ourselves as far as possible to relations holding between particulars, both because the philosophical literature has focused on such relations and because the notions of "exemplification of universals" and of "relations of entailment holding between universals" are sufficiently obscure and controversial to require detailed supplementary discussions. (Also, we shall not always trouble to distinguish between discussion of internal *properties* and of internal *relations*, since whatever doctrine a philosopher holds about the former will apply, *mutatis mutandis*, to the latter).

Two extreme positions have been put forward by philosophers who regard the internal–external distinction as unclear or incoherent. The first is that all of a thing's properties are essential to its being what it is (and, a fortiori, that all its relations are internal to it). This position is associated with idealism and monism, for reasons which will emerge as we proceed. It holds that the connections between each of a thing's properties (including its relational properties) and all of its other properties are so close that the deprivation of a single property would force us to say that, in a nontrivial sense, the thing is no longer what it was.

The second extreme position holds that none of a thing's properties are essential to it (and thus, a fortiori, that no relations are internal to it). This view is put foward by those who make a firm distinction between the thing itself and a description of it. These philosophers say that, although certain properties of the thing are such that a given description could no longer be correctly applied to it were these properties absent, the notion that "the thing would no longer be the same" if these properties were absent is either trivial or misleading. For, in the weakest sense of "same," the absence of *any* of its properties would make the thing no longer the same. Any stronger sense will, however, equate "being the same thing" with "being such that a given description correctly applies to it." But since for each thing there are an infinity of equally correct descriptions, and nothing in the thing itself determines which of these is *the* description, any specification of "essential properties" will be arbitrary.

Both positions hold that the traditional essence–accident distinction, which is drawn by common sense and was first formulated explicitly by Aristotle, must be abandoned. The second position holds that the notion of "essential property" must be seen as a purely conventional notion, without a ground in the nature of the thing itself. It therefore suggests that we replace the notion of a relation being internal to a thing with the notion of a given relational description of a thing (such as "being north of Boston") being internal to (that is, a necessary condition of) another description of the thing (such as "being in Maine"). The first position holds that the notion of "essential property" suggests, wrongly, that there is such a thing as a nonessential property. But since omniscience would see the universe as a seamless web (and, perhaps, as one single individual thing—the Absolute), this suggestion is misleading. Granted, they may say to representatives of the second position, that our present notion of "essential property" is a merely conventional one, we should not be led to conclude that things have no intrinsic natures. They do have intrinsic natures, but these can be known only *sub specie aeternitatis,* as facets of the Absolute. The common-sense essence–accident distinction is natural and inevitable, given the imperfect state of our knowledge. For omniscience, however, this distinction would be pointless.

This brief sketch of the opposing positions suffices to suggest how intimately the issues about internal relations are bound up with a whole range of other philosophical problems—problems about the notions of substance, of essence, and of "bare particulars," about "real" versus "nominal" definitions, about nominalism versus realism, about the way in which we refer to and identify particulars, and about the nature of necessary truth. It is perhaps not too much to say that a philosopher's views on internal relations are themselves internally related to all his other philosophical views.

THE VIEW THAT ALL RELATIONS ARE INTERNAL

The view that all relations are internal, in the form in which it has been discussed in this century, originated in the writings of the absolute idealist school in England and America in the period 1890–1920. In various forms it was held by Bradley, Royce, Bosanquet, and many others. Its most recent sustained defense is found in the work of Brand Blanshard, a follower of Bradley, notably in *The Nature of Thought* (1939). It has obvious historical connections with the doctrines of the seventeenth-century rationalists, notably Leibniz' view that all truths are analytic and Spinoza's assimilation of causal relations to logical relations. Its most important historical antecedent, however, is the philosophy of Hegel. Hegel's insistence that the world was rational through and through, because Reason (or "Spirit") alone was real, was the principal inspiration of the philosophers who adopted the view that all relations were internal. For, if some relations were external, then the universe would be "impenetrable" to reason, in the sense that there would be brute particular facts not deducible from universal truths even by God himself.

A. C. Ewing, in *Idealism* (1934), provides a comprehensive account of the various meanings given to the term "internal" by exponents of absolute idealism and a critical analysis of those arguments in favor of the doctrine that all relations are internal which depend upon an ambiguous use of "internal." As Ewing points out, the meanings given to "internal" ranged from a very weak sense, in which to say that the relation R which X bore to Y was internal to X meant merely that "R makes a real difference to X," to a very strong sense, in which it meant that "from a knowledge of Y and R we could infer with logical necessity that X possesses a certain determinate or relatively determinate characteristic other than the characteristic of standing in the relation in question." Because such ambiguities permeate the discussion of the topic in such writers as Bradley and Royce, we shall not attempt an exegesis of their arguments. Instead, we shall attempt a reconstruction of two particularly persuasive arguments which seem to represent at least part of the common core of the absolute idealists' defense of their position on this subject. The two arguments to be examined by no means exhaust the repertoire of arguments which have been deployed in favor of the view that all relations are internal, but they are the arguments on which criticism of this view has chiefly centered.

Argument from the nature of self-identity. The first argument, which will be called here the argument from the nature of self-identity, was first clearly formulated by a critic rather than a proponent of the view that all relations are internal. G. E. Moore, in a classic attack on this view ("External and Internal Relations"), suggests that "one thing which is always implied by the dogma that 'All relations are internal' is that, in the case of every relational property, it can always be truly asserted of any term A which has that property, that any term which had not had it would necessarily have been different from A." The argument in favor of this view is simply that, as Moore puts it, "if A has P, and x has not, it *does* follow that x is other than A." In other words, it is unquestionably true that

(1) A has P entails that (x does not have P materially implies that x is other than A).

Contemplation of this truth, Moore suggested, led philosophers to say that "A could not be what it is (but would necessarily be something different) did it not have P."

Now, as Moore points out, the argument as it stands is fallacious. (1) does not permit the conclusion that

(2) *A* has *P* materially implies that (*x* does not have *P* entails that *x* is other than *A*).

Only (2) would permit the conclusion that *A* would necessarily be a different particular did it not have *P*. The difference between (1) and (2) may be put by saying that all that (1) tells us is that *A* cannot both have and not have the property *P*, whereas (2) tells us that *A* could not be *A* unless it had *P*. (1) is trivial, whereas (2) blurs the common-sense contrast between essential and accidental properties (and thus between internal and external relations). As Moore puts it, "(1) asserts that if *A* has *P*, then any term which has not, *must* be other than *A*; (2) asserts that if *A* has *P*, then any term which had not, would necessarily be other than *A*." Moore notes that to confuse the two propositions, "you have only to confuse 'must' or 'is necessarily' with 'would necessarily be.'" This confusion, in turn, will lead one to confuse the (physically necessary but logically contingent) fact that *A* has *P* with a statement about what is *logically* necessary for something to be *A*. While not attempting to cite examples of this fallacy in the writings of the absolute idealists, Moore claimed that much of their willingness to adopt the view that all relations are internal was due to their having confused (1) and (2). Whether or not this fallacy played the role in their thought which Moore thought it did is less important, from a historical point of view, than the influence exercised by Moore's diagnosis. Philosophers in general tended to agree with Moore that the absolute idealists had been guilty of this confusion, and his essay was a turning point in discussion of the topic. Defenders of the thesis of the internality of all relations who came after Moore were forced to produce arguments against the main presupposition of Moore's argument—that the common-sense distinction between logically contingent propositions and logically necessary propositions was unobjectionable. Crudely put, one may say that before Moore's essay, defenders of the view that all relations were internal felt able to argue that simple reflection on common-sense criteria for self-identity led to the conclusion they desired. After Moore's essay, they were forced to attempt to undermine common sense by claiming that the distinctions Moore had drawn were, though commonsensical, philosophically indefensible.

Argument from the nature of causality. The above was the strategy adopted by Blanshard in his *The Nature of Thought,* in which he presents the second, far more important and profound, argument in favor of the doctrine that all relations are internal. This may be called the argument from the nature of causality. Moore, like most philosophers in the tradition of British empiricism, had taken for granted a distinction between physical necessity and logical necessity, a distinction between the sense in which it is necessary, given the laws of nature and the past history of the universe, that a given particle be located at a given point in space at a given time, and the sense in which it is *not* necessary, *simpliciter.* Traditional rationalism, on the other hand, had questioned this distinction. Although earlier absolute idealists had also rejected the distinction between two kinds of necessity, they had done so *en passant.* They had treated it as simply one more

consequence of empiricism's uncritical acceptance of a common-sense metaphysics which, they claimed to have shown, was fundamentally incoherent. Blanshard, approaching the matter epistemologically rather than metaphysically, brought forward a battery of arguments designed to show that the acceptance of this distinction was the result of a mistaken Humean analysis of knowledge. By weakening this distinction and claiming that causal necessity (by virtue of which *A* had *P*) could not be separated from logical necessity (by virtue of which *A* was self-identical), he was able to argue that what Moore had viewed as a simple confusion was at worst a confused formulation of a vitally important insight.

In examining this second argument, it will again be convenient to look to its critics rather than to its defenders. Ernest Nagel, in a critique of Blanshard's *The Nature of Thought* entitled "Sovereign Reason," restates and criticizes Blanshard's views on internal relations in a way which brings out very clearly their connection with Blanshard's treatment of causality. Blanshard, in turn, has replied to Nagel in the later chapters (particularly Ch. 12) of his *Reason and Analysis* (1963). A summary of the Blanshard–Nagel controversy will serve two purposes. It will trace the most recent line of defense adopted by defenders of the view that all relations are internal, and it will lead us to an understanding of why some philosophers claim that *no* relations are internal.

Blanshard puts forward, and Nagel quotes as a basis for criticism, the following version of the doctrine that all relations are internal. Despite the ambiguities detected by Ewing, Blanshard holds that "the principal meaning" of this doctrine is clear and formulates it as follows:

(1) that every term, i.e., every possible object of thought, is what it is in virtue of relations to what is other than itself; (2) that its nature is affected thus not by some of its relations only, but in differing degrees by all of them, no matter how external they may seem; (3) that in consequence of (2) and of the further obvious fact that everything is related in *some* way to everything else, no knowledge will reveal completely the nature of any term until it has exhausted that term's relations to everything else. (*Nature of Thought,* Vol. II, p. 452)

Nagel notes, and Blanshard would agree, that everything here turns on the notion of the "nature of a term." If the term's nature includes *all* its properties, then Blanshard is right. Nagel bases his general objections to Blanshard on the claim that this is a perverse use of "nature," since "it is quite clear that just what characters are included in an individual, and just where the boundaries of an individual are drawn, depend on decisions as to the use of language. These decisions, though motivated by considerations of practical utility, are *logically arbitrary*" (p. 275). Nagel, in other words, is saying that "the nature of *X*" consists of just those properties of *X* whose absence would cause us to cease using "*X*" to refer to *X* and that the selection of these properties is determined not by empirical study but by convention. The list of such properties is finite, whereas the list of the properties of *X* is potentially infinite. Nagel thus adopts what has become the standard empiricist view, first clearly formulated by A. J. Ayer in "Internal Relations," that to determine which properties of *X* are internal to it is merely a matter of determining which propositions about *X* are analytic and that determining *this* is simply a matter of consulting linguistic usage. To urge that the nature of a thing includes all its properties would, given this view, be to urge that *all* propositions about *X* are analytic. Both Nagel and Ayer treat this conclusion as a *reductio ad absurdum*.

In examining Blanshard's arguments, Nagel first takes up Blanshard's form of the argument from the nature of self-identity and disposes of it by drawing what is essentially Moore's distinction between the logically contingent fact that *A* has *P* and the logically necessary fact that anything which does not have *P* cannot be identical with *A*. His defense of this distinction is simply that unless the distinction is drawn, we shall wind up with the view that "the nature of *X*" is identical with *X* itself and thus that "the nature of a thing, like the thing itself, would be something that is in principle indefinable and could not therefore be made the basis for bringing into systematic order any of the characters which the thing displays" (p. 276). But from Blanshard's point of view, this reply begs the question, since Blanshard would be quite willing to say that the nature of any given particular is indeed indefinable (by finite minds). For Blanshard the question is merely pushed back to the issue of whether a satisfactory epistemology can be constructed on the basis of the view that all logical necessity has its source in linguistic convention. But this latter issue is just the issue of whether causal relationships (which are agreed on all sides to be matters not of convention but of empirical inquiry) can, in the last analysis, be held to be distinct from logical relationships. If they cannot, then it would seem fair to say that although we must (unfortunately) work with the common-sense distinctions between necessary and contingent truths, essence and accident, physical and logical necessity, and the like, these distinctions are nevertheless mere pragmatic makeshifts (pertaining, in Bradleian terminology, to Appearance rather than to Reality). To invoke them to is to attend not to how things are but merely to how we are forced (by the limitations of our minds and of our everyday language) to talk about them.

Thus the battle between Blanshard and Nagel is truly joined only when Nagel takes up the question of whether "logical necessity is involved in causal relations." Blanshard has, as Nagel notes, two principal arguments for the view that it is so involved. The first is that causal relations must be analyzed either in terms of "mere regularity of sequence" or in terms of "entailment." The failure of the regularity view will, in Blanshard's eyes, constitute a proof of the entailment view. But the entailment view is just that "*A* causes *B*" is a statement about a *logical* relation between *A* and *B*. Now if (as is not implausible) all true relational propositions about particulars are propositions which are true in virtue of causal relations between the particulars mentioned in these propositions, then it follows that all particulars are connected to all others by logical relations and that every such proposition would be seen (by omniscience) to entail a logical truth about every such particular.

Nagel has two objections to this argument. First, the "regularity" and "entailment" views do not exhaust the available analyses of causality; second, "the entailment view contributes *nothing* toward advancing the aims of specific inquiries into the causal dependencies of physical nature." The second objection can be dismissed by Blanshard as irrelevant, since he is quite willing to admit, with Hume, that observation of regular sequence is our only method for determining what causal relations actually hold (except, perhaps, in the case of "direct insight" into certain relations between mental states or events). Blanshard need merely insist that regularity provides *evidence* of an underlying entailment but that the regularity and the entailment must not be confused. Blanshard offers no reply to Nagel's first objection, but one suspects that he would argue that all proposed *via media* analyses of causality in fact boil down to one of the two alternatives he has suggested. Even if this point is granted to Blanshard, however, the whole question of the validity of his attack on the regularity theory remains. We must leave the topic with the remark that Blanshard can, in attacking this theory, take full advantage of the embarrassment encountered by Rudolf Carnap, Nelson Goodman, and others in their attempts to construct an inductive logic on the basis of Neo-Humean "regularities." Further, recent work in inductive logic (such as Goodman's *Fact, Fiction and Forecast*, 1955) and the philosophy of science (the work of Hilary Putnam, Wilfrid Sellars, P. K. Feyerabend, and others) has made it apparent that the distinction between matters of convention and matters of fact is not so clear as Hume and the early positivists believed. This recent work is closely connected with W. V. Quine's skepticism about the analytic–synthetic distinction and related work in the philosophy of language. It is perhaps not too much to say that empiricism is presently in a state of crisis and that the crisis revolves precisely around the validity of the distinctions which empiricists have traditionally invoked against the thesis of the internality of all relations. We must conclude that the question of the validity of Blanshard's first form of the argument from the nature of causality must remain undecided until these issues have been further clarified.

Before leaving the Blanshard–Nagel controversy, however, we must take up the second of Blanshard's arguments in favor of the view that logical necessity is involved in causation. This argument is that philosophical reflection upon the nature of causality leads us to conclude that

> to say that *a* produces *x* in virtue of being *a* and yet that, given *a*, *x* might not follow, is inconsistent with the laws of identity and contradiction. Of course if *a* were a cluster of qualities abstracted from their relations, and its modes of causal behaviour were another set conjoined with the former externally, then one could deny the latter and retain the former with perfect consistency. But we have seen that when we say *a* causes *x* we do *not* mean that sort of conjunction; we mean an intrinsic relation, i.e., a relation in which *a*'s behaviour is the outgrowth or expression of *a*'s nature. And to assert that *a*'s behaviour, so conceived, could be different while *a* was still the same would be to assert that something both did and did not issue from the nature of *a*. *Nature of Thought*, Vol. II, p. 513)

With this argument, as Nagel notes, we are back at the perplexing notion of "the nature of *a.*" Whereas the entailment analysis of the nature of causation can perhaps be stated without using the notion of the "nature of *A*" (although if it were, it might be difficult for Blanshard to infer the thesis of the internality of all relations from the truth of the entailment view), this present argument about the nature of causality makes essential use of this notion. At this point, therefore, Nagel returns to his general line of attack on Blanshard's formulation of the thesis of the internality of all relations and argues that what Blanshard says here is true only if "the nature of *X*" is defined as "all the properties of *X*," a definition which, in Nagel's eyes, is both idiosyncratic and such as to trivialize Blanshard's claim.

The effectiveness of Nagel's reply can be judged only in the light of a general theory about the relation between thought, language, and reality. For, here again, Nagel is taking for granted the view that whether a given property is included within a thing's nature is a question about our language, rather than a question to be settled by further inquiry about the thing itself. Just as judgment of the validity of the first form of Blanshard's argument from the nature of causality must be postponed until certain general philosophical issues have been (at least) clarified, so also judgment of the validity of the second form of this argument must be deferred until questions about the standard empiricist doctrine that all "essences" are "nominal" and that "real essence" is an incoherent notion are settled. For Blanshard can insist that Nagel has begged these latter questions. In *Reason and Analysis* we find Blanshard arguing that Nagel's view that decisions about what characters are included in an individual are "logically arbitrary" leads to the view that, for example, Socrates' snub-nosedness is as good a candidate for an essential property of Socrates as his philosopherhood. Blanshard thinks this a *reductio ad absurdum,* but this rebuttal, once again, merely moves the argument one step further back. Nagel's point is not that we *arbitrarily* select which characteristics of an individual shall count as essential but that the criteria of selection are pragmatic, dictated by our present interests and the modes of classification which we have, in the past, found it convenient to adopt. Nagel would say that a choice about linguistic usage, which is, from a practical point of view, far from arbitrary, is nonetheless *logically* arbitrary, in the sense that a language with alternative conventions is, though inconvenient, perfectly possible. Blanshard's basic disagreement with Nagel consists in his view that such pragmatic considerations are not the last word and his insistence that the goal of thought is the discovery of real essences. Such real essences would be discovered by discovering the chains of entailment that connect all the various universals which characterize (and, in Blanshard's metaphysics, constitute) a particular. In Blanshard's view, to say that analytic propositions are true by convention is thoroughly misleading, for such conventions are the results of attempts to discover such entailments. For Blanshard the identification of the nature of *X* with *X* itself, and of both with the totality of properties which characterize *X*, and of all of these with *X*-as-known-by-an-ideal-knower (one who could grasp the

entailments between all of these properties), is not (as it is for Nagel) a series of confusions but is forced upon us by an analysis of what we mean by "knowing *X*." The validity of Blanshard's second form of the argument from the nature of causality ultimately depends upon the validity of this analysis.

Universals. The nature and depth of the issues involved in the controversy between Blanshard and Nagel may be further clarified by calling attention to one more area of disagreement between them. This concerns the nature and knowledge of universals. Blanshard views a particular as a congeries of universals and views the internal relations between particulars as reflecting the internal relations holding between the universals which constitute them. It is almost a cliché of recent analytic philosophy that to have knowledge of a universal is simply to know the meaning of a word; thus, to be acquainted with all the universals which characterize a particular would be merely to know the meanings of all the words correctly applicable to that particular. Such knowledge would obviously fall far short of telling us about the relations in which that particular stands to other particulars. For Blanshard, however, universals have natures which are not known to those who merely know the meanings of the words which signify those universals. To know the nature of a universal "fully and as it really is" would involve knowing its relations to all the universals which are exemplified in all the particulars which exemplify the first universal. Thus, to know any universal "fully and as it really is" would be possible only for omniscience, just as, and for the same reasons that, knowledge of the real essence of a particular would be possible only for omniscience. Thus, resolution of the controversy about internal relations would require, at a minimum, a decision concerning the adequacy of a nominalistic account of universals. Blanshard views the current antagonism toward idealism (and a fortiori toward the thesis of the internality of all relations) as largely a result of analytic philosophy's "systematic confusion between thought and language," a confusion which leads philosophers such as Wittgenstein to hold (1) that the notion of having a concept or being acquainted with a universal prior to the use of language is incoherent, and (2) that the notion of detecting internal relations between universals apart from considerations of linguistic usage is a relic of a radically mistaken analysis of mental events. If these latter tenets are accepted, clearly Blanshard's arguments cannot even get off the ground. Once again, we must conclude that the thesis of the internality of all relations cannot be profitably discussed until one has taken sides on the most fundamental issues in contemporary philosophy.

THE VIEW THAT NO RELATIONS ARE INTERNAL

When we turn to the view that no relations are internal, we turn from a controversy which reflects profound underlying disagreements concerning the analysis of knowledge to a controversy about much narrower issues concerning the analysis of naming and predication. Those who say that no particular is internally related to any other particular insist that the only entities which can be internally related to one another are *characteristics* of particulars. Following to its logical conclusion Nagel's claim that the assignment of a given description to a given particular is "logically arbitrary," they hold that to say that X would "not be what it is" unless it had P is merely to say that the particular could not be characterized in a given way unless it had this property. But since the particular is sublimely indifferent to how it is characterized, it "is what it is" regardless of whatever properties it may have. To speak of "logically necessary conditions for the self-identity of X" is, at best, to speak elliptically of "logically necessary conditions for correctly describing X as a K," where "K" signifies some kind of thing of which X is a representative, or (more generally) of "logically necessary conditions for correctly describing X as C," where "C" is some general characterization. The whole notion of "properties (and, a fortiori, relations) such that X would cease to be what it is if they were removed" is thus either incoherent or misleading. For "being what it is" is simply too ambiguous a notion; there are indefinitely many kinds to which X belongs and indefinitely many characterizations which apply to it. "Being what it is" is incoherent if it suggests that one of these kinds or characterizations is *intrinsically* privileged and misleading if a user of the phrase has already picked out some such kind or characterization, thus making his choice "privileged" by stipulation. To philosophers who deny the internality of any relations, the whole notion of internal properties and relations is an unfortunate vestige of the Aristotelian notion that there are real essences of particulars to be discovered by empirical inquiry. These philosophers heartily agree with the seventeenth-century rationalists, and with Blanshard, that any Aristotelian attempt to divide intrinsically essential and intrinsically accidental properties is foolish. But whereas Blanshard, sticking to the quest for real essences, insists that this point merely shows that the real essence of an object must include *all* its properties, these philosophers take the point to show the incoherence of the notion of "real essence" and the notion of "internal property."

It may be useful to put the contrast between the roughly Aristotelian common-sense view and the two extreme views in yet another way. If we say that common sense holds that there are both particulars and properties of particulars, then we may say that common sense holds that each particular stands in a necessary relation to some of its properties and in a contingent relation to others. Blanshard dissolves the particular into a congeries of properties, and, because he believes (*a*) that properties (qua universals) have intrinsic natures to be discovered by inquiry (other than inquiry into linguistic usage) and (*b*) that such inquiry would, in principle, discover relations of entailment between all possible properties of all possible particulars, he holds that a particular stands in a necessary relation to *all* its properties. Philosophers who deny both doctrines and who assert (*c*) that "logical necessity" can only characterize relationships between universals, naturally emerge with the conclusion that the whole notion of logically necessary relations between particulars and their properties must be discarded. To put it picturesquely, Blanshard thinks that the dissolution of the traditional essence – accident distinction leaves us with the particular as a node in a network of internal relations between universals. His opponents think that this dissolution leaves us

with "bare" particulars on the one hand (particulars which could logically have *any* properties) and with a network of entailments between universals on the other (a network which is, however, much "looser" than Blanshard's, since between *most* universals no relations of entailment exist).

Concept of bare particulars. As an illustration of the movement toward leaving particulars bare, we may cite Gilbert Ryle, who says, in his article "Internal Relations," that

> for this view [the thesis of the internality of all relations] to be true *or false,* it would have to be significant to predicate a logically proper name or designation of a logically proper name or designation; and it would have to be significant to assert or deny that *this* was *this;* and the question "is anything this?" would have to mean something. . . . "This" is not a predicate, and a sentence in which it pretends to function as one is meaningless. So there *could* be no such dispute as to whether this's being this does or does not depend on its being in one or other of its relations. (p. 165)

This line of thought suggests the general conclusion that there are no analytic propositions which ascribe properties to particulars. For example, it is misleading to call "Socrates was a Greek philosopher" analytic, for what this statement expresses is either (1) the contingent fact that certain features (snub-nosedness, being married to Xanthippe, and so on) were compresent with certain others (being Greek, being a philosopher), or (2) the contingent fact that the word "Socrates" is used to refer to an individual who exhibited certain features.

Even among philosophers who both reject (*a*) and (*b*) and accept (*c*), however, this general conclusion has been a matter of debate. In what follows, we shall consider an attempt to avoid the conclusion that there can be no analytic propositions which ascribe properties to particulars and an attempt to avoid the extreme position that no relations are internal to particulars by providing a "rational reconstruction" of the common-sense view. Such attempts are motivated, at least in part, by philosophical discomfort over the notion of "bare particulars." The nature of this discomfort may be illustrated by considering the question "What, then, *are* these particulars, apart from the properties we ascribe to them?" If particulars really are "bare," then any answer to this question is bound to be either wrong (if it lists some features which are criteria for particularity) or unhelpful (if it consists in saying simply "Well, particulars are just the kind of thing that properties can be ascribed to"). Although the realistic bent of contemporary analytic philosophy makes philosophers hesitate to accept the Bradleian – Blanshardian view that the whole category of (plural) "particulars" belongs to Appearance rather than to Reality, it nevertheless seems that having only bare particulars would be as bad as having no particulars at all.

Internal properties as relative. The most explicit and comprehensive attempt to avoid Ryle's conclusion and still retain most of his premises is found in an article by Timothy Sprigge ("Internal and External Properties"); an examination of Sprigge's treatment of the problem will bring out the underlying issues concerning naming and predication upon whose resolution the present question depends. Sprigge notes that the strength of the Rylean position lies in the fact that

> in sentences expressing particular propositions where the subject word is a name, the subject word has no connotation. Therefore no predicate word can have a connotation which is incompatible with the connotation of the subject word. But a subject–predicate sentence could only express a necessary proposition if the connotation of the subject word were incompatible with the connotation of the negation of the predicate word . . . Of course, this rests upon the questionable view that there may be naming words without connotation—and this indeed is basically the point at issue. (p. 204)

One reason why this latter point is disputable is, as Sprigge says, that "it seems that one must identify a thing by some description. Having been thus identified," he continues, "as answering to that description, is it not in effect defined as the thing having those properties, which properties therefore it necessarily has?" (p. 205). In other words, proper names could not be used unless their users could identify their referents, and how could the users do this save by having a description in mind? Must we not say that the notion that the logician's dogma that "proper names do not connote" is true only of such Russellian "logically proper names" as "this" (which cannot be used save in the presence of their referents)? Sprigge replies to this point by granting it but noting also that since the same particular can be identified by an indefinitely wide range of different descriptions, the point is useless if one is trying to defend the notion of internal properties. In the case of a predicate, rough agreement on criteria for its application is required if the term is to play a useful role. But there seems nothing to prevent every speaker of the language from having a different set of procedures for identifying a particular while nevertheless using the same proper name for it. Too many connotations are, so to speak, as bad as no connotation at all for purposes of formulating necessary truths.

If we follow Sprigge here, we need not be troubled by the spectacle of bare particulars. Every particular we refer to will always be dressed in some description or other, so we need not worry about how they look when undressed. But since each particular can be dressed up in so many ways, we are as far as ever from understanding what an "internal property" might be, unless we relativize the notion and say that certain properties are internal to *X* relative to a person *S* whose personal criteria for identifying *X* include the presence of these properties. Relativizing the notion in this way is, in essence, the basis for Sprigge's "reconstruction" of the notion of internal property. As a sample of the sort of intuition upon which the common-sense distinction between internal and external properties is based, he notes that even though we are driven by the Rylean reasoning outlined above to call all subject–predicate statements about particulars synthetic, we find it hard to imagine the falsehood of, for example, "Scott was, at some time in his life, a man." But what is a synthetic proposition if not one whose falsehood can be imagined? Sprigge proposes that we simply face up to the

fact that there is a class of propositions which, if we *must* choose between calling them synthetic or analytic, must be called synthetic, even though they do not have imaginable contradictories. Specifically, they are such that no program of empirical inquiry could be formulated which would lead us to decide between them and their contradictories. The point is most effectively made in the following passage:

> To ask whether a thing could have been quite different, from what it is, whether Scott could actually have had all the properties of Handel, is on a different level. The questions we have just been asking are all to some degree requests for further descriptions of Scott. But the present question is not one that calls for any investigation of Scott, and it is difficult to accept that a question which calls for no investigation of Scott, to which nothing about Scott is relevant, is really about Scott. (p. 209)

On the basis of these considerations, Sprigge makes the following proposal:

> I suggest that a property is internal to a particular to the extent that no information about that particular is conveyed by one who says that it might have lacked that property. I think that the distinction between internal and external properties is not exact . . . Let *F* be any property of a thing *a*. Then *F* is an external property of *a* if something interesting and true may be said of the form 'if such and such then not-*Fa*'. Otherwise *F* is an internal property. But as from different points of view different things are interesting, so from different points of view different properties are internal and external. (p. 210)

The notion of "internal" is thus not only made a matter of degree but also is relativized to the interests and purposes of those who are discussing *X*. Conceivably, everyone might be interested in *X* for a widely different reason; in this case, it would be quite possible that everyone might identify *X* by means of a widely different, but equally true, description. Then there would be no agreement on internal properties, and an Aristotelian metaphysics would seem unintelligible to us. As it stands, however, we tend to be interested in things for roughly the same reasons and thus to group the same things into the same natural kinds (for example, to regard Scott as "essentially" a man, rather than as a collection of physical particles occupying a given stretch of space time, or as a colorful patch on the landscape of nineteenth-century Scotland). Given this agreement and given our natural taxonomical instincts (our tendency to turn differences of degree into differences of kind whenever possible in order to facilitate inquiry), we can explain the commonsensical character of the distinctions between essence and accident and between internal and external properties (and, a fortiori, internal and external relations).

As an account of the internal–external distinction which avoids both the arbitrariness of Aristotelianism and the counterintuitive character of absolute idealism, Sprigge's proposal is a happy solution. But, like all such solutions, it is no better and no more permanent than the conceptual framework within which it is constructed. There is, to put it mildly, no consensus among philosophers of language as to when a sentence is "about" a given particular, when two sentences are about the same particular, the proper analysis of the notion of "name," the reducibility of names to descriptions, the assimilation of demonstrative pronouns to proper names, the question of whether proper names can be said to have meanings, the utility of the analytic–synthetic distinction, the equation of "necessary truth" with "analytic truth," and a host of related issues. In the absence of a comprehensive philosophy of language in which these issues are clarified and resolved in a systematic way, Sprigge's proposal must be treated as a useful guideline, rather than as a definitive resolution of the issue concerning internal relations. One can imagine, for example, a revivification of the Aristotelian doctrine of predication, according to which "Socrates is a man" exemplifies a radically different sort of predication from "Socrates is a Greek," such an Aristotelian philosophy of language would, when conjoined with a realistic, anti-instrumentalist philosophy of science, produce a view according to which it would make good sense to say that Socrates' humanity really *was* internal to him, not simply relative to our interests but absolutely and intrinsically. Such a view would argue that "man" signifies a natural kind and is thus naturally suited to be a predicate "in the category of substance," whereas "Greek" or "atoms located at p at t" is not, and that this is an empirical truth.

There probably would never have been a problem about internal relations were it not for the efforts of speculative metaphysicians, such as Parmenides, Spinoza, and Hegel, to undermine our common-sense conceptual framework. If one rejects such attempts out of hand, one will treat the adoption of monism and of the thesis of the internality of all relations as a *reductio ad absurdum* of the premises from which these views are derived. Since Moore, the vast majority of Anglo-American philosophers have rejected such attempts and have differed only in their diagnoses of the confusions of falsehoods which engendered metaphysical conclusions. As long as the dogma that logical necessity was a matter of linguistic convention remained unchallenged, a simple and elegant resolution of the problem of internal relations seemed possible. However, recent doubts about this dogma (combined with the realization that Aristotle's distinction between essential and accidental properties is not simply a philosopher's invention but is firmly grounded in common sense) have made the problem look more complex than it appeared in the days of Ayer's *Language, Truth and Logic*. Philosophers who wish, as P. F. Strawson has put it, to substitute a "descriptive" metaphysics for a "revisionary" one are now faced with the problem of reconciling (a) the existence of this common-sense distinction with (b) the standard empiricist view that knowledge of how we speak either does not reveal anything about the nature of the objects we refer to, or at least does so in a very different way than does empirical research directed to those objects themselves, (c) the fact that the meaning we assign to a term is in part a function of the amount of empirical knowledge we possess, and (d) the fact that common sense seems to require a realistic, rather

than an instrumentalistic, view of what it is to "know the nature of an object."

If the difficulties of such a reconciliation prevent "descriptive" metaphysicians from carrying out their chosen task, then the door will be open once again to the two extreme views examined above. It may turn out that common sense is, if not as incoherent as Parmenides and Bradley thought it, at least sufficiently inconsistent as to require the adoption of paradoxical philosophical theses. Whether one then turns to the extreme represented by Ayer's radical conventionalism and instrumentalism, or to the extreme represented by Blanshard's idealistic monism, will be largely a matter of taste. Both views, as suggested above, are parts of internally consistent philosophical systems. Each system retains certain portions of our common-sense framework and insists on these at the expense of other portions. In the absence of a touchstone other than common sense, it is difficult to see how a rational choice between such systems can be made.

Bibliography

Allaire, Edwin B., "Bare Particulars," in *Essays in Ontology.* Iowa Publications in Philosophy, Vol. I. The Hague, 1963. Pp. 14–21.

Alston, William P., "Internal Relatedness and Pluralism in Whitehead." *Review of Metaphysics,* Vol. 5 (1951–1952), 535–558.

Anscombe, G. E. M., "Aristotle," in G. E. M. Anscombe and P. T. Geach, *Three Philosophers.* Ithaca, N.Y., 1961. Gives a sympathetic treatment of Aristotle's distinction between secondary substance and quality.

Ayer, A. J., "Internal Relations." *PAS,* Supp. Vol. 14 (1935), 173–185. Reprinted in Ayer's *Language, Truth and Logic.* London, 1936. Ch. 8.

Blanshard, Brand, *The Nature of Thought,* 2 vols. London, 1939; New York, 1940.

Blanshard, Brand, *Reason and Analysis.* La Salle, Ill., and London, 1962

California, University of, *Studies in the Problem of Relations.* University of California Publications in Philosophy, Vol. XIII. Berkeley, 1928.

Chappell, Vere, "Sameness and Change." *Philosophical Review,* Vol. 69 (1960), 351–362. On criteria of self-identity.

Church, Ralph W., "On Dr. Ewing's Neglect of Bradley's Theory of Internal Relations." *Journal of Philosophy,* Vol. 32 (1935), 264–273.

Ewing, A. C., *Idealism.* London, 1934. This contains the best exposition of the similarities and differences between the exponents of absolute idealism and also of the relation between the doctrine that all relations are internal and other idealistic doctrines.

James, William, *Essays in Radical Empiricism.* New York, 1912. Ch. 3, "The Thing and Its Relations." On Bradley.

Moore, G. E., "External and Internal Relations." *PAS,* Vol. 20 (1919/1920), 40–62. Reprinted in Moore's *Philosophical Studies.* New York, 1922.

Nagel, Ernest, "Sovereign Reason," in his collection of articles *Sovereign Reason.* Glencoe, Ill., 1954.

Rome, Sydney, and Rome, Beatrice, eds., *Philosophical Interrogations.* New York, 1964. Pp. 219–246. Largely a continuation of the debate between Nagel and Blanshard.

Royce, Josiah, *The Spirit of Modern Philosophy.* Boston, 1892. Expounds the relation between early rationalism and Hegel, as it was conceived by the absolute idealists.

Russell, Bertrand, "The Monistic Theory of Truth," in his *Philosophical Essays.* London, 1910. Pp. 150–169. Criticism of absolute idealism.

Ryle, Gilbert, "Internal Relations." *PAS,* Supp. Vol. 14 (1935), 154–172.

Sellars, Wilfrid, *Science, Perception and Reality.* London, 1963. Ch. 9, "Particulars." On criteria for self-identity of particulars.

Sprigge, Timothy, "Internal and External Properties." *Mind,* Vol. 71 (1962), 197–212.

Stace, W. T., *The Philosophy of Hegel.* London, 1924. Reissued New York, 1955. Ch. 2 discusses the relation between early rationalism and Hegel, as it was conceived by the absolute idealists.

Thompson, Manley, "On the Distinction Between Thing and Property," in John Wild, ed., *The Return to Reason.* Chicago, 1953. Another defense of Aristotle's distinction between "secondary substance" and "quality."

Will, Frederick, "Internal Relations and the Principle of Identity." *Philosophical Review,* Vol. 44 (1940), 497–514.

Wollheim, Richard, *F. H. Bradley.* London, 1959. Ch. 3 contains an exegesis of Bradley's treatment of relations.

RICHARD M. RORTY

RELATIVISM IN ETHICS. See ETHICAL RELATIVISM.

RELATIVITY OF KNOWLEDGE. See FUNCTIONALISM IN SOCIOLOGY; HISTORICISM; SKEPTICISM; SOCIOLOGY OF KNOWLEDGE.

RELATIVITY THEORY, PHILOSOPHICAL SIGNIFICANCE OF.

If a physical theory *T* claims that an attribute or relation of a physical event or object is the same in every reference system in which it is specified, then *T* can be said to regard the attribute or relation in question as "invariant" or "absolute" in virtue of thus being independent of the reference system. By the same token, attributes or relations of an event or thing are called "covariant" or "relative" in *T* if *T* asserts that they do not obtain alike with respect to all physical reference systems but depend on the particular system. The physical theories of Einstein, and the variants developed by others, which have each been called the "theory of relativity" are so named because they have relativized some of the attributes and relations (spatial distance, time interval, mass) which the Newtonian theory had asserted to be invariant (absolute). But the theory of relativity has *not* relativized all of the Newtonian invariants; indeed, it has "absolutized" the counterparts of some of the attributes and relations which its Newtonian precursor had affirmed to be relative. Hence, it is wrong to say that the theory of relativity claims everything to be relative. And it is patent that this theory is utterly noncommittal concerning the theses of ethical relativism.

Einstein's special theory of relativity (STR) and general theory of relativity (GTR) have been the most influential of the relativity theories. Hence, the bulk of this article will be devoted to the philosophical highlights of the STR and GTR; A. N. Whitehead's alternative theory of relativity, which was inspired by rival philosophical conceptions, will receive only cursory attention.

Both in Einstein's "Autobiographical Notes" (in P. A. Schilpp, ed., *Albert Einstein: Philosopher-scientist,* pp. 52–53) and in the account of the genesis of the STR which he gave to the Gestalt psychologist Max Wertheimer (see Wertheimer's *Productive Thinking,* New York, 1959, Ch. 10, especially p. 228, note 7), Einstein emphasized that the crucial logical step in his development of the STR was the repudiation of the Newtonian conception of simultaneity. In his fundamental paper of 1905 on the STR ("On the Electrodynamics of Moving Bodies") Section 1 is devoted to the problem of simultaneity within a single inertial system. Only after having given an epochal new philosophical treatment of this problem in Section 1 did he utilize his revolutionary concept of simultaneity in Section 2 to give a statement of the law of light propagation. We shall therefore eschew as unsound, both logically and historically, the customary practice of using optical principles as the axiomatic point of departure for the presentation of the STR. Instead we shall begin with the problem of simultaneity within a single inertial system.

EINSTEIN'S CONCEPTION OF SIMULTANEITY AND SOME PREVALENT MISINTERPRETATIONS

The sense in which two events can be regarded as simultaneous differs according as these events are spatially separated or quasi-coincident. When the two events are spatially quasi-coincident we speak of *local* or contiguous simultaneity; when they are spatially separated we speak of simultaneity *at a distance.*

It may appear at first sight that simultaneity at a distance can easily be based on local simultaneity. Consider two spatially separated events E_1 and E_2 whose effects intersect at a sentient observer so as to produce in him the experience of sensed (intuitive) simultaneity. These effects are then locally simultaneous. From their intersection we should indeed be able to infer that E_1 and E_2 occurred simultaneously if the influence chains emanating from E_1 and E_2 required equal one-way transit times to traverse their respective paths to the observer. But these equal one-way transit times must be furnished by synchronized clocks located at E_1 and E_2, and the synchronism of spatially separated clocks, in turn, depends on a criterion for the distant simultaneity of events occurring at these clocks.

Whitehead's criterion. The above reasoning can show that A. N. Whitehead's attempt to rest the distant simultaneity of physical theory on sensed coincidence is bound to fail. Mere sensed coincidence will not do. One reason is that sentient observers stationed at different space points of the same inertial system will render inconsistent verdicts on the sensed simultaneity of a given pair of separated events. Assume again that E_1 and E_2 are spatially separated events whose effects intersect at a point P_1, producing sensed coincidence in a sentient observer stationed there. Then there will be other points $P_2, P_3, \cdots, P_n$ in the same system such that the same events E_1 and E_2 will not produce sensed coincidence in sentient observers stationed at those points.

To avoid these inconsistencies in a manner consonant with physical theory, the application of Whitehead's criterion would have to be restricted. Simultaneity could be ascribed on the basis of sensed coincidence only restrictedly to those separated events whose simultaneity would be compatible with equal physical one-way transit times and hence appropriate one-way velocities of influence chains issuing from these events and meeting at a sentient observer. If sensed coincidence is to certify simultaneity only with this proviso, Whitehead would have had to utilize the one-way velocities of these influence chains. But one-way velocities involve transit times furnished by synchronized clocks—that is, by clocks which assign the same time number to simultaneous events. He would therefore have had to be in possession of a criterion of clock synchronization or simultaneity which he could derive from sensed coincidence only on pain of becoming involved in a vicious circle. Consequently, sensed coincidence must be rejected as a basis for physical simultaneity at a distance.

Relational conception. Einstein's alternative course involves repudiating certain philosophical and physical assumptions of Newtonian theory. Einstein held that time relations between noncoincident physical events depend for their very existence on the fact that certain physical relations obtain between these events. He thus espoused a relational conception of time (and space); that is, he regarded time (and space) as systems of relations among physical events and things. Time relations are first constituted by the system of physical relations obtaining among events. Hence, the structure of the temporal order will be determined by the physical attributes which enable events to sustain relations of "simultaneous with," "earlier than," or "later than." Specifically, this structure will depend on whether these attributes define temporal relations unambiguously—i.e., so that *every* pair of events is unambiguously ordered in terms of one of the relations "earlier than," "later than," and "metrically simultaneous with." If the temporal order were thus unambiguous, it would be "absolute," for a time relation between any two events that is an unambiguously obtaining factual relation is wholly independent of any particular reference system and hence is the same in every reference system.

If the transitive relation of metrical simultaneity were thus unambiguously fixed by the physical facts, then *as a matter of physical fact* only one particular event at a given point Q could qualify as simultaneous with a given event occurring at a point P elsewhere in space.

Synchronization and clock transport. Is there an actual physical basis for relations of absolute simultaneity among spatially separated events? Suppose that the behavior of transported clocks were of the kind assumed by the Newtonian theory—that is, that if two clocks are initially synchronized at essentially the *same* place A, this *contiguous* synchronism will be preserved after they have been separately transported to some other place B independently of the lengths of their respective paths of transport and of whether or not their arrivals at B coincide. In that case a physical basis for absolute simultaneity would exist in the form of the coincidence of physical events with suitable identical readings of transported clocks of identical constitution. But according to the STR, this physical-clock basis for absolute simultaneity does not exist. Indeed, the STR makes the following assumption: transported material clocks fail to define unambiguously obtaining relations of simultaneity within the class of physical events because relations of simultaneity yielded by clock transport depend on the particular clock used. Let two clocks U_1 and U_2 be initially synchronized at the same place A and then be transported via paths of different lengths to another place B so that their arrivals at B coincide. Then U_1 and U_2 will no longer be synchronized at B. Alternatively, let U_1 and

U_2 be brought to B via the same path (or via different paths of equal length) so that their arrivals do *not* coincide. Their initial synchronization will likewise be destroyed. Thus, a given pair of events at A and B will or will not be held to be simultaneous depending on which of the discordant clocks serves as the standard. This dependence on the particular clock used prevents transported clocks from defining relations of absolute simultaneity within the class of physical events. It also led Einstein to conclude that even within a single inertial system the simultaneity of two spatially separated events E and E^* cannot be based physically on the criterion that the numerical readings on two clocks U_1 and U_2 be the same for event E occurring at the location of U_1 and event E^* occurring at the place of U_2, the clocks having previously been transported to these *separate* places from a common point in space at which they had identical readings.

The behavior which Einstein attributed to transported clocks thus does not make for relations of absolute simultaneity among spatially separated events. This does not, of course, preclude the existence of some other physical relatedness among events which would make for such relations. Yet spatially separated events can sustain physical relations of one kind or another only because of the presence or absence of some actual or at least physically possible physical linkage between them. We must therefore ask under what conditions two such events can be simultaneous if the relations of temporal order between them depend on the obtaining or nonobtaining between them of a physical relation of causal connectibility. Einstein was driven to ask this question because he had postulated that the transport of adjacently synchronized clocks does not furnish a physical basis for the obtaining of relations of simultaneity. He therefore sought to ground the temporal order on physical foundations which are independent of any synchronism of spatially separated clocks.

Topological simultaneity. We are not ready to characterize one of two causally connected (or connectible) events as *the* actual or possible partial or total cause of the other. Hence, the statement we are about to make of the relevance of causal connectibility to simultaneity will use only a symmetric relation of causal connectibility, one that does not involve singling out one of two causally connected events as *the* (partial or total) cause of the other. Since we are concerned with time relations obtaining independently of any clock synchronism, we can now define "timelike separation" as follows: two events will be said to sustain the relation of timelike separation—the relation of being either earlier or later *independently* of any clock synchronization—if and only if they sustain the symmetric relation of causal connectibility or connectedness. Therefore, two noncoincident events will be said to be topologically simultaneous—to lack a timelike separation—and to have a spacelike separation if and only if the specified symmetric causal connectibility does not obtain between them. Two coinciding events are topologically simultaneous but do not, of course, have a spacelike separation.

Thus, the physical basis for the relation of topological simultaneity among noncoinciding events is the impossibility of their being the termini of influence chains. We must now ask, Are the physically possible causal chains of nature such as to define a relation of topological simultaneity among noncoinciding events which is transitive and thus *unique* in the sense that only *one* event at a point Q could be topologically simultaneous with a given event at another space point P? To answer this question, consider four events E_1, E_2, E_3, and E which satisfy the following conditions represented on the accompanying *events* diagram ("world-line" diagram), from which the "arrow" of time has been omitted: (1) E_1, E_2, and E_3 are causally con-

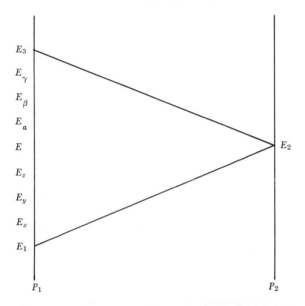

nectible *by a light ray in vacuo*, and E_2 is temporally between E_1 and E_3. (2) E_1, E, and E_3 are causally connectible other than by a light ray, E being temporally between E_1 and E_3; these three events all occur at the *same* space point P_1 of an inertial system, whereas E_2 occurs at a different space point P_2 of that same inertial system. Furthermore, let E_x, E_y, and E_z be events which sustain relations of temporal betweenness to E_1 and E and to one another, as shown on the diagram. Similarly, let E_α, E_β, and E_γ be temporally between E and E_3. The given facts that temporally E_2 is between E_1 and E_3 and that E, E_x, E_y, E_z, E_α, E_β, and E_γ are each between E_1 and E_3 as specified do *not* furnish a basis for any relations of timelike separation or topological simultaneity between E_2 and any one of the events at P_1 lying within the open interval between E_1 and E_3. Whether the latter relations exist will depend, therefore, on whether it is physically possible for there to be causal chains of which E_2 and a particular event in the open interval at P_1 would be the termini.

Limiting assumption. Newtonian physics grants that no light ray or other electromagnetic causal chain could provide a link between E_2 and E_z or E_2 and E_α. But it adduces the second law of motion to assert the physical possibility of other causal chains (such as moving particles) that would indeed furnish these links. It is precisely this latter possibility that is denied by Einstein's STR. The STR enunciates the following topological postulate, to which we shall refer as the "limiting assumption": it is physically

impossible for there to be causal chains that would link E_2 with any event lying *within* the open time interval $\overline{E_1 E_3}$. This physical impossibility obtains independently of any inertial system, and its logical consequences therefore have invariant, or absolute, significance.

Metrical simultaneity. The STR's affirmation of the limiting role of electromagnetic causal chains *in vacuo* within the class of causal chains has a fundamental consequence: topological simultaneity is not a uniquely obtaining relation, because *each* one of the infinity of events at P_1 within the open time interval between E_1 and E_3—not just a *single* one of these events—is topologically simultaneous with E_2. Moreover, this nonuniqueness of topological simultaneity is absolute since it prevails alike in every inertial system, for on Einstein's limiting assumption, *none* of these events at P_1 sustains the relation of timelike separation to E_2—i.e., is either earlier or later than E_2 independently of any clock synchronization. But since *none* of this infinity of events at P_1 is either earlier or later than E_2 in this sense, and since clocks do not furnish consistent relations of simultaneity under transport, an important result follows: no one member of this class of events is *physically* any more entitled than any other to the status of being metrically simultaneous with E_2—that is, to being assigned the same time number by a clock as E_2.

Since all members of our class of events at P_1 are equally candidates for being metrically simultaneous with E_2, some one of these events comes to be metrically simultaneous with E_2 to the exclusion of the others only by convention, or "definition." And this conventional choice of one event E^* in the open interval $\overline{E_1 E_3}$ at P_1 renders the remainder of these events either earlier or later *conventionally* than E_2. The choice of a particular event E^* is effected by means of a rule for setting the clock at P_2 so as to assign to E_2 the same time number that the clock at P_1 assigns to E^*. And the synchronism of the clocks at P_1 and P_2 is decreed by the fact that the clock at P_2 is set on the basis of such a rule. In Newtonian physics there is no scope whatever for choice of the event that can warrantedly be metrically simultaneous with E_2. By contrast, the physical facts postulated by relativity require the introduction, *within a single inertial frame S*, of a convention specifying which pair of topologically simultaneous events at P_1 and P_2 is to be metrically simultaneous. Such a stipulation is necessary in the STR because that theory asserts that the topological simultaneity of noncoincident events or their spacelike separation is *not* a transitive relation. That is, although E_x is topologically simultaneous with E_2 and E_2 is, in turn, topologically simultaneous with E, the events E_x and E are *not* topologically simultaneous; instead, the relation between E_x and E is one of timelike separation, since they are causally connectible by the motion of the pointer of a dial clock. The objection that the ordinary usage of the term "simultaneous" in common-sense discourse entails the transitivity of *every kind* of simultaneity relation is a *petitio principii*. It is tantamount to a linguistic decree that Newtonian beliefs be retained in every physical theory which makes technical use of homonyms of ordinary temporal terms.

In regard to simultaneity, therefore, Einstein's conceptual innovation can be summarized as follows: Time relations among events are assumed to be first constituted by specific physical relations obtaining between them. These physical relations, in turn, are postulated to be such that the topological simultaneity of events at spatially separated points P_1 and P_2 is not a uniquely obtaining relation. Metrical simultaneity is thus left indeterminate by topological simultaneity and by the behavior which the STR postulates for transported adjacently synchronized clocks. Therefore, a conventional choice or synchronization *rule* for which there was no scope in Newton's theory must be invoked over and above the relevant physical facts to assert that a given event at P_2 sustains a uniquely obtaining equality relation of metrical simultaneity to an event at P_1. In this sense the relation of metrical simultaneity is *not* an objectively obtaining physical relation in the STR but depends on a conventional choice. For any given event E_2 at P_2, this conventional choice consists in the selection of a unique event at P_1 as metrically simultaneous with E_2 from within the infinite class of those events at P_1 which are topologically simultaneous with E_2. And this choice is implemented by the rule for setting the clock at P_2. In brief, Einstein's innovation is that the physical relatedness which makes for the very existence of the temporal order has a structure that precludes the existence of objectively and uniquely obtaining relations of metrical simultaneity. Thus, the failure of our measuring operations to disclose relations of absolute simultaneity is only the epistemic consequence of the fact that these relations do not exist.

Frames in relative motion. Einstein's avowal of the conventionality of metrical simultaneity in Section 1 of his STR paper of 1905 explicitly pertains to the situation *within* any given inertial system and makes no reference whatever to the relative motion of different inertial systems. In particular, as is made evident by the above account of the logical status of metrical simultaneity, at this stage there is no commitment whatever to any discordance or *relativity* of metrical simultaneity as between relatively moving inertial frames. Einstein's repudiation of Newton's belief in the uniqueness of distant simultaneity consists in (1) rejecting clock transport as a basis for absolute metrical simultaneity and (2) asserting the nonuniqueness of the *absolute* relation of topological simultaneity. In addition, this denial of uniqueness leaves open the question whether there will be disagreement among relatively moving inertial systems as to the metrical simultaneity of certain pairs of noncoinciding events.

The resulting conventionality of metrical simultaneity does furnish the logical framework within which the *relativity* of simultaneity as between relatively moving inertial systems can first be understood. The nonuniqueness of the invariant relation of topological simultaneity allows each inertial system to adopt its own metrical synchronization rule. Let each system separately adopt for itself the particular, maximally convenient rule selected by Einstein in Section 1 of his fundamental paper, and let the spatial separation of P_1 and P_2 have a component along the line of the relative motion of the inertial frames. Then that relative motion results in the following relativity of simultaneity: each of the relatively moving inertial systems chooses a *different pair of events* as metrically simultaneous from within any given class of topologically simultaneous pairs

of events at P_1 and P_2. This result is embodied in the so-called Minkowski diagram.

Now let the following assignment of time numbers be made to the events at P_1 in our events diagram by means of a local clock stationed there in the given inertial system S: t_1 is the time of E_1, t_3 the time of E_3, and $\frac{1}{2}(t_3 + t_1)$ the time of E. The conventionality of metrical simultaneity then expresses itself as follows: the obtaining of metrical simultaneity within S depends on a choice—*not* dictated by the objective physical facts of the temporal order—of a particular numerical value between t_1 and t_3 as the temporal name to be assigned to E_2 at P_2 by an appropriate setting of a like clock stationed there in S. Thus, depending on the particular event at P_1 that is chosen to be simultaneous with E_2, we set the clock at P_2 upon the occurrence of E_2. Using Reichenbach's notation, the reading t_2 which we impart to this clock as the time of E_2 has the value between t_1 and t_3 given by

$$t_2 = t_1 + \epsilon(t_3 - t_1),$$

where ϵ has the particular value between 0 and 1 appropriate to the choice we have made. For example, suppose that we choose ϵ so that E_y is simultaneous with E_2. Then in system S all of the events between E_1 and E_y, by definition (that is, not objectively), will be earlier than E_2, whereas all of the events between E_y and E_3, by definition, will be later than E_2. Alternatively, we could choose ϵ so that E_y, instead of being simultaneous with E_2 in S, would be earlier than E_2. Or a different value of ϵ might be chosen, so that E_y is later than E_2 in S.

Einstein selected E to be metrically simultaneous with E_2 in S by choosing the value $\epsilon = \frac{1}{2}$ in *each* inertial system in order to obtain descriptively simple laws of nature. This freedom to decree time relations merely reflects the extent to which there is objective indeterminateness of unique metrical time relations between causally nonconnectible events. And this freedom can be exercised only with respect to such pairs of events, since the relation of timelike separation has an objective physical basis in the case of causally connectible events. Once a criterion of metrical simultaneity has been chosen in a given system as indicated, the ensuing assignment of time numbers by synchronized clocks makes it unambiguous which member of any pair of independently time-separated events is the earlier of the two and which the later.

PRINCIPLE OF THE CONSTANCY OF THE SPEED OF LIGHT

Lorentz–Fitzgerald hypothesis. The ether theory of light propagation, which was in vogue prior to the enunciation of the STR, asserts the following: the speed of light in the rest system of the ether is c (186,000 miles per second), independently of the velocity of the light source with respect to the ether system, but the speed of light in any inertial system S moving through the ether differs from c by depending on the motion of S relative to the ether system. To appreciate the observational import of this theory, consider two mutually perpendicular arms of an interferometer in a terrestrial laboratory. These arms are of equal length l as measured by the rods of that laboratory, and one (the "horizontal" arm) points in the instantaneous direction of the earth's motion through the ether. Suppose that light from a source at the point of intersection of the two arms is sent on a round trip along each arm and that the earth moves through the ether with a speed v. Then calculations on the basis of the ether theory show that the round-trip time T_v of light for the vertical arm is

$$T_v = \frac{2l}{\sqrt{c^2 - v^2}},$$

whereas the round-trip time T_h for the horizontal arm is

$$T_h = \frac{2l}{\sqrt{c^2 - v^2}} \cdot \frac{1}{\sqrt{1 - \beta^2}},$$

where $\beta \equiv v/c$. But an experiment performed by Michelson and Morley during the 1880s gave a null result in the sense of showing that T_v and T_h were *equal* instead of differing by a factor of $1/\sqrt{1-\beta^2}$. To explain this equality of the round-trip times within the framework of the ether-theoretic conception of light propagation, H. A. Lorentz and George Fitzgerald independently propounded an auxiliary hypothesis (to be referred to as the L–F hypothesis) which asserted that in virtue of its motion through the ether in the direction of its own extension, the horizontal arm contracted so as to be of length $l\sqrt{1-\beta^2}$ rather than l. The L–F hypothesis explained the null result of the experiment, since T_h becomes equal to T_v when the length l in the expression for T_h is replaced by the contracted length $l\sqrt{1-\beta^2}$.

The L–F hypothesis has been widely accused of being an *ad hoc* modification of the ether theory in the sense that it does not lend itself to testing in any kind of experiment that differs significantly from the Michelson–Morley type. (An experiment is of the Michelson–Morley type if it takes place in an inertial system having a constant velocity v through the ether and if it compares the horizontal and vertical round-trip times for arms having equal lengths l as measured by the rods of the laboratory.) Though frequently cited, the *ad hoc* charge against the L–F hypothesis is untenable if construed as denying the testability of the hypothesis in any kind of experiment differing significantly and interestingly from the Michelson–Morley type. As we shall see, the confirmation of the ether-theoretic L–F hypothesis is logically possible in a kind of experiment that is significantly different from the Michelson–Morley type.

Specifically, for the type of experiment performed by R. J. Kennedy and E. M. Thorndike in 1932 the L–F modification of the ether theory yields *different* observational consequences from those entailed by the original ether theory. Though also employing an interferometer, the Kennedy–Thorndike kind of experiment differs importantly from the Michelson–Morley type. First, the horizontal and vertical arms of the K–T experiment, as measured by laboratory rods, are not equal; instead, they

are as different in length as possible and thus differ observationally with respect to the values of the relevant theoretical variable of length. Second, the interferometer in the K–T experiment, unlike the Michelson–Morley apparatus, does not have a constant velocity v in the ether, since it does not remain in a single inertial system; rather, it is transported to various inertial systems by the diurnal rotation and annual revolution of the earth and therefore takes on different values of the relevant theoretical variable of velocity.

The difference between the vertical and horizontal round-trip times of light entailed by the L–F hypothesis for the K–T experiment is *not* the same as the one entailed by the original ether theory. Specifically, if in the K–T experiment the unequal vertical and horizontal arms have lengths L and l, respectively, as measured by rods in the laboratory, then according to the L–F hypothesis the difference $T_v - T_h$ has the nonvanishing value

$$T_v - T_h = \frac{2(L - l)}{\sqrt{c^2 - v^2}},$$

which *varies* with the diurnally and annually changing velocity v of the apparatus relative to the ether. Were it to occur, the variation of this quantity would enable the K–T experiment to detect any existing velocity v of the apparatus relative to the ether even on the assumption of an L–F contraction. This detection capability is *not* possessed by the Michelson–Morley type of experiment on the assumption of an L–F contraction. Without the L–F hypothesis, however, the original ether theory yields the different nonvanishing, velocity-dependent quantity

$$T_v - T_h = \frac{2}{\sqrt{c^2 - v^2}} \left(L - \frac{l}{\sqrt{1 - v^2/c^2}} \right).$$

Thus, independently of the Michelson–Morley experiment, it is logically possible for a K–T type of experiment to confirm the quantitative predictions of the L–F hypothesis as against those of the original ether theory. And this *logical* fact shows that the L–F hypothesis was not *ad hoc* in the specified sense! (For further details, including useful remarks on the concept of an *ad hoc* hypothesis, made by Carl Hempel in private correspondence see Adolf Grünbaum, "The Bearing of Philosophy on the History of Science," pp. 1408–1412.)

Time dilation. As a matter of *empirical* fact, the K–T experiment of 1932 did not yield observations corresponding to the time difference deduced from the ether-theoretic L–F hypothesis. Just like the Michelson–Morley experiment, the K–T experiment had a negative outcome ether-theoretically: the observations furnished by the K–T experiment corresponded to the velocity-*independent* time difference $T_v - T_h = 2(L - l)/c$. Thus, there is warrant for saying that the K–T experiment failed to produce the kind of positive effect (to within its experimental accuracy) that would have served to *confirm* the L–F hypothesis. But that this particular kind of confirmation failed to materialize does *not* prove that the L–F hypothesis was *falsified* by the null result of the K–T experiment. Assume now that the rates of the clocks in a moving system are reduced by a factor of $\sqrt{1-\beta^2}$ as compared to the ether-system clocks, and adjoin this Lorentz–Larmor auxiliary assumption of "time dilation" to the L–F hypothesis in calculating the quantity $T_v - T_h$ for the K–T experiment. Then we no longer obtain the velocity-dependent time difference yielded by the L–F hypothesis alone, which can be expressed alternatively as

$$T_v - T_h = \frac{2(L-l)}{c\sqrt{1-\beta^2}}.$$

On making the further auxiliary assumption of time dilation, this time difference becomes *independent* of the velocity by acquiring the value

$$T_v - T_h = \frac{2(L-l)}{c}$$

in conformity with the negative outcome of the K–T experiment. Thus, a form of the ether theory which is doubly amended by both the Lorentz–Larmor time-dilation hypothesis and the L–F hypothesis can uphold the latter in the face of the negative result of the K–T experiment.

Superiority of STR. It is clear, therefore, that the justification for rejecting the L–F hypothesis is not that it is *ad hoc* or that the null result of the K–T experiment makes it impossible to maintain. The justification lies, instead, in the philosophical superiority of the STR to the *doubly* amended ether theory, a superiority which obtains even though there is no difference in observational import between these two conceptually rival theories: the STR refuses to postulate the existence of some one preferred inertial ether frame when there is no kind of physical foundation for doing so. This philosophical superiority does not seem to be placed in jeopardy by the fact, noted by P. A. M. Dirac (in "Is There an Aether?," *Nature*, Vol. 168, 1951, 906), that quantum mechanics permits the ether theory to be preserved without the aforementioned two auxiliary hypotheses. Dirac claims that in quantum mechanics the ether can play the physical role of the perfect vacuum of the STR because quantum mechanics allows us to assume that all values of the velocity of the ether are equally probable.

The STR's principle of the constancy of the speed of light—hereafter called the "light principle"—states that the speed of light is the same constant c in all inertial systems, independent of the relative velocity of the source and observer and of direction, position, and time. But the null result of the Michelson–Morley experiment is quite insufficient to provide the requisite empirical support for this light principle, for it sanctions only a much more limited claim: *within* an inertial system, if light rays are jointly emitted from a given point in different directions of the system and are reflected from mirrors at equal distances from that point, as measured by rigid rods, then the rays will return together to their common point of emission.

What is shown by the repetition of this experiment at different times of the year in different inertial systems? Only that there is no difference within *any* given inertial system in the round-trip times for equal distances in

different directions within that system. The null outcome of the Michelson–Morley experiment does not, however, establish the further claim ingredient in the light principle that the round-trip time required by light to traverse a closed path of given length has the same numerical value in different inertial systems, as measured by material clocks stationed in these systems. This latter claim is indeed vouchsafed by the null outcome of the K–T experiment of 1932, although in 1905 Einstein rested it on the more general assumption known as the "principle of relativity," which asserts that there are no preferred inertial systems. Moreover, in addition to the results of the Michelson–Morley and K–T optical experiments, the light principle contains at least the following:

(1) The claim that the velocity of light in any inertial system is independent of the velocity of its source with respect to that system, and

(2) Einstein's limiting assumption regarding light (see above). This assumption is a source of the conventionality of metrical simultaneity within a given inertial system and thus, as outlined above, also enters into the relativity of simultaneity as between different inertial systems.

The conventionality of simultaneity allows but does not entail our choosing the same value $\epsilon = \frac{1}{2}$ for all directions within every system. In each system this choice assures the *equality* of the one-way velocities of light in opposite directions by yielding *equal* one-way transit times $t_2 - t_1$ and $t_3 - t_2$ for equal distances. The ratio of the one-way transit times is $\epsilon/(1-\epsilon)$, and therefore, in the case of $\epsilon \neq \frac{1}{2}$, these one-way times are *unequal*. But no fact of nature independent of our descriptive conventions and convenience would be contradicted if we chose values of $\epsilon \neq \frac{1}{2}$ for each inertial system, thereby making the velocity of light different from c in both senses along each direction in all inertial systems. Of course, for the sake of the resulting descriptive simplicity and convenience, Einstein chose $\epsilon = \frac{1}{2}$ in the formulation of the empirical content of the STR.

Propagation of light. The light principle entails that a single light pulse emitted from the two momentarily coinciding origins of two relatively moving inertial systems S and S' will be propagated in the shape of an expanding sphere about each of these two relatively moving origins. But the particular set of photon events constituting any given *instantaneous* spherical shape of the light wave in system S *cannot* also constitute an instantaneous spherical configuration of the wave about the origin of system S'. The reason is that S and S' disagree as to the simultaneity of two or more events which are spatially separated along the line of their relative motion. Awareness of both this fact and the aforementioned results of optical experiments makes the light principle fully intuitive in the framework of relativistic assumptions. It also provides logical prophylaxis against the ill-conceived and doomed attempt to imagine the above invariance of spherical light propagation on the basis of the Newtonian law of velocity addition, a law repudiated by the STR.

Judgments of length. The so-called Lorentz transformations give the mathematical relations which obtain, according to the STR, between the S-coordinates x, y, z, t of an event and the S'-coordinates x', y', z', t' of that same event. These space-time transformation equations satisfy the light principle, although they are *not* deducible from that principle alone.

The discordance between the simultaneity verdicts of S and S' mentioned earlier issues in the following discrepancy between their judgments as to *spatial* extension: a rod at rest in S' lying in the direction of the velocity v of S' with respect to S and having length l in S' will *not* be of length l in S; instead, the spatial extension in S of the moving rod will depend on the criterion of simultaneity in S and on the magnitude of its velocity v. The Lorentz transformations, which are based on the choice of $\epsilon = \frac{1}{2}$, entail that a rod of length l in S' lying in the direction of the velocity v of S' has the lesser length $l\sqrt{1-\beta^2}$ as measured in S, where it is understood that the length of a *moving* line segment in S is the distance measured in S between *simultaneous projections* of its end points. More generally, as yet unpublished computations which Grünbaum has carried out show that the dependence of the length λ of the moving rod in S on the criterion of simultaneity (value of ϵ) chosen in S is given by

$$\lambda = l\sqrt{1-\beta^2} \cdot \frac{c}{c+v(2\epsilon-1)},$$

an expression which reduces to $\lambda = l\sqrt{1-\beta^2}$ for $\epsilon = \frac{1}{2}$, as required by the Lorentz transformations of the STR. In the case of $\epsilon = \frac{1}{2}$, the systems S and S' agree on the simultaneity of those pairs of events whose spatial separation is *perpendicular* to the line of their relative motion. Therefore, the Lorentz transformations of the STR tell us that S and S' will also agree on the length of any rod whose spatial extension is along a line perpendicular to the line of their relative motion.

GENERAL THEORY OF RELATIVITY

The non-Euclidean geometries were formal systems of pure mathematics until the GTR gave them a place in its account of the physical world. Thus, according to the GTR, the spatial geometry prevailing in the kind of accelerated system constituted by a rotating disk (for example, a merry-go-round) is of the hyperbolic species of non-Euclidean geometry. Einstein's reasoning in support of this conclusion can be seen from the details of the argument which he outlined very briefly in Section 3 of his fundamental 1916 paper on the GTR ("Die Grundlage der allgemeinen Relativitätstheorie").

Einstein's reasoning makes use of the STR results given at the end of our discussion of the comparison of the length measurements made in S and S'. Specifically, suppose that the rectangular axes XY in S are parallel to the rectangular axes X'Y' in S' so that the velocity v of S' relative to S is in the positive X direction. Then, the STR tells us, a rod lying along Y' in S' which is of length a in S' will still be of length a in S' when rotated into the X' direction, whereas the respective lengths that will be ascribed to the rod in these Y and X orientations by the system S will be a and $a\sqrt{1-\beta^2}$. Einstein assumed that (1) the spatial geometry of an inertial system—to be called the "ground system"—with respect to which the disk is rotating uniformly is Euclidean and (2) the STR can be applied to the relations between measurements made on the disk and on the

ground (system S) in the following sense: infinitesimal portions of the periphery of the disk play the role of a rod lying along X' in S', and the diameter of the disk plays the role of a rod lying along Y' in S'. Suppose that a unit rod lying initially along the diameter of the disk is rotated onto the periphery of the disk. In the context of the STR the second of these assumptions entails that in the disk system the rod will remain a unit rod on the periphery, but as judged by the ground system the length of this rod will be changed by the rotation from unity to the lesser value $\sqrt{1-\beta^2}$. If r is the radius of the disk's circular projection onto the ground system, the addition of Einstein's first assumptions now permits us to infer that the unit rod on the disk can be applied $2\pi r/\sqrt{1-\beta^2}$ times to the disk's periphery, for the projection of that rod onto the Euclidean ground system's periphery fits $2\pi r/\sqrt{1-\beta^2}$ times into that periphery, since the projection is of length $\sqrt{1-\beta^2}$ whereas the periphery is of length $2\pi r$. And the number of times which the unit rod on the disk fits into the disk's periphery must be *the same* as the number of times which that rod's projection (shadow) onto the ground-system periphery fits into the projection (shadow) of the disk's periphery. But by Einstein's second assumption, the disk's diameter, as measured by a unit rod on the disk, will have the same length, $2r$, as the diameter of the Euclidean circular projection of the disk onto the ground system. It follows that whereas the ratio of the ground's circumference to the ground's diameter is π, the ratio of the disk periphery, $2\pi r/\sqrt{1-\beta^2}$, to the disk's diameter, $2r$, is $\pi/\sqrt{1-\beta^2}$, a value greater than π, as required by hyperbolic non-Euclidean geometry.

The rotating disk differs from an inertial system (or other gravity-free system) not only in having a non-Euclidean geometry rather than a Euclidean one. On the rotating disk particles are subject to various inertial forces (centrifugal forces, Coriolis forces) which are absent in an inertial system. These inertial forces are not attributable to the gravitational influences of local masses. And Newton's rotating bucket experiment showed that they are also not ascribable to any relative motion of local masses with respect to one another. Newton interpreted the results of this experiment as showing that these forces arise from motion with respect to absolute (matter-empty) space. He therefore regarded them as "fictitious" in the sense of *not* being of gravitational origin.

Mach's program and the GTR. In opposition to Newton, Ernst Mach put forward the program of attributing inertial forces to the *relative* acceleration (e.g., rotation) of a body with respect to the stellar masses. More generally, in the spirit of Berkeley and Leibniz, Mach rejected Newton's absolutistic conception of accelerated motion in favor of the relational conception that both translational inertia and rotational inertia are intrinsically dependent on the large-scale distribution and relative motion of matter. By thus envisioning that the inertial forces on a rotating disk are of gravitational origin, Mach's program involved a modification and extension of the Newtonian concept of gravitation, for the gravitational influences acting on a particle in the disk system were now held to be different from those acting on that same particle in the adjacent ground system. Hence, the gravitational influence prevailing in a given region of space time was no longer an invariant attribute, as it had been in the Newtonian theory, but a covariant attribute.

Einstein noted (in "Prinzipielles zur allgemeinen Relativitätstheorie," *Annalen der Physik*, Vol. 55, 1918, 241 ff.) that both the inertial forces and the metric geometry in a gravity-free system are different from what they are in a system like the rotating disk. He succeeded in functionally relating both the geometry of material rods and clocks and the inertial behavior of particles and light in the context of that geometry to the *same* physical quantities. But it is a widespread error to suppose that the GTR actually carried out Mach's program. To be sure, when Einstein first developed the GTR he sought to implement Mach's idea that a single test particle would have no inertia whatever if the matter and energy of the universe were either annihilated or moved indefinitely far away. But the GTR failed to implement Mach's program in a number of essential respects. For example, according to the GTR the gravitational acceleration of the earth toward the sun is independent of the amount of distant matter isotropically distributed about the sun. Yet on Mach's assumptions about the origin of inertia this acceleration should depend on the total mass distribution.

Thus, there is an important sense in which the GTR has not repudiated the concept of absolute space and has not vindicated the Leibniz–Huygens polemic against Newton and Clarke.

Bibliography

Born, Max, *Einstein's Theory of Relativity*, rev. ed. New York, 1962.

D'Abro, A., *The Evolution of Scientific Thought From Newton to Einstein*. New York, 1950.

Einstein, Albert, et al., *The Principle of Relativity*. New York, 1923. Includes translations of "Zur Elektrodynamik bewegter Körper," originally published in *Annalen der Physik*, Vol. 17 (1905), 891–921; and of "Die Grundlage der allgemeinen Relativitätstheorie," originally published in *Annalen der Physik*, Vol. 49 (1916).

Frank, Philipp, *Einstein, His Life and Times*. London, 1948; New York, 1953.

Grünbaum, Adolf, *Philosophical Problems of Space and Time*. New York, 1963. Part III, Chs. 12–15.

Grünbaum, Adolf, "The Bearing of Philosophy on the History of Science." *Science*, Vol. 143 (1964), 1406–1412.

Reichenbach, Hans, *The Philosophy of Space and Time*. New York, 1957.

Schilpp, P. A., ed., *Albert Einstein: Philosopher-scientist*. Evanston, Ill., 1949.

Törnebohm, Hakan, *A Logical Analysis of the Theory of Relativity*. Stockholm, 1952.

Törnebohm, Hakan, *Concepts and Principles in the Space-time Theory Within Einstein's Special Theory of Relativity*. Goteborg, Sweden, 1963.

Whitehead, Alfred North, *The Principle of Relativity*. Cambridge, 1922.

ADOLF GRÜNBAUM

RELIGION. This article is not a survey of the various forms that religion has taken in human history; rather, it treats the nature of religion as a problem in the philosophy of religion. It will be concerned with attempts to develop an adequate *definition* of religion, that is, to make explicit the basic features of the concept of religion.

GENERAL DEFINITION AND CHARACTERISTICS

Examination of definitions. A survey of existing definitions reveals many different interpretations.

"Religion is the belief in an ever living God, that is, in a Divine Mind and Will ruling the Universe and holding moral relations with mankind."—James Martineau

"Religion is the recognition that all things are manifestations of a Power which transcends our knowledge."—Herbert Spencer

"By religion, then, I understand a propitiation or conciliation of powers superior to man which are believed to direct and control the course of Nature and of human life."—J. G. Frazer

"Religion is rather the attempt to express the complete reality of goodness through every aspect of our being."—F. H. Bradley

"Religion is ethics heightened, enkindled, lit up by feeling."—Matthew Arnold

"It seems to me that it [religion] may best be described as an emotion resting on a conviction of a harmony between ourselves and the universe at large."—J. M. E. McTaggart

"Religion is, in truth, that pure and reverential disposition or frame of mind which we call piety."—C. P. Tiele

"A man's religion is the expression of his ultimate attitude to the universe, the summed-up meaning and purport of his whole consciousness of things."—Edward Caird

"To be religious is to effect in some way and in some measure a vital adjustment (however tentative and incomplete) to whatever is reacted to or regarded implicitly or explicitly as worthy of serious and ulterior concern."—Vergilius Ferm

If we take these definitions as attempts to state necessary and sufficient conditions for something to be a religion, it is not difficult to show that none of them is adequate. With respect to necessary conditions, consider Martineau's definition. It is clear that such a belief does not have to be present in a religion. No polytheistic religion recognizes a single divine ruler of the universe; and there are religions, such as Hinayana Buddhism, in which beliefs in personal deities play no role at all. Bradley and Arnold identify religion with morality, but there are primitive societies in which there is no real connection between the ritual system, with its associated beliefs in supernatural beings, and the moral code. The latter is based solely on tribal precedent and is not thought of as either originating with or sanctioned by the gods. If, as would commonly be done, we call the former the religion of the culture, we have a religion without morality. As for McTaggart and Tiele, it seems likely that if we specify "piety" or "feeling of harmony" sufficiently to give them a clear and unambiguous meaning, we will be able to find acknowledged religions in which they do not play an important role. It would seem that we could avoid this only by construing "piety," for example, to cover any state of feeling that arises in connection with religious activities. It does seem plausible to regard some of the definitions as stating necessary conditions, as in Caird and Ferm. However, it is doubtful that these are sufficient conditions. Does any "ultimate attitude" or any "vital adjustment" constitute a religion? As William James points out (*The Varieties of Religious Experience*, Ch. 2), it seems doubtful that a frivolous attitude toward life constitutes a religion, even if it is the fundamental attitude of a given person. And Ferm's overcarefully worded statement would seem to admit any attitude with respect to anything considered important to the ranks of the religious. This would presumably include one's attitude toward one's wife, toward one's vocation, and, in many cases, toward one's athletic activities. At this point one wonders what has happened to the concept of religion. Many of the definitions are deficient on grounds of both necessity and sufficiency. To return to Martineau, it is quite conceivable that such a belief might be held purely as a speculative hypothesis, without affecting the believer's feelings and attitudes in the way that would be requisite for religious belief. And as for McTaggart, it seems clear that one could from time to time have such a sense of harmony without this being integrated into anything that we would call a religion.

It is noteworthy that most of these definitions stress one aspect or another of religion to the exclusion of others. Thus, Martineau and Spencer represent religion as some sort of belief or other cognitive state; Frazer, as ritual (conceived in a utilitarian fashion); Bradley and Arnold, as a kind of moral attitude and activity; and McTaggart and Tiele as a certain kind of feeling. One might attribute the failings of these definitions to their one-sidedness. One could hardly expect to get an adequate statement of the nature of so complex a phenomenon as religion, essentially involving, as it does, all these forms of human activity by restricting oneself to belief, feeling, ritual, or moral attitude alone. Caird and Ferm escape this particular failing by concentrating on a comprehensive term like "attitude" or "adjustment," which itself embraces belief, feeling, and moral attitude. But, as we have seen, these formulations do not come measurably closer to providing a set of necessary and sufficient conditions.

There are other ways of construing definitions of religion. Instead of taking the above statements as attempts to specify features that are common and peculiar to cases of religion, we might take each of them as an attempt to state the *essence* of religion, that central feature in terms of which all religious phenomena are to be understood. This approach to the matter is explicit in the following statements:

"The essence of religion is a belief in the persistency of value in the world."—Harald Høffding

"The heart of religion, the quest of the ages, is the outreach of man, the social animal, for the values of the satisfying life."—A. E. Haydon

"The essence of religion consists in the feeling of an absolute dependence."—Friedrich Schleiermacher

There are two distinguishable interpretations of claims of this type. They might be interpreted genetically, as accounts of the origin of religion. The claim would then be that what is specified as the essence of religion is the original root from which all phenomena of religion have sprung. Thus, Julian Huxley, like Schleiermacher working with a conception of the essence of religion as a kind of feeling, says, ". . . the essence of religion springs from man's capacity for awe and reverence, that the objects of religion . . . are in origin and essence those things, events, and ideas which arouse the feeling of sacredness" (*Religion Without Revelation*, p. 111). Similarly starting with Høffding's formulation, we might try to show how typical religious doctrines, rites, and sentiments grew out of an original belief in the persistency of value. However, since we know virtually nothing about the prehistoric origins of religion, speculation in this area is almost completely unchecked by data, and it seems impossible to find any rational basis for choosing between alternative genetic accounts.

However, we might also give a nongenetic interpretation. Saying that the essence of religion is a feeling of absolute dependence, for example, might mean that the full interrelatedness of the various features of religion can be understood only if we view them all in relation to a feeling of absolute dependence. This claim would be independent of any view of the origin of religion. The difficulty with this is that there would seem to be several different features of religion that could be taken as central—such as ritual, a need for reassurance against the terrors of life, or a need to get a satisfactory explanation of the cosmos—and it is illuminating to view the rest of religion as related to each of these. How is one to settle on a unique essence?

Characteristic features of religion. Despite the fact that none of the definitions specifies a set of characteristics which is present when and only when we have a religion, or gives us a unique essence, it does seem that they contribute to our understanding of the nature of religion. It appears that the presence of any of the features stressed by these definitions will help to make something a religion. We might call such features, listed below, religion-making characteristics.

1. Belief in supernatural beings (gods).
2. A distinction between sacred and profane objects.
3. Ritual acts focused on sacred objects.
4. A moral code believed to be sanctioned by the gods.
5. Characteristically religious feelings (awe, sense of mystery, sense of guilt, adoration), which tend to be aroused in the presence of sacred objects and during the practice of ritual, and which are connected in idea with the gods.
6. Prayer and other forms of communication with gods.
7. A world view, or a general picture of the world as a whole and the place of the individual therein. This picture contains some specification of an over-all purpose or point of the world and an indication of how the individual fits into it.

8. A more or less total organization of one's life based on the world view.

9. A social group bound together by the above.

Interrelations of characteristics. Religion-making characteristics do not just happen to be associated in religion; they are intimately interconnected in several ways. Some of these connections have been indicated, but there are others. For example, the distinction between sacred and profane objects is based on other factors mentioned. It is not any intrinsic characteristic of a thing that makes it a sacred object; things of every conceivable kind have occupied this position—animals, plants, mountains, rivers, persons, and heavenly bodies. Certain objects are singled out as sacred in a given community because they typically arouse such feelings as awe and a sense of mystery, and thus the members of that community tend to respond to these objects with ritual acts. Again, the emotional reaction to sacred objects may be rationalized by conceiving the object to be the habitation or manifestation of a god. The awe aroused by the wild bull led to its being identified with the wild god of intoxication, Dionysus. The very special impression made by Jesus of Nazareth on certain of his contemporaries was expressed by calling him the Son of God. These examples make it sound as if emotional reactions to sacred objects come first and that these reactions are then explained by positing gods as their causes. But it can also happen the other way round. The acceptance of beliefs about the gods and their earthly habitations can contribute to the evocation of awe and other feelings in the presence of certain objects. The members of a religious community are taught to hold certain objects in awe by being taught various doctrines about the gods. Thus, Christians are taught to regard the cross and the consecrated bread and wine with reverence by being told of the Crucifixion and the Last Supper.

A similar reciprocal relationship holds between ritual and doctrine. A doctrine can be introduced as the justification of an already established ritual. Thus, the myth of Proserpine being carried off to the underworld and remaining there half the year seems to have been introduced as an explanation of a pre-existing magical fertility cult, in which an ear of grain, perhaps called the corn maiden, was buried in the fall and raised sprouting in the spring. On the other hand, changes in doctrine can engender, modify, or abolish rituals. Beliefs about the divine status of Jesus Christ played an important role in shaping the Christmas festival.

Definition in terms of characteristics. If it is true that the religion-making characteristics neither singly nor in combination constitute tight necessary and sufficient conditions for something being a religion, and yet that each of them contributes to making something a religion, then it must be that they are related in some looser way to the application of the term. Perhaps the best way to put it is this. When enough of these characteristics are present to a sufficient degree, we have a religion. It seems that, given the actual use of the term "religion," this is as precise as we can be. If we tried to say something like "for a religion to exist, there must be the first two plus any three others," or "for a religion to exist, any four of these characteristics

must be present," we would be introducing a degree of precision not to be found in the concept of religion actually in use.

Another way of putting the matter is this. There are cultural phenomena that embody all of these characteristics to a marked degree. They are the ideally clear paradigm cases of religion, such as Roman Catholicism, Orthodox Judaism, and Orphism. These are the cases to which the term "religion" applies most certainly and unmistakably. However, there can be a variety of cases that differ from the paradigm in different ways and to different degrees, by one or another of the religion-making characteristics dropping out more or less. For example, ritual can be sharply de-emphasized, and with it the demarcation of certain objects as sacred, as in Protestantism; it can even disappear altogether, as with the Quakers. Beliefs in supernatural beings can be whittled away to nothing, as in certain forms of Unitarianism, or may never be present, as in certain forms of Buddhism. And, as mentioned earlier, in certain primitive societies morality has no close connection with the cultic system. As more of the religion-making characteristics drop out, either partially or completely, we feel less secure about applying the term "religion," and there will be less unanimity in the language community with respect to the application of the term. However, there do not seem to be points along these various dimensions of deviations that serve as a sharp demarcation of religion from nonreligion. It is simply that we encounter less and less obvious cases of religion as we move from, for example, Roman Catholicism through Unitarianism, humanism, and Hinayana Buddhism to communism. Thus, the best way to explain the concept of religion is to elaborate in detail the relevant features of an ideally clear case of religion and then indicate the respects in which less clear cases can differ from this, without hoping to find any sharp line dividing religion from nonreligion. (Cf. Ludwig Wittgenstein's notion of "family-resemblances" among the things to which a term applies.)

An adequate definition of religion should throw light on the sorts of disputes and perplexities that typically produce a need to define religion, such as disputes over whether communism is a religion, and whether devotion to science can be called a man's religion. So long as we are dealing with definitions of the simplistic type that we have criticized, these problems are not illuminated. Each party to the dispute will appeal to a definition suited to the position he is defending, and since none of these definitions is wholly adequate, there is an irreducible plurality of not wholly inadequate definitions to be used for this purpose. Person *A*, who claims that communism is a religion, will give, for instance, Caird's statement as his definition of religion, and person *B*, who denies this, will choose Martineau's. Obviously, the position of each is upheld by his chosen definition. Hence, it would seem that the only way to settle the dispute is to determine which is the correct definition. However, we have seen that this gets us nowhere; no such definition is wholly adequate.

At this point there is a temptation to brand the dispute purely verbal, a reflection of different senses attached to the word "religion." It may seem that the disagreement can be dissolved by persuading all parties to use the word in the same sense. But this is a superficial reaction which does not adequately bring out how much the parties to the dispute have in common. In fact, Martineau and Caird represent two contrasting emphases within a common framework. Suppose that A and B begin with the same paradigm, orthodox Protestant Christianity. But A gives greatest weight to the moral-orientation–emotion elements in this paradigm. As long as anything strongly manifests these elements, as long as it serves as a system of life orientation for the individual who is bound to it by strong emotional ties, he will call it a religion. B, on the other hand, gives greatest weight to the belief in a personal God and the complex of emotions, ritual, and devotional acts that is bound up with that belief. Thus, although they have basically the same concept of religion, they will diverge in their application of the term at certain points. Once we realize that this is the true situation, we can state the problem in a more tractable form. We can enumerate the religion-making characteristics and determine which of them communism has and in what degree. Then we can proceed to the heart of the dispute—the relative importance of these characteristics. Insofar as there is a real issue between A and B, once both are in possession of all the relevant facts, it is whether communism is similar to clear cases of religion in the most important respects, that is, whether the respects in which it is like Protestant Christianity are more important than those in which it is different.

TYPES OF RELIGION

In the case of so complex a concept as religion, it is desirable to supplement the very general portrayal of basic features with some indications of the varying emphases placed on them in different religions. To do this, we must develop a classificatory scheme.

William James has reminded us that in every religion there is some sort of awareness of what is called divine and some sort of response to this divinity. This being the case, a very fruitful way of classifying religions is to ask in the case of each: "Where is the divine (the object of religious responses) primarily sought and located, and what sort of response is primarily made to it?" In answering these questions for a given religion, the religion-making features most stressed in that religion will also come to light. According to this principle of division, religions fall into three major groups: sacramental, prophetic, and mystical.

Location of the divine. In sacramental religion the divine is sought chiefly in things—inanimate physical things like pieces of wood (relics of saints, statues, crosses), food and drink (bread and wine, baptismal water), living things (the totem animal of the group, the sacred cow, the sacred tree), processes (the movements of the sacred dance). This does not mean that the thing itself is responded to as divine, although this can happen in very primitive forms of sacramental religion, called fetishism. Usually the sacred thing is conceived to be the habitation or manifestation of some god or spirit. Thus, the ancient Hebrews treated the elaborate box that they called the Ark of God as the habitation of their god, Jahweh; the Hindus consider the river Ganges sacred to the god Shiva—they believe that Shiva is

in some specially intimate relation to that river, and they bathe in its waters to benefit from his healing power. The Roman Catholic finds the presence of God concentrated in the consecrated bread and wine, which, he believes, has been transformed into the body and blood of Christ. At a more sophisticated level the material thing may be taken as a symbol of the divine rather than as its direct embodiment, as in the definition of a sacrament given in the Anglican Book of Common Prayer, "an outward and visible sign of an inward and spiritual grace."

In prophetic religion the divine is thought to manifest itself primarily in human society—in the events of human history and in the inspired utterances of great historical figures. It is not denied that nature issues from the divine and is under divine control, but it is not in nature that God is most immediately encountered. The divine reality is to be discovered in great historical events—the destruction of cities, the rise and fall of empires, the escape of a people from bondage. The hand of God is seen in these matters because God is encountered more immediately in the lives and the inspired words of his messengers, the prophets, who reveal in their utterances God's nature, his purposes and commands, and derivatively in the sacred books that contain the records of these revelations. Christianity, Judaism, and Islam, the three chief prophetic religions, are sometimes called religions of the book. Here the key term is not "sacrament" but "revelation." Prophetic religion, unlike the others, stresses the *word* as the medium of contact with the divine. (An example is the opening of the Gospel of John.) For the ritualist, and still more for the mystic, whatever words he may use, the consummation of his endeavors is found in a wordless communion with the divine. In prophetic religion, however, the linguistic barrier is never let down; it is not felt as a barrier at all.

The center of mystical religion is the mystical experience, which at its highest development dominates the consciousness, excluding all awareness of words, nature, even of the mystic's own self. In this experience the individual feels himself pervaded and transformed by the divine, identified with it in an indivisible unity. The world and all its ordinary concerns seem as naught as the mystic is caught up in the ineffable bliss of this union. It is not surprising that those who have enjoyed this experience, and those who aspire to it, should take it to be the one true avenue of contact with the divine and dismiss all other modes as spurious, or at least as grossly inferior. Rituals and sacraments, creeds and sacred books, are viewed as paltry substitutes, which are doled out to those who, by reason of incapacity or lack of effort, miss the firsthand mystic communion; or else they are external aids that are of use only in the earlier stages of the quest, crutches to be thrown away when direct access to God is attained.

Response to the divine. In sacramental religion, where the divine is apprehended chiefly in material embodiments, the center of religious activity will be found in ritual acts centering on these embodiments. The sacred places, animals, statues, and such, must be treated with reverence, approached and made use of with due precautions; and around these usages tend to grow prescribed rites. Since the sense of the divine presence in certain objects is likely to be enhanced by participation in solemn ceremonials centering on these objects, the religious activity becomes a self-perpetuating system, embodying what is currently called positive feedback.

In sacramental religion, the ritual tends to absorb most of the religious energies of the adherents and to crowd the other elements out of the center of the picture. Primitive religion, which is strongly sacramental in character, is often unconcerned with moral distinctions; and we might speculate that the progressive moralization of religion is achieved at the expense of ritual preoccupations. We can see this conflict at many points in the history of religions, most notably in the denunciations that the Hebrew prophets directed against the ritual-minded religionists of their day, and in their exhortations to substitute thirst for righteousness for the concern for niceties of ceremony. Even in its highest developments, sacramental religion tends to slacken the ethical tension that is found in prophetic religion. Where sacramentalism is strong in a monotheistic religion, the natural tendency is to take everything in nature as a divine manifestation. If everything is sacred, then nothing can be fundamentally evil; and thus the distinction between good and evil becomes blurred. One of the elements in the Protestant Reformation was a protest against tendencies to blurring of this sort, which took place in the largely sacramental medieval form of Christianity.

The typical response of prophetic religion to the divine is also nicely coordinated with the chief form in which the divine is apprehended. The reaction naturally called for by a message from the divine is acceptance. This involves both an intellectual acceptance of its contents—belief that whatever statements it makes are true—and obedience to the commands and exhortations it contains. Hence, in prophetic religion faith is the supreme virtue, and affirmations and confessions of faith play an important role. This is illustrated by the insistence of such great Christian prophetic figures as Paul and Luther on faith in Christ as both necessary and sufficient for salvation and by the Muslim practice of repeating daily the creed "There is no God but Allah, and Muhammad is his prophet." It is important to realize that faith in this sense means far more than the intellectual assent to certain propositions. It also involves taking up an attitude on the basis of that affirmation and expressing that attitude in action. The Jewish prophet Micah expressed the essence of prophetic religion when he said, "What doth the Lord require of thee, but to do justly and to love mercy, and to walk humbly with thy God?" Thus, it would not be incorrect to say that the emphasis in the prophetic response is ethical, providing we do not separate ethics from the believing acceptance of the divine message that is its foundation.

To understand the typical response of mystical religion, we must remember that for the mystic, immediate identification with the divine is of supreme importance. Therefore he concentrates on an ascetic and contemplative discipline that will be conducive to the attainment and maintenance of that condition. He tends to become involved in abstentions and self-tortures designed to wean him from his attachment to things of this world, and in contemplative exercises designed to withdraw the attention from finite things, leaving the soul empty and receptive to influences from the divine. He will make use of ceremonies and will accede to moral principles insofar as he believes them to be efficacious in furthering his ultimate goal. But ultimately they must go; when union with God has been achieved, they are of no more significance. Thus, like sacramentalism, mysticism tends toward the amoral. Only rarely does either become completely amoral, and then for different reasons. For the sacramentalist, conventional moral distinctions may come to seem unimportant because he views everything as equally saturated with the divine; they seem unimportant to the mystic because every finite object or activity is outside the mystic union, and so all are, in the end, equally worthless. The righteous and the wicked are equally far from the true religious goal. While united with God, one does not act.

Place of doctrine. Finally, we may compare the three types of religion with respect to the status of beliefs and creeds. Since faith is central for prophetic religion and since the word is stressed as the primary medium of divine manifestation, it is not surprising that in prophetic religion, creed and doctrine are emphasized more than in the others. Mystical religion, at its purest, is indifferent to matters of belief and doctrine. The mystical experience and the divinity it reveals are often regarded as ineffable, not to be expressed in human language; hence, mystics tend to reject all doctrinal formulations as inadequate. At best, a mystic will admit that some formulations are less inadequate symbols of the unutterable than are others. Thus, in such predominantly mystical groups as the Sufis and the Quakers, little or no attempt is made to enforce doctrinal conformity. And in an extreme form of mysticism, like that of Zen Buddhism, any doctrinal formulation is discouraged. Sacramental religion occupies a middle ground in this respect. In its more primitive forms, it is often extremely indefinite about belief. It has been said that primitive man "dances out his religion." Certainly the elaboration of ritual in primitive religion far outstrips the associated theory. The primitive will often possess an incredibly detailed set of ritual prescriptions but have only the haziest idea of what there is about the nature or doings of the gods that makes them appropriate. In its more developed forms, sacramental theology becomes more definite, but it is still true that to the extent that a religion is preoccupied with a sacramental approach to the divine, it is more impatient than prophetic religion with doctrinal subtleties.

We can coordinate this classification with the list of religion-making characteristics by pointing out that sacramental religion stresses sacred objects and ritual, prophetic religion stresses belief and morality, and mystical religion places chief emphasis on immediate experience and feeling.

Concrete application. When we come to apply our scheme to particular cases, we must not suppose that any religion will fall completely in one class or another. In fact, it is better not to think of types of religions, but of religious tendencies that enter in varying proportions into the make-up of any actual religion. However, we can usually say that one tendency or another predominates in a given religion. Thus, Buddhism and philosophical Hinduism are predominantly mystical; Judaism, Islam, and Confucianism are primarily prophetic; and popular Hinduism, in company with all polytheistic and primitive religions, is primarily sacramental. Often a religion that begins with a definite bent will admit other elements in the course of its development. Islam, which began as the most severely prophetic of religions, has developed one of the world's most extreme group of mystics in the Sufis, who are completely out of harmony with the spirit of Muhammad, no matter how they may continue to express themselves in his phrases. Again, in Tibet, Buddhism has undergone a development quite foreign to its founder's intentions, blossoming into an extremely elaborate sacramentalism.

Christianity furnishes a good opportunity to study the intermingling and conflict of the different tendencies. It began as an outgrowth of Jewish prophecy, but in the process of adapting itself to the rest of the Western world it took on a considerable protective coloration of both the sacramental and mystical, and these aspects have remained with it throughout its career. Christian mysticism presents a good example of an element existing in a religion that is dominated by another element. As the price of toleration, Christian mystics have had to pay lip service to the official theology and to the prophetic moral element; and as a result, mystic thought and practice in Christianity have seldom received the extreme development found in India. In those cases where the mystical spirit has burst the fetters, as with Meister Eckhart, official condemnation has often resulted.

Looking at Christianity today, it can be said that although it is predominantly a prophetic religion, as compared with Hinduism and Buddhism, with respect to its internal divisions the Catholic wing (both Roman and Greek) tends more toward the sacramental, while the Protestant is more purely prophetic, with mysticism appearing sporadically throughout. In Catholicism the elaborateness of prescribed ceremonies, the emphasis on the necessity of material sacraments for salvation, and the insistence on a special status for consecrated priests are all typically sacramental. In Protestantism the emphasis on the sermon (the speaking forth of the Word of God) rather than on ritual, the emphasis on the Bible as the repository of divine revelation, and the moral earnestness and social concern are all earmarks of the prophetic spirit.

Bibliography

Friedrich Schleiermacher, *On Religion,* translated by John Oman (New York, 1958), and *The Christian Faith,* translated by H. R. Mackintosh (Edinburgh, 1956), contain classic statements of the view that religion is essentially a mode of experience. A more recent statement of this point of view that emphasizes mystical experience is in W. T. Stace, *Time and Eternity* (Princeton, 1952). The moral aspect of religion is stressed in Immanuel Kant, *Religion Within the Limits of Reason Alone,* translated by T. M. Greene and H. H. Hudson (La Salle, Ill., 1934), and in John Baillie, *The Interpretation of Religion* (New York, 1928). Conceptions of religion from the standpoint of philosophical naturalism are to be found in Auguste Comte, *A General View of Positivism* (London, 1865); Ludwig Feuerbach, *The Essence of Christianity,* translated by George Eliot (New York, 1957); George Santayana, *Reason in Religion* (New York, 1905); John Dewey, *A Common Faith* (New Haven, 1934); and Erich Fromm, *Psychoanalysis and Religion* (New Haven, 1950).

Stimulating discussions, not so easily classified, are Henri Bergson, *The Two Sources of Morality and Religion,* translated by R. Ashley Audra (New York, 1935); William James, *The Varieties of Religious Experience* (New York, 1902); Josiah Royce, *The Sources of Religious Insight* (New York, 1912); John Oman, "The Sphere of Religion," in Joseph Needham, ed., *Science, Religion and Reality* (New York, 1925); and Alfred North Whitehead, *Religion in the Making* (New York, 1926). Important discussions from the social sciences include Émile Durkheim, *The Elementary Forms of the Religious Life,* translated by J. W. Swain (London, 1905), and Bronislaw Malinowski, *Magic, Science, and Religion* (New York, 1954). James H. Leuba, *A Psychological Study of Religion* (New York, 1912), and Julian Huxley, *Religion Without Revelation* (New York, 1958), provide extensive critical discussion of a wide variety of definitions, as well as presenting original conceptions.

WILLIAM P. ALSTON

RELIGION, NATURALISTIC RECONSTRUCTIONS OF.

In philosophy a naturalist is one who holds that there is nothing over and above nature. A naturalist is committed to rejecting traditional religion, which is based on beliefs in the supernatural. This does not necessarily carry with it a rejection of religion as such, however. Many naturalists envisage a substitute for traditional religion which will perform the typical functions of religion without making any claims beyond the natural world. We can best classify naturalistic forms of religion in terms of what they take God to be—that is, what they set up as an object of worship. In traditional religion the supernatural personal deity is worshiped because he is thought of as the zenith of both goodness and power. More generally, we can say that religious worship is accorded to any being because it is regarded as having a controlling voice in the course of events and at least potentially exercising that power for the good. This suggests that to find a focus for religious responses in the natural world, we should look for a basic natural source of value. Forms of naturalistic religion differ as to where this is located. Broadly speaking, achievements of value in human life are due to factors of two sorts: (1) man's natural endowments, together with the deposit of his past achievements in the cultural heritage of a society, and (2) things and processes in nonhuman nature on which man depends for the possibility of his successes and, indeed, his very life. Most naturalists locate their religious object primarily on one or the other side of this distinction, although some try to maintain an even balance between the two.

The first factor is stressed most by those who are called religious humanists. This group includes Ludwig Feuerbach and Auguste Comte in the nineteenth century and John Dewey and Erich Fromm in the twentieth. Of these men Comte has been the most influential.

Comte. In Comte's view, it is to humanity that the individual man owes everything that he is and has. It is because he shares in the general biological and psychological capacities of human nature that he is able to live a human life. And the men of a given generation are able to lead a fully human life because of the labors of their predecessors in building up their cultural heritage. Moreover, according to Comte, the service of humanity, in the many forms this can take, is the noblest ideal which could be proposed to an individual; and humanity, unlike an omnipotent God, needs this service. Thus, Comte proposed to set up a religion of humanity with man, viewed as a unitary though spatiotemporally scattered being, as the object of worship.

Unlike many naturalists Comte was not at all vague about the detailed functioning of his proposed religion. He was impressed with the ritual structure of Roman Catholicism and took it as his model. For example, in the analogue of baptism, the sacrament of presentation, the parents would dedicate their child to the service of humanity in an impressive public ceremony. Public observances were to be reinforced by the regular practice of private prayer, on which Comte laid the greatest stress. A person was to pray four times daily, with each prayer divided into a commemorative and a purificatory part. In the first part one would invoke some great benefactor of humanity; by reflecting gratefully on his deeds, one would be inspired to follow his example, and one's love of humanity would thus be quickened. The purificatory part would give solemn expression to the noble desires thereby evoked; in it the individual would dedicate himself to the service of humanity. Other rituals included a system of religious festivals and a calendar of the saints of humanity that provided the material for the prayers on each day of the year.

Some idea of the religious fervor generated in Comte by the contemplation of humanity may be gained from this quotation from *A General View of Positivism:*

> The Being upon whom all our thoughts are concentrated is one whose existence is undoubted. We recognize that existence not in the Present only, but in the Past, and even in the Future: and we find it always subject to one fundamental Law, by which we are enabled to conceive of it as a whole. Placing our highest happiness in universal Love, we live, as far as it is possible, for others: and this in public life as well as in private; for the two are closely linked together in our religion; a religion clothed in all the beauty of Art, and yet never inconsistent with Science. After having thus exercised our powers to the full, and having given a charm and sacredness to our temporary life, we shall at last be forever incorporated into the Supreme Being, of whose life all noble natures are necessarily partakers. It is only through the worship of Humanity that we can feel the inward reality and inexpressible sweetness of this incorporation.   (P. 444)

Comte had considerable influence in his lifetime, and a few functioning parishes of his religion of humanity sprang up. They have not survived, however, and a revival in our time hardly seems likely. In the twentieth century, reeling under the impact of two world wars and the hourly expectation of the death knell of civilization, we are not inclined to grow misty-eyed over humanity. Recent humanists have tended to be more critical in their reverence. The latest trend is to single out the more ideal aspects of man—his aspirations for truth, beauty, and goodness—for religious worship. Or the emphasis shifts from man as he actually exists to the ideals which man pursues in his better moments. Thus, in his book *A Common Faith,* John Dewey defines God as "the unity of all ideal ends arousing us to desire and action" (p. 42).

Dewey. Unlike Comte, Dewey has no interest in developing an organized naturalistic religion. It would seem that religious organization and religious ritual are too closely associated in his mind with the supernaturalism which he rejects. For Dewey the important thing is the religious quality which experience can assume under certain conditions. Any unification of the whole self around the pursuit of an ideal end is religious in quality. Dewey is emphatic in insisting that this is a quality, rather than a kind, of experience. Whenever a person is thoroughly committed to the pursuit of any ideal, be it scientific, social, artistic, or whatever, his experience attains the kind of fulfillment that has always been characteristic of what is most valuable in religion. According to Dewey, in traditional religion this quality has been encumbered and obscured by irrelevant trappings, particularly the theological dogma in terms of which it has been pursued. In the past, self-integration in the pursuit of the ideal has been thought of as service of God, unity with God, or submission to God's will. It is Dewey's conviction that the religious quality can be more effectively sought if the quest is not carried on under this banner. To reflective men, supernaturalistic dogma will always appear dubious at best. If the quest for self-integration in the service of the ideal is too closely tied to theology, it will be endangered when the theology is rejected as rationally groundless. Moreover, insofar as the theology is taken seriously, it diverts attention from the active pursuit of the ideal. Worse, the assurance that the good is already perfectly realized in the divine nature has the tendency to cut the nerve of moral effort; in that case it is not up to us to introduce the good into the world. Thus, Dewey's main concern as a philosopher of religion is to redirect religious ardor into the quest for a richer quality of human life rather than to construct a framework for a naturalistically oriented religious organization.

There is no developed naturalistic philosophy of religion which stresses the nonhuman side of the natural sources of value to the extent to which Comte stresses the human side. (Though we can find this in literature, notably in Richard Jeffries, who had a kind of religious intoxication with inanimate nature without, however, conceiving of it as suffused with a spiritual being or beings. This is a naturalistic counterpart of the nature worship of ancient Greece, just as Comte's religion of humanity is a naturalistic counterpart of an ethical monotheism like Christianity.) However, there is a marked tendency among contemporary naturalists to emphasize the nonhuman side much more than Comte or Dewey. Good examples of this are the liberal theologian Henry Nelson Wieman and the biologist Julian Huxley, who in his book *Religion Without Revelation* has made the most coherent and comprehensive recent attempt to sketch out a naturalistically oriented religion.

Huxley. According to Huxley's conception, religion stems from two basic sources. One is man's concern with his destiny—his position and role in the universe and their implications for his activity; the other is the sense of sacredness. Following Rudolf Otto, Huxley thinks of the sense of sacredness as a unique kind of experience which is an intimate blend of awe, wonder, and fascination; this mode of feeling arises spontaneously in reaction to a wide variety of objects and situations. Religion, then, is a social organ for dealing with problems of human destiny. As such it involves a conception of the world within which this destiny exists, some mobilization of the emotional forces in man vis-à-vis the world thus conceived, some sort of ritual for expressing and maintaining the feelings and attitudes developed with respect to the forces affecting human destiny, and some dispositions with respect to the practical problems connected with our destiny. The sense of sacredness enters into the second and third of these aspects. As Huxley sees it, a way of dealing with problems of human destiny would not be distinctively religious if it did not stem from and encourage a sense of the sacredness of the major elements in its view of the world, man, and human life.

Huxley, as a thoroughgoing naturalist, holds that the supernaturalistic world view in terms of which religion has traditionally performed its functions is no longer tenable in the light of modern scientific knowledge. Moreover, he thinks that it is possible to develop a full-blown religion on a naturalistic basis. As the intellectual basis for such a religion, Huxley puts forward "evolutionary naturalism," a view of the spatiotemporal universe, inspired by modern biology and cosmology, in which the universe is conceived of as an indefinitely extended creative process, always tending to higher levels of development, with all the sources and principles of this creativity immanent in the process. The basic role of man is to be the chief agent of this evolutionary advance on earth through the application of his intelligence to the problems of life on earth and through the building of a harmonious and stable community. A religion based on these conceptions will be focused on an object of worship which is a construct out of all the forces affecting human destiny, including basic physical forces as well as the fundamental facts of human existence and social life. God, then, will consist of all these factors, held together by the feeling of sacredness with which they are apprehended. As a start toward conceiving this assemblage as a unified object of worship, Huxley presents a naturalistic version of the Christian doctrine of the trinity. God the Father is made up of the forces of nonhuman nature. God the Holy Ghost symbolizes the ideals toward which human beings at their best are striving. God the Son personifies human nature as it actually exists, bridging the gulf between the other two by channeling natural forces into the pursuit of ideals. And the unity of all the persons as one God represents the fact that all these aspects of the divine are intimately connected.

Many thinkers, atheists as well as theists, take a dim view of all these proceedings. Since the theists' lack of enthusiasm stems from obvious sources, let us concentrate on the atheists. The issues here are normative or evaluative rather than factual. Comte and Huxley as philosophers of religion are not, with perhaps minor exceptions, making any factual judgments with which other naturalists might disagree because they are making no factual judgments at all beyond their basic commitment to naturalism. If a man like Russell or Sartre disagrees with Huxley, he differs about the value of what Huxley is proposing. His low evaluation may have different bases. First, he may feel that man or the basic forces of nature constitute too pallid a substitute for the God of theism to afford a secure footing for the distinctively religious reactions of reverence, adoration, and worship. A man like Huxley might, for his part,

interpret this as a reflection of a suppressed hankering after the old supernatural deity. Second, Russell or Sartre may turn this charge on Huxley and maintain that one searches for an object of worship within nature only because he has not sufficiently emancipated himself from the old religious orientation and that this religion of evolutionary naturalism represents an uneasy compromise between religious and secular orientations. It seems clear that there is no one objective resolution of such disputes. People differ in such a way that different total orientations will seem congenial to people with different temperaments and cultural backgrounds. It is perhaps unfortunate, on the whole, that many people need to find something fundamentally unworthy in every other religion in order to find a firm attachment to their own religious positions, although it is undoubtedly true that religious discussions are more lively than they would be if this were not the case.

Bibliography

Ames, E. S., *Religion*. New York, 1929.

Comte, Auguste, *A General View of Positivism,* translated by J. H. Bridges. London, 1880. Ch. 6.

Dewey, John, *A Common Faith.* New Haven, 1934.

Feuerbach, Ludwig, *The Essence of Christianity,* translated by George Eliot. New York, 1957.

Fromm, Erich, *Psychoanalysis and Religion.* London, 1951.

Huxley, Julian, *Religion Without Revelation.* New York, 1958.

Russell, Bertrand, *Why I Am Not a Christian and Other Essays.* New York, 1957. Paperback.

Wieman, Henry Nelson, *The Source of Human Good.* Chicago, 1946.

William P. Alston

RELIGION, PHILOSOPHY OF. The main problems and developments in the philosophy of religion are introduced in the articles Philosophy of religion, history of; Philosophy of religion, problems of; and Religion.

The Encyclopedia also features the following separate articles: Agnosticism; Analogy in theology; Atheism; Atheismusstreit; Common Consent Arguments for the existence of God; Cosmological Argument for the existence of God; Creation, religious doctrine of; Degrees of Perfection, Argument for the existence of God; Demiurge; Dogma; Emanationism; Eschatology; Evil, the problem of; Faith; Fideism; God, concepts of; Guilt; Illumination; Immortality; Infinity in theology and metaphysics; Karma; Life, meaning and value of; Life, origin of; Miracles; Moral Arguments for the existence of God; Mysticism, history of; Mysticism, nature and assessment of; Nirvana; Ontological Argument for the existence of God; Pantheism; Pantheismusstreit; Perfection; Physicotheology; Popular Arguments for the existence of God; Providence; Reincarnation; Religion, naturalistic reconstructions of; Religion, psychological explanations of; Religion and morality; Religion and science; Religious Experience, Argument for the existence of God; Religious language; Revelation; Teleological Argument for the existence of God; Theism; Traditionalism; and Why.

The following articles discuss various religions and religious movements: Arius and Arianism; Arminius and Arminianism; Buddhism; Cabala; Christianity; Deism; Gnosticism; Hinduism; Indian philosophy; Islamic philosophy; Jainism; Jewish philosophy; Mani and Manichaeism; Modernism; Patristic philosophy; Pelagius and Pelagianism; Pietism; Reformation; Socinianism; Sufi philosophy; Zen; and Zoroastrianism.

RELIGION, PSYCHOLOGICAL EXPLANATIONS OF.

In the seventeenth and eighteenth centuries the chief impact of science on religion came from the revised picture of the cosmos that emerged from developments in astronomy and physics. In the nineteenth century the impact was from the changed view of the history of life on earth that was presented by geology and evolutionary biology. In the twentieth century the social sciences have had the greatest impact on religion, although of a different nature. Physics and biology worried theologians because they introduced theories about the cosmos, life, and man that were at variance with beliefs intimately bound up with the religious tradition, such as the special creation of man. The impact of the social sciences, on the other hand, comes not from theories that contradict basic religious doctrines but from explanations of religion itself that seem to rob it of its significance.

In the nineteenth and twentieth centuries numerous ideas have been put forward as to the psychological and sociological factors that are responsible for religion. The most important of these are (1) the Marxian theory that religion is one of the ideological reflections of the current state of economic interrelations in a society; (2) the similar, but more elaborately developed, theory of the sociologist Emile Durkheim that religious belief constitutes a projection of the structure of society; (3) the Freudian theory that religious belief arises from projections designed to alleviate certain kinds of unconscious conflict. These are all scientific explanations in that they trace religion to factors wholly within the world of nature, and hence they are, at least in principle, subject to empirical test. Concentration on one of these, the Freudian, will enable us to illustrate the philosophical problems raised by such explanations.

The Freudian explanation. The Freudian account begins with certain similarities between attributes of and attitudes toward a personal deity, on the one hand, and the small child's conception of and mode of relating to his father, on the other. In both cases the superior being is regarded as omnipotent, omniscient, inscrutable, and providential. In both cases the individual reacts to this superior being with utter dependence, awe, fear of punishment, and gratitude for mercy and protection. These parallels suggest, though they do not prove, that the original model for the conception of God is to be found in the infantile conception of one's parents, and that the almost universal inclination to believe in personal deities is to be traced to psychological remnants of the infantile situation. According to Freud, these remnants are mostly the result of the Oedipal conflict. According to his theory, around the age of four the boy (restricting ourselves to the male for simplicity of exposition) comes to desire his mother sexually and

to regard his father as a rival. Reacting more or less to actual indications, the boy becomes so afraid of the father's hostility, and also so afraid of losing his love, that he not only abandons his sexual aims but also represses the entire complex of desires, fears, and conceptions. This complex remains, in greater or lesser intensity, in the unconscious; and it is because a supernatural personal deity provides an external object on which to project it that men have as much inclination as they do to believe in such a being and to accept the attitudes and practices that go with this belief.

To understand what the projection does for the individual, we must recognize that the repressed material involves severe conflict between tendencies to rebel against the father and tendencies to submit to the father, and between the Oedipal desires and the standards that would be violated by satisfying those desires. Projection of this material onto an external deity reduces distress in several ways. First, the externalization of the problem provides some relief. Instead of being plagued by mysterious discomfort, the individual is faced with a clear-cut opposition between various desires of his own and a forbidding external person. Second, there is less conflict because the external figure is so powerful as to seriously weaken the rebellion, and he is so idealized as to render resentment and hostility less appropriate. Third, there are various mechanisms provided for dissipating the guilt over sexual desire for the mother and hostility toward the father. Confession, penance, and renunciations of various kinds afford socially approved means for relieving this guilt and counteracting its crippling influence.

People are more receptive to religious belief at some times than at others. Freud explains this in terms of the mechanism of regression. When a person encounters severe difficulties and frustrations at one stage of life, he tends to regress psychologically to an earlier stage at which these problems did not exist. Thus, when an adult is particularly hard pressed, there is generally some reinstatement of earlier modes of thinking, feeling, and relating to the environment. This means that the Oedipal material in the unconscious will become more intense and closer to the surface, while at the same time the person is more likely to engage in the childish practice of projection.

Thus, according to Freudian theory, an individual's tendency to accept belief in a supernatural personal deity (together with the other aspects of religious activity and involvement) is at least partly caused by a tendency to project a childhood father image existing in the unconscious, this projection normally following a regression set off by a current problem of adjustment and serving to alleviate unconscious conflicts and unconscious guilt. It is clear that, at best, this is only a partial explanation of religious belief. For one thing, it presupposes the prior existence of the religious ideas in the culture; at most, it is an explanation of the individual's readiness to accept these ideas when they are proffered.

Freud tried to supply this lack by developing a parallel theory of the development of religion in society. According to this theory, religion develops as a projection of a psychological complex that results from unconscious racial memories of a primal murder of the tyrannical father figure of a "primal horde." Cultural development is thus treated along the same lines as the development of the individual; something like a "collective unconscious" is posited in which psychic material can be transmitted in an unconscious form from one generation to another. However, these ideas have never won any considerable degree of acceptance, and in discussing Freud we can concentrate on his account of the psychological basis of religion in the individual.

Criticisms of Freudian explanation. With respect to any scientific explanation of religion, there are two questions to be raised. (1) What reason is there to accept it? (2) If it is true, what bearing does it have on the truth, value, or justifiability of religion? It is the second question that specially lies within the province of the philosophy of religion.

It is clear that the Freudian explanation does not imply that the beliefs of religion are false; Freud himself recognized this, though not all Freudians do. But it is often assumed that the success of any explanation of religion in terms of factors within the natural world would show that we do not need to bring anything supernatural into the explanation, and hence would seriously weaken religion's claims to credibility. However, this depends on how these claims were made. If religion is based solely on divine revelation, then the fact that we can give an adequate explanation of religion without bringing in divine activity, revelatory or otherwise, seriously affects—though it does not conclusively disprove—the claim that certain beliefs are true because they are communicated to man by God. But if rational arguments are advanced in support of religious doctrine, such as the classical arguments for the existence of God, then whatever force these arguments have is in no degree lessened by the fact—if it be a fact—that the psychological basis for religion is as Freud supposed. Of course, if the Freudian mechanisms constitute a necessary as well as sufficient condition of religious belief, then it follows that no one has any good reason for these beliefs. If anyone did have a good reason, that would itself be a sufficient condition of the belief, and this would show that it is possible to have the belief without needing to project an unconscious father image. However, it is almost inconceivable that we should show that projection is a *necessary* condition of belief. At most, we could hope to show that there is *some* correlation between degree of unconscious Oedipal conflict and firmness of religious belief. Showing that a certain set of natural factors is *one* of the things that can produce religious belief may well nullify *certain* ways of supporting the beliefs, but it could hardly show that no adequate rational grounds *could* be produced.

There is another way in which it has been thought that the Freudian theory of religion carries with it a negative evaluation of religion. The particular causal factors to which Freud traced religion are of a sort associated with undesirable patterns of organization. To regard religion as caused by these factors is to class it with neurotic and infantile modes of behavior, and as such it is hardly worthy of serious consideration. In this respect, too, the psychoanalytic explanation is typical. One can imagine an explanation that traces religious activity to evaluatively neutral natural factors, such as patterns of neural activity in the brain, but all the explanations in the field trace religion to states and activities that are more or less irrational, immature, or unworthy. Projection is involved in all the theories cited at the beginning of this article; the Marxist theory adds the point that religion is used by the dominant class to provide illusory consolations to those being exploited.

To be clear on this issue, we must distinguish the different forms these claims can take. Psychoanalytic literature is often simply an enumeration of similarities between religion and compulsion neuroses, such as firm attachment to rituals without having a rational explanation of the attachment. However, the similarity in itself proves nothing. A scientist "obsessed with an idea" also exhibits marked similarities to a compulsion neurotic, but this has no implications for the value of his work. The more important claim has to do with the causal factors said to underlie religion. Here, too, we must distinguish between (1) the claim that some neurotic condition is always or generally among the factors producing attachment to a religion and (2) the claim that the causal basis of such attachment is markedly similar to the basis of recognized neuroses. There is no real evidence for the first claim. Controlled studies on the required scale have never been carried out. As for the second, we must ask how similar the causal basis is and what implications we are to draw from whatever degree of similarity exists. The mere fact that religion involves projection as a relief from unconscious conflict is not sufficient ground for labeling religion, in Freud's terms, "the universal obsessional neurosis of mankind." We must distinguish between pathological and healthy resolutions of unconscious conflict.

The anti-Freudian psychoanalyst Jung, in terming religion an alternative to neurosis, expressed his belief that it is a healthy outcome. The basic issue involved here concerns the definition of "neurosis." If we define it in terms of a certain causal basis, then it may be that according to the Freudian theory, religion is, by its very nature, a form of neurosis. But then it remains an open question whether or not it is a desirable, justifiable, or realistic mode of activity. If neurosis is defined in this way, we may have to distinguish between good and bad neuroses. If, on the other hand, we accept common usage and build a negative evaluation into the definition of neurosis (by having as a necessary condition of neurosis that it make a satisfactory adjustment to one's environment difficult), then it would no longer be an open question whether religion, if neurotic, is a good thing. But with this concept of neurosis, we have a much stronger thesis, which calls for evidence that has not yet been provided. No one has shown that in general religious believers are less able to establish satisfying personal relations and less able to get ahead in their work than are nonbelievers. Even if this were shown, there would be further problems of a very sticky sort. The believer might complain that restricting "the environment" to the natural environment is question-begging. He would say that whatever the bearing of religious attachment on getting along in human society, it is essential to adequate adjustment to God and his demands. To ignore this aspect of "the environment" is to employ a criterion of adjustment that presupposes the falsity of religious beliefs.

Similar comments apply to the idea that the psychoanalytic theory implies that religion is infantile and hence unworthy of mature men. It is true that the way a religious man relates himself to God is in many ways similar to the way a small child relates himself to a father. But whether or not this is a mature, realistic mode of activity is wholly a function of whether there really is such a God. If there is, then this is the only reasonable stance to take. Hence, to condemn religion on these grounds is to presuppose the falsity of its beliefs.

Thus, there are many gaps in any line of reasoning which tries to derive a negative evaluation of religion from a causal explanation of religion in psychological or sociological terms. If a person does not feel that he has a firm basis for his religious beliefs, then looking at religion in a Freudian or Marxian light may well lead him to give up his beliefs. More generally, we can say that Freudian or Marxian theory does not provide an intellectual atmosphere in which one would expect religious belief to flourish; but it does not appear that these theories, as so far developed, are in any way logically incompatible with the truth, justifiability, and value of traditional religion.

Bibliography

Important treatments of religion from a psychological point of view include Sigmund Freud, *Totem and Taboo,* translated by A. A. Brill (New York, 1918), *The Future of an Illusion,* translated by W. D. Robson-Scott (New York, 1928), and *Moses and Monotheism,* translated by Katherine Jones (New York, 1939); Carl Jung, *Psychology and Religion* (New Haven, 1938), and *Modern Man in Search of a Soul,* translated by W. S. Dell and C. F. Baynes (New York, 1933); Erich Fromm, *Psychoanalysis and Religion* (New Haven, 1950); A. T. Bosien, *The Exploration of the Inner World* (New York, 1952); and Theodor Reik, *Dogma and Compulsion,* translated by Bernard Miall (New York, 1951). R. S. Lee, *Freud and Christianity* (New York, 1949), and William P. Alston, "Psychoanalytic Theory and Theistic Belief," in John Hick, ed., *Faith and the Philosophers* (New York, 1964), present discussions of the Freudian treatment of religion.

For a sociological point of view, see Émile Durkheim, *The Elementary Forms of the Religious Life,* translated by J. W. Swain (London, 1915); Vilfredo Pareto, *The Mind and Society,* translated by Andrew Bongiorno and Arthur Livingston (New York, 1935), Vol. III; V. F. Calverton, *The Passing of the Gods* (New York, 1934); and G. E. Swanson, *The Birth of the Gods* (Ann Arbor, Mich., 1961).

WILLIAM P. ALSTON

RELIGION AND MORALITY. It would be useless to start with an attempt to define strictly either "morality" or "religion," since each of these words covers a large and ill-defined area. Each involves a more or less clearly articulated set of beliefs, practices, attitudes, and motives. What they have in common is that they are fundamental to the way of life of an individual or of a society, and it is not surprising that they should be closely connected. Indeed, it has often been held that morality is wholly *dependent* on religion, that a man who has no religion cannot have any morality. Even so tolerant and enlightened a man as John Locke held that one is under no obligation to keep faith with atheists, on the grounds that an atheist must be a moral outlaw; and even though this extreme claim would not often now be made, it is still frequently said that all morality *begins* with religion, so that if men had never

been religious they could never have learned morality. The present article will examine the connections between religion and morality, first historically, then conceptually.

MORALITY

A morality, or moral system, contains (1) beliefs about the nature of man; (2) beliefs about ideals, about what is good or desirable or worthy of pursuit for its own sake; (3) rules laying down what ought to be done and what ought not to be done; and (4) motives that incline us to choose the right or the wrong course. Popular or unreflective morality is inclined to lay more emphasis on rules than on ideals. We learn as children that we should be unselfish, that we should not tell lies, and that we should follow a host of detailed rules covering different aspects of life; and for many people morality remains, all their lives, an affair of isolated "do's" and "don't's." Philosophers, on the other hand, attempt to incorporate these miscellaneous rules into a coherent system, although they are divided about the relative importance of rules and ideals.

Deontological and teleological views. On the one hand, deontologists regard rules as fundamental. Moral rules are not rules for achieving ideal ends, dependent for their validity on their success or failure in bringing about these ends, but are worthy of obedience in their own right; and a moral system is a system of rules in which some rules are regarded as depending on others. For example, the rule that one ought to pay debts is not an independent rule but a special case of the more general rule that one ought to keep promises; and the rule that one ought not to kill is a special case of the rule that one ought not to do injury. Teleologists, on the other hand, regard moral rules as rules for producing what is good (health, happiness, knowledge, beauty) and avoiding what is bad (disease, misery, ignorance, ugliness); they are to be judged empirically on the basis of their tendency to promote what is good and prevent what is bad. We are under no obligation to keep promises because "a promise is a promise" if it would clearly be more beneficial to break it.

Most moral systems try to find a compromise between these two extreme views, deontologists allowing that the rule that we should try to maximize human happiness is at least one of the more important rules, and teleologists allowing that there are some rules which we should obey even when the consequences of obeying them are, in the case concerned, likely to be harmful.

Content of morality. So far we have considered only the *structure* of moral systems; we must also consider their *content* and the *motives* that lead us to be moral. As to content, morality is either wholly or almost wholly concerned with relations between men, with how they ought to behave toward each other, with what general rules governing relations between man and man a society ought to adopt. In Hobbes's words, the province of morality is limited to "those qualities of mankind that concern their living together in peace and unity." Moral duties are the duties which arise under such a system of rules, whether we adopt a deontological or a teleological attitude toward these rules. Religious rules we shall find to be different; although where, as in the case of the "higher" religions, the supernatural is thought of as a person or persons with human attributes, religious rules will naturally take on the coloring of moral rules.

The need for morality arises because men are social animals. The human baby cannot survive without the help of its parents; and a small human group such as the family needs mutual support and cooperation for defense against other groups, against other animals, and against the forces of nature. Moreover, everything that we regard as specifically *human,* as distinguishing us from other animals, depends on the use of language and the transmission of skills. Finally, quite apart from the advantages which accrue from society, men normally delight in each other's company. Most of the activities that we prize most highly and regard as valuable for their own sake, not only for their consequences, are, in one way or another, social activities.

But, along with the direct and indirect need for the company of his fellows, man has tendencies that disrupt the society on which his life and happiness depend. When goods are scarce, his limited generosity and his desire to preserve his own life leads each man into competition with his neighbors. If these motives—and we might add pride, jealousy, and sheer stupidity—get the upper hand, there results what Hobbes called a condition of war,

> . . . and such a war as is of every man against every man. . . . In such conditions, there is no place for industry; because the fruit thereof is uncertain; and consequently no culture of the earth; no navigation nor use of the commodities that may be imported by sea; no commodious building; no instruments of moving and removing such things as require much force; no knowledge of the face of the earth; no account of time; no arts; no letters; no society; and, which is worst of all, continual fear and danger of violent death; and the life of man solitary, poor, nasty, brutish and short. (*Leviathan,* Ch. 13)

To avoid this intolerable condition men have devised the systems of rules which we know as law and morality. Though these systems differ widely in detail, their common origin and purpose in the overriding need to preserve social harmony ensure a broad similarity in fundamentals. All moral codes condemn aggression, injustice, and deceit, at least within the social group.

Motives for moral behavior. There are three kinds of motives which lead men to act morally, that is, to obey the moral rules of their society. (1) Enlightened self-interest: We obey moral rules, even when it is irksome or inconvenient to do so, because we know that we shall suffer if we do not. Society enforces its code of rules by such sanctions as disapproval, social ostracism, retaliation, and the penalties of the law; and it is partly fear of such penalties that leads us to obey the rules. But it is not only fear. Most men are intelligent enough to see the advantages that they will gain in the long run by fulfilling their moral obligations. (2) Respect for rules: We are creatures of habit and have been trained to obey the rules of our society from our earliest years. Almost all men have a conscience and, however this has come about (a difficult and controversial question), they sometimes obey the rules for no reason

other than the fact that they just *are* the rules. This attitude is reflected in such sayings as "a promise is a promise," "it just wouldn't be right," and, most revealing of all, "it just isn't done." This last expression is revealing because it points to a failure to distinguish between moral *rules* laying down what we ought or ought not to do and *generalizations* stating what people in fact do or do not do. Very often respect for rules is enhanced or even created by respect for the *author* of the rules: we think it right to obey a rule, even though we do not see the point of obeying it, because it emanates from a source that we recognize as authoritative, worthy of our esteem, and competent to exact our obedience. This attitude will clearly be important when we come to consider religious rules, since to a believer his god is precisely such an authority. (3) "Other-regarding" motives: Under this heading are included love, sympathy, benevolence, and a respect for the rights of others. It is important to distinguish this last motive from respect for rules. If I pay a debt, I may do so out of respect for the rule enjoining the payment of debts or out of respect for my creditor as a person who has a special claim on me. I may, of course, do so from both motives; but they are nonetheless distinct, and this distinction will also turn out to be important.

RELIGION

For most people, belief in God and in an afterlife are the essential ingredients of religion because these are prominent elements in the religions we know best. But if we include these in a definition of religion, we shall find ourselves committed to excluding many primitive and some advanced religions. In Buddhism, for example, there is neither a personal god nor personal immortality. What is essential to religion is (1) belief in supernatural powers, which may be thought of either as persons or impersonally, as "forces"; (2) appropriate emotional attitudes, a sense of the sacred or numinous or uncanny, and an attitude of humility or reverence in its presence; and (3) rites, ceremonies, and other religious duties. Where the supernatural is thought of as a person or persons, these duties are either thought of as duties *toward* supernatural persons or as *enjoined by* them, usually as both. The Mosaic law contains, besides many rules that we should regard as moral (for example, those condemning murder, theft, adultery, and perjury), a vast number of ritual prohibitions. At one time it used to be held that these also had a moral basis, even though it may seem a pointless one to us. It was thought, for example, that the prohibition against eating pork must have been based on the (false) belief that it is unwholesome; but during this century we have come to learn a great deal about primitive religions in all parts of the world, and it has become clear that this is not so.

Primitive religions. Primitive religions used to be regarded as man's first fumbling and, to us, bizarre attempts at what we should call science, history, and morality. Since the publication of Sir Henry Maine's *Ancient Law,* the following account of the relation between morality and religion among primitive peoples (both our own ancestors and peoples still living at a primitive stage of culture) has become an accepted orthodoxy. In primitive communities, it was held, there are rules that are handed on from one generation to another. Some of these rules are what we would call technological—traditional methods of agriculture, hunting, fishing, and carrying on the other useful arts; others are moral, concerned with human relations; others are religious, concerned with the supernatural. No distinction is drawn between technological and religious rules. For example, the Trobriand Islander learns how he must handle his canoe and also what religious rites he must perform before going on a voyage. Similarly, no distinction is drawn between moral and religious rules. Custom is king; and all customs, whether technological, moral, or religious, are thought of as having been ordained long ago by supernatural beings and recorded in the traditions of the community. These supernatural beings are not only the *sources* of all rules; they provide the *authority* and the *sanction* for them. Moral rules are not thought of as obligatory in their own right or as conducive in some direct, nonmagical way to the welfare of the community; they are the commands of supernatural beings, and are worthy of obedience simply because they are his commands. The penalty for disobedience is disaster in this world and damnation in the next. Morality, in this view, is wholly dependent on religion; it is not just that if there had been no religion men would never have learned morality; it is rather that without religion there could be no morality.

If this account of the origins of morality were true, it would be of great historical interest; but it would have no tendency to show that morality is dependent on religion and cannot exist without it. Modern chemistry grew out of the magical, pseudo-scientific theories of the alchemists, but we do not, on that account, regard it as owing its validity to alchemy; and, in general, it is fallacious to argue from the fact that belief *A* has grown out of belief *B* to the conclusion that *A* depends on *B* for its truth. But this received account of the origins of morality and of the ways in which primitive peoples regard their moral rules is seriously mistaken.

In the first place, since many savages have no conception of supernatural *persons,* they cannot possibly regard their rules as emanating from or being enforced by such persons. Second, although religion plays a large part in their lives, it is by no means so all-pervasive as the received theory makes out. Modern anthropologists assure us that savages are fully capable of learning from experience and that their technological practices are, like ours, based on what they have learned about natural phenomena, unconnected with their beliefs about the supernatural. Bronislaw Malinowski wrote of the Trobriand Islanders:

> The savages have a class of obligatory rules, not endowed with any mystical character, not set forth "in the name of God," not enforced by any supernatural sanction but provided with a purely social binding force. . . . There are among the Trobrianders a number of traditional rules instructing the craftsman how to ply his trade. The inert and uncritical way in which these rules are obeyed is due to the general "conformism of savages" as we might call it. But in the main these rules are followed because their practical utility is recognized by reason and testified by experience. Again, other injunctions of how to behave in associat-

ing with your friends, relatives, superiors, equals and so on, are obeyed because any deviation from them makes a man feel and look, in the eyes of others, ridiculous, clumsy, socially uncouth. There are the precepts of good manners, very developed in Melanesia and most strictly adhered to. There are further rules laying down the proceedings at games, sports, entertainments and festivities, rules which are the soul and substance of the amusement or pursuit, and are kept because it is felt and recognized that any failure to "play the game" spoils it. (*Crime and Custom in Savage Society*, pp. 51–53)

When we come to moral rules, however, Malinowski and other anthropologists still sometimes cling to the theory of a religious origin and suppose them to be obeyed for fear of supernatural sanctions, in spite of the fact that their own detailed accounts of the savage's way of life point in a quite different direction. With savages, as with us, moral rules are obeyed partly from a fear of social rather than of supernatural sanctions, partly from habit, and partly from a recognition of the value of these rules to society. This recognition is as rational as is their recognition of the value of technological rules. The main "social binding forces" to which Malinowski refers seem to be loyalty, mutuality of service, regard for the rights of others, a sense of fairness, and fear of reprisal or of social disapproval. These are moral, not religious motives. It is, we are told, rare to find supernatural sanctions invoked unless the rule concerned is not a moral but a religious one.

Religion operates, indeed, in every department of the savage's life, in his work, his play, his relations with others; but within each department, religion is concerned only with what the savage does not understand. His normal routines, based on experience, are liable to interruption by abnormal occurrences (floods, droughts, tempests, earthquakes, and the like) which he cannot control. It is these catastrophes to which he attributes a supernatural origin and which he attempts to ward off by the performance of religious duties.

Similarity of moral codes and diversity of religious beliefs. A further difficulty for the view that morality is based on religion arises from the striking contrast between the similarity of moral and the dissimilarity of religious beliefs, rules, and practices. When a young man is initiated into a tribe, he will receive instruction as to what he must and must not do in religious matters, and this instruction will differ greatly from that given in other tribes. But he will also be given moral instructions, and these are very much the same everywhere. Thus, among the instructions which the Murray Islanders give to their children are "reticence, thoughtfulness, respectful behaviour, prompt obedience, generosity, diligence, kindness to parents and other relatives in deed and word, truthfulness, helpfulness, manliness, discretion in dealing with women, quiet temper. . . . The prohibitions are against theft, borrowing without leave, shirking duty, talkativeness, abusive language, talking scandal, marriage with certain individuals" (A. MacBeath, *Experiments in Living*, p. 329). Similar lists of rules might be cited from many other primitive tribes, and the lists might have come from a present-day pulpit or classroom.

In view of the present popularity of "cultural relativism" (the view that what is right in any society is what is in accordance with its moral code and that these codes differ widely), it may seem surprising to insist that moral rules are everywhere similar. But cultural relativism is itself based partly on a failure to distinguish between moral and religious rules. If these are lumped together, it is easy to pass from the true premise that religious rules are everywhere different to the false conclusion that moral rules are different too. Moreover, the similarity claimed is claimed only for the broadest moral principles, in particular for the condemnation of aggression, injustice, and deceit; and this basic similarity is consistent with a wide divergence in the ways in which these basic principles are applied in practice. There is, for example, in all societies, a general prohibition against homicide; but all societies recognize exceptions. With us, killing in war and, in some countries, as a punishment for major crimes, is not treated as homicide; other societies permit and even enjoin specific forms of homicide that we regard as immoral—the exposure of infants, the killing of the aged, and human sacrifice. The first two practices can be explained (to explain is not to justify) on the grounds that the conditions of life in the communities concerned require them in the interests of society as a whole; the last is an example of a religious duty overriding the moral duty not to take innocent life.

This contrast between the similarity, almost monotony, of moral rules and the great diversity of religious rules, taboos, rituals, and practices is not easily explained on the hypothesis that morality is an offshoot of religion. Why is it that the gods, who are thought of by different peoples as making such widely differing demands in the religious sphere, speak, in the moral sphere, with an almost unanimous voice? This can be explained only on the hypothesis that when men think morally they think as they do when they think technologically—that is, rationally and on the basis of their experience. The human needs that morality serves, nonaggression and cooperation, are everywhere the same; and it is not surprising that intelligent beings, reflecting on their experience, have evolved broadly similar moral codes for meeting them. But, while men and their needs and the conditions in which they live are open to observation, supernatural forces and persons, if any there be, are not. Here men have had to guess, and it is not surprising that many different guesses have been made.

Influence of religion on morality. According to MacBeath, the contrast between the evidence which anthropologists produce for the independence of morality from religion and their frequent theoretical assertions of its dependence upon it can be explained by their failure to distinguish between two different questions: (1) How far and in what ways, if at all, do the beliefs of primitive people about the supernatural, the emotions which it evokes, and the performance of ritual or strictly religious duties directly or indirectly influence their attitude and behavior toward their fellows—that is, the nature and performance of their strictly moral duties? (2) How far, and in what sense, if any, do primitive people regard their moral duties to their fellow men as being also religious duties, in the sense that they are prescribed or sanctioned by their religion?

In answer to the first question, it seems probable that religion has a powerful indirect effect on morality. The religious duties and practices in which the initiate is trained are often painful and arduous, so that purely *religious* training inculcates such valuable *moral* qualities as self-restraint, endurance, and unselfishness. Moreover, religious practices are usually communal and invoke an intensified tribal consciousness. The psychological and social effects of religion may, therefore, be beneficial to morality, and we might expect to find both that communities in which religion plays a large part are more moral than communities in which it does not and also that within each society religious individuals are more moral than those who care little or nothing for religion. Until more evidence is forthcoming, however, it would be rash to conclude that in primitive societies either of these expectations is verified. Evidence for advanced societies is scanty and difficult to assess; the few studies of the influence of religion on moral attitudes and on delinquency that have been made in Europe and in the United States are inconclusive, and they certainly do not support the widespread assumption that this influence must be great. (See Michael Argyle, *Religious Behaviour*, pp. 83–84, 96–100, 121–128.)

Even, however, if a decided affirmative could be given in answer to the first question, this would not tend to show that the same answer could be given to the more fundamental second question. It is one thing to say that religion affects moral character, quite another to say that religion either prescribes or sanctions moral duties, that a man's religion tells him what his moral duties are, provides a justification for performing them, and provides a motive, in the form of supernatural penalties for disobedience. The full claim that morality depends on religion cannot therefore be supported by saying, however truly, that religion has an influence on moral character.

MORALITY AND THE "HIGHER" RELIGIONS

The uncritical attachment to the view that morality is an offshoot of religion and wholly dependent on it is not confined to anthropologists. The culture which has spread all over the world from western Europe during the last five hundred years is often supposed to be a Christian culture; and by this is meant not only that Christianity is its dominant religion but that its dominant ethic is also Christian. For many centuries morality was regarded, along with religion, as the special concern of the Christian church, and, after the Reformation, of the many Christian churches; and Christianity itself sprang from two traditions, the Hebrew and the Greek, in which religion and morality were already closely intertwined. It is not therefore surprising that we should uncritically assume this close association to be in some way necessary.

Christianity and Western ethics. To say that the dominant ethic of the Western world is Christian may mean any of three very different things: (1) the dominant ethic of the great majority of people in the Western world is broadly identical with that to be found in the Christian Bible; (2) the Christian churches have been the main instruments in shaping, propagating, and maintaining moral ideals and standards; or (3) the Christian ethic is derived from and dependent on the religious, nonmoral doctrines and observances of Christianity.

The first of these statements is broadly true. It is only in this century (except for a few years during the French Revolution) that any significant number of people in Europe or people deriving their culture from Europe have expressly repudiated Christianity; radical departures from its moral ideals are, except in the field of sexual morality, rare.

The question raised by the second statement is more complex and controversial. It is, once again, true that until very recently moral instruction has been largely in the hands of clergymen and that the Bible was regarded as the main authority on moral matters; and it has usually been assumed that the Christian religion provided the main *motive* for morality.

Supernatural sanctions and moral behavior. Hope of salvation and fear of damnation are clearly self-interested motives. To tell us that we ought to do good rather than harm to our fellow men or that we ought to obey the rules of our society *because* we shall be rewarded for obedience or punished for disobedience hereafter is to appeal to our regard for our own interest; and this "stick and carrot" approach has been the one most frequent among religious moralists. Nevertheless it may be doubted whether it has in fact been very effective. The Middle Ages are often referred to as the Age of Faith, and there is no doubt that the popular mind entertained a literal and lively belief in heaven and hell. (Whether this is also true of the learned in an age in which any overt denial would have courted the risk of punishment by death it is difficult to say.) Yet the Age of Faith was not notable for its high standard of morality. A lively belief in eternal torment as the punishment for sin existed alongside a cheerful disregard, in practice, of those moral rules for which eternal torment was held to be the punishment.

The paradox is lessened by the fact that when morality is connected with religious faith, the penalties can be evaded. In the fourth century B.C. Plato noticed the same phenomenon.

> Fathers tell their sons and teachers tell their pupils that morality is to be practiced because it earns a man a good reputation. . . . They go on to say that pious and good people are rewarded in heaven with endless good things . . . while the impious and wicked are punished. . . . But preachers also tell them that they have a magic power and that any wrong a man has done can be expiated by means of charms and sacrifices. They produce sacred books which assure us that by means of all sorts of childish performances we can obtain absolution for our sins. (*Republic* 363–364)

Religion and the content of morality. If it is believed that the supernatural sanctions of religion can be bought off by proper observance of purely religious rules, it is not surprising that they carry little weight as a *motive*. Nor is it easy, in a period in which all moral authority is dominated by religion, to determine precisely the extent of the influence of religion on the *content* of men's moral beliefs.

To what extent are men's ideas about what is right and what is wrong shaped by their religious faith? In his essay "Utility of Religion," John Stuart Mill discussed the view, popular in his day, that although religion may be false, it plays an important role in shaping moral beliefs, a view still shared by many anthropologists. His own view was that it is authority, education, and public opinion that really shape our moral, as well as most of our other beliefs.

> Authority is the evidence on which the mass of mankind believe everything which they are said to know, except the facts of which their own senses take cognizance. . . . Over the immense majority of human beings the general concurrence of mankind, in any matter of opinion, is all-powerful. . . . When, therefore, any rule of life and duty, whether grounded or not in religion, has conspicuously received the general assent, it obtains a hold on the belief of every individual.

To education and public opinion (themselves "authorities") Mill attributes a similar power; and since, for centuries, all moral authority was in the hands of the church, it is difficult to say to what extent men owed their morality, such as it was, to their purely religious beliefs. They believed that their morality was Christian in content (in spite of the fact that much of it was manifestly pre-Christian and of nonreligious origin) because they were taught to believe this.

Mill, however, applied his "method of difference" and looked for cases in which authority, education, and public opinion were not wholly in the hands of religion. This was so in ancient Greece, and he might have added ancient Rome and China. In these three civilizations morality and religion were to a large extent independent of each other, and the line between a man's moral duties to his fellow men and his religious duties to the gods or the shades of his departed ancestors was not blurred, as it was by the Jews and Christians. Yet the moral principles of these three civilizations were not, on the whole, lower than ours; indeed they were, in their main outlines, identical.

Mill also took from Jeremy Bentham three examples of moral attitudes, current in the Christian society of his day, which tend to show that religious belief, when not supported by secular authority, education, and public opinion, does not greatly affect the content of morality. (1) According to Christian doctrine all perjury is wrong; yet public opinion (except among the Quakers and a few other sects) upholds the sanctity of oaths only in matters considered to affect the general welfare in an important way.

> The oaths taken in courts of justice and any others which, from the manifest importance to society of their being kept, public opinion rigidly enforces are felt as real and binding obligations. But custom-house oaths, though in a religious point of view equally obligatory, are in practice utterly disregarded even by men in other respects honourable. . . . Utterly false statements are daily and unblushingly sworn at the Custom-house by persons as attentive as other people to all the ordinary obligations of life—the explanation being that veracity in these cases is not enforced by public opinion.

(2) To kill someone in a duel is, from a Christian point of view, murder; but it was regarded by many Christian men as, in certain circumstances, morally obligatory. (3) Illicit sexual intercourse is, from a Christian point of view, as sinful in a man as in a woman; but it has never been so regarded in Christian countries.

Influence of moral ideas on the "higher" religions. So far from morality being everywhere an offshoot of religion, it would seem that what chiefly distinguishes the "higher" religions from the more barbarous and primitive is that religion has become infected with pre-existing moral ideas. As soon as the supernatural comes to be regarded, not as a mysterious and sinister force to be averted by ritual and magic, but as a person to be placated, religious duties begin to take on the color of moral duties, for they become duties toward a person. In none of the earliest cultures were the gods endowed with high moral attributes; nor were they thought to concern themselves much with the behavior of human beings as long as the latter performed their religious duties punctiliously. Religion seems to have been concerned with the averting of disasters and with salvation in the life after death, and both were to be achieved by means of ritual. But between the seventh and the fifth centuries B.C., the concept of god and the function of religion underwent, both in Israel and in Greece, a remarkable change. Rather than morality emerging from religion, it seems that religion took on a moral quality through the attribution to god of such moral characteristics as justice, mercy, and love. It is not so much that the Hebrew prophets revealed to men the previously existing character of god, but that, having come to regard justice, mercy, and love as moral ideals, they ascribed these attributes to god on the grounds that a being worthy of adoration must be morally perfect.

The same hypothesis explains the manner in which creeds and rituals, which are the essence of religion, have, in the "higher" religions, been manipulated into conformity with moral developments that are not religious in origin. Thus, from the time of St. Augustine, if not earlier, it was the universal belief of Christendom that an unbaptized person, however virtuous, had no chance of salvation; and the Athanasian creed makes belief in certain theological dogmas a necessary condition of salvation. Since Christianity was the product of two cultures, the Hebrew and the Greek, in which religion had already been to a large extent moralized, it has always been difficult to reconcile the religious view that our fate in the next world depends on our theological beliefs and on the performance of the proper rituals with the moral view that it should bear some relation to our virtue in this world. Nowadays very few Christians subscribe to the full theological view; but it is difficult to explain this change except on the hypothesis that in our climate of opinion the traditional view seems barbarous and immoral. The change in this climate of opinion was very largely the work of men of the eighteenth-century Enlightenment, some of whom rejected religion altogether while others, clinging to a thin deism, rejected Christianity. Some Protestants, for whom faith has always been more important than works, remain truer to the old unmoralized faith.

CONCEPTUAL CONNECTIONS BETWEEN RELIGION AND MORALITY

Even if it were established, which is far from the case, that historically all morality was an offshoot of religion, this would only show that, *in fact,* moral ideas have never occurred to people who had no religion; it would not tend to show that there was any *necessary* connection between the two, that moral ideas are conceptually dependent on religious ones. What, it is asked, gives a moral rule its validity, its right to claim our obedience? Now, in many cases the validity of a rule is vindicated by showing that it is derived from an authoritative source. This is the case with games, especially highly organized games. If we want to know what are the rules of chess or bridge or football we can appeal to a book of rules which is authorized by a body, sometimes an international body, whose authority to decide what the rules are is in fact unquestioned. It seems to make no sense to say, "I know that such and such a rule is among the rules of the Football Association, but for all that I don't believe that there is such a rule, or I don't see why I should obey it."

A more important example is provided by the legal system of a country. According to English law a policeman who wants to search a man's house must produce a warrant signed by a duly appointed magistrate. To say that he "must" is not to enunciate a law of nature; the sense of "must" is not that of the law that "unsupported bodies must fall to the ground." It is that, according to our rules of law, the policeman's claim to enter my house is invalid and I need not admit him unless he produces the required warrant. What may or must or may not or must not be done, in the legal sense, is determined by the will of the sovereign legislator as interpreted by the highest court in the land. Although questions of difficulty often arise, the question whether someone has a legal right or a legal duty is one to which the answer is verifiable; and it is verified by referring to laws which themselves owe their validity to the source from which they emanate. (It is not always easy to locate that source, especially in a complex constitutional system such as that of United States, but this does not seriously affect the point.) It must be noticed, however, that even when a person discovers that he has a *legal* duty to obey a certain order, he may still regard himself as *morally* bound to disobey it, since there may be a conflict between legal and moral rules.

Morality and law. If we take a deontological view of morality, we tend to think of its structure as being akin to that of a legal system—a system of rules and commands which deserve our obedience if, and only if, they emanate from someone competent to make or give them. It is from thinking along these lines that many people come to believe that morality requires a belief in God. For who, it is plausibly asked, could have a right to issue moral rules but an omniscient and omnipotent creator of the universe? On this view, a man who does not believe in God may indeed recognize and obey the same rules as a man who does; but, unlike the believer, he has no good reason for doing so; he is simply being irrational; and it is from this line of argument that the old view of atheists as moral outlaws stems.

But to make morality dependent on religion in this way is to assume first, that law is a product of the arbitrary will of a lawgiver and second, that morality is analogous to law. Both these assumptions can be questioned. If we adopt the arbitrary-command view of law, we shall have to say that there is nothing intrinsically right or wrong in the acts which are enjoined or forbidden by law. In the case of some laws this seems plausible enough; there seems to be nothing in the nature of things that makes it obligatory for a driver to drive on the left of the road or on the right. It is only after the competent lawgiver has commanded us to drive on one side only that we are under an obligation to do so. But it is not easy to extend this notion to such laws as those forbidding homicide or perjury; so that even when we are considering a legal system it is inadequate to say that it depends for its validity solely on the arbitrary will of a lawgiver.

But even if a legal system were dependent on the arbitrary will of a lawgiver, could this be true of moral systems also? To suppose so is to involve those who believe that morality depends on religion in some very unpalatable consequences. They will have to say that such acts as homicide and perjury are not intrinsically wrong but only become wrong when they are forbidden by God. Some theologians have taken this line. God, they say, makes laws for his creatures of his own free choice. On the alternative and more usual view, God is the promulgator rather than the creator of moral rules. The acts that he forbids are, in themselves, really wrong before he forbids them, but human beings would not know that they were wrong unless God told them so. Any act which contravenes a rule may be considered under either of two aspects: (1) as an act of a particular kind (for example, homicide); and (2) as a breach of the rule. On the first view (that God creates moral rules), an act can be wrong only under the second aspect; disobedience is the only sin; on the second view it is wrong under both aspects. Those who say that morality depends on religion, in the sense that morality requires an author, must take the first view.

On the second view (that the revealed word of God is the source, not of morality, but of moral knowledge) this difficulty does not arise, but there are others no less formidable. There are recognized and agreed ways of discovering what the rules of a game or the laws of a country actually are, but we have no comparable way of finding out what God's moral rules are. Different religions appeal to different books, and to say that such and such a rule must be a genuine divine command because it is in the Bible or in the Koran is to argue in a circle.

The autonomy of morality. Suppose that the above-mentioned difficulty has been surmounted and that I am satisfied that God really has commanded me to act in such and such a manner, it still makes sense to ask whether I *ought* so to act. For the conclusion that I ought so to act will follow from the premise that God commands me to act only on one of two hypotheses. The first is that God's commands are *definitive* of moral obligation, that "I ought to do X" simply *means* "God commands me to do X." Now to take this line is, first, to relapse into the view that God is the author as well as the promulgator of moral laws and, second, to play fast and loose with the meaning of "ought."

For although it may be true that being commanded by God is a sufficient *reason* for an act's being obligatory, it is certainly not what we normally *mean* when we say that someone ought (morally) to do something.

The second hypothesis is that although the validity of God's commands does not depend on their being his commands, it is in fact always the case that he commands us to do what is intrinsically right and to avoid what is intrinsically wrong. But what reason have we to suppose that this is so? It may be said that it is simply obvious; surely God would not command us to do anything wrong. From a practical point of view this reply (supposing that we have got over the difficulty of discovering what God's commands are) is sufficient; but for a theoretical investigation of the relation between religion and morality it is not. What is there in the idea of God that makes it either necessary or at least probable that his moral commands will always be correct? He is, let us say, an omnipotent, omniscient being who created the universe. But such a being might have evil intentions and might deliberately lead us astray. In that case, though it would be imprudent to disobey him, it would not be morally wrong. There is nothing in the idea of an omniscient, omnipotent creator, *taken by itself,* that entails the conclusion that we ought to obey him. This conclusion will follow only if we add moral goodness to our idea of God. If we say that God is necessarily good (an evil creator would not be God at all, but a devil), we are now in a position to conclude that we ought to obey his commands because it would be a contradiction to suppose a good supernatural being to give evil commands. But if we take this line of reasoning, so far from vindicating the view that morality depends on religion, we find that we must base religion on morality. For we must refuse to admit that any being is a proper object of religious adoration until we are satisfied that he is good and not evil, and we must therefore be capable of making moral judgments before we have religious commitments. Since the time of Kant most moral philosophers have taken the view that morality must be "autonomous," that so far from requiring to be based on something else it can admit of no such external basis. The argument for this is quite general: any set of beliefs offered as a possible basis of morality would have to commend itself to our moral judgment before it could be accepted as a valid basis, so that to base morality on it would always be to argue in a circle. The view that morality can be based on religion is just one example of this circular type of argument.

Does morality point to religion? Even though morality is autonomous, both in the sense that its concepts cannot be derived from nonmoral concepts and in the sense that its conclusions cannot be inferences from nonmoral premises, it may still be argued that our moral experience points toward a religious view of the world. The force of such arguments will depend on whether we take a "subjective" or an "objective" view of moral judgments. On the former view, moral judgments are either statements about or expressions of our own moral attitudes, whether or not others share these attitudes. To say that murder is wrong, for example, is to declare one's hostility, perhaps a special "moral" hostility, toward murder; and it seems clear that no form of subjective theory is likely to lead to any religious conclusions. On an objective view of morality, however, the position is different. The hallmark of the objective is that it commends itself in a special way to human reason. To say that something is "objectively real" is to say that its existence is in no way dependent on us; it is *there* to be discovered, not created by our belief in it. Similarly, to say that a statement is objectively true (or false) is to say that its truth (or falsity) is not something that we can create or alter, but something that we apprehend. Now in some cases, particularly mathematics and logic, this claim to objective truth is combined with a claim that at first sight seems inconsistent with it, namely, that the final court of appeal must be a man's own reason. I may, of course, believe that seven 8's are 56 because I have been told that this is so, but in that case, my state of mind is merely one of belief; I am taking it on trust. To claim to know it is to claim that I see that it must be so. But this is no merely subjective appeal, because in claiming that it must be so I am claiming that all rational men must also see it to be so.

Argument from the objectivity of morality. Now moral judgments have seemed to some philosophers to be in the same position as mathematical and logical statements; some moral judgments at least strike us as being objectively valid and yet as appealing to our autonomous reason; and this consideration has been thought to point to a theistic metaphysic in various ways. The argument is similar to the Argument from Design, according to which there is order in the universe (otherwise science would be impossible), and this order presupposes a Great Architect. In the same way, it is said, the fact that there is an objective "moral order" presupposes a Great Moralist. If we consider morality from a deontological point of view, it is a system of objective laws, and laws presuppose a lawgiver. If we consider it from a teleological point of view, the universe has an over-all purpose, and a purpose presupposes a being whose purpose it is.

We have already found reason to reject the first, or deontological, version of this argument. God must be required either as the creator or as the promulgator of the moral law, and neither of these roles is compatible with the autonomy that is a characteristic of genuine moral judgments. The second version is subject to a similar defect. Even if the universe was created by a supernatural being, the difficulty of finding out what his purpose is and what we must do to forward it is as great as that of discovering what the commands of a supernatural lawgiver are. Indeed the difficulties are really identical. Moreover, even if we suppose these difficulties to be surmounted, there remains the objection that we should only be under a moral obligation to forward the purpose which the creator has in mind if that purpose is morally *good.*

One common form of argument from the objectivity of morality to the existence of God has been clearly expressed by Hastings Rashdall:

An absolute Moral Law or moral ideal cannot exist *in* material things. And it does not exist in the mind of this or that individual. Only if we believe in the existence of a Mind for which the true moral ideal is in some sense real, a mind which is the source of whatever is true in our own moral judgments, can we ra-

tionally think of the moral ideal as no less real than the world itself. . . . The belief in God, though not a postulate of there being any such thing as morality at all, is the logical presupposition of an "objective" or absolute morality. A moral ideal can exist nowhere and nohow but in a mind; an absolute moral ideal can exist only in a Mind from which all Reality is derived. (*Theory of Good and Evil,* Vol. II, p. 212)

But this argument turns out to be an illusion based on a trick of terminology. For a precisely parallel argument could be used to prove the existence of the objectivity of mathematics. Suppose there are two large numbers which no one since the world began has ever in fact added together, so that no one has actually entertained the thought "the sum of these particular numbers is such and such." We believe, and rightly believe, that in some sense there certainly *is* such a number and only one such number, that the proposition expressing this thought is objectively true and that any alternative proposition is objectively false. But we would have little tendency to argue from this that there must somewhere be a Mind that has entertained this proposition. In saying that this proposition is objectively true we are saying that anyone who thought it would be thinking truly, not that anyone has actually or ever will actually think it. And when we say that the number which is the sum of our original numbers "exists" or that there "really is" such a number, we would think it odd if anyone were to ask where it existed and how. For these locutions mean only that the proposition which asserts this number to be the sum is true, and that this is an objective truth. There is no question of having to accommodate this number "in" a postulated mind.

If we examine Rashdall's argument, we can see that it is based on taking the notion of the "reality" of moral ideals in a similarly naive way. An objectivist must believe that it is possible, indeed likely, that some moral laws or ideals should "exist" before any human being thinks of them; this is a part of the belief that they are "discovered" rather than made by men. There was a time before the Mosaic law was written when no one had thought of the law that one should love his enemies; but the objectivist must say that this *was* a law from the creation. However, he is clearly not bound to answer the question "Where was this law?" or to postulate a supernatural mind to house it. For what he means by its eternal objectivity is that it is eternally valid. If, in saying that moral laws and moral ideals are "no less real than the world itself," Rashdall means only that moral assertions have the same objectivity, the same appeal to reason, as assertions about the physical world, the objectivist must agree with him; but if he means that they are real *in the same sense* in which physical things are real, namely, in possessing location in space and time, he will reply that this is to misunderstand the nature of laws and ideals. Physical things are precisely what they are not.

A further argument, first used by Kant but repeated in various ways by more recent philosophers, runs as follows. The moral law requires us to achieve certain ends, for example, our own self-perfection and the happiness of others, but these ends can be achieved only in a universe that is propitious. If the universe is hostile, our efforts will be continually frustrated and the demands made upon us by the moral law must be pointless and irrational. Even if we say that our obligation is only to *try* to achieve these ends (there can be no obligation to succeed where success is impossible), the pointlessness of the law remains. To this it may be replied that even if the universe is propitious it by no means follows that it is so because it has a divine creator. To argue in this way is really to fall back on the old Argument from Design.

Bibliography

Argyle, Michael, *Religious Behaviour*. London, 1958.
Bergson, H. L., *Les Deux Sources de la morale et de la religion*. Paris, 1932. Translated by R. Ashley Audra and Cloudesley Brereton as *The Two Sources of Morality and Religion*. New York, 1935.
Burgh, W. G. de, *From Morality to Religion*. London, 1938.
Diamond, A. S., *Primitive Law*. London and New York, 1935.
Kant, Immanuel, *Critique of Practical Reason*. Translated by T. K. Abbot. London and New York, 1898.
Kant, Immanuel, *Religion Within the Limits of Reason Alone*. Translated by T. M. Greene and H. H. Hudson, with new matter by J. R. Silber. New York, 1960.
Lewis, H. D., *Morals and the New Theology*. London, 1947.
MacBeath, Alexander, *Experiments in Living*. London, 1952.
McTaggart, J. M. E., *Some Dogmas of Religion*. London, 1906.
Maclagan, W. G., *Theological Frontiers of Ethics*. London, 1961.
Maine, Henry, *Ancient Law*. London, 1861.
Malinowski, Bronislaw, *Crime and Custom in Savage Society*. London, 1932.
Mill, J. S., *Essays on the Nature and Utility of Religion*, George Nakhnikian, ed. New York, 1958.
Mill, J. S., *Three Essays on Religion*. London, 1874.
Nietzsche, Friedrich, *The Genealogy of Morals*, translated by Francis Golffing. New York, 1956.
Rashdall, Hastings, *The Theory of Good and Evil*. Oxford, 1907.
Sorley, W. R., *Moral Values and the Idea of God*. Cambridge, 1918.
Taylor, A. E., *The Faith of a Moralist*. London, 1930.
Toulmin, S. E., *The Place of Reason in Ethics*. Cambridge, 1950.
Vivas, Eliseo, *The Moral Life and the Ethical Life*. Chicago, 1950.
Westermarck, Edward, *Christianity and Morals*. London, 1939.

PATRICK H. NOWELL-SMITH

RELIGION AND SCIENCE. The purpose of this article is to discuss the present relations between religion and science and to examine respects in which they may be held either to conflict with or to support one another. It is well known that in the nineteenth century scientists and theologians came into open conflict, the sharpness of which is apparent in, for example, T. H. Huxley's lively volumes of essays. It is often said nowadays that the conflict between religion and science is a thing of the past. Science is said to have become less materialistic and hence more favorable to theology, whereas theology has allegedly become more sophisticated and thus less vulnerable to attack by science. Scientists like Arthur Eddington and J. H. Jeans have tried to use the theories of modern physics to support a spiritual interpretation of the universe, whereas among theologians there has been a withdrawal, in that most of them would no longer wish to defend the literal truth of Biblical stories such as that of Adam and Eve or of Noah's ark. Those who still hold that there is a conflict between religion and science are quite

commonly considered naive and old-fashioned. Nevertheless, it will be argued in the present article that although some of the conflicts between religion and science have disappeared, others are still present, and moreover that there are new areas of controversy which were not envisaged by previous generations or at least did not take a prominent place in their thought. It should be understood that in the following discussion "religion" will generally refer to the Christian religion, since Christianity has held a dominant place in the Western religious and intellectual tradition. In most cases it should be possible for the reader who is more interested in some other religion to see for himself whether similar considerations apply. At the end of this article, however, other religions will be briefly discussed, together with the question of whether or to what extent *any* religious outlook might be held to be incompatible with the scientific attitude.

Historical preliminaries. In the history of the conflict between religion and science we find a twofold theme. First, there is the spectacle of religion defending itself against the encroachments of science, and second, there is the spectacle of science hampered and even persecuted by religious organizations. The most celebrated example of religious interference with science is perhaps the humiliation of Galileo. Modern views about the position of the earth in the solar system, about sunspots, about comets, and about meteorology were all arrived at only in the face of theological opposition. In the nineteenth century the propagation of enlightened theories about the geological history of the earth and about the evolution of biological species was greatly hampered because Charles Lyell, Darwin, and others were apprehensive about exciting the animosity of the churches. The progress of medical science was considerably delayed on account of theological opinions about the causes of disease, which was regarded either as a rightful punishment for sins or as the malicious work of Satan. (Against this, of course, must be balanced the good practical effects of the impulse to carry on the healing work of Christ, for instance the founding of hospitals and of orders of nursing sisters.) Not only was the religious theory of the causes of disease inimical to those concerned with the development of theoretical medicine, but the study of anatomy itself was gravely handicapped by religious prohibition of the dissection of the human body. The belief in witches and the cruel use of the text "Thou shalt not permit a witch to live" held up the development of psychiatry, as did the religious opinion that insanity was due to an individual's being possessed by devils.

Happily, all these phenomena are now mainly of historical interest. The scientific spirit is presently so powerful, and scientists are so influential in modern society, that the persecution and intimidation of scientists by religious authorities are things of the past. Moreover, few religious apologists would wish to defend their churches' past hostility toward scientific ideas. They would argue that the persecution of science was a perversion of religion.

In any case, it would be unfair to leave these historical preliminaries without raising the question of whether religion and theology may not in some way have been actively beneficial in the development of science. Even quite mystical notions can clearly be beneficial if they suggest hypotheses to be tested. It is well known that Kepler, in searching for his laws of planetary motion, was motivated by Pythagorean mysticism (for example, at one stage he hoped to fit the planetary orbits around the five regular solids). It could very plausibly be argued that Christian theology was an important condition of the development of modern science, since the idea of God as ruler of the universe made men sympathetic to the idea that God had arranged things in an orderly way and that there were laws of nature which could be discovered if one tried hard enough. However, the assertion that science could not have arisen without the stimulus of theological ideas certainly does not demonstrate that theological ideas are correct. Theology may indeed have been a necessary causal condition of the rise of science, but it does not follow that theology is logically a condition of science. Apart from purely philosophical doubts about the rationality of induction, by now we surely have sufficient scientific evidence of the orderliness of nature to be rationally justified in searching even further for scientific laws and theories.

Finally, it should be noted that in the twentieth century it has frequently been claimed that while there may be a conflict between science and theology, science and religion are nevertheless compatible. This was also the position taken at the end of the nineteenth century by A. D. White in *A History of the Warfare of Science with Theology in Christendom*, in which he argued that a religion that is purified of antiscientific theological ideas will be all the stronger for it. As we shall note later on in this article, some modern philosophers carry this line of thought much further. They try to separate entirely religion and theology in the hope of making religion immune from any scientific criticism and indeed from any intellectual criticism whatever. We shall see that this attempt to remove religion from the intellectual arena is open to grave objections, and for the moment we shall adopt the more usual opinion that religion essentially involves theological ideas and that religion and theology must stand or fall together.

Theology and man's place in the universe. Any religion which, like Christianity, Judaism, and Islam, derives at least part of its authority from a body of scriptural writings that is thought to be divinely inspired, is likely to run into trouble when scriptural pronouncements contradict the findings of science. Thus, in the nineteenth century much ink was shed over the question of the literal truth of the story of the creation in Genesis and of the story of the deluge and Noah's ark, and so on. Some of T. H. Huxley's wittiest polemical essays turn on such issues. Today, however, theologians have generally given up the view of the Scriptures as being literally the word of God and have become content to think of them as inspired by God in some weaker sense, whereby the Scriptures can quite well be supposed to contain the outmoded cosmological, geological, biological, and historical speculations of prescientific man. It is this retreat on the part of the theologians that has made them safe from many of the attacks which T. H. Huxley and his contemporaries used to delight in making against them. This may in part explain the view that science and religion need no longer be in conflict.

Nevertheless, it is far from clear that the theologian has entrenched himself in a position that is safe from all attacks by science. The Christian religion contains at least two fundamental tenets—namely, those of immortality and of the efficacy of prayer—which seem to be particularly hard to reconcile with modern scientific ideas. It also contains tenets which would probably have to be considerably modified in order to be fitted into the modern scientific picture of the world, but which are so constituted that it is possible to suppose that the theologian might eventually be induced so to modify them. It will be convenient to review this latter sort of consideration first.

In its traditional form, Christianity is very much an anthropocentric doctrine. Man plays a central role in the Christian doctrine in a way that he does not, for example, in Hindu or Buddhist theology. The Christian system of ideas must have been more plausible when the earth was thought to be the center of the universe: above us was heaven, and below us was hell. It is true that various sorts of angels were supposed to exist and to be in some ways superior to human beings, but man was considered the lord of the material world. He was made in the image of God, and God became incarnate in the flesh of man. These considerations may pose two problems for theologians.

In the first place, modern astronomy has shown that our planet has no specially distinguished place in the universe. The earth rotates round the sun, which is a medium-sized star situated well away from the center of a vast galaxy of stars. Moreover, this galaxy is only one among countless similar systems of stars. There are probably hundreds of millions of such galaxies, and if certain cosmological speculations were to be accepted, we would have to say that there is an infinite number of them. It is quite probable that in our own galaxy alone there are perhaps hundreds of thousands of stars with planetary systems like that of our sun. Unless we think that the solar system is quite untypical, we must suppose that a fair proportion of these other systems contain planets on which life could develop; and modern speculations on the origin of life strongly suggest that where life can develop it will develop. The inhabitants of a small village may feel insignificant when they are made aware that the population of the earth is approximately three billion persons. Nevertheless, our own numerical insignificance relative to the population of the earth is negligible in comparison with the probable total population of inhabited planets in the universe.

In the second place, evolutionary considerations suggest other ways in which we may not be as important as we are apt to think we are. On our own planet (if we can avoid blowing ourselves up) evolution has perhaps hundreds of millions of years still to run. One who objects to the theological point of view may therefore urge that there may be distant planets on which there are living beings as far superior to *Homo sapiens* as *Homo sapiens* is superior to an insect or a worm. Therefore, is it not presumptuous of the theologian to claim that man is made in the image of God and that God became incarnate in man? The theologian is likely to reply that although life may be incomparably more advanced on other planets than it is on our own, nevertheless the level of human life has a special place in the scheme of things, since it is the first level at which sin appears. Animals (lower in the scale than man) are not sufficiently developed to have the potentiality either for sin or for redemption, and perhaps this is why the incarnation should take place at our level and not at some higher one.

At the very least, however, the theologian must be prepared to consider that the incarnation is not necessarily a unique event, but may have occurred on countless remote planets on which it is probable that intelligent beings exist. In his novel *Perelandra*, C. S. Lewis has suggested that perhaps the inhabitants of other planets have never sinned and thus do not need a redeemer. However, it is surely at least as unlikely that sin should be a purely terrestrial occurrence as that the incarnation should be. The theologian would do better to accept boldly the view (as, for example, E. L. Mascall has done) that there could have been numerous incarnations elsewhere. If this is accepted, however, it suggests the need for a drastic alteration, or at least supplementation, of the dogmas relating to the incarnation. A critic might indeed say that the theologian would have to give up the doctrine of the Trinity in favor of a multiplicity or even a numerical infinity of divine persons. Here, however, he might be underestimating the subtlety of the Christian doctrine of the Trinity. The orthodox view would appear to entail that the same Person of the Trinity could be incarnated over and over again, so that however many incarnations there were, God would still be three Persons. The critic would nevertheless be right in saying that the theologian would still have to revise considerably his views about the second person of the Trinity. The theologian would perhaps accept this contention: he is likely to say that just as science must develop and evolve, so must theology. This is a fair reply to the critic, but it raises a new difficulty, for religion rests heavily upon tradition: far-reaching reformulations of religious dogmas are hard to reconcile with the thought-forms of the sacred and liturgical books.

Religious people often draw attention to their humility. However, as Bertrand Russell has often stressed, there is often an extraordinary vanity mixed with this humility: man was made in the likeness of God, God became man, and God concerns himself with our sins. A criminal feels flattered by the majesty and pomp of the law; although he may be executed, he has his name in the headlines. Similarly, there is something congenial to human vanity even in the thought that God considers us important enough to send us to hell, to say nothing of the belief that those of us who go to heaven find themselves in the very presence of God. The cosmic vanity which accompanies religious thought-forms is amusingly illustrated by a speculation of the well-known cosmologist E. A. Milne in his book *Modern Cosmology and the Christian Idea of God*. Unlike Mascall, Milne is repelled by the thought of multiple incarnations: he says that we cannot consider the possibility that God has suffered vicariously on innumerable remote planets. However, he does consider the possibility that one day we shall be able to establish communication with distant beings and thus be able to preach the gospel to them. We may note in passing that he seems to forget the immense physical unlikeliness of such a system of interstellar and intergalactic communication. For example, to

get a reply from a star a million light-years away we would have to wait two million years. Waiving this point, however, there is something amusing in the idea of human beings teaching theology to perhaps incomparably superior beings in distant places (rather as if a worm were to be made a professor of tunneling).

We have been considering how the realization that there are probably intelligent and even superior creatures on innumerable distant planets may affect theological doctrines. However, similar problems associated with the possibility of superhuman creatures can also arise in a purely terrestrial context, for it is quite likely that we may learn to direct the course of evolution by controlling the mechanisms of heredity. We may perhaps be able to induce favorable mutations in the hereditary material in human egg cells, thus transforming the human species. Some writers on evolution have hailed such a prospect with delight and optimism, but theologians on the whole have reacted with alarm and condemnation. Such experiments with the evolutionary process would indeed constitute a very great moral challenge, but apart from questionable theological premises, it is hard to see how such experiments would be morally wrong. Of course, we can easily feel outraged by the prospect of such evolutionary advances. The idea that we are not at the summit of the evolutionary process is a blow to our vanity. In this instance theological beliefs reinforce our natural human vanity, just as vanity may in part have determined the content of theological beliefs. As T. H. Huxley remarked in a slightly different context, in "The Evolution of Theology," "Men forgive all injuries but those which touch their self-esteem, and they make gods after their own likeness, in their own image make they them."

Therefore, even if theology has come to terms with modern ideas about the past evolution of the human species, as is commonly thought, it may have to face serious unresolved problems in connection with future evolution. It could also be argued that theologians have often been much too sanguine about the question of past evolution. Are modern evolutionary ideas quite so concordant with even a sophisticated theology as is usually supposed? The answer to this question, of course, depends on the particular theology in question. Roman Catholics are certainly allowed to believe in evolution, but there are some reservations. Pius XII, in his encyclical *Humani Generis* (1950), said that it is not permissible to believe that the human race does not descend from a single man. Conjectures about polygenism are incompatible with the doctrine of original sin. "Original sin," he wrote, "is the result of a sin committed, in actual historical fact, by an individual man named Adam, and it is a quality native to all of us, only because it has been handed down by descent from him." It would appear, then, that not only are Catholics committed to a monogenist theory of human evolution, but that they are involved in a serious biological unorthodoxy, for this doctrine of the inheritance of Adam's sinfulness seems to entail the acceptance of at least one instance of the inheritance of acquired characteristics.

When it is claimed that theology and evolutionary theory are compatible, it is always pertinent to inquire just what sort of evolutionary theory is meant. Many attempts to reconcile evolution with theology are in fact successful only in reconciling theology with a pseudoscientific evolutionary doctrine. The same can be said of evolutionary metaphysics of the type expounded by Bergson or, in a more popular form, by George Bernard Shaw, which provides a sort of substitute for religion. These romantic conceptions of evolution must be sharply distinguished from the properly scientific Neo-Darwinian theory, which is based on a mechanistic theory of natural selection that is in accordance with the theories of modern genetics. In modern biology, living creatures tend to be thought of as complicated self-maintaining and self-regulating systems, many of whose characteristics can be simulated by means of physical artifacts. Modern theoretical biology has become more and more a matter of biochemistry. Through the work of A. I. Oparin, Harold Urey, and others, we are also beginning to be able to guess how life could have arisen naturally from inorganic matter. Few modern biologists, therefore, would wish to support the view of the Anglican theologian E. W. Barnes, bishop of Birmingham, England, who as recently as 1933 wrote that "the emergence of life must be regarded as a sign of creative activity" and that "the mystery of life is unsolved, probably unsolvable." It is extremely significant that Barnes, who in addition to being a noted mathematician was well known for his scientific and extremely modernist outlook in theology, should have said this. Even he, it seems, was impelled to believe in "the mystery of life." We must also remember that Roman Catholics hold that evolutionary theory is at the very least incomplete in that it cannot account for the emergence of the souls of men, which are believed to be created through the special agency of God.

Immortality. An important part of Christian belief is the doctrine of personal immortality. Most Christians, however, are committed to belief in the resurrection of the body. However, many Protestants do not take the doctrine of the resurrection of the body very seriously; they either deny it outright or interpret it in some figurative sense. They hold a doctrine of immortality according to which it is a purely immaterial self that survives death.

The doctrine of survival as purely immaterial spirit conflicts with many influential philosophical doctrines. Some philosophers elucidate mind in terms of bodily behavior, and others defend the doctrine that conscious experiences are brain processes. If such views are true, then there is clearly no such thing as an immaterial mind that could survive death. But even if some form of philosophical dualism is accepted and the mind is thought of as something over and above the body, the empirical evidence in favor of an invariable correlation between mental states and brain states is extremely strong: that is, the mind may be thought of as in some sense distinct from the body but also as fundamentally dependent upon physical states. Without oxygen or under the influence of anesthetics or soporific drugs, we rapidly lose consciousness. Moreover, the quality of our consciousness can be influenced in spectacular ways by appropriate drugs or by mechanical stimulation of different areas of the brain. In the face of all the evidence that is being accumulated by modern research in neurology, it is hard to believe that after the dissolution of the brain there could be any thought or conscious experience whatever.

The orthodox doctrine of the resurrection of the body clearly escapes the difficulties associated with the notion of the independent existence of the mind. However, it is beset with equally grave difficulties of another sort. In the early days of the Christian religion, the concept of the resurrection of the body was conceived crudely: the dead were thought to rise from the grave and live again in a heaven somewhere above the clouds. But where, in accordance with modern cosmological views, can the resurrected bodies exist? Any attempt to specify a location (or perhaps some "fifth dimension") seems subject to the sort of embarrassment that typically arises when we try to put the old wine of Christian theology into the new bottles of modern cosmology. There are also philosophical puzzles as to the sense in which the resurrected person would be the same as the earthly person. (For a discussion of philosophical difficulties of this sort, see IMMORTALITY; MIND–BODY PROBLEM; PERSONAL IDENTITY.)

Prayer. A rather different issue, which may lead to conflict between science and religion, is the nature of prayer. At one time the efficacy of prayer was an issue decidable by experiment, as is shown by the Old Testament story of the contest between Elijah and the priests of Baal. Now, however, a more sophisticated attitude is likely to be adopted. The efficacy of prayer is not usually put forward as an empirical issue, for whatever happens is taken to be the will of God, and if a prayer is not answered it is presumably because God, in his own inscrutable way, knows better than we do what is best. Furthermore, the greater people's knowledge of how things actually happen, the less they tend to regard these things as capable of being affected by prayer. Even with all our knowledge of meteorology we cannot be sure what the weather is going to be; nevertheless, changes in the weather no longer strike us as being mysterious. Even many professed Christians have therefore come to feel that there is something about praying for rain that is akin to a belief in magic and superstition. Again, many religious people are not strongly inclined to pray for someone's recovery from disease when they have modern medical knowledge of its diagnosis and prognosis. Some will still continue to pray for a miracle, but many will not do so with any confidence. As weather and disease increasingly come within the scope of scientific law, so a prayer for rain or for the disappearance of a lesion comes more and more to seem like a prayer that the sun should stand still in the sky. Similarly, as our knowledge of human psychology increases, the mental states of human beings also lose their appearance of capriciousness, and the tendency to pray for someone's change of heart may go the way of the tendency to pray for good weather or for good health.

This is not to say, of course, that even the agnostic will regard all prayers as inefficacious. This is because prayer itself is a psychological process which has perfectly natural effects. Thus, one can deny the supernatural efficacy of prayer and still believe that a prayer for recovery can relieve a disease, if, for example, the disease is psychosomatic and the patient both believes in prayer and knows that he is being prayed for. This would be quite unlike the case of a prayer for the recovery of someone who was unaware of the prayer and who was entirely in the company of people who were likewise unaware of the prayer.

However, if prayer is to have supernatural efficacy (which it must have if the usual religious claims about prayer are correct), then its working must be at variance with our scientific beliefs about how things happen. For presumably, all the natural causes and effects of the behavior of the weather or of the human body or brain will be the same after a prayer has been offered as before. How, then, could the weather or the body or brain become different from what it would have been without the prayer? The entire matter is quite inexplicable. A theologian might make a bold reply to this criticism by maintaining that the entire matter is indeed inexplicable and by suggesting that a sufficiently careful meteorological, physiological, or psychological investigation would reveal causal anomalies—that is, actual breaches of scientific law. This, however, would be a retreat to the old conception of the efficacy of prayer as a scientifically testable issue, and the theologian might be reluctant to re-enter the lists in this way.

Mysticism. In regard to the subject of the possibility of interaction between natural and supernatural agents, there is the question of whether religion can be based on mystical experience. It would seem that if mystical experiences are not mere aberrations of feeling, that are explicable in naturalistic terms, then they must be in some way miraculous. If mystical experiences exist and if they are the sort of thing that they are claimed to be, then how can they be explained in terms of modern psychology? In what way is the brain of the mystic affected by the supernatural with which he is in contact? Are the synapses in his brain changed by a purely supernatural agency, or must we believe that his mystical experiences are not correlatable with neuronal changes? Physics and physiology enable us to explain, in outline at least, how we can get in touch with rabbits or even with electrons. "Getting in touch" involves responses to physical stimuli, and it is clear that no naturalistic account could be given of mystical cognition of the supernatural. It would appear that either mystical experiences are not what they are claimed to be or else that there is a clash between the scientific and the theological ways of thinking about the mind.

Separation of religion and science. If the foregoing arguments are correct, it would appear that there are important areas in which science and religion impinge on each other. Some of the battlefields are indeed now deserted, and many of the polemics of nineteenth-century writers are no longer of interest. Nevertheless, it has been suggested in this article that in fundamental ways science does impinge on theology and that some of the conflicts between them are even sharper than they were a hundred years ago. It would be wrong to suppose that the peculiar characteristics of twentieth-century science make it necessarily less inimical to religion than was the science of the nineteenth century. It is true that Eddington and Jeans used to argue, on the basis of modern physics, for an idealist metaphysics, but their arguments would not be accepted by many contemporary philosophers. It is easy (although wrong) for a physicist to come to think of an electron as a mental construction out of sense experiences, but a biologist is not likely to be tempted in this way. For him, the animal is the concrete reality, and any experience which the animal has is something that happens to the animal: the animal can hardly be a construction out of things which happen to the animal.

Eddington, however, compared the scientist to an ichthyologist. Using a net of two-inch mesh, the ichthyologist catches fish that are never less than two inches long. Does this prove that there are no fish in the sea less than two inches long? Clearly not; but his net will never catch them. In the same way it is suggested that there are facts which the scientific method will never "catch."

This is an ingenious suggestion, but it will not help to resolve the sorts of controversy with which we have been concerned. These are not simply cases for scientific agnosticism, but cases in which the scientist would expect things to work out in one sort of way and the religious person would expect it to work out in another sort of way, or in which the religious person is at least likely to be disturbed by positive scientific facts, or the possibility of them. For example, it is hard to see how the idea that there are more things in the universe than science can know of could possibly affect theological worries about life on other planets.

Sometimes the theologian will point to art or morality as being outside the scope of science. However, since art and morality are concerned with evoking feelings and recommending actions, not with the cognition of facts, they would not appear to provide a counterinstance to the omnicompetence of science as a cognitive activity. The theologian, however, may be prepared to maintain that religion is not, in fact, a cognitive activity. An explicitly noncognitivist theory of religion has been put forward by R. B. Braithwaite and, in a slightly different form, by T. R. Miles. Clearly, if religion is essentially noncognitive, then, like morality and art, it cannot possibly conflict with science. These writers eliminate all factual content from religion: they interpret Christian doctrine purely as a collection of stories, myths, or parables that are used to inculcate a certain way of life—"agapeistic behaviour," as Braithwaite calls it. Certainly, if religious belief can be construed correctly in this way, then there can be no logical incompatibility between religion and science. (There may, of course, still be a psychological incompatibility, if the religious myths are uncongenial to the thought-forms of a scientific age.) However, it is unlikely that a religion thus construed is a religion that many religious people would recognize as such. Commonly, a religious creed is construed as making factual assertions. Most Christians would wish to say that in fact Christ rose from the dead, that in fact there is life after death, and so on. Moreover, if religion is not a matter of fact, there is the problem of how to decide rationally between Christianity, say, and Islam. Most religious people would probably not care to assert that the choice must be made on purely ethical or aesthetic grounds.

Other religions. It could plausibly be argued that Christianity is more vulnerable to objections drawn from cosmology, evolutionary theory, and other branches of science than is any other of the great religions. This is because Christianity is the most anthropocentric of the great religions. We have discussed possible ways in which the Christian theologian might react to this sort of challenge. However, in their conception of paradise popular forms of Islam would also appear to suffer from a crudely anthropocentric cosmology. The difficulties with respect to immortality apply to Judaism and Islam as well as to Christianity. Hinduism and Buddhism are easier to reconcile with science inasmuch as they do not give man a special place in the world and still less a place outside the purely natural order. In the case of Buddhism and some popular forms of Hinduism problems arise over the notion of reincarnation, which is contrary to the spirit of modern biology and psychology. Esoteric (Advaita) Hinduism is probably immune from scientific criticism, since its doctrine is on such a transcendental metaphysical level that it has no contact at all with the empirical level. However, such a form of Hinduism is perhaps more a form of metaphysics than of religion. In taking part in religious observances the devotee must abandon his austere metaphysics of nonduality in favor of a pluralism of god or gods and worshipers. In other words, he must return to the phenomenal level of māyā (illusion).

Finally, a critic of religious belief and practice might argue that any religion must inevitably conflict with science. This is because any religion, correctly so-called, relies heavily on the authority of tradition and ancient writings and perhaps of a priesthood. There will therefore be a tension in the mind of one who has leanings toward both science and religion. As a scientist he has scant respect for tradition or for the authority of old writings, and he is used to seeing the scientific theories of one generation rejected by the next. This is not to say that such tension is necessarily unsupportable, since there have always been devout men who have also been eminent scientists. Nevertheless, the tension is likely always to exist in the background, and in view of the great successes of science it may tend to bring about a progressive weakening of religious attitudes.

Bibliography

The history of religious opposition to scientific innovation is well told in J. W. Draper, *The Conflict between Religion and Science* (London, 1876), and A. D. White, *A History of the Warfare of Science with Theology in Christendom* (1896; New York, 1960). A. W. Benn, *The History of English Rationalism in the Nineteenth Century* (New York, 1962), was first published in 1906. Many of T. H. Huxley's essays in his *Collected Essays,* 9 vols. (London, 1894–1897), are concerned with polemics against the religious apologists of his time and provide convincing evidence of the fury with which battle was apt to be fought in those days. Lively and important critiques of religious belief in regard to its relation to science are to be found in Bertrand Russell, *Religion and Science* (Oxford, 1960), and in some of the essays in Russell's *Why I Am Not a Christian* (New York, 1957). See also H. Feigl, "Philosophical Tangents of Science," in H. Feigl and G. Maxwell, eds., *Current Issues in the Philosophy of Science* (New York, 1961). Much of Sigmund Freud, *The Future of an Illusion,* translated by W. D. Robson-Scott (London, 1934), and of "A Philosophy of Life," Lecture XXXV of Freud's *New Introductory Lectures on Psychoanalysis,* translated by W. J. H. Sprott (London, 1933), consists of general philosophical argument and is largely independent of the tenets of psychoanalytic theory.

C. D. Broad's article "The Present Relations of Science and Religion," in *Philosophy,* Vol. 14 (1939), 131–154, evoked a reply by L. J. Walker, S.J., "The Logical Basis and Structure of Religious Belief," in the same volume of the journal (387–409). Broad's article has been reprinted in his *Religion, Philosophy and Psychical Research* (London, 1953). The Catholic attitude toward evolutionary theory was defined by Pius XII in the encyclical *Humani Generis* (1950). This was translated for the London *Tablet,* Sept. 2, 1950, by Ronald A. Knox, and an extract is reprinted in Anne Fremantle, ed., *The Papal Encyclicals in Their Historical Context* (New York, 1956).

The Anglican Theologian E. L. Mascall's *Christian Theology and Natural Science* (New York, 1957) is a noteworthy effort to face some of the chief difficulties which modern science presents to the theologian. Another book of interest by an Anglican priest is A. F. Smethurst, *Modern Science and Christian Belief* (London, 1955). A very readable book on the same theme is the biologist Roger Pilkington's *World Without End* (London, 1960). A very solid work, which incidentally contains much excellent exposition of modern scientific ideas, is E. W. Barnes, *Scientific Theory and Religion* (Cambridge, 1933). Barnes, a modernist Anglican theologian and late bishop of Birmingham, was also a first-rate mathematician, and parts of his book contain some very difficult mathematics. Another book that includes mathematics is the cosmologist E. A. Milne's *Modern Cosmology and the Christian Idea of God* (Oxford, 1952). See also two books by the famous astronomer A. S. Eddington, *The Nature of the Physical World* (New York, 1929) and *The Philosophy of Physical Science* (Cambridge, 1939). Noncognitivist accounts of religious belief are given by R. B. Braithwaite, *An Empiricist's View of the Nature of Religious Belief* (Cambridge, 1955), and by T. R. Miles, *Religion and the Scientific Outlook* (London, 1959). Criticisms of Braithwaite's views are found in J. A. Passmore, "Christianity and Positivism," *Australasian Journal of Philosophy,* Vol. 35 (1957), 125–136, and in Chapter 2 of C. B. Martin, *Religious Belief* (Ithaca, N.Y., 1959). (Chapter 6 of Martin's book contains a valuable discussion of the problem of life after death.) A well-known attempt to construe religious belief as nonempirical is John Wisdom, "Gods," in Antony Flew, ed., *Essays in Logic and Language, First Series* (Oxford, 1951). This article is discussed in Chapter 2 of Martin's book, mentioned above. In this connection also should be mentioned the symposium by Antony Flew, R. M. Hare, Basil Mitchell, and I. M. Crombie, "Theology and Falsification," in A. Flew and A. MacIntyre, eds., *New Essays in Philosophical Theology* (London, 1955). An attempt to reconcile physicalist and religious approaches to the nature of man is given by D. M. Mackay, who is professionally concerned with research in cybernetics and information theory. His idea depends on a notion of "complementarity" whereby science and religion can both give complete but nevertheless complementary accounts of the same things. For references to some of his articles, see his note "Complementary Descriptions," in *Mind,* Vol. 66 (1957), 390–394, which is a reply to a critique of his views by P. Alexander, "Complementary Descriptions," in *Mind,* Vol. 65 (1956), 145–165. R. N. Smart's inaugural lecture, *Theology, Philosophy and the Natural Sciences* (Birmingham, England, 1962), relates the philosophy of religion to both the philosophy of science and the comparative study of religions.

J. J. C. SMART

RELIGIOUS EXPERIENCE, ARGUMENT FOR THE EXISTENCE OF GOD. Arguments from Religious Experience show remarkable diversity, (*a*) in the sorts of experience taken as data for the argument, (*b*) in the structure of the inference itself, and (*c*) in the alleged conclusion, whether to a vague Presence, an Infinite Being, or the God of traditional Christianity.

The following exemplify some versions of the argument:

"At very different times and places great numbers of men have claimed to experience God; it would be unreasonable to suppose that they must all have been deluded."

"The real argument to God is the individual believer's sense of God's presence, the awareness of God's will in tension and conflict with his own will, the peace that follows the acceptance of God's command."

"Experiences of meeting God are self-authenticating: they involve no precarious chain of inference, no sifting of rival hypotheses. They make unbelief logically absurd."

"In itself, religious experience is neither theistic nor pantheistic, Christian nor Buddhist. All these distinctions are *interpretations* of the experience. By itself, religious experience testifies to something far less definite but still infinitely valuable—the insufficiency of all materialisms and naturalisms."

If we compare any of these arguments with the Ontological, Cosmological, and Teleological arguments, important differences in their logic and history can readily be shown. Arguments from Religious Experience are clearly not a priori, like the Ontological Argument, and whereas the Cosmological and Teleological arguments work from premises that affirm highly general facts about the world (that it exists, that it is purposefully ordered), Arguments from Religious Experience rely on far more particularized and elusive premises than these. Not all men have (or are aware of having) distinctively religious experiences, and to those that do have them religious experiences are apt to be short-lived, fugitive sets of events that are not publicly observable.

Despite this slipperiness, the Argument from Religious Experience has attracted some theologians who have been skeptical about the more rationalistic "proofs." In the course of the eighteenth century these proofs received formidable criticism from Kant and Hume. The Ontological Argument was shown to be radically confused over the logic of "existence," and (in Kant's account) the Cosmological and Teleological arguments themselves presuppose the Ontological. Even more important, Kant and Hume together produced a general weakening of confidence that any survey of the observable cosmos (including "the starry heavens above") could yield premises powerful enough to argue to an infinite, unconditioned, all-good deity. Kant turned to "inner" experience, to our awareness of the moral law, and argued that the moral life is intelligible only if we postulate God and immortality.

Although a number of writers followed Kant in arguing from inner moral experience, many others, while accepting the shift from outer to inner, based their inference on a distinctive class of religious experiences. If we describe this shift, in general terms, as a move from objective to subjective, from surveying the world at large for evidences of God to focusing attention on the personal and existential, it clearly was a shift of the greatest moment and one that still helps to determine our contemporary climate of theological thought. We human beings are not stars or electrons—the argument goes—and we cannot experience or guess the role of star or electron in the divine economy. But we *are* persons, and we are directly aware (or some of us are) of a meeting of person with Person in religious experience.

Thinking back, however, to the post-Humean, post-Kantian period, the centering upon inner experience can be seen as one aspect of the romantic movement's protest against the Enlightenment, the new concern for subjectivity, the life of the emotions and intuitions of the individ-

ual. The most important and most seminal single figure here is Friedrich Schleiermacher (1768–1834), with his bold insistence on the primacy of religious feeling—particularly the feeling of utter creaturely dependence—and his distaste for religious doctrines or arguments entertained in a purely intellectual manner, as mere ideas, lacking the life and authority of experience.

OBJECTIONS TO THE ARGUMENT

Prima facie it seemed a reasonable and empirically sound enterprise to establish arguments for God upon claims to have actually experienced him, to have "seen" him, "met" him, encountered him in a personal relation. But there are in fact several directions from which it can be challenged.

Orthodox and neo-orthodox theologians tend to object that the content of religious experience is too *indeterminate* to yield clear knowledge of the God of Christianity. The case for Christianity must not be allowed to rest on the deceptive and elusive emotions of religious people. It rests on the revealed Word of God, on the Person of Jesus Christ as disclosed in the Scriptures, *not* as constructed out of the assorted emotions of the devout. The working of the Holy Spirit cannot be correlated with the experiencing of peculiar feelings, even uplifting ones.

A second familiar objection is that although we certainly do have religious experience, we cannot employ it as the premise of an *argument* to God. The relationship between man and God—an *I–Thou* (in Martin Buber's phrase), personal relationship—is maintained by faith alone. The conception of superseding faith through a *proof* of God's existence forgets the *irreducibly* personal nature of encounter between man and God.

The objector may be making a religious claim, that it is religiously improper to attempt to replace faith by rational argument, or his point may be a logical one, that God—being "pure" person, having nothing bodily or thinglike in his nature—cannot be shown to exist in the way things can be shown to exist.

Suppose, again, we take the Argument from Religious Experience as an explanatory hypothesis; then a skeptical critic may deny that the existence of God is the likeliest, or simplest, or most intelligible, explanation of the experiences. We cannot be intellectually compelled to posit God if more economical and naturalistic explanations can be found—psychoanalytic accounts, it might be, or accounts in terms of individual suggestibility or the influence of religious expectations or tradition.

Last, a critic may concentrate on the conceptual difficulties in the idea of God, for if the argument as a whole is to be sound, its conclusion ("therefore God exists") must be intelligible and free of inner contradictions. This objection may bewilder and disappoint the arguer-from-experience. To him one of the chief apparent advantages in the argument is that its direct appeal to experience bypasses logical or metaphysical complexities. But some element of interpretation, and therefore some application of concepts, must take place when an experience is taken to be an encounter with God. Wherever concepts are handled, they can also be mishandled. Inner contradictions in the claim to experience God could invalidate the interpretation of the experience.

NATURE OF RELIGIOUS EXPERIENCES

What, more exactly, *are* religious experiences? Descriptions of religious experiences can be heavily loaded with doctrinal, even sectarian, interpretation or can be almost entirely free of it. Their impact may fix one's attitudes and evaluations for a lifetime or for only a brief period. They may not only be benign and optimistic, as we have so far assumed, but can also—with no less intensity—be pessimistic and grim. They may involve conversions to a religious orthodoxy or conversions away from one. Consider the following experiences, neither of which is more than minimally interpreted, and both of which are certainly in an important sense religious. The first is from Tolstoy's *War and Peace*, at the point where Prince Andrew has been wounded in the Battle of Austerlitz.

> He opened his eyes, hoping to see how the struggle of the Frenchmen with the gunners ended. . . . But he saw nothing. Above him there was now nothing but the sky—the lofty sky, not clear yet still immeasurably lofty, with grey clouds gliding slowly across it. "How quiet, peaceful and solemn, not at all as I ran," thought Prince Andrew—"not as we ran shouting and fighting. . . . How was it I did not see that lofty sky before? And how happy I am to have found it at last! Yes! All is vanity, all falsehood except that infinite sky. There is nothing, nothing but that. But even it does not exist, there is nothing but quiet and peace. Thank God! . . ."

The second is from Leonard Woolf's autobiographical work, *Sowing* (1960). At the age of eight, the author was sitting in a garden enjoying the fresh air after a train journey. He watched two newts basking in the sun.

> I forgot everything, including time, as I sat there with those strange, beautiful creatures, surrounded by blue sky, sunshine, and sparkling sea. I do not know how long I had sat there, when, all at once, I felt afraid. I looked up and saw that an enormous black thunder cloud had crept up and now covered more than half of the sky. It was just blotting out the sun, and, as it did so, the newts scuttled back into their hole. . . . I felt something more powerful than fear, once more that sense of profound, passive, cosmic despair, the melancholy of a human being eager for happiness and beauty, powerless in face of a hostile universe.

Turning to *theistic* types of experience, we can start from the very basic experience of wonderment, notably wonderment at there being any world at all. This may pass into the sense that the world owes its existence to, and is maintained in existence by, something "beyond," "outside" the world itself, a Being whose nature is utterly remote from the world, yet whose activity and energy are perceptible within the world, as a disturbing, awesome, and thrilling presence. Rudolf Otto's concept of the "numinous" gathers together these ingredients of mystery, dread, and fascination and emphasizes very properly the qualitative distinctiveness and elusiveness of such experi-

ence (*The Idea of the Holy, passim*). No set of categories can neatly contain it: the person who has never known it can barely understand the claims of the person who has.

Religious experiences can be generated by perceptions of individual objects (a grain of sand, a bird), by a train of events, by actions—for instance, the memorable account of Jesus setting his face to go to Jerusalem to his Passion. Even a passage of philosophical reasoning may do this, as when someone contemplates the incompleteness of all explanation, the intellectual opacity of space and time, and feels compelled—with a sense of mystery—to posit a divine completeness and unity.

Closer to the province of morality are experiences of divine discontent, interpreted as intimations of God's existence and call to moral endeavor, the conviction of sin correlative to a sense of God's own holiness, the sense of divine aid in the rectifying of one's moral life, and, in Christian evangelical terms, a sense that one has been redeemed or saved by God's action on man's behalf.

The over-all impression is of the immense diversity of religious experiences. They are indeed linked by complex webs of "family resemblances" (to use Wittgenstein's phrase)—resemblances of attitude, emotional tone, alleged content—but if we ask what all of them have in common, the answer must be meager in content: perhaps only a sense of momentous disclosure, the sense that the world is being apprehended and responded to according to its true colors. What is actually being observed or contemplated can never (logically) be the whole universe, yet the quality of religious experience is such that it does seem to imply something about the whole.

EPISTEMOLOGICAL STATUS OF RELIGIOUS EXPERIENCES

Our sampling of religious experiences may help to deliver us from the dangers of oversimplification, but it cannot by itself determine whether arguments to God based upon them are valid. Clearly, not all the experiences we have mentioned could yield data with which a theistic argument could start. Some, such as that of Leonard Woolf quoted earlier, are decidedly *anti*theistic. But there is a further set of differences among them that must be noted at this stage, differences of an epistemological kind.

When someone speaks of his religious experience, he may be using the word "experience" as it appears in phrases like "business experience," "driving or teaching, etc., experience." He has found the religious pattern of life viable; he has interpreted a multiplicity of events in its categories, and these categories have proved durable. There is the suggestion that the person with religious experience in this sense has been confirming his faith by living it out over a substantial stretch of his life—furnishing data for a pragmatic proof of God's existence.

In other cases the experiences are of much shorter duration, often judgments or quasi perceptions accompanied by certain religious emotions, alleged cognitive acts or intuitions in which the necessity of God's existence is "seen" and an awesome emotive response is elicited simultaneously. Again, the language used may be nearer to that of perceiving—*seeing God* (not just seeing *that* God exists).

There is a claim to knowledge of God by "acquaintance," rather than "description."

Some cases resemble the dawning of an aspect or interpretation, as when we recognize a person in a poor light or make out a pattern in what looked like a maze of lines. It can be like a sudden reading of the expression on a face, the face, as it were, of the universe, or like a realization of *meaning,* as when one sees the point of a poem with which one has long been verbally, but only verbally, familiar. In the light of this disclosure, a new orientation and purposeful organization of life may take place. Energies hitherto dissipated or in mutual conflict are rallied and integrated.

Feelings or emotions may predominate in religious experience, but even so, perception and judgment are almost always involved as well. Feelings are often "feelings *that . . . ,*" surmises, and in that sense feelings involve judgment, have an essential component of belief. Part of what it is to have an emotion is to see and appraise one's situation in a particular way. ("I feel remorse for doing *x*," for example, presupposes "I did *x* freely" and "*x* was morally wrong.") It is only with twinges, *frissons,* aches, and such like that no appraisal of the situation need (logically) be made; these, in any case, could furnish only very weak premises for a theistic argument. Their occurrence can be due to a great variety of causes immanent in one's own organism and one's environment, and they can hardly, without supplementation, force one to posit a *transcendent* cause.

Obviously the structure (and maybe the validity) of an Argument to God from Religious Experience will vary enormously according to what epistemological type of experience is taken as the starting point, and in the literature this is often hard to discern.

VERIFIABILITY OF RELIGIOUS EXPERIENCE

If someone claims to have discovered, perceived, become aware of an ordinary sort of object, we usually know what to do about checking his claim. If we are told that there is a frog in the garden pond, we know what it will be like to confirm this or to find it untrue. We know how to investigate whether it *was* Smith we saw in the dim light, whether we *did* hit the right answer to a sum or cried "Eureka" too soon. But when someone claims to have direct awareness of God, to encounter, see, or intuit the divine, we are not able to suggest a test performance of an even remotely analogous kind. The more developed and theologically sophisticated the conception of deity is, the more it eludes and resists any such check.

This being so, some critics have pointed out a disturbing resemblance between claims to experience God and a certain other range of statements that are not publicly testable—namely, psychological statements such as "I seem to hear a buzzing noise," or "I seem to see a patch of purple." If statements like these cannot be refuted, it is only because they make no assertions about what exists, beyond the experiences of the speaker at the moment he speaks. But the person who says he has direct and certain experience of God wishes to claim irrefutability and to affirm at the same time something momentous about what exists. Can this be done? Or would it take a far more elaborate and many-stranded apologetic to give effective backing to these claims—especially the claims to objectivity?

One might try to obtain this support by compiling records of numerous experiences of the same general kind and treating them as cumulative evidence for the truth of claims to experience God. Without doubt there is an impressive mass of such records within the Judaeo-Christian tradition. Other religious traditions, however, can also produce their own very different records—of the various well-ordered phases in the quest for nirvana or for mystical union with a pantheistic object of worship.

Are these differences, however, real incompatibilities; do they correspond to genuinely different sorts of religious experience? Or are the experiences basically the same, though differently interpreted? On this it is extremely hard to give any confident answer. Part of the difficulty is that most of the developed religions contain several strands in their conceptions of the divine. Christianity, for instance, seeks to unite numinous and mystical views of God: God is "remote" and "other," yet also mystically "near." What can be said again is that any common elements must be very indeterminate in content and able to bear great variety of interpretation—to be taken, among other things, as the disclosure of a state or spiritual goal (nirvana) or of a personal or suprapersonal God. We have seen how an experience may have a minimal—quite undoctrinal—interpretation and yet be religious in a broad sense. But from such an experience alone one can hardly infer anything so definite as the God of theism. Unfortunately, the interpretations that supplement the experience are conceptually intricate and involve all the uncertainty and fallibility of philosophical and theological speculation. In this region we are far removed from the ideals of immediacy, directness, and self-evidence.

Yet a critic who claimed that the Argument from Religious Experience was thereby refuted would be missing the mark. The theist could insist that a much too crude notion of "interpretation" has so far been used, one that suggests, falsely, that there is a merely external and almost arbitrary relation between having and interpreting an experience.

The full impressiveness of the theistic case appears only when we survey the historical development of religious experience in the direction of Christian monotheism. As the idea of deity evolves, from finite and local numen to infinite and omnipresent Lord, from the god of a tribe or nation to the Ruler of all nature, from the deity concealed in holy tent or temple to the one God beyond all phenomena whatever, religious experience is itself simultaneously transformed. It is transformed not haphazardly but so as to produce a crescendo of numinous intensity, a constant refining away of merely superstitious and idolatrous awe at objects unworthy of worship, and the arrival of a distinctive, lofty note of adoration. Experience and interpretation here advance in indissoluble unity. It is argued that this historical development provides material for a more adequate argument to God—one in which the risks of fantasy and subjectivism are much reduced.

Impressive this is, and it may well be the truth of the matter. We must notice, however, that we are now looking at a much more complex piece of argument than the claims of individuals to have direct experience of God. New logical problems appear at several points. Can we be confident, for instance, that an intensification of numinous experience is necessarily a sign that we have a more adequate disclosure of God and not simply that we have constructed a more adequate and awesome *idea* of God? (This is the question that also calls in doubt any purely pragmatic philosophy of religion.) Again, sometimes an artist, or a school of artists, succeeds in progressively clarifying and intensifying an original vision or the expression of some distinctive emotion. But success in this ("now he has brought the theme to full explicitness," for example) is not necessarily correlated with a progress in discovery about the world. Can we be sure that the development of numinous awareness is different in this vital respect?

The person with theistic religious experience is assured that it *is* different. But the sense of assurance, the "Aha!" experience, the penny dropping, the light dawning—these are very unreliable guides to truth, validity, or value. Not the most tempestuous sense of poetic inspiration can guarantee that a good poem is being brought to birth, nor can any of these conviction-experiences by itself authenticate its related judgments. It is enough to recall how often incompatible judgments are made with equal assurance on each side. Yet it is not easy to formulate a version of the Argument from Religious Experience that does not rely crucially on a sense of conviction. Even when appeal is made to the pattern of development toward theism, and thus to a far wider range of phenomena than in any argument from the experience of an individual, still the issue of objectivity—that we are coming to know God, not simply an idea of God—seems to hang upon the fallible, illusion-prone assurance of the subjects. On the other hand, to point this out is to draw attention only to the risk, not to the certainty, of being wrong. A religious person may realize, and be prepared to accept, this measure of risk.

Could we escape the uncertainty, by claiming that *genuine* experience of God is necessarily followed by a godly life, whereas illusory experiences betray themselves by the absence of any practical fruits? Hardly; there might well be a positive correlation between genuine experiences and godliness, but in fact they are not necessarily related. Lapses, moral failures, are always open to human beings, and one cannot rule out by definition the possibility of a man's being both morally remarkable and atheistic.

But, one might argue, is the situation vis-à-vis God any worse in principle than the situation vis-à-vis material objects, such as tables and chairs? Our traffic with these consists in having actual experiences (visual, tactual, etc.) and ordered expectations of future and possible experiences. Where our experience has this sort of structure and can thus be the subject of intelligible discourse, we confer on it the status of objectivity without more ado. But theistic experience certainly occurs, and it too has its structure of expectations.

If we can bring out the difference between these cases (and the peculiar difficulty of the religious case), we shall be showing more clearly than hitherto that the Argument from Religious Experience is most intimately involved in problems of logic and meaning—problems that at first seem alien to its empirical appearance. With a material

object (say, a cube) there are quite intricate but intelligible ways in which we come to see it as a single object out-in-the-world. It is given unity most obviously by possession of perceptible limits and boundaries and by the manner in which its several surfaces can be seen and felt to connect with one another. Moreover, we have mastered the laws of perspective and so can anticipate and understand variations in our perceptions of the object, owing to our own variable positions as observers. Such variations do not, therefore, impugn the assertion that the object exists in the world external to us. With God, who is not a finite material object, there can be no inspecting of boundaries or surfaces. And if part of what we mean by "God" is "an infinitely and eternally loving Being," no conceivable experience or finite set of experiences could by itself entitle us to claim that we had experienced such a being. We might well report experiencing "a sense of immense benevolence toward us," "a sense of complete safety and well-being," but from their intensity alone one could not rigorously conclude, "Therefore I am in touch with an infinitely and eternally loving God." From the intensity of a *human* love one cannot infer, "This love will endure," and without bringing in a supplementary doctrine of God's attributes (not derived from experience) one could no more legitimately do so in the religious case.

Material objects, of course, are sometimes observed in unfavorable perceptual conditions—at a great distance, half-concealed, and so on. Imagination must "fill in" the perceptual gaps as best it can, until conditions improve. Analogous thought models are indeed employed in theological discourse, but they are peculiarly difficult to assess. The Christian theologian is normally most ready to admit that we can neither perceive nor imagine how the various attributes of God unite in a single being (if he is to be called "a being" at all). A fair measure of agnosticism here is compatible with full Christian belief. But it may not be compatible with a reliance upon an Argument to God from Religious Experience, if this is one's chief apologetic instrument. Unless the principles that confer unity and objectivity are able to be collected from the experiences themselves (which seems not to be possible), we have to look elsewhere for them, and the argument is in this respect shown to be inadequate. But it is not, on that account, proved useless, for if it cannot demonstrate the existence of God unaided, it might still function as a necessary auxiliary of other arguments—for example, the Cosmological Argument.

One might be forced to a deeper agnosticism than that to which we have just alluded—deeper in that it dares to affirm scarcely anything at all about the focus (or focuses) of religious experience, whether personal or impersonal. Yet with a minimal ontological commitment it might still set great value on certain religious experiences and seek after them. The attempt to work out a coherent and systematic theological interpretation would be quite abandoned.

This would save *something*, but assessing just how much to expect from a religious agnosticism like this would be a difficult task. The bigger the area of agnosticism, the smaller the area of legitimate religious expectations, such as that of ultimately seeing God "face to face" or of being received by him into glory. As we have more than once observed, the relation between experience and what the experience is taken to be is a most intimate one; the experiences of a Christian and those of a religious agnostic could both be valuable but could not be identical.

PSYCHOLOGICAL EXPLANATIONS

Is it not more enlightened, however, to deny that these experiences really disclose anything about the world? Psychoanalytic research has, after all, revealed many situations in which interior mental events are projected upon the world and are furnished with all the assurance of objectivity, the full sense of "givenness." One does not have to accept the entire Freudian account of religion to see plausibility in its central claim that early parent–child relations of "creaturely" dependence and reverence, with their tensions between love and fear, can yield the unconscious material from which experiences of God–man relations are fashioned. To accept this claim is not necessarily to reduce all religion to neurosis or worse. For it is absurd to class together the person who attains a stable religious solution to his conflicts and the person who retreats to genuine neurosis, developing, say, obsessions, compulsions, or delusions of persecution. Freud certainly went further in his naturalistic explanation of religious experience, being prepared to reduce God to an illusory parent substitute. It may be possible, however, to invert the Freudian account of religious experience and, instead of seeing God as a father substitute, to see human fathers as God substitutes and the human experience of love as training for loving God. The close psychological relation between love of man and love of God would thus have its skeptical sting removed. It may be argued, again, that naturalistic and Christian explanations are compatible: God may elicit from us an effective response to his existence without making use of anything but our natural human equipment of senses, desires, emotions. Even mechanisms of projection can be involved and the projected image of deity be yet a trustworthy symbol of a God who does in fact exist. It is clear from all this that depth psychology does not provide a self-sufficient, decisive refutation of theism.

Nonetheless, depth psychology troubles and disturbs the Arguments from Religious Experience, and so do the very attempts to reconcile it with Christian belief. These virtually admit that the religious experiences might occur much as they actually do occur—without there being a God—in other words, that naturalistic explanations are possible. There seems no way, *at the experiential level*, of settling the really urgent questions, most of all the following: Do we have in theistic experience *mere* projection? Or do we have a projection matched by an objectively existing God?

Bibliography

WORKS ON THE PSYCHOLOGY OF RELIGION

The following works have important implications for the Argument from Religious Experience:

Freud, Sigmund, "Obsessive Acts and Religious Practices" (1907), in *The Standard Edition of the Complete Psychological Works of Sigmund Freud*, translated by James Strachey, ed., in collaboration with Anna Freud, 24 vols. London and New York, 1953–1963.

Freud, Sigmund, *Totem and Taboo* (1913), translated by A. A. Brill. New York, 1927. Also translated by James Strachey. New York, 1952.

Freud, Sigmund, *The Future of an Illusion* (1927), translated by W. D. Robson-Scott. London, 1928; paperback ed., Garden City, N.Y., 1957.

James, William, *Varieties of Religious Experience*. Cambridge, Mass., and London, 1902.

Jung, C. G., *Psychology and Religion*. New Haven, 1938; paperback ed., 1960.

Philp, H. L., *Freud and Religious Belief*. London, 1956.

Thouless, R. H., *An Introduction to the Psychology of Religion*. Cambridge, 1923; reprinted, 1936.

RELEVANT THEOLOGICAL WORKS

Raven, C. E., *Natural Religion and Christian Theology*, Vol. II. Cambridge, 1953.

Schleiermacher, Friedrich, *Die Religion. Reden an die Gebildeten unter ihren Verächtern*. Berlin, 1799. Translated by John Oman as *On Religion: Speeches to Its Cultured Despisers*. London, 1893; reprinted, Gloucester, Mass., 1958; paperback ed., New York, 1958.

Schleiermacher, Friedrich, *Der christliche Glaube*. Berlin, 1821–1822. 2d ed. translated by H. R. Mackintosh and J. S. Stewart as *Christian Faith*. Edinburgh, 1928.

Tennant, F. R., *Philosophical Theology*, Vol. I. Cambridge, 1928.

PHILOSOPHICAL STUDIES

The following works explore the relation between religious experience and religious belief or contain relevant ideas and arguments:

Buber, Martin, *Ich und Du*. Leipzig, 1923. Translated by R. Gregor Smith as *I and Thou*. Edinburgh, 1937.

Campbell, C. A., *On Selfhood and Godhood*. London, 1957. On Rudolf Otto see Lecture 16.

Hick, John, ed., *Faith and the Philosophers*. London, 1964.

Holland, R. F., and Cameron, J. M., "Religious Discourse and Theological Discourse." *Australasian Journal of Philosophy*, Vol. 34 (1956), 147–163, 203–207.

Hook, Sidney, ed., *Religious Experience and Truth*. New York, 1961; Edinburgh, 1962.

Lewis, H. D., *Our Experience of God*. London, 1959.

Lewis, H. D., and Whiteley, C. H., "The Cognitive Factor in Religious Experience." *PAS*, Supp. Vol. 29 (1955), 59–92.

Martin, C. B., *Religious Belief*. Ithaca, N.Y., 1959.

Otto, Rudolf, *Das Heilige*. Breslau, 1917. Translated by John W. Harvey as *The Idea of the Holy*, 2d ed. London, 1950.

Smart, Ninian, *Reasons and Faiths*. London, 1958.

Smith, N. Kemp, "Is Divine Existence Credible?" *Proceedings of the British Academy*, Vol. 17 (1931).

RONALD W. HEPBURN

RELIGIOUS INSTINCT. See COMMON CONSENT ARGUMENTS FOR THE EXISTENCE OF GOD.

RELIGIOUS LANGUAGE. Utterances made in religious contexts are of many sorts. In the performance of public and private worship men engage in acts of praise, petition, thanks, confession, and exhortation. In sacred writings we find historical records, dramatic narratives, proclamations of law, predictions, admonitions, evaluations, cosmological speculations, and theological pronouncements. In devotional literature there are rules of conduct, biographical narratives, and introspective descriptions of religious experience. Philosophical discussions of religious language have concentrated on a restricted segment of this enormous diversity, namely, theological statements, i.e., assertions of the existence, nature, and doings of supernatural personal beings.

There are two reasons for this emphasis. First, the crucial problems about religious language appear in their purest form in theological statements. If we consider a petitionary prayer or a confession, what is puzzling about it is not the act of petition or confession, but the idea of addressing it to God, and God answering it. It is the concept of communication with a supernatural incorporeal person that seems unclear. And this lack of clarity is most apparent in the statement that there exists a God who communicates with men in various ways. We may say that the difficulties in understanding other forms of religious language all stem from obscurities in statements about God.

The second reason for philosophical concentration on theological statements lies in the fact that the philosophy of religion is primarily concerned with questions of justifiability, significance, and value. And it has generally been supposed that whether religion is a justifiable form of human activity largely depends on whether there are sufficient grounds for accepting the theological statements on which it is based. Christianity is a justifiable institution if and only if we are warranted in accepting the proposition that the world is created and governed by an omnipotent, perfectly good personal deity who has revealed himself to men in the Bible. Thus the philosophy of religion is largely taken up with examining the grounds of religious statements. And it is when we do this that we become most acutely aware of the puzzling aspects of religious language. When we make a determined effort to decide whether it is true that God created the physical universe, it is difficult to avoid realizing how unclear what we are saying is, what implications it has, what it logically excludes, and what would count for or against it. Thus the philosophical investigation of religious language focuses on those indeterminacies in theological statements which hamper attempts to find rational grounds for acceptance or rejection.

MEANING OF THEOLOGICAL PREDICATES

Most philosophers who have concerned themselves with the problem have located the difficulties of religious language in the predicates of theological statements. (What does "good" mean in "God is good"?) It may seem that we should start with the subject of the statement, with the concept of God. But there is really no alternative to starting with the predicates. For the only way to make clear what one means by "God" is to provide an identifying description, such as "the creator of the universe"; and to understand that phrase one must understand the predicate "created the universe" as applied to God. Theological predicates can be divided into negative (infinite, nontemporal, incorporeal) and positive. The positive predicates can be concerned either with attributes (good, wise, omniscient) or with actions (makes, forgives, speaks, watches over). Negative predicates present no special difficulty, but in themselves they are clearly insufficient to give any positive conception of the deity. Of the positive attributes we shall concentrate on attributions of action, partly because action terms pose more severe problems, partly

because other attributes are dependent on them. (To say that God is wise is to say that he acts wisely; if we cannot understand what it is for him to perform one or another action, we cannot understand the attribution of wisdom to him.)

Derivation and application. When one reflects on the use of predicates in theological statements one comes to realize two fundamental facts: (1) this use is necessarily derivative from the application of the predicates to human beings and other observable entities; (2) the theological use of predicates is markedly different from the application of predicates to human beings.

Theological predicates are derivative primarily because it is impossible to teach theological language from scratch. How would one teach a child what it means to say "God has spoken to me" without first making sure that the child knows what it is for a human being to speak to him? In order to do so one would have to have some reliable way of determining *when* God was speaking to him, so that when this happens one could say to him, "*That* is what it is for God to speak to you." And even if we admit that God does speak to people from time to time, there is no way for one person to tell *when* God is speaking to another person unless the other person tells him, which would require that the other person have already mastered the theological use of language. Hence there is no alternative to the usual procedure of teaching the theological use of terms by extension from their application to empirically observable objects.

As for the difference in the use of predicates as applied to God and to human beings, there are many ways of seeing that the terms cannot have quite the same meaning in both cases. If, as in classical Christian theology, God is conceived of as not in time, then it is clear that God's performance of actions like speaking, making, or comforting is something radically different from the temporally sequential performance of actions by human beings. St. Thomas Aquinas in his famous discussion of this problem based the distinction between the application of predicates to human beings and the application of predicates to God on the principle that God is an absolute unity and that, therefore, various attributes and activities are not distinguishable in God as they are in men. But even if we allow God to be temporal and straightforwardly multifaceted, we are left with the corporeal–incorporeal difference. If God does not have a body, it is clear that speaking, making, or comforting cannot be the same thing for God as for man.

This leaves us with a serious problem. We must show how the theological use of these terms is derived from their nontheological use. Until we do, it will be unclear just what we are saying about God in such utterances. The usual way of dealing with this problem is by cutting out the inapplicable portions of the original meaning of the terms, leaving the remainder for theology. Thus, since God is incorporeal, his speaking cannot involve producing sounds by expelling air over vocal cords. What is left is that God does something which results in the addressee having an experience of the sort he would have if some human being were speaking to him. The nature of the "something" is deliberately left vague. Since God is a pure spirit, it will presumably be some conscious mental act;

perhaps an act of will to the effect that the addressee shall have the experience of being told such-and-such. More generally, to attribute any interpersonal action to God is to attribute to him a purely mental act which has as its intended result a certain experience, like the one that would result from such an action on the part of a human being.

This account may throw some light on the content of statements about God, but religious thinkers have become increasingly dissatisfied with it. For one thing, it represents theological statements as metaphysical speculations and does little to illuminate the ways they fit into religious activity. Having postulated a pure immaterial substance performing mental acts which, miraculously, have effects in human experience, how do we go about getting into communication with this immaterial substance? Why should it be worshiped at all, and if it should, why in one way rather than another? Moreover, this line of reasoning is not helpful in our efforts to verify theological statements. It offers no hints on how we might determine whether our statements are true, or even whether there is such a being that performs the actions in question.

VERIFIABILITY OF THEOLOGICAL STATEMENTS

Recent discussions have concentrated on the problem of verifiability. In the last few decades a great many philosophers have come to accept some form of the "verifiability theory of meaning," according to which one is making a genuine factual assertion, a real claim as to the way the world is, only if it is possible to conceive of some way in which what he is saying can be shown to be true or false by empirical observation. Applying this theory to theology, it has been argued that since an empirical test is in principle impossible to carry out for statements about a supernatural incorporeal personal deity, these statements cannot be regarded as straightforward factual assertions, but must be interpreted in some other way.

John Wisdom in his influential essay, "Gods," analogizes the function of theology to the following situation. Two people return to a long-neglected garden and find some of the old flowers still surviving among the weeds. One suggests that some gardener has been caring for the plot, and the other expresses doubt about this. On investigation, it turns out that no one in the vicinity has ever noticed anyone working on the garden. Moreover they discover that gardens left to their own devices often take this form. But the first man does not abandon his hypothesis. Instead he expresses his belief that someone who is not discernible by the senses comes and cares for the garden, carrying out designs he and his companion do not fully grasp. At this point the first man has modified his "gardener" hypothesis to the point at which it is no longer susceptible to empirical confirmation or refutation. No matter what is or is not discovered empirically, he will continue to hold it. In this case it seems plausible to say that he is no longer expressing a belief about actual objective events. If he were, he would be able to imagine, however inadequately, some way in which the existence or nonexistence of these events would be revealed to our experience. He is, rather, expressing a "picture preference." It is rewarding to him to think of the situation as if a gardener were coming to take

care of the flowers. If beliefs about God are equally refractory to empirical test, it would seem to follow that they too must be interpreted otherwise than as straightforward matters of fact. (Wisdom, however, does not commit himself to this conclusion.)

In considering the "verificationist" challenge to theology, we must scrutinize both premises of the argument: (1) theological statements are not susceptible to empirical test; (2) if they are not empirically testable they cannot be construed as factual assertions which can be assessed as true or false.

Are they empirically testable? The question of whether theological statements are subject to empirical test is quite complicated. If we rule out mystical experience as a means of observation, then it is clear that statements about God cannot be tested directly. But science is full of hypotheses about unobservable entities—electromagnetic fields, social structures, instincts—which verificationists accept as meaningful because they can be tested indirectly. That is, from these hypotheses we can draw implications which can themselves be tested by observation. The question is whether directly testable consequences can be drawn from theological statements. We can phrase this question as follows: Would we expect any possible observations to differ according to whether there is or is not a God? It would clearly be unreasonable to require of the theologian that he specify a set of observations which would conclusively prove or disprove his assertions. Few, if any, scientific hypotheses could meet that requirement. The most that could reasonably be demanded is that he specify some observable states of affairs which would count for or against his assertions.

One thing that makes this problem difficult is the fact that on this point religious belief differs at different times and places. Supernatural deities have often been thought of as dealing in a fairly predictable way with contingencies in the natural world and human society. Thus in many primitive religions it is believed that the gods will bring abundant crops or victory in battle if they are approached in certain ways through prayer and ritual. Even in as advanced a religious tradition as the Judaeo-Christian, it is believed that God has certain fixed intentions which will result in prayers being answered (when made in the right spirit and under proper conditions) and will result in the final victory of the church on earth.

It would seem that such expectations provide a basis for empirical test. Insofar as they are fulfilled, the theology is confirmed; insofar as they are frustrated it is disproved. However, things are not that simple. Even in primitive communities such tests are rarely allowed to be decisive; the empirical implications are hedged around with a variety of escape clauses. If the ritual dances are held and still the crops fail, there are several alternatives to abandoning traditional beliefs about the gods. Perhaps there was an unnoticed slip somewhere in the ritual; perhaps devils were conducting counter-rituals. More sophisticated explanations are employed in the more advanced religions. For example, God will answer prayers, but only when doing so would be for the true good of the supplicant.

Moreover, as science develops, religion comes to be more concerned with the personal life of the worshiper and less concerned with prediction and control of the course of events. Among religious intellectuals today such predictions as are still made are clearly not testable in practice, because of their lack of specificity ("all things will work together for the good for those who love God"), their enormous scope ("everything in the world contributes to the development of moral personality"), or their inaccessibility ("after death we shall see God face to face"). Nevertheless, it seems that within religion there are strong barriers to completely divorcing belief in God from the expectation of one event rather than another; and so long as there is some connection of belief with testable predictions, however tenuous, it would be a mistake to think of religious statements as absolutely unverifiable in principle.

Are they assertions of fact? As to whether a statement that cannot be empirically tested must not be construed as an assertion of fact, a theologian might well challenge the application of the verifiability theory to theology. If God is supernatural, we should not expect his behavior to be governed by any laws or regularities we could hope to discover. But then we could never be certain that, for example, the statement that God loves his creatures would ever imply that a war should have one outcome rather than another. This would mean that, according to the verifiability theory, it would be impossible for us to make any statements, even false ones, about such a being. But a theory which would prevent us from recognizing the existence of a certain kind of entity, if it did exist, would be an unreasonable theory.

NONASSERTIVE INTERPRETATIONS

Be that as it may, a number of philosophers have been so impressed by these difficulties over verifiability that they have tried to construe theological utterances as something other than straightforward factual assertions. Attachment to the verifiability theory is not the only motivation behind the development of such theories. There are those, like George Santayana, who, without holding that theological sentences are factually meaningless, are convinced that as factual assertions they are false, but still are unwilling to abandon traditional religious discourse. They feel that somehow it has a valuable function in human life, and in order to preserve it they are forced to reinterpret it so that the unwarranted factual claims are expunged. Still another motivation is the hope that this will contribute to the resolution of the problem mentioned earlier, that of specifying the way predicates are used when they are applied to God. As we saw, attempts to give an illuminating definition of theological predicates have not been wholly successful, and this can be taken to indicate that a different sort of approach is needed.

One such line of investigation takes sentences as its units rather than words. It focuses on the kind of linguistic act performed when theological sentences are uttered, rather than on the meaning of words in theological contexts. Instead of asking what "forgives" means when applied to God, we ask what linguistic action is performed when one uses the sentence "God forgives the sins of those who truly turn unto him." It is this sort of question one is ask-

ing when one wonders whether theological sentences make factual assertions and, if not, what they are used to do. If we could answer this question we would have made sufficiently clear how words are being used in theological sentences without having to define special senses for constituent words.

Nonassertive interpretations can be divided into four groups. Statements about God have been interpreted as (1) expressions of feelings of various sorts; (2) symbolic presentations of a variety of vital aspects of experience, from natural facts to moral ideals; (3) integral elements in ritualistic worship; (4) a unique kind of "mythical" or "symbolic" expression, not reducible to any other use of language.

Expressions of feeling. Theological utterances have been interpreted as expressions of feelings that arise in connection with religious belief and activity. Thus we might think of "God made the heavens and the earth" as an expression of the sense of awe and mystery evoked by grandeurs of nature; of "God has predestined every man to salvation or damnation" as an expression of a pervasive sense of helplessness; and of "God watches over the affairs of men" as an expression of a sense of peace, security, at-homeness in the world. This is "poetic" expression rather than expression by expletives. It is like expressing a sense of futility by saying "life's a walking shadow" rather than like expressing futility by saying "Ah, me." That is, the feeling is expressed by depicting a situation which might naturally evoke it; a sense of security, for instance, is evoked by some powerful person looking after one.

Symbolic presentations. Symbolic interpretations of religious doctrines have been common for a long time. The story of Noah and the flood has been regarded by many Christian thinkers not as an account of actual historical occurrences, but rather as a symbolic way of presenting certain religiously important points—that God will punish the wicked, but will also, under certain conditions, show mercy. Many of the traditional ways of speaking about God have to be taken as symbolic. God cannot literally be a shepherd or a rock. The shepherd functions as a symbol of providence and the rock as a symbol for God's role as a refuge and protection in time of trouble. A symbol in this sense is some (relatively) concrete object, situation, or activity which can be taken to stand for the ultimate object of discourse through some kind of association, usually on the basis of similarity. We speak symbolically when what we literally refer to is something which functions as a symbol.

In the traditional use of symbolic interpretation it is, necessarily, only a part of theological discourse which is taken as symbolic. For if we are to hold that the symbolic utterances are symbolizing facts about God, we will have to have some way of saying what those facts are; and we cannot make that specification in symbolic terms, on pain of an infinite regress. But we are now considering views according to which all theological discourse is symbolic, which means that if we are to say what is being symbolized it will have to be something in the natural world that can be specified in nontheological terms. The most common version of such a view is that theological utterances are symbolic presentations of moral ideals, attitudes, or values. This position has been set forth most fully and persuasively by George Santayana, and in a more up-to-date form by R. B. Braithwaite. According to Santayana every religious doctrine involves two components: a kernel of moral or valuational insight, and a poetic or pictorial rendering of it. Thus the doctrine that the physical universe is the creation of a supremely good personal deity is a pictorial rendering of the insight that everything in the world is potentially usable for the enrichment of human life. The Christian story of the incarnation, sacrificial death, and resurrection of Jesus Christ is a way of making the point that self-sacrifice for others is of supreme moral value. It is worthwhile embodying these moral insights in theological doctrine because this vivid presentation, together with the systematic cultivation of feelings and attitudes that accompanies it, provides a more effective way of getting across the insights than would a bald statement.

The way in which interpretations of the first two kinds throw light on the theological use of predicates is analogous to the way in which one explicates the use of words in poetic metaphors. If we consider the metaphor in "sleep that knits up the raveled sleeve of care," it is clear that "knit" is not used simply to refer to a certain kind of physical operation. This utterance has quite different kinds of implications from "she knit me a sweater," in which "knit" does have its usual sense. In the metaphoric statement, "knit" is used in its usual sense to depict a certain kind of situation which, as a whole, is presented as an analogue of the effect of sleep on care. The only way of effectively getting at the function of the word "knit" is by seeing how the whole phrase "knits up the raveled sleeve" is used to say something indirectly about sleep.

In the first two of the four kinds of nonassertive interpretation we are examining, theological statements are essentially metaphors. And if they are correctly so regarded, we get nowhere if we extract the word "made" from the sentence "God made the heavens and the earth" and try to say what it means by itself. What we have to do is take the picture presented by the whole sentence and see how it functions as a way of expressing a feeling of security, or as a way of presenting the insight that everything in the world can be used to enrich human life.

Ritualistic interpretation. The ritualistic interpretation of theological discourse can best be introduced by citing the reply of an intellectually sophisticated high-church Anglican to a question from an agnostic friend. The question was, "How can you go to church and say all those things in the creed?" The reply: "I don't say them; I sing them." In the view under consideration, the corporate practice of worship is the native soil from which talk about God springs. Talk about the attributes, doings, and intentions of a supernatural personal being has meaning as a part of the practice of worship and is puzzling only when it is separated from that context. If we think of an utterance like "God made the heavens and the earth" as the expression of a belief about the way things in fact originated and then wonder whether it is true or false, we will be at a loss. To understand it we have to put it back into the setting where it (or rather a second-person correlate, like "Thou, who hast made the heavens and the earth") does its work. In that setting, these words are not being used to explain anything, but to do something quite different.

Unfortunately, proponents of this view have never been very clear about what this "something different" is. The clearest suggestion they give is that the talk about God serves to provide an imaginative framework for the conduct of worship. It articulates one's sense that something important is going on, and it helps to indicate the appropriateness of one response rather than another. In speaking of the sacrament of communion as the re-enactment of the self-sacrifice of an omnipotent personal deity who took on human form, and in conceiving of it as a cleansing and renewing incorporation of the substance of such a deity, one provides for the activity a pictorial framework that records and nurtures the felt solemnity of the occasion and the attitudes and aspirations kindled by the ceremony. This position presupposes, contrary to the usual view, that ritual worship has an autonomous value, apart from any theological foundation. It is generally supposed that a given ritual has a point only if certain theological doctrines are objectively true. But in the ritualistic interpretation, theological doctrines are not regarded as statements about which questions of truth or falsity are properly raised. Since these doctrines depend for their significance on the ritual, it is supposed that the ritual has some intrinsic value in forming and giving expression to valuable sentiments, feelings, and attitudes.

Myths. Ernst Cassirer has developed the notion that the basis of religious discourse lies in a unique "symbolic form" which he terms "mythical." He maintains that it is found in purest form in the myths of primitive peoples and is based on a way of perceiving and thinking about the world which is radically different from our accustomed mode. In the "mythical consciousness" there is no sharp distinction between the subjective and the objective. No clear line is drawn between symbol and object, between wish and fulfillment, between perception and fantasy. Again, no sharp distinction is made between the object itself and the emotional reaction it evokes; emotional response is taken to be an integral part of the environment. As a result none of our familiar standards of truth or objectivity are applicable. What is most real is what arouses the greatest intensity of emotional response and, particularly, what is felt as most sacred. (The sacred – profane distinction is the fundamental contrast.) The mythical consciousness carries its own special organizations of space and time. For example, there is no distinction made between a position and what occupies it; every spatial position is endowed with a qualitative character and exerts influence as such.

It is the view of Cassirer, and of followers such as Susanne Langer, that sophisticated theology represents an uneasy compromise between mythical and scientific modes of thought, and as such cannot be understood without seeing how it has developed from its origins. It is basically a mythical view of the world, given a "secondary elaboration" in a vain attempt to make it acceptable to the rationalistic consciousness; judged by rationalistic standards it is not only groundless, but meaningless.

Mysticism. Philosophers and theologians in the mystical tradition have put forward versions of this fourth kind of interpretation which do not regard theology as a manifestation of cultural lag. To the mystic the only way to communicate with God is through mystical experience, and this experience reveals God to be an ineffable unity. He can be directly intuited in mystical experience, but since there are no distinctions within the absolute unity of his being, and since any statement we can make predicates of him one thing rather than another, e.g., wisdom as distinguishable from power, no statement can be true of him. The most we can do in language is to direct our hearers to the mode of experience which constitutes the sole means of access. Proponents of this view sometimes speak of theological language as "symbolic," but this differs from our second type of theory in that here there is no way to make explicit what it is that the theological utterances symbolize, and it is therefore questionable whether we should use the term "symbol." A symbol is always a symbol of something. In fact it is difficult to make clear just what, on this view, religious utterances are supposed to be doing. They are said to "point to," "adumbrate," or "indicate" the ineffable divine reality, but all too often these expressions remain uninterpreted.

In recent years two interesting attempts have been made to develop this position further. W. T. Stace, in his book *Time and Eternity* (1952), considers the chief function of religious language to be the evocation of mystical experience, or faint echoes thereof. This seems at first to be a subjectivist account, with the deity omitted, but, as Stace correctly points out, it is an axiom in the mystical tradition that no difference can be found in mystical experience between subject and object, and on these grounds Stace refuses to make the distinction. Although Stace goes along with the mystical tradition in regarding mystical experience as ineffable, he departs from this official position to the extent of giving some indications of the aspects of this experience which different theological utterances evoke. "God is truth" evokes the sense of revelatoriness, "God is infinite" the sense of all-inclusiveness, "God is love" the blissful, rapturous character of the experience, and "God is one" the absolute unity of the experience and the sense of the dissolution of all distinctions.

Paul Tillich, although not squarely in the mystical tradition, is faced with similar problems in the interpretation of religious language. He holds that theological doctrines "symbolize" an ultimate reality, "being-itself," about which nothing can be said literally except that it is metaphysically ultimate. In attempting to clarify the function of religious language, Tillich develops the notion that it is an expression of "ultimate concern," a complex of devotion, commitment, and orientation, focused on something nonultimate—a human being, a nation, or a supernatural deity. Religious statements, which literally refer to such relatively concrete focuses of ultimate concern, express the sense of the sacredness such objects have as "manifestations" of being-itself. But just what it is for such an object to be taken as a "manifestation" or "symbol" of being-itself, Tillich never makes clear.

The basic weakness in these mythical and mystical interpretations is the failure to present any clear hypothesis concerning the function of religious language. Even Cassirer's ideas on "mythical thought" have never been developed to the point of clarifying what contemporary religious believers mean when they talk about God. The other positions are more intelligible, and they all base themselves on important aspects of the use of language in religion. But it seems that each, by inflating its chosen aspect to sole authority, has killed the goose that lays the golden eggs. There is no doubt that in talking about God, religious people express feelings of various sorts, present moral ideals, and articulate what is going on in ritual. But it is not at all clear that they would be using this kind of language if they were not convinced of the truth of the statements they make. Why should I express a feeling of security by saying "God made the heavens and the earth" unless I believe, or at least have some tendency to believe, that as a matter of objective fact the physical universe owes its existence to the creative activity of a supernatural personal deity? Still more, why should I take on the complex of attitudes and activities that goes along with this assertion unless I believe it to be true?

The statement-making function is the cornerstone on which all the other functions depend. And if one is convinced that theological statements are either false or meaningless and still wants to hold to traditional religious formulations, one may *propose* a reinterpretation of theological utterances as expressions of feeling or symbolizations of natural facts. But a proposal for adopting a certain interpretation must be distinguished from a claim that the proposed interpretation correctly reflects the way doctrines are commonly understood.

It would seem that talk about God is much more complex than is recognized by any of the existing theories. The brief discussion given above of empirically testable implications illustrates this point. Theological sentences perform a great many closely interrelated linguistic functions. In saying "God, who created the world, watches over the affairs of men," the believer is committing himself to a certain general view of the ultimate basis of the world, giving voice to certain, perhaps very indefinitely specified, expectations as to how things will ultimately turn out, expressing a basic sense of security in life, committing himself to approach God in prayer and ritual in one way rather than another. And these functions are intimately dependent on each other. What is needed is a description of the relationships among these functions, one sufficiently complex to match the complexity of the subject matter.

Bibliography

St. Thomas Aquinas' historically important discussion of the "analogical" character of theological terms is found in Question XIII of Part I of the *Summa Theologica*. For further discussions in the Thomist tradition see Cajetan, *The Analogy of Names*, translated by E. A. Bushinski and H. J. Koren (Pittsburgh, 1953), and E. L. Mascall, *Existence and Analogy* (London, 1949). Recent discussions by practitioners of analytical philosophy are to be found in Antony Flew and Alasdair MacIntyre, eds., *New Essays in Philosophical Theology* (New York, 1955), and in Basil Mitchell, ed., *Faith and Logic* (London, 1957). See also Alasdair MacIntyre, "The Logical Status of Religious Belief," in *Metaphysical Beliefs* (London, 1957); John Wisdom, "Gods," in Antony Flew, ed., *Essays in Logic and Language*, First Series (Oxford, 1951); C. B. Martin, *Religious Belief* (Ithaca, N.Y., 1959); and I. T. Ramsey, *Religious Language* (London, 1957). Various kinds of symbolic interpretations of religious statements are presented in George Santayana, *Reason in Religion* (New York, 1905); R. B. Braithwaite, *An Empiricist's View of the Nature of Religious Belief* (Cambridge, 1955); W. M. Urban, *Language and Reality* (New York, 1939); Edwin Bevan, *Symbolism and Belief* (Boston, 1957); and Philip Wheelwright, *The Burning Fountain* (Bloomington,

Ind., 1954). Ernst Cassirer's views on mythical language are set forth most completely in Vol. II of *Philosophie der symbolischen Formen,* 3 vols. (Berlin, 1923, 1925, 1929), translated as *The Philosophy of Symbolic Forms* by Ralph Manheim (New Haven, Conn., 1952, 1955, 1957); and in more concentrated form in *Sprache und Mythos* (Leipzig, 1925), translated as *Language and Myth* by S. K. Langer (New York, 1946). For other versions of the view that religious language constitutes an autonomous mode of discourse, see W. T. Stace's *Time and Eternity* (Princeton, N.J., 1952) and Paul Tillich's *Systematic Theology* (Chicago, 1951–1963) and *Dynamics of Faith* (New York, 1957).

WILLIAM P. ALSTON

RENAISSANCE. "Renaissance" is the term customarily employed to designate a cultural movement that began in Italy in the middle of the fourteenth century and spread throughout the rest of Europe. Although the term is well established in the writings of historians, its usefulness has been challenged. Indeed, there has grown up around the concept of the Renaissance an extensive controversy that sometimes threatens completely to divert the attention of scholars from the historical facts. In part, this controversy is simply an acute form of the general problem of periodization in history. The concept of the Renaissance, however, arouses particularly strong opposition because it involves a disparagement of the preceding period, the Middle Ages (*medium aevum*), from which culture presumably had to be awakened.

The idea of a rebirth of literature or of the arts originated in the period itself. Petrarch in the fourteenth century hoped to see an awakening of culture, and many later writers expressed their conviction that they were actually witnessing such an awakening in their own time. Latin was generally the language used by cultivated men to discuss such matters, but no single Latin term or phrase became the standard name for the whole cultural epoch. One of the earliest historians of philosophy in the modern sense, Johann Jakob Brucker, in 1743 referred to the Renaissance only as the "restoration of letters" (*restauratio literarum*), and wrote of the "recovery of philosophy" (*restitutio philosophiae*): even in an earlier German work he used such Latin phrases. Scholars who wrote in Latin never used *rinascentia* as the name for the cultural epoch as a whole. It was the French word *renaissance* that finally acquired this status and was then adopted or adapted into other languages. During the seventeenth century, and fitfully before, French scholars used the phrase *renaissance des lettres* for the humanists' *restitutio bonarum literarum,* taking over in the process the humanist periodization of history. Other writers translated the Latin phrase or phrases into their own vernacular: Edward Gibbon (1787) spoke of the "restoration of the Greek letters in Italy," while Heinrich Ritter, in his history of philosophy (1850), remarked that the *Wiederherstellung der Wissenschaften* derived its name from philology.

Various French authors used the term *renaissance* in titles of their works before Michelet devoted one of his volumes on sixteenth-century France to *la Renaissance* (1855). However, Michelet gave only the sketchiest characterization of the period, and hardly deserves to be credited (if indeed any one person can be) with having "invented" the concept of the Renaissance. Michelet did coin one memorable phrase: he remarked that two things especially distinguished the Renaissance from previous periods—"the discovery of the world, the discovery of man." This phrase was also used by the Swiss cultural historian Jakob Burckhardt for the title of a chapter in his famous work, *The Culture of the Renaissance in Italy* (1860). At his hands, the concept of the Renaissance received what was to become its classic formulation; all subsequent discussion of the concept invariably focuses upon Burckhardt's description of the essential features of life during the Renaissance. Burckhardt, taking the term in its narrow sense of a literary revival of antiquity, conceded that there had been earlier "renaissances" in Europe; but he insisted that a renaissance in this sense would never have conquered the Western world had it not been united with the "already-existing spirit of the Italian people" (*italienischen Volksgeist*). Not until the time of Petrarch, so Burckhardt held, did the European spirit awake from the slumber of the Middle Ages, when the world and man lay "undiscovered."

The relation of the Renaissance to the era that preceded it has been much studied because defenders of medieval culture quickly came to the rescue of their period, stressing its continuity with, or even its superiority to, the Renaissance. However, little has been done to clarify the relation of the Renaissance to the Enlightenment. This is rather surprising, for there was an issue that ran straight through the thought of both these eras: "Can we modern men hope to equal or even excel the achievements of antiquity?" This issue is known to literary historians as the "quarrel of the ancients and moderns." We think of Fontenelle in the seventeenth century as the main champion of the moderns, who had science and truth on their side, as against those writers, with their inflexible rules, who favored the ancients. However, much the same attitude as Fontenelle's is found in the *De Disciplinis* of the Renaissance humanist Juan Luis Vives, who wrote in the early sixteenth century. The Renaissance itself had championed the moderns even before modern science had arisen to prove their case. Renaissance confidence in men's powers was based on art and literature rather than on science, but it was strong nevertheless. Men could respect classical excellence and yet strive to outdo the ancients in every field, including vernacular literature.

Chronological limits. Various events have been taken as marking the beginning of the Renaissance: the crowning of Petrarch as poet laureate of Rome in 1341; the short-lived triumph of Cola di Rienzi in setting up a republican Rome in 1347, an attempt to revive Rome's former greatness; the arrival in Italy of Greek *émigrés* (which actually antedated by a few years the much publicized fall of Constantinople in 1453); the opening up of new trade routes to the East. Each choice represents the selection of a particular field as central in the history of the period: art, architecture, religion, politics, economics, trade, or learning. In certain fields it is hard to maintain any sharp break between conditions in, let us say, 1300 and those in 1350. However, few students of the history of art or of literature are prepared to deny completely the start of new trends in the fourteenth century (at least in Italy). In literature, Petrarch's enthusiasm for Greek antiquity must surely be accepted as inaugurating, in the eyes of men in the fourteenth century, a fresh start. In painting, there is little hesitation about ascribing a similar place to Petrarch's contemporary, Giotto; this ascription dates from the earliest attempt at a history of art, that of Giorgio Vasari (1550). No such figures can plausibly be singled out to mark new beginnings in economic or political history.

Difficulties also surround the choice of an event to mark the end of the Renaissance: the sacking of Rome in 1527, the hardening of the Counter Reformation via the Council of Trent in 1545, the burning of Bruno in 1600, or Galileo's setting of experimental physics on its true path around 1600—any of these might be selected. Once again, however, a periodization that is useful in one field may prove useless in another field. Generally speaking, the era from 1350 to 1600 will include most of the developments commonly dealt with under the heading "Renaissance."

Geographical limits. The shifting locale of the Renaissance presents problems similar to those of its chronological limits. Burckhardt's description focused exclusively on Italy; he implied that the Renaissance, after it had been taken over by the Italian *Volksgeist,* moved on to the rest of Europe. The movement to France is usually said to have resulted from the French invasion of Italy in 1515, which gave the French nobility their first glimpse of the glories of the Italian Renaissance. No comparable event can be singled out for the bringing of the Italian Renaissance to England, unless it be the return from Italy to their native land of the classical scholars Grocyn, Linacre, and Colet in the last decade of the fifteenth century, or perhaps Erasmus' arrival there about the same time. Clearly England did enjoy a renaissance, but it is not easy to fix its dates: English literary historians prefer to discuss the Elizabethan age or the age of the Tudors, thus side-stepping the question of the relation of the English Renaissance to that of the Continent. Still less clear is the coming of the Renaissance to the German lands: German historians treat the sixteenth century as the "time of the Reformation," and tend to discuss the Renaissance chiefly in terms of its impact upon individual reformers.

The Renaissance is sometimes called the "age of adventure." It is not at all clear, however, that the spirit behind men's daring and adventurous actions was entirely new: the two chief incentives toward voyages of discovery, for instance, were commercial acquisitiveness and religious zeal—attitudes by no means foreign to medieval men. It was the shutting off of Venetian trade routes through the Mediterranean by the Turks that forced Europeans to search for new routes to the East, not a new desire for scientific knowledge of geography. The Spanish *conquistadores* may have thirsted for glory, but such a thirst was characteristic of medieval knights as well as of Renaissance humanists. The motives of the Franciscan missionaries were clearly religious and medieval in spirit. Moreover, in the field of domestic trade, the resurgence of economic activity in the fifteenth century which formed the basis for the cultural developments of the Renaissance was less a matter of suddenly effective acquisitiveness than of normal recovery from the slump brought about by the Black Death in 1348.

The new learning. Historians may without hesitation ascribe a rebirth of classical knowledge to the Renaissance period. The discovery of old manuscripts and the invention of printing combined to make the heritage of ancient Greece and Rome available to a far wider audience. The humanists of the fourteenth and fifteenth centuries discovered and preserved many ancient texts that had been neglected for centuries. Of these perhaps the most significant from a philosophical point of view was Lucretius' *De Rerum Natura,* but many other newly discovered texts helped to enrich men's general familiarity with antiquity and to present in full view the setting in which Greek and Roman philosophy originated.

The collecting of manuscripts could be indulged in only by noblemen or well-to-do scholars, but the invention of printing made possible a broader social base for intellectual interests. With the production of vast numbers of newly discovered texts, self-education became a real possibility, as did institutional education on a broad scale. Peter Ramus in France and Philipp Melanchthon in Germany urged the educating of the people, chiefly with the idea of promoting intelligent Christian piety.

Science. Developments in technology and science indirectly provided material for philosophical reflection. The increased use of firearms and cannon in war, for example, made necessary the mathematical study of ballistics; and the scientific work of Benedetti and Galileo drew upon the practical experience of foundries and arsenals. However, Renaissance philosophy of science still took its cue largely from Aristotle: Francis Bacon, dissatisfied with Aristotelian logic and methodology of science, found a replacement not in the actual practices of mechanics and craftsmen but in the rhetorical method derived from Aristotle and applied to the questioning of Nature.

The most spectacular and far-reaching scientific development during the Renaissance was the heliocentric theory advanced by Copernicus, who found hints about Pythagorean cosmology in ancient works. The Copernican theory was surely the most significant revolution ever to take place in science. Far less conspicuous, but still important, were the developments in pure and applied mathematics. Modern notation (such as the use of the "equals" sign) began to be adopted, bringing with it the possibility of greater attention to logical form.

Social values. There have been many attempts, beginning with Michelet and Burckhardt, to capture *the* mind or spirit of Renaissance man. All such attempts seem doomed to failure, for they are bound to oversimplify complex social facts. We may, however, single out four sets of social ideals that were characteristic of various groups during the Renaissance.

The ideals of the feudal nobility, medieval in origin, persisted through the Renaissance among the ruling class, although they underwent considerable refinement. The rude military virtues of camp and field gave way to the graces of the court, which were set forth most admirably in Baldassare Castiglione's book *The Courtier* (1528), one of the most influential treatises on manners ever written. In Castiglione's ideal courtier we may recognize the ancestor of our "gentleman." Works of this sort are presumably also the source of the "universal man," a concept closely associated in modern minds with the Renaissance. In the heroic life idealized by the feudal tradition, love of glory and concern for one's reputation were strong social motives. The humanists' thirst for glory, which Burckhardt emphasized, merely continues this concern but applies it to the achievements of a nonwarrior class, the "knights of the pen." The urban middle class chose, as usual, to emulate the style of life of their superiors: the modern gospel of work as a *raison d'être,* shaping the whole of life, hardly existed during the Renaissance. Few social theorists extolled the virtues of commercial activity until Luther stressed the sanctity of all callings, provided they benefited one's fellow men.

Religion provided the second set of ideals, which centered upon moral salvation and involved a willingness to relinquish the world and all its goods. This mood, exacerbated in some individuals by the terror of imminent death or of eternal damnation, continued unabated throughout the Renaissance; and the entire Reformation movement has been called the "last great wave of medieval mysticism." Although such a religious concern is usually associated by modern secular critics with contempt for this world and with pessimism, it is equally compatible with a cheerful resignation in the face of unavoidable misfortunes and gratefulness for such morally harmless pleasures as life affords. A genuine tension often resulted from the opposing pulls of these religious values and of secular attitudes and this-worldliness: Aristotelian philosophers as well as humanists felt this tension during the Renaissance.

A third set of ideals, that of the ancient sage (Platonic or Stoic), was consciously adopted by Renaissance humanists as an adjunct to Christian exhortation, for many of them felt that Christians could learn much from pagan expounders of virtue. Rarely, if ever, did a humanist attempt to replace the Christian ideal altogether: Burckhardt undoubtedly overstressed the "paganism" of the humanists.

Finally, there was the ideal of a return to nature, a flight from the complexities of sophisticated urban life to pastoral pleasures. This theme has ancient antecedents in the poetry of Theocritus and Vergil, but it emerges into new prominence with Petrarch, who also stressed the benefits of solitude. Passive delight in the beauties of nature can hardly ever be totally lacking in human beings, of course, but during the Renaissance we find an interest in such activities as gardening, the collecting of strange plants and animals, and strolling through woods and fields. Petrarch's famous excursion to the summit of Mont Ventoux turned into an occasion for Christian self-reproach, to be sure, but his letters also abound in references to his gardening and to lone promenades in the countryside near Vaucluse.

Humanism. A major role in the culture of the Renaissance was played by the humanists. All sorts of people call themselves "humanists" today, but in the early days of the Renaissance the name had a clear occupational meaning. During the fourteenth century, the traditional subjects of grammar, rhetoric, and poetry had begun to be called, after a phrase of Cicero, the *studia humanitatis.* The term *umanista* was coined (on the analogy of *artista,* also a product of university slang) to designate a teacher of these subjects in Italian universities. Such studies were by no means new in the fourteenth century; in fact, the humanists were the heirs of a less ambitious but old and respectable medieval profession, that of the *dictator* or teacher of the art of letter-writing (*ars dictaminis*). The Renaissance teachers of "humanities" placed a greater emphasis on ancient models

than had the *dictatores,* but their teaching had much the same objective. Their students often became official letter-writers or speech-makers for popes and princes. Coluccio Salutati and Leonardo Bruni, two of the most influential humanists of the fifteenth century, were chancellors of Florence. The study of Greek philosophy owes much to these two men.

Renaissance humanists did not propound a distinct philosophy but took over from Cicero and Aulus Gellius the ancient ideal of a civilized and urbane way of life that could be formed through acquaintance with Greek literature. With such a program in mind, the humanists began to concern themselves with moral and political philosophy, and this brought them into conflict with the philosophers who taught ethics or politics in the universities. The humanists regarded the Aristotelian Schoolmen as derelict in the performance of their duties, since their teaching (so the humanists claimed) made no differences in the lives of students. The scholastic teachers, in return, regarded the humanists as dilettantes and upstarts, meddling in subjects beyond their depth. The feud of humanists with philosophers began with Petrarch's invective against the secular Aristotelians, the so-called Averroists of his day, and continued through the seventeenth century.

We still tend to see Renaissance Aristotelianism (and medieval Scholasticism as well) through the eyes of these Renaissance humanists. Their bias has crept into most histories of philosophy, largely because the first writers of histories of philosophy shared some of the humanist attitudes. One such early historian was Brucker, whose *Critical History of Philosophy* (1742–1744) has already been mentioned. Brucker presented the Renaissance as a time when human thought emerged slowly into the light (a standard metaphor) from the tiresome labyrinths of medieval Scholasticism. He divided his treatment into various sections, dealing with schools of Greek philosophy that were "restored" during the Renaissance. In spite of his scorn for "more recent Aristotelian–scholastic philosophers," Brucker had great respect for the philosophers who followed the "genuine philosophy of Aristotle": Pomponazzi, Simon Porta, Zabarella, and others. Few modern historians of philosophy pay much attention to these writers. They do, however, characteristically devote lengthy sections to Paracelsus, Jakob Boehme, Robert Fludd, and other "theosophers." According to Brucker, these theosophers "condemn all use of reason in understanding the nature of things," and hence do not belong to the history of philosophy; he includes them only because they have commented incidentally on philosophical matters. Whatever his own philosophical competence may have been, Brucker had one clear advantage over most later historians: he had actually read the Renaissance writers he discussed. Much of Renaissance philosophy still awaits re-evaluation based upon such actual reading of texts.

The general framework of Brucker's treatment of Renaissance philosophy remains a useful way of dealing with most of the thought of the period. The various sects of Greek philosophy were indeed "reborn" during the Renaissance; few of them escaped some sort of revival. There was even what might be called a genuine rebirth of Aristotle, if we mean by this what Brucker probably meant: an

Aristotelianism based directly upon the Greek texts rather than upon Latin or Arabic commentators.

Aristotelianism. It cannot be too strongly emphasized that the main stream of philosophical inquiry during the Renaissance continued to be Aristotelian. The terms employed in philosophical discussion, the problems posed, and the characteristic solutions remain, in basic outline, Aristotelian. Almost all Renaissance philosophers show the influence of their Aristotelian school training, even when they are trying most strenuously to break the shackles of that tradition. The technical terms of philosophy (such as *propositio, entitas, realis, materia, forma, essentia* and many others) originated or became naturalized in the Aristotelian school-tradition, and persisted even in the writings of the most daring innovators, such as Giordano Bruno. The Aristotelian tradition, for reasons already in part suggested, remains the least known and most maligned of all Renaissance schools. Elements of the critical spirit of later medieval philosophy (Scotist and Ockhamist) formed part of the school philosophy of the Spaniard Francisco Suárez and of the Scotsman John Major.

Platonism. Platonism took on new life during the Renaissance, after having been known for centuries chiefly through Aristotle's attacks on it. There was more acquaintance with Plato during the medieval period than is generally recognized, but it is still true that Marsilio Ficino's translations into Latin (first published in 1484) gave the main impetus to the spread of Plato's doctrines. Later editions of Plato often contained Ficino's translations of Proclus and Porphyry, together with his own commentaries, which were strongly colored by his Neoplatonism. Hence, the Platonism that emerged during the Renaissance cannot be distinguished easily from Neoplatonism, for it tends to be otherworldly and religious in tone. The cultural influence of Florentine Platonism emanated from the famous academy founded by Ficino in direct imitation of Plato's school. The society that grouped itself around Ficino aimed at moral improvement and resembled in character certain lay religious societies common in Italy at that time. The whole movement of natural religion was set in motion by Florentine Platonism, as was the renewed study of Pauline theology by such men as John Colet.

Florentine Platonism is well known, by name at least, to most students of the Renaissance. Much less well known is a tradition of reconciling Plato with Aristotle, which also found expression during the period. Byzantine scholars had brought with them to Italy an old battle over the superiority of Plato or Aristotle. During the late Renaissance this battle resolved itself into a truce, with many books written to show that Plato and Aristotle agreed on fundamentals and differed only on words or nonessentials.

Stoicism. Only a few late Renaissance thinkers, such as Justus Lipsius and Guillaume du Vair, committed themselves explicitly to Stoicism, but the influence of Stoic philosophy may be seen at work directly and indirectly (largely via Cicero, Seneca, and the Greek commentators on Aristotle) even during the early Renaissance. Pomponazzi's rigorous moral doctrine, for example, is strongly tinged with Stoic attitudes.

Epicureanism. Rejected with horror by medieval thinkers, who saw him through the eyes of the Church Fathers, Epicurus began to be more sympathetically known as a result of humanist activity in the fifteenth century. Previous to this time, anyone who believed that the soul perished with the body was called an Epicurean, whether he held to any other Epicurean tenet or not. Now it was no longer possible to apply this label so casually. Lucretius' great poem won immediate favor because of its sturdy poetic qualities, but, until Gassendi in the seventeenth century, no one adopted the system of Epicurus in its entirety. Nevertheless, Epicurean influence prior to Gassendi's time did foster a climate less hostile to the concepts of pleasure and utility.

Skepticism. The direct influence of philosophical skepticism in a technical sense began with the first publication of Sextus Empiricus in 1562, from which time skepticism exercised an important influence upon European thought and literature. The religious factionalism or warfare of the sixteenth century had brought about a widespread distrust of dogmatism and fanaticism on the part of such sophisticated minds as Erasmus and Montaigne, whose writings may have contributed to the growth of that spirit of toleration usually associated with the Enlightenment.

The occult tradition. The Renaissance was immensely receptive (perhaps more so than the Middle Ages) to occult and secret lore of all kinds, especially if it claimed to come from the most ancient times and to incorporate the wisdom of the Egyptians, Chaldeans, and Hebrews. When the fashion for reviving ancient thought was at its height, the spurious treatises of "thrice-great Hermes," the so-called Hermetic writings, enjoyed great prestige and blended easily with various other secret teachings, such as that of the Jewish Cabala.

Toward the end of the Renaissance, the vogue for reviving past philosophies began to subside: instead, there began to appear "new" philosophies and "new" systems of thought proudly announced as such, for instance, the *Nova de Universis Philosophia* offered by Francesco Patrizzi or the *Great Instauration* (explicitly opposed to a "restoration") of Francis Bacon. However, most of these efforts at original creation clearly bear the stamp of some ancient sect or sects of philosophy. Even Nicholas of Cusa, the most original systematic mind of the Renaissance, could be called (and indeed once called himself) a Pythagorean. Philosophers hardly ever make a complete break with the past, even when they most loudly claim to be doing so. The great merit of the Renaissance was that thinkers learned what they could from the school of Athens and brought what they learned to bear with fresh vigor upon the problems of human life.

Cardano. No individual completely typifies his age, yet it may be useful to focus for a moment on the way in which the various philosophical traditions converged in a single person. As a case history of this sort, we may take the thought of Girolamo Cardano (1501–1576), an Italian medical man and mathematician. Cardano lived in the late, mature stage of the Renaissance, when the dialogues of Plato and the works of Aristotle were known in their entirety, as were Galen and Hippocrates. The Greek commentators on Aristotle were just being recovered and translated. These works were well known at the universities where Cardano studied: Pavia, a stronghold of humanist learning, and Padua, a center of science and medicine. At Padua the biological and logical aspects of Aristotle's thought were stressed in connection with medical training. Cardano studied under Joannes Montesdoch, a Spaniard, whom he mentions in his writings. There were quite a few such Iberian philosophers studying and teaching in Italy at this time. Aristotelian philosophy was clearly a common European heritage and knew no national boundaries.

A considerable number of Renaissance philosophers were, like Cardano, medical men, and of these quite a few dabbled in mathematics (Galen had urged them to study mathematics for the sake of the training it gave them in sound demonstration). Cardano was, of course, far more successful than most in mathematics: no matter what the true story of his relations with Tartaglia may be, there can be no questioning of Cardano's grasp of algebra, as shown by his solution of cubic equations. Cardano wrote works on medicine, astrology, and mathematics, but his philosophical reputation must rest primarily on two works in natural philosophy: *De Subtilitate Libri XXI* ("On Subtlety," 1550) and its sequel, *De Rerum Varietate* ("On the Variety of Things," 1557). "On Subtlety" attempted a total reconstruction of natural philosophy. Since other philosophers of the period were inspired to embark on similar projects, it is clear that there was widespread dissatisfaction with Aristotle's philosophy of nature even before the attacks of Galileo or Descartes. Aristotle's physical system was to be threatened dramatically by Copernican heliocentrism, which upset the conceptual scheme on which Aristotle's analysis of motion was based. This threat was not explicitly posed, however, until the next century, with Galileo's *Two Chief World Systems*. A Renaissance philosopher such as Cardano did not specifically base his criticisms of Aristotle on the findings of Copernicus or Vesalius: instead, he reproached Aristotle in a general way for having built up "certain general propositions that experiment teaches to be false." Cardano presumably intended to remedy this defect, although it must be confessed that his empiricism is not worked out in philosophical detail. This observation would apply with equal force to most Renaissance nature philosophers, few of whom gave more than perfunctory attention to epistemology.

In developing his own system, Cardano started out by taking as his central category something called "subtlety," which he described as "a certain reason by which sensibilia are with difficulty comprehended by the sense, and intelligibilia by the intellect." Cardano soon abandons this unpromising concept in favor of a revised Aristotelian terminology in which matter, form, soul, principle, and element play roles somewhat analogous to those they play in Aristotle's philosophy. For example, Cardano retains the notion of elements but reduces their number from the traditional Aristotelian four to three by eliminating fire, which he classifies as an "accident." Matter and motion—those central concepts of mechanism—are regarded by Cardano as principles, but they must share this status with form, place, and soul. The last addition puts Cardano into the class of hylozoists, those who believe that all matter is somehow animated, a rather characteristic Renaissance doctrine borrowed largely from Neoplatonism.

Cardano's writings must have appealed to his Renaissance readers: they are lively, detailed, and full of medical and factual information and misinformation. His style contrasts sharply with the dry, logically structured argument of the medievals, which can still be found early in the century in the work of a man such as John Major. Cardano obviously delighted in mathematics and in machinery, in this respect, at least, anticipating Galileo in the generation that followed. The amount of superstitious nonsense incorporated in Cardano's work, however, is still distressingly high, and one can easily understand the impatience of later figures such as Gassendi, Hobbes, and Galileo with their Renaissance predecessors. Cardano wrote a painfully candid autobiography, which appeared in Paris with an evaluation by the French writer Gabriel Naudé (1643). Naudé's judgment on Cardano's character is quite severe. This illustrates a general trend in scholarship: the information current today about many Renaissance thinkers, especially the Italians, comes to us by way of generally hostile French writers of the seventeenth century (Pierre Bayle is exceptional in his lack of polemical intent). If we approach Cardano with the distaste of a Naudé, for example, we too might be inclined to dismiss his work *On Consolation* (1542) as a piece of moralizing cant, when in fact a more humane scholar might consider it a noble document in the light of Cardano's wretched life. Or again, Cardano's passion for gambling could be presented as a despicable and mercenary motive for his interest in games of chance. But a less censorious approach, such as that of Oystein Ore in his *Cardano, the Gambling Scholar* (Princeton, N.J., 1953), will give Cardano the credit he deserves for anticipating the modern conception of probability as the proportion of favorable outcomes to total possible outcomes. Finally, the mere fact that there was enough interest in Cardano's thought still lingering in seventeenth-century France to justify the publication of his entire work (*Opera Omnia*, 10 vols., Lyons, 1663), shows that Naudé's attitude was by no means universal. This comment could also be made of many other Renaissance philosophers who continued to be read in the seventeenth century, even if not all students of that century were as receptive to Renaissance thought as was Leibniz.

(See also FLORENTINE ACADEMY; HERMETICISM; and HUMANISM. See Renaissance in Index for articles on Renaissance figures.)

Bibliography

Everyone interested in the Renaissance should begin by reading two masterpieces of historical writing: Jacob Burckhardt, *Civilization of the Renaissance in Italy* (1st German ed., Basel, 1860), and Johan Huizinga, *The Waning of the Middle Ages* (1st Dutch ed., Haarlem, 1919), both available in various English editions. These works complement each other: Huizinga deals with France and the Low Countries; Burckhardt deals only with Italy and apologizes for having even mentioned Rabelais. No works of comparable standing in cultural history exist for the Renaissance as it affected England, the German lands, or other European countries.

On the concept of the Renaissance, see Wallace K. Ferguson, *The Renaissance in Historical Thought* (Cambridge, Mass., 1948), and Franco Simone, *Il rinascimento francese* (Turin, 1961), which adds new evidence for the seventeenth century in France. Invaluable evidence is contained in Herbert Weisinger's articles, especially "The Self-Awareness of the Renaissance," in *Papers of the Michi-*

gan *Academy of Science, Arts, and Letters*, Vol. 29 (1944), 561–567. See also Augusto Campana, "The Origin of the Word 'Humanist,'" in *Journal of the Warburg and Courtauld Institutes*, Vol. 9 (1946), 60–73, and Hans Baron, "The *Querelle* of the Ancients and the Moderns as a Problem for Renaissance Scholarship," in *Journal of the History of Ideas*, Vol. 20 (1959), 3–22. See also Federico Chabod, "The Concept of the Renaissance," in *Machiavelli and the Renaissance* (New York, 1965).

For general historical background, Edward M. Hulme, *The Renaissance, the Protestant Revolution, and the Catholic Reformation in Continental Europe* (New York, 1914), is convenient. Excellent summaries may be found in *The New Cambridge Modern History*, Vol. I, *The Renaissance, 1493–1520* (Cambridge, 1957).

On humanism, two older works are still basic: Georg Voigt, *Die Wiederbelebung des classischen Alterthums*, 2 vols., 3d ed. (Berlin, 1893), and J. E. Sandys, *A History of Classical Scholarship*, 3 vols. (Cambridge, 1903–1938). All can profit from reading Erwin Panofsky, *Renaissance and Renascences in Western Art* (Stockholm, 1960).

Coming more particularly to philosophy, a useful guide is Paul O. Kristeller and J. H. Randall, Jr., "The Study of the Philosophies of the Renaissance," in *Journal of the History of Ideas*, Vol. 2 (1941), 449–496. Two of the leading present-day historians of Renaissance philosophy are Paul O. Kristeller and Eugenio Garin. Kristeller's major books are *The Classics and Renaissance Thought* (Cambridge, Mass., 1955), revised and enlarged in *Renaissance Thought* (New York, 1961); *Studies in Renaissance Thought and Letters* (Rome, 1956), which brings together many valuable articles; and *The Philosophy of Marsilio Ficino* (New York, 1943). Kristeller's work is solidly based on careful reading of the sources. Garin has dealt with philosophers of the Italian Renaissance extensively in his *La filosofia*, 2 vols. (Milan, 1947), and has compiled useful anthologies, including *Filosofi italiani del quattrocento* (Florence, 1942) and *Il rinascimento italiano* (Milan, 1941). An invaluable anthology, edited by Ernst Cassirer, Kristeller, and Randall, is *The Renaissance Philosophy of Man* (Chicago, 1948).

For French thought during the Renaissance, see Augustin Renaudet, *Préréforme et humanisme à Paris pendant les premières guerres d'Italie (1494–1517)*, 2d ed. (Paris, 1953). For Germany, see Peter Petersen, *Geschichte der Aristotelischen Philosophie im protestantischen Deutschland* (Leipzig, 1921), and Max Wundt, *Die deutsche Schulmetaphysik des 17. Jahrhunderts* (Tübingen, 1939). On Spain see Carlo Giacon, *La seconda scolastica*, 3 vols. (Milan, 1944–1950). On Italy, besides Garin's works, see Giuseppe Saitta, *Il pensiero italiano nell'umanesimo e nel rinascimento*, 3 vols., 2d ed. (Florence, 1961), and Hans Baron, *The Crisis of the Early Italian Renaissance*, 2 vols. (Princeton, N.J., 1955). Important studies are those of Ernst Cassirer, especially *The Individual and the Cosmos in Renaissance Philosophy*, translated by Mario Domandi (New York, 1964).

The Renaissance is a favorite topic for symposia, and the results are sometimes useful: see Tinsley Helton, ed., *The Renaissance* (Madison, Wis., 1961), with contributions by various authorities. Two specialized studies are Carlo Angeleri, *Il problema religiosa del rinascimento* (Florence, 1952), and Georg Weise, *L'ideale eroico del rinascimento e le sue premesse umanistiche* (Naples, 1961). Useful articles appear in *Renaissance Studies* and in *Bibliothèque d'humanisme et de renaissance*.

NEAL W. GILBERT

RENAN, JOSEPH ERNEST (1823–1892), French critic and historian, was born in Tréguier, Brittany. He studied for the priesthood at seminaries in Paris but left the seminary of Saint-Sulpice in 1845 to devote himself to secular teaching and writing. He contributed to the *Revue des deux mondes* from 1851 and the *Journal des débats* from 1853. He received a *docteur ès lettres* in 1852, was elected a member of the Académie des Inscriptions in 1856, and was elected to the Académie Française in 1878. He was appointed professor of Hebrew at the Collège de France in 1862, but the course was then immediately suspended until 1870. In 1884 he became administrator of the Collège de France.

Renan's abandonment of his priestly calling was largely determined by the doubts engendered by his philological study of the Bible. After leaving the seminary, he was strongly influenced by Marcelin Berthelot, the chemist, with whom he maintained a lifelong friendship. Another major influence was German idealism, particularly that of Hegel.

In one sense Renan's life's work can be seen as an attempt to expand the horizons of scientific rationalism by incorporating into it what was valid in idealist philosophy—principally the theme of development, particularly the theme of spontaneous evolution of the human mind. It was the historical aspect and the historical emphasis of Hegel's thought that appealed to Renan, for the cast of his own mind was fundamentally historical, not philosophical. Philosophy for him is not a discipline in its own right, and it is history, not philosophy, that should dominate science; "History is the necessary form of the science of the future." It is evident that Renan used the word "science" in the original sense of "knowledge"; "science" is not to be equated with the natural sciences. On the other hand, his philological and historical method is rationalistic and critical. He was interested, above all, in the evolution of languages and religions as manifestations of the development of the human mind, which is in turn the key to the universe. These manifestations and the universe itself, however, are concrete realities to be discovered through observation, experiment, criticism, and disciplined imagination. They are susceptible to this approach because they are the products of the interplay of natural causes according to constant laws. Renan denied in principle that there is any mystery in the world; what seemed mysterious would yield before the advancing frontiers of knowledge. This is the case in the human no less than in the natural sciences. Renan, in contact with working scientists, rejected the simplistic notions of natural science characteristic of the Positivism of Auguste Comte. He maintained that progress in the natural as well as in the human sciences depends on human judgments of the balance of probabilities on the evidence. He further maintained that all reality is in some degree historical, that the natural sciences (paleontology, for example) reveal the remote parts of history, and that the human and natural sciences can and must therefore be of mutual help.

Just as he banished all traditional metaphysics from philosophy, Renan rejected any supernatural content in religion. The true religion of mankind, in the sense of "a belief accompanied by enthusiasm which crowns conviction with devotion and faith with sacrifice," is that of science (that is, knowledge). Renan's argument runs as follows. The universe is characterized by change according to "laws of progress" under which the human mind becomes increasingly conscious of itself and the ideal is increasingly manifested amid the real: "The goal of the world is the development of mind." At the end of the process God, in the sense not of a creative providence but of an immanent ideal, will be realized. Since this ideal consists in the complete development of consciousness and in the attainment by that consciousness of the full measure of beauty and morality of which it is capable, science must be the great task of mankind. This task must be approached in the spirit neither of mere curiosity nor of mere utilitarianism but in the true religious spirit, seeking revelation of the divine.

The above sketch of Renan's thought is based mainly on his youthful work, *L'Avenir de la science*, written in 1848 but first published in 1890. In his later philosophical writing he modified, but did not abandon, the fundamental position adopted there. Political and social events in France, in particular, damped his optimism and strengthened his skeptical and ironical streak. He began to have doubts about the "religion of science" to which he had turned when he abandoned Roman Catholicism. He became less sure that men had the capacity to attain adequate knowledge, and some of his own writing became tentative, cast at times in the form of dialogue. However, in his professional historical work, which always remained his chief concern, he stood fast by his views on the development of rationality out of instinct and on the progressive realization of God on earth. Even in the new Preface which he added to *L'Avenir de la science* on its publication late in his life, Renan declared that his religion was still "the progress of reason, that is to say, of science." He had been too sanguine, too anthropocentric, and not entirely emancipated from Catholicism; the growth of knowledge had not, in fact, clarified human destiny. He confessed that he did not see how mankind could maintain its ideals if deprived of its illusions, but he retained his faith in knowledge as the supreme pursuit.

Works by Renan

Averroes et l'averroïsme. Paris, 1852.
Essais de morale et de critique. Paris, 1859.
Vie de Jésus. Paris, 1863. Translated by C. E. Wilbour as *The Life of Jesus*. New York, 1864.
Questions contemporaines. Paris, 1868.
Dialogues et fragments philosophiques. Paris, 1876.
Souvenirs d'enfance et de jeunesse. Paris, 1883. Translated by C. B. Pitman as *Recollections of My Youth*. Boston and New York, 1929.
L'Avenir de la science. Paris, 1890. Translated by A. Vandam and C. Pitman as *The Future of Science*. London, 1891.

Works on Renan

Allier, Raoul, *La Philosophie d'Ernest Renan*. Paris, 1895.
Berthelot, René, "La Pensée philosophique de Renan." *Revue de métaphysique et de morale*, Vol. 30 (1923), 365–388.
Charlton, D. G., *Positivist Thought in France During the Second Empire*. Oxford, 1959. See Ch. 6.
Cresson, André, *Ernest Renan: Sa Vie, son oeuvre, avec un exposé de sa philosophie*. Paris, 1949.
Mott, Lewis Freeman, *Ernest Renan*. New York and London, 1921.
Séailles, Gabriel, *Ernest Renan: Essai de biographie psychologique*. Paris, 1895.

W. M. SIMON

RENOUVIER, CHARLES BERNARD (1815–1903), French critical philosopher. He was born in Montpellier and was educated at the École Polytechnique, where he specialized in mathematics and natural science. At the school he came under the influence of the work of Antoine Cournot and of Auguste Comte, who at that time was an in-

structor (*répétiteur*) in higher mathematics there. In 1848 Renouvier published in Paris his *Manuel républicain de l'homme et du citoyen*, a volume addressed to schoolteachers, which urged the preaching of socialism. But his political views were frustrated by the *coup d'état* of Louis Napoleon, and he retired from active participation in politics to write philosophy. Renouvier never held an academic position but worked as a private individual, producing one of the longest series of philosophical works in French history. In 1867 he began the publication, with his friend and collaborator François Pillon, of *L'Année philosophique,* a monthly which propagated Renouvier's philosophical doctrines. These doctrines were chiefly expounded in a series of books, constantly revised by Renouvier, the *Essais de critique générale*, the final edition of which appeared in 1897. He continued writing up to the time of his death, his last work being *Le Personnalisme* (1903). Though his pluralism and his personalism anticipated some philosophical doctrines of the early twentieth century, his main influence was upon his French contemporaries.

Neocriticism. Renouvier's general position is called neocriticism, because it took the method of Kant's critical philosophy as its starting point. But though Renouvier started with Kant's method, he did not accept Kant's conclusions but used them rather as a basis from which to launch a set of ideas often critical of Kant.

Renouvier laid down as an integral part of his philosophy what he called the "law of numbers," according to which every cardinal number is an ultimate individual, finite and irreducible. Mathematics is the paradigm of thinking, and the law of contradiction is more clearly manifested in mathematical operations than anywhere else. But the term mathematics, as Renouvier used it, was restricted to arithmetic, and he derived the nature of numbers exclusively from the cardinal numbers. This led him to deny the existence of any infinite, for he maintained—unable to anticipate the work of Georg Cantor—that an infinite number was a contradiction in terms. Renouvier extended his criticism of the notion of infinity beyond numbers to deny the infinity of space and time as well.

Renouvier recognized that knowledge is relative to its premises and to the person who laid down the premises; nevertheless he could not accept the relativity of logical processes. There is a distinction involved here between logic and the psychology of thought. Just as each number is a distinct and separate entity, so is each human being. And just as the characteristics of each number—duality, triplicity, and so on—can never be reduced to, or "reconciled" with, the characteristics of any other number, so each human being is not exactly like any other and cannot be merged into a general group-consciousness or absorbed into an absolute mind. Knowledge is always the property of individual knowers, and the distinction between knowledge and belief disappears. What an individual knows is what seems reasonable to him, and his contribution to knowledge can never be subtracted. The subtraction can be made verbally, to be sure, but to do so is to alter the character of cognition, which is essentially judgment.

Phenomena. Renouvier also differed from Kant in his doctrine of phenomena. Phenomena are not the appearances of anything other than themselves. They are neither illusions nor purely subjective beings. They are *sui generis*, being whatever we perceive or whatever we make judgments about. He granted that the name is unfortunate except insofar as it indicates appearances. Because there are no things-in-themselves, Renouvier criticized Kant's antinomies, which hold good only if there are noumena. His attack on the first antinomy, for example, was based on its use of the concept of infinity. Since infinity is an inherently inconsistent idea, Renouvier asserted that the world must have had a beginning in time and that space is limited. The domination of the number concept as a conceptual model appears here in full force. For Renouvier, the numbers begin with one, since zero and negative numbers are not really numbers, and spaces are the spaces of individual discrete beings, there being no such entity as number-in-itself or space-in-itself.

There exists within the number series the category of relation. For the numbers are ordered, and order is a kind of relation. All other categories are, for Renouvier, forms of relation, but of relation as discovered within the framework of an individual's consciousness. There turn out to be nine categories—relation, number, position, succession, quality, becoming (*devenir*), causality, purposiveness, and personality. Each has its thesis, antithesis, and synthesis; and all are rooted in the phenomenal world as judged by us. It is uncertain whether Renouvier attempted to derive his categories in the manner of Maine de Biran from personality—our acting as a cause, our seeking ends, our sensory discriminations (which might produce the separateness of quantity and quality), spatial positions, moments in time, and the intervals between them—or whether his assertion that personality is one of the categories is derived from his premise of the law of numbers. In any event, just as each number has its own distinctive quality, its own position in the numeral order, and its many relations to other numbers, determined not only by its own character but also by that of the other numbers, so the human being has his own personality and displays the other categories not only as a distinct entity but also as a perceptive consciousness.

The parallelism between the ways in which a man judges, perceives, and knows and the ways in which he as a person differs from other beings pervades Renouvier's writings. Thus, because one acts to achieve one's purposes, it follows that both causality and purposiveness exist within the human being and must likewise be combined in the phenomenal world. A cause determines the path of an event, but the direction of that event is determined by that which participates in it.

Since no two events are exactly alike, the deterministic factor in nature is mitigated by chance. Renouvier probably got this argument from Cournot, who also insisted upon the probabilistic element in nature. To frame a law or a generalized description depends upon our ability to discover absolutely homogeneous phenomena or groups of phenomena. If this is impossible, then generalizations are at most only probable. But at the same time, each individual phenomenon contributes something to the events of which it is a part, and that contribution in the very nature of things cannot be predicted.

Indeterminism. The problem of causation arises with regard to human beings in the form of the antithesis between free will and determinism. Since every act of consciousness is a relation between a perceiving subject and that which is perceptible, then as soon as a conscious act is formulated and made clear to the perceiving mind, it will be organized in terms of the categories. But there is a choice among the various categories to be applied, for we are not forced either to quantify or qualify, to count or to locate, to assign a date or to recognize a cause. The categories limit the possibilities of judgment but have no inherent order of predominance. In other words, Renouvier held that when we see a phenomenon, for example a tree, we are not forced first to judge it as green, then as distant, old, fan-shaped, simple, or what you will. The order of judgment is determined by us, and we are free, within the range of possible categories, to judge it as we will. The selection of a category or group of categories depends on our free choice in accordance with our interests at the moment of judging.

Freedom cannot be proved, nor can determinism. Both are assumptions utilized in view of their consequences. These consequences may be purely intellectual or may be moral or practical. But freedom itself rests upon the inherent individuality of the human will, an individuality which cannot be completely absorbed into any larger class of beings. Insofar as any being is unique, to that extent it is undetermined or self-determined. And insofar as it is identical with other beings, to that extent the homogeneity of its class accounts for the regularity of its behavior. In short, individuality and freedom are synonymous terms, and Renouvier even called freedom the principle of individuation. The consequence is that just as the personal equation enters into all judgments, so the only certainty we have is the certainty of our judgments. Renouvier put it as follows:

> Certitude is not and cannot be absolute. It is a condition and act of man—not an act and a condition in which he grasps immediately that which could not be immediate, i.e., facts and laws external and superior to present experience, but rather one in which he posits his awareness as it exists and as he maintains it. Strictly speaking, there is no certitude; there are only men who are certain. (*Traité de psychologie rationnelle*, Paris, 1912, Vol. I, p. 366)

But indeterminism is not limited to human judgments. It extends also to history. For since history is in part made up of human behavior, human decisions must be included in its scope, and there is no way of eliminating them. One can, of course, describe the environment of human life, its stability, and its mutability; but if it remains stable, that is because human beings have not changed it, and if it changes, that is due to human acts as much as to natural disasters. Men modify their living conditions, not as a group acting as one man, but as a collection of individuals. Their reasons for doing so may vary, as is inevitable, and of course they are not able to modify their conditions completely. But Renouvier emphasized the importance of human decisions for the way in which men will live, since the ability of human beings to make choices makes it impossible to lay down either a law of universal progress toward the good or one of constant degeneration. Hence Renouvier rejected historical laws, such as those of Comte and Hegel, though he was attracted to meliorism.

Ethics. If there is no historical law dooming mankind to move in any predetermined direction and if history only records actual change, the question arises of the relation of history to ethics. Men make moral judgments and act so as to achieve what they believe to be right. Morals, then, are not the result of history, though what happens in history reflects our moral judgments. Morals are rather the source of historical changes, and if we are to appraise historical events, we shall have to do so in moral terms. This clearly requires a definition of good and evil, and in view of the radical individualism of Renouvier this might seem an insurmountable task. But he identified evil with conflict, conflict both between persons and between groups of persons. For warfare is in essence the prevention by one or more persons of the fulfillment of the volitions of others. Hence tyranny, slavery, and conquest are to be condemned. This assumes that it is possible for a group of enlightened men to respect the individuality of their fellows and for all to live in peace.

In his fictional account of what history might have been, *Uchronie* (1876), Renouvier claimed that the secret of human happiness lies in our recognition of the individual's freedom. If at any epoch men had accepted individual freedom wholeheartedly, he argued, universal peace and harmony would have prevailed. Religious, economic, and national wars would have ended at once; for all men would have taken it for granted that each man has a right to his own religious views, to the satisfaction of his own economic interests, and to his own national loyalties. Renouvier held that education alone could bring this about, though he had no illusions that proper education was ever likely to be instituted. The dogma of historical determinism has had too firm a hold on men's will power and has brought about acquiescence, sloth, injustice, and ignorance.

The basic premises of Renouvier's *Science de la morale* (1869) are that man's nature is rational and that men believe themselves to be free. Their belief in freedom leads men to act for what they judge to be better, and their rationality guides them in their choice of ends. To act morally is to act rationally. By doing so we rise above the beasts; we recognize the humanity in our fellows and respect it. For this reason Renouvier became a bitter opponent of the Catholic church and of monarchy and urged his readers to turn to Protestantism as the religion of individual conscience. To him Protestantism was the religion of a personal God—not an absolute and unchanging Being, omniscient and omnipotent, but finite, limited, free, and the guarantor of our freedom. God's existence is not proved, but it is a reasonable hypothesis drawn from the existence of our moral objectives.

Running through Renouvier's many works are the premises that the plurality of existing things is irreducible; that chance is real and is reproduced in individual freedom of choice; that time and novelty really exist; and that no absolutes or infinites exist.

Works by Renouvier

Essais de critique générale, 4 vols. Paris, 1854–1864.
Science de la morale, 2 vols. Paris, 1869.
Uchronie, l'utopie dans l'histoire. Paris, 1876.
Esquisse d'une classification systématique des doctrines philosophiques, 2 vols. Paris, 1885–1886.
Philosophique analytique de l'histoire. Paris, 1896–1897.
Le Personnalisme. Paris, 1903.

Works on Renouvier

Foucher, Louis, *La Jeunesse de Renouvier et sa première philosophie*. Paris, 1927.
Gunn, J. Alexander, *Modern French Philosophy*. London, 1922. Contains an excellent bibliography.
Hamelin, Octave, *Le Système de Renouvier*. Paris, 1927.
Milhaud, Gaston, *La Philosophie de Charles Renouvier*. Paris, 1927.
Séailles, Gabriel, *La Philosophie de Charles Renouvier*. Paris, 1905.

GEORGE BOAS

RENSI, GIUSEPPE (1870–1941), Italian skeptical philosopher and professor of philosophy at the universities of Messina and Genoa. Rensi first upheld a religiously or theistically oriented idealistic philosophy, defending it in a number of essays and fostering it through his translations of the works of Josiah Royce. He contrasted his theistic "constructive idealism" with the "immanentistic idealism" of Benedetto Croce and Giovanni Gentile; he regarded the latter as a temporary position which, if developed coherently, would have led to constructive idealism. According to Rensi, an idealism that does not arrive at God subtracts reality both from the external world, which then becomes a set of ideas, and from the human spirit, which is then resolved into a set of ideas without a subject.

After World War I, regarded by Rensi as proof of the fundamental irrationality of the world, he began to defend a radical skepticism based on the multiplicity, irreducibility, and irreconcilability of opinions, the reasons used to justify them, and some aesthetic tastes and moral ideas. Rensi held that the traditional objection to skepticism— that it contradicts itself by asserting that there is no truth while dogmatically asserting its own truth—was a purely verbal objection, because the skeptic holds his position against any doctrine taken in itself by showing the contradictions and shortcomings of that doctrine. Therefore the skeptic does not assert that there is no truth but instead that a particular doctrine that claims to possess truth does not and cannot possess truth. Skepticism, in other words, shows the disagreement of reason with itself both within the views of one man and between the views of different individuals. War, the conflict of rights and of political powers, and the contradictory character of philosophies are, according to Rensi, proofs of the intrinsic contradiction in reason. Skepticism does not exclude faith but stems from the preservation of faith. The skeptic is skeptical not because he does not believe but because others believe differently than he; that is, they believe that which he considers absurd.

Rensi had been a socialist in his youth but later came to defend authority. He wished to give to power (and even violence) the function of helping man escape from the chaos of opinions and contrasting interests and of forming a people into an economic, political, and spiritual unity. Authority need not base itself on reason, because it creates for itself the reason of all that it wishes. Although these ideas seem close to those of fascism, Rensi quickly declared himself opposed to fascism and remained so until his death.

According to Rensi, skepticism implies atheism in the field of religion. The refinement of religion that leads to regarding God as inaccessible to the senses and to human powers makes God a nonbeing, the pure and simple negation of every reality accessible to man. From this point of view, both negative theology and mysticism demonstrate atheism. Atheism is still a religion because it is an answer—even if a negative one—to the problem of supreme reality. Unlike other religions, atheism is absolutely disinterested because it contains no egoistic motive and because it places man before the mystery of the All without his being able to expect from the All any help for his own needs.

After 1922, when the absolute idealism of Croce and Gentile assumed the status of an official or semiofficial philosophy in Italy, Rensi accentuated his polemic against it and affirmed the theses most opposed to those of idealism: materialism and pessimism. The Kantian system, considered to be idealistic by the idealists, seemed to Rensi to justify materialism because the Kantian forms of intuition and of thought that condition phenomena, and therefore the totality of nature, are not created by the self but constitute "consciousness in general," which is the intelligibility of the things themselves. According to Rensi, the Kantian doctrine is, therefore, that nature gives reality and knowability to natural things, that things generate of themselves, and of themselves are spatial, temporal, perceptible, and representable; in one word, they are material.

Rensi held that materialism implies pessimism because a material nature deprived of any finality offers man no guarantee and necessarily includes evil, error, and conflicts. For a man who lives in such a nature, morality, when not based on an egoistic calculus or subjected to an imposed code, is a disinterested recognition of evil and a protest against it. It is therefore pure folly. Nevertheless, all of Rensi's works contain a mystical and religious strain, a sense of mystery and of a force which, the triumph of evil in nature and in history notwithstanding, reveals itself in the interiority of man. Rensi condensed this feeling into the phrase "Atoms and the void—and the divine in me."

Works by Rensi

Il genio etico e altri saggi. Bari, 1912.
La trascendenza. Turin, 1914.
Lineamenti di filosofia scettica. Bologna, 1919.
La filosofia dell'autorità. Palermo, 1920.
La scepsi estetica. Bologna, 1920.
Introduzione alla scepsi etica. Florence, 1921.
Apologia dell'ateismo. Rome, 1925.
Realismo. Rome, 1925.
Il materialismo critico. Rome, 1927.
La morale come pazzia. Modena, 1942.

Works on Rensi

Morra, G., *Scetticismo e misticismo nel pensiero di Giuseppe Rensi.* Palermo, 1958.
Nonis, P., *La scepsi etica, di Giuseppe Rensi.* Rome, 1957.

Nicola Abbagnano
Translated by *Nicholas Spadaccini*

REPRESENTATIVE REALISM. See Realism.

RESPONSIBILITY, MORAL AND LEGAL. The term "responsibility" or one of its variants figures in moral discussion in many different ways. Philosophers have traditionally been especially interested in the concept of moral or personal responsibility. It is with the problems connected with this notion that the following discussion is primarily concerned.

Judgments of personal responsibility. F. H. Bradley once claimed that "for practical purposes we need make no distinction between responsibility and liability to punishment." Although it is true that discussions of responsibility have often turned quickly to discussions of blameworthiness and liability to punishment, there is little justification for Bradley's claim. For responsibility is equally relevant to many other forms of social treatment—among others, praise, reward (including special honors such as honorary degrees or titles), legal punishment, legal liability. And, of course, the topic is intimately related to the theological issue of salvation, the allocation of divine rewards and punishments.

Judgments of personal responsibility pertain to this range of practices in a very special way. Unless a person is judged personally responsible for some act or outcome, he would not normally be thought to *deserve* blame, praise, reward, punishment, and so on. Personal responsibility is generally regarded as a necessary condition of the justice of a person's receiving what he deserves. Yet Bradley's error is repeated in many contemporary discussions of "freedom and responsibility" that start with some unilluminating remarks about "responsibility," then move swiftly to examination of blame or punishment. Discussion of responsibility is theoretically fundamental, not ancillary, to accounts of such practices.

Meaning of "moral responsibility." Persons are normally judged morally responsible for their *actions*. But they may be judged responsible for almost anything—events, processes, their own psychological characteristics. Thus, a person may be judged morally responsible for his firm's loss of a contract, the Napoleonic wars, his bad temper, a technique for maintaining the fertility of land, or his friend's divorce. Under what conditions is a person responsible for one of his acts or for some other occurrence? If we can state the necessary and sufficient conditions for judgments of moral responsibility, we shall, in the process, be assigning a sense to the expression. "Moral responsibility," like so many other terms of moral discourse, is inevitably defined persuasively, for one is bound to be influenced in defining it by convictions about the requirements for *deserved* blame, praise, and so on. That is, one is bound to be influenced by convictions, explicit or implicit, about the requirements of justice in such matters.

However, most persons would accept the following form of definition, although those with different moral outlooks would complete it differently: A person is regarded as morally responsible for some act or occurrence x if and only if he is believed (1) to have done x, or to have brought x about; and (2) to have done it or brought it about freely. The completion of this formulation depends on what is meant by a human action; what would count as bringing some outcome about; and, above all, in what sense the terms "free," "freely," or "freedom" are employed. All these conceptions are problematic in ways which lead to very different theories of responsibility. Philosophers have too often supposed that the concept of "freedom" essential to moral responsibility can be fixed independently of what it is to be responsible, and that only after the meaning of "freedom" is specified can we determine whether, and under what conditions, a person is responsible. But in fact what a person means by "free," "freely," or "freedom" will reflect his moral convictions, and especially his views about justice, in the same way and for the same reasons that his conception of "moral responsibility" will reflect these views. As Harald Ofstad has put it, "Ethical systems may determine the sense of 'freedom' we select as relevant" (*Freedom of Decision,* p. 279). One need add only that they not only may, they do.

Freedom and moral responsibility. In his *Nicomachean Ethics,* Aristotle tried to analyze the concept of "voluntary action." Nowhere in his discussion did he clearly take account of the problems that arise if all our decisions and actions are determined by circumstances beyond our control. But he did claim that actions are compulsory "when the cause is in the external circumstances and the agent contributes nothing." It is difficult to say whether, in this and other passages, Aristotle intended to claim that the fact that the cause of action is external *implies* that the agent contributes nothing and is therefore not free in the sense relevant to responsibility. But from the beginning of the Christian era, the view that if decisions and actions are so determined, then persons are not free in the relevant sense, has been forcefully advanced and denied by countless numbers of theologians and philosophers.

The earliest form of the controversy arose in the context of Christian doctrine. In particular the fourth-century Christian theologian Pelagius argued that the doctrines of original sin and grace, and of divine omnipotence and foreknowledge, led to morally repugnant conclusions, primarily the conclusion that although a person's tendencies, decisions, and actions are in no way the fault of the agent, he is nevertheless morally culpable for his actions and, in consequence, justly suffers the torments of hell. If these doctrines are true, Pelagius argued, God is not just. But as God is certainly just, these doctrines must be false. Pelagius insisted that man is possessed of free will in that he has the power of "contrary choice." This power makes it possible for men to sin. In the fifth century St. Augustine countered Pelagius' attack on orthodox doctrine with the claim that though God knows and wills all, he grants to each man who has faith freedom of choice. Though God *knows* what a man will do, he *wills* only hypothetical claims, of the form "*If* this man sins, then he *shall* be punished." Divine decrees of this kind are consistent with freedom of the will. But what about the possession of faith—is this in a man's power? St. Augustine insisted that it was; for to have faith is to believe, and "belief is simply consenting to the truth of what is said, and consent is necessarily an act of will. It follows that faith must be in our power."

Although the terms are often different, the issues generated by this exchange persist. The doctrine of scientific determinism, and not the doctrine of divine omnipotence, is today more commonly thought to pose the chief difficulties. Scientific determinists maintain that external conditions specified in scientific laws are sufficient to produce each human choice and action. But the nature of free choice, the nature of human power and ability, the relevance of necessity to freedom, the role of choice and deliberation, the very possibility of human choice, and many other issues suggested by or actually crystallized in the debate between Pelagius and Augustine are still vigorously debated.

Dilemma of moral responsibility. Efforts to solve the problem of freedom of the will are conveniently considered against the background of the following dilemma.

If determinism is true, then all events, including any person's decisions and actions, are fully determined by circumstances which are ultimately beyond that person's control. If this is so, then that person could not have decided or acted differently. Hence the person was not free.

If determinism is false, then there are at least some events which are not fully determined by antecedent circumstances. To the extent that human decisions and actions are among those events which are not fully determined, those decisions and actions occur by pure chance. But what occurs by pure chance is not within a person's control. Therefore, to the extent that decision and action are not determined, the person is unfree.

But determinism is either true or false. Hence a person is never free with respect to decisions, actions, or the results of actions.

But, it is claimed, a person is morally responsible for an action or occurrence only if he is free in that respect.

Therefore, no one is ever morally responsible for any decision, action, or outcome.

Freedom as the lack of constraint. Some philosophers have argued that determinism does not imply that a person's actions are beyond the person's control. They argue that there is a perfectly clear, ordinary sense to "being able" or "being free" to do something which is compatible with determinism. As Jonathan Edwards, the great American theologian, put it in *Freedom of the Will,* the most sustained, penetrating defense of this position: "Let the person come by his volition or choice how he will, yet, if he is able, and there is nothing in the way to hinder his pursuing and executing his will, the man is fully and perfectly free, according to the primary and common notion of freedom" (Paul Ramsey, ed., 1957, p. 164). The central assumption of Edwards' argument is that the ordinary sense of statements like "Eisenhower could have ordered his troops to take Berlin before the Russians arrived" and "Kennedy was able to call off the invasion of Cuba, but he decided not to do so" is such that these statements are perfectly consistent with determinism. In David Hume's terms, there is an important distinction between an action being caused or determined by antecedent circumstances, and its being constrained or compelled or coerced by antecedent circumstances. Only when an action that is determined is also in some way constrained or compelled is the actor not morally responsible for that act.

Other philosophers have found this position unacceptable for a variety of reasons. Some have argued that the ordinary use of expressions like "was free to," "could have," and "was able to" involves more than lack of constraint. They argue that careful analysis reveals that determinism is indeed inconsistent with statements of the form "X could have done such-and-such." Others have argued that freedom of the will depends upon freedom of decision, not freedom of action; and that if decisions are determined then it surely cannot be the case that one could have decided other than he did. Still others have claimed that there is no reason to accept the authority of common sense or ordinary language in these matters; that it is the philosopher's job to subject our common opinions to the test of careful, reasoned scrutiny, in the manner of Socrates.

Moral judgments and responsibility. Among those who reject common sense as reflected in ordinary language as a basis for philosophical opinion are those who nevertheless endorse the distinction between constrained and nonconstrained causally determined actions but defend it on explicitly moral grounds. Thus, certain philosophers have argued that the aim of holding someone morally responsible should be to influence future behavior in desirable ways—that, indeed, moral responsibility consists in the ability to be influenced by moral judgments. If a judgment of responsibility will not affect behavior in desirable ways, then there is no moral point in holding that person responsible. On this view, most customary excuses will still be acceptable. For it will not, in general, be possible to exert beneficial influence on a person if he did what he did either unintentionally or because no other course of action was possible.

One difficulty with this position is that we are, after all, concerned with persons other than the one whose responsibility is being judged. This concern can be accommodated by taking into account all of the consequences of a given judgment of moral responsibility, and determining whether the consequences are good, or best on the whole. But such a position seems to imply that a person believed to be innocent of an offense might be held morally responsible and be blamed or convicted on the general grounds that it would be socially beneficial to do so. And this seems to conflict with deeply held convictions about the requirements of justice in our commerce with other human beings. Considerations of this sort led Kant to warn against the "serpent-windings" of utilitarianism. Utilitarianism seems to many to imply just such an unqualified appeal to social consequences.

Many thinkers feel that a related consideration has great importance in assigning moral responsibility. They have argued that the claims of justice are satisfied if we justify the rules according to which a person is judged to be morally responsible and blameworthy on the basis of the principle that social utility ought to be maximized, but then apply these rules to particular cases in a way which precludes any further appeal to this principle of utility. In this way, the claims of justice may be satisfied and the problem of freedom bypassed. This view, usually called "rule utilitarianism," has been vigorously discussed by many contemporary moral philosophers. One criticism of it is that the restriction placed on the relevance of the principle of utility cannot itself be justified on utilitarian grounds, and that therefore the principles of justice cannot be explained or defended on a purely utilitarian basis.

Freedom as self-determination. Another gambit directed against the first argument of the dilemma rests on the distinction between self-determined action and action determined by circumstances external to the agent. Thus, F. H. Bradley argued that it is the self that may determine action and that, to the extent that this is so, the person is morally responsible for his actions. He argued that self-determinism does not imply that actions are predictable; actions are, in fact, not predictable, provided that the determining conditions are not entirely "materialistic" because they include "spiritual" or, perhaps, mental causes. The difference between the views of freedom as self-determination and freedom as absence of external constraint is that, although the latter allows that nonconstraining circumstances may be bodily causes external to the agent, the former view rules out this possibility. However, even if one could formulate a clear notion of the self which determines action, there seems to be no reason to suppose that that self, or its determining characteristics, are themselves not determined by circumstances external to the agent. And if this is so, then the action would seem to be determined by circumstances which are ultimately beyond the person's control. In reply to this objection it has been suggested that determinism does not imply that determinants occur *before* that which is determined—and that in the case of human decisions and action, the causal determinants occur simultaneously with the decision that in turn accounts for the action. Thus, the action is determined by a decision that is not itself the result of circumstances beyond the person's control. For, as the determinants are concurrent conditions, in principle they can be affected by prior action. But it is not clear that this view rests on anything more than an *ad hoc* assumption needed to establish the possibility of self-determinism. There is, moreover, much psychological evidence for the view that if one's decisions and actions are determined, then the determinants are circumstances temporally prior to them and external to the agent who decides and acts.

Indeterminism. Philosophers have been equally fertile in rebutting the second argument of the dilemma. Those who believe that only if determinism is false can a person be morally responsible, and thereby are impelled to attack this second argument, are usually called "libertarians" because they believe that the will itself is free in the sense of being undetermined. Libertarians claim that the fact that a decision or action is not fully determined by antecedent conditions does not imply that it occurred by "chance" or "accident" in a way which confers exemption from moral responsibility. But this argument does not refute the claim that an undetermined event is a matter of chance in a way that implies that it occurred by chance or by accident, in the sense of those terms which *is* relevant to moral responsibility. For example, the difference between knocking a flowerpot off a shelf as the result of the fully determined but accidental motion of someone's arm or as a result of an undetermined motion of that arm seems irrelevant to a judgment of responsibility. The two events seem equally to void the responsibility of the agent. Both occurrences seem *accidental* in the relevant sense.

Others—J. D. Mabbott, for instance—claim that the first argument of the dilemma is sound, but it is inconceivable that moral responsibility is inapplicable to the human situation and, therefore, the second argument of the dilemma must be unsound. However, this is hardly an argument; it is rather a dogmatic affirmation of the point at issue. Still another argument is that human beings are so constituted that they necessarily hold others responsible for their actions and necessarily employ concepts in doing so that presuppose indeterminism. This conclusion would seem to rest on dubious psychological assumptions. In any event, if one could develop an account of moral responsibility which does not presuppose that determinism is false, which is morally defensible, and acceptance of which is psychologically possible, this view would be refuted.

Hard determinism. There have been other ingenious efforts to escape the toils of the dilemma. But it has also been argued that persons are indeed never morally responsible. According to this view, which has been called "hard determinism," determinism is true and the first argument of the dilemma is sound. Hard determinists allow that blame and punishment may be useful, but they deny that they are ever morally deserved. Persons who blame or punish should do so only when engaged in moral education or social engineering; and blame and punishment have no special moral significance when they are justified as effective aids in these tasks. As the blame is not moral blame, there is no need to establish that it is *deserved* in virtue of the fact that the person is morally responsible. As John Hospers has put it: "When we view other people's frailties and shortcomings in the light of this perspective, we shall no longer say, 'He deserves what he's getting.' Instead, we shall say, 'There, but for the grace of God (and a favorable early environment) go I'" (*Human Conduct*, p. 521).

Hard determinists forget, however, that the claim that someone deserves what he is getting is not necessarily an expression of moral indignation. It may instead be an expression of the belief that all of the requirements of justice have been satisfied. If it is defensible to suppose that "freedom," used in some sense consistent with determinism, is a requirement of justice, then hard determinism is unacceptable.

The general defect of the dilemma is that it presupposes that the relevant sense of "freedom" can be specified independently of a specific moral outlook, and particularly of a conception of justice. This defect reverses the proper order of moral reflection. The sense in which one can be said to have "acted freely," and therefore to be morally or personally responsible and to deserve blame or praise or punishment or reward, should be specified in the light of one's moral outlook—not independently of it.

LEGAL RESPONSIBILITY AND PUNISHMENT

Many philosophers regard the legal context as paradigmatic for the discussion of moral responsibility. It seems clear that the unfortunate tendency to identify moral responsibility with blame and punishment derives partly from this fact. Nevertheless, the assessment of legal responsibility is so closely related to the assessment of moral responsibility, and legal experts have given such sustained and imaginative attention to the task of articulating criteria which are applicable to complex cases, that a careful study of the relevant aspects of the law will certainly assist the development of an adequate account of moral responsibility. Though problems pertaining to responsibility occur in all branches of the law, criminal law has received the most attention; the topics most frequently discussed in this connection are *mens rea* and criminal insanity.

"Mens rea." The doctrine of *mens rea* requires a certain "mental element" to have been present when the offense was committed. This mental element is usually, but misleadingly, described as "guilty mind." The characterization is misleading, first, because it is generally supposed that the offender need not be aware that he is committing an offense ("ignorance of the law is no excuse"); and, second, because many advocates of *mens rea* do not even require that the offender be morally culpable. On this second point there is, in fact, considerable disagreement. Some argue that unless an offender is morally blameworthy for his offense, he does not deserve to be convicted. Others insist on the distinction between moral responsibility and moral blameworthiness, arguing that a person may be morally responsible and may deserve to be convicted and punished for a crime even though his actions were not blameworthy. Broadly speaking, then, those who subscribe to the doctrine of *mens rea* believe at least that only persons who are morally responsible for their offense deserve conviction and punishment.

Discussions of *mens rea* usually take for granted the possibility of resolving the philosophical perplexities described above. Certain assumptions, generally unexamined, are made, and the work of articulating criteria appropriate to the criminal law goes forward. Those who accept the doctrine of *mens rea* in any of its forms believe that the requirement is satisfied if the offender has committed his offense intentionally. Some also claim that unintentional actions which are performed recklessly or negligently involve the necessary mental element. In general, the person who commits an offense is thought to have satisfied the doctrine of *mens rea* if he knew what he was doing at the time or if he would have known what he was doing had he proceeded with reasonable care and deliberation. The extent to which an offender is able to or actually does exercise deliberate control over his actions and their results seems to be central to the way in which moral responsibility as a condition of deserved conviction and punishment is incorporated into the criminal law. This point is, however, more general than the doctrine of *mens rea* itself—it being possible for someone to have acted intentionally while, by reason of mental defect, not possessing deliberate control over his actions. Before going on to this point, two criticisms of the doctrine of *mens rea* should be considered.

Objections to "mens rea." There are those who argue that, at least for certain criminal offenses, the requirement of *mens rea* ought to be abandoned and that strict liability ought to prevail. That is, for certain offenses it does not matter that the act was unintentional and it does not matter that reasonable care was taken. There are various arguments for strict liability, but, in general, the case for it is specific to the offense.

Though the agent's state of mind would seem not to enter into legal deliberations where strict liability prevails, this is not quite so. For example, it has been held that a bank director is strictly liable for borrowing money in excessive amounts from his own bank. In *State* v. *Lindberg*, 258 U.S. 250 (1922), the director pleaded that he had been assured that the money borrowed did not come from his own bank. Though the director did not borrow the money from his bank intentionally, the act of borrowing was itself intentional. A person cannot be said to have borrowed money which he accepted as a gift; his own intentions as well as the intentions of the donor are controlling. Though borrowing does, therefore, require a certain state of mind, the absence of the "mental element" involved in intentionally borrowing from one's own bank would be sufficient to discharge a person from moral responsibility. Insofar as the doctrine of *mens rea* is designed to satisfy the requirement that only a person who is morally responsible for some act or its result deserves to be held legally responsible and punished, strict liability conflicts with it.

Criteria of "mens rea." The second criticism does not so much repudiate the requirement of *mens rea* in establishing responsibility as it criticizes the effort to develop criteria for *mens rea*. H. L. A. Hart has argued that the practical meaning of *mens rea* is given in what is allowed as excuse or mitigation within the law. In order to determine whether *mens rea* is established, Hart argues, "it is necessary to refer back to the various defenses; and then these general words (like 'mistake,' 'accident,' and so on) assume merely the status of convenient but sometimes misleading summaries expressing the absence of all the various conditions referring to the agents' knowledge or will which eliminate or reduce responsibility." In other words the general "rules" summarize accepted excuses, and there just are no general principles in terms of which we can account for the acceptance of specific excuses. Hart then generalizes his discussion of *mens rea* to pertain equally to the assessment of responsibility in nonlegal contexts.

This thesis encounters many difficulties. For one thing Hart neglects to distinguish adequately between exemption from responsibility and exemption from blame or legal responsibility. Thus, if a person defends himself against moral criticism of his having hit someone else by claiming that he was acting in self-defense, he is in effect accepting responsibility but rejecting blame on the grounds that he was justified in what he did. Second, if proposed as a purely descriptive thesis about our actual use of the language of "excuses," Hart's position begs the prescriptive claim that a general rationale of excuse and mitigation *ought* to be given—that otherwise the acceptance of a certain excuse is morally arbitrary. Those who defend *mens rea* try to meet this obligation by focusing on the element of awareness of what we are doing when we choose and act. Indeed, Hart becomes his own best critic when, in a later essay, he argues that the main rationale for excuse and mitigation within law is respect for "the claims of the individual as such, or at least as a *choosing being.*"

Criminal insanity. A person might intend to kill a particular person after careful deliberation, and do so; and this would be sufficient to satisfy *mens rea*. But if the offender suffered from extravagant delusions of having been persecuted by the person killed, he would normally be thought to be entitled to exemption from criminal liability on grounds of insanity.

The criterion of legal insanity generally adopted within Anglo-American law is the M'Naghten Rule. This rule was formulated by the judges of England in 1843 in response to the public outcry that resulted when Daniel M'Naghten was acquitted, on grounds of criminal insanity, of murdering Sir Robert Peel's private secretary. M'Naghten had mistaken the secretary for Peel and had killed that unfortunate man while suffering from persecutory delusions about Peel's intentions toward him. The judges attempted to provide a morally sound, legally workable criterion for determining whether a person was entitled to acquittal on grounds of criminal insanity. They affirmed that:

> to establish a defence on the ground of insanity it must be clearly proved that, at the time of committing the act, the party accused was laboring under such a defect of *reason,* from disease of the mind, as not to know the *nature and quality of the act he was doing,* or, if he did know it, that he did not *know he was doing what was wrong.* . . . The question has generally been, whether the accused at the time of doing the act *knew the difference between right and wrong.* [Italics added.]

The rule has been the object of vigorous attack and defense ever since its formulation. One type of criticism roughly follows the line of argument expressed by various parts of the dilemma formulated earlier. For example, Barbara Wootton, arguing from a determinist position, has claimed that no acceptable criterion of criminal insanity can be formulated; that efforts to formulate an adequate criterion of mental defect, and, in the final analysis, of responsibility itself, shatter on the rock of the first argument of the dilemma. Consequently, all efforts to assess moral responsibility should be abandoned within the criminal law. The law should be concerned solely with treating the offender. It is clear that this "reform theory" approach to the criminal law would sweep away not only the insanity plea, but *mens rea* as well. Thomas Szasz has, on the other hand, argued that there is no such thing as a mental illness, that the insanity plea is never a valid excuse, and that, therefore, it ought to be abandoned. This argument leads to the same conclusion on policy as that reached by the reform theorists with respect to the insanity plea, but leaves *mens rea* intact. Szasz is not skeptical of moral responsibility as such. Others, like David Bazelon (in his Isaac Ray Award lecture, "Equal Justice for the Unequal"), criticize the M'Naghten Rule as being too narrow—as not embracing all those defects of mind that entitle an offender to exemption on grounds of not having been morally responsible for his offense. It seems clear that many of the issues generated by this debate, as well as those that concern the doctrine of *mens rea*, await an adequate philosophical theory of moral responsibility.

AN APPROACH TO A THEORY OF
MORAL RESPONSIBILITY

An adequate theory of moral responsibility cannot identify moral responsibility with liability to blame or punishment. Moreover, any such theory must explicitly recognize what is, in any event, generally the case: that the meaning assigned to the key concepts in the theory, particularly "freedom," reflects the moral outlook of its author.

The second point is of particular importance. Suppose one reflectively endorses a conception of justice according to which a person deserves blame or praise, reward or punishment, and so on, only if that person's decisions or actions are not determined. Then one should define "freedom" in such a way that "*P* decided (acted) freely" implies "*P*'s decision (action) was not determined." Correspondingly, suppose one endorses a conception of justice according to which a person deserves blame, etc., only if his decisions or actions have some property which may or may not be causally determined by circumstances beyond his control. Then "freedom" ought to be defined in such a way that the meaning of "*P* decided (acted) freely" is consistent with determinism. It is our practical aims and interests which should govern the shape of our language, and not unreflected-upon linguistic habit which should govern the shape of our moral outlook.

Thus, a theory of justice is the essential foundation for a theory of moral responsibility. In this connection it should be remembered that just acts are not always right. (Would it be right to refrain from punishing an innocent person if the consequence was the destruction of human civilization?) Moreover, acts of blame, praise, reward, and punishment which are not just may sometimes be right. (One may be justified in blaming or praising an infant in order to influence his future behavior, but there would be no justice in it.)

Bibliography

Some of the more interesting classical and contemporary discussions (in a vast literature) are cited below.

GENERAL

For broad treatments of responsibility, see Harald Ofstad's *Freedom of Decision* (Oslo, 1960) and Austin Farrar's *The Freedom of the Will* (London, 1958). A number of important papers can be found in the anthologies *Free Will,* Sidney Morgenbesser and James Walsh, eds. (Englewood Cliffs, N.J., 1962); *Determinism and Freedom,* Sidney Hook, ed. (New York, 1958); *Freedom and the Will,* D. F. Pears, ed. (New York, 1963); and *Freedom and Responsibility,* Herbert Morris, ed. (Stanford, 1961). The Morris collection contains many papers particularly relevant to legal responsibility and has an extensive bibliography.

Historically, the most important work is Aristotle's *Nicomachean Ethics.*

DETERMINIST AND LIBERTARIAN DEFENSES

The best traditional defenses of the view that moral responsibility and determinism are compatible are Jonathan Edwards' *Freedom of the Will* (1754), Paul Ramsey, ed. (New Haven, 1957), and David Hume's *An Enquiry Concerning Human Understanding,* Ch. 8. Important contemporary statements of the same position have been made in C. L. Stevenson's *Ethics and Language* (New Haven, 1944), Ch. 14; Moritz Schlick's *Problems of Ethics* (Englewood Cliffs, N.J., 1939), Ch. 7; and P. H. Nowell-Smith's *Ethics* (Oxford, 1957), Chs. 19–21.

The most influential recent defenses of the "libertarian" position are C. A. Campbell's "Is 'Free-Will' a Pseudo-Problem?," in *Mind,* Vol. 60 (1951), 441–465, and Stuart Hampshire's *Thought and Action* (London, 1959). See also J. D. Mabbott's "Free Will and Punishment," in H. D. Lewis, ed., *Contemporary British Philosophy,* 3d Series (London, 1956).

HARD DETERMINISM

For hard determinism, see Holbach's *Système de la nature* (London, 1770) and John Hospers, "Free Will and Psychoanalysis," in Paul Edwards and Arthur Pap, eds., *A Modern Introduction to Philosophy,* 2d ed. (New York, 1965), pp. 75–85. This volume contains an extensive bibliography of material bearing on the topic of the present article on pp. 99–108.

ETHICAL THEORY

Some recent texts which place the problem of moral responsibility in the general context of an ethical theory are Richard Brandt, *Ethical Theory* (Englewood Cliffs, N.J., 1959); A. C. Ewing, *Ethics* (London, 1953); W. Frankena, *Ethics* (Englewood Cliffs, N.J., 1963); and John Hospers, *Human Conduct* (New York, 1961).

PROBLEMS IN THEORY-MAKING

Of the many technical articles dealing with various conceptual problems involved in the development of an adequate theory of moral responsibility, the following are of some interest.

On the difficulties of analyzing such terms as "can" and "ability," see John Austin, "Ifs and Cans," in *Proceedings of the British Academy,* Vol. 42 (1956), 109–132; Richard Taylor, "I Can," in *Philosophical Review,* Vol. 59 (1960), 78–89, and A. S. Kaufman, "Ability," *Journal of Philosophy,* Vol. 60 (Sept. 12, 1963), 537–551.

On the difficulties of analyzing such terms as "intention" and "decision," see Carl Ginet, "Can the Will Be Caused?," in *Philosophical Review* (1962), 49–52; Stuart Hampshire and H. L. A. Hart, "Decision, Intention, and Causality," *Mind,* Vol. 67 (1958), 1–12; G. E. M. Anscombe, *Intention* (Oxford, 1958), and A. S. Kaufman, "Practical Decision," in *Mind,* Vol. 75 (1966), 25–44.

QUESTIONS IN CRIMINAL LAW

For works especially pertinent to the relevance of moral responsibility to the criminal law, see, in addition to the Morris collection (*Freedom and Responsibility*): J. D. J. Edwards, *Mens Rea in Statutory Offenses* (London, 1955); Joel Feinberg, "Problematic Responsibility in Law and Morals," *Philosophical Review,* Vol. 71 (1962), 340–351; and G. L. Williams, *Criminal Law: The General Part* (London, 1953), pp. 28–45, 77–81. See also Henry Hart's "The Aims of the Criminal Law," in *Law and Contemporary Problems,* Vol. 23 (1958), 405–441, which presents a general defense of the claim that moral blameworthiness is an essential condition of criminal liability. For a contrary view, see H. L. A. Hart's "Legal Responsibility and Excuses," in Hook's collection, *Determinism and Freedom;* this article also in part constitutes an amendment to his own earlier essay, "The Ascription of Responsibility and Rights," *PAS,* Vol. 59 (1949), 171–194, where he argues against the possibility of a general rationale of excuse and mitigation.

On the topic of strict liability, see R. A. Wasserstrom's "Strict Liability in the Criminal Law," *Stanford Law Review,* Vol. 12 (1960), 730–745.

The literature dealing with criminal insanity is vast; see Barbara Wootton's *Social Science and Social Pathology* (London, 1959), Ch. 8; Thomas Szasz's *Law, Liberty, and Psychiatry* (New York, 1963); David Bazelon's "Equal Justice for the Unequal" (The Isaac Ray Award lecture). Unfortunately this last work is available only in mimeographed form.

Among scientific writings that have a special relevance are M. Gluckman, *The Judicial Process Among the Barotse of Northern Rhodesia* (Manchester, 1953), and B. F. Skinner, *Science and Human Behavior* (New York, 1953), Chs. 12 and 22.

ARNOLD S. KAUFMAN

REVEL, JEAN-FRANÇOIS, French writer and philosopher, was born in 1924 in Marseilles. Revel studied philosophy at the École Normale Supérieure. He spent three years in Mexico and four in Italy and has been living since 1956 in Paris, having left the academic world for that of journalism and publishing. Revel has written a variety of works ranging from political commentary to a novel; as a philosopher he is best known for two short but pungent books, *Pourquoi des Philosophes?* (1957) and its sequel, *La Cabale des dévots* (1962). In these works Revel launched a most vigorous attack on what he considered the obscurities and pretensions of French academic philosophy and philosophical psychology and sociology. Henri Bergson, Maurice Merleau-Ponty, Pierre Teilhard de Chardin, Claude Lévi-Strauss, and Martin Heidegger and his followers are prominent among those in his line of fire.

Revel is by no means a systematic writer, nor has he so far shown himself to be a substantially creative philosopher in his own right. The main interest and significance of his two books lies less in the details of their polemic than in the fact of their appearance, the nature of the assumptions on which they are based, and the reactions that they have called forth. Revel's general attitude is that of a man of hardheaded everyday good sense. Confronted with the grandiose ornamentation and willful obscurity of both the antiscientific armchair pseudoscience and the vaguely rhapsodical metaphysics that are carried on in the name of philosophy, he can only regard them as some elaborate but pointless intellectual ritual. His own view, reiterated with great force, is that the time for philosophy as system building is past, that those serious questions which remain are the proper concern of the various sciences, and that where science is concerned, there is no competence short of professional competence. To continue to philosophize in the old literary tradition is worse than a waste of time. It can only too easily confuse and mislead the unwary into mistaking long words for great ideas and into reposing in the comfort of a wholly illusory intellectual self-satisfaction.

It would be wrong to overestimate the importance of Revel's attack. He writes with the verve and insight of a well-informed debater rather than on the basis of any detailed or solid theory. Nevertheless, there is obvious point to many of his criticisms. The varied reactions of annoyance, scorn, and enthusiasm that his work has aroused bear witness both to its own impact and to a certain general state of tension both within and about the philosophical world in France. It is of great interest to anyone of the predominantly empiricist tradition of Anglo-Saxon philosophy to see a Frenchman, in the name of science and outraged common sense, accuse French philosophers of having degenerated into purveyors of incantatory verbiage.

Works by Revel

Histoire de Flore. Paris, 1957.
Pourquoi des Philosophes? Paris, 1957; paperback ed., 1964.
Pour l'Italie. Paris, 1958. Translated by A. Rhodes as *As for Italy.* London, 1959.
Le Style du général. Paris, 1959. An essay on Charles de Gaulle.
Sur Proust. Paris, 1961.
La Cabale des dévots. Paris, 1962; paperback ed., 1965.

ALAN MONTEFIORE

REVELATION. The notion of revelation is central to three of the major world religions: Judaism, Christianity, and Islam. Through Christianity in particular it has long been an important element in the religious thought of the West, and the present article will treat it in this context, especially that of Christian theology.

During the twentieth century, but beginning in the nineteenth century, many—especially Protestant—theologians have radically revised their conception of revelation. The view that was virtually axiomatic for all schools of thought a century ago and that still remains the majority position (for it continues both in Roman Catholicism and in sections of conservative Protestantism) may be called the propositional view of revelation.

THE PROPOSITIONAL CONCEPTION

In the propositional view, that which is revealed is a body of religious truths capable of being expressed in propositions. Because a knowledge of these truths is necessary for man's salvation, God has supernaturally made them known. Accordingly, in the words of the *Catholic Encyclopedia*, "Revelation may be defined as the communication of some truth by God to a rational creature through means which are beyond the ordinary course of nature" (Vol. XIII, p. 1).

The fuller significance of this propositional understanding of revelation appears when we view it in relation to three other basic theological categories with which it is closely connected. A particular conception of the nature of revelation involves a particular conception of the nature of faith, as man's response to revelation; of the Bible and its inspiration, as a medium of revelation; and of the character of theological thinking, as thought that proceeds on the basis of revelation.

When revelation is conceived as the divine disclosure of religious truths, faith is necessarily understood as the obedient believing of these truths. Thus faith was defined by the First Vatican Council (1870) as a supernatural virtue whereby "with the inspiration and help of God's grace, we believe that what he has revealed is true, not because its intrinsic truth is seen with the natural light of reason, but because of the authority of God who reveals it" (*Enchiridion Symbolorum*, H. J. D. Denzinger, ed., 29th ed., Freiburg, Germany, 1952, No. 1789).

The Bible finds its place in this system of thought as the book in which divinely imparted truths are written down and thereby made available to all mankind. Indeed, throughout considerable periods of Christian thought the Scriptures have been called the Word of God and have been virtually identified with revelation. The Bible is accordingly thought of as being ultimately of divine authorship; it has been written by human beings, but in the writing of it, their minds were directed by the Holy Spirit. Thus, the First Vatican Council said of the Scriptures that "because they were written as a result of the prompting of the Holy Spirit, they have God for their author" (*Deum habent auctorem;* Denzinger, *Enchiridion Symbolorum,* No. 1787); and in a similar vein, in the twentieth century, the Protestant evangelist Dr. Billy Graham has said, "The Bible is a book written by God through thirty secretaries."

The propositional conception of revelation has also been

integral to an understanding of the structure of theology which until recently has held unquestioned sway in Christian thought since it was established by Thomas Aquinas in the thirteenth century. This hinges upon the distinction between natural and revealed theology. Natural theology comprises all those truths about God, and about the created universe in its relation to God, that can be arrived at by human reasoning without benefit of divine revelation. Accordingly, the core of natural theology consists in the traditional philosophical arguments for the existence of God. Revealed theology, on the other hand, comprises those truths about God, and about the created universe in its relation to God, that are not accessible to right reasoning as such and that can be known to men only because God has chosen to reveal them. (For example, it is held that while the existence of a supreme being is a tenet of natural theology, the further fact, stated in the Trinitarian dogma, that this being is "three Persons in one" belongs to revealed theology.) These various truths constitute the materials with which the theologian works, his primary task being to bring them together into a systematic body of doctrine.

These conceptions of faith, the Bible, and theology are linked together by the propositional character of revelation, with which they are all concerned. The revelation that is imparted by God, believed by men, published in the holy Scriptures, and systematized in the church's dogmas is a body of theological knowledge. This propositional conception of revelation began to form soon after the end of the New Testament period; reached its fullest development in medieval scholastic thought; was largely abandoned by the first Reformers in the sixteenth century, particularly Martin Luther, but became re-established in the Protestant scholasticism of the seventeenth and eighteenth centuries; began to be questioned in the later nineteenth century; and has finally been set aside by considerable sections of Protestant thought in the twentieth century.

THE "HEILSGESCHICHTLICH" CONCEPTION

The fundamental premise of the propositional view has no place in the nonpropositional conception of revelation that has been widely adopted by Christian theologians in the twentieth century. This view maintains that revelation consists not in the promulgation of divinely guaranteed truths but in the performance of self-revealing divine acts within human history. The locus of revelation is not propositions but events, and its content is not a body of truths about God but "the living God" revealing himself in his actions toward man. The nonpropositional view thus centers upon what has come in recent theology to be known as *Heilsgeschichte* ("salvation history") identified as the medium of revelation.

It is not supposed that God has marked his presence by performing a series of miracles, if "miracle" is taken to mean an event that compels a religious response by eluding all natural explanations. It is not characteristic of those theologians who think of revelation in nonpropositional terms to regard the Biblical miracles as constituting theistic proofs. Rather, the *Heilsgeschichte* is the way in which

a certain segment of human history—beginning with the origins of the national life of Israel and ending with the birth of the Christian community as a response to Jesus —was experienced by men of faith and became understood and remembered as the story of God's gracious dealings with his people. What Christianity (and, confining itself to the Old Testament, Judaism) refer to as the story of salvation is a particular stream of history that was interpreted by prophets and apostles in the light of a profound and consistent ethical monotheism. They saw God at work around them in events that accordingly possessed revelatory significance. The *Heilsgeschichte* is thus a portion of history seen "from the inside" by the illumination of a particular religious faith. The publicly observable series of events forming its basis belongs to secular world history and is capable of a variety of political, economic, psychological, and other analyses besides that of theistic faith. As a central instance of this capacity of history to be construed both nonreligiously and religiously, Jesus of Nazareth, who has been seen by those outside the Christian community in various ways—for example, as rabbi, prophet, or political revolutionary—is seen by Christian faith as the divine Son incarnate in a human life, seeking to draw men into a new life in relation to God.

Revelation, understood in this way, presupposes faith as its correlate. That God is at work in a certain situation, which accordingly serves a revelatory purpose, is always a judgment of religious faith. The part played by faith is thus integral to the total event of revelation, if we use "revelation" to refer to the completed communication that occurs when God's approach has met with a human response. In the words of William Temple, whose formulation of this conception of revelation has become classic, ". . . there is event and appreciation; and in the coincidence of these the revelation consists" (*Nature, Man and God*, p. 314).

As in the case of its older rival, the fuller significance of what may be called the *heilsgeschichtlich* conception of revelation can best be indicated by sketching its implications for the understanding of faith, the Bible, and theological thinking. Clearly, in this view faith is not primarily the believing of revealed propositions, but is rather (in its cognitive aspect) a mode of discernment or interpretation in which men are convinced that they are conscious of God at work in and through certain events of both their personal experiences and world history.

The Bible is not a collection of divine oracles, but a record of the events through which God has revealed himself to a special group, a record that itself functions as a further medium of God's self-revelation beyond that group. It has not been written at the dictation of the Holy Spirit, but has been composed by many different writers at different points within the period of the thousand years or so that it documents. It is distinguished from secular records of the same sequence of events by the fact that it is written throughout from the standpoint of faith. The Old Testament is dominated and unified by the God-centered interpretation of Hebrew history taught by the great prophets, in the light of which the story of the nation came to be understood and celebrated and its chronicles edited. The New Testament is dominated and unified by the witness of Jesus' first disciples and of the Christian communities that grew up around them to the life, death, and resurrection of Jesus, whom they had received as the Christ. The faith by which alone the several writers could produce this particular literature constitutes the "inspiration" that has presided over its production.

Finally, there is no body of divinely authoritative theological propositions. Religious doctrines are not revealed, but represent human—and therefore fallible—attempts to understand the religious significance and implications of the revelatory events depicted in the Scriptures. Theologians who regard revelation in this manner have generally abandoned the traditional natural theology, with its theistic proofs, and base their doctrines instead upon faith as it responds to the scriptural records.

SOME QUESTIONS

One of the questions that Christian theologians have repeatedly discussed is whether there is both general and special revelation. Are nature and history as a whole—including the whole religious history of mankind—revelatory of God, as well as the special occasions of the Biblical *Heilsgeschichte*? Many theologians of all communions today hold that God is indeed universally active and that his activity always discloses something of his nature, even though his fullest personal self-revelation has occurred only in the person of Christ.

Another question that has at times been hotly disputed is whether there is an image of God (*imago dei*) in man that constitutes an innate capacity to respond to divine revelation (Emil Brunner) or whether, on the contrary, human nature is so totally corrupted by the Fall that in revealing himself to men God has to create in them a special capacity for response (Karl Barth).

The main philosophical question that arises concerns the criteria by which revelation claims may be judged. For proposition-centered religious thought the answer is provided by natural theology considered as a preamble to revelation. This establishes the existence of God and points, by means of miracles and fulfillments of ancient prophecy, to Christ and the Scriptures as the sources of revealed truth, supplemented in Roman Catholicism by the church as its divinely appointed guardian. For those theologies, on the other hand, that find God at work in historical events whose significance is discerned only by faith, there can be no proof of revelation. Such theologies arise within a community of faith (whether Jewish or Christian) that lives on the basis of what it believes to be an experience of divine revelation. It embodies in its life and literature the "memory" of momentous events in which God has opened a new and better life to mankind. The form of apologetic appropriate to this view is one that defends the right of the believer, as a rational being, given the distinctively religious experience out of which his faith has arisen, to trust that experience and to proceed to live upon the basis of it.

Bibliography

The Biblical basis of the idea of revelation is discussed in H. W. Robinson, *Inspiration and Revelation in the Old Testament* (Oxford, 1946; 4th ed., 1956), and E. F. Scott, *The New Testament Idea of Revelation* (London and New York, 1935).

R. Garrigou-Lagrange, *De Revelatione per Ecclesiam Catholicam Proposita,* 2 vols. (4th ed., Rome, 1945), is a classic Roman Catholic exposition. See also G. H. Joyce, "Revelation," in C. G. Herbermann and others, eds., *Catholic Encyclopedia,* 15 vols. (New York, 1907), Vol. XIII.

John Baillie, *The Idea of Revelation in Recent Thought* (New York, 1956), traces the modern move in Protestantism to a nonpropositional conception of revelation. B. B. Warfield, *Revelation and Inspiration* (New York, 1927), provides a conservative, and C. H. Dodd's *The Authority of the Bible* (London, 1928), a liberal, Protestant view of the place of the Bible in divine revelation. J. K. S. Reid's *The Authority of Scripture* (London and New York, 1958) represents a post-liberal Protestant point of view.

The nonpropositional conception of revelation is expounded in William Temple, *Nature, Man and God* (London, 1934), Ch. 12; Emil Brunner, *Offenbarung und Vernunft* (Zurich, 1941), translated by Olive Wyon as *Revelation and Reason* (London and Philadelphia, 1946); H. R. Niebuhr, *The Meaning of Revelation* (New York, 1941); Karl Barth, "The Christian Understanding of Revelation," in R. G. Smith, ed., *Against the Stream* (New York, 1954); and H. Thielicke, *Offenbarung, Vernunft und Existenz* (Gütersloh, 1936). John Baillie and Hugh Martin, eds., *Revelation* (London, 1937), is a useful symposium.

For a contemporary Jewish discussion, see Abraham Heschel, *God in Search of Man* (New York and London, 1956). For the Islamic conception of revelation, not touched upon in this article, see I. Goldziher, *Die Richtungen der islamischen Koranauslegung* (Leiden, 1920), or A. J. Arberry, *Revelation and Reason in Islam* (New York, 1957); and for Hindu conceptions, K. S. Murty, *Revelation and Reason in Advaita Vedanta* (London, 1961).

For contemporary skepticism concerning revelation, see Julian Huxley, *Religion Without Revelation* (London, 1941; 2d ed., 1957), and Ronald Hepburn, *Christianity and Paradox* (London, 1958).

JOHN HICK

RIBOT, THÉODULE ARMAND (1839–1916), French psychologist, was a professor of psychology at the Sorbonne and from 1889 was the director of the psychological laboratory at the Collège de France. A philosophical disciple of Hippolyte Taine and Herbert Spencer (whose *Principles of Psychology* he translated), Ribot, with Taine, initiated the study in France of a positivistic and physiologically oriented psychology. His interest in philosophy was inseparable from his interest in concrete psychological problems and persisted throughout his life. He founded and edited the *Revue philosophique de la France et de l'étranger,* one of the first French philosophical journals. Ribot influenced not only French positivists and physiological psychologists but even some thinkers who, like Henri Bergson, rejected his epiphenomenalism.

Ribot's work falls into three main periods, but he remained loyal throughout his life to the program expounded in the introduction to his first book, *La Psychologie anglaise contemporaine* (Paris, 1870). He insisted that psychology must be liberated from "the yoke of metaphysics" and stressed the need for an empirical, biological approach to psychology and the limitations of an exclusive reliance on introspection. However, although he insisted on excluding metaphysics from the empirical sciences, he did not dismiss it altogether. The works of Ribot's first period were mainly expository and historical. *La Psychologie anglaise contemporaine* surveyed English associationist psychology from David Hartley to Samuel Bailey. In *La Psychologie allemande contemporaine* (Paris, 1879) he introduced the work of Gustav Fechner, Wilhelm Wundt, Hermann Helmholtz, and others to the French public. *La Philosophie de*

Schopenhauer (Paris, 1874) foreshadowed Ribot's later emphasis on the affective and instinctive basis of personality.

Ribot's second period, characterized by an interest in psychopathology, produced three classic works: *Les Maladies de la mémoire* (Paris, 1881), *Les Maladies de la volonté* (Paris, 1883), and *Les Maladies de la personnalité* (Paris, 1885). Despite a wealth of clinical, empirical material, the underlying motive of these works was philosophical—a positivistic distrust of such reified abstractions as "memory," "will," and "self." These abstractions had played a prominent role in French speculative psychology and in Victor Cousin's eclectic idealism. Ribot showed that the simplicity of such abstract words hides the complexity of the phenomenon named, a complexity revealed by the dissociation found in mental diseases. Ribot was among the first to study dissociations of personality, and his law of regression—that amnesia affects the most recent and least organized impressions and reactions first—was a lasting contribution to psychology.

In Ribot's third period, which began with his *La Psychologie de l'attention* (Paris, 1888), his interest shifted to normal psychological phenomena, particularly to affective phenomena. The major work of this period, *La Psychologie des sentiments* (Paris, 1896), reflects Ribot's biological approach and his epiphenomenalism. Physiological drives underlie our elementary feelings of pleasure and pain, and more complex and evolved stages of these drives underlie more complex emotions. Organic sensibility evolved prior to consciousness, and feelings prior to intellect. Ribot's last work, *La Vie inconsciente et les mouvements* (Paris, 1914), interpreted various manifestations of subconscious activity in terms of motor activity.

Bibliography

Dugas, Laurent, *La Philosophie de Théodule Ribot*. Paris, 1924.
Faguet, Émile, *Propos littéraires*, Fourth Series. 1903.
Krauss, S., *Théodule Ribots Psychologie*. Jena, 1905.
Lamarque, G., *Théodule Ribot: Choix des textes et étude de l'oeuvre*. Paris, 1913.
Taine, Hippolyte, *Derniers Essais de critique et d'histoire*, 6th ed. Paris, 1923.

MILIČ ČAPEK

RICHARD OF MEDIAVILLA, or Richard of Middleton (died c. 1300), *doctor solidus*, was a Franciscan philosopher, theologian, and canon lawyer. Although his date of birth and country of origin are unknown, scholars are generally agreed that he was either French or English. We are certain that in 1283 he was appointed as one of the judges of the works of Peter John Olivi, and we possess three of his sermons, preached in Paris in 1281 and 1283. He was a master of theology in Paris during 1284/1285. In 1288, Richard was one of the tutors of the exiled Prince Louis, son of King Charles II of Sicily and later bishop of Toulouse. Richard's last writings seem to date around 1295, when he completed his commentary on the fourth book of the *Sentences* of Peter Lombard. After 1295 we lose all trace of Richard of Mediavilla.

Richard was scholar in the tradition of Bonaventure and Peckham. He seems to have had a flair for clear and orderly presentation and to have enjoyed wide popularity among his Franciscan confreres. Like many of his fellow Franciscans, he regarded Bishop Tempier's condemnation of 219 propositions in 1277 as definitive. As a result, he set himself to defend, clarify, and organize a philosophy and theology which would vindicate and establish the doctrines contrary to the condemned propositions. He differs from most of his fellow Franciscans, however, in that he is more sympathetic to the Thomistic theory of knowledge.

Richard was one of the first Franciscans to reject the Augustinian theory of divine illumination. For Richard our ideas are solely the result of abstraction from sensible things, though as universals they are strictly intramental. In metaphysics he held that being is predicated analogically, not univocally, of God and creatures. Because every effect somehow bears the trademark of the first cause, God's existence can be proved from the world of nature. Richard found the so-called a priori argument of Anselm unacceptable; he adopted Henry of Ghent's position that essence and existence are only intentionally, not really, distinct. His doctrine of universal hylomorphism—that is, that all creatures are composed of matter and form—coincides with that of Bonaventure. Richard's theory of one substantial form's consisting of multiple grades constitutes the most complete and well-ordered doctrine of the plurality of forms in the Middle Ages. Richard argues to the soul's spirituality from the immateriality of universal concepts. The faculties of intellect and will are not accidents of the soul, nor do they add to its essence; they merely constitute a new relation between the essence of the soul and its acts and objects. Liberty is formally in the will. In common with his Franciscan confreres, Richard asserted that the will is a more noble faculty than the intellect.

Conservative by nature, Richard of Mediavilla was not one to shrink from speaking out. In one remarkable statement we catch a glimpse of his spirit in the search for truth and goodness: "We must start a good war. It is better to fight against falsehood and malice with a certain amount of discord, than, by dissimulating, to give way to malice and falsehood for the sake of harmony" (*Quodlibeta* III, 22).

Works by Richard

Commentarius in Sententias, 4 vols. Brescia, 1591.
Quaestiones Disputatae. Vaticani Latini No. 868. Folios 105–116.
Quodlibeta. Brescia, 1591.

Works on Richard

Hocedez, Edgar, *Richard de Middleton. Sa vie, ses oeuvres, sa doctrine*. Louvain, 1925.
Zavalloni, Roberto, *Richard de Mediavilla et la controverse sur la pluralité des formes*. Louvain, 1951. Has excellent bibliography.

FERDINAND ETZKORN, O.F.M.

RICHARD OF MIDDLETON. See RICHARD OF MEDIAVILLA.

RICHARD OF SAINT VICTOR. See SAINT VICTOR, SCHOOL OF.

RICKERT, HEINRICH (1863–1936), German Neo-Kantian philosopher. Rickert was born in Danzig and received his degree in 1888 from the University of Strasbourg. In 1891 he began lecturing at Freiburg, succeeding

Alois Riehl as professor in 1894. In 1916 he went to Heidelberg as successor to Wilhelm Windelband.

Rickert belonged to the southwestern school of Neo-Kantianism. His main efforts were devoted to a study of the logical and epistemological foundations of the natural sciences and to the historical disciplines in the hope of arriving at a "unity of reality and values." He departed from Wilhelm Dilthey in his criticism of Dilthey's subjective approach to the understanding of historical reality and in his attempt to find a set of more objective criteria; his departure from Windelband consisted in rejecting Windelband's separation of natural and historical disciplines and offering instead a theory that considered all reality to be historical.

Philosophy and natural science. In his early work, particularly in *Der Gegenstand der Erkenntnis* (Freiburg, 1892), Rickert raised the question of the relationship between philosophy and the natural sciences. He denied the universal validity of the method of the natural sciences and attempted to establish the primacy of practical reason as the foundation of his epistemology. He believed that only the Kantian critical method is adequate for explaining the epistemological presuppositions and limitations of the various sciences. While phenomenology may provide a method for describing the contents of consciousness, it fails to account for their intelligibility and relationship to objective reality. Hegelianism, on the other hand, in identifying the real with the rational, leaves out of account or distorts the pluralistic character of reality. Only critical philosophy yields knowledge that is both universal and necessary; it alone can explain the pluralistic, dynamic, and yet rational character of society and history. In view of the lack of philosophical attention to the historical disciplines and because the then prominent philosophical problems of *Weltanschauung* seemed to hinge most directly on distinguishing scientific thinking from historical thinking, Rickert devoted himself thereafter primarily to the problem of historical conceptualization (*Begriffsbildung*).

Individualizing and generalizing thought. On the basis of Windelband's distinction between nomothetic (universal) and ideographic (particular) judgments, Rickert developed his logic of the historical disciplines. At both the scientific and the prescientific stages of conceptualization, he claimed, there are two ways of grasping reality: individualizing and generalizing. Individualizing thought is proper to historical thinking. Instead of fabricating a copy of a historical phenomenon in its complex totality, it establishes the essential relationships that bind the phenomenon to its environment and traces the various stages of its development. Philosophy studies the concept of development, while the objects of historical study are unique developments. Generalizing thought, therefore, is proper to the natural sciences but is inapplicable to history. "Reality," Rickert claimed, "becomes nature if we consider it in regard to what is general; it becomes history if we consider it in regard to the particular or individual" (*Kulturwissenschaft und Naturwissenschaft*, 5th ed., p. 63).

Historical method for Rickert is highly selective, and in the selection of data, value judgments are operative from the very outset. This being the case, the determination of value criteria (*Wertbegriffe*) becomes the primary concern of historical understanding. Generalizing thought is logically free of values (*wertfrei*) because it constructs universally valid concepts. The particular objects to which they apply are interchangeable, and each object, abstracted from all its other relationships, functions only to illustrate the general law. Although in generalizing thought a selective process is at work to determine the common character of a group of particulars, it is the common character, expressed in a formula, that is essential. The aim of generalizing thought is precisely to free its objects from relations of value (*Wertverbindungen*).

"Kulturwissenschaft." Although history is a science of values, this does not mean that the historian may organize his inquiry arbitrarily; in that case history would be mere propaganda. In order for history to be objective, its values (state, law, art, religion) must be universal. The universality of historical values must be established epistemologically, and the relevance of the various social phenomena with respect to these values must be demonstrated empirically. Because history is written by, about, and for civilized men, social activity must be its subject matter. Since social activity can be grasped only by individualizing thought in terms of its significance for universal values, the historian's criterion must be culture, because social activity and value most nearly converge in culture. Culture is most directly concerned with the realization of universal values: "Culture is the common affair in the life of the nations; it is the possession with respect to the values of which the individuals sustain their significance in the recognition of all peoples, and the cultural values which adhere to this possession are therefore those which guide historical representation and conceptual formation in the selection of what is most essential" (*Die Grenzen der naturwissenschaftlichen Begriffsbildung*, 2d ed., p. 509). Thus, believing that his method made of history a logically valid discipline that deals with objective reality, Rickert called the historical sciences *Kulturwissenschaft* (cultural science) in preference to Dilthey's term, *Geisteswissenschaft* (science of the mind or spirit).

Universal history. Far from being a contradiction, universal history is not only possible but is the logical outcome of the search for the value principles (*Wertprinzipien*) according to which the historical process as a whole may be viewed. "The system of values provides the possibility of systematization, and the relationship [of history] to the system of values permits of individualizing treatment" ("Geschichtsphilosophie," p. 400). But precisely because the evaluation of the whole of history is involved, the system of value principles must be purely formal. "We would need something timeless in order to extract an objective sense from the temporal course of history" (*ibid.*, p. 418). Like Kant, Rickert proposed three stages in the development of civilization: dogmatism, skepticism, and criticism, the last of which was the achievement of German idealistic philosophy. While this periodization cannot be verified empirically, it is an example of the critical approach to the question of the unity of historical development. Although it is purely theoretical, it nonetheless gives an axiological grounding to the results of empirical research. In the last analysis, the problem of universal history is to introduce a method whereby the real and the ideal may be theoretically synthesized.

Criticisms. The principal criticism brought against Rickert is that the introduction of a transcendental system of values is unhistorical and leads to the reification of existing values (*Wertabsolutierung*). In isolating universality by viewing it as a distinct realm of thought rather than as a function of all thought, Rickert actually confirmed the positivism and cultural relativism he had sought to overcome. In radically separating the universal from the particular, he was compelled to regard historical data as being identical with those of science, a series of discrete facts that differ only in the relationships in which they are observed. Nevertheless, the fruitfulness of Rickert's theory is borne out by his influence on such contemporaries as Ernst Troeltsch, Friedrich Meinecke, and Max Weber.

Works by Rickert

Die Grenzen der naturwissenschaftlichen Begriffsbildung. Tübingen, 1896–1902; 2d ed., Tübingen, 1913.
Kulturwissenschaft und Naturwissenschaft. Tübingen, 1899; 5th ed., Tübingen, 1921.
Die Probleme der Geschichtsphilosophie. 1905; 3d ed., Heidelberg, 1924.
"Geschichtsphilosophie," in Wilhelm Windelband, ed., *Die Philosophie im Beginn des zwanzigsten Jahrhunderts, Festschrift für Kuno Fischer.* Heidelberg, 1907.
Kant als Philosoph der modernen Kultur. Tübingen, 1924.

Works on Rickert

Becher, E., *Geisteswissenschaften und Naturwissenschaften.* Munich, 1921.
Cohen, M. R., "The Insurgence Against Reason." *Journal of Philosophy,* Vol. 22 (1925), 120–123.
Collingwood, R. G.; Taylor, A. E.; and Schiller, F. C. S., "Are History and Science Different Kinds of Knowledge?" *Mind,* Vol. 31 (1922), 426–466.
Faust, A., *Heinrich Rickert und seine Stellung innerhalb der deutschen Philosophie der Gegenwart.* Tübingen, 1927.
Federici, F., *La filosofia dei valori de Heinrich Rickert.* Florence, 1933.
Gurvitch, Georges, "La Théorie des valeurs de Heinrich Rickert." *Revue Philosophique,* Vol. 124 (1937), 80–85.
Troeltsch, Ernst, "Über den Begriff einer historischen Dialektik. Windelband-Rickert und Hegel." *Historische Zeitschrift,* Vol. 119 (1919), 373–426.

ROBERT ANCHOR

RIEHL, ALOIS (1844–1924), Austrian Neo-Kantian philosopher, was born in Bolzano. Riehl was consecutively *Privatdozent* (1870), extraordinary professor (1877), and professor (1878) at the University of Graz. He moved to the University of Freiburg in 1882, to Kiel in 1895, to Halle in 1898, and to Berlin in 1905.

Riehl's first philosophy was a realistic metaphysics based on Herbart and indirectly on Leibniz, and it is of interest, just as in the case of Kant, to study the relation between Riehl's precritical and critical writings. Between 1870 and 1872 Riehl made his first realistic, monistic, evolutionist decisions within that dogmatic framework. His *Realistische Grundzüge* (Graz, 1870) centered on the problem of sensation, which he originally conceived of as a polycentric reciprocal matrix of consciousness and movement. In *Über Begriff und Form der Philosophie* (Berlin, 1872) he advocated a critical, rational requirement and the scientific character of philosophy, to which he assigned the historical task of leading to ideal ends. In *Moral und Dogma*

(Vienna, 1872) he defended the independence of positive morality from beliefs.

A profound study of Kant freed Riehl from his metaphysical dogmatism. The first volume of his *Der philosophische Kritizismus* (1876) marked an important date in the history of the new Kantianism. This work highlighted the hold on Kant of the spirit of the new positive science (not so much through the influence of Descartes as through that of Locke and Hume). Combating psychological and idealistic "misconceptions" of Kant's views, Riehl proposed that the evolution of Kant's thought be studied, and successive editions of *Der philosophische Kritizismus* benefited from previously unpublished writings of Kant discovered by Kant philologists. Kant, according to Riehl, clarified the method of philosophy; in abandoning metaphysics but not identifying itself with science, philosophy shows itself to be theory of knowledge and the methodology of the natural sciences. It is false, however, to eliminate the thing-in-itself and the presupposition of realism common to the sciences, as Hermann Cohen did. Kant distinguished form from content and sought to determine the formal a priori of nature in general and not the particular laws of nature evident in the real experience of the sciences.

In the second and third volumes of *Der philosophische Kritizismus* (1879 and 1887) Riehl reassessed and amplified his own views. It was not easy: to do so he had to fight with Kant himself (whom Eugen Dühring had blamed for having "two centers of gravity," even reduced to the first *Critique* alone). In Riehl's view, neither dogmatic realism nor idealism, whether phenomenalist, or absolute, or positivistic, was adequate. Riehl sought to bring Kant up to date concerning the "sensible and logical foundation of knowledge" by surveying the great scientific innovations since Kant's day, such as Robert Mayer's principle of the conservation of energy and the Darwinian theory of evolution. Only then could Riehl critically resume his own realistic monism centered on perception. But perception, the first cognition, is not, in Riehl's judgment, the first reality. The two aspects of perception—the mechanical, which can be made objective and is quantitatively determinable by positive science, and the qualitative, which is subjectively immediate and the sole revealer of the real universal reciprocity—are both phenomenon (*Erscheinung*), although not merely appearance (*Schein*); neither of the two aspects makes up "nature in itself." The monistic propensity, leading to the threshold of metaphysics, comes upon reefs which the critique must steer clear of. For example, he desires that his identification of the physical and the psychical should not be confused with materialism, or monadism, or universal psychophysical correspondence, or Spinozistic panpsychism. Again, although Riehl saw mental life as a product of natural evolution, he denied the evolutionary genesis of logical and mathematical concepts.

In 1883, in his inaugural lecture at Freiburg, "Über wissenschaftliche und nichtwissenschaftliche Philosophie," Riehl turned to other fields of philosophy with a progressive valuation (compare a lecture at Princeton, 1913: "Der Beruf der Philosophie in der Gegenwart"). Even in *Der philosophische Kritizismus,* confined to the naturalistic horizon, he had apologized for glancing at "the field of practical philosophy" but had at the end intimated that beyond the realm of science lay the realms of moral action and artistic production (to which he later added religion). It may be asked whether there could be a philosophy of these things if "theoretical" is identical with "scientific" (*wissenschaftliche*). In his later years Riehl struggled with this problem, surrounded too by the other Neo-Kantian movements. "Feeling," which he had acknowledged as another side of experience, might be available for that theoretical purpose, but to be so available its evaluations must be freed from practical empiricism. Heinrich Rickert, who had frequent contact with Riehl, later sought to show Riehl's increasing interest in the world of values, until Riehl finally acknowledged that the role of philosophy is "to raise to conceptual clarity our knowledge of values and their system."

Works by Riehl

Der philosophische Kritizismus, 3 vols. Leipzig, 1876–1887; 2d ed., Leipzig, 1908–1926; 3d ed. Vol. I, Leipzig, 1924.

Friedrich Nietzsche: Der Künstler und der Denker. Stuttgart, 1897.

Zur Einführung in die Philosophie der Gegenwart. Leipzig, 1903.

"Helmholtz in seinem Verhältnis zu Kant." *Kantstudien*, Vol. 9 (1904), 261–285.

"Logik und Erkenntnistheorie." *Kultur der Gegenwart*, Vol. 1 (1907), 73–102.

Philosophische Studien aus vier Jahrzehnten. Leipzig, 1925. Essays.

Works on Riehl

Hofmann, Paul, "Riehls Kritizismus und die Probleme der Gegenwart." *Kantstudien*, Vol. 31 (1926), 330–343.

Jaensch, Erich, "Alois Riehl Der Mann und das Werk." *Kantstudien*, Vol. 30 (1925), III–XXXVI.

Maier, Heinrich, "Alois Riehl." *Kantstudien*, Vol. 31 (1926), 563–579.

Rickert, Heinrich, "Alois Riehl." *Logos*, Vol. 13 (1924–1925), 162–185.

Siegel, Carl, *Alois Riehl: Ein Beitrag zur Geschichte des Neukantianismus. Festschrift der Universität Graz.* Graz, 1932.

Spranger, Eduard, "Alois Riehl." *Forschungen und Fortschritte*, Vol. 20 (June 1944), 129–130.

MARIANO CAMPO
Translated by *Robert M. Connolly*

RIGHTS. Since the seventeenth century, problems connected with rights have steadily engaged the attention of political and legal philosophers. For medieval philosophers the problems of political ethics were problems not of rights but, rather, of the duties a man owed to his lord, his king, his church, or his God, by virtue of his role and function in the universal order. Medieval lawyers, it is true, might challenge encroaching authority by appealing to the ancient and customary privileges or "liberties" appertaining to status or to corporate communities like cities and guilds. In the seventeenth and eighteenth centuries, however, such considerations gave way to notions like "an Englishman's birthright" or, still more personal and universal, "natural rights." Thereafter it was commonly held that it was the proper task of the state and of positive law to safeguard such rights, lists of which were drawn up in documents like the American Bill of Rights and the French

Declaration of the Rights of Man for the guidance and control of governments.

The idea that a man could have a right which, as natural, inalienable, and indefeasible, had some kind of sanctity and validity transcending that of ordinary positive law led philosophers to speculate about what kind of thing a right might be. What sort of assertion is it to say that X has a right to R, and what kind of criteria would have to be satisfied for such a proposition to be true?

Juristic theories of rights. Many philosophers and jurists have treated questions about the nature and criteria of rights as if they asked what facts were referred to when one said "X has a right to R." Spinoza, for instance, tried to give a consistent account, in terms of power, of all instances where rights were ascribed. Thus a man's natural right amounted to the power he could exercise over another; a sovereign's right was the power he exercised by virtue of the combined power of all the individuals who were prepared to support him; and the individual's legal rights were the powers he had by virtue of the sovereign's support in upholding the law. Again, T. H. Green described an individual's right as "a power of acting for . . . what he conceives to be his own good, secured to an individual by the community."

A right, however, is not and does not necessarily imply a power (except, perhaps, in the sense of a legal competence like, for instance, the power to make a will). For a man may have rights he is powerless to enforce if the courts are corrupt or his opponents too powerful to risk offending. One might say perhaps that his rights are hypothetical powers—what he would be able to achieve if he were able and chose to appeal to the courts and if the courts acted according to the law. But this would be the same as saying that his rights are the powers he would enjoy if he had his rights. Rights, in other words, may explain why persons have the powers they do, but they are not identical with these powers.

Legal realists like Jerome Frank, K. N. Llewellyn, or W. W. Cook have maintained that statements ascribing rights really predict what as a matter of fact a court will do or what a man can reasonably expect, given such predictions. However, although it may be of no professional interest to the legal consultant, it is not absurd to say that a man has rights but no expectation of succeeding in court. It would be, for instance, a perfectly intelligible way of complaining of injustice, either in the law or in its administration. As with a power, to decide that a man has a right is under normal conditions to provide a warrant for a prediction and an expectation, but it is not identical with nor a sufficient ground for either of these.

A right is commonly said (by Paul Vinogradoff, for instance) to be a claim upheld by the law. As in the case of "power," however, there is an ambiguity between the positive and the normative sense of "claim." If by a claim were meant a demand actually made, it might be objected both that men possess rights to things they never claim, and that it makes sense to talk of the rights of infants incapable of demanding anything. On the other hand, "to have a claim," as against "to make a claim," means that if one were to make a demand, it would be justified or, at least, defensible. But as with "power," this would then locate the concept not in the language of description but in that of norms. Vinogradoff may well be right in saying that men have acquired legal rights only by claiming them, yet it would be a mistake to confuse a historical fact with an account of the meaning of "rights."

A rather similar confusion underlies the view that a right is an interest protected by the law (Rudolf von Jhering). This view is unsatisfactory whether what is meant by an "interest" is what a man desires or whether it means what it would be to his advantage to have. A man may have rights to what he does not desire. It is not a condition of my having a right to the repayment of a debt, for instance, that I should want it repaid. Equally, however, I may have rights that are not to my advantage. A right to drink myself to death without interference would not be logically absurd. Though, generally speaking, our rights do protect our interests, they are not themselves protected interests.

Rights and duties. Bentham and Austin defined rights in terms of duties. "Every right," says Austin, ". . . rests on a relative duty . . . lying on a party or parties other than the party or parties in whom the right rests" (*Province*, 1954 ed., Footnote p. 285); for Bentham and Austin, a duty exists only where the law imposes (and enforces) a sanction for a breach of it. Bentham wrote in his *Fragment on Government* (1776), "Without the notion of punishment . . . , no notion could we have of either *right or duty*." There are two points here: first, whether duties really depend on consequential sanctions for their meaning or only for their effectiveness, or perhaps for neither; second, whether every right has its correlative duty, such that the right of X can always be stated without alteration of meaning as a duty of Y. As to the first point, there is no internal contradiction in the notion of a duty without a sanction. Indeed, English administrative law has frequently placed statutory duties upon authorities while barring judicial review and providing no alternative remedy or sanction. Outside the sphere of law, it certainly makes sense to talk of moral duties without sanctions. What one ought to do cannot properly be equated with what one must do to avoid a penalty.

The correlation of rights and duties raises more difficult questions. If to ascribe a right is not to attribute a socially supported power or, indeed, to *describe* any actual or hypothetical set of facts about human behavior, can one say that it must be a way of stating the provisions of a system of rules and therefore a way of *prescribing* conduct? Yet a right implies neither what a man must nor what he ought to do, but what he may do if he chooses. It can be reconciled with an exclusively prescriptive conception of law only by identifying every right with an obligation in reverse—"X has a right to \$10 from Y" being exactly equivalent to "Y has a duty to (that is, shall) pay X \$10 if X so chooses."

Since Austin wrote, the concept of a right has been subjected to many patient and subtle analyses. That of Wesley Hohfeld, perhaps the best known, has provided a general framework for later work (Albert Kocourek's, for instance) and has generated a considerable and ingeniously critical literature. Hohfeld distinguished four different concepts of right and identified each with its appropriate "jural correlative." He uses the word "right" specifically for the case in which one says "X has a right (or claim or demand – right, as some writers put it) to \$10 from Y"; this has as its correlative a duty (or one might say, specifically, an obligation of Y to X to do some particular act that X desires him to do). Hohfeld's second concept of right is a "privilege" or a "liberty," the opposite of a duty, and has as its correlative a "no-right." "X has a liberty to do L" entails both that he has no duty to do or not to do L and that Y has no right (that is, no basis of claim) that X shall or shall not do it. Consistent with this, however, is that Y has no duty to refrain from trying to prevent X's doing L. This is the case with two people in legitimate competition. So a no-right is distinct from a duty not to interfere, and correlatively X may possess both a liberty to do L and a right (claim) that Y (and others) should not interfere. The third case Hohfeld distinguishes as a "power," a legal capacity for altering the jural relations of another person, as, for instance, the power to make a will, to transfer ownership by sale, to appoint an agent. The correlative of a power is the "liability" (called by some writers a "subjection" and by Roscoe Pound a "risk") that one's jural relations may be changed, for better or for worse, at the instance of the other person. According to the fourth concept X has an "immunity" (that is, has no liability) when Y is "disabled" from making (has no power to make) changes in X's jural relations.

In this account, the relations that Hohfeld calls correlative are, in fact, identities; a right (claim) is a duty looked at from the standpoint of the other term in the same relationship. However, this does not imply that to every duty there necessarily corresponds a right. What characterizes the right – duty relationship is that Y is obliged to act only because X demands that he should. But there are some duties, such as duties of benevolence, where no one has a corresponding right to demand that they be performed.

A distinction of some importance might be made between first-order relations (that is, claims – duties and privileges – no-rights) and second-order relations (that is, powers – liabilities and immunities – disabilities). Whereas first-order relations can be expressed in terms of prescriptions or the absence of them (permissions), second-order rules and relations define the conditions under which actions shall be legally significant and therefore under which new rules and changes in legal relations can be made. If powers and immunities can be treated as rights at all (and both the power to offer for sale and the immunity of parliamentarians from libel proceedings are commonly referred to as rights), then some rights are neither correlative to sanctioned duties nor expressive of the absence of such duties. Moreover, such rights require a conception of law which is not simply prescriptive and permissive but is also regulative, in the sense that law lays down the conditions under which persons may enter into new binding relations with one another, by contract, marriage, and so on.

Hohfeld believed that although many jural relations could be satisfactorily analyzed only as complex bundles of relations of different types, nevertheless his scheme exhausted all the fundamental types. In fact, however, there are some that do not fit into it very comfortably. What kind of a duty, liability, no-right, or disability would correspond, for instance, to the right to vote? Though it may be possible to break it down into a collection of constituent basic relations, one could do so only at the cost of losing the point of the right, namely, participating in the choosing of a representative.

Because Hohfeld wanted to insist on the differences between natural and legal relations, he sometimes wrote as though there were a world of legal relations alongside the world of natural relations. The Swedish realists Axel Hägerström and Karl Olivecrona, anxious to deny the existence of such a metaphysical world, roundly declared that rights and duties are purely imaginary or fictitious powers or bonds, existing only in men's minds. This, however, is no less misleading than Hohfeld's theory. It is not that rights are illusory things but that they are not things at all or, rather, that accounts of them modeled on accounts of things like chairs, or even relations like proximity or length, are misconceived.

H. L. A. Hart has accordingly argued that it is a mistake to ask for a definition of "a right" (and of such similar words as "duty" and "corporation") because "legal words can only be illustrated by considering the conditions under which statements in which they have their characteristic use are true" ("Definition and Theory in Jurisprudence," p. 60). The expression "a legal right" can be elucidated only by examining the conditions for the truth of a proposition like "X has a legal right to \$10 from Y." These conditions are that (1) there is a legal system in existence, and (2) under the rules of that system some person Y, given the events which have actually happened, is obliged to do or abstain from some action providing X or his agent choose that he should. Under these conditions, the statement "X has a right" is used to draw a conclusion of law in a particular case falling under those rules. This applies, of course, only to a right in the sense correlative to duty. But Hart claims that a similar illustration could be constructed for liberties, powers, and immunities.

Hart's elucidation is limited, however, to particular ascriptions; it throws no direct light, for instance, on the statement in the second amendment to the U.S. constitution that "the right of the people to keep and bear arms shall not be infringed" or on the one in the sixth amendment that "in all criminal prosecutions the accused shall enjoy the right to a speedy and public trial." In both cases, the word "right" is not used to draw a conclusion of law but to state a rule of law.

A general statement of rights differs from a corresponding "conclusion of law" in that a general statement cannot be elucidated in terms of a duty but at best only in terms of an obligation of one class of persons to another, defeasible in particular cases by any of a number of pleas or excuses. A general right is thus a ground of claim, not a license to infer what ought to be done. Nevertheless, A. I. Melden was correct to object to the term "prima facie right," first used by W. D. Ross; for it misleadingly suggests that the genuineness of such rights is in doubt. A right is no less a genuine ground of claim for being rightly overridden in particular instances.

Moral rights and natural rights. The only account a positivist can give of moral rights is in terms of custom or convention. So Bentham and Austin treated moral rights as the correlatives of duties to which sanctions were attached by public opinion (or allegedly by God) rather than by the law. Hegelians like T. H. Green and Bernard Bosanquet have approached the question from a different angle. Morality, they have said, is a developing Idea, manifest in social experience and institutions. It is not simply that whatever public opinion sanctions is moral but that the convictions of a society represent the most advanced stage in the unfolding of a rational morality. Individuals do not make up their own moral convictions; rather, the society's morality forms their moral consciousness. Green admitted that an individual might have a right that was not generally recognized but only if it was a necessary condition for the attainment of some end generally acknowledged as good, to which, therefore, the community was in a sense already committed.

However, reformers very commonly do claim that an underprivileged group has moral rights so far unrecognized. Certainly such a claim is not likely to be politically successful if it cannot be sustained in terms of widely accepted goals or principles. But still, one is not talking nonsense if one says that slaves in ancient Rome had a moral right to freedom even though very few Romans would have understood the claim or acknowledged moral aims that required it. If one accepts the view that a moral claim, judgment, or decision is one that can be supported by some kind of rational argument, then attempts to elucidate "moral rights" in terms of opinion are clearly misplaced.

To ascribe a legal right to a person is, if Hart is right, to reach a conclusion of law, but to ascribe a moral right is not to reach a conclusion about what ought to be done but only to make a relevant claim. Thus A may have a right to gratitude and special consideration from B, whom he has often helped in the past, but B's obligation to A does not mean that his duty in every case is to prefer A's interest to every other. A's right, then, is not a conclusive ground of claim. Indeed, one might want to say on occasion that although A has a right, he would do wrong to press it and that although B has an obligation to A, he would do wrong to let it influence him. A right, in short, is something to be taken into account; it is not a conclusion of moral duty.

There is, however, a long tradition in political philosophy to support the view that there are some rights—natural rights—that all men possess equally and that are in some sense inalienable and indefeasible. According to John Locke, natural rights include the rights to life, liberty, and property. His analysis of these concepts is sketchy, his purpose being to use them as grounds for attacking governmental acts that allegedly infringe them. However, for Locke, as for Hobbes, the natural right to liberty meant at least a liberty to do whatever there was no rule or moral reason against doing.

It is arguable that such a right is in fact a formal principle of procedure in rational and moral argument rather than a right to do anything specific. It places the onus on justifying interference, not on showing why one should be let alone. And this, indeed, is part at least of what is meant by saying that someone is a moral person. For if one denied a man this right, it would be open to others to use him, like their beasts and their tools, for their own purposes and as they chose, without being called upon to show by what right they did so. This would be to acknowledge with Aristotle that some men are slaves by nature. To recognize a man as a moral person is thus to recognize that he has interests and not merely functions and thus to concede at least this minimal right.

The right to freedom couched in this very general form gives no clue, of course, to what might be a good reason for interference. Hart defends, if somewhat tentatively, a more substantial right. To have a moral right, he says, "entails having a moral justification for limiting the freedom of another person and for determining how he should act" ("Are There Any Natural Rights?," p. 183). To have a natural right to freedom entails, first, a liberty to do anything which does not coerce, restrain, or injure another person (for without this limitation the right could not be equal for all). But it also entails a right that everyone else forbear toward oneself in these respects except to prevent one's coercing, restraining, or injuring others. Rights, Hart explains, are claimed mainly in two types of situations: when the claimant has some special justification for interfering himself or when he is resisting someone else's interference. Rights of the first type arise from special transactions or relations—from promises or by special authorization, for instance, or from the relations of persons participating in a common enterprise, each having the right in fairness against the others that as they benefit from his submission to the rules, they shall also submit to them. In Hart's view, the last relation is the moral ground of political obligation and is the element of truth in social contract theories.

General rights, in Hart's view, such as the right to say what one thinks or to worship as one pleases, are really only special exemplifications of the equal right to be free. So to assert a general right is to claim in respect of some particular kind of activity each man's equal right to be free, provided there are no conditions constituting someone else's special right to limit his freedom in that respect. Moreover, Hart maintains that the equal right to freedom is invoked indirectly by every claim to a special right. For my promises and authorizations give others a right to interfere with me not because the purpose of the interference is necessarily good but simply because I have chosen that they may interfere. The limitation on my freedom presupposes my freedom. (This, it might be added, is the core of traditional consent theories of political obligation, for if all men are by nature free and equal, what authority could one man have over another, unless by consent?) Mutual restrictions in a common enterprise also presuppose the equal right to freedom, because only thus can there be fair and equal distribution of restrictions, and therefore of freedoms, among participants.

There is, however, another class of special rights, which Hart mentions but which he does not reconcile with the equal right to freedom—namely, rights arising from special but apparently nonconsensual relations. Locke dealt with the same example of such a right that Hart uses, that of parents to the obedience of their children, by making rationality a condition for the right to freedom and by making the parents' right consensual as soon as children reach the age of reason. It would be more difficult, perhaps, to reconcile with the equal right to freedom the instance suggested by Melden—namely, a parent's right to special favorable consideration from a child—which, it

seems, is neither consensual nor extinguished merely by the child's growing up.

Both Melden and Hart treat ascriptions of moral rights as belonging to a different kind of moral discourse from judgment of what one ought to do. For Hart, to say that every man has an equal and natural right to freedom is not to say that it is never one's duty to restrain another man unless one has his authorization or consent. It is, rather, that on those occasions when a person has such a duty, he does not act as of right, and the person restrained is correspondingly under no obligation to him in particular to submit; he would have as much or as little reason to submit to anyone else whatsoever. So while a man restraining another man from torturing an animal could claim a right to do so only if the man had consented in advance to being restrained by him in particular, he could properly rely, nevertheless, on a general duty to prevent unnecessary cruelty, to override the obligation he owes to the man not to interfere with his freedom. The interference must be justified on its substantial merits, whereas to have a right to act is to have a justification of another kind, irrespective of the moral quality of the act.

If we accept this account, we can also accept the view that at least some natural rights are indefeasible and inalienable. Locke held that it is a man's natural right that his property shall not be interfered with without his consent, but he also held that in an emergency a man's house might be destroyed without his consent to prevent the spread of a fire. According to the Hart–Melden view, this would not be an inconsistency, for the right would remain unimpaired but would be outweighed as a moral consideration by a more urgent duty. So a right becomes a special kind of moral consideration cited to justify restraining or interfering with others or to protest against their interference with oneself; it is different in kind from utilitarian considerations or rules against lying or cruelty, which concern the moral value of the act itself or of its consequences.

Human rights. Hart's account of natural rights deals with those traditionally associated with liberal individualism. Nowadays, however, rights are commonly asserted not only to freedom from interference of various kinds but also to positive benefits (education, a decent standard of living, medical treatment). Rights of this kind are different in that though they appear to make a very definite claim, the correlative duty seems to rest neither on individuals at large (as with freedoms) nor on anyone in particular. To say, as does the 1948 UN Universal Declaration of Human Rights, that "everyone, as a member of society, has the right to social security" (article 22) and "to a standard of living adequate for the health and well-being of himself and his family, including food, clothing, housing" (article 25), is not to say that his government has a duty to provide these things; many who subscribe to this declaration would deny that such services were a government's proper business. Rather, statements of this kind provide, in the words of the Preamble, "a common standard of achievement for all peoples"; that is, they are canons by which social, economic, and political arrangements can be criticized. Human rights, in short, are statements of basic needs or interests. They are politically significant as grounds of protest and justification for reforming policies. They differ from appeals to benevolence and charity in that they invoke ideals like justice and equality. A man with a right has no reason to be grateful to benefactors; he has grounds for grievance when it is denied. The concept presupposes a standard below which it is intolerable that a human being should fall—not just in the way that cruelty to an animal is not to be tolerated but, rather, that human deprivations affront some ideal conception of what a human life ought to be like, a conception of human excellence. It is on the face of it unjust that some men enjoy luxuries while others are short of necessities, and to call some interests luxuries and others necessities is implicitly to place them in an order of priorities as claims. Upsetting that order then demands to be justified. Human rights are the corollary, then, of the equally modern notion of social justice.

Bibliography

RIGHTS IN LAW

Austin, John, *The Province of Jurisprudence Determined.* 1832; London, 1954. The 1954 edition was edited with an introduction by H. L. A. Hart.

Dias, R. W. M., *A Bibliography of Jurisprudence.* London, 1964. Valuable; annotated.

Hägerström, Axel, *Inquiries Into the Nature of Law and Morals,* translated from Swedish by C. D. Broad; Karl Olivecrona, ed. Stockholm, 1953.

Hart, H. L. A., "Definition and Theory in Jurisprudence." *Law Quarterly Review,* Vol. 70 (1954), 37–60.

Hohfeld, Wesley N., *Fundamental Legal Conceptions.* 1919; New Haven and London, 1964. The 1964 edition was edited, with an introduction, by Walter W. Cook. An extensive bibliography of the critical literature on Hohfeld's theories is given in the Dias work cited above.

Jhering, Rudolf von, *Geist des römischen Rechts auf den verschiedenen Stufen seiner Entwicklung,* 3 vols. Leipzig, 1852–1869.

Kocourek, Albert, *Jural Relations,* 2d ed. Indianapolis, Ind., 1928.

Olivecrona, Karl, *Law as Fact.* London, 1939.

Pound, Roscoe, *Jurisprudence.* St. Paul, Minn., 1959. Vol. IV. Includes useful summaries of main juristic theories of rights, with extensive bibliographical references in footnotes.

Ross, Alf, *On Law and Justice.* London, 1958.

Vinogradoff, Paul, "The Foundations of a Theory of Rights," in *Collected Papers.* Oxford, 1928. Vol. II, Ch. 20, pp. 367–380.

MORAL RIGHTS

Benn, S. I., and Peters, R. S., *Social Principles and the Democratic State.* London, 1959. Reissued as *Principles of Political Thought.* New York, 1964.

Bosanquet, Bernard, *Philosophical Theory of the State.* 1899; 4th ed., London, 1923.

Bradley, F. H., *Ethical Studies.* 1876; 2d ed., Oxford, 1927.

Brandt, Richard B., ed., *Social Justice.* Englewood Cliffs, N.J., 1962. Essays by K. E. Boulding, Paul A. Freund, William K. Frankena, Alan Gewirth, Gregory Vlastos.

Green, T. H., *Lectures on the Principles of Political Obligation.* 1882; London, 1941.

Melden, A. I., *Rights and Right Conduct.* Oxford, 1959.

Plamenatz, J., Lamont, W. D., and Acton, H. B., Symposium, "Rights." *PAS,* Supp. Vol. 24 (1950).

Ross, W. D., *The Right and the Good.* Oxford, 1930.

NATURAL RIGHTS

Brown, Stuart M., Jr., "Inalienable Rights." *Philosophical Review,* Vol. 64 (1955), 192–211. One of three articles forming a symposium on natural rights.

Cranston, Maurice William, *What Are Human Rights?* New York, 1963. Preface by Reinhold Niebuhr.

Entrèves, A. P. d', *Natural Law.* London, 1951.

Frankena, William K., "Natural and Inalienable Rights." *Philosophical Review,* Vol. 64 (1955), 212–232.

Hart, H. L. A., "Are There Any Natural Rights?" *Philosophical Review,* Vol. 64 (1955), 175–191.

Hobbes, Thomas, *Leviathan.* 1651; edited with introduction by Michael Oakeshott, Oxford, 1946.

Locke, John, *Two Treatises of Government.* 1690; edited by Peter Laslett, Cambridge, 1960.

Macdonald, M., "Natural Rights," in Peter Laslett, ed., *Philosophy, Politics and Society,* First Series. Oxford, 1956.

Macpherson, C. B., *The Political Theory of Possessive Individualism: Hobbes to Locke.* Oxford, 1962.

Maritain, Jacques, *Les Droits de l'homme et la loi naturelle.* New York, 1942. Translated by Doris C. Anson as *The Rights of Man and Natural Law.* New York, 1943.

Ritchie, David G., *Natural Rights.* London, 1894.

Spinoza, Benedict, *Tractatus Theologico-politicus.* 1670. *Tractatus Politicus.* 1677. Both works translated and edited by A. G. Wernham as *Benedict de Spinoza: The Political Works.* London, 1958.

Strauss, Leo, *Natural Right and History.* Chicago, 1953.

STANLEY I. BENN

RIGNANO, EUGENIO (1870–1931), Italian positivist philosopher, founder (1907) and lifelong editor of the scientific journal *Scientia*. Rignano's first works were sociologically oriented, but he later turned to biology and philosophical biology. His major work, *Psicologia del ragionamento* (1920), places the activity of memory at the basis of all biological and psychic phenomena. Memory is an activity which, through the specific accumulation of concepts, makes possible the progressive adaptation of the organism to the environment, the formation of instincts and emotions, and, in higher organisms, of reasoning. According to Rignano, reasoning is "a series of operations or experiences merely thought out simply"; in other words, a series of operations performed in imagination. The results of these operations are also imagined and are assumed as the conclusions of the reasoning itself. This conception of reasoning, which Rignano derived chiefly from Ernst Mach, was later applied by him to explain the various kinds of reasoning: intuition, reduction, mathematical and mathematico-logical reasoning, intentional reasoning (dialectical or metaphysical reasoning), and pathological forms of reasoning as well. Rignano stressed the distinction between constructive and intentional reasoning. Constructive reasoning is motivated by a desire to discover the truth, and intentional reasoning by a desire to confirm a truth that a person believes he already possesses. Both types of reasoning utilize the same syllogistic form, but constructive reasoning is characteristic of the positivist scientist and intentional reasoning of the metaphysician. Rignano did not distinguish clearly between logical and psychological considerations; rather, he assumed the psychological mechanism as the basis of the logical validity of reasoning processes. The result is that Rignano's account is not very convincing either as logic or as psychology.

Despite his distaste for metaphysics, Rignano in subsequent works elaborated a kind of biological metaphysics based on the hypothesis that at the foundation of life and its evolution there is a "nervous energy" able to mold organic matter and direct it toward an increasing development and a growing adaptation to the environment. According to Rignano, life in its entirety shows a finalistic aspect that would be inexplicable if it were the product of physicochemical forces. This finalism can be explained, however, by assuming that life is a product of psychic, mnemonic energy, which on the basis of past experience envisions ends of future experience and adapts organic material to those ends. It is a kind of vitalism or animism that, according to Rignano, guarantees to evolution a progressive significance. The progress of evolution continues beyond organic life into moral life. The purpose of moral life is to guarantee to all individuals the satisfaction of their needs and to coordinate these needs in harmonious forms that gradually eliminate conflicts.

Works by Rignano

Di un socialismo in accordo con la dottrina economica liberale. Turin, 1901.
La sociologica nel corso di filosofia positiva di Augusto Comte. Palermo, 1904.
Psicologia del ragionamento. Bologna, 1920. Translated by W. A. Holl as *Psychology of Reasoning.* London, 1923.
La vita nel suo aspetto finalistico. Bologna, 1922.
La memoria biologica. Bologna, 1922. Translated by E. W. MacBride as *Biological Memory.* London, 1926.
Che cosa è la vita? Nuovi saggi de sintesi biologica. Bologna, 1926. Translated by N. Mallinson as *The Nature of Life.* London, 1930.
Man Not a Machine. London, 1926.
Problemi della psiche. Bologna, 1928.

NICOLA ABBAGNANO
Translated by *Nicholas Spadaccini*

RILKE, RAINER MARIA (RENÉ) (1875–1926), German poet, was born in Prague, the son of a minor railway official. His mother, who was of upper-middle-class origin, encouraged him in his early ambition to become a poet. The years 1886–1891, which Rilke spent at military academies in Moravia and Austria, had a traumatic effect on him, and not until 1920 was he able to come to terms with his unhappy childhood and family background. His first volume of poetry, *Leben und Lieder*, appeared in Prague in 1895. Desultory studies, mainly in the history of art, at the universities of Prague, Munich, and Berlin were followed by two journeys to Russia in 1899 and 1900 in the company of Lou Andreas-Salomé, a German-Russian to whom Nietzsche had proposed marriage and who later became a follower and friend of Freud. During the second of these journeys he met Tolstoy. On his return Rilke joined an art colony in Worpswede near Bremen, and early in 1901 he married the sculptress Clara Westhoff, one of its members. They had a daughter, but the short-lived marriage was only an interlude in Rilke's essentially solitary and unsettled life. For the next few years, Rilke's attention was centered on Paris and on Rodin, to whose work he devoted a monograph in 1903. Although his job as Rodin's private secretary ended in a quarrel, Rilke never ceased to acknowledge the very direct inspiration he received from close daily contact with the sculptor. The first collection of poems that bears the authentic stamp of greatness, *Neue Gedichte I* (Leipzig, 1907), represents Rilke's aim to render in words the immediacy, concreteness, and intensity ("the inward reality") that he discerned in Rodin's work.

With a single-mindedness that has rarely been paralleled in modern literature, Rilke devoted his whole existence to the poetic task he felt called upon to accomplish, subordinating to it all personal and public considerations. The long list of his patrons, most of whom belonged to the aristocracy of central Europe and a few to the German and Swiss patrician bourgeoisie, testifies to the restlessness of his life, and so do his journeys to Sweden (in 1904, on the invitation of Ellen Key), Italy, north Africa (1910–1911), Spain (1913), and repeatedly to France. The long list of his friends (mainly female) and correspondents, among them Valéry and Gide, includes surprisingly few German writers. Two places were of major importance for the fruition of his poetry: Duino (1910 and 1912), a castle on the Adriatic that belonged to the Princess Marie von Thurn und Taxis-Hohenlohe, where the first Duino Elegy was written, and the little castle of Muzot in the Swiss canton of Valais. It was at Muzot, in February 1922, as the guest of Werner Reinhart, that Rilke, in a storm of inspiration, wrote most of the 55 *Sonette an Orpheus* and several smaller collections of poems; and it was there, above all, that he completed his greatest work, which had been interrupted by World War I—the cycle of ten *Duineser Elegien*, several of which were written in the span of a few days. Rilke died at Valmont, Switzerland, after a protracted and painful illness that was diagnosed as leukemia.

Rilke's mature poetry, written after 1907, displays a consistency of attitude and a coherence of poetic devices that make it representative of a whole era of European thought. Following in the wake of Nietzsche, this poetry is informed by an acute historical consciousness. We live in an age when a "religion" that is based on separating transcendence from immanence is no longer viable:

> . . . All of the living
> Make the mistake of drawing too sharp distinctions.
> Angels (it is said) would be often unable to tell
> Whether they moved among living or dead
>
> (First Elegy)

Our impoverished state is marked by our awareness that "we are not very reliably at home in the interpreted world." Hence, in order to regain for ourselves something that would equal the spiritual and existential fervor that characterized the ages of faith, we must take upon ourselves the task of endowing the world (which, for Rilke, is the world of things and of intimate personal relations) with the inwardness of feeling that other ages directed toward a divinity. Joy, love, and above all suffering and pain should not be diffuse sensations accompanying an unending series of vague hopes and regrets; they must become the objects of a total commitment. Thus, since we are "not yet" strong enough to give ourselves totally in love, we had better follow the example of the lover ("Gaspara Stampa") who drew her strength from an unrequited, "uninterrupted" feeling, or indeed of Narcissus, who used the natural world as a magnifying mirror of his feeling. *Les Saltimbanques*, the traveling *artistes* of Picasso's "blue period" paintings, celebrated in the Fifth Elegy, most fully symbolize our condition. In a world in which all actions are liable to remain uncompleted ("We, though, while we're intent upon one thing, / can feel the cost and conquest of the other"), suffering—the fullest possible realization and appropriation by the self of what is inflicted from without—will be the greater virtue:

Killing merely is a form of our wandering sadness . . .
Pure in the spirit serene
Is what we ourselves endure.

History, for Rilke, is not a social phenomenon but a pageant of situations and persons in whom the ideal of completion and strength of feeling was realized, just as the contemporary world is a series of images that portray our deprivations and stunted responses. To make something of one's fate, of one's experiences, is to give them the permanence (essentially poetic) of a moment of intensity. Similarly, the supreme task, set by the imminence of death, is to repair the adventitiousness of death by drawing it into my life, by making of it "my own death."

The immensity of the task of creating a new spirituality is betrayed by the complex, and quite conscious, ambiguities of Rilke's images of transcendence, chief of which is the image of the Angel, as he appears in the Elegies. He is a messenger (*angelos*) from another sphere; hence, there must be one who sent him. But the Angel comes upon us with a terrible majesty and strength which, to us who are weak, is all his own. In many such astonishing images Rilke expresses the "pure [=necessary] contradiction" that he sees as the root of our being: only by living in total commitment to "the Earth," the here and now, can man transform it into "the heart's inner space," and thus wrest some eventual transition into a "soundless" Beyond—wrest it from he knows not whom. The most accomplished practitioner of such transformations is Orpheus, the poet-maker who, in the creative act, stills all strife by transforming it into song, eternalizes the moment by making of it a monument of inwardness, and transfixes suffering into the eternally valid image of "Lament" (Tenth Elegy).

In a world yearning for the security of faith and finding it in ideology, Rilke's vertiginous images were reduced to prosy precepts for living, becoming thus at once esoteric and banal. Rilke's poetry is not necessarily esoteric, and the creative activity he extolled is closely related to the poetic; but he addressed himself to the single individual. The social sphere of modern life is branded as wholly inauthentic (Rilke either ignored or briefly satirized it); all concerted action is an escape from defective selfhood. He understood and expressed velleities supremely well; his poetry hardly offers a nostrum to cure them.

Works by Rilke

Only the most recent four-volume edition, *Gesammelte Werke*, Ernst Zinn, ed. (Frankfurt, 1955–1961), shows the magnitude of Rilke's work. In addition, some eight collections of his letters are of major importance. The two-volume edition of *Selected Works* (London, 1954–1960) includes J. B. Leishman's brilliant translations of all of Rilke's major poetry.

Works on Rilke

No English biography has appeared since E. M. Butler, *Rainer Maria Rilke* (Cambridge, 1941). H. E. Holthusen, *Rainer Maria Rilke in Selbstzeugnissen und Bilddokumenten* (Hamburg, 1958), is a succinct and discriminating account of the poet's life. See also N. Purtscher-Wydenbruck, *Rilke: Man and Poet* (London, 1949), and E. Buddeberg, *Rainer Maria Rilke—Eine innere Biographie* (Stuttgart, 1955). A brilliant assessment of Nietzsche's influence on Rilke is Chapter 5 of Erich Heller, *The Disinherited Mind* (Cambridge, 1952). E. C. Mason has devoted many studies to a critique of Rilke's work, among them *Lebenshaltung und Symbolik bei R. M. Rilke* (Weimar, 1939) and *Der Zopf des Münchhausen* (Einsiedeln, 1949). Two exegetic works of major importance are Jacob Steiner, *Rilke's Duineser Elegien* (Bern, 1962), and Romano Guardini, *Rilke's Duino Elegies: An Interpretation*, translated by K. G. Knight (London, 1961).

J. P. STERN

RINTELEN, FRITZ-JOACHIM VON, German philosopher of value, was born in Stettin in 1898. He received a doctorate in philosophy in 1924 from the University of Munich, where he began to lecture in 1928. Von Rintelen was appointed professor at the University of Bonn in 1933 and at Munich in 1936, but he was suspended on political grounds in 1941. Since 1947 von Rintelen has been professor of philosophy, psychology, and pedagogy at the University of Mainz. He was a visiting professor at the Universidad Nacional de Córdoba, Argentina, from 1951 to 1952 and at the University of Southern California in 1957.

Von Rintelen has given both a systematic and a detailed historical interpretation of the problem of value. Prior to his dismissal from his professorship at Munich, he had explicated in detail a theory of value (*Wert*) and of meaning (*Sinn*) and had built a philosophical anthropology upon it. Since World War II he has applied this theory to an analysis and penetrating criticism of the irrationalistic, nihilistic, and pessimistic currents in recent European philosophy and literature, showing how the theory resolves the conflicts and paradoxes which he reveals in these currents.

His doctrine of values and of personality is rooted in the realistic tradition of Platonism and Scholasticism but also shows the influence of German idealism. The chief direction of his thought was set in his two academic dissertations, a criticism of the pessimistic philosophy of religion of Eduard von Hartmann and an attempt to extend Ernst Troeltsch's efforts, in the later years of his life, to overcome historical relativism through a theory of values and their operation in history.

Two points in von Rintelen's criticism are particularly salient. The first is his attack upon all dualisms of intellect and will or of mind and life (Max Scheler), all subordination of the rational to a more inclusive irrational, and every combination of an idealistic theory of scientific knowledge with a realism in metaphysics. To these distinctions he opposes an ontological interpretation of value by which these dualistic tensions can be resolved. He rejects von Hartmann's teleology of self-destruction as an ontological impossibility and an aesthetic misreading of the tragedy of our culture; this tragedy cannot be denied, but it implies a transcendent normative meaning to be attained through the reflective transformation of our actions. Thus, there is an inclusive ontological meaning, not attainable through scientific logic but through the value experiences of life, which sustains the human spirit and human life.

Von Rintelen's ontological theory of real value (*Realwert*) was constructed in opposition to psychological, positivistic, and phenomenological definitions. Real value is an objective context of meaning which can be particularized and made concrete through conscious or unconscious strivings. Each actualized value possesses an intrinsic worth varying in intensity with its degree of meaning and a relational worth by virtue of which it enters into a wider order of values. Thus every real value is vertically capable of degrees of normative validity and historically capable of individualization within larger contexts of culture and of personal action. Values are individualized in two spheres corresponding to life and mind in man. In the sphere of nature, objects are primarily existent and only secondarily valued; in that of mind or personality, objects are primarily mental and only secondarily grounded in concrete existence. From this viewpoint human history can be understood as a continually renewed effort to actualize values in terms of a personal regulative ideal of the highest possible fulfillment and in relation to an ultimate *summum bonum,* God, the unique, autonomous, and inclusive real value.

In 1932 von Rintelen published the first volume (ancient and medieval) of a historical study in which the development of this theory of value was to be traced in European thought. This work was left incomplete but was supplemented by specialized historical and systematic articles.

In his later critiques of existentialism and other contemporary intellectual currents, von Rintelen analyzes the plight of man as portrayed in modern philosophy and literature and, by correcting the subjectivism and finitism implicit in this portrayal through his own doctrine of value transcendence, points out the way to "a rewon security of spirit." Outstanding among these works are *Philosophie der Endlichkeit* (1951), which includes analyses of Heidegger, Rilke, Marcel, and Sartre, and *Der Rang des Geistes* (1955), a thorough and distinguished study of Goethe as philosopher, in which the inner tensions or polarities of the poet's thought are examined and Goethe's movement from an eclecticism to a rationally justified theism and an operative human ideal of rational freedom and love is portrayed. In these books von Rintelen shows himself not merely as a constructive philosopher but also as an able critic of literature and culture.

Von Rintelen's thought may thus be considered as a reconstruction of the Christian intellectual tradition in which the inevitable tragedy that inheres in the polarities of human existence may be overcome through a transcendent order of values in which meaning and impulse are harmonized.

Bibliography

Works by von Rintelen are *Pessimistische Religionsphilosophie der Gegenwart: Untersuchung zur religionsphilosophischen Problemstellung bei Eduard von Hartmann und ihre erkenntnistheoretischmetaphysischen Grundlagen* (Munich, 1924); "Der Versuch einer Überwindung des Historismus bei Ernst Troeltsch," in *Vierteljahresschrift für Literaturwissenschaft und Geistesgeschichte,* Vol. 8 (1930), 324–372; *Der Wertgedanke in der europäischen Geistesentwicklung,* Part I, *Altertum und Mittelalter* (Halle, 1932); *Dämonie des Willens* (Wiesbaden, 1948); *Von Dionysos zu Appollon. Der Aufstieg im Geiste* (Wiesbaden, 1948): *Philosophie der Endlichkeit als Spiegel der Gegenwart* (Meisenheim am Glan, 1951), partly translated by Hilda Graf as *Beyond Existentialism* (London, 1963); and *Der Rang des Geistes. Goethes Weltverständnis* (Tübingen, 1955).

For further bibliography and evaluation, see Richard Wisser, "Wertwirklichkeit und Sinnverständnis. Gedanken zur Philosophie von Fritz-Joachim von Rintelen," in Richard Wisser, ed., *Sinn und Sein: Ein philosophisches Symposion F. J. v. Rintelen gewidmet* (Tübingen, 1960), pp. 611–708.

L. E. LOEMKER

RITSCHL, ALBRECHT BENJAMIN (1822–1889), German theologian, was born in Berlin and studied theology at Bonn, Halle, Heidelberg, and Tübingen. He taught theology at Bonn from 1846 to 1864, and at Göttingen for the remainder of his career. Ritschl re-examined Christianity in the light of Neo-Kantianism and historicist principles. After 1875 his influence was widespread in a number of German universities and led to increased interest in religious psychology, comparative religion, and related fields. However, his school came under sharp criticism from orthodox, Pietist, and liberal quarters.

Ritschl undertook to establish Christian theology as an autonomous and systematic discipline. To do this he had first to purge German religious thought of Pietism, Hegelian speculative theism, and the pantheism of Schleiermacher and then to apply the techniques and results of contemporary literary and historical criticism. On the basis of Kant's ascription of priority to practical reason over theoretical reason and his separation of philosophy and religion, Ritschl distinguished between value judgments and theoretical judgments. Unlike Kant, however, Ritschl accorded primacy to religion over philosophy on the grounds that spirit (the noumenal) takes precedence over matter (the phenomenal); also unlike Kant, he accorded moral primacy to the community (the nation) over the individual.

Ritschl believed that the deep-rootedness and continuity of religion, as expressed in dogmas and institutions, testifies to the reality and superiority of the religious need of practical reason in human nature. This need arises out of a basic contradiction between nature and spirit in human nature. The value of religion and particularly of Christianity, Ritschl thought, can be verified by history, which shows that this contradiction seeks a resolution in some form of redemption in the world. The Kantian elements in Ritschl's thinking, in combination with this positivist tendency, led him to believe that history does not merely provide material in support of some arbitrary, nonhistorical preconception but reveals an essential structure of human consciousness and the intrinsic historicity of Christianity.

In attempting to satisfy both the requirements of history and the claims of practical reason, Ritschl adopted the dogmas of redemption and the kingdom of God as embodied in the life of Christ as the pivots of his religious theory. Man seeks to realize his destiny here on earth by leading an ethically self-conscious life, which is the core of religiosity. The acts of love that he performs, the content of the ethical life, represent the human counterpart to redemption, and the community required for their performance represents the terrestrial counterpart to the kingdom of God. God's purpose is thus manifest in history.

Sin, which is only the result of ignorance, is pardonable because it is only a transitory opposition to this purpose. Ritschl therefore rejected the dogma of original sin as unhistorical and hence unverifiable.

Biblical exegesis led Ritschl to believe that the community is both logically and chronologically prior to the church. Only in the community can man find justification and reconciliation in God. Christ was founder of a community and can be comprehended historically only through our knowledge of how that community conceived him.

From his conviction that religious consciousness is universal and characterized by its quest for redemption, Ritschl concluded that Christianity is the superior expression of that consciousness. History, rather than dogma, verifies Christianity, but its validity is thereby strengthened, not relativized.

Although the community takes precedence over the individual, the individual is not thereby depreciated but is provided with a field within which he is able to realize his personality. While the community is prior to the church, this does not devalue the church's interests but emphasizes its actual efficacy as the ecclesiastical form of the community's organization. Religious truths are established in practice rather than by their appearance in the New Testament, but its authority is thereby strengthened, not subverted. Luther is the most significant religious figure since Christ, not because he modernized Christianity but because he recaptured and restored an understanding of the original Christian attitude.

Works by Ritschl

Die christliche Lehre von der Rechtfertigung und Versöhnung, 3 vols. Bonn, 1870–1874. Vols. I and III translated (Vol. I by J. S. Black, Vol. III by H. R. Mackintosh and A. B. Macauley) as *Critical History of the Christian Doctrine of Justification and Reconciliation.* Edinburgh and New York, 1872–1900.
Geschichte des Pietismus, 3 vols. Bonn, 1880–1886.
Theologie und Metaphysik. Bonn, 1881.

Works on Ritschl

Barth, Karl, *Die protestantische Theologie im 19. Jahrhundert.* Zurich, 1947. Translated by B. Cozens as *Protestant Thought: From Rousseau to Ritschl.* New York, 1959. Pp. 390–399.
Ecke, G., *Die theologische Schule Albrecht Ritschls.* Berlin, 1897–1904.
Flügel, O., *Ritschls philosophische Ansichten.* Langensalza, 1886; 3d ed., 1895.
Garvie, Alfred E., "Ritschlianism," in James Hastings, ed., *Encyclopedia of Religion and Ethics.* Edinburgh and New York, 1919. Vol. X, pp. 812–820.
Häring, Theodor, *Zu Ritschls Versöhnungslehre.* Zurich, 1888.
Mackintosh, R., *Albrecht Ritschl and His School.* London, 1915.
Ritschl, Otto, *Albrecht Ritschls Leben,* 2 vols. Freiburg and Leipzig, 1892–1896.
Schoen, H., *Les Origines historiques de la théologie de Ritschl.* Paris, 1893.
Weber, W., *Die Frage der Rechtfertigung in der Theologie Albrecht Ritschls.* Heidelberg, 1940. Dissertation.
Wendland, J., *Albrecht Ritschl und seine Schüler.* Berlin, 1899.

ROBERT ANCHOR

ROBINET, JEAN-BAPTISTE-RENÉ   (1735–1820),

French littérateur and speculative philosopher. Robinet was born in Rennes. He started to become a Jesuit, but with-

drew from the order and went to Holland to devote himself to letters. There he published his principal work, *De la Nature* (4 vols., Amsterdam, 1761–1768), and in 1768, *Considérations philosophiques de la gradation naturelle des formes de l'être, ou les Essais de la nature qui apprend à faire l'homme* (2 vols., Amsterdam and Paris). He eked out an existence by hack work, translating English novels and giving English lessons. He became embroiled with Voltaire by selling the manuscript of *Lettres secrètes* for publication without Voltaire's permission. He went to Paris in 1778 when he was made royal censor and secretary to one of the king's ministers. During the Revolution he returned to Rennes, where he lived quietly. In addition to many minor pieces, he published a translation of Hume (*Essais de morale, ou Recherches sur les principes de la morale,* 1760) and edited a vast compilation, *Dictionnaire universel des sciences morale, économique, politique et diplomatique* (London, 1777–1783, 30 vols. in quarto).

De la Nature caused some stir because of its strange ideas. When it was attributed to François-Vincent Toussaint, Diderot, and Helvétius, Robinet admitted his authorship in a letter to the *Journal des savants.* The many quotations in *De la Nature* testify to its author's vast readings; his thinking, however, is original. It is characterized by a curious mélange of mysticism and scientific spirit. *De la Nature* touches on many subjects, but its announced theme is a modern version of Manichaeanism: there is an equilibrium of good and evil in all substances and their modes. Robinet's purpose is to exculpate God and establish the necessity of evil. Embracing Spinoza's principle that all possibles exist, he attacks Leibniz by asserting that, therefore, there can be only one world and that God had no choice in the matter. "God no more had the power to modify the nature of the world than his own nature."

Robinet argued that behind the apparently random distribution of pleasure and suffering in the world there lies a fluid but fixed order. "The physical economy is such that good and evil are engendered with equal fecundity. They flow naturally from the depth of essences." God can in no way remove evil, for omnipotence does not extend to impossibles or contradictions. The suppression of evil implies contradiction, for good without evil would be infinite. The total quantity of good and evil is at every moment equal. Thus the harmony of the world is always the same, and progress is a myth or an illusion. Despite this equilibrium, God is good and his justice is seen in his not having favored one species at the expense of the others; for man is not king of the universe, as Buffon had claimed, and nothing has been created especially for his use. For human beings, life is a balance of happiness and unhappiness, and they should therefore console themselves by the enjoyment of pleasures. Moderation is the best path in all areas of life. The lower classes must be kept in ignorance, for their own benefit and that of the state; slavery is justifiable. Human nature being what it is, equality and fraternity are impossible.

The universe, for Robinet, is animate. All forms of being, including planets and stars, have the power of reproduction. The individual is unimportant, an instrument nature uses for its procreative purposes; only the species endures. Robinet speculates that nature has developed variations on a single prototype; from stones to men, there is a natural gradation of beings. The "prototype" is "a germ which tends naturally to develop itself. . . . Its energy cannot be repressed. . . . The germ develops, then, and each degree of development gives a variation of the prototype, a new combination of the original plan." The only difference between stone, plant, and animal is "the measure in which they participate in that essence. . . . A stone, an oak, a horse are not men; but they can be regarded as more or less rough types in their relation to a single primitive design. . . ." We must consider the succession of individuals "as so many steps of being [advancing] toward humanity."

Robinet draws close to an evolutionary hypothesis in his concept of nature as experimenting and as developing toward greater complexity; he also considers all species as related. It is not a true evolutionism, however, inasmuch as each trial in the ascending scale of complexity is made *de novo* from the relatively unorganized stage of the original prototype. Species do not themselves have a history but are fixed once they are spewed forth. Robinet also pictures a biological struggle for existence and a natural balance, but does not relate these to transformism.

Robinet's work influenced both Herder and Hegel and is considered of interest in the Soviet Union.

Bibliography

Damiron, M., *Mémoires pour servir à l'histoire de la philosophie au XVIIIᵉ siècle*. Paris, 1858. Vol. II.

Rosso, C., *Moralisti del bonheur*. Turin. 1954.

L. G. CROCKER

ROCHEFOUCAULD, DUC FRANÇOIS DE LA.
See La Rochefoucauld, Duc François de.

ROHAULT, JACQUES (1620–1672), Cartesian experimental physicist, was Claude Clerselier's Cartesian disciple and Pierre-Sylvain Régis's teacher. His *Traité de physique* (Paris, 1671) was a standard text for nearly fifty years. Samuel Clarke, rather than writing a Newtonian physics, translated Rohault's work and added Newtonian footnotes (Latin, 1697; English, 1723).

Rohault presents typical nonoccasionalist Cartesianism based on eight self-evident axioms:

(1) Nothing (that which has no existence) has no properties.

(2) Something cannot possibly be made of nothing, that is, nothing cannot become something.

(3) No thing or substance can be annihilated, that is, be reduced to nothing.

(4) Every effect presupposes some cause.

(5) If we do not cause an effect, it necessarily depends upon another cause.

(6) Everything endeavors to continue in the state in which it is.

(7) Every alteration is made by some external cause.

(8) Every alteration is proportional to the force of the causal agent.

Certain propositions follow logically from these axioms, but Rohault says that such truths of reason have application only if there are existents. First known is the self, whose existence Rohault proves syllogistically:

(*a*) From principle (1) above, whatever has properties is something.

(*b*) Thinking is a property.

(*c*) Whatever thinks, therefore, exists (is something).

(*d*) I think.

(*e*) Therefore, I exist.

Reasoning with these principles about ideas and sensations proves the existence of God and of matter. The essence of mind is thought, and of matter, extension. Rohault states that these substances are completely different but that God so created the human soul that motions caused by material impressions in the body to which it is united give rise in the soul to sensations and some ideas. Neither sensations nor ideas resemble material things. It is simply the nature of sensations to give knowledge of the existence of material things; the nature of some ideas is to give knowledge of the place, situation, distance, magnitude, figure, number, and motion or rest of material things.

Rohault's method in physics is to reason mathematically about experiments before conducting them. His goal is to explain the sensible effects of material things. For this only the primary material properties of size, figure, motion, and arrangement of divisible, impenetrable particles in a plenum are needed; occult qualities are unnecessary.

In the *Entretiens de philosophie* (Paris, 1671), the companion volume to the *Traité*, Rohault explains in mechanical terms Cartesian opinions on animal machines and transubstantiation. Animal behavior, he claims, can be explained if animals are completely material; human behavior, however, requires a rational soul that is immaterial, hence indivisible, hence immortal. Transubstantiation is the point-by-point replacement of bread and wine by Christ's flesh and blood. For Cartesians, sensible qualities in material things are merely powers (determined by particle size, figure, motion, and arrangement) to cause sensations in the mind. Therefore, flesh that occupies the place (is bound by the surfaces) formerly occupied by bread would cause sensations exactly like those that the bread had formerly caused. Consequently, real accidents unsupported by substance are unnecessary. Further physical explanations and assurances that Cartesian principles do not contradict Catholic doctrine occur in the *Oeuvres posthumes de Rohault* (Paris, 1682). Rohault disclaimed metaphysics and said that, accepting the miracle, even his discussion of transubstantiation was only a solution to a problem in physics.

Bibliography

Balz, A. G. A., *Cartesian Studies*. New York, 1951.

Bouillier, F., *Histoire de la philosophie cartésienne*. Paris, 1854.

Damiron, J. P., *Essai sur l'histoire de la philosophie en France au XVIIᵉ siècle*. Paris, 1846.

Mouy, P., *Le Développement de la physique cartésienne 1646–1712*. Paris, 1934.

Watson, R. A., *The Downfall of Cartesianism, 1673–1712*. The Hague, 1966.

RICHARD A. WATSON

ROMAGNOSI, GIAN DOMENICO (1761–1835), was born in Salsomaggiore, near Parma, and studied at the Collegio Alberoni in Piacenza. Through the teaching of Giovanni Antonio Comi, a follower of Leibniz and Wolff,

Romagnosi became acquainted with the doctrines of Condillac and with the writings of Bonnet, which had a decisive influence on him. After his graduation in 1786, he conceived his best-known work, *Genesi del diritto penale* ("Genesis of Penal Law," completed in 1789 and published in Pavia in 1791), in which he claimed that the fundamental right to punish belongs to society. Society alone, and not the individual, can mete out "that amount of evil that is necessary to preserve the well-being of our fellow men" and can oppose the "criminal impulse" with a "moral counterimpulse."

Named mayor of Trent in 1791, Romagnosi remained in that office for ten years, during the period of the French Revolution and the rise of Napoleon. During this time he published, among other works, his *Cosa è l'eguaglianza* ("What Is Equality?," Trent, 1792) and *Cosa è libertà* ("What Is Freedom?," Trent, 1793). After a brilliant political career under the Napoleonic government, he became professor of natural and public law at Parma (1802), but after the restoration he was dismissed from his position and was arrested. The Austrian government also prevented him from accepting a post at the Ionian University at Corfu offered to him by Frederick North, Lord Guilford. Regarded as a master by Italian patriots, Romagnosi died, after a sad but active old age, in Milan. His major works, in addition to the *Genesi*, are considered to be the *Introduzione allo studio del diritto pubblico universale* ("Introduction to the Study of Universal Public Law," Parma, 1805), the *Assunto primo della scienza del diritto naturale* ("A First Thesis on the Science of Natural Law," Milan, 1820), and a series of essays on *incivilimento* (civilizing, or the process of civilization) in 1832.

Although he was influenced by the Enlightenment, Romagnosi remained attached to the historicism of Giambattista Vico and followed a "positive" method of research, advocating the activity of the human spirit rather than sensationalism and substituting for the abstractness of the isolated human individual the concreteness of the nation as the subject of the historical action. In epistemology he refused to reduce all cognitions to "transformed sensations," but at the same time he denied that intelligence is independent of sensitivity: in reality, "discernment" is already present in "feeling." The mind acts by means of its own "rational signs." These cannot be regarded as pre-existing ideas but, rather, as manifestations of mental activity, which, along with the sensory datum, gives form to experience. On the other hand, the correspondence of our prior judgments with the actual signs of things, that is, with experience, constitutes the criterion of the truth of our knowledge, which is sought and found pragmatically.

Romagnosi's civil philosophy is the most interesting part of his work: man is real only in a historically determined society—the "collective person of the society"—which is in a state of constant civilizing progress and whose characteristic traits, elements, and laws Romagnosi sought to define. Romagnosi's doctrine of *incivilimento* constituted a philosophy of history faithful to the concrete development of real events, in contrast with that of Hegel, which Romagnosi opposed as "ultrametaphysical." Society develops through the synthesis of national character (tradition) with stimulation—spontaneous, free, and renewing—according to a law of convenience, with all parts of the nation tending toward an equilibrium of force and utility through the balance of interests and powers. This dialectic of civilization is a work of art, even the highest work of art of a humanity striving for perfection.

Bibliography

Editions of Romagnosi's works are *Opere*, 19 vols. in 24 (Florence, 1832–1837), and *Opere*, 8 vols. in 16 (Milan, 1841–1848; actually 1841–1852), both edited by Alessandro de Giorgi; *Opere scelte*, 3 vols. (Rome, 1936–1937); and *Opere di G. D. Romagnosi, C. Cattaneo, G. Ferrari*, Enrico Sestan, ed. (Milan and Naples, 1957).

Works on Romagnosi are L. G. Confalerione, *G. D. Romagnosi. Notizie storiche e biografiche. Bibliografia e documenti* (Carate Brianza, 1928); Achille Norsa, *Il pensiero filosofico di G. D. Romagnosi* (Milan, 1930); G. A. Belloni, *Romagnosi, profilo storico* (Milan, 1935); E. di Carlo, *Bibliografia Romagnosiana* (Palermo, 1936); Francesco Orestano, *Giandomenico Romagnosi* (Rome, 1935); Giacomo Perticone, *La filosofia "civile" di G. D. Romagnosi* (Florence, 1935); Alessandro Levi, *Romagnosi* (Rome, 1935); Lorenzo Caboara, *La filosofia politica di Romagnosi* (Rome, 1936); and Loris Ricci Garotti, "G. D. Romagnosi nella critica recente," in *Società*, Vol. 14 (1959), 109–140.

EUGENIO GARIN
Translated by *Robert M. Connolly*

ROMANES, GEORGE JOHN (1848–1894), British biologist, comparative psychologist, and student of natural theology. He was born in Kingston, Ontario, but that same year his family inherited a considerable fortune and moved to London. Romanes graduated from Cambridge University in 1870, having taken the natural science tripos after abandoning an early plan to enter the church. His ample private means enabled him to work independently at scientific research, first in physiology and later in comparative psychology. Charles Darwin, with whom he formed a close friendship, encouraged him to apply the doctrine of natural selection to the evolution of mind. This resulted in the publication of *Animal Intelligence* (1881), *Mental Evolution in Animals* (1883), and *Mental Evolution in Man* (1888). As a biologist Romanes was a stanch defender of Darwin's theory, expounding it with characteristic lucidity in *The Scientific Evidences of Organic Evolution* (1882) and extending it in *Darwin and After Darwin* (1893–1897). Like most Victorian intellectuals Romanes was deeply concerned with religion. A *Candid Examination of Theism*, which he published under the pseudonym "Physicus" in 1878, was mainly destructive. After extensive soul searching, however, he later gravitated toward an orthodox point of view. This change is evident in the notes brought out after his death under the title *Thoughts on Religion* (1895).

Romanes' defense of Darwin was mounted not against opponents of evolution but against those whom he called Neo-Darwinians, chiefly A. R. Wallace and August Weismann. They sought to interpret natural selection as the sole causal factor in organic evolution, whereas Darwin had emphatically stated that it was the main, though not the only, factor. Hence, *The Origin of Species* made room for the operation of the Lamarckian factor of use inheritance, whereas the Neo-Darwinians excluded it on a priori grounds. Romanes held that this exclusion in the name of pure Darwinism was unwarranted. Whether there is a transmission of acquired characters can be decided only on empirical grounds, and no conclusive evidence had thus far been produced to lead to the rejection of Lamarckian factors *in toto*. On the contrary, Darwin was right in holding that they "have probably played an important part in the process of evolution as a whole."

The interplay of natural selection and Lamarckian factors is well illustrated, according to Romanes, in the evolution of mind. There is more than an analogy between what happens at the level of organic inheritance according to Lamarck's theory and "the transmission of the effects of culture from generation to generation" at the level of civilized man, for when man invented writing, he produced a vehicle that made possible the "intellectual transmission of acquired experience" and thereby radically altered the rate of his own evolution. Moreover, "in this unique department of purely intellectual transmission, a kind of non-physical natural selection is perpetually taking place among ideas, methods, and so forth, in what may be termed a psychological environment." Romanes undertook to show that a continuity exists between the human and the animal mind. However much they differ in degree, they do not differ in kind—that is, "in origin."

When Romanes wrote *Mental Evolution in Man*, he sought to trace the genesis of all the human faculties except those of morality and religion, which were to be taken up in a subsequent work. But this work was never written. Romanes gradually came to doubt whether man's "religious instincts" could be given a naturalistic explanation. Since religious instincts have arisen in the evolutionary process, must they not point to the reality of some object "towards which the religious side of this animal's nature is directed"? Thus, Romanes' youthful rationalism and skepticism were replaced by a hesitant espousal of theism based on the promptings of emotion and feeling.

Romanes was not a creative scientist or thinker. His major contribution, apart from some original research on the nervous systems of jellyfish, starfish, and sea urchins, stemmed from an ability to discuss competing theories and arguments with clarity, fairness, and accuracy. This ability is evident in his pioneer work on comparative psychology but diminishes when he deals with quasi-metaphysical and theological issues.

Works by Romanes

A Candid Examination of Theism. London, 1878.
Animal Intelligence. London, 1881.
Scientific Evidences of Organic Evolution. London, 1882.
The Mental Evolution in Animals. London, 1883.
Mental Evolution in Man. London, 1888.
Darwin and After Darwin, 3 vols. London, 1893–1897.
An Examination of Weismannism. London, 1893.
Thoughts on Religion. London, 1895.

Works on Romanes

Boring, E. G., *A History of Experimental Psychology*. New York, 1929. Pp. 549 ff.
Romanes, E., *Life and Letters of G. J. Romanes*. London, 1896.
Wallace, A. R., *Darwinism*. London, 1889.
Warden, C. J.; Jenkins, T. N.; and Warner, L. H., *Comparative Psychology*. New York, 1935. Vol. I.

T. A. GOUDGE

ROMAN PHILOSOPHY. See CICERO, MARCUS TULLIUS; LUCRETIUS; MARCUS AURELIUS ANTONINUS; SENECA, LUCIUS ANNAEUS; STOICISM.

ROMANTICISM and "romantic" are protean words, the despair of a rigorous semanticist. They designate a generally accepted period, especially in literature and the arts, of Western cultural history, roughly from the late eighteenth to the mid-nineteenth century. They embrace a cluster or syndrome of ideas about the true, the good, the beautiful, philosophical ideas both in the popular and in the technical sense, ideas endlessly debated in the last few centuries. Although the behavioral scientists groping to establish a rigorous classification of human personality generally eschew the word, "romantic" remains in common use to describe a temperament or personality often, perhaps usually, held to be a constitutional element of an individual and at least in part independent of cultural fashion. In all these senses "romanticism" and "romantic" cover a multitude of particulars which in a given combination can appear very different, if not mutually incompatible. Hence so good a historian of ideas as Arthur Lovejoy urges the use of the plural, *romanticisms*, and can write of the "Chinese origins of *a* romanticism"; and W. T. Jones insists that romanticism can only be understood as a very complex syndrome of "biases" in the direction of what he calls the dynamic, the disordered, the continuous, the soft-focused, the inner, the this-worldly.

THE ROMANTIC TEMPERAMENT

Sensitive, emotional, preferring color to form, the exotic to the familiar, eager for novelty, for adventure, above all for the vicarious adventure of fantasy, reveling in disorder and uncertainty, insistent on the uniqueness of the individual to the point of making a virtue of eccentricity, the typical Romantic will hold that he cannot be typical, for the very concept of "typical" suggests the work of the pigeonholing intellect he scorns. Though his contempt for this world of reason and common-sense calculation may push him toward otherworldliness, the Romantic is too much a man of words and sensations to make a good mystic. He may admire the mystic, especially the exotic mystic from the East, but he himself is a good Westerner. In fact, the difficulties of reconciling the often contradictory particulars of romanticism in respectable generalization come out in any attempt to isolate a romantic personality. William Blake has most of the marks of the Romantic, from the positive one of extreme transcendental yearning to the almost universal romantic negative one of contempt for the "meddling intellect"; yet in his quite otherworldly drawings his symbolic, mystical figures are delineated with a draftsmanship of classical solidity and of firm this-worldliness. There is nothing fuzzy, nothing Turner-like, in Blake's art. William James has the full romantic love for the struggling, the unestablished, the untried; but he cannot be accused of what he himself called "tender-mindedness," of idealistic distrust of the instrument of thought. Nietzsche, who used "romantic" as a term of reproach, who said of Wagner's music that it sweats, and called Mme. de Staël "that prolific ink-yielding cow," shared all the romantic hatreds for the shopkeeper's world of grubbing common sense and above all had the Romantic's desire for *etwas mehr*, the something more of Shelley's "desire of the moth for the star."

However difficult the romantic personality may be to isolate in analysis, it can be recognized all through Western cultural history, and indeed in the active life of enterprise and politics. Euripides and Catullus were surely Romantics. The *Odi et amo* (I hate and I love) of Catullus is a classic assertion of romantic ambivalence; the *rumoresque senum severiorum/omnes unius aestimemus assis* (Let us regard all the gossip of censorious old men as not worth one penny) is a fine assertion of one of the minor marks of romanticism, contempt for the Philistine decencies of the old in spirit. Villon and Rabelais were Romantics, even though they were Frenchmen who, as Frenchmen, so nineteenth-century English and German romanticists thought, should have been incapable of transcending the petty ways of *mesure* and *la raison raisonnante*. In our own day, the romantic temperament crops up everywhere—in artists and poets of course, but also in philosophers. Bergson was a Romantic. But so too, it may be argued, was Whitehead; and there are scientists not untouched by the desire of the moth for the star. In active life, Alexander the Great and Napoleon were Romantics; Frederick the Great and Bismarck were classicists.

There are then, in our Western civilization, presumably always born romanticists and born classicists—or born Dionysians and born Apollonians, to use an expressive dualism especially popular with the Germans from Lessing through Nietzsche to Spengler. (The Germans usually classify themselves as the great Dionysian force in the West.) We can but guess at the distribution of these two types in a general population. Probably the well-defined or extreme temperaments are limited in numbers always; most human beings can adapt to the fashion of their age. In one age, say Vergilian and Horatian Rome, or the France of Louis XIV, the Apollonian is dominant, the Dionysian subdued, even silent. Sometimes in Apollonian ages, however, the Dionysian is the rebel, the man out of tune with his times; Vico, perhaps, should be so listed in the Apollonian early eighteenth century. In another age, and notably in the Romantic Age here considered, the Dionysian is dominant and the Apollonian repressed, sometimes tempted, as was the quite unecstatic J. S. Mill, to romantic depths of understanding.

ROMANTICISM AND THE ENLIGHTENMENT

One type can be dominant, but not in sole and exclusive possession. To the cultural historian, the early and mid-eighteenth century and the early nineteenth can stand for two great antithetical styles or fashions: the first, classical or enlightened; the second, romantic. The years from about 1770 to the first decade of the nineteenth century are obviously years of transition. In a graph, the rising lines of Romanticism cross the descending lines of classicism somewhere in the 1770s in Germany (with the heyday of "Sturm und Drang"), 1798 in England (with the publication of the *Lyrical Ballads*), and 1820 in France (with the publication of *Méditations* by Lamartine). But even after

the triumph of Romanticism as a cultural fashion, individuals and groups continued to display the tastes and attitudes associated with the classicism and rationalism of the eighteenth-century Enlightenment. J. S. Mill tells us in his autobiography that he was influenced by the lyricism and even the transcendentalism of the Lake poets, notably Coleridge; but the influence seems not to have weaned him away from the fundamentals of Benthamite thought. In France the thought of men like Saint-Simon, Louis Blanc, Comte, though some of the externals of romantic fashion are visible among them, is, on the whole, along with that of the French Left generally, true to the traditions of the *philosophes*. Even in Germany, a philosopher like Feuerbach asserts the unromantic doctrines of materialism; and Marxism itself, though it shows romantic marks—the concept of the dialectic, derived of course from Hegel, is essentially romantic in its insistence on change as an overcoming of contradictions—is nonetheless committed to an optimistic and very eighteenth-century stand on the rational organization of man and society.

The romantic generation was indeed very conscious of breaking sharply with its parents and grandparents. Few breaks between cultural generations in the West have been more vigorously asserted than this one. The romantic youth absorbed in the depths of Wordsworth's *Prelude*, or Chateaubriand's *Génie du Christianisme*, or Goethe's *Faust* felt nothing but contempt for the abstract ideas and the confined tastes of his shallow Voltairean grandfather. To a surprising extent, the fashionable Romantic was—or claimed to be—in all things the opposite of the Enlightened. Yet our own generation can hardly avoid holding that the romantic rebellion against its parent was in itself a proof of the filial relation between Romanticism and Enlightenment. Not only were the ideas of men like Rousseau, Vico, Lessing, and even Diderot, all of whom lived at the height of the Enlightenment, seminal to all later Romanticism, but both Enlightenment and Romanticism shared much—a belief in process, change, if not actually progress, a belief in the possibilities of manipulating the environment, indeed a fundamental and very modern relativism never really transcended in the search for eternal verities. Both, whatever their metaphysical position on the problem of determinism, in practice displayed a firm conviction that things not only change, but that they can be changed by human effort. Of many specific doctrines —primitivism, for instance, or individualism in ethics and politics—it is hard to decide whether they are more characteristic of enlightened or of romantic thought.

SOME SPECIFIC ROMANTICISMS: ART AND LETTERS

The romantic touch is extremely visible in all the arts, from painting through architecture to interior decoration. Bright colors, or soft and fuzzy ones; exotic themes, Oriental scenes; crowded and action-filled historical paintings—concretely, almost any canvas by Delacroix—set romantic painting off from the sculptured Roman figures of David. And yet, to point up the coexistence of the romantic and the classic throughout the period, the sharp outlines, the measured realism—the Romantic would hold, the conventionality—of the portraits by Ingres, who survived until 1867, outdo David's in classic firmness. The great romantic style in architecture was the Neo-Gothic, itself a manifestation of the romantic rehabilitation of everything medieval that had been held in contempt by the Renaissance and Enlightenment. Yet Neo-Gothic was never a dominant style, not even in the Nordic lands; moreover, it soon fell into a most unmedieval and unromantic regularity and repetitiveness of detail. But Romanticism did rescue from the neglect in which they had long been left the great medieval cathedrals. In the decorative arts romantic tastes were extremely eclectic, fond of the exotic, addicted to rich dark woods and, in the climax of the Victorian drawing room, to a clutter of display wholly dependent on the existence of inexpensive domestic labor. In music, the romantic at its extreme went in for program music, birdcalls and thunderstorms, vast orchestras, and appropriate dissonances. The difference between the music of Haydn or Mozart and that of Berlioz or Wagner, like that between the painting of David and that of Delacroix, is obvious to the most untutored.

Poetry, the novel, and history are the great romantic literary genres, and in all of them the romantic syndrome is readily recognized. Although Goethe was a complex personality who was frequently in conflict with contemporary representatives of the romantic movement, his *Faust* is in itself a masterly summary of romantic themes: revolt against the dullness, the narrowness of rationalism ("gray dear friend is all theory, green only life's eternal tree"); striving for *etwas mehr,* for the infinite (the essential theme of Faust's bargain with Mephistopheles); contempt for the Philistine, the literal-minded ordinary man (the walk with Wagner); primitivism (Gretchen's innocence); ambivalence ("Two souls, alas, live in my breast"); and much else, right on to the final *chorus mysticus* of Part II. Indeed, this last is a fine touchstone; anyone who finds it nonsense or at least unpalatable is definitely not Romantic:

> Alles Vergängliche
> Ist nur ein Gleichnis;
> Das Unzulängliche
> Hier wird's Ereignis;
> Das Unbeschreibliche
> Hier ist's getan;
> Das Ewig-Weibliche
> Zieht uns hinan.

The three English Lake poets, Wordsworth, Coleridge, and Southey, together pretty well cover the romantic range; and Wordsworth's "The Tables Turned" ("One impulse from a vernal wood," "We murder to dissect," "Enough of science and of art;/Close up those barren leaves") states the central position of the romantic *Weltanschauung* almost as neatly as Goethe's *Gefühl ist alles.* One more figure, one more complex of themes, is needed to round out our concept of romantic poetry: this is the unhappy, misunderstood, heroic Promethean figure, half Shelley and all Byron. In terms of sheer educated fashion, Byron and his whole train of European congeners (imitators would be an unfair word here)—de Musset, de Vigny, Leopardi, Espronceda, Lermontov, and the rest—may stand for the romantic poet.

Forerunners of the romantic novel are clear in the eighteenth-century "Gothic" novel, such as those of Mrs. Ann Radcliffe (so charmingly satirized by the nonromantic Jane Austen in *Northanger Abbey*); in the sentimental novel, such as Rousseau's *Nouvelle Héloïse;* and in the psychological novel of disturbed and disturbing love, such as Choderlos de Laclos's *Liaisons dangereuses* and the novels of the Marquis de Sade. The psychological novel reaches its best in the work of Stendhal, whose heroes foreshadow a long line of adventurers of soul and body, a line by no means extinct today. Yet in terms of the wider public of romantic fashion, Walter Scott's Waverley novels were the great success of their day. They carried their audience back into a simpler, more varied, more interesting past than the present of the Industrial Revolution. They exemplified that other inheritance from the German side of the Enlightenment, the theme, best marked in Herder, of organic historic growth of a folk spirit, a folk character, a product of time, not a product of the planning, present-bound intellect. One lost one's self in Sir Walter's pages, became one with one's own best past. We are a long way from Bolingbroke's definition of history as "philosophy teaching by examples."

HISTORY AND POLITICAL THOUGHT

The writing of serious history received a great impetus from the romantic movement, and in particular from Scott's work. Thierry, Michelet, the Heidelberg school in Germany; in England Hallam, indeed Macaulay, by no means a Romantic in temperament; and in the United States the great New England school of W. H. Prescott, J. L. Motley, and Francis Parkman wrote history for a wide reading public, history with narrative force and movement, history with a message of patriotism, of identification with a folk, yet also history carefully reconstructed by painstaking research. The historian and the critic of art and literature insisted on one of the great romantic themes: continuity, the continuity of life and flow, growth, development; a process, to the Romantic, always denatured, indeed destroyed, by the dividing analytical mind ("We murder to dissect").

The complexities and difficulties of generalizing about Romanticism come out most clearly, perhaps, in the field of political thought. You can, of course, always construct a pair of Procrustean beds: a conservative bed for the Romantics; a liberal, progressive, or radical bed for the Enlightened. Burke and Scott can be squeezed into the first, Paine, Godwin, Jefferson into the second. But the trouble is that you can quite plausibly switch the beds, putting the Romantics into the liberal or progressive bed, the Enlightened into the conservative bed. Shelley, Byron, Benjamin Constant can go into the first; Voltaire (surely no democrat), John Adams, the *idéologues* who rallied to Napoleon can go into the second. But Victor Hugo would have to be divided, his younger self put into the conservative, his older self into the liberal bed.

Critics have indeed tried to fix Romanticism on one side or the other in politics, and—given their premises—not without some success. Probably in the balance Romanticism has worked toward the growth of modern democracy, toward a belief in progress and toward "liberty, equality, fraternity," toward the open society—toward much, in fact, that gets its start from the rationalists of the Enlightenment. Yet the Burkean belief in human fallibility, human blindness of passion, and in tradition-enshrined institutional dikes to restrain these anarchic thrusts (dikes not to be tampered with by the intellect), as well as belief in the folk, in an organic society not the product of planning, is surely also congruous with much of Romanticism. So too is the anti-intellectual strain that comes out much later in theories of racism, elitism, *Blut und Boden*, in Nazism and Fascism.

PHILOSOPHY

Romanticism is more than a fashion in arts and letters, more than an approach to political problems: it is a philosophy, or better, a set of philosophies loosely tied together if only by their common rejection of eighteenth-century rationalism, of refusal to line up, shall we say, on the Locke–Hume axis. Schopenhauer is the arch Romantic, the extreme Romantic, among formal philosophers. The world of phenomena, of sense perception, is to him unreal; the will that moves the universe is real enough, but certainly is not rationally knowable by those it moves; this will is blind, shapeless, evil; life, merely phenomenal though it is, is still for us all painful, wearisome, a long unhappy voyage (note the metaphors of movement); Schopenhauer seems at times to hold that a nirvana of surcease is perhaps attainable; at any rate, this life is hopeless.

Romantic pessimism is not, however, the central theme of philosophy in these years. Hegel, at bottom an optimist, is much more central. In a sense, the great romantic philosophers, most of them Germans, go back to Kant, who always thought of himself as firmly enlightened, and whose brief *Was ist Aufklärung?* is one of the landmarks of the century of prose and reason. The romantic seedling in Kant, however, is his distinction between the noumenal and the phenomenal, and his resolution of the dualism by what amounts to intuition or faith. Fichte and Schleiermacher and the rest developed this essentially romantic reliance on a "faculty" transcending common calculating logic. Hegel accepted, and gave his own turn to, this very old dualism of spirit–matter, real–unreal, and sought to bring them together by his famous and influential concept of the dialectic of thesis–antithesis–synthesis. The dialectic in all its forms displays a most nineteenth-century and romantic general bias toward historicism, process, development—but such a process seen teleologically as an end, a purpose. For Schopenhauer, there was no end save extinction. But for Hegel there was an end, a vague one, a Germanic eternal peace in which change somehow turns out to be, in the workings of the World-Spirit, the real form of permanence.

These philosophers, trained and subtle professionals whom we have no doubt traduced in this brief account, are less definitely to be associated with Romanticism as a broad cultural movement than the popularizers, the essayists, the preachers. To many devotees of Carlyle, Emerson, Ruskin, and to those who listened to bumblers like Bronson Alcott, romantic philosophy became fashionable transcendentalism, an agreeable summary of the less difficult

phases of romantic thought—contempt for the rationalist side of the eighteenth century (indeed, blindness to the existence of any other side of that century), exaltation of intuition, spirit, sensibility, imagination, faith, the unmeasurable, the infinite, the wordless—or at least, only the noblest sounding words. This sort of Romanticism was indeed a solace and an escape, an escape from the difficult and unlovely works that science, technology, and industry were building. But it is by no means the whole of Romanticism, which as a spiritual spur to precisely the kind of invention, adventure, and enterprise, to the preoccupation with change and growth, that was building the new world of the nineteenth century, must be seen as having played, and as continuing to play, an essential part, along with the rational and scientific inheritance from the eighteenth-century Enlightenment, in building our own world of today.

Bibliography

Romanticism is not only a complex cluster of ideas; it is one that arouses strong feelings among critics and historians, and that has had its ups and downs in the estimation of the various cultural generations since the late eighteenth century. The following should set the reader on his way through these thickets of critical and philosophical discussion of Romanticism.

Howard Hugo, ed., *The Romantic Reader* (New York, 1957), is an admirable anthology with a good bibliography of works in English and a useful prologue, "What the Romantics Said About Romanticism." W. T. Jones, *The Romantic Syndrome* (The Hague, 1961), presents a very suggestive analysis, helpful for all study of the history of ideas. Jacques Barzun, *Classic, Romantic and Modern* (Garden City, New York, 1961), contains the ablest defense of Romanticism; see the section "Romantic—A Sampling of Modern Usage" (pp. 155–168). G. A. Borgese, "Romanticism," *Encyclopaedia of the Social Sciences* (New York, 1934), Vol. XIII (VII), a remarkably rich brief account, with full bibliographies up to 1934 in all Western tongues, is sympathetic. Irving Babbitt, *Rousseau and Romanticism* (Boston, 1919; also in paperback), is still the sharpest attack on Romanticism. A. O. Lovejoy, *Essays in the History of Ideas* (Baltimore, 1948), contains several pertinent essays, especially one entitled "On the Discrimination of Romanticisms." Sir Maurice Bowra, *The Romantic Imagination* (Cambridge, Mass., 1949), is a graceful essay by a distinguished English scholar and critic. Walter Jackson Bate, *From Classic to Romantic* (Cambridge, Mass., 1946), is one of the best studies of the complex interweaving of classic and romantic in English literature. Ricarda Huch, *Blüthezeit der Romantik*, 12th ed. (Leipzig, 1922), and *Ausbreitung und Verfall der Romantik*, 10th ed. (Leipzig, 1922), are sympathetic and graceful accounts of the German Romantics. Pierre Lasserre, *Le Romantisme français* (Paris, 1907), is an unsympathetic account of the French Romantics.

CRANE BRINTON

ROMERO, FRANCISCO (1891–1962), Argentine philosopher of transcendence, was born in Seville, Spain, but moved to Argentina as a child. After military and literary careers he turned to philosophy, joining the faculty of the University of Buenos Aires in 1928 and of La Plata in 1929. He renounced his academic posts in 1946 in protest against the government of Juan Perón but resumed them in 1955. Because of his conceptual discipline, scope, originality of thought, and limpid clarity of style, Romero is considered one of the ablest and most satisfying of Latin American philosophers.

The idea of transcendence dominates and unifies Romero's metaphysics and theories of knowledge and values. Transcendence implies at least the diversity achieved by passing beyond a given condition or limit and suggests a universal impetus or agency of such passage, an agency that may be purposive. Opposed to transcendence is immanence, which implies identity and containment within, or return to, a limit. Of the two major forms of transcendence, one is that relation of parts to each other in a structural whole by which novel characteristics emerge that were only latent in the parts considered separately. The other form of transcendence is change and, in particular, evolution in the creative and vitalistic sense of Henri Bergson. Its immanent reduction occurs in the mechanistic evolutionary views of Charles Darwin and Herbert Spencer.

Romero identified reason with immanence; experience, in a broad sense, is related to transcendence. Reason may be either intuitive or discursive. In either case it demands identity and transparency. Identity is found in homogeneity and in permanence; it leads reason to the mechanistic conception of atoms that are similar in kind, endure in time, and are governed by causal laws that presuppose the identification of effects with their causes. Transparency, or clarity, is found in forms emptied of content and in the space in which atoms move and with which they tend to be identified.

Reason is formal only and has no avenue of its own to reality and concrete fact. It is not identical with intelligence, which may criticize it. Where reason fails, experience succeeds. Experience supplies a datum by which knowing must be guided. The objects of experience are not sense data and perceptual objects alone, but also essences and values. In addition, Romero held open the possibility of a metaphysical experience of something ultimate and noumenal but subject to connection with ordinary experience and its phenomenal objects.

Romero divided phenomena into four strata, of which each level is a ground for the next and has greater scope for transcendence than the preceding level. The physical level, that of space and moving atoms, is most pervaded with immanence, but the shift in physical theory from the rigid corpuscle to the *foco activísimo* means a greater emphasis on the role of transcendence even on this level. The vital level is characterized by true duration, a factor of transcendence. The psychical level involves consciousness, which intends, or transcends toward, an object, but there is a countering immanence in the egocentric tendency of the human individual to absorb the object into his own forms and needs. On the spiritual level, the human person, rising above his egocentric needs and attaining a universal subjectivity, contemplates the object disinterestedly in the sphere of knowing and conducts himself altruistically and with regard to general principles in the sphere of action. On the spiritual level transcendence becomes absolute. The person is transcendence incarnate and unqualified. Each level contains and is supported by transcendence, but each is unique and irreducible.

Romero, proceeding cautiously and with an air of hypothesis, proposed that Schopenhauer and Bergson were not wrong in positing a metaphysical datum, but that they misconstrued it. Schopenhauer's will and Bergson's vital impulse are forms of transcendence, which is a more general and basic being than either. Romero did not try to sketch the nature of this being, but he appears to have thought of it as a universal impulse at work in every level of phenomenal transcendence, an impetus that is the essence of reality, the source of value, and possibly the spirit's point of flower, which this being intended from the beginning.

Works by Romero

Lógica. Buenos Aires, 1938. Written with E. Pucciarelli.
Filosofía de la persona. Buenos Aires, 1944.
Papeles para una filosofía. Buenos Aires, 1945.
Teoría del hombre. Buenos Aires, 1952. Translated by W. F. Cooper as *Theory of Man.* Berkeley and Los Angeles, 1965.
Historia de la filosofía moderna. Mexico City, 1959.

ARTHUR BERNDTSON

RORETZ, KARL, Austrian epistemologist, philosopher of culture, and aesthetician. He was born at Schloss Breiteneich in 1881 and studied law, and later philosophy, at the University of Vienna, receiving his doctorate in 1906 with the dissertation "The Problem of Empathy in Modern Aesthetics." In 1922 Roretz became a *Privatdozent* at the university and taught history of modern philosophy until 1938, when he ceased lecturing after the Nazi takeover of Austria. He resumed lecturing in 1945 and continued until his retirement in 1951.

As an epistemologist, Roretz espoused a "critical positivism," a philosophy whose foundation is both scientific and, in Kant's sense, criticist. The outstanding features of his thought are critical reflection, skeptical rationality, intellectual honesty, and independence of mind. He rejected dogmatism and unsupported metaphysical speculation. Like Hans Vaihinger, he regarded metaphysical concepts as self-contradictory fictions. Thus, Roretz held, metaphysics lacks any purely logical meaning.

Roretz' major work, *An den Quellen unseres Denkens* (Vienna, 1937), contains his most acute epistemological analyses. In this monograph he studied "vital concepts," concepts in whose formation an element of will or an element of value plays a decisive part and whose definition is therefore preceded by a decision. Among such concepts are those of art, of ethics, of popular education, and of the slave trade.

Roretz' elegant and penetrating psychological analyses of culture and his critical analyses of values deserve particular consideration. The decline of spiritual values, he contended, is due to internal degeneration or disintegration within the person and the society, and only seldom to external pressure. He also studied the genesis and structure of mass psychological phenomena ("mass illnesses," *Massenerkrankungen*) in religion, politics, economics, art, fashion, and sports—notably such extremely dangerous religious and other spiritual "epidemics" as belief in vampires and devils, witch-hunting, and racial persecution.

As a philosopher of culture, Roretz felt most akin to Nietzsche. Like Nietzsche, he believed in life with a deep conviction. But Roretz' view of life was Kantian, and the meaning of life for him consisted in working at the problems life poses. He advocated a philosophy that interpreted reality from an aesthetic point of view. Such a philosophy, he held, provides an orientation toward life and the world that is biologically optimal. The world appears, in this view, as a drama without metaphysical supramundane or transmundane galleries to which it must play. Roretz professed a deep joy in the variegated splendor of the world. "The meaning of the world," he wrote, "is an aesthetic meaning."

In his studies of what he called intellectual–aesthetic values—aesthetic effects bound up with specific achievements of thought, as in mathematics, strategy, or chess— Roretz made important contributions to aesthetics itself.

His interest in ethical problems was equally great. A convinced humanist and democrat, he supported the Ethical Culture movement and strove for a secular ethics independent of any metaphysical or religious assumptions.

Bibliography

Additional works by Roretz include *Zur Analyse von Kants Philosophie des Organischen* (Vienna, 1922); *Religiöse Epidemien* (Munich, 1925); and *Die Metaphysik—eine Fiktion* (Vienna, 1927).

Also see Franz Austeda, *Dem österreichischen Philosophen K. Roretz zum achtzigsten Geburtstag* (Vienna, 1961), which contains a complete bibliography.

FRANZ AUSTEDA
Translated by *Albert E. Blumberg*

ROSCELIN is commonly regarded as the founder of early medieval nominalism, the first, says the eleventh-century historian Otto of Freising, who set up the *sententia vocum*. Roscelin was born about 1045, probably at Compiègne. He studied there and at Rheims and taught there and at Besançon. He enters history in 1090 against St. Anselm in the Trinitarian debates, which combine an acuteness of argument, an introduction of personalities, a tangle of issues, and a poverty of terms. His contribution may be construed as follows: If individuals are the only real things and species are but words, then theological language, which compares the one divine "nature" to the three persons as substance to properties or even to individuating accidents, would mean that the Incarnation involved God's substance and therefore all three persons; alternatively, would it not be better to speak of them as three distinct things? Roscelin's critics pushed the implications of his dialectic into the theological conclusion of tritheism, yet after a grilling from the Council of Soissons, 1092, he seems to have explained himself, and his teaching career suffered no setback, a fact which witnesses alike to his own irrepressibility and the vitality of the secular schools. He traveled to England, possibly to Rome, and seems to have taught at Loches—he was probably Abelard's *Magister Roz*—and at Tours. He found ecclesiastical preferment and made enemies wherever he went. There is no record of his living after 1120, and John of Salisbury speaks of his teaching having been hooted off and disappearing with him.

What this teaching was cannot be exactly determined. Except for a letter addressed to Abelard, none of his certainly authentic writings remains, and we have to rely on opponents: St. Anselm, who took dialectic in his stride but objected to its elevation as a judge in theology; Abelard, who dismissed pure verbalism as of little account and sought the significant content in universal terms; and John of Salisbury, a man of the school of Chartres and a humanist who thought dialectic without other disciplines was blood-

less and sterile. It is certain that Roscelin attacked the dominant realism of traditional teaching, *doctrina antiqua*, which read genera and species as existing *in re*, not merely in speech (*in voce*), and that he was one of the *moderni* to whom all things were individual. He is credited with saying that a universal was but a *flatus vocis*, a breathing of a word. This, however, is an echo of Priscian, and it is unlikely that Roscelin meant a mere sound effect; in those days no master of standing would have treated a word as a phonetic event without relation to an abstract concept. We have no evidence that Roscelin knew, as did St. Anselm, Aristotle's distinction between first and second substance; it may well have been that his argument stopped short at the simple contrast offered by Porphyry and Boethius between substantial things (*subsistentia*) and mere concepts (*nuda intellecta*) and did not open out into an epistemology. That his influence was not slight seems borne out by the fact that the report of his teaching caused St. Anselm to redraft his *Epistola de Incarnatione*.

Bibliography

Picavet, F., *Roscelin philosophe et théologien d'après la legende et d'après l'histoire*. Paris, 1911.

Reiners, J., *Der Nominalismus in der Frühscholastik*, in the series Beiträge zur Geschichte der Philosophie des Mittelalters, Vol. VIII, No. 5, Münster, 1910.

Wulf, Maurice de, *Histoire de la philosophie médiévale*, 5th ed. Louvain, 1924. Vol. I, pp. 93–107.

THOMAS GILBY, O.P.

ROSENKRANZ, JOHANN KARL FRIEDRICH (1805–1879), German Hegelian philosopher. Rosenkranz was born in Magdeburg. He entered the University of Berlin in 1824. Although he was to become Hegel's most devoted disciple, Rosenkranz was first drawn to Schleiermacher; he heard only an occasional lecture by Hegel and was unimpressed. He began reading Hegel as a student at Halle in 1826 and the following year came under the influence of Karl Daub (1765–1836), a Hegelian theologian at Heidelberg. As a *Privatdozent* and extraordinary professor at Halle, Rosenkranz participated actively in the Hegelian circle there. Called to Berlin, he struck up a friendship with Hegel and joined his birthday celebration a few weeks before Hegel died of cholera in 1831. Rosenkranz himself was stricken almost fatally with the disease, reflecting, as he later reported, that this was carrying discipleship entirely too far. In 1833 he succeeded Herbart as professor of philosophy at the University of Königsberg, where he remained until his death except for a brief political career in Berlin during the revolutionary crisis of 1848/1849.

Rosenkranz wrote over forty substantial works, on systematic philosophy, aesthetics, theology, logic, psychology, literary history, pedagogics, philosophical history and biography, and political and social theory. He also composed poetry and contributed articles on current issues to the newspapers.

Rosenkranz defended the Hegelian system as the authentic expression of the German spirit and the fulfillment of German philosophy. He attacked the "one-sidedness" of the Hegelian left-wing and denied that there was any irreconcilable conflict between Hegel and other major German thinkers, such as Schleiermacher and Kant. Other Hegelians charged that Rosenkranz had interpreted Hegel in a Kantian way, maintaining the duality between thought and being and between the ideal and the actual. Certainly in his view the ideal was always in tension with existing conditions, although it constituted their *telos* and guiding norm. In practice, for example, he held that the church should be independent of the state; because Christianity embodies the highest ideal, the church must be free to hold before the culture its most ideal possibilities. He argued on similar grounds for the freedom of the university from political control.

Underlying religious, political, and intellectual life alike, however, was the *Volksgeist* ("spirit of a people"), interpreted more romantically than in Hegel. It is not the result of the cultural process but the distinctive psychic root of a particular people that gives the people unity as a nation and seeks expression in a total cultural life. A people is free to the extent that it fully embodies this spirit; genuine "public opinion" is the self-understanding of a free people. As a consequence, although Rosenkranz gave mankind precedence over the nation in principle and affirmed the Kantian vision of universal peace, he opposed the supranationalism of the left-wing Hegelians; moreover, he regarded their revolutionary aims as empty abstractions, without relevance to "realities" or to the concrete aspirations of any people, and productive only of despotism. He advocated German unification, under a constitutional monarchy and through Prussian initiative, but only under a constitution which would express the German spirit. Although he vigorously opposed revolutionary change in the Prussian form of government, he just as vigorously, and at personal risk, attacked the repressive policies of its administration. For example, he defended the freedom of the press as the organ of "public opinion"; the local press, in turn, hailed him as "the most popular and liberal man in Königsberg."

Works by Rosenkranz

Encyklopädie der theologischen Wissenschaften. Halle, 1831.
Kritik der Schleiermacherschen Glaubenslehre. Königsberg, 1836.
Psychologie. Königsberg, 1837.
Studien, 5 vols. Berlin and Leipzig, 1839–1848.
Kritische Erläuterungen des Hegelschen Systems. Leipzig, 1840.
Geschichte der Kantischen Philosophie. Leipzig, 1840. Vol. XII of Kant's *Werke,* edited by Rosenkranz and Schubert.
Schelling. Danzig, 1843.
G. W. F. Hegels Leben. Berlin, 1844. Supplement to Hegel's *Werken.*
System der Wissenschaft: Ein philosophisches Enchiridion. Königsberg, 1850.
Aesthetik des Hässlichen. Königsberg, 1853.
Wissenschaft der logischen Idee, 2 vols. Königsberg, 1858–1859.
Hegel als deutscher Nationalphilosoph. Leipzig, 1870.
Neue Studien, 4 vols. Leipzig, 1875–1878.
Politische Briefe und Aufsätze 1848–1856, Paul Herre, ed. Leipzig, 1919.
Die Hegelsche Rechte, Hermann Lübbe, ed. Stuttgart and Bad Cannstatt, 1962. Contains several essays, mostly political, and complete bibliography.

Works on Rosenkranz

Esau, Lotte, *Karl Rosenkranz als Politiker.* Halle, 1935.
Jonas, Richard, *Karl Rosenkranz.* Stuttgart, 1906.
Metzke, Erwin, *Karl Rosenkranz und Hegel.* Leipzig, 1929.

STEPHEN D. CRITES

ROSENZWEIG, FRANZ (1886–1929), religious existentialist, was born in Cassel, Germany. From 1905 to 1912 he studied natural sciences, modern history (under Friedrich Meinecke), and philosophy (under Heinrich Rickert) at the universities of Göttingen, Munich, Freiburg, and Berlin. At Berlin he earned a doctor of philosophy degree in 1912 with a dissertation on Hegel's political doctrines; later, he expanded this study. In the fall of 1913, after a spiritual crisis, he turned to religious, especially Judaic, philosophy. In 1918–1919 he wrote *Der Stern der Erlösung* ("The Star of Redemption"), a three-part religio-philosophical system; in 1920 he founded the Freies Jüdisches Lehrhaus (Independent House of Judaic Studies) in Frankfurt. Two years later he was appointed lecturer for Jewish religious philosophy and ethics at the University of Frankfurt, but the onset of progressive paralysis prevented him from accepting the appointment. Despite his affliction, he continued his scholarly work until his death in Frankfurt.

Hegel und der Staat ("Hegel and the State"), completed in 1914, for which Rosenzweig used both published and unpublished materials, analyzes the development of Hegel's concept of the state and its place in the philosopher's system. For Rosenzweig, the reasons motivating the successive changes in Hegel's political theories are to be found in the philosopher's intellectual progression.

In "Das älteste Systemprogramm des deutschen Idealismus" ("The Earliest Systematic Program of German Idealism," written in 1914), Rosenzweig established that young Schelling was the author of a treatise preserved in Hegel's handwriting. This treatise is Schelling's sole attempt at formulating a unified system, a feat most perfectly realized by Hegel.

Rosenzweig's own philosophy may be defined as religious existentialism. The "Star of Redemption" begins with a critique of the Western philosophic tradition and, especially, of Hegel. Rosenzweig rejected as contrary to experience the attempt to reduce to one basic essence the three elements of reality: God, the world, and man.

In German idealism it is human consciousness and thought from which both God and world are deduced. In addition, consciousness is understood as "consciousness in general," which reduces to insignificance the individual being and his separate consciousness. But thought, Rosenzweig argued, is only one of the components of existence; it does not precede existence. The significance of the individual man stems from his being alive; he is more than a part of nature or the world. In this affirmation of the concrete person in his particularity Rosenzweig resumed the anti-Hegelian revolt of Schopenhauer, Feuerbach, Kierkegaard, and Nietzsche, with its concern for the individual. The experience (*Erfahrung*) of the thinker, intent upon the value and significance of things, must guide him in confronting existence. Experience offers knowledge of God, the world, and man.

Under the influence of the later Schelling, and, to a certain degree, of Hermann Cohen, Rosenzweig links his theory of experience with a theory of conceptual construction; this linkage helps him to discover the interrelationship and interaction of the elements of God, world, and man. By way of an intricate logical construct he arrives at the following statement of relationships in terminology borrowed from theology: creation denotes the action of God upon the world; revelation, the encounter of God and man; and redemption, the relation of man to the world.

In pagan imagery God, the world, and man are separated and independent of each other. The hero of Greek tragedy is isolated from men and alien to the gods; the plastic cosmos is unrelated to man and the gods, who, in turn, have no concern for the world or man. Only Biblical religion teaches the interaction of the elements of reality; in this concept, added to what he calls experience, lie the roots of Rosenzweig's existentialism. According to this view, creation is the process through which God, hitherto hidden in the mythical beyond, appears to give the world reality. But creation implies transitoriness, finiteness, death; the process of creation is renewed and perfected in revelation, through which God, in his love, turns to man; the experience of this love evokes in man the consciousness of being a self and accords man reality. Now his original isolation and dumbness are overcome; his response to God's love is his own love. Man translates his love for God into love for his "neighbor," and by so doing participates in leading the world toward redemption. Through the deeds of love the temporality of life and the finality of death are overcome. Ultimate redemption is anticipated, and a sense of eternity in time experienced, primarily in the rhythm of the days which constitute the sacred calendar in the religions based on revelation, Judaism and Christianity. Both these religions represent, under the aspect of faith, authentic, though different, manifestations of reality, and both are concerned with the existential situation of individual man.

The ideal representative of the "new thinking," as Rosenzweig called his view, is a philosopher-theologian who, while maintaining scholarly objectivity, accepts the subjective, unique self as the new point of departure. The new theology should be existentially orientated, and theological problems should be translated into human terms. In contradistinction to abstract, timeless, purely logical, solitary thinking, the new existential thinking is "grammatical": human language, the word, the name, dialogue, are keys to the understanding of reality; the speaking thinker thinks *for* someone and speaks *to* someone. In such language-bound thinking, utmost importance is accorded to time; past, present, and future are actively involved in the process of thought, a notion found also in Martin Heidegger's philosophy.

In the Judaic field, Rosenzweig advocated a revaluation of the thought of classical Judaism. With Martin Buber he undertook to translate the Old Testament, faithfully transposing into German the style of the original.

Works by Rosenzweig

Hegel und der Staat, 2 vols. Berlin, 1920.
Der Stern der Erlösung. Frankfurt am Main, 1921; 3d ed., Heidelberg, 1954. An English translation, by William W. Hallo, is in preparation.
Briefe, Ernst Simon and Edith Rosenzweig, eds. Berlin, 1935. A selection of letters.
Kleinere Schriften. Berlin, 1937. A collection of papers, including "Das älteste Systemprogramm des deutschen Idealismus" and "Das neue Denken" (1925), a discursive "epilogue" to *Der Stern.*
Das Büchlein vom gesunden und kranken Menschenverstand. Dusseldorf, 1964. Written in 1921. Includes a popular presentation of the chief theme of *Der Stern.* An English version is *Understanding the Sick and the Healthy*, N. N. Glatzer, ed. New York, 1953.

Works on Rosenzweig

Altmann, Alexander, "Franz Rosenzweig on History," in *Between East and West.* London, 1958.
Buber, Martin, "Franz Rosenzweig." *Kant-Studien,* Vol. 35, No. 4 (1930), 517–522.
Freund, Else, *Die Existenzphilosophie Franz Rosenzweigs*, 2d ed. Hamburg, 1959.
Glatzer, Nahum N., *Franz Rosenzweig: His Life and Thought.* New York, 1953.
Guttmann, Julius, "Franz Rosenzweig," in *Philosophies of Judaism,* translated by D. Silverman. New York, 1964. Pp. 367–398.
Löwith, Karl, "M. Heidegger and F. Rosenzweig, or Temporality and Eternity." *Philosophy and Phenomenological Research,* Vol. 3, No. 1 (1942), 53–77.

NAHUM NORBERT GLATZER

ROSMINI-SERBATI, ANTONIO (1797–1855), Italian philosopher, educator, and statesman. Rosmini was born in Rovereto, then part of the Austrian Tyrol. The families of both his parents held patents of nobility under the Holy Roman Empire. A private education begun at an early age and directed to the priesthood established a firm foundation for his later work. Finding Austrian rule oppressive, Rosmini moved to the freer region of Piedmont. He started his career by founding the Institute of Charity, devoted to education and missions. He began to publish prolifically in philosophy, literature, and pedagogy. In politics he became an active exponent of the principles of Neo-Guelphism and reached the peak of his public career as counselor to Pius IX during the period from 1848 to 1853; at the end of this period, more conservative forces came to power. Retiring to private life, Rosmini continued his writing and assumed the direction of his institute. The present article restricts itself to Rosmini's philosophical work.

Although developed in a large number of works, Rosmini's philosophical thought presents a high degree of unity. This unity has two sources: the historical and apologetic intentions which sustain it and the internal development of certain germinal ideas. Rosmini's overt intention was to create a Christian–Catholic apologetics which would meet the demands of modern philosophical thought while remaining faithful to the core of traditional Christian philosophy. Since Augustinian and Thomistic realism predominated in Christian philosophy, Rosmini endeavored to anchor his thought in that tradition, exhibiting an affinity to the Augustinian strain. At the same time, he sought to meet the demands of rationalism and empiricism, and especially of the Kantian attempt at a resolution of the tension between the two. The effort to meet these conditions imparted to Rosmini's thought a high degree of complexity and sophistication.

The point of departure of the Rosminian system is his *Nuovo saggio sull'origine delle idee* (1830), a work of elaborate synthesis. The controlling principle of the synthesis is basically Augustinian, but the work develops around three centers: the idea of being, intellectual perception, and the origin of ideas.

The idea of being. Following Kant, Rosmini accepted a dual order of a posteriori and a priori in the process of knowledge and identified the ground of science with a priori principles of knowledge. Whereas Kant distinguished diverse orders or forms of a priori synthesis, Rosmini reduced that plurality to a single form, the idea of being. Only the idea of being can be thought without reference to any other idea, and only that idea is thought, at least implicitly, in the thinking of any other idea. The idea of being is not the product of the subject, whether empirical or transcendental; it is a datum offered immediately by God to the intelligent subject; it is, moreover, ontologically and functionally constitutive of that subjectivity. The idea of being is both a category and a transcendental operation. It is a category, for the subject knows through the process of the existential judgment, in which being as given in the idea of being is predicated of things. This judgment establishes the subsistence of the object as present and known in the judgment. As a category, the idea of being is the irreducible "other" to any specific content of thought or knowledge. It must also either be a product of the empirical subject or be truly objective. In the first case, the idea of being would be subjective and would render all knowledge subjective; in the second, its objectivity would seem to require the postulation of a "transcendental" subject. Rosmini accepted neither horn of this ostensible dilemma. He held that the human subject is empirical but also capable of a transcendental operation by which it can secure universal and necessary knowledge. It performs this operation through the idea of being; more accurately, this operation is one with the idea of being. As a transcendental operation, the idea of being constitutes the knowing subject ontologically and existentially; it secures the realm of universal and necessary knowledge. Finally, it is transcendent, for it is not the product of the subject, whether empirical or transcendental, but a datum which must be referred to the action of God. It is this last point which relates Rosmini's view to that of Augustine.

Intellectual perception. Although no knowledge is possible except through the idea of being, that idea does not suffice for the effective knowledge of the actual world of determinate forms of subsistence. This world can be known only if sensation has entrance into the realm of the idea of being and vice versa. Sensation is the vehicle of the multiple forms of determinate subsistence of the real world, but it does not present them as being; for them to be presented as being, sensation must be infused by the idea of being. This infusion is achieved concretely in an operation which Rosmini called intellectual perception.

Intellectual perception is rooted in man's fundamental constitution, for he is both sentient and intelligent. Every concrete act of knowing is structured by sensation and intelligence, related in a radical unity. There is neither pure sensation nor pure intellection, or intellectual vision. Intellectual perception, in which these pure elements occur in vital union, places man in authentic contact with the concrete real world. This operation is perception because by it the subject sensibly lays hold of reality, which actually stands before it, as subsistent. It is intellectual because the sensible perception evokes in the indeterminate being, which is already present to the subject in the idea of being, determinations by which the ideas of particular things arise. Intellectual perception is not, manifestly, the synthesis of two antecedently existing elements; it is the complex term of a complex, concrete operation, rooted in the fact that man is a complex principle and subject, both intelligent and sensitive.

Origin of ideas. On the basis of the foregoing points, Rosmini addressed the problem of the origin of ideas. Ideas, except the idea of being, arise through the process of abstraction. Empiricists and sensationists confuse intellectual perception with sensation when they speak of the formation of ideas out of the elements of sensation through abstraction and reflection. The act of reflection is not performed on the simple sense datum but upon objects already known and present through intellectual perception. By noting certain characteristics and averting attention from others, abstraction forms ideas of various degree up to the most general. The idea of being is alone excluded from this account; for it is the presupposition, not the result, of intellectual perception.

Subjective realism. Rosmini proceeded in *Psicologia* (1850) to consider the subject, which is the locus of the process of knowledge. Here again his doctrine reflects his concern to meet both empirical and idealist claims by passing beyond them. He refused to resolve the subject into the transcendental process, as he claimed idealists did, or into the process of sensation, as he said empiricists did. Instead, he offered a "subjective realism" or, better, a "realism of the subject." Its basis is the theory of the "fundamental sentiment," the immediate analogue for which is intellectual perception. The soul, while retaining its classical status as the active principle of vital operations and psychic phenomena, takes on a new dimension; it is the substance-sentiment, the intuitive sense of immanent being which generates subsistence. The reality of the subject is constituted by this immediate, nonobjective, and synthetic sense of self, which draws into a subsistent unity all aspects—sensitive, intelligent, and volitional—of the subject's complex life. This fundamental sentiment is the first and the continuous experience which man has of himself. It always involves, moreover, a relationship to a corporeal term, the body. This specific aspect of the fundamental sentiment, the corporeal sentiment, is characteristic of human nature. By it Rosmini justified the classical doctrine of man's composition out of body and soul. All other sensations are accidental to this fundamental sentiment; it is primitive and incommunicable and constitutes the subject in its unity and complexity.

Rosmini was also able to offer a fresh form of the classical doctrine of the immortality of the soul. Immortality has its basis in the fundamental sentiment of the idea of being; through the corporeal sentiment, the body shares immortality.

The person. Important both in itself and for its function in his social and political thought is Rosmini's central doctrine of the person. A subject has two aspects, nature and person. A subject's nature is the complex and sum of the activities of which the subject is agent. The perfection of the subject in the order of nature is the perfection, in number and in quality, of these activities. "Person" designates the directive unity of these activities and hence is associated in a special way with the will. The will is fundamental because it directs and organizes the activities of a person's nature, and in so doing it exhibits the basic deontic character of the person, its orientation toward a norm, toward the ought. The person emerges as the unique and incommunicable unity of the activities of the nature through a unique and unrepeatable activity of the will. It is not merely an operational or structural unity but a deontic one, basically oriented toward the world of values and norms and hence constitutively moral. The central effort of life is the realization of the developed or explicit person, which is achieved through the exercise of moral decision within the context of nature and its diverse activities. This effort is the basis of Rosmini's distinction between *vita direta* and the *vita riflessa,* which is central to his moral philosophy. The central effort of the moral life is the practice of the *vita riflessa,* the examined life in a creative sense.

The elaboration of the notion of the person gives structure to Rosmini's moral philosophy; his philosophy of right, law, and state; and his theory of education.

Ethics. Personalism enabled Rosmini to overcome the formalism of Kantian ethics. The idea of being is the criterion of the good as well as of truth. In the intimate unity of the person, the speculative act of intellectual perception immediately translates itself into a practical judgment which becomes the legislative principle of action. The truth of being which intellectual perception presents inevitably involves the assenting activity of the will. The will seeks the being of all things in the idea of being, revealed in the deontic order as the good. Rosmini, on Kant's model, tried to distill this insight into a rule: Recognize in action or practice what you have recognized speculatively. The essence of the moral life resides in this act of recognition, reflected prismatically in all the concrete situations in which the agent discovers himself. The obligatoriness of the rule springs from the fact that a hiatus between the speculative and the practical orders, between universal recognition and individual action, is intolerable. The psychological expression of this intolerance is remorse, the characteristic state of a person who deviates from this imperative. The true form of Rosmini's moral philosophy is embodied in another imperative: Be faithful to being; specifically, to the being which is revealed in the idea of being and which is the ground of all.

Fidelity to being was immediately translated by Rosmini into a rule of justice. The idea of being contains all the grades of being. The realm of being thus constitutes at the same time a hierarchy of values. Fidelity to being demands that the rule of justice, "Give to each its due," be inter-

preted in terms of this hierarchy. How is this hierarchy of values to be apprehended? Rosmini's reply is that it is to be apprehended through spontaneous recourse to the intellectual light, the constitutive presence in the subject of the idea of being.

Political philosophy. The concepts of person and justice provide the bases of Rosmini's political philosophy. Abstractly, right is the property of being, for being demands to be recognized and in doing so establishes the moral and the juridical orders. Concretely, right has its locus in the person, because of the person's ontological status as subject. In the person, right becomes a capacity to act eudaemonically, a capacity which is protected by the moral law; the same law imposes on others the obligation to recognize this capacity. Rosmini sought to bring right under the moral law in order to oppose those who would make it rest on force; he made it an endowment of the person to oppose those who would assign its origin to any other source, such as organized society in any of its forms. He distinguished innate natural rights, derived connatural rights, and acquired rights. Property, by means of which the person acquires physicomoral dominion over objects, is the chief acquired right.

While property defines the relation of the person to objects, the social bond relates him to other persons. The basis of the bond of sociality among a plurality of persons is their participation in a common intelligent principle, ideal being. Rosmini placed the forms of social life on a continuum between the terms of the most rudimentary and inclusive—membership in the human race—and the most intimate and exclusive—the conjugal relationship. Civil society falls midway on this continuum. Civil society has only a functional and not a substantive character: it does not originate rights but simply regulates the mode of their enjoyment and exercise. This provides Rosmini with his definition of the state and of government: the state is a regulatory principle of the modality of human rights. A just state achieves a balance between the common good (the good of the members distributively considered) and the public good (that of the social body considered as an organism). Abstractly, the common good is to be preferred to the public good, so as to preclude justification of acts of the state by recourse to the doctrine of "reason of state"; concretely, this preferential status is less determinate.

Being and God. In two extensive works, the *Teosofia* (posthumously published, 1859–1874) and the *Teodicea* (1845), Rosmini drew the widest possible conclusions from his personalistic premises. The theme of the *Teosofia* is the unity of being as prior to any of its modes (the absolute metaformality of being). Being, in this sense, is the basis of all the actual and determinate forms of being and contains within itself all of the principles of that determination *in abstracto* or *virtualiter.* It is not, however, the creative principle by which those forms are reduced to actuality. The need for a creative principle opens the way for the argument of the *Teodicea,* that God necessarily exists. God is the creative principle by which the virtuality of the order of primal being is realized in the actual and concrete modes of existence.

Educational theory. The culmination of Rosmini's thought is considered by many to be his pedagogical theory. The guiding principle of this theory is a summary of his entire philosophy: respect for the human person as the vehicle of divine light and ideal being. Rosmini stressed the unity of educational process and also methodology. The person is the principle of integrity; education is the process of the realization of the person in this sense. The principle of this integration is religion, which gives unity of purpose, unity of doctrine, and unity of powers to the educational process. The supreme law of method, the principle of gradation, ensures the conformity of the process of education to that of life. The process of growth and integration according to this law is from the universal to the particular. The object of the entire process is the free and realized person who fulfills himself in free association with other persons in all social forms and whose freedom rests ultimately upon his foundation in ideal being.

Works by Rosmini

Opere, Enrico Castelli, ed., 28 vols. Rome, 1934——. One hundred volumes planned.
Saggio sull'unità dell educazione. Milan, 1826.
Nuovo saggio sull'origine delle idee. Rome, 1830.
Teodicea. Milan, 1845. Translated as *Theodicy,* 3 vols. New York, 1912.
Psicologia, 2 vols. Novara, 1850. Translated as *Psychology,* 3 vols. 1884–1888.
Del principio supremo della methodica e di alcune sue applicazione in servizio della umana educazione. Turin, 1857.
Teosofia, 5 vols. Turin, 1859–1874.

Works on Rosmini

BIBLIOGRAPHIES

Antologia rosminiana, Vol. 1 (1955).
Caviglione, Carlo, *Bibliografia delle opere di Antonio Rosmini.* Turin, 1925.
Palhories, Fortunat, *La Philosophie de Rosmini.* Paris, 1908.

BIOGRAPHIES

Bertoletti, C. G., *Vita di Antonio Rosmini.* Turin, 1957.
Leetham, Claude, *Rosmini.* London and New York, 1957.
Pagani, G. B., *Vita di Antonio Rosmini,* 2 vols. Turin, 1897. Revised by G. Rossi and G. Bozzetti. Rovereto, 1957. Translated as *The Life of Antonio Rosmini-Serbati.* London, 1907.

PHILOSOPHICAL STUDIES

Bruno, G. F., "Rosmini's Contributions to Ethical Philosophy," in *Archives of Philosophy.* New York, 1916.
Bulferetti, L., *Antonio Rosmini nella Restaurazione.* Florence, 1942.
Capone Braga, Gaetano, *Saggio su Rosmini: Il mondo delle idee,* 2d ed. Florence, 1924.
Caviglione, Carlo, *Il Rosmini vero.* Voghera, 1912.
Chiavacci, C., *Il valore morale nel Rosmini.* Florence, 1921.
Franchi, A., *Saggio sul sistema ontologico di Antonio Rosmini.* Milan, 1953.
Galli, Gallo, *Kant e Rosmini.* Città di Castello, 1914.
Gentile, Giovanni, *Rosmini e Gioberti,* 2d ed. Florence, 1955.
Gonella, G., *La filosofia del diritto secondo Rosmini.* Rome, 1934.
Honan, U., *Agostino, Tommaso e Rosmini.* Milan, 1955.
Morando, Dante, *La pedagogia di Antonio Rosmini.* Brescia, 1948.
Morando, Giuseppe, *Esame critico delle XL proposizione rosminiani condannate.* Milan, 1905.
Nicola, G. B., *Saggi di scienza politica di Antonio Rosmini.* Turin, 1933.

Pignoloni, E., *Il reale nei problemi della Teosofia di Antonio Rosmini.* Milan, 1955.
Prini, Pietro, *Introduzione alla metafisica di Antonio Rosmini.* Milan, 1953.
Riva, C., *Il problema dell'anima intelletiva secondo Antonio Rosmini.* Domodossola, 1956.
Rovea, Giuseppe, *Filosofia e religione in Antonio Rosmini.* Milan, 1952.
Sciacca, M. F., *La filosofia morale di Antonio Rosmini.* Rome, 1938.

COLLECTIONS OF ARTICLES

Atti del congresso internazionale di filosofia "Antonio Rosmini," 2 vols. Florence, 1957.
Crisis (1955), No. 6.
Giornale di metafisica (1955), Nos. 4 and 5.
Humanitas (1955), Nos. 9 and 10.
Rivista della filosofia neoscolastica (1955), Nos. 4 and 5.
Rivista rosminiana (1955), Nos. 3 and 4. Contains an extensive bibliography.
Teoria (1955), Nos. 3 and 4.

A. ROBERT CAPONIGRI

ROSS, WILLIAM DAVID, British Aristotelian scholar and moral philosopher. Sir David Ross was born in 1877 in Scotland and was educated at the Royal High School in Edinburgh, Edinburgh University, and Balliol College, Oxford, where he took firsts in classical moderations and "greats." He was a fellow of Merton College from 1900 to 1902, when he was elected a fellow and tutor of Oriel. He was provost of Oriel from 1929 until his resignation in 1947.

Ross has been prominent in academic and public life. He was vice-chancellor of Oxford University (1941–1944), pro-vice-chancellor (1944–1947), president of the Classical Association (1932), and president of the British Academy (1936–1940). He has been chairman of Council of the Royal Institute of Philosophy continuously since 1940. In 1947 he served as president of the Union Académique Internationale.

Ross was awarded the Order of the British Empire for his work in the ministry of munitions and as a major on the special list during World War I. He was knighted in 1938. During World War II he was a member of the appellate tribunal for conscientious objectors and after the war was honored by the governments of Norway and Poland. Among his many public services were the chairmanships of three government departmental committees (1936–1937) and of the civil service arbitration tribunal (1942–1952). From 1947 to 1949 he was chairman of the important Royal Commission on the Press.

The qualities that made Ross successful in public life are those to which he owes his distinction as a philosopher. He is not only an Aristotelian scholar, but he also has an Aristotelian frame of mind—moderate, critical, balanced, thorough, and, above all, judicious. He values and possesses what Aristotle called "practical wisdom" no less than speculative ability.

Ross edited the Oxford translations of Aristotle, published between 1908 and 1931. He translated the *Metaphysics* and the *Ethics* himself, and he published definitive editions of a number of Aristotle's works. His *Aristotle* (London, 1923) is mainly expository, each chapter being concerned with a major aspect of Aristotle's work; this is still the best all-round exposition in English.

Ross was the leading opponent of the view of John Burnet and A. E. Taylor that the Socrates of Plato's dialogues is never a mouthpiece for Plato's own doctrines. In *Plato's Theory of Ideas* (Oxford, 1951), Ross rejected their contention that the theory of Ideas was originally the work of Socrates and not of Plato. This book traces the development of the theory of Ideas through Plato's thought. It includes a detailed discussion of Plato's cryptic doctrine of "ideal numbers," using Aristotle's account in the *Metaphysics* as a guide to the interpretation of the doctrine.

Ross's main contribution to philosophy, as distinct from philosophical scholarship, is in the field of ethics. In *The Right and the Good* (Oxford, 1930), he argued the case for intuitionism with a lucidity and thoroughness that made the book a classic. For some ten years it was the center of ethical controversy. In his *Foundations of Ethics* (Oxford, 1939) Ross restated his case and replied to his critics.

Ross's approach to ethics is Aristotelian. "The moral convictions of thoughtful and well-educated people are the data of ethics, just as sense-perceptions are the data of a natural science" (*The Right and the Good,* p. 41). He appeals to what we mean by rightness and goodness and assumes that this guarantees the existence of what is meant and is a sure guide to its nature.

The germ of Ross's position is to be found in an article by H. A. Prichard, "Does Moral Philosophy Rest on a Mistake?" (*Mind*, Vol. 21, 1912, 21–152; reprinted in *Moral Obligation*, Oxford, 1949, pp. 1–17). Prichard was a pupil of John Cook Wilson, who also influenced Ross directly, an influence that appears in Ross's opposition to reductionism and in his view that knowledge and opinion are distinct in kind. The other main debt acknowledged by Ross is to G. E. Moore, whose arguments against ethical subjectivism he endorses, although he rejects Moore's "ideal utilitarianism."

Right and good are for Ross distinct, indefinable, and irreducible objective qualities. Rightness belongs to acts, independently of motives; moral goodness belongs to motives. Ross uses "act" for what is done and "action" for the doing of it. Thus, the doing of a right act may be a morally bad action—that is, a right act can be done from a morally bad motive; the inverse also holds. Nor can it ever be morally obligatory to act from a good motive. There are four kinds of good things—virtue, knowledge, pleasure, and the allocation of pleasure and pain according to desert. No amount of pleasure equals the smallest amount of virtue. In *Foundations of Ethics* Ross argued that virtue and pleasure are not good in the same sense—virtue is "admirable," pleasure only "a worthy object of satisfaction." What alone is common to the two senses is that they express a favorable attitude.

Ross's two main targets are ethical subjectivism and "ideal utilitarianism," which "ignores, or at least does not do full justice to, the highly personal character of duty" (*The Right and the Good*, p. 22). Specific duties are of three kinds—reparation, gratitude, and keeping faith. The "plain man" (to whom Ross, as a good Aristotelian, frequently appeals), in deciding what he ought to do, thinks as often of the past (a promise made, a debt incurred) as of

future consequences. Ross does, however, admit among duties the utilitarian general duty of beneficence when it does not conflict with a specific duty. And "even when we are under a special obligation the tendency of acts to promote general good is one of the main factors in determining whether they are right" (*ibid.,* p. 3a).

Conflict of duties is one of the main problems facing an intuitionist, who cannot accept the utilitarian's "Do what will produce the most good." Ross says: "Do whichever act is more of a duty." To make sense of "more of a duty," he draws a distinction between prima-facie and actual duties and holds that conflict can only arise between prima-facie duties. An act is a prima-facie or "conditional" duty by virtue of being of a certain kind (for instance, the repaying of a debt) and would be an actual duty if it were not also of some other morally important kind or did not conflict with another more important prima-facie duty. Thus, if I have promised to lend money to a friend in need, I have a prima-facie duty to hand over the money. But suppose that before I have done so, I find that I need it for the legal defense of my son, charged with a crime of which I believe him innocent. I recognize a conflicting prima-facie duty to help him. Ross maintains that (*a*) one, and only one, of these two prima-facie duties is my actual duty; (*b*) I know each of them to be a prima-facie duty—this is self-evident; (*c*) I can have only an opinion about which is "more of a duty" and therefore my actual duty.

Bibliography

A work by Ross not mentioned in the text is *Kant's Ethical Theory* (Oxford, 1954).

Some works on Ross are J. H. Muirhead, *Rule and End in Morals* (London, 1932); H. J. McCloskey, "Ross and the Concept of Prima Facie Duty," in *Australasian Journal of Philosophy,* Vol. 41 (1964), 336–345; G. E. Hughes, "Motive and Duty," in *Mind*, Vol. 53 (1944), 314–331, W. A. Pickard-Cambridge, "Two Problems About Duty," in *Mind*, Vol. 41 (1932), 72–96, 145–172, 311–340; P. F. Strawson, "Ethical Intuitionism," in *Philosophy*, Vol. 24 (1949), 23–33.

A. K. STOUT

ROUGIER, LOUIS, French philosopher. Rougier, born in 1889, was a pupil of Edmond Goblot; he taught philosophy at the universities of Besançon and Caen. In 1935 he organized and presided over the Paris International Congress of Scientific Philosophy, where the leading spokesmen for logical empiricism, at the time little known in France, presented their views in a body.

From the start, Rougier's thought has been marked by the contemporary upheavals in the sciences of physics, mathematics, and logic. To these developments he devoted several of his early books, including *La Philosophie géométrique d'Henri Poincaré* (Paris, 1920), *La Structure des théories déductives* (Paris, 1921), *La Matière et l'energie selon la théorie de la relativité et la théorie des quanta* (Paris, 1921), and *En Marge de Curie, de Carnot et d'Einstein* (Paris, 1922).

In his view, the upsets in the sciences reinforced the closely pressed critique which he had directed in his doctoral thesis, *Les Paralogismes du rationalisme* (Paris, 1920), against the theory academic philosophers call "rationalism." This is an a priori rationalism, quite different from scientific and experimental rationalism. It asserts the existence of a universal, immutable reason and of eternal, necessary truths, with all the theological, ontological, and epistemological implications that such a thesis requires. According to Rougier, the body of notions and principles that constitute "reason" in the classic sense is simply the characteristic of a certain mental structure, the ontological or metaphysical temperament, which is also the subject of his detailed study *La Scolastique et le thomisme* (Paris, 1925). Besides the temperament dominated by "reason," history discloses other temperaments—animistic, symbolic, scientific—having command of other types of explanation. The human mind possesses an infinite plasticity; it is able to take delight in quite varied forms of intelligibility, without any internal necessity having compelled it to evolve in just the direction that it has. If the laws of logic are necessary truths, it is only because they are tautologies in the sense of Wittgenstein; that is, they are devoid of any information about the universe and hence stripped of any ontological import. Even this logical necessity, as is shown by the existence of a plurality of logics, is relative to a given system of axioms and rules.

This rejection of all a priori synthesis, this radical separation between logico-mathematical statements and empirical statements, and the condemnation it entails of all metaphysics as victim of the imperfections of our natural languages (*La Métaphysique et le langage*, Paris, 1960), closely ally Rougier's philosophy to that of logical empiricism. His long *Traité de la connaissance* (Paris, 1955) offers analyses illustrated with abundant examples from the past and contemporary history of the sciences; in style and ideas it is probably closer than any other French book to the majority of central European and American works on epistemology. Nevertheless, certain features testify to his originality in comparison with the logical empiricism of the Vienna circle. Rougier rejects the physicalist reduction and upholds a plurality of languages. Nor does he agree that all basically unsolvable problems must by their nature alone be regarded as devoid of meaning; besides, meaninglessness is a notion relative to the language chosen. Further, several of the ideas he has developed in works other than the *Traité*, for example his thesis of the diversity of mental structures and the plasticity of the intellect, do not strictly belong to the common stock of the school of logical empiricism, but have been added to it.

Although epistemology and the critique of knowledge are at the center of Rougier's philosophy, he has written in two other fields. One is the history of scientific, philosophical, and religious ideas, to which he has devoted *Celse ou le conflit de la civilisation antique et du christianisme primitif* (Paris, 1926) and *La Religion astrale des Pythagoriciens* (Paris, 1959). The other is contemporary political problems; he has dealt critically with the democratic and egalitarian ideology of the "men of 1789" and their successors in such works as *Les Mystiques politiques et leurs incidences internationales* (Paris, 1935), *Les Mystiques économiques* (Paris, 1949), and *L'Erreur de la démocratie française* (Paris, 1963).

Rougier has sytematically omitted these two aspects of his thought from the account he himself has given of his "philosophical itinerary" (*La Revue libérale*, No. 33, 1961,

6–79), an account which can well serve as an over-all study of his theory of knowledge.

Bibliography

There are no studies of Rougier, but the reader may wish to consult the brief account by A. D. Dandieu in *Anthologie des philosophes français contemporains* (Paris, 1931) followed by a detailed bibliography and two extracts from Rougier's writings.

ROBERT BLANCHÉ
Translated by *Albert E. Blumberg*

ROUSSEAU, JEAN-JACQUES (1712–1778), philosopher, essayist, and novelist, was born at Geneva. His mother having died a few days after his birth, he was brought up by an aunt and an erratic father who taught him to read through the medium of sentimental novels and Plutarch's *Lives*. He had little formal education. After staying for about two years with a country minister at Bossey, he returned to Geneva and lived with an uncle. He was then apprenticed in turn to a notary and an engraver, the latter of whom treated him so brutally that in 1728 he left Geneva to seek his fortune elsewhere.

Rousseau was protected and befriended by Mme. de Warens, a convert to Roman Catholicism, who had left her native canton of Vaud to live at Annecy in Savoy, with financial support from the king of Sardinia and the ecclesiastical authorities. Rousseau's subsequent attachment to her was a decisive factor in his conversion to Roman Catholicism as well as in his emotional development. He made a formal abjuration of Protestantism at the hospice for catechumens at Turin. He then served for a time as a lackey, finally returning to Mme. de Warens in 1729. Thereafter, he led an unsettled life, restless travel alternating with a more stable existence at Chambéry, where Mme. de Warens had established herself. Intellectually, the most important event of this phase of his life was a protracted spell of enthusiastic study under his own direction. A brief experience as a private tutor at Lyons in 1740 helped to create a lifelong interest in education and at the same time convinced Rousseau that he had no aptitude for this profession. As he had acquired some musical competence at Annecy, he set out hopefully for Paris in 1742 with a new system of musical notation. Although this did not bring him the success he hoped for, he was introduced to a number of influential people, including the wealthy Mme. Dupin and her stepson M. de Francueil.

In 1743, Rousseau was appointed secretary to the French ambassador at Venice, M. de Montaigu, but he lost this post the following year because of a quarrel with him. On his return to Paris, Rousseau increased his difficulties by an irregular union with an ignorant servant girl, Thérèse Le Vasseur, in 1745; by her he probably had five illegitimate children, who were all sent to a foundlings' home. He also met Diderot, d'Alembert, and other *philosophes* and was invited to contribute musical articles to the *Encyclopédie*.

Rousseau's literary career began in 1750 with the publication of the *Discours sur les sciences et les arts*, which had previously won a prize at the Academy of Dijon. However, his first real success came with the performance of his opera *Le Devin du village* before Louis XV at Fontainebleau, but his refusal to allow himself to be presented to the king lost him any chance of securing a royal pension. A journey to Geneva in 1754 led to a reconciliation with the republic and a formal return to Protestantism.

After the publication in 1755 of his *Discours sur l'origine de l'inégalité*, Rousseau felt increasingly unhappy in Paris, and in 1756 he installed himself in a small country house, called the Hermitage, which belonged to a rich friend, Mme. d'Épinay. There followed a comparatively short but intense period of literary activity which saw the publication of the *Lettre à d'Alembert sur les spectacles* (1758), *Julie, ou la Nouvelle Héloïse* (1761), *Émile* (1762), and the *Contrat social* (1762).

During this time Rousseau's relations with the Encyclopedists became increasingly strained, with intellectual differences, especially on the subject of religion, being aggravated by personal quarrels with former friends such as Diderot and the Baron von Grimm. In 1762 the condemnation of *Émile* by the Paris Parlement forced him to flee from France and settle in Neuchâtel under the protection of the king of Prussia. In the *Lettre à M. de Beaumont* (1763) Rousseau vigorously defended the "Profession de foi du vicaire savoyard," which had been included in the fourth book of *Émile*, against its condemnation by the archbishop of Paris; this was followed in 1764 by another polemical work, the *Lettres écrites de la montagne*, provoked by increasing opposition from the Genevan authorities to his political and religious views. Alarmed by local hostility, Rousseau decided to leave the Neuchâtel region in 1765, and he accepted an invitation from the philosopher David Hume to make his home in England. His arrival in that country in 1766 and his subsequent residence in Derbyshire were disturbed by the appearance of abnormal emotional and mental reactions, culminating in the irrational conviction that Hume's invitation had been a mere pretext for Rousseau's defamation. After quarreling violently with Hume (who riposted by publishing an account of the affair), Rousseau fled panic-stricken to France in 1767. For the next few years he moved from place to place, oppressed by the thought of universal persecution. He eventually settled in Paris in 1770 and died suddenly on July 2, 1778, less than two months after he had gone to live on the estate of the marquis de Girardin at Ermenonville.

The chief literary activity of Rousseau's last years was the composition of a remarkable series of personal works, the *Confessions*, on which he had worked intensively during his stay in England; the dialogues known as *Rousseau juge de Jean-Jacques*, a curiously pathological document illuminated by some pages of remarkable brilliance and insight; and the beautiful but unfinished *Rêveries du promeneur solitaire*. These writings are remarkable for their lyrical power and sustained efforts at self-analysis.

THOUGHT

From the very first Rousseau's work betrayed the strongly personal emphasis of a writer who felt that he did not truly belong to his immediate environment. Being of Genevan origin, largely self-taught, and endowed with a particularly sensitive temperament, he could never bring himself fully to accept the social and moral implications of French culture, even though he never ceased to admire French taste. In 1749, as he was on his way to Vincennes to visit his imprisoned friend Diderot, he saw in a copy of the *Mercure de France* the subject of the prize essay set by the Academy of Dijon: Whether the restoration of the arts and sciences has contributed to the purification of manners. In the *Confessions* he writes that at that moment he experienced a sudden "illumination" and "inspiration," the dazzling vision of a "new universe," which impelled him to anwer the academicians' question with an emphatic "No!" Although this viewpoint was already familiar to a certain type of traditional Christian moralist, Rousseau struck a new personal note remarkable for its deeply felt sincerity; he always refused to consider himself as a professional man of letters and stressed his role as an independent writer with a message for humanity.

Nature and society. Rousseau's early works (the two discourses and the *Lettre à d'Alembert*) developed the fundamental antithesis which he deemed to exist between contemporary society and the nature of man. European civilization was indicted for having sacrificed the moral demands of human nature to the superficial allure of a purely intellectual culture and thus for having replaced natural by artificial needs. The artificial uniformity of behavior which society imposes on people causes them to ignore "the duties of man and the needs of nature," so that appearance and reality are constantly at variance in modern social life, as for example in the case of an excessive regard for politeness and convention concealing the most ruthless and calculating egoism. Likewise, insisted Rousseau, the sciences and the arts, in spite of their brilliance, are not the genuine expression of fundamental human needs but the result of pride and vanity. The rapid growth of luxury and idleness serves merely to increase the corruption of the contemporary situation. Consequently, as culture appears to attain an ever increasing splendor, genuine human relationships become steadily weaker. Man is alienated from his original nature and prevented from being his real self; a perpetual prey to inner contradictions, he vainly grasps at objects outside himself as he neglects the true lessons of nature in order to pursue the illusions of opinion.

To "society" Rousseau opposed "virtue"—a constant theme of his early works. Virtue confers stability and unity upon human existence because it subordinates idle speculation to the active needs of the moral life. Unlike mere reflection, it induces "strength and vigor of soul," allowing full expression to man's genius and conferring on his existence a solidity and permanence which are quite unlike the ephemeral brilliance of contemporary culture. Whereas society forces man to assume the mask of hypocrisy and deceit as a means of satisfying his selfish interests, virtue, "the sublime science of simple souls," gives him an authentic openness and innocence which allow him to reveal himself to others as he truly is.

A particularly serious feature of modern society is the prevalence of an unnatural inequality based on power and wealth. In the *Discours sur l'origine de l'inégalité* Rousseau examines this phenomenon in the light of man's evolution from the primitive state to his present existence as a political being and concludes that modern conditions represent a fall from happiness into misery. In spite of its historical form, this discourse, as the author himself admits, is a purely hypothetical and imaginative reconstruction that deliberately ignores facts, whether historical or theological, in order to concentrate on the nature of man as it is revealed to Rousseau's intuitive perception. If the state of nature can never be known as a historical fact, it at least serves as a useful concept which enables him to distinguish man's original qualities from fortuitous historical accretions.

Limited and instinctive though the life of primitive man may have been, it was at least a happy one inasmuch as the savage knew how to live in accordance with his own innate needs. Leading an isolated existence in the forests, satisfying his basic appetite for food and sex without difficulty, untouched by modern man's anxiety before illness and death, he was largely self-sufficient; the primordial urge toward self-preservation was effectively counterbalanced by an innate feeling of natural pity which prevented him from inflicting needless pain upon his fellow men. Man was from the outset endowed with free will and perfectibility, but these became active only when the first rudimentary social communities, based mainly on the family, were established, a period which Rousseau treats as the golden age of humanity since it lay halfway between the brutishness of primitive existence and the corruption of political societies. The discovery of agriculture and metallurgy and the distinction between "mine" and "thine" meant that people had to work together, and this inevitably led to the establishment of property. Men then became divided into rich and poor and, later, into powerful and weak, so that the inequality of the social system was at last made permanent through the institution of laws and political organization. In Rousseau's opinion the historical process will culminate in the triumph of despotism, which makes all men once again equal because all have become slaves of one master.

Whereas the early discourses dealt mainly with general principles, the publication of d'Alembert's article "Geneva" in the seventh volume of the *Encyclopédie* in 1757, with its suggestion that the Genevans would benefit from the establishment of a theater, led Rousseau to deal with a specific aspect of his criticism of society. In his various replies to early critics he had already insisted that man, having once left the primitive state, could never return to it; he also maintained that it was the large states, especially the monarchies of Europe, which had traveled furthest on the road to perdition. However, small republics like Geneva, though no longer close to nature, still retained a relative simplicity and innocence and could be protected against further corruption. To introduce the theater into Geneva was, in Rousseau's eyes, to bring an evil product of society into a comparatively unspoiled community. The *Lettre à d'Alembert* also provided him with an opportunity of examining not only the general characteristics of the theater but also the whole question of what amusements are best suited to man's true nature. Starting from the assumption that all valid entertainment must "derive from man's work, relationships and needs," Rousseau insists that it must be an integral part of man's daily life, different from his work and yet inspired by the same spirit. The

theater, however, is primarily an artificial entertainment, the product of idleness and vanity and the fomenter of dangerous passions and emotions; it is always subservient to the impulses which create it and remains incapable of directing people toward moral activity. The theater is typical of a large city like Paris, with its reversal of natural values. Whereas for Rousseau woman is naturally modest and self-effacing, the theater makes her a shameless figure who transforms love into a public spectacle; the very existence of actresses also sets the example of a completely unfeminine way of life that is characteristic of a society in which women set the tone and rule the *salons,* reducing men to a condition of abject and effeminate dependence. By contrast, Rousseau extols the simplicity of the Montagnons, the simple, industrious mountain dwellers whom he remembered from his youth and recalls with heartfelt enthusiasm. Unlike modern men such people relied upon their own creative resources for their work and entertainment. The Genevans, too, through their "societies" and "circles," wisely allowed men and women to indulge in their own separate pastimes. The *Lettre* ends with a remarkable evocation of the kind of national entertainment which, in Rousseau's opinion, would be suitable for a small homogeneous community like Geneva. The Genevans should actively participate in a joyous public entertainment that takes place "beneath the sky" and in the presence of their fellow citizens; in this way the whole community would be inspired by feelings that are both social and human.

Perhaps one of the gravest general aspects of society's harmful influence on the nature of man is its constant tendency to transform *amour de soi* ("self-love") into *amour-propre* ("pride"). Although this antithesis was not peculiar to Rousseau, who had already noted its existence in Vauvenargues, it does occupy a particularly significant position in his social criticism. *Amour de soi* is always good and, in its purest state, quite spontaneous because it expresses the real essence of human existence. It is an absolute feeling or passion which serves as the source of all genuinely natural impulses and emotions; already revealing itself at the instinctive level as the desire for self-preservation, it assumes a much nobler expression as soon as it is combined with reason. Being in complete uniformity with the principle of order, it will affect all the main aspects of human existence as it brings the individual into contact with his own inner self, his physical environment, and his fellow men. Unfortunately modern society has changed this natural *amour de soi,* which makes a man what he truly is, into *amour-propre,* an artificial reaction originating in an anxious reflection which induces a man to be forever comparing himself with others and even finding his sole pleasure in their misfortune or inferiority; through *amour-propre* he is taken outside himself into the realm of illusion and opinion and so prevented from being a complete person.

Education. Having diagnosed the malady of modern civilization, Rousseau was faced with the task of suggesting a cure, and this led him into the domain of education and politics, activities which are, or should be, rooted in man's moral nature. Rousseau was convinced that man's original nature is good, but that it has been corrupted mainly by the historical accident of society. It therefore seemed quite consistent to affirm that men are wicked but that man himself is good. To be good is to exist in accordance with the intrinsic potentialities of one's nature, and *Émile* seeks to trace the natural development of a human being brought up in the country away from the nefarious influence of contemporary social life. From this point of view the work is not just a manual of education but, as Rousseau himself points out, a philosophical treatise on the goodness of human nature. It is less concerned with laying down the practical details of a specific pedagogic method than with describing the fundamental principles which underlie the whole of man's development from infancy to maturity. Rousseau's ultimate object is to teach the art of living, for man's first duty, he says, is to be human.

The educator must realize that "vice and error, alien to man's constitution, are introduced into it from outside"; his first task will be to keep away harmful influences from the young child. This is why *Émile* is set in a rural environment that allows the child to grow in accordance with his own nature. Early education is therefore largely negative insofar as it is mainly concerned with removing obstacles that might hinder this development.

From the first Rousseau stresses the importance of a progressive education: each stage of the process must be carefully adapted to the individual's developing needs and so follow "the natural progress of the human heart." In this respect Rousseau uses in his own way the genetic method of contemporary thinkers like d'Alembert, Condillac, and Buffon, who, in turn, had taken over the notion of the genealogy of ideas developed by Locke in his famous *Essay Concerning Human Understanding*. In *Émile*, however, as in the *Discours sur l'origine de l'inégalité*, Rousseau does not strive to establish an inductive law based on the empirical examination of facts but starts from a fundamental principle (man's natural goodness) which is derived initially from personal intuition, though he believes it to be subsequently verifiable by observation and psychological analysis. *Émile* therefore involves certain metaphysical elements, but these are referred back to the concrete aspects of human nature.

Rousseau maintains that a truly progressive education will recognize that the child has his own special needs as a being who exists in his own right. "Nature wants children to be children before being men. . . . Childhood has its own ways of seeing, thinking and feeling." Since the child's needs are largely physical, negative education "tends to perfect the organs, instruments of our knowledge." Incapable of dealing with abstractions, the child must be educated through contact with things. To him dependence on things will be natural and inevitable; acknowledging only the "heavy yoke of necessity," he will escape the tyranny of any human will. Unlike the despotic power of men necessity is quite compatible with properly controlled freedom since it lets the human being exercise his powers within the limits prescribed for him by nature. "The truly free man" wishes to do no more than this. Well-regulated freedom thus provides the only valid basis and aim of sound education.

Early education, being based primarily on the senses, ignores bookish learning for direct contact with the physical world. Learning through a process of trial and error, the child experiments, as it were, through the medium of facts rather than words. (The sole book Rousseau will allow the child is Defoe's *Robinson Crusoe* and that only because it describes a man's reliance on his own ingenuity and resourcefulness.) Freed from the tyranny of human opinion, the child identifies himself effortlessly with the requirements of his immediate existence; content to be himself and completely absorbed in his present being, he leads a kind of self-sufficient, timeless existence that knows no anxious concern for the future, none of that tormenting foresight which causes modern man to be so unhappily "outside himself." The child is happy because he is unaware of artificial needs or of any serious disproportion between capacity and desire, power and will, and in this respect he resembles the happy savage.

Rousseau recognizes that even at the stage of greatest inner harmony, the child must be prepared for the future, for in him there is a reservoir of potential energy which he does not immediately need. The educator's task is to hold back this energy, this "superfluous aspect of his immediate being," until it can be effectively used. It is particularly important to avoid any precocious excitement of the imagination which may be the source of future unhappiness. These dangers will be largely averted if, after the lesson of necessity, the child learns that of utility, his developing reason being applied only to what interests and helps him. That is why his early judgment must be formed not through words or abstractions but through sensations and feelings.

A truly positive education begins only when the child becomes aware of his relationships with other people, although these early social lessons will be based on sensibility rather than reason, in particular on the innate feeling of pity, with its later concomitants of love and aversion. There are no good or bad passions, says Rousseau. All are good when they are under our control; all are bad when they control us. Through the force of our passions we are impelled beyond ourselves; through the "superabundance of our strength" we are induced to "extend our being." With the growth of sensibility, reason, and imagination the child leaves the self-sufficiency of the primitive stage for a fuller life involving relations with the physical realm of nature and the world of human beings. The educational process must therefore be carefully timed and controlled so that the various potentialities of the human being are brought to fulfillment in an orderly and harmonious manner.

It is clear from the last book of *Émile* that man must be educated for society, though not necessarily for society in its present form. Man's nature is not fully mature until it becomes social. However, the natural man in the state of nature and the natural man in the social state cannot be identical, for whereas the former is predominantly an instinctive, primitive creature living on the spontaneous expression of his innate vitality, the latter is a rational, moral being aware of his obligations to other people, a man called upon to subordinate the impulse of "goodness" to the demands of "virtue." Therefore, only in society can a genuinely human morality become possible. If by "nature" is meant the merely primordial responses of the presocial man, then it is true to say that "good institutions denature man" inasmuch as they raise him up from the absolute self-sufficiency of the isolated primitive state to the level of a moral, relative existence based on an awareness of the common good and the need to live in harmonious relationship with his fellow men. Since morality inevitably involves the problem of man's life as a social being, it is impossible to separate morality and politics, and Rousseau states most emphatically that "those who want to treat morality and politics separately will never understand anything about either." This is a most important aspect of his political thinking. If "nature" intended man for a moral existence, then it also intended him for social life; indeed, only through the individual's participation in the "common unity" can full personal maturity become possible. "Nature" is still the norm, but one that has to be re-created, as it were, at a higher level, conferring on man a new rational unity which replaces the purely instinctive unity of the primitive state.

Political theory. There appears to be no valid reason for finding, as some critics have done, any fundamental contradiction between *Émile* and the *Contrat social*. Such a difficulty arises only when anachronistic attempts are made to explain Rousseau's thought in purely individualist or collectivist terms. If at first sight Émile seems to be an isolated individual, this is mainly because Rousseau wanted to stress the importance of the human being's natural development, and it in no way excludes the idea that all true education must eventually be for society.

In itself the particular form of education, like that of government, must be determined by specific historical and physical conditions, but Rousseau was less concerned with this question than with that of the fundamental principles on which all true education and all true government must be based. In this respect *Émile* and the *Contrat social* are similar since each is a theoretical, normative work. Rousseau points out in his correspondence that the *Contrat social* is a philosophical discussion of political right (the work is actually subtitled *Principes du droit politique*) rather than an examination of any existing form of government. As he says in the Introduction to his work, he is taking "men as they are" and "the laws as they *can* be." He seeks to reconcile "what right permits with what interest prescribes, so that justice and utility are not divided." In Rousseau's eyes this is what distinguishes his approach to political problems from Montesquieu's. Whereas Montesquieu is concerned with "the positive right of established governments," Rousseau, as the theorist of political right, examines the philosophical basis of all legitimate government.

Although the *Contrat social* has often been described as the forerunner of totalitarianism, this interpretation is certainly not consistent with Rousseau's conscious intention, for from the very outset his overriding preoccupation is the same as it was in *Émile*—the problem of *freedom*. No doubt, just as the concept of nature undergoes a radical transformation when it is applied to society, so the natural freedom enjoyed by man in the state of nature differs in important respects from the civic freedom of the social state; both, however, are natural to man at different stages of his development. Man living in society faces a problem which does not affect primitive man—namely, the possible tyranny of his fellow men. Now, a true and just society can never be based on sheer force, for right can never be equated with might. Rousseau vigorously repudiates traditional views which seek to justify the right of conquerors to subject the vanquished to permanent enslavement; no society founded on such a principle can ever be legitimate. Man's participation in society must be consistent with his existence as a free and rational being. Society is therefore unthinkable without a freedom which expresses man's most fundamental attribute. "To give up freedom is to give up one's human quality: to remove freedom from one's will is to remove all morality from one's actions." Moreover, it is with the emergence of society that man comes into possession of his freedom and thus attains the status of a moral being. The institution of any genuine political society must be the result of a social pact, or free association of intelligent human beings who deliberately choose to form the type of society to which they will owe allegiance; this is the only valid basis for a community that wishes to live in accordance with the requirements of human freedom.

However, there still remains the problem of finding a form of association which will continue to respect the freedom that brought it into being. Although man is naturally good, he is constantly threatened by forces which not only alienate him from himself but also transform him into a tyrant or a slave. From this point of view the political problem is not dissimilar from the pedagogic one. How is man to be protected from the tyranny of the human will? Just as the child has to be liberated from dependence upon human caprice in order to confront necessity, so the individual is to be preserved from tyranny by "an excessive dependence" of all citizens on a new kind of necessity, on something that is greater than the citizen himself and yet in one sense a part of his life. Rousseau seeks a form of association in which "each one uniting with all obeys, however, only himself and remains as free as before." In other words, "each one giving himself to all gives himself to nobody." The possibility of inequality and injustice will be avoided through the "total alienation of each associate, with all his rights, to the community"; if such alienation were less than total, it would expose the individual to domination by others. As it is, the citizen does not obey some sectional interest but the general will, which is a "real force, superior to the action of any particular will." Nor, in Rousseau's view, need this arouse any apprehension, for unlike the individual will which concerns itself with specific and perhaps selfish interests, the general will is always directed toward the general good. Moreover, total alienation involves equality in another way; the general will is not simply an external authority which the citizen obeys in spite of himself but the objective embodiment of his own moral nature. In accepting the authority of the general will, the citizen not only belongs to a collective, moral body but also achieves true freedom by obeying a law which he has prescribed for himself. Through the law he escapes from the bondage of appetite in order to follow, as an intelligent being, the dictates of reason and conscience. Submission to a will possessing an "inflexibility which no human force could ever overcome" leads to a freedom which "keeps a man exempt from vice" and to "a morality which lifts him up to virtue." The individual is thereby invested with another kind of goodness, the genuine virtue of the man who is not an isolated being but part of a great whole. Liberated from the narrow confines of his own being, he finds fulfillment in a truly social experience of fraternity and equality with citizens who accept the same ideal.

This conception of political right is essentially democratic insofar as the source of all political authority and, therefore, of all true sovereignty must always lie with the people as a whole. Moreover, such sovereignty is both inalienable and indivisible since, as the basis of freedom itself, it is something that can never be renounced by the people or shared with others. However, Rousseau establishes an important distinction between sovereignty and government. The sovereign, or subjects (for "sovereign and subjects are simply the same people in different respects"), may delegate the executive function of the state to the prince, or government, which thus becomes the agent, or officer, of the people; this is true whatever the form of any particular government, whether monarchy, aristocracy, or republic. If every legitimate government is democratic in essence, this does not mean that democracy, as a definite political institution through which the people themselves carry on the government by assembling as a body, is either possible or desirable in modern conditions. Any specific form of government, as Rousseau was to show very clearly in his *Projet de constitution pour la Corse* (1765) and his *Considérations sur le gouvernement de la Pologne* (probably written about 1770–1771), will depend on a variety of historical and geographical factors.

Law, as the act of the general will and the expression of sovereignty, is of vital importance, for the establishment of sound laws can determine the whole destiny of the state. As Rousseau observes, only the gods themselves would be capable of giving good laws to the human race. That is why the legislator has such an important role in the *Contrat social;* he is invested with a remarkable, almost divine quality. It is from him that the citizen "receives in some way his life and his being"; through the legislator's actions he experiences a genuine transformation of his personal life, forsaking the "physical, independent existence he received from nature" for a moral existence as a social being. This new mode of existence is not something imposed upon him from the outside but a possibility elicited from the depths of his inner self. The legislator is in one respect an almost godlike figure, but his purpose is to serve the essential needs of human nature.

At the end of the final version of the *Contrat social* (though not in the original draft), Rousseau seems to acknowledge that an even more powerful sanction may be required to ensure complete political stability, for he proposes to introduce into the state a kind of civil religion or civic profession of faith to which every citizen, having once given his free assent, must remain obedient under pain of death. This is an aspect of Rousseau's political thought which many commentators have found either shocking or inconsistent. However, it will already be clear that Rousseau is no liberal in the classical political sense since he does not believe in the possibility of any rigid separation of the individual and the state; the development of a full moral life is inconceivable without active participation in society, and the unity and permanence of the state depend, in turn, upon the moral integrity and undivided loyalty of its citizens. This civic profession of faith is deliberately restricted to the "few simple dogmas" which, according to Rousseau, every rational, moral being ought readily to accept: belief in a supreme being, the future life, the happiness of the just, and the punishment of the wicked, together with a "single negative dogma, the rejection of intolerance." Anybody repudiating these principles would presumably be, in Rousseau's opinion, little more than a criminal who, by forfeiting his right to be considered as a responsible human being, threatens the state with anarchy and dissolution. The practical implications of this view may still sound alarming to a modern liberal, but they are not necessarily inconsistent with Rousseau's ideas.

Religion. If the chapter "Civil Religion" seems to strike a new note in the *Contrat social*, it is certainly not incompatible with the religious emphasis of Rousseau's thought, for religion had always played an important role in his work, as the "Profession de foi du vicaire savoyard" made clear. Nature itself must be understood in the widest sense, as the whole realm of being originally created by God, who guarantees its goodness, unity, and order. Rousseau offended traditional Christian orthodoxy with his belief that man needs no intermediary between himself and God and is able to attain salvation by his own efforts. (In spite of his great respect for the figure of Jesus and the message of the Gospels, Rousseau could not accept the notion of the Incarnation as a solution to the problem of human sin.) But Rousseau never doubted the importance of accepting God's existence; man, he believed, is impelled toward God by the evidence of both feeling and reason, for apart from the presence of intelligence in the universe there is also the sensitive man's deep "feeling for nature" and the inescapable conviction of a real bond uniting his immortal soul with the spiritual order which underlies the outward appearance of the physical world. As is well known, Rousseau was the eighteenth-century writer who gave particularly eloquent expression to this aspect of the "feeling for nature." Furthermore, apart from the testimony of reason and sensibility there is also that of the all-powerful conscience, the "divine instinct" or "voice of the soul" which forms the basis of man's moral existence. In moments of doubt and perplexity, when all else fails man, he can always rely for guidance on the promptings of his conscience. This does not mean that reason is thereby excluded, for reason is to be condemned only when it becomes the instrument of blind passion or selfish reflection—in other words, when it fails to recognize its dependence upon other essential elements of human nature. Conscience, however, is an even more important attribute; it is a fundamental feeling that is strikingly effective when reason may be impotent. Even so, conscience, reason, and freedom are all integral elements of man's natural endowment, potentialities that it is his right and duty to develop, for God gave him "conscience to love the good, reason to know it and freedom to choose it." It is only through the harmonious development of all man's faculties that he can come to a full understanding of his own nature and the place allotted to him by God in the universal order.

At first sight Rousseau's philosophy seems to retain many characteristics of the traditional metaphysical outlook, and several critics have stressed his great admiration for Plato and Malebranche. In Rousseau's eyes the universe still possesses a rationality, order, and unity which reflect the wisdom and intelligence of its creator. Yet this cannot be known by reason alone, for although reason has a function in all reflection about the meaning of the world, the heart may often provide surer insights into the ultimate mystery of creation. Moreover, Rousseau's system took the form of a series of basic intuitions which he subsequently linked together into a unified whole. His thought, therefore, is imbued with a strongly personal element which excludes any purely abstract or rationalistic speculation about the ultimate meaning of reality. What concerns him is that part of reality which is identified with the nature of man. The nature of man is, of course, inseparable from nature in the wider sense, but sensibility and feeling, rather than mere reason, are probably the most effective means of penetrating this wider objective realm of being. The thinker concerned with fundamental truths will do well, in Rousseau's view, to concentrate on what is of interest to him, "interest" here being defined not in any narrowly pragmatic or empirical sense but as indicating those matters which appertain to man's original nature. This means that Rousseau finally emerges as a moralist rather than as a traditional metaphysician.

Since reflection on the nature of man involves the ability to distinguish between reality and appearance, between the genuinely original and the merely artificial aspects of existence, the thinker's first task must be to abandon the illusions of opinion for the truths of nature. This explains both the negative, critical aspects of Rousseau's views of modern society and his more positive, constructive efforts to elaborate a philosophy of man. If his interpretation of nature seemed too optimistic to satisfy the demands of contemporary religious orthodoxy, it was also too religious to please the advocates of philosophical skepticism or materialism. Of one thing Rousseau felt quite certain: to ignore or reject the profound moral and spiritual aspects of human existence could have only the most disastrous consequences for the welfare of humanity. The discovery of truth requires an active renewal of the whole man and a reawakened moral consciousness which acknowledges the full implications of man's situation in the universe; the genuine possibilities of human life cannot be separated from the universal order of which they are a part, and man's ultimate felicity is to feel himself at one with a God-created "system in which all is good."

Like so many of his contemporaries Rousseau considered happiness to be the legitimate goal of human endeavor, but he insisted that "enjoyment" must not be interpreted in a shallow or selfish manner. Happiness consists of being oneself and of existing according to one's own nature, but a nature that has been purified of all ex-traneous artificial elements. When truly fulfilled, man will experience satisfaction with himself and a sense of being identified with the pure "feeling of existence"; this, in turn, presupposes the ability to find a true personal unity and plenitude. No doubt, Rousseau's efforts to realize this ideal in his own life were not free from ambiguity and contradiction, as an examination of his personal writings well shows, but his didactic works are consistent in their main objective.

In a corrupt society the recovery of a full human existence can never take the form of a mere return to nature, for the nature of man cannot be equated with the primordial state of nature. Although Rousseau was often nostalgically drawn to the innocence and simplicity of early times, he also treated nature as a dynamic, forward-looking concept. Starting from man as he is, the movement toward nature must be constantly sustained by the vision of what man might be. The achievement of this goal requires a radical transformation of human existence, the rediscovery and re-creation of a new nature. At the same time Rousseau did not believe in the need for any kind of supernatural grace to help man to carry out this task, since nature represented an innate possibility that could be realized through the wise exercise of human freedom alone.

Rousseau's powerful influence on later generations was partly due to this vision of a regenerated human nature, but unlike merely utopian thinkers he seemed to promise a transfiguration of everyday existence, not the pursuit of a hopeless chimera. Indeed, his philosophy revealed a striking, if often elusive, combination of idealistic and realistic elements which constantly seemed to open up the possibility of a better world. Moreover, this optimistic outlook was transmitted through a particularly eloquent and persuasive style, rich in emotional and musical overtones, giving the impression of intense sincerity and convincing the humblest of men that he need never feel ashamed to call himself a human being.

Works by Rousseau

For bibliographical information about the various editions of Rousseau's works, though not about works on Rousseau, the reader is referred to Jean Sénelier, *Bibliographie générale des oeuvres de J.-J. Rousseau* (Paris, 1949), and Théophile Dufour, *Recherches bibliographiques sur les oeuvres imprimées de J.-J. Rousseau*, 2 vols. (Paris, 1925).

COLLECTIONS AND OTHER EDITIONS

Of the collected editions of Rousseau's works, *Oeuvres complètes de J.-J. Rousseau*, 13 vols. (Paris, 1865–1870), and *Oeuvres et correspondance inédites de J.-J. Rousseau*, G. Streckeisen-Moultou, ed. (Paris, 1861), will be superseded by *Oeuvres complètes de Jean-Jacques Rousseau*, Pléiade Bernard Gagnebin and Marcel Raymond, eds. (Paris, 1959——), five vols. projected. Similarly, the *Correspondance générale de J.-J. Rousseau*, Théophile Dufour and P.-P. Plan, eds., 20 vols. (Paris, 1924–1934), with the *Table de la correspondance générale*, P.-P. Plan and Bernard Gagnebin, eds. (Geneva, 1953), will be superseded by the *Correspondance complète de Jean-Jacques Rousseau*, R. A. Leigh, ed. (Geneva, 1965——).

Although the new Pléiade edition of the collected works will henceforth be authoritative, the following separate editions are still important: *Political Writings*, C. A. Vaughan, ed., 2 vols. (Cambridge, 1915); the critical edition of *La Nouvelle Héloïse*, Daniel Mornet, ed., 4 vols. (Paris, 1925); *La Profession de foi du vicaire savoyard*, P. M. Masson, ed. (Paris, 1914); *Les Rêveries du promeneur solitaire,* J. S. Spink, ed. (Paris, 1948). For the *Confessions* see also the edition by Jacques Voisine (Paris, 1964).

Works on Rousseau

Some general bibliographic information about studies of Rousseau's work is to be found in Albert Schinz, *État présent des travaux sur J.-J. Rousseau* (New York and Paris, 1941); Jacques Voisine, "État des travaux sur J.-J. Rousseau," in *L'Information littéraire,* Vol. 16 (May–June 1964), 93–102; and Peter Gay, *The Party of Humanity, Studies in the French Enlightenment* (London, 1964), Ch. 8, "Reading about Rousseau."

A very pleasant introduction to Rousseau is Bernard Gagnebin's *A la Rencontre de Jean-Jacques Rousseau* (Geneva, 1962), a picturesque collection of texts, documents, and illustrative material. Sound general introductions to Rousseau's thought are Daniel Mornet, *Rousseau l'homme et l'oeuvre* (Paris, 1950); E. H. Wright, *The Meaning of Rousseau* (Oxford, 1929), which corrects earlier misinterpretations of Rousseau's idea of nature; and J. H. Broome, *Rousseau: A Study of His Thought* (London, 1963), to which should be added *Rousseau par lui-même,* Georges May, ed. (Paris, 1962), the pioneering article by Gustave Lanson, "L'Unité de la pensée de Jean-Jacques Rousseau," *Annales de la société Jean-Jacques Rousseau,* Vol. 8 (1912), and Ernst Cassirer, *The Question of Jean-Jacques Rousseau,* translated and edited with an introduction by Peter Gay (New York, 1954).

For Rousseau's biography see Jean Guéhenno, *Jean-Jacques,* 3 vols. (Paris, 1948–1952), of which a new edition, entitled *Jean-Jacques, histoire d'une conscience,* 2 vols., was published in 1962. See also F. C. Green, *Jean-Jacques Rousseau: A Critical Study of His Life and Writings* (Cambridge, 1955).

More detailed discussions of various aspects of Rousseau's philosophy are to be found in C. W. Hendel, *J.-J. Rousseau moralist,* 2 vols. (New York and Oxford, 1934; 2d ed., 1 vol., New York, 1962), an important examination of Rousseau's intellectual development; Albert Schinz, *La Pensée de Jean-Jacques Rousseau* (Paris, 1929), which stresses and perhaps exaggerates the basic conflict between the "romantic" and the "Roman" Rousseau but is nevertheless a significant study; Pierre Burgelin, *La Philosophie de l'existence de J.-J. Rousseau* (Paris, 1952), an important modern synthesis of Rousseau's thought; Robert Derathé, *Le Rationalisme de Jean-Jacques Rousseau* (Paris, 1948), a helpful corrective to earlier sentimentalist interpretations of Rousseau; and Jean Starobinski, *Jean-Jacques Rousseau, la transparence et l'obstacle* (Paris, 1957), an original and important study of certain key themes in Rousseau's thought.

Still important for a study of Rousseau's Genevan background is Gaspard Vallette, *Jean-Jacques Rousseau genevois* (Paris, 1908), although the discussion of the Genevan aspects of Rousseau's thought has been modified by more recent criticism, especially by J. S. Spink, *Rousseau et Genève* (Paris, 1934), and François Jost, *Jean-Jacques Rousseau suisse,* 2 vols. (Fribourg, 1961).

Indispensable for any serious study of Rousseau's religious thought is P. M. Masson's *La Religion de J.-J. Rousseau,* 3 vols. (Paris, 1916), in spite of some exaggeration of both its Roman Catholic and sentimental elements; for a corrective see Albert Schinz, *La Pensée religieuse de J.-J. Rousseau et ses récents interprètes* (Paris, 1927). On Rousseau's political thought see Alfred Cobban, *Rousseau and the Modern State* (London, 1934; 2d ed., 1964), and Robert Derathé, *Jean-Jacques Rousseau et la science politique de son temps* (Paris, 1950), which sets Rousseau's political thought in its contemporary philosophical context. For the difficult question of Rousseau's psychology and personality see Louis Proal, *La Psychologie de J.-J. Rousseau* (Paris, 1930), and Suzanne Elosu, *La Maladie de J.-J. Rousseau* (Paris, 1929). More recent discussions of this problem and its bearing on the personal writings are to be found in Ronald Grimsley, *J.-J. Rousseau: A Study in Self-Awareness* (Cardiff, 1961), and Marcel Raymond, *J.-J. Rousseau: La Quête de soi et la rêverie* (Paris, 1962).

The year 1962, being the 250th anniversary of Rousseau's birth, was marked by three important international conferences whose proceedings have been published: *Jean-Jacques Rousseau et son oeuvre, Colloque de Paris, 16–20 Octobre, 1962* (Paris, 1964); *Annales de la société Jean-Jacques Rousseau,* Vol. 35, *Entretiens sur J.-J. Rousseau* (Geneva, 1962); and *Études sur le contrat social de J.-J. Rousseau* (Paris, 1964), proceedings of Dijon conference of May 1962.

It has not been possible to include in this bibliography many important articles on Rousseau. For further information on this and other subjects, the reader is referred to the indispensable *Annales de la société Jean-Jacques Rousseau* (Geneva), published from 1905 on, which contains not only original articles but a full review of Rousseau literature.

RONALD GRIMSLEY

ROYCE, JOSIAH (1855–1916), American idealist philosopher, was born in Grass Valley, California. He received his A.B. degree from the University of California in 1875 and his doctorate from Johns Hopkins University in 1878. In the intervening years he studied in Germany at Leipzig and Göttingen, where he attended the lectures of Hermann Lotze. Royce returned to the University of California in 1878 as an instructor of English. Four years later, with the help of William James and George Herbert Palmer of the Harvard department of philosophy, he was invited to Harvard, where he taught for two years as a replacement for men on leave; in 1885 he received a regular appointment as assistant professor. Until his death Royce was one of the mainstays of the philosophy department in its so-called golden period. During that time he carried on his friendly debate with William James about the merits and demerits of absolute idealism, supervised the doctoral work of George Santayana, and delivered the Gifford lectures at the University of Aberdeen in Scotland. Royce was a prolific writer and was much in demand as a public speaker.

Philosophical orientation. Royce's philosophy is a unique synthesis of the rationalist metaphysic we associate with the system builders in the Western philosophical tradition and the appeal to experience and practice that has been dominant in American philosophy since 1875. Royce is the best American representative of absolute idealism, although there are voluntaristic elements in his position that distinguish it from both the Hegelian position and the systems of the British idealists. Royce's theory of the will and his conception of its role in the knowledge process introduced novel features into the tradition of rationalistic idealism. Royce was aware of this fact and hence called his position absolute voluntarism or absolute pragmatism.

Royce's thought revolves around the problems raised by a religious view of reality. He sought to resolve them through a metaphysical system constructed with the aid of concepts drawn from a wide range of thought and experience. Basic to his position is the concept of the self, an idea which he elucidated in several forms. In his earlier thought the self appears as the Absolute Knower, grasping all truth in one synoptic vision *totum simul.* Later, however, Royce put more emphasis on mediation and on the idea of system. Ultimately, he arrived at the community of interpretation, or social theory of reality, according to which all selves are joined in a Universal Community whose goal is to possess the truth in its totality.

THE NATURE OF BEING

In large measure Royce's idealism consists in his having given to the process of knowing a privileged position in the definition of reality. The nature of Being is to be determined through the elucidation of the process of being known.

Argument from error. The pattern of the approach through knowing was established early in Royce's development. In a paper, "Kant's Relation to Modern Philosophic Progress" (1881), he argued that the proper task of philosophy is to study the nature of experience, especially the role played by the forms of intellectual activity in knowing. In later works he returned repeatedly to the task of defining the relation between sense and understanding, between the perceptual and conceptual poles in experience and knowledge. Strongly influenced by Kant, Royce sought to discover the exact relation between the knowing activity and its matter. He asked how the function of judgment transforms the sensible starting point of all experience into knowledge. Whereas Kant had argued that the past moment and its datum can be brought into the present through the activity of the transcendental subject, Royce regarded the past and future as projections from the present. Knowledge starts with immediate data of sense; these data, as present, are beyond the control of judgment (this is the realistic element in Royce's idealism), but the whole of experience involving reference to a past, a future, and a public object is to be built up from the momentary consciousness. In order to accomplish this construction, judgment and principles of transcendence are required.

Dissatisfied with the view that assigns the status of postulates to the principles needed for transforming immediate data into knowledge, Royce sought to justify those principles. His theory of the Absolute Knower, which he developed in the well-known chapter "The Possibility of Error" in *The Religious Aspect of Philosophy* (Boston, 1885), was intended to show that the conditions for both knowledge and error must themselves be actual; what is actual cannot be explained or justified by what is merely possible or postulated. The argument that is presented for the existence of God or the Absolute Knower may be summarized as follows. Error actually exists; erroneous judgments cannot be made erroneous by finite knowers. In order to be in error, a judgment must fail to agree with its intended object. Yet if the intended object is wholly and completely defined by the isolated judgment, it is difficult to see how the judgment can fail to be true. Royce's central contention is that a judgment can have its own object and at the same time fail to agree with it only if the judgment is not isolated as an entirely enclosed fact but is, instead, part of a system of judgments or an organized body of thought. The isolated judgment cannot have within itself the distinction between its truth and falsity; for that we need an inclusive thought capable of relating the isolated judgment to all other actual and possible judgments about the intended object. In finding error as a fact that we cannot create, we are actually involved in the Infinite Thought. Without that Thought, error is either impossible or unintelligible. This ingenious argument assumes, among other things, that the real individual at which knowledge aims can be identified only at the end of the knowledge process. However, as Peirce and others have shown, there is no need to make this assumption, although without it the argument fails.

Thought and reality. Royce continued to approach the problem of Being—the problem of defining the basic nature of the real—through concentration on the knowledge process. He was also trying to retain critical philosophy and neutralize its negative judgment on the possibility of ontology. His solution was to say that a theory of Being is possible if we can discover the true relation between our ideas and the real world. In *The World and the Individual* (New York, 1901–1902) Royce posed the problem of Being as one of explaining what thought and reality must be like if the former is to attain genuine knowledge of the latter. By means of an extended dialectical argument, Royce examined three classical theories of Being (in his language, theories of "the ontological predicate")—realism, mysticism, and critical rationalism. In subjecting them to critical analysis, he tried to show the element of truth and error in each. From this analysis Royce's own voluntaristic idealism emerged; it was designed to avoid the errors of the other positions while preserving their truth in a new and more comprehensive system that defined Being in terms of purpose fulfilled.

For Royce realism is the doctrine that to be is to be independent of being known. According to realism, the real is just what it is apart from the knower and his acts of knowledge. Royce, however, aimed at exposing this position and hence placed a narrow construction on the term "independent." To be independent is taken to mean that the idea and object are totally externally related. If the idea and object are thus disconnected, he argued, then knowledge becomes inexplicable, and reality is severed from truth. Peirce, among others, objected to this statement of the realist position, describing it as one-sided.

Mysticism is defined as the thesis that to be is to be immediate. Here again, the real is understood as that which falls effectively beyond the power of analytical reason.

Royce's exposition of critical rationalism, which he defined somewhat cryptically with the formula "to be is to be valid," has been charged with ambiguity; Dewey claimed that Royce's entire argument was vitiated by his having confused "possible experience" and "validity" in his presentation of the position. Dewey's claim is not without warrant; Royce combined several ideas under one heading, and it is not clear that they are compatible. Nevertheless, Royce's argument is clear enough in its main outline. The critical rationalist does not accept the independent objects of either realism or common sense and still less allows the immediacy of mysticism. Instead, he defines the real as that which gives warrant or validity to our ideas. To be real in this instance means that an object conforms to certain universal forms or conditions—causal sequence, temporal succession, spatial relations, numerical identity, and so on—that are marked out in advance as the general structure of all experience. For Royce the merit of this position is that it comes closer to defining reality in terms of truth than was possible with either realism or mysticism. Critical rationalism, however, is inadequate because it can define or anticipate only the universal form of experience and cannot reach the determinate individual. Royce's point is that the determinate individual cannot be defined in terms of universal conditions of possible experience alone; in order to have knowledge of an individual, we must appeal to actual, sensible experience. But it is just the need for this appeal that marks the defect of the position; a completed rationalistic idealism would show us how to pass from the idea to its fulfillment in the individual object without having to appeal to a brute, sensible experience that is "given." Critical rationalism, however, is forced to rest with "possible experience," by which Royce meant the universal conditions that any proposed object of knowledge would have to satisfy in order to be an object of experience at all. It is important to notice that the entire discussion is dialectical, in the sense that Royce expounds and criticizes the alternative theories only in relation to his own final view. Competing theories fail or succeed precisely to the extent that they are incompatible with, or contribute to the development of, his voluntaristic idealism.

Voluntaristic idealism. Royce's own view can be summed up in the thesis that to be is to be the individual or determinate fulfillment of a purpose. Distinguishing between the internal and external meaning of ideas, Royce defined an idea as a purpose (internal meaning) seeking its object, or other (external meaning). An idea intends, and thus selects, its object; the object, as the full realization of the idea, must be the determinate individual that allows no other of its kind if it is to be the unique fulfillment of the purpose expressed by the original idea. If we say that Socrates is snub-nosed, our ideas (internal meaning) aim at, or intend, the unique and unduplicable individual Socrates (external meaning). Our ideas are not about just anyone or anything but only about the individual intended; the internal meaning selects the object (external meaning) by reference to which it can be judged true or false. The voluntarism of the position lies in the idea that the other at which all ideas aim is itself the expression of the absolute will or purpose. For Royce it is only in this way that we can explain how an idea can correspond with an object other than itself while that object remains other and yet is the object intended by the idea.

The entire theory is recognizable as a modern version of an ancient doctrine of self-knowledge. We start with an idea that is fragmentary and imperfectly understood, and we seek to find its true meaning in the object that is its individual fulfillment. The object intended exceeds the fragment with which we began; we can discover the true nature of the object and the truth or falsity of our idea only when we have reached the total individual reality that fulfills our purpose. Royce developed this conception of Being into a comprehensive system embracing a doctrine of man, nature, and God. The rational will and its purpose mark the ultimate reality; all finite individuality is what it is in virtue of its fulfilling the purpose of the Absolute Self.

The reality of the infinite. In the essay "The One, the Many and the Infinite" appended to *The World and the Individual*, Royce introduced the topic that was to occupy much of his later thought—the reality of the infinite. He attempted to refute the claim, made by F. H. Bradley in *Appearance and Reality* (1893), that we cannot express in clear concepts the detail of the many facts constituting the Absolute. Since such a claim, if true, would have rendered Royce's entire project pointless, he felt called upon to refute it. To explain how the many develop out of the one, Bradley argued, always leads to an actual infinity, and this is self-contradictory. In the Absolute all is one, but according to Bradley, we are unable to comprehend the unity. Royce denied that an actual infinite is self-contradictory. Through the concept of a self-representative system based on what would now be called a recursive function, he developed a modern version of the actual infinite. The form of the self-representative system was construed as a purpose or an ordering plan and defines once and for all an actual infinity of members. A self-representative system is one that represents itself with all else that it represents. A mirror of the entire universe, for example, would have to include itself among the represented items. By the form of the system, Royce meant the principle or purpose behind it, which in the above example would be mirroring. From the one form or purpose there comes, by the recurrent or self-representative operation, an infinity of detail such that nothing less than that infinity will serve to express all that was meant by the original form. Understanding the self as having the form of a self-representative system, Royce claimed that the multitude of details constituting the concrete individuality of the real world is an expression of that self. Reality is an actual infinite, a unity of one and many. Royce's later doctrine of the community of interpretation represents his final attempt to elaborate the theory.

Logic and mathematics. It is important to note that Royce took very seriously the development of mathematical logic and studies in the foundation of mathematics. He was fond of criticizing pragmatism for neglect of what he took to be a doctrine of absolute truth implied in the new logic of Frege, Russell, Giuseppe Peano, and Schröder. Maintaining that "order is the fundamental category of exact thought about facts," Royce argued for the validity of using technical logical concepts in the construction of a metaphysical theory. Two examples will clarify the point. In the analysis of discrimination, he used the concept of between, arguing that discrimination and comparison are possible because, given any two conceptions, we are always able to find a third conception that is between the other two and expresses some relation in which they stand. This point was later expressed through the logic of triadic relations and the theory of interpretation. An even more striking illustration is found in the use of the limit concept to define the nature of the real as individual. The reality at which the process of knowledge is directed is said to be the "limit" of a series of attempts to apprehend the object. Royce understood "limit," not in the sense of an end term that we can approach at will, but in the sense of a least upper bound, which, in the series $1 + 1/2 + 1/4 \cdots$, for example, is the least number that lies beyond the sum of the series—namely, 2. Thus, the real, individual reality is what is immediately beyond the whole series of efforts to know it.

ETHICAL AND RELIGIOUS DOCTRINES

Royce contributed ideas worthy of consideration to almost every branch of philosophy, not least in ethics.

Loyalty. Royce's *Philosophy of Loyalty* (New York,

1908) is still one of his best-known books. In it he developed the principle of loyalty to loyalty as the basic moral law. He regarded his principle as superior to both Kant's categorical imperative and Mill's principle of utility. Loyalty, by which is meant a freely chosen and practical devotion to a cause or goal, is the highest virtue. Royce was well aware of the existence of evil causes and of the fact that not every cause aims at the loyal spirit. Hence, he argued that loyalty in the ethical sense means devotion to causes that extend the spirit of loyalty and do not contribute to deception, dishonesty, racial and social strife, and so on. Every cause involves some loyalty, but not all causes involve loyalty to loyalty. It is only through loyalty to loyalty itself, the virtue that makes all social life possible, that the self can solve the basic problem of ethics, which is to find a good that is at once objective, in the sense that it constrains our purely individual and subjective interests, and freely chosen, so that the self can acknowledge its obligatory character. Royce followed Hegel in finding the good in a form of self-realization, and he followed Kant in upholding the autonomy of the will.

Philosophy of religion. Royce's interest in the philosophy of religion was a basic factor in the shaping of his philosophical position. Religious issues constitute the foundation of his thought, starting with *The Religious Aspect of Philosophy* (Boston, 1885) and continuing to his last major work, *The Problem of Christianity* (New York, 1913). Royce had a twofold aim in the philosophical treatment of religion. First, he sought to reinterpret classical religious ideas through contemporary experience and current language; second, he attempted to assess their validity by comparing them with the results of metaphysical analysis. Both aims are clearly present in *The Problem of Christianity*, in which he developed an original interpretation of the Christian religion, first, by uncovering the experiential roots of three central ideas—the church, sin, and atonement—and, second, by seeking support for these ideas in his metaphysic of interpretation and community.

Starting with the view that neither perception nor conception alone, nor any indeterminate combination of the two, is able to yield knowledge of selves, Royce went on to develop the theory of interpretation, according to which all our knowledge is mediated through signs. From this view it follows that the human self is not known (either by itself or another) intuitively as a particular datum or as a universal character but only as the goal of an infinite process of interpretation. In requiring comparison with other selves, this process necessitates a community if there is to be self-knowledge. Persons are involved in, and linked together by, a number of different communities—political, legal, economic, moral, religious—each of which is defined by its purpose or the goal for which it exists. The religious or Beloved Community has the special purpose of redeeming man from sin (a moral burden) and from the consequences of the self-centered deeds by which he endangers the community through disloyalty. The three central ideas of Christianity (the church, sin, and atonement) are linked together. The Beloved Community is the locus of the love (in Royce's terms, loyalty) exemplified by the atoning deed of Jesus; the church exists to overcome, through love, the self-centeredness of the individual and to transmute the evil consequences of treachery by a constant renewal of the community of many selves devoted to the cause of charity.

The novel feature of Royce's reinterpretation of Christianity is his attempt to rework the much neglected doctrine of the Spirit, or Third Person, of the ancient Trinitarian tradition. God now appears as the Spirit or Interpreter, linking together a multiplicity of distinct selves in a spiritual unity of love. The Beloved Community, founded by the sacrificial or atoning deed of Jesus, becomes the ultimate instrument of the redemptive process.

Unlike William James, Royce was clearly dissatisfied with a purely practical basis for religious belief. Instead, he made the validity of religion dependent on a metaphysical system. He set forth one such system in *The World and the Individual*, and he returned to the task in *The Problem of Christianity*, in which he dealt with specifically Christian ideas. In the intervening years Royce fell under the influence of Charles Peirce's thought, and he freely acknowledged an indebtedness to Peirce's theory of signs, his analysis of triadic relations, and the idea of the community of knowers engaged in interpreting the meaning of things through an infinite system of signs.

The continuation of the logical and epistemological aspects of Royce's philosophy is to be found mainly in the work of C. I. Lewis, and its metaphysical aspects are developed in the thought of W. E. Hocking. The strong current of pragmatism on the American scene, however, carried philosophical thinking away from the speculative realm and directed it into other channels.

Works by Royce

For a complete list of Royce's writings, published and unpublished, it is necessary to combine the bibliographies in the following works.

Cotton, J. H., *Royce on the Human Self.* Cambridge, Mass., 1954. Pp. 305–311.

Loewenberg, Jacob, *The Philosophical Review*, Vol. 26 (1917), 578–582.

Rand, Benjamin, *The Philosophical Review*, Vol. 25 (1916), 515–522.

Smith, J. E., *Royce's Social Infinite.* New York, 1950. Pp. 171–173.

Works on Royce

Cotton, J. H., *Royce on the Human Self.* Cambridge, Mass., 1954. Well-focused; based on manuscript as well as printed works; aimed at interpreting the whole of Royce's thought in terms of his theory of the self.

Cunningham, G. Watts, *The Idealistic Argument in Recent British and American Philosophy.* London and New York, 1933. A clear and helpful account of Royce's thought, focusing on his attempt to establish the truth of idealism by the argument from error.

Fuss, Peter, *The Moral Philosophy of Josiah Royce.* Cambridge, Mass., 1965. The most incisive account of Royce's ethical philosophy in relation to both his theory of knowledge and the doctrine of the community.

Marcel, Gabriel, *La Métaphysique de Royce.* Paris, 1945. Translated by V. Ringer and G. Ringer as *Royce's Metaphysics.* Chicago, 1956. Four articles on Royce's thought that originally appeared in 1918–1919. The entire range of Royce's philosophy is considered, with indications of Marcel's own existentialism and the resources for it that are to be found in Royce's theory of knowledge and the individual.

Muirhead, John H., *The Platonic Tradition in Anglo-Saxon Philosophy*. London, 1931. A fairly complete, but not especially penetrating, account of all of Royce's works from the earliest essays to *The Problem of Christianity*.

Smith, John E., *Royce's Social Infinite*. New York, 1950. A study of Royce's later thought, stressing the idea of the community and of its relation to Peirce's theory of signs. Considerable emphasis is placed on the logic of interpretation and its use in Royce's final statement of the religious issues.

JOHN E. SMITH

ROYER-COLLARD, PIERRE PAUL (1762–1845), French statesman and professor of philosophy, was born at Sompuis, a village in what is now the department of the Marne. He represented this department in the Chamber of Deputies from 1815 to 1839, usually in the opposition. He is best known as the leader of the *Doctrinaires,* a group whose members derived their political views from what they believed to be immutable and self-evident principles. These principles led to a compromise between absolute and constitutional monarchy, and though the principles were supported by Louis XVIII, they were rejected by his brother and successor, Charles X.

Royer-Collard had little, if any, philosophical training. Nevertheless, from 1811 to 1814 he was professor of philosophy and dean at the Sorbonne. He lectured first on Thomas Reid and later on his own views. Just as his political views were a compromise, so in philosophy he sought a compromise between the left wing of sensationalism and the right wing of authoritarian traditionalism. He found it in the philosophy of Thomas Reid. Royer-Collard rejected sensationalism on the ground that it could not account for judgment, which is always something contributed to sensory material by the active mind. Since the individual mind is active and capable of making judgments, there is no need of a supernatural authority to dictate to it. In place of such an authority he substituted common sense, which is a consolidation of the judgments of all men. But this did not imply a return to tradition except insofar as tradition itself is an expression of common sense. On the contrary, every man has within him the ability to distinguish between right and wrong, truth and falsity, by a power which resembles the natural light of medieval philosophy. If this faculty did not exist, he maintained, one would be stranded in solipsism, for there would be no reason to believe that one man's conclusions would be harmonious with another's.

Common sense, however, does not operate entirely without the guidance of reason. In reaching its decisions, reason utilizes two principles of argument, that of causality and that of induction. The search for causes is intrinsic to thinking itself and will inevitably lead back to the idea of a First Cause. For, following Newton, Royer-Collard believed that one must never accept more causes than are necessary to explain phenomena. However, he does not seem to have had any clear idea of the nature of a causal explanation.

The principle of induction is a necessary accompaniment to that of causality, for it is by induction that one discovers the essential similarities among phenomena that permit one to group them in a single class. It is man's nature to look for these similarities, as it is his nature to look for causes.

Following Reid, Royer-Collard maintained that the distinction between sensation and perception is all-important. Sensation is simply the pleasure found in experience and is purely subjective. Perception is the apprehension of an external object as external. The externality of the object is not proved by reasoning; it is judged by a spontaneous act of the human mind, as in the twentieth-century epistemology of G. E. Moore.

Though only fragments of Royer-Collard's philosophy exist, collected by his admirer Théodore Jouffroy, it is probable that he saw the philosophy of common sense as a support for his political views. Common sense is the basis of communal life; it provides stable theses of morality and religion; it has all the authority of natural law; and to those who accept it, it is incontrovertible. It is, however, generally admitted that the main contribution of Royer-Collard to French philosophy was the introduction into France of Scottish philosophy.

Works by Royer-Collard

Les Fragments philosophiques de Royer-Collard, André Schimberg, ed. Paris, 1913.

Discours prononcé à l'ouverture du cours de l'histoire de le philosophie. A very rare pamphlet in the Bibliothèque de l'Institut.

Works on Royer-Collard

Boas, George, *French Philosophies of the Romantic Period*. Baltimore, 1925. Pp. 157–164.

Garnier, Adolphe, "Royer-Collard," in Adolphe Franck, ed., *Dictionnaire des sciences philosophiques*. Paris, 1875.

Spuller, Eugène, *Royer-Collard*. Paris, 1895.

Taine, Hippolyte, *Les Philosophes classiques de XIXᵉ siècle en France*. Paris, 1857. To be read with caution.

GEORGE BOAS

ROZANOV, VASILY VASILYEVICH (1856–1919), Russian critic and philosopher. Rozanov was born in Vetluga, Russia, and attended secondary schools in Simbirsk (now Ulyanovsk) and Novgorod before entering Moscow University as a student in the faculty of history and philology. After his graduation from the university in 1881, he taught history and geography in a succession of secondary schools in provincial towns and began the writing on religious and philosophical themes which was to gain him a reputation as a brilliant if erratic critic of contemporary culture, both secular and religious. In 1893 a minor government post in St. Petersburg brought him to the center of Russian literary life, and in 1899 he retired to devote full time to writing. He published numerous books and contributed many articles to the Russian reviews of the day, particularly the reactionary *Novoye Vremya* ("New Times"). During the Russian Revolution he took refuge with the religious philosopher Father Paul Florensky in Sergiyevsky Posad (now Zagorsk), near Moscow, where he died.

Rozanov's first major writing and his only strictly philosophical work was an elaborate scholarly treatise entitled *O Ponimanii* ("On the Understanding"), in which he developed a conception of understanding as a unifying mode of cognition that reconciles science and philosophy. He first won public acclaim with his critical study of Dostoyevsky, *Legenda o Velikom Inkvizitore* ("The Legend of the Grand Inquisitor"). In a number of impressionistic, aphoristic works written from 1911 to 1918 he developed most fully the critique of Christianity and the "metaphysics of sex" for which he is best remembered. Chief among these later works are *Opavshiye Listya* (*Fallen Leaves*), *Uyedinyonnoye* (*Solitaria*), and *Apokalipsis Nashevo Vremeni* ("The Apocalypse of Our Time").

Rozanov's mature world view was a mystical theism based on the sanctification of sex. Emphasizing the generative power of sexuality, Rozanov saw in it the aspect of man that relates him most intimately to God. Sexuality is man's "noumenal aspect," of which his other qualities and capacities are manifestations. Rozanov vigorously attacked Christianity for its denial of the flesh in preaching celibacy and fasting and for its failure to recognize the holiness of elementary animal processes. He preferred the religion of the Old Testament because of what he regarded as its greater acceptance of life and greater humanitarianism, and he called for renewed worship of the vital biological forces enfeebled by Christianity.

Works by Rozanov

O Ponimanii. Moscow, 1886.

Legenda o Velikom Inkvizitore. St. Petersburg, 1894.

Religiya i Kultura ("Religion and Culture"). St. Petersburg, 1899.

Priroda i Istoriya ("Nature and History"). St. Petersburg, 1900.

Tyomny Lik: Metafizika Khristianstva. St. Petersburg, 1911.

Uyedinyonnoye. St. Petersburg, 1912. Translated by S. S. Koteliansky as *Solitaria.* London, 1927. The English edition contains an abridged account of Rozanov's life by E. Gollerbach, other biographical material, and matter from "The Apocalypse of Our Time."

Opavshiye Listya. St. Petersburg, 1913. Translated by S. S. Koteliansky as *Fallen Leaves.* London, 1929.

Izbrannoye ("Selections"), George Ivask, ed. New York, 1956.

Works on Rozanov

Edie, James M.; Scanlan, James P.; and Zeldin, Mary-Barbara, eds., *Russian Philosophy,* 3 vols. Chicago, 1965.

Poggioli, Renato, *Rozanov.* New York, 1962.

Zenkovsky, V. V., *Istoriya Russkoy Filosofii,* 2 vols. Paris, 1948–1950. Translated by George L. Kline as *A History of Russian Philosophy,* 2 vols. New York and London, 1953.

JAMES P. SCANLAN

RÜDIGER, ANDREAS (1673–1731), German physician and philosopher, was born in Rochlitz, Saxony. Poverty and bad health allowed him to study only irregularly. In 1692 he served as a tutor in the home of Christian Thomasius. He was compelled to interrupt his studies completely in 1695; not until 1697 could he enter the University of Leipzig, where he studied law and medicine, receiving a master's degree in 1700. He received a doctorate in medicine from the University of Halle in 1703, but he continued to lecture at the University of Leipzig. From 1707 to 1712 he practiced medicine and lectured in Halle, and from 1712 until his death he did so in Leipzig.

The development of Rüdiger's philosophy was greatly influenced by his teachers Christian Thomasius and Franz Budde. However, he soon developed individual views within the Thomasian school. His medical studies centered his interests on natural philosophy and gave his thought a practical bent. Like Budde's, Rüdiger's mind was more systematic than Thomasius'.

Rüdiger's most important work, *Philosophia Synthetica* (1706–1707), is divided into three sections: "Wisdom," "Justice," and "Prudence." The section on wisdom embraces logic and natural philosophy, that on justice covers metaphysics and natural law, and that on prudence covers ethics and politics.

Rüdiger's logic had a clear psychological orientation. He was mainly interested in the origin and development of our ideas, which, he held, come into our minds through the senses, although there are some innate mental elements, too. He criticized Descartes, discussed Gassendi, and drew some inspiration from Locke. Rüdiger stressed the passive element of the mind; reflection, or *sensio interna,* is (contrary to Locke) a passive fact. The standard of truth lies in man's consciousness, in a *recta ratio,* which is not common sense but something that can be acquired only through instruction in logic (*lumen acquisitum*). Logic was therefore more important for Rüdiger than for the other members of the Thomasian school. He developed a refined syllogistic theory, formalizing his acceptance of the mathematical method in philosophy. However, he conceived the mathematical method quite differently from Christian Wolff, as a method for deducing facts from given facts rather than as the drawing of possible conclusions from abstract principles. Rüdiger's philosophy, like that of the Thomasian school generally, was based in large part on the notion of reality and appealed mainly to the senses and to experience, both interior and exterior. He defined "truth" in connection with the possibility of perceiving and "existence" in connection with being perceived—again in the tradition of Thomasian subjectivism.

In natural philosophy, Rüdiger tried to combine the Thomasian and Pietistic animistic or spiritualistic physics with mechanism, but the spiritualistic element predominates. He held that we have no certain knowledge of nature, and generally he refrained from choosing between different hypotheses, for instance, between the Copernican and the Biblical astronomical theories.

The practical bent of Rüdiger's philosophy explains why he discussed metaphysics under the heading of justice. His metaphysical discussions were largely devoted to theology and to man's duties toward God; his discussions of natural law were devoted to our duties toward other men. Metaphysics is the science of reality, and in particular of the *ens realissimum,* rather than the science of possibility. However, according to Rüdiger, we cannot penetrate the essence of things in metaphysics; we can only establish, by means of experience, that things exist and how they exist.

Rüdiger's section on prudence constitutes, in the Thomasian tradition, a kind of anthropology, both private and public. Ethics provides precepts for reaching happiness on earth, and politics provides precepts for governing a commonwealth.

Through his pupil A. F. Hoffmann, Rüdiger exerted a

strong influence on the development of the philosophy of Christian August Crusius, and through Crusius on the whole development of German philosophy.

Works by Rüdiger

Disputatio Philosophica de Eo, Quod Omnes Ideae Oriantur a Sensione. Leipzig, 1704.

Philosophia Synthetica. Tribus Libris de Sapientia, Justitia et Prudentia. Methodo Mathematicae Aemula Breviter et Succinte in Usam Auditorum Comprehense. Leipzig, 1707. Reprinted at Halle, 1711, and at Frankfurt, 1717, as *Institutiones Eruditionis* and at Leipzig, 1723, as *Philosophia Pragmatica. Methodo Apodictica et Quoad Eius Licuit Mathematica Conscripta.*

De Sensu Veri et Falsi. Halle, 1709.

Physica Divina Recta Ira ad Ultramque Hominis Felicitatem Naturalem Atque Moralem Ducens. Frankfurt, 1716.

Klugheit zu Leben und zu Herrschen. Leipzig, 1722.

Christian Wolffens Meinung von dem Wesen der Seele und eines Geistes überhaupt, und Andreas Rüdigers Gegen-Meinung. Leipzig, 1727. A pamphlet attacking Wolff.

Works on Rüdiger

Carls, W., *Rüdigers Moralphilosophie.* Halle, 1894.

Schepers, Heinrich, *A. Rüdigers Methodologie und ihre Voraussetzungen.* Cologne, 1959.

Wundt, Max, *Die deutsche Schulphilosophie im Zeitalter der Aufklärung.* Tübingen, 1945. Pp. 82–97.

GIORGIO TONELLI

RULES. A rule, in the sense to be discussed here, is a prescribed guide for conduct or action; other senses of the word "rule," in which a rule is an empirical regularity or a straight line or the reign of a monarch, will be left out of account.

There are many kinds of rules, corresponding to many senses of the phrase "prescribed guide for conduct or action." The simple verbal definition of what a rule is can satisfactorily include the whole range of rules because it is vague: there are many sorts of action, a variety of kinds of guidance, and different ways of prescribing. The action may be an individual's conjoining two sounds in his speech; it may be an individual's conduct toward other individuals; it may be the disposition of a dispute by a judge; or it may be what card is played next in solitaire or what symbols are set down next by a logician. The guidance may be self-imposed, it may be enforced by the threat of punishment, or it may be a necessary condition for communication or for some action. The guidelines may be prescribed by being formally adopted or explicitly formulated, or the prescription may simply be implicit in the correction and training that is given to persons being initiated into a practice.

For examples of rules that are expressly formulated, one might reach into the U.S. Code, the Ten Commandments, a book of etiquette, the published rules of contract bridge or college football, and a book of recipes. There is considerable variety in the examples found, but still they have instructive features in common: the rules are formulated in verbal expressions, they are formulated by recognized authorities, and the immediate purpose of formulating them is to offer some sort of guidance to conduct and action. The verbal expression of a rule, although itself admitting of considerable variation, can be of great help in recognizing rules. Such an expression, a rule formulation,

identifies a class of actions or a type of conduct and says that such action or conduct is permissible, prohibited, or obligatory. Rule formulations can, of course, vary greatly in clarity and precision, as well as in form. But they always serve to explain rules: If someone asks about a certain rule, or about the rule (to wit, the rule of a recognized authority) governing a certain situation, there is no simpler or more direct way to tell him what the rule is than by giving a verbal formulation of it.

Sometimes, however, rules are not so explicitly presented, and great confusion can result from failing to distinguish rules from the expressions used to formulate them. It is obvious that there cannot be a linguistic expression which formulates a rule unless there is (in some sense) a rule that is so formulated—although the rule need not be actually operative in anybody's behavior. But the converse does not hold. A simple case where a rule is invoked but not formulated would be that of saying to a chess novice when his king is in check, "You must move your king now." Here the verbal expression refers to a particular instance rather than to a class of actions, and hence does not state the rule. No doubt one could, if pressed, state the rule about moving kings when in check, but in more complicated cases this will not always be possible. Every language, for example, depends on and is partly constituted by rules of grammar; but many languages have never been analyzed in even a rudimentary way, and it is not easy to give an accurate formulation of the rules of even one's native language. It follows that there are almost certainly very many rules which have never been formulated.

Since there are rules that have never been formulated, there must be ways to recognize rules other than by there being an explicit statement of the rule. What is necessary for such recognition is that there be a guide for speech or conduct and that this guide be prescribed. In the case of a language whose grammar has never been formulated, the first of these conditions is clearly met: speech is guided by the patterns of sound and syntax that are characteristic of the speakers of one's native language. It is also the case that these patterns are prescribed, since children's deviations from the standard language patterns are corrected by their elders—although, of course, the elders generally do not prescribe the patterns or rules in any formal or explicit manner. Such rules are embedded in the language: although never formulated, they are constantly invoked.

Rules in games and formal systems. Embedded rules are essential to any practice or institution, such as a game. Sometimes the rules of a game are officially articulated by a governing body, as in the case of baseball and bridge. In the case of competitive games, especially where the outcome does not depend on the physical skill of the players, it is sometimes possible to devise an optimum strategy based simply on a clear statement of the rules of the game. Game theory studies such optimum strategies and how they are affected by changes in the rules (see DECISION THEORY). But sometimes no clear statement of the rules is available; and perhaps none is possible. In the case of informal children's games—which seem clearly to be structured, although not so rigidly as baseball or bridge—it may be difficult and unimportant to say just what rules the children are observing in the course of their afternoon's play. What is important is this: if an activity is identified as a game, it must be so identified on the basis of a structure in the activity such as might be described by rule formulations, that is, by explicitly stating what the players may or must or cannot do at certain times or in certain circumstances. If an activity is not implicitly or explicitly governed by rules—that is, if there are not regularities discernible in it, or if the regularities in it are accidental rather than prescribed—it cannot be a game. Games, therefore, are constituted or defined by the rules according to which they are played (although the identity conditions are not so strict that every rule change need result in a new game). The fact that a game inevitably has rules lies behind Wittgenstein's talk of "language-games" and his suggestion that a language is like a game.

Formal systems, or logical calculi, also provide models for languages—again because of the prominent role of rules in them. Such calculi are often considered a sort of game, in which the object is to develop the system in accordance with the stipulated rules; and they are, like games, constituted by rules. Here, however, articulation of the rules is far more important than in the case of games, since there is no antecedent practice in which the rules are manifested. To determine a formal system it is necessary to state precise rules specifying (1) what counts as a symbol, (2) which strings of symbols are permissible (well formed), (3) which permissible strings serve as axioms, and (4) how other permissible strings (theorems) are to be inferred. Sometimes these calculi are called "artificial languages," and in considering them as models of natural languages one must bear in mind two ways in which the role of rules in them is artificial. One is that the rules are exact. The other is that since all the rules are explicitly formulated, the distinction between rules and rule formulations is of little significance.

Rules of natural languages. In the case of a natural language, such as English or German, one may also say that the language is constituted by a set of rules. In this case, however, the distinction between rules and rule formulations is of critical importance, since most such rules have not been explicitly or adequately formulated. In fact, there is not yet an adequate set of rule formulations for any natural language. To say that a natural language is constituted by certain rules cannot be substantiated by arbitrarily specifying what the rules shall be, as in the case of formal systems. In this case the rules must be found rather than made up, for to say that such-and-such rules characterize the English language is not to create a language (nor to say how English should be spoken) but is a report of what rules do in fact guide the linguistic behavior of certain people. It follows that a statement about the rules of a natural language is subject to empirical confirmation or refutation in a way in which the formulation of the rules of a logical calculus is not. The rules of a language are embedded in a certain practice or institution or pattern of behavior, and the purpose of formulating them is to describe that practice; that is, to identify it and characterize it so that, for example, it would be possible for an outsider then to participate in it. Linguists, grammarians, and lexicographers aim to give this sort of description

of languages, and it was the contention of Wittgenstein in his later writings that philosophical remarks are also of this sort.

It might initially seem that rules are essentially and unqualifiedly restrictive, since they determine what cannot or what must be done or said. Consideration of the role of rules in games and languages shows that this supposition is quite wrong. All the rules discussed so far have the effect of opening up new realms of activity, by defining the acts and practices in question, rather than that of restraining men from something they can already do. One cannot play bridge at all, one cannot even renege, except by reference to the rules which define the game; mathematical logic must remain entirely alien to one who won't learn the rules for it; and there are a whole host of common human activities, such as gossiping, telling jokes, giving orders, asking questions, lying, making promises, and so forth—which Wittgenstein referred to as a prominent part of the "natural history" of man—that one can engage in only after mastering a language. The case of language is particularly interesting, since possibilities are opened up not only by following the rules which characterize the language and its subsidiary activities but also by deviating from them. For example, lying involves deliberate deviation from the rule not to assert that S is P unless S is in fact P, a rule without the general observance of which the linguistic activities of reporting and giving testimony would be impossible.

Metaphor, which Aristotle defined as "giving the thing a name that belongs to something else," involves a similar sort of deviation from a lexical rule (see METAPHOR). The importance of rules is never more apparent than when one considers how rules define, or are indispensable to, our linguistic activities.

Moral rules. Moral rules are precepts that ought to be followed, whether they are in fact followed or not. Moral rules, in this sense, are very different from rules which define customs and practices: one can find out empirically what rules people advocate or observe, but, as Hume and G. E. Moore insisted, one cannot determine by such empirical study whether these rules really ought to be followed—that is, whether they are moral rules. Moral rules also differ from rules constitutive of either formal systems or institutions in typically dealing with what must and what cannot be done rather than specifying what may be done: The Ten Commandments, for instance, include only prohibitions and obligations, not permissions. Since most general precepts share these characteristics, philosophers, particularly those who stress deontology in ethical theory, generally distinguish between rules of prudence or etiquette and genuinely moral rules—a distinction very like the one Kant made between hypothetical and categorical imperatives.

Within the class of moral rules it also seems important, especially from the point of view of utilitarianism, to further distinguish between "summary rules," which provide a simple rule of thumb for maximizing utility in most cases, and "practice rules," which are rules one must (logically) follow in order to participate in some ethically valuable practice. If, for example, the precept not to tell lies is a summary rule, a utilitarian may justifiably decide to lie in a given case after considering the effects of the lie on that one case alone; but if the precept is a practice rule, it may be claimed that a utilitarian must also take into account the beneficial consequences of any practice which depends on and is partly constituted by the rule. The view that many moral rules are practice rules is often known as *rule utilitarianism* and is designed to meet traditional criticisms of utilitarianism by severely restricting direct utilitarian consideration of individual cases.

It seems, although the issue is controversial, that moral rules, setting forth obligations and prohibitions rather than permissions, restrict the range of action otherwise open to a person. For instance, the practice of making contracts—that is, the fact that certain constitutive rules are generally observed—enables one to contract to do something which one cannot or will not do; but this possibility of action is severely restricted if one's actions are governed by the moral rule always to fulfill one's obligations. Similarly, our range of expression is greater because we have simple words for sexual organs and acts, but the range is considerably narrowed again by social taboos against using those words. Because they serve as constraints and restraints, moral rules do not enable us to *do* anything we could not otherwise do; they serve, rather, to guide us among existing alternatives and perhaps also enable us to *be* what we could not otherwise be—for example, to be polite, conscientious, or justified. A conscientious housewife does a greater variety of household jobs than one who is not conscientious, but the precept to clean conscientiously does not define these jobs or make them possible. The jobs were possible all along, and the rule to clean conscientiously, if obeyed, makes it *necessary* (in some sense) to do them. This restricts or narrows the previously defined range of possibilities; for if it were not for the rule to clean conscientiously, one could either do these jobs or not. Following such rules makes possible a *quality* of action otherwise inconceivable, but not a greater *variety* of action.

Rules of law. Legal rules sometimes seem like rules of grammar and sometimes like moral rules, and a major dispute in the philosophy of law centers on which of these resemblances deserves greater prominence. Proponents of natural law emphasize that considerations of justice play a large role in the formulation, interpretation, and revision of laws; and they argue that statutes and judicial precedents are, in effect, codified moral rules. From this point of view legal rules are regarded as statements of what *ought* to be and as restraints. Representatives of legal realism and sociological jurisprudence, on the other hand, point out that legal rules characterize the structured aspects of how conflicts are resolved and judicial decisions made. From this point of view, which has been fruitfully adopted by anthropologists who describe the unarticulated legal systems of primitive peoples, legal rules are regarded as constitutive of existing practices and therefore devoid of any special moral force. There is enough variety among legal rules so that both these conceptions of law can find application, the former conception becoming more apt as the rules have to do more with taboos and substantial justice than with procedure. (See LEGAL REALISM and SOCIOLOGY OF LAW.)

Bibliography

The most useful source of instructive remarks about games and practices and about understanding and following rules is Ludwig Wittgenstein, *Philosophical Investigations* (Oxford, 1953). There are general discussions in Max Black, *Models and Metaphors* (Ithaca, N.Y., 1962), and J. Rawls, "Two Concepts of Rules," in *Philosophical Review*, Vol. 69 (1955), 3–32.

On linguistic rules, see *Linguistics Today,* a diverse collection of professional papers edited by A. Martinet and U. Weinreich (New York, 1954), and K. L. Pike, *Language in Relation to a Unified Theory of the Structure of Human Behavior,* 3 parts (Glendale, Calif., 1954–1960).

For an anthropological discussion of a legal system, see M. Gluckman, *The Judicial Process Among the Barotse of Northern Nigeria* (Glencoe, Ill., 1955). Consult also the bibliographies to the articles cited in cross references for further reading on the role of rules in special areas.

NEWTON GARVER

RUMANIAN PHILOSOPHY. Because the Balkan Peninsula was culturally isolated for so long as a result of the Ottoman conquest, philosophy developed tardily in the Rumanian principalities. Between the fifteenth and seventeenth centuries, few philosophical works were translated or copied in Rumania's monasteries; Rumanian monks were interested chiefly in mystical theology, hagiography, and religious folklore. When contact with the West was restored, Italian humanism made a strong impact on some important historiographers. Dimitre (or Demetrius) Cantemir (1673–1723), prince of Moldavia, was an encyclopedic genius who studied logic, metaphysics, and the new natural philosophy and wrote many treatises both in Latin and in Rumanian. His influence, however, was mainly indirect; following his example, scholars began translating texts and textbooks from Greek, German, and French. Historians and educators of the eighteenth and nineteenth centuries read some of the new philosophers and tried to apply their methods. The great historian Nicolae Bălcescu (1819–1859), for example, was influenced by Giambattista Vico. Almost all of the romantic writers borrowed ideas or political programs from Herder, Hegel, or the French encyclopedists. But systematic philosophical endeavor did not begin until the creation of chairs of philosophy at the universities of Jassy and Bucharest and, in particular, with the teaching of Titu Maiorescu (1840–1917) and Dimitrescu-Iaşi (1849–1923). Both were excellent, if unoriginal, professors. More creative, although nonsystematic, was Mihail Eminescu (1850–1889), Rumania's greatest poet. The first philosopher to develop his own philosophical system was Vasile Conta (1845–1882). With his *Theory of the Universal Undulation* (1877), Conta inaugurated the materialistic school, whose members during the 1920s included P. P. Negulescu and the Marxist L. Patraşcanu. The two other main currents of modern Rumanian philosophy are idealism, represented especially by Stefan Zeletin (1882–1934) and Eugeniu Sperantia, and critical realism (I. Petrovici, T. Braileanu). But none of these authors produced an important, original system of philosophy. The contribution of a historian, Alexandru Xenopol (1847–1920), was more significant; his *Théorie de l'histoire* (1908) presented history as a science of causally connected and successive events.

The most creative modern Rumanian philosophers are

those who have not suffered from a sense of inferiority born of cultural provincialism. Although well-acquainted with Western philosophy, they have not attempted to imitate, adapt, or apply the ideas of fashionable German or French philosophers. Constantin Rădulescu-Motru (1868–1954) thought that his system of "energetic personalism" could explain both the evolution of the universe and human creativity. His pupil Nae Ionescu (1890–1940) was responsible for an awakening of interest in metaphysics and religious philosophy. The most gifted and original thinker has been Lucian Blaga (1899–1962), the only Rumanian philosopher to have completed an extremely complex system, including a highly personal metaphysics, a new theory of knowledge, and a detailed morphology of culture. In this ambitious construction Blaga utilized myths, symbols, and ideas from popular Rumanian traditions, both religious and secular. For the first time, the autochthonous heritage of Rumania found philosophical expression. No less interesting is the work of Constantin Noica (born 1911); following Ionescu he has tried to harmonize a Hegelian understanding of history with the Eastern Church's idea of God. Also deserving mention are D. Gusti, founder of Rumanian rural sociology; T. Vianu (born 1897), author of a well-known treatise on aesthetics; the existentialist E. M. Cioran (born 1912); and the logician and philosopher of science Stéphane Lupasco (born 1900). In summation, the Rumanian philosophical genius is best revealed in those thinkers who have tried to synthesize the native spiritual traditions of eastern Europe and the rigorous methodology of the West.

(See Rumanian Philosophy in Index for articles on Rumanian philosophers.)

Bibliography

Botez, Octav, *Alexandru Xenopol, teorician şi filozof al istoriei.* Bucharest, 1928.

Horia, Vintilă, "Introduction à la pensée de Lucian Blaga." *Acta Philosophica et Theologica*, Vol. 2 (1964), 163–174.

Miclea, I., "Conceptii dominante in filozofia românească." *Cultura Creştină*, Vol. 21 (1941), 18–35, 209–221.

Stefanescu, Marin, *Filozofia românească.* Bucharest, 1922.

Mircea Eliade

RUSKIN, JOHN (1819–1900), English critic of art and society, was born in London, the son of a wine merchant. He began writing while at Oxford and in 1843 published, in London, the first volume of *Modern Painters*, four more volumes of which were published during the next 16 years. In 1849 he published *The Seven Lamps of Architecture* and between 1851 and 1853 *The Stones of Venice* (3 vols.). The major part of his work as a young man was criticism of art and architecture, and his subsequent ethical and social writing grew from this root. The beginnings of this important extension of his range can be seen in the famous chapter "The Nature of Gothic" in *The Stones of Venice;* the important connection established there, between art and "the right kind of labour," is developed in *The Political Economy of Art* (printed as *A Joy for Ever,* 1857), *Unto This Last* (1862), *The Crown of Wild Olive* (1866), and *Munera Pulveris* (1863 and 1872). Meanwhile Ruskin continued his criticism of art and architecture,

notably in *The Two Paths* (1859) and in his lectures as Slade professor of art at Oxford, between 1870 and 1879 and in 1883/1884. A volume of essays, *Sesame and Lilies,* appeared in 1865 and an unfinished autobiography, *Praeterita,* between 1885 and 1889. He also published letters on social questions, notably in *Time and Tide* (1867) and *Fors Clavigera* (8 vols., 1871–1884).

Ruskin's social and ethical teaching, though deeply influenced by the work of Carlyle, followed from his understanding of the nature of art. The artist's function is to reveal aspects of the universal truth, which is also beauty. Any corruption of the moral nature of the artist is an inevitable corruption of this revelation, but it is impossible, finally, for an artist to be good if his society is corrupt. The art of any society is, correspondingly, "the exact exponent of its social and political virtues." Where there is a lack of "wholeness" in art (wholeness being a full and deep response to the organic life of the universe), there is a corresponding lack of "wholeness" in society; to recover the one men must recover the other. Just as the beauty of art is the expression of the essential nature of the universe—what Ruskin called "typical beauty"—so the goodness of man is the "exertion of perfect life," which, in comparable relation to the grand design of the created universe, is no more and no less than the "felicitous fulfillment of function" in all living things. From his work on Venice, Ruskin developed a comparative historical approach to the social conditions in which the "exertion of perfect life" can be fostered or damaged. In particular, following the English romantic writers and the architectural critic A. W. Pugin, he saw nineteenth-century industrial civilization as the enemy of wholeness in its rampant individualism, its substitution of "production" for "wealth," and its basic misunderstanding of the nature of work. This kind of social criticism came in many respects to resemble the ideas of some philosophical socialists, and Ruskin's work had an important formative influence on the British labor movement, both directly and through his influence on William Morris, who united Ruskin's ideas with a direct commitment to socialism.

Ruskin's opposition to individualism as a social principle and to competition as a method of political economy was based on his idea of function, the fulfillment of each man's part in the general design of creation. This required a social order based on intrinsic human values, whereas the existing social order, based on the supposed laws of supply and demand, tended to put the economy above men—indeed, to reduce them to mere "labor"—and, by separating work from the pursuit of human perfection, to separate the work from the man, producing only an alienated and fragmented being. Wherever value is understood as "exchange value," rather than as the "intrinsic value" derived from function in the universal design, this corruption of man to a mere tool or machine is inevitable. In particular, the confusion about the nature of value leads to false definitions of both wealth and labor. Labor is degraded whenever it is anything other than the "exertion of perfect life," a creative activity comparable to that of the artist. Wealth is degraded whenever it is confused with mere production, for the meaning of wealth is human well-being, which in material terms is "the possession of useful articles *which we can use."* Even if the existing system always produced useful articles, the kind of society that it also produced made just distribution and wise consumption impossible. Much actual production, and its widespread misuse, could more properly be called "illth" than "wealth," for if it possessed only exchange value and not intrinsic value it corrupted its makers and its users.

The most remarkable aspect of Ruskin's work, then, is the development of a philosophy of art into a moral critique of industrial capitalism. It is a very individual achievement, but it is also part of a general movement of nineteenth-century English thought and has evident connections with Wordsworth, Shelley, Coleridge, and Carlyle, as well as with Morris and the Guild Socialists whom Ruskin so notably influenced.

Works by Ruskin

Works, E. T. Cook and Alexander Wedderburn, eds., 39 vols. London, 1903–1912.

Works on Ruskin

Evans, Joan, *John Ruskin.* London, 1954.
Hobson, J. A., *John Ruskin, Social Reformer.* London and Boston, 1898.
Hough, Graham, *The Last Romantics.* London, 1949.
Quennel, Peter, *John Ruskin, Portrait of a Prophet.* London, 1949.
Whitehouse, J. H., *Ruskin the Prophet.* London, 1920.
Williams, Raymond, *Culture and Society,* Part 1, Ch. 7. London, 1958.

RAYMOND WILLIAMS

RUSSELL, BERTRAND ARTHUR WILLIAM, British philosopher, mathematician, and social reformer, was born in Trelleck, Wales, in 1872. Russell is the grandson of Lord John Russell, who introduced the Reform Bill of 1832 and later twice served as prime minister under Queen Victoria. John Stuart Mill, a close friend of Russell's parents, was his godfather in an informal sense. Russell's parents died when he was a little child. Both of them had been freethinkers, and his father's will had provided that he and his brother were to have as their guardians friends of his father's who shared the latter's unorthodox opinions. As the result of litigation the will was set aside by the Court of Chancery and the two boys were placed in the care of their paternal grandparents. Lord John Russell died two years later, and it was the boys' grandmother who determined the manner of their upbringing. Russell was not sent to school but received his early education from a number of Swiss and German governesses and, finally, English tutors. He entered Cambridge University in October 1890 and studied mathematics and philosophy at Trinity College from 1890 to 1894. He was a fellow of Trinity College from 1895 to 1901 and lecturer in philosophy there from 1910 to 1916. In 1916 Russell was dismissed by Trinity College because of his pacifist activities. He was reinstated in 1919 but resigned before taking up his duties.

What is generally considered Russell's most important work in philosophy was done between 1900 and the outbreak of the first world war. From 1916 until the late 1930s Russell did not hold any academic position and supported himself by writing and public lecturing. During this period

he wrote some of his most influential books on social questions, including *Marriage and Morals* (London, 1929) and his two books on education— *On Education, Especially in Early Childhood* (London, 1926) and *Education and the Social Order* (London, 1932). These views were put into practice in Russell's experimental school, the Beacon Hill School, which he started with his second wife, Dora, in 1927. Russell left the school in 1934 after he and Dora were divorced (the school itself continued until 1943). Russell returned to more concentrated work in philosophy around 1936. He moved to the United States in 1938, teaching first at the University of Chicago and then at the University of California at Los Angeles. In 1940 he accepted an invitation from the Board of Higher Education of New York City to join the department of philosophy at City College. However, he never had an opportunity to take up this appointment, having been found unfit for this position in a remarkable opinion by a judge who felt he had to protect "public health, safety and morals." From 1941 until 1943 Russell lectured at the Barnes Foundation in Philadelphia (these lectures were later expanded into *A History of Western Philosophy*). Dr. Albert Barnes, the head of this foundation, dismissed Russell in January 1943, on three days' notice. In this instance Russell successfully brought action for wrongful dismissal. In 1944 he returned to Cambridge where he had been re-elected to a fellowship at Trinity College.

Russell was a candidate for Parliament on three occasions and was defeated each time: In 1907 he ran at Wimbledon as a candidate of the National Union of Women's Suffrage Societies, in 1922 and 1923 he stood as the Labour party candidate for Chelsea. Russell has twice been jailed—in 1918 for six months on a count of an allegedly libelous article in a pacifist journal and in 1961, at the age of 89, for one week, in connection with his campaign for nuclear disarmament.

In 1908 Russell was elected a fellow of the Royal Society. He became an honorary fellow of the British Academy in 1949, and in the same year he was awarded the Order of Merit. Russell has twice served as president of the Aristotelian Society and has for many years been president of the Rationalist Press Association. In 1950 he received the Nobel Prize for Literature. In making the award, the committee described him as "one of our time's most brilliant spokesmen of rationality and humanity, and a fearless champion of free speech and free thought in the West."

Russell has three children and has been married four times. In 1931, upon the death of his brother, he became the third earl Russell.

Writing in 1935 the German historian Rudolf Metz referred to Russell as "the only British thinker of the age who enjoys world-wide repute." At that time his works could not circulate in Germany, Italy, or Russia. Now they are available in every major and a great number of minor languages (a truncated version of *A History of Western Philosophy* is allowed to circulate even in the Soviet Union). It is safe to say that not since Voltaire has there been a philosopher with such an enormous audience. Russell also shares with Voltaire a glittering and graceful prose style and a delicious sense of humor. It is perhaps Russell's gay irreverence as much as the substance of his heretical opinions that has so deeply offended several generations of moralists and religious conservatives.

In the following section we shall briefly recount some of the highlights and formative influences in Russell's eventful life and sketch his views on political and social issues. Although these views are certainly logically independent of his more technical work as a philosopher, they deal with questions which have traditionally been discussed by philosophers, and they also help one to understand the basic motives inspiring Russell's thought.

LIFE AND SOCIAL THEORIES

Russell's childhood and adolescence were unhappy. The atmosphere in his grandmother's house was one of puritan piety and austerity, and his loneliness, he recalls, was almost unbearable. Only virtue was prized—"virtue at the expense of intellect, health, happiness, and every mundane good." At the age of five Russell reflected that if he lived to be seventy, he had endured only a fourteenth part of his life, and he felt the long-spread-out boredom ahead of him to be unendurable. In adolescence, he remarks, he was continually on the verge of suicide, from which, however, he was "restrained by the desire to know more mathematics." His grandmother had gradually moved from Scottish Presbyterianism to Unitarianism. As a child Russell was taken on alternate Sundays to the parish church and to the Presbyterian church, while at home he was taught the tenets of Unitarianism. When he was 14 he began to question theological doctrines and in the course of four years abandoned successively belief in free will, immortality, and God, the last as the result of reading John Stuart Mill's *Autobiography*. For some time, however, Russell had metaphysical attachments that served as substitutes for religion, and it was not until the end of the first world war that he became a militant opponent of all forms of supernaturalism.

Early Platonism and Hegelianism. Under the influence of J. M. E. McTaggart and F. H. Bradley, Russell came, in his early years at Cambridge, to believe "more or less" in the Absolute and the rest of the apparatus of British Hegelianism. "There was a curious pleasure," Russell wrote in retrospect, "in making oneself believe that time and space are unreal, that matter is an illusion, and that the world really consists of nothing but mind." In a "rash moment," however, he turned "from the disciples to the Master." Hegel's remarks in the philosophy of mathematics he found "both ignorant and stupid," and in other ways Hegel's work appeared a "farrago of confusions." After that Russell was converted by G. E. Moore to a "watered down" version of Plato's theory of Ideas, regarding the subject matter of mathematics as eternal and unchanging entities whose exactness and perfection is not duplicated anywhere in the world of material objects. Eventually Russell abandoned this "mathematical mysticism" as "nonsense." Following Ludwig Wittgenstein he came to believe "very reluctantly" that mathematics consists of tautologies. As to the timelessness of mathematics, Russell now regarded this as resulting from nothing more than that the pure mathematician is not talking about time. Aside

from this, it became emotionally difficult for him to remain attached to "a world of abstraction" in the midst of the slaughter of the Great War. "All the high-flown thoughts that I had had about the abstract world of ideas," he wrote later, "seemed to me thin and rather trivial in view of the vast suffering that surrounded me." The nonhuman world, he added, "remained as an occasional refuge, but not as a country in which to build one's permanent habitation." Since his abandonment of Platonism, Russell writes, he has not been able to find religious satisfaction in any philosophical doctrine that he could accept.

Pacifism. Russell has been interested in social questions throughout his life. He was an early member of the Fabian Society and for some time in the 1890s, under the influence of Sidney and Beatrice Webb, championed imperialism and supported the Boer War. In 1901 he had a quasi-religious experience. He became "suddenly and vividly aware of the loneliness in which most people live" and felt the need to find ways of "diminishing this tragic isolation." In the course of a few minutes he changed his mind about the Boer War, about harshness in the education of children and in the administration of the criminal law, as well as about fierceness in personal relations. This experience led him to write his famous essay "A Free Man's Worship" (1903). Although Russell became a pacifist right then, for another ten years or more he was preoccupied with work in mathematical logic and theory of knowledge. It was not until the war that he became passionately concerned about social issues. It is probable, he observed later, that "I should have remained mainly academic and abstract but for the War." The war, however, "shook him" out of many prejudices and made him reexamine a number of fundamental questions. He recalled:

> I had watched with growing anxiety the policies of all the European Great Powers in the years before 1914, and was quite unable to accept the superficial melodramatic explanations of the catastrophe which were promulgated by all the belligerent governments. The attitude of ordinary men and women during the first months amazed me, particularly the fact that they found a kind of pleasure in the excitement. (*Selected Papers of Bertrand Russell*, p. xi)

He decided that he had been quite mistaken in believing the claims of pacifists that wars were the work of devious tyrants who forced them on reluctant populations. Although he was not then familiar with the theories of psychoanalysis, Russell concluded that the majority of human beings in our culture were filled with destructive and perverse impulses and that no scheme for reform would achieve any substantial improvement in human affairs unless the psychological structure of the average person was suitably transformed.

Russell recalls that his decision to oppose the war was made particularly difficult by his passionate love of England. Nevertheless, he had no doubt as to what he had to do. "When the war came I felt as if I heard the voice of God. I knew that it was my business to protest, however futile protest might be. My whole nature was involved. As a lover of truth, the national propaganda of all the belligerent nations sickened me. As a lover of civilisation, the return to barbarism appalled me" (*Portraits From Memory*, p. 27). Russell remarks that he never believed much tangible good would come from opposition to the war, but he felt that "for the honor of human nature," those who "were not swept off their feet" should stand their ground. He patiently argued in lectures and books that the slaughter of millions of men was not justified by any of the possible gains of a defeat of the Central Powers. Russell's pacifism was not mystical. It was not then and has not been his contention at any time that the use of force is always wrong, that war can never possibly be justified. He maintained that *this* war in *these* circumstances was not worth all the pain and misery, and the lying of all the parties. Consistently with his general position, Russell favored the Allies during the Second World War on the ground that the defeat of the Nazis was essential if human life was to remain tolerable. The Kaiser's Germany by contrast was "only swashbuckling and a little absurd," allowing a good deal of freedom and democracy.

Prior to the war there had been strong pacifist sentiment in all the major Western countries, especially among the intellectuals and the powerful socialist and liberal parties. When war came only a tiny minority of these pacifists remained true to its convictions. Overwhelmed by their need to conform and in many cases by what Russell would have regarded as their own primitive impulses, many of them became the most violent jingoists. Russell was bitterly attacked for his pacifist activities not only, as one might have expected, by conservatives and professional patriots but also by many of his erstwhile friends. H. G. Wells, for example, publicly heaped abuse on Russell when he was already in trouble with the authorities. Russell's political philosophy, according to Wells, amounted to a "tepid voluntaryism," and he (unlike Wells) had no right to speak for British socialism. Wells even abused Russell's work as a mathematical philosopher. Russell, he wrote, is that "awe-inspiring" man who "objected to Euclid upon grounds no one could possibly understand, in books no one could possibly read" (Preface to P. H. Loyson, *The Gods in the Battle*, London, 1917).

At Cambridge, Russell's teacher and friend McTaggart led a move for his ouster. Meetings addressed by Russell were broken up by violent mobs without any police interference. Eventually he was prosecuted by the government. For writing a pamphlet on the case of a conscientious objector he was fined £100. When he would not pay the fine the government sold parts of his library, including rare books on mathematics which Russell was never able to recover. In 1918 he was sentenced to six months' imprisonment for an article in *The Tribunal*, a pacifist weekly, in which he had written that "unless peace comes soon . . . the American garrison, which will by that time be occupying England and France, . . . will no doubt be capable of intimidating strikers, an occupation to which the American army is accustomed when at home." In a fierce denunciation which accompanied the sentence, the magistrate, Sir John Dickinson, referred to Russell's offense as "a very despicable one" and added that Russell "seems to have lost all sense of decency." It should be

added that as the result of the intervention of Arthur Balfour, Russell was treated with consideration while in prison—he finished there his *Introduction to Mathematical Philosophy* and began work on *The Analysis of Mind*.

Attitude toward the Soviet Union. Russell's isolation was not ended with the return of peace. This was due to his failure to support the Bolshevist regime in Russia. Like many Western socialists he at first welcomed the news of the revolution, but, wanting to see things for himself, he visited Russia in 1920 and came back totally disillusioned. Some of Russell's friends argued that any criticism of the revolution would only play into the hands of the reactionaries who wanted to re-establish the old order. After some hesitation Russell decided to publish the truth as he saw it. Russia, he later wrote, "seemed to me one vast prison in which the jailors were cruel bigots. When I found my friends applauding these men as liberators and regarding the regime that they were creating as a paradise, I wondered in a bewildered manner whether it was my friends or I that were mad."

The little book in which he recorded his views of the Soviet Union, *The Theory and Practise of Bolshevism* (1920), was remarkable for, among other things, its prescience. Long before most Westerners had heard of Stalin, Russell predicted, point by point, the reactionary features that came to characterize the Soviet system under Stalin—its militarism and nationalism, the hostility to free art and science, its puritanism, and the gradual ascendancy of bureaucrats and sycophants over the early idealists. Russell was able to reprint the book in 1947 without a single alteration. His isolation after his return from Russia was even greater than during the war. The patriots had not yet forgiven him his opposition to the war, while the majority of his former political friends denounced him for his opposition to the Soviet regime. But Russell has never played to the galleries. As on many other occasions he acted in accordance with his favorite Biblical text—"Thou shalt not follow a multitude to do evil."

Education and sexual morality. Probably the most controversial of Russell's opinions are those relating to education and sexual morality. These were closely connected with his observations of the joy people took in the fighting and killing during the war. Russell wrote that he thought he saw the inward and outward defeats that led to cruelty and admiration of violence and that these defeats were, in turn, largely the outcome of what had happened to people when they were very young. A peaceful and happy world could not be achieved without drastic changes in education. In sexual matters, although not only in these, irrational prohibitions and dishonesty were exceedingly harmful. "I believe," he wrote in *Marriage and Morals*, "that nine out of ten who have had a conventional upbringing in their early years have become in some degree incapable of a decent and sane attitude towards marriage and sex generally" (p. 249). Conventional education was judged to be at fault in a great many other ways as well. Its general tendency was to cramp creative impulses and to discourage a spirit of critical inquiry. While a certain amount of discipline is necessary, very much of the coercion traditionally employed cannot be justified. The child who is coerced "tends to respond with hatred, and if, as is usual, he is not able to give free vent to his hatred, it festers inwardly, and may sink into the unconscious with all sorts of strange consequences throughout the rest of life."

Although puritanical moralists were or professed to be violently shocked by Russell's views on sex and education, it is worth emphasizing that his recommendations are not extreme and that unlike his opponents he stated his position temperately and without recourse to personal abuse. Russell may be characterized as a "libertarian" in education, but he was strongly opposed to the view of other educational pioneers who played down the importance of intellectual training and encouraged originality without insisting on the acquisition of technical skill. Similarly, although he may quite fairly be called a champion of free love, it is grossly misleading to describe Russell as an advocate of "wild living." On the contrary, he disavowed any such intentions. He wrote:

> The morality which I should advocate does not consist simply in saying to grown-up people or adolescents: "follow your impulses and do as you like." There has to be consistency in life; there has to be continuous effort directed to ends that are not immediately beneficial and not at every moment attractive; there has to be consideration for others; and there should be certain standards of rectitude. (*Marriage and Morals*, p. 243)

But this does not mean that we should be "dominated by fears which modern discoveries have made irrational." Russell could see nothing wrong in sexual relations before marriage, and he advocated temporary, childless marriages for most university students. This, he wrote, "would afford a solution to the sexual urge neither restless nor surreptitious, neither mercenary nor casual, and of such a nature that it need not take up time which ought to be given to work" (*Education in the Modern World*, pp. 119–120). It would be wrong to regard Russell as an enemy of the institution of marriage. He did indeed object to keeping a marriage going when no love is left, and, what shocked people a great deal, he remarked that a "permanent marriage" need not exclude "temporary episodes," but he also emphatically affirmed that "marriage is the best and most important relation that can exist between two human beings . . . something more serious than the pleasure of two people in each other's company" (*Marriage and Morals*, p. 115).

Russell's views on sexual morality featured prominently in the New York City case of 1940. When his appointment was announced, Bishop Manning of the Episcopal church wrote an inflammatory letter to all New York City newspapers in which he denounced Russell's subjectivism in ethics and his position on religion and morality. It was unthinkable that "a man who is a recognized propagandist against both religion and morality, and who specifically defends adultery" should be held up "before our youth as a responsible teacher of philosophy." The bishop's letter was the beginning of a campaign of vilification and intimidation unsurpassed in a democratic nation in recent times. The ecclesiastical journals, the Hearst press, and numerous Democratic politicians joined in the chorus of abuse.

Russell was described as "the Devil's minister to men," as an advocate of "the nationalization of women," as "the mastermind of free love and of hatred for parents," and also, needless to say, as an exponent of communism.

The climax of the campaign was a taxpayer's suit by a Mrs. Jean Kay of Brooklyn demanding that Russell's appointment be annulled. The case was heard before Justice McGeehan, who had previously shown his notions of tolerance by trying to have a portrait of Martin Luther removed from a courthouse mural illustrating legal history. In a startling decision, which was bitterly criticized by legal experts as in many respects grossly improper, McGeehan voided Russell's appointment on three grounds: First, Russell had not been given a competitive examination; second, he was an alien and there was no reason to suppose that the post in question could not be competently filled by an American citizen; and, finally, the appointment would establish "a chair of indecency." Elaborate arguments were adduced in behalf of this last claim. Among other things it was maintained that Russell's doctrines would tend to bring his students "and in some cases their parents and guardians in conflict with the Penal Law." In some fashion not explained by the judge, Russell's appointment would lead to "abduction" and rape. Russell's opposition to the laws which make homosexuality a crime was misread as advocacy of a "damnable felony . . . which warrants imprisonment for not more than 20 years in New York State." Evasive actions of the mayor of New York, Fiorello La Guardia, prevented any effective appeal against this monstrous decision, and Russell was never able to take up his position at City College. In 1950, shortly after receiving the Nobel prize, he returned to New York to deliver the Machette lectures at Columbia University. He received a rousing reception which those who were present are not likely to forget. It was compared with the acclaim given Voltaire in 1784 on his return to Paris, the place where he had been imprisoned and from which he had later been banished. As for McGeehan, it is safe to say that he will go down in history as a minor inquisitor who used his one brief moment in the limelight to besmirch and injure a great and honest man.

McGeehan did not pass judgment on Russell's competence as a philosopher, but other opponents of the appointment were not so restrained. Thus, Joseph Goldstein, attorney for Mrs. Kay, described Russell as "lecherous, libidinous, lustful, venerous, erotomaniac, aphrodisiac, irreverent, narrow-minded, untruthful, and bereft of moral fiber." After a few gratuitous lies about Russell's private life, he concluded:

> He is not a philosopher in the accepted meaning of the word; not a lover of wisdom; not a searcher after wisdom; not an explorer of that universal science which aims at the explanation of all phenomena of the universe by ultimate causes . . . all his alleged doctrines which he calls philosophy are just cheap, tawdry, worn-out, patched-up fetishes and propositions, devised for the purpose of misleading the people.

In the present encyclopedia a somewhat different view is taken of the value of Russell's philosophy. Some of his most important theories in epistemology and metaphysics will be discussed in the next section, his contributions to logic and the foundations of mathematics will be covered in the following section, and his views on ethics and religion will be dealt with in the last section. However, a number of Russell's most interesting ideas are not at all or only briefly discussed in the present article. Many of these are treated elsewhere in the encyclopedia. (See ANALYSIS, PHILOSOPHICAL; CORRESPONDENCE THEORY OF TRUTH; EPISTEMOLOGY, HISTORY OF; INFINITY IN MATHEMATICS AND LOGIC; LOGIC, HISTORY OF; LOGICAL PARADOXES; MATHEMATICS, FOUNDATIONS OF; MEMORY; NUMBER; PROPER NAMES AND DESCRIPTIONS; PROPOSITIONS, JUDGMENTS, SENTENCES, AND STATEMENTS; REFERRING; and TYPES, THEORY OF.)

EPISTEMOLOGY AND METAPHYSICS

Russell has exercised an influence on the course of Anglo-American philosophy in the twentieth century second to that of no other individual. Yet, unlike many influential thinkers, he neither founded nor attached himself to any definite movement. Although he wanted above all to be empirical, he has always had reservations of one sort or another to the proposition that all acceptable beliefs can be derived from purely empirical premises, and although his stress on analysis as the proper philosophical method is one of the chief sources of the analytical bent that philosophy currently has in English-speaking countries, he has never accepted the view that philosophy is nothing but analysis.

Early realism. Russell's first distinctive philosophical work was colored by a violent reaction against the absolute idealism then dominant in England, which was ultimately based on the thought of G. W. F. Hegel and whose outstanding British exponent was F. H. Bradley. According to Bradley if we try to think through the implications of any fact whatever, we will inevitably be forced to conclude that everything that there is constitutes a single, immediate unity of consciousness. In Russell's view the main weapon used to bludgeon people into submission to this result was the "doctrine of internal relations," according to which any relational fact—for example, that x is above y—is really a fact about the natures of the terms involved. This doctrine in effect refuses to take relations as ultimate.

It follows from this position that whenever x and y are related, each "enters into the nature of the other." For when x is above y, then being above y is part of the nature of x and being below x is part of the nature of y. Hence, y is part of the nature of x and x is part of the nature of y. Since everything is related to everything else in one way or another, it follows that everything else enters into the nature of any given thing, which is just another way of saying that there is no "other thing" relative to a given thing. In other words, the only thing that exists is one all-comprehensive entity. From the related principle that when we are aware of something, that something enters into the nature of the awareness or of the mind which has the awareness, it follows that it is impossible to conceive of anything which is not included within consciousness. Thus, the one all-comprehensive entity is a unity of consciousness.

Although in his youth Russell, with most of his philosophical contemporaries, was caught up in this philosophy, he and G. E. Moore became disenchanted with it shortly before the turn of the century. Russell came to hold that in sense perception we are as immediately aware of the relations between things as of the things themselves and therefore that any philosophy which denied ultimate reality to relations must be mistaken. Moreover, he came to think that mathematics would be impossible if we held that every relation enters into the nature of its terms; for in mathematics we must understand what our units *are* before we can know anything about their relations to other units. Russell therefore argued for a "doctrine of external relations," according to which relations have a reality over and above the terms they relate and do not enter into the definition of the terms they relate. This led him to a kind of philosophical atomism that thenceforth was characteristic of his philosophy. We may think of the basic core of atomism, which runs through all the shifts in Russell's later philosophizing, as being constituted by the following principles:

(1) There are nonmental facts that are what they are whether or not any mind ever becomes aware of them. This does not follow from the doctrine of external relations, but that doctrine enabled Russell to reject the idealistic argument based on the doctrine of internal relations and thus left him free to hold his native realist convictions with a good conscience.

(2) A particular proposition (for example, that my car is in the garage) can be unqualifiedly true "in isolation." This follows from the thesis that facts are "atomic" in the sense that any given fact could hold, whatever is the case with the rest of the world, together with the correspondence theory of truth—that what makes a true proposition true is its correspondence with an objective fact. Hegelians, on the other hand, had argued that since one could not adequately think about any particular fact without inflating it into the absolute totality of being, whenever one is saying something short of everything, what he is saying is not quite true in any absolute sense.

(3) An important corollary of (2) is the usefulness of analysis as a method in philosophy. If it is possible to get an adequate grasp of the parts of a totality without considering their place in the whole, then it is possible to give an illuminating account of something complex by showing how its simple parts are related to form the whole. Hegelians had argued that analysis cannot get started because we cannot understand what any part is without already seeing how it fits into the whole, which means already knowing everything about the whole. The conviction that analysis is the proper method of philosophy has remained the most prominent strand in Russell's thought.

Intoxicated by his release from idealism, Russell, as he later put it, tended to accept as objectively real anything that the absolute idealists had not succeeded in showing to be unreal. Numbers, points of space, general properties like roundness, physical objects as they appear to sense perception, were all regarded as having an independent existence. Under the influence of Alexius Meinong this extreme realism was reinforced by an extreme form of the referential theory of meaning, the view that in order for a linguistic expression to have a meaning there must be something that it means, something to which it refers. In this stage of Russell's thought, represented most fully by *The Principles of Mathematics* and to a lesser extent by *The Problems of Philosophy*, Russell was inclined to think that the meaningfulness of the sentence "The car is in the garage" required that there be objectively existing referents not only for the words "car," "garage," and "in" but even for the words "the" and "is." An objectively existing "isness" soon proved to be too much for Russell's self-proclaimed "robust sense of reality." He came to think that terms belonging to the logical framework of sentences, such as "the," "is," "or," could perform their function without each being correlated with extralinguistic referents. Nevertheless, a modified form of the referential theory of meaning continued to dominate Russell's thinking.

Logical constructionism. Russell's decisive shift away from the full-blooded realism of *The Principles of Mathematics* came with the development of logical constructionism. The theory can be generally stated as follows. We start with a body of knowledge or supposed knowledge which we feel strongly inclined to accept but which has the following drawbacks: (1) the knowledge claims do not seem to be adequately justified, (2) there are unresolved problems about the natures of the entities involved, and (3) we feel uncomfortable about committing ourselves to the existence of such entities. If we can show that this body of knowledge could be formulated in terms of relations between simpler, more intelligible, more undeniable entities and that when so formulated there is a decisive justification for it, we will have made a philosophical advance. We will have converted the problematic to the unproblematic, the obscure to the clear, the uncertain to the certain. Russell called this technique logical constructionism because the problematic entities were said, in a possibly misleading metaphor, to be "constructed" out of the simpler ones.

Reduction of mathematics to logic. The technique of logical constructionism was first employed in the theory of mathematics worked out by Russell and A. N. Whitehead and published in *Principia Mathematica* (3 vols., 1910–1913). In the *Principia* the authors set out to show that all of pure mathematics can be stated in terms of logic, using no undefined terms other than those required for logic in general—for example, implication, disjunction, class membership, and class inclusion. In the course of carrying out this reduction, various more or less problematic mathematical entities were "constructed" out of what were thought to be less problematic entities. Thus, numbers were defined as classes of classes: Zero is the class of all empty classes. The number 1 is the class of all classes each of which is such that any member is identical with any other member. The number 2 is the class of all classes each of which is such that it includes a member not identical with another member and such that any member is identical with one or the other of these. If one is puzzled about what sort of entity a number is (it does not seem to be in space or time and is not perceivable by the senses) or is uncomfortable about assuming that such queer entities

exist, he will presumably be reassured by the discovery that he can think of numbers as classes of classes of familiar, unproblematic entities. Of course analogous problems may arise with respect to the entities made use of in this first reduction—for example, classes. And in fact various difficulties in doing mathematics in terms of classes led Russell to try to "construct" classes out of "propositional functions." (See the section on logic and mathematics, below.) Starting from a given point we may well have to perform a series of reductions before we get down to maximally intelligible, indubitable entities.

Construction of physical objects. After *Principia Mathematica*, Russell applied the technique of logical constructionism to our knowledge of physical objects, both in physical science and in common sense. Physical theories are formulated in terms of a variety of unperceivable entities—electromagnetic fields, protons, energy quanta, forces exerted at a point, etc. There are serious problems in the philosophy of science both about the content of our concepts of such entities and about the basis for our accepting their existence. We can try to show that such entities can be inferred from what we know about perceivable entities, but how could we get an empirical basis for a principle correlating observed and unobserved entities? Or we can try to show that unobserved entities have to be *postulated* in order to give an adequate explanation of observed happenings, but it seems impossible to show conclusively that no adequate explanation could be given purely in terms of observables. If we apply the constructionist principle, "Whenever possible, substitute constructions out of known entities for inferences to unknown entities," to this problem, we shall try to show that electromagnetic fields can be construed as complexes of less problematic entities related in various ways. Russell has devoted a large proportion of his philosophical energy to trying to show that scientific entities can be constructed out of undeniable data of perception. But it will be easier to illustrate this kind of analysis by taking ordinary physical objects like trees and buildings, for Russell thinks that they raise analogous problems, although in less obvious ways.

There is a long tradition, dominant since the time of Descartes, according to which common sense is mistaken in supposing that we directly perceive physical objects. According to this tradition what we are directly and indubitably aware of in sense perception is something private to the individual observer. There are several sources of this view, the most important of which are, first, the fact that the content of one's perception can change with, for example, changes in perspective, lighting, and physiological condition of the observer, without there being any change in the physical object which, according to common sense, one is perceiving, and, second, the fact that in dreams and hallucinations one can have experiences which are intrinsically indistinguishable from those one has when one is "really" seeing a tree, but in these cases no tree is present. In dreams and hallucinations one is really aware of *something* which is not a physical object and is not perceivable by anyone else. And since these experiences are intrinsically just like those in which a physical object is present, one must be perceiving these private objects in the latter cases as well. This consideration is reinforced by the first, which is designed to show that even where a physical object admittedly is involved, I am often aware of different things without the physical object's undergoing any change.

The conclusion of these arguments is that the colors, shapes, sounds, etc., of which we are directly aware in sense perception (sense data) are private objects which must be distinguished from the entities in the physical world (if any) which we suppose ourselves to be perceiving. This conclusion inevitably gives rise to the question how, if at all, I can start from the private objects of whose existence I can be certain and show that public, physical objects like trees exist. No generally accepted solution to this problem has emerged in several centuries of discussion. Here again Russell tries to avoid the necessity for an inference by showing that the public physical objects can be construed as a complex structure of data of immediate experience. At first Russell aimed at a solipsistic reduction in which a given physical object would be constructed out of the actually experienced data of a single observer, but he soon came to lower his aspiration and to admit into the construction data experienced by others, as well as data which *would* have been experienced by others if they had been in a certain place. The view, then, is that a tree can be regarded as a system of all the actual and possible sense experiences that would be regarded as figuring in perceptions of that tree. This is a form of the position known as phenomenalism, and it is subject to the difficulties to which that position is notoriously subject, particularly the apparent impossibility of specifying which experiences go into defining a particular physical object without referring to that physical object or others in the specification.

Construction of mind. Until about 1920 Russell was a mind–matter dualist. As we have just seen, physical objects were regarded as complex structures of data of the sort given in sense perception. Now, although the mind might be partly constituted by data which are given to "inner sense"—that is, things which are the objects of *introspective* awareness, such as images and feelings—it seemed to Russell, as it had to most philosophers, that in any act of awareness, be it directed to the external or to the internal world, there is in addition to the data of which one is aware a subject or self which has the experience or which performs the act of awareness. But as the spirit of logical constructionism took increasing hold of Russell, he came to feel that there was no real warrant for believing in a subject of awareness which performs acts. He became convinced that one cannot really find any such constituent of the experience; its apparent obviousness is a reflection of the grammar of the sentences in which we speak about such matters—we say "*I* saw a flash of light" rather than "A flash of light occurred." As it presents itself, a minimal piece of consciousness does not involve a relation between two components. It is a unitary whole. Only the flash of light is given. The "I" and the "saw" are added interpretations. If we have no real basis for accepting a subject or mind as an ultimate entity, then the logical constructionist will try to show that it can be exhibited as a complex of entities of which we are directly assured by our experi-

ence. Here Russell followed the lead of William James, who had earlier formulated a view known as neutral monism, according to which both mind and matter consisted of the data of immediate experience. the difference between them lying in the grouping of the constituents. Thus, if I am looking at a tree the visual datum (an irregularly shaped green splotch) of which I am directly aware is both part of my mind and part of the tree. When grouped together with other experiences from this and other perspectives that would be said to be experiences of that tree, it goes to make up a tree; when grouped with other data bound together in a single conscious field, along with other data related to these by memory, it goes to make up a mind. If this theory is acceptable, traditional puzzles about the mind–body relation are dissolved. We are faced not with two radically distinct kinds of stuff but with two different kinds of arrangement of the same elementary components. (That is, some of the components are the same. Russell considers images to be peculiar to mind.) It is in the light of this theory that one should consider Russell's notorious view that what one perceives is always his own brain. Whenever I have any sense perception whatever, I do so because a certain kind of physical activity is going on in my brain. This activity, as a physical process, is to be regarded, like all physical processes, as a construction out of the sort of data given in immediate experience. And since whatever may be the case otherwise, my brain is always active when I perceive, the data of which I am aware enter into the constitution of my brain, whatever other entities they may enter into. Hence the paradoxical view that whenever one is conscious he is aware of his own brain.

When Russell abandoned the subject of experience as an ultimate constituent of the world he rejected sense data and thenceforth spoke simply of sense experiences. But he would have represented his view more clearly by saying that he had given up belief in anything other than sense data. For in the old paradigm of *subject aware of sense data,* it was the subject exercising awareness that was abandoned. In *The Analysis of Mind* Russell set out to construct the conscious mind out of sensations and images. (Insofar as facts regarded as mental do not consist of consciousness, Russell's strategy is to give a behavioristic analysis. Thus, desire, belief, and emotions can be regarded as made up, at least in part, of dispositions to behave in one way rather than another in certain circumstances.) The results are admittedly equivocal. Russell has always been too honest to overlook glaring deficiencies in his analyses. One that has particularly bothered Russell is this: On a common-sense basis it seems clear that one must distinguish between simply having a sensation and taking that sensation as an indication of a tree, and there seems to be an important difference between simply having an image and employing that image in, for example, thinking about a forthcoming election. If this analysis of mind is to be made to work, one must give an account of the reference of perception and thought in terms of the interrelations of data. Thus, we might hold that to take a sensation as an indication of a tree is to be disposed to have the sensation of surprise if certain other sensations were to follow. But apart from difficulties about the nature of these dispositions, which are themselves neither images nor sensations, this is all extremely difficult to work out in detail, and it is equally difficult to make sure that one has shown that it can be done.

It is clear that logical constructionism is based on a tendency opposite to that of the realism briefly espoused by Russell in his youth. Logical constructionism wields Ockham's razor with a heavy hand. We begin with those entities whose existence is indubitable because they are given in immediate experience, and we then try to show that anything we might wish to say about anything else can be stated in terms of relations between these indubitable entities. In other words, anything we want to say about something else is not really about something else. Thus, we try to represent all our knowledge as having to do with as few kinds of entities as possible, thereby reducing the possibility of error.

Logical atomism. Thus far we have concentrated on the epistemological side of logical constructionism, its concern with reducing the number of assumptions we make and with exhibiting clearly the basis for what we claim to know. But it also has a metaphysical side, although Russell wavers about this. Sometimes he talks as if his constructionism is metaphysically neutral. At such times he says that in showing that minds can be constructed out of sensations and images we do not show that there is no ultimate, irreducible subject of awareness; we show merely that everything we *know* about minds can be expressed without assuming the existence of such an entity. At other times, however, he claims that by showing that minds can be constructed out of sensations and images we have shown what minds really are—we have revealed their metaphysical status. And by carrying through constructions of everything that can be constructed out of simpler entities we will have developed a complete metaphysical scheme.

Ideal language. The most systematic presentation of this metaphysical side of logical constructionism is found in the set of lectures *The Philosophy of Logical Atomism,* which Russell gave in 1918. Here Russell makes explicit the principle on which a metaphysical interpretation of logical constructionism depends—namely, isomorphism of the structure of an ideal language and of the structure of reality. If we can determine in outline how the world would be described in an ideal language, we will have, in outline, an account of what the world is like. The restriction to an "ideal" language is essential. Since there are alternative ways of stating the same body of facts, it could not be the case that all these ways reflect the real structure of the world. In this approach to metaphysics the basic metaphysical commitment is to the identity of structure between reality and an ideal language, and one shows one's hand metaphysically by choosing one rather than another set of criteria for an ideal language.

For Russell the most important requirement for an ideal language is an empiricist one, formulated in the "principle of acquaintance": "Every proposition which we can understand must be composed wholly of constituents with which we are acquainted." In other words, we can understand a linguistic expression only if it either refers to something we have experienced or is defined by other expressions which are so used. This principle plays a part in the constructions we have been surveying, as do the considerations we have already made explicit. That is, Russell holds not only that if physical objects were not defined in terms of sense experiences we would have no way of *knowing* anything about them but also—and even more important—we would not be able to *understand* talk about them. In logical atomism this principle is reflected in the requirement that the expressions which figure in the "atomic" sentences in terms of which everything is to be expressed must get their meaning through direct correlation with experience. They will, therefore, be names of particular sense data and terms for properties of sense data and relations between sense data. Russell is forced to exclude the logical framework of sentences from this requirement ("is," "the," etc.), but he is recurrently uneasy about this exclusion and recurrently disturbed by the question how, in that case, we can understand them.

In addition to the need for its undefined terms getting their meaning through correlation with immediately experienced items, the ideal language will have to satisfy some more strictly logical requirements. These will include the absence of vagueness and having one and only one expression for each meaning. But the most important restriction concerns the form of the basic sentences. An atomic sentence will be one that contains a single predicate or relational term and one or more than one name, the whole sentence asserting that the entity named has the indicated property ("This is white") or that the entities named stand in the indicated relation ("This is above that"). If a sentence (1) has this form, (2) contains only terms that get their meaning through correlation with experienced items, and (3) has to do with entities that cannot be analyzed into anything simpler, then it is an atomic sentence. It is clear that for Russell the sentences which satisfy these requirements will all state a minimal fact about a momentary content of sense experience.

Logical atomism can then be presented as the thesis that all knowledge can be stated in terms of atomic sentences and their truth-functional compounds. A truth-functional compound of two sentences is one whose truth or falsity is a determinate function of the truth or falsity of the components. Thus, "I am leaving and you are staying" is a truth-functional compound of "I am leaving" and "You are staying." For the compound is true if and only if both its components are true. There is an empiricist motivation for maintaining this thesis. Atomic sentences, in the sense specified above, can be conclusively verified or falsified by a single experience, and as long as we are dealing only with truth-functional compounds of these no further problem can arise concerning their truth or falsity. Consider a "contrary-to-fact conditional," such as "If I had offered him more money, he would have accepted the job." As it stands this sentence is not a truth-functional compound of its constituents. For in saying it we are presupposing that both its constituents are false, yet this does not settle the question whether the whole statement is true or false. There is a corresponding puzzle about what empirical evidence would settle the question. Obviously I cannot go back in time and offer him more money and see what he will do. If we could find some way to restate this as a (very complicated) truth-functional compound of atomic sentences, it would become clear which experiences would verify or falsify it.

Pluralism and knowledge by acquaintance. The metaphysical correlate of this sketch of the ideal language brings together two of Russell's deepest convictions, the logical independence of particular facts (pluralism) and the dependence of knowledge on the data of immediate experience. In this view reality consists of a plurality of facts, each of which is the sort of fact which could be infallibly discerned in a single moment of experience and each of which could conceivably be what it is even if nothing else were in existence. All the familiar and seemingly relatively simple objects in the world of common sense are really extremely complicated complexes of atomic facts of these sorts.

Russell was well aware that logical atomism in this extreme form was untenable. For example, he insisted that generalizations could not be truth-functional compounds of atomic sentences. The most promising way of so construing them would be to take, for example, "All lemons are yellow" as a conjunction of a large number of atomic sentences of the form "This lemon is yellow," "That lemon is yellow," . . . . But as Russell points out, even if it were possible to list *all* the lemons, the conjunction would say the same thing as the original universal generalization only if we added the conjunct "and that is all the lemons there are." And this last addition is not an atomic sentence. Moreover, Russell had doubts about so-called intensional contexts, such as "Smith believes that the White Sox will win," where the truth or falsity of the compound is clearly independent of the truth or falsity of the components. Whether Smith has this belief does not in any way depend on whether the White Sox win. Russell has always hoped that neutral monism would help him to get out of this difficulty. If we could construct beliefs out of sensations and images we might be able to restate this fact as some truth-functional derivative of atomic sentences.

Later doubts. In the last few decades Russell has come to have more fundamental doubts about logical atomism, including doubts concerning the very notion of a logical atom. How can we ever be sure that we are dealing with something which cannot be further analyzed into parts? How can one be sure that yellowness is an absolutely simple property? More basically, what makes a property *logically* simple? Does the fact that one can explain the word "yellow" to someone by saying "Something is yellow if it has the same color as the walls of your room" show that being the same color as the walls of your room is logically a *part* of yellowness? If so, then yellowness is not absolutely simple. If not, what does count against logical simplicity? Moreover, if there are alternative minimum vocabularies, then a simple, undefined term in one mode of formulation may turn out to be definable in another. Thus, on one systematization "pleasure" might be defined as the satisfaction of desire, whereas on a different systematization "desire" would be defined as the belief that something is pleasant. Russell has given up the belief that we can know that we have gotten down to ultimate simples and even the belief that there must be absolute simples. He

is now disposed to think, in more relativistic terms, of a class of things that can be taken as simple at a given stage of analysis. In those terms he still tends to fall back on sense experiences that are as apparently simple as anything we can find. Such experiences, even if not absolutely simple, can be regarded as being independent of anything except their possible components.

Later developments. Despite Russell's frank admissions that logical atomism does not work as a depiction of the structure of an ideally adequate language, he has not developed an alternative metaphysics. On the principle of isomorphism, if one cannot represent general statements as functions of atomic statements, then one must admit general facts as ultimate constituents of the world. This metaphysical implication does not seem to bother Russell as it once did. This is partly because he has been less preoccupied with metaphysics in recent decades and partly because the principle of isomorphism has been so heavily qualified as to remove most of the cutting edge. In his major philosophical works of the 1940s, *An Inquiry Into Meaning and Truth* and *Human Knowledge,* he is more concerned with the nature of atomic facts thought of as the ultimate pieces of empirical data and the kinds of inferences required to get from these to the rest of what one wants to count as knowledge than he is with inferring a metaphysical structure from the logical form which an adequate statement of our knowledge would assume.

In these works there is a major shift in his view of the structure of atomic facts. Russell had earlier interpreted the word "this" in "This is red" as referring to a particular, something which has qualities and stands in relations but is not itself a quality or relation or set of qualities or relations. This is the traditional concept of substance as the substratum of properties, which was still alive in the realm of sense data even after physical objects and minds were no longer taken to be substances. But eventually the sense datum as substratum of properties went the way of physical objects, minds, and numbers. Here, too, Russell became convinced that there is no empirical warrant for assuming the existence of any such thing. In sense experience I am aware of a variety of qualities and their interrelations, but I am not also aware of something which *has* qualities. The bearer of qualities turns out to be the shadow of the usual grammatical form of the sentences used to report atomic facts. (There is a subject of the sentence—for example, "this"—which does not refer to any quality.) Russell's latest position is that the subject of qualities is simply a construction out of a set of compresent qualities. Thus, in the ideal language "This is red" would be restated as "Red is compresent with . . . ," where in place of the dots we have a specification of the other properties involved in that experience, for example, being round, being in the middle of the visual field, having ragged edges. It might be thought that this necessarily involves giving up the idea of absolute simples, for what takes the place of things in this view is bundles of qualities. But in this theory qualities themselves are regarded as the ultimate particulars (possibly simple) of which the world consists. Thus, in "Red is compresent with . . . ," "red" does not refer to a particular exemplification of redness. If we took that line we would have to suppose that there is something which distinguishes *this* exemplification from other exemplifications of just the same color, and that would have to be something as unempirical as a substratum. Instead, it is taken to refer to the color conceived as a "scattered particular," something which can exist in a number of different places at the same time. And such a particular might well be simple.

Russell has continued to think of common-sense physical objects and the entities of physics as constructions out of entities of the sort which are given in sense experience. But he has come to require less similarity to sense data in the elements of these constructions. His latest view is that although all ultimate entities have basic structural similarities to sense experiences, they need not involve only qualities which are given in sense experience. They may have qualities that it is impossible for us to be aware of. This uncertainty does not carry with it any serious gap in our knowledge, since for physical science it is the structure of external events which is important. In the 1940s Russell became increasingly concerned with the principles which are required to justify inferences from sense experience to unexperienced events and complexes of unexperienced events. The simplest form this takes is, for example, the inference that my desk has continued to exist in my office throughout the night, when no one was observing it. On Russell's view this is an inference from certain sense experiences to structurally similar events spatiotemporally connected with them in certain ways. He feels that the principle of induction by simple enumeration (the more often one has observed A and B to be associated, the more it is likely that they are invariably correlated) is insufficient to justify such inferences. What is needed, he thinks, is a set of assumptions having to do with spatiotemporal connections of events of like structures. In *Human Knowledge* he presents a set of such assumptions. He does not claim that they can be *known* to be true. His point is a Kantian one: we must accept these assumptions if we are to accept the inferences to unobserved events which we all do accept in the course of our daily life.

Russell's entire philosophical career has been dominated by the quest for certainty. In recent years he has been driven to admit that it is less attainable than he had hoped, but nevertheless the desire to approximate it as much as possible has continued to shape his thinking about knowledge and the nature of the world. Because of this desire he has been continually preoccupied with the problem of how to formulate those pieces of knowledge which are rendered indubitable by experience. And because of it he has consistently attempted to analyze anything which appears dubitable into constituents about which there can be no doubt. Even where he has been forced to admit that inferences beyond the immediately given are inevitable, he has striven to reduce the principles of such inferences to the minimum. Russell is distinguished from other seekers after absolute certainty chiefly by the ingenuity of his constructions and by the candor with which he admits the failures of the quest.

LOGIC AND MATHEMATICS

Reduction of mathematics to logic. Russell's main work in logic and mathematics has been concerned with the problem of bringing the two together and with the interpretation of mathematics—arithmetic in particular—as a simple extension of logic, involving no undefined ideas and no unproved propositions except purely logical ones. Russell achieved this synthesis at the beginning of the twentieth century, a little later than Gottlob Frege, but independently of him; in working it out in detail he had the collaboration of A. N. Whitehead. By current standards Russell's work lacks rigor, and in this respect it compares unfavorably with that of Frege; at an early stage, however, Russell did notice a difficulty that had escaped Frege's attention, the paradox about the self-membership of classes, which will be examined later. Because of its complexity it will be best to treat Russell's picture of the logical foundations of mathematics systematically rather than historically, with occasional comments about the actual development of his thought. We shall also separate from the outset two elements of Russell's treatment of his and other paradoxes, the theory of "types" and the theory of "orders," which Russell himself ran together, and thereby give a slightly clearer picture of his intention than his own writings immediately furnish.

Definition of "similarity." Russell took over from Giuseppe Peano the reduction of all other arithmetical notions to complications of the three arithmetically undefined ideas of "zero," "number," and "successor" and defined these in terms of the theory of logical relations between classes or sets. In particular, he defined a number as a class of classes with the same number of members; for example, he defined the number 2 as the class of pairs. This procedure may seem unnatural (do we really mean by "2" the class of two-membered classes?) and circular. To the charge of unnaturalness Russell's answer was that his definition (together with the definitions of addition, etc.) gives all the ordinary results ($2+2=4$, for example) and that for a pure mathematician this is enough; another answer can be given only after it has been made clearer what Russell means by a class. With regard to the charge of circularity, Russell defines the complex "having the same number of members," or "similarity," as he calls it, not in terms of "number" (or of his definition of "number") but in other terms altogether.

At this point some notions from the logic of relations have to be introduced. A relation is said to be one to one if whatever has that relation to anything has it to one thing only and if whatever has anything standing in that relation to it has one thing only standing in that relation to it. (In strictly monogamous countries, "husband of" is a one-to-one relation in this sense.) Here the phrase "one only" does not presuppose the notion of the number 1. The sentence "x stands in the relation R to one thing only" means "For some y, whatever x stands in the relation R to is identical with y." The domain of a relation is the set of objects that stand in that relation to anything (the domain of "husband of" is the class of all husbands); the relation's converse domain is the set of all objects to which anything stands in that relation (the converse domain of "husband of" is the class of individuals that have husbands—that is, the class of wives). A class A is similar to (that is, has the same number of members as) another class if there is some one-to-one relation of which the first class is the domain and the second the converse domain.

One can see that in a monogamous country the class of

husbands will be similar in this sense to the class of wives, but one might think that two sets of objects could have the same number of members without there being any relation at all that pairs them off in the way that "husband of" does in our example. This, however, is a mistake when the term "relation" is understood as widely as it is by Russell. A relation in Russell's sense is, roughly, anything that can be expressed by a sentence with two gaps in it where names might go, and this covers not only obvious relating expressions like "_____ shaves ( )" or "_____ is the husband of ( )" but also ones like "Either _____ is identical with *A*, or *B* is identical with ( )." Take any set of two objects *C* and *D*. The relation "Either _____ is identical with *A* and ( ) with *C*, or _____ is identical with *B* and ( ) with *D*" (where all dashes must be replaced by the same name, and similarly with the bracketed blanks) will be a one-to-one relation in which *A* stands to *C* alone and *B* to *D* alone and in which *C* has *A* alone standing to it and *D* has *B* alone—that is, it will be a one-to-one relation of which the class with *A* and *B* as sole members is the domain and the class with *C* and *D* as sole members the converse domain; there are analogous relations in the case of larger classes. (Where the classes are infinitely large these relations will not be expressible in a language with only finite expressions, and perhaps that means that they will not be expressible in any language. Some philosophers would regard this as a serious difficulty; others would not.)

Axiom of infinity. Similarity, then, or having-the-same-number-of-members, is defined in terms of notions from the logic of relations: one to one, domain, and converse domain. The number-of-members of a given class is the class of classes similar to it, and a class of classes is a number (strictly, a cardinal number) if there is some class of which it is the number-of-members. This last step gives rise to another difficulty: Suppose there are (as there might well be) no more than a certain number *n* of objects in the universe. Then there will be no classes with more than *n* members and so, by the above definition, no cardinal numbers greater than *n*. This makes a great part of arithmetic (for example, the principle that every number has a successor different from itself) subject to the hypothesis (sometimes called the axiom of infinity) that there are an infinite number of objects.

Russell came to accept this last consequence of his definitions, but at an earlier stage he had thought that the axiom of infinity was provable, as follows: If we assume that every property demarcates a class, we must admit that some classes are empty (have no members), for example, there are no objects not identical with themselves. (The number 0 is precisely the class of classes with no members.) Thus, even if the universe contains no ordinary objects at all, there will still be at least one object of a more abstract sort, the universe itself considered as an empty class. And if there is this object there will also be two further objects of a still more abstract sort: the class of classes which has the first empty class as its one member and the empty class of classes. That makes three objects, call them *A*, *B*, and *C*. In addition to these there will be four classes of classes of classes—the class with *B* as its sole member, that with *C* as its sole member, that containing both *B* and *C* as members, and the empty class of classes of classes. And so on ad infinitum.

Russell paradox and the theory of types. Russell was led to abandon the above demonstration (which, as he said, has anyway "an air of hocus-poous about it") by his discovery of the paradox of self-membership, mentioned earlier. If we can concoct classes with some members that are themselves classes, some that are classes of classes, and so on as we please (if, in other words, we can treat classes, classes of classes, etc., as so many sorts of classifiable "objects"), we can, it seems, argue as follows: The most obvious classes do not contain themselves as members—for example, the class of men is not itself a man and so is not itself a member of the class of men (that is, of itself). On the other hand, the class of non-men *is* a non-man (is one of the things that are not men) and thus *is* a member of itself. We can therefore divide classes into two broad classes of classes—the class of classes that are members of themselves and the class of classes that are not. Now take the class of classes that are not members of themselves: is it a member of itself or not? If it is, it must possess the defining property of this class to which *ex hypothesi* it belongs—that is, it must be not-a-member-of-itself. (Thus, if it is a member of itself, it is not a member of itself.) And if it is not a member of itself, *ipso facto* it possesses its own defining property and so *is* a member of itself. (If it is not, it is.) Let *p* be the proposition that our class *is* a member of itself; it follows even from the attempt to deny it, so it *must* be true—but it entails its own denial, so it *must* be false. There is clearly something wrong here.

Russell thought the error lay in treating a class seriously as an object. Perhaps it is an object in a sense, but not in the same sense in which genuine individuals are objects—and classes of classes are different again. They are, as he put it, of different "logical type." In particular, in an intelligible sentence you cannot replace an individual name by a class name or a class name by the name of a class of classes, or vice versa, and still have the sentence make sense. If "Russell is dead" makes sense, "The class of men is dead" does not, and if "The class of men is three-membered" makes sense (even if false), "Russell is three-membered" does not. And where a sentence makes no sense (as opposed to being merely false), its denial makes no sense either. Since "The individual *I* is a member of the class-of-individuals *C*" makes sense, "The class-of-individuals *C* is a member of the class-of-individuals *C*" does not and neither does "The class-of-individuals *C* is not a member of the class-of-individuals *C*"—and so on at higher points in the hierarchy. This being granted, the paradox with which we began simply cannot be intelligibly formulated and thus disappears from the system.

At this point it would be wise to remove a possible source of confusion. The relation of class membership is different from the relation of class inclusion. One class is included in another if all the members of the former are members of the latter; for example, the class of men is included in the class of animals—all men are animals. But the class of men is not a member of the class of animals; that is, the class of men is not an animal (or, more strictly, "The class of men is an animal" is nonsense). The class of men is a member, rather, of the class of classes-of-animals—it is a class of animals. And the class of classes of animals is included in (but is not a member of) the class of classes of living things—any class of animals, in other words, is a class of living things. Inclusion thus relates classes of the same logical type; membership, on the other hand, relates an entity with another entity of the logical type one above its own. The membership of an individual in a class of individuals is membership in a sense different from the membership of a class of individuals in a class of classes, and similarly for inclusion—there is a hierarchy not only of classes but also of membership and inclusion relations.

All this, besides solving a technical problem, is not without some attraction for philosophical common sense. Even apart from paradoxes it seems an artificial "multiplication of entities" to suppose that in addition to the individual objects which form the members of the lowest type of classes there are classes, classes of classes, and so on, and Russell devoted some attention to the problem of showing how what appears to be talk about these rather strange objects is in reality just more and more oblique talk about quite ordinary ones. To see just how he shows this it is necessary to look more closely at what might be called his "straight" language, into which this talk of classes, etc., does not enter and into which, once this talk *has* been introduced, it can always be "translated back."

Logic. From what has been said so far, it is clear that the "logic" to which Russell reduced arithmetic covered, implicitly or explicitly, such subjects as class membership and class inclusion, identity, and some sort of theory of relations. This is that part of logic that we first encounter when we work back to logic from arithmetic. We must now try and work forward to the same point from the fundamentals of logic.

Russell thought of logic as being at bottom "the theory of implication" (to quote the title of one of his early papers). And from the first he considered it important to distinguish implication from inference. He objected to the view that logic is primarily about thinking—conception, judgment, and inference, as some of the traditional logic texts put it. The connection of logic with inference is rather that logic is concerned with that in the real world which makes inference justified, and this is implication. "Where we validly infer one proposition from another," he wrote in 1903, "we do so in virtue of a relation which holds between the two propositions whether we perceive it or not: the mind, in fact, is as purely receptive in inference as common sense supposes it to be in perception of sensible objects" (*Principles of Mathematics,* p. 33).

Material implication. Even in Russell's purely objective, nonpsychological sense "implication" is ambiguous. Implication may be a relation between complete propositions, in which case it is called "material" implication and holds whenever it is not the case that the implying proposition is true and the implied proposition false. Before enlarging and commenting upon this account, certain grammatical and metaphysical clarifications are in order. Russell originally believed that sentences symbolized abstract objects called "propositions" and that material implication was a relation between these objects in exactly the same sense that marriage might be a relation between two people. He later dropped this view and regarded propositions, like classes, as mere "logical constructions," but he still used the old forms of words (as being, no

doubt, accurate enough for practical purposes). In particular, the partly symbolic form "*p* implies *q*" (or "*p* materially implies *q*") freely occurs in all his writings, and we ought to be clear about what he means by it. Generally it is simply a variant of "If *p* then *q*," or completely symbolically "*p* ⊃ *q*" ("*p* hook *q*"), where the phrase "If _____ then ( )"—or the hook—is not a transitive verb expressing a relation between objects but a conjunction, or, as we now say, a "sentential connective." "If *p* then *q*" is thus not a statement about two objects symbolized by "*p*" and "*q*" but rather a complex statement about whatever the statements represented by "*p*" and "*q*" are about. For example, "If James is going to come, John will stay away" is not about two objects symbolized by "James is going to come" and "John will stay away," nor is it about these subordinate sentences themselves; rather, it links these two sentences to make a more complex statement about James and John. And if we say "That James is going to come implies that John will stay away," this is just a verbal variant of "If James is going to come then John will stay away"; that is, the linking expression "That _____ implies that ( )" has the same meaning as the conjunction "If _____ then ( )." The general form "That *p* implies that *q*" thus has the same sense as the form "If *p* then *q*" or "*p* ⊃ *q*," and Russell's "*p* implies *q*" is thus just a loose way of saying "That *p* implies that *q*." In a similar way Russell often uses "*p* is true" and "*p* is false" as variants of "It is the case (is true) that *p*" and "It is not the case (is false) that *p*"; although sometimes he may really be talking about sentences in such a way that the sentence "John will stay away" may be described as true if and only if John will stay away and as false if and only if he will not, and the sentence "James is going to come" may be said to "imply" the sentence "John will stay away" if and only if the sentence "If James is going to come then John will stay away" is true.

The assertion that an implication is true if and only if it is not the case that the implying statement (antecedent) is true and the implied statement (consequent) false is not intended as a definition of the form "If *p* then *q*." It is simply an informal attempt to fix our attention on the relation (or quasi relation) that Russell intends. In his earliest works, like Frege and C. S. Peirce before him, Russell took this relation to be indefinable, and "the discussion of indefinables—which forms the chief part of philosophical logic—is the endeavour to see clearly, and to make others see clearly, the entities concerned, in order that the mind may have that kind of acquaintance with them which it has with redness or the taste of a pineapple" (*Principles of Mathematics,* 1st ed., Preface; 2d ed., p. xv). Later he preferred to take as undefined the conjunction "or" and the negative prefix "it is not the case that" (or just "not") and to define "If *p* then *q*" as an abbreviation of "Either not *p* or *q*"; later still he followed H. M. Sheffer and Jean Nicod in using the stroke form "*p* | *q*" (which is true if and only if the component statements are not both true) and defined "if," "not," and "or" in terms of it. But for Russell the central part of logic has always been the study of implication, whether taken as undefined or not.

Since the form "If *p* then *q*" as understood by Russell is true as long as it is not the case that the antecedent is true and the consequent false, it is automatically true if the antecedent is false (for then it is not the case that the antecedent is true and thus not the case that the-antecedent-is-true-and-the-consequent-false) or the consequent true (for then it is not the case that the consequent is false and thus not the case that the-antecedent-is-true-and-the-consequent-false). In other words, a false proposition materially implies, and a true one is materially implied by, any proposition whatever. But implication is supposed by Russell to justify inference, and the mere fact that "Grass is pink" is false would not seem to justify us in inferring the 25th proposition of Euclid from it, and the mere fact that Euclid's proposition is true would not seem to justify us in inferring it from "Grass is green"—geometry would be much easier if we could do this. Russell's explanation is that the first of these inferences cannot be performed because we cannot get it started (the premise not being true) and that the second inference is justified but we cannot know it to be so unless we already know the conclusion, so that we will not need it. In other words, "Infer a true proposition from anything at all" is a rule with no practical use, but this does not make it logically wrong.

Formal implication and propositional functions. Implications are of practical use when we know their truth without knowing either the falsehood of their antecedents or the truth of their consequents, and this happens most often when a material implication is an instance or particularization of an implication in the second of Russell's senses, a "formal" implication.

Formal implication is not (to use Russell's "realistic" language) a relation between propositions but one between what he calls "propositional functions." One might say roughly that formal implication is a relation between properties and that one property formally implies another if it is never present without the other; for example, being human formally implies being mortal (nothing is human without being mortal). Formal implication is clearly involved in the notion of class inclusion—*A* is included in *B* if being a member of *A* formally implies being a member of *B*. But the notion of a propositional function is wider than that of a property. It is what is meant by an "open sentence," a sentence in which some expression—say, a name—has been replaced by a variable. "Socrates is a man" expresses a proposition; "*x* is a man" expresses a propositional function. Sometimes, more simply, Russell uses the term "propositional function" for the open sentence itself. And the proposition that Socrates is a man may be said to be the *value* of the propositional function "*x* is a man" for the value "Socrates" of the argument *x*. The propositional function "*x* is a man" formally implies "*x* is mortal" if *x*'s being a man materially implies that *x* is mortal whatever *x* may be—that is, if we have "For any *x*, if *x* is a man then *x* is mortal." Russell writes this sort of implication as "$\varphi x \supset_x \psi x$." At one stage he treated this notion, for systematic purposes, as undefined, but even then he regarded it as complex in meaning, being built up from material implication together with the prefix "for any *x*," called a quantifier. Writing this last as "(x)," we may spell out the sense of a formal implication by writing it as "$(x) : \varphi x \supset \psi x$." It should be noted that whereas a propositional function is not a proposition, a formal implication

between such functions *is* a proposition. The propositional function "*x* is a man" is neither true nor false; only its various values are true or false. But "For any *x*, if *x* is human then *x* is mortal" is as it were complete and is as it happens true. The quantifier is said here to "bind" the variable *x*, or, in the terminology Russell took over from Peano, *x* is in this context not a "real" but an "apparent" variable.

A propositional function may also have more than one expression in a proposition replaced by a variable, as in "*x* shaves *y*," "*x* gives *y* to *z*," and "If *x* shaves *y* then *x* does not shave *z*." In such cases the function corresponds to a relation (two-termed or many-termed) rather than to a property, and such functions may again be linked by formal implication, as in "For any *x* and *y*, if *x* is a child of *y* then *x* detests *y*"—that is, "All children detest their parents." Symbolically, we have here the form "$\varphi xy \supset_{x,y} \psi xy$," or "$(x,y) : \varphi xy \supset \psi xy$." Again, formal implication may link a propositional function and a complete proposition, as in "If anything is in that box I'm very much mistaken," which is of the form "For any *x*, if φx then *p*" or "$\varphi x \supset_x p$." Moreover, the expression whose place is taken in a propositional function by a variable need not be a name. It might, for example, be a sentence—"If *p* then *q*" is a propositional function of which "If James is going to be there then John will not come" is the value when "James is going to be there" is the value of the argument *p* and "John will not come" the value of the argument *q*. If we prefix quantifiers to forms of this sort we obtain further formal implications, including the laws of propositional logic themselves—for example, "For any *p*, *q*, and *r*, if *p* implies *q* then if *q* implies *r*, *p* implies *r*," which may be written "$(p,q,r) : (p \supset q) \supset ((q \supset r) \supset (p \supset r))$" or "$(p \supset q) \supset_{p,q,r} ((q \supset r) \supset (p \supset r))$."

A further case of special interest is that in which a variable replaces a verb or equivalent expression, as in "φ(Socrates)," where φ stands indifferently for "is a man," "smokes," "is running," etc. With appropriate quantifiers this function will yield such formal implications as "$(\varphi) : \varphi a \supset \varphi b$," "$\varphi a \supset_\varphi \varphi b$" (roughly, "Whatever *a* does, *b* does," or "Whatever goes for *a* goes for *b*"). However, Russell says not that "φ(Socrates)" and "If φ(Socrates) then φ(Plato)" are functions of the verb or predicate φ but that they are functions of the *function* φx or, as he writes it in this type of context, the function $\varphi \hat{x}$ (the significance of this accenting or "capping" will be indicated later). His aim here is in part to bring out what Peirce and Frege called the "unsaturatedness" of verbs: The function of verbs can be understood only in relation to names and sentences; we use verbs to *make statements* about objects, not to name a special sort of object. The additional associated variables also enable one to represent unambiguously such complexes as "shaving oneself"—if φ is "shaves," shaving oneself is $\varphi \hat{x} \hat{x}$, as opposed to simply shaving ($\varphi \hat{x} \hat{y}$). But Russell was hampered by not having the word "functor" to designate what makes a function out of its argument; it is more natural to speak of "Socrates is a man" as a propositional function of "Socrates," of "*x* is a man" as the same propositional function of "*x*," and of "is a man" as the functor which forms this function in both cases than to speak of "$\hat{x}$ is a man" as a propositional function and to treat it in practice as a functor (Frege and W. E. Johnson were more accurate here, although they, too, lacked the term "functor").

This part of Russell's "philosophical grammar" can now be set out fairly straightforwardly: Sentences may be built out of other units in various ways—out of other sentences by connectives, as in "$p \supset q$," and out of names by verbs, as in "φx," "φxy," and "$\varphi x \supset \psi x$" (which may be conceived of as constructed out of the subsentences "φx" and "ψx" by the connective "$\supset$" or out of the name "x" by the complex verb "$\varphi \hat{x} \supset \psi \hat{x}$," "$\psi$'s-if-it-$\varphi$'s"). The rest of the hierarchy goes on from here—there are, for example, functors that form sentences out of verbs (that is, out of functors that form sentences out of names) and functors that form sentences out of these again, and so on ad infinitum. Functors may require one or more than one argument to make a sentence (the difference between "is a man" and "shaves," in the transitive sense), and when more arguments than one are required they may or may not be of the same type (for example, "If $\hat{x}$ is a man then $\hat{p}$" requires a name and sentence).

Quantification. Of functors that form sentences from verbs, the most important are quantifications, such as "$(x)\hat{\varphi}x$" (which makes a sentence out of the verb whose place in the sentence is kept by "φ"), represented in English by such words as "everything." "Everything" is, or is constructed out of, the universal quantifier; there are many other quantifiers. Russell distinguished one other basic quantifier, "something." "Something is a man" expands in his language to "For some x, x is a man," or symbolically "$(\exists x)(x$ is a man)."

Given the quantifier "something" and negation we can construct the complex "It is not the case that (for some x (x is a man))" or "For no x is x a man." Here we have the philosophical beginnings of the number series. The number 0 makes its appearance as part of a quantification, for we could write the preceding form as "$(0x)(x$ is a man)." And the series can be continued. "Some" means "At least one," and "At most one thing is a man" is "For some x, if anything is human it is identical with x"—that is, "For some x: for any y, if y is human y is identical with x." The combination of "At least one thing is a man" with "At most one thing is a man" gives us "Exactly one thing is a man"; that is, "$(1x)(x$ is a man)." "$(2x)(x$ is a man)" is, similarly, "At least two things are men, and at most two things are men"—that is, "(For some x and for some y, x is a man, y is a man, and y is not identical with x) and (for some x and for some y: for any z, if z is a man z is either identical with x or identical with y)." Apparent occurrences of numbers as objects can be analyzed away in terms of this primary sense; "1 and 1 is 2" for instance, becomes "For any φ and for any ψ, if exactly one thing φ's, exactly one thing ψ's, and nothing does both, then exactly two things either-φ-or-ψ." Numbers are inseparable components of functors of functors of names, or, as Russell would say, functions of functions, but the naturalness of this analysis is disguised in his own work by the fact that before he brings arithmetic into the picture he introduces the language of classes and defines numbers in terms of classes. (The notation "$(0x)\varphi x$," etc., is not Russell's.)

Descriptions. Before going on to Russell's discussion of classes, we should note that "$(x)\hat{\varphi}x$," "$(\exists x)\hat{\varphi}x$," and also "$(0x)\hat{\varphi}x$," "$(2x)\hat{\varphi}x$," and so on, are *functions* of functions of names, not *arguments* of such functions—that is, they are not names. "Something," "nothing," "exactly one thing," etc., are not names, although, like names, they go with verbs to make sentences. They go, so to speak, on the other side of verbs: they "govern" the verbs; the verbs do not govern them. And although Russell's hierarchy of types of functors or "functions" provides innumerable ways of constructing sentences (and so of constructing functions), it provides no way of constructing genuine names. It is of the essence of the expressions represented by Russell's variables of lowest type $(x, y, z$, etc.)—that is, individual names—that they are logically structureless; they pick out individuals, and that is all. But in common speech and in mathematics we do seem to construct names, or at least ways of designating objects, out of expressions of other types: For example, "the man who broke the bank at Monte Carlo" seems to function as a name, yet it seems to be constructed from the verb "broke the bank at Monte Carlo." On Russell's view this appearance is illusory, and sentences in which such apparent names occur can always be replaced by paraphrases expressed entirely in Russell's language of structureless names, functions of functions, etc. However, he regarded it as useful for logical symbolism to reproduce at this point, although with greater precision, some of the devices of common speech and to have, as it were, a secondary language imposed on the primary one.

(Some account of Russell's handling of descriptions—that is, expressions of the form "The so-and-so"—and of other points raised below is given in the article EXISTENCE.) "The φ-er," or "The thing that φ's," when it occurs as the apparent subject of a further verb—that is, in a context of the form "The φ-er ψ's"—is in reality a functor, in some ways like a quantifying expression, of which the verbs "φ's" and "ψ's" are arguments; in fact "The thing that φ's ψ's" amounts precisely to "Exactly one thing φ's, and whatever φ's ψ's," whose first component has been analyzed above and whose second component is a simple formal implication. Expressions of this kind are especially important in mathematics when the contained functor φ is relational in form, as in "The φ-er of y"—that is, "The thing that φ's y." "The square root of y" (the number which yields y when multiplied by itself) is such an expression. Russell called expressions of this kind "descriptive functions." They include most "functions" in the ordinary mathematical sense. It is a little inaccurate, of course, to use name symbols like "y" for numbers, which on Russell's view are not genuine individuals, but once the devices which yield class language and number language have been worked out, Russell's analysis of descriptive functions can be reproduced at the new level in a transposed form. This language of classes and numbers, to which we shall now turn, is itself a case of a secondary language containing apparent names (like "The class of persons that shave themselves") that disappear from the primary-language paraphrase.

Classes, functions, and properties. Russell represented the form "The class of things that φ" as "$\hat{x}(\varphi x)$"—usually read as "the x's such that φx"—and represented "y is a member of the class of φ-ers" as "$y \,\epsilon\, \hat{x}(\varphi x)$." Alternatively we may read "$\hat{x}(\varphi x)$" simply as "φ-er" and "$y \,\epsilon\, \hat{x}(\varphi x)$" as "$y$ is a φ-er." The expression "y is a φ-er" is true if and only if y φ's. One can in fact simply define "$y \,\epsilon\, \hat{x}(\varphi x)$" as "$\varphi y$." Given this definition, other concepts associated with class theory are easily introduced. For example, as noted earlier, "The class of φ-ers is included in the class of ψ-ers" amounts to the formal implication "For any x, if x is a φ-er then x is a ψ-er."

Classes of classes are related to functions of functions as classes are related to functions. To say that a given class—$\hat{x}(\varphi x)$, for example—is a member of the class of two-membered classes (or, as Russell would write it, "$\hat{x}(\varphi x) \,\epsilon\, 2$") is just to say that exactly two things φ—i.e., the class of classes that Russell identifies with the number 2 is just the correlate in the class hierarchy of the function of functions $(2x)\hat{\varphi}x$.

Counting classes. There are two difficulties in Russell's views concerning classes. One is that classes, and, for that matter, numbers, can themselves be counted, as can individuals, but a number of classes would have to be not a class of classes but a class of classes of classes, and a number of numbers would similarly have to be a class of classes of classes of classes. This means that when we say "The number of numbers between 2 and 5 is 2," the first "2" has a sense quite different (belongs to a place quite different in the type hierarchy) from the second; and this seems a little implausible. Russell at this point is content to speak of the "systematic ambiguity" of the key expressions of his symbolic language. Given the proof of "$1 + 1 = 2$," for instance, considered as a statement about numbers of individuals, an analogous proof can always be constructed for the analogous statements about numbers of classes, numbers of numbers, etc., so that in practice it does not matter at which place in the type hierarchy we are working, provided we keep the types going up in order.

Ludwik Borkowski has suggested what may be a better solution: Suppose we always express quantification by a sign followed by a variable; for Russell's "(x)" we might put "$(\forall x)$," by analogy with "$(\exists x)$." We might then use the term "quantifier" not for this expression as a whole but for the initial sign, which can then be described as a functor which constructs a sentence out of a variable followed by a sentence, usually an "open" sentence in which the variable just mentioned occurs. We might then say that the initial sign "$\forall$" or "$\exists$"—or in the case of numerical quantifiers "0" or "1" or "2," etc.—is of the same logical type whatever the type of the variable that comes between it and the sentence following it. For counting properties (and, therefore, classes), we would have prefixes like "(2φ)"—for example, "$(2\varphi)\varphi(\text{Socrates})$" would mean "Socrates has exactly two properties" or, better, "Exactly two things are true of Socrates"; and "(2φ)" is different from "$(2x)$," but the "2" is exactly the same in both contexts.

Counting functions. The other difficulty in Russell's theory is that classes dissolve into functions, but we do not count classes and functions in quite the same way. We would say, for example, that any two-membered class has four sub-classes, in the sense that there are four ways of

selecting members from such a class (both members, the first only, the second only, and neither). The corresponding theorem about functions would seem to be this: If exactly two things φ, then for exactly four ψ's, whatever ψ's φ's. But in fact there will always be vastly more than four ψ's meeting this condition. Suppose, for example, that there are just two men in a room—i.e., $(2x)(x$ is a man in the room)—and that one of them wears spectacles, spats, spotted socks, a red tie, and striped trousers; this much alone gives us five ψ's (namely, "_____ is a man in the room wearing spectacles," "_____ is a man in the room wearing spats," etc.), such that whatever ψ's is a man in the room. The key point here is simply that we count classes as being the same when they have the same members, but we do not count propositional functions as being the same merely because they are satisfied by the same arguments, and all the numerical concepts that are built up from the concept of identity must be similarly adjusted. For instance: "At most one class is a sub-class of $\hat{x}(\varphi x)$" does not mean "For some ψ: for any χ, if $\hat{x}(\chi x)$ is a subclass of $\hat{x}(\varphi x)$, then χ-ing is the same as ψ-ing," but rather it means "For some ψ: for any χ, if $\hat{x}(\chi x)$ is a sub-class of $\hat{x}(\varphi x)$, then whatever χ's ψ's and whatever ψ's χ's." It is the same when we move up a type and count numbers themselves. If we write "$(0x)(\varphi x)$" for "It is not the case that (for some x, φx)" and "$(0'x)(\varphi x)$" for "For any x, if x φ's then x is not identical with itself," we may say that these are different functions of functions—but whatever function either of them applies to the other applies to also; thus, they determine a single class of classes and a single "number," 0. The class and number language which Russell superimposes on his basic one is such that this is the way these quasi entities are counted.

Extensionality. One very radical way of simplifying this whole problem (one which Russell has considered from time to time) is to say that functions (properties, relations, etc.) are to be counted in just the same way that classes are; i.e., that if $\varphi\hat{x}$ and $\psi\hat{x}$ characterize precisely the same objects (are formally equivalent), they are the same function. This is called the principle or law of extensionality; it in effect simply identifies a function with its "extension"—that is, with the class which it determines. The objection to this principle is simply its extreme implausibility in particular cases. For example, it seems obvious that even when two individuals and these two only are the men in a certain room wearing spats and the men in that room wearing spectacles, being a man in the room with spats is something different from being a man in it with spectacles.

Quine's criticism. Logicians such as W. V. Quine, following Ernst Zermelo and John von Neumann, have developed systems in which classes, classes of classes, etc., are treated not as logical constructions but as genuine objects, and Russell's paradox is dealt with not by saying that "x is (is not) a member of x" is meaningless but by denying that "x φ's" always implies that x is a member of the class of φ-ers. This account runs into difficulty when we try to handle certain nonmathematical properties of these supposed objects (see LOGIC, MODAL). Russell's view seems to have the advantage of not unnecessarily "multiplying entities," but Quine argues that Russell succeeds in dispensing with classes only by making genuine objects of properties or functions. This is said on the ground that in the course of his treatment of classes and numbers Russell is compelled to quantify over predicate variables—that is, to employ quantifiers like "$(\exists\varphi)$" (for example, in defining "Exactly as many things ψ as χ" as "*For some relation φ,* whatever φ's anything ψ's and vice versa, whatever is φ'd by anything χ's and vice versa, and whatever φ's or is φ'd by anything φ's or is φ'd by that thing only"). This, Quine says, is to make properties and relations (like φ-ing) the "values of bound variables," and to do this is to treat them as existing.

This amounts to saying that to generalize an expression by quantifying over it is *ipso facto* to make it a name of an object; but this claim may be contested. We do not elucidate "He must have killed him somehow" by translating it "There must be some way in which he killed him" (which, taken literally, suggests that there are objects called "ways") but rather vice versa: we understand "somehow" directly as a generalization of qualifications like "with a knife," and the "way" line of talk is merely a variant of this. Even "something" is often to be understood as a generalized adjective rather than as a generalized individual name—for example, when I say "I am something that Jones is not—logical." It seems more plausible to interpret "I *have* something that Jones has not—logicality" as a verbal variant of the preceding sentence than to say that the latter alone brings out what I am really doing. And the logical rules for such higher-order quantifications are simple—we proceed from the specific case to the generalization, from "I am logical and Jones is not" to "For some A, I am A and Jones is not A," exactly as we do from "I am logical but not intelligent" to "For some individual x, x is logical but not intelligent."

Elimination of abstract terms. Russell might more plausibly be said to "hypostatize" or "reify" abstractions on the ground that there are some contexts from which it seems impossible to eliminate from his basic language his symbols for "abstracts," that is, φx, etc. This part of his system is developed more tidily in Alonzo Church's calculus of λ-conversion, in which the property of φ-ing is represented not by "$\varphi\hat{x}$" but by "$\lambda x\varphi x$," and of "ψ-ing if one φ's" by "$\lambda x\,.\,\varphi x \supset \psi x$." The basic rule of this calculus is that the *application* of $\lambda x\varphi x$ to an object a, symbolized by $(\lambda x\varphi x)a$, is equivalent to the plain φa, and similarly $(\lambda x\,.\,\varphi x \supset \psi x)a$ is equivalent to $\varphi a \supset \psi a$. And where we have a function of functions f, we can in general similarly replace $f(\lambda x\varphi x)$ by $f(\varphi)$—but not always. For instance, it is an obvious law that any such function f which holds for any φ whatever will hold for χ-ing-if-one-ψ's, as in formula F:

$$(f) : (\varphi)\,f(\varphi)\,.\, \supset \,.\,f(\lambda x\,.\,\psi x \supset \chi x).$$

Here the expression with λ seems uneliminable. We cannot replace it with "$\psi \supset \chi$," for this is meaningless—the hook joins sentence forms, not predicate forms. Where we have a specific f the elimination is again possible; for example, if f is the function "applying to exactly two objects," then $f(\lambda x\,.\,\psi x \supset \chi x)$ will amount to $(2y):(\lambda x\,.\,\psi x \supset \chi x)y$ and thus to $(2y)(\psi y \supset \chi y)$. But where the f itself is a variable, as it is in formula F, nothing of this sort is done. We could indeed (following Stanisław Leśniewski) introduce a symbol for the predicate "χ-ing-if-one-φ's" by a special definition; for example

$$[\supset \psi\chi]x =_{\mathrm{Df}} \varphi x \supset \psi x$$

and so replace F with G:

$$(f) : (\varphi)\,f(\varphi)\,.\, \supset \,.\,f([\supset \psi\chi]),$$

but then it would be impossible to eliminate the defined symbol from G in favor of the symbols by which it is defined, and it seems an odd sort of definition that would be thus limited. (Church's use of λ can in fact be regarded as simply a generalization of Leśniewski's procedure.)

The unelirninability of "abstracts" from these contexts is an odd and perhaps awkward fact, but it need not be taken to imply that there are abstract objects, for "abstracts" need not be regarded as a kind of name. In expositions of the λ-calculus it is often said that the form $\lambda x\varphi x$ corresponds to the ordinary-language quasi noun "φ-ing," but this is not strictly correct, as may be seen from the fundamental equation "$(\lambda x\varphi x)a = \varphi a$." If "$\varphi$" here represents not a name but a verb ("φa" means "a φ's"), then so must "$\lambda x\varphi x$" ("$(\lambda x\varphi x)a$" also means "a φ's"), so that if f in $f(\varphi)$ is a function with not names but predicates as arguments, so it must be in "$f(\lambda x\varphi x)$."

Ramified theory of types. We may now describe the added feature which makes Russell's own presentation of his theory of types more complex than the presentation so far given here. Russell divides functions into types not only according to the types of argument which they take but also according to whether they do or do not involve an internal reference to all functions of (what appear to be) their own type. For example, the function "$\hat{x}$ has all the qualities of a great general" has individual-name arguments, just as "$\hat{x}$ is brave" does, but unlike "$\hat{x}$ is brave" it has a "for all φ" within itself—it amounts to "For all φ, if whoever is a great general φ's, then $\hat{x}$ φ's." Russell therefore regards it as of a different type, or, as he often says, of a different order, from "$\hat{x}$ is brave." Functions which do not thus involve a reference to all functions of (what appear to be) their own type he calls "predicative" functions and symbolizes them by putting an exclamation mark or "shriek" after the symbol, as in "$\varphi!x$." Functions cannot in fact (on Russell's view) strictly contain references to all functions of *their own* type or order but references only to ones of orders below their own. A function of individuals, which contains a reference to all predicative functions of individuals, is not itself predicative and cannot be regarded as being among the functions to which it implicitly refers. Having all the properties of a great general, for example, is not itself a property of a great general, at least not in the same sense of "property"—it is a second-order property.

What this means in practice might be illustrated as follows: It seems that if there were no facts about x—that is, if for no φ, φx—then there would be at least one fact about x, namely the fact that there are no facts about it, and hence it cannot be that there are no facts about x. In symbols, from

(1) $$\psi x \supset (\exists \varphi)(\varphi x)$$

it seems possible to obtain

(2) $$\sim(\exists \varphi)(\varphi x) . \supset (\exists \varphi)(\varphi x)$$

by letting $\psi \hat{x}$ in (1) be, in particular, $\sim(\exists \varphi)(\varphi \hat{x})$; and from (2) it follows by a kind of *reductio ad absurdum* that for any given x we have $(\exists \varphi)(\varphi x)$. But on Russell's view this proof will not do, for (1) ought to have been written

(3) $$\psi! x \supset (\exists \varphi)(\varphi! x)$$

and here $\sim(\exists \varphi)(\varphi! \hat{x})$, not being itself predicative, is not a permissible substitution for $\psi! \hat{x}$. It is worth noting, however, that our final conclusion, $(\exists \varphi)(\varphi! x)$, *can* be proved from (3) in a different way—by letting our $\psi! \hat{x}$ be $\chi! \hat{x} \supset \chi! \hat{x}$ ("$\hat{x}$ χ's-if-it-χ's"), which *is* predicative and is true of any x, so that what it implies must be true of any x also. (The new argument is as follows: There is always some fact about x, since at least it is a fact that x is red-if-it-is-red, square-if-it-is-square, etc.)

Axiom of reducibility. Russell lumps together all his type and order restrictions under the general head of avoiding "vicious circles," and the theory of types with the theory of orders worked into it is called the "ramified" theory of types. One trouble with it is that it vitiates certain essential arguments in the higher reaches of mathematics, and to save these Russell introduced an "axiom of reducibility," that to every function of any order there corresponds a predicative function which is formally equivalent to it—that is, which holds for exactly the same arguments as the given function. This means that any argument like our allegedly invalid proof of $(\exists \varphi)(\varphi x)$ above, where it is worth saving, can in principle be replaced by one like our second and valid one; the axiom of reducibility does not itself enable us to find this valid argument but entitles us to proceed as if we had it. It is, however, an intuitively dubious principle and can be dispensed with if we can content ourselves with the theory of types in the "simple" form in which it has been stated in earlier sections.

Semantic paradoxes. It was pointed out by F. P. Ramsey that those paradoxes which Russell lists and which cannot be eliminated (as can, for example, the paradox of the class of all classes not members of themselves) by the "simple" theory of types always contain some implicitly or explicitly "semantic" feature; that is, they all have to do with the relation of language to what it is about and all involve conceptions like truth and meaning. A typical example is the paradox of the liar, of the man who says "What I am now saying is false" and says nothing else but this, so that what he says is true if it is false and false if it is true. Such paradoxes are now generally dealt with by assuming not only a hierarchy of "parts of speech" in one's basic language (this is what the simple theory of types amounts to) but also a hierarchy of languages—a basic language, a "metalanguage" in which we discuss the meaning and truth of expressions in the basic language, a "metametalanguage" in which we deal similarly with the metalanguage, and so on.

It is both easy and necessary to criticize Russell's theories concerning the logical and semantic paradoxes, and his work in logic and the foundations of mathematics generally, but he remains, more than any other one person, the founder of modern logic.

ETHICS AND THE CRITIQUE OF RELIGION

Ethics. Much of Russell's life, as we saw in an earlier section, has been devoted to the advocacy of certain moral and political ideals. In this sense of the word "moralist," in which it has no derogatory implications, Russell has certainly been a moralist and frequently a very passionate one at that. Unlike many other moralists he has also been concerned with what are now referred to as "metamoral" or "metaethical" issues. He has repeatedly addressed himself to questions about the status of moral principles—what, if anything, they mean, what kind of disagreement there is between people who support opposite moral positions, and whether inferences from nonmoral premises to a moral conclusion can ever be valid. In discussing Russell's ethics, we will be concerned only with his metamoral theories.

Early views. In his first important essay on this subject, "The Elements of Ethics" (1910), Russell defended a position closely akin to that of G. E. Moore in *Principia Ethica*. "*Good* and *bad*," he wrote, "are qualities which belong to objects independently of our opinions, just as much as *round* and *square* do; and when two people differ as to whether a thing is good, only one of them can be right, though it may be very hard to know which is right." The goodness or badness of a thing cannot be inferred from *any* of its other properties. "Knowledge as to what things exist, have existed, or will exist, can throw absolutely no light upon the question as to what things are good." Russell was by no means unaware at this time of the wide appeal of the familiar arguments for subjectivism—the "divergence of opinion" on moral questions and the difficulty of "finding arguments to persuade people who differ from us in such a question" ("The Elements of Ethics," in Wilfrid Sellars and John Hospers, eds., *Readings in Ethical Theory*, New York, 1952, pp. 6–7). But he did not then regard these arguments as having any logical force. "Difficulty in discovering the truth," he wrote, "does not prove that there is no truth to be discovered" (*ibid.*, p. 6). Like Moore, he argued that if subjectivism were true it would follow that in a moral dispute there is never really any "difference of opinion" between the disputing parties. If when A says x is good and B says x is bad, A and B were really talking about their respective feelings or desires, they might well both be right at the same time and "there would be no subject of debate between them." At that time Russell regarded this as plainly false. "As a matter of fact," he observed, "we consider some tastes better than others: we do not hold merely that some tastes are ours and other tastes are other people's" (*ibid.*). When "The Elements of Ethics" was reprinted in 1952 in *Readings in Ethical Theory*, the anthology mentioned above, Russell added a footnote in which he explained that "not long after publishing this paper [he] came to disagree with the theory that it advocates." He explains that the change in his views was originally due to Santayana's criticisms in his *Winds of Doctrine,* but he adds that he "found confirmation" for his later position "in many other directions." Russell's later position was first mentioned very briefly in a 1921 preface to a paperback reprint of "A Free Man's Worship"; it was explained in some detail in *What I Believe* (1925) and in *The Outline of Philosophy* (1927), and it received its fullest formulations in *Religion and Science* (1935), *Power* (1938), "Reply to My Critics" (in P. A. Schilpp, ed., *The Philosophy of Bertrand Russell,* 1944), and *Human Society in Ethics and Politics* (1955).

The subjectivity of values. Except on one basic issue, Russell's later position is a point-by-point denial of the earlier theory. "Good" and "bad" are no longer regarded as qualities belonging to objects, and in this respect they are now explicitly contrasted with "square" and "sweet": "If two men differ about values, there is not a disagreement as to any kind of truth, but a difference of taste" (*Religion and Science,* pp. 237–238); "There are no facts of ethics" (*Power,* p. 257); "I see no property analogous to truth that belongs or does not belong to an ethical judgment" ("Reply to My Critics," p. 723). "Taste" in the first of these passages is used in a very broad sense to cover all kinds of psychological states and attitudes, including desires. Russell does not, of course, deny the plain fact that people regard some tastes as better than others and some desires as higher than other desires, but now he is willing to maintain that this merely means that the tastes or desires are their own. "What we 'ought' to desire is merely what someone else wishes us to desire" (*What I Believe,* p. 29).

Russell is quite ready to have his later theory classified as a form of "the doctrine of the subjectivity of values" (*Religion and Science,* p. 237), but it differs in some significant respects from the older theories which have gone by that name. If somebody maintains that pleasure, for example, or the love of God, is intrinsically good, or good "on its own account," this must not be taken to be equivalent to the statement that he approves of it or in some way desires it. Like the advocates of the so-called emotive theory of ethics, Russell maintains that intrinsic moral judgments, grammatical appearances notwithstanding, are not statements or assertions at all but *expressions* of desire. "A judgment of intrinsic value," he writes in *Power,* "is to be interpreted, not as an assertion, but as an expression of desire concerning the desires of mankind. When I say 'hatred is bad,' I am really saying: 'would that no one felt hatred.' I make no assertion; I merely express a certain type of wish" (*Power,* p. 257).

Both here and in his capacity as a reformer Russell places much emphasis on the distinction between purely personal and what he calls "impersonal" desires. A hungry man's desire for food or an ambitious man's desire for fame are examples of the former; a desire for the abolition of the death penalty or the end of racial discrimination, independently of whether the person in question stands to gain from these changes, are examples of the latter. In moral judgments we express certain of our impersonal desires. A king who says, "Monarchy is better than republican forms of government," is using the word "better" in its properly moral sense if he is expressing not just his desire to remain king but a desire that nations have monarchical systems

regardless of his own personal position. Russell occasionally writes as if the desire expressed by moral judgments must be a second-order desire—that is, a desire that everybody have a certain first-order desire—but as several of his own examples make clear, this is not part of his position. What is essential is that the desire be impersonal. In this connection he also observes that the philosophers who stressed the "universality" of moral principles were in a sense quite right. This universality, however, does not consist in any a priori character or logical necessity. What is universal is the *object of the desire* expressed by a moral judgment. "The wish, as an occurrence, is personal, but what it desires is universal. . . . It is this curious interlocking of the particular and the universal which has caused so much confusion in ethics" (*Religion and Science,* p. 236).

As we shall see, Russell has a tendency to overestimate the scope of application of his subjectivism, but in a number of places he points out quite explicitly that large classes of everyday moral judgments and disputes do not come within the purview of the theory. "Ethical controversies are very often as to means, not ends" (*Power,* p. 259). "The framing of moral rules, so long as the ultimate Good is supposed known, is matter for science" (*Religion and Science,* p. 228). It follows from this that if human beings could agree about ultimate ends, all moral disputes would in principle be decidable by an appeal to facts even though the intrinsic judgments would still be not bona fide propositions but expressions of wishes. In fact, however, Russell insists, there is no such agreement about ends. In "The Elements of Ethics" he had conceded that there were *some* ultimate ethical differences but had maintained that people in fact "differ very little in their judgments of intrinsic value." Many of the commonly observed differences are wrongly regarded as ultimate because what are really disagreements about means are mistaken for disagreements about ends. In his subjectivist phase Russell seems to think that differences about ends are not at all uncommon. Behind such disputes as, for example, the subjection of women or the persecution of religious minorities, which do involve questions of means, he writes, "there is generally a difference as to ends," and this sometimes becomes "nakedly apparent," as in Nietzsche's criticisms of Christian ethics. In Christianity, all men are valued equally, but for Nietzsche the majority exists only as means to the superman. This, Russell maintains, is an example of a dispute about ends, and "it cannot be conducted, like scientific controversies, by appeals to facts" (*Power,* p. 259).

In "The Elements of Ethics" Russell had quite properly observed that the mere existence of widespread ethical disagreement (if it is indeed widespread) does not establish any form of subjectivism. Although he has evidently come to believe that ethical disagreement is more widespread than he had thought earlier, he does not offer this as evidence for his new theory. What he does offer as evidence is the undecid*ability* of ethical disputes. He writes:

[The chief ground for adopting this view] is the complete impossibility of finding any arguments to prove that this or that has intrinsic value. . . . We cannot *prove,* to a color-blind man, that grass is green and not red. But there are various ways of proving to him that he lacks a power of discrimination which most men possess, whereas in the case of values there are no such ways . . . since no way can be even imagined for deciding a difference as to values, the conclusion is forced upon us that the difference is one of taste, not one as to any objective truth. (*Religion and Science,* p. 238)

If three men argue, one saying "The good is pleasure," the second "The good is pleasure for Aryans and pain for Jews," and the third "The good is to praise God and glorify him forever," they cannot, as people engaged in a scientific dispute, "appeal to facts," for facts, it seems obvious, "are not relevant to the dispute" (*Power,* p. 257).

Russell's later view agrees with the earlier position on only one significant point, its opposition to naturalism. By "naturalism" is here meant the theory that there *is* a logical connection between some moral judgments and factual premises where the latter are not necessarily confined to empirical statements but may also include metaphysical doctrines. We saw how in "The Elements of Ethics" Russell had insisted that from statements concerning what exists nothing can be inferred about "the goodness of anything." "It is logically impossible," he repeated in the course of expounding his later position, "that there should be evidence for or against" a moral judgment, but now this is maintained because a moral judgment "makes no assertion" and hence possesses neither truth nor falsehood (*Religion and Science,* pp. 236–237).

"Incredibility" of Russell's subjectivism. Rather than attempt a detailed critical evaluation of Russell's subjectivism, we will discuss one objection which has been urged by a number of his critics and which, in one form or another, has been leveled against nearly all forms of subjectivism. It has been argued that a subjectivist cannot consistently make moral judgments. All he can say is that some people have one kind of feeling or attitude while other people feel differently. More specifically, how can Russell's subjectivism be reconciled with his judgments as a moral critic and reformer?

It may be replied that as a matter of pure logic there is no inconsistency between holding that moral judgments are expressions of taste and using moral language to express one's own tastes. Russell, it might be said, would be inconsistent only if he claimed that *his* moral judgments, unlike those of his opponents, are more than expressions of taste. Then he would indeed be like the man who, in the course of an argument about the value of a piece of music, remarked to his opponent "It is all a matter of taste, except that my taste is better than yours." However, while this answer is valid as far as it goes, it does not meet the heart of the objection. For Russell seems to be saying—or at least he would like to be able to say—that his moral judgments (for example, his judgment that democracy is a better system than totalitarianism or that the sexual code advocated in *Marriage and Morals* is superior to that associated with orthodox religion) are in some sense rational or right or well-grounded while the judgments of his opponents are irrational, wrong, or unsupported by the evidence.

Russell apparently did not, when he first advanced his subjectivism, see any serious problem here, but in the 1940s and 1950s he repeatedly expressed dissatisfaction with his own theory on this ground. Thus, in "Reply to My Critics" he writes:

What are "good" desires? Are they anything more than desires that you share? Certainly there *seems* to be something more. Suppose, for example, that some one were to advocate the introduction of bull-fighting in this country. In opposing the proposal, I should *feel,* not only that I was expressing my desires, but that my desires in the matter are *right,* whatever that may mean. As a matter of argument, I can, I think, show that I am not guilty of logical inconsistency in holding to the above interpretation of ethics and at the same time expressing strong ethical preferences. But in feeling I am not satisfied. (*The Philosophy of Bertrand Russell,* p. 724)

To this he adds: "I can only say that, while my own opinions as to ethics do not satisfy me, other people's satisfy me still less." More than a decade later Russell expressed himself even more strongly. In a letter to the *Observer* (October 6, 1957) he comments on Philip Toynbee's review of *Why I Am Not a Christian:* "What Mr. Toynbee says in criticism of my views on ethics has my entire sympathy. I find my own views argumentatively irrefutable, but nevertheless incredible. I do not know the solution."

It is doubtful whether in such comments Russell is really fair to his own subjectivism. Let us recall that the theory was never meant to apply to anything other than what are variously called intrinsic or fundamental value judgments and differences. The questions whether happiness is better than unhappiness and love better than hate are frequently cited as such ultimate moral issues, but it would be hard to find anybody who seriously maintains that suffering is good on its own account or that hate is better than love, although of course people have often maintained that in certain situations and for certain reasons suffering and hate are preferable to enjoyment and love. However, on occasions there do appear to be real value differences of an ultimate kind. Thus, some people would maintain that dignity is "more important" or "nobler" than happiness. Many who do not despise happiness at all would maintain without hesitation that a man who chose to suffer a great deal rather than compromise his integrity (where it is assumed that he would in fact have suffered much less if he had not stood his ground) lived a better life than he would have if he had made the opposite choice. Or, again, there is sometimes disagreement as to whether a person suffering from a fatal illness should be told the truth, although there may be full agreement about the consequences of both telling and not telling him the truth. Russell's subjectivism does apply to this kind of intrinsic moral disagreement, and in such situations he could not, consistently with his theory, claim that the moral judgment he endorses is "more rational" or better supported than that of his opponents.

However, the examples Russell offers when expressing dissatisfaction with his subjectivism are not at all of this ultimate kind, and this applies to all or nearly all the positions he has advocated in his social and political writings. The man who says that the good is pleasure for Aryans and pain for Jews, if he is willing to engage in moral argument at all—if he is not, the problem does not arise—presumably does not *just* say this but proceeds to make all kinds of factual claims about the psychological and physical qualities of Aryans and Jews, respectively, about the laws of heredity, and about various other matters which he regards as justifying his moral position. Similarly, the man who maintains that "the good is to praise God and glorify him forever" presupposes that there is a God, and a God of a certain kind, probably also that he has revealed himself in certain ways, and, if challenged (or perhaps even without being challenged), he will make claims about the hollowness of all earthly satisfactions and the greater reliability, intensity, and duration of the satisfactions derived from glorifying God. Again, a man, who advocates the introduction of bullfighting into the United States would not *just* advance this proposal but would give reasons having to do, perhaps, with the benefits to be derived from engaging in dangerous sports and the special thrills experienced by the spectators. All these supporting factual claims are discussable, and it may be possible to show that they are mistaken or highly implausible. If so, it might well be possible to regard the case of one side in such a dispute as well supported and the other as unsupported by the evidence. In all cases in which the person is willing to support his moral judgment by factual premises, it is perfectly consistent for Russell to assert that one position is "more rational" than the other, where "more rational" does not merely mean that Russell shares the attitude of the person taking this position.

What seems to be amiss here is not Russell's subjectivism but his view (which is not logically implied by it) that the theory applies to cases like the dispute about bullfighting. In his later period Russell seems to be guilty of a gross overestimate of the prevalence of ultimate moral disagreements. It is true, as he observes in *Power,* that behind disagreements about means there is frequently disagreement about ends, but it is very doubtful that the ends in question are in most cases *ultimate* ends. To give a simple illustration of a very common type: two people may offer conflicting moral judgments about a bill to legalize abortion. The man who opposes the legislation may give as his reason (or as one of his reasons) that it would remove one of the conditions restraining unmarried people from engaging in sexual intercourse, whereas the other man might offer this as his reason (or one of his reasons) for supporting the legislation. Although the disagreement may in the immediate context be properly described as one about an end, it is clearly not about an ultimate end. In all likelihood the parties to the dispute would differ about the effects of a freer sex life on personal happiness, on society at large, on the future of religious institutions, and many other things. It is doubtful that either of them would maintain that suffering as such is better than happiness or that hate is better than love.

Even people who advocate what by most contemporary standards would be regarded as "outlandish" moral positions can usually be seen to share many of the intrinsic value judgments of the rest of mankind. Thus, Schopenhauer and other champions of asceticism recommend the suppression of desires, including those that to most human beings seem the most natural and the most innocent, but they do so *not* because in their opinion suppression of these desires would make people unhappy but, on the contrary, because it would enable them to achieve greater happiness or at least because it would reduce suffering to a minimum. In Norman Mailer's bizarre novel *An American Dream* the main character offers a defense of murder, but this unusual position is justified by the argument that "murder offers the promise of vast relief. It is never unsexual." It is accompanied by "exhilaration" which must come "from possessing such strength." It should be noted that murder is here justified not because it causes suffering but because, according to the character, it leads to "exhilaration." In other writings Mailer tells us that the "modern soul marooned in . . . emptiness, boredom and a flat, dull terror of death" would be well advised to pass through "violence, cannibalism, insanity, perversion" and other states and activities that are usually considered highly undesirable, but these recommendations are offered not for their own sake but because they will lead the person "back to life."

As for the really intrinsic clashes of the kind mentioned earlier, to which Russell's subjectivism would apply, one wonders if the consequences of the theory are there really so paradoxical. No doubt people do in such disputes regard their position as superior to that of their opponents—the man who admires integrity will feel contempt for the "cowardly" compromiser, and the compromiser will think the man who chooses to suffer a fool. Here, however, unless there are some *hidden* differences concerning matters of fact, it seems not at all incredible to maintain that calling one position superior simply amounts to expressing one's own preference for it.

None of the above is meant to prove that Russell's subjectivism is a correct account of the logical status of moral judgments, but it would indicate that the favorite objection of his critics can be disposed of without much difficulty.

Critique of religion. No such doubts as Russell has expressed about his subjectivism in ethics mark his views on religion. Unlike many academic philosophers whose position is very similar to his, Russell has not hesitated to express his convictions publicly and without equivocation or compromise. Ever since he abandoned the Platonic theory of ideas, Russell has been a forthright opponent of religion in more senses than one: he regards the basic doctrines of (supernaturalistic) religions as intellectually indefensible, he argues that religious belief has not on balance been a force for good but quite the opposite, and he hopes and believes that religion will eventually die out. "I am myself," he wrote in 1922, "a dissenter from all known religions, and I hope that every kind of religious belief will die out. . . . I regard religion as belonging to the infancy of human reason and to a stage of development which we are now outgrowing" (*Sceptical Essays,* p. 101). In a television interview 37 years later he slightly qualified this prediction. If great wars and great oppressions continue so that many people will be leading very unhappy lives, religion will probably go on, but "if people solve their social problems religion will die out" (*Bertrand Russell Speaks His Mind*, p. 31).

God. Russell has wavered between calling himself an agnostic and describing himself as an atheist. He evidently does not attach too much importance to this distinction, but he has made it clear that if he is to be classified as an agnostic, it would have to be in a sense in which an agnostic and an atheist are "for practical purposes, at one." In the television interview mentioned earlier the interviewer asked Russell, "Do you think it is certain that there is no such thing as God, or simply that it is just not proved?" "No," Russell answered, "I don't think it is certain that there is no such thing—I think that it is on exactly the same level as the Olympic gods, or the Norwegian gods; they also may exist, the gods of Olympus and Valhalla. I can't prove they don't, but I think the Christian God has no more likelihood than they had. I think they are a bare possibility" (*ibid.*, pp. 24–25). He explained his views more fully in an interview published in *Look* magazine in 1953. An agnostic, in any sense in which he can be regarded as one, Russell said, "may hold that the existence of God, though not impossible, is very improbable; he may even hold it so improbable that it is not worth considering in practice" (Leo Rosten, ed., *A Guide to the Religions of America*, New York, 1955, p. 150).

Immortality. On survival, Russell's position is similarly negative. All the evidence indicates that what we regard as our mental life is "bound up with brain structure and organized bodily energy." There is every reason to believe that mental life ceases when the body decays. Russell admits that this argument is "only one of probability" but adds that "it is as strong as those upon which most scientific conclusions are based" (*Why I Am Not a Christian*, p. 51). It is conceivable that evidence from psychical research might change the balance of probability some day, but, writing in 1925, Russell considered such evidence far weaker "than the physiological evidence on the other side." He has not since seen any reason to modify this judgment.

Russell's views on the body–mind problem are known as "neutral monism," and it would be inaccurate to call him a materialist. However, he has always emphasized that as a theory about man's place in the universe his philosophy is closely akin to materialism. "Emotionally," he wrote in 1928, "the world is pretty much the same as it would be if the materialists were in the right" (*In Praise of Idleness*, p. 143). The opponents of materialism, he adds, have been actuated by the desire to prove that the mind is immortal and that the "ultimate power" in the universe is mental and not physical. On both these points, Russell makes clear, he agrees with materialism. When he returned to the subject in 1959 he had not changed his opinion at all. "I still think," he wrote then, "that man is cosmically unimportant, and that a Being, if there were one, who could view the universe impartially, without the bias of *here* and *now*, would hardly mention man, except perhaps in a footnote at the end of the volume" (*My Philosophical Development*, p. 213).

Objections to fideism. Although, needless to say, Russell rejects the traditional arguments for the existence of God and immortality, he greatly prefers the rationalistic theology of such philosophers as Aquinas and Descartes to the fideism of Pascal, Rousseau, Kierkegaard, and their numerous modern followers. "The rejection of reason in favor of the heart," he writes, "was not, to my mind, an advance." He remarks that "no one thought of this device so long as reason appeared to be on the side of religious belief" (*A History of Western Philosophy*, p. 720). There are two fatal objections to the practice of justifying religious belief by an appeal to the emotions of the heart. To begin with, the heart says different things to different men and to the same man at different times, but even if the heart said the same thing to all men this would still not be evidence for the existence of anything outside our emotions, and the fideists, no less than the rationalistic believers, mean to make claims about objective fact, not merely about their own emotions. At bottom, Russell concludes, the only reason offered for the acceptance of the new theology is "that it allows us to indulge in pleasant dreams. This is an unworthy reason, and if I had to choose between Thomas Aquinas and Rousseau, I should unhesitatingly choose the Saint" (*ibid.*, p. 721).

Some unbelievers have gone out of their way to praise the greatness of Jesus and to admit that religious belief, although perhaps not true, is at least of great value to individual believers and to society. Russell makes no such concessions. Although he grants that some of Christ's maxims were indeed admirable (especially those consistently disregarded by Christian dignitaries) he finds much in the teachings of Jesus to be defective, in particular his doctrine of eternal damnation. "Either in the matter of virtue or in the matter of wisdom," Russell concludes, Christ does not "stand as high as some other people known to history"—for example, Buddha and Socrates (*Why I Am Not a Christian*, p. 19).

Harmfulness of religious belief. Russell's views about the nature of the emotions which inspire religious belief ("it is based, primarily and mainly, upon fear") and also about the harmful influence of religious organizations are very similar to those of Hume, Holbach, and other eighteenth-century freethinkers. He has, however, devoted rather more attention to the bad effects of the habit of accepting propositions on faith—in the absence of or even in opposition to the evidence. It is an error, Russell contends, to suppose that a person who does not form his beliefs on the basis of evidence in one domain can remain open-minded and scientific in another. Furthermore, somebody holding comfortable beliefs on faith dimly realizes that they are myths and "becomes furious when they are disputed." Such a person will therefore do his best to suppress all critics who might remind him of the feeble backing of his beliefs. Russell makes it clear that in this context he is not criticizing Christianity only. "The important thing," he writes, "is not what you believe, but how you believe it." The objections to "faith" do not depend on what the faith in question may be. "You may believe in the verbal inspiration of the Bible or of the Koran or of Marx's *Capital*. Whichever of these beliefs you entertain, you have to close your mind against evidence; and if you close your mind against evidence in one respect, you will also do so in another, if the temptation is strong." The person who bases his belief on reason will support it by argument rather than by persecution and will abandon his position if the argument goes against him. If, however, his belief is based on faith, he will conclude that argument is useless and will "therefore resort to force either in the form of persecution or by stunting and distorting the minds of the young whenever he has the power to control their education" (*Human Society in Ethics and Politics*, pp. 207–208).

"The world is horrible." Russell has never denied that in some respects a "godless" philosophy like his has to be gloomy. The beginning of wisdom, he teaches, is acceptance of the fact that the universe does not care about our aspirations and that happiness and unhappiness are not meted out in accordance with what people deserve. "The secret of happiness," he observed during a television program commemorating his 92d birthday, "is to face the fact that the world is horrible." What Russell meant by this becomes clear from a story related by his biographer, Alan Wood. Wood's wife had expressed her opinion that it seemed horribly unjust that the young men who had been killed in the war should not somehow or somewhere have a second chance to achieve happiness. "But the universe *is* unjust," Russell replied, "the secret of happiness is to face the fact that the world is horrible, horrible, *horrible* . . . you must feel it deeply and not brush it aside . . . you must feel it right here"—hitting his breast—"and then you can start being happy again" (*Bertrand Russell: The Passionate Sceptic*, p. 237). Once a person has stopped looking at the universe in terms of anthropomorphic demands, he can concentrate on what is attainable and not waste his time in self-pity and cosmic complaints. For those whose philosophy is shaped not by a respect for facts but by their wishes Russell has always been scathing in his contempt. He expresses his amazement that courage is praised in all types of situations but not when it comes to forming a view about the world. "Where traditional beliefs about the universe are concerned," he writes, "craven fears . . . are considered praiseworthy, while intellectual courage, unlike courage in battle, is regarded as unfeeling and materialistic." Writing in 1957, he notes that this attitude is perhaps less widespread now than it was in his youth, but he adds that it "still inspires vast systems of thought which have their root in unworthy fears." "I cannot believe," he concludes, that there can ever be any good excuse for refusing to face the evidence in favor of something unwelcome. It is not by delusion, however exalted, that mankind can prosper, but only by unswerving courage in the pursuit of truth" (*Fact and Fiction*, p. 46).

Bibliography

BIOGRAPHY

There is a good deal of autobiographical material in Russell's *Portraits From Memory and Other Essays* (London and New York, 1956); in *Fact and Fiction* (London and New York, 1962); in his introduction to *Selected Papers of Bertrand Russell* (New York, 1927); in "My Religious Reminiscences," in *The Rationalist An-*nual*, Vol. 55 (1938), 3–8; in "My Mental Development," in P. A. Schilpp, ed., *The Philosophy of Bertrand Russell* (Evanston and Chicago, Ill., 1944); and in *My Philosophical Development* (London and New York, 1959). Alan Wood, *Bertrand Russell: The Passionate Sceptic* (London and New York, 1956), is the only full-length biographical study of Russell. H. W. Leggett, *Bertrand Russell* (New York, 1950), is a short pictorial biography.

G. H. Hardy, *Bertrand Russell and Trinity* (Cambridge, 1942), traces the controversy between Russell and the fellows of Trinity College over his pacifist activities during World War I. *Rex Versus Bertrand Russell, Report of the Proceedings Before the Lord Mayor* (London, 1916), gives the text of the first of Russell's trials.

D. H. Lawrence, *Letters to Bertrand Russell* (New York, 1948), reproduces Lawrence's letters to Russell during World War I; Russell's letters to Lawrence have not been preserved.

Russell's part in the Beacon Hill School is most fully described in Joe Park, *Bertrand Russell on Education* (Columbus, Ohio, 1963). The Park volume also contains a complete list of Russell's writings on educational topics. Details about the City College case of 1940 can be found in John Dewey and Horace M. Kallen, eds., *The Bertrand Russell Case* (New York, 1941); in a publication by the American Civil Liberties Union entitled *The Story of the Bertrand Russell Case—The Enlightening Record of the Obstruction by Courts and Officials of the Appointment of Bertrand Russell to a Professorship at the College of the City of New York* (New York, 1941); and in Paul Edwards, "How Bertrand Russell Was Prevented From Teaching at City College," which is an appendix to Russell's *Why I Am Not a Christian and Other Essays on Religion and Related Subjects* (London and New York, 1957).

EPISTEMOLOGY AND METAPHYSICS

Principles of Mathematics (Cambridge, 1903) was Russell's first major philosophical work. Its position is one of Platonic realism. In the preface to the second edition (1937) Russell sets forth his later disenchantment with this position. For a nonmathematical exposition of Russell's early realism, see "Meinong's Theory of Complexes and Assumptions," in *Mind*, Vol. 13 (1904), 204–219; 336–354; 509–524. Russell's criticisms of the idealist theory of truth are to be found in "The Monistic Theory of Truth," in *Philosophical Essays* (New York, 1910), a revised version of "The Nature of Truth," in *Mind*, Vol. 15 (1906), 528–533. *Philosophical Essays* also contains two influential essays by Russell attacking the pragmatist theory of truth.

The shift from realism to logical constructionism can be followed in a number of articles, the most important of which is "On Denoting," in *Mind*, Vol. 14 (1905), 479–493. This, together with other important but otherwise largely unavailable essays, is reprinted in Russell's *Logic and Knowledge*, R. C. Marsh, ed. (London, 1956). Russell's "On the Relations of Universals and Particulars," in *PAS*, Vol. 12 (1911–1912), 1–24, reprinted in *Logic and Knowledge*, is a classic presentation of the largely Platonic theory of universals Russell still held at that time. *Problems of Philosophy* (New York, 1912) gives an excellent semipopular account of the general state of Russell's thinking then. Russell's early attempts to represent physical objects as logical constructions can be seen in *Our Knowledge of the External World* (Chicago, 1914) and in two essays, "The Ultimate Constituents of Matter," in *The Monist*, Vol. 25 (1915), 399–447, and "The Relations of Sense-data to Physics," in *Scientia*, No. 4 (1914), both reprinted in *Mysticism and Logic* (London, 1918). Other important essays in this collection are "On Scientific Method in Philosophy" (1914); "On the Notion of Cause," originally published in *PAS*, Vol. 13 (1912–1913), 1–26; and "Knowledge by Acquaintance and Knowledge by Description," originally published in *PAS*, Vol. 11 (1910–1911), 108–128. See also "The Philosophy of Logical Atomism," in *The Monist*, Vol. 28 (1918), 495–527; Vol. 29 (1919), 32–63, 190–222, and 345–380; reprinted in *Logic and Knowledge* (see above). The analysis of basic concepts and principles of physical science is pushed further in *The Analysis of Matter* (New York, 1927). Logical constructionism is applied to mental phenomena in *The Analysis of Mind* (New York, 1921). Russell's increasing concern with psychological aspects of meaning can be traced in "On Propositions, What They Are and How They Mean," in *PAS*, Supp. Vol. 2 (1919), 1–43, reprinted in *Logic and Knowledge*; in Ch. 10 of *The Analysis of Mind*; and in Russell's most extensive work on meaning and empirical data, the rich but chaotic *An Inquiry Into Meaning and Truth* (New York, 1940). Russell's latest thoughts on meaning and various other problems concerning empirical knowledge, particularly in the physical sciences, are given a relatively systematic presentation in *Human Knowledge, Its Scope and Limits* (New York, 1948).

In several works Russell has summarized his philosophy and/or its development. The most important of these are "Logical Atomism," in J. H. Muirhead, ed., *Contemporary British Philosophy*, First Series (London, 1924), reprinted in *Logic and Knowledge* (see above); "My Mental Development," in P. A. Schilpp, ed., *The Philosophy of Bertrand Russell* (see above); and the very interesting recent work *My Philosophical Development* (London and New York, 1959). The last-named work also contains some of Russell's polemics against recent Oxford philosophers and their criticisms of his views. Russell's *A History of Western Philosophy* (London and New York, 1946) and *The Wisdom of the West* (London and New York, 1959), aside from their intrinsic interest, are of great value to students of Russell's thought in showing us his mature evaluations of the great philosophers of past ages.

The critical literature on different aspects of Russell's epistemology and metaphysics is vast. *The Philosophy of Bertrand Russell* (see above) contains a number of excellent discussions, together with Russell's replies. Special mention should also be made of C. A. Fritz, *Bertrand Russell's Construction of the External World* (London, 1952); Erik Götlind, *Bertrand Russell's Theories of Causation* (Uppsala, 1952); J. O. Urmson, *Philosophical Analysis—Its Development Between Two World Wars* (Oxford, 1956); and G. J. Warnock, *English Philosophy Since 1900* (London, 1958). The books by Urmson and Warnock contain detailed appraisals of Russell's logical atomism. Russell's logical atomism as well as his neutral monism and his theories about truth and induction are sympathetically discussed by D. J. O'Connor in Ch. 26 of his *Critical History of Western Philosophy* (New York, 1964). *Rivista critica di storia della filosofia*, Vol. 8, No. 2 (1953), 101–335, and several articles in *Philosophy*, Vol. 35 (January 1960), 1–50, is devoted to Russell's philosophy, including Anthony Quinton's useful sketch of the development of Russell's ideas in epistemology and metaphysics, "Russell's Philosophical Development," 1–13.

LOGIC AND MATHEMATICS

Of Russell's own works on logic and mathematics, see *Principles of Mathematics* (Cambridge, 1903; 2d ed., London, 1937); *Principia Mathematica*, 3 vols., written with A. N. Whitehead (Cambridge, 1910–1913; 2d ed., 1927; paperback ed. up to *56, 1962); *Introduction to Mathematical Philosophy* (London, 1919); and the papers "On Denoting" (1905), "Mathematical Logic as Based on the Theory of Types" (1908), "The Philosophy of Logical Atomism" (1918), and "Logical Atomism" (1924), all of which are reprinted in R. C. Marsh, ed. *Logic and Knowledge* (London, 1956).

On Frege's parallel work, see his *Grundlagen der Arithmetik* (Breslau, 1884), translated by J. L. Austin as *The Foundations of Arithmetic* (Oxford, 1950); and P. T. Geach and Max Black, eds., *Translations From the Philosophical Writings of Gottlob Frege* (Oxford, 1952).

Important critical discussions of Russell's work occur in W. E. Johnson, *Logic*, Pt. II (Cambridge, 1922), Chs. 3 and 6; F. P. Ramsey, *The Foundations of Mathematics* (London, 1931), papers I and II; W. V. Quine, *From a Logical Point of View* (Cambridge, Mass., 1953), essays I, V, and VI; and G. E. Moore, *The Commonplace Book of G. E. Moore, 1919–1953*, Casimir Lewy, ed. (London and New York, 1963), Notebook II, item 4, and Notebook V, item 13.

On formal implication, see A. N. Prior, "The Theory of Implication," in *Zeitschrift für mathematische Logik und Grundlagen der Mathematik*, Vol. 9 (1963), 1–6. On simplifications of type theory, see Alonzo Church, "A Formulation of the Simple Theory of Types," in *Journal of Symbolic Logic*, Vol. 5 (1940), 56–68, and Ludwik Borkowski, "Reduction of Arithmetic to Logic Based on the Theory of Types," in *Studia Logica*, Vol. 8 (1958), 283–295.

ETHICS AND RELIGION

Russell's early views on ethics are in "The Elements of Ethics," Ch. 1 of *Philosophical Essays* (New York, 1910); it has been reprinted in Wilfrid Sellars and John Hospers, eds., *Readings in Ethical Theory* (New York, 1952), pp. 1–34. The fullest statements of his later position are in Ch. 9 of *Religion and Science* (London and New York, 1935) and in *Human Society in Ethics and Politics* (London and New York, 1955). There are critical discussions of Russell's views in Lillian W. Aiken, *Bertrand Russell's Philosophy of Morals* (New York, 1963); in Justus Buchler, "Russell and the Principles of Ethics," in P. A. Schilpp, ed., *The Philosophy of Bertrand Russell* (see above); and in D. H. Monro, "Russell's Moral Theories," in *Philosophy*, Vol. 35 (1960), 30–50.

Russell's earliest views on religion are in "The Essence of Religion," in *The Hibbert Journal*, Vol. 11 (1912), 46–62. His first published discussion of the arguments for the existence of God is contained in Ch. 15 of *A Critical Exposition of the Philosophy of Leibniz* (Cambridge, 1900; 2d ed., London and New York, 1937). His later views are expounded in several of the essays in *Why I Am Not a Christian* (London and New York, 1957) and in Pt. II, Ch. 7, of *Human Society in Ethics and Politics* (see above). The BBC debate with Father F. C. Copleston (1948), "The Existence of God," is available in the British edition, but not in the American edition, of *Why I Am Not a Christian*, but it has been reprinted in Paul Edwards and Arthur Pap, eds., *A Modern Introduction to Philosophy*, 2d ed. (New York, 1965), and in John Hick, ed., *The Existence of God* (New York, 1964). Several chapters in *The Scientific Outlook* (London and New York, 1931) and in *Religion and Science* (see above) contain criticisms of the attempts of certain scientists to derive theological conclusions from physics and biology. Russell's objections to the fideistic position are found in Ch. 12, Bk. 3, of *A History of Western Philosophy* (London and New York, 1946). His objections to William James' defense of religion are contained in Ch. 29, Bk. 3, of the same work and in Ch. 5 of *Philosophical Essays* (see above). Russell's views on religion are criticized in H. G. Wood, *Why Mr. Bertrand Russell Is Not a Christian* (London, 1928); C. H. D. Clark, *Christianity and Bertrand Russell* (London, 1958); G. S. Montgomery, *Why Bertrand Russell Is Not a Christian* (New York, 1959); and E. S. Brightman's contribution to the Schilpp volume, "Russell's Philosophy of Religion," pp. 537–556.

SOCIAL AND POLITICAL THEORY

In addition to the works mentioned in the first section of the present article, the following among Russell's books dealing with social and political questions have been influential: *Principles of Social Reconstruction* (London, 1916); *Roads to Freedom: Socialism, Anarchism and Syndicalism* (London, 1918); *The Problems of China* (New York, 1922); *Power: A New Social Analysis* (London and New York, 1938); *Authority and the Individual* (London, 1949); and *New Hopes for a Changing World* (London and New York, 1951). Ch. 17 of *New Hopes* contains a moving discussion of the problems of growing old and facing death. Russell's fullest discussion of Marxism can be found in *Freedom and Organization 1814–1914* (London and New York, 1934; New York edition entitled *Freedom versus Organization*), which is in effect a history of the main social and intellectual forces of the nineteenth century.

OTHER WRITINGS

Philosophical discussions sooner or later crop up in most of Russell's writings. Some of his most delightful occasional pieces have been collected in *Sceptical Essays* (London and New York, 1927); in *In Praise of Idleness* (London and New York, 1935); and in *Unpopular Essays* (London and New York, 1950). The last of these contains his "Auto-obituary," which was first published in 1936. *Bertrand Russell Speaks His Mind* (London, 1960) is a most interesting volume containing the unedited text of a series of television interviews, dealing with a great variety of topics, which took place in the spring of 1959.

The Basic Writings of Bertrand Russell, 1903–1959, R. E. Egner and L. E. Dennon, eds. (New York, 1961), is a very useful anthology of writings by Russell. The Schilpp volume contains an extremely comprehensive bibliography up to 1944.

(*Life and Social Theories, Ethics and Critique of Religion*)
PAUL EDWARDS
(*Epistemology and Metaphysics*)
WILLIAM P. ALSTON
(*Logic and Mathematics*)
A. N. PRIOR

RUSSIAN PHILOSOPHY. The history of Russian philosophy is comparatively brief. Prior to the time of Peter the Great (1672–1725) philosophical speculation was confined to the interstices of Russian Orthodox theology and homiletics and limited almost exclusively to moral philosophy and philosophical anthropology.

The beginnings of Russian philosophy in a stricter, if not narrowly technical, sense date from the large-scale contact with Western thought and culture initiated by Peter. The subsequent history of Russian philosophical thought exhibits an extraordinary complexity in the sequence and interrelationships of ideas and movements. But with few exceptions, Russian philosophy since the mid-eighteenth century has exhibited a number of distinctive and persistent features. It has been man-centered, nonacademic, closely related to literature (in a broad sense of the term), *engagé*, immoderate, and partisan.

Ethics, social philosophy, and in the nineteenth century the philosophy of history and culture, including philosophy of art, have been the disciplines persistently favored by Russian philosophers. Only recently have they worked in such technical disciplines as logic, theory of knowledge, and philosophy of science. Metaphysics and philosophical theology have been intimately linked to ethics, social philosophy, and philosophy of history.

In contrast to western European, and particularly German, philosophers, Russian thinkers have almost without exception worked outside the universities. During the eighteenth and nineteenth centuries professors of philosophy in Russian universities and theological seminaries, though competent, tended to be more or less faithful disciples of one or another Western master rather than independent thinkers. Even the chief exception, Vladimir Solovyov, left the academic world fairly early, owing to serious differences with school and government authorities.

The major Russian thinkers until well into the twentieth century were, in a broad sense of the word, "critics." Their Western counterparts are thinkers like Kierkegaard, John Stuart Mill, Nietzsche, and Sartre. They generally supported themselves by writing book reviews and occasional articles. The subject of their criticism was not only literature in the narrow sense but also political, social, cultural, and philosophical topics.

Just as Russian philosophers have tended to be literary critics in the above sense, Russian writers have been more than usually concerned with recurrent philosophical and quasi-philosophical problems. Tolstoy, Dostoyevsky, and Pasternak are obvious examples; less well known in this respect are Gogol and, among the poets, A. A. Fet (who translated Schopenhauer) and the symbolists, particularly A. A. Blok and Andrei Bely. And many Russian thinkers who are best known as philosophers or critics have also

been gifted and productive poets, among others, Skovoroda, Radishchev, Khomyakov, and of course, Vladimir Solovyov.

Many Russian philosophers have written with a special intensity, exhibiting an impatience with moderation. This zeal, and the nonacademic status of most Russian philosophers, is closely related to the fact that there was a personal risk involved in professional commitment to the world of speculative thought. Creative thinkers were virtually excluded from academic life. After the Decembrist uprising of 1825 classroom instruction in philosophy was forbidden in Russian universities from 1826 to 1863, and from then until 1889 all that was officially permitted were lecture-commentaries on stipulated Platonic and Aristotelian texts.

The philosophical void in mid-nineteenth-century Russian formal education was partially filled in two related ways. Informal discussion groups, or "circles" (*kruzhki*), were formed during and after the 1830s, and it was in these circles that some of the most gifted Russian university students were initiated into philosophy. These circles also made known to Russian intellectuals both German metaphysics and French social theory.

Second, both inside and outside the circles, major Western works, in the original and in manuscript translation, were eagerly passed from hand to hand and heatedly discussed. For example, students in certain Russian theological schools around 1830 were reading Kant's forbidden *Critique of Pure Reason* in manuscript translation. Soviet students in the 1960s are doing the same sort of thing with forbidden Western works (and even some Eastern ones—those of Georg Lukács, for instance.)

For the reasons sketched above, philosophy in Russia has been regarded as properly an instrumental and engaged, rather than a "pure," discipline. Russian intellectuals, especially in the nineteenth century, viewed ideas as weapons in the struggle for freedom and regarded the study of pure philosophy as an evasion of pressing moral and sociopolitical problems. The Russian intelligentsia subordinated theoretical truth (*istina*) to practical truth–justice (*pravda*). Russian thinkers were engaged in the "quest for truth–justice" (*iskaniye pravdy*).

HISTORICAL BACKGROUND

The cultural roots of medieval Russia lay in Byzantium. During the ninth and tenth centuries the "barbarian" Russians adopted Byzantine religion, plastic art, literature, and the Greek alphabet—all with more or less substantial modifications. After the fall of Constantinople in 1453 and Ivan III's defeat of the Mongols in 1480, Moscow began to assume the Byzantine role as a "third Rome," succeeding Constantinople, the "second Rome." Russian tsars took over the priestly functions that Byzantine emperors had exercised since the time of Constantine. In 1589 the bishop of Moscow was named patriarch of the Orthodox church.

Despite its Byzantine roots, the culture of Muscovy, like that of Kiev before it, remained Slavic on the surface. There was no Russian parallel to the western European use of Latin as a liturgical and learned language, affording a close link with the Greco-Roman world. Old Church

Slavonic, rather than Greek, remained the language of liturgy and learning, and very few Greek writings (these few being chiefly theological or homiletic rather than philosophical) were translated into it.

The first school of humanistic studies in Russia, with a curriculum including both Latin and Greek, was founded in Kiev in 1631. But Russia's renaissance of classical learning—like its massive and fruitful contact with western European culture—was delayed until the time of Peter the Great, receiving special stimulus under Catherine the Great (1729–1796). This period marked the beginning of Russian philosophy as an intellectual discipline distinct from the speculative theology and practical moralizing out of which it had grown.

THE EIGHTEENTH CENTURY

Kiev antedated Moscow as a cultural and political center; the Kiev *collegium* (modeled on Jesuit *collegia* in Poland) predated the Moscow Theological Academy at Zagorsk (1685) by more than half a century. The Ukraine, even after it was brought under the political hegemony of Moscow in the late seventeenth century, remained relatively open to Western influences without losing its ties to Byzantine thought and culture.

Skovoroda. Because of Kiev's special cultural position it was natural that the first Russian philosopher, Gregory Skovoroda (1722–1794), should have spent most of his life in the Ukraine and that he should have been at home in German, fluent in Latin, adequate in Hebrew, rhapsodic about Greek ("the noblest of foreign tongues"), and finally that he should have written his own philosophical works in a rich and powerful Russian prose.

Skovoroda aspired to be a "Russian Socrates"—both a gadfly provoking thoughtless men to scrutinize their lives and an intellectual forerunner of a more profound and systematic "Russian Plato."

Skovoroda's life, like Spinoza's, was marked by loneliness, conflict with ecclesiastical authority, purity of moral passion, and single-mindedness of intellectual commitment. Like Spinoza, he wrote much, circulating his manuscripts among a few friends and disciples, but his works, even more completely than Spinoza's, remained unpublished during his lifetime.

All of Skovoroda's philosophical and theological writings are in dialogue form. They are Socratic in method and theme, although no single figure dominates them as Socrates dominates Plato's earlier dialogues. They are genuinely dramatic, written with wit, imagination, and moral intensity. In these dialogues Skovoroda perceptively criticized both materialism and sense-datum empiricism and developed his own dualistic Platonic metaphysics with a mystical and pantheistic coloring. In deliberate opposition to the Baconian call to "know nature in order to master it," Skovoroda called on each human being to "know himself in order to master himself," putting aside the desire for health, security, comfort, or fame. Skovoroda's position is thus Stoic as well as Socratic. His philosophical anthropology, while essentially Christian and Neoplatonic, anticipated features of nineteenth-century and twentieth-century theories of the unconscious. In a century dominated by

secular rationalism he was probably closest in personality and thought to his younger contemporary William Blake. Like Spinoza, Blake would have appreciated the epitaph Skovoroda wrote for himself: "The world set a trap for me, but it did not catch me."

French influences. Among the cultivated French-speaking Russians of St. Petersburg and Moscow, the dominant intellectual influences in the late eighteenth century were French. The works of Voltaire and the Encyclopedists enjoyed special popularity; but toward the end of the century Freemasonry, principally from German sources, had a parallel impact. The "window upon Europe" that Peter the Great had thrown open by erecting his new capital on the shores of the Gulf of Finland proved an effective medium of cultural and intellectual osmosis.

Natural-law theorists. Diderot's extended visit in 1773 and 1774 to the Petersburg court of Catherine the Great exemplified the penetration into the Russian *grand monde* of the attitudes and doctrines of the *philosophes*. The chief attitudes were skepticism and rationalism (in the sense of hostility toward tradition, "superstition," and "obscurantism"). The chief doctrines were deism, utilitarianism, and natural-law theory. Russian defenders of natural law included V. N. Tatishchev (1686–1750), a learned historian and the first thinker in Russia to outline a utilitarian ethical theory; the anticlerical Prince M. M. Shcherbatov (1733–1790), who upheld a theory of natural religion; and N. I. Novikov (1744–1818), a satirist and sharp critic of serfdom, who was imprisoned for his "subversive" writings in 1792.

Radishchev. The most celebrated of the Russian natural-law theorists was A. N. Radishchev (1749–1802). His *Journey From St. Petersburg to Moscow* (1790), published at a moment when the "enlightened" Catherine was obsessed with the fear that what had happened in Paris in 1789 might happen in Petersburg, brought Radishchev a death sentence, later commuted to a decade of exile. Both as a critic of serfdom and as a martyr for his convictions, Radishchev, even more than Novikov, set a precedent for subsequent oppositionist thinkers, most of whom spent long years in confinement in St. Petersburg or in Siberian exile. More important for the subsequent development of Russian philosophy was the intellectual precedent of combining metaphysical speculation with moral and social criticism. Radishchev's metaphysics and epistemology, as well as his philosophical psychology, were set forth in a long essay "On Man, His Mortality and Immortality" (1796; first Russian publication 1809–1811), a work inspired by Leibniz, Herder, Moses Mendelssohn, and Joseph Priestley. Other Western influences had shaped Radishchev's thought during and after his five-year sojourn in Leipzig, where he studied philosophy, law, and Western languages, namely, the works of Locke, Helvétius, Rousseau, Mably, and Montesquieu. Radishchev followed the Leibniz of the *Nouveaux Essais* in attempting to reconcile empiricism with rationalism; he insisted that all knowledge is based on experience but admitted rational experience (of relations) in addition to sense experience (of things and events). He also held that we cannot know what things are like in themselves, that our conceptions of them are irremediably symbolic.

Other leading eighteenth-century Russian men of learning whose works touched on important philosophical issues were M. V. Lomonosov (c. 1711–1765), the "father of Russian science," and N. M. Karamzin (1766–1826), the "father of Russian history."

THE EARLY NINETEENTH CENTURY

Napoleon's invasion of Russia turned cultivated Russians away from France and toward Germany as a source of values and ideas. By the second quarter of the nineteenth century German philosophy dominated Russian intellectual circles even more completely than it had dominated western European intellectual circles in the years immediately preceding. The influence of Schelling's *Naturphilosophie* and speculative aesthetics was followed by that of Kant's *Kritizismus* and Fichte's voluntaristic philosophy of the *ich*. Kant's works encountered most difficulty with the tsarist censorship; his *Critiques* were confined to manuscript translations until the 1860s. The only published translation of Fichte's work dating from the 1830s was Bakunin's version of "Die Bestimmung des Gelehrten," which appeared in the journal *Teleskop* in 1835.

Although no Russian translations of Hegel appeared until the 1860s, Hegel's influence acquired massive proportions as early as the 1830s. In the 1840s almost all young Russian intellectuals, not only the few academic philosophers, became convinced Hegelians. Cultivated Russians as a group passed through what is probably a unique attachment to Hegel. Hegel's philosophical presence dominated Russian intellectual life for many years; it also operated powerfully to shape Russian philosophical terminology. Russian translations of Hegel are closer to the original than those in any other European language; even the notorious *Aufhebung* has a precise Russian equivalent (*snyatiye; aufheben = snimat*). An unanticipated consequence of the Hegelian coloring acquired by philosophical Russian was a terminological predisposition toward Marxist theory that bore intellectual fruit in the 1890s.

Individualism and antiutilitarianism. During the 1840s two themes emerged in Russian ethics, social philosophy, and philosophical anthropology that were to retain their central importance into the twentieth century—the defense of the freedom and dignity of the human individual and the critique of utilitarian views.

Individualism. The concern for the human individual, person, or personality (*lichnost* has all of these meanings) was shared by Russian conservatives, radicals, and the few liberals; by theists, agnostics, and atheists; by Populists (*narodniki*); and even by a few early Russian Marxists (the Kantian revisionists and the more individualistic of the Nietzschean revisionists).

Russian thinkers tended to see the individual as doubly threatened—by the facts of Russian life and by the theories of Western philosophers. Russian reality (*russkaya deistvitelnost*) was taken by liberals and radicals to include not only such institutions as serfdom and autocracy but also the religiously tinged "conciliarity" (*sobornost*) and the collectivistic peasant village commune (*obshchina*) celebrated by the politically conservative Slavophiles.

By Western theory was meant primarily Hegelian, and later, Marxian, sociohistorical impersonalism or anti-individualism. For example, Belinski, after several years as a devoted Hegelian, broke away from Hegel in the early 1840s as he came to distrust the politically conservative consequences of Hegel's identification of the rational with the real, or actual (*wirklich = deistvitelny*), in human history. He now saw Hegel as reducing the individual person to a mere instrument for the self-realization of absolute *Geist* (*dukh*) through a rationally determined world-historical process. Belinski came to feel, with desperate intensity, that Hegel left no room for the autonomous, artistically creative, or morally responsible individual.

Antiutilitarianism. Utilitarian ethical and social theory (the "ethics and politics of rational egoism") was enthusiastically defended by the "men of the sixties"—Chernyshevski, Dobrolyubov, and, toward the end of his short life, Pisarev, as well as by the Marxianizing nihilist Tkachyov. But this position was repudiated, for a variety of reasons, by almost all other Russian thinkers: by conservative critics, such as Dostoyevsky, Leontyev, and Pobedonostsev; by academic critics, such as Fr. Maltsev; by anti-Hegelian "semipositivist" critics, like Herzen, Kavelin, Lavrov, and Kareyev; and by Hegelian "idealist" critics, such as Chicherin and Solovyov. In their critical response to utilitarianism they again showed themselves closer to their German than to their French and English counterparts.

Schellingians. The most important of the Russian Schellingians were Professor D. M. Vellanski (1774–1847), D. V. Venevitinov (1805–1827), a gifted poet and speculative thinker who died too soon to have written much, and Prince V. F. Odoyevski (1803–1869). Odoyevski, after a period devoted mostly to Schellingian *Naturphilosophie*, turned to philosophical anthropology and the philosophy of history. As a *Naturphilosoph* he foresaw a time when it would be possible to "produce matter out of non-material energy" and to change one chemical substance into another. Odoyevski was one of the first Russian thinkers to formulate the idea of *tselnost*, or wholeness—the "whole man in the whole society in the whole reality"—which became a central theme of the Slavophiles, as well as of such Westernizers as Pisarev and such Populists as Lavrov and Mikhailovski. Odoyevski, in 1844, formulated the first systematic Russian critique of western European culture. He struck yet another Slavophile chord with the claim that the West cannot achieve complete or harmonious development until it finds its own Peter the Great to open a window from Europe to Russia "infusing [western Europe] with the fresh and powerful saps of the Slavic East."

Slavophiles. The Slavophiles (*slavyanofily*), who emerged as the principal rivals of the Westernizers (*zapadniki*) during the 1840s, are often represented as religiously Orthodox and politically conservative in contrast to the anticlerical and politically radical or at least liberal Westernizers. Yet Peter Chaadayev (c. 1794–1856), whose *Philosophical Letters* forthrightly praised Western culture and Roman Catholicism, was a deeply religious and politically conservative thinker; and the revolutionary atheist Michael Bakunin was, during the 1860s, a proselytizing Pan-Slavist. To be sure, for a majority of the Slavophiles

(Khomyakov, Kireyevski, K. Aksakov, and Samarin) and a majority of the Westernizers (Belinski, Herzen, Chernyshevski, and Dobrolyubov) the traditional distinction holds.

Chaadayev. Chaadayev was in many ways a transitional thinker. He combined Skovoroda's religious intensity with Radishchev's critical attitude toward Russian institutions; he anticipated both the Slavophiles' devotion to metaphysics and theology and the Westernizers' admiration for western Europe. Chaadayev admired Schelling (whom he met in Germany in 1825), but he was almost equally influenced by Hegel. His philosophy of history expresses a providentialism reminiscent of Augustine's. Where Augustine saw pride, Chaadayev saw egoism and "fragmenting individualism" as the "original sin" that sets man against man and nation against nation. Russia was particularly guilty of this sin, having separated itself irreconcilably from the West. For these harsh strictures Chaadayev was harshly punished: Nicholas I had him declared officially insane and placed under house arrest.

Khomyakov and Kireyevski. A. S. Khomyakov (1804–1860) was a learned theologian, a perceptive philosophical critic, and a vigorous dialectician; but he wrote comparatively little and did not complete the formulation of his own philosophical position. He sharply criticized the "pure rationalism" of Hegel's system as well as the "pure materialism" of such post-Hegelians as Feuerbach. Both positions were deterministic, denying freedom and subjectivity. Only in *sobornost*—the integral union of man and of men—could freedom and subjectivity be preserved. Khomyakov's emphasis both on integral reason (*razum=Vernunft*), as opposed to fragmented understanding (*rassudok=Verstand*), and on the communal character of the cognitive act was echoed by the other Slavophiles. The exercise of *rassudok* apart from faith, Khomyakov held, separates men; the exercise of *razum*—or reason in faith—brings men together in a communal consciousness.

I. V. Kireyevski (1806–1856) began as a convinced Hegelian, but under the influence of a reconversion to the Russian Orthodox faith of his youth and of the ideas of Khomyakov, he attempted to pass beyond Hegel to "new principles in philosophy." He defended the doctrine that knowing is only a part and function of man's integral activity in the world, an event in a total life process. His notion of integral knowledge was very close to Khomyakov's notion of integral reason; both involved preconceptual and noncognitive elements.

In their philosophy of history and culture the Slavophiles exhibited a common hostility to postmedieval western European civilization. All of them saw Russia as a potential savior of world civilization, destined to overcome the evils that had marred western Europe: fragmenting egoism and individualism, abstract, skeptical rationalism, the devotion to comfort and security. Two instructive instances of Slavophile cultural generalization are provided by Khomyakov's doctrine of freedom and unity and Kireyevski's doctrine of faith and knowledge. According to Khomyakov, Roman Catholicism represented unity without freedom; Protestantism represented freedom without unity; and Russian Orthodoxy represented unity-in-freedom or freedom-in-unity. Kireyevski offered a Hegel-

ian tetrad, rather than a triad, but its resolution is equally predictable: in Scholasticism reason and faith conflict; in the Reformation reason is rejected; in modern (post-Protestant) philosophy faith is rejected. Only in Russian Orthodoxy are reason and faith genuinely reconciled.

The turn to the West. Like the term "Slavophile," the term "Westernizer" is open to misinterpretation. The Westernizers of the 1840s and 1850s were by no means wholly uncritical in their attitude toward western Europe, nor wholly critical of Russia. But they did insist that Russia was a European nation whose backwardness was due to its long isolation from the West. Thus Russia's immediate task was to modernize its economy, social structure, political institutions, and culture in order to take its place in the family of European nations. In philosophy the Westernizers, like the Slavophiles, were German-oriented. Following first Schelling and Fichte, then Hegel, most of them ultimately professed agreement with Feuerbach and the Hegelian left.

Belinski. Like Schelling, V. G. Belinski (1811–1848), a brilliant literary critic and essayist, may be said to have carried on his philosophical education in public, embracing antithetical positions in passionate and rapid succession. In his early Schellingian period he stressed aesthetic activity, celebrating the creative individual who is able to transcend the impure world of sense to contemplate the eternal Idea. Belinski's conversion to Hegelianism was in part a rise to objectivity from the depths of subjectivity and sentimentality. But it also gave Belinski occasion to defend the "rational reality" of the Russian autocracy (1839). By 1840, however, he had fiercely repudiated his own "odious reconciliation with an odious reality." Rejecting Hegelian impersonalism, Belinski defended his own version of ethical individualism: "The fate of the individual person," he declared, "is more important than the fate of the whole world . . . including Hegel's *Allgemeinheit*." Like Herzen, he later turned toward a diffuse utopian socialism as a defense of the human individual, guaranteeing to all men the right to "normal" life and development.

Herzen. A. I. Herzen (1812–1870) moved, in his theory of history, from an early Hegelian rationalism to a "philosophy of contingency," stressing the "whirlwind of chances" in nature and in human life and the "tousled improvisation" of historical development. He was an uncompromising ethical individualist who stoutly and eloquently resisted the fashionable nineteenth-century tendency to subordinate the existing individual to large cultural–historical entities ("society," "nation," "progress," "mankind"). Herzen denied strict ontological determinism, stressing the lived "sense of freedom." In a different vein, anticipating Dostoyevsky, he offered a penetrating analysis of the psychology of the "escape from freedom" and sketched a curiously modern emotive ethical theory.

After 1848, disillusioned with "bourgeois" Europe and the "bourgeois" ideal of many European socialists, Herzen turned to the Russian peasant and the peasant village commune as offering the only hope for the future. In this he anticipated a central doctrine of the later Populists.

Although both Belinski and Herzen are often classified

as materialists (especially by Marxist–Leninist writers), they were not in fact philosophical materialists at all, but—in their maturity—empiricists in epistemology, positivists in methodology, and semipositivists in attitude.

Bakunin. Michael Bakunin (1814–1876) was a leader in the doctrinal peregrinations of a circle that included Belinski and Herzen. Bakunin's essay "Die Reaktion in Deutschland" (1842), written in Germany, was a first statement of "dialectical nihilism." It systematically exploited Hegelian dialectic to justify violent sociopolitical revolution and discredit political compromise. Soon thereafter Bakunin abandoned Hegel and theoretical philosophy altogether, turning to political and propagandistic activity and in middle age embracing materialism, atheism, and anarchist socialism. He collaborated with Sergei Nechaev (1847–1882) in formulating (1869) the doctrine that the "good" end of revolution justifies, even sanctifies, any means that may be necessary to its realization, however repugnant such means may appear in the light of traditional ethical theory.

RADICAL NIHILISM

Herzen, who sometimes called himself a nihilist, used the term in a broad and ambiguous sense that embraced several elements: (1) a methodological nihilism that was close to skepticism; (2) a future-oriented cultural nihilism that merged into an apocalyptic vision of European history; and (3) a political nihilism that saw the Hegelian dialectic as an "algebra of revolution." The second and third types were of only passing significance in Herzen's own intellectual development, but he remained to the end something of a methodological nihilist.

Russian radical nihilism, as a social and intellectual phenomenon of the late 1850s and the 1860s, was primarily political and dialectical, although it included elements of methodological and cultural nihilism. The term itself (*nigilist*) was apparently first used in Russian about 1858 by a Professor Bervi of Kazan University. It became a byword through its subsequent use by N. I. Nadezhin in the politically liberal journal *Vestnik Yevropy* and by the politically moderate Ivan Turgenev in his novel *Fathers and Sons* (1861).

The declared goal of the nihilists was the annihilation of the existing order—social, political, economic, and cultural; the means advocated were drastic, often violent. The outstanding nihilists—Bakunin, Nechaev, Chernyshevski, Pisarev, and Dobrolyubov—shared a basic, often selfless, dedication to destructive revolutionary activity and a disregard, even contempt, for conventional morality. They were enormously impressed by the success of the natural sciences and felt that the development of physics, chemistry, and experimental zoology would ultimately provide answers to all social and moral problems. Pisarev expressed this faith in striking and characteristic words: "It is precisely in the frog that the salvation and renewal of the Russian people is to be found," and he opposed to the frog, as the symbol of applied science and exact useful knowledge, Pushkin (the greatest Russian lyric poet), as the symbol of overrefined and socially useless aestheticism.

The nihilists considered themselves "realists" in two senses—as nonromanticists, or even antiromanticists, and as anti-idealists. The poetry of Pushkin, the plays of Schiller, and the philosophical works of Fichte and Schelling were taken as the archetypes of romanticism. For the nihilists romanticism was by definition "soft," "dreamy," "starry-eyed." They considered themselves "hard," "practical," "realistic." The philosophies of Kant, Fichte, Schelling, and in a more complex way Hegel were taken as exemplars of idealism. Pisarev expressed the two senses of realism in his famous statement, which had almost the force of a manifesto, "Words and illusions perish; facts remain."

Chernyshevski. N. G. Chernyshevski (1828–1889) and N. A. Dobrolyubov (1836–1861) were the first philosophical materialists *stricto sensu* in Russia. Under the influence of Feuerbach, Comte, Fourier, and Mill, Chernyshevski developed, and Dobrolyubov defended, a utilitarian doctrine of rational egoism as the foundation of morality. But Chernyshevski failed in his attempt to reduce altruism to egoism, being forced to distinguish between two types of egoism, one narrowly egoistic, the other in essence altruistic. He also failed to offer a satisfactory account of the source of such nonutilitarian virtues as loyalty and self-respect.

Chernyshevski was concerned not so much to ground as to apply utilitarian principles. His application contrasted sharply with Mill's; it was radical and nihilist where Mill's was liberal and reformist. This divergent application of allegedly identical principles appears to result from a tacit admission of supplementary and incompatible principles: in Chernyshevski the assumption that a moral end justifies "immoral" means and in Mill the contrary assumption. Chernyshevski's radical, or "Machiavellian," utilitarianism was more consistent, if also more repugnant, than Mill's reformist and humanistic utilitarianism. Mill would have been hard pressed to provide a theoretical justification for his refusal to admit "immoral" means, since the only criterion of morality and immorality which he admitted was the greatest-happiness principle. And Chernyshevski could always appeal to the future happiness of millions or billions as a justification for inflicting present pain and even death upon hundreds or thousands. Chernyshevski himself did not put the case quite so bluntly. But this position was openly defended by Chernyshevski's younger contemporary P. N. Tkachyov (1844–1886).

Chernyshevski's philosophy of art, although dogmatic and naive, exercised a vast influence on later Russian radicals. His social philosophy and philosophy of history—particularly his stress on the Russian village commune as a seedbed of socialism and his insistence that Russia could avoid the evils of capitalism and industrialization by moving directly from primitive to advanced socialism—were assimilated and enlarged upon by the Populists during the 1870s and 1880s.

Pisarev. D. I. Pisarev (1840–1868), the *enfant terrible* of the nihilist movement and vigorous popularizer of Darwinian theory, made substantial contributions to literary criticism, social philosophy, and ethics before his premature death. In his early works (1859–1861) he stressed the emancipation of the individual person from social, political, and intellectual constraints and defended the wholeness of human personality against the fragmenting effects of socioeconomic specialization and the warping pressure of artificial moral codes. He defended moral relativism and emotivism: moral judgments, as he put it, are expressions of individual taste, like the preference for port or sherry. During and after his imprisonment in 1862 Pisarev moved toward a utilitarian and "socialist" ethics. But as Pisarev moved from the position of Mill's *On Liberty* toward that of Mill's *Utilitarianism,* his works exhibited a steady loss of philosophical perspicacity. Pisarev's utilitarianism was modified by the principle of "economy of intellectual energies." Where, as in Russia in the 1860s, "intellectual capital" was scarce, Pisarev argued, the greatest-happiness principle required curtailment of such frivolities as abstruse and esoteric art, science, scholarship, and philosophy. Anticipating Tolstoy's moralistic critique of art and science, Pisarev insisted that both be brought into immediate relation to the vital needs of men. If poets, for example, failed to become "Titans, shaking the mountains of age-old evil," they would be as superfluous as "insects burrowing in flower-dust."

RUSSIAN POPULISM

The exclusive emphasis of the "men of the sixties" upon medicine and the exact sciences gave way at the beginning of the 1870s to a belatedly Hegelian stress upon history. The transition to this Populist phase was marked by the publication of two highly influential works—Lavrov's *Istoricheskiye Pisma* ("Historical Letters," 1868–1869) and Mikhailovski's *Chto Takoye Progress?* ("What Is Progress?," 1869). In these and later writings the historical disciplines were singled out as distinct in method and conclusions from the physical sciences and superior to them in relevance and power for the solution of human and social problems.

The Populists—particularly P. L. Lavrov (1823–1900) and N. K. Mikhailovski (1842–1904)—stressed not only Russia's "special path" to socialism but also the debt that the intellectuals owed the common people (*narod*). They rejected the Marxist philosophy of history as defended during the 1890s by G. V. Plekhanov (1856–1918) and V. I. Lenin (1870–1924), opposing to Marx's "objective method" of studying history and society an explicitly "subjective method." "Observation of social phenomena," as Mikhailovski put it, "necessarily involves moral evaluation."

Semipositivism. The Populists appealed unapologetically to ethical criteria in evaluating the relative progressiveness of various cultures, defended individual freedom as an ethical absolute, and stressed the role of strongwilled "critically thinking individuals" in the shaping of history. But at the same time they adopted sociological relativism, endorsed Comte's positivistic critique of speculative philosophy, and tended to emulate the methods of the special sciences. (Lavrov called history the "science [*nauka*] of progress.") The resulting "semipositivism," an eclectic, if not syncretic, position, combined positivistic principles with a very unpositivistic ethical idealism.

Lavrov. Throughout his long life Lavrov was centrally concerned with questions of ethics; in this respect he was close to Leo Tolstoy, whose "panmoralism" ended in a "tyranny of ethics" over art, science, religion, and politics. In Lavrov's view, an elite of "critically thinking individuals" reshapes society in the light of its own moral ideals, thus actualizing truth-justice in historical life. Although the metaphysical problem of free will versus determinism is insoluble, the point of departure in history is "the individual's setting of goals for himself as if he were autonomous."

According to Lavrov, "moral criticism" discovers an equal potentiality for moral growth in all human beings. We have a moral obligation to further the growth of other individuals as much as our own: "Failure to act in the face of the suppression of another's growth is immoral." It was this conviction which impelled Lavrov, after 1870, along the path of revolutionary action.

Mikhailovski. Mikhailovski's chief concern was well expressed by the title of one of his major essays, "The Struggle for Individuality." Following the gifted young biologist N. D. Nozhin (1841–1866), and to some degree Pisarev, Mikhailovski saw increasing socioeconomic specialization and division of labor as threatening the freedom and wholeness of the individual person. Reformulating Comte, he divided history into an early "objectively anthropocentric" stage, the present "exocentric" stage, and a future "subjectively anthropocentric" stage, in which human needs and ideals would be placed frankly at the center of the cosmos. At present, Mikhailovski insisted, the fullest development of individuals is incompatible with the fullest development of societies, conceived on the Neo-Hegelian or Spencerian model of organic growth. And it is the individual, not society, who must never be sacrificed, since he is sacred and inviolable.

Kavelin and Kareyev. Two lesser semipositivists were K. D. Kavelin (1818–1885), who was tutored by Belinski as a young man and wrote lively reminiscences of the latter, and N. I. Kareyev (1850–1931). Both were university professors, moderate in politics and Orthodox in religion. Both emulated Lavrov (without conspicuous success) in attempting to provide a scientific grounding for morality. Repeating a charge that had been made more polemically by Bakunin in the 1860s, Kavelin asserted that science, since it is general and abstract, cannot grasp individuals. But, unlike Bakunin, Kavelin saw this limitation of science as opening a door for Christian morality. Kareyev reformulated Lavrov's theory of the individual, bringing it closer to Kant. Kareyev called his position ethical individualism. Individualism is not egoism, that is, an attack upon other individuals; rather it is a defense against attack on the part of other egoisms. In the name of the absolute value of the human person Kareyev condemned killing of any kind, including euthanasia. On this point he came close to Tolstoy, whose philosophy of history, like those of Hegel and Marx, Kareyev had criticized perceptively and in detail.

METAPHYSICS AND PHILOSOPHY OF RELIGION

Chicherin. B. N. Chicherin (1828–1904) affords an appropriate transition from the semipositivists to the metaphysicians and religiously oriented philosophers of the late nineteenth century. Professor at Moscow University and mayor of Moscow, a devout Christian and cautious liberal, Chicherin was more Kantian even than Kareyev in his ethical individualism. Surprisingly, he was also an orthodox Hegelian in logic, metaphysics, and philosophy of history. On the one hand, he asserted that man as a rational creature and "bearer of the Absolute" is an end in himself and must not be treated as a mere instrument, but on the other, that great men are merely "organs and instruments of a universal spirit." He insisted with Mikhailovski that "not society, but individuals, think, feel, and desire"; hence we must resist any tendency of society (the state?) to grow into an "all-devouring Moloch" that claims to "make mankind happy by putting it in chains."

Dostoyevsky. F. M. Dostoyevsky (1821–1881) was deeply concerned about one "all-devouring Moloch," which he identified with both socialism and Roman Catholicism. In the "Legend of the Grand Inquisitor" and elsewhere in *The Brothers Karamazov,* Ivan Karamazov defends the existing individual against both "totalitarian" and "utilitarian" encroachment, raising up against the abstract calculus of the greatest-happiness principle the absolute value of the life of a little child. Ivan declares, with intense earnestness, that if he were offered the certain choice of making all men happy forever on the condition that one innocent child should suffer briefly now, he would repudiate the offer. *The Brothers Karamazov* dates from 1880. In his earlier works Dostoyevsky had made clear that man neither is nor should be the rational calculator of utilitarian advantage envisaged by the "men of the sixties" (*Notes From the Underground,* 1864) and that on utilitarian principles even murder can be justified (*Crime and Punishment,* 1866). Raskolnikov's unplanned second murder, of the docile Lizaveta, may be interpreted as implying a criticism of the utilitarian emphasis on consequences: this unanticipated consequence of what on utilitarian principles was a "moral" murder, renders it, after the fact, immoral. Dostoyevsky's own position, of course, was both Kantian and Christian in that he ascribed absolute value and inviolability to every human being, even the most "insignificant" and "loathsome."

Tolstoy. L. N. Tolstoy (1828–1910) shared Dostoyevsky's scorn for consequences as determinants of the moral quality of actions. With Kant, Tolstoy stressed intentions; but he insisted, with Schopenhauer, that human individuality is both evil and illusory—not the locus of supreme value. His Schopenhauerian impersonalism was combined with a Rousseauistic anarchism. Following both Schopenhauer and the Buddhists, Tolstoy reduced religion to ethics, and ethics to the principle of nonviolent resistance to evil. He sought to defend the principle by appeals both to the New Testament and to men's rational consciousness; but it remained essentially mystical. At first Tolstoy held, with Rousseau, that men are good and institutions bad; in the end he held that although institutions are indeed bad, men are not so very good, and institutions can be improved only by reforming men's hearts, freeing them from subjection to the "law of violence" and bringing them under the reign of the "law of love."

Leontyev and Rozanov. K. N. Leontyev (1831–1891) and V. V. Rozanov (1856–1919), younger contemporaries of Dostoyevsky and Tolstoy, were highly critical of what Leontyev called the "rose-colored Christianity" of the two novelists. To such humanistic "pseudo Christianity" Leontyev opposed first an aesthetic immoralism and then in his later years a religion of Byzantine severity. Rozanov rejected Tolstoy's asceticism, moving toward a kind of biological mysticism, a "metaphysics of sex." Where Dostoyevsky and Tolstoy placed *agape* at the center of Christianity, Leontyev placed *phobos* and Rozanov *eros.* Leontyev, often called the Russian Nietzsche (although his Nietzschean views antedate Nietzsche's by more than a decade and he died before the German's fame had spread to Russia), was an individualist who condemned European "anthropolatry" and opposed "true Christian humanism" to "European pseudo humanism." To understand his position, and indeed Dostoyevsky's (in *Winter Notes on Summer Impressions,* 1863), we must distinguish two kinds of individualism. The individualism that Leontyev, like Dostoyevsky, attacked was egalitarian, security-minded, and "self-enclosed." The individualism he defended was hierarchical, risk-seeking, and "open." However, Leontyev stopped short of glorifying the strong and passionate individual as Nietzsche did—perhaps because, as a Christian, he felt that any autonomous creation of values by men, even supermen, would be impious or blasphemous.

Rozanov continued Leontyev's de-emphasis of the New Testament; but he found in the Old Testament not so much a wrathful judge as a father, in the sense of a giver of life and founder of families. The union of man and woman, the birth of a child, were for Rozanov mystical and sacred events. The constraints of conventional morality he found not so much reprehensible as negligible: "I am not such a scoundrel," he declared, "as to think of morality; I don't even know whether it is spelled with one *l* or two." His approach to morality, like Kierkegaard's but unlike Nietzsche's, was noncultural and ahistorical.

Solovyov. Both Leontyev and Rozanov were remote from academic and systematic philosophy. Their style was "Nietzschean"—aphoristic, sporadically brilliant, often violent, sometimes shocking. Solovyov and the thinkers influenced by him were conventional and restrained in comparison. Vladimir Solovyov (1853–1900), the most original and influential systematic philosopher of nineteenth-century Russia, resembled thinkers like Pisarev and Mikhailovski in precociousness: Pisarev and Mikhailovski published significant critical studies at the age of 18; Solovyov published a large book (his master's thesis, *Krizis Zapadnoi Filosofii,* "The Crisis in Western Philosophy") when he was 21. He died at 47, the author of ten books as well as many articles and poems.

There is more than a trace of the dogmatism and one-sidedness, as well as the passion, of youth in Solovyov's published treatises. The contrast with his unfinished final work, *Osnovy Teoreticheskoi Filosofii* ("Foundations of Theoretical Philosophy," 1897–1899), is striking. The tone of the later work is mellower, the method more exploratory, the conclusions more tentative, without diminution of wit, perspicacity, or conscientiousness of philosophical analysis. Solovyov's system has been called "the most full-sounding chord in the history of philosophy"; it was a grandiose, if not always fully successful, attempt at what he called an "organic synthesis of religion, philosophy, and science in the interests of the integral life."

It was Spinoza who brought Solovyov to philosophy, and Solovyov's mystically tinged metaphysics of positive total-unity, though inspired by Khomyakov's concept of *sobornost,* was Spinozistic in its pantheism. And despite Solovyov's right-Hegelian deduction of the Trinity, the influence of Schelling overshadows that of Hegel in such conceptions as "world soul," intellectual intuition, and the "second Absolute" or "Absolute in process of becoming" (*werdende Absolut*), as well as in Solovyov's Neoplatonic aesthetics.

Solovyov's critiques of Western positivism and abstract rationalism are pointed and perceptive. He also produced sensitive commentaries on current social and political developments in Russia.

Almost all of the major Russian religious thinkers of the twentieth century were influenced directly by Solovyov, among others, the princes S. N. and E. N. Trubetskoi (1862–1905 and 1863–1920), Nikolai Berdyaev (1874–1948), S. L. Frank (1877–1950), and S. N. Bulgakov (1871–1944). Most of these men, together with N. O. Lossky (1870–1965), who elaborated Solovyov's doctrine of intellectual intuition into an intuitivistic theory of knowledge, spent their later years in exile in western Europe and America.

Philosophers in exile. During the nineteenth century such oppositionist thinkers as Herzen, Bakunin, and Lavrov spent long years of self-imposed exile in western Europe. In the aftermath of the October Revolution, and most massively in 1922, Russian metaphysicians and religious thinkers in turn went into Western exile. Many of them —including Berdyaev, Bulgakov, Frank, and P. B. Struve (1870–1944)—had begun in the 1890s as Marxists but had moved, under Kantian influence, into revisions of Marxism that eventually carried them back to idealism.

Two representative *émigré* thinkers will be singled out for mention here: Berdyaev, the unacademic existentialist, and Lossky, the academic intuitivist.

Berdyaev. Berdyaev called himself, using a term originally applied to Nietzsche, an aristocratic radical. His aristocratic temper left its imprint upon his philosophy. Like his well-born compatriots Herzen and Leontyev, Berdyaev found middle-class, "Philistine" existence aesthetically and morally repulsive. As he himself revealingly expressed it, he went through life "holding his nose." Together with a romantic exaltation of creativity and genius, this aristocratic *hauteur* found philosophical expression in Berdyaev's central categories of objectification and freedom. The objectified world, which is alien, hostile, intolerably banal, is set off sharply from the world of freedom, conceived as the creativity of a spirit that transcends the fallen realm of nature, society, and history. Berdyaev saw the natural world as an obstacle to romantic self-expression; but he failed to face the theoretical difficulties involved in the notion of creativity as an activity of spirit whose product is part of an objectified world that is utterly alien to spirit. Creativity would thus seem doomed not only to what Berdyaev called partial and fragmentary embodiment but to inevitable frustration.

Like Whitehead and other "process philosophers," Berdyaev rejected the category of substance and denied the primacy of being. But, unlike Whitehead, who made becoming (process) primary and interpreted being as an abstract element of process, Berdyaev made freedom primary and related it not to becoming or potentiality, but to the "void of nonbeing" that is its source. Berdyaev admitted that such a doctrine reduces freedom to an "irrational mystery."

Berdyaev was centrally concerned with ethics and philosophical anthropology, a concern that led him both into and out of Marxism. He considered Kant a philosopher of freedom and accepted the Kantian dualism of an order of freedom standing over against the order of natural necessity. But, under Nietzschean inspiration, he rejected Kant's formalism, preferring free creativity and moral passion to moral norm and obligation. He even spoke, in a characteristically paradoxical epigram, of the "sacred duty of lawlessness." Berdyaev's own personalistic ethics was Christian and Dostoyevskian—a morality of love and compassion, grounded in the existential awareness that "all are guilty for all."

Lossky. N. O. Lossky was the chief system-builder among twentieth-century Russian philosophers; he wrote treatises in all of the traditional fields of philosophy except social philosophy and philosophy of history. But his central interest was epistemological. Here he was mainly influenced by Oswald Külpe and Solovyov. His cosmology was Neo-Leibnizian, influenced by A. A. Kozlov (1831–1900). Lossky's monads ("substantival agents") are interdependent and interactive. Human cognition is a special case of such interaction. The object known "enters the knowing subject's consciousness directly." To defend his radical "ideal-realism," Lossky distinguished between the object, the content, and the act of knowing. He admitted that the act is subjective but insisted that both object and content are objective. Lossky, a persistent and conscientious philosophical critic and analyst, rejected the Kantian distinction between analytic and synthetic propositions on the grounds that all propositions regarded subjectively are analytic, but regarded objectively are synthetic. He thus arrived by a path of his own at a problem that has much exercised contemporary Anglo-American analytic philosophers.

MARXISM IN RUSSIA

Marxism became influential in Russia during the early 1890s, when young intellectuals seized upon this new doctrine, as their forebears had seized upon earlier Western philosophies and scientific theories (Hegelianism in the mid-1830s, positivism and utilitarianism in the late 1850s, Darwinism in the 1860s), not primarily as a system of analytical concepts but as a total world view and, in many cases, as a vehicle of secular salvation.

Revisionism. Russian Marxists were thus especially sensitive to the chief systematic gaps in classical Marxist theory —those in epistemology and ethics. The Marxist theory of knowledge was primitive and undeveloped; the Marxist philosophy of history left no room for intrinsic or irreducible ethical criteria. Marx, following Hegel's later views, held, in effect, that whatever is the objective outcome of the immanent dialectic of history is right; and Lenin later held that whatever serves the cause of revolution and the building of socialism is right. From these two criteria, historical and social–strategic, respectively, there is no appeal to any strictly ethical criterion. A number of early Russian Marxists were concerned to discover or devise such a criterion. This concern involved them in both critical scrutiny and theoretical modification of Marxism, that is, in "revisionism" in the double sense of review and reform of doctrine. The doctrines they rejected are more closely associated with the work of Engels than with that of Marx—the epistemological theory of reflection, ontological materialism, and the generalization of the laws of the Hegelian dialectic from human history to the whole of nature. These three doctrines were taken over by Lenin and remain central in contemporary Soviet dialectical materialism.

Two groups of Russian revisionists soon emerged: the "Kantians" in the late 1890s and the "Nietzscheans" in the early 1900s. The Kantian Marxists—Struve, Bulgakov, and Berdyaev—turned to Kant for both an ethic and a theory of knowledge to supplement and "correct" Marxism. The Nietzschean Marxists—S. A. Volski (1880–1936?), A. V. Lunacharski (1875–1933), A. A. Bogdanov (1873–1928), and V. A. Bazarov (1874–1939)—turned to Nietzsche for ethics and social philosophy and to Ernst Mach and Richard Avenarius for theory of knowledge. A third, relatively orthodox group—Plekhanov, L. I. Akselrod-Ortodoks (1868–1946), and A. M. Kollontai (1872–1952), the last two being women—wrote comparatively little on ethics; but their ethical and social views represented an eclectic mixture of Marx, Kautsky, and Spinoza. They were primarily concerned with an ideological defense of the purity of Marxism; most of their intellectual energy was absorbed in criticism of the Kantian and Machian revisions in epistemology. Their epistemological writings, like those of the Kantians and Machians whom they attacked, were derivative from Western sources and of little more than historical interest today.

The Russian revisionist Marxists turned to Kant and Nietzsche both because by the last decade of the nineteenth century Kant and Nietzsche had displaced both Hegel and the anti-Hegelian positivists as the dominant figures in western European philosophy and because there was a genuine doctrinal affinity. Both the Kantian and Nietzschean Marxists rejected what they regarded as the impersonalism or anti-individualism of Marxist social philosophy, the doctrine that the human individual is only a point of intersection of socioeconomic relationships. In a sense, they were repeating Belinski's and Herzen's revolt of the early 1840s against Hegelian world-historical impersonalism. But, unlike Belinski and Herzen, who had forged their own arguments against Hegel, the Russian revisionists sought a prepared theoretical position, in Kant or in Nietzsche, from which to defend the freedom and dignity of the individual person.

The Kantian Marxists attempted to do this through a theoretical justification of "proletarian morality." The Nietzscheans attempted to do it by a critique of repressive normative ethics, both bourgeois and Christian. On this point Nietzsche and Marx concurred; both the proletariat as a class and the superman may be said to stand "beyond (bourgeois–Christian) good and evil."

Kantian and Nietzschean Marxism were eclectic positions, bordering on syncretism. However, their demise— the former about 1903 and the latter about 1917—was due as much to the relentless and, after 1917, institutionalized attack of orthodox Marxist–Leninists as to the doctrinal tensions within the revisionist positions themselves.

Lenin. Even within the orthodox Marxist group, however, revisions cropped up. Plekhanov developed an epistemological theory of "hieroglyphs," which Lenin criticized as a concession to Kantianism. Lenin himself defended a very un-Marxian doctrine of absolute and objective truth. He also revised classical Marxian determinism to emphasize human volition as a factor in shaping historical events. Lenin laid great stress, after 1915, on the Hegelian dialectic; like Bakunin, he focused attention on the conflict rather than the unity of opposites and in particular on the "negation of the negation," for example, the socialist negation of the capitalist negation of feudalism. Again, like Bakunin, Lenin held that the disjunction "idealism or materialism" was both exclusive and exhaustive. It was the attempt of the Russian "Machians" to assert a third (positivist) position, neither idealism nor materialism, that provoked the onslaught of Lenin's *Materialism and Empirio-criticism* (1909).

PHILOSOPHY IN THE SOVIET UNION

After the October Revolution the tension between the two components of Russian Marxism—ontological materialism and Hegelian dialectics—led to a lively philosophical dispute between the "mechanists," headed by L. I. Akselrod, who emphasized materialism and neglected dialectics, and the "Menshevizing idealists" (as they were later called by Stalin), headed by A. M. Deborin (1881–1963), who laid strong emphasis upon dialectics and devoted much energy to the study of Hegel. This struggle culminated in 1930 with the official repudiation of "mechanism," followed a year later by the official repudiation of "Deborinism." The new "orthodox" position established in 1931, an attempt to balance the two elements, marked the beginning of a quarter century of close political control of philosophical discussion in the Soviet Union.

Components of Marxism–Leninism. To understand the philosophical situation in the Soviet Union since the de-Stalinization campaign of 1956, it is helpful to distinguish (with I. M. Bocheński in an article in *Studies in Soviet Thought*, 1962) three components in Marxism–Leninism: the "basic dogmas," the "systematic superstructure," and the "declassified doctrines."

The basic dogmas are formulated in nontechnical terms. They include such theses as that there is a necessary historical development from lower to higher social forms, for example from capitalism to socialism and communism, and that this development takes place through class struggle. Such dogmas remain axiomatic; they can be neither questioned nor reinterpreted. Lenin's blunt warning of 1909 still applies to them: "You cannot eliminate even one basic assumption, one substantial part of this philosophy of Marxism . . . without abandoning objective truth and falling into the arms of bourgeois reactionary falsehood." To call any basic assumption into question is to lapse into revisionism; every such lapse is interpreted as a concession to political reaction and counterrevolution.

The doctrines of the systematic superstructure are formulated in technical, usually Hegelian or quasi-Hegelian language. Among them are such theses as that material reality is riven by objective dialectical contradictions; that accumulated quantitative changes pass over into qualitative changes; and that cognitive acts reflect an objective material reality. All Marxist–Leninists must accept such doctrines, but there is a limited freedom to reinterpret some of them.

New developments. The declassified doctrines are not, strictly speaking, philosophical, but technical and paraphilosophical. They have been "declassified" in the double sense of "exempted from the doctrinal authority of the classics of Marxism–Leninism" and "politically neutralized," or exempted from class partisanship (*partiinost*). It might be more accurate to call them declassified disciplines, for they include such independent fields of study as mathematical logic, cybernetics, and information theory. Recent work in these areas, by Soviet philosophers as well as mathematicians and engineers, has been carried on almost without reference to the classics. There have been competent Soviet studies in such areas as axiomatization, proof theory, and many-valued logic, as well as Russian translations of a number of important works in these fields. However, developments in the declassified disciplines have had limited impact on the systematic superstructure and no effect at all on the basic dogmas.

Modification of the superstructure. There have been two modest post-Stalin amendments in the systematic superstructure of Soviet philosophy. First, the dialectical law of the negation of the negation, a vulgarization of Hegel insisted upon by both Engels and Lenin, has been quietly reintroduced after having been suppressed by Stalin—not so much because it was vulgarized as because it was Hegelian. Contemporary Soviet discussions of this "law" are cautious and tentative; dialectical development is characterized as continuous and progressive rather than explosive.

Second, the doctrine of objective contradictions has been significantly reinterpreted by A. A. Zinoviev and E. Kolman (1958). Kolman even rejected Engels' dialectical formulation of Zeno's paradoxes of motion—the claim that a moving body both is and is not at a given point at a given time—as a violation of the Aristotelian law of noncontradiction. However, Kolman insisted that Engels' statement (in *Anti-Dühring*) was an isolated exception and that in general Engels, like Marx and Lenin, scrupulously avoided making any assertion of the form "*p* and not-*p*."

New openness to other traditions. The greatest change in post-Stalinist Soviet philosophy has not been in doctrine but in an increased openness toward the nonmaterialist Russian intellectual tradition and non-Marxist–Leninist philosophies, both past and present.

Under Stalin, thinkers as diverse as Bakunin, Kavelin, Lavrov, Mikhailovski, Chicherin, Leontyev, Solovyov, and Berdyaev were regularly dismissed as "idealists" and "metaphysicians." (Soviet writers continue to use "idealist" in Lenin's broad sense, equivalent to "nonmaterialist," and "metaphysician" in Engels' narrow sense, equivalent

to "nondialectician.") In recent years there has been some study—consistently critical, to be sure—of certain of these "idealists," for example of Mikhailovski, Solovyov, and Berdyaev. There have been two-volume editions of the works of Skovoroda (1961) and Lavrov (1965). And there have been some attempts to re-evaluate the early Marxist revisionists; for example, certain of Lunacharski's essays, long out of print, are being republished.

The new Soviet willingness to listen to non-Marxist–Leninist ideas led to the invitation in 1958 to A. J. Ayer to publish a paper in the official Soviet philosophy journal *Voprosy Filosofii* and to lecture in Moscow and Leningrad. The paper appeared early in 1962, and Ayer visited the Soviet Union in March of that year. There have also been several recent translations of works by Western thinkers, including Leibniz' selected correspondence, Spinoza's works, Locke's political and philosophical works, selections from Herder, the first volume of a new six-volume edition of Kant, and (in 1965–1966) the first Soviet edition of Hume. Post-Hegelian philosophers are represented by translations of Nicolai Hartmann's *Aesthetics*, Wittgenstein's *Tractatus*, and Russell's *Human Knowledge: Its Scope and Limits*, among others. Studies in the history of ideas have been translated; and critical studies by Soviet writers have been devoted to such thinkers as Kant, Collingwood, Bergson, and Whitehead, none of whom was seriously discussed in Stalin's time.

The quest for truth–justice has been a central theme of Russian philosophizing since the time of Skovoroda. On the question of the relation of the two aspects of *pravda*—theoretical truth and practical justice—one can distinguish two opposed tendencies in Russian philosophical thought that might, for convenience, be labeled "rationalist" and "irrationalist."

The rationalists (for example, the "men of the sixties," Tolstoy, Solovyov, and the Kantian and orthodox Marxists) assume that theoretical truth can and should serve as a support for practical justice in individual and social life. The irrationalists—inconsistently and hesitantly in the eighteenth and nineteenth centuries (Skovoroda, Herzen, the Populists, for example), consistently and decisively in the twentieth century (L. I. Shestov)—assumed the priority of practical justice and were willing to suspend, or even to deny, the claims of theoretical truth. In Shestov's formulation, either one must absolutize theoretical truth, thus relativizing moral values, or else one must relativize theoretical truth, thus absolutizing moral values and redeeming individual existence.

Shestov formulated this "either/or" under the influence of Dostoyevsky and Nietzsche long before he had read Kierkegaard. However, his revolt against reason was also in part a revolt against the Kantian and post-Kantian assimilation of action to speculation, of practical reason to theoretical reason. For Shestov, the common term was deceptive. What the German philosophers had called *praktische Vernunft* is not reason at all. It is not a cognitive capacity, but something instinctive, intuitive, emotive—a mode of value appreciation, of decision, and of action. In this sense, the existentialism of Shestov, even more than that of Berdyaev, represents the logical culmination of the irrationalist tradition in Russian philosophy. The rationalist tradition is today represented by Marxist–Leninists, who remain unalterably opposed to every form of existential philosophy.

(See also COMMUNISM, PHILOSOPHY UNDER. See Russian Philosophy in Index for articles on Russian philosophers.)

Bibliography

Acton, H. B., *The Illusion of the Epoch: Marxism–Leninism as a Philosophical Creed.* London, 1955; Boston, 1957.

Berdyaev, Nikolai, *Russkaya Ideya.* Paris, 1947. Translated by R. M. French as *The Russian Idea.* New York, 1948.

Bocheński, J. M., *Der sowjetrussische dialektische Materialismus (Diamat),* 3d ed. Bern, 1960. Translated from the 3d German edition by Nicolas Sollohub as *Soviet Russian Dialectical Materialism.* Dordrecht, Netherlands, 1963.

Chyzhevski, D. I., "Hegel in Russland," in his *Hegel bei den Slaven.* Reichenberg, Czechoslovakia, 1934; Bad Homburg vor der Höhe, Germany, 1961. Pp. 145–396.

Edie, J. M.; Scanlan, J. P.; Zeldin, M.; and Kline, G. L., eds., *Russian Philosophy,* 3 vols. Chicago, 1965.

Jakowenko, Boris V., *Filosofi russi: saggio di storia della filosofia russa.* Florence, 1925. Translated from the Russian.

Koyré, Alexandre, *La Philosophie et le problème national en Russie au début du XIXe siècle.* Paris, 1929.

Koyré, Alexandre, *Études sur l'histoire de la pensée philosophique en Russie.* Paris, 1950.

Lossky, N. O., *History of Russian Philosophy.* New York, 1951.

Marcuse, Herbert, *Soviet Marxism: A Critical Analysis.* New York, 1958.

Masaryk, T. G., *Die geistigen Strömungen in Russland,* 2 vols. Jena, 1913. Translated by E. and C. Paul as *The Spirit of Russia: Studies in History, Literature, and Philosophy,* 2 vols. New York, 1919; reprinted, New York, 1955.

Scheibert, Peter, *Von Bakunin zu Lenin: Geschichte der russischen revolutionären Ideologien, 1840–1895.* Vol. I: *Die Formung des radikalen Denkens in der Auseinandersetzung mit deutschem Idealismus und französischem Bürgertum.* Leiden, 1956.

Simmons, Ernest J., ed., *Continuity and Change in Russian and Soviet Thought.* Cambridge, Mass., 1955. See especially Pt. IV, "Rationality and Nonrationality," pp. 283–377, with contributions by Theodosius Dobzhansky, Georges Florovsky, Waldemar Gurian, George L. Kline, and Herbert Marcuse, and a summary and review by Geroid T. Robinson.

Utechin, S. V., *Russian Political Thought: A Concise History.* New York, 1964.

Weidlé, Wladimir, *La Russie, absente et présente.* Paris, 1949. Translated by A. Gordon Smith as *Russia Absent and Present.* London, 1952.

Wetter, Gustav A., *Der dialektische Materialismus: Seine Geschichte und sein System in dem Sowjetunion.* Vienna, 1956. Translated by Peter Heath as *Dialectical Materialism: A Historical and Systematic Survey of Philosophy in the Soviet Union.* London and New York, 1958.

Zenkovsky, V. V., *Istoriya Russkoi Filosofii,* 2 vols. Paris, 1948–1950. Translated by G. L. Kline as *A History of Russian Philosophy,* 2 vols. London and New York, 1953.

GEORGE L. KLINE

RUYSBROECK, JAN VAN (1293–1381), Flemish mystic. Ruysbroeck was born in the village of Ruysbroeck, near Brussels. He stood in close relation to German contemplatives of the period, notably Meister Eckhart. In 1343 Ruysbroeck, together with two others, established a community at Groenendael that ultimately came under Augustinian rule. He was the prior of this community.

Ruysbroeck was not a trained theologian and had an imperfect knowledge of Latin. Though he made use in his mystical writings of language drawn from Eckhart, such as the "birth of Christ in the soul" and the "eternal Now," he was sensitive to the kind of allegations of pantheism encountered by Eckhart and in fact directed against Ruysbroeck by Jean de Gerson. In his later writings in particular Ruysbroeck made it clear that he did not believe in the identification of the soul with God in the mystical state, and he criticized those contemplatives who gave up the active life and lapsed into quietism. He thus evolved a practical account of contemplation which connected it with good works.

Ruysbroeck distinguished between different phases of the good life, which should be practiced together. First, there is the active life of doing good works. This by itself will not bring blessedness, since it can mean moral self-reliance rather than dependence on God's grace. But good works are a necessary part of the purification of the soul. Second, there is the practice of the inner virtues—faith, hope, and love. Third, there is the contemplative life, through which the soul may gain union with God. Those who attain this last condition are called "God-seeing." They are not continually immersed, as it were, in this inner blessedness, but find themselves impelled to practice love and good works as a result of it. The practice of good works, suffused by the knowledge of God gained in the state of contemplative union, is what Ruysbroeck referred to as "the common life." This, the ideal he tried to realize in his own monastic community, was interpreted as a reflection of the life of the Trinity, which was united in a common fruition analogous to that enjoyed by the mystic but was also outward-going through the creative power of God, analogous to the work of the monk in serving the society around him.

In order to illustrate the relation of union, yet difference, between the soul and God, Ruysbroeck made use of analogies drawn from human love, as the title of his major work, *The Adornment of the Spiritual Marriage,* indicates. Thus one should "rest in Him whom one enjoys. . . . There love has fallen in love with the lover, and each is all to the other, in possession and in rest" (*The Sparkling Stone,* 13). The love analogy had a certain aptness in bringing out both the sense of union and the necessary theistic distinction between the soul as creature and the Creator. Ruysbroeck also made use of the Neoplatonic doctrine of eternal archetypes or forms, existing in God. Thus the ground of the soul is man's eternal archetype, and in realizing it in its purity and nakedness, the contemplative finds union with God. In this, Ruysbroeck, like other mystics of the period, exhibited the influence of Pseudo-Dionysius. He thus made use too of the notion that creatures proceed from God through the process of creation and return to him through contemplation. But since the creature needs to reflect the love displayed by God in the work of creation, so likewise the mystic must combine his return to God with the outgoing work of love.

Ruysbroeck's works were closely studied by those who belonged to the movement known as the Brethren of the Common Life, started in the latter part of the fourteenth century by Gerhard Groot, who knew Ruysbroeck. Thomas à Kempis belonged to this confraternity. Despite contemporary criticisms of his language as not always squaring with orthodox theology, Ruysbroeck was beatified by the Roman Catholic church.

Bibliography

The definitive edition is B. Ponkens and others, eds., *Ruusbroec Werken*, 2d ed., 4 vols. (Cologne, 1950). English translations include a one-volume edition of *The Adornment of the Spiritual Marriage, The Sparkling Stone,* and *The Book of Supreme Truth,* translated by C. A. Wynschenk Dom and edited with an introduction and notes by Evelyn Underhill (London, 1951), and *The Spiritual Espousals,* translated by E. Colledge (London, 1952). See also Ray C. Petry, *Late Medieval Mysticism* (Philadelphia, 1957).

NINIAN SMART

RYLE, GILBERT, Waynflete professor of metaphysical philosophy in the University of Oxford, was born in 1900. Having read Classical Honour Moderations and the Final School of Literae Humaniores (Greats) he went on to read the then newly established School of Philosophy, Politics and Economics at the Queen's College, Oxford. He became a lecturer at Christ Church in 1924 and in the following year a student and tutor, and he remained there until his appointment as professor at the end of World War II. Ryle was largely responsible for the institution of the new degree of bachelor of philosophy at Oxford. He has been the editor of *Mind* since the retirement of G. E. Moore in 1947.

Ryle's philosophical writings have covered a wide range of topics. They fall mainly within the fields of philosophical methodology, philosophical logic, and the philosophy of mind, but the total spread is very wide and includes some work on the history of philosophy, especially on Plato. Only the fields of moral philosophy, political philosophy, and aesthetics are comparatively neglected. Much of his writing takes the form of articles addressed to the solution of quite specific issues, and it is impossible to discuss here seriatim his "Negation," "Plato's *Parmenides,*" "Conscience and Moral Conviction," and "Heterologicality," to mention the titles of only four such papers.

Probably the best approach to Ryle's philosophical work is through his views on the nature and method of philosophy, which have developed in a consistent way after the end of a short and early flirtation with phenomenology. Many of his articles on specific topics seem to have a clear subordinate aim of illuminating these questions, while such important writings as "Systematically Misleading Expressions," his inaugural lecture, *Philosophical Arguments,* and the book *Dilemmas* are explicitly devoted to them. That *The Concept of Mind* can be regarded as an illustration of his views on philosophical method is a tribute to the consistency of his theory with his practice, though it would be an injustice to treat it merely as such.

Ryle's well-known article "Systematically Misleading Expressions" is important as being easily the first, although incompletely worked out, version of a view of philosophy closely akin to that which Wittgenstein was then beginning to work out independently, and which is often spoken of as having been first suggested by Wittgenstein. This view treats philosophy as the activity of removing fundamental conceptual confusions which have their source in our overreadiness to construe grammatical simi-

larities and differences as indicative of logical similarities and differences. For example, since either unpunctuality or the unpunctual Smith may, with grammatical similarity, be said to be reprehensible, some philosophers are inclined to conclude that similar things are being said of two objects, Smith and unpunctuality; hence, the world is thought to be populated by two kinds of objects, universals and particulars. Again, since "Mr. Baldwin is a statesman" is grammatically similar to "Mr. Pickwick is a fiction," philosophers have been tempted to suppose that the world contained fictions alongside of statesmen. However, Ryle's view is not fully worked out at this stage. Writing in a climate of opinion in which philosophy was widely regarded as the activity of analysis by which the true logical form of facts was explicitly displayed and the test of adequate language was taken to be a one-to-one correspondence with the form of facts, he did not entirely free himself from its influence. As a result, he cannot regard the reformulation of statements in a way that removes misleading grammatical similarities as merely a useful expedient for making ourselves aware of important differences between them; the reformulation is still thought of as the revelation of the true form of the fact, so that "Baldwin is a statesman" is, in an absolute sense, a correct form of utterance, while "Pickwick is a fiction" is incorrectly formulated. This anomalous relic of logical atomism caused Ryle uneasiness even then, and it does not appear again. If we neglect it, we may regard "Systematically Misleading Expressions" as an exposition of a view that Ryle has never abandoned, although he has refined it. One such refinement is found in *Dilemmas*. Here it is claimed that many philosophical problems, if not all, immediately present themselves in the form of dilemmas: we find ourselves holding, without the possibility of sincere repudiation, two or more opinions which seem to be incompatible (that, for example, we often choose responsibly what to do, and that we are what we are through our natural endowment as modified by environment—the problem of free will). Such dilemmas must be overcome by showing that the apparent conflict is a consequence of conceptual confusion rather than by choosing one horn on which to be impaled.

The emphasis is somewhat different in *Philosophical Arguments*. While in "Systematically Misleading Expressions" and in *Dilemmas* the emphasis is on the activity of freeing ourselves from conceptual errors and puzzlement, in *Philosophical Arguments* the more constructive side of the procedure is stressed. By methodically determining what can and what cannot be said without absurdity, which inferences are valid and which are invalid, which grammatical parallels are likely to mislead and which are not, we come to see better the "logical geography" of our conceptual system—how different concepts are related to each other and what are the different roles that they play. There is no essential conflict between the view of Ryle's philosophical procedures as "removing conceptual roadblocks" and "freeing conceptual traffic jams," to echo the metaphor employed in *Dilemmas,* and the more constructive view of them. Thus, it would be idle to ask whether, or at which stages, *The Concept of Mind* is correctly viewed as exposing the confusion of "the ghost in the machine," into which we are led by grammatical analogies, or as mapping the extension and boundaries of such interrelated concepts as "will," "intelligence," "imagination," "thought," and the like; the two aspects are not thus separable.

Ryle often expresses this view of philosophy in terms of the notion of a category mistake, as in *The Concept of Mind*. A category mistake occurs when something is taken to belong to a different category from its true one. Neither in *The Concept of Mind* nor elsewhere is any serious attempt made by Ryle to give a rigorous account of the notion of a category, although there is a historical discussion of it in "Categories," and Ryle sees this notion as akin to Russell's notion of type. Although this is a gap, it is probably of little direct importance to the argument of *The Concept of Mind*. The essential thesis here is that there is a special kind of confusion which can be illustrated by that of taking team spirit as an element in a game as being on equal footing with serving or receiving, of taking a division as a military formation as being on equal footing with its component regiments, of taking Oxford University as an institution as being on equal footing with its component colleges. Ryle then goes on to claim that traditional Cartesian dualism treats the mind as an entity on equal footing with the body and mental activities as being on equal footing with bodily activities, and that this is a confusion of the same kind as those in the three illustrative cases. The language of category mistakes is not essential; Ryle could have used his terminology of 1931 and said that just as the grammatical similarity of "Jones gave an exhibition of dribbling" and "Jones gave an exhibition of ball control" could mislead us into thinking that Jones was giving two independent and simultaneous exhibitions, so the grammatical similarities between our talk of mental and bodily activities could mislead us into thinking that they were independent and simultaneous activities.

Such a misconception Ryle calls the dogma of the ghost in the machine. He attempts to show its falsity in a series of chapters on the main aspects of mental life, in which the arguments fall into two main classes. On the one hand he tries to show that the dogma of the ghost in the machine fails in its explanatory task and is logically incoherent, leading to such logical evils as vicious infinite regresses. On the other hand he tries to show that a satisfactory positive account of mental phenomena can be given, without invoking the ghost, in terms of such things as style of performance, dispositions to certain characteristic performances, and acquired skills. Thus, if a person does a physical action while thinking about what he is doing, we must take it not that the ghost discursively thinks and the bodily machine moves but that the person performs bodily in an appropriate way, while being disposed to perform other actions if the occasion arises.

One chapter in the book is a restatement of the argument of the paper "Knowing How and Knowing That," published in 1946, and it is a plausible inference that this paper was the germ from which the larger enterprise sprang. In that article Ryle suggested that philosophers commonly take it that knowing how to do something is knowing the truth of certain principles and applying them to an activity. He pointed out that although a given cook may learn to cook from a cookbook, the principles of cookery are logically a distillation from the practice of those who know how to cook, just as the principles of valid argument are a distillation from the practice of those who know how to argue. Thus, knowing how to do things, being able to perform intelligently, is logically independent of any interior theorizing; therefore it involves a display of intelligence that others can witness, rather than a mechanical event from which we have to infer a piece of unwitnessable ghostly theorizing. *The Concept of Mind* attempts to extend the same line of thought to other mental phenomena.

It should be noted that Ryle is not content with the "weaker" thesis that overt human actions must not be analyzed as mechanical events brought about by nonphysical, ghostly activities. In fact, he adopts the far stronger thesis that all references to the mental must be understood in terms of, in principle, witnessable activities. We must not only avoid ascribing the skill of a skillful driver to a ghostly "inner" driver, but we must also explain all mental life, including emotion and feeling, in terms of the witnessable. Certainly it is this feature of his book that has led many, with considerable plausibility, to class Ryle as a philosophical behaviorist, though he repudiated this label in advance. Ryle, indeed, sometimes refers to "twinges," "throbs," "flutters," and "glows" in his characterization of feelings in a way hard to reconcile with behaviorism, but it is notoriously difficult to see how such terms are not a relic of the essentially private in Ryle's public world. By adopting this stronger thesis Ryle avoids well-known difficulties about knowledge of other minds and privacy; however, it is not clearly required for the basic program, and much that he has to say is independent of it.

Much of the interest of this modern classic is independent of the question whether Ryle succeeds in demonstrating any general thesis. The detailed discussions of thinking, knowledge, will, emotion, sensation, intellect, and the like have great independent interest. In the course of these discussions Ryle introduces a number of philosophical distinctions, such as those of "task and achievement," "avowal," and "mongrel-categorical," that have become the common tools of modern philosophical discussion. The whole character of philosophical discussion of the mind has been decisively changed, even in quarters where Ryle's conclusions are strongly challenged, by the appearance of *The Concept of Mind*.

Another set of problems to which Ryle has devoted a number of papers are those concerned with the concept of meaning. Here his review of Carnap's *Meaning and Necessity* in *Philosophy*, his "The Theory of Meaning," published in *British Philosophy in the Mid-century*, and his contribution to the symposium "Use, Usage and Meaning" in the *PAS* supplementary volume for 1961 deserve special mention. One main contention in these articles is that it is words that are the bearers of meaning, and whose meanings have to be taught and learned, rather than sentences. To learn a language is to acquire a vocabulary and a syntax; this language is then used in speech, which is an activity that one performs by means of a language. The sentence is a unit of speech, not of language. The theory of meaning is therefore concerned primarily with words, not with sentences; but this theory, Ryle holds, has been often vitiated by a simple model of meaning which he calls the " 'Fido'–Fido" theory, one which seeks always to find as the meaning of a word something that stands to that word rather as the dog Fido stands to the name "Fido." J. S. Mill partly emancipated himself from the theory by distinguishing connotation from denotation, but he continued to say that meaning was connotation and denotation. In the review of Carnap mentioned before, Ryle attempts to show that the " 'Fido'–Fido" theory is still not an outworn fallacy but something that continues to vitiate much sophisticated modern work.

It is notable that the bulk of Ryle's philosophical writing avoids, rather than lacks, any historical discussion. There is the very minimum of reference to even recent learned controversy, and the great philosophers are rarely given even a casual mention. In *The Concept of Mind* the expression "Cartesian dualism" is a nickname for a kind of view which Ryle had once held and to which he thinks many are prone rather than a genuine historical reference. However, this is a policy of segregating the history of philosophy from the treatment of problems, not a sign of lack of interest in the history of philosophy. Ryle's historical interests, though eclectic, are wide. They have, however, centered on Plato; in addition to already published articles on Plato, Ryle has devoted much work to problems arising from the Platonic dialogues, and further publications in that field may be expected.

In conclusion, a word should be said about Ryle's highly individual style, for it is of more than literary interest. It is peculiarly his own, so that it would be impossible for anyone familiar with it not to recognize his work from even a few sentences. One hallmark is the freshness of the vocabulary; although he will liberally coin technical terms when he needs them, he always avoids the well-worn counters of philosophical exchange. Another hallmark is that although the general style is informal, the choice of words is literary rather than colloquial; this is achieved by the use of a vocabulary more novelistic than learned. Although there is much close argument in his writing, the importance of the fresh language, the bold metaphor, and the terse epigram in giving the problem a striking presentation, in bringing down pretentious castles of learned jargon, and in making his own contention memorable is very great indeed.

Works by Ryle

Review of Martin Heidegger's *Sein und Zeit*. *Mind*, Vol. 38 (1929).
"Negation." *PAS*, Supp. Vol. 9 (1929).
"Are There Propositions?" *PAS*, Vol. 30 (1929–1930).
"Systematically Misleading Expressions." *PAS*, Vol. 32 (1931–1932).
"Phenomenology." *PAS*, Supp. Vol. 11 (1932).
"Imaginary Objects." *PAS*, Supp. Vol. 12 (1933).

Locke on the Human Understanding. Oxford, 1933.
"About." *Analysis*, Vol. 1 (1933).
"Internal Relations." *PAS* Supp. Vol. 14 (1935).
"Mr. Collingwood and the Ontological Argument." *Mind*, Vol. 44 (1935).
"Unverifiability-by-me." *Analysis*, Vol. 4 (1936).
"Induction and Hypothesis." *PAS*, Supp. Vol. 16 (1937).
"Taking Sides in Philosophy." *Philosophy*, Vol. 12 (1937).
"Categories." *PAS*, Vol. 38 (1937–1938).
"Plato's *Parmenides*." *Mind*, Vol. 48 (1939).
"Conscience and Moral Convictions." *Analysis*, Vol. 7 (1940).
Philosophical Arguments. Oxford, 1945. Inaugural lecture.
"Why Are the Calculuses of Logic and Mathematics Applicable to Reality?" *PAS*, Supp. Vol. 20 (1946).
Review of Marvin Farber's *Foundations of Phenomenology*. *Philosophy*, Vol. 21 (1946).
"Knowing How and Knowing That." *PAS*, Vol. 46 (1946–1947).
Review of Carnap's *Meaning and Necessity*. *Philosophy*, Vol. 25 (1949).
The Concept of Mind. London, 1949.
" 'If,' 'So' and 'Because,' " in Max Black, ed., *Philosophical Analysis*. Ithaca, N.Y., 1950.
"Logic and Professor Anderson." *Australasian Journal of Philosophy*, Vol. 28 (1950).
"Thinking and Language." *PAS*, Supp. Vol. 25 (1951).
"Feelings." *The Philosophical Quarterly*, Vol. 1 (1951).
"Heterologicality." *Analysis*, Vol. 11 (1951).
"The Verification Principle." *Revue internationale de philosophie*, Vol. 5 (1951).
"Ludwig Wittgenstein." *Analysis*, Vol. 12 (1951).
Contribution to Peter Laslett, ed., *The Physical Basis of Mind*. Oxford, 1951.
"Ordinary Language." *The Philosophical Review*, Vol. 62 (1953).
"Thinking." *Acta Philologica*, Vol. 9 (1953).
"Pleasure." *PAS*, Supp. Vol. 28 (1954).
"Proofs in Philosophy." *Revue internationale de philosophie*, Vol. 8 (1954).
Dilemmas. Cambridge, 1954.
Introduction to D. F. Pears, ed., *The Revolution in Philosophy*. New York and London, 1956.
"Sensation," in H. D. Lewis, ed., *Contemporary British Philosophy*, Third Series. London, 1956.
"The Theory of Meaning," in C. A. Mace, ed., *British Philosophy in the Mid-century*. London, 1957.
"Predicting and Inferring." *Colston Papers*, Vol. 9 (London, 1957).
"On Forgetting the Difference Between Right and Wrong," in A. I. Melden, ed., *Essays in Moral Philosophy*. Seattle, 1958.
"A Puzzling Element in the Notion of Thinking." *Proceedings of the British Academy*, Vol. 44 (1958).
Article on Wittgenstein in *Scientific American* (1959).
"Letters and Syllables in Plato." *The Philosophical Review*, Vol. 59 (1960).
Review of Richard Wollheim's *F. H. Bradley*. *The Spectator* (1960).
"Comment on Mr. Achinstein's Paper." *Analysis* (1960).
"Use, Usage and Meaning." *PAS*, Supp. Vol. 35 (1961).
"La Phénomenologie contre le *Concept of Mind*," in H. Bréra, ed., *La Philosophie analytique*. Paris, 1962.
"Thinking Thoughts and Having Concepts." *Institut Internationale de Philosophie* (1962).
"Abstractions." *Dialogue*, Vol. 1 (1962).

J. O. URMSON

S

SAADIA BEN JOSEPH (882–942), sometimes called al-Fayyumi from the section of Upper Egypt in which he was born, had a brilliant career as the most distinguished intellectual leader of Jewry in his age. He was 23 years old when he left his Egyptian home to play his part on the wider stage of Palestine, Syria, and Babylonia. By this time he had already composed the first known Hebrew dictionary and an important treatise refuting the views of Anan ben David, the founder of the rationalistic Karaite sect. In 921, the rabbis of Babylonia challenged the authority of the Palestinian rabbis to fix the Hebrew calendar. Saadia's defense of the position of the Babylonian rabbis was most effective; he was rewarded by appointment to the rabbinical academy at Sura in Babylonia; and a few years later, in 928, he was the first non-Babylonian ever to be named as the head (*gaon*) of the academy. His tenure of this position was neither calm nor prolonged. Disputes with the exilarch of the Babylonian Jewish community led to the removal of Saadia and his retirement from active participation in the life of the community. His last years saw a burst of literary creativity.

The writings of Saadia truly signalized the birth of a new creative period in Jewish life. He was a pioneering student and productive scholar in many fields of Jewish concern, including Hebrew grammar and philology, Biblical exegesis, and Jewish liturgy. The early attacks on the views of Anan were followed by a long series of writings against Anan's fellow sectarians; since Karaism, a movement which rejected rabbinical and Talmudic law, was at this time the major internal threat to the unity of Jewish life, Saadia's anti-Karaite polemics continued throughout his career. The primary activity of Saadia's public life was in the legal field, and here his contributions were outstanding. In addition to commentaries on Talmudic treatises, Saadia wrote at least ten systematic monographs on a variety of Jewish legal subjects; one of these, *Inheritance,* is preserved in its entirety in the Bodleian Library at Oxford. It was published in 1897 under the editorial care of Joel Mueller. Fragments of others still exist. Saadia was the first to translate the Old Testament into Arabic; this translation, still in use, is notable for its use of paraphrase where a literal translation would have been subject to censure for anthropomorphism. He also composed the earliest known commentary on *Sefer Yetzira* ("The Book of Creation"), an important work of the Jewish mystical tradition.

Thus his major philosophical work, *The Book of Beliefs and Opinions* (Arabic title, *Kitab al-ʿamanat wal-iʿtikadat;* Hebrew title, *Sefer ha-emunoth weha-deoth*), probably completed in 933, is but one of a long list of eminent contributions for which Saadia is remembered. He was probably impelled toward a systematic consideration of the relation between the religious beliefs of Judaism and the opinions arrived at through rational investigation both by the comparable activities of Muslim philosophers—the *Kalam* and other schools—and by the quasi-rational approach characteristic of most of the Karaite spokesmen. In the intellectual milieu of the tenth century, the philosophical issues with which Saadia was concerned were widely and thoughtfully debated. Muslim philosophers of this age had far more of the corpus of Greek philosophical literature available to them than had their compeers in the Christian West. Saadia's *Book of Beliefs and Opinions* may best be described, therefore, as a philosophical apologetics for rabbinite Judaism. The Muʿtazilite school of Muslim philosophers generally presented their systematic treatises in the form of theodicies, treating first of the unity of God and then of his justice. Saadia's philosophical work is similarly patterned but assigns a rather larger share of the discussion to the second, ethical part then to the first, more purely metaphysical and theological one.

Prefaced to the ten sections into which the body of the work is divided is an introductory treatise in which Saadia justifies his engaging in this sort of philosophical enterprise. Here he enters into questions of the sources of human knowledge, the relations of belief and doubt, and the prevalent view that rational speculation necessarily leads to heresy. He argues that not the use of reason, but exclusive dependence on human reason is undesirable. Properly used, in combination with revelation, rational speculation supports revealed religion. From this discussion Saadia moves, in the first major section, to a proof of the doctrine of creation out of nothing and a refutation of 12 contrary views. In the second major section of his book, Saadia discusses the unity of God and demonstrates how the Christian doctrine of the Trinity is based upon a misinterpretation of certain scriptural verses. Treatise three defends the idea of a divine law for God's creatures as a necessary demand of reason and urges the need for prophecy and prophets as the vehicle by means of which the divine law is transmitted to men.

From the fourth treatise to the end of the work, Saadia's concern is more with ethical questions and the consequences for men's future redemption of their obedience or disobedience to the divine precepts delivered by the prophets. In these sections, he defends on rational grounds all of the major doctrines of the Jewish tradition. The tenth and last treatise is of slightly different character; it presents an ethic of the middle way as the proper guide to man's conduct in the affairs of daily life. Thus we may say that Saadia concluded his work on religious philosophy with a secular ethic.

Bibliography

Les Oeuvres complètes de Saadia was edited by J. Derenbourg (6 vols., Paris, 1893–1896). Saadia's *Book of Beliefs and Opinions* may be found in a translation from the Arabic by Samuel Rosenblatt in the Yale Judaica Series, Vol. I (New Haven, 1948).

For material on Saadia, see Jacob B. Agus, *The Evolution of Jewish Thought* (New York and London, 1959); Joseph L. Blau, *The Story of Jewish Philosophy* (New York, 1962); Julius Guttman, *Philosophies of Judaism,* translated by D. Silverman (New York, 1964); Isaac Husik, *History of Medieval Jewish Philosophy* (New York, 1916); Henry Malter, *Life and Works of Saadia Gaon* (Philadelphia, 1921); and *Three Jewish Philosophers. Philo, Saadya Gaon, Jehuda Halevi,* selections with introductions by H. Lewy, A. Altman, and I. Heinemann, eds. (Cleveland and New York, 1960).

J. L. BLAU

SABATIER, AUGUSTE (1839–1901), was perhaps the Protestant theologian most influential in the early twentieth century. Many Catholic modernists as well as Protestant liberals believed that his philosophy of religion had achieved its object, a reconciliation between the essential verities of Christian experience and the demands of science. Sabatier was a professor of reformed dogmatics at Strasbourg and Paris and a sometime journalist and literary critic. He ended his career as dean of the Theological Faculty of Paris.

Sabatier described his theory of religious knowledge as "critical symbolism." By this he meant to indicate that religious doctrine and dogma are attempts to symbolize the primary and eternal religious experience (or consciousness) of the believer. He taught that the doctrines of historical religions are secondary, temporal, and transient symbols of this central religious experience. Christian dogmas, then, are necessarily inadequate attempts to "express the invisible by the visible, the eternal by the temporal, spiritual realities by sensible images." Christ and his disciples through the ages have experienced the divine presence of God the loving Father and with it a sense of moral repentance and an inner energy of the spirit. As with all personal experience, no symbolic structure can act as substitute. Such structures are, in every field, merely hypothetical attempts to grasp experience.

Correspondingly, Sabatier held that the cosmologies, legends, dogmas, and statements about the world and man propagated by historical religions in an attempt to express

and communicate the fact of religious experience can claim only derivative and relative validity. Moreover, they are conditioned by the state of science and philosophy as understood by those who create such religious symbolism. And just as science and philosophy do not give absolute and final truth, neither does religious dogma—hence the decline of older religious symbolism with the progress of science. God lives in man's consciousness, not in dogmas and cosmologies. Man's need for and experience of God's presence prove his existence. Science and philosophy are masters of their own proper domain. Thus, "God is the final reason of everything, but the scientific explanation of nothing."

Sabatier's critical symbolism was exceedingly Protestant in that it rejected Catholic dogmatic absolutism for the absolutism of justification by faith. It appealed to many modern religionists of his day because it seemed to retain valid science and yet avoid positivistic nihilism and agnostic defeatism. Putting personal experience above theories about experience, Sabatier's approach was found congenial in an age that produced Henri Bergson and William James. Like them, Sabatier seemed to give moral claims and value judgments a renewed truth. To know a thing religiously, Sabatier held, is to experience the sovereignty of spirit and to estimate the object known as a means or obstacle to the true moral life of the spirit. Teleology is reintroduced along with objective value, and the meaning of life, as well as the will's freedom to choose good or evil, is made manifest. Sabatier's theories could easily be adapted to the neo-Kantian and neoidealist tendencies at work in philosophy, social science, political ideology, literature, and art at the turn of the century. His continued influence seems assured, for by basing the truth of religion on the personal experience of the believer, he joined the long line of "crisis" and existential theologians of our time.

Works by Sabatier

Esquisse d'une philosophie de la religion. Paris, 1897. Translated by T. A. Seed as *Outlines of a Philosophy of Religion.* New York, 1957.
Essai d'une théorie critique de la connaissance religieuse. Paris, 1899.
Les Religions d'autorité et la religion de l'esprit. Paris, 1903. Translated by L. Seymour as *Religions of Authority and Religions of Culture.* London, 1904.

Works on Sabatier

Michalescu, J., *Darlegung und Kritik der Religionsphilosophie Sabatiers.* Bern, 1903.
Vienot, J., *Auguste Sabatier.* Paris, 1927. Contains the best available bibliography.

JOHN WEISS

SAINT-HYACINTHE, THÉMISEUL DE, French freethinker whose real name was Hyacinthe Cordonnier. Born in 1684 at Orléans, he was unjustly reported to be the son of Bossuet. His ambitious mother induced him to change his name and to become a cavalry officer. Later he devoted himself to the study of ancient and modern languages in Holland, from which he had to flee because of a jealous husband and to which he later returned because he had seduced one of his pupils. He became an editor of the new *Journal littéraire* (1713) and wrote in favor of the moderns. In 1714 his anonymous *Le Chef-d'oeuvre d'un inconnu*, a satire of pedantry, won him notoriety. He eloped to London in 1722 with the daughter of a nobleman. He stayed there for 12 years, became a member of the Royal Society, and began a long and gratuitous quarrel with Voltaire, whom he offended in a satirical play (*Déification d'Aristarchus Masso*, 1732). He returned to Paris in 1734 and later moved to Holland, where he died in 1746.

Three of Saint-Hyacinthe's writings are worthy of mention. The first book, *Le Chef-d'oeuvre d'un inconnu*, is a bizarre work which could easily be a satire on the *explication de texte* method, as it is practiced in some milieus. His last book, *Recherches philosophiques sur la nécessité de s'assurer par soi-même de la vérité* (1743), is a defense of the power of reason to find truth and of its right to do so. He also argues for the moral-sense theory, with which he probably became familiar during his stay in England. His discussion of words as signs of ideas points toward linguistic analysis. Other chapters deal with demonstration and evidence, matter and the soul.

In between these two works, Saint-Hyacinthe wrote his interesting *Lettres écrites de la campagne* (1721). This potpourri is a long conversation treating of many subjects, moral and epistemological. He discusses truth in the light of Locke's definition; evidence for certitude, following the Cartesian *cogito* and the principle of contradiction. He proposes a methodology for discovering the truth that is also Cartesian. Most interesting is his recognition of the nihilistic challenge to moral values which was becoming more vigorous at the time. The longest section of the book expounds the argument that moral nihilism is justified and that all moral values disappear if God does not exist. Saint-Hyacinthe's real purpose was to urge men to believe in God, but the effect of his argument was more likely to lead them to immoralism, for he expounds that doctrine forcefully and endeavors to make it an impregnable position except in the face of God's existence. These little-known pages are notable as the most systematic exposition of moral nihilism before Sade. The *Lettres* had some success, and were translated under the title *Letters Giving an Account of Several Conversations Upon Important and Entertaining Subjects* (2 vols., London, 1731).

Among Saint-Hyacinthe's other publications are the *Lettres à Mme. Dacier* (1715, concerning the *querelle d'Homère*); "Lettre à un ami, touchant le progrès du déisme en Angleterre" (in his edition of *Mémoires concernant la théologie et la morale*, 1732); and the novel *Histoire du prince Titi* (1735).

L. G. CROCKER

SAINT LOUIS SCHOOL, THE. See HARRIS, WILLIAM TORREY.

SAINT-SIMON, CLAUDE-HENRI DE ROUVROY, COMTE DE (1760–1825), French social philosopher and founder of French socialism. Saint-Simon was the eldest son of an impoverished nobleman. He was educated privately by tutors, among them the Encyclopedist d'Alembert.

Beginning a military career at the age of 17, he took part in the American Revolution and was wounded at the naval battle of Saintes in 1782. Despite subsequent disclaimers, Saint-Simon actively supported some of the measures introduced by the French Revolution of 1789. He renounced his title; he also drew up the *cahier* of his locality for the Estates General and presided at the meeting at which his commune elected a mayor. Although his revolutionary zeal earned him two certificates of *civisme*, his activities were not wholly disinterested. He took advantage of the sale at low prices of church and *émigré* property by making considerable purchases. He was arrested in 1793, but since it transpired that a mistake had been made, he was released the following year. He was active in political life under the Directory, among other things participating in the peace negotiations with the English at Lille.

Saint-Simon finally retired from governmental and financial activity and embarked on the career of writer and prophet that continued until the end of his life. He first studied physics for three years, at the same time forming friendships with a number of leading scientists and writers whom he helped to support. Later he traveled extensively, especially in Germany, England, and Switzerland. However, it was not until 1814, when he found an able and enthusiastic collaborator and disciple in the future historian Augustin Thierry, that his writings began to reach a wide public, particularly among the managers and businessmen who had risen to positions of influence during the Napoleonic era. The list of subscribers for his publication *L'Industrie*, the first number of which appeared in 1816, included various prominent industrialists and bankers. The next year Saint-Simon's partnership with Thierry ended, and he began an association with Auguste Comte—an event of considerable significance, for it was in Comte's later work that some of Saint-Simon's fundamental conceptions were given more systematic and trenchant expression than their originator had been able to achieve. The collaboration between these two forceful personalities lasted for seven years but was finally broken by a quarrel in 1824, the year before Saint-Simon's death.

Ideals and reality. "The philosophy of the eighteenth century has been critical and revolutionary: that of the nineteenth century will be inventive and destructive" (*Oeuvres complètes*, Vol. XV, p. 92). This remark accurately reflects the position which Saint-Simon envisaged himself as occupying in the history of political and social ideas. He in no way wished to underestimate the achievements of his Enlightenment predecessors the *philosophes*, who by their bold attacks upon the traditional frameworks of thought and their criticisms of existing institutions had prepared the way for the vast upheaval of the French Revolution. Saint-Simon saw in the writings of such men as Condillac and Condorcet anticipations of his own belief that human affairs should be approached in a scientific, Newtonian spirit of inquiry, and he sympathized with their contention that religious dogmas had over the centuries become the means by which the mass of the people had been held in ignorant and superstitious servitude to their rulers. He also shared the humanitarian and internationalist ideals that had inspired the work of his predecessors. (His subscription to these ideals, apparent in all his main publications, was perhaps most distinctively expressed in *Nouveau Christianisme* [Paris, 1825], an essay that appeared at the very end of his life.)

On the other hand, Saint-Simon's work also pointed forward to the quite new ways of conceptualizing and interpreting social relations that were later to gain wide currency through the writings of Karl Marx. In particular, Saint-Simon exhibited a far firmer grasp of the conditions that determine and mold historical change than had earlier thinkers, and this profoundly affected the form taken by his own practical recommendations. Sincerely held utopian ideals, even when carefully worked out in detailed political programs, were by themselves quite useless, he held, if they did not take account of these conditions. Utopian changes, if put into effect, were likely to result in a vacuum that would eventually be filled by forces as undesirable as those which had been expelled. The destruction of outdated institutions was one thing; their replacement by others of lasting validity, adapted to the technological, economic, and social requirements of the time, was another. This was surely the lesson of the French Revolution. Had not the high hopes and aspirations that marked its beginning ultimately foundered in atrocities, suffering, and tyranny?

Historical change. Despite the importance he assigned to it, Saint-Simon never set out his conception of historical change and development in a precise or systematic form. Like his other contributions to social theory, it was put forward in a somewhat disjointed and piecemeal fashion. Nevertheless, an outline of his view can be extracted from various works, notably from his writings in the periodical *L'Organisateur* (Paris, 1819–1820). Saint-Simon spoke as if he had discovered a necessary law of evolution valid for all societies at all times, but the kernel of what he had to say was actually based upon a single instance, the transformation that had overtaken European society since the feudal period. The chief originality and importance of his analysis of how this change came about lay in his recognition of the role played by the emergence and conflict of classes and of the way in which such conflict issues in new forms of political organization and of ideology adapted to the interests of the socially and economically dominant class. The institutions and beliefs of the Middle Ages fulfilled a perfectly intelligible, and indeed necessary, function from the point of view of the stage of development which society had at that time reached (it is notable that Saint-Simon's approach to medieval history was considerably more sympathetic than that of either his Enlightenment predecessors or his liberal contemporaries). Only later, with the enfranchisement of the communes, the emergence of a class of independent producers, and the subsequent growth of an industrial system of production under the impact of scientific and technological advances, did feudal organization become evidently anachronistic. Then the very features of the framework that had provided medieval society with the protection and unity of purpose it required impeded the free development of the new forces germinating within it. Thus, the seventeenth and eighteenth centuries witnessed the culmination of two major developments. On the one hand, there were increasingly effective attacks by the commons against privileges and institutions that had outgrown their social utility; on the other, the doctrines of the church, which during the Middle Ages had performed valuable services but which had been rendered obsolete by scientific discoveries, were subjected to a series of unanswerable criticisms. The net result was "the ruin of the old system in its parts and as a whole" (*Oeuvres complètes*, Vol. XX, p. 104).

Economic and political program. The lessons Saint-Simon drew from previous developments for his own time were far-reaching. Although the old order was in a general condition of dissolution, it had still not been wholly superseded. Many of the chief centers of power and influence remained in the hands of "more or less incapable bureaucrats" (*ibid.*, pp. 17–26), idlers, and ignoramuses who owed their positions to the accident of birth or inherited wealth and who were in effect no better than destructive parasites. To a considerable extent "men still allow themselves to be governed by violence and ruse" (*ibid.*). In order to remedy this state of affairs, Saint-Simon appealed directly to the leaders of the new class of *industriels*, claiming that the hour had arrived for them to take into their own hands the management of society and thereby complete the revolution that had been maturing for so long. Only if this were done could society be reorganized in a way that would ensure its direction by efficient administrators, men who would see that those who could make a genuinely productive contribution to its advance and prosperity were no longer ignored or exploited and received, instead, their appropriate reward.

Yet, despite his insistence on the need for social justice, Saint-Simon had little faith in political democracy. He envisaged a hierarchical system, characterized by equality of opportunity rather than equality of wealth and run on explicitly elitist lines. The central administration of the community would consist of three chambers—the chamber of invention, the chamber of examination, and the chamber of deputies. Of these the first was to consist of artists and engineers who would propose plans, the second of scientists who would critically assess the proposals and also control education, and the third of captains of industry whose function would be executive and who (Saint-Simon somewhat optimistically assumed) would give just consideration to the interests of all members of the industrial class, workers and managers alike. Saint-Simon appears to have thought that in the type of society he had in mind, which would be rationally planned in a manner advantageous to all, there would be little or no need for the use of force to compel obedience to law and that government in the traditional sense would no longer be required. There is a clear anticipation of the Marxian conception of the withering away of the state.

Ethics and religion. Saint-Simon was always conscious of the importance of moral and social ideals in helping to promote harmony and a sense of purpose in human communities. In medieval times the Christian religion had performed this role, and he thought that there was a place for a comparable system of beliefs, adapted to contemporary knowledge and interests, in any viable modern society. For the creation of such a system he initially looked to philosophy, but in his later years he recommended a return to the fundamental tenets of Christian teaching. The ethical doctrines of Christianity, he held, retained their validity even if the theological and metaphysical dogmas associated with them are no longer acceptable.

Influence. It is impossible in a short space to do justice to the fertility and originality of Saint-Simon's thinking on what he called social physiology. An untidy, impatient, and inelegant expositor of his own ideas, he nonetheless understood the central issues of his time better than many of his contemporaries and exhibited a keener insight into the economic and technical realities that lie beneath the surface of political arrangements and change. Marx indisputably owed a significant debt to him, but Marx was only one among a host of nineteenth-century thinkers who profited in one way or another from Saint-Simon's perceptive and imaginative mind.

Works by Saint-Simon

Oeuvres complètes de Saint-Simon et Enfantin, 47 vols. Paris, 1865–1876.
Lettres d'un habitant de Genève à ses contemporains, A. Pereire, ed. Paris, 1925. Written in 1803.
Textes choisis, J. Dautry, ed. Paris, 1951.
Selected Writings, translated, with an introduction, by F. M. H. Markham, Oxford, 1952.

Works on Saint-Simon

Dondo, M. M., *The French Faust, Henri de Saint-Simon.* New York, 1955.
Durkheim, Émile, *Le Socialisme,* Marcel Mauss, ed. Paris, 1928. Translated by Charlotte Sattler as *Socialism and Saint-Simon.* Yellow Springs, Ohio, 1958.
Manuel, F. E., *The New World of Henri de Saint-Simon.* Cambridge, Mass., 1956.
Plamenatz, J. P., *Man and Society.* London, 1963. Vol. II, Ch. 2.

PATRICK GARDINER

SAINT VICTOR, SCHOOL OF. The Augustinian house of canons at St. Victor in Paris was founded in 1108 by William of Champeaux, the celebrated logician and theologian who retired there from the schools of Paris after undergoing a religious conversion and after Abelard's attacks on his realism. The abbey survived until the French Revolution, but in the twelfth and early thirteenth centuries it was especially famous for its public school and for the distinction of the masters and canons who resided and taught there. From William, St. Victor derived high religious ideals, a leaning toward the conservative theological tradition of the school of Anselm of Laon, and an active interest in the work of other Parisian schools. Its masters mediated between the theological orthodoxy and strictness of the Cistercians—Bernard of Clairvaux was a friend to St. Victor—and the intellectual adventurousness of such secular masters as Abelard. St. Victor in the twelfth century combined Scholasticism and mysticism and exerted a most powerful influence upon the development of both philosophical and theological thought in that century. Not only did it possess among its canons some of the ablest writers of the age but it also attracted as long-staying guests such celebrated teachers as Peter Lombard and Robert of Melun. Besides producing a wealth of literature, its leaders also contributed to the fall of Abelard, to the damping of the enthusiasms of the Chartrains, to the con-

tainment of Gilbert of Poitiers, and to the correction of the Christological errors which abounded in the mid-twelfth century.

Hugh of St. Victor. St. Victor, unlike Chartres, was not devoted to the liberal arts. No commentary upon a non-theological text is known to have been written there, and purely literary writings were even relegated by the greatest Victorine, Hugh (d. 1141), to the position of mere appendices to the liberal arts. The Victories did not encourage profane studies for their own sakes. The extreme, fanatical Walter (d. circa 1180) intemperately denounced the Aristotelian spirit of Abelard, Gilbert of Poitiers, William of Conches, and Peter Lombard. Absalon (d. 1203), too, warned against the dangers found in Aristotle.

Hugh vigorously challenged his humanist contemporaries who in the first half of the twelfth century thought more often of pagan philosophy than of Christ and his saints. Against the Chartrains he insisted upon the disparity between the cosmogony of Plato's *Timaeus* and Christian truth. Nonetheless, in his *Didascalicon* (which contains a program of Christian education) Hugh shows that he was thoroughly immersed in secular studies as the preliminary to divine science, for he considered the arts an indispensable aid to the understanding of Scripture. Hugh sought to pass through knowledge to wisdom and to promote that participation in the divine Wisdom for which man was made. Similarly, Godfrey (d. after 1194) also affirmed that the liberal arts and theology were inseparable and that together they offered a complete education.

Philosophical elements are found scattered in the writings of the Victorines. Inheriting the Boethian–Aristotelian theory of abstraction, Hugh appreciated the necessity for logic without exalting it as highly as did Abelard. In physics Hugh maintained the atomic theory of matter and accepted the principle of the conservation of matter. His psychology was Augustinian, and he found the proof for the existence of the immaterial soul in the fact of its self-consciousness.

Richard of St. Victor. Both Hugh and his disciple Richard (d. 1173) describe the ascent of the soul in contemplation; Richard especially is the theorist of the degrees of love. But whereas Hugh insisted upon the inadequacy of reason and the necessity for faith, Richard, who rivaled Hugh as a spiritual writer, was more scholastic and laid a stronger emphasis upon dialectic to supplement the traditional scriptural and patristic authorities. Inheriting from Anselm of Canterbury his zeal to search for the "necessary reasons" of faith and for an understanding of belief, he accounted for the trinity of persons in God in abstract style with a very original dialectic of mutual love; he was also the first medieval thinker to provide, in one of the great speculative achievements of the period, an empirical basis in the principle of causality for a proof of God's existence.

Victorine theology. Essentially the Victorines provided a theology for contemplatives within the cloister rather than for the schools. Hugh was a systematizer of theology on Augustinian lines, using dialectic when needed. Richard became the mystical doctor of the later Middle Ages. Both Hugh and Richard were Biblical exegetes and spiritual writers, and it is for this that they and such other Victorines as Andrew (d. 1175) and Garnier (d. 1170) and the poet Adam were best known in the Middle Ages. Godfrey was more pronounced in his humanism, combining Chartrain Platonism and Aristotelian dialectic with Victorine spirituality. Achard (abbot 1155–1160) also mingled Augustinian theology with Chartrain Platonism, but all the Victorines concurred in wishing to turn knowledge into wisdom and the reader of the profane sciences into a contemplative. They always returned to the internal and external experiences of the soul, and frequently to the use of allegory and symbolism in the penetration of divine truths. In the early thirteenth century the influence of Pseudo-Dionysius, which had been powerful upon Hugh, prevailed again upon Thomas Gallus, who was a forerunner of the mysticism of the later Middle Ages.

Bibliography

Baron, R., *Science et sagesse chez Hugues de Saint-Victor*. Paris, 1957.

Bonnard, Fourier, *Histoire de l'abbaye royale de Saint-Victor*, 2 vols. Paris, 1904.

Delhaye, P., *Le Microcosmus de Godefroy de Saint-Victor*, 2 vols. Lille and Gembloux, 1951. Text and study.

Dumeige, G., *Richard de Saint-Victor et l'idée chrétienne de l'amour*. Paris, 1952.

Ebner, J., *Die Erkenntnislehre Richards von St. Viktor*. Beiträge zur Geschichte der Philosophie des Mittelalters, Vol. XIX, No. 4. Münster in Westfalen, 1917.

Ethier, A. M., *Le De Trinitate de Richard de Saint-Victor*. Paris and Ottawa, 1939.

Fritz, G., "Richard de Saint-Victor," in *Dictionnaire de théologie catholique*, Vol. XIII. Paris, 1937. Cols. 2676–2695.

Geyer, B., *Die patristische und scholastische Philosophie*. Basel, 1927. Pp. 261–272.

Godfrey of St. Victor, *Fons Philosophiae*, P. Michaud-Quantin, ed. Namur, Belgium, 1956.

Hugh of St. Victor, *Didascalicon*, translated by J. Taylor. New York, 1961.

Kleinz, J. P., *The Theory of Knowledge of Hugh of St. Victor*. Washington, 1944.

Ostler, H., *Die Psychologie des Hugo von St. Victor*. Beiträge zur Geschichte der Philosophie des Mittelalters, Vol. VI, No. 1. Münster in Westfalen, 1906.

Richard of St. Victor, *De Trinitate*, J. Ribaillier, ed. Paris, 1958.

Vernet, F., "Hugues de Saint-Victor," in *Dictionnaire de théologie catholique*, Vol. VII. Paris, 1922. Cols. 240–308.

DAVID LUSCOMBE

SANCHES, FRANCISCO, or Sánchez, philosopher and physician, was born sometime between 1550 and 1552, probably in Braga, Portugal (or perhaps in Túy, Spain), of Spanish New Christian (Jewish forced convert) parents; he died in November 1623, in Toulouse. About 1564 his family left Portugal for Bordeaux, where his father, Antonio, achieved prominence as a physician. Sanches probably studied at the Collège de Guienne (which his distant cousin Michel de Montaigne had also attended), then in Rome, and finally at Montpellier, where he received a medical degree in 1574. He immediately competed for a professorship of medicine, but was turned down. He then moved to Toulouse, where he practiced medicine and wrote. In 1585 he was appointed professor of philosophy at the University of Toulouse, and in 1612 was made professor of medicine.

His published philosophical writings consist of *Carmen de Cometa* (1578); *Quod Nihil Scitur* (1581); *De Longitudine et Brevitate Vitae Liber, In Librum Aristotelis Phy-siognomicon Commentarius,* and *De Divinatione per Somnum, ad Aristotelem* (these three published as *Opera Medica,* Toulouse, 1636); and his letter to the famous mathematician Father Clavius (first published in 1940). In addition there are many medical writings, which appeared in the 1636 edition of his works. The earliest of his writings was apparently the letter to Clavius, a skeptical critique of mathematics dating from 1574/1575, right after the publication of Clavius' edition of Euclid with commentary. The famous skeptical tract *Quod Nihil Scitur* is from the period immediately thereafter (its preface to the reader is dated January 1, 1576). The *Carmen de Cometa* is a critical examination in poetic form (long before Pierre Bayle) of the astrological interpretations of the comet of 1577. The two works dealing with Aristotle carry on this type of rationalistic critique of various Renaissance pseudo-scientific theories, such as those of Cardano. In addition, Sanches mentioned in various writings several major works in progress or preparation, including one on scientific method. This latter work was mentioned by Guy Patin under the Spanish title *Método universal de las ciencias* and was referred to at the end of *Quod Nihil Scitur*. If it ever actually existed, it would probably be the earliest writing in modern times on this subject.

In his philosophical writings, especially in the *Quod Nihil Scitur* ("Why Nothing Can Be Known"), Sanches showed himself to be the most technical exponent of philosophical skepticism in the sixteenth century. Unlike the other skeptics of the period, he developed his skepticism by a systematic analysis of the Aristotelian theory of knowledge. In so doing, he first formulated a type of thoroughgoing Academic skepticism—a denial of the possibility of knowledge—rather than the Pyrrhonian skeptical suspense of judgment on the question of whether anything can be known, and then presented a "constructive skepticism," a way of answering questions through patient, careful empirical research, even though genuine knowledge cannot be obtained.

After announcing that he did not even know if he knew nothing, Sanches then examined the Aristotelian conception of knowledge as a way of expounding the bases of his own total skepticism. Every science, he pointed out, starts with definitions. These do not state the nature of things, but are only nominal; that is, they are arbitrary names assigned to things which have, in fact, no relation to the things named. This nominalistic analysis was then applied to the Aristotelian view that science consists of certain knowledge acquired by demonstrations from true definitions. We do not possess the definitions to begin with and, further, the syllogistic method of demonstration provides no new knowledge. Sanches pointed out the circular reasoning involved in any demonstrative syllogism: the conclusion to be proved is part of the evidence for the premises. One could not have a true definition of the terms involved without already knowing their meaning. Next Sanches showed that, in a formal sense, anything can be proven syllogistically if one starts with the right premises. The fact that a demonstration can be constructed is thus no indication that its conclusion is actually true. The further element of Aristotelian science, that it is true knowledge of things in terms of their causes, was attacked as an unattainable goal. To know a thing in terms of its causes requires infinite erudition, since one would have to know the cause of the cause, the cause of the cause of the cause, and so on.

This attack on the Aristotelian notion of science in the *Quod Nihil Scitur* was coupled with an attack on a form of the Platonic theory of knowledge in Sanches' letter to Clavius. We cannot know about things through mathematical study, since the objects studied by mathematics are not the real, natural ones encountered in human experience, but are rather ideal objects, or perhaps even impossible objects, such as points and lines. The mathematical relations demonstrated about these objects do not explain the causes of anything in experience, unless we independently know the nature of the experienced object, know that it has certain mathematical properties, and know that the principles of mathematics are, in fact, true. Since we cannot gain such knowledge from mathematics, this study can only be considered conjectural or hypothetical, a kind of mental game, until we can independently gain genuine knowledge of things.

Having denied the possibility of scientific knowledge by means of either Aristotelian science or pure mathematics, Sanches proposed his own theory. True science, he insisted, would consist in the perfect knowledge of a thing. It would be the immediate, intuitive understanding of all of the real qualities of an object. Each particular would be understood in and by itself. Generalizations beyond this would never have the complete certitude of particular cases of scientific knowledge, since they would require concepts, abstractions, fictions, and so on.

This perfect knowledge, unfortunately, can be attained only by God. Objects cannot be studied and understood one by one, since they are interrelated and interconnected. Also, there is an unlimited number of different objects, so that complete knowledge is unattainable. In addition, objects are continuously changing, so that they are never in a final or complete form in which we can know them.

However, it is not only the nature of objects that prevents us from gaining true knowledge; our own faculties are also not sufficiently reliable. We gain our ideas of things from information provided by our unreliable senses, which tell us about only the surface characteristics of things, not their true natures. The traditional skeptical evidence, plus Sanches' medical studies, provided him with much detail about the imperfections and limitations of human nature.

Sanches' conclusion was that the only genuine scientific knowledge cannot be attained by human beings. This sweeping negative conclusion, going far beyond the balancing of pros and cons of Montaigne's Pyrrhonism, resulted from a careful epistemological analysis of a theory of the nature of knowledge. Sanches, unlike Agrippa von Nettesheim, tried to state what genuine knowledge would be and then to show why we cannot attain it. Having done this, he did not then follow the destructive tendency of Agrippa or of the followers of Montaigne—that of rejecting all positive steps toward the answering of questions about nature. Since nothing can be known, Sanches advocated a procedure, not to gain knowledge, but to deal constructively with experience. This procedure—patient, careful

empirical research and cautious judgment and evaluation of the data—would not, as Francis Bacon was to claim a generation later, provide us with a key to knowledge of the world. But it would enable us to gain the best information available.

Sanches was probably the first Renaissance skeptic to see science in its modern sense, as the remaining fruitful activity once one has abandoned the search for absolutely certain knowledge about the real nature of things. It is interesting to note, in this regard, that Sanches just barely suggested the fideistic resolution of skepticism (the appeal to knowledge by religious faith) dominant in the writings of Montaigne, Charron, Agrippa, and other sixteenth-century and early seventeenth-century skeptics.

Although Sanches' works are little studied now, it has been claimed that he was quite influential in seventeenth-century thought. Some have seen him as having greatly influenced Descartes, Gassendi, and other early figures in modern philosophy. His *Quod Nihil Scitur* did appear in several seventeenth-century editions (1618, 1636, 1649, and 1665), and it is referred to in many of the discussions of skepticism in the period. The evidence for his direct influence on Descartes, Gassendi, Mersenne, Spinoza, and others is, however, somewhat conjectural and may be difficult to differentiate from that of Sextus Empiricus, Cicero, Diogenes Laërtius, Montaigne, and Charron, who were read by almost everyone in the period. Leibniz, however, does refer directly to some of Sanches' views, both from his *Quod Nihil Scitur* and from his letter to Clavius.

Some have claimed that Sanches was the first modern philosopher, preceding Descartes in the method of doubt and Bacon in the reliance on experience as the source of knowledge. Certainly features of the views of both of these thinkers appeared in Sanches, but the latter was not trying to find, or contending that he had found, an answer to the skeptical attack he had leveled against the possibility of attaining knowledge. What does seem to be original with Sanches is his suggestion that a probabilistic empirical study of experience could replace (but not substitute for) the hopeless quest for knowledge and certainty. In this he may have initiated the modern tradition of constructive skepticism that runs through Mersenne, Gassendi, Glanvill, and Hume to twentieth-century positivistic and pragmatic interpretations of scientific knowledge.

Works by Sanches

Que nada se sabe. Buenos Aires, 1944. Spanish translation of *Quod Nihil Scitur*, with an introduction by Marcelino Menéndez y Pelayo.

Opera Philosophica, Joaquim de Carvalho, ed. Coimbra, Portugal, 1955. Introduction in Portuguese by Carvalho. Best Latin text.

Tratados filosóficos, 2 vols. Lisbon, 1955. Latin–Portuguese edition.

Works on Sanches

Coralnik, A., "Zur Geschichte der Skepsis. I. Franciscus Sanchez." *Archiv für Geschichte der Philosophie*, Vol. 27, N.F. Vol. 20 (1914), 188–222.

Franck, Adolphe, ed., *Dictionnaire des sciences philosophiques*. Paris, 1875. See "Sanchez, François," pp. 1524–1525.

Iriarte, J., *Kartesischer oder Sanchezischer Zweifel*. Bonn, 1935.

Menéndez y Pelayo, Marcelino, "De los orígenes del criticismo y del escepticismo y especialmente de los precursores españoles de Kant," in his *Ensayos de critica filosófica*. Madrid, 1918. Pp. 119–221.

Moreau, Joseph, "Doute et savoir chez Francisco Sanches," in *Aufsätze zur portugiesischen Kulturgeschichte*, 1st series. Portugiesische Forschungen der Görresgesellschaft. Münster in Westfalen, 1960. Vol. I, pp. 24–50.

Moreira de Sá, Artur, *Francisco Sanches filósofo e matemático*, 2 vols. Lisbon, 1947.

Owen, John, *The Skeptics of the French Renaissance*. London and New York, 1893. Pp. 617–646.

Popkin, R. H., *The History of Scepticism from Erasmus to Descartes*, 2d ed. Assen, Netherlands, and New York, 1963. Ch. 2.

Senchet, Émilien, *Essai sur la méthode de Francisco Sanchez*. Paris, 1904.

RICHARD H. POPKIN

SANCTIS, FRANCESCO DE. See under DE SANCTIS, FRANCESCO.

ŚANKARA (c. 788–c. 820) was the most influential metaphysical theologian in the Hindu tradition. A Śaivite Brahmin from Kaladi in Cochin, south India, he filled his short life with remarkable intellectual and religious activity. He became an ascetic when he was a boy, and early went to Banaras for study. His chief works, the commentary on the *Brahma-Sūtra* ("Aphorisms Concerning *Brahman*") and on the ten principal Upaniṣads, were probably compiled in his youth. He traveled extensively throughout India, engaging in disputations with members of rival schools and trying to reform religious life, notably by establishing an order of ascetics and four important monasteries. Near one of these, in the foothills of the Himalayas, he died.

His interpretation of Hindu theology is known as Advaita Vedānta ("Nondualistic" Vedānta), since he formulated Vedānta (literally, "the end of the Veda," or the systematization of scriptural doctrines) in such a way that there is no distinction between the self and God.

The movement he instituted continues, and his followers (the Smārtas, followers of *smṛti*, "tradition") are still numerous. The monastery at Sringeri, whose head leads the south Indian Smārtas, is still a center of learning and pilgrimage. Modern Hindu apologetic, moreover, owes much to Śankara, whose system is the nearest thing to a modern Hindu ideology.

His system depends upon a simple assumption which can be given some scriptural backing (from the Upaniṣads)—that the eternal Self (*ātman*) and *Brahman*, the power underlying and sustaining the empirical cosmos, are identical. This is one interpretation of the famous Upaniṣadic text "That thou art" (*tat tvam asi*). It follows from Śankara's equation that the apparent multiplicity of selves is an illusion, since there is only one ultimate reality, *Brahman*. Likewise, empirical phenomena, since they appear to be different from the one Absolute, are illusory. *Brahman* alone exists; and once this has been realized existentially in inner experience, there occurs *mokṣa*, or release.

Śankara did not attempt, as did Nāgārjuna, to whose thought he owed much, to show the contradictoriness of ordinary concepts about the world and thus to establish an ineffable Absolute dialectically. (Some of his followers, however, adopted this procedure.) Rather, he argued, first, that his interpretation of revelation (*śruti*) was the correct one; and, second, that his solution was not falsified by experience. Thus, his standpoint was in essence theological, although its bold simplicity, and the force of his arguments in its defense, have conferred on it a strong attraction.

Traditionally *Brahman* was characterized as *saccidānanda*—being, consciousness, and bliss. The last of these three expresses the joy and painlessness of *mokṣa*, for this involves realization of one's identity with the divine Absolute. Śankara further argued that in perception one is aware of both appearances and an underlying reality. If that reality is one, however, it follows that the multiplicity of phenomena is illusory. Thus, perception involves an intuition of being but for the rest is misleading. We are intuitively aware of *Brahman* but superimpose upon it characteristics it does not possess. By analogy with illusions, it can be claimed that the whole world as ordinarily encountered is illusory: The experience of release stands to veridical perception as veridical perception does to hallucinations. Consequently, the full understanding of Śankara's system and its verification comes through the nondualistic experience of identity between the Self and *Brahman*. Thus knowledge, at the higher level, is essentially contemplative, rather than theoretical.

This experience of identity was held to be self-authenticating and not directly communicable—rather, it has to be evoked by, for example, the Vedic identity texts which indicate the essential import of revelation. The two-level theory of truth in Advaita was backed by the use of nonfalsification (*abādhitva*) as the criterion of truth. Ordinary, common-sense (*vyāvahārika*) knowledge remains veridical until it is falsified by the higher experience of *Brahman;* illusions, false judgments, and so on at the ordinary level are rightly so called, since they are falsified by later experience. The ordinary distinction between truth and falsity remains applicable at this level.

The *Brahman–ātman* equation on which Śankara's position rests has two sides. In perceptual experience there is an intuition of the outer side; that is, of pure being as underlying appearances. On the inner side, one is aware of the *ātman*, which has the nature of pure consciousness—the second of the three elements in *Brahman*. The notion of an ego underlying psychological states is common enough in the Indian tradition, for all orthodox (Hindu) schools affirm such an entity. But Śankara differed from them in denying the *plurality* of selves. The one Self manifests itself internally as the *sākṣin* or inner witness which illuminates myriads of psychophysical organisms with consciousness. However, it is thereby commonly confused with the empirical ego, and this is the second—the internal—aspect of the grand illusion. Thus both externally, in treating appearances as real, independently of *Brahman*, and psychologically, in supposing that the empirical ego is real, a person is in the grip of ignorance (*avidyā*). This original ignorance is the root of the troubles of living beings, but through spiritual knowledge one removes the veil of nescience and escapes the round of rebirth. Śankara's denial of a plurality of eternal souls brought him closer to Buddhist thought than any school in the orthodox Hindu tradition. For Śankara, individuality properly belongs only to the transmigrating *jīva*, or life monad.

Although the world is, so to say, the product of illusion and ignorance, Śankara did not hold that, strictly speaking, appearances are brought into being by the Absolute or that the Self gives rise to ignorance. The state of affairs is beginningless, and all Śankara was doing was giving an analysis of it. Consequently, questions about the origin of *māyā* (the cosmic illusion) are unanswerable, and the nature of *māyā* is indefinable—it floats, as it were, between existence and nonexistence. But since concepts, like explanations, which are used to deal with phenomena, are necessarily limited to the world of appearances, it is not surprising that the origin of *māyā* is inexplicable. Nevertheless, explanation at the ordinary, common-sense level is in order, and since natural theology is impossible at the higher level, it appears at the lower one. From the standpoint of the ordinary person, immersed in everyday experience, it is correct to view the Absolute as personal God (*Īśvara*) and Creator of the world. Thus Śankara had a two-level theory of *Brahman*. It is qualityless and featureless considered in itself (it is *pure* being, *pure* consciousness, *pure* bliss), but it manifests itself in a lower way as possessing personal characteristics. The former aspect of the Absolute is *nirguṇam*, without attributes; the latter is *saguṇam*, with attributes.

The relation between the *Īśvara* and the impersonal *Brahman* can be illustrated in terms of Śankara's cosmology. He made use here of certain *Sāṃkhya* concepts (see INDIAN PHILOSOPHY: Sāṃkhya and Yoga). The illusion substance, *māyā*, takes the place of *prakṛti*, or nature; but the interplay between the three *guṇas* (qualities or forces which in disequilibrium interact in such a way that the phenomena of the observable world evolve out of the primary substance, nature) within the *māyā* is analogous to the Sāṃkhya scheme. The Lord, in producing the world out of his own substance, himself possesses the *guṇas* and thus is *saguṇam*, while *Brahman* considered in itself is *nirguṇam*. In brief, the Lord as Creator is implicated in his illusory creation and is, from the standpoint of the higher level, himself illusory.

This synthesis between the doctrine of an Absolute and a secondary theism was facilitated by the history of the term *māyā*. Although by Śankara's time it definitely meant illusion, as in a conjuring trick, in its earlier use in the orthodox tradition it meant "creative substance"; that is, the potency by which God is able to produce magical transformations of matter, or the matter he uses in creation. The suggestion of magic accounts for the later meaning of "illusion"; but the association of the term with the creative energy of the Lord made it easier for Śankara to present his picture of *Brahman*, underlying the illusion, as also the creator of the cosmos.

Śankara's view that religion, as well as existence as a whole, can be treated at two levels is one reason for his great contemporary influence, since this key idea (elaborated to include many levels, if necessary) is well suited to express the claims of modern Hinduism to be in the forefront of a movement to synthesize the various great faiths in the world. If otherwise conflicting beliefs, attitudes, and practices can be arranged in a hierarchy of levels, two purposes are achieved. First, contradictions between faiths are removed; and second, certain manifestations of religion can be ranked as higher—thus giving Hindu apologetics a clear mode of procedure.

The doctrine of the two levels and the denial of a plurality of eternal selves indicate Śankara's nearness to

Buddhist Mahāyāna metaphysics. Undoubtedly he was influenced by the Madhyamika school, which was founded by Nāgārjuna. For this reason he was accused of being a crypto-Buddhist. This appearance of unorthodoxy was accentuated by his treatment of revelation (*śruti*). The two-level principle was applied in his exegesis of the scriptures. The so-called "works portion" (*karma-kanda*) of revelation, those passages dealing with ritual and social duties, was consigned to the ordinary level, as were references to *Brahman* as the personal Lord. Thus Śankara's religious aim appeared to transcend orthodox Hinduism, as currently understood. Nevertheless, the impression of neglect of what he considered lower-level religion is somewhat misleading. Śankara not only spent considerable energies in religious reform, but also was a devotional hymn writer. However, personal religion of this kind, although an important preliminary, was of course superseded in the nondual contemplative experience.

However, the crucial question for Advaita is how the unitary Self becomes associated with a multiplicity of empirical egos. The attempted explanation has two stages. First, it must be shown that the Self exists in some sense "in" empirical individuals. Second, some analogy must be produced to show that no contradiction is involved in the notion of one Self in many life monads (*jīvas*). Once such a coherent account is given, the problem of how the Self *comes to be* associated with the life monads can be allowed to evaporate. For, as we have seen, the existence of *māyā* (illusion) and *avidyā* (ignorance) is a beginningless fact of life; and all that need be done is to show that the metaphysical analysis of the situation is correct. The problem is not "How came they to be associated?" but rather "How can they be *dissociated?*"

In the first stage, Śankara argued that we are introspectively aware, by an immediate intuition, of an "I" which is prior to all particular contents of consciousness. This subject is never the object of differentiated experience and is thus pure consciousness. Only in the nondual experience is one able to attain to such a pure consciousness without any overlay of differentiated experience. Assurance that the immediate intuition of the Self is not mistaken can be given by reflecting that the judgment "I doubt the existence of the self" itself presupposes a self to express this doubt. Further, if the self is featureless and without differentiations, one cannot individuate one self from another; there is only one Self.

The second stage in the argument involves the search for suitable analogies. The Self somehow appears refracted by the *upādhis* (limiting conditions) which constitute each empirical ego. But can this happen without its being broken up, so to speak, into fragments and thereby becoming many? One analogy is that of space. We can speak of the space contained in a jug, but this does not entail that there are many spaces—space continues to be a single whole. Only from a certain point of view can it be regarded as limited by the jug. Thus, it is possible to operate with the concept of empirical egos as limiting conditions superimposed on the Self, without running into contradiction. Another analogy used by some Advaitins was that of reflection (*pratibimba*)—the sun, for instance, is mirrored in many pools, but remains the same sun. But this analogy scarcely served the Advaitin purpose well, and was indeed made use of by the Dvaita ("Dualistic") school and others. One can distinguish between the reflections and the source of the reflections, while the whole logic of Śankara's position is to affirm the numerical identity of the Self with what appears to be the plurality of selves.

Provided he can make sense of the relation between the Self and the life monads, Śankara need not say anything further about the origins of this relationship; but he does need to show how release (*mokṣa*) is possible, since the whole point of his teachings is to indicate the path to this goal. This is partly a matter of the right spiritual exercises and reflection upon the higher import of revelation, culminating in an intuitive experience of identity with the Absolute. But there is something of a paradox here. Release does not mean that one *becomes Brahman*. There is no question of changing one's status, but only a change in one's knowledge of that status. Nevertheless, rebirth of the empirical ego ceases upon the attainment of release. It is at this point that there ought to be a causal relation between *Brahman* and the empirical world, but the relation between the two is stated by Śankara in a way which seems to exclude this.

The relation is that of appearance (*vivartta*) to reality. Although this Advaitin "appearance theory" is often counted as one of the classical theories of causation in the Indian tradition, strictly speaking, the relation of cause and effect does not apply to that between *Brahman* and the world of appearances. These concepts belong to the realm of phenomena, which are by definition the objects of empirical or ordinary knowledge. Thus they are not applicable at the higher level. Instead, the Absolute–world relation is conceived by analogy with the perceptual illusion involved in mistaking one object for another; for example, a rope for a snake. The snake appearance is superimposed by the percipient upon the rope and yet would not occur if the rope did not exist. Thus, the *Brahman*–world relation has two features. First, *Brahman* is cause of the world only in the sense that there would be no world appearance without *Brahman* (the converse not holding); and second, the world is an appearance superimposed on *Brahman*. On the other hand, the world of ordinary experience is orderly and not exactly like a dream or a hallucination, experiences which do not fit in with the rest of experience. This orderliness inherent in physical and psychological phenomena means that they are not absolutely nonexistent. The ambiguous status assigned to *māyā* is the reason that Śankara regarded it as indefinable or inexpressible (*anirvacanīya*), and it also accounts for the fact that he did not adopt a subjectivist and solipsistic account of appearances.

The ambivalence between the two levels enabled Śankara to reject the subjective idealist position of the Buddhist Vijñānavādin school (see INDIAN PHILOSOPHY: Buddhism). Moreover, the intuition of pure being and of the Self in outer and inner perception, respectively, implies that running through ordinary experience there is an implicit awareness of the Absolute, so that in an important respect ordinary experience is veridical, even from the higher point of view.

Nevertheless, some later Advaitins—for instance, Prakāśananda in the sixteenth century—developed Śankara's ideas in a subjectivist direction. On the other hand, there has been in recent times a stress (for example, by Radhakrishnan) upon the realism of Śankara's concept of *māyā* and a playing down of the degree to which he suggested that the world is illusory. Other modern Advaitins, such as T. R. V. Murti, have given a somewhat Kantian interpretation to Advaita, in its treatment of lower-level knowledge and in its thesis that concepts of causation apply only within the realm of phenomena. In the medieval period Śankara was strongly criticized by Rāmānuja and Madhva, the main discussion centering on the questions of whether the notion of two levels of truth is coherent or legitimate, and of whether it is consistent to begin from an intuition of the Self and yet to deny a plurality of selves. These criticisms were largely motivated by the desire to defend a theistic position against the undervaluation of personal devotion to God entailed by Śankara's position.

Bibliography

An early and influential Western exposition of Śankara was Paul Deussen, *Das System des Vedānta* (Leipzig, 1883), translated by Charles Johnston as *The System of the Vedānta* (Chicago, 1912).

For a general account of the period, see J. Estlin Carpenter, *Theism in Medieval India* (London, 1921).

Comparative studies are Rudolf Otto, *Mysticism East and West* (New York, 1932); W. S. Urquhart, *The Vedanta and Modern Thought* (London, 1928); and P. T. Raju, *Thought and Reality—Hegelianism and Advaita* (London, 1932).

English translations of important works by Śankara are *The Vedānta Sūtras With the Commentary by Śankarācārya*, translated by George Thibaut, Sacred Books of the East, Vols. XXXIV and XXXVIII (Oxford, 1890 and 1896); *Sarvasiddhāntasamgraha*, translated by Prem Sundar Bose (Calcutta, 1929); *A Thousand Teachings of Sri Śankarachārya* (the *Upadeśasahasri*), translated by Swami Jagadananda (Madras, 1949); *The Great Jewel of Wisdom. (Vivekachūdāmani) Attributed to Shankara Āchārya*, translated by Charles Johnston (New York, 1925).

Also useful are Sarvepalli Radhakrishnan and Charles Moore, eds., *A Source Book in Indian Philosophy* (Princeton, 1957); and Sarvepalli Radhakrishnan, *The Brahma Sūtra* (London, 1960).

Modern interpretations are K. C. Bhattacharyya, *Studies in Vedāntism* (Calcutta, 1909); Kokileswar Sastri, *A Realistic Interpretation of Śankara-Vedānta* (Calcutta, 1931); Sarvepalli Radhakrishnan, *Eastern Religions and Western Thought*, 2d ed. (London, 1940).

On the concept of illusion, see P. D. Devanandan, *The Concept of Māyā* (London, 1951).

See also general histories of Indian philosophy listed in the bibliography to INDIAN PHILOSOPHY.

NINIAN SMART

SANTAYANA, GEORGE (1863–1952), philosopher and man of letters, was born in Madrid. His parents separated within a few years of his birth, and his mother went to live in Boston, Massachusetts, with the children of a previous marriage. Santayana grew up in Ávila under his father's care, but at the age of eight he joined his mother in Boston. He was educated at the Boston Latin School and at Harvard College. After graduating from Harvard in 1886, he studied in Germany for two years and then returned to take his doctorate at Harvard, for which he wrote a thesis on Rudolf Lotze. He subsequently joined the department of philosophy and remained a member of the Harvard faculty until 1912, when a small inheritance permitted him to retire. He lived in England for a number of years and then in

Paris, but in 1925 he finally settled in Rome. During World War II, he took refuge in the convent of an order of English nuns in Rome, and he continued to live there until his death.

Cultural background. Both Santayana's personal life and his philosophical development were decisively influenced by his peculiar position as a Spanish Catholic living and teaching in a predominantly Protestant society with a philosophical and cultural tradition that he felt to be in many respects deeply alien to his own personality. He was always proud—rather defiantly so—of his Catholicism and his Latinity, despite the fact that he was not a believer and was not notably attached to Spain or to Spanish culture. These loyalties expressed instead a deeply rooted hostility to the commercial and democratic ethos of modern industrial society and an equally deep aspiration toward a radically different style of life and thought which, for Santayana, was best exemplified in the classical Mediterranean world. Philosophically, he felt his truest affinities to be with the Greeks and perhaps the Hindus, and among the moderns, with Spinoza, rather than with the empiricism and idealism of German and Anglo-American philosophy. In fact, however, his points of affiliation with the European and American philosophy of the modern period are both numerous and obvious, and it would appear that his debt to the post-Cartesian tradition in modern philosophy is much greater than he was inclined to think. What chiefly set his work apart from the mainstream of twentieth-century philosophy was his highly personal and literary mode of writing and his rather disdainful lack of interest in the methodological questions that were of central importance to the development of phenomenology on the Continent and analytic philosophy in the English-speaking world. When one considers the substantive doctrines to which he was committed, however, and, in particular, the ontological distinctions on which his "Realms of Being" rest, his philosophy emerges as a highly idiosyncratic doctrine of transcendental subjectivity that would scarcely be conceivable apart from the very tradition of modern philosophy which he so violently criticized.

Philosophical development. Santayana's philosophical career falls naturally into two main periods. The first of these is the period in which he published *The Sense of Beauty* (1896) and *The Life of Reason* (1905–1906); its chief distinguishing feature is Santayana's disposition at that time to conceive of philosophy as a kind of descriptive psychology of the higher mental functions. He assumed the broad truth of the doctrine of biological evolution and its relevance to the understanding of mental phenomena, and while he held all knowledge to be representational in nature, he did not question "our knowledge of the external world," nor did he feel the need for any initial withdrawal of belief in such a world in the Cartesian manner. "Mind" is placed firmly in its biological context, and such independence as it enjoys is due not to any special ontological status, but rather to its capacity for giving an ideal and aesthetic meaning to its natural setting and functions.

In the second period, during which he wrote *Scepticism and Animal Faith* (1923) and *Realms of Being* (1927–1940), Santayana came to feel the need for a greater systematic rigor in the exposition of his views and for a purified

and nonpsychological mode of stating the fundamental distinctions on which his philosophy rested. In particular, he felt that in *The Life of Reason* he had not made clear enough that the "nature" described there as having been "drawn like a sponge, heavy and dripping from the waters of sentience" was the idea of nature, not nature itself. He now tried to correct this error by means of a set of ontological—that is, nonpsychological—distinctions between the different kinds of being that are the objects of different kinds of mental activity. Thus, imagination, for example, must be defined by reference to the essences or abstract characters that Santayana now recognized as having a distinct ontological status, rather than the other way around. In carrying out this revision of his earlier views, Santayana was in some measure aligning himself with similar antipsychologistic tendencies at work in the logical realism of Bertrand Russell, as well as in the phenomenology of Edmund Husserl, which he regarded as having a certain affinity to his own views.

Some commentators have felt that this shift from what they describe as Santayana's earlier naturalism to his later "Platonism" amounted to a fundamental change in his general philosophical perspective. Santayana's own statements, however, make it clear that the system presented in *Realms of Being* is to be understood as the ultimate philosophical basis of the naturalistic *Weltanschauung* sketched out in *The Life of Reason,* in which he had paid relatively little attention to technical philosophical issues. It must be admitted that the moral atmosphere of the two works differs, and that in the later one Santayana seems even more the detached spectator of the noncontemplative phases of the "life of reason" than he had before. But this is as much a personal as a philosophical matter, and there is no good reason for denying the fundamental unity of Santayana's thought during the two main periods of its development.

Aesthetics. Santayana's first important philosophical work was *The Sense of Beauty* (1896). In it he attempted to state a complete aesthetic theory, which he later developed further in *Reason in Art* (1905), Volume IV of *The Life of Reason.* In the earlier book, aesthetic theory is characterized as a psychological inquiry whose data are aesthetic judgments considered as "phenomena of mind and products of mental evolution"; the inquiry is to be distinguished both from the actual exercise of critical judgment and from the historical investigation of the evolution of the various art forms. Santayana argued that this inquiry must be carried out independently of metaphysical issues and the "interests of the moral consciousness," and that it must make clear the bases of aesthetic experience in human nature as conceived by natural science and in particular evolutionary biology. To this end, Santayana sketched out a theory of value according to which all preference is an essentially irrational expression of vital interest and the standard of value is the enjoyment or pleasure procurable through different courses of action. Morality is concerned with negative values, namely, the avoidance of pain and suffering, while aesthetic value is concerned with positive enjoyment and stands in the same relation to morality as play does to work.

The pleasure that is distinctively aesthetic, however,

must be further qualified as intrinsic (or immediate) and as "objectified," in the sense of being experienced as a quality of a thing and not as an affection of the organ which apprehends it. Santayana denied that it must have the disinterested character attributed to it by Kant and that it must be universally shared. He defined beauty as "pleasure objectified."

Medium, form, expressiveness. Santayana added to this definition of beauty a threefold distinction between the materials of a work of art, its form, and its expressiveness. Of these, the first two are intrinsic features of the work of art, which thus consists of sensuous elements that have varying degrees of aesthetic value by themselves, and a form or arrangement by means of which these elements are unified and which has its own distinctive value. This synthesis, which constitutes form, is "an activity of the mind." While Santayana throws out suggestions as to how the nature of our perceptual apparatus may determine *which* forms give pleasure, these suggestions are never developed, and there is a heavily mentalistic cast to his whole account of aesthetic experience. This is particularly true of his treatment of expression, which is the power of a work of art to suggest images and ideas that, by becoming associated with it, enhance its value. These associated values may be aesthetic, practical, or moral; or they may be intellectual, as they are in the case of those forms of art, for example, tragedy, which present the ugly as well as the beautiful, and whose value thereby consists in satisfying our desire to know life as a whole. In the end, however, while these distinctions of materials, form, and expression have the validity proper to their spheres, the experience of beauty remains, according to Santayana, unique and unanalyzable.

Function of art. In *Reason in Art* Santayana was concerned with the place of art, as one good among many, within the moral economy of the life of reason. He distinguished between the practical arts and the fine arts and explained the emergence of the latter from the former through the gradual growth of an appreciation of the intrinsic value of what originally had merely instrumental value. Applying this principle, Santayana described the development of music, poetry, and the plastic arts, and in each case attempted to relate the special features of the artistic medium to the mode of abstraction and selectivity that is peculiar to a given art form. He treated all works of art as more or less abstract symbolizations of the natural environment and interests of human beings, and as being animated by an internal "dialectic" of their own through which the moral and dramatic unities of our experience are indirectly expressed. There can be no absolute or universal principles for criticizing works of art, since our critical judgments are simply the corrections or modifications that our aesthetic preference undergoes in the wake of experience; and there is no a priori guarantee that these corrections must be convergent. The ultimate justification of art is simply that it adds greatly to human enjoyment, and thus to human happiness.

"The Life of Reason." Santayana intended *The Life of Reason; or the Phases of Human Progress* (1905–1906) as a naturalistic biography of the human mind, but as he himself pointed out, it was at least partially inspired by He-

gel's *Phenomenology of Mind.* What appealed to Santayana in that work and similar ones in the idealistic tradition was the idea of sympathetically espousing the changing perspectives—scientific, moral, religious, and aesthetic—by which the mind progressively defines its relationship to its natural milieu. By beginning with *Reason in Common Sense,* he hoped to avoid the fundamental error of the idealists, which was to lose all sense of the dependency of this evolution upon a nonmental nature and of its responsiveness to the strains and stresses of our animal being. For the fraudulent dialectical necessity that Hegel had imposed on human history, Santayana proposed to substitute an appraisal—in the broad sense, a moral appraisal—of the contribution made by each of these phases of human development to the ideal of a rational and happy life.

Reason and imagination. In *Reason in Common Sense,* the discovery of natural objects is described as the first and irreversible achievement of human reason operating upon the materials of sense experience. Knowledge of these objects is inevitably representative and indirect, and the relationship of thought to reality must be conceived as an ideal correspondence and not as a material appropriation. Coordinate with these "concretions in experience" are "concretions in discourse," or concepts which sustain among one another all manner of "dialectical" relationships; and the active elaboration of these is the generic activity of imagination. Imagination becomes understanding when, almost by accident, some of its structures prove to be faithful transcriptions of a sequence of natural events; but even when the understanding is most successful, there remain unassimilable traits of experience which, at best, have a tangential relation to the natural order. Toward the free creative activity of the imagination itself, Santayana maintained a dual attitude. It must not, he said, be allowed to impose itself as a literal rendering of what exists, as it all too often attempts to do. When it is allowed to do so, it can only produce a fantastic physics in which dramatic and moral unities are substituted for unities of fact and real process. In another sense, however, the life of reason is the life of the imagination, and its function of idealization and symbolic transformation yields the highest and purest enjoyments of the mental life. Even when the imagination becomes practical, as it does in science, it is the intrinsic aesthetic value of its creations, and not their ulterior practical use, which gives them a place within the life of reason. But at the same time that he praised the imagination, Santayana continually warned against the tendency to confer substantial reality upon the essences it elaborates and to assign to them a causal efficacy within the order of nature. The only power that Santayana was willing to attribute to consciousness itself was that of conferring meaning and ideal unity upon events, and it is in this sense that he described himself as being a materialist.

Religion. If Santayana's theory of the imagination finds its most natural application in his treatment of art, an area in which the claim to any literal validity is reduced to a minimum, the case of religion, which he considers in *Reason in Religion,* Vol. III of *The Life of Reason,* is somewhat different. Religion, Santayana said, is a poetic transformation of natural life in the interest of the moral ordering of that life, even though each religion is typically regarded by its followers as embodying a literal truth. Religion is myth, and it presents "an inverted image of things in which their moral effects are turned into their dramatic antecedents." Because it is myth, religion must not be judged by the inappropriate standard of literal truth, but on the basis of the imaginative richness and comprehensiveness of its reorganization of our moral experience. One's religion is in fact something like one's language or nationality—a native idiom of the moral life which may have its imperfections, but which is both difficult and unwise wholly to abandon. Mystical religions are those that effect vast simplifications of the moral life by excluding all but one element in the natural life, while fanatical religions are those that suppress, on the authority of their own unique truth, all forms of moral poetry other than their own. In Santayana's view, both are inimical to the true value of religion, which is the encouragement it gives us to live in the imagination. True religion stimulates both piety, which Santayana defined as "man's reverent attachment to the sources of his being and the steadying of his life by that attachment," and spirituality, which liberates us from the harsh realities of animal need and desire by interposing an ideal meaning—one that assigns to the goods of this world their proper and subordinate place.

What is paradoxical in Santayana's philosophy of religion is the fact that while he treated all religions as having, at best, a symbolic or expressive truth, he severely condemned the liberals and "modernists" who have attempted, while remaining within the church, to substitute for the literalistic dogmatism of the past a view of religion that in many respects resembles the one held by Santayana himself. It seems inconsistent to deny that a claim to literal truth is essential to religion and at the same time to require that those who surrender this claim must leave the church. This is perhaps a special case of a general paradox resulting from the fact that while Santayana declared "spirit" to be wholly inefficacious, it is an intrinsic feature of the life of reason that spirit should view itself as having efficient power. One may also speculate as to whether Santayana's distaste for views resembling his own, when they become more than the private insights of detached and passive observers and are applied to the task of modifying some institution such as a church, did not itself express a social attitude and a partisanship that cannot claim any special philosophical justification.

Social theory. Santayana's theory of society is stated in *Reason in Society*, Volume II of *The Life of Reason*, and also, in expanded form, in *Dominations and Powers* (1949), his last major work. In the main, social life is assigned a subordinate role within the life of reason. Its principal task and justification is the generation of, and care for, human beings, and it serves ideal ends only incidentally. Society originates in the reproductive instinct, and while this instinct lends itself readily to imaginative development, it finds its ultimate fruition in institutions (the family, the army, the state) that are predominantly practical in nature and, at best, capable of a retrospective idealization. It is, of course, possible for individuals to become associated with one another outside the disciplinary framework of these primary institutions, and when they do so freely, on the basis of a common allegiance to an ideal, they form what

Santayana called a "free," or "rational," society. Patriotism is the loyalty they feel to such societies; but the deepest loyalties of the life of reason are not to anything actual, but to the ideal presences of which, Santayana said, our human partners in the pursuit of the ideal, as well as we ourselves, are at best imperfect symbols. Thus it turns out that the true society—the only society that is a perfect instrument of the life of reason—is the society of the mind and of the essences it entertains.

If Santayana's theory of society expresses, as indeed it does, a profound lack of interest in the practical concerns by which any human society is principally animated, he was nevertheless not without his own strong preferences with regard to a certain ordering of society. A pervasive animus against democracy and liberalism runs through all his discussions of society and is perhaps most noticeable in *Dominations and Powers* (1949). Human society, Santayana argued, is necessarily aristocratic and hierarchical, and egalitarian democracy, which would put an end to the injustice that social inequality so often generates, succeeds only in destroying the interest of life by denying or attempting to suppress our inevitable human diversity. An authentic and "natural" aspiration to some good expresses itself in the form of an authoritative direction of the more passive members of a society and shapes their lives in the light of this aspiration's own moral vision. Accordingly, Santayana frequently tended to identify strong authoritarian government with the natural bent of a self-assertive vitality and uniformly treated liberalism as an incoherent and sterile principle of dissolution, roughly comparable in its inspiration and effect to the Protestant principle in the province of religion. Both liberalism and the Protestant principle are expressions of that romantic individualism which Santayana was willing to tolerate as a kind of playful self-deception of the "inner life," but which he abominated whenever it took itself seriously and became a principle of action directed toward correcting the "natural" order of things.

Morality. Strangely enough, it is in *Reason in Science,* Volume V of *The Life of Reason,* that Santayana's fullest exposition of his views on morality is to be found. In this work he distinguished between "rational" morality and the morality that is either "prerational" or "postrational." Rational morality is no longer the straightforward hedonism of *The Sense of Beauty,* for Santayana now recognized that there must be a principle of selective preference among possible enjoyments. But he still regarded our adoption of such an ideal standard as a matter of temperament and natural inclination; and even the attempt to achieve a comprehensive integration of diverse satisfactions, which is what distinguishes rational morality, is presented as just one possible attitude toward life. Rational morality and the moral philosophy associated with it, Santayana argued, are concerned with what is really good, and they require a highly developed capacity for sympathetic understanding and assessment of all competing goods; but in the end, what is really good can only be what genuinely expresses some vital bias of our natures. By contrast, prerational morality is the unreflective life of primary impulse, which cannot conceive the possibility of alternative goods nor support the discipline entailed by a principled organization of the moral life. Postrational morality, finally, is an essentially religious abandonment of the hope for a rational ordering of human life in favor of some otherworldly ideal. Its sole strength, as Santayana observed, lies in the remnant of natural assertiveness that survives in its condemnation of the works of the natural man and the desperate energy with which a single and exclusive regimen of life is proclaimed to be the sole means of salvation.

Science. Santayana's attitude toward science, as one phase of the life of reason, was an inconsistent mixture of hospitality and indifference. Convinced as he was that all causal efficacy belongs to physical nature, he was strongly inclined to accept the claim of science to exclusive authority in the determination of what is really true. Natural science is at once an extension of common sense and a uniquely successful application of "dialectics," that is, the logical elaboration of terms of thought, or "concretions in discourse," to the study of the physical world. The ideal of such a science would be a closed, mechanistic, and materialistic system, and Santayana believed that progress in the sciences of man, notably psychology, required the adoption of this ideal. But beyond this recognition of the authority of science, Santayana had no detailed interest in its findings and only a very limited belief in its power to contribute to those ideal values that are the true substance of the life of reason. It deals, after all, with only one of many possible worlds; and while the discipline of fact to which it subjects the mind is infinitely preferable to the projection upon the world of some moral fable of our own devising, the highest form of intellectual freedom is still to survey the field of ideal possibilities without any sense of an obligation to describe or a fear of misdescribing any actual state of affairs.

"Scepticism and Animal Faith." In *Scepticism and Animal Faith* (1923), Santayana undertook the extensive recasting of his whole system of thought; to which reference has been made above. The reformulation was to consist in the substitution of a set of ontological distinctions for the introspective psychology of his earlier writings. Properly speaking, this work is an introduction to, and a partial summary of, the main doctrines of *Realms of Being* (1927–1940). It begins with an attempt to radicalize, and thus to overcome, the idealistic skepticism concerning the existence of an external world that has been a central theme of Western philosophy since Descartes. The argument is that if we limit ourselves to what is immediately given (and therefore incapable of being doubted), not only our belief in an external world, but also our belief in the existence of the self, of other selves, and of a past and a future is undermined. All that remain are certain characters or essences that bear no relationship to things or events and cannot properly be said to "exist." Santayana's point is that a genuine skepticism, pushed to its logical extreme, is just as fatal to the "mind" of the idealists as it is to the matter they were prepared to abandon. In a positive sense, the upshot of such skepticism is to reveal essence as the primary and incontestable mode of being; but it is practically and psychologically impossible for human beings to recognize only essential being. "Animal faith" thus supervenes upon the intuition of essence and posits the existence of a world of things and events that transcends immediate intuition. In one sense this belief is quite baseless, since there cannot, in a strict sense, be proof that anything exists; but in another sense this belief is the beginning of wisdom. In this conception there is no great shift away from the view set forth in *The Life of Reason*. The chief difference, however, is that in *Scepticism and Animal Faith* the commitment to existence and to substance (which in the earlier work was presented retrospectively as the first great achievement in the history of consciousness) is first dramatically revoked and then reinstated by the individual mind. But with respect to the logical status and practical necessity of this belief, Santayana's views would not appear to have undergone any significant change.

"The Realms of Being." *The Realms of Being* is a detailed characterization of the four major modes of being or basic categories that emerge from the skeptical self-interrogation of consciousness. The modes of being consist of essence and matter, as noted above, and two derivative modes, truth and spirit.

Essence. The being of essence is first carefully distinguished from certain adventitious notions that have been associated with it in the history of Western philosophy. Among these are the views that attribute causal efficacy or some special moral or aesthetic status to essences as such, and also the views that envisage essence only in the context of some mental activity such as "abstraction" or "imagination." Properly conceived, the being of essence consists simply in the self-identity of its character. Since this intrinsic character involves no reference to any location in space or time, essences are universal and repeatable. They are infinite in number and yet collectively compose one absolute essence in "Pure Being," which is common to all essences. Essences are logically discrete and individual, and one essence can "imply" another only if it is first stipulated that the relationship is that of a whole to one of its parts and that no logical necessity governs the constitution of such wholes. Essences may be exemplified in the realm of matter, but they need not be; and even when they are, the things and events that are the bearers of these ideal characters have a quite different mode of being.

Matter. The "indispensable properties" of the material mode of being are spatial extension and temporal process. Matter exists contingently and is therefore unstable and evanescent; but it also maintains a dynamic continuity, through change and can in this sense be called "substance." It is external to and independent of consciousness; and it is ultimately unknowable, since we know it only through the essences it exemplifies—and these are radically incapable of representing the element of process and diffusion that is peculiar to the realm of matter. Organisms are part of that realm, and the psychological histories (as distinct from the pure consciousness) of human beings can be understood only by reference to the behavioral unity that Santayana calls the "psyche."

Truth. Originally, Santayana had intended to establish only three "Realms of Being," and in fact the Realm of Truth which he later added has obvious affinities with both essence and matter. Truth is the truth about matter, or what exists, and yet it is independent of existence both because "no fact can be a description of itself" and because even if nothing existed, it would still be true that nothing did exist or that just such and such things had existed in the past. Truth is "the sum of all the propositions," and as such it represents a certain selection from the infinite essences or character that things might have had. Truth is timeless and independent of all beliefs. There are no necessary truths, and even the propositions of mathematics are only contingently true since it is simply an accident if they correctly describe the material world.

Spirit. Spirit, as Santayana used the term, is simply pure transcendental consciousness, and as such it must be distinguished from its physical basis (the "psyche") and from particular mental events. The only criterion of the existence of spirit is internal; and it exists contingently. It is entirely passive in its relation to physical nature, and its sole function is pure intuition, which, Santayana says, is "the direct and obvious possession of the apparent without commitments of any sort about its truth, significance, or material existence." The unities of intuition are simply individual essences and are not the product of any mental machinery. By itself, intuition is not cognitive. Considered simply as a skein of meanings, the life of intuition may acquire a unity and a life and even a kind of freedom that lacks the power to intervene in the world but is nevertheless the highest and purest human good.

To some extent, *The Realms of Being* effects a clarification of Santayana's earlier views, although it may be doubted whether he was ever in much danger of being taken for an idealist. Unfortunately, the style of the later book is even more luxuriant than that of *The Life of Reason*, and Santayana's unwillingness to argue technical philosophical issues was still as strong as ever. If what he hoped to present in *Realms of Being* was, as he says, a language in which the great distinctions to which we all have recourse would be clearly marked out, his success must be judged to be only very partial. All doctrines of transcendental subjectivity, including Santayana's, engender immense difficulties which cannot be resolved unless the philosopher is more inclined to meet criticism on some ground other than the assumed truth of his own views. In *Realms of Being*, there are very few signs, of such a disposition on Santayana's part.

Critical works. Santayana was not just a philosopher in his own right but also a critic, both philosophical and aesthetic. Several of his books, among them *Interpretations of Poetry and Religion* (1900), *Three Philosophical Poets* (1910), *Winds of Doctrine* (1913), *Character and Opinion in the United States* (1920), *Platonism and the Spiritual Life* (1927), and *Obiter Scripta* (1936), are made up of critical studies of systems of thought as diverse as the pragmatism of William James and the atomism of Lucretius; and in many ways, Santayana was at his best as a critic. In spite of the severity of his judgments and his tendency to use both philosophers and imaginative writers as stalking horses for his own philosophical purposes, he seldom failed to make some telling observation or incisive criticism that had a validity independent of his own special point of view. At the same time, it must be noted that in

his critical essays he too often affected an Olympian manner which only partially concealed the strongly personal character of his tastes and distastes both for individuals and ideas.

Works by Santayana

MAJOR PHILOSOPHICAL WORKS

The Sense of Beauty. New York, 1896.
The Life of Reason; or The Phases of Human Progress, 5 vols. New York, 1905–1906; one-volume ed., New York, 1954.
Scepticism and Animal Faith. New York, 1923.
Realms of Being, 4 vols. New York, 1927–1940; 1 vol. ed., 1941.
"Three Proofs of Realism," in *Essays in Critical Realism.* New York, 1941.
Dominations and Powers. New York, 1949.

CRITICAL WRITINGS

Interpretations of Poetry and Religion. New York, 1900.
Three Philosophical Poets. Cambridge, Mass., 1910.
Winds of Doctrine. New York, 1913.
Egotism in German Philosophy. New York, 1915.
Character and Opinion in the United States. New York, 1920.
Platonism and the Spiritual Life. New York, 1927.
Some Turns of Thought in Modern Philosophy. New York, 1933.
Obiter Scripta, J. Buchler and B. Schwartz, eds. New York, 1936.
The Idea of Christ in the Gospels. New York, 1946.

OTHER WORKS

Persons and Places, 3 vols. New York, 1944–1953. Autobiography.
The Letters of George Santayana, Daniel Cory, ed. New York, 1955.
The Last Puritan. New York, 1936. Santayana's only novel, which is also a "memoir" of considerable interest.

Works on Santayana

Duron, Jacques, *La Pensée de George Santayana.* Paris, 1950. A massive and detailed study of Santayana's whole philosophy.
Howgate, George W., *George Santayana.* Philadelphia, 1938. A less technical study of Santayana, mainly as a critic and aesthetician.
Munitz, Milton, *The Moral Philosophy of Santayana.* New York, 1939.
Schilpp, P. A., ed., *The Philosophy of George Santayana.* Vol. II in the Library of Living Philosophers. Evanston and Chicago, Ill., 1940. A collection of critical essays by a group of philosophers, among them Bertrand Russell, with an autobiographical statement by Santayana, a detailed reply to his critics, and a detailed bibliography. The most useful single work on Santayana's philosophy.
Singer, Irving, *Santayana's Aesthetics.* Cambridge, Mass., 1957.

FREDERICK A. OLAFSON

SARTRE, JEAN-PAUL, French existentialist, was born in Paris in 1905 and studied at the École Normale Supérieure from 1924 to 1928. After passing his agrégation in 1929 he taught philosophy in a number of *lycées,* both in Paris and elsewhere. From 1933 to 1935, he was a research student at the Institut Français in Berlin and at the University of Freiburg. From 1936 on he published a philosophical novel, *La Nausée* (1938), and a collection of stories, *Le Mur* (1939; *The Wall*), as well as a number of philosophical studies. At the outbreak of war in 1939, he was called up by the French Army and in 1940 was captured by the Germans. Released after the armistice, he returned to Paris, where he continued to teach philosophy until 1944. During these years he completed *L'Être et le néant* (1943; *Being and Nothingness*), his major philosophical work. He was also active in the resistance, and at the end of the war he emerged as the dominant figure in the existentialist movement. During the early postwar years he wrote a number of novels and plays which made him world-famous. As one of the founders (with Simone de Beauvoir and Maurice Merleau-Ponty) of *Les Temps modernes,* a review devoted to the discussion of political and literary questions from a generally existentialist point of view, he took an active part in the ideological controversies of the time. In 1951 he unsuccessfully attempted to found a new political movement that was to be radically to the left but noncommunist. Sartre's political activities, which provided the occasion for acrimonious disputes with his friends Albert Camus and Maurice Merleau-Ponty, have led him into periods of cooperation with the French Communist party, of which, however, he has often been highly critical. His most recent philosophical work, *Critique de la raison dialectique* ("Critique of Dialectical Reason"; 1960) of which only Volume I has appeared, is a restatement of Marxism that is intended to show its underlying harmony with existentialism.

Philosophical orientation. Sartre's philosophical culture appears to have been formed almost entirely within the tradition of Continental rationalism and idealism—that is, the line of thinkers that leads from Descartes to Kant and then from Hegel to the twentieth-century phenomenology of Husserl and Heidegger. Allusions to philosophers outside this tradition are rare in Sartre's writings, and generally he seems not to regard empiricism or positivism—and certainly not materialism—as serious philosophical alternatives. Although a great deal of Sartre's work has been criticism, often extremely violent, of the various forms of dualism and idealism that are peculiar to the Cartesian tradition, it has been, in a profound sense, internal criticism, and his leading ideas, almost without exception, bear the mark of their derivation from one or another of the philosophers he has attacked. At different stages in his career, his thought has seemed to be most strongly influenced first by Husserl, then by Heidegger and Hegel, and finally, during the past decade, by a rather highly alembicated Marx. This is not to deny that Sartre is in many respects an original thinker but, rather, to define the tradition within which his innovations find their place. He has also, of course, drawn extensively on extraphilosophical disciplines like psychology and, to some extent, sociology, but his way of using their results mainly as supporting evidence for conclusions already reached by independent dialectical analysis strongly suggests that in his view the fundamental truths about man and his relation to the world are still the province of a kind of philosophical inquiry that owes very little to the special sciences. As for the physical sciences and mathematics, these find only passing and perfunctory mention in his writings and have clearly had no influence on his thought. By contrast, his very wide literary culture has exerted a constant and powerful influence on his philosophy, and in a sense it can be said that his whole philosophy is an energetic reaffirmation of the primacy of the world of human experience to which literature and art are also addressed.

Central theme. Despite the great diversity of his writings, which range from abstruse ontological dialectic to political journalism and film scenarios, the central theme that runs through all Sartre's work is his passionate interest in human beings. Sometimes he has expressed his sense of the primacy of human existence (conceived as a consciously sustained relationship to oneself, to other human beings, and to the world at large) in a rather exaggerated way—as, for example, when he has a character in the play *Le Diable et le bon Dieu* declare that "only human beings really exist." Yet there can be no doubt of the profoundly moral and, in an authentic sense, humanistic character of his philosophy. While Sartre's deepest interest is in individual human beings, his effort to understand them, to form a general concept of human being, has nevertheless been heavily dependent on a number of other such conceptions, among them the Christian, the Cartesian, and the Hegelian theories of man. All of these Sartre for one reason or another rejects, but he does not regard them as just unfortunate philosophical mistakes. Instead, they express in his view an aspiration of human beings that runs so deep as to be virtually definitive of what it is to be a human being: the aspiration to found one's own individual being in a rational necessity of some sort. Sartre's whole philosophy can be seen as an attempt to describe a mode of being—human being—whose essence is just this aspiration, which he thinks is necessarily doomed to failure. This combination of a rejection of all forms of rationalism, theistic and otherwise, with a recognition of the permanent validity of the demand they express may fairly be regarded as the most characteristic feature of Sartre's thought. It is also the key to his moral philosophy, the fundamental imperative of which is to recognize and accept this unresolvable contradiction that defines human nature.

Stages of development. Although Sartre has attempted, often with great success, to communicate this conception of man through his novels and plays and his political and literary criticism, it is in his philosophical writings that the most detailed exposition and defense of it are to be found. These writings can be conveniently divided into three main groups that roughly coincide with successive periods in Sartre's intellectual development. The first group comprises his contributions to phenomenological psychology, beginning with "La Transcendance de l'égo" (1936) and including *L'Imaginaire* (1940) and *Esquisse d'une théorie des émotions* (1939). The principal work of the second period, in which Sartre emerges as a full-fledged ontologist of human existence, is *L'Être et le néant* (1943); however, with it should be associated *L'Existentialisme est un humanisme* (1946), his somewhat unsuccessful attempt at a simplified statement of the central doctrines of *L'Être et le néant,* as well as a number of critical studies, such as *Baudelaire* (1947), *Réflexions sur la question juive* (1946), and *Saint Genet: comédien et martyre* (1952), in which Sartre's ontological categories are applied to the analysis of human personality. It should be emphasized that there is no sharp break between this period and the earlier one and that many of the ideas that Sartre develops fully in *L'Être et le néant* had begun to emerge in his phenomenological studies. By contrast, the work of his most recent period, in which he has been attempting an extensive restatement of

Marxism that would do justice to the essential insights of his own form of existentialism, seems to involve a much more radical recasting of his whole mode of thought. How extensive this revision will prove to be is hard to judge until the *Critique de la raison dialectique* has been completed.

PSYCHOLOGY

In the three essays that belong to his first period, Sartre is concerned to describe a particular structure of consciousness, very much in the Husserlian manner, without the aid of any master concept of human existence. It is clear, however, that these descriptions are intended as contributions to the working out of such a concept and that Sartre already has a rather clear idea of what its general contours will be. It is obvious, too, that although Sartre is using a descriptive phenomenological method that he learned from Husserl, the results it produces in his hands take him steadily away from Husserl toward a position that has a greater affinity with that of Heidegger.

The self. In "La Transcendance de l'égo," Sartre's first philosophical publication, the divergence from Husserl's views was already abundantly clear. Sartre here argued that Husserl had failed to push his phenomenological reduction far enough; that he had not really succeeded in his aim of "bracketing-off" the world from the sphere of pure consciousness; and that by identifying pure transcendental consciousness with the self, he had produced an inconsistent amalgam of radically disparate elements. According to Sartre, the self, unlike pure consciousness, does not disclose itself exhaustively to immediate intuition and for precisely this reason belongs among the objects that transcend consciousness—that is, in the world. Since the world is constituted by the intentional acts of pure consciousness, the self must also be treated as the result of a synthetic act of organization of this kind and not as itself the agency by which these syntheses are made.

What is not altogether clear in this essay is how radical a revision of Husserl's whole position Sartre felt himself committed to by his own conclusions. It is significant that even at this early, prepolitical stage in his philosophical career, Sartre felt it necessary to answer the Marxist charge that phenomenology is a kind of crypto-idealism that makes man a spectator instead of a deeply committed agent in the historical process. If the self forms part of the world, as Sartre claims to have shown, then it cannot be isolated from history either, and the Marxist charge falls to the ground. But whether the "bracketing-off" operation, even when it is carried out as rigorously as Sartre would wish, is still doomed to break down before the stubbornly unconceptualizable fact of existence Sartre did not make clear.

The emotions. In his essay on the emotions, Sartre presents both Husserl and Heidegger, without any emphasis on their divergencies, as providing the necessary conceptual framework within which psychological phenomena can be adequately understood. Experience, according to the phenomenological view, is not just an aggregate of heterogeneous items of mental content but a structured whole whose two poles are pure consciousness,

as a constitutive, meaning-conferring activity, and the world, conceived as the transcendent correlate of these intentional acts of consciousness. Sartre argues that emotion can be understood only if it is set in the context of this total "human reality." It must, accordingly, be treated as a spontaneous activity of consciousness and not as something that is passively suffered or undergone. Emotion is in fact not a physiological phenomenon but a certain total mode of relating oneself to the world; its peculiar strategy is that of a "magical transformation" of given situations that bypasses the necessity for dealing with them by rational, step-by-step methods. Thus, sadness makes the world appear sad so that it offers no opening to our efforts to change it, and in this way it justifies our passivity by making purposeful effort seem pointless. This self-imposed passivity Sartre calls a "degradation of consciousness," a concept which is a clear forerunner of the "bad faith" that figures so largely in his later work.

This analysis also poses a problem to which, in one form or another, Sartre has felt obliged to return again and again: How can emotion (or any other mental function) be interpreted as a spontaneous and purposive activity without attributing an intolerably sophisticated kind of self-consciousness to those who have the emotion? Sartre's way of meeting this difficulty is to set up an intermediate kind of self-awareness between explicit or reflective consciousness of self (as when I am writing and think to myself, "I am writing") and events of which we are completely unconscious (for example, the circulation of the blood). This intermediary is exemplified by the awareness that I have of what I am doing—my intention—while I am doing it but not thinking about what I am doing. Sartre calls it a "nonpositional" consciousness and argues that strategies of action, such as those which he takes to be characteristic of the emotions, can be attributed to it without any of the incongruities that would result if explicit or verbal self-awareness were required.

The imagination. *L'Imaginaire* is by far the most ambitious of Sartre's studies in phenomenological psychology, and it also makes a much more direct approach to his later ontological themes than the others do. Once again, the point of departure is an alleged misconception of a psychological phenomenon—in this instance, the imagination—that is due to a positivistic refusal to appreciate the importance of the structural organization of our experience. As a result, perception and imagination are confused with one another, and both are conceived as the having of picturelike simulacra of objects before the mind, the only difference between them being caused by superior vivacity, immediacy, and so forth of our perceptions. Against this view, Sartre insists that imagination is an activity of consciousness—an "imaging consciousness"—and that the object of this intentional activity is not some discrete item of psychic content but the very person or thing itself of which we are said to "have an image." Imagination is, in short, an alternative mode of consciousness, addressed to the same objects as perceptual consciousness but—and this is the crucial point in Sartre's theory—to these objects *as they are not,* at least at the time of imagining them. Counterposed to the world, human consciousness sets up, through imagination, alternative "unreal" states of affairs, and the measure of their unreality and of the reality of perceptual objects is the fact that although the latter are never exhaustively given to intuition, imaginal objects are exhausted by our awareness of them. Again, Sartre argues that the self-awareness involved is of the nonpositional kind, and once again, he insists that even when the appearance of passivity in relation to our imaginal experiences seems most undeniable (as, for example, in the case of hallucinations and psychosis), this can be shown to be the work of a spontaneous activity of consciousness that, as it were, imprisons itself. Finally, in answering the question whether imagination is merely a mental function that contingently characterizes human beings but which they might well be without, Sartre explictly identifies imagination with the reality-negating function which he says is essential to human consciousness. Consciousness through imagination "constitutes, isolates, and negates" the world; it can do this only because it is itself nonbeing. Here Sartre initiates his characterization of the ontological status of consciousness that is, he thinks, presupposed by all the descriptions he has given of its distinct functions and that was to be fully worked out in the second main period in his philosophical career.

ONTOLOGY

There can be no doubt that *L'Être et le néant* owes more to the thought of Martin Heidegger than to any other single philosopher. In many respects Sartre's account of "the human reality" is no more than an amplified restatement of the doctrines in Heidegger's *Sein und Zeit*. There are, however, major differences. Heidegger, unlike Sartre, has never been interested in the detailed analysis of the structures of consciousness. Instead, he has described the ontic counterparts of these intentional structures, and in this way he has tried to convey the special character of human being by showing what its "world" is like. In Sartre's view, such a description of the human world must be supplemented by an account of the structure of the consciousness that "founds" this world; he repeatedly criticizes Heidegger for having, in effect, suppressed consciousness. Again, Heidegger has professed himself to be uninterested in any "humanistic" interpretation of his doctrines that would seek to draw ethical consequences from them. By contrast, Sartre is unequivocally committed to the use of his ontological apparatus for the purpose of a general clarification of the human predicament. Finally, Sartre's conclusions with respect to the possibility of a general ontology that would set forth a concept of being as such from which the concepts of conscious and nonconscious being could then be derived seem to be entirely negative. Heidegger, on the other hand, has never declared such a project to be impossible, and in his later writings he has, if anything, given even greater weight to the general concept of being.

The subtitle of *L'Être et le néant* is "Essai d'ontologie phénoménologique." A long tradition of usage that contrasts being—the subject of ontology—with appearance—the subject of phenomenology—might seem to make this collocation of terms highly incongruous. Sartre explains that his kind of ontology, like phenomenology, is purely de-scriptive in character and does not undertake to explain human experience by reference to extraphenomenal realities in the manner of Descartes or Kant. Such explanations are, he says, the work of metaphysics, not of ontology; ontology, as conceived by Sartre, seems to differ from the more familiar kind of phenomenology only by virtue of the superior generality of the concepts it employs— that is, the concepts of being and nonbeing.

Being and appearing. In the introduction to *L'Être et le néant*, entitled "A la Recherche de l'être," Sartre first takes up the claim of contemporary phenomenalism to have overcome the traditional duality of appearance and reality by contructing both the "physical" and the "mental" out of series of "appearances" that are themselves neutral with respect to this distinction. He concludes that such a treatment of the being of objects is entirely justified insofar as it denies that there is any screen of sensations or mental contents behind which reality lurks. Being itself appears. On the other hand, Sartre insists, against the idealists, that being is completely independent of the fact of its appearing and is "transcendent" in the sense that it can never be exhausted by any finite set of its appearances. A question thus arises as to the nature—as Sartre says, the "being"—of this appearing that supervenes upon being and of the relationship between the being of things and the being of their appearing. This is the general problem of the book as a whole.

In order to set up his inquiry in this way, Sartre has to break sharply with Husserl on several points. Most important, in order to establish the transphenomenality of objects, by which is meant their irreducibility to appearances, he drastically reinterprets the Husserlian notion of intentionality. For Husserl intentionality was an internal structure of mental states by virtue of which they were directed toward objects, but it was by no means necessary that these objects should be independent of consciousness. Sartre adds the stipulation that they must be so independent. Otherwise, he argues, objects would owe their being to consciousness, and this he declares to be impossible. His proof is that since objects, whatever their status, are never exhaustively given to an instantaneous intuition, a "constitutive consciousness," as conceived by Husserl, could reproduce this central feature of our consciousness of objects only by intending the infinite series of appearances that compose the object and at the same time not intending all those that are not presently given. This it manifestly cannot do, and thus, Sartre concludes, the transcendence of objects is established.

Being-for-itself and being-in-itself. Just as Sartre presents the transphenomenality of objects as the background against which they appear, he also argues that the being of consciousness is similarly transphenomenal in the sense of not being dependent on its appearing to itself in explicit, reflective self-awareness. Instead, this reflective self-consciousness is said to presuppose the antecedent existence of a prereflective consciousness in much the same way as consciousness of objects is held by Sartre to presuppose their transphenomenal status. The chief characteristic of this being of consciousness—or "being-for-itself," as Sartre calls it—is its activity. It is incapable of being acted on from without, and it consists in and is exhausted by its own intentional, meaning-conferring acts. By contrast, the being of things—"being-in-itself"—is characterized in terms of a complete incapacity for any relationship to itself; it is, in Sartre's highly metaphorical language, "opaque," and it "coincides exactly with itself." All that can strictly be said of it is that it is. In this way, by establishing these two radically distinct types of being and by rejecting both the idealistic and the realistic accounts of their rapport, Sartre has put himself under an obligation to provide a more satisfactory account of the relationship between being-in-itself and being-for-itself and of the relationship of both to the generic concept of being. The last question is not answered until the structures of conscious being have been examined in very great detail, which takes up the major portion of the book.

Conscious being. Sartre's principal clue in his attempt to describe conscious being is the human ability to ask questions and receive negative answers. For him negation is not, of course, just a logical function of judgment. Negative judgments themselves are said to require, as a condition of their being possible at all, an extralogical or ontic counterpart which is nonbeing, and Sartre, accordingly, has to ask what the origin of this nonbeing is. He rejects the Hegelian view that being and nonbeing are logically interdependent in favor of the Heideggerian notion of nonbeing as a kind of circumambient medium in which being is contingently suspended. At the same time, however, he criticizes Heidegger for having failed to show how nonbeing can appear in particularized or local form within the world, and he argues that this is possible only if there is a being that is, or generates its own, nothingness. This being turns out to be human consciousness, whose distinguishing feature is thus to constitute itself by contrast with or as other than its physical milieu, its body, its past, and, indeed, everything whatsoever. By its self-detaching activity, it creates, as it were, a hole in being-in-itself, and the latter, as the horizon that surrounds this focus of negation, becomes a "world." Because consciousness projects being-in-itself against a backdrop of nonbeing, it inescapably apprehends actuality in the context of possibility—that is, of the alternative possibilities of development of which the actual is susceptible. It also apprehends itself as a bridge between the actual and the possible and as having to determine which of these possibilities is to be realized. Finally, human consciousness is free because it is forced to think of itself as—and thus is—other than the world and unincorporable into any causal sequences it may discern within the world. The feeling of anguish, Sartre says, is our experience of this freedom.

The problem of freedom. In the face of this freedom, human beings can adopt either of two fundamentally different attitudes. They can attempt to conceal their freedom from themselves by a variety of devices, the most typical of which is belief in some form of psychological determinism. All of these efforts are doomed to failure, Sartre argues, because human beings can try to conceal their freedom only to the extent that they recognize it. The attempt succeeds only in producing a paradoxical internal duality of consciousness in which consciousness thinks of itself as a thing at the same time that it gives covert recognition to its freedom. This state, which has to be carefully

distinguished both from lying to others and from the Freudian conception of a manipulation of consciousness by subconscious forces, is called "bad faith." Its antithesis is an acceptance of one's own freedom and a recognition that human beings are the absolute origin of, and are solely responsible for, their own acts. On the contrast between these two life-attitudes is based the whole of Sartre's ethic. But while Sartre severely condemns all attempts by human consciousness to objectify itself and put itself on a level with things, he basically defines human being as precisely this self-contradictory effort to achieve the status of a thing while remaining a consciousness that contemplates itself as a thing. Indeed, he goes so far as to define value as this impossible combination of being-for-itself and being-in-itself, and in this impossibility he sees the ultimate reason for the hopeless character of the human enterprise (which he also describes as the attempt to make oneself God). This effort must fail, for while human beings are absolutely responsible for their choices, their existence is not the result of a choice. It is simply a fact, and its uneliminable contingency makes it impossible for human beings to be ontologically self-sufficient in the way that a God must be.

Time. Large sections of *L'Être et le néant* are devoted to discussions of temporality as a structure of conscious being and to analysis of the relationship of one consciousness to another. In his treatment of time, Sartre relies heavily on Heidegger's works and adopts his view of past, present, and future as internal structures of conscious being and thus as so many different ways in which consciousness is what it is not and is not what it is. We are what we were in the past but in the mode of not being it any longer, and we are our future in the mode of not yet being it. Similarly, in the present, consciousness is inescapably tied to the world and to its situation within the world, but once again, it is tied in such a way as to reinforce the distinction between it and the world. For Sartre, temporality in all its dimensions is an activity of consciousness by which the latter negates and transcends itself. There is no place in Sartre's philosophy for time conceived as one dimension of a spatio-temporal continuum which itself exists tenselessly.

Other minds. In his analyses of the reciprocal relationships of consciousnesses, Sartre very clearly goes beyond Heidegger. He argues, first, that it cannot be proved by analogical arguments or otherwise that there are other minds (and to this extent, he thinks, solipsism expresses a truth); rather, it is the case that my own apprehension of my existence is so structured that it presupposes the existence of other conscious beings. This is particularly clear in the case of feelings of shame, which presuppose that my body is accessible to another observer. In general, my experience of myself is inseparable from this public dimension of my existence. In Husserl, Sartre finds this fact recognized only in the form of a logical requirement that has to be met if there is to be an intersubjectively shareable world, not in a way that accounts for our actual encounters with others. Only Heidegger is said to have grasped the relationship of consciousnesses in a way that makes it not just an internal requirement of our conceptual system but a feature of our being that is presupposed by that system. Sartre, however, feels that Heidegger's very general account of *Mitsein* ("being-together") has to be supplemented by an analysis of the experience in which I apprehend myself as I am perceived by another consciousness—that is, as an object, reified and deprived of the transcendence that is central to my own sense of my being. This is the experience of being looked at by someone else. In relation to this intrusive "other," I can adopt either of two courses of action. I can try to dominate it and suppress its transcendence by which my own is threatened, or I can try to make myself into an object to be dominated by the liberty of the other person. In either case, I am destined to fail because I must recognize my liberty (or that of the other) in order to suppress it. What is impossible in either option is a moral consensus that is more than an accidental convergence of independent individual projects.

Action, liberty, and choice. The last section of *L'Être et le néant* deals with human action and human liberty, and it takes the form of an analysis of the relationship between human consciousness and the milieu or situation in which consciousness finds itself. The principal thesis is that this situation, conceived as the intentional object of conscious activity, cannot determine the direction that will be taken or the direction that ought to be taken by the human activity of which it is the premise. Moral autonomy is thus presented as equally inconsistent both with causal determinism and with any kind of natural moral law. It is conscious human being that first isolates particular situations so that they are experienced as incomplete and as calling for complementation through human action; it is only by that same conscious existence that these situations can be assigned the goals toward which they are to develop. It follows that not only the means used to reach a given goal but the goal itself and any general moral principles that may have dictated its selection must be thought of as choices that are subject to no causal influences and no rational controls at all. Such choices are, in the last analysis, "unjustifiable" because the reasoning that is commonly thought of as providing independent guidance for choice is itself an expression of that choice. Such a choice is not, however, to be conceived as a single mental episode; rather, it is human action itself considered as doing one thing rather than another from among the multiple possibilities with which human consciousness endows each actual situation. Taken together, these choices form a system within which particular choices are derivative specifications of what Sartre calls a "total choice of oneself" although they are not deducible from the latter, and even the most extreme passivity or acquiescence is, at bottom, an autonomous choice of this total kind. What I do not choose is the necessity for choosing itself or the situation in which I am obliged to choose. In another sense, however, Sartre argues that by acting in that situation and by conferring on it the meaning it is to have for me, I may be said to accept it and to make myself responsible for it. The individual human person is in fact a choice, and by himself he defines a complete moral universe.

Our choices or "projects" are not necessarily the objects of a reflective self-awareness. Normally, our understanding of our own actions will be in the mode of the nonpositional consciousness previously described. A properly conceived psychoanalytic method would therefore address itself to the task of interpreting the system of choices that our actions express and would reject all reductions of these choices to occult non-choicelike states of the unconscious. Existential psychoanalysis, as conceived by Sartre, must treat empirical needs and desires as simply symbolizations of the total choices by which our relation to being is defined; the meanings it disengages from human behavior must always be treated as internal to the consciousness of the person whose behavior it is, even if only in the mode of "bad faith." In these interpretations, the analyst would be guided, Sartre thinks, by the expressive values of certain qualities in our experience through which the nature of our relationship to being is conveyed. The main example that is offered of this expressive function of qualities is that of "sliminess," whose "metaphysical coefficient" Sartre rather extravagantly declares to be a fear that being-in-itself will absorb being-for-itself.

The general conclusion that Sartre reaches with respect to the relationship between these two kinds of being is that a synthesis of the two that would compose a total being *causa sui* is impossible and that the general concept of being is therefore in a permanent state of disintegration. What is lacking is the kind of mutual entailment by which being-in-itself would presuppose being-for-itself and vice versa, rather in the way that one consciousness, according to Sartre, presupposes the existence of others. But while being-for-itself does presuppose being-in-itself, the latter remains radically independent. The project of constituting an ontologically self-sufficient being is in fact peculiar to being-for-itself, which is thus one of the terms in this relationship between the two kinds of being and the relation itself. It is also a hopeless undertaking because a genuine logical synthesis is precluded by the negating action of human consciousness which perpetually creates anew the distinctions such a synthesis is intended to overcome.

SOCIAL PHILOSOPHY

At the end of *L'Être et le néant*, Sartre promised that it would be followed by a full-scale treatment of the ethical implications of the doctrine of human reality expounded in it. This book has never appeared, and in the light of Sartre's current preoccupations it seems unlikely that it ever will. In recent years, he has turned more and more toward a kind of dialectical sociology that seems very remote from the individualism that was characteristic of his earlier moral theory. He now criticizes severely his own lack of understanding of the way the moral autonomy of the individual is qualified by the fact that he lives in an exploitative society. True moral freedom is now projected into a future that will not be realized until the dialectic of human antagonism has run its course, and of this future Sartre says we can know nothing. Nevertheless, while Sartre is clearly dissatisfied with the virtually total neglect, in his earlier work, of the social aspect of morality, his present description of existentialism as an "enclave within Marxism" substantially exaggerates the degree to which his fundamental position has changed. He is still not a materialist or a determinist in the orthodox Marxist manner, and he is still strongly critical of the refusal by contemporary Marxists to deal with individual personality except in the most crudely schematic way. It is true that he now holds that a material fact—scarcity—is the motor that sets the dialectic of human social relationships going, but he would presumably still want to say that this "natural" fact assumes its human significance only within the context of a conscious project of some sort. Furthermore, Sartre has always recognized that human beings in some sense stand in a passive relation to the products of their own spontaneity, and what he has done in his recent work is simply to give a new emphasis to this kind of passivity which he now conceives in relation to the dual fact of natural scarcity and the resulting dialectic of human antagonism. He still argues that human beings have to be understood by methods that are entirely different from those used in the study of nature, and he still regards scientific inquiry as assuming its full significance only within the context of a dialectical comprehension of man. A final judgment on the degree to which Sartre has really modified his views in the direction of Marxism and not just expanded them to take account of aspects of human life to which Marxist criticism had forcibly drawn his attention must, of course, await the completion of *Critique de la raison dialectique.*

Any appraisal of Sartre's achievement as a philosopher must reckon with the fact that even in his most technical philosophical works he is never really a pure philosopher in the sense of one who is primarily concerned to secure the theoretical underpinnings of some system of ideas. His argumentation is often both skimpy and lacking in rigor; he seems to be unaware of, or unconcerned by, the grossly metaphorical character of many of his leading ideas; and he has allowed free rein to the special bias of his sensibility in a way that is indefensible in abstruse theoretical work. At the same time, his work shows many of the defects that are typical of the grand tradition of philosophical system builders—in particular, an almost total lack of any capacity for critical detachment in relation to his own philosophical theses. His ideas may quite literally be said to define reality for him in a way and to a degree that makes it impossible for him to submit them to any kind of empirical or pragmatic test by which their merits might be compared with those of other philosophical points of view. This is the more unfortunate since it often seems that what Sartre is trying to do, while continuing to use for his own purposes the philosophical vocabulary of rationalism and idealism, is to work out ideas that at many points have clear affinities with tendencies in contemporary pragmatism and sometimes even in analytical philosophy. In any case, after all these criticisms have been registered, the extraordinary fecundity and energy of Sartre's mind must be recognized. Again and again, when he seems most deeply involved in some hopelessly sterile logomachy, he will offer an insight that makes the tortuous complications of his terminology seem a small price to pay in return. In this respect he is like Hegel, whom, among the great philosophers, he may most resemble. Sartre himself will probably not be ranked as a "great philosopher" in the

histories of the future, but he is without doubt an immensely stimulating and acute critical mind.

Works by Sartre

PHILOSOPHICAL

"La Transcendance de l'égo." *Recherches philosophiques,* Vol. 6 (1936), 65–123. Translated by Forrest Williams and Robert Kirkpatrick as *The Transcendence of the Ego.* New York, 1937.

Esquisse d'une théorie des émotions. Paris, 1939. Translated by Bernard Frechtman as *The Emotions: Outline of a Theory.* New York, 1948. Translated by Philip Mairet as *Sketch for a Theory of the Emotions.* London, 1962.

L'Imaginaire: Psychologie phénoménologique de l'imagination. Paris, 1940. Translated by Bernard Frechtman as *The Psychology of Imagination.* New York, 1948.

L'Être et le néant: Essai d'ontologie phénoménologique. Paris, 1943. Translated by Hazel E. Barnes as *Being and Nothingness.* New York, 1956.

L'Existentialisme est un humanisme. Paris, 1946. Translated by Philip Mairet as *Existentialism and Humanism.* London, 1948.

Situations I & III. Paris, 1947, 1949. Two volumes of philosophical and literary essays. The two most important pieces are "La Liberté cartésienne" and "Matérialisme et révolution," both of which have been translated by Annette Michelson in *Literary and Philosophical Essays.* New York, 1955.

Questions de méthode and *Critique de la raison dialectique,* Vol. I. Paris, 1960. Translated by Hazel E. Barnes as *The Problem of Method.* London, 1964.

LITERARY WORK

La Nausée. Paris, 1938. Translated by Lloyd Alexander as *Nausea.* New York, 1949.

Réflexions sur la question juive. Paris, 1946. Translated by George J. Becker as *Anti-Semite and Jew.* New York, 1948.

Baudelaire. Paris, 1947. Translated by Martin Turnell under the same title. Norfolk, Conn., 1950.

Huis clos and *Les Mouches,* in *Théâtre,* Vol. I. Paris, 1947. Translated by Stuart Gilbert as *No Exit* and *The Flies,* in *Two Plays.* New York, 1947.

Le Diable et le Bon Dieu. Paris, 1952. Translated by Kitty Black as *Lucifer and the Lord.* London, 1952.

Saint Genet: Comédien et martyre. Paris, 1952. Translated by Bernard Frechtman as *Saint Genet: Actor and Martyr.* New York, 1963.

Works on Sartre

Ayer, A. J., "Novelist-Philosophers: J. P. Sartre." *Horizon,* Vol. 12 (1945), 12–26, 101–110. Highly critical estimate by contemporary analytical philosopher.

Desan, Wilfred, *The Tragic Finale.* Cambridge, Mass., 1954. Careful explication of some central themes of Sartre's ontology.

Jeanson, Francis, *Le Problème morale et la pensée de Sartre.* Paris, 1947. Preface by Sartre. Probably the best treatment of the ethical aspect of Sartre's philosophy.

Murdoch, Iris, *Sartre: Romantic Rationalist.* New Haven, 1953. Balanced appreciation of Sartre as a philosopher and a man of letters.

Spiegelberg, Herbert, "The Phenomenology of Jean Paul Sartre," in *The Phenomenological Movement,* 2 vols. The Hague, 1960. Vol. II, Ch. 10. A detailed bibliography.

Warnock, Mary, *The Philosophy of Sartre.* London, 1965. An analytical philosopher's view of Sartre.

FREDERICK A. OLAFSON

SATISFIABILITY. See SYSTEMS, FORMAL, AND MODELS OF FORMAL SYSTEMS.

SAVIGNY, FRIEDRICH KARL VON (1779–1861), the founder of historical jurisprudence. Savigny was born in Frankfurt, Germany, into a family that had moved there from Lorraine. Left an orphan at 13, Savigny was brought up by a friend who educated him in ways that recall the experience of young John Stuart Mill. At 17 Savigny entered the University of Marburg; after studying at other universities, he returned to Marburg for his doctor's degree in 1800 and began a long, influential, and distinguished teaching career. At the age of 24 he published *Das Recht des Besitzes* ("The Right of Possession"; Giessen, 1804), and in the following year he began to tour libraries in search of manuscripts for his historical work. In 1810 he accepted a teaching post at the newly founded University of Berlin, which he helped organize and where he became rector. He did much to raise the standards of German universities and to help them achieve a dominant position in the world of scholarship. While teaching, writing, and assisting in the administration of the university until 1842, he also performed judicial tasks, and from 1842 to 1848 he was chancellor of Prussia.

In his stress on continuity and tradition Savigny may have been influenced by Edmund Burke, and in his understanding of the methods and aims of historical research he may have been influenced by Barthold Georg Niebuhr, who also took part in the founding of the University of Berlin and was an admirer of Roman institutions.

Savigny's two *magna opera* were the *Geschichte des römischen Rechts in Mittelalter* (7 vols., Heidelberg, 1815–1834) and the *System des heutigen römischen Rechts* (8 vols., Berlin, 1840–1849). In 1850 his miscellaneous writings, *Vermischte Schriften,* were published at Berlin in five volumes, and in 1851 and 1853 his two-volume work *Das Obligationenrecht als heute römischen Rechts* was published. He was cofounder, in 1815, of the *Zeitschrift für geschichtlichen Rechtswissenschaft.* His massive work on Roman law in the Middle Ages became the source of subjects for countless historical monographs. His students, and their students in turn, dominated historical and legal scholarship and teaching for several generations, and he was universally acknowledged as one of the most influential thinkers and scholars of the nineteenth century.

The main thrust of Savigny's jurisprudential thought, however, is not found in his monumental historical treatises but in a polemical tract published at Tübingen in 1814, *Vom Beruf unserer Zeit für Gesetzgebung und Rechtswissenschaft.* This pamphlet was in rebuttal to A. F. J. Thibaut's *Civilistische Abhandlungen* (Heidelberg, 1814), in which a plan for a single code of laws for all German states was urged.

Savigny argued that law has no abstract origin in nature or mind but is organically connected with the people of a nation and is an expression of its *Volksgeist,* or collective genius. Fundamentally, law is formed by custom and popular faith, "by internal, silently operating powers, not by the arbitrary will of a lawgiver." The "real law" is always "the proper will of the people." Like language and manners, law has movement and development; it grows with a people and dies with it.

In earliest historical times, Savigny claimed, law was no more separable from a people than was its language or its manners. Rights and duties were created and extinguished by symbolic acts, which were the "true grammar" of law in this period. As social existence became more complex and sophisticated, law came to be expressed in abstract forms; jurists became a professional class, and law perfected its language and took a scientific direction. Instead of existing in the consciousness of the people, it now existed in the consciousness of the jurists, who became the representatives of the community, the voice of its *Volksgeist.* Now the law had a twofold existence: the "political" element, or the connection of the law with the general existence of the people, and the "technical" element, or the abstract and scientific existence of the law. From this it follows that the jurist needs a twofold spirit: the historical sense, with which to seize "the peculiarities of every age and every form of law," and the systematic sense, with which to see "every notion and every rule in lively connection and cooperation with the whole" legal order. Through these senses the jurist will acquire mastery over a body of law, obtain for that law a thorough grounding in history, and discover its organic principle. He will be able to separate that which still has life from that which is lifeless "and only belongs to history," and in this way he will arrive at a truly national law—a "living customary law."

Savigny's views contributed in varying degrees to a number of significant results: (1) They helped bring to an end the dominant natural law philosophy that looked to pure reason as the source of law. (2) They delayed the movement for codified legal systems that had started with the Napoleonic codes. (3) They established the historical school of jurisprudence. (4) They laid the basis for the sociological school of legal thought. (5) They retarded the development and acceptance of legislation as a source of law. (6) They contributed to an exaggerated stress on nationalism and to a disparagement of the idea of a common law of mankind as an expression of *Menschengeist.* Perhaps Savigny's most enduring influence is to be found in his idea that law must not be isolated into an autonomous science but must be treated as an aspect of social life, development, and order—as a social, historically conditioned phenomenon.

Bibliography

Kantorowicz, Hermann, "Savigny and the Historical School of Law." *Law Quarterly Review,* Vol. 53 (1937), 326 ff.

Montmorency, J. E. G., "Friedrich Carl von Savigny," in J. Macdonell and E. Manson, eds., *Great Jurists of the World.* Boston, 1914.

Stoll, Adolf, *Friedrich Karl von Savigny,* 3 vols. Berlin, 1927–1939.

Wolf, Erik, *Grosse Rechtsdenker der deutschen Geistesgeschichte.* Tübingen, 1951; 4th ed., 1963. Ch. 12.

Zwilgmeyer, Franz, *Die Rechtslehre Savignys.* Leipzig, 1929. Bibliography on pp. ix–xii.

MILTON R. KONVITZ

SCANDINAVIAN PHILOSOPHY. The term "Scandinavia" means, strictly speaking, only Sweden, Norway, and Denmark. However, as a Nordic country, Finland falls naturally within the same philosophical climate, and in fact the term "Scandinavia," as it is used today, tends to include all the Nordic countries. Consequently, this article will deal with the philosophies of Sweden, Finland, Norway, and Denmark.

SWEDISH PHILOSOPHY

Among the Scandinavian countries Sweden probably has had the strongest philosophical tradition, and its culture has been most strongly influenced by philosophy. Descartes spent the last year of his life in Stockholm, giving lessons in philosophy to Sweden's young queen, and his visit to Sweden may be one of the reasons why, toward the end of the seventeenth century, Cartesian philosophy was influential in both of Sweden's universities, Uppsala and Lund. In the eighteenth century Locke and Hume influenced Swedish philosophy, but by the close of that century Kantianism had been introduced into Sweden by Daniel Boëtius (1751–1810), a professor of philosophy at Uppsala. Although Swedish philosophy remained within the idealist tradition for about a century, its specific Kantian character was of short duration. The powerful and original thinker Benjamin Höijer (1767–1812), in a critique of the Kantian concept of the thing-in-itself, developed a philosophy in many respects kindred to Fichte's philosophy, although on important points Höijer was closer to Schelling. In his later years Höijer's philosophy developed into a position which in many respects can be characterized as Hegelian.

Boström. For more than half a century Swedish philosophy was dominated exclusively by a single thinker, the Uppsala philosopher Christopher Jacob Boström (1797–1866). With Boström, philosophy in Sweden reached its metaphysical and speculative peak. Boström was influenced by both Schelling and Hegel but was a disciple of neither. Not without some justification he has been called Sweden's Plato—although he was, in some respects, closer to Plotinus than to Plato. There is, however, much originality in Boström's philosophy.

Boström argued that being is spiritual. His arguments were, naturally enough, rather speculative, but they were not without some analytic force. Any determination of what is, any thought or any assertion about it, implies consciousness; it implies a relation between consciousness and the object of consciousness, a relation between consciousness and that of which existence is asserted. But a relation between two things is possible only if they have something in common, and the common feature between consciousness and its object can be nothing but consciousness. Moreover, consciousness cannot be a property of a thing; consciousness must be the essence of it. If it were not the essence of a thing but a property of it, it would imply a relation between the property and the thing of which it was a property; such a relation, in turn, implies a common property, a property which of course could be nothing but consciousness.

The empirical world—the world of space and time or, rather, the world in space and time—is the result of the limitations of man's consciousness. The perfect, absolute, and infinite consciousness (God) does not conceive of being through the medium of space and time but as it really is, as a system of ideas. Ideas constitute the substances of the world, the entities of reality. Just as reality is consciousness, ideas are conscious beings; in fact, according to Boström ideas are persons. Saying that reality is a system of ideas is therefore the same as saying that reality is a system of persons. The system of the universe is a hierarchy of ideas, or persons. In this hierarchy the perfect, Absolute idea is that which includes all other ideas; any idea is included in the Absolute idea and also in all ideas that rank higher within the hierarchy, and it includes all ideas that rank lower within the hierarchy. Thus, society is included not only in the Absolute idea but also in the state, and it includes, in turn, the family and man.

Man understands that he is an idea, and the goal of his intellectual life is to understand the essence of himself, an understanding which involves an understanding of other things and therefore also an understanding of the Absolute. The understanding of the ideal world—of what man, family, society, state, and so on, really are—is the goal of man's striving.

Uppsala philosophy. Boströmianism was for Swedish intellectual life almost what Hegelianism was for the intellectual life of Europe. It dominated Swedish metaphysics, ethics, philosophy of law, and philosophy of religion, and until the beginning of the twentieth century it had no rival. The power of Boströmianism was broken only by the equally powerful Uppsala philosophy. This was a strong, novel, and original movement headed by two philosophers of great talent: Axel Hägerström (1868–1939) and Adolf Phalén (1884–1931). On almost all counts Uppsala philosophy was anti-Boströmian. It rejected metaphysics; it rejected subjectivism and idealism; and it argued that moral sentences were nothing but commands and expressions of emotions, lacking all cognitive meaning.

It is interesting to observe the similarity of Uppsala philosophy to logical positivism and to Cambridge analysis. Like logical positivism it was antimetaphysical, and, also like logical positivism, it rejected the supposition that moral sentences have a truth-value. In fact, some of the arguments used for rejecting this supposition were strikingly similar to the arguments used by A. J. Ayer in *Language, Truth and Logic*. And like G. E. Moore it offered arguments for a refutation of idealism. Without violating historical facts, but perhaps simplifying them, it may be said that the modern analytic movement, in Europe at least, arose independently in three places: Cambridge, Uppsala, and Vienna.

Hägerström. In some essays published in 1910 and 1911 Hägerström argued that in a sentence like "This act is wrong," two elements should be distinguished: an objective or a descriptive element and an emotional element. The sentence can therefore be written "This act. Ugh!" Obviously, such an expression cannot meaningfully be said to be either true or false. It is not a statement about the speaker's emotional attitude; it is a way of expressing that attitude.

Consider the sentence "Peace is valuable." It seems to have the same logical structure as the sentence "The book is red." That is, it seems to be a sentence which asserts a proposition. But according to Hägerström to say that it had the same logical structure is to be misled by the grammatical structure of the sentence. What is expressed by the sentence "Peace is valuable" could also be expressed by such sentences as "How nice it is to have peace" or "May we always have peace." Since these sentences have the same logical form as the sentence "Peace is valuable," that sentence clearly does not assert a proposition; it only expresses an emotion. We are deceived by language into believing that there are such things as values and that to say that something is valuable is to ascribe a property—the property of being valuable—to a certain subject. But there are no such things as values, and consequently no such properties as being valuable, capable of functioning as logical predicates.

What is expressed by sentences like "This is what you ought to do" or "This is your duty"? According to Hägerström such sentences are nothing but imperatives. They have the same logical structure as the sentence "Do this!" Just as it would be meaningless to ascribe a truth-value to an imperative, it would be meaningless to ascribe a truth-value to sentences of the type "This is your duty."

One of the consequences of this view is that ethics can be the study neither of which things are good or right and which are bad or wrong nor of the supposed justification of morals. Ethics can be nothing but an investigation into the noncognitive nature of moral sentences.

Hägerström also made revolutionary contributions to legal philosophy. He attacked all then-current theories about the nature of the law and rights and condemned them as meaningless. If it is asserted that in a certain society there exists a right of property, exactly what is asserted? What is meant by the word "right"? Hägerström's answer is that nothing in reality corresponds to a right; no facts are named by that word. The supposed factual basis for a right can be neither a protection guaranteed by an authority nor a command issued by such an authority. It could not be a protection by an authority, such as the state, because the state does not protect a property; it enables the person whose property has been stolen to regain it. But the concept of helping to regain is not identical with the concept of protection. The concept of regaining presupposes that something has been lost—that is, that protection has been lacking or insufficient. Moreover, the child who asserts that a certain toy is his thinks it is his independently of whether the parents (or somebody else) protect this particular toy. And when a country asserts its right to a certain piece of land it does so without necessarily implying that some other country or some organization authorizes it to protect this particular piece of land.

Nor can the meaning of the term "right" be defined in terms of commandments. It is not correct to say, as in fact has been said, that the meaning of a statement of the form "This is A's property" is the fact that the state commands all others to respect A's possession and that it is ready to punish disobedience of this command. A dispute about a property is not a dispute about who is guilty of being disobedient and who is not. The person who believes falsely that he has a right to a certain property is not disobedient. The arguments that will show he is wrong are not arguments that show him to be disobedient to a certain command from the state because, as Hägerström pointed out, a command that does not reach the person for whom it is intended is not a command at all; it is an empty sound.

Hägerström's conclusion that no facts correspond to a right was combined with his studies of the history of legal ideas, especially his studies of Roman law. Through these studies he arrived at the belief that originally a concept like the concept of right was associated with ideas of supernatural and mystical powers. To have a right of property was to have a certain power over the thing of which ownership was claimed. In ancient Rome, if a transfer of property took place (for example, by sale), the transfer was effected by performing a certain ceremony known as the *mancipatio*. The person buying property did so by throwing a piece of copper into a scale and uttering the words "I proclaim that it is mine and that it has been bought by me through this piece of copper." The function of this expression is neither to declare or to describe the speaker's intention nor to report or to predict any factual state of affairs. According to Hägerström the expression functions as a magical formula. The purpose of using it is to bring about a transfer of those supernatural powers which constitute the right in question.

Hägerström 's views on ethics and legal philosophy were rather startling in their day. Nevertheless, they were enormously influential for Scandinavian moral and legal philosophy, and his teaching as well as his published works have been an inspiration for many Scandinavian philosophers.

Phalén. Uppsala philosophy was also revolutionary in epistemology. Its epistemological views were due primarily to Adolf Phalén, according to whom the task of philosophy is to analyze and investigate concepts. He held that many of our common concepts are dialectical, conceived in such a way that two contradictory elements can be found in them. From each proposition applying such a concept two contradictory propositions can be deduced. Phalén tried to show how the concepts presupposed by subjective idealism lead to such contradictions. Subjective idealism rests upon the assumption that perception of objects involves an object in the mind (an idea); in other words, it implies that the object of perception is part of the mind. At the same time, the object of perception must necessarily be something different from the mind which perceives the object. Perception of an object involves a relation between the mind and the object perceived; at the same time the object perceived is regarded as something in the mind—that is, as something which is part of the mind.

The dialectic of the concept of perception may express itself in different ways. Thus, in the act of perception the mind is at one and the same time both active and passive. Perception is a passive reception of ideas, and yet perception implies that the mind perceives, that the mind is active (compare Locke's ideas of sensation and ideas of reflection). Or else the object perceived is both the external object (the external cause of the perception) and the content of the perception (that is, the idea as an effect of the act of perception). These contradictions result from dialectical assumptions involved in the concept of perception. Only by freeing this concept from its subjective presuppositions can contradictions be avoided. That is, perception, understood as the act of acquiring knowledge through the senses, must not be thought of as involving the concept of an idea in a mind.

Phalén regarded the presuppositions of subjective idealism as one of the main sources of most, if not all, the insoluble problems within epistemology. He found an idealist dialectic involved as early as Descartes's notions of innate and adventitious ideas and found the same dialectic in the philosophy of Locke, Berkeley, and Hume. In Kant too the epistemological problem was determined by this dialectic, and by a detailed analysis Phalén tried to show that the movement from Kantian thought to Hegelianism is fully explicable as a logical unfolding of the idealist dialectic in question.

According to Phalén a study of the history of philosophy confirms that many, if not all, of the persistent problems and theories arise from and find their explanation in concepts which determine the development of our thoughts, concepts which he termed "natural categories." To disentangle and to expose the contradictions involved in these categories is, then, the main task of philosophy. As an example of a natural category Phalén took the concept "the present." He tried to prove that it is a dialectical concept and that such opposite theories as Heracliteanism and Platonism, and determinism and finalism, necessarily follow from it. Phalén also made significant and highly interesting contributions by analyzing such concepts as "change," "thing," and "space."

Contemporary Uppsala philosophy. Uppsala philosophy today is alive in the sense that philosophy in Uppsala is still antimetaphysical and analytical, but it is no longer a philosophical school or movement different from the general analytic movement of the Western world. Uppsala philosophy is now probably more influenced by philosophers such as Gottlob Frege, Rudolf Carnap, W. V. Quine, and Bertrand Russell than it is by its great predecessors. Contemporary Oxford philosophy has made almost no impact on Uppsala.

Hägerström's and Phalén's chairs are held by Konrad Marc-Wogau (born 1902) and Ingemar Hedenius (born 1908). In his book *Sensationalism and Theology in Berkeley's Philosophy* Hedenius applied Phalén's theories of the dialectical movement of the concept of perception. In moral philosophy he has received strong impulses from Hägerström but has also removed himself from him. In his work *Rätt och Moral* ("Law and Morals"; Stockholm, 1941) Hedenius criticized Hägerström and his dogmatic followers for not distinguishing between genuine and nongenuine law sentences. Whereas genuine law sentences are imperatives, nongenuine law sentences are statements. They state what, in a certain legal system, the law in fact is.

Marc-Wogau has worked primarily within history of philosophy and epistemology. His *Untersuchungen zur Raumlehre Kants* (dissertation, Uppsala, 1932) and *Vier Studien zur Kants Kritik der Urteilskraft* (Uppsala, 1938) bear witness to the influence of his teachers, Phalén and Hägerström. They illustrate Phalén's dialectical method and support the thoroughgoing nonpsychological interpretation of Kant that Hägerström gave in his *Kants Ethik* (Uppsala, 1902). His detailed analysis of sense-data theories in British philosophy (*Die Theorie der Sinnesdaten*, Uppsala, 1945) reveals, however, that Marc-Wogau is greatly interested in epistemological problems as they are conceived of and analyzed in recent British philosophy. Marc-Wogau, like Hedenius, is now more oriented toward a philosophy descended from Vienna and Cambridge than toward his own predecessors, Hägerström and Phalén.

Other Swedish universities. During the first quarter of the twentieth century the chairs in philosophy at the University of Lund were occupied by Efraim Liljequist (1865–1941) and Hans Larsson (1862–1944). Whereas Liljequist was a Boströmian (Sweden's last Boströmian), Larsson was a Kantian. The reaction against Boströmianism at Lund was never a violent protest: a strong antimetaphysical movement is not congenial to the intellectual climate there. However, the present philosophic situation at Lund cannot be characterized as either metaphysical or antimetaphysical. Rather, it is noncommittal, and its acceptance and rejection of views seem determined by nothing but the weight of the arguments. Among contemporary philosophers at Lund are Gunnar Aspelin (born 1898), professor at Goteborg (Gothenburg) from 1936 to 1949 and at Lund from 1949 to 1963, and Manfred Moritz (born 1909), professor at Lund since 1958. Aspelin has worked primarily within history of philosophy and history of ideas. Moritz has made several studies of Kantian ethics and is also interested in the philosophy of law.

Anders Wedberg (born 1913), professor at the University of Stockholm since 1949, has applied Phalén's methods to the study of the logical structure of Boström's philosophy. In his later works, however, Wedberg has used the tools of symbolic logic. This is the case, for example, in his *History of Philosophy* (in Swedish). In this work his interests lie no longer in the discovery of dialectic concepts but in a formalization of the logical structure of the arguments used by different philosophers—a formalization that proves whether the particular arguments are consistent or not.

In *An Inquiry into the Freedom of Decision*, Harald Ofstad (born 1920), professor at the University of Stockholm since 1954, has made a thoroughgoing study of the problem of the freedom to decide; his thesis is that the issue is a normative one.

The chair at the University of Goteborg is held by Ivar Segelberg (born 1914). His works cover fields as different as Zeno's paradoxes, the concept of a property, and the idea of the self.

FINNISH PHILOSOPHY

Since Finland's life as a nation from the twelfth century until the beginning of the nineteenth century has been connected with and dependent upon Sweden, it is only natural that the development of philosophy in Finland shows a pattern similar to that of philosophy in Sweden.

At Åbo, Finland's earliest center for academic life and a university since 1640, Cartesian philosophy was taught in the middle of the seventeenth century. As in Sweden, Locke, Hume, and Kant influenced philosophic thinking in Finland during the eighteenth century. Whereas idealism in Sweden was primarily influenced by Schelling, however, idealism in Finland was influenced by Hegel (whose thought was introduced by Johan Jacob Tengström in the beginning of the nineteenth century). And although Sweden had a long period of Boströmianism, idealism was never strong in Finland.

In fact, Finland tended to turn away from philosophy as a logical inquiry of concepts and to turn toward empirical studies. Thus, at the end of the nineteenth century and the beginning of the twentieth century, Finnish philosophers engaged in psychological studies. Well known within this group of philosophers is Edward Westermarck (1862–1939), professor of philosophy at Helsinki University from 1906 to 1918, at Åbo from 1918 to 1932 and occupant of a chair in sociology at the University of London from 1907 to 1930. Part I of his first sociological study, *The History of Human Marriage*, appeared at Helsinki in 1889. (The full work was published at London in 1891.) His two-volume work *The Origin and Development of the Moral Ideas* was published in New York in 1906 and 1908. In 1932 his best-known work, *Ethical Relativity* (New York and London), was published, in which Westermarck defined ethical subjectivism and relativism.

In the first half of the twentieth century Ludwig Wittgenstein, logical positivism, and Russell and Whitehead's *Principia Mathematica* came to influence Finnish philosophy, probably more through Eino Kaila (1890–1958), one of Finland's leading philosophers, than anyone else. Kaila was professor at Åbo from 1921 to 1930 and at Helsinki from 1930 to 1948. In 1948 he was appointed a member of the Finnish Academy. His two studies *Über das System der Wirklichkeitsbegriffe* (1936) and *Über den physikalischen Realitätsbegriff* (1944) are in close agreement with the views of logical positivism. This is also true of *Den mänskliga Kunskapen* ("Human Knowledge"; Helsinki, 1939), even though its expository element is more pronounced than its analytic element.

One of Kaila's students is the internationally known philosopher Georg Henrik von Wright (born 1916). After holding a professorship at Helsinki from 1946 to 1948, von Wright was appointed to succeed Wittgenstein at Cambridge. However, he returned to Finland in 1951 to take a chair at the University of Helsinki. In 1958, when he became a member of the Finnish Academy, he resigned his chair. He is greatly interested in applying the system of formal logic to as many philosophical problems as possible. Thus, in his essay "Deontic Logic" (*Mind*, Vol. 60, 1951), he tried to construct a logical system in which deontic concepts are constituents. In *The Logic of Preference* (Edinburgh, 1963), an expanded version of lectures given at the University of Edinburgh the previous year, he claimed that the concept of preference is of pivotal importance to the theory of value in general and that it is a common root of aesthetic, economic, and moral valuations. *The Logic of Preference* is thus to be regarded as a counterpart to "Deontic Logic." One is a study of deontic concepts, the other of axiological or value concepts. Von Wright thus holds that the province of logic is identical with that of descriptive discourse and that the opposing opinion is rooted in misleading analogies and false identifications.

Perhaps even better known are von Wright's studies of the problem of induction and probability. In *A Treatise on Induction and Probability* (London, 1951) his aim was, as he wrote, "to examine, in the light of standards of logical correctness, various types of arguments which can be grouped under the common heading of induction." By formalizing these different arguments, as he also wrote, he reconstructs them, and he reconstructs them in such a way that their bearing, applicability, and relevance become clear.

In 1959 and 1960 von Wright gave the Gifford lectures at the University of St. Andrews. The second series of lectures has been published under the title *The Varieties of Goodness* (London, 1963). It is a conceptual investigation of the different uses of the word "good" and, therefore, of the different forms of goodness. Von Wright distinguished between such forms as instrumental goodness, technical goodness, medical goodness, and utilitarian goodness. Some of these forms have subforms; thus, for example, beneficial goodness is a subform of utilitarian goodness. He does not think, however, that there is such a thing as moral goodness. The moral sense of "good," he maintains, is "a derivation or secondary sense, which must be explained in the terms of nonmoral uses of the word." The principle of justice is "No man shall have his share in the greater good of a community of which he is a member, without paying his due." This principle he regards as the cornerstone of morality.

Two other well-known Finnish philosophers are Erik Stenius (born 1911), professor at Åbo Academy since 1954, and Jaakko Hintikka (born 1911), professor at the University of Helsinki since 1959. Among Stenius' publications is *Wittgenstein's Tractatus: A Critical Exposition of the Main Lines of Thought* (London, 1960). Stenius' interpretation and defense of Wittgenstein's picture theory of language has given rise to lengthy discussion in *Mind* and *Inquiry*. Among Hintikka's publications, *Knowledge and Belief, An Introduction to the Logic of the Two Notions* (Ithaca, N.Y., 1962), is an original, technical, and rather formal analysis of these two epistemological concepts. In his analysis Hintikka constructs such new basic concepts as "defensibility," "indefensibility," and "self-sustenance" to replace the old concepts of "consistency," "inconsistency," and "validity."

DANISH PHILOSOPHY

Søren Kierkegaard wrote somewhere, "Danish philosophy, if there can some day be talk of such a thing . . . ." This implies that there never has been such a thing as Danish philosophy and that it is doubtful that any such thing could ever come into existence. If by philosophy one means a metaphysical system, metaphysical in the sense in which Boström's philosophy is metaphysical, it is probably correct to say that there never was and never will be something called Danish philosophy. But if existentialism counts as philosophy, then certainly Kierkegaard himself ranks as a Danish philosopher. However, to grant that Kierkegaard, as the father of existentialism, is a philosopher is not to grant that existentialism, except in its roots, is a kind of Danish philosophy; in fact, it is not. To attempt to characterize the philosophical temperament of a nation almost inevitably leads to distortion. However, the Danish philosophical temperament (although not Danish philosophy) has tended to be neither metaphysical nor antimetaphysical but nonmetaphysical. Furthermore, Danish philosophy, for better or worse, usually tends to associate itself, if not suicidally to identify itself, with the empirical sciences and mathematics. This characterization of Danish philosophy is true only if one allows for exceptions with respect to both persons and periods (like most other countries, Denmark had a Hegelian period). And despite Kierkegaard, existentialism seems to receive its support not from Danish philosophers but from Danish theologians.

Danish philosophy before Kierkegaard. When Danish philosophy came into being as an independent discipline, it was a result neither of a sudden break with the past nor of the appearance of a single powerful thinker on the Danish philosophical scene. Denmark had neither a Bacon to herald empiricism nor a Descartes to defend the natural light. Nevertheless, by the eighteenth century, empiricism and rationalism both had their place in Danish philosophy. One of the first Danish philosophers to defend empiricism was Jens Schielderup Sneedorff (1724–1764). The source of all knowledge, Sneedorff maintained, is experience. Logic and mathematics are inadequate for experience. At the same time, by experience we get never certainty but only probabilities. Jens Kraft (1720–1765) and Frederik Christian Eilschow (1725–1750) both defended a rationalism patterned after and influenced by the German philosopher Christian Wolff.

Discussion of Kant in Denmark began toward the end of the eighteenth century. But whereas Kant's ethics was regarded with some sympathy, his epistemology had little support. Among thinkers who accepted Kant's moral philosophy at least for a time was Anders Sandöe Ørsted (1778–1860), prime minister (1853) and probably the greatest jurist Denmark has ever had. Ørsted, however, did not remain a devoted Kantian but became a personal friend and a follower of Fichte. Among philosophers who criticized Kant's epistemology were Niels Treschow (1751–1833), a Norwegian philosopher who was a professor at Copenhagen University from 1803 to 1813.

Frederik Christian Sibbern (1785–1872) was appointed as Treschow's successor. At the time of his appointment, Schelling's philosophy had reached Denmark, partly, at least, through Henrik Steffens (1773–1845). Steffens was educated in Denmark but inspired by German philosophy, in particular by that of Schelling. From 1802 to 1804 he lectured in Copenhagen, but because he did not receive a professorship (he was too much of a romantic for Danish philosophical taste) he went to Halle as a professor. He later went to the University of Breslau, and he died while he was professor at the University of Berlin. Before he left Denmark, however, Steffens had exercised a great influence on many members of Denmark's cultural elite (Denmark's greatest poet of the nineteenth century, Adam Oehlenschläger, wrote his famous poem *Guldhornene,* "The Gold Horns," after a 16-hour conversation with Steffens). Sibbern heard Steffens' lectures but remained quite uninfluenced by him. However, ten years later, when Sibbern visited Steffens in Breslau, Sibbern was converted to Schelling's doctrine of the Absolute as the ground of the identity between Nature and Spirit. But whereas both Schelling and Steffens regarded the succession of different individual things in Nature as an expression of a gradually succeeding fulfillment of the Absolute, not as a process in time, Sibbern conceived of the process in time not as an appearance but as a real process.

Individual things, therefore, acquired in Sibbern's thought an importance and a right which they did not possess for Schelling and Steffens. The world, Sibbern maintained, continues to develop; it is a continuing process. And because there will always be new things coming into existence and new experiences, a system comprehending everything is impossible. A philosophical system is an impossibility. Sibbern was therefore critical of Hegel's philosophy.

Hegelianism was introduced into Denmark in the first half of the nineteenth century by Johan Ludvig Heiberg (1791–1860), a poet, literary critic, and man of letters (Sibbern called him a philosophical amateur) and Hans Lassen Martensen (1808–1884), a famous bishop, who became a target for Kierkegaard's attack.

In 1841 a young Hegelian, Rasmus Nielsen (1809–1884), became professor, and when Sibbern retired in 1870 he was succeeded by Hans Broechner (1820–1875), another Hegelian. Nielsen, who was highly gifted and who possessed an unusual ability to inspire his audience, was a great master of Hegelian dialectics. Under the influence of Søren Kierkegaard, however, his views on the relation between religion (Christianity) and philosophy became incompatible with Hegelianism (without thereby becoming compatible with Kierkegaard's views). Broechner also came to differ with Hegel on the relation between religion and philosophy. But whereas Nielsen accepted a modified (or, according to Kierkegaard, a misunderstood) Kierkegaardian view, Broechner accepted D. F. Strauss and Ludwig Feuerbach's critique of Hegel.

Sibbern, Nielsen, and Broechner were all teachers of Nielsen's successor, Harald Høffding (1843–1931). But before Høffding's philosophic career began, the only genius Danish philosophy has been able to foster, Søren Kierkegaard, had lived, worked, and died.

Kierkegaard. Kierkegaard (1813–1855) was an opponent not only of Hegel's philosophy but of any philosophical system. Kierkegaard's concern was existence, existence not as a logical category but existence in the sense in which you and I exist. A philosophical system, to be a system, must have finality (a system which is not final, Kierkegaard maintained, is not a system), but my existence (as well as the existence of the philosopher who thinks out the system) cannot be incorporated into a logical system. According to Kierkegaard, to exist is to be subjective. The objective is the universal, the general, and the timeless. To be objective, therefore, is to abolish existence. To exist is to be subjective, and to be subjective involves a decision. A person may look upon himself objectively; that is, he may in an objective way explain why he is as he is. He observes and understands a certain fact. But the subjective person does not explain why he is as he is. The subjective person affirms himself—he chooses himself. And by choosing himself and taking the responsibility for himself he becomes guilty. Guilt, then, is a necessary condition of existence.

Kierkegaard's last years were devoted to a passionate attack upon official Christendom. Through these attacks he greatly deepened the understanding of what Christianity is—of what it means to be a Christian. A Christian is a man who is redeemed; and a condition of redemption is an infinite despair at not being able to fulfill the Christian claim. The Christianity Kierkegaard attacked, Christianity as it was preached and conceived of in his day, did not preach about or conceive of infinite despair as a condition of redemption.

Probably no other thinker has written with such passion, depth, and originality about human existence and about Christianity as has Kierkegaard. It is no doubt true that whoever today is classified as an existential thinker is in debt to Kierkegaard. But on Danish philosophy and Danish theology Kierkegaard had almost no influence. The intellectual elite read him, few understood him, and only a small number were influenced by him. Rasmus Nielsen, as we have seen, read him and was influenced by him, but, according to Kierkegaard, Nielsen did not understand him. Hans Broechner both read and understood him but did not accept him. Harald Høffding, however, read him, understood him, and was influenced by him; the influence, however, was negative. Because Kierkegaard's writings led Høffding to a deeper understanding of the nature of Christianity, he became repelled by it. If Christianity was what Kierkegaard said it was, then Høffding felt that he had to reject it. But as is well known, Kierkegaard's charge that philosophical systems are irrelevant to human existence and his analysis of Christianity are today shared by many theologians all over the world, Denmark included.

Høffding. The dominant philosopher in Denmark, from the second half of the nineteenth century and almost up to the present, has been Harald Høffding. Høffding's influence is not, even today, exclusively because of his works; it is also, and probably more so, because of the way that his personality impressed his students, the best of whom have occupied chairs of philosophy until recently. With Høffding, Danish philosophy came to be less dependent upon German philosophy, and French and English philosophy became a much greater part of Danish philosophical culture.

Høffding was interested in and contributed to almost all philosophical disciplines. He published works on psychology, epistemology, ethics, and the history of philosophy. Of these works probably his *Dyen nyere Filosofis Historie* (2 vols., Copenhagen, 1894–1895; translated by B. S. Mayer as *History of Modern Philosophy*, London, 1900) is the best known. It is difficult, however, to say which was Høffding's main work and to which philosophical discipline he contributed most significantly. But his contribution to philosophy, not only to Danish philosophy, was considerable. He was deeply concerned with ethics and saw human dignity and human welfare as the only proper goal of human activity, a goal inseparably connected with the progress of scientific knowledge. He had a deep and intimate understanding of the great figures in the history of philosophy. Among the many philosophers he studied and wrote about, he probably rated Spinoza and Kant highest; indeed, his epistemology is akin to Kantianism. Although Høffding saw the progress of science as a condition of the progress of man, it is probably true that psychology was his main interest. He was disposed, therefore, to look at philosophical problems through the eyes of psychology, particularly in his epistemology (and, consequently, in his interpretation of Kant).

Høffding somewhere wrote that an emphasis on psychology and ethics is typical of Danish philosophy. If this is true (which it is only with some modification), then Høffding may be regarded as the most typical Danish philosopher. Nevertheless, there can be no doubt that he must be ranked among the best of Danish philosophers in learning, sound scholarship, and balanced judgment.

Recent Danish philosophy. Among Høffding's successors Frithiof Brandt (born 1892) and Jørgen Jørgensen (born 1894) should be mentioned. Brandt, who occupied a chair at the University of Copenhagen from 1922 to 1958, published a well-known study of Hobbes (his doctoral dissertation), *Thomas Hobbes' Mechanical Conception of Nature* (translated by Vaughn Maxwell and Annie I. Faustbøll, London, 1928). Most of his scholarship, however, has been devoted to the study of Kierkegaard. Psychology has also greatly interested Brandt, and, among other things, he has contributed to the psychology of perception.

Jørgensen's main work is *A Treatise of Formal Logic* (Vols. I–III, Copenhagen, 1931). In this work he shows his extensive knowledge of the development of the philosophy of mathematics and logic. In the early stages of logical positivism he was in sympathy with it, and in 1934 he became a member of the editorial board of the series of monographs *Einheitswissenschaft*. To a great extent it was through Jørgensen that Denmark's epistemological climate in the 1920s changed from a Neo-Kantian viewpoint to a logical-positivistic one. Jørgensen has also been interested in the philosophical aspects of modern quantum mechanics. In his later years, however, he has mainly been occupied with psychology (in 1946 he published at Copenhagen his comprehensive work, *Psykologi paa biologisk Grundlag*, "Psychology Based on Biology"), and he now tends to regard philosophical problems as basically psychological (see his essay "Some Remarks Concerning Languages, Calculuses, and Logic," in Yehoshua Bar-Hillel et al., eds., *Logic and Language, Studies Dedicated to Professor Rudolf Carnap on the Occasion of his 70th Birthday*, Dordrecht, Netherlands, 1962). In general, it may be characteristic not of Danish philosophy as such but of philosophy as it is practiced at the University of Copenhagen that there is a tendency to regard psychological knowledge as a means of solving philosophical problems. However, at Aarhus, Denmark's second university, philosophy is practiced almost exclusively as a conceptual investigation.

NORWEGIAN PHILOSOPHY

Niels Treschow was born in Norway but educated in Denmark. From 1803 to 1813 he held a chair at the University of Copenhagen. Norway's first and for many years its only university, the University of Oslo, was founded in 1813, and Treschow gave up his chair in Copenhagen to become Norway's first professor of philosophy. His return to Norway marks, in a way, the beginning of Norwegian philosophy.

University teaching of philosophy in Oslo was thus inaugurated by a philosopher who was critical of Kant's critical philosophy and who preferred Spinozistic monism to Cartesian dualism. It was introduced, furthermore, by a philosopher who was critical of the existence of universals and emphasized the importance of individuals, who in all their richness could not be regarded as mere instances. Treschow combined the rejection of universals with a theory of evolution. Concepts like "the struggle for existence" and "the survival of the fittest," however, had no place in Treschow's theory. Instead, evolution was connected with a Spinozistic conception of God. Although Treschow continued to publish philosophical works almost until his death in 1833, he taught for only a little more than a year. Toward the end of 1814 he had to give up his chair in order to accept a government post.

Soon after, the Danish philosopher and novelist Poul Martin Møller (1794–1838), who taught philosophy at the University of Oslo from 1827 to 1831, introduced Hegel into Norway. Norway's (and probably Scandinavia's) most faithful Hegelian, Marcus Jacob Monrad (1816–1897), held Treschow's chair from 1845 until his death. Hegelianism was the dominant philosophy in Norway throughout the nineteenth century. With the advent of the twentieth century, Hegelianism finally disappeared and an interest in the sciences arose. In particular, psychology, conceived of and studied as a natural science, was accepted as a proper subject for philosophical studies. A typical Norwegian philosopher of the early twentieth century was Anathon Aall (1867–1943), who was appointed a professor of philosophy at Oslo in 1908. Aall was an anti-Hegelian who regarded psychology as an empirical science. His publications were on the history of philosophy and psychology.

The Hegelian period in Norwegian philosophy (about seventy years) has been called "the dead period," not because it was dominated by Hegelianism but because nothing was published. It was not until the beginning of the twentieth century that Norwegian philosophical works were again published. These were primarily works on psychology (still regarded as part of philosophy) and the history of philosophy. This was true not only of the work of Anathon Aall but also of that of Harald Schjelderup (born 1895), who became a professor of philosophy at Oslo in 1922. Schjelderup's chair later became a chair in psychology.

The philosophical milieu in Norway today is determined by an internationally known and original philosopher (who is also a famous mountain climber), Arne Naess (born 1912). Naess, who became a professor at Oslo in 1939, is the originator of a radical type of empirical semantics and the leader of the so-called Oslo group. For Naess words or sentences do not in themselves mean anything; rather, their meaning is a function of the persons using them and the situation in which they occur. But how does a philosopher find out what in a particular situation a particular person means by a particular word or a particular sentence? Not, it is argued, by his insight; he does not intuit the meaning—only by empirical methods can the meaning of words and sentences be investigated. The Oslo group denies the adequacy of such expressions as "By the sentence *a* is meant the same as is meant by the sentence *b*." An empirical investigation most often results in an expression such as "some occurrences of *a* are synonymous with some occurrences of *b* for some persons in some situations."

The empirical methods applied by the Oslo group employ carefully worked-out questionnaires. By the help of such questionnaires and by teamwork, philosophers of the Oslo group have carried out investigations of such expressions as "truth," "democracy," and "private enterprise." Among members (former or present) of the Oslo group are Harald Ofstad (now professor in Stockholm) and Hermann Tennesen (now in Canada). Not all Norway's philosophers, however, subscribe to empirical semantics. Most important of the nonadherents is Professor Knut Erik Tranøy (born 1918) of the University of Bergen.

If it is correct that Norwegian philosophy has had a dead period, it is equally correct to assert that, primarily because of Arne Naess, Norwegian philosophy is now in the middle of a period of life and growth.

(See Scandinavian Philosophy in Index for articles on Scandinavian philosophers.)

Bibliography

SWEDISH PHILOSOPHY

Boström, C. J., *Skrifter av Christopher Jacob Boström,* H. Edfette and G. J. Keijser, eds., 3 vols. Uppsala, 1883–1906. Translated by Victor E. Beck and Robert N. Beck as *Philosophy of Religion.* New Haven, Conn., 1963.

Hägerström, Axel, "Selbstdarstellung," in Raymund Schmidt, ed., *Die Philosophie der Gegenwart in Selbstdarstellungen,* Vol. VII. Leipzig, 1929.

Hägerström, Axel, *Inquiries into the Nature of Law and Morals,* translated by C. D. Broad, Karl Olivecrona, ed. Copenhagen, 1953.

Hedenius, Ingemar, *Sensationalism and Theology in Berkeley's Philosophy,* translated by Gerda Winqvist, translation revised by Harold H. Borland. Uppsala and Oxford, 1936.

Phalén, Adolf, *Das Erkenntnisproblem in Hegels Philosophie.* Uppsala, 1912.

Phalén, Adolf, *Beitrag zur Klärung des Begriffs des inneren Erfahrung.* Uppsala, 1913.

Phalén, Adolf, *Zur Bestimmung des Begriffs des Psychischen.* Uppsala, 1914.

Phalén, Adolf, "Selbstdarstellung," in R. Schmidt, ed., *Die Philosophie der Gegenwart in Selbstdarstellungen,* Vol. V. Leipzig, 1924.

Phalén, Adolf, "Our Common Notions and Their Dialectical Movement in the History of Philosophy," in *Proceedings of the Seventh International Congress of Philosophy* (1930).

FINNISH PHILOSOPHY

Hintikka, Jaakko, *Distributive Normal Forms in the Calculus of Predicates.* 1953.

Hintikka, Jaakko, "On Wittgenstein's 'Solipsism.'" *Mind,* Vol. 67 (1958), 88–91.

Hintikka, Jaakko, *Two Papers on Symbolic Logic.* 1955.

Hintikka, Jaakko, "On the Interpretation of 'De Interpretatione.'" *Acta Philosophica Fennica* (1962).

Kaila, Eino, *Zur Metatheorie der Quantenmekanik.* 1950.

Kaila, Eino, *Terminalkausalität als die Grundlage eines unitarischen Naturbegriffs.* 1956.

Kaila, Eino, "Die perzeptuellen und konzeptuellen Komponenten der Alltagserfahrung." *Acta Philosophica Fennica,* Vol. 13 (1962).

Stenius, Erik, *Das Problem der logischen Antinomien.* 1949.

Stenius, Erik, *Das Interpretationsproblem der formalisierten Zahlentheorie.* 1952.

Von Wright, Georg Henrik, *The Logical Problem of Induction.* Helsinki, 1941.

Von Wright, Georg Henrik, *Logical Studies.* London, 1957.

DANISH PHILOSOPHY

For the works of Kierkegaard and Høffding, see the articles on them.

Brandt, Frithiof, *Søren Kierkegaard, 1813–1855; His Life—His Works,* translated by Ann R. Born. Copenhagen, 1963. Also translated by R. Drinkuth as *Søren Kierkegaard, 1813–1855. Sein Leben, Seine Werke.* Copenhagen, 1963.

Jørgensen, Jørgen, *The Development of Logical Empiricism.* Chicago, 1951. This is Vol. 2, No. 9, of *The International Encyclopedia of Unified Science.*

NORWEGIAN PHILOSOPHY

For Treschow's works, see the article on him.

Naess, Arne, *Erkenntnis und wissenschaftliches Verhalten.* Oslo, 1936.

Naess, Arne, *Truth as Conceived by Those Who Are Not Professional Philosophers.* Oslo, 1938.

Naess, Arne, *Interpretation and Preciseness; A Contribution to the Theory of Communication.* Oslo, 1953.

Naess, Arne, "Typology of Questionnaires Adapted to the Study of Expression with Closely Related Meanings," in Yehoshua Bar-Hillel et al., eds., *Logic and Language; Studies Dedicated to Professor Rudolf Carnap on the Occasion of his 70th Birthday.* Dordrecht, Netherlands, 1962.

Schjelderup, Harald, *Hauptlinien der Entwicklung der Philosophie von Mitte des 19. Jahrhunderts.* 1920.

Tranøy, Knut Erik, *Wholes and Structures.* Copenhagen, 1959.

JUSTUS HARTNACK

SCEPTICISM. See SKEPTICISM.

SCHELER, MAX (1874–1928), German phenomenologist and social philosopher, was born in Munich. He was a man of intense emotions, superior learning, and endless yearning for new experiences. His father's family, which can be traced to the sixteenth century, was composed largely of jurists and Protestant clergymen from the Bavarian city of Coburg, while his mother was Jewish. The religious conflict of that lineage is reflected throughout his work. The first phase of Scheler's philosophic career was greatly influenced by his liberal and idealist teacher Rudolf Eucken. In 1901 Scheler became *Privatdozent* at the University of Jena. In 1907 he moved to the University of Munich, where his own thought began to take shape. There he met Franz Brentano and several disciples of Edmund Husserl, and under their influence his thinking turned strongly toward the phenomenological movement. He never fully relinquished this influence, although it weakened toward the end of his life. By 1910 Scheler had retired from teaching to live as an independent writer in Berlin. There, while he was entering the second and most fruitful period of his career, he composed either the drafts or final versions of some of his most important works, such as *Über Ressentiment und moralisches Werturteil* ("On Resentment and Moral Value Judgments," 1912) and *Zur Phänomenologie und Theorie der Sympathie-gefühle und von Liebe und Hass* ("Contributions to the Phenomenology and Theory of Sympathy and of Love and Hate," 1913). He also wrote *Der Formalismus in der Ethik und die materiale Wertethik* ("Formalism in Ethics and the Material Value Ethics," 2 vols., 1913–1916), discussing phenomenologically the structure of values as presented to consciousness and criticized Kant's purely formal approach to ethics. After the outbreak of World War I he became an ardent nationalist and sought to justify and glorify German involvement in the war. In 1915 he published the influential *Der Genius des Krieges und der deutsche Krieg* ("The Genius of War and the German War"), and during

the years 1917 and 1918 he carried out a diplomatic mission in Geneva for the German Foreign Office. By 1920 Scheler had repudiated the horrors of war and had become a convert to Catholicism. He presented the philosophic justification of that conversion in *Vom Ewigen im Menschen* (*On the Eternal in Man,* 1921), in which he gave an extensive phenomenological description of the realm of religious essences and values which, according to him, every man is forced to apprehend. It is "a realm of being and value which is in basis and origin utterly different from the whole remaining empirical world." After the war, Scheler accepted the chair of philosophy and sociology at the University of Cologne, at which time he elaborated his sociology of knowledge and produced the *Schriften zur Soziologie und Weltanschauungslehre* ("Contributions to Sociology and to the Study of World Views," 1923–1924), which, in 1926, became *Die Wissenformen und die Gesellschaft* ("Forms of Knowledge and Society"). In 1924, four years before his death, Scheler entered the third period of his life, when he began to turn away from Catholicism and eventually from theism in order to develop a comprehensive anthropology that verged on vitalism and pantheism. At this time the focus of his interest partially shifted to the natural sciences. These endeavors were expounded in *Die Stellung des Menschen im Kosmos* ("The Place of Man in the Universe," 1928) and *Der Mensch im Weltalter des Ausgleichs* ("Man in the Age of Equalization," 1929). He went to the University of Frankfurt early in 1928 and died there during the same year.

Methodology. Scheler strongly emphasized the phenomenological method, which was then being formally developed by Edmund Husserl and which Scheler outlined in *Der Formalismus in der Ethik.* He viewed himself as carrying out the philosophical programs of Nietzsche, Dilthey, and Bergson, and was firmly convinced that phenomenology would bring about a basic transformation in our way of conceiving the world and ourselves. Although his thought is quite unsystematic, Scheler was one of the most insightful, acutely intuitive, and brilliant thinkers of the early twentieth century. His writing abounds in detailed and suggestive descriptions of the subtler states of consciousness, such as sympathy, repentance, resentment, love, and joy. His work has therefore been of significant value in ethics, religion, psychology, and sociology.

Throughout his life Scheler felt a particular kinship to introspective and intuitive philosophers. He preferred Pascal's *logique du coeur* (that is, descriptions of ethical and religious experiences) to inferences and abstract theories about morality and God. Those thinkers in the history of philosophy who demonstrated clear phenomenological orientations—from St. Augustine, St. Francis, and Oriental philosophers to Sigmund Freud—therefore helped to shape Scheler's thinking. Troeltsch quite aptly called him the Catholic Nietzsche. Whatever logical rigor Scheler revealed was mostly the result of the marked influence of Kant. This dual influence of phenomenologically oriented thinkers and of Kant accounts for Scheler's interest in both metaphysics and empirical research. The influence of Scheler, whom Ortega y Gasset greatly admired, helped to spread phenomenology outside Germany into France and the Spanish-speaking countries.

Epistemology. According to Scheler, there is no pure knowledge. Knowledge does not exist for its own sake (that is, for the purpose of contemplation) but always aims at a pragmatic reconstruction of being itself. The phenomenon designated by "knowledge" is not an invariant relationship of man to being, but is to be interpreted pragmatically and instrumentally as a historical, social, and even biologically adaptive form of behavior. According to this analysis, knowledge is divided into three types, determined by function. The first type, scientific knowledge, which has to do with mastery, domination, control, and the accomplishments of technology (*Herrschaftswissen* and *Leistungswissen*), is knowledge of particulars. It is found in the experimental and specialized sciences, consists of observations, and leads to classifications and general laws. Science predicts, and the result—which is also the purpose—of such knowledge is to give man power over nature, society, and history. Our scientific world view is colored not only by the nature of our reason (as Kant held) but also by our motivation for achieving control over nature. Scientific knowledge deals with the sphere of the contingent nature of things (*das zufällige Dasein der Dinge*).

The second type of knowledge resembles what Aristotle called πρώτη φιλοσοφία ("first philosophy")—that is, knowledge of essences (*Wesenswissen* or *Bildungswissen*) and of the categories of being, which are the most general principles of classification. It is knowledge of the universal, acquired through what Husserl called eidetic reduction. Love replaces control as the motive for knowledge of essences. This knowledge does not depend for its existence on real objects; it can be derived from imaginary objects as well. Although knowledge of essences is acquired by observing even a single real or imaginary object, such as a triangle or a just act, it is nonetheless logically independent of induction and therefore true a priori. Furthermore, this second type of knowledge has transcendental or universal application and thereby becomes both the starting point for metaphysics and the foundation for science. Knowledge of essences is a characteristically human activity. The first kind of knowledge, adaptation and control, is found in animals as well as in men, but knowledge of essences is knowledge of reason, and that is the *differentia* of man.

The third type of knowledge is knowledge of metaphysical reality, being itself (*Sein*), and salvation (*Heilswissen* and *Erlösungswissen*). Such knowledge begins with the question of the nature of man (philosophical anthropology) and is possible only through a synthesis of the first two types. Scheler illustrates the subjective orientation that later characterized existential philosophers such as Heidegger: the study of the being of man is the absolute starting point for an understanding of ultimate philosophic questions. The purpose of metaphysical knowledge is to understand being insofar as it resists our drives or is an antithesis, or otherness, to our probing selves. Ultimate being is presumed to contain rational power and an infinite spirit as well as an irrational driving force that appears in the life cycle of individuals. Just as the macrocosm is a replica of the microcosm, so man is a microtheos, a miniature God, and is thereby the primary source of access to

God. The metaphysics of salvation is therefore a kind of meta-anthropology. Understanding of God—the ground of being (*der Grund aller Dinge, Urgrund*)—is to be achieved not through theoretical contemplation, but through active commitment. All men share in the divine nature; they sense it in the drive of sympathy and love toward oneness with the universe, which is the Dionysian way to God. Man is thus a cocreator with God.

Axiology. Through the phenomenological approach to ethics and to values in general—that is, the description of so-called "ethical" states of consciousness and of existence—Scheler hoped to make axiology impervious to the criticisms of relativism in general and of the behavioral sciences in particular. Scheler's work shows important traces of the post-Kantian German tradition of reverence for feeling, as illustrated in Novalis and Schopenhauer. According to Scheler, many emotions have objective referents; the belief that emotions are purely subjective states of consciousness is based on an erroneous description, and consequent misanalysis, of their structure. Some moods, like euphoria and depression, do not refer beyond themselves, but the experience of a value (*Wertfühlen*) is usually an intentional act parallel to perception and conception. Joy about good news, for instance, is an experience with a subjective as well as an objective pole. The object of that experience is seen to be a good thing, which instantiates a value. It follows that there are such things as cognitive emotions and that they point to certain real objects. Scheler was intrigued with Kant's a priori derivation of ethical principles, and he attempted to discover and examine the "real" presuppositions of Kant's position. He did not altogether reject Kant's ethical formalism; instead, he went beyond it. Scheler transmuted Kant's absolutism with respect to values into an axiological objectivism based on the phenomenologically observable fact that the material content of an experience of value is not exclusively the function of the observer's subjectivity and the additional fact that some values are experienced as having characteristics that might best be described and evoked by the word "eternal." Although Scheler owed much to Kant, he disagreed with him on important matters, especially the latter's identification of the a priori with reason. For Scheler, the a priori extends far beyond the uses of reason. Like other phenomenologists, he included the feeling nature of man within the constitution of the mind, and therefore posited what he called an emotional a priori.

In his examination of the structure of the experience of value, Scheler made a number of distinctions, including one between the good, or goods (*Güter*), and the valuable, or values (*Werte*). Values are those essential properties of the objects themselves that entitle us to call them good. Scheler agreed with Kant that the aim of desire (*Ziele*) is *ipso facto* a good (or as William James put it in *The Moral Philosopher and the Moral Life*, "There is some obligation wherever there is a claim"), which is really an emphasis on the content or material aspect of ethics as against its purely formal character. But he disagreed drastically with Kant about the values inherent in these goods and aims. Values are essences given to immediate intuition; they are not, as they were for Plato, removed from the actual objects in which they inhere. In fact, they are disclosed as universal and essential at the same time as they are present in phenomenologically disclosed immediate experience.

Scheler recognized four classes of value: (1) the values of the senses, such as the pleasant and the unpleasant; (2) the values of life, such as the noble (*edel*) and the common (*gemein*); (3) values of the spirit (*geistige Werte*), such as the aesthetic values of the beautiful and the ugly, the correct (*richtig*) and the incorrect (*unrichtig*), and the intrinsic value of knowledge; and (4) religious values, such as the holy and the unholy. Morality itself is not included in this list because to be ethical is in fact to implement one of the above values. These values form a qualitative hierarchy from religious ones, which are the highest, down to sensory ones. Rank is a phenomenologically given fact based on the criteria (reminiscent of Bentham's hedonic calculus) of duration, extent (that is, ability to share), self-sufficiency, satisfaction (*Befriedigung*) or quality (as opposed to intensity), and spirituality (that is, independence from bodily functions).

In contrast to Kant's emphasis on the ought (*Sollen*), Scheler examined the phenomenologically disclosed structure of values themselves (*Werte*). The sense of obligation (*ethischen Tunsollen*) is artificial and disingenuous, while the attraction of the value or the good (*ideales Seinsollen*) is spontaneous and honest. Scheler's general approach to values is best illustrated by his extensive analysis of sympathy in his *Phänomenologie der Sympathiegefühle*. He outlined the structure of sympathy by severing it from related feelings that are often confused with it. We may understand (*Auffassung*) another's emotion, and even feel empathy or experience the contagion (*Mitfühlen*) of his feeling, or we may feel as one (*Einsfühlen*) with him, that is, feel totally identified. In none of these instances do we feel sympathy. Authentic sympathy is not the experience of fusion; it recognizes, meets, and respects unequivocally the subjectivity of another human existence in a genuine encounter. Scheler further illustrated the merits of phenomenology for the study of values through his analytic descriptions of love and hate. To love is to experience spontaneously the movement from a lower to a higher value in the object loved, an experience that leads to a sudden intimation (*Aufblitzen*) of the object's superior value. Love is the adumbration of human possibilities; it is thus the *sine qua non* for sympathy and the basis for the religious ideal of infinite compassion and unqualified acceptance.

Metaphysics. Scheler's metaphysics has epistemological and theological elements. He used the phenomenological method not only to explore the cognitive import of moods and feelings but also to resolve such thorny epistemological problems as the question of the existence of other minds. Scheler's phenomenological solution has seemed to many people exceptionally acute and should be of interest to contemporary analytic philosophers who have been concerned with this question. He discredited all arguments for other minds based on inference, analogy, and empathy, and concluded that we have direct, immediate, and primary access to the minds of other people. Careful description of our consciousness of other bodies discloses that we experience directly the other's pain in his tears and embarrassment in his blushing, even though there

is in addition an inaccessible area (*Intimsphäre*) in every man's soul. Phenomenological analysis of the structure of experience also discloses (as Husserl and Heidegger maintained) that we are confronted by a neutral "sea of being" and that the process of judging data to be either subjective or objective is a constitutive act of our ego.

When Scheler applied phenomenology to religion he achieved significant anti-Thomistic and pro-Augustinian reformulations of traditional theological issues. The phenomenology of religion seeks to understand the ultimate nature of the divine, to study its manifestations in the world of human concerns, and to explore religion through an analysis of the act of faith. The task of the philosophy of religion, which he called *Wesenphänomenologie der Religion*, is to describe phenomenologically, and then generalize (and in this instance, Scheler recognized that he was imitating Rudolf Otto) the manner in which religious experiences or states of consciousness present themselves to us. Proof (*Beweis*) of the existence of God must make allowances for direct intuitive manifestation (*Aufweis*). Scheler discovered that man is in search of an infinity, traditionally called God. Man is a God-seeker (*Gottsucher*). The search leads man to an ineffable numinous experience of an ultimate Personality, appropriately described as *ens a se*, being in itself, which has qualities that can be described metaphorically in the usual religious dogmas, rituals, and myths. To this mystic note Scheler added a touch of personalism: God meets man halfway in response to faith. Traditional metaphysics is therefore but a preliminary to (and sometimes a metaphor for) the understanding of religion. In sum, the phenomenologically disclosed divine attributes are absoluteness, infinite goodness, infinite power, holiness, spirituality, and personality. Crucial to the religious experience is a feeling (isolated by both Schleiermacher and Otto) that man is nothing at all (*Nichtigkeit*). This so-called "creature feeling" (*Geschöpflichkeit*) is the experience of direct contact with the source of one's being; it is the feeling of "infinite dependence" (*Gewirktheitserlebnis*). Man has no choice; he is coerced into responding religiously. If he does so authentically he faces God (*Gott*); if not, he faces an idol (*Götze*). Religious rituals, such as prayer, contrition, reverence, and self-immolation, well up from within man's deepest nature. That a response to these states can be experienced—a response which does not come from the world of everyday experience—is presumably a fact of both historical and personal awareness. The contemporary revival in theology, notably among the group of thinkers sometimes classified as existential theologians, owes a great deal to Scheler's pioneering work.

Anthropology. Personality is perhaps the highest ideal in Scheler's philosophy. According to Scheler, a person is neither a soul substance nor pure spontaneity; he is a unity of activity within the matrix of all-encompassing being, very much as an electron is conceived as an energy cloud. This real unity of activity Scheler called spirit (*Geist*). What distinguishes a person from an animal is his capacity to abstract essence from existence. Man is a unique individual, but he nonetheless consists of both a private and a common factor (*Gesamtperson*). The common part of the person is the foundation for social structures. The person may achieve social union through slavish conformism, through the sharing of experiences (*Miterleben*), through the artificial development of institutions (*Gesellschaft*), and by participating in the higher unity of the church or the state.

Man is also explained in terms other than the purely intuitively discovered essences. For a phenomenologist this is an important concession to nonphilosophical contributions to basic knowledge about human existence. The sciences contribute the realistic aspects (*Realfaktoren*) of our knowledge of man. The real aspects are on the one hand the environmental material conditions studied by such disciplines as geography, climatology, ethnography, and economic geography, and on the other hand the inner biological and psychological drives of man, such as self-preservation and sex. But it is wrong to hold that the spiritual aspects (*Idealfaktoren*) of man are reducible to the realistic or material aspects alone. The work of Scheler's third period was an attempt to reconcile the spiritual realities that so impressed him during most of his turbulent life with the obvious success and popularity of the sciences. The discipline called the sociology of knowledge is the study of the influence that the realistic or material aspect of man has on his spiritual aspect.

The types of inquiry that derive from the social role of knowledge were discussed above. In addition, the sociology of knowledge leads to a classification of five theories of man (or, as Scheler called them, philosophical anthropologies) that dominate our epoch. The first view of man is based not on philosophy or science but on religious faith and derives principally from Jewish and Christian sources. The second view of man arose through the Greek discovery of *Homo sapiens*, or man as a rational animal. Scheler deplored the fact that in European culture the identification of man with *Homo sapiens* is taken as self-evident (except in Dilthey's theories and in Nietzsche's conception of the Will to Power, in which reason becomes rationalization). The third view is the naturalistic, positivistic, and pragmatic theory of *Homo faber*, according to which man is not a being *sui generis* but an extension of nature: man is a large-brained animal capable of using symbols and tools. The fourth conception of man, influenced by Schopenhauer's pessimism, is negative: man is decadent; he has deserted life, has abandoned his holy cosmic sense, and lives in a state of pathological egocentric megalomania. According to this view, intelligence developed in man as a result of his physical inferiority and physiological atrophy. The fifth conception of man is found in the idea of the Superman (*Übermensch*) of Nietzsche's *Also Sprach Zarathustra* and Nicolai Hartmann's *Ethik*.

Works by Scheler

Gesammelte Werke, 4 vols to date. Bern, 1953——.
Über Ressentiment und moralisches Werturteil. Leipzig, 1912. Translated by W. W. Holdheim as *Ressentiment*. New York, 1960.
Zur Phänomenologie und Theorie der Sympathie-gefühle und von Liebe und Hass. Halle, 1913.
Der Formalismus in der Ethik und die materiale Wertethik, 2 vols. Halle, 1913–1916.
Abhandlungen und Aufsätze. Leipzig, 1915.
Der Genius des Krieges und der deutsche Krieg. Leipzig, 1915.
Krieg und Aufbau. Leipzig, 1916.
Vom Ewigen im Menschen. Berlin, 1921. Translated by Bernard Noble as *On the Eternal in Man*. London, 1960.
Schriften zur Soziologie und Weltanschauungslehre. Leipzig, 1923.
Versuche zu einer Soziologie des Wissens. Munich and Leipzig, 1924.
Die Wissenformen und die Gesellschaft. Leipzig, 1926.
Die Stellung des Menschen in Kosmos. Darmstadt, 1928.
Philosophische Weltanschauung. Bonn, 1929. Translated by Oscar A. Haac as *Philosophical Perspectives*. Boston, 1958.
Wesen und Formen der Sympathie. Bonn, 1931. Translated by Peter Heath as *The Nature of Sympathy*. London, 1954.
Die Idee des Friedens und der Pazifismus. Berlin, 1931.
Schriften aus dem Nachlass. Berlin, 1933.

Works on Scheler

Dupuy, Maurice, *La Philosophie de Max Scheler*, 2 vols. Paris, 1959.
Frings, Manfred S., *Max Scheler: A Concise Introduction into the World of a Great Thinker*. Pittsburgh, 1965.
Kränzlin, Gerhard, *Max Schelers phänomenologische Systematik*. Leipzig, 1934.
Schuetz, Alfred, "Max Scheler's Epistemology and Ethics." *Review of Metaphysics*, Vol. 11 (1957), 304–314, 486–501.
Spiegelberg, Herbert, "Max Scheler," in *The Phenomenological Movement*, 2 vols. The Hague, 1960. Vol. I, pp. 228–270.

PETER KOESTENBAUM

SCHELLING, FRIEDRICH WILHELM JOSEPH VON

(1775–1854), German idealist philosopher, was born at Leonberg in Württemberg, the son of a learned Lutheran pastor, Joseph Friedrich Schelling. From his earliest years, he was destined by his family for the ministry. He was educated at the cloister school of Bebenhausen and, from 1790 to 1792, at the theological seminary at Tübingen. There he became friendly with two older students who were to play significant roles in his own life, as well as in cultural history: G. W. Hegel and J. C. Hölderlin, the great romantic poet. The three young men were keen partisans of the French Revolution, and they also enthusiastically discussed the ideas of the philosophers, especially Spinoza, Kant, and Fichte.

For several years Schelling held a position as tutor of the sons of a noble family. Then, in 1798, at the unusually young age of 23, he was called to a professorship at Jena. There the famous Fichte, the leading philosopher in Germany at the time and the idol of Schelling's youth, became his colleague and friend. In 1802 and 1803 Schelling and Hegel jointly edited the *Kritisches Journal der Philosophie*. At that time, though Hegel was five years older than Schelling, he was generally considered to be Schelling's disciple, and Hegel's first book was a comparison of Fichte's and Schelling's philosophies.

In nearby Weimar, Goethe and Schiller were at the peak of their careers. Schelling met them both and became friendly with Goethe. Jena was now the center of German romanticism, and the ideas and personalities of this movement made a profound and lasting impression on Schelling. The romantic movement was, of course, also influenced by his philosophy. In its stress on the importance of the individual and the supreme value of art, and in its antirationalism, organicism, and vitalism, Schelling's transcendental idealism is the epitome of German romantic philosophies.

His friends among the romantics included Ludwig Tieck, who interested Schelling in folklore and mythology; the brilliant young poet Novalis; and August and Friedrich Schlegel, whose translations of Shakespeare made the English playwright one of the main shaping forces of German literature. Schelling was particularly intimate with August and his charming, intellectually gifted wife Caroline. Soon he became informally engaged to Auguste Böhmer, the sixteen-year-old daughter of Caroline by a previous marriage, but she died in 1800 before they could marry. It was rumored at the time that Schelling's amateur medical attentions contributed to her death. Certainly he was impetuous and self-confident to a point that some felt bordered on irresponsibility. This was a personal pattern common among the romantics, who sometimes defended themselves with the words of Schelling, "The beginning and end of all philosophy is—freedom."

In 1803 Caroline divorced August Schlegel and married Schelling. In keeping with the romantic creed, the three remained friends. It seems to have been an ideal marriage in every way. Schelling produced his most successful works during these years, and when Caroline died in 1809 he was grief-stricken; from then on he seemed unable to put his ideas together in a way that satisfied him. He never published another book as long as he lived, though he continued to write and lecture for many years. In 1812 he married Pauline Gotter, a friend of Caroline's.

From 1803 to 1806 Schelling taught philosophy at the new University of Würzburg, and in 1806 he was called to Munich as an associate of the Academy of Sciences and as secretary of the Academy of Arts. He later became secretary of the philosophical section of the Academy of Sciences. These positions were government sinecures that afforded him abundant leisure and also allowed him to lecture at Stuttgart and, from 1820 to 1827, at Erlangen. In 1827 he became a professor at Munich. In 1841 the Prussian authorities, in the hope that he would serve as a counterbalance to the powerful influence of the radical Young Hegelians, appointed him to the position of Prussian privy councilor and member of the Berlin Academy, and he lectured for the next five years at the University of Berlin. He died at the age of 79 at Bad Ragaz, Switzerland.

Of all the major German philosophers, Schelling is the least known in the English-speaking world. His name is familiar as the historic link connecting Kant and Fichte with Hegel, but this description fits only his earlier work. Through his personal association with some of the German romantic writers and his doctrinal influence on the entire German romantic school, as well as through the direct influence of his aesthetics on Samuel Taylor Coleridge and, through Coleridge, his indirect influence on other English poets of the period, he is also known as the philosopher of romanticism. In his last phase, which was partly a conscious reaction to Hegel, he anticipated some of the central ideas of the existentialists, and for this reason there has recently been a revival of interest in his later writings.

The development of Schelling's philosophy can be conveniently divided into four stages—subjective idealism, the philosophy of nature, the philosophy of identity, and the philosophy of the opposition of the negative and the positive. The stages are logically connected with one another, but also are clearly separate, so much so that their author was often accused of inconsistency. For example, Hegel wrote, "Schelling carried on his philosophic education before the public and signaled each fresh stage of his advance with a new treatise."

Subjective idealism. In the first stage Schelling was gradually working himself free from Fichte's subjective idealism to an independent position of his own. The major works of this phase were *Vom Ich als Prinzip der Philosophie, oder über das Unbedingte im menschlichen Wissen* (Tübingen, 1795), in which he posited the ego as the supreme, unconditioned element in human knowledge, and *Philosophische Briefe über Dogmatismus und Kritizismus* (in *Philosophisches Journal*, 1796), in which he compared Spinoza and Fichte. There is little that is original in these works other than the style and the tone. However, Schelling's style is important because its eloquence, its sense of emotional urgency, and its relative freedom from technical jargon—a rare trait in the writings of German idealists—all point to his affinity with the romantic movement and his unique philosophic stress on the importance of aesthetics.

Philosophy of nature. The second stage, the philosophy of nature, was the most famous and the most influential of Schelling's philosophies and remained so until recent years. The first important work of this stage was *Ideen zu einer Philosophie der Natur* (Leipzig, 1797). Against Fichte's conception of the world as the construction of the ego, Schelling now insisted that the world of nature is just as real and just as important as the world of the ego. In fact, it is nature, the objective, that gives to consciousness what consciousness reproduces anew. Originally, consciousness and nature are one and infinite; but consciousness limits itself and presents itself to itself as finite, as different from nature. The essence of the ego is spirit, and the essence of nature is matter, but the essence of matter is force; that is, attraction and repulsion. In force, Schelling finds the common ground of nature and ego. As attraction is objective, it is nature, it is matter; as repulsion it is subjective, it is ego, it is spirit. This duality also governs human perception: as attraction to the self, force governs the streaming of the outer world into the inner world of sensation, and this internal experience of movement constitutes the a priori basis of time; as repulsion, pushing out into the world, force constitutes the a priori basis of space.

Physical sciences. In *Von der Weltseele* (Hamburg, 1798) Schelling dealt with the philosophic problems of the physical sciences. He believed that the fundamental aim of the sciences was the interpretation of nature as a unity, and therefore the proper study of all sciences was force. He tried to show that mechanical, chemical, electrical, and vital forces were all different manifestations of the same underlying force. In the following year, in *Erster Entwurf eines Systems der Naturphilosophie* (Jena and Leipzig, 1799) and in *Einleitung zu dem Entwurf eines Systems der Naturphilosophie oder über den Begriff der spekulativen Physik* (Jena and Leipzig, 1799), he depicted this force as "pure activity." He saw nature as an infinite self-activity, realizing itself in finite matter but forever unexhausted, forever short of completely realizing itself. He felt that he had thus found a parallel in the physical universe for

Kant's idea of the moral universe as practical reason forever striving toward an unattainable ideal. He further developed this phase of his thought in "Allgemeine Deduktion des dynamischen Prozesses" (in *Zeitschrift für spekulative Physik,* Vol. 1, 1800); *Über den wahren Begriff der Naturphilosophie; Darstellung meines Systems der Philosophie* (Jena and Leipzig, 1801); and *Bruno, oder über das göttliche und natürliche Prinzip der Dinge* (Berlin, 1802).

Knowledge. In the *System des transzendentalen Idealismus* (Tübingen, 1800), his most systematic and mature statement, Schelling applied to the philosophy of nature the insights gained from the Kantian and Fichtean philosophy of knowledge. His technique for deriving the world of objects from the world of the ego was to turn consciousness upon itself as the only object of which we have immediate firsthand knowledge. Thus, he found that when we abstract from all objects of knowledge, both within ourselves and in the outside world, we arrive at the pure activity of abstracting, which is pure self-activity. Seen in this light, the consciousness of the not-self is the limit of self-activity, just as the things-in-themselves are at the limits of knowledge in *The Critique of Pure Reason.*

On this foundation, Schelling built a theory of three stages of knowledge, which he described as progressing from sensation to perception, from perception to reflection, and from reflection to will. At first, consciousness of a limit, of the not-self, is felt as a sensation. The limit, where the sensation is felt, is the meeting place of self-consciousness pushing outward and the force of the consciousness of external objects streaming inward. Therefore, all sensation is a feeling of myself as limited. Here we become aware of gravity, of the force of the real objective world in space, and also of intensity, which is the immediate consciousness of the self and its own activity in time. From the perception of the outside world comes reflection, and from reflection on the internal world comes will.

In this way Schelling felt that he had established links among Kant's categories, schemata, and objects of perception. Aside from the technical question of the correctness of this linkage—certainly Kant would have disputed it—it has great historical importance, because this is perhaps the only area in which Schelling decisively influenced the fully matured philosophy of Hegel, who used this reasoning to connect the dialectic of thesis-antithesis-synthesis with Kant's triadic formulation, though the dialectic itself was borrowed by Hegel from Fichte.

Schelling argued that the separation of knowledge from its object occurs only in abstraction. In reality, concepts have no existence apart from their objects, since knowledge is the meeting of objects and self. Therefore, the self is not merely one of the objects of knowledge; it is the condition of all knowledge. And since the essence of the self is pure self-activity, knowledge ultimately derives from willing, which is the action of the self.

Other minds. Schelling now asks two fundamental questions. How do I know there are other intelligences? And how can they act on me? He answers that our consciousness of limitations implies the existence of other selves that act as limiting factors. (Here he takes issue with Kant's teaching that intelligence is limited by something

not itself.) But the other selves can act on me only indirectly, through my representation of their acts. Their action does not compel mine, but limits it; and such limitation is compatible with my freedom. It is the community of interacting intelligences that constitutes the historical life of man. And while nature exists when not perceived by me, it exists then only because it is perceived by other human beings. Objectivity is intersubjectivity.

Will and imagination. Although perception is necessary and limited, will is free and unlimited. The imagination and its ideas mediate between perception and will. As opposed to the conceptions of the understanding, which are finite, the ideas of the imagination are both finite and infinite. An idea's relation to its object is finite, but the activity of the imagination in this relation is infinite. Each idea is subsumed under an ideal, as conceptions are subsumed under their schemata in Kant. The function of the will is to idealize the imagination's ideas. The contradiction thus engendered gives rise to impulse, defined as the desire to restore destroyed identity. Through impulse, there is constant realization of ideals, but the ideas of the imagination are constantly striven after and never attained.

Will and knowledge. The distinction between will and intelligence thus is relative, not absolute. From a higher point of view, they are identical. In intelligence, the I that acts and the I that knows are one. The acting I is an object for itself, while the knowing I merely perceives other objects. In action there is no transition from the world of nature to the world of mind, for the subject has become an object to itself. Any change in the outer world is received as a perception, but every action causes such a change; therefore action is perception. (Here, as elsewhere, Schelling anticipates Gestalt psychology.) Self-determination is the primary condition of all consciousness.

Justice. The object of impulse, which always acts to restore the lost identity of the self and the world, is happiness. But an impulse that transcends its proper limits acts against itself and must be prevented by a sanction not found in nature—a sanction of the will. This sanction of the will is thus the basis of justice, and the law of justice is a second nature that our will sets above the first nature.

The nature of history. The process of history is the gradual realization of law; history can be described as the development of human freedom, as an eternal progress toward the perfect state—a sovereign world federation of all sovereign states—in which all men would be citizens. Thus, history is the realization of freedom through necessity. There is an absolute identity between freedom and necessity, but this identity is forever unconscious, never the object of knowledge but always the object of faith. God is neither personal nor objective, but the revelation of the divine in man. This revelation is never complete. History is a drama in which men are not merely the actors, but also the authors.

Art and aesthetics. If history is a drama for Schelling, nature is a work of art. Like Kant in *The Critique of Judgment,* Schelling believed that organisms and works of art are alike in that they can be properly understood only teleologically; that is, as entities in which the parts serve the whole and the whole is itself purposive. The main difference between art and organisms, according to

Schelling, is that in organisms the activity of the organizing intelligence lies hidden or unconscious, manifest only in the product—the organism itself; but in the work of art the productive activity is conscious whereas the product, the true art work, is unconscious and infinite. The artist never fully understands his art. The purpose of art is neither utility, nor pleasure, nor morality, nor knowledge, but beauty—the realization of the infinite in the finite.

In his aesthetics, which is elaborated in the *System des transzendentalen Idealismus* and his lectures on the philosophy of art, *Über das Verhältniss der bildenden Künste zu der Natur* (Munich, 1807), Schelling is at his most personal, his most impassioned, his most characteristic, and his most original. He held that in art, intelligence for the first time becomes completely self-conscious. In philosophy, it is abstract and limited in the expression of its potential infinity. But in art, which is completely free from abstraction in this sense, intelligence fully realizes its infinite nature. (It is pertinent that Hans Arp, the abstract artist, has written that the works usually called "abstractions" are more accurately referred to as "concretions.") Thus art is the goal toward which all intelligence moves. Art is the true philosophy, because in it nature and history are forever reconciled; but the artist is not therefore a philosopher, since he often lacks a theoretical understanding of his own creation. The theoretical intelligence merely contemplates the world, and the practical intelligence merely orders it; but the aesthetic intelligence creates the world.

Philosophy of identity. The third stage of Schelling's thought was the philosophy of identity, first expounded at length in *Vorlesungen über die Methode des academischen Studiums* (Tübingen, 1803), appropriately written in Spinoza's geometric mode. Here Schelling said that the philosophy of nature and the philosophy of knowledge, taken together, constitute only half the truth and need to be completed by the other half, which unites nature and knowledge in an undifferentiated identity. The production of reality does not rest on the opposition of intelligence and nature, subject and object, but in the identity of all reality as it rises from the absolute. The absolute identity of nature and intelligence is found in their common neutral source, reason. Reason is one and infinite, embracing things-in-themselves and knowledge of things. In reason there is no object, no subject, no space, no time. Its supreme law is the law of identity, $A = A$, which is true regardless of all spatial or temporal considerations. In the formula $A = A$, the distinction between subject and object is formal and relative. Subject and object here concern only the form, and are indifferent as to essence. It was this phase of Schelling's thought that Hegel wittily called "the night in which . . . all cows are black."

Pantheism. The philosophy of identity was a kind of pantheism, but it stressed the aliveness of nature in contradistinction to Spinoza's dead, materialistic, deterministic pantheism. Although Spinoza's influence is evident, it is filtered through the vitalistic interpretations of Herder and Goethe and tempered by the parallel influence of Bruno's vitalistic pantheism. Schelling believed that life was the basis of the inorganic world, and not vice versa.

Nature is inseparable from God, but distinguishable from him. God is not to be comprehended rationally, because his essence is will and he can be apprehended only through the will, in action. For the most part, Schelling's thought here draws from Jakob Boehme, and reintroduces Protestant mysticism into the mainstream of Western philosophy.

God and evil. In *Philosophische Untersuchungen über das Wesen der menschlichen Freiheit* (Landshut, 1809; translated as *Of Human Freedom,* Chicago, 1936) Schelling, like Boehme, distinguishes between God as ground of being and God as perfection. Evil is explained as the ground eliciting the self-will of man in order to awaken him to the distinction between good and evil, which originally were united in one identity. Thus, evil is a necessary stage in the progress toward the total realization of good. Imperfection in being is perfection in the process of becoming. There is a dark ground or negative principle in God, but it exists so that he can become separate from it as a personality.

Positive philosophy. After 1809, the year of his first wife's death, Schelling made the given situation of existence his predominant concern. This final existentialist phase of his philosophy was first propounded in *Die Weltalter* (written in 1811 but not published in Schelling's lifetime), consummated in his lectures at the University of Berlin, and saved for posterity in three volumes, *Einleitung in die Mythologie, Philosophie der Mythologie,* and *Philosophie der Offenbarung,* which were published posthumously in the *Sämmtliche Werke.* In these works he sought to erect a positive philosophy based on the evolution of the divine principle in human history, especially in myths and religions, which he felt opposed and thus completed his own earlier, negative, merely rational philosophy. However, rather than representing a sharp break with his past, this last phase can be considered as the flowering of tendencies he showed as early as 1795, when he wrote, "The main function of all philosophy is the solution of the problem of the existence of the world." It is significant that while the prolific and influential writings of his first three periods were crowded into 14 brief years, from 1795 to 1809, his last period, during which his rate of production slowed and his influence waned, lasted from 1809 to his death in 1854.

God. The root of existence is now found in nonbeing, in God as the ungrounded, the abyss, the eternal nothing. Only against the ungrounded can the ground arise, because nothing can become evident without resistance. Thus God is "eternal contrariety," forever alienating himself from himself. This alienation creates the possibility of the fall. As only the Absolute is real, finite things, which are not real, can exist only in a removal, in a fall from reality. The Absolute creates its own counterpart, freedom, which is both the cause of the fall and the last trace of divinity things bear after the fall. Because of this progression through opposites, Schelling called this fourth phase of his thought the opposition of negative and positive philosophy.

Man. As the creature in whom the fall, and the state of things before the fall, both rise for the first time into consciousness, man is the crown of creation and the most interesting and rewarding object of philosophic attention. Man is free creative activity, the essence of the world. Thus, in his last phase, Schelling was led to a kind of philosophic anthropology, seeking for the essence of man in what he thought was his deepest activity, myth-making and religion. Despite the profoundly mystical flavor of his thought in this period, he still kept contact with his Kantian heritage. In *Philosophie der Mythologie* he explained mythology as a symbolic system of ideas with its own a priori structure as necessary for its functioning as, according to Kant, the a priori structure of the understanding is necessary for logical thought. Cassirer's recent Neo-Kantian formulation of mythology as just such a conceptual structure owes a great deal to Schelling, a debt fully acknowledged in the second volume of *The Philosophy of Symbolic Forms*.

Resemblance to existentialism. What has made this last phase of Schelling's thought most apposite to modern existential philosophy is another question rising from his consideration of man's being in the world. As he put it, "Just he, man, impelled me to the final desperate question: Why is there anything at all? Why not nothing?" It is this question, described as "dreadful" rather than "desperate," that Heidegger took for his central theme in *Being and Time*.

Schelling's resemblance to the modern existentialists is suggestive rather than substantive, but the suggestion is inescapable. Like them, he emphasized that philosophy must deal not only with the "what" of the world, which explains its nature, but also with the "that" of the world— the fact of its existence, of its being there. And like Kierkegaard (who attended some of his lectures in Berlin but was not impressed), Nietzsche, Heidegger, and Sartre, Schelling tried to express the inexpressible pathos of existence in oracular utterances halfway between poetry and metaphysics, the quality of which can be conveyed only by quotation. The world and God have as common ground "the incomprehensible basis of reality." "Existence is self-affirmation." God is "the infinite affirmation of himself." The objective world is the unconscious poetry of the spirit creating itself. Finally, there is a striking formulation of the existential anxiety, which is also an anticipation of the psychoanalytic doctrine of resistance: "The philosopher who knows his calling is the physician who . . . seeks to heal with gentle, slow hand the deep wounds of human consciousness. The restoration is all the more difficult since most people do not *want* to be healed at all and, like unhappy patients, raise an unruly outcry if one even approaches their wounds."

So the problems posed by Schelling over a hundred years ago are still very much alive in the philosophic and literary world of today. At that time his main influence in England was in aesthetics, and his lectures on the philosophy of art were translated as *The Philosophy of Art* in 1845. The continuing, perhaps growing contemporary interest in him is demonstrated by the fact that the first translations into English of any of his books since then— significantly, both from his last, existentialist phase—were published in America in 1936 and 1942.

Works by Schelling

COLLECTED WORKS

Sämmtliche Werke, K. F. A. von Schelling, ed., 14 vols. Stuttgart and Augsburg, 1856–1861.
Werke, M. Schröder, ed., 8 vols. Munich, 1927–1956.

TRANSLATIONS

The Ages of the World, translated by F. de Wolfe Bolman. New York, 1942. Translation of *Über die Gottheiten von Samothrake,* Stuttgart and Tübingen, 1815, a part of *Die Weltalter,* which is mentioned in the text. *The Ages of the World* includes a long, informative introduction on Schelling's philosophy, especially its last phase.
Of Human Freedom, translated by J. Gutmann. Chicago, 1936. Translation of *Philosophische Untersuchungen über das Wesen der menschlichen Freiheit.*
The Philosophy of Art: An Oration on the Relation Between the Plastic Arts and Nature, translated by A. Johnson. London, 1845. Translation of *Über das Verhältniss der bildenden Künste zu der Natur.*

Works on Schelling

Bréhier, Émile, *Schelling.* Paris, 1912.
Cassirer, Ernst, *Das Erkenntnisproblem in der Philosophie und Wissenschaft der neueren Zeit,* Vol. III, *Die Nachkantischen Systeme.* Berlin, 1920. Includes a comprehensive, clear, and sympathetic account of Schelling's epistemology.
Copleston, Frederick C., *History of Philosophy,* Vol. VII. London, 1963. Includes the best account of Schelling's philosophy in English.
Fischer, Kuno, *Geschichte der neueren Philosophie,* Vol. VII, 3d ed. Heidelberg, 1902. Probably the best full-length study of Schelling's life and work.
Hartmann, Nicolai, *Die Philosophie des deutschen Idealismus,* 2d ed. Berlin, 1960. An exhaustive and authoritative work on German idealism.
Hirsch, Eric D., *Wordsworth and Schelling.* New York, 1962. Reviews Schelling's aesthetics and its parallels in Wordsworth.
Jaspers, Karl, *Schelling: Grösse und Verhängnis.* Munich, 1955. A profound and searching analysis from an existentialist point of view.
Kroner, Richard, *Von Kant bis Hegel,* 2 vols. Tübingen, 1921–1924.
Noack, Ludwig, *Schelling und die Philosophie der Romantik.* Berlin, 1859.
Read, Herbert, *The True Voice of Feeling.* London, 1953. Concerned with Schelling's influence on Coleridge. Includes translation of a chapter on philosophy of art by Schelling.
Schneeberger, G., *Schelling: Eine Bibliographie.* Bern, 1954. An extensive bibliography.
Watson, John, *Schelling's Transcendental Idealism.* Chicago, 1882. A clear, careful, scholarly paraphrase of Schelling's *System des transcendentalen Idealismus.*

ADAM MARGOSHES

SCHILLER, FERDINAND CANNING SCOTT (1864–1937), British pragmatist philosopher, was born in Schleswig-Holstein and studied at Rugby and at Balliol College, Oxford. After teaching German at Eton, he returned to Oxford for his M.A. In 1893 he went to Cornell University as an instructor and graduate student. In 1897, without receiving a doctorate, he returned to Corpus Christi College, Oxford, where he was successively assistant tutor, tutor, senior tutor, and fellow and where he received a D.Sc. in 1906. He served as treasurer of the Mind Association and president of the Aristotelian Society (1921), and he was elected a fellow of the British Academy in

1926. From 1926 on, Schiller spent part of each year at the University of Southern California as visiting lecturer and then as professor; in 1935 he moved there permanently.

Pragmatism. Schiller's views, which he called at various times humanism, voluntarism, and personalism, as well as pragmatism, were strongly influenced by William James; and Schiller paid James great tribute, although he claimed to have arrived at his opinions independently. There was, however, an important difference of emphasis between them: James stressed the purposive aspect of thinking, and Schiller, the personal. James also accepted the independence of what is objectively given, whereas Schiller regarded all knowledge, even of "facts," as relatively subjective. Both Schiller and John Dewey were strongly influenced by Hegel and took the process of knowing as central to reality, but the influence of idealism was much stronger on Schiller than on Dewey. And whereas Schiller pursued the subjective and individual aspects of James's psychology, Dewey built upon its objective and social aspects. C. S. Peirce thought that Schiller's philosophy was intermediate between James's and his own.

Schiller's views may best be understood in terms of his opposition to the dominant absolute idealism of the British Hegelians, F. H. Bradley (Schiller's particular bête noire), J. M. E. McTaggart, Bernard Bosanquet, and T. H. Green. To Schiller the absolutism, monism, authoritarianism, rationalism, and intellectualism which these thinkers espoused ignored the basic insight of Protagoras that man is the measure of all things.

Schiller was convinced that all acts and all thoughts are irreducibly the products of individual human beings and therefore inescapably associated with the needs, desires, and purposes of men. Such terms as "reality" and "truth" denote nothing complete and absolute; rather, they are intertwined with human intentions and deeds. Schiller emphasized the effective creativity of the human mind in organizing the universe of human experience and thus in making or remaking "reality." Man makes his truth along with his other values, beauty and goodness. Our axioms are never God-given but are man-made; they are not a priori verities but postulates, or working hypotheses, whose truth grows or diminishes within our experience. The logic we employ in gathering knowledge is dynamic and functional rather than eternally fixed. Our data are not "the given" but "the taken." Thus, in Schiller's view, man's activity is focal both to epistemology and to metaphysics, and there is genuine novelty in our growing universe and no theoretical limit to man's freedom.

Making reality. The absolute idealists maintained that reality is a seamless logical unity, not a mere disjointed plurality; that in the Absolute all separateness vanishes; that nothing finite, nothing that changes, is ever quite real, not even human personality; and that there is something makeshift, transitory, and unsatisfactory about the bits of matter we see, the individual acts we perform, and the private thoughts we think. But, Schiller pointed out, that is all that exists for us. An independent or absolute reality that does not enter into our experience, or explain our knowledge, is irrelevant to us. "Reality" for us is piecemeal, incomplete, and plastic. It is idle to ask "What is

real?" Rather, the only question we can answer is "What can I know as real?"

The reality revealed by our actual active procedures of knowing is not rigid but malleable, not completed but evolving. Because it responds, at least to some extent, to our working and probing, it must somehow be not unrelated to our needs and purposes. The process of knowing, Schiller said, is "*never* one of bringing the mind into relation with a fundamentally alien reality, but always one of improving and extending an already existing system which we know." What we call real is that which, for our own reasons, we evaluate as important. It is the result of the kind of selection by which we reduce the chaos about us to order.

Schiller's critics found intolerable the thesis that we make reality. Bertrand Russell, for example, wrote, "Dr. Schiller says that the external world was first discovered by a low marine animal he calls 'Grumps,' who swallowed a bit of rock that disagreed with him, and argued that he would not have given himself such a pain, and therefore there must be an external world. One is tempted to think that . . . many people . . . had not yet made the disagreeable experience which Grumps made. Meanwhile, whatever accusations pragmatists may bring, I shall continue to protest that it was not I who made the world" ("Professor Dewey's 'Essays in Experimental Logic,'" *Journal of Philosophy,* Vol. 16, Jan. 1919, p. 26).

Schiller found it hard to meet two particular objections to the theory of the making of reality: the world obviously preceded the existence of man, and there are patent limits to man's powers. In his later writings Schiller therefore reluctantly accepted the distinction between "finding" and "making" the real, although he reiterated the meaninglessness of the "real-as-it-is-in-itself." He revived the Greek term *hule* to refer to the indeterminate, formless chaos, to whatever may be beyond man's ability to perceive or manipulate, to the raw malleable material of the cosmos.

Despite its drawbacks, the doctrine of the making of reality provided Schiller with the basis for certain important conclusions. In his view, it provided a perfect accommodation for Darwinian evolution; it supported a belief in the existence of genuinely new things and situations (always a problem for the absolute idealists because they regarded reality as a self-contained whole); it legitimized human progress; it provided a suitable conceptual scheme for the view, which Schiller ascribed to Einstein and other scientists, that to posit "the real" independently of our sensations is to make an intellectual construction; and, most significantly, it was a firm foundation for man's freedom.

Other metaphysical views. Schiller's other metaphysical views may be briefly stated. The function of philosophy, he thought, was to preserve the grand synoptic vision, to be an ultimate synthesis of the special sciences. Metaphysical systems, he held, are quasi-ethical, or even aesthetic, in character; they reflect personality and temperament. Because the individual human person was an ontological ultimate for Schiller, he was a personalistic pluralist. He was also a hylozoist, asserting that all matter is more or less alive.

Truth. Many theories of truth have been propounded

through the centuries, but none has been entirely satisfactory. Schiller pointed out the shortcomings of some, particularly the correspondence and coherence theories. Pragmatists agree that no statement wears its truth like a badge; its truth can be determined only by what follows from it in the course of experience. Truth is only a potential, a valuation applied as the result of a procedure called verifying, or making true. Truth is relative to the evidence and to the purpose of the investigator; no degree of verification will ever establish the absolute truth of a statement. Schiller held that truth is personal and particular, dynamic and progressive, not eternal or absolute but the best solution found so far for any problem. That which thwarts or defeats the purpose of an inquiry we call false; that which furthers it we call true. "Truth is that manipulation of [objects] which turns out upon trial to be useful, primarily for any human end, but ultimately for that perfect harmony of our whole life which forms our final aspiration" (*Humanism*, p. 61).

Nevertheless, Schiller thought the conversion of "The truth is useful" to "The useful is true" to be malicious. Therefore, in Chapter 8 of *Logic for Use* he distinguished seven kinds of truth claims. (1) A postulate is a statement that is "desirable if true," whose truth we try to establish. (2) "A fully verified postulate which serves as principle for a fully established science . . ." and ". . . rests securely on the solid mass of scientific fact it has been instrumental in eliciting" is an axiom. (3) A methodological assumption (determinism, for example) is any guiding principle that appears to be useful in analyzing the flux of events. (4) An assumption of limited usefulness, such as the use of Euclidean geometry in cartography, is a methodological fiction. Finally, truth claims may be, or are, made in (5) fictions, (6) jokes, and (7) lies. Lies are deliberately untrue but may be useful, as in propaganda.

Thus, Schiller held, to claim that all truths work for us in some way and that there is no useless knowledge is far from saying that whatever is useful is true. However, he was aware of difficulties concerning the status of past truth, the usefulness of some parts of pure mathematics, and such questions as whether truth is equivalent to survival value or to social acceptance.

Logic. Since the true is what is true for us as seekers for it, Schiller deplored the divorce of logic from the empirical sciences and from psychology. He criticized traditional formal logic for having been a word game and for having been allied to metaphysics rather than to the empirical sciences and to psychology. For Schiller, as for Dewey, thought arises as an element in the solution of a problem. Thus the activity of reasoning has a biological matrix, and it is conditioned by such factors as interest, purpose, emotion, and satisfaction. Schiller was concerned with showing that meanings had been misunderstood and ignored by logic. Meanings, he pointed out, are acquired only in use; they are plastic and personal, and they occur only in contexts. Traditional logic regarded them as purely verbal and as fixed; it believed that one meaning corresponded to one form, and vice versa. Schiller thought that logic had made the two mistakes of "etherealizing" and "depersonalizing" truth. In its search for formal validity, it had made three fatal abstractions; from actual thinking processes (psychol-

ogy); from purpose, truth, or utility; and from meaning, matter, and context. In two books, *Formal Logic* (1912) and *Logic for Use* (1929), Schiller made an exhaustive study of formal logic, including terms, propositions, definitions, the syllogism, and fallacies. He showed that, even on its own terms, logic was not free from ambiguity—how can there be novelty in the conclusion of a syllogism? What is the precise import of the copula in a proposition? Moreover, logic appealed at several crucial points to such psychological notions as the "necessity" of implication and the "certainty" or "self-evidence" of propositions. Schiller thought that logic should become a systematic evaluation of actual knowing, a study continuous with the sciences. His resolute experimentalism led him to assert, in "Axioms as Postulates" (1902), that even the laws of thought (identity, contradiction, excluded middle) are not principles of being or rules of logic but postulates.

Scientific method. In analyzing the procedures of science, Schiller made several noteworthy contributions. He showed that the concept of "fact" is ambiguous. The "facts" of the scientist are the result of a process of selection, segregation, and evaluation; they are relative to the state of the science, the methods and instruments used, and the aims and bias of the scientist. They are also relative to the hypothesis used, to our own senses, to our memory, and to our words. Schiller also said, "The impossibility of 'breaking' a Law of Nature proves nothing but our determination to uphold a phraseology we have found convenient" (*Formal Logic*, p. 328).

Ethics and religion. Schiller carried his pragmatic approach into ethics and religion. There are no abstract values, he said, but only acts of personal valuation. Moral principles are not a priori presuppositions of right conduct; they are its results. The statements of religion are likewise postulates. (James spoke of the will to believe; Schiller, of the right to postulate.) God is a pervasive principle of goodness, not infinite but finite, struggling to develop; the actions of men therefore make a difference. Man's freedom is correlative to the postulate that man is responsible for his acts and is an agent in the full sense of the term. Schiller shared with James and Bergson an interest in psychical research which stemmed from his desire to examine the methods of science at its periphery and from his postulate of immortality. Schiller was also keenly interested in eugenics. This led him to oppose democracy as a "sham" (*Problems of Belief*, p. 81) and to praise the British fascist Oswald Moseley. His social opinions were generally regarded by his philosophic supporters as a vagary.

Schiller was a prolific writer, a sprightly stylist, and a spirited polemicist who maintained a role of philosophic *enfant terrible* through hundreds of essays and books. He edited and wrote most of a parody of *Mind*, which he called *Mind!*—one of the rare examples of philosophic humor.

Bibliography

Schiller's major books are two collections of essays, *Humanism: Philosophical Essays* (London and New York, 1903) and *Studies in Humanism* (London and New York, 1907). Two later collections are *Must Philosophers Disagree?* (London, 1934) and *Our Human Truths* (New York, 1939).

His major works in logic are *Formal Logic: A Scientific and Social Problem* (London, 1912) and *Logic for Use: An Introduction to the Voluntarist Theory of Knowledge* (London, 1929).

His essay "Axioms as Postulates" appeared in the anthology *Personal Idealism*, Henry Sturt, ed. (London, 1902), pp. 47–133. An early, prepragmatic metaphysics, entitled *Riddles of the Sphinx* and written under the pseudonym of A. Troglodyte (London and New York, 1891), was offered unsuccessfully to Cornell University as a Ph.D. thesis. The essays "Scientific Discovery and Logical Proof" (1917) and "Hypothesis" (1921) were contributed to *Studies in the History and Method of Science,* edited by Charles J. Singer (Oxford, 1918–1921), and may be found in Vol. I, pp. 235–289, and Vol. II, pp. 414–446, respectively. Another work by Schiller is *Problems of Belief* (London, 1924).

A critical study of Schiller's philosophy, with an exhaustive bibliography, is Reuben Abel, *The Pragmatic Humanism of F. C. S. Schiller* (New York, 1955).

REUBEN ABEL

SCHILLER, FRIEDRICH (1759–1805), German poet, playwright, and philosopher, was born in Marbach, Swabia. Duke Karl Eugen of Württemberg, in whose service Schiller's father rose to captain, founded the Karlsschule, in which Schiller was obliged to enroll at the age of 13. He reluctantly gave up his original desire to study theology and, after a false start in the law, turned to medicine. He practiced as an army surgeon for a time, until the success of *Die Räuber* in 1781 decided his vocation as a dramatist. The difficulties of supporting himself by his writing are evident in the haste and volume of his early works, some of which, however, are still performed. In 1790 he married Charlotte von Lengefeld; they had four children. Despite the poverty and chronic sickness that led to his death at the age of 45, Schiller expanded his range to produce major histories of the Dutch rebellion against Spain and of the Thirty Years' War. His historical studies provided the basis of his trilogy *Wallenstein,* as well as of *Don Carlos, Die Jungfrau von Orleans,* and *Wilhelm Tell,* among others. After a period of mutual misunderstanding, Schiller formed a friendship with Goethe, whose character as poet and individual was as much the occasion of Schiller's philosophical quest as the problems raised by Kant's metaphysics and aesthetics. After an interval as professor at Jena, Schiller joined the famous circle at Weimar, where he died.

PHILOSOPHY AND AESTHETICS

There has been in recent years a revival of interest in Schiller as a philosopher. He was not a systematic thinker, and whenever the attempt has been made to accommodate his philosophical efforts in a single scheme, generally on the model of Kant or Fichte, he has invariably suffered by the comparison. Yet he made significant contributions to aesthetics and comparative philosophy even though he abandoned philosophy to return to poetry and drama, having become disillusioned with what he believed to be the excessive claims to certainty and finality of philosophy in his day. Schiller had at first attempted an objective aesthetic theory in the spirit of rationalist philosophy; however, after some notable encounters with Kant, Goethe, and Fichte, his aesthetic theory became an integral account of life and the indispensable role played in it by what Schiller called the aesthetic impulse.

Five stages, not equal in importance, can be traced in the rather loose development of his philosophical and aesthetic writings.

First stage. The first stage of Schiller's development is represented in his writings by two early speeches (1779–1780) made at the Karlsschule in Stuttgart, where he was educated, and in his theses toward the medical doctorate: *Philosophie der Physiologie* ("Philosophy of Physiology," 1779) and *Über den Zusammenhang der tierischen Natur des Menschen mit seiner Geistigen* ("Essay on the Connection Between Man's Animal and His Spiritual Nature," 1780). Although Schiller's initial training was in the tradition of the dominant Leibniz–Wolffian school, his second philosophy teacher, J. F. Abel, introduced him to the Scottish common-sense philosophers and to the English empiricists. The conflict among these schools is best illustrated in the *Philosophische Briefe* ("Philosophical Letters," 1780?–1788) between Julius (who represents Schiller) and Raphael (Abel at first; later Schiller's friend Christian Gottfried Körner, who wrote at least one of the later letters). Julius bemoans the shaking of the old rational certainties by the new thinkers who destroy faith in the rightness of the world's governance without substituting anything equally worthy of faith.

What is most significant in these early writings, apart from the preoccupation with the mind–body problem, is the repeated appearance of Schiller's characteristic method. In a manner prefiguring the Hegelian dialectic, Schiller typically generates the opposed positions of the schools as sharply as possible and then seeks some intermediate view by which they can be reconciled. One example (from *Philosophie der Physiologie*) will suffice: Schiller proposes a mediating force which possesses the exclusive properties of neither matter nor mind but which in some way combines them; this he calls nervous spirit (*Nervengeist*).

Second stage. The second stage began in 1782, when, as a result of the *succès de scandale* of Schiller's first play, *Die Räuber* ("The Robbers," 1781), Duke Karl Eugen prohibited him from writing on any but medical topics. In response, Schiller fled from Stuttgart to Mannheim. This was a period of *Sturm und Drang*, but Schiller combined the self-assertiveness of his new-found freedom with extraordinarily acute self-criticism, as manifested in his own anonymous review (1782) of *Die Räuber* and in the *Briefe über Don Carlos* ("Letters on Don Carlos," 1788). He was concerned with three problems.

First, he questions, especially in *Über das gegenwärtige deutsche Theater* ("The Present-day German Theater," 1782), the validity and autonomy of the art work if it is seen merely as the subjective expression of the artist; for if art is seen in this way, then freedom seems indistinguishable from anarchy. Second, he examines, but cannot yet decide, the issue whether art is subordinate to cognitive and moral criteria. This is taken up in his essay "Die Schaubühne als eine moralische Anstalt betrachtet" ("The Stage as a Moral Institution," 1784) and in the two great "prephilosophical" poems, "Die Götter Griechenlands" ("The Gods of Greece," 1788) and "Die Künstler" ("The Artists," 1789). Third, and most crucial for his own development, is the profound inadequacy he felt in himself compared with the effortless felicity of Goethe's Olympian presence. A letter to Körner of February 2, 1789, illustrates Schiller's feelings: "He has aroused a quite astonishing mixture of hatred and love in me, a feeling not unlike that which Brutus and Cassius must have had for Caesar; I could murder his spirit and then love him with all my heart." From 1789 to 1795 Schiller abandoned poetry and drama until he could resolve these problems of the artist's—especially his own—vocation.

Third stage. The third stage covers the study of Kant, mainly of the *Critique of Judgment*. Schiller's first reaction to this work was dismay at finding that, despite the universality and necessity Kant ascribed to the judgment of taste, he still considered it essentially subjective, as contrasted with the objectivity of cognitive and ethical judgments. Schiller's answer was to attempt "to establish an objective concept of beauty and fully to legitimate it a priori out of the nature of reason" (to Körner, January 25, 1793). This effort is carried out in the "Kallias Letters" to Körner in January and February 1793, but it remained inconclusive, as indeed it must, given the presuppositions of Kant's epistemology, which Schiller on the whole accepted. Schiller finds that the distinction between these judgments is attributable to the dualism of sense and reason in Kant's view of human nature. Kant's rejection of the sensuous aspect as intrinsically inimical and to be suppressed is attacked in *Über Anmut und Würde* ("On Grace and Dignity," 1793). In its stead, Schiller offers, in the first 16 of the *Briefe über die ästhetische Erziehung des Menschen* ("Letters on the Aesthetic Education of Mankind," 1794–1795), an analysis of human nature as comprising three "impulses": the material and formal impulses (*Stofftrieb* and *Formtrieb*), corresponding to Kant's dualism, and a third, the play or aesthetic impulse (*Spieltrieb*), mediating and reconciling them in an integral unity. The famous formulation of the "Kallias Letters," that "beauty is freedom in appearance," reflects Schiller's conviction that Kant has misplaced freedom by locating it in reason alone. Goethe is held guilty (in *Über Anmut und Würde*) of the opposite offense; his genius is taken to be a "mere natural phenomenon," the passive receipt of the Muses' whisperings, not a hard-won conquest over unthinking spontaneity. Goethe acutely remarked to Eckermann many years later that Schiller wrote *Über Anmut und Würde* "to defend himself against me."

But these personal considerations should not be allowed to obscure the far more general dimensions of the problems Schiller was approaching. His theory of aesthetic education, first sketched at this time, has as its objective the harmonious balance not only of the individual's faculties but also of society. In the *Briefe über die ästhetische Erziehung des Menschen*, Schiller's strictures on the social and political institutions of the outgoing eighteenth century are not only dictated by the shock of the Terror but are also remarkable for anticipating the one-sided development and alienation of the individual in an age of specialization.

Aesthetic education (mainly treated in the Thirteenth Letter) is to overcome this fragmentation of life by correcting any excessive commitment in the direction of sense or reason. Where sense predominates in excess, Schiller criticizes the resultant materialism and hedonism. His attack on the exaggerated preconceived teleological principles of the rationalists is coupled with another on Kant's moral rigorism—Schiller denounces the fear that inclination might corrupt duty. The play impulse avoids these extremes of explaining the world exclusively in terms of sense or reason, not by addressing itself to an extrinsic reality by which we are wholly determined but by taking as its object a semblance (*Schein*) of reality which we freely construct ourselves. The related concepts of aesthetic education, play, and semblance, which at this stage seem vague and unspecific, are more unified in Schiller's final position. The advance which characterizes this period is the abandonment of the search for objective beauty as a property of the object ("Kallias Letters") or in the interaction of object and perceiver (*Über Anmut und Würde*); Schiller had now embarked on a very general theory which treats of the aesthetic impulse as the indispensable condition of human nature.

Fourth stage. The views outlined so far undergo a series of changes in the fourth stage so remarkable as to constitute a revolution in Schiller's thought. The key to them lies in his new appreciation of Goethe, epitomized in the *Urpflanze* episode of July 1794. Goethe, explaining his theory of plant morphology to Schiller, sketched a primeval plant as the common ancestor of many subsequent species. In Goethe's words, "He heard and watched everything with great interest and a decided calm; but when I finished he shook his head and said: that is no experience, that is an idea." Schiller had discovered that Goethe, far from being solely dependent upon what nature pleases to give, in fact transmuted the content of his experience, unconsciously supplying the human element of freedom in the transformation of mere perception into a structured whole. This sudden insight into Goethe had far-reaching consequences. In the last 11 of the *Briefe über ästhetische Erziehung des Menschen* there is a shift in the metaphysical foundation on which the aesthetic theory proper is erected. From this period dates Schiller's final abandonment of the rationalistic view that art, to possess any universal significance, must be an imitation of nature.

Rather, the position implied, although it is not made explicit until the fifth stage, is that the external world is known only as man constructs an image of it for himself. We must also note a shift from the argument of the *Briefe über die ästhetische Erziehung des Menschen*, which views the conflict of sense impulse and form impulse as taking place exclusively within the individual, to the position in *Über naive und sentimentalische Dichtung* ("Naive and Sentimental Poetry," 1795), which sees an analogous conflict between classes of individuals.

In the first two parts of *Über naive und sentimentalische Dichtung*, which Thomas Mann has called "the greatest of German essays," Schiller develops a typology of poets. The first purpose of this is to show the existence and equal validity of different modes of perception (*Empfindungsweisen*). The naive poet—Goethe is the exemplar—views the world unconsciously with a spontaneous acceptance of nature as it is or seems to him to be. While the naive poet "*is* nature," the sentimental poet "*seeks* nature"; he sees that the world falls short of an ideal.

If he is repelled by actuality, he is satirical; if he mourns the ideal as lost, he is elegiac; and if he treats the ideal as though it were present, he is idyllic. Schiller indirectly presents himself as a sentimental poet and vindicates his own viewpoint, while at the same time conceding the enviable position of the naive poet.

Speaking thus far only from the standpoint of the poetic typology, Schiller is able to argue, against Kant, that the objectivity, or uniformity, of human response to the environment is not secured by the strict uniformity of the human mind. The different types of poet quite simply *see* the world differently, not, to be sure, with regard to bare factual description but certainly wherever any sort of interpretation or explanation is involved. There were already hints in the Fifteenth Letter that not only was Schiller concerned with the implications in this view for poetry but also that he was prepared to extend this analysis to all forms of explanation, especially philosophical, scientific, and religious. In each case the perspective adopted is colored by different unconscious temperamental dispositions. Thus, Schiller's original effort to show that aesthetic judgment is as objective as cognitive and moral judgments results in his revolutionary conclusion that cognitive and moral judgments are, indeed, as objective (that is, as subjective) as aesthetic judgments.

Fifth stage. In the fifth stage it is the theory of types that provided Schiller's solution to his problems of art and nature, art and cognition, and the artist's vocation. With the development of this theory, Schiller's philosophizing stopped abruptly, with little philosophical elaboration of the solutions implied by his position. The interpretation offered here falls between those interpretations which insist that Schiller's last philosophical writings are entirely of a piece with his earlier idealism and those which claim a sharp turn toward realism in his late works.

Philosophers have always taken it for granted that the scrutiny of first premises—especially of a metaphysical order—is peculiarly their business; and most have further assumed that it is also the philosopher who formulates these premises before they can be scrutinized; but, in Schiller's view, prior to both scrutiny and formulation is their origination—and this, it turns out, is a function of the poet, not of the philosopher. The theory of types in *Über naive und sentimentalische Dichtung* illustrates two major aspects of Schiller's final position. First, there are, as a matter of fact, at least two radically opposed ways of viewing the world, and what has been shown of the poets is also true of men in general—the last part of the essay argues that the typology of poets is only a special case of a still more general theory of human nature. Second, neither of these opposed world views can claim objective validity, either in the strong sense of the rationalists or in the weaker sense of Kant. Of two conflicting hypotheses at least one must be wrong; Schiller's conclusion seems to be that both are wrong. In the essay "Über das Erhabene" ("On the Sublime," 1795 or 1801—the date is disputed), he advises us to take what he calls the uncomprehensibility of nature as a principle of explanation. That is, if we accept the notion that the external world is strictly unknowable ("natural necessity has entered into no compact with man"), then the status of our

hypotheses about the world is that of fictions, inventions, and heuristic devices to answer the questions to which we need answers in order to live; but the validity of these hypotheses will depend upon human criteria of factualness, logic, and plausibility and not upon their agreement with an extrinsic nature.

In "Über das Erhabene" Schiller maintains that man's freedom, his most essential quality, is imposed on him because any account of the world in its totality must transcend his finite experience; and the totality to which his explanations must apply—if their validity is to be objectively verified—is never given. Men are therefore free, within the limitations of what is given, to invent whatever schemes are compatible with those limitations. The philosopher, Schiller has told us (evidently with Fichte in mind), is a caricature compared with the poet, who is the true human being; the philosopher seeks only to make explicit and justify what he already believes, while the poet is not bound by his original endowment of temperament or by the accident of environment. The doctrine of aesthetic education fits this scheme exactly, for Schiller is not committed to a theory of temperament biologically or culturally determined beyond remedy. World views change, and they are changed by men able to liberate themselves from the thralldom of existing attitudes. It is precisely because world views are made, not given, that the makers, the poets, and all men, when they exercise this function, are free.

Schiller's insights, in their final form, have been fruitful in the philosophies of thinkers as diverse as Hegel (especially with regard to method), Nietzsche, Dilthey, James, Jung (who produced variations on Schiller's typology of human nature), Cassirer (the idea of explanatory schemes as symbolic constructs), Marx, Mill, and Dewey (social philosophy).

Bibliography

There is more than one collection of Schiller's works. *Schillers sämtliche Werke, Säkular-Ausgabe,* Eduard von der Hellen, ed., 17 vols. (Stuttgart, 1904–1905), remains the standard edition until completion of the *Nationalausgabe,* publication of which began in Weimar in 1943. *Aesthetic Letters,* translated by Reginald Snell (New Haven, 1954), is a sound translation, unlike the earlier collections, which are unreliable.

For Schiller's letters, see *Schillers Briefe,* Fritz Jonas, ed. (Stuttgart, 1892–1896); Schiller–Goethe *Briefwechsel,* Hans Gräf and Albert Leitzmann, eds. (Leipzig, 1912), and the Schiller–Körner *Briefwechsel,* Karl Goedeke, ed. (Leipzig, 1878).

Bibliographies can be found in Karl Goedeke, *Grundriss zur Geschichte der deutsche Dichtung,* 2d ed. (Dresden, 1903), Vol. V, Part 2, pp. 15–237, and Wolfgang Vulpius, *Schiller-Bibliographie 1893–1958* (Weimar, 1959). Current bibliographies can be found in *PMLA.*

For commentary on Schiller, see Benno von Wiese, *Friedrich Schiller* (Stuttgart, 1959), which embodies the latest scholarship, especially on drama and biography; E. M. Wilkinson, *Schiller. Poet or Philosopher?* (Oxford, 1961), a succinct account of the tension between poetry and philosophy in Schiller; and W. F. Mainland, *Schiller: Ueber Naive und Sentimentalische Dichtung* (Oxford, 1957), the critical edition. S. S. Kerry, *Schiller's Writings on Aesthetics* (Manchester, 1961), omits the last period. For exhaustive listings, see the *Schiller-Bibliographie 1893–1958,* pp. 399–420.

JULIUS ELIAS

SCHLEGEL, FRIEDRICH VON (1772–1829), the leader of the German Romantic movement, was born in Hanover and there received a classical education. He studied law at Göttingen and Leipzig but immediately abandoned it to devote himself to literary pursuits. In the period from 1788 to 1799, his intellectually formative years, Schlegel acquainted himself with all the main currents of contemporary German thought. Kant's *Kritik der Urteilskraft* left a lasting impression on him, but he rejected the critical approach as failing satisfactorily to relate the real and the ideal. While a *Privatdozent* at Jena (1796), Schlegel met Fichte, learned of his theory of the world-creating Ego, and for a time became Fichte's intellectual ally. At Jena he also met Schelling, who introduced him to *Naturphilosophie*. In Berlin in 1797 Schlegel studied the pantheistic mysticism of Schleiermacher, and his attention turned to Spinoza and emanationist philosophy. Finally he was drawn to Leibniz' monadic theory of ideal individuality. All the while Schlegel concerned himself with literature, especially the distinction between ancient and modern; and ultimately it was Schiller's theory of aesthetic consciousness, in which the phenomenal and noumenal worlds converge in pure creative activity, that most deeply influenced his thinking.

Between 1798 and 1808 Schlegel's intellectual tendencies took shape in writings devoted to poetry, criticism, philosophy, and theology. He founded the journal *Athenäum* and, together with his brother August, Ludwig Tieck, and Novalis, contributed essays to it. These articles, formulating the basic conceptions of the German Romantic movement, established Schlegel as its head.

In 1802 Schlegel went to Paris, where he delivered lectures on philosophy, studied Sanskrit, and edited the review *Europa*. Six years later he published *Über die Sprache und Weisheit der Inder,* married Moses Mendelssohn's daughter, converted to Roman Catholicism, and moved to Vienna to assume political duties, first as imperial court secretary to Archduke Charles (1809) and, after the peace of 1814, as Metternich's representative from the Viennese court to the Diet of Frankfurt. When Schlegel returned to Vienna in 1818, he continued his scholarly career and, from 1820 to 1823, edited the Catholic review *Concordia* with Adam Müller. In his two Viennese periods Schlegel gave lectures on modern history (1810) and on ancient and modern literature (1812), and wrote his *Philosophie des Lebens* (1828).

The three leading themes in Schlegel's thought are irony, genius, and dynamic universalism. He renamed the antithetical terms of Schiller's theory of aesthetic consciousness Classic and Romantic, and pursued the theory to its logical extreme. The Classical poet subordinates himself to his material; the Romantic poet dominates it through his personality. Believing with Fichte that speculative understanding is superior to Kant's principle of reflective understanding, Schlegel gave primacy to the creative fancy for which the world is simply an occasion to express itself in all its fullness. The exercise of irony offers the greatest possible expression of freedom, the widest field for creative endeavor, because irony joins jest and earnestness, and artistic feeling for life with a scientific spirit. Since irony strives to rise above all conditions, in the end it must strive to rise above its own art. Thus it reaches its highest level in calculated irrationalism, "transcendental buffoonery," which places the artist at a point outside the world.

In artistic activity the artist becomes increasingly aware of himself as an individual and at the same time, as creator, he discovers the divine element within himself. This constitutes his genius. For this notion Schlegel drew upon Spinoza, Schleiermacher, Leibniz, and the general store of German idealism. Poetry assumes a symbolic significance by expressing the relationship between the artist and the Godhead. Because of the universal character of this relationship, which the artist merely makes explicit, poetry was for Schlegel "eine progressive Universalpoesie." "The peculiar preeminence of man consists in this—that to him alone among all other of earth's creatures, the word has been imparted and communicated. The word actually delivered and really communicated is not a mere dead faculty, but an historical reality and occurrence . . ." (*The Philosophy of History,* p. 86).

The peculiar task of the artist, to articulate the ambiguities and contradictions of a chaotic world, called for an explanatory theory. Schlegel found this in Schelling's dialectical triad of the infinite, the finite, and their final reunion. Its verification, Schlegel believed, is provided by Roman Catholic dogma and the church. Of necessity, therefore, philosophy had to be brought into union with history. The only preconception required for all historical deductions, Schlegel asserted, is a "universal faith in the heavenly Promethean light—or as we should rather say, this spark of our bosoms" (*The Philosophy of History,* p. 73). Schlegel's theory of history reveals the influence of Herder and Goethe, who saw history as the process wherein man strives to realize his essential relationship with the Godhead, a process that can be grasped only symbolically. With Herder, Schlegel believed that nations, by virtue of linguistic unity, are the basic units of history. It is the purpose of states to preserve nations; hence, the true goal of history, for Schlegel, is best facilitated by conservative political principles and institutions, of which the Catholic church is the supreme example. In agreement with Novalis, but unlike Herder, Schlegel regarded the Middle Ages as paradigmatic for the ideal state of society, combining political and religious authority with the integrity of the individual nations.

Vitalized by fancy on the one hand, and by the Godhead on the other, nature becomes the ground of the relationship between man, history, and the divine. Drawing upon Spinoza, Schelling, and Schleiermacher, Schlegel believed that nature so conceived provides the ground for universal identity. History itself supports this belief, he contended, for after coming to know God in his conscience, man next acquired knowledge of God through a mythic representation of nature. The concurrent tradition of all nations leads us to the idea of man's possessing . . . an immediate and intuitive knowledge of God in and out of nature, and . . . an immediate and intuitive knowledge of nature in God" (*Philosophy of Life,* p. 235). Nature is a world of sensuous symbols, and can be grasped only symbolically. Fancy thus assumed a primary role in Schlegel's thought precisely because it reflected ". . . the living powers of the natural world [in] the inward sense of nature, which . . . assures to natural science its . . . true living significance" (*ibid.*, p. 67). Hence, for Schlegel the function of science is not to study the world in abstraction from its symbolizing activity but to seek a union between the world and human life. Where science and life separate, as in Greek philosophy of the fourth century B.C., historical decadence ensues. Where science and life are in union, there is historical growth, for example, at the time of the "transition point between the ancient and the modern world" (*ibid.*, p. 245).

Works by Schlegel

Athenäum (1798–1800). Various articles.
Lucinde: Ein Roman. Berlin, 1799.
Geschichte der alten und neuen Literatur, 2 vols. Vienna, 1815. Translated by J. G. Lockhart as *Lectures on the History of Literature, Ancient and Modern,* 2 vols. Edinburgh, 1818.
Philosophie des Lebens. Vienna, 1828.
Vorlesungen zur Philosophie der Geschichte, 2 vols. Vienna, 1829. Translated by J. B. Robertson as *The Philosophy of History,* 2 vols. London, 1835.
Philosophie der Sprache. Vienna, 1830. Translated, with *Philosophie des Lebens,* by A. J. W. Morrison as *The Philosophy of Life and Philosophy of Language.* New York, 1848.
Prosäische Jugendschriften, 2 vols. Vienna, 1882; 2d ed., Vienna, 1906.

Works on Schlegel

Enders, Karl, *Friedrich Schlegel, Die Quellen seines Wesens und Werdens.* Leipzig, 1913.
Feifel, Rosa, *Die Lebensphilosophie Friedrich Schlegels.* Bonn, 1938.
Gundolf, Friedrich, "Friedrich Schlegels romantische Schriften." *Jahrbuch des freien deutschen Hochstifts* (1927).
Haym, Rudolf, *Die romantische Schule,* 5th ed. Berlin, 1928.
Horovitz, A., "Die Weltanschauung eines Romantikers." *Archiv für Geschichte der Philosophie,* Vol. 27 (1914).
Mann, Otto, *Der junge Friedrich Schlegel.* Berlin, 1932.
Meinecke, Friedrich, *Weltbürgertum und Nationalstaat.* Munich and Berlin, 1928. Pp. 90–99.
Wellek, René, *A History of Modern Criticism,* Vol. II. New Haven, 1955. Pp. 5–35.

ROBERT ANCHOR

SCHLEIERMACHER, FRIEDRICH DANIEL ERNST (1768–1834), was nineteenth-century Protestantism's great systematic theologian. It was he who marked the points of the compass for much of subsequent theology and philosophy of religion. Like St. Augustine, Schleiermacher desired to know God and the soul, and his place in the history of philosophy is due largely to the fact that he was able to state in modern language and concepts the great Augustinian conviction that religious faith is native to all human experience. Therefore, the knowledge of God and the knowledge of the soul are two orders of knowledge that must be distinguished but cannot be separated.

LIFE

Schleiermacher was first and foremost a preacher and theologian, a church statesman, and an educator. He carried out his work as a philosopher in the context of the great idealist systems of Schelling, Fichte, and Hegel, but instead of attempting to imitate these men he applied himself to the critical analysis of religion, both in its personal and societal manifestations, without reducing such experience to some form of philosophic intuition. The upbringing that his father, a Reformed clergyman, gave him and his early education in Moravian institutions set Schleiermacher upon this course. After studying at the university in Halle and taking his examinations for ordination in 1790, he served briefly as a private tutor to the family of Count Dohna in East Prussia and as a minister in the Prussian town of Landsberg. In 1796 Schleiermacher settled in Berlin as a preacher, became a close friend of Friedrich von Schlegel, and emerged as an interpreter of religion to the romantic world view that Schlegel himself epitomized. *On Religion: Speeches to Its Cultured Despisers* (1799) gave Schleiermacher a national reputation at the age of 30. The following year another publication, *Soliloquies,* attested to Schleiermacher's thorough absorption of the spirit of romanticism, but at the same time it indicated the direction that his ethical interests were to take in the future, as in his *Grundlinien einer Kritik der bisherigen Sittenlehre* ("Outline of a Critique of Previous Ethical Theory," 1803). The relation between the religious and ethical dimensions of life constituted a major preoccupation of Schleiermacher's maturity, and it is here that his indebtedness to and divergence from Kant are clearly evident. Of decisive importance during his Berlin sojourn was his embarking upon the translation of Plato, in the course of which his mind became imbued with the philosophy of the author of the *Republic.* By 1804 Schleiermacher was teaching philosophical ethics (philosophy of culture), theology, New Testament, and hermeneutics at Halle. By 1810 he was lecturing as professor of theology at the University of Berlin, where for the remainder of his life he taught dogmatic theology, New Testament theology and criticism, hermeneutics, practical theology, history of philosophy, ethics, and dialectics, to name only the more important of the wide variety of subjects with which he dealt. Concomitantly he held an appointment as preacher at the Dreifaltigkeitskirche, to which he attracted persons from all sections of Berlin, and from this pulpit he wielded a powerful moral influence on the nation. In ecclesiastical politics he labored for the union of the Lutheran and Reformed churches in Prussia, and in national politics he worked not only for stiffer resistance to French expansionism under Napoleon but for internal social reform.

The Christian Faith (Der christliche Glaube nach den Grundsätzen der evangelischen Kirche im Zusammenhange dargestellt) appeared in 1821–1822 and in revised form in 1830–1831. Together with the *Brief Outline of the Study of Theology* (1st edition, 1811) and the two open letters concerning the revised edition of *The Christian Faith* which Schleiermacher wrote to a close friend (*Sendschreiben über seine Glaubenslehre an Dr. Lücke,* 1829), *The Christian Faith* gives us not only Schleiermacher's thought on Christian doctrine and substantive theological issues but also his conception of the organization of the theological disciplines and of systematic theology itself. Schleiermacher made Protestant theology methodologically self-conscious.

PHILOSOPHY OF CULTURE

Schleiermacher criticized Kant for tacitly making ethics into a "highest science" that ignored and devaluated the particular and idiosyncratic in human nature. Ethics, Schleiermacher argued, is the discipline that has for its object "reason in history." Reason never appears except in historical personality—in the personalities of both individual persons and corporate persons. This position leads a significant relaxation of the Kantian separation between practical reason, on the one hand, and the inclinations, temperament, talent, etc., on the other. Schleiermacher viewed these "accidents" and, indeed, the entire spatial, temporal embodiment of reason—apart from which we have no self-consciousness and hence no access to reason—not merely as the "place" of reason in its practical and theoretical functions but also as the organ of reason, by which reason itself is conditioned. The notion of a pure, universal reason could, therefore, be only a regulative concept for Schleiermacher. Insofar as we consider reason in its practical capacity, as a willing or organizing activity, it is not the quest of virtue and autonomous assent to a self-imposed universal law that is foremost in view, but rather the sight of an ethical agent acting according to his own individuated rational nature. Moreover, the individuation of the ethical agent is accomplished not only by the "natural" accidents of time and place but also by the communities, societies, and institutions of which the individual person is the offspring. Schleiermacher presents the ethical agent as an end in himself, that is, as a good, who produces goods according to the peculiar law of his own unique nature. The doctrine of the highest good is formulated through the delineation of the relations of community and reciprocity in which such agents stand to each other, inheriting and endowing, receiving and bestowing. The primary forms in which these relations appear are the family, the nation, the church, the institutions of learning, and what Schleiermacher calls free sociality (*Geselligkeit*).

Nature and society affect reasoning in its theoretical as well as practical operations. When we think, we are conscious of engaging in an activity that is common to all men; nevertheless, our thinking, even at the most abstract level, as in thinking about thought itself, is in actuality predicated upon the specific organization of the physical means of sensation as well as upon the prior existence of a particular system of communication. The speculative activity of reason is thus conditioned by the natural medium in which it is individuated and shaped by the historical, moral character of the primary media (for example, a particular language) through which it maintains itself. Discourse is the means for the sociality of thinking, as Schleiermacher liked to say, and thinking is the inner side of speaking. He defined dialectic as the principles of correctly conducting a dialogue in the realm of pure thinking and taught that all thinking proceeds in the form of dialogue or colloquy. On these grounds, Schleiermacher ruled out the possibility of an intuition of the absolute or of a highest science; the ideal and the real appear only as already informed by each other; pure spirit and matter lie outside of experience. Consequently, the ideal of a universal philosophy, for example, is nullified by the lack of a universal language and the impossibility of such.

The person, as the subject of the activities of thinking/knowing and of willing/doing, is more than a being composed of mind and body, individuated by time and space. A person not only is differentiated from others by nature and history but inwardly differentiates himself and acknowledges such an inward differentiation in all other human beings. That by virtue of which the person makes this inward differentiation is the proprium (*Eigenthümlichkeit*). It is this property in each man that endows him with a life unity, an inalienable identity. Schleiermacher described this proprium as the peculiar organization that reason assumes for itself in each man. However, the life unity, or identity, of the individual person can never come to direct and full expression either in thinking/knowing or in willing/doing, although it accompanies and informs each of these rational activities. The self-consciousness that this sense of identity requires is a self-consciousness to be distinguished—though not isolated—from the forms of self-consciousness in which the subject is responding to or acting upon external objects. Schleiermacher appropriates the word "feeling" for this form of self-consciousness, whose content is the given identity and unity of the self, incapable of being derived from others or surrendered to them. Feeling, thinking, and doing thus make up the three forms of consciousness that constitute the self-consciousness which distinguishes persons. Correspondingly, every person must be seen as a participant in the life of society in both his practical and theoretical functions, but he is also one whose proprium is wholly original. In a person whose feeling form of self-consciousness remains latent or inchoate, the sense of personal identity is deficient and personal consciousness is confused or immature. Such a person fails to contribute to the common or highest good; he is an inert reflection of his world, not one who moves and enriches it; he is a person in the formal sense but is destitute of spiritual life. Since, for Schleiermacher, religion is the most highly and fully developed mode of the feeling form of self-consciousness, all of human culture ultimately depends upon the cultivation of the religious life.

RELIGION

In his earliest published work, the *Speeches,* Schleiermacher made ample use of the romantic preoccupation with the nature and value of individuality, but he qualified the world view of German romanticism in two important respects. First, an individual comes to self-knowledge only in the presence of other persons; hence the need to know and to express the self can be fulfilled only by observing and cultivating the morality of human community and communication. Second, the individual's cultivation of his own humanity—which the romantic accepted as a self-evident imperative—requires that he acknowledge his religious nature, as well as his aesthetic, scientific, and moral nature, and that he cultivate this side of his nature, or self-consciousness, by seeking out religious community. Schleiermacher's thesis, from 1799 to his death, was that man is a religious being. But since the individual must always appropriate his humanity in a fashion that is at once concordant with his generic identity and accordant with his own peculiar identity, religion is as much a problem for the individual as it is a natural endowment. In his mature thinking, as he came to align himself theologically with Augustine and John Calvin, Schleiermacher stressed not only the fact that man is a religious being but also the fact that the most fundamental, pervasive confusion inhibiting human consciousness is religious confusion. Thus, in his Christian theology, he described sin as the failure to maintain a clear distinction between that upon which men are entirely dependent, God, and that upon which men are only relatively dependent, namely, objects within the world.

In *The Christian Faith,* Schleiermacher stated that religion is a determination of feeling. More narrowly defined, it is a feeling of being absolutely dependent, and this feeling, he believed, is one and the same thing with consciousness of being in relation with God. A number of elements in this characterization need to be distinguished if Schleiermacher is to be understood. (1) The feeling of being absolutely dependent is also the feeling of identity, through which the individual is conscious of his inner uniqueness; in describing this feeling as one of being absolutely dependent, Schleiermacher was calling attention to the fact that the identity, or life unity, of the individual is an endowment which cannot be derived from any of the intellectual or volitional relations in which the self stands to other persons and forces, taken either singly or together. In this sense, the individual is utterly dependent, for the particular constitution of his existence, on a "whence" that cannot be rendered conceptually. Hence, the feeling of absolute dependence is not expressive of a felt deficiency or of awe, as it is according to the interpretation of Rudolf Otto in *The Idea of the Holy;* nor is it wholly the same as Paul Tillich's conception of faith as being ultimately concerned about that which concerns us ultimately, since this concern is aroused in part by what Tillich called "nonbeing." (2) The feeling of being absolutely dependent—or "immediate self-consciousness" or "God-consciousness"; Schleiermacher regarded all three terms as equivalent—is discernible only because self-consciousness also involves thinking and willing, which are forms of rational relation between the person and his world, forms involving consciousness of "relative dependence" and "relative freedom." The feeling of being absolutely dependent is distinguishable from the feeling of relative dependence by virtue of the fact that in the latter a person stands in the relations of community and reciprocity with nature and society, while in the feeling of absolute dependence there is no reciprocity present. Consequently, there can be no consciousness of being in relation to God, apart from consciousness of being in relation to the world. (3) The original meaning of the word "God" is not a concept of perfect being, or the like, but the felt relation of absolute dependence. Hence, religion arises not in ideas, nor—for that matter—in willing, but in the immediate consciousness of what Schleiermacher described to Lücke as "an immediate existence-relationship." (4) In fact, then, religion is more than a determination of feeling; it is the

name Schleiermacher gives to the personal self-consciousness in which the feeling of absolute dependence and consciousness of the world coexist and must achieve or receive a living, stable order.

The religion that Schleiermacher described in this way is a purely formal and abstract religion, which exists nowhere in actuality. In conformity with the principles we have outlined above, he insisted that religion always appears in a particular social and historical form. The great religions are religions bearing the stamp of their founders, and he defined Christianity as a monotheistic faith of the teleological variety in which everything is related to the redemption accomplished by Jesus of Nazareth. Everything in the outward, social, and institutional aspect of Christianity is related to its founder, and similarly, everything pertaining to the inner piety of the Christian is related to the historical figure of the redeemer. Thus, while Christianity is, without question, the religion on the basis of which Schleiermacher formed his understanding of all other religions, what is of more importance is that he was the first among modern theologians to perceive that Christianity is historical in two senses. Not only does it have a history, but each Christian becomes a Christian by appropriating to his total self-consciousness the relation to Jesus Christ. Christ must become a part of the self-consciousness, or inner history, of the Christian. There is no part of the relation to God, Schleiermacher stated, in which the relation to Christ is not also actively present. Hence, Schleiermacher revived in his conception of the feeling of being absolutely dependent the Augustinian notion of the inseparability of the knowledge of the soul and the knowledge of God; at the same time he originated the distinctive form of modern Protestant theology—Christocentrism, or Christ as the center of the individual's inner religious consciousness.

Works by Schleiermacher

COLLECTED WORKS AND LETTERS

Aus Schleiermachers Leben in Briefen, 4 vols. Berlin, 1860–1863.
Sämtliche Werke. Berlin, 1835–1864. Published in three divisions: I, theological; II, sermons; III, philosophical and related subjects.
Schleiermachers Briefwechsel mit J. Chr. Gass. Berlin, 1852.

ENGLISH TRANSLATIONS

Brief Outline of the Study of Theology, translated by W. Farrer. Edinburgh, 1850.
The Christian Faith, translated by H. R. Mackintosh and J. S. Stewart. Edinburgh, 1948; New York, 1963.
Christmas Eve: A Dialogue on the Celebration of Christmas, translated by W. Hastie. Edinburgh, 1890.
The Life of Schleiermacher as Unfolded in His Autobiography and Letters, 2 vols., translated by F. Rowan. London, 1860.
"On the Discrepancy Between the Sabellian and Athanasian Method of Representing the Doctrine of a Trinity in the Godhead," translated by Moses Stuart. *Biblical Repository and Quarterly Observer,* Vol. 6 (1835), 1–116.
On Religion: Speeches to Its Cultured Despisers, translated by John Oman. London, 1893; New York, 1958.
Selected Sermons of Friedrich Schleiermacher, translated by Mary F. Wilson. New York, n.d.
Soliloquies, translated and edited by Horace Friess. Chicago, 1926.

CRITICAL EDITIONS

Der christliche Glaube, Martin Redeker, ed., 2 vols. Berlin, 1960. Contains appendices and Schleiermacher's own marginal notations.

Grundriss der philosophischen Ethik, A. Twesten and F. M. Schiele, eds. Leipzig, 1911.

Hermeneutik, nach den Handschriften, Heinz Kimmerle, ed. Heidelberg, 1959.

Kurze Darstellung des theologischen Studiums, Heinrich Scholz, ed. Hildesheim, 1961.

Monologen, F. M. Schiele and Hermann Mulert, eds. Leipzig, 1914.

Reden über die Religion, G. C. B. Pünjer, ed. Braunschweig, 1879.

Schleiermachers Sendschreiben über seine Glaubenslehre an Lücke, Hermann Mulert, ed. Giessen, 1908.

Weihnachtsfeier, Hermann Mulert, ed. Leipzig, 1908.

Works on Schleiermacher

Barth, Karl, *From Rousseau to Ritschl.* London, 1959. A sophisticated chapter on Schleiermacher by his foremost theological critic.

Brandt, Richard, *The Philosophy of Friedrich Schleiermacher.* New York, 1941. The most detailed examination of Schleiermacher's philosophy in English.

Dilthey, Wilhelm, *Leben Schleiermachers,* Berlin, 1870; 2d ed., H. Mulert, ed. Berlin, 1922. The classic biographical work on Schleiermacher, but extends only to the period at Halle. Should be supplemented by Dilthey's articles in his *Gesammelte Schriften,* 2d ed. Stuttgart, 1959–1960. Vols. IV and XII.

Niebuhr, Richard R., *Schleiermacher on Christ and Religion.* New York, 1964. An account of the central ideas in Schleiermacher's theology against the background of his philosophy.

Süskind, Hermann, *Der Einfluss Schellings auf die Entwicklung von Schleiermachers System.* Tübingen, 1909. Valuable account of the early development of Schleiermacher's thinking.

Wehrung, Georg, *Die Dialektik Schleiermachers.* Tübingen, 1920. A scholarly examination of the development of Schleiermacher's lectures on this subject.

RICHARD R. NIEBUHR

CHLICK, MORITZ (1882–1936), one of the founders of modern analytical philosophy and a guiding spirit of the Vienna circle of logical positivists, was born in Berlin. He was a direct descendant on his mother's side of Ernst Moritz Arndt, the famous German patriot and political leader of the war of liberation against Napoleon. At the age of eighteen, Schlick entered the University of Berlin to study physics under Max Planck. He received his doctorate in 1904 with a dissertation on the reflection of light in a nonhomogeneous medium.

Schlick's familiarity with the methods and criteria of research in the natural sciences left him dissatisfied with the epistemological notions both of Neo-Kantianism, which then dominated the German universities, and of Edmund Husserl's phenomenology, which had already become widely known. Instead, Schlick's starting point was the analyses carried out by Ernst Mach, Hermann von Helmholtz, and Henri Poincaré of the basic concepts and presuppositions of the individual sciences. His central interest at the time was the fundamental question of what is to be understood by knowledge.

From 1911 to 1917, Schlick served as lecturer and associate professor at the University of Rostock. In this period he published a series of works, among them his *Allgemeine Erkenntnislehre* (1918; 2d ed., 1925). These

works were devoted partly to a logically precise critical discussion of traditional philosophical conceptions and partly to an elaboration of new criteria for scientific knowledge which attracted considerable attention. In these publications Schlick already presented a first systematic account of his philosophical views.

In 1921 Schlick was named to a professorship at Kiel, and a year later he accepted a call to a chair in philosophy at the University of Vienna. These two years may thus be seen in retrospect as a kind of turning point in the history of philosophy. In 1921 Ludwig Wittgenstein had published his *Tractatus Logico-philosophicus,* and in these same years the first writings of Rudolf Carnap appeared. Under the influence of Wittgenstein and Carnap, Schlick's philosophical views underwent a profound modification, which he later characterized by saying that he no longer saw the goal of philosophy as acquiring knowledge and presenting it as a system of propositions but, rather, as the application of a method. In applying its method, philosophy must take as its aim the discovery and understanding of the meaning of the statements, concepts, and formulations of problems of the special sciences, of philosophy, and of everyday life. When philosophy is understood in this manner, as Schlick emphasized in his French essay "L'École de Vienne et la philosophie traditionelle" (*Travaux du IXième Congrès International de Philosophie,* Paris, 1937), it resembles the method of Socrates, who constantly strove in his conversations to clarify the concepts, assertions, traditional notions, and ordinary modes of expression found in both the philosophy and the practical life of his time.

Schlick taught at the University of Vienna from 1922 until his death in 1936. During these years he twice made trips to the United States as a visiting professor. While in Vienna, Schlick published *Fragen der Ethik* (*The Problems of Ethics,* 1930), as well as numerous papers, most of which were later collected in various volumes. But his views were disseminated most effectively, perhaps, through the discussion society which he founded and which acquired a world-wide reputation as the *Wiener Kreis.* Besides professional philosophers, regular participants in the meetings of the Vienna circle included primarily mathematicians and natural scientists but also psychologists and sociologists. They published a profusion of writings of their own, in which they applied the methods—constantly refined in discussion—of the new Vienna philosophy to the fundamental problems of scientific research. Schlick was responsible for Carnap's appointment as lecturer at the University of Vienna. Another member of the Vienna circle was Kurt Gödel, who in this period published his famous proofs of the completeness of first-order logic and of the incompletability of formal arithmetic. Numerous scholars from Germany, Poland, England, Norway, Sweden, and the United States visited the sessions of the Vienna circle and took part in its discussions. Conflicting views frequently were championed, but the application of the most rigorous logical tools to the positions under consideration was common to all the deliberations. These discussions thus turned out to be a genuine symposium in the classical sense of the term, and the international exchange of views that took place worked a transformation in the philosophical thought of the American and European universities.

On June 22, 1936, while on the way to his lecture in the main building of the University of Vienna, Schlick was fatally wounded by a deranged student. The motives for this act have never been fully clarified. The assailant had been under psychiatric observation for some time because of a previous attempt on Schlick's life. With the death of Schlick, the meetings of the Vienna circle came to a sudden end. The Austrian Ministry of Education, for its part, now embarked on a reactionary cultural policy which barred representatives of scientific, analytic philosophy from all official chairs in the universities. With few exceptions, the participants in the Vienna circle emigrated to England and America. The rigorous scientific requirements of the Vienna philosophy met with widespread sympathy in the West and in Poland and Scandinavia; as a result, philosophy as the "logic of knowledge" experienced a fruitful further development abroad.

In Austria, however, the philosophical movement initiated by Schlick encountered the uncompromising hostility of the state authorities. After the interruption caused by World War II, all the official chairs in the Austrian universities were systematically filled by speculative philosophers generally committed to a theological outlook. Only exceptionally was a representative of scientific philosophy able to qualify as a lecturer. But since lecturers and associate or titular professors, unlike regular professors, are not paid a salary in Austria, the authorities had an effective economic means of compelling the unwanted logical analysts of knowledge to turn elsewhere. In practice, this resulted in a suppression of scientific philosophy which continues to exist to this very day. The necessary consequence of a policy so harmful to science has been a shocking decline in the level of scholarship. Psychologically, the only explanation for this reactionary course of isolating research from the rigorous demands of modern scientific philosophy is the fear that logico-mathematical or empirical scientific analysis might endanger some ideological position. In support of this view is the fact that the eastern European countries, which profess a diametrically opposed ideology, also keep Viennese logical positivism away from their chairs of learning out of the same medieval anxiety that prevails in Austria.

Critique of Kantianism. In his early work *Raum und Zeit in der gegenwärtigen Physik* (1917), Schlick presented a critical examination of the synthetic a priori character that Kantian transcendental philosophy attributed to propositions about space and time. Methodologically following the work of Henri Poincaré and Hermann von Helmholtz, he based his thought primarily on the changes introduced by the theory of relativity into certain of the definitions and principles of classical physics. In conformity with scientific opinion of his time, Kant had sought to establish the absolute validity of Newtonian mechanics by means of the theory of transcendental forms of intuition and of understanding. He regarded the presuppositions and basic principles of classical mechanics as necessary truths about empirical reality, that is, as synthetic a priori propositions. This conception had first been shaken by investigations of mathematicians. In consequence, doubt had also arisen regarding the synthetic a priori character of the general laws of physics. The theory of relativity made a final break with the synthetic a priori characterization of the foundations of Newtonian physics. According to relativity theory, statements about physical states (including propositions about physical space and physical time) are, as a consequence of the methods used by the natural sciences, empirical in character. That is, they are synthetic a posteriori propositions. Meanwhile, Poincaré had pointed to the possibility of interpreting general laws of nature, such as statements about physical space, as conventions or analytic propositions. Thus he had made evident the conventional nature of certain steps in the methodology of empirical research.

This systematic critique, confined at first to the foundations of mathematics and the natural sciences, was generalized by Schlick to all the basic problems of human knowledge. It thus became the basis of his philosophy in this initial period. In the *Allgemeine Erkenntnislehre* (1918), he made a critical study of all the propositions to which Kant and his followers had ascribed a synthetic a priori character. Schlick concluded that in all cases these propositions, where precisely formulated as logically necessary truths, are analytic in character; when, on the other hand, they are interpreted as statements with real content, they are empirical or synthetic a posteriori. There are no synthetic a priori propositions. Later, in his examination of foundational theories in logic and mathematics and of Hilbert's formalism in particular, Schlick conceded that the possibility of synthetic a priori propositions in the realm of logico-mathematical forms must be left open. We are in no position to come to a final decision on this question. But even if necessarily valid propositions with content do exist—perhaps in the sense of the mathematical intuitionists—in the domain of logic and mathematics, they could never, Schlick stressed, be interpreted as absolutely valid statements about the empirically real world.

Critical realism. Schlick's view was that epistemology, in investigating the criteria of reality, is not obliged in the first instance to ask for absolutely true knowledge of reality. The Cartesian method of doubt leads merely to immediate data of experience, the establishment of which in no way suffices to answer the question "What is real?" Instead of seeking absolutely certain knowledge, we must address ourselves to the systems of propositions by the aid of which science seeks to describe reality, and through a critical examination expunge from these systems all propositions that are demonstrably false. The system that remains will then portray reality just as it is. Here, when we speak of the reality depicted by the natural sciences, we mean those phenomena described by true spatiotemporal propositions. Schlick identified the objects of empirical knowledge, thus characterized, with the Kantian thing-in-itself; he called his own philosophical position "critical realism."

According to Schlick, the method by which we arrive at knowledge of the spatiotemporally ordered world has the feature that whereas the truth of propositions about objective, empirical reality can in principle be established only hypothetically, the falsity of such propositions can in some cases be demonstrated beyond question. It is interesting to note that Karl Popper's asymmetrical confirmation theory, which did not appear until some twenty years later, likewise attributes a kind of certainty to the disconfirmation of natural laws in contrast with the fact that full verification is unattainable.

In this first period of his philosophical development, Schlick regarded the controversy between idealism and realism as a factual issue which philosophical reflection could resolve. He believed that critical realism provided the correct answer, and he sought to substantiate this answer by a more precise characterization of what is to be understood by empirical knowledge. Knowledge is "knowledge of sameness." Something is cognized as something else, for example, a whale as a mammal. An especially important form of the knowledge of sameness is re-cognition. Memory outputs over short spans of time are a constitutive element of consciousness. Knowledge of sameness includes not only establishing the sameness or similarity of sense data, memory images, imagined ideas, and the like but also the rediscovery of certain conceptual orderings known, say, from mathematics in the relationships of empirical phenomena. Schlick did not consider the possibility that the study of empirical relationships might lead to the construction of new, hitherto unknown mathematical orders and that in such a case one might arrive at knowledge descriptive of reality that is not knowledge of sameness.

Language and knowledge. The problem of knowledge and its criteria had led Schlick to a further question: how is it possible to express knowledge linguistically? Scientific knowledge and insights, whether logico-mathematical or empirical, are presented in the form of sentences of some language. What conditions must be satisfied by these combinations of linguistic signs if they are to count as analytic or empirical sentences? In this earlier period Schlick's answer was the following: the languages employed in the sciences are designed to make possible the construction of unambiguous expressions that can be true or false. But this property of language presupposes the choice and establishment of rules according to which the linguistic signs are to be employed and to be strung out into expressions and sentences. If in using a language one does not heed the logical and linguistic rules set up for it, sign combinations will occur which, although they may appear on the surface to be sentences with a subject and a predicate, actually violate the rules for combining signs. Consequently, they have no meaning and cannot be either true or false.

Applying this notion to philosophy, Schlick held that the theses of metaphysical systems are just such sequences of signs put together in a way that violates the logical rules of language. For this reason metaphysics is to be denied the status of scientific knowledge. But why does metaphysics disregard the logical rules of scientific languages in its linguistic formulations? Schlick thought the reason lay in the fact that whereas metaphysics endeavors to know reality, it does not seek to know the *relations* between the magnitudes characterizing states of affairs but strives to obtain knowledge of the *content* of phenomena. However, according to Schlick, only relations can be the object of knowledge—relations which reproduce the order of the phenomena and which include particulars on the number, sameness, similarity, and succession of the empirical data, as well as functional connections between measured quan-

tities. The content of phenomena cannot be grasped by means of ordering relations, which are all that are at the disposal of the understanding. In Schlick's opinion, it is only through an intuitive, emotional experience that we can become acquainted with the actual content of reality. Metaphysics desires to know the "content" of real things, and it therefore finds itself compelled to use expressions from scientific languages in a manner contrary to the rules. For this reason the theses of metaphysics cannot have the character of meaningful propositions.

Schlick arrived at these views under the influence of the writings of Bertrand Russell and David Hilbert, both of whom had by this time extensively treated the logical and linguistic foundations of mathematics. They clearly held that in mathematics questions about the logical and linguistic conditions for unambiguous statements must be put with special precision and exactness, but that these questions also affect the foundations of all scientific language systems and hence of scientific knowledge in general. Schlick was the first person to draw, on the basis of these insights into the foundations of logic and mathematics, consequences for epistemology as a whole and to undertake, by logical and linguistic means, the demarcation of a boundary between science and metaphysics.

Philosophy and reality. During his teaching career in Vienna, Schlick subjected the philosophical views he had published before 1922 to a fundamental re-examination. Influenced by Wittgenstein and Carnap, he no longer saw the task of philosophy as the acquisition of knowledge. Instead, philosophy, through the application of logical analysis to the concepts, propositions, and methods of the separate sciences, should aim at reaching an understanding of knowledge as found in the individual disciplines and of its presuppositions. Schlick no longer treated realism and idealism as factually contradictory theses but, rather, as alternative ways of speaking; at most, one could ask which permits a simpler, more easily understood way of talking about the world of experience and about purely conceptual relationships. But if realism and idealism are interpreted as statements about something that exists, the realism–idealism antithesis becomes a "pseudo problem" to which neither a true nor a false answer can be given.

This conception was carried over by Schlick to certain problems in the foundations of physics. In his essay "Die Kausalität in der gegenwärtigen Physik" (1931), reprinted in *Gesammelte Aufsätze* and in *Gesetz, Kausalität und Wahrscheinlichkeit*), he cited the answer given by Werner Heisenberg when he was asked to what extent particles are real or unreal. Heisenberg had replied that whether or not one wished to label particles as really existing was simply a matter of taste (*Die physikalischen Prinzipien der Quantentheorie*, Leipzig, 1930, p. 15). In the systems of propositions that constitute physics, we speak only about the data of observation and the regularities they display, or we construct hypotheses and predictions about the occurrence of observable phenomena. Whether the terms "real" and "unreal" are applied to the observational data, to the hypothetical constituents, or to any other elements of the theories is, so far as the content of the system of propositions is concerned, of no consequence at all. Descriptions in terms of "real" and "unreal" can be omitted without any loss of asserted content. Whether one wishes to make use of these terms is merely a matter of convenience and simplicity in expression.

Philosophical method. Schlick generalized his analysis of modes of speech and ways of formulating questions into a philosophical method. Viewed from his new epistemological standpoint, numerous questions, especially in philosophy, turn out to be anchored in ordinary or scientific forms of speech, or in forms artificially created by metaphysics. The first step in Schlick's method of analyzing knowledge consists in finding out the logical and linguistic rules governing the use of the expressions that occur in the problems, propositions, and forms of speech under study. Such a logical and syntactical critique may show that a certain expression, ordinarily assumed to have an unambiguous meaning, is being applied in accordance with different rules in different contexts and therefore is being used in different senses. A striking example is the concept of space. For a long time only one meaning was attributed to it, and the assumption was that the term "space" as employed in mathematics, physics, and psychology has the same meaning. The logical critique of language reveals that mathematical geometries represent analytic systems of relations, whereas physical space is described by means of a system of empirical laws that have as their content the order schema of possible positions and motions of physical bodies. Empirical sentences with different content describe the geometrical and metrical properties of psychological spaces—visual space, auditory space, tactile space, and the like. Similarly, in the case of such terms as "real," "ideal," "actual," and "imaginary," syntactical analysis yields different meanings corresponding to the different rules that govern the use of these expressions on various occasions. Failure to notice such differences of meaning often gives rise to philosophical problems which are then regarded as insoluble.

Thus the first step in the logical analysis of knowledge is to ascertain the rules for the linguistic use of the expressions under consideration. The second step is to study what meaning is to be ascribed to these expressions in a given complex of questions or system of propositions. Schlick called this the "interpretation" of the expressions, concepts, propositions, questions, or theories. If, for example, the first step in the analysis has shown that the word "real" is used in several senses, then the interpretation must determine which particular meaning the word has in, for instance, the sentence "Only that is real which is immediately experienced," or in the sentence "The real is that which leaves traces behind," or "The real is that which can be described by means of conjugate measured quantities." The connection between the two steps in the method is manifest: the clarification of the possible meanings of an expression must precede the interpretation of it in a given context. According to Schlick, the understanding gained through interpretation is the insight for which philosophy strives.

Schlick applied his philosophical method, among other things, to the physical concepts of causality and energy and to the principles of causality and of the conservation of energy, which were still regarded as synthetic a priori propositions. Interpretation requires that in the case of "universally valid" sentences one must always ask whether one can conceive of conditions under which these sentences would have to be regarded as false. If they can be so regarded, then the empirical character of the sentences in question has been recognized. Schlick was able to specify circumstances whose empirical confirmation is conceivable and under which both the principle of causality and the principle of the conservation of energy (as they are used within physics) would be termed invalid. Accordingly, he expressed the view—at a time when physicists were not yet of this opinion—that the two principles admitted of empirical testing. Subsequent research in physics has confirmed this view. On the other hand, Schlick recognized that the concepts of causality and energy can also be defined in such a way that the principles of causality and of the conservation of energy become analytic sentences. It is this possibility that conventionalism exploits when it declares that general forms of laws are absolutely valid by convention. In a further application of his method, Schlick subjected Hans Driesch's vitalism and the general propositions both of psychology and of Husserl's phenomenology to an analytical critique. He arrived at the general conclusion that if the expressions these theories contain are precisely and properly clarified, the sentences in question take on either an analytic or an empirical character, but they never at one and the same time express synthetic and a priori propositions.

One criterion of meaning Schlick utilized in his analytical procedure was the criterion of verification which Schlick and others attributed to Wittgenstein. By this criterion, general laws of nature can have no significant content because they are not verifiable (or, as it is usually put, are not fully verifiable). This problem gave rise to wide-ranging discussions that went far beyond the Vienna circle. Essentially, Schlick supported Wittgenstein's view that natural laws are not themselves propositions but are to be understood as directives regarding the kind of sentences to be constructed in order to describe or predict individual cases of empirical phenomena. Directives cannot be true or false, so that on this interpretation the verification criterion is not applicable to the laws of nature. On several occasions Schlick characterized this interpretation of natural laws as not entirely satisfactory. But he did not find the opportunity for a definitive exposition of his own position.

Presuppositions and confirmation procedures. Schlick replied to certain criticisms of the philosophy of the Vienna circle. Doubt was expressed that the criteria of the analysis of knowledge are sufficient for distinguishing between analytic and empirical sentences or for drawing a boundary between metaphysics and the individual sciences. Extreme skeptics even questioned the possibility of making such sharp distinctions at all. One argument used by critics concerned the presuppositions that are required whenever one attempts to specify the conditions for determining unambiguously the meaning of concepts and propositions or for deciding unambiguously the truth of analytic and empirical sentences. These presuppositions evade any formal characterization or any determination of their validity, and consequently they have a metaphysical character. Even if these ineluctable presuppositions are limited to the minimal performances of memory necessary for recognizing in a subsequent moment what meaning we have previously assigned to a given expression, the knowledge by recollection we thus presuppose is intuitive in kind and as impossible to check as the theses of metaphysics. Because of these problematical presuppositions, the logical positivist distinctions between analytic and empirical propositions and between scientific and metaphysical propositions cannot possess any validity.

Schlick analyzed these criticisms of recollections that cannot be checked but yet must be presupposed if consciousness, language, thought, and knowledge are to exist. The real problem of the logic of knowledge, he argued, consists in the fact that despite the inexact presuppositions of our methods of knowledge, we nevertheless do obtain exact scientific knowledge. It is wrong to conclude that because the recollections presupposed are unanalyzable and intuitive, the formal logico-mathematical derivations, concept formations, and principles or the empirical criteria of meaning and judgment are inaccurate. The exactness of scientific methods is anchored in proof procedures which guarantee an undeniable advance of knowledge in all the sciences. These procedures distinguish exact scientific knowledge from unverifiable metaphysical speculation. There are no such confirmation procedures for metaphysics, nor does it permit the application of scientific (logical or empirical) criteria of confirmation to its theses and methods. Consequently, in metaphysics there is no such thing as progress of knowledge. Thus the decisive criterion of exactness for the sciences is the advance in knowledge that can be gained through the process of testing, a criterion not satisfied by the speculative methods of metaphysics.

Ethics and value theory. Schlick also applied the method of the analysis of knowledge to problems of ethics and the theory of value. He concluded that the a priori arguments for absolute values do not fulfill the logical criteria of meaning. Only the value-ascribing forms of behavior actually found among people, relative assignments of relative values, can be taken as the basis for ethical and other value systems. In Schlick's view, this sort of value analysis leads to a new kind of empirical foundation for eudaemonism. In his *Fragen der Ethik*, Schlick offered as the fundamental principle of an ethics so based the maxim "Increase your happiness" (*Mehre deine Glückseligkeit*).

Schlick's ethics has been widely criticized as superficial, on the ground that there can be morally objectionable happiness. To understand it correctly, one must take into account how he characterized the happiness which one should strive to increase. By happiness he meant the quiet, joyous assent that accompanies our actions when we carry out for its own sake some activity springing from our talents. This is the kind of activity that is to be evaluated as ethically worthwhile behavior. The joy in such activity resembles the joy of a child at play, and it should be regarded generally as the criterion for emotional and intellectual youthfulness. This youthfulness is not tied to physical age. Anyone who has found the activity proper to himself, and has thus experienced this quiet, joyous happiness, has realized the highest attainable ethical goal and will keep his youthfulness throughout his entire life. On this basis, Schlick rejected all varieties of ethical rigorism,

including the Kantian system. No ethical worth can be attributed to actions undertaken from a mere sense of duty when such actions inspire only distaste and annoyance both beforehand and afterward. On the contrary, acting out of a sense of duty is ethically valuable only if a quiet satisfaction accompanies the action. Moral value, Schlick used to emphasize, attaches only to vital action; the sign of life is youthfulness, but we are young only when we act from joy. When the quiet, inner joyous assent accompanies our action, we fulfill the requirements of the highest principles of ethical value.

Works by Schlick

BOOKS

Raum und Zeit in der gegenwärtigen Physik. Zur Einführung in das Verständnis der Relativitats- und Gravitationstheorie. Berlin, 1917; 2d ed., 1919. Translated by Henry L. Brose as *Space and Time in Contemporary Physics, An Introduction to the Theory of Relativity and Gravitation.* Oxford, 1920.

Allgemeine Erkenntnislehre ("General Theory of Knowledge"). Berlin, 1918; 2d ed., 1925.

Vom Sinn des Lebens. Berlin, 1927.

Fragen der Ethik. Vienna, 1930. Translated by David Rynin as *Problems of Ethics.* New York, 1939.

The Future of Philosophy. Publications in Philosophy of the College of the Pacific, No. 1. Stockton, Calif., 1932. Reprinted in *Gesammelte Aufsätze.*

Gesammelte Aufsätze 1926–36 ("Collected Papers 1926–36"). Vienna, 1938.

Gesetz, Kausalität und Wahrscheinlichkeit ("Law, Causality and Probability"). Vienna, 1948.

Grundzüge der Naturphilosophie, W. Hollitscher and J. Rauscher, eds. Vienna, 1948. Posthumous papers. Translated by Amethe Smeaton as *Philosophy of Nature.* New York, 1949.

Aphorismen. Vienna, 1962.

Schlick also edited, with Paul Hertz, the *Schriften zur Erkenntnistheorie* of Hermann von Helmholtz. Berlin, 1921.

ARTICLES

"Naturphilosophie," in Max Dessoir, ed., *Lehrbuch der Philosophie,* Vol. II, *Die Philosophie in ihren Einzelgebieten.* Berlin, 1925.

"Gibt es ein materiales Apriori?" *Wissenschaftlicher Jahresbericht der philosophischen Gesellschaft an der Universität zu Wien für das Vereinsjahr 1930/31.* Translated by Wilfrid Sellars as "Is There a Factual A Priori?," in Herbert Feigl and Wilfrid Sellars, eds., *Readings in Philosophical Analysis.* New York, 1949.

"Die Wende der Philosophie." *Erkenntnis,* Vol. 1 (1930/1931), 4–11. Reprinted in *Gesammelte Aufsätze.* Translated by David Rynin as "The Turning Point in Philosophy," in A. J. Ayer, ed., *Logical Positivism.* Glencoe, Ill., 1959.

"Die Kausalität in der gegenwärtigen Physik." *Die Naturwissenschaften,* Vol. 19 (1931). Reprinted in *Gesammelte Aufsätze* and *Gesetz, Kausalität und Wahrscheinlichkeit.* Translated by David Rynin as "Causality in Contemporary Physics." *British Journal for the Philosophy of Science,* Vol. 12 (1961), 177–193 and 281–298.

"Positivismus und Realismus." *Erkenntnis,* Vol. 3 (1932/1933), 1–31. Reprinted in *Gesammelte Aufsätze.* Translated by David Rynin as "Positivism and Realism," in A. J. Ayer, ed., *Logical Positivism.*

"Philosophie und Naturwissenschaft." *Erkenntnis,* Vol. 4 (1934), 379–396.

"Über das Fundament der Erkenntnis." *Erkenntnis,* Vol. 4 (1934), 79–99. Reprinted in *Gesammelte Aufsätze.* Translated by David Rynin as "The Foundation of Knowledge," in A. J. Ayer, ed. *Logical Positivism.*

"Facts and Propositions." *Analysis,* Vol. 2 (1935). Reprinted in Margaret MacDonald, ed., *Philosophy and Analysis.* Oxford, 1954.

"Unanswerable Questions?" *The Philosopher,* Vol. 13 (1935). Reprinted in *Gesammelte Aufsätze.*

"Gesetz und Wahrscheinlichkeit." *Actes du Congrès International de Philosophie Scientifique, Paris 1935.* Actualités scientifiques et industrielles, No. 391. Paris, 1936. Pp. 46–57. Reprinted in *Gesammelte Aufsätze* and in *Gesetz, Kausalität und Wahrscheinlichkeit.*

"Sind die Naturgesetze Konventionen?" *Actes du Congrès International de Philosophie Scientifique, Paris 1935.* Actualités scientifiques et industrielles, No. 391. Paris, 1936. Pp. 8–17. Reprinted in *Gesammelte Aufsätze* and in *Gesetz, Kausalität und Wahrscheinlichkeit.* Translated by Herbert Feigl and May Brodbeck as "Are Natural Laws Conventions?," in Herbert Feigl and May Brodbeck, eds., *Readings in the Philosophy of Science.* New York, 1953.

"Meaning and Verification." *Philosophical Review,* Vol. 45 (1936). Reprinted in *Gesammelte Aufsätze* and in Feigl and Sellars, *Readings in Philosophical Analysis.*

"Quantentheorie und Erkennbarkeit der Natur." *Erkenntnis,* Vol. 6 (1936/1937), 317–326. Reprinted in *Gesammelte Aufsätze* and in *Gesetz, Kausalität und Wahrscheinlichkeit.*

"Form and Content, An Introduction to Philosophical Thinking. Three Lectures, Delivered in the University of London in Nov. 1932," in *Gesammelte Aufsätze.*

Works on Schlick

Feigl, Herbert, "Moritz Schlick." *Erkenntnis,* Vol. 7 (1937–1939), 393–419.

Popper, Karl, *The Logic of Scientific Discovery,* translated by the author, with the assistance of Julius Freed and Lan Freed. London, 1959.

Reichenbach, Hans, "Moritz Schlick." *Erkenntnis,* Vol. 6 (1936), 141–142.

Rynin, David, "Remarks on M. Schlick's Essay 'Positivism and Realism.'" *Synthese,* Vol. 1 (1948/1949).

BÉLA JUHOS
Translated by *Albert E. Blumberg*

SCHOLASTICISM. See AUGUSTINIANISM; AVERROISM; MEDIEVAL PHILOSOPHY; OCKHAMISM; SCIENTIA MEDIA AND MOLINISM; SCOTISM; THOMISM.

SCHOLZ, HEINRICH (1884–1956), German theologian and logician. Scholz was born in Berlin. He professed an outspoken Platonism based on a profound knowledge of the history of metaphysics and of the logical works of Leibniz, Bernard Bolzano, and Gottlob Frege. Scholz identified philosophy, in its original Platonic sense as the striving for universal knowledge, with the study of the foundations of mathematics and science. Thus, in *Was ist Philosophie?* (1940; *Mathesis Universalis,* pp. 341–387) he concluded, from Plato's demand for knowledge of geometry and a mathematical astronomy, that the axiomatic method is required for universal knowledge. He regarded mathematical logic as developed by Leibniz, Bolzano, Frege, Russell, and others as the *"epochale Gestalt"* of *metaphysica generalis.* He opposed formalism in logic because it failed to provide for the semantics of formal languages, and he opposed constructivism because of its arbitrary anthropocentric limitations of logic.

Scholz's devotion to logic arose from a concern with metaphysics in theology. He studied theology at Berlin and philosophy at Erlangen, receiving a Dr. phil. from Erlangen with a dissertation on Schleiermacher. He held the chair of systematic theology and philosophy of religion

at Breslau from 1917 to 1919, and then a chair of philosophy at Kiel. In his main systematic theological work, *Religionsphilosophie* (Berlin, 1921), he rejected subjective and existential foundations for religion. God is a transsubjective datum whose being is independent of any "leap of faith"; otherwise truth would be irrelevant to religion: "nothing remains but either to give up the solution to the problem of truth or to enter upon an entirely new course" (*Mathesis Universalis,* p. 13). By a "lucky accident," the discovery of Whitehead and Russell's *Principia Mathematica* in the library at Kiel, Scholz found his new course. From 1923 to 1928 he immersed himself in the study of logic, mathematics, and physics, and of their histories. His thoughts on metaphysics were galvanized, and he developed an enthusiasm for logical calculi rare even among mathematicians; it infused his later lectures and doubtless alienated those readers in Germany who were not quite convinced of the need to analyze Plato and other classical metaphysicians logically. In 1929, his metamorphosis into a logician complete, Scholz assumed a chair of philosophy at Münster, which was transferred to the mathematical faculty in 1943 when he founded the Institut für mathematische Logik und Grundlagenforschung. This institute was inspired by the Warsaw school under Jan Łukasiewicz (whom Scholz later rescued from a Nazi concentration camp). But Scholz did not renounce theology. In "Das theologische Element im Beruf des logistischen Logikers" (1935; *Mathesis Universalis,* pp. 324–340) he likened his motives for undertaking *Grundlagenforschung* to the motives of an Augustinian theologian in search of illumination from the eternal forms. He undertook logical investigations of Anselm's ontological argument ("Der Anselmische Gottesbewies," 1950; *Mathesis Universalis,* pp. 62–74) and of Augustine's arithmetical proof ("Der Gottesgedanke in der Mathematik," 1950; *Mathesis Universalis,* pp. 293–312).

Scholz wrote one of the first competent histories of logic, *Abriss der Geschichte der Logik* (Berlin, 1921; translated by Kurt F. Leidecker as *Concise History of Logic,* New York, 1961), based on the pioneering studies of Louis Couturat and Jan Łukasiewicz. He exhibited what may be called a coincidence of logic and metaphysics through several works that together constitute in effect the first logically competent history of metaphysics. His "Logik, Grammatik, Metaphysik" (1944; *Mathesis Universalis,* pp. 399–438) discusses metaphysics in Aristotle, Leibniz, and Kant. "Die mathematische Logik und die Metaphysik" (*Philosophisches Jahrbuch der Görres-Gesellschaft,* Vol. 51, 1938, 257–291), a 1938 lecture intended to convince a meeting of German Thomists of the importance of mathematical logic, discusses scholastic philosophy, Plato, and Aristotle. He discusses the fundamental importance of the axiomatic method for metaphysics in "Die Axiomatik der Alten" (1930; *Mathesis Universalis,* pp. 27–44), on Aristotle's *Posterior Analytics;* in *Was ist Philosophie?;* and in *Die Wissenschaftslehre Bolzanos* (1937; *Mathesis Universalis,* pp. 219–267). Scholz regarded the *mathesis universalis* of Descartes, Pascal, and Leibniz as of special importance in the history of metaphysics. He developed Leibniz' metaphysical doctrines of identity and possibility in *Metaphysik als strenge Wissenschaft* (Cologne, 1941), a thorough treatment of the logic of identity, and in *Grundzüge der mathematischen Logik,* written in collaboration with Gisbert Hasenjaeger (Göttingen, 1961). In *Grundzüge,* logical truth is defined as that which is identical throughout all possible worlds. Scholz used this definition to explain the a priori (the pre-Kantian *Transzendentale*): possible (not necessarily actual) worlds constitute the logical frame for any description of the real world. Scholz's "Einführung in die Kantische Philosophie," a series of lectures given in 1943 and 1944 (*Mathesis Universalis,* pp. 152–218), was the first systematic treatment of Kant's logical, mathematical, and physical doctrines to call upon both mathematical logic and physics. Of particular interest is Scholz's account of how Kant came to reject the *mathesis universalis* because of Christian Wolff's garbled presentation of Leibniz' mathematical philosophy.

Scholz greatly admired the work of the Vienna circle, particularly that of Rudolf Carnap. However, he held that Platonism, especially in the form of classical mathematics, has been more useful to science than positivism, since it permits theoretical constructions more powerful than any offered by positivism. Positivism retards scientific growth. Thus, according to Scholz, modern relativity theory, even though positivistic tendencies helped lay its observational foundation, is Platonist because of its use of classical analysis. According to Scholz, the logic of Frege and Russell was adequate evidence that Platonism is feasible, and Alfred Tarski's noneffective method of proof and his semantic definition of truth proved that Platonism can be given an absolutely rigorous foundation.

Scholz held that competence in metaphysics requires knowledge of mathematical logic, but he failed to convince most German metaphysicians. His works were ignored, and irrationalism exercised virtual hegemony in Germany during the Nazi era. (Even in the United States, his work was mentioned only in the *Journal of Symbolic Logic.*) Scholz saw language being employed as a poorly controlled, quasi-literary means of expression rather than as a logical tool for grasping objective truth. He therefore engrossed himself in his technical work, the crowning achievement of which was the posthumously published *Grundzüge der mathematischen Logik.* This work deals extensively with the elements of logic; develops propositional logic, quantificational logic, and type-theoretical logic (this last is called "Russell-revised Platonism" because it functions as an ontological foundation for mathematics) in formalized syntactic and semantic metalanguages; and examines the questions of completeness and independence with respect to both effective and noneffective proof methods.

Bibliography

See *Mathesis Universalis,* H. Hermes, F. Kambartel, and J. Ritter, eds. (Basel and Stuttgart, 1961), a selective anthology with a comprehensive bibliography; *Glaube und Unglaube in der Weltgeschichte* (Leipzig, 1911); *Die Religionsphilosophie des Als-ob* (Leipzig, 1921).

An article on Scholz, accompanied by a photograph, is Hans Hermes, "Heinrich Scholz zum 70. Geburtstage," in *Mathematisch-physikalische Semesterberichte,* N.F. Vol. 5 (1955), 165–170.

ECKEHART KÖHLER

SCHOPENHAUER, ARTHUR (1788–1860), was a German philosopher of pessimism who gave the will a leading place in his metaphysics. He was born in Danzig. His father, a successful businessman of partly Dutch ancestry, was an admirer of Voltaire and was imbued with a keen dislike of absolutist governments. When Danzig surrendered to the Prussians in 1793, the family moved to Hamburg and remained there until the father's death (apparently by suicide) in 1805. Schopenhauer's mother was a novelist who in later years established a salon in Weimar, which brought him into contact with a number of literary figures, including Goethe. His relations with his mother, however, were bitter and antagonistic and eventually led to a more or less complete estrangement.

Education. Schopenhauer's early education was somewhat unconventional. He spent two years in France in the charge of a friend of his father, and for another period he accompanied his parents on a prolonged tour of France, England (where he attended school in London for several months), Switzerland, and Austria. After his father's death he was tutored privately in the classics for a time and then entered the University of Göttingen as a medical student, studying, among other subjects, physics, chemistry, and botany. At Göttingen he first read Plato and Kant, and the powerful and lasting impression their writings made upon him directed his interests decisively toward philosophy. In consequence he left Göttingen in 1811 for Berlin, which was at that time the chief philosophical center in Germany, and worked there for two years, attending the lectures of Fichte and Schleiermacher (both of whom he found profoundly disappointing) and making preparatory notes for a doctoral thesis. When the uprising against Napoleon led to the closing of the university, Schopenhauer, for whom nationalist sentiment held little appeal, retired to Rudolstadt to write his thesis, subsequently published there in 1813 under the title of *Über die vierfache Wurzel des Satzes vom zureichenden Grunde (On the Fourfold Root of the Principle of Sufficient Reason).*

Early career. Apart from producing a short book on the perception of color, *Über das Sehn und die Farben* (Leipzig, 1816), which was inspired by a previous essay on the same subject by Goethe, Schopenhauer employed the next four years writing his principal work, *Die Welt als Wille und Vorstellung (The World as Will and Idea).* From the very first stages of the composition of this work, Schopenhauer believed that the ideas he was striving to express were of major importance, and when it was published at Leipzig in 1818 (dated 1819), he was confident that its significance would immediately be recognized. In this expectation he was to be quickly disappointed; the scanty reviews his book received were generally tepid in tone, and the number of copies sold was small. Nevertheless, its publication helped him to obtain the post of lecturer at the University of Berlin, where he chose to give lectures at the same hours as Hegel, who was then at the height of his reputation and popularity. From the start, Schopenhauer advertised his opposition to Hegelian conceptions. He spoke of sophists who, having arisen after Kant, "first exhausted the thinking power of their time with barbarous and mysterious speech, then scared it away from philosophy and brought the study into discredit," and he made it clear that he regarded his own mission as one of repairing the damage that had been done. Schopenhauer's lectures, however, were a failure; Hegel's authority was too firmly established to be undermined in this manner, and Schopenhauer's audience dwindled away.

Later career. Schopenhauer made no further attempt to establish himself academically. From then on he lived a solitary life, profoundly resentful at the lack of the recognition he felt to be his due and confirmed in his opinion that the dominant Hegelian philosophy was the product of a charlatan who, by an artful combination of sophistry and rhetoric, had succeeded in corrupting the intellects of an entire generation. Despite his disappointment, however, Schopenhauer continued to write, producing books that were in effect elaborations and developments of themes already adumbrated in his main work. He published an essay entitled *Über den Willen in der Natur* (Frankfurt, 1836); and a volume on ethics and the problem of free will, *Die beiden Grundprobleme der Ethik* (Frankfurt, 1841), which contained the two essays "Über die Freiheit des Willens" (1839) and "Über die Grundlage der Moral" (1840). In 1844 he brought out a second edition of *Die Welt als Wille und Vorstellung*, greatly expanded by the addition of fifty supplementary chapters. He also contemplated translating Kant's *Critique of Pure Reason* into English and Hume's *Dialogues Concerning Natural Religion* (a work he greatly admired) into German. There can be little doubt that he would have performed both of these tasks well, for his knowledge of English was excellent; but unfortunately nothing came of either project. Finally, Schopenhauer published a collection of essays and aphorisms called *Parerga und Paralipomena* (2 vols., Berlin, 1851), and with this work he began to be widely known. Discussions of his ideas appeared in foreign as well as in German periodicals, and his system was made the subject of lectures in a number of major European universities. By the time of his death in Frankfurt, he had a growing circle of admirers in England, Russia, and the United States, while nearer home the influence of his writings was soon to show itself in the work of such thinkers as Nietzsche and Jakob Burckhardt.

Character. Schopenhauer's personality, which is reflected in much of his writing, was complex and compounded of curiously diverse elements. Although intellectually self-assured to the point of arrogance, he had a brooding, introspective disposition, and he betrayed an extreme susceptibility to irrational fears and anxieties. Thus, he always slept with a loaded pistol near him, and he took compulsive precautions against disease; he once remarked that if nothing alarmed him, he grew alarmed at this very condition—"as if there must still be something of which I am only ignorant for a time." His manner could be truculent and overbearing; as many of his aphorisms make clear, his view of others was colored by a deep suspiciousness and cynicism, and his general outlook on life and existence was unrelievedly pessimistic. Yet this did not prevent him from taking pleasure in many things—art and music, good food and wine, travel, and, despite his notorious essay on the subject, women. And while he detested bores, in company that he found sympathetic he appears to have been a lively and entertaining talker, displaying a sharp, satirical wit.

THE NATURE OF PHILOSOPHICAL THINKING

Schopenhauer's philosophy is best approached from a position that clearly recognizes his indebtedness to Kant, whom he believed to have been indisputably the greatest thinker of modern times. Schopenhauer's chief charge against his own philosophical contemporaries in Germany (Schelling, Fichte, and Hegel)—was that under the pretense of carrying forward and developing Kantian ideas, they had in fact attempted to philosophize in a fashion that Kant himself had ruled out as wholly inadmissible. For if Kant had shown anything, it was that metaphysical speculation in the old "transcendent" sense was useless as a means of achieving knowledge of what lay beyond all human experience. Such knowledge is in principle unattainable, and it followed that any philosopher, whatever his procedure might be, who tried to establish such things as the existence of God and the immortality of the soul was engaged in a hopeless quest. Rationalist metaphysicians like Descartes had employed deductive a priori arguments in an endeavor to prove certain fundamental propositions of theology, and Kant had sufficiently exposed the inadequacy of these arguments by a series of devastating refutations. Yet according to Schopenhauer, Kant's strictures had not prevented some of his self-appointed successors from speaking as if they had mysterious access to truths necessarily outside the range of human cognition—a "little window opening on to the supernatural world," as it were. He suggested, too, that writing in this way appeared more expedient to many academic teachers of philosophy than the honest alternative of expounding truthfully and directly the antidogmatic theses contained in the *Critique of Pure Reason*.

While he accepted Kant's reasons for rejecting metaphysical theorizing in the sense described above, Schopenhauer was nevertheless far from wishing to claim that all philosophical speculation concerning the ultimate nature of the world must be deemed illicit and misconceived. The impulse to seek some general interpretation of reality and of the place of human existence within it was too deeply embedded in the human mind to be totally ignored or set aside. Man, Schopenhauer held, is an *animal metaphysicum*, a creature who cannot avoid wondering at the existence of the world and raising questions concerning its fundamental character and significance—questions which empirical science is unable adequately to resolve, for they lie beyond its sphere. Religion, it is true, attempts in its own way to meet this pervasive need, although not in a manner susceptible to rational justification or certification. For the tenets and concepts of religious faiths, whatever those who subscribe to them may believe to the contrary, can never be more than "allegories" or imaginative figures, and treating them as if they represented literal truths about a higher order of things leads straightway to manifest absurdities and contradictions. By contrast, the concern of philosophical thinking is not with the metaphorical intimation of ideas which are beyond the grasp of the human intellect; rather, such thinking aims at truth *sensu proprio*. It follows, therefore, that any solution of "the riddle of the world" that philosophy purports to provide must not be one that involves overstepping the boundaries within which all human knowledge is set and confined. The determination of exactly where these boundaries lie is accordingly of primary importance as a preliminary to all philosophical inquiry.

PERCEPTION AND THOUGHT

Schopenhauer's theory of knowledge may be said to start with Kant's distinction between *phenomena* (what appears to a perceiving mind) and *noumena* (things as they are in themselves). In our perceptual consciousness of the world, we are in fact aware of it only as mediated through our sense organs and intellect—a point Schopenhauer expressed by saying that, so conceived, the world is "idea" or "representation" (*Vorstellung*). Moreover, everything that presents itself to us in perception necessarily conforms to a certain formal and categorial framework that underlies and finds expression in all departments of our common-sense and scientific knowledge. Thus Schopenhauer was at one with Kant in holding that the human mind cannot (as the British empiricists had suggested) be envisaged as a mere passive recipient of sense impressions, but on the contrary plays an essentially active part in shaping and organizing the sensory material. It is the structure of the intellect, comprising "sensibility" and "understanding," which ensures that this sensory material apprises us of a realm of external objective phenomena, spatially and temporally ordered and standing in determinate causal relations both with one another and with ourselves as percipients. Space and time as forms of sensibility, together with causality considered as the sole category of the understanding (here Schopenhauer diverged from Kant), are therefore "subjective in origin," while at the same time they are necessary conditions of our knowledge of the world as idea. According to Schopenhauer, it is also the case that their valid employment is restricted to this sphere; they have no application to anything not given, or that could not be given, in sense experience.

Schopenhauer distinguished a further class of ideas, namely, what he termed "ideas of Reflection," or sometimes "ideas of ideas" (*Vorstellungen von Vorstellungen*). It is in terms of these that we think about and communicate the contents of our phenomenal experience. In other words, they are the general concepts by virtue of which we can classify phenomena according to common features that are of interest or importance to us, forming thereby a conceptual structure or system which may be said to mirror or copy the empirical world. The function of this system is essentially a practical one; it provides a means of memorizing, and generalizing from, our observations of how things behave under varying conditions, and hence of putting to use what we learn from experience. Schopenhauer insisted, moreover, that this system cannot legitimately be separated from the foundation of empirical reality upon which it is based, and he claimed that concepts and abstract notions that cannot be traced back to experience are comparable to bank notes "issued by a firm which has nothing but other paper obligations to back it with." Consequently, metaphysical theories that pretend to offer an account of the world purely a priori, and that in doing so employ terms or propositions not susceptible to empirical interpretation, are empty of cognitive content; they "move in the air without support." Indeed, such theories

often represent no more than the development, by laborious deductive steps, of the implications of a small group of initial axioms or definitions, yielding systems of empty tautologies.

Thus far, Schopenhauer would appear to have placed fairly stringent limits upon the scope of human inquiry. Attempts to transcend these limits by appealing to the resources of deductive reasoning alone are necessarily impossible, since they involve fundamentally wrong ideas concerning the nature of logical inference. These ideas can never provide us with information of which we were not previously cognizant, for such inference merely makes explicit what is already implicitly asserted in the premises from which it proceeds. Equally, there can be no justification for trying to extend the use of nonlogical, formative principles like the principle of causality in order to establish matters of nonempirical fact, after the manner of some earlier metaphysicians. Schopenhauer even accused Kant of inconsistency in this matter, on the ground that he wrote as though the existence of things-in-themselves, which for Kant are by definition incapable of being experienced, could be validly inferred from the phenomenal data, thereby disregarding his own prohibition. Nonetheless, Schopenhauer considered that the Kantian notion of the thing-in-itself remained a fertile one. Properly conceived, it offered the needed clue to the discovery of a legitimate and correct philosophical interpretation of existence.

THE WILL

According to Schopenhauer, it is not true that the thing-in-itself, the noumenal reality that underlies the world of phenomenal appearances, is beyond the range of all possible human experience. To realize this, it is necessary to take account of the facts of self-consciousness, that is, our own intimate knowledge of ourselves. Self-awareness has two distinct aspects. From one point of view, namely, the standpoint of ordinary perception, I cannot avoid regarding myself as an "object," as much a physical entity as a building or a tree is. In this sense, I necessarily conform to the conditions that constitute the "world as idea" in general; I am a body that occupies space, endures through time, and causally responds to stimuli.

Individual will. My inner experience also assures me that I am nevertheless more than "an object among objects," for I do not appear to myself under this aspect alone. I am also aware of myself from within as a self-moving, active being whose overt perceptible behavior directly expresses my will. This inner consciousness that each one of us has of himself as will is primitive and irreducible. Thus, Schopenhauer claimed that the will reveals itself immediately to everyone as the "in-itself" of his own phenomenal being and that the awareness we have of ourselves as will is quite different from the awareness we have of ourselves as body. At the same time, however, he emphatically denied that the operations of a man's will and the movements he makes with his body are two distinct series of events—events of the first kind being thought of as causally productive of events of the second kind. Schopenhauer believed that dualistic conceptions of the relation of will and body, deriving largely from Descartes, had wrought havoc in philosophy, and he argued instead that a man's body is simply the "objectification" of his will as it appears under the conditions of external perception; what I will and what in physical terms I do are one and the same thing, but viewed from different standpoints.

The will in nature. What has just been discussed represents the cornerstone of Schopenhauer's metaphysic. For it was his contention that we should not assume the above distinction between the phenomenal appearance and the thing as it is in itself to apply only insofar as we ourselves are concerned. On the contrary, just as my own phenomenal being and activity is ultimately intelligible as the expression of my inner will, so may the rest of the phenomenal world be understood to share the same fundamental character that we recognize to be ours. Here was the "great extension" of the concept of will whereby Schopenhauer claimed that all phenomena—human and nonhuman, animate and inanimate—might be interpreted in a way that gave the world as a whole a new dimension of significance and that at the same time was not open to the insuperable objections vitiating traditional metaphysical doctrines. The latter claim may reasonably be doubted. Schopenhauer often displayed considerable perspicacity in detecting errors and inconsistencies in the theories of other philosophers, but he did not always show a comparable critical acumen with regard to his own ideas. Even so, the picture he drew of the world, in accordance with his conception of its inner essence, is not without a certain novelty and horrific fascination, standing as it does at the opposite pole from all those metaphysical systems which have, in one way or another, endeavored to present ultimate reality as if it were the incarnation of rational or moral order. For Schopenhauer, the real was not the rational (as Hegel, for instance, implied that it was); on the contrary, "will" was for him the name of a nonrational force, a blind, striving power whose operations are without ultimate purpose or design. So portrayed, nature in all its aspects, ranging from the simplest physical structures to the most complex and highly developed organisms, takes on the character of an endless, and in the last analysis meaningless, struggle for existence, in which all is stress, conflict, and tension. The mechanistic models, the rationalistic schemes and constructions, in terms of which we find it useful to try to systematize the phenomenal data for scientific and practical purposes, merely serve to disguise from view the true nature of the underlying reality; the proper task of philosophy lies, not in seeking (as so many previous thinkers had sought) to reinforce these misconceptions by consoling and sophistical arguments, but rather in removing the veil of deception and setting the truth in a clear light.

Human nature. As indicated above, Schopenhauer took as the starting point of his theory of the world the nature of man himself, regarded as the embodiment of will. Man is the microcosm in which all that is fundamental to reality as a whole (the macrocosm) may be plainly discerned. And it is in connection with what he wrote about human nature that Schopenhauer's doctrine of the will can perhaps be most profitably considered. For this doctrine, far from being merely an extravagant philosophical fantasy, foreshadows much that was central to the later development of psychological theory; it represents a highly significant contribution with genuinely revolutionary implications.

Will and intellect. What Schopenhauer had to say on the subject of human nature revolved about his conception of the role of the intellect in human behavior. We like to suppose that in principle, everything we do lies within the province of our reason and is subject to our control; only if this is so can we deem ourselves to be truly our own masters. Traditionally, philosophers have given their support to such beliefs; according to Schopenhauer, however, the situation is quite the reverse. For the will is not, as Descartes and others have taught, a sort of instrument or component of the intellectual faculty, mysteriously controlling our actions from on high by means of independent acts of rational choice. As has already been seen, Schopenhauer argued that will and body are simply the same thing viewed under different aspects, and he further claimed that the intellect, far from being the original source and spring of the will and the master of the body, is in fact no more than the will's servant and appendage. From an epistemological point of view, this governance of the intellect by the will manifests itself in the forms of knowledge under which the world appears to us—for example, as a causally governed system. To see things as causes or effects is to see them in terms of their potential uses, that is, as possible means to the gratification of the will.

Motivation. According to Schopenhauer, however, the primacy of will exhibits itself in a number of other important ways. Thus he gave various illustrations, drawn from everyday experience, of the manner in which we are often quite unaware of the true import and significance of our responses to circumstances and situations. Believing ourselves to be activated by some consideration that we find acceptable on moral or other grounds, we miss the real motive and might well be shocked or embarrassed if we knew it. Although we are inwardly and immediately aware of ourselves *as* will, our own consciously formulated conceptions of what we desire or what we are intending are, in fact, a highly unreliable guide when the question under consideration is *what* we will. Sometimes, indeed, Schopenhauer seems to have been making the extreme claim that conscious acts of choice never really determine behavior at all. He suggested in a number of instances that our conduct is not ultimately decided by resolves intellectually arrived at after weighing the pros and cons of alternative courses of action; the real decision is made by the will below the level of rationally reflective consciousness, the sole role of the intellect being to put before the will the various possibilities that lie open to the agent and to estimate the consequences that would ensue upon their actualization. In this sense, we never really form more than a "conjecture" of what we shall do in the future, although we often take such conjectures for resolves; what we have decided to do becomes finally clear to us only a posteriori, through the deed we perform. As it stands, this doctrine gives rise to obvious difficulties. *Some* cases doubtless occur that we should be inclined to describe in some such manner as Schopenhauer recommends, but it does not follow that every case of deliberate action can be so characterized. Indeed, it may be claimed against all positions of this sort that it is only in virtue of our knowledge of what it is to act in accordance with consciously formed choices that the explanation of certain actions in terms of secret or concealed determinations of the will becomes intelligible.

Unconscious mental activity. The above-mentioned difficulties do not invalidate Schopenhauer's exceptionally perceptive and shrewd observations regarding much human motivation. These observations retain their importance even if the more bizarre speculations he based upon them are rejected; and Schopenhauer in fact connected them with a wider theory of human nature that, considering the time in which he wrote, manifested an astonishing prescience. According to this theory, the entire perspective in terms of which we are disposed to view our characters and doings is distorted. We customarily think of ourselves as being essentially free and rational agents, whereas in fact the principal sources and springs of our conduct consist in deep-lying tendencies and drives of whose character we are often wholly unaware. "Consciousness," Schopenhauer wrote, "is the mere surface of our mind, of which, as of the earth, we do not know the inside but only the crust," and in consequence we often put entirely false constructions upon the behavior in which these basic impulses are expressed. He suggested, moreover, that the ignorance we display, the rationalizations which in all innocence we provide, may themselves have a motive, although not one we are aware of. Thus, he frequently wrote of the will as preventing the rise to consciousness of thoughts and desires that, if known, would arouse feelings of humiliation, embarrassment, or shame. Another example of the same process is to be found in instances of memory failure. It is not a mere accident that we do not remember certain things, since there may be powerful inducements for us not to do so; events and experiences can be "completely suppressed," becoming for us as if they had never taken place, simply because unconsciously we feel them to be unendurable. And in extreme cases this can lead to a form of insanity, with fantasies and delusions replacing what has thus been extruded from consciousness.

Sexuality. Freud himself recognized the similarity between ideas like those above and some of the leading conceptions of psychoanalytical theory. Certainly there are striking parallels, and perhaps most obviously between what Schopenhauer had to say about the sexual instinct and the Freudian account of libido. For instance, Schopenhauer claimed that the sexual urge represents the "focus of the will." Apart from the instinct to survive, it is the most powerful motive of all and exercises a pervasive influence in every area of human life. Yet despite this, the amount of attention sexuality had received from most philosophers and psychologists had been remarkably small; it is as though a veil had been thrown over it, through which, however, the subject kept showing through. Nevertheless, Schopenhauer was far from extolling the operations of the sexual drive. Although he thought it necessary to expose honestly the stark reality that human beings seek to hide by falsely romanticizing and idealizing their primitive passions, he also made it clear that he considered sexuality to be a source of great mischief and suffering. Thus he referred to it as a "demon" that "strives to pervert, confuse

and overthrow everything," and spoke of sexual desires as being inherently incapable of achieving lasting satisfaction; according to Schopenhauer, the end of love is always disillusion. In other words, here, as elsewhere, conformity to the dictates of the will ultimately results in unhappiness, which is the universal condition of human existence.

Pessimism and antirationalism. In sum, Schopenhauer's doctrine of the will constituted, in a variety of ways, a reaction against the then dominant eighteenth-century, or "Enlightenment," conceptions of human nature. He not only rejected the Cartesian belief in the primacy of intellect or reason in man, but also, by implication, repudiated the "mechanistic" model according to which writers like Hume sought to explain human personality and motivation in terms of the combination and association of atomistically conceived impressions and ideas. In place of this model, he substituted one of dynamic drive and function that was oriented toward the biological rather than the physical sciences and that stressed the importance of unconscious rather than conscious mental processes. Furthermore, Schopenhauer's writings represent a complete departure from the strain of optimism that underlay so much eighteenth-century thinking about history and society. Schopenhauer utterly rejected such ideas as the inevitability of human progress and the perfectibility of man and replaced them with a picture of mankind in general as doomed to an eternal round of torment and misery. Radical changes in the social structure, however "scientifically" applied, would solve nothing, for the evil condition of life as we find it is merely the reflection of the aggressive and libidinous urges rooted in our own natures. All that can usefully be employed are certain palliatives in the form of social and legal controls which give the individual minimal protection against the incursions of his neighbors; and with such measures men have long been familiar.

ART AND AESTHETIC EXPERIENCE

The pre-eminent position that Schopenhauer assigned to art (certainly no other major philosopher has elevated it to a higher status) is not difficult to understand in the light of his general theory. In this theory, our modes of knowledge and understanding, as well as the activities in which we normally engage, are regarded as being determined by the will. Scientific inquiry was the supreme instance of this, since (Schopenhauer believed) its essential function was one of providing, through the discovery of empirical uniformities, practical techniques for satisfying our wants and desires.

The aesthetic attitude. The artist's concern, however, is not with action, or the possibility of action, at all, but with what Schopenhauer termed "contemplation" or "will-less perception." This type of perception must not be confused with perception of the ordinary everyday kind, wherein things are looked at from the standpoint of practical interest and appear under the aspect of particular phenomenal objects. For it is the mark of aesthetic contemplation that in the enjoyment of artistic experience "we keep the sabbath of the penal servitude of willing"; the world is seen in abstraction from the various aims, desires, and anxieties that accompany our normal apprehension of it, with the result that it presents itself to us in a completely different light.

It is a further consequence of such detachment (and on this point Schopenhauer followed Kant) that all judgments of taste or aesthetic value are disinterested: they cannot have as their basis some titillation of sensual appetite, for instance; nor can they be grounded upon considerations of social utility, or even of moral purpose. To speak of a natural scene or of a work of art or literature as "beautiful" is to judge it in and for itself, and quite outside the framework of cause and consequence within which our ordinary perceptual judgments have their natural place and from which they derive their significance.

The aesthetic object. The claim that aesthetic awareness presupposes a distinctive attitude of mind and attention is clearly separable from the contention, also advanced by Schopenhauer, that in such awareness the content of our experience is of a radically different kind from that involved in ordinary sense perception. Surprising as it may seem in the light of some of his earlier pronouncements, Schopenhauer held that the subjective conditions which define and universally determine our perception at the everyday level are wholly in abeyance in the case of aesthetic apprehension, and that to this complete "change in the subject" there is a corresponding change in the object. As aesthetic observers, we are no longer confronted with a multiplicity of individual things and events that are spatiotemporally and causally interrelated, but instead are presented with the "permanent essential forms of the world and all its phenomena," which Schopenhauer termed the "Ideas" (*Ideen*). This conception of fundamental Ideas, which Schopenhauer adapted from Plato to serve the purposes of his own, very different, theory of art, helps us to understand why he regarded art not merely as a kind of knowledge, but as a kind of knowledge vastly superior to any found in the sphere of the natural sciences. In his view, the natural sciences can never do more than discover regularities at the stage of phenomenal appearance, whereas works of genuine art exhibit to the beholder the nature of the archetypal forms of which the particular phenomena of sense perception are necessarily incomplete and inadequate expressions. Artistic productions may, in fact, be said to be the vehicles through which the artist communicates his profound discoveries and insights and thereby enables others to share his vision.

The notion that the proper objects of artistic perception are Platonic Ideas in the sense described above gives rise to obvious objections. It certainly fits somewhat uneasily into Schopenhauer's system insofar as that originally seemed to be based upon the postulate that phenomenal representation and noumenal will between them exhaust the field of possible human knowledge. And quite apart from this, the theory of Ideas raises problems on its own account. It appears paradoxical, for instance, to suggest that a picture of, say, apples in a bowl is not a picture of things of the sort we can all see and touch in the ordinary way, but of something set mysteriously apart from these and situated in a realm beyond the range of normal vision. Even so, it is at least to Schopenhauer's credit that he recognized some of the difficulties presented by much that we are prone to think and say about artistic portrayals of

experience. The concept of perception, for instance, seems to play a significantly different role in the context of aesthetic appraisal and criticism from the role it plays in other contexts. Again, the specific sense in which certain art forms (painting, for example) are concerned with "representing" reality is notoriously difficult to analyze. The claim that the artist sees something literally distinct from what we ordinarily see is, no doubt, hard to defend; on the other hand, the (different) claim that he sees and is able to portray ordinary things in unfamiliar ways, and under fresh and revealing aspects, appears to contain an obvious truth. Schopenhauer himself never clearly distinguished between these two claims. Theoretically he subscribed to the first, but much that he said in his discussion of concrete cases accords better with the second. Not only did he often stress the particularity of the artist's observation of phenomena; he also suggested that the artist's unique mode of presenting individual objects, scenes, or situations succeeds in illuminating for us whole ranges of our experience to which we have previously been blind. He argued, however, that it would be a mistake to suppose that we can ever convey by verbal description what we learn from our direct acquaintance with particular works of art. For what these works communicate will in the end always elude anything we try to say about them. "The transition from the Idea to the concept," he wrote, "is always a fall."

Music. Schopenhauer thought that all forms of artistic activity—with one important exception—could be understood and explained in terms of his theory of Ideas. The exception was music. Music is not concerned with the representation of phenomena or the fundamental forms that underlie phenomena, but has as its subject the will itself, the nature of which it expresses directly and immediately. Thus, of all the arts, music stands closest to the ultimate reality of things which we all bear within ourselves and speaks "the universal imageless language of the heart." Schopenhauer's ideas, in this instance and in general, produced a deep impression upon Richard Wagner, who in his opera *Tristan und Isolde* tried to realize in musical form the leading conceptions of Schopenhauer's theory of the world. It is a curious irony that Schopenhauer, far from reciprocating Wagner's admiration, spoke of his music with actual distaste.

ETHICS AND MYSTICISM

Although the world, viewed from a purely contemplative standpoint, presents a spectacle that can be aesthetically enjoyed, it does not follow that the operations of the agency which underlies all that we perceive can afford us any kind of moral guidance or solace. On the contrary, the ethical significance of existence lies in its ultimate horror. Unlike many other metaphysicians, Schopenhauer concluded from his system, not that we should gratefully seek to make our lives conform to the pattern implicit in the nature of reality, but rather that true salvation consists in a total rejection of this pattern. The moral worth of individuals lies in their capacity to liberate themselves from the pressures and urges of the rapacious will.

Inalterability of character. It is not altogether easy to see how liberation is possible. Schopenhauer had claimed that human beings, like everything else in nature, are in essence expressions of will. How, then, can they become otherwise? Furthermore, he insisted upon a strictly deterministic interpretation of human character and action, one that makes the type of freedom of choice postulated by traditional libertarian doctrines inconceivable. What a person does is always and necessarily a manifestation of his inner disposition, which remains fixed and is unalterable by any resolutions he may form to be different. The individual discovers what he is really like by observing his behavior over the course of his life. He will find that this behavior conforms to certain invariant patterns of reaction and response, so that if the same circumstances recur, his conduct in the face of them will be the same as it was before. Such consistent behavior patterns are the outward manifestation of the individual noumenal essence, or timeless character, which each man is in himself—a conception Schopenhauer claimed to have derived from Kant's discussion of the foundations of moral responsibility, though the consequences he drew from it were in fact far removed from any drawn by Kant. Nor can some of these consequences be said to have been logically very happy; for instance, Schopenhauer seems to have employed the notion of a man's character so elastically that it ruled out the possibility of any imaginable state of affairs falsifying his thesis concerning its innate and unchangeable nature.

Ethical variation. Schopenhauer's claim that a man cannot change his character at will does not, however, commit him to the view that the dispositions of different individuals do not show significant ethical variations. For an explanation of the fact that there are good as well as evil persons in the world, he returned to the fundamental tenets of his metaphysic. It is a feature of the good, as contrasted with the self-centered or egotistical, individual that he comprehends himself and his relations with others from a "higher" standpoint, which enables him to recognize, however obscurely or inarticulately, the common unitary nature shared by all things. Egoism rests upon the assumption that the individual is a self-sufficient unit, to which all else is foreign. But the individual appears to be set apart from his fellows by an impassable gulf only when apprehended in accordance with the spatiotemporal scheme that informs our everyday "will-governed" way of looking at things. A profounder insight, such as is exhibited intuitively in the behavior of the just and compassionate man who "draws less distinction between himself and others than is usually done," involves awareness of the illusory character of the phenomenal world. Those who possess this awareness no longer see their fellow creatures as alien objects to be overcome or manipulated in pursuit of their own egocentric aims, but rather as "themselves once more," homogeneous with their own being and nature. Thus, in the last analysis, the distinction between virtue and vice has its source in radically different modes of viewing those around us; and this distinction could, Schopenhauer believed, be adequately explicated and justified in the terms provided by his own philosophical system.

Denial of the will. Schopenhauer frequently quoted the Brahman formula, *tat tvam asi* ("that thou art"), when discussing the metaphysical unity of things that underlies the realm of appearance. Indeed, all his writings on ethical and related subjects show affinities with the doc-

trines advanced in the Upanishads and in Buddhist texts—affinities which he freely acknowledged. Like the Indian teachers, he considered all human life to be enmeshed in suffering, and following them, he often used the word *māyā* to refer to the illusory phenomenal world to which, as empirical individuals, we belong. Total release from the enslavement of the will, as compared with the identification of himself with others that is displayed in the conduct of the morally good man, in fact occurs only when a person finally ceases to feel any attachment to earthly things and when all desire to participate in the life of the world completely vanishes. Such an attitude of mind, which Schopenhauer attributed to ascetics and mystics of all times, becomes possible when a man's will "turns and denies itself," and when what in the eyes of ordinary men is the very essence and substance of reality appears to him as "nothing." But Schopenhauer was insistent that this "turning of the will," which is a highly mysterious process, is not something a man can bring about through his own deliberate volition, since the process involves the complete "abolition" of his previous personality. This "turning of the will" comes to him, as it were, "from outside" and springs from an insight which wholly transcends the will and the world. Such mystical insight, moreover, is necessarily incommunicable and indescribable; all knowledge, including that attainable by philosophy, here reaches its limit, and we are left with only "myths and meaningless words" which express no positive content. "The nature of things before or beyond the world, and consequently beyond the will," Schopenhauer declared at the close of his main work, "is open to no investigation." The end of philosophy is silence.

IMPORTANCE AND INFLUENCE

Schopenhauer's critics have not failed to draw attention to discrepancies and inconsistencies in his system. These certainly exist, and his natural clarity of expression, which contrasts so sharply with the obscure and cloudy terminology favored by his philosophical contemporaries in Germany, makes them comparatively easy to detect. On the other hand, these discrepancies should not be allowed to stand in the way of a proper appreciation of what was important and influential in Schopenhauer's thought. The nineteenth century witnessed a decline in the fascination that achievements in physics and mathematics had previously exercised over philosophy, and there was a tendency in speculative thought to explore new ways of interpreting and conceptualizing human life and experience. In this development Schopenhauer played a central role. Both through his theory of will, with its psychological implications, and also through the new metaphysical status he gave to art, he helped to bring about a profound shift in the intellectual and imaginative climate. In this connection, the impression made by his ideas upon novelists like Tolstoy, Conrad, Proust, and Thomas Mann is particularly noteworthy. Among philosophers, the impact of Schopenhauer's thought was weaker and certainly never approached that produced by Hegel's writings; while in more recent times, when philosophical speculation in general has been at a discount, he has attracted little interest. Yet such neglect is undeserved, and the significance of his contribution should not be underestimated. He realized more fully than the majority of his contemporaries the implications of the Kantian critique of traditional metaphysics, and some of the things he himself had to say about the nature of a priori knowledge have a strikingly modern ring. Again, it is worth emphasizing his "instrumentalist" view of human thinking, which anticipated William James and the American pragmatist school, and also his highly perceptive attacks upon the Cartesian theory of personality and self-consciousness, which in important respects foreshadowed present-day approaches to problems in the philosophy of mind. (In particular, his theory of the double knowledge we have of ourselves as agents in the world has interesting contemporary analogues.) Finally, it should be remembered that possibly the greatest philosopher of modern times, Ludwig Wittgenstein, read Schopenhauer and was influenced by him. The extent of this influence appears most clearly in the notebooks Wittgenstein kept during World War I (*Notebooks 1914–1916,* translated by G. E. M. Anscombe, Oxford, 1961), but signs of it are also to be found in the *Tractatus Logico-philosophicus* (translated by D. F. Pears and B. F. McGuiness, London, 1961), particularly in the sections on ethics and the limits of language in the latter part of the work.

Works by Schopenhauer

The most recent edition of Schopenhauer's collected works in German is *Sämtliche Werke,* A. Hübscher, ed., 2d ed., 7 vols. (Wiesbaden, 1946–1950).

There are two English translations of *Die Welt als Wille und Vorstellung: The World as Will and Idea,* translated by R. B. Haldane and J. Kemp, 3 vols. (London, 1883), and *The World as Will and Representation,* translated by E. F. J. Payne, 2 vols. (Indian Hills, Colo., 1958). Translations of other writings of Schopenhauer include *On the Fourfold Root of the Principle of Sufficient Reason and On the Will in Nature,* translated by K. Hillebrand (London, 1888); *The Basis of Morality,* translated by A. B. Bullock (London, 1903); *Selected Essays of Schopenhauer,* translated by T. B. Saunders (London, 1951); *Essay on the Freedom of the Will,* translated by K. Kolenda (New York, 1960); and *The Will to Live: Selected Writings of Arthur Schopenhauer,* Richard Taylor, ed. (New York, 1962).

Works on Schopenhauer

Modern commentaries on Schopenhauer are scarce, but F. C. Copleston, *Schopenhauer, Philosopher of Pessimism* (London, 1946), provides a careful and levelheaded survey from a critical and explicitly Roman Catholic point of view. There is also an interesting discussion of Schopenhauer's philosophy by Richard Taylor in D. J. O'Connor, ed., *A Critical History of Western Philosophy* (New York, 1964). The view of Schopenhauer presented in the present article is given at greater length in Patrick Gardiner, *Schopenhauer* (Harmondsworth, England, 1963).

Among earlier works, the following may be mentioned as dealing with particular aspects of Schopenhauer's thought and influence: G. Simmel, *Schopenhauer und Nietzsche* (Leipzig, 1907); R. A. Tsanoff, *Schopenhauer's Criticism of Kant's Theory of Experience* (New York, 1911); and A. Baillot, *Influence de la philosophie de Schopenhauer en France* (Paris, 1927). See also William Caldwell, *Schopenhauer's System in Its Philosophical Significance* (Edinburgh, 1896); and Israel Knox, *The Aesthetic Theories of Kant, Hegel, and Schopenhauer* (New York, 1936). For interpretations by writers deeply influenced by Schopenhauer's philosophy, see Friedrich Nietzsche, "Schopenhauer als Erzieher," in *Unzeitgemässe Betrachtungen* (Leipzig, 1873–1874); and Thomas Mann's introduction to *The Living Thoughts of Schopen-*

hauer (London, 1939). Schopenhauer's influence upon Wittgenstein is considered in G. E. M. Anscombe, *An Introduction to Wittgenstein's Tractatus* (London, 1959), Ch. 13, and Erik Stenius, *Wittgenstein's Tractatus* (Oxford, 1960), Ch. 11.

The most complete life of Schopenhauer is W. Schneider, *Schopenhauer, eine Biographie* (Vienna, 1937). In English, see William Wallace, *Life of Schopenhauer* (London, 1890); and Helen Zimmern, *Arthur Schopenhauer: His Life and Philosophy* (London, 1876; rev. ed., London, 1932).

PATRICK GARDINER

SCHRÖDINGER, ERWIN (1887–1961), Austrian physicist, was born in Vienna and studied physics and mathematics with Franz Exner, Rudolf Hasenöhrl, and Wilhelm Wirtinger. After brief appointments at Jena, Stuttgart, and Breslau, he became (1922) professor of mathematical physics at Zurich. It is here that he developed his wave mechanics in the fall of 1925. Schrödinger succeeded Max Planck at Berlin in 1927, only to leave in 1933, shortly after Hitler's rise to power. After a few years in Oxford and Graz (which he had to leave in 1938, when Austria was made part of the Third Reich) he accepted an invitation by Eamon de Valera to Dublin's newly founded Institute for Advanced Studies. Schrödinger received the Nobel prize in physics (jointly with Paul Dirac) in 1933. He returned to Austria in 1956.

Thought. Though the ideas of Werner Heisenberg and Schrödinger are now usually regarded as complementary aspects of one and the same point of view, they arose from different motives and were originally incompatible. Schrödinger was strongly influenced both by Boltzmann's physics and by his philosophy. "His line of thought," he said in his address to the Prussian Academy in 1929, "may be called my first love in science. No other has ever thus enraptured me and will ever do so again." In 1922, five years before Heisenberg's uncertainty relations saw the light, Schrödinger criticized "the *custom,* inherited through thousands of years, of thinking *causally,*" and he defended Boltzmann's conjecture (which had been elaborated by Exner and Hasenöhrl) that the observed macroscopic regularities might be the result of an interplay of inherently indeterministic microprocesses. (This, he reports later, "met with considerable shaking of heads.") Yet "the inherent contradictions of atomic theory" (which played such a central role in Bohr's work and which were to some extent regarded by him as something positive) "sounded harsh and crude" to Schrödinger "when compared with the pure and inexorably clear development of Boltzmann's reasoning." He even "fled from it for a while" into the field of color theory. It was mainly the work of Louis de Broglie which encouraged Schrödinger to return to the theory of the atom and which finally led him to develop his wave mechanics.

There can hardly be a greater disparity than that between the procedures of Heisenberg and Schrödinger. Heisenberg had participated in the various attempts to adapt the classical theories to the new experimental situation and to arrive at what Bohr called a "rational generalization of the classical mode of description." In the course of these endeavors he concentrated on observable magnitudes and had explicitly refrained from giving an account of the internal processes of the atom. Schrödinger, on the other hand, proceeded to do just this. His reasoning is realistic throughout. Briefly, the argument is as follows: Classical geometrical optics can be summed up in Fermat's principle, according to which a beam of isolated light rays transverses an optical system in such a manner that each single ray takes the shortest possible time to arrive at its destination. This formal principle can easily be explained by reference to the way in which wave fronts are accelerated or retarded when passing media of different refractive index and turn in consequence. The classical mechanics of mass points can be formulated in a manner that makes it formally identical with Fermat's principle: The path of a system of mass points is such that a certain integral, depending on this path, assumes an extreme value. "It seems" (so Schrödinger describes his train of thought in his Nobel address) "as if Nature had effected exactly the same thing twice, but in two very different ways—once, in the case of light, through a fairly transparent wave mechanism; and on the other occasion, in the case of mass points, by methods which were utterly mysterious, unless one was prepared to believe in some underlying undulatory character in the second case also." Now, if this analogy is correct, then we have to expect diffraction phenomena in regions comparable to the wave length of the hypothetical matter waves. The breakdown of the ordinary Hamiltonian formalism inside the atom indicates that such regions may be of the size of the atom, so that the atom itself becomes "really nothing more than the diffraction phenomena arising from an electron wave that has been intercepted by the nucleus of the atom." Calculations carried out on this basis led to all the features known from experiment and later on produced a coherent theory that could in principle be applied to any possible situation. In this theory the collection of particle coordinates forming the initial condition of classical point mechanics is replaced by a "wave function" whose development in time is given, in a perfectly causal fashion, by the so-called time dependent *Schrödinger equation*. The similarity to classical mechanics where we start out with an objective state of affairs which then develops causally in time cannot be overlooked. However, this appearance of objectivity and causality soon turned out to be deceptive. For example, the theory cannot give a satisfactory account of such phenomena as the tracks of particles in a Wilson chamber. There are other difficulties, too, which after considerable discussion led to a new interpretation of the wave function (Max Born's interpretation) that closed the gap that apparently existed between matrix mechanics and wave mechanics (both theories were also shown to be mathematically equivalent). In this new interpretation the waves are not real and objective processes but only indicate the probabilities of the outcome of certain experiments. The general transformation theory, then, altogether robbed the wave function of its realistic connotation and turned it into a purely formal instrument of prediction.

Schrödinger, though aware of the difficulties of his original ideas, never acquiesced in the interpretation transferred upon it by the Copenhagen school. He attacked this interpretation both on physical and on philosophical grounds. On the physical side he doubted the consistency of the various approximation methods which were used to establish a connection between theory and fact. Philosophically, he objected to the tendency "to forgo connecting the description [of what is observable] with a definite hypothesis about the real structure of the universe." He also pointed out that strictly speaking the connection between theory and experiment had been established only at very few points and that "the tremendous amount of empirical confirmation" could be accepted only at the expense of consistent procedure and mathematical rigor. It is unfortunate that his criticism had only very little influence and that the clarity, simplicity, and consistency of a Boltzmann, which it intended to achieve, has now largely become a thing of the past.

Bibliography

All the writings of Schrödinger which are of interest for a wide audience are contained in *Science, Theory, and Man* (New York, 1957). For a more recent criticism of orthodox quantum theory, see "Are There Quantum Jumps?," in *The British Journal for the Philosophy of Science*, Vol. 3 (1952), 109–123 and 233–242. See also "Die gegenwärtige Lage in der Quantentheorie," in *Naturwissenschaften* (1935). Schrödinger's views on various philosophical and religious topics not directly related to physics are presented in *My View of the World* (Cambridge, 1964).

PAUL K. FEYERABEND

SCHULTZ, JULIUS (1862–1936), German philosopher, dramatist, historian, and philologist, was born in Göttingen. From 1888 until 1927 he taught at a high school in Berlin. Among Schultz's numerous writings dealing with philosophy, the most important are *Die Maschinentheorie des Lebens* (1909) and *Die Philosophie am Scheidewege* (1922).

Schultz's starting point is the question How must we conceive of consciousness, on the one hand, and the object, on the other, if we wish to understand from their combined action the world of phenomena? To answer the psychological part of this question, Schultz first studied the axioms and categories of ordinary and of scientific thinking in order to see what attitude toward the phenomena is forced upon our understanding by its own innermost essence. At the same time he found a solution to the epistemological problem, namely, that if we desire not only to describe the world scientifically but also to understand it uniformly and completely, we must reduce all qualitative differences to quantitative ones. Accordingly, we must interpret the world of sense as a world of motion and explain all the happenings in the world in a mechanistic-dynamistic manner.

In epistemology, Schultz acknowledged special indebtedness to Kant and Hans Vaihinger, whose views he interpreted and developed in a psychologistic fashion. His philosophy of nature is characterized by the attempt to outline a thorough and systematic causal-mechanistic world view. The nucleus of this view is a "machine theory of life," which Schultz developed on a broad scientific basis. The theory explains the phenomena of life with the help of the postulate of "biogenes." These are defined as unobservable molecules of submicroscopic size, which are not themselves alive but which build up the living forms. Schultz conceived of the "biogenes" in such a manner that from their joint action one can understand all the processes of life in their goal-directedness and wholeness, and thus both the forms as well as the functions of organisms. In this biomechanistic conception, organic forms are extremely complicated physicochemical systems. The goal-directed course of living processes arises out of the meaningful arrangement of these systems, and their structure and behavior are explained by strictly causal natural laws, making unnecessary the assumption of immaterial vital forces.

Schultz also contributed to the typology of philosophical thought. He sought to reduce all philosophical standpoints to two basic conceptions of the world and of life, corresponding to two different types of men. The first type pays homage to the value of conservation and prefers purposeful, useful activity; as a thinker, this practical-minded man professes an ethics of duty and believes in progress and in the efficacy of metaphysical forces. The second type prefers the value of formation and as an aesthete or theorist playfully seeks a sympathetic understanding of forms, which he desires to behold in their abundance. He professes an ethics of character, or ethics of the beauty in life, and believes in an eternal recurrence of coming into being and ceasing to be. As an advocate of determinism and causality, he envisages a mechanistic picture of the world in order to understand it in its depth. Schultz himself preferred the second standpoint, which determined his attitude in the philosophy of history. In particular, he took a pessimistic view of the future development of culture. He feared that man would become part of a machine, a socialized worker-ant—organized for common work down to the last detail, but, as in the early ages, without a history.

Bibliography

Schultz's main philosophical works are *Psychologie der Axiome* (Göttingen, 1899); *Die Bilder von der Materie* (Göttingen, 1905); *Die drei Welten der Erkenntnistheorie* (Göttingen, 1907); *Die Maschinentheorie des Lebens* (Göttingen, 1909; 2d ed., Leipzig, 1929); *Die Philosophie am Scheidewege* (Leipzig, 1922); *Leib und Seele* (Berlin, 1923); *Das Ich und die Physik* (Leipzig, 1935).

His chief historical work is *Wandlungen der Seele im Hochmittelalter*, 2 vols. (Breslau, 1936; 2d ed., 3 vols. Breslau, 1940).

For Schultz's philosophical autobiography see Raymund Schmidt, ed., *Die Philosophie der Gegenwart in Selbstdarstellungen* (Leipzig, 1922), Vol. III, pp. 177–198. For a complete biography and bibliography see Erwin Ditz, *Julius Schultz' Maschinentheorie des Lebens*, Vol. XIV in *Studien und Bibliographien zur Gegenwartsphilosophie* (Leipzig, 1935).

FRANZ AUSTEDA
Translated by *Albert E. Blumberg*

SCHULZE, GOTTLOB ERNST (1761–1833), skeptic and critic of Kantian philosophy, was born in Heldrungen, Thuringia. He was professor at Wittenberg and Helmstedt and later at Göttingen, where one of his students was Arthur Schopenhauer. His influence is due chiefly to his writings, in which he developed his critical–skeptical position. Schulze's main work, and the one which made him famous, was *Aenesidemus*. In this work, which first appeared anonymously and without the place of publication, Schulze presents objections to the Kantian critique and to K. L. Reinhold's intended vindication of the critical philosophy. Schulze's arguments against the critical philosophy led him to share Hume's skepticism, of which he gave a concise presentation.

The *Aenesidemus* tries to show that Hume's skepticism has not been refuted by the critical philosophy. However, Schulze's position is not that of absolute skepticism: the validity of formal logic and the principles of identity and contradiction are not subject to doubt. He defined skepticism as the doctrine "that philosophy can establish neither the existence nor the non-existence of things-in-themselves and their qualities. Also the limits of our cognitive capacity cannot be fixed and ascertained on the basis of generally valid principles. . . . But the reality of presentations and the certitude of mental events immediately given through consciousness no skeptic has ever doubted" (*Aenesidemus*, p. 24). On the other hand, "skepticism does not declare the metaphysical questions to be eternally unanswerable and in principle not liable to a solution" (*ibid.*). Through progressive development it is possible to approach a solution of the problems concerning the existence or nonexistence of things-in-themselves and the limits of our cognitive capacities.

Thus the possibility of perfecting human cognition so as to attain clarity and certitude in particular metaphysical questions was not denied by Schulze. However, his objection to the critical philosophy was not limited to the question concerning the possibility of progress in metaphysics; he also attempted to show the self-contradictory nature of Kant's critical philosophy. The critical philosophy argues that since general and necessary knowledge is possible only through synthetic a priori judgments, such judgments must represent reality. Furthermore, such judgments are possible only on the assumption of a pure capacity of understanding; hence, such a capacity must exist. In interpreting Kant, Reinhold generalized this mode of argumentation, formulating the fundamental principle that the presentation of any object implies the distinction between consciousness of the subject, of the object, and of the relation obtaining between them. From these indispensable components of the presentation Reinhold concluded the reality of corresponding objects. However, from the fact that presentations always contain the notions of subject, of object, and of their relation to each other it is illegitimate, according to Schulze, to conclude the objective reality of corresponding objects. The transition from thought to being is grounded in ontological thinking, which Kant himself showed to be defective in his criticism of the classic proofs for the existence of God and of dogmatic metaphysics. Since one cannot argue from the conditions of thought to the reality of objects, the problem of philosophy is, according to the critical philosophy, to search for the competence and the legitimacy of our thought to determine objects of reality. The task of the Kantian critique is to show the objective validity of our judgments. However, the indispensable conditions of thought constitute subjective necessity, from which objective validity cannot be derived.

Furthermore, "it is presupposed that each part of human cognition must be grounded in reality as its cause. Without such an assumption the doctrine of the *Critique* concerning the origin of the necessary judgments has no meaning whatsoever" (*ibid.*, pp. 137 f.). The conclusion from the necessary judgments in our consciousness as to the reality of objects is based on the principle of causality. Existing objects constitute the causes of our cognition. The category of causality is thus employed with reference to noumena. Also, in the conception of sensibility as a faculty of receptivity, the existence of things-in-themselves that have the capacity to affect our sensibility is presupposed. Here again the concept of causality is applied to noumena, while, according to the critical philosophy, causality as a category of understanding is confined to the realm of phenomena. Reinhold's doctrine that things-in-themselves, although not cognizable, are nonetheless thinkable, is untenable. Since the things-in-themselves are thought to be the cause of cognition, they are cognized as having the capacity to affect the knowing and thinking capacity. The thing-in-itself must be cognizable, or it cannot be considered as a cause of cognition. Likewise, the concept of causality cannot be employed for proving the reality of the subject as a thing-in-itself. Schulze understood the Kantian solution of the question "How are synthetic a priori propositions possible?" as consisting in the derivation of these propositions from the subject as their cause: "The *Critique* derives the necessary synthetic propositions from the subjective mind (*Gemüth*) and its a priori determined cognitive processes . . . by the application of the principle of causality, which does not harmonize with its own principles delimiting the area of application of the categories" (*ibid.*, pp. 153 f.). Moreover, the conclusion from the propositions to the reality of a capacity in the mind does not explain the process of cognition. Nothing is gained by proposing that the perception of the material given is due to a receptive capacity, for a problem is not explained by reducing it to something unknown. The problem of cognition of experience is not solved by a reduction of cognition to a receptive capacity which is no less problematical.

Schulze considered the a priori concepts as existing in time "prior" to the cognition of objects. This account of the a priori concepts as innate ideas and as inherent qualities of the subjective mind is a misunderstanding of the Kantian position that has been common to numerous interpreters of Kant until the present. Schulze thus failed to understand the essence of the critical philosophy, which does not aim at deriving the synthetic propositions from the subject as a thing-in-itself. Kant was not concerned with the psychological process of cognition but with objective cognition, as manifested in the scientific process. The problem is how synthetic a priori propositions are possible in mathematics and science, and not how the human mind as a subject conceives such propositions. The objectivity of the judgments is vouchsafed by the scientific laws determining objects which arise through these laws. This is implied in the Kantian principle of the "possibility of experience." Scientific experience is possible only through synthetic propositions. Since without synthetic propositions there would be no scientific experience at all, their legitimacy is vouchsafed by the function they fulfill for experience. Furthermore, Schulze held the difference between synthetic and analytic propositions was not an objective distinction, and, psychologically considered, it

depends on subjective circumstances whether a proposition is synthetic or analytic for a particular individual at a certain moment. Schulze's criticism of Kant implied the notion of the subject and predicate of the proposition as individually given and fixed entities, so that the synthetic proposition connects elements which can be thought of in themselves. Hence, the concepts of the subject and the predicate must be thought of as separately given, and the question is how their connection can be of a necessary nature. Schulze did not realize that for Kant the concept of the subject arises by its determination through the synthetic proposition. In the proposition "S is P," S is an unknown before its determination through P. The investigation of S is a "doubt-inquiry process" (Dewey's expression); S acquires determination only through the predicate. Schulze's criticism is thus predicated upon an understanding of the critical philosophy as subjective idealism with the notion of a priori concepts as innate ideas, which leads to dogmatic assumptions concerning the application of the concept of causality to things-in-themselves. The a priori concepts in the critical philosophy are not to be understood as constituent features of the subjective human mind but as creative functions of thought in the process of ordering experience.

Schulze was also critical of Kant's conception of moral theology. He raised objections to the Kantian doctrine of the postulates (God, freedom, immortality) as formulated in the *Kritik der praktischen Vernunft*. From the sense of the moral command in us, the categorical imperative, there can be no conclusion as to the reality of a most perfect being. As ideas of reason, God, freedom, and immortality are endless tasks for human activity, but by the conception of these ideas as postulates their real existence as objects is posited. "The Kantian moral theology postulates *more* than what practical reason demands for the satisfaction of its requirements . . ." (*ibid.*, pp. 440 ff.). In his criticism of the postulates Schulze has partly anticipated the Neo-Kantianism of the Marburg school. Hermann Cohen, for example, although motivated by different considerations, has pointed out that the regulative ideas of reason do not require the support of the doctrine of postulates.

Schulze's contribution to the development of Kantian idealism consists in his exposing the contradictions and inconsistencies involved in both dogmatic–realistic and subjective–idealistic interpretations of the critical philosophy, but his attempt at a vindication of Hume's skepticism proved ineffective for further development of Kantian idealism. Philosophical thought took the course not back to Hume but to a more consistent critical idealism eliminating the concept of a thing-in-itself (as in Maimon) and to speculative idealism as it developed in the post-Kantian metaphysical systems. However, by his valuable criticism of the doctrine of the faculties of the soul Schulze anticipated Johann Friedrich Herbart and influenced Eduard Beneke (1798–1854).

According to Schulze, a phenomenon of the life of the soul is not explained by attributing it to a "faculty." Such an attribution does not explain, but merely gives another name to the same thing. The task of psychology as a science is, rather, a detailed description of actual mental occurrences and their systematic classification. By such a method, general concepts of psychological phenomena can be attained; but they should not be attributed to "faculties" of the soul, which is a metaphysical concept.

Works by Schulze

Grundriss der philosophischen Wissenschaften, 2 vols. Wittenberg, 1788–1790.

Aenesidemus, oder über die Fundamente der von dem Herrn Professor Reinhold in Jena gelieferten Elementarphilosophie. Nebst einer Vertheidigung des Skepticismus gegen die Anmassungen der Vernunftkritik. 1792. Re-edited by the Kantgesellschaft, in the series of rare philosophical works edited by Arthur Liebert. Berlin, 1911.

Kritik der theoretischen Philosophie, 2 vols. Hamburg, 1801.

Enzyklopädie der philosophischen Wissenschaften. Göttingen, 1814.

Über die menschliche Erkenntnis. Göttingen, 1832.

Works on Schulze

Cassirer, Ernst, *Das Erkenntnisproblem in der Philosophie und Wissenschaft der neueren Zeit,* Vol. III. Berlin, 1920.

Erdmann, Johann Edward, *Versuch einer wissenschaftlichen Darstellung der Geschichte der neueren Philosophie.* Riga and Dorpat, 1848–1853. Vol. III.

Fischer, Kuno, *Geschichte der neueren Philosophie,* 3d ed. Heidelberg, 1900. Vol. VI.

Kroner, Richard, *Von Kant bis Hegel,* 2 vols. Tübingen, 1921.

Wiegershausen, Heinrich, *Aenesidem-Schulze, der Gegner Kants und seine Bedeutung im Neukantianismus.* Berlin, 1910. This is *Kantstudien,* Supp. No. 17.

SAMUEL ATLAS

SCHUPPE, ERNST JULIUS WILHELM (1836–1913),

German philosopher, was born in Brieg, Silesia. He studied at the universities of Breslau, Bonn, and Berlin, and he took his doctorate at Berlin in 1860. He taught at grammar schools in Silesia and then held a chair of philosophy at the University of Greifswald from 1873 to 1910.

Epistemology. In his main work, *Erkenntnistheoretische Logik* (Bonn, 1878), largely anticipated by his earlier book *Das menschliche Denken* (Berlin, 1870) and summarized in his later *Grundriss der Erkenntnistheorie und Logik* (Berlin, 1894; 2d ed., Berlin, 1910), Schuppe was concerned with the epistemological bases of knowledge generally and of logic in particular. Schuppe held that a theory of knowledge should avoid hypotheses such as the transcendent reality postulated by realists and metaphysicians, but that it should equally avoid one-sided objective or subjective foundations of knowledge, whether materialist, positivist, or idealist.

In keeping with these requirements, Schuppe developed the notion of conscious immanence (*Immanenz, Bewusstsein, Ich*) in which subject and object form a unity. This immanence of consciousness, or ego, is a fact (*Tatsache*) which is given with certitude and can therefore serve as a starting point for epistemology. Only abstractly can the ego be divided into subject and object; concretely it is a correlation of the two. This is not to say that the object is a psychic entity, but merely that there is no being not related to a subject. To ignore the correlation would be to incur a contradiction because a supposed unthought entity is nevertheless implied in the thought of the epistemologist.

To account for the distinction and division of conscious-ness and content (*Inhalt*), and of contents among themselves (subjective elements such as acts are distinct from objects of acts, however much both may have to be considered contents for an abstract subject), Schuppe presented a theory of "common" content: Objective content is a given which can be shared by several, whereas subjective content (sensation, for example) is unique and private. The need for this division led to a theory of consciousness in general (*Bewusstsein überhaupt*) as distinguished from the consciousness of a concrete individual subject. Individuality is based on content not shared by others. Other minds, which are presupposed by the notion of consciousness in general, are known, Schuppe claimed, by inference mediated by one's own body; but he also asserted that they can be regarded as immediately perceived. Schuppe denied the claim that other minds are immanent contents of one's mind—like any other object—as being tantamount to solipsism. Schuppe drew upon the ontic fact of a plurality of minds as a basis for consciousness in general.

Schuppe held that thought is also a "component" of the content of consciousness, along with the sense component; it "accedes" to perceptual data. Accordingly, objects of cognition can be considered as constituted by an interaction of an original given of sense, by itself an abstraction, with performances of thought (*Denkarbeit*). In fact Schuppe came to regard thought as the central function of consciousness: To think is to appropriate content, to receive an impression in its positive determinacy, to fixate it as identical. This primary performance of appropriation is thought-in-general, which is prior to judgment. Schuppe argued that at this stage there is only one datum to be appropriated but that for judgment two contents, subject and predicate, are required. (Here Schuppe was influenced by a grammatical notion of judgment.) Continuing to develop his notion of content, Schuppe introduced an analysis of content in which thought stands for the identification of two contents (an instance of the principle of identity, with the principles of contradiction and limitation as corollaries) and, somewhat surprisingly, for the establishment of causal connection between them. Identity and causality are the categories that constitute objective content. (Here Schuppe was guided by a metagrammatical or transcendental notion of judgment, interpreting the category as the predicate of the unified contents.)

Ontology. With this basis of transcendental thought, Schuppe's "espistemological" logic was not so much concerned with the "forms" of formal logic as with the establishment of a priori truths about the object of knowledge. Thus the logic constitutes a theory of objects, an ontology. Schuppe analyzed the given into its elements (temporal and spatial determinateness, sense impression) and conceptual moments (genera and species), and distinguished several kinds of union (*Zusammengehörigkeit*) among them. In a transcendental progression Schuppe established number, space region, thing, organism, and artifact; and genera, species, and matter. He avoided any reference to a transcendent cause. Understandably, he presented a coherence theory of truth.

Logic. Schuppe sought a transcendental genealogy as a basis for logic. This project involved a certain deviation from the traditional understanding of formal logic. He rejected the isolation in logic of a purely formal realm, denying in fact that purely formal theorems are significant. He regarded propositions as assertions of categorial unification. Logic must be concerned with the realm of material content in which unity is asserted and must examine the various types of union of content, that is, the "real" genera of content, which, in the case of objects of appearance, are grounded in the causal context. This doctrine has ramifications in many areas of logic, for example, in the theory of definition.

Schuppe's theoretical philosophy can be regarded as a doctrine of the constitution of knowledge and its objects by transcendental synthesis. In view of its intuitive starting point and its analysis of given content, however, it seems to be a compromise between a logico-transcendental theory and a theory of reflective intuition. The agency responsible for the grounding of objectively constituted content is both a transcendental principle and an existent consciousness. The normative element of a transcendental theory is merged with the factual basis of a subjective ontology. Schuppe's philosophy thus stands between transcendental critique and ontological philosophy of immanence. Although it leans heavily on Kant, it anticipates much of Husserl's phenomenology and constitutes an example for a theoretical understanding of the interplay of factuality and logico-transcendental thought.

Practical philosophy. Schuppe's *Grundzüge der Ethik und Rechtsphilosophie* (1881, reprinted 1963) offers an independent compromise between a normative position, based on the will as a form of consciousness in general, and a eudaemonistic one, based on pleasure. He also wrote several studies in the philosophy of law, such as *Der Begriff des subjektiven Rechts* (Breslau, 1887), and joined the philosophical discussion concerning the new German civil code (*Das Gewohnheitsrecht*, Breslau, 1890; *Das Recht des Besitzes*, Breslau, 1891).

Bibliography

In addition to the works by Schuppe already cited, see *Allgemeine Rechtslehre mit Einschluss der allgemeinen Lehren vom Sein und vom Wissen*, edited and with an introduction by Wilhelm Fuchs (Berlin, 1936).

For works on Schuppe, see R. Hermann, *Schuppes Lehre vom Denken* (Greifswald, 1894); Gunther Jacoby, *Wilhelm Schuppe*, No. 45, *Greifswalder Universitätsreden* (Greifswald, 1936); L. Kljubowski, *Das Bewusstsein und das Sein bei Wilhelm Schuppe* (Heidelberg, 1912); Rudolf Zocher, *Husserls Phänomenologie und Schuppes Logik* (Munich, 1932).

KLAUS HARTMANN

SCIACCA, MICHELE FEDERICO, a founder of the Gallarate movement, professor of theoretical philosophy at the University of Genoa, and the founder and editor of the journals *Giornale di metafisica* and *Humanitas*. Sciacca was born in 1908. He started as a historian of ideas, writing important works on Reid (1935), Plato (1939), and St. Augustine (1939); a massive review of Italian thought, *Il XX secolo* (2 vols., Milan, 1941); and a review of recent European thought, *La filosofia oggi* (Milan, 1945).

Although Sciacca studied under Antonio Aliotta, his major stimulus came from Giovanni Gentile, from whom Sciacca derived his basic axiom that concrete being must be act, never fact. Sciacca has developed this principle in his own fashion under the influence of Plato, St. Augustine, Antonio Rosmini, and Maurice Blondel.

Sciacca's latest position has been one of "integralism." The central notion of integralism is interiority, according to which the ground of all forms of being and existence lies in the activity of the subject. Sciacca asserts that the existent, or act, cannot be a fact among facts; its existence resides wholly in its own self-generative actuality. Against existentialism he asserts that the being of the existent cannot be pure possibility or nothingness; it must be being. The whole concern of integralism is to establish the character of the being that the existent is. Sciacca holds this being to be objective interiority, which he delineates in his most original speculative work, *Interiorità oggettiva* (Milan, 1951). Interiority is the positing by the existent of itself as act. So defined, it cannot be conceived as purely immanent, in the manner of Gentile. It must posit itself with reference to a transcendent and objective reality and define itself within this horizon. The basic structural principle of interiority is truth, or the subject's affirmation of the ground of its existence in the very act of existing. The immanent ground of the subject and of all existence is a transcendent being, not abstract but more concrete and existentially real than the subject—God. In affirming the existence of God, the subject also affirms its own being, the innermost character of its own act of existing.

Sciacca's basic insight is thus that the being of the subject cannot be mere possibility, nothingness, or facticity but must be act; that this act is the affirmation of its own actuality through the affirmation of its transcendent ground; and that the absolute existent is present in concrete human existence. It is this presence of the Absolute that establishes the human existent as a person.

In *Morte ed immortalità* (Brescia, 1954), Sciacca holds that the affirmation of God within human existence that constitutes the human subject cannot be a merely transitory relationship and that immortality is therefore the logical extension of interior objectivity.

Bibliography

Works on Sciacca include the following: Sante Alberghi, "Sul pensiero di M. F. Sciacca," in *Giornale critico della filosofia italiana*, Series III, Vol. 4 (1950), 841–893; A. Robert Caponigri, "The Existence of God: Proof From Truth," in *Saggi in onore di M. F. Sciacca* (Milan, 1960), pp. 53–78; Cornelio Fabro, "La verità integrale dell'uomo integrale," in *Divus Thomas*, Series III, Vol. 27 (1950), 511–519; Augusto Guzzo, Romeo Crippa, and A. Arata, eds., *Michele Federico Sciacca* (Turin, 1951), which contains a complete bibliography of Sciacca's writings and of writings about him; and "Note critiche sul neo-spiritualismo," in *Giornale di metafisica*, Vol. 9, No. 2 (1956), which contains contributions by various authors.

A. ROBERT CAPONIGRI

SCIENCE, PHILOSOPHY OF. The Encyclopedia has two survey articles on philosophy of science, PHILOSOPHY OF SCIENCE, HISTORY OF and PHILOSOPHY OF SCIENCE, PROBLEMS OF. It also contains the following articles: CONFIRMATION: QUALITATIVE ASPECTS; CONFIRMATION: QUANTITATIVE ASPECTS; CONTRARY-TO-FACT CONDITIONAL; CONVENTIONALISM; CRAIG'S THEOREM;

EXPLANATION IN SCIENCE; INDUCTION; LAWS AND THEORIES; LAWS OF SCIENCE AND LAWLIKE STATEMENTS; MEASUREMENT; MILL'S METHODS OF INDUCTION; MODELS AND ANALOGY IN SCIENCE; OPERATIONALISM; PROBABILITY; RELIGION AND SCIENCE; SCIENTIFIC METHOD; SENSATIONALISM; WHY. Other articles are listed under LOGIC AND FOUNDATIONS OF MATHEMATICS; PHYSICAL SCIENCES; POLITICAL AND SOCIAL THEORY; and at the end of the articles BIOLOGY and PSYCHOLOGY. See Philosophy of Science, History of, and Philosophy of Science, Problems of, in Index for thinkers who have devoted special attention to problems in the philosophy of science.

SCIENCE AND RELIGION. See RELIGION AND SCIENCE.

SCIENTIA MEDIA AND MOLINISM. The *scientia media* is a key term in the theology of Luis de Molina (1535–1600) and in the variants of his teaching introduced by the later Jesuits, especially Robert Bellarmine, Leonard Lessius, Francisco Suárez, and Gabriel Vasquez, in the attempt to resolve the apparent contradiction between the doctrines of grace and of free will.

Molina, a Spanish Jesuit who taught at Coimbra and Evora in Portugal, published his famous *Liberi Arbitrii cum Gratiae Donis, Divina Praescientia, Providentia, Praedestinatione et Reprobatione Concordia* at Lisbon in 1588. The publication of the *Concordia*, as it came to be called, soon led to a controversy that divided the theologians and philosophers of Spain. Generally, the position of Molina was enthusiastically supported by members of his own order and just as vigorously denounced by the Thomists.

For Molina the essential problem was to maintain both man's freedom and the efficacy of grace. Given the fact of God's foreknowledge, Molina wished to preserve such a foreknowledge without lapsing into determinism, to show that although God knows infallibly what an individual will freely do, such an infallible knowledge in no way determines the will of the individual. Molina argued that there is a cooperation or concursus of man's free will with the divine grace, in contrast to the Thomist view that man's will was physically predetermined to act freely by God. Molina held that this was only a disguised form of determinism. The Thomists maintained that Molina denied the universal divine causality.

The central point in Molina's solution of this problem is based upon the *scientia media*. This, according to Molina, is a form of the divine knowledge that lies between the two forms of God's knowledge that Aquinas had described in the *Summa*. Aquinas maintained that God's knowledge may be one of "vision," a knowledge of that which exists, has existed, or will exist. Alternatively, God's knowledge may consist of the purely possible, a knowledge of "simple understanding," of things and events which have not existed, do not exist, and will not exist. The *scientia media* for Molina is a mean between these two forms of knowledge and is the knowledge that God has of conditional future contingent events; thus, God foreknows from all eternity what an individual would do under certain circumstances if offered his grace. Aquinas held that nothing

lies outside the divine causality and that God's knowledge, or vision, of the future free acts of the individual entails an act of will by God that predetermines that our acts are free. Molina insisted that God's knowledge is prior to the decree of his will and that his foreknowledge does not predetermine our free acts. God, knowing infallibly what an individual will do under certain circumstances if offered his grace, decrees the circumstances and the grace necessary to effect the cooperative action of the individual. Hence, the infallibility and efficacy of grace is due to the infallibility of God's knowledge, the *scientia media,* not to anything in the grace itself.

The distinction between sufficient and efficacious grace throws further light on these contrasting positions. Like the Thomists, Molina accepted the necessity of grace for salvation, the absolute gratuity of grace, and that sufficient grace is given to all men. However, Molina denied the need for any distinction between sufficient and efficacious grace. He claimed that sufficient grace becomes efficacious if the will of the individual accepts it. Thus, God foreknew St. Paul's consent before he decreed the grace necessary for conversion. The concurrence of the simultaneous act of the individual and the grace of God replaced the notion that the decree of God is prior to the act of the individual and predetermines it. Thomists objected that this made the efficacy of the divine grace dependent on man rather than on God. Molina declared that the efficacy of grace was unimpaired, for its efficacy or infallibility was extrinsic to the act of the individual and intrinsic in God's foreknowledge. In effect, Molina endeavored to preserve more fully the freedom of the individual without destroying the power of grace; the Thomists were more concerned with preserving the power of grace without destroying the freedom of the individual.

Later Molinism. Later Molinism is identified largely with what is termed "congruism," a theological doctrine reflecting especially the views of Bellarmine and Suárez. Congruism retains the principal features of Molina's theology but modifies it in certain respects. Efficacious grace is equated with *gratia congrua* and sufficient grace with *gratia incongrua*. This distinction emphasized more strongly that grace was efficacious when it was congruous with those circumstances and the disposition of the individual that would enable him to will a certain act freely but infallibly. Grace was inefficacious when it was not congruous with the circumstances and disposition of the individual. The efficacy of the *gratia congrua* is intrinsic to the *scientia media* and extrinsic to the will of the individual. *Gratia incongrua* is grace that is sufficient for a salutary act but which the individual will reject.

On predestination the Molinists agreed with the Thomists that God wishes all men to be saved and that he extends sufficient grace to all, that contrary to Pelagianism predestination is wholly gratuituous, and that some individuals are elected in preference to others solely as God wills. However, they tended to modify the Thomist view of an absolute predestination to glory irrespective of foreseen merits. Many of the Molinists argued that predestination is conditional upon the future actions of the individual and becomes absolute only with the foreseen merits of the individual. In contrast to the Thomists, who argued for the priority of predestination to glory to the predestination of efficacious grace, the Molinists held that God foresees in the *scientia media* that some will cooperate with his grace and predestined them to glory by offering them his grace.

The differences between Molina and his successors are more often subtle than essential. Although the debate on Molinism has continued for over three centuries, Molinism is clearly compatible with faith and continues to have many supporters. Like Thomism it has its difficulties and its critics. The difference between the two schools remains essentially one of the relative emphasis to be placed upon grace or freedom.

(See also BELLARMINE, ST. ROBERT; SUÁREZ, FRANCISCO.)

Bibliography

Bonet, A., *La filosofía de la libertad en los controversias teologicas del siglo XVI. y primera mitad del XVII*. Barcelona, 1932.

Boyer, C., "Providence et liberté." *Gregorianum* (1938), 194–208.

Kleinhappl, Johann, *Der Staat bei Ludwig Molina*. Innsbruck, 1935.

Pegis, Anton C., "Molina and Human Liberty," in *Jesuit Thinkers of the Renaissance*. Milwaukee, 1939. Pp. 75–132.

Rasolo, Louis, "Le dilemme du concours divin." *Analecta Gregoriana*, Vol. 80 (1956).

Romeyer, B., "Libre arbitre et concours selon Molina." *Gregorianum* (1942), 169–201.

Stegmüller, Francis, ed., *Geschichte des Molinismus*, I: Neue Molinaschriften, Münster, 1935.

Vansteenberghe, E., "Molinisme," in *Dictionnaire de Théologie Catholique*, Vol. X. Paris, 1929. Cols. 2184–2187.

JOHN A. MOURANT

SCIENTIFIC EXPLANATION. See EXPLANATION IN SCIENCE.

SCIENTIFIC LAWS. See LAWS AND THEORIES; LAWS OF SCIENCE AND LAWLIKE STATEMENTS.

SCIENTIFIC METHOD. The term "method," strictly speaking, "following a way" (from the Greek μέτα, "along," and ὁδός, "way"), refers to the specification of steps which must be taken, in a given order, to achieve a given end. The nature of the steps and the details of their specification depend on the end sought and on the variety of ways of achieving it. The "method" of science will therefore vary according to whether its end is taken to be the conquest of nature, for instance, or the discovery of truth and in the light of different theories about the relation between those ends and man's primitive condition of impotence and ignorance. The term "scientific method," if applied to scientific investigation in general or to something allegedly embodied in the practice of every branch of science, can only refer to the lowest common denominator of a range of methods devised to cope with problems as diverse as classifying stars and curing diseases. If such a lowest common denominator exists—that is, if some recognizable characteristics are shared by the extremes of the continuum of methods plausibly called "scientific"—it can amount to little more than fidelity to empirical evidence and simplicity of logical formulation, fidelity to the evidence taking precedence in cases of conflict. However,

these two overriding requirements for scientific activity do not constitute a specification of steps to be taken by scientists, and even the primary requirement (fidelity to empirical evidence) must be given up if mathematics is to be regarded as a science.

The branch of the philosophy of science known as methodology takes upon itself the examination and critical analysis of the special ways in which the general structure of theory finds its application in particular scientific disciplines. This conception of methodology allows for variation of method not only from one discipline to another but also from one epoch to another in the history of the same discipline. The philosophical study of this plurality of methods is not mainly prescriptive; the philosopher does not, as a rule, tell the scientist what to do, neither laying down the ends he should seek nor specifying the steps which must be taken to achieve them. Methodological argument arises not so much from doubt about what the scientist should do as from doubt about what he is doing. A clarification of this question does, however, have prescriptive overtones. Some disciplines—notably the so-called behavioral sciences—have historically been in doubt about their own status as sciences, and they have come under attack as unscientific. If it could be shown that the method of science depended on quantitative measurements, for example, and if these disputed sciences could devise quantitative methods of their own, their claim to be *called* sciences would be strengthened. (But this yearning for scientific respectability might lead—some critics claim that it has led—to spurious quantification and other artificial activities.)

Methodology as analytic rather than prescriptive is comparatively recent; it probably originates with John F. Herschel (*Preliminary Discourse on the Study of Natural Philosophy*, London, 1830). This development corresponds to the emergence of science as an autonomous activity separate from the pursuit of knowledge in general, a historical process which is often said to have begun with Galileo, although there is mounting evidence that it was well advanced in the late Middle Ages. The ideas of method current in the seventeenth and eighteenth centuries were devoted to showing how philosophy should conduct itself in order to become scientific, that is, exact; thus, Descartes's work on the subject is entitled *Discourse on the Method of Rightly Conducting the Reason and Seeking Truth in the Sciences*. By the time of Newton concern was narrowed to the objects of *natural* philosophy, and Newton's methodology (summed up in his "Rules of Reasoning in Philosophy") is less a speculative recommendation than an account of principles implicit in his own work. It is often more rewarding to look at what the scientist does than to listen to what he says about it; Newton, for example, claimed not to make hypotheses, and yet some of his fundamental propositions are clearly hypothetical. We must distinguish, however, not only between what the scientist does and what he says he is doing but also between these and what the philosopher says the scientist is doing or ought to be doing; and we must distinguish further between "doing" in the sense of turning stopcocks, giving injections, and inventing particular working hypotheses, on the one hand, and "doing" in the sense of discovering laws, building theories, and changing the condition of man, on the other hand. The former refers to the daily activity of individual scientists, the latter to the long-range activity of science as a collective enterprise; and a method implicit in the collective activity, different elements of which may have been contributed by different individuals—one forming a hypothesis, another devising empirical tests, etc.—will not necessarily assist any one individual in specifying his own course of action. A confusion between the private and cooperative aspects of science has led many people to expect too much of the scientific method as a guide in their personal lives.

Historical development. The idea of method has not been stable in its historical development. It is possible, nevertheless, to identify three main tendencies, associated with three periods of philosophical activity in the field, according to which scientific method consists of (1) principles laid down as regulative for the acquisition of knowledge of the world in general (ancient philosophy), (2) principles laid down as regulative for the acquisition of the special kind of natural knowledge known as scientific (early modern philosophy), and (3) principles abstracted from the practice of persons successfully engaged in the acquisition of scientific knowledge (the last hundred years). This abstraction is not merely a description of the behavior of scientists; it involves an assessment of what that behavior signifies, a grasping, as Karl Popper expresses it, of the "rules of the game of empirical science." The methodological principles in question (for example, a preference for simple formulations) must be sharply distinguished in each case from the metaphysical principles which constitute the ground of the knowledge acquired (for example, a belief that sense data are ultimate) and from the logical principles which dictate its structure when acquired (for example, a demand for consistency). Failure to make these distinctions has often confused the discussion of methodology, which deals always with the *activity* of acquiring knowledge.

Of course, the anticipated structure of the finished product and the nature of the foundations on which it rests may be expected to have great influence on the steps taken to arrive at it, and yet the three sets of principles referred to often seem to have surprisingly little to do with each other. Aristotle is a good case in point. For him the metaphysical principles on which the possibility of natural knowledge rests were, to simplify matters somewhat, that there exist individual substances, that these fall into types, and that these types are characterized by an intelligible essence embodied in each individual of the type. The logical principles which order such knowledge prescribe a descent from universals of great generality referring to a small number of classes, perhaps a single one, to particulars of complete specificity referring to large numbers of individual objects. The methodological principles, however (which are not gathered in any one place but which can be reconstructed from various passages in the *Posterior Analytics,* the *Physics,* and the biological writings), make recommendations about observation, classification, and definition, insist on the limitation of subject matter (physics, for example, is to be kept distinct from biology), and call for finite chains of demonstration. Aristotle himself

was a great scientist as well as a great philosopher; he exemplified the truth that whatever philosophical theory is adhered to, the practice of science constrains the investigator to observe certain autonomous canons. These canons form the object of methodological inquiry, and it is clear from the biological writings that Aristotle was prepared to separate questions about the conditions of investigation into particular animal structures from questions about the way in which knowledge so gained is to be organized and related to first principles. Thomas Aquinas, who was no scientist, was content with the assimilation of methodology and logic: "Logic," he said, "teaches method for all scientific inquiry." But logic in theory is one thing, and logic in its application to the world quite another.

That application requires, first, close observation of events and a language for their unambiguous description. Aristotle made notable advances in both respects but failed to relate them to his theory of scientific knowledge, which remained for the most part purely logical. Medieval philosophers—for example, Roger Bacon—stressed the necessity of an empirical approach to balance purely rational considerations, without, however, following their own advice to any great extent. For along with the growing interest in empirical investigation, which reached its most rapid development in the seventeenth century, there went a growing interest in rational construction—mathematics—which developed most rapidly at the same time. The complement to accurate observation and description, in the application of logic, is the construction of the logical system itself in such a way as to render it capable of absorbing and transforming empirical propositions, that is, to provide science with its own mathematical apparatus. This process naturally has an effect, in turn, on the language of observation, which will concentrate on those aspects of events which lend themselves to mathematical manipulation. The growth of science was most spectacular when these two interests reached an equilibrium; the mainstream of its history passes through Galileo and Newton, not through Francis Bacon on the empiricist side or Descartes on the rationalist side. In the *Principia* Newton characterized the "whole burden of philosophy" as involving a progression from observation of the phenomena of motions to investigation of the forces of nature, and then demonstration, from these forces, of the other phenomena associated with the theory. This characterization expresses the balance admirably: investigation is the province of empiricism; demonstration, of rationalism. "Scientific method," if it has any univocal meaning, means the right mixture of observation and experiment on the one side, and theory construction on the other. It would be a mistake, however, to conclude that the proportions should be equal. For both Galileo and Newton a little experimentation went a long way, and the really hard work lay in getting the theory to fit it. There is no reason to suppose that the situation has changed since then, and this should give pause to contemporary practitioners of sciences in which the data are piling up without any sign of fundamental theoretical clarification.

Bacon and Descartes. Before leaving these historical considerations, some further attention should be paid to the methods of Descartes and Francis Bacon. Each created a methodological tradition which still persists, although neither tradition is the one mainly followed by the subsequent development of science; Galileo and Newton practiced better methods than Bacon and Descartes were able to prescribe. The Baconian method, described in *Novum Organum,* was an inductive one, rising from particulars enumerated in "Tables of Instances" to true definitions (or "forms") of various observable phenomena (or "natures"). By the form of heat, for example, Bacon meant the essential characteristics which hot things have in common; the use of his method led him to conclude that heat is a rapid expansive motion of minute particles which get in one another's way. (Unfortunately, he also concluded that the general direction of this motion is upward.) The intermediate steps of the method are of critical importance. The presentation of instances to the understanding, in the tables, is done selectively: There is, first, a "Table of Essence and Presence," listing cases where the nature in question is positively observed; next, there is a "Table of Deviation, or of Absence in Proximity," listing cases where we might expect the nature but where it is not in fact observed; third, there is a "Table of Degrees, or of Comparison," listing cases where the nature is observed with greater or less intensity. The tables are followed by a process of "Exclusion, or Rejection of Natures," in which spurious phenomena (those which cannot, in the light of the tables taken together, be considered as genuine cases of the nature in question) are eliminated. The next step Bacon called the indulgence of the understanding, or the commencement of interpretation, or the "First Vintage": it is, in effect, the advancement of a hypothesis about the form. The significance of this step is that no method is given for arriving at the hypothesis; it is assumed that the understanding naturally has a hypothesis ready and that its anxiety to test this hypothesis needs to be indulged. Bacon cannot, therefore, be considered, as simply a proponent of induction —without too much distortion, he can be regarded as a forerunner of the so-called hypothetico-deductive method. The two features of his approach which prevent it from accurately representing the pattern of modern science are, first, that it is almost entirely qualitative, and second, that it is embedded in an uncritical natural history. The tables are preceded, in fact, by an indiscriminate amassing of possibly relevant data into a "Natural and Experimental History, sufficient and good." The lack of empirical justification for earlier theories led Bacon to overcompensate. He said, with remarkable insight, that the true scientist is like the bee, which goes to nature for its raw material but works it into a new product, rather than like the empiricist ant, which merely collects, or the rationalist spider, which merely spins out its own substance—but in his own work antlike qualities predominated.

Descartes, on the other hand, was less impressed by the lack of empirical foundations for earlier theories than by the implausibility of their first principles. His method was one of systematic doubt, together with the systematic organization of whatever withstood that doubt. The origin of what was to be doubted was not of much concern; the end in view was the sound scientific one of saying how the world must be if it is to be as it is, but this was qualified by the assumption that, God not being a deceiver, we see the world as it is without the necessity of too much detailed investigation. Descartes recognized, as did Bacon, the likelihood that the understanding will jump to hasty conclusions, but these, he maintained, should be held suspect not because they may be unfaithful to the evidence but because they may be unclear or indistinct. And, like Bacon, Descartes believed that although the scientific method is not for everybody, any reasonably intelligent person can solve the salient problems for himself if only he follows it correctly.

Method in science: Galileo and Newton. The advance of science was not secured by reasonably intelligent persons following the methods of Bacon or Descartes; it was secured by very exceptional persons following their own methods. Why were Galileo and Newton better scientists than Bacon and Descartes? First, their greatest work was done in tackling limited problems, not in seeking the grand design of understanding or power. Galileo is popularly remembered for the law of falling bodies, which established a simple relation between the position of a body and the time at which it is at that position. These two things define a modest and limited chain of inference, which works both ways: where tells when, when tells where. They are abstracted from all the other truths about the body in question, truths which Aristotle or Bacon might have taken pains to note, and the relation between them is the very paradigm of scientific explanation—a self-contained logical relationship empirically demonstrated as valid under given conditions. Galileo wrote,

> Anyone may invent an arbitrary type of motion and discuss its properties, but we have decided to consider the phenomena of bodies falling with an acceleration such as actually occurs in nature. . . . And this, at last, after repeated efforts we trust we have succeeded in doing. In this belief we are confirmed mainly by the consideration that experimental results are seen to agree with and exactly correspond with those properties which have been, one after another, demonstrated by us. (*Dialogues Concerning Two New Sciences,* p. 160)

Second, the guiding principles of this limited activity are not laid down a priori but are learned from the experience of scientific inquiry. Newton formulated his guiding principles in the "Rules of Reasoning in Philosophy," already referred to:

Rule I: We are to admit no more causes of natural things than such as are both true and sufficient to explain their appearances.

Rule II: Therefore to the same natural effects we must, as far as possible, assign the same causes.

Rule III: The qualities of bodies, which admit neither intension nor remission of degrees, and which are found to belong to all bodies within the reach of our experiments, are to be esteemed the universal qualities of all bodies whatsoever.

Rule IV: In experimental philosophy we are to look upon propositions collected by general induction from phenomena as accurately or very nearly true, notwithstanding any contrary hypotheses that may be imagined, till such time as other phenomena occur, by which they may either be made more accurate or liable to exceptions. (*Mathematical Principles of Natural Philosophy*, pp. 398–400)

Newton's own use of hypotheses (for example, the inverse-square law of attraction), to which he was blind only because his fertile scientific imagination made it effortless, has already been referred to. Along with some other implicit elements of his own practice—such as his willingness to abandon lines of inquiry which led to inconsistencies—it would not be difficult to enlarge the "Rules" into a succinct definition of scientific method, drawing at the same time on some of the other considerations adduced earlier in this article. Such a definition would recommend for the solution of any scientific problem, first, an immersion in observed fact; second, the accurate definition of universal categories for the description of the regular features of what is observed; third, the inductive generalization of simple universal laws expressing such regularities; fourth, the entertainment of explanatory hypotheses; fifth, the detailed comparison of the consequences of the hypotheses with the inductive generalizations, rejecting the consequences of the hypotheses in favor of the inductive generalizations in cases of conflict; sixth, the axiomatic organization of the hypotheses which survive this test and the demonstration of the rest of the theory as following from them. Newton's was the first *fully developed* scientific theory, and an examination of the circumstances of its creation shows that all these methodological principles were called into play.

Possibility of prescriptive methodology. This article began on a note of skepticism about the possibility of a prescriptive methodology for science in general. There are several reasons for this skepticism. In the first place, in Newton's time there was only one developed science, physics; the late eighteenth century saw the emergence of chemistry, the nineteenth of biology and psychology, the twentieth of the social sciences, and these have brought with them new problems of method not amenable to the comparatively simple analysis which is appropriate to physics. The range of meaning of "science" has been widened and is a matter of dispute not to be settled by methodological prescriptions. The question whether or not history is a science, for example, cannot be arbitrarily decided by pointing out that it is neither experimental nor predictive.

In the second place, the critical step in the method, even for physics, is only apparently covered by the prescription. Bacon's assumption that there was really nothing problematic about the "First Vintage" has not been improved upon; there is still no systematic way of generating hypotheses. This is the problem known as the "logic of discovery," and although a great deal of intensive work has been bestowed on it, no clear and generally applicable pattern has emerged. John Stuart Mill's "methods of experimental inquiry," for example, while sometimes spoken of as methods of discovery, are methods for the discovery of causal connections—that is, for the verification of laws—but not for the discovery of hypotheses.

In the third place, it is no longer clear that the function of science is mainly the construction of theories like Newton's, which explain observed events by reference to unobserved things and properties (forces, for example, and, in later theories, fundamental particles). In the nineteenth century, under the influence of Ernst Mach and Karl Pearson, a view came into prominence according to which science is merely an accurate and economical description of the world, whose practical task is to enable the scientist to make predictions; according to Mach it did not matter what method the scientist followed to do this, so long as the predictions came out right, that is, with a high probability. So-called black box theories for the analysis of complex phenomena, which have become important in connection with the development of cybernetics, preserve almost nothing of the traditional structure and method of science, but it would be presumptuous to claim that they are unscientific.

The sensationalism of Mach has had important methodological consequences in that it has stimulated a renewed interest in the nature of the empirical evidence on which science rests. The work of members of the Vienna circle on protocol sentences, for example, is a direct result of it. A certain mistrust of the superstructure of scientific theory, remote from its empirical foundations, has been characteristic of the whole positivist movement, and the crisis in physics precipitated by the development of relativity theory and quantum theory suggests that there is some justification for such an attitude. An important reaction to this crisis was the methodological doctrine of P. W. Bridgman, known as operationism or operationalism, according to which concepts employed in scientific theories must be defined in terms of actual operations carried out by scientists in measuring their quantitative values. Thus, the concept of simultaneity was defined by Einstein through the measurement of distances from a centrally placed observer who receives light-signals from two distant points at the same time. But Bridgman's elaboration of this principle, in which length was defined as the laying down of meter sticks, etc., turns out to be more an injunction against metaphysics than a regulative principle for scientific practice (it certainly cannot be said to be descriptive of scientific practice); this tendency for methodological considerations to pass over into metaphysical or epistemological ones is characteristic of contemporary work in the field. The conventionalism of Pierre Duhem and Jules Henri Poincaré has had very little to do with the actual acceptance or rejection of theories by working scientists, and the same can be said of the traditional dispute between the inductive and hypothetico-deductive models of theory, represented today (to oversimplify matters somewhat) by the confrontation between the inductive logic of Carnap, according to which the important thing about scientific propositions is that they are *confirmable* on the basis of available evidence, and the theory of Popper, according to which the important thing about them is that they are potentially (although not actually) *falsifiable*. This argument is an argument about the meaning of the term "probability" rather than about the specification of steps to be taken by scientists in the solution of their problems.

Methodology in this stricter sense is not dead; significant work is going on in techniques of statistical inference, in the handling of large quantities of data, in decision theory, and so forth, which has genuine implications for scientific practice. But the philosophical content of the discipline has changed; the search for a unique scientific method seems less urgent than it once did, because by now it is clear that in general it has already been discovered, while in detail there is no such thing. The general conclusion is that the method of science is a mixture —the proportions of which vary from one science to another—of logical construction and empirical observation, these components standing in a roughly dialectical relation. The details, on either side of this division, remain the object of a range of inquiries from the study of laboratory techniques to pure axiomatics.

Bibliography

CLASSIC DISCUSSIONS

Aristotle, *Analytica Posteriora,* in J. A. Smith and W. D. Ross, eds., *Works,* 12 vols. Oxford, 1910–1952. Vol. I.

Bacon, Francis, *Novum Organum,* T. Fowler, ed. Oxford, 1878–1879.

Bacon, Roger, *Opus Majus,* translated from the Latin by R. B. Burke. Philadelphia, 1928.

Descartes, René, *Discourse on Method,* translated by N. Kemp Smith, in *Descartes' Philosophical Writings.* New York, 1953.

Galilei, Galileo, *Discorsi e dimonstrazioni matematiche intorno a due nuove scienze.* Leiden, 1638. Translated by Henry Crew and Alfonso de Salvio as *Dialogues Concerning Two New Sciences.* New York, 1914.

Newton, Sir Isaac, *Mathematical Principles of Natural Philosophy,* translated by Andrew Motte, Florian Cajori, ed. Berkeley, 1934.

EARLY MODERN WORKS

Duhem, Pierre, *La Théorie physique. Son objet. Sa structure.* Paris, 1906. Translated by P. P. Wiener from the 2d French ed. as *The Aim and Structure of Physical Theory.* Princeton, 1954. The classic statement of conventionalism.

Herschel, Sir John Frederick William, *A Preliminary Discourse on the Study of Natural Philosophy.* London, 1830. The first modern account of scientific method.

Jevons, William Stanley, *The Principles of Science: A Treatise on Logic and Scientific Method.* London, 1873. A standard contemporary account, with a strong emphasis on logic.

Mach, Ernst, *Contributions to the Analysis of Sensations,* translated by C. M. Williams. Chicago, 1897. A leading statement of the antimetaphysical views of the positivists.

Mill, John Stuart, *A System of Logic, Ratiocinative and Inductive, Being a Connected View of the Principles of Evidence and the Methods of Scientific Investigation.* London, 1843. A comprehensive treatment from a radically inductivist standpoint.

Pearson, Karl, *The Grammar of Science.* London, 1892; 3d ed., London, 1911. An early positivist treatment.

Whewell, William, *The Philosophy of the Inductive Sciences, founded upon their History.* London, 1840; new ed., 1847. A survey of the methods of the various sciences at that time.

MODERN DISCUSSIONS

Blake, R. M.; Ducasse, C. J.; and Madden, E. H., eds., *Theories of Scientific Method: The Renaissance Through the Nineteenth Century.* Seattle, 1960. A useful summary of some leading historical ideas.

Bridgman, P. W., *The Logic of Modern Physics.* New York, 1927. The manifesto of operationalism.

Carnap, Rudolf, *The Continuum of Inductive Methods.* Chicago, 1952.

Hanson, Norwood Russell, *Patterns of Discovery.* Cambridge, 1958. An account of the methodological development of some theories of classical and modern physics.

Nagel, Ernest, *The Structure of Science.* New York, 1961. A comprehensive and thorough treatment of current issues.

Popper, Karl, *The Logic of Scientific Discovery.* London, 1959.

PETER CAWS

SCOT, MICHAEL (fl. 1217–c. 1240), astrologer, alchemist, and translator of Arabic and Hebrew works into Latin. Born in Scotland late in the twelfth century, he spent most of his active life in Toledo, Palermo, and mainland Italy—perhaps at Rome. He first appears with any degree of certainty at Toledo in 1217, when he finished a translation of al-Bīṭrogī's (Alpetragius') *Liber Astronomiae* ("On the Spheres"). The next certain date is 1220, when he is reported to have completed a Latin translation of Aristotle's *Historia Animalium,* probably at Toledo. He seems to have become favorably known at the papal court, for he was offered the archbishopric of Cashel in Ireland in 1225. He refused the office because of his ignorance of Gaelic. Probably during this period he produced the translation of Aristotle's *De Caelo et Mundo,* along with several other physical works of Aristotle with their Arabic commentaries by Averroës. It was these commentaries that were to be so influential among the Schoolmen for the next several generations. About 1228, as nearly as can be judged, Scot entered the service of Emperor Frederick II in Sicily, or at his court at Palermo, as his official astrologer. While there, he wrote his compendious *Liber Introductorius,* a general survey of the whole science of astrology, and the *Liber Particularis,* similar in content but much briefer, intended for popular use. He also composed a *Physiognomia,* a general handbook of physiological science. All three works were dedicated to the emperor and brought Scot a wide reputation. From this second, Sicilian period of his life comes the *Abbreviatio Avicenne de Animalibus,* probably done in 1231, in answer to Frederick's request for more scientific information about the animal kingdom. It was also during this period that Scot wrote *De Arte Alchemie* in which he reported having witnessed and himself verified alchemical experiments performed by Arabs, Jews, Spaniards, and north Africans.

Because of his renown many other works have been ascribed to him, such as a commentary on John of Holywood (Sacrobosco) entitled *De Sphera* and a Latin translation of Maimonides' *Guide of the Perplexed,* but these attributions lack any proof or, indeed, likelihood. Scot's great contribution remains his work of translation from Arabic and Hebrew sources of Aristotle's zoological works, the work of al-Bīṭrogī, the commentaries of Averroës on Aristotle, and the zoological work of Avicenna. Dante consigns him to hell as a magician.

Bibliography

The biography by J. Wood Brown, *Life and Legend of Michael Scot* (Edinburgh, 1897), must be used with care. For more recent and reliable treatments, see Lynn Thorndike, *History of Magic and Experimental Science During the First Thirteen Centuries of Our Era,* 2 vols. (New York, 1923——), Vol. II, pp. 307–337; C. H. Haskins, *Studies in the History of Mediaeval Science* (Cambridge, 1927), pp. 272–298; and G. Sarton, *Introduction to the History of Science* (Baltimore, 1931), Vol. II, Ch. 2, pp. 579–582, with a bibliography of editions.

S. HARRISON THOMSON

SCOTISM, the philosophical system named after John Duns Scotus (c. 1265/1266–1308), represents one of the two main trends in Scholasticism, the other being Thomism. Scotism played a vital role in the shaping of Christian thought and developed principally within the Franciscan order, gradually replacing the older school of Alexander of Hales and St. Bonaventure. The intrinsic value of the Scotistic synthesis and the growing prestige of Duns Scotus, whose penetrating analysis and constructive criticism won recognition both inside and outside the Franciscan order, were the decisive factors in the establishment of Scotism as a distinct movement. Yet it was not until the end of the fifteenth or the beginning of the sixteenth century that a Scotistic school, which received its official confirmation at the general chapter of the Franciscan order held at Toledo, Spain, in 1633, was actually established. The chapter's decree gave a vigorous impulse to Scotistic studies, which were further stimulated by Luke Wadding's edition of all Scotus' works, published in 1639. The introduction of the *Opus Oxoniense* (Scotus' commentary on the *Sentences* of Peter Lombard) as an official text along with Aquinas' *Summa Theologica* in many universities and other higher centers of learning also contributed to the spread of Scotism.

The golden age of Scotism must be placed between the sixteenth and eighteenth centuries, when Scotistic chairs were established in principal universities of Italy, France, England, Poland, Spain, and Latin America, and even at the University of Kiev in Russia. In the seventeenth century Scotism had attained such popularity that a Louvain professor, John Caramuel, could affirm that "the Scotistic school is more numerous than all other schools taken together." This statement should not surprise anyone who is acquainted with the remarkable growth of the Franciscan order at that time. Moreover, Scotus had many followers even outside his own order, especially among the Augustinians and the Jesuits.

The decline of Scotism, as of Scholasticism in general, began in the eighteenth century and became even more noticeable in the following century with the suppression of religious orders in many European countries. When the need was seen in the nineteenth century for a revival of Scholasticism, the leaders of this movement concentrated their efforts on the restoration of Thomistic philosophy, in order to present the intellectual world with a unified, homogeneous system. This fact partly explains the emphasis placed by Catholic authorities on the teachings of St. Thomas and the consequent neglect of Scotistic studies even among Catholic scholars. However, as a result of more serious and objective studies, there are clear indications of a growing interest among both scholastics and nonscholastics in the teachings of Scotus. The day may not be far when the full value of the Scotistic synthesis will be appreciated. The critical edition of Scotus' *Opera Omnia* currently in progress may be a first step in this direction.

Doctrine. The characteristic features of Scotism, as contrasted with Thomism, may be reduced to the following points. The primary and proper object of the human intellect is being as being and not merely the essence of material things. The concept of being is univocal, since it is the most common notion that can be predicated of God and creatures, substance and accidents, and may be considered apart from the intrinsic modes that determine a being in its concrete reality, such as finiteness and infinity, being *in se* and being *in alio*. Man's intellect has a direct, intuitive knowledge of the singular material object, and not merely an indirect knowledge of it gained by reflecting upon the material image (that is, *per conversionem ad phantasmata*), as Aquinas teaches. While material bodies are composed of matter and form as substantial principles, prime matter is not pure potentiality but has an act of its own, the act of being matter. The principle of individuation is not matter but a positive perfection called *haecceitas*, or "thisness," which belongs to both material and spiritual substances. In man there is, in addition to the soul, the *forma corporeitatis*, that is, that by which the body is a body independently of the informing act of the soul. Between the soul and its powers, as well as between the powers themselves, there is only a formal distinction. This formal distinction, which obtains between entities that are not exactly the same and yet cannot be separated from one another, also obtains between being and its transcendentals, between animality and rationality in man, between common nature and *haecceitas*, between essence and attributes in God, and between the divine attributes themselves.

The unique and absolute infinity of God is the attribute that best distinguishes him from creatures and constitutes his absolute perfection. While creation is primarily an act of the divine will, so that things exist and are good because God wills them, creation is also a rational act based on the divine intellect. Because of the essential contingence of creatures, God can dispense man from those precepts of the natural law that concern his duties toward his fellow men but not from those concerning his relationship to God. Man's ultimate end consists in love of, rather than in knowledge of, God, for it is the will and not the intellect that is the superior power in man.

Scotists. Among the many Scotists who distinguished themselves because of either their teaching or writings, the following deserve special mention: Francis Mayron (d. after 1328), a most devoted pupil of Scotus', who introduced the *Actus Sorbonicus*, or full-day disputation, into the University of Paris; John de Bassolis (d. about 1347), whom Scotus esteemed so much that he described his presence as being equivalent to an entire audience; Peter of Aquila (d. 1361), who was called "Scotellus" because of his fidelity to Scotus' teaching, which he condensed in a valuable compendium; Nicholas de Orbellis (d. 1455), whose commentary on the *Sentences* of Peter Lombard appeared in several editions; William of Vaurouillon (d. 1463), one of the most prominent fifteenth-century Scotists, known for his commentary on the *Sentences* and for his *Vademecum* containing the opinions presented anonymously by Scotus; and Francis Lychetus (d. 1520), whose commentaries on the *Opus Oxoniense* and other works by Scotus have greatly contributed to the understanding of the Scotistic doctrine.

Also worthy of mention are Luke Wadding (d. 1657), editor of Scotus' complete works, with commentaries by outstanding Scotists (12 vols., Lyons, 1639); Francis Macedo (d. 1681), author of more than seventy volumes, who was called *omniscius* because of his encyclopedic knowledge; Claudius Frassen (d. 1711), a profound scholar known for his *Scotus Academicus* (4 vols., Paris, 1672–1677; 12 vols., Rome, 1900–1902); Jerome of Montefortino (d. 1738), whose work *Ioannis Duns Scoti Summa Theologica* (6 vols., Rome, 1900–1903) presents Scotus' teaching in the general framework of Aquinas' *Summa Theologica;* Parthenius Minges (d. 1926), known for his many studies on Scotus and especially for his work *Ioannis Duns Scoti Doctrina Philosophica et Theologica* (2 vols., Quaracchi, Italy, 1930); and Carlo Balić (b. 1899), president of the commission for the critical edition of Duns Scotus' *Opera Omnia.*

Bibliography

Bertoni, Alexandre, *Le bienheureux Jean Duns Scot; sa vie, sa doctrine, ses disciples.* Levanto, Italy, 1917. Pp. 433–580.

Bettoni, Efrem, *Duns Scoto.* Brescia, 1946. Translated and edited by Bernardine Bonansea as *Duns Scotus: The Basic Principles of His Philosophy.* Washington, D.C., 1961.

Ryan, John K., and Bonansea, Bernardine M., eds., *John Duns Scotus, 1265–1965,* Vol. III of *Studies in Philosophy and the History of Philosophy.* Washington, D.C., 1965. Symposium of 15 articles by outstanding Scotists in commemoration of the seventh centenary of the birth of Duns Scotus.

Scaramuzzi, Diomede, *Il pensiero di Giovanni Duns Scoto nel Mezzogiorno d'italia.* Rome, 1927.

Wadding, Luke, *Scriptores Ordinis Minorum,* new ed. Rome, 1906. See also Joannes Hyacinthus Sbaralea, *Supplementum,* new ed. Rome, 1908.

BERNARDINE M. BONANSEA, O.F.M.

SECONDARY QUALITIES. See PRIMARY AND SECONDARY QUALITIES.

SELF. See PERSONAL IDENTITY.

SELF-CONSCIOUSNESS. See CONSCIOUSNESS.

SELF-PREDICTION.

In recent years philosophers have produced arguments designed to prove that not all human behavior can be predicted or otherwise known in advance, and these arguments have been taken to be relevant to the problem of freedom of the will as well as to the question whether there can be genuine behavioral sciences. Specifically, it is argued that in certain circumstances it is logically impossible that one should come to know decisions, and actions for whose occurrence decisions are necessary conditions, in advance of the occurrence of such decisions. This has been interpreted as a refutation of determinism.

Two antipredictive arguments will be presented separately, and later their import when taken together will be discussed. The first concerns the scientific defectiveness of predictions which influence the predicted event, and the second concerns the logical impossibility of a person's knowing now what he will decide only at some future time.

Influence of predictions. It is a familiar fact that some prophecies and predictions are self-fulfilling in the sense that the prediction itself produces the predicted event—for example, when all the stock market tip sheets predict that stock *x* will drop sharply in the next few weeks. We also know, for similar reasons, that some predictions are self-

defeating. For example, Jones predicts that he will, as usual, take the easy way out of a difficulty, but then, to prove to himself that he can do better, he does just the opposite. This prediction affected his deliberation and caused him to make a decision opposite to the one he had predicted. Now, the argument which follows does not maintain that a person's predictions of his own future decisions are necessarily or always self-defeating; instead, it maintains that it is logically impossible that by considering causes a person should come to know that his final prediction of what he will decide is *not* self-defeating, and it maintains that the attempt to achieve such knowledge involves an infinite regress. In other words, this antipredictive argument purports to prove that predictions of one's own future decisions on the basis of antecedent causal conditions cannot possibly be scientifically complete.

It is necessary to state some assumptions and restrictions required by the argument. The first assumption is that decisions are events and hence are the sorts of things that can be caused; many philosophers would reject this assumption. Second, the argument concerns only causal *knowledge* of future decisions, by which is meant predictions derived with scientific adequacy from what one knows to be all the relevant antecedent causes of the decision, as distinct from predictions not known to be based on all the relevant causes and which consequently yield only a likelihood of the decision's occurrence. Finally, the argument aims to prove only that it is logically impossible for a person to have causal knowledge of his *own* decision in advance of making such a decision.

Let us assume, then, that some set of circumstances C is causally sufficient for a person S to make decision D and that S has unlimited knowledge of past circumstances and relevant causal laws. Can S come to know that C is sufficient for D? S may come to make a prediction P that past circumstances C are sufficient for D. We have supposed that as a matter of fact C *is* causally sufficient for D, but S nevertheless cannot *know* that this is so unless he also knows that there are no contrary causes. That is, before S can know that C is sufficient for D he must also know that there is no other circumstance which, together with C, is sufficient for not-D. One such probable cause of not-D is the prediction itself. Therefore, S cannot know that C is sufficient for D unless he knows that it is false that

(1) C plus P are causally sufficient for not-D.

S has been allowed unlimited knowledge of past circumstances and relevant causal laws, hence S can know that (1) is false, that is, he can know that making the prediction will not cause him to make a different decision. It does not follow, however, that S now can know that C is sufficient for D, for the same problem recurs: S's knowledge that (1) is false, which we will call P_1, is a new datum and is itself a possible cause of not-D. Therefore, S cannot know that C is sufficient for D unless he knows that it is false that

(2) C plus P_1 are causally sufficient for not-D.

And S's knowledge that (2) is false, or this knowledge plus his feelings or attitudes toward (2), constitute a further possible contrary cause, P_2. Thus, an infinite regress arises, within which the agent's prediction on the basis of some evidence C or his revision of the prediction or his final thoughts about the prediction are relevant data in addition to the data upon which the prediction was based. *S*'s calculating of causes cannot possibly "catch up" with the number of possible causes which must be examined if the prediction is to be scientifically complete, for the final results obtained cannot themselves also be part of the basis of one's prediction.

When one attempts to predict a supernova, it is true that in this case, too, the final prediction arrived at is necessarily excluded from the data upon which the prediction is based. However, although it is logically possible that predictions or thoughts about predictions can produce or impede a supernova, it is not scientifically possible that they do so. Therefore, the infinite regress argument is no obstacle to knowledge of, for example, scientific laws or stellar events but concerns only particular events which can be produced or prevented by human agency. And it is clearly applicable to attempted predictions of one's own decisions because we know that speculations and predictions about what one is likely to decide are always among the conditions most likely to be determinative of what one will in fact decide.

Counterarguments favoring determinism. The view that this first antipredictive argument casts doubt on determinism may be challenged in a number of ways:

(*a*) The argument presents no obstacle to the existence of a complete causal explanation of one's own past decisions.

(*b*) There is no logical obstacle to a person's predicting a future decision of someone other than himself, although such prediction does confront a methodological difficulty. That is, suppose that *A* predicts a future decision of *B*'s and resolves not to tell *B* the prediction. Then it appears that *A* must also predict something about himself; namely, that he will not later decide to revoke his past decision and tell *B*, after all—and this, according to the infinite regress argument, *A* cannot possibly do. One complication here is the question whether the regress argument precludes *A*'s predicting that he will make no decisions at all during a certain future period; *if* the regress argument does not preclude this, then *A* can predict that he will not change his mind and tell the original prediction to *B*. But in any case the solution seems to lie in having *A* make his prediction of *B*'s decision from a dungeon or a distant planet or in such a way that he has no time to communicate with *B* in advance of *B*'s making his decision; that is, perhaps it is sufficient that it be physically (although not logically) impossible that *A* should ruin the impeccable scientific basis of his prediction by telling *B*.

(*c*) The regress argument shows no peculiarity of human or even of sentient beings. For it is easy to imagine a simple machine, for which no one would dream of claiming free will or moral responsibility, the behavior of which could not possibly be predicted in circumstances similar to those previously described. We need only suppose that the machine can do two things, *x* and *y*, that a prediction of either of these things, punched into a card, can be inserted in the machine, and that we announce our predictions of what the machine will do by inserting appropriately punched cards into the machine. The machine is built to do *x* when fed the prediction "machine will do *y*" and to do *y* when fed the prediction "machine will do *x*." The

situation in which a prediction of a person's decision is defective is fully as artificial as this, and in each situation the prediction is defective for the same reason. In each case, given the causal hypothesis, one can in principle make a scientifically impeccable prediction of what will occur only if neither the person nor the machine is allowed to be influenced by the prediction. Meaning "*y*" when one inserts the card saying "machine will do *x*" into the machine is equivalent to telling a person he will decide not-*D* when one knows that telling him this will cause him to decide *D*.

It can be argued that the first antipredictive argument shows only that given the causal hypothesis, it is still possible to make predictions competently and incompetently and that one of countless ways in which one can make predictions incompetently is to allow one's prediction to disturb the system that one is trying to predict. However, although it may be the case that the self-defeating prophecy and the self-fulfilling prophecy are equally explicable and, in general, equally avoidable phenomena, it appears that the special situation in which the self-defeating prophecy is unavoidable is important to us—namely, the situation in which we attempt to predict our own decisions. The regress argument also poses a methodological problem for social scientists who wish to circulate predictions of human behavior, but it does not show that there is any event which in principle cannot be predicted.

Logical impossibility of self-prediction. The second antipredictive argument appears to follow from the analytic truth that one cannot know now what, by hypothesis, one will not know until some later time. Thus, one form of this argument (see Karl Popper, "Postscript: After Twenty Years") maintains that exact historical prophecy is incompatible with the fact of advancing knowledge. That is, it is impossible to predict the future decisions and actions of people because these future decisions and actions will be formed and done on the basis of knowledge which, by hypothesis, no one now possesses.

Another form of the argument maintains that it is logically impossible for a person to know what he will decide to do before he actually makes his decision (see Stuart Hampshire, *Thought and Action*; Carl Ginet, "Can the Will Be Caused?"; and D. F. Pears, *Freedom and the Will*). It is claimed that if a person knows or thinks he knows what he will try to do tomorrow, then either he has already decided what he will try to do or he believes that what he will try to do is not up to him. In neither of these two cases can he decide what he will try to do, for in each case there is nothing for him to decide. Decision is making up one's mind about what one will try to do or about what one will acquiesce in; therefore, to say that one will decide tomorrow appears to entail that there is something one will know then and which, by hypothesis, one does not know now.

However, there is a difficulty here. What is it that one knows as a result of decision and that one cannot know prior to the decision? From the fact that a person has decided to do something, it does not follow that he knows what he will do or try to do in the future. Decision does not give one knowledge of anything that will occur in the future because the mere fact that a person has decided does not ensure that he will not falter, change his mind, or die tomorrow. Hence, it appears to be mistaken to assume that because decision entails ignorance prior to decision, this ignorance is of something which one will know later as a *result* of decision; what one comes to know when one decides is nothing in addition to the decision itself and not any fact about the future. The reason for this appears to be that "decision" is an intentional concept.

Sometimes a person claims to know what a future decision of his will be, and various explanations of his supposed mistake can be made: (*a*) He has already decided, and he confuses with the act of decision itself some future reaffirmation, announcement, or implementation of his decision. (*b*) He has tentatively decided and plans at the last moment to reappraise his decision, but he thinks that he knows the result of that reappraisal because of his tentative decision. In this case, if he does not deliberate again at the last moment, then he merely reaffirms what he has already decided, and if he does deliberate again, then it is impossible that he should know in advance the result of his deliberation, even though this new decision agrees with his earlier tentative decision. (*c*) He construes a future reaffirmation of a decision already made to be a new decision because its time, place, or context differs from that in which he first decided. (*d*) He confuses a guess, likelihood, or probability with *knowledge* of his future decision.

It has also been claimed (for example, by Richard Taylor, in "Deliberation and Foreknowledge") that if a person knows or thinks he knows what he will do in the future, then it is impossible for him to deliberate about what he will do, for deliberation also presupposes ignorance. "Jones is deliberating whether to do *x*" entails "Jones does not know whether or not he will do *x*." But here a distinction must be made between the agent's belief or knowledge that he will do a particular act in the future and the agent's belief or knowledge that this particular act he will do is in some sense not up to him. If a person believes that he will do *x*, he cannot deliberate whether to do *x*, even though he believes that he will do *x* freely, that what he does is up to him. On the other hand, if a person believes that what he will do is not up to him, then he cannot deliberate whether to do *x*, even though he lacks knowledge or belief about what he will do. Hence, although it has been claimed that both foreknowledge and lack of freedom preclude deliberation and decision, these claims nevertheless require separate argument, and only foreknowledge is relevant to self-prediction and the paradoxes thereof.

It might be thought that the two antipredictive arguments are not truly distinct, and indeed some philosophers have written as though these arguments were but two approaches to the same logical point. But they are distinct, except insofar as they can be put to similar purposes. The first argument applies to all predictions which can causally influence the events predicted, whether these events happen to be decisions, revolutions, or stock market trends. It is thus broader in scope and does not require that the event also be of that special sort which, in certain circumstances, is logically impossible to know in advance. The second argument attacks the very idea of foreknowledge, however obtained, of occurrences that entail prior igno-

rance and does not, as does the first argument, attack the scientific adequacy of predictions that can influence the predicted events.

Logical impossibility of causing decisions. Many philosophers would maintain that if some set of antecedent conditions is causally sufficient for the occurrence of an event, then it is logically possible that the event be predicted or known prior to its occurrence. From this claim, together with the second antipredictive argument, can be constructed the following argument which attempts to prove that it is logically impossible that decisions have causes (see Ginet, *op. cit.*): If it is logically possible for a decision to be caused, then it is logically possible for a person to know what his own decision will be before he makes his decision; it is not logically possible for a person to know what his own decision will be before he makes his decision; therefore, it is not logically possible for a decision to be caused.

This argument is, in the following way, of more apparent relevance to the traditional problem of freedom of the will and in particular to a theory of human agency: Let us suppose that decisions are necessary conditions for the occurrence of certain actions, and let us suppose further that decisions are part of the causes of such actions. If so, then any set of causes sufficient for the occurrence of such an action must include a decision as part of the set, for whatever is sufficient for something to occur must include everything necessary for that thing to occur. But the decision, by the preceding argument, is uncaused, and therefore no set of causes existing prior in time to the decision can be sufficient for the occurrence of the action. The decision can thus be viewed as a partial, uncaused cause of the action, which, together with ordinary causes, is sufficient for the occurrence of the action.

Difficulties of the following sort have been raised against the argument which maintains that it is impossible that decisions be caused: First, it has been doubted that it follows from the causal hypothesis that it is possible for a person to predict his own decisions; for the possibility of predictability in principle need not include the possibility of predictability in all possible circumstances (see A. J. Stenner, "On Predicting Our Future"). As we have seen, it is not obvious that paradoxes arise when we suppose someone to predict decisions of persons other than himself. Second, a premise of this argument maintains that from the hypothesis that decisions are caused, it follows that one could in principle make a scientifically adequate prediction, based on knowledge of antecedent causes, of one's own future decision. But the first of the two antipredictive arguments claims that this does not follow at all, because it is impossible to establish that one's prediction has no contrary influence on the predicted event. That is, the first antipredictive argument, if sound, shows that the causal hypothesis does not entail the apparent absurdity that in principle one could, by considering antecedent conditions and relevant causal laws, come to know one's own decisions in advance.

Bibliography

Canfield, J., "Knowing About Future Decisions," *Analysis*, Vol. 22, No. 6 (1962), 127–129.

Ginet, Carl, "Can the Will Be Caused?" *Philosophical Review*, Vol. 71, No. 1 (1962), 49–55.

Hampshire, Stuart, and Hart, H. L. A., "Decision, Intention and Certainty." *Mind*, Vol. 67, No. 265 (1958), 1–12.

Hampshire, Stuart, *Thought and Action*. London, 1960.

Herbst, P., "Freedom and Prediction." *Mind*, Vol. 66 (1957).

Lyon, A., "The Prediction Paradox." *Mind*, Vol. 68 (1959), 510–517.

MacKay, D. M., "Brain and Will" (BBC Third Program, 1957), printed in Paul Edwards and Arthur Pap, eds., *A Modern Introduction to Philosophy*. New York, 1965.

MacKay, D. M., "On the Logical Indeterminacy of a Free Choice." *Mind*, Vol. 69 (1960).

Murdoch, Iris; Hampshire, Stuart; Gardiner, Patrick; and Pears, D. F., "Freedom and Knowledge," in D. F. Pears, ed., *Freedom and the Will*. London, 1963. Pp. 80–104.

Popper, Karl, "Postscript: After Twenty Years," in his *Logic of Scientific Discovery*. London, New York, and Toronto, 1959.

Stenner, A. J., "On Predicting Our Future." *Journal of Philosophy*, Vol. 61, No. 14 (1964), 415–428.

Taylor, Richard, "Deliberation and Foreknowledge." *American Philosophical Quarterly*, Vol. 1, No. 1 (1964).

ANDREW OLDENQUIST

SELLARS, ROY WOOD, American critical realist, taught philosophy at the University of Michigan. Sellars was born in 1880. Although he was never as well known outside philosophical circles as some of his contemporaries, since the publication of his first book, *Critical Realism*, in 1916, Sellars has maintained a substantial reputation among his fellow philosophers as a vigorously independent thinker. His thought is rigorous and critical; he has never yielded to the fashionable movements of the day but has steadfastly pursued his own original insights into basic philosophical problems.

The core of Sellars' philosophy is epistemological. He is concerned with showing that the critical realism of the philosopher is related to the "natural realism" of the "plain man." The philosopher reflects on the plain man's uncritical view of knowledge, which he clarifies and refines so that it is philosophically justifiable, but he does not vitiate its essential insistence upon the independence of the object of knowledge. The most significant element in Sellars' vindication of realism is his revision of the theory of perception, which he describes as a process of interpretation of sensa, as mediated by factors both external and internal to the perceiving subject. This view of perception avoids both the simplistic claim of natural realism that things reveal themselves directly in perception and the subjectivist claim that the objects of perception are ideas rather than things. Knowledge, too, is a complex process and occurs at various levels of complication. Its ultimate biological source is to be found in the adjustment of the organism to its environment; its ultimate outreach is in scientific knowledge, which replaces the relativity of individual perspectives by close approximations to exact measurement. Whether on the implicit organic level or on the highly explicit and self-critical scientific level, we know that we know when the content of our beliefs corresponds to the externally observed state of affairs.

Working from this epistemological position, Sellars developed an evolutionary cosmology and a materialistic ontology, carrying on his insight that there are levels, or "gradients," of being. Even the higher levels like life and mind, which emerge under most favorable conditions, are, however, physical systems. Sellars' materialism is nonreductive, but he insists that "life is not a nonnatural force coming from outside, but a term for the new capacities of which nature has found itself capable." On the valuational side, Sellars argues from these positions to a humanistic theory of ethics and religion (he was one of the major contributors to the composition of the Humanist Manifesto of 1933) and to a politics of democratic socialism.

Works by Sellars

Critical Realism. Chicago, 1916.

The Next Step in Democracy. New York, 1916.

The Next Step in Religion. New York, 1918.

Evolutionary Naturalism. Chicago, 1922.

Religion Coming of Age. New York, 1928.

The Philosophy of Physical Realism. New York, 1932.

Works on Sellars

Bahm, Archie; Chisholm, R. M.; and others, "A Symposium in Honor of Roy Wood Sellars." *Philosophy and Phenomenological Research*, Vol. 15 (1954), 1–97.

Reck, Andrew, *Recent American Philosophy*. New York, 1964.

J. L. BLAU

SEMANTICS. The term 'semantics', although relatively new, refers to a variety of disciplines and has both a broad and a narrow use within some of these. A single rubric for these diverse disciplines is perhaps warranted by their common concern with signs and meanings, but in some instances the differences are more striking than the similarities—contrast, for example, the rigorous work of Alfred Tarski on the definition of truth with the somewhat fanciful formulations of Alfred Korzybski. Thus, classification and selection must precede exposition.

The study of signs has been called 'semiosis' or 'semiotics' (C. W. Morris, *Foundations of the Theory of Signs*); however, even among specialists 'semantics' is the commonly employed generic name for the field, especially if the subject is restricted, as this article will be, to linguistic signs—that is, symbols. Symbols occur in at least three distinguishable groups of relations: (*a*) they are related to other symbols; (*b*) they are related to things other than symbols by such relations as referring, denoting, meaning, connoting; and (*c*) they are related to things other than symbols by such relations as using, uttering, responding to, noticing. The broad field of semantics is divided (*ibid.*) into three subjects on the basis of these groups; the first is *syntax*, the second *semantics*, and the third *pragmatics*. The narrower field of semantics is sometimes further divided (W. V. Quine, "Notes on the Theory of Reference") into two subjects: the theory of reference (denotation, extension) and the theory of meaning (connotation, intension). Cutting across these categories is Carnap's distinction between *descriptive* semantics, or the empirical investigation of natural languages, and *pure* semantics, the analytical study of artificial languages.

Descriptive semantics (much of which is comprehended in the empirical science of linguistics), the deeper results of pure semantics (whose formulation involves a considerable amount of logic and set theory), and the somewhat extravagant claims of Korzybski and some of his followers (which cannot be squeezed into the classification just given) will not be treated here. (For descriptive semantics, see SEMANTICS, HISTORY OF; for pure semantics, see SYSTEMS, FORMAL, AND MODELS OF FORMAL SYSTEMS.) Further, the imperative, interrogative, and exclamatory forms of expression will be disregarded and exclusive attention given to the declarative. With these omissions acknowledged we can properly limit our attention to the more elementary and fundamental aspects of semantics, beginning—after a few introductory observations—with syntax, passing next to semantics and then to pragmatics, and concluding with a few remarks on the philosophical significance of recent accomplishments in these disciplines.

Failure to distinguish explicitly between mention and use of words seldom corrupts ordinary discourse; it would be pedantic to demand that

Ghost Town has more letters than citizens

give way to

'Ghost Town' has more letters than Ghost Town has citizens.

In semantics, however, where language is mentioned as frequently as it is used, it is important to distinguish clearly between an expression mentioned and the name used to mention that expression (see Quine, *Mathematical Logic*, Sec. 4); indeed, much work in semantics is vitiated by the tendency to ignore this distinction.

It is usually convenient, and sometimes necessary, to distinguish the language which is the object of semantical investigation (the one mentioned) from that in which the investigation is carried out (the one used); the former is known as the *object language* and the latter as the *metalanguage* (Rudolf Carnap, *Introduction to Semantics*). In much of the early literature the object language was relatively simple in structure and the metalanguage the investigator's natural language, supplemented by a few special symbols. The exposition here will follow this practice, although at present languages of formidable structure are being investigated in a completely formalized metalanguage. (See remarks in Carnap, "Replies and Systematic Expositions," pp. 914–915.)

SYNTAX

Many of the notions studied and some of the results obtained within syntax can be exemplified by a relatively simple object language L. We begin with a description and classification of its symbols:

(*a*) *Variables* are the lower-case Latin letters 'x', 'y', and 'z', with or without numerical subscripts; thus, there are denumerably many variables.

(*b*) *Logical constants* are an identity sign '$=$', two quantifiers '$\wedge$' and '$\vee$'—universal and existential, respectively—and three sentential connectives, '$\sim$' for negation, '$\rightarrow$' for the (material) conditional, and '$\wedge$' for conjunction.

(*c*) *Descriptive constants* are two individual constants,

'a' and 'b', and three (one-place) predicates, 'F', 'G', and 'H'. (The distinction between logical and descriptive constants has resisted analysis and remains somewhat arbitrary [see Quine, "Carnap and Logical Truth"]; it reflects, however, an intended difference in semantical treatment, which will become apparent in the details of the truth-definition for L given below.)

(*d*) *Punctuation symbols* are '(' and ')'.

To aid the intuition of the uninitiated reader and to facilitate illustrations later, translations of the symbols of L into its metalanguage M will be given. For simplicity (which could lead to confusion) we let the variables of M include those of L, and we take each variable as a translation of itself; we treat punctuation symbols similarly—retaining the freedom to replace them with ordinary punctuation of English. The logical constants '$=$', '$\wedge$', '$\vee$', '$\sim$', '$\rightarrow$', and '$\wedge$' are translated, respectively, as 'equals', 'all', 'some', 'not', 'if . . . then . . .', and 'and' (or a stylistic variant of any of these words); the descriptive constants 'a', 'b', 'F', 'G', and 'H' have as translations, respectively, 'Socrates', 'Plato', 'is a spinster', 'is a woman', and 'is married'.

Linear strings of symbols of L, such as '$\rightarrow F\wedge x$' and '$xF\wedge\sim$', are expressions of L; well-formed expressions, which are to be terms and formulas, are distinguished from those that are ungrammatical. A *term of L* is either a variable or an individual constant of L. It is more difficult to define *formula of L*. A (recursive) characterization given by the following clauses is adequate and intuitive:

(A) A predicate of L followed by a term of L is a formula of L.

(B) The result of flanking '$=$' with terms of L is a formula of L.

(C) The result of prefixing '$\sim$' to a formula of L is a formula of L.

(D) The result of flanking '$\rightarrow$' or '$\wedge$' with formulas of L and enclosing the result in a pair of parentheses is a formula of L.

(E) The result of prefixing to a formula of L the quantifier '$\wedge$' or '$\vee$' followed by a variable of L is a formula of L.

This characterization is exhaustive; that is, nothing is a formula of L which is not obtained by successive applications of (A)–(E).

By employing in M variables (specifically, Greek letters) and some device, such as display or quasi-quotation marks (corners, '⌜' and '⌝'; Quine, *Mathematical Logic*, Sec. 6), to indicate when a symbol of L is being used autonymously (Carnap, *Logical Syntax of Language*, Sec. 42)—that is, as its own name—clauses (A)–(E) can be expressed more perspicuously. For example, by employing display, (D) gives way to

(D') If ϕ and ψ are formulas of L, then

$$(\phi \rightarrow \psi)$$

and

$$(\phi \wedge \psi)$$

are formulas of L.

By employing quasi-quotation marks, clause (E) gives way to

(E') If ϕ is a formula of L and α is a variable of L, then ⌜$\wedge\alpha\phi$⌝ and ⌜$\vee\alpha\phi$⌝ are formulas of L.

In the display or within the corners a symbol of the object language is being used to mention itself; thus, for example, the reading of

$$\ulcorner \wedge \alpha \phi \urcorner$$

is

the result of writing '$\wedge$', followed by α, followed by ϕ.

Given that M includes the apparatus of elementary set theory, the recursive characterization of a formula can be replaced by an explicit definition. First one defines the set of *atomic formulas of L* by means of clauses (A) and (B), above. Then one indicates what it means to say a set is closed under certain grammatical operations—for example, by saying that a set K is closed under *negation* if $\ulcorner \sim \phi \urcorner$ belongs to K whenever ϕ does, and that it is *closed under conjunction* if $\ulcorner (\phi \wedge \psi) \urcorner$ belongs to K whenever ϕ and ψ do. The definition of a formula can now be given: ϕ is a formula of L if and only if ϕ is an element of every set K such that the set of atomic formulas of L is included in K and K is closed under negation, conjunction, conditionality, and quantification (universal and existential). From this definition the clauses (A)–(E) are immediately provable, and the exhaustiveness of these clauses is obtained precisely rather than by the informal comment that followed them. Further, a simple induction principle is obtained from the definition. To show that all formulas have some property it is sufficient to consider the set defined by that property and show that this set includes the set of atomic formulas of L and is closed under the relevant operations. In this manner one can prove, for example, that if ϕ is a formula of L, then there exists a finite sequence of formulas of L whose last term is ϕ and each of whose terms is either an atomic formula of L or a negation, conjunction, conditional, or quantification (universal or existential) of preceding terms of the sequence.

A *sentence of L* is a formula of L in which no variable is *free*, this latter notion being characterized by the following clauses:

(F) If ϕ is an atomic formula of L and α is a variable of L, then α is free in ϕ if and only if α occurs in ϕ.

(G) If ϕ is a formula of L and α is variable of L, then α is free in $\ulcorner \sim \phi \urcorner$ if and only if α is free in ϕ.

(H) If ϕ and ψ are formulas of L and α is a variable of L, then α is free in $\ulcorner (\phi \rightarrow \psi) \urcorner$ if and only if α is free in either ϕ or ψ.

(H') If ϕ and ψ are formulas of L and α is a variable of L, then α is free in $\ulcorner (\phi \wedge \psi) \urcorner$ if and only if α is free in either ϕ or ψ.

(I) If α and β are variables of L and ϕ is a formula of L, then α is free in $\ulcorner \wedge \beta \phi \urcorner$ if and only if α is different from β and free in ϕ.

(I') If α and β are variables of L and ϕ is a formula of L, then α is free in $\ulcorner \vee \beta \phi \urcorner$ if and only if α is different from β and free in ϕ.

According to the above definition, '$\vee x(Gx \wedge Hx)$' is a sentence of L, but '$(\vee x Gx \wedge Hx)$', although a formula of L, is not a sentence of L; the translation of the former is 'Some woman is married', and that of the latter is 'Something is a woman, and x is married'.

The preceding syntactical considerations are formation rules; further relations of symbols to symbols are given by

transformation rules—rules of deduction (Carnap, *Introduction to Semantics*). Rules of transformation, which characterize such notions as *derivability* and *theorem* but which are not essential for our subsequent considerations, will not be given here (see LOGIC, MODERN). Specifying the formation rules of L—that is, defining such basic syntactical notions as *term of L, formula of L,* and *sentence of L*—generates a *syntactical system*.

The characterization of L, although typical of much of the literature in which one finds the construction of a syntactical system, is not completely rigorous; indeed, the word 'symbol', the initial technical term, is at best ambiguous. Its ambiguity is brought out by the distinction between *symbol-event* and *symbol-design* (*ibid.*). This distinction is not peculiar to formal languages; it can be seen, for example, in the response to a request for the number of letters in 'cattle': the response 'six' refers to symbol-events, and 'five' refers to symbol-designs. Presumably the former are particular occurrences in space time, whereas the latter are sets of sufficiently similar occurrences. Clearly this distinction, or one like it, must be carried over from symbols to expressions. Most work in syntax and semantics has proceeded on the assumption that symbols and expressions are best construed fundamentally as designs (*ibid.*), but there is some significant work by philosophical nominalists based on the view that they are events (see Nelson Goodman and W. V. Quine, "Steps Toward a Constructive Nominalism," and R. M. Martin and J. H. Woodger, "Toward an Inscriptional Semantics"). There are difficulties, frequently overlooked or ignored, in the notion of a symbol or expression as a set of spatial-temporal events, and some authors seeking complete rigor along classical, Platonist, rather than nominalist, lines adopt as symbols arbitrary abstract entities suited to purposes of formalization. (See, for example, Alfred Tarski, "A Simplified Formalization of Predicate Logic With Identity.")

Another inelegance typical in the literature and mirrored in the exposition above is the assertion that an expression is a *linear string* of symbols. (One manifestation of this lack of rigor is the unexplained term 'occurs' in clause (F) of the characterization of a free variable.) There are several precise ways to introduce expressions. One is to develop within the metalanguage an axiomatic theory of concatenation and to treat expressions of the object language as concatenations of the symbols of the object language (see Tarski, "The Concept of Truth in Formalized Languages," p. 173). Another is to use arithmetization, in which concatenation is handled as an arithmetical operation and axioms required for the preceding method are obtained as theorems of arithmetic (see Kurt Gödel, "Über formal unentscheidbare Sätze der Principia Mathematica und verwandter Systeme I"). Still another is to treat expressions as dequences of the abstract entities that are the symbols of the object language; here concatenation is simply the set-theoretical concatenation of sequences (see Tarski, "A Simplified Formalization").

SEMANTICS

Definition of truth. A syntactical system L becomes a semantical system when rules are given in its metalanguage M which determine a necessary and sufficient truth-condition for every sentence of the system. These rules, often embodied in a recursive definition, lead to a definition of truth. A condition of adequacy for such a definition is expressed by means of the so-called material criterion (see Tarski, "The Semantic Conception of Truth and the Foundations of Semantics" and "The Concept of Truth"; see also CORRESPONDENCE THEORY OF TRUTH). The material criterion is given by the schema

> . . . is true in *L* if and only if _____.

An instance of this schema is any sentence of *M* formed by replacing '. . .' with a quotation-mark or structural-descriptive name of a sentence of *L* and replacing '_____' with a translation in *M* of that sentence. The adequacy condition requires the provability in *M* on the basis of the truth-definition and the ordinary principles of logic of every instance of the material criterion. For example, the sentence

(1) '$\forall x(Gx \wedge \sim Hx)$' is true in *L* if and only if some woman is not married

is an instance of the criterion, and the adequacy condition requires its provability in *M*.

Formal correctness. The definition of truth must be not only materially adequate but also formally correct (Tarski, "The Semantic Conception of Truth" and "The Concept of Truth"); that is, it must not lead to contradiction. It is just at this point that a distinction such as that between an object language and its metalanguage becomes essential. This is demonstrated by the so-called Liar paradox, whose formulation is facilitated by instances of the material criterion. Suppose a language *S* (serving as its own metalanguage) contained a predicate 'is true in *S*', together with the usual apparatus of syntax, such as elementary logic and names for expressions of *S*; let the following two sentences be sentences of *S*: The next sentence of *S* is true in *S*. The previous sentence of *S* is not true in *S*.

Given an adequate definition in *S* of 'true in *S*', the following instances of the material criterion are true in *S*:

(2) 'The next sentence of *S* is true in *S*' is true in *S* if and only if the next sentence of *S* is true in *S*.
(3) 'The previous sentence of *S* is not true in *S*' is true in *S* if and only if the previous sentence of *S* is not true in *S*.

Empirically the reader can verify the truth of

(4) The next sentence of *S* is identical with 'The previous sentence of *S* is not true in *S*'.
(5) The previous sentence of *S* is identical with 'The next sentence of *S* is true in *S*'.

From (2)–(5) the explicit contradiction

> The previous sentence of *S* is true in *S* if and only if the previous sentence of *S* is not true in *S*

follows by the elementary principles of identity and sentential logic. (Indexical terms, defined below, and empirical premises, which were employed in the preceding for-

mulation, are inessential to the Liar paradox. See Tarski, "The Semantic Conception of Truth," note 11.)

The standard procedure for obtaining a formally correct definition of truth for a language *S* is to exclude from *S* the expression 'is true in *S*'. This expression and its definition are put into a metalanguage for *S*—a language essentially richer than *S* (see Tarski, "The Semantic Conception of Truth" and "The Concept of Truth").

Truth in a model. Several methods of providing an adequate truth-definition for formalized languages of specified structure are now standard in the literature; the treatment here will be similar to that used by Tarski and R. L. Vaught in "Arithmetical Extensions of Relational Systems." Its main departure from the classical treatment will be to define not truth but the more general notion of truth in a model, where a model is a partial specification of a possible world; truth is then simply truth in that model which is a partial specification of the actual world. A *model* for the language *L* is an ordered couple of entities $\langle DR \rangle$. The first member, *D*, is any nonempty set; it is the domain of the model (the domain of discourse), which comprises the values of the variables of *L*. The second member, *R*, is a function which assigns denotations to the descriptive constants of *L*; it assigns to each individual constant of *L* an element of *D* and to each predicate of *L* a set of elements of *D*—that is, a subset of *D* (which may be empty or be *D* itself).

An explicit definition of truth of a sentence of *L* in a model for *L* is achieved through the auxiliary notion of *satisfaction* in a model—the fundamental semantical notion in this procedure. Somewhat more intuitive than this relative notion of satisfaction in a model is the absolute notion of satisfaction; satisfaction is a relation between arbitrary objects and arbitrary formulas of a language. Informally the relation between satisfaction and truth can be illustrated as follows: the object Socrates satisfies the formula '*x* is wise' if and only if the result of replacing '*x*' in that formula with a name of Socrates, say 'Socrates', is a true sentence. Formally it is convenient to characterize satisfaction as a relation between a formula and an assignment of objects to variables, and this convenience will be employed in defining the relative notion of satisfaction in a model; the definition is given recursively with the aid of some elementary set-theoretical notions. (Here, as in the preceding examples, the recursive characterization can be eliminated in favor of an explicit definition; the details, however, are somewhat more complex than those given in the earlier illustration. See Tarski, "The Concept of Truth," p. 193, note 1.)

A function *f* is said to be a *value assignment* on (a non-empty set) *D* if *f* correlates each variable of *L* with an element of *D*.

The *value* of a term ζ of *L* *with respect to* a model $\langle DR \rangle$ for *L* and a value assignment *f* on *D*—succinctly, $\mathrm{Val}^f_{\langle DR \rangle}(\zeta)$—is $f(\zeta)$ if ζ is a variable and $R(\zeta)$ if ζ is an individual constant.

Given that $\langle DR \rangle$ is a model for *L* and *f* is a value assignment on *D*, the notion of *satisfaction* in $\langle DR \rangle$ is completely characterized by the following clauses:

(J) If π is a predicate of *L* and ζ is a term of *L*, then *f* satisfies $\ulcorner \pi \zeta \urcorner$ in $\langle DR \rangle$ if and only if $\mathrm{Val}^f_{\langle DR \rangle}(\zeta) \in R(\pi)$.

(K) If ζ and η are terms of *L*, then *f* satisfies $\ulcorner \zeta = \eta \urcorner$ in $\langle DR \rangle$ if and only if $\mathrm{Val}^f_{\langle DR \rangle}(\zeta)$ equals $\mathrm{Val}^f_{\langle DR \rangle}(\eta)$.

(L) If ϕ is a formula of L, then f satisfies $\ulcorner\sim\phi\urcorner$ in $\langle DR\rangle$ if and only if f does not satisfy ϕ in $\langle DR\rangle$.

(M) If ϕ and ψ are formulas of L, then f satisfies $\ulcorner(\phi\rightarrow\psi)\urcorner$ in $\langle DR\rangle$ if and only if, if f satisfies ϕ in $\langle DR\rangle$, then f satisfies ψ in $\langle DR\rangle$.

(N) If ϕ and ψ are formulas of L, then f satisfies $\ulcorner(\phi\wedge\psi)\urcorner$ in $\langle DR\rangle$ if and only if f satisfies ϕ in $\langle DR\rangle$ and ψ in $\langle DR\rangle$.

(O) If ϕ is a formula of L and α is a variable of L, then f satisfies $\ulcorner\wedge\alpha\phi\urcorner$ in $\langle DR\rangle$ if and only if every value assignment g on D such that $g(\beta)$ is $f(\beta)$, for every variable β of L other than α, satisfies ϕ in $\langle DR\rangle$.

(P) If ϕ is a formula of L and α is a variable of L, then f satisfies $\ulcorner\vee\alpha\phi\urcorner$ in $\langle DR\rangle$ if and only if there is an assignment g on D such that $g(\beta)$ is $f(\beta)$ for every variable β of L other than α which satisfies ϕ in $\langle DR\rangle$.

Considered informally, clause (J) states that a simple subject–predicate formula is satisfied if the subject is characterized by the predicate, or, more precisely, if the denotation of the formula's subject term (an object specified by either f or R) is an element of the denotation of its predicate term (a set of objects specified by R). Clause (K) asserts that an identity formula is satisfied if the two terms that flank the identity sign denote the same object. Clauses (L)–(N) give to negation, the (material) conditional, and conjunction their familiar truth-conditions. Clauses (O) and (P), certainly less perspicuous than the preceding clauses, respectively state—speaking loosely—that the universal quantification of a formula is satisfied by an object if the formula quantified is satisfied by every object and that the existential quantification of a formula is satisfied by an object if the formula quantified is satisfied by some object. Perhaps examples will be better than looseness as an aid to intuition. A simple quantification '$\wedge xFx$' is to be satisfied by an object if and only if the formula 'Fx' is satisfied by every object. Clearly this is achieved by clause (O), for every object in the domain of discourse will be brought into consideration by running through all assignments which differ from a given assignment at most in the value assigned to 'x'. To comprehend the significance of the requirement that only assignments which coincide appropriately with the given assignment are brought into consideration, an example with two variables is required. Consider the formula

(6) $\qquad\qquad \wedge x(Fy\rightarrow Fx),$

a model in which the denotation of 'F' is the set of benevolent persons, and an assignment f such that $f($'y'$)$ is Hitler. Under this interpretation, (6) asserts that everyone is such that he is benevolent if Hitler is. Thus, f should satisfy (6), and indeed this is the result obtained by the clauses above, for by clause (O) we consider only assignments which assign Hitler to 'y' and by clause (M) each of these satisfies '$(Fy\rightarrow Fx)$'. However, if clause (O) read

> If ϕ is a formula of L and α is a variable of L, then f satisfies $\ulcorner\wedge\alpha\phi\urcorner$ in $\langle DR\rangle$ if and only if every value assignment with respect to $\langle DR\rangle$ satisfies ϕ in $\langle DR\rangle$,

then by specifying a value assignment which correlated with 'y' a benevolent person and with 'x' a malevolent

person one would show, by clause (M), that the given value assignment f did not satisfy formula (6).

A definition of truth in a model is now quite straightforward: a sentence ϕ of L is true in a model $\langle DR\rangle$ for L if every value assignment on D satisfies ϕ in $\langle DR\rangle$.

For a definition of truth itself we consider an ordered couple $\mathscr{M}=\langle DR\rangle$, in which D is the set of actual objects and R assigns to the descriptive constants 'a', 'b', 'F', 'G', and 'H', respectively, Socrates, Plato, the set of spinsters, the set of women, and the set of married persons. It is clear that $\mathscr{M}$ is a model for L. A sentence of L is said to be true (in L) if it is true in $\mathscr{M}$. The (material) adequacy of this definition can be illustrated by a proof in M (left to the reader who enjoys elementary logical manipulations) of the instance (1), cited earlier, of the material criterion. (A proof of adequacy—that is, a proof that every instance of the criterion is provable in M—requires an inductive argument of the meta-metalanguage. Perhaps it is worth noting that only by supplementing semantic analysis with empirical knowledge can one have grounds for asserting that '$\vee x(Gx\wedge\sim Hx)$' is true in L.)

The principle of excluded middle for L is forthcoming on the basis of the preceding definitions; indeed, it holds not only for the particular model $\mathscr{M}$ but also for arbitrary models.

> If ϕ is a sentence of L and $\mathscr{N}$ is a model for L, then either ϕ is true (in L) in $\mathscr{N}$ or the negation of ϕ is true (in L) in $\mathscr{N}$.

The principle is an immediate consequence of the fact that if there are no free variables in a formula (as is the case for a sentence), then either every value assignment satisfies it or none does; this fact is a corollary to the fact, established by induction over formulas (see above under "Syntax"), that if two value assignments coincide for the free variables of a formula, than either both satisfy it or neither does.

Logical truth. The preceding analysis of truth in a possible world (a model) is easily extended to provide a definition of logical truth—which is simply truth in all possible worlds (all models). It is interesting to approach this notion through an intermediary. We say that a formula ϕ of L is valid in D if ϕ is true in $\langle DR\rangle$ for every function R such that $\langle DR\rangle$ is a model for L. For example, '$(\vee xFx\rightarrow\wedge xFx)$' is valid in any set that has exactly one element.

Universal validity (David Hilbert and Wilhelm Ackermann, *Principles of Mathematical Logic*)—that is, logical truth (Carnap, *Meaning and Necessity*)—is simply validity in every nonempty set. For example, the formula '$(\wedge xFx\rightarrow\vee xFx)$', the converse of that cited above, is universally valid. (Some philosophers prefer to have universal validity comprehend the empty domain, which can be achieved by simple modifications in the preceding analysis. See, for example, Donald Kalish and Richard Montague, "On Tarski's Formalization of Predicate Logic With Identity," Sec. 2; Quine, "Quantification and the Empty Domain"; and Andrzej Mostowski, *Sentences Undecidable in Formalized Arithmetic*.)

Truths about a formalized object language that are provable in its metalanguage, such as the principle of excluded middle for *L*, are *metatheorems*. The now classical results of early work in semantics include some metatheorems involving validity. For example, if a formula of *L* not containing '=' is valid in a set, then it is valid in every nonempty set of smaller cardinality; further, if any formula of *L* is valid in a denumerably infinite set, then it is universally valid.

Analyticity and synonymy. Despite the adverse comments of some philosophers (for example, in P. F. Strawson, "Truth"), the analysis of the notion of satisfaction in a model is generally recognized as a monumental contribution to philosophical analysis. (See, for example, the remarks in R. M. Martin, "On Carnap's Conception of Semantics," pp. 366 and 384, and the concluding remarks in Quine, "Notes on the Theory of Reference.") But this analysis, which provides an account not only of the notions of truth in a model, truth, and logical truth but also of such related concepts as denotation and definability (see Tarski, "The Concept of Truth," p. 194, note 1), does not seem to involve the notion of meaning, commonly thought to be the subject of semantical investigation. The above concepts, however, do not exhaust the basic semantical notions that are of interest to philosophers and are investigated within pure semantics; indeed, an important notion that has not been mentioned is that of analyticity, a notion seemingly pregnant with meaning.

To initiate an analysis of analyticity consider *L* under its intended interpretation—that given by its translation into *M* and the model *M*. The sentence

(7) $\qquad \Lambda x(Fx \rightarrow \sim Hx)$,

read (in *M*) as 'No spinster is married', is true in *L*. Yet it is not what a philosopher would consider an empirical truth—a synthetic statement. Clearly anyone who sought to determine the truth-value (the truth or falsity) of (7) by an empirical investigation, say by interviewing women and following the question 'Are you a spinster?' with the question 'Are you married?', would be considered not only foolish but also foolhardy. Moreover, (7) is not a logical truth; (7) is true in *M*, but it is not true in all models for *L*. The truth of (7) seems to rest essentially neither on facts nor on structure but on meaning: the meaning of 'spinster' seems to comprehend, in some way, being unmarried. In other words, the philosopher's (alleged—see Quine, "Two Dogmas of Empiricism") distinction between analytic and synthetic truths cannot be identified with the distinction in *L* between logical and nonlogical truths. Some supplementation of the preceding notions is required if an adequate analysis of analyticity is to be obtained within pure semantics.

One approach to the problem is that given by means of *meaning postulates* (Carnap, "Meaning Postulates"). A meaning postulate is a sentence of a formalized language which provides, in some sense, an intended meaning relation between predicates of that language. Thus, to give a complete semantical system for a formalized language one must give not only a truth-definition (providing a truth-condition for each sentence of the language) but also a list of meaning postulates (providing intended meaning relations between predicates of the language). For example, to complete the semantics of *L* the preceding analysis is to be supplemented by the stipulation that

(8) $\qquad \Lambda x(Fx \rightarrow Gx \wedge \sim Hx)$

be a meaning postulate. This stipulation indicates the intention to understand 'spinster' so that spinsters are unmarried women.

On the basis of meaning postulates some models are considered inadmissible; put affirmatively, a model for *L* is *admissible* if and only if every meaning postulate of *L* is true in it. Logical truths are still those sentences true in every model. Analytic truths are those sentences true in every admissible model; that is to say, a sentence of *L* is *analytic* in *L* if it is true in every model for *L* in which each of the meaning postulates of *L* is true. (Clearly all logical truths are analytic; a synthetic—that is, empirical—sentence is one such that neither it nor its negation is analytic.) Given the meaning postulate (8) and the above definition, it is clear that (7) is an analytic sentence of *L*.

It is a short step from analyticity to synonymy: synonymy is simply analytic coextensiveness. For example, two formulas ϕ and ψ of *L* whose only free variable is '*x*' are synonymous in *L* if both $\ulcorner \Lambda x(\phi \rightarrow \psi) \urcorner$ and $\ulcorner x(\psi \rightarrow \phi) \urcorner$ are analytic in *L* (Quine, "Carnap and Logical Truth," p. 403, and "Two Dogmas of Empiricism," p. 29). Thus, meaning, at least as it manifests itself in analyticity and synonymy, is given an analysis in terms of truth (in a model).

Even among those philosophers who have neither distaste for formalizations nor dissatisfaction with the semantical concept of truth, there are many who find completely inadequate the characterization of analyticity and synonymy by means of the truth-notion and meaning postulates. Their objections are varied and deep. The deepest objection traces the difficulty back to the thesis that no fundamental distinction can be drawn between empirical and nonempirical statements (Quine, "Carnap and Logical Truth" and "Two Dogmas of Empiricism," and Morton White, "The Analytic and the Synthetic: An Untenable Dualism").

More heuristic and more germane to our present purpose is the point of view that countenances meanings but objects to making sameness of meaning, synonymy, a matter of stipulation. To put the objection in another form, the preceding analysis leaves analyticity as applied to a meaning postulate an undefined notion. If one is to take some meaning concept as primitive, perhaps synonymy is a more natural candidate than analyticity. Given the notion of synonymy, it is for some a short step to analyticity: an analytic sentence is one obtained from a logical truth by interchange of synonyms (Quine, "Two Dogmas of Empiricism," p. 23, and "Carnap and Logical Truth," p. 403). For an analysis of synonymy one must pass from the theory of reference—that part of semantics surveyed so far—to the theory of meaning.

Sense and denotation. Quine has proposed that semantics be thought of as comprising two disciplines: (*a*) a theory of reference (denotation), which involves individuals (of a domain of discourse), sets of these individuals (and relations among them, for languages richer than *L*), and truth-values, and (*b*) a theory of meaning, which (if it exists) requires additional entities, such as concepts of individuals, properties, and propositions. This suggestion stems from a denial of the thesis (Bertrand Russell, *Introduction to Mathematical Philosophy*, p. 174) that meaning can be identified, directly or by any ingenious or complex construction (for example, Goodman, "On Likeness of Meaning," or Carnap, *Meaning and Necessity*, p. 14), with reference (denotation). Any simple identification of meaning with denotation can easily be impugned. Interchange of synonyms cannot make a difference in meaning. Yet this principle—the substitutivity of synonyms—fails if meaning is identified with denotation. The passage from the trivial assertion

(9)   The morning star is the morning star

to the informative assertion

(10)   The morning star is the evening star

certainly involves a radical change in meaning, but the latter is obtained from the former by interchange of terms with the same denotation (Gottlob Frege, "Über Sinn und Bedeutung"). A slightly richer example seems to present even more serious trouble to an analysis that depends solely on denotations, for in the passage from

(11)   Everyone who accepts the principle of self-identity believes that the morning star is the morning star

to

(12)   Everyone who accepts the principle of self-identity believes that the morning star is the evening star

not only meaning but also truth-value has changed. Here is an example that seems to run counter to the plausible and penetrating insight that what a complex expression denotes is to be a function of what its component expressions denote when they are within it (*ibid.*). (In this case one is to take as the complex expression a sentence which denotes a truth-value and to take as its components names which denote the thing named.)

The writings of Frege contain suggestions which have led not only to a resolution of the difficulties imposed upon a semantical theory by the foregoing examples but also to investigations in the theory of meaning which give some promise of results as substantial and significant as those already obtained in the theory of reference. One of Frege's proposals is that a semantical analysis associate with a term two entities—both a sense (connotation, intension) and a denotation (referent, extension); for example, a predicate is to be associated with a property as well as a class, an individual constant with an individual concept as well as an individual, and a sentence with a proposition as well as a truth-value. (See Alonzo Church, "The Need for Abstract Entities in Semantic Analysis," and Carnap, *Meaning and Necessity*. Frege was never this explicit concerning the sense of an expression.) Further, he distinguished, in a natural language and only by examples, between two types

of sentential contexts, ordinary and oblique; his most frequent examples of the latter are 'that' clauses, such as '. . . says that . . .', '. . . believes that . . .', '. . . knows that . . .'. ('It is necessary that . . .' is an important oblique context not considered by Frege; 'It is not the case that . . .' is an ordinary context. See Frege, "Über Sinn und Bedeutung," and Quine, "Reference and Modality.") Terms with the same sense must have the same denotation, but terms with the same denotation need not have the same sense; meaning is identified with the sense of a term, not the denotation. These distinctions and principles are sufficient to account for the difference in meaning between (9) and (10)—granted, of course, that the concept of the morning star is different from that of the evening star. To account for the change of truth-value in passing from (11) to (12), Frege held that in an oblique context a term refers to, denotes, its sense rather than its denotation. The occurrence of 'the evening star' in (12) and that of 'the morning star' in (11) which it replaced are in an oblique context. In that context 'the morning star' and 'the evening star' do not denote the same thing (again granted that these terms differ in sense), and hence there is no difficulty in holding that (11) denotes truth and (12) falsehood.

Formal developments of Frege's suggestions have come only recently and have not yet successfully been carried very far; indeed, the rigorous working out of a semantics of sense and denotation is a much more formidable task than the seemingly simple insights which motivated it would suggest.

The precise characterization of that which is the sense of an expression constitutes a fundamental problem; here the most fruitful suggestion has its inception in Carnap's *Meaning and Necessity*, Sec. 40, and its development in David Kaplan's *Foundations of Intensional Logic*. Consider L again. Our previous semantical analysis provided denotations for the individual constants, predicates, and sentences of L. A semantics of sense and denotation must also provide a sense for these expressions. Carnap's idea is that the sense of an expression of L is to be a function from models for L to denotations of expressions of L. (Such functions were first studied, for rather different purposes, by Tarski in "Some Notions and Methods on the Borderline of Algebra and Metamathematics." There and in more recent model-theoretic work they are called *elementary* or *arithmetical* functions.) The intuition behind this suggestion can be grasped most easily in connection with sentences. To understand a sentence is to know under what conditions it would be true and under what conditions it would be false; that is to say, to know the sense (meaning) of a sentence is to know not its actual truth-value but its truth-value in each possible world. This idea becomes precise, in connection with L, when we characterize a sense of a sentence of L (that is, a proposition) as a function which assigns to each model for L a truth-value. Similarly a sense for an individual constant of L (that is, an individual concept) is to be a function which assigns to each model for L an individual in the domain of that model, and a sense for a predicate of L (that is, a property) is to be a function which assigns to each model for L a subset of the domain of that model.

The syntactical structure of a formalized language whose

semantics is to comprehend both senses and denotations poses another fundamental problem; here the most successful effort has its inception in Church ("A Formulation of the Logic of Sense and Denotation") and its partial development in Kaplan (*Foundations of Intensional Logic*). There are serious, but perhaps not insuperable, difficulties in allowing the syntax or semantics of an expression in a formalized language to depend on its (linguistic) context, that is—as is the case in Frege's informal treatment of oblique contexts—in allowing equivocation. Thus, Church suggests that instead of allowing a single expression to be equivocal—denoting its denotation in some contexts and its sense in others—we avoid this equivocation by adding another term. For example, the name 'Socrates' will have a sense and a denotation, but every occurrence of this term will refer to its denotation, Socrates. In addition, the language should contain a term, say 'Socrates', which is to have as its denotation the sense of 'Socrates'. Of course, if the analysis is to be systematic, the term 'Socrates' has a sense as well as a denotation, and hence another term is required, say 'Socrates', whose denotation is the sense of 'Socrates', and so on. Church, in his formal theory of sense and denotation, achieves the required multiplicity of terms by a syntax embodying a type structure (see TYPES, THEORY OF).

Naming functions. It remains an open question whether a truth-definition—no details of which will be given here (see Kaplan, *Foundations of Intensional Logic*)—combining the semantical and syntactical ideas adumbrated above will lead to an adequate analysis of analyticity and synonymy or resolve the various puzzles introduced by oblique contexts. The main difficulty perhaps lies in a truth-condition for sentences involving quantification into additional oblique contexts (Quine, "Quantifiers and Propositional Attitudes").

Consider the sentence

(13) $\forall x$(George IV wondered whether x wrote *Waverley*).

The truth-condition for (13) seems to involve a concept of Sir Walter Scott rather than the individual himself—that is, the author of *Waverley*—for certainly the king would not have wondered whether the author of *Waverley* wrote *Waverley*. But a rigorous formal analysis in terms of concepts has yet to be given. Other promising suggestions for the analysis of quantification into such oblique contexts are to be found in the arguments of Quine, who claims not to understand sentences such as (13), and the insights of Montague and Kalish, who agree that the truth-condition for (13) involves more than the relevant denotations but that this something more is an implicit choice of names rather than a concept (sense) (Quine, "Quantifiers and Propositional Attitudes"; Montague and Kalish, "That"). Montague and Kalish, like Frege, recognize an equivocation, but they place it not in the names that occur in the oblique context but in the subordinating conjunction that forms the context. In (13) the term 'wondered whether' is ambiguous until a name is chosen for each individual of the domain of discourse. For instance, if N_0 and N_1 are functions which assign names to each individual of the

domain of discourse, then the ambiguous sentence (13) gives way to two unambiguous sentences:

(14) $\forall x$(George IV wondered whether$_{N_0}$ x wrote *Waverley*).

(15) $\forall x$(George IV wondered whether$_{N_1}$ x wrote *Waverley*).

Given, for example, N_0(Scott) = 'Scott' and N_1(Scott) = 'the author of *Waverley*', (14) is true and (15) false, for the truth-condition of the former would be related to George's doubts concerning the truth-value of the result of replacing 'x' in 'x wrote *Waverley*' with N_0(Scott), that is, 'Scott wrote *Waverley*', whereas that of the latter would be related to his doubts concerning the truth-value of the result of replacing 'x' in 'x wrote *Waverley*' with N_1(Scott), that is, 'the author of *Waverley* wrote *Waverley*'.

Modal operators. Each of the preceding semantical methods, that of sense and denotation and that of naming functions, introduces complexities known to be unnecessary for an interesting and, for many purposes, adequate treatment of oblique contexts formed by modal operators, such as 'it is logically necessary that', 'it is physically necessary that', 'it is morally obligatory that'. The analyses (Jaakko Hintikka, "The Modes of Modality"; S. A. Kripke, "Semantical Considerations on Modal Logic"; and Richard Montague, "Logical Necessity, Physical Necessity, Ethics, and Quantifiers") can be illustrated by considering L again, supplemented by an operator '$\square$', whose translation is 'it is logically necessary that', and the formation rule that $\ulcorner\square\phi\urcorner$ is a formula if ϕ is. The notion of a model for L remains unchanged, and the characterization of satisfaction is that of clauses (J)–(P) above, together with an additional clause for the interpretation of '$\square$'. Of the variety of interpretations considered, a simple and rather intuitive one is contained in the clause

(Q) If ϕ is a formula of L, then f satisfies $\ulcorner\square\phi\urcorner$ in $\langle DR \rangle$ if and only if f satisfies ϕ in $\langle DS \rangle$ for every function S such that $\langle DS \rangle$ is a model for L.

Truth in a model is now defined as before. Clause (Q) has the natural consequence that $\ulcorner\square\phi\urcorner$, where ϕ is a sentence of L that does not contain the modal operator '$\square$', is true in a model $\langle DR \rangle$ if and only if ϕ is valid in D. Physical and moral necessity can be treated similarly; for the former, of course, only all physically (rather than logically) possible worlds (on a given domain), and for the latter only all morally acceptable ones, would be brought into consideration (see Montague, "Logical Necessity").

PRAGMATICS

In contrast to the literature dealing with (pure) semantics, there is no well-established body of literature that can be identified as work in (pure) pragmatics; indeed, Carnap, in "Testability and Meaning," suggested that pragmatics is only a descriptive (empirical) study, although later, in "On Some Concepts of Pragmatics," he acknowledged an urgent need for theoretical work. But he did not make explicit what the nature of this work was to be. Yehoshua Bar-Hillel ("Indexical Expressions") identified pragmatics with the study of formal languages containing indexical terms—that is, languages having such features as tensed verbs and first-person and second-person pronouns. (The phrase 'indexical terms' was coined by C. S. Peirce.) Such languages have been investigated by A. N. Prior (*Time and Modality*), and indexical terms were given considerable attention by Russell (*An Inquiry Into Meaning and Truth*) under the rubric 'egocentric particulars' and by Hans Reichenbach (*Elements of Symbolic Logic*) under the rubric 'token-reflexive words'. Specification of the fundamental semantical relation for this study—that of satisfaction in an indexed family of models at an index (the analogue of satisfaction in a model)—as well as its precise characterization in some special cases, was first given by Montague; its precise characterization for certain other cases was the joint work of Montague and Nino Cocchiarella. Technical results concerning this notion occur in both Cocchiarella (*Tense Logic: A Study of Temporal Reference*) and some unpublished work of Dana Scott. Pragmatics, so conceived, is simply the extension of the semantical truth-definition to formal languages containing indexical terms—a conception easy to reconcile with C. W. Morris' classification, for the truth-value of a sentence with an indexical term seems to be related to both the person asserting the sentence and his space-time position. (Another line of development is to be found in Martin, *Toward a Systematic Pragmatics* and *Intension and Decision*.)

To illustrate this conception of pragmatics, giving some of its details and perhaps indicating its significance, we shall consider a formalized language L^* obtained from L by the addition of tense operators and another pair of quantifiers. '**P**' and '**F**' will be the tense operators. If ϕ is a formula of L^*, then $\ulcorner\mathbf{P}\phi\urcorner$ is read 'It was the case that ϕ', and $\ulcorner\mathbf{F}\phi\urcorner$ is read 'It will be the case that ϕ'; we can read ϕ itself as 'It is now the case that ϕ'. The quantifiers 'Λ' and 'V', which are to range over objects actual at a given time, are to be supplemented by the quantifiers 'Λ^p' and 'V^p', which are to range over possible objects.

For the semantics of L^* a new notion is required, that of a *history*; intuitively regarded, a history is a possible universe with a past, a present, and a future. We want to define here not truth in a model but, instead, truth in a history at a given time.

A model for L^* is an ordered triple $\langle DBR \rangle$, where D is a subset (perhaps empty) of a nonempty set B, and R is a function which assigns to each individual constant of L^* an element of B and to each predicate of L^* a subset of B. B is the set of possible objects of the model—that is, the set of things some or all of which are to be actualized in this history. D is the set of objects considered to be actual at some time. Formally a history for L^* is an indexed set of models for L^* all having a common set of possible objects.

As the index set for this illustration we take the integers; hence, only discrete time is considered. Thus, H is said to be a history for L^* if H is a function which assigns to each integer a model for L^* in such a way that all these models have the same set of possible objects.

As before, the notion of truth is approached by means of the notion of satisfaction. Given that H is a history for L^*, that i is an integer, that $H(i)$ is $\langle DBR \rangle$, and that f is a value assignment on B, the notion of satisfaction is characterized (in part) by the following clauses (some details, analogous

to those of the characterization of satisfaction, are left to the reader):

(R) If π is a predicate of L^* and ζ is a term of L^*, then f satisfies $\ulcorner\pi\zeta\urcorner$ in H at i if and only if $\mathrm{Val}^f_{H(i)}(\zeta) \in R(\pi)$.

(S) If ϕ is a formula of L^* and α is a variable of L^*, then f satisfies $\ulcorner\mathrm{V}\alpha\phi\urcorner$ in H at i if and only if there is a value assignment g on B such that $g(\alpha) \in D$ and $g(\beta)$ is $f(\beta)$ for every variable β of L^* other than α which satisfies ϕ in H at i.

(T) If ϕ is a formula of L^* and α is a variable of L^*, then f satisfies $\ulcorner\mathrm{V}^p\alpha\phi\urcorner$ in H at i if and only if there is a value assignment g on B such that $g(\beta)$ is $f(\beta)$ for every variable β of L^* other than α which satisfies ϕ in H at i.

(U) If ϕ is a formula of L^*, then f satisfies $\ulcorner\mathbf{P}\phi\urcorner$ in H at i if and only if there is an integer $j < i$ such that f satisfies ϕ in H at j.

(V) If ϕ is a formula of L^*, then f satisfies $\ulcorner\mathbf{F}\phi\urcorner$ in H at i if and only if there is an integer $j > i$ such that f satisfies ϕ in H at j.

A sentence ϕ of L^* is said to be *true* in a history H for L^* at an integer i if every value assignment on B satisfies ϕ in H at i, to be *valid* in a history H for L^* if true in H at every integer, and to be *universally valid* (logically true) if valid in every history for L^*.

Those who work in pure semantics are subjected to a constant polemic by some of their philosophical colleagues; the contention is not that there is no interest in their formalizations and truth-definitions but that there is no philosophical interest in them. Frequently the point is made that philosophical problems are generated in and by ordinary language and must therefore find their resolution therein (see, for example, Strawson, "Carnap's Views on Constructed Systems Versus Natural Languages in Analytic Philosophy"). Put this way, the point is dull—even fatuous (see Carnap, "Replies and Systematic Expositions," Sec. 19)—but it can be sharpened by the demand that the formal language in which the original problems are restated be in some sense adequate to the statement of those problems. And it must be admitted that philosophically interesting portions of ordinary language have resisted any natural translation into classical formalisms. Perhaps the remedy lies in the richer languages now being investigated.

Certainly ordinary language is shot through with oblique contexts, and these contexts occur regularly in the expositions and polemics of philosophers. Although these contexts have resisted straightforward translation into languages comparable to L (see, for example, Kalish and Montague, *Logic: Techniques of Formal Reasoning*, Ch. 6, Sec. 5), there are good grounds for the claims that they will yield to a more sophisticated treatment, such as the one suggested by Montague and Kalish in "That" (and illustrated by 14 and 15 above), and that faithful representations will be found in a Fregean system of sense and denotation developed along the lines of Church ("A Formulation of the Logic of Sense and Denotation") and Kaplan (*Foundations of Intensional Logic*).

Another prominent feature of ordinary discourse is names which are not names of anything, such as 'Pegasus'. Classical formalisms provide for the symbolization of definite descriptions such as 'the winged horse' (see, for example, Kalish and Montague, *Logic,* Ch. 7) and hence can handle some nondenoting expressions (see PROPER NAMES AND DESCRIPTIONS), but they have no direct counterpart of nondenoting names. This variance from ordinary language is easily removed; indeed, L^* is a formalism accommodating nondenoting names (individual constants). Neither the syntactical devices of tenses and two pairs of quantifiers nor the semantical notion of an indexed set of models is required for this accommodation. (See Hintikka, "Existential Presuppositions and Existential Commitments," and Hugues Leblanc and Theodore Hailperin, "Nondesignating Singular Terms," for syntactical treatments of the point and Scott, "Existence and Descriptions in Formal Logic," for a model-theoretic one.) Although the sentence '$\Lambda y \forall x\ x = y$' is a logical truth of L^* (as is the sentence '$\forall^p x\ x = a$'), the sentence '$\forall x\ x = a$' is not. The latter is true in a history at a given time (an index) if the individual constant 'a' denotes an object actual at that time; thus, L^* provides a natural translation of 'Socrates exists (now)'. Further, utilizing the tense operators of L^*, we can contrast reality with fiction: the sentence '$\mathbf{PFV}x\ x = a$', which asserts that 'a' denotes a possible object that is actual at some time, is a natural translation of 'Socrates is real', and its negation, which asserts that 'a' denotes a possible object that is never actual, is a translation of 'Socrates is a fiction (unreal)'.

Perhaps the most conspicuous feature of ordinary language absent from standard formalizations is tense. Here pragmatics provides the corrective. Consider the sentence

(16) There was once a president whose memory is now despised.

It is not clear that this sentence can be translated into a tenseless language, even if that language has names for all moments of time. But it has a natural representation in L^*. For the purpose of this example let 'Fx' and 'Gx' of L^* be read, respectively, as 'x is a president' and 'the memory of x is despised'. Then (16) passes into

$$\forall^p x(\mathbf{P}(\forall y\ y = x \wedge Fx) \wedge Gx).$$

The formulation of philosophical positions, as well as the translation of isolated English sentences, seems to require tenses. Their role in epistemological considerations is illustrated by the claim that sentences such as

(17)   There is a canoid patch,
(18)   There was a canoid patch,

in contrast to

There will be a canoid patch,

can be known (with empirical certainty) on the basis of the present testimony of sense and memory. This position cannot be expressed in a tenseless language, for to substitute for (17) or (18) a sentence of the form

There is a canoid patch at _____,

where '_____' is replaced by the name of a moment of

time, would be completely inadequate: no sophisticated epistemologist has ever claimed that his knowledge of his position in time was based (solely) on the present testimony of his senses and memory.

It would not be overly optimistic to see in semantics, especially in pure pragmatics developed along the lines illustrated above, the possibility of a precise formulation of some of the perdurable problems of metaphysics and epistemology and thereby, finally, a step toward their solution.

Bibliography

Bar-Hillel, Yehoshua, "Indexical Expressions." *Mind,* Vol. 63 (1954), 359–379.

Carnap, Rudolf, *Logische Syntax der Sprache.* Vienna, 1934. Translated by Amethe Smeaton as *Logical Syntax of Language.* London and New York, 1937.

Carnap, Rudolf, "Testability and Meaning." *Philosophy of Science,* Vol. 3 (1936), 419–471, and Vol. 4 (1937), 1–40.

Carnap, Rudolf, *Meaning and Necessity.* Chicago, 1947; 2d, enl. ed., 1956.

Carnap, Rudolf, *Introduction to Semantics.* Cambridge, Mass., 1948.

Carnap, Rudolf, "Meaning Postulates," in *Meaning and Necessity,* 2d ed., above. Supplement B, pp. 222–229.

Carnap, Rudolf, "On Some Concepts of Pragmatics," in *Meaning and Necessity,* 2d ed., above. Supplement E, pp. 248–250.

Carnap, Rudolf, "Replies and Systematic Expositions," in P. A. Schilpp, ed., *The Philosophy of Rudolf Carnap,* below. Sec. III, pp. 859–1013.

Church, Alonzo, review of 2d printing of 1st ed. of W. V. Quine, *Mathematical Logic. Journal of Symbolic Logic,* Vol. 12 (1947), 56.

Church, Alonzo, "A Formulation of the Logic of Sense and Denotation," in Paul Henle, H. M. Kallen, and S. K. Langer, eds., *Structure, Method, and Meaning: Essays in Honor of Henry M. Sheffer.* New York, 1951.

Church, Alonzo, "The Need for Abstract Entities in Semantic Analysis." *Proceedings of the American Academy of Arts and Sciences,* Vol. 80 (1951), 100–112.

Cocchiarella, Nino, *Tense Logic: A Study of Temporal Reference.* Doctoral dissertation, University of California, Los Angeles, 1966.

Frege, Gottlob, "Über Sinn und Bedeutung." *Zeitschrift für Philosophie und philosophische Kritik,* Vol. 100 (1892), 25–50. Translated by Herbert Feigl as "On Sense and Nominatum," in Herbert Feigl and W. S. Sellars, eds., *Readings in Philosophical Analysis.* New York, 1949. Also translated by Max Black as "On Sense and Reference," in Peter Geach and Max Black, eds., *Translations From the Philosophical Writings of Gottlob Frege.* Oxford, 1952.

Gödel, Kurt, "Über formal unentscheidbare Sätze der Principia Mathematica und verwandter Systeme I." *Monatshefte für Mathematik und Physik,* Vol. 38 (1931), 173–198.

Goodman, Nelson, "On Likeness of Meaning." *Analysis,* Vol. 10 (1949), 1–7.

Goodman, Nelson, and Quine, W. V., "Steps Toward a Constructive Nominalism." *Journal of Symbolic Logic,* Vol. 12 (1947), 105–122.

Hilbert, David, and Ackermann, Wilhelm, *Principles of Mathematical Logic,* ed. with notes by Robert E. Luce, translated by Lewis M. Hammond, George G. Leckie, and F. Steinhardt. New York, 1950. Translation of *Grundzüge der theoretischen Logik,* 2d ed. Berlin, 1938.

Hintikka, Jaakko, "Existential Presuppositions and Existential Commitments." *Journal of Philosophy,* Vol. 56 (1959), 125–137.

Hintikka, Jaakko, "The Modes of Modality." *Acta Philosophica Fennica,* Vol. 16 (1963), 65–81.

Kalish, Donald, and Montague, Richard, *Logic: Techniques of Formal Reasoning.* New York, 1964.

Kalish, Donald, and Montague, Richard, "On Tarski's Formalization of Predicate Logic With Identity." *Archiv für mathematische Logik und Grundlagenforschung,* Vol. 7 (1965), 81–101.

Kaplan, David, *Foundations of Intensional Logic.* Doctoral dissertation, University of California, Los Angeles, 1964.

Kripke, S. A., "Semantical Considerations on Modal Logic." *Acta Philosophica Fennica,* Vol. 16 (1963), 83–94.

Leblane, Hugues, and Hailperin, Theodore, "Nondesignating Singular Terms." *Philosophical Review,* Vol. 68 (1959), 239–243.

Martin, R. M., *Toward a Systematic Pragmatics.* Amsterdam, 1959.

Martin, R. M., *Intension and Decision.* Englewood Cliffs, N.J., 1963.

Martin, R. M., "On Carnap's Conception of Semantics," in P. A. Schilpp, ed., *The Philosophy of Rudolf Carnap,* below. Pp. 351–384.

Martin, R. M., and Woodger, J. H., "Toward an Inscriptional Semantics." *Journal of Symbolic Logic,* Vol. 16 (1951), 191–203.

Montague, Richard, "Logical Necessity, Physical Necessity, Ethics, and Quantifiers." *Inquiry,* Vol. 4 (1960), 259–269.

Montague, Richard, and Kalish, Donald, "That." *Philosophical Studies,* Vol. 10 (1959), 54–61.

Morris, C. W., *Foundations of the Theory of Signs.* Chicago, 1938. This is Vol. I, No. 2, of *International Encyclopedia of Unified Science.*

Mostowski, Andrzej, *Sentences Undecidable in Formalized Arithmetic.* Amsterdam, 1957.

Prior, A. N., *Time and Modality.* Oxford, 1957.

Quine, W. V., *Mathematical Logic.* New York, 1940; rev. ed., Cambridge, Mass., 1951.

Quine, W. V., *From a Logical Point of View.* Cambridge, Mass., 1953; 2d, rev. ed., 1961.

Quine, W. V., "Two Dogmas of Empiricism," in *From a Logical Point of View,* above. Article II, pp. 20–46.

Quine, W. V., "Notes on the Theory of Reference," in *From a Logical Point of View,* above. Article VII, pp. 130–138.

Quine, W. V., "Reference and Modality," in *From a Logical Point of View,* above. Article VIII, pp. 139–159.

Quine, W. V., "Quantification and the Empty Domain." *Journal of Symbolic Logic,* Vol. 19 (1954), 177–179.

Quine, W. V., "Quantifiers and Propositional Attitudes." *Journal of Philosophy,* Vol. 53 (1956), 177–187.

Quine, W. V., "Carnap and Logical Truth," in P. A. Schilpp, ed., *The Philosophy of Rudolf Carnap,* below. Pp. 385–406.

Reichenbach, Hans, *Elements of Symbolic Logic,* New York, 1947.

Russell, Bertrand, *Introduction to Mathematical Philosophy.* London, 1919.

Russell, Bertrand, *An Inquiry Into Meaning and Truth.* New ork, 1940.

Schilpp, P. A., ed., *The Philosophy of Rudolf Carnap.* La Salle, Ill., 1964.

Scott, Dana, "Existence and Descriptions in Formal Logic," in *Philosopher of the Century.* London, 1966.

Strawson, P. F., "Truth." *Analysis,* Vol. 9 (1949), 83–97.

Strawson, P. F., "Carnap's Views on Constructed Systems Versus Natural Languages in Analytic Philosophy," in P. A. Schilpp, ed., *The Philosophy of Rudolf Carnap,* above. Pp. 503–518.

Tarski, Alfred, "The Semantic Conception of Truth and the Foundations of Semantics." *Philosophy and Phenomenological Research,* Vol. 4 (1944), 341–375.

Tarski, Alfred, "Some Notions and Methods on the Borderline of Algebra and Metamathematics." *Proceedings of the International Congress of Mathematicians,* Vol. 1 (1952), 705–720.

Tarski, Alfred, *Logic, Semantics, Metamathematics.* Oxford, 1956.

Tarski, Alfred, "The Concept of Truth in Formalized Languages," in *Logic, Semantics, Metamathematics,* above. Article VII, pp. 152–278.

Tarski, Alfred, "A Simplified Formalization of Predicate Logic With Identity." *Archiv für mathematische Logik und Grundlagenforschung,* Vol. 7 (1965), 61–79.

Tarski, Alfred, and Vaught, R. L., "Arithmetical Extensions of Relational Systems." *Compositio Mathematica,* Vol. 13 (1957), 81–102.

White, Morton, "The Analytic and the Synthetic: An Untenable Dualism," in Sidney Hook, ed., *John Dewey: Philosopher of Science and Freedom.* New York, 1950. Pp. 316–330.

DONALD KALISH

SEMANTICS, HISTORY OF. The scope of this article is in part determined by the following restrictions. (1) Although the development of semantics in the twentieth century equals or surpasses all that was done earlier, it receives very little attention here because the major theories and theorists of this period are thoroughly discussed in other articles. (2) The only semantic theories considered are those developed by Western philosophers; thus, no account is taken of the theories of meaning propounded, for example, by ancient Hindu philosophers or by European grammarians or linguists. (3) Since semantic theories concerning nonlinguistic signs tend to involve considerations of theories of knowledge generally, they are not discussed here except as they may occasionally bear directly on a theory of linguistic meaning. On the other hand, much of what philosophers have had to say about language is discussed here, whether or not it can be precisely described as semantics.

The contents of this article are arranged as follows.

ANTIQUITY
    The cosmologists
    The Sophists
    Conventionalism and naturalism
    Plato
    Aristotle
    The Stoics
    The Epicureans
THE MIDDLE AGES
    St. Augustine
    Boethius
    St. Anselm
    Abelard
    Impositions and intentions
    "Scientia sermocinalis"
    The properties of terms
    Syncategoremata
    Speculative grammar
THE RENAISSANCE AND ENLIGHTENMENT
    Semantics, logic, and epistemology
    Bacon
    Hobbes
    The "Port-Royal Logic"
    Locke
    Leibniz
    Berkeley
    Maupertuis and his critics
    Condillac
    Lambert, Hamann, and Herder
    The "idéologues"
    Universal grammar
THE NINETEENTH AND TWENTIETH CENTURIES
    Bentham
    Humboldt
    Johnson
    Mill
    Peirce and the pragmatists

Frege
Mauthner
Husserl and Meinong
Developments in the twentieth century

ANTIQUITY

The cosmologists. Since the earliest Greek philosophers were primarily cosmologists, their views on language are not the most fully developed (or best preserved) of their doctrines. Sources very late in antiquity attributed to Pythagoras (fl. 530 B.C.) the view that although the soul assigned names to things, it did so not arbitrarily but on the basis of a natural connection between them, somehow like that between mental images and their originals. Modern historians sometimes credit Heraclitus (fl. 500 B.C.) with having thought a great deal about language, but most of the fragments offered in evidence have to do with the *logos,* which surely is to be interpreted as the guiding principle of nature rather than as word or language. While we have nothing of his explicitly on language, it seems likely that Heraclitus did attach philosophical significance to the puns or contradictions in terms on which some of his paradoxical remarks depend.

Semantic theory seems to have made its first definite appearance in philosophy in the monism of Parmenides (fl. 475 B.C.), who maintained that only what was true was expressible. He evidently based this remarkable doctrine on the argument that a statement is false if and only if it contains a false name, but a false name is by definition a name lacking a real bearer and hence a name that names or expresses nothing. (His monism of course entailed that there was only one real name-bearer.) Thus he described several words, such as "becoming" and "perishing," as "mere names that mortals have established, believing them to be true"—that is, believing that there really are such processes, which Parmenides denied.

The Sophists. Language first became a subject of specialized inquiry among the Sophists, who, unlike their philosophical predecessors, were more interested in man than in the cosmos. That orientation alone would probably have drawn them to the study of language, but there was also the fact that they earned their livings teaching people to speak well. Economic as well as philosophical considerations therefore probably played a part in leading them to include at least grammar as an important part of their work. Protagoras (fl. 445 B.C.), the first of the Sophists, may also be considered the first grammarian. He distinguished the tenses and something like grammatical moods (classifying sentences as answers, questions, commands, and wishes), and he classified nouns as masculine, feminine, and "inanimate" (a division based on semantic rather than syntactic considerations, since it depended on the particular sex or lack of sex in the things the nouns were used to name). Grammar developed rapidly among the Sophists. Among the more philosophically interesting parts of grammatical theory to be found in Plato, who doubtless learned much of it from the Sophists, are distinctions between subject and predicate, between substantive and adjective, between the active and passive voices, and

among types of discourse—political, rhetorical, conversational, dialectical, and technical.

The Sophists originated semantical as well as grammatical inquiries. Prodicus (fl. 435 B.C.), who Plato thought was the best of the Sophists on language, seems to have operated on the hypothesis that there were no genuine synonyms, that where there were two words, there were two meanings. In Plato's dialogues Prodicus is depicted drawing instructive distinctions between "enjoyment" and "pleasure," "esteem" and "praise," "fearlessness" and "courage," for example; and he insisted on the study of "the right use of words" as the beginning of education. Protagoras, Prodicus, and Hippias (fl. 435 B.C.) are all credited with treatises on "the correctness of names," and Socrates (died 399 B.C.) is depicted discoursing on that subject in Xenophon's *Memorabilia* (III, xiv, 2–7).

Semantics may have become a theoretical issue for the first time in the paradoxical arguments propounded by Gorgias (fl. 435 B.C.) in support of his third nihilistic thesis. The three theses were (1) nothing exists; (2) even if something existed, it would be unknowable; (3) even if something existed and were knowable, it would be incommunicable. Gorgias gave four arguments for thesis (3) along the following lines. Suppose there really are things and they can be perceived by our senses. Then (*a*) some of those things will be perceivable by one sense only and others by another sense only; and since one sense cannot perceive objects proper to another sense, a system of audible signs will not permit communication regarding things perceivable only by sight, and so on for the other senses. In any case, (*b*) those supposed things are not identical with any signs one might use to communicate about them, and so one could never convey the things themselves to another person but only the signs. Moreover, (*c*) even if one could produce signs exactly representing those supposed things, he could not communicate those signs to another person, for the signs themselves are things, and no one can have in his mind the same things that someone else has in *his* mind at the same time. Finally, (*d*) any signs we might use would have to be formed as a result of our perception of those supposed things, but since genuine knowledge of a cause cannot be gained from its effect, no knowledge of those things could be communicated by means of any signs. Occasionally in arguments (*a*), (*b*), and (*c*) Gorgias seems, like Swift's Laputans, to have sophistically confused talking about things with handing them around; but not all his paradoxes of communication are transparent, and some passages in Plato and Aristotle suggest that Gorgias' arguments may have helped to shape their semantic theories.

Conventionalism and naturalism. The oldest surviving arguments in support of a particular semantic theory may be those attributed very late in antiquity to Democritus (fl. 420 B.C.), perhaps presented originally in his book *On Words.* He is supposed to have offered the following four considerations in support of his position that the relation between names and things named is conventional ($\theta\acute{\epsilon}\sigma\epsilon\iota$) rather than natural ($\phi\acute{\upsilon}\sigma\epsilon\iota$): (*a*) the occurrence of homonyms, that is, one and the same name for things different in nature; (*b*) the occurrence of synonyms, that is, different names for one and the same thing; (*c*) the occurrence of name-changes while the thing named remains the same in nature; (*d*) the nonoccurrence of verbal analogies corresponding with real analogies, for instance, there is a verb analogous to the noun "understanding" but none analogous to "justice."

In all probability no philosopher ever held a thoroughgoing semantic naturalism, although there are traces of tendencies in that direction in the doctrine attributed to Pythagoras and in the assumptions that appear to underlie the work of Prodicus and Gorgias. The opposition of naturalism and conventionalism as semantic theories forms the point of departure for the development of Plato's semantics of names in the *Cratylus*. Much of the significance of the *Cratylus* and of ancient philosophy of language generally has been obscured, from antiquity onward, by the confusion of this semantic issue with a dispute over the origin of language in which "naturalism" and "conventionalism" were the principal doctrines. In that dispute, however, it was not the naturalist but the conventionalist position that was preposterous, conventionalism in that context being the claim that language first arose as a result of agreements among men or because some especially powerful individual compelled those around him to use his names for things. There are, of course, implications for semantics in theories about the origin of language, but neither Plato nor any other ancient philosopher of the first rank failed to distinguish between the two inquiries.

Plato. The oldest surviving work of any kind on language is Plato's *Cratylus* (probably written about 388 B.C.). The main topic of this dialogue is the nature of the relation between names and things named.

The "Cratylus." At the beginning of the *Cratylus* a kind of semantic naturalism is attributed to Cratylus and a kind of semantic conventionalism to Hermogenes. All that is said about naturalism at the outset is that it seems unintelligible, and the first serious undertaking is a discussion of the conventionalism advanced by Hermogenes in these words:

> I cannot be persuaded that there is any correctness of name other than convention [ξυνθήκη] and agreement [ὁμολογία]. For it seems to me that whatever name anyone gives to a thing is the correct one, and if someone changes that name for another, the later one is no less correct than the earlier—just as when we change the names of our slaves. For no name has been generated by nature for any particular thing, but rather by the custom [νόμῳ] and usage [ἔθει] of those who use the name and call things by it. (384 C–D)

There is nothing in this conventionalism we have not already seen in the Democritean arguments except the claim that "whatever name anyone gives to a thing is the correct one," and Socrates immediately asks whether this claim is intended to apply to private persons as well as to nations (385A). Hermogenes fails to appreciate the difference, and when, as a result, Socrates is on the point of showing that this subjectivist claim destroys the possibility of distinguishing between true and false statements, Hermogenes tries to salvage it by suggesting an analogy

between arbitrary individual name-giving and different natural languages (385D–E). The picture presented is that of a conventionalist who recognized that the existence of different autonomous natural languages was strong confirmation of his position and was then so carried away as to produce a doctrine of autonomous idiolects, evidently reasoning as follows: Just as the Greek word for horse is no more and no less correct than the Persian word for horse, so there is no basis for correcting a Greek who should decide to use the Greek word "anthropos" where other Greeks use "hippos," and vice versa.

The conventionalism presented as a basis for discussion in the *Cratylus* is entirely plausible except for the obviously untenable doctrine of autonomous idiolects. One consequence of the doctrine is that at any given time a given thing (or type of thing) has just as many correct names as there are people who name it differently (385D). This suggests some sort of Protagorean skepticism in its author, but Hermogenes is ready to agree that "things have some fixed reality of their own, not relative to us or caused by us" (386D). Socrates uses this admission to show the necessity of objectively correct names. There are real things, he says, and real things are not subject to our whims. We recognize that we cannot do certain jobs involving real things simply by fiat. We must make the correct moves, using the correct tools, and the correct tools for a given job cannot be generally described as the first ones anyone may choose (386E–387B). Now in the use of language, names are our tools, and we employ those tools in doing two essential jobs plainly involving real things: "teaching" (communicating the truth) and "classifying things according to their natures" (387B–388B). If "whatever name anyone gives to a thing is the correct one," we clearly have no chance of succeeding in communicating the truth to one another or in developing classification schemes that will "carve reality at the joints."

The destruction of the doctrine of autonomous idiolects leaves a gap in conventionalism, a gap that was there in any case but that would not have been so easily seen if Plato had not thus deliberately marred this conventionalism in order to call attention to it. Not just anyone is an arbiter of the correctness of names; but then "who *does* provide us with the names we use?" (388D). The answer is derived from the sounder portions of Hermogenes' conventionalism, in which he claimed that custom or law generates our names for things. This suggests that the arbiter of custom, or the law-giver (νομοθέτης), may be identified as the name-maker (ὀνοματουργός) (388D–389A). The "law-giver" is Plato's personification of a recognized stipulative linguistic authority, more nearly like the French Academy or the *Oxford English Dictionary* than like an individual—Solon, for instance.

This refurbished conventionalism is adequate as far as questions of pronunciation, word order, and usage are concerned; these can be settled by having recourse to the recognized authority. The question raised by the criticism of autonomous idiolects, however, was not "how do we determine which names are *accepted*?" but, rather, "how do we determine which names are *correct*?" Plato took the two questions to be distinct and made his most important contribution to the semantics of names in answering the second of them. The development of his answer may be traced out as follows.

If the refurbished conventionalism is to do any more than offer an account of the phenomena of a language, it must be augmented by part of Cratylus' naturalism, which was originally stated in these three claims: "(*a*) for each of the things that really exist there is a correctness of name that has been produced by nature; (*b*) that is not a name which some people agreeing together to give as a name do give as a name, uttering a bit of their voice in accordance therewith; but (*c*) there is a kind of correctness of names that is the same for all, both Greeks and barbarians" (383A–B).

At the beginning of the dialogue this position was taken to be unintelligible because it was thought to be in competition with conventionalism as an account of the phenomena of a language. Claim (*b*) does seem to justify the view that the theory is just a wrong-headed account of that kind. Temporarily ignoring claim (*b*), Socrates proceeds to show that this naturalism makes sense as an account of the conceptual underpinnings of all languages. The fact that the word for horse in Greek is "hippos" and in Latin "equus" shows that different linguistic authorities are operative in different natural languages. Both those words are perfectly acceptable, intertranslatable names for horse; and what makes them so is the fact that each of them embodies in different marks (or sounds) a single "ideal name," which belongs to horse "by nature," whose correctness has been produced by nature, and which is the same for all, both Greeks, who say "hippos," and "barbarians,"· who say "equus" (389C–390A). That single ideal name cannot be the type of which occurrences of "hippos" or of "equus" are the tokens, since it is "the same for all." Nor can it be identified with what Plato called the form of horse, for although the form of horse may be the ideal *horse,* there is nothing of which it could conceivably be a *name.* Instead, the ideal name embodied as well in "equus" as in "hippos" is the correctly framed concept *horse,* and the difference between the two words is merely the difference between two equally good notations. To say that the concept is framed correctly is to say that it is the concept of the form rather than of individuals participating in that form; to say that its correctness has been produced by nature is to say that it somehow resembles the form. The correctly framed concept *horse* is a logically proper name of the form of horse; it is the ideal name for which all the words correctly translatable into English as "horse" are various notations.

Plato goes on to develop and apply this theory along the following lines. If we should come across a natural language the speakers of which owned horses and cows but had only one name for both species, or had no single name for horse, using instead an indifferently ordered string of names for legs, head, tail, and so on, then we should have a genuine case of incorrect names. The speakers of that language would be laboring under the influence of incorrectly framed concepts, concepts that fail to carve reality at the joints. Thus, we avoid incorrect names (such as "phlogiston") to the extent to which philosophy and science

(personified by Plato as "the dialectician") have provided us with a correct conceptual schema (390C–E). But the embodiment even of correctly framed concepts in the evolving phenomena of a natural language will sooner or later lead to the development of homonyms and synonyms, which, although not incorrect, are infelicitous for the purposes of science and philosophy. Such infelicities could be avoided if we were to construct a precise, consciously designed concept-notation for the use of philosophers and scientists (421E–423E, 424D–425A). And even if we do not or cannot actually construct it, the notion of a perfectly systematic embodiment of correctly framed concepts may serve as an ideal against which to measure the adequacy of technical language (435C). Thus, the frequently recurring project of an ideal language is to be found for the first time in the very first extant treatise on language.

Perhaps the single most unusual feature of this remarkable semantic theory is the doctrine of the ideal name. Within the *Cratylus* itself the identification of the ideal name with the correctly framed concept is not explicit, although it is clearly implied. That implication is strengthened by the many passages in other dialogues in which Plato did treat concepts as a kind of name—for instance, *Theaetetus* 189E, 206D; *Sophist* 263E; *Philebus* 38E–39A; *Phaedrus* 276A.

Cratylus' naturalism and Hermogenes' conventionalism are so expressed in the dialogue as to give every appearance of being simply Plato's devices for raising semantic questions. Each of them contains an obvious, completely gratuitous overextension. (Later in the dialogue [428A ff.] Cratylus' claim [*b*] goes the way of Hermogenes' autonomous idiolects.) Neither position alone is remotely plausible or likely to have been actually held by any philosopher, but each of them contains an essential ingredient of Plato's own semantics of names.

The "Parmenides" and the "Sophist." Plato's other major contributions to semantics occur in the later dialogues *Parmenides* and *Sophist,* in which he goes beyond the doctrine of the *Cratylus* in undertaking the connected tasks of (1) giving an account of the semantics of such names as lack existent bearers, (2) refuting the Parmenidean doctrine that false statements express nothing, and (3) giving an account of the semantics of simple statements.

(1) In *Parmenides* 160B–161A there is an attempt to state three necessary conditions for the meaningfulness of a denial of existence. (The example actually employed is the hypothesis "if a One does not exist," which is eminently generalizable.) If we are meaningfully to say of *x* that it does not exist, then (*a*) "there is knowledge of" *x* (since "otherwise the very meaning of . . . '[*x*] does not exist' would be unknown"); (*b*) *x* is "something different from other things"; (*c*) "this non-existent [*x*] has the characters of being *that,* and *something,* and of *being related to this,* or *to these,* and all other such characters. . . . If it does not exist, there is nothing against its having many characters; indeed it must [have many characters] if it is *this* [*x*], and not another, that does not exist. If what is [said] not to exist is neither *the* [*x*], nor *this,* and the statement is about *something else,* we ought not so much as to open our lips . . . ." These three interdependent condi-

tions do not seem inconsistent with the semantics in the *Cratylus,* and much of what was to be brought out later in the *Sophist* is already implicit in them—for instance, the distinction between existential and predicational occurrences of "is" ("if it does not exist, there is nothing against its having many characters").

(2) When Parmenides or Plato speaks of expressing nothing, he means saying nothing *meaningful,* rather than saying nothing *at all.* This is implied in Parmenides' fragments and is quite plain in Plato, when he says, for example, "Must we not assert that [a man] is not even expressing anything when he sets about uttering the words 'a thing that is not'?" (*Sophist* 237E; *Cratylus* 429E). Those words constitute what Parmenides called a false name. A true, or meaningful, name is one having an identifiable existent bearer, a name that signifies something real; and there is no sharp semantical distinction between true names and true statements—"If we are speaking the truth, evidently the things we are speaking of must be" (*Parmenides* 161E). Thus the Parmenidean doctrine is that false statements are meaningless, or that truth and meaningfulness are indistinguishable. Although its scope was never restricted, the doctrine makes most sense when applied to statements of the form "*x* exists," with which Parmenides was preoccupied. Such a statement, he would say, either is true or expresses nothing. In order to preserve the possibility of falsity, even in the limiting case of such statements, Plato had to question the Parmenidean dictum and establish that *what is not* has being in some respect (*Sophist* 241D), which he does in the complex, important doctrine of the interweaving of the Forms (252E–259C). However, his most direct answer to the Parmenidean doctrine is developed in his semantics of statements, an account based directly on the ontological theory just mentioned, since ". . . any discourse we can have owes its existence to the weaving together of Forms" (260A).

(3) "Now, remembering what we said about Forms, . . . let us consider words in the same way. . . . Words that when spoken in succession signify something, do fit together, while those that mean nothing when they are strung together do not" (261D–E). "Now a statement never consists solely of names spoken in succession, nor yet of verbs apart from names" (262A). Thus "the simplest and shortest possible kind" of statement is exemplified in "Theaetetus sits" or "Theaetetus flies," "because . . . it gives information about facts or events; . . . it does not merely *name* something but *gets you somewhere* by weaving together verbs and names. Hence we say it *states* something . . ." (262D). "Whenever there is a statement, it must be *about* something . . ." (262E). Both the examples above are about one and the same existent thing, the bearer of the name "Theaetetus," but the second is a combination of name and verb in which "what is different is stated as the same or [as is actually the case in this example] what is not as what is," and anything "answering to that description finally seems to be really and truly a false statement" (263D).

In the *Parmenides* and *Sophist,* then, Plato not only extended semantics for the first time beyond the consideration of names to that of statements but, in doing so, also distinguished between meaningfulness and truth, showing

for the first time that truth depends not merely on names but on certain syntactically regular combinations of verbs and names. It should be noted, however, that he does seem to have taken meaningfulness as the necessary and sufficient condition of grammaticalness.

Plato's semantics of statements may be better appreciated against the background of the semantical doctrines of his contemporaries Antisthenes the Cynic (fl. 390 B.C.) and Stilpo the Megarian (fl. 340 B.C.). Beginning with the familiar "two names, two bearers" view, Antisthenes managed to reject all predication, on the grounds that what the subject named was one thing and what the predicate named was quite another, and to accept only identity statements of the form "*x* is *x*" or analogies of the form "*x* is like *y.*" Stilpo, too, rejected predication, perhaps on ontological grounds, since he insisted on "the unity of being" and may have thought that this could be expressed only in strict identity statements.

Aristotle. Aristotle's primary interest in language was naturally that of a logician, and while his writings contain many passages on semantic questions, there is relatively little developed theory. His semantics of words (he treats of more than just names) is like Plato's in many respects and is to be found mainly in *De Interpretatione,* Chapters 1–3. There he presents, with little or no argument, the following account of signification.

Although there are different natural languages, the men who use them are confronted with the same extramental things. The mental modifications arising from that confrontation are *likenesses* (ὁμοιώματα) of the things, and they are thus the same for all men too. Within a given natural language, written words are conventional *symbols* (σύμβολα) of spoken words. (Aristotle was no doubt unaware of ideographic notations.) The spoken words are, in turn, related to the mental modifications, first of all as *symptoms,* or natural signs (σημεῖα), of them—that is, of the presence of mental modifications in the speaker. More important, the spoken words are related to the mental modifications in the same way that written words are related to spoken words, as *symbols* of them. Just as written words constitute a conventional notation for (or embodiment of) spoken words, so do spoken words for mental modifications. Discussions of these passages have almost invariably failed to recognize the first of the two relations between spoken words and mental modifications as distinct and have confused the second relation with that of name to bearer.

It seems that, according to this account, words signify things in virtue of serving as symbols of mental modifications resembling those things. What sorts of "things" can words thus be made to signify? Not much is said on that question in *De Interpretatione,* but in *Categories* (Ch. 5) and *Sophistical Refutations* (Ch. 22), for example, various words are said to signify (σημαίνειν) "a certain *this,*" "a qualification," "a substance of a certain qualification," "passivity," "a certain relation to something else," "a quantity," and so on. More important, "'man' and every common name signifies not a certain *this,* but a quality or a relation or a mode (or something of the sort)" (*Sophistical Refutations* 178b38).

Ambiguity, Aristotle maintained, is theoretically unavoidable, for since "names and the sum-total of formulas [λόγοι] are finite while things are infinite in number . . . the same formula and a single name must necessarily signify a number of things." This will, however, give us no trouble unless "we think that what happens in the case of the names happens also in the case of the things, as people who are counting think of their counters," which *are* in a one-to-one correspondence with the things counted (*Sophistical Refutations* 165a5). Although this passage is part of a warning against sophisms of ambiguity, when taken together with the preceding passage it seems to constitute an injunction against seeking *the* bearer of a common name, as Plato and so many of Aristotle's successors did.

A single individual is the bearer of many names in that they are all correctly predicable of it, but "we do not identify having one meaning with being predicable of one thing, since on that assumption even 'musical' and 'white' and 'man' [all of which are predicable of Socrates] would have one [and the same] meaning" (*Metaphysics* 1006b15).

The principal kinds of words recognized by Aristotle were the name (ὄνομα) and the verb (ῥῆμα—"predicate" is possibly a more accurate translation). He described them both as the smallest conventionally significant units, incapable of being true or false independently. A name without a bearer, such as "unicorn," is neither "false" (as some of his predecessors had claimed) nor nonsignificant; and a name combined with "is," "was," or "will be" always produces something true or false. A verb uttered by itself is a name, but it additionally signifies time and "some combination, which cannot be thought of without the components." Because of the latter additional signification, a verb "is always a sign (σημεῖον) of things being said of something else" (*De Interpretatione* 16b24, 16b7).

"Non-man" names nothing definite and so is not strictly a name; analogously, "does not walk" holds indifferently of all sorts of existents and nonexistents. These negated words Aristotle put into the separate categories of "indefinite names" and "indefinite verbs." "Inflections," such as "man's," are not names either, since they produce nothing true or false when combined with "is," "was," or "will be"—nor is "walked" a verb; it is an "inflection," because it signifies additionally "a time outside the present." In "complex names," such as "lifeboat," the parts are significant, but not independently, since, for example, "life" in this occurrence cannot be given an ordinary interpretation (*De Interpretatione*, Chs. 2 and 3). Finally, there are "connections" (σύνδεσμοι), words and phrases that "make many things one" (*Rhetoric* III, 12; 4), which seem to include particles, conjunctions, prepositions, and idiomatic phrases of several sorts and which in one passage of doubtful authorship are said to be nonsignificant (ἄσημοι) (*Poetics*, Ch. 20). (The "connections" are almost certainly the direct ancestors of Priscian's "syncategoremata," which figured prominently in medieval semantics.) This loosely organized classification, vaguely consistent at best, is based on a tangle of semantic and syntactic considerations, but it does contain important advances—for instance, in the treatment of names without bearers and complex names.

Aristotle's semantics of sentences is concentrated in but by no means confined to *De Interpretatione*, Chapters 4–8. Names have no significant parts and complex names no independently significant parts, but a sentence (λόγος) must have independently significant parts. (This is surprising in view of the fact that in a highly inflected language such as Greek there are frequent occurrences of one-word sentences—"I-walk," "he-walks," and so on.) "Every sentence is significant—not as a tool but . . . by convention," he maintained (16b33), apparently dissociating his view from Plato's in *Cratylus* 386D ff. Plato, however, was talking about names, not sentences, and Aristotle here seems to have gratuitously set aside an insight into the semantics of sentences that was later to be developed by the Stoics. Some sentences, such as "prayers" and future contingents, are neither true nor false according to Aristotle, and he set the pattern for nearly all logicians thereafter when he put such sentences aside and attended solely to the always true or false "statement" (λόγος ἀποφαντικός).

Aristotle maintained that among the independently significant parts of a statement there must be either a name or an indefinite name and a verb or an inflection of a verb arranged in such a way that the whole "signifies something about something." It is only in such a combination that there is truth or falsity, and, as Aristotle put it in the early chapters of *De Interpretatione*, it looks as if he took the combination in question to be one of *words*. In *Metaphysics* 1027b23, however, he said that "falsity and truth are not in things . . . but in *thought*; while with regard to *simple* concepts and essences falsity and truth do not exist even in thought . . . but . . . the combination and the separation are in thought and not in things," and he suggested something similar in *De Interpretatione*, Chapter 14 (and elsewhere), as well (cf. Plato, *Republic* 382B). There is no evidence that Aristotle distinguished consistently or clearly between sentences and what later philosophers called propositions or judgments, but such passages indicate at least his sense of the difficulty in locating truth in strings of words, or in a direct relation between strings of words and arrangements of things.

Aristotle seems sometimes to have considered the communicative capacity or public character of a locution as a criterion of its having independent significance. Thus in *Metaphysics* 1006a21 he remarked that if a man "really is to *say anything*," he must "say something that is significant *both for himself and another*"; and in support of his claim that when a verb is uttered by itself it is really a name and signifies something, he noted that on such an occasion "the speaker arrests his thought and the hearer pauses."

The Stoics. The nature of the Stoics' philosophy of language is the most tantalizing problem in the history of semantics. We know enough of it to say that it was by far the most intricate and probably the most insightful theory of its kind in antiquity and for centuries afterward; but we cannot be certain what its details were, and even its leading principles are sometimes obscured by vague or conflicting testimony. Those Stoics who had most to say about language were, naturally, the logicians, and the difficulty of determining the exact character of what they had to say stems from the fact that none of the many works of the Stoic logicians is extant. The best surviving sources (which date from almost five hundred years after the period of greatest development in Stoic logic and semantics) are Sextus Empiricus, *Outlines of Pyrrhonism,* Book II, and *Adversus Mathematicos,* Book VIII; and Diogenes Laërtius, Book VII. Under these circumstances it is seldom possible to assign a particular doctrine to a particular Stoic, but much of the best of their logic and semantics is very likely to be the work of Chrysippus (c. 280–206 B.C.).

Under the Stoic division of philosophy into physics, ethics, and logic, logic was divided into rhetoric and dialectic, and dialectic further divided into an account of language (περὶ τῆς φωνῆς) and an account of things signified (περὶ τῶν σημαινόμενων). Both these subdivisions contain material relevant to semantics. In their account of language the Stoics distinguished vocal sound generally, "which may include mere noise," from the sort that is articulate (ἔναρθρος), that is, capable of being embodied in written symbols (ἐγγράμματος). Articulate sound, in turn, may be nonsignificant—for instance, "blityri"—or significant (σημαντική); but for any articulate sound to be considered a *sentence* (λόγος) it must be significant *and* a product of someone's reason (Diogenes Laërtius 7.55–57).

Within that same branch of their dialectic the Stoics recognized five kinds of words and distinguished their semantic or syntactic functions. They were the first who clearly separated (1) names, such as "Socrates," from (2) appellatives (προσηγορίαι), such as "man." (Cf. Aristotle's similar but significantly different distinction in *De Interpretatione,* Ch. 7.) A name *"points out* a kind proper to an individual,"* while an appellative "*signifies* a common kind." (3) A verb *"signifies* a predicate"; (4) a conjunction *"binds together* the parts of a sentence"; (5) an article (possibly also what would now be called a relative pronoun) serves to *"distinguish* the gender and number of nouns" (Diogenes Laërtius 7.58). Thus the function of conjunctions and articles is purely syntactic, the semantic function of (proper) names is different from that of appellatives (or common names), and the appellative and the verb—the standard ingredients of the simplest kind of logicians' sentence—have one and the same kind of semantic function. The appellative occurring in a sentence signifies a subject and the verb a predicate or "something attachable (συντακτόν) to the one or more subjects."

Obviously the division between the accounts of language and of things signified was not exclusive, but the transition from the one account to the other as the Stoics conceived of them may be seen in the claim that all we *utter* (προφέρειν) is sounds, while what we *express* (λέγειν) is matters of discourse (πράγματα), or *lekta*—"expressibles" (Diogenes Laërtius 7.57). It is the doctrine of the *lekton* around which the Stoics organized their account of things signified. In its novelty, importance, and difficulty that doctrine overshadows all the considerable remainder of their philosophy of language.

The lekton. Probably the clearest introduction of the notion of the lekton is the one to be found in these passages from Sextus:

The Stoics . . . said that three things are linked together: (1) what is conveyed by the linguistic sign [τὸ σημαινόμενον], (2) the linguistic sign itself [τὸ σημαῖνον], and (3) the object or event [τὸ τυγχάνον]. Of these the linguistic sign is the sound—e.g., "Dion"; what is conveyed by the sign is the matter of discourse indicated thereby, which we apprehend over against and corresponding to our thought (while the barbarians do not understand, although they do hear the sound); and the object or event is the extra-mental entity—e.g., Dion himself. Two of these are corporeal—viz. the sound and the object or event—and one is incorporeal—viz. the matter of discourse conveyed by the linguistic sign, the lekton. . . . (*Adversus Mathematicos* 8.11–12)

They also say that the lekton comes into being as corresponding to a rational presentation [λογικὴν θαντασάν], and that a rational presentation is one presenting something that can be set forth in a sentence. (*Adversus Mathematicos* 8.70)

The kind of lekton associated with the name "Dion" was said to "stand in need of completion," and the only categories cited for such completable lekta were subjects and predicates. In order to be "set forth in a sentence," the completable lekta must enter into the composition of a lekton "complete in itself." The kind of complete lekton regularly associated with a standard subject-predicate sentence was called a statement (ἀξίωμα), and truth or falsity was ascribed to it, not to the sentence. Statements naturally received most attention from the Stoic logicians, but they recognized many other varieties of complete lekta as well. The fact that they did so strongly suggests that they had developed other categories of completable lekta too, for most of the other complete lekta cannot be analyzed into subject and predicate. Among the other varieties were commands, prohibitions, yes–no questions, questions requiring more than "yes" or "no," curses, prayers, doubts ("Can it be that life and pain are akin?"), and quasi statements ("How like to Priam's son the cowherd is!") (*Adversus Mathematicos* 8.71–73; Diogenes Laërtius 7.65–68).

Since these are categories of incorporeal lekta rather than of sentences, they cannot be identified with strictly grammatical categories. Moreover, although some of the distinct lekta do correspond to grammatically distinct sentences—for instance, the two kinds of questions—many of them do not. The Stoics' own example of the kind of lekton called a doubt was expressed in what is grammatically a yes–no question; commands and prohibitions get expressed in declarative as well as in imperative sentences, and occasionally both may be expressed in one and the same sentence, for example, "Abstain from strong drink." Thus Plutarch reports, in his attack on the Stoics, that "they themselves maintain that those who forbid *say* one thing, *forbid* another, and *command* a third. For he who says 'you ought not to steal' forbids stealing and commands not stealing at the same time as he says you ought not to steal" (*On the Contradictions of the Stoics* 1037d). As many as three different complete lekta may, then, be associated with a single sentence, and those lekta are obviously not to be identified as thoughts or intentions on the part of the speaker or hearer. Nor does it seem likely, despite Plutarch's way of presenting the doctrine, that all the complete lekta associated with a given sentence must be expressed whenever the sentence is uttered. Besides being far-fetched, that requirement would ignore the sense of express*ibility* built into the Stoics' technical term "lekton." Instead, the Stoic doctrine seems to be that a number of distinct linguistic jobs—such as stating, commanding, prohibiting—can be performed by means of a single sentence, depending on which of the complete lekta associated with that sentence is actually communicated on a given occasion of its use. Thus the three lekta associated with the example given by Plutarch may be presented as (1) the statement that one ought not to steal, (2) the command not to steal, and (3) the prohibition of stealing. It seems to be a discovery of the Stoics (and their greatest contribution to semantics) that the explication of meaning involves not only the things we talk about and the thoughts we express but also the jobs we do by means of language alone.

The Epicureans. Of the Stoic semantic triad—linguistic sign, what is conveyed thereby (the lekton), and external object or event—the Epicureans accepted only the first and third, ascribing truth and falsity directly to spoken sentences (Sextus Empiricus, *Adversus Mathematicos* 8.13). This rejection of the lekton is typical of the Epicureans' mistrust of any doctrine that went beyond the evidence of the senses. Plutarch describes them as "completely doing away with the category of lekta, leaving only words and objects and claiming that the intermediate things conveyed by the signs simply do not exist" (*Adversus Coloten* 1119F), but there is also a vague suggestion that they may have found it convenient to provide "lekta" as dummy referents in one important kind of case. "They deprive many important things of the title of 'existent,' such as space, time, and location—indeed, the whole category of lekta (in which all truth resides); for these, they say, are not *existents* [ὄντα], although they are *something* [τινά]" (*Adversus Coloten* 1116B). In stating their atomist metaphysics, the Epicureans were of course obliged to use such words as "space" and "time," and it looks as if they may have clumsily attempted to provide referents for them by associating only such words, or sentences containing such words, with lekta. However, even if they did maintain that there are two kinds of referents for words, real things and lekta, the latter to be invoked only in case the former are unavailable and the words are indispensable, there is nothing of the *Stoic* lekton in their doctrine.

Aside from this putative special use of special lekta, the Epicureans' philosophy of language seems to have remained remarkably faithful to their fundamental sensationalism. Epicurus (341–270 B.C.) had originally stressed the importance of beginning the study of physics (one of the main branches of Epicurean, as of Stoic, philosophy) by ascertaining the ultimate referents (ὑποτεταγμένα) of words, "so that our proofs may not run on untested indefinitely nor the terms we use be empty. The primary intent (ἐννόημα) of every term employed must be clearly seen and ought to need no explication" (Diogenes Laërtius 10.37–38); and he went on to claim that these ultimate referents must then be "our sensations," "present impressions," "actual feelings." These are always veridical since their immediate causes are the *eidola,* and thus "the agent productive of each of them is always entirely presented and, as being presented, is incapable of being productive of the presentation without being in very truth as it appears. . . . Thus the visible object not only appears but

actually is as it appears. . . . The presentations that occur are, then, all true" (Sextus Empiricus, *Adversus Mathematicos* 7.203–204). The square tower in the distance appears round, but its round appearance is itself a physical object, an *eidolon* detached from the tower and impinging on the apparatus of sight. If I say, then, "the tower is round," I may (and in this case I shall) be mistaken, since the tower is not the immediately presented object. But if I say "the appearance (or presentation) of the tower is round," I cannot be mistaken (at least not in that same way). Although this is a move in the direction of protocol sentences, it does not rest on a distinction between sense-datum and physical-object sentences, since for the Epicureans the protocol sentence was only a more correctly framed physical-object sentence.

No full account of this Epicurean reductivism is extant, but its principle is clearly operative not only in their physics but in their ethics as well, where one pervasive maxim for the avoidance of fear is to reduce the mysterious (for example, in natural phenomena) to what is actually presented and to describe it in terms precisely associated with the features of the actual presentation (see, for instance, Diogenes Laërtius 10.78 ff.).

Epicurus' followers evidently took the nature of the relation between words and sensations as a major topic for psychological theory. The notion of *prolepsis* is at the center of the Epicurean psychology, and in at least one of its many guises prolepsis seems to be the act of associating a word with a *typos,* or outline left in the mind as the result of repeated similar presentations. One example of prolepsis is the identification "such and such a thing is a man"—"for no sooner is the word 'man' uttered than we think of the typos of man in accordance with the prolepsis, the senses having led the way. As a result, the immediate referent of every name is apparent. . . . Nor would we have given a name to anything if we had not first come to know the typos of it in accordance with prolepsis" (Diogenes Laërtius 10.33). The typos, then, is the immediate referent (τὸ πρώτως ὑποτεταγμένον) of every name. When a name is used and understood, an act of prolepsis at once brings the corresponding typos to mind. (Since nothing but sensation can produce a typos, the need for some other sort of referent in the case of words such as "space" and "time" is apparent.) If this was indeed the core of the Epicurean semantics of words, it must be judged inferior to many other theories of its kind in antiquity.

Epicurus himself and the Epicureans generally had a good deal to say about the origin of language, and what they said usually makes better sense than most such accounts in antiquity. Lucretius (99–55 B.C.) is especially good on this topic, which he treated at some length in Book V of his poem. Among his more novel and interesting achievements is an extended series of arguments against the theoretical possibility that language (as distinguished from *a* language) might have been *invented* (*De Rerum Natura* 5.1041 ff.).

THE MIDDLE AGES

St. Augustine. Most of what St. Augustine (354–430) had to say about language and meaning was said not for its own sake but in support or elucidation of some theological doctrine. Partly for that reason, perhaps, his semantic doctrines had less effect on philosophy of language in the Middle Ages than might be expected, considering his enormous influence on medieval philosophy in general.

The short treatise *Principia Dialecticae* (probably written around 384, when Augustine was a professor of rhetoric) contains what may be the only instance of a semantic inquiry pursued by Augustine without a motive. In it he distinguishes four principal semantic elements: (1) the word (*verbum*), a spoken articulate sound, classifiable as a vocable of some language; (2) the expressible (*dicibile*), "whatever is sensed in the word by the mind rather than by the ear and is retained by the mind"; (3) the ordinary use of the word (*dictio*), (opposed, for instance, to the use of the word as a sign for itself), which involves "both [1] the word itself and [2] that which occurs in a mind as the result of the word" when the word occurs "not on its own account but on account of something else that is to be signified"; (4) the signified thing (*res*), which may be "something understood, or sensed, or inapprehensible"—the last category reserved for, for instance, God and formless matter (Ch. 5). Of these four elements, (2) and (3) together seem to represent different aspects of the Stoic lekton; but whatever their origin, their inclusion here indicates a level of sophistication in semantics that was not to be attained again for at least eight hundred years.

Chapter VII of the *Principia Dialecticae* is devoted expressly to the "import" (*vis*) of words. In it Augustine maintains that "the import of a word is that whereby the extent of its efficacy is recognized [*qua cognoscitur quantum valeat*], and it is efficacious to the extent to which it can affect a hearer." Import is a broader notion than signification and includes several sorts of effects a given word may have because of its sound, its degree of familiarity to the hearer, its degree of admissibility into polite conversation, its being recognized by the learned hearer as a dactylic foot or as some particular part of speech, and so on. The paradigm case of signification is described as occurring "on an occasion when a sign has been comprehended through a word [and] the mind regards [*intuetur*] nothing other than that very thing the sign it comprehends is a sign of. Suppose, for example, that Augustine has been named and someone to whom I am known thinks of nothing other than myself, or that some other man named Augustine comes to mind if the name happens to be heard by someone who does not know me but knows that other man." The most remarkable and apparently novel features of this brief account are (*a*) the extension of the notion of meaning in Augustine's doctrine of "import" and (*b*) the orientation of his account of meaning around the effects words have on their hearers. The remainder of the treatise deals with simple and conjoined words and sentences, etymology, and various types of ambiguity and obscurity.

The longest of Augustine's discussions of semantic questions occurs in the dialogue *De Magistro* (389), which is designed ultimately to support the Augustinian doctrine of "divine illumination" as the sole genuine source of truth. Thus the first 11 chapters are supposed to show that "we learn nothing through those signs that are called words" (Ch. X), while chapters XI–XIV develop the thesis that Christ, the truth, teaches us inwardly while men by

their use of outward signs merely prompt us to raise questions. The argument in support of the negative conclusion is an outstanding example of overemphasis on the word as the unit of signification. "When words are uttered, either we know or we do not know what they signify. If we know, then we do not learn but are reminded. If, on the other hand, we do not know, then we are not even reminded (though we may be prompted to ask)" (Ch. XI). Therefore, "we learn nothing through those signs that are called words"—as if one's knowing what the words mean in "armadillos are mammals" precluded one's learning anything through hearing that sentence uttered. At this crucial juncture in the dialogue Augustine's ulterior motive seems to have distorted his judgment.

Perhaps the most interesting point in the early chapters of *De Magistro* is one that bears on the best-known Augustinian passage on language, the description of his learning to speak in *Confessions* (397), 1.8, made famous by Wittgenstein's use of it in *Philosophical Investigations* (Sec. 1). The passage in the *Confessions* can hardly be considered a theoretical statement at all, since Augustine's main aim in it is to describe a milestone on his descent "into the stormy fellowship of human life," but it does contain a brief, uncritical account of one way in which a child might be shown "the things of which words are signs." That this account cannot be considered important in the context of Augustine's own views on language is plain from the fact that he had already criticized just such an account on theoretical grounds in *De Magistro*. In an attempt to refine the original suggestion of the dialogue that a sign cannot be a sign "unless it signifies something" (Ch. II), Augustine asks to be shown "that one thing itself, whatever it is, which is signified by these two words," *ex* and *de*, Latin prepositions there taken to be synonymous. After several obviously unsuitable suggestions, the tentative conclusion is reached that not only in these problematic cases but also in every case of attempting to show "the thing signified," all that can be shown is further signs, such as other words, pointing, pantomiming. This criticism is of course not the same as Wittgenstein's, nor is it particularly far-reaching in its own right, since it is soon modified to allow that we can in certain cases display the very thing signified without the use of further signs—for instance, if the thing signified is something we are able to do (such as walk) and we are not in the act of doing it when asked to display the thing signified (Ch. III).

A rather fully developed semantic theory appears in the *De Trinitate* (399–419), especially in 9.7–12 and 15.10–16, although it is presented no more for its own sake than is the theory in *De Magistro*. The theory appears as the explanatory half of an ingenious analogy designed to clarify (*a*) the relation between the First and Second Persons of the Trinity, (*b*) the two natures of the Second Person, and (*c*) the identification of the Second Person as the Word. The analogical points may be ignored for present purposes and the semantic doctrine sketched as follows. "Word" has at least two senses. "In one sense, those things are called words that occupy intervals of time with syllables, whether they are pronounced or only thought. In another sense, everything that is known is said to be a word impressed on the mind as long as it can be brought out of memory and defined . . ." (9.10). (Augustine actually introduces a third sense involving the love of what is known, but it seems pointless except for purposes of the analogy.) The second kind of "word," which Augustine describes more generally as a "locution" when the demands of the analogy are not uppermost in his mind, occupies the central position in the doctrine. "The word that sounds outwardly is a sign of the word that gives light inwardly, and the name 'word' is better suited to the latter; for what is uttered by the mouth of the flesh is the articulate sound of the word [*vox verbi*]; . . . [thus] our word becomes an articulate sound . . . by taking on [articulate sound], not by consuming itself so as to be changed into it" (15.11).

The doctrine of the inward locution sometimes bears a striking resemblance to Plato's doctrine of ideal names in the *Cratylus,* although a direct historical connection seems unlikely. "For of necessity, when we say what is true—i.e., say what we know—the knowledge itself, which we retain in memory, gives birth to a word that is altogether of the same kind as the knowledge from which it is born. For the thought formed by the thing that we know is a word that is neither Greek nor Latin nor of any other language. But since it is necessary to convey it into the knowledge of those with whom we speak, some sign is adopted by which it is signified" (15.10; cf. *Sermo* 225.3). According to this doctrine, then, it seems that one's saying "armadillos are mammals" embodies in sounds one's inward locution to that effect, which itself differs from one's knowledge that armadillos are mammals only in being brought out of memory into conscious thought. Augustine sometimes suggests that the inward locution, then, is not itself verbal; words used in the mind are not essentially different from words outwardly pronounced, as Augustine's first division claims. Indeed, the inward locution is evidently less a mental entity than the state of consciousness into which a mental entity, namely, a known truth, must be brought if it is to be given verbal expression.

Boethius. As an original contributor to semantics, Boethius (480–524) is much less interesting than Augustine. Since, however, his translations and commentaries constituted the sole source of Aristotelian logic for the medievals until the twelfth century, Boethius' influence over the development of semantics in the Middle Ages is powerful where Augustine's is slight.

Most medieval semantic theories take as their starting point Boethius' translation of the rudimentary account in Aristotle's *De Interpretatione,* Chapter 1. No doubt the traditional misreading of those passages during and after the Middle Ages is largely the result of the fact that in his otherwise faithful rendering Boethius obliterated the Aristotelian distinction between symbols and symptoms, translating both σύμβολα and σημεῖα as *notae.* Another of the principal difficulties in Aristotle's account—the apparent interposition of "mental modifications" between words and things—had been discussed at least as early as the third century by Alexander of Aphrodisias, whose confusing resolution of the difficulty was transmitted to the medievals in Boethius' second commentary on the *De Interpretatione.* Alexander had asked whether Aristotle's account forces us to consider the mental modifications as

names of things. In order to avoid that consequence he had developed the view that although "a name is imposed on a thing" and "although spoken words are names of things, nevertheless we use spoken words not in order to signify things, but in order to signify those mental modifications that are produced in us as a result of the things. Therefore, since spoken words are uttered for the purpose of signifying those entities, he [Aristotle] was right to say that they are primarily the signs [*notas*] of those entities" (413A–B; all references in this section are to J. P. Migne, ed., *Patrologia Latina,* Vol. 64).

Perhaps the most influential doctrine (at least in the late Middle Ages) that can be traced directly to Boethius' treatment of *De Interpretatione,* Chapter 1, is that of the three discourses: written, spoken, and mental. Citing Porphyry (c. 233–c. 305) as his authority, Boethius reported that "among the Peripatetics there were said to be three discourses [*orationes*]—one written in letters, another uttered in speech, and a third put together in the mind. Now if there are three discourses, the parts of discourse are no doubt likewise threefold; for since the noun and the verb are the principal parts of discourse, there will be some nouns and verbs that are written, others that are spoken, and still others that are silent and employed by the mind" (407B–C). Here, as in his transmission of the Aristotelian account itself, the vagueness of Boethius' presentation is as important historically as its content. Are there two completely different sets of nouns and verbs, one for writing and one for speech? And is this mental discourse nothing more than silently running over a sentence in Latin or English, or is it a nonverbal operation, reminiscent of Augustine's "inward locution"? The fact that mental discourse is said to have nouns and verbs of its own suggests the former view, if either; but since Aristotle had maintained that the mental modifications were the same for all (regardless of their native tongue), and since Boethius offers this doctrine of the three discourses in explanation of Aristotle's account, there is some basis for the second view as well. These were among the difficulties discussed in the medieval development of the doctrine.

The medieval distinction between words of first and second "imposition," a genuine prefiguring of the twentieth-century distinction between object language and metalanguage, also has its roots in Boethius' transmission of older doctrines. In his commentary on Aristotle's *Categories* he presents the distinction very much as he found it in Porphyry's *Expositio* of the same work (A. Busse, ed., pp. 57–58). "The first imposition [*positio*] of a name is made with respect to the *signification* of the word, the second with respect to its *form*" (159C). Thus, whenever some extralinguistic entity is called a man, it is a case of first imposition. "But when the word 'man' itself is called a noun, no reference is made to the signification of the word [Boethius has 'noun'], but to its form, in virtue of which it admits of inflection by means of [grammatical] cases" (159B–C). Thus "noun" in its ordinary use is a word of second imposition.

In this primitive form the distinction seems to apply only to the grammarian's kind of interest in discourse. Boethius, however, took the position that "the whole art of logic is concerned with discourse" (161C–D). How does the philosopher's interest in language differ from the grammarian's? Very much as the economist's interest in money differs from the numismatist's, for Boethius compares the signification of a word to the buying power of a coin and its grammatical form to the "bronze stamped with a design." Consider "an utterance that designates nothing, such as 'gargulus.' Although the grammarians, considering its form, contend that it is a noun, philosophy does not recognize it as a noun unless it is imposed in such a way as to designate a conception belonging to a mind (in which same way it can signify some real thing)" (408c–D). Apparently, then, second imposition needs to be more broadly conceived, or a philosopher's kind of second imposition must be added to the kind described by Boethius. The resolution of such difficulties was among the goals of the later doctrine of the impositions and "intentions" of words.

By far the most influential of Boethius' bequests to the Middle Ages was his formulation of the problem of universals in his second commentary on Porphyry's *Isagoge*. Needless to say, a great many semantic issues were discussed in the long controversy over universals, and a few of the more important ones will be noted below. Boethius' formulation of the problem, however, was oriented around questions of metaphysics rather than of semantics and so may be passed over here.

St. Anselm. One of the semantic problems recognized by the early medievals in the few logical works of Aristotle available to them was the problem of paronyms, or denominatives. Its principal source is the following passage in the *Categories*, Chapter 8 (10a27 ff.). "These, then, that we have mentioned are qualities, while things called paronymously because of these or called in some other way from them are qualified. Now in most cases, indeed in practically all, things are called paronymously, as the pale man from paleness, the grammatical from grammar, the just from justice, and so on."

St. Anselm (1033–1109) remarks at the end of his dialogue on denominatives—*De Grammatico*—that the semantics of denominatives was a favorite topic among dialecticians of the eleventh century, evidently because of the difficulty of developing a satisfactory account of denominative words that occur both as concrete nouns and as adjectives. (Anselm's chief example is *grammaticus*, but because the English word "grammatical" is not a denominative of this sort, "illiterate" will be used here.) Thus, the opening question of Anselm's dialogue is whether "illiterate" signifies a substance or a quality. This seems to be a narrow, perhaps artificial problem, but under his characteristically ingenious treatment it leads to results of general importance.

The superficially most plausible solution to the problem is that such a word sometimes signifies a substance—as in "not every illiterate is stupid"—and sometimes a quality (illiteracy)—as in "not every illiterate person is stupid." This solution is shown to fail, however, at least in its second half, for if we tried to use "illiterate" alone in speaking about the quality—as in "illiterate is a deplorable condition"—"not only the grammarians would be upset, but even the peasants would laugh" (Ch. XI). "Illiterate," we must recognize, "does not signify a person and illiteracy as a unit [*ut unum*] but signifies illiteracy directly

[*per se*] and a person indirectly [*per aliud*]" (Ch. XII). Another way to put the distinction between the two kinds of signification is to say that "illiterate" is *significative* of illiteracy and *appellative* of a person. "I now describe a name as appellative of each thing itself that is called [*appellatur*] by that name in the speaker's usage; for there is no speaker's usage in which 'illiteracy is illiterate' occurs, . . . but rather 'the person is illiterate' . . ." (*ibid.*).

The remainder of the dialogue refines and generalizes this account in the course of dealing with various objections to it. Anselm's most original and important contributions seem to be those developed mainly in the last two chapters (where the discussion centers around *albus*—"white"—rather than *grammaticus*). The Master of the dialogue has suggested that "white" signifies (rather than appellates) nothing but being in possession of whiteness (*habens albedinem*). This is disturbing to the Student, who feels the need of a signified *thing*. "White," he is willing to grant, "does not determinately signify this or that possessing entity, such as a body," but he wants to insist that it "indeterminately signifies something possessing whiteness." His principal argument is that " 'white' signifies either something possessing whiteness or nothing; but one cannot conceive of nothing as possessing whiteness; therefore it is necessary that 'white' signify something possessing whiteness" (Ch. XX).

In reply Anselm takes the position that while it may always be the case that what is signified somehow depends for its being on some real thing, it cannot always be the case that what is signified is a thing. His arguments for this position display an interesting use of the principle of substitutivity.

If "white" signified a thing at all, it would signify something white. Now the signification of a word is what its definition presents, and what is presented by the definition may be substituted for the word itself. "So wherever 'white' is used it is taken correctly as 'something white' " (Ch. XXI). Then "Socrates is white" may be rewritten as "Socrates is something white." But "wherever 'something white' is used it is also correctly said twice—'something something white'—and wherever it is said twice, there also three times, and so on indefinitely" (*ibid.*). Thus the plausible "Socrates is something white" would become the nonsensical "Socrates is something something white" and would ultimately lose all semblance of a statement.

Instead, in "Socrates is white," "white" appellates something white—Socrates himself—but what it signifies is being in possession of whiteness. Nor will it do to introduce a signified thing at *this* point, for if we take something in possession of whiteness to be what "white" signifies, we shall have to grant that something in possession of whiteness is that which is white. "If, therefore, 'white' is 'that which is white,' it is also 'that which is that which is white'; and if it is that it is also 'that which is that which is that which is white,' and so on indefinitely" (*ibid.*). The nonsense-engendering substitutions cannot be made within "being in possession of whiteness," however, since the denominative "white" does not itself occur in it. Thus "it is clear enough that 'white' does not signify something in possession of whiteness . . . , but only being in possession of whiteness—i.e., [the categories] *quality* and *possession* [and not the category *substance*]—and quality and possession by themselves make up no *something*" (*ibid.*). This argument is described as holding good for all single words that, like "white," signify "a plurality [of categories] out of which no one thing is made up" (*ibid.*).

Although the special consideration of denominatives apparently lost its vogue soon after Anselm, many of the problems dealt with in his *De Grammatico* remained current and can be found two centuries afterward at the center of the theory of the properties of terms (see below).

Abelard. The extensive logical writings of Peter Abelard (1079–1142) are best known for the theory of universals developed in them. That theory is important in the history of semantics because (*a*) it explicitly approaches the problem of universals as a semantic rather than a metaphysical problem and because (*b*) in doing so it introduces many of the elements of the semantic theories developed by the terminist logicians of the thirteenth and fourteenth centuries.

Regardless of how the problem of universals is approached, it involves a consideration of the semantics of words, especially of common names. Nevertheless, many of the countless medieval theories, in their preoccupation with the Porphyrian–Boethian questions about the existential status of genera and species, slighted or ignored the semantic issues. Abelard, on the other hand, began by adding a new semantic question to the three traditional metaphysical questions. "Could a universal consist of the signification of a concept [*significatione intellectus*] when the things named were destroyed, as [in winter] when there are no roses to which the name 'rose' is common?" (*Logica* "*Ingredientibus*," B. Geyer, ed., p. 8).

Having associated universals with words, Abelard asked "whether they are associated *only* with words or with things as well" (p. 9). Applying the Aristotelian criterion *predicability of more than one thing*, he showed in a series of elaborate arguments that a universal cannot be identified as (1) a single thing or (2) a collection of things (pp. 10–16). His principal objection really avoids the issue of whether or not it makes sense to speak of a thing or a collection as predicable at all and concentrates instead on the impossibility of predicating a thing or a collection of more than one thing. Thus "it remains for us to ascribe universality of that sort to words [*vocibus*] alone" (p. 16). As Abelard came to realize, words considered as utterances or inscriptions are themselves things. Accordingly he eventually distinguished between utterances [*voces*] and words [*sermones*] and organized his theory of universals around words in this strict sense—*sermo = vox + significatio*—which he described as products of human arrangements rather than mere natural effects (*Logica* "*Nostorum Petitioni Sociorum*," B. Geyer, ed., p. 522).

The only kind of word to which universality can conceivably be ascribed is the kind of word apparently predicable of more than one thing, that is, a common name in the nominative case. But that ascription cannot mean that the common name has some universal thing as its bearer, for, as he had shown, "universal thing" is a contradiction in terms. Nor can some particular thing be picked out as its bearer, for although it *may be* Socrates alone of whom the statement "a man is sitting in this house" is true, we can-

not *infer* from it that Socrates is sitting in this house (p. 18). These considerations led Abelard to base the ascription of universality not on what the words name (*nominare*)—for example, "man" names each and every individual thing that is a man—but on their "mode of signification"; for although they name things that are discrete, they do so not "discretely and determinately" but "confusedly" (p. 29).

Abelard's explanation of this notion of confused naming, which was to play an important part in thirteenth- and fourteenth-century theories of the properties of terms, seems incomplete but runs along the following lines. "To signify is to establish [*constituere*] a concept" (p. 136), and "when I hear 'man' . . . I do not recall all the natures or properties that are in the things subject [to that name]; instead, as a result of [hearing] 'man' I have a conception of animal, rational, and mortal, though not of subsequent accidents as well, [a conception that is] confused rather than discrete" (p. 27). Thus Abelard's answer to his additional semantic question is a qualified "yes." In winter the name "rose" lacks universality in that there are no things of which it is predicable, that is, "it is devoid of nomination" (*nominatione*). "Nevertheless, it is still significative then in virtue of the concept [*ex intellectu*]; . . . otherwise there would not be the proposition 'no rose exists'" (p. 30).

Other medieval theories of universals, such as Ockham's, center on semantic doctrines; but Abelard's "sermonism" was perhaps the most important medieval influence on the development of semantics during the succeeding two centuries of the high Middle Ages. Topics and terminology remained relatively stable in that remarkable period in the history of semantics, although many philosophers and every logician contributed to the discussions. For that reason the remaining material on the Middle Ages is oriented mainly around *topics* in medieval semantics, and no attempt is made to mention every man who discussed them.

Impositions and intentions. The pervasive medieval distinctions between two levels of signification have attracted some attention in the twentieth century because of their resemblance to the object language–metalanguage distinction. Historically there were two such distinctions, both based on the observation, found already in Porphyry, that while some signs signify nonsigns, others are signs of signs.

The original distinction was drawn with respect to conventional signs, specifically, with respect to names (nouns and adjectives) in a natural language. Such signs acquired their signification only as a result of having been imposed by the users of the language. The primary, or first, imposition was on extralinguistic entities, and names such as "man" and "white" were classified as names of first imposition. As the language developed, other conventional signs were imposed on conventional signs as such; thus, names such as "noun" and "plural" are of second imposition. Names such as "utterance" and "mark" do signify conventional signs, but not as such (since there are of course nonsignificant utterances and marks); they are therefore names of first imposition. Most medieval logicians, presumably in avoidance of an infinite regress, were careful not to define names of second imposition as names of names of first imposition. Thus "name of second im-position" is itself a name of second imposition. But even those who, like Abelard (*Logica "Ingredientibus,"* B. Geyer, ed., p. 112), did define second imposition in terms of first seem never to have recognized a "third" imposi-tion. (The imposition distinction, therefore, cannot reason-ably be described as prefiguring a hierarchy of types.) The use made of the imposition distinction was apparently rather meager. Aristotle's categories were, for example, often said to be names of first imposition, while the subject matter of his *De Interpretatione* was described as names of second imposition. The distinction, although it was refined and discussed well into the fifteenth century, seems to have acquired what importance it had mainly from its connection with the later and better known of the two distinctions between levels of signification.

Concepts in their capacity as natural signs were called intentions and described in the doctrine of the three dis-courses as mental terms. It was only natural, then, to dis-tinguish levels of signification among intentions as among conventionally significant extramental terms. This distinc-tion, probably stemming from Avicenna (see Carl Prantl, *Geschichte der Logik im Abendlande*, 2.328), classified as first intentions all those naturally significant of entities other than intentions as such, while those that did natu-rally signify intentions as such were second intentions. The concept *humanity* is of course a first intention, but so is the concept *mental entity*. The concepts of the predicables —*genus, species, differentia, property, accident*—are sec-ond intentions, as is the concept *predicable* itself; no "third" intentions were ever recognized.

Thus first and second intentions and impositions were fundamentally parallel distinctions in separate domains. However, their development in the thirteenth and early fourteenth centuries was complicated (and sometimes confused) by two factors. First, there were, of course, ex-tramental terms imposed on first and second intentions, such as "humanity" and "genus." Such names were all of first imposition (since no intention was a conventional sign), but they were sometimes further described as names of first or second intention. Second, even more complicat-ing was the fact that the first and second intentions them-selves were considered to be terms in mental propositions. Thus, while in the written proposition "*animal* is a genus" the subject and predicate terms are both of first imposition, in the corresponding mental proposition that *animal* is a genus the subject term is a first intention and the predicate term is a second intention.

Of the two distinctions between levels of signification, the intention distinction had much more philosophical importance. The confusing interrelations of the two dis-tinctions are perhaps best exhibited in William of Ockham (died 1349), particularly in *Summa Logicae*, I, 11–12. Logicians after Ockham—for instance, Albert of Saxony (died 1390), Pierre d'Ailly (1350–1421), Paul of Venice (died 1428), and Paul of Pergula (died 1451)—exhibited a tendency to simplify them by reverting to the treatment of impositions and intentions as strictly separate, parallel distinctions. Post-medieval scholastics—for example, John of St. Thomas (1589–1644)—were inclined to apply the intention distinction indifferently to extramental as well as

to mental terms and to ignore the imposition distinction; it is in this simplified form that the "medieval" distinction between levels of signification is usually discussed in recent literature.

"Scientia sermocinalis." Almost everything genuinely novel in medieval logic is to be found in the theories of the properties of terms and of the functions of syncategore-matic words developed by the logicians of the high Mid-dle Ages. One reason why logic set off along that line of logicosemantic inquiries is that medieval logicians, es-pecially through the formative period ending about 1250, thought of their subject as the science of language (*sci-entia sermocinalis*).

That classification itself marked a break with the Aristo-telian–Boethian tradition in that it was precise where the tradition had been vague. The notion of predication was unquestionably an essential part of the subject matter of logic, but Aristotle and Boethius had treated it in ways that often suggested that predicates might be extralinguistic and even extramental entities. This crucial vagueness, which was to some extent also the source of the medievals' concern with universals, left open the possibility that logic might be essentially a science of reality, resembling or subsumed under metaphysics.

However, in the earliest complete European logic we have after Boethius—the *Dialectica* of Garland the Comput-ist (died before 1102)—that possibility was already noted and explicitly ruled out. Predication, Garland maintained, occurs only in a proposition, and the only constituents of propositions are utterances; thus, only utterances may be predicated. The five predicables (genus, species, differ-entia, property, accident), the elementary subject matter of medieval logic, are, in virtue of being predicables, utter-ances and no more; and the ten categories (substance, quality, and so on) are likewise categories of utterances only—for instance, noun and adjective (*Dialectica*, L. M. de Rijk, ed., p. 3).

The attempt to establish logic as a science of linguistic entities only may be called sermocinalism. During the years 1150 to 1250, when medieval logic was acquiring its distinctive character, sermocinalism held undisputed sway as the philosophy of logic, but it did so in the refined and strengthened form given it in the writings of Peter Abe-lard. Garland had attempted to make utterances (*voces*) the elements of logic, which he thought of as the science of language. Abelard, recognizing that utterances are physical events which are, as such, of no interest to logicians, re-placed the overly simple utterance with what he called the *sermo*, defined as the utterance taken together with its signification. Logicians in the second half of the twelfth century seem to have been unanimous in their adoption of this refinement. An anonymous *Dialectica seu Logica* supported the rejection of utterances as the elements of logic with the following interesting argument, somewhat reminiscent of Aristotle's doctrine of complex names. "Some utterances are significant; some are not. . . . This division . . . is exhaustive but seems not to be exclusive, since the same utterance may be both significant and not significant. For example, the utterance 'king' [*rex*] is significant as a word, but since it is also part of a word, a syllable of a word—as in 'smoking' [*sorex*, shrew]—it is in that case and on that account not a significant utterance" (Martin Grabmann, *Bearbeitungen,* Berlin, 1937, p. 30).

Having more precisely identified the elements of logic as linguistic entities, Abelard suggested that logic as the science of language should determine significations on the basis of the application of utterances, determining the proper application of utterances on the basis of the investigations of the natural sciences (*Dialectica,* pp. 286–287). One reason for this suggestion seems to have been his concern with propositions true *gratia terminorum,* analytically true on semantic rather than on syntactic grounds— for instance, "if there is paternity, there is filiation" or "if it is a body, it is corporeal" (see pp. 284–286).

To most medieval philosophers Abelard's emphasis on the importance of signification as well as of utterance might have suggested that mental entities of some sort were to be considered the elements of logic. He explicitly rejected this possibility, however, and in doing so made his most important contribution to sermocinalism. He argued that a proposition true *gratia terminorum* could not be verified by an appeal to the status of mental entities. "When we say 'if it is man it is animal,' if we refer to the connection of the *understanding* of the propositions, as if we were concerned with the *concepts,* there is no truth to the conditional, since the one *concept* may occur entirely without the other" (p. 154). What we are concerned with, Abelard maintained, is the connection between the *term* "animal" and the *definition* of the term "man"—namely, the inclusion of the term "animal" within the string of terms making up the definition of the term "man." As a result of this move, sermocinalism was directed not only against the notion of logic as a science of reality (*scientia realis*) but evidently also against the notion of it as the science of reason (*scientia rationalis*).

The philosophy of logic that eventually challenged sermocinalism concentrated its opposition on this last point. Since it was explicitly drawn from the philosophy of Avicenna, the rival doctrine may conveniently be called Avicennianism. Although as many of Avicenna's writings as were available to the medievals had been translated into Latin around the middle of the twelfth century, Avicennianism as a philosophy of logic seems not to have come into prominence until Albert the Great (1193–1280) adopted it around the middle of the thirteenth century. By that time, however, medieval logic was firmly committed to its distinctive line of development as the *scientia sermocinalis.* As a result, the main impact of Avicennianism as an alternative to sermocinalism was felt less on the work of the logicians than on the metaphysicians' discussions of the nature of logic.

The central doctrine of Avicennianism is presented in the frequently quoted passage from Avicenna's *Philosophia Prima:* "The subject matter of logic, as you know, is intentions understood *secondarily,* which are applied to intentions *primarily* understood . . ." (I, 2, f70vA). Logic was the science of reason, Avicenna claimed, for "the relation of this doctrine [logic] to internal thought, which is called internal speech, is just like the relation of grammar to outward signification, which is called speech" (*Logica* f3rA). Thus grammar, not logic, was the sermocinal science, according to Avicennianism, and the rise of specu-

lative grammar that was to follow may in part be attributed to this point of view.

The properties of terms. Until about the middle of the twelfth century the subject matter of medieval logic was drawn from Aristotle's *Categories* and *De Interpretatione,* together with a set of books by Porphyry and Boethius that were centered more or less closely on those two books of Aristotle. Later in the Middle Ages this collection of books, or the kind of logic these books contained, became known as *logica vetus,* the old logic. When the remaining four books of Aristotle's Organon began to circulate in western Europe during the twelfth century, they, or their contents, became known as *logica nova,* the new logic. The only completely new kind of material in the *logica nova* was the treatment of fallacy in Aristotle's *Sophistical Refutations,* which excited a tremendous interest in *sophismata,* fallacies resulting from the misuse of or natural ambiguities in various devices of ordinary discourse. Largely because of this lasting interest, medieval logicians of the late twelfth and early thirteenth centuries gradually developed an original logicosemantic inquiry. In order to distinguish this genuinely medieval contribution from Aristotle's contributions to logic, thirteenth-century philosophers began to speak of it as the *logica moderna,* lumping the *logica vetus* and *logica nova* together as *logica antiqua.* Perhaps the *logica moderna* was aimed originally at nothing more than providing *ad hoc* rules of inference to cover problematic locutions in ordinary discourse, but, although it retained that aim throughout its three-hundred-year history, its principal aim soon became the development of a reasonably general account of the different ways in which words are used to stand for things and to operate on other words.

The earliest known fully developed productions of the "modernist" or "terminist" logicians are the logical treatises of William of Sherwood (died 1266/72), Peter of Spain (died 1277), and Lambert of Auxerre (fl. 1250), evidently written at Paris about the middle of the thirteenth century. At that time the *logica moderna* seems to have been thought of as having two branches, an account of "the properties of terms" (*proprietates terminorum*) and an account of the signification and function of "syncategorematic words" (*syncategoremata*). The two branches naturally differed in detail, but both accounts employed the same principles of explanation and had the same aims. Most nouns, pronouns, verbs, participles, and adjectives were considered to be categorematic words, words capable of serving as terms (that is, as subjects or predicates); and the syncategorematic words were those which can occur in a statement only together with categorematic words. The two branches of the *logica moderna* were thus theoretically exhaustive of the kinds of words occurring in various roles in statements.

The modernists of the thirteenth century regularly recognized four properties of terms: (1) signification—the word's meaning, broadly conceived, or the range of conventional uses of the word (a property of every categorematic); (2) supposition—the conventional interpretation of a word on a particular occasion of its use, a modification of its signification resulting from its syntactic context, if any, and other considerations (a property only of nouns, pronouns, and "substantive expressions," that is, other categorematics employed as substantives and particularly as subjects); (3) copulation—virtually the same as supposition, except that it is a property only of verbs, participles, and adjectives, especially when they occur as predicates; (4) appellation—"the present correct application of a term" (Sherwood), a property only of nouns, adjectives, and participles; for instance, in 1965 Chicago is an appellatum of "city" but Nineveh is not.

Obviously these four properties are not on an equal footing. The supposition, copulation, or appellation of a term was considered a function of its signification; Vincent of Beauvais (died 1264) even designated signification the genus of which the other three are species (Carl Prantl, *Geschichte der Logik*, Vol. III, p. 83, n. 319). Moreover, copulation and appellation are of distinctly secondary importance. By the middle of the fourteenth century only signification and supposition were regularly recognized as properties of terms, and throughout the history of the *logica moderna* it was the supposition (*suppositio*) of terms on which the inquiry centered. For that reason the best way of quickly acquiring a broad but accurate idea of the modernists' account of the properties of terms is to examine their divisions of supposition. (The recognition and treatment of the divisions of course differed from one modernist to another, but the following selection includes all the major divisions and many of the more interesting minor divisions.)

The supposition of a term was divided initially into *proper* and *improper* supposition. A term had improper supposition when it was used figuratively, and several varieties of improper supposition were distinguished: antonomastic, synecdochic, metaphoric, ironic, and metonymic. The proper supposition of a term was divided into *formal* and *material* supposition, the latter being the use of a term to refer to itself, either as type or as token—for instance, "*man* is a noun," "'*man is an animal*' is a true statement," "*man* is a monosyllable," "*man* has three letters." Formal supposition was *personal* if the term was used to refer to individuals bearing the form signified by the term, *simple* if the reference was to the form itself, as in "*man* is a species." The initial division of personal supposition was sometimes based on the division of terms as *common* or *discrete*, depending on the possibility of using them to refer to more than one individual at a time. Thus, the subjects of the statements "*Socrates* is running" and "*that man* is running" have discrete personal supposition.

The portions of supposition theory dealing with the divisions of the personal supposition of common terms were more fully developed than the rest, not only because they were intrinsically more interesting but probably also because they provided the most points of contact between the *logica antiqua* and the *logica moderna*. In those portions of supposition theory, far more than in the others, the emphasis lay on the application of the theory to the evaluation of inferences, especially such inferences as involved Aristotle's four categorical propositions (or near relatives of them) but could not be adequately evaluated within the *logica antiqua*.

A common term was said to have *determinate* personal supposition when it was used to refer to some one individual without identifying the supposited individual, as in "a *man* is running" or in "some *man* is running." A statement including a "distributive sign" (such as "every" or "no") was, on the other hand, bound to include one or more common terms having *confused* personal supposition, terms used to refer to more than one individual at once or to one individual many times (as in "every man sees a *man*," where the second occurrence of "man" has confused supposition even if it is being used to refer to only one individual). If the confused supposition included each and every individual bearing the form signified by the common term, it was designated *distributive*, as in "every *man* is an animal," "no *man* is an *ass*." If the confused supposition did not plainly include that totality, it was designated *merely confused* (*confusa tantum*), as in "every man is an *animal*," "every man sees a *man*."

The modernists observed that in many cases of distributive confused supposition it was possible to make a "descent" under the term having such supposition, instantiating as in "every man is an animal, therefore this man is an animal"; "no man is an ass, therefore no man is this ass." They described such cases as *mobile* but paid at least as much attention to the *immobile* distributive supposition produced by the use of "exclusives" or "exceptives" together with distributive signs. Thus, in "only every man is running" the distributive supposition of the common term is immobilized by the exclusive "only," so that one cannot infer "therefore only this man is running." It was also recognized that the inclusion of the distributive sign within the scope of the exclusive or exceptive was not always dependent on their relative positions in the statement, since from "every man except Socrates is running" one cannot infer "therefore this man except Socrates is running" (although this unacceptable inference is uninterpretable rather than invalid).

Supposition theory was an attempt to develop a unified treatment of a great number of semantical and logical topics that are still of interest, although now for the most part they are treated in separate inquiries. It is therefore especially intriguing and difficult to discover just what that unifying notion—supposition—amounted to. One broad description that plainly holds good for most of the divisions of supposition is that they are syntax-dependent referential functions of a term's signification. Any description in terms of syntax and semantics will, however, fail to cover all the divisions of supposition and will miss what is distinctive in it. In the case of improper supposition, for example, while the circumstances under which a term is used clearly do determine whether or not it is being used figuratively, it will not do to limit those circumstances to the syntactic context of the term's use. Again, supposition theorists frequently remarked on the fact that the supposition apparently determined by the syntax often differs from the supposition intended by the framer of the statement. The man who visits his friend's garden and says "this plant grows in my garden" says what is false "with respect to discourse" (*de virtute sermonis*), but the circumstances of his utterance show that he intends to use the word "plant" as in the statement "such a plant grows in my garden." The correct analysis of the suppostion of "plant" takes it to have the supposition determined for it *not* by that syntactic context but by the clearly discernible "intention of the framer" (*intentio ponentis*). Finally, among later supposition theorists it was a matter of controversy whether terms occurring in statements written in a closed book had any supposition at all, and those few who held that they did then have supposition seem to have been motivated by a misguided concern that otherwise certain true statements in a closed book, such as "God exists," might cease to be true while the book remained unread.

The consensus of the modernists seems to have been that a term had one or another kind of supposition only on an occasion of its actually being used in referring (or understood to have been used in referring) to some entity or entities, the particular kind of supposition being determined by a number of the circumstances of the occasion and its syntactic context being the most important but not in itself the decisive circumstance.

Syncategoremata. Within the *logica moderna* the investigation of syncategorematic words complemented the investigation of the categorematic words under the doctrine of "the properties of terms." Something closely resembling the modernists' notion of syncategoremata seems to have been operative in Aristotle and the Stoics, but the medievals evidently acquired the technical term and the rudiments of the notion directly from Priscian (fl. 500), who had reported that "according to the dialecticians [not identified], there are two [principal (?)] parts to a sentence—the noun and the verb—since they alone and of themselves make a sentence; but they called the other parts *syncategoremata*—that is, consignificants" (*Institutio de Arte Grammatica*, M. Hertz, ed., in H. Kiel, *Grammatici Latini*, Leipzig, 1855, Vol. II, p. 54).

Interest in the syncategoremata as such began in connection with the twelfth-century interest in fallacies of ambiguity as it became plain that the crucial ambiguity was often located elsewhere than in subjects and predicates. The grammatical basis of distinction provided by Priscian seems to have been adopted at first and occasionally even narrowed so that only the "indeclinables"—prepositions and conjunctions—were considered to be syncategoremata (see the anonymous late twelfth-century *Fallacie Parvipontane*, L. M. de Rijk, ed., in *Logica Modernorum*, Vol. I, p. 559; also see Abelard, *Dialectica*, L. M. de Rijk, ed., pp. 118–121). The notion of syncategoremata that became important in the *logica moderna*, however, was not founded on a strictly grammatical distinction. Abelard's treatment of "alone" in "a man alone is capable of laughter" (*Logica "Ingredientibus,"* B. Geyer, ed., p. 483) prefigured the pattern that was to be followed by the modernists. He pointed out that if "alone" is taken to be part of the subject, the statement is about a man who happens to be by himself, while if "it is attached to *the predication*" it denies the capacity for laughter to all nonmen, as if to say: 'a man is capable of laughter in such a way that nothing else is capable of laughter.' "

When the investigation of syncategorematic words appeared as a separate inquiry in the treatises on syncategoremata by William of Sherwood and Peter of Spain (first half of the thirteenth century), the distinguishing characteristic of syncategorematic words was the fact that they had some effect on the relation between the categorematic

words—that is, the predication or the "composition"—or on the relation between two predications or compositions. Thus Sherwood's inventory of syncategoremata, most of which became standard, included the verbs "begins" and "ceases" and the noun "nothing" as well as grammarians' syncategoremata such as "every," "both," "except," "alone," "is," "not," "necessarily," "if," "unless," "and," and "or." The standard syncategoremata, then, cannot be completely described as a selection of logical operators, although they plainly included such a selection. Nor was the investigation of them aimed primarily at uncovering their strictly formal properties. Many of the rules put forward in connection with one or another syncategorema were rules of inference—such as "When there are two distributions over one and the same part of a locution, the first immobilizes the second" (Sherwood)—but just as many were semantic rules—such as "The sign 'every' or 'all' requires that there be at least three appellata [for the term to which the sign is attached]" (Sherwood)—and there seems to have been no clear distinction drawn between the two sorts of rules.

The modernists' treatises on syncategoremata presupposed the doctrine of the properties of terms, as is shown by the rules given just above, and much of their discussion of the function of such words is in terms of the various modifications of supposition produced within the scope of one or another syncategorema. (The problem of determining the scope of syncategoremata, especially in contexts including more than one, was particularly important in these investigations.) In this way the syntactic and semantic questions about syncategoremata were essentially interconnected. Sherwood at least among the older modernists was sometimes concerned to discuss the *signification* of syncategoremata—"every," for example, was said by him to signify universality—but that seems to have been a feature of his unusual doctrine that in order to be significant a word had to signify some *form*. Most writers on syncategoremata took up Priscian's really unjustified translation of the Greek *syncategoremata* as "consignificants" and used it as the basis for their view that "strictly speaking, a syncategorema signifies nothing, but when added to another word it makes that word signify something, or makes it supposit for something or some things in some definite way, or exercises some other function having to do with a categorema" (William of Ockham, *Summa Logicae*, I, 4; cf. the remarks of John of Salisbury in *Metalogicon*, Book I, Ch. 16).

The initial impetus to the study of syncategoremata came from the twelfth-century interest in fallacies, and the investigation continued to be associated with fallacies or with sophismata throughout its development. Observations about syncategoremata were only incidental in the twelfth-century treatises on fallacies, but the novel emphasis of the *logica moderna* on the syncategoremata themselves is evident in the development of a new sort of treatise—"On Exponibles"—in the first half of the thirteenth century. "An exponible proposition is a proposition having an obscure sense that stands in need of exposition because of some syncategorema located in it explicitly or implicitly or in some word" (*Tractatus Exponibilium*, doubtfully ascribed to Peter of Spain, in J. P. Mullally, ed., *The Sum-*

mulae Logicales of Peter of Spain, p. 104). The exponibles did not involve fallacious arguments nor were they, strictly speaking, ambiguous. They were simply subjects for analysis, an analysis that was to explicate the force of some syncategorema in some particular context. For example, "'Man *inasmuch as* [*inquantum*] he is rational is not capable of braying'—that is, [1] no man is capable of braying and [2] every man is rational and [3] no rational entity is capable of braying and [4] because an entity is rational it is not capable of braying" (p. 115).

Sophismata. The sophismata which played an increasingly important role in investigations of syncategoremata from the thirteenth through the fifteenth centuries may be characterized as falling somewhere between fallacies of ambiguity and exponible propositions. In the independent treatises on syncategoremata prevalent in the thirteenth century, the sophismata served as the illustrations of the principles uncovered in the investigation and characteristically took the form of an assertion (the sophisma proper) followed by a proof, a counterargument, and an adjudication of the apparent paradox by an appeal to the principles. For example, "Suppose that exactly one individual of each species of animal is running. Then [*a*] every animal is running. (Proof: a man is running; a lion . . . ; a goat . . . ; and so on with respect to the individuals; therefore every animal is running.) But [*b*] every man is an animal; therefore every man is running. [Solution:] [*a*] is ambiguous since [because of 'every'] the word 'animal' can distribute for the remote parts (or the individuals belonging to genera)—in which case it is false, since it is then distributed for all its individuals—or for the genera of the individuals (or for the proximate parts)—in which case the minor [*b*] is plainly not accepted. . . ." (William of Sherwood, *Syncategoremata,* J. R. O'Donnell, ed., in *Medieval Studies,* Vol. III, p. 49).

The continuity of the development of the *logica moderna* was enhanced by the fact that from the twelfth century through the fifteenth century the same sophismata were treated from varying points of view, but at the same time the number and intricacy of the sophismata were constantly increasing. As a result the modernists of the fourteenth century frequently produced treatises entitled *Sophismata* in which large numbers of them were grouped according to the syncategoremata at issue in them, and the investigations that had begun in separate treatises on syncategoremata were pursued in the *Sophismata* and *Exponibilia* of the late Middle Ages.

Speculative grammar. The notion that grammar and philosophy were intimately related was one of the most pervasive of the assumptions that determined the character of medieval thought. It is probably to be explained by the facts that grammar was one of the very few inquiries to survive antiquity intact and that the only ancient philosophy available during the early Middle Ages was Aristotle's *Categories* and *De Interpretatione,* works of a decidedly grammatical cast. The usual view of the connection between the two subjects was the one expressed most memorably by John of Salisbury—"Grammar is the cradle of all philosophy" (*Metalogicon,* Book I, Ch. 13)—and the *logica moderna,* by far the most impressive medieval contribution to semantics, is a clear example of the influence of gram-

mar on philosophy. The influence ran the other way, however, in the development of "speculative grammar" (*grammatica speculativa*), or the doctrine of the "modes of signifying" (*modi significandi*), a movement that began somewhat later and subsided somewhat earlier than the *logica moderna.* Although there were some connections between the two movements—for instance, Roger Bacon (1214/20–1292), one of the first of the speculative grammarians, or "modists," also contributed to the *logica moderna*—they tended to be mutually independent and to some extent theoretically opposed developments in the history of semantics.

The most important single factor in the rise of speculative grammar in the early thirteenth century was the enthusiasm for the notion of a *science,* then being rediscovered in the *Posterior Analytics* of Aristotle and in his Arabic commentators. For a time it was the aim of every study to achieve the status of an Aristotelian science, a body of necessary knowledge deductively demonstrated, and two facts seemed to stand in the way of certifying grammar as a science. For one thing, as it had been presented by Priscian and Donatus, grammar was simply a set of observations about correct constructions without any attempt at explanation of the correctness; but only knowledge "by causes" qualified as scientific. For another, even Peter Helias (fl. 1150), who in his commentaries on Priscian had been the first medieval to attempt explanations of grammatical facts, had maintained that there were as many grammars as there were languages; but a unified subject matter was a prerequisite of a science.

Thus a science of grammar was not to be found in the grammatical authorities, and it seemed one never would be found as long as grammar was conceived of as something to be discerned only in the investigation of actual languages. Robert Kilwardby (died 1279) set the stage for speculative grammar when he argued that "since a science remains the same for all men and its subject matter remains the same, the subject matter of grammar must remain the same for all men. But grammatically ordered speech or articulate utterance that can be put into a grammatical pattern is *not* the same for all men, and for that reason it will not be the subject matter of grammar [as a science]" (Commentary on Book I of Priscian's *Ars Minor*). No science of languages was possible, but grammar might become the science of language, the *scientia sermocinalis,* if the variable external trappings were ignored and one concentrated on the conceptual underpinnings—which, as Aristotle had pointed out, *were* the same for all men. Thus Roger Bacon was led to proclaim that "with respect to its *substance* grammar is one and the same in all languages, although it does vary *accidentally*" (*Grammatica Graeca,* E. Charles, ed., p. 278), and this became the often repeated fundamental assumption of the speculative grammarians.

As it developed, speculative grammar took the form of an attempt to provide an Aristotelian ontology of language, finding analogues in the various parts of speech for matter, form, substance, process, and so on. As Siger of Courtrai (died 1341) put it, "grammar is the *scientia sermocinalis,* which considers discourse and its properties [*passiones*] in general for the purpose of expressing principally concepts of the mind by means of interconnected discourse" (*Summa Modorum Significandi*, G. Wallerand, ed., p. 93). Siger then cited Avicenna for the Aristotelian doctrine that concepts are the same for all men because they are the result of experiencing extramental entities, which are the same for all men. Thus, the ontology that applies to the extramental entities must apply as well to the concepts derivative from them (if they adequately copy the extramental entities) and, in turn, to the discourse employed to express those concepts (if it is to be adequate for that purpose). "Therefore *modes of being,* or properties of things . . . , precede a *mode of understanding* as a cause precedes an effect . . ." (*ibid.*). In the same way a mode of designating (*modus signandi*) follows a mode of understanding, "since a thing is understood and also conceived of before it is designated by means of an *utterance* [*vox*], for utterances are signs of passions, as is said in *De Interpretatione,* Ch. 1" (p. 94). When the understanding assigns a given concept to an utterance, the merely physical utterance becomes a word (*dictio*).

Up to that point the semantic theory underlying speculative grammar might fairly be described as a technical restatement of Aristotle. It was only with the introduction of its "modes of signifying" that the theory acquired its novelty and notoriety. (It was repeatedly attacked and ridiculed by logicians and grammarians of the late Middle Ages and even more strongly assailed by the Renaissance humanists.) As an utterance becomes a word by means of a mode of designating, so a word becomes one or another part of speech by means of a mode of signifying. The modes of signifying, however, are not modes of the utterance of the word but are "certain concepts of the understanding itself" (*ibid.*). The kind of concept in question seems to be one that links the word to some Aristotelian mode of being. Thus, the kind of concept involved in the mode of *designating* is the kind that supplies a *significatum* for the utterance "horse," transforming it from a mere sound into a word, while the mode of *signifying* consists in the recognition that it is *substance* that is signified by the word "horse." And when the understanding adds to that *general* mode of signifying—*substance*—the *specific* mode of signifying—*quality*—then "horse" has been transformed in turn from a mere word to a substantive and from a mere substantive to a noun (pp. 94–95). Along these same lines, the utterance "horse" will eventually be accounted for as a *common concrete* noun, and similar patterns of modes of signifying are invoked in order to account for the other parts of speech.

Aristotelian ontology was employed by the speculative grammarians not only as the link between grammatical forms and modes of extralinguistic being but also as a picture of intralinguistic relations. Thus, verbs stood at the pinnacle of the linguistic microcosm because just as the other animals are submissive to man, so the inflections of the other parts of speech in a sentence are ultimately submissive to the verb. The infinitive of a verb, however, was analogous to primary matter in substances. And just as the organisms capable of fewest adaptations are ranked lowest in the kingdom of nature, so the indeclinables, the syncategoremata, are the most inferior parts of speech (pp. [52]–[54]).

THE RENAISSANCE AND ENLIGHTENMENT

Semantics, logic, and epistemology. As the Middle Ages gave way to the Renaissance in the late fifteenth century, logic (on which semantics had been centered) first lost its medieval attainments and then subsided into inactivity until the middle of the nineteenth century. What little there was in the way of logical inquiry from about 1450 to about 1850 was carried on under the view of logic as the art (or science) of reason, the idea of *scientia sermocinalis* having been ridiculed into oblivion by the Renaissance humanists. Aside from the work of late Scholastics, such as the *Ars Logica* of John of St. Thomas (1589–1644), and an occasional deliberate attempt at revival, such as the *Logica Fundamentis Suis a Quibus Hactenus Collapsa Fuerat Restituta* (1662) of Arnold Geulincx (1624–1669), there were no further developments of the logicosemantic theories of the *logica moderna*.

Philosophers retained their interest in semantics, however, after losing interest in and even all knowledge of the kind of logic with which it had been associated. Epistemology dominated the philosophy of the Renaissance and the Enlightenment (for present purposes, roughly 1500–1800) as logic had dominated medieval philosophy, and the development of semantics during this period centered on epistemology. As a consequence, much of the development took place in the context of discussions of nonlinguistic signs, such as representative ideas, and will not be directly considered here.

Perhaps partly because logic had lost its identity as an inquiry into language, the interest of philosophers in language was more intense and diversified during this period (and especially in the eighteenth century) than at any earlier time. Some of this interest was manifested in widespread speculation about the origin of language and in projects for a universal language or a "real characteristic." Although works on these subjects are typical of the period and often contain material of value for the history of semantics, they can be considered here only as they bear directly on a theory of meaning or philosophy of language selected for discussion.

Bacon. Francis Bacon (1561–1626) produced comparatively little that can be described as philosophy of language, but the occasional novel insights and the programmatic character of what he did produce helped to give it a considerable influence over philosophy of language in the Enlightenment. Almost everything of his that is relevant to the history of semantics is to be found in the "Art of Elocution or Tradition" (in the *Advancement of Learning* and the *De Augmentis Scientiarum*) and the doctrine of the "Idols of the Market Place" (in the *Novum Organum* and the *De Augmentis Scientiarum*).

The first of these is plainly Bacon's revised version of the medieval *trivium*—grammar, logic, rhetoric—although he nowhere says so. In the later Middle Ages these subjects had sometimes been designated the *artes sermocinales,* and in the *De Augmentis Scientiarum* Bacon said that the subject matter of the *ars tradendi* was *sermo.* This inquiry into "tradition"—that is, discourse or communication—had three branches, concerning "the organ," "the method," and "the illustration" of tradition; and most of the work of the three branches was explicitly associated with grammar, logic, and rhetoric, respectively. For present purposes the first of these three branches is much more important than the other two.

In his scheme of "Human Philosophy" the Art of Tradition occurred as "the fourth kind of Rational Knowledge" (Spedding, Ellis, and Heath, eds., 3.383–4), because reason was "as it were the soul of discourse," according to Bacon. "Nevertheless, in treating of them reason and discourse ought to be separated, no less than soul and body" (1.651). He began his separate treatment of discourse by identifying speech and writing as the most familiar organs of discourse and stressing their connection with reason by citing with approval the traditional version of Aristotle's doctrine: "Words are the images of cogitations, and letters are the images of words" (3.399; but cf. 3.284, 3.85–86). But his interest in less familiar organs of discourse prompted him to frame a set of general conditions for an organ of discourse: "Whatever can be broken down into differences sufficiently numerous for explicating the variety of notions (provided those differences are perceptible to sense) can become a vehicle of cogitations from one man to another" (1.651; cf. 3.399). An organ of discourse can be used to *communicate* nothing but notions, but it will contain elements that *express* not only notions but also things. In the most familiar arrangement of organs of discourse, words (by which Bacon meant only articulate sounds [2.411–412]) are expressed by letters—that is, phonograms. Letters, in turn, may be expressed by ciphers—that is, cryptograms—and both letters and ciphers may be designated "nominal characters." But he recognized another kind of "notes of things, which signify things *without* the aid or intervention of words," either "on the basis of congruity" or "arbitrarily." As examples of the former sort he cited hieroglyphics and gestures, gestures being "transitory hieroglyphics," the "words" for which hieroglyphics may be the "letters," and he classified them together as "emblems"—that is, sensible images to which intellectual conceptions could be reduced by analogy (1.652–653; 649). As examples of the latter sort he cited "real characters" such as Chinese ideograms, which "have nothing emblematic in them, but are simply surds, no less than the elements of letters themselves; . . . there ought to be as many of them as there are radical words" (1.653). Despite that disadvantage, real characters could and, Bacon thought, did function as an organ of discourse beyond the limits of a single natural language just because they signified "things and notions" without the intervention of words (1.652). Although he was convinced that there were no more convenient organs of discourse than words and letters, Bacon listed the study of the notes of things among his desiderata (1.653). Acting on this suggestion, the Royal Society commissioned some of its members to look into the project of a universal real character, the eventual result being John Wilkins' *Essay towards a Real Character and a Philosophical Language* (1668), one of many such attempts during this period.

As another part of the inquiry into organs of discourse Bacon proposed a "philosophical grammar," and this desideratum likewise had an extensive but un-Baconian influence. Some of what he had to say about philosophical grammar was reminiscent of the medieval speculative grammar—for instance, it was to be "a kind of grammar that would carefully inquire not into the analogy of words to one another, but into the analogy between words and things or words and reason" (1.654)—and this is what seems to have caught the imagination of his many successors in the Enlightenment who produced works in philosophical or "universal" grammar. What Bacon really had in mind was probably something more nearly like the comparative philology characteristic of the nineteenth century: "But the noblest kind of grammar would, I think, result if someone well taught in many languages, learned as well as vulgar, would treat of the various properties of *languages*, showing in what respects each excels and in what respects it is deficient" (*ibid.*; cf. 3.230, 3.401). He did, however, go on to suggest that one might combine all the best properties uncovered in that analysis into "a very finely formed image and remarkable model of speech itself for expressing the mind's meanings aright" (1.654).

In his sketch of a philosophical grammar Bacon emphatically disapproved of what he believed Plato had been attempting in the *Cratylus*, an inquiry into "the imposition and original etymology of names . . ." (*ibid.*; cf. 3.531), but his own concern in the doctrine of the "Idols of the Market Place" closely parallels Plato's real concern in the *Cratylus*, that is, distinguishing between correct and incorrect names. "The idols imposed on the understanding through words are of two kinds. Either they are names of things that are not (for just as there are things that lack a name because they have not been observed, so there are names that lack things, resulting from a fantastic supposition); or they are names of things that are, but confused, ill-defined, and rashly and irregularly abstracted from the things . . ." (1.171). As an example of the first he gave "prime mover"; his example of the second kind was "humid," which, as his discussion of it shows, is less objectionable on these grounds now than it was in seventeenth-century English.

Hobbes. Thomas Hobbes (1588–1679) conceived of his systematic philosophy as beginning with an investigation into language and produced different versions of the investigation in *Human Nature* (1650), Chapters 5 and 13; *Leviathan* (1651), Chapters 4–7; and *Elementa Philosophiae Sectio Prima: De Corpore* (1655; English 1656), Part I, "Computatio Sive Logica." (The latest of those versions is also in most respects the fullest and is used as the basis of the following account.)

Philosophy, Hobbes observed, depends on ratiocination, or "computation" (Molesworth edition, 1.3). In reasoning regarding particular things "we add and subtract in our silent thoughts, without the use of words" (*ibid.*; see 3.32); but in most instances, and certainly in philosophizing, "men owe all their true ratiocination to the right understanding of *speech*" (1.36), such ratiocination being "nothing but reckoning, that is adding and subtracting, of the consequences of *general names* . . ." (3.30). In the second chapter of his *Logic*, devoted specifically to "names," Hobbes produced a novel combination of several elements in the Aristotelian–Scholastic account of the semantics of names. Ratiocination of every kind depends on memory, and the intelligent use of memory requires what Hobbes called "*marks,* namely, sensible things taken at pleasure, that, by the sense of them, such thoughts may be recalled to our mind as are like those thoughts for which we took them" (1.14). It is possible, Hobbes thought, for a man to "spend all his time partly in reasoning and partly in inventing marks for the help of his memory, and advancing himself in learning"—that is, to devise and profitably use a private language—but if science and philosophy are to develop, there must be "certain *signs* by which what one man finds out may be manifested and made known to others" (*ibid.*). Signs that do "signify the cogitations and motions of our mind" are "*words* so and so connected," or what Hobbes called "*speech,* of which every part is a *name*" (1.15). The use of names as marks, he held, was logically prior to their use as signs, since "names, though standing singly by themselves, are marks . . . ; but they cannot be signs otherwise than by being disposed and ordered in speech . . ." (*ibid.*). He recognized the syntactic disposition of names in speech as necessary but not sufficient for "declaring our conceptions to others." Speech cannot "perform that office alone without the help of many circumstances," such as "time, place, countenance, gesture, the counsel of the speaker" (2.274). We must "consider the drift, and occasion, and contexture of the speech, as well as the words themselves" (4.23).

When names are ordered in speech so as to be signs rather than marks, "it is manifest they are *not* signs of the things themselves" but signs only of our conceptions (1.17). Hobbes seems to have been following Aristotle's lead here, but more faithfully than most, since he went on to say, "That the sound of this word 'stone' should be the sign of a stone, cannot be understood in any sense but this, that he that hears it collects that he that pronounces it thinks of a stone" (*ibid.*). Thus, even though indirectly and only in virtue of signifying that the speaker is thinking of a stone, the name "stone" ordered in speech *is* a sign of a stone. At any event, Hobbes nowhere suggested that "stone" occurring in speech was a *name* of some mental entity. On the contrary, in going on to show that "it is not at all necessary that every name should be a name of some thing," Hobbes began by pointing out that " 'man,' 'tree,' 'stone' are *names* of things themselves" (*ibid.*), though they may be used as *signs* of our conceptions of men, trees, and stones and as *names* of "fictions and phantasms of things," such as images in dreams. "Moreover, that which neither is, nor has been, nor ever shall, or ever can be, has a name, namely, 'that which neither is, nor has been,' &c.; or more briefly this, 'impossible' " (*ibid.*). For "a name is not taken in philosophy, as in grammar, for one single word, but for any number of words put together to signify one thing" (1.23), Hobbes having decided "to apply the word 'thing' to whatsoever we name; as if it were all one whether that thing be truly existent, or be only feigned" (1.18).

Much of Hobbes's investigation of names was presented in the form of discussions of traditional classifications of names. His treatment of them sometimes presents the half-understood remnants of complex medieval theories—for instance, his treatment of names of first and second intention (1.20–21)—but there are occasional interesting novelties as well. In his discussion of common and proper

names he put forward his strict nominalism: "this word 'universal' is never the name of any thing existent in nature, nor of any idea or phantasm formed in the mind, but always the name of some word or name" (1.20); at another point he remarked that the univocal–equivocal distinction "belongs not so much to names as to those that use names" (1.23); and he based the distinction between simple and compound names not on appearances but on considerations of analyzability, so that in the context of a discussion of man "body" is a simple name while "man" is a "more compounded name," being equivalent to "animated rational body" (1.23–24). He encountered important difficulties in his discussion of names of "certain and determined" and of "uncertain and undetermined" signification (1.21–23), which is evidently a badly distorted remnant of supposition theory. In the course of that discussion Hobbes was led to claim, for example, that *particular* names—such as "some man"—"are of *uncertain* signification, because the hearer knows not what thing it is the speaker would have him conceive" (1.22), as if the "uncertainty" in, say, "some man will marry my daughter" were the sort that could always be resolved by asking the speaker "*which* man?" Even worse confusion resulted from his attempt to show that such quantifiers as "every" and "some" were unnecessary for purposes of reasoning. Such words, he maintained, "which denote universality and particularity, are not names; so that 'every man' and 'that man which the hearer conceives in his mind' are all one; and 'some man' and 'that man which the speaker thought of' signify the same. From whence it is evident, that the use of signs of this kind, is not for a man's . . . getting of knowledge by his own private meditation (for every man has his own thoughts sufficiently determined without such helps as these) but . . . for the teaching and signifying our conceptions to others . . ." (*ibid.*).

In his treatment of propositions Hobbes sometimes spoke as if only such propositions as "Cicero is Tully" were true—for instance, "that proposition only is true in which are copulated two names of one and the same thing" (1.57)—but usually his description of a true proposition was more moderately and more accurately expressed along such lines as these: "A *true* proposition is that, whose predicate contains, or comprehends its subject, or whose predicate is a name of every thing, of which the subject is a name . . ." (1.35; cf. 4.23–24). He produced a detailed analysis of falsity as reducible to combinations of names of different sorts of entities (1.57–62). His truth theory was, however, quite radical in other respects. The "first truths," he claimed, "were arbitrarily made by those that first of all imposed names upon things, or received them from the imposition of others. For it is true [for example] that *man is a living creature,* but it is for this reason, that it pleased men to impose both those names on the same thing" (1.36). This suggests an identification of the proposition with a particular sequence of words, but Hobbes elsewhere gave the impression of having been on the point of drawing a clear distinction between propositions and the vehicles of their expression—for instance, "every proposition may be, and uses to be, pronounced and written in many forms. . . . And therefore, whensoever they [students of philosophy] meet with any obscure proposition, they ought to reduce it to its most simple and categorical form . . ." (1.39).

Hobbes rejected the analysis of contingent categorical propositions into their corresponding hypothetical forms, pointing out that while this analysis was allowable for *necessary* categoricals, "in contingent propositions, though this be true, 'every crow is black,' yet this, 'if any thing be a crow, the same is black' [i.e., '$(x)(Cx \supset Bx)$'], is false" (*ibid.*).

In several places Hobbes discussed the various uses of speech—for example, *Human Nature*, Chapter 13—and at one point argued against the notion that a promise simply by its form of words creates an obligation (2.18–20).

The "Port-Royal Logic." René Descartes (1596–1650) had very little to say about language, but Antoine Arnauld (1612–1694) took an avowedly Cartesian approach to semantic questions in the *Port-Royal Grammar* (*Grammaire générale et raisonnée*, with Lancelot, 1660) and the *Port-Royal Logic* (*Logique ou l'art de penser*, with Nicole, 1662). The latter book had a tremendous influence; it marks, better than any other, the abandonment of the medieval doctrine of an essential connection between logic and semantics. Disdain for medieval theories was emphatically expressed in it—"No one, thank God, is interested in . . . second intentions" (*Premier Discours*)—but at several points the theories were still employed (for instance, in 1.2 and 2.10) and elsewhere in the book they were supplanted by innovations that sometimes obscured what had been clear in the *logica moderna*.

In words reminiscent of Hobbes's on this point, Arnauld remarked that if logic considered only an individual's reflections on his ideas, the investigation of language would form no part of it. But we must use "exterior signs" for communication, "and since this custom is so strong that even when we think by ourselves things are presented to our mind only together with the words with which we are accustomed to adorn them in speaking to others, it is necessary in logic to consider the ideas joined to words and the words joined to ideas" (Introduction; cf. Descartes, *Principles*, Part I, Principle 74). Arnauld of course argued (1.1) against Hobbes's anti-Cartesian suggestion that reasoning might be "nothing more than the uniting and stringing together of names or designations by the word 'is,'" so that all we could ever conclude is "whether or not there is a convention (arbitrarily made about their meanings) according to which we join these names together" (*Objections to Descartes's Meditations*, 3.4).

Signs and signification were frequently discussed in the *Port-Royal Logic*, sometimes with interesting results; the most fundamental questions were, however, treated with the kind of inattention to detail that came to characterize most of the many semantic theories of the Enlightenment. "The sign," said Arnauld, "comprises two ideas—one of the thing that represents, the other of the thing represented—and its nature consists in exciting the second by means of the first" (1.4). In the case of words, the "thing represented" was identified as a "thought" or an "idea." Even proper names were defined as those "that serve to mark . . . the ideas that represent only one single thing," and "general words" were said to be those "that are joined

to universal and general ideas" (1.6). The doctrine is so far consistent and recognizably Cartesian, even if crude. But it is complicated, no doubt inadvertently, by many suggestions of a different sort of signification for words. Thus, on a single page Arnauld began by calling words "sounds that are intended to signify *ideas*," went on to speak of "things and modes" as "the *objects* of our thoughts," and ended by defining names as "the words intended to signify both *things and modes*" (2.1); and he nowhere provided an account that might justify this extended use of "signify." He may have been assuming a transitivity of signification—words signifying ideas representing things—but Locke was the first to attempt to spell out such a theory.

Arnauld warned against the "great equivocation in the word 'arbitrary' when we say that the signification of words is arbitrary," pointing out that while "it is purely arbitrary to join one idea to one sound rather than to another," nevertheless the ideas, "at least those that are clear and distinct," are not arbitrary. The result of correct reasoning is "a solid, effective judgment regarding the nature of things based on the consideration of the ideas of them a man has in mind, which ideas it has pleased men to mark by means of certain names" (1.1). But, on the other hand, one of his reasons for rejecting Aristotle's categories was that they were "arbitrary names that form no clear and distinct idea in the mind" (1.3).

Arnauld also explicitly rejected Aristotle's definition of a verb, putting in its place one that not only captured the essence that Aristotle missed but was also much simpler: "a word that signifies affirmation" (2.2). Evidently he did not mean that it signified the idea of affirmation (as would the noun "affirmation"), but he did not work out the definition in a way that tied it to the rest of his signification theory.

Like so many other philosophers of the period, Arnauld believed that "the best means of avoiding the confusion of words to be found in ordinary languages is to make a new language and new words that would be attached only to the ideas we want them to represent." He differed from most, however, in suggesting that this be accomplished simply by a conscientious, systematic use of precise nominal definitions attached to already extant vocables of ordinary languages (1.12).

One of the more interesting notions in Arnauld's doctrine of signification was introduced in his observation that "it often happens that besides the principal idea (which is regarded as its *proper* signification) a word excites several other ideas that may be called *accessory*." Sometimes the accessory ideas are attached to the words "as the result of common usage," as in "you lied," the *proper* signification of which is the idea that you knew the contrary of what you said, the ideas of contempt and outrage being *accessory* (1.14). In some respects this is reminiscent of Augustine's doctrine in *Principia Dialecticae*, especially when Arnauld uses it to argue (against Cicero) that certain words may, in virtue of their accessory ideas, be described as unchaste (*ibid.*). Accessory ideas may also be attached for the purpose of a single use of a word, and on that basis Arnauld attempted an explanation of the varying signification of the demonstrative pronoun "this," here as elsewhere in the book applying his semantic doctrines to the elucidation of the formula of transubstantiation—"this is my body" (1.15). His notion of accessory ideas might have been (but was not) used to advantage in his discussion of problems of identity of reference, where he argued that when the mind frames the proposition "that Rome, which was of brick before the time of Augustus, was of marble when he died, the word 'Rome,' which appears as only one subject, nevertheless marks two subjects that are really distinct but reunited under a confused idea of Rome that prevents the mind from perceiving the distinction of subjects" (2.12). The suggestion is that the proposition should be rejected by anyone having a clear and distinct idea of Rome, which is preposterous. Even if the *proper* signification of "Rome" was taken to be only the idea of buildings, surely such *accessory* ideas as location, population, and institutions could have been invoked to warrant the continuing use of the single proper name.

Like Hobbes, Arnauld recognized complex terms expressed in a single word, but instead of Hobbes's criterion of analyzability Arnauld employed the notion of accessory ideas attaching to the word under certain circumstances. Thus, the term "king," which is simple *"in expression,"* was "a term complex *in sense*" when uttered in seventeenth-century France, "because in pronouncing the word 'King' we not only have in mind the general idea corresponding to that word; we also mentally join to it the idea of Louis XIV, who is now King of France. There is an infinity of terms in ordinary human discourse that are complex in this respect" (1.8).

Arnauld's analysis of the semantics of sentences clearly illustrates the importance of the loss of supposition theory. In one badly confused but typical passage he claimed that "when one says that men are animals, the word 'animal' no longer signifies all animals, but only the animals that are men" (2.17). Not only does this transform predication into identity, it also violates his own doctrine of signification. Again, in discussing "some man is just" Arnauld maintained that "just" there "signifies only the justice that is in some man," the result being that "some man is identified with some just [thing]" (2.18).

A complete chapter of the *Port-Royal Logic* is devoted to the discussion of propositions such as "this is Alexander" (pointing to his portrait), which he described as "expressions in which one uses the name of the thing to mark the sign," seldom if ever causing any difficulty in actual use, and propositions such as Joseph's explanation of Pharaoh's dream—"the seven full sheaves are seven full years of plenty"—"expressions in which, the sign being marked by its own name or by a pronoun, one affirms of it the signified thing." One result of this novel approach to metaphor is his formulation of a rule governing the appropriateness of the second sort of proposition: "the mind of those to whom one speaks must already regard the sign as a sign and be concerned to know of what it is a sign" (2.14).

"Comprehension" and "extension." Certainly the most influential semantic doctrine of the *Port-Royal Logic* was Arnauld's introduction of a distinction between the "comprehension" and the "extension" of a term. (In the nineteenth century Sir William Hamilton renamed the former "intension.") The principle of such a distinction had been employed in the medieval distinction between simple and personal supposition, and even the distinction itself had occasionally been anticipated in one form or another (for instance, by Cajetan), but Arnauld's introduction of it seems to have been original and certainly was the first instance of a systematic use of it. It is difficult, however, to say exactly what Arnauld intended by the distinction, for its exposition is obscured by his generally confused account of signification. He first advanced the distinction as one pertaining to "universal ideas" (or terms). "I call the *comprehension* of the idea the attributes it comprises in itself that cannot be removed from it without destroying it, as the comprehension of the idea of the triangle comprises extension, figure, three lines, three angles, the equality of those three angles to two right angles, etc. I call the *extension* of the idea the subjects with which that idea agrees, . . . as the idea of triangle is extended to all the various species of triangle." And Arnauld went on to say that the idea could be restricted in its extension by "applying it to only some of the subjects with which it agrees, without thereby destroying it," for example, by attaching to it "an indistinct and indeterminate idea of a part, as when I say 'some triangle' " (1.6). If, however, the extension consists of species and not of the individuals, which is what Arnauld maintained, then such a device for restricting extension is always to be read as "some (species of) triangle," which produces an absurdity. Because of his theory of signification there would be theoretical difficulties for Arnauld in simply identifying the term's extension with the individuals in question, but for the most part he seems to have had that identification in mind rather than the one he laid down.

Individual terms, too, were said to have comprehension and extension. In the phrase "Julius Caesar, the greatest commander the world has ever seen," the comprehension of that individual term is "explicated" in one of countless possible ways. But the extension of an individual term cannot be restricted, Arnauld maintained, and thus every singular proposition is universal (1.8, 2.3).

Locke. In the third book of his *Essay Concerning Human Understanding* (1690) John Locke (1632–1704) produced the first modern treatise devoted specifically to philosophy of language. No work had a greater influence over the development of semantics during the Enlightenment than did Book III of this work, "Of Words"; yet its semantic theories were neither novel in principle nor clearly and thoroughly developed. To go no further back, many of its principles had been anticipated in Kenelm Digby's *Two Treatises* (1664), in Richard Burthogge's *Organum Vetus et Novum* (1678), and in Hobbes's works. Of course Locke's "Of Words" acquired importance simply by being a part of the enormously influential *Essay,* but the source of its special influence lay in the fact that Locke had expressly connected semantic inquiry with theory of knowledge. He had set out to investigate "our knowledge," and along the way he found himself unexpectedly compelled to investigate "the force and manner of signification" of words (3.9.21), having discovered that "there is so close a connexion between ideas and words . . . that it is impossible to speak clearly and distinctly of our knowledge, which all consists in propositions, without considering, first, the nature, use, and signification of Language" (2.33.19). The new epistemological orientation of semantic inquiries, apparent even in the logic books of the period, was first explicitly established in Locke's *Essay*.

Locke evidently thought of the material of Book III as serving two purposes in his philosophy. On the one hand, he characterized his new "way of ideas" as nothing more than "the old way of speaking intelligibly" (third letter to Stillingfleet), which he reduced to a few commonsensical maxims for the avoidance of "jargon," very much in the spirit of Bacon's treatment of the "Idols of the Market Place." The semantic theory in Book III was developed in part as a support for these "remedies of the . . . imperfections and abuses of words" (3.11), and Locke's preoccupation with that practical aim may help to explain some of the imprecision and inconsistency in his theoretical statements. He did, however, clearly recognize a more strictly theoretical purpose in the semantic inquiries of Book III, one which he summarized in his description of the third branch of science—"Σημειωτικὴ, or *the doctrine of signs*" (4.21.4), the consideration of ideas as the signs of things and of words as the signs of ideas.

Locke's account of words as the signs of ideas shows little of the sensitivity to the complexities of language that had characterized the work of many of his predecessors, including Hobbes. Except for one very short, cryptic chapter on "particles" (by which he evidently meant syncategorematic words but perhaps also verbs), the semantics of words in Book III is exclusively a semantics of "names"—names of "simple ideas," of "mixed modes," and of "natural substances"—with no suggestion that anything has been left out of consideration (3.4.1).

The development of his fundamental thesis regarding the signification of these names begins with his observing that "words being voluntary signs, they cannot be voluntary signs imposed by [a man] . . . on things he knows not." Now what a man knows is in his mind, but all that is in a man's mind is his own ideas. Therefore, "words, in their primary or immediate signification, stand for nothing but *the ideas in the mind of him that uses them*" (3.2.2). This is not markedly different from the starting point of many earlier semantic theories, but Locke's initially uncompromising development of it led to some extreme consequences. Men, he observed, "suppose their words to be marks of the ideas also of other men" or "to stand also for the reality of things." Faithful to his fundamental thesis, Locke nevertheless insisted that "it is a perverting the use of words, and brings unavoidable obscurity and confusion into their signification, whenever we make them stand for anything but those ideas we have in our own minds" (3.2.4–5). Thus, the basic semantic relation in Locke's account of language is that of a word used by some speaker as a proper name for some idea in that speaker's mind. It seems to follow from this doctrine that as long as one does use words in this (the only approved) way, one cannot misuse them; and Locke does sometimes suggest that in the early chapters of Book III (see, for instance, 3.2.3). Those chapters indeed present a classic formulation of what Wittgenstein was later to criticize as the notion of a "private language."

Establishing words as proper names of ideas in the speaker's mind fulfills the first of Locke's two principal conditions "for the perfection of language" (3.1.3). The second was the devising of "general words," which he thought men accomplished by using words "for signs of general ideas." It was evident, Locke observed, that general words "do not signify barely one particular thing; for then they would not be general terms but proper names." His account of the signification of general words is, however, severely damaged by the inclusion in those same passages of his declaration of a thoroughgoing nominalism: "things themselves . . . are all of them particular in their existence, even those words and ideas which in their signification are general" (3.3.11–12).

Although many of his most careful theoretical statements ruled out any extension of the signification of a word beyond an idea in the speaker's mind, Locke here (and frequently in the later chapters of Book III) was apparently assuming that by virtue of signifying an idea, a word also (secondarily and indirectly, perhaps) signified whatever the idea signified. However, he never examined that assumption or even recognized it to be one. When he came to apply his theory to the discussion of various sorts of names, he often relaxed or ignored the strictures laid down in the general theory developed in the first three chapters. Thus, in his chapter on the "names of our ideas of substances" he found it convenient to say "By the word *gold* here, I must be understood to design [that is, designate] a particular piece of matter; v.g., the last guinea that was coined. For if it should stand here in its ordinary signification, for that complex idea which I or anyone else calls gold, i.e. for the nominal essence of gold, it would be jargon" (3.6.19).

When, on the other hand, Locke did apply his semantic theory strictly, he was likely to produce such surprising results as his doctrine that every generalization about a substance, such as "all gold is fixed," means either "that fixedness is a part of the definition, i.e., part of the nominal essence the word gold stands for; and so this affirmation 'all gold is fixed,' contains nothing but the signification of the term gold. Or else it means, that fixedness, not being a part of the definition of the gold, is a property of the substance itself, in which case it is plain that the word gold stands in the place of a substance. . . . In which way of substitution it has so confused and uncertain a signification that, though this proposition—'gold is fixed'—be in that sense an affirmation of something real, yet it is a truth will always fail us in its particular application [since we know only our idea of gold and not "the real essence" of gold], and so is of no real use or certainty" (3.6.50; compare his interesting treatment of "trifling propositions" in 4.8).

Locke's strictly subjectivist, nominalist theory of signification in the opening chapters of Book III, which gave him so much trouble in its application, may represent nothing more than his overzealous attempt to state precisely such characteristically commonsensical observations as can be found in his *Conduct of the Understanding*, Section 29, where he advised "those who would conduct their understanding right, not to take any term . . . to stand for anything, till they have an *idea* of it. A word may be . . . used as if it stood for some real being; but yet if he that reads cannot frame any distinct idea of that being, it is certain to him a mere empty sound without a meaning."

(Locke's influence is frequently discussed in the remainder of this article. See, for instance, the sections on Leibniz, Berkeley, and Condillac and on universal grammar.)

Leibniz. Gottfried Wilhelm Leibniz (1646–1716) developed some of his views on language specifically as criticisms of Locke in his *Nouveaux Essais sur l'entendement* (finished after 1709; first published 1765). One example of this *ad hoc* development is his rejection of Locke's account of "general words" as no more than devices for avoiding the proliferation of proper names. Leibniz argued that they were necessary ingredients in the "essential constitution" of languages and went so far as to claim, in an exact reversal of Locke's position, that "it is certain that all *proper* or *individual* names were originally *appellative* or general" (3.1.3; see 3.3.5). Even in the *Nouveaux Essais*, however, most of Leibniz' views on language can be traced to considerations that lie at the center of his own philosophy.

Universal characteristic. Perhaps the most important of the central considerations of Leibniz' philosophy is his lifelong preoccupation with the idea of a "universal characteristic," which cannot be examined here except as it bears directly on his philosophy of language. Leibniz' earlier doctrine of the characteristic (c. 1679) was "that a kind of alphabet of human thoughts can be worked out and that *everything can be discovered and judged by a comparison of the letters of this alphabet and an analysis of the words made from them*" (Gerhardt edition 7.185). Descartes, on the other hand, had maintained that such a language (he never knew of Leibniz' scheme, of course) depended on the prior establishment of "the true philosophy" (letter to Mersenne [1629], in Adam and Tannery edition 1.76). Leibniz' initial response was that while the establishment of the characteristic "does depend on the true philosophy, it does not depend on its completion"; for as long as we have the true "alphabet of human thought" to begin with, we can complete the true philosophy simply by correctly manipulating the characteristic (Couturat edition, pp. 27–28). (The many artificial languages projected during the Enlightenment may be classified as "Cartesian" or "Leibnizian," depending on whether they were put forward solely as devices for recording and communicating knowledge or also as heuristic devices. It is the Leibnizian rather than the Cartesian projects that bear a significant resemblance in principle to the formalized languages for logic developed after the middle of the nineteenth century.) Writing some years later (1697) and in a context where the issue between his own and Descartes's views was not explicit, Leibniz did nevertheless acknowledge that "genuinely real, philosophic characters must correspond to the analysis of thoughts. It is true that such characters would presuppose the true philosophy, and it is only now [when he believed himself to have discovered the principles of the true philosophy] that I should dare to undertake the construction of them" (Gerhardt edition 3.216).

By a "real" characteristic Leibniz meant a symbolism that was in some important respect naturally (rather than conventionally) associated with what it symbolized. Although a thoroughly real characteristic could be developed only in an artificial language, Leibniz observed that natural languages were in certain respects real characteristics. It was on the basis of that observation that he became the first major philosopher after Epicurus to suggest an appeal to ordinary language as a philosophical technique. His general attitude is expressed in the *Nouveaux Essais:* ". . . I truly think that languages are the best mirror of the human mind and that an exact analysis of the signification of words would make known the operations of the understanding better than would anything else" (3.7.6). Part of what he meant by "exact analysis" closely resembled Plato's use of etymology in the *Cratylus*. In his preface to a 1670 edition of Nizolius (in which he has a great deal to say about language) Leibniz argued that "the good grammarian and the philosopher too can, so to speak, deduce the use of a word from its origin by means of an unbroken sorites of metaphors" (Gerhardt edition 4.140). But he also viewed ordinary language in its unanalyzed state as having a special philosophic value: "Whatever cannot be explicated by means of popular terms (unless like many kinds of colors, odors, and tastes, it consists in immediate sensation) is nothing, and should be kept away from philosophy as if by a kind of purifying incantation" (4.143). Not every ordinary language was equally valuable as a touchstone for philosophy: "No language in Europe is better suited than German for this certifying trial and examination of philosophical doctrines by means of a living language, for German is richest and most nearly complete in real characters [*in realibus*], to the envy of all other languages. . . . On the other hand, the German language is easily the least well suited for expressing fabrications [*commentitia*]" (4.144; cf. Duclos edition 6.2.10 ff.). Leibniz' praise of German for its high proportion of real characters was very likely based simply on the fact that it contains words of Germanic origin where English and the Romance languages are likely to have words of Greek and Roman origin—for instance, *Unabhängigkeit* and "independence"—a feature of the German language which no doubt does provide its native speakers with comparatively easy access to many abstract notions.

Leibniz also recognized a more pervasive kind of "realness" in natural languages which might be called *syntactic,* in contrast with the historically more familiar kind just discussed. It constituted the essential ingredient in his doctrine of "expression" and thus formed part of his metaphysics (monads *express* the universe) as well as of his philosophy of language. In *What Is an Idea?* (1678) he offered this account:

That is said to *express* a given thing in which there are relations [*habitudines*] that correspond to the relations belonging to the thing expressed. But these expressions are of different kinds—e.g., the model of a machine expresses the machine itself; the projective delineation of a thing in a plane expresses the solid; discourse expresses thoughts and truths; characters express numbers; an algebraic equation expresses the circle (or some other figure)—and what is common to these expressions is the fact that we can pass from the mere consideration of the expressed relations to a knowledge of the corresponding properties of the thing being expressed.

Leibniz drew the conclusion that "it is clearly not necessary that that which expresses be similar to that which is expressed as long as a certain analogy of [internal] relations is preserved" (Gerhardt edition 7.263–264). What he was proposing, however, was clearly a novel approach to resemblance as a basis for semantic relations, suggesting for the first time that in complex signs the "realness" of the symbolism may consist in the resemblance between the *schemata* of the expression and of what is expressed rather than in a resemblance between the *elements* of those two schemata. This was brought out most clearly in his *Dialogue* (1677)—for example, in the observation that "even if the *characters* are arbitrary, still *the use and interconnection* of them has something that is not arbitrary—viz. a certain proportion between the characters and the things, and the relations among different characters expressing the same things. This proportion or relation is the foundation of truth" (7.192).

In describing this schematic resemblance as the foundation of truth, Leibniz stated the principal thesis in his novel doctrine of propositions as extralinguistic, extramental schemata. Although such a notion of propositions had been hinted at by Hobbes, Leibniz was evidently the first to make it explicit; and, as it happened, he developed his doctrine in conscious opposition to Hobbes's view of truth as dependent on words and hence arbitrary. It had been standard philosophical usage from the beginning of the Middle Ages to use the word "proposition" for whatever was either true or false, and the principal refinement of this usage before Leibniz had been the medieval distinction of "mental" propositions from propositions spoken or written. Leibniz' first objection against what he called Hobbes's "super-nominalism" might be interpreted as going no further than that, as in his observation that "truths remain the same even if the notations vary" (*Preface to Nizolius* [1670], in Gerhardt edition 4.158). He subsequently recognized, however, that those "truths" could not be identified with true propositions that had been, were, or would be actually in someone's mind—for instance, in the *Dialogue* of 1677: "A. . . . Do you think that all propositions are thought? / B. I do not. / A. You see, therefore, that truth does belong to propositions or thoughts, but to *possible* [propositions or thoughts], so that this at least is certain, viz. that *if* anyone should think in this [or a contrary] way, his thought would be true [or false]" (7.190).

Once Leibniz had distinguished propositions from actual thoughts and from combinations of words, he was in a position to reject the traditional account of truth as "the conjunction or separation of signs according as the things themselves agree or disagree among themselves," in which account "by 'the conjunction or separation of signs' one must understand what is otherwise called a proposition." Leibniz' attack on this tradition contrasted its technical terminology with ordinary usage in order to show that it concealed rather than resolved problems:

An epithet—e.g., "the wise man"—does not make a proposition, and yet it is a *conjunction* of two terms.

Negation, moreover, is something different from *separation,* for saying "the man" and after an interval pronouncing "wise" is not to deny. Finally, *agreement* [or *disagreement*] is not, strictly speaking, what one expresses by means of a proposition; two eggs have agreement and two enemies have disagreement. The manner of agreeing [or disagreeing] at issue here is quite extraordinary [*toute particulière*]. Thus I think this definition completely fails to explicate the point at issue. (*Nouveaux Essais* 4.5.2)

And Leibniz went on from this criticism of the traditional doctrine of propositions to present once again his own view of them as entities distinguishable both from words and from actual ideas (*Nouveaux Essais* 4.5.2).

"Leibniz' Law." Leibniz' famous principle of substitutivity, known in recent literature as Leibniz' Law, has frequently been used as a starting point by twentieth-century writers on semantics. Leibniz employed the principle as part of the primitive basis of his logical calculus and put forward several versions of it in papers written from 1679 through the early 1690s. The various versions may be accurately synthesized as follows: Those entities are the same, one of which may be everywhere substituted for the other, preserving the truth(-value) (see 7.219; 7.228; 7.236). Although Leibniz did not identify the entities in question and sometimes discussed the principle as if it applied, for example, to geometrical figures, the context generally makes it plain that its principal intended application was to terms in propositions actually expressed in some notation. His discussion of the principle in the papers in which he applied it took no account of contexts in which the principle does not apply, but at least one passage in his later writings shows that he had by then recognized that cases of what the medievals had called material supposition did not fall under the principle. "Indeed, one sometimes speaks of words *materially* without being able in that context [*cet endroit-là*] to substitute in place of a word its signification, or its relation to ideas or to things. This occurs not only when one speaks as a grammarian but also when one speaks as a lexicographer, in giving the explication of a name" (*Nouveaux Essais* 3.2.6). Recent criticism of Leibniz' Law has often begun with the complaint that he failed to notice just such exceptions.

Berkeley. Locke had argued that a word was significant solely in virtue of standing for an idea in the mind of the user of the word. When George Berkeley (1685–1753) began philosophizing, he accepted that doctrine as axiomatic. In several early entries in his private *Philosophical Commentaries* (1707–1708) he presented it as part of the basis of his otherwise anti-Lockean position—for instance, "All significant words stand for Ideas" (Luce and Jessop edition 1.45; see 1.39, 1.43, 1.53). Even before ending the *Commentaries,* however, Berkeley had rejected Locke's semantics too and had begun to replace it with a doctrine of great importance in the development of his own philosophy and in the history of semantics.

The actual turning point was apparently reached in his discovery that some words that should have been paradigm cases for Locke's semantics had no precisely correspondent ideas. "Qu: How can all words be said to stand for ideas? The word Blue stands for a Colour without any extension, or abstract from extension. But we have not an idea of Colour without extension; we cannot imagine Colour without extension" (1.62). In this passage Berkeley questioned for the first time not only Locke's semantics but also (indirectly) his doctrine of abstract ideas. He very soon saw that the connection between the two was essential. Given Locke's semantics, together with the facts that a general word was significant and that no concrete particular idea corresponded to it, one was forced to introduce a Lockean abstract idea simply in order to give a general word something to stand for. (As Berkeley pointed out [2.36], Locke had virtually admitted as much in the *Essay* [3.6.39].) Berkeley's alternative account in the Introduction to *The Principles of Human Knowledge* (1710), Section 11, was that "a word becomes general by being made the sign, not of an abstract general idea but, of several particular ideas, any one of which it indifferently suggests to the mind" (2.31; see 2.127). Berkeley's account thus involved abandoning Locke's semantic principle that there be a single idea to serve as the name-bearer for each significant word.

In the history of semantics, however, as in the history of philosophy in general, Berkeley's rejection of abstract ideas is more important than his alternative account of the signification of general words. The rejection was based not only on the well-known exposition of the internal inconsistency—as in *Principles,* Introduction, Section 13 (2.32–33)—but also on his many and varied attacks on their semantic foundation. Since Locke's commitment to the view that each word had to stand for one idea in order to be significant was what had compelled him to introduce abstract ideas, Berkeley set out to show, by means of various sorts of counterinstances, "that words may be significant, although they do not stand for ideas. The contrary whereof having been presumed seems to have produced the doctrine of abstract ideas" (3.292–293; see 1.70).

He seems to have found at least four sorts of counterinstances, the first and most obvious consisting of words that stand for something other than ideas. Words such as "volition," "I," "person," and the "particles" (or syncategorematic words) are significant in virtue of standing for "spirits" or their activities (the particles standing for "the operations of the mind") (1.65, 1.80, 1.81; see 3.292). But in Berkeley's immaterialism there were no entities other than spirits and ideas for which words could stand, and so there could be no other counterinstances consisting simply of words that stood for non-ideas. He was thus led to investigate the relation "stands for" more closely than its relata. In a move reminiscent of supposition theory he attacked Locke's account of "understanding propositions by perceiving the agreement or disagreement of the ideas marked by their terms," claiming that when he asserted of a particular dog "Melampus is an animal" he had not two ideas but "only one naked and bare idea, viz. that particular one to which I gave the name Melampus." Nor does "animal" in that proposition "stand for any idea at all. All that I intend to signify being only this, that the particular thing I call Melampus has a right to be called by the name animal." But it would not do, he pointed out, to say that "animal" here stood for the same idea as did "Melampus,"

since that would make the proposition a tautology (2.136–137; cf. 1.69, 8).

The principal effect of this second sort of counterinstance was to raise some serious doubt regarding the nature of the relation "stands for," and Berkeley's remaining counterinstances took the almost unprecedented step of suggesting that that relation was not always an essential ingredient in significance. Words that might in certain occurrences be said to stand for ideas are very often used in reasoning and in ordinary conversation as uninterpreted (but interpretable) "counters." A word used in that way does *not* in each of its occurrences stand for an idea in the mind of the user or, for that matter, raise a corresponding idea in the mind of the hearer or reader (2.37, 3.291–292, 8.25, 8.27).

Finally, a word sometimes occurs in a context such that one would miss rather than grasp its significance by taking it to stand for the idea to which it is customarily attached. "For example, when a Schoolman tells me *Aristotle hath said it,* all I conceive he means by it, is to dispose me to embrace his opinion with the deference and submission which custom has annexed to that name" (2.38). What is more, a word may occur in a context that precludes the possibility of taking it to stand for an idea without thereby being rendered insignificant—for example, the subject term in "the good things which God hath prepared for them that love him are such as eye hath not seen nor ear heard nor hath it entered into the heart of man to conceive." It was Berkeley's view that the significance of propositions such as these last two was to be found not in the ideas the words might otherwise be said to stand for but in the purpose, or "design," of the proposition. The design of this last example cannot be "to raise in the minds of men the abstract ideas of thing or good nor yet the particular ideas of the joys of the blessed. *The design is to make them more cheerful and fervent in their duty*" (2.137 [italics added]; see 2.293, 3.292). Words, he held, "have other uses besides barely standing for and exhibiting ideas, such as raising proper emotions, producing certain dispositions or habits of mind, and directing our actions . . ." (3.307). Thus, in his attacks on the semantic foundation of Locke's doctrine of abstract ideas Berkeley came nearer than anyone since the Stoics to abandoning, or at least supplementing, the attempt to account for all linguistic meaning in terms of the relation between names and their bearers.

As for Locke's semantics, Berkeley had reduced it to the unexceptionable principle of common sense that had no doubt prompted Locke's theoretical claims, namely, we ought not to use words without knowing their meaning (1.78; 2.76). But he took Locke's call for a new "doctrine of signs" quite seriously, summarizing his own (mostly anti-Lockean) semantic theory under that heading in *Alciphron* (1732), Dialogue VII, Section 14 (3.307). Like Bacon, Hobbes, and Locke before him, Berkeley thought of himself as providing philosophical remedies for the abuse of words, but he differed from them in making this the core of his philosophy, announcing that "the chief thing I do or pretend to do is only to remove the mist or veil of Words" (1.78; see 2.40). He set out explicitly to do just that at many points throughout his writings, but nowhere in a more concentrated form than in the Introduction to the *Principles*.

In keeping with that aim Berkeley frequently urged his readers to contemplate ideas apart from words, maintaining that "if men would lay aside words in thinking 'tis impossible they should ever mistake save only in Matters of Fact" (1.84; see 2.40). He felt, therefore, that it was "absurd to use words for the recording our thoughts to ourselves: or in our private meditations" (1.62) and introduced his "Solitary Man" for the purpose of examining that pristine state of mind in a concrete example, "to see how after long experience he would know without words" (1.71; see 2.141–142). Such passages taken together suggest an anticipation of Wittgenstein's attack on the notion of a private language, but Berkeley had second thoughts about the absurdity of the private use of words and seems to have concluded that "the Solitary Man would . . . find it necessary to make use of words to record his Ideas if not in memory or meditation yet, at least, in writing without which he could scarce retain his knowledge" (1.75).

Berkeley's ingenious linguistic analogy in his account of sense experience, the "Universal Language of Nature," was first put forward in his *New Theory of Vision* (1709) and developed in several later works. Speaking strictly, it belongs to his theory of knowledge rather than to his philosophy of language, but in the course of developing the analogy he often made interesting observations about language conceived in the ordinary sense (see, for instance, 1.228–233, 1.264–265).

Maupertuis and his critics. In the latter half of the eighteenth century philosophical interest in language was concentrated among French philosophers. Under the influence of Condillac and the British empiricists they eventually came to consider the analysis of signification their most important task. Among the earliest figures in this development was Pierre Louis Moreau de Maupertuis (1698–1759), who first published his brief *Réflexions philosophiques sur l'origine des langues et la signification des mots* in 1748. To some extent his position resembled those taken by Berkeley and by Condillac in his first book, *Essai sur l'origine des connaissances humaines* (1746); but Maupertuis seems to have written his *Réflexions* before he knew their work. Partly because of the author's fame as a scientist, the *Réflexions* attracted considerable attention and was commented on by Turgot (1750), Condillac (1752), Diderot (1753), Voltaire (1753), and Maine de Biran (1815), among others.

Maupertuis conceived of the question of the origin of language very much as philosophers since Descartes had been conceiving of the question of the origin of knowledge. It was intended to give rise not to speculations about prehistoric man but rather to an analysis of the hypothetical circumstances of a man with fully developed faculties who has suddenly been deprived of all his memories and of all human society. Would such an individual frame a language at all? If he did so, what would be the stages of its development? By asking and answering such questions as these within the framework of his "metaphysical experiment," Maupertuis expected to gain insight into the nature of language and its relation to the acquisition of knowledge. He began by imagining himself in the condition of the adult newborn. As soon as he had had two perceptions,

I should see that the one was not the other, and I should try to distinguish between them. And since I should have no ready-made language, I should distinguish between them by means of any marks whatever and might be satisfied with the expressions "A" and "B" as standing for the same things I now mean when I say "I see a tree," "I see a horse." Receiving new perceptions afterwards, I could designate them all in that way. . . . (*Réflexions*, Sec. 7)

It is not clear whether his saying "A" to himself in this protolinguistic context is really separable from his act of individuating the perceptual event of his seeing a tree, but Maupertuis did consider "A" and "B" as signs of his perceptions and thus presented a nearly classic case of what Wittgenstein later described as a "private language." The first development beyond those initial "signs" was recognized by Maupertuis as sufficiently radical to be described as "another language." In Section 8 he wrote:

For example, in the preceding perceptions I should recognize that each of the first two had certain characteristics that were the same in both and that I could designate those by a single sign. Thus I should change my first simple expressions "A" and "B" into these: "CD" and "CE," which would differ from the first only in that new convention, and which would correspond to the perceptions I now have when I say "I see a tree," "I see a horse."

Maupertuis's analysis proceeded in this way until he had introduced devices for discriminating kinds of perception, numbers of objects perceived, remembered and anticipated perceptions, and so on. His purpose in doing so, however, was to provide the background for a new philosophic method, which he applied most notably in his analysis of "the force of the proposition 'there is . . . .'" Although in saying "there is a tree" I may seem to be making a claim that goes beyond the evidence of my perceptions, once language has been reconstructed on the basis of my perceptions alone, I am in a position to see that "there is a tree" is no more than an abbreviation for "I shall see a tree every time I go to that place." This latter proposition in turn is reducible to the sequence "I was in a certain place," "I saw a tree," "I returned to that place," "I saw that same tree again," and so on (Secs. 24–28).

Eight years after writing the *Réflexions* and having meanwhile read the French translation of Berkeley's *Dialogues* (1750), Maupertuis readily admitted the similarity of his metaphysics to Berkeley's and rested his claims of independent importance on having introduced an analysis of language as the means to that end. "The point is that this philosopher [Berkeley] attacks the system of our errors only by parts. He demolishes the structure at the top, and we undermine its foundations. This is a structure quite different from that famous tower the erection of which on the Plains of Shinar was prevented by the confusion of tongues; this one is not erected *except by* abusing or forgetting the meaning of words" (*Reply to Boindin*, Sec. II, in *Oeuvres*, 1756 ed.). Berkeley's own attitude was, of course, much the same; but the *Dialogues* alone among his major works fails to bring that out.

Several of Maupertuis's critics, most notably Turgot, attacked the hypothesis on which he rested his inquiry:

"A solitary man such as Maupertuis imagines . . . would not try to find marks with which to designate his perceptions. It is only when confronted with other people that one looks for such marks. From this there follows what is obvious in any case, that the first purpose and first step of language are to express objects and not perceptions" (*Remarques critiques*, Sec. 7). Only Maine de Biran among Maupertuis's critics defended his use of the private-language hypothesis (*Note sur les Réflexions*, Sec. V).

Condillac. Étienne Bonnot de Condillac (1715–1780) wrote his first book, *Essai sur l'origine des connaissances humaines* (1746), in an effort to do what he felt Locke might have done if he had not "realized too late" the importance for epistemology of the material in Book III of his *Essay*, "Of Words" (Locke's *Essay* 3.9.21). Locke had "treated only in his third Book what should have been the subject matter of the second" (*Essai*, G. Le Roy, ed., 1.5a). Condillac acknowledged its historical value: Locke seemed to him to have been "the first to have written on this material as a genuine philosopher. I felt, nevertheless, that it had to form a considerable portion of my own work, both because it can be viewed in a novel, more extended way and because *I am convinced that the use of signs is the principle that discloses the source [développe le germe] of all our ideas*" (1.5b; italics added). Condillac thus became the first modern philosopher to found his theory of knowledge, and consequently his entire philosophy, on considerations of signification and language, considerations that occupied him throughout his career and that shaped French philosophy for at least fifty years afterward.

Like Locke, Condillac denied that the ideas produced in sensation alone constitute a kind of knowledge, but he began his divergence from Locke in his account of the acquisition of knowledge on the basis of such ideas. "The *sole* means of acquiring knowledge is to trace our ideas back to their origin, to observe their generation, and to compare them under all possible relations. This is what I call *analysis*" (1.27a). Analysis consists in discriminating and ordering elements that are presented confusedly and simultaneously and thus requires the introduction of interrelatable signs for those elements. On these observations Condillac based his leading principle that "every language is an analytic method and every analytic method is a language" (2.419a).

This has the look of a vicious circle. Analysis is said to be a necessary condition of knowledge, and language to be necessary for analysis; but surely knowledge is also necessary for the formation of a language. Condillac attempted to break this circle by introducing the notion of an innate language, which he called the language of action. "The elements of the language of action are born with man, and those elements are the organs given us by the author of our nature. Thus there is an innate language although there are no innate ideas. Indeed, it was necessary that the elements of some sort of language, prepared in advance, should precede our ideas, since without signs of some kind it would be impossible to analyze our thoughts . . ." (2.396b). In its most rudimentary form this "language" consists simply in overt reactions: "our external conformation is set to represent everything that takes place in our soul" (*ibid.*). Involuntary expressions of fear, pain, desire, and so on are not elements of analysis for the individual

producing them, but observers of his responses can, as a result of observing the order of events making up his responses, see analyzed for them what is simply gross experience for the respondent. "Men begin to 'speak' the language of actions as soon as they feel anything, and they speak it then without having any plan of communicating their thoughts. They form the plan of speaking it in order to make themselves understood only when they notice that they have been understood . . ." (2.397a). The usefulness of results gained by this means stimulates a natural feedback process of development on "the principle of analogy," and the language of action is made more effective by the gradual transformation of "natural" and "accidental" signs into "signs of institution," the most convenient of which are articulate sounds (1.60b–62a). The origin of language, discussed as an independent topic by many of his contemporaries and successors, is thus an essential consideration in Condillac's epistemology.

Signs of institution, including, of course, words, are themselves natural in the sense that as a language develops, they are framed on analogy with more primitive elements in that same language (and ultimately with elements of the language of action). The principle of analogy is in fact a necessary ingredient in any usable language (compare Bacon's doctrine of "emblems"). "Imagine an absolutely arbitrary language, such that analogy had determined neither the choice of words nor their various senses. That language would be an ununderstandable gibberish" (2.471a). If the principle of analogy remained unimpaired in ordinary languages, "we would reason as nature teaches us to reason, moving effortlessly from discovery to discovery." But every ordinary language has been impaired to some extent by the intrusion of words that have the roots of their analogy in other languages. (A similar line of reasoning had led Leibniz to praise the German language as a natural "philosophical characteristic.") Perhaps, then, the principle of analogy can be retained in a perfectly unadulterated form only in a highly artificial language, such as algebra, which Condillac describes as "the language of mathematics."

Since language of some sort is a necessary condition of knowledge, it is a mistake to maintain, as Locke had done, that the primary purpose of language is to *communicate* knowledge. "The primary purpose of language is to analyze thought. In fact we cannot exhibit the ideas that coexist in our mind successively to others except in so far as we know how to exhibit them successively to ourselves. That is to say, we know how to speak to others only in so far as we know how to speak to ourselves" (1.442a). It is a consequence of this view that the art of thinking, or logic, reduces to the art of speaking.

> Although a thought is not a succession in the mind, it has a succession in discourse, where it is decomposed into as many parts as there are ideas making it up. Then we can observe what it is we do when we think, we can give an account of it, we can, consequently, learn how to conduct our reflective thought. In this way thinking becomes an art, and that art is the art of speaking. (1.403b)

Condillac's view of the connection of thought and language was reinforced by his observations on "abstract general ideas." "When, for example, I think about *man,* I cannot consider anything in that word except a common denomination, in which case it is perfectly plain that my idea is in some way circumscribed in that name, that it extends to nothing beyond the name, and that, consequently, it is only that name itself" (2.401b). Thus the clarity and precision of abstract ideas "depends entirely on the order in which we have produced the denominations of classes. Therefore, there is only one means of determining ideas of this sort, and that is to produce a well-made language" (*ibid.*). Abstract general ideas, however, are the principal ingredients of reasoning, and Condillac was even ready to say that "to speak, to reason, to produce abstract or general ideas for oneself, are at bottom one and the same thing" (2.402a). His consideration of abstract ideas, then, was one more "proof that we reason well or badly only because our language is well or badly made" (*ibid.*).

All intellectual progress, on Condillac's view, depended on and in part consisted in establishing a "well-made language," and "a science, properly treated, is nothing other than a well-made language" (1.216a). The one perfectly well-made language so far established, he thought, was mathematics, which he examined from this point of view in his last book, *La Langue des calculs* (1798). One reason why Condillac was prepared to identify a science with a well-made language is to be found in his doctrine of propositions. All that remains to be done in a science once the appropriate language has been established is the mechanical exposition of the truths proper to that science. The exposition is mechanical because "a proposition is only the unfolding of a complex idea in whole or in part," and since a proposition "in which one and the same idea is affirmed of itself" is an identical proposition, "every truth is an identical proposition" (2.748a). An identical proposition may, however, be instructive for some persons, namely, those who observe "for the first time the relation of the terms out of which it is formed. . . . Thus a proposition may be identical for you and instructive for me" (2.748b). Nevertheless, "if in all the sciences we could equally trace the generation of the ideas and everywhere apprehend the true system of the things, we should see one truth give birth to all the rest, and we should find the abridged expression of all we know in this identical proposition: *the same is the same*" (2.749b).

Condillac's influence extended not only to philosophers but also to the great chemist Antoine Lavoisier (1743–1794), who in his *Méthode de nomenclature chimique* (with Morveau, 1787) and *Traité élémentaire de chimie* (1789) wholeheartedly adopted Condillac's notion of a science as a well-made language. Operating under this notion, Lavoisier introduced such technical terms as "phosphoric acid" and "sulphuric acid" in a successful attempt to initiate the development of the language of modern chemistry on Condillac's principle of analogy.

Lambert, Hamann, and Herder. In the century between Leibniz and Humboldt, philosophy of language in Germany was concentrated in the writings of three men: Johann Heinrich Lambert (1728–1777), Johann Georg Hamann (1730–1788), and Johann Gottfried Herder (1744–1803).

Lambert was a distinguished mathematician and the first man to follow Leibniz' lead in his contributions to logic, the most important of which was the earliest attempt at a calculus of relations. His work in the philosophy of language appeared in his *Neues Organon* (1764), especially Part III, "Semiotik, oder die Lehre von der Bezeichnung der Gedanken und Dinge."

In philosophy of language, as in logic, the principal influence on Lambert was that of Leibniz, as may be seen in his preoccupation with the effect of language on thought and knowledge and with the possibility of controlling and improving that effect. Various natural languages impose various structures on our knowledge, but every natural language is fundamentally the product of prephilosophical, prescientific mankind. When we attempt to use such a language in advanced intellectual activities, we must submit our thought to the tyranny of usage (III, 1). We are thus led to seek an artificial language that from its inception could be entirely subjected to the needs of the intellect. Lambert's attitude toward such artificial languages differed, however, from Leibniz' and constitutes a significant development in this line of thought. Great men, he observed, have worked at the project of a simple, perfectly regular and precise rational language, but without notable success. In any case, the adoption of such a language would be practically impossible (III, 2, 330). If we then revert to natural languages, however, we find that, strictly speaking, we cannot adopt any single one of them as a foundation for knowledge. There are, in the first place, conflicting usages even within a single natural language, some of which would have to be more or less arbitrarily ruled out; and, in the second place, any set of usages finally adopted would inevitably continue to undergo changes within the natural language of which they were a part.

Once we recognize that we do thus necessarily deviate to some extent from any given language in adapting it to intellectual purposes, it is apparent that we ought to do so consciously and under the guidance of pre-examined criteria. The criteria developed and employed by Lambert were, he observed, the sort that might have served as the operative rules of a philosopher's artificial language. In fact, he seems to have elevated Leibniz' projected "universal characteristic" to the status of an ideal language, the principles of which are approximable to varying degrees but never fully realizable. He described his detailed examination of language as one that made a point of not distinguishing sharply between "actual and possible languages," meaning thereby that his approach to natural language was a mixture of description and prescription in which he attempted to point out those aspects of the actual language which were already accommodated to certain requirements of the ideal and to suggest ways in which those aspects might be enhanced and extended without introducing radical reforms that had little chance of acceptance.

The fundamental criterion employed by Lambert in his evaluation of sign systems in general and of natural languages in particular was the interchangeability of "the theory of the signs" and "the theory of the objects" signified, the degree of interchangeability marking the extent to which the signs approximated the fundamental ideal of being "scientific" (III, 23–24)—he cited musical notation as an example of a particularly close approximation. It seems evident that this fundamental criterion, which with its many corollaries pervades Lambert's philosophy of language, constituted his adaptation of Leibniz' doctrine of "expression."

Besides systematic general chapters on various aspects of language, Lambert's "Semiotik" includes specific examinations of the character and function of various parts of speech and of the philosophical significance of etymological and syntactic interrelations among words.

Lambert and Hamann shared the conviction that the character of language was a topic of the greatest importance for philosophy, but they differed in almost every other important respect. Hamann's writings are undisciplined, obscure, and strongly colored by religious mysticism. Philosophically he was a forerunner of romanticism and existentialism, consciously rejecting most of the attitudes of the Enlightenment.

To the extent to which Hamann's philosophy exhibits a structure, it centers on his views on language, so much so that he himself called it verbalism (*Schriften*, C. H. Gildemeister, ed., 5.493–495). In almost everything he had to say about language, however, he opposed his contemporaries—Lambert (and the Leibnizian tradition) implicitly, Herder explicitly. The fundamental thesis of Hamann's verbalism is that ordinary natural language does and should take philosophical precedence over all technical or abstract language. Occasionally he wrote as if his basis for this claim was that God had employed such language as the instrument of revelation (*Schriften*, F. Roth and G. A. Wiener, eds., 1.85–86, 1.99), but he seems to have had more generally evaluable reasons for it as well. He evidently felt that the opposition between the rationalists and the empiricists of the Enlightenment was irresolvable largely because of the reliance of both parties on introspection. The special importance of ordinary language in this connection was that it constituted a medium in which the operations of reason and experience were united and made publicly accessible. The operations of reason, indeed, consisted entirely in linguistic operations (Roth and Wiener, 6.15 and 6.25; Gildemeister, 5.515, 7.9). Philosophy, however, had traditionally adulterated what should have served as its principal source and instrument. Hamann brought this out in a characteristic attack on Kant's abstract, technical language in the first *Critique:*

> While geometry fixes and fictionalizes the ideality of its concepts of points without parts, of lines and planes conforming to ideally divided dimensions, by means of empirical signs and figures, metaphysics misuses all the word-signs and figures of speech of our empirical knowledge as mere hieroglyphs and types of ideal relations and as a result of this learned mischief transforms the straightforwardness [*Biederkeit*] of language into such a senseless, whirling, unsteady, indeterminable something ($= x$), that nothing remains but a windy murmuring, a magical shadow-play, at best . . . the talisman and rosary of a transcendental superstition regarding *entia rationis,* their empty sacks and slogan. (Roth and Wiener, 7.8)

It was not only Kant's misuse of language that attracted Hamann's criticism but more especially his utter neglect of language as a topic for inquiry, which from Hamann's point of view vitiated Kant's claim to have provided a critique of reason. To point up the folly of such neglect, he tried to show that at various crucial junctures in his argument (as in the deduction of the categories) Kant had uncritically relied on certain linguistic conventions and that what he had called paralogisms and antinomies of reason really had their roots in the misuse of language.

Hamann based his doctrine of the pre-eminence of ordinary language not only on its value as a subject for philosophical inquiry but also on the fact that it alone among types of language was "objectively given." As such it served as the "womb" of reason and of all specialized, abstract languages designed to aid the operations of reason. Moreover, since ordinary language thus constituted the ultimate link between language and reality, all such abstract languages must be held finally accountable to it, that is, translatable into it.

As a philosopher of language, Herder is best known for his prize essay on the origin of language (1771), a topic with which this article is generally not concerned. Herder's essay, however, occupies a position of special importance among hundreds of similar productions by eighteenth-century philosophers, for it began the trend away from the speculative problem of origin and toward the scientifically more accessible problems of the development of language. (It was praised for that reason by several of the great linguists of the nineteenth and twentieth centuries, such as Grimm, Benfey, Sapir, and Jespersen.)

Ostensibly Herder was adjudicating between two rival accounts of the origin of language, but his real purpose was to dismiss the problem as senseless. The two theories at issue were those of special divine creation and of deliberate human invention of language, the former as represented in J. P. Süszmilch's work and the latter associated primarily with Rousseau's second *Discours.* Herder took reason to be the defining characteristic of man and argued in support of Hamann's position that the operation of reason and the use of language were inseparable. He then drew the obvious conclusion that if God had created what was genuinely man, He had created a language-using animal and no special divine creation of human language was conceivable. By the same token, animals correctly describable as men could not conceivably have invented language. Thus the question of how and when men came to use language was misconceived, although the question of how primitive human languages developed was well worth considering. Hamann ridiculed Herder's argument, with justification. It seems probable, however, that the argument was intended as irony, to deflate the pretensions of the theorists rather than to refute the theories.

The "idéologues." Antoine Louis Claude Destutt de Tracy (1754–1836) devised the name *idéologie* for the new "science of the analysis of sensations and ideas." One section of the Second Class of the Institut National (founded in 1795) was devoted to that science in lieu of the prescientific inquiry known as metaphysics, and Destutt de Tracy and other philosophers associated with the work of that section became known as *idéologues.* For about eight years, until Napoleon abolished the Second Class of the Institut in the reactionary atmosphere of the First Empire, the *idéologues* were the dominant philosophical group in France. They thought of themselves as working in a field that had been opened by Locke and first thoroughly explored by Condillac, whose most original contribution was considered to be his discovery that language was as essential to the more fundamental processes of thought and analysis as it was to communication. Although part of at least Destutt de Tracy's interest in language was directed specifically to *grammaire générale* (see below), the *idéologues* followed Condillac in considering language a topic of importance in every area of philosophical inquiry.

The *idéologues* resented being thought of as disciples of Condillac, however, and while they did, professedly, share some of his broad philosophical convictions, much of what they had to say about language (as about other topics) involved substantial revision or outright rejection of Condillac's specific doctrines. There seems to have been some tendency for the revisions to take the form of a generalization of Condillac's doctrines, notably from a concern with language to a concern with signs of all sorts. Thus, in a representative passage of his *Rapports du physique et du moral* (delivered in 1796), Pierre Jean Georges Cabanis (1757–1808) purported to be defending and explicating Condillac's central claim that every language was an analytic method by arguing that "one distinguishes among sensations only by attaching to them signs that represent and characterize them; one compares them only in so far as one represents by signs either their resemblances or their differences." Of course, Cabanis pointed out, taking this account as explicative of Condillac's claim required taking "language" in "the broadest sense," as meaning "the methodological system by means of which one pins down [*fixe*] one's own sensations" (*Oeuvres,* Claude Lehec and Jean Cazeneuve, eds., p. 157).

The question of the nature and epistemological function of signs (including linguistic signs) took on critical importance for the *idéologues* as a result of Destutt de Tracy's *Mémoire sur la faculté de pensée* (delivered in 1796), prompting them to set "the influence of signs on the faculty of thought" as the subject for the first essay competition sponsored by the section on the analysis of sensations and ideas. The best entries were *Des Signes envisagés relativement à leur influence sur la formation des idées* by Pierre Prévost, *Introduction à l'analyse des sciences, ou de la génération, des fondements, et des instruments de nos connaissances* by P.-F. Lancelin, and *Des Signes et de l'art de penser, considérés dans leurs rapports mutuels* by Marie-Joseph Degérando (1772–1842). Degérando's essay won the prize and was published in an expanded four-volume version in 1800. In it some of the principal issues in the philosophy of language of the seventeenth and eighteenth centuries were subjected to a final scrutiny, partly as a result of the historically apt questions provided by the *idéologues* as a guide for the essayists:

(1) Is it really the case that sensations can be transformed into ideas only by means of signs? Or, what comes to the same thing, do our first ideas depend essentially on signs? (2) Would the art of thinking be perfect if the art of signs were perfected? (3) In those sciences in which there is general agreement as to the truth, is this because of the perfection of the signs employed in them? (4) In those branches of knowledge that provide inexhaustible fuel for dispute, is the division of opinion a necessary effect of the inexactitude of the signs employed in them? (5) Is there any means of correcting badly made signs and of rendering all sciences equally susceptible of demonstration? (*Mémoires de l'Institut National des Sciences et Arts. Sciences morales et politiques,* 1.i–ii)

Question (1) was on a thesis of *idéologie* itself, as may be seen in the passage from Cabanis quoted above. Degérando's answer was complex, but it was sufficiently affirmative to mark him an *idéologue*. On the one hand he felt that the mind needed no signs but merely an act of attention in order to pin down its sensations. On the other hand, "I shall give the name ['sign'] to every sensation that excites an idea in us in virtue of the association obtaining between them. Note carefully that it is not the sensation as such to which the name is given; it gets the name only in respect of the function it performs. Thus I shall say, for example, that the smell of a rose is the sign [not of the rose but] of the ideas of color and of form that the smell excites" (1.62–63). He distinguished between such prelinguistic signs and linguistic signs by pointing out that while the former "excite" ideas in us but attract attention to themselves, the latter lead our attention away from themselves to the ideas they have been made to signify, a formulation that constituted a refinement of the traditional distinction between natural and conventional signs.

In his detailed answers to questions (2) and (5) Degérando carefully criticized the many attempts at universal characteristics, calculi of reason, and philosophical languages that had been made by philosophers of the Renaissance and the Enlightenment. He laid down five criteria for such systems: (*a*) unambiguous relations between signs and signified ideas; (*b*) relations among signs exactly analogous to relations among signified ideas; (*c*) simplicity, that is, minimum number of primitives (*conditions premières*), each sign as abbreviated as possible, perspicuity of the sign system as a whole; (*d*) distinctness among signs of different sorts and among syntactic relations of different sorts; (*e*) as many distinct sorts of signs as distinct sorts of ideas to be signified (4.353–355). The only hopes of satisfying such criteria, he maintained, lay along four different lines, or "systems for philosophical language." Having examined each in detail, he concluded that all were in some respects unacceptable. Like Lambert, however, he suggested that a judicious application of the principles of such systems might produce some improvement in natural languages for philosophical purposes (4.355–415).

Perhaps even more important historically than his arguments against the feasibility of such artificial languages was his attack on the attitudes underlying them. It had usually been assumed that such a language would be international, and, indeed, if it were not, it would fail to achieve a good part of its purpose. But, Degérando maintained, there was no feasible means by which to establish it internationally, and even if it were established, it would soon be modified into separate dialects in various localities

(3.557). Worst of all, the notion is pernicious, for such a language could at best be the instrument of communication exclusively among the learned and would thereby tend to separate them further from those they ought to instruct (3.572).

The fundamental mistake giving rise to all such schemes, according to Degérando, is the confusion of "the *method of reasoning* employed by the mathematicians with the *mechanical processes* of their calculations. Their method, as I have shown . . . , they do have in common with the metaphysicians," but the mechanical processes of their perfectly satisfactory artificial languages are the result of "the relative simplicity of the ideas on which they operate" (4.447–451). Other *idéologues,* particularly Destutt de Tracy, joined in this thoroughgoing repudiation of artificial languages for philosophy (see, for instance, *Mémoires de l'Institut,* Vol. III).

Questions (3) and (4) together called for an examination of Condillac's contention that a science was to be identified with a well-made language. Cabanis, himself a scientist, and Destutt de Tracy had frequently made significant use of this doctrine, but Degérando rejected it in a way that seems symptomatic of the end of the Enlightenment conception of a science. Some of the basis for his answers to these questions is evident in his answers to questions (2) and (5). "A well-made language," he maintained, "proclaims and presupposes a science that is already well advanced," thus adopting the Cartesian position on this issue rather than the Leibnizian. "We shall say that the great art of perfecting a science consists above all in making better observations and only *then* adopting a better language—i.e., one that is better suited to the observations that have been assimilated" (3.150–151). "The nomenclature of a science is related to the science itself as monuments are related to history: it preserves what is, but it can neither predict what is not yet nor unfold the future" (3.199).

Degérando resembled other *idéologues* more closely, however, in his view that improvements in philosophy—that is, in the analysis of sensations and ideas—did depend on a thorough examination of the natural language in which it was carried out. His own rather novel, never-realized scheme for accomplishing this was the construction of a philosophical dictionary.

> It has been recognized that we can have clear ideas only in possessing a well-made language, and that a language can be well-made only in so far as we have reformed the most familiar operations of the mind from the very outset, only in so far as we have grasped the relation that interconnects them all. That being the case, we have felt the need of remaking the language in its entirety and, in some sense, recommending the education of the human mind. The surest and perhaps the most truly efficacious means of accomplishing this great project would be, I think, the formation of a philosophical dictionary truly worthy of the name— one, that is to say, that would in some sense be a genealogical tree of our ideas and of the signs we use. Such a dictionary would be a sequence of definitions strictly bound to one another. Each notion would be defined in it by showing how it was acquired, or at least how it should have been acquired. The mind

would find itself naturally led to *create* the words rather than seeking merely to *explain* them to itself. . . . The dictionary I propose would have an aim altogether different [from that of ordinary dictionaries]. In it one would seek to explain not so much how we speak as how we think; the conventions of the language would be presented in it as *results,* not as *principles.* . . . [This dictionary would not be arranged in alphabetical order but] it would be a book, a history. The order of facts would be the only order observed in it. It would not . . . be designed to be consulted occasionally, but it would have to be the object of a connected reading. . . . A definition would never be offered in it except in accordance with one general rule—that of determining an idea by means of tracing it back to the ideas that must have preceded it in the age when language was instituted among men. . . . The dictionary would thus in some sense embrace the history of mankind and would serve as a natural introduction to all the sciences. The study of it would be necessary for all who wished to think well, and its formation would be one of the noblest undertakings of philosophy. (4.80 ff.)

What little influence the *idéologues* had is somewhat more noticeable in British than in Continental philosophy of the nineteenth century, partly because of the interest of some of the Scottish common-sense philosophers in their work.

Universal grammar. Among the most important and distinctive influences on the philosophy of language of the Enlightenment was the development of universal grammar. In the broadest sense of the term it was, as defined by James Harris (1709–1780), "that grammar which without regarding the several idioms of particular languages only respects those principles that are essential to them all" (*Hermes, or a Philosophical Inquiry concerning Language and Universal Grammar,* 1751, Book I, Ch. 2). Although it resembles the speculative grammar of the Middle Ages in some of its basic assumptions, universal grammar seems to have had an independent origin that may with reasonable accuracy be dated 1660, the year in which Arnauld and Lancelot published the *Port-Royal Grammar—Grammaire générale et raisonnée.*

Lancelot was a grammarian in the scholastic (rather than humanist) tradition who provided the subject matter that Arnauld presented in accordance with Descartes's method, believing that he was thereby "developing in grammar a branch of Cartesianism" (p. 137). In grammar, as in every subject, the method consisted fundamentally in "beginning with the most general and simplest matters in order to proceed to the least general and most complex," and in the study of language one therefore had to begin with principles and elements common to all languages in order to proceed to the study of one's own and other particular languages. Thus, universal grammar, as Arnauld (and many of his successors) conceived of it, was an investigation of language (*langage*) designed as a propaedeutic to the study of languages (*langues*). In practice, however, the elements and principles of universal grammar tended to be those of traditional Latin grammar, and thus many of the so-called universal grammars, at least before Condillac, are of little value either to linguists or to philosophers.

More important than the content of the early treatises on universal grammar, however, is the connection they established between grammar and philosophy, especially in France, where universal grammar dominated linguistic studies for 150 years following the *Port-Royal Grammar*. César Chesneau Dumarsais (1676–1756), the foremost of the universal grammarians between Arnauld and Condillac, maintained that "grammarians who are not philosophers are not even grammarians" (*Véritables Principes de la grammaire*, 1729, 1.201), and men engaged in the inquiry at that time styled themselves *grammairiens-philosophes*. Dumarsais seems often to have thought of "philosophy" in connection with grammar as no more than a certain scientific attitude (see, for instance, his article "Grammairien" in the *Encyclopédie*), but he also held some of the views that were to serve as the basis for a more strictly philosophical grammar, as can be seen in his explanation that "grammar has a necessary connection with the science of ideas and reasoning because grammar treats of words and their uses and words are nothing but the signs of our ideas and our judgments" (*ibid.*).

The *grammairiens-philosophes* began to be more markedly philosophers than grammarians beginning with the articles on grammatical topics in the *Encyclopédie*. Although Dumarsais was in general charge of them, several were written by philosophers such as Voltaire, Diderot, and Turgot; and the articles as a group contain less information on the announced topics than they do discussions of philosophical questions more or less vaguely associated with those topics. Nicolas Beauzée (1717–1789), one of the authors of those articles, defended the new approach to grammar in his *Grammaire générale* (1767): "Why should one think metaphysics out of place in a book on universal grammar? Grammar ought to expose the foundations—the general resources and the common rules—of language, and language is the exposition of the analysis of thought by means of speech. No aim is more metaphysical or abstract than that" (*Préface*, p. xvii).

In the works of Condillac, the emphasis was no longer on the propriety of taking a philosophical approach to grammar but rather on the fundamental importance of universal grammar as an inquiry serving the purposes of philosophy itself. In the "Motif des études" introducing his course of studies for the prince of Parma, Condillac described grammar as "a system of words that represents the system of ideas in the mind when we wish to communicate them *in the order and with the interrelations we apperceive.*" Consequently, as he remarked in the "Objet de cet ouvrage" preceding his *Grammaire* (1775), he regarded grammar "as the primary division of the art of thinking. In order to discern the principles of language we must observe how we think; we must seek those principles in the analysis of thought. But *the analysis of thought is quite complete in discourse,* with more or less precision depending on the greater or less perfection of languages and the greater or less exactness of mind on the part of those who speak them. This is what makes me think of languages as so many analytic methods."

Condillac's elevation of universal grammar to the status of a fundamental philosophical inquiry marked the beginning of a new phase in the development of universal gram-

mar, but his view of it was no more than a natural consequence of the then well-established belief that the construction of an absolutely universal grammar for all languages was a feasible undertaking. If language depicted thought and all languages shared a set of elements and principles, then the study of those common elements and principles would provide a science of human thought.

For Condillac's successors, the *idéologues*, who took the analysis of sensations and ideas to be the whole of philosophy, universal grammar became *the* philosophical method. As Destutt de Tracy put it, "this science may be called *idéologie* if one attends only to the subject-matter, *universal grammar* if one has reference only to the method, or *logic* if one considers only the goal" (*Élémens d'idéologie*, 1801, 1.5). It was in accordance with this conception of philosophy that the traditional chairs of logic and metaphysics in the *écoles centrales* of France were replaced in 1795 with chairs of universal grammar, which "by offering instruction in the philosophy of language would serve as an introduction to the course in private and public morality" (*Élémens, Préface*, p. xxiii).

Destutt de Tracy devoted the second part of his *Élémens d'idéologie*, some 450 pages, to a presentation of universal grammar suited to the purposes of the new course. Although he did occasionally cite parallel examples in other European languages and stress the value of knowing several languages, his principal interest was in what might fairly be described as the analysis of ordinary French. As an *idéologue* he was committed to provide analyses that would in every case disclose the signified idea (or sensation). His first step in establishing the conditions for such an analysis was to insist that the unit of signification was not the word or phrase, no matter how complex, but only the proposition, the linguistic device expressive of a judgment. If one simply utters the words "Peter," "to be not tall," we say that it means nothing, it makes no sense, although if one merely changes the form of the verb so that one says "Peter is not tall," thereby expressing a judgment, we can discern in what he says signs of his having an idea of Peter and an idea of his height (2.29–33). Thus Destutt de Tracy committed himself to providing ideological analyses only if the linguistic entity to be analyzed occurs within a proposition. Even so, locating the signified idea sometimes required considerable ingenuity, as in his attempt to analyze all "conjunctions" in such a way as to show not only two propositions related by each conjunction but also the idea signified by each.

One can say as much regarding the conjunctions we use in asking questions, even though they might at first seem not to connect two propositions, because the first is suppressed. Thus when I say "how did you get in again?," "why did you leave?," I am really expressing these ideas: "I want to know [*Je demande*] *how* you got in again," "I want to know *why* you left." And when we unfold the sense of those conjunctions the result is: "I want to know *a thing that is the manner in which* you got in again," "I want to know *a thing that is the reason for which* you left." (2.136)

In Destutt de Tracy considerations of grammar were entirely subject to the demands of ideological analysis, as is plain not only in the structure of his final analyses above but also in his readiness, quite unusual even among *grammairiens-philosophes*, to revise the classifications of traditional grammar (treating the "adverbs" *comment* and *pourquoi* as "conjunctions") when philosophical considerations seemed to call for their revision. When his volume devoted to universal grammar appeared in 1803, the experimental substitution of universal grammar for logic and metaphysics in the schools had already been abandoned, along with the *idéologues'* highest hopes for revolutionizing philosophy.

In Germany, Wolff and Lambert had taken notice of universal grammar, but the movement had no appreciable impact on philosophy. In England it affected mainly the work of Harris, of James Beattie (1735–1803), and of John Horne Tooke (1736–1812), all of whom developed universal grammar far less as a philosophical than as a philological inquiry. By the beginning of the nineteenth century, universal grammar was rapidly going out of fashion as a branch of philosophy, even in France, despite the last efforts of the *idéologues*.

THE NINETEENTH AND TWENTIETH CENTURIES

Bentham. Jeremy Bentham (1748–1832) did almost all his work in philosophy of language during the last twenty years of his life, primarily under the influence of Locke, the *idéologues*, and the universal grammarians. In a passage distinctly reminiscent of Locke's call for the development of "the doctrine of signs," Bentham expressed his own conviction that "a demand exists for an entirely new system of *Logic*, in which shall be comprehended a *theory of language*, considered in the most general point of view" (*Works*, John Bowring, ed., 8.119–120). His belief in the importance of a theory of language within a system of logic seems to have made an impression on Mill and may mark the beginning of the return to a view of the interrelations of logic and language more like that prevailing in the later Middle Ages than like that of the eighteenth century.

Universal grammar constituted a part of Bentham's plan for fulfilling the demand he had recognized, and his account of its subject matter is modeled explicitly on what he considered the "pioneering" work of John Horne Tooke (see, for instance, 8.187–188). Unlike Tooke, however, Bentham was inclined to consider it a branch of philosophical rather than philological inquiry and echoed the *idéologues* in his claim that within "the field of universal grammar it is not enough for a man to look into the books that are extant on the subject of grammar, whether particular or universal—he must look into his own mind" (10.193). He also followed the *idéologues*, Degérando in particular, in rejecting Condillac's view that languages and analytic methods were identifiable. On the one hand, he held, the analysis of experience on the most primitive level was dependent on the prelinguistic faculty of attention; on the other hand, "every name, which is not, in the grammatical sense, a *proper* name, is the sign and result" of an act of *synthesis* rather than of analysis (8.75; 8.121–126). Bentham did, however, cite Lavoisier's Condillac-inspired reform of the language of chemistry as a prime example of the practical value of the philosophy of language (3.273).

On more strictly semantic questions Bentham occasionally wrote as if he had simply absorbed and to some extent clarified the doctrines of Locke's Book III, but when his most distinctive refinements of Locke are brought together, they mark a genuine advance in the history of semantics. He was in general agreement with Locke that "language is the sign of thought, an instrument for the communication of thought from . . . the mind of him by whom the discourse is uttered [to another mind]. . . . The immediate subject of a communication made by language is always the state of the speaker's mind." The crucial doctrine of immediate signification, which in Locke had been obscured by his vacillating treatment of it, was explicated by Bentham as follows:

> In both these cases ["I am hungry," "That apple is ripe"], an object other than the state of my own mind is the subject of the discourse held by me, but in neither of them is it the *immediate* subject. In both of them the *immediate* subject is no other than the state of my own mind—*an opinion entertained by me in relation to the ulterior object or subject. . . .* [Language] may be the sign of . . . other objects in infinite variety, but of this object [the utterer's state of mind] it is always a sign, and it is only through this that it becomes the sign of any other object. (8.329–331)

Since, however, "communication may convey information purely, or information for the purpose of excitation" (8.301), the immediately signified state of the speaker's mind may be either "the state of the *passive* or *receptive* part of it, or the state of the *active* or *concupiscible* part" (8.329). Bentham described the use of language as a medium of communication as its "transitive" use. "By its *transitive* use, the collection of these signs is only the vehicle of thought; by its *intransitive* use, it is an instrument employed in the creation and fixation of thought itself." Consequently the transitive use of language "is indebted for its existence" to the intransitive use (8.228–229, 8.301).

Partly because he had begun with "thoughts" rather than Lockean ideas as the immediate significata of linguistic signs, and perhaps also because of the similar position taken in Destutt de Tracy's universal grammar, Bentham recognized not words but propositions as the elements of significance.

> If nothing less than the import of an entire proposition be sufficient for the giving full expression to any [but] the most simple thought, it follows that, no word being anywhere more than a fragment of a proposition, *no word is of itself the complete sign of any thought*. It was in the form of entire propositions that when first uttered, discourse was uttered. . . . *Words may be considered as the result of a sort of analysis*—a chemicological process for which, till of a comparatively much later period than that which gave birth to propositions, the powers of the mind were not ripe. (8.320–323; italics added)

"In language, therefore, the *integer* to be looked for is an entire proposition" (8.188).

Many of Bentham's predecessors, but especially Locke, had inveighed against the philosophers' tendency to "take words for things." Bentham's refinement and extension of this notion into a doctrine of "linguistic fictions" is his most distinctive contribution to philosophy of language. He began by taking the evidently unprecedented step of defining extralinguistic elements in terms of the functions of certain elements of language.

> An *entity* is a denomination in the import of which every subject matter of discourse, for the designation of which the grammatical part of speech called a noun-substantive is employed, may be comprised. . . . A *real* entity is an entity to which, on the occasion and for the purpose of discourse, existence is really meant to be ascribed. . . . A *fictitious* entity is an entity to which, though by the grammatical form of the discourse employed in speaking of it, existence be ascribed, yet in truth and reality existence is not meant to be ascribed.

Thus the noun-substantive "motion" in "that body is in motion" is the name of a fictitious entity, since "this, taken in the literal sense, is as much as to say—Here is a larger body, called a motion; in this larger body, the other body, namely, the really existing body, is contained." While he insisted that linguistic fictions stood in need of what he called exposition, he also maintained that they were contrivances "but for which language . . . could not have existence" (8.195–199).

The mode of exposition to which linguistic fictions were to be subjected was called paraphrasis, which "consists in taking the word that requires to be expounded—viz. the name of a *fictitious* entity—and, after making it up into a *phrase,* applying to it another phrase, which, being of the same import, shall have for its principal and characteristic word the name of the corresponding *real* entity" (8.126–127). Since all words designative of nonphysical entities involved linguistic fictions, most of the work of philosophy, Bentham thought, would consist in such exposition of language.

In his *Principles of Morals and Legislation,* Chapter X, Bentham recommended a method of starting philosophical inquiry that was later to be employed and advocated by J. L. Austin. "I cannot pretend," Bentham said of his catalogue of motives in that chapter, "to warrant it complete. To *make sure* of rendering it so, the *only* way would be to turn over the dictionary from beginning to end; an operation which, in a view to perfection, would be necessary for more purposes than this" (italics added).

Humboldt. The special historical importance of the work of Wilhelm von Humboldt (1767–1835) lies in the fact that it incorporates the transition from the eighteenth-century philosophy of language to the nineteenth-century science of linguistics. It does so not only in respect of the philosophical doctrines presented in it but also because Humboldt coupled those doctrines with empirical investigations of the sort he considered to be demanded by his philosophy of language.

His most important work—*Ueber die Kawi-Sprache auf der Insel Jawa* (published 1836–1839)—begins with the lengthy philosophical essay "Ueber die Verschiedenheit des menschlichen Sprachbaues und ihren Einflusz auf die geistige Entwickelung des Menschengeschlechts." In it he developed his single most influential and original notion—that language is to be viewed not as a finished product but as a continuous process (*Sie selbst ist kein Werk, ergon, sondern eine Tätigkeit, energeia*), as the totality of instances of speech (or of the understanding of speech). Written words constitute language only when they are read and to the extent to which they are understood (*Gesammelte Schriften,* A. Leitzmann, ed., 7[No. 1].46 ff.). The rules of syntax and the individual words of a language are, then, the products of analysis, having real existence only insofar as they are embodied in instances of actual speech. Thus, as Destutt de Tracy and Bentham had observed from other points of view, "we cannot possibly conceive of language as beginning with the designation of objects by words and thence proceeding to their organization. In reality, discourse is not composed from words that preceded it. On the contrary, the words issued from the totality of discourse" (7[No. 1].72 ff.; cf. 7[No. 1].143).

The essential role played by language in fixing and organizing thoughts had been recognized long before Humboldt, but he extended that recognition into the bold new doctrine that language activity was the medium of contact between the mind and reality. "Man lives with the world about him principally, indeed . . . exclusively, as language presents it to him." Humboldt felt that this conception of language held the solution to the post-Kantian problems regarding subjectivity and objectivity.

> In speech the energy of the mind breaks a path through the lips, but its product returns through our own ears. The idea is [thus] translated into true objectivity without being withdrawn from subjectivity. Only language can do this. . . . [Moreover,] just as the particular sound mediates between the object and the man, so the whole language mediates between him and the nature that works upon him from within and without. He surrounds himself with a world of sounds in order to assimilate the world of objects. (7[No. 1]. 55 ff.)

Somewhat as Hamann had done, Humboldt thus believed that philosophy reduced to the philosophy of language, and that he had "discovered the art of using language as a vehicle by which to explore the heights, the depths, and the diversity of the whole world" (letter to Wolfe, 1805).

The differences among natural languages were philosophically as well as scientifically important in Humboldt's view, and he was opposed to the prevailing eighteenth-century type of universal grammar, which achieved its universality at the expense of linguistic differences that happened not to fit the grammatical schema adopted by the grammarian-philosopher. He proposed instead, and provided examples of, a genuinely comparative grammar, insisting that the comparative grammarian avoid adopting the grammar of Latin or of his native language as the schema within which to organize the forms of other languages ("Ueber das Entstehen der grammatischen Formen und ihren Einflusz auf die Ideenentwickelung," in *Gesammelte Schriften* 4.285 ff.). Each natural language, he believed, was characterized by its own "inner form," expressive of the psyche of the nation within which it had developed and which it bound together. The distinctive inner form manifested itself in the root words as well as in the patterns of word combinations peculiar to the language. This doctrine, which powerfully influenced the development of linguistics, was in Humboldt's presentation of it little more than a consequence of the traditional semantic doctrine that speech reflected not objects but man's view of objects, coupled with the novel romanticist conviction that the reactions of men to the world around them were not everywhere the same. Not only were the grammatical differences among languages to be respected and studied in their own right, but the separate vocabularies were also to be re-examined with a view to discovering not interlinguistic synonymy (which, strictly speaking, was illusory) but the nuances of meaning that gave expression to different world views (7[No. 1].59 ff.; 89 ff.; 190 ff.).

Humboldt's immediate influence was not on philosophers but on other founders of the science of linguistics, particularly on Franz Bopp (1791–1867). What influence his work eventually had on philosophy of language, at any rate outside Germany, seems to have been transmitted indirectly through the work of nineteenth- and twentieth-century linguists.

Johnson. Alexander Bryan Johnson (1786–1867), the earliest American philosopher of language, was an isolated figure in the history of semantics. Locke and the Scottish common-sense philosophers strongly influenced his work, and he had learned something of the *idéologues* through Dugald Stewart's account of them. He seems, however, to have had little or no knowledge of his other predecessors and contemporaries. Johnson's work on language, published in three successive versions and under various titles in 1828, 1836, and 1854, went unnoticed for a hundred years and has had no appreciable influence since its republication during the 1940s. As the circumstances of his work would lead one to expect, it was unusual for its time both in its insights and in its mistakes.

The mistake that led to most of the others and to some of his principal insights as well occurred in his account of the semantics of words, in which he identified the signification(s) of a word with the thing(s) to which the word is applied. "Every word," he argued, "is a sound, which had no signification before it was employed to name some phenomenon." Consequently, "words have no inherent signification, but as many meanings as they possess applications to different phenomena. *The phenomenon to which a word refers, constitutes in every case, the signification of the word*" (*Treatise on Language*, Lectures VI and V; italics added). The phenomena available as referents (or meanings) were exhaustively divided by Johnson into "sights, sounds, tastes, feels, smells, internal feelings, thoughts, and words" (Lecture XI). The word "table," for example, signifies both a sight and a feel, "two distinct existences" bearing a single name. In this way "language implies a oneness to which nature conforms not in all cases," and men are prone to "make language the expositor of nature, instead of making nature the expositor of language" (Lecture III). Johnson made this common human failing his constant theme and provided several examples of philosophical and scientific difficulties that he felt were obviated by exposing a confusion of this sort as their

source. Philosophers, he suggested, might append to every "nominal unit that aggregates objects generically different" a capital letter—for instance, S, sight; F, feel—indicative of the phenomenon signified on each occasion. By that means Hume, for example, might be seen to be announcing an "unconscious quibble," when he says, 'The table (S) which we see, seems to diminish (S) as we recede from it, but the real table (F) suffers no diminution (F).' The whole zest of the proposition consists in the sensible duality of each of the nominal units table and diminution. . . . We play bo-peep with words, by neglecting to discriminate the intellectually conceived oneness of diminution, and its physical duality" (*The Meaning of Words*, pp. 89–92).

In his account of the semantics of propositions Johnson remained faithful to the identification of meaning and referent with disastrous results, the most obvious of which was the confusion of meaningfulness (or meaninglessness) with truth (or falsity). "No proposition," he held, "can signify more than the particulars to which it refers" (Lecture VIII). He saw that one difficulty with this doctrine was that under it "the proposition that all men must die seems equivalent only to the proposition that all men have died." In his attempt to preserve the "universal application" of such general propositions, he adopted the indirect criterion of the failure of their negations to refer to any sensible particular. Thus "the proposition that all men will die, possesses a universal application for the reason that to say, some men will not die, *refers to no sensible particulars, and hence is insignificant*" (Lecture IX; italics added).

It was, however, this same approach to the semantics of propositions that led Johnson to develop and make critical use of a verifiability criterion of meaningfulness. Chemists, he remarked, had an indisputable right to "say simply that they can produce hydrogen gas, and oxygen, from water, and vice versa," but what they say instead is "that water is nothing but a combination of these gases. The assertion is true, *so long as it means [merely] the phenomena to which it refers;* but it produces wonder, because we suppose it has a meaning beyond the phenomena" (Lecture VII; italics added). Similarly, "if you inquire of an astronomer whether the earth is a sphere, he will desire you to notice what he terms the earth's shadow in an eclipse of the moon, the gradual disappearance of a ship as it recedes from the shore, &c. After hearing all that he can adduce in proof of the earth's sphericity, *consider the proposition* ['the earth is a sphere'] *significant of these proofs. If you deem it significant beyond them, you are deceived by the forms of language*" (Lecture VIII; italics added). In his verifiability criterion of meaningfulness and in his related discrimination of significant and insignificant questions (Lectures XIX ff.), Johnson anticipated some of the fundamental semantic principles of the pragmatists and positivists.

Mill. Many of the remarkable developments in semantics in the late nineteenth and early twentieth centuries took place under the influence of or in reaction against the doctrines of John Stuart Mill (1806–1873). He presented his "philosophy of language" (a designation he seems to have made current) in Book I and Chapters III–VI of Book

IV of *A System of Logic* (1843), acknowledging the influence of the medieval logicians and Hobbes in particular, but also of Locke, Dugald Stewart, and others in the tradition of British empiricism. Like most of his empiricist predecessors in France and England, Mill believed that a philosophical inquiry into language had a high therapeutic value for philosophy itself, viewing metaphysics as "that fertile field of delusion propagated by language" (1.7.5).

By way of explaining his return to the practice of associating semantical inquiries with logic, Mill argued that since "language is an instrument of thought," not only in the reasoning process proper but in the antecedent operations of classification and definition, "logic . . . includes, therefore, the operation of Naming" (Introduction, Sec. 7). It is not clear whether Mill intended to *identify* the ratiocinative use of language with naming or to claim that all language *stems from* the operation of naming, but he did revert to the tradition of considering "names" as the elements of his semantic theory. And since he took it to be obvious that "a proposition . . . is formed by putting together two names" (1.1.2), it seemed equally obvious that "the import of words [or names] should be the earliest subject of the logician's consideration: because without it he cannot examine into the import of propositions" (1.1.1).

Names. In his account of the import of names, Mill began by taking the unusual tack of defending "the common usage" against the view of "some metaphysicians," arguing that words are "names of things themselves, and not merely of our ideas of things." (Although there are passages in Hobbes and Locke, for example, that can be interpreted as expressions of that view, neither they nor, it seems likely, anyone else held quite the view Mill was criticizing.) "It seems proper," Mill claimed, "to consider a word as the *name* of that . . . concerning which, when we employ the word, we intend to give information." When, however, "I use a name for the purpose of expressing a belief, it is a belief concerning the thing itself, not concerning my idea of it," even when the belief in question is one concerning some idea of mine (1.2.1).

A name, in Mill's adaptation of scholastic terminology, was said to *denote,* individually and collectively, the things of which it was the name, "the things of which it can be predicated." But, as Mill observed, "by learning what things it is a name of, we do not learn the *meaning* of the name" (1.2.5). A name happens "to fit" a given thing "because of a certain *fact.* . . . If we want to know what the fact is, we shall find the clue to it in the *connotation*" of the name (1.5.2). The connotation of the name is the "attribute" or set of attributes possession of which by a given thing is the fact in virtue of which the name fits the thing, and "the *meaning* of all names, except proper names [which have no meaning] and that portion of the class of abstract names which are not connotative [such as 'squareness,' which *denotes* a single attribute], resides in the connotation" (1.5.2). Mill recognized the connection of this distinction with the doctrine of denominatives (see the discussion of Anselm above), and in a note to 1.5.4 he indicated its relations to Hamilton's intension–extension distinction (see below).

Connotation and denotation. Mill believed that the connotation–denotation distinction was "one of those

which go deepest into the nature of language" (1.2.5). He made considerable use of it himself, and it played an important part in philosophical discussions for at least 75 years afterward. It is, however, a notoriously unclear distinction, especially in Mill's own treatment of it. With regard to denotation, for example, he claimed that a "concrete general name" such as "man" denotes Socrates—that is, is a name of, is predicable of that individual—but he claimed also that it denotes *the class* of which that individual is a member, which (at best) introduces a crucial ambiguity into the notion of denotation. With regard to connotation, the most serious difficulty centers on the notion of "attributes," which Mill suggested at one point was to be identified with what medieval logicians meant by "forms" (1.2.5n). In an evidently more careful account he declared that "the meaning of any general name is some outward or inward phenomenon, consisting, in the last resort, of feelings; and these feelings, if their continuity is for an instant broken, are no longer the same feelings, in the sense of individual identity. What, then, is the common something which gives a meaning to the general name? Mr. [Herbert] Spencer can only say, it is the similarity of the feelings: and I rejoin, the attribute is precisely that similarity. . . . The general term *man* does not connote the sensations derived once from one man. . . . It connotes the general type of the sensations derived from all men, and the power . . . of producing sensations of that type" (2.2.4n). The only plausible interpretation of this doctrine seems to bring it very close to Hobbes's (or Locke's) actual account of words as signs of our ideas (despite Mill's attack on its weakest version: words are *names* of our ideas), for in the end Mill's semantics of words appears to be founded on the familiar view that words are signs of extramental entities (denotation) only in virtue of being signs of mental entities of some sort (connotation). Mill surely would have recoiled at the suggestion that his doctrine of the connoted attribute as a "general type" of sensations committed him to an acceptance of extramental metaphysical entities.

After a detailed, ingenious investigation of the semantics of many-worded connotative concrete individual names (1.2.5), frequently discussed by his successors, Mill turned to the semantics of propositions. His account of the meaning of names and his view that the meaning of a proposition is a function of the meanings of the names that serve as its terms led naturally to his view that "when . . . we are analyzing the meaning of any proposition in which the predicate and the subject, or either of them, are connotative names, it is to the *connotation* of those terms that we must exclusively look, and not to what they *denote*." The view of Hobbes—that the predicate term is to be considered a name of whatever the subject term names—"is a mere consequence of the conjunction between the two attributes," the connotations of the two terms, and is adequate only in case both terms are nonconnotative names (1.5.2). Thus, "all men are mortal" asserts that "the latter set of attributes *constantly accompany* the former set." And on the basis of the account of attributes introduced above, "we may add one more step to complete the analysis. The proposition which asserts that one attribute always accompanies another attribute, really asserts thereby no other thing than this, that one phenomenon always accompanies another phenomenon; in so much that where we find the latter, we have assurance of the existence of the former." He was, however, careful to note that "the connotation of the word *mortal* goes no farther than to the occurrence of the phenomenon at some time or other" (1.5.4).

When he came to discuss "real" (as opposed to "verbal") propositions, however, Mill disclosed that with respect to real propositions the account just cited was only one of "two formulas" in which "their import may be conveniently expressed." The account in terms of companion sets of attributes is suited to the view of real propositions "as portions of speculative truth." But they may be viewed also "as memoranda for practical use," and Mill's consideration of them in this light prefigured some elements of pragmatist theories of meaning. "The practical use of a proposition is, to apprise or remind us what we have to expect in any individual case which comes in the assertion contained in the proposition. In reference to this purpose, the proposition, All men are mortal, means that the attributes of man are *evidence of*, are a *mark of*, mortality; . . . that where the former are we . . . [should] expect to find the latter." The two formulas for expressing the import of real propositions are, Mill maintained, "at bottom equivalent; but the one points the attention more directly to what a proposition means, the latter to the manner in which it is to be used" (1.6.5).

Mill agreed with the majority of his philosophical contemporaries in deploring attempts to devise a formalized language for philosophy and suggesting that philosophers reform the natural languages for their uses. He was in a minority, however, in urging philosophers to have a healthy respect for natural languages. One of the "inherent and most valuable properties" of a natural language is "that of being the conservator of ancient experience"—"Language is the depository of the accumulated body of experience to which all former ages have contributed their part, and which is the inheritance of all yet to come." Consequently, "it may be good to alter the meaning of a word, but it is bad to let any part of the meaning drop" (4.4.6). Mill was emphatic about the special respect with which words of uncertain connotation were to be treated, and he laid down as a principle for the guidance of philosophers that "the meaning of a term actually in use is not an arbitrary quantity to be fixed, but an unknown quantity to be sought" (4.4.3). The attitude toward natural languages enjoined on philosophers by Mill was in part the attitude adopted by J. L. Austin and other twentieth-century philosophers of ordinary language.

Peirce and the pragmatists. In a tradition stemming from Locke, Charles Sanders Peirce (1839–1914) characterized logic "in its general sense" as "*semiotic* (σημειωτική), the quasi-necessary, or formal, doctrine of signs" (*Collected Papers* 2.227) and went much further than anyone before him had tried to go toward the development of a completely general theory of signs. (Insofar as Peirce's semiotic deals with nonlinguistic signs, it lies outside the scope of this article, but his elaborate, varying terminology makes it difficult to present a single standard version of even that portion of the theory which is directly relevant to his treatment of linguistic meaning.)

Peirce seems sometimes to have thought of semiotic as a generalized version of the medieval trivium, describing its three branches as "pure grammar," "logic proper," and "pure rhetoric" (2.228–229). The first branch was to investigate the necessary conditions of meaningfulness, the second was to investigate the necessary conditions of truth, and the third was "to ascertain the laws by which in every scientific intelligence one sign gives birth to another, and especially one thought brings forth another" (2.229). These branches, with their subject matter somewhat differently described, were to become well known in twentieth-century philosophy under the designations "syntactics," "semantics," and "pragmatics" respectively—designations introduced by Charles W. Morris (*Foundations of the Theory of Signs*, 1938) and used extensively by Rudolf Carnap and others.

"Semiosis" was Peirce's name for an instance of signification, which he described as involving three principal elements: the *sign*, "something which stands to somebody for something in some respect or capacity" (its "ground"); the *object*, that for which the sign stands; and the *interpretant*, another sign, equivalent to or "more developed" than the original sign and caused by the original sign in the mind of its interpreter (2.228). The notion of the interpretant is the distinctive element in Peirce's general account of signification and the one that played the central role in his pragmatism (or "pragmaticism"), which he often described as consisting entirely in "a method for ascertaining the real meaning of any concept, doctrine, proposition, word, or other sign" (5.6).

Some of Peirce's predecessors had already suggested that the meaning of a word could be determined only on a given occasion of its occurrence within a propositional context, but in Peirce the traditional primacy of the semantics of words over the semantics of propositions was so thoroughly overturned that his theory of linguistic meaning is almost exclusively a theory regarding the meaning of whole propositions. According to that theory, a proposition, like every other sign, has an object—some state of affairs, factual or otherwise. The *meaning* of a proposition, however, he identified not with its object but with one particular kind of effect of the proposition on an interpreter, namely, its "*logical*" (as opposed to "emotional" or "energetic") *interpretant* (5.476).

Peirce's definitive account of the logical interpretant appeared in the 1905 paper "What Pragmatism Is" (5.411–434), in which he attempted as well to explain the distinctive and often misinterpreted "futuristic" aspect of pragmatist meaning theory.

> The rational meaning of every proposition lies in the future. How so? The meaning of a proposition [that is, its logical interpretant] is itself a proposition. Indeed, it is no other than the very proposition of which it is the meaning: it is a translation of it. But of the myriads of forms into which a proposition may be translated, what is that one which is to be called its very meaning? It is, according to the pragmaticist, that form in which the proposition becomes applicable to human conduct, . . . that form which is most directly applicable to self-control under every situation and to every purpose. This is why he locates

the meaning in future time; for future conduct is the only conduct that is subject to self-control.

The only form of the proposition that would satisfy all these conditions was "the general description of all the experimental phenomena which the assertion of the proposition virtually predicts. For an experimental phenomenon is the fact asserted by the proposition that action of a certain description will have a certain kind of experimental result; and experimental results are the only results that can affect human conduct." Thus, as Peirce finally conceived of it, the meaning of a proposition is evidently to be explicated in the form of a true conditional with the original proposition as antecedent and, as its consequent, a conjunction of propositions constituting "the general description of all the experimental phenomena which the assertion of the [original] proposition virtually predicts."

Among the more striking problems in this account are (1) the difficulty of applying it to propositions other than those which occur within the context of an experimental science and (2) the fact that the meaning of a proposition is said to consist in other propositions, the meanings of which are presumably explicable in the same fashion, ad infinitum. Peirce was aware of both these problems. His response to (1) was generally to minimize the differences between the context of an experimental science and other contexts within which propositions occur, although he did occasionally, especially in his later writings, acknowledge the perhaps insuperable difficulties in employing this as a completely general theory of linguistic meaning. With regard to (2) Peirce was at first inclined to claim that a proposition (or any other sign) was, indeed, imperfectly significant if the series of its interpretants was finite ("Sign," in Baldwin's *Dictionary*). Later, however, the notion of "the *ultimate* logical interpretant" was introduced. "The real and living logical conclusion" of the series of logical interpretants is an expectation (on the interpreter's part) of certain phenomena "virtually" predicted by the assertion of the original proposition. This expectation Peirce frequently referred to as "habit." "The deliberately formed, self-analyzing habit—self-analyzing because formed by aid of analysis of the exercises that nourished it—is the living definition, the veritable and final logical interpretant" (5.491; cf. 5.486). Habit, which Peirce sometimes described as a "readiness to act in a certain way under certain circumstances and when actuated by a given motive," was not itself a sign and so stood in no need of interpretants of its own.

It was on this very point that Peirce thought his own doctrine differed from that of William James (1842–1910). "In the first place," he wrote, "there is the pragmatism of James, whose definition differs from mine only in that he does not restrict the 'meaning,' that is, the ultimate logical interpretant, as I do, to a habit, but allows percepts, that is, complex feelings endowed with compulsiveness to be such" (5.494). James's own definition of "pragmatism" in Baldwin's *Dictionary* identified it as "the doctrine that *the whole meaning* of a conception *expresses itself* in *practical consequences* either in the shape of conduct to be recommended or in that of experiences to be expected, if the conception be true . . ." (italics added), but in doing so he evidently believed he was promulgating "Peirce's

principle . . . that *the effective meaning* of any philosophic proposition can always be *brought down to* some *particular consequence,* in our *future practical experience,* whether active or passive" (*Collected Essays and Reviews,* R. B. Perry, ed., p. 412; italics added). James's conception of pragmatism as a theory of meaning (and of truth) was, however, unquestionably broader and less carefully qualified than Peirce's and may fairly accurately be summarized in his own characteristic observation that concepts and propositions "have, indeed, no meaning and no reality if they have no use. But if they have any use they have that amount of meaning. And the meaning will be true if the use squares well with life's other uses" (*Pragmatism,* p. 273).

Pragmatism first became generally known in the form given it by James and in the still wider "humanism" of F. C. S. Schiller, and it was in those forms that it was subjected to intense criticism at the beginning of the twentieth century by F. H. Bradley and G. E. Moore, among others. Peirce's more intricate and interesting theory of meaning was not really considered in its own right until some years afterward, perhaps beginning with the publication of C. K. Ogden and I. A. Richards' very influential *The Meaning of Meaning* in 1923, in which some ten pages were devoted to an exposition of Peirce's semiotic.

At the same time a pragmatist theory of meaning more complex and no less broad than James's was being developed in the "instrumentalism" of John Dewey (1859–1952). Dewey discussed meaning of every imaginable sort and in countless contexts, with the result that it is difficult to elicit from his many writings a genuinely representative doctrine specifically of linguistic meaning. Perhaps the least misleading single source is Chapter 5 of his *Experience and Nature,* first published in 1925. His position there was as follows:

The sound, gesture, or written mark which is involved in language is a particular existence. But as such it is not a *word,* and it does not become a word by declaring a mental existence; it becomes a word by gaining meaning; and it gains meaning when its use establishes a genuine community of action. . . . Language and its consequences are characters taken on by natural interaction and natural conjunction in specified conditions of organization. . . . Language is specifically a mode of interaction of at least two beings, a speaker and a hearer; it presupposes an organized group to which these creatures belong, and from whom they have acquired their habits of speech. It is therefore a relationship, not a particularity. . . . The meaning of signs moreover always includes something common as between persons and an object. When we attribute meaning to the speaker as *his* intent, we take for granted another person who is to share in the execution of the intent, and also something, independent of the persons concerned, through which the intent is to be realized. Persons and thing must alike serve as means in a common, shared consequence. This community of partaking is meaning.

Even when, as in these passages, Dewey seems to have been considering linguistic meaning specifically, there is a real possibility that his intentions were much broader, for his conception of language was itself considerably broader than that of most philosophers. He was, for example, prepared to say that "because objects of art are expressive, they are a language. Rather they are many languages. For each art has its own medium and that medium is especially fitted for one kind of communication. . . . The needs of daily life have given superior practical importance to one mode of communication, that of speech" (*Art as Experience*, 1935, p. 106).

Pragmatist theories of meaning, beginning with Peirce's 1878 paper "How to Make Our Ideas Clear," are alike in little more than their tendency to associate the meaning of a proposition with the conditions of its verification, but in that respect they may be said to have inaugurated twentieth-century developments of empiricist and operationalist theories of meaning.

Frege. The contributions of Gottlob Frege (1848–1925) to logic, philosophy of mathematics, and semantics were largely unappreciated at the time of their publication, primarily during the last quarter of the nineteenth century. Their influence (direct or indirect) on recent philosophy has been so great, however, that Frege might fairly be characterized as the first twentieth-century philosopher. In his *Begriffsschrift* (1879) he developed "a formalized language of pure thought modeled on the language of arithmetic," which has been recognized as the first really comprehensive system of formal logic. In his other two major works, *Die Grundlagen der Arithmetik* (1884) and *Die Grundgesetze der Arithmetik* (1893–1903), he tried to show "that arithmetic is founded solely upon logic."

Philosophical problems encountered by Frege in those highly technical undertakings were explored by him in several papers that have had a wider influence than his books have had. As the topics of the books might lead one to expect, his philosophical papers are concerned almost exclusively with one or another aspect of systems of signs. Of these papers, the one that has had most effect on the development of semantics is "Ueber Sinn und Bedeutung" (1892, translated in P. T. Geach and Max Black, *Translations From the Philosophical Writings of Gottlob Frege*, 1952), although the doctrine presented in it may prove to be historically less important than the doctrine of "functions" developed in other papers.

There is a broad and not wholly misleading similarity between Frege's distinction of sense (*Sinn*) and reference (*Bedeutung*) and such distinctions as comprehension–extension (Arnauld), intension–extension (Hamilton), connotation–denotation (Mill), depth–breadth (Peirce). It seems possible, however, that Frege developed his distinction independently; in any case, the details of his doctrine are quite novel. Most important, perhaps, was his discovery of special contexts rendering the application of any such distinction problematic.

Sense and reference. Frege's development of the doctrine of sense and reference began, characteristically, in a consideration of the relation of identity: "=." He noted that "$a = a$ and $a = b$ are obviously statements of different cognitive value," which they would not be if we were to take the relation to hold "between that which the names 'a' and 'b' designate" or refer to (Geach and Black, p. 56). Consequently, "it is natural now, to think of there being connected with a sign (name, combination of words, letter), besides that to which the sign refers, which may be called

the reference of the sign, also what I should like to call the *sense* of the sign, wherein the mode of presentation is contained. . . . The reference of 'evening star' would be the same as that of 'morning star,' but not the sense" (p. 57).

Frege first applied his distinction to proper names, by which he meant any "designation of a single object." In keeping with Arnauld's similar distinction but in opposition to Mill's, Frege ascribed sense as well as reference to such designations. "A proper name (word, sign, sign combination, expression) *expresses* its sense, *stands for* or *designates* its reference. By means of a sign we express its sense and designate its reference" (p. 61). The sense of "Aristotle" "might, for instance, be taken to be the following: the pupil of Plato and the teacher of Alexander the Great" (p. 58n).

Certain expressions, such as "the least rapidly convergent series," have a sense, he maintained, but no reference at all. "In grasping a sense, one is not certainly assured of a reference" (p. 58). An expression that has a reference "must not be taken as having its ordinary reference" when "standing between quotation marks" (pp. 58–59). Such observations had been made before, but Frege seems to have been the first to try to show what that extraordinary reference might be and, more important, to recognize that many different linguistic contexts affected the reference of expressions included within them, especially indirect discourse and subordinate clauses following such verbs as "hear," "conclude," "perceive," and "know." He claimed, for example, that "in reported speech, words . . . have [not their customary but] their *indirect* reference," and that "the indirect reference of a word is . . . its customary sense" (p. 59). His account of the effect of such contexts on reference has not been widely accepted, but the problems raised by it have stimulated the widespread interest of twentieth-century philosophers in such now familiar topics as synonymy, opacity of reference, Leibniz' Law, and what, following Brentano (see below), have come to be called intentional contexts.

Frege was concerned with saying what sort of entities sense and reference were. In the case of a proper name his description of the reference was relatively unproblematic: "a definite object (this word ['object'] taken in the widest range)"— (p. 57)—so wide that "$2 + 2$" and "4," for example, were two proper names with one and the same "object" as their reference. Regarding the sense of a proper name, he found it easier to say what it was not: "The reference of a proper name is the object itself which we designate by its means; the idea, which we have in that case, is wholly subjective; in between lies the sense, which is indeed no longer subjective like the idea, but is yet not the object itself" (p. 60). Thus, there is "an essential [subjective–objective] distinction between the idea and the sign's sense." Frege seems not to have completely depsychologized the notion of the sense of the sign, however, since he suggested that it may be an element in mankind's "common store of thoughts which is transmitted from one generation to another" rather than "a part or a mode of the individual mind" (p. 59).

In Frege's discussion of the sense and reference of declarative sentences, the doctrine of the sense was relatively straightforward while the account of the reference became problematic. A sentence, he held, "contains a thought," and by "a thought" he meant "not the subjective performance of thinking but its objective content, which is capable of being the common property of several thinkers" (p. 62 and note). The two sentences "the morning star is a planet" and "the evening star is a planet" contain different thoughts, as may be seen from the fact that "anybody who did not know that the evening star is the morning star might hold the one thought to be true, the other false. The thought, accordingly, cannot be the reference of the sentence, but must rather be considered its sense" (p. 62). We are content to consider only the sense of sentences as long as we are not concerned to judge of their truth or falsity, but "in every judgment, no matter how trivial, the step from the level of thoughts to the level of reference (the objective) has already been taken" (p. 64). What we seek in judgment is the truth-value of the sentence. "We are therefore driven into accepting the truth-value of a sentence as constituting its reference. . . . Every declarative sentence concerned with the reference of its words is therefore to be regarded as a proper name, and its reference, if it has one, is either the True or the False" (p. 63).

As his use of the phrase "driven into accepting" indicates, Frege was well aware that this was a startling doctrine of the semantics of sentences. Much of the remainder of his paper on sense and reference was devoted to considerations that he felt tended to support it, among them Leibniz' Law; for "what else but the truth-value could be found, that belongs quite generally to every sentence if the reference of its components is relevant, and remains unchanged by substitutions of the kind in question?" (p. 64).

The doctrine that sentences are proper names, whether or not of the True and the False, had an important negative effect in that its rejection by Wittgenstein (see, for instance, *Tractatus* 3.143) and by Russell under Wittgenstein's influence (see, for instance, "Logical Constructions," Lecture I) helped to shape the course of philosophy of language in the twentieth century.

It is quite likely, however, that Frege's assimilation of declarative sentences to proper names was not quite so thorough or simple as his presentation of it in "Ueber Sinn und Bedeutung" suggests. Some of his remarks in an earlier paper, "Funktion und Begriff" (1891), at least raise the possibility that he may have denied proper-name status to sentences actually being used in making assertions (rather than considered as examples). In order to make what he took to be the indispensable "separation of the act from the subject-matter of judging" he introduced his assertion sign—"⊢"—"so that, e.g., by writing

$$\vdash 2 + 3 = 5$$

we *assert that* $2 + 3$ equals 5. Thus here we are *not just writing down a truth-value*, as in

$$2 + 3 = 5,$$

but also at the same time *saying that it is the True*." And in a note to this passage he maintained that "'⊢$2 + 3 = 5$' does not *designate* [that is, refer to] anything; it *asserts* something" (p. 34; italics added).

Mauthner. Of the several late nineteenth-century philosophers writing in German whose work centered on a concern with language, the most unusual was Fritz Mauthner (1849–1923). His principal work, *Beiträge zu einer Kritik der Sprache,* fills three large volumes and went through three editions, the first in 1901–1902. In his thoroughgoing attempt to transform all philosophy into philosophy of language, in his criticisms of Kant, and in his penchant for paradox he resembled Hamann, whom he admired, and also, to some extent, Humboldt. He seems, however, to have been most powerfully influenced by the positivism of Ernst Mach and especially by Hume's skepticism, adopting as his philosophical watchword "Back to Hume!"

Part of what Mauthner meant by that is apparent in the epistemological doctrine on which he founded his critique of language: "Our memory [with which he identified our knowledge] contains nothing but what our poor fortuitous senses [*Zufallsinne*] have presented to it" (*Beiträge* 3.536). By calling our senses "fortuitous" he was calling attention to the fact that if we had been otherwise equipped with senses, we might have framed a very different view of the world. Language, however, depicts not the world but a world view. Therefore, any attempt to infer propositions regarding reality from facts of language is a form of "word-superstition." Moreover, each man's individual senses present a world view unique in certain ultimately undeterminable respects, and so communication by means of language, even if it purports to be no more than an exchange of views, is fundamentally illusory. "No man knows the others. . . . With respect to the simplest concepts we do not know of one another whether we have the same representation associated with one and the same word." From such avowedly Lockean observations Mauthner drew the typically paradoxical conclusion that "by means of language men have made it forever impossible to get to know one another" (1.54). Thus he characterized language as "nothing other than just the community or the mutuality of world-views." It is not a tool for the communication or acquisition of knowledge; indeed, it is not a tool or an object of any sort but merely a practice, a use. And "because it is no object of use but use itself, it perishes without use" (1.24). But of all Mauthner's many characterizations of language the one most suggestive of distinctively twentieth-century attitudes is this: "Language is merely an apparent value [*Scheinwert*], like a rule of a game [*Spielregel*], which becomes more binding as more players submit to it, but which neither alters nor comes into contact with [*begreifen*] the world of reality" (1.25).

Philosophy, in Mauthner's view, had to become a critique of language if it was to be anything at all, and in that guise its principal function was to be therapeutic. "Philosophy . . . cannot wish to be anything more than critical attention to language. Philosophy can do no more with respect to the organism of language or of the human spirit than can a physician with respect to the physiological organism. It can attentively observe and designate the developments with names" (1.657). "If I want to ascend into the critique of language, which is at present the most important undertaking of thinking mankind, I must do away with language behind me and before me and in me, step by step—I must break in pieces each rung of the ladder as I tread on it" (1.1–2). It comes as no surprise to learn that the end of this therapeutic process was to be silence, the silence of mystical contemplation.

In the course of the long process, however, Mauthner found occasion to make many insightful observations on traditional problems of the philosophy of language. As several of his contemporaries and immediate predecessors had done, he recognized not the word but the sentence (*Satz*) as the unit of meaningfulness and described the meaning of the word as a function of its use in a given sentence. Another position that was not new but to which he gave an especially forceful presentation was the rejection of the view "that because there is a word, it must be a word *for* something; that because a word exists there must exist something real corresponding to that word." This form of word superstition he regarded as "mental weakness" (2d ed., 1.159). It is probably only coincidence, but the name theory of linguistic meaning against which Mauthner inveighed bears a strong resemblance in some respects to the theories of Meinong and Husserl then being published and to the early views of Russell and Wittgenstein. Mauthner also opposed efforts at universal grammar (such as some of Brentano's followers were then engaged in) and mathematical logic, maintaining that all formalization of language obliterated or obscured far more than it clarified. Thus, he noted that "if someone says 'cheese is cheese' . . . this utterance is *not* an instance of the general formula 'A = A' " (3.366), a formula "so empty that outside logic it must arouse the suspicion of insanity" (*Wörterbuch der Philosophie*, article "A = A").

Perhaps more than any other philosopher of language Mauthner had an appreciation of the history of the subject; at one time, in fact, he planned a fourth volume of his *Beiträge* that was to present the approach to the critique of language throughout the history of philosophy. Even as it stands, however, his work is filled with references to his predecessors and evaluations of their work from the viewpoint of the critique of language. Aristotle, for example, comes off badly, but Locke ranks very high. Indeed, Mauthner took "the English" to task for abandoning the work of Locke, for failing to see that "the content of their famous 'understanding' is simply the dictionary and grammar of human language" (*Beiträge* 3.535).

Mauthner's own effect on the history of the philosophy of language is still difficult to assess. Wittgenstein certainly knew of his work (see, for instance, *Tractatus* 4.0031). Whether or not Wittgenstein's turn in the direction of some of Mauthner's doctrines in *Philosophical Investigations* was coincidence or derived in part from Mauthner's influence remains an open question.

Husserl and Meinong. The students of Franz Brentano (1838–1917), among whom were Husserl, Meinong, Marty, and Twardowski, were alike at least in taking Brentano's concept of intentionality as a point of departure in their own philosophizing. Brentano had introduced intentionality in his *Psychologie vom empirischen Standpunkt* (1874) as the differentia of "mental states," a characteristic "which the schoolmen of the middle ages called the intentional (or mental) inexistence of an object and which we . . . describe as *the relation to a content*, or *the direction to an object* (by which we need not understand a reality), or *an immanent objectivity*. Every mental state possesses in itself something that serves as an object, although not all possess their objects in the same way" (*Psychologie* 2.1.5; italics added). The "intending" of an object by a mental state, the "directedness" of a mental state, bears a close enough resemblance to what is called significance in other contexts that much of what Brentano and his followers had to say in working out their central doctrine of intentionality has some relevance to semantics, broadly conceived. More specifically, the notion of intentionality underlies the considerable discussion in semantics of "intentional contexts," produced as a result of the ordinary use of such "intentional words" as "believe," "want," and "ascribe." For present purposes, however, our attention is confined to what Brentano's two best-known students, Husserl and Meinong, had to say expressly about language and linguistic meaning. The doctrines of both men passed through several stages of development and contain many complexities, only a few of which can be noted here.

The philosophy of language of Edmund Husserl (1859–1938) was developed at various places in his work but is concentrated in the first and fourth essays in his *Logische Untersuchungen* (1900–1901; rev. ed. 1913–1921). The first, entitled "Expression and Meaning" (2.23–105), was designed partly as a general preparation for intensive work in phenomenology as conceived by Husserl. It opens with an investigation of signs in general and proceeds to the consideration of expressions, signs that may be said to have meanings (*Bedeutungen*) and not merely to indicate something. The three ingredients of meaningfulness, or "the meaning-situation" are (1) a "meaning-endowing act," or "meaning-intention" on the part of the producer of the expression, which may be associated with a "meaning-fulfilling act" on the part of an interpreter of the expression; (2) the *content* of these acts, or the *meaning* of the expression; (3) the *object* of these acts, or, in Husserl's broader terminology, the *objectivity* that is meant by the expression. To talk about what is expressed by a given expression may be to talk about any one of these ingredients. (To some extent Husserl avoided the usual sort of technical distinctions among semantical relations, specifically rejecting Frege's sense–reference distinction as a violation of the ordinary use of the words *Sinn* and *Bedeutung*, words which Husserl used interchangeably [2.53].) Somewhat more precisely, an expression used in ordinary circumstances for purposes of communication may be described as "manifesting" the psychical experience of its producer —that is, the meaning-endowing act—which is a necessary condition of its status as an expression. This manifesting function of an expression would, however, be lacking in the case of an expression used in an unoverheard monologue. The manifesting and the more strictly expressing functions differ also in that, for example, the expression "the three altitudes of a triangle intersect in a point" manifests a distinct mental state or act each time it is used in ordinary circumstances for purposes of communication, although what it expresses, in the stricter sense, remains the same on all occasions of such use.

Some of Husserl's main points in "Expression and

Meaning" are summarized in sections dealing with "equivocations" associated with discussions of meaning and meaninglessness (2.52–61). "A meaningless expression is, properly speaking, not an expression at all." Thus "green is or" (Husserl's example) only gives the appearance of an expression (2.54). Meaningfulness, however, entails reference (*Beziehung*) to an object, regardless of whether that object exists or is "fictive." "Consequently, to use an expression with sense and to refer to an object (to present an object) are one and the same." Nevertheless, Husserl was careful to point out, the object of an expression is not to be confused with its meaning (*ibid.*). As a result, "objectlessness" of an expression is not "meaninglessness" (where "objectlessness" indicates only the lack of a real object). Neither the name "golden mountain" nor the name "round square" is meaningless, although both are objectless, the second one necessarily so (2.55). After a rather obscure passage (2.56–57) in which Husserl was evidently criticizing (without mentioning) pragmatism for identifying meaning with meaning-fulfilling acts, he devoted an entire section to the criticism of Mill's doctrine of connotation and denotation, with particular attention to Mill's view of "non-connotative names" as meaningless. A proper name, Husserl objected, is not a mere sign but an expression. It can, like any other expression, function as a mere sign—for instance, in a signature—but it ordinarily does much more. He felt that if Mill's distinction between what a name denotes and what it connotes were carefully separated from the merely related distinction between what a name names and what it means, some of the confusion in Mill's doctrine would be dissipated (2.57–61).

In his fourth Logical Investigation, "The Distinction of Independent and Dependent Meanings and the Idea of a Pure Grammar" (2.294–342), Husserl pursued the analysis of meaning undertaken in the earlier treatise. Of most historical interest is his attempted refurbishing of the Enlightenment project of a universal grammar, an enterprise furthered by Anton Marty (1847–1914), another of Brentano's students, in his *Grundlegung der allgemeinen Grammatik und Sprachphilosophie* (1908). In his treatise Husserl developed a notion of "pure logic" as "the pure formal theory of *meanings*" and insisted that we could not understand the functioning of even our own language if we did not first construct a "pure-logical grammar," the subject matter of which would be the "ideal form" of language. At a later stage of his career, however, Husserl abandoned this "ideal-language" approach to considerations of semantics and syntax and urged the return to living history and actual speech—the return to the *Lebenswelt*—for the materials of philosophy.

Husserl's influence in all respects has been felt more strongly in Europe than in England and America. Some of his work in philosophy of language has been investigated and developed further by, among others, Maurice Merleau-Ponty.

Alexius Meinong (1853–1920) developed his theory of linguistic meaning as an integral part of the "theory of objects" in which he worked out his version of the doctrine of intentionality. His most complete presentation of it may be found in his *Ueber Annahmen* (1902; rev. ed. 1910).

Meinong began, in the traditional way, by developing a semantics of words. His assimilation of it to his theory of objects gave rise to no particularly novel features. "Whoever happens to pronounce the word 'sun,'" he declared, "normally gives *expression* [*Ausdruck*] thereby, whether or not he wishes to do so, that a definite presentation—it may be a presentation of perception or one of imagination—is taking place within him. What kind of presentation it is is determined principally on the basis of what is presented in it—i.e., its object—and this object is precisely that which the word 'sun' *refers to* [*bedeutet*]" (*Ueber Annahmen*, pp. 19–20; italics added). He summed up his account of the "expression" and "reference" of words (which he presented explicitly as opposed to Husserl's doctrine of *Ausdruck* and *Bedeutung*) by saying that "a word always 'refers to' the object of the presentation that it 'expresses' and, conversely, expresses the presentation of the object that it refers to" (p. 20). (The obvious similarities to Frege's doctrine of sense and reference, even as to the same unusual use of *bedeuten,* may be coincidental. There are, of course, clear differences as well, especially as regards Frege's treatment of "sense" and Meinong's treatment of "expression.") Meinong concluded his rather brief account of the meaning of words by refining his original distinction to the point of recognizing a "secondary" as well as the "primary" expression and reference described above (pp. 20–23).

He then undertook to apply his "antithesis of expression and reference" to the semantics of sentences, and he first applied it in an effort to provide a more satisfactory criterion of sentencehood than that provided by traditional grammar. The phrase "the blue sky" and the sentence "the sky is blue" have, he maintained, one and the same object as their reference. If, however, "I say 'the sky is blue,' I thereby *express* an opinion [*Meinung*], a judgment, that can in no way be gathered from the words 'the blue sky'" (p. 25; italics added). The phrase expresses the kind of experience described by Meinong as the pure presentation or idea, the *Vorstellung* proper, while the sentence expresses a different fundamental kind of experience, the judgment (*Urteil*). The judgment differs from the pure presentation giving rise to it in two respects that might be described as "intentional"—conviction and a determinate position as regards affirmation and negation (p. 2). Sentences, he claimed, might also be used to express "assumptions" (*Annahmen*), which, because they have to be either affirmative or negative assumptions, share the second defining characteristic of judgments but lack the first, conviction (p. 4).

Meinong's most important contribution to semantics, partly because of its effect on the development of Russell's theory of descriptions, was his doctrine of "objectives," particularly in his application of it in the treatment of negative sentences, which he recognized to be crucial cases for his doctrine. Suppose that a magistrate judges that on a given occasion there was no disturbance of the peace. On the Brentano–Meinong view of mental states, there must be an object of that judgment. Putting it another way, there must be a reference for the sentence "there has been no disturbance of the peace," which expresses the magistrate's judgment. It cannot be the disturbance of the peace on the occasion in question, for, by the hypothesis, there is no such object. According to Meinong it can, however, be "the non-existence of a disturbance of the peace" or "that there has been no disturbance of the peace." Meinong held that it makes no sense to say that that nonexistence *exists*, but we may say that "it is the case." This entity, the being of which is being the case, is the "objective" to which the sentence refers. The objective *may* be a fact—if, for example, it is a fact that there has been no disturbance of the peace—but false judgments also have their objectives (2d ed., p. 43). That regarding which the judgment is made—a disturbance of the peace—is the object (proper) of the judgment; what is judged in it—that there has been no disturbance of the peace—is its objective (2d ed., p. 52).

The objectives of negative sentences and the objects of denials of existence, such as "a *perpetuum mobile* does not exist," "must have properties, and even characteristic properties, for without such the belief in non-existence can have neither sense nor justification; but the possession of properties is as much as to say a manner of being [*Sosein*]," which of course is not to be confused with existence. "In this sense 'there are' also objects that do not exist, and I have expressed this in a phrase that, while rather barbarous, I am afraid, is hard to improve upon—viz. 'externality [*Aussersein*] of the pure object'" (p. 79). Meinong believed that he had formulated an important principle in this doctrine, "the principle of the independence of manner of being from existence," which he illustrated and summarized in the following famous passage: "Not only is the often cited golden mountain golden, but the round square, too, is as surely round as it is square. . . . To know that there are no round squares, I have to pass judgment on the round square. . . . Those who like paradoxical expressions can therefore say: there are objects of which it is true that there are no objects of that kind" (*Ueber Gegenstandstheorie*, 1904, pp. 7 ff.).

Meinong's influence on the development of semantics is best exhibited in Russell's series of articles on him in *Mind*, 1899–1907.

Developments in the twentieth century. In two respects language has become the center of attention for English-speaking philosophers during the first two-thirds of the twentieth century. First, a large and apparently still increasing number of philosophers have been interested in investigating language, natural and artificial, from various points of view—an activity describable as philosophy of language. Second, many philosophers, whose main interest has not been philosophy of language but, say, epistemology or ethics or metaphysics, have found it helpful to approach those inquiries by way of an investigation of language—an approach sometimes described as linguistic philosophy. Not surprisingly, many linguistic philosophers have contributed to the philosophy of language as well. The language-centered activity of philosophers has been so far-reaching and so diverse in this century that an account of it would approximate a history of twentieth-century philosophy. Even if we restrict our attention to semantics proper within the philosophy of language, we find, as Ryle has remarked, that "preoccupation with the theory of meaning could be described as the occupational

disease of twentieth-century Anglo-Saxon and Austrian philosophy." The foundations, and in many instances the patterns, of these complex developments can be discerned in the preceding sections of this article, and the details can be found in the many articles of the *Encyclopedia* devoted to the writers, the problems, and the movements associated with philosophy of language and linguistic philosophy in the twentieth century. The concluding section of this article is no more than a brief, necessarily incomplete, survey intended primarily as a guide to detailed discussions elsewhere.

At the turn of the century some of the stage-setting for developments to come was provided by F. H. Bradley (1846–1924) and John Cook Wilson (1849–1915). Although Bradley was an idealist and Cook Wilson a critic of idealism, the two men agreed in rejecting traditional treatments of judgments, particularly the subject–predicate analysis. Because both viewed logic as concerned with thought rather than with language, they saw no reason to tie logical analysis to grammatical forms. They diverged, however, in their attitudes toward ordinary language, Bradley holding that the ordinary expression of a judgment, such as "the sugar is sweet," was "riddled with contradictions" in virtue of its inescapable commitment to abstractions and relations. Cook Wilson, on the other hand, having decreed logical analysis free from considerations of ordinary language, nevertheless insisted that for the student of logic "everything depends" on determining "the *normal* use of . . . a linguistic expression" and warned that "distinctions current in language can never be safely neglected" by philosophers.

Moore, Russell, and Wittgenstein. Foremost among the early anti-idealists were the young G. E. Moore (1873–1958) and Bertrand Russell. In opposition to Bradley, they developed a doctrine of propositions which for a time they shared and which both later repudiated in divergent ways. Moore's method of conceptual analysis indirectly gave a special impetus to the development of linguistic philosophy, for the elusive character of concepts as the subjects for analysis led philosophers attracted by Moore's analytic approach to philosophical problems to apply the technique to linguistic expressions of concepts. Although Moore would not have described himself as an "ordinary language" philosopher, his technique of refuting philosophical statements has been accurately characterized as "pointing out that these statements *go against ordinary language*" (see Norman Malcolm, "Moore and Ordinary Language," in P. A. Schilpp, ed., *The Philosophy of G. E. Moore*, 1942). Russell's own contributions to philosophy of language are as complex and as far-reaching in their influence as those of any single writer of the twentieth century. All the following sources, among others, contain important material: "On Denoting"; the series of articles entitled "The Philosophy of Logical Atomism"; "On Propositions: What They Are and How They Mean"; Chapter 10, "Words and Meaning," in *The Analysis of Mind*; Chapter 4, "Language," in *Philosophy*; and *An Inquiry Into Meaning and Truth*. For an excellent critical survey see Max Black, "Russell's Philosophy of Language," in *Language and Philosophy*; anything briefer would be more misleading than helpful.

One of Russell's principal rivals in extent of influence over philosophy of language and linguistic philosophy in this century is Ludwig Wittgenstein (1889–1951). He and Russell, his teacher, were strong influences on each other during Russell's logical atomism period, just prior to the publication of Wittgenstein's *Tractatus Logico-philosophicus* in 1921. The theory of meaning presented in the *Tractatus* may be characterized in such passages as these: "The proposition is a picture of reality. The proposition is a model of reality as we think it (4.01). . . . I conceive the proposition—like Frege and Russell—as a function of the expressions contained in it" (3.318). The elements of a proposition he called "names," and as for the meaning of names, "The name means the object. The object is its meaning" (3.203). Russell believed that Wittgenstein, like himself at that time, was "concerned with the conditions for a logically perfect language" postulated as an *ideal,* and that language fulfills its function "in proportion as it approaches to the ideal language which we postulate." The *Tractatus* does contain passages—such as 3.323-3.325—conducive to such an interpretation (and Wittgenstein's 1929 paper "Logical Form" certainly does describe philosophy as concerned with the construction of an ideal language). There are, however, likewise indications in the *Tractatus* of the attitudes toward ordinary language that Wittgenstein was to develop in his later philosophy— such as 4.002 and 5.5563. (Commentaries on the *Tractatus* have recently been published by G. E. M. Anscombe, Erik Stenius, George Pitcher, Alexander Maslow, and Max Black.)

Logical positivism. The philosophy of Russell and the early Wittgenstein had considerable influence on the growth of logical positivism, which was associated at first with the Vienna circle. Among the more prominent members of the group were Moritz Schlick (1882–1936), Otto Neurath (1882–1945), Friedrich Waismann (1896–1959), and Rudolf Carnap. Much of the controversy within and surrounding logical positivism focused on "the principle of verifiability," the identification of the meaning of a proposition with its method of verification. Although the principle bears a clear resemblance to pragmatist meaning theories, the positivists believed (evidently mistakenly) that it was to be found in Wittgenstein's writings and his discussions with members of the circle.

Carnap's work, doubtless the most impressive of the positivists' contributions to semantics, developed away from his early identification of meaning with translatability into experience and toward a commitment to "formal semantics" or "logical syntax," represented in, for instance, *Logische Syntax der Sprache* (1934), *Introduction to Semantics* (1942), and *Meaning and Necessity* (1947). This development took place largely under the influence of the logician Alfred Tarski, whose own best-known contribution to semantics is presented in the 1944 paper "The Semantic Conception of Truth and the Foundations of Semantics." Karl Popper, another philosopher who came under Tarski's influence and who was in close contact with the Vienna circle, felt that the positivists' preoccupation with the problem of meaning was misguided. His own "thesis of refutability" was interpreted by Carnap as a reworking of the verifiability principle and helped to con-

vince him that "testability" rather than verifiability was the criterion of meaningfulness.

In England a positivist view of language was presented with great impact by A. J. Ayer in *Language, Truth and Logic* (1936). Waismann, who of all the positivists stood closest to Wittgenstein, settled in England, where his gradual development away from positivist conceptions of language culminated in the long series of articles entitled "Analytic–Synthetic" (*Analysis*, 1949–1952).

The influence of positivism. In the late 1930s, many of the European positivists settled in the United States, where Charles W. Morris attempted to synthesize positivist and pragmatist meaning theory in, for instance, *Signs, Language and Behavior* (1946). (See Gustav Bergmann, *The Metaphysics of Logical Positivism,* 1954, especially Chapter 2, "Semantics"; and Max Black, "Carnap on Semantics and Logic," in *Problems of Analysis,* 1954, and "The Semiotic of Charles Morris," in *Language and Philosophy,* 1949.) A more thoroughgoing and philosophically more influential assimilation of pragmatist and positivist meaning theory is to be found in the later work of C. I. Lewis (1883–1964), especially in *An Analysis of Knowledge and Valuation* (1946).

Carnap's direct influence may be seen in *Semantics and Necessary Truth* (1958) by Arthur Pap (1921–1959) and in the formal semantics of Richard Martin as developed in *Truth and Denotation* (1958), *Toward a Systematic Pragmatics* (1959), *The Notion of Analytic Truth* (1959), and *Intension and Decision* (1963). A somewhat different approach to formal semantics has been taken by some logicians, notably Alonzo Church in such papers as "A Formulation of the Logic of [Frege's] Sense and Denotation" in Henle, Kallen, and Langer, *Structure, Method and Meaning* (1951), and "The Need for Abstract Entities in Semantic Analysis" (1951), in Fodor and Katz, *The Structure of Language* (1964).

Partly as a result of Carnap's difficulties with the intricacies of the distinction between analytic and synthetic statements and the related concept of synonymy, many philosophers, especially in the United States, have developed semantic theories centering on discussions of those topics. Among those philosophers Willard Van Orman Quine and Nelson Goodman have been most influential. (See, for instance, Goodman and Quine, "Steps Toward a Constructive Nominalism," 1947; Goodman, "On Likeness of Meaning," 1949; Quine, *Word and Object,* 1960). Quine has recently been attracted to the behaviorist view of language put forward by the psychologist B. F. Skinner in *Verbal Behavior* (1957).

The Meaning of Meaning (1923), by C. K. Ogden and I. A. Richards, is not generally thought of as being in the mainstream of philosophers' discussions, largely because its authors were not professional philosophers and did not intend their book primarily for an audience of philosophers. While its main impact did fall outside philosophy, it had a marked effect on the development of philosophical semantics, especially in the United States. Charles Morris was evidently influenced by its blend of pragmatism and behaviorism, and the authors' stress on the difference between "descriptive" and "emotive" language had widespread philosophical consequences. (See, for example,

C. L. Stevenson, "Persuasive Definitions," *Mind,* 1938, and *Ethics and Language,* 1944; Black, Stevenson, and Richards, "A Symposium on Emotive Meaning," *Philosophical Review,* 1948; Karl Britton, *Communication,* 1939.)

Language and human nature. Outside philosophy proper, Ogden and Richards' work may be seen as a major contribution to the tradition that considers the study of meaning to have a crucial bearing on human happiness or sanity. The modern resurgence, if not the origin, of this tradition is to be found in the writings of Lady Victoria Welby (1837–1912)—such as *What Is Meaning?* (1903) and *Significs and Language* (1911). Its most enthusiastic proponents have been the "general semanticists" Alfred Korzybski (1879–1950) and his followers, the best-known of whom are Stuart Chase and S. I. Hayakawa. (For a philosophical critique of *The Meaning of Meaning,* see Max Black, "Ogden and Richards' Theory of Interpretation"; see also his "Korzybski's General Semantics." Both are in Black's *Language and Philosophy.*)

A broad philosophical approach to language as a source of insights into human nature was not uncommon among European philosophers of the late nineteenth century and is still occasionally to be found in the work of Continental existentialists and phenomenologists, such as Heidegger, Merleau-Ponty, and Gusdorf. The only twentieth-century representative of this approach who has so far had an appreciable effect among English-speaking philosophers is Ernst Cassirer (1874–1945). The first volume of his *Philosophie der symbolischen Formen* (1923; translated 1953) is devoted to language, and the long first chapter of that volume consists of a selective survey of the history of philosophical inquiries into language. W. M. Urban was influenced by Cassirer in the writing of his *Language and Reality* (1939); Susanne Langer applied some of Cassirer's principles in *Philosophy in a New Key: A Study in the Symbolism of Reason, Rite, and Art* (1942). (See W. M. Urban, "Cassirer's Philosophy of Language," in P. A. Schilpp, ed., *The Philosophy of Ernst Cassirer,* 1949.)

The later Wittgenstein. Between 1930 and 1947 Wittgenstein lectured at Cambridge, developing a position antithetical in most respects to the *Tractatus.* (Some stages in this development are presented in records of his lectures, published in 1958 as *The Blue and Brown Books;* the final results appear in his *Philosophical Investigations,* 1953.) Much of Wittgenstein's later philosophy rests on his rejection of two semantic doctrines: (1) "the naming theory of linguistic meaning," the view that propositions are composed of names the meanings of which are to be identified as the objects named and (2) "the private-language theory," the view that to understand a word is to contemplate some mental entity accessible only to oneself. His rejection of (1) is perhaps summed up in these passages from the *Investigations:* ". . . the word 'meaning' is being used illicitly if it is used to signify the thing that 'corresponds' to the word. That is to confound the *meaning* of a name with the *bearer* of the name. . . . For a *large* class of cases—though not for all—in which we employ the word 'meaning' it can be defined thus: the meaning of a word is its use in the language. And the *meaning* of a name is sometimes explained by pointing to its *bearer*" (Part I, Secs. 40 and 43). As may be seen in preceding sections of

this article, Wittgenstein in the *Tractatus* and Russell in his logical atomism period had been somewhat old-fashioned (perhaps unknowingly) in their adoption of a naming theory of linguistic meaning. The development of semantics had already been tending away from that view in various directions. In his rejection of the private-language theory, however, Wittgenstein came closer to opposing what was still a widespread doctrine, and this thesis of his later philosophy has prompted much more controversy than the first.

Perhaps the most widely influential aspects of Wittgenstein's later philosophy were the closely interrelated rejection of the philosophers' quest for an ideal language and certification of "ordinary language": "On the one hand it is clear that every sentence in our language is 'all right as it is.' That is, that we are not *striving after* an ideal, as if our ordinary vague sentences had not yet got an irreproachable sense, and a perfect language had yet to be constructed by us.—On the other this seems clear: Where there is sense, there must be perfect order. And so there is perfect order even in the vaguest sentence" (Part I, Sec. 98). On Wittgenstein's later philosophy see, for instance, Norman Malcolm, "Wittgenstein's *Philosophical Investigations,*" in *Knowledge and Certainty* (1963), and David Pole, *The Later Philosophy of Wittgenstein* (1963).

"Ordinary-language" philosophy. "Ordinary-language" philosophy, associated originally with Oxford, must be considered the mainstream of developments stemming in large part from Wittgenstein's later philosophy. It owes something to G. E. Moore's analytic method as well, and such semi-independent sources as the work of J. L. Austin (1911–1960) and of John Wisdom have also contributed to its development. With the notable exception of Austin, ordinary-language philosophers have not, for the most part, been oriented toward a philosophical interest in language for its own sake any more than was Wittgenstein. They have instead been primarily linguistic philosophers, turning toward ordinary language as a source of philosophical data and sometimes also of criteria. As linguistic philosophers, however, such men as Gilbert Ryle, P. F. Strawson, J. O. Urmson, and Norman Malcolm have been led to write also on language itself. (For a bibliography of such writings, see C. E. Caton, *Philosophy and Ordinary Language,* 1963. On the nature of the philosophical appeal to ordinary language, see Malcolm, "Philosophy for Philosophers," *Philosophical Review,* 1951; Kurt Baier, "The Ordinary Use of Words," *PAS,* 1951; Ryle, "Ordinary Language," *Philosophical Review,* 1953; A. G. N. Flew, "Philosophy and Language," *Philosophical Quarterly,* 1955.)

At least one prominent contemporary philosopher of language, Max Black, seems to have benefited equally from the work of Bertrand Russell and from the ordinary-language movement. (See, for instance, his *Problems of Analysis,* 1954, and *Models and Metaphors,* 1962.) Others, such as P. T. Geach (*Reference and Generality,* 1962) and L. J. Cohen (*The Diversity of Meaning,* 1963), seem in their discussions of language to be combining to some extent the approaches of ordinary-language philosophers and of formalists.

The Norwegian philosopher Arne Naess has developed and employed questionnaires for the purpose of determining meanings by interviews with the people who make ordinary use of the language. He has made ingenious applications of his technique to philosophical problems (see, for example, "Toward a Theory of Interpretation and Preciseness" [1949], in Linsky, *Semantics and Philosophy of Language*, 1952), but his influence has so far been limited almost entirely to his Norwegian collaborators.

Descriptive linguistics and generative grammar. The influence of contemporary linguistics is a significant factor in the recent development of the philosophy of language. A notable case in point is Paul Ziff's *Semantic Analysis* (1960), which makes a philosophical application of the techniques of morphological analysis presented in Zelig Harris' *Methods in Structural Analysis* (1951). The work of descriptive linguists such as Harris (or Sapir and Bloomfield before him) has, however, been of less interest to philosophers generally than the "generative" or "transformational" grammar developed more recently by Noam Chomsky and such associates as P. M. Postal and R. B. Lees. (See, for instance, Chomsky's *Syntactic Structures*, 1957; *Current Issues in Linguistic Theory*, 1964; and *Aspects of the Theory of Syntax*, 1965.)

The respects in which generative grammar differs fundamentally from modern descriptive linguistics may also be those features of it that are most attractive to philosophers of language. It is, for example, oriented toward the construction of explanatory (rather than merely descriptive) theories of languages that will, ideally, be inferable from a general explanatory theory of *language*, a "universal grammar." Chomsky in particular has emphasized the essential correctness of the insights of certain grammarian-philosophers and linguists of past centuries—men such as Arnauld, Cordemoy, Du Marsais, Beattie, and Humboldt. Their projects failed for a lack of appropriate technical devices, Chomsky believes, and not because they were fundamentally misconceived: ". . . a real understanding of how a language can (in Humboldt's words) 'make infinite use of finite means' has developed only within the last thirty years, in the course of studies in the foundations of mathematics. Now that these insights are readily available it is possible to return to the problems that were raised, but not solved, in traditional linguistic theory, and to attempt an explicit formulation of the 'creative' processes of language. There is, in short, no longer a technical barrier to the full-scale study of generative grammars" (*Aspects of the Theory of Syntax*, p. 8).

The new grammar may be said to have produced its own grammarian-philosophers. Some of their work may be examined in *The Structure of Language: Readings in the Philosophy of Language* (1964), an extensive anthology edited by Jerry Fodor and Jerrold Katz. In their Preface to that book Fodor and Katz state their beliefs that "current philosophizing has failed to provide either an adequate understanding of language or convincing answers to philosophical problems about language" and that "only an approach which integrates with empirical linguistics can succeed where current philosophy of language fails." Positivism and ordinary-language philosophy are, in their view, the only varieties of philosophy of language currently available, and while "Positivism has given us a theory which fails to be a description of natural language,

Ordinary Language philosophy has given us particular descriptions which fail to be a theory." The character of semantics in a linguistics-oriented philosophy of language is described by Fodor and Katz in "The Structure of a Semantic Theory": ". . . the speaker's knowledge of his language takes the form of rules which project the finite set of sentences he has fortuitously encountered to the infinite set of sentences of the language. . . . The problem of formulating these rules we shall refer to as the *projection problem*. . . . The significance of transformational grammars for our present purposes is that they provide a solution for the grammatical aspect of the projection problem." The subject matter of semantics, on this view, is whatever portion of the projection problem is insoluble within a transformational grammar. In the formula adopted by Fodor and Katz, "linguistic description minus grammar equals semantics." Thus, for example, "one facet of the speaker's ability which a semantic theory will have to reconstruct is that he can detect nonsyntactic ambiguities and characterize the content of each reading of a sentence."

Bibliography

There is at present no thorough general study of the history of semantics. Much relevant information may be found, however, in works on the history of logic, particularly in I. M. Bocheński, *A History of Formal Logic*, translated by Ivo Thomas (Notre Dame, Ind., 1961); Philotheus Boehner, *Medieval Logic* (Manchester, 1952); L. M. de Rijk, *Logica Modernorum*, Vol. I (Assen, 1962); William and Martha Kneale, *The Development of Logic* (Oxford, 1962); Benson Mates, *Stoic Logic* (Berkeley and Los Angeles, 1953); E. A. Moody, *The Logic of William of Ockham* (New York and London, 1935), and *Truth and Consequence in Medieval Logic* (Amsterdam, 1953); and Carl Prantl, *Geschichte der Logik im Abendlande*, 4 vols. (Leipzig, 1855–1870).

Surveys less thorough than this article are contained in Ch. 7, "Language," of Janet and Séailles's *History of the Problems of Philosophy*, translated by A. Monahan and edited by H. Jones (New York, 1902), and in Ch. 1, "The Problem of Language in the History of Philosophy," of Vol. I, *Language*, of Ernst Cassirer's *The Philosophy of Symbolic Forms*, translated by R. Manheim (New Haven, 1953).

The following selection of books and articles is arranged in four parts corresponding to the four parts of the article.

ANTIQUITY

Allen, W. S., "Ancient Ideas on the Origin and Development of Language." *Transactions of the Philosophical Society* [of Great Britain] (1948), 35–60.

Billiesich, F., *Epikurs Sprachphilosophie*. Landskron, 1912.

De Lacy, Estelle, "Meaning and Methodology in Hellenistic Philosophy." *The Philosophical Review*, Vol. 47 (1938), 390–409.

De Lacy, Phillip, "The Epicurean Analysis of Language." *The American Journal of Philology*, Vol. 60 (1939), 85–92.

Demos, Raphael, "Plato's Philosophy of Language." *The Journal of Philosophy*, Vol. 61 (1964), 595–610.

Deuschle, Julius, *Die Platonische Sprachphilosophie*. Marburg, 1852.

Goldschmidt, Victor, *Essai sur le "Cratyle."* Paris, 1940.

Lersch, Laurenz, *Die Sprachphilosophie der Alten*, 3 vols. Bonn, 1838–1841.

Luce, J. V., "The Theory of Ideas in Plato's *Cratylus*." *Phronesis*, Vol. 10 (1965), 21–36.

Moravcsik, Julius, "Being and Meaning in the 'Sophist.'" *Acta Philosophica Fennica*, Fasc. 14 (1962), 23–78.

Robinson, Richard, "The Theory of Names in Plato's *Cratylus*." *Revue internationale de philosophie*, Vol. 9 (1955), 221–236.

Robinson, Richard, "A Criticism of Plato's *Cratylus.*" *The Philosophical Review*, Vol. 65 (1956), 324–341.

Schoemann, G. F., *Die Lehre von den Redetheilen nach den Alten.* Berlin, 1862.

Steinthal, Hugo, *Die Geschichte der Sprachwissenschaft bei den Griechen und Römern.* Berlin, 1863.

Weltring, G., Das Σημεῖον *in der Aristotelischen, stoischen, Epikureischen, und skeptischen Philosophie.* Bonn, 1910.

THE MIDDLE AGES

Arnold, Erwin, "Zur Geschichte der Suppositionstheorie, die Wurzeln des modernen Subjektivismus." *Symposion, Jahrbuch für Philosophie*, Vol. 3 (1952), 1–34.

Boehner, Philotheus, "Ockham's Theory of Truth." *Franciscan Studies*, Vol. 5 (1945), 138–161.

Boehner, Philotheus, "Ockham's Theory of Signification." *Franciscan Studies*, Vol. 6 (1946), 143–170.

Boehner, Philotheus, "Ockham's Theory of Supposition and the Notion of Truth." *Franciscan Studies*, Vol. 6 (1946), 261–292.

Boehner, Philotheus, "A Medieval Theory of Supposition." *Franciscan Studies*, Vol. 18 (1958), 240–289.

Carreras y Artau, Joaquín, *De Ramón Lull á los modernos ensayos de formación de una lengua universal.* Barcelona, 1946.

Grabmann, Martin, "Die Entwicklung der mittelalterlichen Sprachlogik (Tractatus de Modis Significandi)," in his *Mittelalterliches Geistesleben*, 3 vols. Munich, 1926. Vol. I, Ch. 4.

Grabmann, Martin, *Thomas von Erfurt und die Sprachlogik des mittelalterlichen Aristotelismus; Sitzungsberichte der Bayerischen Akademie der Wissenschaften* (Philosophisch-historische Abteilung), Jahrgang 1943, Heft 2.

Heidegger, Martin, *Die Kategorien- und Bedeutungslehre des Duns Scotus.* Tübingen, 1916.

Henry, D. P., "Saint Anselm's Nonsense." *Mind*, Vol. 72 (1963), 51–61.

Manthey, Franz, *Die Sprachphilosophie des hl. Thomas von Aquin und ihre Anwendung auf Probleme der Theologie.* Paderborn, 1937.

Prior, A. N., "The Parva Logicalia in Modern Dress." *Dominican Studies*, Vol. 5 (1952), 78–87.

Roberts, Louise Nisbet, "Supposition: A Modern Application." *The Journal of Philosophy*, Vol. 57 (1960), 173–182.

Rotta, P., *La filosofia del linguaggio nella patristica e nella scolastica.* Turin, 1909.

Saw, Ruth Lydia, "William of Ockham on Terms, Propositions, Meaning." *PAS*, Vol. 42 (1941/1942), 45–64.

Thomas, Ivo, "Saint Vincent Ferrer's *De Suppositionibus.*" *Dominican Studies*, Vol. 5 (1952), 88–102.

Thurot, Charles, *Notices et extraits des manuscrits latins pour servir à l'histoire des doctrines grammaticales au moyen âge.* Vol. 22, Part 2 of Notices et extraits des manuscrits de la Bibliothèque Impériale. Paris, 1868.

Wallerand, G., "Étude sur Siger de Courtrai," in *Les Oeuvres de Siger de Courtrai (Étude critique et textes inédits).* Vol. VIII of *Les Philosophes belges.* Louvain, 1913.

RENAISSANCE AND ENLIGHTENMENT

Acton, H. B., "The Philosophy of Language in Revolutionary France." *Proceedings of the British Academy*, Vol. 45 (1959), 199–219.

Cohen, L. Jonathan, "On the Project of a Universal Character." *Mind*, Vol. 63 (1954), 49–63.

François, Alexis, "La Grammaire philosophique," in F. Brunot, *Histoire de la langue française des origines à 1900.* Paris, 1932. Vol. VI, Part 2, Book 2.

Friedrich, Hugo, "Die Sprachtheorie der französischen Illuminaten des 18. Jahrhunderts, insbesondere Saint-Martins." *Deutsche Vierteljahrsschrift für Literaturwissenschaft und Geistesgeschichte*, Vol. 13 (1935), 293–310.

Funke, Otto, *Studien zur Geschichte der Sprachphilosophie: I. Zur Sprachphilosophie des 18. Jahrhunderts: J. Harris' "Hermes"; II. Zur Sprachphilosophie der Gegenwart.* Bern, 1927.

Funke, Otto: *Zum Weltsprachenproblem in England im 17.*

Jahrhundert: G. Dalgarno's *"Ars signorum" (1661) und J. Wilkins' "Essay towards a Real Character and a Philosophical Language."* Anglistische Forschungen, No. 69. Heidelberg, 1929.

Furlong, E. J., "Berkeley's Theory of Meaning." *Mind*, Vol. 73 (1964), 437–438.

Harnois, Guy, *Les Théories du langage en France de 1660 à 1821.* Paris, 1929.

Hunt, H. J., "Logic and Linguistics: Diderot as 'Grammairien-philosophe.'" *The Modern Language Review*, Vol. 33 (1938), 215–233.

Kuehner, Paul, *Theories on the Origin and Formation of Language in the Eighteenth Century in France.* Philadelphia, 1944.

Maynial, Édouard, "Les grammairiens-philosophes du XVIIIᵉ siècle: La Grammaire de Condillac." *Revue Bleue*, 4th series, Vol. 19 (1903), 317–320.

Oesterle, John A., "Another Approach to the Problem of Meaning." *The Thomist*, Vol. 7 (1944), 233–263. Supposition theory in John of St. Thomas.

O'Flaherty, James C., *Unity and Language: A Study in the Philosophy of Johann Georg Hamann.* Chapel Hill, N.C., 1952.

Pott, August, "Zur Geschichte und Kritik der sogenannten allgemeinen Grammatik." *Zeitschrift für Philosophie und Philosophische Kritik*, Vol. 43 (1863), 102–141.

Robert, Louis, *Les Théories logiques de Condillac.* Paris, 1869.

Russell, L. J., "Note on the Term Σημειωτική in Locke." *Mind*, Vol. 48 (1939), 405–406.

Sahlin, G., *César Chesneau du Marsais et son rôle dans l'évolution de la grammaire générale.* Paris, 1928.

Salvucci, Pasquale, *Linguaggio e mondo umano in Condillac.* Urbino, 1957.

Trendelenburg, Adolf, "Ueber Leibnizens Entwurf einer allgemeinen Characteristik," in his *Historische Beiträge zur Philosophie*, Vol. III. Berlin, 1867.

Unger, Rudolf, *Hamanns Sprachtheorie im Zusammenhang seines Denkens.* Munich, 1905.

Wallace, Karl R., *Francis Bacon on Communication and Rhetoric.* Chapel Hill, N.C., 1943.

THE NINETEENTH AND TWENTIETH CENTURIES

Bronstein, Daniel, "Inquiry and Meaning," in P. P. Wiener and F. H. Young, eds., *Studies in the Philosophy of Charles Sanders Peirce.* Cambridge, Mass., 1952. Pp. 33–52.

Buchler, Justus, "What Is the Pragmaticist Theory of Meaning?," in P. P. Wiener and F. H. Young, eds., *Studies in the Philosophy of Charles Sanders Peirce.* Cambridge, Mass., 1952. Pp. 21–32.

Burks, Arthur W., and Weiss, Paul, "Peirce's Sixty-six Signs." *The Journal of Philosophy*, Vol. 42 (1945), 383–388.

Dewey, John, "Peirce's Theory of Linguistic Signs, Thought, and Meaning." *The Journal of Philosophy*, Vol. 43 (1946), 85–95.

Farber, Marvin, *The Foundation of Phenomenology: Edmund Husserl and the Quest for a Rigorous Science of Philosophy.* Cambridge, Mass., 1943.

Findlay, J. N., *Meinong's Theory of Objects.* London, 1933.

Lovejoy, Arthur O., "What Is the Pragmaticist Theory of Meaning? The First Phase," in P. P. Wiener and F. H. Young, eds., *Studies in the Philosophy of Charles Sanders Peirce.* Cambridge, Mass., 1952. Pp. 3–20.

Mohanty, J. N., *Edmund Husserl's Theory of Meaning.* The Hague, 1964.

Morris, Charles W., "Signs About Signs About Signs." *Philosophy and Phenomenological Research*, Vol. 9 (1948/1949), 115–133.

Ogden, C. K., *Bentham's Theory of Fictions.* New York and London, 1932.

Ogden, C. K., and Richards, I. A., "Some Moderns—1. Husserl, 2. Russell, 3. Frege, 4. Gomperz, 5. Baldwin, 6. Peirce," in *The Meaning of Meaning.* New York and London, 1923. Appendix D.

Rynin, David, "Introduction" and "Critical Essay," in his edition of Alexander Bryan Johnson's *A Treatise on Language.* Berkeley and Los Angeles, 1947.

Walker, Jeremy D. B., *A Study of Frege.* Oxford, 1965.

Weiler, Gershon, "On Fritz Mauthner's Critique of Language." *Mind*, Vol. 67 (1958), 80–87.

Wienpahl, P. D., "Frege's Sinn und Bedeutung." *Mind*, Vol. 59 (1950), 483–494.

The development of philosophy of language, like the development of philosophy generally in this century, has taken place at least as much in articles as in books, and the use of anthologies is consequently almost indispensable in the study of it. All the following anthologies contain material useful for the study of philosophy of language in the twentieth century: *Logical Positivism*, A. J. Ayer, ed. (Glencoe, Ill., 1959); *Philosophical Analysis*, Max Black, ed. (Ithaca, N.Y., 1950); *Philosophy and Ordinary Language*, C. E. Caton, ed. (Urbana, Ill., 1963); *Ordinary Language*, V. C. Chappell, ed. (Englewood Cliffs, N.J., 1963); *Logic and Language*, A. G. N. Flew, ed. (1st series, New York, 1951; 2d series, 1953); *The Structure of Language*, J. Fodor and J. Katz, eds. (Englewood Cliffs, N.J., 1964); *Classics in Semantics*, D. E. Hayden and E. P. Alworth, eds. (London, 1965); and *Semantics and Philosophy of Language*, L. Linsky, ed. (Urbana, Ill., 1952).

William P. Alston, *Philosophy of Language* (Englewood Cliffs, N.J., 1964), provides a good introduction to the subject as it has developed in this century. John Passmore, *A Hundred Years of Philosophy* (New York, 1957), provides an excellent history of this period and its immediate background, with considerable detail regarding developments in philosophy of language. More specialized and also to be recommended are G. J. Warnock, *English Philosophy Since 1900* (New York and London, 1958), and J. O. Urmson, *Philosophical Analysis: Its Development Between the Two World Wars* (New York and London, 1956).

NORMAN KRETZMANN

SENECA, LUCIUS ANNAEUS, was born at Córdoba, Spain, about the beginning of the Christian era into a provincial middle-class family of pronounced intellectual leanings. His father was an accomplished rhetorician, and Seneca's education at Rome naturally included a thorough grounding in rhetoric. He was, however, equally attracted to philosophy and received instruction from several masters who professed various forms of the currently popular Stoic eclecticism. In the course of a normal political career his distinction as an advocate incurred the displeasure of Emperor Caligula, and he was all but condemned in 39. We are told that only his ill health, which presaged an early death, saved him. In 41 he was banished to Corsica by Claudius on a charge of adultery with the emperor's niece, an exile he seems to have borne with little fortitude. Recalled to Rome in 49 to become tutor to the young Nero, he was from his pupil's accession in 54 until 62 one of the emperor's two chief advisers. Then, feeling his power slipping away, he retired from public life. In 65 he was accused of participation in a conspiracy to depose Nero (some said he was to succeed to the throne) and, on the imperial command, embraced the suicide which his philosophy permitted him as a final release from the ills of this world. Personally acquainted with the extremes of failure and success in public life, Seneca was well qualified to discuss the moral problems which confronted the Roman ruling classes.

Seneca's works include the twelve *Moral Essays* of widely differing lengths expounding various aspects of ethical theory or giving advice on particular moral problems (written between 37 and 65). The 124 *Moral Letters*, a kind of correspondence course in right thinking and acting addressed to a novice in Stoicism, were written toward the end of his life. Roughly contemporaneous with the *Letters* is the "Physical Problems," which deals with Stoic explanations of natural phenomena and is often heavily laced with moral reflections. There are also nine tragedies, poetic dramas based loosely on Greek models; these powerful studies of emotional stress are intended to be read, not performed. The *Apocolocyntosis* is a brutal satire on the deification of the emperor Claudius. Several philosophical works, both physical and ethical, are lost or fragmentary. All his speeches have perished.

Seneca's style, noted for its rhetorical finish, epigrammatic brevity, and mordant wit, occasionally carries these characteristics to excess but is neither as overpowering nor as tedious as its severer critics suggest.

Philosophy. Seneca was, in general, a faithful adherent of Stoicism, but he more than once asserts his right to adopt any views of previous philosophers that seem correct to him. He frequently quotes Epicurus with approval, and he is even able to suggest that the apparently contradictory aims of opposing schools may, in the end, come to the same thing, thus exemplifying the eclectic and synthesizing spirit of the philosophy of the period. He also draws heavily on the popular ethical preaching of the Cynics. It is often difficult to distinguish this element from his orthodox Stoicism because of the community of ideas between them, but Seneca probably owes to the Cynics the urgent, evangelizing tone which characterizes his work.

His main philosophical aim was to lead men toward virtue, to convey to them the knowledge of the nature of the world and their place in it which would enable them to conduct their lives in accordance with the will of God. Logic and physics have their place, but only to provide a foundation. They must not usurp the place of ethics, which is the true end of philosophy. "There is no philosophy without goodness, and no goodness without philosophy." This emphasis on ethics at the expense of logical studies and physical theories, which formed such an important part of early Stoic teaching, was no major innovation, since they had always effectively been subordinate to ethics.

Widsom is the key to goodness. The truly wise man, with his understanding of the universe, will value only that which is in itself truly valuable, namely, virtue. He will realize that all the external goods and ills of this world are transitory. They cannot detract from a man's true worth, which is within him. Only when he loses this can he truly be said to have been harmed. To achieve this state of self-sufficiency, we must rid ourselves of our emotions, which are essentially mistaken judgments of the value to be attached to externals and are constant incitements to vice. In this elimination of the emotions the will plays a vital part. Wisdom and goodness demand a conscious harmonization of our own wills with the divine will of the universe. Once this is achieved, we will always choose what is right and reject what is wrong, thus producing actions which are not only right in themselves but which are also chosen for the right motives, a vital feature of true moral action. The man who achieves this state will be a truly godlike creature, utterly immune to the blows of Fortune.

There is nothing either original or striking in this. It is standard Stoic doctrine, some of it, indeed, going back before the earliest Stoics to Socrates. What is striking is the power with which the message is expounded. Seneca's primary aim is to persuade us to act and think rightly, not to prove that certain ethical propositions are true. To achieve this, he depicts with extreme vividness the benefits of virtue and the disadvantages of vice. He is at his best when enlarging upon the disastrous effects of the emotions. Pain, pleasure, fear, desire—all are equally to be avoided. He examines with almost clinical precision the vicious effect of the passions on men and then proceeds to explain how they may be brought under control and finally conquered, illustrating his argument with a wealth of examples, cautionary or encouraging.

This method obviously does not lend itself to the exposition of an all-embracing and coherent philosophical system. Indeed, lack of consistency and logical development, both between different works and within the same work, have long been major criticisms of Seneca. This cannot be denied, but it can be explained. Seneca was a practical moral teacher, a kind of spiritual guide or father confessor to his friends. In a favorite metaphor, he was a "physician" of the soul. Thus, he concentrates on particular moral or psychological problems (he would not have distinguished between them) and provides particular answers to suit both the problem and the person who raises it. The stance taken and the arguments produced vary according to the stage in the Stoic faith which his questioner has reached. This practical aim is brought out in his emphasis on the value of moral "progress." This was an early modification in Stoic teaching which Seneca eagerly adopted. While not deserting the fundamental and austere concept of the true "Sage," it recognized the importance and relative moral worth of determined effort to attain that ideal, thus bridging the abyss between the perfect "Sage" and the great mass of "fools," a compromise vital to Seneca's practical aims.

Seneca has nothing to offer the philosopher who studies the structure of language or intellectual processes, but the acuteness of his psychological insights and the sanity of his particular moral advice make him of the greatest interest to those concerned with the human heart and its strivings after virtue.

Bibliography

The complete Latin text is published by Teubner in six volumes (Leipzig, 1902–1923). Translations (with facing Latin text) of the *Moral Essays, Moral Letters,* tragedies, and *Apocolocyntosis* (with Petronius) are in the Loeb Classical Library. There is a translation of the "Physical Problems" by J. Clarke and A. Geikie, *Physical Science in the Time of Nero* (London, 1910).

For discussion of Seneca, see Samuel Dill, *Roman Society: From Nero to Marcus Aurelius* (London, 1905; paperback ed., New York, 1956), pp. 289–333, and P. Grimal, *Sénèque* (Paris, 1957), which has a good bibliography. A critical bibliography is in A. L. Motto, "Recent Scholarship on Seneca's Prose Works (1940–1957)," in *Classical World,* Vol. 54 (1960/1961), 13–18, 37–48, 70–71, 111–112 (addendum on 1957–1958).

James R. G. Wright

SENSA. A distinction is often drawn in philosophy between two types of objects of awareness in perception. First, there are physical objects or substances (such as chairs, books, rocks, and water) and living organisms (animals, plants, and human beings insofar as they are perceptible, that is, their bodies). A common technical term for all these is *material objects.* Second, there are data of immediate awareness, which we shall refer to as "sensa" (singular, sensum), such as color patches or shapes, sounds, smells, and tactile feelings. This distinction is usually fourfold: (a) in status—material objects are external, located in physical space, and "public" (observable by different persons at once), while sensa are private and are usually held to have no external physical existence; (b) in extent—material objects may at one time correspond to several sensa and normally persist throughout the occurrence of many sensa; (c) in directness—the perception of material objects is indirect, that is, it involves inference from or interpretation of sensa that are "given" directly to consciousness; (d) in certainty—one is always certainly aware of sensa but not necessarily so of material objects.

There is no universally accepted term for sensa; "sensations" and "sense data" are commonest but indicate a further subdivision. "Sensation" is customarily used by scientists and psychologists and carries with it the suggestion that sensa are the immediate mental effects of brain activity resulting from the excitation of a sense organ by external stimuli. It and the less specialized term "sense impression" may be used interchangeably for the whole experience of awareness of sound, color, and the like, or for any sensum (such as a sound or a color patch) distinguished within it. The term "sense datum" (plural, "sense data") apparently originated with G. E. Moore but was introduced in print by Bertrand Russell in 1912. It later became particularly associated with the sense-datum theory of Moore, C. D. Broad, and H. H. Price, while Russell developed different views and came to use other terms. Sense data are not meant to carry any implications of causal theory, and awareness of them is called sensing (the term "sense datum" is used for the sensum only, not for the whole experience). With the development of the sense-datum theory, controversy arose between those who regarded sense data as objects distinguishable from the act of awareness of them (act/object analysis) and those who denied this and claimed that sensing is really of "sense contents" (adverbial analysis). But the terminology is generally fluid—for instance, some modern neurologists use the term "sense data" instead of "sensations" in causal contexts. Similar concepts are found in earlier writers, though their language is different. Locke's "ideas of sense," Berkeley's "ideas" or "sensible qualities," and Hume's "impressions" are all forms of sensa.

SENSATIONS

It has often been maintained, by philosophers as well as by psychologists, that perceiving consists in the synthesis and interpretation of sensations. But it must be realized that the occurrence of sensations in all perception is only a hypothesis and not an obvious feature of experience. In ordinary language, one may speak of having or feeling sensations of thirst, cold, or pressure and may refer to itches or pains as sensations. But the technical use of the word "sensations" involves a considerable extension of meaning, since one then speaks of visual or auditory sensations (that is, colors or sounds), while such locutions have no place in ordinary speech. We do not have green sensations in our eyes, nor do we normally feel or have sounds in our ears. Admittedly we do have afterimages, spots before the eyes, or ringing in the ears; but these are special cases because, unlike the objects or data of normal perception, the images, spots, or ringing "follows us around" and cannot be avoided by moving the head, closing the eyes, or stopping the ears. Indeed, in normal perception we are conscious not of colored shapes or of sounds as such but of material objects, or at least of ostensible material objects. Admittedly we may sometimes be aware of sounds, smells, tastes, or feelings of pressure, as distinct from objects or object properties, but it is doubtful how far these can be said to be sensations. Sounds and smells seem public and external: two or more people may hear the same sound or smell the same smell and agree on its source; sounds travel, and a smell may fill a room. Tastes are a borderline case—private and in the mouth, yet in a sense external to the skin and membranes—while feelings of pressure or warmth are partly sensations proper and partly seem to be awarenesses of heavy or warm objects. On the other hand, colors and colored shapes normally seem quite external, public, and at a distance from us.

Sensations in this technical sense (private mental objects of immediate awareness) are thus mainly hypothetical occurrences. Their postulation can be justified only by its success in explaining the facts of perception, and it rests on two grounds. First, there is the causal argument—perception of objects depends on and is conditioned by a chain of causal processes; for example, light waves or sound waves stimulate the appropriate sense organ, causing impulses to travel along nerves to the brain and activate the appropriate receiving area. Perception cannot, therefore, be direct contact or confrontation with external objects—all immediate awareness must result from the causal process and be an awareness of mental sensations due to brain activity. Since they are thus separated from the external object in time and space, sensations cannot be identified with its properties, though they may resemble them. Second, there is the psychological argument—many characteristics of perception show that it is not a direct intuitive awareness but involves interpretation of sensations. Thus, error and illusion are really misinterpretations; perception of motion, depth, and distance involves the use of sensory "cues"; and perceptual identification and discrimination are interpretative, not immediate, since they can be improved by learning and experience. (Both these arguments are discussed at greater length under PERCEPTION. Here we may simply note some relevant difficulties.)

The extent of sensations. Even if the causal argument forces us to distinguish between external material objects and the immediate objects of awareness caused by brain activity, it does not follow that the latter must be sensations, such as colors or sounds. They may be percepts, that is, mental contents that correspond to whole material objects, though here the psychological argument comes in, suggesting that percepts are the products of interpretation. Supporters of the theory of sensations, no doubt influenced by discoveries concerning the atomic structure of matter, at one time even claimed that the basic sensations are "atomic," that they are sensory point-elements, each cor-

responding to a different nerve cell—a patch of red color would thus be made up of many sensations of red. This view has now been completely abandoned, largely as the result of the experiments of the Gestalt psychologists, which show that our primary awareness is of organized wholes or figures (*Gestalten* in German), and not of elements into which these wholes might theoretically be analyzed. But even though sensations are not now thought of as minute elements that we synthesize, nonatomic sensations (colored patches of a larger size, or patterns of them, as well as sounds, smells, and so on) may still be regarded as data that we interpret in perception.

Awareness and interpretation of sensations. The awareness of sensations or, for that matter, of percepts must itself be explained: the danger is that it will be construed as analogous to perceiving; for example, that seeing objects will be explained as seeing sensations caused by them, which is a circular explanation and can thus lead to an infinite regress—seeing sensations must require seeing further sensations, and so on. (Compare the duplication objection to representative realism in REALISM). It is therefore necessary to maintain that the awareness of sensations or percepts ("having sensations") is a special kind of direct awareness different from perceiving, an amendment explicitly adopted by the sense-datum theory.

The problems of the psychological argument are (*a*) that interpretation of anything would commonly be regarded as presupposing consciousness of what is interpreted, and we are normally conscious neither of having sensations (as opposed to perceiving objects) nor of interpreting them; and (*b*) that the nature of the interpretation of sensations is controversial—a range of theories is possible because it is not introspectable. The sensationalists (James Mill, J. S. Mill, and others who derived their inspiration from Hume) claimed that perceiving is the association of various sensations. "Association" is a vague term and was explained as the customary linking of ideas or sensations that are similar, contiguous in space and time, and so on. Bradley and other idealists successfully attacked the sensationalist view as inadequate to explain the facts of perception; instead, they claimed that the interpretation is an inference leading to a judgment, supposing that the possibility of error in perception required this. But this overintellectualized perceiving; inferences and judgments are not the only forms of mental activity liable to error.

ARGUMENTS FOR THE INTRODUCTION OF SENSE DATA

During the last fifty years, philosophers have made little use of the concept of sensation in their theories but have instead talked of sense data or sense contents. Though the same things—color patches, sounds, smells, and tastes—have been put forward as examples both of sensations and of sense data, the new terminology marks several changes. Recognition of the visual depth or stereoscopic qualities of sense data means that one visual sense datum or color patch is usually held to correspond to the whole of the visible part of an ostensible object (so that one may have striped or variegated sense data). Little detailed attention has been paid to psychological phenomena, except for discussion along traditional lines of error and illusion and their bearing on whether perceiving is a form of judgment. There has also been almost a revulsion from causal arguments, clearly influenced by their tendency to involve one in the notorious difficulties of representative realism. Instead, a fresh start has been made in the conviction that philosophy has its own distinct contribution to make in the logical and introspective analyses of perception and in the consideration of relevant epistemological issues, that is, of the extent to which perception provides knowledge of external reality. Nevertheless, with some adjustment the new arguments might be supplemented by and in turn supplement the causal and psychological arguments for sensations.

Sense data are defined as whatever is "given" or "directly present" in perceiving; they are the object of *sensing,* of "direct" or "immediate" or "actual" awareness in perception. The claim that this awareness occurs within perceiving is essential to the analysis. To most of its exponents it seems a clear fact of our experience as percipients, one revealed by reflective examination. "Direct" is explained by Price (in *Perception*) as meaning intuitive or "not reached by inference, nor by any other intellectual process." This formal definition was often supplemented by a kind of ostensive one: Moore, J. R. Smythies, and others gave instructions for looking at an object or scene and picking out the sense datum, such as a colored shape. (Misleadingly, afterimages were sometimes offered as examples of sense data, but their difference from normal perception has already been noted; misleadingly also, some talked of seeing or hearing sense data.)

This definition of sense data naturally raises the question "Why not say that tables, chairs, and other material objects are given or directly seen?" In answering this, these philosophers produce various arguments for distinguishing sense data from material objects.

The certainty argument. The certainty argument was stressed by Price and by Russell in his search for "hard data," though it is also found in other sources. Directness or givenness implies certainty—what is given must be limited to what we are absolutely certain of. But in any perceptual situation we cannot be sure that we are aware of any particular material object. For example, an object that seems to be a tomato may in fact be something quite different—a wax imitation, perhaps, or a reflected patch of light, or a hallucination (that is, not be a material object at all). Yet whatever the illusion may be, there can be no doubt, when we seem to see a tomato, that there is given a red, round, bulgy patch of color, a sense datum. Another version of this argument is the method of reduced claims; by confronting him with possible sources of error, you force the person concerned to reduce his claim from "I see a tomato" to what he actually and directly sees or, rather, senses: "I see a red, round color patch."

The partitive argument. When we observe a tomato or a bell, what we "actually see"—the "objective constituent" of the situation, what is given or sensed—is the colored shape that seems to be its front surface. This is a sense datum. We assume that the object has other surfaces and has other characteristics, such as causal properties, three-dimensionality, and persistence in time; and if we loosely say that we see a bell, we imply that we are perceiving an object possessing these properties, although we do not directly see or sense them. This argument, which stresses extent of sense experience rather than certainty, was preferred by Broad and Moore but seems inferior in suggesting that sense data are those parts of an object that we "actually see" on a given occasion—which raises difficulties with respect to illusions.

The argument from the content of illusions. When a drunkard sees a hallucinatory pink elephant or sees two bottles when only one is present, what is the elephant or second bottle if it is nothing material? The sense-datum theorist answers, "A private object of awareness, a sense datum," and applies this also to cases of the relativity of perceiving: for example, when a round plate looks elliptical to a person standing at one side, the elliptical appearance cannot be the plate, which is round; it is an elliptical sense datum private to that person. Indeed, it is argued that at all times we are directly aware only of sense data, since there is no qualitative jump between the cases where one *cannot* be directly aware of an object, and so *must* be sensing sense data, and the normal cases where we *think* we are directly aware of an object. This gradation or lack of jump is particularly clear in the case of relativity, as when we gradually move from where the plate looks round to where it looks elliptical, but it also applies to many hallucinations where the illusory sensa are integrated with a genuine background. In short, perceiving a material object involves sensing sense data related or "belonging" to it; when the plate looks round to me and elliptical to you, I am sensing a round sense datum belonging to it and you are sensing an elliptical one.

THE FULL SENSE-DATUM THEORY

The fundamental conception of sense data, as directly given elements of experience, spread far beyond epistemology. Both the atomic facts of the logical atomists and the supposedly incorrigible basic or protocol propositions of the logical positivists had as their prime examples simple statements about sense data (or sensa generally), such as "This is red." But the conception was also developed into a full theory of perception by consideration of the following topics, even though disagreements led to variant accounts.

The general nature of sense data. The arguments for the introduction of sense data, if valid, show that sense data are given and provide examples of them. Further alleged properties emerge from the discussion of illusions and relativity, namely, that sense data (1) are private, each sensed by only one percipient (see argument from the content of illusions); (2) are transitory existents, lasting only while they are sensed, so that they are usually claimed to be events rather than things or properties; (3) are distinct from the percipient and seem to be external (in contrast with sensations); (4) are without causal properties, for sounds (as opposed to sound waves) cannot act on other things, nor can colors or tastes, though the sensing of them may affect a person; (5) cannot be other than they appear to be, or the certainty argument is undermined.

Despite wide agreement on most of these points, a considerable divergence of view arose about (3) and (5). Point (3)—that sense data are distinct from the percipient and seem to be external—involves what came to be called the act–object analysis of sensing. Largely on phenomenological grounds—on how direct experience of color patches, sounds, and such seem to the person concerned—Price and others claim that sense data have distinct existence, that they are objects distinguishable from the act of awareness of them. But some philosophers maintain that the data are only "sense contents" and do not exist apart from the sensing of them any more than does a pain or sensation. This view is formulated in the so-called adverbial analysis of sensing, namely, that "I sense a red color patch" is properly to be regarded as a statement of *how* I sense or, to put it in a different way, "red color patch" is an internal accusative of the verb "sense," just as "waltz" is an internal accusative of "dance" in "I danced a waltz."

There is agreement on point (5)—that sense data cannot appear to be what they are not, for example, sense data cannot appear elliptical when they are round. (Even this is dubious—an apparently pink expanse may, on examination, be found to consist of red dots on a white background.) But some say that sense data can fail to appear as they are (do not reveal their full properties at first sight); thus, one may see that a colored datum is striped without noting how many or how thick the stripes are. Others deny this, claiming that a closer look results in a fresh datum. In fact, the theory cannot deal satisfactorily with the phenomenon of attention. A thing may look quite different on careful examination from the way it looks at a casual glance, and the difference seems to be a matter of how attentively we look, a matter of changes in our mode of observation. In line with this evidence, one should say that sense data may reveal their full properties only on a closer examination, but then one is suggesting that sensing may at times be casual and inattentive and is thus undermining the fundamental claim that sensing is certain and incorrigible.

The relation of sensing to perceiving. The distinction between sensing and perceiving is threefold. First, perceiving is the awareness of some material object; except in certain kinds of illusion this awareness is the result of the object in question (or light or sound from it) acting on the percipient's sense organs. Sensing is the awareness of private sense data that differ from material objects and do not affect the sense organs. Second, sensing is claimed to be direct, immediate, and incorrigible, a form of knowing. Owing to illusions, perceiving cannot be this; it is fallible and indirect. Third, the indirectness of perceiving is said to consist in its being mediated by sensing; perceiving involves sensing, contains sensing within it.

Various views are possible about the nature of this mediation of perceiving by sensing, but they are best expressed as theories of perceptual consciousness. The same kind of consciousness of a tomato, for example, seems present in normal perception, when one sees a tomato as a tomato; in an illusion, when what one sees as a tomato is a piece of wax; and in a hallucination, when no corresponding material thing is there. The kind of consciousness present in these three cases may be called perceptual consciousness and is more conveniently dis-

cussed than perceiving, where the implication that there is an object acting on the sense organs complicates the issue.

Some, such as Brand Blanshard (*The Nature of Thought*, London, 1939, Ch. 2), claim that perceptual consciousness consists in sensing a datum and judging or inferring that it belongs to a material object. Price, however, argued that this is too intellectual and does not fit the facts. We unquestioningly accept or take for granted rather than infer or judge, and therefore he defined perceptual consciousness as sensing a sense datum (or data) and taking for granted that it (or they) belong to a material object. Others have said that we *refer* the sense datum to a material object, but "refer" is vague.

Two points of interest arise here. First, philosophers have most often said that we accept or judge that the sense datum *belongs* to a physical object. This seems obvious only about smells or tastes, and one would on first thought say we assume that the visual sense datum or color patch is the tomato. There is a reluctance on the part of sense-datum theorists to allow this, presumably because they are influenced by the partitive argument or by their knowledge that *ex hypothesi* the sense datum cannot possibly be the physical object. But there seems to be no reason why the ordinary man, whose mental processes are being described, may not mistakenly assume this; one would, for example, say "That patch of white over there on the hill is a sheep" (admittedly, the patch as "public" is hardly a sense datum, but it is the nearest one can get to a sense datum by ordinary examples). Second, to say that we judge or infer that a sense datum belongs to (or is) a physical object is implausible, for it implies we are conscious of it first as a datum, which is not true to the facts: there is no passage of mind from datum to object, as in inference. Even to say we subconsciously judge or infer is unsatisfactory, for it seems extravagant to suppose that we constantly do subconsciously what we never do consciously. Price attempts to overcome this by maintaining that to take for granted that *A* is or belongs to *B*, one does not need to distinguish them at the time—indeed, the contrary is implied. Sensing thus comes to be regarded as a sort of sensory core within perceptual consciousness, surrounded, as it were, by the further activity of taking for granted. The two states of mind, sensing the red sense datum and consciousness of the tomato, arise together and simultaneously and can be distinguished only by subsequent analysis.

Even this account may be criticized on the grounds that it still does not do justice to the evidence of experience, namely, that perceptual consciousness is one unitary and unanalyzable state of mind, not two. No subsequent analysis of experience reveals sensing as an element within perceptual consciousness. Analysis or reflective examination can result in a "reduced" or critical phenomenological mode of observation in which one distinguishes sounds or colored shapes as such without attributing them to objects, but if this is sensing—and it seems to be the nearest one can get to it—then it is a quite different state of mind from normal perceiving. There is no ground for supposing that this, achievable only by an effort of analysis, occurs as part of normal unconsidered perception. In general, therefore, the attempt to establish sensing sense data as an omnipresent basic element in perceiving faces the same difficulties that faced the claim that perceiving is the interpretation of sensations.

Another way of seeing the error is to consider the normal usage of "taking for granted." Price's analysis is at first sight closest to "Y saw the book and took for granted that it belonged to B," but then Y is referred to as conscious of the book, while the average percipient is not conscious of sense data as sense data; he is conscious only of the material object. This difficulty can be avoided by the formulation "X took for granted that A was B"; for example, that the piece of wax was a tomato, or that the visitor was the man he was expecting. In each case both A and B denote the same entity (the wax or the visitor). A describes this entity in a way that the speaker knows to be correct; B describes it as X saw it. Similarly, one might say, "He took for granted that the sense datum (A) was a material object (B)." But this will not really save the analysis in which the datum and the physical object are alleged to be two quite different entities; to fit the analysis the first phrase (A) must also be a description of the alleged object of awareness of X, not of the speaker. Price seems to be making the mistake of offering as a description of a percipient's actual mental content what is in fact a description of the situation that can be made only by someone correcting the percipient's error.

The relation of sense data to physical objects. One of the vaunted advantages of the sense-datum analysis of perception is its neutrality with respect to the traditional realist theories of knowledge. (Idealism was ruled out by the original claim that sense data are distinct from the sensing of them.) Indeed, sense data were even said to be neutral in that so far as the analysis is concerned, they can be mental or physical or neither. Consequently, it is possible to state the various theories of knowledge in terms of sense data. Naive realism reduces to the view that sense data are parts of the surface of material objects; representative realism would claim that sense data are mental existents caused or generated by cerebral activity ultimately due to material objects and that sense data resemble the properties of these objects. (The second view and, if not too naive, the first also, could admit "wild sense data"—hallucinations that are not part of or caused by physical objects.)

Moore at times toyed with supposing that sense data are parts of the surface of objects (and even seriously discussed whether they might be identical with objects), though this must have been due to his affection for the partitive argument. The other arguments for sense data and general considerations about illusion do not allow this; for example, a round dish cannot have an elliptical sense datum as part of its surface. Representative realism is a more likely possibility: neurologists such as Smythies advocate this theory in terms of sense data, and Broad proposed something not unlike it. Most of the philosophers have, however, rejected it in view of its traditional difficulty—if our observation is limited to sense data while material objects are only assumed causes of sense data, then these objects are in fact never observed and therefore may, for all we know, not really exist.

A more common view is that sense data belong to material objects in the special sense that the latter are composed of "families" of sense data. This "family" relationship is not literally one of whole and part, as in naive realism; the material object is supposed to be a complex system or pattern of groups or sequences of sense data. But if a physical object is simply a family of sense data, then when no sense datum occurs—when the object is unobserved—the object must cease to exist. This is felt to be too paradoxical, and two main lines of development within this view have been put forward: (1) phenomenalism, in which the object is regarded as a family of actual and possible sense data—when unobserved, it consists solely of possible sense data (for this and its more sophisticated and widely adopted linguistic variant, see PHENOMENALISM); (2) a compromise theory put forward by Price in which the material object, while mainly such a family, contains a physical occupant that persists, even while it is unobserved, as the source of all its causal properties. The notion of a physical occupant has some analogies to Kant's notorious thing-in-itself, and this view has not obtained widespread acceptance.

This divergence of view reflects a central dilemma in the sense-datum theory. If the theory maintains that sense data belong to material objects or that the latter in some way consist of them, then it is difficult to explain (*a*) the persistence of such objects when unobserved; (*b*) the privacy that all versions attribute to sense data—how can a public object be a family of private sense data?; (*c*) the conditioning or even generation of sense data by the sense organs and nervous system, which is required by the physiological facts, by the occurrence of hallucinations or color blindness, and by the effects of attention and learning on perception. (Most sense-datum theorists admit the generation as well as the conditioning.) But if one does not say that sense data belong to or constitute material objects, the distinctness and apparent depth of sense data (at least of visual ones) is difficult to explain; and, more important, sense data tend to become mental entities like sensations. This, together with the privacy and the generation by the brain, leads one into representative realism.

One attempt to escape this dilemma is to say that sense data are extended and located in their own private "sensible" space along the lines first suggested by Bertrand Russell in his *Mysticism and Logic* and *Our Knowledge of the External World*. There is one such sensible space, with its own extension and dimensions, for every point in physical space, and the latter in fact becomes the system of points at which sensible space occurs. A physical object is thus, as it were, spread over physical space in a series of "perspectives" or "unperceived aspects," in the special sense that from different points in physical space, granted that sense organs and brain function properly, sense data may occur in sensible space but also belong to the object as appearances of it and reproduce its characteristics in a way modified both by the viewpoint and by the nature of the sensory apparatus.

This theory is very complex, which means that any summary of it is necessarily garbled. Two of the complexities are that a special interpretation is needed of what we normally call the volume occupied by a physical object and that account must be taken of the different senses, for sight, sound, and touch at least each have their own specific spaces. (Russell later spoke of sensible space as a construct of these spaces, but a construct cannot be the space in which immediately given sense data are located.) A further difficulty is that a given sensible space cannot really be at a point. Not only are the hands, say, at some distance from the eyes, but the brain and the sensory activity associated with perception of an object at one time and place are also really spread over an area. However, the major objection is once again the causation and conditioning of sense data by sense organs and nervous system. How do they influence or produce data in sensible space, or modify the appearance in sensible space of an object in physical space? As soon as one tries to fit in the causal processes, it is difficult to avoid straightforward representative realism, in which all this elaboration becomes unnecessary; perspectives become otiose, except as mere possibilities, or turn into light waves and sound waves. Hence, Russell's later views gradually approach representative realism (for example, in *Human Knowledge,* 1948).

There does, in fact, seem to be no satisfactory way out of this dilemma for the sense-datum theory. Upholders of it must embrace one horn or the other—they must maintain pure phenomenalism or representative realism. Each has its well-known difficulties, but the second, though once thought hopeless, is now perhaps more easily made plausible than the first.

DIFFICULTIES CONCERNING SENSE DATA

A number of difficulties have been noted already in the full theory, but others lie even in the arguments for sense data.

The certainty argument. Various objections may be made to the certainty argument. First, so far as introspective examination is concerned, our awareness is, as we have mentioned, of putative objects, not of color patches —one sees a tomato or something looking like one. Awareness of color patches as such is a different kind of observation from normal perceiving, not a sensory core within it. One may more readily be said to be directly aware of sounds or smells as such; but even then, as we saw concerning sensations, one is aware of them as public and external, not private.

Second, the assumed link between immediacy and certainty is questionable. If immediacy is put forward as an introspective characteristic of the awareness of sense data, nothing follows about its certainty because any awareness we point to as direct may be mistaken. On the other hand, if immediacy and certainty are linked conceptually, as the premise of the certainty argument suggests—if they are defined in terms of each other—then it may be that what seems to be immediate, and hence certain, awareness is not immediate. This point may be illustrated in various ways. The certainty argument claims that sensing reveals existents—that when we look at an (apparent) tomato, we cannot doubt that something red and round and bulgy *exists*. Strictly speaking, however, we are certain only of something red-looking; it may in fact be orange that looks red in this light. Indeed, as J. L. Austin pointed out, even statements about how a thing looks may have to be re-

tracted. Further, the controversy over whether sense data can fail to appear as what they are throws further doubts on the incorrigibility claim, and the alternative adverbial analysis, that sense data are only sense contents, challenges the view that something exists distinct from the percipient's experience of it.

Third, the certainty argument is too ready to deny that we see physical objects in cases of illusion and distortion and to assume that we are aware of the same kind of existent in both perception and hallucination. Both these assumptions may plausibly be denied. When we look at the putative tomato, even if it is a piece of wax or a reflection of a tomato or an image on a screen, we are still seeing a material object—wax, or the tomato "in" (via) the mirror, or a screen illuminated in a certain way. There is no need to suppose that we are aware of something else, a sense datum. On the other hand, the common explanation of hallucinations would be that they are unusually vivid mental images confused with perceptions. Such images, like afterimages, seem to be private, but one should not assume that they are identical with what we are aware of in normal perception. The sense-datum theory can, however, reply that hallucinations are normally quite indistinguishable by the victim from normal perception and may also be integrated with a perceived background—for instance, the apparition may walk across the room and cast shadows—so if the hallucinatory images are private, so must be the data of the background. Although two entities are not necessarily identical because they are generally indistinguishable, identity may be the most plausible explanation of their indistinguishability, and the integration is very difficult to explain except on the sense-datum theory or on some form of representative realism. All the same, the sense-datum theory, if treated as an explanatory hypothesis, has the disadvantage of being very uneconomical in postulating so many distinct entities (the sense data).

The partitive argument. The partitive argument can be dismissed quite briefly, apart from its other troubles already mentioned. From the fact that we do not actually see the whole of an object at once, it does not follow that we do not then see the object, any more than the fact that we cannot visit all of New York at once means that we cannot visit it at all. Consequently, there is no ground for regarding what we actually see of an object as something different from it (a sense datum) or the actual seeing as some special direct awareness (sensing).

The argument from the content of illusions. The argument from the content of illusions presents problems similar to those of the certainty argument. The alternative to the sense-datum answer concerning what the drunkard sees in hallucinations is "a mental image," and in double vision "one bottle looking double." Neither answer is wholly satisfactory, since the first cannot explain the integration of the image with a real background, and the second has been accused of evading the issue—looking double is not like looking blue or looking elliptical, for it involves an extra apparent object, not a differing quality of the one object. Ordinary cases of relativity are much more easily dealt with. When one sees a round dish that looks elliptical, one is simply seeing the dish and not some elliptical existent; the theory oddly assumes that things cannot look other than they are. This assumption is linked with the notion of immediacy: it is gratuitously supposed that in seeing the dish as elliptical, one is immediately aware of an elliptical existent. However, this begs the question by equating immediacy with incorrigibility, so that what looks elliptical is said to be elliptical. Furthermore, there is no cogent ground in experience or in the argument for supposing that nonhallucinatory sense data are private to a person: the elliptical shape of the plate or even the second bottle might also be sensed by others. The privacy is best supported by arguing that sense data are "generated" by brain processes (as in the causal argument for sensations).

Other difficulties. Various other criticisms of sense data have been put forward, especially by Gilbert Ryle and J. L. Austin. First, sensing is either seeing under another name—in which case there is the reduplication or regress noted concerning sensations—or else it is a myth. The notion of a mistakeproof awareness, Ryle claimed, arises from misunderstanding the character of perception words, which are achievement words or indicate the scoring of an investigational success. One cannot perceive unsuccessfully any more than one can win unsuccessfully, but that is a linguistic or conceptual matter; it does not mean that if one looks or plays, one is bound to see or to win. Second, the theory, in speaking of sense data as existents, is simply reifying (treating as things) the sounds, smells, or looks of things. Ryle claimed a linguistic origin for this: by wrongly speaking of "seeing looks" or "smelling whiffs," which are pleonastic usages like "eating nibbles," the theory tends to treat looks and whiffs as the sort of things we can see or smell—that is, as objects. And fails to see that the point of such words is to show how we are perceiving objects. (He could hardly condemn hearing sounds, even if the other examples are correct.) Third, Austin attacked the tendency of G. E. Moore, A. J. Ayer, and others to distinguish different senses of the word "see": the normal sense (seeing objects) and the restricted "direct" or "actual" seeing (sensing, which is incorrigible). He claimed that the second sense is a myth: the basic fact is that one may describe the object one sees in various ways, depending on how advertent one is; for example, as a tomato or as a red object. But in these two cases it is the same thing described in different ways, not two different things; nor does it follow that there are two kinds of seeing or two senses of the word "see."

Austin had other alleged linguistic grounds for the theory's mistakes, such as confusion of illusion with delusion, but it is doubtful whether the several different linguistic origins that he and Ryle claimed for the theory are really genuine and important. The reflective examination of experience seems a more likely origin for the theory, in view of the stress laid on it by the sense-datum philosophers. They have been so struck by the apparent immediacy of perceiving, by its apparently direct confrontation with a "given," that they have readily assumed that it does involve such an immediate awareness or confrontation; and because (on account of illusions) they cannot identify immediate awareness with the perception of a physical object, they have supposed it to be an inner awareness of special data—the sensing of sense data.

FURTHER DEVELOPMENTS

Sense contents. As we have seen, the adverbial analysis of sensing claims that sensa no more exist as entities distinct from the sensing of them than do itches or pains; consequently, they are often referred to in this analysis as sense contents. Important advocates of this approach have been C. J. Ducasse and A. J. Ayer, and under its influence Moore modified and Russell abandoned an earlier faith in an act – object analysis (that sense data are separate entities distinct from the act of sensing). Russell's conversion to the adverbial analysis was brought about by his conclusion that the subject of awareness is a logical fiction; since the act – object analysis presupposes a subject of the act of awareness, it had to be dismissed (*Analysis of Mind*, p. 141). Probably few would follow him on this; it is, at any rate, not clear that the adverbial analysis can dispense with the subject, nor is it clear why one should wish to. Moore's *Refutation of Idealism* relied on the act – object analysis, but he later had doubts about this. He tended to see the problem as whether sense data have any existence when unperceived, or rather, unsensed; that is, whether their *esse* is *percipi* or *sentiri*. He regarded this as an open question, producing various arguments on either side at different times. Actually, the two questions are not quite identical: the adverbial analysis implies that sense data or sense contents cannot exist unsensed, while the act – object analysis is neutral on this.

It seems clear that whether sense data exist unsensed is not a question that can be settled by sensing them. Consequently, some would say it is a purely conceptual matter, one of how sense data are to be defined or how the general theory is to be framed. But factual issues are relevant and present a dilemma similar to the one of the relation of sense data to physical objects. If one accepts that sense data are generated by the brain, then it seems that they cannot exist unsensed. Even if they are only conditioned by the nervous system, they must appear different from what they really are in the unconditioned, unsensed state, thus undermining the certainty argument. On the other hand, to say that a physical object is a family of sense data is scarcely meaningful if sense data do not exist unsensed; therefore, Russell at one period claimed that they do exist unsensed, calling them sensibilia in this state. More usually, however, phenomenalism is maintained; sense data do not exist unsensed, but possible ones or possibilities of sensation do.

So far as introspection is concerned, decision between the analyses depends on which sense is considered. Visual sense data, such as color shapes, would seem clearly to be distinct and to require an act – object analysis. (Afterimages are more doubtful, but anyhow are a special case.) Much the same applies to sounds and smells, which are normally experienced as external: on the other hand, tactile and other bodily (somatic) sense data, such as pains or feelings of warmth or pressure, and the sensations of movement (kinesthetic data) seem clearly adverbial, as perhaps is taste; but there are marginal cases. Explanation of this variation is difficult for the theory, which would be more plausible if it could give one account of all sense data; it is also difficult to square the distinctness claimed in the act – object analysis with the privacy always claimed. Another possible line, which seems required for dreams and mental images and for hallucinations where no distinct objects are present, would be to say that while sense data seem to the person to be distinct, they are actually contents of adverbial experiences, as are sensations. However, this would undermine the claim of the theory to rely on introspective analysis.

Sense-datum language. One suggestion that has been made is that the sense-datum philosophers have not, as they at first thought, produced a new theory of perception; they have simply introduced a new and more convenient terminology for discussing the facts of ordinary perceiving. This was accepted for a time by those who sought to see all philosophy as dealing with language and by those who, impressed by the difficulties the sense-datum theory encountered, sought to salvage something from the wreck. It is not popular now, for those with a linguistic bias have turned to the examination of ordinary language rather than to the advocacy of new terminologies, while the general decline of support for sense data has proceeded beyond this halfway house. Another reason for supposing that the sense-datum theory was only a terminology was the view that theories must be verifiable by observation of predicted consequences, which the sense-datum theory is not, but this seems to confuse a philosophical theory with a scientific theory.

Considered simply as a terminology, the language of sensing and sense data was claimed to have certain advantages; for example, that it is (*a*) noncommittal—one can describe the contents of one's experience independently of the physical objects they are thought to refer to—and (*b*) neater than ordinary language, for one can avoid periphrases like "there appears to be a red, bulgy tomato-like object" merely by listing the data sensed. But these are only slight advantages, and it seems that they are far outweighed by the fact that a sense-datum language cannot be truly neutral. It has been so long associated with the sense-datum theory that it must inevitably beg the question by suggesting that the data are private, transitory existents; that one is not "actually seeing" physical objects; or that in describing the scene in terms of visual and tactile data, one has described the experiences of normal perception and not of the different "reduced" phenomenological observation.

Bibliography

SENSATIONS

Readers are advised to consult the historical surveys and then follow up any particular treatment that interests them with the aid of the references given. On the psychological side, see Edwin Garrigues Boring, *Sensation and Perception in the History of Experimental Psychology* (New York, 1942) and *A History of Experimental Psychology*, 2d ed. (New York, 1950); on the philosophical side, most useful is David Walter Hamlyn, *Sensation and Perception* (London and New York, 1961). A stimulating but idiosyncratic discussion is given in Bertrand Russell, *The Analysis of Mind* (London, 1921). Also, many of the books listed below under sense data discuss sensations. Gilbert Ryle's article "Sensations," in Hywel David Lewis, ed., *Contemporary British Philosophy*, 3d series (London, 1956), attacks the whole concept; a careful study of a limited field is David Malet Armstrong, *Bodily Sensations* (London, 1962).

SENSE DATA

The following contain statements of the sense-datum theory.

Pioneer work is found in George Edward Moore, *Some Main Problems of Philosophy* (introductory lectures of 1910/1911; London, 1953) and his more difficult *Philosophical Studies* (London, 1922). He kept returning to the problems of perception, not always consistently; for the advanced student, Alan Richard White, *G. E. Moore* (London, 1960), is a useful guide with a full bibliography. Bertrand Russell was another pioneer in his lucid elementary *Problems of Philosophy* (London, 1912) and his more significant *Mysticism and Logic* (articles of 1914; London, 1918) and *Our Knowledge of the External World* (London, 1914), but he tended to subordinate the topic of sense data to his special perspective theory. Clear and systematic is Henry Habberley Price, *Perception* (London, 1932), which develops a full sense-datum theory. Another well-known account is Charlie Dunbar Broad, *The Mind and Its Place in Nature* (London, 1925); earlier and fuller statements of his views, with more attention to causal problems are in his *Scientific Thought* (London, 1923) and *Perception, Physics and Reality* (Cambridge, 1914). Alfred Jules Ayer gives several clear discussions, mainly from a phenomenalist point of view, in *The Foundations of Empirical Knowledge* (London, 1940), *Philosophical Essays* (London, 1954), and *The Problem of Knowledge* (London, 1956). For a modern version of representative realism stated in terms of sense data, see John Raymond Smythies, *Analysis of Perception* (London, 1956).

There are many criticisms of the sense-datum theory. A general introductory survey, chiefly of Price's version, and extended criticisms are given in Rodney Julian Hirst, *The Problems of Perception* (London, 1959). Gilbert Ryle's criticisms are found in his *The Concept of Mind* (London, 1949) and *Dilemmas* (Cambridge, 1954); John Langshaw Austin's are in his lively defense of a common-sense approach, *Sense and Sensibilia* (London, 1962); Roderick M. Chisholm has some succinct criticisms in his more technical *Perceiving* (Ithaca, N.Y., 1957); Harold Arthur Prichard, *Knowledge and Perception*, W. D. Ross, ed. (London, 1950), attacks Russell and the view that sensing is a form of knowing. Martin Lean, *Sense Perception and Matter* (London, 1953), attacks Broad's version; and valuable is H. H. Price's "The Nature and Status of Sense-data in Broad's Epistemology," in Paul Arthur Schilpp, ed., *The Philosophy of C. D. Broad* (New York, 1959). On Moore, besides A. R. White's book, senior students should see P. A. Schilpp, ed., *The Philosophy of G. E. Moore* (Evanston and Chicago, 1942), particularly C. J. Ducasse, "Moore's Refutation of Idealism"; O. K. Bouwsma, "Moore's Theory of Sense-data"; and Paul Marhenke, "Moore's Analysis of Sense Perception"; and Moore's replies to them.

Among many critical articles, notable are Roderick Firth, "Sense-data and the Percept Theory," in *Mind*, Vol. 58, No. 232 (1949), 434–465, and Vol. 59, No. 233 (1950), 35–56, attacking the sense-datum analysis of perceptual consciousness; Winston H. F. Barnes, "The Myth of Sense-data," in *PAS*, Vol. 45 (1944/1945); and Anthony M. Quinton, "The Problem of Perception," in *Mind*, Vol. 64, No. 253 (1955), 28–51, criticizing the concept of sense data and the arguments for them; also a more advanced discussion of the earlier versions of the sense-datum theory in the symposia "The Status of Sense-data," in *PAS*, Vol. 14 (1913/1914), 355–406, and "The Nature of Sensible Appearances," in *PAS*, Supp. Vol. 6 (1926), 142–205.

SENSE-DATUM LANGUAGE

The linguistic interpretation of sense data is developed in George A. Paul, "Is There a Problem About Sense-data?," in *PAS*, Supp. Vol. 15 (1936), and A. J. Ayer, "The Terminology of Sense-data," in *Mind*, Vol. 54, No. 216 (1945), 289–312, reprinted in his *Philosophical Essays* (London, 1954); there is a useful discussion of it in the symposium "Seeming," in *PAS*, Supp. Vol. 26 (1952), 195–252.

SENSE CONTENTS (ADVERBIAL ANALYSIS)

The most important advocate of this approach is C. J. Ducasse, *Nature, Mind and Death* (La Salle, Ill., 1951), largely identical with his contribution to *The Philosophy of G. E. Moore*. Brief statements may be found in A. J. Ayer, *Language, Truth and Logic*, 2d ed. (London, 1947) and *Philosophical Essays* (London, 1954). A fuller discussion, with emphasis on the differences between the senses, is C. D. Broad, "Berkeley's Argument About Material Substances," in *Proceedings of the British Academy*, Vol. 28 (1942), 127 ff., and his *Scientific Thought* (London, 1923).

R. J. HIRST

SENSATIONALISM, the doctrine that all knowledge is derived from sensations, takes several closely related forms. As a psychological theory it stresses the origins of knowledge and the processes by which it is acquired; it seeks to reduce all mental contents to unitary sensations and has close connections with associationism. It is sometimes, as by its acute but sympathetic critic James Ward, called presentationism. As an epistemological theory it tends toward the view that statements purporting to describe the world are analyzable into statements concerning the relations between sensations and that this analysis elucidates the meanings of the original statements. It is sometimes regarded as a form of empiricism and adopted with antimetaphysical intentions.

Sensations are usually regarded as occurrences in us, either caused by external objects (Epicurus and Locke) or not meaningfully attributable to external causes (James Mill and Condillac). By some they are explicitly likened to feelings or emotions (Anaxagoras and Hartley), and by others to images (Mach); the more modern forms, however, probably depend, even if not explicitly, on taking them all as analogous to feelings.

There is a tendency to associate sensationalism with the nineteenth and twentieth centuries, as a development of the work of the empiricists of the seventeenth and eighteenth centuries, but it actually has a long history. A study of its development takes us back to the pre-Socratics, and although in its modern forms it usually leans heavily on the distinction between sensation and perception, there were views which can be called sensationalist long before the distinction was made (for example, Protagoras held them). The distinction between sensation and perception is used because it is believed that although perception involves interpretation and, thus, the possibility of error, sensation does not. Sensationalism is therefore sometimes looked upon as the end point of the empiricists' quest for certainty and a sure foundation for knowledge.

The Greeks. The Greeks had no linguistic means of distinguishing between sensation and perception, but they do not appear to have considered this a serious lack. The pre-Socratics were apparently interested in perception mainly from the physiological and physical point of view; they wanted to describe processes, which they tended to see as purely mechanical (this is especially true of Empedocles and the atomists), involving the meeting of effluences from the sense organ and the external object. But Anaxagoras introduced a feature which has some significance for an understanding of sensationalism—namely, the idea that perception involves pain. This facilitates the assimilation of all sensations to feelings referred to below.

Protagoras. Protagoras, accepting the Heraclitean view that all is change or becoming and having concluded that

"man is the measure of all things," found it easy to regard our constantly changing sense experiences as the objects of knowledge and to hold that all the so-called qualities of things, not merely the secondary qualities as the atomists believed, were relative to the perceiver. This turned attention to epistemological questions connected with the nature of perception.

Plato. Perhaps Plato and Aristotle were primarily reacting against this view of Protagoras in their discussions of perception. Plato's argument in the *Republic* is that sense experience does not give knowledge but only opinion, since knowledge must be certain and cannot be of what is constantly changing—that is, sensations or the sensible world. According to some scholars—D. W. Hamlyn, for example—another view can be extracted from the later dialogue the *Theaetetus*, but this is highly controversial. Protagoras was referring to knowledge of a familiar, everyday sort. The view allegedly to be found in the *Theaetetus* is that the senses can give us this rudimentary empirical knowledge; they give us direct acquaintance with the outside world and even without interpretation can therefore give us knowledge. There is no distinction to be made, as far as the sensible world itself is concerned, between what is and what appears. Because sense experience is caused by the external world, it can be regarded as infallible. But this step is suspect both on general grounds and in relation to Plato's own insistence that the categories of right and wrong are contributed by the mind. His thought seems to be that if judgment is made by the mind and if saying that something is wrong is making a judgment, then bare sense experience, being prior to judgments of it, cannot ever be said to be wrong. It should, of course, be added that it cannot be said to be right either.

Aristotle. Aristotle, in attempting to refute the sensationalism of Protagoras, stressed the element of judgment in perception and almost arrived at the distinction between sensation and perception. At the same time he appears to admit an important feature of sensationalism. Each sense has its proper object or special sensible; the proper object of hearing is sound and that of sight is color. But there are also common sensibles, qualities of objects which are not specially related to any one of the five senses but which are related to the common nature of them all, which he referred to as the common sense. These qualities are, roughly, the primary qualities motion, rest, shape, size, and number. Because there is a necessary connection between each sense and its special sensible, it is impossible for the senses to make mistakes about them; for example, hearing cannot err about the fact that it is concerned with sound and not color. This, however, does not entail any incorrigibility in the deliverances of the senses as is required by sensationalism. It simply means that each sense is necessarily concerned with its special sensible. Aristotle's claims about incorrigibility probably arise, as Hamlyn says, from an unresolved conflict between his view of the senses as both active and passive. (The senses can make mistakes only if they are active and make judgments; as mere passive receptors, they cannot. If we fail to distinguish in this way, we may think of the senses as judging infallibly.) In *De Memoria et Reminiscentia* Aristotle outlined some principles of association which look forward to later accounts.

Epicurus. Epicurus, who believed that sense perception is the source of all knowledge, held a causal theory of perception. He did not distinguish between sensation and perception and regarded what were later called sensations as incorrigible because caused. He was an atomist and attempted a mechanical account of perception. The Stoics opposed this account and again stressed the importance of at least rudimentary judgment in perception. Their conception of *phantasiae* roughly corresponds to the conception of sensations as images; they held that these were not necessarily veridical although some of them were intuitively certain.

The Scholastics. Problems of perception were not central in medieval philosophy except as they bore on the relation between empirical and other varieties of knowledge.

Augustine. Augustine is important on the subject of perception perhaps only because he saw that it is not meaningful to talk of sensations as either true or false; these terms can be applied only to judgments. He simply assumed that sense impressions correspond to the external world but regarded the knowledge thus obtained as of the lowest kind.

Aquinas. Aquinas followed Aristotle in his views on perception to the extent of holding that it involves the reception of a sensible form without matter, but this produces a change in the soul, not merely, as for Aristotle, in the sense organ. Sensory images (*phantasmata*) are received passively, but they are images of external objects. They have the peculiarity that we are not aware of them. The mind abstracts universal qualities from these and uses them in making judgments. The senses and the intellect are closely connected: *Nihil est in intellectu quod non prius in sensu* ("Nothing is in the intellect which was not first in the senses"). Because our perceptions involve judgments, they may or may not be veridical, but the *phantasmata* are not appropriately called either. This, with the fact that the *phantasmata* are images *of* something, prevented Aquinas from being a sensationalist, but he was very close to being one in spirit and utterance.

Ockham. Although William of Ockham differed from Aquinas in many ways, he also distinguished a sensible and an intellectual element in cognition. Those cognitions which involve only immediate experiences are said to be perfect. Error arises in judgment, but when we are directly apprehending something, we are not in error.

The seventeenth and eighteenth centuries. Sensationalism proper can perhaps be regarded as the product of a steady development of empiricist ideas from the seventeenth century to the nineteenth. Hobbes is sometimes credited with its inception, but his sensationalism is rudimentary. He did have some conception of the association of ideas and, of course, contributed to the foundations of empiricism.

Largely because of the climate of scientific opinion, involving as it did a growing belief in the importance of observation and experiment, the philosophers of the seventeenth century were much concerned with problems of perception. They were especially interested in the elimination of errors arising from sense experience and in the

attempt to make our knowledge of the natural world as reliable as possible. The rationalists attempted to show that knowledge could be based on indubitable truths of reason, independent of sense experience. The empiricists sought a hard core of indubitable truths involved in sense experience upon which all knowledge could be based.

Galileo. Galileo distinguished between primary and secondary qualities and thought that secondary qualities existed only as sensations in us. They are, however, caused by primary qualities in objects, especially by shape and motion.

Hobbes. Under the influence of Galileo, Descartes, Mersenne, and Gassendi, Hobbes developed the philosophy of motion into what must be the most thoroughgoing materialism there has ever been. For him all our inquiries must start from sense experience, but there are certain principles—for instance, that motion cannot be understood to have any other cause besides motion—which we know independently of sense experience and upon which other knowledge depends. Nothing exists but matter in motion, so sensations are material changes in us which somehow mediate between motions in the external world and the minute motions of our bodily parts. Hobbes assumed the existence of external motions causing our sensations; knowledge of these "objects" can come only through sensations. This does not entail the empiricist view that all knowledge is reducible to knowledge of sensations; Hobbes was in general rationalist, for he held that certain truths of reason are essential even for that knowledge of the natural world which depends upon sensation.

Locke. Locke's work marks the beginning of the growth of sensationalism proper, although he was not himself a sensationalist just because he did not develop his particular form of empiricism consistently. His "ideas of sensation" are close to what were later called simply sensations, but his representative theory of perception and his assertion of the existence of substance entail that in spite of explicit claims he relied on knowledge which did not come entirely through sensation.

Berkeley. Berkeley attempted to remove this inconsistency in his attack on material substance and representative perception. Whether we view his reliance on God as the unempirical importing of a concept merely for the purpose of filling an embarrassing gap—that is, to allow us to hold that objects continue to exist when no human being is perceiving them—or as the attempt to delineate a concept which is logically necessitated by our experience, Berkeley's account of ideas brings us very near sensationalism. There is no talk of external objects which are composed of any material different in kind from what we directly know—that is, ideas. Later sensationalism can be regarded as comparable to Berkeley's system without God, with all its problems as well as its advantages.

Hume. Hume continued this development, in one direction by rejecting mental substance, which was retained by Berkeley, as well as material substance. The world for us, as far as we can justifiably say in philosophical contexts, consists of impressions and ideas, and knowledge is of relations between these. Hume was not, however, as great a skeptic as is often alleged. We have, naturally, certain beliefs—for example, in the external world and in causal efficacy—which cannot be rationally supported. When philosophy fails to provide this rational support, so much the worse for philosophy. If Hume had not been affected by the common view that knowledge implies certainty, he would no doubt have admitted these "natural" beliefs as knowledge and thus have been farther from sensationalism in his official theory than he actually was.

Sensationalism in its fullest sense is best seen in the works of Hume's lesser-known contemporaries David Hartley and Étienne Bonnot de Condillac. Hartley's work was later developed by James Mill, and its most thoroughgoing exponent in the nineteenth century was perhaps Ernst Mach.

Hartley. Hartley was a medical man; his interests were largely physiological, and his work stimulated the development of a school of psychology. His basic concepts were sensations and the association of ideas, for which he admitted a debt to Locke and Newton. All mental occurrences originate in sensations caused by vibrations of minute particles of the brain set off by external stimulation. Simple ideas are "copies" of sensations—that is, physiologically they are tiny vibrations corresponding in character to the original vibrations and left behind by sensations when the stimulus is withdrawn. Complex ideas are built up from these by association according to certain discoverable principles. The vibrations occur in a subtle elastic fluid in the medullary substance of the nerves and brain. This mechanical account is reminiscent of Hobbes's view and admittedly owes a debt to Newton's mechanistic philosophy. The conception of the association of ideas springs from Locke, and the consequent contention that ideas are copies of sensations echoes Hume's account of impressions and ideas. Hartley's theory leads to the conclusion that we are aware only of occurrences within ourselves but that these depend for their character on the external world. There is a twofold correspondence, between ideas and sensations and between sensations and stimuli.

James Mill. James Mill accepted Hartley's basic conceptions and developed the psychological side of the theory. Hartley had expressed in terms of vibrations two principal determinants of the strength of association—the vividness of the sensations and the frequency of their conjoint occurrence. Mill discussed these principles in some detail, without Hartley's preoccupation with vibrations, contrasting his principles of association with Hume's and using some rather unsatisfactory arguments for preferring his own. In place of Hume's contiguity in time and place, causation, and resemblance, Mill put synchronous order and successive order, which include causation as a special case, and vividness and frequency, which include resemblance as a special case. He went farther than Hartley in considering the relation of sensations to the external world; external objects for him are "clusters of sensations." Most of our beliefs about them depend on sight and sensations of color, with which we associate the other properties we attribute to them.

Condillac. While Hartley was writing in England, Condillac was developing similar ideas in France. He was a disciple of Locke, and his first book was largely an exposition of Locke's philosophy. In his *Traité des sensations*, he developed his own psychological theory, largely in opposition to the various current conceptions of innate ideas. He set out to show that all knowledge is "transformed

sensation" and does not depend upon anything else, even, as Locke would have had it, reflection. He examined the nature and power of each of the senses by imagining a statue which has all the human faculties but has never had a sense impression. He then allowed its senses to be activated, one by one and in various combinations, and asserted that the results showed how all knowledge can gradually be constructed. He concluded that men consist of their experiences and that what they perceive is their own mental occurrences. Unlike Hartley, he did not try to give a mechanical account of these occurrences, being more concerned with psychology than physiology, and he admitted the reality of the soul. He had a considerable influence on the beginnings of British psychological thought through James Mill and J. S. Mill, Alexander Bain, and Herbert Spencer.

Mach and twentieth-century empiricism. Whereas Hartley, Condillac, and the Mills were interested in sensations mainly in relation to psychology, ethics and politics, Ernst Mach's interest sprang from an attempt to provide an analysis of the methods of the physical sciences. His sensationalism was associated with a search for a solid foundation for scientific statements and with a desire to free science of all metaphysics. He held that only statements which are directly verifiable in sense experience can finally be accepted as conclusions in the sciences. He concluded that all scientific statements are analyzable into statements about the relations between our sensations and that nothing can be said, scientifically, about anything beyond this. In a sentence reminiscent of James Mill he said, "The world is my sensation." It follows, also, that the various branches of science do not differ in subject matter but only in their approach to the subject matter, which is—alike for all—sensations; this was the basis of the "unity of science" movement and the logical positivism of the Vienna circle.

Mach's work was very much in harmony with the spirit of his time, especially in relation to the physical sciences, and has had an important influence on later philosophical thought. He admitted a debt to Berkeley and Hume and a number of his philosophically minded scientific contemporaries. His idea that the world is composed of "elements" which can be regarded either as sensations or the constituents of physical objects has close connections with Russell's neutral monism and logical atomism, and his description of the aims of science is similar to that of pragmatism and operationism. In one way or another, most empiricist thought about science during the twentieth century has been influenced by his work. Recent philosophical theories of perception involving sense data or sensa are in the direct line of descent insofar as they stress the mind dependence of sense data, our direct awareness of or acquaintance with them, and the alleged incorrigibility of certain sorts of statements about them. Such theories can be regarded as attempts to refashion Mach's form of sensationalism in order to avoid some of the obvious objections to it.

Sensationalism and related theories all suffer from one defect, which renders the whole approach suspect; under the heading "sensations" they class together things which it is important to distinguish—for example, such sensible qualities as colors and sounds; bodily aches and pains; desires and emotions; and such feelings as dizziness, anger, and jealousy. We would not normally be prepared to class all these as experiences, but certain empiricist contentions—for example, that we know colors only through their effects on us—can make it seem superficially plausible to call them all sensations. Just because this blurs the distinctions between various things included under the heading, sensationalism as a general theory gains plausibility. Toothaches and certain feelings have an air of immediacy and unmistakability which may lead us to suppose that color sensations, since they, too, are sensations, are ultimate and incorrigible data for the construction of a world picture. I can be certain that I have a toothache, and no one can be better justified than I in asserting or denying this. If color sensations can be assimilated to toothaches, there might seem to be some hope of arriving at incorrigible statements about the external world. Hence, the importance of the clue afforded by Anaxagoras' view that perception involves pain. A close examination of experiences of color and other sorts of experience reveals that the necessary assimilation is seriously misleading; moreover, it brings in its train enormous difficulties for an account of science. On one hand, incorrigibility can be achieved, if at all, only with the loss of the publicity of the statements concerned; on the other hand, it is difficult or impossible to show how scientific problems could ever arise if sensationalism were correct, since there is no reason that any particular combination of sensations should or should not follow any other.

In fact, the word "sensation" suffers from ambiguities similar to those involved in the word "idea" as used by Locke and Berkeley; as "sensation" must do even more work than "idea," the ambiguities are correspondingly more serious. The view of science which springs from sensationalism (see MACH, ERNST; and PEARSON, KARL), according to which science describes but does not explain, suffers further from insufficient consideration of the nature of description and its relation to explanation and from a failure to appreciate the difficulties involved in the idea of describing sensations.

Bibliography

GENERAL

Armstrong, D. M., *Bodily Sensations*. London, 1962. Consideration of the logic of sensations.

Boring, E. G., *Sensation and Perception in the History of Experimental Psychology*. New York, 1942. Useful discussions of some of the ideas of sensationalism from the point of view of psychology.

Copleston, F. C., *History of Philosophy*. London, 1946——. Seven volumes published thus far.

Hamlyn, D. W., *Sensation and Perception*. London, 1961. Excellent historical survey with a useful bibliography.

Hirst, R. J., *The Problems of Perception*. London, 1959. Account of philosophical problems connected with sensationalism.

Passmore, J. A., *A Hundred Years of Philosophy*. London, 1957.

THE GREEKS

Aristotle, *De Anima*, translated by K. Foster and S. Humphries, with the commentary of St. Thomas Aquinas. London, 1951.

Aristotle, *Works*, J. A. Smith and W. D. Ross, eds., 12 vols. Oxford, 1910–1952. See Vol. VIII, *Metaphysics*, especially Γ, 5

(1928), and *De Memoria et Reminiscentia*, in Vol. III (1931). These works contain most of Aristotle's important views on sensation.

Burnet, John, *Early Greek Philosophy*. London, 1892.

Cornford, F. M., *Plato's Theory of Knowledge*. London, 1935. Contains Plato's *Theaetetus*, which considers the place of perception in knowledge, with a commentary.

Gulley, Norman, *Plato's Theory of Knowledge*. London, 1962. Authoritative and readable treatment.

Kirk, G. S., and Raven, J. E., *The Presocratic Philosophers*. Cambridge, 1957. This and Burnet, *op. cit.*, give accounts of pre-Socratic views on sensation.

Plato, *The Collected Dialogues*, Edith Hamilton and Huntington Cairns, eds. New York, 1961. See the *Republic*, *Protagoras*, *Theaetetus*, and *Timaeus*.

Randall, J. H., *Aristotle*. New York, 1960.

THE SCHOLASTICS

Aquinas, Thomas, *Summa Theologica* (selections) in *Basic Writings of St. Thomas Aquinas*, annotated by Anton C. Pegis, ed., 2 vols. New York, 1945. Vol. I, Questions 78–86.

Aquinas, Thomas, *Commentary on Aristotle's De Anima*. See Aristotle, *De Anima* (above).

Copleston, F. C., *Aquinas*. London, 1955. Most easily accessible account of Aquinas' thought.

Fremantle, Anne, ed., *The Age of Belief*. New York, 1955. Selections from the writings of the Scholastics, with commentary.

Gilson, Étienne, *Christian Philosophy in the Middle Ages*. London, 1953. Valuable general account.

THE SEVENTEENTH AND EIGHTEENTH CENTURIES

Bacon, Francis, *Novum Organum* (1620), translated by G. W. Kitchin. Oxford, 1855.

Bower, G. S., *Hartley and James Mill*. London, 1881.

Condillac, É. B. de, *Essai sur l'origine des connoissances humaines*. Amsterdam, 1746.

Condillac, É. B. de, *Traité des sensations* (1754). Translated by G. Carr as *Treatise on Sensations*. London, 1930. This and above work influenced British empiricism.

Galileo, *Il Saggiatore* (1623). Translated in part by Stillman Drake in *Discoveries and Opinions of Galileo*. New York, 1957.

Hartley, David, *Observations on Man*. London, 1749. An early version of sensationalism which influenced both philosophers and psychologists.

Hobbes, Thomas, *Leviathan* (1651), Michael Oakeshott, ed. New York, 1947; paperback ed., 1962.

Hobbes, Thomas, *De Corpore* (1655), translated as *Elements of Philosophy Concerning Body*. London, 1839.

Locke, John, *Essay Concerning Human Understanding* (1690), A. C. Fraser, ed. Oxford, 1894.

Mill, James, *The Analysis of the Phenomena of the Human Mind*, J. S. Mill, ed. London, 1829. Development of Hartley's sensationalism.

THE NINETEENTH AND TWENTIETH CENTURIES

Alexander, Peter, *Sensationalism and Scientific Explanation*. London, 1963. Criticism of the sensationalist account of science.

Ayer, A. J., *Foundations of Empirical Knowledge*. London, 1940. One version of the sense-datum theory.

Ayer, A. J., *Philosophical Essays*. London, 1954.

Ayer, A. J., ed., *Logical Positivism*. Glencoe, Ill., 1959.

Bain, Alexander, *The Senses and the Intellect*. London, 1855.

Broad, C. D., *Scientific Thought*. London, 1923. Another modern sense-datum theory.

Clifford, W. K., *Lectures and Essays*. London, 1879.

Carnap, Rudolf, *The Unity of Science*, translated by Max Black. London, 1934.

Feigl, Herbert, and Sellars, Wilfrid, eds., *Readings in Philosophical Analysis*. New York, 1949. Useful collection of papers, many of which represent modern developments from sensationalism.

Frank, Philipp, *Modern Science and Its Philosophy*. Cambridge,

Mass., 1949. Historical account of the development of logical positivism.

George, W. H., *The Scientist in Action*. London, 1936. Science seen as the relating of pointer readings.

Herbart, J. F., *A.B.C. of Sense-Perception*. New York, 1896.

Herbart, J. F., *Lehrbuch zur Psychologie*. Königsberg, Germany, 1816. Translated by M. K. Smith as *Text Book of Psychology*. London, 1891.

James, William, *Essays in Radical Empiricism*. London, 1912.

Kraft, Victor, *The Vienna Circle*. New York, 1953.

Mach, Ernst, *Populärwissenschaftliche Vorlesungen*. Leipzig, 1894. Translated by T. J. McCormack as *Popular Scientific Lectures*. Chicago, 1898. Mach's works are classics of modern sensationalism.

Mach, Ernst, *Die Analyse der Empfindungen*. Jena, 1906. Translated by C. M. Williams as *The Analysis of Sensations*. Chicago, 1914.

Mill, J. S., *An Examination of Sir William Hamilton's Philosophy*. London, 1865.

Moore, G. E., *Philosophical Studies*. London, 1922.

Moore, G. E., *Some Main Problems of Philosophy*. London, 1953. This and above work contain another variety of sense-datum theory.

Neurath, Otto; Carnap, Rudolf; and Morris, C. W., eds., *International Encyclopedia of Unified Science*. Chicago, 1938–1962.

Pearson, Karl, *The Grammar of Science*, 3d ed. London, 1911.

Poincaré, Henri, *La Science et l'hypothèse*. Paris, 1902. Translated by W. J. Greenstreet as *Science and Hypothesis*. London, 1905.

Poincaré, Henri, *La Valeur de science*. Paris, 1905. Translated by G. B. Halsted as *The Value of Science*. London, 1907.

Price, H. H., *Perception*. London, 1932. Perhaps the most detailed and elegant version of the sense-datum view.

Russell, Bertrand, *Our Knowledge of the External World*. London, 1914.

Russell, Bertrand, *The Analysis of Mind*. London, 1921.

Russell, Bertrand, "The Philosophy of Logical Atomism," in R. C. Marsh, ed., *Logic and Knowledge*. London, 1956.

Schilpp, P. A., ed., *The Philosophy of Bertrand Russell*. Evanston, Ill., 1946.

Ward, James, *Psychological Principles*. Cambridge, 1918. Attack on sensationalism in psychology.

PETER ALEXANDER

SENSATIONS. See SENSA.

SENSE DATA. See SENSA.

SENSIBILIA. See PHENOMENALISM.

SENTENCES. See PROPOSITIONS, JUDGMENTS, SENTENCES, AND STATEMENTS.

SERVETUS, MICHAEL, Spanish theologian and physician, was born in Spanish Navarre in 1511 and was burned at the stake in Geneva in 1553. In the history of medicine he is remembered for having been the first to publish a description of the pulmonary circulation of the blood, and in the history of theology, he is noted for his systematic refutation of the Nicene doctrine of the Trinity. In philosophy, he developed a Christocentric pantheism that included elements from the Neoplatonic, Franciscan, and cabalistic traditions. It should be pointed out, however, that he believed that natural philosophy should be grounded in empirical investigation.

After studying the three Biblical languages as well as mathematics, philosophy, theology, and law at the universities of Zaragoza and Toulouse, Servetus, in the capacity of secretary, accompanied Juan de Quintana, the Franciscan confessor of Emperor Charles V, to the latter's coronation in Bologna. Breaking with the imperial court, he went on his own to Basel, where he sought out John Oecolampadius, and then went on to Strasbourg, where he had some contact with Martin Bucer and, in particular, Wolfgang Capito. In nearby Hagenau he had printed his *De Trinitatis Erroribus* (1531) and, in response to Bucer's critique, the more moderate and more Christologically oriented *De Trinitate* (1532). In Strasbourg Servetus met Kaspar Schwenkfeld, from whom he may have taken over a heretical idea about the celestial flesh of Christ. In Strasbourg he may also have come in contact with the Anabaptists, whose views on baptism he was later to espouse. By way of Basel, where he tried to get Erasmus' approval of his *De Trinitate*, he went to Lyons, where he worked as a proofreader and began his study of medicine under the Neoplatonizing Symphorien Champier. Next he went to Paris, where by chance he met John Calvin and got into trouble with the medical faculty over his views on astral influences. His *Apologetica Disceptatio pro Astrologia* (1538) marks an important turning point in Servetus' evaluation of the place of Greek philosophy. Whereas before he had regarded the influence of philosophy on theology as corrupting, he was now prepared to speak of "*divinus* Plato," on whose authority he defended astrology. After establishing himself in Vienne as physician to the archbishop, he engaged in correspondence with Calvin and composed the recently discovered and identified *Declaratio Jesu Christi Filii Dei* (c. 1540). Out of this grew his more massive *Restitutio Christianismi* (1553). Through the machinations of Calvin himself, Servetus was apprehended and tried for heresy, first in Catholic Lyons and then, after his escape, in Calvinist Geneva, where, after refusing to recant, he was burned at the stake.

Servetus' view of nature, history, and salvation was centered on the figure of Jesus Christ, whom he considered to be in a quite physical sense the Son of God. Servetus declined, however, to call the earthly Son eternal and declined to call either the Word or the Spirit *personae;* rather, he called them, neutrally, *res*—that is, in a modalist sense, the faces, forms, images, or manifestations of God. He mistakenly regarded the traditional *hypostasis (persona)* and *substantia* as equivalent, and hence, to avoid what he considered an un-Biblical tritheism, he called the Father or Jehovah alone God. Before the Incarnation the Word was Elohim, or Uncreated Light. Indeed, this Light, or alternatively Christ (as distinguished from the earthly Son, Jesus), was also "the eternal sea (*pelagus*) of ideas." The Spirit has always been a Power of God, working outwardly in the world as his breath (*flatus*) and inwardly as the agitation, or motion, of the human spirit at regeneration.

The way in which the Uncreated Light became the Second Adam in Mary was for Servetus paradigmatic of the process by which creative Light was ever penetrating matter to form minerals, plants, animals, and all created things. For Servetus "even the treasures of natural science are hidden in Christ." Connected with his speculation on Light was Servetus' concept of the Shadow, according to which he was able to regard all of the Old Testament and all religion outside the Bible as a shadowing forth of the

Son that was to be born of Mary. He cherished the old Law as a pregnant woman bearing the embryonic Christ until the fullness of time.

Servetus rejected post-Constantinian (post-Nicene) Catholicism because of its alleged tritheism and its use of political force in the realm of conscience. He also opposed the Reformation churches because of their use of force, their denial of free will in accepting redemptive grace, and their neglect of sanctification, which he understood as communicated in an almost physical sense through the believers' baptism at the age of thirty (in imitation of Jesus). Nevertheless, in common with the Spiritual Libertines and some Anabaptists, Servetus held to the provisional death of every soul with the body pending the general resurrection. Under the influence of Joachimite speculation, he believed that the true church would be restored in the year 1560.

Works by Servetus

The two works on the Trinity have been translated by E. M. Wilbur as *Two Treatises on the Trinity*, Harvard Theological Studies (Cambridge, Mass., 1932), Vol. 16. See also Charles D. O'Malley, *Michael Servetus: A Translation of His Geographical, Medical and Astrological Writings* (Philadelphia, 1953).

Works on Servetus

For literature on Servetus, see Roland Bainton, *Hunted Heretic: The Life and Death of Michael Servetus, 1511–1553* (Boston, 1953), which includes a bibliography; Wolrad Emde, "Michael Servetus als Renaissancephilosoph und Restitutionstheologe," in *Zeitschrift für Kirchengeschichte*, Vol. 50 (1941), 96–131, especially good on *Restitutio Christianismi;* and Marcial Solana, *Historia de la filosofía española* (Madrid, 1941), Vol. I, pp. 629–681, especially good on *De Trinitate*.

GEORGE HUNSTON WILLIAMS

SETH, ANDREW. See PRINGLE-PATTISON, ANDREW SETH.

SET THEORY. The theory of sets was developed by Georg Cantor in the short period from 1874 to 1897. In spite of the opposition of most contemporary mathematicians until the 1890s, it had attained recognition as a distinct and important branch of mathematics by the turn of the century. The rapidity of its subsequent development, in both its foundations and its applications, may be gathered from the following statement in the beginning of the most comprehensive contemporary encyclopedia of mathematics (Nicholas Bourbaki, *Théorie des ensembles*, Paris, 1954, p. 4): "It is now well known that current mathematics, almost in its entirety, can be derived from a single source, from the theory of sets."

The relations between set theory and logic are particularly close. Logicism of the Bertrand Russell variety, which considers mathematics to be but an elaborate extension of logic, regards set theory as the connecting link.

The theory of abstract sets, in which the nature of the members of a set is not specified, is distinguished from the theory of sets of points, in which the members are (real or complex) numbers or points or systems of these. The latter theory is fundamental to the theory of functions, to (set-theoretical) topology, and to other branches of mathematics. This article deals chiefly with abstract set theory.

The original impetus to the development of set theory came in part from philosophy—in particular, from the problem of the actual infinite, as it eventually appeared in Bernard Bolzano's posthumous *Paradoxien des Unendlichen* (1851). The impetus came more strongly from certain problems in the theory of real functions raised in the 1870s by Cantor, Hermann Hankel, H. J. S. Smith, and others. Richard Dedekind's profound theory of the positive integers (1888) also played a role in the subsequent development of set theory.

Between 1882 and 1895, Cantor proposed various definitions for the concept of a set, the final one being "A set [*Menge*] is a collection into a whole [*Zusammenfassung zu einem Ganzen*] of definite, distinct objects of our intuition or our thought. The objects are called the members [*Elemente*] of the set." The term "definite" means that given a set *s*, it should be at least intrinsically determined for any object whether that object is a member of *s* or not; "distinct" stresses that any two members of a set are different, as contrasted with a sequence, in which the same member may occur repeatedly.

The chief ingredient of the definition, "collection into a whole," is hardly more than tautological with regard to "set." Although in 1895 the set concept still appeared to be self-evident, it was obvious a few years later that the definition leaves room for logical antinomies such as those of Cesare Burali-Forti and Bertrand Russell. It is therefore not feasible to develop set theory on the basis of Cantor's definition.

In the main, three different ways to remedy the situation have been proposed, all of which came independently and about the same time (1908). The most radical is that of intuitionism, particularly the neo-intuitionism of L. E. J. Brouwer and his followers; very little of set theory would be left on this view. Another is the type-theoretical approach in the sense of Russell, W. V. Quine, and others, an approach generally combined with logicism in regard to the nature of mathematics. In the third approach axiomatic restriction of the set concept replaces a direct definition. (Such restriction implicitly directs the exposition in the following section. In the concluding section the purpose and the effect of axiomatization are explained.)

CLASSICAL (CANTORIAN) SET THEORY

Fundamental concepts. The primitive (dyadic) relation of set theory is that between a set and its members. It is called the membership relation and is denoted by ϵ; we read $a \,\epsilon\, s$ as "a is a member of the set s," "s contains a," etc. The domain of the membership relation—that is, the class of those objects that can serve as members of a set—may either coincide with the counterdomain, which is the class of sets, or contain additional objects ("individuals," but not in the proper logical sense). The latter was Ernst Zermelo's original approach (1908), but since the 1920s the preference in general has been to restrict the domain to sets, which satisfies the normal needs of mathematics. Only for very special purposes, discussed below, does one use individuals or "extraordinary sets" (for instance, sets that contain themselves as members).

A set, then, should be an object that contains members. This rule has a single exception, to be mentioned presently.

Equality. Three attitudes are possible with regard to equality (=) between sets. First, the equality relation may be regarded as belonging to the underlying logic (for example, the first-order functional calculus with equality). Second, equality may be considered as a second primitive (dyadic) relation, in addition to membership. Third, equality may be defined either by requiring that equal sets belong to the same sets (classes) or by regarding sets as equal if they contain the same members. In any case the principle of extensionality is usually adhered to. This means that a set is determined by the totality of its members; hence, it can be denoted by its members, a, b, c, $\cdots$, in the form $\{a,b,c,\cdots\}$.

Subsets. A set s is called a subset of a set t—in symbols, $s \subseteq t$—if each $x \epsilon s$ belongs to t; in particular, a set s is a proper subset ($s \subset t$) if s does not contain all the members of t. However, this definition, which presupposes the existence of s and t, does not secure the existence of subsets of a given set. The normal way of securing their existence is by "comprehension"; that is to say, given t and a predicate P that is meaningful for all $x \epsilon t$, there exists the subset t_p of those $x \epsilon t$ that satisfy P.

The empty set. If P means "is a member of t," we obtain $t_p = t$. But for the predicate "is not a member of t" we obtain, as the corresponding subset, a set which contains no member at all. For this reason, and for many others, an *empty set*, $\emptyset$, which has no members, is admitted. By the principle of extensionality there exists only one empty set. We have $\emptyset \subseteq s$ for any set s. Accordingly, a finite (see below) set F of n members has just 2^n subsets, which evolve by distributing two values, such as "yes" and "no," independently to the members of F.

Union and intersection. Given a set S of sets a, b, c, $\cdots$, the two fundamental operations of Boolean algebra yield the union $\cup S$ and the intersection $\cap S$ of the members of S. The union $\cup S$ contains the elements that belong to at least one $x \epsilon S$, corresponding to logical disjunction; the intersection $\cap S$ contains those that belong to each $x \epsilon S$ and thus corresponds to logical conjunction. We may write $\cup S$ as $a \cup b \cup c \cup \cdots$ and $\cap S$ as $a \cap b \cap c \cap \cdots$.

Equivalence. Next to membership and equality the most important relation of the theory of plain sets (explained below) is that of equivalence ($\sim$). The relation $s \sim t$ obtains if there exists a mapping φ of s onto t such that by φ, to each $x \epsilon s$ corresponds a single $y \epsilon t$ and vice versa. Clearly, equivalence is a reflexive, symmetrical, and transitive relation. Equivalence can be reduced to membership as follows: Let S, T be "disjoint" sets (sets without common members) and P the set of all pairs $\{s,t\}$ with $s \epsilon S$, $t \epsilon T$. Then P may have subsets $\bar{P}$ such that each member of $S \cup T$ belongs to a single member of $\bar{P}$; if so, each $\bar{P}$ is a mapping of S onto T, and hence $S \sim T$.

Finite and infinite sets. It is essential to distinguish between finite sets (including $\emptyset$) and infinite sets. This may be done in various ways, the relations between which (with or without the axiom of choice—see below) are an important object of study. Either "finite" or "infinite" is defined, and the other concept is taken as its negation. Two distinct standard definitions are the following:

(*a*) The set s is finite ("inductive") if there is a nonnegative integer n such that s contains just n members; other-wise s is infinite. (The explicit reference to integers can be eliminated by Russell's definition of "inductive cardinals.")

(*b*) The set s is infinite ("reflexive") if s is equivalent to a proper subset of s; otherwise s is finite.

Since it is easy to show that an inductive set is not reflexive, the equipollence of (*a*) and (*b*) depends on proving that every noninductive set is reflexive; in this proof the axiom of choice is used.

Denumerable sets. A set d is called denumerable if d is equivalent to the set N of all positive integers. The set d is infinite even in the stronger sense of "reflexive" because N is equivalent to, for instance, the proper subset N_0 obtained by dropping the number 1, as is shown by relating $n \epsilon N$ to $(n+1) \epsilon N_0$. Every infinite subset of d, as well as the union of finitely or denumerably many denumerable sets, is clearly denumerable. Hence, the sets of all rational, and even of all algebraic, numbers are denumerable.

A more profound theorem states that any infinite set has a denumerable subset. If "infinite" is taken in the sense of "noninductive," the axiom of choice is required for the proof.

Transfinite cardinals. In the discussion so far nonequivalent infinite sets have not appeared, and the notion of infinity may still prove trivial. Therefore, the real birth of set theory must be seen in Cantor's proof, in 1874, that the set N of integers and the continuum are nonequivalent sets. Cantor later generalized his method of proof, by the diagonal procedure, so as to show the existence of infinitely many nonequivalent infinite sets. In this context "continuum" refers not merely to the linear continuum, the set of all points of a segment or line or the set of the corresponding real numbers, but to a continuum of any finite number of dimensions, or even of denumerably many dimensions; all these sets prove to be equivalent.

The existence of nonequivalent infinite sets enables us to introduce transfinite cardinal numbers. Just as the same finite cardinal, or nonnegative integer, corresponds to equivalent finite sets, so we may ascribe to an infinite set a transfinite cardinal and to all equivalent sets the same cardinal. There are various nonelementary methods—for example, "abstraction"—for explicitly defining cardinals. For most purposes, however, the "functional" definition by equality is sufficient: The cardinals of sets are equal if and only if the sets are equivalent. The cardinal of denumerable sets is denoted by $\aleph_0$ (read aleph-zero).

Ordering of cardinals. Cardinals can be ordered according to magnitude by the following definition: The cardinal $\mathbf{s}$ of S is less than the cardinal $\mathbf{t}$ of T (or $\mathbf{t}$ is greater than $\mathbf{s}$) if S is equivalent to a subset of T but T is not equivalent to any subset of S. This order is evidently asymmetrical and transitive; $\aleph_0$ is the least transfinite cardinal. By the diagonal method it can be proved that for any finite or infinite set S, the "power set" of S—that is, the set whose members are all the subsets of S—has a greater cardinal than S (Cantor's theorem). In particular, the continuum can be represented as the power set of a denumerable set.

Continuum problem. The question whether the continuum has the cardinal *next* to $\aleph_0$ (this assumption being Cantor's continuum hypothesis) has no answer. Therefore, the cardinal of the continuum is denoted not by $\aleph_1$ but usually by $\aleph$ without index. In the case of the power set of a denumerable S one speaks of the continuum problem, and in the case of any infinite S of the generalized continuum problem. As far back as the second International Congress of Mathematicians, at Paris in 1900, David Hilbert named the continuum problem as first among many important unsolved problems of mathematics; in spite of enormous efforts, including those of Hilbert, a final solution was not reached until 1963.

Comparability. The question of the comparability of cardinals—that is, whether of two different cardinals one is less than the other—cannot be answered at this point in the article. But it can be proved that two sets each of which is equivalent to a subset of the other have the same cardinal (equivalence theorem); hence, if S is equivalent to a subset of T, the cardinal of S is less than or equal to the cardinal of T.

Arithmetic of cardinals. Addition, multiplication, and exponentiation in the domain of cardinals are easily defined, and they satisfy the formal laws valid in ordinary arithmetic. Not only may the terms, factors, etc., be transfinite, but sums and products of infinitely many terms are defined that have nothing to do with the quasi-infinite series, etc., of analysis defined by limit processes. A few of the results thus obtained are

$$1+2+3+\cdots+n+\cdots=\aleph_0.$$
$$\aleph_0+\aleph_0+\cdots(=\aleph_0\cdot\aleph_0)=\aleph_0.$$
(1) $\qquad\qquad$ $c+n=c+\aleph_0=c$, for every transfinite cardinal c.

(2) $\qquad$ $\aleph+\aleph+\aleph+\cdots=\aleph\cdot\aleph_0=\aleph.$

(3) $\qquad$ $\aleph\cdot\aleph(=\aleph^2)=\aleph^n=\aleph^{\aleph_0}=\aleph.$
$$2^{\aleph_0}(=2\cdot2\cdot2\cdot\cdots)=\aleph_0{}^{\aleph_0}=\aleph(>\aleph_0).$$
$$2^\aleph=\aleph_0{}^\aleph=\aleph^\aleph>\aleph.$$

Generally, 2^c is the cardinal of the power set of a set of the cardinal c; hence, $2^c>c$.

The seemingly self-evident proposition that a product of cardinals equals 0 if and only if one of the factors is 0 possesses special significance. The part "if" is trivial on a suitable definition of multiplication (Cartesian product, see below), and the part "only if" coincides (if the number of factors is infinite) with the axiom of choice (see below).

Unlike these "direct" operations, the inversions, namely subtraction, division, etc., cannot be carried out generally in the domain of cardinals, as follows from the equalities (1) to (3) and similar ones. These equalities also show the invalidity of the ordinary inequalities of arithmetic; for instance, although $\aleph_0<\aleph$, we have $\aleph_0+\aleph=\aleph+\aleph$ and $\aleph_0\cdot\aleph=\aleph\cdot\aleph$. Such deviations from arithmetic—and, even more, those presented below—contributed to the initial rejection of set theory.

Ordered sets and order types. The transition from sets to their cardinals disregards not only the nature of the members but also their order, if any; for this transition the members serve as mere unordered units. Yet for applications within and outside of set theory it is important to consider not only such "plain" sets but also ordered sets for which, in addition to the membership relation, an order relation $\prec$ between the members of the set is defined. As is usual in mathematics, $\prec$ is assumed to be an irreflexive, asymmetrical, transitive relation such that between any two

different members a, b of an ordered set s one of the statements $a\prec b$, $b\prec a$ holds true. (If the latter condition is not satisfied the set is called a partially ordered set.) We read $a\prec b$ as "a precedes b" or "b follows a." The subset of s that contains all members preceding an $a\in s$ is called a section of s.

The order relation can be reduced to the membership relation in the sense that the following can be proved: For any plain set s there exists a set O_s such that each member of O_s in a certain sense "orders" s. Yet this proof does not guarantee that s can be ordered, because O_s may be empty. If s is infinite (and O_s is not empty), O_s is also infinite. Two ordered sets are considered equal if they contain the same members in the same order. In simple cases an ordered set may be denoted by its members, included in parentheses and in a succession that hints at the order; for instance,

$$(\cdots,5,3,1,2,4,6,\cdots)$$

means the set of positive integers so ordered that the odd numbers precede the even ones, even numbers being arranged according to increasing magnitude and odd according to decreasing magnitude.

The similarity between ordered sets is defined in full analogy with the equivalence between plain sets. We have $s\simeq t$ (s is similar to t) if there exists a "similar mapping" ψ of s onto t such that where x_1 and x_2 are different members of s, and y_1 and y_2 are their respective images by ψ in t, from $x_1\prec x_2$ in s follows $y_1\prec y_2$ in t (and hence also vice versa). Similarity is a reflexive, symmetrical, and transitive relation. Similar sets are certainly equivalent. Unlike equivalence, similarity between infinite ordered sets may be destroyed by the addition of a single member to one of the sets; for instance, an ordered set with a first member cannot be similar to one without a first. Similarity can also be reduced to the membership relation.

In the same way as the concept of cardinal is obtained from equivalence, the concept of order type is obtained from similarity. Again the simplest method, if not an explicit one, is the "functional" definition: To every ordered set we ascribe an order type, and the types of two sets are equal if and only if the sets are similar. Accordingly, the sets

$$(1,2,3,4,\cdots)\qquad\text{and}\qquad(\cdots,4,3,2,1)$$

have different types, though they contain the same members; the type of the first is denoted by ω, the type of the second by $*\omega$. The cardinal of both types—that is, of sets of these types—is clearly $\aleph_0$.

For finite (ordered) sets, cardinal and order type practically coincide because every alteration of the order produces a similar set. Therefore, the numbers 0, 1, 2, $\cdots$ may be conceived of as cardinals or as order types, depending on the context. Ordering the order types "according to magnitude" is impossible, as is shown by simple examples, such as ω and $*\omega$.

Given a plain infinite set s, not only infinitely many ordered sets with the same members correspond to s, but even infinitely many types do—although different sets may have the same type. To the set of all positive integers, whose cardinal is $\aleph_0$, belong $2^{\aleph_0}=\aleph$ different types.

The addition of finitely or infinitely many types, given in

a definite order, can still be defined without restriction, and the cardinal of the sum equals the sum of the cardinals of the single terms. In general this addition is not commutative; for instance, $w+1 \neq 1+\omega$ because $1+\omega=\omega$ whereas $\omega+1$ has a last member. Multiplication, however, can in general be reasonably defined only for finitely many factors.

Well-ordered sets, ordinals, alephs. By far the most important among ordered sets, both for the theory and for its applications, are the sets called well-ordered; their importance was recognized by Cantor from the first. There are various equipollent definitions. For instance,

(*a*) An ordered set is well-ordered if every (ordered) nonempty subset has a first member (the most used but not the logically simplest definition).

(*b*) An ordered set w is well-ordered if every subset that is not "confinal" with w has an immediately following member in w.

(*c*) An ordered set is well-ordered if it has no subset of the type $*\omega$.

For practical reasons the empty set and sets with a single member are also considered to be well-ordered.

Every finite ordered set is well-ordered. Conversely, it can be proved that every well-ordered set which keeps this property when its order relation is inverted ($b \prec a$ instead of $a \prec b$) is finite. This constitutes a new definition of finiteness.

The order types of well-ordered sets w are called ordinal numbers, or ordinals. The type ω is an ordinal, but $*\omega$ is not. We can arrange ordinals according to magnitude in a natural way by calling the ordinal of any section of w less than ($<$) the ordinal of w. The type ω is the least transfinite ordinal.

The striking properties of well-ordered sets and ordinals are inductivity and comparability.

Transfinite induction. Mathematical induction lies at the bottom of Peano's (and Dedekind's) axioms for integers and is the standard tool used for proof and definition in the theory of numbers. A far-reaching generalization of mathematical induction is at the disposal of the theory of well-ordered sets. It is called transfinite induction, and its use for the purpose of proof is expressed by the following, almost self-evident, theorem: Let W be a well-ordered set and $T(w)$ a predicate defined for $w \epsilon W$. If the truth of $T(w)$ for all w which precede any definite $w_0 \epsilon W$ implies its truth for w_0 itself, then $T(w)$ is true for all $w \epsilon W$.

Definition by means of transfinite induction is far more complex. For instance, the exponentiation of ordinals may be defined by reducing α^β to the values of $\alpha^{\bar\beta}$ for all $\bar\beta < \beta$, including $\alpha^0 = 1$.

Comparability. Comparability is expressed by the following theorem, which can be proved by induction: Of two well-ordered sets that are not similar, one is similar to a section of the other. Hence, either two ordinals are equal or one is less than the other. This comparability of the ordinals also involves the comparability of the cardinals of (infinite) well-ordered sets, which are called alephs. Similarity of w_1 to a section of w_2 means a fortiori that w_1 is equivalent to a subset of w_2; hence, by the equivalence theorem, the cardinal of w_1 is less than or equal to the cardinal of w_2.

The least aleph is $\aleph_0$, which is followed by $\aleph_1, \aleph_2, \cdots$, $\aleph_\omega, \cdots$. Cantor's continuum hypothesis maintains that $\aleph = \aleph_1$. The first real progress toward a solution was Gödel's proof, in 1938, that $\aleph = \aleph_1$ cannot be disproved. The full solution of the problem was reported by Paul J. Cohen in 1963 (see below).

The well-ordered set of the ordinals (ordered by magnitude) that belong to a certain aleph—that is, to sets whose cardinal is this aleph—is called a number class. The set of all denumerable ordinals is the lowest nontrivial number class; it still hides many unsolved problems.

There exists no set that contains all ordinals (Burali-Forti's antinomy), all cardinals, or all alephs.

The theory of well-ordered sets is crowned by the well-ordering theorem, conjectured by Cantor but first proved by Zermelo in 1904. It states that every (plain or ordered) set "can be well-ordered"; more precisely, for any set s there exist well-ordered sets which contain the members of s. (The proof is suggested below.) From this theorem follows the comparability of cardinals, for now every cardinal proves to be an aleph, and alephs are comparable. In particular, $\aleph$ must be an aleph, and the problem of ascertaining its place in the series $\aleph_0, \aleph_1, \aleph_2, \cdots$ is but another expression of the continuum problem.

Applications of set theory. It may appear that the creation of set theory originated from the wish to introduce infinitely great magnitudes (cardinals, ordinals) into mathematics and philosophy. This was the case only to a very restricted extent. The major impulse came from the theory of real functions, and another came from geometry; in both cases it proved imperative to characterize certain sets of points for which the rough distinction between finite and infinite was inadequate. The theory of integers and "chains" had a share.

In conformity with its origins, the main applications of set theory to this day are found in analysis, geometry, and topology. The modern theory of real functions is completely permeated by the methods and results of the theory of sets of points; in particular, the concepts of measure (integral) are set-theoretical. Such notions as "curve" and "dimension" are based on set theory. Most geometrical and topological studies either use the theory of ordered sets or employ plain sets complemented by space-theoretical primitive concepts, such as neighborhood and distance. In the former case the most spectacular among the early achievements was Cantor's full characterization, in 1883, of the linear continuum by concepts of pure order and hence independently of the concept of time—a problem attacked without success for two thousand years. It turns out that "density" cannot serve even as a first approach and that "continuity" (in the sense that no jumps or gaps occur) is not sufficient either; the decisive novelty is the property that a denumerable subset (say, of the rational numbers or points) is densely contained in the continuum, which property completes the characterization of the linear continuum.

The concept of dimension is invariant with respect not to one-to-one mappings but to continuous mappings. A set-theoretical analysis of such concepts as curve was found to be a necessity after Peano's discovery of a plane "curve" that passes through every point of a two-dimensional domain, such as a square. (For the significance of set theory in algebra, see below.)

Within applied mathematics, the theory of probability in particular owes much of its modern progress to set theory. Even in astronomy, physics, and chemistry, set-theoretical tools find their use.

Above all, set theory, being the most general branch of mathematics and being closely connected with logic, fulfills the task of methodically investigating and providing a foundation for the primary concepts of mathematics, such as number, function, mapping, and order. Thus, it serves as a universal basis of mathematics. Refuting attacks by prominent scholars, David Hilbert in 1925 called set theory the most admirable blossom of the mathematical mind and altogether one of the outstanding achievements of man's purely intellectual activity.

AXIOMATIC SET THEORY

Zermelo's axiomatization. Having overcome the opposition of the mathematical world, set theory enjoyed a decade of universal recognition, application, and admiration. But early in the twentieth century antagonists of a new persuasion arose, among them such outstanding French mathematicians as Henri Poincaré, Émile Borel, and H. L. Lebesgue, who had previously contributed to some extent to the expansion of set theory and the application of its methods. Their arguments, not very convincing in themselves, attracted the attention of mathematicians and philosophers in view of the logical, and partly of the semantical, antinomies that emerged around the turn of the century and that seemed to be rooted in the basic concepts of set theory. In 1908 there began a consistent attack on the part of neo-intuitionists.

In its most radical form, the Dutch, this attack appears dogmatic and remains limited to a narrow circle, although since 1950 interesting ties between neo-intuitionism and the theory of general recursive functions have become evident. But more general doubts about the soundness of nondenumerable sets, transfinite cardinals, higher number classes, etc., have spread and are at present supported by the arguments of such important philosophers and logicians as Hao Wang and Paul Lorenzen. However, the overwhelming majority of mathematicians, even those who are theoretically impressed by the critical arguments, continue to apply the methods of set theory. Very few, if any, have followed the example of Hermann Weyl, who confessed that he avoided certain analytical research subjects because they were immersed too deeply in set theory. On the other hand, type theory and the *Principia Mathematica* of A. N. Whitehead and Bertrand Russell, as well as the subsequent logicistic theories of Quine and others, can by no means be considered antagonistic to set theory. However, they do maintain that the logical foundation on which the theory was constructed at the turn of the century is insufficient and has to be fundamentally altered.

A turning point, the effect of which is still felt, came in 1908, when Zermelo showed that without changing its traditional logical basis one could, with the aid of one or two undefined (primitive) relations, deduce set theory from a small number of primary assumptions (axioms). This would obviate the need for a definition of the set concept, which in view of the antinomies seems impracticable. With the addition, in the 1920s, of some improvements and one or two new axioms to Zermelo's original seven, this axiom system has proved sufficient to develop classical set theory, with none of the known antinomies being derivable from it.

The exposition of set theory given earlier implicitly follows the lines of Zermelo and his successors. The development of the theory from the axioms will now be sketched explicitly in its main features, and one of the axioms, the axiom of choice, will be dealt with in some detail because of its general logical (and mathematical) importance.

As has already been explained, the membership relation ϵ serves as the primitive concept of the system, possibly in combination with equality. Usually only sets are admitted as objects of the (nonempty) domain. The equality between sets satisfies the principle of extensionality; this may be expressed in various ways—for instance,

Axiom 1. Two sets are equal if they contain the same members.

The first step toward forming sets is contained in

Axiom 2. For any two different objects (sets) a, b, there exists the set $\{a,b\}$ which contains just a and b.

Comprehension is expressed by

Axiom 3. For a set s and a "definite" predicate P, there exists the set s_p which contains just those $x \epsilon s$ which satisfy P.

The set s_p is a subset of s. From this axiom follows the existence of the empty set $\emptyset$ and, for any a, of the unit set $\{a\}$. The sharpening of the notion of a "definite predicate" has a complex history, but Thoralf Skolem's contribution (1922/1923) was the decisive one. The tools of modern logic make the task far simpler than it was half a century ago. In brief, one focuses on a monadic predicate that is meaningful for all members of s, corresponding to an elementary well-formed formula of the first-order functional calculus with a single free variable (built up from atomic ϵ-statements).

Axiom 4. For any set s, there exists the union of the members of s—that is, the set containing just the members of the members of s.

Axiom 5. For any set s, there exists the power set of s—that is, the set whose members are just all the subsets of s.

Since the ordinary way of securing subsets is given by axiom 3, there is a nonpredicative, and hence nonconstructive, interdependence between axiom 3 and axiom 5. For instance, the power set of s may enter the predicate that determines a subset of s. Here, at least, metaphysical assumptions seem to influence the assessment of the system, for the interdependence looks far less dangerous to Platonic realism than to constructivist attitudes.

Axioms 2 through 5 permit, among other operations, formation of the intersection and of the Cartesian product—the latter, initially, when the factors of the product are pairwise disjoint (see below). They also permit definition of equivalence and order, but not of cardinals and order types, for which one uses equivalent or similar sets.

Our axioms do not, however, guarantee the existence of

infinite sets. For this purpose a special postulate is needed, such as

Axiom 6. There exists a set Z with the properties (a) $\emptyset \in Z$ and (b) if $x \in Z$, then $\{x\} \in Z$.

These properties do not determine Z, but one can easily conclude that there is a least set Z_0 with the properties (a) and (b); its members are just the different sets

$$\emptyset, \{\emptyset\}, \{\{\emptyset\}\}, \cdots,$$

If $\emptyset$ is denoted by 1 and, generally, $\{a\}$ by $a+1$, it can be seen that Z_0 is essentially the set $\{1,2,3,\cdots\}$ of all positive integers. This set is infinite and even reflexive.

Axiom of choice. If $S = \{s, s', s'', \cdots\}$ is a set of pairwise disjoint nonempty sets, the subsets of the union $\cup S$ contain certain members out of $s, s', s'', \cdots$. The apparently innocent question whether among these subsets there are any that contain a single member out of each member of S has turned out to be one of the central problems of twentieth-century logic and mathematics. One can prove without difficulty that there exists a set whose members are all subsets of $\cup S$ having the property mentioned, namely the Cartesian product of the members of S. Although it is evident that the Cartesian product is empty if $\emptyset$ is a member of S, it is not possible to prove the inverse, that there exists at least one such subset of $\cup S$ if no member of S is empty. One therefore introduces the following:

Axiom 7 (axiom of choice). If S is a set of pairwise disjoint nonempty sets, the Cartesian product of the members of S is not empty. Every member of the Cartesian product is called a selection set of S.

Clearly, axiom 7 yields a new kind of subset (of $\cup S$), whose existence seems not to follow from axiom 3.

The axiom admits of gradations, chiefly according to the cardinality of S and/or its members. Although the case of finite S is trivial (provable), the case where all members of S are finite is especially interesting and important. Russell "illustrated" this case by pointing to an infinite set of pairs of stockings (as opposed to pairs of shoes, for which a selection set can be defined as the set of all left shoes—that is, by comprehension).

In many important cases the condition that the members of S be pairwise disjoint is inopportune. Then the selection sets of S are replaced by single-valued choice-functions $f(s)$ such that $f(s) \in s$ for each $s \in S$.

Bertrand Russell, on good ground, called axiom 7 the "multiplicative principle" (1906). Zermelo, who in 1904 first introduced the statement for the purpose of proving the well-ordering theorem—but without assuming the disjointness of the members—called it the "axiom of choice"; this name, though less fortunate than Russell's, has stuck. It derives from the idea that in order to secure a member of the product, one "chooses" from each member of S a single member and unites the chosen members into a selection set.

For sixty years the most important unsolved problem connected with the axiom of choice was its independence. It was reasonably assumed that it is impossible by means of the other axioms to prove the axiom of choice, even in its weakest form, when S is denumerable and the members of S are pairs. However, this impossibility was proved (since 1922) by using assumptions which are not pertinent, such as that of the existence of individuals or extraordinary sets. Only by Paul J. Cohen's method of 1963 did it become possible to prove the axiom's independence without special assumptions. Its consistency was proved in 1938 by Kurt Gödel.

Because it is a purely existential statement, the axiom of choice is rejected as meaningless by intuitionists. A more reserved attitude is taken in *Principia Mathematica*, where the axiom appears as a hypothesis, and all statements depending on it are specially marked. Yet today the axiom is used almost universally by mathematicians because of its important and indispensable role in almost all parts of mathematics, from arithmetic (definition of finiteness) and algebra (since Ernst Steinitz' pioneer work on abstract algebra in 1910) to analysis and topology.

The original task of the axiom, which led to its explicit formulation, belongs to set theory: the axiom's use in proving the well-ordering theorem, and thereby the comparability of cardinals. Actually, not only do these two statements follow from the axiom of choice, but the converse is also true. They thus constitute three equipollent principles, and when one of them is accepted the other two can be deduced. There are many other equipollent statements—for instance, certain maximum principles that are useful in algebra.

Investigations have also been made of "non-Zermelian" systems of set theory in which the negation of the axiom of choice is assumed. Such systems, though apparently consistent, yield paradoxical results—more paradoxical than certain implications of the axiom of choice (for instance, that half of a sphere's surface is congruent to a third of it).

Further axioms. In the 1920s it was found necessary to add two further axioms to the seven listed. The original axioms do not secure, for instance, the existence of a set that contains both Z_0 and, together with any member Z, the power set of Z; the union of the members of such sets would have a cardinal that exceeded the cardinals of all sets secured so far. Therefore, a new axiom, of "replacement" (Abraham Fraenkel, 1921), or "substitution" (Thoralf Skolem, 1922), was introduced.

Axiom 8. For any set s and any single-valued function (predicate) f with a free variable x, there exists the set that contains just the members $f(x)$ with $x \in s$.

Soon after, it was found by John von Neumann that this axiom, beyond providing very comprehensive sets, has a more general significance. In particular, it makes possible a direct definition of ordinals, and thereby also of alephs, by transfinite induction, without resorting to the method of abstraction.

Another, far stronger axiom has been proposed, by Alfred Tarski, among others, to secure so-called inaccessible numbers.

Extraordinary sets (which were first observed by Dmitry M. Mirimanoff) have already been mentioned. Examples are a set that contains itself as a member and a set s which, together with another set t, satisfies $s \in t$ and $t \in s$. In order to exclude such (certainly unnecessary and undesirable) sets, von Neumann (1925) and, later, others proposed the addition of an axiom (of "foundation" or "restriction") of the following type:

Axiom 9. Every nonempty set *s* contains a member *t* such that *s* and *t* have no common member.

Von Neumann's and Bernays' axiomatizations. The axiom systems mentioned in what follows are highly developed and are useful for mathematics, but they are far more complicated than the various types of Zermelian systems and are technically very intricate. Therefore, only their *raisons d'être* and their distinctive properties will be described, together with a few details of general mathematical interest.

Restrictions on set formation. Although Zermelo's axiom system has proved perfectly adaptable to its purpose of developing classical set theory while avoiding antinomies, it has a defect that is disturbing from the philosophical rather than the mathematical viewpoint. The avoidance of logical antinomies is effectuated by restricting the formation of sets, as indicated by the axioms. Only axioms 4 through 6 (and 8) have "expansive" power, and axiom 3, in particular, yields not the set of all objects with a given property but only subsets of sets secured previously.

The question arises whether this restriction of the formation of sets, although sufficient for avoiding antinomies, is necessary for this purpose—in other words, whether the axioms do not limit the concept of set more than is necessary. To be sure, this question was of less concern at the beginning of the century, when, under the alarming impact of the antinomies, the problem was to guarantee a sufficient restriction of the concept.

Von Neumann's system. In the early 1920s von Neumann became aware that the logical antinomies (those of Russell and Burali-Forti, or simply that of the set of all sets) are generated not by the extreme comprehensiveness, as such, of the sets but by these sets' being admitted as members of sets. Hence, one could presumably proceed to the very boundary of what is still allowable by admitting the comprehensive sets but excluding them from membership in other sets. One then has to distinguish between two kinds of primitive concepts, the "sets," which may serve as members of other sets, and the "classes," to which such membership is denied. Membership of a set and membership of a class thus become different primitive relations. The papers of von Neumann (1925–1929) are highly involved and technical, in part because he replaced set with function, which does no harm but makes comprehension more difficult.

Bernays' system. Bernays, in an important series of papers (1937–1954) and a still farther-reaching monograph (1958), developed an axiomatic system that fundamentally retained von Neumann's ideas but formally approached Zermelo's attitude; in addition, he raised and answered many new questions. Von Neumann and Bernays have abandoned predicate variables, which appear above in the form of "predicate" and "function" in axioms 3 and 8. The axiom system thus becomes "finite"—at the cost of an increasing number of primitive concepts and relations. The theory of ordinals, which had been initiated by von Neumann by means of the axiom of replacement, was largely expanded by Bernays.

As Leopold Löwenheim and Thoralf Skolem discovered and von Neumann later elaborated, the notion of transfinite cardinals undergoes a relativization; two sets whose cardinals are different within a certain axiomatic system may both from the outside prove denumerable because the mappings required for this purpose are not available within the system. Yet the encouragement that intuitionists initially drew from this paradox seems not to be justified, for even the contrast between finite and infinite, so fundamental to intuitionism, is weakened and relativized by the same arguments.

Gödel's consistency proof. In 1938, Bernays' axiomatization of set theory was slightly modified by Gödel so as to enable a proof of the consistency of the (generalized) continuum hypothesis. The proof was achieved by the addition of a special postulate (of "constructibility") to the axiom system. However, the postulate is not to be viewed as one of the axioms of set theory.

Present status of set theory. Far from finally solving the continuum problem, Gödel's proof made painfully clear the awkward situation in which set theory, and mathematics in its entirety, finds itself today. It was conjectured that the negation of the continuum hypothesis is also consistent with the axioms of set theory. The continuum hypothesis thus would play a role analogous to that of Euclid's axiom of parallels. It would be independent of the recognized principles of mathematics, and there would exist two different kinds of mathematics, "Cantorian" and "non-Cantorian," just as geometry bifurcates into Euclidean and hyperbolic geometries at Euclid's axiom. In Cantorian mathematics $2^{\aleph_0} = \aleph_1$; in non-Cantorian mathematics $2^{\aleph_0} > \aleph_1$. This conjecture was finally proved in 1963 by Cohen, who thus solved, although in the negative, the continuum problem eighty years after it had been raised by Cantor's work.

The situation regarding the axiom of choice is similar. Since it is independent, its negation yields "non-Zermelian mathematics" as against more normal Zermelian mathematics.

This is not all, for unfortunately the analogy is not perfect. The continuum is essentially the set that contains all subsets of the set N of all integers. Not just inveterate Platonists but most mathematicians will admit that the concept "subset of N" is meaningful and that the set $\mathbf{N}$ of all these subsets either has or does not have the property that every nondenumerable subset of $\mathbf{N}$ is equivalent to $\mathbf{N}$, which expresses $\aleph = \aleph_1$. As Gödel put it (in "What Is Cantor's Continuum Problem?," *American Mathematical Monthly*, Vol. 54, 1947, 515–525), the axioms of set theory "describe some well-determined reality; in this reality Cantor's conjecture must be either true or false, and its undecidability from the axioms as known today can only mean that these axioms do not contain a complete description of that reality" (p. 520).

Thus, the modern development of set theory seems to shatter mathematics altogether, at least in its analytical parts. New axioms apparently need to be introduced, corresponding to a deeper understanding of the primitive concepts underlying logic and mathematics. Yet nobody has so far succeeded in discovering even a direction in which such axioms might be sought.

Bibliography

The excellent international journal *Fundamenta Mathematicae*, published in Warsaw since 1919, is devoted entirely to set theory and its applications.

CLASSICAL SET THEORY

Cantor, Georg, *Gesammelte Abhandlungen mathematischen und philosophischen Inhalts,* Ernst Zermelo, ed. Berlin, 1932; reprinted, Hildesheim, 1962. With a biography of Cantor by A. A. Fraenkel.

Fraenkel, A. A., *Einleitung in die Mengenlehre,* 3d ed. Berlin, 1928; reprinted, New York, 1946. Also treats axiomatic set theory.

Fraenkel, A. A., *Abstract Set Theory.* Amsterdam, 1953; 3d ed., 1965.

Halmos, P. R.,*Naive Set Theory.* Princeton, N.J., 1960.

Hausdorff, Felix, *Grundzüge der Mengenlehre.* Leipzig, 1914; reprinted, New York, 1949. Still one of the best books on set theory.

Hausdorff, Felix, *Mengenlehre,* 2d ed. Berlin and Leipzig, 1935. Translated by J. R. Aumann et al. as *Set Theory,* 2d ed. New York, 1962. A shortened version of *Grundzüge der Mengenlehre.*

Kamke, Erich, *Mengenlehre,* 4th ed. Berlin and Leipzig, 1962. Translated by Frederick Bagemihl as *Theory of Sets.* New York, 1950.

Kuratowski, Kazimierz, and Mostowski, Andrzej, *Teoria Mnogości* ("Theory of Sets"). Warsaw and Wrocław, 1952.

Sierpiński, Wacław, *Leçons sur les nombres transfinis.* Paris, 1928; reprinted, 1950.

Sierpiński, Wacław, *Cardinal and Ordinal Numbers.* Warsaw and New York, 1958.

Young, W. H., and Young, Grace C., *The Theory of Sets of Points.* Cambridge, 1906.

AXIOMATIC SET THEORY

Bernays, Paul, "A System of Axiomatic Set Theory." *Journal of Symbolic Logic,* Vols. 2, 6, 7, 8, 13, 19 (1937–1954). Series of seven papers.

Bernays, Paul, and Fraenkel, A. A., *Axiomatic Set Theory.* Amsterdam, 1958.

Cohen, P. J., "The Independence of the Continuum Hypothesis," I and II. *Proceedings of the National Academy of Sciences,* Vol. 50 (1963), 1143–1148, and Vol. 51 (1964), 105–110.

Fraenkel, A. A., and Bar-Hillel, Yehoshua, *Foundations of Set Theory.* Amsterdam, 1958. Also covers logicism, intuitionism, metamathematical approaches.

Gödel, Kurt, *The Consistency of the Axiom of Choice and of the Generalized Continuum-hypothesis With the Axioms of Set Theory.* Princeton, N.J., 1940; rev. ed., 1953.

Keene, G. B., *Abstract Sets and Finite Ordinals.* Oxford and London, 1962.

Quine, W. V., *Set Theory and Its Logic.* Cambridge, Mass., 1963.

Suppes, Patrick, *Axiomatic Set Theory.* Princeton, N.J., 1960.

ABRAHAM A. FRAENKEL

SEXTUS EMPIRICUS, the codifier of Greek Skepticism, lived in the last half of the second century and the first quarter of the third century A.D. He seems to have been a Greek, if his subtle handling of the Greek language is any indication, though we do not know where he was born or where he died. He knew Rome, Athens, and Alexandria with some intimacy, but we do not know where he taught.

He was head of a Skeptical school, probably in some great city, and he was succeeded as head of that school by Saturninus, a contemporary of Diogenes Laërtius (who wrote about Sextus). He learned much from the empiricist skeptical doctor Menodotus of Nicomedia, who was born about fifty years before Sextus. Sextus himself was a medical doctor, as were Menodotus, his teacher, and Saturninus, his successor. We are not sure whether his Latin name "Empiricus" is a proper name or an appellation designating him as an "empirical" medical doctor (as against the "methodical" school). He criticized the empirical school of medicine for dogmatically denying that we can have knowledge of hidden causes and seemed, at least on this point, to go along with the methodical school, which refused to dogmatize about the impossibility of such knowledge. Whatever his affiliation, he was a central figure among the late Skeptical medical doctors, who terminated the history of Greek Skepticism.

Sextus, besides possessing a large fund of knowledge on medical matters, had a clear, plain prose style, an almost mechanically orderly mind, and a somewhat dry but gratifying sense of humor. He was a careful student of the history of Skepticism, having worked scrupulously upon texts no longer available to us; and his codification is a careful and ambitious attempt to define and illustrate Greek Skepticism.

His extant works constitute the only lucid, complete, and firsthand summary of Greek Skepticism available to us. They are usually divided into two works, the *Outlines of Pyrrhonism (Hypotyposes)* and the *Against the Dogmatists (Adversus Mathematicos).* The *Hypotyposes* seems to be a compilation of introductory lectures, explicit and simple in nature. It is divided into three books, the first of which defines the key terms of Skepticism, while the other two make use of these terms to attack dogmatism (especially the dogmatism of the Stoics). Noteworthy here is the attack on the validity of the syllogistic proof. Sextus tried to show that any syllogism is an example of a vicious circle, since the truth of the conclusion (for example, "Socrates is mortal") must already be known if the truth of the major premise ("All men are mortal") has been ascertained.

The *Adversus Mathematicos* contains 11 books, five of which use the method defined and exemplified in the *Hypotyposes* in order to refute "philosophers" (logicians, physicists, and ethicists), and six of which use that method to refute "scientists" (grammarians, rhetoricians, geometricians, arithmeticians, astronomers, and musicians).

The key terms. *Skepsis,* or Skepticism, is a term applied by Sextus to the oral teachings of Pyrrho and to the goals and method implicit in those teachings. On the one hand, Skepticism is distinct from dogmatism (the metaphysics of Plato, Aristotle, Zeno, and Epicurus) because the Skeptic does not claim to have certain knowledge of hidden or "nonevident" things, as the dogmatist does; on the other hand, Sextus held, Skepticism is distinct from the Academic philosophy of men like Carneades and Clitomachus, because these men dogmatically asserted that (1) knowledge is impossible; (2) some beliefs are more probable than others; (3) a strong inclination can accompany some of our (more probable) beliefs; and (4) probability should be a guide to living. The Skeptic suspended judgment on the question of whether knowledge is impossible, refused to recognize any one belief as being more probable than any other, and consequently did not believe that a strong inclination or assent should accompany any of our beliefs. The Skeptic, as against the dogmatist and the Academician, took arguments for and against nonevident things as equally probable or improbable, no one being more or less worthy of assent than another. He was an open-minded "inquirer."

The *arche,* or motivating force, behind Skepticism was the hope of attaining unperturbedness, *ataraxia.* Endless battles between dogmatists, and passionate, stubborn adherence to, or disbelief in, a given doctrine had disturbed men for centuries. And all this had been the case because there had been no publicly accessible criterion for deciding or proving who was right. Skepticism was one of the eudaemonistic philosophies of late antiquity, having as its ultimate goal (like Stoicism and Epicureanism), not pure theoretical knowledge, nor simply a disinterested negation of all claims to knowledge, but happiness, peace of mind in day-to-day activities.

Ataraxia, then, is the third and last stage of the doubting process, according to Sextus. The first stage is antithesis, the presenting of claims about the same nonevident subject and putting these claims into opposition with each other, so that mutually contradictory claims appear equally probable (or improbable). In this stage the *tropoi,* or "ways of arguing," are used. The second stage is the suspension of judgment (*epoche*), which follows the awareness of antithesis. Instead of assenting to, or denying, any one of the claims relative to the subject at hand, we put together all those mutually inconsistent claims and withold judgment on each and all of them. When we have achieved *epoche,* the last stage, unperturbedness follows, as the shadow follows the body. When we realize that—as Sextus put it—"reason is such a trickster," we find peace.

Obviously the basic step in that process is the first, antithesis. To facilitate this step, the Skeptics from Aenesidemus through Agrippa to Sextus himself devised various tropes, or modes, of argument. The first ten tropes of Aenesidemus set in opposition to each other claims about external objects (the tower seen from a distance as round, as opposed to the same tower seen as square from close up) as well as claims about moral laws (the Scythians sacrifice human beings to Artemis, while Greeks forbid human sacrifice). Later Skeptics, like Agrippa, set up further modes of argument, more drastic and far-reaching than the first ten.

Epoche has to do only with nonevident, hidden things like the Stoic's *pneuma,* the fiery world stuff, or like ultimate good and evil. It has to do with claims that go behind or beyond the phenomena, beyond the appearances of our senses and feelings and everyday actions. Words like "substance," "essence," "soul," when applied to entities forever inaccessible to decisive observation or experience, are thought of as "indicative signs" (*endeiktikon*). But words or experiences, when treated merely as "commemorative" (*ypomnestikon*) of other experiences (the scar being a sign of the wound we remember receiving), are untouched by the whole doubting process. This, according to Sextus, is as it must be if we would continue to live and avoid paralysis in everyday life.

This refusal to paralyze and even destroy everyday life with doubt took two forms for Sextus. First of all, it made him an empiricist scientist (unlike the ancient "theoretical," or "logical," school of medicine, which involved a priori theorizing on the hidden causes of diseases). As a physician he confined himself to observing symptoms, describing syndromes, and tentatively pointing out observed relationships among these symptoms and syndromes. He would not make transphenomenal hypotheses; he made strictly tentative descriptions and predictions, dealing only with commemorative signs.

Second, the refusal to doubt phenomena also took the form of what Sextus called the "doctrinal rule" of Skepticism. This rule stated that one must live in accordance with appearances, that is, in accordance with sense experiences, one's physical needs (thirst, etc.), and the customs and laws of one's country. Only by so living could the unperturbedness that was the *arche* of epistemological doubt be realized. But the Skeptic (as against the Academic, who reasoned by way of probabilities) did not give any strong assent to these appearances; he simply allowed them to carry him along, without being duped by the "proofs" that this "trickster reason" could, if given the chance, concoct.

In saying this, Sextus not only distinguished his doctrine from the probabilism of Carneades and from the various dogmatisms thriving toward the end of the second century; but he reminded us that he was discussing a philosophy and a philosopher deeply interested in happiness in action, not simply in knowledge. Still, after observing this, one must not forget that by far the larger part of the works of Sextus involved dialectic, philosophical argumentation, as well as definition. Unlike the nondialectical thought of Pyrrho, the thought of Sextus was that of a lover of logic as well as of observation. In the writings of Sextus the epigrammatic moralism of Pyrrho and the scrupulous epistemology of Aenesidemus and the New Academy were brought together; and any discussion of Greek Skepticism as a whole is incomplete if it leaves out either of these two tendencies.

Bibliography

The most reliable text is Sextus Empiricus, *Opera,* edited by H. Mutschmann, with revisions by J. Mau, 3 vols. (Leipzig, 1954–1958). Another edition, with English translation, by R. G. Bury is *Sextus Empiricus,* in the Loeb Classical Library, 4 vols. (London, 1917–1955).

Victor Brochard, *Les Sceptiques Grecs* (Paris, 1923), is a very full account but tries to make too much of Sextus as a positivistic logician. One of the most searching analyses of Sextus' work is Albert Goedeckemeyer, *Die Geschichte des griechischen Skeptizismus* (Leipzig, 1905). Werner Heintz, *Studien zu Sextus Empiricus* (Halle, 1932), is an extremely useful commentary on the text, while Mary Mills Patrick, *Sextus Empiricus and Greek Scepticism* (Cambridge, 1899), is uneven but useful.

Sextus Empiricus is also a source for Stoic logic. This aspect of his work is fully discussed in Benson Mates, *Stoic Logic* (Berkeley, Calif., 1953; paperback edition, Berkeley, Calif., 1961). See also R. Chisholm, "Sextus Empiricus and Modern Empiricism," in *Philosophy of Science,* Vol. 8 (1941), 371–384; and Benson Mates, "Stoic Logic and the Text of Sextus Empiricus," in *American Journal of Philology,* Vol. 70 (1949), 290–298.

PHILIP P. HALLIE

SHAFTESBURY, THIRD EARL OF (ANTHONY ASHLEY COOPER),

was the first philosopher to use the term "moral sense." He was born in London in 1671, the son of the second earl and a grandson of the first; he died in 1713. The first earl of Shaftesbury (1621–1683) was a Whig leader who enjoyed the extremes of political fortune, sometimes holding high office, sometimes a prisoner in the Tower, and finally dying in exile. He assumed responsibility for rearing his grandson and placed John Locke, who was his physician and confidential friend, in charge of the boy's education. Locke engaged Elizabeth Birch to be the boy's teacher. She could speak both Latin and Greek with the greatest fluency, and thanks to her instruction Shaftesbury could read these languages with ease by the time he was 11 years old. He also spent three years at Winchester, but he did not like the school and persuaded his father to let him travel abroad. Accompanied by a tutor, he spent the years 1686–1689 on the Continent, where he acquired a knowledge of French and developed a connoisseur's taste for sculpture, painting, and music. At the age of 24 he was elected to Parliament as a member for the borough of Poole. He served for three years, until the dissolution of 1698. His asthma decided him against seeking re-election. Although he was in bad health, he maintained a formidable schedule of study and writing. When he succeeded to the earldom in 1699, he faithfully attended the meetings of the House of Lords despite the painful effect of the London air on his lungs. In 1709 he married Jane Ewer, by whom he had a son. His health finally forced him to seek the warmer air of Italy, to which he retired in 1711. He died in Naples.

In style Shaftesbury's writings are very much the communications of one refined soul to others of similar refinement. Elegance is aimed for in every phrase, and no regard is paid to the pedestrian reader who is eager for close reasoning and precise conclusions. Nonetheless, the respect which Shaftesbury's writings were accorded in the eighteenth century and the influence of his championing of freedom of thought must not be forgotten.

Shaftesbury's work does not present a philosophical system, and a comprehensive view of his doctrines may be gained only by a judicious reading of his essays. They are "An Inquiry Concerning Virtue or Merit" (first published in 1699), "A Letter Concerning Enthusiasm" (London, 1708), "Sensus Communis, An Essay on the Freedom of Wit and Humour" (London, 1709), "The Moralists, A Philosophical Rhapsody" (London, 1709), and "Soliloquy, or Advice to an Author" (London, 1710). These essays were republished as a collection with the title *Characteristics of Men, Manners, Opinions, Times* in three volumes (London, 1711). For the collection Shaftesbury wrote a long introductory essay, "Miscellaneous Reflections on the Preceding Treatises."

In his writings Shaftesbury argues for freedom of thought, for an enlightened, even lighthearted, view of religion, and for regarding man as naturally virtuous. He favors freedom of inquiry because he believes that the best in thought and manners can be discovered only by trying all things. Although excesses may occur, they are best remedied by letting them run their course, for as long as the mind is free, it will correct itself. The only help for faulty reasoning is more reasoning. When some authority specifies what must be thought and endeavors to force conformity, the very fettering of reason encourages excess. Shaftesbury would extend freedom of thought even to allowing wit and ridicule in the examination of religious doctrines. He would permit humor in the discussion of religion because he believes that there is no better test of the truth of some claim than to see whether it can withstand ridicule. But more especially, Shaftesbury favors a good-humored attitude on the part of those who consider religious questions because he believes that our notions of

God are projections of our own humor. As we are, so shall we think God to be. Now, according to Shaftesbury's way of viewing the matter, God must necessarily be good-humored. But we can never understand this quality unless we possess it ourselves. Hence, the necessity for permitting good humor in the discussion of religion.

Shaftesbury believed that we cannot understand qualities of mind and character which we do not possess ourselves. This topic is the theme of his "Soliloquy, or Advice to an Author," in which he argues that an author's best foundation for rendering a just account of human nature is thorough knowledge of himself. Shaftesbury is sure that no author who knows himself can possibly believe that all human actions stem from selfish motives. The exposition of this view is part of his attack on Hobbes's account of human nature as unrelieved selfishness.

Although he favored freedom of inquiry in religious matters, Shaftesbury has no particular set of religious doctrines for which he wishes to argue. He views God as a good-tempered, benevolent being who orders the world, and he remarks that holding such a theistic view may be helpful to the practice of virtue, although he does not think that it is necessary to virtuousness. But what must have really aroused Shaftesbury's contemporaries was not any one of his actual religious opinions but his calm assumption that any list of possible world views must include atheism, which he defines as believing that there is no "designing principle or mind" responsible for nature. If atheism is a possible view, then it is discussible, and discussibility implies a respectability which the religious zealots found it hard to admit.

In his discussion of morality Shaftesbury advances two principal theses. The first is that morality may exist independently of religion, and the second is that man is naturally virtuous. On the one hand, he wishes to show that morality need not be subject to the supervision of religious authorities, and, on the other, he wishes to show that when religion and morality are separated, a selfish interest in one's own welfare is not all that is left to provide a foundation for morality. There is more to accounting for the possibility of morality than a simple choice of either religion or Hobbes.

Shaftesbury argues for the separability of religion and morality by showing that religion presupposes morality. If we are to fear the wrath of God, then there must be some principle by which we regulate our fears. It is unthinkable to Shaftesbury that there be no principle by which God bestows rewards and punishments and that we are justly blamed only for doing what is blamable. Thus, if we are to fear God's blame, we must already know what is blameworthy. Shaftesbury supposes, of course, that nothing is blameworthy simply because it displeases God. God and men must share a sense of deformity which enables them to identify the morally odious. There is no divine monopoly here.

The best argument for the separability of morality and religion would, of course, be to show that morality may arise independently of religion. Here is the importance of Shaftesbury's claim that virtue is natural. How does he endeavor to establish this claim? Shaftesbury knows that Hobbes has gone before him and that in order to show that human nature provides a foundation for virtue, he must first clear away Hobbes's account of human nature as thoroughly selfish. He argues that Hobbes has given no more than one picture of human nature and that we must consider whether it is the most plausible one that can be found. Why should selfishness or self-interest be the only natural passion? By asking this question, Shaftesbury makes room for at least the possibility that a "social feeling or sense of partnership with mankind" may be natural. And, he argues, the social feeling must be natural, for how could there be society if this feeling did not exist first? If society is a set of conventional arrangements, as Shaftesbury believes it is, then the existence of society implies the pre-existence of a disposition among men to make conventions. Thus, the selfish picture of human nature cannot be the whole story, for if selfishness were the only natural feeling, there would be no society. What is more, since the existence of a social feeling is sufficient to account for the origin of society, appeals to the religious sanctions for society are necessarily subsequent to the actual foundation of society and are therefore of secondary importance.

Virtue, for Shaftesbury, is the pursuit of the public interest. "There is no real love of virtue without the knowledge of public good." We are disposed to act virtuously by our affection for virtue. In Shaftesbury's philosophical heirs, Francis Hutcheson and Hume, this affection for virtue is called the "moral sense." Shaftesbury does use the term "moral sense," and he is presumably the first to introduce it into moral philosophy, but he does not himself make much of it. He is also the first to liken this sense to a sense of harmony in music and a sense of proportion in architecture and art. The following quotation may be taken as characteristic of Shaftesbury's exposition of the doctrine of the moral sense:

> In a creature capable of forming general notions of things, not only the outward beings which offer themselves to the sense are the objects of the affection, but the very actions themselves and the affections of pity, kindness, gratitude and their contraries, being brought into the mind by reflection become objects. So that by means of this reflected sense, there arises another kind of affection towards those very affections themselves, which have been already felt, and are now become the subject of a new liking or dislike. ("Inquiry Concerning Virtue or Merit")

The appeal to a "reflected sense" in this account marks Shaftesbury's debt to Locke.

When Shaftesbury declares that men are naturally virtuous, he must not be taken as claiming that all men are actually virtuous. He allows that the affection for virtue may very well be opposed by contrary affections. He supposes, however, that a person who is aware of the superior pleasures to be found in virtuous action will naturally prefer virtue to mere self-interest. He argues, too, that religious opinions can affect virtue only by raising affections that are contrary to or incompatible with virtue. Since the affection for virtue is natural, religion is unnecessary to its presence in us. However, theistic opinions about a benevolent God may reinforce the affection. But

so may the good example of others and rewards and punishment.

It is in moral philosophy that Shaftesbury parts company with Locke, and it is Locke's attack on innate ideas that Shaftesbury objects to. Not that Shaftesbury is a partisan of innate ideas as such, but he does see Locke as claiming that there is nothing essential in human nature and that all that a man is, must be impressed upon him from without. But morality, then, can be only the product of external authority ultimately imposing its will simply because it has the power to do so. For Shaftesbury this is unthinkable. Hence, he opposes Locke and grounds morality on an affection for virtue which is an inherent part of human nature.

Bibliography

The latest edition of the *Characteristics* is that prepared by John M. Robertson (London, 1900). Robertson's introductory essay may also be consulted. A short biography of Shaftesbury written by his son, the fourth earl, and Shaftesbury's philosophical notes and letters are published in *The Life, Unpublished Letters, and Philosophical Regimen of Anthony, Earl of Shaftesbury*, edited by Benjamin Rand (London, 1900).

See also Thomas Fowler, *Shaftesbury and Hutcheson* (London, 1882); R. L. Brett, *The Third Earl of Shaftesbury: A Study in Eighteenth Century Literary Theory* (London, 1951); and Dorothy B. Schlegel, *Shaftesbury and the French Deists* (Chapel Hill, N.C., 1956).

ELMER SPRAGUE

SHELLEY, PERCY BYSSHE (1792–1822), is usually thought of as a romantic and lyric poet rather than as a philosophical one. He was, however, the author of a number of polemical prose pamphlets on politics and religion; and both his prose and his poetry reflect a coherent background of social and metaphysical theory.

In general, Shelley's beliefs are those of the radical English intelligentsia of the period immediately before and after the French Revolution, and in particular of William Godwin, who became his father-in-law. It has often been said that Shelley was really antipathetic to Godwin's atheism and determinism and that he gradually threw off Godwin's influence in favor of a more congenial Platonic transcendentalism. This view, however, seems to rest on a misunderstanding of both Godwin and Shelley.

Attack on Christianity. In *The Necessity of Atheism*, for which he was expelled from Oxford in 1811, Shelley argued, on Humean lines, that no argument for the existence of God is convincing. He developed this position in *A Refutation of Deism* (1814), a dialogue which purports to defend Christianity against deism, but which actually presents a strong case against both and in favor of atheism. In both these works, and in some of his essays (many of which were not published in his lifetime), Shelley was concerned with what he later called "that superstition which has disguised itself under the name of the system of Jesus." In the longer *Essay on Christianity*, published posthumously, he explained what he thought that system really was: an allegorical expression of the virtues of sympathy and tolerance, and of an anarchistic belief in the equality of men and in the wickedness of punishment and all other forms of coercion. Christ, Shelley claimed, had "the imagination of some sublimest and most holy poet";

he was also a reformer who, like most reformers, practiced a little mild deception by pandering to "the prejudices of his auditors." The doctrine of a personal God, in particular, is not to be taken as "philosophically true," but as "a metaphor easily understood."

The natural and the moral order. Shelley explained this coupling of poetry and religion, and the view that both are essentially allegory, in *A Defence of Poetry* (1821). It is the function of both poetry and religion to provide men with a coherent view of the world that will help them to understand both themselves and their fellow men, and to provide it in a form that will kindle the imagination as well as the intellect—that is, through metaphor. There is a natural order in the universe, which science and philosophy reveal; there is also a moral order, which men themselves must impose. The metaphor of a personal God is meant to impress this twofold order on men's minds. Since this metaphor had, unfortunately, been perverted by a superstitious interpretation, Shelley himself preferred such symbols as the World Soul or the Spirit of Intellectual Beauty.

Anarchism. The details of the moral order itself are made clear in Shelley's political pamphlets. Shelley began to write these when, as a youth of 19, he set out to settle the Irish question by instructing the Irish in the fundamental principles of Godwinian anarchism. Godwin's main thesis was that social institutions, and particularly the coercive ones imposed by governments, fasten blinkers on men's minds which prevent them from seeing their fellows as they really are. The ultimate solution is a community small enough for each member to know the other members as individuals. Such intimate personal knowledge will bring understanding and sympathy, so that men will be prepared to cooperate for the common good, without the coercion of law. As Shelley put it, "no government will be wanted but that of your neighbour's opinion." Men will indeed value their neighbors' opinions, but they will not take their neighbors' opinions on trust. To do so would be useless, because even a true opinion is of little value unless one understands the grounds for holding it. It is only when men see things as they are, in all their intricate interconnections, that they will feel the right emotions and thus lead happy and virtuous lives.

Political pamphleteering. In accordance with these general principles, Shelley urged the Irish not to seek emancipation by means of violence, but to agitate for freedom of assembly, freedom of the press, and parliamentary representation as the first steps toward the ideal society. It was also in accordance with these principles that Shelley wrote his *Letter to Lord Ellenborough* (1812), in which he protested vehemently against the sentence passed on the publisher of Paine's *Age of Reason*. Both this pamphlet and the *Address on the Death of Princess Charlotte* (1817), in which he suggested that Englishmen would do better to mourn for their lost liberties than for even the most beautiful and blameless of princesses, were eloquent attacks on judicial persecution and on the suppression of free speech. In another pamphlet, *On the Punishment of Death* (left unpublished), he opposed capital punishment. In the long essay *A Philosophical View of Reform,* another of the unpublished manuscripts found among Shelley's journals, he

recapitulated the common radical objections to priests, kings, and the aristocracy, and gave his support to such measures as a more democratic suffrage and a capital levy on unearned wealth.

Unity of the world. Shelley's writings on politics and religion provide meanings for many of the symbols and metaphors to be found in his poetry. His frequent references to life and the world around us as "a painted veil," an illusion through which we must penetrate to the reality behind (this reality being the "one" that remains when "the many change and pass"), is probably to be interpreted as a Godwinian allegory. Godwin had said that men see life as if through a veil—the veil of their own prejudices, which are imposed by social institutions. The constant theme of Godwin's novels was that men must transcend these prejudices in order to understand and love their fellow men. Shelley's idealization of love, which has been taken as a departure from Godwin, is actually his attempt to present this Godwinian theme in a form that will kindle the imagination. It is, moreover, quite in accord with Godwin's views to say that once the veil is removed, the world will be seen as a unity—both in the sense in which science may be said to be a unity (the truth about one field of study cohering with and illuminating the truth about another), and in the sense that a true understanding of our fellow men will give rise to virtuous behavior. This seems to be what Shelley had in mind when he spoke of "the indestructible order" that it is the business of poetry to reveal. There is no need to suppose that he thought of this order as being imposed upon the world by a moral being.

The universal mind. It is true that Shelley was also influenced by Plato, Spinoza, Berkeley, and (in spite of his derogatory remarks about Kant in *Peter Bell the Third*) by the newer type of idealism which was beginning to be made fashionable by Coleridge. In *On Life* he suggested that there are no distinct individual minds, but one universal mind in which all minds participate. As early as 1812 he had identified this "mass of infinite intelligence" with Deity. In this, Shelley was certainly departing from the doctrine of materialists like Holbach; but Godwin, although he was not an idealist, was hardly a materialist either. Godwin would certainly have said that when men see things as they are, they hold the same opinions and, in a sense, think the same thoughts. Each man, seeing things from his own point of view, grasps only part of the truth. He will come nearer to grasping the whole of the truth as he comes to understand and sympathize with the minds of other men. In a sense, the truth as a whole is the property not of any one mind but of the sum of all minds. Probably Shelley himself meant little more than this.

"Prometheus Unbound." Shelley's beliefs find expression in his poetry in a way that is seen fairly clearly in *Prometheus Unbound* (1820), which can be interpreted as a Godwinian allegory. Prometheus, chained to his rock, is suffering mankind, and as the discoverer of fire, he is also knowledge and the civilizing arts. These discoveries, in themselves, are not enough to liberate man from the oppressive rule of Jupiter, which is built "on faith and fear." Prometheus is freed when, instead of cursing his oppressor, he begins to pity and so to understand him. This reflects the favorite Godwinian theme that the oppressor, no less than the oppressed, is the victim of social institutions. A better order is possible only when men come to understand this fact and substitute mutual sympathy for recrimination and punishment. It is also necessary to understand the secrets of Demogorgon, who personifies the natural forces which control the universe, and to cooperate with the Hours, who, with their chariots, personify Godwin's conviction of the inevitability of gradualism.

Works by Shelley

The definitive edition of Shelley's writings is *The Complete Works of Shelley*, R. Ingpen and W. E. Peck, eds., 10 vols. (London and New York, 1926–1930). A useful collection is *Shelley's Prose, or The Trumpet of a Prophecy*, D. L. Clark, ed. (Albuquerque, N.M., 1954).

Works on Shelley

A detailed biography is N. I. White, *Shelley*, 2 vols. (New York, 1940). Works dealing especially with his thought are C. Baker, *Shelley's Major Poetry* (New York, 1948); H. N. Brailsford, *Shelley, Godwin, and Their Circle* (London, 1913); P. Butter, *Shelley's Idols of the Cave* (Edinburgh, 1954); A. M. D. Hughes, *The Nascent Mind of Shelley* (Oxford, 1947); D. King-Hele, *Shelley: His Thought and Work* (London, 1960); A. Sen, *Studies in Shelley* (Calcutta, 1936); and M. T. Wilson, *Shelley's Later Poetry* (New York, 1959).

D. H. MONRO

SHESTOV, LEON (1866–1938), Russian philosopher and religious thinker, was born in Kiev. His real name was Lev Isaakovich Schwarzmann. Shestov studied law at Moscow University but never practiced it. He lived in St. Petersburg from the late 1890s until he migrated to Berlin in 1922; he later settled in Paris. He gave occasional lectures in Berlin, Paris, and Amsterdam and made two lecture tours in Palestine, but he held no regular academic position.

Shestov called Shakespeare his "first teacher of philosophy"; in his later years he interpreted Hamlet's enigmatic "the time is out of joint" as a profound existential truth. Shestov apparently turned to philosophy relatively late, perhaps in 1895, when he reportedly underwent a spiritual crisis. He himself never referred to such a crisis; in general, his works are less confessional and autobiographical than those of most existential thinkers. However, they are neither impersonal nor unimpassioned; intensity and *engagement* (in a religious and moral rather than a political sense) are hallmarks of his thought.

Shestov was perhaps most strongly influenced by Pascal, Dostoyevsky, and Nietzsche. He discovered Kierkegaard quite late and found his position highly congenial, but he had worked out his own existentialist position independently of Kierkegaard. Shestov's philosophical works are written in an aphoristic, ironic, questioning style reminiscent of Pascal's *Pensées* and Nietzsche's *Beyond Good and Evil*. Shestov believed, with Kierkegaard, that subjective truth borders on paradox. "People seem shocked," he once wrote, "when I enunciate two contradictory propositions simultaneously . . . . But the difference between them and me is that I speak frankly of my contradictions while they prefer to dissimulate theirs, even to themselves. . . . They seem to think of contradictions as the *pudenda* of the

human spirit . . ." (quoted in de Schloezer, "Un Penseur russe . . . ," pp. 89–90).

Shestov was not a systematic thinker. He attacked the views of others, sometimes massively; but he was content to suggest or sketch his own position. His writings focus positively on the question of religion and morality or religiously based morality; negatively on the critique of theoretical and practical rationalism. Among the rationalists whom he attacked by name are Parmenides, Plato, Aristotle, Plotinus, Spinoza, Kant, Hegel, and Husserl.

The basic either/or of Shestov's thought is suggested by the title of his major work in philosophy of religion: *Afiny i Ierusalim* ("Athens and Jerusalem"). Athens is the home of reason, of a philosophical rationalism which insists on a neat and knowable cosmos ruled by eternal and unalterable laws. Jerusalem is the home of faith, of an existential irrationalism which stresses contingency, arbitrariness, mystery, and pure possibility. For God "all things are possible," even what Descartes had called a logical absurdity, that is, causing what has in fact happened not to have happened.

Sometimes Shestov's attack on reason took the form of questioning reason's theoretical competence. Thus, he complained that theorists of biological and cosmic evolution, with their loose talk about "millions and billions of years" and about "eternal nature," were perpetrating a "monstrous absurdity."

More frequently Shestov made the rather different claim that rational knowledge neglects what is essential—the individual, contingent, incomprehensible, and mysterious. "However much we may have attained in science," he wrote, "we must remember that *science cannot give us truth* . . . . For truth lies in the singular, uncontrollable, incomprehensible, . . . and 'fortuitous' . . ." (*In Job's Balances*, p. 193). "We live," Shestov declared, "surrounded by an infinite multitude of mysteries" (*Afiny i Ierusalim*, p. 25).

Most frequently Shestov attacked the moral consequences of theoretical reason, its erosion and subversion of human values. Reason exhibits necessity and imposes nonfreedom. Faith assumes contingency and makes freedom possible. Rationalists recognize an eternal structure of being, a system of necessary laws which antedates any possible cosmic lawgiver. The necessity of such laws requires obedience. What is nonnecessary, whether contingent or arbitrary, admits of free decision and creativity. Shestov repudiated all obedience to necessity in the sense of acceptance of necessary evil, injustice, and inhumanity. There are scales, he declared, upon which human suffering weighs heavier than all the necessities of theoretical reason; such are "Job's balances."

In particular, Shestov rejected the Greek view, which he traced back to Anaximander, that coming to be (*genesis*) is a kind of affront to the gods, a cosmic *hubris*, justly rewarded by the punishment of passing away (*phthora*). He called this the "dreadful law which inseparably links death to birth." "In man's very existence," Shestov added, "thought has discovered something improper, a defect, a sickness, or sin, and . . . has demanded that this be overcome at its root [by] a renunciation of existence . . ." (*Kirgegard i Ekzistentsalnaya Filosofiya*, p. 8).

In such passages Shestov may appear to have confused natural (descriptive) laws with moral (prescriptive) ones. However, his point could be made in terms of such a distinction; descriptive laws, insofar as the regularities which they describe are universal and necessary and not merely local or statistical, demand unconditional acceptance and thus in a sense function prescriptively.

In any case, Shestov wished to assert that rationalists, in absolutizing theoretical truth, inevitably relativize human life. In yielding to "self-evidence," they accept the "horrors of human existence" as something necessary and legitimate. Shestov, in contrast, was quite prepared to relativize theoretical truth if that was the price to be paid for absolutizing moral and religious values and thus "redeeming" the existing individual.

The Nietzschean strain in Shestov's thought appears most clearly in his denial of the validity of universal norms. Such norms function to limit and repress creativity. "The fundamental property of life," he wrote, "is daring; all life is creative daring and thus an eternal mystery, irreducible to anything finished or intelligible" (*In Job's Balances*, p. 158). Under the tyranny of ethical rationalism (a part of the general tyranny of reason, which develops naturally out of the initial autonomy of reason), we come to fear chaos because it is a loss of order. But "chaos is not a limited possibility; it is an unlimited opportunity" (*ibid.*, p. 226).

For Shestov the decisive either/or—reason and necessity or faith and freedom—is not a choice, as rationalists would claim, between sanity and insanity. It is a choice between two kinds of madness (the distinction is reminiscent of Kierkegaard's distinction between "objective" and "subjective" madness). The first kind of madness is that of theoretical reason, which takes as ultimate, eternal, and universally obligatory those objective truths which rationalize and legitimize the "horrors of human existence." The second kind of madness is the Kierkegaardian leap of faith which ventures to take up the struggle against rationalized and legitimized horror at the point where such struggle is "self-evidently" doomed to defeat. Between these two kinds of madness, Shestov's own choice is clear and final.

Works by Shestov

Dostoyevski i Nitshe: Filosofiya Tragedii. St. Petersburg, 1903. Translated by R. von Walter as *Dostojewski und Nietzsche: Philosophie der Tragödie.* Cologne, 1924. Also translated into French as *Dostoevski et Nietzsche (La Philosophie de la tragédie).* Paris, 1926.

Apofeoz Bespochvennosti: Opyt Adogmaticheskovo Myshleniya ("The Apotheosis of Groundlessness: An Essay in Undogmatic Thought"). St. Petersburg, 1905. Translated by S. S. Koteliansky as *All Things Are Possible.* London, 1920. With a foreword by D. H. Lawrence.

Na Vesakh Iova. Paris, 1929. Translated by A. Coventry and C. A. Macartney as *In Job's Balances.* London, 1932.

Kirgegard i Ekzistentsalnaya Filosofiya (Glas Vopiyushchevo v Pustyne). Paris, 1939. Translated by T. Rageot and Boris de Schloezer from the manuscript as *Kierkegaard et la philosophie existentielle (Vox Clamantis in Deserto).* Paris, 1936; reprinted 1948. English translation by Mrs. E. A. Hewitt forthcoming 1966.

Afiny i Ierusalim. Paris, 1951. Translated from the manuscript by Boris de Schloezer as *Athènes et Jerusalem: Essai de philosophie religieuse.* Paris, 1938.

Works on Shestov

Schloezer, Boris de, "Un Penseur russe: Léon Chestov." *Mercure de France,* Vol. 159 (1922), 82–115.

Zenkovsky, V. V., *Istoriya Russkoi Filosofii,* 2 vols. Paris, 1948, 1950. Translated by G. L. Kline as *A History of Russian Philosophy,* 2 vols. London and New York, 1953. Pp. 780–791.

GEORGE L. KLINE

SHĪRĀZĪ, ṢADR AL-DĪN. See MULLĀ ṢADRĀ.

SHPET, GUSTAV GUSTAVOVICH, (1879–1937), Russian philosopher and major exponent of the phenomenology of Husserl in Russia. Shpet did his undergraduate work at Kiev University under the Russian Neo-Kantian philosopher and psychologist G. I. Chelpanov, and he subsequently followed his teacher to Moscow University for advanced work. In 1910 he became an instructor in philosophy at the latter institution. During the ensuing two decades he gained considerable renown, rising in 1918 to the position of professor of philosophy at Moscow University and publishing many works in epistemology, history of philosophy, aesthetics, and psychology. His last philosophical works appeared in 1927. In 1933–1934 he published a number of Russian translations of Byron, Thackeray, and Dickens. His name ceased to appear in Soviet reference books after the early 1930s. He died in a Siberian prison camp.

Shpet's critical attitude toward speculative metaphysics was shown in his earliest work, *Problema Prichinnosti u Yuma i Kanta* ("The Problem of Causality in Hume and Kant," Kiev, 1907), published while he was still a student; and subsequently his constructive philosophical views were elaborated from a strongly antimetaphysical and antireligious standpoint. He viewed the history of philosophy as a dialectical progression from folk wisdom, or lore (*mudrost*), through metaphysics to "rigorous science." In the final stage, philosophy is not derived from the conclusions of particular sciences—this results in a narrow "physicism," "psychologism," or the like—but is rather a "basic science" underlying all the special sciences.

Shpet's view of the phenomenological character of this basic science was best expounded in his chief philosophical work, *Yavleniye i Smysl* ("Appearance and Meaning," Moscow, 1914). Closely following Husserl, Shpet presented a conception of philosophy as a study of the pure data of consciousness—phenomena and the "meanings" which phenomenological reduction discloses in them. Shpet emphasized the social character of consciousness. The immediate experience from which the philosopher must take his start, he maintained, is sociocultural in nature; and in addition to the consciousness that an individual ego possesses, there also exist forms of "collective consciousness." Shpet's subsequent elaboration of these themes led him into the areas of social psychology, aesthetic experience, and the function of language as the bearer of meanings in social intercourse. His interest in the philosophical analysis of consciousness drew him to William James, and as early as 1911 he edited a Russian translation of James's *A Pluralistic Universe.*

Shpet wrote a number of works in the history of Russian philosophy. His *Ocherk Razvitiya Russkoy Filosofii*

("Outline of the Development of Russian Philosophy," Petrograd, 1922) is a pioneering study of early Russian philosophy, noted for its caustic judgments. He also published individual studies of P. D. Yurkevich, Alexander Herzen, and Peter Lavrov.

Additional Works by Shpet

Istoriya kak Problema Logiki ("History as a Problem in Logic"). Moscow, 1916.

Esteticheskiye Fragmenty ("Aesthetic Fragments"), 3 vols. Petrograd, 1922–1923.

Vvedeniye v Etnicheskuyu Psikhologiyu ("Introduction to Ethnic Psychology"). Moscow, 1927.

Vnutrennaya Forma Slova ("The Internal Form of the Word"). Moscow, 1927.

Works on Shpet

V. V. Zenkovsky, *Istoriya Russkoy Filosofii*, 2 vols. Paris, 1948–1950. Translated by G. L. Kline as *A History of Russian Philosophy*, 2 vols. New York and London, 1953.

JAMES P. SCANLAN

SIDGWICK, HENRY (1838–1900), English philosopher and educator. He was born in Yorkshire and attended Rugby and Trinity College, Cambridge. After a brilliant undergraduate career, he was appointed a fellow at Trinity in 1859. He had already begun to have religious doubts, and in the years following 1860 he studied Hebrew and Arabic intensively, hoping to resolve these doubts through historical research. At the same time Sidgwick was teaching philosophy, and he had for many years been a leading member of the small group that met for philosophical discussions with John Grote. Gradually he came to think that if answers to his religious questions were to be found at all, they would be found through philosophy—but he never fully quieted his doubts. In 1869 he resigned his fellowship because he felt he could no longer honestly subscribe to the Thirty-nine Articles, as fellows were required to do. His college promptly appointed him to a lectureship, and when religious tests were dropped, he was reappointed fellow. In 1876 he married Eleanor Balfour, sister of Arthur Balfour. He succeeded T. R. Birks as Knightbridge professor of moral philosophy in 1883, and continued actively teaching in the moral sciences course until his death.

Work and activities. Philosophy was only one of Sidgwick's many interests—he also wrote on education, literature, political theory, and history of political institutions. He was active in the cause of women's education at Cambridge and had a large part in the founding of Newnham College for women, to which he devoted considerable time and money. Another main interest was psychical research—he performed some experiments with F. W. H. Myers as early as 1873, and in 1882 he helped found the Society for Psychical Research. He served twice as the society's president, and investigated and reported on many alleged psychical phenomena, very few of which, however, he believed to be both genuine and significant.

Sidgwick's most important work is *The Methods of Ethics* (1874). His other philosophical writings, although interesting for the light they throw on his moral philosophy, are too slight, too occasional, or too little original to be of independent significance; but the *Methods* has been held by C. D. Broad and other writers to be the greatest single work on ethics in English—and possibly in any language. Sidgwick's work in economics and political science is generally thought not to be of comparable importance.

Philosophical method. *The Methods of Ethics* exemplifies Sidgwick's views on the nature of philosophy. The philosopher's aim is not to discover new truths; rather, it is to give systematic organization to knowledge that we already possess. Theoretical philosophy attempts to unify the knowledge obtained through the sciences, so that all of it may be seen as a whole and all the methods used in science may be seen as parts of one method. Practical philosophy has a similar task to perform with our common moral knowledge of what ought to be and what ought to be done, and with the methods we use in obtaining this knowledge.

In carrying out the task of practical philosophy, Sidgwick offered a resolution of a perennial controversy that had been particularly sharp in the middle years of the nineteenth century—that between utilitarians, such as J. S. Mill, and intuitionists, such as Whewell. However, he found himself unable to reach a solution to another central controversy, that between those who held that morality is independent of religious belief and those who held that without religion no coherent morality is possible. A brief summary of the course of the argument of *The Methods of Ethics* will make these points plain. Sidgwick took a method of ethics to be a reasoned procedure for reaching specific decisions about what one ought to do. The methods used by common sense, he argued, may be reduced to three. One method takes excellence or perfection as an ultimate goal, and claims that we have intuitive knowledge of a variety of independently valid moral principles and maxims. We reach specific conclusions by subsuming particular cases under the relevant principles. According to the other two methods, we are to infer the rightness or wrongness of acts from the amount of happiness they would cause. According to one method, we calculate the consequences to the agent alone. According to the other, we consider the consequences for eveyone affected by the act. Moral rules and principles, for these two methods, are only useful indications of the effects that certain kinds of actions may generally be expected to have. After discussing some basic ethical concepts, Sidgwick examined each method separately and then considered their mutual relations. He concluded that the first method, intuitionism, and the third, utilitarianism, supplement one another, and that their conclusions form a systematic whole. Thus, it is reasonable to act as those conclusions dictate. The remaining method, egoism, can also be systematically developed, and it is reasonable to act according to its conclusions. Either of the two views thus reached dictates obligations that are binding quite independently of any religious sanctions.

However, empirical evidence alone does not show that the conclusions of the egoistic method will always agree with those of the intuitional–utilitarian method. Using methods that are perfectly reasonable, we are sometimes led to serious contradictions. Unless we can find some evidence for the existence of a moral power that will repay self-sacrifice and punish transgression, we will be unable to bring all our practical beliefs and methods into any coherent system. The mere fact that the existence of a power that rewards and punishes behavior is needed to make our practical beliefs coherent does not justify the assertion that there is such a power. Sidgwick personally held that the theistic view is natural for man, but he despaired of finding any evidence to support it and refused to use it in his philosophy. The consequence of the existence of these practical contradictions is (as Sidgwick put it in the melancholy concluding words of the first edition of the *Methods*) that "the prolonged effort of the human intellect to frame a perfect ideal of rational conduct is seen to have been foredoomed to inevitable failure."

Basis of classification. Sidgwick's classification of the methods implicit in common-sense morality rests on two considerations. First, the methods reflect two sides of human nature. Those taking happiness as the final end reflect the sentient side of man, the capacity for enjoying and suffering, while the method taking excellence as the final end reflects the fact that man is also an active being, with a need to do as well as a need to feel. Second, the classification indicates an epistemological distinction that Sidgwick constantly took as basic, the distinction between propositions that we are entitled to assert only because we have correctly inferred them from others that we know, and propositions that we are entitled to assert because we know them without any inference, directly or "intuitively." The intuitional method claims that we have noninferential knowledge of moral principles, while the other methods emphasize the ways in which moral rules and maxims are arrived at by inference.

Noninferential truth. If there is inferential knowledge, Sidgwick believed, there must be noninferential knowledge; and since he also held that there are no infallible sources of noninferential knowledge, the problem arises of how to test claims to possess noninferential truth or claims to have found self-evident propositions. Sidgwick proposed four tests that apparently self-evident propositions must pass before we can be justified in accepting them: (1) the terms in which they are stated must be clear and precise; (2) their self-evidence must be very carefully ascertained; (3) they must be mutually consistent; and (4) there must be general agreement of experts on their truth. Sidgwick argued at great length that common-sense moral principles, which according to traditional intuitionism are self-evident, fail to pass these tests. Hence, if they are true principles, as we all take them to be, they must be inferential and dependent, not self-evident and independent.

Self-evident moral principles. What do common-sense moral principles depend on? There are four principles that do pass Sidgwick's tests and that he accepted as self-evident. (1) Whatever action anyone judges right for himself, he implicitly judges to be right for anyone else in similar circumstances. (2) One ought to have as much regard for future good or evil as for present, allowing for differences in certainty. (3) The good enjoyed by any individual is as important as the good enjoyed by any other. (4) A rational being is bound to aim generally at good.

Principle of benevolence. From the principles that the good of each person is equally important and that a rational being must aim generally at good, Sidgwick deduced an abstract principle of benevolence. Common-sense moral-

ity, he argued, appeals to this principle to settle cases in which its usual rules give no answers, and allows its rules to be overridden by the principle if they conflict with it. These facts indicate that common sense considers its rules to depend for their validity on this principle. However, the abstract principle of benevolence is also at the center of utilitarianism, and common-sense morality—the stronghold of traditional intuitionists—is thus seen to be fundamentally utilitarian. The utilitarian, in turn, can have no objection to any of the self-evident principles, and the two methods can thus be completely synthesized. Even the egoist can accept three of the self-evident truths; his rejection of the fourth is an indication of the basic contradiction in the realm of practical reason.

Criticisms of utilitarianism. Sidgwick is usually considered a utilitarian, and he frequently referred to himself as one. However, his views differ considerably from those of the earlier utilitarians.

Empiricism. Sidgwick rejected the empiricist epistemology that J. S. Mill developed and that seemed to underlie Bentham's thought. Empiricism, as Sidgwick understood it, holds that the basic premises from which all knowledge is built are cognitions of particular facts and that these cognitions alone are infallible. Sidgwick argued that these cognitions are not infallible and that empiricism cannot give a satisfactory account of the principles of inference that guide the construction of knowledge from the basic data. Metaphysically, he rejected not only materialism but also the reductive sensationalism to which he believed the empiricist epistemology led. Following Thomas Reid, he held to what he called a common-sense dualism of mind and matter, although he found the connections between the two most obscure.

Definition of ethical terms. Sidgwick also rejected what he took to be the traditional utilitarian attempt to define ethical concepts like "good" and "ought" in terms of nonethical concepts like "pleasant" or "conducive to most pleasure" and in this way to justify the construction of a purely factual, scientific morality. No reduction of "ought" to "is," of ideal to actual, had yet been successful, he held, although he hesitated to say that no reduction could possibly succeed. However, he did affirm that it is impossible to make an ethical first principle true by definition. To define "good" as "pleasure" is self-defeating if you wish to hold, as a first principle that the good is pleasure, since what you hold as a principle would then be a tautology, and a tautology cannot be an ethical first principle. Recognition of these points, Sidgwick believed, would force the utilitarian to admit the need of a basic intuition in his philosophy.

Motivation. Sidgwick rejected the motivational theories of Bentham and the Mills. He did not think that we always necessarily act to obtain what we take to be our own pleasure or our own good.

The relevance of psychology. Sidgwick strongly objected to the tendency, which he attributed to Mill, to substitute psychological (or perhaps, with Comte, sociological) investigation into the origins of ideas and beliefs for properly philosophical investigation of their applicability or truth. Quite aside from his doubts as to the adequacy of the associationist psychology that the earlier utilitarians accepted, Sidgwick held that psychological discoveries about the antecedents and concomitants of ideas and beliefs are, in general, irrelevant to questions of their truth and validity—and psychology can tell us only about antecedents and concomitants. It cannot supersede the deliverances of direct introspective awareness on the question of what our ideas now are.

Determinism. Sidgwick agreed with the earlier utilitarians that there seems to be overwhelming evidence in support of a deterministic view of human action. However, he held that this evidence must be balanced against the fact that in the moment of choosing between alternative actions we inevitably think ourselves free to choose either alternative. He argued that the issue is, therefore, not yet settled, but he held that it is not important for ethical theory that it should be.

Independence of politics. Sidgwick held that utilitarianism does not necessarily lead to reforming radicalism in politics. He pointed out the strong utilitarian element to such conservative thinkers as Hume and Burke, and he argued at great length that a utilitarian would be extremely cautious in recommending important changes.

Agreements with utilitarianism. Sidgwick's position was, of course, utilitarian in its major ethical aspects. He held that the only ultimate or intrinsic good is desirable or pleasant states of consciousness; that acts are objectively right only if they produce more good than any other alternative open to the agent; and that moral rules, such as those of truth-telling or promise-keeping, are subordinate to the principle of utility and are dependent on it for whatever validity they possess. He also held that the value of character and motive is derived from, and to be judged in terms of, the consequences of the actions to which they tend to lead. Sidgwick's disagreements with the traditional forms of utilitarianism are part of his attempt to show that the utilitarian view of morality is independent of metaphysical doctrines, psychological theories, and political platforms and therefore is capable of being what he argued it is—the position toward which common-sense morality in every age and in every society has tended.

Works by Sidgwick

The Methods of Ethics. London, 1874. Extensively revised for the editions of 1877, 1884, and 1890. The sixth edition (1901) was the last revised by Sidgwick; it contains an autobiographical sketch of great interest.
Principles of Political Economy. London, 1883, 1887, 1901.
Outlines of the History of Ethics. London, 1886. Many subsequent editions.
Elements of Politics. London, 1891 and 1897.
Practical Ethics. London, 1898.
Philosophy, Its Scope and Relations. London, 1902.
Lectures on the Ethics of Green, Spencer, and Martineau. London, 1902.
Development of European Polity. London, 1903.
Miscellaneous Essays and Addresses. London and New York, 1904.
Lectures on the Philosophy of Kant, James Ward, ed. London, 1905.

Works on Sidgwick

Bradley, F. H., "Mr. Sidgwick's Hedonism," in his *Collected Essays.* Oxford, 1935. Vol. I. Polemic against Sidgwick.
Broad, C. D., *Five Types of Ethical Theory.* London, 1930. This and the two following works are useful and lengthy discussions of Sidgwick.

Broad, C. D., *Ethics and the History of Philosophy.* London, 1952.
Broad, C. D., *Religion, Philosophy, and Psychical Research.* London, 1953.
Havard, W. C., *Henry Sidgwick and Later Utilitarian Political Philosophy.* Gainesville, Fla., 1959.
Hayward, F. H., *The Ethical Philosophy of Sidgwick.* London, 1901. Not very useful.
Sidgwick, A., and Sidgwick, E. M., *Henry Sidgwick: A Memoir.* London, 1906. The standard biography, written by his brother and his widow. It contains letters, unpublished papers, and a complete bibliography of his writings.

J. B. SCHNEEWIND

SIGER OF BRABANT, also known as Siger de Brabant and Sigerius de Brabantia, thirteenth-century scholastic philosopher. The facts of Siger's life are extremely few (the dates of his birth and death are not known), and those believed to be authentic are almost entirely linked with his stormy professional career as master of arts at the University of Paris during the third quarter of the thirteenth century. The background leading to this career was the introduction to the Latin world, between 1150 and 1250, of Greek works of philosophy and science accompanied by their Greek, Alexandrian, and Arabic commentaries. Since these writings presented apparently well-reasoned conclusions which were occasionally in direct conflict with established Christian doctrines, upheavals and significant readjustments became necessary in Western Latin philosophy. To mention but two instances, these newly introduced writings presented arguments for the eternity of the world and arguments against the immortality of the individual soul. In the most general terms, Greek necessitarianism was counterposed to the Christian contingent universe.

Siger himself was closely involved with the severe problems of readjustment in the faculty of arts at Paris, particularly after 1255, when the works of Aristotle were officially admitted to the curriculum. In 1266 he was mentioned by the papal legate as one of the prime movers of intellectual disturbance in the faculty of arts. In 1270 the archbishop of Paris, Étienne Tempier, condemned 13 philosophical theses, several arising from the use of Averroës in the interpretation of Aristotle but all associated with the recently acquired Greek thought. Some of these condemned propositions can be found in writings attributable to Siger and, interestingly enough, can also be located in many other contemporary philosophers, including Thomas Aquinas—a clear indication of the powerful impact of the Greek and Arabic traditions on Western Latin speculation.

In 1272, on the occasion of the election of a new rector for the faculty of arts, Siger was singled out in a document cautioning against "imprudence" in the teaching of philosophy, that is, the improper teaching of Aristotle. However, many masters in the faculty of arts seem to have continued to insist on their intellectual autonomy, so much so that in 1277 the archbishop was impelled to make public a list of 219 condemned propositions, which appear again, for the most part, in the faculty's analysis of Aristotelian writings, that is, the insistence on the rigor of Aristotle's reasoning even when such reasoning leads to conclusions incompatible with basic tenets of Christian faith. Some months later Siger and a certain Bernier de Nivelles were summoned before the French Inquisition, but they apparently avoided this judicial action by leaving Paris. The rest of Siger's life is obscure. There is a tradition that he went to Italy and was murdered in Orvieto about 1285, but the evidence is not solid.

Doctrine. The presentation of Siger's philosophical views cannot be dissociated from the problems engendered for Western Latin thinkers by the introduction of the corpus of Greek thought during the late twelfth and early thirteenth centuries. This corpus contained conclusions that were seriously at variance with cardinal points of Christian belief and thus were the cause of much speculative re-evaluation. Siger's authentic writings are, for the most part, the normal publications of a master of arts active in teaching: commentaries on Aristotelian works and special treatises on unusual problems arising in the commentaries. His interpretations are meticulous and his decisions cautious where Aristotle, as is frequently the case, speaks in laconic fashion. Siger recognized, nevertheless, that there are some conclusions rigorously derived in Aristotle that conflict with Christian faith. For example, following Aristotelian principles, Siger argued to the conclusions that God is ignorant of the truth-value of future contingent propositions, that chance is the foundation of the possibility of free will, and that no case can be made in Aristotelian writings for the possibility of personal immortality. In such intellectual situations, however, Siger maintained that the truth of such propositions must be immediately ceded to the declarations of faith. This pattern of holding to Aristotle's logical rigor, yet simultaneously insisting on the certain veracity of the dictates of Christian faith, can be found in many masters of arts in the late thirteenth and early fourteenth centuries. Such masters have often been called Averroist, but it is probable that Greek thought as such, and not merely Averroës' commentaries on Aristotle, is responsible for the far-reaching conflicts and subsequent intellectual re-evaluations of the later Middle Ages.

Furthermore, when the question of the firm authenticity of Siger's writings arises, a vital historical question is activated. Dante places Siger in heaven, and even has him identified by Thomas Aquinas:

> This figure, which your eyes encounter as they return toward me, is the light of a spirit who, wrapt in grave thought, found death slow in coming. This is the eternal light of Siger, who, when he taught in the Street of Straw, established unwelcome truths. (*Paradiso* X, 133–138)

Scholars who have wished to make Dante the apogee of medieval literature and, concomitantly, to show that he reflects the assumed apogee of medieval philosophy, Thomas Aquinas, have thus been faced with a difficult problem of interpretation. Siger, in the authentic writing *De Anima Intellectiva*, sustains Averroës' analysis of Aristotle's doctrine of the soul—that the active aspect of the intellect is a single separable principle available for all men alike. Whether this is a correct reading of the sense of Aristotle himself is subject to critical analysis; such a reading, however, clearly offends the Christian (Thomist) doctrine of the soul as an individuality capable of continued

subsistence following its separation from the corrupted physical body.

Controversy about this problem has been evident for decades: there are, on the one hand, unorthodox but definitely authentic writings by Siger, and, on the other, writings of less certain attribution setting forth more orthodox positions, such as the plurality of individual intellective souls and the probability of their survival following the dissolution of bodies. One scholarly position, exemplified by F. Van Steenberghen, has maintained that if Dante is to be understood as holding a Thomist philosophical position, then Siger ought not to be located in heaven, unless at some point in his career he had changed his views on such matters as the nature of the intellective soul. Such a modification would strengthen claims for the authenticity of the less certain commentaries and would place him properly in Dante's "Thomist" heaven. Yet fourteenth-, fifteenth-, and sixteenth-century philosophical writings by Siger's successors have been carefully scrutinized by scholars for any indication of changes in his thinking, and nothing has yet been found to suggest a shift from the views set forth in the well-authenticated works. All firm evidence delineates him as a typical master of arts of the thirteenth century: acute and logically sound, yet at the same time thoroughly alive to, and possibly uncomfortable with, the serious discrepancies between conclusions founded on the Aristotelian texts and propositions reflecting the spiritual demands of Christian faith.

Works by Siger

Mandonnet, P., ed., *Siger de Brabant et l'averroïsme latin au XIIIᵉ siècle*, 2d ed., 2 vols. Louvain, 1911 and 1908. Vols. VI and VII in the series *Les Philosophes belges*.

Van Steenberghen, F., *Siger de Brabant d'après ses oeuvres inédites*, 2 vols. Louvain, 1931 and 1942. Vols. XII and XIII in the series *Les Philosophes belges*.

Works on Siger

Gilson, Étienne, *Dante the Philosopher*. New York, 1949.

Gilson, Étienne, *History of Christian Philosophy in the Middle Ages*. New York, 1955.

Graiff, C. A., *Siger de Brabant. Questions sur la métaphysique*. Louvain, 1948.

Nardi, B., *Sigieri di Brabante nel pensiero del rinascimento italiano*. Rome, 1945.

Van Steenberghen, F., *Les Oeuvres et la doctrine de Siger de Brabant*. Brussels, 1938.

STUART MacCLINTOCK

SIGN AND SYMBOL. In thinking about language and linguistic meaning, one cannot but be struck by the fact that many nonlinguistic phenomena seem to be akin to language in significant respects. On the one hand, there are gestures, bell ringings, whistles, and so on which have conventional signification not totally unlike that of words and sentences. On the other hand, there are cases in which something means or indicates something else quite apart from any conventions, as when a certain kind of noise in the engine indicates that the valves are defective. There are also many intermediate cases. It may be useful to look at language in the light of its similarities to and differences from more or less closely allied phenomena.

General concept of a sign. We may consider the following list.

(1) A rapid pulse is a *sign* of fever.

(2) A hum like that *indicates* a loose connection in the wiring.

(3) Pottery fragments are a *sign* of human habitation.

(4) When he starts working nights, it *means* he is tired of you.

(5) That is a *diagram* of a high compression engine.

(6) That is a *picture* of Aunt Susie.

(7) In your dream the spider is a *symbol* of your sister.

(8) The elephant *represents* the Republican party.

(9) That whistle *means* that the train is about to start.

(10) By raising his hand, he *indicated* that he understood perfectly.

(11) On this team "45" is the *signal* for an end run.

(12) "Pinochle" is the *name* of a game.

(13) "Thermometer" *denotes* an instrument for measuring temperature.

(14) "Winnie" is a *nickname* for Winston Churchill.

Many thinkers—most notably, C. S. Peirce—have supposed that all of the above are species of a single genus, for which the term "sign" can be employed. That is, in each of these cases what we have is one thing serving as a sign of something else, and the various italicized expressions indicate different ways in which one thing can be a sign of something else—that is, different kinds of signs.

It is clear that general sign theory can be correct only if "sign" is given some technical sense, for there is no ordinary sense of the term in which it can be applied to every one of the above cases. It makes no sense to say of a diagram that it is a sign of a high compression engine or to say of the word "pinochle" that it is a sign of a certain game. (The same is true of any other word we might use for the genus—for example, "represents." To say that a rapid pulse represents fever, if the statement is to make any sense at all, is to say something quite different from (1). And "That whistle represents that the train is about to start" is of doubtful significance.) In what special sense, then, is "sign" being employed?

Peirce gives many definitions of "sign," the most intelligible of which is "a sign . . . is something that stands to somebody for something in some respect or capacity" (*Collected Papers*, Vol. II, Par. 228; in subsequent references to Peirce we shall follow the custom of giving the volume number followed by a paragraph number after a decimal, as 2.228). What Peirce (along with all other general sign theorists) is actually defining is "Someone takes *x* to be a sign of *y*" rather than "*x* is a sign of *y*." An appropriate reaction on the part of an interpreter is neither a necessary nor a sufficient condition for the truth of the latter, though it is, of course, for the truth of the former. It is not a necessary condition, for if a rapid pulse *is* a sign of fever, it is whether or not anyone ever realized this. It is not a sufficient condition, for even if people generally react to walking under a ladder as if it were a sign of impending ill fortune, that does not make it a sign of impending ill fortune. Henceforward, we shall tacitly understand the problem to be one of specifying what it is for someone to take *x* to be a sign of *y*.

If we proceed in this way, we are putting the weight on "stand for." Here, too, it may be doubted that the term applies widely enough in any ordinary sense. Does (4) imply that his working at night stands for his being tired of you? Whatever we decide about that, we still have to ask whether there is any interesting single sense in which one thing stands for another in each case. Attempts to exhibit such a sense have usually taken one of two forms, which we may label "ideational" and "behavioral." The germs of both are to be found in Peirce himself. According to the ideational sense, "*x* stands for *y* (for a person *P*)" is taken to mean "When *P* becomes aware of *x*, it calls *y* to mind." According to the behavioral sense, it is to be construed as "When *P* perceives *x*, he is led to make some behavioral response appropriate to *y*." There are grave difficulties with both approaches. The ideational account will have to be heavily qualified in order to be at all plausible, since I could realize that the elephant represents the Republican party (that the elephant "stands for the Republican party for me") without its being true that the Republican party is called to mind every time I see an elephant, and even if this is not generally true. The formulation will have to be modified to include some specification of the conditions under which such callings-to-mind take place. The trick is to do this without weakening the criterion to the point that anything becomes a sign of anything. We would run this danger if we said that what is required is that *x* call *y* to mind when the person is in the proper state. Moreover, it would seem that this account of "stand for" would let in all cases of association of ideas as cases of signs. Suppose that because of strong impressions formed in my early childhood, the sight of a screen porch regularly calls up the memory of my grandmother. Does this warrant our saying that a screen porch stands for my grandmother for me? This may not be a difficulty, since as long as we are devising technical terms, we can decide doubtful cases like this as we see fit.

Behavioral interpretation of "sign." The behavioral account runs into even more difficulties. It is obvious that in many cases like those on our master list, I can take *x* as a sign, indication, representation, signal, and so on of *y* without ever overtly responding to *x* in any way appropriate to *y*. Thus (14), suppose that whenever I hear "Winnie" (used as a nickname for Winston Churchill), it is in such sentences as "Winnie is a great man" or "If it hadn't been for Winnie, Britain would have folded," never in such sentences as "Winnie is coming into the room now." That is, the word always occurs in discourse about its referent (while far away), never in announcements of his impending presence. In that case I would never overtly respond to the utterance of the name in any way like that in which I would respond to the person. Again (5), it would be very odd for one to respond overtly to a diagram of a high compression engine in anything like the way he responds to the engine itself, however clearly he recognizes that the former is a diagram of the latter. This crude behavioral interpretation does seem to fit some of the other cases better, for example, (1)–(4) and (9)–(11). If one recognizes a rapid pulse as a sign of fever, we would expect him to react to it in ways he would take to be appropriate—call a doctor, administer aspirin, and so on. Again, if one takes (9) to be true, that would seem to carry with it reacting to the whistle in any way one would react to the train's being about to start—for instance, hurrying to get on it. But even in these cases we have to remember that a person might take x to be a sign of y, even though he is not disposed to respond to y in any way whatsoever; in this case there will be no "appropriate" response to transfer partially. One might realize the significance of the whistle even though the impending departure of the train has no practical significance for him, just as one might realize that a certain noise indicates an improperly seated valve even though he has no disposition whatsoever to do anything about it.

More sophisticated versions of the behavioral interpretation try to take account of these points by focusing on implicit responses or on the production of a disposition to respond if certain other conditions are satisfied. One who focuses on implicit responses is the psychologist Charles Osgood. In his view, even though x may not elicit any overt y-appropriate responses, it will elicit internal responses which are either like internal responses to y or are incipient overt responses of the sort made to y. Thus, the name "Winnie" may call up feelings similar to those called up by the man himself, and the diagram may elicit faint beginnings of muscular movements which would be involved in working on the engine. (Osgood will still have to find some way of dealing with cases in which someone who takes x to be a sign of y is not given to making any response to y at all. Perhaps this can be taken care of by bringing in cognitive responses—thoughts of y, which are so subtle that at least we will never have reason to think that they are absent.) In taking this line, Osgood is postulating processes for which we do not have any evidence at present, and it remains to be seen to what extent such evidence will be forthcoming. Moreover, insofar as emotional responses and even cognitive responses are admitted into the class of implicit responses, one wonders what has happened to the behavioral orientation of the position.

The switch from overt response to disposition to respond is associated chiefly with Charles Morris. In (8), even though the train whistle may not stir me into activity if I have no intention of catching the train or if I am already on it, still, if it is a sign of impending departure for me, we can at least say this: that if I intended to ride the train and were not already on it, the whistle would lead me to move hurriedly in its direction. This might be put by saying that the whistle produces in me a disposition to hurry toward the train if I want to catch it and am not already on it. The claim then would be that taking x as a sign of y always involves the production of one or more such dispositions in the sign interpreter. This approach is not subject to some of the difficulties that plague the others, but there are still problems. For one thing, it is not clear how we could put any limit on the number of dispositions produced by a given sign. It would presumably be just as true to say that the whistle produced in me a disposition to light a fuse if I wanted to blow up the train, a disposition to wave if I cannot resist waving to departing trains, and so on, indefinitely. Once we are no longer restricted to actual facts about the sign interpreter, we can think of an indefinite number of responses which the sign would produce if one or another nonexistent condition were satisfied. Perhaps that indicates that there is something

odd about saying that the sign *produces* such dispositions. Second, as long as we have to admit intentions, desires, beliefs, and the like into the conditions involved in the dispositions, the behavioral character of the analysis is called into question.

Symbols and indices. The difficulty in isolating a generic feature which is common to all the items on the list may well lead us to abandon the attempt. It still seems that they are all closely allied in some way, but this may be because of what Wittgenstein called "family resemblances" rather than because of the common possession of a generic feature. That is, it may be that there are a number of features, each of which is possessed by several items and several of which are possessed by each item, without its being the case that there is any one feature or set of features possessed by all the items. Even if this is the case, it will be useful to trace similarities and differences in various subclasses of the larger class. In so doing, distinctions between signs and symbols will be among the points revealed.

Our original list could be subdivided in different ways. We might distinguish between humanly devised signs—(3), (5), (6), (8)–(14)—and natural signs—(1), (2), (4), (7). According to this principle of division, (2) is natural even though it has to do with the operations of an artifact, for the hum was not instituted by human contrivance to be a sign; it has that status regardless of our plans. It would seem, however, that the most penetrating classification will be achieved by attending to the kind of justification which would be given for each statement on the list. Looking over the list with this in mind we can see a fundamental difference between (1)–(4) and (8)–(14).

For a statement in the first group to be true, it must be the case that examples of x and y (taking the form of each statement to be "xRy") are regularly correlated, that always or usually when there is an x, there is also a y in some more or less exactly specifiable spatiotemporal relation to the x in question. Statement (1) is justified only if it is generally the case that when a person has a rapid pulse, that person also has a fever. Statement (2) is justified only if it is generally the case that when a hum like this one emanates from a piece of electrical apparatus, there is a loose connection in the wiring of that piece of apparatus at that time. Statement (3) is justified only if it is generally true that for any place at which pottery fragments are found, human beings inhabited that place at some earlier time.

What is required for the truth of statements of the second group, by contrast, is the fact that there exists a regular practice of using the "sign" in a certain way. If one were challenged in one of these statements, he would defend himself by alleging that in (9) a whistle like that is regularly used by engineers (or by this engineer or by engineers on this line) to indicate imminent departure, that in (11) on this team "45" is the agreed signal for an end run, or that in (13) "thermometer" is regularly used in the English-language community to denote instruments of that sort. (The task of making explicit what it is to use x in a certain way, what aspects of the employment of "signs" are crucial here, is a very difficult task which lies outside the limits of this article. See MEANING.) Moreover, this is all that would be required for justification. It would not also be necessary to show that x's are regularly correlated with *y*'s in some ways. In some of these cases such correlations do not, in fact, hold. To say that cases of "thermometer" are correlated with instruments for measuring temperature could mean only that generally when "thermometer" is uttered, there is some instrument for measuring temperature in the vicinity at that time. But we can see that this is false by reflecting on the frequency of the occurrence of "thermometer" in sentences like "Thermometers are very useful" and "I need to buy a thermometer," sentences which one can utter with perfect propriety in the absence of thermometers. In other cases such correlations will normally hold, but they are not strictly required for the truth of the statement. Thus, such whistles may well be regularly followed by the immediate departure of the train, and the utterance of "45" by the quarterback in appropriate circumstances may well be universally followed by an (at least attempted) end run. But suppose that engineers on this line were in the habit of dawdling at the station after giving the signal for departure, at least to the extent that it is not generally true that such a whistle generally is immediately followed by departure. And suppose that this football team gets things confused so often that it is not generally true that the call "45" is actually followed by an end run. Sentences (9) and (11) could still be true. It may well be that statements like (9) and (11) could be true only if some correlations of these sorts hold to a certain minimum extent. If there were no significant correlation between numbers barked out by quarterbacks and subsequent offensive operations, then perhaps it could not be true that any number is a signal for any particular play. But the fact remains that appropriate correlations are not required in each case for the truth of such statements.

Thus, it looks as if there is a sharp distinction between the two groups of facts. One is a matter of certain *de facto* correlations holding and not a matter of the *x*'s being used in a certain way. (For that group the *x*'s are not used at all; they happen.) The other is a matter of the way the *x* in question is used and not a matter of correlations in which it stands with the *y*. These two groups of signs bear a striking resemblance to two of the three categories in Peirce's most important threefold classification of signs—"icon," "index," and "symbol." Peirce's most readily intelligible definition of "index" is "a sign which refers to the Object that it denotes by virtue of being really affected by that Object" (2.248); he defines "symbol" as "a sign which is constituted a sign merely or mainly by the fact that it is used and understood as such" (2.307). These seem equivalent to our two groups, except that for the first we have broadened the notion of being affected by the object into the notion of any fixed spatiotemporal relation to the object.

Comment may be in order concerning the relation of this definition of "symbol" to the more common one according to which a symbol is something with a conventional significance or something which has meaning by convention. The two can be taken as equivalent provided we do not take the term "convention" literally. Many writers who stress the conventional character of language say things which, taken literally, are plainly false—for example, that words get their meaning because users of the language agree to use them in certain ways, that it is by arbitrary fiat

that words mean what they do, that words are adopted by common convention, and so on. There is every reason to think that agreements, fiats, and conventions, in any literal senses of these terms, play a very small role in the origin and development of languages. Talk of this sort is best regarded as a pseudohistorical way of expressing truths about the contemporary status of language which are expressed more soberly by talk of current practices of using words in certain ways, just as the social contract theory of the origin of society is a pseudohistorical way of expressing certain truths about current political arrangements.

Icons. Peirce defines his third type of "sign," icon, as "a sign which refers to the Object that it denotes merely by virtue of characters of its own" (2.247). It seems clear that *x* can have any signlike relation to *y* by virtue of "characters of its own" only if *y* shares some of those characters, as when *x* is taken as a sample of a certain cloth by virtue of similarities to other pieces of that cloth, so that the signifying is on the basis of similarity rather than on causal or conventional connections. Do the remaining items on our list fall into this category? Leaving (7) aside for the moment, it is certainly true that similarity plays an important part in (5) and (6), though in (5) the relevant similarity is more abstract, holding between certain aspects of the structure of the diagram and the engine rather than between their gross external appearances. However, it is easy to see that more than similarity is required for the truth of (5) and (6). Other pictures may look more like Aunt Susie than this one, even in the relevant respects, and still be pictures of someone else. What is crucial is the fact that this picture, unlike the others, was painted with Aunt Susie sitting as model and was produced as her portrait. We might think of (6) as an impure icon; similarity plays a role but only in connection with circumstances of production and the intentions of the producer and consumer. This might lead us to say that it is an index and a symbol as well as an icon. With (5) the impurity stems most prominently from the fact that because of the operation of certain conventions, we look to certain features of the diagram rather than others to tell what it is a diagram of, how to read off the engine from the diagram. These conventions are such, let us say, that the color of the markings is irrelevant, as is the shape of each element. Words are used to indicate what each element in the diagram stands for; the iconic element comes from the way in which the spatial relations between the elements of the diagram are taken to tell us something, by way of similarity, about the spatial relations between the corresponding elements of the engine.

Example (7) is more difficult to analyze. Of course, this difficulty stems partly from indeterminacies in the Freudian theory of symbols, including dream symbols. Presumably, the basis of the connection is an association of ideas, based on a similarity in emotional reaction to sisters and to spiders. But to fully spell out what is involved, we would have to have a clear account of what it is for the spider to function as a symbol of the dreamer's sister in the dream, and for that we need further development of the theory. One reason this case is instructive is that it reveals Peirce's use of "symbol" to be a technical one. Indeed, this can be seen from the fact that in Peirce's sense of the term, words are all symbols, whereas we ordinarily distinguish between expressing sòmething in words and putting it into symbols—for example, those of symbolic logic or those of mathematics. Dream symbols and religious symbols are something else again. It may be that religious symbols are the closest thing we have to a pure Peircean icon. In a certain religion, fire may be reacted to as a symbol of life or of the mutability of things just on the basis of a felt similarity, even if no adherent of the religion ever made this explicit (in verbal symbols). But here, too, it is notoriously difficult to get a clear picture of what is going on.

Reduction of symbols to indices. Despite the fundamental differences between indices and symbols, there have often been attempts to reduce symbols to indices, or at least to show that they are more closely related than they would appear to be at first sight. Thus, we might be able to show that it is essential to words that they function as reliable indications of the presence of something, even if it is because of the existence of certain conventions that they are taken to be such indications. John Locke thought of words as signs of ideas in the mind of the speaker; according to his view, it is essential for a word having the meaning it has to function regularly as a sign in this way. The more up-to-date version of this position would replace ideas with neural processes in the brain. This has been called the "thermometer view of man"; linguistic utterances constitute the external registering of invisible internal goings-on. Quite apart from such speculative hypotheses as these, it is undoubtedly true that linguistic utterances do serve as indications of various things. Thus, if a man says, in a disconsolate tone, "The war in Vietnam is going badly," I may take this as an indication that he is interested in international affairs, that he has a favorable attitude toward our intervention in Vietnam, that he has heard of Vietnam, that he knows the English language, and so on. The fact that verbal utterances do function as signs in so many ways undoubtedly adds to the temptation to suppose that language can be adequately treated as a body of signs of a certain kind.

From our list it is clear that the class of symbols will include many items which would not ordinarily be said to belong to any language. The relation of linguistic and nonlinguistic symbols is a complex one (for a brief discussion see LANGUAGE).

Bibliography

C. S. Peirce's development of the general theory of signs is to be found in his *Collected Papers*, 6 vols. (Cambridge, Mass., 1931–1935), Vol. II. The enterprise is continued with a behavioral emphasis in Charles Morris, *Signs, Language, and Behavior* (New York, 1946), and in Charles Osgood, *Method and Theory in Experimental Psychology* (New York, 1953), Ch. 16. Interesting discussions of the varieties of symbolism are to be found in Susanne K. Langer, *Philosophy in a New Key* (New York, 1948); in Part II of W. M. Urban, *Language and Reality* (New York, 1939); and in Philip Wheelwright, *The Burning Fountain* (Bloomington, Ind., 1954). Ch. 4–6 of H. H. Price, *Thinking and Experience* (London, 1953), contain penetrating comments on the distinction between signs and symbols.

WILLIAM P. ALSTON

SIGWART, CHRISTOPH (1830–1904), German philosopher and logician, was born and died in Tübingen. He studied philosophy, theology, and mathematics there and taught in Halle from 1852 to 1855, before joining the theological seminar in Tübingen in 1855. He accepted a professorship at Blaubeuren in 1859 and returned to Tübingen as professor of philosophy, a position he held from 1865 to 1903. His doctoral dissertation was on Pico della Mirandola. He also wrote on Schleiermacher, Spinoza, Zwingli, and Giordano Bruno, as well as on ethics. His most important work was the two-volume *Logik,* a comprehensive treatise on the theory of knowledge.

The aim of logic, Sigwart maintained, is normative rather than descriptive. Logic is a regulative science whose aim should be to present a useful methodology for the extension of our knowledge. It is "the ethics rather than the physics of thought" and concerns itself not with an account of psychological processes but with finding the rules in accordance with which thought may achieve objective validity. Like ethics, logic is concerned with the question "What ought I to do?" The adequacy of thought lies not in its correspondence with an antecedently objective reality but in its satisfaction of human purposes. The overriding purpose of reasoning is to reach ideas that are necessary and universal for us, for human beings. Objective validity is essentially a matter of intersubjective agreement. The possibility of discovering the rules for necessary and universally valid thinking, however, depends also on an immediate awareness of self-evidence, a property that is possessed by necessary judgments. The experience of self-evidence is a postulate beyond which we cannot inquire. Logic strives to disclose the conditions under which this feeling occurs.

In Sigwart's philosophy there is a voluntarist element combined with respect for natural science, both of which evidently impressed William James. (James quoted from Sigwart in his essay "The Dilemma of Determinism.") Sigwart held that an activity of free and conscious willing is presupposed not only by ethics and metaphysics but by logic as well. Free will is presupposed by any distinction between correct and incorrect reasoning, since thinking must be a voluntary activity and not necessitated. The will is supreme in the realm of theory as well as in that of practice. The ultimate presupposition of all experience, and therefore of all thinking too, is not merely Kant's "I think," which can accompany all ideas, but also "I will," which governs all acts of thought.

Sigwart's classification of the forms of judgments and categories presents judging as the basic cognitive function. Judgments are divided into simple narrative judgments, expressive of an immediate recognition ("This is Socrates"), and complex judgments, presupposing twofold and higher syntheses ("This cloud is red"). The discussion of existential judgments agrees with Kant in denying that existence, or "to be," adds anything to the content of an idea.

Sigwart was also interested in the work of men outside his own country; for example, the *Logik* contains a lengthy discussion of Mill on induction. Sigwart's ethical and metaphysical views were somewhat conventional: he held that progress in the development of the social order is an inevitable fact of history, and he argued that the attempt to make all our knowledge coherent inevitably leads to the idea of God.

Works by Sigwart

Spinozas neuentdeckter Traktat von Gott, dem Menschen und dessen Glückseligkeit. Gotha, 1866.

Logik, 2 vols. Tübingen, 1873 and 1878. 5th ed., Tübingen, 1924, contains Heinrich Maier's biography of Sigwart and a bibliography. Translated by Helen Dendy as *Logic,* 2 vols. London, 1890.

Vorfragen der Ethik. Freiburg, 1886.

Works on Sigwart

Häring, T. L., *Christoph Sigwart.* Tübingen, 1930.

Levinson, R. B., "Sigwart's Logic and William James." *Journal of the History of Ideas,* Vol. 8 (1947), 475–483.

ARNULF ZWEIG

SIMMEL, GEORG (1858–1918), German philosopher and sociologist, was born in Berlin and resided there except for the last four years of his life. He was educated there, and in 1881 he received his doctorate from the University of Berlin. Three years later he began to teach at that university as a *Privatdozent* and from 1900 he was associate professor without faculty status. Although successful as a lecturer and a writer, he was never promoted to a full professorship at Berlin, nor was he able to secure such a position at any other leading German university. Only in 1914, when his career was almost ended, was he offered a chair in philosophy at the provincial University of Strasbourg. However, World War I disrupted university life there, so that Strasbourg benefited little from Simmel's teaching. Just before the end of the war, Simmel died of cancer.

Simmel's failure as an academic was connected with the nature of his interests, his style of lecturing and writing, and his philosophic position. He had many influential friends—he knew and corresponded with Max Weber, Heinrich Rickert, Edmund Husserl, Adolf von Harnack, and Rainer Maria Rilke—and his applications for openings were always well supported by the testimony of his crowded lecture halls and the success of his many writings, both technical and popular. However, from the strait-laced viewpoint of the German academic hierarchy Simmel was suspect. He seemed to be interested in everything: he wrote books or essays on Rembrandt and Goethe, on Michelangelo, Rodin, and Stefan George; on Florence, Rome, Venice, and the Alps; on the philosophy of money, adventure, love, landscapes, and the actor; on ruins, handles, coquetry, and shame; as well as on the more standard philosophic subjects of ethics, philosophy of history, Kant, Schopenhauer, and Nietzsche, and, at the end of his life, metaphysics. Throughout his career he made contributions of lasting importance to sociology, a subject that had not yet achieved academic respectability. His style, too, was not that expected of a professor of philosophy. It was insightful rather than expository; digressive rather than systematic; witty rather than solemn. Because Simmel's position on any particular point was frequently not easy to see, he was often considered to be a critic whose primary impulse was analytic, if not destructive. By some he was thought to have no philosophic position at all.

Other, more sympathetic, readers of his work called him a *Kulturphilosoph,* primarily on the basis of his preoccupation with the objects of culture. Yet because toward the end of his career Simmel began to sketch a philosophic position having a conception of human life at its center, he is also referred to as a *Lebensphilosoph.* Both of these activities, however, are but two sides of the same lifelong dual concern: to illuminate the objects of culture by showing their relation to human experience and to shed light upon the nature of human life by seeing it in relation to its products.

Simmel conceived of human life as being a process and as being, necessarily, productive. By calling life a process (which he expressed by partially defining life as "more-life"), Simmel sought to convey the view that life has the characteristics of what the Greeks called "becoming": it is continuous and continuously changing; strictly speaking, it can only be lived (experienced), not known. However, this same life produces objects that are not in constant flux, that have form and hence are intelligible. (In virtue of this productiveness of human life, Simmel completed his definition by saying that life is "more-than-life.") These products constitute the realm of culture and include not only works of science, history, and art, but social and political institutions and religious theories and practices as well. These objects stand in a twofold relationship to human life: their genesis lies in human experience and, once in existence, they are independently subject to being experienced in various ways. Simmel's philosophy dealt in detail with both of these relationships.

To account for the existence of the objects of culture, Simmel made use, in his own particular way, of the categories of form and content. He posited a realm of contents (rather like Santayana's realm of essences) as the material that enters into all experience. Contents, however, are not experienced as they are in themselves; they are shaped by the experiencing psyche. Experience (Simmel here followed Kant) is formative; to see how form arises thus requires an understanding of the natural history of experience.

Simmel conceived of a stage in human life in which all needs are instantly satisfied, in which there is no gap between desire and fulfillment. Such a stage of life would be prior to experience and hence prior to any differentiation of subject and object. In that stage there would be neither self nor sugar but only sweetness. However, the world is clearly not so organized that life could actually be lived in this way, and in the gap between need and fulfillment both experience and form are born. In becoming conscious, we distinguish between ourselves as subject and that which we experience as objects.

Experience, however, is not all of a piece: we experience in different modes. It is one thing to know an object, another to appreciate it as beautiful, and still another to revere it as an object of worship. In Simmel's view, the *contents* experienced in each of the three cases may be the same, although they are not the same *in* experience. The *objects* of the three experiences differ in that the contents are given shape—are objectified—by means of three different ways of experiencing. The same contents differ in form.

For the most part, men act to fulfill their needs. Their experience gives shape to contents only to the extent to which the immediate requirements of a situation demand it. In the scholastic language Simmel sometimes adopted, both the *terminus a quo* (the origin) and the *terminus ad quem* (the goal) of the objects produced by ordinary experience—of whatever mode—remain within the biography of the individual producing them. As a result of this subservience to the needs of individuals, form in ordinary experience is not pure, and the objects that are formed in this way are not yet properly the objects of culture. As long as life sets the goals of action (characteristic of the phase of life Simmel called teleological or pragmatic), knowledge is tentative and limited—not yet science; art is homespun and primitive—not yet fully aesthetic; religion is simple and sporadic—not yet embodied in a theology and in institutions. The form is proto-form and the objects are proto-culture.

However, the bonds of the teleology of life can be broken. The *terminus ad quem* of men's actions need not reside within their lives: they can act for the sake of a form, a type of action Simmel called free action. Instead of knowing for the sake of acting, some men act in order to know; instead of seeing for the sake of living, some men—artists—live in order to see. In acting for the sake of a form, experience in the relevant form is refined; the structure inchoate in ordinary experience is made explicit and worked out. Form proper is born and the objects of culture are produced.

There are many kinds of form; there is and can be no definitive list. Knowledge, art, religion, value, and philosophy are among the important forms (or "world forms," as Simmel called them) by means of which men have shaped the realm of contents. Reality, too, is only one such form and enjoys no privileged status; the objects of reality constitute the world of practice—those objects which we perceive and manipulate in our daily lives. There are other forms and other worlds, however; one of the tasks of the philosopher is to distinguish and analyze them.

Human life is not self-sufficient; it needs things outside itself to exist and to continue to exist. The objects life forms first come into being to meet its needs; but, because they are objects, they continue to exist independently of life and to make their demands upon the race that has produced them. Men work out the forms implicit in the various modes of ordinary experience; they become artists, historians, philosophers, and scientists. But once works of art, history, philosophy, or science exist, they make a second demand upon men: they are the objects by whose assimilation men become cultivated. Here Simmel saw a source of inevitable conflict. Men differ from each other, and the way in which each person can fulfill himself is peculiar to him. Thus, to fulfill himself each person must utilize a different selection of already existing objects of culture. However, not every road, not just any selection, leads to the assimilation of these objects. To properly understand the objects an individual requires in order to become cultivated, he may need to learn to apprehend a vast number of other objects not so required. In order to serve life, *his* life, an individual may have to make his own needs subservient to those of forms. This is the tragedy of culture.

In his philosophic position Simmel attempted to do

justice to the antitheses that have occupied philosophers since the pre-Socratics. Life as a process is the pole of flux and becoming; it can be lived, but not known. Form is stable and has structure; it is the pole of being and is intelligible. Life is one; experience in all modes is the experience of the same subject. Forms and worlds are many; they are severed from the life that produced them and take on existence independent of it. Neither Being nor Becoming, neither the One nor the Many, holds exclusive sway. The tension between the poles of these antitheses is a permanent feature of the world.

This position underlies the greatest part of Simmel's work. His writings in *Kulturphilosophie* are explorations into the nature of different forms and of different works, whether of philosophy or of art. They are investigations into the relationships between the lives and works of men like Rembrandt and Goethe. In sum, his essays in the philosophy of culture are a series of applications of his philosophy of life.

Bibliography

IMPORTANT WORKS BY SIMMEL

Die Probleme der Geschichtsphilosophie. Eine erkenntnistheoretische Studie. Leipzig, 1892; 2d ed. (completely revised), 1905.
Einleitung in die Moralwissenschaft. Eine Kritik der ethischen Grundbegriffe, 2 vols. Berlin, 1892–1893.
Philosophie des Geldes. Leipzig, 1900.
Kant. Sechzehn Vorlesungen gehalten an der Berliner Universität. Leipzig, 1903.
Die Religion. Frankfurt am Main, 1906. Translated by Curt Rosenthal as *Sociology of Religion.* New York, 1959.
Soziologie. Untersuchungen über die Formen der Vergesellschaftung. Leipzig, 1908. Partly translated, with other essays, by Kurt H. Wolff in *The Sociology of Georg Simmel.* Glencoe, Ill., 1950.

COLLECTIONS OF ESSAYS BY SIMMEL

Philosophische Kultur. Gesammelte Essays. Leipzig, 1911.
Zur Philosophie der Kunst. Philosophische und kunstphilosophische Aufsätze, Gertrud Simmel, ed. Potsdam, 1922.
Fragmente und Aufsätze aus dem Nachlass und Veröffentlichungen der letzten Jahre, Gertrud Kantorowicz, ed. Munich, 1923.
Brücke und Tür. Essays des Philosophen zur Geschichte, Religion, Kunst und Gesellschaft, Michael Landmann and Margarete Susman, eds. Stuttgart, 1957.

WORKS ON SIMMEL'S PHILOSOPHY

Aron, Raymond, *Essai sur la théorie de l'histoire dans l'Allemagne.* Paris, 1938. Includes a discussion of Simmel's philosophy of history.
Gassen, Kurt, "Georg-Simmel-Bibliographie," in Kurt Gassen and Michael Landmann, eds., *Buch des Dankes an Georg Simmel.* Berlin, 1958. Excellent bibliography.
Jankélévitch, Vladimir, "Georg Simmel, philosophe de la vie." *Revue de métaphysique et de morale,* Vol. 32 (1925), 213–257, 373–386.
Mandelbaum, Maurice, *The Problem of Historical Knowledge: An Answer to Relativism.* New York, 1938. Includes a discussion of Simmel's philosophy of history.
Weingartner, Rudolph H., *Experience and Culture: The Philosophy of Georg Simmel.* Middletown, Conn., 1962.
Wolff, Kurt H., ed., *Georg Simmel, 1858–1918. A Collection of Essays with Translations and a Bibliography.* Columbus, Ohio, 1959.

RUDOLPH H. WEINGARTNER

SIMON, RICHARD (1638–1712), French Biblical scholar. Born in Dieppe, he studied with the Oratorians and the Jesuits and at the Sorbonne, specializing in Hebrew and Near Eastern studies. Before being ordained a priest in 1670, he taught philosophy at an Oratorian college. He soon became one of the foremost experts in Hebrew, Judaism, and Eastern Church history. Influenced by Spinoza's critique of the Bible and by the theory of his friend and fellow Oratorian, Isaac La Peyrère, that there were men before Adam, Simon began developing his views about the Bible and church doctrine. His first published work, a defense of the Jews of Metz (1670), attacked Christian anti-Semitism. It was followed by a study of the Eastern Church, another of Jewish ceremonies and customs, and an attack on the monks of Fécamp. His most important and revolutionary work, *Histoire critique du vieux testament,* was printed in 1678. Bossuet caused it to be banned immediately, and almost all copies were destroyed. A few reached England, and the work was published in French with an English translation by Henry Dickinson (1682). The scandal forced Simon to leave the Oratory and become a simple priest. Thereafter he argued with various Protestant and Catholic thinkers and wrote many works on the history of religion and on the Bible, which culminated in his translation of the New Testament (Trévoux, 1702). Bossuet caused this work to be banned also.

Simon's revolutionary contention was that no original text of the Bible exists, that the texts we possess have developed and have been altered through the ages, and that it is therefore necessary to apply the method of critical evaluation to Biblical materials to establish the most accurate human form of the revelation. This method involves philology, textual study, historical researches, and comparative studies. Protestants saw that Simon's claim that there is no perfect copy of Scripture fundamentally challenged their position that truth is found only by examining the Bible. Catholics feared that he was undermining all bases of Judaeo-Christianity by raising problems about all its documents and traditions. Simon contended that he was merely trying to clarify religious knowledge by showing its foundations and development and the need for a tradition to interpret and understand it.

Whether intentional or not, Simon's method launched the whole enterprise of Biblical higher criticism, which was often directed toward undermining confidence in the uniqueness and ultimate truth of the Judaeo-Christian revelation.

Additional Works by Simon

Histoire critique du vieux testament. Paris, 1678. 2d ed., Amsterdam, 1680. Translated by Henry Dickinson as *A Critical History of the Old Testament.* London, 1682.
Lettres choisies de M. Simon, 4 vols. Amsterdam, 1730.

Works on Simon

Bredvold, Louis I., *The Intellectual Milieu of John Dryden.* Ann Arbor, Mich., 1956. Ch. 4.
Hazard, Paul, *La Crise de la conscience européene,* 2 vols. Paris, 1935. Translated by J. Lewis May as *The European Mind 1680–1715.* London, 1964. Part II, Ch. 3.
Steinmann, Jean, *Richard Simon et les origines de l'exégèse biblique.* Paris, 1959.

RICHARD H. POPKIN

SIMON MAGUS, the earliest Gnostic leader known to us, was a native of the Samaritan village of Gitta. He is first mentioned in Acts (8.4–8.25), where he appears as a wonder-worker who had gained a considerable following in Samaria and who sought to augment his stock in trade by purchasing the power of conferring the Holy Spirit from the apostles. The identity of the Simon of the book of Acts and the founder of the Gnostic sect has been questioned, but Irenaeus, among others, has no doubt of it. According to Hippolytus, Simon died in Rome when he failed, in an abortive attempt at a miracle, to rise from the pit in which he had been buried alive. In the pseudo-Clementine literature Simon serves as the target for veiled Jewish–Christian attacks on Paul and Marcion. According to Origen, in his time the Simonians numbered only thirty, but Eusebius, years later, still knew of their existence.

The Simonian theory is of special interest not only as one of the earliest Gnostic systems but also as providing an illustration of the ways in which such systems developed and were modified. Assessment of the evidence is complicated by the meagerness of our sources and by various problems of evaluation and interpretation, but in general we may distinguish three main stages. Simon himself appears to have been a "magician" of the common Hellenistic type, who claimed to be a divine incarnation. His teaching would be not so much Gnostic in the second-century sense (that is, the Gnosticism of the heretical Christian systems) but rather a form of syncretistic gnosis into which he sought to incorporate Christian elements. The accounts of Justin and Irenaeus introduce his companion, the ex-prostitute Helen, whom he declared to be the first conception (*Ennoia*) of his mind, emanating from him like Athena from the head of Zeus. A notable feature here is the blending of Biblical elements with elements from Homer and Greek mythology.

Descending to the lower regions, Ennoia generated the angels and powers by whom this world was made but was then detained by them and compelled to suffer a round of incarnations (thus she is, *inter alia,* Helen of Troy) until Simon himself came to redeem her. The problem here is to know how much can be credited to Simon himself and how much to reflection among his followers.

A third and more philosophical stage is represented by the "Great Affirmation" preserved by Hippolytus, which probably has nothing to do with the original Simon but may be the work of later disciples attributed, as was often the case, to the master himself. Here the primal ground of being is fire, from which emanate three pairs of "roots," or Powers, which are the origin of all existence: Mind and Thought, Voice and Name, Reason and Desire (text in W. Völker, *Quellen zur Geschichte des christlichen Gnosis,* Tübingen, 1932, pp. 3 ff.). In this scheme, elements from Greek philosophy (Heraclitus, Plato, Aristotle) are blended with Biblical and Homeric elements into a thoroughly Gnostic system. It is of interest to note that Simonianism provides one of the sources of the later Faust legend.

Bibliography

GENERAL WORKS

Grant, R. M., *Gnosticism and Early Christianity*. New York, 1959. Pp. 70 ff.

Jonas, Hans, *The Gnostic Religion*. Boston, 1958. Pp. 103 ff.

Leisegang, H., *Die Gnosis*. Stuttgart, 1955. Pp. 60 ff.

Wilson, R. McL., *The Gnostic Problem*. London, 1958. Pp. 99 ff.

SPECIALIZED WORKS

Casey, R. P., "Simon Magus," in F. J. F. Jackson and Kirsopp Lake, eds., *The Beginnings of Christianity*, Vol. V. London, 1933. Pp. 151 ff.

Cerfaux, L., *Receuil Cerfaux*, 2 vols. Gembloux, 1954. Vol. I, pp. 191 ff.

Haenchen, E., "Gab es eine vorchristliche Gnosis?" *Zeitschrift für Theologie und Kirche*, Vol. 49 (1952), 316 ff.

Haenchen, E., *Die Apostelgeschichte*. Göttingen, 1959. Pp. 250 ff.

Hall, G. N. L., "Simon Magus," in James Hastings, ed., *Encyclopaedia of Religion and Ethics*. Vol. XI, pp. 514 ff. Deals fairly extensively with the "Great Affirmation."

Headlam, A. C., "Simon Magus," in James Hastings, ed., *Dictionary of the Bible*. Vol. IV, pp. 520 ff. On p. 527 Headlam lists four points in the later Faust legend which point back to the legend of Simon Magus.

Lietzmann, H., "Simon Magus," in August Pauly and Georg Wissowa, eds., *Realencyclopädie der classischen Altertumswissenschaft*, 2d series. Vol. III, Cols. 180 ff.

R. McL. Wilson

SIMPLICITY is a term that enters into philosophic discourse in many ways. It may refer to simple (as opposed to compound) ideas or to simple constituents of the world; it may refer to some simple (as opposed to complex) characteristic of the structure of the world, or of our description of that structure; or it may refer to some formal characteristic of logical systems, or merely to the notation in which we express them. We shall be concerned in this article only with simplicity as ascribed to the natural world and to our descriptions of the world—in other words, with the notion of simplicity in the context of natural science. It is this aspect of simplicity which has recently received serious attention from philosophers.

Simplicity is very frequently said to be a desirable characteristic of the concepts, laws, and theories of natural science. If we ask why this should be so, three different kinds of answer suggest themselves.

Pragmatic convenience. In the absence of any other considerations, pragmatic convenience might well commend itself as sufficient reason for the preference and search for simplicity, but in itself it is a difficult notion to make philosophically precise or even interesting. Convenience is a characteristic which depends greatly on the psychological make-up and circumstances of different people, on the logical and material tools available to them, on the purposes they have in view, and on many other factors. Furthermore, even if it were possible to provide some objective and unique definition of convenience, this would not necessarily be correlated with the acceptability of scientific concepts and theories. True and useful theories are occasionally highly inconvenient. Clearly, other factors are involved here, and some of these factors are concerned with other aspects of simplicity.

Belief that nature is simple. The belief that nature is simple has certainly been held in various forms and at various periods in the history of science; maxims such as "Nature works by the shortest route" and "Nature does nothing in vain" have frequently been influential in the construction of theories. Is there any evidence for the truth of this belief? A cursory glance at the history of science indicates many occasions on which the search for simplicity has been successful, and the choice of the simplest hypothesis in particular situations has been fruitful. But it also indicates other occasions on which simple theoretical systems have broken down and complex theories have been accepted. This much is evident to a merely intuitive understanding of simplicity; and if we ask more precisely what is meant by the doctrine that nature is simple, it must be noted that in the history of science, for any given analysis of the concept (and we shall consider some examples below) there have always been counterexamples, so that the belief in simplicity is not entirely justified as an induction from past experience.

There are other, and more fundamental, objections to regarding belief in the simplicity of nature as an induction. First, it can be argued (as George Schlesinger has done) that the sample of laws we have is not unbiased, for it represents just that aspect of nature which has been found sufficiently simple to be manageable to the human mind, and no conclusion can be drawn from it to the rest of nature. Second, if we try to make an induction from past experience of simplicity to the future, we are involved in a logical circle. S. F. Barker pointed out that the induction is of a kind which involves passing from the statement "All observed *X*'s are *Y*'s" to the statement "All *X*'s are *Y*'s," and the justification of that particular inductive conclusion itself rests on the fact that it is in some sense simpler than any other hypothesis consistent with the same evidence.

Thus, if the doctrine of the simplicity of nature is to be saved, it seems it can only be in the form of some metaphysical faith in an unapparent but perhaps very fundamental simplicity, and while such a belief may function as a spur to research, it cannot be said to be confirmable or refutable by empirical evidence.

Criterion of choice between scientific theories. If it could be shown that nature is simple, this would provide a justification for choosing simple theories. Even if this cannot be shown, however, there may still be reasons, stronger than mere convenience, for preferring simple theories. Of course, there are other criteria for satisfactory theories, some of which may take precedence over simplicity—for example, logical consistency, past confirmation and absence of refutation, coherence with wider domains of theory, intuitive plausibility, and so on. But there may be some choice-situations in which only invocation of a simplicity criterion will give a unique decision. In other words, while other criteria may be necessary for acceptability, it may sometimes be the case that only the addition of simplicity makes the set of criteria sufficient for a unique choice. This is the case, for example, in Hans Reichenbach's theory of inductive posits, and it seems also to lie behind the preference for simple curves which are fitted to data points. Here one out of a potential infinity of curves is chosen, its uniqueness consisting in the fact that in some intuitive mathematical sense it is the simplest.

EXPLICATIONS OF SIMPLICITY

It is apparent from the foregoing discussion that the question of the definition or explication of simplicity is problematical. There are many different senses of the notion, several of which have already been implied. Also, not all these senses are correlated with one another—a concept or theory may be simple in some subjective sense, for example, but its mathematical expression may be highly complex. In order to go further in evaluating simplicity as a characteristic of scientific concepts, we must examine some of its more closely specified senses. We shall find that not many such definitions have been attempted, and that there are serious objections to be brought even against these. The subject is therefore unfortunately not yet in a state which allows us to pursue the more fundamental problems on the basis of any generally accepted explication of various kinds of simplicity.

Objective-logical simplicity. The attempted explications we shall consider can all be classified initially in the category which R. S. Rudner called objective-logical simplicity. That is to say, they concern concepts of simplicity which are nonsubjective and nonpsychological, and which refer to the logical (not merely notational) structure of our descriptions of the world, not directly to simplicity characteristics of the world in itself. There are, first of all, two deceptively simple characterizations of simplicity in this category which can at once be dismissed as inadequate. First, it might be suggested that the simpler of two theories is that which contains fewer nonnecessary postulates. But any postulate set can be reduced to one member by conjunction and, even if this is forbidden by some *ad hoc* device, the same system can often be formulated by means of many different but equivalent postulate sets. Moreover, it is intuitively clear that some single postulates are more simple than others, and the measure of simplicity should take account of this. Again, the simplicity of the consequences of a given postulate set is not necessarily best measured by the simplicity of the set itself.

This brings us to the second preliminary suggestion: that simplicity can be measured by the number of extralogical primitives in the system. This seems to be conformable with Ockham's injunction that entities (individuals, predicates) should not be multiplied unnecessarily. We cannot, however, base a measure of simplicity on the number of individuals presupposed by a system, since this is usually not known and may be infinite; and, as Nelson Goodman has shown in his paper "The Logical Simplicity of Predicates," even the proposal to count predicates will not do just as it stands because the predicate sets of a given system may be transformable in such a way that an equivalent system can be found with a different number of predicates.

The proposal to count extralogical predicates is actually a proposal for the measure of simplicity of a language basis, not of a particular theory or postulate set in that language. It is clear that there are two different concep-

tions of simplicity here, both of which need clarification before the total intuitive notion of simplicity can be explicated. Attempts to define simplicity have so far fallen roughly into two groups, according to which of these two conceptions is in mind. We shall begin by considering three proposals for the definition of simplicity of statements in a given language.

Jeffreys' proposal. Harold Jeffreys' aim is to explain the preference for simple laws in science by showing that a confirmation theory can be developed in which simple laws have the highest prior probability. He therefore has first to define a simplicity ordering of all possible laws. Only a denumerable set of possible laws can be considered, since no nondenumerable set satisfies two of the conditions of such a confirmation theory—namely, that the prior probability of any law must be nonzero and that, if the number of laws is infinite, the prior probabilities form terms of a convergent series whose sum is unity. Jeffreys argues that physics, including quantum physics, does in fact contemplate only a denumerable infinity of possible laws—namely, differential equations of finite order and degree (ignoring the absolute values of their coefficients) and the quantum equations which are systematically formed from these. The problem is therefore reduced to finding a simplicity ordering for differential equations. The details of Jeffreys' suggested ordering vary in different publications, but essentially he proposes that the complexity of a law should be defined as the sum of the absolute values of the integers (degrees and derivative orders) contained in it, together with the number of its freely adjustable parameters. Thus $y^2 = ax^3$ would have complexity 6; $d^2y/dx^2 + 2.345y = 0$, complexity 4; and so on.

Several objections have been made to this method of ordering. Among the most important are the following.

(1) Counterintuitive examples are easily constructed: for example, it is not clear that the second of the two expressions above ought to have the same complexity value as $y = ax^2$, which appears simpler.

(2) Robert Ackermann has objected that the ordering does not take explicit account of simple transcendental functions such as $y = \sin x$; or, if these are supposed to be measured in terms of their differential equations, then such a large number of possible laws would have very low complexity that the measure would become useless in choice situations.

(3) Many laws in science contain in a nontrivial manner parameters which range over the real numbers, but sets of such laws are not denumerable and therefore not accounted for in Jeffreys' ordering.

(4) Limitation to differential equation form unduly restricts the possibilities in physics, let alone the other sciences.

These objections are quite fundamental, and although attempts might be made to overcome some of them, it is not clear that Jeffreys' method can ever yield a satisfactory general explication. Furthermore, even if a simplicity ordering could be produced, the further difficulties involved in Jeffreys' confirmation theory as a whole are such that it is very doubtful whether the preference for simplicity could ever be said to be justified in terms of it.

Popper's proposal. Karl Popper's discussion of simplicity not only proposes an ordering of laws and theories but also suggests a justification of the preference for simplicity in terms of his criterion of falsifiability. Briefly, his argument is as follows: we prefer theories which have greatest content—that is to say, theories which say most about the world, restrict the possibilities in the world to the greatest extent, and are therefore more falsifiable. But the order of falsifiability, he claims, is identical with the order of simplicity. Hence, we are justified in preferring simple theories. The argument leads to exactly the opposite conclusion from that of Jeffreys when the relation between probability and simplicity is considered. For Jeffreys, it is self-evident that we prefer theories which have greatest prior probability, and he therefore seeks to show that these can also be taken to be the simplest. But for Popper falsifiability is all-important and theories with greater content have lower prior probability in all confirmation theories. Popper therefore denies that simplicity is correlated with high probability and seeks to show that it is identical with falsifiability. He exhibits this in two sorts of cases. First, he shows that a simplicity ordering of equations similar to that of Jeffreys is also a falsifiability ordering, since an equation of low degree and order with a small number of parameters requires fewer data points to falsify it if it is false and therefore is more restrictive on the possibilities in the world and is more falsifiable. For example, a straight line represented by $y = ax + b$ can be falsified if false by three points, whereas a circle $x^2 + y^2 = a^2$ cannot be falsified if false by fewer than four points. Hence, the straight line is both simpler and more falsifiable than the circle. Second, if one law is included in another more general law, as for example "All planets move in circles" is included in "All heavenly bodies move in circles," the more general law is both more falsifiable and simpler in the sense that it requires fewer specifications of particular objects. That is, the definition of "heavenly body" is shorter than that of "planet."

Most of the objections that have been made against Jeffreys' simplicity ordering can also be made against Popper's falsifiability ordering. Furthermore, if "number of points required to falsify a suggested law" is taken to define simplicity, counterexamples can be adduced, for the intuitive simplicity of curves is not always correlated with this definition. As for measuring the simplicity of a law by its generality, this can be shown to break down in very elementary cases. For example, given the evidence that all observed X's are Z's, the generalization "All X's and all Y's are Z's" is more falsifiable than "All X's are Z's," which it includes, but "All X's are Z's" is more simple and would generally be adopted as the best hypothesis on the basis of the evidence. As Nelson Goodman pointed out, the amount of content of a theory indicates the theory's power rather than its simplicity, and power and simplicity in intuitive senses are not always correlated. They are not correlated, for example, in cases where two theories have the same content, but one is expressed in more economical language than the other—and such linguistic simplicity is not irrelevant. For example, "The sum of the product of two and three, and the product of three and one, and two, equals twelve" has the same content as "$2 \cdot 3 + (3 + 1) \cdot 2 = 12$" but can hardly be said to be simpler. Nor is it the case, as Goodman's example shows, that the theory with more content is always the more acceptable in scientific practice.

Kemeny's proposal. In the article "Two Measures of Simplicity," John G. Kemeny suggested a logical measure of complexity of a set of statements or theory in terms of the number of ways it could come out true in an n-member universe. Suppose, for example, we are given a universe containing two individuals, a and b, and two extralogical predicates, P and Q, such that each of a and b has either P or not-P, and Q or not-Q. In this universe and this language there are 16 distinct possibilities of predicating the individuals. A "theory" is a set of statements asserting relations between the predicates which limits the total number of possibilities in some way. "All individuals are either P or Q," for example, reduces the possibilities to nine, and "All individuals are P" reduces them to four. According to Kemeny's measure, the complexity of the first theory is greater than that of the second. Kemeny then removed the reference to a particular n-member universe by requiring that a more complex theory is one which comes out true in more ways in any n-member universe where n is sufficiently large.

This definition of complexity shares with Popper's the merit that it suggests a justification for the preference for simplicity (regarded as the inverse of complexity) in terms of the degree of restriction placed on the universe—that is, in terms of a theory's falsifiability. But it is, of course, equally open to the objections that content does not always correlate with our intuitions of simplicity and that content is not always the best measure of acceptability. Kemeny's proposal also suffers from the restriction to a finite world: it cannot, for instance, deal with metrical predicates, and it is not easy to see how it could be applied to realistic choice-problems in science, in most of which an infinity of possibilities is involved.

Goodman's proposal. The first three proposals exhaust the detailed attempts to define simplicity as a measure of statements or theories. As we have seen, there are serious objections both to the suggested explications of simplicity as such and to the consequent attempts to justify on their basis the actual choice-preferences of scientists. These difficulties have in fact led some writers (for example, Mario Bunge and Robert Ackermann) to reject altogether both the possibility and the value of trying to define this notion of inductive simplicity. The fourth definition of simplicity—contributed by Nelson Goodman—differs from the other three in being a measure of the simplicity of linguistic predicate bases, not of statements. Goodman himself said (in "Recent Developments in the Theory of Simplicity") that an adequate explication of economy of bases requires the definition of both simplicity and power.

Goodman's method is essentially a refinement on the proposal merely to count the extralogical predicates in the language basis. Consider a language containing one two-place predicate $R(x,y)$. The predicate R can always be replaced by two one-place predicates, $P(x)$ and $Q(x)$ —where P is "is a member of the domain of R," and Q is "is a member of the converse domain of R." It is not the case, however, that two one-place predicates can always be replaced by one two-place predicate, except under special conditions of symmetry or self-completeness (the condition that there are pairs of individuals always associated by *R*). Goodman's general definition of complexity depends on the principle that if every set of predicates of one kind is replaceable by some set of predicates of another kind, then the first kind cannot be more complex than the second—in other words, a set of predicates which is always replaceable is in general simpler than that by which it is replaced. The definition has been worked out in considerable axiomatic detail, but it only takes account of the logical relations between predicates of a language, and not of particular nonlogical relations between predicates such as are asserted by theories. It is therefore difficult to see how it can be generally applicable to the choice between different theories on the basis of their simplicity, since alternative theories may be expressed in the same language having the same logical simplicity.

It must finally be concluded that, although various senses of simplicity are important criteria for scientific theories, the general problem of the explication of kinds of simplicity and of the relation between simplicity and the acceptability of scientific theories still calls for a great deal more investigation.

Bibliography

Ackermann, Robert, "Inductive Simplicity." *Philosophy of Science,* Vol. 28 (1961), 152–161.

Ackermann, Robert, "A Neglected Proposal Concerning Simplicity." *Philosophy of Science,* Vol. 30 (1963), 228–235.

Barker, S. F., *Induction and Hypothesis.* New York, 1957. Chs. 5 and 9.

Barker, S. F., "On Simplicity in Empirical Hypotheses." *Philosophy of Science,* Vol. 28 (1961), 162–171.

Barker, S. F., "The Role of Simplicity in Explanation," in H. Feigl and G. Maxwell, eds., *Current Issues in the Philosophy of Science.* New York, 1961. P. 265.

Bunge, Mario, "The Weight of Simplicity in the Construction and Assaying of Scientific Theories." *Philosophy of Science,* Vol. 28 (1961), 120–149.

Bunge, Mario, "The Complexity of Simplicity." *Journal of Philosophy,* Vol. 59 (1962), 113–135.

Bunge, Mario, *The Myth of Simplicity.* Englewood Cliffs. N.J., 1963.

Caws, Peter, "Science, Computers and the Complexity of Nature." *Philosophy of Science,* Vol. 30 (1963), 158–164. A discussion of optimum scientific complexity relative to the complexity of nature.

Goodman, Nelson, "On the Simplicity of Ideas." *Journal of Symbolic Logic,* Vol. 8 (1943), 107–121.

Goodman, Nelson, "An Improvement in the Theory of Simplicity." *Journal of Symbolic Logic,* Vol. 14 (1949), 228–229.

Goodman, Nelson, "The Logical Simplicity of Predicates." *Journal of Symbolic Logic,* Vol. 14 (1949), 32–41.

Goodman, Nelson, "New Notes on Simplicity." *Journal of Symbolic Logic,* Vol. 17 (1952), 189–191.

Goodman, Nelson, "Axiomatic Measurement of Simplicity." *Journal of Philosophy,* Vol. 52 (1955), 709–722.

Goodman, Nelson, "The Test of Simplicity." *Science,* Vol. 128 (1958), 1064–1069.

Goodman, Nelson, "Recent Developments in the Theory of Simplicity." *Philosophy and Phenomenological Research,* Vol. 19 (1959), 429–446.

Goodman, Nelson, "Safety, Strength, Simplicity." *Philosophy of Science,* Vol. 28 (1961), 150–151.

Hillman, D. J., "The Measurement of Simplicity." *Philosophy of Science,* Vol. 29 (1962), 225–252. A revised formulation of Goodman's method.

Jeffreys, Harold, *Scientific Inference,* 2d ed. Cambridge, 1957.

Jeffreys, Harold, *Theory of Probability,* 2d ed. Oxford, 1961.

Jeffreys, Harold, and Wrinch, D., "On Certain Fundamental Principles of Scientific Inquiry." *Philosophical Magazine,* Vol. 42 (1921), 369–390.

Kemeny, J. G., "A Logical Measure Function." *Journal of Symbolic Logic,* Vol. 18 (1953), 289–308.

Kemeny, J. G., "The Use of Simplicity in Induction." *Philosophical Review,* Vol. 62 (1953), 391–408.

Kemeny, J. G., "Two Measures of Simplicity." *Journal of Philosophy,* Vol. 52 (1955), 722–733.

Popper, K. R., *The Logic of Scientific Discovery.* London, 1959. Ch. 7 and Appendix *viii.

Post, H. R., "Simplicity in Scientific Theories." *British Journal for the Philosophy of Science,* Vol. 11 (1960), 32–41. Linguistic simplicity as optimum coding.

Post, H. R., "A Criticism of Popper's Theory of Simplicity." *British Journal for the Philosophy of Science,* Vol. 12 (1961), 328–331.

Reichenbach, Hans, *Theory of Probability.* Berkeley, 1949.

Rudner, R. S., "An Introduction to Simplicity." *Philosophy of Science,* Vol. 28 (1961), 109–119. Introduction to the symposium of articles by Ackermann, Barker, Bunge, and Goodman.

Schlesinger, George, *Method in the Physical Sciences.* London, 1963. Ch. 1.

Suppes, Patrick, "Nelson Goodman on the Concept of Logical Simplicity." *Philosophy of Science,* Vol. 23 (1956), 153–159.

Svenonius, Lars, "Definability and Simplicity." *Journal of Symbolic Logic,* Vol. 20 (1955), 235–250. On the simplicity of predicate bases.

MARY HESSE

SIMPLICIUS, sixth-century Neoplatonist and commentator on Aristotle, studied in Alexandria under Ammonius and in Athens under Damascius. The School at Athens was closed in 529, and Simplicius withdrew to Persia. When he returned, his paganism barred him from lecturing. His surviving commentaries (on Aristotle's *Categories, Physics, De Caelo,* and *De Anima*) are both more learned and more polemic than would have been suitable for students. His chief importance in the history of philosophy probably lies in his being a source of our knowledge of other ancient philosophers, notably the pre-Socratics.

Simplicius takes for granted the metaphysics of Neoplatonism as it had been systematized in the Athenian School of the fifth century. He accepts the usual three hypostases but follows Iamblichus and Damascius in making much of the distinction between each hypostasis and, indeed, between each self-subsistent reality as it is undifferentiated (remaining in the One) and as it is differentiated or pluralized (proceeding). (See, for example, *In De Caelo,* pp. 93–94, Heiberg.) It is one of the concepts or devices by which he carries out the task that dominates his work, to reconcile Plato and Aristotle. They appear to disagree, for instance, about motion: a self-moving or an unmoved mover, the motion or immobility of reason, and so on. According to Simplicius, Plato is usually writing of the primary kind of motion, and Aristotle of the secondary, or proceeding, kind. Simplicius' interpretation of the *De Anima* is based on that of Iamblichus, which took it as a valid description of the embodied soul, to be supplemented by a metaphysical account of the "separate" intellect.

In natural philosophy, Simplicius, like other Neoplatonists, is more ready to criticize Aristotle, so that the result is more often a compromise, rather than a reconciliation, with Plato. Aristotelian matter had long been identified with Plato's not-being; Simplicius has little to add here to Plotinus and Porphyry. But the problems of space, motion, place, and allied concepts had repeatedly been examined and were already beginning to suggest relational definitions foreign to Aristotle's physics. In an excursus on the notion of place (*In Physica,* Vol. XI, pp. 601–645, Diels) Simplicius describes some interesting and original views of Damascius, which he reconciles with Aristotle only by implying, implausibly, that the two are complementary. A similar but less scientific treatment of time as a kind of metaphysical cause of the existence of motion and things in motion depends on the distinction already referred to between remaining in the One and proceeding; the latter aspect accounts for flowing time, which is the measure of succession.

Simplicius also wrote an extant commentary on the Stoic Epictetus' *Enchiridion* (or handbook of ethics). In moral philosophy the Neoplatonists borrowed much from Stoicism, and while well expressed, most of the commentary is commonplace for the period. However, it does contain a semipopular presentation of Neoplatonic theology or metaphysics (pp. 95–101, Dübner), and this has been claimed as a survival of Alexandrian Platonism in which (as in the Middle Academy) the highest hypostasis is not the One, but Intellect. The text is not unambiguous but dubiously supports the claim.

Bibliography

Diels, Hermann, ed., *Simplicius in Physicorum, Libros I–IV,* in *Commentaria in Aristotelem Graeca,* Vol. XI. Berlin, 1882.

Diels, Hermann, ed., *Simplicius in Physicorum, Libros V–VIII,* in *Commentaria in Aristotelem Graeca,* Vol. X. Berlin, 1895.

Dübner, F., ed., *Commentarius in Epicteti Enchiridion,* in *Theophrasti Characteres.* Paris, 1877.

Heiberg, J. L., ed., *Simplicius in de Caelo,* in *Commentaria in Aristotelem Graeca,* Vol. VII. Berlin, 1894.

Jammer, Max, *Concepts of Space.* Cambridge, Mass., 1954.

Praechter, Karl, "Simplicius," in August Pauly and Georg Wissowa, eds., *Realencyclopädie der klassischen Altertumswissenschaft,* Series 2, Vol. V. Stuttgart, 1927.

Sambursky, S., *Physical World of Late Antiquity.* London, 1962.

A. C. LLOYD

SKEPTICISM, as a critical philosophical attitude, questions the reliability of the knowledge claims made by philosophers and others. Originally the Greek term *skeptikos* meant "inquirers." Philosophical skeptics have been engaged in inquiry into alleged human achievements in different fields to see if any knowledge has been or could be gained by them. They have questioned whether any necessary or indubitable information can actually be gained about the real nature of things. Skeptics have organized their questioning into systematic sets of arguments aimed at raising doubts. Extreme skepticism questions all knowledge claims that go beyond immediate experience, except perhaps those of logic and mathematics. A limited or mitigated skepticism in different degrees questions particular types of knowledge claims made by theologians, metaphysicians, scientists, or mathematicians which go beyond experience, but it admits some limited probabilistic kinds of knowledge. Some skeptics have held that no knowledge beyond immediate experience is possible, while others have doubted whether even this much could definitely be known. The arguments advanced by skeptics from Greek times onward, and the use to which these arguments have been put, have helped to shape both the problems dealt with by the major Western philosophers and the solutions they have offered.

HISTORY OF SKEPTICISM

Skeptical tendencies appear in some pre-Socratic views. The metaphysical theory of Heraclitus that everything is in flux and that one can't step twice into the same river was taken as indicating human inability to discover any fixed, immutable truth about reality. The purported development of this theory by Cratylus to the view that since everything is changing, one can't step once into the same river, because both that river and oneself are changing, leads to a broader skepticism. Cratylus apparently became convinced that communication was impossible because, since the speaker, the auditor, and the words were changing, whatever meaning might have been intended by the words would be altered by the time they were heard. Therefore, Cratylus is supposed to have refused to discuss anything and only to have wiggled his finger when somebody said something, to indicate that he had heard something but that it would be pointless to reply, since everything was changing.

Xenophanes questioned the existence of any criterion of true knowledge in his observation that if, by chance, a man came across the truth, he would be unable to distinguish it from error.

More serious skeptical doubts were raised by some of the Sophists. Gorgias is reported to have doubted whether anything exists, and to have offered an argument that if anything did happen to exist, we could not know it; and if we did know it, we could not communicate it.

The relativism involved in the famous saying of the great Sophist Protagoras, "Man is the measure of all things," indicates another skeptical tendency. Plato's discussion of Protagoras' view shows that it was taken as a denial that there is absolutely true knowledge, and that each man's views are equally valid versions of what is going on. No further standards of judgment exist.

Academic skepticism. Although Pyrrho, from whom the Pyrrhonians get their name, lived before the major Academic skeptics, skepticism as a philosophical methodology was first formulated by the leaders of Plato's Academy in the third century B.C. Beginning with Arcesilaus (c. 315–c. 240 B.C.), the Academics rejected Plato's metaphysical and mystical doctrines. Instead they concentrated on what they thought was involved in the Socratic remark "All that I know is that I know nothing," and on the questioning method and tactics of Socrates as portrayed in the Platonic dialogues. Although we do not possess the writings of Arcesilaus, or of the reputed greatest member of the school, Carneades (c. 213–128 B.C.), later writings by Cicero, Sextus Empiricus, and Diogenes Laërtius give a fairly good idea of the kinds of arguments they developed. The attack of Arcesilaus was directed primarily against the

Stoics, and that of Carneades against both the Epicureans and Stoics. The Stoics had claimed that there were some perceptions which could not possibly be false either per se or as signs of the true nature of reality. Arcesilaus and Carneades pointed out that there was no criterion for distinguishing a perception of this kind from one that appeared to be so, or was thought to be so. Carneades insisted that there were no intrinsic marks or signs which these so-called real perceptions possessed and which illusory ones did not, and that no justifiable criterion existed for separating one type from the other. Therefore, he contended, we must suspend judgment about whether reliable representations of objects actually exist. This state of affairs, the Academics maintained, showed that no assertions about what is going on beyond our immediate experience are certain. The best data that we can acquire, they said, only tell us what is reasonable or probable, but not what is true. Carneades seems to have developed a verification theory and a probabilistic view resembling those of twentieth-century pragmatists and positivists. The view attributed to Carneades thus constituted a kind of mitigated skepticism.

The Academic skeptics dominated the Platonic Academy until the first century B.C., when, during the period that Cicero studied there, it was taken over by the eclectic philosophers Philo of Larissa and Antiochus of Ascalon. Cicero's *De Academica* and *De Natura Deorum* describe both the traditional skeptical views and those of the newer teachers. St. Augustine's *Contra Academicos* was an attempt to answer the skepticism described by Cicero.

The Pyrrhonian school. In the Roman period, the main center of skeptical activity shifted from the Academy to the Pyrrhonian school, probably connected with the methodic school of medicine at Alexandria. The Pyrrhonians attributed their origins to the views of Pyrrho of Elis (c. 360–c. 270 B.C.). Pyrrho left no writings but was, rather, the model of the skeptical way of life. The stories about him indicate that he tried to avoid committing himself to doctrines about the nature of reality while living according to appearances and attempting to attain happiness, or at least peace of mind. His student Timon (c. 320–c. 230 B.C.) attacked a great many views, including those of the Academic skeptics, mainly by satire while developing a practical, moral way of living according to human necessities without making any grandiose commitments or claims.

Pyrrhonism, as a theoretical formulation of skepticism rather than merely an emulation of Pyrrho, is supposed to have begun with Aenesidemus, who probably taught in Alexandria in the first century B.C. He is reported to have attacked both the Academics and the dogmatic philosophers; the Academics because they were sure that what is probable and what is improbable are distinguishable, and the dogmatic philosophers because they thought they had discovered the truth. Aenesidemus and his successors, using the achievements of the Academics, developed "tropes," or ways of carrying on skeptical argumentation in order to produce *epoche* (suspension of judgment) about matters dealing with what is nonevident. The fullest presentation of this type of skepticism that we possess is that of Sextus Empiricus (second or third century), one of the last Pyrrhonian teachers. In his *Pyrrhoniarum Hypotyposes* and *Adversus Mathematicos*, Sextus set forth the Pyr-

rhonian tropes in groupings of ten, eight, five, and two, each set indicating why one should suspend judgment about all claims to knowledge extending beyond immediate experience. The most famous of these sets was the ten tropes (attributed to Aenesidemus). The first four of these ten deal with contradictions involved in trying to perceive the real nature of things. Animals perceive things differently; different men perceive things differently; man's senses perceive the same object in various ways; and man's circumstances also seem to alter what he perceives. Have we any way of being sure that man, and not some other animal, perceives the world correctly? And have we any way of telling which men, or which of our senses, or under what circumstances we are able to, perceive the true nature of things? Others of the ten tropes suggest that the object may be difficult or impossible to perceive correctly because it or our perceiving organs change or are affected by circumstances, frequency of occurrence, or customs of the society in which the observations take place.

In further analyses, Sextus brought forth Pyrrhonian arguments to cast doubt on any claims by dogmatic philosophers to have gained knowledge of the naturally nonevident world (that is, of any reality that is not now being, and cannot at some time be, observed). Any criterion, such as logical inference or presumed causal connection, used to judge what is naturally nonevident can be challenged by asking if the criterion itself is evident. The fact that there are disputes about everything that is not observable shows that it is not obvious what criterion should be adopted. The dogmatist is faced either with begging the question by using a questionable criterion to establish the standard of what is true, or with an infinite regress involving finding a criterion for judging his criterion, and a criterion for this, and so on. In attacking the various forms of the dogmatic claim to know what is nonevident, Sextus presented fully developed or in embryo almost all of the arguments to appear later in the history of skepticism. Sextus also presented a battery of Pyrrhonian arguments against the Stoic contention that there are indicative signs in experience that indubitably reveal what is the case beyond experience.

The point in all this argumentation, Sextus stated, was to lead mankind to the Pyrrhonian goal of *ataraxia* (unperturbedness). As long as people try to judge beyond appearances and to gain knowledge in the dogmatist's sense, they will be frustrated and worried. By setting forth the evidence pro and con, without even judging if it is good or satisfactory evidence, they will be led to suspension of judgment and peace of mind, and thereby will be cured of the dogmatist's disease, rashness.

Sextus reported (he carefully avoided saying that he asserted anything) that the Pyrrhonians did not hold to the negative dogmatic conclusions of the Academics, in that they did not deny that knowledge of the nonevident was possible. Instead, they suspended judgment on the question. In response to opponents who tried to portray the Pyrrhonian attitude as a definite view, Sextus said that it was like a purge that eliminates everything, including itself.

The Pyrrhonians replied to the charge that their attitude would make living impossible by stating that they were not in any way doubting the world of appearances, and that one could live peacefully and undogmatically in that world by following natural inclinations (without judging that they were right or wrong) and experience and what it suggests, in terms of patterns (what the Pyrrhonians called "suggestive signs") and the laws and customs of society.

The Pyrrhonian movement continued until the third century as both a philosophical and a medical one (medical skeptics cast doubt both on the claim that diseases have causes and on its denial). It questioned theories in physics, logic, mathematics, astrology, grammar, and other disciplines. The movement died out in the late Hellenistic period and had little influence thereafter as religious views became predominant.

The medieval period. As the Roman Empire became Christianized, the major remaining indication of skeptical influence was St. Augustine's discussion of Academic skepticism. His *Contra Academicos* was the last major attempt before the Renaissance to come to grips with skeptical questions in epistemology. Augustine was strongly attracted to Cicero's views and to the Platonism of the Middle Academy. Part of the resolution of his personal religious crisis was his realization, presented in *Contra Academicos* and other early writings, that skepticism can be completely overcome only by revelation. From this standpoint philosophy becomes faith seeking understanding.

In the Christian Middle Ages it was mainly Augustine's version of, and his answer to, skepticism that was discussed. Two medieval Latin translations of Sextus exist, one from the late thirteenth century and the other at least a century later, but there is no evidence that they were at all widely read or taken seriously.

In the Islamic world, where there was more direct access to classical writings, there are more indications of skeptical currents, especially among the more extreme antirational Spanish Muslim and Jewish theologians. The arguments of al-Ghazālī and Yehuda Halevi against the possibility of rational scientific and theological knowledge about the real nature of the universe, and especially against the claims of the Aristotelians of the period, are often very similar to classical Academic and Pyrrhonian attacks. (And al-Ghazālī's skeptical rejection of rational knowledge of necessary connections in the world is very close to that of Malebranche and Hume.) However, the use made of skepticism by Arabic and Jewish authors was radically different from that of the classical writers. Al-Ghazālī and Yehuda Halevi were concerned to bring men to a mystical and nonrational appreciation of religious truths by making them see the intellectual bankruptcy of the rational theologies then current. Al-Ghazālī's great treatise that led to the end of the golden age of Islamic philosophy and science was entitled *Autodestruction of the Philosophers.* (This same type of view reappeared in the late Christian Middle Ages in Nicholas of Cusa's theory of learned ignorance.)

Renaissance and Reformation. The rediscovery of the classical skeptical texts during the Renaissance vitally affected the development of modern thought. The writings of Sextus and Cicero's *De Academica* began to arouse interest again. Present evidence indicates that the Greek text of Sextus, probably brought to Europe from Constantinople, was known in manuscript at least as early as 1441,

and that various humanistic scholars used materials from Sextus. In 1562 Henri Estienne (Stephanus) published at Paris a Latin translation of the *Pyrrhoniarum Hypotyposes,* and in 1569 Gentian Hervet published a Latin translation of *Adversus Mathematicos* at Antwerp. The Greek texts were first printed at Cologne, Paris, and Geneva in 1621. There is also indication that some of Sextus' works were translated into English in the 1590s, but this translation has not been found. A fragment from Sextus was later published as "The Skepticke," attributed to Sir Walter Raleigh. A complete English translation of the *Hypotyposes* appeared in Thomas Stanley's *History of Philosophy* (4 vols., London, 1655–1662). A partial French translation was done by Samuel Sorbière in the 1630s, but it was not published. Another unpublished French translation from the seventeenth century was discovered in a collection of manuscripts acquired by the University of California at Los Angeles. The first complete French translation, by Claude Huart, did not appear until 1725.

Religious controversy. At first Renaissance interest in both Academic and Pyrrhonian views appeared principally in theological discussions. Erasmus, in *In Praise of Folly,* after ridiculing various Scholastics, remarked that he preferred the Academics because they were "the least surly of the philosophers." Later, in his *De Libero Arbitrio* (Basel, 1524), attacking Luther's view, Erasmus contended that the problem of free will was too complex for humans to comprehend, and Scripture too difficult to interpret on these matters. Therefore, he recommended the skeptical attitude of suspension of judgment, along with acceptance of the church's view. Luther furiously attacked this skeptical defense of Catholicism in his *De Servo Arbitrio* (Wittenberg, 1525) and insisted that a Christian cannot be a skeptic; that he must be certain, not dubious, since salvation is at stake. Erasmus could remain a genial doubter if he wished, but Luther warned him that Judgment Day was to follow, and "Spiritus sanctus non est Scepticus."

In the dispute between Erasmus and Luther a fundamental problem that was to awaken a vital concern with skepticism was raised, the problem of determining the criterion of ultimate religious knowledge. At Leipzig, Luther had challenged the church's criterion: that of the pope, the councils, and tradition. At the Diet of Worms he had proposed a subjective, private one instead, that of the dictates of the Holy Spirit to each man's own conscience. The ensuing battle to justify either the church's or the reformers' criterion made this classical skeptical problem a living issue. The recently rediscovered texts of Sextus, Cicero, and others played a major role in this battle. A skeptical crisis developed which modern philosophy would seek to resolve. Erasmus' solution, that of suspending judgment and accepting the Catholic view on faith or tradition, was later developed into what is sometimes called Christian Pyrrhonism.

The new skepticism. At the outset of the sixteenth century Gian Francesco Pico della Mirandola (the nephew of the famous humanist) and Henricus Cornelius Agrippa von Nettesheim used the skeptical arguments to attack the Scholastics, the new Renaissance scientists, the alchemists, the cabalists, and others and, by undermining all confidence in man's alleged rational achievements, to lead him to true religion. Renaissance changes in man's conception of the cosmos further intensified the emerging skeptical crisis. Voyages of exploration and new astronomical theories and discoveries destroyed many of the medieval beliefs about the nature and content of the cosmos. Reports of explorers concerning the superior moral character of savages cast doubt on previously accepted moral theories. The rediscovery of classical theories made many thinkers dubious about scholastic methods and conclusions. A wide spectrum of creative theories emanating from Iberia—cabalism, mysticism, and other doctrines—added to the unsettling ferment. Servetus and Vesalius revolutionized views about anatomy. Paracelsus challenged accepted medical theories and practices. The revival of interest in Hebrew, in Jewish views, and in early and deviant Christian theories raised still further problems. Most crucial of all, almost every accepted theological doctrine was now questioned, and a wide variety of other possibilities were offered.

In this atmosphere a series of new skeptical writings appeared. Some plainly and simply urged, because of the bankruptcy of human reason, acceptance of the wise conclusion of the ancient skeptics as well as acceptance of traditional religion. Pedro Valencia's *Academica* (Antwerp, 1596) offered a survey of ancient skepticism, claiming it would make one realize that the Greek philosophers had not found the truth, and that one should turn away from the philosophers to God and recognize that Jesus is the only sage.

Hervet. Gentian Hervet, secretary to the Cardinal of Lorraine and a veteran of the Council of Trent, pointed out in the preface to his Latin translation of Sextus that the importance of this ancient work was its demonstration that human reason is incapable of opposing or resisting the arguments that can be raised against it. God's revelation is our only source of certainty. Therefore, he contended, the arguments of Sextus provided a powerful answer to Calvinism. The Calvinists claimed to have a new theory about God. By showing that all human claims to knowledge are dubious, Hervet contended that those of Calvin are dubious as well. When man realized the vanity of all attempts to comprehend the universe, he would become humble and recognize that God can be known only by faith, not by the reasoning of the reformers. Hervet's employment of Pyrrhonism against Calvinism was soon to be shaped into a skeptical machine of war for use by the Counter Reformation.

Sanches and Montaigne. The most philosophical statements of the new skepticism and its relevance to the problems of the day were offered by Michel de Montaigne and his distant cousin Francisco Sanches. Sanches (c. 1550–1623), an Iberian refugee from the Inquisition, taught philosophy and medicine at Toulouse. In his *Quod Nihil Scitus,* written in 1576 and published in 1581, he used the classical skeptical arguments to show that science, in the Aristotelian sense of giving necessary reasons or causes for the behavior of nature, cannot be attained. He then argued that even his own notion of science—perfect knowledge of an individual thing—is beyond human capabilities because of the nature of objects and the nature of man. The interrelation of objects, their

unlimited number, and their ever-changing character prevent their being known. The limitations and variability of man's senses restrict him to knowledge of appearances, never of real substances.

Sanches' first conclusion was the usual fideistic one of the time, that truth can be gained only by faith. His second conclusion was to play an important role in later thought: just because nothing can be known in an ultimate sense, we should not abandon all attempts at knowledge but should try to gain what knowledge we can, namely, limited, imperfect knowledge of some of those things which we become acquainted with through observation, experience, and judgment. The realization that *nihil scitur* ("nothing is known") thus can yield some constructive results. This early formulation of "constructive" or "mitigated" skepticism was to be developed into an important explication of the new science by Marin Mersenne, Pierre Gassendi, and the leaders of the Royal Society.

The most influential version of the new skepticism in setting the problems for modern philosophy was Montaigne's. His rambling essay *Apologie de Raimond Sebond,* written shortly after he read Sextus and went through his own personal *crise pyrrhonienne,* summed up the skeptical currents of the sixteenth century and showed why all of man's rational achievements up to that point were seriously in doubt. Starting from a quibble about the validity of the arguments of the fifteenth-century Spanish theologian Sebond (Raymond de Sabunde), Montaigne moved to a general skeptical critique of the possibility of human beings understanding anything. He kept repeating that only through faith and revelation can real knowledge be gained. Montaigne used a vast variety of ancient skeptical arguments, often modernizd by new examples. He stressed the skeptical difficulties involved in judging the reliability of sense experience. He pointed out the personal, social, and cultural factors that influence people's judgments. And he showed that the criteria employed to determine standards of judgment are themselves open to question and doubt, unless God gives us some indubitable first principles and makes our faculties reliable. Unaided by divine grace, all of man's achievements, even those of the most recent scientists, become dubious. All we can do, Montaigne asserted, is follow the Pyrrhonian suspension of judgment, live according to nature and custom, and accept what God chooses to reveal to us.

The seventeenth century. Montaigne's skepticism, both as set forth in the *Apologie* and in the more didactic presentations of his disciples, Pierre Charron's *De la Sagesse* (Bordeaux, 1601) and Jean-Pierre Camus' *Essay sceptique* (Paris, 1603), became most popular in the early seventeenth century, especially among the avant-garde intellectuals in Paris. The so-called *libertins,* including Gabriel Naudé, Mazarin's secretary; Guy Patin, rector of the Sorbonne medical school; and François de La Mothe Le Vayer, teacher of the dauphin, espoused Montaigne's attitude and were often accused of being skeptical even of fundamental religious tenets. Others, like François Veron, used the arguments of Sextus and Montaigne to challenge the Calvinist claim of gaining true knowledge from reading Scripture. Counter Reformers, by raising skeptical epistemological problems about whether one could determine what book is the Bible, what it actually says, what it means, and so on, forced Calvinists to seek an indisputable basis for knowledge as a prelude to defending their theological views.

Gassendi and Mersenne. Perhaps the most forceful presentation of skepticism in the early seventeenth century is Pierre Gassendi's earliest work, *Exercitationes Paradoxicae Adversus Aristoteleos* (Grenoble, 1624). Gassendi challenged almost every aspect of Aristotle's view, as well as many other theories. He applied a battery of ancient and Renaissance skeptical arguments, including that "No science is possible, least of all in Aristotle's sense." In this work Gassendi indicated in embryo what became his and Marin Mersenne's constructive solution to the skeptical crisis, the development of an empirical study of the world of appearances rather than an attempt to discover the real nature of things.

In the 1620s works challenging the prevalent skeptical tendencies began to appear. Some authors simply stated that Aristotle would have resolved the difficulties by applying his theory of sense perception and knowledge to the problems raised. Others, like François Garasse, decried the irreligious tendencies they discerned in all this doubting. Still others, like Francis Bacon, tried to overcome the skeptical difficulties by appealing to new methods and new instruments that might correct errors and yield firm and unquestionable results. Herbert of Cherbury, in *De Veritate* (1624), offered an elaborate scheme for overcoming skepticism which combined Aristotelian and Stoic elements, and ultimately appealed to common notions, or truths known by all men, as the criteria by which reliable and indubitable judgment would be possible. Mersenne, in many writings of the 1620s and 1630s, used skeptical materials (as did Gassendi) to attack the alchemists, the cabalists, and other Renaissance pseudo scientists, and he tried to mitigate the force of the skeptical challenge by pointing out how, in fact, worthwhile "knowledge" is gained. Mersenne granted that the problems raised by Sextus could not be answered and that, in a fundamental sense, knowledge of the real nature of things cannot be attained. However, he insisted, information about appearances and deductions from hypotheses can provide an adequate guide for living in this world and can be checked by verifying predictions about future experiences. Gassendi, in his later works, developed this constructive skepticism as a *via media* between complete doubt and dogmatism, and offered his atomic theory as the best hypothetical model for interpreting experience. Mersenne and Gassendi thus combined skepticism about metaphysical knowledge of reality with a way of gaining useful information about experience through a pragmatic scientific method.

Descartes. René Descartes, raised in the skeptical atmosphere of early seventeenth-century France, insisted that it was possible to overcome all doubt and to find an absolutely certain basis for knowledge. By applying the skeptical method more thoroughly than the skeptics had, he claimed, an indubitable truth, as well as an indubitable criterion of true knowledge and a whole system of truths about reality, could be found. Descartes started by rejecting all beliefs rendered dubious by the skeptical problems

about sense experience, the possibility that all that we know is part of a dream (a theory that appeared in Cicero and Montaigne), and the possibility that there may be a demon who distorts our judgment (a new skeptical possibility which he introduced). In the process of trying to doubt everything, Descartes claimed, one basic indubitable truth—"I think, therefore I am"—is encountered. The very act of doubting one's own existence makes one aware of the truth that one exists. By examining what characteristics make this truth indubitable, the criterion of true knowledge, that whatever ideas are clearly and distinctly perceived are true, is discovered. This criterion then enables one to find true first principles among one's ideas and to use these principles to prove that there is a God, that God is not a deceiver, that he guarantees that whatever we clearly and distinctly perceive really is true, and that there is an external world. The Cartesian "way of ideas," then, takes skepticism as its point of departure, uses it to reveal a basis of certitude, and then further uses it to gain indubitable metaphysical knowledge from our clear and distinct ideas.

Replies to Descartes. Descartes's dramatic resolution of the skeptical crisis generated a new era of skeptical argumentation. The skeptics sought to show that Descartes had not really conquered skepticism, while his dogmatic opponents tried to show that he was actually a skeptic in spite of himself. To refute Descartes, traditional skeptical arguments had to be refashioned and redirected. In the objections to Descartes's *Meditations* (Paris, 1641), Gassendi, Mersenne, and others argued that either fundamental skeptical difficulties remained in the Cartesian system or that Descartes had not really established anything absolutely certain. During the rest of the seventeenth century skeptical challenges were raised about what, if anything, had actually been proved by the *cogito*, about whether Descartes's criterion was of any value, and about whether the "truths" Descartes enunciated about the mathematical–physical universe were actually certain or ever true. Gassendi, and later Pierre-Daniel Huet, charged that either the *cogito* stated an uninteresting truism or it was fraught with problems. Huet's *Censura Philosophae Cartesiana* (Paris, 1689) and his unpublished defense of it raised doubts about each element of the proposition "I think, therefore I am" until it became "I may have thought, therefore perhaps I may be." Gassendi, Huet, and others questioned whether Descartes's criterion could determine what was true or false. Could we really tell what was clear and distinct, or could we only tell that something appeared clear and distinct to us? Would we then need another criterion to tell when the first actually applied, and so on? Mersenne pointed out that even with the criterion we could not be sure that what was clear and distinct to us, and hence true, was really true for God. Hence, in an ultimate sense, even the most certain Cartesian knowledge might be false. Gassendi, in what Descartes called "the objection of objections," pointed out that for all anyone could ascertain, the whole Cartesian system of truths might be only a subjective vision in somebody's mind and not a true picture of reality. Huet argued that since all the fundamental Cartesian data consisted of ideas, and ideas are not real physical things, the Cartesian world of ideas, even if clear and distinct, cannot represent something quite different from itself.

Followers of Descartes. As Cartesianism was attacked from many sides, adherents modified it in various ways. The radical revision of Nicolas Malebranche, designed partially to avoid skeptical difficulties involved in connecting the world of ideas with reality, was immediately attacked by the skeptic Simon Foucher. The orthodox Cartesian Antoine Arnauld claimed that Malebranchism could only lead to a most dangerous Pyrrhonism. Foucher, who wished to revive Academic skepticism, applied various skeptical gambits to Malebranche's theory, one of which was to be important in subsequent philosophy. He argued that the skeptical difficulties which Descartes and Malebranche used to deny that sense qualities (the so-called secondary qualities—color, sound, heat, taste, smell) were features of real objects, applied as well to the mathematically describable primary qualities like extension and motion, which the Cartesians considered the fundamental properties of things. These mathematical qualities, as perceived, are as variable and as subjective as the others. If the skeptical arguments are sufficient to cause doubt about the ontological status of secondary qualities, Foucher contended, they are also sufficient to lead us to doubt that primary ones are genuine features of reality.

English skepticism. While the French skeptics were busily challenging the new dogmatism of Descartes, in England a somewhat different kind of skepticism was developing. As a result of theological controversies, some Anglican writers, starting with William Chillingworth, tried to distinguish unanswerable, hyperbolic, and metaphysical doubts, of the sort raised by Sextus and Descartes, from reasonable ones that could be dealt with in terms of probabilities and common sense. They pointed out that absolutely certain knowledge about the world is unattainable. However, there is information that can be called knowledge in the sense that it cannot reasonably be doubted. Bishop John Wilkins and Joseph Glanvill, two early members of the Royal Society, distinguished between infallibly certain and indubitably certain knowledge. Infallibly certain knowledge cannot be attained by human beings because their faculties may be corrupt or defective, and any of the necessary connections they think they discover in the world may be mere concomitancies which could be otherwise. However, in ordinary life there are many indubitable beliefs that no reasonable man questions. In terms of this distinction Wilkins, Glanvill, and their colleagues built up a theory of empirical science and jurisprudence for studying nature and deciding human problems within the limits of "reasonable doubt." Their limited skepticism appears in the Anglo-American theory of legal evidence and in the theory of legal evidence and in the theory of science of the early Royal Society. They believed that by applying their probabilistic empirical method to religious questions they could justify a tolerant, latitudinarian form of Christianity. John Locke to some extent followed their views in rejecting total skepticism as unreasonable and in appealing to common-sense standards to answer or avoid traditional skeptical difficulties.

Other resolutions of skepticism. Other answers were offered to the skeptics and to their challenge of some of the basic tenets of the new philosophy. Hobbes had admitted the force of the problem of finding *the* criterion for judging what was genuinely true, and he insisted that the solution was ultimately political—the sovereign would have to decide. Pascal in his scientific works gave one of the finest expositions of the hypothetical probabilistic nature of science and mathematics. In his *Pensées* he stated the case for ultimate and complete skepticism as strongly as it ever has been done. But, he contended, no matter how much reason leads us to doubt, "I lay it down as a fact that there never has been a real complete skeptic. Nature sustains our feeble reason, and prevents it raving to this extent." (Arnauld, in the *Port-Royal Logic,* similarly called the Pyrrhonists a sect of liars, since they could not believe what they said.) Pascal portrayed man as both a natural and instinctive believer and "a sink of uncertainty and error." His solution lay in turning to God, not in any philosophical answer. Spinoza, on the other hand, with his completely rational vision of the world, could not regard skepticism as a serious problem. If one had clear and adequate ideas, there would be no need or excuse for doubting. Doubt was only an indication of lack of clarity, not of basic philosophical difficulties.

The philosopher who took the skeptics most seriously was Leibniz, a close friend of Huet and Foucher and a correspondent of Pierre Bayle's. Many of Leibniz' most famous statements of his views are answers to these skeptics. Leibniz believed that his system of logic, epistemology, and metaphysics was impervious to their criticisms. Foucher tried to show him that he failed to take seriously the skeptical challenge to the very principles of reasoning that he employed and to the traditional assumptions about the nature of knowledge that he accepted. Bayle, in the article "Rorarius" in his *Dictionnaire historique et critique,* offered the first major critique of Leibniz' theory of the pre-established harmony, showing it had been no more successful in resolving skeptical difficulties than had previous metaphysical systems and was at least as implausible as the others.

Bayle and the Enlightenment. At the end of a century of attempts to deal with the skeptical crisis, perhaps the most incisive of the modern skeptics, Pierre Bayle, summed up the seventeenth-century intellectual situation in his monumental *Dictionnaire historique et critique* (2 vols., Rotterdam, 1697–1702), in which he opposed "everything that is said and everything that is done." Bayle's *Dictionnaire* is biographical, and most of the important discussion occurs in long, digressive footnotes to lives of often very insignificant figures. Bayle was a master dialectician who delighted in offering skeptical challenges to philosophical and theological theories, ancient or modern, from Thales to Leibniz, Locke, and Newton. Using all the gambits of the skeptical tradition, Bayle sought to show that most theories "are big with contradiction and absurdity" and that man's efforts to comprehend the world in rational terms always end in perplexities, bewilderment, and insoluble difficulties. He thereby developed a most extreme skepticism, questioning the knowledge claims of theology, metaphysics, mathematics, and the sciences. In notes B and C to his article "Pyrrho," and in his clarification of the article in the Appendix, Bayle argued that the new philosophy cast all in doubt. It had started from the doubts of Sextus Empiricus, and in spite of Descartes's efforts and those of his successors, it was ending in a complete skeptical debacle. Using Foucher's argument and some ammunition from Malebranche, Bayle contended that the doubts accepted by modern philosophers about the real external existence of secondary qualities applied to the primary ones as well, so that we cannot tell what characteristics the external world might have, nor even if there is one.

Gassendi and Huet had challenged whether the Cartesian criterion could ever be successfully applied. Bayle challenged whether it was even the criterion of knowledge. He argued for the possibility of a proposition's being clear and distinct and yet demonstratively false. (Many theologians and philosophers tried to refute this challenge by showing that rational discourse would be destroyed if no standards existed.)

The point of his skeptical attack, Bayle insisted, was to make men see that philosophy was an unsatisfactory guide and could only lead to doubts. Then, perhaps, they would abandon reason and turn to faith. Bayle's presentation of what this turn to faith involves has none of the fervor of Pascal. It usually seems to be just a tepid statement of the unintelligibility and amorality of a faith that is to be accepted blindly. What he himself believed is almost impossible to determine in the morass of doubts. Bayle also employed his skepticism as a justification for complete toleration. If all theories about the ultimate nature of reality are questionable, can there be any basis for persecuting people for accepting one rather than another? People accept views on the basis of what their consciences force them to believe. An erring conscience would have the same effect as a correct one in compelling assent. Since right or true belief cannot be distinguished from false ones, there is no justification for persecuting people for their beliefs.

Bayle's *Dictionnaire* was the *coup de grâce* to the seventeenth century's attempt to find a new metaphysical basis for certain knowledge. Among major philosophers, only George Berkeley thought the skeptical crisis could still be resolved through another metaphysical scheme. By denying the ontological distinction between ideas and things, and thereby removing the basis for many of the skeptical arguments, Berkeley thought he could refute the skeptics and establish the reality of human knowledge. To his chagrin, he was soon classed as just one more ingenious skeptic, as well as a visionary with a strange spiritualistic metaphysics. Almost everyone else seemed willing to accept Bayle's demolishing of the quest for metaphysical certainty. His skeptical arguments were soon applied to traditional religion by Voltaire and others. But in place of Bayle's doubts or his appeal to faith, they offered a new way of understanding man's world—that of Newtonian science—and professed an inordinate optimism about what man could comprehend and accomplish through scientific examination and induction. Though Bayle remained the heroic figure who had launched the Age of Reason by criticizing all the superstitions of past philosophy and theology, the leaders of the Enlightenment, both in France and in the British Isles, felt that his skepticism was passé and only represented the summit of human understanding before "God said, Let Newton be, and all was light." Various simple answers were now offered to skepticism, some by the Scottish moral theorists and some by overzealous dogmatists like Jean Pierre de Crousaz, who accused skepticism of being responsible for everything evil, including even financial crises.

Hume. In the euphoric intellectual atmosphere of the eighteenth century, David Hume still worried about skepticism. An avid reader of Bayle, Hume seems to have lived through his own personal skeptical crisis as he wrote his *A Treatise of Human Nature*. Hume sometimes held a most extreme skeptical position, going at least as far as Bayle in questioning even the knowledge claims of science, mathematics, and logical reasoning, and sometimes held a limited, mitigated skepticism allowing for probabilistic standards for evaluating beliefs about what is beyond immediate experience. When Hume examined the general nature of all beliefs, he tended toward complete skepticism. When he examined metaphysics and theology, in contrast with science, he tended toward a positivistic, limited skepticism. And when he developed his own views about human nature and conduct, his doubts tended to recede and his positive views became more pronounced.

Hume had a Newtonian vision that if the "experimental method of reasoning" were applied to moral subjects, the character of man's intellectual endeavors would be clarified and the limits of human capacities would be made apparent. The enthusiasm of Hume's Preface indicates his optimism about constructing "a science of man." His analysis revealed a skepticism about man's ability to gain knowledge about anything beyond the immediately obvious or demonstrable relationships of his ideas. In the course of the *Treatise* and the *Enquiry Concerning Human Understanding,* Hume showed that no truths about matters of fact could be established deductively or inductively. Since any conceivable (imaginable) state of affairs is possible, Hume argued that no genuine demonstrative evidence could establish that something must be, and could not be otherwise. Inductive reasoning, Hume pointed out, is inconclusive, since its evidential value rests upon the assumption that nature is uniform, that the future will resemble the past. This assumption cannot itself be justified. Our information about the world beyond what is immediately perceived, except for "forced" beliefs, is the result of causal reasoning from a present impression to its supposed cause or effect. In analyzing such "reasoning," Hume showed that we are unable to discover any necessary connections among experienced events or any justifiable basis for applying data about the constant conjunctions of past events to future ones. When we examine why we believe that certain relationships exist between matters of fact, we see that customs or habits, rather than rational evidence, lead us to the views we hold. The quest for a justifiable basis for belief always reveals how unjustified are our beliefs about matters not immediately experienced. In Book I, Part IV of the *Treatise,* the last chapter of the *Enquiry,* and the *Dialogues Concerning Natural Religion* Hume undermined the reliability of rational and empirical arguments in philosophy and theology, and raised doubts concerning the merits of logical argumentation about the existence of an external world, of the self, and of God.

When we examine what we believe and what leads us to believe it, we find that "Philosophy would render us entirely Pyrrhonian, were not Nature too strong for it." The skeptical problems notwithstanding, we are naturally constrained to believe all sorts of things. Under normal conditions we find that we are led by nature to believe that the future course of events will resemble the past course, and on this we base our so-called "reasonable" or "scientific" views and expectations about the world. But nature does not refute complete skepticism. It only prevents us from believing in, or accepting, the doubts that result from skeptical reasonings.

Hume showed that man was caught between a total Pyrrhonism that he could not refute and a natural compulsion to believe in the future course of events, the reality of an external world, the existence of some kind of personal identity, and possibly in some kind of intelligent force in the world. These metaphysical and theological views were indefensible but unavoidable. The Humean skeptic could only accept the situation and explore the reasons for doubting when he felt inclined to, at other times accepting what he found he had to believe. In a sense, Hume's skepticism was a more consistent and forceful statement of the original Pyrrhonian view. Though less detailed and thorough than Bayle's dialectical demolishment of a wide variety of knowledge claims, Hume's version centered the skeptical attack on the issues that were to dominate subsequent philosophy—the problems of induction, causality, external existence, the nature of the self, and the proofs of the existence of God. And Hume showed what was actually involved in the Pyrrhonian statement that the skeptic accepts beliefs by habit and custom, and according to nature. The skeptic could not suspend judgment on all questions without going mad, since "Nature, by an absolute and uncontrolable necessity has determin'd us to judge as well as to breathe and feel" (*Treatise of Human Nature*, Book I, Part 4, Sec. 1). More than any of his predecessors, Hume explored the nature of beliefs and the factors that induce people to accept them.

Reid and the common-sense school. In an era when most of his philosophical contemporaries were overly optimistic about human capabilities to comprehend the world, Hume's skepticism was largely ignored, while his psychological, historical, political, and antireligious works were taken as a great contribution to the Age of Reason. One of the first to appreciate Hume's skeptical arguments was Thomas Reid, who studied Hume's writings for 25 years before publishing his answer, *Inquiry into the Human Mind on the Principles of Common Sense* (Edinburgh, 1764). Reid discerned that both Berkeley and Hume had shown that the basic principles of modern philosophy led systematically to total skepticism about man's ability to attain any certainty or even probability about the world. The answer to this development, Reid contended, was not to ignore or scoff at the arguments of Berkeley and Hume but to reconsider the assumptions on which modern philosophy is based. When the conclusions of philosophy run counter to common sense, there must be something wrong with philosophy. Since nobody could believe and act by complete skepticism, the fact that this skepticism was the consistent issue of the Cartesian and Lockean way

of ideas only showed the need to start anew. Reid offered his common-sense realism as a way of avoiding Hume's skepticism by employing as basic principles the beliefs we are psychologically unable to doubt.

Hume was unimpressed by Reid's argument. Reid, he believed, had seen the problem but actually had only offered Hume's own solution, that nature does not allow us to live as if all were in doubt, even though we are unable to resolve all doubts theoretically. The Scottish common-sense school of Oswald, Beattie, Stewart, Brown, and others kept reiterating its claim to having refuted Hume's skepticism by appealing to natural belief, while at the same time conceding that Hume's fundamental arguments could not be answered. Thomas Brown, an early nineteenth-century disciple of Reid, admitted that Reid and Hume differed more in words than in opinions, saying, " 'Yes.' Reid bawled out, 'we must believe in an outward world'; but added in a whisper, 'we can give no reason for our belief.' Hume cries out, 'we can give no reason for such a notion'; and whispers, 'I own we cannot get rid of it' " (Sir James Mackintosh, *Dissertation on the Progress of Ethical Philosophy*, 2d ed., Edinburgh, 1837, p. 346).

The German Enlightenment and Kant. The Scottish school was perhaps the first to make Hume's version of modern skepticism the central view to be combated if philosophy was to make coherent sense of man's universe. The more fundamental attempt, for subsequent philosophy, to deal with Hume's skepticism was developed in Germany in the second half of the eighteenth century and culminated in Kant's critical philosophy. Such leaders of the Prussian Academy as Jean Henry Samuel Formey, Johann Bernhard Mérian, and Johann Georg Sulzer had long been arguing against Pyrrhonism. They were among the first to read, translate (into French and German), and criticize Hume's writings. They saw in the skeptical tradition up to Bayle and Huet, and in Hume's version of it, a major challenge to all man's intellectual achievements. Although their answers to skepticism were hardly equal to the threat they saw in it, these writers helped revive interest in and concern with skepticism in an age that thought it had solved, or was about to solve, all problems. Others in Germany contributed to an awareness of the force of skepticism: Johann Christoff Eschenbach by his edition of the arguments of Sextus, Berkeley, and Arthur Collier, Berkeley's contemporary, against knowledge of an external corporeal world; Ernst Platner by his skeptical aphorisms and his German edition of Hume's *Dialogues on Natural Religion* (1781); hosts of German professors by dissertations against skepticism; and the translators of the Scottish critics of Hume.

The culmination of this German concern with skepticism occurred when Kant was awakened from his dogmatic slumbers by reading Hume and his opponents. Kant saw that Hume had fundamentally challenged the Enlightenment hope that all skeptical disputes could be settled by what Locke had called "the physiology of the understanding," and that the question "How is knowledge possible?" had to be re-examined. Kant's solution can be considered as an attempt to establish a middle ground incorporating complete skepticism about metaphysical knowledge and a conviction that universal and necessarily certain knowledge existed about the conditions of all possible experience. He assumed that knowledge is possible, and hence that total skepticism is false. The problem was then to explain how this universal and necessary information could be attained, in the face of Hume's arguments. In the view that knowledge begins with experience, but does not come from it, Kant believed he had found a revolutionary new answer to the skeptical crisis. Space and time are the necessary forms of all possible experience, and the categories and the logical forms of judgment are the conditions of all knowledge about experience. Mathematical knowledge is possible because it is not derived by induction from experience but is the way the world must be experienced. A science of nature is possible because all experience must be ordered and organized according to certain categories.

By transcendental analysis we can uncover the universal and necessary conditions imposed on all experience and judgment. But these conditions provide no means for gaining knowledge either about the contents of experience (as opposed to its form) or about what transcends experience, a supposed real world, a self, and God. The contents of experience can be learned only empirically and inductively, and such information is only probable. Metaphysical knowledge cannot be attained, since there is no way of telling if the conditions of experience apply beyond the limits of all possible experience, and no way of telling what to apply them to.

Skeptical rejoinders to Kant. Kant and his disciple Karl Friedrich Staüdlin (who wrote the first systematic history of skepticism, from Pyrrho to Kant) regarded Kant's critical philosophy as the finale of man's long struggle with skepticism. Kant's contemporaries and successors, however, saw his effort as beginning a new phase in skeptical thought and providing a new road to Pyrrhonism. From three different sides Kant was attacked by skeptical critics, each employing a portion of the earlier skeptical tradition as a way of showing that Kant had failed to resolve the skeptical crisis. G. E. Schulze (also known as Aenesidemus-Schulze, after the title of his major work of 1792) argued that Kant had not succeeded in establishing any genuine truths about objective reality, since as Kant himself had shown, there is no way of extending information about the conditions of thought to real objects, or things-in-themselves. But without any such extension, the objective validity of our judgments cannot be determined. At best, all that can be established is the subjective necessity of certain of our views, which is essentially what Hume had shown. So Schulze, by insisting on the inability of the Kantian analysis to move from subjective data about what people have to believe to any objective claims about reality, contended that Kant had not advanced beyond Hume's skepticism, and that this failure of the Kantian revolution actually constituted a vindication of Hume's views.

Salomon Maimon challenged Kant's theory from within and developed a view which he called "rational skepticism." In contrast with Hume, Maimon agreed with Kant that there were rational a priori concepts, such as those involved in mathematics. In opposition to Kant, Maimon held that the applicability of transcendental concepts to experience was itself something based on inductions from experience. Since such inductions could only be probable, no universal and necessary knowledge about experience could be gained. Kant had assumed that such knowledge existed, and examined *how* this was possible. Maimon asked *whether* it was, and showed that the evidence was always experiential. Inductively it might become more and more probable that a priori concepts applied to experience, but, because of Hume's critique of induction, we must remain skeptical on this score. Maimon ruled out metaphysical knowledge as unattainable, on both Humean and Kantian grounds.

Thus Maimon developed a mitigated Kantianism (to some extent like that of the Neo-Kantian movement a century later) in which the reality of a priori forms of thought is granted but in which the relation of these forms to matters of fact is always in question. Knowledge (that is, propositions that are universal and necessary, rather than ones that are just psychologically indubitable) is possible in mathematics but not in sciences dealing with the world. Unlike the logical positivists, who were to claim that mathematics was true because it consisted only of vacuous logical tautologies, Maimon contended that mathematics was true because it was about creations of our mind. Its objective relevance was always problematical. This turn to human creativity as the basis of truth was soon to be expanded by Fichte as a new road to knowledge of reality and a means of transcending skepticism.

Maimon's partial skepticism exposed some of the fundamental limitations of Kant's critical philosophy as a solution to the skeptical crisis. Another skeptical critique was offered by the religious thinker Johann Georg Hamann, who accepted Hume's and Kant's arguments as evidence that knowledge of reality cannot be gained by rational means but only by faith. Hamann exploited the skeptical thought of these philosophies to press for a complete antirational fideism. He used Hume's analyses of miracles and of the evidence for religious knowledge to try to convince Kant of the futility of the search for truth by rational means. During the height of nineteenth-century positivism, materialism, and idealism, Hamann's type of fideism was revitalized by Kierkegaard and Lamennais, who used it as a critique of French liberal, empirical, and Enlightenment views and as a new defense of orthodoxy and political conservatism. Kierkegaard brilliantly combined themes from Sextus, Hume, and Hamann to attack the rationalism of the Hegelians, to develop a thoroughgoing skepticism about rational achievements, and to show the need for faith in opposition to reason. Fideism has become a major element in twentieth-century neo-orthodox and existentialist theology, which tries to show that the traditional skeptical problems still prevent us from finding an ultimate basis for our beliefs except by faith.

Idealism. In the mainstream of philosophy after Kant, although skepticism continues to play a vital role, few philosophers have been willing to call themselves skeptics. The German metaphysicians, from Fichte and Hegel onward, sought to escape from the skeptical impasse produced by Hume and Kant and to reach knowledge of reality through the creative process and the recognition of historical development. They attempted to portray skepticism as a stage in the awareness and understanding of the process of events. For Fichte skepticism made one recognize the need for commitment to a fundamental outlook about the world. The commitment to see the world in terms of creative thought processes led to a revelation of the structure of the universe as an aspect of the Absolute Ego.

For Hegel skepticism was the nadir of philosophy, actually its antithesis. According to Hegel, human knowledge is a historically developing process. At each stage of the process both our knowledge and the world itself are limited and contain contradictions, which are overcome at the next stage. Only the final, Absolute stage, when no further contradictions can be developed, permits genuine knowledge that is not partly true and partly false. Then, presumably, skepticism is no longer possible. The English Hegelian F. H. Bradley, in his *Appearance and Reality* (London, 1893), used the traditional skeptical arguments to show that the world was unintelligible in terms of empirical or materialistic categories, and hence that one had to go beyond the world appearance to find true knowledge.

Recent assimilation of skepticism. The empirical and positivistic critique of speculative metaphysics, launched in the late nineteenth and early twentieth centuries by Ernst Mach, Bertrand Russell, Rudolf Carnap, and others, included a skepticism about the possibility of any metaphysical knowledge (amounting in some formulations almost to the Academic skeptical view that no knowledge beyond appearances is possible). Logical positivism and the later linguistic philosophy have tried to obviate the skeptical problems by restricting the use of the term "knowledge" to logically true tautologies, empirically verifiable facts, or ordinary common-sense beliefs and assertions. Similarly, pragmatists from William James onward have sought to eliminate skeptical difficulties by limiting the meaning of "true knowledge" to hypotheses that are pragmatically confirmed or verified. In such views, metaphysical assertions are no longer ranked as false or dubious but as nonsense, or non-assertions. They can be evaluated as poetic utterances, or appreciated for their emotive qualities, but they have no truth value.

Many other major views of the last hundred years, whether intentionally or not, have included or taken for granted various aspects of traditional skepticism. Empiricists, from John Stuart Mill onward, have not claimed to have found any means of attaining certain knowledge beyond the world of experience or appearance, except in terms of logical and/or mathematical tautologies. And the information about the world of experience, they have granted, is only probable. The sciences have systematized our understanding of these data but have not thereby shown that they are necessarily true. On the contrary, the probabilistic nature of science has been used by Russell and others as a constant warning against various dogmatic views. Russell, in his discussions of induction, has repeatedly stressed the logical force of the arguments offered to develop an extreme or complete skepticism.

James, Sigmund Freud, Karl Mannheim, and Charles Beard, while they have provided much insight into why we hold the views we do, have at the same time spawned newer forms of relativistic skepticism. By revealing the economic, social, and psychological factors that have led us to our beliefs, they have made it difficult, if not impossible, for us to consider the truth of what we believe apart from how or why we believe it. Truths, in the views of these writers, become relative to the person holding them and to the conditions under which they are held, rather than absolute assertions about the nature of things.

In a world in which most thinkers are covertly skeptical about the possibility of attaining knowledge concerning reality, there have been few overt skeptics recently. Since for many the impasse reached by Humean and Kantian thought is taken as the end of the quest for certain knowledge of reality, the skeptical problems seem out-of-date and irrelevant. When they are transferred from their original locus into questions about experience or common-sense belief, they appear odd and sometimes easily answerable, although these are hardly the same problems. The continuing appearance of refutations of skepticism by contemporary philosophers indicates, perhaps, that to some extent they are still haunted by the problems that no longer seem soluble.

Recent skeptics. Besides those contemporary fideists who employ skepticism as a road to religious faith, one might include as overt skeptics among twentieth-century thinkers such diverse figures as Fritz Mauthner, George Santayana, and Albert Camus, and as quasi skeptics figures like Hans Vaihinger, Alain, and possibly Karl Popper. Mauthner, in the early part of the century, developed a type of skepticism from his work on the analysis of language. Any language, he contended, is both social and individual, and shows only what linguistic conventions are used at given times and what features of experience they name in various ways. Each language expresses a *Weltanschauung*, and what is considered as true in a language is always relative to this outlook. When one attempts to ascertain what is true, one is thrown back on data about linguistic conventions and cannot proceed to any independent evaluation of the actual correspondence of assertions to objective states of affairs.

Mauthner's critique of language led him into complete skepticism about the possibility of genuine knowledge. Even his critique, he realized, was an attempt "to say the unsayable," and thus silent mystic contemplation was all that was really possible. In the light of his studies of atheism and religion, Mauthner called himself a "godless" mystic; "godless" because, according to his critique of language, "God" was as unwarranted a substantive name as any other.

A kind of naturalistic skepticism was offered by George Santayana, especially in his *Scepticism and Animal Faith* (New York, 1923). Santayana insisted that "nothing given exists as it is given," and that all our beliefs about what is given are open to question. He contended that he was carrying skepticism further than Hume. had, in that he questioned both Hume's description of what is given and his psychological interpretations of experience.

When the full force of complete skepticism is realized, Santayana claimed, one can appreciate what is in fact absolutely indubitable, the immediately experienced or intuited qualities that Santayana called "essences." The interpretation of these essences leads to various questionable metaphysical systems. A thoroughgoing skepticism makes one realize the unjustifiable assumptions involved in interpreting the realm of essences, and also that we do interpret them and thereby construct meaningful pictures of the world. Santayana called the process of interpretation "animal faith," which is consistent with complete skepticism and involves following natural and social tendencies and inclinations.

> I have imitated the Greek sceptics in calling doubtful everything that, in spite of common sense, anyone can possibly doubt. But since life and even discussion forces me to break away from a complete scepticism, I have determined not to do so surreptitiously nor at random, ignominiously taking cover now behind one prejudice and now behind another. Instead, I have frankly taken nature by the hand, accepting as a rule in my farthest speculations the animal faith I live by from day to day. (*Scepticism and Animal Faith*, 1955, p. 308)

This animal faith is guided by biological events, which bring one to beliefs about reason, experience, and art, all of which may be illusory but which lead to various "realms of being" that can be studied, appreciated, and lived in.

Another form of twentieth-century skepticism is that of such existentialist thinkers as Albert Camus. Camus built on the fideistic skepticism of Kierkegaard and Leon Shestov and the skepticism regarding religion and objective values of Nietzsche. In his *Myth of Sisyphus* he portrays man as trying to measure the nature and meaning of an essentially absurd universe by means of questionable rational and scientific criteria. Camus regards the skeptical arguments used by Kierkegaard and Shestov as showing the contradictory nature of human rational attempts to understand the world as decisive, but he rejects their fideistic solution: overcoming the skeptical crisis by "a leap into faith." Instead, he accepts Nietzsche's picture of the ultimate meaninglessness of the world because "God is dead." For Camus, the basic absurdity of the human situation, of man constantly seeking for understanding and meaning in an unintelligible and meaningless world, must be recognized and accepted. In this situation knowledge in the traditional sense is unattainable, and no justifiable, or even plausible, *modus vivendi* between man's desires for understanding and worthwhile goals and the absurd conditions of his existence can be found. The mythological Sisyphus, eternally pushing a huge rock uphill, only to have it fall to the bottom again, typifies the human situation. Sisyphus "knows the whole extent of his wretched condition." He does not expect to find truth, nor does he expect to end his struggle. He finds no ultimate point or value in his situation, but he perseveres with a "silent joy," realizing that his struggle has meaning only for him, in terms of his human condition, and not in any objective frame of reference. The struggle is neither sterile nor futile for him, though it is meaningless in terms of understanding or possible achievement.

This type of skepticism, now quite popular, is allied with a kind of futilitarianism, reflecting the feeling that the optimism of the Enlightenment and the nineteenth century are illusions. The spiritual collapse of hopes for progress, peace, and human happiness in the course of the catastrophes of the twentieth century has led many intellectuals to a fundamental skepticism about man's capacity to know and understand his world, and about the merits of the ideals he has been striving for. This collapse, coupled with a strong skeptical current running from Bayle, Hume, and Voltaire to Bertrand Russell and others about the value of the religious and moral traditions of the Western world, has turned many philosophers away from any serious quest for genuine knowledge about the nature of reality and has led to the denial of grandiose knowledge claims and any metaphysical or theological system. The turn toward the intensive examination of ordinary belief and language, and of man's personal involvement in his allegedly absurd, meaningless situation, is in many ways like the intellectual atmosphere in which skepticism thrived both in Hellenistic times and in the late Renaissance. Well-structured worlds had collapsed, and with the collapse of all the frames of reference no goals any longer seemed obvious or certain. In those periods, as today, the questioning of basic assumptions deepened the disillusionment with traditional *Weltanschauungen* and led to a quest for new bases of certainty, knowledge, and values.

THE VALUE OF SKEPTICISM IN PHILOSOPHY

Skepticism has been continually attacked and "refuted" in the history of philosophy and has only occasionally been set forth as a serious view. Opponents have argued from Greek times to the present that skepticism is untenable and that it flies in the face of common sense and ordinary beliefs. As Hume admitted, one of the characteristics of skeptical argumentation is that "it admits of no answer, and produces no conviction."

The skeptics from Sextus Empiricus to Montaigne, Bayle, Hume, and Santayana have pointed out that the strength of skepticism lies not in whether it is tenable as a position but in the force of its arguments against the claims of dogmatic philosophers. To avoid leaving his opponents the opportunity to challenge the consistency of skepticism, Sextus carefully avoided stating the view as anything other than a chronicle of his personal feelings at given moments. Montaigne indicated that the Pyrrhonians needed a nonassertive language to state their case, since as soon as they asserted anything, opponents could claim that they had violated their own views. Bayle and Hume pointed out that skepticism, if stated and argued for consistently, would be self-refuting *but* that this self-refutation would not take place until skepticism *and* the opposing dogmatic views had all been undermined.

However, skepticism has not functioned in philosophy as merely one more position alongside idealism, materialism, and realism. Instead, it has been like an anonymous letter received by a dogmatic philosopher who does hold a position. The letter raises fundamental problems for the recipient by questioning whether he had adequate grounds for his assertions and assumptions or whether his system is free from contradictions or absurdities. The recipient may try to fend off the attack by challenging whether any philosopher could write the letter without opening himself to similar attacks. By imputing an author, the dogmatist may show the problem involved in consistently stating skepticism, but he does not thereby reply to the arguments in the letter. Skeptical arguments are usually parasitical, in that they assume the premises of the dogmatist and show problems that ensue, on the standards of reasoning of the dogmatist.

For the dogmatist, the skeptical arguments, regardless of whose they are, pose basic difficulties; and if he sees their relevance to his own views, it is he who must deal with them if he wants to be satisfied that his system is tenable. Sextus set forth his arguments primarily in terms of Stoic and Epicurean views; Montaigne, both in terms of these and of scholastic and Platonic ones; Gassendi, in terms of Cartesian, scholastic, and Renaissance naturalistic ones; Bayle, in terms of the systems current in his day—scholastic, Cartesian, Leibnizian, Lockean; and Hume, mainly in terms of Lockean and Cartesian ones. The upholders of these systems then had the problem of refuting these arguments within their systems, regardless of who in fact posed the problems and whether he believed what he appeared to be saying.

The historical skeptics did not say that they personally regarded everything as doubtful. They distinguished believing various matters from having sufficient reasons for believing them. Regardless of the legends about Pyrrho, the skeptical authors seem to have followed Huet's view that it is one thing to philosophize and another to live, and that many propositions may be philosophically dubious but acceptable or even indubitable as living options. The problem posed by skeptical probing was not what do, or what must, people believe but, rather, what evidence is there for beliefs, and is this evidence adequate?

From Greek times onward, skepticism has functioned as a gadfly to dogmatic philosophy and as a challenge to keep it honest. The skeptical critique has thrived on the desire to find a coherent and consistent account of our knowledge and beliefs about the world. Had there never been disillusionment about what was accepted as true, skepticism would probably not have arisen. Nevertheless, skepticism has led to continual re-examination of philosophical claims and to new dogmatic systems trying to avoid difficulties in others. This in turn has led to new skeptical attacks and ingenious new criticisms or new versions of criticism. Thus skepticism has been a major dynamic force in intellectual history. And even if many philosophers are now willing to accept Hume's friend Thomas Blacklock's observation that "the wise in every age conclude, what Pyrrho taught and Hume renewed, that dogmatists are fools," human folly keeps the quest for knowledge of the ultimate nature of reality going and skeptics keep challenging the latest claims to such knowledge. Without skepticism, we probably could not distinguish enthusiasm, prejudice, or superstition from serious or meaningful beliefs. As Shaftesbury said, after living with Bayle for a while, any views he had that could survive the continuous skeptical onslaught, he regarded as being as valuable as the purest gold. Each age is able to assess the views which are valuable to it only if they are subjected to the same challenge.

(See also APPEARANCE AND REALITY; CERTAINTY; DOUBT; ETHICAL RELATIVISM; FIDEISM; ILLUSIONS; INDUCTION; IRRATIONALISM; NIHILISM; OTHER MINDS; PARADIGM-CASE ARGUMENT; and SOLIPSISM. See Skepti-

cism in Index for articles on individual skeptics and on philosophers especially concerned with rebutting skeptical arguments.)

Bibliography

The following works deal with the history and nature of skepticism. In addition, see bibliographies to articles on specific skeptical thinkers.

Allen, Don Cameron, *Doubt's Boundless Sea: Skepticism and Faith in the Renaissance.* Baltimore, 1964.

Atlas, Samuel, *From Critical to Speculative Idealism: The Philosophy of Salomon Maimon.* The Hague, 1964.

Bartholmèss, Christian, *Huet, évêque d'Avranches, ou le scepticisme théologique.* Paris, 1850.

Bevan, Edwyn, *Stoics and Sceptics.* New York, 1959.

Boas, Georg, *Dominant Themes of Modern Philosophy.* New York, 1957.

Bredvold, Louis I., *The Intellectual Milieu of John Dryden.* Ann Arbor, Mich., 1931.

Brochard, Victor, *Les Sceptiques grecs.* Paris, 1887.

Busson, Henri, *Le Rationalisme dans la littérature française de la Renaissance.* Paris, 1957.

Dąmbska, Izydora, *Sceptycyzm Francuski XVI i XVII Wieku.* Torun, Poland, 1958.

Goedeckemeyer, Albert, *Die Geschichte des griechischen Skeptizismus.* Leipzig, 1905.

Gregory, Tullio, *Scetticismo ed empirismo: Studio su Gassendi.* Bari, 1961.

Hallie, Philip P., ed., *Scepticism, Man, and God. Selections From the Major Writings of Sextus Empiricus.* Middletown, Conn., 1964. Edited, with introduction, notes, and bibliography by Philip P. Hallie; translated by Sanford G. Etheridge.

Maccoll, Norman, *The Greek Sceptics From Pyrrho to Sextus.* London and Cambridge, 1869.

Menéndez Pelayo, Marcellino, *Obras completas*, Vol. XLIII, *Ensayos de crítica filosófica.* Santander, 1948. Ch. 2, "De los orígenes del criticismo y del escepticismo y especialmente de los precursores españoles de Kant," pp. 117–216.

Owen, John, *Evening With the Skeptics.* London, 1881.

Owen, John, *The Skeptics of the French Renaissance.* London and New York, 1893.

Patrick, Mary Mills, *The Greek Sceptics.* New York and London, 1929.

Popkin, Richard H., "David Hume: His Pyrrhonism and His Critique of Pyrrhonism." *Philosophical Quarterly*, Vol. 1 (1950–1951), 385–407.

Popkin, Richard H., "Berkeley and Pyrrhonism." *Review of Metaphysics*, Vol. 5 (1951–1952), 223–246.

Popkin, Richard H., "David Hume and the Pyrrhonian Controversy." *Review of Metaphysics*, Vol. 6 (1952–1953), 65–81.

Popkin, Richard H., "The Sceptical Crisis and the Rise of Modern Philosophy." *Review of Metaphysics*, Vol. 7 (1953–1954), 132–151, 307–322, 499–510.

Popkin, Richard H., "The Skeptical Precursors of David Hume." *Philosophy and Phenomenological Research*, Vol. 16 (1955), 61–71.

Popkin, Richard H., *The History of Scepticism From Erasmus to Descartes.* Assen, Netherlands, 1960; New York, 1964. Contains lengthy bibliography on skepticism from 1500 to 1650.

Popkin, Richard H., "Scepticism and the Counter-reformation in France." *Archiv für Reformationsgeschichte*, Vol. 51 (1960), 58–88.

Popkin, Richard H., "Scepticism in the Enlightenment," in T. Bestermann, ed., *Studies on Voltaire and the 18th Century*, Vol. XXVI. Geneva, 1963. Pp. 1321–1345.

Popkin, Richard H., "Traditionalism, Modernism and Scepticism of René Rapin." *Filosofia*, Vol. 15 (1964), 751–764.

Popkin, Richard H., "The High Road to Pyrrhonism." *American Philosophical Quarterly*, Vol. 2 (1965), 1–15.

Richter, Raoul, *Der Skeptizismus in der Philosophie*, 2 vols. Leipzig, 1904–1908. A history and examination of skepticism from ancient times to the end of the nineteenth century.

Robin, Léon, *Pyrrhon et le scepticisme grec.* Paris, 1944.
Russell, Bertrand, *Sceptical Essays.* New York, 1928.
Saisset, Émile, *Le Scepticisme: Aenesidème, Pascal, Kant.* Paris, 1865.
Santayana, George, *Scepticism and Animal Faith.* New York, 1923; reprinted New York, 1955.
Staüdlin, Karl F., *Geschichte und Geist des Skepticismus,* 2 vols. Leipzig, 1794.
Tafel, J. F. I., *Geschichte und Kritik des Skepticismus und Irrationalismus.* Tübingen, 1834.
Villey, Pierre, *Les Sources et l'évolution des essais de Montaigne.* Paris, 1908.
Zeller, Eduard, *The Stoics, Epicureans, and Sceptics,* translated by O. J. Reichel, rev. ed. London, 1880.

RICHARD H. POPKIN

SKOLEM-LÖWENHEIM THEOREM. See LOGIC, HISTORY OF; SYSTEMS, FORMAL, AND MODELS OF FORMAL SYSTEMS.

SKOVORODA, GREGORY SAVVICH (1722–1794), Ukrainian poet, fabulist, philosopher, and religious thinker. Skovoroda was educated at the Kiev Theological Academy. As a young man he traveled in eastern and western Europe and paid brief visits to St. Petersburg and Moscow, but eighteenth-century European culture left few traces on his thought. He taught, mainly literature, at Pereyaslavl (Pereyaslav-Khmelnitski) about 1755 and at the Kharkov Collegium from about 1759 to 1765, but he fell out with his ecclesiastical superiors and was dismissed. He spent his last thirty years as a mendicant scholar and "teacher of the people."

Skovoroda's disciple, M. I. Kovalinski, has left an engaging account of Skovoroda's manner of life:

> He dressed decently but simply; . . . he did not eat meat or fish, not from superstitious belief but because of his own inner constitution; . . . he allowed himself no more than four [hours a day] for sleep; . . . he was always gay, good-natured, easy-going, quick, restrained, abstemious, and content with all things, benign, humble before all men, willing to speak so long as he was not required to . . . ; he visited the sick, consoled the grieving, shared his last crust with the needy, chose and loved his friends for the qualities of their hearts, was pious without superstition, learned without ostentation, complaisant without flattery. ("The Life of Gregory Skovoroda," translated by G. L. Kline, in *Russian Philosophy,* Vol. I, p. 20)

Skovoroda aspired to be a "Socrates in Russia" both as a moralist, a gadfly provoking thoughtless and selfish men to scrutinize their lives, and as an intellectual forerunner, clearing the path for the more profound and systematic philosophizing of a future "Russian Plato." In many ways he was not only the last, but also the first, of the medievals in Russia. His metaphysics and philosophical anthropology are explicitly Christian and Neoplatonic, and his philosophical idiom is studded with Greek and Church Slavonic terms and constructions. He knew both German and Latin (he left over a hundred Latin letters and poems) and had some knowledge of Greek and Hebrew, but he wrote all of his philosophical works in Russian. As it happened, few

of his own philosophic coinages were accepted by later Russian thinkers.

All of Skovoroda's philosophical and theological writings are in dialogue form. They are Socratic in method and in theme, genuinely dramatic and dialogic, written with wit, imagination, and moral intensity. They offer an acute critique of both ontological materialism and sense-datum empiricism, and they outline a dualistic cosmology with a pantheistic (or "panentheistic") and mystical coloring. One of Skovoroda's favorite metaphors for the relation of appearance to reality is that of a tree's many passive, shifting shadows to the firm, single, living tree itself.

In deliberate opposition to the Baconian summons to "know nature in order to master it," Skovoroda urged individuals to "know themselves in order to master themselves" and to put aside desires for comfort, security, fame, and knowledge. His position is thus Stoic as well as Socratic. Seneca, no less than Socrates, would have savored the epitaph which Skovoroda wrote for himself: "The world set a trap for me, but it did not catch me."

Works by Skovoroda

Hryhori Skovoroda: Tvori v Dvokh Tomakh ("Gregory Skovoroda: Works in Two Volumes"), O. I. Biletski, D. K. Ostryanin, and P. M. Popov, eds. Kiev, 1961. Text in Russian and Latin; Introduction, commentary, notes, and translation of Latin text in Ukrainian.
"A Conversation Among Five Travellers Concerning Life's True Happiness" (abridged translation by George L. Kline of "Razgovor pyati putnikov o istinnom shchastii v zhizni," *Tvori v Dvokh Tomakh,* Vol. I, pp. 207–247) in James M. Edie, James P. Scanlan, Mary-Barbara Zeldin, and George L. Kline, eds., *Russian Philosophy,* 3 vols. Chicago, 1965. Vol. I, pp. 26–57.

Works on Skovoroda

Chyzhevsky, D., *Filosofiya H. S. Skovorody* ("The Philosophy of G. S. Skovoroda"). Warsaw, 1934. In Ukrainian.
Ern, V., *Grigori Savvich Skovoroda: Zhizn i Ucheniye* ("Gregory Savvich Skovoroda: His Life and Teaching"). Moscow, 1912.
Zenkovsky, V. V., *Istoriya Russkoi Filosofii,* 2 vols. Paris, 1948–1950. Translated by George L. Kline as *A History of Russian Philosophy,* 2 vols. London and New York, 1953. Pp. 53–69.

GEORGE L. KLINE

SMITH, ADAM (1723–1790), one of the most influential political economists of Western society, first became known as a moral philosopher. Smith was born in Kirkcaldy, Scotland. His father died shortly before he was born, and his mother's loss doubtless explains the lifelong attachment that flourished between her and her son. Smith entered the University of Glasgow in 1737, where he attended Francis Hutcheson's lectures. In 1740 he entered Balliol College, Oxford, as a Snell exhibitioner. He remained at Oxford for seven years and then returned to Kirkcaldy. In 1748, he moved to Edinburgh, where he became the friend of Hume and Lord Kames. In 1751 he was elected professor of logic at the University of Glasgow, and in the next year he exchanged logic for the professorship in moral philosophy, an appointment which he held for the next ten years.

The *Theory of Moral Sentiments,* drawn from his course of lectures, was published in 1759. The work received wide acclaim and so impressed the stepfather of the young duke of Buccleuch that he invited Smith to become the duke's tutor, with the promise of a pension for life. Smith resigned his professorship at Glasgow and accompanied the duke on a visit to the Continent which lasted from 1764 to 1766. His tutoring duties ended, he returned again to Kirkcaldy, where he spent the next ten years in retirement at work on *The Wealth of Nations,* which was published in 1776 and for which he became famous. In 1778 he was appointed a commissioner of customs for Scotland. He died in 1790 and was buried in the Canongate churchyard, Edinburgh.

The greater part of the *Theory of Moral Sentiments* is an account of moral psychology. Only after he has settled the psychological questions does Smith turn, in the last seventh of the work, to moral philosophy. The mainstay of Smith's moral psychology is sympathy. Sympathy is our fellow feeling with the passions or affections of another person. Smith characterizes the mechanism of sympathy in this way: "Whatever is the passion which arises from any object in the person principally concerned, *an analogous emotion* springs up at the thought of his situation, in the breast of every attentive spectator." The important phrase here is "at the thought of his situation." Sympathetic feelings may seem to arise from our seeing the expression of a certain emotion in another person, but Smith argues that if the appearance of grief or joy, for example, arouses similar feelings in us, it is because these feelings suggest to us the general idea of some good or evil that has befallen the person in whom we observe them. What is more, there are some passions whose expression excites disgust rather than sympathy until we are acquainted with their cause. The furious behavior of an angry man, for example, is more likely to exasperate us against him than against his enemies. Thus, Smith concludes that sympathy does not arise so much from the view of the passion as from the view of the situation which excites it, and he reinforces this claim by noting that we sometimes feel for another a passion which he himself seems to be altogether incapable of, as when we feel embarrassed at someone's behaving rudely although he has no sense of the impropriety of his behavior.

Sympathy is the basis for our judgments of both the propriety and the merit of other people's feelings and the actions which follow from them. When the original passions of the principal person are in perfect accord with the sympathetic emotions of the spectator, the passions of the principal appear to the spectator as just and proper. Smith even goes as far as to say that to approve of the passions of another as suitable to their objects is the same as to observe that we entirely sympathize with them. Indeed, even though our own emotions may make it impossible for us to have on occasion a certain sympathetic emotion, we may "by general rules" recognize the appropriateness of some person's having a given emotion because, for example, we could sympathize with the other person's joy but for our own grief.

Although our sense of the propriety of some piece of conduct arises from our sympathy with the affections and motives of the agent, our sense of merit (that is, our sense of a certain action's making the agent worthy of a reward) stems from our sympathy with the gratitude of the person affected by the action. When we see someone aided by another, our sympathy with his joy at the receipt of the aid animates our fellow feeling with his gratitude toward his benefactor.

Having shown how sympathy gives rise to the senses of propriety and of merit in our judgment of the passions and conduct of others, Smith turns to showing how these sentimental mechanisms may be employed in our judgment of ourselves. We must take care to avoid a self-interested partiality in our judgments. According to Smith, impartiality can be achieved only if we look at our own behavior as though it were someone else's. Thus, we may judge ourselves from the same point of view that we judge others, and our approval or disapproval of our own conduct will depend on whether we can sympathize with the sentiments from which our actions flow. Conscience, "the judge within us," enables us to make a proper comparison between our own interests and the interests of others. With its aid we may approach the ideal of the man of perfect virtue, who is possessed of both a command of his own feelings and a sensibility for the feelings of others.

We may guard against self-deceit by keeping before us the general rules for what is appropriate in human conduct. These rules have their basis in the sentiments which certain kinds of behavior evoke, and our own respect for the rules should follow from the correspondence between them and our own feelings as we observe the conduct of others. Smith stresses that the rules are generalizations from particular instances in which conduct has excited the sense of propriety and merit in mankind. A just regard for these general rules is a sense of duty. By acting from a sense of duty, one can make up for any lack of the appropriate sentiment on a given occasion. Of all the general rules, those which define justice have the greatest exactness.

Throughout his discussion of our moral psychology, Smith assumes the general acceptance of beneficence and justice as social virtues. He glides quickly over the problem of their description, and he introduces sympathy into his moral psychology as a kind of absolute without considering whether someone might sympathize with "wrong" affections.

In his moral philosophy Smith treats of two questions: Wherein does virtue consist? What power or faculty of the mind recommends virtue to us?

The different accounts of virtue may be reduced to three principles. First, virtue is the proper government and direction of all our affections (propriety). Second, virtue is the judicious pursuit of our own private interest (prudence). Third, virtue lies in the exercise of only those affections which aim at the happiness of others (benevolence). These principles make it evident either that virtue may be ascribed to all our affections when properly governed (as the principle of propriety implies) or that virtue is limited to one of two classes of our affections, either the prudent ones or the benevolent ones.

After surveying the various systems of morals, Smith offers the following conclusions. The systems based on propriety give no precise measure of it. Smith remedies this defect by pointing out that the standard of what is appropriate in sentiments and motives can be found no-where but in the sympathetic feelings of the impartial spectator. The most that can be claimed for the definition of virtue as propriety is that there is no virtue without propriety, and where there is propriety, some approbation is due. But those who make propriety the sole criterion of virtue can be refuted by the single consideration that they cannot account for the superior esteem granted to benevolent actions. On the other hand, however, neither prudence nor benevolence can be allowed to be the sole criterion of virtue, for whichever we choose, we make it impossible to explain our approbation of the other. Smith's implied conclusion is that there can be no single criterion of virtue and that each of the three principles which he notes must be allowed its just scope.

When Smith turns to the question of what power or faculty of the mind recommends virtue to us, he remarks that this question is of purely speculative interest and has no practical importance whatsoever. Several candidates had been proposed by Smith's predecessors as the source of virtue, notably self-love, reason, or some sentiment. Smith rejects self-love as the ultimate basis of behavior, and hence as the basis of virtue, on the ground that its proponents have neglected sympathy as a cause of action. For Smith, sympathy is not a selfish principle. Smith also rejects reason as a source of the distinction between virtue and vice because reason cannot render any action either agreeable or disagreeable to the mind for its own sake. The first perceptions of right and wrong must be derived from an immediate sense of the agreeableness or disagreeableness of actions. Thus, Smith is left with the conclusion that there must be some sentiment which recommends virtue to us.

Smith considers the proposal that there is a special sense of virtue, the moral sense, as proposed by his former teacher Hutcheson. But Smith regards the moral sense as objectionable on two counts. First, no one seemed to be aware that he had a moral sense before the moral philosophers began to talk about it; and if the moral sense is a genuine sense, this state of affairs seems very odd indeed. Second, Smith finds that sympathy, a recognized human phenomenon, is the source of a range of feelings which provide a foundation for virtue. Therefore, since a sentimental basis for virtue is already provided by nature, there is no need to invent one in the form of a moral sense.

An Inquiry into the Nature and Causes of the Wealth of Nations is partly a description of the actual conditions of manufacture and trade in Smith's own time, partly a history of European economics, and partly recommendations to governments. Smith opposes the mercantilist beliefs that money is wealth and that the best economic policy for a country is the retention within its borders of as much gold and silver as possible. He argues, rather, that wealth is consumable goods and that the wealthiest country is one that either produces itself or can command from others the greatest quantity of consumable goods.

The development of a full-blown economic system requires some people in a society to possess a supply of either raw materials or manufactured goods greater than is required to fulfill their own immediate needs. The surplus stocks provide the opportunity for trade among people with various needs. Where the demand for a certain kind of thing is great enough to assure a producer that his other wants may be supplied in exchange for producing this certain good, he will specialize in its production. This kind of division of labor will continue, according to Smith, until some laborers are producing a very small part of a manufactured product because the master finds that a division of labor enables his workers to produce a greater quantity of goods in a shorter time.

Smith believes that the general welfare will be best served by permitting each person to pursue his own interest. Sympathy, which figured largely in Smith's account of moral psychology, is not mentioned in his economics. Self-interest is the motive required to explain economic action. Smith argues, "Every individual is continually exerting himself to find out the most advantageous employment for whatever capital he can command." Since the most advantageous employment of capital is to be found in producing and selling the goods which satisfy the greatest needs of a people, the capitalist is bound to work to satisfy those needs. Intending only his own gain, he contributes nonetheless to the general welfare. Thus, the capitalist is "led by an invisible hand to promote an end which was no part of his intention."

Smith was instrumental in bringing his contemporaries to see the modern European economic system for the first time, and we are the heirs of their vision. Of course, Smith is guilty of oversimplifications and omissions, but his work is nonetheless a model of both observation and systematization in the social sciences.

Bibliography

The edition of *The Wealth of Nations* prepared by Edwin Cannan (New York, 1904) is recommended. See also William R. Scott, ed., *Adam Smith as Student and Professor, With Unpublished Documents* (Glasgow, Scotland, 1937), a biographical account, and Eli Ginzberg, *The House of Adam Smith* (New York, 1934), which is the classic analysis of Smith's economics based on consideration of his predecessors and contemporaries. For Smith's moral philosophy, see James Bonar, *Moral Sense* (London, 1930), Chs. X and XI.

ELMER SPRAGUE

SMITH, JOHN (c. 1616–1652), moral and religious philosopher of the Cambridge Platonist school, was born at Achurch, near Oundle, in Northamptonshire. Very little is known with certainty about his origins. It would seem that his father was a locally respected small farmer, that both of his parents were elderly when he was born, that he lost his mother in his early childhood and his father soon after. His short life was a continual struggle against poverty and ill health. In 1636 he was somehow enabled to enter Emmanuel College, where he came under the influence of Benjamin Whichcote. Although he was about the same age as his fellow Platonist Ralph Cudworth, Cudworth was already a fellow of Emmanuel before Smith took his B.A. in 1640; Smith was very likely his pupil and certainly came under his influence. The influence may have been in some measure reciprocal.

Smith took his M.A. degree in 1644; the same year he was elected a fellow of Queen's College, Cambridge, having been declared by the London Assembly of Divines a suitable person to replace one of the fellows who had been ejected by the Puritan Parliament. He taught Greek, Hebrew, and mathematics. Like his master Whichcote he had gifts of character and personal warmth, which won for him not only the respect but also the affection of pupils and friends. The funeral sermon preached by Simon Patrick on his death on August 7, 1652, is, even allowing for the extravagance of phrase common to such occasions, an impressive tribute to his intellectual and personal gifts. He published nothing, but after his death a series of *Discourses* which he had delivered as dean of his college in the chapel of Queen's was collected, edited, and published by John Worthington. Another volume was promised but never appeared.

Matthew Arnold described Smith's *Discourses* as "the most admirable work left to us by the Cambridge School." This is the judgment of a man whose interests lay in religion and culture rather than in philosophy. As a philosopher Smith will not stand comparison with Cudworth or More. Basically, he was an eloquent apologist for the liberal theology of the Cambridge school. The flow of that eloquence, however, is interrupted, in the Cambridge Platonist manner, by quotations in a variety of tongues from Plato, especially the *Phaedo* and the *Republic,* and the Neoplatonists, the Hebrew Scriptures, the Talmud, and, the sole contemporary, Descartes. Smith's reasoning is by no means close. "It is but a thin, airy knowledge," he writes in the first *Discourse,* "that is got by mere speculation, which is ushered in by syllogisms and demonstrations." God's nature, he thinks, is to be understood by "spiritual sensation" rather than by verbal description; Smith's object is to arouse such a "spiritual sensation" in men's souls, and philosophy is only ancillary to that task.

Thought. The first six of the *Discourses* Smith composed as a continuous essay. They were to be the first segment of a book which he did not live to complete. As editor, Worthington broke up the essay into chapters and added, from Smith's papers, four sermons to act as a substitute for the unwritten segments of the essay. Smith's general thesis is the Platonic one that goodness and knowledge are intimately united; only the purified soul can achieve true knowledge. Every soul, he thought, has within it innate concepts of religion and morality. Ordinarily obscured by sensuality, they nevertheless act as a guide to the direction in which purification is to be sought. Such principles Smith thinks of as innate ideas. Knowledge, in his view, is derived by reflection of the character of our souls; it does not arise out of sensory experience. One can see why he admired the Neoplatonists and welcomed the teachings of Descartes. He did not live long enough to share in the revulsion against Descartes's teachings as mechanistic, which Henry More and Cudworth were to exhibit; indeed, in his *Discourses* he draws on Descartes's physiology.

According to Smith, the three great enemies of religion are superstition, legalism, and atheism. Superstition consists of treating God as a capricious power who has to be cajoled by flattery, bribery, or magical spells. Legalism conceives of religion as laying down doctrines which should simply be accepted as rules for governing our conduct. It can take a variety of forms; "Scripture-Christianity" is quite as legalistic as Jewish formalism if it consists of picking out of the Scriptures a set of doctrines on the acceptance of which salvation is supposed to depend. Smith attacks this sort of Christianity with particular vigor, especially in his Sermon "Pharisaical Righteousness" (*Discourses* VIII).

As for atheism, Smith, unlike Cudworth and More, did not have Hobbes to contend with. He knew of atheism only as it appears in the writings of the Epicureans; much of his (very brief) argument against atheism is directed against the Epicurean version of atomism. He regards the belief in God as a "natural belief" which scarcely needs to be defended. He is much more preoccupied with the belief in immortality, perhaps because Richard Overton in a notorious pamphlet, *Man's Mortality* (1643), published in London although as if from Amsterdam, had denied that man is by nature immortal, arguing that the soul and the body are so compounded that they die and are resurrected together. Smith defends what Overton had rejected—the traditional distinction between soul and body—calling upon Descartes for support.

If men are led to doubt the immortality of their souls, Smith argues, this is only because they are conscious that their souls do not deserve to be immortalized. Once they improve the quality of their lives, they will come to be conscious of their souls as exhibiting a kind of goodness that is obviously destined to be eternal. Similarly, if questions arise about God's nature, these can be settled, as Plotinus had suggested, only by reflection on the workings of our own souls in their most godlike moments. God is the perfect soul, the perfectly loving soul, the perfectly rational soul; that this is God's nature we see by reflection upon our own perfections and imperfections.

It is easy to see why men as different as John Wesley and Matthew Arnold expressed admiration for Smith and sought to introduce his writings to a wider audience. Smith's appeal to inwardness, to the capture of the soul by God, recommends him to the evangelical; his rejection of merely creedal religions, the moral emphasis of his teaching, recommends him to the liberal theologian.

Bibliography

The *Select Discourses* were first published and edited by John Worthington in 1660 (London). The best edition is that edited by Henry Griffin Williams for the Cambridge University Press in 1859. Various extracts have been published, for example, by John Wesley in Vol. XI of his Christian Library (London, 1819–1827). A selection with the title *The Natural Truth of Christianity,* edited by W. M. Metcalfe (Paisley, 1882), includes an introductory commendation by Matthew Arnold.

For works on Smith, see bibliography to CAMBRIDGE PLATONISTS; Rufus Matthew Jones, *Spiritual Reformers in the Sixteenth and Seventeenth Centuries* (London, 1914), Ch. 16; the Address to the Reader prefixed to John Worthington's edition of the *Discourses* (reprinted in the 1859 edition); John K. Ryan, "John Smith, Platonist and Mystic," in *The New Scholasticism,* Vol. 20, No. 1 (1946), 1–25; and J. E. Saveson, "Descartes' Influence on John Smith, Cambridge Platonist," in *Journal of the History of Ideas,* Vol. 20, No. 2 (1959), 258–263.

JOHN PASSMORE

SMUTS, JAN CHRISTIAAN (1870–1950), South African statesman, soldier, and scholar, introduced the concept of "holism" into philosophy. Smuts was born on a farm near Riebeek West, Cape Colony (now Cape of Good Hope Province). He graduated from Victoria College, Stellenbosch, in 1891 and from Cambridge in 1894, where he studied law. At both places his record was brilliant, but he had the reputation of being a bookish recluse who made few friends. Returning home in 1895, he was admitted to the bar, entered political life, and during the Boer War commanded a force against the British with the rank of general. However, when World War I broke out in 1914 he became a staunch defender of the Allied cause. In 1918 he published a pamphlet entitled *The League of Nations: A Practical Suggestion,* which helped to form Wilson's ideas. From 1919 to 1924, and again from 1939 to 1948, he was prime minister of South Africa. In the intervening period he completed his only philosophical work, *Holism and Evolution* (New York, 1926). Smuts was a dominant figure in the politics of his country for over half a century and an influential figure on the world scene. His enemies considered him arrogant and ruthless, more interested in ideas than in people. Yet the theme of his politics, as of his philosophy, was the integration of parts into wholes.

This theme is central to *Holism and Evolution,* where it is used to integrate the results of the sciences, especially the biological sciences, and where it becomes the basis of "a new *Weltanschauung* within the general framework of Science." The background was supplied by the theory of evolution, so interpreted as to preclude mechanistic or materialistic formulations of it. Such formulations, Smuts held, are incompatible with the fact that evolution is creative, having successively brought into existence items that are genuinely novel and that were not even potentially existent before they appeared on the scene. These items he called "wholes." Their appearance was explained by postulating a primordial whole-making, or "holistic," factor in the universe. This factor he also called a "creative tendency or principle" operative throughout the history of nature.

Smuts apparently wished to distinguish wholes in the strict sense from mere aggregates, mechanical systems, and chemical compounds. In a true whole the parts lose forever their prior identity. In aggregates, mechanical systems, and chemical compounds, however, the identity of the parts or elements is not lost but is always recoverable. There are certain entities, such as biochemical systems, which appear to have an intermediate status. For they display "a mixture of mechanism and holism." These systems form "the vast ladder of life." At the bottom of the ladder, mechanistic features predominate; at the top, holistic features predominate. True wholes, free of any admixture of mechanism, are exemplified in minds or psychic structures, which first appear among higher organisms, and in human personality, "the supreme embodiment of Holism."

Smuts sometimes spoke of atoms and molecules as wholes, presumably using the term in other than the strict sense he had defined. The broader use allowed him to affirm that the factor of holism is "responsible for the total course of evolution, inorganic as well as organic. All the great main types of existence are due to it." Long before organisms or minds arose, the holistic factor was producing elementary wholes of a purely physical kind. Later,

through a series of "creative leaps," it became more fully embodied in biological structures, minds, and persons. Indeed, "it is in the sphere of spiritual values that Holism finds its clearest embodiment," for in this sphere love, beauty, goodness, and truth have their source.

Smuts nowhere attributed to the holistic factor any teleological orientation. Nor did he apply to it any personal or spiritual categories. It was represented as an ultimate principle, metaphysical rather than religious, at work and still working in the cosmos.

There is a considerable resemblance between Smuts's philosophical views and those of Bergson and C. Lloyd Morgan. All three philosophers stressed the creativity of evolution, its engendering of novelties whose presence invalidates mechanistic materialism. All were critical of Darwinism and opposed it with arguments and assertions couched in highly general terms. Smuts differed from the other two philosophers in refusing to state explicitly that the holistic factor is spiritual or akin to mind. But at bottom it remains as inscrutable as Bergson's *élan vital* or Morgan's directing Activity.

Bibliography

McDougall, William, "The Confusion of the Concept." *Journal of Philosophical Studies,* Vol. 3 (1928), 440–442.
Morgan, C. Lloyd, review of *Holism and Evolution. Journal of Philosophical Studies* (1927), 85–89.

T. A. GOUDGE

SOCIAL CONTRACT is the name given to a group of related and overlapping concepts and traditions in political theory. Like other such aggregations in philosophy and intellectual history, it has at its center an extremely simple conceptual model, in this case that the collectivity is an agreement between the individuals who make it up. This model suggests that it is proper to ask whether the agreement was or is voluntary in character and whether, therefore, the individual can decide to withdraw either because he no longer agrees or because the conditions which are or were understood in the agreement are not being maintained. It suggests furthermore that the individual should be thought of as logically prior to the state or to society, and that it is meaningful to speculate on situations in which individuals existed but no collectivity was in being. From a historical point of view, it is therefore relevant to discuss periods of time during which no collectivity existed, when what is traditionally called a "state of nature" prevailed, and to contrast these periods with times when by agreement the collectivity had come into existence, that is, with what is traditionally called a "state of society."

The concept of a prepolitical state of nature that can be brought to an end by agreement can thus be applied to geographical areas of human society as well as to periods of time. Individuals in such areas must be considered, as Thomas Hobbes himself said, "to have no government at all and to live at this day in that brutish manner." Although this may seem to be the least persuasive of the elements belonging to the social contract, its parallel in relationships between politically constituted societies or states, that is to say, in the international state of nature, is perhaps the most useful and persistent. It seems still to command allegiance in the study of international relations. The actual process of agreeing ("contracting," "compacting," "covenanting") to end the state of nature and establish a state of society has been the subject of extensive analysis and elaboration by political and social theorists. Distinctions have been drawn, more precisely perhaps by academic commentators in modern times than by contractarian writers themselves, between a social contract and a governmental contract.

The social contract proper (*pactum societatis, pacte d'association, Gesellschaftsvertrag*) is thought of as bringing individuals together in society, and the governmental contract (*pactum subjectionis, pacte du gouvernement, Herrschaftsvertrag*) as establishing a formal government. As might be expected, the nature and form of the contract or contracts has been thought of in a variety of ways. In some systems the contract is a once-and-for-all, irrevocable act understood to have been performed in the remote past (Richard Hooker), but in others it appears as a continuing understanding that is perpetually being renewed and is regarded rather as a trust than as a contract (Locke). The parties to the various contracts differ also: Sometimes agreements are made between individuals only, sometimes between individuals and governments or sovereigns, sometimes between a body of individuals acting as a fictitious person (*persona ficta*) and either the sovereign or a member of the body. In such ways as these a whole set and succession of interrelated contractual agreements have occasionally been presumed, as in the case of the seventeenth-century German political theorist Samuel Pufendorf and his followers in the eighteenth century.

The theory of a social contract belongs with the individualist attitude to state and society; indeed the simple conceptual model of agreement for the collectivity in all its possible shapes seems to inform the entire individualistic outlook. Contractual political theory is, therefore, universally associated with the rights of the individual person, with consent as the basis of government, and with democratic, republican, or constitutional institutions. It has also been regarded as a part of early capitalist individualism, and in Victorian England a great watershed was held to exist between a condition in which status ruled relationships and one in which contract ruled them. Notwithstanding this assumption, the social contract is perfectly reconcilable with the most absolute of despotic rule and with the complete negation of constitutionalism or the rule of law. Hobbes is the classic case here, for his two alternative accounts of how society and government came simultaneously into being are designed to tie every citizen to unquestioning obedience to a supreme, irresistible, indivisible sovereign whose dictates are the law. Spinoza makes a rather similar use of contractual principles, but the political theory of Rousseau, although expounded in contractual form, has collectivist tendencies, since it endows political society with the capacity to make men moral. Rousseau's major political work, *Du Contrat social*, must be looked upon as the point of departure of the quite separate and traditionally quite irreconcilable outlook whose model is the theory of the general will (see GENERAL WILL, THE).

Explanatory value. If the collectivity is understood as embodying agreement, it does not necessarily follow that any such agreement between parties ever actually took place in historical time. Nor does it follow that there may be men in the world still living in a prepolitical, precontractual situation or that those now within constituted society could ever revert to the nonpolitical condition. A contractarian political theory, therefore, can be entirely hypothetical, analyzing state and society as if agreement must always be presumed. Such an argument can provide a penetrating critique of existing arrangements and of their rationale: It can be used in a reformist direction, to suggest what ought to be the aims and ends of statesmen. No reversion to a literal state of nature need be implied by criticism of this kind, only that this or that action or abuse requires a remedy in accordance with the suggested criterion of an assumed agreement.

In this hypothetical form the contract theory is still of importance to political philosophy. It has recently been used by John Rawls in his articles "Justice as Fairness" and "Distributive Justice" to develop an account of justice alternative to the utilitarian (previously assumed to have outmoded contractarianism). Contemporary appreciations of the great contractarian writers (for example, by Howard Warrender, C. B. Macpherson, and A. G. Wernham), especially of Hobbes but also of Locke, Spinoza, and Hume, and even of Rousseau, have tended to insist that the classic theories are hypothetical, which makes it possible to free the theories to a surprising extent from the lumber which had attached to them—the unacceptable histories of the human race, the fanciful anthropology and sociology. Moreover, the assumptions of natural law can thus be put aside.

Natural law. The reinterpretation of social contract theory is an important example of the way in which past political theory can enter into present theoretical analysis independently of chains of influence and continuous traditions. Still, the reinterpretation may lead to a serious distortion of the truth about the actual contents of contractarian treatises on politics. All the many members of the school of natural law, including those named above, did in fact assume that their contractual claims were literal as well as hypothetical. They all made dogmatic statements about the history of humanity and the condition of savages. Moreover all of them, though here writers like Hobbes and Hume are in special categories, subscribed to the general system of natural law in one form or another.

The concept of natural law provided the fixed and enduring framework within which the contract ending the state of nature could be concluded, and subsequent breaches or revisions of the contract could be related to the original act. Therefore, natural law had to be assumed if the contract was to be taken at all literally. The duty to keep promises, on which any contract rests, could hardly come into being with the contract itself, and this duty must persist should the contract be broken, if only to make a new one possible. When the Commons of England in January 1689 accused their former king, James II, of "breaking the original contract betwixt King and people," they did so in the secure belief that this was an offense which was and always would be punishable under natural law. It is understandable, then, that the history of the idea of a social contract has been largely the same as that of natural law itself.

History. The origins of social contract theory and of natural law can be sought in the Roman Stoicism of Cicero and in the system of Roman law. The development of social contract into a standard feature of the Western Christian attitude can be seen in the Middle Ages, and its apotheosis can be observed in the period between the Reformation and the eighteenth century. It is usual in fact to insist that the rise of the contractarian attitude to predominance in European political thought came about because of the Reformation. Certainly the justification of the right of a Protestant minority in a Catholic country, and of that of a Catholic minority in a Protestant country, to its own form of religious worship came about because of the gradual acceptance of contractarian notions by Reformation and post-Reformation political and legal thinkers and even by some politicians and sovereigns. The slow and hesitant growth of religious toleration would undoubtedly have been even more retarded if natural law and the social contract had not been at hand to provide a definition of the individual citizen, his individual rights, and the nature of his relationship to political authority. Accordingly, we find that the French religious wars of the 1560s, 1570s, and 1580s, together with the revolt of the Dutch against the throne of Spain, which began in 1568, brought about the elaboration of contractarian ideas. In both these cases embattled Calvinists were asserting their political as well as their religious rights against Catholic authorities, but in England at the same time it was the Catholics who needed contractarian justification for their rights, even finally their rights to resist government.

The *Monarchomachi* ("bearers of the sword against monarchs"), as the French writers were called, developed the contract between people and sovereign in various directions, and in the famous *Vindiciae Contra Tyrannos* (1579) it justified a recognizably revolutionary doctrine. In Holland the contract was codified further and became in the works of Althusius and Grotius an informing principle of political life as well as of the relations between sovereign and people. (Grotius' great work, however, the *De Jure Belli ac Pacis* of 1625, acquired and retains its fame because of its application of natural law and contractarian principles to international law.)

All these ideas and all these experiences—particularly the experience of religious separatism developing into civil war—can be seen at work in Hobbes, the most impressive of all contractarian theorists. In Hobbes's *Leviathan* (1651), the state of nature was a state of war, a propertyless anarchy brought to an end only by the contract of absolute submission. Hobbes made such devastating use of the destructive potentialities of the social contract in criticism of the conventional thinking about natural law that all succeeding systems can be looked upon to some extent as commentaries upon him. This is truest of Spinoza (*Tractatus Theologico-politicus*, 1670; *Tractatus Politicus*, 1677) and until recently was thought to be true of Hobbes's eminent and enormously influential successor in England, John Locke.

Locke's *Two Treatises of Government* (written 1679–1683, published 1689) are now known to have been written as an attack on Filmer, not on Hobbes, and Locke's relatively peaceful and sociable state of nature, brought to an end by a very limited contract, has only a somewhat distant relationship with Hobbes's "war of all against all." It is interesting that Filmer should have been the most effective critic of the concept of a state of nature and of the possibility and relevance of contract and that his traditional, patriarchal authoritarianism was to a large extent immune from contractarian notions.

It was not traditionalism, however, which broke down contractarian assumptions within a generation of the death of Locke in 1704, but rather the rapid defeat of the natural law outlook by utilitarian criticism in England and by general will notions in France and elsewhere. Contract lost its persuasiveness as the rationalist outlook on the nature of law gave way to the historical outlook early in the nineteenth century. The development of observational anthropology and empirical sociology in more recent times makes it entirely unlikely that contract in anything but a strictly hypothetical form will ever be adopted again by political theorists.

This conventional account of the history of contract could be corrected and extended by reference to the simple model of the collectivity as agreement with which this article began. This is so obvious an image that it can be found in some form in any political system, even in the refusal of Socrates to escape from his prison and avoid the poison on the ground that he owed obedience to his native city because of the benefits he had received as a citizen. It seems likely that every political theory must be contractual, at least to some degree, in this very wide sense.

Nevertheless, since contract proceeds by abstracting the individual from society, and then by reassembling individuals again as society although they are by definition asocial abstractions, the general contractual social and political scheme seems incurably faulty, quite apart from the empirical objections to it on the part of contemporary social scientists.

Bibliography

The standard account in English is J. W. Gough, *The Social Contract* (1st ed., Oxford, 1936; rev. ed., 1957). Ernest Barker analyzes classical notions of contract very succinctly in a compilation he edited for the World's Classics series entitled *Social Contract: Essays by Locke, Hume, and Rousseau* (Oxford, 1948); he has also translated the relevant part of Otto Gierke's monumental general treatise, *Das Deutsche Genossenschaftsrecht* (1913), as *Natural Law and the Theory of Society*, 2 vols. (Cambridge, 1934). In addition, see A. G. Wernham, ed., *Spinoza, Political Works* (Oxford, 1958); Peter Laslett, ed., *John Locke, Two Treatises of Government* (Cambridge, 1960); Howard Warrender, *Political Philosophy of Hobbes* (New York, 1957); and C. B. Macpherson, *Political Theory of Possessive Individualism: Hobbes to Locke* (New York, 1962).

More recent theoretical analyses of contract are Margaret Macdonald, "The Language of Political Theory," in Antony Flew, ed., *Logic and Language*, First Series (Oxford, 1956), and the essays in the collection *Philosophy, Politics and Society*, Peter Laslett and W. S. Runciman, eds. (Oxford, 1957——), especially those by John Rawls.

PETER LASLETT

SOCIALISM. This article is concerned with "socialism" from the time at which, so far as anyone knows, the word was first used in print to describe a view of what human society should be like. This was in 1827, in the English

Co-operative Magazine, a periodical aimed at expounding and furthering the views of Robert Owen of New Lanark, generally regarded as the father and founder of the cooperative movement. (Owenite cooperation, incidentally, was an institution different from, and far more idealistic than, the distributive stores which in the Victorian age took over the name.) Some historians have traced the ancestry of socialism much farther back: for example, to primitive communist societies, to the Jesuits of Paraguay, to the ideal communities described by Thomas More and others, to the Diggers of Cromwell's army, and even to Plato's *Republic.* Although there are elements of socialism to be found in all these, particularly in More's *Utopia,* the scope of this article is limited to socialism in modern times and to the sense in which the word is normally used, omitting both distant possible origins and, of course, bastard movements like the National Socialism (Nazism) of twentieth-century Germany and Austria which, save for the bare fact that they enforced central control of social policy, had nothing of socialism in them.

Origin of socialism. The seedbed of socialism, as of so much else in modern thought, was the French Revolution and the revolutionary French thinkers who preceded it—Voltaire, Rousseau, and the Encyclopedists. Rousseau was no socialist, but from his cornucopia of seminal though sometimes unclear and inconsistent thought socialists drew the ideas of men born free but everywhere in chains, of a "general will" making for perfection in society, of the importance of education, and a host of others. From the Encyclopedists they learned to question all institutions in the light of reason and justice, and even from "Gracchus" Babeuf to demand equality for the downtrodden and to seek it by means of dedicated conspirators. Owen himself was no revolutionary; insofar as his ideas can be traced to anyone but himself, they probably came from early reading of the William Godwin who wrote *Political Justice;* Owen envisaged a society consisting of small, self-governing, cooperating communities, established by the free and rational consent of all, of whatever class or station. Originally, the word "socialism" appears to have laid particular emphasis on communal cooperation in contrast to the more-or-less liberalism that was coming to be the creed of the industrial revolution—hence Owen's rather contemptuous dismissal of Bentham and the utilitarians. The idea of socialism came rapidly to fit the aspirations of the working classes and their radical champions not only in its country of origin but far beyond it.

Socialist tenets. During its lifetime of nearly 150 years, a period which has seen vast changes not merely in the industrial and political organization of society but also in men's minds, their modes of thought, and their interpretation both of themselves and of what they have seen around them, "socialism" has naturally borne many meanings, and dozens of views have been held and expressed about the form of society that socialists hope to see and about the means by which it should be attained and secured. Long before Marx and Engels introduced the great schism between what they called utopian and scientific socialism, there were wide differences of opinion; and the differences are no less wide today. George Bernard Shaw, for example, in *The Intelligent Woman's Guide to Socialism and Capitalism,* laid down absolute equality of money incomes

as a *sine qua non*—a dictum accepted by few of his fellow socialists, and not by Shaw himself in any practical sense. There are many other definitions that could be quoted. Nevertheless, the word is certainly not meaningless. It describes a living thing which grows and changes as it lives; and it is possible to discern certain beliefs that are fundamental to all who can be called socialists, as well as to note the divergences in what may be called secondary beliefs and to relate these, in part at least, to the conditions of the time.

Critique of existing society. The first of the fundamental beliefs of socialists is that the existing system of society and its institutions should be condemned as unjust, as morally unsound. The institutions which are thus condemned vary from time to time and from place to place according to circumstances, the greatest stress being laid sometimes on landlordism, sometimes on factory industry, on the churches, the law, or the political government, or a combination of these (as William Cobbett, in an earlier century, denounced "The Thing"), depending on what seems to be the most potent engine or engines of oppression. This condemnation may be associated with the values of revealed religion, as in the case of the various forms of Christian socialism, or may positively repudiate those values, as Marx did; in either case the emphasis is on injustice. Proudhon's dictum, "Property is theft," expresses this condemnation most concisely. Many socialist movements, such as the Saint-Simonians in the 1830s and the Fabians half a century later, attacked the existing system for its economic and social inefficiency as well; but this criticism was less fundamental. Socialists like Fourier in France and William Morris in England laid much more stress on freedom, happiness, and beauty than on material wealth. Even the economists among them, however, long asserted that granted decent (that is, socialist) distribution of the product of industry and agriculture, there would easily be "enough to go round" and to provide everyone with a standard of living recognized to be reasonable. By the mid-twentieth century the enormous multiplication of potential demand, coupled with realization of the existence of hundreds of millions living far below European standards of life, had referred that type of prophecy to the far-distant future.

A new and better society. The second fundamental of socialism is the belief that there can be created a different form of society with different institutions, based on moral values, which will tend to improve mankind instead of, as now, to corrupt it. Since it is living men who are to create the new institutions—men who must, therefore, recognize and follow the appeal of moral value—this belief is in effect an assertion of the perfectibility, or at least near-perfectibility, of man. It was most dogmatically stated by Owen, in books like *A New View of Society;* and the history of socialism shows that it can survive innumerable disappointments. It is not the same as a belief in "progress," which has been held by many who were not socialists; it is more like *Magna est veritas et praevalebit* ("The truth is great and will prevail")—truth being here equated with justice.

Does justice, in social institutions, imply equality? Does it also imply democracy? For socialists, the answer to both these questions has generally been positive but the answer has not been absolute. Equality of rights—yes; equality before the law—yes, again. We have already observed, however, that complete equality of income was not a universal socialist tenet; and from the very earliest days there were sharp differences among socialists on the relationship between work and income. On the dictum "From each according to his ability" they more or less agreed. But some added "to each according to his needs"; others countered with "to each according to his effort—or his product." This debate, in which sides were taken, on the whole, in accordance with the temperament and/or environment of the individual and in which many intermediate positions were adopted, remained unresolved throughout the history of socialism—not surprisingly, since the problem of controlling the level of incomes has defeated all except completely static societies. On the question of democracy, again, the great majority of socialists have been democrats in the ordinarily accepted sense of the word. But some rejected any formal democratic process in favor of a communal consensus resembling the Quaker "sense of the meeting" (or Rousseau's general will). Owen, in practice, was an autocratic egalitarian; and post-Marxist socialism has evolved a procedure known as democratic centralism, which bears little relation to what any pre-Marxist would recognize as democracy.

Deep differences arose early on the kind of institution which would be best suited for a world devoted to justice. There was one main difference at first: some put their faith in small communities of neighbors, as far as possible self-sufficient, cooperating freely with other similar communities in such functions as exchange of goods, and relying to the minimum on any regional or central authority for such necessities as defense and the supply of credit; others looked rather to a development of science, technology, and large-scale industrial production and banking to increase rapidly the supply of material goods and thereby the prosperity of a socialist economy through centralized planning techniques. Of these two schools—whose views have necessarily been greatly simplified for the compass of this article—the first, or "utopian," is best known from the writings of Owen, Fourier, and Proudhon, and the second, or "scientific," from those of Saint-Simon and his followers. The first clearly derived from rural society: Owen's villages of cooperation and Fourier's phalansteries were based upon small-scale agriculture, with such industrial and craft production as could conveniently be carried on in villages or small communities. This was the kind of society envisaged, much later, in William Morris' *News from Nowhere;* and much later still, there were curious echoes of it in Lenin's dreams of cheap electricity transforming the life of the Russian peasantry and even in the Chinese "great leap forward," with a piece of factory in every backyard. The weakness of this school is that its fear of size, of external authority, and of the apparatus of the state and of central government, whatever concessions it may in theory make to "natural necessities," such as the conduct of a national railway system, are liable to lead in practice as well as in theory to anarchism and the repudiation of any government at all—which in the modern world means chaos. The second school, that of large-scale production and planning, was, from the beginning, in harmony with the way the world was tending. Its dangers are today only too obvious, and the recurrent malaise of large-scale in-dustry in times of prosperity, the demands for "shares in control," and the like, show the vacuum created by the nonfulfillment of the utopian ideals of a just society.

Revolution. Whatever form of institution the several schools of socialism envisaged for the future, all agreed that what was required was a fundamental transformation of society amounting to revolution, a program of action to effect such a transformation, and a revolutionary will so to transform it existing in the members of present-day society. This is the third fundamental socialist assumption; how it is to be put into effect has been the subject of much division of opinion. As socialism was generally believed to have a strong rational basis, it was natural that all schools of socialists should set great store by education, persuasion, and propaganda; Owen, indeed, carried the trust in rationality so far that he could not believe that anyone, whatever his condition or his preconceived opinions, could fail to be converted by "Mr. Owen's powers of persuasion," if only Mr. Owen could employ them sufficiently often and at sufficient length. Others, less confident, sought to achieve their end by preaching and by working upon groups already conditioned by the circumstances of their working lives to accept the whole or a part of the socialist gospel—the most obvious of these being, of course, the trade unions and other organizations of the working class. In this spirit Marx looked upon the British trade unions that supported the International Working Men's Association (the "First International") as "a lever for the proletarian revolution." Strikes, threats of strikes, and other forms of what much later came to be known as "direct action," supplemented persuasion by inducing the ruling classes to make concessions which could not otherwise have been wrung from them. The practicability, either of persuasion or of group action, depended very largely on the political conditions of time and place. And although there was a running argument between gradualists, who believed that revolutionary change could be brought about peacefully and piecemeal, and revolutionaries, who thought head-on collision between the holders of power and their victims was inevitable in the long run if not immediately, the difference was not as absolute as was often supposed. In Britain, after the defeat of Chartism had registered the end of insurrectionism in any form, after the press had been freed and the franchise widened, the organizations of the working class leaned to peaceful evolution far more than to violence—the "inevitability of gradualism" was an accepted belief long before Sidney Webb put it into words in the 1920s. In tsarist Russia, at the other extreme, a generally authoritarian government, operating a police state, appeared to bar the door to anything but physical revolution. There were many possible in-between positions; and the role of the convinced individual socialist varied similarly, from that of open persuader, adviser, and organizer, like Keir Hardie at the end of the nineteenth century, to that of secret conspirator, like Auguste Blanqui in France after 1848 and organizers of communist cells in our own day.

Internationalism. One other characteristic should briefly be mentioned. Socialism was initially a world philosophy, not concerning itself with race or nation, not advocating the brotherhood of man so much as assuming it. The opening of the *Communist Manifesto,* "Workers of the world, unite," crystallized this into words; the nationalism of Poles, Irish, Italians, Hungarians, was only an aspect of the struggle against corrupt institutions. Later, of course, nationalism grew so strong that it clashed, sometimes violently, with other fundamentals of socialism; nevertheless, the idea remained potent for generations, and it may still be suggested that socialist movements that have become exclusively nationalist have ceased to be socialist at all.

Marxian socialism. The *Communist Manifesto* marks a great divide between pre-Marxian and post-Marxian socialism. Marx and Engels dismissed all their predecessors as utopians and formulated a system of socialism which they claimed was "scientific." There is no room here to expound Marxist philosophy or Marxist economics; but it must be pointed out that neither "utopian" nor "scientific" is an accurate description. Marxist socialism accepted the fundamentals as set out above; it differed from most of its forerunners in that it did not, save in a few very vague allusions, seek to describe the new, uncorrupt institutions that would appear after the revolution; it assumed—and what could be more utopian?—that after the proletariat had conquered, it would make all anew and "the government of man be replaced by the administration of things."

"Scientific," in Marxist language, meant not so much acceptance of technology and large-scale production—although this was included—as the proving, by logical argument and study of history, of two quite simple propositions: first, that under the existing capitalist system, the proletariat, the laboring class, is systematically and continuously robbed of its just share of the fruits of production; second, that "changes in the modes of production and exchange," and not any other factor, such as "man's insight into eternal truth and justice," are leading inevitably to a reversal of the system that will remove the bourgeois capitalist class from the seats of power and replace it by the organs of the proletariat. This is the base on which the whole enormous superstructure of Marxism is founded; it is not science, but messianic prophecy. It is easy to understand, however, the compelling effect that this fundamentally simple appeal had to the downtrodden at various times and in various places. At the same time, Marx's powerful and penetrating analysis, which discredited a great deal of current economic and historical theory, profoundly attracted many of the best brains among those who were dissatisfied with the human results of the existing system, and the teaching of the Marxists that morality in action was relative to the needs of the time, even if slightly inconsistent with their denunciation, on grounds of injustice, of slavery and wage slavery, gave their followers both the inspiration of those who were fighting a continuing battle and the sanction to use any and every method that could advance their cause. Marx did not invent the conception of classes, but Marxists fought the class war.

The work of Marx and Engels has had as great and lasting an effect on the thinking of non-Marxists, particularly after the Russian Revolution, as has that of Freud on non-Freudians. This article cannot deal with the developments in socialist thought, Marxist or non-Marxist, in the post-Marxian era. These are of enormous importance for the study of history and present-day politics; but they are concerned principally with method and strategy. The fundamental tenets of socialism as a view of society have remained substantially unaltered, although the process of translating them has been far more lengthy and complicated than the nineteenth century ever foresaw.

Bibliography

By far the most complete work on socialism is G. D. H. Cole, *History of Socialist Thought*, 7 vols. (London, 1953–1960), last volume published posthumously. Each volume except the last has a full bibliography for every chapter.

Earlier books are Max Beer, *History of British Socialism* (London, 1929); Édouard Dolléans, *Histoire du mouvement ouvrier*, 2 vols. (Paris, 1936–1939); Sir Alexander Gray, *The Socialist Tradition—Moses to Lenin* (London, 1946); Élie Halévy, *Histoire du socialisme européen* (Paris, 1948); Thomas Kirkup, *History of Socialism*, rev. ed. by E. R. Pease (London, 1913); H. W. Laidler, *Social Economic Movements* (New York, 1944), first issued as *History of Socialist Thought* (New York, 1927); and Paul Louis, *Histoire du socialisme en France*, rev. ed. (Paris, 1950).

For documents, see Raymond Postgate, *Revolution, 1789–1906*, reissued, with a new introduction (New York, 1964).

MARGARET COLE

SOCIAL SCIENCE EXPLANATIONS OF RELIGION. See RELIGION, PSYCHOLOGICAL EXPLANATIONS OF.

SOCIAL SCIENCES. See POLITICAL AND SOCIAL THEORY.

SOCIETY. A group of perennial problems in social philosophy arises from the concept "society" itself and from its relation to the "individual." What is the ontological status of a society? When one speaks of it as having members, is that to recognize it as a whole with parts, or is the relation of some different kind? Or is this a case of what Whitehead called the fallacy of misplaced concreteness?

Social action and social relations. "Society" is used both abstractly and to refer to entities which can be particularized, identified, and distinguished from each other as social systems or organizations. The phrase "man in society" is an instance of the more abstract use, for it refers neither to some particular form of association nor to a particular collectivity in which individuals find themselves. It refers, rather, to the social dimension of human action—to a certain generalized type of human relationship. Purely spatial or physical relations between human beings, like contiguity, are not social; for social relations give to human actions a dimension possessed neither by the mere behavior of things nor, indeed, of animals.

Max Weber defined a social action as one which, "by virtue of the subjective meaning attached to it by the acting individual (or individuals), . . . takes account of the behavior of others and is thereby oriented in its course" (*Theory of Social and Economic Organization*, p. 88). That is to say, the agent understands his own action as having a particular point, which in turn depends on an understanding of what another individual or other individuals have done in the past (as, for instance, in an act of vengeance), are doing now, or are expected to do in the future (as, for instance, in a proposal of marriage). So, said Weber, the efforts of two cyclists to avoid hitting one another would have a social character, whereas the collision between them would not. An action would not be social merely because it was the effect on an individual of the existence of a crowd as such. For instance, laughing less inhibitedly in a crowd than one would when alone would not be an action oriented to the fact of the existence of the crowd "on the level of meaning"; while the crowd may be one of the causes of the action, the point or meaning of the action does not presuppose some conception of, say, the crowd's purposes or the reasons for its presence. Nor would merely imitative behavior be social; one could learn to whistle by imitating a man, a bird, or a whistling kettle. Learning and performance need neither an understanding of what is imitated as an action nor an orientation toward expected future action of the model. However, says Weber, if the action is imitated because it is "fashionable, or traditional, or exemplary, or lends social distinction . . . it is meaningfully oriented either to the behavior of the source of imitation or of third persons or of both" (*ibid.,* pp. 112–114). Weber then goes on to define "social relationship." This would exist wherever, among a number of actors, there existed a probability that their actions would be social actions.

Weber's concept of the "meaning" of an action is rather obscure. It may be a meaning "imputed to the parties in a given concrete case," or it may be what the action means "on the average, or in a theoretically formulated pure type—it is never a normatively 'correct' or metaphysically 'true' meaning" (*ibid.,* p. 118). This concept is connected with Weber's much criticized conception of empathic understanding (*Verstehen*). But this connection is not strictly necessary, for the meaning we give to the actions of others depends not so much on an attempted reconstruction of what is in their minds as on a knowledge of the norms and standards regulating their behavior in a given context. Thus I know what a man is about when he presents a bank teller with a signed paper of a certain size, shape, and color, not because I can reconstruct his state of mind in imagination but because I can recognize the procedures for cashing checks.

Weber insists that it is the probability itself of a course of social action that constitutes the social relation, not any particular basis for the probability. Yet we can rely on situational responses (like the bank teller's, for instance) very largely because we expect them to conform to norms and procedures, by which such responses are deemed appropriate or otherwise. Assuming, as many sociologists would, that even war is a social relation, the acts of opposing commanders are mutually oriented by an understanding of the aims and practices of warfare and by the supposition that the other's actions will be appropriate, not only in terms of means and ends but also in consideration of whatever rules of war may be current. Thus we can move from the concept of social relations as frameworks for interaction to Talcott Parsons' conception of a social system constituted by differentiated statuses and roles.

Societies as organizations. The concept of "a society" implies a system of more or less settled statuses, to each of which correspond particular patterns of actions appropriate to a range of situations. By virtue of qualifying conditions a man enjoys a status; in virtue of that status he has a role to play. These concepts, however, are meaningful only in the context of rules or norms of conduct—a man's role is not simply what he habitually does (for this may be no more socially significant than a tic), nor even what he is expected to do, if an expectation is only what one might predict about his future conduct from a knowledge of his past. His role is what is *expected of* him, in the sense of what is required of him by some standard. The role of secretary to an association, for instance, requires that he read the minutes of the last meeting, because the rules of procedure assign this action to whosoever enjoys this status. Less formally, a father's role may be to provide the family with an income, and failure to do so will be regarded not merely as falsifying predictions but also as disappointing reasonable or legitimate expectations—reasonable, because grounded on an understanding of the norms constituting the structure of the family. Indeed, though what we knew of some particular father might give us good grounds for predicting that he would neglect his role, that would not mean that its requirements did not apply to him. Of course, when we speak of "the family" or "the modern state," we commonly have in mind ideal types or paradigms. There may be significant deviations from these in practice. Any particular family may have its own standards, deviant from the social norm, according to which the role of father does not include providing the family income.

Looked at in these terms, a society is an aggregate of interacting individuals whose relations are governed by role-conferring rules and practices which give their actions their characteristic significance. Thus, to demand money with menaces is one thing if done by a common blackmailer or footpad, another if done by a tax collector.

Nevertheless, the act of John Smith, tax collector, is still the act of John Smith, who acts also in different roles in other situations—as father, member of Rotary, and so forth. So one may take two views of a society. On the one hand, one may see it, as a biographer might, as an aggregate of life histories of its individual members, each, in the course of his life, acting in a variety of roles which explain (but only partially) what he does. Or one may adopt the sociological standpoint. A society is then a pattern of roles, and what President Brown does is less important than that it instantiates the role of president.

Individualist and holistic accounts. Are there any statements about societies, or what Durkheim termed "social facts," that are not ultimately reducible to statements about individuals? According to an extreme individualist or nominalist, such as Thomas Hobbes, social wholes have no substantial reality; propositions attributing properties or actions to a collectivity can be reduced, without residue, to a series of propositions about the relations and actions of individuals: "A multitude of men are made one person, when they are by one man, or one person, represented. . . . and *unity,* can not otherwise be understood in multitude" (*Leviathan,* Michael Oakeshott, ed., Ch. 16, p. 107). Karl Popper's methodological individualism is as uncompromising. So-called social wholes, he declares, are theoretical constructs; "social phenomena, including collectives, should be analysed in terms of individuals and their actions and relations" (*Conjectures and Refutations,* p. 341).

There is no agreement, however, on whether such analysis is possible. Some philosophers, while admitting that every action is the action of an individual, nevertheless deny that "statements which contain societal terms" can be reduced "to a conjunction of statements which only include terms referring to the thoughts and actions of specific individuals" (Maurice Mandelbaum, "Societal Facts," p. 482). While the "societal fact" of cashing a check can be expressed in terms of what individuals do, nevertheless the description will always contain societal terms like "bank" and "money," which cannot themselves be translated without remainder into wholly individual terms. Furthermore, such societal facts, it is said, interact with individual behavior; a banking system can have an effect on a concrete individual. For it is clearly true that for every individual, the institutions and mores of his society present themselves as independent and external facts, just as much as his physical environment does. And if that is true for every individual, it is true for the totality of individuals composing the society. That is not to say that a totality is a thing independent of individuals or that it has a group mind; it is only to say that for any participant or for any observer of an individual's actions, it makes sense to talk of him confronting and confronted by independent social facts (Gellner elaborates this point). Moreover, the principle that social action can ultimately be explained by referring to the dispositions of individuals to behave in certain ways in given circumstances overlooks the possibility that these dispositions may themselves depend on social facts.

The view that social facts are not reducible to individual facts is commonly called holism. In its more extreme forms it relies heavily on biological organic analogies. An organism, it is said, is prior to its constituent parts in the sense that any understanding of their nature and function presupposes an understanding of the whole organism. The whole organism is more than the mere sum of its parts, since no account in terms of the parts considered separately could add up to some of the things that could be said about the whole. (The same might be said, however, of some of the properties of a triangle that arise from the three sides considered in relation to one another.) Just as the liver is a more significant object considered as an organ of a working body than as a detached piece of tissue, so the acts of individuals are significant or intelligible only when considered as the acts of role-bearers or as manifesting characteristics of their social or cultural environment. So drinking wine has a different range of social meaning in England from the one it has in France. The thought-experiment of the social contract theorists, who put man into an asocial state of nature the better to understand his real purposes in society, was radically misconceived, precisely because it abstracted man from the very context in which alone he would be a man but still attributed human properties to him.

According to the Hegelians (Bosanquet, for example), so far are we from being able to reduce social facts to individual facts that it is the individual himself who must be explained as an expression of the concrete social universal —an idea manifesting itself organically in its differentiated parts, as the idea of an oak tree is differentially but organically manifest in its leaves, bark, trunk, and so forth, all in a sense different from one another yet all linked by the idea of the oak and collectively differentiated thereby from the corresponding parts of an elm. "Man" is an abstraction —we are men as we are Germans, Englishmen, Frenchmen; that is, we instantiate the spirit of our own society.

Holistic organicism of this kind has laid great stress on history. Social wholes, it is said (by Savigny, for instance), are not like mechanical wholes. Mechanical wholes can be understood by reducing them to their smallest constituent parts which conform in their behavior to general laws from which the varying behavior of the aggregates can be deduced. A social whole, on the contrary, is *sui generis,* to be understood not by analysis but by studying it *as* a developing whole. Consequently, there can be no general theory of social action, and history is the only legitimate mode of sociological inquiry.

According to Popper, these arguments are totally misconceived. There is simply no way of studying wholes as wholes; any attempt at understanding implies abstracting from a particular configuration of properties and circumstances those which seem significant for the particular study and relating them to general laws and hypotheses that are valid for all cases, irrespective of time, in which the stated initial conditions are satisfied. A law of development could be a statement about the general tendencies of certain types of society, given certain initial conditions; but it is a misunderstanding of the nature of both scientific and historical inquiry to propose a study of a society as a whole, partly because a social whole is a theoretical construct and partly because to attribute to it its own peculiar law of growth, in some sense true regardless of, or despite, any initial conditions whatsoever, is to make any explanatory statement about its behavior impossible. (See also HOLISM AND INDIVIDUALISM IN HISTORY AND SOCIAL SCIENCE.)

Community and association. The individualist account of social action is most persuasive when the form of social organization under consideration is a joint-stock corporation or a trade association. There is little temptation to attribute group personalities to such bodies, except in a strictly legal sense, and therefore little resistance to treating them as nothing but procedural forms. Their members and officials are clearly identified individuals with limited common interests. These interests explain their interaction, without suggesting that the association is anything more than a means for promoting them. Moreover, such interests remain intelligible even abstracted from the context of the society.

Ferdinand Tönnies distinguished this type of organization, which he called a *Gesellschaft* (association), from its polar opposite, the *Gemeinschaft* (community). Paradigms of the latter type are the family, the village, the tribe, and the nation. These are much less formally organized than a joint-stock company. They have no clearly defined, limited aim; qualifications for membership may be poorly defined, depending very largely on subjective criteria. Yet individuals do not deliberately join such bodies—more usually they are born into them or acquire membership by residence. At the same time, membership in such a community may mean much more to the individual. So far from his using the organization as a means for the pursuit of personal interest, privately conceived, what he conceives to be his interest may depend very much on the influence of the collectivity upon him. He may feel bound to it by ties and responsibilities not of his own choosing which nevertheless demand his respect. Moreover, such communities appear to have a lifespan greater than that of any generation of individual members, which cannot be explained, as might that of a corporation, by the continuities of constitutional procedures. It is, rather, that from generation to generation there passes an attachment to a common set of symbols and a common history, a participation in what Durkheim termed "collective representations" in a collective consciousness—a common culture, in short—which enables members to identify one another where other criteria are uncertain, which gives the society its cohesion, and which provides the standards by which its members' actions are regulated and assessed.

A functionally inclusive collectivity. "Boundary maintenance," to use Talcott Parsons' term, is a necessity for every society. To possess an identity, a society must furnish criteria whereby its members can identify one another, since their actions and attitudes toward one another will be different from those toward outsiders. But Parsons also conceives of boundary maintenance by social subsystems within a broader system. Thus he defines "a society" as a collectivity "which is the primary bearer of a distinctive institutionalized culture and which cannot be said to be a differentiated subsystem of a higher-order collectivity oriented to most of the functional exigencies of a social system" (*Theories of Society*, Vol. I, p. 44). Such a collectivity is organized by political, economic, familial, and similar subsystems. Parsons distinguishes polity and society, but he asserts that "the boundaries of a society tend to coincide with the territorial jurisdiction of the highest-order units of political organization" (*ibid.*, p. 46). For, in Parsons' view, a society's existence depends so crucially on commitment to common values and on the maintenance of order between its individual and collective components that the political boundary tends to settle automatically the limits of the society.

The relation between state and society presented no problems for the Greeks. Political, religious, cultural, and athletic activities were largely undifferentiated and occurred within the single organizational structure of the polis. The first serious problems in this respect emerged with the Christian dichotomies between God and Caesar, church and state, the *Civitas Dei* and the *Civitas Terrena*. The medieval view was that, ideally, there was one universal community of mankind with two modes of organization, or "subsystems," church and empire. Reality never corresponded very closely to this ideal. It became irretrievably divorced from it with the rise of the nation-state and the Reformation. Since then, when men have talked of the society to which they belong, they have thought primarily (like Parsons) of the social order contained within the boundaries of a state and sustained by its organized power.

Nevertheless, liberal thinkers have striven hard to maintain the conceptual distinction between state, or polity, and society. One reason has been to resist the claim that the state could be the only focus of loyalty, competent by

virtue of an overriding authority to lay down the terms on which other associations might function. (See SOVEREIGNTY and STATE for fuller discussions of these problems.) On the other hand, there has emerged a new totalitarianism which identifies state and society. Every form of economic, religious, artistic, or scientific activity thereby acquires a political dimension, promoting or impeding the public good as embodied in state policy. Hegel provided a metaphysical justification for this kind of doctrine when he distinguished between, on one hand, civil society—a level of social organization including the market economy and the forces of civil order—and, on the other, the transcendent state—"the realized ethical idea or ethical spirit," "the true meaning and ground" of lower forms of social organization like the family and civil society (*Philosophy of Right*, Secs. 257, 256). By contrast, not only do liberals insist on the subordination of the state to society; they have also tended, according to Sheldon S. Wolin, to depreciate the political and to attach increasingly to other social subsystems, like the business corporation or the voluntary association, concepts like statesmanship, authority, and legitimacy, which have been considered hitherto characteristic of the state. Meanwhile, Wolin argues, the concept of an organization directed to the most general interests of the community tends to get lost, to be replaced by a model of conflicting pressure groups operating within a very nebulously defined arena. If Parsons is right, our notion of a society as the most inclusive framework of social interaction depends on the political not only for its boundary maintenance but also for its very identity. There may be a danger that in pressing the antitotalitarian, pluralistic account so far that it dissolves the state, it will lose thereby its capacity to define the society.

Bibliography

Bendix, Reinhard, *Max Weber—An Intellectual Portrait*. New York, 1960.

Black, Max, ed., *The Social Theories of Talcott Parsons*. Englewood Cliffs, N.J., 1961.

Bosanquet, Bernard, *The Philosophical Theory of the State*, 4th ed. London, 1923.

Durkheim, Émile, *Les Règles de la méthode sociologique*. Paris, 1895. Translated by S. A. Solovay and J. H. Mueller as *Rules of Sociological Method*. Glencoe, Ill., 1938. Edited by G. E. G. Catlin.

Durkheim, Émile, *De la Division du travail social*, 5th ed. Paris, 1926. Edited and translated by George Simpson as *The Division of Labor in Society*. Glencoe, Ill., 1947.

Gellner, Ernest, "Holism Versus Individualism in History and Sociology," in Patrick Gardiner, ed., *Theories of History*. Glencoe, Ill., 1959. Pp. 489–503.

Hegel, G. W. F., *Grundlinien der Philosophie des Rechts*. Berlin, 1821. Translated with notes by T. M. Knox as *Hegel's Philosophy of Right*. Oxford, 1942.

Hobbes, Thomas, *Leviathan*. London, 1651. Edited with Introduction by Michael Oakeshott. Oxford, 1946.

MacIver, R. M., and Page, C. H., *Society; An Introductory Analysis*. New York, 1949.

Mandelbaum, Maurice, "Societal Facts," in Patrick Gardiner, ed., *op. cit.* Pp. 476–488.

Parsons, Talcott, *The Structure of Social Action*. Glencoe, Ill., 1949. Includes extended discussions of the views of Alfred Marshall, Vilfredo Pareto, Émile Durkheim, and Max Weber.

Parsons, Talcott, *The Social System*. Glencoe, Ill., 1951. Parsons' intricate style and elaborate terminology will deter any but the most determined.

Parsons, Talcott; Shils, Edward; Naegele, K. D.; and Pitts, J. R., eds., *Theories of Society*, 2 vols. New York, 1961.

Popper, Karl R., *The Poverty of Historicism*. London, 1957.

Popper, Karl R., *The Open Society and Its Enemies*, 2 vols., 4th rev. ed. London, 1962.

Popper, Karl R., "Prediction and Prophecy in the Social Sciences," in his *Conjectures and Refutations*. London, 1963. Ch. 16. Also in Patrick Gardiner, ed., *op. cit.* Pp. 276–285.

Simmel, Georg, *The Sociology of Georg Simmel*, translated and edited by K. H. Wolff. Glencoe, Ill., 1950. An anthology of Simmel's principal works on sociological theory.

Stark, Werner, *The Fundamental Forms of Social Thought*. London, 1962. A study of the traditional organicist–mechanistic dichotomy and an attempt to overcome it.

Tönnies, Ferdinand, *Gemeinschaft und Gesellschaft*. Leipzig, 1887. Translated by C. P. Loomis as *Fundamental Concepts of Sociology*. New York, 1940. Reissued as *Community and Association*. London, 1955.

Watkins, J. W. N., "Historical Explanation in the Social Sciences," in Patrick Gardiner, ed., *op. cit.* Pp. 503–514.

Weber, Max, *Grundriss der Sozialökonomik—III Abt: Wirtschaft und Gesellschaft*. Tübingen, 1925. Part I edited and translated by Talcott Parsons and A. M. Henderson (with Introduction by Parsons) as *Theory of Social and Economic Organization*. New York, 1947.

Wolin, Sheldon S., *Politics and Vision*. Boston, 1960.

STANLEY I. BENN

SOCINIANISM, an evangelical rationalist movement, was one of the forerunners of modern Unitarianism. Three phases can be distinguished: (1) the thought of Laelius Socinus (1525–1562) and his nephew Faustus Socinus (1539–1604); (2) the thought and institutions of the Minor (Reformed) church of Poland, especially as embodied in the Racovian Catechism (1605), which represented a fusion of Faustus' theology with that of the local anti-Trinitarian and partly Anabaptist Minor church; and (3) the rationalist theology of the Socinianized Minor church. This last phase was especially important after the Socinianized Minor church was crushed in Poland in 1658 and the spirit of Socinianism became influential in the Netherlands among the Remonstrants; in the British Isles, in the seventeenth century, among certain Anglican divines and nonconformist intellectuals; and, in the eighteenth century, among the Arminian divines of New England, who were forerunners of the Unitarian congregationalists.

Socinian evangelical rationalism originated from an amalgam of the rationalist humanism of Juan de Valdés, Florentine Platonism, and Paduan Aristotelianism; in Poland it was augmented by certain Calvinist and Anabaptist ingredients. In all three phases Socinianism was characterized by (1) a rationalist interpretation of Scripture (which was nevertheless accepted as true and authoritative), with a predilection for the pre-Mosaic and the New Covenantal parts of the Bible; (2) an acceptance of Jesus as the definitive word or revelation of God but nevertheless solely a man, not divine but chosen by God to rule as king, priest, and prophet over the world and the church; (3) belief in the principle of pacific separation of church and state; (4) acceptance of the doctrine of the death of the soul with the body with, however, selective resurrection and immortality for all those who persevered "through the power of the Spirit" in observing all of Jesus' earthly commandments.

Laelius and Faustus Socinus. Laelius Socinus, born in Siena, was a well-to-do student with a wide and critical interest in theology. He established contact and became friendly with several reformers, notably Philipp Melanchthon, John Calvin, and Johann Bullinger, and also with the Rhaetian heretic Camillo Renato. Himself suspected of heresy, Laelius was obliged to prepare a Confession of Faith (in which, however, he reserved the right to further inquiry), one of the few extant documents from his hand. At his death he left his library, and perhaps some unpublished papers, to his nephew.

Faustus Socinus, born in Siena, was a student of logic and law, a member of the local academy, and an indifferent poet. He first clearly manifested his rejection of traditional Christian doctrines in a letter of 1563, in which he argued against the postulate of natural immortality. In 1570 he wrote his first major work, *De Auctoritate Sacrae Scripturae*, and in 1578 he issued his basic treatise on Christology and soteriology, *De Jesu Christu Servatore*. Because of the latter work he was invited to Transylvania to defend the legitimacy of prayer addressed to the ascended Christ against the faction in the Unitarian Reformed church led by Francis Dávid. On the journey he was persuaded to make Poland his permanent home. There he became a major defender of the Minor church, although he declined on principle to become a communicant member of it, refusing to submit to believers' baptism by immersion. Socinus was co-commissioned with local pastors to revise the Latin *Catechesis* (1574) of Racov, the communitarian settlement and spiritual center of the Minor church, northeast of Cracow. The radical revision was published in Polish in 1605, a year after Socinus' death, as the *Racovian Catechism*, the first Latin edition of which (1609) was dedicated to James I of England.

The Socinianized Minor church. The Socinianized Minor church, centered in Racov, had an academy that at one time attracted a thousand students and a publishing house that turned out tracts and books in a score of languages; it became in fact more a school than a church. Among the faculty of the academy and the pastorate of the synod, which met annually in Racov, the most prominent were Socinus' own grandson, Andreas Wiszowaty (died 1678), who wrote *Religio Rationalis;* Stanislas Lubieniecki (died 1675), who wrote *Historia Reformationis Polonicae;* Samuel Przypkowski (died 1670), who wrote *Vita Fausti Socini;* and quite a few converts from German Protestantism who resettled in Poland and were rebaptized: Christoph Ostorodt (died 1611); Johann Völkel, who wrote *De Vera Religione* (1630); Johann Crell (died 1631), who wrote *De Uno Deo Patre* and a defense of Socinus against Grotius, *De Satisfactione;* and Christoph Sand (died 1680), who compiled the *Bibliotheca Antitrinitariorum*.

Spread of Socinianism. Well before the crushing of the Minor church in 1658, Socinians were established in the Netherlands. At Amsterdam the basic works of the movement, the eight-volume *Bibliotheca Fratrum Polonorum*, edited by Wiszowaty, were printed in 1688. In England, Socinian rationality, latitudinarianism, Unitarianism, and mortalism (psychopannychism) variously appealed to Arminian prelates, Oxford rationalists (like William Chillingworth), Cambridge Platonists (like Benjamin Whichcote), philosophers and scientists (like Isaac Newton and John Locke), and to the first avowed native Socinians, Paul Best, John Biddle ("the father of English Unitarianism"), and Stephen Nye, whose *History of Unitarianism commonly called Socinianism* set off the Trinitarian controversy in the Established church in 1687.

Bibliography

Chmaj, Ludwik, *Faust Socyn.* Warsaw, 1963.
Kühler, W. J., *Socinianisme in Nederland.* Leiden, 1912.
McLachlan, H. John, *Socinianism in Seventeenth-century England.* Oxford, 1951.
Wilbur, Earl M., *A History of Unitarianism: Socinianism and Its Antecedents.* Cambridge, Mass., 1945.

GEORGE HUNSTON WILLIAMS

SOCINUS, LAELIUS AND FAUSTUS. See SOCIN-IANISM.

SOCIOLOGY, FUNCTIONALISM IN. See FUNC-TIONALISM IN SOCIOLOGY.

SOCIOLOGY OF KNOWLEDGE. The sociology of knowledge is concerned with determining whether man's participation in social life has any influence on his knowledge, thought, and culture and, if it does, what sort of influence it is.

Development. Although the term "sociology of knowledge" was coined in the twentieth century, the origins of the discipline date back to classical antiquity. Plato, for instance, asserted that the lower classes are unfit to pursue the higher kinds of knowledge, because their mechanical crafts not only deform their bodies but also confuse their souls. Plato also held the more refined doctrine of the correspondence of the knower (or more precisely, the faculties and activities of the knower's mind, which are in part determined by society) and the known. This latter theory became part of the Platonic tradition and ultimately stimulated some modern pioneers in the sociology of knowledge, notably Max Scheler. Both theories anticipated an essential claim of the sociology of knowledge—that social circumstances, by shaping the subject of knowing, also determine the objects which come to be known.

In the Middle Ages, patterns of life were fixed and defined, and patterns of thought tended to be equally so; ideas appeared as absolute, and the factors that conditioned them remained hidden. As soon, however, as rifts developed in the social fabric, awareness of these factors re-emerged. Machiavelli's remark in the *Discourses* that the thought of the palace was one thing, the thought of the market place quite another, revealed this new awareness.

In the following centuries, the stream of ideas which was to lead to the modern sociology of knowledge was divided between rationalism and empiricism. The rationalists regarded mathematical propositions as the archetype of truth. As mathematical propositions do not change in content from age to age and from country to country, the rationalists could not concede that different societies might

have different systems of knowledge, all equally valid. But if truth was one, error could be multiform, and its roots could be sought in social life—for instance, in the machinations of privileged classes in whose interest it was to keep the people in ignorance. Bacon's doctrine of "idols," or sources of delusion, set forth in his *Novum Organum,* illustrates this tendency. The rationalists thus became the first "unmaskers" of "ideologies."

According to the empiricists, the contents of the mind depend on the basic life experiences, and as these are manifestly dissimilar in dissimilarly circumstanced societies, they almost had to assume that reality would offer a different face in each society. Thus, Vico asserted that every phase of history has its own style of thought which provides it with a specific and appropriate cultural mentality. The treatment of the Biblical account of creation by the two schools shows their contrast. Voltaire called it a piece of stultifying priestcraft which no rational person anywhere would accept: how could the light exist before the sun? Herder answered that for a desert nation like the ancient Hebrews the dawn breaks before the solar disk appears above the horizon. For them, therefore, the light *was* before the sun.

Though the problems of the genesis of error and the genesis of truth should be kept apart, the overly sharp distinction between them and the partisan handling of them before the end of the eighteenth century prevented any tangible progress. And even though Kant achieved a synthesis of rationalism and empiricism, the sociology of knowledge failed to gain from his advances. Kant's whole approach prevented such a gain: the problem of knowledge arose for Kant from the meeting of the *individual* mind with the *physical* world. The social element was missing at either pole. The sociology of knowledge explains Kant's narrowness itself as socially determined. The decay of feudal society and the emergence of a class of independent producers (peasants and artisans) had created the desire to "liberate" man from the "artificial restrictions" of social life. A presocial, asocial, or antisocial type of man was thought possible and even superior to social man. The primacy of being was ascribed to the individual, and society was considered to be no more than a collection of individuals linked by contract. In these circumstances, no one could see the influence of social forces on the human mind.

The nineteenth century brought a strong reaction against this radical individualism. As the forces of social control reasserted themselves, man was once again conceived of as essentially a social creature. The result of this new trend was Marx's mislabeled "materialistic interpretation of history." Marx wrote in his *Introduction to the Critique of Political Economy:* "It is not men's consciousness which determines their existence, but on the contrary their social existence which determines their consciousness." For Marx, the real "substructure" upon which the intellectual "superstructure" rests is a special set of human relationships. Though his definition of these relationships is too narrow, and though he has been variously interpreted, Marx's formulation provided the starting point in the development of the modern sociology of knowledge.

Social origin of ideas. While there is general agreement among scholars in the field that social relationships provide the key to the understanding of the genesis of ideas, there are also far-reaching disagreements among several distinct schools, within which there are again individual differences. An attempt will be made here only to characterize the three most important basic attitudes.

Materialist school. A materialist group of writers emphasizes that human beings are creatures of nature before they are creatures of society and tends to see human beings as dominated by certain genetic drives, with decisive consequences for their emergent mentalities. Nietzsche, for instance, ascribed to man an elementary will to power; if this will is frustrated by a barrier, self-consolatory ideas are apt to appear. Christianity is one such idea; it is essentially a philosophy of "sour grapes," a "slave morality." It assures the defeated that they are really superior to those who have defeated them.

Vilfredo Pareto's *Trattato di sociologia generale* is the most elaborate statement of this position. According to Pareto, men act first and think of reasons for their action only afterward. These reasons he calls "derivations" because they are derived from, or secondary to, the "residues," or quasi instincts, which in fact determine human modes of conduct and, through them, human modes of thought as well. This school continued the line initiated by the rationalists. Theirs is a doctrine of ideologies which devalues thought while it accounts for its formation.

Idealist school. A second group of writers asserts that every society has to come to some decision about the Absolute and that this decision will act as a basic premise that determines the content of the culture. Juan Donoso Cortés tried to explain the classical Greek world view as the product of heathen preconceptions about the Absolute, and the medieval world view as the product of Christian–Catholic preconceptions. An ambitious presentation of this theory is Pitirim Sorokin's *Social and Cultural Dynamics.* He distinguishes three basic metaphysics that, prevailing in given societies, color all their thinking. If a realm beyond space and time is posited as the Absolute, as in ancient India, an "ideational" mentality will spring up; if the realm inside space and time is posited as the Absolute, as in the modern West, a "sensate" mentality will come into being; and if, finally, reality is ascribed both to the here and now and to the beyond, as in the high Middle Ages, an "idealistic" mentality will be the result. Sorokin's doctrine is itself idealistic in character and finds its ultimate inspiration in a religious attitude.

Sociologists of knowledge. The third group of writers occupies the middle ground. These writers do not go beyond the human sphere but divide it into a primary and conditioning half and a secondary and conditioned one. There is, however, great diversity of opinion over exactly which social facts should be regarded as conditioning thought. Marx, for instance, held that relations of production, which themselves reflect still more basic property relations, were primary, but many other factors, such as power relations, have been singled out by other thinkers. Still others regard the social constitution as a whole as the substructure of knowledge, thought, and culture. A typical representative of this numerous group is W. G. Sumner. In his classic *Folkways,* he suggested that wherever men try to live together, they develop mutual adjustments which harden into a set of customs, supported and secured by social sanctions, which permanently coordinate and control their conduct. These habits of action have as their concomitants habits of the mind, a generalized ethos that permeates the mental life of the society concerned. This theory can be sharpened by formulating it in axiological terms. A society is a society because, and insofar as, it is attuned to certain selected and hierarchically ordered values. These values determine what lines of endeavor will be pursued both in practice and in theory.

This third group represents the sociology of knowledge in the narrower and proper sense of the word. The theory just summed up has received some empirical confirmation through the discovery that societies do gain mental consistency to the degree that they achieve better human coordination and integration.

Relation of a society to ideas expressed in it. The problem next in importance to the identification of the substructure of knowledge is the explanation of its relation to the superstructure. Here again there are three schools which may, but do not always, correspond to those already discussed. One tendency is toward causalism. The positivists Gustav Ratzenhofer and Hippolyte Taine, for example, expected of the future a science of culture no less deterministic than the sciences of matter. But though the term "determination" is frequently and generally used in all the literature of this school, it hardly ever means strict determination. While this first school concedes, in principle, no independence to the mind and its contents, a second, Platonic tendency ascribes complete independence to the mind. To Scheler, Florian Znaniecki, and others, thinking means participating in eternal pre-existent ideas. If these ideas are to become active in the world, they must ally themselves to a social movement seeking appropriate ideas. Max Weber has called this doctrine the doctrine of elective affinity. The third theory argues in terms of interdependence and appears regularly in connection with functionalism (see FUNCTIONALISM IN SOCIOLOGY). If society is to function as a unity, its modes of acting and thinking must be in, or on the way to, agreement. Neither substructure nor superstructure is given ontological priority, but there is a tendency to see thought in action as prior to thought as theory.

Extent of influence. Another problem concerns the extent of the influence of social factors on ideas. Here opinions range from the view that these factors influence only a few political slogans to the view that their influence is all-pervading. An important systematic dividing line separates the authors who assert that the categories of thought themselves are socially determined from those who deny that they are.

Epistemological significance. The main philosophical importance of the sociology of knowledge consists in its claim to supplement, if not to replace, traditional epistemology. If society partially or totally determines knowing and thinking, how does this affect their validity? All sociologists of knowledge are inclined to stress that initially the human mind is never aware of more than a sector of reality and that the selection of a sector to be investigated is dependent on the axiological system which a given society has made its own. From this point they diverge once again into three schools, and once more there is no simple correlation with the tendencies previously identified.

Effect of social factors on thought. Some writers, like Pareto, hold that, in the last analysis, only the senses are reliable sources of knowledge. They tend to split the mental universe into a scientific and a nonscientific department and accord the ideas belonging to the latter at best conventional status, but no truth-value in the narrower sense of the term. The axiological system of society, insofar as it is not taken up with scientific and technological pursuits, appears as an opaque and distorting medium that interposes itself between the intellect and reality. The effect of society on the mind is thus something negative, to be regretted and, if possible, overcome.

Whereas this group denigrates the social element in human beings, and hence in human knowledge, another, including Émile Durkheim and Karl Mannheim, sees it as supreme. The latter group conceives the individual as the most likely source of error and society as the most reliable source of truth, if for no other reason than because personal blunders are neutralized in a common attitude. They regard society as the test of the validity of a belief: it is valid if those who hold it manage to operate smoothly within their social system. But if the true is what works and if different societies work differently (as manifestly they do), then truth is once again merely convention. At any rate, there can be no general truths.

The third group, including Max Weber and Scheler, considers that the social influence on mental activity consists essentially in giving directions. What knowledge will be sought in a society depends on the axiological system which reigns in that society. In its most radical form, this doctrine sees our very awareness of facts as socially determined: only those aspects of reality which are marked by their possession of some value, social in origin, will be noticed and enter into the canon of knowledge. There appears, however, no cogent reason why a person should not see a thing thus selected for study on an axiological basis as what it really is. It can therefore be said that every society has its own truth, without giving the word a relativistic tinge. Any human being who integrates himself, factually or intellectually, with a certain society and accepts its constitutive values will have to agree that, from the chosen angle, the world does, and must, look as it is described by the searchers and thinkers of that society. Hence sociality is neither a truth-destroying nor a truth-guaranteeing, but merely a truth-limiting factor. The resulting limitations can, in principle, be overcome by combining the valid "aspectual" insights of all societies into a comprehensive whole.

Knowledge of nature and knowledge of culture. An important distinction sometimes made is that between knowledge of nature and knowledge of culture. The facts of nature do not change from age to age and from country to country; the facts of culture do. Knowledge of the form-

er, therefore, need not be marked by relativity. The Paretian theory, by making physical knowledge the model of all knowledge, does less than justice to the study of cultures; the theory of Mannheim and Durkheim, by making cultural knowledge the model of all knowledge, is apt to fall into the opposite mistake (though its best protagonists have managed to avoid this). The theory of Max Weber and Scheler escapes both weaknesses. In every society's axiological system, some interest in nature, especially in methods of dominating nature, will be present, and insights gained in the pursuit of this domination will be comparable, transferable, and absolute in the sense of binding on all human beings. Other values will vary from society to society; insights gained in pursuit of them will be correspondingly incomparable, nontransferable, and relative (even though they can all be fitted together as alternative actualized possibilities inherent in one creature, man).

Because man must take the facts of nature as he finds them, while the facts of culture are his own work, the social determination of knowledge will be different in the two instances. In scientific research, only the origin of an insight will be determined by the social factor (say, a pressing social need); in cultural studies, however, both the origin and the content will be socially determined. In the case of science, tendencies arising from the social sphere induce a person to open his eyes and see; in the case of cultural studies, they induce him to open his eyes and decide what he shall see. These considerations go far toward overcoming the conflict between the unduly negative and the unduly positive epistemological versions of the sociology of knowledge and show the superiority of the third approach.

Sociology of knowledge as a science. In conclusion, it should be emphasized that the sociology of knowledge is not only a substantive philosophical discipline but also an analytical tool that can be used by the descriptive sciences concerned with the observable products of the mind. Because it can throw light on the genesis, and often on the content, of concrete thought structures, the sociology of knowledge may enable the historian or the anthropologist to achieve a deeper understanding of the facts before him. Considered from this angle, the sociology of knowledge appears, above all, as a hermeneutic method and need not become involved in the difficult ontological problems which the social "determination" of knowledge, thought, and culture is otherwise bound to raise.

Bibliography

DEVELOPMENT

Barth, Hans, *Wahrheit und Ideologie.* Zürich, 1945. Important, particularly with regard to Nietzsche.

Grünwald, Ernst, *Das Problem der Soziologie des Wissens.* Vienna and Leipzig, 1934. First comprehensive critical survey.

Lukács, Georg, *Geschichte und Klassenbewusstsein.* Berlin, 1923. Most distinguished Marxist study of this century.

Stark, Werner, *Montesquieu: Pioneer of the Sociology of Knowledge.* London, 1960.

Stark, Werner, "The Conservative Tradition in the Sociology of Knowledge." *Kyklos,* Vol. 13 (1960), 90–101.

Stark, Werner, "Die idealistische Geschichtsauffassung und die Wissenssoziologie." *Archiv für Rechts- und Sozialphilosophie,*

Vol. 46 (1961), 355–374. This paper and the preceding one attempt to balance the picture of the doctrine's development.

MAIN TRENDS

Adler, Franz, "A Quantitative Study in Sociology of Knowledge." *American Sociological Review*, Vol. 19 (1954), 42–48. From the viewpoint of logical positivism.

Alpert, Harry, *Emile Durkheim and His Sociology*. New York, 1939.

Eisermann, Gottfried, "Vilfredo Pareto als Wissenssoziologe." *Kyklos*, Vol. 15 (1962), 427–464.

Lieber, Hans-Joachim, *Wissen und Gesellschaft*. Tübingen, 1952. Good all around, mainly on Scheler and Mannheim.

Mannheim, Karl, *Ideologie und Utopie*. Bonn, 1929. Translated by Louis Wirth and Edward Shils as *Ideology and Utopia*. London, 1936. Basic; from the historicist point of view, with comprehensive bibliography.

Mannheim, Karl, *Essays on the Sociology of Knowledge*, Paul Kecskemeti, ed. London, 1952.

Maquet, Jacques J., *Sociologie de la connaisance*. Louvain, 1949. Translated by John F. Locke as *The Sociology of Knowledge*. Boston, 1951. On Mannheim and Sorokin.

Rüschmeyer, Dietrich, *Probleme der Wissenssoziologie*. Cologne, 1958. Strong bias toward naive empiricism.

Scheler, Max, ed., *Versuche zu einer Soziologie des Wissens*. Munich and Leipzig, 1924. Decisive pioneering effort.

Scheler, Max, *Die Wissensformen und die Gesellschaft*. Leipzig, 1926. Basic; from the phenomenological point of view.

Znaniecki, Florian, *The Social Role of the Man of Knowledge*. New York, 1940.

PHILOSOPHICAL ASPECTS

Child, Arthur, "The Problem of Imputation in the Sociology of Knowledge." *Ethics*, Vol. 51 (1940–1941), 200–219.

Child, Arthur, "The Theoretical Possibility of the Sociology of Knowledge." *Ethics*, Vol. 51 (1940–1941), 392–418.

Child, Arthur, "The Existential Determination of Thought." *Ethics*, Vol. 52 (1941–1942), 153–185.

Child, Arthur, "The Problems of Imputation Resolved." *Ethics*, Vol. 54 (1943–1944), 96–109.

Geiger, Theodor, *Ideologie und Wahrheit*. Stuttgart and Vienna, 1953. Rationalistic approach.

Horowitz, Irving, L., *Philosophy, Science, and the Sociology of Knowledge*. Springfield, Ill., 1961. Methodological problems.

Schelting, Alexander von, *Max Webers Wissenschaftslehre*. Tübingen, 1933. Basic.

Stark, Werner, "The Sociology of Knowledge and the Problem of Ethics," in *Transactions of the Fourth World Congress of Sociology*, Vol. IV. London, 1959.

GENERAL SURVEYS

De Gré, Gerard L., *Society and Ideology*. New York, 1943.

Merton, Robert K., "The Sociology of Knowledge," in Georges Gurvitch and Wilbert E. Moore, eds., *Twentieth Century Sociology*. New York, 1945.

Stark, Werner, *The Sociology of Knowledge*. London, 1958. Attempt at a total evaluation.

WERNER STARK

SOCIOLOGY OF LAW. The demands that law be in some degree legitimate, that it express community aspirations with fidelity, and that it lend itself to the effective solution of practical problems have long encouraged reflection on the limits, potentiality, and validity of law, including the social and psychological foundations of obedience. Although important foundations for the sociology of law were laid in the nineteenth century, a special-ized concern with it is a twentieth-century development. Legal sociology has its main roots in jurisprudence rather than in the work of sociologists. The "sociological school" of legal theory, associated with the names of Rudolf von Jhering (1818–1892), Oliver Wendell Holmes, Jr. (1841–1935), Léon Duguit (1859–1928), Eugen Ehrlich (1862–1922), and Roscoe Pound (1870–1964), was developed by jurists who felt the need to look beyond the traditional confines of legal scholarship. The sociologists Émile Durkheim (1858–1917) and Max Weber (1864–1920) made important contributions to the sociology of law, but with certain exceptions, such as Durkheim's influence on Duguit, the writings of sociologists have not had a large influence on the development of a sociological orientation among students of jurisprudence.

This history has suggested a distinction between sociological jurisprudence and sociology of law. Sociological jurisprudence obeys a practical impulse; it seeks to infuse legal policy and decision making with the perspectives, insights, and specific knowledge of the social disciplines, including history, psychology, sociology, and economics. The nature of law is taken as unproblematic. The goal is the improvement of the quality of justice and the strengthening of the capacity of law to meet human needs.

In principle, sociology of law has a wider compass. Its interests may extend to any aspect of law and society, regardless of practical import. On the other hand, sociological jurisprudence is itself a school of thought, stressing basic ideas and principles. It cannot be identified with any particular set of practical reforms or inquiries. Therefore, the association of sociology of law and sociological jurisprudence is likely to continue.

Sociological postulates. There are four starting points or postulates in the sociological orientation toward law. Three are descriptive; one is normative.

Law within society. First, it is postulated that legal norms and institutions are embedded in a social matrix. This premise seeks to infuse the study of law with a historical and functional perspective. The aim is to view law not as an isolated system but as an integral part of culture and society. Legal ideas, such as property, contract, and fault, are studied for their changing social content and for the light they cast on the social order. Important studies of law and social history include Henry Maine's *Ancient Law* (1861), Karl Renner's *The Institutions of Private Law and Their Social Functions* (1929), Max Weber's *Economy and Society* (1922), and James Willard Hurst's *Law and Economic Growth* (1964).

From the standpoint of sociological jurisprudence, the social history of law provides a platform from which to criticize present-day law. Historical study is in part the discovery of anachronisms. When these are revealed, the authority of existing rules, especially the reasoning behind them, is undermined. For sociology of law a larger concern is the identification of major legal trends, particularly those which reflect broader social changes and which may point to emergent or incipient law. The idea of incipient law calls attention to imminent (and sometimes immanent) legal change, to change that is implicit in the evolving social order. Roscoe Pound's emphasis on the "socialization of law" refers to such a development, as does A. V.

Dicey's study *Law and Public Opinion in England* (1905).

Law as social. Second, it is held that law is itself a social phenomenon. The sociological perspective not only seeks to place law "in context"; it also insists on the study of "law in action." This requires that the legal order be seen as a mode of organization and decision. Law is more than a set of principles and rules. It is a kind of activity carried on by living men in living institutions. Therefore, the personal and social characteristics of lawyers, judges, police, and administrators must be studied, as well as the social dynamics of the organizations in which they work. This is an important emphasis in contemporary legal sociology, as represented in studies of the legal profession, of the administration of criminal justice, and of the behavior of juries.

State law not unique. Third, it is claimed that law is not uniquely associated with the state. Like jurisprudence itself, sociology of law encourages the quest for a general theory of law. It seeks to identify attributes that transcend particular contexts. This generalizing impulse, together with the effort to see law "in society," tends to blur the distinction between state law and other forms of social control. Thus, Ehrlich held that law is endemic in custom and social organization; it is most truly found in the actual regularities of group life. State law is only a part, and not necessarily the most important part, of the sociolegal order. Weber defined the legal norm as one likely to be enforced by a specialized staff applying coercive sanctions. In this way he hoped to distinguish law from other social phenomena. However, he emphasized that coercion may be psychological rather than physical, and his definition allows for extrastate law, such as church law or the law of any other association binding on its own members.

A useful theory of law would see it as appearing in all institutions that rely for social control on formal authority and rule making. This does not mean that law loses its distinctive character or becomes equivalent to social control. We see legal experience wherever there is a system of order that contains specialized mechanisms for certifying rules as authoritative and for safeguarding rule making and rule applying from the intrusion of other forms of decision and control. On this view, law is not equivalent to custom; neither is it restricted to state action.

This approach departs somewhat from the traditionally antiformalist posture of legal sociology. Historically, the sociological school tended to depreciate formal legal systems as significant social realities. It did so by giving primacy to other sources of social order, by criticizing the "unrealism" of legal rules and concepts, and by seeking the legal outside of its conventional sphere. The antiformalist and pluralist emphases are still strong, but they are mitigated by a growing sensitivity to legal ideals, such as due process, and by a better understanding of what legal authority is and the variety of settings in which it is found.

Law and social purpose. Finally, it is held that law should yield to social purpose. This normative proposition reflects the strongly instrumentalist orientation of sociological jurisprudence. Instrumentalism is the enemy of legal isolation, for it demands that received law be justified by its responsiveness to social needs, claims, and interests.

Furthermore, the demand that law yield to social purpose quickly turns attention to the role of social knowledge in law. For if laws are instruments, they are open to interpretation and revision in the light of changing circumstances. This gives the social scientist a legitimate place in the legal dialogue.

Analytical issues. Although a great deal of sociological work can be done without confronting the difficulties that inhere in the concept of law, in the long run some basic intellectual problems must be faced. Two issues will be touched on here.

Law as a normative concept. Social scientists are accustomed to treating norms and ideals as facts. But they are disinclined to evaluate these facts. To engage in evaluation, it is thought, will inevitably involve the social scientist in the preconceptions of his own society and his own time; moreover, any tendency to break down the wall of separation between fact and value is intellectually dangerous. This point of view has created a mood favorable to legal positivism and opposed to a normative concept of law. For the latter the legal system is more than a set of related norms to be treated as unassessable factual givens. Law is not a brute datum of social power but a mode of decision making guided by distinctive standards and ideals, capable of self-fulfillment or corruption. There are, on this view, standards latent in any purported legal order that offer principles of criticism for the assessment of specific legal norms as well as official conduct. A recent statement of the normative concept of law is found in Lon L. Fuller's *The Morality of Law* (1964).

A normative approach invites attention to the *competence* of the legal system, especially its capacity to restrain arbitrary power, to adapt a received tradition to emergent social needs, and to enhance the role of reason in legal judgment. The aim set for sociological inquiry is to specify the elements of this competence and to consider the conditions that subvert or sustain it.

The outstanding issue is whether the criteria of legal achievement are imposed by the preference of the analyst. Or are they in some sense objectively latent in the legal process, founded in the distinctive social functions of law? The latter view presumes that government by law is logically similar to love, friendship, education, and other social phenomena whose nature encompasses the realization of values.

Law and nature. A normative concept of law is associated with the natural-law perspective in jurisprudence. This is so because the basic quest of natural law is for legally authoritative principles of criticism to test and limit sovereign will. If such a test is always to be available, then something beyond positive law must serve as a source of authority. If the appeal is to "nature," as distinguished from an appeal to supernatural authority or to the *Volksgeist*, then the problem of law and social knowledge is posed again.

In sociological jurisprudence there is no resistance to the reconstruction of law in the light of social analysis. On the contrary, this is the heart of the program. However, the implications for the theory of law have not been worked out. Is the appeal to knowledge merely a way of criticizing law from the outside, with only such authority as can be won through the political process? Or is legal judgment in some special way committed to accepting and incorporating knowledge about man and human institutions? If there is such a commitment, what machinery is available for taking account of social knowledge while preserving the continuity and legitimacy of legal decision? These questions suggest that despite the long dispute over natural law, it remains unsettled how much and in what way the legal validity of law is affected by scientifically warranted conclusions regarding human and social nature.

Bibliography

Cohen, Julius; Robson, R. A. H.; and Bates, Alan, *Parental Authority: The Community and the Law*. New Brunswick, N.J., 1958. An example of recent empirical research on legal norms.

Durkheim, Émile, *De la Division du travail social*. Paris, 1893. Translated by G. Simpson as *The Division of Labor in Society*. Glencoe, Ill., 1952.

Ehrlich, Eugen, *Grundlegung der Soziologie des Rechts*. Munich, 1913. Translated by W. L. Moll as *Fundamental Principles of the Sociology of Law*. Cambridge, Mass., 1936.

Friedmann, Wolfgang, *Law in a Changing Society*. Berkeley, 1959.

Gurvitch, Georges, *Sociology of Law*. New York, 1942.

Pound, Roscoe, *Jurisprudence*, 5 vols. St. Paul, Minn., 1959. Contains extensive commentary and bibliography pertaining to sociological jurisprudence.

Rheinstein, Max, ed., *Max Weber on Law in Economy and Society*. Cambridge, Mass., 1954.

Sawer, Geoffrey, *Law in Society*. Oxford, 1965.

Stone, Julius, *Human Law and Human Justice*. Stanford, 1965. This and the following book critically review many jurisprudential writers and issues, including much of relevance to legal sociology.

Stone, Julius, *Social Dimensions of Law and Justice*. Stanford, forthcoming.

Timasheff, N. S., *An Introduction to the Sociology of Law*. Cambridge, Mass., 1939.

PHILIP SELZNICK

SOCRATES (c. 470–399 B.C.), of Athens, was perhaps the most original, influential, and controversial figure in the history of Greek thought. Very little is known about his life. He died by drinking hemlock after having been condemned to death for "not believing in the gods the state believes in, and introducing different new divine powers; and also for corrupting the young," according to the indictments recorded in Plato's *Apology* and Xenophon's *Apology*. Philosophy before him was "pre-Socratic"; he was the "hinge," or the orientation point, for most subsequent thinkers and the direct inspiration of Plato. There is no agreement, however, on the exact nature of Socrates' philosophical contribution or on whether anything certain can be said of the historical Socrates. This controversy is known as the Socratic problem, which arises because Socrates wrote nothing on philosophy, unless, perhaps, jottings of self-examination not for publication (cf. Epictetus, *Discourses* II, 1, 32). Not only a historical problem is involved in the nature of the evidence, but also a philosophical puzzle in the character of Socrates embedded in Plato's dialogues.

Two extreme answers which would put an end to further controversy have been put forth in this century. Professors John Burnet and A. E. Taylor have argued that the Socrates of Plato's dialogues, and only he, is the historical Socrates, and agnostics suggest that we know nothing of Socrates, the earliest reports being versions of a literary myth of no greater historical validity than stage Agamemnons.

There are two arguments for the latter view. (1) None of the primary evidence is historical in purpose or character. Aristophanes' comedy *The Clouds* (423 B.C.) is a satire on intellectuals, and Socrates, the chief character, is a mere type. The Socratic dialogues of Socrates' friends and admirers (Plato and the fragmentary minor Socratics—for example, Antisthenes and Aeschines) were not intended as biography but as live philosophy, mostly written well after Socrates' death, where "Socrates" illustrates the writers' arguments, which differ from one another. Xenophon also knew Socrates, but much in his memoirs is probably secondhand and tainted with the suspect fancies of Greek apologetics. It is demonstrable that the first two chapters of Xenophon's *Memorabilia* are a reply to a literary pamphlet written some time after 394 by the Sophist Polycrates. This pamphlet put a fictitious prosecuting speech into the mouth of Anytus, one of Socrates' accusers. Aristotle, who was not born until 15 years after Socrates' death, probably derived his historical assessment from the earlier suspect literature; anyway, his "historical" comments are often protreptic interpretations for his own philosophy. The frequent references in later antiquity must derive from these suspect sources or from an oral tradition hardening into collected "Sayings of Socrates" (see Hibeh Papyrus 182), an equally untrustworthy source. (2) All the evidence is riddled with contradiction, and not only of details. The whole presentation of one reporter is scarcely consistent with that of another; indeed, the Socratics were bitterly critical of one another. There are no objective facts against which to resolve these inconsistencies.

It should, however, be protested against extreme agnosticism that contradiction among the reports cannot by itself prove them all wholly mythical. Doubt thrown on part of a historical anecdote does not necessarily invalidate the whole. It does not follow from two contradictory pieces of evidence that neither of them can be true or be explained. We are looking for a common stimulus to divergent interpretations where cancellation by naive abstraction proves nothing. Contradiction should lead to a critical examination of the value of a piece of evidence against the background and context of the individual reporter. Second, literary genres are never mutually exclusive. None of the evidence can be thus dismissed. Who can say that Plato's Socrates is a figment of his literary imagination or that Aristophanes did not reflect current opinions of Socrates? *The Clouds* itself helped to create a historical prejudice about Socrates which was later used against him at his trial; Plato's *Apology* is geared to this historical atmosphere. Polycrates' fictional speech probably embodied another part of the historical prejudice, and Xenophon's account is not invalidated because it is a reply to a fictional speech although its value for us is limited by our knowledge of Xenophon. Aristotle can be shown to have distinguished (*Metaphysics* 987a29 ff. and 1078b9 ff.) between the Platonic and the historical Socrates in the history of a subject, the theory of Forms, on which twenty years in the Platonic Academy must have made him expert. There is no reason to suspect misrepresentation.

It seems to follow that while the skeptics are right in not accepting any evidence per se as having firsthand historical certainty, all the evidence has a right to be regarded as historical interpretations of varying value, from which it may be difficult but not impossible to separate historical plausibility. It is clear this could not be done by simple corroboration but by an estimate of the peculiarities of each reporter's view of Socrates. Only by an intensive study of Plato and the others may we hope to gauge the "lenses" through which they saw Socrates and thus interpret their evidence. Then and only then may corroboration play a significant part.

The question arises whether one reporter should take precedence over the rest. The likeliest candidate is Plato, but he should not be taken as absolutely as Burnet and Taylor take him. For although they argued that it was unlikely that Plato would misrepresent his revered master, it is still more improbable that a man of Plato's ability could postpone his own philosophical progression and, contrary to his Socrates' methods, preach another's philosophy until after he was sixty, when the character of Socrates retired into the background of Plato's dialogues. Nor is it easy to see why a historical criterion should work for Plato's Socrates and not for other writers of the same genre. But it is impossible to believe that the development of "Socrates'" doctrine in the course of the dialogues, which were written after his death, can be other than Plato's; Aristotle was right to make his distinction. Plato's Socrates, too, is an interpretation. Weight should be given, however, to Plato's sincere attachment to Socrates and to his insight into Socrates' thought. Also, although Socratic doctrine must still be disentangled from a study of the development of Plato's thought (and probably never will be to everybody's satisfaction), Plato does give by far the most coherent and convincing picture of Socrates' personality. That Plato thought this personality of prime philosophical importance is the most fruitful thing we know of the historical Socrates. From such principles a plausible account of Socrates may be attempted.

Early life and personal circumstances. Our sources insist that Socrates was remarkable for living the life he preached. But information is sparse. He was the son of Sophroniscus (only in later sources described as a stonemason), of the deme Alopeke, and Phaenarete, a midwife, an occupation translated by Socrates into philosophical activity. The father was a close friend of the son of Aristides the Just, and the young Socrates was familiar with members of the Periclean circle. Later, he was obviously at home in the best society, but he had no respect for social status. His financial resources were adequate to entitle him to serve as a hoplite in the Peloponnesian War, where his courage in the campaigns of Potidaea, Delium, and Amphipolis is offered as evidence that there was a complete concord between his words and character. His later absorption in philosophy and his mission made him neglect his private affairs, and he fell to a level of comparative poverty, which was in tune with his arguments on the unimportance of material goods and his own simple needs. He was probably more in love with philosophy than with his family, but that his wife Xanthippe was a shrew is a late tale and that he was not without interest in parental and filial duties is obvious in his thought for his sons' future in Plato's *Crito*. But all personal considerations, including his own life, were subordinated to "the supreme art of philosophy"; tradition holds that by refusing to compromise his principles, he deliberately antagonized the court which was trying him for impiety and forced an avoidable death penalty. Plato's *Crito* and *Phaedo*, set during Socrates' last days, give a moving and convincing picture of a man at one with himself.

Contemporary philosophy. In Plato's *Phaedo* (96A) Socrates describes his youthful enthusiasm for philosophies that concentrated on physical descriptions of the universe, which were then in vogue, and his subsequent disillusionment with all material explanations of causation. Although the tone and context of Plato's theory of Forms forbid literal acceptance of the whole passage, the general outline is probably correct. The contemporary Ion of Chios recorded that as a young man Socrates was a pupil of Archelaus. Archelaus' teacher, Anaxagoras, was linked with Socrates' name to stir a prejudice which persisted from Aristophanes' *Clouds* to the trial. But by the time we have any descriptive picture of Socrates, he had abandoned any interest in physics and was immersed in ethical and logical inquiries. It is more helpful to see Socrates against the background of the Sophists. Almost the only information to be derived with any certainty from *The Clouds* is that Socrates (then about 47) was regarded as a Sophist. Polycrates was still attacking him as such after his death, and Plato and Xenophon go to great pains to distinguish him from other Sophists. The Sophists were itinerant professors teaching for a fee the skill (*sophia*) of *arete* (excellence, in the sense of how to make the best of yourself and get on). Socrates was the Athenian Sophist inasmuch as his life was dedicated to the same new intellectual inquiry into education—the science of effecting *arete*. He might claim that he took no fees and gave no formal instruction, but he would start and dominate an argument wherever the young and intelligent would listen, and people asked his advice on matters of practical conduct and educational problems. Sophists frequently studied language and rhetoric as an obvious key to private and political success; Socrates' interest in words and arguments was notorious. Plato lightheartedly compared him with Prodicus, the specialist in subtle discriminations of the meanings of apparently synonymous words. The terrorist government of Thirty banned any public utterance by him. His very method of argument, dialectic, characterized by destructive cross-examination, could be confused with, and sometimes in Plato falls to the level of, the combative eristic technically practiced by Sophists, who concentrated almost exclusively on technique. The similarities are real. The distortion arises from seeing Socrates simply as the Athenian counterpart of the Sophistic phenomenon. Plato suggests that he differed fundamentally in moral purpose and intellectual standards and so should be contrasted to them.

Political and social influence. Like all generalizations, the classification of Socrates as a Sophist carries such half-truths as the charge, reflected in Polycrates' pamphlet, that Socrates was politically dangerous, the enemy of democracy, and the inspiration of the notorious politicians Alcibiades and Critias. The politician Anytus could not formally bring this charge at the trial since the effective deployment of political attack in the courts was barred by the amnesty decree of 403. But the anti-Sophistic prejudice was real enough in the sensitive restored democracy, which remembered its earlier animosity against supposed political interference by freethinking, unscrupulous Sophists in Pericles' circle.

Nevertheless, in the strict sense the political influence of Socrates is a mirage. The only two public acts recorded by his apologists (see Plato's *Apology* 32Bf.) were refusals to involve himself in state actions he thought wrong; both were courageous personal protests of no political significance. In the *Apology* (31D; cf. *Gorgias* 521C–E, 473E) Socrates explicitly denies political participation. Nor was he a power behind the scenes, for his friends Critias and Charmides when in power tried ineffectively to muzzle his caustic comments (Xenophon, *Memorabilia* I, 2, 32 f.). The association with Alcibiades is testified to by the rash of "Alcibiades dialogues" by the Socratics, and Socrates could not fairly disown his influence by simply denying that he was responsible because he had no financial contract or profession as a teacher. But his influence was always personal, not political. No characteristic political philosophy emerged from the Socratics; even Plato may have conceived his doctrine of philosopher-kings through pondering the injustice of Socrates' conviction and death rather than from what Socrates had said (*Epistle* VII 324C–326B).

However, in the wider Greek sense of "political" there was reason for fearing Socrates as a social force. Where *arete*, education, and state were fused in one image (see Plato, *Protagoras* 325C–326E), an educator critical of received assumptions was a revolutionary. Socrates not only publicly raised such fundamental questions as "What is *arete*?" and "Who are its teachers?," but also by discrediting through their own representatives the accepted educational channels and by creating a climate of questioning and doubt, he was suspected by conservative minds of the dangerous game of discomfiting all authority before a circle of impressionable youths and subtracting from the state the stability of tradition (see the encounter with Anytus in *Meno* 90A–95A). It was also apparent that the values by which Socrates lived, his indifference to material wealth and prosperity, and his freedom from desire and ambition were themselves a living criticism of the actual social and economic structures of Athens. In fact, Socrates claimed the right of independent criticism of all institutions and of politicians who did not seem to know what they were doing or compromised their principles; the Athenian democracy was distinguished merely by relying on a majority of ignoramuses. But he did not oppose the authority of law, and in Plato's *Crito* he rejected his friends' plan to smuggle him out of the country by putting forward a theory of social contract imbued with the true Athenian's emotional regard for his country as for a parent. He claimed that he

had ruined himself financially in service to the state; yet his unsettling effect on the young and his persistent criticism were intolerable to any establishment. A gadfly, however patriotic (*Apology* 30E), will, if it does not go away by itself, eventually be removed as a poisonous nuisance. That Socrates was not attacked until he was seventy argues that his influence was not so wide as has been suspected (that is, that many did not take him seriously), unless he was saved by the power of his friends or by the charm and sincerity of his own personality.

Religion. The charge made against Socrates of disbelief in the state's gods implied un-Athenian activities which would corrupt the young and the state if publicly preached. Meletus, who brought the indictment, counted on an anti-intellectualist smear that had precedents in the impiety trials of Pericles' friends. The prejudice against Socrates, who was neither a heretic nor agnostic as some Sophists undoubtedly were, had persisted from *The Clouds* and was perhaps fostered by the conduct of Alcibiades in the scandalous parody of the Mysteries in 415 B.C. But Socrates provoked hostility. Two outbursts of feeling are recorded in court. One was at the mention of Socrates' daimonion (hinted at in the charge as a notorious religious innovation), a divine sign apprehended by him alone as a voice from god forbidding a contemplated action. Plato and Xenophon played this feature down, but it was regarded as unique in Socrates (Plato, *Republic* 496C) and was quite distinct from other accepted forms of religious communion. The claim set him dangerously apart from his fellows. The second instance involved the pronouncement of the Delphic oracle to his friend Chaerephon. The oracle said that no man was wiser than Socrates, and Socrates had the audacity to use this as justification of his mission as examiner-extraordinary of the views and conduct of every notable in Athens, claiming that in exposing their false conceit, he proved the god right—he at least knew that he knew nothing. Although this was characteristic Socratic irony—the expression of only half-serious suggestions with a curious mixture of humility and presumption—Socrates clearly thought his mission was divinely inspired, and this involved criticism of the received mythology enshrined in the work of the poets and religious experts. In Plato's *Euthyphro* Socrates challenged both popular conceptions of piety and that of the fanatic who preaches strict interpretation of "scriptural authority." His logical and moral objections to the confused and scandalous standards of anthropopathic deities were aimed at a truer redefinition of piety. He was no mystic. Religion appears to have been a branch of ethics for him, and conscious right conduct in religious matters he held to be dependent on a rational inquiry into what piety was. Yet, the accounts portray, besides the restless searcher for understanding, a man of sincere practice in traditional cult forms, with a simple faith in the providence of a divinity that was good and without contradiction. It was apparently possible for Socrates to contain his religious purification within the terms of the Olympian pantheon.

The philosophical personality. The political and religious attack on Socrates by his enemies, although understandable, conveys an unsatisfactory picture of the intellectual dynamite which released Plato. Socrates' friends and followers placed his contributions in the fields of morals and logic, but they present a philosophical personality, not a philosophical system. The most striking feature of the evidence is that it required the invention of a new literary and philosophical genre, the Socratic dialogue, to convey his influence. The difference between Xenophon and Plato is as much one of form as of content. The shrewd moral confidant of Xenophon's anecdotal account could have been only of local interest; the character of Socrates in the organic dialogues of Plato has stimulated all Western philosophy. In the dialogues the common Socratic element is not quotation of doctrine, which varies, not the philosophy of Socrates, but Socrates philosophizing.

Socrates philosophized by joining in a discussion with another person who thought he knew what justice, courage, or the like is. Under Socrates' questioning it became clear that neither knew, and they cooperated in a new effort, Socrates making interrogatory suggestions that were accepted or rejected by his friend. They failed to solve the problem but, now conscious of their lack of knowledge, agreed to continue the search whenever possible. These discussions, or "dialectics," whereby Socrates engaged in his question-and-answer investigations, were, for Plato at least, the very marrow of the Socratic legacy. For those who had not heard Socrates at it, the "Socratic dialogue" was invented.

Plato revealed the advantages of dialectic by contrasting the method with contemporary Sophistic education typified by the set lecture of dictated information or expounded thesis and the eristic technical exercise of outsmarting opponents. For Socrates knowledge was not acceptance of secondhand opinion which could be handed over for a sum of money like a phonograph record (or encyclopedia) but a personal achievement gained through continual self-criticism. Philosophy involved not learning the answers but searching for them—a search more hopeful if jointly undertaken by two friends, one perhaps more experienced than the other but both in love with the goal of truth and reality and willing to subject themselves honestly to the critical test of reason alone.

Socrates was the first openly to canvass this conception of the operation of philosophy and is still the best illustration of it. He thought himself uniquely gifted to stimulate the operation in others. He disclaimed authority on his own part, pleading the ignorance of the searcher; this did not prevent him from directing the argument, which is a different matter from feeding information. An intellectual midwife (Plato, *Theaetetus* 149; already in *The Clouds*), he tested the wind eggs of others and assisted fertile production. Wind eggs predominated, and the *elenchus* (cross-examination) exposing them followed a set pattern: the subject claims knowledge of some matter evidenced in a proposition defining what is usually an ethical term; a series of questions from Socrates elicits a number of other propositions which, when put together, prove the contrary of the original definition. But obstetrics is essentially a personal affair; what is really tested is the person and his false conceit. The premises and argumentation of the *elenchus* are tailored to each individual, even to the extent, in the case of a hostile witness, of fallacious argument. At this point the establishment of truth is not at stake; the ques-

tion of whether the person will destroy for himself the main blockage of his thought, his false confidence, is the issue. Socrates' zeal for this demolition work produced such aporia (the perplexity of no way out) that he was accused of simply numbing his victims like a sting ray. Plato had to point out, in the illustration with commentary of Socratic *elenchus* which forms the first half of *Meno*, that false conceit was paralysis, and that Socratic disillusionment was the stimulus, of philosophy. "The life not tested by criticism is not worth living" (*Apology* 38A).

Even so, the destructive logic could have stifled, sterilized, and offended more than it did had it not been for an element Plato termed *eros*, denoting not only the passionate attachments Socrates inspired but also that quality of passion in the enthusiasm of a great teacher who fires his associates with his own madness. The young especially felt a personal attraction which was not, despite some ribald stories, physical—Socrates was a popeyed man with a flattened snub nose and could be compared to a Silenus (Plato, *Symposium* 215)—but for his character and his conversations.

Plato's picture is vivid: of a genial but disturbing personality, a social grace and disreputable appearance; a placidity radiating a calm like that found at the center of a storm; the puckish humor and wit offsetting the sharpness of mind and clarity of thought and tireless concentration; the freshness and unexpectedness of his arguments, his power of not exhausting a subject but of opening it up; the warmth of his attachments, his eccentricities, mischievousness, simplicity, deviousness, modesty, and presumption; the knack of bringing a gathering or person to life and leaving it exhausted; the practical example of his life and the uncompromising idealism of his death; a man whose talk foreigners came to Athens to hear; whose homely, not to say vulgar, instances could suddenly uncover penetrating and embarrassing truths; talk with which the best brains in Athens literally fell in love, a talk and beauty of inner man, which they took to be the touchstone of truth and right; above all, the affection in Plato's writing—this picture astonishingly still conveys the magnetism of the personality. And Plato would have us believe that Socrates, as the human embodiment of a philosophical attitude directed by a passionate love of truth and knowledge, finally inspired in his associates the love of *sophia* itself. This claim, of course, may still be tested by the reader of Plato's dialogues.

Philosophical doctrines. Our knowledge of Socratic doctrine is severely limited by his own refusal to formulate his inquiries into a system and by the personal variations of his interpreters. There are indications, however, that the expert skill (*sophia*) for which he so "lovingly" searched in the operation of "philosophy" gained a new meaning through him. His version of *sophia*, unlike that in most pre-Socratic thought, was concerned almost exclusively with the ethics of human conduct (this is the evidence of both Aristotle and the Socratics). "Socrates was the first to call philosophy down from the heavens" (Cicero, *Tusculan Disputations* V, 4, 10). His opposition to the contemporary cult of successful living was based on a new concept of the psyche, to which he assigned for the first time moral and intellectual status, making it the dominant factor in human conduct. This conception was quite different both from popular ideas on the soul and from the psychology of philosophers like Heraclitus (Fr. 119) and the Pythagoreans (see Empedocles, Fr. 115). Socrates advocated the Delphic motto "Know thyself" and suggested that introspection showed how man achieves his real personality—the perfectly efficient realization of his being (*arete*)—when the psyche is in control of the physical and the intellectual and moral part of the psyche is in control of the rest of it (see *Meno* 88E). Happiness (*eudaimonia*), then, depends not on external or physical goods but on knowingly acting rightly. The proper condition of the psyche is thus of prime importance, and the task of philosophy is its care, training, or doctoring (Plato, *Apology* 29Df.). As there is only one proper condition, being good implies the capacity for any virtue; although different virtues are distinguishable, virtue is a unity and a form of knowledge.

Socrates was a man of essentially practical aims who dismissed physics and theoretical mathematics as useless (Xenophon, *Memorabilia* IV, 7). Through his new interpretation of human fulfillment, he was seeking a way by which *arete* and right action could be guaranteed. His own character probably suggested the importance of self-control. Only a man in control of himself is in control of his actions; the self-discipline of moral reason frees a man from the slavery of distracting appetites so that he can do what he wishes—that is, pursue true happiness. Above all, only rationally controlled action is not self-defeating. No one voluntarily makes a mistake. By "voluntarily" he meant consistently with one's true will—that is, to be really happy. Socrates was, of course, familiar with the experience of yielding to temptation, but he explained that in such cases one does not really believe that what one does is bad and does not really know that what is rejected is good. For Socrates "good" was a term of utility signifying advantage for the doer. Thus, he argued that no one would deliberately choose what will harm him or knowingly reject what will benefit him most. If a wrong choice is made, it must be an intellectual mistake, an error which the man who knows could not make. *Arete,* according to another Socratic epigram, is (that is, depends on) knowledge. Socrates was thus hunting for a practical science of right conduct which through its rational organization was infallible, predictable, and teachable. It is this search which the earliest Socratic dialogues of Plato are probably testing.

Clearly, the key to such a science is the interpretation of knowledge, and the evidence here displays a confusion over different types of knowing. Socrates is sometimes represented as comparing his moral expert with other experts of practical skills, suggesting the slogan "Efficiency (*arete*) is know-how," but he seems to have recognized the moral inadequacy of mere technical expertise. Most frequently, Socrates wanted to know what a thing is (*arete,* justice, or the like) on the assumption that it is impossible to be good (just, or the like) on purpose unless one first knows what it is. If one knows what it is, one can say what it is (unlike the Sophists, who professed to teach *arete* but could not coherently state what *arete* was). Now, since he held that a correct rational account (*logos*) of what good is was not only a necessary, but even a sufficient, condition of being good, the prime practical

business of the philosopher involved the examination of moral terms and the attempt to define them. This is the evidence of Aristotle (*Metaphysics* 1078b17ff.) and the main activity of the Socrates in the early Platonic dialogues. ("What is courage, piety, beauty, justice, *arete*?" he asked in the *Laches, Euthyphro, Hippias Major, Republic* I, *Protagoras,* and *Meno*.)

The failure of the attempt is of much interest. The Platonic Socrates rejected as inadequate definition by instance or enumeration and answers which were too narrow or too wide. The equivalence sought appears to be more than mere verbal identification. Above all, Socrates was not seeking the conventional meaning of the word but what the thing really is—the essence of what is denoted by the word. He seems to have been groping for an analytical formula of the type "Clay is earth mixed with water," which explicates the essential nature or structure of the thing in question. The hope was that if one could recognize for certain with one's mind what was the essential ingredient which made all just acts just, one could recognize any instance and also reproduce an example at will and so act justly. The success of this attempt at real definition was precluded by certain assumptions about the kind of answer and confusion over the type of question involved (see R. Robinson, *Plato's Earlier Dialectic,* 2d ed., Ch. 5); yet even if Socrates had been able to explicate "justice" to his own satisfaction, the question of how knowledge of its description could prescribe our conduct would have remained. The analogies to which Socrates was addicted tended to obscure the idiosyncrasies of moral terms. Nevertheless, a dialogue like *Euthyphro* is still an excellent introduction to the problem of definition.

In the *Metaphysics* (1078b17ff.) Aristotle qualified Socratic definitions as universal. If Socrates did search (as he did in the early dialogues) for a single ingredient which was the same in all instances and for an explanation of them, he was at least logically committed to a theory of universals, which, however, was probably not systematically investigated until Plato constructed, partly from Socratic "definitions," his theory of Forms. Aristotle should be believed when he stated that Socrates did not himself make the universals or definitions exist apart, as the Platonic Socrates did later in the middle dialogues.

Aristotle also said that induction (*epagoge*) and syllogizing are characteristic of Socrates (*loc. cit.*). Induction probably does not mean the full inductive procedure of the scientist, but merely argument from analogy—by all accounts, one of Socrates' notorious habits, which he most dangerously employed. Syllogizing is "adding together" premises to discover deductively a conclusion; in the aporetic dialogues it is the method by which Socrates elicited conclusions which destroy as contradictories the originally proposed definitions. But if he did hope to construct a science of living, the syllogisms would have been the necessary arguments developing the premises of the real definitions of "what-a-thing-is" into a rational system or science.

Socrates' championship of reason took deep root in Greek thought, possibly all the more so because he did not expound a system. He himself was probably concerned simply with continually testing in public the possibility in action of his rationally dominated ethic, but he never really doubted that it was possible. If he overstressed the power of reason in psychology, this may be partly attributed to his own unique strength of character, which conformed his actions to his thinking. It is also attributable to the paradoxical fusion of *eros*-passion with the rational in him. His reason was infused with desire for the end of good and truth, which attracted his mind by its beauty so that he was in love with it. Plato, too, was infected; with rational detachment he demonstrated the Socratic willingness to "follow the argument (logos) wherever it might lead" in the dialogues. We are also shown how the logos led Socrates to a martyrdom which Plato used to canonize him in emotionally moving prose. It must have been the fusion of logos and *eros* that was so highly infectious; the Socratic evidence is inexplicable unless it was the gift of the historical Socrates. However, what really matters now is not such a historical supposition, but that the Platonic Socrates' love of *sophia* (philosophy) is still contagious. Yet, the incarnation of philosophy in Plato could not have come so convincingly alive had there not been a man who was regarded by Plato as "the finest, most intelligent, and moral man of his generation" (Plato, *Phaedo* 118) and who was also the greatest of mental midwives.

The Socratics. Socrates established no school. The logos led his associates in different directions, and each was critical of the others. Plato cultivated the seeds in ethics, logic, and epistemology that flowered into a rational system. Of the minor Socratics our evidence is sparse. Antisthenes, stressing the self-sufficiency of virtue and its dependence on knowledge, developed the aspect of self-discipline and freedom from convention. His ascetic tendencies were sneered at by the hedonist Aristippus of Cyrene. Socrates' views on pleasure are hard to discover (see, for example, the hedonistic calculus in Plato, *Protagoras* 351B ff.), but Aristippus' insistence on the intelligent control of pleasure as distinct from slavish adherence or abstinence does not clash with what we hear of Socrates in Plato's *Symposium*, for example. Euclides of Megara may have fused Socratic and Eleatic elements; his school was notorious for an interest, possibly stimulated by Socrates, in the methodology of argument. Phaedo, who wrote at least one Socratic dialogue (Diogenes Laërtius, II, 105, and Cicero, *Tusculan Disputations* IV, 37, 80), founded a school in Elis; Simmias and Cebes were active in Thebes; their doctrines are not known. Aeschines of Sphettus (an Athenian deme), probably a contemporary of Plato, wrote dialogues admired by the ancients for their style and for the fidelity of the portrait of Socrates; indeed, a malicious tale accused him of passing off material of Socrates' obtained from Xanthippe as his own. The Stoic Panaetius classed his dialogues as "genuine," together with those of Plato, Xenophon, and Antisthenes. Aeschines' portrait possibly had the smallest ingredient of orginality; it would still be limited by his own capacities and insight. Enough survives of Aeschines' *Alcibiades* and *Aspasia* to give a tantalizing glimpse of these works. Socratic themes briefly appear, but the fragments are too truncated to allow Socrates' personality to emerge, and they are of more historical than philosophical interest. Like Xenophon, Aeschines had no subsequent philosophical influence.

Socrates' influence spread far beyond his contemporaries. The ancients regarded him as the root of most subsequent philosophy. The main stem rose through the Platonic Academy (not least Socratic in its skeptical Middle and New periods), from which Aristotle himself came. From Antisthenes a link (possibly tenuous) was traced through Diogenes to Cynicism. Through Socratic elements in Cynicism and the Platonic Academy, Stoicism tried to graft itself onto the Socratic tradition, although it was later Stoics like Panaetius and Epictetus who expressly admired the influence of Socrates. Even the hedonistic Cyrenaic school stems from Aristippus. It is possible that Socrates' philosophy may still be growing. "Even now although Socrates is dead the memory of what he did or said while still alive is just as helpful or even more so to men" (Epictetus, *Discourses* IV, 1, 169).

Primary Sources

In this section and the next sections works are listed to follow the development of themes in the text.

Aristophanes, *The Clouds*, V. Coulon, ed., translated by H. van Daele, Vol. I, 6th ed. Les Belles Lettres. Paris, 1958. Greek text with English translation by B. B. Rogers. Loeb Classical Library. Cambridge, Mass., and London, 1924.

Plato, *Dialogues*, John Burnet, ed. Oxford Classical Texts, 1902–1906. Translated by B. Jowett, 4th ed., rev., 4 vols. Oxford, 1953.

Xenophon, *Memorabilia*, translated by E. C. Marchant. Loeb Classical Library.

Xenophon, *Apology* and *Symposium*, translated by O. J. Todd. Loeb Classical Library, 1922.

Aeschines, *Fragmenta*, H. Krauss, ed. Leipzig, 1911.

Aischines von Sphettos, H. Dittmar, ed. Berlin, 1912.

Antisthenes, *Fragmenta*, A. Winkelmann, ed. Zurich, 1842.

Aristippus, *Fragmenta*, E. Mannebach, ed. Leiden and Cologne, 1961.

Aristotle. See T. Deman, *Le Témoignage d'Aristote sur Socrate*. Paris, 1942.

Diogenes Laërtius, *Lives of Eminent Philosophers*, 2 vols. Loeb Classical Library. See Book 2, 18 ff.

Socratic Problem

Magalhães-Vilhena, V. de, *Le Problème de Socrate*. Paris, 1952. This book and the following work give a good conspectus of the literature.

Magalhães-Vilhena, V. de, *Socrate et la légende platonicienne*. Paris, 1952.

Vogel, C. J. de, "The Present State of the Socratic Problem." *Phronesis*, Vol. 1 (1955), 26 ff.

HISTORICITY OF PLATONIC SOCRATES

Burnet, John, *Greek Philosophy, Thales to Plato*. London, 1914.

Burnet, John, "The Socratic Doctrine of the Soul." *Proceedings of the British Academy*, Vol. 7 (1915–1916).

Taylor, A. E., *Varia Socratica*. Oxford, 1911.

Taylor, A. E., *Socrates*. London, 1935.

SKEPTICS

Dupréel, E., *La Légende socratique*. Brussels, 1922.

Gigon, O., *Sokrates*. Bern, 1947.

Gigon, O., *Kommentar zu Xenophons Memorabilien*. Basel, 1953——. Vol. I (1953) and Vol. II (1956) have been published thus far.

Joel, K., *Der echte und der Xenophontische Sokrates*. Berlin, 1893–1901. For Xenophon.

Chroust, A.-H., *Socrates, Man and Myth*. London, 1957. For Polycrates.

Other General Constructions

Zeller, Eduard, *Die Philosophie der Griechen.* Leipzig, 1875, 1922. Translated by O. Reichel as *Socrates and the Socratic Schools.* London, 1885. See Part 2, Section 1.

Maier, Heinrich, *Sokrates.* Tübingen, 1913.

Stenzel, Julius, "Sokrates," in August Pauly and Georg Wissowa, eds., *Realencyclopädie der classischen Altertumswissenschaft,* second series, Vol. III, Part 1 (1927), Cols. 811 ff.

Ritter, C., *Sokrates.* Tübingen, 1931.

Festugière, A.-J., *Socrate.* Paris, 1934.

Jaeger, Werner, *Paideia,* 3 vols. Berlin, 1936–1947. Translated under the same title by Gilbert Highet. Oxford, 1939–1944. See Vol. II.

Versényi, Laszlo, *Socratic Humanism.* New Haven, 1963.

WITH SPECIAL REFERENCE TO PLATONIC SOCRATES

Diès, A., *Autour de Platon.* Paris, 1927.

Field, G. C., *Plato and His Contemporaries.* London, 1930.

Hackforth, Reginald, *Composition of Plato's Apology.* Cambridge, 1933.

Robinson, Richard, *Plato's Earlier Dialectic,* 2d ed. Oxford, 1953.

Gould, John, *The Development of Plato's Ethics.* Oxford, 1955.

I. G. KIDD

SOHRAWARDĪ, SHIHĀB AL-DĪN YAḤYĀ (c.549 H./ A.D. 1155-587 H./A.D. 1191),

was born in Sohraward, ancient Media, in northwestern Iran. He died in Aleppo, in the full bloom of youth, a victim of the vindictiveness of the doctors of the Law and of the fanaticism of Ṣalāḥ al-Dīn (the "Saladin" of the Crusaders). It is important that this philosopher not be confused with two other Sufis with similar names (Shihāb al-Dīn 'Omar and Abu'l-Najīb Sohrawardī).

A guiding thought dominates Sohrawardī's work: to restore the philosophy and theosophy of the sages of ancient Persia. Three centuries before it was effected in the works of the great Byzantine philosopher Georgius Gemistus Pletho, the conjunction of the names of Plato and Zoroaster was realized in the works of this thinker of Islamic Persia. Broadly outlined, this work (where the influence of Hermeticism and late Neoplatonism was also joined) brought forth an interpretation of the theory of Platonic Ideas in terms of Zoroastrian angelology. If his design reconciled itself with difficulty to the spirit of legalistic Islam, of religion and the Law, it was not, on the other hand, contrary to a spiritual Islam, bringing into play all its resources and profoundly influencing it. This employment in effect imposed on philosophy an exigency that assured it thenceforth of a completely characteristic place in Islam. Sohrawardī did not separate philosophy and spirituality; a philosophy that does not terminate in or at least tend toward a mystical and spiritual experience is a vain undertaking. Seeking out a mystical and spiritual experience without a preliminary philosophical position puts one in great danger of losing one's way. The influence of this doctrine has been considerable, especially in Iran, and endures even to the present.

The key word in Sohrawardī's entire work is (in Arabic) *Ishrāq.* Literally, it means the illumination of the sun when it arises (*Aurora consurgens*). Transposed to the spiritual plane, it means a type of knowledge which is the very *Orient* of knowledge. Sohrawardī's principal work is entitled *Ḥikmat al-Ishrāq,* "Oriental" philosophy or theosophy (the term *ḥikmat ilāhīya* being the exact equivalent of the Greek *theosophia*). It deals with a philosophy that is Oriental because it is illuminative and illuminative because it is Oriental. Between these two terms there is reciprocity rather than opposition (as C. Nallino believed). The disciples and perpetuators of Sohrawardī are known as the *Ishrāqīyūn* or *Mashriqīyūn,* the "Orientals." Sohrawardī himself is designated as pre-eminently the *shaikh al-Ishrāq.* Prior to Islam, these "Orientals" are to him essentially the sages of ancient Persia. Their "philosophy of enlightenment" originated with the concept of *Xwarnah* (Light-of-Glory in the Avesta and Mazdaistic cosmology; *Khorreh* in Persian). In its turn, this concept dominates the entire work of the *shaikh al-Ishrāq.* "Oriental" knowledge, which is its subject matter, is essentially a discovered "presential" knowledge (*'ilm hoḍūrī*), and intuitive perception, such as knowledge of oneself, in opposition to a type of re-presentative knowledge (*'ilm ṣūrī*), through the intermediary of a Form or a *species.*

This is why an entire section of our shaikh's work (among approximately fifty titles, a trilogy, each of whose constituent elements is composed of a logic, a physics, and a metaphysics) is dedicated to freeing philosophy from all accumulated obstacles attributable to the abstractions of the Peripatetics and the scholastic scholars of Islam (the *Mutukallimūn*). This preliminary study was crowned with the work cited above, where, from the analysis of the concept of being as Light, the theory of the procession of beings of Light is disengaged (complex angelic hierarchies, deduced somehow from the esoteric interpretation of the laws of optics). To the structure of these hierarchies correspond those of the plans of the universe, which are "symbolic of each other." Sohrawardī, more particularly, seemed to have been the first to found, systematically, an ontology of the *mundus imaginalis* (*'ālam al-mithāl*), a world of the Image and a world of the Souls (the *malakūt*), acting as an intermediary between the world of pure Intelligences (the *jabarūt*) and the sensible world. This is a world without which the visionary experiences of the prophets and mystics, as well as the suprasensible events that the philosophy of the Resurrection treats, would remain unexplained. From this another complete section of Sohrawardī's works, deliberately written in Persian, was introduced, especially to this world, as the first phase of spiritual initiation. It forms a cycle of symbolic tales in which Sohrawardī consciously followed Avicenna (Ibn Sīnā). He knew very well what he owed to Avicenna and why he was able to go further than he: Avicenna also had formulated the project of an "Oriental" philosophy, but he could not realize it, not having known its true source.

Thus did the work of the *shaikh al-Ishrāq* give rise in Islam to a current of philosophy and spirituality distinct from the three currents that are usually considered, that of *Kalām* (the rational scholastic scholars), that of the *falāsifa* (philosophers known as the Hellenists), and Sufism. It is currently said that the *Ishrāq* is to the philosophy of the *falāsifa* what Sufism is to the theology of the *Kalām.* By doing this, Sohrawardī defended the cause of philosophy against the pious agnosticism of the literalist theologians, as well as against that of certain Sufi pietists. It was only because his work was ignored for so long a time in the West (where one was accustomed to assessing Islamic philosophy from the viewpoint of what was known of it by Latin Scholastics) that an exaggerated importance was attached to Averroës, whose work was considered as having attained the self-proclaimed pinnacle and terminal point of philosophy in Islam. Neither the Peripateticism of Averroës (with which the ontology of *Malakūt* was lost) nor the critique of the philosophy of Ghazālī has had any influence on Oriental Islam, notably on Iranian philosophy. Even there, what develops is a "Sohrawardian Avicennism" to which is joined the influence of Ibn 'Arabī (of Andalusia, died A.D. 1240, one of the greatest mystical theosophists of all time), which spread forth into the "prophetic philosophy" of Shī'ism. The influence of Sohrawardī's doctrines was later dominant in the School of Ispahan, in the sixteenth and seventeenth centuries, in the Iran of the Safavids (with the great names of Mīr Dāmād, Mollā Ṣadrā Shīrāzī, Moḥsen Fayẓ, Qāẓī Sa'id Qommī, and so forth), as it was also later preponderant in India in those circles influenced by the generous religious reform of Shāh Akbar. It still makes itself felt in Iran at the present time.

Bibliography

For an edition of the works of Sohrawardī, see *Opera Metaphysica et Mystica*, Vol. I, Henry Corbin, ed. (Istanbul and Leipzig, 1945), and *Oeuvres philosophiques et mystiques* (which is *Opera Metaphysica et Mystica*, Vol. II), Henry Corbin, ed. (Teheran and Paris, 1952). The two volumes contain a long introduction in French.

See also Henry Corbin, *Histoire de la philosophie islamique*, Vol. I (Paris, 1964), pp. 284–304 and the detailed bibliography on pp. 360–361, and *Terre céleste et corps de résurrection: de l'Iran mazdeen a l'Iran shi'ite* (Paris, 1961), which contains translations of several of Sohrawardī's works.

HENRY CORBIN

SOLGER, KARL WILHELM FERDINAND (1780–1819), German romantic philosopher, was born in Schwedt. He studied jurisprudence, philology, and philosophy at the University of Halle and at Jena, where he heard Schelling lecture. After some time in the Prussian civil service, he lectured on philosophy at the University of Frankfurt an der Oder (1809), where he met Ludwig Tieck, the writer. From 1811 until his death he was a professor at the University of Berlin.

Like many romantics, Solger was preoccupied with the polarity of the finite and the infinite. Man is finite but filled with a desire for the infinite. The world in which he finds himself is fragmented. Grasping splinters of reality, common understanding operates in terms of polarities— concrete and universal, appearance and concept, body and soul, individual and nature. Only in the infinite Idea are polarities reconciled. Common understanding is tied to the finite. Man must escape from its rule if he is to recognize the infinite Idea. God made a sacrifice of himself to create the finite, and man must sacrifice himself and the phenomenal to return to the infinite. In this annihilation the Godhead reveals itself. The reconciliation of the finite and the infinite is the goal of the philosopher when he tries to capture truth in his systems; it is the duty of the moral man who confronts it as a task; it is achieved by the artist who,

in creating the beautiful, reveals the Idea in the phenomenal.

The philosophy of art was at the center of Solger's philosophical program. Enthusiasm and irony are the two mainsprings of artistic creation. Enthusiasm, like Plato's Eros, ties man to the reality in which he has his ground. The enthusiast is possessed by the Idea. Irony recognizes the negativity of phenomenal reality and negates it. Thus it pushes away the veil that normally hides the Idea from us.

For Solger, as for Plato, philosophy is fundamentally conversation. It is a joint struggle for something that is dimly apprehended and yet escapes adequate articulation. Truth is never a possession; it only reveals itself in the process of striving for it. Thus, the most adequate vehicle for the expression of philosophical thought is the dialogue.

Works by Solger

Erwin, Vier Gespräche über das Schöne und die Kunst, 2 vols. Berlin, 1815.

Philosophische Gespräche. Berlin, 1817.

Nachgelassene Schriften und Briefwechsel, L. Tieck and F. von Raumer, eds. Leipzig, 1826.

Vorlesungen über Aesthetik, K. W. L. Heyse, ed. Leipzig, 1829.

The Complete Correspondence (between Solger and Ludwig Tieck), P. Matenko, ed. New York, 1932.

Works on Solger

Allemann, Beda, *Ironie und Dichtung*. Pfullingen, 1956.

Boucher, Maurice, *K. W. F. Solger, ésthetique et philosophie de la présence*. Paris, 1934.

Hartmann, Hans, *Kunst und Religion bei Wackenroder, Tieck und Solger*. Erlangen, 1916. A dissertation.

Hegel, G. W. F., *Sämmtliche Werke*. Stuttgart, 1927–1930. Vol. XII, pp. 100–106, 221; Vol. XX, pp. 132–202.

Heller, J. E., *Solgers Philosophie der ironischen Dialektik*. Berlin, 1928.

Kierkegaard, Søren, "Om Begrebet Ironi." *Samlede Vaerker*, 15 vols. Copenhagen, 1901–1906. Vol. XIII, pp. 376–387.

Müller, Gustav, "Solger's Aesthetics—A Key to Hegel." *Corona, Studies in Celebration of the 80th Birthday of Samuel Singer*. Durham, N.C., 1941.

Schönebeck, Erich, *Tieck und Solger*. Berlin, 1910. A dissertation.

Walzel, Oskar, "'Allgemeines' und 'Besonderes.'" *Deutsche Vierteljahrsschrift*, Vol. 17 (1939), 152–182.

Wildbolz, Rudolf, *Der philosophische Dialog als literarisches Kunstwerk*. Bern and Stuttgart, 1952.

KARSTEN HARRIES

SOLIPSISM. The term "solipsism" (Latin *solus*, alone, plus *ipse*, self) would generally suggest any doctrine that attaches prime importance to the self. If we ask about the kind of importance, we are led at once into a variety of possibilities among which there are three chief elements. The first is the notion of self-seeking, of interest especially to moralists and psychologists. This we may call "egoism." The second is the notion of the self as the supposed total of existence, which is a notion for metaphysicians to examine. This may be called "reality solipsism." The third is the notion of the self and its states as the only object of real knowledge and the origin of any problematic knowledge of other existence. This, which is an epistemological notion of interest to specialists in theory of knowledge, we may call "knowledge solipsism." Since these three notions are prima facie different, we may use them as a convenience for dividing a complex topic, although in some way or other each takes the self to be basic or to be of chief importance.

If there is any other feature shared by all forms of solipsism, it is the requirement that "the" self is not just the solipsist's own; that the word "self" or "I" is not to be confined to a single, fixed reference. The doctrine is general in the sense that "the" self is that of any person who is supposedly following the argument and thinking the singular word "I." However paradoxical this requirement may seem or actually be, and however it is eventually to be accommodated, it is a feature that has not been denied in any formulation of solipsism. Since all forms depend upon the revolving pronoun "I," solipsism could probably be given the generic label "egoism"—as it was, in fact, prior to 1870, when usage began to reserve the word for the first of the three emphases listed above.

EGOISM

Self-seeking may be considered as theory or as practice. As practice alone, self-seeking would be of little intellectual interest except to psychologists and writers of fiction. When it has been treated by philosophers, it has ceased to be considered merely as practice and has become illustrational, suggestive of a doctrine favoring it or a contrary one condemning it.

Apparently the earliest use of a cognate of the English term "solipsist" is ascribable to an apostate Jesuit, Giulio Clemente Scotti, in a work of 1652 titled *La Monarchie des solipses,* which depicts a kingdom of self-seekers. The work was a satire on the Jesuits, and for some time thereafter in France, Jesuits were subject to the epithet *solipsistes.*

Philosophically more interesting questions arise on the matter of principle. It is doubtful whether self-seeking, understood without any restriction, can be viewed as a coherent moral principle at all. For wherever one person's self-seeking conflicts with another's, the principle would enjoin both, and by implication countermand itself. To become coherent it would evidently have to be restricted to something short of extreme egoism.

Of course egoism must be distinguished from metaphysical and epistemological doctrines, which are philosophically more technical. For one thing, to urge self-seeking is plainly different from denying that there is any reality but oneself. Indeed, these two doctrines are incompatible; the latter doctrine, which is metaphysical, would make the former unintelligible, since insofar as the former has validity, other selves must be supposed to exist. The doctrine of self-seeking is also different again from the epistemological doctrine, for neither of these doctrines purports to carry any commitment respecting the other. That all three forms have in fact shown some tendency to occur together does not obliterate their differences.

(For further discussion of egoism, see EGOISM AND ALTRUISM.)

METAPHYSICAL SOLIPSISM

Of the two other kinds of solipsism—the metaphysical and epistemological—the metaphysical is both the more familiar and the more provocative. It has seldom been identified by more than a short phrase like "Only I exist" or "Self is the whole of reality." To see more clearly what it is and why any theorist should ever have been taken with it, one must identify it more fully and note how it has arisen as a temptation.

The reasoning behind the doctrine may be put as follows. Every claim concerning the existence or nonexistence of anything is grounded in experience and could not possibly extend beyond it. An existential claim which seemed to reach beyond experience could have no basis or reference; it would apparently be unintelligible and not strictly a claim at all. But experience is essentially immediate; in itself it is never mistaken (only inferences from it can be mistaken), and it is had by one person only and is private to him. Hence, existential claims can never truly, and perhaps never with full intelligibility, claim more than the existence of the experiencing self and its states, and indeed perhaps never claim more than this as of the moment of the experience.

Now this metaphysical doctrine is remarkable because, although it is so audacious that a philosophical novice can do little more than gasp at it, philosophers themselves have treated it with deference. They have frequently said of it that it is implausible but incapable of being refuted.

Descartes. The doctrine of metaphysical solipsism is not ancient. Despite an early version of the *cogito ergo sum* in St. Augustine (*City of God* XI, 26), Descartes must be considered responsible for the introduction of solipsism as a recognized problem. As he made clear in his *Meditations,* where he early expressed a doubt whether there are "sky, air, earth, colors, shapes, sounds" or any existences at all but "inventions of my mind," he·used the doubt as a device for presenting his own method of proof—his own style of certifying the items of knowledge that we gain by a careful use of our faculties. At the end of the work he pointedly rejected the solipsistic doubt as being extravagant and ridiculous. Yet what he himself expressly maintained was not the same as what he unwittingly stirred up for later philosophers. The reality solipsism to which he assigned a purely rhetorical role survived to disturb many later philosophers who unhesitatingly rejected his method; and although they did not actually espouse solipsism, they frequently believed that it might be true.

Locke and Kant. Locke unintentionally helped the metaphysical doctrine of solipsism along. His pronouncement that knowledge is "nothing but the perception of the connection of and agreement, or disagreement and repugnancy of any of our ideas" (*Essay Concerning Human Understanding,* IV, 1.2) has turned out to be both an empiricist maxim and a sanction of doubt. For ideas have almost inevitably been taken as being in the thinker's mind alone, so that communication between minds becomes at best a form of inference or guesswork for both parties. Locke's maxim was endorsed by an untroubled Berkeley but also by an apparently troubled Hume, and if Hume, in his reliance upon the force of natural belief (*Treatise,* Book I) can be said to have found an answer to solipsistic doubt, the answer is not one that has satisfied posterity any more than it satisfied Immanuel Kant. In Kant's opinion the theoretical plausibility of skeptical doctrines like solipsism was "a scandal to philosophy" which in part led him to develop his own system of philosophy (see the preface to *Critique of Pure Reason,* 2d ed.). Kant intended to demonstrate once and for all that if the "given" of immediate experience is characterized in such a way as to yield doubt of a real world and of other selves, then it is characterized erroneously, and that a correct analysis of it yields assurance rather than doubt. But again, as in the case of Descartes, the consequences were not without irony.

Fichte and others. Fichte, claiming to be a faithful Kantian, elaborately conceded that solipsism was acceptable in theory and proposed its avoidance through the exercise of "faith" in the practices of actual life (*The Vocation of Man,* Chs. 5 ff.). In this respect Fichte was rather like Hume, and their point of view has become predominant. It has recently been advocated, for instance, by F. C. S. Schiller (*Humanism,* Ch. 14), by Santayana (*Scepticism and Animal Faith,* Ch. 3), and by Russell (especially in *Human Knowledge,* Pt. III, Ch. 2). Russell's approach is distinguished by a search for definite principles of inference by which we may justify each step we take beyond solipsism, in actual life. Whereas Hume sought the most plausible generic account of our beliefs about enduring objects independent of our minds, so Russell sought the most plausible principles for a type of justification of them.

The opinions stated above have been more or less concessive. Since the big issue concerning metaphysical solipsism is whether it can or cannot be refuted in theory, it is instructive to consider the chief criticisms directed against it by the few writers who hold that it is demonstrably faulty.

Criticisms. One kind of criticism is simply that reality solipsism denies established fact. In this instance, one may cite G. E. Moore's attack on skepticism in general, when he claimed that he could give a conclusive ostensive proof that such doctrines were wrong. He held his hand above a desk and then said that it was certain that he had done so and thus that there were hands and desks and other things ("Proof of an External World"). Another kind of criticism is more concerned with mistaken details in the solipsist's reasoning. Bradley, for instance, maintained that immediate experience, which solipsism purports to analyze, is experience of the "this-mine" and that it offers no justification for the view that the "mine," or ego, includes or owns the "this" (*Appearance and Reality,* Ch. 21). Similar objections were advanced by Josiah Royce and, more fully and formidably, by Wilhelm Schuppe. It has also been argued, in slightly varying ways, that solipsism of the sort Bradley and Royce prefer can be no better than radical empiricism—that is, no better than the doctrine that immediate experience is the source of all knowledge—and that it must therefore fail, since radical empiricism cannot account for our possession of concepts and of the resources of logic.

Obviously, this last sort of objection needs merely a further detail in order to become embarrassingly trenchant. Suppose that it be added explicitly that solipsism presupposes meanings and logical relations for its own assertion. The objection has now become a charge of incoherence. Thus, L. S. Stebbing has argued that "the premises for an argument leading to solipsism are invariably derived from knowledge which is inconsistent with solipsism" ("Communication and Verification," p. 28). Again, W. B. Gallie, Norman Malcolm, and Rush Rhees have maintained that meanings are social and that a meaningful assertion must be of such a nature that it is subject to possible check or correction by other persons. Criticism of this kind is familiar to those influenced by the later work of Wittgenstein. (See PRIVATE LANGUAGE PROBLEM.) In Wittgenstein's earlier *Tractatus Logico-philosophicus,* although solipsism is said not to make propositional sense and to be misleading when offered as an assertion, yet the author's position is that in some sense "*the limits of my language* mean the limits of my world" (5.6) and that "what the solipsist *means* [intends] is quite correct; only it cannot be *said*" (5.62). Further, solipsism, if its implications are strictly carried out, is said to coincide with pure realism (5.64). It is Wittgenstein's later work, instead, which is responsible for much of the present-day attack on solipsistic tendencies. (For other developments of the "nonsense" charge, see essays by Castelli and Pastore in *Il solipsismo.*)

Russell's criticism. The above objections are intended to head off the metaphysical doctrine in general. They are more sweeping than Russell's charge (in *Human Knowledge*) against the subspecies of solipsism that requires a fixed self. Russell's point is that the metaphysical doctrine is not a single doctrine unless it is true. If it is not true, then the sentence "I alone exist" has as many interpretations as persons reading it; and conversely, if the doctrine is single and unambiguous, it has to be false. To trim away the ordinary-language grammar of persons and all assumptions by which a strict solipsism would be embarrassed, it is necessary, according to Russell, to set aside all inference and to understand solipsism as solipsism-of-the-moment —that is as the claim that only whatever is noticed in immediate experience exists. Russell thinks that this claim may be true, although he himself chooses not to accept it.

The Wittgensteinians and others. Plainly, the type of criticism offered by Stebbing, Gallie, several Wittgensteinians, and others is more radical. It applies even where Russell's does not. This type of criticism maintains that solipsism could not be true because it is logically incoherent and unintelligible. To be intelligible it would have to be false, and to be true it would have to be senseless. If it were not a doctrine to which this complaint is applicable, it would not be solipsism.

If the defender of solipsism (even a partial defender like Russell) is to meet this objection, he must show that the doctrine is normally put into countersolipsistic language only for the sake of convenience, and that it can be expressed, or thought about, without dependence upon common language. Now it might seem that this is as reasonable as the opposite; for unless we are to prejudge the question, surely the solipsist must be allowed to offer the thesis that other persons and things are bits, phases, or projections of "me." Accordingly it would seem that he has a rule for reinterpreting all reference to other beings and that there is thus the possibility of a language which a solipsist could employ.

The language of solipsism. The difficulty, however, is that solipsism must lift itself by its own bootstraps in a way in which a rejection of it need not. Prior to the introduction of solipsism, we have a common language with conventions and rules requiring that the pronoun "I" be used in contrast with the conceivable applications of "it," "he," "they," "you," and so on. Now when a doctrine is introduced with the claim that it requires a language with not merely new and superficially different conventions but radically *contrary* ones, we have a right to wonder what they are, in what terms they could possibly be stated, ar.d what a lengthy message in that language (not just "I am all there is" or "You are my projection") would look like when it depicted facts and circumstances that a person could identify. But in the case of a solipsist language, we could never know these things, for it would be a fundamentally different language in a way that precludes such understanding. It is not just that there might be such a language that we, with our poor faculties, are unable to conceive; rather, such a language appears to be impossible. For in order to be stated intelligibly, it would require the connected contrasting concepts of grammatical persons (I, you, he, and so on), and yet in its very thesis it rejects their meaningfulness. If this is correct, the defender of solipsism cannot protest that his adversaries beg the question. For the question is one that is *impossible* to beg. The issue is like that concerning basic logical principles. If a man says, "I reject the fundamental principles and truths of logic, and you cannot argue against me without begging the question," we have a right not only to reply, "Oh, then we *can*?" but also to conclude that he is incoherent. This kind of incoherence seems to be the target of Russell's joke about Mrs. Christine Ladd-Franklin, who, professing to be a solipsist, was surprised that there were no others. (This point about persons says nothing of time concepts, which may pose a further handicap, so that solipsism-of-the-moment may well be the faultiest version instead of the most formidable.)

EPISTEMOLOGICAL SOLIPSISM

Whereas the metaphysical brand of solipsism has had no outright advocates, the epistemological brand has had many. In some degree or style it has been espoused by almost every major philosopher since Descartes. After all, it is easy to believe that knowledge about what exists is empirical and that all empirical knowledge originates in inner cognitive states of persons.

The epistemological doctrine holds that the self is the origin of knowledge of existence. In holding this, it does not assert that there is one and only one self which is this source. Instead, it maintains either or both of two theses: first, that knowledge about existence and nonexistence of everything outside the self originates in immediate experience, or "the given," which is not strictly shared; and second, that to any given person, the intelligibility of existential claims originates in his own immediate experience. The term "methodological solipsism" (coined by Hans Driesch and adopted by Rudolf Carnap and others) is normally used for a provisional reality solipsism combined with the first thesis above.

The second thesis above is worth citing because it reflects part of the empiricist syndrome that persisted from Locke to the logical positivists. But in itself it is so elastic in meaning, and perhaps so unmomentous as well, that it may be set aside in favor of attending to the first thesis.

Now the first thesis—namely, that existential knowledge arises from immediate and thus unshared experience—is initially so plausible and seemingly so innocent that its popularity could be no surprise. Its tendency to suggest reality solipsism is so strong that little effort is required to explain the long sufferance accorded that latter doctrine as well.

It is again ironic that an epistemological thesis that has been urged by generations of philosophers who have been eager to avoid the puzzles of metaphysics should almost always have been voiced with a metaphysical overtone. Locke's maxim cited above, that knowledge is nothing but the perception of relations between our ideas, is but an early example which led directly to paradox in Berkeley (his theistic "proof" combined with his *esse est percipi*) and to indecisions in Hume. Another unfortunate case is J. S. Mill's endorsement of Hamilton's view that what is "mediately known is, in truth, not known to be" (*Examination of Sir William Hamilton's Philosophy*, Ch. 10). Von Schubert-Soldern, stressing the same point, led many to suppose he was an out-and-out solipsist (*Grundlagen einer Erkenntnistheorie*). In listing truths to which he thought reality solipsism obliquely bears witness, Bradley wrote that "though my experience is not the whole world, yet that world appears in my experience and, so far as it exists there, it *is* my state of mind" (*Appearance and Reality*, Ch. 21). In Santayana and in much of Russell the ambiguity is well known. A characteristic formulation is also found in W. T. Stace, who, in developing a kind of epistemological solipsism, wrote that "the initial position of every mind must be solipsistic," and that, although a search may eventually reveal "very good reason to believe in the existence of other minds," in the meanwhile "each of us must begin from within his own consciousness" as a "solitary mind" (*Theory of Knowledge and Existence*, Ch. 5, pp. 65 ff.). Overtones of this occur even in the early work of Carnap (*Logische Aufbau der Welt*; cf. *Unity of Science*, pp. 46–47). Traces are evident in Ernst Mach, C. I. Lewis, C. D. Broad, P. W. Bridgman, and, despite his cautions, A. J. Ayer. One may be allowed the conclusion, perhaps, that particular advocacies of knowledge solipsism do not differ from one another in having or not having resemblance to reality solipsism, but rather in the degree of that resemblance.

The question is whether epistemological solipsism contains this ambiguity inherently. Does that doctrine say merely that whoever finds out an empirical fact for himself does so on his own? This would be too trivial. If it is saying that experience contains essentially an immediate element, it is merely a thesis of classical empiricism. In holding the self and its own states to be the sole objects of certain knowledge, what is it asserting if not a doctrine that is provisionally metaphysical? We need not suppose it an accident that epistemological solipsism, despite the assurances of its advocates, has always looked more or less like solipsism of the metaphysical sort. The very formulation of knowledge solipsism seems implicitly metaphysical.

In any case, there are at least two points in regard to

which the epistemological doctrine is far from convincing. One is the principle that experience is essentially immediate experience, with all the limitations this suggests. The other, closely related to it, is the principle that there are qualities or features of immediate experience necessarily describable only in a private language—or at least that there is the possibility of such a language. Recent criticism has opened both of these principles to serious doubt.

Bibliography

GENERAL STUDIES

Ferrater Mora, José, "Solipsismo," in *Diccionaria de filosofia.* Buenos Aires, 1958.

Hoernlé, R. F. A., "Solipsism," in J. Hastings, ed., *Encyclopaedia of Religion and Ethics.* New York and Edinburgh, 1908–1926.

Mazzantini, Carlo, "Solipsismo," in *Enciclopedia filosofica.* Venice and Rome, 1957.

Tufts, J. H., "Solipsism," in J. M. Baldwin, ed., *Dictionary of Philosophy and Psychology.* New York, 1901–1905.

METAPHYSICAL SOLIPSISM

Bradley, F. H., *Appearance and Reality.* Oxford, 1893. Ch. 21.

Castelli, Enrico, and Pastore, Annibale, et al., *Il solipsismo, alterita e communicazione.* Rome, 1933.

Moore, G. E., *Philosophical Papers.* London, 1959. Especially "Defense of Common Sense" (1925) and "Proof of an External World" (1939).

Pastore, Annibale, *Il solipsismo.* Turin, 1924.

Royce, Josiah, "Self-consciousness, Social Consciousness, and Nature." *Philosophical Review,* Vol. 4 (1895), 465–485, 577–602.

Russell, Bertrand, *Human Knowledge.* London, 1948. Part III, Ch. 2.

Russell, Bertrand, *Our Knowledge of the External World.* London, 1914 and 1923. Lectures III and IV.

Santayana, George, *Scepticism and Animal Faith.* New York, 1923. Ch. 3.

Schiller, F. C. S., *Humanism,* 2d ed. London, 1912. Ch. 14.

Schlick, Moritz, "Meaning and Verification," in *Philosophical Review,* Vol. 45 (1936), 339–369; reprinted in H. Feigl and W. Sellars, eds., *Readings in Philosophical Analysis.* New York, 1949. Especially Sec. 5. Also in Schlick's *Gesammelte Aufsätze.* Vienna, 1938.

Schubert-Soldern, Richard von, *Grundlagen einer Erkenntnistheorie.* Leipzig, 1884.

Schuppe, Wilhelm, "Der Solipsismus." *Zeitschrift für Immanent Philosophie,* Vol. 3 (1898).

"Solipsism," in J. O. Urmson, ed., *Concise Encyclopedia of Western Philosophy.* London, 1960.

EPISTEMOLOGICAL AND LINGUISTIC ISSUES

Ayer, A. J., *Foundations of Empirical Knowledge.* London, 1940. Ch. 3.

Ayer, A. J., *Problem of Knowledge.* London, 1956. Ch. 5.

Ayer, A. J., *Privacy.* London, 1959; also in *Proceedings of the British Academy,* Vol. 45 (1959), 43–65.

Bouwsma, O. K., "Descartes' Scepticism of the Senses." *Mind,* Vol. 54 (1945), 313–322.

Carnap, Rudolf, *Der Logische Aufbau der Welt.* Berlin, 1928.

Carnap, Rudolf, "Die physikalische Sprache als Universalsprache der Wissenschaft." *Erkenntnis,* Vol. 2 (1932). Translated by Max Black as *Unity of Science.* London, 1934.

Feigl, H., "Physicalism, Unity of Science and the Foundations of Psychology," in Paul A. Schilpp, ed., *The Philosophy of Rudolf Carnap.* La Salle, Ill., 1963–1964. Pp. 227–267.

Gallie, W. B., "Solipsistic and Social Theories of Meaning." *PAS,* Vol. 38 (1937–1938), 61–84.

Lewis, C. I., *An Analysis of Knowledge and Evaluation.* La Salle, Ill., 1946. Book II, especially Ch. 7, Sec. 11; Ch. 9, Sec. 8; Ch. 11, Sec. 5.

Mach, Ernst, *Popular Scientific Lectures.* La Salle, Ill., 1943. Especially the ninth and eleventh lectures.

Malcolm, Norman, "Russell's *Human Knowledge.*" *Philosophical Review,* Vol. 59 (1950), 94–106.

Malcolm, Norman, "Wittgenstein's *Philosophical Investigations.*" *Philosophical Review,* Vol. 63 (1954), 530–559.

Malcolm, Norman, "Knowledge of Other Minds." *Journal of Philosophy,* Vol. 55 (1958), 969–978.

Rhees, Rush, "Can There Be a Private Language?" *PAS,* Supp. Vol. 28 (1954), 63–94. Symposium with Ayer.

Ryle, Gilbert, *The Concept of Mind.* London, 1949. Especially Ch. 1.

Stace, W. T., *Theory of Knowledge and Existence.* Oxford, 1932. Ch. 5.

Stebbing, L. S., and Russell, L. J., "Communication and Verification." *PAS,* Supp. Vol. 13 (1934), 159–193.

Stebbing, L. S., "Constructions." *PAS,* Vol. 34 (1934), 1–30.

Strawson, P. F., Critical notice of Wittgenstein's *Investigations. Mind,* Vol. 63 (1954), 70–99.

Strawson, P. F., *Individuals.* London, 1959. Part I, Ch. 3.

Weinberg, Julius, *An Examination of Logical Positivism.* London, 1936. Ch. 7.

Wisdom, John, *Other Minds.* Oxford, 1953.

Wittgenstein, Ludwig, *Tractatus Logico-philosophicus.* London, 1922 and 1933. Passages 5.6–5.641. New translation by D. F. Pears and B. F. McGuinness. London, 1961. A survey of useful comments on the relevant passage in this work will be found in Max Black, *A Companion to Wittgenstein's Tractatus* (Cambridge, 1964), pp. 307–311.

C. D. ROLLINS

SOLOVYOV, VLADIMIR SERGEYEVICH (1853–1900), Russian philosopher, religious thinker, poet, and literary critic. The son of Sergey M. Solovyov, a noted historian, Solovyov was related through his mother to Gregory Skovoroda. He experienced a mystical "vision of the divine Sophia" at the age of nine. He passed through a phase of violent atheism and materialism in the late 1860s, when these currents dominated Russian intellectual life. When he was 18, a reading of Spinoza introduced him to speculative philosophy and probably reinforced his proclivity for mysticism and pantheism. Post-Kantian German philosophy, however, was the chief formative influence on his thought.

Solovyov entered Moscow University, where his father was a professor, in 1870. He studied first in the faculty of mathematics and physics and then transferred to that of history and philology. He graduated in 1873 and spent a year at the Moscow Theological Academy. He completed his M.A. in philosophy with a bulky thesis, *Krizis Zapadnoy Filosofi* ("The Crisis of Western Philosophy"; Moscow, 1874). In 1875 he went abroad to continue his studies. He took no formal courses but did research at the British Museum, where he experienced a second vision. He then went on to Egypt, where he had his last such vision.

Solovyov returned to Russia in 1876 but severed his connection with Moscow University in 1877 over a question of university policy. He moved to St. Petersburg, where he lectured at the university and also took his doctorate (1880). There, in the fall of 1877, when he was only 24, he gave a series of lectures on *Bogochelovechestvo* ("Godmanhood") which presented a complete system of speculative cosmology and philosophical theology. The lectures were attended by Dostoyevsky and Tolstoy among others and were enthusiastically received. Solovyov quickly established himself as the first major figure in Russian academic philosophy, but on the accession of Alexander III in 1881, he gave a public lecture at the university condemning capital punishment and urging the tsar to pardon his father's assassins. The audience responded warmly, but the university authorities rebuked Solovyov and ordered him not to lecture until further notice. In November 1881 he resigned his post and never taught again. During the 1890s he wrote a series of articles on philosophical concepts and individual thinkers for the Russian Brockhaus–Yefron encyclopedia, *Novy Entsiklopedicheski Slovar,* including the articles on beauty, cause, experience, freedom of the will, metaphysics, nature, space, time, Plato, Plotinus, Proclus, Nicholas of Cusa, Malebranche, Kant, Hegel, and Comte.

There is more than a trace of the dogmatism and one-sidedness, as well as the intensity, of youth in "The Crisis of Western Philosophy," "Lectures on Godmanhood," *Filosofskie Nachala Tselnovo Znaniya* ("Philosophical Principles of Integral Knowledge"; Moscow, 1877), and Solovyov's doctoral dissertation, *Kritika Otvlechënnych Nachal* ("Critique of Abstract Principles"; Moscow, 1880). Solovyov made such hasty generalizations as the claim that English minds are philosophically shallow and incapable of Russo-German speculative profundity, citing as evidence such "coarsely realistic" English terms as "something," "nothing," "somebody," and "nobody," which in Russian are *nechto* ("some-what"), *nichto* ("no-what"), *nekto* ("some-who"), and *nikto* ("no-who").

Solovyov's last works are not marred by such features. His unfinished work, *Osnovy Teoreticheskoi Filosofii* ("Foundations of Theoretical Philosophy"; 1897–1899), is a series of Cartesian meditations, mellow in tone, exploratory in method, tentative in conclusions yet undiminished in wit, perspicacity, or analytic vigor and conscientiousness. There is also much less dogmatism and juggling with concepts in Solovyov's last completed work, *Tri Razgovora* (1900; *Three Conversations*), a carefully constructed Platonic dialogue which presents four distinct points of view; of these, the two most pronounced and sharply opposed are a Tolstoyan ethic of nonresistance to evil ("The Prince") and Solovyov's own Neo-Hegelian critique of this position ("Mr. Z.").

In his early works Solovyov was often more Platonic than Plato and more Hegelian than Hegel; he wrote, for example, that "the general formulas of Hegelianism will remain as the eternal formulas of philosophy" (*Sobraniye Sochinenii,* Vol. I, p. 282, note). His Hegelian terminology has raised almost insuperable obstacles for English translators innocent of Hegel, since many of his renderings of Hegelian terms, like the German originals, have no satisfactory English equivalents.

In this early period Solovyov was fascinated by the notion of the organic. He claimed that mankind is as truly an individual organism as any particular human being, that mankind seems abstract to particular men, but a particular man seems abstract to his component cells (which possess some degree of awareness). Solovyov also habitually constructed triads; there was, for example, the triad of making, knowing, and doing (or "creativity, knowledge, and practical activity"), whose respective subjective bases are feeling, thought, and will and whose objective principles are beauty, truth, and goodness. The human activities corresponding to making are *mistika* ("mysticism"), fine art, and applied art; those corresponding to knowing are philosophy, theology, and science; and those corresponding to doing are ecclesiastical, political, and economic institutions. In purged and unified form, making becomes "free theurgy" or "integral creativity," knowing becomes "free theosophy" (in a technical sense, not that of the theosophists) or "integral knowledge," and doing becomes "free theocracy" or "integral society." The philosophy which is synthesized with theology and science is itself a synthesis of *mistitsizm* ("mysticism"), rationalism, and empiricism and is related to creativity and moral practice. The authentic and primordial form of "integral knowledge" is intuitive—an *umstvennoye sozertsaniye,* translating Schelling's *intellektuelle Anschauung.*

Solovyov distinguished three levels of psychic structure—spirit, intellect, soul—with corresponding modes of activity or actualization—will, representation, feeling—and corresponding ideal objects—good, truth, beauty. In "Lectures on Godmanhood" he explicitly related these Hegelian triads to the Trinity. "What the absolute wills as good," he wrote, "is the same as what it represents as truth and feels as beauty" (*Russian Philosophy,* Vol. III, p. 69). God the Father is characterized primarily by will, God the Son (Logos) by representation, and God the Holy Spirit by feeling. At first sight it seems puzzling that "spirit" should characterize God the Father and "soul" God the Holy Spirit. Solovyov's difficult and controversial doctrines of the "world soul" and "divine Sophia" were intended in part to show why and how this is the case.

The Absolute is a "living organism," a divine *vseyedinstvo* ("total-unity"), but the "fallen" natural world "represents a positing of all that is, in which each, in itself or through its own will, asserts itself apart from the others and in opposition to them (evil) and thereby undergoes the external actuality of the others as opposed to its own will (suffering)" (*ibid.,* p. 78). This "chaos of discordant elements," each one alien and impenetrable to all the others, exhibits externality, or spatiality. "Every entity finds in all other entities a permanent and coercive limit to its actions" (*ibid.,* p. 80).

Earlier, Solovyov had taken a Leibnizian view of the reciprocal externality of material entities, characterizing matter as "a product of forces or, to be more precise, the relative boundary of their interaction. Thus atoms either do not exist or they are immaterial, dynamic units, living monads" (*Sobraniye Sochinenii,* Vol. I, p. 271).

In *Foundations of Theoretical Philosophy* Solovyov's speculative focus narrowed and his boldness of imaginative construction was tempered by what he called the "conscientious quest for valid truth to the finish." He agreed with Descartes and, in anticipation, with Edmund Husserl and C. I. Lewis that "so long as knowledge covers only the present fact, it is a party to all the latter's certitude; between . . . *pure consciousness* and its object not the neenest shaft of skepticism can be thrust" (*Russian Philosophy,* Vol. III, p. 109). Solovyov insisted that immediate experience provides no basis for distinguishing between veridical and illusory perceptions or even between dreaming and waking states:

> In pure consciousness there is no distinction between the seeming and the real. . . . But when the reflection that accompanies consciousness takes this absolute self-validating character of subjective immediacy as an indication of an external reality, then there arise those errors of judgment which since ancient times have given cause for skepticism. (*Ibid.,* p. 112)

Solovyov acknowledged that all men have an instinctive belief in the reality of the external world and of other persons, but he insisted that the task of philosophy is to justify this belief. Furthermore, contrary to Descartes, the self is not given in immediate awareness. The *res cogitans* is "an impostor without a philosophical passport. Formerly he occupied a humble cell in a scholastic monastery, as some *entitas, quidditas,* or even *haecceitas.* Hastily changing clothes, he escaped from the monastery, proclaimed *cogito ergo sum,* and held for a time the throne of modern philosophy" (*ibid.,* pp. 118–119). Solovyov held that the attempt to ground personal identity on the continuity of memory is abortive, for "from the fact that I distinctly remember now everything that happened yesterday it by no means follows that this yesterday is not today's illusion" (*ibid.,* p. 129).

"If truth," Solovyov concluded, "were a fact of immediate consciousness it need not and could not be sought, and hence there could be no philosophy. But, to the distress of some and the delight of others, there *is* philosophy. . . . There is consciousness of fact and there is an aspiration for cognition of truth" (*ibid.,* p. 134). Solovyov intended to rebuild his speculative system on purged and strengthened theoretical foundations. He did not live to complete the task.

Works by Solovyov

Sobraniye Sochinenii ("Collected Works"), 9 vols. St. Petersburg, 1901–1907; 2d ed., 10 vols., 1911–1914.
Chteniya o Bogochelovechestve. 1878. Reprinted in Vol. III of *Sobraniye Sochinenii.* Abridged translation by George L. Kline as "Lectures on Godmanhood," in James M. Edie, James P. Scanlan, Mary-Barbara Zeldin, and George L. Kline, eds., *Russian Philosophy,* 3 vols. Chicago, 1965. Vol. III, pp. 62–84.
Osnovy Teoreticheskoi Filosofii. 1897–1899. Reprinted in Vol. IX of *Sobraniye Sochinenii.* Part I translated by Vlada Tolley and James P. Scanlan as "Foundations of Theoretical Philosophy," in *Russian Philosophy,* 3 vols. Chicago, 1965. Vol. III, pp. 99–134.
Opravdaniye Dobra: Nravstvennaya Filosofiya. Moscow, 1897. Translated by N. A. Duddington as *The Justification of the Good: An Essay in Moral Philosophy.* London, 1918.
Tri Razgovora o Voine, Progressi, i Kontse Istorii, i Kratkaya Povest ob Antikhriste, Moscow, 1900. Translated by A. Bakshy as *Three Conversations Concerning War, Progress, and the End of History, Including a Short Story of the Antichrist.* London, 1915.
Smysl Lyubvi. 1892–1894. Reprinted in Vol. VII of *Sobraniye Sochinenii.* Translated by Jane Marshall as *The Meaning of Love.* London, 1945; New York, 1947.
A Solovyov Anthology, compiled by S. L. Frank, translated by N. A. Duddington. London and New York, 1950.

Works on Solovyov

Lopatin, L. M., "Filosofskoye Mirovozzreniye V. S. Solovyova." Read in Moscow, 1901. Translated by A. Bakshy as "The Philosophy of Vladimir Soloviev." *Mind,* Vol. 25 (1916), 425–460.
Lossky, N. O., *History of Russian Philosophy.* New York, 1951. Pp. 81–133.
Masaryk, T. G., *Die geistigen Strömungen in Russland,* 2 vols. Jena, 1913. Translated by E. Paul and C. Paul as *The Spirit of Russia,* 2 vols. London and New York, 1919. Vol. II, pp. 225–286.
Zenkovsky, V. V., *Istoriya Russkoi Filosofii,* 2 vols. Paris, 1948–1950. Translated by George L. Kline as *A History of Russian Philosophy,* 2 vols. London and New York, 1953. Pp. 469–531.

GEORGE L. KLINE

SOMBART, WERNER (1863–1941), German economic and social theorist, was born in Ermsleben near the Harz Mountains. He was professor of economics at the University of Breslau from 1890 to 1906 and at Berlin University from 1906 to 1931. Sombart made a strong impact on German economic thought and policies; he played a leading role in the Verein für Sozialpolitik and the Deutsche Soziologische Gesellschaft, and he was joint editor with Max Weber and Edgar Jaffe of the journal *Archiv für Sozialwissenschaft und Sozialpolitik.*

Sombart's interests covered economic and social history and theory, sociology, and the methodology of the social sciences, although his contributions to methodology were more polemical than constructive. Together with Dilthey, Rickert, Jaspers, and Max and Alfred Weber, he helped to establish modern German historical and cultural sociology. Sombart was a highly prolific writer, and few of his writings are free from marks of careless workmanship, though nearly all sparkle with suggestive ideas.

Study of capitalism. Sombart concentrated on the study of the development and the structural make-up of European industrial society and in particular on the development of capitalism and the transition from capitalism to socialism. In his early work he was influenced by Marx, but in his mature period he sought to go beyond Marx's theoretical and historical edifice and fundamentally to undermine the Marxist *Weltanschauung.*

Sombart's magnum opus was *Der moderne Kapitalismus,* whose first and second versions (1902 and 1916–1927) both demonstrated methodological and substantive advances. In contrast to Max Weber's comparative–institutional approach, Sombart conceived of the European capitalist system as a "historical individual," that is, the collective expression of the values of the expansive "Faustian" spirit of enterprise and the acquisitive bourgeois spirit. He traced the development of capitalism through early, high (mature), and late periods, each representing different cultural attitudes and styles. The basic qualities of each period were seen as determined by its system of economic values (*Wirtschaftsgesinnung*)—which he understood as being in continuous interpenetration with the other areas of cultural and social activity; by the forms of its legal and social organization; and by its technology and methods. In a dialectical process of transition, one period generates another as its antithesis. His emphasis on the concrete historical elements caused Sombart to neglect the theoretical and analytical structure of economics, which he regarded as supplementary to his own kind of investigation. Thus, economists tend to regard Sombart's work as history, but historians do not.

Sombart supported his study of capitalism by a large number of sociological monographs on such subjects as the city, precious metals, the location of industry, Jews, fashion, advertising, the bourgeois, the proletariat, war and capitalism, and luxury and capitalism. Following the Russian and German revolutions at the end of World War I, Sombart sharply dissociated himself from Marxian socialism, which, like capitalism, he regarded as "uninhibited Mammonism," the victory of evil forces (utilitarianism and hatred) over idealism and love. He advocated "German socialism" or "anticapitalism," based on the rejection of materialism, "technomania," and belief in progress. His specific prescriptions became increasingly totalitarian.

Social philosophy. In social and cultural philosophy Sombart stressed the idea of an "economic system" (*Wirtschaftssystem*) whose forms and organization are the creation of the mind and reflect the clusters of cultural values (*Wirtschaftsgesinnungen*) mentioned above. The concept of *Wirtschaftssystem* is related to that of structure and to Max Weber's "ideal types." Originally Sombart conceived of this concept in terms of the early psychology of Dilthey and, like Max Weber, took account of the subjective intentions of historical agents. Later, however, he turned to an almost phenomenological interpretation of the "objective" meaning of cultural systems. Like Weber, Sombart regarded the "ideal type" both as a conceptual tool for evaluating historical processes and as a reflection of the essential structure of historicultural reality. Sombart, however, emphasized the "realist" function and interpreted history as an expression of the national spirit rather than a multicausal sequence. In the first edition of *Der moderne Kapitalismus* this attitude led him to a naturalistic confusion of theory and history, which was assailed by Max Weber. Though Sombart was an economist by profession, he regarded economic laws as determined by the exigencies of the spirit of the age, and like Comte and the German historical school, he rejected the claim of economics to be an independent discipline. In his *Die drei Nationaloekonomien*, which he regarded as the theoretical key to his work, he distinguished between ethical (*richtende*), analytical (*ordnende*), and interpretive (*verstehende*) economics. He rejected the first because science should be ethically neutral, the second because it fastened on applied science only and opened the door to the mechanical methods of the natural sciences, which cannot lead to the required understanding of meanings, of cultural institutions, and of motivations (*Sinn-, Sach-,* and *Seelverstehen*). His insistence on the exclusion of value judgments, on the one hand, and on an intuition of essences, on the other hand, led Sombart into unresolved intellectual difficulties and caused him finally to stress the superiority of biased observation over the limited vistas of scientific thought. Sombart came to regard the dispute over methods as a contest between German (heroic–spiritual) and Western (utilitarian–mercenary) thought. He reproached Western philosophy for the "deconsecration of the mind," a destructive tendency to resolve the spiritual realm of ideas into their psychological and sociological elements.

Accordingly, Sombart saw sociology as more than a limited specialized discipline; to him, it was a universal discipline whose aim is to explain the whole of human relationships and cultural categories. He viewed society as a creation of the mind, and accordingly, his "noo-sociology" embraced religion, art, the law, and the state, as well as economics. In his final work, *Vom Menschen*, Sombart assigned the same universal function to philosophical (*geistwissenschaftliche*) anthropology, which was to be developed into a "basic science" coordinating all knowledge concerning human groups and peoples, both their structures and their origins. This work, a bitter indictment of civilization, was, however, merely programmatic.

Sombart exerted considerable influence upon a generation of German economists and sociologists, but his chief significance lies in his suggestive contributions to the morphology and genesis of capitalism and to the history of economic and social ideas.

Works by Sombart

Sozialismus und soziale Bewegung im 19. Jahrhundert. Jena, 1896; 10th ed. entitled *Der proletarische Sozialismus*, 2 vols. Jena, 1924. Translated by M. Epstein as *Socialism and the Social Movement in the 19th Century.* London, 1898.

Der moderne Kapitalismus, 2 vols, Munich, 1902; 7th ed., 6 vols., Munich, 1928. Condensed translation by F. L. Nussbaum as *A History of the Economic Institutions of Modern Europe.* New York, 1933.

Das Proletariat. Frankfurt, 1906.

Die Juden und das Wirtschaftsleben. Munich, 1911. Translated by M. Epstein as *The Jews and Modern Capitalism.* London, 1913; paperback, with introduction by B. Hoselitz, New York, 1962.

Der Bourgeois. Munich, 1913. Translated by M. Epstein as *The Quintessence of Capitalism.* London, 1915.

Studien zur Entwicklungsgeschichte des modernen Kapitalismus, 2 vols. Munich, 1913. Translated by W. R. Dittmar as *Luxury and Capitalism.* New York, 1938.

Die drei Nationaloekonomien. Munich, 1930.

Die Zukunft des Kapitalismus. Berlin, 1932. Translated as *The Future of Capitalism.* Berlin and London, 1932.

Deutscher Sozialismus. Berlin, 1934. Translated by Karl F. Geiser as *A New Social Philosophy.* Princeton, 1937.

Vom Menschen. Berlin, 1938.

Noo-Soziologie, Nicolaus Sombart, ed. Berlin, 1956.

Works on Sombart

Plotnik, Martin J., *Werner Sombart and His Type of Economics.* New York, 1937. Has good bibliography.

Weippert, Georg, *Werner Sombarts Gestaltidee des Wirtschaftssystems.* Göttingen, 1953.

H. O. PAPPÉ

SOPHISTS. The term "sophist," when used historically, refers to certain Greeks in the fifth and early fourth centuries B.C. who became famous as itinerant teachers, men such as Protagoras, Hippias of Elis, Prodicus of Ceos, and Thrasymachus. These men, whose center of operations was Athens, are sometimes said to constitute the first or old Sophistic movement. The second or new Sophistic movement was a vast one, affecting the whole Greek-speaking world; it began in the second century A.D., with the aim of reviving the literary glories of the classical period. But by that time, the term "sophist" meant merely "teacher of rhetoric," and the movement as a whole is of no interest for the history of philosophy. Before the middle of the fifth century B.C. the word *sophistes* was used in a nontechnical sense to mean "wise, prudent, or statesman-like," and also "skilled at one's craft," but the range of people to whom the term was actually applied suggests strongly that it was more or less confined to the seers, prophets, and sages of early Greek communities, men like Orpheus, Musaeus, Pythagoras, and those of the group known as the Seven Wise Men.

The true nature of the fifth-century Sophistic movement has been the subject of much discussion, and there is no single clear view that holds the field. Plato in the *Sophist* propounds a series of highly unflattering definitions, and while occasionally (as at 231B) he allows that the Sophists have some good features, in general he does not treat them as genuine seekers after truth, but as men concerned only with making money and securing success in argument by any means whatsoever and teaching their pupils to do likewise. Aristotle followed Plato in taking the Sophist to be "one who makes money by sham wisdom" (*Sophistical Refutations* 165a22), and the authority of Plato and Aristotle together gave the name "sophist" the bad sense that it now bears, that of "a quibbler" or "cheat" in argument. Both clearly agreed, however, that the Sophists had brought a powerful destructive criticism to bear upon many traditional ideas, especially in morals and politics. This has led to the comparison of the Sophistic movement with that of the Enlightenment in the eighteenth century, and consequently it has been regarded as liberating men's minds from the shackles of religion and tradition. (It was not so regarded, however, in Diderot's *Encyclopédie;* in the article "Sophiste," for example, the earlier view prevailed. The more sympathetic view probably appeared first in Hegel.) In the minds of those who did not love the Enlightenment this comparison caused the Sophists to be seen as the corrupters of youth and the destroyers of Greece, initiating or at least encouraging the decline from the great classical age of the fifth century. The historian George Grote, himself a radical and a reformer, in the famous Chapter 67 of his *History of Greece* dealt decisively with this view; he claimed that the Sophists were the regular teachers of Greek morality in their day, neither above nor below the standard of the age, the general effect of their teaching being good.

Since Grote's day the importance of the Sophists as educators has been generally recognized, but there has been disagreement as to *what* they taught. One view, propounded by Heinrich Gomperz, regards them as teaching the art of public speaking with a view to securing political success and nothing more. Most would now recognize that this is too narrow. They taught and discussed many other things as well—grammar, linguistic theory, moral and political doctrines, doctrines about the gods and the nature and origin of man, literary analysis and criticism, mathematics, and at least in some cases, the elements of physical theory about the universe.

But were they philosophers? Hegel, in his *Lectures on the History of Philosophy,* regarded them as subjective idealists, and as such, they represented, in his view, the antithesis to the thesis of the pre-Socratics, who had ignored the subjective, self-determining element in their approach to reality. Eduard Zeller (in *Philosopie der Griechen,* 6th ed., Leipzig, 1920, Vol. I, pp. 1278 ff.), while dropping Hegel's triadic dialectic, still took essentially the same view in that he regarded them as characterized by relativism and skepticism and a revolt against physical science. Grote, in his zeal to defend the Sophists, maintained that they were not a sect like, for instance, the Eleatics and also that they held no particular doctrines in common. This last contention, although still frequently repeated, is fairly certainly an exaggeration, and Zeller's view is probably closer to the truth.

Plato on the Sophists. The key to the problem lies in a right understanding of Plato's judgment of them. The basic position shared by all the Sophists, so far as we know, was the attempt to explain the universe in terms of its phenomenal aspects alone, without any appeal to outside principles or to a real world other than phenomena. Their revolt was not against the tradition of the pre-Socratics as a whole: all the major Sophists retained considerable interest in physical science. What they did revolt against was the Eleatic tradition, which not only found true reality outside phenomena but refused the claim that the phenomenal world was real at all. It was this aspect of Sophistic thought that Plato found intolerable: they rejected just what he regarded as of the highest value and reality (see, e.g., *Phaedo* 101E). For Plato the phenomenal world of the Sophists *was* a sham world, and anyone who spoke about it without going beyond it for its ground and explanation could not possibly be seeking the truth. If such a person taught others to do likewise, then he deserved all the contempt that Plato's considerable literary powers could arouse against him. But in the modern world, where the majority of scholars are not Platonists and, for the most part, do not even wish to look for reality in the direction where Plato believed it lay, it is something of a paradox that the Platonic condemnation of the Sophists has remained largely unquestioned. The time is long past when the rejection of any transcendent reality can be taken as evidence that the search for truth has been abandoned.

Sophist view of reality. In fact there is abundant evidence that the Sophists were genuinely concerned with the truth as they saw it. Their individual accounts of the status of the phenomenal world clearly varied. The evidence is often scanty and unclear, but Protagoras, Gorgias, Hippias, and Prodicus all seem to have recognized the more or less contradictory character of phenomenal experience and to have been prepared to accept or explain this as in some way a feature of reality nonetheless (For summary statements of their particular views, see GORGIAS OF LEONTINI; HIPPIAS OF ELIS; PRODICUS OF CEOS; and PROTAGORAS OF ABDERA.) Others proposed different solutions. Thus Aristotle portrayed Antiphon (Fr. 15) as denying in advance the prior reality of forms, whether Platonic or Aristotelian, when he argued that if a rotting bed were to put forth a shoot, this would be wood and not a bed (*Phys-*

ics 193a9), while a pupil of Gorgias, Lycophron, avoided the apparent need to say that a phenomenal object is both one and many by proposing to delete the verb "to be," and to say, for example, "Socrates white" instead of "Socrates is white" (*Physics* 185b25).

On society and morality. Of extreme interest and importance are the social, moral, and political doctrines developed by the Sophists. The belief in a golden age in the past when all things were better than in the present (sometimes called primitivism) was widespread in the fifth century B.C., and the only common alternative view was that of a cyclical pattern in human history. Belief in continuing progress was exceptional or nonexistent before the Sophists. But Protagoras in a famous myth of the origins of society saw human history in terms of the progressive development of arts and crafts for the supplying of human needs, with government in settled communities and organized living marking a vast step forward. Critias, who became one of the Thirty Tyrants of Athens at the end of the Peloponnesian War but who nonetheless ranked as a Sophist, supposed that men only emerged from savagery with the help of the civil state and penal laws, as well as through the deliberate invention of the gods in order to inspire fear in the evildoer. Prodicus was another to offer a sociological account of the development of religion, although it is not clear to what extent his general view was antiprimitivist.

The belief that virtue can be taught was universal among the Sophists, so much so that some have regarded it as their sole distinguishing feature (in particular, Werner Jaeger). The effect of this doctrine upon Athenian society was revolutionary, since it implied that anyone, after instruction, might become qualified for the exercise of power, and it left no special place for privilege by birth or the inheritance of a special family or class tradition. It is not surprising that Protagoras was probably the first man ever to explore the theoretical basis of democratic government. Moreover, it was natural to hold that the teaching of virtue involves explanation. If what is virtuous can be explained, then what cannot be explained may not deserve to rank as virtue. This way of arguing provided a weapon against traditional morality which was eagerly seized upon, especially by the young, at a time when social change required the adaptation, in any case, of much of the traditional morality of Greece. Sometimes these arguments were perverse and seemed to traditionalists to be directed only at victory in debate—such arguments Plato called "eristic." At other times a special technique was used, called "antilogic," which consisted in drawing out the latent contradictions in popular or other beliefs. More positively, the Sophists exerted a permanent influence on political and forensic debate by insisting that moral contentions be supported by reasons, and by showing ways in which these could be given. Socrates functioned as a Sophist when he spoke in this way, just as much as did those who took money for their instruction.

Nature and convention. One particular antithesis was of great importance in Sophistic arguments on morality—the opposition between nature and convention as standards of right and wrong. It is uncertain who invented this antithesis, if indeed any one person did so. But it figured promi-

nently in Sophistic debates, sometimes allowing an appeal from human laws to supposedly higher laws of nature, but sometimes also placing human laws above those implied by nature. Protagoras' myth suggests that he preferred the second view. Antiphon, in a series of papyrus fragments recovered in the twentieth century, opposed two kinds of justice according to this antithesis. He may have preferred natural justice, according to which all men are to be treated alike, but it is possible that he was merely discussing the opposition without taking sides.

The most revolutionary supporters of the law of nature were Thrasymachus (in the first book of Plato's *Republic*) and Callicles (in the *Gorgias*). Thrasymachus' argument has not always been correctly appreciated. He has been treated as an immoralist because he argued that no one should pursue anything but his own interest, and since justice embodied in the laws of a state imposes the interests of another—namely, the stronger, who is sovereign—it is silly to obey them unless forced to do so. Callicles took a similar view, supporting it in a slightly different way. The historical significance of both lies in the insistence that any obligation, to be binding, must spring from within, and in this they are the remote ancestors of Kant's doctrine of the autonomy of the will. On the other hand, in an anonymous treatise preserved by Iamblichus, which apparently dates from the period of the first Sophistic, existing laws are defended as the source of all our security, and so as superior to natural laws.

Bibliography

Testimonia and fragments of the works of the Sophists may be found in H. Diels and W. Kranz, *Fragmente der Vorsokratiker,* 6th ed. (Berlin, 1952), Vol. II; K. Freeman, *Companion to the Presocratic Philosophers* (Oxford, 1946); and K. Freeman, *Ancilla to the Presocratic Philosophers* (Oxford, 1948). There is an Italian translation and commentary by M. Untersteiner, *Sofisti: Testimonianze e frammenti,* 4 vols. (Florence, 1949–1962).

For secondary studies on the Sophists, see H. Gomperz, *Sophistik und Rhetorik* (Leipzig, 1912); W. Jaeger, *Paideia* (Berlin, 1934), translated under the same title by G. Highet (Oxford, 1939), Vol. 1, Bk. 2, Ch. 3, being the best treatment so far available. Both M. Untersteiner, *I Sofisti* (Turin, 1949), translated by K. Freeman as *The Sophists* (Oxford, 1954), and E. Dupréel, *Les Sophistes* (Neuchâtel, 1948) contain much speculation not generally accepted by other scholars. See also G. B. Kerferd, "The Doctrine of Thrasymachus in Plato's *Republic,*" in *Durham University Journal,* Vol. 40 (1947–1948), 19 ff., and G. B. Kerferd, "The First Greek Sophists," in *Classical Review,* Vol. 44 (1950), 8 ff.

G. B. KERFERD

SOREL, GEORGES (1847–1922), French pragmatist philosopher and social theorist. Sorel was born in Cherbourg and was trained at the École Polytechnique. He served as an engineer with the French roads and bridges department for 25 years in Corsica, the Alps, Algeria, and Perpignan before retiring at the age of 45 to devote himself to scholarship. In the following 30 years he produced a series of highly curious books on the philosophy of science, the history of ideas, social theory, and Marxism, of which one, *Réflexions sur la violence* (1908; *Reflections on Violence*), immediately became world famous. Before and after his retirement Sorel's life was quite uneventful, for despite his hatred of the bourgeois, his conduct was a model of provincial respectability. Nevertheless, he never married his lifelong companion, Marie David, to whom he dedicated his work after her death in 1897. Sorel's Roman ideas on the importance of chastity, marriage, and the family were no match for his family's objections to Marie's proletarian origins.

Economic and political views. Sorel's first books, on the Bible and the trial of Socrates, were written while he was still in charge of irrigation around Perpignan. They are works of erudition, marked by a streak of passionate eccentricity. Soon after retiring to the suburbs of Paris, Sorel discovered the work of Karl Marx and edited (1895–1897) a magazine, *Le Devenir social,* that introduced theoretical Marxism to France. At the same time Sorel collaborated with Benedetto Croce and Antonio Labriola in propagating Marx's ideas in Italy. (Italy was always Sorel's second intellectual home, although he never visited it or even left French territory, and much of his work has been published only in Italian.) Sorel soon became dissatisfied with Marxism's scientific pretensions and joined with Croce, Eduard Bernstein, Tomáš Masaryk, and Saverio Merlino in precipitating the revisionist crisis. The other revisionists drew reformist conclusions from their critique of Marxism and abandoned revolutionary activity, but Sorel did the opposite. He transferred his interest from orthodox socialism to the most revolutionary wing of the French labor movement, the anarchosyndicalists. He argued that this was consistent because the syndicalists did not use Marxism as science but as myth. It was to account for this mythical character of extremist social doctrines that Sorel elaborated one of his most influential theories.

By the eve of World War I, Sorel had lost faith in syndicalism, and for a time he associated with such extreme right-wing groups as the monarchists and ultranationalists, as well as with groups of Catholic revivalists. Silent during the war, Sorel emerged after the Bolshevik Revolution to devote his last energies to the defense of the cause of Lenin, as he understood it. He supposed that it meant transfer of power away from central authority to the workers' and peasants' soviets and thus that it was in the federalist spirit of Proudhon rather than in the spirit of Marx.

Years earlier, Sorel had predicted an important political career for Mussolini, who, in turn, called *Reflections on Violence* his bedside book. Yet despite tenacious legend, Sorel had no influence over either fascism or communism. He himself disclaimed any part in Mussolini's nationalist doctrines, and Lenin denied drawing ideas from "that confusionist." Apologists of later revolutionary movements, notably African and Asian nationalism, have echoed Sorel's doctrines, and students of all such movements still find useful his conceptions of myth and violence. Croce said that Sorel and Marx were the only original thinkers socialism ever had.

Philosophy of science. Sorel accepted Jaurès's scornful description of him as "the metaphysician of socialism," for he thought of himself as primarily a philosopher, though not of socialism alone. Socialism engaged no more of his attention than the philosophy of science or the history of Christianity. Sorel's philosophy of science was technological rationalism: Scientific laws were accounts of the working of experimental machinery into which a part of nature,

after being purified to make it homogeneous with the man-made mechanism, had been incorporated. There was no cause to suppose that such machines were models of nature's hidden mechanisms, and in fact there was no sign that determinism of any sort operated in nature left to herself. Determinism existed only where men created it, in machines that did violence to nature by shutting out chance interference. Thus, science is concerned with "artificial nature," the man-made phenomena of experiment and industry. It has nothing to say about "natural nature," where hazard, waste, and entropy are uncontrolled, where our knowledge is limited to statistical probability and our intervention to rule of thumb. Sorel accepted the pessimistic conclusions often drawn at that time from the second law of thermodynamics, to the effect that there was absolute chance in nature and that the universe was "running down" to heat-death.

It was against that malevolent nature of chance and waste that humanity struggled in a hopeless effort of "disentropy," seeking to establish regions of determinism (experimental science) and of economy of forces (productive industry). Being a professional engineer, Sorel could work out these ideas in great technical detail. He even applied them to mathematics, saying that geometry was about architecture, not nature.

Social theory. Sorel's social theory derived from his philosophy of science. There are "entropic" trends in society comparable to those in nature. Culture is constantly threatened by a relapse into barbarism and disorder that would make history sheer meaningless succession. Against perpetual decadence men struggle heroically to establish limited zones of law, order, and cultural significance. To succeed in this for a time, they must do violence to their own natures by imposing on themselves a hard discipline and accepting moral isolation amid their mediocre fellows. This means living in conformity to "the ethic of the producers" and seeing the good life to be a cooperative creative enterprise carried on in a self-reliant spirit. Against this ethic stands "the ethic of the consumers," which takes the good to be things to be obtained rather than a way of acting. In the consumers' view typical goods are welfare, prosperity, distributive justice, and the classless society, things to be aimed at for the future and enjoyed if secured. Sorel replied that enterprises undertaken in that spirit were based on envy and inevitably fell under the control of adventurers (usually intellectuals) who duped the masses. He cited as instances slave revolts, peasant wars, Jacobinism, anti-Semitism, and contemporary welfare-state socialism.

In contrast, producers' movements concentrated on building the independent institutions that embodied their morality of productivity and solidarity. Such movements might be concerned with religious, artistic, scientific, or industrial activities, and Sorel took capitalism and syndicalist socialism as successive and equally admirable types of an industrial producers' movement. The workers were in revolt against capitalism not because of exploitation or inequality of riches (such matters concerned consumers only) but because the bourgeoisie had become unenterprising, cowardly, hypocritical—in a word, decadent. Until some more youthful, vigorous movement wrested social pre-eminence from the bourgeoisie (and Sorel did not think that socialism was the only contender), Western history would be a meaningless sequence of parliamentary deals and predatory wars. All movements "ran down" in the end, as their nerve failed, even (or especially) without challenge from a new movement. This succession of periods of heroic creativity and decadent barbarism did not constitute a true historical cycle, but Sorel adopted the accounts of the heroic and decadent phases of society given by Giambattista Vico in his cyclical theory. Sorel and Croce stimulated the revival of interest in Vico, and Sorel regarded his own social theory as a Viconian revision of Marxism.

Violence. Sorel is remembered less for his general philosophical system than for two notions lifted from it, violence and myth. Sorel found the syndicalists using violence during industrial strikes, and he set out to answer the common charge that a movement that resorted to violence was *ipso facto* evil and retrograde. He pointed out that Christianity and French republicanism, for example, had welcomed violent confrontations in order to mark clearly their rejection of the social milieu and their refusal to compromise. In such cases violence was a sign of moral health which frightened away lukewarm supporters and gave notice of earnest determination to adopt a new way of life. Physical violence—head breaking and bloodshed—was only one extreme of a range of vehement attitudes of which the other extreme was "a violence of principles," such as parading the least acceptable part of one's doctrines (in the Christian religion, miracles) to discourage one's "reasonable" friends. Sorel's theory of violence was intended to cover that whole range of attitudes, and the only special stress on physical violence was the statement that without being at all typical of social relationships, physical violence is a logical extreme from which no rising movement will shrink in certain unfavorable circumstances. Such circumstances would be confrontation with the armed force of a state that preached pacifism and social unity while it sought to smother a rebellious minority. The classic case was primitive Christianity, which could have secured tolerance within Roman polytheism but enthusiastically courted violent persecution to mark its unbridgeable differences with paganism. Parliamentary democracy was an even greater threat to independent social movements than polytheism had been to Christianity, because it claimed to have devised, in parliament, a perfect market where all social demands could be reconciled by elected representatives, thus ensuring social harmony. A movement that refused to come to that market because it wanted things other than parliamentary seats and budget subsidies would have to be unequivocal, vehement, and even violent to escape from the nets of democratic prejudice. Most shocking of all, violence might be exercised not only against supposed enemies but against the men of good will, the peacemakers sent to befriend the minority and corrupt it into conformity.

Sorel's theory of violence caused scandalized misunderstanding among respectable people and some morbid enthusiasm among protofascists. Yet Sorel had not defended indiscriminate violence. He had said that since violence is ubiquitous in society, in the form of war and the enforcement of law and order, one could not selectively deplore violence on the part of an opposition without first looking to see who that opposition was. One should ask if it were associated, as so often in the past, with a progressive and heroic morality obliged to be ruthless to force recognition of its independence and to signify its rejection of mediocrity. Sorel noted that such movements built up sanguinary legends about how much violence they had known. Just as strikers exaggerated police brutalities committed on "our martyred dead," so the early Christians had endured far too little persecution to justify the tradition that the church was nourished by the blood of martyrs. Such violent tales were only symbolically true; a few clashes that proved a willingness to go to extremes had revealed the Christian community to itself and its enemies.

Last, Sorel argued (in 1908, when the seeds of world war, Bolshevism, and fascism were germinating) that Edwardian democrats were deluding themselves in thinking that civilized men had progressed beyond the stage at which they would use violence to promote or oppose causes. Violence would never be outgrown (and if it were, that would not be progress) because it was not, absolutely and in itself, brutish. It could be lucid, noble, and applied to the defense of high purposes; it could mark the birth of a new civilizing agency. Of course, it could also be bestial and oppressive, in which case Sorel called it force.

Myth. Sorel found that myth was being used by the syndicalists, and he recalled similar uses from history. In no sense did he urge political activists to adopt extremist beliefs they knew to be false. That ambiguity, of which Sorel was accused, was really in the sociological facts themselves, he said. One found movements uttering views about the future without trying to establish their prophecies as scientifically plausible, without even caring to argue whether the forecasts were sound. They cared for those visions of the future passionately, but they cared for them only as inspiring pictures of what the world would be like if the new morality won all men's hearts. Such visions were myths, a present morality stated in the future tense. The case in point was the general strike. Syndicalists said socialism would come if all workers went on strike at once, whereupon the capitalist state would be paralyzed. Parliamentary socialists replied, reasonably enough, that for the workers to strike all at once and successfully defy the state, they would have to be ardent socialists to a man and the regime ripe for overthrow. But in that event socialism would already have arrived, and the general strike would not be needed. It was not a means to anything because it presupposed that all the problems were solved. Precisely this, answered Sorel, is the social function of the general strike. It is the dramatic picture of a morality triumphant. It is not a plan or scientific forecast, and therefore rational criticism of it is pointless. Besides, intellect has nothing better to put in its place, because the future is radically unpredictable and there is no science of the unknowable. A myth, being the expression of the aspirations of an enthusiastic mass of men and women, could well foreshadow something like itself, at least something equally sublime, whereas scientific blueprints for the future foreshadowed nothing but disappointment, the rule of intellectual planners, and the spread of the consumer outlook among those who waited for the planned good time to start. Granted that prevision is impossible, there are only two sorts of attitude toward the future—myths and utopias. Myths command respect as the product of intense social wills that could achieve something in history; utopias deserve scorn as the divagations of solitary intellectuals.

Sorel's tolerant view of myths and his anxiety to protect their improbabilities from rational examination were dependent on his conviction (drawn from Henri Bergson's philosophy) that the future is undetermined and thus totally unknowable. Few philosophers accept that position, and they would thus feel entitled to be more critical of myths than Sorel allowed. Yet he provided social theory with a valuable new concept—the galvanizing mass faith about which even its own believers are ambivalent, half admitting it to be improbable and yet clinging to it as the dramatic epitome of the cause they live for.

Works by Sorel

Contribution à l'étude profane de la Bible. Paris, 1889.
Le Procès de Socrate. Paris, 1889.
La Ruine du monde antique. Paris, 1901.
Essai sur l'église et l'état. Paris, 1902.
Saggi di critica del marxismo. Palermo, 1902.
Introduction à l'économie moderne. Paris, 1903.
Le Système historique de Renan, 4 vols. Paris, 1905–1906.
Insegnamenti sociali della economia contemporanea. Palermo, 1907.
Réflexions sur la violence. Paris, 1908. Translated by T. E. Hulme and J. Roth as *Reflections on Violence.* New York, 1914.
Les Illusions du progrès. Paris, 1908.
La Décomposition du marxisme. Paris, 1908.
La Révolution dreyfusienne. Paris, 1909.
Matériaux d'une théorie du prolétariat. Paris, 1919.
Les Préoccupations métaphysiques des physiciens modernes. Paris, 1921.
De l'Utilité du pragmatisme. Paris, 1921.
D'Aristote à Marx. Paris, 1935.
Variot, Jean, *Propos de Georges Sorel.* Paris, 1935. Sorel's conversations.

Works on Sorel

V. Delesalle, *Bibliographie sorélienne* (Leiden, 1939), lists hundreds of articles and reviews by Sorel scattered through dozens of journals, including material of philosophical interest, and records the extensive literature on Sorel up to 1939; J. H. Meisel, *The Genesis of Georges Sorel* (Ann Arbor, Mich., 1951), adds later items. Of the many hundreds of studies, the most instructive are Richard Humphrey, *Georges Sorel, Prophet Without Honor* (Cambridge, Mass., 1951); Victor Sartre, *Georges Sorel* (Paris, 1937); Michael Freund, *Der revolutionäre Konservativismus* (Frankfurt, 1932); Giuseppe Santonastaso, *Georges Sorel* (Bari, Italy, 1932); Pierre Andreu, *Notre maître, M. Sorel* (Paris, 1953); Jean Deroo, *Le Renversement du matérialisme historique* (Paris, 1942); Max Ascoli, *Georges Sorel* (Paris, 1921); Georges Guy-Grand, *La Philosophie syndicaliste* (Paris, 1911); Gaétan Pirou, *Georges Sorel* (Paris, 1927); Georges Goriely, *Le Pluralisme dramatique de Georges Sorel* (Paris, 1962); Fernand Rossignol, *La Pensée de Georges Sorel* (Paris, 1948); various authors, special issue of *Fédération* (November 1947).

NEIL McINNES

SORLEY, WILLIAM RITCHIE (1855–1935), British philosopher, worked chiefly in the fields of ethics and metaphysics. Born in Selkirk, Scotland, he became a fellow of Trinity College, Cambridge, in 1883 and was professor of moral philosophy at the University of Cambridge from 1900 until his retirement in 1933. He developed a form of

idealism that lies closer to the Neo-Kantianism of Wilhelm Windelband and the Baden school than does most British idealism. This relationship emerges both in Sorley's preoccupation with the idea of value and in his interest in the history of philosophy.

Sorley's first book, *The Ethics of Naturalism* (Edinburgh, 1885), was polemical in tone and announced his own dissatisfaction with naturalism and his preference for a spiritual interpretation. This work was followed by *Recent Tendencies in Ethics* (Edinburgh, 1904). Sorley's reputation was by now well established, and an invitation to give the Gifford lectures afforded him the opportunity to give an extended statement of his philosophy that was published in *Moral Values and the Idea of God* (Cambridge, 1918).

In this work, Sorley's starting point is derived from a suggestion he found in Lotze, namely, that instead of constructing a metaphysic and then drawing its consequences for ethics, the correct procedure is to take moral experience and its interpretation in ethics as themselves our principal clues to the nature of reality, and so to base our metaphysic upon them.

What is distinctive in moral experience for Sorley is the idea of value. Whereas the natural sciences disregard value, the historical sciences take account of it, and in the manner of some of his German contemporaries, Sorley enlarges on the difference between the historical and the natural sciences. He finds this most strikingly shown in the fact that the historical sciences deal with individual cases, whereas the natural sciences look for general causal connections.

Individuality, although perhaps not fully manifested short of the whole of reality, is certainly more clearly a characteristic of persons than of things. It is in personal life that values are present, and persons may be called "bearers" of value. Sorley distinguishes between instrumental and intrinsic values. The former belong to things, the latter only to persons. Things may be good in an instrumental sense, but only a person can be intrinsically good.

We cannot, however, rest content with a dualism in which persons and things, values and facts, are left unrelated to each other. The naturalism that Sorley had attacked earlier is criticized anew on the grounds of its abstraction. It disregards values, but values and the persons who bear them are as much a part of reality as are the events of nature. In particular, it is claimed that our moral experience has as much claim to be heard as does our experience of the natural world.

Even if we reject naturalism and turn to philosophies of a spiritual or idealist type, we still find that various solutions are offered. Sorley tries to steer a middle course between the extremes of monism and pluralism, and he finds his solution in a philosophy of ethical theism. The idea of a personal God who is the creator of the natural world with its causal connections as well as the supreme source and bearer of values can best satisfy all the facts of experience. This God sufficiently unifies the scheme of things to overcome the disjunction between fact and value, and yet, since he is less than an all-inclusive absolute, he allows for that relative independence and diversity that seem to be a presupposition of genuinely personal and individual experience as Sorley understands it.

Sorley admits that the presence of evil in the world creates difficulties for any theistic solution, but he claims that objections based on the fact of evil are not fatal, if we bear in mind that the solution offered is not a rigid monism. God limits himself by his creation, for moral values can be realized only by free beings, and the gift of freedom makes possible evil as well as good. But Sorley maintains that in spite of the evil that may, and does, arise, such a world is not only better than any world that lacked freedom but can alone be the setting for the creation of value.

He also wrote *A History of English Philosophy* (Cambridge, 1920).

JOHN MACQUARRIE

SOTO, DOMINIC DE, Dominican scholastic theologian, was born at Segovia, Spain, in 1494 and died at Salamanca in 1560. He studied at Alcalá de Henares and became a professor of philosophy there after advanced studies at the University of Paris. Entering the Dominican order in 1524, Soto taught theology from 1525 onward at the University of Salamanca. He was very active in the deliberations of the Council of Trent. Soto's writings include two commentaries on Aristotle (*In Dialecticam Aristotelis,* Salamanca, 1543; *In Libros Physicorum,* Salamanca, 1545). Theological works containing some philosophical thought are *Summulae* (4 vols., Burgos, 1529); *De Natura et Gratia* (Venice, 1547); and the treatise *De Justitia et Jure* ("Justice and the Law"; Salamanca, 1556).

One of the founders of the school of Spanish Thomism, Soto had his own opinions on many philosophical questions. Like Duns Scotus, he denied the usual Thomistic distinction between essence and existence. In theory of knowledge, he also showed the influence of Scotism, teaching that the primary object of human understanding is indeterminate being in general. His psychology followed that of Aquinas, with strong emphasis on the intellectual functions: the intellect is a nobler power than the will. Soto is an important figure in the philosophy of law and politics. He violently criticized the theory of the state of pure human nature, as popularized by Cajetan and Suárez. Unlike his teacher, Francisco de Vitoria, Soto taught that law stems from the understanding rather than from the will of the legislator; he clearly differentiated natural law, which depends on the real natures and relations of things, from positive law, which results from a decision of the legislator (*De Justitia* I, 1, 1). In political philosophy he represents a growing tendency toward democratic thinking in Renaissance scholasticism: both civil and ecclesiastical power derive ultimately from God, but the civil power proceeds through the medium of society; the people concretize the authority received from God in the persons whom they designate as rulers. Soto is also regarded as one of the founders of the general theory of international law.

Bibliography

De Justitia et Jure has been translated into Spanish by Jaime T. Ripoll as *Tratado de la justicia y del derecho,* 2 vols. (Madrid, 1926).

For literature on Soto, see A. J. Carlyle, *History of Medieval Political Theory* (Edinburgh, 1950), Vol. VI, pp. 254–258; T. Davitt, *The Nature of Law* (St. Louis, 1951), pp. 161–177; and

Beltrán de Heredia, "El maestro Domingo (Francisco) de Soto," in *La ciencia tomista,* Vol. 43 (1931), 357–373.

VERNON J. BOURKE

SOUL. See IMMORTALITY; PSYCHE; PSYCHOLOGY.

SOUND, according to Aristotle's *De Anima* (418a12) and Berkeley's *First Dialogue,* is the special, or proper, object of hearing. G. J. Warnock, in his *Berkeley,* interprets this as meaning that sound is the "tautological accusative" of hearing: Sounds can only be heard and must be heard if anything is heard.

Hearing receives attention in philosophy mainly for its differences from seeing. Two respects in which listening and hearing differ from looking and seeing are (1) that there is nothing analogous, in seeing, to hearing *the sound of* something, and (2) that, in telling where something is, there is nothing analogous, in listening, to our having to look in the right direction.

Warnock's explanation of the first of these differences is that we establish the presence and existence of an object by sight and touch, and then proceed to distinguish the object thus established from its smell and taste and the noises it makes. He mentions, as reasons for not ascribing such primacy to hearing, that inanimate objects often do not make any noises, that animate ones make them only intermittently, and that it is often difficult to tell where a sound is coming from. There would be a further reason if, as P. F. Strawson maintains (in *Individuals,* p. 65), a universe in which experience was exclusively auditory would have no place at all for spatial concepts. This reason would be decisive if in a nonspatial world there could be no concept of an object (*Individuals,* Ch. 2). Strawson asserts that we can discover some spatial features of things by listening (for instance, sounds seem to come from the left or right), but denies that such expressions as "to the left of" have any intrinsically auditory significance. In accordance with this, G. N. A. Vesey labels knowing where a sound comes from by listening "borrowed-meaning" knowledge.

Berkeley makes use of the fact that we talk of hearing sounds caused by things, together with the principle that "the senses perceive nothing which they do not perceive immediately: for they make no inferences," to gain acceptance of the view that we cannot properly be said to hear the causes of sounds.

We can see directly (otherwise than by reflection) only what is on the same side of our heads as our eyes. Knowing in what position we have had to put our heads—in what direction we have had to look—to see an object, we know in what direction the object is. Hearing is not limited in this fashion, and so we identify the position of a merely seen object and a merely heard object very differently. Furthermore, if Strawson and Vesey are right about spatial expressions not having an intrinsically auditory significance, we cannot hear that one object is to the left of another as we can see that one object is to the left of another. It might be concluded that knowledge that the source of a sound is to one's left, gained by listening, must be mediated knowledge—that is, must have involved the making of an inference. To be valid, this conclusion would require the further premise that acquiring a perceptual capacity is invariably a matter of learning to interpret one thing as a sign of another. An alternative hypothesis would be that the only interpretation involved is at the physiological level; that is, that differences in the stimuli to the two ears which, in a person whose experience was exclusively auditory, would have no counterpart in experience, would, in a person who knew what it was to see and feel things as being on his left or right, subserve his hearing things as being on his left or right.

B. O'Shaughnessy ("The Location of Sound") asserts that hearing where a sound comes from is noninferential and immediate. He contends that the seeming mysteriousness of the fact that listening can tell us where a sound is coming from is the result of our thinking of what is heard as a complex of two elements, "the sound itself" and "its coming from the left" (defining "the sound itself" as what is auditory—evidence of a "metaphysical theory of the sensory substratum"), and then having to think of its coming from the left *either* as "part and parcel of the sound" *or* as something we experience "other than and additional to the sound itself" but somehow related to it. That the sound is coming from the left, O'Shaughnessy holds, is neither part of the sound, nor something else we experience; nor is it something "we simply know." The mistake lies in our thinking of what is heard as a complex, and O'Shaughnessy sees this as a result of our having "the idea that a thought or meaning is a complexity."

Sound is a Lockian secondary quality. Hylas, in Berkeley's *First Dialogue,* accordingly distinguishes between sound as it is perceived by us ("a particular kind of sensation") and sound as it is in itself ("merely a vibrative or undulatory motion in the air"). Consideration of this philosophical position would not seem to raise issues peculiar to sound.

Bibliography

Jonas, Hans, "The Nobility of Sight: A Study in the Phenomenology of the Senses." *Philosophy and Phenomenological Research,* Vol. 14, No. 4 (June 1954), 507–519.

Malpas, R. M. P., "The Location of Sound," in R. J. Butler, ed., *Analytic Philosophy,* Second Series. Oxford, 1965. Pp. 131–144.

O'Shaughnessy, B., "An Impossible Auditory Experience," *PAS,* Vol. 57 (1956–1957), 53–82.

O'Shaughnessy, B., "The Location of Sound," *Mind,* Vol. 66, No. 264 (October 1957), 471–490.

Strawson, P. F., *Individuals.* London, 1959, Ch. 2.

Vesey, G. N. A., "Knowledge Without Observation." *Philosophical Review,* Vol. 72, No. 2 (April 1963), 198–212.

Warnock, G. J., *Berkeley.* Harmondsworth, England, 1953. Pp. 33–36.

G. N. A. VESEY

SOUTH AMERICAN PHILOSOPHY. See LATIN AMERICAN PHILOSOPHY.

SOVEREIGNTY.

Analysis of sovereignty brings one into contact with nearly all the major problems in political philosophy. At least seven related concepts may be distinguished:

(1) A person or an institution may be said to be sovereign if he or it exercises authority (as a matter of right) over every other person or institution in the legal system, there being no authority competent to override him or it. For some writers, though not for all, this concept also implies unlimited legal competence; for, it is said, an authority competent to determine the limits of its own competence must be omnicompetent. (2) Difficulties arising from the first concept have led some writers to ascribe sovereignty to a constitution or basic norm from which all other rules of a system derive validity. (3) Sovereignty is sometimes ascribed to a person, or a body or a class of persons, said to exercise supreme power in a state, as distinct from authority, in the sense that their wills can usually be expected to prevail against any likely opposition.

The state itself is often said to be sovereign. This may mean any of at least four distinct (though possibly related) things: (4) that the state as an organized association will in fact prevail in conflict with any person or any other association in its territory; (5) that the rights of all such associations and persons derive from the legal order that is supported by the state or that (according to Hans Kelsen) *is* the state; (6) that the state is a moral order with claims to obedience and loyalty which have precedence over all others; (7) that the state is autonomous vis-à-vis other states; according to some theories, the state has only such obligations, whether in law or in morals, as it chooses to recognize.

Classical and medieval theories. Aristotle regarded legislative authority as supreme in a state and classified states according to whether it was located in a monarch, in an oligarchical assembly, or in an assembly of the whole people. But to speak of a "supreme legislative authority" is a little misleading here; for the Greeks, legislation was the local application of a divinely ordained order, rather than the authoritative creation of new laws. The Roman concept of imperium was nearer sovereignty: the princeps (ruler) personally embodied the supreme authority of the Roman people. He was *legibus solutus* (not bound by the laws), at least in the sense that no one could question his enactments. Still, there were strong elements of natural law in Roman jurisprudence; the emperor was supreme because his function was to command what was *right* and for the public good.

There was rather less room for sovereignty in medieval political thought. According to Aquinas, for instance, the king was not only subject to divine and natural law but for most purposes to the custom of his realm as well. Medieval statutes commonly purported to restore laws that had been abused, rather than to innovate. In Aquinas' view the Roman maxim *Quod principi placuit legis habet vigorem* ("What pleases the prince has the force of law") was valid only if the prince's command was reasonable. According to Henry de Bracton, "the king ought to have no equal in his realm . . . [but] he ought to be subject to God and the law, since law makes the king . . . there is no king where will rules and not the law" (*De Legibus et Consuetudinibus Angliae,* G. Woodbine, ed., New Haven, 1915–1942, Vol. II, pp. 32–33). Similarly, the *plenitudo potestatis* ascribed to the pope usually meant that supreme ecclesiastical authority was undivided, or that he held a reserve jurisdiction in secular matters—not that he was *legibus solutus.*

Alongside the doctrine of royal supremacy was another

that derived royal authority from the people corporately. According to Marsilius of Padua, supreme authority rested in the *legislator,* which was either the whole organized community or an assembly (not necessarily elected) that spoke for it. Marsilius' stress on legislation as the will of a supreme authority brought him closer than his predecessors to Bodin and Hobbes.

Bodin: paradox of lawful sovereignty. Jean Bodin's *Six Livres de la république* (1576) is generally considered the first statement of the modern theory that within every state there must be a determinate sovereign authority. Writing during the French religious wars, he insisted that an ordered commonwealth must have a sovereign competent to overrule customary and subordinate authorities. Sovereignty is "a supreme power over citizens and subjects unrestrained by law"; it is "the right to impose laws generally on all subjects regardless of their consent." Law is "nothing else than the command of the sovereign in the exercise of his sovereign power." Accordingly the sovereign could be subject to no one else, for he makes the law, amends it, and abrogates it for everyone. Nevertheless, he is subject to the laws of God and of nature. For instance, he may not seize his subjects' property without reasonable cause and must keep his promises to them. Moreover, he must respect the fundamental laws of the constitution, like the succession law, for sovereignty, as a *legal* authority, stems from these.

In defining sovereignty as a supreme power unrestrained by law, while yet admitting these limitations, Bodin is not as inconsistent as he is commonly said to be. Within the legal system, sovereignty may be unlimited; yet the sovereign may be bound in morals and religion to respect the laws of God and nature. Bodin's suggestion that sovereignty can be limited by constitutional laws raises more serious difficulties; for if "law is nothing else than the command of the sovereign, in the exercise of his sovereign power," how can any law be beyond his power to amend? The qualification, "in the exercise of sovereign power," may be important. Constitutional laws seem to be what H. L. A. Hart calls "rules of recognition" (see his *Concept of Law*), that is, they are rules that lay down the criteria of validity for rules of substance; they constitute the sovereign office, designate who shall occupy it, and identify his acts as those of a sovereign authority. For the sovereign to interfere with them, Bodin said, would be for him to undermine his own authority. If the acts of the sovereign are those done "in the exercise of sovereign power," that is, in accordance with the rules of recognition, it would be logically impossible to act in a valid sovereign way inconsistently with these rules. Nevertheless, the sovereign could still amend them so long as he used the unamended procedures to do so. Yet Bodin regarded the rules constituting the sovereign office as unamendable in principle; should the prince infringe them, "his successor can always annul any act prejudicial to the traditional form of the monarchy since on this is founded and sustained his very claim to sovereign majesty" (all quotations from *Six Books*, Bk. I, Ch. 8).

Bodin's reasoning, though confused, bears closely on certain recent constitutional controversies in the United Kingdom and Commonwealth countries, which have hinged on the contention that a sovereign legislature, though admittedly competent to prescribe its own powers and procedures, must yet do so only by the procedures currently laid down. Such procedures, it is argued, are among the criteria for identifying the legislature and for determining what constitutes one of its acts. Bodin's analysis of sovereignty also suggests how an omnicompetent authority like the British Parliament can yet limit its omnicompetence, as it purported to do in the Statute of Westminster of 1931. In that statute it renounced supreme authority over the dominions by making their advice and consent part of the procedure for any future legislative acts affecting them.

Hobbes: sovereignty and supreme power. Where Bodin was concerned mainly with supreme legal authority, Hobbes was more concerned to show a necessary relation between order, political power, sovereign authority, and political obligation. Hobbes argued that since no man can safely rely on his own strength or wits alone, men's obligations under the law of nature to forbear from harming one another must be subject to mutual guarantees; otherwise, for anyone to forbear in the competitive struggle would be to endanger his life. There is no reliable guarantee unless all parties agree not to exercise their "natural right to all things," but to submit unconditionally to a sovereign authorized to act on behalf of each of them, with the power to make them keep their agreements. Mutual forbearance would then be a duty. Sovereignty, therefore, is necessary for a social order among equals. Sovereignty cannot be made effectively subject to conditions without depriving it of its point; for on whom could be conferred the authority to judge whether such conditions had been violated? If on the individual subjects, no one individual could rely on the submission of any other. If on the sovereign, the conditions themselves would be merely formal. And there could be no independent arbiter, for any independent arbiter who could impose his ruling would himself be sovereign. Sovereignty is likewise indivisible, for if anyone had the power to mediate effectively in conflicts of authority, he would be sovereign. The united strength of all is therefore the sovereign's to use as he thinks fit. His duties under God and natural law are strictly God's business. The subject, having freely surrendered the right to interpret the law of nature for himself, must accept the sovereign's pronouncements on what is right and wrong. He could, however, be under no obligation to take his own life or to submit willingly if the sovereign should seek to kill him. Both commitments would be unnatural, being contrary to the supreme end, which is to avoid sudden death; and having no sanction in reserve, the sovereign would have no way of enforcing either obligation.

The sovereign remains one only so long as "the power lasteth, by which he is able to protect" his subjects. The purpose of submission is protection; protection requires overwhelming power; so overwhelming power is the actual condition for supreme authority. Conversely, supreme authority, brooking no rivals, commanding the power of everyone, wields supreme power. Further, natural law enjoins us to keep our covenants, above all the covenant establishing the civil order. In its concrete political expression, natural law is identical with the command of the sovereign and therefore with the civil law. So the sovereign authority is also the supreme moral authority.

John Austin and the imperative theory of law. The imperative theory of law expounded by Hobbes was developed by Bentham to disarm opponents of legal reform who treated natural law and morality as built-in justifications of the unreformed common law. For if, as Bentham argued, law were simply whatever the sovereign commanded, or, in the case of the common law, what he chose not to rescind, then it might be reformed by command in accordance with rational principles of utility. In the hands of Bentham's disciple John Austin the theory of sovereignty became a tool for juristic analysis. "Law properly so-called" was distinguished from rules of other kinds as a "rule laid down for the guidance of an intelligent being by an intelligent being having power over him." Within any legal system there must be one supreme power, "a *determinate* human superior, *not* in a habit of obedience to a like superior (receiving) *habitual* obedience from the *bulk* of the society" (*Province*). His will was the ultimate validating principle of law; otherwise the quest for validity would lead to an infinite regress. Austin avoided it by resting sovereignty on the sociological fact of obedience.

The English Parliament, which is subject to legal limitation or restraint by no other authority is, prima facie, the paradigm of a sovereign legislature. Yet if its will is law, that is because law makes it so. Moreover, it is the law that defines the conditions for determining what that will is. For an institution has a will only by analogy; it is constituted by the decisions of individuals playing roles defined by rules. A change in the rules might change the will, though the individual decisions remained the same. Austin himself falters, admitting that to identify the members of the sovereign Parliament would require a knowledge of the British constitution. Habitual obedience, in short, may be rendered not to determinate individuals but to an institution, which is a legal creation. In the United States supreme legislative authority rests in the constitutional amending organ—composed of the two houses of Congress, each acting by a two-thirds majority, plus three-quarters of the states, acting through their legislatures or by conventions. So complex, discontinuous, and impersonal an authority cannot enjoy habitual obedience; its authority, like its very being, presupposes the law. To say that the law is what it commands, simply because it is formally competent to annul any rule, is to use "command" in a very strained sense.

In any case, there could be a constitution without an amending organ that nevertheless could allocate areas of competence to a number of organs. All authorities would then be limited. If one could still speak of sovereignty, it would be divided among them, with no "determinate human superior"; each would be supreme in its own sphere. The notion that sovereignty must be indivisible and omnicompetent is a corollary, then, of the false theory that every law is an enforceable command. Federal states retain their character not because their component institutions obey a sovereign authority able to enforce its will but because there is a general disposition to conform to accepted rules and in cases of dispute to accept the arbitration of the courts. The latter, however, being formally incompetent to legislate, cannot themselves be the requisite Austinian common superior.

The imperative theory was in part an attempt to determine the conditions that a legal system must satisfy if rules valid within the system are to be identifiable and conflicts of rules resolved. An alternative answer, however, is that every system must have what Hans Kelsen called a *Grundnorm* (a basic law), which is "the supreme reason of validity of the whole legal order" and which gives it its systematic unity. In these schematic analyses of legal systems, the basic law (usually a constitution) and the Austinian sovereign have very similar functions. Some writers indeed have transferred the concept of sovereignty from rulers to constitutions, thus abandoning the imperative theory. This either leaves a purely structural analysis of a legal order or it substitutes for Austin's "habitual obedience" respect for the constitution as the sociological starting point.

Sovereignty and political power. As Austinian analyses of sovereignty became metalegal and remote from political facts, attempts were made to split, not indeed the sovereign, but the concept of sovereignty into two types: legal and political (or practical). The first would be attributable to the supreme legislature; the second to the class or body in the society that "could make [its] will prevail whether with or against the law" (Bryce) or "the will of which is ultimately obeyed by the citizens" (Dicey). In a democracy this would normally be the people, or the electorate.

The notion of sovereignty as supreme power in the latter sense, however, suggests certain problems. First, one must generally take account not only of what one can do by oneself but also of other people's possible resistance or cooperation. No one can ever do just what he wants; even the supreme army commander must keep the troops loyal. Every social choice is between only those alternatives that the powers of other men leave open. Political decisions reflect not only actual pressures but also those that might be anticipated were things decided differently. Again, a group may exercise very great power in that policy sphere in which it has an interest as a group; but in others its members' interests may be diverse and conflicting, and there may be quite different configurations of interests and pressures. This does not mean that there could never be a particular group strong enough to get its way regardless of counterpressures, and with group interests spanning most of the important areas of policy. Even so, many political scientists see decisions emerging not from the domination of any one particular will or group interest but rather from an interplay of interests and pressures. In their view, the concept of supreme power simply suggests the wrong model. At best the concept would mean that in the search for explanations one need not look outside the internal politics of the supreme group; other groups could safely be ignored. (For criticisms of theories attributing supreme power to the people, the electorate, or the majority, see DEMOCRACY.)

Sovereignty as moral supremacy: Rousseau. The transposition of the concept of sovereignty from the context of seventeenth-century and eighteenth-century despotisms to the modern, popularly based state accounts for many of the perplexing features of the concept. The sovereign was then a king by divine right who at his strongest was subject to very few restraints and no legal limitations and to whom, it was said, his subjects owed unconditional obedience as a moral and religious duty.

Rousseau shifted sovereignty from the king to the people, which was now to exercise supreme power, somewhat paradoxically, over itself. For Rousseau, the citizens of a state had put themselves freely but unconditionally "under the supreme direction of the general will." And he radically altered the emphasis of the old doctrine that the people is the source of supreme authority by suggesting that the general will would be authentic and binding only if every citizen participated equally in expressing it. Moreover, since its object was the common good, there could be no higher claim on the citizen; he realized his own highest ends in total submission to it. As a legislating participant and a beneficiary of the moral order sustained by the general will, he attained freedom, not in the unrestricted slavery of impulse and appetite, but in obedience to a moral law that he prescribed to himself. It is true that Rousseau did not identify the will of all with the general will. The latter would be expressed only if the citizens addressed themselves to the question Wherein does the common good lie?, not to the question What would suit me personally? Democracy, too, can be corrupt, and the state in decay.

From Rousseau on, to ascribe sovereignty to the people was not (or not only) to state a political fact or a legal theory but to make a moral claim. Moreover, Rousseau reshaped the whole conceptual order of politics when he wrote that "the public person" created by the act of political association "is called by its members *State* when passive, *Sovereign* when active, and *Power* when compared with others like itself. Those who are associated in it take collectively the name of *people,* and severally are called *citizens,* as sharing in the sovereign power, and *subjects,* as being under the laws of the state" (*Social Contract,* Bk. I, Ch. 7). It was the citizen, not the king, who might say, henceforth, *L'état, c'est moi.* Consequently, the object of the state, if not corrupted by tyrants or by selfish sectional interests, was a good in which all its members might participate on terms of justice and equality. Its sovereignty amounted to a claim to override, in the name of the public interest, all lesser associations and interests.

The state and Hegelian idealism. Rousseau was hostile to sectional associations as rivals to the general will; Hegel accepted them as partial expressions of, or vehicles for, the more inclusive Idea which was the state. The state's sovereignty lay in its moral pre-eminence over all other forms of human association. As the highest stage in the moral evolution of man, the state embodied concretely, as a living institution, man's autonomous, rational will. Man progressed dialectically through the conflict of states, the most vigorous and forward-looking state taking the leadership of humanity from the aging and debilitated and setting its own mark on a new age. The state was sovereign, therefore, in its relations with other states because it owed them nothing; its highest moral commitment was to its own survival as the agent of history, which alone could judge its works.

Critics. The Hegelian view of sovereignty was challenged early in this century by political and legal theorists and historians, like Otto von Gierke, Hugo Krabbe, Léon Duguit, F. W. Maitland, J. N. Figgis, and H. J. Laski. They substituted a pluralistic for the monistic model of the state. They held that state and society must be distinguished; that society is made up of many associations, each serving its own range of human needs and interests. They denied that the state's moral purpose, whether ideal or actual, gives it a special claim on the allegiance of its members, overriding the churches' claim on those of them who are believers, or the unions' on those of them who are workers. In a given situation, a church might mean even more to believers than the state. Moreover, the suggestion that the corporate legal status and existence of associations depends on state recognition was vigorously repudiated. Associations came into existence to fulfill needs the state could not satisfy. According to Duguit, the existence and corporate rights of associations and, indeed, law itself were social facts which the state simply registered; it did not create them. According to Figgis and Laski, the state's claim to regulate the constitutions, aims, and internal relations of other associations was an invasion of their corporate moral autonomy. Each was strictly sovereign in its own sphere. The pluralists conceded that the state must continue, but as an umpire, maintaining the minimal conditions of order, determining conflicts of jurisdiction, and protecting members of one association from the encroachments of another. Hobbes would certainly have interpreted this as an admission of the need for a single sovereign authority; for as arbiter, the state must have the power to judge what is an encroachment and therefore the powers of review and disallowance. Enjoying an overriding authority, the state could not be merely one among others. Despite Duguit, the law must ultimately be determined by *state* officials. For Kelsen, who identified state and law, corporations are necessarily subsystems *within* the state system, since their rules have legal effect only by the state's extending recognition to them. But, of course, the same could conceivably be said, in reverse, of other associations. For instance, the state could just as well be seen from a religious standpoint as encapsulated within the greater religious and moral order sustained by the church.

Sovereignty in international relations. Is state sovereignty consistent with international law? In Hobbes's view, states confront one another in the posture of gladiators—lacking a common superior, they could not be subject to any law. Austin regarded international law as any kind of positive morality; without a sovereign, it could not be "law properly so-called." Attempts have been made to get around this difficulty by what Georg Jellinek termed "auto-limitation": international law is binding because sovereign states have imposed it on themselves. The relation between international law and a municipal legal order can be expressed, in Kelsen's terms, as follows: seen from the standpoint of a municipal legal order, international law is validated in a self-subsistent municipal legal system by the *Grundnorm* of that system, in other words, by being received into the system. Kelsen repudiated this conclusion, however, because he wanted to maintain that there is one all-inclusive world of law and that international law itself provides the principles validating the laws of so-called sovereign states as subsystems. But one could as well describe the one world of law from the standpoint of any legal system one chose, on the condition that it recognized other legal systems. For each system could encapsulate the rest, including international law.

Article 2 of the United Nations Charter claims that the organization is based on the sovereign equality of all members. This must surely mean that states are sovereign if, unlike colonies or trust territories, they are not liable to have any binding obligations laid upon them by other states without their consent. If international law is really a legal system, however, it cannot mean that a state has obligations only if, and for as long as, it chooses. For then there is no law. The notions of unlimited competence or overriding authority associated with "sovereignty" in a state's internal relations are out of place here. A sovereign state in international law must therefore be a particular kind of legal personality, like corporations in municipal law, with characteristic powers, rights, immunities, and obligations, including those implied in the principle of equality—namely, freedom from interference in its domestic jurisdiction, and, in the absence of an international legislature, immunity from new obligations except by consent. Nevertheless, states are considered bound by the established law and custom of nations, and the obligations of new states date from their inception and do not wait upon any consent or deliberate act of acceptance.

Finally, the alleged equality of sovereign states is not, of course, equality in power. Sovereignty in law is consistent with a large measure of actual control over a state from outside, though a minimum of independence might be a qualifying condition for sovereign status. Even the most powerful state, however, cannot ignore altogether the need to placate its friends and to avoid provoking its foes to the point of inconvenient obstruction. Freedom to act is relative in international as in internal affairs.

Bibliography

Dias, R. W. M., *A Bibliography of Jurisprudence.* London, 1964. A valuable annotated bibliography. For sovereignty, see Chs. 4 and 14.

HISTORY OF THE CONCEPT

Bennett, W. H., *American Theories of Federalism.* University, Ala., 1964. Largely concerned with the concept of sovereignty in history of U.S. constitutional theories.

Cohen, H. E., *Recent Theories of Sovereignty.* Chicago, 1937. Contains an extensive bibliography.

Galizia, Mario, *Teoria della sovranità dal medioevo alla rivoluzione francese.* Milan, 1951.

McIlwain, Charles H., *The Growth of Political Thought in the West.* New York, 1932.

Merriam, Charles E., *History of the Theory of Sovereignty Since Rousseau.* New York, 1900.

Riesenberg, P. N., *The Inalienability of Sovereignty in Medieval Political Thought.* New York, 1956.

STUDIES DISTINGUISHING TYPES OF SOVEREIGNTY

Benn, S. I., "The Uses of 'Sovereignty.'" *Political Studies,* Vol. 3 (1955), 109–122.

Bryce, James, *Studies in History and Jurisprudence.* Oxford, 1901. Vol. II.

Dicey, A. V., *Law of the Constitution,* E. C. S. Wade, ed., 10th ed. London, 1959.

Rees, W. J., "The Theory of Sovereignty Restated," in P. Laslett, ed., *Philosophy, Politics and Society,* 1st Series. Oxford, 1956.

THE CONCEPT IN IMPERATIVE THEORIES OF LAW

Austin, John, *Lectures on Jurisprudence,* R. Campbell, ed., 5th ed. London, 1885.

Austin, John, *The Province of Jurisprudence Determined,* edited with an introduction by H. L. A. Hart. London, 1954. First published in 1832.

Bodin, Jean, *Six Livres de la république.* Lyon, 1576. Translated and abridged by M. J. Tooley as *Six Books of the Commonwealth.* Oxford, 1955.

Burns, J. H., "Sovereignty and Constitutional Law in Bodin." *Political Studies,* Vol. 7 (1959), 174–177.

Hart, H. L. A., *Concept of Law.* Oxford, 1961.

Hobbes, Thomas, *Leviathan,* edited with an introduction by M. Oakeshott. Oxford, 1946. First published in 1651.

Kelsen, Hans, *Das Problem der Souveränität und die Theorie des Völkerrechts.* Tübingen, 1920.

Kelsen, Hans, *General Theory of Law and State.* Cambridge, Mass., 1945.

Marshall, G., *Parliamentary Sovereignty and the Commonwealth.* Oxford, 1957.

Spinoza, Benedict, *Tractatus Theologico-politicus.* Amsterdam, 1670.

Spinoza, Benedict, "Tractatus Politicus," in his *Opera Posthuma.* Amsterdam, 1677. This work and the one above may be found in translation in A. G. Wernham, ed., *Benedict de Spinoza: The Political Works.* London, 1958.

Warrender, Howard, *Political Philosophy of Hobbes.* Oxford, 1957.

SOVEREIGNTY AS MORAL SUPREMACY

Bosanquet, Bernard, *Philosophical Theory of the State,* 4th ed. London, 1923. First published in 1899.

Green, T. H., *Lectures on the Principles of Political Obligation.* London, 1941. First published in 1882.

Hegel, G. W. F., *Grundlinien der Philosophie des Rechts.* Berlin, 1821. Translated with notes by T. M. Knox as *Hegel's Philosophy of Right.* Oxford, 1942.

Rousseau, J.-J., *Le Contrat social.* Amsterdam, 1762. Available in French in C. E. Vaughn, ed., *Political Writings of Jean-Jacques Rousseau.* Oxford, 1962. Translated and edited by F. Watkins in *Rousseau: Political Writings.* Edinburgh, 1953.

PLURALIST CRITICS OF SOVEREIGN-STATE THEORY

Duguit, Léon, *Les Transformations du droit public.* Paris, 1913. Translated by H. J. Laski and F. Laski as *Law in the Modern State.* New York, 1919.

Figgis, J. N., *Churches in the Modern State.* London, 1913.

Gierke, Otto von, *Das deutsche Genossenschaftsrecht,* 4 vols. Berlin, 1868–1913. Part of Vol. III translated with an introduction by F. W. Maitland as *Political Theories of the Middle Ages.* Cambridge, 1900. Part of Vol. IV translated with an introduction by Ernest Barker as *Natural Law and the Theory of Society, 1500 to 1800.* Cambridge, 1934.

Krabbe, Hugo, *Lehre des Rechtssouveränität.* Groningen, Netherlands, 1906.

Krabbe, Hugo, *Die Moderne Staats-Idee.* The Hague, 1915. Edited and translated by G. H. Sabine and W. J. Shepard as *The Modern Idea of the State.* New York, 1922.

Laski, Harold J., *Studies in the Problem of Sovereignty.* New Haven, 1917.

Laski, Harold J., *The Foundations of Sovereignty and Other Essays.* New York, 1921.

Laski, Harold J., *Grammar of Politics,* 5th ed. London, 1948.

STANLEY I. BENN

SPACE. When men began to think about the nature of space, they thought of it as an all-pervading ether or as some sort of container. Since a thing can move from one part of space to another, it seemed that there was something, a place or a part of space, to be distinguished from the material objects which occupy space. For this reason places might be thought of as different parts of a very subtle jelly-like medium within which material bodies are located.

History of the concept of space. Some of the Pythagoreans seem to have identified empty space with air. For more special metaphysical reasons Parmenides and Melissus also denied that there could be truly empty space. They thought that empty space would be nothing at all, and it seemed to them a contradiction to assert that a nothing could exist. On the other hand, there seems to be something wrong with treating space as though it were a material, which, however subtle, would still itself have to be *in* space. Democritus and the atomists clearly distinguished between the atoms and the void which separated them. However, the temptation to think of space as a material entity persisted, and Lucretius, who held that space was infinite, nevertheless wrote of space as though it were a container. Yet he seems to have been clear on the fact that space is unlike a receptacle in that it is a pure void. Since material bodies, in his view, consist of atoms, there must be chinks of empty space even between the atoms in what appear to be continuous bodies.

Plato's views on space have to be gotten mainly from the obscure metaphors of the *Timaeus*; he, too, appears to have thought of space as a receptacle and of the matter in this receptacle as itself mere empty space, limited by geometrical surfaces. If so, he anticipated the view of Descartes, where the problem arises of how empty space can be distinguished from nonempty space. Even if, like Lucretius and other atomists, we make a distinction between the atoms and the void, what is this void or empty space? Is it a thing or not a thing?

Aristotle. Aristotle tried to dodge the difficulty by treating the concept of space in terms of place, which he defined as the adjacent boundary of the containing body. For two things to interchange places *exactly,* they would have to be identical in volume and shape. Consider two exactly similar apples which are interchanged in this way. The *places* are not interchanged; rather, the first apple is now at the very same place at which the second apple was and vice versa. We seem, therefore, to be back at the notion of space as a substratum or ether, but it is probable that Aristotle was trying to avoid this and that he meant to define place by reference to the cosmos as a whole. Aristotle thought of the cosmos as a system of concentric spheres, and the outermost sphere of the cosmos would, on his view, define all other places in relation to itself. In the Aristotelian cosmology each of the various "elements" tends toward its own place. Thus, heavy bodies tend toward the center of the earth, and fire goes away from it. This is not, however, for any other reason than that the center of the earth happens to be the center of the universe; the places toward which the elements tend are independent of what particular bodies occupy what places. In more recent times we view these as two different and

seemingly irreconcilable ways of thought—the notions of space as a stuff and of space as a system of relations between bodies.

Descartes and Leibniz. Descartes held that the essence of matter is extension, and so, on his view, space and stuff are identical, for if the essence of matter is to be extended, then any volume of space must be a portion of matter, and there can be no such thing as a vacuum. This raises the question of how we can distinguish one material object (in the ordinary sense of these words) from another. How, on Descartes's view, can we elucidate such a statement as that one bit of matter has moved relative to another one? In what sense, if matter just *is* extension, can one part of space be more densely occupied by matter than another? Descartes considered these objections but lacked the mathematical concepts necessary to answer them satisfactorily. We shall see that a reply to these objections can be made by denying that space is the same everywhere, and this can be done by introducing the Riemannian concept of a space of variable curvature.

As against Descartes, Leibniz held a relational theory of space, whereby space is in no sense a stuff or substance but is merely a system of relations in which indivisible substances, or "monads," stand to one another. Few philosophers have followed Leibniz in his theory of monads, but in a slightly different form the relational theory of space has continued to rival the Cartesian, or "absolute," theory. The issue between the two theories has by no means been decisively settled, at least if we consider not space but space-time. It is still doubtful whether the general theory of relativity can be stated in such a way that it does not require absolute space-time.

Kant. In his *Prolegomena,* Immanuel Kant produced a curious argument in favor of an absolute theory of space. Suppose that the universe consisted of only one human hand. Would it be a left hand or a right hand? According to Kant it must be one or the other, yet if the relational theory is correct it cannot be either. The relations between the parts of a left hand are exactly the same as those between corresponding parts of a right hand, so if there were nothing else to introduce an asymmetry, there could be no distinction between the case of a universe consisting only of a left hand and that of a universe consisting only of a right hand. Kant, however, begged the question; in order to define "left" and "right" we need the notions of clockwise and counterclockwise rotations or of the bodily asymmetry which is expressed by saying that one's heart is on the left side of one's body. If there were only one hand in the world, there would be no way of applying such a concept as left or clockwise. The relationist could therefore quite consistently reply to Kant that if there were only one thing in the universe, a human hand, it could not *meaningfully* be described as either a right one or a left one. (The recent discovery in physics that parity is not conserved suggests that the universe is not symmetrical with respect to mirror reflection, so there is probably, in fact, something significant in nature analogous to the difference between a left and a right hand.)

Later, in his *Critique of Pure Reason,* Kant argued against both a naive absolute theory of space and a relational view. He held that space is something merely subjective (or "phenomenal") wherein in thought we arrange nonspatial "things-in-themselves." He was led to this view partly by the thought that certain antinomies or contradictions are unavoidable as long as we think of space and time as objectively real. However, since the work of such mathematicians as Weierstrass, Cauchy, Dedekind, and Cantor, we possess concepts of the infinite which should enable us to deal with Kant's antinomies and, indeed, also to resolve the much earlier, yet more subtle, paradoxes of Zeno of Elea.

Newton's conception of space. Newton held absolute theories of space and time—metaphysical views which are strictly irrelevant to his dynamical theory. What is important in Newtonian dynamics is not the notion of absolute space but that of an inertial system. Consider a system of particles acting on one another with certain forces, such as those of gravitational or electrostatic attraction, together with a system of coordinate axes. This is called an inertial system if the various accelerations of the particles can be resolved in such a way that they all occur in pairs whose members are equal and lie in opposite directions in the same straight line. Finding an inertial system thus comes down to finding the right set of coordinate axes. This notion of an inertial system, not the metaphysical notion of absolute space, is what is essential in Newtonian dynamics, and as Mach and others were able to show, we can analyze the notion of an inertial system from the point of view of a relational theory of space. Psychologically, no doubt, it was convenient for Newton to think of inertial axes as though they were embedded in some sort of ethereal jelly—absolute space. Nevertheless, much of the charm of this vanishes when we reflect that, as Newton well knew, any system of axes which is moving with uniform velocity relative to some inertial system is also an inertial system. There is reason to suppose, however, that in postulating absolute space Newton may have been partly influenced by theological considerations that go back to Henry More and, through More, to cabalistic doctrines.

We can remove the metaphysical trappings with which Newton clothed his idea of an inertial system if we consider how in mechanics we determine such a system. But even before we consider how we can define an inertial system of axes, it is interesting to consider how it is possible for us to define any system of axes and spatial positions at all. As Émile Borel has remarked, how hard it would be for a fish, however intelligent, which never perceived the shore or the bottom of the sea to develop a system of geometrical concepts. The fish might perceive other fish in the shoal, for example, but the mutual spatial relations of these would be continually shifting in a haphazard manner. It is obviously of great assistance to us to live on the surface of an earth which, if not quite rigid, is rigid to a first order of approximation. Geometry arose after a system of land surveying had been developed by the Egyptians, who every year needed to survey the land boundaries obliterated by the flooding of the Nile. That such systems of surveying were possible depended on certain physical facts, such as the properties of matter (the nonextensibility of chains, for example) and the rectilinear propagation of light. They also depended on certain geodetic facts, such as that the tides, which affect even the solid crust of the earth, were negligible. The snags that arise when we go beyond a

certain order of approximation were unknown to the Egyptians, who were therefore able to get started in a fairly simple way. It might be tempting to say that it was fortunate that the Egyptians were unaware of these snags, but of course in their rudimentary state of knowledge they could not have ascertained these awkward facts anyway. When, however, we consider geodetic measurements over a wide area of the globe we need to be more sophisticated. For example, the exact shape of the earth, which is not quite spherical, needs to be taken into account. Moreover, in determining the relative positions of points which are far apart from one another it is useful to make observations of the heavenly bodies as seen simultaneously from the different points. This involves us at once in chronometry. There is thus a continual feedback from physics and astronomy. Increasingly accurate geodetic measurements result in more accurate astronomy and physics, and more accurate astronomy and physics result in a more accurate geodesy.

Such a geodetic system of references is, however, by no means an inertial one. An inertial system is one in which there are no accelerations of the heavenly bodies except those which can be accounted for by the mutual gravitational attractions of these bodies. It follows, therefore, that the directions of the fixed stars must not be rotating with respect to these axes. In principle we should be able to determine a set of inertial axes from dynamical considerations, even if we lived in a dense cloud, as on Venus, and were unaware of the existence of the fixed stars. This may have influenced Newton to think of space as absolute. However, Newton was not on Venus, and he could see the fixed stars. It is therefore a little surprising that he did not take the less metaphysical course of supposing an inertial system to be determined by the general distribution of matter in the universe. This was the line taken in the nineteenth century by Ernst Mach and is referred to (after Einstein) as Mach's principle. It is still a controversial issue in cosmology and general relativity. Mach's principle clearly invites, though it does not compel, a relational theory of space, such as Mach held. The origin of the axes of an inertial system in Newtonian mechanics was naturally taken to be the center of gravity of the solar system, which is nearly, but not quite, at the center of the sun. In fact, it is continually changing its position with reference to the center of the sun. Now that the rotation of the galaxy has been discovered, we have to consider the sun as moving around a distant center. We shall here neglect the possibility that our galaxy is accelerating relative to other galaxies. In any case, once we pass to cosmological considerations on this scale we need to abandon Newtonian theory in favor of the general theory of relativity.

The philosophical significance of the foregoing discussion is as follows: When we look to see how inertial axes are in fact determined we find no need to suppose any absolute space. Because such a space would be unobservable, it could never be of assistance in defining a set of inertial axes. On the other hand, the complexities in the determination of inertial axes are such that it is perhaps psychologically comforting to think of inertial axes, or rather some one preferred set of such axes, as embedded in an absolute space. But Newton could equally have taken up the position, later adopted by Mach, that inertial systems are determined not by absolute space but by the large-scale distribution of matter in the universe.

SPACE AND TIME IN THE SPECIAL
THEORY OF RELATIVITY

We have already noticed the dependence of space measurements on time measurements which sometimes obtains in geodesy. This situation is accentuated in astronomy because of the finite velocity of light. In order to determine the position of a heavenly body we have to make allowance for the fact that we see it in the position it was in some time ago. For example, an observation of a star which is ten light-years away is the observation of it in its position of ten years ago. Indeed, it was the discrepancy between the predicted and observed times at which eclipses of the satellites of Jupiter should occur which led Olaus Roemer to assign a finite, and approximately correct, value to the velocity of light. The correction of position and time on account of the finite velocity of light presupposes in any particular case our knowing what this velocity is, relative to the earth. This would seem to depend not only on the velocity of light relative to absolute space (or to some preferred set of inertial axes) but also on the earth's velocity relative to absolute space (or to the preferred set of inertial axes). The experiment of Michelson and Morley showed, however, that the velocity of light relative to an observer is independent of the velocity of the observer. This led to the special theory of relativity, which brings space and time into intimate relation with one another. For present purposes it is necessary to recall only that according to the special theory of relativity events which are simultaneous with reference to one inertial set of axes are not simultaneous with reference to another inertial frame. The total set of point-instants can be arranged in a four-dimensional space-time. Observers in different inertial frames will partition this four-dimensional space-time into a "space" and a "time," but they will do so in different ways.

Before proceeding further it is necessary to clear up a certain ambiguity in the word "space." So far in this article space has been thought of as a continuant. In this sense of the word "space" it is possible for things to continue to occupy space and to move from one point of space to another and for regions of space to begin or cease to be occupied or to stay occupied or unoccupied. Here space is something which endures through time. On the other hand, there is a different, timeless use of the word "space." In solid geometry a three-dimensional space is thought of as timeless. Thus, if a geometer said that a sphere had changed into a cube, he would no longer be thinking within the conceptual scheme of solid geometry. In geometry all verbs must be tenseless. In this tenseless way let us conceive of a four-dimensional space-time, three of whose dimensions correspond roughly to the space of our ordinary thought whereas the other corresponds to what we ordinarily call time. What we commonly think of as the state of space at an instant of time is a three-dimensional cross section of this four-dimensional space-time.

Taking one second to be equivalent to 186,300 miles,

which is the distance light travels in that time, any physical object, such as a man or a star, would be rather like a four-dimensional worm—its length in a timelike direction would be very much greater than its spacelike cross section. Thinking in terms of space-time, then, two stars which are in uniform velocity with respect to each other and also with respect to our frame of reference will appear as two straight worms, each at a small angle to the other. An observer on either star will regard himself as at rest, so he will take his own world line—the line in space-time along which his star lies—as the time axis. He will take his space axes as (in a certain sense) perpendicular to the time axis. It follows that observers on stars which move relative to one another will slice space-time into spacelike cross sections at different angles. This makes the relativity of simultaneity look very plausible and no longer paradoxical. As Hermann Minkowski observed, the relativity of simultaneity could almost have been predicted from considerations of mathematical elegance even before the experimental observations which led to the special theory of relativity. Indeed, Minkowski showed that the Lorentz transformations of the theory of relativity can be understood as simply a rotation of axes in space-time. (In trying to picture such a rotation of axes it is important to remember that Minkowski space-time is not Euclidean but semi-Euclidean.) In Minkowski's words, "Henceforth space by itself, and time by itself, are doomed to fade away into mere shadows, and only a kind of union of the two will preserve an independent reality." We must not forget that space-time is a space in the mathematical sense of the word "space," not in the sense in which space is a continuant. Thus, certain objectionable locutions are often used in popular expositions. For example, we sometimes hear it said that a light signal is propagated from one part of space-time to another. The correct way to put the matter is to say that the light signal *lies* (tenselessly) along a line between these two parts of space-time. Space-time is not a continuant and is not susceptible of change or of staying the same.

EUCLIDEAN AND NON-EUCLIDEAN SPACE

Geometry, as we observed earlier, developed out of experiences of surveying, such as those of the ancient Egyptians. The assumptions underlying the surveying operations were codified by Greek mathematicians, whose interests were mainly theoretical. This codification was developed by Euclid in the form of an axiomatic system. Euclid's presentation of geometry shows a high degree of sophistication, though it falls considerably short of modern standards of rigor. Euclid's geometry was a metrical one. There are, of course, geometries which are more abstract than metrical geometry. The most abstract of all is topology, which deals with those properties of a space which remain unchanged when the space is distorted, as by stretching. Thus, from the point of view of topology a sphere, an ellipsoid, and a parallelepiped are identical with one another and are different from a torus. Metrical geometry uses a bigger battery of concepts—not only such notions as those of betweenness and of being longer than (which itself goes beyond topology) but also those of being, say, twice or three and a half times as long as.

Euclid regarded one of his axioms as more doubtful than the others. This is the axiom which is equivalent to the so-called axiom of parallels. It will be more convenient to discuss the axiom of parallels than Euclid's own axiom. The axiom of parallels states that if C is a point not on an infinite straight line AB, then there is one and only one straight line through C and in the plane of AB which does not intersect AB. Geometers made many efforts to deduce the axiom of parallels from the other, more evident ones. In the seventeenth and eighteenth centuries Gerolamo Saccheri and J. H. Lambert each tried to prove the axiom by means of a *reductio ad absurdum* proof. By assuming the falsity of the axiom of parallels they hoped to derive a contradiction. They did not succeed; in fact, Saccheri and Lambert proved a number of perfectly valid theorems of non-Euclidean geometry, though they were not bold enough to assert that this was what they were doing.

János Bolyai and N. I. Lobachevski replaced the axiom of parallels with the postulate that *more than one* parallel can be drawn. The type of geometry which results is called hyperbolic. Another way to deny the axiom of parallels is to say that *no* parallel can be drawn. This yields elliptic geometry. (Some adjustments have to be made in the other axioms. For instance, straight lines become finite, and two points do not necessarily determine a straight line.) It is easy to prove (by giving a non-Euclidean geometry an interpretation within Euclidean geometry) that both hyperbolic and elliptic geometries are consistent if Euclidean geometry is. (And all can easily be shown to be consistent if the theory of the real-number continuum is.) A priori, therefore, there is nothing objectionable about non-Euclidean geometries. Unfortunately, many philosophers followed Kant in supposing that they had an intuition that space was Euclidean, and mathematicians had to free themselves from this conservative climate of opinion.

The question then arose whether our actual space is Euclidean or non-Euclidean. In order to give sense to this question we must give a physical interpretation to our geometric notions, such as that of a straight line. One way of defining a straight line is as follows: Suppose that rigid bodies A, B, C have surfaces S_A, S_B, S_C, such that when A is applied to B, then S_A and S_B fit; when B is applied to C, then S_B and S_C fit; and when C is applied to A, then S_C and S_A fit. Suppose also that S_A, S_B, S_C can all be slid and twisted over one another—i.e., that they are not like cogged gears, for example. Then S_A, S_B, S_C are all by definition plane surfaces. The intersection of two planes is a straight line. (In the above we have used the notion of a rigid body, but this can easily be defined without circularity.) With the above definition of a straight line and the like we can make measurements to tell whether the angles of a triangle add up to two right angles. If they make more than two right angles, space is elliptic; if less than two right angles, space is hyperbolic; and if exactly two right angles, space is Euclidean. However, such experiments could not determine the question to any high degree of accuracy. All that this method shows is that, as every schoolboy knows, physical space is *approximately* Euclidean.

To make measurements which could settle the question to any high degree of accuracy we should have to make them on an astronomical scale. On this scale, however, it is not physically possible to define straight lines by means of the application of rigid bodies to one another. An obvious suggestion is that we should define a straight line as the path of a light ray in empty space. One test of the geometry of space might then come from observations of stellar parallax. On the assumption that space is Euclidean, the directions of a not very distant star observed from two diametrically opposite points on the earth's journey round the sun will be at a small but observable angle. If space is hyperbolic, this angle, which is called the parallax, will be somewhat greater. If space is elliptic, the parallax will be less or even negative. If we knew the distance of the star, we could compare the observed parallax with the theoretical parallax, on various assumptions about the geometry. But we cannot know the distances of the stars except from parallax measurements. However, if space were markedly non-Euclidean, we might get some hint of this because the distribution of stars in space, calculated from parallax observations on Euclidean assumptions, would be an improbable one. Indeed, at the beginning of this century Karl Schwarzschild made a statistical analysis of parallaxes of stars and was able to assign an upper limit to the extent to which physical space deviates from the Euclidean.

A good indication that space, on the scale of the solar system at least, is very nearly Euclidean is the fact that geometrical calculations based on Euclidean assumptions are used to make those predictions of the positions of the planets which have so strongly confirmed Newtonian mechanics. This consideration points an important moral, which is that it is impossible to test geometry apart from physics; we must regard geometry as a part of physics. In 1903, Poincaré remarked that Euclidean geometry would never be given up no matter what the observational evidence was; he thought that the greater simplicity of Euclidean, as against non-Euclidean, geometry would ensure our always adopting some physical hypothesis, such as that light does not always travel in straight lines, to account for our observations. We shall not consider whether—and if so, in what sense—non-Euclidean geometry is necessarily less simple than Euclidean geometry. Let us concede this point to Poincaré. What he failed to notice was that the greater simplicity of the geometry might be bought at the expense of the greater complexity of the physics. The total theory, geometry plus physics, might be made more simple even though the geometrical part of it was more complicated. It is ironical that not many years after Poincaré made his remark about the relations between geometry and physics he was proved wrong by the adoption of Einstein's general theory of relativity, in which over-all theoretical simplicity is achieved by means of a rather complicated space-time geometry.

In three-dimensional Euclidean space let us have three mutually perpendicular axes, Ox_1, Ox_2, Ox_3. Let P be the point with coordinates (x_1, x_2, x_3), and let Q be a nearby point with coordinates $(x_1 + dx_1, x_2 + dx_2, x_3 + dx_3)$. Then if ds is the distance PQ, the Pythagorean theorem

$$ds^2 = dx_1{}^2 + dx_2{}^2 + dx_3{}^2$$

holds. In a "curved," or non-Euclidean, region of space this Pythagorean equation has to be replaced by a more general one. But before considering this let us move to four dimensions, so that we have an additional axis, Ox_4. This four-dimensional space would be Euclidean if

$$ds^2 = dx_1{}^2 + dx_2{}^2 + dx_3{}^2 + dx_4{}^2.$$

In the general case

$$ds^2 = g_{11}dx_1{}^2 + g_{22}dx_2{}^2 + g_{33}dx_3{}^2 + g_{44}dx_4{}^2$$
$$+ 2g_{12}dx_1dx_2 + 2g_{13}dx_1dx_3 + 2g_{14}dx_1dx_4$$
$$+ 2g_{23}dx_2dx_3 + 2g_{24}dx_2dx_4 + 2g_{34}dx_3dx_4.$$

The g's are not necessarily constants but may be functions of x_1, x_2, x_3, x_4. That it is impossible to choose a coordinate system such that for a certain region g_{12}, g_{13}, g_{14}, g_{23}, g_{24}, g_{34} are all zero is what is meant by saying that the region of space in question is curved. That a region of space is curved can therefore in principle always be ascertained by making physical measurements in that region—for instance, by testing whether the Pythagorean theorem holds. There is, therefore, nothing obscure or metaphysical about the concept of curvature of space. The space-time of special relativity, it is worth mentioning, is semi-Euclidean and of zero curvature. In it we have

$$g_{11} = g_{22} = g_{33} = -1, \qquad g_{44} = +1,$$

and g_{12}, g_{13}, g_{14}, g_{23}, g_{24}, g_{34} are all zero.

According to the general theory of relativity, space-time is curved in the neighborhood of matter. (More precisely, it has a curvature over and above the very small curvature which, for cosmological reasons, is postulated for empty space.) A light wave or any free body, such as a space satellite, is assumed in the general theory to lie along a geodesic in space-time. A geodesic is either the longest or the shortest distance between two points. In Euclidean plane geometry it is the shortest, whereas in the geometry of space-time it happens to be the longest. Owing to the appreciable curvature of space-time near any heavy body, a light ray which passes near the sun should appear to us to be slightly bent—that is, there should be an apparent displacement of the direction of a star whose light passes very near the sun. During an eclipse of the sun it is possible to observe stars very near to the sun's disk, since the glare of the sun is blacked out by the moon. In the solar eclipse of 1919, Sir Arthur Stanley Eddington and his colleagues carried out such an observation which gave results in good quantitative accord with the predictions of relativity. In a similar way, also, the general theory of relativity accounted for the anomalous motion of the perihelion of Mercury, the one planetary phenomenon which had defied Newtonian dynamics. In other cases the predictions of Newtonian theory and of general relativity are identical, and general relativity is, on the whole, important only in cosmology (unlike the special theory, which has countless verifications and is an indispensable tool of theoretical physics).

IS SPACE ABSOLUTE OR RELATIVE?

The theory of relativity certainly forces us to reject an absolute theory of space, if by this is meant one in which

space is taken as quite separate from time. Observers in relative motion to one another will take their space and time axes at different angles to one another; they will, so to speak, slice space-time at different angles. The *special* theory of relativity, at least, is quite consistent with either an absolute or a relational philosophical account of space-time, for the fact that space-time can be sliced at different angles does not imply that it is not something on its own account.

It might be thought that the *general* theory of relativity forces us to a relational theory of space-time, on the grounds that according to it the curvature of any portion of space-time is produced by the matter in it. But if anything the reverse would seem to be the case. If we accept a relational theory of space-time, we have to suppose that the inertia of any given portion of matter is determined wholly by the total matter in the universe. Consider a rotating body. If we suppose it to be fixed and everything else rotating, then we must say that some distant bodies are moving with transitional velocities greater than that of light, contrary to the assumptions of relativity. Hence, it is hard to avoid the conclusion that the inertia of a body is partly determined by the local metrical field, not by the total mass in the universe. But if we think of the local metrical field as efficacious in this way, we are back to an absolute theory of space-time. Furthermore, most forms of general relativity predict that there would be a curvature (and hence a structure) of space-time even if there were a total absence of matter. Indeed, relativistic cosmology often gives a picture of matter as consisting simply of regions of special curvature of space-time. (Whether this curvature is the cause of the existence of matter or whether the occurrence of matter produces the curvature of space-time is unclear in the general theory itself.) The variations of curvature of space-time enable us to rebut the objection to Descartes's theory that it cannot differentiate between more and less densely occupied regions of space. Nevertheless, there are also difficulties about accepting such a neo-Cartesianism. We must remember that quantum mechanics is essentially a particle physics, and it is not easy to see how to harmonize it with the field theory of general relativity. One day we may know whether a particle theory will have absorbed a geometrical field theory or vice versa. Until this issue is decided we cannot decide the question whether space (or space-time) is absolute or relational—in other words, whether particles are to be thought of as singularities (perhaps like the ends of J. A. Wheeler's "wormholes" in a multiply connected space) or whether space-time is to be understood as a system of relations between particles. This issue can be put neatly if we accept Quine's criterion of ontological commitment. Should our scientific theory quantify over point-instants of space-time, or should we, on the other hand, quantify over material particles, classes of them, classes of classes of them, and so on? The latter involves a commitment to particle physics, but if a unified field theory is successful, our ontology may consist simply of point-instants, classes of them, classes of classes of them, and so on, and physical objects will be definable in terms of all of these. So far neither Descartes nor Leibniz has won an enduring victory.

Bibliography

An excellent, mainly historical, account of the philosophy of space is given in Max Jammer, *Concepts of Space* (Cambridge, Mass., 1954; rev. ed., New York, 1960). Ch. 1, "The Concept of Space in Antiquity," is particularly valuable as a guide to the very scattered and obscure references to space in Greek philosophy. Also useful is John Burnet, *Early Greek Philosophy*, 3d ed. (London, 1920). For Descartes, see his *Principles of Philosophy*, Part II, Secs. 4–21. For Leibniz, see especially his correspondence with Clarke, third paper, Secs. 3–6, and fifth paper, Secs. 32–124. The Leibniz–Clarke correspondence has been edited, with introduction and notes, by H. G. Alexander (Manchester, 1956). See also Bertrand Russell's *The Philosophy of Leibniz* (London, 1900). Newton's metaphysical views on space are to be found in the Scholium to the definitions of the *Principia* (*Mathematical Principles of Natural Philosophy*, translated by Florian Cajori, Berkeley, 1934). For Kant's example of the left hand and the right hand, see his *Prolegomena to Any Future Metaphysics*, translated by P. G. Lucas (Manchester, 1953), Sec. 13. Kant's most characteristic doctrines about space are to be found in his *Critique of Pure Reason*, in Secs. 2–7 of the "Transcendental Aesthetic" and in the "First Antinomy." In N. Kemp Smith's translation (London, 1929) these passages will be found on pp. 67–82 and 396–402. A criticism of Kant, Zeno, and other philosophers is to be found in Bertrand Russell's *Our Knowledge of the External World*, Lecture VI, "The Problem of Infinity Considered Historically" (London, 1914). See also Adolf Grünbaum, "A Consistent Conception of the Extended Linear Continuum as an Aggregate of Unextended Elements," in *Philosophy of Science*, Vol. 19 (1952), 288–306. For Mach's criticism of Newton, see especially Secs. 2–6 of his *Science of Mechanics*, translated by J. T. McCormack, 6th ed. (La Salle, Ill., 1960).

On a fairly elementary level, and although somewhat out of date in places, Émile Borel, *Space and Time* (New York, 1960)—a translation, by Angelo S. Rappoport and John Dougall, of the French edition published in 1922—can be recommended. So can the more difficult *Philosophy of Space and Time*, by Hans Reichenbach (New York, 1958), and *Philosophical Problems of Space and Time*, by Adolf Grünbaum (New York, 1963). See also Grünbaum's paper "Geometry, Chronometry and Empiricism," in Herbert Feigl and Grover Maxwell, eds., *Minnesota Studies in the Philosophy of Science*, Vol. III (Minneapolis, 1962). A criticism of Grünbaum's views is given by Hilary Putnam in his paper "An Examination of Grünbaum's Philosophy of Geometry," in Bernard Baumrin, ed., *Philosophy of Science, the Delaware Seminar*, Vol. II (1962–1963; published New York, 1963). Chs. 8 and 9 of Ernest Nagel's *Structure of Science* (New York, 1961) are very useful. An interesting dialogue by A. S. Eddington, "What Is Geometry?," is a prologue to his *Space, Time and Gravitation* (Cambridge, 1920). On relativity, see Hermann Minkowski, "Space and Time," in Albert Einstein, et al., *The Principle of Relativity* (New York, 1923); Hans Reichenbach, "The Philosophical Significance of Relativity," and H. P. Robertson, "Geometry as a Branch of Physics," both in P. A. Schilpp, ed., *Albert Einstein: Philosopher-scientist*, 2d ed. (La Salle, Ill., 1951); and Adolf Grünbaum, "The Philosophical Retention of Absolute Space in Einstein's General Theory of Relativity," in *Philosophical Review*, Vol. 66 (1957), 525–534 (a revised version appears in J. J. C. Smart, ed., *Problems of Space and Time*, New York, 1963). See also J. A. Wheeler, "Curved Empty Space-time as the Building Material of the Physical World: An Assessment," in Ernest Nagel, Patrick Suppes, and Alfred Tarski, eds., *Logic, Methodology, and Philosophy of Science* (Stanford, Calif., 1962), pp. 361–374.

For a discussion of the asymmetry between clockwise and counterclockwise rotations in relation to the nonconservation of parity, which has some relevance to Kant's problem of the left and right hands, see the brilliant popular exposition by O. R. Frisch, "Parity Is Not Conserved, a New Twist to Physics?," in *Universities Quarterly*, Vol. 11 (1957), 235–244, and the article by Philip Morrison, "Overthrow of Parity," in *Scientific American*, Vol. 196 (April 1957). For Poincaré's views, see *Science and Hypothesis* (New York, 1952), especially pp. 72–73. In connection with the sharpening of the issue between absolute and relational theories of space and time into an issue of ontology, see W. V. Quine, *Word and Object* (Cambridge, Mass., and New York, 1960), especially Sec. 52, "Geometrical Objects." A book of readings on space and time is J. J. C. Smart, ed., *Problems of Space and Time* (New York, 1964).

I should like to thank Professor B. C. Rennie, who read an earlier draft of this article and made helpful comments.

J. J. C. Smart

SPANISH PHILOSOPHY

SPANISH PHILOSOPHY properly begins with Ramón Lull (c. 1232–1316), who was the first to use a Spanish tongue (Catalan, for Lull came from Majorca) to discuss philosophy and was perhaps the first European to use a national, rather than a classical, language for that purpose. Castilian was not used as a philosophical medium until the time of Pérez de Oliva (1495–1532). Nevertheless, philosophy written in Spain in Latin and Arabic during preceding centuries (and, in the case of Latin, for three centuries after Lull) is commonly claimed as part of the national tradition. Some historians even see a characteristic Spanish style of thought that has recurred from Seneca to today, as though Roman, Arab, Jew and modern Spaniard had found in the peninsula an abiding intellectual climate. If there is any such constant climate, it shows itself less in a special sort of thinking than in a perennial opposition to philosophizing, in a perpetual difficulty in naturalizing philosophy in Spain. This question has received much attention from Spanish writers since 1865 and particularly since the Generation of 1898 began to meditate on the "tragic enigma" of Spanish history. For these writers, one aspect of Spain's alleged failure or misfortune was the absence of a continuous philosophical tradition and the conviction of successive Spanish ruling classes that philosophy as such is foreign to the national genius.

Two explanations have been offered. The first is psychological. José Ortega y Gasset termed the national character "orgiastic"; Miguel de Unamuno termed it "African." Both meant that the Spaniard was gifted for intuition and for a poetic vision of God and the world but was much less capable of abstract reasoning. Therefore his culture was exuberant, imaginative, passionate, and spasmodic but seldom philosophical. The other explanation is historical. Through external causes, philosophy in Spain fell victim to political oppression by foreign despots (Moroccan, Hapsburg, and Bourbon) or by patriots anxious to root out that foreign influence (crusaders, inquisitors, and fascists). Witch hunts, book-burning, and denunciation of philosophy as seditious, irreligious, or unpatriotic prevailed from the Arab invasion to the Counter Reformation and on down to recent times. This repeated stunting of speculation in Spain in the long run isolated the country from the mainstream of Western thought, and since the seventeenth century the gap has been unbridgeable. Spain was forced by the Counter Reformation to remain in the scholastic path of Suárez while the rest of Europe took the road opened up by Descartes.

Hispano-Romans. Spaniards were prominent in the silver age of Latin Literature. Martial, the two Senecas (father and son), and Lucan (the last three born in Córdoba) were Spaniards, and Marcus Aurelius came from a Hispano-Roman family. All lived and wrote in Rome, yet they have been held to show a typically Spanish cast of thought. In particular, the stoicism of the younger Seneca (c. 4 B.C.–c. A.D. 65) is regarded by some as "the very philosophy of the Spaniard." He was not a speculative philosopher; he preached a rigid morality compressed into striking maxims; his taste for declamation and word play often got the better of reasoned argument—three features that have been said to be typically Spanish. In Lucan, Martial, and Quintilian can be seen even more plainly a foretaste of the weaknesses of later Spanish writing: deliberate obscurity and an immoderate use of formal artifice.

St. Isidore. St. Isidore, bishop of Seville from 596 to his death c. 636, was one of the encyclopedists of late antiquity. His twenty-volume *Etymologiae* ("Etymologies"), a compendium of the surviving learning in philosophy, history, and language, was studied until the end of the Middle Ages.

Hispano-Arabs. The schools of Arab Spain were dominated by Oriental Arab philosophy, which was mainly a commentary on Aristotle and the Neoplatonists Proclus and Plotinus. Hispano-Muslim speculation was seldom original or independent, being a conservative Islamic scholasticism, the main theme of which was rational interpretation of the Koran in an effort to reconcile faith and reason. It began long after the Arab conquest and flourished only under the Almohade dynasty in the twelfth century. By the end of that century there was a violent religious reaction leading to persecution, ransacking of libraries, burning of books, and the exile of such thinkers as Averroës and Maimonides. Thereafter the Persian mysticism of al-Ghazālī (who wrote a *Destructio Philosophorum*) triumphed throughout Arab Spain, and Andalusian philosophy died out. The holy war against the advancing Christians during much of the next three centuries created a climate of military asceticism and mystic fervor incompatible with philosophical reflection.

The most important result of the Hispano-Arab schools was the transmission of Greek thought to western Europe. From the eleventh century, that intermediary role was progressively taken over by the Christian translation schools in Toledo and Seville, which later eclipsed Córdoba. From Toledo, then a renowned philosophical center, the lost Greek learning, obscured by Neoplatonist and Arab glosses, spread through Europe.

Avempace, or ibn-Bājja (1090–1138), opposed to the mystic spirituality of the Sufis a rational mysticism of Neoplatonist stamp. Abubacer, or ibn-Ṭufayl (c. 1105–1185), was a disciple of Avempace, a rationalist, mystic, and Neoplatonist interpreter of Aristotle. He wrote a philosophical novel about the intellectual development of a castaway on a desert island which, under the title *Philosophus Autodidactus*, became famous in Europe six centuries later, after Gracián's *El criticón* but before Defoe's *Robinson Crusoe*, two works on a similar theme.

Averroës, or ibn-Rushd (1126–1198), the most celebrated of the Hispano-Arab thinkers, in the Middle Ages was called The Commentator. His commentary on Aristotle was ranked on a par with the original until Aquinas denounced that ranking as error, and Averroism remained an opposition undercurrent in the Schools until the sixteenth century. From the high offices of judge and physician to the caliph, Averroës several times fell into disgrace and at last was driven into exile in Morocco. As a result of that persecution, the original of much of his work has been lost, but Hebrew translations survive. Apart from the paraphrases of, and gloss upon, Aristotle, he wrote a *Destructio Destructionis*, a defense of philosophy against al-Ghazālī's *Destructio Philosophorum*, as well as treatises on the rerelation of philosophy to theology. It was on this latter point that Averroës was long influential, for he elaborated the doctrine of "double truth." A sacred text, he said with the Koran in mind, had various meanings, depending on the profundity of the interpretation. It could mean all things to all men and, further, a proposition true in theology could be false in philosophy and vice versa. This notion became a prominent feature of Latin Averroism.

Averroës' characteristic tenets were the eternal nature of matter and movement and the unity of the human intellect. The first theory asserted that nothing came from the void, so neither matter nor form had been created. Movement was continual and matter eternal. The second asserted that human intellect was an immaterial, unique, and eternal form with which individual minds had various and varying relations. There was no individual knowledge, only the knowledge of the whole human race, and no personal immortality, only that of the impersonal mind of the species. These doctrines were condemned by the Catholic church in 1240 and again in 1513.

Medieval Jewish philosophers. In Andalusia, medieval Jewish philosophy was contemporary with and largely dependent on Hispano-Arab thought. Written mostly in Arabic, it was translated into Hebrew much later. In addition to Neoplatonist mysticism, it contained elements of the secret doctrine of the Cabala, but its main purpose was scholastic—the reconciliation of Talmudic teaching with Hispano-Arab Aristotelianism.

Avicebrón, or ibn-Gabirol (c. 1021–1058/1070), became known to Christendom for his *Fons Vitae*. He held that all substances were composed of matter and form and could be classed in order of increasing perfection, with the soul at the summit. The soul was material but not necessarily corporeal. Jehovah's will was the principle of the universe, a doctrine that led to a type of Judaic pantheism.

Moses Maimonides (1135–1204), a contemporary and compatriot of Averroës, was, like him, a physician and theologian. He suffered persecution, forced conversion to Islam, and exile. Apart from books on medicine and Talmudic learning, Maimonides wrote philosophical works designed to harmonize faith, represented by the Old Testament, with reason, represented by Aristotle. The best known of these, the *Guide for the Perplexed,* was a veritable *summum* of Judaic scholasticism. For Maimonides, knowledge of God was the supreme aim of both philosophy and religion, and the only perplexity related to how to harmonize the principles of those two disciplines. The rational proof of God's existence that this implied extended only to negative knowledge. We could know what God was not, not what he was, for the essence of God was inaccessible. Maimonides differed with Averroës on two major points. He did not accept the doctrine of the double truth, which led to an allegorical reading of the Bible, although he said the sacred text had to be read philosophically rather than literally. Second, he did not merge individual personality totally in the mind of the species, holding that the individual could, by means of philosophy, acquire a measure of separate identity that would be partly saved, or counted to his credit, after death. Maimonides' influence extended down to Spinoza and later Jewish thinkers.

Peter of Spain. Apart from the translations of the Toledo school of Dominicus Gondissalvus, Spaniards made little contribution to Christian Scholasticism. An exception was Peter of Spain (Pope John XXI in 1276–1277), whose *Summulae Logicales* became a famous logic textbook. One thing from it endures today: such mnemonics for syllogistic forms as Barbara and Celarent.

Lull. The outstanding Spanish thinker of the Middle Ages was Ramón Lull (Raymond Lully, also Lulio, Lullus, and Lulle), a Franciscan visionary from Palma de Majorca who led an extraordinarily active life and is thought to have been stoned to death in north Africa in 1316. Lull was obsessed with unity—the unity of religions, of political systems, of languages, of sciences, and of concepts—an idea he pursued with a naive and utopian enthusiasm. Distressed by the struggle between Islam and Christianity that rent his homeland, Lull argued that the Muslims could be overcome not by force but by reason. This could come about only if the Christian faith were stated rationally, in the form of irrefutable propositions.

This notion of scientific apologetics would be uninteresting, were it not for Lull's thoroughness. Not only did he imagine a reconciliation of faiths in a universal religion; not only did he dream (like his contemporary, Dante) of political unity in a universal empire; not only did he propose a world language six centuries before Esperanto and Volapük; but he argued that all sciences and forms of reasoning must be unified, too, so as to facilitate and guarantee men's religious, cultural, and political unity. He tried to show how that could be done, by the Tree of Science and the Great Art. The Tree of Science was a classification of all branches of knowledge, duly arranged in a hierarchy under the domination of theology. The content of this thirteenth-century encyclopedia is now without interest, but the scheme for a rational unification of the sciences anticipated Bacon, Comte, and the positivists. The *Ars Magna,* or Great Art, similarly anticipated Descartes's *mathesis universalis,* Leibniz' *caractéristique universelle,* and the symbolic logics of today. Lull's idea was to reduce all possible relations between concepts to "typical figures" so that, given a subject, one could find all possible predicates, and vice versa. Each term was represented by a letter of the alphabet, and by grouping the letters in all possible combinations, one would have an *ars combinatoria* which not only gave a mnemonic but also actually permitted discoveries of new propositions. Symbols of concepts could be set out on a series of concentric rings, and by revolving the rings separately one would find new combinations and discover problems at the same time as their solutions. Lull meant to use this systematic algebraic logic to convince the infidels of the truth of Christianity, but the logic clearly had other applications. The Art of Lull, as it was called, was well known to the Renaissance and was experimented with by Giordano Bruno, the Cartesians, and Leibniz.

Lull's system was applied by his fellow Catalan Raymond de Sabunde (c. 1385–1436) to combat the Averroist doctrine of the double truth. Philosophy and theology could not be at odds, he argued, because the content of the two revelations—the *liber scriptus,* or Bible, and the *liber vivus,* or Nature—was identical, as he tried to prove by showing a one-to-one correspondence of their concepts. Known later under the appropriate title of *Natural Theology,* Sabunde's one book was admired by Montaigne (who translated it) and by Hegel.

Renaissance philosophers. Spain was little affected by the Renaissance and had only a few humanist thinkers who rebelled against Scholasticism. One was Juan Luis Vives (1492–1540), one of the greatest Renaissance empiricists, but it is significant that he lived mostly outside Spain. He studied in Paris, taught at Oxford and Louvain, and died in Bruges. He wrote much on ethics and pedagogy, advocating state (instead of church) action for relief of the poor, defending the education of women, and attacking scholastic logomachy. In philosophy he denounced universal concepts as having corrupted medieval science, recommended observation and experiment, practiced a more critical methodology, and held that each man was endowed with a faculty of personal judgment, which he was free to exercise without recourse to authority. This "judgment" was one of the first appearances of a faculty later called natural light or common sense.

Francisco de Vitoria (1480–1546), a Dominican theologian who taught at Salamanca, is credited as the founder of international law, which he applied to the defense of the Indians against Spanish oppression. Throughout the sixteenth century the tradition of Spanish medicophilosophers was maintained, notably by Juan Huarte (c. 1529–1588), whose *Exámen de los ingenios para las ciencias* ("Examination of Minds," Baeza, 1575) had dozens of editions and translations (the German one by Lessing) and was perhaps the first rudimentary essay in psychophysiology and psychotechnics.

Counter Reformation philosophers. The characteristic Spanish thought during the Renaissance was neither humanism nor natural philosophy but a reaction against both—a last determined defense of Scholasticism. This movement reached its apogee in the Council of Trent (1545–1563) and ended with the death of Suárez in 1617. It was centered in Salamanca and Alcalá, and later at Coimbra in Portugal, and was dominated by Jesuits. It provided the philosophy of the Counter Reformation, and in Spain it succeeded in annulling the influence of Erasmus.

Francisco Suárez (1548–1617) was the most notable of the Neo-Scholastic theologians. His ambition (very largely realized, for the seminaries used his work for centuries) was to summarize the whole of Scholasticism and to restate the church's philosophy in clear, definitive form so that it could face a long siege by modern thought. His works filled 26 volumes, of the which *Disputationes Metaphysicae* (1597) are the keystone. Suárez' enormous feat of summing up Scholasticism included certain departures from the Thomist tradition. The most important was the clear separation of metaphysics from theology. Aquinas had thought that philosophy could only confirm, complete, or illustrate theology; but Suárez held that theology required a previous independent metaphysics as foundation. He set out, therefore, to make metaphysics a systematic discipline, instead of the commentary on Aristotle it had been until then. He first discussed being in general, then being as cause (adopting the classic fourfold division of causes but noting two sorts of efficient cause, the necessary and the free), and finally being in its most general characters or categories (finite and infinite, substance and accident, etc.).

In his *Tractatus de Legibus* ("Treatise on Laws," Coimbra, 1612) Suárez developed the concept of international law introduced by Vitoria and replied to the theory of a divine right of kings put forward by James I of England. In the *Tractatus* and in *Defensio Fidei Adversus Anglicanae Sectae Errores* ("Defense of the Faith," 1613), he argued that God gave sovereignty to the community and not just to the monarch. Suárez was striking a blow for Pope Paul V against Anglicanism, but he also advanced the democratic case against absolutism.

The vast renown of Suárez in succeeding centuries (as much in Protestant countries as in Catholic) was due to his success in embalming Scholasticism in its perfect and most luminous form. In that state, it was consecrated by every seminary that sought to stand against the rise of modern philosophy. Yet through the study of Suárez in Germany some of the ideas of Scholasticism passed, in new guise, into modern thought. In Spain his death marked the end of philosophical speculation for centuries, and his Thomism reigned unchallenged.

Balmes. In the long period when philosophy was absent from Spain, the name of Jaime Balmes stands out. A Catalan priest, politician, and journalist, Balmes managed during a brief and active life (1810–1848) to compose a popular work on logic, *El criterio* (Barcelona, 1845), two systematic expositions of Scholasticism, and two apologetic works. His ambition was to restore philosophical discussion in Spain, but he was unaware of developments in Germany at that time and was hostile to French and Protestant thought; he could therefore, do little to bring his country back into intellectual contact with its neighbors. Balmes' common-sense philosophy has been compared with that of Vives and Thomas Reid, but the Catalan practiced a more arbitrary intuitionism and peremptory assertion. It was his philosophy of history that was most influential in Spain. In *El protestantismo comparado con el catolicismo en sus relaciones con la civilización europea* ("Protestantism Compared With Catholicism in Their Relations With European Civilization," 4 vols., Madrid, 1842–1844) Balmes replied to Guizot's liberal *Histoire générale de la civilisation en Europe* by arguing that in the breach between Spain and the modern world, Spain was right and the rest of Europe wrong. Spain remained loyal to the tradition of culture founded on religious unity, which the Reformation had betrayed. Balmes' polemical positions were taken over by traditionalists, who made him Spain's national philosopher, but his bid to revive philosophy in Spain came to nothing.

Krausism. The effort to revive philosophy was soon renewed, but once again it misfired. This time it led to one of the most curious freaks in the history of philosophy, Spanish Krausism. Julián Sanz del Rio (1814–1869), a doctor of canon law, was named professor of the history of philosophy at the new University of Madrid in 1843, on condition that he leave at once for Germany to study the latest European thinking. During a stay in Heidelberg, Sanz del Rio contrived to overlook all the great German philosophers from Kant to Schelling and fell entranced before the harmonious rationalism of an obscure minor figure, Karl C. F. Krause (1781–1832). Krause was a mystic and spiritualist whose doctrines are commonly held to be incomprehensible, save that they include a religion of humanity and a millenary prophetism reminiscent of his contemporary, Comte. Sanz del Rio returned to preach this doctrine in Spain, both in his teaching and in books that were free adaptations of Krause. The most notable was *Ideal de la humanidad para la vida* (Madrid, 1860). Despite opposition from the church (the book was put on the Index), from the Balmesian traditionalists, and from the state (Sanz del Rio was dismissed from the university in 1868 and other Krausists were jailed and persecuted), Krausism was the dominant philosophy in Spain for a generation and remained an active influence until 1910.

Spanish Krausism was less a philosophy than a cult, a rationalist religion that can be regarded as a forerunner of the Modernist movement in Catholicism. Its adherents behaved like members of a freemasonry, and it is doubtful whether many of them understood Sanz del Rio's obscure books on his even more obscure master. Nevertheless, Spanish Krausism meant a boundless confidence in reason, in the perfectibility of man, and in social progress, as well as the quest for a "reasonable" style of living that would be infused with the conviction of working for a better world. It produced a type of thinking that was nebulous, enthusiastic, grave, sincere, and optimistic. In religion it was allied with liberal Catholicism and the demand for a rational, rather than a revealed or authoritarian, dogma. In politics it was necessarily liberal, for it recognized no authority other than reason and noted that free exercise of reason was impossible under Caesarist or arbitrary governments, which were all that Spain knew. Its social impact was considerable, but as an attempt to Europeanize Spanish thinking it was doomed to failure because it had taken as its European model the worst sort of post-Schelling metaphysics.

Recent Spanish philosophers. From the unpromising background of Spanish Scholasticism, traditionalism, Krausism, and authoritarianism there arose with the twentieth century two thinkers who rapidly won world-wide consideration, Unamuno and Ortega. Unamuno succeeded where Balmes and Sanz del Rio failed, in that he acquainted Spain with contemporary European philosophy and awakened interest abroad in Spanish thought. Ortega maintained and greatly developed that acquaintance and that interest, until both were aborted by the Spanish Civil War.

Unamuno. Miguel de Unamuno (1864–1936) was professor of Greek at Salamanca from 1891 to 1936, with interruptions due to political persecution. He was not, strictly speaking, a philosopher. Indeed, how to regard Unamuno's sort of literary production is, in itself, a philosophical problem, and one that has recurred in regard to existentialist writers like Albert Camus and Jean-Paul Sartre. In essays, poems, plays, and novels, Unamuno dealt unphilosophically with the great subjects—life, death, immortality, tragedy, and the place of reason or philosophy in human conduct. He claimed to cover what is regarded as the idealist philosopher's province but did not accept the constraints of logic and argument any more than he accepted the authority of religion. He wrote as though there were a third, and higher, way of treating those great questions. Man, he said, hungers for immortality, and neither reason nor religion can assuage the metaphysical anguish caused by the prospect of death. The sole recourse is to a vital and irrational faith which has no base in philosophy or theology but manifests itself as charity, anguish, and a sense of the tragic and mysterious. Unamuno's irrationalism was more arbitrary than that of philosophers like William James and Henri Bergson, who also considered conceptual knowledge inadequate to meet the problems of life. His literary imagination was more luxuriant than theirs and deserves comparison with Kierkegaard and Dostoyevsky. In the end, Unamuno made no contribution to formal philosophy; but his claim to apprehend immediately (rather than to know conceptually) the human situation taken as an urgent and anxious problem makes him a forerunner of the vitalists and the existentialists. His main works with some philosophical relevance were *Del sentimiento trágico de la vida* (Madrid, 1913; translated by J. E. C. Flitch as *The Tragic Sense of Life*, London, 1921) and *Vida de Don Quijote y Sancho* (Madrid, 1905; translated by H. P. Earle as *The Life of Don Quixote and Sancho*, New York, 1927).

Ortega. José Ortega y Gasset (1883–1955) was the greatest thinker Spain had produced in centuries and, unlike his predecessors, he had the gifts of the founder of a school. Professor of metaphysics at Madrid from 1910 to 1936, he was energetic and courageous as teacher, journalist, editor, publisher, and politician—in short, as an intellectual leader. As a metaphysician he sought the ultimate or radical reality in which the being of things was rooted. His first thoughts on that subject revealed his Neo-Kantian training at Marburg, for he wrote, "The definitive being of the world is neither matter nor mind nor any determinate thing but a *perspective*" (*Meditaciones del Quixote*, in *Obras completas*, Vol. I, p. 321; *Meditaciones* published separately, Madrid, 1914; translated by E. Rugg and D. Moran as *Meditations on Quixote*, New York, 1961). However, in developing this theory of reality as points of view, he stressed the mutual dependence of the two terms of the perspective, the subject and the object. The object had no being apart from a knower, but neither did the subject have existence, save among things. Radical reality was the matrix in which both coexisted: "I am I plus my circumstances." This, Ortega held, disposed of both idealism and realism, which he defined respectively as the independence of minds and of things. Gradually conation played a more important role in Ortega's conception of this matrix of experience, and he then called it life (*El tema de nuestro tiempo*, Madrid, 1923; translated by J. Cleugh as *The Modern Theme*, New York, 1933). Ultimate reality was human life, but Ortega at once marked his difference with vitalism by insisting on the rationality of the *élan vital* at the human level. He called this theory ratio-vitalism, the conciliation of rationalism and irrationalist biologism. His doctrine was more rationalist than vitalist because he used "life" and "vitality" to denote what pragmatists like John Dewey would call intelligence or practical reason.

In turn, vital reason took on a temporal extension, and life came to mean a man's life or existential career. That is, Ortega moved away from biologism and took more account of social and historical circumstances. Thus he came to call vital reason "historical reason" and to speak of the ego's vocation and of the pressure on it to form a "life project." He said, "Man does not have a nature but a history"; his being is infinitely plastic, for he chooses at every moment from among the possibilities that solicit him. There has been dispute about whether Ortega or Heidegger was the first to use this vocabulary. In any case, Ortega, one of the greatest writers in Castilian, filled books of essays with brilliant metaphors as he exposed every facet of a theory that seemed to lend itself better to fine writing than to close argument.

The Madrid school. The teaching and example of Ortega called up the richest flowering of philosophical talent in Spain's history. Dozens of writers, whether influenced by Ortega's Neo-Kantian, his ratio-vitalist, or his existentialist views, applied themselves to every sort of problem, from logic to the philosophy of law. This vigorous, fruitful movement was scattered by the Spanish Civil War and its aftermath, so that its history now belongs as much to Latin America as to Spain. In Spain itself, where Thomism has dominated philosophical teaching since 1939, writers profoundly influenced by Ortega range from Catholic spiritualists like García Morente (*Fundamentos de la filosofía*, Madrid, 1943) and Xavier Zubiri (*Naturaleza, historia, Dios*, Madrid, 1944) to men of a liberal Catholic temper, such as Julián Marías (*Introducción a la filosofía*, Madrid, 1947) and Luis Diez de Corral (*El rapto de Europa*, Madrid, 1954). All these Orteguists have come under sustained and forceful criticism from Spanish Thomists for having sought to present as acceptable to Spaniards a philosophy that is in fact "incompatible with Catholicism." (See the works of Santiago Ramírez: *La filosofía de Ortega y Gasset*, Barcelona, 1958; *Un orteguismo católico*, Salamanca, 1958; *La zona de seguridad*, Madrid, 1959.) The upshot of this large and confused debate could well decide the future of philosophy in Spain by revealing whether Ortega succeeded in establishing his thought as a native, although minority, tradition.

(See Spanish Philosophy in Index for articles on Spanish philosophers.)

Bibliography

The standard histories of Spanish philosophy are as uneven as their subject and have not been translated. They include Adolfo Bonilla y San Martín, *Historia de la filosofía española hasta el siglo XII*, 2 vols. (Madrid, 1908–1911), which was brought up to date by the Asociación española para el progreso de las ciencias as *Historia de la filosofía española*, 2 vols. (Madrid, 1957), and Mario Méndez Bejarano, *Historia de la filosofía en España* (Madrid, 1925). For the age of Suárez, see Marcial Solana, *Historia de la filosofía española, época del renacimiento, siglo XVI*, 3 vols. (Madrid, 1941); for Krausism, Juan López Morillas, *El krausismo español* (Mexico City, 1956); for the modern period, J. Carro, *Filosofía y filósofos españoles (1900–28)* (Madrid, 1929).

Julián Marías, *Historia de la filosofía* (Madrid, 1941), is written from a Spanish point of view and thus gives more information on Spanish thinkers than is usual. The same author's *La filosofía española actual* (Buenos Aires, 1948) and *La escuela de Madrid* (Buenos Aires, 1959) cover contemporary philosophers.

J. B. Trend, *The Origins of Modern Spain* (New York, 1934), and Pierre Jobit, *Les Éducateurs de l'Espagne contemporaine* (Paris, 1936), give adequate treatment to Spanish philosophers. Extremely useful is Alain Guy, *Philosophes espagnols d'hier et aujourd'hui*, 2 vols. (Toulouse, 1956).

NEIL MCINNES

SPANN, OTHMAR (1878–1950), Austrian philosopher and sociologist, was born in Vienna and educated at the universities of Vienna, Zurich, and Tübingen. He was a professor at Brünn from 1909 to 1919, when he was appointed to a chair of economics and sociology at Vienna.

Spann contrasted his "neoromantic universalism"— called neoromantic by Spann to indicate his debt to Adam Müller—with "individualism," that is, with the doctrine that society derives its character from the independently existing qualities of the individual men composing it. He classified as individualist such allegedly erroneous doctrines as the economic liberalism of Adam Smith and David Ricardo, utilitarianism, the various "social contract" theories, "natural law" theories of social life, egalitarianism, anarchism, Machiavellianism, and Marxism. As this heterogeneous grouping suggests, Spann was less interested in discussing the individual merits and faults of these doctrines than in placing them with respect to his total intellectual system. Such an aim was entirely consistent with his universalistic tenet that wholes are logically prior to and more real than their parts. Particular intellectual doctrines, on this view, can be understood only in relation to the total world view to which they belong.

Spann's main application of universalism was in his theory of society, widely acclaimed by fascists. What is spiritual (*das Geistige*) in an individual is never due to himself alone but is always "an echo of what another spirit excites in him." The development and persistence of spirituality must be understood in the context of personal relations falling under the heading of what Spann called *Gezweiung*. Individuals so related form a genuine whole, the reality of which is presupposed by, rather than a result of, the spiritual characteristics of the related individuals. Examples of *Gezweiung* are the relations between artist and public, mother and child, teacher and pupil. Spann was not merely making the formal logical point that if, for instance, one calls a man "a teacher," one implies that he has a pupil, and vice versa. He was saying something about the quality of the teacher's and the pupil's experiences; the teacher "learns by teaching," and the pupil incorporates some of the teacher's spiritual qualities into his own soul.

Spann held that it is the prior existence of such institutions as art, the family, and education that makes possible relations of *Gezweiung*. These institutions have both a higher degree of reality and a higher value than do individuals. One does not understand what education is unless one understands that there can be more and less satisfactory instances of the teacher–pupil relationship and that

there could be no actual instance beyond conceivable improvement. Therefore, a knowledge of the ideal must precede understanding of particular cases, and the study of social institutions must be normative.

An institution is itself only a partial whole (*Teilganz*) belonging to a higher reality, society. Society, too, has a normative aspect; it involves a hierarchy of values in terms of which the *Teilgänze* are mutually related. There must be a corresponding hierarchy among the social sciences; particular social institutions and aspects can be studied only in the context of a general theory of society.

Spann's emphasis on hierarchy was reinforced by his insistence that all *Gezweiung* involves a relation between a leader and one who is led. It belongs to the nature of society that there should be "obedience of those low in the spiritual scale toward those more highly developed." In Spann's theory distributive justice, based on the idea of inequality of function, replaces liberty as the fundamental social value.

Spann's stress on inequality is reflected in his political program. His doctrine of estates (*Stände*) was intended to combine decentralization with a strengthening of authority in order to check socially deleterious individualist tendencies. Each industry would be directed by the "mentally most highly developed individuals" from labor unions and employers' unions, which would send representatives to a central representative *Ständehaus*. Property would be owned communally by the various estates, and each industry's legal problems would be handled by its own special courts.

Works by Spann

Die Haupttheorien der Volkswirtschaftslehre auf lehrgeschichtlicher Grundlage. 1910. Translated from the 19th German edition by Eden Paul and Cedar Paul as *Types of Economic Theory.* London, 1930. This translation also appeared under the title *History of Economics.* New York, 1930.

Kurzgefasstes System der Gesellschaftslehre. Berlin, 1914.

Fundament der Volkswirtschaftslehre. Jena, 1918.

Der wahre Staat. Leipzig, 1921.

Gesellschaftsphilosophie. Jena, 1932.

Kämpfende Wissenschaft. Jena, 1934. Collected papers.

Erkenne Dich selbst! Eine Geistesphilosophie als Lehre vom Menschen und seiner Weltstellung. Jena, 1935.

Naturphilosophie. Jena, 1937.

Kategorienlehre, 2d ed. Jena, 1939.

Works on Spann

Gerber, Carl, *Der Universalismus bei Othmar Spann in Hinblick auf seine Religionsphilosophie.* Berlin, 1934.

König, Albert, *Emit Brunners Staatsauffassung und der Universalismus Othmar Spanns.* Bleicherode, 1938.

Räber, Hans, *Othmar Spanns Philosophie des Universalismus. Darstellung und Kritik.* Jena, 1937.

Wagner, H. G., *Essai sur l'universalisme économique. Othmar Spann.* Paris, 1931.

Wrangel, Georg, *Das universalistische System von Othmar Spann.* Jena, 1929.

PETER WINCH

SPAVENTA, BERTRANDO (1817–1883), Italian Hegelian philosopher, was born at Bomba in Abruzzo, educated in the seminary at Chieti, and taught for a time in the seminary at Monte Cassino before moving to Naples in

1840. There he became one of a small circle of liberal students associated with Ottavio Colecchi (1773–1847), who taught privately in opposition to the "official" philosophy of Pasquale Galluppi. Colecchi was himself a devotee of Kant, but he read all the German idealists carefully and in the original. Spaventa, like the other young men in Colecchi's circle, was convinced that the real meaning of Kant's work was to be found in the later idealists, especially in Hegel, and the Hegelian interpretation of the *Critique of Pure Reason* always remained the nodal point of his own speculations.

Spaventa's younger brother, Silvio, was imprisoned at Naples for his part in the revolution of 1848, and Bertrando was forced to take refuge at Turin for ten years. This was the period during which most of his ideas took shape. By 1850 he had renounced the priestly office to which he had, with great reluctance, been ordained some years earlier in the hope that by preferment he could relieve the poverty of his family. In Turin he turned his hand to political journalism, writing philosophical and historical polemics against the church and particularly against the Jesuits. He was already an enthusiastic student of Giordano Bruno and Tommaso Campanella.

The "circulation of Italian philosophy." The first fruits of Spaventa's labors were his "Studi sopra la filosofia di Hegel" (in *Rivista italiana*, N.S., November 1850, 1–30, and December 1850, 31–78) and his "I principî della filosofia pratica di Giordano Bruno" (in *Saggi di filosofica civile*, Genoa, 1851). His studies of Hegel were specifically concerned with the *Phenomenology,* but they contained the germ of Spaventa's most original and fruitful conception, which he termed "circulation of Italian philosophy." This germ was the claim, first voiced by Silvio Spaventa about 1844, that the real tradition of Italian philosophy had been cut off and driven into exile by the Counter Reformation, so that "Not our own philosophers of the last two centuries, but Spinoza, Kant, Fichte, Schelling, and Hegel, have been the real disciples of Bruno, Vanini, Campanella, Vico and other great thinkers." In this view of the history of philosophy Spaventa's patriotism was neatly reconciled with his political and intellectual liberalism. He could use it both against the defenders of the *status quo* and against the patriotic chauvinism of Rosmini and Vincenzo Gioberti, who believed that their native tradition enshrined a truth that had become corrupted in the rest of Europe. Spaventa himself held at this time that, on the contrary, nothing of value had survived in contemporary Italian philosophy.

He began to shift from this position toward his doctrine of a completed circle when he studied Rosmini's work in connection with an article on Kant which he wrote in 1855. He decided then that everything good in Rosmini's theory of knowledge had been stolen from Kant. This unjust judgment at least involved the admission that there were valuable elements in Rosmini's thought. When Spaventa began, in 1857, to work on a critical survey of Galluppi and Gioberti in connection with a projected study of Hegel's *Phenomenology,* his attitude changed dramatically, and he ended by writing in 1858 one massive volume of a planned two-volume work, *La filosofia di Gioberti* (Naples, 1863). The view which he now took was that all the fruits of Eu-

ropean speculation from Descartes to Kant were to be found in the work of Galluppi and Rosmini when it was rightly understood, and that Gioberti was even moving at the end of his life toward a critical reconstruction of his system that would have made it clearly the culmination of post-Kantian speculation.

Thus, in its fully developed form, the thesis that Spaventa proclaimed to the new nation when he returned as professor at Bologna in 1860, and at Naples from 1861 onward, was that the metaphysics of modern idealism was born in Bruno, that Campanella's theory of knowledge foreshadowed all the problems of rationalism and empiricism which were finally resolved by Kant, and that the achievement of the Germans had been anticipated by Vico and had at last returned to be integrated with its sources in Galluppi, Rosmini, and Gioberti. As history, this thesis becomes more dubious with every succeeding clause. It must be taken rather as an account of the historical genesis of Spaventa's own idealism and as a model of how an idealist of the Hegelian type must strive, in studying the history of philosophy, to integrate different aspects of the truth as they appear. From this standpoint we can see how the emphasis on concrete experience that Spaventa found in Bruno and Campanella led him to feel that the rather abstract formalism of Kant's transcendental unity of apperception must be integrated with Rosmini's theory of the self as rooted in a "fundamental feeling"; once this was done, the Rosminian–Giobertian doctrine of knowledge as the intellectual intuition of Being could be jettisoned. Spaventa's most fundamental philosophical insight is to be found in his critical analysis of the difficulties that arise from an intuitive theory of knowledge.

Later studies. The "circulation of Italian philosophy" and the critical reconstruction of Gioberti is, properly speaking, a sort of Italian version of the coming to consciousness of the Absolute in Hegel's *Phenomenology;* Spaventa is remarkable among the Hegelians of his generation in that he regarded the *Phenomenology* as being of equal importance with the *Logic* in Hegel's system and as the key to a right interpretation of the system. He always rejected the religious interpretation of Hegel given by the "Right" and defended at Naples by his better-known colleague Augusto Vera. To admit that the Idea was really superior to and independent of the laborious progress of the Spirit in history would have entailed falling back into just the sort of Platonic intuitionism that Spaventa had so trenchantly criticized. The Being from which Hegel's *Logic* begins must therefore be taken as the thinking being of the Absolute Spirit itself which emerges at the end of the *Phenomenology.* Thus a completely human or immanent interpretation of the *Logic* as an actual process of thinking, rather than as an ideal pattern of thought, can be given.

Just how the *Philosophy of Nature* fits into Hegel's system thereby becomes even more obscure; Spaventa did not concern himself with this problem as such, but his ready acceptance of the Darwinian theory forced it on him in another way when the positivists began to produce evolutionary explanations of the Kantian a priori. Pointing to the vicious circle involved in a causal explanation of our belief in causes, Spaventa began in his last years to work out a phenomenalist account of experience that would do justice to the positivist claims while remaining firmly founded on Kant's first *Critique*. He died, however, before his work was finished. *Esperienza e metafisica* was published at Turin in 1888.

Spaventa was never widely understood or appreciated in his own lifetime. His most sympathetic follower was Donato Jaja (1839–1914), who inspired Giovanni Gentile to collect and republish Spaventa's scattered essays, along with some unpublished manuscripts. As a result of Gentile's work, Spaventa's true stature and importance have been recognized; and in Gentile's own "actual idealism" the three distinct strands of Spaventa's thought—the Italian tradition, the Hegelian dialectic, and critical phenomenalism—are woven into a single synthesis.

Additional Works by Spaventa

Saggi di critica filosofica. Naples, 1867.
Scritti filosofici, Giovanni Gentile, ed. Naples, 1900. Contains biography and full bibliography to 1900.
Principi di etica. Naples, 1904. A study of Hegel's ethics.
La filosofia italiana nelle sue relazione colla filosofia europea. Bari, 1908.
Logica e metafisica. Bari, 1911.

Works on Spaventa

Cubeddu, I., *Bertrando Spaventa*. Rome, 1964. The most comprehensive monograph on Spaventa.
Grilli, M., "The Nationality of Philosophy and Bertrando Spaventa." *Journal of the History of Ideas*, Vol. 2 (1941), 339–371.

H. S. HARRIS

SPECIOUS PRESENT. See TIME, CONSCIOUSNESS OF.

SPECULATIVE SYSTEMS OF HISTORY. Behind the construction of speculative systems of history there has in general been the conviction that the human past may be approached and studied at two quite different levels. At the first of these levels it is possible to explore in detail particular periods or sections of the past; to undertake the examination and explanation of specific incidents, episodes, or developments; and to seek to understand and assess the characters or motives of the agents engaged. Such tasks may be said to be the preserve of the ordinary practicing historian, working with his attention fixed firmly upon the empirical data and under the necessity at all times of being prepared to substantiate the accounts he provides by reference to the sources and authorities at his disposal. By so following the canons of accepted historical procedure, he may be able to offer more or less adequate pictures of what happened within selected areas of inquiry and to show why in the known circumstances the events portrayed took place when and how they did.

But while the importance and interest of this type of inquiry has not been denied, it has nonetheless sometimes been claimed that we cannot finally remain satisfied with such a limited and piecemeal mode of interpreting the facts of human history. Something more is required than the bare narration and analysis of particular historical situations and processes if what men have thought and done in the past is to appear as other than a mere sequence of occurrences, lacking in rational system or coherent design. Such a mere sequence would constitute an affront not only to our intellects but to our moral sensibilities as well. Immanuel Kant, writing toward the close of the eighteenth century, gave expression to an attitude of this sort when he referred to "a certain repugnance" that may assail us when we survey "the conduct of men as it is exhibited on the great stage of the world." According to Kant, we are apt to be oppressed by the apparent futility and childishness that is characteristic of much human behavior. He suggested that the philosopher's sole resource lay in trying to find "a universal purpose of nature in this paradoxical movement of human things" and in asking himself "whether in view of this purpose a history of creatures who proceed without a plan of their own may nevertheless be possible according to a determinate plan of nature." Other thinkers, before and after Kant, have experienced a dissatisfaction broadly similar to his. They have argued, for example, that a restriction of attention to the fragmentary details of the past can in the end lead only to a sense of disillusion and ultimate unintelligibility. The bits and pieces, if they are to be truly comprehended and understood, must be seen in relation to a wider context, and this requires a synoptic vision of history as a whole—a vision, moreover, that presents the historical process as manifesting some kind of discernible "meaning" or "significance" or "order." For in this way alone can it appear acceptable to us as self-respecting rational beings.

Words like "significance" and "order" are vague and indeterminate and are clearly susceptible to various interpretations. Such variety of interpretation is reflected in the very dissimilar forms that the attempts to provide unitary all-embracing theories of the historical process have in fact taken. For it would be a mistake to suppose that these theories have all conformed to one basic pattern or that the thinkers who have put them forward have shared a single unchanging conception of what they were trying to achieve. Diversity rather than uniformity of aim and result has characterized the development of speculation about history. Nor is this feature surprising if one takes into account the shifting views of human nature, the varying political and social ideals, and the divergent metaphysical, epistemological, and methodological assumptions which have inspired the creation of different historical systems. Nevertheless, it is convenient for the purposes of exposition to make a broad provisional division between two main types of theory, despite the difficulty in particular cases of deciding to which category a work properly belongs. We shall therefore distinguish between "teleological" and "scientific" systems and begin by considering the first of these.

TELEOLOGICAL THEORIES

The suggestion that the course of human history may be understood teleologically—that is to say, in terms of some underlying purpose or plan—is very old. As has been indicated, Kant appealed explicitly to this idea, but in doing so he was in a sense only resuscitating under a new guise a conception that had long been familiar and that—at any rate so far as European speculation was concerned—largely derived from theological sources. Christianity, insofar as it presents history as a drama which has a divinely appointed beginning and end and proceeds through stages marked by events of supreme religious significance, may be said to be the forerunner of many subsequent attempts to interpret the past teleologically; and from St. Augustine in the fifth century to Bossuet in the seventeenth, a number of Christian writers in fact tried to give detailed expression to the notion that the historical process conforms to a providentially ordered design. Pressed to its limit, as in Bossuet's *Discours sur l'histoire universelle* (1681), this view of history takes the form of exhibiting the rise and fall of states and empires as dependent in the last analysis upon the secret direction of a divine intelligence. It tends, too, to represent the evils and disasters which befall men—plagues, wars, famines, and the like—as being either fit and deserved punishments for previous misdeeds or the necessary means toward the promotion of some greater good that can finally be seen to justify them.

Eighteenth-century secular theorists. Bossuet compared the relation between his own enterprise and histories in the ordinary sense to that which subsists between a general map and maps of particular areas or districts: in the general map "you learn to place these parts of the world in their totality." His successors envisaged their task similarly, although the assumptions upon which he based his system no longer seemed adequate to their more secular eyes. If the ultimate sense and direction of history as a whole presented a problem, it did not follow that the key to its solution should be sought among the unprovable postulates of religion. Rather, the key should be looked for in an empirical spirit, by focusing attention upon the concrete ascertainable facts. Yet it is a noteworthy and curious fact that, despite such claims, the notion of some kind of underlying metaphysical purpose continued to find a place in the work of many historical theorists. It might be that this purposive principle was regarded as being in some sense implicit, or "immanent," in the historical development of peoples, determining the necessary stages of that development while at the same time having its source in man's own character and make-up rather than being imposed from outside: such was Vico's conception. Again, with some writers the concept of nature was given a partially teleological connotation. The idea of what is natural to man and society formed a bridge between the facts of history as empirically known and understood, on the one hand, and the "intended" or ideal direction in which it was assumed that history could be seen to be moving, on the other. "Nature has begun all things, and always aright," wrote Condillac; and a similar belief was expressed in Kant's essay on universal history, though hedged round with reservations and qualifications deriving from the "critical" theory of human knowledge he had propounded elsewhere. Thus Kant posited as an "a priori guiding thread" the suggestion that nature has implanted certain capacities in men and has ensured the ultimate realization of these capacities through those very antisocial and competitive human propensities which at first sight seem to have been the scourge of mankind. The conflicts to which the pages of history bear ample witness prevent stagnation and drive men unwittingly forward toward the creation of ever-improving social institutions and toward making arrangements favorable to the development of their original endowments.

Hegel. Some of Kant's ideas were incorporated by Hegel in what was perhaps the most complex, ambitious, and influential contribution to teleological speculation in history. The most historically conscious of all the great classical philosophers, Hegel treated his philosophy of history as forming the apex of a metaphysic that is impregnated throughout with historical conceptions. According to him, history is essentially concerned with what he termed "spirit" (*Geist*). The essence of spirit is to be found in the notion of freedom; and the actual history of mankind is interpreted as exhibiting different stages in the progressive unfolding of this rational idea. The various phases of the realization of the concept of freedom follow one another according to dialectical laws of transition and find embodiment in the concrete legal, political, and religious institutions peculiar to particular nations and societies. It would be wrong, however, to attribute to Hegel the view that such changing forms of social organization necessarily arise as a consequence of men's translating into reality plans and ideals consciously meditated in advance. On the contrary, he spoke of the private aims and selfish passions of men as being the most effective springs of human action; and in a famous phrase he referred to the "cunning of reason" which, using these aims and passions as its instruments, arrived at results undreamed of, or at best only dimly descried, by individual historical agents. Thus it is from the standpoint of historical retrospect and reflection alone that the true significance of events appears; the events are then seen to be indicative of a purpose "higher and broader" than any conceived by those who actually participated in them.

The claim that human history evolved, and necessarily evolved, according to a pattern determined by the implications of a particular rational idea or scheme would seem to presuppose some a priori insight into the ultimate nature of things that transcends the limits of empirical observation and inquiry. Yet Hegel sometimes spoke as if this were not so, suggesting that it was not his intention to anticipate the findings of historical investigation and research and contending that history must be taken "as it is—we have to proceed historically, empirically." In the light of such remarks it might seem reasonable to interpret his procedure as involving no more than the postulation of a certain framework of description within which the past can be conveniently, even illuminatingly, portrayed and "mapped." Hegel himself somewhat condescendingly allowed that even "the average and mediocre historian" is not a mere passive recipient of data but brings his own categories to the interpretation of his material; and it might be argued that Hegel's own aim in presenting history in terms of the development and extension of human freedom was simply to provide a more perspicuous and fruitful mode of conceptualizing the past than had previously been employed. Similarly, his references to "spirit" and to the operations of reason in history might be held to be susceptible to a straightforwardly empirical interpretation that begs no metaphysical questions. It remains doubtful, however, whether Hegel would in fact have acquiesced in an account of his intentions that proceeded along these rather unspectacular lines. Though he insisted upon the importance of empirical confirmation, this insistence did not prevent him from talking as if the course history takes was metaphysically ordained from the start, the logical outcome of a pre-existent idea at the heart of reality. In this connection, the English philosopher R. G. Collingwood, who was prepared to go further than most in stripping Hegel's system of its mystical elements (he treated the claim that history is a rational process as essentially meaning that history is the product of human thought expressing itself in action), admitted that what Hegel wrote at times recalled "the theological view of the Middle Ages," where the plans executed in history are the plans of God, not those of men.

SCIENTIFIC THEORIES

Whatever may be said of systems like that of Hegel, there nevertheless have been speculative thinkers who have expressly excluded from their programs any reference to transcendent purposes or principles, claiming that their theories are hypotheses securely grounded upon empirical fact and arrived at in accordance with the rigorous application of inductive methods. Such systems belong to the second type distinguished earlier and labeled, for want of a better term, "scientific." Hobbes in the seventeenth century had already envisaged the possibility of investigating human affairs according to procedures analogous to those that were beginning to be used with startling effect in the sphere of physical nature. It was only later, however, that this revolutionary suggestion took specific shape in the belief that the construction of a science of history in parallel with the existing natural sciences, was a feasible project. To many Enlightenment and post-Enlightenment thinkers, indeed, it seemed (in view of their preoccupation with problems relating to man and society) that the creation of such a science was a theoretical and practical necessity. If physical nature was, as Newton and others had apparently shown it to be, subject to discoverable laws of universal validity, it seemed perverse to these thinkers to imagine that the phenomena of which the stream of history is composed—both the "macroscopic" events like wars, revolutions, and the rise and fall of societies and the "microscopic" actions of individual human beings—do not exhibit the operation of similar regularities and uniformities. Indeed, an inquiry directed toward the discovery of such laws seemed to be an essential prerequisite to the construction of any serious program concerned with questions of social reform and reorganization.

Historical data. While there may have been widespread agreement about the need for a science of history in the general sense discussed above, there was manifestly less consonance of opinion regarding the particular form such a science might be expected to take. For example, what kind of laws would it comprise? To what types of historical phenomena would those laws apply, and in what manner could they be said to determine the course of events? The answers varied. To some thinkers it seemed self-evident that collective or "group" phenomena, such as cultures, nations, or social classes, represented the primary and irreducible data of historical theory; to others, by contrast, it appeared clear that laws relating to such phenomena must be derivable in principle from more fundamental principles relating to individual human psychology.

Laws in history. Ambiguities also seemed to emerge in the interpretation of the notion of law itself, a point that has been stressed by later critics. Karl Popper has claimed, for instance, that in the case of Auguste Comte and John Stuart Mill, both of whom were firm believers in the potential value of scientific method for the understanding of society, the "laws of succession" they postulated were not laws in the proper sense at all. Comte's famous "law of the three stages," for example, according to which human history passes from a theocratic stage dominated by kings and priests through an intermediary metaphysical one to a final stage in which society is organized scientifically, may be objected to on the grounds that, as stated at least, it does no more than postulate the existence of a certain historical trend. It is thus a singular categorical statement, and not of the universal hypothetical form held to distinguish statements of law in the scientific sense. Similar objections have been brought against Mill's references to "empirical laws," according to which different stages of society succeed one another, and to a "law of progress," which will enable us "to predict future events" (cf. Karl Popper, *The Poverty of Historicism*, p. 27).

Progress. Mill's use of the term "progress" raises a further point. Few of those who have wished to substantiate the thesis that history necessarily moves along a certain course have seriously entertained the possibility that the direction it takes might be other than a desirable one. This is true even of the Marxian system, the scientific objectivity of which has been so insistently emphasized by its adherents. Although Marx was profoundly influenced by the Hegelian view of history as a dynamic process whose forward movement is dialectically generated by conflicts between opposed or contradictory principles, he translated the Hegelian categories into a form that, he believed, deprived them of their unacceptably metaphysical or "idealist" implications. So reinterpreted, they could function as the framework of a theory in which the ultimate causes of historical change were located in the concrete realities of man's material existence. Technical developments in the means men use to satisfy their needs produce successive conflicts between economically determined groups or classes, with the previously oppressed class rising in each case to a position of dominance and creating new social forms. The foreseeable culmination of the process lies in the emergence of a classless society made possible by the victory of the proletariat. Yet the realization of this state of affairs, which is in the long run inevitable, should be hastened, not merely passively awaited; it is to be actively striven for as a human goal of pre-eminent worth and importance. Marx's justification for making such a claim has often been questioned in the light of the apparent skepticism with which he approached moral valuations in some of his writings. Moral and political ideals, according to these writings, belong to the ideological "superstructure" and are really no more than the reflections and expressions of fundamental class interests. However, so far as the nature of history itself was concerned, it would seem that for Marx no sharp line could be drawn between fact and value, the distinction between the two not having the force it has come to acquire in the eyes of many contemporary philosophers. The conceptions of what ought to be and of what necessarily will be were for him intimately fused; moreover, the type of future society he envisaged would be one which finally liberated men from the brutalizing forces that had previously thwarted the free and full development of their potentialities. It was therefore not only irrational, but also morally reprehensible or wicked, to try to obstruct the unalterable march of events.

Cyclical theories. Marx was not alone in assuming the inevitability of progress. Various theorists who radically diverged from him in other respects shared his view consciously or unconsciously. It would be wrong, though, to give the impression that all thinkers who have sought to interpret history in terms of a law-governed system have presented it as a unilinear progression or advance. While there was nothing new in the notion that the historical process conforms to a cyclical pattern rather than to that of a single forward movement—it is to be found, for instance, in Renaissance writers and was at the center of Vico's thought—the idea received fresh impetus from the popularity of vitalistic theories in biology toward the end of the nineteenth century and was dramatically revived, first by Oswald Spengler in his *Decline of the West,* and later in Arnold Toynbee's *A Study of History.* In the former book one-track views of historical development are totally rejected and history is regarded as offering the spectacle of a series of self-contained "cultures," each following a predictable path of growth and decay analogous to that exhibited in the evolution of particular living organisms. Although Toynbee attacked his predecessor for the essentialist and quasi-mystical conceptions that underlie Spengler's identification of different cultural units, in his own treatment of "civilizations" as the basic objects of historical study Toynbee often seems to have held a comparable, though less uncritical, preoccupation with biological models.

CRITICISMS AND APPRAISALS

Toynbee's vast system represents without doubt the most considerable contribution the twentieth century has made in the field of historical speculation. As such it has become a center of argument and controversy, bringing to a focal point much of the general opposition toward speculative projects and schemes that has been so markedly displayed in recent years. This opposition has to a large extent been prompted by the belief that the various attempts which have in fact been made to elicit comprehensive laws or patterns of historical development can be shown to involve radical misunderstandings or confusions. One example of this type of criticism has already been referred to, namely, the allegation that certain writers tend to assimilate laws to trends.

Unsound criteria. Even if there are many cases where misunderstandings cannot be demonstrated, other difficulties, no less damaging, are still held to present themselves. The claim, for instance, that it is possible to generalize concerning the various cultures or societies that have emerged during the course of history, and thereby to confirm inductively the existence of some evolutionary cycle to which each is necessarily subject, has also been attacked. Specifically, the objection is that the procedure for identifying particular cultures has not been made clear; in practice proponents of the view in question tend to rely upon an "intuitive" criterion of identity that already presupposes the validity of the generalizations they seek to establish; thus their method turns out to be circular.

Vague and unsystematic laws. In other cases it is urged that statements are formulated which purport to be laws but which, although not open to the charge just mentioned, are nevertheless so vague and imprecise as to make it hard to see what information they provide. At best, they can perhaps be construed as heuristic principles, suggestive of the lines along which laws with a determinate empirical application might be framed; at worst, they appear to be reducible to empty truisms. And, even if this were not so, the propositions in question—lacking as they do the characteristic of being systematically interconnected within the structure of a complex theory—would in any event hardly qualify as laws in the scientific sense. Here, once more, the vaunted analogy with the procedures of natural science seems to break down.

Use of unclarified concepts. Objections such as those above have been primarily of philosophical origin, and they accurately reflect the empiricist and antispeculative trend that has been a general feature of the development of philosophy in the present century. Many of the more influential participants in that development are distinguished for their contributions to the study of scientific methodology, and it is natural that some of them should have given critical attention to the works of writers who have claimed scientific respectability for their historical interpretations. Apart from this, the analytical temper of contemporary philosophers has rendered them acutely sensitive to the theoretical confusions that may be generated by the mishandling or misunderstanding of abstract concepts. Such philosophers have consequently viewed with suspicion the part played by notions like class, culture, or forces in the construction of systems of history, seeing in these notions a frequent source of spurious explanations and of conjectures wholly unwarranted by the evidence. The conclusion commonly drawn has been that theories purporting to demonstrate the operation in history of laws as inexorable as those supposed to govern the worlds of physics and biology stand on no firmer ground than, and indeed share much in common with, the more openly metaphysical or teleological interpretations that they were intended to supersede.

Oversimplification and inaccuracy. Hostility toward the speculative enterprise has not, however, been confined to philosophers. The reaction of many modern historians has been equally unsympathetic, although the grounds of their opposition are perhaps of a more complex character. In part, it may be attributed to a pervasive tendency for the historical studies to move in the direction of increased specialization and toward an ever growing preoccupation with the details of the past. One symptom of this tendency has been a disposition to regard all "general" history, of whatever form or kind, with distrust, because it is thought to entail inevitable distortion or simplification. It is noteworthy that some of the main criticisms historians have leveled against Toynbee have been accusations of inaccuracy and of neglect of salient facts in the overriding interests of theory.

Misconceptions of the historian's task. Another complaint, also sometimes made, is that the speculative historian, in his search for patterns and general laws, unjustifiably transgresses the limits of his own craft and profession: the proper task of the historian is to describe and explain the past in its concrete particularity, not to propound abstract hypotheses concerning the workings of society. This objection at first sight seems to be misplaced and to be answerable by reference to the distinction drawn in the introduction to the present article; one need only admit the existence of two separate levels of inquiry, different in scope and aim but not therefore mutually incompatible. Nevertheless, it does perhaps point to an issue involving genuine disagreement. For the fact remains that a number of speculative theories have been put forward in a manner implying criticism of history as it is ordinarily conceived and written and suggesting that the historian customarily works in the light of inadequate or outdated assumptions that stand in urgent need of replacement. The claim that these assumptions should be replaced by some all-embracing scheme or system, constructed on allegedly scientific principles and related to history proper as a theoretical, or "pure," scientific discipline is related to its "applied" counterparts, is precisely what has appeared unacceptable to many historians. They have rejected the claim, not merely on the grounds that it represents an unwarranted interference "from outside" with the historian's conduct of his professional activity but also because it involves a profound misunderstanding of the very nature and subject matter of history. The latter thesis was indeed argued for at length early in the present century by Benedetto Croce and later by Collingwood, both of whom were, significantly, practicing historians as well as philosophers. Thus Collingwood maintained that history is an autonomous discipline, radically different from natural science and employing categories and procedures uniquely fitted to the interpretation of its material. It followed, according to him, that scientifically inspired attempts to subsume that material under general laws and formulas were misconceived, springing from a wrong-headed naturalistic approach altogether out of place in the historical sphere. Since Collingwood wrote, a number of his specific contentions and arguments have been challenged. But the central tenets of his position, in particular his insistence upon the irreducibility of historical modes of thinking to scientific ones, continue to be given serious attention and have been persuasively restated by various thinkers in recent years.

Positive contributions of speculative theories. Taken together, the objections which have been urged against speculative systems of history constitute a formidable array. Yet it would be rash to conclude, as some have done, that such systems add up to no more than a series of aberrations, ultimately devoid of intellectual value or consequence. The main issue of principle raised—the question

of whether a science of history and society in some shape or form is a realizable possibility—is by no means dead; it might be said, for instance, that ideals of the type that earlier led to the construction of the great classical systems are still operative today in much sociological and anthropological inquiry, although channeled toward comparatively restricted and empirically determinate objectives. Nor would it be wise, so far as the actual practice and study of history is concerned, to underestimate the influence that the theories of Marx and others have exercised upon the development of historiography. Although such systems may not have measured up to the grandiose claims made on their behalf by their creators, they have often left in their wake procedural suggestions and interpretative ideas of great originality which opened the eyes of historians to new ways of looking at their subject and which subsequently proved immensely fertile and illuminating when introduced at the level of ordinary explanation and research. And here, perhaps, is a consideration worth remembering by those who may be tempted to resist proposals for large-scale methodological reform or innovation in history in the name of certain definitive "presuppositions of historical thought." If these presuppositions have not in fact preserved an immutably fixed and constant form in the past, but have been subject to periodic shift and revision, why should they be presumed immune to future change?

Bibliography

PRIMARY SOURCES

The following list includes some of the most important and influential contributions to the field:

Bossuet, J. B., *Discours sur l'histoire universelle.* Paris, 1681; reprinted Paris, 1925.

Comte, Auguste, *Cours de philosophie positive*, Émile Littré, ed., 4th ed., 6 vols. Paris, 1877. Translated by Harriet Martineau as *The Positive Philosophy of Auguste Comte*, 3d ed., 2 vols. London, 1893.

Condorcet, A. N. de, *Esquisse d'un tableau historique des progrès de l'esprit humaine.* Paris, 1795. Translated by June Barraclough as *Sketch for a Historical Picture of the Progress of the Human Mind.* London, 1955.

Hegel, G. W. F., *Vorlesungen über die Philosophie der Geschichte*, E. Gans, ed. Berlin, 1837. Translated by J. Sibree as *Lectures on the Philosophy of History.* London, 1857; reprinted with introduction by C. J. Friedrich, New York, 1956.

Kant, Immanuel, "Idee zu einer allgemeinen Geschichte in weltbürgerlicher Absicht." *Berliner Monatsschriften* (November 1784), 386–410. Translated by W. Hastie as "The Idea of a Universal Cosmo-political History," in Kant's *Eternal Peace and Other International Essays.* Boston, 1914.

Marx, Karl, and Engels, Freidrich, *Selected Works*, 2 vols. Moscow, 1950.

Mill, J. S., *A System of Logic.* London, 1943.

Spengler, Oswald, *Der Untergang des Abendlandes*, 2 vols. Munich, 1918–1922. Translated by C. F. Atkinson as *The Decline of the West*, 2 vols. London, 1926–1928.

Toynbee, Arnold, *A Study of History*, 10 vols. Oxford, 1934–1954.

Vico, Giambattista, *Scienza nuova*, 3d ed. Naples, 1744. Translated by T. G. Bergin and M. H. Fisch as *The New Science of Giambattista Vico.* Ithaca, N.Y., 1948.

COMMENTARIES AND CRITIQUES

Sampson, R. V., *Progress in the Age of Reason.* London, 1956. This work affords a useful general account of the development of speculative theories of history in the eighteenth and nineteenth centuries.

Twentieth-century appraisals of the speculative enterprise, written from varying philosophical standpoints, are to be found in the following works:

Berlin, Isaiah, *Historical Inevitability*. London, 1954.

Berlin, Isaiah, "History and Theory: The Concept of Scientific History." *History and Theory*, Vol. 1 (1960), 1–31.

Cohen, M. R., *The Meaning of Human History*. La Salle, Ill., 1947.

Collingwood, R. G., *The Idea of History*. Oxford, 1946.

Croce, Benedetto, *Teoria e storia della storiografia*. Bari, 1917. Translated by Douglas Ainslee as *History: Its Theory and Practice*. New York, 1921.

Dray, William, *Philosophy of History*. Englewood Cliffs, N.J., 1964. Chs. 5–8.

Hayek, F. A. von, *The Counter-revolution of Science*. Glencoe, Ill., 1952.

Hook, Sidney, *The Hero in History*. New York, 1943.

Popper, Karl R., *The Open Society and Its Enemies*, Vol. II. London, 1945.

Popper, Karl R., *The Poverty of Historicism*. London, 1957.

Walsh, W. H., *Introduction to Philosophy of History*. London, 1951.

Winch, Peter, *The Idea of a Social Science*. London, 1958.

BOOKS BY HISTORIANS

Barraclough, Geoffrey, *History in a Changing World*. Oxford, 1955.

Butterfield, Herbert, *Christianity and History*. London, 1950.

Carr, E. H., *What Is History?* New York, 1962.

Geyl, Pieter, *Debates With Historians*. New York, 1958.

Trevor-Roper, H. R., *Men and Events*. New York, 1957.

PATRICK GARDINER

SPENCER, HERBERT (1820–1903), English philosopher who attempted to apply evolutionary theory to all branches of knowledge. Spencer was born in Derby. His father, William George Spencer, was a Quaker teacher with a keen and independent mind, but in spite of his father's intellectual inclinations Spencer had an education that was exceptionally free of restraint. Unlike Mill, who began to learn Greek when he was 3, Spencer was allowed to study whatever he wished. At the age of 12 he knew little of Latin or Greek, history, English, or arithmetic. He was, however, interested in the sciences and had picked up some knowledge of physics, chemistry, and anatomy. When he was 13, Spencer was sent to his uncle, Reverend Thomas Spencer, at Hinton Charterhouse, near Bath, to begin his formal education. But he found the discipline too severe and ran away, returning to Derby after walking 115 miles in three days without sleep and with scarcely any food. However, he was returned to his uncle and, finally, by the age of 16 he had acquired some knowledge of mathematics even though he was still very ignorant of language and history.

At 17 he became assistant schoolmaster at Derby but left after three months to become a civil engineer with the London and Birmingham Railway. During this period he began to show interest in education, politics, and religion, and in 1840 he wrote to his father that he intended to pursue these subjects. This also seems to have been one of the few times that Spencer was interested in a young woman, but nothing came of it.

With the construction of the Birmingham and Gloucester Railway in 1841, the engineers, including Spencer, were discharged. He returned home intending to develop several inventions and also to continue his interests in natural history, sculpting, and, curiously enough, phrenology. These interests were interrupted when, in the following year, he became active politically and was appointed honorary secretary of the Derby branch of the Complete Suffrage Movement, which was allied to the Chartist agitation. During this time he unsuccessfully attempted to publish several reviews and articles. He also became an assistant editor of the *Pilot*, an official newspaper of the suffragist movement, but he soon resigned. Kant interested him, but he complained that the reading was difficult and unrewarding.

In 1848 Spencer's fortunes were considerably brightened when he became the subeditor of the *Economist* and became acquainted with such important figures as John Chapman, George Henry Lewes, Thomas Carlyle, George Eliot, and Thomas Henry Huxley. In 1850 Spencer published his first book, *Social Statics*, which, nine years before the publication of the *Origin of Species*, advocated a theory of evolution similar to that of Darwin although with a strong Lamarckian bent.

In 1854, in spite of his lack of any systematic learning, Spencer began to write his second book, *The Principles of Psychology*, which he published himself in 1855. In 1859 Darwin's work was published, and Spencer became so enthusiastic about it that he decided to write a series of volumes which would apply the conception of evolution to all the sciences. In this way he hoped to develop an all-inclusive philosophical theory, a synthetic philosophy, as he called it, which would incorporate all scientific data and use a scientific methodology. From 1860 to 1893 Spencer worked on this project, producing volumes on metaphysics, biology, psychology, sociology, and ethics. In spite of occasional inaccuracies about scientific details, Spencer's work obtained world recognition.

Spencer never married, perhaps because of ill health or because his books did not bring him any financial rewards until his later years. He died after a lengthy period of illness.

Theory of knowledge. The significant points of Spencer's philosophy are to be found in the *First Principles* (1862) and the six-part *Principles of Ethics* (1879–1893). He began by accepting the views of William Hamilton and J. S. Mill that knowledge is concerned strictly with empirical subject matter. However, he did not take this to mean that we are inevitably involved in some form of solipsism. In agreement with Kant, Spencer acknowledged the existence of two domains, that which we name experience and that which has traditionally been named reality. The experience we undergo is the result of the interaction between reality and the particular human organism, but even though we are required to acknowledge the existence of the external stimulant, we can never know exactly what it is like in its own right. This is a unique case in that, although we can investigate the effects of the stimulant, the cause is inherently unknowable.

Religious knowledge. Since we cannot know the nature of reality apart from its effects, we are led to a belief in some Unknowable; this does not mean, however, that we are committed to a belief in the existence of God. First of all, our complete dependence on sensory data for knowledge makes it impossible for us to tell whether this Unknowable is at all comparable to any kind of divine substance. We are never in the position to test whether our idea of what the Absolute is corresponds to what it actually is. Second, reasoning, which for Spencer is no more than an advanced physical ability by which an organism can meet environmental problems, cannot cope with data that are not reducible to observables. When such an endeavor is made, reasoning, like any machine whose function is abused, breaks down. Consider what occurs when we attempt to analyze a concept whose reference is taken to be necessarily outside of the domain of experience—the concept of God. All questions are either unanswerable or productive of paradoxes. If there is a God, then how did he come into existence? If he was created by something else, then who created that? And so forth into an infinite regress. Could God have created himself? If so, then out of what elements did he create himself? If there were elements out of which he created himself, then who created these elements? If he created himself out of nothing, then how can something come out of nothing? None of these questions can be answered by an appeal to some possible empirical datum, nor can they be answered by any pure logical analysis without at once involving further unanswerable questions. Thus, for Spencer theism fails as a means of giving us insight into the nature of the Unknowable and its relation to us.

Pantheism also fails. The fact that pantheism treats God as an immanent rather than an external power does not eliminate the questions that are raised with theism. It is still impossible to imagine the universe arising uncaused out of nothing. We should be required, in this view, to think of the universe as existent in some potential form prior to its becoming actual; and even if it were meaningful to speak of a potential universe, the question would still remain how a potential universe could have been created.

Are we then necessarily led to atheism? Spencer denies this as well. The fact that we do not know whether a God exists does not mean that therefore no God exists. The rejection of theism and pantheism entails only that we can have no knowledge about the Unknowable, not that the Unknowable does not exist. At most we can simply say that we do not know whether there is a God. Agnosticism, Spencer concludes, is the only reasonable belief in regard to religious and metaphysical issues.

Spencer therefore rejected all known theological schemes and was also highly critical of the various absurdities and abuses he believed existed in all religious institutions. Many religions, he claimed, still cling to beliefs that arose strictly because of wrong inferences about natural phenomena. Thus the notion of a soul, or of a ghost, arose because primitive men could not account for dreams, shadows, and reflections. All such phenomena led to the belief that men were dual personalities, one of which remains unchanged regardless of changes in the visible man. From this conception there gradually developed the theory that there were eternal, unchanging, omnipotent personalities. In this way, Spencer declared, men came to believe in gods; and, for similar reasons, the Judaeo-Christian God has many strictly human traits. Spencer deplored this religious anthropomorphism which depicted God as filled with hatreds and desires that were appropriate only to human beings. He also strongly disapproved of the attempt by the church to fight scientific doctrines, especially those of Copernicus and Darwin. But in spite of these objections he felt that religion could serve as a means of fostering friendship and cooperation among human beings and also of guaranteeing the retention of the most worthwhile values of the past. Furthermore, religion could be useful as a way of developing interest in the various enigmas that are found in the universe, a means of motivating men to initiate scientific inquiries.

Scientific knowledge. The fact that we can never know what the Unknowable is in itself does not imply, according to Spencer, that we cannot have any genuine knowledge. The domain of phenomena is characterized by features which are not controllable by our desires or even by our manipulations. Certain relationships consistently appear in spite of our objections or antagonistic attitudes. Also, in all objects, including ourselves, there are varying degrees of energy—or force, as Spencer called it. These aspects of reality are manifestations of the Unknowable, and information about them is the only kind of knowledge human beings can obtain or ought to seek.

It is clear that knowledge, for human beings, is not a study of the Unknowable but rather of the manifestations of the Unknowable among phenomena. Out of this concern with phenomena and the force implicit in them there arises science, which, according to Spencer, is simply a more sophisticated, more precisely stated form of ordinary knowledge. The task of science is to accumulate data and then to discover general laws, accomplishing this task by assigning the investigation of specific aspects of phenomena to specific disciplines. Thus, the study of matter is the purpose of physics, and from this discipline has come the recognition of those universal characteristics of force which are described in the laws of the conservation of energy, the indestructibility of matter, and gravitation. Similarly, the science of biology studies living beings and has discovered laws of development and evolution. The other sciences have made analogous discoveries. But we ought not to think that these laws are simple empirical generalizations, for they describe the ways in which the Unknowable makes its appearance in the phenomenal world. Therefore they have an urgency, a necessity attached to them that is not to be found in ordinary, purely statistical laws. Thus, even though Spencer began by adopting a Kantian position, unlike Kant he did not attribute the necessary relationships that are taken to be in nature to the peculiar formation of the human mind. We do not impose forms and categories on what is observed. On the contrary, the external stimulant itself imposes upon us restrictions and limitations which we cannot ignore or change. Newton's laws are not characteristic of our kind of mind, for surely we can conceive of a world in which other laws would hold and, after sufficient time, would seem to be just as necessary. We can also imagine minds being changed by operations or accidents, but such changes do not entail an accompanying reconstruction of nature. Thus, if there are any necessary relationships, they must be due to something external to ourselves.

Similarly, Spencer rejected the whole Kantian analysis of space and time. He agreed that space and time cannot be regarded as objective in the same way that phenomena are, for if they were, then they ought, like all things, to possess attributes. But neither space nor time can be said to have any observable attributes, so they are not objective. Nor are they subjective, for if they were, Spencer maintained, then they would not exist; and to allege that nonexistents exist would be a contradiction in terms. Furthermore, historically, space and time have been defined differently. They are not, therefore, innate concepts in the mind. Along with force, causation, motion, substance, and matter they are, in Spencer's analysis, concepts whose explication can never be completely given. Since, like the Unknowable, they relate to the realm which we can never know, all attempts at their definition must be unsuccessful and scientists must use such concepts with the recognition of the limitations involved. For all practical purposes we can regard time as an abstract abbreviatory term summarizing all sequences of phenomena and space as a term summarizing all coexistences.

Evolution. Although science is concerned with the discovery of general laws, its results are departmentalized; it does not attempt to discover or speculate about relationships that will hold for all subject matters. Therefore scientists are not philosophers, for only philosophers deal with the formulation of theories that hold for everything. In the past their theories were metaphysical and were rightfully rejected, but Spencer believed that the new Darwinian hypothesis could become the nucleus of a genuine philosophical theory. The law of evolution, Spencer proclaimed, would be the first philosophical world view that would incorporate scientific data and would be substantiated by purely inductive procedures.

With this pronouncement Spencer then essayed to show how every state of being—both mental and physical—is characterized by the same evolutionary principle. Everything, from single entities to classes, develops from a simple, almost primitive stage in which only elementary functions are performed to a state in which more complicated functions arise. The growth and transformation that are described so clearly in biology and anthropology are processes found everywhere, but this does not mean that there is some Hegelian end which is gradually making its appearance. Spencer consistently denied that his evolutionary theory was to be construed teleologically, claiming that so far as we can ever tell, there are no final goals that everything is striving to attain. There are beginnings, middles (or periods of equilibrium), and ends; but all these processes take place in a finite space and a finite time. A person is born; he matures; he dies. Similarly, a society begins, reaches a stage of equilibrium, and is destroyed by something internal or external. All around us we can see the workings of the law of evolution and dissolution, but we can never know whether the universe as a whole is undergoing this process. Such a question is directed to-ward the domain of the Unknowable and therefore can never be answered. That evolution applies to phenomena only in a relative sense—in a sense that there are finite and not absolute ends—is expressed in Spencer's famous formula of evolution: "Evolution is an integration of matter and concomitant dissipation of motion; during which the matter passes from a relatively indefinite, incoherent homogeneity to a relatively definite, coherent heterogeneity; and during which the retained motion undergoes a parallel transformation" (*First Principles,* 6th ed., para. 144).

Having formulated his theory, Spencer undertook to substantiate it by showing its application in all fields of inquiry. In his *Principles of Biology* (1864–1867) Spencer presented a detailed examination of how, under the influence of environmental conditions, organisms that are almost without any structure gradually become differentiated. Whereas in primitive organisms the entire body carries out all the functions, in the more advanced organisms there is a "physiological division of labour" as special organs evolve to fulfill specific functions and homogeneity gives way to heterogeneity. Thus the amoeba has little coherence among its parts; and there is comparative homogeneity throughout; but in such a highly developed form as man there are distinct parts that have highly specialized functions and yet are integrated to form a unified whole. Similarly, the heart, which is initially no more than an enlarged blood vessel, eventually becomes the four-chambered structure found in human beings. Accepting a Lamarckian viewpoint, Spencer further argued that the use or disuse of an organ could cause its function to be modified in future generations. The eye came about when light kept striking a particularly sensitive cell, causing it to operate in a certain way. This new cellular behavior was inherited by later organisms.

Intelligence. Spencer sought to define intelligence as a characteristic acquired by a live object with a highly complex physical structure, reacting and interacting with a harsh environment. Intelligence is a set of tendencies and behavior patterns by which human beings endeavor to adapt themselves to environmental difficulties. More specifically, it is a mechanism by which mind acquires the ability to produce ideas about future possible events. However, intelligence is not given all at once. At first, animals depend solely upon the sensations they receive when their skins are acted upon by the environment. Eventually parts of the skin become specialized to perform gustatory, visual, auditory, and olfactory functions; animals can then respond to environmental forces with which they are not in direct physical contact. An amoeba reacts only when it is touched, but more advanced organisms can respond to objects at a distance. In the next stage of development the sensations caused by these specialized stimuli become fused into an integrated whole which we call experience or consciousness. This kind of fusion serves to shorten the time needed for evaluating sensory data and making appropriate responses. Finally, this basic stimulus-response kind of experience itself evolves. From this fusion of basic sensations there arises a new and better way of giving the organism its desired equilibrium—the ability of mind to produce ideas depicting future possibilities. Whereas the lowest form of animal knows only the passing moment, man can imagine both future and past times and thus learn to meet difficulties before they actually occur.

Sociality and sympathy. Feelings, too, arise through evolution. Life seeks to survive, and feelings of pleasure are necessary to sustain this urge. If the organism experienced no rewards for maintaining its own life and reproducing its kind, if there were no sense of accomplishment, then the urge to survive might easily be extinguished. Therefore, behavior that contributes to survival is accompanied by the feeling of pleasure, and behavior that endangers survival is accompanied by the feeling of pain. Similarly, feelings of sociality and sympathy developed in human beings because in the struggle for survival men came to recognize that human cooperation is necessary, and the pleasures that accrue to the feeling of sociality were the rewards that guaranteed the continuation of such cooperation.

The development of the feelings of sociality and sympathy led to the emergence of a new kind of entity, society, which is the subject of sociology and ethics. Here, too, the principle of evolution holds. Society, like other organisms, has its period of infancy, of maturity, and of death. Spencer, however, unlike Hegel, did not push the organic theory of the state to its extreme. He maintained that there are important differences between an organism and a society. In an organism, consciousness is to be found in one particular area, the brain, and not in any of the parts. On the other hand, in a society, consciousness is to be found only in the individual parts. Furthermore, the cells of an organism are subordinated to the organism as a whole, but a society exists solely for the benefit of its members. For this reason Spencer opposed all forms of socialism and was a firm believer in the principle of laissez-faire. In fact, he argued that if socialism were ever to arise in a state, it would lead to a very strict military despotism.

Even though Spencer believed that all societies must eventually die because of some external or internal disturbance, he was not a pessimist. He maintained that Western civilization, at least, was just entering its most mature stage of development. Sympathy and understanding were increasing. Nations were becoming less prone to resort to war in order to settle their differences. Freedom of speech, religion, and the press were being guaranteed. Society was no longer as rigidly stratified, and men could more easily move up the social ladder. Even representative government was gradually becoming universal. In fact, Spencer believed that with the proper indoctrination a society of the very highest order could continue for a very long time. Accepting the fallacious Lamarckian theory, Spencer imagined that if a code of ethics were taught to men for several successive generations, the code would become congenital. Every individual, Spencer argued, inherits some predispositions from his predecessors, and later generations are therefore more advanced intellectually than earlier ones.

Ethics. In accordance with his view that societies exist only for the benefit of their individual members, Spencer developed a strict utilitarian system of ethics. Good is what gives men pleasure in the long run. Ethics is the science of conduct, and conduct deals with the adjustment of acts to ends. The lower animals find their satisfaction in using the environment to their best advantage; human beings find their satisfaction, or happiness, in a similar way. Appropriate adjustments result in pleasure; inappropriate adjustments result in pain. We ought, Spencer declared, to look to our own pleasures, but we ought to do this by using intelligence, which gives us some insight, no matter how small, into what the future may bring; present pleasures may be outweighed by possible future pains. Unlike primitive men, Spencer maintained, we have the ability to form ideas about remote ends, and disaster befalls us more easily when we refuse to entertain such ideas or to construct them in accordance with the scientific data available to us. In fact, the whole conception of a moral consciousness is no more than a rule that a mind imposes upon itself to the effect that it ought always to consider the consequences of its actions, to examine whether more or fewer possible benefits to itself and to society would result. The notion of duty is also a rule emphasizing the need to consider future benefits in contrast with present temptations. Without the feeling of duty we would simply act for ourselves alone and, in this way, in the long run act against our own best interests.

This account of duty also gives Spencer what he believes is a means of eliminating the traditional contradiction between egoism and altruism. At first all men were primarily interested in themselves, as was necessary in a world where men could scarcely keep themselves alive. In fact, even in a more advanced society egoism serves some good, since the person who is very interested in himself and takes care of himself is very often healthier than others and is, therefore, better able to care for others. But, in any case, as society advanced, egoism became modified by the recognition that, if we wish to attain the objects that can afford us pleasure, we ought to help others because they, in turn, will help us. Thus, according to Spencer, egoism and altruism are mutually compatible. We are concerned with the welfare of others because their welfare affects our own.

Education. Spencer's utilitarianism and his biological analysis of human behavior led to concrete educational proposals. Since men are in constant struggle with environmental forces, they ought, first and foremost, to be taught the subjects that will help them most in this struggle. A knowledge of science, therefore, is crucial because it is the primary means by which men may be able to avert possible natural disasters. After the sciences, one ought to study psychology, education, and the social sciences because these will give insight into ways of resolving family and social problems. Finally, one ought to study art because it produces the kind of satisfaction that needs no justification nor analysis in terms of future satisfactions. It is an immediate good in itself, producing an immediate feeling of mental well-being.

Spencer was highly critical of the study of Greek and Latin and languages in general because it seemed to lead to rote learning and a conditioned acceptance of authority as the ultimate criterion of truth. Learning should begin by introducing the child to actual experimental situations from which he should deduce the law involved. The child should be taught to regard the world as a place in which he must make his own decisions in accordance with the best available scientific data. Therefore, teachers should encourage initiative and the free expression of ideas, and they can best do this by being actively engaged in inquiry and study. A teacher who is interested in his work, according to Spencer, will be more apt to produce research-oriented students.

Although Spencer's philosophy was influential during its time, it has not proved to be as significant as it originally seemed to be. Like Hegel's evolving Absolute, Spencer's evolutionary theory covered too much. It did little to explain why evolution took one direction rather than another. Unlike scientific laws, his principle of evolution did not permit any genuine predictions. Any change whatsoever could be interpreted as a step in the evolutionary process, and, therefore, no falsification of the principle could ever occur. Thus, the charge of tautology which Spencer directed against metaphysics, namely, that empirical data were not relevant to either the confirmation or the disconfirmation of its theories, could also be made against his own theory. Furthermore, Spencer's claim that he was employing inductive procedures shows that he harbored a confusion between induction and deduction. He apparently believed that there could be sufficient empirical evidence from which one could deduce that there exist certain fundamental laws of nature. It is fairly clear that the theory of evolution had the same logical status for Spencer as the dialectic had for Hegel: no evidence was to be allowed to repudiate the doctrine.

The Unknowable is also open to criticism. First of all, it is paradoxical to defend science, with its demand that all assertions be at least potentially verifiable, and, at the same time, to insist on the existence of an entity which is inherently incapable of ever being inspected. Second, even though the Unknowable is supposed to be unknowable, Spencer finds no difficulty in attributing characteristics to it: it exists, and it is the cause of the domain of phenomena. But since, in Spencer's view, all descriptions and statements of cause refer only to relations among phenomena, one ought not to be able even to speak of the Unknowable as a cause of phenomena. It has no function in a theory of knowledge.

Spencer's social and ethical theories have also been challenged. His laissez-faire doctrines are simply not defensible in a world as highly industrialized as ours. Spencer believed that an industrial society would foster self-reliant, humane, and individualistic human beings, but he ignored the brutalities and injustices that could arise in such societies unless appropriate controls were introduced. In his ethical views, Spencer's hedonism is open to the same criticism as that made against Bentham and Mill, and there is the same difficulty in determining how mathematical techniques are to be applied to pleasure and pain. When does a pleasure begin and when does it end? Is anticipation of a pleasure part of the pleasure itself? If so, then what mathematical values are to be assigned to it? Are there great as well as small anticipations? How are these to be measured? In fairness to Spencer, it ought to be pointed out that he was aware of how difficult it is to construct a hedonistic calculus; but his view that a maxi-

mum of pleasure will accompany a maximum of social and physical adjustment was not more enlightening. Adaptability frequently is not accompanied by pleasure, and it is questionable whether such adjustment ought to be aimed at by human beings. History abounds with examples of men who rightfully fought against the accepted conventions and mores of their time. Spencer himself exemplifies the spirit of opposition to convention.

The importance of Spencer, however, lies in his insistence on the use of scientific knowledge and methodology for philosophical analysis and in his championing of individual rights. As if anticipating twentieth-century totalitarianism, he warned against allowing governments to encroach upon private rights and permitting military organizations to become too influential. In an age in which imperialism and expansionism were popular concepts endorsed by both the press and the general public, Spencer did not hesitate to voice his strong objections. Finally, Spencer's encyclopedic knowledge must be admired. In spite of gaps in his background reading, he was actively involved in inquiries into almost all significant areas of learning. In all these areas he made some original—even if not, perhaps, everlasting—contributions. It is a feat that few philosophers have ever performed.

Works by Spencer

Essays on Education. London, 1861.
First Principles. London, 1862; 6th ed. reissued 1937.
Principles of Biology, 2 vols. London, 1864–1867.
Principles of Psychology, 2 vols., 2d ed. London, 1870–1872.
Principles of Sociology, 3 vols. London, 1876–1896.
Principles of Ethics, 2 vols. London, 1879–1893.
Man Versus the State. London, 1884.
Autobiography. London, 1904. Published after his death.
The Study of Sociology. Ann Arbor, Mich., 1961. Introduction by Talcott Parsons.

Works on Spencer

Asirvatham, E., *Herbert Spencer's Theory of Social Justice.* New York, 1936.
Bowne, B. P., *The Philosophy of Herbert Spencer.* New York, 1874.
Diaconide, E., *Étude critique sur la sociologie de Herbert Spencer.* Paris, 1938.
Duncan, David, *Life and Letters of Herbert Spencer,* 2 vols. New York, 1908.
Elliot, Hugh, *Herbert Spencer.* New York, 1917.
Hudson, W. H., *An Introduction to the Philosophy of Herbert Spencer,* 2d ed. London, 1904.
Royce, Josiah, *Herbert Spencer.* New York, 1904.
Rumney, Judah, *Herbert Spencer's Sociology.* London, 1934.
Taylor, A. E., *Herbert Spencer.* New York, 1928.
Watson, J., *Comte, Mill, and Spencer.* Glasgow, 1895.

JACK KAMINSKY

SPENGLER, OSWALD (1880–1936), was born at Blankenburg, Germany. Spengler is known almost entirely for his contribution to philosophy of history. After studying at the universities of Munich, Berlin, and Halle—chiefly natural science and mathematics, although he also read widely in history, literature, and philosophy—Spengler obtained a doctorate in 1904, with a thesis on Heraclitus, and embarked upon a career as a high school teacher. In 1911 he abandoned teaching to take up the penurious life of a private scholar in Munich, where the first volume of his only considerable work, *Der Untergang des Abendlandes* (*The Decline of the West*), gradually took shape. This volume was published in 1918 at the moment of his country's defeat in World War I. Its pessimistic conclusions so exactly suited the prevailing mood that its author rocketed to instant but short-lived fame.

An ardent nationalist, Spengler has sometimes been accused, especially because of his reactionary and quite undistinguished political writings after 1923, of having helped to prepare the way intellectually for fascism. He actually opposed Hitler's rise, but chiefly on the ground (as he put it) that what Germany needed was a hero, not a heroic tenor. He died in Munich in 1936, bitterly resentful of the drastic decline his reputation had suffered. It is doubtful that Spengler would have been greatly mollified by the revival of interest in his work that followed World War II, for this was due as much to the general stimulus given to speculation about history by Arnold Toynbee's popular *A Study of History* as to any belated recognition of the independent merits of Spengler's views.

History as comparative morphology. *The Decline of the West*, although fascinating in stretches, is an unsystematic, repetitive, obscurely written book. Its style is oracular rather than analytical; it offers more "insights" than arguments. Yet its major claims are reasonably clear. From the outset it calls for a "Copernican revolution" in our way of viewing human history that will at once undermine both the traditional ancient–medieval–modern framework generally employed by empirical historians (a framework which Spengler finds provincial) and the prevailing linear interpretation of most Western philosophers of history, whether progressive or regressive (which he finds naive). According to Spengler, history, steadily and objectively regarded, will be seen to be without center or ultimate point of reference. It is the story of an indefinite number of cultural configurations, of which western Europe is only one, that "grow with the same superb aimlessness as the flowers of the field." The careers of such cultures, he contends, constitute the only meaning to be found in the course of history as a whole; they are pockets of unconnected significance in a wilderness of human life, most of which is "historyless." All that philosophical study of history can attempt is a "comparative morphology of cultures"—an inquiry into the typical form of their life, their rhythms, and possibly their laws—aimed at giving categories and an interpretative framework to empirical historiography. In outline at least, this is the aim of Spengler's two massive volumes.

But what exactly are the cultures that provide subject matter for the morphological approach to history? In view of the common complaint that Spengler "biologizes" history, it should be noted that he represents cultures as spiritual phenomena, although rooted in a definite "natural landscape." A culture is the spiritual orientation of a group of people who have achieved some unitary conception of their world which informs all their activities—their art, religion, and philosophy, their politics and economics, even their warfare—and which is expressible in a distinctive concept of the space in which they are to live and act.

This concept of space functions as the culture's "prime symbol" and is the key to the understanding of its history.

Thus, classical man, to whom Spengler applies Nietzsche's term "Apollinian," is said to have conceived of himself as living in a local, finite space, a visible, tangible here-and-now, of which the life-sized nude statue and the small columned temple are eminent expressions. The concept shows itself equally in such things as the circumscribed political life of the city-state and the practice of burning rather than burying the dead, as if the idea of eternity could not be squarely faced. By contrast, modern Western man conceives of himself as living in a space of boundless extent, his whole culture expressing a Faustian urge to reach out and fill it with his activity. Thus, the spires of Gothic cathedrals soar skyward, Western painting develops distant perspectives, music produces the expansive form of the fugue. Also typically Faustian are long-distance sailing and long-range weapons, the conquest of space by telephone, and the insatiable ambitions of Western statesmen (for whom, like Cecil Rhodes, "expansion is everything").

Other cultures each have their characteristic space concept. The ancient Egyptians saw their world in one dimension, and their architecture, which assumed the basic form of a corridor enclosed in masonry, expressed the notion of "moving down a narrow and inexorably prescribed life-path." The Russians, whom Spengler classifies as non-Western, have a "flat plane" culture, which, when free to do so, expresses itself in low-lying buildings and an ethics of undiscriminating brotherhood. The Arabian culture of the Middle East, which Spengler calls Magian, views the world mysteriously, as a cavern in which "light . . . battles against the darkness." Its architecture is consequently interior-oriented; its religion, magical and dualistic. Altogether, Spengler claims to identify nine (possibly ten) such cultures, which have emerged at various times from "the proto-spirituality of ever-childish humanity." But he does not rule out the possibility of others being discovered.

Spengler's concept of human cultures has some affinity with Hegel's concept of the state. Both envisage an organic unity of human attitudes and activities that express a definite form of the human spirit. Spengler never wrote the promised metaphysical work that might have made clearer the general status of "spirit" in his philosophy of history. But his concept of it certainly differs from Hegel's, for he denies that the spirituality of successive historical units taken together reveals the developing nature of spirit itself. The units have no rational connection with one another, Spengler maintains, denying categorically that one culture can ever really understand, learn from, or (strictly speaking) be influenced by another. The divergence of his approach from Hegel's is even greater in his account of the typical career of a culture. Whereas Hegel attempted to represent not only the succession of historical units, but also the succession of stages within each unit, as a rationally (that is, dialectically) ordered sequence, Spengler finds, instead, a pattern analogous to the life cycle of a plant or animal. Like biological organisms, cultures grow old. The qualitative changes that accompany the "aging" will be as apparent, to a historian possessing "physiognomic tact," as is a culture's original orientation.

Cultural cycle. Spengler often speaks of the aging of cultures in terms of the succession of the four seasons. They have their spring in an early heroic period when life is rural, agricultural, and feudal. In the Apollinian culture this was the Homeric period; in the Faustian it was the high Middle Ages. This is a time of seminal myths, of inspiring epic and saga, and of powerful mystical religion. With summer comes the rise of towns not yet alienated from the countryside, an aristocracy of manners growing up beside an older, lustier leadership, and great individual artists succeeding their anonymous predecessors. In the Apollinian culture this was the period of the early city-states; in the Faustian it was the time of the Renaissance, of Shakespeare and Michelangelo, and of the Galilean triumphs of the uncorrupted intellect. Autumn witnesses the full ripening of the culture's spiritual resources and the first hints of possible exhaustion; it is a time of growing cities, spreading commerce, and centralizing monarchies, with religion being challenged by philosophy and tradition undermined by "enlightenment." In the classical world this was the age of the Sophists, of Socrates and Plato; in the West it was the eighteenth century, which reached the apogee of creative maturity in the music of Mozart, the poetry of Goethe, and the philosophy of Kant. Transition to winter is characterized by the appearance of the megalopolis, the world city, with its rootless proletariat, plutocracy, esoteric art, and growing skepticism and materialism. It is an age, furthermore, of imperialism, of increasing political tyranny, and of almost constant warfare, as political adventurers skirmish for world empire. In general, culture loses its soul and hardens into mere "civilization," the highest works of which are feats of administration and the application of science to industry.

Faustian culture is, according to Spengler, presently well into its autumn period, at a point roughly equivalent to 200 B.C. in the Apollinian culture. An early sign of our advanced cultural age is the career of Napoleon, who is morphologically contemporary with Alexander the Great; our Julius Caesar is yet to come. The moral is plain.

> We are civilized, not Gothic or Rococo, people; we have to reckon with the hard cold facts of *late* life, to which the parallel is to be found not in Pericles' Athens but in Caesar's Rome. Of great painting or great music there can no longer be, for Western people, any question. . . . Only *extensive* possibilities are open to them.

Young Faustians who wish to play a significant role in the gathering winter should, in other words, either join the army or enroll in a technological institute. Spengler hopes that enough of his countrymen will heed his advice to ensure that the Faustian equivalent of the Roman Empire will be German.

Cultural cycle and determinism. Clearly, Spengler regards comparative morphology as a basis for predicting the future of a culture, given the stage it has reached. Spengler, in fact, represents his study as the first serious attempt to "predetermine history," and he offers comparative charts in support of his claim that the life cycle of a culture takes about one thousand years to work itself through.

It is nevertheless misleading to call Spengler's account of history deterministic without qualification. Unlike Toynbee's, for example, it offers no explanation of the origin of cultures; the sudden rise of a new "world experience" is left a cosmic mystery. Nor do Spengler's cultures disappear on schedule after reaching the stage of civilization; civilizations may last indefinitely, as the examples of India and China show. Even while alive, the working out of a culture's "destiny" leaves open many alternative possibilities; the themes, Spengler says, are given, but not the modulations, which "depend on the character and capacities of individual players." Thus, Germany was bound to be united in the nineteenth century; how it would be united depended on what Frederick William IV would do in 1848 and Bismarck in 1870. Spengler's historical "laws" are thus not envisaged as determining, but only as limiting, the actions of individuals. This is part of the rationale of his political activism.

The notion, furthermore, of a developing culture's being a *self*-determining system is qualified by Spengler's recognition of two ways in which its normal development may be frustrated. Thus, he claims that the Mexican culture had perished through external assault, "like a sunflower whose head is struck off by one passing." Spengler also concedes that a culture can sustain spiritual damage from too close proximity to a stronger one, resulting in what he calls pseudomorphosis. What originally led him to elaborate this idea was the confused development of the Magian culture, which came to life on the ground of the Apollinian before the older culture had passed away. In such cases, Spengler observes, the younger culture "cannot get its breath, and fails not only to achieve pure and specific expression-forms, but even to develop fully its own self-consciousness." The Russian culture—which, according to Spengler, was "prematurely born"—has similarly been deformed by intrusions of the Faustian culture, first in the "reforms" of Peter the Great and again in the Bolshevik Revolution. Since weaker cultures take on only certain outer forms of dominant ones, however, Spengler would deny that the doctrine of pseudomorphosis contradicts his claim that one culture never really influences another.

Difficulties in Spengler's theory. Like all large synoptic systems, Spengler's theory of history has been criticized for rearing its speculative superstructure on too shaky an empirical foundation. Even Toynbee has not escaped this charge, and in breadth of historical knowledge (if not always in perceptiveness) Spengler is vastly the inferior of the two. His knowledge of his cultures is much more uneven; all he really knows well is the Apollinian and Faustian. More important, what he does say at the detailed level all too often gives the appearance of special pleading. In some cases his morphological judgments are just a bit too ingenious to be convincing, as when he declares that Rembrandt's brown is the color of Beethoven's string quartets. In other cases dubious value judgments seem to be traceable chiefly to the requirements of the overarching thesis, as when the Roman Empire, being a winter phenomenon, is represented as culturally sterile, in spite of Vergil, Horace, and Ovid. In still other cases critics have suspected Spengler, if not of falsifying, then at least of suppressing, known historical facts, as when he claims that classical man, by contrast with Magian man, was polytheistic, ignoring the almost uniform monotheism of the great Greek philosophers. Highhanded treatment of the details is made easier by the fact that what passes for empirical verification in Spengler's work is really only casual exemplification of his general ideas; he makes no attempt to test systematically, and possibly to falsify, a precisely articulated hypothesis about cultural development. And when the details become intransigent, much can be explained away as pseudomorphosis. Thus, high-rise buildings in Russia are called Western-inspired, and Hadrian's Pantheon (the "first mosque") is labeled an irruption of the Magian.

Even if Spengler's actual procedure were scientifically more acceptable, there would remain the basic weakness of any attempt to generalize about the whole of history from a mere eight to ten instances of cultural development, two of which are conceded in any case to be abnormal. Spengler's defenders, of course, have often denied the relevance of this sort of criticism. What he attempted, they claim, was not social science, not even philosophy of history in the sense of arguing to general conclusions from philosophical premises in the manner of Kant and Hegel. It was, rather, a vision of events, whose truth is the truth of poetry. From this standpoint Spengler's charts and tables are an unfortunate lapse that should not be taken too seriously; part of the value of his work lies in its imaginative imprecision. Certainly, Spengler himself declared that whereas nature should be studied scientifically, history should be studied poetically. As a defense against the empirical objection, however, this will not do. For poetry is not predictive. Spengler's theory is distinctive in insisting that the significant features of history are those which are focused by the historian's aesthetic judgment. But classification and simple induction of the sort characteristic of the underdeveloped sciences is as essential to his final conclusions as is aesthetic insight.

The weakness of Spengler's inductions might not have been so serious had he not been an uncompromising holist as well. He offers no explanation of the changes his cultures undergo; he makes no attempt to isolate the factors that might throw light on their "mechanism" and that might have afforded reasons for expecting such developments to continue. In fact, part of the function of the puzzling contrast he draws between the "causality" of nature and the "destiny" of history is to persuade us not to look for this sort of thing. Spengler seems to think of causality rather narrowly as a matter of physical interaction. His own model for historical development is the biological destiny of a seed, its tendency to grow into a plant of a definite kind, barring accidents and in spite of deformations—it being assumed that this is not explicable mechanistically. It is ironical that although Spengler himself, in elaborating this concept of explanation, claimed to be resisting inappropriate scientific approaches to history, it is precisely because of this approach that some critics have charged him with scientism. Idealist philosophers of history, for

example, have regarded Spengler as a cryptopositivist because, in searching out the life cycle of cultures without trying to understand in detail and from the inside why the human participants acted as they did, he treats what he originally defined spiritualistically as if it were part of nature. The causation of action by human reason, these critics would say, is central to all explanations of historical change. By ignoring this, Spengler's theory falls into incompatible parts.

Many critics have held that an even more obvious contradiction vitiates much of what Spengler had to say about specifically historical understanding. According to him, the reason cultures never really influence one another is that they are never able to grasp one another's prime symbol—a doctrine of cultural isolation that Spengler extended even to such apparently recalcitrant subjects as mathematics (to Apollinians and Faustians, he says, number means entirely different things). But the notion that we can never understand what is culturally alien to us surely raises barriers to the sort of understanding claimed by Spengler himself; comparative morphology presupposes a correct grasp of what is being compared. Spengler tries to meet this difficulty with the *ad hoc* claim that a few intuitive geniuses may rise above the barrier of cultural relativism. Yet the fact that he offered his book to the general public surely betrays confidence in a rather wider distribution of transcultural insight than is strictly compatible with the impossibility of cultures' learning from one another. Nor is it helpful to suggest that cultures may learn without being influenced, for the reason for denying influence was the impossibility of understanding. The difficulty is compounded by Spengler's sometimes also denying that we can understand what is culturally "out of phase" with us, even though it belongs to the past of our own culture. Thus, we are told that although Tacitus knew of the revolution of Tiberius Gracchus two and a half centuries earlier, he no longer found it meaningful. Together, Spengler's two limitations on the understanding lead to the conclusion that we can understand only ourselves. This is scarcely a promising position from which to develop a theory of historical inquiry.

Bibliography

The first volume of Spengler's *Der Untergang des Abendlandes*, subtitled *Gestalt und Wirklichkeit* (Munich, 1918), was revised in the definitive Munich edition of 1923. The second volume, *Welthistorische Perspektiven*, had been published there the previous year. A good English translation by C. F. Atkinson is available under the title *The Decline of the West* (London, 1932), and there is an abridged edition of this prepared by Helmut Werner and Arthur Helps (New York, 1962).

For an introductory discussion of the background and influence of Spengler's work, as well as a select bibliography, see H. S. Hughes, *Oswald Spengler: A Critical Estimate* (New York, 1952). For further references see Patrick Gardiner, ed., *Theories of History* (Glencoe, Ill., 1959), p. 524. For criticism from the standpoint of both idealist philosophy of history and empirical historiography, see R. G. Collingwood, "Oswald Spengler and the Theory of Historical Cycles," in *Antiquity*, Vol. 1 (1927), 311–325, 435–446.

W. H. DRAY

SPINOZA, BENEDICT (BARUCH) (1632–1677), rationalist metaphysician, is of all philosophers the one whose life has least apparent connection with his work. The objectivity and impersonality of his philosophical style betray a rare concern for truth and clarity, and for nothing else. As a Jew, Spinoza had relatively few ties with his Dutch neighbors; as a Jew expelled from the synagogue for his unorthodoxy (1656), he had few ties with his Jewish neighbors. He had a rabbinical education and then went to a German tutor, Van Den Ende. He lived in Amsterdam, his birthplace, until 1660 and then in Rijnsburg and Voorburg, earning his living by grinding and polishing lenses and discussing philosophical problems with his friends, both in conversation and in correspondence. He published an account of Descartes's philosophy (*Renati Descartes Principiorum Philosophiae, Pars I et II,* Amsterdam, 1663) and the *Tractatus Theologico-politicus* (Amsterdam, 1670), the latter anonymously. He refused the chair of philosophy at Heidelberg in 1673 because he thought it would have cost him his independence and tranquillity. He died of consumption, aggravated by the dust from lens grinding.

Spinoza's manifest determination to think through his own thoughts, in relative isolation from others, accounts both for his independence from external influences apart from purely philosophical ones and for his almost total lack of influence for long after his death. The *Ethics* appeared in a collection of works published immediately after his death, and the *Tractatus de Intellectus Emendatione* was not discovered for publication until the late eighteenth century. Spinoza tried to protest the political assassination of Jan De Witt in 1672, but a friend prevented him—and probably thereby saved his life—by locking him up. Spinoza corresponded with and met Leibniz, who had read the *Tractatus Theologico-politicus*. He also corresponded with Henry Oldenburg and Christian Huygens. If every fact that we now possess about Spinoza's life were lost to us, his writings would be no more difficult to interpret than they are now, for the difficulties are considerable.

Fortunately, on at least one point Spinoza enlightened us: his motives. Like Hobbes, he was aware of the uncertainty that accompanies all worldly pursuits; like Hobbes he saw in such pursuits an endless and unsatisfying search, a perpetual transition from one object of desire to the next; but unlike Hobbes, he did not take it for granted that such a continuous restlessness constitutes the core of the human condition. He tells us in the *Tractatus de Intellectus Emendatione* that he resolved to search for a good that would so fill the mind that all dependence on contingent circumstance and uncertainty would end. He follows Plato and Aristotle in rejecting wealth, reputation, and pleasure as candidates for the role of such a good. He concludes that the supreme good consists in the enjoyment of a human nature which, because it is perfectly aware of its place in and its unity with the whole natural scheme of things, accepts the inevitability and necessity of that natural order. The knowledge requisite to attain such an awareness includes natural science, an understanding of politics, morals, education, and the material and technological bases of social life. "We must in no way despise technology. . . ." Spinoza's philosophy is itself a part of this practical knowledge to be acquired with a view to attaining the supreme good. But since the supreme good is ultimately

defined in terms of the philosophical conclusions reached within Spinoza's system, this is of little interpretative value. It is thus brought home at the outset that the self-enclosed character of Spinoza's thought constitutes the central difficulty in interpreting it. Not that Spinoza was uninfluenced by or was not reacting to either his immediate or his more distant predecessors. Spinoza may be partially expounded as the critic of Descartes, the critic of Hobbes, and even as a dissident follower of Maimonides (see JEWISH PHILOSOPHY); but what his criticisms amount to is clear only from within his own system. Some commentators have evaded this difficulty by separating strands in Spinoza's thought and treating them in isolated fashion, and to some extent a procedure of this kind is inevitable. But insofar as the commentator abstracts, he tends to falsify. How, then, can one think himself inside the system without surrendering the possibility of judging it in terms other than its own? Interestingly and surprisingly, an answer to this question is also contained within Spinoza's system, for his system contains an account of the nature of the "outsider."

Suppose, he said in a letter, that a parasitic worm living in the bloodstream tried to make sense of its surroundings: from the point of view of the worm, each drop of blood would appear as an independent whole and not as a part of a total system. The worm would not recognize that each drop behaves as it does in virtue of the nature of the bloodstream as a whole. But in fact the nature of the blood can be understood only in the context of a larger system in which blood, lymph, and other fluids interact; and this system in turn is a part of a still larger whole. If we men begin with the bodies that surround us in nature and treat them as independent wholes, the relation between which is contingent and given, then we shall be in error precisely as the worm is in error. We must grasp the system as a whole before we can hope to grasp the nature of the part, since the nature of the part is determined by its role in the total system. This epistemological point is found elsewhere in seventeenth-century writers, notably in Pascal. It marks a decisive break with Cartesian mechanistic rationalism (the machine which is the body in the Cartesian system can be thought of as an independent whole and not as a part of a larger system of nature) and with Hobbesian empiricism (the worm is essentially an empiricist). Thus, the image formed by the person who does not grasp the system of nature is like that of the parasitic worm; to have grasped the system of nature is to move not from part to whole but from whole to part. The whole is a single system which has two names, "God" and "Nature." But the point of the two names cannot be grasped until the unity of Spinoza's exposition of the system is understood, and this unity resides in the system's deductive and quasi-geometrical character.

IDEAL OF RATIONAL UNDERSTANDING

Spinoza's use of a deductive geometrical method of exposition is easily misunderstood. It is not just that he shares with Descartes, Hobbes, and Leibniz an interest in geometrical problems and a high regard for the power of geometrical methods, nor is it only a preference for deductive methods in the interests of clarity which leads him to write as he does. Rather, it is that the content of Spinoza's philosophy requires a deductive mode of exposition in the strictest sense of "requires." That is, the criterion of truth and certitude set out in the philosophy is such that unless Spinoza's philosophy were expounded deductively, it could not possess the truth and certitude which he wishes to claim for it. If, in Spinoza's view, a proposition is to be true and certain, its truth and certainty can be exhibited only when that proposition is shown to be part of a total deductive system of such propositions, the truth of each of which depends upon its connection with all the others. Spinoza's deductive system is presented as geometrical because Euclidean geometry provided for him, as for his contemporaries, the paradigm case of an axiomatized system. As with all such systems, the axioms and the primitive terms can be understood only in terms of the propositions which are consequently derived, just as the consequent propositions must be referred back to the axioms and primitive terms. Furthermore, when such a system is an attempt to set forth the total character of the universe, the system takes on a specially self-enclosed character.

Any criticism of any part of such a system is inevitably a criticism of the whole. Spinoza's confidence in his manner of exposition was probably reinforced not only by mathematical parallels but also by the fact that he wrote in the academic Latin of the day, a language whose vocabulary had been purged of ambiguity to an unusually high degree. Those characteristics of academic Latin which ensured that by the seventeenth century no genuine poet could use it lent to those who wrote in it an illusion of quasi-mathematical precision. There is, of course, more than one way to approach Spinoza's philosophy; but the unusually close links between its form and its content suggest that if one begins by setting out the form which, in Spinoza's view, all rational understanding must take, then the way in which form determines content (as well as vice versa) will become clear.

To explain anything is to know its cause. The cause of any being is that which not only brings that being into existence but also makes that being what it is and not another thing. Not only does the cause of a being make that being what it is, it also necessarily produces the effect that it does. There is, therefore, in Spinoza an intimate relationship between essence (what something is) and cause (what makes it what it is). This concept of cause is a scholastic one put to new purposes. The relationship between cause and essence was anticipated in medieval scholastic philosophy in discussions of the divine causality of the real essence of created beings; but since for the Scholastics the causality which mattered was that of finite *contingent* existence, that causality which brings into being one actual, existent world out of all the possibilities open to God, there was not for the Scholastics the intimate and necessary connection between the concept of cause and that of essence which there was for Spinoza.

The properties of any being are divided into those which that being possesses essentially and necessarily and those which it possesses accidentally and contingently. To understand any being, to have genuine knowledge of it, is to know its essential properties. (This is also a radically re-

vised scholastic concept. For the Scholastics the world is a collection of finite, created substances; and according to them, the explanation of the existence of those substances which happen to exist is to be found in the creating will of God. For Spinoza, however, a plurality of substances is ruled out by his concept of rational understanding.) According to Spinoza's ideal of rational understanding, to explain is to show the necessary connection of essential properties with the substance of which they are properties, that is, to show that they *are* essential properties. If a property is contingent and accidental, then it can only be due to the action of some second substance on the first, and we explain the existence of the property by exhibiting it as necessarily connected with the essence of that substance. Thus, an explanation terminates in showing how a substance is the cause of its own essential properties, solely by being the substance that it is. To explain is to exhibit as *causa sui*. But from this it follows that there is and can be only one ultimate explanation, only one cause, only one substance. Suppose there were two substances. The properties which constitute their relationship or lack of it could not be necessary and essential properties of either. Thus, the relationship would be unintelligible; and for Spinoza it is unintelligible that there could be such a relationship. It follows that all rational understanding consists in showing how some feature of the universe necessarily has the role it has as some kind of essential property of the one substance which is *causa omnium rerum* and *causa sui* at one and the same time. Thus, the necessity for the existence of only one total explanation dictates that a true philosophy will consist of one set of necessarily connected propositions, any one of which or any subset of which is justified by exhibiting its place in the deductive order. The same necessity dictates that there can be only one substance in the universe, and that all relations are internal and necessary, none external and contingent. Thus, Spinoza's method of exposition and the content of his metaphysics are inexorably linked.

Spinoza's originality here lies in the way in which he uses Aristotelian and Cartesian notions in combination, criticizing each in the light of the other. From Descartes he accepts the deductive ideal; from Aristotle, the concept of substance and the concept of an essential property. He assumes with Aristotle that all propositions are of subject–predicate form, but, contrary to Aristotle, he believes that in every case to attach a predicate to a subject is to assign a property to a substance. In his Cartesian preoccupation with necessary truth Spinoza neglects the kind of logical investigation that Aristotle undertook in the *De Interpretatione*, in which the analysis of sentences led him to accept contingent statements; and in failing to distinguish the identifying from the describing functions of expressions (also investigated in *De Interpretatione*), he cannot distinguish between a substance incorrectly identified and a substance incorrectly described. Hence, description and identification are totally assimilated; and if anything is really a property, then to ascribe it to its subject will be to utter a necessary truth. But to say—as this might suggest—that Spinoza's monism springs from conceptual confusion is not to say that he made a simple mistake; it is, rather, to point out the consequences of failing to make certain conceptual distinctions, consequences which can be appreciated only when they are developed as fully as Spinoza developed them.

Spinoza's program is a priori in the sense that it sets an ideal of understanding before the intellect; it does not start from any one particular puzzlement or inadequacy. It is this a priori program which impresses upon the intellect a single pattern of understanding and explanation. For Spinoza there are not sciences, there is science; and there are not alternative deductive forms in which understanding can usefully be expressed. There is *one* deductive form in which all understanding *must* be expressed. To interpret Spinoza, therefore, as the ancestor of modern conceptions of science can be dangerously misleading.

"DEUS SIVE NATURA"

The unity of Spinoza's system is not only the product of his deductive ideals; it is also in part the outcome of his theological preoccupations. These preoccupations have been grotesquely underestimated both by those who have wanted to see in Spinoza an anticipation of their own atheism and materialism, and by those who have wanted to condemn Spinozism as atheistic, as did Moses Mendelssohn in the eighteenth century, when he defended his dead friend Lessing against the charge of Spinozism. But such writers as Novalis, Goethe, Coleridge, and Edward Caird, who have stressed the theological content of Spinoza's thought, have been almost as misleading.

It is true that Spinoza follows his native Judaism in affirming the existence and the unity of God. It is true that in a letter to Oldenburg he affirms the identity of his doctrine with that of St. Paul and "I might dare to say with that of all the ancient Hebrews. . . ." It is true that the first book of the *Ethics* is entitled "De Deo." But since "God" is the name of the one substance whose other name is "Nature," the contrast between God and the world, a contrast which is at the heart of both Judaism and Christianity, is obliterated. The one substance can have nothing outside itself to limit it. It is and therefore must be undetermined from outside itself and unbounded; hence, Spinoza calls it infinite. Thus, not only the unity and existence but also the infinity of God are preserved in Spinozism, although all three, it is clear, are given a new sense.

Spinoza has, of course, no need of a proof of the existence of God apart from his proof of the existence of the one substance. But in his demonstration that to perceive the essence of the one substance is to perceive the necessity of its existence, he reproduces a form of the Ontological Argument which Descartes used to prove the existence of God—that the essence of God (or of substance) entails its existence. Moreover, he does not rest his case for the identity of God and nature solely upon the deduction of the necessity of there being only one substance. He produces detailed arguments to show that an infinite and necessary divine being could not exist alongside a finite and contingent nature external to the divine being. If it did, it would then be the case that God was limited and therefore determined by something other than himself. And if God were so limited, he would be finite and unfree. Equally, if God were limited by a purely contingent being, his relationship

to that being could only be contingent, and therefore not all the properties of God would be necessary ones. But all these conclusions are absurd, for a God who is finite or unfree, or of whom any contingent truths are true, *ex hypothesi* could not be God. Thus, there can be nothing which falls outside the divine being and which is not necessitated by it.

It will, perhaps, clarify Spinoza's conception of God if we consider first what he rejects of traditional theology and then that in which he purports to agree with it. On a traditional Jewish view—in a scholastic work such as Moses Maimonides' *Guide of the Perplexed*—the only ground of creation lies in the free and mysterious will of God, and there is no necessity that what has actually been created should have been created; there is simply the divine fiat. On this view, explanation terminates with a brute fact, the fact that God created thus and not otherwise; and for Spinoza there are no ultimate brute facts, let alone this   e. Both his ideal of understanding generally and his conception of the divine lead straight to a rejection of the orthodox doctrine of creation. Nonetheless, Spinoza is prepared to conceive of God as the creator of the world—in a sense which the orthodox Jew or Christian might well take to be Pickwickian—provided God is understood to be the immanent and continuing cause of the world and not its transient first cause. He thus rejects the view, found among many of his contemporaries and notably in Newton's *Scholium*, that God is the first, efficient, external cause of the world's being and motion but that thereafter the world continues according to divinely ordained mechanical laws. The scientist looks and need look only as far as those laws; the theologian looks beyond, to the lawmaker. This deistic compromise allows science and theology their own territories; Spinoza's doctrine of the one substance insists upon a unitary doctrine in which every issue between them must be resolved. At least two questions arise for Spinoza which cannot arise for deism. How is the origin of motion to be accounted for, if not along Newtonian lines? And what attitude is to be taken toward the Biblical accounts of divine creation? Answers to these questions are indeed furnished in Spinoza's writings.

The second orthodox theological doctrine which Spinoza rejects is belief in divine teleology. It is not just that he rejects all forms of the Argument from Design; he rejects the very conception of God's having purposes, designs, or desires for the world. To suppose this is to suppose that God wishes to bring about some state of affairs which does not yet exist; and to suppose this is to suppose that there is something which God at present lacks but which he needs or desires. This is absurd. God *ex hypothesi* can lack nothing. The rejection of this doctrine has further consequences. If God has no purposes, a fortiori he can have no moral purpose for mankind. At once traditional Jewish morality is brought in question, and with it the status of the Scriptures. Spinoza provides answers to these questions in his analysis of religion.

What of orthodoxy does Spinoza accept? He is, as has already been shown, prepared to say of God much of what orthodoxy says—that God is free, infinite, and a necessary being; he is also prepared to say, like some orthodox theologians, that when we ascribe predicates to God, we must do so in quite a different sense from that in which we would ascribe them to anything else. This is partly because "God" is the name of the whole intelligible system of which all finite beings are mere parts; but for Spinoza this also rests partly upon a view that the divine essence can be considered apart from its relation to its attributes: in the *Tractatus Theologico-politicus* he says of the divine names that Jehovah is a name which points to "the absolute essence of God without reference to created things," and *El Shaddai* and the other divine names point to attributes.

Anticipations of Spinoza's type of pantheism can be found in the Jewish mystical traditions. When both Jewish and Christian Scholastics spoke of God's knowledge of his creatures, they found it difficult to hold that his creatures were external objects to God, about whom God could know contingent truths. In answer to this problem a sixteenth-century cabalist, Moses Cordovero, wrote in words which are almost reproduced by Spinoza (*Ethics* II, Prop. VII, *Scholium*): "But the creator is Himself knowledge, the knower and the object known. His knowledge does not arise from His directing His thoughts to things outside of Him, since in comprehending and knowing Himself, He comprehends and knows everything that exists" (*A Garden of Pomegranates*). Thus, Spinoza could and did legitimately claim to be developing one strain in the Jewish theological tradition.

OPPOSITION TO DUALISM

"The mind and the body are one and the same thing. . . ." The unity of the one substance is incompatible with any dualism, and Spinoza's theology therefore attacks the dualism of God and the created world. The second great dualism under attack from Spinoza is that of body and mind. Spinoza has sometimes been presented as primarily continuing and correcting Descartes, but here he is explicitly detaching himself from the Cartesian tradition. It is certainly true that the study of Descartes was seminal for Spinoza, and there are obvious debts both of doctrine and of terminology. Nonetheless, Spinoza's philosophy is in one crucial respect at the opposite pole from that of Descartes. Descartes presents an epistemology from which he derives a metaphysics; Spinoza presents a metaphysics without which his epistemology could scarcely be intelligible. This difference is in the end what determines their difference on the body–mind problem. For Descartes the question "What certain truths can I grasp?" leads to a differentiation between the clear and distinct apprehension which I have of my own existence as a conscious thinking thing and the guarantees which I possess of the existence of extended material substance, guarantees which I possess only because a perfect being—God—would not allow me to be deceived in my sense experience. The status of mind is necessarily quite different from that of body; I am a mind but only have a body. This leads to a deep inability to connect mind and body in the Cartesian tradition. When Malebranche sees mental events and bodily events as two independent series of events which God providentially synchronizes so that my decision to move my hand and the hand's subsequent move-

ment follow from each other just *as if* the one caused the other, he is truer to Descartes's original position than Descartes is in his resort to the pineal gland. The role of God in Descartes's system of thought is essentially that of filling epistemological gaps. (Thus Descartes, the nominally orthodox Catholic, treats God with a great deal less respect than does Spinoza, the explicitly heretical Jew.)

Both the nature of the role assigned to God's mysterious action and the purely contingent character of the explanation involved rule out any such solution for Spinoza. But he does not need a solution of this or any other kind, since according to his premises the problem cannot, so he believes, arise. Spinoza is neither an occasionalist like Malebranche, nor an epiphenomenalist who sees mental events as the effect of bodily causes, nor an interactionist envisaging reciprocal causality between body and mind. Body and mind are not causally related at all; they are identical, because thought and extension are two attributes under which the one substance is conceived. Spinoza's doctrine of substance and attributes is not merely an assertion of the unity of the single substance but an attempt to explain the relationship between that unity and the multiplicity of finite beings.

Substance and attributes. Substance is that which is in itself and is conceived through itself; it can be conceived independently of the conception of anything else. To be conceivable is not to be imaginable, for imagination is very low and unreliable in the grades of experience and knowledge. To be conceivable is to be capable of being thought without contradiction. And since for Spinoza what can exist in itself and what can be conceived by itself are one and the same, to know what can and must be thought is also to know what can and must exist. But substance is not characterless; to grasp its essence is to perceive its attributes. Spinoza defines an attribute as "that which intellect perceives in substance as constituting its essence" (*Ethics* I, Def. IV). Each of the attributes of the one substance is infinite, expresses the eternal and infinite essence of the one substance, and is conceived through itself. Although there can be no plurality of substances, there must be an infinity of attributes, each distinctly conceivable from all the others.

The argument which carries us from the one substance to a plurality of attributes seems little better than a linguistic conjuring trick. Sometimes the attributes are spoken of merely as aspects under which we conceive the one substance; sometimes they are spoken of almost as if they possess an independent reality. The argument here appears to be of the form that because we can think of X as Y and of X as Z, we can therefore think of Y and Z as identical in some sense (but also as different). Clearly, where X is the name of a substance and Y and Z are names of properties, this is false. The fact that two properties are properties of the same thing in no sense makes them identical.

Why is Spinoza deceived by so obvious a fallacy? The answer surely lies in the fact that the premises from which he starts never permit him to formulate clear criteria of identity and difference. Two distinct reasons for this failure to formulate the needed criteria can be detected. One is the metaphysical desire to exhibit everything as the same in respect of its being a manifestation of the one substance. The other is the assimilation of causal and logical relations. To say of one thing that it is the cause of another is, for Spinoza, to point to a relation of entailment. But Spinoza has no clear theory of entailment, of logical necessity, or of analytic truth. These are notions upon which he habitually relies without ever passing beyond formulations which blend Cartesian references to clarity of conception with scholastic phrases of the "in itself" and "through itself" variety. Yet unless a clear meaning can be assigned to the notion of a relation which is both causal and logical, Spinoza cannot hope to identify clearly the terms of this relation. His use of the word "idea" helps him to avoid clarity at this point. Sometimes an "idea" appears to be a proposition, sometimes a concept, and sometimes a concept or proposition as it is entertained in thought.

When we pass from the one substance to its attributes, therefore, there is no way of making the transition intelligible. Indeed, grave difficulties occur. Since the one substance cannot be bounded in any way, it follows that the number of its attributes cannot be bounded. "The more reality or being anything has, the more attributes it possesses" (*Ethics* I, 9). But of the infinite number of infinite attributes, each of which is a necessary expression of the one substance, there are only two which we grasp, thought and extension. Why only two? If everything is a necessary consequence of the nature of the whole, there ought to be available a demonstration of how it is necessarily true that, as Spinoza says (*Ethics* II, Axiom 5), "We feel and perceive no particular things save bodies and modes of thought." It is worth noting that Spinoza originally avoids the need for proof on this point by introducing this proposition as an axiom. But one of his correspondents, Ehrenfried von Tschirnhaus, asked him if it can be proved "that we cannot know any attributes of God other than thought and extension." Spinoza's answer is that in thinking we can grasp no more than the essence of mind and "that the essence of mind is the idea of the body, which idea does not involve or express any of God's attributes except for extension and thought." But this is merely repeating the assertion for which proof has been requested.

Extension. The twin attributes under which we conceive the one substance are, then, to be thought of as different ways of envisaging one and the same reality. All reality can be thought of as a series of *res extensae*, physical bodies ordered in causal series, or equally as a series of ideas ordered in intelligible logical sequences. The two sequences will correspond exactly, not because of any external contingent correspondence between them but because they are the same causal sequence viewed in two different ways. The manner in which we think of extended substance is due to our modes of thinking or, rather, to our modes of imagining, rather than to the nature of extension as it is in itself. For we think of extended substance as divided into separate bodies which occupy a limited area in space and endure for a limited amount of time, but extension itself cannot be thought of as other than enduring always and existing everywhere. We may in our imagining conceive of extended substance as made up of separate bodies. "It is mere folly or insanity to suppose that extended substance is made up of parts or bodies really distinct from each

other" (Ep. 29). And the manner in which we think of thought will depend upon the grade of thinking to which our particular finite mind has attained.

Immediately below the infinite attributes in the metaphysical hierarchy come infinite modes, which are eternal, just as the attributes of which they are the modes of existence are eternal. The infinite and eternal mode of extension Spinoza calls motion-and-rest. And finally on the Spinozistic scale there are modes of extension which are finite. The finite modes, which constitute individual bodies, of the kind of which the universe of ordinary physical objects is made up, are configurations of fundamental particles (*corpora simplicissima*) moving together in different ways.

It is at this point, rather than in his conception of total explanation, that Spinoza anticipates in the most striking way the development of theoretical physics. For Spinoza, motion-and-rest is an eternal mode; he treats movement as ultimate, rest as a special case of movement, and the system of moving bodies as one in which each state of the system must be explained in terms of prior states of the system rather than in terms of the initial activity of a Prime Mover outside the system. Moreover, the explanation of change is in terms of different distributions of motion-and-rest among the ultimate particles, which thus come to resemble points at which energy is concentrated in the system. Thus, they are more like the quanta of modern physics than the atoms of classical physics. The configurations which compose individual physical objects as we know them are part of a hierarchy of such systems in which there is an ascent from the ultimate particles at one end of the scale to that total configuration which is the entire physical universe and which Spinoza presents as a single individual in which all the other entities are parts, under the title "the face of the whole universe" (*facies totius universi*).

It is worth emphasizing not only the kinship of this physical theory to theories which date from the close of the nineteenth century but also the extent to which this part of Spinoza's doctrine is independent of the rest. Some sense can perhaps be made of the metaphysical monism as an ideal of total explanation; and some sense can certainly be made of the physical theory. But how the precise content of the physics derives from the metaphysics not only cannot be understood, but also is unintelligible even in Spinoza's own terms. He says explicitly that finite things cannot follow from any infinite attribute of God but only from such an attribute as it is affected by some finite mode (*Ethics* I, 28), and this line of argument seems to involve him in both asserting and denying that the finite can follow from the infinite. Since, according to Spinoza, everything that is must follow from God and his infinite attributes, if there are finite modes, they also must follow from an infinite cause. If not, how do they come into being? How could there ever be any finite modes to affect the infinite attributes?

Individuals, then, are configurations which maintain themselves in being and possess a drive toward self-preservation (*conatus in suo esse perseverandi*). The hierarchy of individuals is a hierarchy of power; the higher an individual is on the scale, the less it is acted on by external forces and the more its changes come from within itself. No physical event is external to the *facies totius universi*, so that it is necessarily highest on the scale. Moreover, in the hierarchy of individuals, the more an individual is acted upon by others without its *conatus in suo esse perseverandi* being defeated, the higher it is on the scale. In Spinoza there is an equation between being more or less active as a causal agent upon others, being more or less in interaction with others, and being more or less real. The basis of this hierarchy is the more fundamental equation of ultimate reality with ultimate causality. The hierarchy that emerges in the end is the Aristotelian one: the inorganic, the vegetative, the animal, and the human. The human body is more real than animal bodies because it maintains itself in being more effectively and also interacts more with its environment.

Thought. Corresponding to the infinite mode of extension, motion-and-rest, is the infinite and eternal mode of thought, intellect. Just as the infinite mode of extension covers all that is physical, so the infinite mode of intellect covers all that can be thought. There is a hierarchy of ideas, just as there is a hierarchy of bodies, and just as there is a highest-order body, the *facies totius universi,* so there is a highest-order idea, the infinite idea of God. Neither ideas nor bodies belong to the one substance, conceived as the cause of all (*natura naturans*), but to the finite modes of the infinite attributes, which come into existence through the mediation of the infinite modes. The relationship between ideas and bodies can be envisaged from the standpoint of either. Every body has an idea corresponding to it, which is its soul (*anima*). The human body's idea alone is worthy of being called a mind (*mens*). Or, from the standpoint of the idea, every idea has that of which it is an idea (*ideatum*), its body. The human mind is the idea of the human body.

What can this mean? In any ordinary sense of "idea," even in a Cartesian sense, this saying appears largely enigmatic. Surely, we are inclined to say, my mind contains the ideas of many things other than my body. Spinoza's answer is that if I have an adequate idea of something other than my own body, then this idea is not just something in *my* mind, but insofar as my mind apprehends it, my mind becomes more than merely *mine*. It is, rather, the infinite and eternal mode of intellect which is at work.

The whole paradox would not have arisen had Spinoza distinguished logical from psychological statements as we customarily distinguish them. The word "idea" bedevils everything. For Descartes and for Locke in their very different ways an idea is at least something belonging to an individual mind. And this use of "idea" creates for them an epistemological problem: how can we know that there are independent external realities that correspond to our ideas? This is certainly a misleading question which drives Descartes to the Ontological Argument and Locke to something he knows not what; but for Spinoza the question cannot even arise. Ideas and that of which they are ideas do not have to be brought together because they have never been separated. An idea and its *ideatum* are the same thing viewed in two ways. But because Spinoza uses the misleading vocabulary of Descartes and Locke, his avoidance of their question does not save him from

unintelligibility. Instead, this unintelligibility is pushed a stage further back, onto the word "idea" itself. But in order to understand Spinoza's use of this term, we must look to his systematic theory of knowledge.

THEORY OF KNOWLEDGE

In the *Ethics* Spinoza distinguishes three levels at which the mind operates. He gives a Hobbesian or empiricist account of the first, a corrected Cartesian account of the second, and blends his own metaphysics with traditional theology for the third. Thus, for Spinoza the empiricist versus rationalist controversy does not arise, for the two parties to it are describing different phenomena.

Confused ideas. The first level is that of vague or confused experience, where notions are formed by whatever causal associations our bodies enter into. There is a physiological explanation for the formation of such notions. Whatever ideas we form at this level are essentially images (*imaginationes*) rather than thoughts (although Spinoza uses the word *cogitatio* to cover all the contents of the mind) and are essentially passive rather than active. The connections between one image and another are those of mechanical association rather than of any logical connection.

Out of the modification of the body which results from recurrent interaction with other bodies, general ideas are formed. The repetition of similar experiences when similar interactions occur results in the abstraction of a composite image, and this is what constitutes a general idea. Likewise, it is by physiological processes of association that ordinary language is built up, the recurrent association of one image with others resulting in the one coming to be taken as a sign for the others. How far we share general ideas and the meanings of ordinary language depends, therefore, upon how far we share experiences, upon how far our bodies have undergone similar modifications. Ordinary language, reflecting as it does the changes and chances of causal interaction, cannot furnish us with a precise instrument of thought. Moreover, what is founded on sense experience and expressed in ordinary language cannot be genuine knowledge. In so arguing, Spinoza makes use of Hobbes's nominalist account of language and knowledge, but for purposes quite other than those for which Hobbes used it. Spinoza takes this account to be an account not of the rational man's use of language but of ordinary, prerational, confused discourse. In criticizing Hobbes, Spinoza is mainly in the right. Indeed, he is insufficiently radical. A merely naturalistic, causal account of language and belief omits the rule-governed character of language, for a rule of language is not just a record of regular sequences which a majority of language users happen to follow but at once an expression of standards of meaningfulness and a means of generating a wide range of significant utterances for the person who knows how to utter and to follow them. An empiricist, nominalist, Hobbesian account of language can give no account of the logical connections in language and makes meaning dependent on reference, while in fact it is necessary to understand reference in the light of a more general doctrine of meaning; and on a Hobbesian account we cannot explain how we can both understand and utter meaningful assertions about what we have never experienced and perhaps never will experience. But this last consideration, although important for the refutation of Hobbes, is quite alien to Spinoza, whose account of the second level of the mind leaves experience behind altogether.

Adequate ideas. As bodies interact with each other, similarities between the experiences of interaction of different bodies result in the building up of certain universal notions. These notions are the general ideas referred to above and are the work of imagination out of intellect. Nonetheless, such are the interactions of bodies that quite inescapably we build up certain "common notions" which have two characteristics: *all* men share them, and they are adequate ideas of characteristics possessed by *all* bodies. What is universally the case in the mode of extension will universally have its counterpart in the mode of thought. Thus, what is true of all bodies will be impressed upon every mind. What are these ideas, and what does it mean to call them adequate?

Common notions are ideas of characteristics that every individual thing that participates in the mode of extension must necessarily possess. The most elementary spatial and physical properties of bodies are the subject matter of common notions, and upon them is built the whole scheme of scientific knowledge. Euclidean geometry, with its elementary concepts of line and point, is one example of a science which makes use of common notions. To call an idea adequate is to say that it stands in a certain logical relation to other ideas and that we can see the necessity that it should be thus and not otherwise. Moreover, we cannot have an adequate idea without being conscious that the idea is adequate. If we know, we necessarily know that we know. I can never be puzzled as to whether I know; but I can, because I possess not only adequate ideas but also ideas of those ideas, realize that in the light of the criteria which adequate ideas provide, many of my other ideas are found wanting. They lack clarity, they are confused; I cannot perceive any necessary relationship between them and my other ideas. Thus, I can study what I already know and hence derive a method for knowing more, for replacing confusion with clarity and the perception of necessity. The task of correcting the understanding depends, then, upon my original possession of at least one adequate idea to furnish me with a criterion of adequacy, necessity, and truth. But how do I know that this original idea is adequate? For Spinoza this question simply cannot arise because "Truth is the criterion of itself and of the false, as light manifests itself and the dark" and "Truth is its own norm." A true idea is always and necessarily self-evident; to call an idea true is to say that it exhibits the logical necessity of the relationship between the characteristics of that of which it is an idea. Our idea of extension is true insofar as it states what properties any extended thing necessarily possesses.

It follows both from Spinoza's physiological account of the origin of our ideas and from his logical elucidation of the concept of truth that no idea can be wholly false. For if our ideas originate in and reflect the interactions of our bodies, every idea must have to some extent, no matter how confused it may be, its *ideatum*. By *ideatum* Spinoza means that in the mode of extension to which the given idea is the counterpart in the mode of thought. Equally, if the truth of an idea resides in its logical relationships with other ideas, every idea by virtue of being an idea must stand in some such relationships with other ideas, no matter how confusedly. It follows that although ideas may be wholly true, to be false is to be less than true, not to be wholly other than true. Our ideas are in a hierarchy, with the physiologically produced images at the bottom and those ideas which form part of a logically interlocking system in which the necessity of the relationship of every item to every other item is manifest at the top. There can be only one such system, for any system which covered less than everything would leave its relationship to what was outside it unintelligible and unexplained, and therefore it would not be a system of ideas whose every feature was manifestly logically necessary. In other words, the necessity of the single total system of ideas is the same as the necessity for there being one, and only one, substance. Rational inquiry (for Spinoza there can be no ultimate distinction between the natural scientist, the philosopher, and the theologian) will always attempt to approach this ideal, as indeed Spinoza attempts to approach it in the *Ethics*, but there is a very good reason why one can never hope to attain it with any completeness. My ideas can only be the counterparts of those interactions in which my body participates. If I could extend my ideas so that they embraced the entire universe in the mode of thought, it could only be because my body was coextensive with the physical universe. In other words, "I" would be God and "my" body would be nature.

Intuitive ideas. The total system of ideas is the *infinita idea Dei* (infinite idea of God), and only God possesses a totally adequate idea of himself. Insofar as I approach the possession of such an idea, I necessarily approach the condition of God and I necessarily become God to some extent. Hence the aptness of Novalis' tag about Spinoza as "the God-intoxicated man." This third and highest grade of knowledge, which is that of the divine mind, Spinoza calls *scientia intuitiva* (intuitive knowledge).

Spinoza and Descartes. Spinoza's originality is nowhere more apparent than in the difference from Descartes which is apparent in his theory of knowledge. Descartes is a deeply inconsistent thinker in that he declares clarity and distinctness to be the criteria of truth but still seeks a guarantee that his clear and distinct ideas do in fact correspond to what is the case in the realm of physical bodies. The inconsistency resides in the attempt *both* to find a guarantee for the truth of an idea in the idea itself and its relationship with other ideas *and* yet to mean by "truth" roughly a sort of correspondence to an external reality. This inconsistency could be avoided either by abandoning the criteria of clarity and distinctness or by rejecting the dualism of thought and extension. Most empiricist thinkers have chosen to abandon the criteria of clarity and distinctness; Spinoza chose to reject the dualism of thought and extension.

The price which empiricism paid for its choice was to divorce the realm of necessity from that of knowledge and thus to render unintelligible the way in which advances in knowledge could alter our views as to what statements express necessary truths. ("A straight line is the shortest distance between two points" was until recently taken to be a necessary truth; the physics of relativity have shown it to be empirically false.) The price which Spinoza had to pay for his rejection of Cartesian dualism was the assimilation of all truth to necessary truth. By accepting this in the way he does, Spinoza avoids the characteristic difficulties of Cartesianism. As has already been noted, he does not have to build an epistemological bridge between ideas and the physical world and he does not have to invoke God, as Descartes does, in the role of metaphysical bridge builder. Second, he is not involved in the circularity of the *Cogito*. Descartes accepts the *Cogito* because it is clear and distinct, and he accepts the criterion of clarity and distinctness because he finds that these properties appertain to his grasp of the *Cogito*. Third, Descartes's demonstration of how we can come to grasp the truth involves him in the desperate task of explaining how, according to his account, error can be possible. His explanation is that intellectual error is a consequence of the will's mistakenly accepting or rejecting what the intellect presents to it. But this suggests that we can either choose to believe or choose not to believe a given proposition. Spinoza avoids any suggestion of this by an account of truth which allows for error and falsity from the outset. Since error and falsity are a privation of truth, in recognizing what is true, we also gradually come to recognize what is false. Moreover, since the sequence of ideas in my mind is a counterpart of the causal sequence of modifications of my body as it undergoes and initiates changes, there can be no question of real alternative possibilities of acceptance or rejection of an idea that is arising, and therefore no question of choice.

The way in which Spinoza makes this last point has led to a charge of inconsistency, formulated by Stuart Hampshire, as follows. Spinoza's theory of knowledge entails that all mental life is determined. Yet the announced aim of his philosophy is practical, to correct the understanding, and by attaining the crown of the intellectual life, to attain to beatitude. But if it is determined, as a physical sequence is determined, that we should think what and as we do, then how can we hope to change and improve our intellectual life? The inconsistency here is apparent rather than real. Certainly, unless certain conditions are satisfied, I cannot possibly change intellectually—and in the case of most men these conditions are not satisfied. Spinoza is clear on this. But if my mind is determined in a certain way, then it will be determined in such a way that I not only can and do, but also must, improve and correct it. This determination of the mind will accompany a certain determined sequence of modifications of the body. What appears under the aspect of thought as my decision to improve my understanding will appear under the aspect of extension as a set of physiological changes. But in order to elucidate the relationship between the mental and the physiological any further, Spinoza's psychology must be set out more systematically.

PSYCHOLOGY

Spinoza's psychology is parallel to his theory of knowledge, and for a very good reason. Both the ordinary concept of an emotion and the ordinary concept of the will are, according to Spinoza, confused notions. In reality they are only ideas, functioning in various ways and viewed under various aspects. Thus, both Spinoza's theory of knowledge and his psychology are accounts of those elusive entities, ideas. Corresponding to the three stages of confused experience and images, scientific understanding, and *scientia intuitiva* are the stages which constitute human bondage, human freedom, and the intellectual love of God. These are psychological stages in that they are distinguished as different conditions of the mind. Spinoza's basic psychological concept is equally physiological: the human being, like any other being, is a unity inspired by a *conatus in suo esse perseverandi* (a drive toward self-preservation). Modifications of the body impinge upon the mind in the form of confused ideas which we experience differently, depending upon whether or not the individual's power of preserving itself is increased or diminished. If it is maintained or increased, what we experience is pleasure (*laetitia*); if it is decreased, what we experience is pain (*tristitia*). Pleasure is distinguished from mere pleasurable sensation (*titillatio*); and pain is sadness rather than physical pain. Pleasure and pain are thus outcomes of external causes impinging upon the individual *conatus*. Desire is *conatus* consciously directed toward some specific object. Spinoza then explains the individual emotions as involving different combinations of desire, pleasure, and pain, further differentiated by their association with other ideas. But, before discussing Spinoza's view of the emotions further, one precaution must be taken.

There is no single word in Spinoza which means what we mean by "emotion." The words which are liable to be translated by "emotion" are *affectus* and *passio*, but both of these words have a meaning defined by their place in the Spinozan system. An *affectus* is a modification, initially one of the body. A *passio* is something undergone, a modification effected by an external cause, as contrasted with one initiated from within the individual. "Affect, which is called a passion of the soul, is a confused idea by which the mind affirms of its body a power of endurance greater or lesser than before, and by which the mind is determined to think one thing rather than another" (*Ethics* III). The idea is said to be confused because from it we gain no insight into the genuine cause of the affect. Just as our general ideas at the level of confused experience are formed by mechanical association, so also are our desires. By association that which has been customarily linked with pleasure becomes an object of desire, and that which has been customarily linked with pain becomes an object of aversion. When the ordinary, and not philosophically enlightened, man explains his preferences, he gives reasons which have nothing to do with the true causes of his desire or aversion; this is what Spinoza means when he calls the ideas of such a man confused. In regard to the association of one idea with another or with feelings of pleasure, such an agent is completely passive; he regards himself as an agent, but he is merely reflecting the causal interchange between his own *conatus* and external powers. It would be wrong to think of Spinoza as asserting that feelings are merely associated with ideas; for Spinoza feelings *are* ideas. What does he mean? An affect is a modification of the body; every modification of a body has an idea as its counterpart. An inadequate idea and an adequate idea are alike in being counterparts of such a modification, and they do not differ in their relation to action. An idea, although it may be passive in respect of the agent's initiation, is never just a passive image. To have an idea is always to move or to be moved in a certain way. All thinking is action; all movement has its accompaniment in idea. Hence, it is less odd than it would be outside the context of Spinoza's system to assert that an affect is an idea. As it is with feeling and emotion, so it is more obviously with will. "There is in the mind no act of will save that which an idea as idea involves" (*Ethics* II, 49), and, in the same passage, "A particular act of will and a particular idea are one and the same." Spinoza believes that the popular conception of the will as active is a product of the mistake of supposing the intellect to be passive. Men argue mistakenly that since thought cannot move us to action, and we *are* moved to action, something else—the will—must so move us. Spinoza's assertion that ideas are active and move us to act places him against all those who have wanted to mark an ultimate dichotomy between fact-stating and action-guiding discourse.

Spinoza's treatment of particular emotions is often detailed and subtle. He is aware of the possible complexity of the emotions due to a multiplicity of associations and of that intertwining of pleasure and pain which results in such phenomena as ambivalence. Just as Spinoza is a nominalist in his treatment of *experientia saga* in the theory of knowledge, so he is also a nominalist in his treatment of the emotions. These only are particular emotions. "There is in the mind no faculty of understanding as such, or desiring as such, or loving as such." Moreover, one man's experience of emotion need not resemble another's; what constitutes the two emotions the same emotion is their common relationship to pleasure and pain as defined in terms of *conatus*. All emotion, reflecting as it does the striving of the individual to maintain itself in being, as this is reflected in the seeking of pleasure and the avoidance of pain, has reference to the individual self. We are pleased at the happiness of others because we, by having regard to and for the happiness of others, increase our own powers. We wish other men to be rational because there is a general advantage in men's being rational. This at first sight resembles a Hobbesian egoism, but Spinoza's account of motivation at the level of the passions differs from a Hobbesian egoism in two striking ways. To maintain myself in being is to maintain in being what is part of the eternal order of things. "The power whereby each individual thing and therefore man maintains his being is the power of God or nature" (*Ethics* IV, 4). Moreover, the necessity of the self-maintaining character of the individual follows from the axioms of the system; it is not just contingently true that men regard their own self-interest. This is in a way true also of Hobbes, but the detail of the Hobbesian theory of human nature is independent of Hobbes's physical theorizing in a way which is not true of Spinoza's system.

Similarity to Freud. The derivation of the psychology from the metaphysical axioms makes it as dangerous to compare Spinoza with Freud as it is to compare him with modern theoretical physicists. But the resemblance is nonetheless not an illusory one. The Spinozan *conatus* is one ancestor of the Freudian *libido;* and the Spinozan thesis of confused ideas which men cite as reasons for what they seek and avoid, items which in fact are not the causes which move them, is the ancestor of the Freudian thesis of rationalization. Spinoza and Freud were both interested in the plasticity of the emotions. Spinoza also anticipated Freud in the view that to become aware of the causes which move us is no longer to fall victim to them; but whereas Freud regarded his assertions as empirical and contingent, derived from and confirmed by observation, for Spinoza the parallel assertions are a priori truths. Nonetheless, the comparison of Freud and Spinoza suggests that one way of regarding rationalist metaphysical systems may be as deductive frameworks from which possible scientific theories can be derived. The vindication of a given metaphysical system would then lie in its providing us with concepts by means of which we may frame theories and explanations. A system such as that of Spinoza, with implications for both psychology and physics, compatible with empirical findings in these fields, and suggestive of possible new observations and inquiries, would rank higher than a system which was either barren of such consequences or whose consequences were incompatible with the empirical findings.

Human bondage and freedom. If human bondage consists in being moved by causes of which we are unaware because our ideas are confused, the transition to freedom is made solely by our ideas becoming adequate. When our ideas are adequate, we are no longer moved by something external to us; what initiates our movement is within us, and by definition we are free. The view that we become free by understanding the causes of our actions requires elucidation in two ways. First, Spinoza is not involved in denying the occurrence of the familiar experience of being able to identify the emotions which move one but of still being subject to them. To understand the cause of our actions is not to identify an emotion in common-sense fashion, for such an emotion is a confused idea. It is to replace the confused idea with an adequate idea. Hence, we no longer have the same emotion. To have adequate ideas is, moreover, to grasp and to be guided by "the law of one's own nature." "An emotion which is a passion ceases to be a passion as soon as we form a clear and distinct idea of it" (*Ethics* V, 3).

We are delivered from the bondage of passion by understanding because "The mind has greater power over the passions, and is less subject to them, in so far as it understands all things as necessary." We see the true causes of things being as they are and cannot then want them otherwise. It is not that we cease to have the desires which we formerly had. "For all desires by which we are determined to any action may arise as well from adequate as from inadequate ideas" (*Ethics* V, 4, *Scholium*). But these desires now are aimed at a goal which is common to all men and which is constant for each man. Consequently, one is rescued both from struggle with others and from the condition in which "we are in many ways driven about by external causes, and like the waves of the sea driven by contending winds, we are swayed hither and thither, unconscious of the issue and our destiny."

It is crucial for Spinoza that rational understanding is not merely a means to something else. It is at once means and end. The goals which understanding reveals are the goals of freedom and rationality, and these are one and the same. This freedom, which consists in knowing the causes which move one, and thus making the causes internal and not external to the agent, is of course not only compatible with but also requires complete determinism. Belief in free decision is among the illusions, the confused ideas, which the free man has discarded. From this there follow large consequences for the understanding of moral predicates.

MORALITY, RELIGION, POLITICAL PHILOSOPHY

According to Spinoza, the elements of the ordinary man's conventional moral code are a belief in free will, a use of praise and blame depending on this belief, and a use of such predicates as "good" and "evil" in the belief that they denote characteristics of that to which they are ascribed. In fact, Spinoza thinks, men call good whatever gives them pleasure, and evil whatever gives them pain, and these predicates express characteristics of those who use them and not of the objects about which they are used. But in fact all conventional use of moral predicates is out of place, for such a use presupposes that things could be other than they are, that men could have failed where they have succeeded and succeeded where they have failed, and that the world could be improved. To suppose this is to fail to see that everything occurs necessarily; it is to imply a contingency in the universe which the free man knows to be an inadequate idea. The *conatus suo esse perseverandi* is the foundation of virtue, in the true sense of that word, for "by virtue and power I understand the same thing" (*Ethics* IV, Def. 8). There is a link between the ordinary conventional use of moral predicates and what the free man knows, for the ordinary use of "good" and "evil" which refers to pleasure and pain refers to the effects of the *conatus*, before we are conscious of the true nature of pleasure, pain, and desire. After we become conscious of it, we equally seek to maintain the power of our being; but we now know what that power truly consists in, namely, knowledge. The virtuous life, the life of knowledge, can be described in terms both of attitudes and emotions and of goals.

There is no pain in the life of the free man, a fact which follows logically from the definitions of pain and of freedom. For when we are free, we are moved only by causes internal to our being; and pain is caused by the impinging upon us of external causes which decrease our power and vitality. Consequently, freedom and pain are incompatible. As we free ourselves from the impact of the external, as our ideas become adequate, so our ideas become part of the infinite idea of God; and even then, although they cease to be only the ideas of a particular body, the fundamental relationship between thought and extension is still preserved. For the essence of body is also imperishable and eternal (*Ethics* V, 22 and 23). In becoming God, the mind loses all distinction of subject and object: "the love of God to man and the intellectual love of man to God are one and the same."

In reaching this point, Spinoza's philosophy reaches its final goal. It has specified a good, the intellectual love of God, with which the mind can be filled and thus be impervious to change and circumstance. The distinction between true and illusory goods has been finally made.

Views on religion. It is clear that Spinoza's conception of the religious life is at odds with that of all traditional religion, particularly with the Judaism which excommunicated him. In Spinoza's own view, however, there can be no clash between philosophy and revelation. The Old Testament is to be interpreted in two ways: as allegories of intellectual truth, and as fitted for the social, moral, and intellectual needs of a primitive people. The Hebrew prophets could not have spoken other than as they did; the philosophically enlightened man cannot accept what they said, if he is asked to treat it as a literal truth. But the unenlightened modern man needs allegory, anthropomorphism, threat, bribes, and promises to keep him law-abiding and to support him emotionally, just as much as the audience of the prophets did. It would be wrong, therefore, to try to deprive him of it. Spinoza's great emphasis is not upon skepticism about popular religion but upon the need to preserve freedom of inquiry for those who wish it.

Political philosophy. In Spinoza's political philosophy too the necessity of freedom is central. As in every other part of his philosophy he uses Hobbes in an attempt to go beyond him. He accepts as completely as Hobbes does the fact that politics is entirely a matter of power. He also accepts a Hobbesian version of the social contract in which we hand over power to a sovereign in return for a restraint upon the anarchy which threatens all possibility of peace and survival. It is not surprising that he accepts the Hobbesian equation of "have a right to" with "have the power to," for this is consistent with his own critique of conventional morality. But we can see the beginnings of the breach with Hobbes when we consider that, although both held that when a contract is no longer to our advantage, we are therefore under no obligation to keep it ("to be under obligation" means "to find advantages in"), the Spinozan and Hobbesian conceptions of advantage are at opposite extremes. For Hobbes, advantage lies in satisfying as many of one's desires as possible without being preyed upon by others. For Spinoza, advantage lies in escaping from the bondage of just those desires which Hobbesian man aspires to satisfy. Consequently, Spinoza wishes to see a state in which civil peace secures above all freedom for diverse opinions, provided only that these do not lead to seditious acts. The imposition of irrational beliefs upon unwilling subjects, so he argues, produces precisely the civil strife which men wish to avoid. This is quite unlike Hobbes, who sees opinion as a source of contention and who thinks that we hand over to the sovereign and to his magistrates the right to set standards for the expression of opinions and even for the meaning of words.

This difference is rooted in the contrast between Hobbes's view that reason is merely a means to the ends set by the desires and Spinoza's that the desires must be transformed by the ends which rational inquiry sets for rational men. It is, therefore, not surprising that while Hobbes sees security in monarchy, Spinoza, after comparing different types of constitutions, concludes that the best type is a democracy in which the owners of property rule. Here there is an interesting coincidence between systems and environment. For if Hobbes's system points toward monarchy, so did his social experience of the English Civil War. Spinoza's ideal is clearly not merely a product of abstract reasoning but also of the tolerance of Amsterdam and its mercantile bourgeois democracy.

For a century after his death Spinoza's thought was substantially ignored. From the time of Goethe, and as a result of the influence of Goethe and of Schelling, he has been continually reinterpreted. The two most prevalent interpretations of Spinoza are equally enthusiastic and equally incorrect. For Goethe and Coleridge, Spinoza was a pantheist and mystic; for G. V. Plekhanov, Spinoza was a monistic materialist. The one tradition underlines *Deus,* the other *Natura;* both miss the essential Spinozan point which lies in the *sive* (the equation). Equally, idealist commentators, such as Edward Caird and H. H. Joachim, or an analytical philosopher like Stuart Hampshire, are apt to import into Spinoza interests which were not his. The corrective to these interpretations lies in stressing Spinoza's attempt to achieve complete deductive unity in the metaphysics. From the axioms and definitions to the final consequences, the system stands or falls as a whole. If this is not the right way to do philosophy, we can understand why this is so only by a study of the system as a whole. What Spinoza has left us is, because it is the most complete and hard-headed exposition of rationalist metaphysics, the best evidence we have of its impossibility. (See also SPINOZISM.)

Works by Spinoza

Spinoza Opera, C. Gebhardt, ed., 4 vols. Heidelberg, 1924.

TRANSLATIONS

The Chief Works of Spinoza, translated by R. H. M. Elwes, 2 vols. London, 1883; New York, 1955 and 1956.
The Principles of Descartes' Philosophy, translated by H. H. Briton. Chicago, 1905.
Short Treatise on God, Man and His Well-being, translated by A. Wolf. London, 1910.
Ethics, translated by W. H. White and A. H. Stirling. Oxford, 1927.
Correspondence of Spinoza, translated by A. Wolf. London, 1928.
The Political Works, edited and translated by A. G. Wernham. Oxford, 1958.

Works on Spinoza

Caird, Edward, *Spinoza.* Edinburgh and London, 1902.
Hallett, H. F., *Benedict de Spinoza, The Elements of His Philosophy.* London, 1957.
Hampshire, Stuart, *Spinoza.* Harmondsworth, 1951; London, 1956.
Joachim, H. H., *A Study of Spinoza's Ethics.* Oxford, 1901.
Joachim, H. H., *Commentary on Spinoza's Tractatus de Intellectus Emendatione.* Oxford, 1940.
Oko, Adolph S., *The Spinoza Bibliography.* Boston, 1964.
Parkinson, G. H. R., *Spinoza's Theory of Knowledge.* Oxford, 1954.
Pollock, F., *Spinoza: His Life and Philosophy.* London, 1880.
Roth, Leon, *Spinoza, Descartes and Maimonides.* Oxford, 1924.
Roth, Leon, *Spinoza.* London, 1954.
Saw, R. L., *The Vindication of Metaphysics: A Study in the Philosophy of Spinoza.* New York, 1951.

Strauss, L., *Die Religionskritik Spinoza als Grundlage seiner Bibelwissenschaft.* Berlin, 1930.
Wolfson, H. A., *The Philosophy of Spinoza,* 2 vols. Cambridge, Mass., 1954; New York, 1958.

ALASDAIR MACINTYRE

SPINOZISM. The term "Spinozism" has almost invariably been used, by both defenders and detractors, to refer to doctrines held or allegedly held by Spinoza. Unlike "Platonism," for example, it has not generally been used to refer to a developing doctrine arising out of Spinoza's philosophy. In the seventeenth and eighteenth centuries the term was frequently used to disparage various types of atheistic doctrines that were held to be attributable to Spinoza. For almost a century after his death, his work was neglected by philosophers, execrated by orthodox theologians of diverse denominations, and slighted even by freethinkers. It is not always possible, however, to distinguish between those genuinely opposed to Spinoza's alleged atheism and those who really espoused atheism while pretending to disparage it.

Bayle and the "philosophes." Spinoza's early reputation rested almost entirely on the long article in Bayle's *Dictionnaire philosophique* (1697), for some time the only readily accessible account of Spinoza's system. Bayle, like many others, admired Spinoza's life but abhorred his doctrine. In Spinoza he saw an application of his own thesis that atheism may coexist with the highest moral excellence. All agree, he wrote, that Spinoza was a "sociable, affable, friendly, and thoroughly good man. This may be strange, but no stranger than to see a man lead an evil life even though he is fully persuaded of the truth of the Gospel." But Bayle described Spinoza's philosophy as "the most absurd and monstrous hypothesis that can be envisaged, contrary to the most evident notions of our mind." Bayle's antagonism to Spinoza's philosophy arose primarily from his dissatisfaction with monism as a solution to the problem of evil. That such an extreme evil as war could exist among men who are but modes of one and the same infinite, eternal, and self-sufficient substance seemed particularly outrageous to him.

Voltaire, like Bayle, expressed esteem for Spinoza's life but had misgivings about his philosophy, although he did accord a measure of praise to the *Tractatus Theologico-politicus.* Voltaire's understanding of Spinoza's *Ethics,* however, may be questionable, for he quoted from the inaccurate, popularized version by the count de Boulainvilliers, published under the title *Réfutation de Spinoza* (Brussels, 1731). According to Voltaire, Spinoza's system was built on complete ignorance of physics and was the most monstrous abuse of metaphysics. In regarding the universe as a single substance Spinoza was, as he put it in his *Le Philosophe ignorant* (Geneva, 1766), "the dupe of his geometrical spirit."

Diderot, in the *Encyclopédie,* also closely followed Bayle's article in his criticism of Spinoza's philosophy, yet his own views unmistakably reveal Spinozist elements in denying the existence of a being outside, or separate from, the material universe. "There is," he wrote in *Entretiens entre d'Alembert et Diderot,* "no more than one substance in the universe, in man or in animal." Diderot's monism was not quite the same as Spinoza's metaphysical monism, for it was more pragmatic in nature. His "one substance" was merely material substance, not substance in Spinoza's sense of "that which is in itself, and conceived through itself . . . (and) of which a conception can be formed independently of any other conception (*Ethics*, Part I, Definition 3). The universe, for Diderot, was monistic in its material unity. Nonetheless, Spinoza's metaphysical monism could be considered as the logical basis for Diderot's materialist monism.

Germany. While Voltaire's and the Encyclopedists' interpretation of Spinoza was gaining currency in France, attempts were being made in Germany to reappraise his philosophy. This re-examination was an integral part of the German Enlightenment which, while sharing with its French and English counterparts the affirmation of the individual's right to question established truths, also sought to link this affirmation with religious faith rather than with skeptical disbelief. In the course of this quest Spinoza's image underwent a distinct change. From Hume's ironically labeled "universally infamous" atheist, Spinoza became Novalis' *gottbetrunkener Mensch*. A number of leading German thinkers came increasingly to see in Spinoza's pantheism a profoundly religious conception and interpretation of the cosmos.

To some extent, the reversal in Spinoza's fortunes was also a corollary of the developments in science. Few of Spinoza's contemporaries who accepted the new scientific theories realized their theological implications. The intellectual reorientation in eighteenth-century Germany, on the other hand, was accompanied by a corresponding change in theological thinking. In the light of these changes Spinoza's philosophy appeared much less inimical to the essential truths of religion.

"Pantheismusstreit." Probably the strongest factor contributing toward the revival of interest in Spinoza's thought was the controversy that raged over Gotthold Lessing's alleged Spinozism. This dispute, sparked by the disagreement between Moses Mendelssohn and F. H. Jacobi, came to involve almost every notable figure in the German literary world. Jacobi, in his account of a conversation with Lessing, claimed that the latter had been a Spinozist. According to this account Lessing said that the orthodox conceptions of deity were no longer satisfactory for him and that, if he were to call himself after any master, he knew of no other than Spinoza. Although Jacobi conceded that Spinoza's philosophy was logically unanswerable, he found it unacceptable on religious grounds; in religion, he felt, he had to take refuge in an act of faith, a "salto mortale" as he called it. Lessing sardonically replied that he was unable to trust his old limbs and heavy head for such a leap.

It should not, however, be inferred that Lessing's philosophical outlook was in every detail or even in essentials merely a reflection of Spinozist ideas. Lessing was far too independent a thinker to be subject to any single pervasive influence. He was also far less metaphysically oriented than Spinoza, and his faith in man's perfectibility was tempered by a shrewder realization of man's limitations than that of his world-shunning precursor. Nor must it be assumed that Lessing's exchanges with Jacobi can be taken at their face value. Lessing was fully aware of Jacobi's misconceptions in his approach to Spinoza and hardly took him seriously. He may have been speaking with tongue in cheek, and it would therefore be unwise to attach too great an importance to the views he espoused.

Lessing did succeed in eliciting Jacobi's admission that Spinoza's philosophy was the most rigorous and consistent intellectual enterprise ever attempted and in inducing him to study it more deeply. Although Jacobi's further studies did little to alter his conviction that Spinoza was an atheist and that final truths were to be found in the philosophy of the heart rather than in that of the understanding, they nonetheless helped to focus attention on Spinoza to an unprecedented degree. Two men in particular, Herder and Goethe, who were both on intimate terms with Jacobi, were the most directly affected. Herder openly called himself a Spinozist, although his ontology and cosmology had much more in common with Shaftesbury's and Leibniz' than with Spinoza's. Yet he insisted that by substituting his concept of *Kraft* for Spinoza's substance he was not fundamentally departing from Spinozist premises. Herder clearly did not realize how very different were his metaphysical presuppositions in postulating an ever-changing *Kraft* in place of Spinoza's unchanging substance and hence how profoundly at variance was his brand of monism with that of his great precursor, despite superficial similarities. Goethe, too, in his autobiography and in his correspondence with Jacobi, acknowledged a far greater debt to Spinoza than he really owed. In Book XIV of his *Dichtung und Wahrheit* he paid his eloquent tribute to Spinoza's influence:

> After I had looked around the whole world in vain for a means of developing my strange nature, I finally hit upon the *Ethics* of this man . . . . Here I found the serenity to calm my passions; a wide and free view over the material and moral world seemed to open before me. Above all, I was fascinated by the boundless disinterestedness that emanated from him. That wonderful sentence "he who truly loves God must not desire God to love him in return" with all the propositions on which it rests, with all the consequences that spring from it, filled my whole subsequent thought.

Yet Goethe's pantheism had far greater affinity with Herder's—and thus with Shaftesbury's and Leibniz'—than with Spinoza's. Like Herder's confessed Spinozism, Goethe's was much more the result of a poetical imagination and of an emotional craving than of logical analysis and philosophical understanding. Indeed, although Hegel regarded Spinoza's philosophy as philosophy par excellence and although Fichte and Schelling took it as their starting points, the general nature of the Spinozist revival in Germany was literary rather than philosophical.

England. Much the same was true of the Spinozist renaissance in England and to a lesser extent in France during the nineteenth century. Admittedly, deism in England had already displayed marked Spinozist characteristics, even if one cannot agree with Leslie Stephen that the "whole essence of the deist position may be found in Spinoza's *Tractatus*." Few deists were consciously aware of the Spinozist heritage, and it was not until German thought had begun to make itself felt in the English literary world that Spinozism acquired significance as a subject of intellectual discourse.

Samuel Taylor Coleridge was undoubtedly the chief link in this transmission. To judge from Henry Crabb Robinson's account, Coleridge, when receiving from him Spinoza's *Ethics,* kissed Spinoza's face on the title page, said the book was his gospel, but—almost in the same breath—proclaimed his philosophy false and hence incapable of affecting in the slightest his faith "in all the doctrines of Christianity, even of the Trinity." The ambivalence in Coleridge's attitude toward Spinoza, whom he praised as the "Hercules' pillar of human reason" and simultaneously assailed for his moral and religious views, followed a pattern characteristic of many Spinozists before him, most notably Jacobi. Like Jacobi, Coleridge paid tribute to the rigor of Spinoza's logic and commended his works as "medicinal" reading, while deploring their inadequacy as a philosophical basis of religious belief. Spinoza's *unica substantia,* Coleridge maintained, was not an object at all but a mere notion, a subject, of the mind. Spinoza committed the "most grievous error" of seeing God "in his *Might* alone . . . and not likewise in his moral, intellectual, existential and personal Godhead." In the *Biographia Literaria* Coleridge related that he had talked much to Wordsworth about Spinoza, which would help to account for the undeniably Spinozist elements in Wordsworth's poetry. But like Coleridge and other English writers of this period, Wordsworth added nothing new to the conception of Spinozism.

Nineteenth-century France. The reception of Spinoza in nineteenth-century France also witnessed no startling reinterpretations except that, as in Germany, the charge of atheism appeared to many to be quite unfounded. Like Lessing, Herder, and Goethe, Victor Cousin and his followers decisively dismissed the accusations to which Spinoza's *Ethics* had been subjected by orthodox Christians. Nonetheless, Théodore Jouffroy and Émile Saisset, both disciples of Cousin, had serious misgivings about Spinoza's pantheism, for it seemed to absorb the individual in too determinate a manner in the cosmic forces of the whole and thus to threaten the very possibility of human freedom. Paul Janet echoed these misgivings and declared that "the genius of Spinoza was therefore not well adapted to the French mind." But Jouffroy's detailed attention in his lectures at the Sorbonne to Spinoza's thought, and Saisset's publication of a French translation of Spinoza's works, helped to create an intellectual climate in which Spinoza's philosophy could no longer be ignored or lightly dismissed. Thenceforth very many French writers of note, from Edgar Quinet, Lamartine, and Jules Michelet to Georges Sand, Renan, and the Saint-Simonians felt impelled to grapple with Spinozist ideas.

Russia. The spread and proliferation of interest in Spinozism could not help making its imprint on Russia, a country whose thinkers had for some time been increasingly fascinated by Western philosophical thought. Even more remarkable is the extent to which Russia maintained its preoccupation with Spinoza despite—or perhaps because of—the Bolshevik Revolution. No other pre-Marxian philosopher, with the possible exception of Hegel, has received as much attention in the Soviet Union. From 1917 to 1938, 55,200 copies of Spinoza's works were published in the Soviet Union, compared to 8,000 in the period from 1897 to 1916. Prerevolutionary literature on Spinoza had for the most part been critical and negative, but what non-Marxists considered Spinoza's chief philosophical defects later appeared to many Soviet writers as his strong points. Spinoza's political doctrines particularly appealed to the Marxists. Georgi Plekhanov came to see in Spinozism, when freed from its theological wrappings, a historical forebear of dialectical materialism, and he spoke of Marxism as a "variety of Spinozism." Following Marx and Engels, many Soviet writers credited Spinoza with having correctly solved the fundamental ontological problem concerning the relation of consciousness to being, and of thought to things. Indeed, admiration for Spinoza prompted some to call him "Marx without a beard." Spinoza's rejection of an act of creation, his denial of a continuing intervention in the governance of the world by a supernatural being, his acceptance of nature as something ultimate, self-caused, and "given," without limits of time or space, were all features not lost upon dialectical materialists. No less congenial was the determinism and naturalism of Spinoza's ethical and social philosophy which, while insisting on the possibility of arriving at objective and absolute truth, had analyzed the moral concepts of good and evil in terms of human desire and judgment. Finally, and most important, the allegedly passive role of thought in Spinoza's system, which several prerevolutionary writers had critically commented upon, was regarded in the Soviet Union as the most convincing proof of Spinoza's profound understanding of the historical process. Even if it is conceded that the Marxists revealed as many differences of emphasis in their positive appraisal of Spinoza's thought as did the non-Marxists in their negative approaches, the essentials of Spinoza's doctrines substantially engaged Russian philosophical thinking since the nineteenth century.

Spinozism, then, embodies no single consistent school of thought. Many who professed to admire and accept Spinoza's philosophical premises were as apt to misunderstand and misinterpret them as those who despised them. Yet despite the diversity of meaning that the term underwent in different intellectual contexts and periods, its catalytic significance cannot be gainsaid.

Bibliography

Bayle, Pierre, *Dictionnaire historique et critique,* 2d ed. Rotterdam, 1702.

Coleridge, Samuel Taylor, *Biographia Literaria.* London, 1817.

Colie, R. L., "Spinoza and the Early English Deists." *Journal of the History of Ideas,* Vol. 20 (1959), 23–46.

Diderot, Denis, *Oeuvres complètes,* J. Assezat and M. Tourneux, eds. Paris, 1875–1877. Vol. II.

Dilthey, Wilhelm, "Aus der Zeit der Spinoza-Studien Goethes." *Archiv für Geschichte der Philosophie,* Vol. 7 (1894), 317–341.

Goethe, Johann Wolfgang von, *Aus meinem Leben: Dichtung und Wahrheit,* 4 vols. Tübingen and Stuttgart, 1811–1833.

Herder, Johann Gottfried von, *Gott, einige Gespräche.* Gotha, 1787. Translated with an introduction by F. H. Burkhardt as *God, Some Conversations.* New York, 1940.

Jacobi, Friedrich Heinrich, *Ueber die Lehre des Spinoza.* Breslau, 1785.

Jakobi, Max, ed., *Briefwechsel zwischen Goethe und F. H. Jakobi.* Leipzig, 1846.

Janet, Paul, "Spinoza et le Spinozisme." *Revue des deux mondes,* Vol. 70 (1867), 470–498.

Janet, Paul, "Le Spinozisme en France." *Revue philosophique,* Vol. 13 (1882), 109–132.

Kline, G. L., *Spinoza in Soviet Philosophy.* London, 1952.

Lévy-Bruhl, Lucien, "Jacobi et le Spinozisme." *Revue philosophique,* Vol. 27 (1894), 46–72.

Metzger, Lore, ed., "Coleridge's Vindication of Spinoza: An Unpublished Note." *Journal of the History of Ideas,* Vol. 21 (1960), 279–293.

Morley, Edith J., ed., *Henry Crabb Robinson on Books and Their Writers,* 2 vols. London, 1938. These volumes contain the references to contemporary English books and their writers in Crabb Robinson's diary, travel journals, and reminiscences.

Rehorn, Karl, *G. E. Lessings Stellung zur Philosophie des Spinoza.* Frankfurt, 1877.

Stephen, Leslie, *History of English Thought in the Eighteenth Century.* London, 1876. Ch. 1, Par. 33.

Suphan, Bernhard, *Goethe und Spinoza, 1783–86.* Berlin, 1882.

Voltaire, *Le Philosophe ignorant.* Geneva, 1766. Cited from Voltaire, *Mélanges.* Paris, 1961.

FREDERICK M. BARNARD

SPIR, AFRIKAN ALEXANDROVICH

SPIR, AFRIKAN ALEXANDROVICH (1837–1890), Russian metaphysician. Born in Yelizavetgrad (Kirovograd) in the Ukraine, the son of a Russian doctor and a mother of Greek descent, Spir became interested in philosophy when, at the age of 16, he read Kant's *Critique of Pure Reason,* a work which was to have a profound influence on him. He received no formal education in philosophy, however, and consequently never gained entry into philosophical circles, either in his native country or in Germany, where he settled in 1867. Spir attended a naval cadet school. He received both the Order of St. George and the Order of St. Andrew for his services as a naval officer. Before leaving Russia, he freed all his serfs and gave them land and lodging. He also gave away most of his money and lived on the income from the remainder. In 1869 Spir wrote that only two human activities have real worth—socially useful work and intimate discourse among people who think alike, yet in his lifetime Spir was denied both of these; indeed, few philosophers have been so isolated or ignored.

During the 15 years Spir lived in Germany he published many articles and several books, including his major philosophical work, *Denken und Wirklichkeit* ("Thought and Reality"; Leipzig, 1873), but notices and reviews were few. Bad health cut him off even further from the world. Hoping for a more receptive audience among French-speaking readers, Spir moved to Switzerland in 1882, but his work remained unknown and his views not understood. He died in Geneva, a Swiss citizen, just as his writing was beginning to attract attention.

Spir's later writings are on the whole restatements and clarifications of the metaphysical views presented in *Denken und Wirklichkeit,* which he felt might have been neglected because of its difficulty. In *Denken und Wirklichkeit* Spir argued that the task of philosophy is to seek absolutely true knowledge. In order to carry out this task, two immediately certain facts must be recognized: consciousness and the supreme law of thought, the principle of identity. This principle is the expression of a norm, of the a priori concept of the unconditioned, that is, of an object which is its own essence and is self-identical. To deny this concept is to deny that it can be conceived and, hence, that it can be denied. The principle of identity is seen to be the one synthetic a priori principle.

To the subjective necessity of this norm is added an objective proof: All our experience disagrees with it and, therefore, it cannot be a mere generalization from experience. Finally, the principle of identity adds something to experience: All phenomena are organized as if they were self-identical; therefore the principle of identity is the condition of all the regularity of experience.

The unconditioned is, then, the norm, true essence, or God. The unconditioned, however, is not the source or ground of the conditioned: The norm cannot be the source of the abnormal, which contains elements of falsity foreign to the absolute. The relation of the absolute to the phenomenal can best be described analogously, as the relation of an object to its false idea. Having no relation to true being, the phenomenal world simply cannot be explained, its principle can only be thought of as its very abnormality, as its nonself-identity, as becoming. Hence the phenomenal world has no beginning and no end. On the other hand, since it is conditioned by becoming, it strives for and evolves to what it is not, the normal. In man, empirical nature has evolved to consciousness, to the awareness of its abnormality. In this awareness man recognizes a norm. Thus he rises above empirical nature and sees the law of his true being as the law not of nature but of the norm, as the laws of morality and logic. Thus morality rises above natural science and, since the moral law is the norm, morality becomes religion.

Works by Spir

Gesammelte Werke von A. Spir, 2 vols., 4th ed. Leipzig, 1908–1909.

Recht und Unrecht. Leipzig, 1879. Translated into English by A. F. Falconer as *Right and Wrong.* Edinburgh, 1964.

Works on Spir

Jodl, Friedrich, "African Spir." *Zeitschrift für Philosophie,* Vol. 98 (1891).

Lapshin, I. I., "A. Spir, sa vie, sa doctrine." *Bulletin de l'Association russe pour les recherches scientifiques à Prague,* Vol. 7, No. 42 (1938).

Lessing, Theodor, *African Spirs Erkenntnislehre.* Erlangen, 1899. Dissertation.

Zacharoff, Andreas, *Spirs theoretische Philosophie.* Jena, 1910. Dissertation.

MARY-BARBARA ZELDIN

SPIRITO, UGO

SPIRITO, UGO, Italian idealist philosopher, was born in 1896 at Arezzo. He began his academic career as assistant to Giovanni Gentile at Rome and first established his reputation as an acute interpreter and trenchant defender of "actual idealism." He was also one of the founders of "corporative" economic studies in fascist Italy and has always maintained an active interest in economics and in political and social science.

Spirito held that Gentile's "pure act" was not merely a philosophical concept but was also necessarily a concept of philosophy itself as an activity. This belief led Spirito in

1929 to proclaim the identity of philosophy and science, because all actual knowledge must be the solution of a determinate historical problem and neither philosophy nor science as they occur in actual experience can claim an absolute status independent of the history of their genesis and of the progress of further research. According to Spirito, the actual unity of philosophy and science is what is realized in the process of scientific research; his claim that the "pure act" is the conscious achievement of this unity led to the conception of life as research, set forth in his best known book *La vita come ricerca*. In this work the absolute philosophical knowledge of traditional metaphysics was presented as the ideal limit toward which scientific research must forever tend but which it can never attain.

In later works, Spirito was led to an ever more strictly negative or critical conception of the task of philosophy because of the difficulty of defining this ideal goal and the paradox involved in discussing it without knowledge of it (which could only come from the secure possession of an eternal standpoint). The philosopher must confine himself to the task of identifying and exposing all claims to absolute knowledge and all forms of antihistorical dogmatism or superhistorical metaphysics wherever they occur. Such claims will otherwise impede the free advance of positive research, which includes all types of inquiry leading to the acquisition of knowledge, whether theoretical or practical. In aesthetics, for example, the philosopher must concentrate on removing prejudices created by definitions and philosophies of art; he must leave to artists, critics, and competent students the construction of the positive science of aesthetics.

This negative conception of the philosopher's task necessarily presupposes a positive philosophy of scientific research itself as a cooperative and progressive solution of problems that organized social groups of researchers define for themselves. Theoretical problems are solved when science replaces personal opinion. Similarly, practical disagreements will be properly resolved only when scientific planning replaces the selfish initiatives of private individuals. The ideal of social competence must replace the ideal of personal culture in ethics and education, for only through commitment to membership in the community of positive research can an objective criterion of moral and practical values be found without recourse to any metaphysical or religious absolutes. Thus, Spirito has inverted the conception of the relation between philosophy and science and between technical competence and general culture, which he found in Croce and Gentile. He is now one of the leaders of a new Hegelian left in Italy.

Works by Spirito

Opere complete, 12 vols. (as of 1965). Florence, 1950——.
Scienza e filosofia. Florence, 1933.
La vita come ricerca. Florence, 1937.
La vita come arte. Florence, 1941.
La vita come amore. Florence, 1953.
Critica della democrazia. Florence, 1963.

H. S. HARRIS

The Encyclopedia of Philosophy

The Encyclopedia of Philosophy

The
ENCYCLOPEDIA
of
PHILOSOPHY

PAUL EDWARDS, *Editor in Chief*

VOLUME EIGHT

Macmillan Publishing Co., Inc. & The Free Press
NEW YORK
COLLIER MACMILLAN PUBLISHERS
LONDON

MACMILLAN PUBLISHING CO., INC.
COLLIER-MACMILLAN CANADA LTD.

MANUFACTURED IN THE UNITED STATES OF AMERICA

REPRINT EDITION 1972

The Encyclopedia of Philosophy

S

[C O N T I N U E D]

SPRANGER, (FRANZ ERNST) EDUARD (1882 –
1963), German philosopher and educator, was born in
Grosslichterfelde, Berlin. He studied both mathematics and
science at a *Realschule* and the humanities at a classical
Gymnasium. At the University of Berlin he studied under
Wilhelm Dilthey and Friedrich Paulsen and earned his
right to lecture with *Wilhelm von Humboldt und die Hu-
manitätsidee* (Berlin, 1909), a classic in the history of
German humanism. He was called to the University of
Leipzig as professor of philosophy in 1911 and to Berlin as
professor of philosophy and pedagogy in 1920. He spent
the most creative years of his career and exercised his
greatest influence on the *Geisteswissenschaften* and on all
levels of German education while at Berlin. In 1933 he
submitted his resignation in protest against interference
with university freedom by the new National Socialist
government but was persuaded by many followers to
retain his influential university position. In 1937/1938
he lectured in Japan. He was arrested and imprisoned
in 1944 but was released upon the intercession of the
Japanese ambassador. Appointed rector of the University
of Berlin by the Allied military government in 1945, he
found it impossible to accept interference by the East
Berlin authorities and in 1946 accepted a professorship
in philosophy at Tübingen, where he lectured until
his retirement.

Spranger sought to further two projects begun by his
teacher, Wilhelm Dilthey. One was an "understanding"
(*verstehende*) psychology that would approach human life
not with scientific abstractions but perceptively and with
an appreciation of cultural values; the other was an attempt
to provide a normative interpretation of the *Geisteswissenschaften*. The interdependence of these two problems led
Spranger to a Hegelian position (toward which Dilthey
himself had begun to turn before his death), and he became a leading figure of the German Neo-Hegelian revival
of the 1920s.

In his chief work, *Die Lebensformen* (Halle, 1914; translated by J. W. Pigors as *Types of Men,* Halle, 1928), Spranger undertook a typological analysis of personality through
the use of the method of *Verstehen*. He held this method to
be empirical in that it results in "an at least minimally
categorialized after-experience." It is essentially an aesthetic perception of cultural forms in individual life and is
motivated by a Platonic *eros*—a love for the personal values involved; this, Spranger insisted, does not interfere
with its objectivity. Six forms of value—all of which are
objectively rooted in the historical and cultural order, and
each of which may dominate a person's life and evoke a
reordering of the others in subordination to itself—determine six types of personality in modern culture—the
theoretical, economic, aesthetic, social, political, and religious—which center respectively in the values of truth,
utility, beauty, love, power, and, in religion, in the devotion to a vital totality of value. The moral is not a distinct
type of value but enters into all valuations. Spranger schematized these types into an ideal order without denying
individual freedom in value selection.

Spranger's *Psychologie des Jugendalters* (Leipzig, 1924;
8th ed., 1926) applied his method and conclusions to the
problems of youth. Four important attainments mark
the sound growth of the adolescent: the discovery of
self, the development of a life plan, the ordering of the
self into the different spheres of human relations, and
the awakening of the sexual life and *eros*. The six personality types developed in the *Lebensformen* can serve as a
schema for comprehending the individual person in exploring these critical developments.

Spranger's analysis of the *Geisteswissenschaften* found
application in his discussions of the ethical bases of modern culture and education. It combined criticism of the
historical philosophies of society and culture with the
development of a modified Hegelian theory of objective
spirit. Subjective and objective spirit are in close interaction within every historically relative situation. To them
Spranger added a third dimension of spirit, the normative.
This, the relativized absolute spirit of Hegel, comprised
the factors which serve a regulative role in history through
art, religion, and philosophy. Responsibility for the actualization of the normative, however, lies in the individual; no cultural content becomes meaningful except "insofar as it is again and again created out of the attitude and
the conscience of the individual soul."

After World War II Spranger turned to religious themes,
particulary in *Die Magie der Seele* (Tübingen, 1947). This
"magic of the soul," which is essential to the life of a culture, is constituted by the religious consciousness and
serves not to meet immediate external goals but to aug-

ment the powers of the person himself. Faith is a "withdrawal into inwardness."

Spranger's work in the philosophy of education kept the classical humanistic ideal alive and exercised a liberating effect on all levels and dimensions of education. It found notable expression in classic studies of great figures in education—von Humboldt, Rousseau, Friedrich Froebel, Pestalozzi, and Goethe. Spranger was also involved in most of the ethical and cultural problems of German life, addressing himself to such challenges as labor education, vocational education, personal and vocational guidance, and juvenile delinquency. The eloquence of Spranger's lectures and writings, his personal warmth, felt by a wide circle of friends of all ages, and his combination of keen perception with deep moral concern made him one of the most admired and influential of German thinkers. His deep sense of the German tragedy, and his long preoccupation with its moral and historical causes and the moral cost of redemption, won for him, before he died, the most distinguished honors that his country could bestow.

Bibliography

Among Spranger's other works are *Wilhelm von Humboldt und die Reform des Bildungswesen* (Berlin, 1910); *Goethes Weltanschauung. Reden und Aufsätze* (Leipzig and Wiesbaden, 1942); *Gibt es ein Kulturpathologie?* (Tübingen, 1947); and *Aus Friedrich Froebels Gedankenwelt* (Heidelberg, 1951).

For a complete bibliography of Spranger's works, see Theodore Neu, *Bibliographie Eduard Spranger* (Tübingen, 1958).

For recent discussions of Spranger's thought and influence, see H. W. Bähr, ed., *Erziehung zur Menschlichkeit—Festschrift für Eduard Spranger zum 75. Geburtstag* (Tübingen, 1957); and Hans Wenke, ed., *Eduard Spranger, Bildnis eines geistigen Menschen unserer Zeit* (Heidelberg, 1957).

L. E. Loemker

STACE, WALTER TERENCE, Anglo-American empiricist philosopher, was born in 1886 in London. He graduated from Trinity College, Dublin, in 1908 and from 1910 to 1932 served in the civil service in Ceylon. During this period he published *A Critical History of Greek Philosophy* (London, 1920) and *The Philosophy of Hegel* (London, 1924). In 1932 he retired from the civil service to teach philosophy at Princeton University, where he remained until his academic retirement in 1955. He was president of the American Philosophical Association in 1949.

Stace's *The Theory of Knowledge and Existence* (Oxford, 1932) is the definitive statement of his general position on philosophical method. His argument rests on the claim that on strict empirical grounds the solipsist position is logically unassailable. Whereas philosophers such as George Santayana, starting with the same claim, appealed to a doctrine of "animal faith" and emphasized the irrational element in belief in an external world, Stace carefully and in detail offered an analysis of the steps whereby we construct our conception of an external physical world out of the available data. He often spoke of his doctrine as a theory of "fictions," but in print he preferred the word "constructions." The point is that the construction of the fiction of an external world is neither irrational nor animal. It is a step-by-step inference which, although it fails to provide a logical answer to solipsism's claims, does satisfy

human demands for reasons for belief. Ultimately our reasons for belief rest, according to Stace, upon two general claims which can be empirically supported—the claims that men's minds are similar and that they labor together in common. These two empirical facts, and not logical proofs, support our common-sense beliefs. This thesis lies at the heart of most of Stace's later work.

Stace in this earlier period was an advocate of the sense-datum theory. In spite of continued association of his name with Hegel, he was chiefly indebted to Hume, G. E. Moore, and Bertrand Russell. His main object of attack was Russell's *Our Knowledge of the External World*, which, according to Stace, constantly violates the principle of empiricism. In 1934 he published one of his best-known articles, "The Refutation of Realism" (*Mind*, Vol. 43, 1934, pp. 145–155), in response to Moore's influential "The Refutation of Idealism." Moore's argument was based upon a distinction between sense data and our awareness of them. Stace replied that one can grant the distinction and still deny any force to the claim that sense data exist when not being perceived. He generalized the claim that there can be no good reason for believing any version of the proposition that entities exist unperceived. They may so exist, but it is absurd to claim that this can be empirically proved. It follows that where "such proof is impossible, the belief ought not to be entertained."

This argument seems, on the face of it, to contradict the thesis of *The Theory of Knowledge and Existence*. Stace always subsequently maintained, however, that his article had been misunderstood because it was not recognized as irony. He also insisted that Moore's article had been intended as humorous. The irony of his own consisted in showing that the simplest natural belief cannot be supported by strict logical proofs.

Stace's next major work was *The Concept of Morals* (New York, 1937). In one sense the main argument of the book might be, and has been, characterized as a version of subjectivism because it associates a general theory of the meaning of moral judgments with a general theory of man's wants and approvals. Perhaps the most permanently valuable aspect of the argument, however, is the attempt to disassociate the view he is defending from the label "subjectivist." Stace held that the proper contrast between subjectivism and objectivism is between views which make reasoned adjudication of ethical disputes impossible, and views which provide rational grounds for holding that one moral claim can be correct and its rivals mistaken. According to Stace, what makes his view objectivist in this significant sense is the connection between it and a general theory of man's nature, including his desires, wants, and approvals. The result is a modified version of utilitarianism based upon the same two principles emphasized in the theory of knowledge, the similarity of men's minds and the fact that they labor together in common.

In two articles ("Positivism," *Mind*, Vol. 53, 1944, pp. 215–237; and "Some Misinterpretations of Empiricism," *Mind*, Vol. 67, 1958, pp. 465–484) Stace distinguished empiricism from recent positivistic tendencies. The intention of both is to attack the attempt on the part of more recent logical empiricists, who, Stace claimed, associate empiricism with the demand for strict logical proofs.

In September 1948 Stace published in *The Atlantic Monthly* (pp. 53–58) an article entitled "Man Against Darkness." The thesis of the article, which Stace considered neither very original nor very shocking, was that the world view endorsed by the physical sciences since the time of Galileo is incompatible with Christianity's traditional world view. The violent reaction to this article stunned him. There followed *The Gate of Silence* (Boston, 1952), a book-length poem; *Philosophy and the Modern Mind* (New York, 1952), a careful historical study of the thesis which had been popularly stated in "Man Against Darkness"; and *Time and Eternity* (Princeton, 1952), an essay in the philosophy of religion which many consider his most profound work.

No doubt partially because of the years he had lived in Ceylon, Stace was attracted to Hinayana Buddhism, and both *The Gate of Silence* and *Time and Eternity* reveal the extent of that influence on his later metaphysical thought. The theme of paradox runs throughout these works: "Men have always found that, in their search for the Ultimate, contradiction and paradox lie all around them. . . . Either God is a Mystery or He is nothing at all" (*Time and Eternity*, p. 8).

Thus, Stace now held that belief must transcend the confines of strict logic, and the rigorous empiricist ended by courting mysticism. Fully aware of this fact, Stace set himself to what he conceived to be his final philosophical task—the reconciliation of empiricism and mysticism. The result was *Mysticism and Philosophy* (New York, 1960). He claimed (1) that the mystical experience is a fact, is unique, and is the same in all cultures; (2) that the interpretations of the mystical experience vary widely from culture to culture; and (3) that a genuine empiricism cannot ignore the mystical experience simply because it is logically paradoxical.

Throughout the somewhat otherworldly philosophical reflection of his later life, Stace has retained an interest in practical problems. His *The Destiny of Western Man* (New York, 1942) was an expression of horror against the irrational totalitarianism which swept Europe in the 1930s. In February 1947 he published an article in *The Atlantic Monthly*, vigorously attacking the legal basis of Zionist arguments. In recent years he has been concerned with the universal condemnation of colonialism, insisting that high generalizations be checked against the evidence. In a letter to the *New York Times* (Feb. 4, 1964), he wrote that colonialism ". . . civilized half the world at the cost of the loss of some *amour propre*, of some snobbishness, of some arrogance, of some hard feeling, but—in the case of the Romans and British, at any rate—of very little real cruelty, injustice or tyranny."

Bibliography

An additional work by Stace is "The Metaphysics of Meaning," in *Mind*, Vol. 44 (1935), 417–438.

Works on Stace are A. J. Ayer, "The Principle of Verifiability," in *Mind*, Vol. 45 (1936), 199–203, a reply to Stace's "The Metaphysics of Meaning"; C. J. Ducasse, a review of *Mysticism and Philosophy*, in *Journal of Philosophy*, Vol. 59 (1962), 323–335; H. H. Price, "Mr. Stace on the Construction of the External World," in *Mind*, Vol. 42 (1933), 273–298; and Ralph E. Stedman and H. B. Acton, "Mr. Stace's Refutation of Realism," in *Mind*, Vol. 43 (1934), 349–353. On *The Theory of Knowledge and Existence*, see the critical notice by F. C. S. Schiller in *Mind*, Vol. 42 (1933), 94–100, and the review by L. Susan Stebbing in *Philosophy*, Vol. 8 (1933), 354–357.

JAMES WARD SMITH

STAËL-HOLSTEIN, ANNE LOUISE GERMAINE NECKER, BARONNE DE (1766–1817), French novelist and essayist, was born in Paris, the daughter of Suzanne Curchot and Jacques Necker, finance minister to Louis XVI.

In 1786 she married Eric Magnus, baron of Stäel-Holstein, the Swedish ambassador to France, from whom she separated in 1797. In the year of her marriage she published her first novel, *Sophie*, and four years later a tragedy, *Jeanne Grey*. Her interest in philosophy began with a study of Rousseau, whose fervent admirer she remained throughout her life. She incurred the hostility of Napoleon Bonaparte both by her frank criticism and by her liberalism, and her advocacy of a constitutional monarchy led to her being exiled in 1802. She made her first trip to Germany at this time, a trip which was the occasion of her book *De l'Allemagne*. This work was sent to the printer in 1810, but it was condemned by the censor and did not appear until 1813. After years of traveling, Mme. de Staël returned to Paris, where she remained until her death.

The philosophical ideas of Mme. de Staël are to be found mainly in two books, *De la Littérature considérée dans ses rapports avec les institutions sociales* (1800) and *De l'Allemagne*. In the former she attempted to show the influence of religion, morals, and laws on literature and that of literature upon religion, morals, and laws. This book presupposed the perfectibility of man, as Mme. de Staël admitted, but human progress was not automatic; to come into being it required the constant and deliberate aid of education (*les lumières*), which could be provided only through literature. A second premise was that of national characters, the Greek being given to art, emulation, and amusement; the Roman, to dignity, gravity of speech, and rational deliberation. Later she contrasted the Northerner and the Southerner, in *De l'Allemagne* exemplified respectively by the German and the Frenchman. Nevertheless, there is nowhere in Mme. de Staël's writings the notion of national souls or collective spirits (*Geister*). People to her were individuals, and whatever community of interests and talents they showed was to be attributed to the influence of other individuals.

Mme. de Staël never questioned the absolute value of personal liberty. This belief she attributed to Protestantism, her family religion. To her, Protestantism rested on the principle of personal interpretation, and the source of one's convictions was to be looked for in the heart, just as it was in the teachings of Rousseau's Savoyard vicar. She held that individual differences in temperament were irreconcilable, and believed that only statistics could help a statesman solve his people's ethical problems. It may have been this firmly rooted idea which made her fear the natural scientist as the tool of despots. The scientist, who rejects everything which cannot be reduced to mathematics, is always willing to pursue his own ends, regardless of the vital interests of his fellow men.

The chief contribution of *De l'Allemagne* to philosophy was that it acquainted Mme. de Staël's countrymen with the works of Kant, Fichte, Schelling, and Friedrich Schlegel. She presented their ideas simply and sketchily but on the whole correctly. In this way she helped break the hold which the sensationalism of the school of Condillac had had upon the French. Mme. de Staël wrote no book which can be considered as technical philosophy, but she represents the mind which has absorbed a philosophy as a technique of thinking and as a corrective to authoritarianism.

Works by Mme. de Staël

Oeuvres complètes, 17 vols. Paris, 1820–1821.
Lettres sur les ouvrages et le charactère de J.-J. Rousseau. Paris, 1788.
De l'Influence des passions sur le bonheur, 2 vols. Lausanne, 1796. A defense of reason as a critical agent.
De la Littérature considérée dans ses rapports avec les institutions sociales. Paris, 1800.
De l'Allemagne, 3 vols. London, 1813.

Works on Mme. de Staël

Blennerhasset, Charlotte, *Frau von Staël, ihre Freunde und ihre Bedeutung in Politik und Literatur,* 3 vols. Berlin, 1887–1889. Translated by J. E. Gordon Cumming as *Mme. de Staël, Her Friends and Her Influence on Politics and Literature.* London, 1889.
Gautier, Paul, *Mme. de Staël et Napoléon.* Paris, 1902.
Ollion, E., *Les Idées philosophiques morales et pedagogiques de Mme. de Staël.* Mâcon, 1910. Thesis.
Herold, J. Christopher, *Mme. de Staël, Mistress to an Age.* Indianapolis, Ind., 1958. A popular but well-documented biography.

GEORGE BOAS

STAHL, GEORG ERNST (1660–1734), a leading German medical scientist and chemist of his day. Stahl was appointed professor of medicine at the University of Halle in 1694, and from 1716 until his death he served as personal physician to Frederick William I of Prussia. His numerous medical writings had a strongly doctrinal tendency, which made them the source of lively, often bitter, controversy. His famous phlogiston theory, an erroneous explanation of the nature of combustion and calcination, was nonetheless, before Antoine Lavoisier's discoveries, instrumental in placing chemistry on a scientific basis. The same may be said of his studies concerning the properties and composition of acids, alkalis, and salts.

Led by his medical, rather than chemical, interests to philosophy, Stahl elaborated (particularly in his *Theoria Medica Vera,* 1707) a rigorous position of animism, affirming that the animal organism was formed, governed, and preserved by an immaterial principle, or soul. If Stahlian thought was indebted to the *archei* of J. B. van Helmont's occultist biology, and more broadly to both Neo-Aristotelian and Neoplatonic versions of animism in the late Renaissance, his notion of soul, reflecting the impact of post-Cartesian dualism, was typical of his own period. He conceived of it as essentially a rational and spiritual substance distinct from matter, but simultaneously he assigned to it the ability to control the organism by an "unconscious" mode of activity. Thus, the soul not only thinks and wills but, having constructed its body, also excites, regulates, and sustains all involuntary and vital

processes. It does so by the intermediary of movement, which Stahl regarded as an immaterial entity, for matter itself is held to be essentially passive and inert. The soul, by a specific energy, is supposed to communicate the "spiritual act" of movement to the organism in pursuance of its own aims.

This rather obscure view of things (which Leibniz, among others, criticized) was not improved by Stahl's manner of expression, a mixture of dogmatic haughtiness and repetitious turgidity. If he failed, moreover, to consider properly the various contradictions and difficulties peculiar to his position, this was due largely to his lack of interest in metaphysics as such. His animism was intended less as a philosophical contribution than as a theoretical standpoint from which to perceive and evaluate the phenomena of disease and health in accordance with an expectative approach to therapeutics. Even more significantly, it represented a protest against the dominant iatromechanist and iatrochemical schools, which at the time tended to see animate beings too naively and rigidly in terms of facile mechanical analogies and unexplained chemical reactions. But although Stahl's animism had the merit of emphasizing the presence of an irreducible "life force" having no equivalent in the machine, the omnipresent role allowed to this life force at the expense of a purely organic dynamism proved untenable.

The influence of Stahlianism was checked during the first half of the eighteenth century by the success of the mechanistic and empirical doctrines of Hermann Boerhaave and Friedrich Hoffman. Subsequently, Stahl's medical philosophy was reinterpreted at the important Faculty of Montpellier, with the general result that its spiritualist aspect was abandoned as unscientific while its insistence on a metamechanical "vital principle" in the organism was adopted as profoundly valid. Stahl thereby came to be recognized as the founder of the vitalistic school of modern biology.

Works by Stahl

Oeuvres médico-philosophiques et pratiques, 5 vols. Paris, 1859–1863.

Works on Stahl

Gottlieb, B. J., *Bedeutung und Auswirkungen Stahls auf den Vitalismus.* Halle, 1943.
Lemoine, Albert, *Le Vitalisme et l'animisme de Stahl.* Paris, 1864.
Metzger, Hélène, *Newton, Stahl, Boerhaave et la doctrine chimique.* Paris, 1930.

ARAM VARTANIAN

STALLO, JOHN BERNARD (1823–1900), American educator, jurist, and philosopher of science. He was born at Damme in southern Oldenburg, Germany and immigrated in 1839 to Cincinnati, where, except for three years in New York, he resided until 1885. In that year he was sent on a diplomatic assignment to Italy and remained there until his death. From 1839 to 1847 Stallo taught languages, physical science, and philosophy at Jesuit schools in Cincinnati and New York. In 1849 he was admitted to the bar, and thereafter he practiced law in Cincinnati, serving two years as a judge and 17 years as examiner of teachers for the public schools.

During his early years Stallo was an adherent of the German *Naturphilosophie,* and in 1848 he published an exposition of this system under the title *General Principles of the Philosophy of Nature.* The book was neither very original nor very influential. In later years he regretted its publication and came to look upon "the spell of Hegel's ontological reveries" as "one of the unavoidable disorders of intellectual infancy."

From the time he left St. John's College (now Fordham University), where he had been professor of physics, chemistry, and mathematics, Stallo continued his interest in the development of physical science. In 1865 and 1868 he published two popular articles in German relating to the philosophy of science. These were followed (1873–1874) by four highly original papers in *Popular Science Monthly* under the general title "The Primary Concepts of Physical Science." Somewhat reworked and greatly expanded, they reappeared in book form in 1882 as *The Concepts and Theories of Modern Physics,* a classic contribution to the philosophy of science.

Philosophy of science. In his introduction to *The Concepts and Theories of Modern Physics,* Stallo attempted to forestall possible misinterpretation of the book, pointing out that it was intended as a contribution neither to physics nor to metaphysics, but rather to the theory of knowledge. In spite of this explanation, however, the chorus of critical comment which greeted the book was based principally on the very misapprehensions Stallo had anticipated. He was thus induced to write a comprehensive reply to his critics which was published in the second and later American editions. In this reply he revealed the principal source of his penetrating and original critique of contemporary physical theory, which was the discovery by students of comparative linguistics that every distinct form or system of speech involves a distinct metaphysical theory. With this principle in mind, he had examined the concepts of physics and had found that despite the anti-metaphysical tendencies of scientists themselves, their theoretical writings preserved a number of concealed ontological assumptions. These he proposed to make evident, in order that the contradictions between classical theory and new data might be resolved.

Stallo's critique was indeed unique, and it is doubtful whether it could have been offered at the time by anyone but an amateur of his particular background and interests. German philologists (for example, Hermann Paul, Karl Brugmann, and Max Delbruck), because of their sensitivity to philosophical problems, had done the most important work in relating linguistics to epistemology, and Stallo was closely conversant with German scholarship. Because of his former professorship in physical science, he was also thoroughly familiar with the literature of that field, even with the current scientific periodicals. Finally, his early preoccupation with philosophy had put him in a position to assess with nearly professional skill the metaphysical dangers of an uncritical accumulation of scientific data. Since he was free of any professional allegiance to the prevailing doctrines in either philosophy or physics, but had a profound knowledge of both, he was able to sound a well-timed alarm. The fact that his warning fell for the most part on deaf ears, and that the revolution in physical concepts which he foresaw was actually precipitated in quite another way than by his theoretical critique, does not detract from the philosophical interest and importance of his ideas.

Stallo's book was published in the same year that A. A. Michelson first disclosed the results of his delicate experimental attempt to discover any variation in the speed of light with respect to the direction of the earth's motion. This and similar experiments laid the foundation for a revolutionary revision of physical concepts in the next few years, and shortly after Stallo's death such a revision was substantially carried out through the labors of H. A. Lorentz, Max Planck, and Albert Einstein. In the light of these events, it is interesting to recall the chief ontological errors against which Stallo published his warning to scientists: that of the hypostasis of concepts, that of disregard of the twofold relativity of all physical phenomena, and that of confusing the order of understanding with the order of nature.

The fundamental dichotomy of matter and motion in the atomicomechanical hypothesis that underlay the physics of Stallo's period required assumptions that he recognized to be in direct conflict with an increasing number of established facts in physics, chemistry, and astronomy—especially the assumptions of absolutely equal and rigid irreducible particles and of the essentially kinetic character of all energy. The contradictory properties required of the ether by physicists and chemists in his time afforded Stallo a clear example of the trouble to come, as did the existing difficulties in the mechanical theory of heat and the phenomena of specific heats.

Stallo's critique was by no means entirely destructive for he also set forth certain basic principles that he considered essential to a proper structure of physical concepts. Some of these principles are strikingly in accord with conclusions later reached by physicists, when they were forced by their own data to undertake the reconstruction of physical theory. Thus, Stallo declared that every object known to the intellect is, by the very act of its apprehension, affected by the determinations of the cognizing faculty—a remark strikingly akin to the principle of indeterminacy as now accepted. This constituted the first aspect of his "twofold relativity." The other aspect was even more closely linked to the basic assumption of Einstein's special relativity theory, promulgated five years after Stallo's death, for Stallo had already declared that no object can be known save through its relation to other objects and that the only properties or attributes a thing can possess are these relations. Stallo also stressed the selective aspect of cognition and the necessarily varying classifications of objects by different departments of knowledge, thus affording a constructive epistemological antidote to the apparent contradictions existing between different sciences that employ what is apparently the same concept—an appearance that Stallo and many others would regard as a linguistic illusion concerning the nature of things and properties.

Stallo extended his critique to certain developments in contemporary mathematics, but there it was by no means satisfactory, for he considerably underestimated the utility of non-Euclidean geometry and the theory of aggregates in the reconstruction of physical theory.

Influence. The principal influence exerted by Stallo's work was upon later philosophers of science, rather than the scientists (or philosophers) of his day. Ernst Mach's views were already formed before he saw Stallo's book. Émile Meyerson took it into account in his *Identity and Reality* (1908). P. W. Bridgman was acquainted with Stallo's work when he set forth the principles of operationalism in 1927, and he placed it in a class with the writings of W. K. Clifford, Ernst Mach, and Henri Poincaré on matters of scientific philosophy. Shortly before his death Bridgman wrote an extended criticism and appreciation of Stallo as the introduction to a modern edition of the *Concepts,* but in some respects that essay labors under the basic misapprehension of his purposes that Stallo attempted to forestall in the preface to the first edition of his book.

Works by Stallo

General Principles of the Philosophy of Nature. Boston, 1848.
"The Primary Concepts of Modern Physical Science." *Popular Science Monthly* (Oct. 1873–Jan. 1874).
The Concepts and Theories of Modern Physics. New York, 1882; 2d ed., with answer to critics, 1885. Reprinted in various years, New York and London, and with critical introduction by P. W. Bridgman, Cambridge, 1960. Translated into French as *La Matière et la physique moderne,* with preface by C. Friedel. Paris, 1884; 4th ed., 1905. Translated into German by H. Kleinpeter as *Die Begriffen und Theorien der modernen Physik,* with foreword by Ernst Mach. Berlin, 1901; 2d ed., 1911.
Reden, Abhandlungen und Briefe. New York, 1893.

Works on Stallo

Drake, S., "J. B. Stallo and the Critique of Classical Physics," in H. M. Evans, ed., *Men and Moments in the History of Science.* Seattle, Wash., 1959.
Kleinpeter, H., "J. B. Stallo als Erkenntniskritiker." *Vierteljahrsschrift für wissenschaftlichen Philosophie,* Vol. 25, No. 4 (1901), 401–440.
McCormack, T. J., "John Bernard Stallo." *Open Court,* Vol. 14, No. 5 (May 1900), 276 ff.
Ratterman, H. A., *Johann Bernhard Stallo, deutschamerikanischer Philosoph, Jurist und Staatsmann.* Cincinnati, 1902.
Youmans, W. J., "Sketch of John B. Stallo." *Popular Science Monthly* (Feb. 1889).

STILLMAN DRAKE

STAMMLER, RUDOLF (1856–1938), German Neo-Kantian legal philosopher. His first major work, *Die Lehre vom richtigen Recht,* outlined his philosophy of law, which was elaborated in subsequent works. Stammler sought to apply Kant's distinction between pure and practical reason to the law. The embodiment of pure reason in legal theory is the concept of law, which Stammler defined as "combining sovereign and inviolable volition." The counterpart of practical reason is the idea of law, that is, the realm of purposes realized by volition. But whereas for Kant practical reason was not, like pure reason, a matter of intellectual perception, but of morality, Stammler sought to formulate a theoretically valid idea of justice. He based it on the community of purposes and the fact that man is a reasonable being, an end in himself. From this he derived two "principles of respect" and two "maxims of participa-

tion." The former are that no one's volition must be subject to the arbitrary desire of another and that any legal demand must be of such a nature that the addressee could be his own neighbor. The latter are that no member of a legal community must be arbitrarily excluded from the community and that a legal power may be exclusive only insofar as the excluded person can still be his own neighbor.

For Stammler these were not merely formal principles; they could be used to solve actual legal problems. He attempted, for example, to apply them to the legality of cartels and to the solution of disputes between upper and lower riparian owners over the use of water. His solutions were generally those of a moderate liberal.

Max Weber has shown in "Rudolf Stammlers Überwindung des materialistischen Geschichtsauffassung" (*Gesammelte Aufsätze zur Wissenschaftslehre,* Tübingen, 1922, pp. 291–359) that Stammler's alleged formal categories are in fact categories of progressive generalizations, the more general being relatively more formal than the less general. Stammler's main error was his attempt to make the idea of justice a matter of theoretical knowledge; it was therefore inevitable that he should confuse principles generally acceptable to a moderate liberal with universally valid principles of justice. His idea of justice is therefore a cross between a formal proposition and a definite social ideal, kept abstract and rather vague by the desire to remain formal. Stammler's chief merit remains his reintroduction of legal philosophy as a vital aspect of the study of law.

Works by Stammler

Wirtschaft und Recht. Halle, 1896. Law and economics are related as form and matter.
Die Lehre vom richtigen Recht. Halle, 1902. Translated by I. Husik as *The Theory of Justice.* New York, 1925.
Theorie der Rechtswissenschaft. Halle, 1911.
Lehrbuch der Rechtsphilosophie. Berlin and Leipzig, 1922.

WOLFGANG FRIEDMANN

STATE. Before the sixteenth century the word "state" was used to refer to the *estates* of the realm or to kingly office or dignity, but not to an independent political community. Machiavelli was largely responsible for establishing this modern usage. The change, however, was not in words only but also in ways of thinking about political organization and political relations. In feudal society a man figured in a network of quasi-contractual relations in which his political rights and duties were closely linked to land tenure and fealty. He was his lord's man and his king's man. The powers of kingship were only with difficulty distinguished from property rights. From the twelfth century on, the conceptions of Roman law began once more to influence political thought. Public authority was more sharply distinguished from private rights; the peculiar position of the king among his barons, which feudal writers recognized but found difficult to conceptualize, came to be expressed in Roman terms—the *princeps* was said to speak on behalf of the whole people and to exercise *imperium,* as distinct from a feudal privilege, because his care was for the whole *respublica.* However, so long as barons could still simultaneously hold fiefs from different kings in different lands, the notion could not develop of the territorially defined state, making an exclusive claim to the allegiance of all who resided within its borders. The idea that men could be not only subjects of their king but also citizens of their state became possible with the consolidation of national monarchies in England, France, and Spain. Its development was assisted in the thirteenth century by the quickening of interest in Aristotle's ideas about the city-state and, in the early sixteenth century, by the Renaissance interest in the ancient Roman republic. Classical elements, then, were grafted onto the late medieval stock to produce the Renaissance state.

With the declining influence of such customary forms of regulation as feudal and manorial ties, the guild, and the family, the state became an indispensable category for any kind of speculative thought about society. Moreover, as the grip of custom slackened, men came to think that law might be made by an authoritative will rather than discovered by the understanding or known by tradition. The political order, as the authority structure through which law was created and which therefore conferred legal status and rights on all other forms of association, gained a corresponding pre-eminence. Out of the split in the universal church and the consequent alliance for mutual survival between protestant princes and religious reformers, there emerged the idea of a national church closely related to the state, further stressing that the state was a community or polity and not simply an aggregation of men who happened to owe allegiance to a common overlord. The consolidation of national states created a new state of nature—a world peopled by sovereign states recognizing no overriding authority and only tenuously subject, if at all, to a common law. Suárez, Vitoria, Grotius, and Pufendorf, the pioneers of international law, explored the relations between states in such a world; what was implied for the internal structure of a state was worked out by Jean Bodin and Thomas Hobbes. (See SOVEREIGNTY for a fuller treatment of the views of Bodin and Hobbes.)

Identity of the state. Since the seventeenth century, political philosophers have been largely preoccupied with the relations of the state and the individual, with the citizen's rights, if any, against the state, with the right of the state to punish, to promote morality, or to regulate the affairs of other associations such as families, trade unions, and churches. These matters have been all the more troublesome because there is disagreement about the proper analysis of propositions about the state. For instance, what does it mean to say that a state has acted in a certain way, made a decision, adopted a policy, assumed responsibility, and so on? These are not statements about every one of its citizens, nor are they simply statements about the acts of certain individuals who govern the state; for not all the actions of the man who for the time being is president are acts of the United States, nor is an act of the state always attributable to one man in particular. Hobbes was certainly mistaken when he argued that what made an aggregate of many men into one corporate person was that one man acted for the rest: "The *unity* of the representer, not the *unity* of the represented . . . maketh the person *one*" (*Leviathan* I, 16).

Again, what kind of sustained identity has the state, that one can speak of its enduring through many generations of natural lives? It is tempting to meet such a question with an organic analogy: Although the cells die and are replaced, the organism survives; although an action of an organism requires nothing more than the coordinated operations of its organs, it is not identical with the actions of any one or of all of them (unless their functions as elements in an organism are presupposed in the descriptions of their actions). The organism, it is often said, is a form of life transcending its parts; purposes are attributed to it that are not the purposes of any one of its parts or of all of them taken severally. Many writers, notably the Hegelians, have described the state in this way, exalting the interests of the state at the expense of the interests of its members considered as individuals.

A quite different account of the state has been given by writers who have employed atomic or contractual models, with explanatory analogies drawn from joint-stock corporations, clubs, or perhaps from mechanical contrivances. Thus, Hobbes talks of the state as an *artificial* man, contrived by an agreement of self-determining individuals. It can have no purposes not ultimately reducible to the purposes of individuals; its acts are those of a sovereign authorized to act on their behalf. The contractual analogy in Hobbes and Locke is a device for explaining how and under what conditions the acts of one or a few ruling individuals could be attributed to a body composed of a multitude of free and autonomous persons, all with their own separate interests, yet each committed by his own consent to a public interest in which he has a personal stake.

The problem of meaning, however, must be distinguished from the moral problem of obligation. The notion of corporate action does not necessarily entail consent or authorization on the part of individual members, although it could be argued that without consent the individual could have no moral commitment or responsibility. Acts of the state are acts of persons in an official capacity, acting according to procedures and within the competence prescribed by the rules of its constitution. A president's actions are those of the United States only when they form part of a particular procedural routine; they then indicate appropriate responses by other officials. When the president acts in nonofficial roles—as father or as member of his golf club—his actions are incidents in what a Wittgensteinian would call different "games" and therefore have appropriately different implications. The enduring identity of a state can be correspondingly analyzed in terms of the endurance of its procedural order. The Constitution of the United States has had an unbroken history since its adoption in 1788; the changes it has suffered have all been valid according to the criteria it prescribes for itself.

This sort of analysis explains the personality and life of a state without resorting to organic analogies or to metaphysical notions of an order of being where a whole is greater than the sum of its parts. However, it does not deal with all the problems. Despite several revolutions since 1789, there is a sense in which the French state has a continuous history, unlike the Austro-Hungarian state that was destroyed after World War I and replaced by a number of successor states. If the population of an area continues to be governed undivided, as an independent political unit, there seem to be grounds for saying that it remains the same state, despite changes in regime. In the case of France, although formal continuity of legitimization broke down between, for instance, the Second Empire and the Third Republic, there is a continuity of tradition and, despite deep cleavages, a sense that however bitterly rival groups contend, they are nevertheless committed by their awareness of history and common culture to remaining in political association. A struggle to control or reconstruct the machinery of government is not necessarily, then, an attempt to break up the political association, as it was in the Austro-Hungarian empire. (For a fuller discussion of the relation between state and nation, see NATIONALISM.)

The state as an association. To call the state an association is to put it on the same footing as clubs, churches, and trade unions. There are features of the state, however, which, although no one of them is peculiar to the state alone, together make it a rather special case. For instance, because men do not usually become or remain members of a state by choice, and because a state exercises exclusive authority over everyone in a given territory, the concept of membership is hazier than in the case of voluntary associations. The state insists that not only its citizens but also everyone else in its territorial jurisdiction shall conform to its rules. Indeed, the notion of a citizen suggests a certain minimum degree of active participation. This may be restricted, as it was in Athens, to a relatively small number of the resident native population. In that case, would the association include only the citizens? Are the rest outsiders on whom the state imposes its will, much as a trade union might insist that nonunionists shall not work for lower wages than its members? Or are citizens and noncitizens merely two classes of members, one with rights of participation, such as the right to vote, the others with private rights only?

Unlike trade unions, literary societies, joint-stock corporations, and guilds, the state's range of interests is very wide and, in principle, unlimited. This, too, is connected with its nonvoluntary character. Even allowing for migration and naturalization, men do not easily join or leave a state, and when they do, it is usually only with its permission. And whether they join it or not, they are subject to it if they reside in its territory. Consequently, the state does not need to define the terms and aims of their membership. Neither is there any higher authority which can rule, as the state's judicial authorities may do in relation to other associations, that a proposed act falls outside its terms of association and therefore infringes its members' rights. This indeterminacy of scope is a characteristic that the state shares with the family and even with some churches. Such associations have no defined set of aims: the behavior norms they sustain may govern a very wide, if fluctuating, segment of the social life of their members. And in the last hundred years the effective sphere of the state has encroached increasingly on the spheres of other associations.

The state and conflicts of interests. The state's territorial inclusiveness and the uncertain limits to its concern have led many political philosophers to assign to it a unique role among the forms of human association. Plato's *Republic* sketched an ideal state in which men's conflicting interests and energies were harnessed and reconciled by philosopher-rulers who would integrate them

into a single-minded unity, the principles of which could be discovered by a philosophical insight. Aristotle claimed that, at its best, the Greek *polis* was the most perfect association because, while including lesser associations like the family and the village, it was large enough to provide within itself everything necessary for the good life for man. For Aristotle, citizenship was a matter not of passively enjoying rights but of participating energetically in the many-sided life of the *polis*. The Greek writers had in mind a small state, a face-to-face community capable of satisfying emotional needs that the impersonal mass state of the twentieth century cannot. Nevertheless, the same completeness that Aristotle found in the *polis* has often been attributed to the modern state.

Rousseau, though tempted to identify the modern state with the *polis*, hesitated to do so unconditionally. He believed that the state was sufficient for the expression of all human excellencies. The vocation of the citizen was the highest to which a man could aspire. Participating in the expression of the general will for the common good of the whole association, the citizen rose above private interest and became a moral person, "substituting justice for instinct in his conduct. . . . man, who so far had considered only himself, finds that he is forced . . . to consult his reason before listening to his inclination" (*Social Contract* I, 8). Membership of the state was for Rousseau, as for Plato and Aristotle, a moral education; bad laws corrupted nature, good laws provided conditions for moral development and nobility of soul. Not only was nothing needed beyond the state but also, Rousseau suspected, lesser associations, by setting up partial or sectional interests as objects of loyalty, frustrated the public interest and corrupted the state. Nevertheless, the ideal state of Rousseau's *Social Contract* remained a city-state, small enough for everyone to know everyone else. The attempt by others to extend the conception to the nation-state led to confusion in theory and, in practice, to Jacobin totalitarianism.

Hegel transformed Rousseau's doctrine by substituting for personal, face-to-face relations a metaphysical dependence of parts on the whole. The state was the concrete universal, the individual a mere partial expression of it. Sectional associations had a function in organizing human interests. They operated, however, on a lower plane of reality than the state, a plane that Hegel termed "civil society." This was not a different order from the state but the same social organization viewed from the standpoint of the subjective ends that individuals set themselves. It was the plane of the free market economy motivated by the pursuit of profit and sectional advantage, where competitive conflicts are checked, ordered, and adjusted by the police. Nevertheless, unknowingly and despite themselves, individuals promoted ideal ends. Interests that from the subjective point of view of civil society were sectional and egoistic appeared objectively in the state as moments or partial expressions or functions of the greater whole. The state would then rightly regulate although not supplant such interests. (For a fuller discussion of Hegel's theory of the state, see SOVEREIGNTY.)

For Plato and Rousseau the conflict of interests was a pathological symptom in a state; for Hegel it was an unreality masking a fundamental unity that the state would safeguard if necessary. For all three there was a transcendent public interest in which the apparent interests of individuals are dissolved and fused.

There is, however, another view that takes the conflict of interests as a fundamental fact of nature; it can be controlled but never finally superseded. Machiavelli, Hobbes, and Bentham were in this tradition. The state existed to regulate competition, since without it individual objectives would be mutually frustrating. The harmony it achieved, however, was artificial; the state remedied a desperate situation by altering the conditions under which men sought their own interests, deflecting them from antisocial ends by fear of punishment. Marx and Engels, agreeing that the state suppressed conflict, saw it as a strictly coercive instrument maintained by the dominant economic class to safeguard its privileges. But they believed that with the advent of a classless society, scarcity would give way to abundance, and conflict to harmony. The state would then wither away, to be replaced by a new administrative order without organized violence. The state, then, was a response to a pathological although historically necessary condition. Ultimately, however, the evolution of society would bring about the changes in man which would make Rousseau's vision possible. For Augustine the earthly state was the palliative for sin; for Marx it was the palliative for class conflict. But for both there was a condition of ultimate redemption, where the coercive state would have no place.

For John Locke civil society (equivalent in Locke's terms to the state) existed to safeguard the natural rights of individuals, which they could not successfully preserve in the state of nature. Nevertheless, because Locke considered man rational by nature and therefore ideally capable of living in peace according to the law of nature, the condition of conflict was pathological, not natural. However, the norm was not participation in a transcendent good but a condition in which each man enjoyed his own area of legitimate privacy, troubled by neither private nor public intrusions. For Locke, as for Hobbes, the state's ends were reducible to those of individuals. Bentham put this quite unequivocally: "This public interest . . . is only an abstract term; it represents only the mass of the interests of individuals" (*Principles of the Civil Code, Works,* Vol. I, p. 321). The state had and could have no moral function except to arrange that as many people as possible should obtain as much as possible of whatever it was that they wanted. For some purposes all that was needed was for the state to uphold property and the sanctity of contract; economic motives in a free market would do the rest. But Benthamite utilitarianism was committed to active state policies wherever, as in public health, laissez-faire would not work. The Benthamite state was readily convertible to a Fabian policy of social engineering. But the objective would still be, in Roscoe Pound's phrase, "such an adjustment of relations and ordering of conduct as will make the goods of existence . . . go round as far as possible with the least friction and waste" (*Social Control Through Law,* New Haven, Conn., 1942, p. 65).

The view that politics is a matter of who gets what is substantially that of the group theorists in political science, such as A. E. Bentley and, more recently, Harold Lasswell,

David Truman, and Robert Dahl. In their accounts, the state is dissolved into a "political process" which can be analyzed without residue in terms of the competitive pressures of interests. Whereas Locke and Rousseau would have agreed that the public interest was the proper end of state action (although possibly disagreeing in their accounts of it), many modern political scientists, Glendon Schubert for instance, have rejected the concept of public interest as being so vague as to be useless or as being a device of politicians for advocating policies actually pursued for quite other reasons. Policy decisions, they argue, are the resultants of competing interests—there is no single interest that everyone would acknowledge, nor one that would be to everyone's advantage. Thus, there can be no public interest that the state ought to pursue.

An analysis like Schubert's depends, on the one hand, on the identification of interest and desire and, on the other hand, on interpreting "public" to mean "enjoyed by everyone." This was clearly not Rousseau's meaning. A citizen's interest was in being a man of a certain kind with characteristic excellences, attainable only in a healthy state. He might misguidedly desire what was not in his interest; so might all the citizens, for the will of all was not necessarily the same as the general will. But as long as their vision was clear, conflict was impossible because the public interest was whatever would be to *anyone's* advantage, insofar as he was capable of human excellence.

Political scientists mistrust such a theory, partly because it tends to describe the actual state as if it were the ideal and partly because it is evaluative, whereas they want theories to be descriptive and explanatory. What is in a man's interest, they say, is simply what he strives to get, irrespective of why he does so or with what wisdom. However, treating the state as simply an arena for sectional pressures has the drawback of disregarding or misconstruing the widespread opinion that to act in the public interest is to be impartial between competing groups—that the state (or its rulers) is therefore in a special position as arbiter between group interests. This frequently gives state decisions a moral authority that a mere political barometer, responding to the greatest pressures, could never enjoy, and it provides politicians and public servants, potentially at least, with a range of motives that are quite unlike interests as usually understood.

Sheldon S. Wolin, in *Politics and Vision,* has recently advanced the somewhat paradoxical thesis that despite the vast extension of governmental activity, there has been a steady depreciation of politics and the political order since the seventeenth century. This has been matched, he asserts, by a corresponding heightening of regard for nonpolitical institutions and associations—for society as distinct from the state. This "groupism" is regrettable, in Wolin's view, because the specialized roles adopted by the individual are no substitute for citizenship. Citizenship, as the individual's most general role, calls on him to choose regardless of special interests. As a member of a society bounded for most purposes by the state's frontiers, he is confronted with this demand only as a member of the state. As a trade unionist, for instance, he shares sectional loyalties with coworkers and is led to strive for advantages at the expense of other groups. To be conscious of oneself as a citizen, however, is to enjoy an integrative experience, which "demands that the separate roles be surveyed from a more general point of view." The political art, in Wolin's opinion, is that "which strives for an integrative form of direction, one that is broader than that supplied by any group or organization." Wolin comes close indeed to the view of Rousseau and Hegel that there is a concrete morality in the state. As a citizen one is asked to judge what would be to the advantage of *anyone,* their special circumstances aside. In this manner one approaches a moral judgment, an impartial assessment of claims in matters of general concern.

A further disadvantage of a fragmented vision of the political process is its tendency to miss the influence of the state, both as an idea and as a tradition, on the life of the society. As a trade union or a church is not simply an arena for its own sectional interests, so each state embodies a set of values and objects of loyalty which may greatly influence what its members consider their interests to be. Its manners and traditions leave their mark on them. Associations that participate in its political processes reflect its style, its modes of organization, and its procedures. Moreover, the state lays down terms on which its members deal with one another and with foreigners, establishing an area within its borders in which trade, communications, and movement are free, and regulating traffic that crosses them. Because of its regulative power, the texture of social relations is far closer within its boundaries than across them. It thus supplies not only a legal but also a general conceptual framework for much of our social thought and action. Thus, where we speak of Australian primary producers' associations, Australian football teams, and the Australian Political Studies Association, we speak not of the Australian state but of Australia. This seems to support the Hegelian view of the state as a national community within which certain particular functions are promoted by sectional associations operating within it. But then one must distinguish the state in this sense from its governmental authority structure, which would be but one of its organs alongside trade unions, graziers' associations, and the like. For voluntary and sectional associations are not, like departments of state, of the navy, or of the post office, subordinate parts of the governmental structure, nor are their actions the acts of the state. This distinction would be quite consistent with a generalized although conditional duty on the part of sectional associations to submit to governmental authority. However, it would not be a duty owed by subordinate agencies to a superior but rather one owed by members of a society in which an authority is recognized as arbiter and coordinator of interests and as initiator of policies of general concern. This would also be consistent with the moral right of associations to defy the government should these functions be abused. The fact that the government is the executive agent of the politically organized state does not mean that its own views of the public interest or of a just settlement of conflicting claims must always and necessarily prevail.

The word "nation" is often used to refer to the state-community; so, in slightly different contexts, is the word "country." Both words, however, have other meanings and overtones, "nation" being used of cultural groups which can transcend state frontiers or which may be minorities within a state, "country" referring more particularly to the state's territory or to the state as an international personality. (For a fuller discussion of the relations of state and nation, see NATIONALISM.)

Limits of state action. Liberal political philosophers have tried to define necessary limits beyond which the activities of the state must not extend. Some, like Locke, account for the existence of the state in terms of some specific function, such as the safeguarding of natural rights. They then infer, by analogy with the statement of aims in the articles of association of a club or joint-stock company, that the state would be exceeding its competence if it did more than that. Others have tried to define an area of private action which the state ought not invade. According to J. S. Mill, for instance, the state is never justified in restraining the action of a normal adult solely on the grounds that it is in his interests that it should. Some, like T. H. Green and Ernest Barker and, in a more sophisticated form, F. A. Hayek, have claimed that the state as a coercive organization has intrinsic limitations. Although it can hinder hindrances to the good life, it cannot force men to live that life; any form of activity, such as religion, art, or science, whose value lies in spontaneity or freedom of belief must therefore fall outside its scope. Barker argued that because the state's essential mode of action was through general rules, it was not apt for any field that, like industry, required *ad hoc* discretionary decisions. Such an argument depends, however, on a very doubtful kind of essentialism. The state has no one *modus operandi.* For the varied range of activities that states have undertaken in the last one hundred years, they have devised an equally varied range of techniques. They encourage the arts as well as censoring them. Nearly all modern states have very extensive responsibilities in education, industrial management, health insurance, and medical services, all of which have at one time been private undertakings and none of which involves coercion except in very remote or indirect ways. It does not follow from the state's monopoly of legitimate coercion that it can do nothing for which coercion is inappropriate. Nor need we suppose that, if there are indeed forms of social activity that the state has at present no satisfactory means of regulating, encouraging, or promoting, it may not yet invent them. Therefore, one cannot say in advance whether a given task would be more properly left to individual initiative or organized by governmental agencies. That depends on what can be done with the techniques available.

Bibliography

Virtually all the works listed in the bibliography to SOVER-EIGNTY are also relevant to this topic. The works listed here are therefore additional references.

HISTORICAL TREATMENTS

Cassirer, Ernst, *The Myth of the State.* New Haven, Conn., 1946.

Jouvenel, Bertrand de, *Du Pouvoir. Histoire naturelle de sa croissance.* Geneva, 1945. Translated by J. F. Huntington as *On Power: Its Nature and the History of Its Growth.* Boston, 1962.

Nisbet, Robert, *The Quest for Community.* New York, 1953. Republished as *Community and Power.* New York, 1962.

Plamenatz, John, *Man and Society,* 2 vols. London, 1963.

Wolin, Sheldon S., *Politics and Vision.* Boston, 1960.

ANALYTICAL WORKS

Benn, S. I., and Peters, R. S., *Social Principles and the Demo-cratic State.* London, 1959. Republished as *Principles of Political Thought.* New York, 1964.

Jouvenel, Bertrand de, *De la Souveraineté.* Paris, 1955. Trans-lated by J. F. Huntington as *Sovereignty: An Inquiry Into the Political Good.* Cambridge (England) and Chicago, 1957.

Jouvenel, Bertrand de, *The Pure Theory of Politics.* Cambridge, 1963.

Mabbott, J. D., *The State and the Citizen.* London, 1948.

THE APPROACH OF MODERN POLITICAL SCIENTISTS

Bentley, A. F., *The Process of Government.* Chicago, 1908.

Dahl, Robert A., *Modern Political Analysis.* Englewood Cliffs, N.J., 1963.

Friedrich, Carl J., *Man and His Government.* New York, 1963. Includes extensive bibliography.

Friedrich, Carl J., ed., *The Public Interest.* New York, 1962. This is Vol. V of American Society of Political and Legal Philoso-phy, ed., *Nomos.*

Lasswell, Harold D., and Kaplan, Abraham, *Power and Society: A Framework for Political Inquiry.* New Haven, Conn., 1950.

Schubert, Glendon, *The Public Interest.* Glencoe, Ill., 1960.

WORKS IN THE CLASSICAL LIBERAL TRADITION

Barker, Ernest, *Principles of Social and Political Theory.* Ox-ford, 1951.

Bentham, Jeremy, *Works,* John Bowring, ed., 11 vols. London, 1843.

Bentham, Jeremy, *A Fragment on Government* (London, 1776), W. Harrison, ed. Oxford, 1948. This volume also contains *Intro-duction to the Principles of Morals and Legislation.*

Bentham, Jeremy, *Traités de législation, civile et pénale,* E. Dumont, ed., Paris, 1802. Translated by R. Hildreth as *The Theory of Legislation.* Boston, 1840; London, 1864.

Hayek, F. A., *The Constitution of Liberty.* London, 1960.

Locke, John, *Two Treatises of Government* (1690). Peter Laslett, ed. Cambridge, 1960.

Mill, J. S., *On Liberty* (1859) and *Considerations on Represent-ative Government* (1861), R. B. McCallum, ed. Oxford, 1946; London, 1947.

Popper, Karl, *The Open Society and Its Enemies,* 2 vols., 4th rev. ed. London, 1962.

MARXIST VIEWS

Bottomore, T. B., and Rubel, M., editors and translators, *Karl Marx: Selected Writings in Sociology and Social Philosophy,* 2d ed. London, 1961. Includes selected bibliography of Marx's writ-ings.

Engels, Friedrich, *Der Ursprung der Familie, des Privateigen-thums und des Staats.* Zurich, 1884. Translated by Lewis H. Morgan as *Origin of the Family, Private Property and the State,* 4th ed. London, 1946.

Lenin, V. I., *Gosudarstvo i Revoliutsiia.* Petrograd, 1918. Translated as *State and Revolution* in *Selected Works,* J. Fine-berg, ed., Vol. VII. London, 1946.

Marx, Karl, and Engels, Friedrich, *Die deutsche Ideologie* (1845–1846), in *Marx–Engels Gesamtausgabe.* Berlin, 1932. Part I, Vol. V. Parts I and III were edited by R. Pascal and translated by William Lough and Charles P. Magill as *The German Ideology.* London, 1938.

Marx, Karl, and Engels, Friedrich, *Manifest der kommunisti-schen Partei.* London, 1848. Edited with introduction by Harold J. Laski as *Communist Manifesto: Socialist Landmark.* London, 1948.

CATHOLIC THEORIES OF NATURAL LAW

Entrèves, A. P. d', *La dottrina dello stato; elementi di analisi e di interpretazione.* Turin, 1962.

Maritain, Jacques, *Man and the State.* Chicago, 1951.

FASCIST VIEWS

Gentile, Giovanni, *Genesi e struttura della società.* Florence, 1946. Translated and edited by H. S. Harris as *Genesis and Struc-ture of Society.* Urbana, Ill., 1960. The views of the official philos-opher of Italian fascism from the standpoint of "actual idealism."

STANLEY I. BENN

STATEMENTS. See PROPOSITIONS, JUDGMENTS, SEN-TENCES, AND STATEMENTS.

STEBBING, LIZZIE SUSAN (1885–1943), English logician and philosopher, was born in London. A very delicate child, she received a discontinuous education until she went to Girton College, Cambridge, in 1906. While at Cambridge she happened to read Bradley's *Ap-pearance and Reality,* which led to her interest in philoso-phy. She became a pupil of the logician W. E. Johnson. From 1913 to 1915 she lectured in philosophy at King's College, London; and she became a lecturer at Bedford Col-lege, London, in 1915 and a professor in 1933.

In London Miss Stebbing's philosophical development was stimulated by the meetings of the Aristotelian Society, which were often attended by Russell, Whitehead, and G. E. Moore; and she always acknowledged the philosoph-ical influence of Moore as particularly strong. In 1931 she published *A Modern Introduction to Logic* and in 1937 *Philosophy and the Physicists,* which were by a consider-able degree the most substantial of her books. She wrote numerous papers, the best of which are to be found in *Mind* and the *Proceedings of the Aristotelian Society.*

In philosophy Susan Stebbing's main interests lay in the metaphysical questions posed by logic and in the founda-tions of science. Much of her work in these topics is con-tained in *A Modern Introduction to Logic.* The book's merit does not lie in any originality in formal logic, or even in its method of presenting formal structures, but rather in its clear exposition of the logical theories of the early twentieth century, together with a stimulating, lucid, per-ceptive account of the metaphysical problems the new logical techniques either dispersed or clarified, and of the metaphysics that lay behind these logical theories. It was the first book on modern logic which introduced together and comprehensively both the formalism and its related philosophical problems. It is probably still the best intro-duction for a reader prepared to give serious thought to such problems.

In the professional journals Miss Stebbing published papers on a range of topics closely related to those of *A Modern Introduction to Logic,* but her interests were not confined to such purely academic, though deeply absorb-ing, matters. She wrote several books on what one might call logic in practice. (Her book *Thinking to Some Purpose* is a good example both in its title and in its content.) She was strongly convinced of the importance of rationality and clarity in the conduct of human affairs and of the immense importance of knowledge. She attempted, therefore to expose the artifices by which hard facts are obscured in soft language, either so that the unscrupulous may deceive us or so that we may hide from ourselves what we do not wish to see. Her books in this field are especially valuable for their actual examples of irrationality and emotional persuasion in high places and on vital matters.

This commitment to rational clarity was combined with her more purely professional interests and skills in *Philosophy and the Physicists*. In the course of writing books with the ostensible aim of popularizing contemporary science, Sir James Jeans and Sir Arthur Eddington had argued that modern physics shows the world to be quite other than the sort of place it seems to be, not merely physically but also metaphysically. Both argued for idealist views of physics and, consequently, for a comfortable if imperfectly clear form of theism. In much of her book Miss Stebbing exposed the fallacies, needless obscurities and mystifications with which the pages of Jeans and Eddington abound. *Philosophy and the Physicists* is an excellent piece of rational cool criticism, but a significant characteristic of the book is its implicit faith that we need not seek protection behind intellectual smoke screens and, indeed, that this sort of evasion prevents any really dignified adjustment to the human situation based on knowledge and reason. Susan Stebbing deeply believed that such an adjustment is possible.

Bibliography

Books by Susan Stebbing are *A Modern Introduction to Logic* (London, 1931; 2d ed., revised, London, 1933); *Philosophy and the Physicists* (London, 1937); *Thinking to Some Purpose* (London, 1939); and *Ideals and Illusions* (London, 1941).

The Aristotelian Society collected the material for *Philosophical Studies: Essays in Memory of L. Susan Stebbing* (London, 1948), a volume of essays that contains an appreciation by John Wisdom and a full bibliography of Miss Stebbing's writings.

G. C. NERLICH

STEFANINI, LUIGI (1891–1956), Italian personalist philosopher, taught at Messina and Padua. He was a founder of the Gallarate movement and the founder and first editor of the *Rivista di estetica*. Much of Stefanini's own philosophy is to be found in his work on the history of philosophy. He tried to demonstrate by careful historical analysis that authentic religious and metaphysical needs are adequately met by certain historical positions, especially those of St. Augustine and St. Bonaventure. His guiding principle, "paradigmatism," is of Platonic and Neoplatonic origin and may be stated thus: that which is created in the image of another (as is man) has as its constitutive imperative, or life vocation, the expression in itself of its transcendental model.

Stefanini professed in turn Christian idealism, spiritualism, and personalism. His Christian idealism was based on a critique of Giovanni Gentile's claim that the self generates the self and the world and hence is the paradigm of the world. Stefanini held that the self apprehends itself not as self-generating but as created and therefore has its paradigm in an other. Art is an immediate expression of that other and provides an approach to the Christian experience, in which the image of God in the human subject is remodeled on the higher paradigm of Christ.

Stefanini's spiritualism began in a critique of historicism, phenomenology, and existentialism. All of these, he claimed, divide the transcendental from the existential. He sought to heal this split by the analysis of the self. The self is not existence as given (*Dasein*) but existence that utters

itself. The self is spirit, or word, and this word does not utter, but alludes to, the Absolute; in this way it reveals its dependence. The purest form of this allusion to the Absolute is the Word of God, Christ. The vocation of the Christian is to utter that Word in himself.

Stefanini called his most mature thought "personalism." The self is central to every form of participation and is the only ultimate point of reference. But the self cannot sustain itself; it rests upon the other, and the transcendent is therefore the principle of the self's being. The self realizes itself as a person by its relation to the transcendent. It seeks to realize the transcendent in itself according to the limits and form of its own being.

Works by Stefanini

Idealismo cristiano. Turin, 1926.
Platone, 2 vols. Padua, 1932–1935.
Spiritualismo cristiano. Brescia, 1942.
La metafisica della persona. Brescia, 1948.
La metafisica dell'arte. Brescia, 1949.

Works on Stefanini

Bortolaso, Giovanni, "Uno spiritualista cristiano: Luigi Stefanini." *Civiltà cattolica* (1956), No. 1, 295–304.

Carlini, Armando, "Incontri e scontri con Stefanini e con Sciacca." *Giornale critico della filosofia italiana*, Series III, Vol. 4 (1950), 841–893.

Chaix-Ruy, Jules, "Les Philosophes italiens d'aujourd'hui." *Revue thomiste*, Vol. 55 (1947), 407 ff.

De Ruggiero, Guido, "Stefanini." *La critica* (1934), 383 ff.

Luigi Stefanini. Filosofi d'oggi series. Turin. Contains a complete bibliography.

A. ROBERT CAPONIGRI

STEFFENS, HENRICH (1773–1845), philosopher, scientist, and novelist and short-story writer of Danish and German descent. Steffens was born in Stavanger, Norway, the son of a physician in the service of the Dano-Norwegian monarchy. From 1790 to 1794 Steffens studied natural science, especially mineralogy and geology, in Copenhagen. He next studied natural history in Kiel, where he became interested in philosophy. In 1798 he moved to Jena, drawn not least by the natural philosophy of Friedrich Schelling, whose *Erster Entwurf eines Systems der Naturphilosophie* had appeared in 1797. In Jena, Steffens met Schelling, Goethe, and August Schlegel; and in Berlin in 1799 he met Friedrich Schlegel and Friedrich Schleiermacher.

In 1802 Steffens returned to Copenhagen to lecture on natural philosophy. Through his large audience he influenced the development of the romantic movement in Denmark, but he failed to obtain the university position he had hoped for, and in 1804 he accepted a chair in natural philosophy and mineralogy at the University of Halle. In 1811 he was appointed professor of physics in Breslau, where he remained, except for a brief period of service as a volunteer in the war against Napoleon in 1813–1814, until 1832. In that year Steffens became professor at Berlin, where he lectured on natural philosophy, anthropology, and geology until his death.

Steffens' philosophy was markedly influenced by Spinoza and by Spinozistic pantheism, as well as by Schelling. Schelling's *Von der Weltseele, eine Hypothese der höheren Physik zur Erklärung des allgemeinen Organismus* ("On the World-soul, a Hypothesis of Higher Physics in Explanation of the General Organism") appeared in 1798, and in Steffens' *Beiträge zur innern Naturgeschichte der Erde* ("Contributions to the Inner Natural History of the Earth"; 1801) the influence of Schelling is readily discernible. The title of Schelling's work gives an indication of the substance and trend of Steffens' philosophical thinking; it is a blend of natural science and speculative philosophy imbued with the general spirit of the romantic movement, somewhat less speculative than that of Schelling.

Steffens viewed the history of nature as a development or evolution from inorganic stages to organic and animate forms, governed by a divine purpose. His pantheism found characteristic expression in the view that nature itself is creative, the acme of the natural creative process being the free individual human personality, or spirit. According to Steffens' *Anthropologie* (1822) man is a living unity of spirit and nature—a microcosm, in the sense that the history of mankind mirrors the development of nature itself. He found in myths and mythological traditions a true, though symbolically expressed, understanding and knowledge of nature; however, he believed that a proper scientific study of nature was a necessary prerequisite for a correct interpretation of the meaning of myths.

Works by Steffens

Beiträge zur innern Naturgeschichte der Erde. Freiburg, 1801.
Grundzüge der philosophischen Naturwissenschaft. Berlin, 1806.
Anthropologie. Breslau, 1822.
Was ich erlebte, 10 vols. Breslau, 1840–1844. Steffens' autobiography; an important source for the study of the romantic movement in Germany.

Works on Steffens

Petersen, Richard, *Henrich Steffens.* Copenhagen, 1881.
Waschnitus, Victor, *Henrich Steffens.* Neumünster, Germany, 1939.

KNUT ERIK TRANÖY

STEINER, RUDOLF (1861–1925), German philosopher and occultist, was born in Kraljevic, Hungary, of Catholic parents. His early education was obtained at technical secondary schools and the Polytechnic Institute of Vienna. Steiner's anthroposophical teaching, presented as "spiritual science," is an extraordinary synthesis of "organic" ideas in nineteenth-century German thought with theosophical material and fresh occult intuitions. In 1902 Steiner became a lecturer and general secretary of the Theosophical Society's German branch, but his earlier thought had been basically formed between 1890 and 1897, years devoted to the study and editing of Goethe's scientific writings at the Goethe-Archiv in Weimar. In this time, and during a period (1897–1900) as editor of the *Magazin: Monatschrift für Litteratur,* he developed his own views of evolution, natural organization, and science through confrontation with the ideas of Darwin, Haeckel, Nietzsche, and contemporary German philosophies.

Steiner presented his synthesis as a modern scientific and monistic world conception, despite the range of esoteric content it eventually included. His early work, *Philosophie der Freiheit* (1896), contained no occult material, but it left room for inclusion of such material by the theories of knowledge and of spiritual freedom which it expounded: Mechanistic science gives only abstract knowledge of some uniform relations in nature. The model for fuller knowledge of individual beings is the organic idea of a self-evolving and self-directing organism, which Goethe saw in the "primal plant." The method for generalizing such knowledge is one of intuitive thinking. Steiner espoused a "monism of thought": a valid world image is ever building as individual spirits live in (*miterleben*) the organic world process.

Heralding Nietzsche's independence of thought, Steiner followed him in rejecting both natural teleology and objective moral laws. Yet he maintained that Nietzsche was always protestingly and tragically dashing his free spirit against an alien culture and a limited science of nature. Nietzsche's doctrine of "eternal recurrence," however, was a factor which led Steiner to give sympathetic attention to Indian thought. Nature is, after all, but one manifestation of spiritual reality, which reveals itself more directly in thought and in art. Among Indian ideas which Steiner adopted while a theosophist is the fourfold construction of man on earth as having the physical, the ether, the astral bodies, and the "I," with their respective powers of development and transformation.

After 1907 conflict with Annie Besant's pro-Hindu policies led Steiner to withdraw from the Theosophical Society, but he continued on an independent line of esoteric thinking, to which in 1913 he gave the name "anthroposophy." Natural evolution, he then taught, has thus far been a progression of bodily organizations into which "pure spirit" descends through successive reincarnations with the aim of producing individual self-consciousness. Reaching its apogee in the Renaissance, this development showed its dangerous limitations in nineteenth-century individualism. The societal remedy, Steiner declared in 1919, was not the collectivism of a totalitarian state but a "three-fold social organism," in which the juridical, spiritual, and economic spheres of life are independently organized as three autonomous interacting systems. Equality is a concept applying particularly to the juridical sphere of rights (which includes just compensation for work), liberty to the spiritual domain, and fraternity or voluntary cooperation to the economic organization of production.

Steiner's own interest lay primarily in the liberty of the spiritual sphere, which included great reaches of "cosmic memory." In future stages of evolution, spirit, without loss of self-consciousness, must ascend again through knowledge of its cosmic relations to its universality and transcendence over matter. Special organs ("the lotuses") must be cultivated to apprehend the higher worlds of spirit and the traces left by their events in the cosmic ether. These include the anti-Lucifer impulses given by Buddha, Zarathustra, Plato, and Christ and the regenerative solar influence of the blood shed in the mystery of Golgotha.

After World War I Steiner was able to establish a cultural center, the Goetheanum, in Switzerland at Dornach, near Basel. His movement spread from Germany to England, the United States, and other countries. Anthroposophy was practiced at various levels of initiation; those not ready for the higher insights could participate in the preliminary disciplines. These included eurythmic dance, mystery plays, organic agriculture and therapy, and distinctive educational measures in a number of notable elementary schools, beginning with the Waldorf School in Stuttgart. While the higher aim of Steiner's pedagogy was to develop special powers of spiritual insight, the cultivation of moral balance, a harmony of virtuous dispositions intermediate between excesses and defects, was considered a prerequisite.

Bibliography

The writings of Rudolf Steiner are extensive. His autobiography, *Mein Lebensgang* (Dornach, 1925), was translated by Olin D. Wannamaker as *The Course of My Life* (New York, 1928).

Of basic interest to students of general philosophy are *Philosophie der Freiheit* (Berlin, 1896), translated as *Philosophy of Spiritual Activity* (2d ed., rev. and enl., London, 1916); *Goethes Weltanschauung* (Stuttgart, 1897); and *Friedrich Nietzsche: Ein Kämpfer gegen seine Zeit* (1895; expanded 2d ed., Dornach, 1926).

For further developments of his thought in various directions, see *Knowledge of the Higher Worlds and Its Attainment* (London and New York, 1923); *The New Art of Education* (London and New York, 1928); *The Problems of Our Time* (London and New York, 1919); and *The Writings and Lectures of Rudolf Steiner*, compiled by P. M. Allen (New York, 1956).

A collected edition of Steiner's major writings was begun in observation of the centennial of his birth. Vol. I in English has appeared as *Cosmic Memory: Prehistory of Earth and Man*, Rudolf Steiner Publications (West Nyack, N.Y., 1961); it is a translation by Karl E. Zimmer of *Aus der Akasha-Chronik*. Four additional volumes have been published. For additional information, the reader may consult the *Bibliographie der Werke Rudolf Steiners*, prepared by Guenther Wachsmuth (Dornach, 1942).

A secondary work of interest is J. W. Hauer, *Werden und Wesen der Anthroposophie* (Stuttgart, 1922).

HORACE L. FRIESS

STEPHEN, LESLIE (1832–1904), English man of letters, was the son of James and Jane Venn Stephen, both of whom came from families in the innermost group of the reforming Evangelicals who formed the so-called Clapham Sect. He attended Eton, briefly and unhappily, and then went to Trinity Hall, Cambridge, where he was made a fellow in 1854. Fellows had then to be ordained in the Church of England, and Stephen took holy orders and eventually became a priest, although he was not deeply religious. At the same time, religious doubt and disaffection began to trouble him. In 1862, as a result of these doubts, he resigned his fellowship, and in 1864 he left Cambridge for good. By 1865 he had completely lost all religious belief. He settled in London and began writing for various journals. Thereafter he wrote continually, copiously, and on a very wide range of topics.

In 1867 he married Thackeray's daughter Harriet Marian. She died in 1875, leaving him with one child. Three years later he married Julia Jackson Duckworth, a widow. They had four children, one of whom became the writer Virginia Woolf. Mrs. Stephen died in 1895.

Stephen was for many years editor of the *Cornhill Magazine*. In 1882 he accepted an invitation to edit the newly projected *Dictionary of National Biography*. The success of the project was largely due to his lengthy period of arduous service in this position (he wrote 387 of the biographies himself). Stephen was knighted in 1901.

Stephen was not a considerable innovator, in philosophy, in historical method, or in literary criticism. He had, however, very great gifts of rapid narration and clear and lively exposition. His work on the history of thought is based on massive reading and wide acquaintance with the social, political, and religious aspects of the periods of which he wrote. If it is neither original in its criticism nor profound in its understanding of positions, it is still useful and has not been entirely superseded because of its grasp of the broader contexts of thought and the skill with which it brings out the continuities from one period to another and from earlier formulations of problems to later ones.

It was Stephen who made Thomas Huxley's coinage "agnostic" an English word, and the problems and beliefs springing from his agnosticism underlay both his major historical works and his philosophical writings. He rejected theism of the sort he had originally been taught because he rejected the doctrine of original sin and because the problem of evil seemed to him insoluble. To evade this problem by confessing the transcendence and incomprehensibility of God was, he thought, to change from a believer into a skeptic, and in that case the part of honesty was simply to avow oneself an agnostic. But true Victorian that he was, he felt that morality, by this view, becomes gravely problematical. If there is no deity to sanction moral principles, why will—why should—men obey them?

To answer these questions was part of Stephen's aim in his investigations of eighteenth-century thought. He dealt more systematically with them, and with others, in his least successful and most tedious book, *The Science of Ethics*. The agnostic, he held, must place morality on a scientific basis, and this means that there must be nothing in his ethics that is outside the competence of scientific inquiry. Brought up on John Stuart Mill and profoundly influenced by Darwin, Stephen attempted to cut through what he impatiently dismissed as academic debates about morality by showing that moral beliefs were the result neither of excessively rational utilitarian calculation nor of mysterious intuition but of the demands of the social organism in its struggle for survival. Since the healthy survival of the social organism must increasingly coincide with conditions that bring the greatest happiness to the greatest number of those individuals who are the "cells" in the "social tissue," utilitarianism is not entirely false. But its atomistic analysis of society is erroneous, and its criterion of rightness is neither adequate nor entirely accurate. The healthy survival of society, and of oneself as part of it, can alone serve as sanction for morality, and the rules for that health, which are mirrored in our instincts and our deepest habits and appear in consciousness as intuitively known moral rules, can be put on a scientific basis only when we come to possess, as we do not yet, a scientific sociology.

Works by Stephen

Stephen's works are far too numerous to be listed completely here. *Essays on Freethinking and Plainspeaking* (London, 1873) and *An Agnostic's Apology and Other Essays* (London, 1893) contain most of his better-known popular essays. *The Science of Ethics* (London, 1882) is his only purely philosophical work. His important historical studies are *History of English Thought in the Eighteenth Century* (2 vols., London, 1876; 3d ed., 1902); *The English Utilitarians* (3 vols., London, 1900); and *Hobbes* (London, 1904). To these the lectures in *English Thought and Society in the Eighteenth Century* (London, 1904) provide a valuable supplement.

Works on Stephen

The standard biography is F. W. Maitland's charming *Life and Letters of Leslie Stephen* (London, 1908), which contains an adequate bibliography of Stephen's work. Noel Annan, in *Leslie Stephen* (London, 1952), studies Stephen as a representative Victorian thinker and as a link between the Clapham Sect and the Bloomsbury Group.

J. B. SCHNEEWIND

STERN, LOUIS WILLIAM (1871–1938), German philosopher and psychologist, was born in Berlin and received his Ph.D under Hermann Ebbinghaus in Berlin in 1892. From 1897 to 1915 he taught philosophy and psychology at the University of Breslau, and in 1915 he moved to Hamburg, where, in 1919, he helped to found the University of Hamburg. He was forced into exile in 1933 by the Nazi government and became professor of psychology and philosophy at Duke University. He died in Durham, North Carolina.

As a psychologist Stern revolted against the elementarism (the belief in the adequacy of analysis of consciousness into its elementary parts) current in Germany before the general acceptance of Gestalt psychology. In his early studies of the perception of change and motion, he employed phenomenological methods and anticipated some later developments in Gestalt psychology. He soon gave up psychophysical experimentation, however, and pioneered in various fields of applied psychology, such as psychology of childhood, forensic psychology, intelligence testing (he introduced the concept of the intelligence quotient), and vocational psychology. Stern's work in psychology was always timely and often ahead of his times; he therefore earned a reputation as a psychologist which he never enjoyed as a philosopher, for most of his philosophizing was either opposed to, or out of touch with, contemporary movements. Some resemblance to *Lebensphilosophie* can be discerned, but he had little contact with Wilhelm Dilthey and his circle. Stern's philosophy must be understood in conjunction with his own psychological work, as providing the presuppositions for his lifelong scientific focus on the individual person—not on elements in his behavior and not on abstract universal laws relating them, but on the unique man. Even against Gestalt psychology, which likewise rejected elementarism, Stern's motto was: "No *Gestalt* without a *Gestalter*." The *Gestalter* was the person.

Stern called his philosophy critical personalism to distinguish it from other personalistic theories, such as animism, vitalism, and Cartesianism, which were based upon the familiar dualism of mind and body. For him the person was an integral totality (*unitas multiplex*) whose defining property was purposive activity. What is not a person is a thing. A thing is not a whole but merely an aggregate; not autonomous but determined from without; not concretely individual but fragmentary or abstract. The person–thing distinction does not correspond to the mind–body distinc-

tion; rather, Stern held, the person is "psychophysically neutral," and both mind and body are thinglike abstractions from the original concreteness of a person sufficiently complex to be called an organism. Only some persons are conscious; indeed, only some of them are living. The person–thing distinction is repeated hierarchically, and the world is a system of persons included in and inclusive of others. A thing is a person seen from the standpoint of the supervenient person; that is, a person which includes other persons as parts.

With this conception, which suggests Aristotle, Leibniz, and Gustav Fechner, Stern formulated his theory of teleomechanics as a way of avoiding an ontological dichotomy between teleology and mechanism. Mechanical uniformities, patterns of thing-behaviors, are derivative from teleological activities of supervenient personal beings in which the things are components. By this theory Stern attempted to derive the formal concepts and principles of the thing-world as we know it, such as magnitude, uniformity, class, causality, space, and time. By making these concepts and principles derivative, not fundamental, Stern's theory gave metaphysical priority to teleological and irreducibly individualistic notions.

Since the concrete substances of the world are teleological both as goal-setting and as goal-realizing, Stern identified the concept of intrinsic value with that of genuine, or personal, being. There are values corresponding to every level of person, indeed to every individual in the hierarchy of persons. But whereas in the theory of teleomechanism persons become things in the context of supervenient persons and thereby have at most extrinsic value, Stern later explored interpersonal relations in which the autonomy of each person is preserved and heightened through those relations which constitute a higher person. To the teleomechanical (cosmological) relation between persons Stern now added the introceptive (axiological) relation, by which ends and intrinsic values of other persons as such are utilized by each person as factors in his own selfhood and autonomous self-determination and growth. In the formation of more inclusive and autonomous persons, the value of the whole suffuses the included persons with a radiative value (*Strahlwert*) instead of depersonalizing them as merely instrumentally valuable.

Stern's studies of love, religion, art, history, and ethics are deep and perceptive applications of his account of introception and radiative values. The theory of radiative value is especially fruitful in his accounts of symbolism and expression in many fields, and in his theory of introception he attempted to rationalize the value-oriented assessment of total personality characteristic of his psychology of individual differences.

Stern's personalism differs from that of personal idealism in that it is neither theistic nor idealistic, nor so radically pluralistic. It has closer resemblances to Jan Christiaan Smuts's holism and to some phases of Max Scheler's theory of value.

Bibliography

Works by Stern are *Person und Sache*, 3 vols. (Leipzig, 1906–1924); *Personalistik als Wissenschaft* (Leipzig, 1932); and *Allgemeine Psychologie auf personalistischer Grundlage* (The Hague, 1936), translated by H. D. Spoerl as *General Psychology from the Personalistic Standpoint* (New York, 1938). An autobiographical essay may be found in Carl Murchison, *History of Psychology in Autobiography* (Worcester, Mass., 1930), Vol. I, pp. 335–388.

LEWIS WHITE BECK

STEWART, DUGALD (1753–1828), with whom the Scottish philosophy of common sense acquired the dignity of an institution, was born in Edinburgh. At the University of Edinburgh, where his father was professor of mathematics, he studied logic and moral philosophy under teachers influenced by Thomas Reid's *Inquiry into the Human Mind on the Principles of Common Sense* (1764). From the classes in natural philosophy Stewart carried away the greatest admiration for "the inductive method" preached by Bacon. In 1771 he went to Glasgow, partly in order to hear Reid's lectures. He returned to Edinburgh to deputize for his ailing father, became conjoint professor of mathematics in 1775, and took over the duties of the chair until his appointment in 1785 as professor of moral philosophy. In 1792 he published the first volume of the *Elements of the Philosophy of the Human Mind* (the second in 1814, the third in 1827), the *Philosophical Essays* in 1810, and *The Philosophy of the Active and Moral Powers of Man* in 1828. These are his most important works.

Philosophy of mind. Stewart saw himself as following Reid in a Baconian reformation of the philosophy of mind. Natural philosophy became science, he held, when inquiry, freed from metaphysical conjecture, was directed toward discovering by observation and experiment the laws governing the connection of physical phenomena. The science of nature has advanced by bringing these uniformities, by the same method, under laws of higher generality, reaching in some cases laws of great explanatory power capable of unifying widely different areas of phenomena. (Stewart left a small place in his account of the procedure of science for the use of analogy and for hypotheses recommending themselves by virtue of their simplicity.) The transformation of the philosophy of mind is to be similar. It requires that the phenomena of consciousness be approached without conjecture and that the laws of their connection be inductively established. The aim of a science of mind is to arrive at a knowledge of the "general laws of our constitution" which would correspond to Newtonian principles in physics and, like them, would make possible the deductive explanation of a great range of phenomena.

The science of mind necessarily presupposes what Reid called—unhappily, in Stewart's opinion—"the principles of common sense." He had several objections to this description of our intuitive convictions about ourselves and about the world. "Common sense" in common usage means much the same as "mother wit" and is used not to refer to these intuitive convictions but to practical sagacity in everyday life. Moreover, the expression has connotations which render it peculiarly unfit for the technical use to which Reid assigned it: They make his appeal to common sense against philosophical paradox and skepticism sound like an appeal to the vulgar against the learned. Instead of "the principles of common sense," Stewart preferred to speak of "the fundamental laws of human belief." It is reason, not common sense, which authorizes

the truths to which Reid appeals, and these truths are not properly termed "principles." Principles allow inferences, but nothing follows from these truths: "From such propositions as these—*I exist; I am the same person to-day that I was yesterday; the material world has an existence independent of my mind; the general laws of nature will continue, in future, to operate uniformly as in time past*—no inference can be deduced, any more than from the intuitive truths prefixed to the *Elements* of Euclid" (*Works*, Vol. III, p. 45). In Stewart's opinion, the special character of all mathematical reasoning is that, governed by axioms, it proceeds entirely from definitional premises; the demonstrated "truth" of a mathematical proposition is, accordingly, its demonstrated connection with its premises. Mathematical axioms and the fundamental laws of belief, although different kinds of intuitive truth, are alike in another respect, Stewart held. As axioms govern mathematical reasoning, so these laws are governing presuppositions, some of them of all our thinking, others of all our thinking within wide areas. They inevitably carry with them the tacit consent of mankind, and the denial of any of them is quite unlike the repudiation of the stubbornest, most widespread prejudice: If we suspected that a man was seriously prepared to act on this denial, we would think he was losing his reason.

Unity of the philosophical sciences. Stewart borrowed from Hume and Reid an idea which became vividly real to his imagination, that of the unity of the "philosophical sciences" (such as logic, moral and political philosophy, and aesthetics) in their common dependence on the philosophy of mind. He never traced with any precision the articulations between root and branches. He saw the need for a study of human nature "*considered as one great whole*"—since the philosophy of mind was not to be developed in isolation from the disciplines it was to unify—but his studies of human nature are fragmentary and keep to its surface. Though nothing of positive philosophical interest emerged from the idea of a unified totality of the philosophical sciences, Stewart's good sense and great caution at least held him back from any totalitarian excesses: he kept intact, for instance, the necessary discontinuities between psychology on the one hand and on the other, logic, ethics, and metaphysics.

Language. Stewart wrote at length about language. In agreement with Reid he held that a "natural" language of gesture, facial expression, and tone of voice, its signs "instinctively" understood, made possible the formation of language whose signs are established by convention. He criticized Reid for his unguarded inferences from the scaffolding of speech to beliefs that had framed it. He stressed the dependence of meaning, and the grasp of meaning, on context. Words in isolation often have no more significance than the letters composing them. Philosophers readily imagine that they have split up unitary acts of understanding into a complexity of related ideas when all they have done is something like parsing, mistaking "*grammatical elements of speech*" for ideas. He argued that we "*think* as well as *speak* by means of words," or at least by using signs of one sort or another, whenever our thinking contains any element of generality. He constantly emphasized the need for watchfulness in a philosophical approach to the language we all employ in speaking of the mind. Its development from our ways of speaking about material things, the ease with which theories can be read off from the metaphors must be kept in view, and the theory-canceling variety and inconsistency of the metaphors.

Theism and morality. The substantival mind, the soul, oneself, is not, according to Stewart, something of which we are introspectively conscious; our knowledge of it is wholly "relative," derived from the phenomena of consciousness which refer themselves to it as their subject. We have the same sort of knowledge of material substance. Stewart's repeated polemics against materialism tended to be methodological rather than metaphysical; any proposal to substitute a physiological for an introspective psychology (supported by wide study of the diverse manifestations of human life) struck, he thought, at the foundations of the science of mind. He did, however, maintain that the immateriality of the mind, "which is involved in the only conceptions of matter and mind that we are capable of forming," has an important place among the considerations that should lead us to expect life after death. It establishes a presumption of immortality, and it enables us to counter objections to the possibility of an existence apart from the body. Other considerations turn on the principle that, as experience shows, our nature is adapted to the nature of things. There are tendencies deeply rooted within our nature which require a future life for their realization.

Along with a version of the Argument from Design, containing little that is not commonplace, Stewart had a supporting argument for the existence of God in which part of Hume's account of causation figures. Hume rightly explained physical causation in terms merely of constant conjunction. But since every change must be the result of real agency, and since will alone is capable of this, we are obliged to infer from the changes in the physical world the universal agency of God. We are ourselves self-determining, and therefore morally responsible, agents. The irreducible notions of right and wrong, Stewart considered, may be ascribed legitimately but not very illuminatingly to reason or to a moral sense. What matters is a recognition of the objectivity of right and wrong. The substantial universality of moral principles will be discerned when it is realized that the same principle can govern different conduct in different circumstances or where "speculative opinions" differ.

Stewart put the whole of his philosophy to moral use. In the judgment of an eminent contemporary, he was "one of the greatest of didactic orators," and his teaching acquired a widened authority as providing a context of stability for ideas of social progress and political liberalism which he himself encouraged. Linked with Reid's teaching, it had a very considerable influence in America. In France their ideas were a major force in the reaction effected by Pierre-Paul Royer-Collard, Théodore Jouffroy, and Victor Cousin against characteristic eighteenth-century modes of philosophical thought.

Bibliography

Stewart's *Collected Works*, edited by Sir William Hamilton, with a memoir by John Veitch, was published in 11 volumes (Edinburgh, 1854–1860); Vols. X and XI were brought out by Veitch.

There are chapters on Stewart in James McCosh, *The Scottish Philosophy* (London, 1875), and Henry Laurie, *Scottish Philosophy in Its National Development* (Glasgow, 1902). Terence Martin, *The Instructed Vision* (Bloomington, Ind., 1961), deals with the influence of the common-sense school on the American mind. See also Victor Cousin, *Philosophie écossaise*, 3d ed. (Paris, 1857), and T. T. Segerstedt, *The Problem of Knowledge in Scottish Philosophy* (Lund, Sweden, 1935).

S. A. GRAVE

STIRNER, MAX (1806–1856), was the nom de plume of the German individualist philosopher Johann Kaspar Schmidt. Born in Bayreuth, Bavaria, Schmidt had a poor childhood. His academic career was long and fragmented. From 1826 to 1828 he studied philosophy at the University of Berlin, where he fell under the influence of Hegel. After brief periods at the universities of Erlangen and Königsberg, he returned to Berlin in 1832 and with some difficulty gained a certificate to teach in Prussian Gymnasiums. Several years of poverty and unemployment followed, until Schmidt found a position as teacher in a Berlin academy for young ladies run by a Madame Gropius. After this he lived something of a double life: the respectable teacher of young ladies had for another self the aspiring philosophical writer who assumed the name of Stirner.

The immediate stimulus that provoked Stirner to write his one important book, *Der Einzige und sein Eigentum* (Leipzig, 1845; translated by Steven T. Byington as *The Ego and His Own*, New York, 1907), was his association with the group of young Hegelians known as Die Freien (the "free ones"), who met under the leadership of the brothers Bruno and Edgar Bauer. In this company Stirner met Marx, Engels, Arnold Ruge, Georg Herwegh, and many other revolutionary intellectuals. In the same circle he also met Marie Dahnhardt, whom he married in 1843 and who left him in 1847. Before the publication of his book Stirner produced only a few brief periodical pieces, including an essay on educational methods printed by Karl Marx in *Rheinische Zeitung*.

Thought. *Der Einzige und sein Eigentum*, a treatise in defense of philosophic egoism, carried to its extreme the young Hegelian reaction against Hegel's teachings. In part it was a bitter attack on contemporary philosophers, particularly those with social inclinations. Stirner's associates among Die Freien were rejected as strongly as Hegel and Feuerbach.

Stirner's approach was characterized by a passionate anti-intellectualism which led him to stress the will and the instincts as opposed to the reason. He attacked systematic philosophies of every kind, denied all absolutes, and rejected abstract and generalized concepts of every kind. At the center of his vision he placed the human individual, of whom alone we can have certain knowledge; each individual, he contended, is unique, and this uniqueness is the very quality he must cultivate to give meaning to his life. Hence, he reached the conclusion that the ego is a law unto itself and that the individual owes no obligations outside himself. All creeds and philosophies based on the concept of a common humanity are, in Stirner's view, false and irrational; rights and duties do not exist; only the might of the ego justifies its actions.

There is much in common between Stirner's embattled

ego and Nietzsche's superman; indeed, Stirner was seen as a forerunner of Nietzsche during the 1890s.

Stirner has often been included with the anarchist philosophers, and he has much in common with them. However, he differs from writers like Godwin, Proudhon, and Kropotkin in that the idea of a system of natural law, or immanent justice, which human law negates, is essential to their points of view. Stirner, however, rejected the idea of any such law, and in this respect he stands nearer to certain existentialists and the nihilists. Furthermore, while the anarchist seeks freedom as his ultimate goal, Stirner regarded such an aim as always being limited by external necessities; in its place he sought uniqueness or "ownness." "Every moment," he said, "the fetters of reality cut the sharpest welts in my flesh. But *my own* I remain."

Stirner agreed with the anarchists, however, in regarding the state as the great enemy of the individual who seeks to fulfill his "own will." The state and the self-conscious and willful ego cannot exist together; therefore the egoist must seek to destroy the state, but by rebellion rather than by revolution. This distinction is essential to Stirner's doctrine. Revolution, in overthrowing an established order, seeks to create another order; it implies a faith in institutions. Rebellion is the action of individuals seeking to rise above the condition they reject; it "demands that one rise, or exalt oneself." Revolution is a social or political act; rebellion is an individual act, and therefore appropriate to the egoist. If rebellion prospers, the state will collapse.

In rebellion the use of force is inevitable, and Stirner envisaged "the war of each against all," in which the egoist fights with all the means at his command. This viewpoint led Stirner to justify and even to exalt crime. Crime is the assertion of the ego, the rejection of the sacred. The aim of egoist rebellion is the free wielding of power by each individual.

In Stirner's view the end of this process is not conflict but a kind of dynamic balance of power between men aware of their own might, for the true egoist realizes that excessive possessions and power are merely limitations on his own uniqueness. His assertion is based on the absence of submissiveness in others; the withdrawal of each man into his uniqueness lessens rather than increases the chance of conflict, for "as unique you have nothing in common with the other any longer, and therefore nothing divisive or hostile either." Stirner argued that far from producing disunity among individuals, egoism allows the freest and most genuine of unions, the coming together without any set organization of the "Union of Egoists," which will replace not only the state with its political repression but also society with its less obvious claims.

Later years. *Der Einzige und sein Eigentum* is not just a most extreme expression of individualism, it is also the single manifestation of Stirner's own revolt against a frustrating life that finally submerged him. In his totally undistinguished later years he embarked on a series of unsuccessful commercial ventures and translated English and French economists. His remaining book, *Die Geschichte der Reaktion* (Berlin, 1852), lacked the fire of discontent that made his earlier work so provocative. Stirner's last years were shadowed by declining powers and haunted by creditors; he died poor and forgotten in 1856.

Bibliography

For further information on Stirner, see Victor Basche, *L'Individualisme anarchiste: Max Stirner* (Paris, 1904); James Gibbons Huneker, *Egoists* (New York, 1921); and John Henry Mackay, *Max Stirner, sein Leben und sein Werk* (Berlin, 1898).

George Woodcock

STÖHR, ADOLF (1855–1921), Austrian philosopher, psychologist, and linguist, was born at St. Pölten and studied law and philology, then botany, and finally philosophy, at the University of Vienna. In 1885 he was appointed *Privatdozent* in theoretical philosophy at the same university, rising to associate professor in 1901 and to full professor of the philosophy of the inductive sciences in 1911. He published some thirty works in logic, natural philosophy, psychology, and philosophy.

Language and thought. Stöhr developed his system of logic in the closest connection with the psychology of thought processes and linguistics. His work deals in great detail with the dependence of thought upon language (what he calls the glossomorphy of thought), and he warned against the dangerous consequences that flow from confusing forms of speech with forms of thought. Not only do we make use of language to fix our thoughts and to communicate our knowledge; we also think in our language, so that the structure of our thought reflects the logical forms of our language. When the course of thought becomes automatic, the result may be that self-critical thought is replaced by an "idle flow of speech" ("glossurgy"), which is frequently even self-contradictory.

Through such reflections Stöhr began the "critique of language" pursued later with such success by other important thinkers. With the aid of this critique, he sought above all to oppose the misuse of language in philosophy and to unmask the muddled philosophical thinking that gives rise to the reification of concepts, metaphors, and allegories. Because "our language compels us to designate consciousness as if it were constructed of a subject, of mental acts and of physical objects" (as in the sentence "I see an object"), the illusion arises that "thoughts have the form (*morphe*) of the language (*glossa*)." The final outcome is that fictions are taken for facts; metaphors, for that which is actually meant. Thus the fact of the psychological "I" is confused with the fiction of the mental "subject," and the fact of phenomenal matter as a complex of visual and tactile sensations is confused with the materialistic fiction of a metaphysical matter (*Wege des Glaubens*, pp. 20 ff.).

Metaphysics. Stöhr distinguished three roots of metaphysical thinking: wonder at the facts (the "theorogonous" metaphysics of the "constructing imagination"); pain (the "pathogonous" metaphysics of the "suffering heart"); and glossomorphic confusion (the "glossogonous" metaphysics of the "rolling word"). Metaphysics can supply no universally valid knowledge because the transcendental is in principle unknowable; one can only "have faith" in the existence of something beyond experience. This metaphysical faith is the expression of a subjective reaction of the heart and is "lived." Knowledge cannot engender faith, and faith cannot substitute for knowledge; for the two are of an entirely different nature" ("Ist Metaphysik möglich?," p. 30). "Everyone proceeds along that path of faith which his whole constitution obliges him to take. There is neither an inductive nor a deductive proof for or against a faith" (*Wege des Glaubens*, p. 36).

Stöhr rejected both "pathogonous" and "glossogonous" metaphysics, and thus the whole of metaphysics in the traditional sense, with its claim to knowledge of the transcendental. Anyone who pretends to provide such knowledge is philosophizing both "pathogonously" and "glossogonously." Anyone who is unable to find the meaning of life in life itself, in the work and tasks of life, and therefore suffers in being alive, seeks that meaning beyond the world and life. Since he would like to convince others of the truth of his outlook on life and the world, which is directed to the beyond, he intentionally or unintentionally misuses language in order to offer rhetorical pseudo solutions to metaphysical pseudo problems as if they were genuine solutions to real problems.

Stöhr himself professed "theorogonous" metaphysics. He defined it as "the satisfaction of an artistic propensity by means of the elegant construction of a world view"—which, of course, must not contradict the facts. "Thus metaphysics, in contrast to the empirical sciences, does not grow through apposition, but continuous building, rebuilding and building anew" (*Lehrbuch der Logik*, p. 304). Stöhr constructed his own view of nature in this manner, not dogmatically but as an exercise, assigning more importance to the creation than to the validity of a system. (He often said in discussion: "I am only playing with these ideas. I do not say that this is the way things are. I do not say even that this is the way they probably are. All that I say is that this is the way they may be.")

Natural philosophy. Stöhr attempted to explain the structure of matter and the peculiarities of organic happenings in conformity with his undogmatic approach. Since for him mechanism was the sole intelligible conception of nature, he sought to understand both the organic world and the inorganic world with the help of mechanistic conceptual models. Stöhr proved to be as original a thinker in the philosophy of nature as in logic and psychology. That many of his ingenious solutions to problems are today outmoded by the progress of the sciences does not alter the epistemological excellence of his clear and exact style of thought.

Bibliography

Stöhr's major works include *Umriss einer Theorie der Namen* (Leipzig and Vienna, 1889); *Alegbra der Grammatik* (Leipzig and Vienna, 1898); *Philosophie der unbelebten Materie* (Leipzig, 1907); *Der Begriff des Lebens* (Heidelberg, 1909); *Lehrbuch der Logik* (Leipzig and Vienna, 1910); "Ist Metaphysik möglich?" in *Jahrbuch der philosophischen Gesellschaft an der Universität zu Wien 1914 und 1915* (Leipzig, 1916), pp. 25–36; *Psychologie. Tatsachen, Probleme und Hypothesen* (Vienna and Leipzig, 1917; 2d ed., 1922); and *Wege des Glaubens* (Vienna and Leipzig, 1921). Works on Stöhr include Franz Ferdinand Worlitzky, *Über die Philosophie Adolf Stöhrs*, a dissertation (Vienna, 1925), and Franz Austeda, "Der Oesterreicher Adolf Stöhr—einer der bedeutendsten Denker unseres Jahrhunderts," in *Neue Wege*, No. 104 (Vienna, 1955), 3–5.

Franz Austeda
Translated by *Albert E. Blumberg*

STOICISM is that Hellenistic philosophy which sought to make the personal and political lives of men as orderly as the cosmos. In the course of its five-hundred-year history as an organized movement, some of its leaders devoted themselves mainly to understanding the macrocosm, and others emphasized the ethical, political, and religious life of man the microcosm. But all the Stoics believed that the fundamental injunction laid on man is to follow the law of nature, and in the development of Stoicism this injunction acquired a systematic meaning.

Unfortunately, we have only tiny fragments of the writings of the Early Stoa; we have reason to believe that these writings must have been remarkable both in their logical and cosmological insights and in their ethical and political aspects. The Roman Stoics, many of whose works we do have, usually minimize the logic and physics of the Stoics, and commentators like Cicero, Plutarch, Sextus Empiricus, and Diogenes Laërtius, though they cast much light on both the theoretical and practical aspects of early Stoicism, obviously fail to give us a full account of the foundations of Stoicism. As a result, understanding the whole movement is not only a difficult scholarly labor but also one requiring imagination.

Early Stoa. Heraclitus of Ephesus was the father of Stoic physics; his subordination of the individual to the logos or law of nature, his concept of reason as a creative fire (pneuma) residing in the individual and in the universe at large, and his belief in eternal change are essential to all Stoic physics. The Megarians, with their elaborate techniques of refutation and their love of paradox and rigorous inference, gave the Stoics their start in logic. And the Cynics, with their cosmopolitanism, their love of nature as superior to local convention or political power, and above all their belief in the *autarkeia* or autonomy of the virtuous man, did much to create the Stoic ethic. Nor must we neglect the powerful influence exercised on the Stoics by the image of Socrates, whose life and death were emblems of rational self-control.

By 300 B.C., when Zeno started lecturing formally on the Painted Porch (*Stoa Poikile*) in Athens (where the paintings of Polygnotus were), he had absorbed these influences. His school flourished during the period when the city-state was losing its ascendancy in Greek life, when the Greek popular religions were waning, and when scientific research of various sorts was going on in Alexandria, Antioch, and Pergamum. Moreover, all the leading Stoics before Christ were from outside Greece. In short, Athens was no longer the center of world culture; science, religion, and politics were becoming truly international, and Stoicism was one of various expressions of this internationalism.

The Early Stoa blossomed in the third century B.C. and had as its main leaders Zeno of Citium, on Cyprus (c. 336–c. 264); Cleanthes of Assos, in Asia Minor (c. 331–c. 232); and Chrysippus of Soli, in southeastern Asia Minor (c. 280–c. 206). Under their guidance, Stoicism developed its basic doctrines. Though interested in metaphysics, Zeno apparently emphasized *ischus kai kratos*, strength of character in ethical and political action. Of the three Cleanthes was the poet and religious visionary, and Chrysippus was, more than any of them, responsible for developing Stoicism into a system, so that he came to be called "the second founder of Stoicism." But it is hard to distinguish sharply among their contributions, and so they are usually thought of as a creative team which gave Stoicism its basic form and content.

Middle Stoa. In the second and first centuries B.C. the transitional Middle Stoa flourished. In about 156, Diogenes of Seleucia, then leader of the Athenian Stoa, came to Rome as part of a delegation to persuade the Romans to exempt Athens from a fine. He came with Critolaus the Peripatetic and Carneades the Skeptic; the latter outshone him, but the severe, gray-eyed Cato attacked all three of the Athenian philosophical leaders for undermining military virtue; still, the tide of Stoicism was rising in Italy, and the Roman Empire would for centuries ride upon it.

The two most distinguished members of the Middle Stoa were Panaetius of Rhodes (185–c. 110), who profoundly influenced the young Scipio and thus reached the flower of the Roman intellectuals, and Posidonius of Apamea (c. 135–c. 51), the Chrysippus of the Middle Stoa. They brought some aspects of Platonism into Stoicism: Posidonius, the pupil of Panaetius, faces back to the time when the Stoa was building a universal system; Panaetius faces forward to the time when Stoicism became involved in the military, social, and political life of Rome. He helped soften the asceticism of the Early Stoa, attached more value to external goods than the Early Stoa did, and spoke in terms of gradual moral progress or discipleship, not the pure ideal of the wise man. Posidonius, on the other hand, brought rigor and detail to the Stoic system. For instance, he developed a golden age theory of history, describing in detail the time when the wise man ruled originally and men lived happy lives following nature. He also developed the Stoic belief in the fundamental indivisibility of the cosmos.

Late Stoa. The Late Stoa, which flourished and died in the first and second centuries A.D., was Roman. Epictetus, Seneca, and the emperor Marcus Aurelius carried on the work of Panaetius and made the Stoic more a tranquil, useful member of society than a scientist or an ascetic. Of these three Seneca (c. 4 B.C.–A.D. 65) was the most sympathetic to Posidonius the cosmologist, though he never trusted logical theory much. This minister of Nero and writer of tragedies developed the two poles of Stoic ethics, inward tranquillity and social duty.

Epictetus (c. 50–c. 138), a freed slave of a member of Nero's bodyguard, developed the distinction between things in our power (the power to give or withhold assent and to use external impressions) and things not in our power (external impressions, our body, and the rest of the inexorable world). He believed in innate moral predispositions which could be actualized by education or left to decay.

Marcus Aurelius (121–180), the last of the great Stoics, distrusted pure logic and cosmology more than any other leading Stoic. An emperor from 161 until his death, he gave equal weight to the two focuses of Stoic ethics, inward self-control and useful citizenship in the cosmopolis that is the universe.

In the sixteenth century, elements of Stoicism occurred in the thought of men like Justus Lipsius, Michel de Mon-

taigne, Guillaume du Vair, and George Chapman. But as Hiram Haydn points out in *The Counter-Renaissance,* given all the other elements in their thought, they were not in any sense pure Stoics, since there was a large degree of Christian theology in their thought. They were "Stoics" mainly because they emphasized following the laws of nature as much as they emphasized Christian doctrine.

THE SYSTEM OF STOICISM

Some Stoics compared their logic to the wall, their physics to the tree, and their ethics to the fruit of a fertile field. This figure is useful as an aid to understanding a philosophy that employs images so centrally, and that is often inconsistent or, at least to us, opaque. Stoic logic protects the physics and ethics of Stoicism, laying down rules for the validation of truth claims. Physics, protected by these rules, displays the structure of the cosmos. And ethics, the practice for which the field was cultivated, shows men how to imitate and participate in that structure.

Logic. The Greek word *logos* and the logic that articulates its demands had to be translated by the Romans with the phrase *ratio et oratio* ("reason and speech"). Logic is concerned with three aspects of the word: sound (*phone*), significance (*lekton*), and the object signified by significant sound (*ektos hypokeimenon*). Some *lekta* are assertions; others are questions, commands, and the like. Stoic logic dealt primarily with assertions and apparently emphasized one particular way—the connective "if . . . , then . . ." (*synemmenon*)—of relating *lekta*. They saw such conditionals as truth-functional complexes—that is, as having their truth-value determined solely by the truth-values of their components. The Stoics systematically laid down the truth-values of components that made whole conditionals true or false, and they did the same for conjunctions and alternations. For instance, they discovered what we now call the "material conditional"—that is, the kind of conditional which is false only when its "if" clause is true and its "then" clause is false. But their zeal was too great; they offered other kinds of conditionals with other truth conditions, and the Skeptics attacked them for not having one agreed-upon analysis of the all-important conditional. The Stoics claimed that all valid syllogistic arguments could be reduced to a certain set of five so-called undemonstrated arguments (very much like our modern elementary valid argument forms). They were the first systematic nonsyllogistic logicians.

But even a primarily deductive logic like the Stoics', which emphasized the firm connections between *lekta* in order to emphasize the firm connections between parts of this single universe, had to have a way of validating particular claims about the external object (*to ektos hypokeimenon*). The criteria that a particular truth claim must meet became a great issue for the Stoics, since without such criteria their claims in physics were undefended. The difference between a mind picture (*phantasia*, say, a flash of light we make no claims about), casual assent to a mind picture (*synkatathesis,* the belief that there seems to be a white light there), comprehension (*katalepsis,* the conception of a white light which we remember), and science (*episteme,* a consistent system of conceptions about light) is one of degree to the Stoics. Zeno is said to have shown the difference between these degrees of knowledge by likening sensations to extended fingers, casual assent to a loosely closed hand, lucid conception to a fist, and science to his left hand firmly closed around his right fist. At the base of this analysis lay the *phantasia kataleptike,* or apprehensive perception. Sometimes the Stoics said that the criterion such a perception meets is that of clarity (*enargeia*), but they soon learned that some clear perceptions prove false. Sometimes they said that such a perception is one the wise man calls truthful, but the Skeptics attacked this as question-begging, since we recognize the wise man by his ability to recognize the *phantasia kataleptike.* Sometimes the Stoics resorted to general consent as a proof, but the Skeptics attacked this as proving only universal belief, not actual truth. Finally the Stoics turned to probability (*to eulogon*) as the test for the true mind picture. A perception is true if it fits in with others and is useful to believe in. But this was a capitulation to Skeptics like Carneades, who adopted this sort of approach as an alternative to dogmatic belief.

Despite its weaknesses, however, Stoic logic is a monument to the Stoics' intense desire to find the truth and their confidence that they would find it. Subsequent philosophies were to use large pieces of the Stoics' wall in constructing and defending their own assertions.

Physics. The physics of the Stoics was, on the whole, identical with their theology, in which the formative power that makes each thing what it is and harmonizes all things was God. The key words in the Stoic vocabulary are all basically synonymous: God, Zeus, creative fire, ether, the word (logos), reason of the world, soul of the world, law of nature, providence, destiny, and order. The Stoics were monists. There is in their physics no qualitative difference between God and the rest of the universe; God is only the most tense (cohesive) creative aspect of the universe. The stuff which he informs comes from him, is sustained by him, and differs from him only by being more relaxed and less creative. By looking at the Stoic universe both chronologically and as a whole, we can learn much about the Stoic concept of order, which is central to their ethics.

For the Stoic, things do not happen in time; time is a dimension of things. And the eternal course of the universe is, by the nature of things, cyclical, not progressive or regressive. Each cycle is called a *periodos,* or *magnus annus,* and every *periodos* begins with the logos, or the creative fire, passes through the creation and organization of the four elements (water, earthly fire, air, and earth), and ends with a conflagration, a return to the fire from whence all came. This return begins early in the *periodos* and accelerates (entropy increases) until the universe is where it began. And every *periodos* is identical in all details with every other; there is an eternal recurrence of all things. Time being what it is and the *logos spermatikos,* or lifegiving word, containing its own purposes and powers, these changes are autonomous, not stimulated or bounded from without, since space, like time, is only a dimension of body. In short, all change is immanent in God and unchanging in its laws. We now have two of the basic aspects of the Stoic notion of order, autonomy and uniformity.

Considered as a whole (in a late stage of the *periodos*), the universe is a vast rational (orderly) animal, perfectly spherical in shape, a plenum held together and shaped by the *tonos* (strain or tension) that is God himself. Individual things are of four types: those with the least tension holding them together—rocks, for example; those with more tension—plants; those with a rudimentary soul (psyche)—animals; and, finally, the creatures which most closely approximate the total universe of which they are a part—rational beings. These alone are possessed of reason; these alone have a spark of the very divinity that created them. There are two types of such beings, men on earth and gods, who take the form of stars in heaven. The ruling part (*to hegemonikon*) of this universe is the pneuma, or creative fire. Some Stoics—Cleanthes, for example—took the sun to be the pneuma. Beyond the circling outermost heaven, or ether, is the indefinite spaceless void (since there is no space without body). A circle of air lies this side of heaven; inside this circle of air lies a circle of vapor and water. At the very center lies the earth, which is the kernel of the universe and residence of man.

The Stoics defined God as "a rational spirit having itself no shape but making itself into all things." One of their many proofs of his existence was by consent. There is an innate disposition to believe in God; the universal belief in God attests to the existence of this disposition or preconception; to ignore it is to cripple reason; to use it is to believe in God. We have seen how the Skeptics attacked this; they also denied that there is as a matter of fact such common consent to God's existence. Another proof is usually ascribed to Chrysippus. If there exists something greater than human reason can devise, this thing must be the work of some reasoning being that is greater than man, of God or gods. The Skeptics accused this argument of circularity, since it assumed that there was a creative force to be identified with God (or the gods). Why couldn't the structure of the universe emerge from the ordinary course of things? One of the Stoics' most famous proofs was from providence. Only a providential God could produce such beauty, such interlocking purposes as the universe reveals. To this the Skeptics never tired of opposing accounts of disaster and the like. But the Stoics held this proof dear and pointed out that imperfections of detail are essential to perfection of the whole, like darkness in a picture. So important to the Stoic is the belief in *pronoia,* or *providentia,* especially regarding God's benevolent care for mankind, that when Aristarchus of Samos dared to suggest that the sun, not the earth, was stationary at the center of the spheres, the Stoics attacked him for impiety and did much to discredit the idea.

Ethics. The fruits of the tree, ethics, can now be described: Live according to the benevolence and orderliness of the universe. The consequence of such a life is *apatheia,* or *euthymia,* spiritual peace and well-being; another term for this ultimate desideratum was *eudaimonia,* the happy condition of the daimon, or soul, when it resembles the deity. Having achieved this ultimate goal, one's life is as autonomous, as uniform, and as benevolent as God himself.

The means to the achievement of this goal was virtue. All the cardinal virtues are of a piece, impossible without the others, and they are all basically attitudes, not just actions. One is intelligence (knowing what is good and bad); another is bravery (knowing what to fear and what not to fear); a third is justice (knowing how to give everyone what properly belongs to him); and the fourth, competing with the first for importance in the list, is self-control (knowing what impressions to assent to, what passions to moderate or extinguish). At first, there seemed to be for the Stoic a sharp distinction between the virtuous man (the wise man) and the rest (the fools), but as Stoicism modified its ideals, many things once considered totally indifferent to the wise man came to be spoken of as "advantages" to be used (though not to be *needed*). Health, property, and honor were among these advantages; their opposites were disadvantages to be avoided (but not at all costs), and the things totally indifferent (adiaphora) to the wise man became things like the paying of a debt with one piece of money rather than another. By inserting these three categories between the cardinal virtues and their opposites, Stoicism became a philosophy that could appeal to more kinds of men.

The Stoics had two main ways of enjoining men to be wise, the study of physics and ethics and the frequent reference to the wise man, the undisturbed man. In time, the Stoics gave up hope of finding him and spoke in terms of apprenticeship to wisdom, of degrees of wisdom. But the imitation of the wise man was always an important means to wisdom. Before studying Zeno's books and agreeing to take over the Painted Porch, Cleanthes is said to have followed Zeno around for a long time to observe his actions.

The Stoic ethic had as an essential part a broad political theory: the belief that all rational beings, even slaves and foreigners, bore within them a spark of the creative fire. This belief took the form of their doctrine of natural law. The Stoic had more to do than simply seek his own *eudaimonia;* he must, like all other individuals in nature, be of service to his fellow creatures, to his brothers under the fatherhood of God, the *logos spermatikos.* Regardless of national conventions or laws, regardless of property, race, rank, or birth, he must always be cognizant of the creative fire each rational being possesses. The complex Stoic concept of duty (*kathekon*) to be found in Cicero's *De Officiis* makes all Stoic virtues far more than a means to individual spiritual well-being. Unlike the Epicurean, the Stoic had as his absolute duty the promotion of a cosmopolis that would be the very image of the rationally ordered physical world.

Bibliography

ANCIENT WORKS

Arnim, H. von, ed., *Stoicorum Veterum Fragmenta*, 3 vols. Leipzig, 1903–1924. The basic source book on the Early Stoa.

Cicero, Marcus Tullius, *De Officiis*, translated by W. Miller. London, 1913. Very detailed summary.

Cicero, Marcus Tullius, *De Natura Deorum*, translated by H. Rackham. New York, 1933. Very detailed summary.

Diogenes Laërtius, *Lives of Eminent Philosophers*, translated by R. D. Hicks, 2 vols. New York, 1925. Vol. II, Book vii, "Zeno." The usually garrulous Diogenes here gives us an extraordinarily detailed account of Stoic logic.

Sextus Empiricus, *Outlines of Pyrrhonism*, translated by R. G. Bury, Vol. I. Cambridge, 1955. Book II.

Sextus Empiricus, *Against the Logicians*, translated by R. G. Bury, Vol. II. Cambridge, Mass., 1957. The best source on Stoic logic is Sextus Empiricus, the Skeptic.

MODERN WORKS

Arnold, E. Vernon, *Roman Stoicism*. London, 1958. One of the fullest accounts of Stoicism but mistitled, since it is richer on Greek Stoicism than on Roman.

Bréhier, Émile, *Études de philosophie antique*. Paris, 1955. Chs. 11–13 contain some of the most incisive remarks to be found on Stoic logic and physics.

Mates, Benson, *Stoic Logic*. Berkeley and Los Angeles, 1961. Clear and useful on formal logic but neglects both the criteria for true perception and the relationship of logic to Stoic metaphysics.

Pohlenz, M., *Die Stoa*. Göttingen, 1948. Often beautifully written and full of penetrating summary insights.

Sambursky, Samuel, *Physics of the Stoics*. New York, 1959.

Zeller, Eduard, *The Stoics, Epicureans, and Sceptics,* translated by O. J. Reichel. London, 1870; New York, 1962. This old whetstone, on which twentieth-century scholars of Stoicism have sharpened their tools, is, despite the many criticisms leveled at it for minimizing Stoic logic and the like, one of the most useful summaries of Stoicism available.

PHILIP P. HALLIE

STOUT, GEORGE FREDERICK (1860–1944), English philosopher and psychologist. Records of Stout's early life are scant. He was born in South Shields, Durham. A clever boy at school, he went in 1879 to St. John's College, Cambridge, where he obtained first-class honors in the classical tripos with distinction in ancient philosophy and followed this with first-class honors in the moral sciences tripos with distinction in metaphysics. In 1884 he was elected a fellow of his college, and in 1891 he succeeded Croom Robertson as editor of *Mind.* He was appointed Anderson lecturer in comparative psychology at Aberdeen in 1896; Wilde reader in mental philosophy at Oxford in 1899; and professor of logic and metaphysics at the University of St. Andrews in 1903. He remained at St. Andrews, where he was instrumental in establishing a laboratory of experimental psychology, until his retirement in 1936. In 1939 he went to Sydney, Australia, to live with his son Alan, who had been appointed to the chair of moral and political philosophy at the University of Sydney. He spent the remaining years of his life joining vigorously in the discussions of a lively circle of younger philosophers at that university.

Stout's position in the history of philosophy and psychology is at the end of the long line of philosophers who, by reflective analysis, introspection, and observation, established the conceptual framework of what became in his time the science of psychology. He was a pupil of James Ward but not a mere disciple. He assimilated the essentials of Ward's system into his own philosophy of mind, but in the assimilation he transformed and extended them so that he created an entirely original and distinctive philosophy. Although he was formidable in polemical discussion, his bent was to constructive thinking. He assimilated many systems, boasting in later years, "I have got them all in my system" (idealism, realism, rationalism, and empiricism). He acknowledged indebtedness to philosophers as diverse as Spinoza and Hobbes and to the last was preoccupied with the ideas of his contemporaries Russell, Moore, and Wittgenstein, and he was far from being unsympathetic to the increasingly influential schools of psychology: behaviorism and the hormic and gestalt psychologies.

In Stout's work there is a progressive development of three main theses: the doctrine concerning thought and sentience; the concept of the embodied self; and a doctrine concerning "conative activity." These central theses entail in their elaboration the reinterpretation of many of the concepts important, historically and analytically, in the philosophy of mind. It is difficult to distinguish clearly, although the attempt is rewarding, between changes (or developments) in Stout's views and changes merely in his terminology. In his earlier writings, for example, he was content to describe the ultimate data of our knowledge of the external world as "sensations." Later he followed Ward in using the term "presentations," and finally he accepted "sense data" and "sensa" to facilitate discussion with the exponents of the prevailing phenomenalism of the day. The readiness to change his terminology was most striking in his many attempts to convey his distinctive doctrine of thought reference.

Thought and sentience. Since the time of Berkeley there has been a widely accepted doctrine that cognition begins with simple sensations which are mental states and "in the mind"; that these sensations and their corresponding images are associated in order to form complex ideas; that some of these sensations and images are projected so as to appear as phenomena of the external world; and that these sensations are the ultimate basis of our beliefs about and our knowledge of the external world. Against this Stout set up the proposition that sense experience involves "thought reference" to real objects. As Descartes had held that "thought" (as he used the term) implies a thinker, so Stout held that "thought" (in the same sense) implies something real and objective which is thought about.

This thesis, prominent in his *Analytic Psychology*, was expressed in terms of the concept of "noetic synthesis." In his characteristic conciliatory way he conceded the abstract possibility of "anoetic sentience" (sense experience without thought reference), but in subsequent writings he was inclined to deny both the occurrence of anoetic sentience and (to coin a phrase for him) "nonsentient noesis" (imageless thought or any form of thought reference independent of sense experience). In the elaboration of this thesis he offered a paradoxical theory of error—one difficult to refute or prove—to the effect that there can be no complete error, no sheer illusion, no pure hallucination. All errors are misinterpretations of fact. This thesis was later expressed in terms of "original meaning," in saying that every sense experience is apprehended as "conditioned by something other than itself," or as an "inseparable phase of something other than itself." It was developed with subtlety and in detail in the genetic psychology of the *Manual of Psychology*.

Following Ward, Stout attempted to give a natural history of the development of human awareness of the world which also offered grounds for our knowledge of what the world is really like. The central thesis here is that we must accept as primary not only the particular sense data of experience but also the categories or ultimate principles of unity: space, time, thinghood, and causality. These are not so much a priori cognitions as dispositions to organize experience in certain ways. We do not, for instance, have a priori knowledge that every event has a cause, but we have a disposition to look for causes. So, *mutatis mutandis,* with the other categories.

The embodied self. Stout, like Ward, accepted a two-dimensional, tripartite devision of mental functions into cognition, feeling, and conation; and he distinguished self, attitude, and object in each function. However, in the analysis of every concept in this scheme Stout modified every idea he took from Ward. He was more thoroughgoing in his adoption of Brentano's principle that the essential component which distinguishes a mental function from a nonmental one is the attitude or way in which the subject is concerned with its objects. His most fundamental divergence from Ward was in his account of the knowing, feeling, and willing subject (self or ego). His differences from Ward are set out in detail in his important article "Ward as a Psychologist" (*Monist,* January 1926). Here he opposed to Ward's account of the pure ego his own view that the self as first known in sensible experience is that thing whose boundary from other things is the skin.

The *Manual of Psychology* contains a puzzling and confusing chapter, "Body and Mind," that combines a critique of the classical theories of interactionism, epiphenomenalism, and parallelism, all of which presupposed Cartesian dualism, with a defense of a version of parallelism which did not. This chapter puzzled students until, many years later, Stout was able to set out more clearly (especially in the Gifford lectures) his basic philosophical thesis. This was a rejection of a dualistic ontology (that there are two sorts of substance, material things and minds) and a defense of a dualism of attributes—physical and mental—combined in a single entity, the embodied mind, which has both physical and mental attributes united somewhat as the primary and secondary characteristics are united in a material object as it is apprehended in naive perceptual situations. This view of the self entailed a corresponding reanalysis of the mental attitudes of cognition, feeling, and conation.

Stout discarded the dualism of substances but retained the dualism of qualities in his account of mental dispositions. These came to be described as "psychophysical dispositions" in accounts of the instincts, sentiments, attitudes, and other proposed ultimate sources of behavior. In this he anticipated and inspired the hormic psychology of William McDougall and, less directly, the theory of personality elaborated by Gordon Allport. McDougall was to describe the ultimate springs of human conduct in terms of certain innate primary psychophysical dispositions to perceive and attend to certain objects, to feel emotional excitement in the presence of such objects, and to experience an impulse to act in certain ways in regard to those objects. Allport later defined these sources of behavior as mental and neural "states of readiness" for such experiences and activities. In Stout these concepts are embodied in a more radical account of conative activity and conative dispositions.

Conation. Although he accepted the classical tripartite division of mental functions, Stout accorded a certain priority to conation, so much so that he encouraged what has been described as the "conative theory of cognition," such as that developed by his contemporary Samuel Alexander. (The last paper published by Stout was "A Criticism of Alexander's Theory of Mind and Knowledge," *Australian Journal of Psychology and Philosophy,* September 1944.) The term "conative activity" covers all psychophysical processes which are directed to a goal (whether anticipated or not). It includes such cognitive processes as observation, recollection, and imagination, which are directed to the attainment of clearer and fuller perception of things present, the reconstruction of the past, and the comprehension of future possibilities. Conation is divided into practical and theoretical conation. Practical conative activity is directed to producing actual changes in the objects and situations with which the subject has to deal in the real world. Theoretical conation is directed to the fuller and clearer apprehension of such objects and situations. Stout's account of theoretical conation was in effect his account of attention. Attention is theoretical conation, although it incorporates practical conation through determining sensory–motor adjustments and the manipulation of instruments which facilitate clarity of perception.

Traditional accounts of association and reproductive and productive thinking were similarly revised and restated in conative terms. The law of association by contiguity was reformulated as the law of association by continuity of interest. One basic idea in all later theories of productive or creative thinking derives from Stout's account of "relative suggestion," an expression introduced by Thomas Brown which led to confusion between Stout's usage and Brown's.

In his treatment of all these concepts, Stout advanced beyond Ward and contributed significantly to the transition of psychology from a branch of philosophy to a science of human experience and behavior. These contributions were largely ignored, however, because of the powerful movements in psychology which were adverse to what had come to be described as "armchair psychology," that is, the purely formal analysis of psychological concepts. Stout's influence on philosophical thought outside his own circle of associates was also limited because of the reaction against "speculative" philosophy and the increasing restriction of philosophical discussion to analysis, more especially to the analysis of linguistic usage.

Stout's philosophy was, mistakenly, treated as being in the tradition of metaphysical speculation and the creation of systems in the grand manner. His final position is most fully set out in the two volumes of Gifford lectures. These embody many clarifications of concepts in the philosophy of mind and some acute criticism of earlier expositions of materialism and of contemporary phenomenalism. They contain the only records of Stout's views on aesthetics and ethics and his more tentative speculations concerning God, teleology, and the nature of material things. There is probably no philosopher who in his own thinking so smoothly made the transition from the prevailing idealism of the late nineteenth century to the prevailing critical, nonspeculative philosophy of the mid-twentieth century. Something of the idealist tradition is preserved in his sophisticated defense of philosophical animism, but more important are his detailed contributions to the transition from the philosophy of mind of the nineteenth century to that of the twentieth.

Works by Stout

Analytic Psychology, 2 vols. London and New York, 1896.

A Manual of Psychology. London and New York, 1899; 4th ed., rev. by C. A. Mace, London, 1929; 5th (and last) ed., London, 1938. The 5th edition contains an appendix on gestalt psychology by R. H. Thouless and a supplementary note by Stout.

Studies in Philosophy and Psychology. London and New York, 1930.

Mind and Matter. London and New York, 1931. Vol. I of the Gifford lectures.

God and Nature, Alan Stout, ed. London, 1952. Vol. II of the Gifford lectures with a memoir by J. A. Passmore and a full bibliography.

Works on Stout

Broad, C. D., "The Local Historical Background of Contemporary Cambridge Philosophy," in C. A. Mace, ed., *British Philosophy in the Mid Century.* London, 1956; 2d ed., New York, 1966.

Hamlyn, D. W., "Bradley, Ward and Stout," in B. B. Wolman, ed., *Historical Roots of Contemporary Psychology.* New York, 1966.

Mace, C. A., "George Frederick Stout." *Proceedings of the British Academy,* Vol. 31.

Mace, C. A., "The Permanent Contributions to Psychology of George Frederick Stout." *British Journal of Educational Psychology,* Vol. 24, Part 2 (June 1954).

Passmore, J. A., *A Hundred Years of Philosophy.* London, 1957. Pp. 192–202 and *passim.*

C. A. MACE

STRATO AND STRATONISM. Strato of Lampsacus succeeded Theophrastus as head of the Peripatetic school at Athens about 286 B.C., and he remained its president until his death in 269 B.C. He wrote on logic, theology, ethics, and medicine, but it is above all to his physical doctrines that he owes his fame and importance because it was with these doctrines that he made fundamental changes in the teaching of Aristotle. He rejected the doctrine of different natural directions of movement, according to which earth and water move toward the center of the universe and air and fire in the opposite direction, and he supposed that since all bodies are heavy in varying degrees, all movement is naturally downward. Whereas Aristotle had treated empty space only as conceptual and not as actually occurring, Strato accepted it as possible within the cosmos but not outside it. Normally, such empty space is discontinuous and is within bodies. This explains how light and heat can pass through certain apparently solid bodies. If it becomes continuous, as in a vacuum, then it is forcibly filled by adjacent bodies.

With the aid of this doctrine of space and of other particular physical doctrines, Strato was able to eliminate teleology, which was a distinctive feature of Aristotelian physics, in favor of a blind necessity. This involved the rejection of any divine agency in the organization of the universe, but Strato did not substitute a necessity which was merely mechanical, as the atomists tended to do. He should rather be seen as reverting to the innate dynamism typical of the systems of thought of the earlier pre-Socratics (compare Wehrli, Frs. 33–34). He considered the soul as a kind of breath (*pneuma*) spreading through the body from a central position in the head. Sensation was wholly dependent upon the intellect, which for Strato was even more important than for Aristotle, but there was for Strato no possibility of the separate existence of the intellect nor of the survival of the soul after death.

Stratonism. Inevitably the radical departures from Aristotle initiated by Strato provoked a reaction, above all by Clearchus of Soli, who defended the power of the soul to leave the body. More surprisingly, Stratonism itself seems to have had virtually no influence on subsequent philosophic thought, whether inside or outside the school of Aristotle. It is instead among the scientists of Alexandria, among such men as Hero and the physician Erasistratus, that the positivism of Strato bore fruit. Aristarchus of Samos was a pupil of his and through Aristarchus Archimedes also came under his influence.

Bibliography

Fragments of Strato's writings, edited by F. Wehrli, may be found in *Die Schule des Aristoteles*, No. 5, *Straton von Lampsakos* (Basel, 1950).

Works on Strato are G. Rodier, *La Physique de Straton de Lampsaque* (Paris, 1890); H. Diels, "Über das physikalische System des Stratons," in *Sitzungsberichte der Berlin Akademie* (1893), 101–127; and Theodor Gomperz, *Greek Thinkers*, Vol. IV, translated by G. G. Berry (London, 1911), Ch. 43.

G. B. KERFERD

STRAUSS, DAVID FRIEDRICH (1808–1874), German theologian, historian of religion, and moralist, was born at Ludwigsburg in Württemberg. He studied from 1821 to 1825 at Blaubeuren, where he fell under the influence of the Hegelian theologian F. C. Baur, and at the Tübingen Stift from 1825 to 1831. He next attended the University of Berlin, where he heard lectures by Hegel and Friedrich Schleiermacher. In 1832 he went to the University of Tübingen as lecturer, remaining there until 1835, the year of the publication of the first volume of his most important work, *Das Leben Jesu kritisch bearbeitet* (2 vols., Tübingen, 1835–1836; translated from the 4th German edition by George Eliot as *The Life of Jesus Critically Examined*, London, 1848). The universal storm of public indignation which this book occasioned resulted in his dismissal from the university and his permanent retirement from academic life. Master of a clear and forthright prose style, Strauss had no difficulty supporting himself as a journalist and popular exponent of the view that religion—Christianity in particular—is an expression of the human mind's capacity to generate myths and treat them as truths revealed by God to man.

When he began his study of the Gospels, Strauss was neither a liberal nor a materialist. His original interests had been those of a Hegelian idealist; he had meant to study the available records of Jesus' life in order to distinguish their historically valid content from the theological accretions that had become associated with them during the first two centuries of the Christian era. His investigations convinced him, however, that the principal importance of the Gospels was aesthetic and philosophical, not historical. On the one hand, the Gospels provided insight into the Messianic expectation of the Jewish people in the late Hellenistic period; on the other hand, they reflected a memory of the exceptional personality of a great man, Jesus. Thus envisaged, the Gospels were a synthesis of notions peculiar to the Jews regarding the nature of world history and of certain moral teachings associated with the name of a purely human, yet historically vague, personality, presented in an aesthetically pleasing form for members of a new religious community that was both Jewish and Greek in its composition. For Strauss, the Gospels were, in short, interesting primarily as evidence of the workings of consciousness in the sphere of religious experience: they showed how the mind could fabricate miracles and affirm them as true, contrary to the Hegelian dictum, then regarded as an established truth, that the real was rational and the rational was real.

Had Strauss halted at this point, his work might have been ignored as merely another vestige of the free thought of the Enlightenment. Instead, he went on to argue that even if the historicity of the account of Jesus' life in the Gospels were denied, it need not follow that the Gospels were a product of conscious invention or fraud. He held, rather, that they could be said to belong to a third order of mental activity, called by Hegel unconscious invention or myth and defined by him as an attempt to envision the Absolute in terms of images derived from sensible experiences. As unconscious invention, the Gospels were to be viewed as poetic renderings of man's desire to transcend the finitude of the historical moment, as evidence of the purely human desire to realize the immanent goal of Spirit in its journey toward the Hegelian Being-in-and-for-itself. Thus, although Strauss had denied that the Gospels were evidence of the direct intrusion of the divine into history or even of the true nature of Jesus' life, he had, in his own view, at least salvaged them as documents in the history of human expression. In doing so, of course, he had reduced them to the same status as the pagan myths, legends, and epics.

In a second work, *Die christliche Glaubenslehre* (2 vols., 1840–1841), Strauss tried to clarify the theoretical basis of his original historical inquiry. He argued that Christianity was a stage in the evolution of a true pantheism that had reached its culmination in Hegelian philosophy. What the poet and mystic took for God was nothing but the world—specifically, man in the world—conceived in aesthetic terms. Science studied the same phenomena that are governed by physical laws, and philosophy was, as Hegel had taught, mind reflecting on these prior activities of thought and imagination.

Das Leben Jesu became a *cause célèbre* in a Germany growing increasingly reactionary both politically and intellectually. The attack launched against Strauss from all quarters soon made him a symbol to German liberals; he was regarded as a martyr of science and freedom of thought. Accordingly, Strauss was drawn into political as well as theological polemics. In 1848 he published at Halle a defense of bourgeois liberalism, *Der politische und der theologische Liberalismus*. He later turned to the study of philosophical materialism (that of Lange and of Darwin) and to the production of a series of historical works on leading advocates of freedom of thought in European history (for example, a long biography of Ulrich von Hutten, 1858, and a study of Voltaire, 1870). As he progressed, he repudiated the Hegelianism of his first book. In a preface to a later edition of *Das Leben Jesu,* he stated that he had undertaken it to show "to those to whom the conceptions . . . as to the supernatural character . . . of the life of Jesus had become intolerable . . . [that] the best means of effectual release will be found in historical inquiry." Abandoning the last residues of his earlier idealism, he argued that "everything that happens, or ever happened, happened naturally." He still recognized the aesthetic value of the Gospel account, but he now saw it as providing the image of the good life that had finally become possible on this earth because of the triumphs of science and industrial technology and the advance of political liberalism. It was this position that won for him the enmity of both Marx and Nietzsche. To Marx, he was the bourgeois *idéologue* par excellence, who tried to combine Christian sentimental ethics and the practices of capitalism in a single package. For Nietzsche, Strauss represented the German *Bildungsphilister* who made a show of intellectual radicalism but always left the conventional morality intact.

Strauss remained to the end of his life the spokesman of popular religious criticism, materialistic in his intention but Hegelian in method, a combination which allowed him to accommodate almost any position that appealed to him. After 1850 his political and social criticism became increasingly conservative—aristocratic, monarchical, and nationalistic. In part this transformation was due to the suspicion that popular democracy would be in general as unable to recognize genius as it had been unable to recognize, in particular, the value of Strauss' own works; but this transformation was also a result of his attempt to move from Hegelianism to positivism. In the second half of the eighteenth century, positivist social thought had become—as, for example, in Hippolyte Taine—a kind of crude determinism, hostile to any revolutionary impulse.

To the young Hegelians, who were already becoming aware of the methodological limitations of Hegel's late thought, *Das Leben Jesu* provided an impulse to the critical, empirical study of the historical milieus within which *Geist* supposedly manifested itself, and it thus prepared them to accept Leopold von Ranke's historicism. To German liberals, Strauss remained a symbol of the risks that had to be run by any German who presumed to espouse radical causes. The later Marxists regarded Strauss as merely a confused bourgeois who had blundered onto forbidden ground. For them, the way to a true revision of Hegelianism was provided by Feuerbach. Feuerbach saw that the true importance of Strauss' *Das Leben Jesu* lay in a problem that remained implicit in the work and was hardly touched upon by Strauss himself: the psychological problem about the nature of the mythmaking mechanism that distinguishes man from the rest of nature. It was Feuerbach, then, rather than Strauss, who posed the question with which German philosophy had to come to terms in the 1840s—the question of the relation between human consciousness and its material matrix.

Works by Strauss

Gesammelte Schriften, Eduard Zeller, ed., 12 vols. Bonn, 1876–1878.
Ulrich von Hutten, 2 vols. Leipzig, 1858. Translated by Mrs. G.

Sturge as *Ulrich von Hutten, His Life and Times.* London, 1874.
Hermann Samuel Reimarus. Leipzig, 1862.
Kleine Schriften biographischen, literarischen, und kunstgeschichtlichen Inhalts. Leipzig, 1862.
Der Christus des Glaubens und der Jesus der Geschichte. Berlin, 1865.
Kleine Schriften, Neue Folge. Berlin, 1866.
Voltaire: sechs Vorträge. Leipzig, 1870.
Ausgewählte Briefe. Bonn, 1895.

Works on Strauss

Barth, Karl, *Die protestantische Theologie im 19. Jahrhundert.* Munich, 1947. Translated by Brian Cozens as *Protestant Thought from Rousseau to Ritschl.* New York and London, 1959.
Feuter, Eduard, *Geschichte der neueren Historiographie,* 3d ed. Munich and Berlin, 1936.
Nietzsche, Friedrich, *Unzeitgemässe Betrachtungen, Erstes Stück.* Leipzig, 1873. Translated by A. M. Ludovici as *Thoughts out of Season.* New York, 1924.
Schweitzer, Albert, *Von Reimarus zu Wrede.* Tübingen, 1906. Translated by W. Montgomery as *The Quest for the Historical Jesus.* London, 1910.
Zeller, Eduard, *David Friedrich Strauss in seinem Leben und seinen Schriften,* 2 vols. Heidelberg, 1876–1878.

HAYDEN V. WHITE

STRAWSON, PETER FREDERICK, British philosopher, was born in 1919 and educated at Christ's College, Finchley, and St. John's College, Oxford. He holds the B.A. and M.A. degrees and is a fellow of University College, Oxford.

Language and logic. Strawson is a leading member of the circle of philosophers whose work is sometimes described as "ordinary language philosophy" or as "Oxford philosophy." Of his early work, the most influential and most controversial is the famous article "On Referring" (*Mind*, 1950), a criticism of the philosophical aspects of Russell's theory of definite descriptions. According to Russell's theory any sentence of the form "The f is g"—for example, "The king of France is bald"—is properly analyzed as follows (in terms of our example): "There is a king of France. There is not more than one king of France. There is nothing which is king of France and which is not bald."

Strawson argues that this analysis confuses referring to an entity with asserting the existence of that entity. In referring to an entity, a speaker presupposes that the entity exists, but he does not assert that it exists, nor does what he asserts entail that it exists. Presupposition is to be distinguished from entailment. In asserting something of the form "The f is g," a speaker refers or purports to refer to an entity with the subject noun phrase, and to do so involves presupposing that there is such an entity, but this is quite different from asserting that there is such an entity.

According to Strawson this confusion between referring and asserting is based on an antecedent confusion between a sentence and the statement made in a particular use of that sentence. Russell erroneously supposes that every sentence must be either true, false, or meaningless. But, Strawson argues, sentences can be meaningful or meaningless and yet cannot strictly be characterized as true or false. Statements, which are made using sentences, but which are distinct from sentences, are, or can be, either true or false. The sentence "The king of France is bald" is indeed meaningful, but a statement made at the present time using that sentence does not succeed in being either true or false because, as there is presently no king of France, the purported reference to a king of France fails. According to Russell the sentence is meaningful and false. According to Strawson the sentence is meaningful, but the corresponding statement is neither true nor false because one of its presuppositions—namely, that there is a king of France—is false.

In another well-known article of this early period, "Truth" (*Analysis*, 1949), Strawson criticizes the semantic theory of truth and proposes an alternative analysis to the effect that "true" does not describe any semantic properties or, indeed, any other properties at all, because its use is not to describe; rather, we use the word "true" to express agreement, to endorse, concede, grant, or otherwise accede to what has been or might be said. Strawson explicitly draws an analogy between the use of the word "true" and J. L. Austin's notion of performatives. Like performatives, "true" does not describe anything; rather, if we examine its use in ordinary language, we see that it is used to perform altogether different sorts of acts.

This article gave rise to a controversy with Austin, a defender of the correspondence theory. The gist of Strawson's argument against the correspondence theory is that the attempt to explicate truth in terms of correspondence between statements on the one hand and facts, states of affairs, and situations on the other must necessarily fail because such notions as "fact" already have the "word–world relationship" built into them. Facts are not something which statements name or refer to; rather, "facts are what statements (when true) state."

In his first book, *Introduction to Logical Theory* (New York and London, 1952), Strawson continued his investigation of the logical features of ordinary language by studying the relations between ordinary language and formal logic. The book, he says, has two complementary aims: first, to compare and contrast the behavior of ordinary words with the behavior of logical symbols, and, second, to make clear the nature of formal logic itself. It is in the first of these two enterprises that he has shown the more originality and aroused the more controversy. The theme of this part of the book is that such logical systems as the propositional and predicate calculi do not completely represent the complex logical features of ordinary language and indeed represent them less accurately than has generally been supposed. He argues that the logical connectives, especially "∨," "⊃," and "≡," are much less like "or," "if," and "if and only if" than is often claimed. In his discussion of predicate logic (Chs. 5 and 6), he continues the themes of "On Referring," arguing that certain orthodox criticisms which are made of traditional Aristotelian syllogistic fail because of a failure to appreciate the fact that statements made in the use of a sentence of the form "All *f*'s are *g*" presuppose the existence of members of the subject class. Thus, for example, the question whether it is true that all John's children are asleep does not even arise if John has no children. Once it is seen that statements of the form "All *f*'s are *g*" have existential presuppositions, it is possible to give a consistent interpretation of the traditional Aristotelian system. The failure to understand this

and the misconception regarding the relation of the predicate calculus to ordinary language are in large part due to the same mistakes that underlie the theory of descriptions: the failure to see the distinction between sentence and statement; the "bogus trichotomy" of true, false, or meaningless; and the failure to see the distinction between presupposition and entailment. The final chapter of the book contains a discussion of probability and induction in which Strawson argues that attempts to justify induction are necessarily misconceived, since there are no higher standards to which one can appeal in assessing inductive standards. The question whether inductive standards are justified is as senseless as the question whether a legal system is legal. Just as a legal system provides the standards of legality, so do inductive criteria provide standards of justification. Underlying this point is the fact that inductive standards form part of our concept of rationality. It is, he says, a necessary truth that the only ways of forming rational opinions concerning what happened or will happen in given circumstances are inductive.

Metaphysics. In the middle 1950s Strawson's concerns shifted from investigations of ordinary language to an enterprise he named descriptive metaphysics. This enterprise differs from "revisionary metaphysics" in that it is content to describe the actual structure of our thought about the world rather than attempting to produce a better structure, and it differs from ordinary conceptual analysis in its much greater scope and generality, since it attempts to "lay bare the most general features of our conceptual structure."

These investigations resulted in the publication of a second book, *Individuals* (London, 1959). The book is divided into two parts. Part One, entitled "Particulars," deals with the nature of and preconditions for the identification of particular objects in speech; Part Two, "Logical Subjects," concentrates on the relations between particulars and universals and on the corresponding and related distinctions between reference and predication and subjects and predicates. The first important thesis of the book is that from the point of view of particular identification, material objects are the basic particulars. What this means is that the general conditions of particular identification require a unified system of publicly observable and enduring spatiotemporal entities. The material universe forms such a system. Material objects can therefore be identified independently of the identification of particulars in other categories, but particulars in other categories cannot be identified without reference to material objects. This provides us, then, with a sense in which material objects are the basic particulars as far as particular identification is concerned.

A second thesis, one of the most provocative of the book, concerns the traditional mind–body problem. In Chapter 3, entitled "Persons," Strawson attacks both the Cartesian notion that states of consciousness are ascribed to mental substances, which are quite distinct from but nonetheless intimately connected to bodies, and the modern "no-ownership" theory, according to which states of consciousness are not, strictly speaking, ascribed to anything at all. Both views, he argues, are ultimately incoherent. The solution to the dilemma posed by these views is that the concept of a person is a primitive concept. It is a concept such that both states of consciousness and physical properties are ascribable to one and the same thing—namely, a person. The concept of a mind is derivative from the primitive concept of a person, and the concept of a person is not to be construed as a composite concept made up of the concept of a mind and the concept of a body. The recognition of the primitiveness of the concept of a person enables us to see both why states of consciousness are ascribed to anything at all and why they are ascribed to the very same thing to which certain physical states are ascribed.

Most of Part Two of *Individuals* is devoted to an investigation of the problems of the relations of subjects and predicates. Strawson considers two traditional ways of making the distinction between subject and predicate: a grammatical criterion in terms of the different kinds of symbolism for subject and predicate expressions and a category criterion in terms of the distinction between particulars and universals. He investigates the "tensions and affinities" between these two criteria, and he concludes that the crucial distinction between the way a subject expression introduces a particular into a proposition and the way a predicate expression introduces a universal into a proposition is that the identification of a particular involves the presentation of some empirical fact which is sufficient to identify the particular (this harks back to the doctrine of what is presupposed by identifying references in "On Referring" and *Introduction to Logical Theory*), but the introduction of the universal term by the predicate term does not in general involve any empirical fact. The meaning of the predicate term suffices to identify the universal which the predicate introduces into the proposition. One might say that identifying reference to particulars involves the presentation of empirical facts; the predication of universals involves only the presentation of meanings. This enables us to give a deeper sense to Frege's notion that objects are complete—in contrast to concepts, which are incomplete—and it enables us to account for the Aristotelian doctrine that only universals and not particulars are predicable.

In tone, method, and over-all objectives, *Individuals* stands in sharp contrast to Strawson's earlier work. Piecemeal investigation of ordinary language occurs here only as an aid and adjunct to attacking large traditional metaphysical problems. One might say that *Individuals* employs essentially Kantian methods to arrive at Aristotelian conclusions. Yet much of the book is at least foreshadowed by Strawson's earlier work, particularly "On Referring" and certain portions of his first book. The notion of descriptive metaphysics itself has been as influential as the actual theses advanced in *Individuals*. More than any other single recent work, this book has resurrected metaphysics (albeit descriptive metaphysics) as a respectable philosophical enterprise.

(For further discussion of Strawson's theories, see PERFORMATIVE THEORY OF TRUTH and PERSONS.)

Additional Works by Strawson

"Necessary Propositions and Entailment Statements." *Mind* (1948).

"Ethical Intuitionism," in Wilfrid Sellars and John Hospers, eds., *Readings in Ethical Theory*. New York, 1952.

"Particular and General." *PAS*, Supp. Vol. 27 (1953–1954).

"Critical Notice of Wittgenstein." *Mind* (1954).

"Presupposing: A Reply to Mr. Sellars." *Philosophical Review* (1954).

"A Logician's Landscape." *Philosophy* (1955).

"Construction and Analysis," in A. J. Ayer et al., *The Revolution in Philosophy*. London, 1956.

"In Defense of a Dogma." *Philosophical Review* (1956). Written with H. P. Grice.

"Singular Terms, Ontology and Identity." *Mind* (1956).

"Logical Subjects and Physical Objects." *Philosophy and Phenomenological Research* (1956–1957).

"*Logic and Knowledge* by Bertrand Russell." *Philosophical Quarterly* (1957).

"Metaphysics," in D. F. Pears, ed., *The Nature of Metaphysics*. London, 1957. Written with H. P. Grice and D. F. Pears.

"Professor Ayer's *The Problem of Knowledge*." *Philosophy* (1957).

"Proper Names." *PAS*, Supp. Vol. 31 (1957).

"Propositions, Concepts and Logical Truths." *Philosophical Quarterly* (1957).

"Singular Terms and Predication." *Journal of Philosophy* (1961).

"Social Morality and Individual Ideal." *Philosophy* (1961).

"Freedom and Resentment." *Proceedings of the British Academy* (1962). Annual philosophical lecture.

"Determinism," in D. F. Pears, ed., *Freedom and the Will*. London, 1963. A discussion with G. J. Warnock and J. F. Thomson.

"Identifying Reference and Truth Values." *Theoria* (1964).

"Truth: A Reconsideration of Austin's Views." *Philosophical Quarterly* (1965).

Works on Strawson

Aune, Bruce, "Feelings, Moods and Introspection." *Mind* (1963).

Ayer, A. J., "The Concept of a Person," in *The Concept of a Person and Other Essays*. London, 1963.

Bradley, M. C., "Mr. Strawson and Skepticism." *Analysis* (1959).

Caton, C. E., "Strawson on Referring." *Mind* (1959).

Coval, S. C., "Persons and Criteria in Strawson." *Philosophy and Phenomenological Research* (1964).

Geach, P. T., "Mr. Strawson on Symbolic and Traditional Logic." *Mind* (1963).

Jarvis, Judith, "Notes on Strawson's *Logic*." *Mind* (1961).

Lewis, H. D., "Mind and Body." *PAS* (1962–1963).

Pears, D. F., review of *Individuals*. *Philosophical Quarterly* (1961).

Quine, W. V., "Mr. Strawson on Logical Theory." *Mind* (1953).

Russell, Bertrand, "Mr. Strawson on Referring." *Mind* (1957).

Sellars, Wilfrid, "Presupposing." *Philosophical Review* (1954).

Urmson, J. O., review of *Individuals*. *Mind* (1961).

Williams, B. A. O., review of *Individuals*. *Philosophy* (1961).

JOHN R. SEARLE

STUMPF, KARL (1848–1936), German psychologist and philosopher, was born in Wiesentheid, Bavaria. He studied law at Würzburg, but under the influence of Franz Brentano his interests turned to philosophy and psychology. In 1868 he took a degree at Göttingen, under Lotze, with a dissertation on the relation between Plato's God and the Idea of the Good. In 1869 he entered the Catholic seminary in Würzburg, where he studied St. Thomas and the Scholastics. A year later, having lost his faith in orthodox Christianity and having abandoned the idea of becoming a priest, he left the seminary and became docent at Göttingen, where he taught for three years. His acquaintances included the philosopher and psychologist Gustav Fechner, who used Stumpf as a subject for his experiments in aesthetics. Stumpf's passionate fondness for music motivated his pioneering research in the psychology of sound perception. In 1873 he became professor of philosophy at Würzburg and in 1879, at Prague. His associates included Ernst Mach and Anton Marty. In 1884 he moved to Halle, where Husserl (who later dedicated his *Logische Untersuchungen* to Stumpf) became his student. Stumpf moved to Munich in 1889, but his heretical religious views made him uncongenial to some of his orthodox colleagues and to the authorities. He therefore accepted a professorship in Berlin in 1894. There he founded the Phonogram Archive, devoted to collecting recordings of primitive music, and the Psychological Institute, and for a time he directed research in Kant and Leibniz at the Academy of Sciences. Besides Husserl, his most famous student was Wolfgang Köhler, the Gestalt psychologist. William James, who praised Stumpf's *Tonpsychologie* very highly, was a friend and correspondent.

Stumpf contributed greatly to the development of psychology from a branch of philosophy into an empirical science. His own experimental work was largely concerned with acoustical phenomena, but he also wrote on other topics in psychology, such as the theory of emotions. As a philosopher, Stumpf was an empiricist who preferred Locke and Berkeley to the tradition of German idealism. He praised Kant for emphasizing the concepts of necessity and duty but rejected the view that the categories are a priori (by which Stumpf meant innate) and not derived from perceptions. The category of substance, or "thing," he maintained, is a concept that can be traced back to such actual experiences as that of perceiving the close interpenetration of the parts of a whole. The constituent characteristics of a sensory feeling, such as quality and intensity, form a whole rather than a mere aggregate. Experience includes the perceiving of relations; it does not consist merely of individual sensations that need to be related by the understanding. In the realm of mental functions, all simultaneous states of consciousness and intellectual and emotional activities are perceived as a unity. The concept of a substance, whether of a physical or a psychical substance, is not that of a bundle of qualities, as with Hume, but is a unity of qualities and relations. As for the concept of cause, Stumpf believed that both Kant and Hume were wrong; we can sometimes actually perceive a causal nexus as opposed to a mere sequence, and this experience is the origin of the category of cause. For example, when our thought processes are governed by some interest or mood, we do not first experience the interest and only subsequently its effects; rather, we are aware of the interest and its effects all at once. Thus we directly experience causality in our own internal activity. Without this we would not be conscious of reality. We transfer this awareness of causality to natural phenomena, although this projection is superfluous for scientific purposes where only lawlike sequences of events are needed.

Stumpf accepted a dualism of mind and nature but regarded the task of philosophy as the investigation of what mind and nature have in common. Philosophy is the science that studies the most general laws of the psychical and of the real. To be real means to have effects. The reality of our own mental states is the first datum. We recognize the reality of external objects as they affect us, having first acquired the idea of causality internally.

From Brentano, Stumpf took the fundamental notion of self-evidence. We experience the self-evidence of such judgments as $2 \times 2 = 4$, and this self-evidence cannot be further reduced. It is the subjective aspect of truth. Truth itself is that property of contents of consciousness whereby they compel assent. Truth is a function of that which is thought, not a function of the thinker. Stumpf explicitly rejected the positivist and pragmatist theories of truth.

Knowledge is of two sorts, a priori and a posteriori. A priori knowledge consists of deductions from self-evident propositions and from bare concepts. It ought to be expressed in hypothetical propositions, since no determination of fact is here made. Mathematical knowledge is of this type. If there are more geometries than one, all are a priori; only their applicability to objective space is an empirical question. A priori knowledge may be secured from any concept. The mere concept of three tones implies a definite order according to which a tone of one pitch must be located between the other two. The concept of a tone series contains the possibility of its continuation ad infinitum. These are propositions that we know but that neither have nor require proof. They are analytic, not only known by means of our concepts but known because they are about our concepts. A posteriori knowledge, on the other hand, is of facts and laws. Both sensory contents and mental activities or functions are experienced directly. Stumpf introduced the term *Sachverhalte* (state of affairs) into philosophy, although he claimed only to have replaced Brentano's notion of "content of judgment" with the term.

Stumpf rejected the idea of vitalism or of any sort of life force, although he did not oppose empirical psychovitalism, the view that feelings, thoughts, and volitions can be stimuli for physical nerve processes. He argued that evolution did not dispose of the problem of teleology, since life itself, whose origin from nonliving atoms is so mathematically improbable, requires an explanatory hypothesis.

Works by Stumpf

Über den psychologischen Ursprung der Raumvorstellung. Leipzig, 1873.

Tonpsychologie, 2 vols. Leipzig, 1883 and 1890.

Leib und Seele. Leipzig, 1903.

Erscheinungen und psychische Funktionen. Berlin, 1907.

Philosophische Reden und Vorträge. Leipzig, 1910. Contains various papers on evolution, the aesthetics of tragedy, and child psychology.

Die Anfänge der Musik. Leipzig, 1911.

Empfindung und Vorstellung. Berlin, 1918.

Franz Brentano. Munich, 1919.

Spinozastudien. Berlin, 1919.

Autobiography in Raymund Schmidt, ed., *Die Philosophie der Gegenwart in Selbstdarstellung,* Vol. V. Leipzig, 1924. Pp. 205–265. Gives the best summary of his philosophical views. An English translation is available in Charles Murchison, *Psychology in Autobiography,* Worcester, Mass., 1930. Vol. I, pp. 389–441.

William James. Berlin, 1927.

Erkenntnislehre, 2 vols. Leipzig, 1939–1940.

Works on Stumpf

Boring, E. G., *History of Experimental Psychology.* New York and London, 1929. Gives fullest account of Stumpf's psychology and his classification of experiences in relation to that of Husserl and Brentano.

Spiegelberg, Herbert, *The Phenomenological Movement,* 2 vols. The Hague, 1960. Vol. I.

Titchener, E. B., *Experimental Psychology.* New York and London, 1905. Vol. II, pp. 161–163. Stumpf's psychophysics.

Titchener, E. B., "Prof. Stumpf's Affective Psychology." *American Journal of Psychology,* Vol. 28 (1917), 263–277. Stumpf's theory of emotions.

ARNULF ZWEIG

STURZO, LUIGI (1871–1959), Italian political figure and philosopher who elaborated a systematic historical anthropology. Sturzo was born in Caltagirone, Sicily. He was ordained a priest in 1894 and received a doctorate in philosophy from the Gregorian University in Rome in 1898. He taught philosophy at the seminary in Caltagirone from 1898 to 1903. Sturzo served as mayor of Caltagirone from 1905 to 1920. He founded the Italian Popular party in 1919 and served as its political secretary from 1919 to 1923. As early as 1926, in *Italy and Fascism,* Sturzo exposed the total economic concentration of power in the ruling radical right and the method of violence by which the power elite governed. His major works were written in exile in the period from 1924 to 1946 in Paris, London, and New York and were first published in translations. In recognition of his historic role in the birth of the Italian Republic, Sturzo was named a senator for life in 1952.

In philosophy Sturzo elaborated a "dialectic of the concrete" based primarily on the thought of St. Augustine, Leibniz, Giambattista Vico, and Maurice Blondel. He opposed this dialectic to both absolute idealism, which he regarded as a necessitarian monism, and scholastic realism, which he considered a spectatorlike abstractionism. At the basis of his thought is historical man projected into "the fourth dimension, that of time." Man is at one and the same time individual and social, free and conditioned, structural and in process; he is a singular history in process rather than a nature fixed in essence. Man is never pure becoming, however, but a radical tendency toward reason in action.

Organically, man is constitutionally relational in his total organic connections. Socially, he is a manifold and simultaneous projection of collective purposes which are made concrete in social structures that embody his many needs in a dynamic interplay of primary and subsidiary associations.

When collective purposes become institutionalized and each social form presses for exclusive domination, conflicts are engendered. If one form gains such domination, forces of renewal and reform are unwittingly released. Thus, driven by precarious and incomplete achievements, man advances by conquering new dimensions of experience, both personal and collective.

The most radical novelty and the most powerful solvent of conflicting interests is the concrete ingression of the divine into the total human process. This "historicization of the divine" in its empirical reality is both singular and collective and constitutes the driving force of human progress.

Although he recognized the recurrence of regression, Sturzo professed an enlightened optimism, similar to that of Teilhard de Chardin, born out of his vision of one mankind moving toward ever greater socialization through the growth of international consciousness as revealed in the rationalization of force and the repudiation of war.

Works by Sturzo

Opera Omnia, edited under the auspices of the Istituto Luigi Sturzo. Bologna, 1953—. Of a projected 30 vols., 12 have been published.

The following works were first published in Italian in *Opera Omnia,* First Series.

La comunità internazionale e il diritto di guerra (1928). Vol. II. 1954. Translated by Barbara B. Carter as *The International Community and the Right of War.* London, 1929.

La società: Sociologica storicista (1935). Vol. III. 1960. Translated by Barbara B. Carter as *The Inner Laws of Society.* New York, 1944.

Chiesa e stato: Studio sociologico-storico (1937). Vols. V–VI. 1959. Translated by Barbara B. Carter as *Church and State.* New York, 1939.

La vera vita (1943). Vol. VII. 1960. Translated by Barbara B. Carter as *The True Life.* Washington, 1943.

Del metodo sociologico. Bergamo, Italy, 1950.

Works on Sturzo

De Rosa, Gabriele, *Storia del partito popolare.* Bari, 1959.

Di Lascia, Alfred, "Sturzo." *Cross Currents,* Vol. 9 (1959), 400–410.

Pollock, Robert C., ed., "Luigi Sturzo: An Anthology." *Thought.* Vol. 28 (1953), 165–202. Pollock's commentary is invaluable.

Timasheff, Nicholas S., *The Sociology of Luigi Sturzo.* Baltimore, 1962.

Walsh, John, and Quick, Joan, "A Sturzo Bibliography." *Thought,* Vol. 28 (1953), 202–208.

ALFRED DI LASCIA

SUÁREZ, FRANCISCO (1548–1617), Spanish scholastic philosopher and theologian, "Doctor Eximius," was born at Granada. His father was a wealthy lawyer, and Francisco was the second of eight sons, six of whom entered the religious life. In 1564 he applied for admission to the Jesuit order. Perhaps because of ill health he showed little promise at first, and he failed to pass the examinations. Suárez appealed the verdict of his examiners, but his second examinations were not much better than the first. The provincial agreed, however, to admit Suárez at a lower rank. Shortly after his admission to the order, he began his study of philosophy. He showed little promise in the next few months and considered abandoning his studies for a lesser occupation in the order. However, he was persuaded by his superior to continue his studies, and within the next few years he became an outstanding student. Completing his course in philosophy with distinction, he transferred to the theology curriculum at the University of Salamanca and soon became an outstanding theologian.

In 1571 he was appointed professor of philosophy at the Jesuit college in Segovia and shortly thereafter was ordained to the priesthood. From 1576 to 1580 he served at the University of Valladolid and was then honored with an appointment to the chair of theology at the Jesuit college in Rome. Five years later he was transferred to a similar chair at the University of Alcalá. He had now achieved considerable reputation as a theologian and in 1593 was singled out by Philip II of Spain for appointment to the chair of theology at the University of Évora in Portugal. The years at Évora saw the publication of such major works as the *Disputationes Metaphysicae* (1597); the *De Legibus ac Deo Legislatore* (1612); the *Defensor Fidei*

(1613), a refutation of the *Apologia* of King James I of England; and the *Varia Opuscula Theologica* (1599), which embodied Suárez' contributions to the congruist movement. In 1616 Suárez retired from active teaching; he died the following year.

At the time of his death, Suárez' reputation as a philosopher and theologian was extraordinary, and his metaphysics dominated thought at Catholic and many Protestant universities for the next two centuries. Descartes is said to have carried a copy of the *Disputationes* with him during his travels. The *Ontologia* of Christian Wolff owed much to Suárez, and Leibniz read him avidly. Schopenhauer declared that the *Disputationes* was an "authentic compendium of the whole scholastic wisdom." After Aquinas, to whom he owed much, Suárez is generally recognized as the greatest of the Scholastics. His philosophy will be considered under two headings, the metaphysics (including epistemology) and the philosophy of law.

Metaphysics. The metaphysics of Suárez is basically Aristotelian and Thomistic yet also highly original. It reveals remarkable erudition and a profound knowledge of his medieval predecessors. Some of the outstanding features of Suárez' metaphysics may be shown in a brief exposition of his views on the nature of metaphysics, the theory of distinctions, the principle of individuation, the problem of universals, the knowledge of singulars, the doctrine of analogy, the existence of God, and the problem of freedom.

Nature of metaphysics. Suárez defined metaphysics as the science of being qua being. Taken as a noun, being signifies a real essence; taken as a participle, being refers to the act of existing. A real essence is noncontraditory, and by real Suárez means that which can or actually does exist in reality. Being may also be distinguished as real being and conceptual being. Real being may be immaterial, material, substantial, or accidental. The concept of being is analogical, derived from knowledge of the various kinds of real being; it is not univocal. The metaphysician is concerned primarily with immaterial being, and metaphysics is necessary for an understanding of sacred theology.

Theory of distinctions. Like his predecessors Suárez held that in God essence and existence are one. Aquinas held that in finite beings essence and existence are really distinct. Suárez, however, maintained that the distinction is solely one of reason, a mental or logical distinction, for to assert a real distinction presupposes a knowledge of existence, and this would entail an essence of existence. To the Thomist objection that the denial of real existence destroys the contingency of created beings, Suárez replied that it is unnecessary to add a real distinction to establish the contingency, for it is in the nature of created being to be contingent. The emphasis upon essence in contrast to existence led Étienne Gilson to refer to Suárez' metaphysics as "essentialistic" in contrast to the "existentialistic" metaphysics of Aquinas.

Principle of individuation. The principle of individuation is neither the *materia signata* of Aquinas nor the *haecceitas* of Scotus, although Suárez agreed with Scotus that "individuality adds to the common nature [essence] something which is mentally distinct from that nature . . . and which together with the nature constitutes the individual metaphysically." In composite substances both form and matter individuate, for the essence of the individual is made up of both matter and form, with form the principal determinant. Individuals may be distinguished on the basis of their matter—for example, quantity—but their individuation is determined by form and matter, not by our mode of cognition.

Problem of universals. Universals have no existence either in reality or in individuals. There are only individuals; universals do have a foundation in reality, however, for the mind abstracts them from the likenesses of individuals. Suárez criticizes the Ockhamists for insisting that universals are only words or mental constructs, but it is difficult to dissociate his position from theirs, for he strongly insists that there are as many essences as individuals and that each individual being is an individual essence.

Knowledge of singulars. With Scotus, Suárez maintained that the intellect has a direct knowledge of singulars. "Our intellect knows the individual material object by a proper species of it . . . our intellects know individual material objects without reflection." Suárez maintained that the active intellect can have this kind of knowledge, for there is nothing contradictory about such knowledge and it is in conformity with experience. Furthermore, it is the function of the active intellect to make the passive intellect as similar as possible to the representation of the phantasms. Unlike Aquinas, Suárez maintained that the passive intellect can abstract the universal and that the active intellect can know the individual material object.

Doctrine of analogy. Suárez rejected the Scotist doctrine of the univocity of being. Like Aquinas he accepts the analogicity of being, but he insists that there is only an analogy of attribution—not of proportionality—which possesses an element of metaphor. "Every creature is being in virtue of a relation to God, inasmuch as it participates in or in some way imitates the being of God."

Existence of God. A metaphysical rather than a physical proof is needed to establish the existence of God. The major defect in the Aristotelian argument from motion is the principle that "everything which is moved is moved by another." For this principle Suárez substituted the metaphysical principle that "everything which is produced is produced by another." From this principle he argued that there must be an unproduced or uncreated being, for an infinite regress either of a series or a circle of finite beings cannot be accounted for. And even if an infinite series were accepted, such a series would depend on a cause external to it. From the conclusion that there exists an uncreated being, Suárez proceeded to demonstrate that there is only one such being. Regarding the nature of such a being, its perfection, wisdom, infinitude, and so on, he followed Aquinas.

Problem of freedom. Like Molina, Suárez was convinced that the Thomist doctrine that God physically predetermines the free act of the individual nullified man's freedom. Suárez maintained that through the *scientia media* God knows from all eternity what an individual will do if his grace is extended to him, and he consequently gives sufficient grace to effect the congruent action of the individual's will with his grace. (For a detailed discussion of *scientia media* and congruism, see SCIENTIA MEDIA AND MOLINISM.)

Philosophy of law. Although Aquinas' influence on Suárez is apparent, Suárez was a highly original and influential thinker in the philosophy of law. He effected the transition from the medieval to the modern conception of natural law, and his influence is particularly noticeable in the work of Hugo Grotius.

Nature of law. Suárez maintained that Aquinas' definition of law as "an ordinance of reason directed to the common good" placed an inordinate emphasis on reason or intellect. Suárez did not deny that reason has a part in the law, but he did hold that obligation is the essence of law and that obligation is essentially an act of will. He defined law as "an act of a just and right will by which a superior wills to oblige his inferior to do this or that."

Eternal law. Like Aquinas, Suárez distinguished between eternal, divine, natural, and human law. However, the treatment of each is based on Suárez' contention that law is fundamentally an act of will. Eternal law is the divine providence which extends to all creatures and from which the other laws are derived. Defined as "a free decree of the will of God, who lays down the order to be observed," it is immutable and has always existed with God. It differs from the other laws, whose origins depend upon their promulgation; the eternal law receives its promulgation only through the other laws. Man's knowledge of such a law is limited and is reflected in his acceptance of the divine law, the discovery of the natural law, and his promulgation of the human law.

Divine law. Divine law is the direct revelation of God—the Mosaic law. The power and the will of God are the source of man's obligation to obey the divine law. In contrast, the power and the obligation of the human law are directly the will of the legislator, although indirectly the will of God.

Natural law. Natural law receives considerable attention from Suárez. This law is the participation of the moral nature of man in the eternal law. The natural law is based on the light of reason, but it is the work of the divine will and not the human will; its ultimate source is God, the supreme legislator. The natural law is not identified with man's nature; it transcends his will. The precepts of the natural law are the general and primary principles—to do good and avoid evil; the more definite and specific principles—that God must be worshiped; and certain moral precepts that may be deduced from the primary principles—that usury is unjust, adultery wrong, and so on. There is no dispensation from the natural law; its precepts are immutable. Thus, the introduction of private property did not reflect a change in the natural law, for although the natural law conferred all things upon men in common, it did not positively enjoin that only this form of ownership should endure.

Human law. Human law must be based on either the divine law or the natural law and is best exemplified in political philosophy. Following Aristotle, Suárez held that man is a social animal. He rejected the view that political society is artificial, the result of a social contract or an enlightened egoism. The state is natural, and the legislative power is derived from the community and exists for the good of the community. The ultimate source of such power is God, who bestows it as a natural property upon the community. Such power is actualized only upon the

formation of a political society. The form of government is essentially a matter of choice by the people. The modernity of Suárez is revealed in his rejection of the medieval ideal of the imperial power. He accepted the sovereignty of individual rulers and was skeptical of the feasibility of a world state. In discussing the rule of tyrants, he distinguished between a legitimate ruler who behaves tyrannically and a usurping tyrant. Revolt against the latter is self-defense; it is even legitimate to resort to tyrannicide provided that the injustice is extreme and the appeal to authority impossible. In the case of the legitimate ruler, the people have a right to rebel, for they bestowed the power upon the ruler. Tyrannicide is rejected here, and the rules of a just war must be followed. Suárez maintained that war is not intrinsically evil; just and defensive wars are permissible, and considerable attention is given to the conditions for waging a just war. Suárez also rejected the extremist views of papal power over temporal rulers, but he argued for the spiritual supremacy and jurisdiction of the papacy. This implied that the papacy has an indirect power to direct secular rulers for spiritual ends.

Bibliography

MODERN EDITIONS

Works mentioned in text and others are to be found in the *Opera Omnia*, 28 vols. (Paris, 1856–1878). The *Disputationes Metaphysicae* have recently appeared in a Latin and Spanish edition (Madrid, 1960–1964). For the philosophy of law see especially the *Selections From Three Works of Francisco Suárez, S.J.* (*De Legibus, Defensor Fidei,* and *De Triplici Virtute Theologica*), 2 vols. (Classics of International Law, No. 20, Oxford, 1944). There is an introduction by J. B. Scott.

BIBLIOGRAPHICAL WORKS

McCormick, J. J., *A Suarezian Bibliography.* Chicago, 1937.
Mugica, P., *Bibliografica suareciana.* Granada, 1948.
Scorraille, R. de, *François Suarez de la compagnie de Jésus, d'après ses lettres, ses autres écrits inédits et un grand nombre de documents nouveaux,* 2 vols. Paris, 1912–1913. The most authoritative bibliographical study.

METAPHYSICAL AND EPISTEMOLOGICAL STUDIES

Alejandro, J. M., *La gnoseologica del Doctor Eximio y la accusación nominalista.* Comillas, Spain, 1948.
Breuer, A., *Der Gottesbeweiss bei Thomas und Suarez.* Fribourg, Switzerland, 1930.
Conza, E., *Der Begriff der Metaphysik bei Franz Suarez,* Leipzig, Germany, 1928.
Descoqs, P., "Thomisme et Suarezisme." *Archives de philosophie,* Vol. 4 (1926), 434–544.
Dumont, P., *Liberté humaine et concours divin d'après Suarez.* Paris, 1960.
Grabmann, M., "Die Disputationes Metaphysicae des Franz Suarez," in *Mittelalterliches Geistesleben,* 3 vols. Munich, 1926–1956. Vol. I, pp. 525–560.
Hellín, J., *La analogía del ser y el conocimiento de Dios en Suárez.* Madrid, 1947.
Mahieu, L., *François Suarez, sa philosophie et les rapports qu'elle a avec la théologie.* Paris, 1921.
Mullaney, T., *Suárez on Human Freedom.* Baltimore, Md., 1950.

PHILOSOPHY OF LAW STUDIES

Perena Vicente, L., *Teoría de la guerra en Francisco Suárez,* 2 vols. Madrid, 1954.
Recaséns Siches, L., *La filosofia del derecho en Francisco Suárez.* Madrid, 1927.

Rommen, Heinrich, *Die Staatslehre des Franz Suarez.* Munich and Gladbach, 1927.

COLLECTED ESSAYS

Estudios eclesiásticos, Vol. 22, Nos. 85–86 (1948).
Gemelli, A., ed., *Scritti vari*. Milan, 1918.
Pensamiento, Vol. 4, special issue (1948).

JOHN A. MOURANT

SUBCONSCIOUS. See UNCONSCIOUS; UNCONSCIOUS, PSYCHOANALYTIC THEORIES OF THE.

SUBJECT AND PREDICATE. The contrast between subject and predicate is a significant one in at least four different realms of discourse: grammar, epistemology, logic, and metaphysics. A large number of philosophical problems have to do with how the distinction on one level is related to that on some other level; whether there really are four such distinct realms and, if so, how they bear on one another are matters of controversy.

Grammar. In the realm of grammar, subject and predicate are sentence parts; they are, therefore, words or groups of words, and their definition and identification is a matter of syntax. In the simplest case, where the sentence consists of just two words, such as

(1)   Bats fly,
(2)   Fraser swims,

the subject is the noun and the predicate is the verb. Very few sentences are so simple, but an indicative sentence with just one noun and one verb remains a good paradigm for the grammatical categories of subject and predicate because we can see in it the form of the sentence stripped down to its essentials: if either of the two words were omitted, we would no longer have an indicative sentence. Furthermore, very many sentences of English, as well as of other familiar European languages, break neatly and obviously into two parts corresponding to the noun and the verb in the paradigm, and modern linguistic analysis of sentence syntax generally begins by viewing a sentence as a noun phrase plus a verb phrase:

$$S \rightarrow NP + VP$$

Although subject–predicate sentences are very common in English and in other languages, this form of sentence is not the only one, other forms being exemplified in English by normal idiomatic expressions for commands, requests, salutations, and so on. These other forms of sentence, however, have traditionally been assimilated to the subject–predicate form through the assumption of an "unexpressed subject" or some other missing element. It once seemed reasonable to try to save appearances in this way because subject and predicate seemed to be universal grammatical categories, found not only in the European languages but also, for example, in Sanskrit. Recent familiarity with a wider variety of languages has shown that these categories are by no means universal, and it is doubtful whether any grammatical categories or linguistic forms are universal. Some linguists have proposed that topic and comment are found universally, although subject and predicate are not. These categories, however, do not

have to do just with the arrangement of words in sentences but rather with *knowing* what is being discussed and *understanding* what is said about it; hence topic and comment are not purely grammatical categories. The present situation in linguistics may therefore be summed up by saying that subject and predicate are useful grammatical concepts but do not represent universal grammatical categories.

In philosophy the grammatical distinction between subject and predicate has been prominent at least since Plato, who, in the *Sophist*, distinguished nouns and verbs as two classes of names. It is fair to say, however, that in that discussion, as well as in subsequent ones, philosophers have been interested in this grammatical distinction primarily because of the use they might make of it in treating problems of epistemology, logic, and metaphysics.

Epistemology. In epistemology the contrast between subject and predicate is a contrast between that part of a sentence which serves to identify or designate what is being discussed and that part which serves to describe or characterize the thing so identified. The categories of subject and predicate have more claim to universality at the level of epistemology (semantics) than at the level of grammar (syntax). It is here that the hypothesis about topic and comment, mentioned earlier, has its significance, for the fact that every language has some grammatical device or other for identifying a subject, or topic, and predicating something of it, or commenting on it, largely accounts for our remarkable ability to translate the content of any message from one language to another.

The epistemological sense of subject and predicate has much in common with the grammatical sense: sentences (1) and (2) can be taken as paradigms for both senses, and the grammatical subject very frequently identifies the subject of discourse. Nevertheless, the two senses are not identical. They diverge, for example, in sentences with a dummy subject. In "It is raining" the expletive "it" is the grammatical subject of the sentence, but since it does not designate anything at all, it does not designate or identify what the sentence is about. Other instances are more relevant to philosophical issues and may be controversial. Consider

(3)   What is not pink is not a flamingo.
(4)   What is not just is not to be done.

There is no difficulty with (4), for it says something about unjust acts, and hence its grammatical and epistemological subjects coincide. But (3) seems to be about flamingos rather than about nonpink things, even though it has the same grammatical form as (4). Perhaps this is because we directly recognize and classify things as flamingos and as unjust acts, and even as pink, whereas in order to call something "not pink" one would normally first recognize it as gray or blue or some other color. If this is correct, the epistemological subject of (3) is mentioned in the grammatical predicate rather than in the grammatical subject.

Another instance of the divergence of the epistemological and grammatical senses is in relational sentences, such as

(5)   Andrew was hit by Bernard.
(6)   The cat is between the bird and the snake.

Sentences (5) and (6) may be taken to be about the two persons and the three animals, respectively, and what is said about their epistemological subjects is that a certain relation is true of them. Treating (5) and (6) as having multiple subjects in this manner is much more congenial than is a grammatical analysis to what Russell, among others, has said about the importance of relations (see RELATIONS, INTERNAL AND EXTERNAL).

It should be noted that what counts as the epistemological subject of a statement may be determined in part by the context in which it is made: if Bernard is the "topic" of conversation, (5) would naturally be construed as a "comment" about him, but other conversations in which (5) occurs will be focused differently. The importance of context in determining what counts as a subject differentiates the epistemological conception of subject from all the others.

Predicates as well as subjects have required special treatment in epistemology. Kant distinguished real predicates from grammatical or logical predicates, a real predicate being one which says something about the subject—that is, one which attributes some property to the subject. Kant's contention that "exists" is not a real predicate but only a grammatical or logical one provides the basis for his refutation of the Ontological Argument. Statements of identity have also been held by Frege, Russell, Wittgenstein, and others not to be genuine predications—or at least not to be straightforward ones. Hence, in

(7)   Tully is Cicero

the words "is Cicero" would not express an epistemological predicate, although they assuredly constitute the grammatical predicate. These are matters which are still not so clear as they might be.

Some very important topics in semantics and the philosophy of language are connected with the epistemological contrast between subject and predicate. In order to know what a person is talking about, I must know to what (or to whom) certain words in his utterances refer; the problem of how words can have such reference is an important one (see REFERRING). In order to understand what is said about the subject under consideration, I must further know what is signified or entailed or meant by certain other words the person uses, whence arises another important problem, how words come to have sense or connotation. The distinction between two such modes of meaning, characteristic respectively of subjects and of predicates, has a long history and is still a live issue. Plato, in the *Theaetetus* and the *Sophist,* distinguished the mode of meaning of nouns from that of verbs. More recently Mill's distinction between connotation and denotation and Frege's distinction between sense and reference have taken up the same theme and made it central to the philosophy of language (see MEANING and PROPER NAMES AND DESCRIPTIONS).

Logic. In formal logic there has been a distinction between subject and predicate ever since Aristotle's pioneering work in the field, but a dispute about the nature and scope of the distinction separates traditional from modern logicians. Aristotle would regard sentences (1) and (2) as both having subject–predicate form, but only (1) could serve as a paradigm for his formal logic. In traditional formal logic what is important about the subject term in the paradigm is, roughly, that it comes at the beginning of the sentence and indicates what (or who) is being discussed and that its quantity can be expressed by "some" or "all" preceding the noun. The pattern involved is

$$S \text{ is } P,$$

and since every proposition must have a topic about which something is asserted, this pattern is held to be manifested universally in categorical propositions. In modern logic, on the other hand, what is important about the subject term is that it is a proper name and stands for an individual, and so only sentence (2) can serve as a paradigm of the subject–predicate form. The pattern involved is

$$Fa$$

(where "F" stands for some attribute and "a" is a proper name); this pattern never applies to general propositions, since fully general propositions contain quantifiers, variables, and predicate terms but no proper names. According to this view general propositions pertain just to predicates and are not subject–predicate propositions at all. Russell's famous attack on "subject–predicate logic" was an attack on the view that every proposition must have a logical subject.

From a formal point of view the issue can be seen as a dispute about whether the principle of transposition (or contraposition) applies to subject–predicate propositions. In traditional logic it does, for the complement of a predicate can serve as a subject. This is not the case in modern logic, however, where only singular terms count as subjects and where transposition applies only to complex propositions compounded with the "if–then" sentence connective. There is a related divergence in the treatment of existence. Kant, a typical traditional logician in this respect, called existence a "logical" predicate, although not a "real" one; in effect, the grammatical analysis of assertions of existence into subject and predicate is carried over into logic. In modern logic, on the other hand, existence is generally represented through quantification, rather than through a predicate (see EXISTENCE and LOGIC, MODERN).

Epistemological and metaphysical considerations are involved in this dispute about how to represent subjects and predicates in formal logic. Roughly speaking, traditional logic seems to favor some sort of realistic view of universals, since terms representing universals can serve as both logical subjects and logical predicates. In the notation of modern logic, on the other hand, only singular expressions can serve as logical subjects, and this rule seems to give prominence to individuals rather than to universals. But a variety of epistemological and metaphysical views can consistently be advanced by both traditional and modern logicians, and the ascendancy of modern logic can be attributed to its greater flexibility, adaptability, and power as a calculus, rather than to epistemological and metaphysical views associated with it. It seems prudent, therefore, to keep matters of perspicuous symbolism and logical transformation separate from other considerations.

To illustrate the problems about the relation of logical structure to epistemological structure, one might consider

(8)   All ravens are black.

The epistemological subject of (8) is ravens, and hence one would go about confirming the proposition by examining ravens and finding them black. If, using the rule of transposition, we derive from (8) the logically equivalent form

(9)   All nonblack things are nonravens,

one is tempted to assume that the epistemological subject and predicate of (8) have been similarly transposed, so that nonblack things is the epistemological subject of (9). This assumption gives rise to the so-called paradox of confirmation (see CONFIRMATION: QUALITATIVE ASPECTS), for it then appears as though we might confirm (8) and (9) by examining nonblack things and finding them not to be ravens, contrary to our normal procedure for confirming such simple generalizations. One solution is to hold that transposition does not apply to the epistemological structure of a proposition, that the epistemological structure of a proposition is therefore not always parallel to its logical structure, and that the epistemological subject of (9) is the same as that of (8)—that is, ravens. But the desire to have epistemological structure unambiguously represented in logical notation is a powerful consideration for some philosophers, and hence the matter is still controversial.

Metaphysics. The distinctions between subject and predicate in grammar, epistemology, and logic have given rise to a variety of metaphysical doctrines. These doctrines deserve separate consideration because although they are closely related to the distinctions already sketched and are suggested by them, none follows from them.

Plato noted that applying different predicates to a subject often entails a change in the subject, whereas applying a predicate to different subjects does not entail a change in the predicate. He took this changelessness to be a mark of reality (as well as epistemological priority), and hence his theory of Forms gives great ontological prominence to predicates (concepts, universals—i.e., that which a grammatical predicate stands for). This bold thesis opened a long and continuing dispute about the nature of universals (see UNIVERSALS), the problem being to determine what ontological commitments, if any, are entailed by our use of predicative expressions (in the epistemological sense).

Aristotle, in contrast to Plato, gave ontological standing to subjects as well as to predicates. Discussing substance (see SUBSTANCE AND ATTRIBUTE) in his *Categories,* he defined "first substances" as things satisfying two conditions: (*a*) being subjects but never predicates and (*b*) not being in or of something else (as a color or surface must be the color or surface of some other thing). He then defined "second substances" as things satisfying the second condition but not the first. First substances are individuals. Second substances are species or universals and hence incorporate an element of Plato's metaphysics (although not all universals are substances). An attractive feature of

Aristotle's metaphysical treatment of subjects is that it fits his conception of subjects in epistemology and logic: what we talk about and investigate (especially in biology, Aristotle's scientific forte) are individuals and species, and his logic allows both individual names and universal terms, including species names, to occur as logical subjects. But, in spite of its merits, Aristotle's metaphysical conception of subjects is often regarded as unsatisfactory, largely because of qualms about putting individuals and species in one basket, about distinguishing predicates which stand for substances from those which do not, and about the usefulness of traditional logic.

Leibniz' doctrine of monads builds on Aristotle's conception of individual substance. But Leibniz considered Aristotle's definition inadequate, and he defined a monad or individual substance as a subject that contains all its predicates—that is, as an individual from whose "notion" it is possible to deduce all that may ever be truly predicated of it. Few philosophers have thought there were any such substances. One difficulty may be that Leibniz attributed to his monads, which are epistemological subjects, the sort of identity that characteristically belongs to a predicate—namely, a definite set of entailments which define it.

Whereas Leibniz had only one kind of substance, Hegel allowed only one individual substance, the Absolute. The Absolute is the ultimate subject of every statement and resembles Leibniz' monads in that it contains all its predicates in the same sense as the monads are supposed to. Other philosophers have not been convinced of the existence of such a universal subject; Russell, who acknowledges Hegelian idealism to be a plausible account of the metaphysical implications of traditional logic, regards the doctrine as a *reductio ad absurdum* argument against a logic that analyzes every proposition as having a subject and a predicate.

Another interesting element of idealism is the concept of the concrete universal. Like the idea of a monad, this concept is an attempt to overcome the subject–predicate dualism by amalgamating features of both subjects and predicates in a single sort of entity. Whereas a monad is a subject with characteristics of a predicate (in that its identity is determined by what is logically contained in it, or entailed by it), a concrete universal is a predicate treated as a concrete individual thing.

One philosopher who accepted the subject–predicate dualism as a basis for his metaphysics was Frege. There are, he maintained, two radically different sorts of things, objects and concepts. Objects are complete, or "saturated," and stand on their own, so to speak; we have names for them and talk about them, but the name of an object can never be a grammatical or logical predicate. Concepts, or, more generally, what Frege called "functions," are incomplete, or "unsaturated"; they require an object to complete them and hence cannot stand alone, and a concept term is always a predicate, never a subject. Frege's dualistic view has been very influential with other philosophical logicians, including Russell, Wittgenstein, Carnap, and P. T. Geach, but difficulties in Frege's formulation of it have impeded its general acceptance. One difficulty is that even Frege wished to talk about concepts, and hence he had to suppose that each concept has a special object associated with it which serves only as an object to talk about when we mean to discuss the concept. A more serious difficulty is that the object–concept dualism does not fit with Frege's semantic distinction between sense and reference, which also arises from a consideration of subjects and predicates. One might expect that reference would be the mode of meaning characteristic of names of objects, and sense the mode of meaning characteristic of concept terms; however, both names and concept terms have both sense and reference. Frege had powerful reasons for what he said, but the final impression is that his two distinctions are distressingly unrelated; hence, the philosophers most influenced by him have differed from him. Russell, for example, vigorously rejected Frege's distinction between sense and reference (in his essay "On Denoting"), and Wittgenstein in his *Tractatus Logico-philosophicus*, although indebted to Frege when he characterized his metaphysical objects, left no room for any other entities corresponding to Fregean functions.

Many analytic philosophers, including Carnap, Ernest Nagel, and Max Black, hold that neither grammatical nor logical categories have metaphysical implications. P. F. Strawson, however, has revived the issue among them by considering the implications and presuppositions of grammatical, logical, and epistemological subjects in his metaphysical essay *Individuals*. On balance, metaphysical skepticism must probably be considered as controversial as any of the metaphysical doctrines proposed.

Bibliography

For the linguistic aspects consult a standard work, such as Leonard Bloomfield, *Language* (New York, 1933), or R. A. Hall, Jr., *Introductory Linguistics* (Philadelphia, 1964). Russell's strictures against subject–predicate logic can be found in his discussions of Aristotle and Hegel in his *History of Western Philosophy* (New York, 1945), and his *An Inquiry Into Meaning and Truth* (New York, 1940) contains discussions of both logical and epistemological aspects of the question, as well as comments on Wittgenstein. Russell's paper "On Denoting" can be found in *Logic and Knowledge* (London, 1956), together with other relevant papers. Frege's views are readily accessible in *Translations from the Philosophical Writings of Gottlob Frege*, P. T. Geach and Max Black, eds. (Oxford, 1952). Wittgenstein's *Tractatus Logico-philosophicus* has had a more profound influence with respect to semantics and logical form than any other twentieth-century work. Mill's discussion of connotation and denotation can be found in Book I of his *System of Logic*.

The chief works by Aristotle are *On Interpretation, Categories,* the opening paragraph of *Prior Analytics,* and Book Zeta of the *Metaphysics;* by Hegel, *The Phenomenology of the Mind,* especially the Preface; by Leibniz, *Monadology;* by Carnap, P. A. Schilpp, ed., *The Philosophy of Rudolf Carnap* (La Salle, Ill., 1963), the autobiographical essay and the replies; by Black, *Models and Metaphors* (Ithaca, N.Y., 1962); by Geach, *Reference and Generality* (Ithaca, N.Y., 1962).

G. E. M. Anscombe and P. T. Geach, *Three Philosophers* (Oxford, 1961), contains useful comments on the relevant views of Aristotle and Frege. One of the best recent discussions of the influence of grammar on metaphysics is Morris Lazerowitz, "Substratum," in Max Black, ed., *Philosophical Analysis* (Englewood Cliffs, N.J., 1950). For further references, see the articles cited in text and articles on the philosophers mentioned.

NEWTON GARVER

SUBJECTIVISM IN ETHICS. See ETHICAL SUBJECTIVISM.

SUBSTANCE AND ATTRIBUTE. The concepts of substance and attribute are the focus of a group of philosophical problems which have their origins in Greek philosophy and in particular the philosophy of Aristotle. The concepts are, of course, familiar to prephilosophical common sense. Yet although we are acquainted with the distinction between things and their properties and are able to identify the same things among the changing appearances they manifest in time, these common-sense notions give rise to a group of philosophical problems when we come to scrutinize them. Thus we may wonder what it is that remains the same when, for example, we say that the car has new tires and lights and does not run as smoothly as it used to, but is still the same car; or when we say that although we could hardly recognize him, this man is the same one we went to school with thirty years ago.

It is interesting to note that the principal term for substance in the writings of Aristotle is *ousia,* a word which in earlier Greek writers means "property" in the legal sense of the word, that which is owned. (This sense is familiar in English in the old-fashioned expression "a man of substance.") The word *ousia* also occurs in philosophical writings before Aristotle as a synonym for the Greek word *physis,* a term which can mean either the origin of a thing, its natural constitution or structure, the stuff of which things are made, or a natural kind or species. The Latin word *substantia,* from which the English term is derived, is a literal translation of the Greek word *hypostasis* ("standing under"). This term acquired its philosophical connotations in later Greek and occurs principally in controversies among early Christian theologians about the real nature of Christ. A third philosophical term, *hypokeimenon* ("that which underlies something"), is used by both Plato and Aristotle to refer to that which presupposes something else.

There is, however, little of philosophical importance to be learned from the etymology of the terms in which problems are formulated and discussed. We shall first consider the questions to which the concepts of substance and attribute give rise in some of the philosophers for whom they have been important. We may then ask which of these questions remain as live philosophical issues at the present time and what answers can be given to these surviving questions.

Aristotle. Aristotle's account of substance has been the most influential in the history of philosophy. His account is, however, obscure and probably inconsistent. The difficulties of elucidating and reconciling the various parts of his doctrine have been part of the cause of its influence—it has offered a continuing challenge to commentators and critics from Aristotle's time to the present. "Substance in the truest and primary and most definite sense of the word is that which is neither predicable of a subject nor present in a subject; for instance, the individual man or horse" (*Categories* 2A11). The explanation is obscure, but the examples cited leave no doubt of what Aristotle means here: Substance in the most basic sense of the word is the concrete individual thing. However, he goes on at once to mention a second sense of the word: "Those things are called substances within which, as species, the primary substances are included; also those which, as genera, include the species. For instance the individual man is included in the species 'man' and the genus to which the species belongs is 'animal'; these, therefore,—the species 'man' and the genus 'animal'—are termed secondary substances." These secondary substances are predicable of a subject. "For instance, 'man' is predicated of the individual man" (*Categories* 2A21–22), as when we say "Socrates is a man." Aristotle seems to have the idea here that essences or natures are substances, and the more qualities they comprise, the more substantial they really are; he explains, "Of secondary substances, the species is more truly substance than the genus, being more nearly related to primary substance" (*Categories* 2B7). For example, the species *Canis domesticus* shares more qualities in common with the individual dog Tray than does the genus *Canis.* This notion of essences as substances is treated at length by Aristotle in the *Metaphysics* and seems to be his preferred sense of the term. The intimation that the more qualities something has, the more substantial it is, has the advantage of suggesting that being a substance is a matter of degree and not an all-or-nothing matter. This hint, which Aristotle does not develop, contains an important idea, as will be seen later. But the doctrine of secondary substances has little else to recommend it and involves a serious logical confusion between the relations of class membership and class inclusion, as well as the notorious difficulties of the doctrine of essences.

Aristotle's main purpose in the *Categories* is to contrast the independent way of existing proper to substances with the parasitic mode of being of qualities and relations. Substances can exist on their own; qualities and relations, only as the qualities of or relations between substances. The key to this distinction is given by the phrase "present in a subject." (The Greek word for "subject" here is *hypokeimenon,* literally "underlay.") Substances are never "present in a subject." This does not mean, as Aristotle explains, that a substance is never "present in" something else as a part of a whole. On the contrary, he cites heads and hands (*Categories* 8B15) as substances although they are parts of bodies. Rather, *x* is present in *y* when it is "incapable of existence apart from" *y.* This notion introduces a third sense of substance as that which is capable of independent existence. This sense is of considerable importance in later philosophy, but Aristotle does not develop it. He uses it chiefly to emphasize the distinction between substances on the one hand and their qualities and relations on the other. A quality—"red," "sweet," or "virtuous"—cannot exist apart from an *x* which has the quality. Relations like "larger than" or "to the left of" cannot occur in the absence of the *x* and *y* which they relate. It is true, of course, as Aristotle's critics have pointed out, that it is no more possible for a substance to exist without qualities than for qualities to exist without a substance. However, it is possible to point to prima facie examples of qualities existing without substances—the blue of the sky, for instance, or a red afterimage floating in my visual field. Surely the sky is not a substance, nor is my visual field. However, one cannot point to any instances of substances existing without qualities. Even if it makes sense to suppose that such a thing could occur, it is clearly incapable of being identified. Aristotle does not consider these problems. What he seems to have meant, although he does not express himself clearly, is that what is capable of independent existence is the concrete individual thing, a substance

with its qualities and in its network of relations to other substances. But even here there is an obvious difficulty. Once we introduce the notion of relations involving other substances, we put a restriction on independent existence.

A fourth criterion of substance is that "while remaining numerically one and the same, it is capable of admitting contrary qualities" (*Categories* 4A10). This Aristotle calls "the most distinctive mark of substance." This notion is developed, more by later philosophers than by Aristotle himself, into the conception of a center of change and so of a substratum that underlies and supports its qualities. Finally, Aristotle emphasizes the notion of substance as a logical subject, "that which is not asserted of a subject, but of which everything else is asserted" (*Metaphysics* 1029A8), and he links this sense of the term with the concept of substratum. This logical criterion has been criticized as making the notion of substance dependent on the structure of Greek (and some other Indo-European languages), in which subject–predicate sentences are a standard mode of expression, and upon a restricted and now outmoded view of logic in which all statements canonically expressed are in a form in which a predicate is affirmed of a subject. It is not the case that sentences in all languages fall into a subject–predicate form or that this form of expression is adequate for a developed logic.

Other philosophers. The various notions of substance as (1) the concrete individual, (2) a core of essential properties, (3) what is capable of independent existence, (4) a center of change, (5) a substratum, and (6) a logical subject are never thoroughly worked out and reconciled in Aristotle. He appears to emphasize now one and now another mark of substance as of paramount importance. The quotations cited above have been chiefly from the *Categories;* the topic is taken up and discussed at length in the *Metaphysics.* The discussion is tentative and not finally conclusive, but Aristotle seems to favor alternative (2), substance as essence, as his preferred sense. But the whole treatment is important not for the answers that he gives but for the questions that he raises. Discussions of substance in later philosophers have tended, with few exceptions, to take over one or more of the six senses proposed by Aristotle as the clue to the problem.

Atomists and medievals. Of the philosophical theories of antiquity, one other is of some consequence. Ancient atomism, founded by Leucippus and Democritus, developed by Epicurus, and expressed in its most attractive form in the *De Rerum Natura* of the Roman poet Lucretius, suggests that the truly real and substantial elements of nature are the atoms out of which everything is composed. It is these that are fundamental, unchangeable, and, in the last resort, capable of independent existence. The problem of substance and attribute was not much discussed by the ancient atomists, but their theories provide material for an answer to the question raised by Aristotle.

During the Middle Ages, discussion of this problem was very naturally centered upon the theological repercussions of rival theories. In particular, the doctrines of the Incarnation of Christ and of transubstantiation depended for their rational justification upon a plausible theory of substance. But these theological outworks produced no new basic insights that can be regarded as an improvement on the work of Aristotle. Indeed, they are just variations upon Aristotelian themes.

Descartes. The revival of philosophy in the seventeenth century in a form that was relatively independent of the religious framework of medieval philosophy produced several systems for which the notion of substance is fundamental. In the work of Descartes the concepts of substance and attribute become associated naturally with those of the conscious self and its states, and the problem of substance becomes associated with the problem of personal identity. Descartes had been thoroughly trained in the form of Aristotelian scholasticism current in his day, and his notions of substance are in part derived from this and in part inconsistent with it. He gives a formal definition of substance as follows: "Everything in which there resides immediately, as in a subject, or by means of which there exists anything that we perceive, i.e. any property, quality, or attribute of which we have a real idea is called a *Substance;* neither do we have any other idea of substance itself, precisely taken, than that it is a thing in which this something that we perceive or which is present objectively in some of our ideas, exists formally or eminently. For by means of our natural light we know that a real attribute cannot be an attribute of nothing" (*Philosophical Works,* translated by Haldane and Ross, 2d ed., Cambridge, 1931, Vol. II, p. 53). In other words, what we are directly aware of are attributes of things and not the things themselves. But it is a logically self-evident principle (known by "the natural light" of reason) that an attribute must be an attribute of something, and the something is a substance—known by this inference and not directly. So far Descartes does not depart from scholastic doctrine, but he goes on to affirm that substances have essential attributes. For example, thought is the essential attribute of mind, and extension is the essential attribute of matter. But he does not explain what a substance is apart from its essential property. What is the mind apart from thinking or matter apart from extension? Unless this question is answered, how can Descartes answer the later empiricist criticism that the concept of substance is meaningless because empty of content?

In another context (*ibid.,* p. 101) he gives an alternative definition of substance. "Really the notion of *substance* is just this—that which can exist by itself, without the aid of any other substance." This second definition is a bad one, being circular in expression; but clearly Descartes has in mind both here and in the quotation above simply the Aristotelian criteria (3) and (5). On the basis of these definitions, Descartes postulates three types of substance: material bodies, minds, and God. But the first two, being in a certain sense dependent on God for their existence, clearly have a lower grade of substantiality. Descartes's conception of substance and attribute is made impossible to understand by the vagueness of the notion "attribute" by which he seeks to clarify the idea of substance. If "attribute" means "property or relation," it simply is not true that all attributes are attributes of substances. For example, a color may have properties that are not properties of the colored thing. It is true of the color *red* that it is produced by light of wavelength about 7000 angstrom units, but this is not true of red objects. In any case, it seems that Des-

cartes has simply defined "substance" and "attribute" relative to each other so that his explanation is circular and thus uninformative: attributes are what qualify substances and substances are what have attributes.

Spinoza. Descartes's second account of substance as that which is capable of independent existence was taken up and developed by Spinoza in his *Ethics.* Spinoza was a student of Descartes and may be regarded as one who developed some of Descartes's ideas to consistent but surprising conclusions. Reflecting on Descartes's second account of substance, Spinoza showed that if by "substance" we mean, according to his definition, "that which is in itself and is conceived through itself," it is easy to show that there can be only one such being, the whole universe. Thus Spinoza equated substance with God and nature, the three terms being synonymous for him. This "hideous hypothesis," in Hume's ironical phrase, has won for Spinoza the inconsistent titles of atheist and pantheist. What he did, in fact, was to demonstrate the alarming consequences for religious orthodoxy of Descartes's second definition and to indicate obliquely that substantiality in this sense is a matter of degree. Nothing in the universe is completely independent of its environment, although some things are more independent than others. A human being has a certain degree of independence of his environment but can exist only within a certain range of temperature, pressure, and humidity, and with access to air, food, and water. Other things may be more or less independent of their surroundings, and the extent of their freedom in each case is an empirical question. Spinoza did not draw this conclusion, but it is implicit in his development of Descartes.

Leibniz. Another rationalist philosopher, Leibniz, makes the concept of substance fundamental to his philosophical system. He uses two of the Aristotelian criteria of substance, substance as a center of change and substance as a logical subject, but adds the concept of simplicity. The basic elements of Leibniz' metaphysical system were what he called monads. In his *Monadology* he defines "monad" as "nothing but a simple substance. . . . By 'simple' is meant 'without parts.'" That there are such simple substances follows, for Leibniz, from the admitted fact that there are compound things, which can be nothing but collections of simple things. Leibniz seems here to have been influenced by the arguments of the ancient materialists for the existence of atoms. His monads, however, were supposed to be immaterial substances, centers of change and thus subjects of predicates. Unfortunately, by describing his substances in this way, he deprives the term of meaning just as Descartes had done. He does indeed affirm that his monads are centers of activity, but this activity is manifested only in their tendency to move from one state to another. But if the essence of something is to be the x which undergoes changes and of which predicates can be affirmed, it can have no positive character of its own. In Russell's words, "substance remains, apart from its predicates, wholly destitute of meaning" (*The Philosophy of Leibniz,* p. 50).

Locke, Berkeley, Hume. Leibniz had criticized the British empiricist philosopher John Locke for professing to find substance an empty concept. The weakness of Locke's criticisms of the concept was that he concentrated his attack on the notion of a substratum of qualities. This is not the most important of the Aristotelian senses of the term. But if "substratum" can be shown to be an empty notion, it is easy to raise skeptical doubts about some of the associated senses, particularly those of substance as a center of change, as the concrete individual, and as a logical subject. Locke points out that we find in experience groups of qualities which occur together in time and place. We therefore presume these qualities to belong to one thing and come to use one word, "gold," "apple," or "water" (whatever it may be) to refer to the collection of properties "which indeed is a complication of many ideas together." Further, "not imagining how these simple ideas *can* subsist by themselves, we accustom ourselves to suppose some *substratum* wherein they do subsist, and from which they do result, which we therefore call *substance*" (*Essay concerning Human Understanding,* Book II, Ch. 23). Substance, then, is not a positive concept but merely an "obscure and relative" notion of "the supposed but unknown support of those qualities we find existing, which we imagine cannot exist *sine re substante* without something to support them." Since Locke has already tried to show that all our meaningful concepts originate in experience, substance is an awkward counterexample to his theory of knowledge. Indeed, he would probably have rejected it altogether but for certain associated moral and theological doctrines which his cautious and conformist temperament made him forbear to reject outright. Moreover, he seems to have been unable to reject Descartes's principle that attributes must inhere in a substance, although he does not submit this supposed logical truth to any rigorous examination.

However, Locke's empiricist successors, Berkeley and Hume, were fully aware of the importance of Locke's criticism and his reduction of the notion to "an uncertain supposition of we know not what." Berkeley's attack on the concept of material substance owes much to Locke, and Hume was content to write off the whole idea as an "unintelligible chimaera." Moreover, Hume extended the skepticism of Locke and Berkeley in respect of material substance to question, on analogous grounds, the existence of spiritual substances or selves. It is clear that a mind whose function is merely to be the bearer of states of consciousness is as vacuous a notion as Locke's material "we know not what."

Kant. Immanuel Kant's *Critique of Pure Reason* (1781) transformed the notion of substance, as it did so many other philosophical concepts. In Kant's view, "substance" does not refer to a feature of the objective world independent of human thinking. On the contrary, the unity and permanence of substances are features contributed by the human understanding to the world of phenomena. This represents a very radical revision of the concept of substance. Substance shrinks from being a fundamental feature of the objective world to an aspect under which men cannot help classifying their experience—and they cannot help themselves not because of the nature of external reality but because of the structure of their own cognitive apparatus.

Modern criticism. Since Kant's day the permanent and valuable features of philosophy have been those that have grown out of the immense development of the formal and natural sciences from the end of the eighteenth century to the present, a development that has shown the falsity of the scientific assumptions on which the Kantian revolution was built. For example, Kant believed that Newtonian physics, Euclidean geometry, and Aristotelian logic were finally and beyond all question true of the world, and some features of his system depend on these assumptions. This development has presented the problem of substance as a problem soluble, if at all, in the light of empirical evidence drawn from the relevant sciences. It has, moreover, made clear that there is no one problem of substance but a number of subproblems that can be treated independently. These problems can still be stated in something like their original Aristotelian form, but we may find ourselves looking in different areas of knowledge for their answers. There is no one unitary science, such as metaphysics or ontology, that can be looked to for a solution. For example, the notion of substance as a logical subject of predicates (as when we say of a piece of gold, "*It* is heavy," "*It* is yellow," "*It* is malleable," "*It* melts at 1063° C.," and so on) is now seen to be a problem of interest to formal logic and to linguistics. It is a technical question of logic whether all sentences about individual things can be (or must be) expressed in subject–predicate form. And it is a technical question of linguistics whether all languages use such a form to express these notions, or indeed have a subject–predicate syntax at all. (The answer in both cases seems to be "No.")

Independent existents. The question "What, if anything, is capable of independent existence?" can be seen, insofar as it relates to material things, to be a question to which physics, chemistry, and biology give us the answers. (If the question is asked about the existence of nonmaterial things such as numbers or propositions, we have first to make clear what is meant by "existence" in such contexts.) We see that "independent" is not a term with a clear meaning but, rather, is an elliptical expression. "X is capable of independent existence" means "X is capable of existing without regard to features $y_1, y_2, \cdots, y_n$ of its environment." Since these conditions are so numerous, it is easier to express the concept negatively: "X is not independent" means "X is incapable of existing apart from conditions $z_1, z_2, \cdots, z_n$" or "$z_1, \cdots, z_n$ are necessary conditions for the existence of X." On this interpretation, a substance in the sense of something that is capable of completely independent existence is something for whose existence there are no necessary conditions. The specific values of the variable z will vary with the value of X. For example, if X is a piece of ice or a lump of metal, one of the z's will be temperature; if X is a green plant, the z's will include light and oxygen; and so on. It may well be that nothing in the universe is independent of all conditions, but whether this is so is an empirical question.

Essences. Aristotle's favorite, but least satisfactory, account of substance was that of substance as essence, an essence being a set of qualities that conjointly embody the nature of the thing they qualify, are grasped by intellectual intuition, and are expressed in the definition of the thing. But developments in the sciences (especially in biology) and in the philosophy of science over the past century have shown that this notion is illusory. Definitions, in the contemporary view, are either descriptions of current linguistic usage or recommendations for linguistic conventions. They cannot seek to explicate the essential nature of the definiendum because naturally occurring objects have no such invariable natures. Definitions in formal sciences like mathematics and logic do delineate the invariant properties of the definienda precisely because they are proposals for conventions.

Substratum. There remains for consideration substance in the senses of (*a*) a center of change, (*b*) a substratum of qualities, and (*c*) the concrete individual thing. Senses (*a*) and (*b*) are closely akin and are both vulnerable to the empiricist line of criticism made famous by Locke. We may regard a particular thing as qualified by different properties at different times (for example, when an insect changes from egg to caterpillar to pupa to moth), or as qualified by a group of qualities at the same time (for example, when we say that a lump of sugar is white and sweet and soluble). Both of these ways of looking at substance lead to the unanswerable question "What is it that is the bearer of the qualities in each case?" But the answer to this cannot even be as satisfactory as Locke's "something we know not what," for by thus separating the subject (or hypothetical bearer of the qualities) from its predicates, we effectively prevent ourselves from saying anything about it. For to say anything about it is merely to assign to it one more predicate. This way of explaining substance makes it an empty concept.

Yet the obvious alternative to this blind alley seems no more promising. Suppose that when we say "Some apples are red" we do not mean what contemporary logic teaches us to mean: There is an x that has both the property of being an apple and the property of being red. Suppose that instead we mean: That set of particular properties which we call "apple" includes the further property of being red. Then the relation "being predicated of" turns out to be nothing more than the familiar relation of being a member of a group. This conclusion looks innocuous until we realize that this interpretation would make all subject–predicate affirmations either necessarily true or logically false. For the proposition "The set of properties Q_1, $Q_2, \cdots, Q_n$ contains the property Q_n" is a logically true statement. And if we amend it to make it informative thus: "The set of properties $Q_1, \cdots, Q_n$ contains the property Q_{n+1}" we do not have an informative proposition but, rather, a logically false one.

The way out of this dilemma is not to ask such misleadingly general questions as "What is the locus of change?" or "What is the bearer of properties?" We can ask for the detailed history of a particular thing, an insect, a plant, a man or what not, and the answer will be given to us by the relevant sciences—embryology, anatomy, physiology. We can ask for the detailed structure of a particular thing, a piece of gold, a moth, a man, or what not; again the relevant science—physics, chemistry, anatomy—will give us the answer if the answer is known. But we cannot ask for the history or structure of things in general, for there is no science of things in general.

Concrete individuals. A similar criticism awaits the last of the Aristotelian answers to the question about substance: A substance is a concrete individual thing. We cannot sensibly ask what makes things-in-general concrete individuals. The notion of a concrete individual thing is clear in its standard cases, like men, tables, mice, or stones. But it is unclear in its nonstandard applications. Is a cloud a concrete individual or is it just the particles that make it up that can be so called? Is a rainbow? Or a dream table? Can electrons be called individual things when it is impossible in principle to identify them and trace their continuous histories? Examples such as these show the futility of trying to find a general formula that will clarify the notion of a concrete individual thing. We can, of course, ask the psychologists what perceptual characteristics of things lead us to class them as individuals. That a set of jointly occurring properties stands out in our perceptual field, that it moves as one, that it persists through time—all these and other characteristics will lead us to regard a thing as a thing. But there is no decisive test which will enable us to decide, if we are doubtful, whether a certain x is really a concrete individual or not. In borderline cases this must be a matter for decision, not diagnosis.

Bibliography

BOOKS

Aristotle, *Metaphysics* and *Categories* (Oxford translations). Oxford, 1908 and 1928.
Blanshard, Brand, *The Nature of Thought.* London, 1939. Ch. 3.
Broad, C. D., *An Examination of McTaggart's Philosophy.* Cambridge, 1933. Vol. I, Ch. 7.
Leibniz, G. W., *Monadology*, Robert Latta, ed. Oxford, 1898.
Locke, John, *An Essay concerning Human Understanding*, J. Yolton, ed. London, 1962. Book II, Ch. 23.
Russell, Bertrand, *The Philosophy of Leibniz.* Cambridge, 1900.
Russell, Bertrand, *The Analysis of Matter.* London, 1927. Ch. 23.
Russell, Bertrand, *An Inquiry Into Meaning and Truth.* London, 1940.
Russell, Bertrand, *Human Knowledge.* London, 1948.
Shoemaker, Sydney, *Self-Knowledge and Self-Identity.* Ithaca, N.Y., 1963.
Strawson, P. F., *Individuals.* London, 1959.

ARTICLES

Anscombe, G. E. M., "Aristotle," in *Three Philosophers.* Oxford, 1963.
Anscombe, G. E. M., and Körner, S., "Substance." *PAS*, Supp. Vol. 38 (1964).
Basson, A. H., "The Problem of Substance." *PAS* (1948/1949).
Bennett, Jonathan, "Substance, Reality, and Primary Qualities." *American Philosophical Quarterly* (1965).
Cousin, D. R., "Aristotle's Doctrine of Substance." *Mind* (1933).
Kneale, William, "The Notion of a Substance." *PAS* (1939/1940).
Lazerowitz, Morris, "Substratum," in Max Black, ed., *Philosophical Analysis.* Ithaca, N.Y., 1950.
Mei, Tsu-Lin, "Chinese Grammar and the Linguistic Movement in Philosophy." *The Review of Metaphysics*, Vol. 14 (1961). An original and penetrating critique of the notions of subject and predicate.
Sellars, Wilfrid, "Substance and Form in Aristotle." *Journal of Philosophy* (1957).
Stebbing, L. Susan, "On Substance." *PAS* (1929/1930).

D. J. O'CONNOR

SUFI PHILOSOPHY. Beginning about 800 the term "Sufi" (*Ṣūfī*) was applied to Muslim mystics who, as a means of achieving union with Allah, adopted ascetic practices, including the wearing of garments made of coarse wool (*ṣūf*). In a short time, however, the term "Sufi" came to designate all Muslim believers in mystic union, without regard to whether their doctrines and their quests were associated with asceticism.

Sufism (or Sufiism) arose and flourished as a result of several influences: (1) A mystic tinge in Muhammad's teachings; (2) the contact of some of the faithful with Gnosticism, Neoplatonism, Pseudo-Dionysius' mystical writings, and perhaps Buddhism (which was flourishing in Turkestan and nearby areas); and (3) the social upheaval in Arab lands after Muhammad's death, which drove some Muslims to the inner life as an escape from the outer world's hardships. In addition, Sufism was partly a quietistic reaction against the extravagance and worldliness of a few communal leaders, Muhammad's immediate successors, who wallowed in luxury and pomp.

Among the principal teachings of Sufism are the following:

(1) Absolute Being (God) is also Absolute Beauty.

(2) Since beauty tends toward manifestation, Absolute Being developed the phenomenal world.

(3) To win a sense of direct communion with the Absolute Being behind the phenomenal world, one should practice the quietistic virtues (poverty, austerity, humility, fortitude, and discipline), devote oneself to the ways of inwardness (withdrawal, silence, solitariness, and self-examination), and keep in mind a constant awareness of God (with faith, awe, and desire).

(4) It is useful to utter certain slogans (such as "Allah is here!") as reminders of the mystic belief and aim and as aids to concentration on the quest for unification.

(5) If one follows these directions with sufficient perseverance, one will advance through the standard mystic stages of concentration, apprehension of the oneness of everything, sudden and unpredictable illumination, blissful ecstasy, sense of union with the Deity, sense of one's own nothingness, and sense of the nothingness beyond nothingness.

Although asceticism had appeared in the prehistory of Sufism (650–750), philosophy in a strict sense had played little or no role. The first period of Sufism proper (c. 750–1050), when the name Sufi gained currency, was characterized by an evolution of the otherworldly bent from the mere practice of asceticism toward the joining of such practice with pantheistic speculations and mystical meditations. The pantheistic speculations had their root in immanentist passages in the Qur'an (Koran), such as "Wheresoever you turn is the face of Allah" (ii, 109). In this formative period of Sufism, Rābi'a al-'Adawīya (717–801), a freed slave girl who came to be known in the West as "the Muslim Saint Teresa," introduced the vocabulary of love and wine as symbols of the blissful ecstasy of direct mystical apprehension of God.

In the same early period as Rābi'a, two Sufis were executed by the orthodox for referring to themselves as identical with the Deity. First of the two martyrs was Abū Yazīd (d. 875), variously called Bayazid or al-Bistami, a Persian ecstatic who exclaimed, with searing fervor, "How great is My Majesty!" He introduced the doctrine of *fana'* (probably derived from "nirvana"), or annihilation—that is,

the passing away of individual consciousness in a state of union with God—which has played a significant role in Sufi thought. The second martyr, al-Hussayn ibn-Mansur al-Hallāj (854–922), "the Saint of Baghdad," having experienced an intense sense of unification with Allah, proclaimed, "I am the Truth." Both took their fate with stoic equanimity.

From a fairly early date Sufi convents were founded, where neophytes and experienced devotees together participated in simple living, recitation of mystical religious and philosophical classics, and performance of mystic rituals. One of the earliest of these convents was established at Ramleh (southeast of present-day Tel Aviv) about 775. Celibacy was not a requirement for membership in a Sufi convent; some members lived with their families outside the convent but came to the convent regularly.

The second period of Sufism (c. 1050–1450) provided a needed sanctuary against the apparent blasphemy of self-identification with Allah. Abū Ḥamid al-Ghazālī (1058–1111) fused mysticism with Muslim traditionalism by de-emphasizing the pantheistic aspects of Sufism. His success was so great that he is sometimes said to have made Islam a mystic faith. "Strive," he said, "to know how to attain to the Divine Presence and the contemplation of the Divine Majesty and Beauty." He added, however, that "to be a Sufi means to abide continuously in God and to live at peace with men." From a religious viewpoint this was a far less dangerous teaching than Hallāj's "I am the Truth."

Other key figures of this medieval period were Farid ad-Dīn 'Attar (died c. 1230), ibn-al-'Arabī (1165–1240), and Jalal ad-Dīn Rūmī (1207–1273). 'Attar's *Parliament of the Birds,* an allegory describing the quest of the birds (Sufis) for their leader (God), was translated in abridged form by Edward Fitzgerald. In the verses of the *Parliament,* devotees were summoned to the high goal as follows:

> Come you lost Atoms to your Centre draw,
> And *be* the Eternal Mirror that you saw:
> Rays that have wander'd into Darkness wide
> Return, and back into your Sun subside.

Of ibn-al-'Arabī, who was born in Spain and settled in Damascus, some 150 works are extant, including a compendium of Sufi doctrine entitled *Meccan Revelations.* One of ibn-al-'Arabī's main contributions was his crystallization of the idea, which had long been forming in Sufism, of the universal man, corresponding to the idea of the logos in Western thought. The universal man, the archetype of the universe (as the macrocosm) and of man, contains the Platonic essences and serves as a model to which men can strive to conform. Since Dante's eschatology resembles ibn-al-'Arabī's in some features, a few scholars have suggested a direct influence of the latter on Dante.

Rūmī's *Masnawi* ("Rhyming Couplets"), in Persian, is a series of mystic tales, ruminations, invocations, and so forth, expounding and illustrating the doctrines mainly of pantheism and transmigration: "I am the mote in the sunbeam, I am the ball of the sun, I am the glow of the morning, I am the breath of evening"; "I die as a stone and become a plant, I die as a plant and become an animal, . . . dying as a man I shall come to life as an angel, . . . and in the end I shall become the Nothing." Rūmī instituted the devotional dances now associated with the whirling dervishes. These dances, consisting of accelerated movements of head and feet (sometimes in rotations of the whole body), are aimed at "remembering" one's inner self, God, and the identity of the two, in a state of ecstatic trance and exaltation.

The symbolism of love and wine used earlier by Rābi'a as a rhetorical device (the religious experience coming first and the language of pleasure then expressing it) was, in this era and later, sometimes given an opposite twist, so that the extolling of the virtues of the grape by Omar Khayyam, and of the sweets of love by Hafiz, were taken by their Sufi readers to refer to "the mysterious force in the grape" and "the love of the essence of life" (the language of pleasure coming first and the mystic interpretation of it following).

The medieval period was marked by the establishment of the great Sufi orders, of which about one hundred still exist, with an estimated several million adherents. Chief founders of these orders were 'Abd al-Qadir (1078–1166), whose followers have their headquarters in Baghdad; Shihāb al-Dīn al-Suhrawardī (1155–1191), who was executed at the instance of the orthodox and whose order is influential in Iran; Nur ad-Dīn al-Shadhili (1196–1258), who was persecuted in his native Tunis but found many disciples in Egypt; and Rūmī, whose Mevlevis (disciples of *Mawlana,* "our master"—i.e., Rūmī), with headquarters at Konya, south of Ankara, have the whirling dance as their most characteristic feature. Besides the members of the orders, there have appeared, over the centuries, numbers of unorganized wandering Sufi mendicants (*faqīr* in Arabic, *darwīsh* in Persian), some genuinely pious, whereas others, who were fraudulent beggars, brought disrepute to Sufism.

The modern period of Sufi philosophy and practice (c. 1450–1850), sometimes referred to as the period of the poets (although poets abounded in the second period as well), begins with Mawlana Nur ad-Dīn Jāmī (1414–1492) of Persia, who is known mainly for his narrative poem *Yusuf and Zulaykha.* He also wrote prose biographies of earlier Sufi teachers and a theosophical treatise, *Law'iḥ* ("Flashes of Light"), arguing that union with God can be achieved only by realizing the delusion of self as well as of the phenomenal world with its vanities:

> Set enmity between the world and me,
> Make me averse from worldly company:
> From other objects turn away my heart,
> So that it is engrossed with love of Thee.

In India, Kabir (1435–1518), a weaver in Benares, combined the tenets of Brahmanism, Vaisnavism, and Sufism. In his poems he referred to God interchangeably as Rama, Hari, or Allah. Although representing God as omnipresent, Kabir defended the individuality of the human soul, which, however, can attain unification with God through love.

In this period, obscurantism, association of miracle legends with the early Sufi saints, use of charms and amulets, and Cabalism became prevalent in Sufism, especially in Egypt but also generally throughout the Muslim world.

In the fourth, or contemporary, period (since 1850), Muhammad Amin al-Kurdi al-Shafi'i al-Naqshabandi of Iraq (d. 1914) prepared a manual of mystic instructions in Arabic which was widely reprinted. Among the directions which he gave for attempting to attain mystic unification with Allah were these: Be seated; close the eyes; make your humility perfect; imagine that you are dead and the mourners have departed, leaving you alone to face the Judgment; concentrate all your senses; expel all preoccupations and wayward impulses of the heart; and direct your perception toward God.

Sir Muhammad Iqbal (1877–1938), a Punjabi Muslim who studied philosophy at Cambridge (under J. M. E. McTaggart) and at Munich and taught philosophy at the Government College in Pakistan, is best known as a poet, having been compared with Rabindranath Tagore. He described the mystic initiate as proceeding through four stages: belief in the Unseen, search after the Unseen, knowledge of the Unseen gained by looking into the depth of one's own soul, and realization. Total union with the Unseen he rejected as inconsistent with monotheism. In his later years he repudiated both Sufism and the Vedantism which he had previously espoused.

Also prominent among recent Sufis is Inayat Khan (1882–1926), of Baroda in northwest India, who came to London in 1910, lectured there on Sufi philosophy, and founded the *Sufi Quarterly.* His *Sufi Message,* containing transcripts of his lectures, has recently been published in London for the International Headquarters of the Sufi Movement in Geneva. Inayat Khan's message stresses the spiritual and the beautiful in life: "Why was I born, O God, if not to find Thee?" Its technical philosophical content is minimal.

Bibliography

The chief works on Sufism are Arthur J. Arberry, *An Introduction to the History of Sufism* (London, 1943) and *Sufism, An Account of the Mystics of Islam* (London, 1950); Reynold A. Nicholson, *Studies in Islamic Mysticism* (Cambridge, 1921) and *The Idea of Personality in Sufism* (Cambridge, 1923); Idries Shah, *The Sufis,* with an introduction by Robert Graves (New York, 1964); and Margaret Smith, ed., *The Sufi Path of Love, An Anthology of Sufism* (London, 1954).

Also useful are the articles on Sufism in various encyclopedias, especially the article "Tassawuf" ("Sufism"), in M. T. Houtsma et al., eds., *The Encyclopaedia of Islam,* 4 vols. (London, 1913–1936), also published in French and German; and the article in James Hastings, ed., *Encyclopedia of Religion and Ethics,* 13 vols. (New York, 1908–1926).

Works by or about individual Sufis include Margaret Smith, *Rabi'a the Mystic and Her Fellow Saints in Islam* (Cambridge, 1928); A. E. Affifi, *The Mystical Philosophy of Muhyid Din-ibnul 'Arabi* (Cambridge, 1939) and the chapter "Ibn Arabi and the Sufis" in Seyyed Hossein Nasr, *Three Muslim Sages* (Cambridge, Mass., 1964); Jalal ad-Dīn Rūmī, *Masnavi i Ma'navi, The Spiritual Couplets,* translated by E. H. Whinfield (London, 1887); *Rumi, Poet and Mystic, 1207–1273; Selections From His Writings,* translated by R. A. Nicholson (London, 1950); *Poems of a Persian Sūfī, Being the Quatrains of Bābā Tāhir,* translated by A. J. Arberry (Cambridge, 1937); Muhammad Iqbal, *The Secrets of the Self,* translated by R. A. Nicholson (London, 1920; rev. ed., Lahore, 1940; reprinted 1944); and *The Sufi Message of Hezrat Inayat Khan,* 11 vols. thus far (London, 1960——).

Two periodicals have specialized in Sufism: *Sufi Quarterly*

(London, 1925–1933) and *The Sufi* (London, 1951–1952, only two issues published).

Further sources are cited in Gustav Pfanmüller, *Handbuch der Islam-Litteratur* (Berlin, 1923), pp. 265–292; in J. D. Pearson, *Index Islamicus, 1906–1955* (Cambridge, 1958), pp. 72–82; and in the 1956–1960 *Supplement* (published 1962) to Pearson's *Index Islamicus*, pp. 25–28.

WILLIAM GERBER

SUHRAWARDI, SHIHABODDIN. See SOHRAWARDĪ, SHIHĀB AL-DĪN YAHYĀ.

SUICIDE. The prohibition of suicide, or self-killing, can be looked upon as a matter of natural aversion, primitive superstition, religious belief, or philosophical argument; but there has always been a current of libertarian opinion which has succeeded in removing most of the penal sanctions against suicide. Suicide differs from euthanasia in that the latter is either an assisted suicide or a killing by another for humanitarian reasons and by merciful means, generally with the consent of the person killed, in which case it is referred to specifically as voluntary euthanasia.

Views on suicide. Although the laws of ancient Thebes and Athens expressed man's natural repugnance to suicide by deprivation of funeral rites and symbols of degradation, the philosophical position of the ancient world was not wholly opposed to suicide. Socrates, as reported by Plato, thought that man was, as it were, the property of the gods, so that self-killing would bring down their wrath; but the permission of the gods could be made manifest by a "visible necessity of dying," as had been imposed on Socrates himself. Plato admitted other exceptions to the prohibition of suicide—any shame of extreme distress and poverty or affliction by any extraordinary sorrow or inevitable turn of fortune. These exceptions were so wide as to destroy the practical effect of the general rule, but Aristotle repeated the prohibition without the exceptions. He thought of suicide as an act of cowardice and an offense against the state, but the reason he gave for the latter position —that what the law does not command, it forbids—is palpably false.

Epicurus held that if life ceases to be a pleasure, the remedy for a free man was to end it; and the Stoics, too, regarded it as part of human freedom that a man continued to live by his own consent. This view greatly affected Roman philosophy. Seneca argued eloquently in favor of suicide as an escape from suffering and from the decay of old age, but he admitted the general duty to live for others, such as a child or wife. Cato the Younger, Pliny the Elder, Epictetus, and Marcus Aurelius took much the same position. Cicero, however, gave both religious and social reasons for rejecting suicide.

It seems that the earliest rejection of suicide in Jewish thought was by Josephus, the commander of a defeated army. His soldiers wished to kill themselves to avoid surrender, but Josephus opposed them. His two main arguments were that suicide is a crime remote from the common nature of all animals and that the soul is a depositum received from God, so that a man acts wickedly in casting it from his body. The later general opinion in Europe that suicide was wrong was the work of the Christian church, particularly of St. Augustine. Many Christians had committed suicide to avoid the sins of the world, and the only logical answer was an argument that suicide was itself a greater sin than any that could be avoided by it. Augustine invoked the sixth commandment, which he regarded as applicable to self-murder (though this interpretation was hardly consistent with the number of suicides reported without disapprobation in the Old Testament). He also thought that the suicide deprived himself of the opportunity for penitence and acted ignobly in trying to escape the ills of life. In order to justify some historic suicides, Augustine suggested that they had been specially commanded by God. St. Thomas Aquinas added three further arguments. The suicide, he thought, acted contrary to natural inclination, natural law, and the charity a man owes to himself; he deprived society of his activity, and he usurped the function of God.

Montaigne was the first explicitly to question the Christian attitude that came to rest on Augustine's and Aquinas' arguments. After presenting arguments for and against suicide, he concluded that the most excusable incitements to suicide were pain and the fear of suffering a worse death. John Donne's *Biathanatos,* published posthumously in 1644, expressed the opinion that the prohibition of suicide was merely part of the economic enslavement of laborers, who could not be allowed to escape from the tasks expected of them. Montesquieu's discussion was much better reasoned than Donne's. In his *Persian Letters* (1721) he presented both sides of the case in arguments attributed to imaginary correspondents. The degradation of the corpse of the suicide was unjust because a person should not be compelled to labor for a society of which he no longer consented to be a member, and the act of suicide does not "disturb the order of Providence" any more than any other human act altering the modifications of matter. When the soul is separated from the body, there is no less order and regularity in the universe. On the other hand, a being is compounded of two parts, body and soul, and the necessity of preserving their union is the greatest mark of submission to the decrees of the Creator. In *The Grandeur and Declension of the Roman Empire* Montesquieu expressed admiration for the Roman practice of suicide, which "gave every one the liberty of finishing his part on the stage of the world, in what scene he pleased." This attitude he compared unfavorably with the then current practice of kings and generals who submitted tamely to execution or imprisonment when fortune turned against them.

Voltaire was even more explicit. Why, he asked, should the suicide of a general be contrary to Christianity when killing in war was not? Some argued that the ancient heroes who committed suicide—Brutus, Cato the Younger, Cassius, Marc Antony and the rest—lacked true courage, but the truth was that a violent death calmly determined was so far from being a mark of pusillanimity that it was a victory over nature.

Hume's *Essay on Suicide* (published posthumously in 1783) elaborated Montesquieu's arguments. Man's life was of no more importance to the universe than that of an oyster. If the disposal of human life were reserved to the Almighty, almost any action would become an encroachment on his privilege. "If I turn aside a stone which is falling on my head, I disturb the course of nature and I invade the peculiar province of the Almighty by lengthening out my life beyond the period, which, by the general laws of matter and motion, He has assigned to it." As to the social argument, Hume said, "A man who retires from life does no harm to society; he only ceases to do good; which, if it is an injury, is of the lowest kind." Moral duties imply reciprocity; when I withdraw myself altogether from society, I am no longer bound. And where my life is a positive burden to society, my withdrawal from it is not only innocent but laudable.

Charles Moore wrote *A Full Inquiry Into the Subject of Suicide* to combat Hume, and this work is still one of the fullest surveys of philosophical and religious thought up to that time (1790). Moore believed that suicide is wrong because it may counteract some hidden design of Providence, but he allowed himself to say,

> The most excusable cause seems to be an emaciated body; when a man labours under the torture of an incurable disorder, and seems to live only to be a burden to himself and his friends. This was thought to be a sufficient apology for the action in ancient days and can only be combated in modern ones by the force and energy of that true religion, which both points out the duty and reward of implicit resignation.

In the nineteenth century Schopenhauer, the philosopher of pessimism, repeatedly discussed the subject of suicide. He regarded suicide as an "error" on the ground that it affords only an apparent and not a real release from the sufferings of life. Such a release is only apparent because the will as a thing-in-itself is outside of space and time, and the person committing suicide cannot destroy the will itself but only "its manifestation at this place and time" (*The World as Will and Idea*, Vol. I, Book 4, para. 69). At the same time Schopenhauer vigorously opposed the view that suicide was either a sin or a crime. It is preposterous to view suicide as a crime when "it is quite obvious that there is nothing in the world to which every man has a more unassailable title than to his own life and person" ("On Suicide," in *Studies in Pessimism*, p. 25). Schopenhauer inveighed at some length against the "vulgar bigotry" prevailing in England which made it impossible for Hume to publish his *Essay on Suicide* in his lifetime and which condoned ignominious burial of suicides and the seizure of their property. The clergy should be challenged, Schopenhauer remarked, "to explain what right they have to go into the pulpit, or to take up their pens and stamp as a crime an action which many men whom we hold in affection and honor have committed; and to refuse an honorable burial to those who relinquish this world voluntarily" (*ibid.*, p. 26).

Mme. de Staël took the orthodox view for moral and spiritual reasons, and William James thought that the rejection of suicide was implicit in the belief that life was worth living.

Some contemporary writers support the extreme individualist or libertarian position, allowing suicide at will; notable among these is H. Romilly Fedden. Harry Roberts, a physician, advocated the Stoic attitude largely as an argument for legalizing euthanasia. Most modern writers who support the morality of suicide are similarly influenced by sympathy toward those suffering from painful and incurable disease, and psychological and sociological studies also suggest that suicide is a problem of psychiatry or social engineering rather than of abstract morals. A study by E. Stengel and Nancy Cook indicated that the great majority of so-called attempted suicides were not in fact single-minded efforts at self-destruction but had a hidden "appeal character"; in other words, the suicide seemed to gamble with his life, consciously or subconsciously hoping that either the attempt would succeed or, if it failed, his life would be improved as a consequence of the attempt.

If any consensus can be found among those who discuss the topic today, it is in favor of the proposition that the law should not attempt to punish a person who attempts to commit suicide. Greater understanding of the plight of the would-be suicide and of the uselessness of punishment led to the abolition of the crime of attempted suicide in England in 1961, a step that had been proposed by a commission on suicide appointed by the archbishop of Canterbury in 1959. This step had been taken in France as long ago as 1790, under the influence of Montesquieu, Diderot, and Voltaire. Other European countries have followed this lead, and in many of the states of the United States, too, attempted suicide ceased to be punishable during the nineteenth century, either as a matter of law or in the practical application of the law.

Views on euthanasia. Religious and ethical differences still affect the treatment of those who assist the suicide, particularly in the case of the doctor who assists his suffering patient to commit suicide. (Closely analogous is the case of the doctor who himself kills his patient, perhaps with the patient's consent, for humanitarian reasons; in law this is murder on the part of the doctor, not suicide on the part of the patient, but from the ethical point of view there is little difference. Both are forms of what is commonly called euthanasia.) Orthodox religious opinion allows altruistic suicide, at least within the Roman Catholic doctrine of double effect, where the good result flows not from the suicidal death but from the act that brought it about—for example, when the injured member of a stricken expedition goes off into the desert to give his companions a better chance of survival. This, however, does not mean that religious opinion condones suicide as a means of escape from one's own suffering. Although it is now universally conceded to be useless and harmful to punish those who attempt suicide for any reason, because the punishment of one who attempts suicide can only increase his depression and render a renewed attempt more likely, prevailing opinion still holds that it is right and efficacious to punish those who assist suicide (or who kill with consent), even though they act from the strongest humanitarian motives. This seems to show that the more relaxed attitude toward the person who attempts his own suicide is based on limited pragmatic considerations and does not signify any abandonment of the traditional condemnation or any adoption of the position that the law should not, merely on religious grounds, repress a practice freely consented to that does not harm others.

The arguments against euthanasia are partly religious,

partly pragmatic. The Reverend Joseph V. Sullivan presents the Roman Catholic point of view. Supreme dominion over life belongs to God alone, and it is never lawful for man on his own authority to kill the innocent directly. The mental agony of approaching death is "part of the sacrifice that God demands for the sins and faults of life. . . . Some suffering is necessary; God knows how much each man needs." Norman St. John-Stevas has repeated these arguments: "Suffering for the Christian is not an absolute evil, but has redeeming features. It may be an occasion for spiritual growth and an opportunity to make amends for sin." Since no one suggests that euthanasia be made compulsory for those who do not want it, the religious arguments hardly seem to be relevant to the proposal that euthanasia should cease to be punishable as a matter of secular law.

However, pragmatic arguments are also advanced, notably by Yale Kamisar. Kamisar finds in euthanasia a number of indirect evils: the difficulty of ascertaining the patient's real consent, which leads to the danger of abuse; the risk of an incorrect diagnosis; the risk of administering euthanasia to a person who could later have been cured by new medical developments; and the "wedge" argument (condoning euthanasia would lead to general disrespect for the sanctity of human life).

Glanville Williams challenges these arguments, pointing out that there are cases where the patient's consent is clear. The other dangers are inherent in medical operations generally, and one can make a mistake by not acting as much as by acting. The "wedge" argument does not explain why wholesale killing in war has no serious effect upon the value generally attached to the preservation of life. The same position had previously been taken by Joseph Fletcher.

Antony Flew advances two main moral reasons in favor of euthanasia: that it is cruel to prevent sufferers from getting the quick death for which they ask and that a true estimate of the value of human beings would lead to the conclusion that the wishes, interests, and aspirations of every human being ought to be taken into account by every other human being who has dealings with him. Sidney Hook argues that the only rationally acceptable philosophy is that there is no ethical value in living just any sort of life; the only life that is worth living is the good life.

We may define the good differently, but no matter what our conception of the *good* life is, it presupposes a physical basis—a certain indispensable minimum of physical and social well-being—necessary for even a limited realisation of that good life. Where that minimum is failing together with all rational probability of attaining it, to avoid a life that at its best can be only vegetative and at its worst run the entire gamut of degradation and obloquy, what high-minded person would refuse the call of the poet *mourir entre les bras du sommeil*? We must recognise no categorical imperative "to live," but "to live well."

Eliot Slater has expressed the view, as a biologist, that the current attitude toward death is irrational, even neurotic.

If the aged and the sick did not die within no long span after they had ceased to be self-supporting, the burden on society would become disastrous. The position of the biologist asked to contemplate the death of the individual is that this is an end devoutly to be wished. Death plays a wholly favourable, indeed an essential, part in human economy.

Intermediate between those who condemn euthanasia and those who approve it are those who think that the law, at least, should adopt a neutral attitude. This is the position of H. L. A. Hart.

The only ground common to all shades of opinion is that the physician, whether or not he may rightfully help to shorten life, may rightfully desist from attempting to prolong the life of a patient in great pain and may rightfully supply or administer pain-killing drugs even though he realizes that their effect may be not only to kill pain but also to shorten life.

Bibliography

The listing of books and articles below follows the order of the discussion in the text of this article.

ON SUICIDE

Plato, *Laws*, translated by A. E. Taylor. London, 1934. Book 9.
Aristotle, *The Nicomachean Ethics*, translated by J. A. K. Thomson. London, 1953. Book 5, Sec. 11.
Seneca, *Letters to Lucilius*, translated by E. P. Barker. Oxford, 1932. See especially Letter 70.
Josephus, Flavius, *The Jewish War*, translated by R. Traill. London, 1851. Book 3, Ch. 8, Sec. 5.
Augustine, *The City of God*, translated by G. E. McCracken. London, 1957. Book 1.
Thomas Aquinas, *Summa Theologica*, translated by J. Rickaby under the title *Ethicus*. London, 1892. Second Part, Second Number, Question 64, Art. 5.
Montaigne, Michel de, *Essays*, translated by John Florio. London, 1928. See Book 2, Ch. 3, "A Custom of the Isle of Cea."
Donne, John, *Biathanatos*. London, 1644.
Montesquieu, Baron de, *Complete Works*, English translation. London, 1777. Vol. III, pp. 86–87, *The Grandeur and Declension of the Roman Empire,* and pp. 335–337, *Persian Letters*, Nos. 76–77.
Voltaire, *Works*, translated by T. Smollett, 4th ed. Dublin, 1772. See Vol. XVII, pp. 165 ff., "Of Suicide."
Hume, David, *Philosophical Works*, T. H. Green and T. H. Grose, eds. London, 1874–1875. Vol. II, pp. 406 ff., *Essay on Suicide.*
Moore, Charles, *A Full Inquiry Into the Subject of Suicide.* London, 1790.
Staël, Mme. de, *Réflexions sur le suicide.* London, 1813.
Schopenhauer, Arthur, *Studies in Pessimism*, translated by T. B. Saunders, 2d ed. London, 1891.
Schopenhauer, Arthur, *The World as Will and Idea*, translated by R. B. Haldane and J. Kemp. London, 1883.
O'Dea, James, *The Philosophy of Suicide.* New York, 1882.
Westcott, W. Wynn, *Suicide.* London, 1885.
James, William, *Is Life Worth Living?* Philadelphia, 1896.
Gurnhill, James, *The Morals of Suicide.* London, 1900–1902.
Bayet, Albert, *Le Suicide et la morale.* Paris, 1922.
Hook, Sidney, "The Ethics of Suicide." *International Journal of Ethics*, Vol. 37 (1927), 173 ff.
Dublin, Louis I., and Bunzel, Bessie, *To Be or Not to Be.* New York, 1933.
Roberts, Harry, *Euthanasia and Other Aspects of Life and Death.* London, 1936.
Fedden, H. Romilly, *Suicide.* London, 1938.
Stengel, E., and Cook, Nancy, "Recent Research Into Suicide

and Attempted Suicide." *Journal of Forensic Medicine*, Vol. 1 (1954), 252–259.

Landsberg, Paul Louis, *The Experience of Death. The Moral Problem of Suicide*, translated by Cynthia Rowland. London, 1953.

Williams, Glanville, *The Sanctity of Life and the Criminal Law*. New York, 1957; London, 1958. Also discusses euthanasia.

St. John-Stevas, Norman, *Life, Death and the Law*. London, 1961. Also discusses euthanasia.

Report of a Committee Appointed by the Archbishop of Canterbury, *Ought Suicide to Be a Crime?* London, 1959.

ON EUTHANASIA

Sullivan, Joseph V., *Catholic Teaching on the Morality of Euthanasia*. Washington, 1949.

Kamisar, Yale, "Some Non-religious Views Against Proposed 'Mercy-killing Legislation.'" *Minnesota Law Review*, Vol. 42 (1958), 969 ff. Reply by Glanville Williams, Vol. 43 (1958), 16 ff.

Fletcher, Joseph, *Morals and Medicine*. Princeton, N.J., 1954.

Flew, Antony, "The Principle of Euthanasia." *The Plain View*, Vol. 4 (1957), 189–190.

Slater, Eliot, "The Fear of Death." *British Medical Journal* (1958), Vol. 1, 885 ff.

Hart, H. L. A., *Law, Liberty and Morality*. Oxford, 1962.

GLANVILLE WILLIAMS

SULZER, JOHANN GEORG (1720–1779), Swiss aesthetician, was born in Winterthur. After studying in Zurich under J. J. Bodmer, he became a tutor in a private home in Magdeburg in 1743. He then went to Berlin, where he became acquainted with Maupertuis and Leonhard Euler. In 1747 he was appointed professor of mathematics at the Joachimsthaler Gymnasium and in 1763 he moved to the new Ritterakademie. Illness forced him to resign in 1773, but in 1775 he was appointed director of the philosophical section of the Berlin Academy, to which he had been elected in 1750.

Sulzer's *Allgemeine Theorie der Schönen Künste* ("General Theory of the Fine Arts") was originally planned as a revision of Jacques Lacombe's *Dictionnaire portatif des beaux-arts* (1752), but it developed into an original encyclopedia covering both general aesthetics and the theory and history of each of the arts and of literature. The edition of 1796–1798, completed with biographical supplements by Christian Friedrich von Blankenburg, is still the best *summa* of German Enlightenment aesthetics and theory of art, as well as being an original contribution to aesthetics.

Sulzer's style, his psychological interests, and his unsystematic method were typical of the "popular philosophers." Because of his lack of system, and because his ideas are spread through the various articles of his encyclopedia, it is difficult to reduce his views to an organic and systematic whole.

Sulzer's aesthetics was inspired by Leibniz, A. G. Baumgarten, G. F. Meier, Moses Mendelssohn, Joseph Addison, Edwards Young, and others. But the psychological character of Sulzer's work is even stronger than that of Baumgarten, Meier, or Mendelssohn. He was the first to find the source of beauty in the perceiving subject only, abandoning every residue of French classicism still present in his German predecessors.

Following Leibniz, Sulzer held that the essence and perfection of the soul consists in its activity of representation. The soul is representing sensibly when it is representing a multiplicity of partial representations taken as a whole. If it is representing every part of a representation as a distinct unit, it is thinking. Sensible representation is more effective than thought, and leads more readily to action. Thus the "lower faculty" of representation of traditional German psychology became more important relative to intellect in Sulzer than in Baumgarten or Meier.

Aesthetics, for Sulzer as for Baumgarten and Meier, was the theory of sensible representation. It explained how to arouse the soul to greater activity. This activity would make sensible representations more lively, and because the activity of representation was intimately connected with the feeling of pleasure, more pleasurable and beautiful.

By studying the psychological constitution of the soul it would be possible to deduce the general rules of the different arts—the more special rules can neither be deduced nor taught. The most important rule concerns the harmony of unity and multiplicity in the beautiful object as it arises out of the representative action of the soul. The object must conform to a spontaneous (*ungezwungen*) order and it must be coherent (*zusammenhängend*).

Sulzer held that beauty is judged by a special feeling—taste—which he sometimes seems to have held to be a function of a faculty different from intellect and the faculty of moral feeling but closely connected with both, particularly with the latter through the moral value of beauty. Taste itself is a transition between thinking and feeling.

Beauty, according to Sulzer, is a product of genius which is the highest stage of the spontaneous representative state of the soul. Genius is a natural force within the soul, and it acts unconsciously in a rational way. It does not, contrary to Baumgarten and Meier, create a new world. Art is an imitation of nature not because it copies nature, but because the artist of genius imitates nature's creative process. He creates nothing outside of nature, but something new within the natural world. In general, art is the expression of a psychological state of man; it imitates human nature in that it expresses nature through the representation of an object.

Sulzer, influenced by Winckelmann, held that some works of art represent an ideal—that is, they express sensibly a general concept not mixed with anything particular.

In the theory of the individual arts Sulzer's most important contributions were in the aesthetics of music. Music, according to Sulzer, was the expression of passion. Opera, which is a union of all the arts, is the highest form of drama. Besides influencing musical theoreticians, Sulzer's aesthetics influenced Kant and Schiller; and although Sulzer was attacked by Goethe in 1772, his work was the foundation of the aesthetics of the *Sturm und Drang*.

Works by Sulzer

Versuch einiger moralischer Betrachtungen über die Werke der Natur. Berlin, 1745.

Untersuchungen über die Schönheit der Natur. Berlin, 1750.

Allgemeine Theorie der Schönen Künste, 2 vols. Leipzig, 1771–1774; 4th enlarged edition with supplements by C. F. von Blankenburg, 4 vols., Leipzig, 1796–1798.

Vermischte philosophische Schriften, 2 vols. Leipzig, 1773–1781.

Works on Sulzer

Dahne, M., *J. G. Sulzer als Pädagoge*. Leipzig, 1902.

Gross, H., *Sulzers Allgemeine Theorie der schönen Künste*. Berlin, 1905.

Heym, L. M., *Darstellung und Kritik der ästhetischen Ansichten J. G. Sulzers*. Leipzig, 1894.

Leo, Johannes, *Zur Entstehungsgeschichte der "Allgemeinen Theorie der schönen Künste" J. G. Sulzers*. Heidelberg, 1906.

Palme, A., *J. G. Sulzers Psychologie und die Anfänge der Dreivermögenslehre*. Berlin, 1905.

Tumarkin, Anna, *Der Asthetiker J. G. Sulzers*. Frauenfeld and Leipzig, 1933.

Wolf, R., *J. G. Sulzer aus Winterthur*. Zurich, 1860.

GIORGIO TONELLI

SUMNER, WILLIAM GRAHAM (1840–1910), American social philosopher, economist, and cultural anthropologist. Sumner graduated from Yale in 1863 and continued his studies at Geneva, Göttingen, and Oxford, with the aim of entering the Episcopal ministry. He did so in 1867, having returned to America the preceding year. Increasingly, however, this calling conflicted with his wider interests, and when in 1872 he was offered the chair of political and social science at Yale University, he gladly accepted it. He soon gained a considerable reputation as a teacher, publicist, and local politician, but his chief claim to renown derived from his studies in social development, culminating in his masterpiece, *Folkways* (1907).

Two conflicting impulses—polemical and scientific—dominated Sumner's approach to the study of society. It was undoubtedly the polemical impulse which fed the scientific. Dissatisfaction with the reformist dogmatism of his age prompted his search for a scientific basis for his own no less dogmatic advocacy of laissez-faire. In place of "political engineering" based on a facile and sentimental philosophy, Sumner advocated "social evolutionism" free from moralizing preconceptions.

Sumner identified the basic social forces with certain group habits, or "folkways," which, he held, operate on a subsconscious level and reflect the spontaneous and the primary needs and interests of a given society, such as hunger, sex, vanity, and fear. These needs and interests, rather than conceptually formed purposes, determine the course of social development. Once the folkways attain persistence and stability, they become reinforced by more conscious processes, such as religious sanctions. Through repeated transmission they assume the status of sociomoral traditions, or "mores." The mores, supported by group authority, then function as the chief agencies of "legitimation"; they determine what shall be deemed right or wrong, or socially acceptable or unacceptable. The mores form the matrix into which an individual is born, and they pervade and control his ways of thinking in all the exigencies of life. The individual becomes critically conscious of his mores only when he comes into contact with another society with different mores or, if he lives in a society at a higher level of civilization, through literature.

Attempts to change a particular set of mores meet with considerable resistance, for they present themselves "as final and unchangeable, because they present answers which are offered as 'the truth'" (*Folkways*, Ch. 2, Sec. 83). Hence, Sumner argued, it was not likely that they could be substantively affected by revolutions or other predetermined acts or changed "by any artifice or device, to a great extent, or suddenly, or in any essential element" (*ibid.*, Sec. 91). Legislation by itself can do little to bring about a transformation of social and moral values. To be truly effective, legislation must grow out of a people's mores; only then is it in keeping with their basic "interests." Nonetheless, Sumner did not deny the significance of legislation, as some commentators have suggested. Indeed, he believed it had a highly educative role, even when it was ineffective in achieving its intended ends. For "it is only in so far as things have been transferred from the mores into laws and positive institutions that there is discussion about them or rationalizing upon them" (*ibid.*, Sec. 80). These unintended consequences, far from being a threat to the established system of mores, constitute a vital component of that system, since it is through such a "rationalizing" process that the mores develop "their own philosophical and ethical generalizations, which are elevated into 'principles' of truth and right" (*ibid.*, Sec. 83).

Although Sumner had little faith in the efficacy of social and economic change produced by state intervention, he was by no means a fatalist or a blind defender of the *status quo*. A relativist in the tradition of Montesquieu and Herder, a conservative in the tradition of Burke and Alexander Hamilton, an individualist in the tradition of Jefferson and Wilhelm von Humboldt, a historicist in the tradition of Savigny and the romanticists, a Spencerian and Darwinist by confession, Sumner believed that man could mold his social life only by paying heed to the "organic" nature of social growth, that he could modify its operative values only "by slow and long continued effort" (*ibid.*, Sec. 91).

Starting from premises not unlike those of Marx, Sumner was, in a sense, a social determinist. However, he recognized the dynamic role of beliefs and the operative value of ideas and, like Marx, he denied their independence from or superiority to material interests. Material interests constituted both the primary source and the ultimate sanction of social action. Although they drew opposite inferences from their shared premises, and although they were both mistaken in their several dogmatisms and prophecies, Sumner and Marx nevertheless laid bare in an equally fearless manner many features of social development which their generation ignored.

Works by Sumner

A History of American Currency. New York, 1874.

Andrew Jackson as a Public Man. Boston, 1882.

What Social Classes Owe to Each Other. New York, 1883.

Alexander Hamilton. New York, 1890.

The Financier and the Finances of the American Revolution, 2 vols. New York, 1891.

A History of Banking in the United States. New York, 1896.

Folkways. Boston, 1907.

Earth-hunger and Other Essays, A. G. Keller, ed. New Haven, 1914.

The Forgotten Man, and Other Essays, A. G. Keller, ed. New Haven, 1918.

Works on Sumner

Ball, H. V.; Simpson, G. E.; and Ikeda, K., "Law and Social Change: Sumner Reconsidered." *American Journal of Sociology*, Vol. 67, No. 5 (March 1962).

Barnes, H. E., *An Introduction to the History of Sociology.* Chicago, 1948. Ch. 6, "William Graham Sumner; Spencerianism in American Dress."

Ellwood, C. A., *A History of Social Philosophy.* New York, 1939. Ch. 28, "William Graham Sumner and Laissez Faire."

Hofstadter, Richard, *Social Darwinism in American Thought.* Boston, 1955. Ch. 3, "William Graham Sumner."

Keller, A. G., *Reminiscences (Mainly Personal) of William Graham Sumner.* New Haven, 1933.

Starr, H. E., *William Graham Sumner.* New York, 1925.

FREDERICK M. BARNARD

SUSO, HEINRICH (1295/1300–1366), Rhineland mystic, was born at Constance and early entered the Dominican order. A mystical experience at the age of 18 set him on the path of asceticism, but a later one, between 1335 and 1340, led him to abandon self-mortification and to embark on an active career as preacher and spiritual adviser. As a result of attacks on some of his teachings and on his personal character, he was transferred to Ulm in 1348.

During his period of studies in Cologne, Suso had come into contact with Tauler and also came under the influence of Eckhart. Indeed, in *Das Büchlein der Wahrheit (The Little Book of Truth,* c. 1327) he was bold enough to defend Eckhart against the doctrinal charges leveled against him, setting Eckhart's disputed doctrines alongside other quite orthodox statements made by him and providing interpretations which did not entail pantheistic conclusions.

Although Suso made use of the Eckhartian-sounding distinction between the undifferentiated Godhead and God as manifested in the persons of the Trinity, he did not hold that there was an ontological distinction within the divine Being. Rather, he held that the distinction was an intellectual one, made from the human point of view and dependent on our mode of trying to understand God's nature. Although Suso also used extreme Neoplatonic language in speaking of God as Nothing, he made it clear that this was simply to say that, because of God's complete simplicity, we cannot ascribe predicates to him in the sense in which they are applied to creatures. Suso went on to try to explain the contrasting and paradoxical multiplicity of God's nature, as exhibited in the Trinity, by the usual concept of eternal procession. Like his doctrine that the distinction between the Godhead and God as the Trinity is not an ontological one, the notion of procession should be taken in a way that does not imply the priority of God considered as a simple Nothing over God considered as the Father, Son, and Holy Spirit. Thus, Suso drew a strong distinction between the procession occurring within the divine Being and the creation of the world. The latter is a free act of God, and creatures owe their being to him; thus God is ontologically prior to the world. On the other hand, the internal dynamics of the Trinity are a perfect and eternal feature of God's life.

The idea of God as Nothing reflected, as did similar doctrines held by other medieval mystics, not only a view about predication in theology but also about the mystical experience itself. Thus, Suso characteristically spoke of that state in which the contemplative is taken out of himself and is made calm in the ground of the eternal Nothing. The fact that the contemplative experience is free from images and discursive thought is a sufficient explanation of the negative language used. Suso generally avoided the suggestion that the soul is merged with the Godhead and described the union as one of wills in which, however, the soul retains its identity. Nevertheless, there were times when he, orthodox as he generally was and wished to be, spoke of a substantial identification with the Godhead. Some explanation of this apparent inconsistency is found in his assertion that in the mystical state the individual is no longer aware of his own identity. It is afterward, and through going beyond a merely phenomenological description of the experience, that the mystic is able to give what he considers to be the correct theological account of it.

Suso's chief works were the autobiographical *Das Buch von dem Diener (The Life of the Servant)*; the *Horologium Sapientiae,* which also occurs in a somewhat different German version as *Das Büchlein der ewigen Weisheit (The Little Book of the Eternal Wisdom)*; and *Das Büchlein der Wahrheit (The Little Book of Truth).* The second of these, which is a dialogue about and meditation on the sufferings of Christ, attained a wide circulation, almost rivaling that of Thomas à Kempis' *The Imitation of Christ.* Because of the degree of openness in the description of his inner life, Suso's writings constitute a valuable source for the study of Christian mysticism.

Bibliography

The German writings can be found in Karl Bihlmayer, *Heinrich Suso: deutsche Schriften* (Stuttgart, 1907). The *Horologium Sapientiae* was edited by J. Strange (Cologne, 1861). Useful translations are J. M. Clark, *Little Book of Eternal Wisdom and Little Book of Truth* (London, 1953) and *The Life of the Servant* (London, 1952). For a general introduction, see J. M. Clark, *The Great German Mystics* (Oxford, 1949), Ch. 4.

NINIAN SMART

SWEDENBORG, EMANUEL (1688–1772), scientist, Biblical scholar, and mystic, was a member of a famous Swedish family of clergymen and scholars; his father was a prominent bishop and a prolific writer. Swedenborg studied the classics and Cartesian philosophy at Uppsala and became interested in mathematics and natural science. In 1710 he went abroad, spending most of the next five years in England, where he learned the Newtonian theories and developed a modern scientific outlook. After his return to Sweden in 1715, Swedenborg was appointed an assessor in the College of Mines by Charles XII. He held this office until 1747, when he resigned in order to devote his time to the interpretation of the Scriptures.

Philosophy of nature. Swedenborg's many writings are characterized by great scholarship and by a fervent search for a synthesis of ancient wisdom and modern experience, empirical science, rationalistic philosophy, and Christian revelation. After some minor treatises on geological and cosmological problems, he published his first important work in 1734, *Opera Philosophica et Mineralia* (3 vols., Dresden and Leipzig); the first part of this work, *Principia Rerum Naturalium,* contains his philosophy of nature. Here Swedenborg utilized the concept of the mathematical point, which he described as coming into existence by motion from the Infinite. This point forms a nexus, or connection, between the Infinite and the finite world, and by its motion it creates aggregates of elements that build up the Cartesian vortexes, which are interpreted as the fundamentals of nature. The original motion in the Infinite, however, is not a mechanical motion but a kind of Leibnizian *conatus*, a motive force in nature that corresponds to will in human minds. In the first point there is a corresponding tendency, which transmits itself to the subsequent aggregates in this great chain of being.

The outlines of Swedenborg's natural philosophy are derived from Descartes, Leibniz, and other rationalists, but in the *Principia* Swedenborg was also inspired by empirical philosophy, especially that of Locke. A similar English influence can be observed in Swedenborg's cosmology, which is set forth in the *Principia* and in a short hexaemeron entitled *De Cultu et Amore Dei* (London, 1745). In these works Swedenborg presents a nebular hypothesis according to which the planets are formed of solar matter. It has been maintained that the planet theory of Kant and Laplace might have been derived from Swedenborg via Buffon, but most probably the similarities between Swedenborg and Buffon depend on their common source of inspiration, Thomas Burnet's *Telluris Theoria Sacra* ("The Sacred Theory of the Earth," 1681). This treatise was widely known (even Coleridge admired it), and there is no doubt that it guided Swedenborg in his cosmology. Swedenborg's cosmology was essentially mechanistic, but like the great speculative philosophers of the seventeenth century, he attempted very early to find a theory that could combine these scientific hypotheses with Christianity.

Together with this mechanistic outlook there are several elements in Swedenborg's philosophy of nature that anticipate the organic theories set forth in his anatomic and psychological works. These works include *Oeconomia Regni Animalis* (2 vols., London and Amsterdam, 1740–1741), *Regnum Animale* (3 vols., The Hague and London, 1744–1745), and many other posthumously published treatises on the animal kingdom. The main problem concerning Swedenborg here is the relationship between soul and body. Since he was not satisfied by any of the current philosophical hypotheses, he turned to the study of contemporary microanatomy and physiology. His own theory, which is sometimes called the *harmonia constabilita* (coestablished harmony), is similar to Leibniz' theory of pre-established harmony. The two models are not identical, however, since there is a component of successive growing in Swedenborg's notion which is missing in the pre-established harmony.

In his physiological research Swedenborg starts with the study of the blood, which in its relation to the organization of the human body corresponds in some important ways to the role of the mathematical point as a nexus between the spiritual and the physical worlds. Swedenborg distinguishes several degrees of purity in the blood, with the highest degree corresponding to the Cartesian spiritous fluid. This fluid functions both as a concrete communication line between soul and body and as an abstract principle, a formative force of the body (*vis formatrix*). Swedenborg combined this concept of life force with Aristotle's concept of form and developed a teleological system very much like Leibniz' monadology.

Doctrine of series and degrees. Swedenborg's system may be called the doctrine of series and degrees. The degrees are distinct links in the universal chain and form connected series of several kinds. Three of these series— the mineral kingdom, the plant kingdom, and the animal kingdom—belong to the earth. In these great series there are also subordinate series, down to the lowest elements. Each series has its first substance, which is dependent on the first series of nature. The first series of nature is an organic development of the concept of the mathematical point. Here, Swedenborg comes very close to the Neoplatonic conception of a world soul, a creative intellect from which the material world is called forth by the process of emanation. It seems probable that Aristotle's notion of the hierarchy of organisms was a decisive influence in the structuring of this gigantic system, in which Swedenborg has tried to arrange all series and degrees in a fixed order that determines all their interrelations. Swedenborg refused to follow Leibniz and Wolff in calling his first substances monads because he did not look upon them as absolutely simple. For him they are created not directly from the Infinite but via the first substance of nature, in the same way that, according to the *Principia*, all natural elements are produced indirectly via the mathematical point.

The first substance of the series, its *vis formatrix*, determines the development of the whole series. There exists nothing in nature that does not belong to such a series. In the *Oeconomia* the human series consists of four degrees, the soul (*anima*), the reason (*mens rationalis*), the vegetative soul (*animus*), and the corresponding sense organs of the body, but in the theosophic writings after 1745 the series is reduced to three degrees with the *animus* subordinated to the *mens rationalis*. Nor is there any first substance of nature in these later works. The chain of the series extends up to God, who himself becomes the highest series.

Psychology. The philosophy of the theosophic period thus presents a kind of Neoplatonic emanation system, although in his earlier works Swedenborg was more influenced by contemporary philosophy. In his psychology he also turned to Locke, and his epistemology coincides with Locke's *tabula rasa* theory. According to Swedenborg, there are no innate ideas in the *mens rationalis*. He also thought, however, that all a priori knowledge is in the *anima* but that after the Fall of man the soul (*anima*) was separated from the body; this synthetic source of knowledge—in some ways corresponding to Locke's notion of intuitive knowledge—was thereby closed for ordinary men. If we could return to Adam's integrity before the Fall, it would be opened up anew. This dream of regaining paradise haunted Swedenborg in the decade before 1745, and he attempted to devise several methods for discovering this lost knowledge.

Doctrine of correspondence. One of the best-known elements in Swedenborg's philosophy is his doctrine of correspondence. This doctrine parallels the speculations about *harmonia constabilita,* but it also has other connections with contemporary thought. The meaning of the term "correspondence" is stated in a short manuscript written in 1741 and entitled *Clavis Hieroglyphica* ("A Hieroglyphic Key," London, 1784). This work is an attempt to illustrate how linguistic terms may be used with three different meanings—the natural, the spiritual, and the divine. Later, this doctrine becomes the fundamental exegetic principle of the theosophic works. Swedenborg's doctrine of correspondence is an attempt to describe and explain the relations between the spiritual world and our material universe by means of linguistic analogies, the construction of which may be illustrated by the following example from *Clavis Hieroglyphica.*

(1) There is no motion without *conatus,* but there is *conatus* without motion. For if all *conatus* were to break out into open motion the world would perish, since there would be no equilibrium. (2) There is no action without will, but there is will without action. If all will were to break out into open action man would perish, since there would be no rational balance or moderating reason. (3) There is no divine operation without providence, but there is indeed a providence not operative or effective. If all providence were operative and effective, human society would not be able to subsist such as it now is, since there would be no true exercise of human liberty. (*Psychological Transactions by Emanuel Swedenborg,* pp. 162–163)

The notions conatus, will, and providence correspond; so do world, man, and human society. By such means, the principles of the philosophy of nature are given a wider field of application, so that they reveal heavenly and divine secrets. Fundamentally, this doctrine may be interpreted as a variation of the Platonic theory of the relations between the world of ideas and the world of senses, but it is important to stress that Swedenborg looked upon his system primarily as a synthesis of ancient wisdom and contemporary thought.

The *Clavis Hieroglyphica* is related to the interpretations of hieroglyphics that were made during the Renaissance. This is apparent in Swedenborg's use of excerpts from Christian Wolff's *Psychologia Empirica* (1732) where the famous German rationalist discusses the Egyptian hieroglyphs and their mystic signification and gives examples from Comenius and others. More important, Wolff inspired speculation about the universal philosophical language, *mathesis universalium* (Swedenborg) or *characteristica universalis* (Leibniz). In a posthumously published manuscript (Stockholm, 1869), Swedenborg tried to formulate his psychophysical conclusions in algebraic formulas of sorts, and he declared his conviction that such an attempt might eventually succeed. But in the meantime he introduced in the *Clavis Hieroglyphica* what he called a key to natural and spiritual arcana by way of correspondences and representations. Thus, there is no doubt that the doctrine of correspondence must be regarded as Swedenborg's contribution to the solution of the problem of the philosophical language. It should be noted, however, that he seems to have been influenced by Malebranche in respect to the correspondent relations between the mind and the cerebral base. Swedenborg also follows another fundamental thought of Malebranche, according to which the omnipotence of God functions in conformity with an eternal order (*l'ordre immuable*); this idea becomes prominent in Swedenborg's theosophic writings.

Theosophic works. Swedenborg's scientific and theosophic works are closely related. The decisive difference is that Swedenborg after a profound spiritual experience in 1745 directed his reasoning exclusively toward the interpretation of Scripture according to the doctrine of correspondence. His first exegetic work is *Arcana Coelestia quae in Genesi et Exodo Sunt Detecta* (8 vols., London, 1749–1756), and it was followed by many others. In all his exegetic treatises Swedenborg also gives vivid descriptions of his experiences in the spiritual world. Apart from these descriptions we meet with the same main theories, although they have been developed into an emanationist theology. Like most of his contemporaries, Swedenborg had always been certain of the existence of spirits and angels, and in the exegetic works he went so far as to describe a comprehensive spiritual system. The spirits live in cities where they have an active social life with social functions (even marriage) corresponding to earthly conditions. The relegation of spirits to heaven or hell from the intervening spiritual world depends on the spirits themselves, since their utmost desire (*amor regnans*) leads them into suitable company.

Christ and the doctrine of atonement play a very insignificant role in Swedenborg's theology, and he dismissed the Trinity dogma. Christ is the *Divinum Humanum,* a manifestation in time of God himself. Swedenborg's theology is extremely intellectual and totally dependent on the interpretation of the divine word as the mediating link between the Creator and man. In the course of time decadent churches have destroyed the original meaning of this word, and Swedenborg saw his mission as the restoration of its primary sense. He identified his own exegetic activity with the return of Messiah and the foundation of the New Jerusalem. However, Swedenborg did not aspire to effect conversions but confined himself to explaining the spiritual meaning of the Scriptures. He felt he had been commanded to do this in his decisive vision of 1745.

Conclusion. This is not the place to discuss the difficult problem of Swedenborg's mental status. For many modern observers it is only too easy to look upon his theosophy as the result of a pathological development of a pronouncedly schizoid personality whose intense desire for synthesis could not be satisfied within the boundaries of science and normal experience. But this must remain speculation. What is certain is that hundreds of thousands of followers have seen in him a prophet and visionary explorer of divine secrets. He has had a wide influence in several fields of thought and art, especially in romantic and symbolist literature; for poets like Baudelaire and Strindberg he was a teacher and predecessor. Swedenborg is, of course, not a philosopher in the modern meaning of the word, but he is an interesting representative of the mystical trend in eighteenth-century thought.

Bibliography

Swedenborg's manuscripts are deposited in the library of the Royal Academy of Science in Stockholm. The greater part of them have been published (as photolithographs of the original or in edited translations or both) by the New Church societies, especially the Swedenborg Scientific Association in the United States, which is a great aid to scholars. Swedenborg wrote in Latin, but almost all of his works are available in English translations; a detailed but unfortunately obsolete bibliography is J. Hyde, *A Bibliography of the Works of Emanuel Swedenborg Original and Translated* (London, 1906).

The following English translations of his many philosophical and scientific works can be recommended: *The Principia; or, The First Principles of Natural Things, Being New Attempts Toward a Philosophical Explanation of the Elementary World,* translated by A. Clissold, 2 vols. (London, 1846); *The Infinite and the Final Cause of Creation, Also the Intercourse Between the Soul and the Body,* translated by J. J. G. Wilkinson (London, 1908); *Psychologica, Being Notes and Observations on Christian Wolff's "Psychologia Empirica" by Emanuel Swedenborg,* translated and edited by A. Acton (Philadelphia, 1923); *The Economy of the Animal Kingdom, Considered Anatomically, Physically, and Philosophically by Emanuel Swedenborg,* translated by A. Clissold, 2 vols. (London, 1845–1846); *The Fibre,* Vol. III of *The Economy of the Animal Kingdom, Considered Anatomically, Physically, and Philosophically by Emanuel Swedenborg,* translated and edited by A. Acton (Philadelphia, 1918); *A Philosopher's Note Book. Excerpts From Philosophical Writers and From the Sacred Scriptures on a Variety of Philosophical Subjects; Together With Some Reflections, and Sundry Notes and Memoranda by Emanuel Swedenborg,* translated and edited by A. Acton (Philadelphia, 1931); *The Brain Considered Anatomically, Physiologically, and Philosophically by Emanuel Swedenborg,* translated and edited by R. L. Tafel, 2 vols. (London, 1882–1887); *Three Transactions on the Cerebrum. A Posthumous Work by Emanuel Swedenborg,* translated and edited by A. Acton, 2 vols. (Philadelphia, 1937–1940); *Psychological Transactions by Emanuel Swedenborg,* translated and edited by A. Acton, 2d ed. (Philadelphia, 1955); *Rational Psychology. A Posthumous Work by Emanuel Swedenborg,* translated and edited by N. H. Rogers and A. Acton (Philadelphia, 1950); *The Animal Kingdom Considered Anatomically, Physically, and Philosophically by Emanuel Swedenborg,* translated by J. J. G. Wilkinson, 2 vols. (Boston, 1858); *The Animal Kingdom,* Parts 4 and 5, translated and edited by A. Acton (Bryn Athyn, Pa., 1928); *The Five Senses,* translated and edited by E. S. Price (Philadelphia, 1914); and *The Worship and Love of God,* translated by F. Sewall and A. H. Stroh (Boston, 1925).

The vast literature about Swedenborg is of unequal quality. An excellent survey is given in M. Lamm, *Swedenborg* (Stockholm, 1915); it has been translated by Ilse Meyer-Lüne as *Swedenborg: Eine Studie über seine Entwicklung zum Mystiker und Geisterseher* (Leipzig, 1922), and into French by E. Söderlindh as *Swedenborg* (Paris, 1936). This is still the best work available. In Ernst Benz, *Emanuel Swedenborg: Naturforscher und Seher* (Munich, 1948), there is more stress on theology and church history, but in general the author follows Lamm. A popular biography is S. Toksvig, *Emanuel Swedenborg, Scientist and Mystic* (New Haven, 1948). A modern solid monograph, although inspired by New Church teachings, is C. O. Sigstedt, *The Swedenborg Epic* (New York, 1952). An analysis of *De Cultu et Amore Dei,* which also deals with many of the philosophical and scientific problems in the rest of Swedenborg's production up to 1745, is I. Jonsson, *Swedenborgs Skapelsedrama "De Cultu et Amore Dei"* (Stockholm, 1961), written in Swedish with a summary in English.

Swedenborg's correspondence has been published in translations and with very informative commentaries in A. Acton, *The Letters and Memorials of Emanuel Swedenborg* (Bryn Athyn, Pa., 1948).

The biographical sources are collected in R. L. Tafel, *Documents Concerning the Life and Character of Emanuel Swedenborg,* 3 vols. (London, 1875–1890).

Among the many useful studies by A. H. Stroh may be mentioned "The Sources of Swedenborg's Early Philosophy of Nature," Vol. III of *Emanuel Swedenborg: Opera Quaedam aut Inedita aut Obsoleta de Rebus Naturalibus,* published by the Royal Swedish Academy of Science (Stockholm, 1911), and "Swedenborg's Contributions to Psychology," in *Transactions of the International Swedenborg Congress* (London, 1911).

INGE JONSSON

SWEDISH PHILOSOPHY. See SCANDINAVIAN PHILOSOPHY.

SWIFT, JONATHAN (1667–1745), British clergyman, moralist, satirist, poet, and political journalist, was born in Dublin, a few months after his father's death. He was educated at Kilkenny Grammar School and received his M.A. *speciali gratiâ* from Trinity College, Dublin, in 1686 and M.A. from Hart Hall, Oxford, in 1692. Periodically, from 1689 to 1699, he acted as secretary to Sir William Temple at Moore Park, Surrey. Ordained deacon and priest in the established church of Ireland, he was left by Temple's death in 1699 to make a career for himself. As domestic chaplain to the earl of Berkeley, lord justice of Ireland, he returned to Dublin and was granted the D.D. degree in 1701 by Trinity College.

In 1704 there appeared anonymously (his customary mode of publishing) *A Tale of a Tub* and *The Battle of the Books,* brilliant satires upholding the ancients against the moderns; assaulting both Catholic and Puritan theologies while upholding the *via media* of the Anglican church; and castigating the shallowness of contemporary scholarship and literature. Thereafter Swift associated with the Whiggish wits in the circle of Addison and Steele, contributing to the *Tatler* and laughing the astrologer John Partridge out of business in the hilarious *Bickerstaff Papers* (1708–1709). Gradually, however, when the Whig ministry displayed no interest either in the welfare of the Irish church or in Swift's own ecclesiastical preferment, he veered toward the Tories. His literary friends now included Pope, John Gay, William Congreve, Matthew Prior, and John Arbuthnot, many of whom later joined with him in the famous Scriblerus Club dedicated to eternal warfare against the dunces.

In 1710 Swift assumed the editorship of the *Examiner,* thus becoming party spokesman for the new Tory ministry of Robert Harley and Lord Bolingbroke. He shortly resigned this post to work on *The Conduct of the Allies* (1711), a pamphlet designed so to sway public opinion as to bring about the end of the "Whiggish" War of the Spanish Succession, an event which occurred in 1713 with the Treaty of Utrecht. Swift was unable, however, to reconcile the ever increasing animosities between Harley (now Lord Oxford) and Bolingbroke, each of whom was surreptitiously treating with both Jacobite and Hanoverian claimants to the British crown. The death of Queen Anne in 1714 and the accession of George I (of Hanover) led to the downfall and disgrace of the Tory party. Swift, having been installed the previous year as dean of St. Patrick's Cathedral in Dublin, retired to Ireland, a country whose people he despised. A fascinating record of events and personalities of the turbulent years of ecclesiastical and political intrigues, 1710–1713, is preserved in his letters to Esther Johnson, known as the *Journal to Stella.*

During the long years of "exile," Swift, paradoxically, became the national hero of Ireland, rising to her defense against the ruthless exploitation by the English. Two works are especially notable in this campaign. First, there was *The Drapier's Letters to the People of Ireland* (1724), which caused the king of England, the prime minister, and the Parliament to back down from the insult to the people of Ireland in the proposed coining of William Wood's copper halfpence. And second, there was *A Modest Proposal For preventing the Children Of Poor People From Being a Burthen to Their Parents or Country, And For making them Beneficial to the Publick* (1729), which employed shock technique to apprise the Irish people of the fact that slaughtering and dressing infants for the dinner tables of English absentee landlords was really little different from prevailing conditions, which allowed them to die of starvation. In the *Proposal* and other politico-economic publications Swift advocated what was later to be called the boycott. In 1726 the immortal social and political satire *Gulliver's Travels* was published in London. Minor works—economic, political, and satirical—continued to appear until about 1739. In 1742 Swift's health had deteriorated to the extent that, for his own protection, he was declared of unsound mind and memory and incapable of caring for himself or his estate. Today it is recognized that Swift was suffering from labyrinthine vertigo (Ménière's disease), a purely physical disease, and that in modern terminology he was not insane. He lingered on until 1745, when he died in his 78th year and was buried in St. Patrick's Cathedral, ironically leaving most of his estate for the founding of a hospital for the insane. His last words were "I am a fool." He had prepared for himself an epitaph in Latin which is translated "When savage indignation can no longer torture the heart, proceed, traveller, and, if you can, imitate the strenuous avenger of noble liberty." "Savage indignation" and the fight for "noble liberty" are truly the prime characteristics of Jonathan Swift.

Religion and morality. Never professing to be a philosopher, Swift was nevertheless a serious thinker on the problems of religion and morality; however, because of his pervasive use of irony, his writings in this area have not infrequently been misunderstood and maligned. Swift always maintained, and quite properly, that he was not attacking religion but the corruptions and excesses of religion and the abuses of reason. As dean, he performed all the functions of that office and was in every respect a sincere Christian. In his surviving sermons, only 11 of which are unquestionably authentic, he takes a common-sense (derived from the funded experience of mankind) approach to theology. The lingering Trinitarian controversy, which caused such bitterness and name-calling among the "orthodox" that Parliament prohibited further publication on the subject, Swift found thoroughly repugnant. In *A Letter to a Young Gentleman, lately enter'd into Holy Orders* (1720), Swift advised that the Christian mysteries should not be explicated by divines but should remain incomprehensible, for otherwise they would not be "mysteries." Though God-given, man's reason is not infallible, because of the interests, passions, and vices of the individual. Although there is clearly a skeptical bent in Swift, he is not to be regarded as a skeptic. Mysteries (for instance, the Trinity) are to be accepted on faith (which is above reason) and asserted on the authority of the Scriptures. As Swift stated in a private letter, "The grand points of Christianity ought to be taken as infallible revelations." It was this orthodox insistence on revelation that made Swift the intractable enemy of the English deists, who maintained that knowledge is prior to assent or faith.

Swift's religious antirationalism, anti-intellectualism, and fideism are well illustrated in his writings against the deists: John Toland, Matthew Tindal, and Anthony Collins were his chief butts. Collins who, in his *Discourse of Free thinking* (1713), had twice taunted Swift by name, is subjected to Swiftian irony in *Mr. C——n's Discourse of Freethinking; put into plain English by way of Abstract, for the Use of the Poor* (1713). Grossly unjust to Collins though it is deliberately intended to be, Swift's work is a witty exploitation of antirationalistic and anti-intellectualistic arguments. The optimistic apriorism inherent in deism was repugnant to Swift, who as an essentially Christian pessimist was always less concerned with philosophical and theological niceties than with the practical problems of morality.

Swift's vital interest in morality is observable in *An Argument against Abolishing Christianity* (1711). This masterpiece of irony attacks the rationalistic deistical concept of a self-sufficient religion of nature that needs no special revelation by assuming the position that "real" Christianity is no longer capable of justification to a sophisticated age. However, "nominal" Christianity is justifiable on grounds of expediency: it may help to preserve pride, wealth, and power and, possibly, to prevent a drop in the stock market of as much as one per cent. *A Project for the Advancement of Religion and the Reformation of Manners* (1709) urges Queen Anne to lead a moral crusade against existing vices in the nation. That Swift was not ironic but completely earnest in this project is certain because of the abhorrence of human vices and the necessity for reformation he expressed in many other writings.

Believing that man is not *animal rationale* but merely *rationis capax,* Swift discerns a negative philosophy of history in man's tendency to degenerate after a certain degree of order and virtue has been achieved. In this restrictive sense only is he to be called a Christian misanthrope or simply a misanthrope. Swift devoted his life to exposing cruelty, inhumanity, inordinate love of power, pride, corrupt politics, and political oppression and to inculcating integrity and virtue in its major aspects of magnanimity and heroism—yet with no illusion that human nature is capable of reaching virtue in an eminent degree. This satiric–moralistic aim, enhanced by Swift's comic vision, finds its most brilliant literary achievement in *Gulliver's Travels,* a work which always has, and always will, vex, shock, divert, and entertain the world.

Modern Editions of Swift

The Letters of Jonathan Swift to Charles Ford, D. Nichol Smith, ed. Oxford, 1935.
The Prose Works of Jonathan Swift, Herbert Davis, ed., 13 vols. (14 projected). Oxford, 1939——.
Journal to Stella, Harold Williams, ed. Oxford, 1948.
The Poems of Jonathan Swift, Harold Williams, ed., 3 vols. Oxford, 1958.
The Correspondence of Jonathan Swift, Harold Williams, ed., 5 vols. Oxford, 1963–1965.

Modern Works on Swift

Davis, Herbert, *The Satire of Jonathan Swift.* New York, 1947.
Ehrenpreis, Irwin, *The Personality of Jonathan Swift.* London, 1958.
Ehrenpreis, Irwin, *Swift: The Man, His Works, and the Age,* Vol. I, *Mr. Swift and His Contemporaries.* London, 1962.
Ferguson, Oliver W., *Jonathan Swift and Ireland.* Urbana, Ill., 1962.
Gilbert, Jack G., *Knaves, Fools, and Heroes: Jonathan Swift's Ethics.* Unpublished Ph.D. dissertation, University of Texas, 1962.
Landa, Louis, "Swift, the Mysteries, and Deism." *Studies in English,* University of Texas, 1944. Pp. 239–256.

Landa, Louis, *Swift and the Church of Ireland.* Oxford, 1954.

Looten, C., *La Pensée religieuse de Swift.* Paris, 1935.

Quintana, Ricardo, *The Mind and Art of Jonathan Swift,* 2d ed. New York, 1953.

Quintana, Ricardo, *Swift: An Introduction.* London and New York, 1955.

Wedel, T. O., "On the Philosophical Background of Gulliver's Travels." *Studies in Philology,* Vol. 23 (1926), 434–450.

Williams, Kathleen, *Jonathan Swift and the Age of Commerce.* Lawrence, Kans., 1958.

Ernest Campbell Mossner

SWINESHEAD, RICHARD, or Suisset, was a member of Merton College in 1348 and was one of the leading Oxford mathematicians and logicians of the mid-fourteenth century. His name was often coupled with William Heytesbury, a fellow Mertonian. Swineshead wrote a commentary on the *Sentences,* a number of logical works (including *De Insolubilibus* and *Obligationes*), a treatise on movement (*De Motibus Naturalibus*), and a book of mathematical calculations. This last, *Liber Calculationum,* was his most important work and earned him the title of "Calculator"; it shows the very strong influence of one of the outstanding Mertonians of the earlier fourteenth century, Thomas Bradwardine. Swineshead followed Bradwardine in combining the study of theology, logic, and mathematics.

Little is yet known of Swineshead's general outlook. He appears to have applied dialectical arguments to matters of theology to show that they were not demonstrable, as, for example, in disputing the proofs for God's unicity and omnipotence. His study of movement dealt with motion from four aspects (generation, alteration, increase and diminution, and local movements) and with the problem of determining a maximum and minimum by the method of arithmetical calculations. Bradwardine seems to have been the originator of this approach in his *Tractatus Proportionum,* where he treated the relationship of speed, force and resistance in terms of proportions rather than by simple multiplication of whole numbers. It was in Swineshead's *Liber Calculationum* that the full influence of Bradwardine's new method was shown. The work comprised a series of *sophismata* ("discussions") covering virtually every aspect of the science of calculations and became a standard work. It was particularly concerned with the problem of local movement, for the solution of which Swineshead enunciated 49 rules to cover its different cases. Swineshead, however, remained primarily the expositor of an already developed method; his work evinced none of the originality which was to be found in the so-called Paris School of Jean Buridan and his followers, above all Nicholas Oresme. His work on calculations, like that of his contemporary Heytesbury, would have been inconceivable without Bradwardine.

Swineshead broached a number of other scientific matters, among them the problem of the quantity of matter, or the nature and cause of rarity and density. This, too, he treated in his *Liber Calculationum.* He concluded that density was determined by the relation of the quantity of the subject—the volume—to its mass. Thus, in common with the majority of fourteenth-century thinkers, he saw the quantity of matter as a particular kind of quantity to be considered in its own right.

Works by Swineshead

Calculationes. Venice, 1520.

Liber Calculationum. Padua, 1450.

Works on Swineshead

Maier, A., *Die Vorläufer Galileis im 14. Jahrhundert.* Rome, 1949.

Maier, A., *Zwei Grundprobleme der scholastischen Philosophie.* Rome, 1951.

Maier, A., *An der Grenze von Scholastik und Naturwissenschaft.* Rome, 1952.

Maier, A., *Metaphysische Hintergründe der spätscholastischen Philosophie.* Rome, 1956.

Maier, A., *Zwischen Philosophie und Mechanik.* Rome, 1958.

Gordon Leff

SYLLOGISM. See Logic, traditional; Logical terms, glossary of.

SYLVESTER OF FERRARA, FRANCIS (c. 1474–1528), a leading Thomistic commentator, sometimes listed under Francis, sometimes under his family name Silvestri, and cited in the Latin literature as Ferrariensis. He was born in Ferrara, Italy, entered the Dominican order in 1488, and took his magistrate in theology at Bologna in 1507. He later taught philosophy and theology at Bologna and other cities in northern Italy. Sylvester's "Commentary on *Summa Contra Gentiles*" has been printed with the definitive edition of that work of St. Thomas in the Leonine edition of *Opera Omnia S. Thomae* (Vols. XIII–XV, Rome, 1918–1926). Among his other philosophical writings are two commentaries on Aristotle: *Annotationes in Libros Posteriorum* (Venice, 1535), and *Quaestionum Libri de Anima* (Venice, 1535).

A critic of Scotist and Ockhamist thought, Sylvester of Ferrara held some highly personal views, modifying Thomism in directions different from those of his contemporary Cajetan. In psychology and epistemology, Sylvester taught a theory of intellectual abstraction by compresence in which the actual object of understanding is quite different from the intelligible determinant which is impressed on the possible intellect (*species impressa* is not the *intelligibile*). The agent intellect performs two distinct actions, one on the phantasm and the other on the possible intellect. He modified Aquinas' view that the proper object of the understanding is the universalized nature of sensible things, by teaching that the possible intellect forms a proper concept of the singular. In metaphysics, he also modified Thomism, saying that pure essences—for example, the natures of angels—may be multiplied numerically in existence, although how this is done is unknown. Concerning the individuation of bodies, Sylvester held that this is accomplished by matter as marked by definite dimensions (*materia signata quantitate determinata*).

Perhaps Sylvester is best known for his explanation of metaphysical analogy as that general characteristic of beings whereby they all somewhat resemble each other and yet are different. Contrary to the theory of Cajetan that all analogy reduces to that of proportionality, Sylvester argued that in every instance of analogy there is a first analogate which determines the meaning of the other analogates (*analogia unius ad alterum*). In endeavoring to harmonize various texts of St. Thomas, Sylvester may have minimized the essential character of analogy, moving in the direction of attribution and metaphor.

Among present-day followers of Sylvester's theory of analogy are such important Thomists as F. A. Blanche, J. M. Ramirez, and N. Balthasar.

Bibliography

For a concordance to the Latin text of the Commentary on *Summa Contra Gentiles*, use *Indices . . . in Commentariis . . . Caietani et . . . Ferrariensis*, in Vol. XVI of the Leonine edition of *Opera S. Thomae* (Rome, 1948). See also G. P. Klubertanz, *St. Thomas on Analogy* (Chicago, 1960), pp. 10 ff., and F. A. Blanche, "Sur le Sens de quelques locutions concernant l'analogie," in *Revue des sciences philosophiques et théologiques,* Vol. 10 (1921), 52–59 and 169–193.

VERNON J. BOURKE

SYMBOL AND SIGN. See SIGN AND SYMBOL.

SYMBOLIC LOGIC. See LOGIC, HISTORY OF; LOGIC, MODERN.

SYNONYMITY has been a major topic in philosophy since the publication of Rudolf Carnap's *Meaning and Necessity* in 1947, though it was discussed earlier in the writings of W. V. Quine and C. I. Lewis. After Quine and Morton White launched their attacks on the tenability of the analytic–synthetic distinction, around 1950, the two topics became closely linked.

Synonymity and the analytic–synthetic distinction. Analytic statements, in Quine's account, fall into two classes. Those of the first class, exemplified by (1), are logically true.

(1) No unmarried man is married.

Quine has no objection to the notion of analytic truth as used here, for he has what he regards as an acceptable account of the notion of logical truth in terms of which the notion of analytic truth is partially explicated. "The relevant feature of this example is that it not merely is true as it stands, but remains true under any and all reinterpretations of 'man' and 'married.' If we suppose a prior inventory of *logical* particles, comprising 'no,' 'un-,' 'not,' 'if,' 'then,' 'and,' etc. then in general a logical truth is a statement which is true and remains true under all reinterpretations of its components other than the logical particles" (all quotations from Quine are from "Two Dogmas of Empiricism").

All logical truths are analytic. The problems which beset analyticity, however, concern those purported analytic truths which are not logical truths. These are typified by

(2) No bachelor is married.

This is not a logical truth, for it does not remain true under every reinterpretation of its nonlogical components, "bachelor" and "married." If (2) is nevertheless to be considered analytic, it is because we can turn it into the logical truth (1) by replacing synonyms with synonyms. Thus, since "bachelor" and "unmarried man" are synonyms, we may replace the former with the latter in (2) in order to arrive at (1), a truth of logic.

It might appear that a generalization of the above considerations would yield a satisfactory account of the notion of an analytic statement. The generalization would go as follows: a statement is analytic if and only if it either (1) is a logical truth or (2) is transformable into a logical truth by the substitution of synonyms for synonyms. This account is rejected by Quine and White on the ground that synonymity (or synonymy, as Quine prefers) is no clearer a notion than analyticity. In Quine's words, "We still lack a proper characterization of this second class of analytic statements, and therewith of analyticity generally, inasmuch as we have had in the above description to lean on a notion of 'synonymy' which is no less in need of clarification than analyticity itself."

Interchangeability criterion of synonymity. A natural response to Quine is that we can give an acceptable account of synonymity in terms of interchangeability. The suggestion is that the synonymity of two linguistic forms consists simply in their interchangeability in all contexts without change of truth-value—interchangeability, in Leibniz' phrase, *salva veritate.* Benson Mates has offered an argument to show that if two expressions are synonymous they are interchangeable everywhere *salva veritate.* Following Frege, Mates assumes that the meaning of a declarative sentence is a function of the meanings of the words which compose the sentence. Furthermore, two declarative sentences having the same meaning will necessarily have the same truth-value. It follows from these two assumptions that the replacement of a word in a sentence by another word synonymous with it cannot change the meaning of that sentence and hence cannot change its truth-value. Thus, if two words are synonymous they are interchangeable everywhere *salva veritate.*

In spite of the reasonableness of the above argument, the proposed interchangeability criterion soon runs into difficulty. Consider the synonymous pair "bachelor" and "unmarried man." The following statement is true:

(3) "Bachelor" has fewer than ten letters.

But the result of replacing the word "bachelor" by its synonym "unmarried man" is the false statement

(4) "Unmarried man" has fewer than ten letters.

This case can presumably be set aside on the ground that quoted expressions should themselves be understood as words functioning as names for their quoted contents. The interchangeability test is then interpreted as not applying to words such as "bachelor" when they appear as fragments of other words, such as " "bachelor." " This makes the account of synonymity rest on the notion of wordhood, but Quine does not object on this account.

Perhaps Quine does not take seriously enough the difficulties involved here. Consider the synonymous pair "brothers" and "male siblings." Replacement of the former by the latter in

(5) *The Brothers Karamazov* is Dostoyevsky's greatest novel

turns a true statement into one which is not true,

(6) *The Male Siblings Karamazov* is Dostoyevsky's greatest novel.

Quine cannot object to this replacement for the same reason he objects to substitution of synonyms for synonyms within the context of quotation marks, for he cannot reasonably claim that titles are all single words.

The most serious problem connected with the interchangeability criterion is that the requirement is, apparently, too strong. Problems about wordhood aside, it is doubtful that paradigmatic synonym pairs like "bachelor" and "unmarried man" can pass the test. Consider the statement

(7) Jones wants to know whether a bachelor is an unmarried man.

Suppose it true, as it may well be, of some man named "Jones." Replacement of synonym for synonym here yields a statement which is no doubt false,

(8) Jones wants to know whether a bachelor is a bachelor.

Carnap's "intensional isomorphism." Carnap intended the concepts of intensional isomorphism and intensional structure to be explications of the ordinary notion of synonymity. Intensional isomorphism is explained in terms of logical equivalence (L-equivalence) when the usual application of the latter notion is extended beyond full sentences to cover various sentence parts. For example, two names "a" and "b" are L-equivalent if and only if "$a = b$" is logically true (L-true). Two (one-place) predicate expressions "P" and "Q" are L-equivalent if and only if "$(x)(Px \equiv Qx)$" is L-true. (This means that it is L-true that whatever has the property P also has the property Q, and conversely.) An analogous definition extends the notion of L-equivalence to many-place predicates (expressions for relations). Expressions for which the relation of L-equivalence has been defined in this manner are called "designators." If two designators are L-equivalent they are said to have the same intension.

Intensional structure is explained thus: "If two sentences are built in the same way out of corresponding designators with the same intensions, then we shall say that they have the same intensional structure" (all quotations from Carnap are from *Meaning and Necessity*). For example, consider the expressions "$2 + 5$" and "II sum V." These occur in a language S in which "2," "5," "II," and "V" are designations for numbers and "+" and "sum" signs for arithmetical operations. We suppose that according to the semantical rules of S, "2" is L-equivalent to "II" (and thus the two have the same intension), "5" is L-equivalent to "V," and "+" is L-equivalent to "sum." With regard to this example Carnap says, ". . . we shall say that the two expressions are *intensionally isomorphic* or that

they have *the same intensional structure*, because they are not only L-equivalent as a whole, both being L-equivalent to '7,' but consist of three parts in such a way that corresponding parts are L-equivalent to one another and hence have the same intension." In our example corresponding parts correspond spatially, but this is not a necessary condition. Thus, Carnap regards "$5 > 3$" as intensionally isomorphic to "Gr(V,III)" because the (two-place) predicates ">" and "Gr" are L-equivalent and so are "5" and "V" and "3" and "III." The (two-place) predicates "correspond," regardless of their positions in the sentences. The sentence "$(2+5) > 3$" is intensionally isomorphic to "Gr(Sum(II,V),III)" because "$2+5$" is intensionally isomorphic to "Sum(II,V)" and the predicate expressions are L-equivalent, as are "3" and "III." On the other hand "$7 > 3$" is not intensionally isomorphic to "Gr(Sum(II,V),III)" even though "Gr" is L-equivalent to ">," "3" to "III," and "Sum(II,V)" to "7." They are not intensionally isomorphic because "Sum(II,V)" is not intensionally isomorphic to "7," although these expressions have the same intension (are L-equivalent). Intensional isomorphism of two expressions requires the intensional isomorphism of all corresponding subdesignators.

Objections. Consider Carnap's extension of the use of "$\equiv$" so as to hold between predicators. According to this extension, if A_i and A_j are two predicators of degree 1, the following abbreviation is allowable:

$$A_i \equiv A_j \qquad \text{for } (X)(A_i X \equiv A_j X).$$

Now let us assume as L-true a sentence of the following form:

(1) $$A_i \equiv A_j.$$

This sentence will be intensionally isomorphic to

(2) $$A_i \equiv A_i.$$

But (1) is not intensionally isomorphic to

(3) $$(X)(A_i X \equiv A_i X),$$

which is the definitional expansion of (2). Sentence (1) will not be intensionally isomorphic to (3), because (3) contains a designator, "(X)," which cannot be matched to a designator in (1). The point of this criticism is that an expression can be intensionally isomorphic to another expression without being isomorphic to a third expression which has the same meaning as the second according to a definition. For this reason intensional isomorphism seems not to be an adequate explication of synonymity.

In "A Reply to Leonard Linsky," Carnap says that the ordinary notion of synonymity is imprecise. He concludes that more than one explicans must be considered. He proposes a series of seven possible explicata, at least some of which would not be affected by the above criticism.

The most serious argument against Carnap's program is that of Benson Mates: Let "D" and "D'" be abbreviations for two intensionally isomorphic sentences. Then the following are also intensionally isomorphic:

(1) Whoever believes that *D* believes that *D*.
(2) Whoever believes that *D* believes that *D'*.

Now the following sentence is true:

(3) Nobody doubts that whoever believes that *D* believes that *D*.

But (4), which is intensionally isomorphic to (3), is very likely false:

(4) Nobody doubts that whoever believes that *D* believes that *D'*.

If anybody even doubts that whoever believes that *D* believes that *D'*, then (4) is false, and the consequence is that two intensionally isomorphic sentences will differ in truth-value. But since two synonymous sentences cannot differ in truth-value, it follows that intensional isomorphism is not adequate as an explication for synonymity.

According to Hilary Putnam, Carnap believes that his theory in its present form cannot refute Mates's criticism. However, other philosophers (notably Alonzo Church) disagree with Putnam and (apparently) Carnap over the soundness of Mates's argument.

Goodman's theory. One of the most widely discussed contributions to the topic of synonymity is Nelson Goodman's "On Likeness of Meaning." His view is particularly attractive to nominalistic philosophers who would avoid "abstract" entities, such as thoughts, senses, and meanings, in their semantical theories. Goodman proposes to explicate the notion of synonymity solely in terms of words and their "extensions"—the objects to which they apply. His account is confined to predicate expressions.

Suppose we say that two predicate expressions have the same meaning if and only if they have the same extensions—are true of the same things. A fatal objection to this view is that there are clear cases where two words have the same extension but do not have the same meaning. "Centaur" and "unicorn," for example, have the same (null) extension, yet they differ in meaning.

We thus see that any simple identification of sameness of meaning of two expressions with sameness of extension must fail. But Goodman argues that we can still give an extensional account of sameness of meaning; although two words may have the same extension, certain predicates composed by making identical additions to these two words may have different extensions. "Centaur" and "unicorn" have the same (null) extension, but there are centaur pictures that are not unicorn pictures. Thus, "centaur picture" and "unicorn picture" have different extensions. Goodman concludes that "difference of meaning among extensionally identical predicates can be explained as difference in the extensions of certain other predicates. Or, if we call the extension of a predicate by itself its *primary* extension, and the extension of any of its compounds a *secondary* extension, the thesis is formulated as follows: two terms have the same meaning if and only if they have the same primary and secondary extensions." Suppose that in accordance with our nominalistic inclinations we ex-

clude thoughts, concepts, attributes, meanings from the extensions under consideration. This means that when considering the identity of meaning of, for example, "centaur" and "unicorn" we will ignore such secondary extensions as those of "thought of a unicorn" and "thought of a centaur" or "concept of a unicorn" and "concept of a centaur." "If the thesis is tenable, we have answered our question by stating, without reference to anything other than terms and the things to which they apply, the circumstances under which two terms have the same meaning" (all quotations from Goodman are from "On Likeness of Meaning").

Let us see how Goodman's solution works. The predicates "(is the) morning star" and "(is the) evening star" have the same (primary) extension but differ in meaning. This difference is explained by Goodman as being due to a difference in the secondary extensions of these predicates. There are morning-star pictures that are not evening-star pictures and vice versa.

Now consider any predicates "*P*" and "*Q*." Consider the actual ink marks which constitute any inscription of the phrase "a *P* that is not a *Q*." Such an inscription will itself be part of the (secondary) extension of the predicate "*P*," for it will be part of the extension of the expression "*P*-description." But no inscription of the phrase "a *P* that is not a *Q*" will be part of the extension of the expression "*Q*-description." It follows from this that "*P*" and "*Q*" have different (secondary) extensions and hence that they are not synonymous. Since "*P*" and "*Q*" are any predicate expressions, no two predicates are synonymous. For example, any inscription of the phrase "a centaur that is not a unicorn" will be part of the extension of the expression "centaur description," but it will not be part of the extension of the expression "unicorn description." Hence, "centaur" and "unicorn" have different secondary extensions (though they have the same primary extension), so they differ in meaning.

Ordinary-language view. The discussions of the interchangeability criterion of synonymity and of Goodman's extensional criterion lead to the same radical conclusion. No two expressions are synonymous. Many philosophers regard this result as a *reductio ad absurdum* of the proposed criteria. Goodman seems to regard the result as a *reductio ad absurdum* of what is "commonly supposed" about synonymity. It is not clear whether he thinks that these views are commonly supposed only by the philosophers who discuss such questions or that they are held by those who in ordinary language sometimes declare two words to be synonymous. What is "commonly supposed," according to Goodman, is that (1) some predicates are synonymous with others and (2) synonymous expressions can replace each other "in all nonextensional contexts without change of truth-value."

Goodman holds that the two requirements are incompatible, and we can see why. "A *P* that is not a *Q*" is a *P*-description, not a *Q*-description; "a *Q* that is not a *P*" is a *Q*-description, not a *P*-description. On the supposition that "*P*" and "*Q*" are synonymous the following two statements have the same truth-value, if the interchangeability criterion is correct.

(1) "A *P* that is not a *Q*" is a *P*-description.
(2) "A *P* that is not a *Q*" is a *Q*-description.

However, the first statement is true and the second false. Thus, the predicates "*P*" and "*Q*" are not interchangeable everywhere, even in extensional contexts. But since "*P*" and "*Q*" are any predicates, no predicates are interchangeable everywhere. It follows from this that either no predicates are synonymous or synonymous predicates are not interchangeable everywhere.

In the face of this dilemma Goodman takes the alternative of declaring that "the relation of exact synonymy between diverse predicates is null." This is to say that no two predicates (or expressions of any kind, presumably) are "exactly synonymous." To many it has seemed more reasonable to abandon the interchangeability criterion. If no two expressions are synonymous or mean exactly the same thing, it is hard to see how the expressions "synonymous expressions" and "mean exactly the same thing" could have any currency in our language. Is it really credible that whenever we say two expressions are synonymous we are wrong? Is it not much more likely that the philosophers who discuss these issues have supposed that our concepts are governed by criteria which in fact do not apply? Consider a dictionary of synonyms. Is it credible that it is wrong in every entry because no two terms are synonymous? Surely not.

The above, or something like it, represents the response of the ordinary-language philosophers to the radical conclusions discussed in the earlier parts of this article. Such philosophers observe that a pair of terms may be regarded as synonymous "for certain purposes." This requires that they be interchangeable not everywhere but only in contexts relevant to the given discussion. It is wrong, these philosophers argue, to treat language as though it were a calculus governed by exact rules. But it is one thing to complain that the philosophers have distorted our actual use of the concept of synonymity and quite another to supply a careful and complete account of what that use is. Such an account remains to be given.

Bibliography

Several of the papers cited below are reprinted in *Semantics and the Philosophy of Language,* edited by Leonard Linsky (Urbana, Ill., 1952).

ANALYTIC–SYNTHETIC DISTINCTION

Quine, W. V., "Two Dogmas of Empiricism," in *From a Logical Point of View.* Cambridge, Mass., 1953. Ch. 2.
White, Morton, "The Analytic and the Synthetic," in Linsky, *Semantics* (above). Ch. 14.
White, Morton, *Towards Reunion in Philosophy.* Cambridge, Mass., 1956.

INTERCHANGEABILITY

Frege, Gottlob, "On Sense and Reference," in Max Black and P. T. Geach, eds., *Translations From the Philosophical Writings of Gottlob Frege.* New York, 1952.
Mates, Benson, "Synonymity," in Linsky, *Semantics* (above). Ch. 7.
Quine, W. V., "Notes on Existence and Necessity," in Linsky, *Semantics* (above). Ch. 5.

INTENSIONAL ISOMORPHISM

Carnap, Rudolf, *Meaning and Necessity.* Chicago, 1947.
Carnap, Rudolf, "A Reply to Leonard Linsky." *Philosophy of Science,* Vol. 16, No. 4 (1949), 347–350.
Church, Alonzo, "On Carnap's Analysis of Statements of Assertion of Belief." *Analysis,* Vol. 10 (1950), 97–99.
Church, Alonzo, "Intensional Isomorphism and Identity of Belief." *Philosophical Studies,* Vol. 5, No. 5 (1954), 65–73.
Lewis, C. I., *An Analysis of Knowledge and Valuation.* La Salle, Ill., 1946.
Lewis, C. I., "The Modes of Meaning," in Linsky, *Semantics* (above). Ch. 3.
Linsky, Leonard, "Some Notes on Carnap's Concept of Intensional Isomorphism and the Paradox of Analysis." *Philosophy of Science,* Vol. 16, No. 4 (1949), 343–347.
Putnam, Hilary, "Synonymity and the Analysis of Belief Sentences." *Analysis* (April 1954), 114–122.
Sellars, Wilfrid, "Putnam on Synonymity and Belief." *Analysis* (1955), 117–120.

GOODMAN'S THEORY

Goodman, Nelson, "On Likeness of Meaning," in Linsky, *Semantics* (above). Ch. 4.
Goodman, Nelson, "On Some Differences About Meaning." *Analysis* (March 1953), 90–96.
Rudner, Richard, "A Note on Likeness of Meaning." *Analysis,* Vol. 10 (1950), 115–118.
Thomson, James, "Some Remarks on Synonymy." *Analysis,* Vol. 12 (1952), 73–76.

ORDINARY-LANGUAGE VIEW

Rollins, C. D., "The Philosophical Denial of Sameness of Meaning." *Analysis,* Vol. 11 (1950), 38–45.
Shwayder, David, "Some Remarks on 'Synonymity' and the Language of Semanticists." *Philosophical Studies,* Vol. 5, No. 1 (1954), 1–5.

LEONARD LINSKY

SYNTACTICAL AND SEMANTICAL CATEGORIES. The basis for any theory of syntactical categories is the linguistic fact that in all natural languages there are strings of (one or more) words which are mutually interchangeable in all well-formed contexts *salva beneformatione*—that is, with well-formedness (grammaticality, syntactical correctness) being preserved in the interchange—and that there are innumerable other strings which do not stand in this relation. Any theory of semantical categories rests on a similar fact, with *well-formed* replaced by *meaningful* or *semantically correct,* and *beneformatione* by *significatione.*

The relation between "well formed" and "meaningful" is, in general, complex, and neither term is simply reducible to the other. The English expression "Colorful green ideas sleep furiously" (to use an example given by Noam Chomsky) is, at least *prima facie,* syntactically well formed. Yet it is semantically meaningless, even though certain meanings can be assigned to it by special conventions or in special contexts. In contrast, many everyday utterances are syntactically ill formed (because of false starts, repetitions, and the like) but semantically perfectly meaningful, again at least *prima facie.*

Chomsky and his followers have recently stressed that for natural languages well-formedness and meaningfulness are mutually irreducible, but this view has not gone unchallenged. For constructed language systems, particularly those meant to serve as languages of science, it has generally been assumed that the notions of well-formedness and meaningfulness coincide.

Since the time of Aristotle it has been customary among philosophers to explain the linguistic facts about interchangeability by resort to ontological assumptions. Certain strings of words, it is said, are not well formed (or meaningful) because the entities denoted by the substrings (the meanings, denotata, etc., of these substrings) do not fit together. Edmund Husserl, one of the authors who dealt most explicitly with interchangeability, coined the term "meaning categories" (*Bedeutungskategorien*). He maintained that we determine whether or not two expressions belong to the same meaning category, or whether or not two meanings fit together, by "apodictic evidence." But his examples and terminology—for instance, the use of the expression "adjectival matter" (*adjektivische Materie*)—indicate that his apodictic evidence was nothing more than a sort of unsophisticated grammatical intuition, which he hypostatized as insights into the realm of meanings. Husserl certainly deserves great credit for distinguishing between nonsense (*Unsinn*) and "countersense" (*Widersinn*), or, in modern terms, between strings that violate rules of formation and strings that are refutable by the rules of deduction. But he is also responsible for the initiation of a fateful tradition in the treatment of semantical (and syntactical) categories. This tradition assumes—sometimes without even noticing the problematic status of the assumption, more often with only the flimsiest justification—that if two strings are interchangeable in some one context *salva beneformatione*, they must be so in all contexts.

This article will discuss the chief modern contributions to the theory of syntactical and semantical categories. It will first outline the achievements of the Polish logician Stanisław Leśniewski and his pupil Kazimierz Ajdukiewicz. It will then evaluate the contributions by Rudolf Carnap and, in particular, stress the added flexibility gained by his decision not to adhere to Leśniewski's "main principle." Finally, the synthesis by Yehoshua Bar-Hillel of the insights of Ajdukiewicz and Carnap into a theory of syntactical categories and the demonstration by Noam Chomsky of the essential inadequacy of categorial grammars for a description of the syntactical structure of natural languages will be mentioned.

LEŚNIEWSKI

In 1921, Leśniewski made an attempt to simplify Russell's ramified theory of types (see TYPES, THEORY OF) but was not satisfied with the outcome. A type theory, however simplified and otherwise improved, remained for him an "inadequate palliative." He therefore began, the following year, to develop a theory of semantical categories that had greater appeal to his intuitive insights into the syntactical and semantical structure of "proper" language. For this purpose he turned from Russell to Husserl, of whose teachings he had learned from his teacher and Husserl's pupil, Kazimierz Twardowski, and, in particular, to Husserl's conception of meaning categories. As a prototype of a proper language, to which his theory of semantical categories was to be applied, Leśniewski constructed the canonical language L. Husserl's tacit assumption that if two strings are interchangeable in some one context *salva beneformatione*, they must be so in all contexts was elevated to the rank of the "main principle of semantical categories." Today Leśniewski's term "semantical categories" must be regarded as a misnomer, since the categorization was based on purely syntactical considerations. At the time, however, Leśniewski, like many other authors, believed that well-formedness and meaningfulness are completely coextensive for any proper language.

According to Leśniewski, each string, whether a single word or a whole phrase, of a proper language, and hence of his canonical language L, belongs to at most one category out of an infinitely extensible complex hierarchy. Strings are understood as tokens rather than as types. Moreover, two equiform tokens may well belong to different categories. This homonymy, however, never leads to ambiguity, since in any well-formed formula the context always uniquely determines the category of the particular token. In fact, Leśniewski exploited this homonymy for systematic analogy, with an effect similar to that obtained by Russell's exploitation of the typical ambiguity of strings (qua types).

Leśniewski excluded from the hierarchy only strings outside a sentential context, terms inside quantifiers binding variables, and parentheses and other punctuation signs. Defined constants were automatically assigned to categories by means of "introductory theses," as Leśniewski called those object-language sentences which, in his view, served to introduce new terms into an existing language. He gave rigid directives for the formation of introductory theses, assignment to a category being valid only after these theses were specified. The constructive relativity thus introduced was intended to take the place of the order restrictions by which Russell had sought to avoid the semantical antinomies.

In his canonical language Leśniewski worked with two basic categories, "sentences" and "nominals," and a potential infinity of functor categories. He admitted only indicative sentences; interrogatives, imperatives, hortatives, and the like were excluded. He explicitly rejected any categorial distinction between proper names and common nouns or between empty, uniquely denoting, and multiply denoting nominal phrases, although he later drew these distinctions on another basis. In the notation subsequently devised by Ajdukiewicz the category, say, of the sentential negation sign (that is, of a functor which, from a sentence as argument, forms a complex expression itself belonging to the category of sentences) is denoted by its "index" "s/s". The denominator of this "fraction" indicates the category of the argument and the numerator that of the resulting string. The index of such binary connectives as the conjunction sign is "s/ss". With "n" as the category index of nominals, "n/n" is assigned to "attributive adjectives" (but also to "nominal negators" like "non-_____"), "s/n" to "predicative intransitive verbs," "s/nn" to "predicative transitive verbs," "$s/n//s/n$" to certain kinds of "verbal adverbs," etc.

AJDUKIEWICZ

With the help of this notation Ajdukiewicz was able to formulate, in 1935, an algorithm for the determination of the syntactical structure of any given string in certain languages and, in particular, of its "syntactical connexity"—that is, its well-formedness. These languages had to embody, among other conditions, the Polish notation, in which functors always precede their arguments (thereby freeing parentheses from their customary duty as scope signals and making them available for other duties) and had to be "monotectonic," in H. B. Curry's later terminology—i.e., to allow just one structure for each well-formed formula. These conditions of course excluded the natural languages from coming under Ajdukiewicz's algorithm.

To illustrate: Let

Afagbc

be a string in a given language fulfilling the above conditions. Let "*n*" be the index of "*a*", "*b*", and "*c*", let "*s/n*" be the index of "*f*", let "*s/nn*" be the index of "*g*", and let "*s/ss*" be the index of "*A*". The index string corresponding to the given string is, then,

$$\begin{array}{cccccc} A & f & a & g & b & c \\ s/ss & s/n & n & s/nn & n & n. \end{array}$$

Let the only rule of operation be the following: replace $\alpha/\beta\beta$ (where α and β are any index or string of indexes) by α (always applying the rule as far "left" as possible). One then arrives in two steps at the "exponent" "*s*", thus verifying that the given string is a sentence with the "parsing" $(A(fa)(gbc))$. The whole derivation can be pictured as follows:

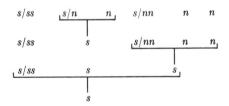

In 1951, Bar-Hillel adapted Ajdukiewicz's notation to natural languages by taking into account the facts that in such languages arguments can stand on both sides of the functor, that each element, whether word, morpheme, or other appropriate atom in some linguistic scheme, can be assigned to more than one category, and that many well-formed expressions will turn out to be syntactically ambiguous or to have more than one structural description. These changes greatly increased the linguistic importance of the theory of syntactical categories and initiated the study of a new type of grammars, the so-called categorial grammars.

Ajdukiewicz never questioned the validity of Leśniewski's main principle. Neither did Alfred Tarski at first. It was taken for granted in the main body of Tarski's famous 1935 paper, "Der Wahrheitsbegriff in den formalisierten Sprachen" ("The Concept of Truth in Formalized Languages," whose Polish original dates from 1931). The

appendix to this paper voiced some doubts as to its intuitive appeal, but these doubts probably derived more from a growing preference for set-theoretical logics over type-theoretical ones than from straight linguistic considerations.

CARNAP

Rudolf Carnap, in *Der logische Aufbau der Welt* (1928), had few misgivings about applying the simple theory of types to natural languages. Like Russell, he made a half-hearted attempt to provide a quasi-linguistic justification for the type hierarchy, and his notion of "spheres" (*Sphären*) occupies a position approximately midway between Russell's types and Leśniewski's semantical categories. Carnap's explanation of certain philosophical pseudo problems as based on a "confusion of spheres" (*Sphärenvermengung*) antedates Gilbert Ryle's discussion of "category mistakes" in his *Concept of Mind* (London, 1949) by over twenty years. Both explanations rest on an uncritical implicit adherence to the "main principle," even though Leśniewski's formulation was not known to Carnap at the time he wrote his book, probably because Leśniewski's publications prior to 1929 were all in Russian or Polish. On the other hand, neither Leśniewski, Ajdukiewicz, nor Tarski quotes Carnap's book in their pertinent articles. Ryle, in his book, does not mention any of these publications.

Carnap was apparently the first logician to use the term "syntactical categories," in 1932. At that time he believed that all logical problems could be treated adequately as syntactical problems, in the broad sense he gave the term.

He was also the first to free himself from the main principle. It eventually occurred to him that this principle embodied an arbitrary restriction on freedom of expression. Any attempt to impose this restriction on natural languages resulted in an intolerable and self-defeating proliferation of homonymies, similar to the outcome of the attempt by Russell and some of his followers to impose type-theoretical restrictions on natural languages, other than the tolerable "typical" ambiguities. In some cases it sounded rather natural to invoke equivocation (which is, of course, a "nontypical" ambiguity)—in the tradition of Aristotle, who used this notion to explain the deviancy of "The musical note and the knife are sharp." But in innumerable other cases there were no independent reasons for such invocation, and the induced artificialities exploded the whole structure. For instance, very strong reasons seem to be required if one were to assign the string "I am thinking of" to a different type or syntactical category each time the string following it belonged to a different type or category. For one may have after "I am thinking of" such varied strings as "you," "freedom," "the theory of syntactical categories," and "the world going to pieces."

In 1934, in *Logische Syntax der Sprache*, Carnap took implicit account of the possibility that two strings might be interchangeable in some contexts but not in all. He coined the term "related" for this relation and used "isogenous" for the relation of total interchangeability. Languages in which all strings are either pairwise isogenous or unrelated have, in this respect, a particularly simple structure. But there is no reason to assume that natural languages will exhibit this particularly simple structure. In fact, observing the main principle becomes a nuisance even for rich constructed language systems; as Carnap showed, the principle is not observed in some of the better-known calculi (perhaps contrary to the intention of their creators) with no real harm done.

BAR-HILLEL AND CHOMSKY

The relation "related" is clearly reflexive and symmetrical; hence, it is a similarity relation. The relation "isogenous" is, in addition, transitive; hence, it is an equivalence relation. Starting from these two relations, Bar-Hillel, in 1947, developed a theory of syntactical categories, illustrated by a series of model languages, all of which were, in a certain natural sense, sublanguages of English. In 1954, Chomsky developed a more powerful theory by taking into account, in addition, relations between the linguistic environments of the strings compared.

Recently, primarily owing to the insights of Chomsky and coming as a surprise to most workers in the field, it has become clear that interchangeability in context cannot by itself serve as the basic relation of an adequate grammar for natural languages. It may play this role for a number of constructed languages, and it certainly does so, for example, in the case of the standard propositional calculi. More exactly, it provides a satisfactory basis for what have become known as "phrase-structure languages," or what Curry calls "concatenative systems."

A phrase-structure language is a language (a set of sentences) determined by a phrase-structure grammar, the grammar being regarded as a device for generating or recursively enumerating a subset of the set of all strings over a given vocabulary. A phrase-structure grammar, rigorously defined, is an ordered quadruple $\langle V,T,P,S \rangle$, where V is a finite vocabulary, T (the terminal vocabulary) is a subset of V, P is a finite set of productions of the form $X \rightarrow x$ (where X is a string over $V-T$, the auxiliary vocabulary, and x is a string over V consisting of at least one word), and S (the initial string) is a distinguished element of $V-T$. Any terminal string (string over T) that can be obtained from S by a finite number of applications of the productions is a sentence. When the X's in all the productions consist of only one word the grammar is called a context-free, or simple, phrase-structure grammar.

Interchangeability in context seems also to be adequate for describing the surface structure of all English sentences but not for describing their "deep structure." It is powerful enough to enable us to analyze correctly the sentence "John loves Mary" (S) as a concatenate of a noun phrase (NP), consisting in this particularly simple illustration of a single noun (N), and a verb phrase (VP), consisting of a transitive verb (Vt) and another noun phrase itself consisting of a noun. Two customary representations of this analysis are the "labeled bracketing,"

$$({}_S({}_{NP}({}_N\text{John})({}_{VP}({}_{Vt}\text{loves})({}_{NP}({}_N\text{Mary}))))),$$

and the "inverted tree,"

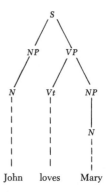

(both representations are simplified for present purposes). Interchangeability in context is likewise powerful enough to provide "Mary is loved by John" with the correct structure,

$$({}_S({}_{NP}({}_N\text{Mary})({}_{VP}({}_{\text{Pass}Vt}{}^{\text{is}}({}_{Vt}\text{love})\text{-ed by})({}_{NP}({}_N\text{John}))))).$$

However, these analyses will not exhibit the syntactically (and semantically) decisive fact that "Mary is loved by John" stands in a very specific syntactical relation to "John loves Mary," namely that the former is the passive of the latter. No grammar can be regarded as adequate that does not, in one way or another, account for this fact. Transformational grammars, originated by Zellig Harris and considerably refined by Chomsky and his associates, appear to be in a better position to describe the deep structures of these sentences and of innumerable others. Such grammars adequately account for the relation between the active and passive sentences and explain the fact that one intuitively feels "John" to be in some sense the subject of "Mary is loved by John," a feeling often expressed by saying that "John," though not the "grammatical" subject, is still the "logical" subject of the sentence. Transformational analysis shows that "John," though indeed not the subject in the surface structure of the given sentence, is the subject of another, underlying sentence of which the given sentence is a transform.

It has recently been proved that categorial grammars and context-free phrase-structure grammars are equivalent, at least in the weak sense of generating the same languages qua sets of sentences over a given vocabulary, though perhaps not always assigning the same structure(s) to each sentence. These sets can also be generated (or accepted) by certain kinds of automata, the so-called push-down store transducers. The connection that this and other results establish between algebraic linguistics and automata theory should be of considerable importance for any future philosophy of language.

DEVELOPMENTS IN THE 1960s

The early 1960s witnessed a revival of interest in the semantic categorization of expressions in natural languages, mostly under the impact of the fresh ideas of Chomsky and his associates. The whole field of theoretical semantics of natural languages is still very much in the dark, with innumerable methodological and substantive problems unsolved and sometimes hardly well enough formulated to allow for serious attempts at their solution. However, there is now a tendency to include indexes of semantical categories in the lexicon part of a complete description of such languages. These indexes, after application of appropriate rules, determine whether a given string is meaningful and, if it is, what its meaning is in some paraphrase of standardized form or, if it is not, how it deviates from perfect meaningfulness. In addition to semantical category indexes there are morphological, inflectional, and syntactical category indexes that determine whether the given string is morphologically and syntactically completely well formed, that present its syntactical structure in some standardized form, or that indicate the ways in which it deviates from full well-formedness.

Whether at least some semantical categories can, or perhaps must, be considered in some sense universal (language-independent) is a question that, like its syntactical counterpart, is now growing out of the speculative stage, with the first testable contributions beginning to appear. Very recent investigations by Uriel Weinreich (1966) have cast serious doubts on the possibility of making a clear distinction between syntactical and semantical categories. Should these doubts be confirmed, the whole problem of the relation between these two types of categories will have to be re-examined. (See also CATEGORIES; SEMANTICS, HISTORY OF.)

Bibliography

Ajdukiewicz, Kazimierz, "Die syntaktische Konnexität." *Studia Philosophica*, Vol. 1 (1935), 1–27.

Bar-Hillel, Yehoshua, *Language and Information*. Reading, Mass., 1964.

Carnap, Rudolf, *Logische Syntax der Sprache*. Vienna, 1934. Translated by Amethe Smeaton as *The Logical Syntax of Language*. London and New York, 1937.

Carnap, Rudolf, *Der logische Aufbau der Welt*, 2d ed. Hamburg, 1961.

Chomsky, Noam, "Formal Properties of Grammars," in R. Duncan Luce, R. R. Bush, and E. Galanter, eds., *Handbook of Mathematical Psychology*, Vol. II. New York, 1963. Ch. 12.

Chomsky, Noam, *Aspects of the Theory of Syntax*. Cambridge, Mass., 1965.

Curry, H. B., *Foundations of Mathematical Logic*. New York, 1963.

Husserl, Edmund, *Logische Untersuchungen*, 2d ed., Vol. II. Halle, 1913.

Luschei, E. C., *The Logical Systems of Leśniewski*. Amsterdam, 1962.

Suszko, Roman, "Syntactic Structure and Semantic Reference." *Studia Logica*, Vol. 8 (1958), 213–244, and Vol. 9 (1960), 63–91.

Tarski, Alfred, *Logic, Semantics, Metamathematics*, translated by J. H. Woodger. Oxford, 1956. Contains a translation of "Der Wahrheitsbegriff in den formalisierten Sprachen."

Weinreich, Uriel, "Explorations in Semantic Theory," in Thomas A. Sebeok, ed., *Current Trends in Linguistics*, Vol. III. The Hague, 1966.

YEHOSHUA BAR-HILLEL

SYNTAX AND SYNTACTICS. See SEMANTICS.

SYNTHETIC STATEMENTS. See ANALYTIC AND SYNTHETIC STATEMENTS.

SYSTEMS, FORMAL, AND MODELS OF FORMAL SYSTEMS.
Formal systems are idealized, abstract languages originally developed by modern logicians as a means of analyzing the concept of deduction. Models are structures which may be used to provide an interpretation of the symbolism embodied in a formal system. Together the concepts of formal system and model constitute one of the most fundamental tools employed in modern mathematical theories of logic. Recently they have become the cornerstone of a burgeoning study which not only includes the foundations of mathematics and the metamathematical analysis of the several deductive sciences but has even played some role in the analysis of empirical theories. A full understanding of all the varied applications which have been made of the concepts of formal system and model requires a detailed mathematical knowledge, especially of algebra and the theory of sets. Such a knowledge is not here presupposed. We shall, however, attempt to deal with the most basic areas in discursive terms, calling on a few simple mathematical notions for occasional aid. The introduction of symbolism to a certain extent will be unavoidable.

TRUTH, CONSEQUENCE, AND DEDUCTION

The primary function of language is to formulate and convey information about the world we live in. The principal linguistic unit designed to convey information is the (declarative) sentence. The information we possess about the world may be gauged by the extent to which we are able to separate those sentences which are true from those which are not.

The most basic method of determining the truth or falsity of a given sentence is through direct investigation of its subject matter. It often happens, however, that such an investigation is either impractical or inconvenient, and we may then seek to determine the truth or falsity of a given sentence P by comparing it with certain other sentences, say $Q_1, Q_2, \cdots, Q_n$, whose truth-values are already known to us. The passage from $Q_1, \cdots, Q_n$ to P is called inference.

Aristotle's great contribution to the study of logic was his recognition that the validity of an inference can be certified by comparing the forms of the hypotheses $Q_1, \cdots, Q_n$ to the form of the conclusion P. Roughly, by the form of a sentence is meant the pattern whereby the sentence is built up from its elementary components—nouns, verbs, etc.—and the distribution within the sentence of certain key logical words, such as "and", "not", and "all". By saying that validity can be determined by form we mean that if $P', Q_1', \cdots, Q_n'$ are sentences obtained, respectively, from $P, Q_1, \cdots, Q_n$ by a transformation which leaves the forms of sentences unchanged, and if P is validly inferable from $Q_1, \cdots, Q_n$, then P' is also validly inferable from $Q_1', \cdots, Q_n'$.

A sentence which can be validly inferred from a given set of sentences is called a logical consequence of those sentences. Thus, P will be a logical consequence of $Q_1, \cdots, Q_n$ if every form-preserving transformation from $Q_1, \cdots, Q_n$ to the true sentences $Q_1', \cdots, Q_n'$ transforms P into a sentence P' which is also true. Thus,

$Q_1, \cdots, Q_n$, as well as P, need not themselves be true when P is a logical consequence of $Q_1, \cdots, Q_n$. However, since the identity transformation (which leaves each sentence unchanged) is form-preserving, we see that whenever P is a logical consequence of true sentences $Q_1, \cdots, Q_n$ it must be true.

The relation between form and validity described above is not intended as a definition of validity but is simply one of its properties; the discovery of this relation, at least in a special case, goes back to Aristotle. (A definition will be given later.)

Aristotle's detailed analysis of the consequence relation was limited to the syllogistic case, which deals with inferences from two hypotheses to a conclusion, the three sentences having certain very special forms. Since there is only a small number of syllogistic forms, Aristotle was able to indicate which ones are valid simply by giving a complete list.

When, in the mid-nineteenth century, mathematicians took up the investigation of logic by means of methods rooted in their own discipline, they soon perceived that besides the syllogisms there was an unlimited number of inferential forms of increasingly complex character, so that no complete list of valid forms could possibly be set down.

How, then, was one to identify a valid inference? Borrowing a basic idea of the axiomatic method, first successfully applied by Euclid to geometry, the mathematical logician attempted to organize a theory of the consequence relation in the form of a deductive system. In constructing a deductive system a limited number of sentences are designated as "logical axioms"; these are selected from among logically valid sentences—that is, sentences with the property that not only they but all sentences having the same form are true. Then a limited number of "transformation rules" are provided, each of which allows passage from a fixed number of sentences of specified form to a new sentence whose form is related to theirs. Finally, starting with any hypotheses $Q_1, \cdots, Q_n$, one proceeds in a step-by-step fashion to combine these hypotheses and the logical axioms by repeated use of the transformation rules, so as to arrive at some new sentence P.

The whole series of steps leading from $Q_1, \cdots, Q_n$ to P is called a deduction (or derivation), and P is said to be deducible (or derivable) from $Q_1, \cdots, Q_n$. If the transformation rules are properly chosen, then whenever P is deducible from $Q_1, \cdots, Q_n$ it will also be a consequence of them; hence, such a system of axioms and rules provides a means of identifying valid forms of inference and is said to be sound. It was the hope of the early mathematical logicians that a suitable system of this kind would generate all valid forms of inference; such a system would be called complete.

When we deal with any of the natural languages there is a fundamental obstacle we must overcome in order to establish a deductive system of the kind we have described, and that is the difficulty in specifying what a sentence is, or even in describing the totality of words that may appear in sentences. Natural languages are too rich in modes of expression, too scarred by accidents of past growth, too much in continual process of change to lend themselves to the kind of precise formulation and analysis that was contemplated by the mathematical logicians.

Therefore, as in any branch of applied mathematics, idealized, abstract systems were created with the intention of approximating at least some limited portion of the natural systems under investigation. These idealized logical systems are specified by means of four components: (*i*) a list of symbols (generally classified into several sorts), (*ii*) formation rules for constructing sentences (and often auxiliary linguistic components) from these symbols, (*iii*) logical axioms, and (*iv*) transformation rules. Because all components of such a system are specified simply in terms of the formal relations among symbols, without any reference to meanings that might be attached to these symbols, we speak of a formal system, or sometimes a formal deductive system. The list of symbols and the formation rules determine what may be called the grammar of the formal system; the axioms and transformation rules constitute its deductive apparatus.

A formal system, as we have seen, is a device for explicating the notion of consequence. Although the system itself is formulated without reference to meanings conveyed by the symbols and sentences of which it is constituted, the motive underlying its employment—and hence the criterion by which it must be judged—is an attempt to certify the truth of certain sentences based on a knowledge of the truth of others. And the concept of truth is very much involved with meanings.

It is the method of making precise the notion of truth and such related semantical notions as satisfaction and denotation that requires our consideration of the concept of a model for a formal system. Historically, mathematical analysis of the semantical aspects of logic came later than the corresponding work on formal aspects. One reason for this is that mathematically the semantical notions generally require a relatively complex conceptual framework of set theory for their formulation whereas the formal notions have a simpler, algebraic character. But a full understanding of logic requires a study of both kinds of concepts and an investigation of the relations between them.

A MINIATURE THEORY: THE SYSTEM I

The ideas described in intuitive fashion in the preceding section must now be made precise by concrete examples. In order to concentrate on the logical and metamathematical concepts and notation which are our principal concern, we shall begin with a formal system whose structure and content are extremely limited. In subsequent sections we shall consider successive complications which must be dealt with in order to handle systems adequate for the analysis of significant mathematical theories.

(*Ii*) In what we shall call System *I* only four symbols will be employed: an identity symbol, $\approx$, and three individual constants, c_1, c_2, and c_3.

[The particular shapes of the several symbols employed in this or any other formal system are of no interest, so we never bother to describe or exhibit these symbols. The symbol "$\approx$" is our name for the identity symbol of System

I, but the identity symbol itself may have any shape whatsoever. Similarly, we employ "c_1", "c_2", and "c_3" as names for three other symbols with whose forms we have no concern, except that we shall understand that they are distinct from one another and from the symbol $\approx$. A similar understanding will be implicit in our description of other formal systems.]

(*Iii*) There is only one formation rule for System *I*: If c_i and c_j are any individual constants, then $c_i \approx c_j$ is a sentence of the system.

[When we write "$c_i \approx c_j$", as above, we are referring to the string of three symbols consisting of c_i followed by $\approx$ followed by c_j. (In some works this string is denoted by "$c_i \frown \approx \frown c_j$", where the symbol "$\frown$" denotes the operation of concatenation.) A similar understanding holds hereafter whenever a string of symbol-names is used.]

Our specifications (*Ii*) and (*Iii*) complete the description of the grammar of System *I*; (*Iiii*) and (*Iiv*) will define its deductive apparatus.

(*Iiii*) Three sentences of System *I* are chosen as logical axioms: $c_1 \approx c_1$, $c_2 \approx c_2$, and $c_3 \approx c_3$.

[It is easy to see that there is a total of nine sentences in System *I* and that therefore one-third of all sentences are axioms.]

(*Iiv*) The System *I* has two rules of inference. The rule of symmetry (Rule *S*) allows us to pass from any sentence $c_i \approx c_j$ to the sentence $c_j \approx c_i$ (where c_i and c_j are any individual constants). The rule of transitivity (Rule *T*) allows us to pass from any pair of sentences $c_i \approx c_j$ and $c_j \approx c_k$ to the sentence $c_i \approx c_k$ (where c_i, c_j, and c_k are any individual constants).

[An application of Rule *S* to any given sentence results in interchanging the first and last of its symbols—the result being again a sentence. Rule *T* can be applied only when the last symbol of one of two sentences is the same as the first symbol of the other; the result of the application is again a sentence. The symbols c_i, c_j, c_k may all be distinct, or two or three of them may be the same.]

Parts (*Ii*) to (*Iiv*) constitute a complete specification of our formal system. To develop the formal system we consider any set Γ of its sentences and define a formal deduction from Γ to be a finite column of sentences each of which either is an element of Γ or a logical axiom or else is obtained from an earlier sentence of the column, or from two earlier sentences, by Rule *S* or Rule *T*. When Γ is empty such a column is called a formal proof. If A is the last line of some deduction from Γ, we say that A is formally deducible from Γ, or that Γ yields A, and indicate this by the notation "$\Gamma \vdash A$". In those cases where Γ is empty we say that A is a formal theorem and write simply "$\vdash A$".

If System *I* were a "serious" formal system, we would begin to establish particular formal theorems by finding formal proofs for them, and we would deduce particular sentences A from especially interesting sets Γ of hypotheses by finding formal deductions from Γ for A. As it happens, however, System *I* is of such a simple nature that these enterprises would hardly afford much interest.

It is easy to see, for example, that the only formal theorems are the three logical axioms themselves; if we start with these axioms, any application of Rule *S* or Rule *T* only

leads back to them. Similarly, the conditions under which we can have $\Gamma \vdash A$ are extremely simple.

Let us turn, now, to the semantical aspect of the language of System *I*. First we must say exactly what we mean by a model for System *I*: This will be a system with four components, $\langle M, a_1, a_2, a_3 \rangle$. The first component, M, is to be any (nonempty) set of objects of any kind whatsoever. The other components, a_1, a_2, and a_3, are to be elements—any elements—of the set M; they may be distinct, or two of them may be the same, or all three may be the same. Often we use a single symbol to denote a model—we will let $\mathbf{M} = \langle M, a_1, a_2, a_3 \rangle$. The set M is called the universe (sometimes also universe of discourse or domain) of the model $\mathbf{M}$. The objects a_1, a_2, a_3 are called the distinguished elements of the model $\mathbf{M}$.

Given any model $\mathbf{M}$, we adopt a fixed procedure for using $\mathbf{M}$ to interpret the grammar of System *I*, as follows: The individual constants, c_1, c_2, and c_3, are used to denote, respectively, the distinguished elements a_1, a_2, a_3 of the model; using the symbol "$d_\mathbf{M}$" for the operation of denotation with respect to the model $\mathbf{M}$, we can express this by writing "$d_\mathbf{M}(c_1) = a_1$, $d_\mathbf{M}(c_2) = a_2$, $d_\mathbf{M}(c_3) = a_3$". Then if $c_i \approx c_j$ is any sentence of System *I*, we specify that it will be true of the model $\mathbf{M}$ if $d_\mathbf{M}(c_i)$ is the same element of M as $d_\mathbf{M}(c_j)$ and that it will be false of the model $\mathbf{M}$ if $d_\mathbf{M}(c_i)$ is different from $d_\mathbf{M}(c_j)$. Using T and F to stand for truth and falsity and denoting the truth-value of a sentence A for the model $\mathbf{M}$ by the expression "$V_\mathbf{M}(A)$", we can write "$V_\mathbf{M}(c_i \approx c_j) = T$" if $d_\mathbf{M}(c_i) = d_\mathbf{M}(c_j)$ and "$V_\mathbf{M}(c_i \approx c_j) = F$" if $d_\mathbf{M}(c_i) \neq d_\mathbf{M}(c_j)$. When A is a sentence and $\mathbf{M}$ is a model such that $V_\mathbf{M}(A) = T$ we say that $\mathbf{M}$ satisfies A.

[We use the symbol "$=$", as is usual throughout mathematics, to indicate that the two expressions between which it is placed denote the same thing. Similarly, "$\neq$" is used to indicate that the expressions on both sides of it denote two different things.]

In terms of the notion of truth relative to a given model we can define the notions of logical validity and logical consequence as follows: We say that a sentence A is valid, and write "$\models A$", when and only when we have $V_\mathbf{M}(A) = T$ for every model $\mathbf{M}$. (In other words, A is valid if and only if every model satisfies it.) And if Γ is any set of sentences, we say that A is a consequence of Γ (or that Γ implies A), and write "$\Gamma \models A$", when and only when we have $V_\mathbf{M}(A) = T$ for all those models $\mathbf{M}$ such that $V_\mathbf{M}(C) = T$ for every C in Γ. (In other words, A is a consequence of Γ if and only if A is satisfied by every model which satisfies all sentences of Γ.)

For example, if N is the set of natural numbers, 0, 1, 2, $\cdots$, and $\mathbf{N}$ is the model $\langle N, 3, 8, 3 \rangle$, then the sentence $c_1 \approx c_3$ is true of $\mathbf{N}$—that is, $V_\mathbf{N}(c_1 \approx c_3) = T$—but $c_1 \approx c_3$ is not logically valid because $V_\mathbf{M}(c_1 \approx c_3) = F$ where $\mathbf{M} = \langle N, 3, 6, 7 \rangle$. On the other hand, the sentence $c_1 \approx c_1$ is valid, since for any model $\mathbf{P} = \langle P, a_1, a_2, a_3 \rangle$ we have $V_\mathbf{P}(c_1 \approx c_1) = T$, since $d_\mathbf{P}(c_1) = a_1$ and, of course, $a_1 = a_1$. In the same way the sentences $c_2 \approx c_2$ and $c_3 \approx c_3$ can be seen to be valid.

Again, although we have both $V_\mathbf{N}(c_1 \approx c_1) = T$ and $V_\mathbf{N}(c_1 \approx c_3) = T$ for the model $\mathbf{N}$ above, we do not have $\{c_1 \approx c_1\} \models c_1 \approx c_3$, because $V_\mathbf{M}(c_1 \approx c_1) = T$ whereas $V_\mathbf{M}(c_1 \approx c_3) = F$. On the other hand, we do have $\{c_3 \approx c_1\} \models$

$c_1 \approx c_3$, for if P is any model $\langle P, a_1, a_2, a_3 \rangle$ for which $V_\mathsf{P}(c_3 \approx c_1) = T$, then $d_\mathsf{P}(c_3) = d_\mathsf{P}(c_1)$—that is, $a_3 = a_1$—but then, of course, $a_1 = a_3$, and hence $V_\mathsf{P}(c_1 \approx c_3) = T$. In the same way we can show that $\{c_i \approx c_j\} \models c_j \approx c_i$ for any individual constants c_i and c_j.

As a final example we note that if c_i, c_j, and c_k are any individual constants we must have $\{c_i \approx c_j, c_j \approx c_k\} \models c_i \approx c_k$. Suppose that M is any model $\langle M, a_1, a_2, a_3 \rangle$ such that M satisfies $c_i \approx c_j$ and $c_j \approx c_k$. This means that $d_\mathsf{M}(c_i) = d_\mathsf{M}(c_j)$ and $d_\mathsf{M}(c_j) = d_\mathsf{M}(c_k)$—that is, $a_i = a_j$ and $a_j = a_k$. But then, of course, $a_i = a_k$, and hence $V_\mathsf{M}(c_i \approx c_k) = T$—that is, M satisfies $c_i \approx c_k$.

Both the deductive apparatus (*I*iii and *I*iv) of System *I* and the semantical notions of model, truth-value, validity, and consequence are based on the grammar (*I*i and *I*ii) of the system. But the definitions of the semantical notions make no mention of the deductive apparatus, and the definition of the deductive concepts (such as formal deduction and formal theorem) make no reference to the semantical concepts. Nevertheless, there is the closest connection between these two categories of ideas. Indeed, as we have indicated informally in the preceding section, the utility of a deductive apparatus derives precisely from the fact that whenever a sentence A is formally deducible from a set Γ of hypotheses, A is also a consequence of Γ in the semantical sense. Let us now examine this assertion in the case of System *I*.

In our consideration of examples of logically valid sentences we noted that each sentence of the form $c_i \approx c_i$ (where c_i is any individual constant) is valid. But these are just the sentences chosen as formal axioms in (*I*iii). Thus, if M is any model and A any formal axiom, we have $V_\mathsf{M}(A) = T$. Furthermore, in our consideration of examples of sentences that are implied by (i.e., are consequences of) given sets of sentences we observed that if A is obtained from B by Rule S and M is any model for which $V_\mathsf{M}(B) = T$, then $V_\mathsf{M}(A) = T$. Finally, we observed that if A is obtained from B and C by Rule T and M is any model such that $V_\mathsf{M}(B) = T$ and $V_\mathsf{M}(C) = T$, then $V_\mathsf{M}(A) = T$.

With these observations at hand, suppose now that Γ is any set of sentences whatsoever and that X is any formal deduction from Γ. Then X is a finite column of sentences each of which is either an element of Γ or an axiom or else is obtained from previous lines of the column by Rule S or Rule T.

Let M be any model which satisfies all sentences of Γ, so that $V_\mathsf{M}(C) = T$ for all C in Γ. We can consider in turn each sentence B of the column X and inquire about the truth-value $V_\mathsf{M}(B)$. By hypothesis, if B is in Γ, we know that this value is T. Also, as we have observed above, $V_\mathsf{M}(B) = T$ if B is an axiom. Next, if we come to the first sentence B (in the column X) which is obtained from earlier lines by Rule S or Rule T, those earlier lines must be axioms or elements of Γ and so have value T; hence, $V_\mathsf{M}(B) = T$ in this case. Now that this line of X is seen to be satisfied by M, we can proceed to the next line of X which is obtained from earlier lines by Rule S or Rule T and conclude in the same way that it must be satisfied by M. Continuing line by line through the column X, we finally see that M must satisfy every line of x, particularly the last line, A.

The argument above shows that whenever a sentence A is deducible from a set Γ of sentences, if M is any model which satisfies all sentences of Γ, then M satisfies A. In symbols, whenever we have $\Gamma \vdash A$ we also have $\Gamma \models A$. This substantiates by precise argument our earlier contention that deducibility of A from Γ may properly serve as evidence that A can be validly inferred from—that is, is a logical consequence of—Γ. Of course, our argument has established this relationship only for the very simple System *I*. However, the same sort of argument applies to each of the systems that have been studied by logicians, for in each case the choice of formal axioms and transformation rules is guided by the desire that the axioms be easily seen to be logically valid and that the rules be easily seen to preserve satisfaction by an arbitrary model M.

Is the converse relation true? That is, is every consequence of an arbitrary set of sentences deducible from that set in the system *I*? In other words, is our formal deductive system complete?

For many systems the question of completeness is much harder to answer than the question of soundness, but in the case of System *I* we can provide an affirmative answer rather easily. In fact, let us suppose that Γ is any set of sentences and that $c_i \approx c_j$ is a sentence which is not deducible from Γ. We shall show that $c_i \approx c_j$ cannot be a consequence of Γ. That is, we must exhibit a model M such that $V_\mathsf{M}(A) = T$ for all A in Γ but $V_\mathsf{M}(c_i \approx c_j) = F$.

To begin, we observe that c_i and c_j must be distinct constants, for if they were the same, then $c_i \approx c_j$ would be one of our axioms and therefore would certainly be deducible from Γ (because it would be the last line of a one-line deduction from Γ). Since we are given that $c_i \approx c_j$ is not deducible from Γ, we conclude that $c_i \neq c_j$.

Altogether we have three individual constants, c_1, c_2, and c_3, in System *I*. We have just seen that c_i and c_j are two of them; let c_k be the third. Thus, for the remainder of this argument i, j, and k are the numbers 1, 2, and 3 in some order.

Now let us choose M to be some set of two elements, say {Paris, London}. We shall take a_i to be Paris and a_j to be London. As soon as we decide which element of M to choose as a_k we will have determined a model $\langle M, a_1, a_2, a_3 \rangle$. In fact, we shall choose a_k as follows: If $c_i \approx c_k$ is deducible from Γ, we take a_k to be Paris; if $c_i \approx c_k$ is not deducible from Γ, we take a_k to be London.

Let M be the model $\langle M, a_1, a_2, a_3 \rangle$ defined above. We shall show that M has the desired property of satisfying all sentences of Γ but does not satisfy the sentence $c_i \approx c_j$. The latter fact is obvious, for $d_\mathsf{M}(c_i) = $ Paris and $d_\mathsf{M}(c_j) = $ London—and, of course, Paris $\neq$ London—so $V_\mathsf{M}(c_i \approx c_j) = F$. Let us show, therefore, that we must have $V_\mathsf{M}(A) = T$ for every sentence A in Γ.

Two cases arise for consideration. Let us first consider the case where $\Gamma \vdash c_i \approx c_k$—that is, where $c_i \approx c_k$ is deducible from Γ. Here we have chosen c_k and c_i both to be Paris, so we have $V_\mathsf{M}(c_i \approx c_k) = T$ and $V_\mathsf{M}(c_k \approx c_i) = T$. We also have, obviously, $V_\mathsf{M}(A) = T$ if A is any of our three axioms $c_1 \approx c_1$, $c_2 \approx c_2$, and $c_3 \approx c_3$. In fact, there are just four sentences A in System *I* for which we have $V_\mathsf{M}(A) = F$; these are $c_i \approx c_j$, $c_j \approx c_i$, $c_k \approx c_j$, and $c_j \approx c_k$. And none of these can be in Γ, as the following argument shows.

We know that $c_i \approx c_j$ is not in Γ, for otherwise it would certainly be deducible from Γ, and our hypothesis is that it is not. Furthermore, $c_j \approx c_i$ cannot be in Γ, for then we could deduce $c_i \approx c_j$ from Γ by Rule S, again contrary to hypothesis. Next we note that $c_k \approx c_j$ cannot be in Γ, for if it were—since we are considering the case where $c_i \approx c_k$ is deducible from Γ—we could deduce $c_i \approx c_j$ by applying Rule T, whereas our hypothesis is that $c_i \approx c_j$ is not deducible from Γ. Finally, $c_j \approx c_k$ cannot be deducible from Γ, for if it were, then we could deduce $c_k \approx c_j$ by Rule S—and we have just seen that $c_k \approx c_j$ is not deducible from Γ.

We have considered all four sentences A of System I for which $V_M(A) = F$ and found that none of them can be in Γ. Hence, for every A in Γ we have $V_M(A) = T$, as claimed. Of course, we have considered only the case where $c_i \approx c_k$ is deducible from Γ; we must now consider the contrary case.

Suppose that $c_i \approx c_k$ is not deducible from Γ, so that we have selected c_k to be London. With this determination of c_k we see that the sentences $c_k \approx c_j$ and $c_j \approx c_k$, as well as the three logical axioms, are satisfied by M whereas the sentences $c_i \approx c_j$, $c_j \approx c_i$, $c_k \approx c_i$, and $c_i \approx c_k$ are not. Exactly as in the previous case, we conclude that neither $c_i \approx c_j$ nor $c_j \approx c_i$ can be in Γ. Of course, $c_i \approx c_k$ cannot be in Γ in the case we are considering, for if it were, it would be deducible from Γ, which our case precludes. Finally, we conclude that $c_k \approx c_i$ is not in Γ, for then $c_i \approx c_k$ would be deducible by Rule S. Thus, in the second case as well as the first we see that any sentence of Γ must be satisfied by M.

This concludes our proof that if $c_i \approx c_j$ is not deducible from Γ, it cannot be a consequence of Γ. In short, the formal deductive System I is complete.

A THEORY OF IDENTITY WITH CONNECTIVES

The miniature System I considered in the preceding section permits us to assert the identity of objects (otherwise undescribed in the system) denoted by the symbols c_1, c_2, and c_3. However, even if we confine our interest to these objects and to questions concerning their identity, there are many propositions expressible in English that cannot be expressed with the very limited vocabulary available in the grammar of System I. In the simplest case we might wish to assert that two of the objects are not identical —that is, that they are distinct. Again, we might wish to assert that a given object is identical to one of the others without specifying which one is involved. Sentences like "not $a_1 \approx a_2$" and "$a_1 \approx a_2$ or $a_1 \approx a_3$" are compounded of sentences of System I by means of words, such as "not" and "or", called sentential connectives.

There are five sentential connectives generally considered in the formal deductive systems studied by logicians: "not", "or", "and", "if . . . then", and "if and only if". In order to provide a theory of identity that incorporates such connectives we shall enrich the grammar of the System I by adding five new symbols, $\neg$, $\vee$, $\wedge$, $\rightarrow$, and $\leftrightarrow$. To aid in their employment we shall also introduce symbols that function as left and right parentheses, $\dashv$ and $\vdash$. The resulting system will be called I_s. [The symbol "$\dashv$" is our name for the symbol which functions as a left parenthesis in I_s. As usual, we say nothing about the appearance of the symbol denoted by "$\dashv$"; it may or may not be the traditional "(".]

$(I_s i)$ The System I_s has eleven distinct symbols:

$$\approx, c_1, c_2, c_3, \neg, \vee, \wedge, \rightarrow, \leftrightarrow, \dashv, \vdash.$$

The first of these is called the identity symbol, the next three are called individual constants, the next five are called sentential connectives, and the last two are called parentheses. In the order shown, the connectives are called the symbols for negation, disjunction, conjunction, conditional, and biconditional.

Although I_s contains only a finite number of symbols, in forming the sentences of this system it is contemplated that each connective may be used repeatedly (without limit on the number of occurrences in a single sentence). Hence, unlike the original System I, System I_s contains infinitely many sentences. In order to describe the totality of these sentences one generally resorts to a recursive definition of the notion of sentence, as follows.

$(I_s ii)$ The System I_s has two formation rules. (a) If c_i and c_j are any individual constants then $c_i \approx c_j$ is a sentence. (b) If A and B are any sentences then $\neg A$, $\dashv A \vee B \vdash$, $\dashv A \wedge B \vdash$, $\dashv A \rightarrow B \vdash$, and $\dashv A \leftrightarrow B \vdash$ are also sentences.

[The sentences specified in (a)—the sentences of the original System I—are called the atomic sentences of System I_s. Rule (b) indicates how new sentences can be constructed from given ones; a sentence so constructed is called a compound sentence of System I_s. The two rules (a) and (b) are intended to constitute an exhaustive description of the sentences of I_s, so the string of symbols $c_1 \neg \dashv$, for example, is not a sentence. In order to make this explicit some authors add to rules (a) and (b) a clause (c) such as "No string D of symbols is a sentence unless its being a sentence follows from (a) and (b)." However, this leaves ambiguous the sense in which "follows from" is used. Another approach is to specify that a string of symbols is a sentence when and only when it is in every class G of strings such that (a) all strings $c_i \approx c_j$ are in G, and (b) whenever A and B are strings in G so are the strings $\neg A$, $\dashv A \vee B \vdash$, $\dashv A \wedge B \vdash$, $\dashv A \rightarrow B \vdash$, and $\dashv A \leftrightarrow B \vdash$. However, this involves the notion of an arbitrary class of strings, which certain authors prefer to exclude from the definition of "sentence." Still another method, which utilizes the notion of a finite sequence of strings in place of a class of strings, is to specify that a string of symbols is a sentence of I_s when and only when it is the last string of some finite sequence W of strings such that each string of W is either (a) a string $c_i \approx c_j$ or (b) a string $\neg A$, $\dashv A \vee B \vdash$, $\dashv A \wedge B \vdash$, $\dashv A \rightarrow B \vdash$, or $\dashv A \leftrightarrow B \vdash$ compounded from strings A and B which appear earlier in the sequence W. If one wishes to avoid using (implicitly or explicitly) any such concept as *follows from, class,* or *finite sequence,* one can simply leave clauses (a) and (b) as originally given, but then there seems no way of making clear the intention of limiting the sentences of I_s to those obtainable by use of (a) and (b).]

The list of symbols $(I_s i)$ and the formation rules $(I_s ii)$ constitute a full description of the grammar of the System I_s, and we turn now to a description of the deductive apparatus of this system. In this connection two remarks are appropriate. First, we shall require infinitely many sentences to serve as logical axioms of I_s, but we shall be able to describe them by means of a finite number of "schemata." Second, although the logical axioms of I_s will include those of the original system, I, the rules of inference of I will not be included among those of I_s; instead, there will be special axiom schemata of I_s which correspond to the two rules of inference of I.

($I_s$iii) If A, B, C are any sentences of I_s, the following compound sentences will be logical axioms of I_s:

(1) $\{A \rightarrow \{B \rightarrow A\}\}$,
(2) $\{\{A \rightarrow \{B \rightarrow C\}\} \rightarrow \{\{A \rightarrow B\} \rightarrow \{A \rightarrow C\}\}\}$,
(3) $\{\{\neg B \rightarrow \neg A\} \rightarrow \{A \rightarrow B\}\}$,
(4) $\{\{A \rightarrow B\} \rightarrow \{\{B \rightarrow A\} \rightarrow \{A \leftrightarrow B\}\}\}$,
(5) $\{\{A \leftrightarrow B\} \rightarrow \{A \rightarrow B\}\}$,
(6) $\{\{A \leftrightarrow B\} \rightarrow \{B \rightarrow A\}\}$,
(7) $\{\{A \vee B\} \leftrightarrow \{\neg A \rightarrow B\}\}$,
(8) $\{\{A \wedge B\} \leftrightarrow \neg\{A \rightarrow \neg B\}\}$.

For any individual constants c_i, c_j, and c_k the following sentences will be logical axioms of the System I_s:

(9) $c_i \approx c_i$,
(10) $\{c_i \approx c_j \rightarrow c_j \approx c_i\}$,
(11) $\{\{c_i \approx c_j \wedge c_j \approx c_k\} \rightarrow c_i \approx c_k\}$.

This completes the list of axioms of I_s.

($I_s$iv) There is only one rule of inference for the System I_s: If A and B are any sentences of I_s, we say that B is obtained from A and $\{A \rightarrow B\}$ by the rule of detachment (also called *modus ponens*).

Specifications (I_si) to ($I_s$iv) complete the description of the deductive System I_s. The notions of formal deduction, formal proof, deducibility, and formal theorem are all taken over from the corresponding notions of the System I, except, of course, that the axioms and rules of I_s are employed in place of those of I. For example, if Γ is any set of sentences of I_s, then by a formal deduction from Γ we mean a (finite) column of sentences each of which is either an element of Γ or a logical axiom of I_s or else is obtained from two earlier sentences of the column by the rule of detachment. If A is the last line of such a column, we say that A is deducible from Γ, or that Γ yields A, and we indicate this by the notation "$\Gamma \vdash A$". When Γ is empty a deduction from Γ is called a formal proof of the System I_s; we write "$\vdash A$" in place of "$\Gamma \vdash A$" and say that A is a formal theorem of I_s.

As a simple example we have $\{c_1 \approx c_2\} \vdash c_2 \approx c_1$, because the three-line column

$$c_1 \approx c_2$$
$$\{c_1 \approx c_2 \rightarrow c_2 \approx c_1\}$$
$$c_2 \approx c_1$$

is a formal deduction from the one-element set $\{c_1 \approx c_2\}$. (The first line is an element of this set, the second is an axiom of schema 10, and the third is obtained by detachment from the others.)

From the fact that $\{c_i \approx c_j\} \vdash c_j \approx c_i$ (which is as easily derived for any i and j as for the special case $i = 1$ and $j = 2$ above) the Rule S of System I may be obtained as a derived rule of inference for the System I_s. That is, in seeking to establish that a certain sentence A is deducible from a given set Γ we may construct a column X of sentences which is like a deduction from Γ except that we allow uses of Rule S as well as the rule of detachment. Such a column can always be transformed into a genuine deduction X' by the insertion of certain additional lines in a manner suggested by our

three-line deduction of $c_2 \approx c_1$ from $\{c_1 \approx c_2\}$. That is, each time a sentence $c_j \approx c_i$ appears in X as a result of applying Rule S to an earlier line $c_i \approx c_j$ we form X' by inserting the axiom $\{c_i \approx c_j \rightarrow c_j \approx c_i\}$ before $c_j \approx c_i$ and then justify the line $c_j \approx c_i$ by the rule of detachment instead of by Rule S.

It can also be shown that $\{c_i \approx c_j, c_j \approx c_k\} \vdash c_i \approx c_k$ in the system I_s, and therefore Rule T of the System I is also a derived rule of I_s. Among the many derived rules for the System I_s, which help in establishing that particular sentences are consequences of given sets of sentences, are the following:

(a) If $\Gamma \vdash A$ and if $\Delta \vdash C$ for every C in Γ, then $\Delta \vdash A$.

(b) If $(\Gamma, A) \vdash B$, then $\Gamma \vdash \{A \rightarrow B\}$.

(Here "(Γ, A)" denotes the set obtained from Γ by adding A as an element.)

Rule (b) is called the rule of deduction.

In order to gauge the significance of the deductive System I_s we must examine the semantical aspect of the language based on the grammar determined by (I_si) and ($I_s$ii). As in the case of the System I, the fundamental notion is that of a model M, say $\langle M, a_1, a_2, a_3 \rangle$, where M is a nonempty set and a_1, a_2, a_3 are elements of it. When the grammar of I_s is interpreted with respect to such a model M we again assign to each atomic sentence $c_i \approx c_j$ a truth-value, T or F, in the same way as for the System I—namely, we set

$$V_M(c_i \approx c_j) = T \qquad \text{if } a_i = a_j,$$
$$V_M(c_i \approx c_j) = F \qquad \text{if } a_i \neq a_j.$$

These rules of interpretation indicate our intention of using the symbol $\approx$ to express the relation of identity. But we must now indicate the manner in which we intend to interpret the sentential connectives by supplying additional rules which assign a unique truth-value to every sentence of I_s. These new rules are recursive in character, in conformity with the recursive definition employed for the concept of a sentence of I_s.

If A is any sentence of I_s, we specify a truth-value for the compound sentence $\neg A$ (constructed from A) according to the following rule.

$$V_M(\neg A) = T \qquad \text{if } V_M(A) = F;$$
$$V_M(\neg A) = F \qquad \text{if } V_M(A) = T.$$

This specification is exhibited by the first truth table.

$V_M(A)$	$V_M(\neg A)$
T	F
F	T

Similarly, if A and B are any sentences of I_s, we specify truth-values for the sentences compounded from them by the connectives $\vee$, $\wedge$, $\rightarrow$, and $\leftrightarrow$ by means of the second truth table.

$V_M(A)$	$V_M(B)$	$V_M(A \vee B)$	$V_M(A \wedge B)$	$V_M(A \rightarrow B)$	$V_M(A \leftrightarrow B)$
T	T	T	T	T	T
T	F	T	F	F	F
F	T	T	F	T	F
F	F	F	F	T	T

For instance, if $V_M(A) = F$ and $V_M(B) = T$, this table indicates that $V_M(B \leftrightarrow A) = F$ and hence $V_M(B \to \dotplus B \leftrightarrow A \dotplus) = F$.

The method of interpreting the language of I_s described above provides a unique truth-value for each sentence with respect to any given model. For example, suppose $M = \langle M, a_1, a_2, a_3 \rangle$ is the model obtained by letting M = the set of all men, a_1 = Socrates, a_2 = Aristotle, and a_3 = Socrates. Let $N = \langle N, b_1, b_2, b_3 \rangle$, where N = the set of all cities, b_1 = Athens, b_2 = Athens, and b_3 = Ithaca. The sentence $\dotplus c_1 \approx c_2 \to \dotplus c_1 \approx c_3 \vee c_2 \approx c_3 \dotplus \dotplus$ is true of M but false of N, whereas the sentence $\dotplus c_1 \approx c_2 \vee c_1 \approx c_3 \dotplus$ is true of both M and N.

Having determined the method of assigning a truth-value $V_M(A)$ for each sentence A of I_s with respect to any model M, we can now specify the semantical notions of validity and consequence for I_s in a manner identical to that employed for the System I. A sentence A is called a consequence of a set Γ of sentences when and only when $V_M(A) = T$ for all those models M such that $V_M(C) = T$ for every C in Γ. (We also express this condition by saying that Γ implies A and use the notation "$\Gamma \models A$" to indicate it.) If a sentence A is a consequence of the empty set of sentences, we say that A is valid and use the notation "$\models A$".

As with the System I so also with I_s: the deductive apparatus ($I_s$iii) and ($I_s$iv) is justified by its relation to the semantical notions arising from the interpretation of its grammar with respect to models. In particular, a formal deduction from a set Γ, whose last line is a sentence A, may be used as evidence for asserting that Γ implies A, as can be shown by the identical argument used to demonstrate the corresponding proposition for the System I. (Recall that this fact—namely, that whenever we have $\Gamma \vdash A$ we also have $\Gamma \models A$—entitles us to say that the deductive System I_s is sound.) Thus, we see that for the special case where Γ is empty a formal proof of I_s may be taken as evidence that its last line is logically valid. In other words, whenever we have $\vdash A$ we also have $\models A$. Of course, the demonstration of these properties rests on the facts that each axiom of I_s is valid and that the rule of detachment always leads from valid sentences to another sentence which is valid—facts easily checked by means of truth tables.

The question whether, conversely, $\vdash A$ whenever $\models A$—or, more generally, whether $\Gamma \vdash A$ whenever $\Gamma \models A$—is the question of completeness for the deductive System I_s. This question has an affirmative answer for I_s just as it did for I. But whereas we were able to give a detailed demonstration of the completeness of the System I, a corresponding demonstration for I_s requires a technical background beyond that presupposed for this article.

Consistency and satisfiability. In order to give some idea of how the completeness of the System I_s may be established, it is useful to introduce two new notions, one syntactical in character and the other semantical, which in a certain sense are dual to the notions of deducibility, $\vdash$, and implication, $\models$.

A set Γ of sentences of I_s is said to be inconsistent if there is some sentence A for which we have both $\Gamma \vdash A$ and $\Gamma \vdash \neg A$. If there is no such A we say that Γ is consistent. These notions are defined in terms of the deductive apparatus of I_s; that is, the definitions depend on the axioms and rules of inference of I_s but make no reference to the interpretation of the language of I_s by means of models.

A set Γ of sentences of I_s is said to be satisfiable if there is some model M which satisfies every sentence of Γ—that is, such that $V_M(C) = T$ for every sentence C in Γ. This notion is defined in terms of the semantical notion of the truth-value of a sentence for a given model but makes no reference to the deductive apparatus of I_s.

Actually the notion of consistency is very closely connected to the notion of deducibility, for given any set Γ and sentence B, we can show that $\Gamma \vdash B$ if and only if the set $(\Gamma, \neg B)$ (obtained from Γ by adding $\neg B$ as an element) is inconsistent. Indeed, if $\Gamma \vdash B$, then Γ, $\neg B$ is certainly inconsistent since in this case we clearly have both $(\Gamma, \neg B) \vdash B$ and $(\Gamma, \neg B) \vdash \neg B$. A proof that, conversely, we must have $\Gamma \vdash B$ whenever $(\Gamma, \neg B)$ is inconsistent is somewhat more involved, and we shall defer it to the end of this section.

It turns out that the same close relation which connects deducibility with consistency also connects the semantical notions of implication with satisfiability. In other words, for any set Γ and sentence B we have $\Gamma \models B$ if and only if the set $(\Gamma, \neg B)$ is not satisfiable. Indeed, that Γ, $\neg B$ is not satisfiable means that there is no model M which satisfies all the sentences of $(\Gamma, \neg B)$—put another way, it means that any model which satisfies all sentences of Γ does not satisfy $\neg B$. But that M does not satisfy $\neg B$ means that $V_M(\neg B) = F$, and hence $V_M(B) = T$—that is, M satisfies B. Thus, the condition "$(\Gamma, \neg B)$ is not satisfiable" means that every model M which satisfies all sentences of Γ must also satisfy B—and this is just what it means to say that $\Gamma \models B$, that Γ implies B.

The fact that the same relation holds between deducibility and consistency as between implication and satisfiability suggests that there is a close connection between consistency and satisfiability just as there is one between implication and deducibility. In fact, we can infer that every satisfiable set Γ is consistent from the previously indicated proposition that the deductive System I_s is sound. To see this, assume that Γ is inconsistent, so that we have some sentence A for which both $\Gamma \vdash A$ and $\Gamma \vdash \neg A$ hold. Since I_s is sound we conclude that both $\Gamma \models A$ and $\Gamma \models \neg A$ hold. In other words, if M is any model that satisfies all sentences of Γ, it will satisfy both A and $\neg A$. However, no model can satisfy both A and $\neg A$, for if $V_M(A) = T$, then $V_M(\neg A) = F$. Hence, there can be no model M which satisfies all sentences of Γ; that is, Γ is not satisfiable. Since this conclusion follows from our assumption that Γ is inconsistent, we see that every satisfiable set of sentences is consistent.

By a similar argument we can show that the question of the completeness of the deductive System I_s is equivalent to the question whether every consistent set of sentences of I_s is satisfiable. To show this, we may start with any consistent set Γ and add further sentences of I_s to it until we obtain a maximal consistent set Γ^* such that any further addition results in an inconsistent set. It can be shown that such a set Γ^* must contain A or $\neg A$ (but not both) for any sentence A of I_s. We obtain a model M which satisfies all sentences of Γ^* (and hence of Γ) by taking M to be the set of the three numbers 1, 2, and 3; taking a_1 to be 1; taking a_2 to be 1 or 2 according as $c_1 \approx c_2$ is or is not in Γ^*; taking a_3 to be 1 if $c_3 \approx c_1$ is in Γ^*, 2 if $c_3 \approx c_1$ is not in Γ^* but $c_3 \approx c_2$ is, and 3 if neither $c_3 \approx c_1$ nor $c_3 \approx c_2$ is in Γ^*; and finally, taking M to be the model $\langle M, a_1, a_2, a_3 \rangle$. Indeed, for this model M it can be shown that we have $V_M(A) = T$ for all sentences A in Γ^* and $V_M(A) = F$ for all sentences A of I_s which are not in Γ^*.

Decision methods. From the proof of the completeness of the deductive system it follows that if C is any sentence which is not a formal theorem of the deductive System I_s, then $V_M(C) = F$ for a model whose domain M consists of just the three numbers 1, 2, and 3. This observation leads to a decision method for I_s—that is, an automatic method which decides, in a finite number of steps, whether any given sentence of I_s is or is not a formal theorem. Given any sentence B, we can consider in turn each of the 27 models M whose domain M consists of the numbers 1, 2, and 3, and by means of the truth tables for the sentential connectives we may compute the corresponding truth-value $V_M(B)$ in each case. If this value comes out T in all 27 cases, then B must be a formal theorem. If, on the other hand, we have $V_M(B) = F$ for one of these models M, then B is not a formal theorem (by the soundness of I_s).

It is obvious that if every sentence of I_s is deducible from some set Γ, then Γ is inconsistent. The converse is equally true. To see this, suppose that we have both $\Gamma \vdash A$ and $\Gamma \vdash \neg A$ for some sentence A and that B is any sentence of I_s whatsoever. Since $\{\neg A \to \{\neg B \to \neg A\}\}$ is an axiom (by schema 1), we may infer from $\Gamma \vdash \neg A$, by detachment, that $\Gamma \vdash \{\neg B \to \neg A\}$. Then, using the axiom $\{\{\neg B \to \neg A\} \to \{A \to B\}\}$ of schema (3), a second use of detachment gives $\Gamma \vdash \{A \to B\}$. But since, by hypothesis, $\Gamma \vdash A$, a third use of detachment gives the desired $\Gamma \vdash B$.

With this result, that any sentence is deducible from an inconsistent set, it is easy to demonstrate (as was claimed above) that whenever $(\Gamma, \neg B)$ is inconsistent we must have $\Gamma \vdash B$. Indeed, from the inconsistency of $(\Gamma, \neg B)$ we can, as we know, infer $(\Gamma, \neg B) \vdash \neg c_1 \approx c_1$. Then by the derived rule of deduction we obtain $\Gamma \vdash \{\neg B \to \neg c_1 \approx c_1\}$. Making use of the formal axiom of schema (3), $\{\{\neg B \to \neg c_1 \approx c_1\} \to \{c_1 \approx c_1 \to B\}\}$, we then use detachment to obtain $\Gamma \vdash \{c_1 \approx c_1 \to B\}$. Finally, since $c_1 \approx c_1$ is an axiom (schema 9), we obtain the desired $\Gamma \vdash B$ by another use of detachment.

FIRST-ORDER THEORY OF IDENTITY

We now come to a most important extension of our language. Thus far the grammars of System I and System I_s permit us to make statements about the designated elements a_1, a_2, and a_3 of a model $\langle M, a_1, a_2, a_3 \rangle$ but provide no way for us to make general statements about arbitrary elements of M or existential statements about some unspecified elements of M. To accomplish this aim we must extend our System I_s, enriching its vocabulary by the addition of variables and quantifier symbols. The resulting System I_1, called a first-order deductive system, is of the kind that has received most study by mathematical logicians.

$(I_1 i)$ The symbols of the System I_1 include the eleven symbols of System I_s,

$$\approx, c_1, c_2, c_3, \neg, \vee, \wedge, \to, \leftrightarrow, \{, \};$$

two new symbols, $\forall$ and $\exists$, called quantifier symbols; and an infinite sequence of new symbols, $v_1, v_2, v_3, \cdots$, called

individual variables. The individual constants, c_1, c_2, and c_3, together with the individual variables, are called individual symbols.

[Unlike its predecessors, the System I_1 has infinitely many symbols. Although in recent years there has been some investigation of first-order systems containing only a finite number of variables, the organization of the deductive apparatus for such systems has proved exceedingly difficult and is still only imperfectly understood.]

In giving the formation rules for the System I_1 we shall, for the first time, have to deal with the complexity arising from the fact that sentences are constructed from components which are strings of symbols in grammatical categories other than that of sentences. Before we proceed to details it would be well to indicate the intuitive ideas by illustration.

Suppose that M is a model $\langle M, a_1, a_2, a_3 \rangle$ about which we wish to assert that every element of M is identical to a_2. In the language of I_1 this can be expressed by the sentence $\{\forall v_1\} v_1 \approx c_2$, which corresponds to the English sentence "For all v_1, v_1 is identical to c_2." The part $\{\forall v_1\}$, corresponding to the English phrase "For all v_1," is called a universal quantifier; the part $v_1 \approx c_2$, corresponding to the English phrase "v_1 is identical to c_2," is called a sentential formula. Notice that when the model M is used to interpret the language of I_1 the constant c_2 is used as a name for the model element a_2 but the variable v_1 is not a name for any fixed element of M. The formula $v_1 \approx c_2$, like its English counterpart "v_1 is identical to c_2," does not have a fixed truth-value, T or F, determined by the model M. Hence, although it resembles a sentence, the formula $v_1 \approx c_2$ is not in fact a sentence.

$(I_1 ii)$ If v_i is any variable of I_1, then $\{\forall v_i\}$ is called a universal quantifier and $\{\exists v_i\}$ is called an existential quantifier. Certain strings of symbols, to be called sentential formulas (or simply formulas), are selected according to the following recursive definition: If u and w are any individual symbols (constants or variables), then $u \approx w$ is a formula; if A and B are any formulas, then so are $\neg A$, $\{A \vee B\}$, $\{A \wedge B\}$, $\{A \to B\}$, $\{A \leftrightarrow B\}$; if A is any formula and Q is any quantifier, then QA is a formula. Certain formulas are called sentences of I_1, as follows: A formula A is called a sentence when and only when each occurrence of a variable v_i in A occurs in a part of A having the form QB, where B is a formula and Q is one of the quantifiers $\{\forall v_i\}$ or $\{\exists v_i\}$. In general, if A is any formula of I_1, an occurrence of a variable v_i in A is said to be bound if it occurs in a part of A having the indicated form QB; any occurrence of v_i in A which is not bound in this sense is said to be free. These two kinds of occurrences of variables in formulas will play a role in our description of the deductive apparatus of the System I_1, to which we now turn.

In the System I_1 formulas may serve as formal theorems even if they are not sentences—that is, even if they contain free occurrences of variables—and, more generally, a formula may be deducible from a set of formulas when all, some, or none of the formulas involved are sentences. This is in accord with normal mathematical practice. For example, the formula $v_1 \approx v_1$, or its English equivalent, "v_1 is identical to itself," expresses a logically valid proposition because it is true (in an arbitrary model M) no matter what element of the model is associated with the variable v_1; hence, we would want this formula to be a formal theorem and, indeed, will make it one of our axioms. Again, we may recognize intuitively that the English sentential formula "There is something different from v_2" is a logical consequence of the formula "c_3 is different from v_2" because the truth of the first formula follows from that of the second independently of the model element associated with the variable v_1; hence, we shall want to have the formula $+\exists v_1 + \neg v_1 \approx v_2$ deducible from $\neg c_3 \approx v_2$ in System I_1.

(I_1*iii*) If A, B, C are any formulas of I_1, then a formula compounded from them by one of the axiom schemata (1) to (8) of the System I_s will be an axiom of I_1. Corresponding to the axiom schemata (9) to (11) of the System I_s will be schemata of I_1 which allow the occurrence of individual variables, as well as of constants. Thus, if u, w, and t are any individual symbols of I_1, the formulas

(9') $u \approx u$,

(10') $+ u \approx w \to w \approx u +$,

(11') $+ + u \approx w \wedge w \approx t + \to u \approx t +$

will be axioms. Finally, we need some new axiom schemata in order to deal with the quantifiers. To describe these we need the notion of substitution for the free occurrences of a variable v_i in a formula A. In fact, if u is any individual symbol, we shall let $A_u{}^{vi}$ be the formula resulting from A when the symbol u is substituted for all free occurrences of v_i in A, provided that no such substituted occurrence of u becomes bound in the resulting formula. (If a substituted occurrence becomes bound we say that there is a "collision of bound variables," and in that case we do not define the notation "$A_u{}^{vi}$".) The remaining axioms can now be described by means of four schemata.

(12) $+ +\forall v_i + A \to A_u{}^{vi} +$ is an axiom whenever A, v_i, and u are such that the notation "$A_u{}^{vi}$" is defined.

(13) $+ +\forall v_i + +B \to C + \to + B \to +\forall v_i + C + +$ is an axiom whenever B and C are formulas and v_i is a variable with no free occurrence in B.

(14) $+ A_u{}^{vi} \to +\exists v_i + A +$ is an axiom whenever A, v_i, and u are such that the notation "$A_u{}^{vi}$" is defined.

(15) $+ +\exists v_i + +B \to C + \to + +\exists v_i + B \to C + +$ is an axiom whenever B and C are formulas and v_i is a variable with no free occurrence in C.

(I_1*iv*) The System I_1 has two rules of inference. One is the rule of detachment, which permits us to obtain the formula B from two formulas A and $+A \to B +$. The other, the rule of generalization, permits us to obtain the formula $+\forall v_i + A$ from the formula A, where v_i is any variable.

When it comes to employing the rules of inference in formal deductions we must limit our use of the rule of generalization in a manner not encountered in our earlier deductive systems. The notions of formal proof and formal theorem are entirely analogous to the corresponding concepts for the earlier systems: A formal proof is a finite column of formulas each line of which either is an axiom or else is obtained from earlier lines of the column by one of the two rules of inference; the last line of such a column is a formal theorem of the System I_1. However, by a formal deduction from a set Γ of formulas we mean a finite column each line of which is either an element of Γ or a formal theorem (not necessarily axiom) of I_1 or else is obtained from earlier lines of the column by detachment (but not

generalization); the last line of such a column is said to be deducible from Γ. As with earlier systems, we use the notations "$\vdash A$" and "$\Gamma \vdash A$" to indicate, respectively, that A is a formal theorem and that A is deducible from Γ.

In order to understand this special role of the rule of generalization in the deductive System I_1 and, more generally, to justify the entire deductive apparatus of this system, it is necessary to consider the way in which the formulas of I_1 are interpreted with respect to a model **M**. In general, we can say that the meanings of the identity sign, $\approx$, and the connectives, $\neg$, $\vee$, $\wedge$, $\to$, and $\leftrightarrow$, are the same as those specified for the System I_s, whereas the quantifiers $+\forall v_i+$ and $+\exists v_i+$ correspond in meaning to the English phrases "For all v_i in the model" and "For some v_i in the model." However, when we come to the technical specification of these meanings we shall see that the presence of freely occurring variables in the formulas of I_1 requires an element not present in the earlier systems.

The sentence $c_1 \approx c_3$ does not have a truth-value by itself, but when a model $M = \langle M, a_1, a_2, a_3 \rangle$ is given, the sentence determines a unique truth-value, $V_M(c_1 \approx c_3)$, which is T when $a_1 = a_3$ and F when $a_1 \neq a_3$. Suppose, however, we consider the formula $v_5 \approx c_3$. There is no definite truth-value $V_M(v_5 \approx c_3)$, because the variable v_5, unlike the constant c_3, is not the name of a definite element of the set M. Thus, when **M** is given we can say only that the formula $v_5 \approx c_3$ has a truth-value "which depends on the value of the variable v_5." That is, in order to specify a definite truth-value for the formula $v_5 \approx c_3$ we must not only give a particular model **M** but also assign to the variable v_5 a particular element of the domain M of that model.

In general, a formula A of I_1 takes on a definite truth-value for a model **M** only when values are assigned to each variable which occurs freely in A. However, as a convenient device for treating all formulas uniformly we introduce the notion of a simultaneous assignment of values to all variables of the System I_1. If **M** is any model, an **M**-assignment is a function (i.e., an abstract operation) which associates an element of the domain M of **M** with each variable v_i of I_1. If ϕ is a particular **M**-assignment, we write "$\phi(v_i)$" for the element of M which ϕ associates with v_i. It is also convenient to use the notation "$\phi(c_i)$" for the distinguished element a_i of **M** ($i = 1$, 2, or 3).

For each model **M** and each **M**-assignment ϕ we specify a truth-value $V_M(A, \phi)$ for every formula A of I_1 by the following recursive definition.

In the case of atomic formulas,

$$V_M(u \approx w) = T \qquad \text{if } \phi(u) = \phi(v)$$
$$V_M(u \approx w) = F \qquad \text{if } \phi(u) \neq \phi(v),$$

where u and v are any individual symbols.

Next, for formulas compounded by connectives—formulas of the form $\neg A$, $+A \vee B +$, $+A \wedge B +$, $+A \to B +$, or $+A \leftrightarrow B +$—we specify truth-values by means of the same truth tables employed in interpreting the System I_s. For example, $V_M(A \wedge B, \phi) = T$ if $V_M(A, \phi) = T$ and $V_M(B, \phi) = T$; and $V_M(A \wedge B, \phi) = F$ if either $V_M(A, \phi) = F$ or $V_M(B, \phi) = F$.

Finally, for formulas compounded by means of quantifiers the specification is as follows: $V_M(+\forall v_j + B, \phi) = T$ if $V_M(B, \psi) = T$ for every **M**-assignment ψ such that $\psi(v_j) = \phi(v_j)$

for all variables v_j other than v_i; and $V_M(\dashv \forall v_i \vdash B, \phi) = F$ if $V_M(B, \psi) = F$ for some such ψ. Also, $V_M(\dashv \exists v_i \vdash B, \phi) = T$ if $V_M(B, \psi) = T$ for some M-assignment ψ such that $\psi(v_j) = \phi(v_j)$ for all variables v_j other than v_i; and $V_M(\dashv \exists v_i \vdash B, \phi) = F$ if $V_M(B, \psi) = F$ for all such ψ.

It can be demonstrated that if ϕ and ϕ' are two M-assignments such that $\phi(v_i) = \phi'(v_i)$ for all those variables v_i which occur freely in a given formula A, then $V_M(A, \phi) = V_M(A, \phi')$. In particular, if A is a sentence—that is, if it contains no freely occurring variables—then $V_M(A, \phi) = V_M(A, \phi')$ for any M-assignments ϕ and ϕ' whatsoever; in such a case we may use the simpler notation "$V_M(A)$" for this truth-value.

An M-assignment ϕ is said to satisfy a formula A if $V_M(A, \phi) = T$. A formula A is M-valid if every M-assignment satisfies A, and A is logically valid if it is M-valid for every model M. We use the notations "$\models_M A$" and "$\models A$" to indicate, respectively, that A is M-valid and that A is logically valid. If for any model M and for any M-assignment ϕ which satisfies every formula of Γ we also have ϕ satisfying A, then we say that A is a logical consequence of Γ and write $\Gamma \models A$.

The deductive System I_1 is sound in the sense that whenever we have $\Gamma \vdash A$ we also have $\Gamma \models A$ and whenever we have $\vdash A$ we also have $\models A$. The proof of this follows mainly the lines of the corresponding proofs for the System I and the System I_s, but variations are needed, based on the restricted use of the rule of generalization in formal deductions. First, examining each axiom schema in turn, we show that every axiom is logically valid. Next we show that if ϕ is any M-assignment which satisfies formulas A and $\dashv A \rightarrow B \vdash$, then it also satisfies the formula B obtained from them by the rule of detachment. The same is not true for the rule of generalization. However, if M is any model for which A is M-valid, then each formula $\dashv \forall v_i \vdash A$ obtained from A by the rule of generalization will also be M-valid. These facts enable us to show that every line of any formal proof is logically valid and then that every line of any formal deduction from a given set Γ is satisfied by any M-assignment ϕ which satisfies all formulas of Γ. The soundness of the deductive System I_1 then follows. The fact of soundness can also be expressed in the dual form stating that any set Γ which is satisfiable (by some model M and M-assignment ϕ) is also consistent.

The deductive System I_1 is also complete, in the sense that whenever we have $\models A$ we also have $\vdash A$ and whenever we have $\Gamma \models A$ we also have $\Gamma \vdash A$. Dually the completeness can be expressed in the form stating that every consistent set Γ is satisfiable.

As in the case of the System I_s, the soundness and completeness of the deductive System I_1 contribute toward a decision method for this system. In fact, it can be shown that if A is any formula of I_1 which is not logically valid and n and p are, respectively, the number of freely occurring variables and the number of quantifier occurrences in A, then $\neg A$ is satisfiable in a model whose domain consists of the numbers $1, 2, \cdots, n + p + 3$. Since the question whether a given formula is satisfiable in such a model can be decided by a finite computation of truth-values, the satisfiability of $\neg A$ in such a model leads to an automatic method to decide in a finite number of steps whether any given formula of I_1 is or is not a formal theorem.

OTHER FIRST-ORDER THEORIES

The three theories so far considered have involved increasingly rich modes of expression, but all were designed for discourse about models consisting of a set of objects (the domain of the model) and three distinguished elements of this set. More generally, in various mathematical or scientific theories we are interested in structures consisting of a domain in which certain sets, relations, and operations, as well as certain elements, are distinguished. Such a structure is called a relational system. A typical example is the structure $N = \langle N, +, \times, <, 0, 1 \rangle$, where N is the set of all natural numbers, $0, 1, 2, \cdots$; $+$ and $\times$ are the usual operations of addition and multiplication; $<$ is the usual relation of ordering by magnitude; and $0, 1$ are the first two elements of N in that ordering. The type of the structure N consists of all structures whose first component is a set A, whose next two components are binary operations on A, whose next component is a binary relation on A, and whose last two components are elements of A. Similarly, each relational system determines a type of such systems.

Corresponding to each such type we may construct a first-order formal deductive system capable of interpretation with respect to any structure of that type. All these systems share the identity symbol, the quantifier symbols, the connectives, the parentheses, and the list of variables. In addition, we must provide individual constants corresponding to each distinguished element, n-place predicate symbols corresponding to each distinguished n-place relation, and n-place operation symbols corresponding to each distinguished n-ary operation. For example, in the case of structures of the type of N we would provide individual constants c_0 and c_1, operation symbols $\oplus$ and $\otimes$, and a two-place predicate symbol L. We shall now indicate how a first-order deductive system J_1 can be obtained for this type of relational system.

($J_1 i$) The symbols of J_1 are the identity symbol, individual variables, parentheses, connectives, and quantifier symbols of I_1 together with the symbols c_0, c_1, $\oplus$, $\otimes$, and L mentioned in the preceding paragraph.

($J_1 ii$) The formation rules of the System J_1 (as of any system possessing operation symbols) require that we deal with a new grammatical category, the terms, in addition to the categories of quantifiers and sentential formulas which were present in I_1. The terms are defined recursively as follows: (a) Any individual symbol by itself is a term. (b) Whenever s and t are terms the strings $\dashv s \oplus t \vdash$ and $\dashv s \otimes t \vdash$ are also terms. This notion of term is then used in the recursive definition of sentential formula for the System J_1 by specifying, first, that if s and t are any terms, then $s \approx t$ and Lst are atomic formulas and, second, that compound formulas are to be constructed by means of connectives and quantifiers in exactly the same way as for the System I_1. Finally, the distinction between free and bound occurrences of variables in formulas and the specification of sentences as formulas which possess no freely occurring variables are exactly the same as in the System I_1.

An example of a sentence of J_1 is the following:

(*) $\quad +\forall v_1 + +\neg v_1 \approx c_0 \rightarrow +\exists v_2 + +v_1 \otimes v_2 + \approx c_1 +.$

After we have given the rules for interpreting the grammar of J_1 we shall see that this sentence, when interpreted with respect to the particular model N, expresses the proposition that if x is any natural number other than 0, there is a natural number y such that the product of x and y is the number 1. Of course, the sentence (*) is false of N, as we see by taking x to be 2 and reflecting that there is no number y in N such that $2 \times y = 1$. However, the same sentence (*) is true of the model $R = \langle R, +, \times, <, 0, 1 \rangle$, where R is the set of all rational numbers (ratios of integers).

To turn to the deductive apparatus of the System J_1, the list of axiom schemata ($J_1 iii$) can be taken over bodily from the schemata (1) to (15) of ($I_1 iii$), except that the identity schemata (9′) to (11′) must be supplemented by the following schemata, which relate the identity symbol to the predicate symbol L and the operation symbols $\oplus$ and $\otimes$. For any terms u, u', v, and v' the following formulas are axioms:

(16) $\quad + +u \approx u' \wedge v \approx v' + \rightarrow +Luv \leftrightarrow Lu'v' + +$;
(17) $\quad + +u \approx u' \wedge v \approx v' + \rightarrow +u \oplus v + \approx +u' \oplus v' + +$;
(18) $\quad + +u \approx u' \wedge v \approx v' + \rightarrow +u \otimes v + \approx +u' \otimes v' + +$.

($J_1 iv$) The rules of inference for J_1 are exactly those of I_1—detachment and generalization. These rules also enter into the definition of formal proof and formal deduction (from a given set Γ) in the same way as for the System I_1. As in previous systems, we use the notations "$\vdash A$" and "$\Gamma \vdash A$" to indicate, respectively, that A is a formal theorem and that A is deducible from Γ.

In semantical interpretation of the grammar determined by ($J_1 i$) and ($J_1 ii$) the principal difference from the rules of interpretation of the System I_1 involves the method of taking account of the grammatical category of terms. Given a model of the type of N—take N itself, for example—and given an N-assignment ϕ, we determine for each term t a value $V_N(t, \phi)$ which is an element of the domain N of the model (rather than a truth-value, which is the value determined by a formula). The recursive definition of these values is as follows:

(a) $\quad V_N(v_i, \phi) = \phi(v_i), \quad V_N(c_0, \phi) = 0, \quad V_N(c_1, \phi) = 1$;

(b) if s and t are any terms, then

$$V_N(+s \oplus t+, \phi) = V_N(s, \phi) + V_N(t, \phi),$$
$$V_N(+s \otimes t+, \phi) = V_N(s, \phi) \times V_N(t, \phi).$$

(On the right side of the last two equations we are simply adding and multiplying the numbers which are the values of the terms s and t under the assignment ϕ.) Once the values of terms have been determined as above, a second recursive definition giving the values of formulas begins by specifying that for any terms s and t, the value $V_N(s \approx t, \phi)$ is T or F according as $V_N(s, \phi) = V_N(t, \phi)$ or not, and the value $V_N(Lst, \phi)$ is T or F according as $V_N(s, \phi) < V_N(t, \phi)$ or not. Then, having in this way assigned values to each atomic formula, we proceed to assign values to formulas compounded

by connectives or quantifiers, using exactly the same rules as employed for the System I_1. Once $V_N(A, \phi)$ is determined for all formulas A, the definitions of validity ($\models A$) and of logical consequence ($\Gamma \models A$) may be copied from those of I_1.

Like systems previously considered, J_1 turns out to be both sound and complete, so that for any set Γ and any formula A we have $\Gamma \vdash A$ if and only if we have $\Gamma \models A$. A similar result applies to formal systems corresponding to any type of relational system. However, unlike the situation encountered in the case of the System I_1, these results do not in general lead to a decision method for arbitrary first-order systems. In fact, for the System J_1 it can be proved that there does not exist any automatic method to decide in a finite number of steps whether a given formula A is or is not a formal theorem; the same is true of any first-order system that has a predicate or operation symbol of more than one place and formal theorems that are just the logically valid formulas of the system.

The precise formulation of the general notion of a decision method, which underlies this last result, rests on the concept of a recursive function or the closely related concept of a Turing machine, which is a kind of idealized computing machine. These notions, in turn, arise from the study of certain formal deductive systems (for definitions, see RECURSIVE FUNCTION THEORY).

FORMAL SYSTEMS FOR ARITHMETIC

The formal deductive System J_1 has as its formal theorems precisely those formulas of its grammar which are logically valid. In particular, a sentence of J_1 will be a theorem if and only if it is true of every model having the same type as the system N of natural numbers. Suppose, however, we are interested in the system N itself and wish to find the sentences that are true of it. How do we proceed?

The usual method is to seek out a suitable set P of sentences which we take as nonlogical axioms, in addition to the axioms of the System J_1. Then, taking the same rules of inference as for J_1, we arrive at a formal deductive System K_P. If the sentences A of P are chosen so that $V_N(A) = T$, then every theorem B of K_P will also have this property. In fact, it is easy to see that a sentence (of the grammar of J_1) will be a theorem of K_P when and only when it is a logical consequence of P—that is, when and only when $P \models B$.

One can find simple sets P of axioms for arithmetic from which one can formally infer, in the resulting System K_P, all of the theorems which have historically been demonstrated informally by the methods of so-called elementary number theory. Such, for example, is the following variant of Peano's axiom system, which we shall call P_0:

(P1) $\quad \neg +\exists v_1 + +v_1 \oplus c_1 + \approx c_0 +.$
(P2) $\quad +\forall v_2 + +\neg +\exists v_1 + +v_1 \oplus c_1 + \approx v_2 \rightarrow v_2 \approx c_0 +.$
(P3) $\quad +\forall v_1 + +\forall v_2 + + +v_1 \oplus c_1 + \approx +v_2 \oplus c_1 + \rightarrow v_1 \approx v_2 +.$
(P4) $\quad +\forall v_1 + +v_1 \oplus c_0 + \approx v_1.$
(P5) $\quad +\forall v_1 + +\forall v_2 + +v_1 \oplus +v_2 \oplus c_1 + + \approx$
$\quad\quad\quad\quad + +v_1 \oplus v_2 + \oplus c_1 +.$
(P6) $\quad +\forall v_1 + +v_1 \otimes c_0 + \approx c_0.$

$(P7)$ $\vdash\forall v_1\vdash\vdash\forall v_2\vdash\vdash v_1\otimes\vdash v_2\oplus c_1\vdash\vdash\approx$
$\quad\quad\quad\vdash\vdash v_1\otimes v_2\vdash\oplus v_1\vdash.$

$(P8)$ $\vdash\forall v_1\vdash\vdash\forall v_2\vdash\vdash Lv_1v_2\leftrightarrow$
$\quad\quad\quad\vdash\exists v_3\vdash\vdash\vdash v_1\oplus v_3\vdash\oplus c_1\vdash\approx v_2\vdash.$

$(P9)$ $\vdash\vdash A_{c_0}{}^{v_1}\wedge\vdash\forall v_1\vdash\vdash A\rightarrow A_{\vdash v_1+c_1}{}^{v_1}\vdash\vdash\rightarrow\vdash\forall v_1\vdash A\vdash,$

where A is any formula of the grammar of J_1.

[*P9* is a schema expressing the principle of mathematical induction.]

Despite the fact that all "ordinary" theorems about natural numbers can be proved in this System K_{P_0}, one can construct a sentence D_0 of the grammar of J_1 which is true of N but not provable in K_{P_0}. (The description of D_0 is quite lengthy and complex.) It is natural, then, to form the axiom system P_1 from P_0 by adding the sentence D_0 as an axiom. However, the same method for constructing D_0 from P_0 enables us to construct a sentence D_1 belonging to the grammar of J_1 which is true of N but not provable in K_{P_1}. Indeed, we can continue in this way to obtain an axiom system P_n for every natural number n, each obtained from the preceding axiom system P_{n-1} by the addition of a certain sentence D_{n-1} which is true of N but not provable in $K_{P_{n-1}}$. We can then let P^* be the axiom system obtained from P_0 by simultaneous addition of all the infinitely many axioms $D_0, D_1, D_2, \cdots$. But we can still find a sentence D^* which is true of N but not provable in K_{P*}.

Is there any set of axioms which is complete for the true sentences of N? There is, if we declare, for instance, that every sentence true of N shall be an axiom. But in this case there is no automatic method to tell whether or not any given sentence is an axiom.

The celebrated incompleteness result of Kurt Gödel asserts that if Q is any system of axioms which are true of N such that there is an automatic method to tell whether any given formula of J_1 is or is not in Q, then there are true sentences about N which cannot be proved in K_Q (see GÖDEL'S THEOREM).

A similar incompleteness result holds if in place of the system N we consider the system R of rational numbers: No system of axioms for which there is an automatic decision method can yield as theorems all and only those sentences of J_1 which are true of R. On the other hand, if we pass to the system R_e of real numbers (i.e., all numbers which can be expressed by means of infinite decimal expressions), there is a complete axiom system for its true sentences, and, indeed, there is a decision method to tell whether any given sentence of J_1 is or is not true of R_e.

SKOLEM–LÖWENHEIM RESULT

In the preceding section we considered a particular structure N and inquired about the set of all sentences which are true of N. It often happens in mathematics, however, that we start with some fixed set of sentences Γ and seek to determine the totality of structures which satisfy all of the sentences of Γ. In particular, we may inquire under what conditions an axiom system Γ determines a unique model which satisfies it.

As an example, consider the axiom system Γ_0 consisting of the two axioms $\vdash\forall v_1\vdash v_1\approx c_0$ and Lc_0c_0. We can easily construct a model M, of the same type as N, which satisfies Γ_0. In fact, let M be the set whose only element is Socrates, let $\circ$ be the only binary operation possible on M (so that Socrates $\circ$ Socrates = Socrates), and let U be the unique nonempty binary relation on M (so that Socrates is in the relation U to himself). Then if we take M to be the structure $\langle M, \circ, \circ, U, \text{Socrates}, \text{Socrates}\rangle$, M will have the same type as N and will satisfy both sentences of Γ_0.

Of course, there are many other models with the same properties. Instead of starting with Socrates we could start with any object whatsoever and construct a one-element model M' in the same way. Although literally different models, M and M' are "essentially the same"; the mathematician uses a technical concept, isomorphism, to describe the relation of M to M'. In the same way it can be shown that given any model L whatsoever, it is possible to construct many isomorphic models L' all satisfying the same sentences as L.

Is there any other set of sentences which, like Γ_0, determines a unique model satisfying it—except for isomorphic copies? The answer is affirmative. Indeed, if we start with a structure M whose domain is finite, we can always find a set Γ of sentences such that every model satisfying Γ must be isomorphic to M. On the other hand, if Δ is a set of sentences which is satisfied by at least one infinite model (that is, one model whose domain is infinite), then it is also satisfied by a large class of models no two of which are isomorphic.

To formulate the sharpest form of this result it is necessary to employ the notion of transfinite numbers. Just as the natural numbers can be used to indicate the cardinality of finite sets, so can the transfinite numbers be used to indicate the cardinality of infinite sets. Two sets (whether finite or infinite) have the same cardinality when and only when the members of one can be put in a one-to-one correspondence with those of the other. It is known that there are infinitely many different transfinite numbers. The set of natural numbers has the smallest of these as its cardinality.

A strong form of the Skolem–Löwenheim theorem states that if Γ is any set of first-order sentences which is satisfied by one infinite model, then it is also satisfied by models of every transfinite cardinality. No two models with different cardinality can be isomorphic.

The study of the logic of identity is generally considered to have begun with Leibniz. However, his work was not conveyed through the construction of any formal deductive system such as I but consisted in the formulation of individual principles expressed in the form of valid formulas or rules of inference.

The notion of a formal deductive system, like most important scientific concepts, was the product of an evolutionary process. Mathematico-symbolic notation was introduced into the study of logic by George Boole in 1847. Contributions during the latter half of the nineteenth century, principally those of Charles Sanders Peirce and Gottlob Frege, led to the formulation, in 1910, of *Principia Mathematica*, by Alfred Whitehead and Bertrand Russell; this work contains the essentials of a formal deductive system, although the several parts are not clearly distinguished from one another and are not all explicit.

Emil Post, in 1921, published the first fully rigorous account of the logic of sentential connectives, providing a formal deductive system, a precise account of the semantical interpretation of its grammar, and demonstrations of its soundness and completeness.

Beginning in the 1920s, the study of formal deductive systems of first-order logic was carried out widely. In Norway, Thoralf Skolem developed the earlier ideas of Leopold Löwenheim, which resulted in the following form of the theorem that bears their name: If Γ is any set of first-order sentences all of which are satisfied by some infinite model, then there is a model satisfying Γ which has the minimum transfinite cardinality (i.e., the same cardinality as the set of natural numbers). Alfred Tarski later extended this result to the form we gave earlier; a proof appears in Leon Henkin's "The Completeness of the First-order Functional Calculus." Recent extensions of this work into simultaneous consideration of two transfinite cardinal numbers were initiated by Robert Vaught.

A great many logical studies were begun in Poland in the 1920s. Especially noteworthy were the investigations by Alfred Tarski ("Fundamentale Begriffe der Methodologie der deductiven Wissenschaften") in which he studied the consequence relation axiomatically, instead of by defining it, as we did above. In 1934, Tarski gave the first comprehensive and mathematically precise analysis of the semantical concepts for languages of first order and related kinds (see his "Der Wahrheitsbegriff in den formalisierten Sprachen").

In Germany in the 1920s, David Hilbert, in collaboration with such men as Wilhelm Ackermann and Paul Bernays, undertook research designed principally to establish the consistency of axiom systems for the system N of natural numbers (*Grundlagen der Mathematik*). They sought a proof which could be carried through in a very simple, constructive part of mathematics, but in 1931, Kurt Gödel ("Über formal unentscheidbare Sätze der Principia Mathematica und verwandter Systeme I") showed that such a proof was impossible. An interesting consistency proof for an axiom system such as the P_0 discussed above was given by Gerhard Gentzen in 1936. One of those working in the directions suggested by Hilbert was the French logician Jacques Herbrand, who, in 1930, effected an interesting reduction of first-order logic to the logic of sentential connectives.

The completeness of a formal system for first-order logic was established by Kurt Gödel in 1930 ("Die Vollständigkeit der Axiome des logischen Funktionenkalküls"). His 1931 paper established the incompleteness of various formal systems for the arithmetic of natural numbers. The proof of the incompleteness of formal systems for the arithmetic of rational numbers was given by Julia Robinson in 1949; she later extended this result to certain algebraic number systems. The completeness of a certain first-order system for the arithmetic of real numbers, as well as a decision method for this system, was published by Tarski in 1948 (*A Decision Method for Elementary Algebra and Geometry*), some 18 years after the work was first done and written for publication. In 1936, Alonzo Church proved the nonexistence of a decision method for first-order systems of logic ("Correction to a Note on the Entscheidungsproblem").

There has been considerable investigation into questions of definability in first-order logic, stemming from a fundamental discovery of Evert Beth's in 1953 ("On Padoa's Method in the Theory of Definition"). Beth's theorem, in turn, is now seen to be a simple consequence of the "interpolation theorem" established by William Craig in 1957: If A and C are first-order formulas such that $\vdash A \rightarrow C$, then there is a formula B in which there occur only predicate symbols which occur both in A and in C, such that $\vdash A \rightarrow B$ and $\vdash B \rightarrow C$. Craig's theorem has also had important application to problems in what has come to be called the theory of models—the study of the interrelations between the form of a sentence and the properties of the class of models which satisfy it.

In addition to formal systems of first-order logic there are systems of logic of second and higher order. These include new types of variables which range over sets and relations of model elements (and sets of sets, etc.), as well as the individual variables of first-order systems. Included in Gödel's 1931 paper is a proof of the incompleteness of any sound formal system of second- or higher-order logic for which one can automatically decide whether a given sentence is an axiom. In 1951, Henkin showed that by extending the notion of model for such systems completeness can be achieved ("Completeness in the Theory of Types").

This article has been confined to formal systems based on the classical logic of two truth-values. There have, however, been many studies of nonclassical logic. Systems based on three or more truth-values have a long history, and various systems of constructive logic have been developed, most notably by the intuitionists. Algebraic interpretations of formal systems have been developed. Systems of logic with infinitely long formulas have also been studied.

Bibliography

The reviews in the *Journal of Symbolic Logic* provide a complete survey of the literature on formal systems.

Addison, John; Henkin, Leon; and Tarski, Alfred, eds., *Proceedings of the International Symposium on the Theory of Models, Berkeley, 1963*. Studies in Logic and the Foundations of Mathematics. Amsterdam, 1965.

Beth, Evert, "On Padoa's Method in the Theory of Definition." *Indagationes Mathematicae*, Vol. 15 (1953), 330–339.

Beth, Evert, *The Foundations of Mathematics*. Studies in Logic and the Foundations of Mathematics. Amsterdam, 1959. Interesting collection of diverse topics.

Boole, George, *The Mathematical Analysis of Logic, Being an Essay Toward a Calculus of Deductive Reasoning*. London and Cambridge, 1847.

Church, Alonzo, "Correction to a Note on the Entscheidungsproblem." *Journal of Symbolic Logic*, Vol. 1 (1936), 101–102.

Church, Alonzo, *Introduction to Mathematical Logic*, Vol. I. Princeton, N.J., 1956. Detailed treatment of sentential and first-order logic, with a wealth of historical detail.

Craig, William, "Linear Reasoning: A New Form of the Herbrand–Gentzen Theorem." *Journal of Symbolic Logic*, Vol. 22 (1957), 250–268.

Frege, Gottlob, *Die Grundlagen der Arithmetik, eine logisch-*

mathematische Untersuchung über den Begriff der Zahl. Breslau, 1884; reprinted, 1934.

Gentzen, Gerhard, "Die Widerspruchsfreiheit der reinen Zahlentheorie." *Mathematische Annalen,* Vol. 112 (1936), 493–565.

Gödel, Kurt, "Die Vollständigkeit der Axiome des logischen Funktionenkalküls." *Monatshefte für Mathematik und Physik,* Vol. 37 (1930), 349–360.

Gödel, Kurt, "Über formal unentscheidbare Sätze der Principia Mathematica und verwandter Systeme I." *Monatshefte für Mathematik und Physik,* Vol. 38 (1931), 173–198. Translated by John van Heijenoort in *A Source Book in Mathematical Logic.* Cambridge, Mass., forthcoming.

Halmos, Paul, *Algebraic Logic.* New York, 1962.

Henkin, Leon, "The Completeness of the First-order Functional Calculus." *Journal of Symbolic Logic,* Vol. 14 (1949), 159–166.

Henkin, Leon, "Completeness in the Theory of Types." *Journal of Symbolic Logic,* Vol. 15 (1950), 81–91.

Herbrand, Jacques, "Sur la Non-contradiction de l'arithmétique." *Journal für die reine und angewandte Mathematik,* Vol. 166 (1931), 1–8.

Heyting, Arend, *Intuitionism, an Introduction.* Studies in Logic and the Foundations of Mathematics. Amsterdam, 1956.

Hilbert, David, and Ackermann, Wilhelm, *Grundzüge der theoretischen Logik,* 3d ed. Berlin, 1949. 2d ed. translated by Lewis M. Hammond as *Principles of Mathematical Logic.* New York, 1950. Contains a fairly concise treatment of sentential and first-order logic.

Hilbert, David, and Bernays, Paul, *Grundlagen der Mathematik,* 2 vols. Berlin, 1934–1939.

Karp, Carol, *Languages With Expressions of Infinite Length.* Studies in Logic and the Foundations of Mathematics. Amsterdam, 1964.

Leibniz, G. W. von, "Specimen Calculi Universalis," in *Philosophische Schriften,* C. J. Gerhardt, ed., Vol. 7. Berlin, 1890. Pp. 218–221.

Löwenheim, Leopold, "Über Möglichkeiten im Relativkalkül." *Mathematische Annalen,* Vol. 76 (1915), 447–470.

Peirce, Charles Sanders, "On the Algebra of Logic." *American Journal of Mathematics,* Vol. 3 (1880), 15–57.

Post, Emil, "Introduction to a General Theory of Elementary Propositions." *American Journal of Mathematics,* Vol. 43 (1921), 163–185.

Quine, W. V., *Mathematical Logic,* rev. ed. Cambridge, Mass., 1951. In the first half is a concise treatment of sentential and first-order logic.

Robinson, Julia, "Definability and Decision Problems in Arithmetic." *Journal of Symbolic Logic,* Vol. 14 (1949), 98–114.

Rosser, J. B., and Turquette, A. R., *Many-valued Logics.* Studies in Logic and the Foundations of Mathematics. Amsterdam, 1952.

Russell, Bertrand, and Whitehead, A. N., *Principia Mathematica,* 3 vols. Cambridge, 1910–1913.

Skolem, Thoralf, *Logisch-kombinatorische Untersuchungen über die Erfüllbarkeit oder Beweisbarkeit mathematischer Sätze nebst einem Theoreme über dichte Mengen.* Skrifter Utgitt av Videnskapsselskapet i Kristiania, I. Matematisk-naturvidenskapelig Klasse 1920, No. 4 (1920).

Tarski, Alfred, "Fundamentale Begriffe der Methodologie der deductiven Wissenschaften." *Monatshefte für Mathematik und Physik,* Vol. 37 (1930), 361–404. Translated by J. H. Woodger in *Logic, Semantics, Metamathematics.* Oxford, 1956.

Tarski, Alfred, "Der Wahrheitsbegriff in den formalisierten Sprachen." *Studia Philosophica,* Vol. 1 (1936), 261–405. Translated by J. H. Woodger, *op. cit.*

Tarski, Alfred, *A Decision Method for Elementary Algebra and Geometry.* Santa Monica, Calif., 1948.

Vaught, Robert, "A Löwenheim–Skolem Theorem for Two Cardinals." *American Mathematical Society Notices,* Vol. 8 (1961), 239.

LEON HENKIN

T

TAGORE, RABINDRANATH (1861–1941), Indian writer and philosopher. Romain Rolland, referring to the Orient and the Occident, said that Tagore contributed more than anyone else toward "the union of these two hemispheres of spirit." Sarvepalli Radhakrishnan called Tagore "the greatest figure of the Indian renaissance."

Tagore was born in Calcutta, studied in London, returned to India, and was married in 1883. He founded Visvabharati, a university at Santiniketan (near Bolpur), became India's most popular poet, won the Nobel Prize for literature in 1913, and was knighted in 1915. He visited and lectured in Canada, the United States, South America, England and several countries of Europe, the Soviet Union, Turkey, Iran, Ceylon, China, and Japan. He was in personal contact with Bergson, Croce, Einstein, Russell, and other leading intellectual figures of his period.

Tagore wrote about fifteen books of philosophical lectures and essays, about one hundred books of verse (mostly in Bengali, and partly translated by himself from his own Bengali version into English), about fifty plays (in some of which he acted the main role), and about forty works of fiction. His main writings of philosophical interest are *Sadhana, The Realisation of Life* (1913), *Personality* (1917), *Creative Unity* (1922), *The Religion of Man* (1931), all published in London and New York, and *Man* (1937), published in Madras. His best-known poems appear in *Gitanjali* ("Song Offerings"), translated by the author from the original Bengali, with an introduction by W. B. Yeats (1913), *The Crescent Moon,* likewise translated by the author from the original Bengali (1913), and *Fruit-Gathering* (1916), all published in London and New York. He produced some drawings and paintings, beginning about his seventieth year, and planned and produced ballets.

Tagore's basic philosophical position is one which recognizes the useful insights of the main opposing views on a given question. For example, concerning the transcendence or immanence of God, Tagore accepted, on the one hand, the value of the doctrine of Brahman as "the absolute Truth, the impersonal It, in which there can be no distinction of this and that, the good and the evil, the beautiful and its opposite, having no other quality except its ineffable blissfulness in the eternal solitude of its consciousness"; but he also felt, on the other hand, that "whatever name may have been given to the divine Reality it has found its highest place in the history of our religion owing to its human character, giving meaning to the idea of sin and sanctity, and offering an eternal background to all the ideals of perfection which have their harmony with man's own nature" (*The Religion of Man*).

Similarly, he combined the best insights of humanists, who exalt man, and of otherworldly seekers of the World Force, who belittle man; of naturalists, who deny spirit, and extreme partisans of spirit, who cut man off from nature; of individualists and universalists; of determinists and defenders of free will; of hedonists and ascetics; and of romanticists and realists.

In his social philosophy, as well as in his metaphysics, Tagore attempted to synthesize polar opposites. Neither wholly conservative nor wholly liberal, he favored gradual reform. This evolutionary note is reflected in his views on the economic order, public health, education, the social structure, national politics, and international affairs.

Tagore's emphasis on the mediating unity which embraces variety appears, for example, in *Sadhana*, where he wrote: "Facts are many, but the truth is one. . . . Man must clearly realise some central truth which will give him an outlook over the widest possible field. And that is the object which the Upanishad has in view when it says, Know thine own Soul. Or, in other words, realise the one great principle of unity that there is in every man."

In May 1930, Tagore delivered the Hibbert lectures at Oxford. In the following year, the lectures were published in expanded form as a book, *The Religion of Man*. Tagore's mediationism appears in the book in such passages as the following: "The final freedom which India aspires after . . . is beyond all limits of personality, divested of all moral or aesthetic distinctions; it is the pure consciousness of Being, the ultimate reality. . . ." The yogi has claimed that through intensive concentration and quietude we do reach "that infinity where knowledge ceases to be knowledge, subject and object become one—a state of existence that cannot be defined. . . . India attunes man to the grand harmony of the universal, leaving no room for untrained desires of a rampant individualism to pursue their destructive career unchecked, but leading them on to their ultimate modulation in the Supreme."

Bibliography

The philosophical works by Tagore which are mentioned above, as well as others, have been published in various editions, in English and in translation into European languages.

Works on Tagore's philosophy include the following (arranged in chronological order): Sarvepalli Radhakrishnan, *The Philosophy of Rabindranath Tagore* (London, 1918; reissued Baroda, 1961); Sachin Sen, *The Political Thought of Tagore* (Calcutta, 1947); B. G. Ray, *The Philosophy of Rabindranath Tagore* (Bombay, 1949); V. S. Naravane, *Rabindranath Tagore, A Philosophical Study* (Allahabad, n.d.); and Sasadhar Sinha, *Social Thinking of Rabindranath Tagore* (New York, 1962).

Of the many biographies of Tagore, mention may be made of Krishna Kripalani, *Rabindranath Tagore, A Biography* (Oxford and New York, 1962).

WILLIAM GERBER

TAINE, HIPPOLYTE-ADOLPHE (1828–1893), philosopher, psychologist, historian, and critic. Taine and Ernest Renan were the leading French positivistic thinkers of the second half of the nineteenth century. As a result of Taine's great independence of mind, his life was not always comfortable. Discriminatory treatment from the authorities of the Second Empire led to his withdrawal from teaching from 1852 to 1863, when he was appointed an examiner at Saint-Cyr. The next year he became a lecturer at the École des Beaux Arts; from his lectures there came his famous *Philosophie de l'art*. At the intervention of the Catholic clergy, a French Academy award for his *Histoire de la littérature anglaise* was denied him, and he was elected to the academy only in 1878, after the fall of the Second Empire. By that time he had antagonized both liberals and Bonapartists by his ruthless destruction of the revolutionary and Napoleonic legends. Nevertheless, his influence was great and diversified. His positivistic and physiological approach to psychology was adopted by Théodule Ribot, Pierre Janet, and others, and his opposition to centralization and to revolutionary experiments attracted Catholic traditionalists like Paul Bourget and Maurice Barrès, who, however, ignored his severe condemnation of the old regime and his outspoken sympathies for Protestant and parliamentary England.

Although Taine's philosophical views were formed early in life under the joint influence of Spinoza, Hegel, and classical science, they were first systematically expounded in his *De l'Intelligence*. The theory of mind presented in this book is based on Taine's general monism and determinism. Thus in the Preface to the fourth edition (Paris, 1883), he stated his opposition to faculty psychology on the grounds that words like "capacity," "self," "reason," and "memory" suggest by their simplicity the existence of indivisible mental entities and thus prevent us from grasping the enormous complexities of the underlying psychological mechanisms. The self is nothing but a series of mental events. In his attack on the substantialization of the self and the reification of abstractions, Taine drew on psychopathology and neural physiology. Psychopathology shows how mental disease can dissociate the components of a complex phenomenon which appears subjectively as simple; neural physiology reveals the enormous complexity of the neural mechanism that underlies mental phenomena. Taine held a double-aspect theory of the relation between introspective data and public physical events; the mental and the physical are two sides of the same process, "two translations of the same text" (*De l'Intelligence*, Book 4, Ch. 2). Taine's use of physiological analysis, his strictures on introspection, and his mechanistic determinism place him among the naturalists.

Like most of his contemporaries, Taine regarded classical science as complete, and its picture of nature as definitive. Like Spencer, Wilhelm Ostwald, and others, he regarded the law of conservation of energy as ultimate, as "the immutable ground of being," and the equivalence of cause and effect as a consequence of this law.

Taine applied his rigorous determinism to all phenomena—physical, mental, and social. There is little in his writings dealing directly with physical phenomena, but there is no question that the determinism of classical physics was for him an ideal model to which other sciences should conform. Thus in the Introduction to his *Histoire de la littérature anglaise,* he proposed that every social phenomenon should be explained as the result of race, environment, and time—that is, of the particular psychosocial state of a society. Taine had already applied this method in previous essays, and he applied it in his *Philosophie de l'art* and later in his major historical work, *Les Origines de la France contemporaine,* inspired by his reflections on the French defeat in 1870. The thesis of this monumental and controversial work is that there was one persistent theme—excessive centralization—underlying all the violent upheavals of modern France. Introduced by the Bourbons, it was strengthened by the French Revolution, which destroyed the natural provinces and replaced them by departments which were mere administrative appendixes of the central government; in the hands of Napoleon the centralized administrative structure was an efficient tool of internal control and external conquest, but it became an unwieldy bureaucratic machine as soon as it was deprived of Napoleon's ruthless energy.

Taine's detailed study of social conditions under the old regime, of revolutionary excesses, and of mob psychology after 1789 strengthened the inclination to pessimism present in his previous writings. This inclination found its most eloquent expression in the following passage: "Man is a nervous machine, governed by à mood, disposed to hallucinations, transported by unbridled passions, essentially unreasonable" (*History of English Literature*, Vol. II, p. 173). In *De l'Intelligence* Taine had said that every image tends to acquire a hallucinatory intensity unless checked by the inhibiting influence of other images. Thus mental equilibrium and social stability are mere "happy accidents." Civilization is a mere surface beneath which lurk irrational drives always ready to break through.

Works by Taine

Essais de critique et d'histoire. Paris, 1858.
Histoire de la littérature anglaise, 4 vols. Paris, 1863–1864. Translated by H. van Laun as *History of English Literature,* 2 vols. Edinburgh, 1873.
Nouveaux Essais de critique et d'histoire. Paris, 1865.
Philosophie de l'art. Paris, 1865; 2d ed., enlarged, Paris, 1880. First edition translated by J. Durand as *The Philosophy of Art.* New York, 1865.
De l'Intelligence, 2 vols. Paris, 1870. Translated by T. D. Hayes as *Intelligence*. London, 1871.

Les Origines de la France contemporaine, 5 vols. Paris, 1876–1893.

Derniers Essais de critique et d'histoire. Paris, 1894.

Works on Taine

Barzelotti, Giacomo, *Ippolito Taine.* Rome, 1896.

Bourget, Paul, *Essais de psychologie contemporaine.* Paris, 1883. Vol. I.

Chevrillon, André, *Taine: Formation de sa pensée.* Paris, 1932.

Faguet, Émile, *Politiques et moralistes du XIXᵉ siècle.* 3d series. Paris, 1900.

Giraud, Victor, *Essai sur Taine: Son oeuvre et son influence.* Paris, 1901.

Kahn, Sholem J., *Science and Aesthetic Judgment: A Study in Taine's Critical Method.* New York, 1953.

Lacombe, Paul, *La Psychologie des individus et des sociétés chez Taine.* Paris, 1906.

Lacombe, Paul, *Taine, historien et sociologue.* Paris, 1909.

MILIČ ČAPEK

TANABE HAJIME (1885–1962), Japanese philosopher of science, esteemed as second only to Nishida Kitarō for his originality and influence. He was born in Tokyo and retired at the war's end to Karuizawa where he died. In 1913 he became a lecturer on the philosophy of science at Tōhoku University in Sendai. He later taught at Kyoto University and became the most famous successor of Nishida. Through his teaching and books he contributed to the formation of the Kyoto school of philosophy, which was dominant in Japan until 1945. He studied at the universities of Berlin and Freiburg from 1922 to 1924, and on his return he published *Kanto no mokutekiron* (*Kant's Teleology;* Tokyo, 1924). Tanabe's major work of these years was *Suri tetsugaku* ("A Study of the Philosophy of Mathematics"; Tokyo, 1925), which established him as the leading philosopher of science in Japan. It shows the influence of Hermann Cohen of the Marburg Neo-Kantian school and of Nishida's intuitionism.

In 1927 Tanabe began a transition from Husserl's phenomenology and Heidegger's existentialism to Hegel's dialectic, developing his line of thought through the 1930s. In two essays, *Shakai sonzai no ronri* ("The Logic of Social Being"; Kyoto, 1936) and *Shu no ronri* ("The Logic of the Species," published in the philosophical journal of Kyoto University, 1939), he opposed Nishida's "logic of field." The species that Tanabe speaks of is the nation, the mediating element between the individual and generic mankind in the philosophy of history. Tanabe held that Nishida had neglected the role of the species and had therefore lost sight of the historical being in mankind, or at least had reduced it to mere individuality. Rejecting the political implications—the glorification of the state—contained in the logic of the species, Tanabe developed the *shu no ronri no benshōhō,* the "dialectic of the logic of the species" (he published a book with that title in Tokyo in 1947). He had earlier proposed the "absolute dialectic"—"absolute criticism," in effect a denial of all former philosophical positions—which was a result of his *zangedō toshite no tetsugaku,* "philosophy as repentance." In the book exploring this latter line of thought (Tokyo, 1946), he had advocated a clean sweep of former nationalism.

Basically Tanabe was looking for a mystical integration of Christian love and Buddhist "nothingness" that would save mankind from the horrors of the atomic age. Some of Tanabe's postwar works, such as *Jitsuzon to ai to jissen* ("Existence, Love and Praxis"; Tokyo, 1947) and *Kirisutokyō no benshōhō* ("The Dialectic of Christianity"; Tokyo, 1948), testify to his quest for the "absolute nothingness," which is not ontological nihilism but rather the oriental negation of the phenomenal world in favor of something inexpressible in philosophic language. Nevertheless, to the end Tanabe sought to philosophize, not to become a religious thinker. He even thought his "absolute nothingness" could help to solve the sociopolitical problems of postwar Japan.

This line of thought must be evaluated in the light of the years of turmoil he endured before and after World War II. His originality is most evident in his concept of the logic of the species, but his most important contribution to twentieth-century Japanese philosophy will remain what he did in the philosophy of science, especially in mathematics.

Bibliography

See *Tanabe Hajime zenshū* ("The Complete Works of Tanabe Hajime"), 15 vols. (Tokyo, 1964), and *Tanabe tetsugaku* ("Tanabe's Philosophy"; Tokyo, 1951). Tanabe's "Memento Mori," a Zen Buddhist philosophical meditation on how, facing an age of death, we must think of life, has been translated by V. H. Viglielmo and published in *Philosophical Studies of Japan,* Vol. I (1959), 1–12. See also Gino K. Piovesana's *Recent Japanese Philosophical Thought, 1862–1962* (Tokyo, 1963), pp. 145–158.

GINO K. PIOVESANA, S.J.

TAOISM. See CHINESE PHILOSOPHY; LAO TZU; MYSTICISM, HISTORY OF.

TARSKI, ALFRED, Polish-American mathematician and logician, was born in Warsaw in 1902, received his doctorate in mathematics from the University of Warsaw in 1924, and two years later was named docent. In 1939 he immigrated to the United States. Appointed lecturer in mathematics at the University of California (Berkeley) in 1942, he has served at that institution as professor of mathematics since 1946.

MATHEMATICS

Tarski has worked in both pure mathematics, especially set theory and algebra, and mathematical logic, especially metamathematics. This article will not discuss his mathematical contributions, although some of them (in particular his famous theorem, established jointly with Banach, on the decomposition of the sphere, as well as his theory of inaccessible cardinals) have a definite bearing on the epistemology of mathematics. (See S. Banach and A. Tarski, "Sur la décomposition des ensembles des points en parties respectivement congruentes," *Fundamenta Mathematicae,* Vol. 6, 1924, 244–277.)

It should be noted that in these papers Tarski has not criticized the assumptions of set theory. Like most mathematicians he has simply accepted them as true. This attitude and a systematic use of set-theoretic concepts have profoundly influenced his work in logic and metamathematics. Unlike the followers of David Hilbert and of L. E. J. Brouwer, Tarski has not refrained from the use of infinitistic set-theoretical concepts. He finds a definition or a theorem to be acceptable if it is expressed or proved on the basis of set theory. This attitude, of course, is completely different from that of Hilbert's formalism or Brouwer's intuitionism (see MATHEMATICS, FOUNDATIONS OF).

As a consequence of this methodological attitude, Tarski has gained much freedom in introducing new notions and thus has put himself in a much more advantageous position than the adherents of Hilbert or Brouwer. Consider the following very simple but typical example. In *Logic, Semantics, Metamathematics* (p. 38) Tarski defines the set of consequences of a given set of axioms as the smallest set containing the axioms and closed with respect to the rules of proof, and on this definition he bases the whole theory of the consequence relation in the propositional calculus. A follower of Hilbert or Brouwer would never accept such a definition because he would regard the clarification of the notion of set (involved in this definition) as the ultimate aim of his activity.

The free use of set theory has enabled Tarski to extend the field of application of metamathematics (see, for instance, his investigations of "infinitary languages," discussed below) and has formed a natural basis for the development of his semantic method. This method can indeed be formulated only in a language that has considerable deductive strength and is provided with means to express definitions of a very complicated structure. The general theory of sets satisfies both these requirements.

Obviously Tarski's methodological attitude is rejected by the adherents of finitism and by all logicians who seek in metamathematics a justification or explanation of set theory.

METAMATHEMATICS

Metamathematics is a branch of mathematical logic which studies formal theories and solves problems pertaining to such theories. Tarski has contributed so much to this field that he deserves to be regarded, with Hilbert, as its cofounder.

Axiomatic theory of formal systems. In his early papers Tarski presented an axiomatic theory of arbitrary formal systems. A "theory" for him is a set (whose elements are called formulas) and a function (called the consequence function) which correlates a set of formulas with each such set; this new set is called the set of consequences of the first set. The consequence function is not wholly arbitrary; it must satisfy certain axioms which will not be reproduced here. Several metamathematical notions, such as consistency, completeness, and independence, can be defined for theories in this abstract sense. All formal theories that were known in 1930 can be subsumed under this scheme. While this is no longer true today (see below), a relatively small rectification of Tarski's axioms would suffice to restore the universality of his scheme.

Systems based on propositional logic. Besides discussing the most general scheme of formal theories, Tarski axiomatically described theories based on the classical propositional logic. Here the assumptions must, of course, be specialized. It is assumed, for example, that certain operations are defined on the set of formulas (the joining of two formulas by means of a connective). An example of an important property of consequence that Tarski took as an axiom is the deduction theorem. Its importance is that it provides the possibility of defining the consequence function in terms of one fixed set S_0 of sentences, specifically the set of consequences of the empty set. In concrete cases, S_0 consists of logical tautologies expressible in the given theory. In what follows, we shall speak of theories as being based on a logic L if S_0 is the set of tautologies of the logic L.

Description of systems. Tarski calls a set X of formulas a system if it is deductively closed, that is, if it is equal to its set of consequences. In "Grundzüge des Systemenkalküls" he formulated a general program aimed at describing all systems of a given theory. Tarski showed in this paper that in order to achieve this aim it is sufficient to describe all complete systems, and he illustrated his program in several simple but interesting cases of decidable theories. Many ideas developed in this paper were later incorporated by Tarski in the general theory of models.

SEMANTICS

In the early 1930s Tarski formulated the semantic method, which is his most important achievement in logic. The essence of the method consists in discussion of the relations between expressions and the objects they denote.

Tarski himself says that his semantics is a modest discipline. Yet the philosophical claims of semantics were ambitious from the start. Tarski's aim was "to construct—with reference to a given language—*a materially adequate and formally correct definition of the term 'true sentence,'*" a problem "which belongs to the classical questions of philosophy."

Almost from the beginning the methods of semantics exerted a profound influence on philosophers engaged in the construction and study of exact scientific languages. Semantics opened new possibilities in these studies, which formerly were limited to purely syntactic problems and thus were unable to express relations between languages and extralinguistic objects. Semantics offered a natural tool for the discussion of such relations. The price one had to pay was the use of a much stronger metalanguage than the one sufficient for syntax. At any rate, semantic methods became an accepted tool in the study of scientific languages: "Contemporary studies in the methodology of science are primarily concerned with the syntax and semantics of the language of science" (R. M. Martin, *Truth and Denotation*, Chicago, 1958, p. 16).

Tarski published little concerning the applicability of semantics to the study of empirical languages (see, however, his remarks in "The Semantic Conception of Truth and the Foundations of Semantics"). Rather, he limited himself to applications of his method to logic and mathematics. His most outstanding contributions in these areas will be described briefly.

Interpretations of propositional calculi. The propositional calculus provides us with simple examples of semantic notions. Thus, the two-element Boolean algebra is an interpretation of the calculus; the propositional connectives are interpreted as functions whose arguments and values range over the algebra. We may accordingly conceive of the propositional calculus as a language that describes the two-element algebra. Instead of the two-element algebra we may take any other matrix for the propositional calculus. Thus, a formal calculus may have (and in general does have) many interpretations. Tarski early became acquainted with these notions through his collaboration with Jan Łukasiewicz, who in the 1920s initiated the metatheoretical investigation of propositional calculi. In a joint publication Tarski and Łukasiewicz gave a general set-theoretical definition of a matrix and showed its usefulness in various special problems.

Models. Models play the same role for theories based on (extensions of) the first-order functional calculus as that played by matrices for propositional calculi. If a theory T has as its primitive constants k predicates with $r_1, \cdots, r_k$ arguments, then a model for T is defined as an ordered $k+1$-tuple $\langle A, R_1, \cdots, R_k \rangle$, where R_i is a relation with r_i arguments ranging over A $(i = 1, \cdots, k)$. A model determines a partition of sentences into two sets, one consisting of sentences which are true in the model and the other of sentences which are false in the model. A formula which contains free variables is by itself neither true nor false in the model, but if arbitrary elements of A are correlated with the free variables of the formula, it becomes either true or false. In the first case we say that the elements of A correlated with the free variables satisfy the formula in the model. We have here an analogy with the situation in the propositional calculus: if a matrix is given and if its elements are correlated in an arbitrary way with the free variables of a formula, then the formula has a value which is an element of the matrix. This analogy between models and matrices was stressed in "The Concept of Truth in Formalized Languages," in *Logic, Semantics, Metamathematics,* pp. 152–278. (This is an English translation of an earlier paper.)

The notion of a model and some related semantic notions were known to mathematicians and logicians long before the work of Tarski. No one, however, was concerned to strive for such a degree of precision as Tarski maintained. The fruits of Tarski's approach are first, a precise set-theoretical description of the semantic notions, together with a meticulous discussion of the language in which these definitions are expressible; second, the discovery of general properties of these notions which sometimes are very startling; and third, the discovery of a broad field of applications.

The semantic notions, which before Tarski were used in solving relatively special problems concerning consistency and independence, now turned out to be powerful tools in dealing with many metamathematical investigations. For a philosopher the most important application of the semantic method is Tarski's theory of truth. (For a discussion of this topic, see CORRESPONDENCE THEORY OF TRUTH.)

Logical consequence. Logical consequence is defined as follows: a sentence F is a logical consequence of a set X of sentences if F is true in every model in which all sentences of X are true. For theories based on first-order logic this notion is coextensive with the syntactic notion of derivability (Gödel's completeness theorem). For theories based on the higher-order logics or on the various extensions of first-order logic, these notions are essentially different. Analyzing the intuitions underlying the notion of consequence, one arrives with Tarski at the conclusion that it is the semantic and not the syntactic notion which adequately describes the notion that is intuitively given. At the same time, many logics in which the consequence functions are defined semantically turn out to be free from defects resulting from the incompleteness phenomenon discovered by Gödel. This shows the essential gains brought by the acceptance of the semantically defined notion of logical consequence. What is lost is the finitary ("combinatorial") description of the consequence function.

Definability. Like the notion of consequence, definability can be treated syntactically and semantically. Although investigations in both these directions were pursued in special cases before Tarski, it is only following Tarski's work that we can speak of a systematic theory of definability.

Syntactic theory of definability. Let T be a formal theory among whose constants there is a one-place predicate C. We say that C depends on other constants of T if there is a formula F free of C with exactly one free variable x such that the equivalence $C(x) \equiv F$ is provable in T. In special cases this notion was used long before Tarski; but Tarski was the first to formulate this notion precisely and in the general case, to discuss its properties, and to discover a far-reaching parallelism between the notions of consequence and definability. One of the most interesting results of his theory is a general formulation of a method (due in principle to A. Padoa) allowing one to establish the independence of a constant. Tarski also showed the universality of this method in cases in which the theory under consideration is based on second-order logic or its extensions; the case of theories based on first-order logic was decided much later by E. W. Beth.

Semantic notion of definability. Let M be a model as defined above. A subset S of A is called definable in M if there is a formula F with exactly one free variable such that an element a of A satisfies F in M if and only if a is an element of S. The formula F is called a definition of S in M.

The determination of the class of definable sets is an interesting problem which occupies a central place in investigations concerning the so-called hierarchies of sets. Without going into details, the aim of these investigations is to discuss sets obtainable from simple sets (which constitute the lowest level of the hierarchy) by means of fixed operations which lead to higher and higher levels. Hierarchies of this kind are discussed in mathematics (the Borel and the projective hierarchies) and in metamathematics (the arithmetical, the hyperarithmetical, and the analytic hierarchies). Tarski and Kazimierz Kuratowski in a joint paper described a method which in many cases allows one to infer directly, from the form of definition of a set, to which level of a given hierarchy this set belongs. Their method introduced essential simplifications into the theory of hierarchies.

The importance of these investigations for metamathematics will be clear if we reflect that, for example, Gödel's incompleteness theorem is an obvious corollary of the fact that the set of (numbers of) sentences derivable from the axioms of arithmetic does not belong to the lowest level of the arithmetical hierarchy. Tarski's work on definability is thus closely connected with problems of incompleteness. The most important result in this field is his theorem on truth, which says that under very general assumptions the set of (numbers of) sentences that are true in a model M is not definable in M. Gödel's incompleteness theorem for arithmetic and many related results are immediate corollaries of this theorem ("On Undecidable Statements in Enlarged Systems of Logic and the Concept of Truth," 1.939). Tarski's semantic theorem, however, requires for its formulation as well as for its proof a much stronger logical basis than the syntactic theorem of Gödel.

General theory of models. Notions closely related to models (as defined above) appeared in abstract mathematics independently of the logical investigations. Mathematicians were led to notions of this degree of generality by the development of abstract algebra. Tarski developed these algebraic investigations and tied them to metamathematics.

It is easy to explain the close connections between the general theory of models and the theory of systems. If we consider a theory whose consequence function is defined semantically, then every system is determined by the class of those models in which all sentences of the system are true. Conversely, every model determines a (complete) system consisting of sentences which are true in the model. However, different models may yield one and the same system.

Tarski and his students exploited these relationships especially for the case in which the theory under consideration is based on first-order logic. In this case it is irrelevant whether we accept the semantic or the syntactic notion of consequence, and we thus have the advantage of being able to use on the one hand the connection between systems and models and on the other the various properties of the consequence function that result from its syntactic definition. One of these properties is the so-called compactness of the consequence function, which states that if a set X of sentences is contradictory, then the same is true of a finite subset of X.

In his publications on the theory of models, which date as far back as 1949, Tarski sought to develop the theory in purely mathematical terms and avoided notions current in logic but less so in mathematics. Consequently his papers on the theory of models are more accessible to mathematicians than to logicians. The details of his highly technical works on the theory of models cannot be related here, and we must content ourselves with the brief indications given above. (For further information, see SYSTEMS, FORMAL, AND MODELS OF FORMAL SYSTEMS.)

Generalizations of first-order logic. As was stated earlier, the general setting of model theory is meaningful for theories which are not necessarily based on first-order logic. Tarski suggested two important generalizations of first-order logic and showed that the model-theoretic approach to these logics leads to important discoveries.

The first of these logics is one with infinitely long formulas ("A Sentential Calculus With Infinitely Long Expressions"). Such formulas are, of course, abstract entities definable only in strong systems of set theory; nev-

ertheless, Tarski showed that most of the questions formerly raised exclusively for theories based on ordinary logic are also meaningful for this abstractly described logic. The mathematically important work "Some Problems and Results Relating to the Foundations of Set Theory" resulted from a negative solution of the analogue of the compactness problem ("Some Model-Theoretical Results Concerning Weak Second Order Logic," *Notices of the American Mathematical Society* 5, Abstract 550–6) for logics with infinitely long formulas.

Another important logic introduced by Tarski is weak second-order logic, that is, second-order logic in which the set variables are restricted to finite sets. For this logic as well, the semantic notion of consequence is definable only in a fairly strong system of set theory. Thus weak second-order logic, like the preceding one, is only an abstract construction. Tarski established various metamathematical properties of this logic (for instance, the analogue of the Skolem-Löwenheim theorem) and showed that they imply important mathematical consequences in algebra.

FURTHER CONTRIBUTIONS

Decision problem and undecidable theories. The decision problem for a theory T is the question whether there exists an algorithm allowing one to decide whether a sentence of T is or is not provable in T. Tarski discussed this problem for a large number of theories using the so-called method of the elimination of quantifiers, which originated with Thoralf Skolem ("The Concept of Truth in Formalized Languages," in *Logic, Language, Metamathematics*, p. 204). The most important result in this direction was a positive solution of the problem in the case in which T is the first-order theory of the field of real numbers (*A Decision Method for Elementary Algebra and Geometry*). This result found numerous applications in algebra and geometry.

A theory for which the decision problem does not admit a positive solution is called undecidable. It was related above how Tarski deduced the incompleteness (and hence the undecidability) of arithmetic from his general theorem. His further efforts were directed toward establishing the undecidability of various very weak but mathematically interesting theories. To this end he introduced the important notion of essential undecidability. A theory is said to be essentially undecidable if all consistent extensions of it are undecidable. Tarski showed in *Undecidable Theories* (1953) that a theory which has a joint consistent extension with an essentially undecidable theory based on a finite number of axioms is itself undecidable, although in general not essentially undecidable. This theorem provided a basis for numerous undecidability results obtained partly by Tarski and partly by his collaborators.

Intuitionist and modal logics. Of the numerous papers that Tarski devoted to the propositional calculus, only those on the intuitionistic and modal propositional calculi can be mentioned here. In "Sentential Calculus and Topology" (*Logic, Semantics, Metamathematics*, pp. 421–454) he established a startling connection between intuitionistic logic and topology: he constructed matrices for the intuitionistic propositional calculus, using as elements closed subsets of a topological space. In his further work on this calculus, done jointly with J. C. C. McKinsey, he no longer used topological notions but worked instead with certain algebraic structures. The class of all subsets of a topological space and the class of all closed subsets of such a space are examples of such structures, which Tarski and McKinsey called closure algebras and Brouwerian algebras respectively. Using them, they established several properties of the intuitionistic and modal propositional logics.

Cylindric algebras. The above papers give a good illustration of Tarski's growing tendency to deal with metamathematical problems by means of algebraic tools. Another example is his work on cylindric algebras. These algebraic structures are related to the predicate calculus with identity in the way Boolean algebras are related to the usual propositional calculus. Logics with infinitely long expressions can also be investigated by means of suitable cylindric algebras.

Calculus of binary relations. The calculus of binary relations was created by Ernst Schröder but soon fell into oblivion. Tarski gave axioms for this calculus, investigated its relations to the predicate calculus, and initiated extensive work on the models of his axioms. Of the several applications of the calculus found by Tarski, the axiomatization of set theory without variables, the existence of undecidable subsystems of the two-valued propositional calculus, and a general method of reduction of the number of primitive terms of a theory should be mentioned.

PHILOSOPHY

In the rich bibliography of Tarski's publications there are almost no philosophical papers. The exceptions are "The Establishment of Scientific Semantics" and "The Semantic Conception of Truth and the Foundations of Semantics," which deal with the philosophical significance of semantics. A partial exception is Tarski's paper on the notion of truth (in *Logic, Semantics, Metamathematics*, pp. 153–278), although the bulk of it is devoted to a systematic exposition of semantics.

Tarski, in oral discussions, has often indicated his sympathies with nominalism. While he never accepted the "reism" of Tadeusz Kotarbiński, he was certainly attracted to it in the early phase of his work. However, the set-theoretical methods that form the basis of his logical and mathematical studies compel him constantly to use the abstract and general notions that a nominalist seeks to avoid. In the absence of more extensive publications by Tarski on philosophical subjects, this conflict appears to have remained unresolved.

Bibliography

Tarski's scientific writings consist of more than one hundred articles and books, plus many abstracts and reviews. Among these the most important for logic and philosophy are the following:

"Sur les truth-functions au sens de MM. Russell et Whitehead." *Fundamenta Mathematicae*, Vol. 5 (1924), 59–74.

"Grundzüge des Systemenkalküls." *Fundamenta Mathematicae*, Vol. 25 (1935), 503.

"Der Wahrheitsbegriff in den formalisierten Sprachen." *Studia Philosophica*, Vol. 1 (1935/1936), 261–405.

"Über unerreichbare Kardinalzahlen." *Fundamenta Mathematicae*, Vol. 30 (1938), 68–89.

"On Undecidable Statements in Enlarged Systems of Logic and the Concept of Truth." *Journal of Symbolic Logic*, Vol. 4 (1939), 105–112.

"On the Calculus of Relations." *Journal of Symbolic Logic*, Vol. 6 (1941), 73–89.

"The Semantic Conception of Truth and the Foundations of Semantics." *Journal of Philosophy and Phenomenological Research*, Vol. 4 (1944), 341–375. Reprinted in H. Feigl and W. Sellars, eds., *Readings in Philosophical Analysis*. New York, 1949. Pp. 52–84.

"On Closed Elements in Closure Algebras." *Annals of Mathematics*, Vol. 45 (1944), 141–191, and Vol. 47 (1946), 122–162. Written with J. C. C. McKinsey, with remarks by Tarski, 163–165.

"Some Theorems About the Sentential Calculi of Lewis and Heyting." *Journal of Symbolic Logic*, Vol. 13 (1948), 1–15. Written with J. C. C. McKinsey.

"Some Notions and Methods on the Borderline of Algebra and Metamathematics," in *Proceedings of the International Congress of Mathematicians*. Cambridge, Mass., 1950. Pp. 705–720.

A Decision Method for Elementary Algebra and Geometry. Santa Monica, Calif., 1948; 2d ed., Berkeley and Los Angeles, 1951.

Undecidable Theories. Amsterdam, 1953. Written with A. Mostowski and R. M. Robinson.

Logic, Semantics, Metamathematics. Oxford, 1956. Tarski's papers on logic from 1923 to 1938, collected and translated by J. H. Woodger.

"A Sentential Calculus With Infinitely Long Expressions." *Colloquium Mathematicum*, Vol. 6 (1958), 165–170. Written with Dana Scott. Remarks by Tarski, 171–176.

"Cylindric Algebras," in *Proceedings of Symposia in Pure Mathematics: II Lattice Theory*. Providence, R.I., 1961. Pp. 83–113. Written with Leon Henkin.

"Some Problems and Results Relating to the Foundations of Set Theory," in *Proceedings of the 1960 Congress on Logic, Methodology, and Philosophy of Science*. Palo Alto, Calif., 1962. Pp. 125–135.

"From Accessible to Inaccessible Cardinals." *Fundamenta Mathematicae*, Vol. 53 (1964), 225–308. Written with H. J. Keisler.

ANDRZEJ MOSTOWSKI

TAULER, JOHANNES (c. 1300–1361), German mystic. About the age of 15, he entered the Dominican order at Strasbourg and probably studied in the Dominican *studium generale* at Cologne, where he may have been taught by Meister Eckhart. He was certainly influenced by the latter and by the contemplative movement known as the *Gottesfreunde* ("Friends of God"). He was in Strasbourg at the time of Pope Innocent XXII's interdict on the city for taking the wrong side in the war between different sections of the Holy Roman Empire, but there is no good evidence for the story that during the Black Death he defied the interdict by administering sacraments to the dying. He remained a loyal and orthodox member of the church. Much legendary material surrounds his life, and various spurious works are attributed to him. It was on the basis of these sources that some earlier scholars mistakenly thought of Tauler as a precursor of the Reformation.

In his sermons, Tauler geared mystical teachings, which made use of Eckhartian and Neoplatonic concepts, to practical purposes. He was deeply committed to the view that mystical experiences are a nourishment to the soul in supporting the individual in a life of active love and that there are behavioral criteria for estimating their worth. He believed that in this active life we may possess God through a fusion of the divine and human wills. However, far from reducing contemplative religion to the exercise of good works, Tauler believed that the love of God and the love of men go together and that the former finds its consummation in the inner union of the soul with the Creator.

In principle, all men should be capable of this return of the soul to its Source (the notion of return was typical of the Neoplatonic tradition with which Tauler was acquainted). Two qualifications, however, must be made. First, the way of return, according to Tauler's account, involves great heroism and suffering. The creaturely side of man must be crucified. Self-mortification is a sign of burning love of God, and eventually the friend of God may acquire a real desire for, rather than an aversion to, suffering. In this emphasis on suffering, Tauler was strongly Christocentric in his preaching. But second, the fall of man has so tainted the human being that the divine light, which illuminates the contemplative and brings about the return to God, is something that man cannot achieve on his own. It is the gift of divine grace. Thus, the culmination of the mystic's quest is not a personal achievement of the mystic, but an enjoyment granted from beyond.

The importance of the need for grace gave Tauler's mysticism a firmly orthodox character. Nevertheless, he maintained that the operation of divine grace requires a right attitude on the part of men. Tauler speaks of God as a fisherman who lets down a baited hook into the ocean. Those fish who are not disposed toward the bait will not be hooked. This simile had its basis in Tauler's account of human psychology.

According to his psychology, three aspects of the soul can be distinguished. At the deepest level is the Ground of the soul—otherwise referred to as the Spark, the Apex (*Punkt*), and God in the soul—a concept deriving from Eckhart's teaching. However, Tauler is eager to assert that the Ground is God-given and is not an intrinsic, natural property of the individual. At another level, the soul possesses intellect, sense faculties, and will. Third, there is what Tauler refers to as the heart (*das Gemüt*). The attitude of the individual toward the divine Being is determined by whether his heart is turned toward the Ground or away from it. If the former, God will descend, draw the spirit up to himself, and unite it with him. Man's choice is therefore essentially a choice of disposition. Once this choice has been made, God through his grace will conform the human will to his own. Thus, the end of the contemplative life is a state in which the mystic is, so to speak, "taken over" by God, so that all his actions express God's purposes rather than his own.

Bibliography

Tauler's works include *Twenty-five Sermons*, translated by Susanna Winkworth, 2d ed. (London, 1906); *The Sermons and Conferences of John Tauler*, edited and translated by Walter Elliott (Washington, 1910); *Die Predigten Taulers*, F. Vetter, ed. (Berlin, 1910); and *Johannes Tauler—Predigten*, G. Hofmann, ed. (Freiburg, 1961).
See also J. M. Clark, *The Great German Mystics* (Oxford, 1949).

NINIAN SMART

TAUTOLOGY. LINGUISTIC THEORY OF THE A PRIORI; LOGIC, MODERN; LOGICAL TERMS, GLOSSARY OF.

TAYLOR, ALFRED EDWARD (1869–1945), British philosopher, was born at Oundle, Northamptonshire, and educated at New College, Oxford. His teaching experience was unusually varied: he was a fellow of Merton College, Oxford, 1891–1898; lecturer at Owens College, Manchester, 1898–1903; professor of logic and metaphysics at McGill University, Montreal, 1903–1908; professor of moral philosophy at St. Andrews University, 1908–1924; and professor of moral philosophy at Edinburgh, 1924–1941. His interests were also varied; not only was he an authority on Greek philosophy but he also made extensive contributions to current thinking on ethics, metaphysics, and the philosophy of religion. Taylor's thought was within the tradition of British Neo-Hegelianism, but as his philosophy developed, other influences came in also, though he remained firmly attached to a theistic and spiritualist interpretation of reality.

In the field of Greek philosophy, Taylor is noted chiefly for his work on Plato. He gives a full-scale exposition of Plato's thought in *Plato: The Man and His Work* (London, 1926) and a detailed study of Plato's cosmology in *A Commentary on Plato's Timaeus* (Oxford, 1928). Even in these works Taylor's own philosophical interests assert themselves, notably in his attempt to minimize alleged differences between the Platonic and Biblical ways of understanding creation and in his contention that the Demiurge of Plato is a creator in the full sense of the word.

Taylor's philosophy found early expression in *The Problem of Conduct* (London, 1901) and in *Elements of Metaphysics* (London, 1903). At this stage he was influenced primarily by F. H. Bradley and English idealism. Later, Platonism, Thomism, and even Bergsonism became important additional influences on his mature thought as expressed in *The Faith of a Moralist* (London, 1930), a work based on his Gifford lectures of 1926–1928.

Here Taylor claims that if we take moral experience seriously, we must recognize that it points beyond itself to, and is completed in, religion and that we are thus led to theism. Moral experience does deserve to be taken seriously, for facts and values are given together and never occur in separation in our concrete experience of the world. A naturalistic philosophy that allows reality to fact but denies it to value is guilty of a false abstraction. This argument about the concreteness of experience is a necessary prolegomenon to Taylor's position as a whole, for if the values of the moral life were divorced from the facts of the world, then no argument from moral experience to the nature of reality could succeed.

Taylor's attempt to move from the facts of moral experience to a religious metaphysic turns on two main considerations. The first concerns the nature of the good at which the moral life aims. Is it a temporal good or is it an eternal good? Taylor contends that even to be able to ask this question and to be aware of the temporal dimension of our existence is to have begun to transcend the form of temporality. Further reflection shows that no merely temporal goods can satisfy the demands of man's nature. Such goods are defective in various ways; for instance, they can be attained only successively and cannot be enjoyed simultaneously. One might answer, of course, that this merely shows that human aspirations are doomed to frustration, but Taylor rejects this and claims that the facts of moral striving point to an eternal good.

The second consideration concerns the question of how such an eternal good is to be attained. Can man of himself attain to an eternal good? Taylor answers in the negative, for he sees sin and guilt as inhibiting the moral life and preventing man from reaching his goal. But again he does not accept this frustration as final. Man's unavailing endeavors to reach toward the eternal good are met by what Taylor calls the initiative of the eternal. This is the divine grace that reaches down to man and enables his moral fulfillment. Thus, the moral life finds its completion in religion; if we deny this, we are bound to say that the moral life is self-stultifying. To take its demands seriously is to believe that it makes sense, and according to Taylor, it makes sense only in the light of a theistic world view.

The individual destined for an eternal good and enabled by divine grace to move toward that good is also assured of immortality. Hence, from consideration of the implications of the moral life alone we arrive at a kind of minimal theology, so to speak, of God, grace, and immortality. But Taylor, who was himself a devout churchman of the Anglican communion, asks whether this minimal theology does not, like morality, point beyond itself for completion. The concreteness that characterizes Taylor's starting point is apparent again in his conclusions, as he argues that a bare philosophical theism needs to be embodied in an actual historical religion. Although the philosopher does not appeal to revelation, his analysis can, Taylor believed, bring us to the point at which we see the need for a concrete revelation to complete the bare schema of philosophical theology. Philosophy makes it reasonable to expect that there would be such a revelation, and Taylor thinks that Christian revelation especially fulfills this expectation. He continued to wrestle with the problems of religion, which provide the themes for two of his last books, *The Christian Hope of Immortality* (London, 1938) and *Does God Exist?* (London, 1943).

Bibliography

Additional works by Taylor are *Varia Socratica* (Oxford, 1911); *The Laws of Plato* (London, 1934); *Philosophical Studies* (London, 1934); and *Aristotle* (Edinburgh, 1943).

W. D. Ross, "Alfred Edward Taylor, 1869–1945," in *Proceedings of the British Academy*, Vol. 31 (1945), 407–424, contains a bibliography of Taylor's writings.

JOHN MACQUARRIE

TEILHARD DE CHARDIN, PIERRE (1881–1955), paleoanthropologist and Roman Catholic priest who advocated a doctrine of cosmic evolution, was born in Sarcenat, France. At the age of 18 he entered the Jesuit order and remained a faithful member of it for the rest of his life. By the time he was ordained, his interest in science and the reading of Bergson resulted in his becoming a fervent evolutionist. Association with the Bergsonian scholar Édouard Le Roy also deeply influenced his thought. It became one of Teilhard's aims to show that evolutionism does not entail a rejection of Christianity. He likewise sought to convince the church that it can and should accept the implications of the revolution begun by Darwin, but he met with uniform opposition from ecclesiastical superiors.

In 1926 he was expelled from the Catholic Institute in Paris, at which he had taught after returning from service in World War I. Until 1946 he was "exiled" in China, where he participated in paleontological researches which led to the discovery of Peking man. He also completed the manuscript of his major work, *Le Phénomène humain* (*The Phenomenon of Man*); but despite repeated applications to Rome he was refused permission to publish it. After his death the appearance of the work, along with his other essays, gave rise to controversies both inside and outside the church.

The evolutionism that Teilhard advocated is all-embracing and characterizes much more than living things. Teilhard contended that long before living things appeared on the earth, the basic stuff of the cosmos was undergoing irreversible changes in the direction of greater complexity of organization. Hence, nonliving nature is profoundly historical. It is not a system of stable elements in a closed equilibrium. On the contrary, it conforms at all stages to a "law of complexification," comparable in importance to the law of gravity and illustrated by the vast array of organic forms which have appeared in evolutionary history. The most recent of these forms is man.

When viewed "from without" by the physical sciences, man is a material system in the midst of other material systems. But each individual man experiences himself "from within" as a conscious being. Consciousness is thus directly identifiable as "spiritual energy." Teilhard maintained that *all* constituents of the cosmos, from elementary particles to human beings, have "a conscious inner face that everywhere duplicates the material external face." Since this is so, the physical evolution of the cosmic stuff will at the same time be an evolution of consciousness. The more highly integrated a material system, the more developed its psychical interior will be. Thus, in the human brain an intense concentration, or "involution," of cells has led to the emergence of self-conscious thought, the most advanced stage reached by evolution thus far.

But greater developments are in store from the evolutionary convergence of disparate cultures and forms of consciousness. Man is now a single, interbreeding species expanding on the finite, spherical surface of the planet and still showing signs of biological immaturity. Furthermore, his capacity for self-conscious thought and the production of cultures has added a new "layer" to the earth's surface, which Teilhard calls the "noosphere," distinct from, yet superimposed on, the biosphere. The noosphere, or "thinking layer," forms the unique environment of man, marking him off from all other animals. The evolutionary convergence which it makes possible will be manifested externally in the unification of all human cultures into a single world culture. Paralleling this, a movement toward psychical concentration will occur, so that the noosphere will become involuted in a Hyperpersonal Consciousness "at a point which we might call *Omega*." Here evolution will reach the terminal phase of convergent integration.

Teilhard's concept of Point Omega is obscure, like other aspects of his evolutionism, because it is essentially the expression of a mystical vision. Omega is not identical with God but, rather, is God insofar as he determines the direction and goal of cosmic history. Hence, the evolutionary process is orthogenetic, although neither vitalistic nor wholly devoid of chance events. The integration of all personal consciousnesses at Omega will be achieved, Teilhard urged, through love, which forms *le Milieu divin,* the spirit of Christ at work in nature.

Teilhard's doctrine tends to become pantheistic in certain of its formulations. On the whole, it is difficult to reconcile Teilhard's views either with orthodox Christian teaching or with a scientific theory of evolution. Yet the prose poetry of *The Phenomenon of Man* has stirred the imagination of theologians, philosophers, and scientists, even when it has not won their assent.

Works by Teilhard de Chardin

Oeuvres, 9 vols. Paris, 1955——. Ten volumes are projected.
Le Phénomène humain. Paris, 1955. Translated by Bernard Wall as *The Phenomenon of Man.* New York, 1959.
Lettres de voyage. Paris, 1956. Translated by René Hague and others as *Letters From a Traveller.* London, 1962.
Le Milieu divin. Paris, 1957. Translated by Bernard Wall and others as *The Realm of the Divine.* New York, 1960.
L'Avenir de l'homme. Paris, 1959. Translated by Norman Denny as *The Future of Man.* New York, 1964.
Hymne de l'univers. Paris, 1964. Translated by Simon Bartholemew as *Hymn of the Universe.* London, 1965.

Works on Teilhard de Chardin

Cuénot, Claude, *Pierre Teilhard de Chardin, les grandes étapes de son évolution.* Paris, 1958. Translated by Vincent Colimore and edited by René Hague as *Teilhard de Chardin: A Biographical Study.* Baltimore, 1965.
Francoeur, R. T., ed., *The World of Teilhard.* Baltimore, 1961.
Raven, C. E., *Teilhard de Chardin: Scientist and Seer.* London, 1962.
Tresmontant, C., *Pierre Teilhard de Chardin, His Thought.* Baltimore, 1959.

T. A. GOUDGE

TELEOLOGICAL ARGUMENT FOR THE EXISTENCE OF GOD. The Teleological Argument for the existence of God is a member of the classic triad of arguments, which is completed by the Ontological Argument and the Cosmological Argument. Stated most succinctly, it runs:

The world exhibits teleological order (design, adaptation).

Therefore, it was produced by an intelligent designer.

To understand this argument, we must first understand what teleological order is.

Teleological order. Generally speaking, to say that a group of elements is ordered in a certain way is to say that they are interrelated so as to form a definite pattern, but the notion of a definite pattern is vague. Any set of elements is interrelated in one way rather than another, and any complex of interrelations might be construed by someone as a definite pattern. Certain patterns are of special interest for one reason or another, and when one of these is exhibited, the complex would ordinarily be said to be ordered. Thus, when the elements form a pattern in whose perception we take intrinsic delight, we can speak of aesthetic order. When there are discernible regularities in the way, certain elements occur in spatiotemporal proximity, we can speak of causal order. The distinctive thing about teleological (Greek, *telos,* "end" or "goal") order is that it introduces the notion of processes and structures being fitted to bring about a certain result.

The usual illustrations of teleological order are from living organisms. It is a common observation that the anatomical structures and instinctive activities of animals are often nicely suited to the fulfillment of their needs. For example, the ears of pursuing, carnivorous animals, like the dog and the wolf, face forward so as to focus sounds from their quarry, while the ears of pursued, herbivorous animals, like the rabbit and the deer, face backward so as to focus sounds from their pursuers.

Examples of instinctive behavior are even more striking. The burying beetle deposits its eggs on the carcass of a small animal and then covers the whole "melange" with dirt to protect it until the young hatch out and find an ample supply of (hardly fresh) meat at hand.

If we are going to distinguish teleological order from causal order, we shall have to make explicit the tacit assumption that the result which the structure or process in question is fitted to bring about is of value. Otherwise, *any* cause–effect relationship would be a case of teleological order. It is just as true to say that wind is fitted to produce the result of moving loose dirt into the air as it is to say that the mechanism of the eye is fitted to produce sight. The latter would be counted as an example of "design," whereas the former would not, because we regard sight as something worth having, whereas the movement of dirt through the air is not generally of any value. This has the important implication that insofar as it is impossible to give an objective criterion of value, it will not be an objective matter of fact that teleological order is or is not exhibited in a given state of affairs.

It is important to note that the term "design," as used in this argument, does not by definition imply a designer. If it did, there could be no argument *from* design to the existence of God; we would have to know that the phenomena in question were the work of a designer before we could call them cases of design. We must define "design" in such a way as to leave open the question of its source. We have design in the required sense when things are so ordered that they tend to perform a valuable function. We might put this by saying that things are ordered as they would be if some conscious being had designed them, but in saying this we are not committing ourselves to the proposition that a mind *has* designed them. The equivalent terms "adaptation" and "teleological order" are not so liable to mislead in this way.

Arguments for the existence of God have been based on kinds of order other than the teleological. Exhortations to move from a consideration of the starry heavens to belief in God constitute an appeal to aesthetic order. It is sometimes claimed that we must postulate an intelligent creator to explain the regularity with which the solar system operates. Here it is causal order which is involved. Arguments like these are often not clearly distinguished from those based on teleological order, to which we shall confine our attention.

Arguments from particular cases of design. The simplest form of the argument is that in which we begin with particular cases of design and argue that they can be adequately explained only by supposing that they were produced by an intelligent being. Thus William Paley, an eighteenth-century philosopher, in a classic formulation of the argument concentrated on the human eye as a case of design, stressing the ways in which various parts of the eye cooperate in a complex way to produce sight. He argued that we can explain this adaptation of means to end only if we postulate a supernatural designer. This is the heart of the teleological argument—the claim that adaptation can be explained only in terms of a designer. It always rests, more or less explicitly, on an analogy with human artifacts. Thus, Paley compared the eye to a watch and argued as follows: If one were to find a watch on a desert island, one would be justified in supposing that it was produced by an intelligent being. By the same token (the adjustment of means to ends) one is entitled, upon examination of the human eye, to conclude that it was produced by an intelligent being.

If it is asked why we should take artifacts as our model, the answer would seem to be this. Artifacts are certainly cases of design. In a watch, for example, the structure is well suited to the performance of a valuable function: showing the time. With artifacts, unlike natural examples of design, we have some insight into what is responsible for the adjustment of means to end. We can understand it because we can see how this adjustment springs from the creative activity of the maker, guided by his deliberate intention to make the object capable of performing this function. Hence, in natural cases of adaptation where the source of the adaptiveness is not obvious, we have no recourse but to employ the only way we know of rendering such phenomena intelligible—supposing them to stem from conscious planning. Since we do not observe any planner at work, we must postulate an invisible planner behind the scenes.

Criticisms. The comparison to artifacts was attacked by David Hume in his *Dialogues Concerning Natural Religion,* in which he suggested that the production of artifacts by human planning is no more inherently intelligible than the production of organisms by biological generation. Why, asked Hume, should we take the former rather than the latter as the model for the creation of the world? Even if we admit that the world exhibits design, why are we not as justified in supposing that the world was generated from the sexual union of two parent worlds as in supposing that it was created by a mind in accordance with a plan? In answer to Hume it might be argued that creation gives a more satisfactory and a more complete explanation than generation because the generation consists of a reproduction of the same kind of thing and hence introduces another entity that raises exactly the same kind of question. If we are initially puzzled as to why a rabbit has organs that are so well adapted to the satisfaction of its needs, it does not help to be told that it is because the rabbit sprang from other rabbits with just the same adaptive features. If, on the other hand, we could see that the rabbit had been deliberately constructed in this way so that its needs would be satisfied, we would be making progress. To this Hume would reply that the mind of the designer also requires explanation. Why should the designer have a mind that is so well fitted for designing? Thus, this explanation also leaves problems dangling, but at least it is not just the same problem. If we were to reject every explanation that raised fresh problems, we would have to reject all of science.

Darwinian theory of evolution. The development of the Darwinian theory of evolution opened up the possibility of a more serious alternative to the theistic explanation. According to this theory, the organic structures of today developed from much simpler organisms by purely natural processes. In this theory (as developed since Darwin) two factors are considered to play the major role: mutations and overpopulation. (A mutation occurs when an offspring differs from its parents in such a way that it will pass this difference along to its offspring, and they will pass it along, and so on. It is a relatively permanent genetic change.)

The way these factors are thought to work can be illustrated by taking one of the cases of adaptation cited above. If we go back far enough in the ancestry of the dog, we will discover ancestors that did not have ears facing forward. Now let us suppose that a mutation occurred which consisted of an ear turned somewhat more forward than had been normal. Granting that organisms tend to reproduce in greater numbers than the environment can support, and hence that there is considerable competition for the available food supply, it follows that any feature of a given organism that gives it any advantage over its fellows in getting food or in avoiding becoming prey will make it more likely to survive and pass along its peculiarity to its offspring. Thus, within a number of generations we can expect the front-turned-ear proto-dogs to replace the others and be left in sole possession of the field. Since mutations do occur from time to time, and since some of them are favorable, we have a set of purely natural factors by whose operation the organic world can be continuously transformed in the direction of greater and greater adaptation.

The Darwinian theory aspires to do no more than explain how more complex organisms develop from less complex organisms. It has nothing to say about the origins of the simplest organisms. However, no matter how simple the organism, its structure must be fitted to the satisfaction of its needs, or it will not survive. Therefore, Darwinian theory is not a complete explanation of the existence of teleological order in the world; it merely tells us how some cases develop from other cases. Hence, it alone is not an alternative to the theistic explanation, but in principle there is no reason why it should not be supplemented by a biochemical theory of the origin of life from lifeless matter. No such theory has yet been completely established, but progress is being made. When and if this is done, there will be an explanation of design in living organisms for which there is empirical support, and it can no longer be claimed that theism represents the only real explanation of such facts.

What follows from the argument. The other major deficiency in Paley's form of the argument is that, even if valid, it does not go very far toward proving the existence of a theistic God. The most we are warranted in concluding is that each case of design in the natural world is due to the activity of an intelligent designer. Nothing is done to show that all cases of design are due to one and the same designer; the argument is quite compatible with polytheism or polydaemonism, in which we would have one supernatural designer for flies, another for fish, and so on. Even if there is one, and only one, designer, nothing is done to show that this being is predominantly good rather than evil; neither is anything done to show that he is infinitely powerful or wise, rather than limited in these qualities. Of course the theist might seek to supplement this argument by others, but by itself it will not bear the weight.

Argument from the universe as a whole. No argument that, like the Teleological Argument, is designed to show that facts in nature require a certain explanation, can establish the existence of a deity absolutely unlimited in power, knowledge, or any other respect. By such reasoning we can infer no more in the cause than is required to produce the effect. This deficiency is irremediable. However, there is a simple way of eliminating competing scientific claims—by starting from the universe as a whole rather than from individual instances of design within the universe. There are different ways of doing this. We might think of the whole universe as instrumental to some supreme goal, or we might think of the universe as a unified system of mutually adjusted and mutually supporting adaptive structures.

Taking the whole universe as instrumental to some supreme goal would give us the strongest argument, for here the analogy with consciously designed artifacts is strongest. An artifact like a house, ship, or watch is designed for the realization of goals outside its internal functioning; it is intended to be used for something. Therefore, if the analogy with artifacts is the main support for the notion that the universe was the result of conscious planning, that support would be firmest if grounds were presented for thinking that the universe as a whole was well fitted to be used for something. And if this something were of maximum value, we would then have a basis for attributing supreme goodness to the designer.

However, this alternative is rarely taken, largely because it is difficult to decide on a suitable candidate for, in Tennyson's words, the "far-off divine event, toward which the whole creation moves." The most common suggestions are the greater glory of God and the development of moral personality. But in regard to the first, no one can really understand just what it would mean for a God who is eternally perfect to receive greater glory, and in regard to the second, even if we can overcome doubts that moral development is worth the entire cosmic process, it would seem impossible ever to get adequate grounds for the proposition that everything that takes place throughout all space and time contributes to this development.

The second interpretation, that the universe is a unified system of mutually adjusted and mutually supporting adaptive structures—has been tried more often. So conceived, the argument will run as follows.

(1) The world is a unified system of adaptations.

(2) We can give an intelligible explanation of this fact only by supposing that the world was created by an intelligent being according to some plan.

(3) Therefore, it is reasonable to suppose that the world was created by an intelligent being.

The famous formulation of the argument in Hume's *Dialogues* makes explicit the analogy on which, as we have seen, step two depends. Hume's formulation, which is substantially equivalent to the above, runs as follows.

(1) The world is like a machine.

(2) Machines are made by human beings, in accordance with plans.

(3) Like effects have like causes.

(4) Therefore, the world probably owes its existence to something like a human being, who operates in accordance with a plan.

Types of adaptation. If one is to think of the whole universe as a system of connected adaptations, he will consider kinds of adaptation other than that exemplified by the fitness of organisms to the conditions of life; this kind alone will not bear the whole weight. F. R. Tennant, who has developed the weightiest recent presentation of the teleological argument in his *Philosophical Theology*, discusses six kinds of adaptation:

(1) The intelligibility of the world. The world and the human mind are so related that we can learn more and more without limit.

(2) The adaptation of living organisms to their environments. This is the kind on which we have been concentrating.

(3) The ways in which the inorganic world is conducive to the emergence and maintenance of life. Life is possible only because temperatures do not exceed certain limits, certain kinds of chemical processes go on, etc.

(4) The aesthetic value of nature. Nature is not only suited to penetration by the intellect; it is also constituted so as to awaken valuable aesthetic responses in man.

(5) The ways in which the world ministers to the moral life of men. For example, through being forced to learn something about the uniformities in natural operations, men are forced to develop their intelligence, a prerequisite to moral development. And moral virtues are acquired in the course of having to cope with the hardships of one's natural environment.

(6) The over-all progressiveness of the evolutionary process.

Tennant admits that no one of these forms of adaptiveness is a sufficient ground for the theistic hypothesis, but he maintains that when we consider the ways in which they dovetail, we will see theism to be the most reasonable interpretation. Thus, the adjustment of lower organisms to the environment takes on added significance when it is seen as a stage in an evolutionary process culminating in man, which in turn is seen to be more striking when we realize the ways in which nature makes possible the further development of the moral, intellectual, and aesthetic life of man.

When the argument takes this form, it is no longer subject to competition from scientific explanations of the same facts. If our basic datum is a certain configuration of the universe as a whole, science can, by the nature of the case, offer no explanation. Science tries to find regularities in the association of different parts, stages, or aspects within the physical universe. On questions as to why the universe as a whole exists, or exists in one form rather than another, it is silent. Ultimately this is because science is committed to the consideration of questions that can be investigated empirically. One can use observation to determine whether two conditions within the universe are regularly associated (increase of temperature and boiling), but there is no way to observe connections between the physical universe as a whole and something outside it. Therefore, there is no scientific alternative to the theistic answer to the question "Why is the universe a unified system of adaptations?"

Alternative explanations of adaptation. What alternatives to the theistic explanation of adaptation are there? In the literature on the subject one often encounters the suggestion that we have this kind of universe by chance. If we dismiss the animistic notion of chance as a mysterious agent, the suggestion that we have this kind of universe by chance boils down to a refusal to take the question seriously. It may be said that the fact that the universe as a whole exhibits teleological order is not the sort of thing that requires explanation. It is difficult to see what justification could be given for this statement other than an appeal to the principle that sense observation is the only source of knowledge and/or meaning.

One cannot perceive by the senses any relation between the physical universe as a whole, or any feature thereof, and something outside it on which it depends. Hence, an extreme form of empiricism would brand the question posed by the Teleological Argument as fruitless or even meaningless. If, on the other hand, the question is taken seriously, any answer will be as metaphysical as the theistic answer, for it is really a question as to what characteristics are to be attributed to the cause (or causes) of the universe. Do the relevant facts about the world most strongly support the theistic position that the cause is a perfectly good personal being who created the universe in the carrying out of a good purpose? Or is there some other view that is equally, or more strongly, supported by the evidence? The Manichaeans held that the physical universe was the work of a malevolent deity and that man must separate himself from the body in order to escape this diabolical power and come into contact with the purely spiritual benevolent deity. It has also been held in many religions that the universe is the joint product of two or more deities who differ markedly in their characteristics. In Zoroastrianism it is held that the world is the battleground of a good deity and an evil deity, the actual state of affairs bearing traces of both. Indian religious philosophy typically regards the universe as resulting from a nonpurposive manifestation of, or emanation from, an absolute unity that is not personal in any strict sense.

Extent of adaptiveness in the universe. To evaluate the Teleological Argument in the light of competing explanations, we must ask whether the extent of adaptiveness in the universe is sufficient to warrant the theistic conclusion. As the problem is formulated in Hume's *Dialogues,* is there a close enough analogy between the universe and a machine? This requires judging the relative proportion of adaptive features to nonadaptive or maladaptive features. In addition to taking account of Tennant's enumeration of the ways in which the shape of things is instrumental to

the realization of valuable ends, we must look at the other side of the picture and try to form an adequate impression of (1) the ways in which the shape of things is neutral, providing neither for good nor for evil, and (2) the ways in which the shape of things frustrates the search for value.

As for (1), as far as we can see, the distribution of matter and the variety of chemical elements in the world, to take two examples at random, could have been very different from what they are without reducing the chances of sentient beings leading satisfying lives.

As for (2), we begin to trespass onto the problem of evil, except that here we are interested in suffering and frustration not as possible disproofs of theism but as affecting the cogency of the Teleological Argument for the existence of God. There are many ways in which the organization of the world makes for disvalue rather than value in the lives of men and other sentient creatures. One need only mention the numerous sources of disease, the incidence of malformed offspring, the difficulty of attaining optimum conditions for the development of healthy personalities, and the importance of antisocial tendencies in human nature. It is quite possible, of course, that all the things which seem to be unfortunate features of the world as it exists are necessary elements in the best of all possible worlds (see EVIL, THE PROBLEM OF). If we already believe that the world is the creation of a perfect deity, that carries with it the belief that these apparent evils are necessary even though we cannot see how they are. However, if we are trying to establish the existence of a perfect deity, we have to proceed on the basis of what we can see. And since, so far as we can see, the world would be better if the features listed above were altered, we cannot argue that the state of adaptiveness in the world requires explanation in terms of a perfectly good, omnipotent deity. But we have already seen, on other grounds, that the Teleological Argument cannot be used to establish the existence of a being unlimited in any respect.

The serious problem that remains is whether the total picture of adaptation and maladaptation, so far as we have it, gives sufficient support to the hypothesis that the world represents the at least partial implementation of a plan that is at least predominantly good. To resolve this problem we must weigh opposite factors and arrive at a final judgment of their relative importance. Unfortunately there are no real guidelines for this task. No one knows how much adaptation, relative to maladaptation, would warrant such a conclusion; and even if he did, he would not know what units to employ to perform the measurement. What is to count as one unit of adaptation? Do we count each individual separately, or is each species one unit? How can we compare the value of human knowledge with the disvalue of disease? It would seem that on this issue different positions will continue to be taken on the basis of factors outside the evidence itself.

(For the history of the Teleological Argument, see PHYSICOTHEOLOGY.)

Bibliography

In the Middle Ages there was general acceptance of an Aristotelian physics, according to which even purely physical processes were explained in terms of the natural tendency of a body toward an end. (Fire naturally tends to come to rest at the periphery of the universe.) Given this background, it was argued that the consideration of any natural processes led to the postulation of a designer. The argument in this form is found in Thomas Aquinas, *Summa Theologica*, Part I, Question 2, Article 3. Contemporary Thomistic statements try to adjust this line of thought to modern physics. See G. H. Joyce, *The Principles of Natural Theology* (New York, 1951); Réginald Garrigou-Lagrange, *God, His Existence and His Nature*, 2 vols. (St. Louis, 1934–1936); and D. J. B. Hawkins, *The Essentials of Theism* (New York, 1949).

The influential presentation by the eighteenth-century thinker William Paley is to be found in his *Natural Theology: Or, Evidences of the Existence and Attributes of the Deity, Collected from the Appearances of Nature* (Indianapolis, 1964). Important recent formulations include F. R. Tennant, *Philosophical Theology,* 2 vols. (New York, 1928–1930), Vol. II, Ch. 4, and A. E. Taylor, *Does God Exist?* (New York, 1947).

Acute criticisms of the argument are to be found in David Hume, *Dialogues Concerning Natural Religion;* Immanuel Kant, *Critique of Pure Reason*, Book II, Ch. 3; C. D. Broad, *Religion, Philosophy, and Psychical Research* (London and New York, 1953); John Laird, *Theism and Cosmology* (New York, 1942); and J. J. C. Smart, "The Existence of God," in Antony Flew and Alasdair MacIntyre, eds., *New Essays in Philosophical Theology* (New York, 1955).

WILLIAM P. ALSTON

TELEOLOGICAL ETHICS. The common feature of all teleological theories of ethics is the subordination of the concept of duty, right conduct, or moral obligation to the concept of the good or the humanly desirable. Duty is defined as that which conduces to the good, and any statement enjoining a particular course of conduct as a duty or moral obligation is regarded as acceptable only if it can be shown that such conduct tends to produce a greater balance of good than do possible alternatives. Nonteleological theories, which hold that the concept of duty is logically independent of the concept of good and thereby deny the necessity of justifying duties by showing that they are productive of good, are called deontological theories.

Classical, medieval, and early modern philosophers seem to have taken the premises of the teleological outlook for granted. Like Socrates in the *Republic,* they often accepted head-on the challenge to prove that a life of justice was better and happier than a life of injustice. Whatever doubts they may have had about the logical necessity of meeting this challenge were not clearly voiced. It was not until Kant that a deontological theory of ethics was unambiguously formulated.

Critics of teleological ethics often initiate their attack by citing real or hypothetical cases in which the public welfare seems to require the violation of some generally accepted moral rule. An example would be the case of a sheriff who must choose between turning a man accused of a crime over to a lynch mob or precipitating a riot that will certainly result in a large number of deaths. If, the critics argue, the teleological principle were valid, the moral rule (in the example given, the sheriff's duty to protect those in his custody) would have to be violated. But, they continue, to condone the violation of the rule is to flout our sense of justice.

In general, answers to this kind of criticism take one of the following forms: (1) Teleological ethics does not require the violation of moral rules. The good itself requires that each of us adhere strictly to his duty. This appears to be the answer of Bentham, Mill, and most of the other classical utilitarians. In the case cited, it might be argued that the sheriff's firmness would, by increasing respect for the law and discouraging would-be lynchers in the future, have favorable long-range social consequences more than sufficient to offset the evils attending the riot. (2) Teleological ethics does occasionally require violation of moral rules, but occasional violations of moral rules can themselves be justified on moral grounds. This argument has been defended in the twentieth century by F. C. Sharp and J. J. C. Smart. Assume that in the example cited the sheriff's firmness would have no desirable future consequences or that such consequences would be negligible. His only choice, then, would be between a greater and a lesser evil: the death of many or the death of one. Justice clearly requires that he choose the lesser evil.

Bibliography

For criticism of teleological ethics, see bibliography to DEON-TOLOGICAL ETHICS. See also UTILITARIANISM and ENDS AND MEANS.

See also Jeremy Bentham, *Deontology; or the Science of Morality: In Which the Harmony and Coincidence of Duty and Self-interest, Virtue and Felicity, Prudence and Benevolence, are Explained and Exemplified* (London, 1834); John Stuart Mill, *Utilitarianism* (London, 1861), Chapter 5, "On the Connection between Justice and Utility"; F. C. Sharp, *Ethics* (New York, 1928); and J. J. C. Smart, *An Outline of a System of Ethics* (Melbourne, 1961).

ROBERT G. OLSON

TELEOLOGY. The term "teleology" locates a series of connected philosophical questions. If we grant that there is such a thing as purposive or goal-directed activity (as we must, since, for example, a political campaign aimed at victory represents a clear, uncontroversial case), we may ask the following questions: (1) By what criteria do we identify purposive activity? (2) What is the nature of the systems that exhibit purposive activity? (3) Does the nature of purposive activity require us to employ special concepts or special patterns of description and explanation that are not needed in an account of nonpurposive activity? And if we grant that there are objects and processes which perform functions (again, as we must, since no one would deny, for instance, that the human kidney performs the function of excretion), we may ask: (4) By what criteria do we identify functions? (5) What is the nature of the systems which exhibit functional activity? (6) Does the description of functions require special concepts or special patterns of analysis?

These six questions have been formulated with the help of a distinction between purposive and functional activity. Although the distinction is not always drawn in discussions of teleology, it is desirable for a number of reasons. It seems, at least prima facie, that the criteria of functional activity are quite distinct from the criteria of purposive activity: urine excretion, for example, seems to be a function by virtue of its role in the economy of a living organism, whereas activity seems to be purposive in virtue of the manner in which it is controlled. Thus, it seems at least logically possible that a purposive activity could perform no function, and that a function could be performed without purposive activity. Moreover, in view of this fundamental conceptual difference between purpose and function, we should expect the analysis of purposive and functional activity to show differences in logical pattern. On the other hand, it also seems clear that there are close connections between function and purpose; thus the final question: (7) What is the relation between ascriptions of function and ascriptions of purpose?

PURPOSIVE ACTIVITY

Criteria. A number of writers have proposed definitions of "goal-directed" or "purposive" action that leave open the question of whether the action is intentional or in any way involves consciousness. R. B. Braithwaite suggests, as a behavioral criterion of goal-directed activity that either may or may not be goal-intended, "persistence toward the goal under varying conditions." This is a condensed version of very similar criteria offered by R. B. Perry, E. S. Russell, and A. Hofstadter. All presuppose that a goal may be identified and that both persistence and sensitivity to varying conditions may be located by reference to the goal. E. C. Tolman adds the requirement that purposive activity show "docility," that is, some improvement in reaching the goal in the course of successive trials. But docility, however important it may be in the total picture of biological purposiveness, is surely not part of the criterion of purposiveness. Any abilities that are in fact learned could, in logical principle, be innate.

This criterion, in Braithwaite's form, is of course susceptible of considerable refinement; Braithwaite himself (in *Scientific Explanation*), for example, proposes a way of identifying variations in conditions as relevant variations for applying the criterion. Further possible refinements will be discussed in the next section.

The apparent circularity in the criterion—defining "goal-directed" in terms of a "goal"—is not serious. The location of persistence, sensitivity, and a goal may proceed together by a method of successive approximations. For example, a pattern of animal behavior may appear persistent and lead to a tentative identification of a goal, and the identification may be checked by looking for sensitivity to conditions or further evidence of persistence. A hypothesis about any one of the three—goal, persistence, sensitivity—can be confirmed by investigating either of the other two.

It seems clear that there are behavioral criteria for identifying purposive action, not only of human beings but also of other animals and of artifacts such as self-guided missiles. A pilot who watches a rocket approach in spite of his evasive maneuvers would rightly have no doubts about either the goal-directedness of the rocket's movements or the identity of its goal. No doubt the actual criteria of purposiveness that have been proposed suffer various shortcomings. In particular, they seem to lay down a necessary but not a sufficient condition. However, most philosophers would regard the program of seeking behavioral criteria as sound.

Nature of systems showing purposive activity. Is it possible for the philosopher, as distinct from the biologist, psychologist, or communications engineer, to say anything illuminating about the nature of the systems—men, mice, and missiles—that engage in purposive activity? He can at least examine more closely the behavioral criteria of purposiveness, in order to see whether there might be covert reference to the nature of the system in the criteria's actual application. A critic of the behavioral criteria might remark that a river is persistent in reaching the sea and is sensitive to the conditions necessary for reaching the sea—it detours all obstacles—but we would not call the flowing of a river purposive, nor would we call the sea or reaching the sea its goal. In short, the critic might say, a river is not the sort of thing to which we ever ascribe purposiveness.

Directive correlation. A number of philosophers, including Braithwaite, Ernest Nagel, George Sommerhoff, and Morton Beckner, have proposed ways of avoiding the difficulty about rivers and the like. Although there are differences in their accounts, they all adopt the strategy of regarding an activity as purposive only when its goal-seeking character is the outcome of relatively independent but dovetailing processes. Sommerhoff, for example, defines "purposive behavior" with the help of a concept he terms "directive correlation." Two variables, such as the position of a moving target and the direction in which an automatic target-tracking mechanism points, are said to be directively correlated with respect to a goal state (in this case, the state in which the mechanism points at the target) whenever: (1) The two variables are independent in the sense that any value of one is compatible with any value of the other. (2) The actual value of both, at a given time, is at least in part causally determined by the prior value of a "coenetic" (steering) variable (in the example, the coenetic variable is the same as one of the directively correlated variables, namely, the position of the moving target). And (3) the causal determination is such that the actual values of the directively correlated variables are sufficient for the realization of the goal state. Sommerhoff then defines "purposive behavior" as directively correlated behavior in which the coenetic variable is identical with one of the directively correlated variables.

Stipulations (2) and (3) make the notion of two processes dovetailing so as to achieve a goal as precise as the notion of causal determination; and stipulation (1) specifies that the processes must be independent. The requirement of independence rules out such cases as the river, for the direction in which a river flows is not independent of the lay of the land.

Sommerhoff's analysis is not without difficulties (see Nagel and Beckner), but it is undoubtedly correct in general approach. A system *S* that could exhibit directive correlation would satisfy a number of prior conceptions about purposive behavior; for instance, that *S* would employ information about its environment, particularly about an aspect of the environment associated with the goal, and that the behavior of *S* would be dependent upon a specialized physical hook-up, such as some sort of circuitry.

It is now possible to suggest a schema for constructing a criterion of purposive activity that includes both a necessary and a sufficient condition and that incorporates some reference both to the empirical character of the activity and to the nature of the system that engages in it. Activity is purposive if and only if it exhibits sensitivity and persistence toward a goal as a result of directive correlation.

Need for special concepts or patterns of description and explanation. Purposive activity, in the analyses of Braithwaite and Sommerhoff described above, does not involve a special kind of causality but only a special organization of ordinary causal processes. If these analyses are correct, both living organisms and artificial machines are capable of purposive activity. If, therefore, special concepts or patterns of description and explanation are not needed in the case of purposive machines, it would appear that they are equally unnecessary in the case of organisms. Many philosophers have drawn this conclusion, and it must be admitted that accounts like Braithwaite's and Sommerhoff's constitute powerful arguments in its support.

There is room for some doubt, however. Even if we grant that purposive activity can be *defined* in terms that are equally applicable to organic and inorganic systems, it does not follow that all purposive activity can be *explained* on the model of inanimate activity. The most serious doubt concerns those purposive activities which may be described as the acts of agents, such as acts deliberately undertaken for the sake of a consciously envisaged end. Suppose, for example, that some or all of these acts of agents are in principle unpredictable—a view accepted by some philosophers. Then, if they can be explained at all, their explanation is essentially *post hoc*. The pattern of such explanation is not yet properly understood; nevertheless, there is at least some doubt that it can dispense with the conception of following a rule. But these considerations raise questions that cannot be pursued here.

FUNCTIONS

Criteria. When we assert truly—for example, that a function of the kidney is the excretion of urine—precisely what relations must hold between the kidney and excretion? It has been proposed, for example by Nagel, that teleological terms like "purpose" and "function" can be eliminated in the following way: an expression such as "A function of the kidney is the excretion of urine" is translated into the nonteleological expression "The kidney is a necessary (or necessary and sufficient) condition of urine excretion." In general we may interpret Nagel as proposing a translation schema—For "F is the function of A," write "A is a necessary (or necessary and sufficient) condition of F"—that dispenses with teleological language and which also provides part of a criterion (a necessary condition) for identifying functions.

At best, however, Nagel's schema must be modified, for the possession of kidneys is neither a necessary nor a sufficient condition of urine excretion. It is obviously not sufficient; but it is also not necessary, since urine can also be excreted by various artificial devices. (If it is objected that these devices are themselves a sort of kidney, then the statement that a kidney is necessary for excretion reduces to a tautology.) Moreover, the translation schema is much less plausible when applied to organic functions that are ordinarily accomplished in distinct ways. Temperature regulation, for example, is a function of man's body hair; but hair is not necessary for heat regulation, since the function may be performed by other physical and physiological mechanisms. When we ascribe a function to the kidney or to body hair, we seem to be saying no more than that these structures *contribute to* certain processes; we leave open the question whether they are necessary or sufficient for the processes. The relation "contributing to" may be defined without employing teleological language. Let F be a process, some or all of which takes place in system S; and let A be a part of, or a process in, S. Finally, let the terms "S-like," "F-like," and "A-like" refer respectively to all those entities which answer to the definition of the terms employed in specifying S, F, and A. (In the example "A function of the kidney in vertebrates is the excretion of urine," all vertebrates are S-like, all cases of urine excretion are F-like, and all kidneys are A-like.) Then "A of S contributes to F" if and only if there exist S-like systems and states or environments of these S-like systems in which F-like processes occur and the possession of A-like parts or processes is necessary for the occurrence of F-like processes.

On this definition, we may say that in general a man's kidney contributes to the excretion of urine and that body hair contributes to heat regulation. And if we adopt the translation schema "For 'F is the function of A in S,' write 'A contributes to F in S,'" we may say, even in the case of a man whose bad kidneys have been bypassed to an artificial kidney, that the function of his flesh-and-blood kidneys is still the excretion of urine; they merely fail to perform it.

Nature of systems showing functional activity. Nagel's translation schema and the above modification of it provide a way of translating a teleological statement T_1 into a statement T_2 that does not employ explicitly teleological terms. Therefore, the satisfaction of T_2 by a given A, F, and S is a necessary condition of F's being a function of A. It is, however, not a sufficient condition; we may not in general translate T_2 into T_1. We would not say, for example, that the function of the ground is to hold up the rocks even though, in our technical sense, the ground contributes to the holding up of rocks. It would seem that out of the whole set of "contributing" cases, only a very restricted subset could be regarded as functions.

How may this subset be specified? We ordinarily attribute functions to two sorts of systems, artifacts and living things. We may consider first a simple artifact such as a cooking pan. We ascribe a function to the whole pan: cooking. Moreover, we also ascribe functions to parts and properties of the pan insofar as they contribute to its usefulness in cooking. For example, it is natural to think of the handle as providing a grip, of the rivets as fastening on the handle, and so on. In short, whenever we are prepared to acknowledge a single function F, we are also prepared to acknowledge a hierarchy of functions, with F at the top and the functions at each lower level contributing to all those above them.

The assignment of functions to living organisms proceeds on the same principle. There are two organic processes which are regarded as fundamental, the maintenance of life and reproduction. Alternatively, these two processes may be thought of as contributing to a single process, the maintenance of a species, which stands at the top of all functional hierarchies. The fundamental processes thus play a defining role in the identification of functions. The following schema lays down a necessary and sufficient condition of functional activity: F_1 is a function of A in S if and only if A contributes to F_1 in S; and F_1 is identical with or contributes to F_2 in S, where F_2 is either a purpose for which the artifact S is designed or the process of maintenance of the species of which S is a member.

The concept of an artifact may be interpreted quite broadly in order to include not only things like cooking pans but also all cultural products, such as works of art, language, and legal institutions. It makes sense, for example, on the above analysis and on this interpretation of "artifact," to ask "What is the function of Ophelia in *Hamlet*?" and "What is the function of verb inflections in Japanese?" The justification for regarding maintenance of the species as a fundamental function, serving a logical role in functional analysis, is examined below.

Need for special concepts or patterns of analysis. The definition of functional activity offered above provides a way of interpreting ascriptions of functions without using explicitly teleological expressions. However, there is a sense in which many of the concepts that are employed in the ascription of functions are implicitly teleological. Consider, for example, the concept of an "escape reaction." It is applied to a great variety of animal movements, such as flying up, forming dense schools, withdrawing into burrows, jumping into water, and gathering under the mother. These diverse reactions probably have no relevant feature in common other than a functional one; they all, in the technical sense, contribute to the avoidance of death by predation. Such functional concepts are common in the theory of animal behavior, in all branches of natural history, in physiology, and indeed in everyday language. The terms which we most commonly use, for example, in describing machines are defined functionally.

The view that teleological language can be eliminated from the language of science may be true; again, the most difficult cases concern human agency. But the program of eliminating teleological expressions even from biological theory must involve more than the elimination of such terms as "function," "purpose," "goal," and "in order to." If there is any point in eliminating these terms, there is just as much point in eliminating all concepts that are defined functionally, for "The function of this movement is to escape from a predator" is equivalent in asserted content to "This movement is an escape reaction." It is obviously true that the movement in question can be described, without employing the term "escape reaction," as a movement that contributes to the avoidance of a predator. But if we eliminate the term "escape reaction," we have excised from the language the term that applies not only to this movement but to all the diverse movements, in a variety of taxonomic groups, that serve this function.

The ascription of functions, therefore, does not require either an explicit or an implicit teleological vocabulary. It should be recognized, however, that the elimination of implicitly teleological expressions (concepts that are defined functionally) would result in a language for biological theory that would bear very little resemblance to the existing language.

Moreover, the difference would not be superficial; the rejection of functional concepts would amount to the re-

jection of a powerful and fruitful conceptual scheme. Our picture of living organisms as organized functional hierarchies is an essential part of the theory of natural selection; it is the foundation of physiology and morphology; and it is the basis of the medical view of disease as derangement of function. It is the fruitfulness of this conceptual scheme, embodied in a network of connected functional concepts, that constitutes the justification for assigning to maintenance of the species its central logical role in the ascription of functions.

RELATION BETWEEN ASCRIPTIONS OF FUNCTION AND OF PURPOSE

We have drawn a sharp distinction between functional activities, which contribute to a "fundamental" process, and purposive activities, which are persistent, flexible patterns of directively correlated behavior. It is clear, however, that function and purpose are closely connected —so closely, indeed, that many writers have failed to see the distinction. These connections may be described as follows:

(*a*) Whenever we construct an artifact as an aid to our own purposive activities, we are willing to ascribe functions to the artifact and to its parts and properties.

(*b*) Many but by no means all organic functions are served by purposive activities. For example, temperature regulation in the mammals involves directive correlation, whereas the excretion of urine does not.

(*c*) Conversely, *every* organic mechanism which provides an organism with the means of purposive activity serves the function of maintenance of the species. This is an empirical fact. It does not mean, however, that each case of purposive activity, when it occurs, performs a function. A purposive activity that is ordinarily adaptive (functional under normal circumstances) can lead to disaster when the circumstances are abnormal. For example, the homing of a male moth on a female, directed by the attractant secreted by the female, is ordinarily both purposive and functional. But it can lead the moth to his death when the attractant is placed on a surface covered with an insecticide.

Bibliography

Beckner, Morton, *The Biological Way of Thought*. New York, 1959.

Braithwaite, R. B., "Teleological Explanations." *PAS*, N.S. Vol. 47 (1947), i–xx.

Braithwaite, R. B., *Scientific Explanation*. Cambridge, 1953.

Hofstadter, A., "Objective Teleology." *Journal of Philosophy*, Vol. 38, No. 2 (January 1941), 29–39.

Nagel, Ernest, "Teleological Explanation and Teleological Systems," in H. Feigl and M. Brodbeck, eds., *Readings in the Philosophy of Science*. New York, 1953. Pp. 537–558. A revised and enlarged version of this article appears in Nagel's *The Structure of Science*. New York, 1961. Pp. 401–428.

Perry, R. B., "A Behavioristic View of Purpose." *Journal of Philosophy*, Vol. 18, No. 4 (February 1921), 85–105.

Russell, E. S., *The Directiveness of Organic Activities*. Cambridge, 1945.

Sommerhoff, George, *Analytical Biology*. London, 1950.

Tolman, E. C., *Purposive Behavior in Animals and Men*. New York and London, 1932.

MORTON BECKNER

TELESIO, BERNARDINO (1509–1588), Renaissance philosopher, was born at Cosenza, in Calabria, Italy. He studied philosophy, physics, and mathematics at the University of Padua, and received his doctorate in 1535. In Padua he became acquainted with the teaching of Aristotle and the two main Aristotelian schools, the Averroistic and the Alexandrist. Following the trend of the time, he devoted himself especially to the study of nature; but far from accepting the Aristotelian doctrine, he reacted vigorously against it. Telesio pursued his literary activity mostly at Naples, where he was a guest of the Carafa family, and at Cosenza. He enjoyed the friendship of several popes, and Gregory XIII invited him to Rome to expound his doctrine. He never engaged in any formal teaching, for he preferred to discuss his ideas in private conversations with friends.

Telesio is the author of the nine-book *De Rerum Natura Iuxta Propria Principia* ("On the Nature of Things According to their Principles," 1586) and of several philosophical opuscules. He proposed to interpret nature by following the testimony of the senses, rather than to attempt an explanation through the "abstract and preconceived ideas" of the Aristotelians. Nature must be studied in itself and in its own principles, which are matter and the two active forces of heat and cold. Matter is the passive, inert substratum of all physical change and is substantially the same everywhere. Unlike Aristotelian prime matter, which is pure potency, it is concrete and actual, and hence it can be directly perceived by the senses. Heat and cold are the two opposing forces responsible for all natural events; the first is represented by sky and the second by earth. Heat is also the source of life in plants and animals, as well as the cause of biological operations and some of the lower psychological functions in man. The whole of nature is animated and endowed with sensation in varying degrees (panpsychism). In addition to the vital principle there is present in man and animals "spirit," a very subtle material substance that emanates from the warm element and is generated with the body. Spirit is properly located in the brain and has the function of anticipating and receiving sense impressions. It has both an appetitive power and an intellective power of its own that correspond to the sensitive appetite and the cogitative power (*vis cogitativa*) of the Aristotelians.

Besides body and spirit, man has a *mens,* or *anima superaddita,* which is created by God and informs both body and spirit. This is roughly equivalent to the spiritual soul of Platonic–Augustinian tradition, whose operations transcend those of spirit and reach up to the divine. Apart from the natural drive or instinct of self-preservation, which Telesio attributed to all beings—including inorganic matter—man can also strive after union with God and contemplate the divine. This inner tendency of the *mens,* along with the need for proper sanctions in a future life in order to correct injustices, was one of the arguments used by Telesio to prove the immortality of the soul, which is known by revelation but can also be demonstrated by reason.

For Telesio self-preservation was man's supreme good. Just as in man there is a twofold intellect, one pertaining to the spirit and the other to the soul, so also there is in him a twofold appetitive power. The sensitive appetite tends toward temporal goods and its own preservation in this life; rational appetite or will tends toward immortal goods and its own preservation in a future, eternal life. Virtues are powers or faculties that enable man to achieve self-preservation; they are not merely habits, as Aristotle taught. There are virtues of the spirit and virtues of the soul. Among the virtues, sublimity and wisdom occupy a high place. Sublimity is not merely a particular virtue but virtue as a whole. It stands at the summit of all virtues and somehow includes all of them, for it directs all man's operations toward his supreme good. Wisdom helps man to attain to the knowledge of God as creator of the universe and can reach out to the knowledge of the divine substance itself.

Although Telesio did not specifically treat the problem of God's existence (it was beyond the scope of his study), he touched incidentally upon Aristotle's argument from motion and criticized it on the ground that movement is an intrinsic property of heat, the first active principle of material beings. Accordingly, there is no need for an extrinsic agent to set the bodies in motion. Besides, an immovable mover that sets the heavens in motion, as conceived by Aristotle, is a contradiction. The existence of God is better proved from the wonderful order of the universe, which can only be the work of a divine mind.

As evidenced by this summary exposition of Telesio's thought, it would be wrong to call him a naturalistic philosopher, if the term "naturalism" is taken to mean a purely materialistic approach to reality. In his *De Rerum Natura* Telesio claimed to investigate the nature of things according to their intrinsic principles, and only incidentally spoke of their extrinsic causes. He gave us a philosophy of nature along the general lines of Aristotle's *Physics,* although from a different point of view and following a more scientific method; he did not intend to present a philosophy of reality as a whole. Briefly, he discussed nature or the world as it is in its concrete reality, not as it came about or in reference to the end for which it was made. His approach to man, knowledge, and morality was on the same plane. One should not be surprised, then, to find in his *De Rerum Natura* no special treatment of God, the spiritual soul, man's ultimate end, and other doctrines commonly held by Christian philosophers. His pertinent statements were nevertheless more than sufficient to show the personal convictions of their author. Thus, in his dedicatory letter to Ferdinand Carafa, duke of Nocera, he wrote: "Our doctrine, far from contradicting the senses and Holy Scripture . . . so agrees with them that it seems to stem directly from these two sources."

Telesio was called "the first of the moderns" by Francis Bacon, who claimed that Telesio was the first to raise the banner against Aristotle. This same phrase has been used in connection with Telesio by some modern historians of philosophy to indicate his revolt against the traditional teaching of the Catholic church. The truth is that Telesio was neither a mere critic of Aristotle nor an antagonist of the church, to which he always professed loyalty. His modernity consists, rather, in the emphasis he placed on sense experience in the study of nature, thus paving the way for the scientific method of Galileo Galilei and his followers and opening a path in philosophy that was soon to be followed by Tommaso Campanella, Francis Bacon himself, and Thomas Hobbes. It must be admitted that Telesio often discussed scientific problems with a philosophical method. The result was that his *De Rerum Natura,* a pioneering work of unquestionable value, was neither a scientific study nor a philosophical treatise, but a hybrid combination of science and philosophy not quite in agreement with the rigorous empirical method he professed to follow. This weakness in Telesio's system was pointed out by his contemporary Francesco Patrizi, the Neoplatonist.

Works by Telesio

De Rerum Natura. Naples, 1586. New edition, Vincenzo Spampanato, ed., 3 vols. Vol. I, Modena, 1910; Vol. II, Genoa, 1913; Vol. III, Rome, 1923.
Varii de Naturalibus Rebus Libelli, Antonio Persio, ed. Venice, 1590. Various philosophical opuscules.
Solutiones Thylesii (and two other opuscules), in Francesco Fiorentino, *Bernardino Telesio,* 2 vols. Florence, 1872–1874. Works contained in an appendix.

Works on Telesio

Abbagnano, Nicola, *Telesio.* Milan, 1941.
Di Napoli, Giovanni, "Fisica e metafisica in Bernardino Telesio." *Rassegna di scienze filosofiche,* Vol. 6 (1953), 22–69.
Gentile, Giovanni, *Bernardino Telesio.* Bari, 1911.
Soleri, Giacomo, *Telesio.* Brescia, 1944.
Troilo, Erminio, *Bernardino Telesio,* 2d ed. Modena, 1924.
Van Deusen, Neil, *Telesio, the First of the Moderns.* New York, 1932.
Van Deusen, Neil, "The Place of Telesio in the History of Philosophy." *The Philosophical Review,* Vol. 44 (1935), 417–434.

BERNARDINE M. BONANSEA, O.F.M.

TENNANT, FREDERICK ROBERT (1866–1957), philosopher of religion and theologian, spent most of his life in Cambridge, England, and was educated at Cambridge University. He was a fellow of Trinity College and university lecturer in the philosophy of religion. His writings are in two main areas. In the strictly theological field he produced several influential studies of the concepts of sin and the fall of man, in which he diverged widely from the traditional Augustinian doctrines. In the philosophy of religion and the philosophy of science (in both of which his thought shows the influence of his Cambridge contemporary James Ward) Tennant's magnum opus is the two-volume *Philosophical Theology,* which develops, from foundations in the sciences, the thesis that there is "a theistic world-view commending itself as more reasonable than other interpretations or than the refusal to interpret, and congruent with the knowledge—i.e. the probability—which is the guide of life and science" (Vol. II, p. 245).

Tennant described his method as empirical rather than a priori. He meant (1) that his epistemology was based on a psychological examination of the cognitive capacities of the human mind, and (2) that his theistic argument was inductive, treating the existence of God as a hypothesis which goes beyond but builds upon the hypotheses of the special sciences.

Tennant argued in *Philosophy of the Sciences* that all knowledge, other than that in logic and mathematics, consists in probable interpretative judgments whose verifi-

cation to the human mind is ultimately pragmatic. Thus, science and natural theology share a common method and status: ". . . inductive science has its interpretative explanation-principles, . . . and its faith elements with which the faith of natural theology is, in essence, continuous" (p. 185). So Tennant can speak of theology as "the final link in a continuous chain of interpretative belief" (p. 184) and can say that "theistic belief is but a continuation, by extrapolation, or through points representing further observations, of the curve of 'knowledge' which natural science has constructed" (pp. 185–186). (For Tennant's conception of faith as the volitional element in the acquisition of all knowledge, scientific no less than religious, see FAITH.)

Tennant rejected religious experience—both the special experiences of the mystic and the less special religious experience of the ordinary believer—as a valid ground for belief in God, and he rested his entire case upon what he called the wider, or cosmic, teleology.

The version of the Argument to Design in Volume II of Tennant's *Philosophical Theology*—taking account as it does of Hume's critique of the much simpler arguments of the eighteenth-century teleologists culminating in William Paley's *Natural Theology,* and taking account also of relevant developments in nineteenth-century and early twentieth-century science including the work of Darwin —is probably the strongest presentation that has been written of this type of theistic reasoning. Serious discussions of the Teleological Argument should deal with it in the form provided by Tennant rather than in the relatively cruder versions of earlier centuries or of contemporary popular apologetics.

Tennant begins by making it clear, in accordance with his general theory of knowledge, that the argument is to provide "grounds for reasonable belief rather than rational and coercive demonstration." It employs a concept of probability which is not that of mathematics or logic but "the alogical probability which is the guide of life" and which, Tennant had already claimed in Volume I, is the ultimate basis of all scientific induction.

The argument itself does not rely (as did Paley's) on particular instances of apparent design in nature or on the arithmetical accumulation of these. Tennant allowed that each separate case of adaptation may be adequately explicable in purely naturalistic as well as in teleological terms. But he held that "the multitude of interwoven adaptations by which the world is constituted a theatre of life, intelligence, and morality, cannot reasonably be regarded as an outcome of mechanism, or of blind formative power, or of aught but purposive intelligence" (*Philosophical Theology,* Vol. II, p. 121).

His detailed argument contains the following strands:

(1) The basic instance of order is that the world stands in relation to human thought as something "more or less intelligible, in that it happens to be more or less a cosmos, when conceivably it might have been a self-subsistent and determinate 'chaos' in which similar events never occurred, none recurred, universals had no place, relations no fixity, things no nexus of determination, and 'real' categories no foothold" (p. 82).

(2) The internal and external adaptation of animal or-

ganisms can be accounted for in terms of an evolutionary process operating by means of natural selection; but how, other than by a cosmic purpose, is that process itself to be accounted for? Here "The discovery of organic evolution has caused the teleologist to shift his ground from special design in the products to directivity in the process, and plan in the primary collocations" (p. 85).

(3) The emergence of organic life presupposes complex and specific preparatory processes at the inorganic level. Why has a universe of matter produced life and intelligence? If there were millions of universes, we might expect this to happen in a few of them. But there is only one universe. "Presumably the world is comparable with a single throw of dice. And common sense is not foolish in suspecting the dice to have been loaded" (p. 87).

(4) Nature produces in great abundance beauty which seems to exist only for the enjoyment of man. "Theistically regarded, Nature's beauty is of a piece with the world's intelligibility and with its being a theatre for moral life; and thus far the case for theism is strengthened by aesthetic considerations" (p. 93).

(5) Nature has produced man, with his ethical sense. If we judge the evolutionary process not by its roots in the primeval slime but by its fruits in human moral and spiritual experience, we note that "The whole process of Nature is capable of being regarded as instrumental to the development of intelligent and moral creatures" (p. 103).

(6) These five aspects of nature can individually be understood naturalistically. Nevertheless, taken as a whole they suggest a cosmic purpose which has used nature for the production of man. The more we learn of the complex conditions which had to come about before man could exist, "the less reasonable or credible becomes the alternative theory of cumulative groundless coincidence" (p. 106).

Having thus sought to establish theism as the most reasonable explanation of the world as a whole, Tennant discussed the problem of evil considered as challenging the theistic hypothesis, and he offered a theodicy which is typical of the thought of many British theologians on this subject in the twentieth century. This type of theodicy has an ancestry going back through Schleiermacher to the early Hellenistic thinkers of the Christian church, especially Irenaeus, and it stands in contrast to the Augustinian and Latin tradition. For Tennant the possibility of the moral evil of sin was involved in the creation of free and responsible personal beings and was justified by the fact that only free persons can be the bearers of moral and spiritual values. Tennant saw the natural evil of pain in its many forms as a necessary concomitant of man's existence in a world which has its own stable structure and laws of operation; and it is justified by the fact that only in such an environment can the higher values of the human personality develop.

The same aspects of Tennant's thought constitute its strength from one philosophical point of view and its weakness from another point of view. He presented theology as an extension of science and theism as a hypothesis which is arguable in essentially the same sort of way as, for example, organic evolution. To some it will seem that by thus assimilating religious to scientific theorizing, Tennant

made theology intellectually respectable; and this was his own view of the matter. To others, however, it will seem that Tennant was presenting religious belief in false colors. From their point of view, having excluded the true basis of religious faith in religious experience, Tennant attempted in vain to infer religious conclusions from nonreligious data, and by thus setting theistic belief upon a wrong and inadequate foundation, he has weakened rather than strengthened it.

Works by Tennant

The Origin and Propagation of Sin. Cambridge, 1902.
The Sources of the Doctrines of the Fall and Original Sin. Cambridge, 1903.
The Concept of Sin. Cambridge, 1912.
Miracle and Its Philosophical Presuppositions. Cambridge, 1925.
Philosophical Theology, 2 vols. Cambridge, 1928 and 1930.
Philosophy of the Sciences. Cambridge, 1932.
The Nature of Belief. London, 1943.

Works on Tennant

Broad, C. D., "Frederick Robert Tennant, 1866–1957." *Proceedings of the British Academy,* Vol. 44 (1960).
Buswell, J. Oliver, *The Philosophies of F. R. Tennant and John Dewey.* New York, 1950.
Scudder, D. L., *Tennant's Philosophical Theology.* New Haven, Conn., 1940.
Smart, Ninian, "F. R. Tennant and the Problem of Evil," in his *Philosophers and Religious Truth.* London, 1964.

JOHN HICK

TERESA OF ÁVILA, ST. (1515–1582), Spanish mystic, was born of an aristocratic family in Ávila. In 1535 she entered a Carmelite convent there and four years later was prostrated by a long illness, probably of psychological origin. However, she had already felt the call to contemplation, and at about the age of 40, after a long struggle, she received a second "conversion," which turned her toward an intense practice of contemplation. Her order was relatively lax in its rules, and she felt impelled to begin a reform. In 1562 a reformed convent was established in Ávila under her direction. After five years, despite ill health and official opposition, she began energetically to spread the reform to other parts of Spain. She died in 1582, after a three-year illness. Her main works were her *Life* (1562–1565), *The Way of Perfection* (1565), and *The Interior Castle* (1577). The first is a full account of her inner experiences, and the last gives a more systematic description of the contemplative life.

Her account of the stages of mysticism, in the *Life,* uses the analogy of watering a garden by various means. Once the weeds have been uprooted, irrigation is needed. Those who bring the water from a well are compared to beginners in prayer and meditation. It is a laborious activity, involving the taming of the senses so that they are no longer distracting. The second stage of meditation is reached with the prayer of quiet. This is compared to irrigating the garden by a water wheel. The third mode of watering is by a running brook: this corresponds to a state of contemplation in which effort is no longer needed, as if the work were done by the Lord. It is, according to St. Teresa, "a celestial frenzy," in which the faculties of sense perception no longer function. The soul no longer wishes to live in the world but solely in union with God. The intellect is worth nothing, for ordinary modes of understanding are considered irrelevant or nonsensical. In the fourth stage, which is compared to a shower falling on the garden, the soul is totally passive and receptive, all its faculties somehow united with God. The soul cannot properly understand what is occurring, but afterward it is certain that there has been a union with God.

In *The Interior Castle* St. Teresa supplements her earlier account, comparing the contemplative life to entering a castle or palace in which there are many rooms. These are arranged concentrically in six rings of rooms, or "mansions," round an inner chamber where the king lives. To enter this castle, prayer is needed. Ordinary Christians can enter the first three mansions through humility, meditation, and exemplary conduct; and the attainment of the third mansion represents the life achievement of many worthy Christians. But more remains in the spiritual life than such a virtuous existence. The fourth mansion corresponds to the "second water" of St. Teresa's earlier simile. In the fifth the soul seems to be asleep and unconscious both of the external world and of itself (although such language is analogical; the contemplative is not literally asleep). The soul is illuminated in this state by God. The sixth mansion is like a couple's first sight of one another at a betrothal. Finally, the soul enters the holy of holies. It seems as if this place is dark, because of the overpowering strength of the divine light. Here the soul has a direct vision of God, like the beatific vision to be enjoyed hereafter in heaven. Throughout these descriptions St. Teresa makes frequent use of the imagery of love and of marriage. The distinction between the "betrothal" and the "marriage" is found also in the writings of St. John of the Cross, a friend and follower of St. Teresa.

The detail and sensitivity of St. Teresa's autobiographical reports have given her a special importance in the history of mysticism.

Bibliography

St. Teresa's works are collected in Spanish as *Obras de Santa Teresa de Jesús*, P. Silverio, ed., 9 vols. (Burgos, 1915–1926); they appear in English as *Collected Works*, translated and edited by E. Allison Peers, 3 vols. (London, 1946). Also see E. Allison Peers, *Studies of the Spanish Mystics*, Vol. I (London, 1927).

NINIAN SMART

TERTULLIAN, QUINTUS SEPTIMIUS FLORENS

(c. 160–c. 220), African Church Father, was born in Carthage and was converted to Christianity about 193. He made early use of his training in rhetoric and Roman law in two apologetic works, *Ad Nationes* and *Apologeticum*, written in 197. These owe much to earlier Greek Christian apologies and to the writings of Varro, an Augustan polymath who analyzed religion along Stoic lines; *Ad Nationes* seems to have been a first draft of the *Apologeticum*. Tertullian was the first Christian theologian to write in Latin, and most of his works deal with moral and theological issues; all contain elements of polemic either against various aspects of Greco-Roman culture or against Christian heresies. Tertullian's works can be dated by cross references, allusions to current events, and by his gradual

movement toward the ascetic–apocalyptic sect of the Montanists, advocates of the "new prophecy"; he became a Montanist about 206 and later became the leader of a Montanist group in Carthage. Nothing is known of his life after the time of his last literary work, written about 220.

His writings are vigorously, even violently, individualistic in style and often in content; he loved paradox and contradiction, going so far as to claim in *De Carne Christi* (Ch. 5) that the incarnation of Christ *"certum est quia impossibile"* ("is certain because impossible"). This claim seems to be based on a line of argument found in Aristotle's *Rhetoric* (Book 2, Ch. 23, Sec. 22): it is likely that unlikely things should happen. Tertullian's philosophical theology is derived largely from his Greek Christian predecessors (St. Justin Martyr, Tatian, St. Theophilus, Irenaeus); his own contributions are chiefly Stoic in origin. For him philosophy is partly, or sometimes, an enemy of religion ("What does Jerusalem have to do with Athens?"), sometimes an ally ("Seneca is often one of us").

Only two of Tertullian's nonapologetic works are primarily concerned with philosophical themes. One is the early treatise *Adversus Hermogenes*, in which he attacks the doctrine that matter is eternal and claims that Hermogenes derived this belief from Platonic and Stoic sources. His own arguments against the eternity of matter are partly a revision of a lost book by Theophilus, as the common Genesis text indicates. Hermogenes argued that the immutable God cannot have created the world from himself or have begun to create it *ex nihilo;* therefore he must have made it from matter, to which its imperfections are to be ascribed. God continually "creates," influencing matter as a magnet influences iron. In reply, Tertullian insisted primarily on God's freedom from "necessity." God created by his free will and therefore was not limited by matter.

His other work of philosophical interest is the Montanist treatise *De Anima* (c. 210–213), which is intended to prove that Platonic teaching is false. The soul is actually corporeal and originates from a "soul-producing seed" at the moment of conception. It is not pre-existent and does not transmigrate—an argument directed not only against Platonists but also against Christian heretics, chiefly Gnostic. Tertullian also discusses the human embryo and other related topics. His work is largely based on a treatise on the soul by the Greek physician Soranus, who wrote at Rome early in the second century. From Soranus, Tertullian derives most of his discussions of Plato, the Stoics, Aristotle, Heraclitus, and Democritus.

Tertullian's importance thus lies in his mediation of earlier conceptions, Christian and pagan alike, and for his translation of Greek ideas into Latin.

Additional Works by Tertullian

Tertullian: Apologetical Works, R. Arbesman, E. J. Daly, and E. A. Quain, eds. New York, 1950. Includes English translations of the *Apologeticum* and *De Anima*.

Quinti Septimi Tertulliani Opera, 2 vols., in J. G. P. Borleffs, E. Dekkers, et al., eds., *Corpus Christianorum, Series Latina*. The Hague, 1953–1954.

Works on Tertullian

Becker, C., *Tertullians Apologeticum: Werden und Leistung*. Munich, 1954.

Evans, E., *Tertullian's Treatise Against Praxeas.* London, 1948.

Evans, E., *Tertullian's Treatise On the Incarnation.* London, 1956.

Evans, E., *Tertullian's Treatise On the Resurrection.* London, 1960.

Koch, H., "Tertullianus" in A. Pauly and G. Wissowa, eds., *Real-Encylopädie der classischen Altertumswissenschaft.* Vol. VA (1934), Cols. 822–844.

Lortz, J., *Tertullian als Apologet,* 2 vols. Münster in Westfalen, 1927–1928.

Moffatt, J., "Aristotle and Tertullian." *Journal of Theological Studies,* Vol. 17 (1915–1916), 170–171.

Short, C. de L., *The Influence of Philosophy on the Mind of Tertullian.* London, 1933.

Waszink, J. H., *Tertullian De Anima.* Amsterdam, 1947. Extremely important.

Waszink, J. H., *The Treatise Against Hermogenes.* Westminster, Md., 1957.

ROBERT M. GRANT

TETENS, JOHANN NICOLAUS, German philosopher and psychologist. He was born in Tetenbüll, Schleswig, in 1736 or in Tönnig, Schleswig, in 1738, and died in 1807. He studied at the universities of Rostock and Copenhagen and became a *Magister* at Rostock University in 1759. From 1760 until 1765, when he became director of the local Gymnasium, he taught physics at Bützow Academy. He was full professor of philosophy at the University of Kiel from 1776 to 1789, during which period he also carried out an official study of the local hydraulic installations on the North Sea coast. From 1789 until his death he had a brilliant career as a high financial official in Copenhagen.

Tetens was strongly influenced by J. C. Eschenbach, his teacher of philosophy at Rostock. Eschenbach was an eclectic who accepted some Leibnizian and Wolffian tenets but sided with the Pietists against Wolff; nevertheless he seems to have been influenced more by the Berlin Academy and by Locke's empiricism than by C. A. Crusius. Tetens likewise was influenced by Locke and, after their publication, by Leibniz' *Nouveaux Essais.* Among his contemporaries he was influenced by David Hartley, Abraham Tucker, J. G. Sulzer, Helvétius, and Charles Bonnet. Tetens was one of the first in Germany to discuss Hume at length. J. H. Lambert's *Architektonik* and Kant's *Inaugural Dissertation* later played important roles in the development of Tetens' own views.

Tetens hoped to reform German metaphysics by using the critical approach of the new empirical psychology. He wished to restore metaphysics in a new form that would meet the criticisms based on the skeptical and psychological orientations of the English and French schools, then widely influential in Germany. On the other hand he defended phenomenalism against the adherents of the schools of common sense and of "popular philosophy."

In his first significant work, *Ueber die allgemeine spekulativische Philosophie* ("On General Speculative Philosophy," Bützow and Wismar, 1775; reprinted Berlin, 1913), Tetens discussed the weaknesses of traditional metaphysics and proposed some remedies. He held that to reform metaphysics, the sources and development of metaphysical concepts must be investigated. The means of inquiry was "inner sense," or introspection. He tried to give purely psychological answers to psychophysiological problems on the one hand and to metaphysical problems on the other.

In this spirit, Tetens' major work, *Philosophische Versuche über die menschliche Natur und ihre Entwicklung* ("Philosophical Essays on Human Nature and Its Development," 2 vols., Leipzig, 1777; reprinted Berlin, 1913), was an extended inquiry into the origin and structure of knowledge. He distinguished three faculties of the human mind: understanding, will, and feeling of pleasures and pains. He stressed the independence of the third faculty from the first two. The three may be reducible to one, but if so, according to Tetens, we cannot know it.

The mind is essentially active. Even sensation implies a reaction of the subject to the thing sensed. There are three fundamental activities of representation: perception, reflection (or abstraction from perceptions), and fiction (or the construction of new ideas out of perceived and abstracted representations).

Relations are established among perceived things by means of "primary original notions of relationships," or "forms"; one such form is causal connection. The three activities of representation together with the forms bring about the "concept of an object." Tetens proposed a rule for deciding whether something exists subjectively or objectively—we attribute a sensation to a thing if the sensation is contained as a part in the entire sensation of the thing.

Tetens distinguished rational knowledge from sensible knowledge by its being general and necessary. Metaphysical first principles are undeniable because they are rooted in the essence of the ego. They are like natural laws to which the intellect is subjected. The intellect—or common sense—and reason are governed by different kinds of laws, and the confusion between the two kinds of laws brings them into conflict.

Tetens discussed with great insight many other extremely complicated problems in metaphysics, ethics, the philosophy of education, and the philosophy of language. His *Philosophische Versuche* exerted a tremendous influence on Kant while he was writing the *Critique of Pure Reason,* and the many similarities between their doctrines are evident. Tetens' doctrines may be compared to Kant's even in their speculative power and importance.

Bibliography

Brenke, M., *J. N. Tetens' Erkenntnistheorie vom Standpunkte des Kritizismus.* Rostock, 1901.

Fuchs, Arnold, *J. N. Tetens' pädagogische Anschauungen.* Langensalza, 1918.

Golembski, W., "Die deutsche Aufklärungsphilosophie als Quelle des Transzendentalismus, I, Die Ontologie des J. N. Tetens." *Bulletin International de l'Academie Polonaise des Sciences et des Lettres* (1934), 167–173.

Lorsch, J., *Die Lehre vom Gefühl bei Tetens.* Giessen, 1906.

Schinz, M., *Die Moralphilosophie von Tetens.* Leipzig, 1906.

Seidel, Arthur, *Tetens Einfluss auf die kritische Philosophie Kants.* Leipzig, 1932.

Sommer, R., *Grundzüge einer Geschichte des deutschen Psychologie und Aesthetik von Wolff–Baumgarten bis Kant–Schiller.* Würzburg, 1892. Pp. 260–302.

Störring, G., *Die Erkenntnistheorie von Tetens.* Leipzig, 1901.

Uebele, W., "Herder und Tetens." *Archiv für Geschichte der Philosophie,* Vol. 18 (1905), 216–249.

Uebele, W., *J. N. Tetens nach seiner Gesamtentwicklung betrachtet mit besonderer Berücksichtigung des Verhältnisses zu Kant.* Berlin, 1911.

GIORGIO TONELLI

THALES OF MILETUS, since early antiquity regarded as the founder of the Ionian school of natural philosophy. Evidence suggests that he was a Milesian of Greek origin who flourished around 580 B.C. and that his field of distinguished activities included practical and political matters. There are indications that he visited Mesopotamia and Egypt, that he predicted the possibility of an eclipse in 585 B.C., and that he proposed a simple doctrine on the origin and nature of the world.

The most ancient references to Thales depict him as a man of exceptional wisdom. Later commentators associate him with specific discoveries in physics, metaphysics, astronomy, geometry, and engineering. Modern studies have hailed him as a proponent of the rational approach. However, recent conservative reconstructions of Thales' ideas have called for the abandonment or modification of earlier estimates. In the absence of primary sources, several scholars have argued that the earliest testimony of Herodotus, Plato, and Aristotle must be preferred to later reports stemming from the doxographic tradition. Such a preference is necessary, they maintain, since Thales left no written documents, and most of the post-Aristotelian compilers depended for their comments on Aristotle's reports. When the ancient evidence is carefully examined, these commentators hold, a believable picture of Thales' thought emerges. The following is an outline of his thought, based on the early sources.

Thales was very much concerned with the political conditions and developments in Asia Minor during his time: as an advisor he showed foresight in urging the Ionians to form a confederation against the Persians. As a "learned person" (*sophos*) he showed remarkable vision, correctly anticipating a solar eclipse during a battle between the Lydeans and the Persians. As an engineer he made the Halys River passable for King Croesus by diverting its waters.

In his speculations Thales asserted with unprecedented boldness that the world originated in water and was sustained by water and that the earth floated on water. Inasmuch as there is natural change everywhere, he went on to claim, the world is animated, and even apparently inanimate objects possess *psyche,* the principle of self-motion.

A fuller interpretation of the above necessarily takes one outside the area of the historically confirmable; yet one must propose some interpretation beyond the hard evidence if later fabrications are to be discarded. On the basis of Aristotle's cautious remarks it can be inferred that Thales thought of the world as perfectly understandable through the idea of water—an element essential to life (and thus to self-motion), versatile, common, and powerful enough to account for every physical phenomenon.

While there is very little else that may be safely associated with Thales' life and thought, post-Aristotelian commentators persist in crediting him with many specific discoveries. They suggest that he discovered the solstices and measured their cycles, that he discovered the five celestial zones (arctic, antarctic, equator, and the tropics), the inclination of the zodiac, the sources of the moon's light, and more. He is said to have explained the rise of the Nile as due to the etesian winds, and in geometry, to have discovered proofs for the propositions that the circle is bisected by its diameter, that the angles at the base of an isosceles triangle are equal, that two triangles are identical when they have one side and the angles formed by it with the other sides equal, and that in two intersecting straight lines the opposite angles at the intersection are equal. He was supposedly responsible for the axiomatization of the field of geometry, and he was further credited with measuring the height of the pyramids and the distance of ships at sea.

Most of these unsubstantiated ascriptions must be judged as unhistorical and inconsistent with the temper of the Milesian's thought. Thales was the last representative of a tradition that respected myth, was fond of intuitions, and did not concern itself with proofs. To be sure, he was also the founder of a new approach, that of attempting to comprehend the world through reason alone.

Bibliography

Burnet, John, *Early Greek Philosophy*, 4th ed. London, 1930. Pp. 40–50.

Dicks, D. R., "Thales." *Classical Quarterly*, Vol. 9 (1959), 294–309.

Diels, H., and Kranz, W., *Die Fragmente der Vorsokratiker*, 7th ed. Berlin, 1954. Vol. I, pp. 67–81.

Guthrie, W. K. C., *A History of Greek Philosophy*, 4th ed. Cambridge, 1962. Vol. I, pp. 45–72.

Hölscher, V., "Anaximander und die Anfänge der Philosophie." *Hermes*, Vol. 81 (1953), 252–277, 385–417.

Kirk, G. S., and Raven, J. E., *The Presocratic Philosophers*. Cambridge, 1957. Pp. 74–88.

Snell, Bruno, "Die Nachrichten über die Lehre des Thales und die Anfänge der griechischen Philosophie und Literaturgeschichte." *Philologus*, Vol. 96 (1944), 170–182.

P. DIAMANDOPOULOS

THEISM signifies belief in one God (*theos*) who is (*a*) personal, (*b*) worthy of adoration, and (*c*) separate from the world but (*d*) continuously active in it.

According to theism, God is a Subject possessing not only mind but also will. Being fully personal, he can be conceived through images drawn from human life and can be addressed as "thou" in prayer. Theists regard this personal God of religion as the *ultimate* reality. In this they differ from such thinkers as Sankara, Hegel, and F. H. Bradley, for whom personal images of God are intellectually immature depictions of a suprapersonal Absolute.

Theists claim that God merits adoration (or worship) on two grounds. First, he is wholly good. Second, he excels men in power. According to theism proper (or theism in the strict sense), God is *infinitely* powerful both in himself (as self-existent Being) and, consequently, in his relation to the world.

Theists hold that God is, in his essence, separate from the world. This belief distinguishes theism from pantheism, according to which the world is a part, or mode, of God. According to theism proper, God created the world *ex nihilo*. Admittedly "theism" is also sometimes applied in a loose sense to the view that God imposes form on pre-existent matter. But this application is valid only if the other requirements of theism are satisfied.

Theism always involves the belief that God is continuously active in the world. In this it differs from deism. According to deism—a word first applied to a group of eighteenth-century English thinkers—God, having made the world at the beginning of time, left it to continue on its own. Theists (notably Aquinas), on the other hand, maintain that every item in the world depends for its existence on the continuous activity of God as the Creator, so that *ex parte Dei* "creation" and "preservation" are identical.

Because deists remove God from continuous contact with the world, they are hostile to the orthodox Christian claim that God has supernaturally revealed himself in a series of events which reached their fulfillment in the Incarnation. Hence Toland, claiming the support of Locke, interpreted Christianity as the reaffirmation of the truths of natural religion. Certainly the Christian does not claim that the facts of revelation (or, a fortiori, the dogmas based on them) can be deduced, or in any way established, by pure reason; but he can validly claim that the idea of such a revelation is *compatible with* theistic (as it is not with deistic) premises.

Theistic belief raises the following questions, which (among others) constitute the "philosophy of theism," or theism *simpliciter*, in a secondary, speculative sense: How can finite terms refer to God if he is infinite? Is it possible to demonstrate, or at least to justify belief in, God's existence by reason? Is there a mode of experience which is specifically "religious"? In what sense (or senses) can one speak of a divine "providence"? Is the belief in a God who is both omnipotent and good compatible with the fact of evil?

Philosophical theism has often been attacked. At the end of the Middle Ages, William of Ockham denied that reason could prove God's existence. This denial was repeated by Kant. In this century Barthians, existentialists, and empiricists have rejected the possibility of speculative metaphysics in any form. Yet many philosophers and theologians (for example, Étienne Gilson, Jacques Maritain, E. L. Mascall, and A. M. Farrer) still maintain that theistic reasoning is both possible and necessary. (See ANALOGY IN THEOLOGY; CREATION, RELIGIOUS DOCTRINE OF; EVIL, THE PROBLEM OF; GOD, CONCEPTS OF; INFINITY IN THEOLOGY AND METAPHYSICS; PROVIDENCE; and the articles on individual arguments for the existence of God listed under GOD, ARGUMENTS FOR THE EXISTENCE OF.)

Bibliography

Farrer, A. M., *Finite and Infinite*. London, 1943.
Gilson, Étienne, *God and Philosophy*. New Haven and London, 1941; paperback, New Haven, 1959.
Maritain, Jacques, *The Range of Reason*. New York, 1952.
Mascall, E. L., *Existence and Analogy*. New York, 1949.

H. P. OWEN

THEODICY. See EVIL, THE PROBLEM OF; LEIBNIZ, GOTTFRIED WILHELM.

THEODORIC OF CHARTRES (or Thierry of Chartres) was a twelfth-century philosopher and younger brother of Bernard of Chartres. He appears first as a master in 1121, when he spoke in support of Peter Abelard at the latter's trial for heresy at Soissons. In the 1130s he was teaching the arts in Paris, and in 1142 he became chancellor at Chartres. He attended the trial of Gilbert of Poitiers at Rheims in 1148 and shortly afterward became a monk. The date of his death is unknown.

Theodoric's rhetorical teaching survives in a commentary on Cicero's *De Inventione*. Three versions of his exposition of Boethius' *De Trinitate* and a fragmentary exposition of Boethius' *De Hebdomadibus* are also extant, as is a commentary on the beginning of the book of Genesis (the *De Sex Dierum Operibus*). In the last-named work Theodoric's Platonizing cosmology and his mathematical bent found their expression. In his *Heptateuch,* a bulky collection of the sources for each of the seven liberal arts, Theodoric revealed his fidelity to the ancients. Grammar was represented by the works of Donatus and Priscian, rhetoric by Cicero, astronomy by Ptolemy; but the place of honor went to Boethius for his writings on music, arithmetic, geometry, and, especially, dialectic. Theodoric reproduced Boethius' translations and commentaries on the whole of Aristotle's *Organon,* with the exception of the *Posterior Analytics*.

Theodoric regarded the arts as the indispensable instrument of philosophy, which consisted of physics, mathematics, and theology. He based his Trinitarian speculation upon arithmetic, applying the Pythagorean–Platonic dialectic of unity–multiplicity to St. Augustine's dictum that the Father is unity, the Son equality, and the Spirit the agreement of unity and equality. Unity can only engender its equality; both are one substance but have different properties and are called persons by the theologians. Theodoric's argument emphasized the unity of the Trinity but made difficult a numerical distinction between the divine persons. The dialectic of unity–multiplicity was perhaps more appropriately used to explain the relationship of the Creator to creation. Unity is God and is immutable and eternal; the principle of multiplicity is the domain of creation. Unity is the *forma essendi* of creatures, their unique and entire being, totally and essentially omnipresent. Things are not pantheistically identified with the One; multiplicity is distinct from, and subordinate to, unity. The divine unity in an ineffable way absorbs the forms of all beings in itself, but only images of these forms are joined to matter. Theodoric's thought here moves close to his brother's theory of native forms.

Although Theodoric stressed the universal causality and omnipresence of the Creator, he presented creation as an ordered system of secondary causes. Matter was created by God from nothing, but the fashioning of the world out of the four elements occurred by the action of the circular motion of heaven and of the diffusion of heat in the underlying elements. The four elements of matter (which Genesis collectively designates by the names of heaven and earth) arranged themselves into four concentric spheres. The heaven of air and fire enveloped the water and the earth and, being supremely light, tended to move by turning about. Fire became ardent and illumined the air and heated the water, vaporizing it to reveal islands on the earth and to incubate life in the water and on land. The mechanistic character of this explanation is supplemented by a recognition of the role of spirit, which fills and animates the world. Through the "seminal reasons" introduced by God into creation, nature is capable of its own continuation after the completion of the work of six days.

Theodoric's doctrine of creation represents an adventurous application of the teachings of the Platonic *Timaeus* to the Biblical account.

Theodoric was a bold speculator, molded by and helping to mold the Platonic tradition of Latin Christendom. He seems also to have been the first medieval schoolman to have commented on the recently rediscovered *Prior Analytics* and *Sophistic Refutations* of Aristotle. Moreover, it was to him that Hermann of Carinthia sent his translation of Ptolemy's *Planisphere*, just as Bernard of Tours dedicated his *De Mundi Universitate* to Theodoric. Other disciples and admirers included Clarembald of Arras and John of Salisbury and, in the fifteenth century, Nicholas of Cusa.

Bibliography

Commentary and text of works by Theodoric are *De Septem Diebus et Sex Operum Distinctionibus*, N. M. Haring, ed., in "The Creation and Creator of the World According to Thierry of Chartres and Clarenbaldus of Arras," in *Archives d'histoire doctrinale et littéraire du moyen âge*, Vol. 22 (1955), 137–216; and the following additional articles by Haring: "The Lectures of Thierry of Chartres on Boethius' *De Trinitate*," in *Archives* . . . , Vol. 25 (1958), 113–226; "A Commentary on Boethius' *De Trinitate* by Thierry of Chartres," in *Archives* . . . , Vol. 23 (1956), 257–325; and "Two Commentaries on Boethius (*De Trinitate* and *De Hebdomadibus*) by Thierry of Chartres," in *Archives* . . . , Vol. 27 (1960), 65–136.

Extracts of Theodoric's commentary on Cicero's *De Inventione* were edited by P. Thomas, "Un Commentaire du moyen âge sur la rhétorique de Cicéron," in *Mélanges Charles Graux* (Paris, 1884), pp. 41–45; by W. H. D. Suringar, *Historia Critica Scholiastarum Latinorum*, Vol. I (Leiden, 1834), pp. 213–252; and by R. Ellis, "Petronianum," in *The Journal of Philology*, Vol. 9 (1880), 61.

On the above extracts see P. Delhaye, "L'Enseignement de la philosophie morale au XIIᵉ siècle," in *Mediaeval Studies*, Vol. 11 (1949), 77–99, Appendix C, 97–99; and F. Masai, "Extraits du commentaire de Thierry de Chartres au *De Inventione* de Cicéron," in *Scriptorium*, Vol. 5 (1951), 117–120, 308–309. There is an edition of the Prologue to the *Heptateuch* by E. Jeauneau in *Mediaeval Studies*, Vol. 16 (1954), 171–175; there is a summary of the contents of the Prologue in A. Clerval, *Les Écoles de Chartres* (Paris, 1895), 220–240.

A biography of Theodoric is A. Vernet, "Une Épitaphe inédite de Thierry de Chartres," in *Receuil de travaux offerts à M. Clovis Brunel*, 2 vols. (Paris, 1955), Vol. II, pp. 660–667.

Theodoric's doctrines are discussed in Étienne Gilson, *History of Christian Philosophy in the Middle Ages* (London, 1955), pp. 145–148; J. M. Parent, *La Doctrine de la création dans l'école de Chartres* (Paris and Ottawa, 1958), *passim*; and W. Jansen, *Der Kommentar des Clarenbaldus von Arras zu Boethius 'De Trinitate'* (Breslau, 1926), *passim*.

DAVID LUSCOMBE

THEOLOGY. See GOD, CONCEPTS OF; PHILOSOPHY OF RELIGION, HISTORY OF; PHILOSOPHY OF RELIGION, PROBLEMS OF; PHYSICOTHEOLOGY; RELIGION; see also articles listed under GOD, ARGUMENTS FOR THE EXISTENCE OF.

THEOPHRASTUS (c. 371–c. 286 B.C.), pupil of Aristotle and his successor as head of the Peripatetic school, was born in Eresus, a town in Lesbos. He wrote much and was also responsible for the preservation and transmission to posterity of Aristotle's works. Whether or not he actually edited them or revised them is a matter of controversy, but it is possible that for some time Aristotle's treatises remained in a somewhat fluid state within the school and that various versions were current.

The surviving works of Theophrastus comprise two botanical works, *Historia Plantarum* (*Enquiry into Plants*), in nine books, and *De Causis Plantarum* ("Etiology of Plants"), in six books, which together provided a full system of botany for the first time; and a series of small scientific treatises, some surviving in fragmentary or summary form only—"On Fire," "On Stones," "On Tiredness," "On Smells," "On Weather Signs," "On Sweat," "On Winds," "On Dizziness," "On Swooning," and "On Paralysis"; the essay "On Metaphysics"; and the famous *Characters*, which deals with thirty moral types based on the kind of classification given in Aristotle's *Nicomachean Ethics*.

In addition to these works, Diogenes Laërtius (*Lives*, Book V, 42 f.) lists over two hundred titles. Among the more important of these was the historical work "On the Opinions of the Physical Philosophers," in 18 books, which Hermann Diels in 1879 showed was the source of the greater part of later doxographical statements about the pre-Socratics. From this work we have one extract, *De Sensu* ("On Sensation"), but Diels's study gives us a fair idea of the arrangement and contents of the whole. A right assessment of Theophrastus' investigations here is fundamental for our understanding of the pre-Socratics. On one (extreme) view (McDiarmid), virtually all of Theophrastus' judgments and material were derived from Aristotle, but more probably Theophrastus, although writing within the framework of Aristotle's system of thought, had direct access to many of the original sources. He was certainly not uncritical in his treatment of doctrines in the fragment "On Sensation," so that he was probably critical elsewhere in his approach as well.

Much interest attaches to Theophrastus' general attitude toward the teaching of Aristotle. For a long time he was treated simply as the faithful but rather uninspired follower of the master, and it is only recently that his importance as an independent thinker has begun to be appreciated. Throughout his works Theophrastus is critical of a number of major Aristotelian doctrines, some of which are basic to Aristotle's thinking, but he stopped short of the fundamental reconstructions that some of his criticisms might seem to require. In logic he introduced the five indirect moods for the first figure of the syllogism, moods that later became the fourth figure. He improved Aristotle's proof of the conversion of universal negative propositions and maintained against the master the convertibility of universal negative propositions of possibility. He is credited with introducing the doctrine of hypothetical and disjunctive syllogisms but may have done no more than mention them. All these developments are attributed in the ancient sources to both Theophrastus and Eudemus, and they may have been jointly responsible for them.

In physics, Theophrastus' position is not altogether clear. He seems to have accepted from Aristotle the existence of a single first principle ("On Metaphysics," I.6), but he was dissatisfied with the theory of the prime mover (*ibid.*, II.7–9) and the universal application of teleology (*ibid.*, IV.14–15, IX.28–32); and he supposed that change occurred in every category, not merely in those of substance, quantity, quality, and place (Wimmer, Fr. 19). He rejected the Aristotelian doctrine of space (Fr. 21) and found difficulties in the Aristotelian doctrine of the intellect (nous). In his botanical works he stressed the importance of empiricism, and it is this side of Aristotle's thinking that seems to have especially appealed to him.

Works by Theophrastus

Works and Fragments, *Theophrasti Eresii Opera Quae Supersunt Omnia*, F. Wimmer, ed. (Teubner series). Leipzig, 1854–1862. With Latin translation (Didot series). Paris, 1866.
De Sensu, in Hermann Diels, *Doxographi Graeci*. Berlin, 1879. Also with English translation in G. M. Stratton, *Greek Physiological Psychology Before Aristotle*. London, 1917.
Enquiry into Plants, A. F. Hort, ed., 2 vols. London, 1916. Loeb Classical Library.
Metaphysica, W. D. Ross and F. H. Fobes, eds. Oxford, 1929.
Characters, R. G. Ussher, ed. London, 1960.

Works on Theophrastus

Barbotin, E., *La Théorie aristotélicienne de l'intellect d'après Théophraste*. Paris, 1954.
Bocheński, I. M., *La Logique de Théophraste*. Freiburg, Switzerland, 1947.
McDiarmid, I. B., "Theophrastus on the Presocratic Causes." *Harvard Studies in Classical Philology*, Vol. 61 (1953), 85–156.
Regenbogen, O., "Theophrastos," in A. Pauly and G. Wissowa, eds., *Realencyclopädie der classischen Altertumswissenschaft*, Supplementband VIII (1940).
Steinmetz, P., *Die Physik des Theophrastos von Eresos*. Bad Homburg, 1964.

G. B. Kerferd

THEORIES. See Laws and theories.

THEORY OF TYPES. See Russell, Bertrand Arthur William (section on logic and mathematics); Types, theory of.

THEOSOPHY. See Steiner, Rudolf; Swedenborg, Emanuel.

THINKING. Thinking is an essentially human activity occurring in two basic forms. We may think in order to attain knowledge of what is, must, or may be the case; we also may think with a view to making up our mind about what we will or will not do. Following Aristotle, these two forms of thought may be called, respectively, contemplation and deliberation. Both forms may be carried on well or badly, successfully or unsuccessfully, intelligently or stupidly. When contemplation is successful, it terminates in a conclusion; successful deliberation terminates in a decision or resolution. Again following Aristotle, the form of reasoning involved in contemplation may be called theoretical, and the form involved in deliberation may be called practical. Obviously, our day-by-day reasoning in ordinary life is an untidy mixture of both these basic forms.

Less generally, thinking is commonly understood as a largely covert activity, something done mainly *in foro interno*. This activity is also conceived of as intentional in Franz Brentano's sense of "being directed towards an object." For whether we are trying to solve a logical puzzle or are in the process of making up our minds about what to say to a noisy, officious neighbor, we are thinking about

something or other. This object (or subject) of our thinking may be either abstract or concrete. We may think about courage, justice, or humanity just as easily as we think about our neighbors and friends, our flowers and the evening sunset. In thinking about these various objects, whether abstract or concrete, we are also necessarily thinking something about them. We think of them as having various features, as doing something or other, or as being related in this or that way to other things of various sorts. For convenience, we may express the last fact about thinking by saying that our specific thoughts have contents as well as objects. We may think that the rain is welcome, that Mary is enchanting, that debts ought to be paid, or that triangularity entails trilaterality.

Another distinctive feature of particular thoughts is that the language used to describe them is nonextensional in a rich sense that is commonly called intentional. As Roderick Chisholm has pointed out, this type of discourse has three distinguishing marks. For one thing, some sentences used to describe thoughts or to ascribe them to thinkers may contain a substantive expression (a name or description) in such a way that neither the sentence nor its negation implies either the existence or the nonexistence of that thing to which the substantive expression truly applies. An example of such a sentence, which illustrates that one may think about nonexisting objects, is "Tommy is thinking about Santa Claus." Second, a noncompound sentence about thinking may contain a propositional clause in such a way that neither the sentence nor its negation implies either the truth or the falsity of the propositional clause. An example of such a sentence, emphasizing that one may think what is false, is "It occurred to Jones that demons cause schizophrenia." Finally, a sentence like "Mary thought that the author of *Waverley* wrote *Ivanhoe*" has the peculiarity that although Scott is the author of *Waverley*, one cannot infer that Mary thought that Scott wrote *Ivanhoe*. This last mark of intentionality implies that although things or events have many names and may be described in many different ways, the fact that a person thinks of them in connection with one name or description does not imply that he thinks of them in connection with some other name or description.

From these few remarks about the nonextensional character of discourse about thoughts, several important conclusions about the nature of thinking may immediately be drawn. First, of all the logically equivalent linguistic forms that may be used to describe either the object or the content of a man's thought, only one such form is in most cases strictly applicable. This suggests that thinking something about a particular subject generally involves conceiving of the subject under a certain name or description and attributing something to the subject according to a fairly specific form of attribution. To the extent that the name or description and the attribution are expressible in certain specific words, it will not, in general, be true that an expression or description of the thought in some other words will be equally accurate. The force of this point may be put by saying that at least some thoughts are essentially conceptual, tied to a particular mode of conceiving of a thing or attribute, and felicitously expressed only in specific verbal forms.

Another consequence of these considerations is that certain thoughts have a particular logical form. This emerges not only from the fact that in most thoughts a subject (or object) is in some way characterized, so that the thinking may involve the idea of, schematically, *S*'s being *M,* but also from the possibility that certain logical forms may be involved in a thought while equivalent forms are not. Thus, from "Jones thought that it will rain or snow," it does not follow that Jones thought that it will not both not rain and not snow, even though what is thought in these two cases is logically equivalent by virtue of De Morgan's laws. (One reason that this implication does not hold is that Jones may never have heard of these laws.)

Taking all of what has been said about particular thoughts into account, it appears that as ordinarily conceived, the thoughts involved in both contemplation and deliberation have the following basic features. First, they are characteristically, but perhaps not necessarily, carried on *in foro interno.* Second, they are directed toward an object or a number of objects, and they either attribute something to, or deny something about, this object or objects. Third, the language used to describe them is nonextensional in the sense of possessing at least one of the three intentional marks mentioned above. Fourth, thoughts are often conceived in relation to, and are felicitously expressible by, specific verbal forms; that is, they are often essentially linguistic or conceptual. Finally, particular thoughts have some kind of logical form; they may be categorical, hypothetical, disjunctive, universal, particular, and the like. In general, it may be said that the philosophical task of analyzing the concept of thinking must yield an explanation of exactly what sort of activity thinking is and of how and to what extent it can possess the features just mentioned.

Traditional theories. A survey of the full range of views on thinking that have been influential in the history of philosophy would reveal, roughly speaking, that most important theories of thinking have been variants of one or more of the following basic views: Platonism, Aristotelianism, conceptualism, imagism, psychological nominalism, and behaviorism. A brief description and criticism of these may thus serve as a useful introduction to the philosophical theory of thinking.

According to the Platonist, thinking is either a dialogue in the soul involving mental words that refer to Forms (such as Redness, Triangularity, Flying) and, possibly, to individuals (such as Socrates) or a spiritual activity of inspecting or recollecting Forms and discerning their natures and interrelations (see UNIVERSALS). According to Aristotelianism, thinking is an act of the intellect in which a thing's essence, or intelligible form, actually qualifies the intellect; to think about humanity is for one's intellect to be informed by—literally, to share—the essence humanity. To the extent that one thinks something about humanity—for instance, that it involves animality—one's intellect is also informed by this other essence, the latter being perhaps part of the former. For conceptualists (the rationalists, for example, and Kant) thinking is an activity of bringing concepts or ideas before the mind, these being either innate and applicable to the world in virtue of God's grace (Descartes, Leibniz) or else formed by abstraction

from sense experiences and thus actually sharing the abstract features of those experiences (Locke and, for empirical concepts only, Kant). For imagists (Berkeley, Hume) thinking is basically a sequence of episodes involving images; these images are tied to certain "habits," which are the inveterate tendencies of the mind to move from one image to another. To think about triangularity, according to this view, is to imagine some particular triangle while disposed to pass on to other images "of the same sort." According to the psychological nominalist (such as Hobbes when he speaks of reasoning) thinking is literally a dialogue in the soul (or, better, in the head) involving the use of verbal images, or mental words, which denote things or classes of things. In this view a complete thought is a mental utterance of a sentence, such as "Tom is tall." Finally, according to behaviorism, thinking is either thoughtful overt speech—thoughtful in the sense that it is in accordance with various principles of relevance, evidence, or inference that the agent is prepared to cite in explanation of his behavior—or a changing series of dispositions to behave intelligently that the agent can at any time avow.

Some basic difficulties. One perennial problem peculiar to the Platonic approach is that of accounting for one's ability to learn about the Forms and thus of learning to think. The trouble is that Forms are conceived of as independent of the changing world in which we live, and Plato's suggestion (in the *Phaedo*) that man was born with an ability to "recollect" the Forms experienced in another life is scarcely acceptable to a contemporary thinker. Also, since Forms are conceived of as distinct from the common domain of sense experience, there is a profound difficulty about how to justify knowledge of the Forms. Plato had argued in the *Theaetetus* that true knowledge "can give an account of itself," but it seems that a satisfactory answer has not been given to the question of how agreement in argument or a man's ability to answer objections brought against his view shows knowledge of an independent world of Forms. In recent years this problem has been posed, for instance by W. V. Quine, as a demand that the Platonist provide clear, objective criteria for the identity of such strange otherworldly entities as propositions and attributes.

A basic problem for the Aristotelian is to account for the logical form of a thought—that is, for the fact that one may think "If *p* were the case, *q* would be the case" or even "It will either rain or snow." The reason for difficulty here is that there are no intelligible forms corresponding to subjunctive conditionality, to disjunction, or, indeed, to any other logical relation, and it is by no means clear how the intelligible essences that do inform the intellect can be joined to constitute a thought about something conditional or disjunctive. Also, since all general ideas are presumably to be extracted from the sensible forms of experienced objects, thought about what is unobservable, like electrons and negative charges, seems to be impossible as well.

Apart from their highly questionable theories of intelligible essences, one basic drawback common to the Platonic and the Aristotelian views of thinking is their difficulty in accounting for a man's ability to think about particular, nonabstract objects. In the *Sophist*, Plato does, it is true, suggest that some of the mental words of a soul's dialogue may refer to particulars such as Socrates, but his general position is that the objects of thought must be unchanging, intelligible objects, which are universal rather than particular. In arguing that the individuality of a thing is determined by its matter, which is essentially a potentiality rather than an actuality, Aristotle was committed to a similar view, although his medieval heirs argued that particulars could be thoroughly conceived of if, like angels and gods, they constituted the only possible members of a species. Duns Scotus, philosophizing as a modified Aristotelian, attempted to get around this difficulty by arguing that particulars are merely congeries of universals. This view, although common in the objective idealism of the nineteenth century, faces a serious problem of distinguishing actual from merely possible particulars or, as Leibniz would have expressed it, of distinguishing a world containing a certain actual particular from a merely possible world containing a "compossible" particular. This Leibnizian type of objection tends to be expressed today by saying that the language used to characterize actual, as opposed to merely possible or fictional, particulars is essentially token reflexive, involving an implicit reference to the speaker: adequate identification of a particular concrete thing cannot be given wholly in context-independent general terms (see Hampshire and Strawson).

A difficulty common to conceptualism and Aristotelianism is that in most of their forms they involve an untenable theory of concept formation—namely, abstractionism. As Peter Geach has pointed out, this theory fails even for the favorite examples of the abstractionist since one cannot abstract the concept of color from an experience of scarlet, the latter not being redness plus a differentia. Conceptualists also share with Aristotelians the difficulty already noted of giving an adequate account of the logical form of various thoughts. Kant, a conceptualist, went further than most in the attempt, but he was forced to bring in a priori categories and to insist that men are born with an innate ability to think according to such patterns as "All . . . are . . ." and "Either . . . or . . . ." His approach in this regard was unsatisfactory not only because it is out of line with the well-attested fact that one must *learn* to think according to certain patterns but also because there are no special patterns in accordance with which all men *must* think. (On the last point see B. J. Whorf.)

Imagism shares with Aristotelianism and conceptualism the difficulty of accounting for the logical forms of thought, but it faces the added difficulty of explaining our ability to think of things never perceived, like infinity and million-sided polygons. Although psychological nominalism escapes these difficulties with ease, it runs headlong into the objection that we do not constantly mutter words to ourselves throughout every thinking moment. This objection is not meant to imply that we never think in words; its point is, rather, that we do not always do so and that it is not essential to our thinking one thing rather than another that we experience some verbal imagery. The final alternative, behaviorism, is simply Procrustean as a theory of thinking, for it ignores the plain fact that we do commonly think to ourselves *in foro interno*. As a result of this failure, the behaviorist is unable to account satisfactorily for the changes in behavior and behavioral dispositions that are frequently brought about by our silent deliberation and contemplation.

Merits of traditional theories. Although each theory just discussed has serious drawbacks and can therefore be said to fail in some measure or other, each nevertheless has some hold on the truth. Thus, the Platonist's idea that thinking is a kind of dialogue in the soul is not entirely empty, for while all thinking is not inner speech pure and simple, it is still true that it is generally like inner speech in crucial respects and that it is felicitously expressed in verbal discourse. The implication that thinking may be carried out *in foro interno* and yet not be mere inner speech is also shared by conceptualism and imagism. The latter has the added advantage of accounting for the occasional utility of imagistic thinking, as in pondering the location of a town on a map, the kind of angle formed by certain intersecting lines, and so on (see H. H. Price). Psychological nominalism actually accounts for most features of conceptual thinking except for the possibility of its occurring without verbal imagery. The forms of thought are explained by reference to the forms of the sentences used in inner speech, the object and content of a thought are explained with reference to the words used, and so on. Behaviorism, finally, although not without its shortcomings, does have the advantage of accounting for the important fact that some episodes of thinking, such as resolves and decisions, essentially involve behavioral dispositions: If a man is not moved, or disposed, to do A when he believes he is in circumstances C, he is not, *ceteris paribus,* resolved or decided to do A in C (see INTENTION). The crucial importance of this tie-up between certain forms of thought and behavioral dispositions is that it shows how an explanation of behavior in terms of reasons (rather than causes) can be acceptable. Without this tie-up we would have to say that a man's reasons for acting are strictly irrelevant to the question of why he so acted, for the intellect could not then "move a man to act."

Toward an adequate account. A useful way of working out an account of thinking free from the drawbacks of traditional theories is to examine Ryle's influential critique of all theories which insist that thinking must be done *in foro interno.* According to his argument in *The Concept of Mind,* all such theories are based on the mistaken idea that nonhabitual, intelligent human behavior is always guided by silent thought, whose presence explains why the behavior occurs and why it is intelligent. In Ryle's opinion this persistent idea is plainly untenable and leads to a vicious regress. This regress occurs because thinking is itself an activity that is admittedly done well or badly, intelligently or stupidly. This being so, the idea in point would imply that the intelligent character of thinking requires explanation by further thinking, which in turn guides the first thinking and explains why it occurs, why it is intelligent, and the like. Since this further thinking will itself be done well or badly, intelligently or stupidly, it will also require explanation by a third line of thinking and so on without end.

In rejecting this traditional idea, Ryle argues that reference to interior and anterior acts of thinking is not in any way needed for the explanation of most intelligent behavior. In his view a form of behavior, especially verbal behavior, may be regarded as intelligent, thoughtful, or even rational if it is done in accordance with certain principles of inference, evidence, relevance, and so on. That the behavior is in accordance with these principles does not mean that they are rehearsed in thought while the behavior is being carried out. On the contrary, it means only that the behavior conforms to, or is in line with, these principles and that the agent is disposed to cite or at least to allude to them if called upon to explain his behavior. Thus, if a man calculates out loud, then—assuming that this calculation is done in accordance with principles in the above sense—there is no need to introduce any further thought episodes to account for the fact that he arrives at a certain conclusion or resolution; the steps that led him to the conclusion or resolution are already laid bare. If the calculation shows intelligence or ingenuity, it does so by virtue of the relations between the overt steps; going from a premise to a conclusion is not proved reasonable or unreasonable, rational or irrational, by reference to something other than the premise and the conclusion. When we have the premise and the conclusion, we have all we need to decide whether the inference was reasonable. Even if we were to allude to interior steps of reasoning in order to explain a man's actions, we would have to appraise those steps in light of the same principles. Therefore, it may, in fact, be said that purely overt calculation or deliberation is itself a process of thinking and that thinking is not something that is necessarily done silently in the soul. In other words, overt thinking is just as useful a mode of thinking as any other, and there is no need, even no point, in always hunting for hidden acts of thought.

Criticism of Ryle's approach. Although there is considerable plausibility to Ryle's approach, it must be granted that not all the calculation or deliberation that accounts for a man's actions is done out loud or on paper. In fact, nothing is more obvious than the fact that a good share of one's calculation is not done overtly and that reference to silent thought is constantly and legitimately made in order to account for activities that would otherwise remain inexplicable. Thus, a man may make a move in chess after sitting in silent anguish for long minutes at the board; and the intelligence of this move will remain a stubborn question mark until, perhaps after the game, he outlines the strategy behind it. The same is true in countless other cases. On being asked a question, the mathematics student may close his eyes for a minute before giving the answer, and when the answer is given, he can usually follow it with a proof, a line of reasoning he will claim to recall having thought out *in foro interno.*

Ryle was, of course, aware of these cases in *The Concept of Mind,* and he attempted to account for them by arguing that a man can learn to mutter to himself as well as mutter out loud. Thus, when pressed, Ryle could not entirely dispense with the traditional conception of covert thinking; in regarding it as "inner speech" he was, in fact, squarely in the tradition of Hobbes, and his view is thus subject to the same fundamental difficulty—namely, that to most it seems plainly false that inner speech occurs whenever one can correctly be said to think *in foro interno.*

The analogy theory. Although Ryle's view of thinking does not, as a whole, succeed, in the opinion of the present writer it does come close to the truth. For while silent thought need not be inner speech, it may still be an activity that is at least formally analogous to speech. In what sense "formally analogous"? In the sense in which chess played with pennies and nickels is formally analogous to chess played with standard pieces or in which the Frenchman's "Il pleut" is formally analogous to the Englishman's "It is raining": the same basic moves are made, but the empirical features of the activities are different. Thus, while the thought *p* is empirically different from the act of saying that *p* (in that the former need not even involve verbal imagery), it may still be regarded as formally the same: both are activities that conform to the same principles and have many of the same implications. This sort of formal identity among empirically different activities is, of course, hard to state clearly, but at least an intuitive sense of what is meant by speaking of such an identity can be conveyed by the following analogy. Saying that *p* is a formal analogue of thinking that *p* in the way that playing "Texas chess" (with automobiles on certain counties) is a formal analogue of playing ordinary chess (with ivory pieces on checkered boards). What is essential in both cases is that formally analogous activities are carried on in accordance with the same basic principles—the principles or rules of chess, on one hand, and various principles of inference and relevance, on the other.

This theory of thinking, which may be called the analogy theory, does more than merely correct the shortcomings of Ryle's view. It also seems to account for all of the distinctive features of conceptual thinking that were mentioned earlier. Since it also appears to possess none of the drawbacks of traditional theories, it is perhaps the most satisfactory account of thinking yet developed by philosophers.

Bibliography

CONTEMPORARY DISCUSSIONS

Bergmann, Gustav, "Intentionality," in *Meaning and Existence.* Madison, Wis., 1960.

Chisholm, Roderick, "Sentences About Believing." *PAS,* Vol. 56 (1955–1956), 125–148.

Chisholm, Roderick, and Sellars, Wilfrid, "Intentionality and the Mental," in *Minnesota Studies in the Philosophy of Science,* Vol. II, Herbert Feigl and Grover Maxwell, eds. Minneapolis, Minn., 1958.

Ginnane, W. J., "Thoughts." *Mind,* Vol. 49 (1960), 372–390.

Hampshire, Stuart, *Thought and Action.* London, 1959.

Kenny, Anthony. *Action, Emotion, and Will.* London, 1963.

Price, H. H., *Thinking and Experience.* London, 1953. An extremely valuable discussion of traditional theories of thinking.

Quine, W. V., *Word and Object.* Cambridge, Mass., 1960.

Ryle, Gilbert, *The Concept of Mind.* London, 1949.

Strawson, P. F., *Individuals.* London, 1959.

Whorf, B. J., *Language, Thought, and Reality.* Cambridge, Mass., 1956.

TRADITIONAL THEORIES

Detailed information on traditional theories may be found in F. C. Copleston, *A History of Philosophy,* 7 vols. (New York, 1959).

Specific reference may be made, however, to the following classics, which are published in numerous editions: Aristotle, *De Anima* and *Nicomachean Ethics*, Book 5; George Berkeley, *Principles of Human Knowledge*, Introduction; René Descartes, *Meditations* and *Principles of Philosophy;* Thomas Hobbes, *Leviathan*, Part I, Ch. 5, and *Elements of Philosophy*, Chs. 2–3; David Hume, *Enquiry Concerning Human Understanding*, Secs. 2–4, and *Treatise of Human Nature*, Secs. 1–4; Immanuel Kant, *Critique of Pure Reason* and *Critique of Practical Reason;* G. W. Leibniz, *Leibniz Selections,* P. P. Wiener, ed. (New York, 1951); John Locke, *Essay Concerning Human Understanding*, Book II, Chs. 1, 2, 7, 8; Plato, *Phaedo, Republic, Sophist,* and *Theaetetus.*

PSYCHOLOGICAL STUDIES

Bartlett, F. C., *Thinking.* London, 1953.
Bruner, J. S., Goodnow, J. J., and Austin, G. A., *A Study of Thinking.* New York, 1956.

THE ANALOGY THEORY

Aune, Bruce, "On Thought and Feeling." *Philosophical Quarterly,* Vol. 13 (1963), 1–12.
Aune, Bruce, *Epistemology and the Philosophy of Mind.* New York, 1966. Ch. 8.
Geach, Peter, *Mental Acts.* London, 1957.
Sellars, Wilfrid, "Physical Realism." *Philosophy and Phenomenological Research,* Vol. 15 (1954), 13–32. An illuminating discussion of conceptualism and recent Platonism.
Sellars, Wilfrid, *Science, Perception, and Reality.* London, 1964. "Being and Being Known" is an up-to-date critique of Aristotelianism. See also "Empiricism and the Philosophy of Mind" and "Philosophy and the Scientific Image of Man."

BRUCE AUNE

THOMAS À KEMPIS (1379/1380–1471), writer on asceticism and probable author of *The Imitation of Christ,* was born in Kempen, near Düsseldorf, Germany. He belonged to the Brethren of the Common Life, a group which was much influenced by Jan van Ruysbroeck and whose organization centered on the Windesheim community. The major part of Thomas' life was spent at the Augustinian monastery of St. Agnes, near Zwolle.

Thomas' writings on the interior life and ways of practicing virtue are not philosophical or theoretical but are purely practical in intent. This is true also of *The Imitation of Christ,* about whose authorship there has been much dispute. It is not altogether certain that the work, really a set of four treatises, should be attributed to Thomas. The oldest manuscripts date from about 1422 and contain only the first book, and the first complete edition goes back to 1427. Since the work is not quoted earlier than the fifteenth century, it seems likely that it originated during Thomas' lifetime. Moreover, the style is remarkably like that of writings which can certainly be ascribed to him (a statistical investigation has also supported this). For these reasons we can rule out certain speculative attributions (to Jean Gerson and to John Gersen, in the thirteenth century). On the other hand, the first attribution of the book to him occurred rather late, in the second edition of an account of the Windesheim community written in the latter part of the fifteenth century. The fact that Thomas signed a manuscript of the *Imitation* is not conclusive, for he was, like his fellow monks, a copyist and also signed a Bible. But the balance of probability is that Thomas himself compiled the work anonymously, and he certainly incorporated into it materials not original to himself, especially in the first book.

The wide circulation of the book was partly due to the efforts of the copyists at Windesheim, but it was also due to the kind of piety it recommended. The second part of the full title (*Of the Imitation of Christ and of Contempt for All Worldly Vanities*) indicates that its teachings were adapted to the monastic life—and indeed it was primarily intended as a handbook for monks. But its tender concentration on the figure of Jesus made attractive its doctrine of resignation—the surrendering of all worldly concerns to the service of, and imitation of, Christ. Moreover, it gave very concrete guidance on many problems—for example, how to distinguish the results of grace from natural acts and propensities. The most notable feature of the book, however, is its uncompromising and uncomfortable insistence on self-mortification as preparation for grace and the presence of the true Lover of the soul, Christ. The "imitation" of Christ that Thomas recommends is not a simple copying of Jesus but acting by analogy with Jesus, whose life was mainly characterized, according to Thomas, by suffering and self-sacrifice.

The first book has mainly to do with the moral reform of the individual. The second concerns the preparation for the interior or illuminative life. The third consists in a dialogue between Christ and the soul which gives a further exposition of ascetic practices, and one or two passages give a hint of the kind of mystical experience awaiting those who truly love Christ. The fourth book is a manual for those who receive Holy Communion.

There is very little theology in the *Imitation.* Thomas seems to have been reacting against the speculations of academic theology, for he wrote: "Of what use is your highly subtle talk about the blessed Trinity, if you are not humble?" and "I would rather feel compunction than be able to produce the most precise definition of it." The strongly practical bent of the work, in any event, gave it a continuing relevance to the Christian life and enabled it to achieve the status of a classic ranking, in Christian piety, with *Pilgrim's Progress.*

Works by Thomas

Opera et Libri Vite Fratris Thome a Kempis, P. Danhausser, ed. Nuremberg, 1494. Critical edition by M. J. Pohl, 7 vols. Freiburg im Breisgau, 1902–1922.
Prayers and Meditations on the Life of Christ, translated by William Duthoit. London, 1904.
The Founders of the New Devotion, translated by J. P. Arthur. London, 1905.
The Chronicle of the Canons Regular of Mount St. Agnes, translated by J. P. Arthur. London, 1906.
Meditations and Sermons on the Incarnation, Life and Passion of Our Lord, translated by Dom Vincent Scully. London, 1907.
Sermons to the Novices Regular, translated by Dom Vincent Scully. London, 1907.
The Imitation of Christ, translated by Ronald Knox and Michael Oakley. London, 1959. The freshest and most direct translation.

Works on Thomas

Huijben, Jacques, and Debougnie, Pierre, *L'Auteur ou les auteurs de L'Imitation.* Louvain, 1957. On the question of authorship of the *Imitation.*

Scully, Dom Vincent, *Life of the Venerable Thomas à Kempis*. London, 1901.

Yule, George Udney, *The Statistical Study of Literary Vocabulary*. Cambridge, 1944. On the question of the authorship of the *Imitation*.

NINIAN SMART

THOMAS AQUINAS, ST. (c. 1224–1274), Catholic theologian and philosopher, was born at Roccasecca, Italy, the youngest son of Landolfo and Teodora of Aquino. At about the age of five he began his elementary studies under the Benedictine monks at nearby Montecassino. He went on to study liberal arts at the University of Naples. It is probable that Aquinas became a master in arts at Naples before entering the Order of Preachers (Dominicans) in 1244. He studied in the Dominican courses in philosophy and theology, first at Paris and, from 1248 on, under Albert the Great at Cologne. In 1252 he was sent to the University of Paris for advanced study in theology; he lectured there as a bachelor in theology until 1256, when he was awarded the magistrate (doctorate) in theology. Accepted after some opposition from other professors as a fully accredited member of the theology faculty in 1257, Aquinas continued to teach at Paris until 1259.

Aquinas then spent almost ten years at various Dominican monasteries in the vicinity of Rome, lecturing on theology and philosophy (including an extensive study of the major works of Aristotle) and performing various consultative and administrative functions in his order. In the fall of 1268 Aquinas returned for his second professorate in theology at the University of Paris. He engaged in three distinct controversies: against a group of conservative theologians who were critical of his philosophic innovations; against certain radical advocates of Aristotelianism or Latin Averroism; and against some critics of the Dominicans and Franciscans and their right to teach at the university. Many of Aquinas' literary works were in process or completed at this time. It is thought that he was provided with secretarial help in this task, partly in view of the fact that his own handwriting was practically illegible. Called back to Italy in 1272, Aquinas taught for a little more than a year at the University of Naples and preached a notable series of vernacular sermons there. Illness forced him to discontinue his teaching and writing toward the end of 1273. Early in 1274 he set out for Lyons, France, to attend a church council. His failing health interrupted the trip at a point not far from his birthplace, and he died at Fossanova in March of that year.

The writings of Thomas Aquinas were produced during his twenty years (1252–1273) as an active teacher. All in Latin, they consist of several large theological treatises, plus recorded disputations on theological and philosophical problems (the "Disputed Questions" and "Quodlibetal Questions"), commentaries on several books of the Bible, commentaries on 12 treatises of Aristotle, and commentaries on Boethius, the pseudo-Dionysius, and the anonymous *Liber de Causis*. There are also about forty miscellaneous notes, letters, sermons, and short treatises on philosophical and religious subjects. Although Aquinas' philosophic views may be found in almost all his writings

(thus the "Exposition of the Book of Job" reads like a discussion among philosophers), certain treatises are of more obvious interest to philosophers. These are listed in detail at the end of this article.

General philosophical position. In the main, Aquinas' philosophy is a rethinking of Aristotelianism, with significant influences from Stoicism, Neoplatonism, Augustinism, and Boethianism. It also reflects some of the thinking of the Greek commentators on Aristotle and of Cicero, Avicenna, Averroës, ibn-Gabirol, and Maimonides. This may suggest that we are dealing with an eclectic philosophy, but actually Aquinas reworked the speculative and practical philosophies of his predecessors into a coherent view of the subject which shows the stamp of his own intelligence and, of course, the influence of his religious commitment.

One of the broad characteristics of Aquinas' work in philosophy is a temperamental tendency to seek a middle way on questions that have been given a wide range of answers. This spirit of moderation is nowhere better illustrated than in his solution to the problem of universals. For centuries philosophers had debated whether genera and species are realities in themselves (Plato, Boethius, William of Champeaux) or mere mental constructs (Roscelin, Peter Abelard). What made this odd discussion important was the conviction (certainly shared by Aquinas) that these universals (such as humanity, justice, whiteness, dogness) are the primary objects of human understanding. Most thinkers in the Middle Ages felt that if something is to be explained, it must be treated in universal terms. Therefore, the problem of universals was not simply an academic question.

Aquinas' position on this problem is now called moderate realism. He denied that universals are existing realities (and frequently criticized Plato for having suggested that there is a world of intelligible Forms), but he also insisted that men's universal concepts and judgments have some sort of foundation in extramental things. This basis for the universality, say of humanity, would consist in the real similarity found among all individual men. It was not that Aquinas attributed an actual, existent universal nature to all individual men: that would be an extreme realism. Rather, only individuals exist; but the individuals of a given species or class resemble each other, and that is the basis for thinking of them as universally representative of a common nature.

Thomas' spirit of compromise as a philosopher was balanced by another tendency, that toward innovation. His original Latin biographers all stress this feature of his work. Thomas introduced new ways of reasoning about problems and new sources of information, and he handled his teaching in a new way. In this sense Thomas Aquinas was not typical of the thirteenth century and was perhaps in advance of his contemporaries.

Faith and rational knowledge. As Aquinas saw it, faith (*fides*) falls midway between opinion and scientific knowledge (*scientia*); it is more than opinion because it involves a firm assent to its object; and it is less than knowledge because it lacks vision. Both are intellectual acts and habits of assent: in the case of faith a person is not sufficiently moved by the object to accept it as true, so, by an act of will, he inclines himself to believe. Knowledge implies assent motivated by a personal seeing of the object without any direct influence from will. Where objects of belief have to do with divine matters which exceed man's natural cognitive capacity, the disposition to believe such articles of religious faith is regarded as a special gift from God. Reason (*ratio*) is another type of intellectual activity: simple understanding and reasoning differ only in the manner in which the intellect works. Through intellection (understanding) one knows simply by seeing what something means, while through reason one moves discursively from one item of knowledge to another. (These functions of believing and knowing are treated in many places by Aquinas: *Summa Contra Gentiles* III, 147; *In Boethii de Trinitate*, Ques. II and III; *Summa Theologiae* I, Ques. 79–84.)

Aquinas thought that philosophy entailed reasoning from prior knowledge, or present experience, to new knowledge (the way of discovery) and the rational verification of judgments by tracing them back to more simply known principles (the way of reduction). Where the basic principles are grasped by man's natural understanding of his sensory experiences, the reasoning processes are those of natural science and philosophy. If one starts to reason from judgments accepted on religious faith, then one is thinking as a theologian. Questions V and VI of *In Boethii de Trinitate* develop Aquinas' methodology of the philosophical sciences: philosophy of nature, mathematics, and metaphysics. He distinguished speculative or theoretical reasoning from the practical: the purpose of speculation is simply to know; the end of practical reasoning is to know how to act. He described two kinds of theology: the philosophical "theology," metaphysics, which treats divine matters as principles for the explanation of all things, and the theology taught in Scripture, which "studies divine things for their own sakes" (*In Boethii de Trinitate* V, 4 c).

Thus philosophy, for Aquinas, was a natural type of knowledge open to all men who wish to understand the meaning of their ordinary experiences. The "philosophers" whom he habitually cited were the classic Greek, Latin, Islamic, and Jewish sages. Christian teachers mentioned by Aquinas were the "saints" (Augustine, John of Damascus, Gregory, Ambrose, Dionysius, Isidore, and Benedict); they were never called Christian philosophers. The word "theology" was rarely used by Aquinas. In the first question of his *Summa Theologiae* he formally calls his subject sacred doctrine (*sacra doctrina*) and says that its principles, unlike those of philosophy, are various items of religious faith. Thus, Thomas Aquinas was by profession a theologian, or better, a teacher of sacred doctrine who also studied and wrote about philosophy. He obviously used a good deal of pagan and non-Christian philosophy in all his writings. His own understanding of these philosophies was influenced by his personal faith—as almost any man's judgment is influenced by his stand for or against the claim of religious faith—in this sense Thomism is a "Christian philosophy." Aquinas did not ground his philosophical thinking on principles of religious belief, however, for this would have destroyed his distinction between philosophy and sacred doctrine, as presented in the opening chapters of the first book of *Summa Contra Gentiles*. One of the clearest efforts to maintain the autonomy of philosophy is found in Aquinas' *De Aeternitate Mundi* (about 1270), in which he insists that, as far as philosophical considerations go, the universe might be eternal. As a Christian, he believed that it is not eternal.

Among interpreters of Aquinas there has been much debate whether his commentaries on Aristotle deal with his personal thinking. It is generally agreed even by non-Thomists (W. D. Ross, A. E. Taylor) that these expositions are helpful to the reader who wishes to understand Aristotle. It is not so clear whether the mind of Aquinas is easily discernible in them. One group of Thomists (Étienne Gilson, Joseph Owens, A. C. Pegis) stresses the more obviously personal writings (such as the two *Summa*'s) as bases for the interpretation of his thought; another school of interpretation (J. M. Ramírez, Charles De Koninck, J. A. Oesterle) uses the Aristotelian commentaries as the main sources for Aquinas' philosophic thought.

Theory of knowledge. The Thomistic theory of knowledge is realistic. (This theory is presented in *Summa Theologiae* I, 79–85; *Quaestiones Disputatae de Veritate* I, 11; *In Libros Posteriorum Analyticorum* I, 5; II, 20.) Men obtain their knowledge of reality from the initial data of sense experience. Apart from supernatural experiences which some mystics may have, Thomas limited human cognition to sense perception and the intellectual understanding of it. Sense organs are stimulated by the colored, audible, odorous, gustatory, and tactile qualities of extramental bodies; and sensation is the vital response through man's five external sense powers to such stimulation. Aquinas assumed that one is cognitively aware of red flowers, noisy animals, cold air, and so on. Internal sensation (common, imaginative, memorative, and cogitative functions) works to perceive, retain, associate, and judge the various impressions (phantasms) through which things are directly known. Man's higher cognitive functions, those of understanding, judging, and reasoning, have as their objects the universal meanings that arise out of sense experience. Thus, one sees and remembers an individual apple on the level of sensation—but he judges it to be healthful because it contains vitamins, or for any other general reason, on the level of intellectual knowledge. Universals (health, humanity, redness) are not taken as existing realities but are viewed as intelligibilities (*rationes*) with a basis in what is common to existents. As a moderate realist, Aquinas would resent being classified as a Platonist; yet he would defend the importance of our knowledge of the general and common characteristics of things.

Although human cognition begins with the knowing of bodily things, man can form some intellectual notions and judgments concerning immaterial beings: souls, angels, and God. Aquinas taught that man does this by negating certain aspects of bodies (for instance, a spirit does not occupy space) and by using analogy. When the notion of power is attributed to God, its meaning is transferred from an initially physical concept to the analogous perfection of that which can accomplish results in the immaterial order. Thomas did not think that men, during earthly life, can know the nature of God in any adequate, positive way.

Discursive reasoning was taken as an intellectual

process moving from or toward first principles in logical processes of demonstration (the ways of discovery and reduction, described above). In one way, sense experience is the first principle (starting point) for all of man's natural knowledge. This is one aspect of Aquinas' empiricism. Following Aristotle's *Posterior Analytics,* Thomas taught that many sensations combine to form a unified memory, and many memories constitute sense experience. From this manifold of experience, by a sort of sensory induction, there arises within human awareness a beginning (*principium*) of understanding. Such first principles are not demonstrated (they naturally emerge from sense cognition), but they become the roots for consequent intellectual reasoning. A doctor who tries a variety of remedies to treat headaches eventually notices that one drug works well in almost all cases—at some point he grasps the universal "Drug *A* is a general remedy for headache." From this principle he proceeds rationally to order his practice. If he becomes a teacher of medicine, he uses such a theoretical principle to instruct others. This is the basis of the life of reason.

Philosophy and the physical world. In his exposition of the *Liber de Causis* (Lect. 1), Aquinas described a sequence of philosophic studies: logic, mathematics, natural philosophy (physics), moral philosophy, and, finally, metaphysics. The first kind of reality examined in this course would be that of the physical world. (At the start of the next century, Duns Scotus criticized Thomas for attempting to base his metaphysics and his approaches to God on physics.) Interpreters still debate whether Aquinas himself felt that this was the order to be followed in learning philosophy, or whether he was merely reporting one way that the "philosophers" had taught it. In any case, the philosophical study of bodies, of mobile being in the Aristotelian sense, was important to Aquinas. One group of his writings (*De Principiis Naturae,* parts of Book II of the *Summa Contra Gentiles,* the treatise *De Aeternitate Mundi*) offers a quite personal treatment of this world of bodies. Another set of writings (the commentaries on Aristotle's *Physics* and *De Generatione et Corruptione*) shows how indebted Aquinas was to Aristotle in his theory of physical reality.

Matter and form. The philosophy of nature (*phusis*) was understood as the study of a special kind of beings, those subject to several kinds of change. Physical beings have primary matter as one component and, depending on their species or kind, substantial form as their other integral principle. Neither matter nor form is a thing by itself; matter and form are simply the determinable and determining factors within any existing physical substance. Like Aristotle, Aquinas took it that there are many species of bodily substances: all the different kinds of inanimate material (wood, gold, water, etc.) and all the species of plants and animals. Within each such species there is one specifying principle (the substantial form of wood, potato plant, or dog), and the many individual members of each species are differentiated by the fact that the matter constituting dog *A* could not also constitute dog *B* (so viewed, matter is said to be quantified, or marked by quantity).

Change. Being mobile, physical beings are subject to four kinds of change (*motus*): of place (locomotion), of size (quantitative change), of color, shape, and so on (qualitative change), and of species of substance (generation and corruption, substantial change). Basically, prime matter is that which remains constant and provides continuity during a change from one substance to another. When a pig eats an apple, that part of the apple really assimilated by the pig becomes the very substance of the pig; some factor in the apple, the prime matter, must continue on into the pig. All four types of change are explained in terms of the classic theory of four causes. The final cause is the answer to the question "why" something exists or occurs; the agent or efficient cause is the maker or producer of the change; the material cause is that out of which the change comes; and the formal cause is the specifying factor in any event or existent. So used, "cause" has the broad meaning of *raison d'être.*

Space and time. Certain other points in Aquinas' philosophy of nature further illustrate the influence of Aristotle. Place, for instance, is defined as the "immobile limit of the containing body" (*In IV Physicorum* 6). Moreover, each primary type of body (the four elements still are earth, air, fire, and water) is thought to have its own "proper" place. Thus, the place for fire is "up" and that for earth is "down." Some sort of absolute, or box, theory of space may be presupposed; yet in the same passage Aquinas' discussion of the place of a boat in a flowing river indicates a more sophisticated understanding of spatial relativity. Time is defined, as in Aristotle, as the measure of motion in regard to "before" and "after." Eternity is a type of duration differing from time in two ways: the eternal has neither beginning nor termination, and the eternal has no succession of instants but exists entirely at once (*tota simul*).

Encouragement of science. Doubtless Aquinas' philosophy of the physical world was limited and even distorted by certain views and factual errors derived from Aristotle and from thirteenth-century science. Apart from the mistaken hypothesis that each element has its proper place in the universe, Thomas also used the Eudoxian astronomy, which placed the earth at the center of a system of from 49 to 53 concentric spheres. (Besides the Commentary on *De Caelo* II, 10, and the Commentary on *Meteorologia* II, 10; see *Summa Contra Gentiles* I, 20, and *Summa Theologiae* I, 68, 4 c.) At times Thomas showed an open mind on such questions and an ability to rise above the limitations of his period. His Commentary on Aristotle's *Metaphysics* (Lect. 1 on Book III and Lect. 9 on Book XII) provides a key instance. Pointing out that astronomers differ widely on the number and motions of the planets, Aquinas recommended that one study all the reports and theories of such scientists, even though these scientific explanations are not the last word on the matter and are obviously open to future revision. He further compared the study of physical science to the work of a judge in a court of law. One should listen to, and try to evaluate, all important testimony before attempting to formulate one's own judgment on the problems of contemporary science. This is Aquinas at his best, hardly a philosophical dogmatist.

Human functions and man's nature. Anthropology, or psychology, in the classical sense of the study of man's psyche, forms an important part of Aquinas' philosophy.

His view of man owed much to the Aristotelian treatise *On the Soul*, to the Christian Platonism of Augustine and John of Damascus, and to the Bible. This part of Aquinas' thought will be found in *Scriptum in IV Libros Sententiarum* ("Commentary on the *Sentences*") I, Dists. 16–27; *Summa Contra Gentiles* II, 58–90; *Quaestio Disputata de Anima;* the *Libros de Anima;* and *Summa Theologiae* I, 75–90.

Aquinas' usual way of working out his theory of human nature was first to examine certain activities in which man engages, then to reason to the kinds of operative powers needed to explain such actions, and finally to conclude to the sort of substantial nature that could be the subject of such powers. He described the biological activities of man as those of growth, assimilation of food, and sexual reproduction. A higher set of activities included sensory perception, emotive responses to what is perceived, and locomotion: these activities man shares with brute animals. A third group of activities comprises the cognitive functions of understanding, judging, and reasoning, as well as the corresponding appetitive functions of affective inclination toward or away from the objects of understanding. To these various functions Aquinas assigned generic powers (operative potencies) of growth, reproduction, sensory cognition and appetition, physical locomotion, and intellectual cognition and appetition (will).

Re-examining these functional powers in detail, Aquinas distinguished five special sense powers for the cognition of physical individuals: sight, hearing, smell, taste, and touch. These functions and powers are called external because their proper objects are outside the mental awareness of the perceiver: this is essential to epistemological realism. Following these are four kinds of internal sensory activities: the perceptual grasping of a whole object (*sensus communis*), the simple retention of sensed images (imagination), the association of retained images with past time (sense memory), and concrete discrimination or judgment concerning individual things (cogitative sense, particular reason). Still on the level of sensory experience, Aquinas (here influenced by John of Damascus) described two kinds of appetition (emotion): a simple tendency toward or away from what is sensed as good or evil (this affective power is called the concupiscible appetite), and a more complicated sensory inclination to meet bodily threats, obstacles, and dangers by attacking or avoiding them or by putting up with them (this affective power is called irascible appetite). Eleven distinct kinds of sensory passions (emotions) are attributed to these two sensory appetites: love, desire, delight, hate, aversion, and sorrow to the concupiscible; fear, daring, hope, despair, and anger to the irascible. Much of this psychological analysis is quite sophisticated, employing data from Greek, Roman, and early Christian thought and also using the physiological and psychological treatises of Islamic and Jewish scholars. It also forms the basis of the analysis of human conduct in Thomistic ethics.

On the higher level of distinctively human experience, Aquinas found various other activities and powers. These are described in his commentary on Book III of Aristotle's *De Anima*, in the *Summa Contra Gentiles* (II, 59–78), and in Questions 84–85 of the *Summa Theologiae*. The general capacity to understand (*intellectus*) covers simple apprehension, judging, and reasoning. The objects of intellection are universal aspects (*rationes*) of reality. Since universal objects do not exist in nature, Aquinas described one intellectual action as the abstraction of universal meanings (*intentiones*) from the individual presentations of sense experience. This abstractive power is called agent intellect (*intellectus agens*). A second cognitive function on this level is the grasping (*comprehensio*) of these abstracted meanings in the very act of cognition; this activity is assigned to a different power, the possible intellect (*intellectus possibilis*). Thus, there are two quite different "intellects" in Thomistic psychology: one abstracts, the other knows. No special power is required for intellectual memory; the retention of understandings is explained by habit formation in the possible intellect.

Will. Affective responses to the universal objects of understanding are functions of intellectual appetition. Considered quite different from sensory appetition, this is the area of volition, and the special power involved is the will (*voluntas*). Aquinas distinguished two kinds of volitional functions. First, there are those basic and natural tendencies of approval and affective approach to an object that is judged good or desirable without qualification. In regard to justice, peace, or a perfectly good being, for instance, Aquinas felt that a person's will would be naturally and necessarily attracted to such objects. This natural movement of the will is not free. Second, there are volitional movements toward or away from intellectually known objects that are judged as partly desirable or as partly undesirable. Such movements of will are directed by intellectual judgments evaluating the objects. In this case volition is said to be "deliberated" (specified by intellectual considerations) and free. It is in the act of decision (*arbitrium*) that man is free. Aquinas did not talk about "free will"; the term *libera voluntas* is found only twice in all his works, and then in a nontechnical usage; rather, he spoke of free choice or decision (*liberum arbitrium*). Man, by virtue of his intellectual powers, is free in some of his actions.

Soul. Although Aquinas sometimes spoke as if these various "powers" of man were agents, he formally stressed the view that it is the whole man who is the human agent. A human being is an animated body in which the psychic principle (*anima*) is distinctive of the species and determines that the material is human. In other words, man's soul is his substantial form. Some of man's activities are obviously very like those of brutes, but the intellectual and volitional functions transcend materiality by virtue of their universal and abstracted character. Aquinas took as an indication of the immateriality of the human soul the fact that it can understand universal meanings and make free decisions. The soul is a real part of man and, being both immaterial and real, it is spiritual. From certain other features of man's higher activities, especially from the unity of conscious experience, Aquinas concluded to the simplicity and integration of man's soul: it is not divisible into parts. This, in turn, led him to the conclusion that the soul is incapable of corruption (disintegration into parts) and thus is immortal.

Since Thomas thought the soul incapable of being partitioned, he could not explain the coming into being of new human souls by biological process. He was thus forced to the view that each rational soul is originated by divine creation from nothing. Human parents are not the total cause of their offspring; they share the work of procreation with God. This view explains why Aquinas put so much stress on the dignity and sanctity of human reproduction, which he regarded as more than a biological function. When he claimed, in his ethics, that the begetting and raising of children is the primary purpose of married life, he was not thinking of simple sexual activity but of a human participation in God's creative function. This does not mean that man is the highest of God's creatures; Aquinas speculated that there are other kinds of purely intellectual beings with activities, powers, and natures superior to those of men. These are angels. Thomas Aquinas is called the Angelic Doctor in Catholic tradition because of his great interest in these purely spiritual but finite beings. They would constitute the highest realm of the universe.

Metaphysics and real being. Aquinas devoted much thought to the question "What does it mean to be?" Many Thomists think that his greatest philosophical ability was shown in the area of metaphysics. His general theory of reality incorporates much of the metaphysics of Aristotle, and some interpreters have seen Thomistic metaphysics as but a baptized Aristotelianism. Recent Thomistic scholarship has selected two non-Aristotelian metaphysical teachings for new emphasis: the theory of participation and the general influence of Platonic metaphysics (L. B. Geiger, Cornelio Fabro, R. J. Henle), and the primacy of *esse*, the fundamental act of being (Gilson, Jacques Maritain, G. P. Klubertanz). Because *esse*, which simply means "to be," is sometimes translated as "existence," this second point of emphasis is called by some writers the existentialism of Thomistic metaphysics. It has little, however, to do with present-day existentialism. A major treatment of metaphysical problems is to be found in Aquinas' long Commentary on Aristotle's *Metaphysics*, but here again the problem is to decide how much is Thomistic. Some very competent scholars (Pegis, Gilson) regard this work as a restatement of Aristotelianism; others (De Koninck, Herman Reith) consider the Commentary to be a key exposition of Aquinas' own metaphysics. It is admitted by all that there are some explanations in it that are not found in Aristotle.

Metaphysics, for Aquinas, was the effort to understand reality in general, to find an ultimate explanation of the manifold of experience in terms of the highest causes. His predecessors had variously described the subject matter of this study as existing immaterial substances, as the most universal and common aspects of being, as the first causes of all things, and as the divine being in itself. Commenting on these opinions in the Prologue to his Commentary on the *Metaphysics,* Aquinas remarked: "Although this science considers these items, it does not think of each of them as its subject; its subject is simply being in general." In this sense, he called the study of being "first philosophy."

Analogy. It is distinctive of Aquinas' thought to maintain that all existing realities, from God down to the least perfect thing, are beings—and that "being" has in this usage an analogical and not a univocal meaning. In a famous passage (*In I Sententiarum* 19, 5, 2, ad 1) Aquinas de-

scribes three sorts of analogy: one in which a given perfection is present in one item but only attributed to another; one in which one perfection exists in a somewhat different way in two or more items; and one in which some sort of remote resemblance or community is implied between two items which have no identity either in existence or in signification. "In this last way," Aquinas adds "truth and goodness, and all things of this kind, are predicated analogously of God and creatures." In later works the notion of proportionality is introduced to develop the concept of the analogy of being. Vision in the eye is a good of the body in somewhat the same way that vision in the intellect is a good of the soul. Similarly, the act of being in a stone is proportional to the act of being in a man, as the nature of a stone is proportional to the nature of man. Whereas some interpreters feel that the analogy of proportionality is the central type of analogy of being, others insist that Aquinas used several kinds of analogy in his metaphysics.

Being and essence. One early but certainly personal presentation of the metaphysics of Aquinas is to be found in the brief treatise *De Ente et Essentia*, which was strongly influenced by Avicenna. His usage of basic terms of analysis, such as being (*ens*), essence (*essentia*), nature, quiddity, substance, accident, form, matter, genus, species, difference, immaterial substance (*substantia separata*), potency, and act, is clearly but rather statically defined in this *opusculum*. Additional precisions, particularly on the meaning of element, principle, cause, and *esse*, are to be found in the companion treatise, *De Principiis Naturae*. A more dynamic approach to being and its operations is offered in the *Quaestiones Disputatae de Potentia Dei* and in Part I of the *Summa Theologiae*.

Fundamental in the metaphysical thinking of Aquinas is the difference between *what* a being is and the fact *that* it is. The first is a question of essence; the second is the act of being, *esse*. Essences are many (various kinds of things—stones, cows, air, men) and are known through simple understanding, without any necessity of adverting to their existence or nonexistence. For a thing *to be* is entirely another matter; the fact that something exists is noted in human experience by an act of judgment. Many essences of things are material, but there is nothing about *esse* that requires it to be limited to materiality. This proposition (to be is not necessarily to be material) is the "judgment of separation" (*In Boethii de Trinitate* V, 3). Many Thomists now regard it as a fundamental point of departure for Aquinas' metaphysical thinking.

There are also certain most general features of real beings which transcend all division into genera and species; these are convertible with metaphysical being. In other words, they are coextensive and really identical with being. Such transcendentals are thing (*res*), something (*aliquid*), one, true, good, and (according to some interpreters) beautiful. The more important of these transcendentals suggest that every being is internally undivided but externally distinct from all else (*unum*), that every being has some intelligible meaning (*verum*), and that every being is in some way desirable (*bonum*). The theory of transcendentals is much more expanded and stressed in later scholasticism than in Aquinas' own writings. He barely touches upon it in Questions I and XXI of *De Veritate* and in the discussion of God's attributes in *Summa Theologiae* (I, Ques. 6, 11, 16).

Potency and act. Potency and act are important principles in Aquinas' metaphysical explanation of the existence and operation of things. In *De Potentia Dei* (I, 1) Aquinas pointed out that the name "act" first designated any activity or operation that occurs. Corresponding to this sort of operational act is a dual meaning of potency (or power). Consider the activity of sawing wood: the passive potency of wood to be cut is required (water, for instance, cannot be sawed); also required is the active potency of the sawyer to do the cutting. In addition, in the same text, Aquinas says that the notion of "act" is transferred to cover the existence of a being. Essential potency, the metaphysical capacity to exist, would correspond to this act of being (*esse*). In this way the theory of act and potency was applied to all levels of being. At the highest level, God was described as Pure Act in the existential order, but this did not prevent Aquinas from attributing to God an active potency for operating.

Finality. Still another dimension of metaphysical reality, for Aquinas, was that of finality. He thought of all activities as directed toward some end or purpose, a basic assumption in Aristotle. But Aquinas developed this tendential, vector characteristic of being and applied it to the inclination of possible beings to become actual. The finality of being, in Thomism, is that dynamic and ongoing inclination to be realized in their appropriate perfections that is characteristic of all realities and capacities for action. In this sense the finality of being is an intrinsic perfectionism in the development of all beings. Aquinas also held that all finite beings and events are tending toward God as Final Cause. This is metaphysical finality in the sense of order to an external end. This theme runs through Book III of *Summa Contra Gentiles.*

Philosophy and God. The consideration of the existence and nature of God was approached by Aquinas both from the starting point of supernatural revelation (the Scriptures), which is the way of the theologian, and from the starting point of man's ordinary experience of finite beings and their operations, which is the way of the philosopher: "The philosophers, who follow the order of natural cognition, place the knowledge of creatures before the divine science; that is, the philosophy of nature comes before metaphysics. On the other hand, the contrary procedure is followed among the theologians, so that the consideration of the Creator precedes the consideration of creatures" (*In Boethii de Trinitate,* Prologue). In the same work (II, 3 c) we are told that the first use of philosophy in sacred doctrine is "to demonstrate items that are preambles to faith, such as those things that are proved about God by natural processes of reasoning: that God exists, that God is one," and so on.

Aquinas recognized two types of demonstration, one moving from cause to effects and the other from effects back to their cause. The arguments that he selected to establish that God exists use the second procedure and are technically called *quia* arguments. In other words, these proofs start with some observed facts of experience (all Aquinas' arguments to God's existence are a posteriori)

and conclude to the ultimate cause of these facts. Well aware of his debt to his predecessors, Aquinas outlined three arguments for the existence of God in *De Potentia Dei* (III, 5 c). The first shows that, since the act of being is common to many existents, there must be one universal cause of all (Plato's argument, Aquinas noted); the second argument starts from the fact that all beings in our experience are imperfect, not self-moved, and not the source of their actual being, and the reasoning concludes to the existence of a "mover completely immobile and most perfect" (Aristotle's argument); the third argument simply reasons from the composite nature of finite beings to the necessary existence of a primary being in which essence and the act of existing are identical (Avicenna's proof). Aquinas felt that these two pagan philosophers and an Islamic thinker had successfully established the conclusion "that there is a universal cause of real beings by which all other things are brought forth into actual being."

The "Five Ways." The most famous of the arguments are the "Five Ways" (*Quinque Viae*) of reasoning to the conclusion that God exists (*Summa Theologiae* I, 2, 3, c). All these ways employ the principle of causality and start from empirical knowledge of the physical world. They are not entirely original with Aquinas, depending not only on Plato, Aristotle, and Avicenna but also on Augustine and especially on Moses Maimonides. The First Way begins with the point that things in the world are always changing or moving and concludes to the existence of one, first, moving Cause. The Second Way argues from the observation of efficient production of things in the universe to the need of an existing, first, efficient Cause. The Third Way reasons from the contingent character of things in the world (none of them has to be) to the existence of a totally different kind of being, a necessary one (which has to be). The Fourth Way argues from the gradations of goodness, truth, and nobility in the things of man's experience to the existence of a being that is most true, most good, and most noble. The Fifth Way starts from the orderly character of mundane events, argues that all things are directed toward one end (the principle of finality), and concludes that this universal order points to the existence of an intelligent Orderer of all things. At the end of his statement of each "way," Thomas simply said, "and this is what all men call God," or words to that effect. Obviously, he presupposed a common meaning of the word "God" in the dictionary or nominal sense. There is disagreement among interpreters as to whether the "ways" are five distinct proofs or merely five formulations of one basic argument. Most Thomists now favor the second view.

Aquinas favored the argument from physical motion (*prima autem et manifestior via est*). The *Summa Contra Gentiles* (I, 13) offers an extended version of this first argument and frankly indicates its relation to the ideas in the last books of Aristotle's *Physics*. The other four ways are but briefly suggested in the *Summa Contra Gentiles*. In another, much neglected, work (*Compendium Theologiae* I, 3) the first way is stated clearly and concisely. Before attempting to establish in detail the various attributes of God, such as divine unity, one should consider whether he exists. Now, all things that are moved must be moved by other things; furthermore, things of an inferior nature are moved by superior beings. (Aquinas' examples are chosen from thirteenth-century physics and astronomy, in which the four basic elements were thought to be under dynamic influence of the stars, and lower celestial bodies were considered to be moved about by those at a greater distance from the earth. How much of the force of this argument may depend on outmoded science is a matter of debate in present-day Thomism.

Aquinas next argues that the process in which *A* moves *B, B* moves *C,* and so on cannot be self-explanatory. His way of saying this is "This process cannot go on to infinity." He concludes that the only possible explanation of the series of physical motions observed in the universe requires the acceptance of the existence of a different sort of "mover"—a being that is not moved by another, in other words, a first mover. This would have to be a real being, of course, and of a quite different nature from bodily things. He eventually suggests that this "first mover existing above all else" is what Christians call God.

In the same passage from the *Compendium,* two other facets of the argument from motion are introduced. First, Aquinas claims that all causes observed as acting in the physical universe are instrumental in character and must be used, as it were, by a primary agent. This primary agent is again another name for God. To suppose that the universe is self-explanatory is, to Aquinas, like thinking that a bed could be constructed by putting the tools and material together, "without any carpenter to use them." This is an important case of the conception of God as a divine craftsman. In the second place, this text suggests briefly that an infinite series of moved movers is an impossibility; the length of the series has nothing to do with its explanatory function, if all its members be finite. Finally, any such series requires a first mover (primary in the sense of causality, not necessarily of chronological priority). This first mover would be a Supreme Being. It is obvious that many of the attributes of God are already implied in the argument for divine existence.

Knowledge of God. Regarding the nature and attributes of God, Aquinas' greatest emphasis fell on how little we really know about the Supreme Being. In a series of articles (*Summa Theologiae* I, 86 – 88) on the objects of human knowledge, he reiterated his position that man is naturally equipped to understand directly the natures of material things; further, that man is aware of his own psychic functions as they occur but that all man's understanding of the nature of his own soul, of immaterial substances such as angels, and of infinite immaterial being (God) is achieved by dint of discursive and indirect reasoning. There is, of course, a wide gap between material and immmaterial substances. Yet both these types of finite beings fall within the same logical genus, as substances, and thus bodies and created spirits have some aspects in common. On the other hand, God is an immaterial being of an entirely different nature from that of bodies or even of created spirits. Between God and creatures there is no univocal community: that is to say, God does not fall within the same genus, either real or logical, as any other being. Hence, God's nature transcends all species and genera. Man's natural knowledge of God's nature is therefore very imperfect, achieved by negating various imperfections found in finite

beings: thus, God is not in time, not in place, not subject to change, and so on. Furthermore, man may reach some semipositive knowledge of God by way of analogy: thus, God is powerful but not in the finite manner of other beings; he is knowing, willing, and so on.

Providence. Divine providence is that attribute of God whereby he intelligently orders all things and events in the universe. As Aquinas explained it in the *Summa Contra Gentiles* (III), God both establishes the plan (*ratio*) in accord with which all creatures are kept in order and executes this plan through continued governance of the world. Literally, providence means "foresight," and this required Aquinas to face certain problems traditionally associated with any theory of divine foreknowledge. First of all, he insisted that such a view of divine providence does not exclude chance events from the universe. In one sense, a chance event occurs apart from the intention of the agent. However, what is intended by one agent may involve another agent who is unaware of the intention of the first. Hence, a plurality of real but imperfect agents sets the stage for chance: God knows this and permits it to occur.

Evil. In the *Quaestiones Disputatae de Malo* and elsewhere Aquinas agreed with Augustine that evil (both physical and moral) is a privation of goodness, of perfection, in being or in action. This does not deny the fact that evil really occurs but asserts that it is like a wound in being (the phrase is Maritain's); and, like any defect, evil is important by virtue of what is lacking. As to why a perfectly good God will allow evil to occur, Thomas argued that the possibility of evil is necessary so that many goods may be possible. "If there were no death of other animals, there would not be life for the lion; if there were no persecution from tyrants, there would be no occasion for the heroic suffering of the martyrs" (*Summa Theologiae* I, 22, 2, ad 2).

Freedom. Aquinas also did not admit that divine foreknowledge is opposed to the exercise of human freedom. His explanation of this point (in *Summa Theologiae* I, 103, 7 and 8) is complicated and not easy to state briefly. In effect, human freedom does not imply absolute indeterminism (action that is uncaused). What a man does freely is caused by himself, as a knowing and willing agent. God makes man capable of choosing well or ill, permits man to do so freely, and knows what man will accomplish. What appears to be necessitated from one point of view may be quite contingent and free from another viewpoint. From God's vantage point in eternity, human actions are not affairs of past or future but are events within the all-inclusive present of a divine observer who witnesses these events but does not determine them.

Ethics and political philosophy. The foregoing problems and considerations fall within Aquinas' speculative philosophy. His practical philosophy, aimed at the intelligent performance of actions, is divided into ethics, economics (treating problems of domestic life), and politics. In all three areas the thinking is teleological; finality, purposiveness, and the means–end relation all are aspects of Thomistic teleology. Rationally controlled activities must be directed to some goal; they are judged good or bad in terms of their attainment of that goal and in terms of the means by which they attain (or fail to attain) that end.

Aquinas dealt with the theoretical analysis of ethical activities in a long series of works: the *Scriptum in IV Libros Sententiarum,* Book III; *Summa Contra Gentiles* III, 114–138; the *In X Libros Ethicorum; Quaestiones Disputatae de Malo;* and the *Summa Theologiae,* Part II. Most of these works take the approach of moral theology, viewing moral good and evil in terms of accord or discord with divine law, which is revealed in Scripture and developed and interpreted in Christian tradition. Thomas himself did not consider moral theology to be a part of philosophy, and it will not be further considered here, except as throwing incidental light on his ethical position.

Voluntary action. Aquinas' ethics consists of a study of good and evil in human conduct, from the point of view of man's achievement of ultimate happiness. Not all the actions in which man is involved are truly human but only those accomplished under control of man's intellect and will. The primary characteristic of human conduct, according to Aquinas, is not so much freedom as voluntariness. His description of voluntary activity is a development of the teaching of Aristotle. Several factors are required for a voluntary action. There must be sufficient knowledge on the part of a moral agent that a given action is within his power; he cannot be entirely ignorant of the kind of action that he is performing or of the means, circumstances, and end of his action. Violence, under certain conditions, modifies the voluntariness of one's actions—as do certain kinds of uncontrollable feelings. Furthermore, as Aquinas saw it there are two opposites to what is voluntary. The "involuntary" is a contrary: it represents a diminution of voluntariness. Thus, an action that is partly involuntary is also partly voluntary and is, to a greater or lesser extent, imputable to the agent. On the other hand, the "not-voluntary" is the contradictory of what is voluntary, and an agent who is not voluntary is not morally responsible for his action.

Natural law. Most surveys of ethical theories classify Aquinas' ethics as a natural law theory. He described natural law as a rational participation in the eternal law of God and suggested that all men have a sufficient knowledge of what is morally right (the *justum*) to be able to regulate their own actions. In a famous passage (*Summa Theologiae* I–II, 94, 2) Aquinas explained the way in which he thought that rules of natural law are known. The judgment of *synderesis* (an intellectual quality enabling any man to intuit the first principle of practical reasoning) is simply the proposition "Good should be done and sought after; evil is to be avoided." (Most modern Thomists take this rule as a formal principle in the Kantian sense, requiring further knowledge to fill in the content of specific moral rules.) Aquinas then proceeded to describe three kinds of inclinations natural to man: that of man's substantial nature toward the conservation of its own existence and physical well-being, that of man's animal nature to seek such biological goods as sexual reproduction and the care of offspring, and that of man's reason whereby he tends toward universal goods, such as consideration of the interests of other persons and the avoidance of ignorance. All three kinds of inclinations are presented as natural and good, provided they are reasonably pursued. They form the bases from which one may conclude to a number of rules of natural moral law. Aquinas never attempted to make an exhaustive listing of the precepts of such a law; nor did he consider such a codification advisable.

In point of fact, the natural law approach to moral theory is not the only, and not the best, classification of Aquinas' ethics. Particularly in view of various shifts in the meaning of "law" since the time of Aquinas (notably a growing stress on law as a fiat of legislative will), it can be positively misleading to limit Aquinas' ethics to a natural law position. He defines law in general as "any ordinance of reason that is promulgated for the common good by one who has charge of a community" (*Summa Theologiae* I–II, 90, 4 c). "Reason" is the key word in this definition. Right reason (*recta ratio*) is the justification of ethical judgment in Aquinas' thought. "In the case of volitional activities, the proximate standard is human reason (*regula proxima est ratio humana*) but the supreme standard is eternal law. Therefore, whenever a man's action proceeds to its end in accord with the order of reason and of eternal law, then the act is right; but when it is twisted away from this rightness, then it is called a sin" (*ibid.,* 21, 1 c).

Reason, goodness, and justice. Thomistic ethics requires a person to govern his actions as reasonably as he can, keeping in mind the kind of agent that he is and the position that he occupies in the total scheme of reality. Man's own good is achieved by the governance of his actions and feelings under rational reflection—and God does not require anything else. "For we do not offend God, except by doing something contrary to our own good" (*Summa Contra Gentiles* III, 121–122). It is a part of being reasonable to respect the good of others. The moral good, then, is not so much what men are obligated to do by an all-powerful legislator; rather, it is that which is in accord with the reasonable perfecting of man. In becoming a better agent within himself, man is making himself more fit for ultimate happiness and for the vision of God. This kind of ethics resembles a self-perfectionist theory, without idealist overtones.

Aquinas based much of his teaching on ethical rules on the theory of natural justice found in Book V of the *Nicomachean Ethics.* All things have specific natures which do not change: dogs are dogs and stones are stones. Certain functions are taken as natural and appropriate to given natures: eating is an act expected of a dog but not of a stone. Human nature shares certain functions with the higher brutes but is distinguished by the performance of rational activities. Some of these typical functions are always the same in relation to man's nature and ethical rules pertaining to these do not change. Aquinas' example of such an immutable rule of justice is simply "Theft is unjust." Other ethical judgments, however, are not essential to justice (for example, detailed ordinances which contain many variable factors); these secondary rules are by no means absolute and immutable. Examples would be rules concerned with taxation, buying and selling, and other such circumstantially variable regulations. Moral law is composed of both types of rules and is neither absolute nor immutable in all its requirements.

Conscience. In *De Veritate* (XVII) Aquinas referred to moral conscience as a concrete intellectual judgment whereby the individual agent decides for himself that a given action or feeling is good or bad, right or wrong, to be done or not to be done. Conscience was not considered a special power or moral sense, nor was it viewed as the source of universal moral convictions. For Aquinas it was simply a man's best practical judgment concerning a concrete moral problem. As such, moral conscience is a person's internal guide to good action; one acts immorally in going against his conscience, for it is his best judgment on a matter. If it is not his best judgment, then the person is clearly required to make a better effort to reach a conscientious decision. Reasonable consideration of a proposed action includes thinking of the kind of action that it is (the formal object), the purpose to which it is directed (the end), and the pertinent circumstances under which it is to be performed. These three moral determinants were used by Aquinas to complete the theory of right reasoning in *De Malo* (II, 4 c, ad 2, ad 5).

Family. Aquinas also considered man in his social relations. In the *Summa Contra Gentiles* (III, cc. 122–126) the family is regarded as a natural and reasonable type of small society, designed to provide for the procreation and raising of children and for the mutual good of husband and wife. (The material on matrimony in the so-called *Supplement* to the *Summa Theologiae* was excerpted from Book IV of the *Scriptum in IV Libros Sententiarum* and does not represent Aquinas' mature thought.) The main reason why people get married, Aquinas thought, is to raise children, so his approach to the family was child-oriented. There should be but one husband and wife in a family; they should stay together until the children are fully grown and educated; the should deal honestly and charitably with each other as marriage partners. Many of Aquinas' arguments for monogamy and the indissolubility of the marriage bond are but restatements of similar reasonings in Aristotle's *Politics*.

Political theory. Aquinas' family, living in southern Italy, had been closely allied with the imperial government: his father and at least two of his brothers were in the service of Emperor Frederick II. Aquinas thus grew up with monarchic loyalties. On the other hand, early in life he joined the Dominicans, a religious community remarkable for its democratic and liberal practices. As a result Aquinas' political philosophy (in *De Regno*, in *In Libros Politicorum,* and in *Summa Theologiae*, I–II, *passim*) stressed the ideal of the limited monarchy, or that kind of state which Aristotle had called the *politeia.* The purpose of the state is described as to provide for temporal peace and welfare. Political society is quite different from ecclesiastical society (the church), whose end is otherworldly. Here again Aquinas always stressed the central role of reason: "Divine justice (*ius divinum*) which stems from grace does not cancel human justice which comes from natural reason." There is no detailed theory of government in Aquinas' writings.

Art and aesthetics. In his theory of art Aquinas was quite abstract and intellectualistic, taking Aristotle's *Rhetoric, Poetics,* and *Nicomachean Ethics* (Book VI) as his major sources. He used a new awareness of the spiritual and moral dimensions of the beautiful, found seminally in the mystical Neoplatonism of Dionysius the Pseudo-Areopagite, to develop the fragmentary aesthetics of Aristotelianism. Most of these precisions are found in Aquinas'

commentary on the fourth chapter of Dionysius' *De Divinis Nominibus.*

Art is understood to be a special habit, or acquired skill, of the practical intellect, which is simply man's possible intellect applied to problems of action. Prudence, the key practical habit in moral discourse, is defined as right reason in doing things (*recta ratio agibilium*). Similarly, art is defined as right reason in making things (*recta ratio factibilium*). These two practical habits are not confused. Elsewhere it is explained: "The principle of artifacts is the human intellect which is derived by some sort of similitude from the divine intellect, and the latter is the principle of all things in nature. Hence, not only must artistic operations imitate nature but even art products must imitate the things that exist in nature" (*In I Politicorum* 1). Some artifacts are merely useful; others may be beautiful; and still others may exist only in the order of thought (Aquinas took seriously the dictum that logic is an art).

He regarded the beautiful and the good as really identical but insisted that they differ in their formal meanings (*rationes*). Where the good is simply that which all desire, the beautiful is that which gives pleasure when perceived (*quod visum placet*). Three aspects of the beautiful are distinguished: integrity (*integritas sive perfectio*), due proportion (*debita proportio sive consonantia*), and brilliance (*claritas*). Each of these aesthetic factors is taken as capable of variation in degree and appeal.

These notions on the general meaning of beauty were used not to describe the attraction of a life of sacrifice but of spiritual perfection as a member of a religious community, such as the Dominicans. "In fact," Aquinas wrote, "there are two kinds of beauty. One is spiritual and it consists in a due ordering and overflowing of spiritual goods. Hence, everything that proceeds from a lack of spiritual good, or that manifests intrinsic disorder, is ugly. Another kind is external beauty which consists in a due ordering of the body" (*Contra Impugnantes Dei Cultum et Religionem* 7, ad 9). He was actually defending the practice of begging, as used in the mendicant orders. Aquinas agreed that there is something distasteful about begging but argued that it is an admirable exercise of humility, when religiously motivated. Here again the concept of purpose, teleological order, is central.

Metaphysical participation recurs as a key theme in Aquinas' discussion of the manner in which the manifold of creation shares in the transcendent beauty of God. All lower beauties are but imperfect manifestations of one highest *pulchritudo*. This is Dionysian mystical aesthetics and is presented in *In Dionysii de Divinis Nominibus* (IV, 5–6).

Authority and influence. Aquinas has been given a special position of respect in the field of Catholic scholarship, but this does not mean that all Catholic thinkers agree with him on all points. Within three years of his death a number of propositions closely resembling his philosophic views were condemned as errors by Bishop Tempier of Paris. This episcopal condemnation was formally revoked in 1325. Thomistic thought met much criticism in the later Middle Ages. Since the Renaissance nearly all the popes have praised Aquinas' teaching; the one who provided for the first collected edition of his works (St. Pius V) also did the same for St. Bonaventure, a Franciscan, and proclaimed both Doctors of the Church. In the ecclesiastical law of the Catholic church, revised in 1918, canon 589:1 states that students for the priesthood are required to study at least two years of philosophy and four of theology, "following the teaching of St. Thomas." Further, canon 1366:2 directs professors in seminaries to organize their teaching "according to the method, teaching and principles of the Angelic Doctor."

Actually, Thomism has never been the only kind of philosophy cultivated by Catholics, and from the fourteenth century to the Enlightenment, Thomism was rivaled and sometimes obscured by Scotism and Ockhamism.

In 1879, with the publication of the Encyclical *Aeterni Patris* by Pope Leo XIII, the modern revival of Thomism started. While this document praised Thomism throughout, Pope Leo added this noteworthy qualification: "If there be anything that ill agrees with the discoveries of a later age, or, in a word, improbable in whatever way—it does not enter Our mind to propose that for imitation to our age" (Étienne Gilson, ed., *The Church Speaks to the Modern World,* New York, 1954, p. 50; see THOMISM for further details on the history of Thomism.)

In 1914 a group of Catholic teachers drew up a set of 24 propositions which, they felt, embodied the essential points in the philosophy of Aquinas. The Sacred Congregation of Studies, with the approval of Pope Pius X, published these "Twenty-four Theses" as clear expressions of the thought of the holy Doctor. (Original Latin text in *Acta Apostolicae Sedis,* Vol. 6, 1914, 384–386; partial English version in Charles Hart, *Thomistic Metaphysics,* Englewood Cliffs, N.J., 1959, *passim.*)

The first six theses attempt a formulation of the general metaphysical position of Aquinas. All beings are composed of potential and actual principles, with the exception of God, who is pure act. The divine *esse* (act of being) is utterly simple (that is, without parts or constituents) and infinite in every way. Other beings are composite; their acts of existing are limited in character and merely participated. In general, metaphysical being may be understood in terms of analogy: God's being and that of created things do not belong within the same genus, but there is some remote resemblance between divine and nondivine beings. To satisfy competing theories of analogy which developed in Renaissance Thomism, the theses describe this metaphysical analogy in terms of both attribution (following Suárez) and proportionality (following Cajetan). The real distinction between essence and *esse* is stressed in the fifth thesis, while the difference between substance and accidents is stated in the sixth (accidents *exist in* some substance but never, in the natural course of things, exist by themselves). Marking a transition to special metaphysics (cosmology and philosophical psychology), the seventh proposition treats a spiritual creature as composed of essence and *esse,* and also of substance and accidents, but denies that there is any composition of matter and form in spirits.

A series of theses (VIII to XIII) describe bodily beings as constituted of prime matter and substantial form, neither of which may exist by itself. As material, bodies are extended in space and subject to quantification. Matter as quantified is proposed as the principle which individuates bodies. The location of a body in place is also attributed to quantity. Thesis XIII distinguishes nonliving from living bodies and makes the transition to a group of propositions concerned with human nature and its activities. The life principle in any plant or animal is called a soul, but, in the case of the human animal, the soul is found to be a principle of a very special kind. Theses XIV to XXI focus on the vital nature and functions of man. His soul is capable of existing apart from the human body; it is brought into existence directly by God's creative action; it is without constituent parts and so cannot be disintegrated, that is to say, the human soul is immortal. Moreover, man's soul is the immediate source of life, existence, and all perfection in the human body. Subsequent propositions emphasize the higher human functions of cognition and volition, and they distinguish sensitive knowledge of individual bodies and their qualities from intellectual understanding of the universal features of reality. Willing is subsequent to intellectual cognition, and the free character of volitional acts of choice is strongly asserted.

The last three theses offer a summary of Aquinas' philosophic approach to God. The divine existence is neither directly intuited by the ordinary man nor demonstrable on an a priori basis. It is capable of a posteriori demonstration using any of the famous arguments of the Five Ways; these arguments are briefly summarized. Thesis XXIII reaffirms the simplicity of God's being and maintains the complete identity between the divine essence and *esse.* The final thesis asserts the creation by God of all things in the universe and stresses the point that the coming into existence and the motion of all creatures are to be attributed ultimately to God as First Cause.

These 24 theses represent a rigid and conservative type of Thomism. Many modern Catholic philosophers, while recognizing that these propositions do express some of the basic themes in the speculative thought of Aquinas, doubt that it is possible to put the wisdom of any great philosopher into a few propositions and prefer to emphasize the open-minded spirit with which Aquinas searched for information among his predecessors and approached the problems of his own day. After all, it was Aquinas who remarked that arguments from authority are appropriate in sacred teaching but are the weakest sort of evidence in philosophic reasoning.

Works by Thomas Aquinas

COLLECTED EDITIONS

Opera Omnia, 25 vols. Parma, 1852–1873. Reprinted New York, 1948–1950. A noncritical but almost complete edition.

Opera Omnia, 34 vols. Paris, 1871–1882. A noncritical but almost complete edition.

S. Thomae Aquinatis, Opera Omnia. Rome, 1882——. This is the incomplete Leonine edition of the Latin works (many Latin works are published separately in Turin). Vols. I–III contain some of the commentaries on Aristotle, notably that on the *Physics;* Vols. IV–XII contain the *Summa Theologiae,* with Cajetan's Commentary; Vols. XIII–XV contain the *Summa Contra Gentiles,* with the Commentary by Sylvester of Ferrara; Vol. XVI is the Index. Announced for publication next are the *Quaestiones Disputatae,* the *Commentary on Job,* and the *Commentary on the Nicomachean Ethics.*

INDIVIDUAL WORKS

Scriptum in IV Libros Sententiarum (1252–1257), Pierre Mandonnet and M. F. Moos, eds., 4 vols. Paris, 1929–1947. No English version.

De Ente et Essentia (1253), Ludwig Baur, ed. Münster, 1933. Translated by Armand Maurer as *On Being and Essence.* Toronto, 1949.

De Principiis Naturae (1253), J. J. Pauson, ed. Fribourg, 1950. Translated by V. J. Bourke in V. J. Bourke, ed., *The Pocket Aquinas.* New York, 1960. Pp. 61–77.

Contra Impugnantes Dei Cultum et Religionem (1256), R. M. Spiazzi, ed., in *Opuscula Theologica,* Vol. I. Turin, 1954. Translated by J. Proctor as *An Apology for the Religious Orders.* Westminster, Md., 1950.

Quaestiones Disputatae de Veritate (1256–1259), R. M. Spiazzi, ed. Turin, 1949. Translated by R. W. Mulligan and others as *Truth,* 3 vols. Chicago, 1952–1954.

Quaestiones Quodlibetales (1256–1272), R. M. Spiazzi, ed. Turin, 1949. No English version.

In Librum Boethii de Trinitate Expositio (1257–1258), Bruno Decker, ed. Leiden, 1959. Partially translated by Armand Maurer as *Division and Methods of the Sciences.* Toronto, 1953.

In Librum Dionysii de Divinis Nominibus (1258–1265), Ceslas Pera, ed. Turin, 1950. Partially translated by V. J. Bourke in *The Pocket Aquinas.* New York, 1960. Pp. 269–278.

Summa de Veritate Catholicae Fidei Contra Gentiles (1259–1264), Vols. XIII–XV of the Leonine edition. Rome, 1918–1930. Also published in a one-volume "manual" edition. Turin and Rome, 1934. Translated by A. C. Pegis, J. F. Anderson, V. J. Bourke, and C. J. O'Neil as *On the Truth of the Catholic Faith,* 5 vols. New York, 1955–1957.

De Emptione et Venditione (1263), translated and edited by Alfred O'Rahilly as "Notes on St. Thomas on Credit." *Irish Ecclesiastical Record,* Vol. 31 (1928), 164–165. Translation reprinted in *The Pocket Aquinas.* New York, 1960. Pp. 223–225.

Quaestiones Disputatae de Potentia Dei (1265), R. M. Spiazzi, ed. Turin, 1949. Translated by Lawrence Shapcote as *On the Power of God.* Westminster, Md., 1952.

Commentaries on Aristotle (1265–1273), listed in next section.

De Regno (1265–1266), Jean Perrier, ed. Paris, 1949. Translated by G. B. Phelan and I. T. Eschmann as *On Kingship.* Toronto, 1949.

Compendium Theologiae (1265–1269), R. A. Verardo, ed. Turin, 1954. Translated by Cyril Vollert as *Compendium of Theology.* St. Louis, 1957.

Summa Theologiae (1265–1273), Vols. IV–XII of the Leonine edition. Rome, 1918–1930. Reprinted Turin, 1934. Translated by the English Dominican Fathers as *The Summa Theologica,* 22 vols. London, 1912–1936. Revision of part of the English Dominican Fathers' translation appears in *Basic Writings of Saint Thomas Aquinas,* A. C. Pegis, ed. New York, 1945.

Quaestiones Disputatae de Spiritualibus Creaturis (1267), L. W. Keeler, ed. Rome, 1938. Translated by John Wellmuth and Mary Fitzpatrick as *On Spiritual Creatures.* Milwaukee, 1949.

Quaestio Disputata de Anima (1269), R. M. Spiazzi, ed. Turin, 1949. Translated by J. P. Rowan as *The Soul.* St. Louis, 1949.

Quaestiones Disputatae de Malo (1269–1272), R. M. Spiazzi, ed. Turin, 1949. Partially translated by A. C. Pegis as *On Free Choice.* New York, c. 1945.

Quaestiones Disputatae de Virtutibus (1269–1272), R. M. Spiazzi, ed. Turin, 1949. Partially translated by J. P. Reid as *The Virtues in General.* Providence, R.I., 1951.

In Job Expositio (1269–1272), in Vol. XVII of Leonine edition. Rome, 1962. No English version.

In Evangelium Joannis Expositio (1269–1272), Raphael Cai, ed. Turin, 1952. No English version.

De Unitate Intellectus (1270), L. W. Keeler, ed. Rome, 1936. Translated by Sister Rose E. Brennan as *The Unicity of the Intellect.* St. Louis, 1946.

De Substantiis Separatis (1271), F. J. Lescoe, ed. West Hartford, Conn., 1962. Translated by F. J. Lescoe as *Treatise on Separate Substances.* West Hartford, Conn., 1960.

De Aeternitate Mundi (1271), R. M. Spiazzi, ed. Turin, 1954.

Translated by Cyril Vollert as *On the Eternity of the World.* Milwaukee, 1965.

In Librum de Causis (1271), H. D. Saffrey, ed. Fribourg, 1954. No English version.

COMMENTARIES ON ARISTOTLE

In Libros Posteriorum Analyticorum, in Vol. I of the Leonine edition. Rome, 1882. Translated by Pierre Conway. Quebec, 1956.

In Libros de Anima, R. M. Spiazzi, ed. Turin, 1955. Translated by Kenelm Foster and Silvester Humphries as *Aristotle's De Anima With the Commentary of St. Thomas.* London and New Haven, 1951.

In Libros de Caelo et Mundo, in Vol. III of the Leonine edition. Rome, 1886. Also edited by R. M. Spiazzi. Turin, 1952. No English version.

In X Libros Ethicorum, R. M. Spiazzi, ed. Turin, 1949. Translated by C. I. Litzinger as *Commentary on the Nicomachean Ethics,* 2 vols. Chicago, 1964.

In Libros de Generatione et Corruptione, in Vol. III of the Leonine edition. Rome, 1886. Also edited by R. M. Spiazzi. Turin, 1952. No English version.

In Libros Peri Hermeneias, in Vol. I of the Leonine edition. Rome, 1882. Also edited by R. M. Spiazzi. Turin, 1955. Translated by Jean Oesterle as *Aristotle on Interpretation—Commentary by St. Thomas and Cajetan.* Milwaukee, 1962.

In Libros de Memoria et Reminiscentia, et de Sensu et Sensato, R. M. Spiazzi, ed. Turin, 1949. No English version.

In XII Libros Metaphysicorum, R. M. Spiazzi, ed. Turin, 1950. Translated by J. P. Rowan as *Commentary on the Metaphysics of Aristotle,* 2 vols. Chicago, 1961.

In Libros Meteorologicorum, in Vol. III of the Leonine edition. Rome, 1886. Also edited by R. M. Spiazzi. Turin, 1952. No English version.

In VIII Libros Physicorum, in Vol. II of the Leonine edition. Rome, 1884. Also edited by P. M. Maggiolo. Turin, 1954. Translated by R. J. Blackwell and others as *Commentary on Aristotle's Physics.* London and New Haven, 1963.

In Libros Politicorum, R. M. Spiazzi, ed. Turin, 1951. Translation of Book III, Lectures 1–6 by E. L. Fortin and Peter D. O'Neill in Ralph Lerner and Muhsin Mahdi, eds., *Medieval Political Philosophy.* New York, 1963. Pp. 297–334.

Works on Thomas Aquinas

GUIDES

Bergomo, Petri de, *Tabula Aurea in Omnia Opera S. Thomae Aquinatis.* Bologna, 1485. Reprinted in Vol. XXV of *S. Thomae, Opera Omnia.* Parma, 1873.

Deferrari, Roy J.; Barry, Sister M. Inviolata; and McGuiness, Ignatius, *A Lexicon of St. Thomas Aquinas, Based on the Summa Theologica and Selected Passages of His Other Works.* Washington, 1949.

Indices . . . in Summam Theologiae et Summam Contra Gentiles, in Vol. XVI of the Leonine edition. Reprinted with some omissions in *Editio Leonina Manualis.* Rome, 1948.

Schütz, Ludwig, *Thomas-Lexikon.* Paderborn, 1895. Reprinted New York, 1949. The most useful concordance.

STUDIES

Anderson, J. F., *An Introduction to the Metaphysics of St. Thomas Aquinas.* Chicago, 1953. Collection of basic texts with clear explanations; useful for the theory of analogy.

Bourke, V. J., *Aquinas' Search for Wisdom.* Milwaukee, 1965. A factual biography excluding pious legends and situating Aquinas' thought in the context of his life.

Callahan, Leonard, *A Theory of Esthetic According to St. Thomas.* Washington, 1927. Rethinks the original theory but also interprets the fragmentary maxims of Aquinas on beauty and art.

Chenu, M. D., *Towards Understanding Saint Thomas.* Chicago, 1964. Masterful introduction to the advanced study of the works of Thomas Aquinas.

Copleston, F. C., *Aquinas*. London, 1955. This is a well-written exposition of the philosophy of Aquinas, with some effort to meet the criticisms of British analysts.

De Koninck, Charles, "Introduction à l'étude de l'âme." *Laval théologique et philosophique*, Vol. 3 (1947), 9–65. Reprinted in Stanislas Cantin, *Précis de psychologie thomiste*. Quebec, 1948. LXXXIII, 173.

Descoqs, Pedro, *Thomisme et scolastique*. Paris, 1927. Representative Suarezian criticism of the metaphysics of Aquinas; insists that there are other valid positions in philosophy.

Duns Scotus, John, *De Primo Principio*, translated and edited by Evan Roche. St. Bonaventure, N.Y., 1948. Important for fourteenth-century criticism by Duns Scotus of the general metaphysics and natural theology of Aquinas.

Fabro, Cornelio, *La nozione metafisica di partecipazione secondo S. Tommaso*. Milan, 1939; 2d ed., Turin, 1950. Outstanding study of the metaphysics of Thomism, stressing the Platonic elements.

Garrigou-Lagrange, Réginald, *Reality: A Synthesis of Thomistic Thought*. St. Louis, 1950. Adapted from a long article in the *Dictionnaire de théologie catholique*, this work represents a most conservative type of Thomism.

Geiger, L. B., *La Participation dans la philosophie de saint Thomas*. Paris, 1942. Excellent discussion of the Platonic themes in Aquinas' metaphysics; with Fabro and Geiger it has become clear that Thomism is not a "baptized" Aristotelianism.

Gilby, Thomas, *The Political Thought of Thomas Aquinas*. Chicago, 1958. Work of popularization which offers, however, a rather balanced view of the monarchic and democratic elements in Aquinas' ideas on government.

Gilson, Étienne, *The Christian Philosophy of St. Thomas Aquinas*. New York, 1956. With "Catalogue of St. Thomas's Works" by I. T. Eschmann. A highly esteemed exposition: the French original followed the order of the *Summa Contra Gentiles;* this English revision stresses the idea that Thomism is a Christian philosophy.

Grabmann, Martin, *Die Werke des hl. Thomas von Aquin*, 3d ed. Münster, 1949. The most complete study of the chronology and authenticity of the writings of Aquinas.

Henle, R. J., *Saint Thomas and Platonism*. The Hague, 1956. Good example of a careful textual study using the method of parallel passages taken in chronological sequence.

Jaffa, H. V., *Thomism and Aristotelianism. A Study of the Commentary by Thomas Aquinas on the Nicomachean Ethics*. Chicago, 1952. A sharp criticism of Aquinas as an interpreter of Aristotle's practical philosophy.

Klubertanz, G. P., *St. Thomas Aquinas on Analogy*. Chicago, 1960. Advanced and difficult study of all that Aquinas has written on metaphysical analogy; stresses the pluralism inherent in the theory; several types of analogy are at work.

Kluxen, Wolfgang, *Philosophische Ethik bei Thomas von Aquin*. Mainz, 1964. Important discussion of the relation between moral theology and ethics.

Maritain, Jacques, *Art and Scholasticism*. New York, 1930. An almost classic account of the aesthetic theory of Aquinas, with some adaptation to artistic problems in the twentieth century.

Maritain, Jacques, *The Angelic Doctor: The Life and Thought of St. Thomas Aquinas*, rev. ed. New York, 1958. Popular work stressing papal approval of Thomistic philosophy and the special status of Aquinas in Catholic educational programs.

Meyer, Hans, *The Philosophy of St. Thomas Aquinas*. St. Louis, 1944. In the guise of an exposition of Aquinas' thought, this is actually a trenchant critique of Thomism.

Oesterle, John A., *Ethics: Introduction to Moral Science*. Englewood Cliffs, N.J., 1957. Representative textbook emphasizing the autonomy and strictly philosophical character of Thomistic ethics.

Owens, Joseph, *An Elementary Christian Metaphysics*. Milwaukee, 1963. Advanced textbook in the tradition of the Christian philosophy interpretation of Aquinas.

Pieper, Josef, *Guide to Thomas Aquinas*, translated by Richard and Clara Winston. New York, 1962. A readable and elementary introduction by a noted German Thomist.

Rahner, Karl, *Geist im Welt. Zur Metaphysik der endliche Erkenntnis bei Thomas von Aquin*. Innsbruck and Leipzig, 1939. Outstanding German study of the theory of knowledge.

Ramírez, J. M., *De Auctoritate Doctrinae Sancti Thomae Aquinatis*. Salamanca, 1952. Representative of the well-informed and broadminded views of some Spanish Dominicans on the status of Thomism in Catholic philosophy.

Rommen, Heinrich, *The State in Catholic Thought*. St. Louis, 1945. Situates Thomistic political philosophy in the broader context of Catholic thinking as a whole.

Reith, Herman, *The Metaphysics of St. Thomas Aquinas*. Milwaukee, 1958. Standard exposition, not difficult to read. Includes 200 pages of quotations from many works of Aquinas.

Ryan, J. K., "St. Thomas and English Protestant Thinkers." *New Scholasticism*, Vol. 22, No. 1 (1948), 1–33; No. 2 (1948), 126–208. Excellent survey of the reactions to, and criticisms of, Aquinas in post-Reformation British thought.

Smith, Gerard, *Natural Theology: Metaphysics II*. New York, 1951. On Aquinas' philosophical approach to God; Ch. 16 discusses divine foreknowledge and human freedom.

Ude, Johannes, *Die Autorität des hl. Thomas von Aquin als Kirchenlehrer*. Salzburg, 1932. Basic study of the question "Must Catholics agree in philosophy and theology with Thomas Aquinas?" The answer is "No."

Walz, Angelus, *Saint Thomas d'Aquin*, French adaption by Paul Novarina. Louvain and Paris, 1962. One of the best biographies; this French printing has much more information than the English version, *Saint Thomas Aquinas*, translated by S. T. Bullough. Westminster, Md., 1951.

Wittmann, Michael, *Die Ethik des hl. Thomas von Aquin*. Munich, 1933. Good historical study of Thomistic ethics in relation to Aristotle, the Stoics, and the Fathers of the Church.

Works on Thomism

Bourke, V. J., *Thomistic Bibliography, 1920–1940*. St. Louis, 1945.

Bulletin thomiste (since 1921). Le Saulchoir, Belgium. (This Dominican study center moved after World War II to Étiolles, Soisy-sur-Seine, France.) Offers very complete listings and evaluations of works on all aspects of the life, writings, thought, and historical relations of Aquinas. The bulletin is numbered in three-year cycles but appears periodically in smaller fascicles. (For American readers there is a Canadian suboffice: Centre annexe du Bulletin thomiste, Institut d'Études Médiévales, 831 avenue Rockland, Montreal.)

Mandonnet, Pierre, and Destrez, Jean, *Bibliographie thomiste*. Le Saulchoir, Belgium, 1921; rev. ed., M. D. Chenu, ed., Paris, 1960.

Répertoire bibliographique. Annual supplement to *Revue philosophique de Louvain* (Belgium).

Wyser, Paul, *Thomas von Aquin* and *Der Thomismus*, fascicles 13–14 and 15–16 of *Bibliographische Einführungen in das Studium der Philosophie*. Fribourg, Switzerland, 1948 ff.

VERNON J. BOURKE

THOMASIUS, CHRISTIAN (1655–1728), philosopher and jurist and the first important thinker of the German Enlightenment. He was born in Leipzig, the son of the Aristotelian philosopher Jakob Thomasius, who had been a teacher of Leibniz. Christian, after studying philosophy and law at the universities of Leipzig and Frankfurt an der Oder, began lecturing at Leipzig in 1682. His theological enemies forced him to move in 1690 to the Ritterakademie in Halle, became professor of law there in 1694, and later was Geheimrat (privy counselor) and rector of the university.

Law and theology. Thomasius followed his father, as well as Grotius and Pufendorf, in the study of natural law. He sought a foundation for law, independent of theology, in man's natural reason. Like Pufendorf he opposed the orthodox Lutheran view that revelation is the source of law and that jurisprudence is subordinate to theology. He held that law is based on common sense and on truths common to all religions. On the other hand, many precepts traditionally held to be absolute were only the result of the historical development of a given nation, subject to change and justifiable only in terms of the characteristics of that nation. Thomasius asserted the right of free and impartial interpretation of the Bible and of God's laws, reacting against orthodox Lutheran exegesis and the intricacies and dogmatism of scholastic theology. He condemned fanaticism and the persecution of heretics and preached toleration of differing religious beliefs.

Thomasius opposed the episcopal system of church government, which asserted the rights of consistories and of theological faculties in church affairs, and supported a territorial system of church government, in which the government would have control of church administration but not of dogma. In dogma neither state nor consistories and faculties should have power; the latter should make decisions concerning dogma, but individual churches and Christians should be free to accept or reject them. Thomasius thus sought to break the power of the governing bodies of the church, which were dominated by intolerant orthodox Lutherans, and to subordinate the church to the government, which by natural law should be supreme within the state. It was these doctrines that forced Thomasius' expulsion from Leipzig and led to his reception at Halle by the Prussian government, which was more liberal in religious matters.

Education and the nature of man. Thomasius held that philosophy should be practical and should concentrate on man, his nature, and his needs. He opposed the Aristotelian scholasticism of orthodox Lutheranism because its abstractions and speculative complexities were useless in life. His *Introductio ad Philosophiam Aulicam* ("An Introduction to Philosophy for the Courtier," Leipzig, 1688) was in the tradition of Renaissance humanistic pedagogy. It advocated a worldly education intended to produce "courtiers" (politicians, diplomats, and bureaucrats) rather than the "pedantic" scholastic education of the universities. The German states established after the Thirty Years' War were organizing centralized governments and modern administrations on the French model, and they needed officials with the practical education Thomasius advocated. Thomasius' model was the education given in the German *Ritterakademien* (schools for the nobility), and he himself introduced this practical, worldly education into the teaching of the Halle faculty of law.

The *Introductio* was intended as the first of a series of texts furthering Thomasius' educational goals. In it Thomasius advocated eclecticism and disapproved of sectarianism and quarrels between schools of thought. He held that philosophy should be independent of revealed theology and founded on the observation of reality. Metaphysics was harmful and should be confined to a short terminological excursus. For Thomasius theoretical philosophy comprised natural theology, physics, and mathematics. The *Introductio* presented his theory of man and covered psychology and theory of knowledge, knowledge being obtained through the senses only. Thomasius was a

nominalist, and he was skeptical about rationally proving God's existence. He closed with a summary of logic, both practical and theoretical. Thomasius continued the educational program of the *Introductio* in his *Einleitung zu der Vernunfft-Lehre* ("Introduction to Logic," Halle, 1691), *Einleitung zur Sitten-Lehre* ("Introduction to Ethics," Halle, 1692), *Ausübung der Vernunfft-Lehre* ("Practical Logic," Halle, 1693), and *Ausübung der Sitten-Lehre* ("Practical Ethics," Halle, 1696), all of which introduced the use of German into university teaching.

In the *Introductio* and other works Thomasius' eclecticism and opposition to dogmatism, his empiricism, his concentration on description of human nature and the giving of advice for practical behavior, are evident. His eclecticism and opposition to dogmatism was connected with the tradition of Peter Ramus that survived in the school of Comenius and with Thomasius' philosophical individualism. He often presented his doctrines as only hypothetical and spoke of "my own" philosophy, renouncing absolute truth. Thomasius' concentration on the practical was influenced by such writers as Pierre Charron and Baltasar Gracián. Besides his texts he wrote special works on "prudence" (*Klugheit, prudentia*), giving advice for persons in different situations and positions.

Thomasius held that logic should be simple, should avoid the scholastic syllogistic treatment, and should be based on personal experience. Its goal should be not only the demonstration but also the discovery of truth. In line with his empiricism and opposition to dogmatism, Thomasius wrote much on probability and combined his discussion of logic with psychology and sociology.

Thomasius believed that Christian ethics must be based on rational love. Love, in its different forms, is the basic impulse in man. The will is independent of reason and is the origin of evil.

Pietism. About 1694 Thomasius underwent a personal religious and philosophical crisis. Influenced by certain Pietist thinkers, he lost faith in the natural goodness and intellectual power of man and held that virtue and truth could be reached only through God's grace, man being otherwise vicious and blind. He solemnly disavowed his former errors in a public confession. By 1705 Thomasius showed a renewed faith in human freedom and goodness and in the natural light. The period from 1694 to 1705 is known as Thomasius' Pietist period, but his acceptance of Pietism was eased by substantial similarities between his own views and those of the Pietists. Both opposed "pedantry," Aristotelianism, Lutheran orthodoxy, the episcopal system of church government, and intolerance; both were also eclectic and empirical and avoided scholastic abstractions and theological subtleties. A personal acquaintance with the Pietist A. H. Francke played an important part in Thomasius' temporary conversion to other Pietist views.

Metaphysics. Thomasius' two works on metaphysics were published at Halle during his Pietist period, the *Confessio Doctrinae Suae* in 1695 and the *Versuch vom Wesen des Geistes* ("An Essay on the Essence of Spirit") in 1699. Like Paracelsus, Valentin Weigel, Jakob Boehme, and others before him, Thomasius presented a mystical or theosophical variety of animism or vitalism. The world, both spiritual and material, is animated by a spirit created by God. Truth can be found only in the Bible as made clear by divine illumination. Although such views were held by some Pietists, they were not confined to them, and Thomasius continued to hold them after his Pietist period. Perhaps Thomasius' metaphysics was influenced not only by Pietism but also by the school of Comenius, who influenced Thomasius in other ways, and by the Hermetic school of medicine and chemistry, which had a mystically based experimental attitude. The latter possibility especially would explain Thomasius' combination of empiricism and a mystical metaphysics advanced only as a hypothesis.

Influence. Thomasius' most important followers were either Pietists or their sympathizers, and his views soon became the official Pietist philosophy. The theologian Joachim Lange in particular stressed Thomasius' Pietism and held that divine illumination was the only source of truth. By 1710 Thomasius' followers had displaced the Aristotelians in nearly all the German universities. Lange led the first attacks against the new doctrines of Christian Wolff, but Thomasius, true to his spirit of toleration, did not participate in the attack. Wolffianism became dominant after 1730, but a few Pietist centers remained. Later, the work of the Pietists A. F. Hoffmann and C. A. Crusius helped to bring about the renewal of German philosophy after 1760, which culminated in the critical philosophy of Kant.

Additional Works by Thomasius

Institutiones Iurisprudentiae Divinae. Frankfurt and Leipzig, 1688.
Die neue Entfindung einer wohlgegründeten und für das gemeine Wesen höchstnötige Wissenschaft. Das Verborgene des Hertzens anderer Menschen auch wider ihren Willen aus der täglichen Conversation zu erkennen. Halle, 1692.
Kleine deutsche Schriften. Halle, 1701.
Fundamenta Iuris Naturae et Gentium. Halle, 1705.
Kurtzer Entwurff der politischen Klugheit. Halle, 1705.

Works on Thomasius

Battaglia, Felice, *Cristiano Thomasius.* Rome, 1935.
Bienert, Walther, *Der Anbruch der Christlichen deutschen Neuzeit dargestellt an Wissenschaft und Glauben des Christian Thomasius.* Halle, 1934.
Bloch, Ernst, *Christian Thomasius.* Berlin, 1953.
Fleischmann, Max, ed., *Christian Thomasius, Leben und Lebenswerk.* Halle, 1931.
Jaitner, W. R., *Thomasius, Rüdiger, Hoffmann und Crusius.* Bleicherode, 1939.
Kayser, R., *Christian Thomasius und der Pietismus.* Hamburg, 1900.
Neisser, Liselotte, *Christian Thomasius und seine Beziehung zum Pietismus.* Munich, 1928.
Schneiders, Werner, *Recht, Moral und Liebe. Untersuchungen zur Entwicklung der Moralphilosophie und Naturrechtslehre des 17 Jahrhunderts bei Christian Thomasius.* Münster, 1961.
Schubert-Fikentscher, Gertrud, *Unbekannter Thomasius.* Weimar, 1954.
Wolf, Erik, *Grotius, Pufendorf, Thomasius.* Tübingen, 1927.

GIORGIO TONELLI

THOMAS OF YORK (1220/1225–1260/1269), English metaphysician and theologian, joined the Franciscan order by 1245, and he became doctor of theology at Oxford in 1253. He was fifth lecturer to the Oxford Franciscans (1253/1254) and sixth lecturer at the Cambridge convent (1256/1257). Thomas was the protégé of both Adam Marsh and Robert Grosseteste, whose tradition he followed. He wrote a treatise, *Manus Quae Contra Omnipotentem* ("The Hand Which Is Raised Against the Almighty"), supporting St. Bonaventure in the battle between seculars and mendicants at Paris.

His major work, *Sapientiale,* written between 1250 and 1260 and never finished, is the earliest known metaphysical *summa* of the thirteenth century. It makes use of all the major writers of antiquity, as well as the Muslim and Jewish philosophers (particularly Avicebrón and Maimonides), the Church Fathers, and his immediate predecessors at Paris and Oxford. Although he presents all the important opinions on each point, he is not a mere compiler but an original and profound philosopher who had mastered the entire corpus of knowledge available.

In the *Sapientiale* he treats all the standard metaphysical problems, both general and specific (a distinction he seems to have been the first to make), from an essentially Augustinian standpoint. His theory of matter is eclectic: there is a universal matter which is pure potentiality, and matter understood simply as privation. Heavenly bodies, for example, lack the second kind. Because in act they are already everything they are capable of becoming, they are free of any privation. He subscribes to a modified form of Grosseteste's light metaphysics, including a form of corporeity which is present in every body. However, since form is the principle of individuation, there must be a plurality of forms in any given body. (Thomas does not explicitly raise this question, but it is implicit in much that he says.) He is very clear, though, that the soul cannot be a form perfecting that of the body. It is itself composite and is related to the body "as a pilot is to a ship." The soul is able to gain knowledge by abstracting universals from singulars through sense (the complete universal can be known from one singular), but it gains more certain knowledge from above, receiving ideas from Ideas through interior illumination.

Thomas maintained the distinction in creatures between essence and existence, the latter characterized by composition from matter and form, and the mark of a creature's contingency. His emphasis on the contingency of creation prevented his arriving at a clear-cut assertion of the efficacy of natural causes, although he usually seems to favor this position.

Finally, Thomas was a vigorous proponent of what had become the typical Franciscan position since Grosseteste, denying the eternity of the world, of time, of matter, and of motion, and refusing any accommodation to the Aristotelian or Averroistic schools.

Bibliography

An edition of the *Sapientiale* is being prepared by R. J. O'Donnell, C.S.B. Pending its appearance, see D. E. Sharp, *Franciscan Philosophy at Oxford in the Thirteenth Century* (Oxford, 1930), pp. 49–114; Felix Treserra, "De Doctrinis Metaphysicis Fratris Thomae de Eboraco," in *Analecta Sacra Tarraconensis,* Vol. 5 (1929), 33–102; and A. B. Emden, *A Biographical Register of the University of Oxford to A. D. 1500* (Oxford, 1957–1959), Vol. III, pp. 2139–2140.

RICHARD C. DALES

THOMISM. The epithet "Thomist" has been applied since the fourteenth century to followers of St. Thomas Aquinas; the earlier "Thomatist," occasionally used, was dropped toward the end of the fifteenth century. The term has a different implication according to the three main historical periods that can be distinguished. First, until the beginning of the 1500s, during a period of vigorous Scholasticism and competition among several schools, Thomism stood in metaphysics for the doctrine of a composition of essence and existence in all created beings; and in noetics it opposed both nominalism and the Neoplatonic concept of illumination by the Ideas. Second, from the sixteenth until the eighteenth century Thomism flourished in the golden age of Spanish Scholasticism. (At this time Thomists unreservedly applied to theology the metaphysical concept of the premotion of all secondary causes by the first cause.) Third, beginning about the middle of the nineteenth century there was a revival of Thomism that was authoritatively endorsed by the Catholic church. Since then it has been claimed for Thomism that it represents the *philosophia perennis* of the West; Thomists have engaged in many-sided dialogue with thinkers from other traditions and disciplines and have been constructive in applying Thomistic principles to modern social and political problems.

We shall take these periods in order, noting beforehand that a unified philosophy, inspired by the writings of Thomas, persists throughout. In the philosophy of Thomas phenomenology is not divided from ontology; the world is real and composed of many real and distinct things, all deriving from one fount and all related by the analogy of being. Man is a single substance composed of body and soul; his knowledge begins from experience of the material world, and his understanding is developed through reason; his free activity determines his personal and eternal destiny.

Thirteenth to sixteenth century. When Thomas died in 1274, much of his teaching was still regarded as startling. Despite the affection in which he had been held (this was greater in the faculties of arts than in those of divinity) and despite his writings against the Latin Averroists, there developed a bitter opposition expressed in criticism and censure. It came from the representatives of the traditional Augustinian theology and was reinforced by the Franciscan masters. Conservative, yet by no means obscurantist, they included Thomas in their suspicions of what can be simplified as the "this-worldliness" of the new Aristotelianism. Étienne Tempier, bishop of Paris, was commissioned by Pope John XXII (Peter of Spain, the famous logician, who was an able natural philosopher) to investigate the charges against the new philosophy; he exceeded his instructions and in 1277, in a scissors-and-paste syllabus, he condemned 219 propositions, about a dozen of which can be traced to Thomas. In the same year Robert Kilwardby, the ex-provincial of the English Dominicans and now the archbishop of Canterbury, forbade the teaching of Thomas at Oxford, and his successor, John Peckham, acridly continued the same policy; they led the group called the *Cantuarienses*. As is evidenced in William de La Mare's list of correctives (*correctoria*) issued to be appended to Thomas' writings, many of the points at issue were highly technical, and some of them may now seem even trivial; the debate, much of which Thomas himself anticipated in his *Quaestiones Quodlibetales*, revolves round what to him were contrasts—but to his critics were conflicts—between nature and grace, reason and faith, determinism and freedom, the existence of the universe from eternity and its beginning in time, the soul as biological form and as spirit, and the role of the senses and of divine enlightenment in the acquisition of knowledge.

Although the censures had no force outside Paris and Oxford and the criticisms were more moderate in substance than they were in tone (they judged Thomas to be dangerous rather than heretical), his fellow Dominicans were quick to rally to his defense, to get the condemnations reversed and to correct the corrections, which they called corruptions. Thomas' old master, Albert the Great, so much the leader of the new movement that it has been called Albertino-Thomism, interposed at Paris; Pierre of Conflans, archbishop of Corinth, and Giles of Lessines remonstrated with Kilwardby; and Richard Clapwell, prior of Blackfriars, Oxford, progressively adopted Thomas' positions and stoutly maintained them against Peckham. The school was strengthened by a brilliant group of English and French Dominicans, and it was adopted by the Dominican order at successive general chapters. It could always count on support from the Roman Curia, which was favorably inclined toward Greek philosophy. The Ecumenical Council of Vienne (1311–1312) endorsed man's psychophysical unity, and in 1323 John XXII canonized Thomas and solemnly commended his doctrine. Henceforth he was a received authority.

Among the Thomists of these first fifty years John of Paris and Thomas Sutton were outstanding; other noteworthy teachers were Raymond Martin, a contemporary of Thomas who worked on the frontiers of Arabic science, William of Macclesfield, William of Hothun (archbishop of Dublin), Thomas Joyce (Jorz), Robert of Orford, Rambert of Bologna, Bernard de la Treille (Bernard of Trilia), Hervé de Nedellec, Nicholas Trivet, James of Lausanne, Ptolemy of Lucca, Peter de la Palu, James of Metz (uneasily attached to the school), and Remigio de Girolami, the master of Dante. In their hands the distinctions between essence and existence, matter and form, and substance and accident became sharper, although some of these scholars were reluctant to go beyond Aristotle to support, as Thomas did, the concept of an act of a form. Of particular interest is a German group deriving more directly from Albert than from Thomas and imbued with strains of Neoplatonism from Proclus and Avicenna; within this group were Ulrich of Strasbourg, Dietrich of Vrieberg (Freiburg), Berchtold of Mosburg, and, most famous of all, Meister Eckhart, whose Thomism is not generally considered to have been unequivocal. All these men were Dominicans; the secular master Peter of Auvergne and the Augustinian friars Giles of Rome and James of Viterbo can also be ranged with them.

As the later Middle Ages drew on, the enterprise of integrating a wide-ranging philosophy in theology was succeeded by more piecemeal investigations, and the schools settled down to their own party lines with a sharpened logic but some loss of originality. In the rivalry between the Dominicans and the Franciscans. Thomism was matched against Scotism, and this set the tone of its development: in fact, however, as Dominic de Soto later acknowledge, the agreements between the two were more important than their differences. Moderate realism was represented at all the universities and adhered to at Louvain, at Cologne, and later at Heidelberg. Thomism itself must be reckoned a minority movement, and some prominent Dominicans did not belong to the school. Durandus of Saint-Pourçain steadily ran counter to Thomas' teaching, and the Cambridge Dominican Robert Holkot did not fall in with it. A central figure is John Capreolus, called the *Princeps Thomistarum,* whose writings are a mine of information on the disputes with Scotists and Ockhamists. Although Capreolus chose Thomas' "Commentary on the *Sentences*" for his expositions rather than the better organized *Summa Theologiae,* together with Serafino Capponi de Porrecta he bequeathed to their order the habit of systematically articulating the whole corpus of Thomas' teaching. Less confined to the classroom and closer to life and the historical movement of ideas was St. Antoninus, archbishop of Florence, the moralist who is a major authority for medieval economics.

The influence of the Renaissance was already beginning to make itself felt, and the first period of Thomism closed nobly in north Italy with Bartholomew of Spina, Crisostomo Javelli, Francis Sylvester (or Ferrariensis), and Thomas de Vio (or Cajetan). The last two, the classical commentators on the *Summa Contra Gentiles* and the *Summa Theologiae* respectively, were friends and opponents, particularly on the metaphysics of analogy. Both were responsive to the renewed vitality of Latin Averroism, and for them the unity of their school lay more in an inner consistency of approach than in a common subscription to a list of propositions, such as marked later scholasticism when it had retreated or been banished from the profane world into the ecclesiastical academies. Cajetan, the master of a nervous style which fitted the subtle analysis at which he excelled, was a good scholar and a man of affairs. His standing in the school is second only to that of Thomas himself, although there is some question whether he was not a better Aristotelian than a Thomist. It is alleged that his emphasis on existence as the act of substance rather than on *esse* as the act of being may have encouraged the habit of discussing essences apart from existence, which was treated as a predicate.

Sixteenth to nineteenth century. The second period, conterminous with the golden age of Spain, also had its origins in Burgundy and also declined through an inability to adjust to an expanding world outside its frontiers. In the fifteenth century Dominic of Flanders developed Thomas' exposition of the *Metaphysics,* and Peter Crockaert of Brussels, the master of Francisco de Vitoria (the father of international law), was the first of a great line of masters associated with the University of Salamanca. It was the faculty of this university that intervened with the Spanish government to humanize colonial policy. They forsook the crabbed angularities of fifteenth-century Scholasticism for a more flowing baroque style; at the same time, however, they found what they regarded as the formal logic of Aristotle to be a sufficient instrument for their debates, and the

advances made on it (the *subtilitates anglicanae*) were neglected. Although they are chiefly famous as Tridentine divines, the theological questions that they considered— the relations of efficacious grace and free will, of authority and conscience—occasioned sustained philosophical discussion.

Among these sixteenth-century authors, the following are well worth study: Melchior Cano for scientific method and Bartholomew de Medina, Dominic de Soto, and Martin de Ledesma for moral theory. Dominic Báñez is much admired for his high Thomism in metaphysics and natural theology. These were Dominicans, but the best-known writer of the group is the Jesuit Francisco Suárez, who is impressive by virtue of the breadth of his interests and the organization of his voluminous writings, although strict Thomists would reckon him an eclectic and would think that he achieved his clarity by too concrete a habit of thought. The Jesuits were at this time taking the lead in higher education, and of all the orders they were the most aware of contemporary scientific research. Courses of philosophy began to be given apart from theology, and the teamwork of the Jesuits at Coimbra produced the volumes entitled *Conimbicenses* (1592), and of the Carmelites at Alcalá de Henares those entitled *Complutenses* (1624). In twentieth-century Thomistic studies John of St. Thomas has perhaps been more influential than Cajetan, and his *Cursus Philosophicus,* digested in Josef Gredt's *Elementa Philosophica,* may be recommended as of lasting value.

Yet by the end of the seventeenth century Thomism was important only in the centers of ecclesiastical learning; it was part of the establishment, more honored, perhaps, than listened to. Its monument is the Casanata Library in Rome, founded with two chairs of Thomist exegesis. Its philosophy served mainly as a prolegomenon to theological studies and was conducted in the "essentialist" temper of Leibniz and Wolff. In this spirit Antoine Goudin wrote his significantly titled *Philosophia Juxta D. Thomae Dogmata* (Milan, 1676), which by 1744 had gone through 14 editions. Salvatore Roselli's six-volume *Summa Philosophiae* (Rome, 1777) was written in response to the reiteration of the Dominican commitment to Thomas' doctrine made by the master general, John Thomas Boxadors. Both works influenced the revival of Thomism in the next century. But few Thomists took part in the dialogue of philosophers from Descartes to Hegel, and the writings of the school were studied only by those with antiquarian tastes or a special interest in the history of philosophy.

Nineteenth and twentieth centuries. The situation began to change about the middle of the nineteenth century. A circle of teachers at Piacenza, Naples, and Rome who were dissatisfied with the eclectic doctrines which then served for clerical studies and were critical of the developed Kantianism of Georg Hermes, the accommodated Hegelianism of Anton Günther, the antirationalism of traditionalism, and the ontologism of Antonio Rosmini began to look to the synthesis of Thomas. The Dominicans themselves had remained faithful to Thomas, but their temper was somewhat rabbinical and concentrated on the letter of the text; and except in Spain and southern Poland they had been scattered in the troubled times after the French Revolution. At the beginning of the nineteenth century a secular canon, Vincenzo Buzzetti, inspired two brothers, Serafino and Domenico Sordi, who later became Jesuits, and Giuseppe Pecci, the brother of the future Leo XIII, to the work of the restoration of Thomism. They were joined by Gaetano Sanseverino, who contributed the five-volume *Philosophia Christiana* (Naples, 1853), and were supported by the influential Jesuit periodical *Civiltà cattolica*. The movement gathered strength with the affirmation of the rights of reason at the First Vatican Council (1869–1870) and with the teaching of two great professors at the Gregorian University, Matteo Liberatore and Josef Kleutgen, and of two Dominican cardinals, the Corsican Thomas Zigliara and the Spaniard Zefirín Gonzales. Finally, Leo XIII's encyclical *Aeterni Patris* (1879) sounded the recall to Thomas' basic doctrines in order to meet modern needs. Succeeding popes have reinforced this recommendation, not without embarrassment to those not wedded to Thomas' system, and even to those Thomists who would not have philosophy inculcated according to administrative needs. In practice, however, and despite the scares of the Modernist movement and the antimetaphysical temper of the last twenty years, the injunctions have not proved irksome; and many forward-looking thinkers have discovered that Thomas was a benign and generous patron of their studies.

A history of Neo-Thomism—the title is not relished by many in the school who do not see themselves committed to an absolute system—remains to be written. A summary of its extensive literature and of its work in universities and higher centers of study must needs be partial and even random. One characteristic of Neo-Thomism has been its willingness to assimilate influence from outside its own tradition, which is a tribute to the depth and versatility of its principles. Another is that it has not been preoccupied with ecclesiastical matters; it inspired the social teaching of Leo XIII, with the result that many laymen and statesmen have consulted it in developing the ideals and practice of Christian democracy. Nor has the conduct of speculation been reserved to clerics, and in recent years Thomism has no names more eminent than those of Jacques Maritain and Étienne Gilson. Although it appeals primarily to Catholics, its adherents are not necessarily Catholics, or even Christians. It presents no fixed image of conformity.

The Spanish works of high Thomism (the names of Norberto del Prado and Jaime Ramírez may be mentioned) have seemed to stand apart from the streams of contemporary thought, and the chief agencies that have taken Thomism into the world debate have been the University of Louvain and the French Dominicans. The Institut Supérieur at Louvain was founded in 1889 by Désiré Mercier, later cardinal, to bridge the gap between modern science and philosophy, particularly with respect to the problem of knowledge. In connection with this effort, the work of Joseph Maréchal was noteworthy. The French Dominicans have made contributions important both in critical research and in the popularization of Thomistic philosophy, and they have been alert to consider the most seemingly disparate interests; their periodicals, the *Revue des sciences philosophiques et théologiques* and the *Revue thomiste,* provide probably the best index to the activities

of the school. From the universities of Munich and Münster has come important work, and the names of Martin Grabmann and Otto Geyer are illustrious. Other outstanding figures are Réginald Garrigou-Lagrange of the University of St. Thomas in Rome and R. Welty and I. M. Bocheński of the University of Fribourg. A strong stream of Thomism is evident in the work of A. E. Taylor at Edinburgh, Kenneth Kirke at Oxford, E. L. Mascall at London, and Mortimer Adler at Chicago. Distinguished work comes from the Medieval Institute in Toronto, and there are flourishing centers of Thomistic study in Washington, River Forest, Ill., St. Louis, Montreal, and Sydney. The enumeration, however, is incomplete and perhaps invidious. The bibliographies of the *Bulletin thomiste* bear witness to a world-wide interest in Thomistic thought on the part of both philosophers and theologians.

Bibliography

Bourke, V. J., *Thomistic Bibliography, 1920–1940.* St. Louis, 1945.

Dezza, Paolo, *Alle origini del Neotomismo.* Milan, 1940.

Gilson, Étienne, *History of Christian Philosophy in the Middle Ages.* London and New York, 1955. Pp. 277–294, 361–436, 471–485. This work contains excellent bibliographies.

Mandonnet, Pierre, and Destrez, Jean, *Bibliographie thomiste.* Paris, 1921.

Roensch, F. J., *The Early Thomistic School.* Dubuque, Iowa, 1964.

Wulf, Maurice de, *Histoire de la philosophie médiévale,* 5th ed. Paris and Louvain, 1925. Vol. II, pp. 33–51, 112–151, 197–203, 272–277.

THOMAS GILBY, O.P.

THOREAU, HENRY DAVID (1817–1862), once described himself as "a mystic, a transcendentalist, and a natural philosopher." If this description does some justice to the extent of Thoreau's eclecticism, it nevertheless obscures those characteristics which made him important during his lifetime and still remain significant today. For Thoreau was an anarchist and revolutionary who created a highly articulate literature of revolt. Born at Concord, Massachusetts, the son of a pencil maker, Thoreau emerged from Harvard in 1837 with testimonials signed by Dr. George Ripley, Ralph Waldo Emerson, and the president of the university, all of whom attested, in glowing terms, to his moral and intellectual integrity. After a brief skirmish with school teaching, Thoreau became infected with the ideas of the New England transcendentalists, gave up all plans of a regular profession, and devoted himself to literature and the study of nature. His remarkable practical skills and intimate knowledge of the Concord countryside enabled him to earn his living independently, largely through pencil making and surveying, for the rest of his life.

From 1841 to 1843 Thoreau resided with Emerson. This brought his intellectual development roughly into line with the ideas of transcendentalists like Amos Bronson Alcott, Margaret Fuller, and Ellery Channing, all of whom he came to know well. Thus, philosophically, Thoreau's reaction against the still fashionable sensationalism of Locke and the theistic utilitarianism of William Paley was aided by ideas derived from the Scottish philosophers of common sense, who, in turn, formed a bridge to the idealism of Coleridge, Carlyle, and the Germans. Emerson also directed Thoreau to the English metaphysical poets and to Goethe. But despite this deep and undeniable cultural *rapprochement* it would be a misunderstanding to see Thoreau merely as Emerson's most eccentric disciple. Thoreau's individuality was maintained even at the intellectual level. He also studied New England history and legend, the life of the Indian, and early accounts of American travel and exploration; he probably had a better knowledge of the Greek and Latin classics than Emerson and certainly knew more about Oriental scriptures, of which he possessed an excellent collection. Above all, Thoreau's knowledge of natural history, motivated not so much by a desire for scientific understanding as by a need for concrete communion with nature, marks him off from the rest of Emerson's circle.

Nature and society. Thoreau's writings everywhere bear the stamp of aboriginal practicality that also made him unique as a person. Society and nature were not for Thoreau, as they were for so many romantic thinkers, dialectical opposites whose inner identity was simply in need of philosophical explication. For him they involved a genuine contrast that he had personally experienced as a professional "saunterer" in and around Concord. Nature represented for Thoreau an "absolute freedom and wildness," whereas society provided "a freedom and culture merely civil." In his writing, as in his life, he attempted to implement the view that man should be regarded "as an inhabitant, or a part and parcel of Nature, rather than a member of society." It is only through a sustained involvement with the vast "personality" of nature that man can simplify his existence, clarify his senses, drive life into a corner, and reduce it to its lowest terms, thus achieving in practice a purer and tougher form of that self-reliance extolled, somewhat abstractly, by Emerson.

With these objects in mind, in the spring of 1845 Thoreau began building himself a hut on the shore of Walden Pond, a small lake then about a mile and a half south of Concord village. There he lived alone, with occasional visits to the village and from friends, until September 1847. His mode of life at the pond is described in *Walden, or Life in the Woods* (1854). For Thoreau Walden was an experiment in individualistic anarchism, just as Fruitlands and the Brook Farm community were for other transcendentalists attempts to revert to more "natural" modes of communal existence. But Thoreau had little confidence in collective protests against the existing social order, inspired by the doctrines of François Fourier. For him individual communion with nature was more fundamental than relationships with other men, even in societies where the worse forms of economic alienation have been overcome. For, unlike any social experience, the experience of nature becomes as much a discipline for the moral will as a stimulant to creative imagination. But essentially it is the spontaneity of wildness or nature that is to be favorably contrasted with the politico-economic organization of advanced European and New England societies. For, wrote Thoreau, "all good things are wild and free." The creative spontaneity of nature that is so crucial for man's spiritual well-being is embodied in all enduring products of culture—in the *Iliad* and *Hamlet,* in religious scriptures,

in music, and especially in mythologies of all kinds. Commerce—"that incessant business"—and its political manifestations are indeed "vital functions of human society," yet a bare minimum of time should be consciously spent on them. They are "*infra*-human, a kind of vegetation," whose operations, like those of the human body, should be performed for the most part automatically, unconsciously. Far from viewing economic success alone as the sign of achievement or virtue, Thoreau believed that "to have done anything by which you earned money merely is to have been truly idle, or worse."

Despite the acquisitive basis of New England society, Thoreau saw a vision of true freedom in the expansion of the western frontier. For him the West was identical with the wild, and "wildness is the preservation of the world." These ideas, which constitute Thoreau's most persuasive expressions of revolt against bourgeois society, are best seen in his essays "Walking" (1862) and "Life Without Principle" (1863).

Revolution and reform. Thoreau's essay "Civil Disobedience" (1849) has been the most influential of his works because of its overt political implications. It was, for example, a reading of this essay in 1907 that helped Gandhi develop his own doctrine of passive resistance. Here Thoreau advocates active rebellion against the state. This involves what he calls "action from principle" on the basis of an intuitive perception of what is right, which is roughly equivalent to acting on the dictates of one's own conscience. He boldly asserts that "the only obligation which I have a right to assume is to do at any time what I think right." Action thus motivated "changes things and relations" and is therefore "essentially revolutionary." Radical social reforms, like the abolition of slavery (for which Thoreau agitated throughout his life), can be effected not by petitions to elected representatives of government or by other indirect democratic means but only when each right-minded individual takes direct action on his own part. This would consist in withdrawing his allegiance "in person and property" from the government that supports or permits the abuse in question. Such is the form of "peaceful revolution" Thoreau himself attempted to put into practice by refusing to pay taxes. Despite its localized New England context and its relative lack of theoretical sophistication, it is possible to see Thoreau's doctrine of civil disobedience as historically linked, through the revolutionary element in European idealism, with the larger protest against the established order represented more notably by Kierkegaard's *The Present Age* (1846) and the *Communist Manifesto* (1847). Like Marx, Thoreau sought the dismantling of existing institutions in an attempt to discover an economy which would provide full human satisfaction. Yet like Kierkegaard he insisted on maintaining the uniqueness of the individual as the ultimate source of value; he attempted, however, to overcome the isolation his radical views forced upon him by means of a dialogue not with God but with nature.

Bibliography

The most complete edition of Thoreau's works is that published by Houghton Mifflin in 20 volumes: *The Writings of Henry David*

Thoreau (Boston, 1906). H. S. Salt, *Life of Henry David Thoreau* (London, 1890; reissued in an abridged version, 1896), is indispensable for an understanding of Thoreau's personality. For other details see Floyd Stovall, ed., *Eight American Authors: A Review of Research and Criticism* (New York, 1956; reprinted, 1963).

MICHAEL MORAN

THOUGHT, LAWS OF. See LAWS OF THOUGHT.

THUCYDIDES (c. 460–c. 399 B.C.), Athenian historian, student of politics, and general. There is little certain knowledge about the life of the author of *The Peloponnesian War*. He came of a prominent conservative family which may have been of Thracian origin and which held property in Thrace. There is indirect evidence that through his father, Olorus, he was related to Miltiades and to Cimon, two of the architects of the Athenian empire. In 424 Thucydides was elected to the office of general and commanded Athenian forces in Thrace, where he operated gold mines and where he apparently had influence among the people. After losing the city of Amphipolis to the enemy, he was sent into exile and remained away from Athens for twenty years. According to his own account, he spent much of this time among the Spartans and their allies and so was able to collect data about the war from both sides of the battle lines. At the conclusion of peace in 404 he returned to Athens and probably died there about the turn of the century. There is also a tradition that he died in Thrace.

Thucydides was a political observer, not a speculative philosopher. Nevertheless, his work builds self-consciously on a clearly defined philosophical position, an antimetaphysical naturalism and positivism which he probably learned from the practitioners of Hippocratic medicine and from the Sophists, who dominated the higher education of fifth-century Athens. His method of analysis shows the influence of both.

The Peloponnesian War, Thucydides' only extant work, is a detailed account of the "world war" of 430–404 B.C. which destroyed the polis as the sovereign unit of ancient Greek political order. It is usually called a history, and Thucydides is universally known as one of the great Greek historians. His scholarly objective, however, much more resembles that of the modern political scientist than that of the modern historian. Thucydides himself called his book a *syngraphe*, which Voegelin translates as "write-up," an expression which, in approaching the conception of "case study" as used in modern social science, renders more adequately the meaning of the word than the usual "history." For it was Thucydides' intention in describing the dynamic pattern of a classic case of imperial growth and decline, the case of the Athenian empire, to reveal the character of democratic empire as such, as a type of political order, as well as to describe the unique aspects of Athenian experience.

The choice of a detailed description of a particular to reveal the universal well illustrates Thucydides' positivism. Reality consists for him in a visible process, the movements of the phenomenal world, rather than, as for his Ionian and Eleatic philosophical forebears, in some invisible, essential substratum of prime matter or of

thought "underlying" the sensible world. Observation discloses in the flux an order of recurrent forms, which permit both classification and prognosis, using procedural principles and a technical vocabulary which are as applicable to politics as to medicine. Concepts such as prophasis (exciting cause), which the Hippocratics had developed for the study of disease, Thucydides employs to explain the outbreak of war as a concomitant of one phase of the growth of empire.

Natural forces embedded in the empirical process, rather than transcendent principles, cause the movements of the phenomenal world. In politics these are, first, the universal drives for security, prestige, and economic gain ("three of the strongest motives, fear, honour, and interest"). Thucydides shows their role in the political decision-making of the war by imaginatively recreating numerous and lengthy speeches and diplomatic exchanges, replete with the typical naturalistic arguments of Sophistic rhetoric.

The rational or irrational ordering of "the three greatest things" is environmentally determined, a product of social and political structure and of chance occurrences. It is Thucydides' thesis that an individualist and democratic order, which is marked by legal and political equality and freedom of occupation, manner of life, and education, releases vast social energies which, at the outset, are harnessed by rational leadership in such a way as to produce a socially diffused satisfaction of the three strongest passions through the creation of empire. Fundamentally unstable, however, democratic empire in its second phase falls into extreme irrationality, touched off by "accidental" events like the plague or war losses, against whose ill psychological effects the system can muster no immunizing antibodies. Massive frustration and political destruction are the end result. Both Pericles, the embodiment of rational leadership, and Alcibiades, the irrationalist, are dependent, not independent, variables of the total Athenian situation.

By giving less freedom to the individual, a closed society like Sparta, based on the principle of status and governed by unquestioned tradition, develops less creative initiative, less intelligence, and less energy than a democracy and, hence, only a modest empire. But its traditional norms are a more stable vehicle of rationality than Athenian enlightened self-interest.

As an environmental determinist, Thucydides wrote for those who "desire an exact knowledge of the past as an aid to the interpretation of the future," not its control. Like the Hippocratic doctors, his emphasis was on description and prognosis rather than on therapy.

Bibliography

Modern editions of *The Peloponnesian War* are edited by J. S. Jones, 2d ed., 2 vols. (Oxford, 1942), and by Otto Luschnat (Leipzig, 1960——). There are English translations by Benjamin Jowett, 2d ed., 2 vols. (Oxford, 1900), and by Richard Crawley (London, 1910; revised by Richard Feetham, Chicago, 1952). See also reissue of Hobbes's translation; David Grene, ed., 2 vols. (Ann Arbor, Mich., 1959).

Works on Thucydides are William T. Bluhm, *Theories of the Political System* (Englewood Cliffs, N.J., 1965), Ch. 2; Charles N. Cochrane, *Thucydides and the Science of History* (London, 1929); Francis M. Cornford, *Thucydides Mythistoricus* (London, 1907);

John H. Finley, Jr., *Thucydides* (Cambridge, Mass., 1942); Jacqueline de Romilly, *Histoire et raison chez Thucydide* (Paris, 1956); Leo Strauss, *The City and Man* (Chicago, 1964), Ch. 3; and Eric Voegelin, *Order and History,* Vol. II, *The World of the Polis* (Baton Rouge, La., 1957), Ch. 12.

William T. Bluhm

THÜMMIG, LUDWIG PHILIPP (1697–1728), German Wolffian philosopher, was professor of philosophy at Halle from 1717 until 1723 when he was expelled with Wolff. On Wolff's recommendation he was appointed professor of philosophy at the Collegium Carolinum in Kassel, but he ended his career as an instructor of pages. His early death prevented him from regaining a decent position when Wolff's fortunes improved.

Thümmig was one of Wolff's earliest pupils, and his *Institutiones Philosophiae Wolffianae* (2 vols., Frankfurt and Leipzig, 1725–1726) was intended as a short and more readily understandable presentation, closer to the doctrines of traditional philosophy, of the doctrines presented in Wolff's German works. The work was written in Latin to prevent misunderstandings arising out of Wolff's new German terminology. The order of presentation of the main subjects covered, and the sharp separation between the topics treated in the discussions of the main branches of philosophy, were probably suggested by Wolff and were later adopted by him in his own Latin works. Unlike Wolff in his German works, Thümmig discussed cosmology before psychology, and divided psychology into empirical and rational branches. This order became traditional in the Wolffian school and was adopted by Wolff himself in his Latin works.

Thümmig used the traditional language and manner of exposition to make Wolff's doctrines more acceptable. He introduced non-Wolffian elements into his solution to the problem of pre-established harmony. He also differed from Wolff in regarding the study of natural law as a theoretical science (*scientia legum naturalia*) but ethics and politics as practical sciences whose purpose was to reach an agreement between man's real condition and the natural law.

Bibliography

Thümmig's works include *Demonstratio Immortalitas Animae ex Intima Eius Natura Deducta* (Halle, 1721), and *Meletemata Varii et Rarioris Argumenti.* Braunschweig and Leipzig, 1727.

For a discussion of Thümmig, see Max Wundt, *Die deutsche Schulphilosophie im Zeitalter der Aufklärung* (Tübingen, 1945), pp. 212–214.

Giorgio Tonelli

TILLICH, PAUL (1886–1965), German–American theologian, was born in Starzeddel in eastern Germany, the son of a Lutheran pastor. He received a theological and philosophical education and was ordained in the Evangelical Lutheran church in 1912. He served as an army chaplain during World War I and then taught theology and philosophy at Berlin, Marburg, Dresden, and Frankfurt. On Hitler's advent to power in 1933, Tillich immigrated to the United States, serving as professor of systematic theology and philosophy of religion at Union Theological Seminary from 1933 to 1956. From 1956 until his death he held chairs at Harvard and at the University of Chicago.

Anxiety. Tillich's religious thought has been enormously influential, particularly in English-speaking countries. He was strongly influenced by existentialism, and he held, as did Kierkegaard, that religious questions are appropriately raised only in relation to problems that are inherent in the "human situation" and that theological claims are not mere responses to theoretical puzzles. Thus, Tillich presents Christian doctrines as resolutions of practical problems. His discussion of anxiety in *The Courage to Be* is a good example of his method. He first analyzes thoroughly and with great sensitivity what he considers the three great anxieties of modern man—the anxiety of death, that of meaninglessness, and that of guilt. These three forms of anxiety are three modes of response to various kinds of threats from nonbeing, threats to which existence as such is subject. As a practical solution to this practical problem, theology presents God. By participating in God, who is the infinite power to resist the threat of nonbeing, man acquires the courage to exist fully, even in the face of such anxiety. Similarly, when a person becomes deeply aware of historical existence as full of ambiguities, he becomes filled with perplexities and despair. The Christian answer is the notion of the Kingdom of God, which is the meaning, fulfillment, and unity of history.

Knowledge of reality. Tillich's concern was with the religious significance of the "human situation," and he held that religious questions arise out of human problems. In a similar vein, the only basis for an understanding of the ontological structure of reality is the analysis of human existence, of man's encounter with his environment. We can grasp the being of other things only by analogy with man. Tillich, in the first volume of his *Systematic Theology,* sees man as ". . . that being in whom all levels of being are united and approachable." But man is not merely ". . . an outstanding object among other objects." He is the ". . . being who asks the ontological question and in whose self-awareness the ontological answer can be found." Man can proceed in this way ". . . because he experiences directly and immediately the structure of being and its elements"—because ". . . the interdependence of ego-self and world is the basic ontological structure and implies all the others." Man is a self; ". . . therefore selfhood and self-centeredness must be attributed . . . to all living beings and, in terms of analogy, to all individual *Gestalten* even in the inorganic realm." In accordance with this view, Tillich takes concepts that he supposes to have their primary application to human existence—individualization and participation, dynamics and form, freedom and destiny—and designates them as the elements constituting ontological structure, applying them to being as such.

Faith. Tillich conceives of faith or, as he calls it, "ultimate concern" as a way of organizing human experience and activity. In his view, faith is an unconditional surrender to something and the willingness to recognize it as an absolute authority; an expectation that one will in some way receive a supreme fulfillment through encounter and commerce with it; a discovery that everything in one's life and one's world is significant only insofar as it is in some way related to it; and experiencing it as holy—that is, reacting to it with an intimate blend of a sense of awe, mystery, and fascination.

Every human being, Tillich believed, has such an ultimate concern, but the objects of the concern vary enormously. Supernatural beings, historical persons whether religious or secular, nations, social classes, political movements, cultural forms like painting and science, material goods, social status—any of these may be the object of an ultimate concern. But despite what Tillich said, it would seem that such orientation around a single object is a rare achievement. Most people, it would seem, have several major interests. Moreover, there is a crucial difference between concern with an object, whether existent or thought to exist, and concern for the realization of some end. The significance of taking an end, like social status, as having authority is not clear. Nevertheless, Tillich's analysis of religiosity is a penetrating one, and it reveals the important resemblances between religiosity and nonreligious modes of personal organization.

God. Tillich tried to show that the religious life is more than an organization of human feelings and attitudes and that it involves a reference to a reality outside itself, a reference that can be validated. Although Tillich did not, like Kierkegaard, deny the religious relevance of rational investigation, and although he did think that ontology gives some support to religion, he did not believe in the validity of traditional metaphysical proofs of specifically religious doctrines and in particular of the existence of a personal God. Tillich did not, in fact, accept the notion of a personal deity. For him the doctrine of a supernatural person, like all religious doctrines, is to be conceived as an attempt to symbolize an ultimate reality, "being-itself," which is so ultimate that all that can literally be said about it is that it is ultimate. If the God of theism is a person, the often repeated charge that Tillich is really an atheist thus seems justified; yet Tillich can point out that in the past Christian theology has repeatedly found difficulty in the notion that God is a person in any straightforward or literal sense.

The Ultimate. Tillich defended his view that religious faith is objectively valid by claiming that an ultimate concern must necessarily have what is metaphysically Ultimate as its object. It is not clear, however, that if a concern is ultimate (in the sense of being the dominant interest of a person), the object of the concern is necessarily Ultimate in the relevant sense; that is, that the object of the concern is that on which all else depends for its being. Tillich has argued elsewhere that one can be ultimately concerned only with what is metaphysically Ultimate. Nothing can properly be of ultimate concern unless it is the ultimate determiner of the reality and meaning of our existence, and only being-itself occupies this position. From this conclusion it is only a short step to say that in ultimate concern one is always really concerned with being-itself, whether one realizes it or not.

Religious symbols. But if being-itself is always the object of ultimate concern, what is the status of the various nonultimate entities on which ultimate concern seems to be focused? According to Tillich, as we have seen, the object of an ultimate concern is generally something relatively concrete, such as a person or a social group, and not, at least not consciously, some ineffable metaphysical Ultimate. Tillich claims that these concrete objects function as symbols of the Ultimate. They manifest the Ultimate to those who experience them as holy, and for those persons they *point to* the Ultimate; through them the individual participates in the Ultimate. Thus, ultimate concern has in a sense a double object. Unfortunately, Tillich never gave an intelligible account of these closely interrelated concepts of symbolizing and pointing to, which are so crucial for his position. Pointing to the Ultimate cannot consist in calling the Ultimate to mind, for admittedly most people have no such concept. The main difficulty is that being-itself is given such a fundamental position in Tillich's metaphysical scheme that one necessarily is related to being-itself at every moment in any way in which anyone could conceivably be related to it. Thus, if it is possible to speak of beings participating in being-itself, then each being necessarily so participates at every moment of its existence. There seems to be no room for any special contact with being-itself that could be generated by religious symbols when they are "pointing to it."

Defense of Christianity. As a Christian theologian, Tillich wanted to demonstrate that among ultimate concerns the Christian concern is the most adequate. He sometimes said that some ultimate concerns are "idolatrous" because they are directed at finite objects rather than at the Ultimate. But by his own principles Tillich could not say this, because every case of ultimate concern involves a concrete object that manifests or points to the Ultimate. If it did not so function, it would not be a case of ultimate concern. The only possible way of showing that one ultimate concern is more adequate than another would be to show that it served better as a symbol of being-itself. But since nothing can be said literally about being-itself except that it is Ultimate, a feature that nothing else can share, it is not clear how this could be done. Tillich's own argument for the superiority of Christianity seems itself to be in symbolic terms. He said that by dying on the cross, Jesus Christ, who is the basic symbol of being-itself in Christianity, underlined the fact that symbols have their significance not in themselves but as manifesting the Ultimate.

Works by Tillich

Translations of important works include *The Religious Situation,* translated by H. R. Niebuhr (New York, 1956), and *The Interpretation of History,* translated by N. A. Razetski and E. L. Talmey (New York, 1936).

Tillich's magnum opus is *Systematic Theology,* 3 vols. (Chicago, 1951–1963). Vol. I contains most of the philosophically interesting sections. *The Courage to Be* (New Haven, 1952) is an existentially toned account of the spiritual situation of contemporary man. *The Dynamics of Faith* (New York, 1957) is the best popular account of Tillich's position. *Biblical Religion and the Search for Ultimate Reality* (Chicago, 1955) defends the thesis that ontological speculation has relevance to Biblical religion. *Theology of Culture,* R. C. Kimball, ed. (New York, 1959), is a collection of Tillich's writings on the mutual relevance of theology and various aspects of culture.

On the notion of a religious symbol, see "The Religious Symbol," in *Journal of Liberal Religion*, Vol. 2, No. 1 (Summer 1940), 13–33, and "Theology and Symbolism," in F. E. Johnson, ed., *Religious Symbolism* (New York, 1955), pp. 107–116.

Works on Tillich

For discussions of Tillich's works, see C. W. Kegley and R. W. Bretall, eds., *The Theology of Paul Tillich* (New York, 1952); W. P. Alston, "Tillich on Idolatry," in *Journal of Religion*, Vol. 38 (1958), 263–267; Paul Edwards, "Professor Tillich's Confusions," in *Mind*, Vol. 74 (1965), 192–214; and W. P. Alston, "Tillich's Conception of a Religious Symbol," in Sidney Hook, ed., *Religious Experience and Truth* (New York, 1961), pp. 12–26.

WILLIAM P. ALSTON

TIME. Time has frequently struck philosophers as mysterious. Some have even felt that it was incapable of rational discursive treatment and that it was able to be grasped only by intuition. This defeatist attitude probably arises from the fact that time always seems to be mysteriously slipping away from us; no sooner do we grasp a bit of it in our consciousness than it has slipped away into the past. We shall see, however, that this notion of time as something which continually slips past us is based on a confusion.

ST. AUGUSTINE'S PUZZLES

The apparent mysteriousness of time can make puzzles about time seem more baffling than they are, even though similar ones arise in the case of nontemporal concepts. St. Augustine, in his *Confessions*, asks, "What is time?" When no one asks him, he knows; when someone asks him, however, he does not know. He knows how to use the word "time" and cognate temporal words, such as "before," "after," "past," and "future," but he can give no clear account of this use. Trouble arises particularly from the form in which he puts his question: "What is time?" This looks like a request for a definition, and yet no definition is forthcoming. However, most interesting concepts cannot be elucidated by explicit definitions. Thus, to explain the meaning of the word "length," we cannot give an explicit definition, but we can do things that explain how to tell that one thing is longer than another and how to measure length. In the same way we can give an account of our use of the word "time" even though we cannot do so by giving an explicit definition. In short, this puzzle of St. Augustine's is not of a sort that arises peculiarly in the case of time. Beyond pointing this out, therefore, it is not appropriate here to go further into the matter.

Augustine was also puzzled by how we could measure time. He seems to have been impressed by the lack of analogy between spatial and temporal measurement. For example, you can put a ruler alongside a table top, and the ruler and the table top are all there at once. On the other hand, if you measure a temporal process, you do it by comparing it with some other process, such as the movement of the hand of a watch. At any moment of the comparison, part of the process to be measured has passed away, and part of it is yet to be. You cannot get the thing to be measured before you all at once, as you can with the table top. Moreover, if we compare two temporal processes —say, my walking twenty miles last week with my walking twenty miles today—we compare these with two different movements of my watch hand, whereas we can compare two different table tops with the same ruler. Augustine is led to see a puzzle here because he demands, in effect, that nonanalogous things should be talked about as though they were analogous.

In any case, the two things are not, in fact, quite as nonanalogous as they appear to be at first sight. If we pass to a tenseless idiom in which material things are thought of as four-dimensional space-time solids, the difference becomes less apparent. For in the case of the tables we compare two different spatial cross sections of the four-dimensional object which is the ruler with spatial cross sections of the two tables. Augustine seems to have been influenced by the thought that the present is real, although the past and future are not (the past has ceased to exist, and the future has not yet come to be); consequently, the measurement of time is puzzling in a way in which the measurement of space need not be (where the whole spatial object can be present now). This thought—that the present is real in a way in which past and future are not real—is part of the confusion of the flow or passage of time.

THE MYTH OF PASSAGE

We commonly think of time as a stream that flows or as a sea over which we advance. The two metaphors come to much the same thing, forming part of a whole way of thinking about time which D. C. Williams has called "the myth of passage." If time flows past us or if we advance through time, this would be a motion with respect to a hypertime. For motion in space is motion with respect to time, and motion of time or in time could hardly be a motion in time with respect to time. Ascription of a metric to time is not necessary for the argument, but supposing that time can be measured in seconds, the difficulty comes out very clearly. If motion in space is feet per second, at what speed is the flow of time? Seconds per what? Moreover, if passage is of the essence of time, it is presumably the essence of hypertime, too, which would lead us to postulate a hyper-hypertime and so on ad infinitum.

The idea of time as passing is connected with the idea of events changing from future to past. We think of events as approaching us from the future, whereupon they are momentarily caught in the spotlight of the present and then recede into the past. Yet in normal contexts it does not make sense to talk of events changing or staying the same. Roughly speaking, events are happenings to continuants—that is, to things that change or stay the same. Thus, we can speak of a table, a star, or a political constitution as changing or staying the same. But can we intelligibly talk of a change itself as changing or not changing? It is true that in the differential calculus we talk of rates of change changing, but a rate of change is not the same thing as a change. Again, we can talk of continuants as coming into existence or ceasing to exist, but we cannot similarly talk of a "coming-into-existence" itself as coming into existence or ceasing to exist. It is nevertheless true that there is a special class of predicates, such as "being past," "being present," "being future," together with some epistemological predicates like "being probable" or "being foreseen," with respect to which we can talk of events as changing.

Significantly enough, these very predicates do not apply to continuants. We do not, for example, naturally talk of a table or a star as "becoming past" but of its "ceasing to exist." There is something odd about the putative properties of pastness, presentness, futurity, and the like, whereby events are supposed to change.

Token-reflexive expressions. Leaving aside the epistemological predicates, we may suspect that the oddness arises from the fact that the words "past," "present," and "future," together with "now" and with tenses, are token-reflexive, or indexical, expressions. That is, these words refer to their own utterance. Let us indicate tenselessness in a verb by putting it in italics. Thus, if we say, "Caesar *crosses* the Rubicon," we do not indicate whether the crossing is something before, simultaneous with, or after our assertion. Tenseless verbs occur in mathematics where temporal position relative to our utterance is not even in question. Thus, we can say, "2 + 2 *is* equal to 4" not because we wish to be noncommittal about the temporal position of 2 + 2 as being 4 but because it has no temporal position at all.

The token-reflexiveness of the word "past" can be seen from the fact that a person who said that a certain event *E* is past could equally well have said, "*E is* earlier than this utterance." Similarly, instead of saying, "*E* is present," he could say, "*E is* simultaneous with this utterance," and instead of "*E* is future," he could say, "*E is* later than this utterance." "*E was* future" is more complicated. It means that if someone had said, "*E* is future" or "*E is* later than this utterance," at some appropriate time earlier than our present utterance (the utterance which we now refer to as "this utterance"), he would have spoken truly. Thus, if we say that in 1939 the battle of Britain was in the future, we are putting ourselves into the shoes of ourselves as we were in 1939, when, given a certain amount of prescience, we might have said truly, "The battle of Britain *is* later than this utterance." Apart from this imaginative projection, we are saying no more than that the battle of Britain *is* later than 1939.

It follows that there is a confusion in talking of events as changing in respect of pastness, presentness, and futurity. These are not genuine properties, as we can see if we make the token-reflexiveness explicit. "*E* was future, is present, and will become past" goes over into "*E is* later than some utterance earlier than this utterance, *is* simultaneous with this utterance, and *is* earlier than some utterance later than this utterance." This is about as near as we can get to it, and it will be seen that we have to refer to three different utterances. A failure to recognize the token-reflexiveness of words like "past," "present," and "future" can lead us to think wrongly of the change from future to past as a genuine change, like the change in position of a boat which floats down a river.

Nevertheless, there is probably a deeper source of the illusion of time flow. This is that our stock of memories is constantly increasing, and memories are of earlier, not of later, events. It is difficult to state this matter properly, since we forget things as well as acquire new memories. With a very old man there may well be a net diminishing of his stock of memories, and yet he does not feel as if time were running the other way. This suggestion is therefore a

tentative and incompletely worked out one. The subordinate question of why our memories are of the past, not of the future, is an extremely interesting one in its own right, and we shall see that it can be answered.

Tenses. Not only words like "past" and "future" but also tenses can be replaced by linguistic devices containing tenseless verbs and the phrase "this utterance." Thus, instead of saying, "Caesar crossed the Rubicon," we could have said, "Caesar *crosses* the Rubicon earlier than this utterance." For the present and future tenses we use "simultaneous with this utterance" and "later than this utterance." Of course, this is not a strict translation. If I say, "Caesar *crosses* the Rubicon earlier than this utterance," I am referring to my utterance, whereas if you say, "Caesar crossed the Rubicon," you are implicitly referring to your utterance. Nevertheless, a tensed language is translatable into a tenseless language in the sense that the purposes subserved by the one, in which utterances covertly refer to themselves, can be subserved by the other in which utterances explicitly refer to themselves.

A second qualification must be made. In the case of spoken language the token or "utterance" can be taken to be the actual sounds. In a written language the "token," the configuration of ink marks, is something that persists through time. By "this utterance" we must therefore, in the case of written language, understand the coming-into-existence of the token or perhaps the act of writing it. It has sometimes been objected that this account will not stand, since "this utterance" means "the utterance which is *now*," which reintroduces the notion of tense. There does not seem to be any reason, however, why we should accept this charge of circularity. We have as good a right to say that "now" means "simultaneous with this utterance" as our opponent has to say that "this utterance" means "the utterance which is now." The notion of an utterance directly referring to itself does not seem to be a difficult one.

Duration. The philosophical notion of duration seems to be heavily infected with the myth of passage. Thus, Locke (*Essay,* Book II, Ch. 14, Sec. 1) says that "duration is fleeting extension." More recently, Bergson has made the notion of duration (*durée*) central in his philosophy. According to him, physical time is something spatialized and intellectualized, whereas the real thing, with which we are acquainted in intuition (inner experience), is duration. Unlike physical time, which is always measured by comparing discrete spatial positions—for example, of clock hands—duration is the experienced change itself, the directly intuited nonspatial stream of consciousness in which past, present, and future flow into one another. Bergson's meaning is unclear, partly because he thinks that duration is something to be intuitively, not intellectually, grasped. It is closely connected in his thought with memory, for in memory, he says, the past survives in the present. Here he would seem to be open to the objection, urged against him by Bertrand Russell in his *History of Western Philosophy,* that he confuses the memory of the past event with the past event itself or the thought with that which is thought about.

Even though the Bergsonian notion of duration may be rejected because of its subjectivism and because of its close connection with the notion of time flow or passage, there is nevertheless a clear use of the word "duration" in science and ordinary life. Thus, in talking about the duration of a war, we talk simply about the temporal distance between its beginning and its end.

McTaggart on time's unreality. The considerations thus far adduced may well be illustrated by considering how they bear on McTaggart's well-known argument for the unreality of time, which was put forward in an article in *Mind* (1908) and in his posthumous *Nature of Existence*. For McTaggart, events are capable of being ordered in two ways. First, they can be ordered in respect to past, present, and future. He calls this ordering of events "the *A* series." Second, events can be ordered in respect to the relations "earlier than" and "later than." He calls this "the *B* series." McTaggart then argues that the *B* series does not by itself give us all that is essential to time and that the *A* series is contradictory. Neither leg of his argument can stand criticism. His reason for saying that the *B* series misses the essence of time is that time involves change and yet it always is, was, and will be the case that the Battle of Hastings, say, is earlier than the Battle of Waterloo. We have already seen, however, that it is not just false but also absurd to talk of events' changing. The Battle of Hastings is not *sempiternally* earlier than the Battle of Waterloo; it simply *is* (tenselessly) earlier than it. The notion of change is perfectly capable of being expressed in the language of the *B* series by saying that events in the *B* series *differ* from one another in various ways. Similarly, the proposition that a thing changes can be expressed in the language of the *B* series by the statement that one spatial cross section of it *is* different from an earlier one, and the proposition that it does not change can be expressed by saying that earlier and later cross sections *are* similar to one another. To express the notion of change, we are therefore *not* forced to say that events change. Nor, therefore, are we forced into referring to the *A* series, into saying that events change (in the only way in which we can plausibly say this) in respect to pastness, presentness, and futurity. Nevertheless, if we do retreat to the language of the *A* series, we can perfectly well do so without contradiction. Just as McTaggart erred by using tensed verbs when talking of the *B* series, he in effect made the correlative error of forgetting tenses (or equivalent devices) when talking of the *A* series. For the contradiction which he claimed to find in the *A* series is that since any event is in turn future, present, and past, we must ascribe these three incompatible characteristics to it. But an event cannot be future, present, or past *simpliciter* but only with reference to a particular time—for example, one at which it was future, is present, and will be past. If we restore the tenses, the trouble with the *A* series disappears. Unsuccessful though McTaggart's argument is, it provides an excellent case study with which to elucidate the relations between tensed and tenseless language.

SPACE-TIME

The theory of relativity illustrates the advantages of replacing the separate notions of space and time by a unified notion of space-time. In particular, Minkowski showed that the Lorentz transformations of special relativity correspond to a rotation of axes in space-time. He showed how natural the kinematics of special relativity can seem, as opposed to Newtonian kinematics, in which, in effect, we should rotate the time axis without correspondingly rotating the space axes. Since the theory of relativity it has become a commonplace to regard the world as a four-dimensional space-time manifold. Nevertheless, even in the days of Newtonian dynamics, there was nothing to prevent taking this view of the world, even though it would not have been as neat as it is in relativity theory. If we pass to the four-dimensional way of looking at things, it is important not to be confused about certain conceptual matters. Confusion will arise if we mix the tenseless way of talking appropriate to the four-dimensional picture with our ordinary way of talking of things as enduring substances, "the permanent in change."

In ordinary language we use the word "space" itself as the name of a continuant. We can say, for example, that a part of space has become, or has continued to be, occupied. Space-time, however, is a "space" in a tenseless sense of this word, and since time is already in the representation, it is quite wrong to talk of space-time as itself changing. Thus, in some expositions of relativity we find it said that a certain "world line" is a track along which a material body moves or a light signal is propagated. The body or light signal, however, cannot correctly be said to move through space-time. What should be said is that the body or the light signal *lies* (tenselessly) along the world line. To talk of anything's moving through space-time is to bring time into the story twice over and in an illegitimate manner. When we are talking about motion in terms of the space-time picture, we must do so in terms of the relative orientations of world lines. Thus, to say that two particles move with a uniform nonzero relative velocity is expressed by saying that they *lie* (tenselessly) along straight world lines which are at an angle to one another. Similarly, the recent conception of the positron as an electron moving backward in time is misleading, since nothing can move, forward or backward, in time. What is meant is that the world lines of a positron and electron, which are produced together or which annihilate one another, can be regarded as a single bent world line, and this may indeed be a very fruitful way of looking at the matter.

In popular expositions of relativity we also read of such things as "our consciousness crawling up the world line of our body." This is once more the confusion of the myth of passage and, hence, of the illegitimate notion of movement through space-time. It is instructive to consider how H. G. Wells's time machine could be represented in the space-time picture. A moment's thought should suffice to indicate to us that it cannot be represented at all. For if we draw a line extending into the past, this will simply be the representation of a particle which has existed for a very long time. It is not surprising that we cannot represent a time machine, since the notion of such a machine is an incoherent one. How fast would such a machine flash over a given ten-second stretch? In ten seconds or minus ten seconds? Or what? No sensible answer can be given, for the question is itself absurd. The notion also involves the contradiction, pointed out by D. C. Williams in his article "The Myth of Passage," that if I get into a time machine at

12 today, then at 3 P.M., say, I shall be *both* at 3 P.M. today *and* at, say, minus a million years B.C.

ABSOLUTE AND RELATIONAL THEORIES

Isaac Newton held to an absolute theory of space and time, whereas his contemporary Leibniz argued that space and time are merely sets of relations between things which are "in" space and time. Newton misleadingly and unnecessarily expressed his absolute theory of time in terms of the myth of passage, as when he confusingly said, "Absolute, true and mathematical time, of itself and from its own nature, flows equably without relation to anything external." The special theory of relativity has made it impossible to consider time as something absolute; rather, it stands neutrally between absolute and relational theories of space-time (see SPACE). The question as between absolute and relational theories of space-time becomes especially interesting when we pass to the general theory of relativity. According to this theory, the structure of space-time is dependent on the distribution of the matter in the universe. In most forms of the theory there is nevertheless a residual space-time structure which cannot be thus accounted for. A curvature is usually attributed to space-time even in the complete absence of matter, and the inertia of a body, according to this theory, depends in part on this cosmological contribution to the local metrical field and hence not solely on the total mass of the universe, as a purely relational theory would require. Research on this question is still going on, and until it has been decided, Mach's principle (as Einstein called it), according to which the spatiotemporal structure of the universe depends entirely on the distribution of its matter, will remain controversial. But even if Mach's principle were upheld, it might still be possible to interpret matter, in a metaphysical way, as regions of special curvature of space-time.

TIME AND THE CONTINUUM

An absolute theory of space-time, as envisaged above, need not imply that there is anything absolute about distance (space-time interval). Because of the continuity of space-time any space-time interval contains as many space-time points as any other (that is, a high infinity of them); space and time do not possess an intrinsic metric, and there must always be an element of convention in our definitions of congruence in geometry and chronology, as Grünbaum has pointed out, influenced by Riemann. This means that the same cosmological facts can be expressed by means of a variety of space-time geometries, provided that they have the same topological structure. (Topology is that part of geometry which treats only of those properties of a figure which remain the same however that figure is transformed into a new one, with the sole restriction that a point transforms into one and only one point and neighboring points transform into neighboring ones. Thus, the surface of a sphere and that of a cube have the same topology, but that of a sphere and that of an infinite plane do not.)

Zeno and Cantor. The continuity of space and time can be properly understood only in terms of the modern mathematical theory of infinity and dimensionality. Given the concepts available to him, Zeno rightly rejected the view that an extended line or time interval could be composed of unextended points or instants. (See Aristotle, *Physics* 231a20–231b18 and *De Generatione et Corruptione,* 316a15–317a17.)

In modern terms we may say that not even a denumerable infinity of points can make up a nonzero interval. Cantor has shown, however, that there are higher types of infinity than that which belongs to denumerable sets, such as the set of all natural numbers. Cantor showed that the set of real numbers on a line, or segment of a line, is of a higher type of infinity than is the set of natural numbers. Perhaps the right cardinality of "dimensionless points" *can* add up to a nonzero length. This answer is on the right track. Nevertheless, the cardinality of a set of points does not by itself determine dimensionality. For example, Cantor showed that there is a one-to-one mapping between the points of a plane and the points of a line. However, a mathematical theory of dimension has been developed which accords with our intuitions in assigning 0, 1, 2, 3, and so on, dimensions respectively to points, lines, planes, volumes, and so on, and which also assigns dimensions to other sorts of sets of points. For example, the set of all rational points on a line has dimension 0. So does the set of all irrational points. In these cases an infinity of "unextended points" does indeed form a set of dimension 0. Since these two sets of points together make up the set of points on a line, it follows that two sets of dimension 0 can be united to form a set of dimension 1. Strictly speaking, it is even inaccurate to talk of "unextended points." It is sets of points that have dimension. A line is a set of points, and the points are not parts of the line but members of it. The modern theory of dimension shows that there is no inconsistency in supposing that an appropriate nondenumerable infinity of points makes up a set of greater dimensionality than any finite or denumerable set of points could.

The theory of the continuum implies that if we take away the lower end of a closed interval, we are left with an open interval, an interval without a first point. In fact, Zeno's premises in his paradox of the dichotomy do not lead to paradox at all but are a consistent consequence of the theory of the continuum. Motion is impossible, according to the paradox of the dichotomy, because before one can go from *A* to *B*, one must first get to the halfway mark *C*, but before one can get to *C*, one must get to the halfway mark *D* between *A* and *C*, and so on indefinitely. It is concluded that the motion can never even get started. A similar argument, applied to time intervals, might seem to show that a thing cannot even endure through time. The fallacy in both cases comes from thinking of the continuum as a set of points or instants arranged in succession. For if a continuous interval had to consist of a first, second, third, and so on point or instant, then the dichotomy would provide a fatal objection. However, points or instants do not occur in succession, since to any point or instant there is no *next* point or instant. Such considerations enable us to deal with Zeno's paradox of Achilles and the tortoise, in which similar difficulties are supposed to arise at the *latter* end of an open interval.

Kant's antinomies. A related paradox is Kant's first antinomy, in his *Critique of Pure Reason.* As was shown by

Edward Caird in his commentary on Kant's *Critique,* the antinomies (or paradoxes which Kant had constructed about space, time, and causality) were quite as important as Hume's skeptical philosophy in arousing Kant from his "dogmatic slumbers." Kant's first antinomy relates to both space and time; here we shall concentrate on it as it relates to time. There are two antithetical arguments. The first states that the world had a beginning in time, whereas the second, with equal plausibility, seems to show that the world had no beginning in time. The first argument begins with the premise that if the world had no beginning in time, then up to a given moment an infinite series of successive events must have passed. But, says Kant, the infinity of a series consists in the fact that it can never be completed. Hence, it is impossible for an infinite series of events to have passed away.

It can be seen that Kant's argument here rests partly on the myth of passage. Kant thinks of the world as having come to its present state through a series of past events, so that an infinite succession would therefore have had to be completed. Otherwise, he would have been just as puzzled about the possibility of an infinite future as about an infinite past, and this does not seem to have been the case. Just as the sequence 0, 1, 2, . . . can never be completed in the sense that it has no last member, the sequence . . . , −2, −1, 0 cannot be completed in the sense that it has no first member. This is not to say, of course, that an infinite set need have either a first or last member. Thus, the set of temporal instants up to, but not including, a given instant, has neither a first nor last member. However, Kant is clearly thinking not of the set of instants but of a sequence of events, each taking up a finite time. The set of instants does not form a sequence since there are no instants that are next to one another. Kant's definition of infinity, besides being objectionably psychologistic, is clearly inapplicable to infinite sets of entities which do not form a sequence, such as the points on a line or a segment of a line. Concerning an infinite set of events which form a sequence, however, Kant is not justified in supposing that its having a last member is any more objectionable than its having a first member. There is a perfect symmetry between the two cases once we rid ourselves of the notion of passage—that is, of the one-way flow of time.

Now let us look at Kant's antithetical argument. He argues that the world cannot have had a beginning in time, so that, contrary to the thesis of the antinomy, there must have been an infinity of past events. His reason is that if the world had begun at a certain time, all previous time would have been a blank and there would be no reason that the world should have begun at the time it did rather than at some other time. Previously, Leibniz had used the same argument to support a relational theory of time. If time is constituted solely by the relations between events, then it becomes meaningless to ask questions about the temporal position of the universe as a whole or about when it began. In an absolute theory of time (or of space-time) Kant's problem remains, but further discussion of it cannot be pursued here since it would involve us in a metaphysical discussion of causality and the principle of sufficient reason.

THE DIRECTION OF TIME

We have just seen that Kant was puzzled about the infinity of the past in a way in which he was not puzzled about the infinity of the future. It has been suggested that the myth of passage had something to do with this inconsistency. If we reject the notion of passage, we find ourselves with a new, though soluble, problem. This is the apparent temporal asymmetry of the universe, which contrasts sharply with its large-scale spatial symmetry. For example, if we look out at the galaxies, they appear to be distributed evenly in all directions, and yet a time direction seems to be specified by the fact that they are all receding from one another, not approaching one another. On a more mundane level the temporal asymmetry of the universe strikes us forcibly in many ways. For example, there is nothing in our experience analogous to memory but with respect to the future. Nor is there anything like a tape recording or a footprint of the future—that is, there are no *traces* of the future. A memory is indeed a special case of a trace. This asymmetry about traces explains how we can be so confident about the past history of the human race and about the past evolution of living creatures, whereas it would be a bold man who would try to guess the political history of even the next hundred years or the organic evolution of the next few millions. The question "Why are there traces only of the past, not of the future?" is thus a fundamental one.

We must first rule out a purely verbalistic answer to this question. Someone might say that traces are always of the past, never of the future, because it is part of the meaning of the word "trace" that traces are of earlier, not of later, events. This would be to suppose that our question is as stupid as the question "Why are bachelors always male, never female?" This account of the matter is not good enough. Admittedly, in our language as it is, the expression "female bachelor" is a self-contradictory one. Nevertheless, it is quite easy to imagine a variant of English in which "bachelor" simply meant "not yet married person" and according to which spinsters could therefore be called "bachelors." Let us call a spinster a "female analogue" of a bachelor. We can now silence the verbalistic objection to our question about why traces are always of the past, never of the future, by recasting it in the form "Why are there no future analogues of traces?"

Temporal asymmetry and physical laws. The temporal directionality of the universe or, at the very least, of our present cosmic era of the universe would therefore appear to be a deep-lying cosmological fact, which is not to be glossed over by verbalistic explanations. How is it to be explained? We must first dismiss the suggestion that the asymmetry lies in the laws of physics. The laws of classical dynamics and electromagnetism, as well as of quantum mechanics, are all expressed by time-symmetrical differential equations. In other words, if $f(t)$ is a solution to these equations, so is $f(-t)$—at least if we may ignore some possible implications of an experiment carried out in 1964 by James H. Christenson, James W. Cronin, Val L. Fitch, and René Turlay on the decay of K_2^0 mesons. It follows that if a cinematographic film were taken of any process describable by means of these laws and then run backward, it would still portray a physically possible process. It is true that phenomenological thermodynamics would provide a contrary case, since its second law does contain time explicitly. Thus, if you put a kettle full of ice on a hot brick, you find that the system turns into one in which a kettle full of water sits on a cool brick. A film of this process cannot be reversed to show a process which is possible in phenomenological thermodynamics; we cannot have a system of a kettle filled with water on a cool brick turning into one in which the water has frozen and the brick has become hot. In spite of all this we must still assert that the laws of nature are time symmetrical. This is because phenomenological thermodynamics provides only an approximation of the truth (it is refuted by the phenomenon of Brownian motion, for example) and, more importantly because the detailed explanation of the facts of which phenomenological thermodynamics treats at the surface level is to be found in statistical thermodynamics. Statistical thermodynamics bases itself on the laws of mechanics, which are time symmetrical.

According to statistical thermodynamics, the situation in which the water in our kettle freezes while the brick gets hotter is indeed a physically possible one, though it is an almost infinitely unlikely one. Why it is unlikely has to do not with the laws of nature themselves but with their boundary conditions. There is indeed a puzzle here, because if we reverse all the velocities of a closed system, we get a configuration which, according to statistical mechanics, is as likely as the original one. Therefore, the process seen on our reversed cinematographic film should be as likely as the original one. The answer to this objection (the reversibility objection) lies in the fact that corresponding to a given macroscopic description (cold kettle on hot brick, say), there is a whole ensemble of possible microstates. It follows that though any microstate is as probable as any other, this is not so with macrostates, and given the information that a body is in a macrostate *A*, it is highly probable that it will turn into a macrostate *B* rather than vice versa if *B* corresponds to an ensemble of microstates which is vastly more numerous than the ensemble of microstates corresponding to *A*.

An analogy with a pack of cards will help to make this clear. Consider a well-shuffled pack of cards. Any order of the cards is as probable as any other provided that the order is precisely described. Given any one such order *P*, it is, of course, just as probable that in shuffling, *P* will turn into the order (call it *Q*) in which the pack is arranged in suits as that *Q* would turn into *P*. But if *P* is described simply as haphazard, there is a vast number of states other than *P* which are also haphazard. Thus, although a shuffling which turns *Q* into *P* is no more probable than one which turns *P* into *Q*, there are far more shufflings which turn *Q* into a state abstractly described as haphazard than there are shufflings which turn a particular haphazard state—say, *P*—into *Q*.

Suppose we started with our cards arranged in suits, the state *Q*. If we shuffled them, they would soon get into what we should call a well-shuffled state. Nevertheless, if we went on shuffling long enough, we should eventually get

back to the unshuffled state *Q*. This illustrates the following interesting point. Let us for the moment toy with the almost certainly false cosmological hypothesis that the universe is a finite nonexpanding collection of particles without spontaneous creation or annihilation. Then, just as with our pack of cards, such a universe will eventually return to any given state. The universe will get more and more shuffled until we get the so-called heat death, in which everything is a featureless uniformity and will then become less and less disordered. In the era in which, as we should put it, the universe was getting less disordered, time would seem to run in the opposite direction to that in which it seems to run to us. (Thus, denizens of this era would still say that the universe was getting more disordered.) Indeed, there would be an infinite sequence of cosmic eras, much as is supposed in some Buddhist cosmologies, except that time would seem to run in opposite ways in alternate eras. In a sufficiently large view there would be temporal symmetry in this universe, though not on the scale of any single cosmic era. This is what makes the hypothesis of a finite nonexpanding universe philosophically instructive, even though it is probably contrary to fact.

Trace formation and entropy. We are now in a position to deal with the formation of traces. Although a wide, relatively isolated part of the universe is increasing in its state of being shuffled, or, to use the more precise notion developed by physicists, in its entropy, subsystems of the wider system may temporally decrease in shuffling, or entropy. Thus, an isolated system, such as that consisting of a cube of ice in a beaker of water, may well have lower entropy than its surroundings. This reduction of entropy is bought at the expense of a more than compensating increase of entropy in the surroundings. There will, for example, be an increase of disorderliness in the system containing the coal and air that react chemically and drive the generators that provide the electric power that drives the refrigerator that makes the ice cube. (The system consisting of coal and oxygen is a more highly ordered one than is that which consists of the ashes and used up air.) Eventually our ice cube melts and becomes indistinguishable from the water in which it floated.

Branch systems. The formation of a trace is the formation of a subsystem of temporarily lower entropy than that of its surroundings, and the trace is blotted out when the entropy curve of the subsystem rejoins that of the larger system. A footprint in sand is a temporarily highly ordered state of the sand; this orderliness is bought at the expense of an increased disorderliness (metabolic depletion) of the pedestrian who made it, and this extra orderliness eventually disappears as a result of wind and weather. Reichenbach calls such systems of temporarily lower entropy "branch systems." It is an observable fact, and one to be expected from considerations of statistical thermodynamics, that these branch systems nearly all (in practice, quite all) go in the same direction. This direction defines a temporal direction for the universe or at least for our cosmic era of it.

On investigation it will be seen that all sorts of traces, whether footprints on sand, photographs, fossil bones, or the like, can be understood as traces in this sense. Indeed, so are written records. The close connection between information and entropy is brought out in modern information theory, the mathematics of which is much the same as that of statistical thermodynamics. A coherent piece of prose is an ordered part of the universe, unlike a completely random sequence of symbols.

It is possible that the formation of branch systems may be linked to deeper cosmological facts. Thomas Gold has argued persuasively that the formation of such a system is possible only because the universe provides a sink for radiation, and this is possible, again, only because of the mutual recession of the galaxies. It may therefore ultimately be the expansion of the universe which accounts for the direction of time. Beyond noting this interesting suggestion of a link between the small-scale and large-scale structure of the cosmos, we can for our present purposes take the formation of branch systems for granted without linking it to uncertain cosmological speculations.

Popper's account. The theory of branch systems outlined above has been developed rigorously by Reichenbach and Grünbaum, whose work partly goes back to that of Ludwig Boltzmann. (A rather similar account of temporal direction has been independently given by O. Costa de Beauregard.) We must now consider a different account of the direction of time, one which was conceived by K. R. Popper.

Slightly changing Popper's example, let us consider a spherical light wave emitted from a source, as when a small electric bulb is turned on. Consider how this process would look in reverse. We should have a large spherical wave contracting to a point. This would be causally inexplicable. In order to get a spherical light wave coming in from the depths of an infinite space, we should have to suppose a coordinated set of disturbances at every point of a vast sphere, and this would require a *deus ex machina*. Moreover, this would still not provide the reverse of an outgoing wave expanding indefinitely. Thus, although the contracting wave is as much in accordance with the laws of optics as is the expanding one, it still is not compatible with any physically realizable set of initial conditions. Once more, as with the Reichenbach–Grünbaum solution, we see that temporal asymmetry arises from initial, or boundary, conditions, not from the laws of nature themselves.

Popper's criterion of temporal direction does not shed light on the concept of trace, as does the criterion of branch systems. And traces, particularly memory traces, give us our vivid sense of temporal asymmetry in the world. It is also interesting that if we consider a finite but unbounded nonexpanding universe, a contracting spherical wave would be physically realizable. Just as an expanding series of concentric circles which are on the earth's surface and have their original center at the North Pole would become a series of circles contracting to the South Pole, so in a symmetrical finite but unbounded universe a spherical wave expanding from a center would eventually become a contracting wave, shrinking to the antipodal point of the point of emission. If we included the facts of radiation in our finite nonexpanding universe, we should have to suppose a finite but unbounded space, and

Popper's criterion of temporal direction would become inapplicable. Including such facts would therefore also not conflict with our supposition of alternate cosmic eras in such a universe. In such a universe the Reichenbach–Grünbaum account of temporal direction for particular cosmic eras would still be applicable.

We must stress that Reichenbach and Grünbaum are not trying to give an analysis of the ordinary language concept of earlier and later. This is learned to some extent ostensively, and we may perfectly well know how to use words like "earlier" and "later" without knowing anything about entropy or branch systems. As Wittgenstein might have said, "We know the language game." What Reichenbach and Grünbaum are concerned with is a deeper problem: What are the general features of the universe which enable us to play the language game? Indeed, if the universe did not contain traces, it would be impossible for there to be any thought at all.

TIME AND FREE WILL: THE SEA FIGHT TOMORROW

It is sometimes thought that the picture of the world as a space-time manifold is incompatible with free will. It is thought that if one of my future actions exists (tenselessly) in the space-time manifold, then it is fated that I will do this action, and I cannot be free not to do it. To evade this conclusion, philosophers have sometimes been inclined to reject the theory of the manifold and also to deny that propositions about the future have to be either true or false. This view can be contested at several levels. First, the fact that one of my future actions exists in the space-time manifold does not mean that I am fated to do it, in the sense that I come to do it independently of what I do in the meantime. It will still be my choice. Second, the doctrine of the space-time manifold does not even imply the weaker doctrine of determinism. Determinism asserts that the laws of nature connect earlier and later spatial cross sections of the manifold in a determinate way, whereas indeterminism denies this. Thus, according to determinism, a complete knowledge of one spatial cross section of the universe would enable a superhuman calculator (who knew enough laws of nature) to deduce what other spatial cross sections would be like. Indeterminism, being only a denial of a certain sort of connectedness between elements of the manifold, is quite compatible with the theory of the manifold as such. Third, it could be argued that free will is perfectly compatible with determinism anyway. On three counts, therefore, we may assert that the theory of space-time has, in fact, nothing at all to do with the question of free will.

Aristotle canvassed some of these matters in his well-known passage about the sea battle (*De Interpretatione*, Ch. 9). Aristotle held that it is necessary that either there will be a sea battle tomorrow or there will not be but that it is not necessary that there will be a sea battle tomorrow nor is it necessary that there will not be a sea battle tomorrow. He held, however, that all present and past events are necessary, as are some future ones, like an eclipse of the moon. It is quite clear, therefore, that Aristotle's notion of necessity here is not the modern notion of logical necessity. Nor by "necessary" can he even mean "predictable" or "retrodictable." Since past events, though not all retrodictable, may have at least left traces, perhaps Aristotle may have meant by "necessary" something like "knowable in principle." But how about past events whose traces have been blotted out? It is hard to give a coherent interpretation of Aristotle here, and certainly to try to give one would be to go into metaphysical subtleties not especially connected with time. Some commentators have interpreted Aristotle as saying that the proposition "There will be a sea battle tomorrow" is neither true nor false. It would seem, however, that this was not Aristotle's view.

Finally, it must be pointed out that the difference between past and future is very misleadingly expressed by the common remark that we can change the future but not the past. It is true that we can affect the future and we cannot affect the past. We cannot, however, *change* the future, for the future is what it will be. If I decide to take the left-hand fork in a road instead of the right-hand one, I have not changed the future, for in this case the future *is* my going left. To talk of changing the future is indeed to relapse into the error of talking of events' changing and of the notion of passage.

Bibliography

GENERAL WORKS

An important book is Hans Reichenbach, *The Philosophy of Space and Time* (New York, 1958), which is a translation of a book published in German in 1928. Reichenbach partially modified his ideas in this book in his later work *The Direction of Time* (Berkeley, 1957). A wide-ranging book on the philosophy of time is *The Natural Philosophy of Time* by the cosmologist G. J. Whitrow (London and Edinburgh, 1961). Other important books are Adolf Grünbaum, *Philosophical Problems of Space and Time* (New York, 1963), and O. Costa de Beauregard, *La Notion du temps* (Paris, 1963) and *Le Second Principe de la science du temps* (Paris, 1963). See also Adolf Grünbaum's long essay "The Nature of Time" in R. G. Colodny, ed., *Frontiers of Science and Philosophy* (Pittsburgh, 1962).

A valuable essay is Wilfrid Sellars' "Time and the World Order" in Herbert Feigl et al., eds., *Minnesota Studies in the Philosophy of Science*, Vol. III (Minneapolis, 1962). An earlier essay of considerable value is the article "Time" by C. D. Broad in *Encyclopedia of Religion and Ethics*, Vol. XII (Edinburgh and New York, 1921; reissued, New York, 1951). Several of the essays in *The Problem of Time*, University of California Publications in Philosophy, Vol. 18 (Berkeley, 1935), are of interest.

A book of readings on space and time is *Problems of Space and Time*, edited, and with an introduction, by J. J. C. Smart (New York, 1964). The history of philosophical thought about time is presented in M. F. Cleugh, *Time and Its Importance for Modern Thought* (London, 1937).

ST. AUGUSTINE'S PUZZLES

Augustine's reflections on time are to be found in his *Confessions*, Book XI, Chs. 14–28; a good translation is A. C. Outler, *St. Augustine: Confessions and Enchiridion*, Vol. VII of the Library of Christian Classics (Philadelphia, 1955). Augustine much influenced Wittgenstein. For evidence of this see Ludwig Wittgenstein, *The Blue and Brown Books* (Oxford, 1958), p. 26. W. H. Watson, a physicist who had attended lectures on philosophy by Wittgenstein, quotes a passage from Augustine on time (in order to show what a typical philosophical problem is like) in the first chapter of his *On Understanding Physics* (Cambridge, 1938). Part of the article by J. N. Findlay, "Time: A Treatment of Some Puzzles," in A. G. N. Flew, ed., *Logic and Language*, First Series (Oxford, 1951), discusses Augustine's puzzles. See also Ronald Suter, "Augustine on Time, With Some Criticisms from Wittgenstein," *Revue internationale de philosophie*, Vol. 16 (1962), 319–332.

THE MYTH OF PASSAGE

On the topic of the myth of passage see especially D. C. Williams' brilliant criticism in "The Myth of Passage" in *Journal of Philosophy*, Vol. 48 (1951), 457–472. In Ch. 35 of C. D. Broad, *Examination of McTaggart's Philosophy*, Vol. II (Cambridge, 1938), Part 1, are relevant arguments against the notion of passage, even though in the end Broad does not free himself from it. An earlier view of Broad's is given in his *Scientific Thought* (London, 1923). On Broad's changing views about time see C. W. K. Mundle, "Broad's Views About Time" in P. A. Schilpp, ed., *The Philosophy of C. D. Broad* (La Salle, Ill., 1959). A criticism of the notion of passage is in J. J. C. Smart, "The River of Time" in A. G. N. Flew, ed., *Essays in Conceptual Analysis* (London, 1956), and "Spatialising Time," in *Mind*, Vol. 64 (1955), 239–241. A contrary point of view is defended by A. N. Prior, "Changes in Events and Changes in Things" (The Lindley Lecture, University of Kansas, 1962); "Time After Time" in *Mind*, Vol. 67 (1958), 244–246; and "Thank Goodness That's Over" in *Philosophy*, Vol. 34 (1959), 12–17. A reply by Jonathan Cohen to the last article is to be found in the same volume.

J. M. E. McTaggart's argument for the unreality of time is to be found in his *Philosophical Studies* (London, 1934), Ch. 5 (originally published as an article in *Mind*, 1908), and *Nature of Existence*, Vol. II (Cambridge, 1927), Ch. 33. For criticisms of this see C. D. Broad's *Examination of McTaggart's Philosophy*, Paul Marhenke's article in the book *The Problem of Time*, D. W. Gotshalk's "McTaggart on Time" in *Mind*, Vol. 39 (1930), 26–42, and part of D. F. Pears's article "Time, Truth and Inference," in A. G. N. Flew, ed., *Essays in Conceptual Analysis*. On the other side see Michael Dummett, "A Defense of McTaggart's Proof of the Unreality of Time" in *Philosophical Review*, Vol. 69 (1960), 497–504, and L. O. Mink, "Time, McTaggart and Pickwickian Language" in *Philosophical Quarterly*, Vol. 10 (1960), 252–263.

On tenses and similar token-reflexive expressions see Hans Reichenbach, *Elements of Symbolic Logic* (New York, 1947), Sec. 50–51; Nelson Goodman, *The Structure of Appearance* (Cambridge, Mass., 1951), Ch. 11; and Bertrand Russell, *An Inquiry Into Meaning and Truth* (New York, 1940), Ch. 7. Also Yehoshua Bar-Hillel, "Indexical Expressions," in *Mind*, Vol. 63 (1954), 359–379; Jonathan Cohen, "Tense Usage and Propositions," in *Analysis*, Vol. 11 (1950–1951), 80–87; R. M. Gale, "Tensed Statements," in *Philosophical Quarterly*, Vol. 12 (1962), 53–59, together with ensuing discussion notes on this. The article by Sellars, *op. cit.*, has much on tenses. Zeno Vendler, "Verbs and Times," in *Philosophical Review*, Vol. 66 (1957), 143–160, shows that tenses have more functions than one might first suppose. A tense logic is worked out by A. N. Prior in his *Time and Modality* (Oxford, 1957); R. M. Martin, in his review of this book in *Mind*, Vol. 68 (1959), 271–275, questions whether this is legitimately part of logic. See also Jonathan Cohen's critical notice of the same book in *Philosophical Quarterly*, Vol. 8 (1958), 266–271. A tenseless language is advocated by W. V. Quine, *Word and Object* (Cambridge, Mass., 1960), Sec. 36. Tensed language is advocated by J. N. Findlay, "An Examination of Tenses," in H. D. Lewis, ed., *Contemporary British Philosophy* (New York, 1956).

Other articles are R. G. Collingwood, "Some Perplexities About Time," in *PAS*, Vol. 26 (1925–1926), 135–150, and the symposium, "Time and Change" by J. Macmurray, R. G. Braithwaite and C. D. Broad in *PAS*, Supp. Vol. 8 (1928), 143–188. On the status of the past see A. J. Ayer, "Statements About the Past," in his *Philosophical Essays* (London, 1954), and G. E. Hughes's inaugural lecture at Victoria University, *On Having the Past All Over Again* (Wellington, New Zealand, 1951).

See also Richard Taylor, "Spatial and Temporal Analogies and the Concept of Identity," in *Journal of Philosophy*, Vol. 52 (1955), 599–612, and "Moving About in Time," in *Philosophical Quarterly*, Vol. 9 (1959), 289–301; and Bernard Mayo, "Objects, Events, and Complementarity," in *Philosophical Review*, Vol. 70 (1961), 340–361.

F. H. Bradley's argument for the unreality of space and time is given in his *Appearance and Reality*, 2d ed. (Oxford, 1930), Ch. 2. Henri Bergson's accounts of time and duration are given in his *Time and Free Will* (New York, 1910), *Matter and Memory* (New York, 1911), and *Introduction to Metaphysics* (London, 1913). Like Bergson's, A. N. Whitehead's metaphysics took for granted a form of the myth of passage. His views are to be found especially in *An Enquiry Concerning the Principles of Natural Knowledge* (Cambridge, 1920), Chs. 3–6, and parts of *Process and Reality* (Cambridge, 1929). See also V. C. Chappell, "Whitehead's Theory of Becoming," in *Journal of Philosophy*, Vol. 58 (1961), 516–528.

SPACE-TIME

Hermann Minkowski's classic paper "Space and Time" can be found in *The Principle of Relativity*, a collection of papers by Einstein and others, translated by W. Perret and G. B. Jeffery, with notes by Arnold Sommerfeld (New York, 1923). Popular accounts can be found in A. S. Eddington, *Space, Time and Gravitation* (Cambridge, 1920), and Moritz Schlick, *Philosophy of Nature* (New York, 1949), Ch. 7. Milič Čapek, in his *The Philosophical Impact of Contemporary Physics* (Princeton, N.J., 1961), criticizes the theory of the space-time manifold and defends the concept of becoming.

ABSOLUTE AND RELATIONAL THEORIES

A relational theory of space and time is defended by Leibniz. See especially his third and fifth papers in H. G. Alexander, ed., *The Leibniz–Clarke Correspondence* (Manchester, 1956). On space-time in the general theory of relativity see Adolf Grünbaum's paper "The Philosophical Retention of Absolute Space in Einstein's General Theory of Relativity" in J. J. C. Smart, ed., *Problems of Space and Time*, and references given therein, and J. A. Wheeler, "Curved Empty Space-time as the Building Material of the Physical World," in Ernest Nagel, Patrick Suppes, and Alfred Tarski, eds., *Logic, Methodology and Philosophy of Science* (Stanford, Calif., 1962).

TIME AND THE CONTINUUM

A good discussion of the paradoxes of Zeno will be found in Adolf Grünbaum, "Modern Science and the Refutation of the Paradoxes of Zeno," in *Scientific Monthly*, Vol. 81 (1955), 234–239, which should be read together with Grünbaum's paper "A Consistent Conception of the Linear Continuum as an Aggregate of Unextended Elements" in *Philosophy of Science*, Vol. 19 (1952), 288–306. Since 1951 many articles on Zeno's paradox of Achilles and the tortoise have appeared in *Analysis*. See also V. C. Chappell, "Time and Zeno's Arrow," in *Journal of Philosophy* Vol. 59 (1962), 197–213, and Harold N. Lee, "Are Zeno's Paradoxes Based on a Mistake?," in *Mind*, Vol. 74 (1965), 563–570. Also of interest is Paul Benacerraf, "Tasks, Super-tasks and the Modern Eleatics," in *Journal of Philosophy*, Vol. 59 (1962), 765–784. A useful account of Zeno's paradoxes is to be found in Kathleen Freeman, *Pre-Socratic Philosophers: A Companion to Diels, Fragmente der Vorsokratiker*, 3d ed. (Oxford, 1953).

Kant's antinomies about space and time occur in *The Critique of Pure Reason*. There is a translation of this book by Norman Kemp Smith (London, 1929). Zeno's and Kant's antinomies are discussed by Bertrand Russell in lectures 6 and 7 of *Our Knowledge of the External World* (London, 1922). See also C. D. Broad, "Kant's Mathematical Antinomies," in *PAS*, Vol. 55 (1954–1955), 1–22. The commentary by Edward Caird, mentioned in the present article, is *The Critical Philosophy of Immanuel Kant* (Glasgow, 1889).

THE DIRECTION OF TIME

Besides Reichenbach's book *The Direction of Time* and the book by Grünbaum, *op. cit.*, see especially Adolf Grünbaum's paper "Carnap's Views on the Foundations of Geometry" in P. A. Schilpp, ed., *The Philosophy of Rudolf Carnap* (La Salle, Ill., 1962), which, despite its title, contains a thorough discussion of the present problem, and Grünbaum's essay "The Nature of Time." See also Erwin Schrödinger's fine paper "Irreversibility" in *Proceedings of the Royal Irish Academy*, Vol. 51 (1950), 189–195, and Norbert Wiener, "Newtonian and Bergsonian Time," which is Ch. 1 of *Cybernetics*, 2d ed. (New York, 1961). Also see Ludwig Boltzmann, "On Certain Questions of the Theory of Gases," in *Nature*, Vol. 51 (1895), 413–415. Reichenbach's book depends to a great extent on Boltzmann's ideas. There is a readable treatment of some of these issues in the final appendix of Schlick's *Philosophy of Nature*. A different solution to the problem is to be found in notes by K. R. Popper in *Nature*, Vol. 177 (1956), 538, Vol. 178 (1956), 382, Vol. 179 (1957), 1,297, and Vol. 181 (1958), 402–403, in connection with which see the note by E. L. Hill and Adolf Grünbaum, in *Nature*, Vol. 179 (1957), 1,296–1,297. See also O. Costa de Beauregard, "L'Irreversibilité quantique, phénomène macroscopique," in A. George, ed., *Louis de Broglie* (Paris, 1953). Grünbaum has examined Popper's view in his essay "Popper on Irreversibility" in Mario A. Bunge, ed., *The Critical Approach to Science and Philosophy, Essays in Honor of Karl Popper* (New York, 1964). There are two beautiful articles entitled "The Arrow of Time" by the cosmologist Thomas Gold in *La Structure et l'évolution de l'univers*, proceedings of the 11th Solvay Conference (Brussels, 1958), 81–91, and in *The American Journal of Physics*, Vol. 30 (1962), 403–410. "The Direction of Time" by Max Black in his *Models and Metaphors* (Ithaca, N.Y., 1962), is written from the point of view that scientific considerations are irrelevant to the problem of the direction of time. The problem about traces is well posed by C. Ehrenfels in Ch. 1 of his *Cosmogony* (New York, 1948).

A readable discussion of the experiment by James H. Christenson, James W. Cronin, Val L. Fitch, and René Turlay, which suggests a possible violation of time symmetry in the laws of nature themselves, can be found in Eugene P. Wigner's article "Violations of Symmetry in Physics" in *Scientific American*, Vol. 213 (December 1965), 28–42.

TIME AND FREE WILL: THE SEA FIGHT TOMORROW

On fatalism see R. D. Bradley, "Must the Future Be What It Is Going To Be?," in *Mind*, Vol. 68 (1959), 193–208; Richard Taylor, "Fatalism," in *Philosophical Review*, Vol. 71 (1962), 56–66, with the discussion on this by Bruce Aune in the same volume, 512–519; and A. J. Ayer, "Fatalism," in his *The Concept of a Person and Other Essays* (London, 1963). On the sea battle see Aristotle, *De Interpretatione*, Ch. 9. Extensive notes and a translation can be found in J. L. Ackrill's *Aristotle's Categories and De Interpretatione* (Oxford, 1963). This passage has also been translated and discussed by G. E. M. Anscombe in "Aristotle and the Sea-Battle" in *Problems of Space and Time*. See also Colin Strang, "Aristotle and the Sea Battle," in *Mind*, Vol. 69 (1960), 447–465. Many journal articles on the subject, following on D. C. Williams' interesting "The Sea-Fight Tomorrow," appear in Paul Henle, Horace M. Kallen, Susanne K. Langer, eds., *Structure, Method, and Meaning* (New York, 1951). See especially the discussion note "Professor Donald Williams on Aristotle" by Leonard Linsky and the rejoinder by Williams in *Philosophical Review*, Vol. 63 (1954), 250–255, and Richard Taylor, "The Problem of Future Contingents," and Rogers Albritton's reply in *Philosophical Review*, Vol. 66 (1957), 1–46. The seventeenth-century English philosopher Thomas Hobbes also wrote on the sea-fight; see his *Works*, William Molesworth, ed. (London, 1839), Vol. IV, p. 277, and discussion by A. G. N. Flew, "Hobbes and the Seafight," *Graduate Review of Philosophy*, Vol. 2 (1959), 1–5.

J. J. C. SMART

TIME, CONSCIOUSNESS OF. William James's discussion of the perception of time in *Principles of Psychology* (Vol. I, Ch. 15) provides a convenient starting point for a discussion of the consciousness of time. James's main concern was to give an empiricist account of our temporal concepts. This is clear from the Lockian question with which he started: "What is the *original* of our experience of pastness, from whence we get the meaning of the term?" (p. 605) and from his answer that the "prototype of all conceived times is the specious present, the short duration of which we are immediately and incessantly sensible" (p. 631). A contemporary empiricist might formulate James's thesis thus: that all other temporal concepts can be defined in terms of the relation "earlier than" and that this relation is sense given or can be ostensively defined so that even if a person does not use the term "specious present," he is obliged to say that some earlier events are still, in some sense, present to us when we are sensing a later event.

Consider why James used the term "specious present" in describing such facts. He quoted with approval a passage by E. R. Clay, who invented this term; the quotation shows that they both assumed that the philosophically correct use of "present" is to refer to the boundary, conceived of as a durationless instant, between past and future. They pictured time as a line of which the specious present is a segment whose later boundary is the real present and hence concluded that the specious present and its contents are really past. James used two phrases which suggest that the specious present also includes a bit of the future; one, when he said that it has "a vaguely vanishing backward and forward fringe" (p. 613) and, two, when he said that it is "a saddle-back from which we look in two directions into time" (p. 609). This view is implied by nothing else he said, so we shall ignore the paradoxes it would needlessly generate and concentrate on what James said frequently: that we are continuously directly perceiving or intuiting a past duration and its contents.

James illustrated the concept of the specious present by citing experiments carried out by Wilhelm Wundt and his pupil Dietze designed to measure the duration of the longest group of sounds which a person can correctly identify without counting its members. According to Wundt, this duration is 6 seconds; according to Dietze, it is 12 seconds. James equated this period (6 to 12 seconds) with the duration of the specious present (and failed to add the qualification "for hearing"). The ability which Wundt and Dietze were investigating is a familiar one. Hearing a series of sounds as a melody or as a sentence involves recognizing them as forming a temporal pattern, or Gestalt. Another familiar experience is sometimes cited in this context: The chiming of a clock may not be noticed until it has stopped, yet we can still attend to the sounds and, one is inclined to say, inspect them; we can notice facts about them—for example, that there are five or ten chimes. Since James applied the concept of the specious present by reference to such auditory experiences, he was committed to saying that a sound which audibly terminated 5 or 10 seconds ago is still being directly perceived. Now, this seems inconsistent. "I am now directly perceiving (or sensing) X" seems to imply "X is now present and exists simultaneously with my perceiving (sensing) it."

This criticism was made by H. J. Paton (*In Defence of Reason*, pp. 105–107) against the account of the specious present given by Russell and Broad. Russell and Broad had, however, applied the concept of the specious present differently from James. They appealed to the fact that we see things moving, that we see the second hand of a watch moving in a way that we cannot see the hour hand moving. They took this to imply that we simultaneously sense the second hand (or, rather, the corresponding sensa) occupying a series of adjacent positions. To this Paton replied, "If in a moment I can sense several different positions of the second-hand, then these different positions would be sensed as being all at the same moment. . . . What I should sense would be not a movement, but a stationary fan covering a certain area and perhaps getting gradually brighter towards one end. . . . You can't see a sensum that isn't there. If you see it, it is there at the time you see it." Paton concluded that awareness of the positions of the second hand prior to the present instant must be ascribed to memory. Paton, however, overlooked a fact about vision. What he failed to find when he looked at the second hand is found when we look at things which move (traverse a given optical angle) more quickly. If, in the dark, you watch someone rotating a lamp at the appropriate speed, you see a moving ring of light or if, in daylight, you hold a bright object—for instance, a watch—and move it fairly quickly across your visual field while gazing at a point in the middle of its path (place 1), you can still, momentarily, see a streak in place 1 when the watch is seen, out of the corner of your eye, to have halted at place 2. Such facts provide a second way of applying the concept of the specious present.

Our philosophical problem is to analyze and describe the experiences in question in a way which avoids contradictions and which, if we are empiricists, is consistent with saying that temporal relations are given in experience. We shall examine several alternative accounts of the relevant facts but first note that the account one finds appropriate will depend on one's philosophical standpoint, especially concerning the nature of the mind and of perception. Obviously, it makes a difference whether one conceives of the self as, for example, an immaterial substance which transcends time or as a physical organism, whether one holds a realist or a representative theory of perception. Paton assumed, as did Russell and Broad, that what we see are sensa, conceived of as entities numerically distinct from physical objects, and Paton asserted that sensa can exist only at the moment at which they are sensed. Whether this dictum need be accepted will be discussed later.

Our problem is also phenomenological. The specious present doctrine dissolves into a platitude unless we draw a distinction between what is "sensed" (or "immediately experienced" or "directly perceived") and what is "perceived" (or "perceptually accepted, recognized, or judged"). No one doubts that we perceive things changing, that it is correct to speak of "seeing" a thing move, and so on. The phenomenological question is whether, in such cases, the very recent positions or states of things are still being sensed. In posing the problem in this way, we are not committed to a representative theory of perception or to a sensum terminology. As we are using "to sense" and kindred verbs to say that we perceive more than we sense—that we see an orange as juicy and solid when all that we sense is its front surface—does not entail that the things we sense are numerically distinct from the things we perceive—the orange.

ATTEMPTED SOLUTIONS

Time as the fourth dimension. A simple solution seems to be open to anyone who accepts the thesis that the physical world is a four-dimensional manifold. If, accordingly, we (learn to) think of physical objects as four-dimensional solids in describing which tenseless verbs must be used, it is a corollary that what is visually sensed is not an instantaneous cross section of the four-dimensional manifold, but a short slice thereof, about one-tenth of a second long in the time dimension. Suppose you see a meteor flash across the sky. If you hold a realist theory of perception, you would say that what you sense is a short slice of the history of the four-dimensional meteor. If you identify conscious states with brain processes, you would say that what you sense is a short slice of certain of your four-dimensional brain cells. And in these sentences "short slice of the history of" would be used literally, since you are presumably following mathematicians like Hermann Minkowski in treating time as if it were another spatial dimension, which is "at right angles to each of the other three" (whatever this may mean apart from indicating what sort of diagrams to draw).

This account would satisfy the empiricist insofar as it implies that temporal intervals and relations are sense given in the same sense as that in which spatial intervals and relations are sense given. This account, however, does not seem viable. If the physical world were a four-dimensional manifold, it would be logically impossible for its contents—four-dimensional solids—to move or otherwise change unless they did so in a time which is distinct from the one which has been spatialized (and such motion would not concern us since we do not observe motions of four-dimensional solids). The four-dimensional conceptual scheme would permit no use for the basic concepts in terms of which we do (and must?) interpret our experience—notably, our concept of a physical thing as a three-dimensional entity which can move and change, our concept of a physical event as a change in one or more such physical things, and our concept of physical causation as a relation between such physical events. Now, it is a ground-floor empirical fact that we observe things moving and changing. Anyone who adopts the four-dimensional world theory is therefore obliged to tell us what it is that moves or changes. Since he is treating the physical world as changeless, the only answer he can give is that it is our states of consciousness that change as we become successively aware of adjacent cross sections of the four-dimensional world. But this makes sense only if we, the observers, are not in space time (and one would still have to acknowledge a [real] time dimension other than the one which has been spatialized, in which our states of consciousness are successive). Our first account of the specious present could be accepted by a dualist if he could show that it is possible to dispense with our concepts of physical things, events, and causes. We may well doubt whether he can do this, for even the physicists cannot formulate many of their questions without using our conceptual scheme.

Augustine and C. D. Broad. James followed Clay in assuming that the philosophically correct use of "present" is to refer to a durationless instant. We christen this "the punctiform present (PP) assumption." Anyone who makes this assumption is committed to saying that apart from its later boundary the specious present is really past, and he is thereby disposed to say (1) that the contents of the specious present consist of images or "representations" of what has just been sensed and (2) that what these images represent is known only by memory. Here we have a second way of describing the relevant experiences.

This way of thinking is found in Augustine's classical discussion of time (*Confessions*, Book XI, Secs. 10–28). Augustine claimed that no one would deny that the present has no duration, and surprisingly, until recently no one has. Augustine combined the PP assumption with another which he deemed self-evident—that everything which is past or future does not (now) exist. He proceeded logically to the conclusions that when a person perceives or measures time, what he is attending to is "something which remains fixed in his memory" and therefore that time is not "something objective" (Sec. 27). He ended by, in effect, defining "past" in terms of human memories and "future" in terms of human expectations (Sec. 28). (These conclusions suited Augustine, for his purpose in discussing time was to show that it is meaningless to ask what God was doing before he made heaven and earth; see Sections 10–13, 30.) Idealists may be happy to accept Augustine's conclusion that time is unreal (subjective), but many philosophers and psychologists who do not accept this conclusion have found themselves in a quandary as a result of taking for granted Augustine's premises. Their quandary is that however one applies the concept of the specious present, if its contents are described as sensa or images, the sensa or images which a person has at any durationless instant are present at (that is, simultaneous with) that instant, but then whatever relations may hold between such sensa or images, temporal precedence cannot be among them, for this relation holds between things which are not simultaneous. One is then driven to say that awareness of the nontemporal features of one's sensa or images somehow stimulates one to construct ideas of temporal relations which are not sense given. James quoted several psychologists who got into this quandary, but he showed no sign of recognizing its (for him) unacceptable implications—that it obliges one either to deny the objective reality of time or to appeal to an intuition or a priori knowledge of time.

The paradoxical implications of Augustine's premises are clearly exhibited in C. D. Broad's account of time in his *Examination of McTaggart's Philosophy.* Broad here abandoned the account of the specious present he had given in *Scientific Thought,* where he had spoken of an event's being present throughout a finite process of sensing. He now asserted that it is only "instantaneous event-particles" which are "present in the strict sense," and he spoke of events (event-particles) becoming (coming into existence) and passing away (ceasing to exist). He was thus committed to the strange metaphysical theory according to which each event-particle is created and annihilated at "successive" instants, and the answer to the question "What exists at present?" would have to be "A set of simultaneous event-particles," though during the time it takes you to utter this phrase, an infinite number of such sets would have been born and died.

Why has the PP assumption been treated as self-evident by so many eminent thinkers? No one has claimed that the correct (strict) use of "here" is to refer to a Euclidean point; why have so many philosophers assumed that the correct (strict) use of "now" or "present" is to refer to a durationless instant? That it rejects, by implication, the PP assumption is a merit of the now popular token-reflexive analysis of sentences containing "now" or "present" or a verb in the present tense. In this analysis "now" is rendered "simultaneous with this utterance," and uttering a sentence takes a second or two. But this analysis is open to two objections: (1) that when one says "It is (now) raining," one is not referring to one's own utterance and (2) that when one refers to "the present war," the duration of the war does not coincide with one's utterance. To remedy these objections, we need to jettison the traditional over-simplified assumption that the only temporal relations are earlier than, simultaneous with, and later than (the only relations which could hold between durationless instants); we need to recognize the numerous perceptible temporal relations between durations or processes (for example, sounds), the relations which are formally analogous to those which can hold between two segments of varying lengths belonging to the same straight line (coincidence, adjacence, partial and complete overlapping). We may then say "It is (now) raining" equals "The falling of rain (here) overlaps temporally with this" where "this" refers to the duration of the speaker's so-called specious present.

An empiricist solution. The first solution we considered could be accepted only by a dualist who holds that minds are not in space time (and Descartes's problems concerning the connection between mind and body would become much more acute, since one's body is being conceived of as a four-dimensional solid). The second solution we considered is consistent only with either a form of idealism which denies the objective reality of time or a form of rationalism which treats our knowledge of time as a priori. If we reject the premises used by Augustine and many others, we can find a solution which is consistent with empiricism and with the views that time order is an objective feature of the world and that we, whatever else we may be, are physical creatures. Consider first the proposition that what is past or future cannot (now) exist. We may reply that "existence" should be predicated, in any tense, only of things (continuants), not of events, which happen or occur, and not of processes, which go on. Admittedly, past or future events are not now happening, and past or future processes are not now going on, but, of course, many of the things, including people, which existed at past times and which will exist at future times exist now.

We must also reject the PP assumption and may define "present" as the duration of the speaker's specious present. But can we, for this purpose, employ either or both of the methods of interpreting "the specious present"? James's method would make "the specious present" 6 to 12 seconds long; Russell's would make it about one-tenth of a second, so we can scarcely combine these interpretations. In Wundt's experiments, cited by James, the subjects were attending to sounds which had audibly terminated, though they were still presented in the sense that the subject could still "hear" them. If we say that a sound which has audibly terminated is still present, this would be inconsistent, for "it *has* audibly termina*ted*" implies "it is past." We ought surely to describe the duration of the specious present, as interpreted by James, as "the span of immediate memory for hearing," and to call this a *specious* present is appropriate.

Does a similar objection arise if we define "present" as the duration of what is visibly sensed, when, for example, we see a meteor? Can we describe this experience by saying that we simultaneously sense the meteor occupying a series of different places throughout a fraction of a second? Those who accept the PP assumption will say, "No. When the meteor has visibly reached place 2, it is no longer in place 1, where it was one-tenth of a second earlier, and we cannot sense a thing occupying a place in which it no longer is; thus, the fading sensation of the meteor must be ascribed to (immediate) memory." But why the "must"? In discussing such phenomenological problems, for which ordinary language was not designed, it is not decisive to appeal to the "correct" (normal) use of language, but note that "remember" is not used in the way prescribed by our critic. In our earlier example, moving a watch across one's field of vision, we should say that the streak at place 1 is *seen*, not that it is merely *remembered*.

The experiences we have in seeing such movements can be described by saying that visual sensations linger and very rapidly fade. (This fact rarely obtrudes on us because we follow a moving object in which we are interested by head or eye movements and do not attend to the resultant blurring of background objects.) But are we *obliged* to describe the facts by saying that a moving object can be simultaneously seen (sensed) in a series of different positions? We are obliged to do this if we adopt a realist theory of perception. Consider the case of the moving watch. The realist holds that what is sensed is a surface of the watch, and as we conceive such a physical object, it cannot occupy different regions of space at the same time; thus, the realist must describe this experience by saying that, for a very short time, a person still senses (very indistinctly) the watch at place 1 when it has visibly reached place 2. But this argument is not sufficient if one adopts a representative theory of perception, or phenomenalism. For then one may, apparently, say that what one senses is a contemporary instantaneous streaky sensum at place 1. But can one consistently say this? To say this involves conceiving a sensum as an entity which exists only at a durationless instant. This generates paradox since one will have to say that we *falsely* believe that we see something moving and that this belief is somehow generated by our sensing a compact series of instantaneous and stationary sensa the later members of which differ in their spatial relations from the earlier; one will also be unable to give an empiricist account of how we come by the notions earlier and later. To try to get out of this quandary, the user of the sensum language may amend his account and say that what we sense is the contemporary instantaneous state of a sensum; then he is conceiving of a sensum as a continuant (albeit a short-lived one)—that is, as something which endures and can change. Those who use sensum language usually do talk of sensa moving and changing.

Since sensa may be and often are conceived of as short-lived continuants, the user of the sensum language is free to drop the PP assumption. The latter implies that the phenomenological objects (images or sensa) which a person has or is aware of at any durationless instant, must be present at—that is, simultaneous with—that instant, and this implies that temporal precedence cannot be sense given. If, however, a sensum is conceived of as a continuant, we may say that the *same* sensum is present throughout a short period, that successive states or positions of the sensum are present at a given instant, and that a person can still sense a visual sensum where it was one-tenth of a second ago. Paton's statement "You can't sense a sensum that isn't there. If you see it, it is there at the time you see it" was intended to refute the possibility that one can simultaneously sense a sensum occupying a series of adjacent positions, but such dicta cannot be treated as synthetic a priori propositions. Philosophers make the rules of the sensum language as they go along, and there seem to be no clear and accepted rules for translating "visual sensations linger and fade" into this language. If we use this language, we are free to adopt rules which allow empiricists to say what they need to say—that is, that temporal relations between different sensa and different states of the same sensum are sense given.

Few philosophers would now accept Kant's view that time (conceived of as an infinite continuum) is an intuited datum or his view that our knowledge of time is a priori (*Critique of Pure Reason,* "Transcendental Aesthetic," II, Sec. 4). Most philosophers would now agree with James that time is a notion that we construct from temporal relations which are sense given. Such philosophers must surely accept the thesis that temporal relations are sense given *within* the present and that this duration of which we are in James's words "incessantly sensible" ought to be called "the *conscious* present." Clay and James called this duration "the specious [that is, pseudo] present" because they assumed that only its later boundary should be called "the real present."

Final considerations. The besetting sin of philosophers, scientists, and, indeed, all who reflect about time is describing it as if it were a dimension of space. It is difficult to resist the temptation to do this because our temporal language is riddled with spatial metaphors. This is because temporal relations are formally analogous to spatial relations—for example, the formal resemblance between the overlapping of two sticks and the overlapping of two sounds disposes us to forget that in the latter case "overlapping" is used metaphorically. If we picture the passing of time in terms of movement along a line, we are led to ask "What moves?" and are disposed to answer, like Husserl, "Events keep moving into the past" and to forget that "move" is now being used metaphorically, that events cannot literally move or change. As J. J. C. Smart asserted, things change, events happen ("The River of Time," **Mind,** Vol. 58, 1949, 483–494). Those who spatialize time, conceiving of it as an order in which events occupy different places, are hypostatizing events. The temptation to hypostatize events is presumably the result, at least in part, of

the linguistic fact that the terms, which can be said to stand in temporal relations like simultaneous with and earlier than, are event expressions. Those who ponder about time are forever using event expressions as their main nouns, and they frequently seem to forget what events are—changes in three-dimensional things. What we perceive and sense are things changing. Time is a nonspatial order in which things change.

This conclusion is deflationary. Poets, mystics, and metaphysicians naturally prefer more exciting ways of talking about time. It is ironical that although Henri Bergson forcibly criticized the spatialization of time, he based his metaphysical theories largely upon describing time in spatial images and metaphors. Bergson argued that our spatialized concept of time is an intellectual construct which misleadingly represents real concrete time (*durée*), which is grasped by, and belongs only to, inner consciousness (*Time and Free Will*). In describing *durée*, however, he said things which are difficult to reconcile and, in some cases, to interpret at all. *Durée* is said to *flow* (p. 221), yet its different moments are said to *permeate* one another (pp. 110 and 133) and to be *inside* one another (p. 232). Bergson did not recognize that these are as much spatial metaphors as is describing time as linear. It was his own metaphors and his implicit use of the PP assumption which led Bergson to his paradoxical conclusions—for example, that "duration and succession belong not to the external world, but [only] to the conscious mind" (p. 120). We cannot prevent metaphysicians who are so inclined from trying to reduce things to events or processes or to expand things into four-dimensional solids, but such intellectual acrobatics are unnecessary, apart from the paradoxes which they generate. Our consciousness of time's "flow" is our consciousness of things changing.

Bibliography

The interest of twentieth-century philosophers in time stems largely from the writings of Henri Bergson, who held that understanding the nature of time is the key to the main problems of philosophy. His first important book, *Essai sur les données immédiates de la conscience* (Paris, 1889), was translated by F. L. Pogson as *Time and Free Will* (London and New York, 1910). This contains what purports to be a phenomenological description of time consciousness, but from the start Bergson's language is permeated with idealist metaphysics. Edmund Husserl discussed problems concerning awareness of time in his *Vorlesungen zur Phänomenologie des inneren Zeitbewusstseins* (Halle, 1928), which has been translated by J. S. Churchill as *The Phenomenology of Internal Time-consciousness* (Bloomington, Ind., 1964). In *An Outline of Philosophy* (London, 1927), pp. 204–205, and *The Analysis of Mind* (London, 1921), pp. 174–175, Bertrand Russell presented, very briefly, the kind of solution argued for above, but he did not acknowledge any of the difficulties that others have found in this concept. C. D. Broad has made two detailed attempts to analyze the concept of the specious present, in *Scientific Thought* (London, 1923), pp. 346–358, and *Examination of McTaggart's Philosophy*, Vol. II (Cambridge, 1938), Ch. 35. He used similar diagrams in each book, but what these are said to symbolize differs greatly in each. His earlier account can be criticized for its use of the concept of momentary acts of sensing, but this could have been remedied. In his later account he ended by describing the specious present doctrine as a verbal trick for trying to reconcile contradictory propositions. It looks as if Broad was converted by the sort of criticism made by H. J. Paton in his paper "Self-Identity," *Mind,* Vol. 38 (1929), 312–329, later reprinted in his *In*

Defence of Reason (London and New York, 1951). J. D. Mabbott criticized his own odd interpretation of the specious present doctrine in "Our Direct Experience of Time," *Mind,* Vol. 60 (1951), 153–167. C. W. K. Mundle challenged Mabbott's interpretation and discussed several alternatives in "How Specious Is the 'Specious Present'?," *Mind,* Vol. 63 (1954), 26–48, and later critically examined three different accounts of time contained in Broad's writings in "Broad's Views About Time," in P. A. Schilpp, ed., *The Philosophy of C. D. Broad* (New York, 1959). The thesis criticized above, that the physical world should be conceived as a four-dimensional manifold, is argued in J. J. C. Smart's *Philosophy and Scientific Realism* (London and New York, 1963).

C. W. K. MUNDLE

TIMON OF PHLIUS, the most famous student of Pyrrho of Elis, was born at Phlius about 320 B.C. and died in Athens about 230 B.C. He was orphaned early in life and after a career as a stage dancer became a student of Pyrrho. He lived in Elis with his wife and children until poverty forced him to leave with them for Chalcedon. Here he gained a reputation as a Sophist and accumulated considerable wealth. He then moved to Athens, where he remained until his death. He was fond of gardens and solitude, but his love of wine, his need for money, and his restless, even bitter, wit made him quite unlike his ascetic teacher Pyrrho. He was especially fond of ridiculing Arcesilaus, the head of the Skeptical New Academy (although he gave an encomium at his burial). His bitterness led him even to self-ridicule; because he had only one eye he called himself "Cyclops."

Although little of his work is extant, he wrote epic poems, tragedies, satires, 32 comic plays, twenty thousand lines of prose, and iambic verse. His most famous works, the *Indalmoi* ("Images") and the *Silloi* ("Lampoons"), survive as fragments in the writings of Diogenes Laërtius and Sextus Empiricus. The *Silloi* are satirical poems in hexameter verse parodying Homer and depicting philosophers past and present as arrogant, bickering talkers, sometimes duped by their own lies, as in the case of the arrogant Aristotle, and sometimes duping only others, as in the case of Plato. Above all philosophers Timon admired Pyrrho for relentlessly pointing out the contradictions into which philosophers fall and for being a thinker "whom no mortal can resist." His works spread the fame of Pyrrho across the Greek-speaking world.

For Timon, doubt had none of the elaborate dialectic that the New Academy and Aenesidemus were to bring to it, nor did it have the calm, the *ataraxia,* that it had for Pyrrho. Like Pyrrho, Timon praised unperturbedness as the great virtue that followed doubt "like a shadow," although his writings do not exemplify it. He often simply collated opposing arguments and then railed bitterly at the arguers. He was more of a wit than a dialectician. To those who claimed that we can find truth by having our senses cooperate with our understanding he often responded that "birds of a feather flock together," meaning that the illusions of the senses and the illusions of judgment are merely assembled, not eliminated, by such cooperation. He preferred such figures of speech to elaborate dialectic.

Timon clearly recognized man's unavoidable needs (such as for food) and defended the validity of customary, habitual patterns of action. In the *Indalmoi* he wrote, "The

apparent is omnipotent wherever it goes." In another work he wrote, "I do not lay it down that honey is sweet, but I admit that it appears to be so." Phenomena, like our needs and habits, deserved our assent, at least if we would achieve unperturbedness and happiness. His philosophy was a practical one that attacked pretentious reasoning by means of humor and bite in order to leave room for the simple, basic necessities of life, like food, drink, and privacy.

Bibliography

ANCIENT

Diogenes Laërtius, "Pyrrho" and "Timon," in *Lives of Eminent Philosophers,* translated by R. D. Hicks. London, 1925. Vol. II.
Sextus Empiricus, translated by R. G. Bury. London, 1955. Vols. I and III.

MODERN

Bevan, E., *Stoics and Sceptics.* New York, 1959.
Brochard, V., *Les Sceptiques grecs.* Paris, 1923.
Goedeckemeyer, A., *Die Geschichte des griechischen Skeptizismus.* Leipzig, 1905.

PHILIP P. HALLIE

TINDAL, MATTHEW (1657?–1733), English jurist, Whig propagandist, and deist, was born at Beer Ferris, Devonshire, the son of John Tindal, a minister. After an early education in the country, he proceeded to study law at Oxford, first at Lincoln College and later at Exeter College. In 1678 he was elected to a law fellowship at All Souls' College. In 1679 he received the B.A. and the B.C.L. degrees and in 1685 the D.C.L. In 1685 he was also admitted as an advocate at Doctors' Commons, a society of ecclesiastical lawyers, with a pension of £200 a year for the remainder of his life. While at Oxford and under the influence of the high churchman George Hickes, he defected from the Church of England and became a Roman Catholic for a brief period, but he recanted in 1688. Soon thereafter, he began to publish a long series of tracts and books, culminating in 1730, when he was over seventy years old, with *Christianity as Old as the Creation.* Frequently called "the deist's Bible," this work elicited more than 150 replies, including Bishop Butler's famous *Analogy of Religion* (1736).

At Oxford, Tindal's enemies accused him of gluttony but granted that he was so abstemious in the drinking of wine that he frequently outsmarted them in argument. Dr. Edmund Gipson, bishop of London, however, won a posthumous "victory" over Tindal when he managed to acquire the manuscript of a second volume of *Christianity as Old as the Creation* and deliberately burned it. The same forged will (probably by Eustace Budgell) that made this action possible also deprived Tindal's nephew of his property.

Tindal died stoically in 1733 and was buried in Clerkenwell Church, London. Without question the most learned of the English deists, Tindal consistently referred to himself as a "Christian deist."

Early political publications. Tindal did not begin to publish until he was middle-aged. A first series of tracts, *Essay of Obedience to the Supreme Powers* (1694), *Essay* on the Power of the Magistrate and the Rights of Mankind in Matters of Religion (1697), The Liberty of the Press (1698), and Reasons against restraining the Press (1704), all showed low church and Miltonic influences. Tindal first gained notoriety with The Rights of the Christian Church Asserted, against the Romish, and all other Priests who claim an Independent Power over it (1706), which brought over twenty answers. A sequel, A Defence of the Rights of the Christian Church (1709), was condemned by the House of Commons and burned in 1710 by the common hangman. These early works are strongly Whiggish, anti-authoritarian, and anticlerical in tone; they argue for freedom of the press and for general toleration (except for atheists)—principles that were to be even more forcefully urged in Christianity as Old as the Creation. For his radical political view that although the magistrate has power to legislate in the area of religion, he has no authority to compel conformity and that persecution of nonconformity not only violates natural law but is also futile, Tindal, like many other deists, was branded by the orthodox as "Spinozan."

"The deist's Bible." *Christianity as Old as the Creation: Or, The Gospel A Republication of the Religion of Nature* appeared in 1730 with subsequent editions in 1731, 1732, and 1733; in 1741 it was translated into German by Johann Lorenz Schmidt, a writer in the Leibniz–Wolff tradition. Although the work makes frequent mention of Locke, it is fundamentally rationalistic, and it is the rationalistic side of Locke that is emphasized—that morality is capable of demonstration and is therefore true, that whatever is known to be true on the basis of reason cannot be falsified by revelation, that the Bible must be read like any other book, that without reason any religion can be held to be true because of the power of tradition.

As is implied by the subtitle, Tindal's thesis is an elaboration of the proposition from Dr. Thomas Sherlock, bishop of Bangor and later of London, quoted on the title page: "The Religion of the Gospel is the true original Religion of Reason and Nature. . . . And its Precepts declarative of that original Religion, which was as old as the Creation." Citation from the rationalistic orthodoxy of such latitudinarians as Archbishop Tillotson, Samuel Clarke, and Thomas Sherlock, a deceptive device frequently employed by the deists, provides some indication of how close in thought rationalistic orthodoxy and rationalistic deism actually were.

Tindal's use of Sherlock's thesis, developed in a dialogue between A (Tindal) and B (an objector to, and a questioner of, A), is entirely negative. The Scriptures, with all the ambiguities that have confused the Church Fathers, the Schoolmen, and modern theologians, are really a work of supererogation. Although never stated in so many words, it is clear that Tindal's radical anticlericism challenged the validity of all historical religions and established churches.

On the critical and historical side, the Scriptures are examined and attacked by Tindal in great detail to expose the imperfect morality of certain Old Testament heroes and, to some extent, of certain parables of the New Testament. Even worse, according to Tindal, priestcraft and tradition, working together, have corrupted the texts and confused the people. Churches have used the teachings of the New Testament to acquire new members and have then used the teachings of the Old Testament to keep members in line. Tindal was incensed that priests first tempt men to examine their faith and then punish them for so doing if, perchance, their interpretations differ from those established by tradition and authority. This side of Tindal's work greatly influenced Voltaire.

On the philosophical side it is Tindal the rationalist, rather than the critic and moralist, who was the "Christian deist," for Tindal, like Lord Herbert of Cherbury before him, took what Alexander Pope was to call "the high Priori Road." God is conceived of as the God of reason, and because human nature is inalterable, man's reason has known His being and attributes from the beginning of time. Rational man, then, reasons downward from the divine perfections to morality and religion. All men, whether of the highest intellect or the meanest capacity, declares Tindal, are equally capable of knowing the immutable law of nature or reason and the religion of nature. In this respect Tindal is close to the more "orthodox" theologians of the waning rationalist or latitudinarian school in Britain represented by Archbishop Tillotson, Samuel Clarke, and Thomas Sherlock. The book concludes with Tindal's statement of his three basic notions about natural religion. First, there are things which show, by their inner nature, that they are the will of an infinitely wise and good God (for example, the relations between God and man, the immutability of morality). Second, there are things that have no worth in themselves, which are to be considered solely as means (forms of worship, positive regulations and precepts); these are to be used as men see fit in their quest for happiness. Third, there are things (the vested interests of priestcraft, miracles, "enthusiasm") so indifferent that they cannot be considered as either means or ends, and if emphasis is placed on them in religious matters, the worst sort of superstition ensues—and superstition is the enemy of true religion.

Tindal does not consider the fact that many people are totally incapable of right reason, a point that was dutifully reported by many of his opponents. The philosophical argument of Bishop Butler repudiated rationalism as the chimerical building of the world upon hypothesis in the manner of Descartes. The paradoxical and abusive Bishop Warburton was content to dismiss Tindal's apriorism as "the silliest, and most wretched Error, in an age of Paradoxes." Tindal is the last and most influential of the British deists who sought to keep the movement on a high intellectual level.

Bibliography

There is no collected edition of the works of Tindal. Early documents and "lives" include A Copy of the will of Dr. Matthew Tindal, with an account of what pass'd concerning the same, between Mrs. Lucy Price, Eustace Budgell esq.; and Mr. Nicholas Tindal (London, 1733); Memoirs Of The Life and Writings of Matthew Tindall, LL.D. With A History Of The Controversies Wherein he was Engaged (London, 1733); and The Religious, Rational and Moral Conduct of Matthew Tindal, LL.D., late fellow of All Souls', by a member of the same college (London, 1733).

There are no full-scale modern treatments of Tindal, but the following works are of some importance: Alfred O. Aldridge,

"Polygamy and Deism," in *Journal of English and Germanic Philology,* Vol. 48 (1949), 343–360; Rosalie L. Colie, "Spinoza and the Early English Deists," in *Journal of the History of Ideas,* Vol. 20 (1959), 23–46; Arthur Friedman, "Pope and Deism," in James L. Clifford and Louis A. Landa, eds., *Pope and His Contemporaries: Essays Presented to George Sherburn* (Oxford, 1949), pp. 89–95; Ernest Sirluck, "*Areopagetica* and a Forgotten Licensing Controversy," in *Review of English Studies,* Vol. 11 (1960), 260–274; Norman L. Torrey, *Voltaire and the English Deists* (New Haven, 1930), Ch. 5. See also the general bibliography under DEISM.

ERNEST CAMPBELL MOSSNER

TOLAND, JOHN (1670–1722), English deist, philosopher, diplomat, political controversialist, secular and Biblical scholar, and linguist. Christened "Janus Junius" in the Roman Catholic church, Toland later took the name of John. He was born near Londonderry, Ireland, possibly of partial French extraction. At the age of 16 he ran away from school to become a Protestant Whig. In 1687 he turned up at Glasgow University and in 1690 was awarded an M.A. at Edinburgh University. For two years he studied at the University of Leiden under Friedrich Spanheim the younger, and in 1694 he settled at Oxford for some time to carry on research in the Bodleian Library. "The Character you bear in Oxford," he was informed by a correspondent, "is this; that you are a man of fine parts, great learning, and little religion." The stream of books and pamphlets, mostly anonymous or pseudonymous, which followed has been estimated by various authorities to range from thirty to one hundred. His most famous work, *Christianity not Mysterious: Or, A Treatise Shewing That there is nothing in the Gospel Contrary to Reason, Nor above it: And that no Christian Doctrine can be properly call'd A Mystery,* appeared in 1696, when he was but 25 years old, elicited some fifty refutations and prosecution in both England and Ireland. In Ireland it was condemned by Parliament and ordered to be burned by the common hangman; an order was issued for the author's arrest. In England it was presented as a nuisance by the grand jury of Middlesex and roundly denounced in Parliament and in pulpit. In 1697, Toland replied to the Irish condemnation with the *Apology for Mr. Toland* and in 1702 to the English with *Vindicius Liberius: Or, Mr. Toland's Defence of himself.*

Politics. Toland's political publications are numerous. He was always the defender of toleration and the opponent of superstition and enthusiasm, a consistent Whig and a Commonwealth man. Outspoken and not very politic, he dedicated several of his tracts to the Whig deist Anthony Collins, who held similar convictions. Among Toland's more important political publications are the *Life of John Milton* (1698) and *Amyntor: Or, a Defence of Milton's Life* (1699), both of which have religious as well as political overtones. In 1701 the *Art of Governing by Parties* and *Anglia Libera: Or, the Limitation and Succession of the Crown of England explain'd and asserted* were published; the latter, supporting the Act of Settlement, was well received by Sophia, electress of Hanover. As a result Toland became secretary to the embassy to Hanover under Lord Macclesfield and presented a copy of the act and the book to Sophia. She was not, however, entirely pleased with his *Reasons for addressing his Majesty to invite into England their Highnesses, the Electress Dowager and the Electoral Prince of Hanover* (1702). Nevertheless, the electress was instrumental in introducing Toland to the court of Berlin and to her daughter Sophia Charlotte, wife of Frederick, the first king of Prussia. For the queen he composed *Letters to Serena* (1704) and *An Account of the Courts of Prussia and Hanover* (1705). At the invitation of the electress, Toland met Leibniz and held numerous discussions with him in the presence of the queen. The two philosophers, though disagreeing on certain fundamentals, respected each other, kept up a correspondence for years, and to some extent were mutually influenced.

Career. Toland's chaotic career worsened throughout his life. He had early been under the political patronage of the third earl of Shaftesbury and later under that of Harley, Lord Oxford. For the earl of Shaftesbury he had written political tracts, but Toland lost his friendship by publishing one of the earl's works, *An Inquiry Concerning Virtue,* without authorization. For Harley he wrote political tracts and brought out an edition of James Harrington's *The Commonwealth of Oceana* with a biography but lost his friendship in 1714 with the *Art of Restoring* and *The Grand Mystery Laid Open,* wherein he implied distrust of his patron's loyalty to the Hanoverian succession. Of necessity, he became a Grub Streeter and lost everything in the South Sea Bubble of 1720. As a result he either wrote or revised someone else's text of *The Secret History of the South-Sea Scheme.* The following year his health went into a rapid decline, abetted by the inept treatment of a physician, which inspired the indomitable Toland, ill as he was, to write a tract entitled *Physic without Physicians* ("They learn their Art at the hazard of our lives, and make experiments by our deaths"). In 1722 he died in extreme poverty.

"Christianity not Mysterious." Like Hume in "Of Miracles" (1748), Toland found an appropriate quotation for his title page from Archbishop Tillotson: "We need not desire a better Evidence that any Man is in the wrong, than to hear him declare against Reason, and thereby acknowledge that Reason is against him." The first edition appeared anonymously, but the second edition of the same year (1696) bore Toland's name.

Always professing some form of theism here and in subsequent writings, Toland, in his work, has affinities with the rationalistic religious common notions of Lord Herbert of Cherbury and with the empiricism and common-sense approach of John Locke in *An Essay Concerning Human Understanding* (1690) and *Reasonableness of Christianity* (1695). He remained, however, fundamentally a rationalist in the line of Bruno, Descartes, Spinoza, and Leibniz.

Drawing freely upon Lord Herbert, the Cambridge Platonists, and Locke, though without naming names, Toland set out to prove that no Christian doctrine is mysterious —that is, above reason: "Could that Person justly value himself upon his being wiser than his Neighbors, who having infallible Assurance that something call'd a Blictri had a Being in Nature, in the mean time knew not what this Blictri was?" Faith and revelation involve both knowledge and assent, but revelation must rely upon the evidence of faith. In the Gospels, Toland correctly points out, "mystery" does not designate what cannot be known by man but, rather, what is revealed only to the chosen few. Faith, the hallmark of Puritanism, is consequently of no avail without the confirmation of reason.

Like many of the deists Toland argued that priestcraft introduced mysteries and then fostered them by ceremonies and discipline. Unlike Bishop Warburton, that eighteenth-century colossus of controversy who is alleged to have said, "Orthodoxy is my doxy; heterodoxy, another man's doxy," Toland ends *Christianity not Mysterious* with "I acknowledge no Orthodoxy but the Truth."

It was widely believed that Toland was a disciple of Locke, and he had been described to Locke by William Molyneux in 1697 as "a candid Free-Thinker, and a good Scholar." However, when *Christianity not Mysterious* aroused such a stir, Locke, who seems hardly to have realized the logical consequences of his own Arminianism (witness his prolonged controversy with Bishop Stillingfleet), repudiated any approval of his so-called disciple.

Biblical criticism. Oddly enough, Toland's Biblical criticism first appears in the seemingly innocuous *Life of John Milton,* wherein, suggesting that the *Eikon Basilike* was not written by Charles I but was a priestly forgery, he proceeds to remark that many supposititious pieces under the name of Christ and his apostles had been accepted in the period of primitive Christianity. Divines rushed in where scholars feared to tread, charging Toland with attacking the authenticity of the Gospels. Toland speedily responded with *Amyntor,* which contains a catalogue of apocryphal pieces 22 pages in length and is one of the earliest examinations of scriptural canon by an Englishman. Though in no sense definitive, Toland's catalogue forced the issues of the canon and of early church history upon the scholars. Christ did not, he declares, institute one religion for the learned and another for the vulgar.

Toland's exploration of early Jewish religion and of the Druids' religion—he was an adept in the Celtic language—led him to the conviction that the simplicity of reason has been corrupted by the machinations of priestcraft. *Letters to Serena* explores somewhat unsystematically the beginnings of religion, examining the origin and force of prejudices, the history of the immortality of the soul among the heathens, the origin of idolatry, and motivations of heathenism. These and other explorations embryonically anticipate Hume in the *Natural History of Religion* (1757) and the *Dialogues concerning Natural Religion* (1779).

Toland argued that belief, prejudice, and superstition are ingrown from infancy. "You may reason yourself into what religion you please; but, pray, what religion will permit you to reason yourself out of it?"

He found a perfect example of surviving simple intuitive religion in a French letter written in 1688 from Carolina: "We know our Saviour's precepts without observing them, and they [the Indians] observe them without knowing him." As Toland put it elsewhere, "Those who live according to Reason . . . are Christians, tho' they be reputed Atheists." In "Hodegus," an essay of 1720, he interprets Old Testament miracles by a naturalistic method, thereby anticipating Reimarus and the German rationalistic school of Biblical exegesis.

Philosophical development. Toland's rationalism led him to translate and to defend Giordano Bruno's Latin treatise of 1514 on the infinite universe and innumerable worlds. In turn, he proceeded into a variety of naturalistic monism, which eventuated in pantheism. In the *Letters to Serena* he attacked Spinoza for his disavowal of the necessity of motion to matter, but in later works he had lavish praise for much of Spinozism. *Socinianism truly stated: being an example of fairdealing in theological Controversy,* a work of 1705 in which is found the first use of the word "pantheist," is essentially pantheistic.

Toland's final statement, however, if it is to be taken seriously, was published in 1720 in Holland; termed "Cosmopoli," it was issued under the pseudonym Janus Junius Edganesius (indicating Inis-Eogan or Eogani Insuli, the northernmost peninsula of Ireland and the place of Toland's birth). *Pantheisticon: sive Formula celebrandae Sodalitatis,* the work referred to and translated into English in 1751, has been variously interpreted as a serious exposition of the philosophy of pantheism, a literary hoax, a sort of litany in derision of Christian liturgies, a mask to disguise atheism, a modernized version of the secret doctrines of Freemasonry, and a device to stimulate new thinking. The work consists of a dialogue between the president of a pantheistical society which acknowledges no other God than the universe and its members, who respond to his endeavors to inspire them with the love of truth, liberty, and health, cheerfulness, sobriety, temperateness, and freedom from superstition.

It is sufficiently evident that Toland was not a really original thinker but one who reflected many influences. Born Roman Catholic, he became Protestant. He was a latitudinarian, a freethinker, a deist, a materialist, and a pantheist. In a Latin epitaph that he composed for himself, he laid claim to the knowledge of ten languages. He was a prolific writer on many subjects, sometimes confused and contradictory, sometimes foreshadowing aspects of modern thought. In his life of 52 years his restless, inquiring mind was ever active, his accomplishments were manifold, and he was an internationalist of consequence in the Age of Enlightenment.

Additional Works by Toland

Other works of Toland not named above but worth mentioning include *Adeisidaemon, sive Titus Livius a Superstitione Vindicatus* (The Hague, 1709); *Nazarenus, or Jewish, Gentile, and Mahometan Christianity* (London, 1718); *Tetradymus,* containing "Hodegus," "Clidophorus," "Hypatia," and "Mangoneutes" (London, 1720); and *The Miscellaneous Works of Mr. John Toland, Now first published from his Original Manuscripts,* with a life by Pierre Des Maizeaux, ed., 2 vols. (London, 1747), a reprint, with some additions, of *A Collection of Several Pieces by Mr. John Toland,* 2 vols. (London, 1726).

Works on Toland

Cragg, G. R., *From Puritanism to the Age of Reason.* Cambridge, 1950. Ch. 7.

Dyche, Eugene I., "The Life and Works and Philosophical Relations of John (Janus Junius) Toland, 1670–1722." *Abstracts of Dissertations, The University of Southern California.* Los Angeles, 1944, pp. 64–69.

ElNouty, Hassam, "Le Panthéisme dans les lettres françaises au

XVIIe siècle: Aperçus sur la fortune du mot et de la notion." *Revue des sciences humaines*, Vol. 97 (1960), 435–457.

Heinemann, F. H., "Prolegomena to a Toland Bibliography." *Notes and Queries*, Vol. 185 (1943), 182–186.

Heinemann, F. H., "John Toland and the Age of Enlightenment." *Review of English Studies,* Vol. 20 (1944), 125–146.

Heinemann, F. H., "Toland and Leibniz." *Philosophical Review,* Vol. 54 (1945), 437–457.

Heinemann, F. H., "John Toland, France, Holland, and Dr. Williams." *Review of English Studies,* Vol. 25 (1949), 346–349.

Heinemann, F. H., "John Toland and the Age of Reason." *Archiv für Philosophie*, Vol. 4 (1950), 35–66.

An Historical Account of the Life and Writings of the late eminently famous Mr. John Toland. London, 1722. "By one of his Intimate Friends."

Lange, Friedrich A., *History of Materialism.* New York, 1950.

Lantoine, Albert, *Un Précurseur de la franc-maçonnerie, J. Toland.* Paris, 1927.

Nourrison, Jean Felix, *Philosophies de la nature. Bacon–Bayle–Toland–Buffon.* Paris, 1887.

See also the general bibliography under DEISM.

ERNEST CAMPBELL MOSSNER

TOLERATION is a policy of patient forbearance in the presence of something which is disliked or disapproved of. Toleration must thus be distinguished from freedom or liberty precisely because it implies the existence of something believed to be disagreeable or evil. When freedom or liberty is said to prevail, no criticism, moral or otherwise, is entailed of the people who are said to be free or of the use to which such people put their freedom. Indeed, there are some writers who would reserve the words "liberty" and "freedom" for the rightful exercise of human choice, thinking, with the poet Milton, that "only the good man can be free." Toleration, on the other hand, has an element of condemnation built into its meaning. We do not tolerate what we enjoy or what is generally liked or approved of. We speak of freedom of speech, of worship, and of movement—speech, worship, and movement being good or ethically neutral things. But when we speak of toleration, we speak of the toleration of heretics, dissenters, or atheists, all of whom were once thought to be wrongdoers, or we speak of the toleration of prostitution, gambling, or the drug traffic, all of which are still generally regarded as evils. To tolerate is first to condemn and then to put up with or, more simply, to put up with is itself to condemn.

T. S. Eliot once surprised his readers by saying, "The Christian does not wish to be tolerated." He did not mean, as some supposed, that the Christian yearned for martyrdom. He meant that the Christian did not wish to be put up with. The Christian wanted something better—to be respected, honored, loved. And what Eliot said in the name of Christians would doubtless also be said by Jews, Muslims, Mormons, Negroes, or any other minority group which finds itself tolerated by a larger society. Toleration is always *mere* toleration. It is less than equality just as it is distinct from liberty, and it is sharply at variance with fraternity. For these reasons toleration is far from an ideal policy; it is contaminated, so to speak, by that very implication of evil which its meaning contains.

Toleration must also be distinguished from indifference. A man who has no feelings about something is indifferent to it, not tolerant, for if he has no feelings, he cannot be said to dislike or disapprove of it. He cannot claim to put up with what troubles him in no way. It has sometimes been said by critics of religious toleration that such toleration is evidence of indifference to religion and that indifference to religion is bad. Here one must distinguish a logical connection from a historical one. It may well be a historical fact that the growth of religious toleration as a government policy in France and England during the eighteenth century was due to a diminution of religious fervor, to an increase in worldliness, and in a word, to indifference. Even so, however, the toleration must be distinguished from the indifference, for the words have significantly different meanings. There have been many men, like Hobbes, who were personally indifferent to religion but opposed to religious toleration, and many, like Locke, who had strong religious beliefs but who favored religious toleration.

Alternatives to toleration. The alternative to toleration is often said to be persecution. This is a misleading dichotomy. Persecution is by definition always wrong. Moral condemnation is part of the meaning of the word. Yet who is to say that the alternative to toleration is always a wrong policy? Is the suppression of the drug traffic, for example, wrong? Is it persecution? It would be perverse to say that everything that is not tolerated is persecuted. Persecution is one alternative to toleration. However, there is another alternative which must be expressed in more neutral language, though, of course, it is one of the central difficulties of all social theory that neutral language is not always at one's disposal. Almost all the words we use in discussing social and political problems have a normative element in them. We might be wise, for lack of a better term, to rely on the word "suppression" as the alternative to "toleration." To ask whether the persecution of religious dissenters was justifiable in thirteenth-century Europe is to prejudice the issue from the outset by speaking of persecution. But one might have an impartial discussion about whether the suppression of religious dissent was justifiable at that time and place, for even those who practiced it would agree to calling it suppression.

Many writers have opposed policies of toleration, but few have ventured to defend intolerance. This is clearly because intolerance in private life is considered a moral defect or weakness, a defect allied to arrogance, narrow-mindedness, and impatience. Hence, intolerance has an unpleasant ring. James Fitzjames Stephen frankly advocated intolerance in opposition to John Stuart Mill's policy of toleration, but though Stephen's arguments were of a kind more likely to appeal to the majority, his success with the public was conspicuously less than Mill's; manifestly, Stephen had made an infelicitous choice of language. Most supporters of what Stephen called intolerance have preferred to speak of order, discipline, authority, or control in putting forward a case for suppression against one of toleration.

Pagan and Christian attitudes. The central problem of toleration in Western history was for centuries the problem of religious toleration. This is one of the consequences the West has faced because its religion is Christianity. Polytheistic religions are by nature more tolerant. The

Greeks, for example, were conservative in the matter of religious ceremonies and institutions, but they admitted a great variety of theological beliefs. Where there were many gods, there could be many dogmas. And although Socrates and the Pythagoreans were persecuted, it was not on religious grounds but because they were accused of threatening the morality and political security of the community. The Romans were less steady in their policy, alternating between policies of general permissiveness and repression of particular sects—notably, but not exclusively, the Christians. Roman toleration was limited by at least one specifically religious notion, namely, the belief that the traditional deities would punish a whole people for the offense of those who failed to worship them.

The early Fathers of the Christian church, having themselves been cruelly persecuted by the Romans, were in favor of religious toleration as a principle. But as soon as Constantine made Christianity a state religion, the pagans, who had once been the persecutors, became the persecuted. Nevertheless, it may be recorded that the Christian repression of paganism never went to the cruel lengths to which Roman repression had gone. St. Augustine, an early advocate of suppressing heretics, went out of his way to say that the death penalty for heresy was wrong. The comparatively few pagans who were put to death by the Christian emperors were usually executed on charges of sorcery rather than of worshiping false gods.

This policy of moderate repression continued throughout the early Middle Ages. In the late Middle Ages, the Renaissance, the Reformation, and the Counter Reformation, toleration was virtually repudiated on principle by European Christians. The few Christians who continued to favor religious toleration are conspicuous for that very reason. They include the Anabaptists in Germany, the Arminians in Holland, Zwingli in Switzerland, Castellio in France, Socinus in Poland. But the main Protestant churches, whether Lutheran, Calvinist, or Anglican, were not conspicuously more tolerant than the Catholic church. The Catholic church's chief instrument of religious discipline was the Inquisition, which freely employed torture as well as the death penalty in its endeavors to recover erring souls for God.

Christian arguments in defense of repression are several. Some writers repeat the old pagan argument that God is offended by heretical practices and is likely to inflict disasters on the whole community as a punishment. Other writers stress the point that heresy is a crime, a form of revolt against lawful authority, a culpable betrayal of promises made (even if only by proxy) at baptism. Crime, it is argued, cannot be tolerated. A more sophisticated argument maintains that the authority of the church is as essential to the continued existence of civil society as is that of the state; hence, those men who defy the church are akin to those who repudiate their duty to the king. Thus, members of such religious sects as the Cathari, Waldenses, and Albigenses are regarded by certain Catholic theorists as seditious rebels who have put themselves in a state of war with the sovereign power. The true religion seals men together in the safety of the commonwealth; dissent and heresy are therefore likely to open the way to anarchy. Furthermore, it is held by all these Christian writers that

to tolerate heresy is to do no service to the man concerned, for to leave him alone in his error is to leave him in a state of sin, faced with the prospect of eternal damnation in the life to come. It is thus thought to be no real cruelty to inflict painful penalties, even death itself, on an erring man if by so doing one is sparing him the far greater torments of hell.

Philosophical arguments for toleration. The philosopher who is best known for having addressed himself to the Christian arguments for suppression was the Englishman John Locke. In the seventeenth century Christians were generally beginning to lose confidence in the old policy of repression, although it was still being practiced. The unity of Christendom was plainly ended and not likely to be recovered. Protestantism in its various forms had come to be almost as great a power in the world as Catholicism. The old notion of one true faith against heresy had lost its meaning. Besides, although Protestantism in its leading forms did not preach toleration, it preached a gospel which led inexorably to the demand for toleration; the Protestant doctrine that every man must be a priest unto himself gave the dissenter just as good grounds as the orthodox believer for claiming that his faith was true. Confidence in the utility—and justice—of suppressing unorthodox opinions was shaken by such writers as Pierre Bayle (1647–1706), who in his *Pensées sur la comète* (1682), argued that morality is independent of religion.

Locke's plea for toleration, set forth in his *Epistola de Tolerantia,* published in 1688, was not the first such plea, but it was the earliest systematic argument in its favor. Locke's first point is that repression is not an effective policy. Force can be used to make a man go through the motions of a given form of Christian worship, but force cannot make a man entertain any faith or belief in the privacy of his soul. What force can do is make a man pretend to be an orthodox believer. And such a policy, says Locke, is not only useless but also morally harmful since it is bound to breed hypocrisy. Locke thus totally rejects the Catholic argument that force—let alone torture and death—can bring any man to salvation.

Second, Locke rejects the traditional argument that a man's obligation to the church is equal to his obligation to the state and that civil society will lapse into anarchy if religious dissent is tolerated. Locke describes the church as a "voluntary society" which has a mission in the world quite independent of the functions of the state. The church exists to save men's souls, and it can fulfill this mission only by persuasion, by essentially nonviolent means. The state, on the other hand, exists to protect men's rights—their lives, liberties, and estates—so that the use of force as an ultimate sanction is a necessary part of the state's function. The state has no concern with the salvation of men's souls, just as the church has no concern with the use of force. Nor has the state any knowledge of what the true religion is. The Persian ruler believes it is Islam; the Spanish ruler believes it is Catholicism; the English king believes it is Anglicanism. They cannot all be right. Therefore, that a religion is established is no evidence that it is the true religion. Each man has his own faith, and every person's conscience is entitled to the same respect.

Locke's theory of toleration was intimately connected

with his theory of freedom. Since he held that one of the most fundamental reasons for the existence of the state was the preservation of man's natural right to liberty, he argued that the government was entitled to use force against an individual only when it was necessary to protect the rights of others. Certain things, Locke agreed, could not be tolerated: (1) the propagation of "opinions contrary to human society, or to those moral rules which are necessary to the preservation of civil society"; (2) any claim "to special prerogative opposite to the civil right of the community"; (3) the activity of "persons who are ready on any occasion to seize the government, and possess themselves of the estates and fortunes of their fellow subjects"; (4) transferring allegiance to a foreign prince; and (5) denying the existence of God.

Locke's reason for withholding toleration from atheists was the rather quaint one that a man who did not believe in God could not take a valid oath and that oaths and covenants were "the bonds of human society." Locke was unwilling to extend toleration to Roman Catholics, not on religious grounds but because he held, with some reason, that Roman Catholics were not loyal subjects of the English crown, since they owed their first allegiance to a foreign prince, the pope.

Locke's argument for toleration, which seemed distinctly avant-garde when it was first published, eventually came to be regarded as common sense. Indeed, even Catholic teaching on the subject of toleration moved toward Locke's position. Later Catholic apologists distinguished between (1) theological dogmatic toleration, (2) practical civil toleration, and (3) public political toleration. The first, theological dogmatic toleration, was resisted as firmly as ever. The teaching of the Catholic church was held to be the absolute and certain truth; thus, to tolerate any opinion at variance with it would be to tolerate falsehood, and the clear duty of the rational mind to uphold truth and deny falsehood imposed an equally categorical duty to deny any religious or moral teaching at variance with the teaching of Rome, which is infallible. However, what is called practical civil toleration was gradually accepted by Catholics. First, it was said to be the Christian's duty to distinguish between the error and the man who erred. Error was always to be opposed, but the man who erred was to be regarded, in full Christian charity, as a fellow man and, therefore, not to be persecuted. On public political toleration, later Catholic theory was somewhat ambiguous. This was because of the need to claim for Catholic minorities in Protestant states the utmost possible toleration without equally committing Catholic governments to tolerating Protestant minorities. Thus, the principle of public political toleration was admitted to vary between its application in a secular state and in a "truly Christian state."

The outstanding exponent of the case for greater toleration in the nineteenth century was John Stuart Mill. In many ways his argument followed the lines laid down by Locke, but Mill put fewer limitations on toleration than did Locke. He was more insistent that the only justification for interfering with any man's liberty was a reasonable assurance that some danger or threat to the liberty of another was involved. Again, where Locke was exclusively concerned with the protection of individual liberty from the interference of state and church, Mill was increasingly concerned with the limitations on human freedom that stemmed from unwritten law—the pressure of convention and public opinion. Mill wanted to see toleration extended from the realm of politics to that of morals and manners, to all self-regarding actions, as he called them. Mill, as a Victorian, lived, of course, in a society which not only frowned on things like free love, adultery, and Sabbath-breaking but also vigorously applied the social sanction of ostracism to any who committed these sins. Mill felt that people were more oppressed and hemmed in by the unwritten laws than they were by laws enforced by the state and that human freedom and variety could not flourish in a repressive atmosphere. Mill demanded toleration because he held that liberty, individuality, and variety were of the highest ethical value; they were what made man "nobler to contemplate."

Mill's ablest critic, James Fitzjames Stephen (in his book *Liberty, Equality, Fraternity,* written in reply to Mill's essay *On Liberty*), argued that intolerance was a necessary preservative of society. The modern liberal state was possible precisely because society was able to discipline itself through unwritten laws. It was a good thing for men to be compelled by social intolerance to keep laws of conduct which the wisdom of the ages had shown to be good. Mill's claim that there was a class of self-regarding actions which had a right to be tolerated because they did not affect others was, in Stephen's view, unfounded; almost everything a man did affected someone else. Suicide, intemperance, debauchery, and so forth were not things which injured the agent alone. The class of self-regarding actions was virtually an empty one. And since almost all conduct was other-regarding, society had a right to interfere as widely as it did. Stephen argued that the general run of men did not have the wit to think out moral codes of their own or the strength of character to obey such codes if they established them. Hence, some form of external sanction was needed if morality was to be upheld. Stephen also rejected Mill's view that variety was a good thing in itself. Goodness, he agreed, was varied, but that did not mean that variety itself was good; a nation in which half the population was criminal would be more diversified than a wholly honest one, but it would not be a better nation. Dissent for its own sake Stephen condemned as frivolous and sentimental Bohemianism. Eccentricity was a mark of weakness rather than of strength; and constraint, far from being an evil, was a great stimulus to exertion. Stephen even held that the intolerance which went with the Puritan spirit had been one of the chief factors enabling England to surge ahead of other nations in making industrial and social progress.

Political toleration. With the rise of totalitarian governments in the twentieth century, the problem of toleration took on a new aspect. For democratic and freedom-loving governments the toleration of intolerance became an acute problem. In 1936 the British government introduced a ban on political uniforms because of the disturbances caused by Oswald Mosley's fascist movement and its black-shirted adherents; an attempt was made under Wilson's Labour government in 1965 to proscribe acts of racial discrimination. After World War II the United States was troubled by the difficulty of deciding how much toleration could be safely extended to communists when several communists proved to be Russian or Cuban agents and when all communists seemed to have a more pronounced loyalty to the Soviet Union than to the United States. The position of the communists in twentieth-century America was thought to resemble that of the Catholics in seventeenth-century England, and many Americans recalled Locke's view that such persons had forfeited their right to toleration. Other Americans argued that repression was futile; the interdiction of open communist organizations would do little to protect the state from secret and more sinister communist activities. Hence, an abridgment of political toleration would do no good to anyone, for it would simply create martyrs without eliminating spies. Thus, the argument both for and against political toleration in the twentieth century cannot be said to have differed greatly from the debate concerning religious toleration that exercised the minds of earlier generations.

Bibliography

Bonet-Maury, G., *Histoire de la liberté de conscience en France.* Paris, 1909.

Creighton, M., *Persecution and Tolerance.* London, 1895.

Devlin, P. A., *The Enforcement of Morals.* Oxford, 1965.

Hart, H. L. A., *Law, Liberty and Morality.* Oxford, 1963.

Jordan, W. K., *The Development of Religious Toleration in England.* London, 1932–1940.

Lecky, W. E., *History of the Rise of Rationalism in Europe.* London, 1877.

Lecler, J., *Histoire de la tolérance au siècle de la Réforme.* Paris, 1955.

Locke, John, *Epistola de Tolerantia.* Gouda, 1688.

Luzzatti, L., *La libertà di conscienza.* Milan, 1909.

Mill, John Stuart, *On Liberty.* London, 1859.

Ruffini, F., *La libertà religiosa.* Florence, 1901.

Seaton, A. A., *The Theory of Toleration Under the Later Stuarts.* Oxford, 1911.

Stephen, J. F., *Liberty, Equality, Fraternity.* London, 1861.

Voltaire, F.-M. de, *Traité sur la tolérance.* Paris, 1763.

MAURICE CRANSTON

TOLETUS, FRANCIS (1532–1596), the first important Jesuit philosopher, was born in Córdoba, Spain. He studied philosophy at the University of Valencia and theology at the University of Salamanca under Dominic de Soto. While a professor of philosophy at Salamanca, Toletus entered the Jesuit order (1558). He taught philosophy at the order's Roman College from 1559 to 1563 and theology from 1563 to 1569. In 1593 Toletus became the first Jesuit cardinal. He died in Rome.

Toletus' Latin philosophical works include commentaries on the logic, physics, and psychology of Aristotle; Toletus' commentary on Thomas Aquinas' *Summa* (*Enarratio in Summam Theologiae Divi Thomae*) also contains philosophical material. In all these works his views are Thomistic with many personal modifications. In the theory of knowledge, Toletus taught that individual things are directly apprehended by the intellect, that the primary object of knowledge is a sort of particularized form (*species specialissima*) and not being in general (*Physica*, Venice, 1600, p. 12), that intellectual abstraction is simply a precision from accidents and a consideration of the substance of anything (*De Anima*, Venice, 1575, p. 170), that the agent intellect may be fundamentally the same power as the possible intellect (*De Anima*, Venice, 1586, pp. 144–146). His metaphysics is distinguished by a theory of triple acts in the same being: formal, entitative, and existential (*Physica*, p. 33). The existential act is limited in two ways: by the receptive potency and by its efficient cause (*Enarratio*, Vol. I, p. 118). He denied that essence and existence are really distinct principles (*Physica*, p. 34; *Enarratio*, Vol. I, p. 79), and that matter is pure potency; it has its own actuality (*Physica*, pp. 32–36), but form is the principle of individuation (*De Anima*, p. 163). The number of the categories (ten) in Aristotle's logic is merely probable. It is possible rationally to demonstrate the existence of God but the famous "five ways" of Aquinas are incomplete; they do not establish the key attributes of God (*Enarratio*, Vol. I, 69).

Bibliography

The Latin philosophical works are collected in *Omnia quae Hucusque Extant Opera* (Lyons, 1586). See also *Enarratio in Summam Theologiae Divi Thomae*, 4 vols. (Rome, 1869–1870).

Works on Toletus include L. Morati, "Toledo, Francisco de," *Enciclopedia filosofica* (Venice and Rome, 1957), Vol. IV, Cols. 1216–1217 (an excellent entry to which the present account is indebted); C. Giacon, *La seconda scolastica* (Milan, 1944), pp. 25–44. 51–65.

VERNON J. BOURKE

TOLSTOY, COUNT LEO NIKOLAEVICH (1828–1910), Russian novelist, social and moral–religious reformer, and Christian anarchist, was born on the family estate of Yasnaya Polyana in central Russia. Orphaned by the age of nine and brought up by elderly female relatives and private tutors, Tolstoy studied jurisprudence and Oriental languages at the University of Kazan from 1844 to 1847 but left without taking a degree. He served in the artillery in the Caucasus in 1851–1852 and in the Crimean War (1853–1855), during which he took part in the siege of Silistra and the defense of Sevastopol. In 1857 and 1860–1861 he traveled abroad, visiting Germany, Switzerland, France, Italy, and England and holding conversations with Proudhon in Brussels. In 1862 he married Sophia Andreyevna Bers, 16 years his junior, who bore him 13 children. In the remaining 48 years of his life Tolstoy did not leave Russia and spent most of his time on the estate at Yasnaya Polyana.

Tolstoy's creative life is normally divided into two parts—the period in which he wrote his great novels (1852–1876) and the period in which he was predominantly occupied with moral and social reform (1879–1910). The two periods were separated by an intense spiritual and emotional crisis (1876–1879), during which Tolstoy reached the verge of suicide. To the first period we owe, among other writings, his *Childhood* (1851–1852; this and other dates being the times of writing given in the carefully annotated Russian edition of the complete works), *Boyhood* (1852–1854), and *Youth* (1855–1857), the *Sevastopol Stories* (1855–1856), *The Cossacks* (1852–1863), *War and Peace* (1863–1869, 1873), and *Anna Karenina* (1873–1877). The crisis that made Tolstoy a "Tolstoyan" at the age of 50 is described in *A Confession*

(1879–1882). He sought the meaning of life and found it in the simple Christianity of the Gospels, which he regarded as containing the basis for creating the Kingdom of God on earth and, hence, as a guide to social action. He now preached humility, absolute rejection of all forms of violence and coercion, vegetarianism, the renunciation of luxury and, as far as possible, of sexual relations, the evil of property, and the moral value of manual labor. He placed his own property in the hands of his wife in the 1880s, and some of it—for example, the copyright to all his works after 1881—he renounced completely. He saw his own past life as devoted first to "the service of ambition, vanity and lust" and then to an equally selfish "correct, honorable family life," both of which must be rejected for the brotherhood of man. In 1884 he relinquished the use of his title and took up regular manual work, plowing, making shoes, and the like, to the distress of his family. The religious and ethical teaching that he now proclaimed was expounded in a flood of essays, stories, letters, and pamphlets, most of them banned from publication in Russia by the censorship. These included *What I Believe* (1882–1884), *What Then Must We Do?* (1882–1886), *The Kingdom of God Is Within You* (1890–1893), *The Christian Teaching* (1894–1896), and the exposition of his moral views on art, *What Is Art?* (1897–1898). The break between the two periods of Tolstoy's creative life is not absolute: his diaries and some of his moralistic stories of the late 1850s and early 1860s—*Lucerne, Three Deaths,* and *Polikushka*—as well as his educational writings of 1862 and 1873, presage the views of his later period; while a number of stories of the later period—*Memoirs of a Madman* (1884–1887), *The Death of Ivan Ilyich* (1881–1886), *Kreutzer Sonata* (1887–1889), *The Devil* (1889–1890), and "Master and Man" (1894–1895)—combine with their moral purpose ample evidence of his continued gift for detailed observation and description, especially of emotions. The only long novel of his later period, *Resurrection* (1889–1899), is generally considered very bad.

Tolstoy was not a philosopher; he had no genuine conception of a philosophical problem or of a technical philosophical argument; he was primarily a practical moralist and "sage." For the philosopher, four aspects of Tolstoy's work are of some, though mostly marginal, interest. First, he was a pedagogical reformer who founded a school for peasants on his estate in 1859 and published a journal setting forth his educational theories in 1862; later he produced some additional writings on educational theory. Second, in the novel *War and Peace*, especially in the second part, Tolstoy attempted to espouse a philosophy of history, summing up his reactions to questions discussed by Russian intellectuals in the early 1860s and suggested to him by his reading of Joseph de Maistre and the Slavophile M. P. Pogodin's *Historical Aphorisms*. Third, there was his general Christian anarchist "philosophy," as expounded in his later years. Fourth, in his later period Tolstoy repudiated the vanity of literature for its own sake and the value of almost all of his own earlier writing and propounded in *What Is Art?* an aesthetic theory which was much discussed by philosophers and literary men in the first half of the twentieth century.

Educational theories. Tolstoy's pedagogical writings stressed that the natural criterion for pedagogy was freedom and the only method was experience. The school at Yasnaya Polyana was based on the principles that children were free to come and go as they pleased and that no form of violence or coercion could be used to make them study. At his best, Tolstoy propounded a Socratic concept of education, in which there was equality and critical interplay between teacher and pupil, who were joined in a common search for knowledge. The child was not to have formulas, dogmas, the teacher's conceptions, or external "civilized" values thrust upon him; he was encouraged to follow the natural bent of his curiosity. While Tolstoy believed that education was a form of improvement, he also believed that peasants should be educated to be peasants; he did not see education as a means for inducing social mobility or producing social change, save in the direction of creating simpler, more natural, and more moral relations among men. Characteristically, on finding that his informal and voluntary methods did not produce progress in Russian grammar, Tolstoy decided that grammar was not a proper subject for elementary education and should be deferred to the university level. On the same basis, but with subtler arguments, he advocated that the teaching of history be similarly deferred to the tertiary level.

Philosophy of history. In *War and Peace*, Tolstoy was trying to do something of greater philosophical interest than his educational work. History, he sought to show, is not made by great historical personages, nor can it be summed up in laws analogous to those of science. The real stuff of historical events is not decisions, orders, large projects, and plans, let alone laws or social movements. An actual battle, for instance, consists of the vast interplay of small, specific personal actions and emotions which take place almost or entirely unconsciously. The individual who plays a part in historical events never himself understands their significance; he cannot foresee the full effects of his actions, and he cannot say what the outcome would have been if one action had been left undone. There is a flow of historical events made up of an infinity of individual actions; the flow can be observed, but it cannot be charted, determined by free will from outside, or reduced to laws. Not the people who seek to control this flow, but those who surrender themselves to it, in an almost elemental way, understand most about what is going on.

Religious anarchism. "Faith," Tolstoy is reported to have said in conversation, "is not so much the knowledge of truth as loyalty to it." In *A Confession*, Tolstoy made it clear that his Christian teaching was the response to an overwhelming emotional need and not the product of metaphysical speculation. The choice before him during his emotional crisis was whether to live or to die, and he could live only if he could be persuaded that life had meaning. The meaning of life could not be based on personal satisfaction and enjoyment, since death destroyed all such satisfaction and made it meaningless. (Tolstoy could not believe in an individual immortality which would produce personal pleasures after death.) Life, he decided, could have meaning only on the basis of two beliefs: that God exists and that we need to renounce completely the welfare of the individual personality and seek the meaning of our life in its divine origin, which is expressed in love of other men.

From Rousseau, and from his own experiences in Russia, Tolstoy had acquired the greatest suspicion of civilization, culture, and intellectualism. In *A Confession* he claimed to have found the elements of his teaching among "poor, simple, uneducated people," untouched by civilization, among "wanderers, monks, dissenters, peasants." He found his religion not in the writings of the theologians but in the simple stories and simple exhortations of the Gospels. True social Christianity, as Tolstoy saw it, rested positively on love and negatively on five commandments expressed in the Sermon on the Mount: do not be angry; do not lust; do not take oaths; do not judge or resist evil; do not fight. Tolstoy took these to imply absolute nonviolence and only passive resistance to violence. These views influenced Gandhi, with whom Tolstoy corresponded. In the period when he was writing the *Kreutzer Sonata,* he interpreted "Do not lust" as an injunction implying complete celibacy, even in marriage; but he soon amended this view to the position that chastity was an ideal toward which people should strive to the extent made possible by their nature and their circumstances. The taking of oaths and the possession of property he opposed more consistently, and under his influence Tolstoyan agricultural communities holding all property in common were founded, first in Russia and then in England, America, and Holland, though all eventually failed. In Israel the earliest collective settlements were founded under the theoretical influence of the Jewish Tolstoyan A. D. Gordon; they have survived and retain some of the Tolstoyan "religion of labor."

Tolstoy's opposition to all forms of coercive government was uncompromising. "The temptation of government," or the temptation of acting wickedly in the name of the common good, seemed to him the worst of the five temptations; it was the temptation that led Caiaphas to demand the death of Christ. All government is a conspiracy to commit crimes against the governed by violence or threat of violence.

The philosophical basis of Tolstoy's teaching on these questions was fairly slender and uncritical. He distinguished man as a spirit, man as a soul, from the animal personality (the spatiotemporal body of man), which dies at death. The purpose of man's spirit is to merge itself in God by merging itself in other men: man is worthless as an individual and is truly alive only as a manifestation of the divine impersonal force, which is love. Man must therefore renounce the personal life, in which he loves himself alone and seeks maximum enjoyment for himself, and learn to love all men. This does not mean renouncing his animal personality, his attributes in time and space, which will not melt away: it means making the animal personality a tool of the spirit. In *What I Believe* Tolstoy appeared to suggest that there is no personal immortality but that man becomes immortal only through merging his personality into humanity as such. A few years later, in *On Life,* Tolstoy was more ambiguous, arguing that man has a real or special self which is immortal. But as in all views of this type, there was no real examination of the concept of spirit or spiritual self, no genuine discussion of arguments that

might be brought against the existence of God or of a divine purpose in life, no proper consideration of the logical standing of moral injunctions and of the basis on which they can be justified. In the earlier part of his second period, Tolstoy simply took his departure from an interpretation of the Gospels; later, as he devoted more attention to Oriental religions, he came to feel that what he regarded as the sound Christian teaching was not peculiar to Christianity but common to all religions. At no stage did he regard Christ as peculiarly divine, and from the beginning Tolstoy's teachings were condemned and persecuted by the Russian Orthodox church, whose dogmas, institutions, and authority he rejected. In 1901 he was formally excommunicated by the Holy Synod.

Aesthetics. In an essay on Guy de Maupassant (1893–1894), written as a preface to a Russian edition of the Frenchman's works, Tolstoy argued that there are four tests that must be fulfilled for a work to be a work of art. The author must have "genius"—the faculty of intense, strenuous attention applied according to the author's taste to this or that subject and enabling the author to see things in some new aspect overlooked by others. The author must give the work beauty of expression, and he must express himself with sincerity, with an earnestness that has burned itself into the material. Finally, there must be "a correct, that is, a moral relation of the author to his subject." Tolstoy elaborated this view in *What Is Art?*, in which he specifically linked his conception of art with his general conception of the good society. In the process he reached some eccentric judgments on past writers that have made his theory seem necessarily absurd to some, simply because it leads to such conclusions. All art, he said, is worthless if it swings away from morality; Greek drama is "wild, coarse and meaningless"; Michelangelo's "The Last Judgment" is foolish; *King Lear* is a clutter of improbabilities; Ibsen, Wagner, and Strauss are mere imitators. But behind these ex cathedra pronouncements there is a developed, if not very subtle or closely examined, view of art. Tolstoy argued that art cannot be the search for beauty, for two reasons—because beauty is selfish, a subjective pleasure, and therefore worthless, and because there is no common standard of pleasure or beauty, which means that beauty cannot be a standard of art. Art, Tolstoy claimed, is the transfer or communication of feelings, but only certain kinds of feelings, those feelings which are moral. The contagiousness of art, its success in communicating the author's emotion to the reader, depends on novelty and originality of feeling, clarity of expression, and the sincerity of the author; the worth of the feelings communicated depends for Tolstoy entirely on their approximation to his own belief in the brotherhood of men and their sonship in God. Tolstoy was willing to grant that the morality of an artistic work must be judged in relation to the morality of the time in which it was produced; but it must be judged in relation to the highest morality of the time, and this for Tolstoy is always "the religious perception of the age." The autonomy of art, its separation from religion, Tolstoy said, is a stultifying and immoral romantic conception which arose in the Renaissance; true art will always be infused with moral and religious feeling. The common people have such feelings, and if art does not appeal to the common people, then it cannot be appealing to noble emotions, that is, cannot be true art.

For some time Tolstoy's *What Is Art?* has provided the rather crude *locus classicus* for a moral theory of art. But the concept of art as communication of emotion has since been taken up by other more professional philosophers. Tolstoy's belief in the simple religious virtues and the sound artistic taste of the common people has rightly been questioned, and he has been attacked for ignoring completely the element of learning that is involved in reaching an appreciation of artistic work and for failing to appreciate the conflict of moral values even within religious traditions. The moral aspect of his theory—for him the most important—merges into general problems about moral philosophy, moral evaluation, and the concept of goodness, problems which Tolstoy himself never saw as requiring genuine philosophical discussion or criticism.

Works by Tolstoy

The definitive Russian edition of Tolstoy's works is *Sochineniya,* edited by Tolstoy's friend and disciple V. G. Chertkov and others, 90 vols. (Moscow, 1928–1958); it contains drafts, variants, and all the extant diaries and notebooks, with commentary. An additional (unnumbered) index volume was published in Moscow in 1964; it contains a full chronological list of Tolstoy's writings.

There are two collections of Tolstoy's writings in English, each containing some material omitted in the other: *Works,* translated by Leo Wiener, 24 vols. (Boston and London, 1904–1905); and *Works,* translated by Louise and Aylmer Maude, 21 vols. (Oxford, 1928–1937), known as the Oxford centenary edition. *A New Light on Tolstoy—Literary Fragments, Letters and Reminiscences Not Previously Published,* translated by P. England (New York and London, 1931), contains material not elsewhere available in English, notably three chapters of "The Decembrists."

Works on Tolstoy

Among biographies of Tolstoy are Aylmer Maude, *The Life of Tolstoy,* 2 vols. (Oxford, 1930), also included in the Oxford centenary edition of the *Works,* and Ernest J. Simmons, *Leo Tolstoy* (Boston, 1946), a useful one-volume biography.

Critical studies include Isaiah Berlin, *The Hedgehog and the Fox* (London, 1957), a study of Tolstoy's views on history; A. H. Craufurd, *The Religion and Ethics of Tolstoy* (London, 1912); H. W. Garrod, *Tolstoy's Theory of Art* (London, 1935); Georg Lukács, *Studies in European Realism,* translated by E. Bone (London, 1950), containing a Marxist discussion of Tolstoy's work and its relation to feudalism; Theodore Redpath, *Tolstoy* (London, 1960), a slim but intelligent critical study, emphasizing his literary work and containing a useful select bibliography.

For a discussion of Tolstoy's views on the meaning of life, see LIFE, MEANING AND VALUE OF.)

EUGENE KAMENKA

TÖNNIES, FERDINAND (1855–1936), German sociologist and social philosopher. Tönnies was born in Eiderstedt, Schleswig-Holstein. His family were originally Dutch settlers who had been farmers in the Schleswig-Holstein area for over two hundred years. On the farm of his birth and in the surrounding countryside, Tönnies came to know traditional peasant culture at first hand. When Tönnies was nine years old his family moved to the small town of Husum, where an established writer, Theodor Storm, exerted an important influence on him. From his oldest brother, who was engaged in trading with English merchants, Tönnies learned about a world he considered more rational and individualistic than that of the peasants he knew so well.

Before Tönnies reached the age of 17 he graduated from the Gymnasium and began his university studies in classical philology and philosophy, first at the University of Jena and later at Leipzig, Bonn, Berlin, and Tübingen. He received his doctorate in philosophy from Tübingen in 1877. Thereafter his life was devoted to the study of social philosophy and the social sciences. In 1881 he became a lecturer at the University of Kiel, where he remained until his dismissal by the Nazis in 1933. Tönnies was conservative by temperament and in his daily behavior, but he participated in such liberal movements of his time as cooperatives and progressive labor movements. Although it is not easy to specify the political orientation of so independent and original a thinker as Tönnies, his son-in-law, Rudolf Heberle, classifies him as a socialist who was more Fabian than most German intellectuals but more Marxian than the Fabians.

Tönnies was influenced in his writing and thinking by his fellow Schleswig-Holsteiner, the philosopher Friedrich Paulsen; by Adolph Wagner, the economist; and by Wilhelm Wundt, the social psychologist and philosopher. Tönnies' own thinking on state socialism did not contradict Wagner's views concerning the state's increasing control of life. In his quest for the psychological underpinning for his sociological concepts he was influenced by Wundt's concepts of purposeful will (*Zweckwille*) and instinctive will (*Triebwille*). He was also profoundly influenced by the philosophy of Hobbes. As early as 1877 Hobbes's advocacy of state omnipotence, as well as his social contract theory, absorbed Tönnies' interest. Marx, too, exerted an effect on his thinking. Like Marx, he considered economic institutions to be important in social change. Unlike Marx, he did not believe in economic determinism because he believed that religion and other noneconomic influences were too important to ascribe change to a single source. Whereas Marx attached great importance to technology, Tönnies acknowledged its importance but gave primacy to such economic activities as trade and trading relationships. Other influences upon Tönnies' thinking and writing came from Sir Henry Maine; Lorenz von Stein, an earlier teacher at Kiel; the German natural rights philosophers and thinkers of the romantic school; and such English and American writers as L. H. Morgan.

The historical and romantic schools of thought proffered opposing theories about the early forms of communal and "natural" groupings and later forms of pluralities. A synthesis of the opposing theories of society—the historic-organic theory and the rationalist natural law theory—became Tönnies' masterpiece, *Gemeinschaft und Gesellschaft (Community and Society,* 1887). Its subtitle, "A Treatise on Communism and Socialism as Empirical Patterns of Culture," reveals some of the major problems with which it dealt. Tönnies demonstrated that neither Hobbes's nor Aristotle's interpretations of man and society were wrong because each emphasized different aspects of social life. Aristotle was correct, Tönnies claimed, in saying that man was by nature a social being who lived in traditional communities and other pluralities which had evolved naturally; Hobbes was correct in seeing man as rationally forming contractual arrangements that resulted in associations and organizations. The traditional forms of social organization were *Gemeinschaft*-like and might be considered ends in themselves, but the contractual agreements could be considered as means to ends, and to be *Gesellschaft*-like.

Gemeinschaft is an ideal type (or what Tönnies termed a "normal concept") in which natural, or essential, will (*Wesenwille*) has primacy. Natural will has primacy when association is based upon relationships which have one or more of the following characteristics: they are ends in and of themselves, they are spontaneous and affective, and they are the outcome of interaction between incumbents of status roles such as mother and child, which traditionally or out of habit exhibit these qualities. Such pluralities as families, friendship groups, clans, peasant neighborhoods, and religious sects are *Gemeinschaft*-like. *Gemeinschaft* exists at one end of a polar continuum that has *Gesellschaft* at the other end. *Gesellschaft* is that social form in which rational will (*Kürwille*) has primacy. The prototype of *Kürwille* directs the actions of traders bargaining with one another. When it has primacy, social relations and facilities become means to ends which are sharply differentiated so that they may be chosen and employed in conformity with the norms of rationality and efficiency in both the technical and economic sense. Thus, modern governmental bureaucracies and manufacturing concerns are *Gesellschaft*-like.

The four concepts *Gemeinschaft, Gesellschaft, Wesenwille* and *Kürwille* are at the center of almost all of Tönnies' writings, which give special attention to social custom or codes, stratification, and public opinion. Tönnies' influence in the social sciences was great, and it extended to such men as Max Weber and Émile Durkheim, themselves influential and seminal scholars. Almost every social scientist who has used a typology acknowledges an indebtedness to Tönnies, and so general has the use of Tönnies' concepts become, that they are often used as straightforward sociological terminology, without credit being given to their originator.

Bibliography

Tönnies' *Gemeinschaft und Gesellschaft* (Leipzig, 1887; 8th ed., 1935) was translated and edited by Charles P. Loomis as *Community and Society* (New York, 1957), which contains a bibliography of Tönnies' works and secondary literature on him. Tönnies' *Die Sitte* (Frankfurt, 1909) was translated by A. Farrell Borenstein as *Custom: An Essay on Social Codes* (New York, 1961). Other works by Tönnies are *Hobbes, Leben und Lehren* (Stuttgart, 1896), *Marx, Leben und Lehren* (Berlin, 1921), and *Kritik der öffentlichen Meinung* (Berlin, 1922). The most complete bibliography of Tönnies' writings was prepared by Else Brenke as part of *Reine und angewandte Soziologie, eine Festgabe für Ferdinand Tönnies, zu seinem 80. Geburtstage* (Leipzig, 1936). Among secondary writings on Tönnies are Rudolf Heberle, "The Sociology of Ferdinand Tönnies," in *American Sociological Review*, Vol. 2, No. 1 (1937); H. E. Stoltenberg, *Wegweiser durch Tönnies: Gemeinschaft und Gesellschaft* (Berlin, 1919); and Nicholas S. Timasheff, *Sociological Theory—Its Nature and Growth* (New York, 1955), pp. 97 ff.

CHARLES P. LOOMIS

TOTALITARIANISM. See the article on FASCISM.

TOUCH. Two bodies are said to be touching if there is no spatial gap between some point on the surface of one and some point on the surface of the other. If one of the touching bodies is that of a sentient being, it may be aware of certain properties of the other body: for instance, that it is hot or cold, rough or smooth, wet or dry, hard or soft, sweet or sour. The sentient being is said to be aware of an object's sweetness or sourness by taste. (Aristotle attributes our distinguishing taste from touch to the fact that only a part of our flesh is sensitive to flavor.) The remaining properties the sentient being is said, in common speech, to be aware of by touch. Accordingly, touch appears in the traditional list of senses, with sight, hearing, etc.

Aristotle. Aristotle remarks that in the case of touch the contraries hot–cold, dry–moist, and hard–soft do not seem to have a single subject in the way in which the single subject of the properties acute–grave and loud–soft is sound, which is perceived by hearing. This may lead one to say that there are really a number of different senses that are mistakenly referred to as one sense, touch, perhaps because the body of a sentient being must touch an object in order for it to be aware by any of them of that object's properties. Or one may say that there is a single subject of the different contraries, namely, a material thing, and that there is only one sense, touch, whereby we are aware of the different properties of which the material thing is a subject. If one takes the latter course, it may appear that touch is the only sense whose proper object is the material world.

Locke, Berkeley, and Condillac. To Locke, it seemed that "the idea most intimately connected with and essential to body, so as nowhere else to be found or imagined, but only in matter" was the idea of solidity. This idea is received by touch and "arises from the resistance which we find in body to the entrance of any other body into the place it possesses."

As Locke held it to be by touch that we receive the idea of solidity, the idea essential to body, so Berkeley, in his *Essay Towards a New Theory of Vision*, held it to be touch alone that directly acquaints us with the external world. He abandoned this view in *The Principles of Human Knowledge*, maintaining that the objects of touch are as much sensations as are the objects of sight.

Locke regarded solidity as a "simple idea": "If anyone asks me what this solidity is, I send him to his senses to inform him." Later philosophers have tried to explain what is involved in the sensation of solidity. Condillac distinguished it from the sensations of sound, color, and smell, since a person knows his own body by it. If a person presses his hand against his chest, his hand and chest "will be distinguished from one another by the sensation of solidities which they mutually give each other." Thus, involved in the notion of a sensation of solidity is the notion of the recognition as such of a feeling given to a part of the body. If organic sensations were not localized in the body, a person could never know his own or any other body by touching it, for "it is only with extension that we can construct extension, just as it is only with objects that we can construct objects."

H. H. Price. H. H. Price carried the analysis a step further. He divided touch "into three distinct types of sensation: contact sensation proper, muscular sensation, and the sensation of temperature." The perception of solidity involves both contact sensation proper and muscular sensation. The latter is "essentially a modification of the voluminous life-feeling [that] might also be described as our sense of embodiment." Muscular strain is felt at a place in the body and as having vectorial character, that is, originating from or tending toward a certain direction. A person experiences the solidity of something when the resistance he feels on pressing it "is actually felt as coming from within the closed boundary which contact-sensation reveals. . . . Thus the tactual conception of Matter is strictly speaking tactuo-muscular or contactuo-muscular."

Local sign theory. The analyses of both Condillac and Price specify organic sensations as being localized. As Condillac expressed it, to know its body the child must "perceive its sensations, not as modifications of its soul, but as modifications of the organs which are their occasional causes." Condillac cannot explain "how the self which is only in the soul appears to be found in the body . . . it is enough that we observe this fact." The alternatives are either that a person is born with the capacity to locate organic sensations or that he acquires this capacity. Most philosophers hold the capacity to be acquired, although they differ widely in the accounts they give of how it is acquired; whether by the person's learning to interpret some feature of the sensation as a sign of its location (the so-called local sign) or in some other way.

Movement and touch. Perhaps the most important recent contribution to the problem of how touch mediates awareness of its objects was made by David Katz in "Der Aufbau der Tastwelt." Summarizing Katz's conclusions, Merleau-Ponty expresses the crux of the matter as being that "the movement of one's body is to touch what lighting is to vision. . . . When one of my hands touches the other, the hand that moves functions as subject and the other as object. There are tactile phenomena, alleged tactile qualities, like roughness and smoothness, which disappear completely if the exploratory movement is eliminated. Movement and time are not only an objective condition of knowing touch, but a phenomenal component of tactile data. They bring about the patterning of tactile phenomena, just as light shows up the configuration of a visible surface."

Body – object relation. With the view that the objects of touch are physical objects may be contrasted the view that we are not aware of the object we touch but of a relation holding between our body and that object. It is a fact that how warm an object feels to an observer depends causally on the warmth of the part of the observer's body with which he is touching it. We notice the temperature of a hand that is colder or warmer than our own. Aristotle explains this in terms of his theory of sensation as the assimilation in form of the organ to the object. D. M. Armstrong mentions it, together with the fact that a person can say immediately with what portion of his body he is in contact with an object perceived by touch, in support of his theory that all immediate tactual perception involves perception of a relation holding between the observer's body and the object he is touching. As evidence for his theory, Armstrong holds that "hardness and softness as immediately perceived by touch, are obviously relative to the hardness or softness of our flesh." It is unclear from this evidence whether Armstrong is justified in claiming more than that how things feel to us depends on the condition of the part of the body with which we feel them.

Bibliography

Aristotle, *De Anima*. Book II, Ch. 11.
Armstrong, D. M., *Bodily Sensations*. London and New York, 1962. Chs. 3–5.
Berkeley, George, *An Essay Towards a New Theory of Vision*. Dublin, 1709. Secs. 45–49.
Condillac, E. B. de, *Treatise on the Sensations*. Paris and London, 1754. Part II, Chs. 1–5.
Katz, David, "Der Aufbau der Tastwelt." *Zeitschrift für Psychologie*, Vol. 11 (1925).
Locke, John, *An Essay Concerning Human Understanding*. London, 1690. Book II, Ch. 4.
Merleau-Ponty, Maurice, *Phenomenology of Perception*. London and New York, 1962. Pp. 313–317.
Price, H. H., "Touch and Organic Sensation." *PAS*, Vol. 44 (1943/1944).
Vesey, G. N. A., *The Embodied Mind*. London, 1965. Ch. 4. Contains an exposition and criticism of the local sign theory and references to other work on the subject.
Warnock, G. J., *Berkeley*. Harmondsworth, England, 1953. Ch. 3.

G. N. A. VESEY

TOYNBEE, ARNOLD JOSEPH, the foremost contemporary representative of what is sometimes termed "speculative philosophy of history." In some respects he occupies a position analogous to that of Henry Thomas Buckle in the nineteenth century. Like Buckle, he has sought to discover laws determining the growth and evolution of civilization and to do so within the context of a wide comparative survey of different historical societies; like Buckle again, the results of his investigation have become a storm center of controversy and criticism. To support his hypotheses, Toynbee has, however, been able to draw on a vast fund of material of a kind unavailable to his Victorian predecessor, and the imposing examples and illustrations in which his work abounds make Buckle's much-vaunted erudition look strangely threadbare. As a consequence, Toynbee's historical theory is worked out in far greater detail; in fact, it represents a highly articulated and complex structure with many ramifications and appendages. Moreover, the materialist optimism underlying Buckle's linear conception of history as a continuous progressive development is wholly absent from Toynbee's analysis of the rise and decay of different cultures, while, in place of Buckle's positivistic rationalism, there runs through all Toynbee's work, especially his later books, a strain of mysticism and religious idealism.

Born in 1889, Toynbee was educated at Balliol College, Oxford, and was a tutor there from 1912 to 1915. Subsequently, he became professor of Byzantine and modern Greek language, literature, and history at London University (1919–1924) and then for thirty years held the post of director of studies in the Royal Institute of International Affairs. He has written on a wide variety of topics concerning Greek history, international politics, and contemporary affairs, but his main work has been his *A Study Of History,* the first ten volumes of which were published between 1934 and 1954. Since then, two other volumes have appeared, the last, entitled *Reconsiderations,* being largely an attempt to meet points raised by his numerous critics and, where he has thought it necessary, to qualify previous claims in the light of their objections. Toynbee has always listened carefully to those who have disagreed with him, although he has apparently never felt that their observations justified any major revision of his views.

"A Study of History." Toynbee claims that his project was first suggested to him when, at the beginning of World War I, he became aware of certain striking affinities between the courses taken by the Graeco-Roman and modern European civilizations. It occurred to him that similar parallels might be discernible elsewhere, that there is, as he puts it, "a species of human society that we label 'civilisations'" and that the representatives of this species which have thus far appeared on this planet may exemplify in their various histories a common pattern of development. With this idea forming in his mind, Toynbee came across Oswald Spengler's *Decline of the West,* in which he found many of his own intimations affirmed and corroborated. Nevertheless, it seemed to Toynbee that Spengler's account was defective in important ways. The number of civilizations examined (eight) was too small to serve as a basis for safe generalization; little attempt was made to explain why cultures rise and decline in the manner described; and, in general, Spengler's procedure was marred by certain a priori dogmas that distorted his thinking, leading him to display at times a cavalier disregard for the facts. What was required was a more empirical approach, one in which it was clearly recognized that a problem of explanation existed and that the solution of this problem must be in terms of verifiable hypotheses that can stand the test of historical experience.

The pattern of history. Toynbee has repeatedly referred to his own method as essentially "inductive." His aim (initially, at least) was to "try out the scientific approach to human affairs and to test how far it will carry us." In undertaking this program, he has been insistent upon the need to treat as the fundamental units of study "whole societies," as opposed to "arbitrarily insulated fragments of them like the nation-states of the modern West." In contrast with Spengler, he claims to have identified 21 examples (past and present) of the species "civilization," though he has admitted that even this number is inconveniently small for his purpose—"the elucidation and formulation of laws." He has argued, however, that a significant degree of similarity is discernible between the careers of the societies he has examined and compared; certain stages in their respective histories can be seen to conform to a recognizable pattern too striking to be ignored, a pattern of growth, breakdown, and eventual decay and dissolution. Within this pattern certain recurrent "rhythms" may be detected. When a society is in a period of growth, it offers effective and fruitful responses to the challenges that present themselves; when in decline, on the other hand, it proves incapable of exploiting the opportunities and of withstanding or overcoming the difficulties with which it is confronted. Neither growth nor disintegration, Toynbee holds, is nec-

essarily continuous or uninterrupted. In disintegration, for instance, a phase of rout is frequently succeeded by a temporary rally, followed in turn by a new, more serious relapse. As an example he cited the establishment of a universal state under the Augustan Pax Romana as a period of rally in the career of the Hellenic civilization, coming between a time of troubles which, in the form of revolutions and internecine wars, preceded it and the first stages of the Roman Empire's final collapse, which followed in the third century. Toynbee contends that clearly comparable rout-rally rhythms have manifested themselves in the disintegration of many other civilizations, such as the Chinese, the Sumerian, and the Hindu. In these, too, we encounter the phenomena of increasing standardization and loss of creativity that were apparent when the Graeco-Roman society was in decline.

Historical models. Toynbee's tendency to interpret the history of other civilizations in terms suggested by that of the Hellenic culture is marked, and many of his opponents have claimed that it has led him into imposing artificial schemes upon the past and into postulating parallels by no means borne out by the historical material. In his most recent work Toynbee has shown himself to be sensitive to criticism of this kind. He has maintained, however, that for an investigation of the kind he envisaged it was at least essential to start with a model of some sort, his chief doubts being whether the model he chose was ideally suited to his purpose and whether a future student of the comparative history of civilizations would not be better advised to employ a diversity of specimens, rather than a single example, to guide his inquiries.

However, it is not clear that in proposing this amendment to his original procedure, Toynbee has fully appreciated the principal points at issue. He still seems to be searching for some single pattern of interpretation to which the histories of particular societies can be seen to stand as specimen cases, and in so doing, he overlooks two considerations, both of which have been stressed by various critics.

First, he continues to leave obscure the question of how the identity of a given civilization is to be determined. This is by no means a trivial matter, since in his practice Toynbee has often given the impression of identifying civilizations by reference to the very principles of development which in other places he has claimed to have elicited purely through an empirical survey of their actual careers. He thereby exposes himself to the charge of treating as factual discoveries what are no more than disguised tautologies.

Second, it has been argued that insofar as the term suggests an explanatory device capable of rendering intelligible a certain range of phenomena, Toynbee's references to models in the context cited are misleading. To maintain that a number of other societies have tended to follow a path significantly similar to the course taken by a selected specimen is by itself to explain nothing; at best, it is to point out that there is something *requiring* explanation— namely, the existence of the similarities in question. But although such an objection has force, Toynbee has, in fact, attempted to account for the correlations he believes himself to have discovered. He is not, as some have alleged, content simply to enumerate like instances and has always taken the problem of seeking explanations seriously. Thus, when trying to account for the disintegration of civilizations, he has invoked such notions as the "intractability of institutions" and the "nemesis of creativity," as well as pointing to the development of "internal" and "external" proletariats and of "dominant," as opposed to "creative," minorities. Whether the explanations he has sought to provide are plausible or convincing is, of course, another matter. Frequently, they seem to involve an appeal to laws too vague to afford adequate support, and at other times Toynbee enlists the services of highly dubious or irrelevant analogies. He also tends to treat literary or folk myths as if they in some way gave evidential backing to his generalizations.

Order or chaos. In defending his position, Toynbee has frequently attacked what he calls "antinomian historians," upholders of "the dogma that in history no pattern of any kind is to be found." He has argued that to deny the existence of patterns is implicitly to deny the possibility of writing history, for patterns are presupposed by the whole system of concepts and categories a historian must use if he is to talk meaningfully about the past.

But patterns of what sort? Toynbee sometimes implies that it is essential to choose between two fundamentally opposed views. Either history as a whole conforms to or manifests some unitary order and design, or else it is a "chaotic, disorderly, fortuitous flux" which defies intelligible interpretation. As examples of the first he cites the "Indo-Hellenic" conception of history as "a cyclic movement governed by an Impersonal Law" and the "Judaeo-Zoroastrian" conception of it as governed by a supernatural intellect and will. A combination of these ideas appears to underlie Toynbee's own picture of the human past as it finally emerges in *A Study of History*, particularly in the later volumes, where the suggestion that the rise and fall of civilizations may be susceptible to a teleological interpretation is explicitly put forward.

It would seem, however, that Toynbee has posed his dilemma in altogether too simple terms. There are a number of familiar ways in which historians may be said to reduce the material of history to order and coherence, none of which involves the acceptance of all-embracing beliefs regarding the historical process as a whole of the type he instances. Of course, if the notion of the intelligibility of the past is initially defined in a manner that presupposes the validity of such beliefs, it is possible to accuse historians who deny that it is necessary or even legitimate to adopt them of making nonsense of their subject. But why, it may be asked, should such a stipulation be accepted?

Repudiation of older schemes. In fact, Toynbee does not really intend to advance so exclusive a claim. He does not deny that historians may be able to make sense of particular segments of human history without being committed to universalistic positions of the sort mentioned, imperfect and incomplete though such explanations must ultimately be judged to be. He does, however, strongly suggest that the piecemeal approaches and categories of traditional history leave much to be desired, applying to them terms like "archaic," "infantile," and "crude." Here, possibly,

lies the true source of his objections to "antinomianism." He wishes to condemn the old structures and clichés, the worn axioms unconsciously assumed in conventional historical thought. In particular, he is critical of the lines along which historians have been prone to cut up the past, both geographically and temporally. He distrusts the artificial cohesion they have projected into certain periods through the use of comprehensive simplifying labels like "the Renaissance" and "the Middle Ages," and he questions the unity and self-sufficiency implicit in their conception of "European history."

It is, of course, perfectly acceptable to appraise and seek to revise the conceptual schemes of previous historians in the light of fresh empirical knowledge and discoveries, but it is quite another thing to propound a general theory of historical development which appears in its final form to rely heavily upon extrahistorical considerations and preconceptions of a metaphysical or religious kind. Toynbee has perhaps never sufficiently appreciated the force of this distinction; even so, it would be churlish not to recognize the imaginative fertility, the sheer inventiveness, which is so marked a feature of his system, whatever its shortcomings in other respects. *A Study of History* is rich in methodological suggestions and contains a profusion of original interpretative concepts and frameworks. Whether any of these will be found of value by future historians or social scientists remains to be seen.

Freedom and law in history. A word may be said about Toynbee's views regarding the future of Western civilization and their relation to his general theory. He frequently speaks as if Western society were in an advanced state of breakdown; at the same time he repeatedly shows himself unwilling to draw the conclusion that it is in fact doomed to final disintegration, and he speaks of the possibility of a "reprieve" granted by God. The "determinism" implicit in his thought when he is seeking to apply "the scientific approach to human affairs" tends thus to conflict with the "libertarian" principles to which he claims to subscribe when discussing the nature of human actions and which are connected with his own metaphysical and religious beliefs. The later volumes of the *Study* display a persistent uneasiness over this apparent contradiction, yet it cannot be said that the efforts he has made in these volumes to reconcile the roles of law and freedom in history have proved satisfactory. Rather, they serve to highlight the logical difficulties that had already revealed themselves at earlier stages in Toynbee's work.

Works by Toynbee

A Study of History, 12 vols. Oxford, 1934–1961.
A Study of History: Abridgment of Volumes I–X, D. C. Somervell, ed. Vols. I–VI, Oxford, 1946; Vols. VII–X, 1957.
Civilisation on Trial. Oxford, 1948.
An Historian's Approach to Religion. Oxford, 1956.

Works on Toynbee

Dray, W. H., "Toynbee's Search for Historical Laws." *History and Theory,* Vol. 1 (1960), 32–54.
Geyl, Pieter, *Debates With Historians.* London, 1955.
Montagu, Ashley, ed., *Toynbee and History: Critical Essays and Reviews.* Boston, 1956.
Samuel, Maurice, *The Professor and the Fossil: Some Observa-*

tions on Arnold J. Toynbee's "A Study of History." New York, 1956. A criticism of Toynbee's views on the Jews.

Trevor-Roper, H. R., "Arnold Toynbee's Millenium [*sic*]," in his *Men and Events.* New York, 1957.

Walsh, W. H., "Toynbee Reconsidered." *Philosophy*, Vol. 38 (1963).

PATRICK GARDINER

TRACY, DESTUTT DE. See DESTUTT DE TRACY, ANTOINE LOUIS CLAUDE, COMTE.

TRADITIONALISM

TRADITIONALISM was a philosophy of history and a political program developed by the Counterrevolutionists in France. It was ultramontane in politics and antiindividualistic in epistemology and ethics.

It was the common belief of both those who favored the French Revolution and those who opposed it that the revolution was prepared by the *philosophes.* Voltaire and Rousseau were invoked by both parties as having been either the initiators of much-needed reforms or the corrupters of youth. The intellectual differences among the *philosophes* were minimized. The Revolutionary party believed that Voltaire and Rousseau were the leaders of two schools of thought, both of which removed the seat of authority from the group—society or the nation or the church —to the individual, and that the two schools disagreed only on the question of whether authority was vested in the reason or in feeling (*sentiment*). The Voltairians were said to be individualistic rationalists; the Rousseauists individualistic sentimentalists. In short, the Voltairians were supposed to believe that any individual, by the use of reason alone, could reach all attainable truth in any field; the Rousseauists, that one had only to look into his "heart" to achieve the same result. Oversimplified as this was as history, it was common belief.

The philosophy of Comte Joseph de Maistre (1753–1821) and of his alter ego, Vicomte de Bonald (1754–1840), was developed in conscious reaction to individualism. De Maistre and Bonald were rationalistic, but they maintained that the reason to be trusted was that of the group, not that of the individual. The common reason, like the common sense, was lodged in a superindividual being, manifested in tradition and expressed in language. The superindividual being was the Roman Catholic church, the authority of which was binding not only on its avowed members but on all men. The church alone had direct access to the source of truth (God) and for 1,800 years had remained steadfast and unshaken in its dogmas. Since truth must be one and everlasting, the traditionalists were persuaded by a simple conversion of the proposition that where there was a single and everlasting set of ideas, it must be true. "No human institution has lasted eighteen centuries," de Maistre wrote in *Du Pape* (3 vols., Lyons, 1821). Therefore, he inferred, the church must be superhuman or divine.

Human nature can be understood only by seeing humanity as an integral part of the church. The human individual is but a fragment of a whole. He is completely dependent on society for his bodily welfare and even for his thoughts, for his thoughts are internal speech, and no language is either that of a single individual or created by an individual. Combating the theory that language was invented, de Maistre argued, as Rousseau and Thomas Reid had done before him, that thought is required for invention and language must therefore have existed before it could be invented. Language is the thought of the race expressing itself. It is also rational—we cannot express emotions and sensations linguistically. We speak our thoughts; we speak *of* our feelings and emotions. Since the traditionalists were French, they turned to the history of France for their evidence and found it in the antiquity of the Capetian dynasty, founded, in their view, by Louis the Pious in the ninth century, if not by Charlemagne; in the genesis of French from Latin; and in the primacy of Catholicism in France, which was converted from paganism by Dionysius the Areopagite, the first pagan to be converted by St. Paul.

The supremacy of the pope in both religious and secular affairs was emphasized by de Maistre. Although there might be two swords, the spiritual and the temporal, the latter was wielded, in the language of Boniface VIII, at the pleasure and sufferance of the priest (*ad nutum et patientiam sacerdotis*). This factor of the traditionalists' teachings led to ultramontanism, which, when vigorously preached by Lamennais in the nineteenth century, was condemned by the pope.

Another type of traditionalism was espoused by Pierre Simon Ballanche (1776–1847). In his major work, *Palingénésie sociale* (1827–1829), Ballanche developed a philosophy of history based on man's fall from primordial innocence. However, he maintained that there could be steady progress toward universal rehabilitation. In upholding the possibility of human progress, Ballanche differed from Bonald and de Maistre, for whom time and change, variety and multiplicity, were inherently evil. To Ballanche they were the only condition of redemption. He was convinced of the ultimate perfection of mankind, at which time all that is potential in the human essence would be realized. All men were to be rehabilitated, regardless of their present merits. There was no eternal hell. Even religion would progress, in that God would reveal its truths bit by bit as man became worthy of receiving them. Each man would have to make himself worthy by listening to his heart, an appeal to personal interpretation that was considered heretical.

Although Ballanche agreed with Bonald and de Maistre that the understanding of history could come only from seeing the designs of God in every historical event, he did not believe that government should be theocratic. On the contrary, the two swords must be wielded by two separate powers. The secular power, however, should not be in the hands of the people; they should be permitted to voice their aspirations only so that the sovereign might accept them.

It remained for Félicité Robert de Lamennais (1782–1854) to carry traditionalism to its logical conclusion. Beginning with the strictest form of ultramontanism, he developed into a heresiarch, never realizing that he was moving away from the course of reason. If the pope was the head of the church and the church was superior to the state, then the pope should be recognized as the one sovereign and autonomous being on earth. The sole test of certitude, Lamennais maintained, lay in the racial reason, and this collective reason was tradition. Tradition gives society its unity, and its unity fosters civilization. However, society to Lamennais was not France; it was humanity. And since civilization was Catholicism, national boundaries were artificial and should be eliminated except for practical purposes. The common sense of mankind, in which he believed as did the Stoics, was nothing that could be substantiated by the reason. It was the reason. One must submit to tradition in order to avoid the divisive effects of sectarianism. When the state put obstacles in the way of such submission, then rebellion was legitimate. However, this involved freedom of conscience, of the press, and of education, if it was to be practiced. It was at this point that Gregory XVI in his encyclical *Mirari Vos* intervened to silence Lamennais.

Traditionalism as a body of doctrine was condemned in 1855 in a decretal against Augustine Bonnetty (1798–1879), a priest. The theory directly condemned was the *fidéisme* of the Abbé Bautain (1796–1867), which Bautain had retracted in 1840. Since the identity of reason, common sense, and tradition demanded prerational assertions, faith seemed to be the only thing left to which the traditionalist might appeal. However, this raised faith to a position above that of reason, contrary to the doctrine of the church. The rationalistic position of the church was confirmed at the third session of the Vatican Council in 1870.

Bibliography

Ballanche, Pierre Simon, *Oeuvres complètes*, 4 vols. Paris, 1830. See especially *Palingénésie sociale* (first published in 2 vols., Paris, 1827–1829); *Le Vieillard et le jeune homme* (first published Paris, 1819); *Vision d'Hébal* (first published Paris, 1831).

Boas, George, *French Philosophies of the Romantic Period.* Baltimore, 1925. Ch. 3.

Denziger, Heinrich, *Enchiridion Symbolorum et Definitionum*, 13th ed. Freiburg, 1921. No. 1613 *et seq.*; No. 1649 *et seq.*

Ferraz, Marin, *Histoire de la philosophie en France au XIXe siècle: Traditionalisme et ultramontanisme.* Paris, 1880.

Gunn, J. Alexander, *Modern French Philosophy.* London, 1922. Ch. 7.

Laski, Harold, *Authority in the Modern State.* New Haven, Conn., 1919. On the condemnation of traditionalism.

GEORGE BOAS

TRAGEDY. Philosophers from Aristotle to the present day are almost unanimous in subscribing to the doctrine that the term "tragedy" denotes a class of works of art, distinguishable from all other classes, whose members possess certain common properties by virtue of which they are tragic and, hence, that these properties are necessary and sufficient, essential, or defining properties of tragedy; that without a definition of tragedy, critical discourse about particular tragedies cannot be shown to be either intelligible or true; and, consequently, that the major task of a philosophy of tragedy is to provide such a theory. Literary critics and writers of dramatic tragedies who theorize about tragedy, such as Dryden, Corneille, Racine, and Arthur Miller, concur with philosophers in this doctrine.

Is there a theory (a poetics, true statement, or real definition) of tragedy? Can there be such a theory? Need there be such a theory in order to guarantee the intelligibility of critical talk about why X is tragic or whether X is tragic? These shall be our focal questions in examining the major historical theories of tragedy.

ARISTOTLE

"Tragedy, then, is an imitation of an action that is serious, complete, and of a certain magnitude; in language embellished with each kind of artistic ornament, the several kinds being found in separate parts of the play; in the form of action, not of narrative; with incidents arousing pity and fear effecting the proper purgation of these emotions" (*Poetics*, 1449B; Butcher translation).

Aristotle's definition is the most famous ever given, and the major part of the *Poetics* is an explication of it. First, Aristotle states that tragedy is a mode or species of imitation which differs from the other modes of poetic imitation (comedy, epic, dithyramb, and music) in that it imitates the actions of men who are better than or like us, and that it imitates by means of language, rhythm, and harmony, in the medium of representation.

Aristotle, however, does not define "imitation" (*mimesis*), which is the genus of tragedy. Exegetes of Aristotle dispute its meaning: "replica," "reproduction," "ideal representation," "re-creation," among others, have been suggested. But the only meaning, vague as it is, which seems warranted by the *Poetics*, especially by the discussion of the origin of poetry in man's instinct to imitate, is that imitation is the creation of a likeness which is not necessarily an exact copy.

"Action" is not defined either. All that seems clear is that it implies personal agents with distinctive qualities of character and thought, and that it has to do with what men do and suffer. By "serious action" Aristotle means a passage, which is necessary or probable, from happiness to misery and which is worth while; it is not an action that necessarily ends unhappily or in death.

"Action" leads to "plot," which is one of the central concepts of the *Poetics*, yet one that is not even articulated in Aristotle's explicit definition of "tragedy." By "plot" Aristotle means the arrangement of the incidents of the story. Fundamentally, plot is an imitation of the action. As such, it is central to tragedy, more important than the other qualitative or formative elements: characters, thought, diction, melody, and spectacle. According to Aristotle, plot is the most important element of tragedy because (1) it imitates what in life is most important for tragedy, namely, the actions of men or the passage from happiness to misery; (2) because it induces pity and fear and the tragic effect, purgation; and (3) because it may contain (as the best tragedies do) the most powerful elements of emotional interest in tragedy, namely, reversal of the situation (*peripeteia*) and recognition (*anagnorisis*).

Neither "pity" nor "fear" is defined. All Aristotle says is that pity is aroused by unmerited misfortune, and fear by the misfortune of one like ourselves. "Reversal of the situation" denotes a change of the action to its opposite, as in *Oedipus Rex*, in which the messenger attempts to cheer Oedipus and instead produces the opposite effect by revealing who Oedipus really is. "Recognition" refers to the change from ignorance to knowledge. The best form of recognition is one that coincides with a reversal of the situation, as in *Oedipus Rex*. Further, there are various kinds of recognition, ranging from "recognition by signs," such as scars or tokens (the least artistic), to "recognition . . . from the incidents themselves" (the most artistic), as is also exemplified in *Oedipus Rex*.

"Purgation" (*katharsis*) is the most debated term in the *Poetics*. Explanations of the term range from expulsion of harmful emotions to purification of them. F. L. Lucas suggests that purgation is the partial removal of excess humors, and thereby the restitution of the passions to a healthy balance which effects the pleasure of emotion relieved (*Tragedy*, pp. 38 ff.). Whatever the exact meaning the term has for Aristotle, the effect of tragedy upon its audience, and hence the function of tragedy, is an intrinsic part of its definition.

The best tragic plots are complete, whole, and of a certain magnitude. Briefly, this means that a good plot has a causally related beginning, middle, and end, and a length that allows the hero to pass, by a series of probable or necessary stages, from happiness to misfortune, or vice versa. Good plots also possess unity—a unity of action, not of the hero and not of time and place. Aristotle says nothing about unity of place, and insofar as time is concerned, he says only that tragedy, unlike epic, tends to confine itself within or nearly within the period of 24 hours. Further, good plots can indicate what may happen as well as what did happen. Indeed, this concern for the possible (provided the possible is probable or necessary) distinguishes poetry from history, making poetry more philosophical and elevated than history. For the statements of poetry are universal, that is, they are about what *A* or *B* will probably or necessarily do, rather than about what *A* or *B* did do. Finally, the worst plots are episodic, that is, they are plots in which the sequences are not probable or necessary.

Character is subordinate to plot. Indeed, tragic plots determine their chief characters. Characters should manifest good moral purpose, act appropriately (for example, men, but not women, should be valorous), be true to life, and be consistent. But in order that the tragedy may achieve the tragic effect, the tragic hero must also be highly renowned and prosperous, although not eminently good or just, and in fact must display some error of judgment or fault (*hamartia*) that causes his misfortune; however, he need not have any vice or depravity as the cause of his downfall. Hence, the tragic plot cannot present a virtuous man brought from prosperity to adversity, nor a bad man proceeding from adversity to prosperity, nor an utter villain being defeated, for none of these inspires pity or fear.

As his explication reveals, Aristotle offers two definitions of tragedy, which he subdivides into tragedy and good tragedy. Every tragedy is an imitation of the passage from happiness to misery and contains the requisite pity and fear, *hamartia,* purgation, thought, melody, representation, and spectacle. Every good tragedy is characterized by all these but has reversal and recognition (together); unity of action; good, appropriate, true, and consistent characters; and a fine use of language, especially metaphor. That Aristotle does offer these two definitions, and hence two sets of criteria for tragedy, can be seen in the fact that, for him, a certain vehicle may be a tragedy even though it has

no reversal, but it cannot be a tragedy if it has no pity and fear.

Is Aristotle's theory true? Does it cover all tragedies, or even the Greek ones? Philosophers and critics after Aristotle challenge his description of Greek tragedy and of tragedy altogether. Critics (for example, H. D. F. Kitto, in *Greek Tragedy*) point out that *hamartia* does not characterize Oedipus or Medea, as it does Creon in *Antigone,* and that awe rather than pity or fear is inspired by *Agamemnon.* Some critics question the priority of plot, the subordination of character to plot, and the denigration of spectacle. They also challenge the concept that *hamartia,* purgation, and the tragic hero as a relatively good man are necessary properties or even members of a disjunctive set of sufficient properties of tragedy, for there are tragedies without *hamartia* or purgation, and tragedies with a wicked hero or an eminently just one. Many critics and philosophers argue that Aristotle's list of formative elements leaves out the essential property of the hero's *areté* (excellence), as well as the elements of conflict, doom, regeneration, spiritual waste, and a just punishment, without which there can be no tragedy. Contemporary writers of tragedy, for example, Samuel Beckett and Eugene Ionesco, perhaps echoing the views of Schopenhauer, even go so far as to suggest through their work that tragedy need have no hero, plot, or imitation of a serious action, but only the bare presentation of the underlying "absurdity" of life.

Aristotle seems to be on safer ground with his list of evaluative criteria. In the sense in which *hamartia,* purgation, the tragic hero, and so forth are challengeable properties of tragedy, Aristotle's criteria of great tragedy—the unity of action, wholeness, completeness and magnitude of plot, consistency of character, and the coincidence of reversal of the situation with recognition—remain intact. "*Oedipus Rex* is a great tragedy because of (among other reasons) its relentless unity of action and plot and its messenger scene of reversal and recognition" is unchallengeable in the way that "*Oedipus Rex* is a tragedy because Oedipus is a relatively good man whose error or frailty leads to his downfall, which induces pity and fear and their purgation" is not unchallengeable. Nevertheless, Aristotle's list of evaluative criteria, brilliant as it is, cannot be said to sum up a real or true definition of great tragedy; his criteria are neither necessary nor sufficient for great tragedy.

MEDIEVAL, RENAISSANCE, AND NEOCLASSIC THEMES

A. C. Bradley, in his celebrated essay "Hegel's Theory of Tragedy" (in *Oxford Lectures on Poetry*), writes, "Since Aristotle dealt with tragedy, and, as usual, drew the main features of his subject with those sure and simple strokes which no later hand has rivalled, the only philosopher who has treated it in a manner both original and searching is Hegel." Accurate as this assessment of Hegel may be, it would be wrong to infer from it that there is little or nothing of philosophical interest written about tragedy from Aristotle to Hegel. For there are original ideas about tragedy in the medieval period as well as ideas derived from the *Poetics* during the Renaissance and neoclassic periods which, because they represent variant uses of the concept of tragedy, are extremely important for philosophy.

The great medieval contribution to the theory of tragedy is the tradition that is reflected in the writings of Boccaccio, Chaucer, and later medieval authors, according to which tragedies are nondramatic narratives such as those in *De Casibus Illustrium Virorum*—stories of the falls of illustrious men. Central in these tales is a total reverse of fortune that comes upon a man of high degree who is in apparent prosperity. Chaucer's monk sums up this medieval notion of the tragic in the *Canterbury Tales*. A tragedy is a story

> Of him that stood in greet prosperitee
> And is y-fallen out of heigh degree
> Into miserie, and endeth wrecchedly.
> (*Canterbury Tales* B, 3165–3167)

Scholarly views about the significance of the fall differ. Lily Campbell, for instance, argues (in *Shakespeare's Tragic Heroes*) that these medieval tales function as *exempla* which, by pointing out man's uncertainty in and possible fall from prosperity, warn all men of the fickleness of fortune, and, by ascribing the cause of the fall to vice, of divine justice in the world. Consequently, for her, medieval tragedy, like all tragedy, not only presents evil but explains it. English Renaissance tragedy, including that of Shakespeare, incorporates this medieval view but also constitutes a shift from the mere presentation of the fall of princes to the justification of evil in the retribution of God against those who bring evil upon themselves in their exercise of passion. Tragedies thus become *exempla* of moral philosophy, admonishing men to attend to the lessons of the consequences of evil in order to avoid ruin and misery. Renaissance theorists of tragedy fused the medieval notion of tragedies as *exempla* with the Aristotelian doctrine of drama as lively imitation, the latter teaching us (delightfully) how not to live.

But Willard Farnham, in *The Medieval Heritage of Elizabethan Tragedy*, interprets the significance of the fall differently. Without acceptance of the world, he claims, there can be no tragedy, only surrender. In spite of their scorn for the world, these medieval tales of the fall of illustrious princes transcend moralizing about man's evil to become absorbed emotionally and sympathetically in the sufferings of these princes. According to Farnham, affirmation of the grandeur of man, not denigration of him, is central to these tales of woe, and it is this affirmation that also characterizes Elizabethan tragedy, as indeed it does all tragedy. Thus, for Farnham, neither medieval nor Renaissance tragedy is an explanation or justification of evil; it is an espousal of life in spite of evil.

Shakespearean and French classical tragedy, along with the ancient Greek, are universally acknowledged as the great moments in the history of dramatic tragedy. Shakespearean tragedy derives in part from the medieval type. The tragedies of Corneille and Racine, however, are partly rooted in Greek drama (and Roman, which was modeled on the Greek) and in an extensive interpretation (or misinterpretation) of Aristotle's *Poetics*.

The *Poetics* was not known in the West until the Italian Renaissance. The first critical edition with a commentary was Francisco Robortello's (1548). From the time of Robortello to that of Coleridge (and later, too) certain views about tragedy, either Aristotelian or those attributed to Aristotle, were vehemently debated. The most notorious issue, of course, concerned the three unities. But imitation, purgation, probability and necessity, and action also figured prominently in the long discussion.

J. C. Scaliger first formulated the three unities of action, time, and place. L. Castelvetro and others repeated them as being necessary for tragedy. But it was the French theorists, and especially Corneille (after *Le Cid*) and Racine, who codified the unities and rendered them sacrosanct in their tragedies. They based the concept that the action of a tragedy must coincide temporally with the performance itself and that it must occur in one place on an interpretation of Aristotle's notions of probability and necessity as verisimilitude—that is, on the way things are likely to work in nature. To create and preserve belief in the action on the stage, strict limitations of time and place must be preserved. The audience cannot be expected to retain belief in the action if it covers years or occurs in many different places.

According to French classical theory, however, the three unities are not the main requirement of tragedy. The stress was laid on imitation of a serious action, which was conceived of as a representation of human action during a particular crisis of duty or honor versus love, or of passion versus will or reason (as in Racine's masterpiece, *Phèdre*). The tragic hero is not so much renowned and prosperous as he is noble, in the quite literal sense of belonging to the nobility. The action is confined to the crisis; no complicated or double plots are tolerated, and no mixture of the serious and the comic is allowed. Nor can there be scenes of violence on the stage. The action also inspires pity and fear and their purgation, which effects both pleasure and moral instruction. Finally, insofar as Aristotle's linguistic embellishments are concerned, only verse, with no prose, can be present.

The fact that these characteristics were considered to be defining properties of all tragedy, and not simply of French or Greek tragedy, can be seen in Voltaire's indictment of the tragedies of Shakespeare—especially *Hamlet,* which Voltaire castigated as a "monstrous farce."

Dryden, Johnson, and Coleridge answered the French theorists by challenging, in effect, their restrictive defining criteria in order to force an enlargement of the concept of tragedy so that it would include Shakespeare. In his *Essay of Dramatic Poesy* (1668), Dryden first paid tribute to the three unities, not because they produce verisimilitude but because they effect an aesthetic unity; then he rejected the three unities, as well as the French conception of serious action, in favor of Shakespearean tragedy, with all its irregularities, mixture of the comic and serious, use of prose, and violation of the rules, on the ground that Shakespearean tragedy possesses a variety whose liveliness pleases as the French, in all its rigidity, does not. Johnson supplemented Dryden's attack by dismissing credibility as being basic to verisimilitude and the two unities of time and place, and argued that delusion, not belief, governs our response to the drama; and in order to justify Shakespeare's irregularities, he substituted truth to nature ("just representations of general nature") for truth to conventional rules. Coleridge ended the debate by rejecting both the French insistence upon the rules and Johnson's notion of delusion. Shakespeare's dramas, he argued at length, have their own unity, which is organic, not mechanical like that of the French tragedies. We respond to these dramas, as we do to all poetry, not with belief or disbelief (delusion) but with the suspension of disbelief that constitutes poetic faith. With Coleridge, the tragedies of Shakespeare enter among the paradigms of tragedy.

HEGEL, SCHOPENHAUER, AND NIETZSCHE

Before Hegel, German critics and philosophers theorized about the nature of tragedy. Lessing conceived of tragedy as fundamentally a revelation and justification of the divine order in the universe, whereas Schiller contended that moral resistance to suffering, not suffering by itself, is primary in tragedy. F. Schlegel emphasized the struggle in tragedy between man and fate which results in man's physical defeat, yet also his moral victory, and A. W. Schlegel insisted upon the ultimately inexplicable character of the tragic in the world. Goethe's brilliant insight that catharsis is best understood as expiation and reconciliation on the part of the hero rather than as purgation on the part of the public should also be noted.

Hegel, Schopenhauer, and Nietzsche proclaimed metaphysical theories of tragedy. Unlike Aristotle, who did not subscribe to any tragic event in the world which is imitated by dramatic tragedy but only to the passage in human affairs from happiness to misery, these three philosophers concur in their basic doctrine that dramatic tragedy depicts and rests upon some tragic fact in the world. For Aristotle, tragedy existed only in art, whereas for these three philosophers, there is tragic art primarily because there is tragedy in life. Hegel makes this explicit in his assessment of the life and trial of Socrates:

> In what is truly tragic there must be valid moral powers on both sides which come into collision; this was so with Socrates. . . . Two opposed rights come into collision, and the one destroys the other. Thus both suffer loss and yet both are mutually justified. . . . The one power is the divine right, the natural morality . . . objective freedom. The other . . . is the right . . . of subjective freedom. . . . It is these two principles which we see coming into opposition in the life and philosophy of Socrates. (*Lectures on the History of Philosophy*)

Hegel. In his most important work on tragedy, *The Philosophy of Fine Art,* Hegel singles out *Antigone* as the best illustration of the dramatic representation of the tragic fact of collision and reconciliation. Two great forces are present in the play: public law and order, and familial love and duty. Both are good, both are integral aspects of a moral society (hence of absolute justice), and both are recognized to be such by Creon and Antigone. But both forces are pushed to their extremes by the protagonists so that they negate each other, thereby violating the absolute nature of justice. And because of this violation, both Creon and Antigone are condemned. Only absolute justice is vindicated.

For Hegel the tragic hero, in drama as in life, is identical with the finite force he represents. Indeed, his tragic flaw consists in this identification, since it renders him one-sided and hence incompatible with the demands of absolute justice. His one-sidedness makes his action and condemnation inevitable.

Dramatic tragedy intensifies, unifies, and embellishes upon the tragic fact, through plot, character, language, and scenic representation. It also produces the requisite pity fear, and purgation. But, Hegel argues, dramatic tragedy excites and purifies us by more than the sufferings of the hero, for our fear and pity are directed ultimately toward the might of absolute justice that rules the world, the comprehension of which brings us the feeling of reconciliation—according to Hegel, the true tragic effect.

All dramatic tragedies share the basic elements of collision and reconciliation. Ancient dramatic tragedy, however, differs from modern tragedy in regard to the modes of conflict and resolution. Because character is subordinate to ethical forces in ancient dramatic tragedy, the conflict is always of two ethical principles, even in *Oedipus Rex,* in which, Hegel strainingly (and obscurely) suggests, the conflict is between what one consciously wants to do and what one unconsciously has done. Resolution, and with it triumphant vindication of the ethical absolute, is achieved either by the downfall of the hero, as in *Antigone;* the surrender or sacrifice of the hero, as in *Oedipus Rex;* the harmonization of interests, as in *Eumenides;* or the reconciliation in the soul of the hero, as in *Oedipus at Colonus.* In modern dramatic tragedy, in which the ethical forces are played down or not present at all, or other forces are at work, and the subjectivity of character is paramount, the conflict centers in the hero himself. He is inwardly torn and thereby destroys himself. *Hamlet,* for example, is tragic not because Hamlet violates morality but because his noble nature prevents him from acting, and this, together with external circumstances, brings about his doom. Pure reconciliation is also played down or eliminated altogether in much modern tragedy. It is present in *Hamlet,* but not in *Richard III,* where it is replaced by "criminal justice"; nor is it to be found in many social tragedies, which create only sadness at misfortune and hence, for Hegel, are not really tragic at all.

Schopenhauer. For Schopenhauer, the tragic fact in the world that is represented by dramatic tragedy, and without which there could be no such art form, is the terrible side of life—"the unspeakable pain, the wail of humanity, the triumph of evil, the scornful mastery of chance, and the irretrievable fall of the just and innocent" (*The World as Will and Idea,* Book III). It is this tragic fact that hints at the nature of the world, the ceaseless and futile strife of the irrational will; it also hints at the only way to escape from the struggle, namely, by the complete renunciation of the will. Man, thus, can overcome the tragedy involved in volition not, as Hegel claims, by a mastery of the dialectic of negation but only by a total surrender of the will to live.

Dramatic tragedy mirrors the tragic fact of life and at the same time projects the way out. By centering on the real tragic flaw, which is not the individual sin of the tragic hero but the original sin of being born at all, it demonstrates that "the representation of a great misfortune is alone essential to tragedy."

Great misfortune is represented in three ways: by a character of extraordinary wickedness, such as Richard III, Iago, Shylock, or Creon in *Antigone,* who authors his own misery; by blind fate, such as that which permeates *Oedipus Rex* or *Romeo and Juliet,* in which chance and error dominate man; and by ordinary, decent characters in ordinary circumstances who hurt each other simply through the ways in which they are juxtaposed with one another. This third kind, exemplified best by Goethe's *Clavigo,* is the greatest dramatic tragedy because it depicts the tragic fact of life as it threatens or is actually experienced by most of us, who are neither monstrous nor placed in extraordinary circumstances. This type of tragedy, Schopenhauer concludes, leaves us shuddering as "we feel ourselves already in the midst of hell."

Nietzsche. For Nietzsche, too, human suffering is basic to tragedy, but in his view it yields neither despair nor resignation, as it did for Schopenhauer, nor can it be overcome by reason and knowledge, as Socrates maintained. It can be transcended, but only by an affirmation of the life force that lies behind it, the belief that "despite every phenomenal change, life is at bottom joyful and powerful" (*The Birth of Tragedy,* vii). It is this affirmation that constitutes the "tragic myth," the fundamental truth about man, without which dramatic tragedy is impossible.

Suffering and affirmation derive from more fundamental forces in the world, (namely, the Dionysian and Apollonian), for nature rests upon the duality of "intoxication" and "dream," of "individuality" and "unification." The world is a constant struggle between the irrational, absurd, and ecstatic, on the one hand, and the rational, intelligible, and harmonious on the other. Dramatic tragedy joins these two forces, and in this process the tragic hero, in spite of his terrible suffering and his fall, affirms his annihilation by accepting his consequent unification with the Dionysian forces.

Thus, dramatic tragedy is a ritualistic affirmation of life. The horrors of human experience are rendered palatable by the principles of artistic order and beauty, as well as triumphant through the necessary destruction of human individuality. In Greek tragedy both the chorus and the hero represent this fusion of the Dionysian and the Apollonian. Apollo is the artistic victor, but Dionysus is the metaphysical one. The serenity traditionally attributed to Greek tragedy, consequently, must give way to the orgiastic joy of man's identification with nature, which is the hidden reality of Greek tragedy.

Dramatic tragedy, as myth and ritual, also includes the spectator. He, too, is part of the pattern of unification with the Dionysian forces. Like the hero and the chorus, he shares in the affirmation of life that is presented in the annihilation of the hero. The tragic effect, therefore, is not purgation, purification, resignation, or detachment but joyful participation in the tragic ritual, which alone offers "metaphysical solace" for our existence in an absurd world.

SOME CONTEMPORARY THEORIES

Theories of tragedy abound in modern thought. Among the influential ones are those of A. C. Bradley, J. W. Krutch, F. L. Lucas, E. M. W. Tillyard, Una Ellis-Fermor,

and Peter Alexander. For Bradley the essence of tragedy, both human and dramatic, is the irretrievable self-waste or destruction of value in the conflict of spiritual forces in the world. Dramatic tragedy involves the requisite action or conflict: a hero who need not be morally good but must be touched by human excellence and who, because of his one-sidedness (tragic flaw), is partly responsible for his inevitable suffering and fall; and the tragic effect, which includes awe and admiration as well as pity and fear. But plot, character, and, of course, dialogue and spectacle are tragic only because they entail or are entailed by the essential self-waste of good, a loss that cannot be ultimately justified or explained.

Krutch, in his jeremiad *The Modern Temper,* denies the possibility of tragedy except in those ages (for example, the Periclean and Elizabethan) when man accepts as real his own nobility and importance in the universe. Tragedy, thus, is not a representation of noble actions but of actions considered to be noble. Without this projection—"the tragic fallacy"—there can be no tragedy. Tragedy may contain calamity, but it must show man's greatness in overcoming it. When calamity becomes an end in itself, thereby inducing misery and despair, as it does in modern tragedy (especially in Ibsen), the term "tragedy" loses its correct meaning, for tragedy cannot denigrate man; it must exalt him.

Lucas defines tragedy as "a representation of human unhappiness which pleases us notwithstanding, by the truth with which it is seen and the fineness with which it is communicated. . . . Tragedy, in fine, is man's answer to this universe that crushes him so pitilessly. Destiny scowls upon him: his answer is to sit down and paint her where she stands" (*Tragedy,* p. 78).

Tillyard distinguishes between three types of tragedies: those of suffering, sacrifice, and regeneration. The tragedy of suffering (such as Webster's *The Duchess of Malfi*) involves the suffering of a strong character who is not greatly responsible for his plight and who protests against it as he reflects upon it and its place in the universe. The tragedy of sacrifice, which is rooted in religion, has for its characters a god, a victim, a killer, and an audience, and for its aim the riddance of a taint on the social organism (as in *Oedipus Rex*). The tragedy of regeneration (such as Aeschylus' *Oresteia*) is one of spiritual renewal after disintegration; it symbolizes the life cycle from birth to destruction that leads to re-creation, and it is the "centrally tragic" (*Shakespeare's Problem Plays,* p. 14).

Una Ellis-Fermor, in *The Frontiers of Drama,* describes tragedy as an interim reading of life between religion, on the one hand, and Satanism, or pessimistic materialism, on the other. Basic to tragedy is the equilibrium of the evil that is observed and the good that is guessed at. Dramatic tragedy includes great strength of emotion, revealed through character, action, and thought, directness of presentation, and catastrophe. What is central, however, is the balance between an intense awareness of pain or evil, which is clearly revealed, and an intuitive apprehension of a transcendent realm of values. This balance is achieved by the chorus and outer action, as in *Agamemnon;* by inner and outer action, as in *Hamlet;* or by form and action, as in *Oedipus Rex.* In each case evil is affirmed, but it is transcended by a higher good which induces exultation, not despair or faith. The balance is destroyed when evil is denied, as in Milton's *Samson Agonistes;* or is seen as remedial, as in Elmer Rice's *The Adding Machine;* or is affirmed as ultimate, as in Marlowe's *Dr. Faustus.* These dramas, therefore, are not really tragedies.

Finally, Peter Alexander, in *Hamlet: Father and Son,* rejects the traditional conception according to which tragedy includes *hamartia* and purgation, and defines tragedy instead as the dramatization and celebration of the virtues of men—their glory, achieved through affliction and calamity. *Areté,* not *hamartia,* therefore, is central. Tragedy includes suffering and calamity, but these need not be created and sustained by human frailty or wickedness. Love, honor, and duty can also effect suffering and catastrophe. Thus, *hamartia* as the tragic flaw that justifies the hero's fall and punishment is not basic or even necessary in tragedy. Nor is catharsis the rational acceptance of the fall of the hero as a result of his tragic flaw; rather, catharsis is an active mastery over life's pain, which is intelligible only if tragedy glorifies human virtues.

Is there, then, a true theory of tragedy? Do any of the critics or philosophers provide a true statement of the necessary and sufficient properties of all tragedies, their common, essential nature, by virtue of which all of them are tragic? Does any formula cover all tragedies—Greek, Elizabethan, French, and modern—without leaving out any of their tragic properties?

The fundamental disagreements among the theorists themselves about the nature of tragedy seriously call into question such a formula, for, as we have amply seen, the theorists disagree not only about the essence of tragedy but even about its necessary properties. Do all tragedies have a hero? Do all tragic heroes possess the tragic flaw? Are all tragic heroes responsible for their fate? Do all of them suffer terribly, fall, and die? Are all touched by greatness? Do all get their just deserts? Do all tragedies commemorate human excellence? Do all end unhappily? Do all stir us deeply? Is the action in all of them inevitable? Are there collision and conflict in all? Do all induce catharsis in any of its numerous senses—purgation, purification, moderation, redemption, active mastery of pain, reconciliation, and so forth—or do all produce any other uniform reaction in their spectators? There is much basic disagreement over all these properties.

Perhaps, as all the theorists imply, the disagreements can be resolved by further examination of dramatic tragedies and of the human situation. But neither of these yields a true theory of tragedy. Research into all existing dramatic tragedies and the probing of their shared properties reveal no essences. What, for example, do *Oedipus Rex, Oedipus at Colonus, Medea, Hamlet, Phèdre, Hedda Gabler, The Weavers,* and *The Three Sisters,* to mention only a very few tragedies, have in common that makes them tragic and distinguishable from other works of art? Perhaps they share some similarities, but no set of necessary and sufficient properties is common to all. Nor will further examination of the human situation furnish us with a theory of tragedy, because there is no tragic fact in the world about which a theory of tragedy could be true or which would corroborate such a theory. There may be

spiritual waste, loss of greatness, suffering, struggle, defeat, *areté,* regeneration, explicable or inexplicable evil, and catharsis. But whether any of these, or a collection of them, is tragic cannot be determined by any investigation. In spite of the enormous effort expended by the great theorists, one cannot but conclude that there is no established true theory of tragedy.

Can there be a true theory of tragedy? It seems that there cannot be, for underlying every theory of tragedy is the assumption that tragedy has a set of necessary and sufficient properties. This assumption is equivalent to the doctrine that the concept of tragedy or the term "tragedy" and its adjectival derivatives have a set of necessary and sufficient conditions for their correct, intelligible use, and this doctrine is false. That it is false has already been disclosed by the logical behavior of the concept of tragedy, whose use has not and cannot have a set of essential conditions of employment.

It is the disagreements among the theorists about the necessary and sufficient properties of tragedy that furnish the clue to the logical behavior of the concept of tragedy and the consequent impossibility of a theory, for these disagreements are not primarily over the application of accepted criteria for the correct use of the concept but over the very criteria themselves. What is central in the disagreements about the theories of tragedy are the debates over which criteria shall determine the correct use of the concept of tragedy.

Tragedy is not definable (in the theory sense of a true, real definition) for another reason, namely, that its use must allow for the ever present possibility of *new* conditions. It is simply a historical fact that the concept, as we know and use it, has continuously accommodated new cases of tragedy, and, more important, the new properties of these new cases. One cannot state the necessary and sufficient conditions for the correct use of a concept whose very use entails the requirement that the concept be applicable to new conditions.

Each theory of tragedy expresses an honorific redefinition of tragedy that restricts the use of the term to a selection from its multiple criteria. It is this selection that gives point and value to all the theories of tragedy, for each serves, through its specific selection, as a recommendation to concentrate upon certain preferred criteria or properties of tragedy that are neglected, distorted, or omitted by other theories. If we attend to these criteria or properties instead of to the unsuccessful attempts of essentialist definitions, we shall have much to learn from the individual theories about what to look for in tragedies as well as how to look at them.

Does criticism need a theory of tragedy in order to give intelligible reasons for any particular drama's being tragic? If so, then discourse about the tragic is unintelligible, since there is not and cannot be such a theory. But such discourse is intelligible; hence, the reasons for describing something as tragic must depend upon something other than a theory. The critic, for example, says, "*Hamlet* is tragic because it has P," whatever P may be; "because it has P" is intelligible not because P is necessary or sufficient for tragedy but because P is a member of an open set of acknowledged (yet debatable) traditional properties or of argued-for new properties of the tragic. The reasons require properties, but none of these properties need be necessary or sufficient; hence, none need depend for its cogency upon a theory of tragedy.

Bibliography

Alexander, Peter, *Hamlet: Father and Son*. Oxford, 1955.

Aristotle, *The Poetics,* translated with a commentary by S. H. Butcher. London, 1911.

Bradley, A. C., *Shakespearean Tragedy*. London, 1904.

Bradley, A. C., *Oxford Lectures on Poetry*. London, 1909.

Campbell, Lily B., *Shakespeare's Tragic Heroes: Slaves of Passion*. Cambridge, 1930.

Castelvetro, Lodovico, *Poetica d'Aristotele vulgarizzata ed esposta*. 1570.

Coleridge, S. T., *Coleridge's Shakespearean Criticism*, T. Raysor, ed., 2 vols. Cambridge, 1930.

Corneille, Pierre, *Examens* and *Discours*. 1660.

Dixon, W. Macneile, *Tragedy*. London, 1929.

Dryden, John, *Essays of John Dryden*, W. P. Ker, ed., 2 vols. Oxford, 1926.

Ellis-Fermor, Una, *The Frontiers of Drama*. London, 1945.

Farnham, Willard, *The Medieval Heritage of Elizabethan Tragedy*. Oxford, 1956.

Goethe, J. W. von, "Nachlese zu Aristoteles Poetik." 1827.

Harrison, Jane, *Themis*. Cambridge, 1912.

Harrison, Jane, *Ancient Art and Ritual*. New York, 1913.

Hegel, G. W. F., *The Philosophy of Fine Art,* translated by F. P. B. Osmaston, 4 vols. London, 1920.

Henn, T. R., *The Harvest of Tragedy*. London, 1956. Contains good summaries of classical theories of tragedy as well as an excellent bibliography.

Johnson, Samuel, *Johnson on Shakespeare*, W. Raleigh, ed. Oxford, 1908.

Kitto, H. D. F., *Greek Tragedy*. London, 1950.

Krutch, J. W., *The Modern Temper*. New York, 1929.

Lessing, G. E., *Hamburgische Dramaturgie*. Hamburg, 1767–1769. Translated by H. Zimmern, with introduction by V. Lange, as *Hamburg Dramaturgy*. New York, 1962.

Lucas, F. L., *Tragedy*, rev. ed. London, 1957.

Margoliouth, D. S., *The Poetics of Aristotle*. London, 1911.

Murray, Gilbert, *The Classical Tradition in Poetry*. Cambridge, 1927.

Nietzsche, Friedrich, *The Birth of Tragedy*, translated by F. Golffing. New York, 1956.

Quinton, A., "Tragedy." *PAS*, Supp. Vol. 34 (1960).

Raphael, D. D., *The Paradox of Tragedy*. Bloomington, Ind., 1960.

Schiller, Friedrich, *Essays Aesthetical and Philosophical*. London, 1916.

Schlegel, A. W., *A Course of Lectures on Dramatic Art and Literature,* translated by J. Black and A. Morrison. London, 1846.

Schlegel, F., *Lectures on the History of Literature, Ancient and Modern,* translated by J. Lockhart. Edinburgh, 1818.

Schopenhauer, A., *The World as Will and Idea,* translated by R. B. Haldane and J. Kemp. New York, 1961.

Tillyard, E. M. W., *Shakespeare's Problem Plays*. London, 1957.

Wellek, René, *A History of Modern Criticism*, Vols. I and II. London, 1955. An indispensable analysis and survey of all the important theories of tragedy from Dryden to Schopenhauer.

MORRIS WEITZ

TRANSCENDENTALISM. See GERMAN PHILOSOPHY; KANT, IMMANUEL; NEO-KANTIANISM; NEW ENGLAND TRANSCENDENTALISM.

TRANSCENDENTAL LOGIC. See KANT, IMMANUEL.

TRESCHOW, NIELS (1751–1833), Norwegian philosopher, defended a monism strongly influenced by Spinoza and Liebniz. Treschow was born at Drammen, Norway. He studied at the University of Copenhagen, where he became a professor in 1803. In 1813 he left Denmark to become the first professor of philosophy at the University of Oslo, but he held the post for only one year before entering government service.

Treschow's philosophical views are based on an idea of the unity of all things and on a concept of God similar to that of Spinoza. However, Treschow wanted to combine the idea of God's immanence, the idea that God is in all things, with the idea of God's transcendence, the idea that God is above all things. God is not the unity of all things but rather that which makes all things into a unity; as such, God is not an abstraction but a real individual, "unchangeable, eternal, and independent" (*Om Gud, Idee- og Sandseverdenen*, Vol. I, p. 81). The nature of God is manifest in our consciousness. God, or the One, "stands in the same relation to the manifold produced by it as does our mind to its thoughts, feelings, and decisions" (*ibid.*, p. 115). Our consciousness "pictures the Absolute One."

In his psychology also, Treschow tried to uphold a Spinozistic view, opposing the Cartesian dualism of soul and body. "Man may indeed be considered composite," Treschow said, but not a composite of soul and body, for these are both different aspects of the same thing as it is a possible object of the inner and outer sense (see *Om den Menneskelige Natur*, p. 11).

Treschow also commented on the problem of universals and individuals. He criticized the tendency of abstract philosophers to give priority to universals and to regard individual things and events as instances and exemplifications of universals. The concrete individual, he held, is prior in existence and in knowledge. Only individuals exist, and universals are merely means toward the recognition and description of individual things. An individual thing cannot be fully grasped, however, since this would involve recognizing what is at the basis of all its various states, the idea which expresses all these states.

Since only individuals are real, universal concepts, or concepts of species of things, are "artificial," and so also is any classification of things into more or less fixed kinds. The "specific nature of man" is in a way a fiction, but man has developed gradually from some animal in which the specifically human dispositions potentially inhered, and the natural history of man is part of the history of the whole of nature. In his philosophy of history Treschow tried to substantiate his claim that man descended from some species of animal. Man's gradual development is due to the interaction of external and internal conditions. The fact that the individual physically and mentally goes through the various phases of the historical development of the species was to Treschow another proof of the primacy of the individual.

Works by Treschow

Gives der Noget Begreb Eller Nogen Idee om Enslige Ting? ("Are There Concepts or Ideas About Particular Things?"). Copenhagen, 1804.

Elementer til Historiens Philosophie ("Elements of the Philosophy of History"). Copenhagen, 1811.

Om den Menneskelige Natur, Især fra Dens Aandelige Side

("Human Nature, Especially Its Mental Aspects"). Copenhagen, 1812. The first Scandinavian work on empirical psychology.

Om Gud, Idee- og Sandseverdenen ("On God and the Worlds of Ideas and Sensations"), 3 vols. Christiania, 1831–1833.

Works on Treschow

Høffding, Harald, *Danske Filosofer* ("Danish Philosophers"). Copenhagen, 1909.

Schmidt-Phiseldech, K., *Niels Treschows Historiefilosofi.* Copenhagen, 1933.

Svendsen, P., *Gullalderdrøm og Utviklingstro* ("The Dream of the Golden Age and the Belief in Evolution"). Oslo, 1940.

Winsnes, A. H., *Niels Treschow. En Opdrager til Menneskelighet* ("Niels Treschow. An Educator to Humanity"). Oslo, 1927.

ANFINN STIGEN

TROELTSCH, ERNST (1865–1923), German theologian and social scientist. Troeltsch was born near Augsburg in Bavaria. He studied Protestant theology at the universities of Erlangen, Göttingen, and Berlin, and after three years as a Lutheran curate in Munich, he returned to the University of Göttingen as a lecturer in theology. He became extraordinary professor at Bonn in 1892, and in 1894 ordinary professor of systematic theology at Heidelberg, a position which he held for 21 years. He also served as a member of the Bavarian upper legislative house. In 1915 he moved to a chair of philosophy in the University of Berlin, serving concurrently as a member of the Prussian Landtag and as undersecretary of state for religious affairs.

Troeltsch contributed to the philosophy and sociology of religion and also to cultural and social history, ethics, and jurisprudence. His work raised in many related fields the much-debated questions of the extent and limitations of the historicosociological method. He played a leading role in the clarification of the conception of historicism and made important contributions to the study of methodology in the historical sciences. By recognizing the impact of sociological and historical thinking on the shaping of modern mentality, Troeltsch became involved in the intractable problems of the relation between absolute ethical and religious values and historical relativity. He remained uncompromisingly sincere in revealing the difficulties of this approach and admitted to not being able to surmount them or to reconcile conflicting results in an all-embracing theory.

Troeltsch's intellectual development was bound up with his recognition of the importance of historical change. He chose theology as the field in which, in his own words, "one had access to both metaphysics and the extraordinarily exciting historical problems." The historical theology devoid of metaphysics of his teacher Albrecht Ritschl stimulated him to radical doubt of the validity of Ritschl's own procedure, although with Ritschl Troeltsch accepted the Kantian primacy and underivative character of the basic structure of human morality. He argued that moral awareness was basic to the human constitution and that it was only during the course of historical development that morality and religion became connected and interdependent. To understand Christian ethics as the supreme manifestation of such historical combination was nevertheless his aim in *Grundprobleme der Ethik* (written 1902; in *Gesammelte Schriften,* Vol. II). Troeltsch was aware of the problems arising from two basic assumptions: (1) the Kantian thesis that the formal necessities and laws of morality are irreducible and (2) the equally basic assumption of materialist ethics that what we study are the manifestations of a grown and growing morality in religious, social, and political consciousness. Thus Kant's formalism changed in Troeltsch's hands from a means of critical analysis to an attempt to provide an ontology of personality. The point of reference for an understanding of the moral person is no longer the will as such, but morality as realizing itself through persons in history.

Troeltsch's major work is *Die Soziallehren der christlichen Kirchen und Gruppen* (Tübingen, 1912, translated by Olive Wyon as *The Social Teaching of the Christian Churches,* London and New York, 1931). It is a collection of many detailed studies in Christian social ethics published earlier in the *Archiv für Sozialwissenschaft und Sozialpolitik,* with new chapters on Calvinism, the sects, and mysticism. The work is unified by the sociological formulation of the entire history of the Christian churches.

It is easy to see how Troeltsch maneuvered himself into what has been described as the "crisis of historicism." For despite his insistence on the formal a priori of morality and the necessity of thinking of some values and norms as transcending historical change and accident, Troeltsch could not avoid the suggestion that the explanation of a given phenomenon can be adequately provided only by an account of its genesis.

Troeltsch faced the problems his position posed for Christian ethics and theology, with their claims to historically unique or historically transcendent values. In *Die Trennung von Staat und Kirche* ("Separation of State and Church") he spoke of the polymorphous truth of the churches. This conception was still present in his later attempts to reconcile the absolutist claims of Christian revelation—which as monomorphous truth belongs strictly to the early church—with the later developments of the three great Christian forms of social expression: the church, the sects, and mysticism.

Troeltsch made reliable and learned contributions to the history of ideas, notably his analysis of the role of Protestantism in the formation of the modern world and his searching studies of the differentiation of Protestantism into Calvinism and Lutheranism with their important differences in ethos. He was in basic agreement with his friend Max Weber, whose theses he summarized and elaborated. His important contributions to the conception of group personalities are generally recognized in sociology, philosophy, and jurisprudence. His work on the great social groups—family, guild, state, and church—owed much to Otto von Gierke's *Genossenschaftsrecht,* but Troeltsch went beyond Gierke's emphasis on corporative formations to a study of their personal aspect.

Troeltsch's political thought emerged from his wide learning in the history of ideas. After World War I he was among those German thinkers who realized that Germany's disastrous estrangement from the West was based on a divergence in political philosophy. He urged a return of German political thinking to the position of the eighteenth-century Enlightenment, before the romantic glorification of the state. He thought that this position was compatible with Western thought, as rooted in Stoic and

Christian ethics with their essential respect for the individual person that grew into the modern democratic idea of the rights of man. Troeltsch made the point that German political thinking had yet to learn from the West not to despise arrogantly the serious possibilities of compromise.

In 1922 Troeltsch collected his writings on the philosophy of history under the title *Der Historismus und seine Probleme* ("Historicism and Its Problems"). Material toward a projected second volume is contained in *Christian Thought, Its History and Application* (London, 1923, Friedrich von Hügel, ed.; published in German under the title *Der Historismus und seine Überwindung*, Berlin, 1924).

Works by Troeltsch

Gesammelte Schriften, 4 vols. Tübingen, 1922–1925. Does not contain all the works.
Vernunft und Offenbarung bei J. Gerhard und Melanchthon. Göttingen, 1891.
Die Absolutheit des Christentums und die Religionsgeschichte. Tübingen, 1902.
Psychologie und Erkenntnistheorie in der Religionswissenschaft. Tübingen, 1905.
Protestantisches Christentum und Kirche in der Neuzeit. Leipzig and Berlin, 1906.
Die Trennung von Staat und Kirche. Tübingen, 1907.
Die Bedeutung des Protestantismus für die Entstehung der modernen Welt. Munich, 1911. Translated by W. Montgomery as *Protestantism and Progress.* London, 1912.
Die Bedeutung der Geschichtlichkeit Jesu für den Glauben. Tübingen, 1911.
Augustin, die christliche Antike und das Mittelalter. Munich, 1915.
Spektator-Briefe, Aufsätze über die deutsche Revolution und die Weltpolitik 1918/1922. Tübingen, 1924.
Deutscher Geist und Westeuropa. Tübingen, 1925.
Vorlesungen über "Glaubenslehre." Munich, 1925.

Works on Troeltsch

Alberca, Ignacio Escribano, *Die Gewinnung theologischer Normen aus der Geschichte der Religion bei E. Troeltsch.* Munich, 1961.
Bodenstein, Walter, *Neige des Historismus, Ernst Troeltschs Entwicklungsgang.* Gütersloh, 1959.
Kaftan, Theodor, *Ernst Troeltsch.* Schleswig, 1912.
Kasch, Wilhelm F., *Die Socialphilosophie von Ernst Troeltsch.* 1963.
Köhler, Walther, *Ernst Troeltsch.* Tübingen, 1941.
Rintelen, Fritz-Joachim von, "Der Versuch einer Überwindung des Historismus bei Ernst Troeltsch." *Deutsche Vierteljahrsschrift,* Vol. 8 (1930), 324–372.
Scheler, Max, "Ernst Troeltsch als Soziologe." *Kölner Vierteljahrshefte für Soziologie* (1923/1924).
Tillich, Paul, "Ernst Troeltsch." *Kant-Studien,* Vol. 29 (1924), 351–358.
Vermeil, Edmond, *La Pensée religieuse d'Ernst Troeltsch.* Paris, 1922.
Wichelhaus, Manfred, *Kirchengeschichtsschreibung und Soziologie im neunzehnten Jahrhundert und bei Ernst Troeltsch.* Heidelberg, 1965.

EVA SCHAPER

TRUTH. See COHERENCE THEORY OF TRUTH; CORRESPONDENCE THEORY OF TRUTH; PERFORMATIVE THEORY OF TRUTH; PRAGMATIC THEORY OF TRUTH.

TRUTH-TABLES. See LOGIC, MODERN; LOGICAL TERMS, GLOSSARY OF.

TSCHIRNHAUS, EHRENFRIED WALTER VON (1651–1708), or Tschirnhausen, German mathematician and physicist, was born in Kieslingswalde, near Görlitz, and became count of Kieslingswalde and Stolzenberg. He studied mathematics at Görlitz and at the University of Leiden, where the Cartesian philosophers Adriaan Heereboord and Arnold Geulincx were teaching. After serving with the Dutch in 1672 during a war with France, Tschirnhaus studied further in Leiden and in Germany, and in 1674 he traveled to London, Paris, Rome, Sicily, and Malta. He met Spinoza in Holland, English scientists in London, and he undoubtedly met Cartesian philosophers and scientists such as Jacques Rohault and Pierre-Sylvain Régis in Paris. Tschirnhaus finally settled down in Kieslingswalde. He established several factories for manufacturing glass and for grinding magnifying glasses, and was associated with J. F. Böttger in the development of Meissen porcelain. Tschirnhaus published various essays on mathematics and optics in the *Acta Eruditorum* from 1682 to 1698, and a philosophical treatise, *Medicina Mentis* (Amsterdam, 1687; 2d ed. revised, Leipzig, 1695; reprinted with introduction by W. Risse, Hildesheim, 1964), on methodology, logic, and theory of knowledge, which also explained some of his geometrical discoveries.

Medicina Mentis followed Tschirnhaus' scientific interests; but some general features of the treatise were derived from Cartesianism, Spinoza, English empiricism, and, in some respects, from Leibniz. Tschirnhaus' "mental medicine" was intended as a method of discovering rational truth as a basis of a happy life. Only true knowledge can tame the passions, which are the source of error and therefore of unhappiness.

Knowledge comes only from the senses, but purely sensible knowledge—which Tschirnhaus called imagination—is passive, approximate, and relative, and must be governed by rigid precepts. Reason abstracts from imagination, producing universal and strict concepts. The intellect considers things "as they exist in themselves"; that is, it penetrates their "real nature" and connects in one whole the real thing and its sensible and abstract representations. Reason operates by analysis, intellect by synthesis.

Only intellectual knowledge can reach truth and be communicated. Falsehood arises when intellect works like imagination. The criterion of truth is "what can be conceived"—that is, ideas insofar as they may be connected or not connected with one another. This criterion does not rest simply on an abstract rule to be applied in each case, but on the possibility of connecting ideas in a comprehensive system. But for Tschirnhaus this system was not, as for the rationalists, a closed and independent cognitive order. He considered the intellectual faculty to be the source of logical truth. But metaphysical truth comes from experience, and it is truth insofar as it has been deduced from experience by reasoning conforming to logical standards, and insofar as it is confirmed "through evident experiments."

Intellectual knowledge operates by elaborating simple concepts, or "definitions"; by deducing simple properties, or "axioms," from them; and by connecting the definitions in all possible ways to produce "theorems." Tschirnhaus held that definition is real. It is a knowledge of causes that enables us to reproduce the object. In its highest stages intellectual knowledge is knowledge of the natural world. Science is a whole, and should conform to the methodological ideal of mathematical clarity. Physics is the foundation of the other sciences. By demonstrating the rationality and necessity of all events, physics leads us to recognize divine providence. Human freedom arises from the command of God.

Although Tschirnhaus' *Medicina Mentis* was quite famous in its own day and its methodology was an important source of Wolff's ideas, it exerted no direct influence on the German Enlightenment.

Bibliography

Campo, Mariano, *Cristiano Wolff e il razionalismo precritico.* Milan, 1939. Vol. I, Part 1, Ch. 2.

Klüger, Richard, *Die pädagogischen Ansichten des Philosophen Tschirnhaus.* Leipzig, 1913.

Kunze, A., "Lebensbeschreibung des E. W. von Tschirnhaus und Wurdigung seiner Verdienste." *Neues Lausitzer Magazin,* Vol. 43 (1866).

Radetti, G., "Cartesianesimo e spinozismo nel pensiero di E. W. von Tschirnhaus." *Rendiconti della Classe di Scienze morali, storiche e filologiche della Accademia Nazionale dei Lincei,* Sec. 6, Vol. 14, Nos. 5 and 6 (1938), 566–601.

Reinhardt, K., *Beiträge zur Lebensgeschichte von E. W. von Tschirnhausen,* Meissen, Germany, 1903.

Verweyen, Johannes, *E. W. von Tschirnhaus als Philosoph.* Bonn, 1906.

Weissenborn, H., *Lebensbeschreibung des E. W. von Tschirnhaus.* Eisenach, Germany, 1866.

GIORGIO TONELLI

TUNG CHUNG-SHU (c. 179–c. 104 B.C.), probably the most influential Confucian scholar of the Han dynasty (206 B.C.–A.D. 220), laid an institutional basis for the Confucian orthodoxy and for the recruitment of able scholars as government officials through the examination system. He was an expert in the Kung-yang commentary of the Confucian classic *Spring and Autumn,* and he gave the classic a new interpretation that combines the ethical and political teachings of Confucius with the supernatural view of the metaphysicians.

After having received the degree of eruditus (*po-shih*) in the Confucian classics, Tung Chung-shu became a public instructor during the reign (156–140 B.C.) of Emperor Ching. It has been recorded that he lectured from behind a curtain, and although he had many students, few were admitted to his presence. He was also said to have been so engrossed in his scholarly pursuits that for three years he did not even once visit his garden. As a result of his responses to the written inquiries addressed to the scholars of the realm by Emperor Wu (reigned 140–87 B.C.), Tung Chung-shu attracted imperial notice and was appointed minister successively to two royal princes. However, he was not successful in his political career and spent the remaining years of his life in teaching and writing. In addition to his several memorials to the throne, he is known for his work on the *Spring and Autumn,* entitled *Ch'un-ch'iu Fan-lu* ("Copious Dew in Spring and Autumn"), a curious admixture of moral and metaphysical essays in 17 chapters. He had numerous followers and his influence lasted well beyond his lifetime.

Tung Chung-shu's main contribution as a Confucian philosopher lies in his study of the *Spring and Autumn* which, according to him, teaches "compliance with Heaven's will and imitation of the ancients." To do so is "for the people to follow the sovereign, and for the sovereign to follow Heaven." Thus, the basic principle in government is to subject the people to the sovereign's domination, and the sovereign to Heaven's will. In Tung's concept, Heaven (*T'ien*) is not the all-mighty anthropomorphic god of the ancient Chinese but the physical universe itself. Somewhat akin to the Western concept of nature, it is nevertheless endowed with intellect and purpose. The ruler, as Heaven's representative on earth, should administer his kingdom in accordance with Heaven's will. As Heaven is inherently good and benevolent, so should the sovereign be. His virtuous rule will be marked by order and harmony in the universe. On the other hand, any evil act of his will cause catastrophes (such as floods and fires, earthquakes and mountain slides) and anomalies (such as comets, eclipses, and the growing of beards on women) sent by Heaven as a warning to men. "The origin of catastrophes and anomalies," he wrote in "Copious Dew," "is traceable to misrule in the state. First, Heaven sends catastrophes to admonish the people. When this goes unheeded and no changes are made, Heaven would then frighten the people with prodigies. If men are still unawed, ruin and destruction will finally befall the empire."

Although he was an avowed monarchist, Tung Chung-shu's strange science of the catastrophes and anomalies had the effect of curbing misgovernment on the part of the ruler. The idea has so embedded itself in the minds of the Chinese people that even in more enlightened and rational times, Confucian scholar-officials found Tung's concept useful as a means of remonstrance against the ruler's misuse of despotic power. But Tung Chung-shu is chiefly remembered today for his historical role in exalting Confucianism as China's official state doctrine, which was to mold the nation for more than two thousand years from the Han dynasty to the present age.

Bibliography

Tung Chung-shu's *Ch'un-ch'iu Fan-lu* ("Copious Dew in Spring and Autumn") is available in Chinese in the Szu-pu Pei-yao edition (Shanghai, 1935).

For literature on Tung Chung-shu, see Wing-tsit Chan, *A Source Book in Chinese Philosophy* (Princeton, N.J., 1963), pp. 271–288, which contains an introduction and selections in English translation. See also Fung Yu-lan, *A History of Chinese Philosophy,* translated by Derk Bodde, 2 vols. (Princeton, N.J., 1952–1953), Vol. II, pp. 7–87.

LIU WU-CHI

TURGOT, ANNE ROBERT JACQUES, BARON DE L'AULNE (1727–1781), French statesman, economist, and philosopher of history. Born in Paris, Turgot began formal theological training in 1743, anticipating a career in the church. As a young scholar at the Sorbonne (1749–1751) he showed brilliant promise in several writings on the philosophy of history. In 1752 he left the service of religion to become a magistrate, and from 1753 to 1761 he fulfilled the legal and administrative duties of a master of requests. His writings in this period included contributions to the *Encyclopédie* in metaphysics, linguistics, science, economics, and political theory, as well as short writings over a similarly broad range of fields, but his contemplated major work on the history of human progress never materialized. From 1761 to 1774 he served as the enlightened intendant (royal administrator) of Limoges; in this period and later, economic subjects predominated in his writings. Appointed minister of marine by Louis XVI in 1774, he was very shortly afterward transferred to the crucial position of comptroller general of finance. In this post Turgot instituted economies, corrected abuses in the taxation system, established free grain trade within France, and suppressed the guilds and the labor services. Opposition at court and in the Parlement of Paris, and the withdrawal of royal support, led to his resignation after twenty months (1776), thus ending the last attempt at thoroughgoing reform of the *ancien régime* in France before the Revolution.

Economic and social theories. Turgot's economic theories are expressed most fully in his *Réflexions sur la formation et la distribution des richesses* (1766, published serially 1769–1770; translated as *Reflections on the Formation and the Distribution of Riches*, New York, 1898). In this and other works his basic principles are essentially physiocratic: the sole ultimate source of wealth is land, and only the growth and the unhindered flow of capital can create prosperity. Assuming that the French economy would continue to be largely agrarian, Turgot advocated a gradual simplification and moderation of taxation, looking toward the day when only landowners would be taxed, on the basis of a careful assessment of their profits, and when restrictions and impositions upon commerce and industry might be altogether abolished.

Turgot's general political thought, based on a belief in paternalistic, enlightened monarchy, is of less interest than his two *Lettres à un grand vicaire sur la tolérance* ("Letters to a Grand Vicar on Toleration," 1753, 1754; in *Oeuvres*, Vol. I) concerning governmental toleration of religion. In these letters he defended a broad toleration of different faiths but maintained that the state may offer special protection to the "dominant" or most numerous religion, as a useful guide to men in their uncertainties. He nevertheless held that some sects—those too rigid, irrational, morally or socially burdensome, or politically subversive—are not worthy of such protection, but should simply be tolerated; Roman Catholicism, he noted, might be considered by some to be such a sect. The dogma of infallibility is dangerous if it is false, and "it is certainly false or inapplicable when the exercise of infallibility is confided to those who are not infallible, that is to princes and governments" (*Oeuvres*, Vol. I, p. 425). Intolerance, unworthy of a gentle and charitable Christianity, must in any case be eradicated, for the rights of society are not greater than those of individuals, and individual conscience is no proper concern of government.

Philosophy of history. To the philosopher, Turgot's importance may well derive from his early writings on the theory of history, notably his *Tableau philosophique des progrès successifs de l'esprit humain* ("Philosophic Panorama of the Progress of the Human Mind," 1750; in

Oeuvres, Vol. I), and his "Plan de deux discours sur l'histoire universelle" ("Plan of Two Discourses on Universal History," c. 1750; in *Oeuvres,* Vol. I). Upon the basis of contemporary psychological sensationalism, and with a nod to Providence, Turgot constructed a broad theory of human progress reflecting past theories and foreshadowing later ones.

In contrast to the phenomena of the world of nature, trapped in unprogressive cycles of birth and death, Turgot postulated the infinite variability and indeed the perfectibility of mankind. In the past and in the future, as knowledge and experience accumulate, man's reason, passions, and freedom permit him to escape from the repetitive cycles of external nature. Movement and change give rise to new relationships, and thus all experience is instructive; even passion and error, calamity and evil providentially contribute to mankind's advance. Indeed, the ambitions and the vices of men and the barbarities of warfare, however morally reprehensible, may often rescue mankind from stagnation or mediocrity.

The vital medium of progress, wrote Turgot, is the process of human communication. Ideas deriving from sensations are developed through the use of signs, pictures, and especially language, by which knowledge and experience are transmitted and augmented from generation to generation. Since above all it is the man of genius who can grasp the implications and make articulate the lessons of experience, it is society's duty to encourage natural genius and to heed its advice. "Moral" circumstances, such as the cultivation of genius, are more important in determining the extent and nature of progress than are such physical circumstances as climate.

Progress is uneven throughout man's history. Moreover, it varies necessarily in the different areas and aspects of human activity, such as science, technology, morality, and the arts. Progress in the arts, for example, is always radically limited by the nature of man himself, since the goal of the arts is pleasure alone, whereas speculative scientific knowledge can be as infinite as the natural universe. And each area of activity has its own rules of progress. In his discussion of scientific progress, Turgot suggested three historical stages of development (anticipating Auguste Comte's system): the anthropomorphic or supernatural, the abstract or speculative, and the empirical–mathematical.

For Turgot the broad tempo of progress was increasing in the mid-eighteenth century; indeed, despite instances of momentary or partial decadence, any wholesale retrogression of mankind was now impossible. Surely, he wrote, the general momentum of science, buttressed by mathematics, was irreversible. Yet Turgot, especially in his later years, had frequent doubts, and he was well aware of the forces of error and evil in the world, both in the past and in the happier future. The historical continuity so much stressed in his writings in fact ruled out any immediate, thorough renovation of mankind. Certainly the future would not bring the radical break with a deplorable past that was intimated in the thought of many another writer of the Enlightenment. Because the element of empiricism was seldom wholly absent in Turgot, his historical thought, although undoubtedly optimistic, was never unreservedly utopian.

Bibliography

Turgot's works were published as *Oeuvres de Turgot et documents le concernant,* Gustave Schelle, ed., 5 vols. (Paris, 1913–1923).

For literature on Turgot, see Douglas Dakin, *Turgot and the Ancien Régime in France* (London, 1939), which has an extensive bibliography; Edgar Faure, *La Disgrâce de Turgot* (Paris, 1961), which also has an extensive bibliography; and Frank E. Manuel, *The Prophets of Paris* (Cambridge, Mass., 1962), Ch. I, pp. 11–51.

HENRY VYVERBERG

TWARDOWSKI, KAZIMIERZ (1866–1938), had a twofold role in the recent history of philosophy. He had a decisive influence on Polish philosophy in the twentieth century; and at the turn of the century he contributed to the transformation of European philosophy in its search for new, intellectually responsible methods of philosophical inquiry. His conception of philosophy and his specific contributions to epistemology, philosophical psychology, and theory of science helped to pave the way for the emergence of phenomenology and of some forms of analytic philosophy.

Twardowski was born in Vienna. He studied philosophy at the University of Vienna, where he came under the influence of Franz Brentano. In 1892 he received a Ph.D. degree from the university and became a lecturer there in 1894. In 1895 he was appointed to a chair of philosophy at the University of Lwów, where he taught until 1930.

Like Brentano, he wanted philosophy to be scientific, which to him meant a rejection of grandiose but nebulous speculation, an unrelenting war on conceptual confusion and linguistic obscurity, and a painstaking analysis of clearly defined problems, which through elimination of conceptual sloppiness, leads to empirically verifiable conclusions. No wholesale condemnation of metaphysics was intended by these methodological injunctions. Nevertheless, Twardowski was increasingly aware of the boundary beyond which the method of philosophy, as conceived by him could not reach and beyond which a philosopher qua philosopher should remain silent.

More specifically, the basic philosophical science, avoiding both irresponsible speculation and skepticism, was to be the Brentanist "descriptive psychology," understood as a sort of empirical inquiry, but distinct from experimental psychology. Twardowski, however, went well beyond Brentano and contributed to the demise of psychologistic accounts of meaning and of psychologism in general. In an early and influential book, *Zur Lehre vom Inhalt und Gegenstand der Vorstellungen,* Twardowski introduced a sharp distinction between the mental act, its content, and its object. The distinction between content, which is mental and a part of a person's biography, and object, which is not, was overlooked by Brentano and the early Meinong but became crucial for Twardowski and led him to a general theory of objects of thought. These ideas influenced Meinong, Husserl, and to some extent Schlick, and through them much of early twentieth-century philosophy. The difficulties of Twardowski's theory of objects, with its attending danger of overpopulating the Platonic heaven, led later to Stanisław Leśniewski's "ontology" and Tadeusz Kotarbiński's "reism." Twardowski's conclusions, far from supporting psychologism, implied a sharp separation of logic and philosophy from psychology. Moreover, the actual procedure of this "psychological investigation" did not look much like psychology either. Phenomenologists have seen in it the germ of the ideas which reappeared both in the later Husserl and in the realist branch of phenomenology. Up to a certain point, it is equally plausible to construe Twardowski's contributions as an early attempt to develop a philosophical psychology, in the sense of an examination of the logical geography of mental concepts.

Twardowski's later work included a further analysis of mental concepts; the formulation of a nonpsychologistic and non-Platonizing account of logic, based on the distinction between acts and their products; the extension of a similar line of reasoning to a general theory and classification of the sciences; and an examination, on several occasions, of various methodological issues of psychology. This included a critique of reductive materialism, and a defense of introspection as a source of knowledge. One of his most influential works, "O tak zwanych prawdach względnych," was a lucid critique of relativism.

A strong sense of the scholar's social responsibilities, heightened by the special circumstances of Polish history, led Twardowski to devote more and more time to educational activities, to the detriment of his own work, but to the lasting benefit of Polish philosophy.

As a teacher, Twardowski transformed Polish philosophy and endowed it with a distinct style. He did not preach any particular *Weltanschauung,* and his influence—not unlike that of G. E. Moore—was due less to his specific doctrines than to his way of doing philosophy, his qualities of character, his intellectual integrity, and the impact of his personal example. The school that he created was not linked by a common allegiance to any philosophical creed, but rather by a common acceptance of rigorous standards of professional excellence. Most of his pupils went their own independent ways, representing a wide spectrum of philosophical opinion, but they never ceased to express their gratitude to him. The best-known among them, Jan Lukasiewicz, Leśniewski, Kazimierz Ajdukiewicz, and Kotarbiński, differed from Twardowski methodologically in their emphasis on the philosophical relevance of symbolic logic. Twardowski's influence, transmitted by his numerous students—philosophers and nonphilosophers—went far beyond academic circles and, fostering the ethos of free and responsible inquiry in all areas of intellectual life, became a significant factor in the history of Polish culture.

Twardowski organized the teaching of philosophy in Poland, initiated regular meetings of philosophers, founded the first Polish psychological laboratory (1901), the Polish Philosophical Society (1904), and in 1911 the quarterly journal *Ruch Filozoficzny,* which he edited until his death. In 1935 he became the chief editor of *Studia Philosophica,* a periodical publishing works of Polish philosophers in foreign languages. He was also active as the editor of several different series of original works and translations, many of them inspired by him, such as Władysław Witwicki's masterful translations of Plato.

Works by Twardowski

Idee und Perzeption. Vienna, 1892.

Zur Lehre vom Inhalt und Gegenstand der Vorstellungen. Vienna, 1894.

Wyobrażenia i pojęcia. Lwów, 1898.

"O tak zwanych prawdach względnych," *Księga Pamiątkowa Uniwersytetu Lwowskiego.* Lwów, 1900. Translated into German by M. Wartenberg as "Über sogenannte relative Wahrheiten." *Archiv für systematische Philosophie,* Vol. 8, No. 4 (1902), 415–447.

Zasadnicze pojęcia dydaktyki i logiki. Lwów, 1901.

"Über begriffliche Vorstellungen," in *Beilage zum XVI Jahresbericht der Philosophischen Gesellschaft a. d. Universität zu Wien.* Leipzig, 1903.

O filzofji średniowiecznej. Lwów, 1910.

O metodzie psychologji. Warsaw, 1910.

O czynnościach i wytworach. Cracow, 1911.

O psychologji, jej przedmiocie, zadaniach i metodzie. Lwów, 1913.

Rozprawy i artykuły filozoficzne. Lwów, 1927.

Wybrane pisma filozoficzne, T. Czeżowski, ed. Warsaw, 1965.

Works on Twardowski

Discussions of Twardowski in English include T. Czeżowski, "Tribute to Kazimierz Twardowski on the 10th Anniversary of His Death," in *Journal of Philosophy,* Vol. 57 (1960), 209–215; T. Czeżowski, "Kazimierz Twardowski as Teacher," in *Studia Philosophica,* Vol. 3 (1948), 13–17; J. N. Findlay, *Meinong's Theory of Objects* (London, 1938); Roman Ingarden, "The Scientific Activity of Kazimierz Twardowski," in *Studia Philosophica,* Vol. 3 (1948), 17–30; Z. A. Jordan, *Philosophy and Ideology* (Dordrecht, Netherlands, 1963).

A bibliography of writings by and on Twardowski until 1938, compiled by D. Gromska, can be found in *Ruch Filozoficzny,* Vol. 14 (1938), 14–39. Additional bibliography can be found in Z. A. Jordan's book.

GEORGE KRZYWICKI-HERBURT

TYCHE. See MOIRA/TYCHE/ANANKE.

TYNDALL, JOHN (1820–1893), British physicist and natural philosopher, was born in Leighlin Bridge, Ireland. While teaching surveying and mathematics at Queenwood College in Hampshire, he became determined to get a higher education. He went to the University of Marburg in 1848, studied mathematics, physics and chemistry, and obtained his Ph.D. two years later. He experimented on diamagnetism in Germany and returned to Queenwood for two years. In 1853 he was appointed professor of natural philosophy at the Royal Institution. After the death of Michael Faraday in 1867, Tydall became resident professor and superintendent at the institution until his retirement in 1887. He did important research on diamagnetism, glaciers (Tyndall was an accomplished mountaineer and did this work in the Alps), the absorption of radiant heat by gases and vapors, and spontaneous generation. Tyndall showed that some microorganisms were more resistant to heat than had been realized, and he demonstrated in numerous experiments that life could not be generated in a sterilized medium exposed to sterile air.

Tyndall was a competent and original scientist, but his greater fame stemmed from his outstanding success as a lecturer and writer popularizing scientific subjects for lay audiences. In 1874 Tyndall delivered the Presidential Address to the British Association for the Advancement of Science (Belfast Address). This address provoked much public controversy.

Tyndall had been interested in philosophy all his life, and he was much influenced by the work of Fichte. He defended determinism and agnosticism and wrote extensively on questions concerning the mind–body relationship, the problem of the compatibility of science and religion, and other aspects of religious belief. (Three articles on prayer and on miracles are reprinted in *Fragments of Science,* Vol. II.) Many of Tyndall's philosophical ideas are brought together in the Belfast Address, which was both a powerful plea for the freedom of scientific inquiry and a presentation of a naturalistic philosophy. Tyndall began with a thumbnail sketch of the history of thought, stressing the positive role of Greek atomism and the negative influence of the Aristotelian tradition. He then examined Bishop Butler's *Analogy of Religion,* in which the bishop presented arguments for a complete separation of our "living powers," or "ourselves," and our bodies, or "bodily instruments." Arguing from the identity of action, for example, of the eye and eyeglasses, the bishop claimed that "our organized bodies are no more a part of ourselves than any other matter around us." Tyndall imagined a dialogue between a Lucretian and the bishop. The Lucretian queries whether one can form a mental picture of the self apart from the organism and suggests that consciousness is very much dependent on the state of the brain. Tyndall's bishop counters by asking how sensation, thought, and emotion can arise from dead atoms: "Are you likely to abstract Homer out of the rattling of dice, or the Differential Calculus out of the clash of billiard-balls?" How does materialism explain *Vorstellungs-Kraft,* or the ability to conceptualize and the power of the imagination? Tyndall commented, "I hold the Bishop's reasoning to be unanswerable," and he asserted that it is vain to attempt to comprehend the connection between psychic and physical events.

Tyndall surveyed the Darwinian theory of evolution, remarking that it rejects the "notion of creative power" and refers the "choicest materials of the teleologist" to natural causes. To account for the concomitant evolution of mind Tyndall relied on Herbert Spencer's theory of the development of the senses and intelligence through the interaction between organism and environment and on the "hereditary experience theory," according to which constantly experienced relations become automatic in thought ("forms of intuition") and are inherited.

Considering the origin of life in respect to the theory of evolution, Tyndall commented that the idea of the supernatural creation of one or a few primordial forms is as anthropomorphic as the idea of the creation of many. Even though there is no evidence at present for spontaneous generation, one who believes in the continuity of nature must proceed with the "vision of the mind." Tyndall saw life and mind as latent in the cosmos: "By a necessity engendered and justified by science I cross the boundary of the experimental evidence, and discern in that Matter which we, in our ignorance of its latent powers, and notwithstanding our professed reverence for its Creator, have hitherto covered with opprobrium, the promise and potency of all terrestrial life."

At the close of his address Tyndall emphasized that feeling has origins as ancient and as worthy as the origins of intelligence and that religious sentiment, which is "mischievous if permitted to intrude on the region of objective *knowledge,* over which it holds no command," dignifies and completes man in the region of poetry and emotion. Science, which must be free to investigate cosmological questions, is but one of the human activities leading to the whole man. He exhorted his listeners to prefer "commotion before stagnation" and not to "purchase intellectual peace at the price of intellectual death."

The address received a great deal of adverse criticism in the pulpit and the press. In its defense Tyndall wrote two articles which appear in the *Fragments.*

Bibliography

Fragments of Science, A Series of Detached Essays, Addresses and Reviews was published in two volumes (Popular Uniform Edition, New York and London, 1915). These volumes form Vol. I and Vol. II of the *Selected Works of John Tyndall,* 6 vols. (New York and London, 1872 ff.).

The standard biography is A. S. Eve and C. H. Creasey, *Life and Work of John Tyndall* (London, 1945).

ARTHUR E. WOODRUFF

TYPES, THEORY OF. In the spring of 1901, while working on *The Principles of Mathematics,* Bertrand Russell realized that the foundations of mathematics were threatened by the appearance of what he called The Contradiction. Russell's paradox—the name under which The Contradiction later became generally known—was of a logical rather than a mathematical nature and was not related at all, for example, to the paradoxes of the Infinite which had so much concerned Bernard Bolzano. Russell's paradox involved one of the most elementary logical relations, that of class membership. In analyzing Georg Cantor's famous proof that there is no greatest cardinal number, Russell was led to consider classes that were not members of themselves. When he then asked whether the class of all such classes was a member of itself, he was easily able to demonstrate that it *was* a member of itself if and only if it *was not* (see LOGICAL PARADOXES).

While investigating ways of overcoming this paradox that would conform with logical common sense but leave intact as much of mathematics as possible, Russell hit upon the idea that the error in the train of thought leading to The Contradiction was the treatment of classes as being on a par with their members. In particular, classes of individuals are not themselves individuals, and classes of classes of individuals are not themselves classes of individuals. To ask whether a class is a member of itself is a meaningless question, and each of the two grammatically possible answers is a pseudo statement—a sentence which, despite its grammatical form, is neither true nor false. If classes are conceived of as belonging to one and only one type of class in a potentially infinite hierarchy of such types and if the membership of each class is required to be homogeneous, with its type therefore completely determined by any of its members, then The Contradiction disappears.

The idea that not all objects are to be regarded as belonging to one level was, of course, not entirely original with Russell. Among nineteenth-century logicians it had been envisaged by both Gottlob Frege and Ernst Schröder, although neither tried to develop it into a full-fledged theory or, of course, realized its connection with the problem of avoiding the logical paradoxes.

SIMPLE THEORY OF TYPES

The intuitions underlying Russell's theory of logical types seem to be of a definitely ontological character. Nevertheless, Russell has repeatedly insisted that the essence of his theory consists in the fact that not all expressions in a natural language, say English, can replace a given expression in a given significant sentence and preserve the significance of the resulting expression. This is an extraordinary understatement, whether intended or not. The linguistic fact cited by Russell may indeed be taken in a sense as the basis for theories of syntactical and semantical categories (see CATEGORIES; SYNTACTICAL AND SEMANTICAL CATEGORIES). But a "theory of logical types," as this expression actually is used by Russell and later authors, is based upon certain much more specific assumptions (even though there does not appear to be a perfect consensus among logicians as to its precise meaning).

Roughly speaking, that a language contains a type theory seems to mean at least that a hierarchy exists among the entities countenanced in this language, so that a given string of elements of this language—words, morphemes, atomic symbols or the like—will be regarded as well formed only if, among other conditions, certain restrictions are observed as to the kinds of entities that are denoted by some substrings or that fall within the range of the variables occurring in the string. A typical illustration is a membership sentence of the form ". . . ϵ _____". This will not be well formed unless the expression to the left of "ϵ" denotes an entity (or, if it is a variable, ranges over entities) occupying a position in the hierarchy exactly one step lower than the position occupied by the entity denoted by the expression to the right of "ϵ". Generally, but by no means always, there are expressions that occur only to the left but never to the right of "ϵ" (or fulfill some parallel condition in other formalisms). Such expressions denote the entities of the lowest type in the hierarchy, the individuals. Entities denoted by expressions of the next-higher type are classes of individuals; then come classes of classes of individuals, etc., ad infinitum.

Thus, in a language embodying a theory of types the counterpart of the English sentence "The number 3 is a member of the class of all pairs of natural numbers" turns out to be ill formed rather than false, as it would be in a language system embodying a set theory (in the technical sense of this expression). Clearly this result could not have been derived from grammatical observation of English speech. It is equally implausible that in order to ensure the well-formedness and truth of its formalized counterpart, the English sentence "The natural number 3 is *not* a member of the class of all pairs of natural numbers" would first have to be reinterpreted to mean "It is not the case that the English sentence 'The natural number 3 is a member . . .' is well formed" and thereby be turned into a metalinguistic sentence.

It has become customary of late to speak of types of expressions rather than of (or in addition to) types of entities denoted by these expressions. Russell himself, when it was pointed out by Max Black (1944) that his prior usage led to difficulties and even to paradoxes, accepted the new mode of speech, though for the wrong reasons (see below).

For the sake of illustration let us consider a rather rich language embodying a type hierarchy, Rudolf Carnap's Language II (1937). The *individual-expressions* of this language are all numerical expressions—that is, expressions denoting natural numbers. The language also contains *predicate-expressions* and *functor-expressions* of various kinds (as well as other kinds of expressions, which will be disregarded here). A particular predicate-expression can have *argument-expressions* of only a certain type, and a functor-expression can have argument-expressions and *value-terms* of only a certain type. The type of an expression is determined as follows: Every individual-expression is assigned to type 0. If the n terms of an argument-expression respectively have types $t_1, t_2, \cdots, t_n$ in that order, then the argument-expression is assigned to type $t_1, t_2, \cdots, t_n$. If an argument-expression α_1 is of type t_1 (notice that these symbols are syntactical variables for type designations) and if the predicate-expression π_1 has to form with α_1 the well-formed sentence $\pi_1(\alpha_1)$, then π_1 will be assigned to type t_1. The sentence $\pi_1(\alpha_2)$ will then be well formed if and only if α_2 belongs to type t_1. For $\varphi_1(\alpha_1) = \alpha_2$ to be well formed (where φ_1 is a functor-expression, α_1 is of type t_1, and α_2 is of type t_2) $\varphi_1(\alpha_1)$ must be assigned to the same type as α_2—i.e., to t_2—and φ_1 will be assigned to type $(t_1 : t_2)$. In that case $\varphi_1(\alpha_3) = \alpha_4$ will be well formed if and only if α_3 is of the same type as α_1 and α_4 is of the same type as α_2. In Language II, "=" itself is not regarded as a predicate-expression and is not assigned to any type. In other languages, such as the one adopted in *Principia Mathematica,* "=" is treated as a predicate-expression exhibiting a kind of systematic ambiguity. This is known as *typical ambiguity* because the various occurrences of "=" are assigned to various types, all of the form (t_i, t_i), where t_i is the type of the expressions to the left and right of "=". Adoption of the device of typical ambiguity calls for special care.

For certain purposes it is useful to assign *level-numbers* to well-formed expressions. This is done by the following rules: An individual-expression is assigned the level-number 0. An argument-expression is assigned the highest level-number of its terms. The level-number of a predicate-expression is greater by 1 than that of its argument-expression, and the level-number of a functor-expression is greater by 1 than the maximum of the level-numbers of its argument-expression and its value-expression.

The range of expressions assigned to types is much larger in some other languages than in Language II. For example, in one of Alonzo Church's systems (1940) there are two basic types: ι, the type of individual-expressions, and o, the type of sentences (Church himself uses different terminology). Functors from entities of type t_1 to entities of

type t_2 are assigned to type $(t_2 t_1)$. The negation connective is considered to be a functor from sentences to sentences and is therefore assigned to type (oo). The disjunction connective is considered to be a functor from sentences to functors from sentences to sentences—an innocuous but, for certain purposes, efficient variant of the usual conception of this connective as a functor from pairs of sentences to sentences—and therefore assigned to type $((oo)o)$. Rather than adopt the device of typical ambiguity, Church allows infinitely many different identity symbols. Type symbols are carried as right subscripts; for instance, the official symbol for the negation connective is "N_{oo}". Various inoffensive conventions are invoked to alleviate the burden imposed on the notation.

RAMIFIED TYPE THEORY

Both of the type-theoretical language systems sketched above exhibit a so-called *simple* hierarchy. It was to such a hierarchy that Russell looked in 1903 to provide a solution for The Contradiction. But other solutions attracted his attention, and when he finally fell back on type theory, in 1907, he gave it the form of a *ramified* hierarchy, in which the type, or rather *order,* of a predicate-expression was determined not only by the type of its argument-expressions but also by the form of its definition.

There were two main reasons for Russell's adopting a ramified type theory. First, under the influence of Henri Poincaré, Russell began to take constructivist locutions seriously. Neither Russell nor Poincaré wanted to go so far as to believe that certain classes were created in time out of other, already existing classes (though other authors expressed their belief in just that way, whatever they meant thereby). Yet the construction metaphor did suggest to them that they should restrict (in effect, though not literally) the condition "Fx" occurring in their law of comprehension,

$$(\exists y)(x)(x \in y \equiv Fx),$$

in such a way that the "new" class y should not belong to the range of the bound variables occurring in "Fx". Poincaré claimed that unless this restriction was made, one would fall into a vicious circle, and Russell concurred.

Second, other paradoxes of a vaguely logical character, later called "semantic paradoxes," were discovered between 1902 and 1907. Their discovery caused a revival of interest in the classical paradox of the Liar. The simple theory of types was unable to cope with such paradoxes, but Russell believed that they could be explained as resulting from a violation of the hierarchy of orders introduced by the ramified theory of types.

The ramified theory did not, however, allow the development of classical mathematics, and for this purpose Russell found himself forced to stipulate his famous axiom of reducibility (see RUSSELL, BERTRAND, section on logic and mathematics). Although the resulting system may be free of contradiction, it loses its constructivist appeal; thus, the first motive for its adoption no longer holds. The second motive also turned out to be shaky. Giuseppe Peano, even before the appearance of the ramified theory of types, had pointed to the semantic ("linguistic") character of Richard's paradox, suggesting that it and its cognates should be dealt with by linguistics, not logic. But Russell missed the point, mainly because he failed to distinguish clearly between attributes and open sentences (by using for both notions the term "propositional function"). Leon Chwistek (1924–1925) and F. P. Ramsey (1925) both advocated abandoning the axiom of reducibility. Chwistek took a course which Russell, in the Introduction to the second edition of *Principia Mathematica* (1925), called "heroic" and which at any rate was highly idiosyncratic and was never widely understood. Ramsey's approach led to the development of the "modern" theory of types developed by Kurt Gödel, Alfred Tarski, Carnap, and Church.

Some authors, such as Hao Wang and Paul Lorenzen, have continued to take seriously the constructivist idioms. Their efforts to overcome the shortcomings of a ramified type theory without an axiom of reducibility have been partially successful, and Lorenzen, in particular (1965), has been able to reconstruct on this basis large parts of classical mathematics, including almost all of analysis. However, Wang works with cumulative types and types of transfinite order (see below), whereas in Lorenzen's latest efforts hardly a trace is left of the original ramified type hierarchy.

Opinions as to the intuitive appeal of the simple type theory have always been rather divided. Some authors have regarded such a hierarchy as a necessary ingredient in any acceptable language; others have taken it as a device that should be judged purely by its value in avoiding antinomies as weighed against the inconveniences, if any, brought about by its use. Russell's own position over the years has been somewhat ambivalent. For logicists, who desired to "reduce" mathematics to logic, the adoption of a type theory had various technical disadvantages, such as an infinite reduplication of numbers in every level from the second onward (since cardinal numbers are defined as certain classes of classes) and the existence of infinitely many null classes and of infinitely many universal classes. These disadvantages, although not fatal, were sometimes bothersome and often counterintuitive enough to balance the intuitive appeal of the assumptions leading up to them.

In Russellian type theories it is impossible to prove the existence of infinite classes, since the classical methods, already used by Bolzano, violate the type restrictions. (Though it is easy, in such theories, to prove the existence of Λ, the null class of individuals, of $\{\Lambda\}$, the class containing this class as its only member, of $\{\{\Lambda\}\}$, and so on, the infinite class that would contain all these entities is, of course, illegitimate.) Russell therefore had to stipulate a special axiom of infinity for this purpose. Since he could not convince himself of its logical character, under his own interpretation ("There exist infinitely many individuals in the universe"), he had to be satisfied with proving many important theorems only hypothetically, on the assumption that the axiom of infinity is true. (However, in such languages as Carnap's Language II, where the individual-expressions are taken to denote positions in some given order rather than physical entities, a statement of infinity can be shown to be analytic; thus, the question whether such a statement is provable from other axioms or must be

taken as a special axiom becomes subsidiary. As a matter of fact, the axiom is provable in Language II.)

LIBERALIZED TYPE THEORIES

Some authors have been attracted to type theories not because of their dubious ontological appeal but rather because of the fact that the standard proofs for various antinomies cannot be expressed in them. Such authors are in a position to liberalize some of the stipulations of these theories, thereby gaining additional freedom. This may be reflected in additional elegance, even in additional power, while the attractive features can sometimes be shown to be retained.

Of the two most important liberalizations, one permits types of transfinite order and the other dispenses with the exclusiveness of the types and works with cumulative types—each type includes all lower types, and all entities belonging to a given type also belong to all higher types.

By allowing for variables of type ω, for instance, it becomes possible to talk about all entities of finite type, which is, of course, impossible in a Russellian type theory. However, care must be taken not to reintroduce the standard antinomies.

By allowing for cumulativeness one obtains additional advantages over the ordinary theory of types. Thus, the standard Wiener–Kuratowski reduction of relations to classes threatens to run afoul of the requirement of the homogeneity of classes; special measures are required to counter this threat. Cumulative types permit this reduction without further ado.

W. V. Quine (1963) has shown how, by carrying out this liberalization, one can arrive by easy stages at a theory that is indistinguishable from Zermelo's set theory (see SET THEORY), thereby adding considerably to the clarification of the relationship between two of the most important recent approaches to the foundations of mathematics.

Quine had earlier (1937) presented a different way of departing from Russell's type theory while still avoiding the paradoxes. Russell's approach had weakened logic by forcing it into a *many-sorted* frame—a system containing different "sorts" of variables with exclusive sets of constants that can be substituted for them. Quine was able to restore the strength of logic by returning to general variables but, at the same time, requiring that in the axiom of comprehension the formula "Fx" be *stratified*—i.e., that there be a way of assigning integers to the variables occurring in it (with all occurrences of the same variable indexed the same way, of course) in such a way that "ϵ" is always flanked by variables with consecutive ascending indices. Russell's paradox is then avoided not because "$x \notin x$" is ill formed but because it is unstratified; the existence of the troublesome class is accordingly not forthcoming by application of the axiom of comprehension.

The resulting system is known as *NF* (for "new foundations," the first words in the title of the paper in which Quine first propounded the system). Only a sketch of it is presented here. In comparison with a cumulative theory of types, *NF*, though no longer containing types at all in any serious sense of the word, is both less and more liberal. The existence of classes corresponding to heterogeneous relations can in general not be proved. On the other hand, no axiom of infinity is needed, and the existence of a unique universal class is easily forthcoming.

But *NF* has strange features: Cantor's theorem to the effect that the class of all subclasses of any given class is of greater cardinality than this class itself does not hold in general; the class of unit subclasses of the universal class is of smaller cardinality than the universal class; the relation of smaller to greater among cardinals fails to be a well-ordering, causing all models of *NF* to become nonstandard; the axiom of choice can be disproved in *NF*; finally, proof by mathematical induction is greatly handicapped.

As far as the constitution of mathematics is concerned, many of these shortcomings can be overcome by restricting oneself to Cantorian classes—that is, to those classes for which Cantor's theorem does hold. But the existence in *NF* of non-Cantorian classes is more than a strange luxury. With their help important theorems can be proved that say nothing of non-Cantorian classes and therefore hold also for the normal Cantorian ones. There exists here an interesting analogy to the situation in analysis, where recent research by Abraham Robinson (1965) has shown that nonstandard analysis can be used to prove important theorems in standard analysis.

By enlarging the universe of *NF* to contain ultimate classes—classes that are not members of anything—in addition to membership-eligible classes, or sets in what is now becoming a technical sense of this word, a new system is created that is free of most of the shortcomings of *NF*. (The idea of ultimate classes was introduced by John von Neumann in 1925, following earlier hints by Cantor in a letter of 1899, first published in 1932, and by Julius König in 1905.) The new system is called *ML*, after Quine's *Mathematical Logic* (1940), the book in which it was originally introduced, in a somewhat different form. In *ML* there are no non-Cantorian classes, and the axiom of choice, in the form "Every class of exclusive sets has a selection class," can no longer be disproved along the lines of *NF*. Cantor's theorem holds in full generality. Cantor's paradox cannot be derived because the class of all sets is not a set but an ultimate class, and the class of all classes does not exist.

ML is more elegant and powerful than *NF*, but its consistency might therefore look more doubtful. However, Wang was able to prove, in 1950, that *ML* is consistent if *NF* is.

FURTHER CONSISTENCY RESULTS

According to one of Gödel's well-known results, the consistency of no type theory can be proved within itself. J. G. Kemeny (1949), however, proved that the consistency of simple type theory (without the axiom of infinity) can be proved in Zermelo's set theory, thereby showing that type theory is, in this important sense, weaker than Zermelo's set theory. The consistency of ramified type theory (with an axiom of infinity but without an axiom of reducibility), has been demonstrated by various methods.

It follows from Gödel's incompleteness theorem (see GÖDEL'S THEOREM) that the theory of types is not complete with respect to truth under all *principal* interpretations—

that is, those interpretations in which the range of each first-level *n*-ary predicate variable is the set of *all* sets of ordered *n*-tuples of individuals (and similarly for higher-level predicates). But Leon Henkin (1949) succeeded in proving that the theory of types is complete with respect to truth under all *sound* interpretations, principal and secondary (an interpretation is called secondary if the ranges mentioned are arbitrary subsets of the sets mentioned). In other words, all sentences that are true in every *general* model (a model is called general if it corresponds to a sound interpretation) are provable in the theory of types; this is not the case, however, for all sentences true in every standard model (a model is called standard if it corresponds to a principal interpretation).

Investigations into the model theory of higher-order logic began only recently. David Kaplan and Richard Montague (1965) have attacked the problem in full generality and in particular have tried also to accommodate transfinite types and nonlogical predicates of higher-level objects. Among other results, they have defined an interesting notion of isomorphism which is also applicable to higher-order structures.

TYPE THEORY AND NATURAL LANGUAGES

It would have been philosophically significant had it proved possible to establish that all languages worthy of the name must contain a type hierarchy, or at least that no satisfactory foundation of mathematics is possible without one. But nothing of the sort has been shown. There are a large number of constructed languages without type hierarchies, and in some of them satisfactory foundations for mathematics have been provided. The attempt to impose a type hierarchy upon natural languages seems misguided and linguistically pointless. The concerns of Russell and other authors about how to formulate the theory of types in English (or any other natural language) without violating the theory in its very formulation (e.g., by speaking of all types) are now no more than interesting curiosities. At one time (1944) Russell was induced by these worries to give up talking about types of extralinguistic entities altogether and to be satisfied with assigning types solely to linguistic entities.

The situation may be different with respect to syntactical and semantical categories. Consider, for example, the problems of demarcating, in natural languages, well-formed strings from ill-formed ones and meaningful strings from meaningless ones; of clarifying the relationships between the two dichotomies; of investigating the limits of the usefulness of these dichotomies; and of determining the region in which it becomes more useful to employ comparative or even quantitative concepts. Such questions not only are highly important for the understanding of the workings of natural languages but are doubtless also of great significance for the treatment of many philosophical problems. Yet it is difficult to see what help could be extended here by the concept of types. It would only confuse an already highly complex issue.

That so many authors have thought otherwise, at one time or another, may be explained by the fact that they, under the impact of Russell and Ludwig Wittgenstein, believed that there exists an ideal language and that this language contains a type hierarchy, as did *Principia Mathematica;* in addition, these authors greatly underestimate the difficulty of reformulating, in the language of *Principia Mathematica* or any other ideal language, problems originally stated in some natural language.

Bibliography

Andrews, Peter, *A Transfinite Type Theory With Type Variables.* Amsterdam, 1965.

Black, Max, "Russell's Philosophy of Language," in P. A. Schilpp, ed., *The Philosophy of Bertrand Russell.* Evanston, Ill., 1944. Pp. 227–255.

Carnap, Rudolf, *The Logical Syntax of Language,* translated by Amethe Smeaton. London and New York, 1937.

Church, Alonzo, "Schröder's Anticipation of the Simple Theory of Types." Cambridge, Mass., 1939. Preprinted for the Fifth International Congress for Unity of Science.

Church, Alonzo, "A Formulation of the Simple Theory of Types." *Journal of Symbolic Logic,* Vol. 5 (1940), 56–68.

Chwistek, Leon, "The Theory of Constructive Types." *Annales de la Société Polonaise de Mathématique,* Vol. 2 (1924), 9–48, and Vol. 3 (1925), 92–141.

Fraenkel, A. A., and Bar-Hillel, Yehoshua, *Foundations of Set Theory.* Amsterdam, 1958.

Gödel, Kurt, "Über formal unentscheidbare Sätze der Principia Mathematica und verwandter Systeme I." *Monatshefte für Mathematik und Physik,* Vol. 38 (1931), 173–198. Translations in Martin Davis, ed., *The Undecidable* (Hewlett, N.Y., 1965); and John van Heijenoort, ed., *A Source Book in Mathematical Logic* (Cambridge, Mass., forthcoming).

Henkin, Leon, "Completeness in the Theory of Types." *Journal of Symbolic Logic,* Vol. 15 (1950), 81–91.

Kaplan, David, and Montague, Richard, "Foundations of Higher-order Logic," in Yehoshua Bar-Hillel, ed., *Proceedings of the 1964 International Congress for Logic, Methodology and Philosophy of Science.* Amsterdam, 1965. Pp. 101–111.

Kemeny, J. G., *Type Theory Versus Set Theory.* Dissertation, Princeton University, 1949.

Lorenzen, Paul, *Einführung in die operative Logik und Mathematik.* Berlin, Göttingen, and Heidelberg, 1955.

Lorenzen, Paul, *Differential und Integral.* Frankfurt, 1965.

Poincaré, Henri, "Les Mathématiques et la logique." *Revue de métaphysique et de morale,* Vol. 13 (1905), 815–835, and Vol. 14 (1906), 17–34, 294–317.

Quine, W. V., "New Foundations for Mathematical Logic." *American Mathematical Monthly,* Vol. 44 (1937), 70–80. Reprinted, with additions, in *From a Logical Point of View,* 2d ed. Cambridge, Mass., 1961.

Quine, W. V., *Mathematical Logic.* New York, 1940; rev. ed., Cambridge, Mass., 1951.

Quine, W. V., *Set Theory and Its Logic.* Cambridge, Mass., 1963.

Ramsey, F. P., "New Foundations of Mathematics." *Proceedings of the London Mathematical Society,* Vol. 25 (1925), 338–384. Reprinted in *The Foundations of Mathematics and Other Logical Essays.* London, 1931.

Robinson, Abraham, *Non-standard Analysis.* Amsterdam, 1966.

Russell, Bertrand, *The Principles of Mathematics.* Cambridge, 1903; 2d ed., London, 1937.

Russell, Bertrand, "Mathematical Logic as Based on the Theory of Types." *American Journal of Mathematics,* Vol. 30 (1908), 222–262. Reprinted in *Logic and Knowledge.* London, 1956.

Russell, Bertrand, "Reply to Criticisms," Schilpp, *op. cit.*

Specker, Ernst, "The Axiom of Choice in Quine's 'New Foundations for Mathematical Logic.'" *Proceedings of the National Academy of Sciences,* Vol. 39 (1953), 972–975.

Specker, Ernst, "Typical Ambiguity," in Ernest Nagel et al., eds., *Logic, Methodology, and Philosophy of Science.* Stanford, Calif., 1962. Pp. 116–124.

Tarski, Alfred, *Logic, Semantics, Metamathematics,* translated by J. H. Woodger. Oxford, 1956.

Wang, Hao, *A Survey of Mathematical Logic.* Amsterdam, 1963.

Whitehead, A. N., and Russell, Bertrand, *Principia Mathematica,* 3 vols. Cambridge, 1910–1913.

YEHOSHUA BAR-HILLEL

U

UEXKÜLL, JAKOB JOHANN, BARON VON
(1864–1944), student of animal behavior and theoretical
biologist, was born in Estonia. He graduated from the University of Dorpat (Tartu) in 1884 and continued his studies
there until 1903, when he moved to Heidelberg. Field work
took him to various countries and regions, including central
Africa. In 1925 he was appointed director of the Institut für
Umweltforschung at Hamburg and was made honorary
professor at the university. He died in Italy, at Capri.

In von Uexküll's books, scientific material was interlaced with much philosophical discussion. Underlying this
discussion was an explicitly Kantian conception of knowledge. Von Uexküll held that this conception was most in
accord with the discoveries of animal psychology concerning the function of sensory stimulation and orientation in
living organisms. His investigations in this area led him to
conclude that every animal lives in a unique "environing
world" (*Umwelt*) which is determined by its type of organization and especially by its receptors and effectors. These
organs determine what can become a stimulus or sign for
the animal. They also determine what modes of response it
can carry out. The sum of possible stimuli for each animal
is its "sign-world" (*Merkwelt*), and the sum of possible
responses is its "action-world" (*Wirkwelt*). Together these
two domains make up the *Umwelt*. The correlate of the
Umwelt is the *Innenwelt,* created by the animal's internal
"directing" apparatus. Thus, orientation involves a self-regulating behavior cycle in which the animal selects
stimuli from the influences of the outer world and responds to them in such a way as to maintain its adjustment
to its environment.

Man, like all other living things, has his own *Umwelt*.
This, von Uexküll thought, was the profound truth that
Kant expounded in a misleading, because nonbiological,
way in the Transcendental Aesthetic of the *Critique of
Pure Reason*. Human sensibility determines the character
of the world we perceive in space and time. Hence, for
man "all reality is subjective appearance," and it is on this
fundamental principle that the science of biology must
proceed. Nevertheless, von Uexküll held, it is possible for
man to reconstruct by means of inferences from observation something of the *Umwelten* of organisms other than
himself. One finds in his books fascinating descriptions of
how the same segment of nature presents itself to a dog, a
fly, a starfish, or a paramecium, so that each lives in a
world quite unlike that of the others. The human *Umwelt*
is thus only one of a vast number of experienced universes.

There is one feature which von Uexküll thought can be
ascribed to all these universes—they all have a structure;
they exhibit conformity to plan (*Planmässigkeit*). This
feature occurs everywhere in the organic world; in the
action of genes, in embryological processes, in physiological functions, and so on. It is so pervasive as to warrant the
contention that special planning forces (*planmässige
Krafte*) are at work in living things. These forces are quite
different from physicochemical agencies. Hence, the project of seeking a mechanistic explanation of life is doomed
to failure. It does not follow that some kind of vitalism or
finalism must be espoused, for the forces may be conceived as natural powers, "life-energies" (*Lebensenergien*)
which can exist only in an organized state. What they are
in themselves, however, or precisely how they act on matter, we do not know.

Like many German biologists of his day, von Uexküll
was unsympathetic to the idea of evolution and was contemptuous of Darwinism. He thought that the term "evolution" was a complete misnomer, for it means "unfolding" (*Entfaltung*), that is, a process in which the forming of
folds becomes less and less. But the history of living things
has been a steady increase of "folds," a growth in the complexity of organic plans. Darwinism, "which is more a
religion than a science," tries to get rid of the idea of planning forces by attributing evolution to the interplay of
random natural powers (*planloser Naturkräfte*). This has
given rise to hopeless confusions within the theory. Fortunately, "Mendelism came, and swept the whole theory
away."

The best feature of von Uexküll's books is their discussion of the empirical details of animal behavior. His philosophical arguments have little finesse, and those that attempt to base biology on a Kantian view of knowledge do
not face even the obvious objections to such an enterprise.
His opposition to Darwinism was not derived from a careful study of it, and his announcement of its disappearance
is now just a historical curiosity.

Works by von Uexküll

Umwelt und Innenwelt der Tiere. Berlin, 1909.
Theoretische Biologie. Berlin, 1920. Translated by D. L. Mackinnon as *Theoretical Biology*. New York, 1926.

Streifzüge durch die Umwelten von Tieren und Menschen. Berlin, 1934. In collaboration with G. Kriszat.

Works on von Uexküll

Bertalanffy, Ludwig von, "An Essay on the Relativity of Categories." *Philosophy of Science,* Vol. 22 (1955), 243–263.
Schubert-Soldern, Richard von, *Mechanism and Vitalism,* translated by C. E. Robin. Notre Dame, Ind., 1962.

T. A. GOUDGE

UGLINESS. Aesthetics has often been described as the philosophical study of beauty and ugliness. It is important at the outset to see what is involved in this familiar definition, for it embodies a view of ugliness and of its role within aesthetic theory which has been the major source of contention in historical debates on the concept. The first thing to note about this view is that it takes ugliness to be a category that properly falls within aesthetic theory. Ugliness designates aesthetic disvalue as beauty designates positive aesthetic value. The two therefore constitute a value polarity analogous to right and wrong in ethics or to truth and falsehood in epistemology. Just as the field of ethics comprises responsible human actions of which some are evil and blameworthy, so, among perceptual objects, there are some which have negative aesthetic value. This does not mean that such objects simply lack the characteristics by virtue of which things are beautiful; it means, rather, that they possess recognizable properties that are the opposites of those found in beautiful objects.

The relation between beauty and ugliness has commonly been conceived in hedonistic terms, that is, whereas a beautiful object is a source of pleasure in the spectator, an ugly object arouses its opposite, pain. Plato, in numerous instances, takes beauty to be characteristically pleasurable (*Hippias Major* 297–299, *Philebus* 50–52, *Laws* II). Aristotle perpetuates this view, and in his study of specific art forms (notably tragedy) he holds that it is the proper function of these forms to create pleasure. Yet it is clear in his classic *Poetics* that he is troubled by the seeming conflict between this view of art and the empirical fact that works of art often represent objects and events that are ugly. Aristotle raises the question first in regard to the type of visual art that depicts things "which in themselves we view with pain" (IV). He does not doubt, however, that the painting itself arouses pleasure, a phenomenon that is explained by our intellectual interest in recognizing the object. Comedy, moreover, "imitates" men who are ignoble and therefore ludicrous; and though this is a kind of ugliness, the comedy is, for reasons that Aristotle does not specify, kept from being painful (V). Finally, though the protagonist is a good man who suffers adversity, tragedy is not merely shocking (XIII).

Thus Aristotle initiated the controversy over the "paradox of tragedy" that has survived to the present day. As has been shown, this paradox is not the sole instance of the problem of ugliness in art, but it states the problem most acutely, both because tragedy is almost the only artistic genre whose subject matter is necessarily sorrowful or pathetic and because of the pre-eminent value that has traditionally been claimed for works in this genre. Why do we esteem narratives of evil and suffering? The poetic values of tragic literature, the ennobling courage of the hero, the insight and wisdom gained by the spectator—these are among the usual solutions of the paradox. All of them consider the ugly as only a single aspect of the work of art, for they all undertake to show that within the work as a whole the ugliness is somehow transcended. Hence they presuppose that some objects, such as the preartistic model of tragic plot, are "painful in themselves," and therefore ugly.

Throughout aesthetic theory, ugliness is discussed mainly by those philosophers who deny precisely this assumption. They wish to hold that ugliness does not exist, and since their thesis runs counter to ordinary belief, they are constrained to justify it. In Augustine, the unreality of ugliness is enjoined by his most fundamental philosophical doctrines. Stated theologically, the world and everything in it have been created by an infinitely good God, as an expression of his goodness; stated metaphysically, existence is not neutral with respect to value and disvalue, but is rather an embodiment, through and through, of positive value. In such a world view, the apparent presence of evil of any kind poses a problem, and Augustine considers sin and blindness just such problems. But aesthetic disvalue is a particular issue for him because his conception of reality is conspicuously aesthetic. All things are images of the ideas of form and harmony that exist in the mind of God, and together they make up an internally ordered unity. The categories of Greek aesthetic theory are thus writ large in his metaphysics.

To say that a thing can exist at all only if it possesses form, and that, indeed, its existence cannot be conceived of apart from form, implies the solution of Augustine's problem. Objects are beautiful by virtue of their form, but if this is so, then ugliness does not exist, since sheer formlessness cannot exist. The opposite of beauty is not anything real, but merely the absence or "privation" of positive value. But now the argument seems to prove almost too much, for it appears to deny the possibility of the very facts—that is, apparently ugly objects—which gave rise to it in the first place. Augustine therefore employs the notion of "degrees" of value characteristic of metaphysical optimism and idealism. An object may not have the form appropriate to things of its kind, but this lack constitutes a relative deficiency of beauty, not sheer ugliness. Moreover, such objects must be seen not in isolation but as parts of the universe as a whole. Seeming ugliness sets off, and thereby enhances, the beauty of the world. Augustine uses the same argument in the case of objects, such as dangerous animals, which are not in any clear way lacking in form, but are considered ugly because they are displeasing or offensive to the sight.

However, when "form" has been construed less broadly than it was by Augustine, it has been used to differentiate beauty from genuine ugliness. During the sixteenth and seventeenth centuries, numerous treatises were devoted to particular arts, on the model of the *Poetics*. The properties of form that a work must possess in order to achieve beauty are specified precisely and narrowly. These include the "unities" in drama (Corneille) and the "correct" anatomical proportions in the visual arts (Dürer). A work of art that lacks these properties is still recognizably a drama or a sculpture and therefore has some organization or structure. Yet it is not only deficient in beauty but really ugly.

This assured and unequivocal way of distinguishing ugliness was called into question, however, by the rebellion against the "rules" of form that was carried on throughout the eighteenth century. The rules were found to be too parochial and constricting. Yet the distinction between beauty and ugliness might still have been drawn, by reference to felt experience rather than to the object, if the hedonistic theory of value had been consistently preserved. But examination of aesthetic experience (of the sublime) reveals that it engenders feelings which are akin to pain. Sublime objects are overwhelming, menacing, intractable to understanding and control. And yet such experiences, because they are intensely moving, are of great value. Thus, both formalism and hedonism, which had traditionally sustained the duality of beauty–ugliness, are impugned. More fundamentally still, the eighteenth century first established aesthetics as an autonomous and systematic discipline. The question "What counts as a properly aesthetic phenomenon?" was then raised explicitly for the first time. The answer to this question, as we shall see, ultimately determines whether ugliness is a category of aesthetic disvalue. In all these ways, the eighteenth century provided impulse and direction to the vigorous prosecution in recent thought of what was first called, at the close of that century, "the theory of ugliness" (Friedrich von Schlegel, 1797).

According to two of the most influential answers to the question raised above, the aesthetic is to be found either (1) wherever some conceptual theme is embodied in an object that can be grasped by sense and imagination or (2) wherever some sensory structure expresses to the observer its distinctive feeling-quality. Any object of either kind is said to possess beauty. Ugliness, traditionally, is the "opposite" of aesthetic value. But what would be the opposites of these two conceptions of the aesthetic? In the first case, the opposite would be found in some sensory presentation devoid of intellectual significance or, alternatively, in pure concepts, such as certain of those of science and philosophy, which are beyond imagination. Such objects, however, do not exemplify aesthetic disvalue; rather they fall wholly outside of the realm of the aesthetic as it is defined according to this theory. In the second case, similarly, a thing completely lacking any emotional tone—if any such thing exists—is simply nonaesthetic.

This conclusion, however, fails to take into account ugliness in the usual sense—that is, what we perceive as being displeasing or revolting. W. T. Stace, a recent exponent of the first theory mentioned above, which he took over from Hegel, suggests that what is thus excluded from the aesthetic should be called "the unbeautiful"—"the mere negative absence of beauty"—rather than the ugly. Ugliness itself is a "species" of beauty that is present whenever such concepts as evil and disaster enter into the aesthetic object. The pain that such concepts arouse in us is moral, not aesthetic, and it is usually overcome by the aesthetic pleasure we gain from the total object. Bernard Bosanquet develops the second theory, derived from Benedetto Croce, by arguing that most of what is usually found to be ugly is deemed so because of "the weakness of the spectator." Either the work of art makes very great demands on his emotional capacities or, as in satiric comedy, it offends his moral beliefs; the "weakness," however, is remediable. Such a work of art is therefore more properly considered an instance of "difficult beauty" than of ugliness. Are there any objects at all that come within the realm of the aesthetic and are genuinely (or, as Bosanquet says, "invincibly") ugly? Bosanquet is "much inclined" to think that there are none. Given his view that the expressive is the aesthetic, and that "every form expresses" and is therefore beautiful, it is difficult to see how there could be any such object. He holds, however, that ugliness is to be located in what is only incipiently and partially expressive, that is, in a work of art that suggests some feeling but does not coherently elaborate and fulfill the suggestion, as in sentimental or "affected" art.

The traditional polarity of beauty–ugliness marks the distinction between aesthetic value and disvalue. Both the above theories conceive of the aesthetic in such a way that they leave little or no room for disvalue. Yet both Stace and Bosanquet regard the aesthetic experience as pleasurable. At the same time, they want to make room for art that is tragic, demonic, "difficult" (Stace, for example, cites the sculpture of Jacob Epstein). Therefore, as has just been shown, they seek to reconcile the painfulness of such art with the positive value that it necessarily possesses as an aesthetic object. In the case of Bosanquet, however, the question should be raised whether the expression of feeling is universally accompanied by pleasure. Historically, the concept of "expression" has tended to accommodate emotions of every kind within art, even those, as in an art of violence or outrage, which are "darkest." Successful artistic expression can render such emotions more, rather than less, concentrated and painful, and if it be urged that pleasure is taken in the unity and power of the artist's conception, there are, according to Bosanquet's theory, many nonartistic aesthetic objects that are intensely expressive and for which this explanation will not hold. Since there is no necessary or logical connection between "expression" and "pleasingness," it must be decided empirically whether, even when "the weakness of the spectator" is overcome, his experience of the expressive object has a positive hedonic tone. Stace's view that the painfulness of the theme of a work of art is moral, not aesthetic, seems more like definitional legislation than an insight into aesthetic experience. Moral perplexity and frustration are integral to such art as tragedy, and their painfulness enters into our perception of the total work of art. Stace's view, too, is a defense of hedonism. Yet there is no reason a priori to hold to hedonism in aesthetics, and indeed these difficulties cast doubt on such a theory. The term "ugliness," in the sense of what is preponderantly painful, may still be used to designate one kind of aesthetic object without any implications of disvalue. So considered, "X is ugly but aesthetically good" is not self-contradictory and may indeed be something that we want to and have to say. Those modern artists who have vigorously repudiated the pleasingness of beauty as the goal of their creative efforts have made this way of speaking sound less implausible than it once did.

The graver and more basic question is whether ugliness, in the broader sense of negative aesthetic value, is, for aesthetic theory, otiose. Doubtless, we also want to say sometimes that the work of art is bad. Bosanquet, however, takes genuine ugliness to be at least partially expressive, and if we follow this lead, badness must be construed as a deficiency or relatively slight degree of aesthetic goodness. The work achieves less than it promises; the nonartistic object is lacking in vitality or charm. According to this view, then, there is no opposite to aesthetic value, but only, as Augustine said, a "privation" of it. On the other hand, this may be thought to be a gratuitous misreading of those properties which are commonly held to constitute ugliness or which are adduced as reasons for judging a thing ugly. Muddy orchestration or incoherent plot structure are, significantly, opposites to orchestral clarity or unity of plot, and they are equally real and present to awareness. In the absence of compensating virtues, objects that possess them are "positively bad."

No matter whether the denial of negative value should, finally, be tolerated or rejected, it is fair to say that this denial is less vexing in aesthetics than in ethics or epistemology. The explanation lies, in large part, in Bosanquet's notion of "the weakness of the spectator." The determination of beauty and ugliness is much more closely tied to the perceptual and emotional capacities of the spectator and to the attitudes which affect them than it is to moral and cognitive values. This leads us to think that the experience of negative value (though not that of positive value) results from a failure to see what is yet there to be seen. Thus, the transvaluation of what had previously been accounted ugly, which is endemic to the history of art and taste, is characteristically credited with being an enlargement of sympathy and a refinement of discrimination. The more obdurate cognitive and moral judgments of falsehood and evil, however, are not characteristically altered in this way. Can any limits, therefore, be set to what sensibility finds to be aesthetically good? To define the field of the aesthetic in such a way that all things are seen to possess positive value formalizes the endless catholicity of aesthetic interest. Freed from the exigencies of morality and the biases of perceptual habit, the aesthetic approach to the world, at the hypothetical limit, fixes upon any tone or shade the quality of any ambience. In Keats's words, it "has as much delight in . . . an Iago as an Imogen." But if everything engages and rewards aesthetic perception, then either "aesthetic disvalue" is a self-contradiction or else it denotes nothing.

Bibliography

Bosanquet, Bernard, *Three Lectures on Aesthetic.* London, 1923. Lecture III is the starting point for any serious discussion of the problem of ugliness.

Chapman, Emmanuel, *Saint Augustine's Philosophy of Beauty.* New York, 1939. Those of Augustine's writings on aesthetics which have survived are scattered among several different treatises. This convenient volume locates these passages.

Pepper, Stephen C., *The Basis of Criticism in the Arts.* Cambridge, 1946. Contrasts the meaning and status of ugliness in some of the major aesthetic theories. In the author's own view, ugliness is a moral rather than an aesthetic category.

Rosenkranz, Karl, *Ästhetik des Hässlichen,* Koenigsberg, 1853. The classic post-Hegelian study of ugliness. Addicted somewhat to multiplying conceptual distinctions but a thoughtful and suggestive analysis. Argues that art would be unduly narrow if it did not include the ugly and that ugliness is not simply a device to enhance beauty.

Santayana, George, *The Sense of Beauty.* New York, 1936. An influential contemporary statement of hedonist aesthetics.

Stace, W. T., *The Meaning of Beauty.* London, 1929.

Véron, Eugène, *Esthétique.* Paris, 1878. Translated by W. H. Armstrong as *Aesthetics.* London, 1879. An early and forceful statement of the theory that the artist seeks emotional self-expression rather than beauty and will therefore exploit rather than mitigate the ugliness of his subject.

JEROME STOLNITZ

ULRICH (ENGELBERT) OF STRASBOURG (fl. 1248–1277),

scholastic philosopher and theologian, priest, and author. A member of the Dominican priory at Strasbourg in the German province, Ulrich studied under Albert the Great at Cologne, together with Thomas Aquinas and Hugh of Strasbourg, between 1248 and 1254. During those years Ulrich heard Albert expound the Dionysian corpus and the *Ethics* of Aristotle. As a lecturer in theology at Strasbourg, Ulrich acquired considerable fame for his learning; among his illustrious disciples was Lector John of Fribourg.

The ancient catalogues attribute to Ulrich commentaries on Aristotle's *Metheora* and *De Anima,* Peter Lombard's *Sentences,* and the book of Ecclesiastes. However, his only extant work is a remarkable compendium of theology entitled *De Summo Bono,* planned and probably written in eight books. Only the first book and fragments of others have been published, and the known manuscripts end with Book VI, tr. 5. This compendium was composed between 1262 and 1272 and marks a notable advance over the earlier *summas* of William of Auxerre, Alexander of Hales and Albert the Great. It is divided into (1) introduction to theology, (2) essence of the supreme Good, (3) Trinity in general, (4) the Father and creation, (5) the Son and incarnation, (6) the Holy Spirit and sanctification, (7) sacraments, and (8) ultimate beatitude.

The doctrinal framework of Ulrich's thought is predominantly Augustinian and Neoplatonic, depending largely on Pseudo-Dionysius, Avicenna, *Liber de Causis,* and Albert. For Ulrich man has a rational predisposition for knowing the existence of God as the supreme cause. This knowledge is rendered more precise, although not comprehensive, by the traditional three ways: (1) negating imperfections found in creatures (for example, as creatures are finite, God is infinite); (2) seeing God as the ultimate cause of all perfections; and (3) recognizing the transcendence of those perfections in God. God created the universe in a hierarchical order ranging from the first luminous intelligence through lesser intelligences, man, animals, plants, elements, and material principles. In all creatures there is a real distinction between essence and existence, and in all material substances there is only one substantial form. Created intellectual substances, seeing the eternal Ideas in God, illuminate lesser intelligences to know truth. The human mind has four immediately evident (*per se nota*) rules by which it can investigate theology, the science of the faith: God is the supreme Truth and cause of all truth; primary Truth can neither deceive nor be deceived, therefore his Word should be believed; we should believe everything clearly revealed by God through his spokesmen; Scripture is true precisely because God gave it to us in that way. Unlike these rules, the articles of faith are not immediately evident, but in the light of faith and these rules, the articles of faith become objects of scientific study.

For five years (1272–1277) Ulrich was provincial of the German province before the General Chapter of Bordeaux assigned him to Paris to lecture on the *Sentences* and to obtain his degree in theology. He died, probably in 1278, before becoming a master; in the manuscripts he is designated a bachelor in theology.

Bibliography

Daguillon, Jeanne, *Ulrich de Strasbourg, O.P., la "Summa de Bono,"* Lib. I. Paris, 1930. Bibliothèque Thomiste, Vol. XII.

Glorieux, Palémon, *Répertoire des maîtres en théologie de Paris au XIIIᵉ siècle*, 2 vols. Paris, 1933–1934. Vol. I, pp. 145–151.

Grabmann, Martin, "Studien über Ulrich von Strassburg," in *Mittelalterliches Geistesleben; Abhandlungen zur Geschichte der Scholastik und Mystik*, 3 vols. Munich, 1926–1956. Vol. I, pp. 147–221.

Quétif, Jacques, and Échard, Jacques, *Scriptores Ordinis Praedicatorum Recensiti*, 2 vols. Paris, 1719–1721. Vol. I, p. 256.

Théry, Gabriel, "Originalité du plan de la Summa de Bono d'Ulrich de Strasbourg." *Revue Thomiste*, Vol. 27 (1922), 276–297.

JAMES A. WEISHEIPL, O.P.

ULTIMATE MORAL PRINCIPLES: THEIR JUSTIFICATION.

The problem of how, if at all, we could set about justifying assertions about what we ought to do in various practical situations is one which has been the major concern of moral philosophers. Such basic questions are indeed endemic in most branches of philosophy. We ask not only if we can ever know what we ought to do but whether we can justify our claims to knowledge of an external world, how we can know the truth of statements about the past, or whether we can ever be sure of the existence of minds other than our own. But in ethics the problem seems more recalcitrant and, indeed, to many nonphilosophers at least, more real. For while skepticism about the existence of an external world or of other minds may seem difficult to refute, to most it is impossible to embrace, whereas skepticism about the possibility of claiming knowledge of any objective truths about what we ought to do is not so rare, either among men in general or those who would wish to characterize themselves as philosophers.

It is not, of course, surprising that this should be so. Ethical attitudes vary much more, from society to society and even between individuals, than do our beliefs about the external world or other people's feelings. The patent fact of ethical disagreement forces us to re-examine the bases of our moral beliefs. Furthermore, the disagreements we encounter concerning moral issues often seem to involve deep matters of principle which leave no common ground between the disputants. This is sometimes referred to as the problem of disagreement about ultimate moral principles. It is this problem—whether ultimate moral principles are susceptible of rational justification—which will be examined in this article.

Most philosophers would agree that the particular way in which a philosophical problem is formulated will make a great deal of difference to what solution is possible to it or, indeed, whether any solution is possible. It will be necessary therefore to set out in detail what is meant by a disagreement about ultimate moral principles and to defend this way of expressing the issue against certain objections before a possible solution is set out.

Moral principles. A "man of principle" is sometimes thought of, with distaste, as a man who acts in accordance with a fixed set of rules, ignoring the complexities of the situation and failing to adapt his behavior to changing circumstances. The morality of principles and rules is sometimes contrasted with the morality of sensibility, which emphasizes such virtues as sympathy and integrity as against a rigid code of behavior. In either kind of morality, however, particular judgments will have to be made, based on a view of the situation in which the agent acts, and some factors in the situation will have to be regarded as reasons for acting in one way rather than another. There is, therefore, a more general sense of "moral principle," which can be regarded as common to both views, in which a moral principle indicates some factor which is generally relevant to what ought to be done.

Moral principles can then be regarded as statements picking out those factors of situations which can be appealed to as moral reasons. "Lying is wrong" suggests that the fact that a statement is known to be false is a reason for not making it to someone. "Adultery is wrong" suggests that the fact that someone is married is a reason for his refraining from sexual intercourse with any person who is not his spouse. And, again, "One ought to be kind" suggests that there are reasons for performing kind actions rather than unkind ones. Asserting a moral principle of this kind and denying the suggestion about reasons results in paradox. Thus, for example, if somebody says "Lying is wrong, but the fact that a statement constitutes a lie is no reason whatsoever for not making it," he seems to have taken back in the second half of his sentence what he asserted in the first.

If saying that someone ought to do something commits one to claiming that there is some fact in the situation which is a reason for doing the thing in question, then this reason must be subject to the requirement which reasons in general must satisfy: that anything which is a reason in any one case must be a reason in every case unless there are other special reasons for ignoring it. This applies to reasons generally, not just to moral reasons. For example, if the fact that it is raining is a reason for saying Smith will get wet, it is a reason for saying anyone else will unless there are some relevant differences in their cases, such as being indoors or carrying an umbrella. It is this which leads to the claim that moral principles must be universal, at least to the degree that they pick out factors which are universally relevant to what we ought to do, although not necessarily universally determining what we ought to do in every particular case. Thus it would seem that the correctness of the universal moral principle involved—or, in other words, that what is appealed to as a reason should indeed be a reason—is a necessary although not a sufficient condition of the correctness of the particular judgment about what ought to be done.

Justification of moral judgments. If the correctness of universal moral principles is a condition of the correctness of particular moral judgments, then obviously the first question we must ask in investigating how our particular moral judgments can be justified is, How can we justify claiming that certain moral principles are correct? There are, however, some objections to this way of treating the problem which must be considered.

It may be pointed out that value judgments in other areas do not seem to require justification by reference to some universally relevant factors. And if we are willing to allow that in other realms of value there are judgments which do not require to be backed by universal principles, why not in morals? For example, there are very considerable difficulties in representing judgments about the value of a work of art as being backed by or dependent on principles at all. It may be impossible, when we say some work of art is good, to indicate any feature the possession of which is bound to make any other work of art good. (One might be tempted to say that beauty is such a feature. But this is unconvincing because one is using the term either narrowly, in which case there are plenty of good works of art which one would never describe as beautiful, or so widely that it means only "good in the way that a work of art is good.") Surely, however, it must be agreed that the goodness of anything, including a work of art, depends on what qualities it has, however difficult it may be to say in a given case precisely what qualities it has which make it good. And in order to begin to justify the judgment that something is good, one must refer to its qualities; one cannot draw anyone's attention to the goodness itself. If it is proper to refer to these qualities to back one's claim that the object is good, then it is at least to the point to ask why something else, which has the same qualities, is not good. If such a question is to the point, it shows that we accept that the possession of certain qualities is being put forward as a general reason for saying that the object is good.

However, even if this is correct, it is clear that the features by virtue of which any given work of art is judged to be good tend to be many, complicated, and organically related. Although any feature pointed to in support of a judgment that a work of art is good must also be relevant to the criticism of other works of art, there may be in every other case many other relevant factors which alter the situation completely. The same thing might be claimed for moral cases. It may be said that every human situation is infinitely complicated, so that however many relevant features one may pick out in a particular case, there will always be a host of others which can be set against them. Such considerations would lead not so much to a denial of the universality of morally relevant features as to doubt about the utility of stating the problem in terms of principles. To this there are two answers.

First, it would be against common sense to claim, for example, that the wanton murder of children is not wrong. Even where other features which are regarded as morally relevant are also present—such as that one had promised one's old mother on her deathbed to try to exterminate the Jews—few would regard them as justifying child murder. So anyone who persists in claiming that it is always possible that such actions as child murder may be justified because of the complex character of every particular hu-

man situation is, at best, someone who has an unusual moral outlook, and this means that his very claim that every situation is so complicated that no general principles can be admitted is dependent on his having a different set of moral principles from most people's. So even to consider whether this objection is correct, we still have to ask which general principles are justifiable.

Second, we have already remarked that moral principles will be a necessary but not a sufficient condition of the correctness of our particular moral judgments. Although on their own they may never be sufficient to solving all moral problems, they will certainly be necessary to our having any moral problems at all. This may be illustrated in terms of a case mentioned by Sartre. A young man has a dilemma. Should he join the French resistance, or should he stay at home and look after his aging mother? Sartre points out that no rehearsal of general principles would ever serve to solve such a problem. This is no doubt true, but it does not show that the correctness of such principles is not relevant. For why is the young man worried about only those two possibilities? There are plenty of other things he could do. He could learn tightrope walking or set up as an ice-cream vendor or enlarge his earlobes with brass rings. But these are obviously of no importance, whereas looking after the old mother and joining the resistance are important. Why is Sartre's case serious and dramatic and the other suggestions frivolous and silly? Why does it matter what the young man does, to himself or to anyone? There can surely be no problem at all unless such things as joining the resistance (defending one's country) or looking after the old mother (kindness to a dependent) are morally relevant features of the situation—unless they are things which it is reasonable to consider in deciding what to do. And if there are morally relevant features in the situation, there are corresponding moral principles. If these principles are not correct (and, indeed, there are those who would question patriotic principles), then there is no problem, or at least not the same problem.

A different kind of objection can be disposed of very briefly. It is that as a matter of experience, we do not think in terms of principles. Rather, on particular occasions we simply know instinctively what is right. Now this may very well be true or perhaps true for a number of people. However, the question at issue is not a psychological one about the kind of process that goes on before a moral judgment is made; it is a philosophical one about how we may justify making the moral judgments we do make, by whatever psychological process we make them. Whatever goes on in the heads of mathematicians, it is still Euclid's proofs alone which can justify Euclid's theorems.

Ultimate moral principles. Moral principles in the sense adumbrated above will be of varying degrees of generality, and some will be held to be more fundamental than others. For example, the principle that one ought not to commit adultery may be defended on the ground that adultery is inimical to the stability of the family. In terms of reasons for acting, this can be put as follows. The fact that someone is married is held to be a reason for his refraining from sexual intercourse with anyone other than his spouse. But why is this a reason? Because, it might be said, *in fact* sexual infidelity is apt to break up the unity of the family. Such an argument would, of course, presuppose that the fact that something is apt to disrupt the family is a reason for avoiding it or, in other words, that one ought not to disrupt the family. Thus the principle "One ought not to commit adultery" would be regarded as less fundamental than the principle "One ought not to disrupt the unity of the family." In the process of trying to justify particular moral judgments, we will usually find ourselves trying to show that certain necessary conditions of their correctness, our moral principles, have further necessary conditions in terms of more fundamental moral principles. The process will usually be much more complicated than I have represented it; in justifying a less fundamental moral principle, we will usually find a variety of more fundamental moral principles coming into play. But however complicated such a process may be, it is obvious that we cannot suppose it to go on forever. At some point we should reach some principles which we regard as the most fundamental. For example, we might want to say that we do not claim that one ought to be kind because this follows from some further principle; we ought to be kind because we ought, and that is an end to the matter. These we may call ultimate moral principles, and their correctness is a necessary condition of the correctness of all other moral judgments. Unless some such ultimate moral principles can be shown to be justifiable, no other moral judgments can be shown to be justifiable.

Some philosophers hold that this representation of the matter is utterly mistaken and, indeed, that it is precisely because of this "justificationist" view that so many philosophers despair of finding an answer and become ethical skeptics. If, it is argued, moral principles are regarded not as first premises from which a moral system is deduced but as conjectures which can be altered and amended by subsequent moral experience, we at least have a method of correcting our moral attitudes which will justify us in claiming that they are more or less rationally defensible. It will not be possible to do this view justice in a small space. It can only be said here that the major difficulty with this view is that the test of the moral principle is taken to be the particular judgments we are inclined to make, particular judgments which conflict with the supposed principle and thus refute it. But what is now the test of the correctness of the particular judgment? The suggested method would seem to be a way of finding out, by examining someone's particular judgments, what his moral principles are rather than a way of finding out which moral principles are correct. Furthermore, it has not been claimed in this article that moral principles are first premises from which whole moral systems can be deduced but only that moral principles are statements of relevant moral factors. Their correctness is a necessary, not a sufficient, condition of the correctness of moral judgments.

However, the charge is certainly well founded that this way of setting out the problem is a most plausible invitation to ethical skepticism. For it would on the face of it appear that the very statement of the problem precludes its solution. If we look on more and more general moral principles as representing a regress of necessary conditions of the correctness of moral judgments, then either this regress is viciously infinite or there is a point at which it must stop. But any attempt to justify some principle as a stopping point would appear to start the whole process off

again. To acquiesce in some stopping point would be to accept an ultimate principle and, it would seem, to accept that nothing further could be said in its justification. It looks then as if this way of putting the problem makes inevitable the conclusion that ultimate principles are unjustifiable.

Autonomy and objectivity of moral principles. One way to put the problem is to regard it as a conflict between the autonomy and the objectivity of moral principles.

The demand that ethics be regarded as autonomous originated with Kant, in the view that an action is not moral unless it is determined by the agent's rational will rather than by something external to that will, such as a desire, or the will of another (a king, a friend, the state, God). Here the concern is with the determination of action, not directly with the determination or, rather, justification of moral judgment. The autonomy of moral principles, with which we are concerned, is not, however, entirely unconnected with Kant's sense of autonomy. It is the idea that a moral judgment can never depend for its correctness entirely on factors which are nonmoral; that is, that in the justification of any moral judgment one must have recourse to a moral principle, which must in turn be justified in terms of some more general moral principle and so on. In other words, a moral judgment or principle is never deducible from any set of premises which contain no moral judgment or principle.

The demand that morality be regarded as objective was also emphasized by Kant. A moral act for Kant was one that could be willed by an autonomous, rational will; its character as a moral act depended not on the particular nature or desires of the willing agent but on the nature of a rational will as such. For Kant a maxim is objective when it is valid for any rational being. Again, Kant's concern was with the determination of action rather than the justification of judgment. But once again our sense of objectivity is not unconnected with Kant's. When someone's judgment is stigmatized as subjective rather than objective, this means that some idiosyncratic factors such as the hopes and fears or special interests of the speaker have affected his judgment; an objective judgment, however, is one not affected by such idiosyncratic factors but one which any reasonable and unbiased person would form in the circumstances. Obviously, we can speak of objective matters only in respect of matters which are publicly determinable, where we can talk of what would be judged by any reasonable and careful observer rather than what appears to be the case to some individual because of some peculiarities of his own. Thus, we might say with Kant that objectively true judgments are those which are "valid for all rational beings" rather than what merely seems to be so to certain individuals. The demand of objectivity in ethics may then be put at its most minimal as the demand that the truth of any moral judgment shall not depend on the peculiarities of the person making it but, rather, that it shall be determinable by any rational observer who is apprised of the facts. Its truth will not depend on the fact that it is judged so by some one person rather than another but on objective considerations.

The conflict between the demands of objectivity and autonomy is now not difficult to see. For how can ultimate principles, which cannot be based on any further considerations, be based on objective considerations? How can we claim that they are matters which are publicly determinable when it would seem that, if they were autonomous, no considerations beyond themselves would make their truth determinable at all?

Henry Sidgwick, impressed by the utilitarian moral system but despairing of the kinds of argument put forward by earlier utilitarians such as Bentham and Mill to justify their ultimate principle, substituted instead the doctrine of intuition, a doctrine which was accepted by many other philosophers who were very far from being utilitarians. It was thought that the problem of justification in ethics was parallel to similar problems in other fields of knowledge and that in each case one would find oneself with incorrigible starting points, truths known directly, without inference or the necessity or possibility of further justification. Thus, in our knowledge of the world we might be thought to begin with direct awareness of our experience; in mathematics, with the direct perception of mathematical relationships. In ethics we begin simply with the perception of universal ethical relationships, between what is right or fitting and certain states of affairs. Whatever the difficulties in this general epistemological theory, in ethics there is the additional difficulty that the common-sense roots of the problem of justification—the inescapable fact of disagreement on fundamental ethical matters—are untouched by the doctrine of intuitionism. The appeal to intuition in the face of this disagreement leaves no way of rationally resolving it. (See ETHICAL OBJECTIVISM; ETHICS, PROBLEMS OF; MORAL SENSE.)

Transcendental arguments. It is possible, however, that an account of the justification of ultimate principles can be given which avoids both an infinite regress of justifying principles and any arbitrary stopping point. Kant's demands for autonomy and objectivity amount to the requirement that a morally good action be rationally chosen in accord with a law which is valid for all rational beings universally and which is determined by nothing beyond itself. The difficulties in making the demands of autonomy and objectivity compatible, so that this requirement becomes a feasible one, seem capable of only one kind of solution, which was the one adopted by Kant. If moral principles cannot be justified by considerations outside themselves yet must be regarded as objectively justifiable, then it seems that certain moral principles must somehow be demanded by the formal character of morality itself; certain rules must be required by any morality that is to satisfy the two demands.

Kant's particular solution has not seemed very satisfactory, but if a solution is to be found at all, it must be in the same direction. To put the point in more contemporary language, the only kind of solution which seems possible is one that shows that certain moral principles must be regarded as correct if moral discourse is to be possible at all, at least as an autonomous and objective form of practical discourse. An argument to this effect may be called a transcendental argument. If such arguments can be constructed, it should be easy to see how they solve the problem we have been considering. For a principle can be shown to be objectively true, without appealing to factors outside itself, if it can be shown that the form of discourse

of which the principle is an example is impossible without presupposing the principle. That is, by showing that no one can claim to be using a form of autonomous, practical, and objective discourse unless he at the same time accepts the principle in question.

Three arguments of this kind can be advanced to establish three ultimate principles, which we may call the principles of impartiality, rational benevolence, and liberty. It is important that throughout it should be borne in mind that these arguments are intended to establish ultimate principles—that is, factors of the most general moral relevance, which will be necessary, but by no means sufficient, to establishing any correct moral theories, rules, or particular judgments. Even given that these arguments establish the ultimate principles of impartiality, rational benevolence, and liberty, there will still remain the difficult problem of their application in practice.

Impartiality. As far as we are concerned with a form of discourse in which we objectively judge actions right or wrong, so that a correct practical judgment is one that could in principle be reached by anybody, such judgments must be made in terms of features which the actions or the situations in which they are done possess and not on any other factors arbitrarily introduced by the person making the judgment. Thus, any feature picked out as relevant must be one which is always relevant unless there is some special explanation, for a feature which is relevant in one case and not in another, where there is no further difference, is one that is not relevant at all in any ordinary sense and forms no guide to action. It follows that any action which it is right or wrong for one person to do is right or wrong for every person to do unless there are some special factors present in the other cases. And from this demand of universality it follows, insofar as morality is practical, that one ought to act in accordance with it: What anyone ought to do in any given set of circumstances is what anyone else ought to do, as long as his case is not relevantly different, and anything one ought to do on any given occasion is what one ought to do on every occasion unless again there are factors present which are relevantly different. That one ought to treat similar cases similarly is obviously a general case of the particular requirement of justice toward men, that any form of treatment which is thought to be right for one man must be right for all others, unless the others are significantly different.

Rational benevolence. The principle of rational benevolence is that stated by Sidgwick, that one ought in action to consider the interests of all beings in the universe. That this is a most impractical injunction is important; but not fatal, for how in practical situations we may apply any ultimate principle is another, though admittedly difficult, question.

The principle may be justified as follows. The demand of objectivity is that what is right or wrong should be determinable at least in principle by all rational beings. This requires that moral discourse should be a form of public discourse, in which the relevance and force of any consideration is dependent on its content and not on the will or status of whoever puts it forward. That is, the remark of any rational being may be relevant to the question whether some action is right or wrong. The ideal of this form of discourse therefore requires that it should be possible for any rational being to participate in it as an interlocutor; if any is excluded arbitrarily then all may be, and the form of discourse as a public institution would be impossible. This does not mean that other forms of discourse may not be constructed in which certain possible interlocutors are excluded by fiat, but this would not then be the fully rational, autonomous, and objective form of discourse we require. A parallel may be found in scientific discourse. As far as it is objective, considerations must be dealt with on their merits and not in terms of the will or status of whoever puts them forward. If any arbitrary exclusion of possible interlocutors is made, then we do not have public objective scientific discourse but a sort of game in which arbitrarily selected players alone are entitled to make certain moves and in which what is determined in the outcome is who has won rather than what is true.

If moral discourse is to be public and objective, then it must allow for the participation of any possible rational interlocutor. Now let us define an interest as that which any rational being should seek for himself insofar as he considers the effects of his actions on himself and not on others except insofar as what affects others also affects him (for example, if it is rational for anyone to avoid pain, then it is in my interest to seek those actions which avoid pain to myself but not necessarily those which avoid pain to others except insofar as the pain of others causes pain to me or prevents my achieving some other end which it would be rational for me to choose for myself). Now it is by definition necessary that every rational being should seek his own interests as far as possible. It would be irrational for any being to participate in a form of discourse the practical effect of which would be to deny his interests; hence, it would be irrational for anyone to adopt moral discourse without further justification if from the beginning his interests were to be ruled out. But this means that anyone who wishes to adopt moral discourse must allow that any possible interlocutor must not have his interests ruled out of consideration from the beginning, and any rational being is in principle a possible interlocutor. It follows that as far as public objective moral discourse is to be possible, it is presupposed that what is determined by such means will not neglect the interests of any rational being—that is, that in deciding what I ought to do, or what anyone ought to do, the interests of all rational beings whatsoever must be taken into account.

Liberty. The principle of liberty is that one ought not to interfere, without special justification, in the chosen course of any rational being or impose on any rational being conditions which will prevent him from pursuing his chosen courses of action. Moral discourse is a form of discourse in which we try to guide action rationally. We try to determine action on the basis of a rational consideration of the nature of the action and its context, not by some other means such as violence. Any interference with the chosen course of a rational being is a determination of his action by force or at least a limit imposed by force on the extent to which his actions may be rationally determined. Such interference must then be presupposed as absent in public objective practical discourse in which action is determined by reason, and hence in using such discourse, in partici-

pating in it as an institution, one is presupposing that one ought not to interfere by force, but only by rational persuasion, in the chosen course of any rational being.

The arguments given for these three principles are very much oversimplified, and it could not be claimed that they have the force of demonstrations. But enough has been said to show that the type of argument they represent is at least a possible one and hence that the apparent conflict between autonomy and objectivity is not a real one and that the problem of the justification of ultimate principles may not be insoluble.

Completeness and application of principles. Two important problems remain. The first we may deal with briefly. It is one which was very important to Kant, with regard to both theoretical and practical principles. How can we be sure that we have achieved completeness in any list of principles? If ultimate principles can be established only by transcendental arguments, we have at least some clue to the answer to this problem; for the rest it might be argued that the problem is not so urgent as some have thought.

A transcendental argument is one which depends on an account of what is necessary to a given form of discourse; in ethics we are concerned with what is necessary to a form of discourse which is practical, universal, objective, and autonomous. We are, that is, dependent on a consideration of the formal characteristics of the form of discourse. This gives at least some negative criterion for deciding what principles may be justified as ultimate. Thus, it would be most implausible to suggest, for example, that "One ought not to drink alcoholic liquor on Sundays" could be justified as an ultimate moral principle. For it is reasonably obvious that no direct connection could be established between the purely formal characteristics of any form of discourse and such particular matters as are picked out by the concepts of the principle in question. Such a principle would have to be, if justifiable at all, one which would depend on matters beyond the purely formal characteristics of practical reason. However, it is always possible, though in this case surely a fantastic suggestion, that someone with sufficient ingenuity might show that some apparently low-level principle is in fact justifiable as an ultimate one by a transcendental argument. And this may disturb us, for how can we be sure that we are not failing to take account of such principles all the time? We should not, however, be much disturbed, for two reasons. First, if a principle is a necessary condition of the possibility of moral discourse, one would expect to find it as a pervasive explicit or implicit principle of most moral codes (allowing for the resources of human confusion), and this is true for the three principles—justice, benevolence, and liberty—we have mentioned. Second, when it is suggested that there is a reason for acting in one way rather than another, the suggestion requires justification, in the absence of which the suggestion may be reasonably ignored. The onus of proof is on anyone who suggests that a certain principle is correct; until such proof is at least suggested, the fear that there may be quite unknown principles, which are not generally accepted but which could, with sufficient ingenuity, be justified transcendentally, is an idle one.

The second difficulty which we face at this point is of

the utmost importance; indeed, one might fairly say that out of it all the really important and difficult questions of substance in ethics arise. It is the problem of the application of these principles to particular situations, both in themselves and in relation to one another. Unless it is possible to show that these principles can be rationally applied, then no amount of rational demonstration of the ultimate principles will enable us to show that the particular moral judgments we make can be rationally justified.

In this article it has been argued that any account of how particular judgments about what ought to be done can be justified will need to examine principles which are necessary but not sufficient to justify particular judgments. These principles will pick out factors of general moral relevance, and the principles in turn will require justification. This may then require reference to more general principles, but some principles which are incapable of further justification will be reached in this way, and these we have called ultimate principles. It would seem that ultimate principles could never be justified objectively, but it is suggested that arguments which show them to be necessary if objective practical discourse is to be possible would justify them and that such arguments are possible. It is, however, emphasized that since ultimate principles are necessary but not sufficient to the justification of particular judgments, we have not by this suggestion solved the whole problem of how ethical disagreement can be rationally resolved. We have only removed one ground for saying that they can never be rationally resolved.

Bibliography

For an account of objectivity and autonomy, and an attempt to justify certain factors as ethically relevant from a consideration of the formal character of practical reason, see Immanuel Kant, *The Moral Law: Kant's Groundwork of the Metaphysic of Morals,* translated by H. J. Paton (London, 1964).

Attempts to justify ultimate principles are to be found in Jeremy Bentham's *Introduction to the Principles of Morals and Legislation* in *A Fragment on Government, and an Introduction to the Principles of Morals and Legislation,* W. Harrison, ed. (Oxford, 1948); J. S. Mill's *Utilitarianism* in *Utilitarianism, Liberty, and Representative Government,* No. 482A in Everyman's Library; Henry Sidgwick's *Methods of Ethics* (London, 1907; reprinted 1962).

More recent attempts to justify some factors as of ultimate ethical relevance are to be found in Kurt Baier's *The Moral Point of View: A Rational Basis for Ethics* (Ithaca, N.Y., 1958), especially Chs. 7–8, and Baier's two articles in *Philosophical Studies,* Vol. 4 (1953)—"Good Reasons," 1–15, and "Proving a Moral Judgment," 33–44; J. N. Findlay's *Values and Intentions* (London, 1961), his "Morality by Convention," in *Mind,* N.S. Vol. 53 (1944), 142–169, and his "Justification of Attitudes," in *Mind,* N.S. Vol. 63 (1954), 145–161; Philippa Foot's "Moral Arguments," in *Mind,* N.S. Vol. 67 (1958), 502–513, and her "Moral Beliefs," in *PAS,* N.S. Vol. 59 (1958/1959), 85–104; A. P. Griffiths' "Justifying Moral Principles," in *PAS,* N.S. Vol. 58 (1957/1958), 103–124; D. L. Pole's *The Conditions of Rational Enquiry* (London, 1961), especially Ch. V; M. G. Singer's *Generalisation in Ethics* (London, 1963); S. E. Toulmin, *An Examination of the Place of Reason in Ethics* (Cambridge, 1950; reprinted 1958).

A. PHILLIPS GRIFFITHS

UNAMUNO Y JUGO, MIGUEL DE (1864–1936), Spanish philosopher of life. Unamuno's concern was neither with the problems of linguistic clarification and conceptual analysis nor with speculative metaphysical constructions but, rather, with coming to terms with life both intellectually and emotionally. The symbols he used are related to Spanish life and destiny and his way of thinking was Spanish, but his message is universal. He expressed himself symbolically, through poetry, religious writings, and the novel, and through the general evocative and emotive character of his prose. However, his efforts to give literal articulation to the mystery and anguish of his existence make him a philosopher rather than exclusively a novelist or poet. The style of philosophy that Unamuno represents must at all times emanate from the world situation and the life situation of the individual philosopher. It follows that Unamuno's philosophy is to be found not only in his writings but also in his general mode of life, particularly in his conspicuous political actions at a time of serious turmoil in Spain.

In view of this it is quite proper to call Unamuno an existentialist. First, his philosophy clearly wells up from his own human situation in space and time. Second, his writings tend to be emotive rather than intellectual. He wished to express not exact ideas but feelings; and feelings are often more accurately expressed in the turgid and quasi-sentimental language of Unamuno than in logical exegesis. Third, his subject matter was existential—death and anxiety, doubt and faith, guilt and immortality. Fourth, he traced the sources of his thought to such existentialist precursors as Pascal and Kierkegaard and found kinship with anyone who stressed intuition and subjectivity in the life of man and in the construction of world views—with men like Schopenhauer, Nietzsche, and William James. Finally, Unamuno's philosophy, like Kierkegaard's, was deliberately unsystematic, an expression of his wrestling with existence, and any systematic account of that expression must falsify or at least distort the facts of experience.

LIFE

Don Miguel de Unamuno y Jugo was born in the Basque city of Bilbao. He studied philosophy and classics at the University of Madrid and moved to Salamanca in 1891 as professor of Greek at the university there. He was associated with the university for most of the rest of his life, being appointed rector in 1901 and named rector for life in 1934. Unamuno's first published work, *En torno al casticismo* ("On Purism," 1895), was a historical and political work which questioned and examined the place of Spain in the modern world. His first novel, *Paz en la guerra* ("Peace in War," 1897), sometimes called the first existentialist novel, was based on his early memories of the siege of Bilbao in 1873. In the novel *Amor y pedagogía* ("Love and Pedagogy," 1902) Unamuno tried to show the basic failure of science in dealing with human and humanistic problems. *Amor y pedagogía* describes a man's attempt to educate his family scientifically and the dismal failure of this attempt. *Vida de Don Quijote y Sancho* (*Life of Don Quixote and Sancho,* 1905) foreshadowed many of the themes of Unamuno's masterpiece, *Del sentimiento trágico de la vida en los hombres y en los pueblos.* The *Vida de Don Quijote* is a plea for salvation through the anguish and passion experienced by the man of flesh and blood. *Del sentimiento trágico de la vida (The Tragic Sense of Life)*, which appeared in 1913, expresses Unamuno's intemperate longing for eternal life and his desperate search for some solace in the exploration of the tension and conflict that exists between faith and reason. The novel *Niebla (Mist)* was published in 1914, and in 1917 Unamuno's modern version of the problem of Cain, *Abel Sánchez*, appeared. In 1924 Unamuno was deported to Fuerteventura in the Canary Islands for his unrelenting attack on the totalitarianism of General Primo de Rivera. He managed to escape to France and remained in exile until 1930, when Rivera's dictatorship fell. Unamuno was reinstated as rector of the University of Salamanca the next year.

From 1931 to 1933 Unamuno served in the Cortes, the constituent assembly of the Spanish republic, as an independent Republican deputy. His last and greatest novel appeared in 1933. *San Manuel bueno, mártir* ("Saint Emanuel the Good, Martyr") describes the agony of a priest who finds it impossible to believe. Unamuno's independence, individualism, and patriotism led to his being dismissed from his rectorship in 1936. He at first favored the nationalists in the Spanish Civil War, but he came to feel that neither side was working for the best interest of either Spain or humanity. During the last year of his life he was under house arrest in Salamanca.

CENTRAL THEMES

To characterize Unamuno's basically unsystematic philosophical position is difficult. A few themes can be isolated from his philosophy, however, and may be generalized as follows:

(1) Unamuno's interest was primarily in the individual rather than in social reality, and thus his philosophy extols the agony and the importance of the individual. In this context Unamuno's Spanishness becomes not a social ideal but the expression of his individuality.

(2) He emphasized the importance of personal integrity. Truthfulness to oneself and total honesty in ideals are the hallmarks of the philosophical man.

(3) He saw his function—and that of philosophers generally—as that of a Socratic gadfly to the community. The philosopher is needed to reawaken us to our genuine nature, to our authentic problems, and to the honest attempts to resolve them.

(4) Much of Unamuno's life was spent in agony over the conflict between faith and reason. Reason alone—which Unamuno invariably associated with skepticism—cannot lead to any kind of fundamentally hopeful knowledge. Faith can do so, but faith exists only in the shadow of the despair that is reason; it has no independent and positive existence. Faith can never totally dispel reason, and reason always leads to despair. The logic of the heart is hopeful and gives meaning to life, but it is never strong enough fully to set aside the darkness of the logic of the head.

(5) Unamuno's general conception of religion was related to the tension between faith and reason. Although Catholicism did not fully satisfy either his emotions or his reason, Unamuno felt that religion is a necessity of life. We must risk faith in the way that Pascal wagered, James

willed, and Kierkegaard leaped. We must, for profoundly pragmatic reasons, live as if God does in fact exist.

(6) The above views led to the doctrine that commitment is one of the central features of the authentic life. An authentic life is dedicated to and identified with an ideal, an ideal that genuinely emanates from the depths of each man. The truth of such a commitment can be vindicated and confirmed only by the heart; but since reason casts permanent doubt on that commitment, a blind, courageous leap of faith is needed for authentic human existence.

(7) Life thus becomes a vague, brittle, and tenuous cluster of experiences between two awesome, incomprehensible, and impenetrable barriers of nothingness: birth and death. Only through a foundationless but fervid commitment can man escape, at least temporarily, the despair of meaninglessness.

(8) Unamuno loved Spain and was an impartial observer and recorder of the Spanish temperament. According to Unamuno, the Spaniard—like his paradigm Don Quixote—wants adventures, willingly risks revolution for the establishment of utopian societies, and is impractical. But there is also a practical side to the Spaniard, symbolized by Sancho Panza, which often degenerates into blind formalism, intolerance, religious bigotry, and unprincipled commercialism.

Unamuno's commitment to Spain embraced his commitment to the Catholic church. However, it was only his heart that pulled him toward the church; his reason pulled him away from it. This excruciating tension between his fervent emotional need and hope for the presence of an enveloping and supporting God and for certainty with respect to the immortality of the soul on the one hand, and the fact that he found this world picture rationally untenable on the other hand, was central to Unamuno's philosophy.

GOD AND EXISTENCE

The problem of human existence, in Unamuno's famous formulation, is *el sentimiento trágico de la vida* (the tragic sense of life); it is the fact that there is sorrow which has no resolution and evil which has no redemption. We should weep, not because it helps but precisely because it avails us nothing. If we recognize the pervasiveness of hopelessness and despair, we can at least experience the brotherhood of man. Without disease or defect (be it sin in paradise, a weak species of ape like man, or immunization—the momentary creation of an illness for the sake of health) there can be no progress. Philosophy in this sense is eminently practical: *Primum vivere, deinde philosophari*—"man philosophizes in order to live." "He philosophizes either in order to resign himself to life or to seek some finality in it, or to distract himself and forget his griefs, or for pastime and amusement" (*The Tragic Sense of Life*, p. 29).

The most attractive solution to the problems of human existence, to "the tragic sense of life," is the hope for eternal life expressed in man's perennial hunger for immortality. This hunger has two dimensions—it refers either to the nondestruction of the soul or to the merger of the soul with the universe or the totality of being. In connection with the first of these dimensions, Unamuno seems to have held that the destruction of a man's consciousness is an a priori impossibility: we cannot even conceive of the nonexistence of consciousness, since that conception is itself an act of consciousness. In connection with the second, he concluded that man is nothing if he is not everything—to exist is yearning to reach all space, all time, all being. To be a man is to seek to become God. Unless man is God, he is not even man: "Either all or nothing!" was Unamuno's motto.

Catholicism promises immortality, but modern rationalism denies it. As a consequence, fundamental doubt sets in, doubt that is both passionate and rational. Such tense but mature insight, however, does lead to some solace: "But here, in the depths of the abyss, the despair of the heart and of the will and the skepticism of reason meet face to face and embrace like brothers" (*ibid.*, p. 106). Man must reach the depths of despair, doubt, and agony in order to arrive at the solid "foundation upon which the heart's despair must build up its hope." Furthermore, the agony that arises out of the tensions of passionate doubt and total rational skepticism when both are focused on the problem of eternal life may also form "a basis for action and morals."

Tension is the essence of life, and the tension that leads to agony is also the tension that allows man to feel his existence; pure consciousness deserves only suicide. Life, to be felt as real, *as there,* as existing, must be a life of passion. This truth is well illustrated by love, which for Unamuno is basically sexual love. In the tensions and paradoxes of love—as well as in compassion and pity—man experiences the richness, concreteness, and fullness of his existence. Consciousness, in this sense, is knowledge through participation; it is "co-feeling."

The hope for immortality is supported by the notion of God. The traditional arguments for the existence of God prove nothing other than that we have the idea of God. The God who is the idea of excellence and the first mover is a fleshless and passionless abstraction and cannot soothe the anguish of man's existence. This abstraction is not what the heart craves. The strongest conclusion of reason is that we "cannot prove the impossibility of His existence." Belief in God is an expression solely of man's longing for the rich and concrete experience of his existence and of his determination to live by this longing and make it a basis for action. Man's agonizing hunger for the divine—even though it cannot be satisfied directly—leads to hope, faith, and charity, and eventually to his sense of beauty and of goodness.

There are other typically existentialist themes in Unamuno's philosophy:

(1) Man is painfully aware of his contingency. That he exists or that he is the particular person he happens to be is neither necessary nor permanent.

(2) To assuage his anguish, man must feel his existence, even if he is led to suffering. He must learn to experience his uniqueness by expanding the range and the self-consciousness of his perceptions of the world.

(3) All existence is a mystery: consciousness is a mystery, contingency is a mystery, absurdity is a mystery, and anguish is a mystery.

(4) Love is the basic force of human existence. It encompasses all the conative relations of man to being and enables him to overcome the anguish of his contingency by giving him the rich feeling of his own existence.

(5) The central temporal dimension of human existence is the future, which leads to a desire for immortality and to a concern with death. This focus on the future is expressed in Unamuno's use of *esperar:* it means both the joys of hope and the anguish of eternal waiting. The structure of the future expresses both man's determination to continue to live and his permanent dissatisfaction and despair concerning existence.

(6) Goals are self-created and are permanent commitments.

(7) Finally, Unamuno's views on the nature of language foreshadow those of Merleau-Ponty and Heidegger. Language is a mode of being. Living, not only knowing, is expressed in certain basic forms, one of which is language. Language thus is not symbolic but the actual embodiment of an idea. Without language an idea could not exist.

EPISTEMOLOGY AND METAPHYSICS

Truth, according to Unamuno, is subjective; it exists only as it is manifested in authentic belief. Belief, in turn, is an expression of man's total being and consequently is realized in action. Objective truth is, strictly speaking, a meaningless conception. Through its identity with belief and action, truth is ultimately an act of will. It is a will to create; and the will as creator wants and loves at the same time. Because of this personal and volitional factor in truth, the opposite of truth is not error but the lie. This subjective view of truth gives a distinct idealistic, even mystical, cast to Unamuno's thought. All knowledge about man and the world is subjective in the sense that it begins with first-person experience. To think of truth as transcending first-person experiences is, strictly speaking, a contradiction, because the very program of transcending first-person experiences is a first-person project and concept and a construction. There is, however, another kind of truth, illustrated by mathematics, which is the function of reason alone, whereas true belief is a function of man's whole being.

Unamuno followed Heraclitus in holding that reality is a state of permanent flux, so that no two experiences are ever the same. There are two metaphysical alternatives. Reality may be a vast sea of consciousness with my subjectivity at the center. There is no easy way to distinguish this consciousness from a mere dream. Its sole foundation is the fact that I experience it and that I will it to be real. Unamuno ultimately rejected this view. The other view is that the focus of our being may be outside ourselves. We may identify ourselves with the realities of other people, with trees, flowers, and mountains. This orientation, to which Unamuno did not accede fully but which he preferred, is close to objective idealism and to naturalism. In either view, man and world are intimately meshed.

Works by Unamuno

Obras completas, Manuel García Blanco, ed., 7 vols. Madrid, 1950–1959.
En torno al casticismo. Madrid, 1895.

Paz en la guerra. Madrid, 1897; 3d ed., Madrid, 1931.

Amor y pedagogía. Barcelona, 1902; 2d ed., Madrid, 1934.

Vida de Don Quijote y Sancho, según Miguel de Cervantes Saavedra, explicada y comentada. Madrid, 1905; 2d enlarged ed., Madrid, 1914. Translated by H. P. Earle as *Life of Don Quixote and Sancho According to Miguel de Cervantes Saavedra Expounded With Comment.* New York, 1927.

Poesías. Bilbao, 1907.

Por tierras de Portugal y España. Madrid, 1911.

Rosario de sonetos líricos. Madrid, 1911.

Contra esto y aquello. Madrid, 1912; 4th ed., Buenos Aires, 1941.

El espejo de la muerte. Madrid, 1913.

Del sentimiento trágico de la vida en los hombres y en los pueblos. Madrid, 1913. Translated by J. E. Crawford Flitch as *The Tragic Sense of Life in Men and in Peoples.* London, 1921.

Niebla. Madrid, 1914. Translated by Warren Fite as *Mist. A Tragi-comic Novel.* New York, 1928.

Ensayos, 7 vols. Madrid, 1916–1918.

Abel Sánchez. Madrid, 1917. Translated by Anthony Kerrigan in *Abel Sanchez and Other Stories.* Chicago, 1956.

Andanzas y visiones españolas. Madrid, 1922; 2d ed., Buenos Aires, 1941.

De Fuerteventura á París. Paris, 1925.

La agonía del cristianismo. Madrid, 1931. Translated by K. F. Reinhardt as *The Agony of Christianity.* New York, 1960.

San Manuel ,bueno, mártir y tres historias más. Madrid, 1933.

Epistolario á Clarín. Madrid, 1938.

La ciudad de Henoc. Comentario 1933. Mexico City, 1941.

Poems, translated by Eleanor Turnbull. Baltimore, 1952.

Cancionero, diario poético. Buenos Aires, 1953.

Teatro. Barcelona, 1954.

Cincuenta poesías inéditas (1899–1927). Madrid, 1958.

Works on Unamuno

Ferrater Mora, José, *Unamuno,* translated by Philip Silver. Berkeley and Los Angeles, 1962.

Meyer, François, *L'Ontologie de Miguel de Unamuno.* Paris, 1955.

Oromí, Miguel, *Pensamiento filosófico de M. de Unamuno.* Madrid, 1943.

Rudd, Margaret Thomas, *The Lone Heretic.* Austin, Texas, 1963.

PETER KOESTENBAUM

UNCERTAINTY RELATIONS. See QUANTUM MECHANICS, PHILOSOPHICAL IMPLICATIONS OF.

UNCONSCIOUS. Under the impact of new developments in science, ideas in all fields are undergoing rapid change. This is especially true of the twentieth-century conception of the "unconscious," the term being used here in a general sense for all those mental processes of which the individual is not aware while they occur in him.

The present interest in the unconscious is a result of the advance of science and psychology during the past hundred years, and to understand this interest requires some knowledge of the history of ideas. But the timing of this outburst of interest, its intensity (which is greatest in the English-speaking countries and least in Russia and China), and the particular conception of the unconscious which is now dominant are mainly due to one man, Sigmund Freud. His high degree of success in creating widespread appreciation of the power of the unconscious makes the improvement of his conception of it a matter of great importance. Fortunately, a historical survey can not only put recent sectarian conflicts in perspective but can also throw light on aspects of the unconscious which have long

been recognized by philosophers and humanists but which receive inadequate emphasis in Freudian theory.

There have been few peoples since, say, 3000 B.C. that have not possessed myths expressing a sense of the power of divine or natural agencies to influence the individual without his being aware of that influence. Before the emergence of clear conceptions regarding nature and man there prevailed a sense of the continuity of phenomena, and it was taken for granted that man was part of a totality in which anything might influence anything else. This assumption of continuity is evident in much Eastern thought. Western recognition, from around A.D. 1600, of unconscious mental processes, at first philosophical but gradually becoming more scientific, may be superficially regarded as the rediscovery of something that had long been taken for granted in certain Eastern traditions and also in some Greek and Christian writings. Plotinus held that "the absence of a conscious perception is no proof of the absence of mental activity," Augustine was interested in memory as a faculty extending beyond the grasp of the conscious mind, Thomas Aquinas developed a theory of the mind covering "processes in the soul of which we are not immediately aware," and most mystics assumed that insights might be gained by a process of inner reception in which the conscious mind is passive.

But these early ideas lack an essential feature of the modern concept of the unconscious that became possible only after Western thought had set out on the search for precision and scientific validity and, in doing so, had separated the conscious mind from material processes; that is, this became possible only from about 1600 on, or after Descartes. For the ultimate purpose of the concept of unconscious mental processes is to link conscious awareness and behavior with its background—a system of processes of which one is not immediately aware—and to establish this connection without losing the benefits of scientific precision. Here lies the weakness of the concept of the unconscious: it cannot be made fully acceptable to the scientific age until some science or union of sciences has provided an adequate conception of the unity and continuity of conscious thought, unconscious cerebral processes, physiological changes, and the processes of growth. In fact, the idea of the unconscious (or some equivalent) can acquire scientific status only after a unified picture of the human organism has repaired the intellectual lesions created by Cartesian and other dualistic or specialized methods.

Descartes to Freud. It is useful, if oversimplified, to consider that Descartes, by his definition of mind as awareness, provoked as a reaction the Western "rediscovery" of unconscious mental processes. During the two and a half centuries between Descartes's *Discourse on Method* (1637) and Freud's first interest in the unconscious, many philosophers, psychologists, biologists, novelists, and poets recognized that mental activity of various kinds occurs without awareness. This view was reached through introspection, through observation, or through attempts to create a theory of the working of the mind. By the last decades of the nineteenth century it was so widespread in Germany and Britain, and to a lesser extent in France, that one can say that by then the existence of the unconscious mind had become a common assumption of educated and psychological discussions; however, its structure, mode of operation, and role in illness were left for the twentieth century to explore.

Here we can consider only a few names out of many, selected either because they were influential or because their ideas represent an advancing understanding.

Our survey opens at the moment when Cartesian thought was acquiring influence. Ralph Cudworth, English divine and philosopher, wrote in 1678:

> There may be some vital energy without clear consciousness or express attention—Our human souls are not always conscious of whatever they have in them—that vital sympathy, by which our soul is united and tied fast to the body, is a thing that we have no direct consciousness of, but only in its effects—There is also a more interior kind of plastic power in the soul . . . whereby it is formative of its own cogitations, which it itself is not always conscious of . . . . (*True Intellectual System of the Universe,* Book I, Ch. 3)

Many other thinkers of the seventeenth and eighteenth centuries expressed similar ideas, at first mainly in relation to the cognitive aspects, such as perception and memory. Leibniz introduced the notion of a quantitative threshold. For him ordinary perceptions were the summation of countless small ones, each of which we are not aware of, because they lie below this threshold.

Two eighteenth-century figures were among the first to direct attention to the emotional aspects of the unconscious mind. Rousseau tried to explore the unconscious background of his own temperament and to discover the reason for his fluctuating moods ("It is thus certain that neither my own judgment nor my will dictated my answer, and that it was the automatic consequence of my embarrassment"), and J. G. Hamann, a German religious philosopher, studied the deeper levels of his own mind as evidenced in his experience of conversion, in the emotional life, and in imaginative thinking ("How much more the formation of our own ideas remains secret!").

Between 1750 and 1830 a number of German philosophers and poets increasingly emphasized the emotional and dynamic aspects of the unconscious. Herder stressed the role of unconscious mental processes in relation to the imagination, dreams, passion, and illness. Goethe expressed in poems and *aperçus* his sense of the fertile interplay of conscious and unconscious in the creative imagination, "where consciousness and unconsciousness are like warp and weft." Fichte treated the unconscious as a dynamic principle underlying conscious reason. Hegel based his philosophy on the conception of an unconscious historical process becoming in the individual a partly conscious will. For Schelling unconscious nature becomes conscious in the ego.

Many of the romantic writers and poets, particularly in Germany and England, echoed what was in the air: a vivid sense of the powerful, dark, yet creative aspects of the unconscious mind. Thus, J. P. F. Richter wrote: "The unconscious is really the largest realm in our minds, and just on account of this unconsciousness the inner Africa, whose unknown boundaries may extend far away."

Another sequence of German thinkers made the idea of the unconscious a commonplace of European educated circles by about 1880: Schopenhauer, C. G. Carus, Gustav Fechner, Eduard von Hartmann, and Nietzsche. Schopenhauer took the idea of a mainly unconscious will in nature and in man as his central theme. Carus, physician and friend of Goethe, opened his *Psyche* (1846) with the words: "The key to the understanding of the character of the conscious life lies in the region of the unconscious" and presented Goethe's favorable view of the unconscious. Fechner, like Freud (who expressed a debt to him), regarded the mind as an iceberg largely below the surface and moved by hidden currents. He used the concept of mental energy, a topography of the mind, an unpleasure–pleasure principle, and a universal tendency toward stability. Von Hartmann's *Philosophy of the Unconscious* (1869) gave a survey of a vast field of unconscious mental activities, and this book enjoyed a great success in Germany, France, and England. He discussed 26 aspects of the unconscious and converted the Goethean ideas of Carus' *Psyche* into a grandiose metaphysical system. Nietzsche, in his penetrating insights into the unconscious, reflected what was already widespread but gave it a new intensity. "The absurd overvaluation of consciousness . . . . Consciousness only touches the surface . . . . The great basic activity is unconscious . . . . Every sequence in consciousness is completely atomistic . . . . The real continuous process takes place below our consciousness; the series and sequence of feelings, thoughts, and so on, are symptoms of this underlying process. . . . All our conscious motives are superficial phenomena; behind them stands the conflict of our instincts and conditions."

Nietzsche had cried, "Where are the new doctors of the soul?" Soon after, Freud started on his task: to begin afresh, unprejudiced by all this speculation, and to try to identify the precise structure of unconscious processes and their role in particular mental disturbances, so that lesions of the mind might be repaired by systematic techniques. We are not here concerned with his methods of therapy or with their degree of efficacy but with his steadily developing and often modified theory of the unconscious mind.

Freud was not the first to develop a systematic theory of conflicts in the unconscious. J. F. Herbart had put forward a theory of the operation of unconscious inhibited ideas and their pressure on consciousness, and of the resulting conflict between conscious and unconscious ideas at the threshold of consciousness. But he had little immediate influence. Meanwhile, a school of medical thought was developing in England that treated the patient as a unity, took for granted the interplay of unconscious and conscious, and sought to use this way of thinking in its approach to mental illness. William Hamilton, student of medicine and metaphysics, lectured on the role of the unconscious, particularly in relation to emotions and action, thus providing the background for the psychiatrist H. Maudsley and the naturalist W. B. Carpenter. Maudsley's *The Pathology of Mind* (1879) expresses this English school of thought about the unconscious and is included in the references given by Freud in his *Interpretation of Dreams* (1900), while Carpenter's *Principles of Mental Physiology* (1876) discusses "unconscious cerebration." A group of physicians in Germany were pursuing similar lines of thought, but for these figures and for the French interest in hypnotism, which exerted a strong influence on depth psychology, the reader must turn to histories of psychiatry.

During the 1870s several theories of unconscious organic memory were developed, and between 1880 and 1910 physicians and philosophers in many countries were concerned with various aspects of the unconscious (see references given in the surveys cited below).

Freud. Sigmund Freud, even late in life, had no idea how extensive attention to the unconscious had been. Today we need to see him in perspective in order to strengthen what was weak in his ideas and so to advance toward a complete theory of the unconscious mind in health as well as in sickness. A more detailed survey of Freudian theory and method is given elsewhere (see FREUD, SIGMUND; PSYCHOANALYTIC THEORIES, LOGICAL STATUS OF; UNCONSCIOUS, PSYCHOANALYTIC THEORIES OF THE); here we can treat only those aspects of his ideas which are directly relevant to the theory of the unconscious.

For Freud all mental processes are determined by natural laws, ultimately by those governing chemical and physical phenomena; they are associated with quantities of psychic energy that strive toward release and equilibrium; the primary driving force is instinctual energy (libido, a concept that was at first narrowly, then more widely interpreted) expressing an often unconscious wish, and moving from unpleasure to physical pleasure (pleasure principle); the predominant energy is sexual, but other forms are present, and Freud later assumed two basic instincts, sexuality in a broad sense and aggression (Eros and Thanatos). The establishment of civilized life involves restraints on sexual activity, and the unconscious proper (in Freudian theory the accessible unconscious being called the preconscious) consists of instinctual energies, either archaic or repressed during the life of the individual, particularly in childhood (universal incestuous desires of the earliest years, adolescent frustrated dreaming, aggressive impulses, etc.); these are available only through the use of special techniques. A genetic or developmental approach to mental illness is therefore essential. Forgetting is an active process in which painful memories are repressed. The Freudian unconscious is a pool of mainly repressed energies, distorted by frustration and exerting a stress on conscious reason and its shaping of the patterns of daily life. The strain produced by this stress, present in some degree in all civilized men and women, is seen in neurosis. It is only by exceptional luck in heredity or experience that civilized man can avoid this tragic and potentially universal feature of modern life, the major influence of the unconscious being antagonistic to reason. This doom and neurosis he can escape (wholly, Freud thought at first; later he had doubts) by becoming aware of his situation and gaining insight into the particular traumatic experiences which created his neurosis. Freud began with an unquestioning conviction that insight brought recovery. The interpretation of dreams (which are symptoms and express wish fulfillment) and the process of free association can render accessible the regions of the unconscious producing the neurosis and can make possible a cure. Myths express for communities what dreams do for the individual. Later, Freud developed his ego theory, dividing the mind into three areas: the id, or basic instincts; the ego, or rational part of the mind which deals with reality; and the superego, a differentiated part of the ego which results mainly from the child's self-identification with his parents. This triple division overlaps awkwardly with the unconscious–conscious dichotomy, and here the theory becomes obscure. It left Freud unsatisfied—indeed, late in his life he stated that understanding of the deepest levels of the mind was not yet possible.

These are, in condensed form, the main ideas which make up the core of the Freudian theory of the unconscious, leaving aside his many applications of it. The theory, in its most characteristic form, is a description of the pathology of civilized man, although for Freud this implied little restriction, since all suffer in some degree from the neurosis of civilization.

When this theory is reviewed today, most agree that Freud's general conception of a repressed unconscious, and its relation to child sexuality, aggression, defense mechanisms, sublimation, and so forth, is a permanent contribution of the highest importance. On the other hand, his sharp categories (conscious–unconscious, wishful–realistic, stages of sexual development, etc.) are merely, as he himself recognized, provisional steps toward the truth. But his theory suffers from a more radical weakness than these.

Freud's attitude toward the unconscious has been regarded as biological. But it was not so in a genuine sense, for all viable organisms display an organizing principle, not yet understood, which ensures that everything occurs in support of the continuation of life. This coordinating and formative principle underlies all organic properties, including the processes of the human unconscious, such as the imaginative and inventive faculties without which civilization could not have developed. It has been widely recognized that this factor—although it had been emphasized in earlier views of the unconscious, for example, by Cudworth, Goethe, Fichte, Schelling, Coleridge, and Carus—is not adequately represented in the Freudian theory, perhaps because it was neglected by the physicochemical approach to organisms dominant when Freud was shaping his ideas. His theory of the mind is overly analytic or atomistic and must be complemented by a general and powerful principle of coordination.

Adler, Jung, and Rank. The lack of a general principle of coordination was recognized by three of Freud's colleagues, Alfred Adler, Carl Gustav Jung, and Otto Rank, who, from different points of view, stressed the potential integration and self-organizing power either of the unconscious or of the mind as a whole. Adler treated the person as a unity; he did not regard the unconscious–conscious division as basic and held that the inaccessible unconscious contains elements which have never been repressed but which are simply not yet understood and are unconsciously assumed in the endeavor to adapt socially and to overcome supposed or real weaknesses.

The individual's aspiration or unconscious need to realize a potential unity was more deeply appreciated by Jung. He created the concept of the collective unconscious, which is not a "group mind" but the deepest level in the individual mind, consisting of potentialities for ways of thinking shared by all men because their genetic constitutions are closely similar and their family and social experiences share certain universal features. In a given society the collective unconscious contains particular traditional symbols or archetypes which organize thought and action. This sociological concept of the deeper mental levels involves a historical background in which ritual, myth, symbol, and religious attitude play organizing and integrating roles that contribute to the strength and stability of the psyche and that are subject to an underlying tendency developing a differentiated unity in the person (individuation). The tension of superficially opposed aspects in the unconscious mind produces autonomous foci of energy, acting as complexes. The ultimate aim for Jung was not discovery of truth but acceptance of the role of deep psychology in the present historical situation: assistance in the search for life-enhancing significance in the fate of living in a scientific age at a time when traditional sources of strength have been weakened but a fully comprehensive scientific truth is not yet in sight. In this search, psychology enters realms that previously belonged to history, philosophy, and religion. Jung's ideas form part of a discursive communication of attitudes, rather than being steps toward an ultimately confirmable theory of unconscious mental processes.

Rank stressed the role of religious and aesthetic traditions in shaping the unconscious, and he saw in the life will a factor making for integration. The writings of these three display agreement that Freud, particularly in his early work, overemphasized the role of genital sexuality, unduly neglected the historical background of the individual unconscious, and failed to allow for the role of factors making for coordination both within each Freudian level of the mind and between the various levels.

The future of the concept. It has been observed (by Ira Progoff and others) that, mainly in their later years, Freud, Adler, Jung, and Rank all looked toward a future theory of the mind based on what perhaps can best be called the organic core of the mind (similar to Jung's objective psyche and psychoid) and capable of covering all human mental faculties, man's cultural history, his imagination, his mental illnesses and health. This still lies ahead. It seems that no important basic advance has been made in the theoretical understanding of the unconscious mind since then; certainly no one has yet made a satisfactory synthesis of the reliable features of their views. Thus, there has been a pause in the advance of the theory of subjective deep psychology. Freud hoped for assistance from the neurophysiology of the brain, but this has not yet come.

We should now consider what the unconscious has stood for in the minds of different groups. The mystics saw it as the link with God; the Christian Platonists as a divine creative principle; the romantics as the connection between the individual and universal powers; the early rationalists as a factor operating in memory, perception and ideas; the postromantics as organic vitality expressed in will, imagination, and creation; dissociated Western man as a realm of violence threatening his stability; physical scientists as the expression of physiological processes in the brain which are not yet understood; monistic thinkers as the prime mover and source of all order and novelty in

thought and action; Freud (in his earlier years) as a melee of inhibited memories and desires the main influence of which is damaging; and Jung as a prerational realm of instincts, myths, and symbols often making for stability. It is natural to seek a common principle underlying these partial truths, but we do not possess the unified language in which to express it scientifically.

The formulation of a valid theory of the integrated human mind and of its various pathologies would imply the possibility of a transformation in man and his unconscious toward a more harmonious condition accompanied by the development of a social order that does not bring with it inescapable neurosis. This may seem a distant hope. But recent advances in biology and medicine have opened new vistas of improvement, and no survey of the idea of the unconscious would be complete without a glance into this possible future for theory and practice, for therein may lie the deepest reason for the fascination which the idea has for so wide a public.

This sketch of the idea of the unconscious has neglected its recent applications to religion, art, the history of science, philosophy, literature (Proust believed that the reality of experience lies in the unconscious), ethics and justice. In all these realms the main effect has been to broaden, deepen, and loosen traditional conceptions. But the unification of scientific principles, so badly needed today, still lies ahead. In this an improved conception of the unconscious must play a crucial role.

Bibliography

HISTORICAL SURVEYS

It is remarkable that no authoritative critical study has yet been made of all ideas of the unconscious from earliest times to the present; the following works are useful historical surveys:

Ellenberger, H., "The Unconscious Before Freud." *Bulletin of the Menninger Clinic,* Vol. 21 (1957), 3.

Margetts, E. L., "Concept of Unconscious in History of Medical Psychology." *Psychiatric Quarterly,* Vol. 27 (1953), 115.

Whyte, L. L., *The Unconscious Before Freud.* New York, 1960; paperback ed., 1962.

Zilboorg, Gregory, *History of Medical Psychology.* New York, 1941.

COMMENTARIES

Drews, A. C. H., *Psychologie des Unbewussten.* Berlin, 1924.

Geiger, Moritz, "Fragment über den Begriff des Unbewussten und die psychische Realität." *Jahrbuch für Philosophie und phänomenologische Forschung,* Vol. 4 (1921), 1–137.

Jones, Ernest, *The Life and Work of Sigmund Freud,* 3 vols. New York, 1953–1957.

MacIntyre, Alasdair C., *The Unconscious; A Conceptual Analysis.* New York, 1958.

Miller, J. G., *Unconsciousness.* New York, 1942.

Northridge, William L., *Modern Theories of the Unconscious.* London, 1924.

Progoff, Ira, *Death and Rebirth of Psychology.* New York, 1942.

Taylor, W. S., "Psycho-analysis Revised or Psychodynamics Developed?" *American Psychologist* (November 1962), 784.

ORIGINAL WORKS

Carus, C. G., *Psyche.* Pforzheim, 1846; 3d ed., Stuttgart, 1860.

Cudworth, Ralph, *True Intellectual System of the Universe.* London, 1678.

Freud, Sigmund, *Die Traumdeutung.* Vienna, 1900. Translated by James Strachey as *The Interpretation of Dreams*, in *Standard Edition of the Complete Psychological Works*, James Strachey, gen. ed., 24 vols. New York, 1953–1964. Vols. IV and V.

Freud, Sigmund, "The Unconscious," in *Collected Papers*, James Strachey, ed., 5 vols. London, 1924–1950. Vol. IV, *Papers on Metapsychology and Papers on Applied Psychoanalysis*, p. 98.

Hartmann, Eduard von, *Die Philosophie des Unbewussten*, 3 vols. Berlin, 1869. Translated by W. C. Coupland as *The Philosophy of the Unconscious*. London, 1884.

Jung, C. G., *Wandlung und Symbole der Libido*. Leipzig, 1912. Translated by Beatrice M. Hinkle as *Psychology of the Unconscious*. London, 1916. Rev. ed. and new translation by R. F. C. Hull from the 4th ed. (1952), *Symbole der Wandlung*, as *Symbols of Transformation*, published as Vol. V of *Collected Works*, Herbert Read et al., eds. London and New York, 1956.

Jung, C. G., *Über die Psychologie des Unbewussten*. Zurich, 1943. Translated by R. F. C. Hull as *Two Essays on Analytical Psychology*, Vol. VII of *Collected Works*. London and New York, 1953; paperback ed., New York, 1956.

Leibniz, G. W., *Die philosophischen Schriften*, C. J. Gerhardt, ed., 7 vols. Berlin, 1875–1890. Vol. V, p. 48, Vol. VI, p. 600.

Schopenhauer, Arthur, *Die Welt als Wille und Vorstellung*. Leipzig, 1819. Translated by R. B. Haldane and J. Kemp as *The World as Will and Idea*, 3 vols. London, 1883–1886.

LANCELOT LAW WHYTE

UNCONSCIOUS, PSYCHOANALYTIC THEORIES OF THE.

Discussions of the unconscious have largely focused on the concept, not on the theory. Freud himself, in his papers of 1900, 1912, and 1915, followed this practice. The original problems have thus been obscured and our perspective of psychoanalysis distorted. In order to clarify the problem we must concentrate on the phases of the problem facing Freud and on the theories he proposed to solve it. We shall then find that we are dealing not with the mere existence of an entity which is untestable or conceptually impossible but with a theory containing a very unusual sort of term, one that does not stand for anything inspectable; this situation is unusual in the lower reaches of science and in ordinary life, but it is a commonplace in high-level explanatory theories. For empirical science is concerned not with establishing the mere existence of entities but with their testable activities—not just with the concept itself but with the theory. Pasteur, for example, showed not simply that germs exist but that there are germs which manufacture poisons. Likewise, it would be pointless to prove the existence of the unconscious, even if such a proof were possible; for Freud, the theory of the unconscious concerned sources, activities, and end products.

Freud's problem. We can begin not with the earliest phase of Freud's problem, which was to understand hysterical manifestations, but with the next form of the problem, which gave rise to the theory of the unconscious. The theory arose very simply from the case of a patient who went into a hypnotic trance of her own accord (Breuer and Freud, *Studies in Hysteria*). Under hypnosis she and other patients recounted tales of traumata which made their physical disorders (paralyses, for example) understandable—but only on the hypothesis that these symptoms were *motivated*. And this required further hypotheses: that the traumatic situations the patients described distressed them and that their motives were also distressing and were forgotten to avoid the distress.

The hypothesis of the unconscious seems to have en-tered the scene here (though such a hypothesis was in some sense widely recognized long before Freud—see L. L. Whyte, *The Unconscious Before Freud*). Freud postulated that memories of forgotten events remain somewhere in the mind and that their sole function is to fill gaps between conscious events (Freud, *The Interpretation of Dreams*, Standard Edition, Vol. V, p. 168). Since, on this hypothesis, the unconscious is passive, the hypothesis seems to be untestable. But with Freud's addition that the forgotten motive and the distress connected with it actually produce the nervous complaint, the hypothesis becomes—like Pasteur's theory of the germ—a dynamic theory with observable consequences. In short, the theory of the unconscious is that, when unconscious, a motive and the distress it would give to consciousness together give rise to symptoms or inhibitions.

This gives us a way of approaching the problem—to see whether such a theory is testable, rather than primarily to investigate the existence of such unconscious occurrences. Although the question of existence is a genuine one and deserves attention, to place it at the center of a methodological discussion of psychoanalysis is to lose sight of the main problem.

A theory of the unconscious lacking hypotheses about the mode of activity of the unconscious is untestable. It should now be clear that Freud's hypothesis of the unconscious is a component of a theory, not an isolated theory; we can thus examine whether the hypothesis is testable.

Assuming the theory, certain inferences may be drawn which should test it. For instance, if a patient could be persuaded or educated out of a sense of shame, he should be able to recover the memory of the motive, and the paralysis should cease—but such a test could probably not be carried out. Another possibility is to force the patient to re-experience the motive and the distress connected with it under hypnosis, thus accustoming him to the situation and enabling him to recover the lost memory, so that paralysis will cease. Since Freud in fact adopted this procedure, the theory of the unconscious in that form is undoubtedly testable and was indeed satisfactorily tested on many occasions, as well as satisfying the test. This theory is amenable to laboratory testing with hypnotized subjects.

Whereas only controlled experiment may persuade orthodox experimentalists that a hypothesis is testable, the clinical method of testing is, methodologically speaking, equally valid, provided it is carried out with a predicted end that will refute the hypothesis if it fails to materialize.

Early psychoanalysis. Curiously enough, the most easily testable theory of the unconscious was put forward by Freud before psychoanalysis entered the scene. Why did psychoanalysis seem to make the theory untestable? To answer this we must examine the reasons for the transition from hypnosis to psychoanalysis. Freud abandoned hypnosis for the purely practical reasons that not everyone can be hypnotized and that he was not a good hypnotist. For a short time he tried the method of placing his hands on the patient's forehead and saying that the forgotten ideas would be remembered when the pressure was removed (*Studies in Hysteria*, p. 110). But forcing and hypnosis were not always successful, since they both involved making a patient conscious of an idea that was greatly distressing. Freud then introduced the method of free association (see *An Autobiographical Study*), with better results, and with it psychoanalysis can be said to have been born (although Freud's methods were somewhat different from present ones). What was Freud's theory at that point? Had the theory of the unconscious undergone any change?

Essentially, the theories of forcing and of free association were the same: that one could work from a conscious idea to an unconscious, distressing idea by focusing attention progressively on the links of a chain of intermediate ideas of which the first few are conscious. This hypothesis was sometimes fruitful, for at times unconscious ideas were recovered in this way. Methodologically, this means the theory is testable.

On the one hand, the theory of the unconscious remains broadly unchanged; it still contains the hypothesis that there is a motive, that the motive is distressing, that there is forgetting, and that all these together cause the disturbance complained of. But on the other hand the theory is changed in detail. The earlier version was simply that the motive and the distress it caused were forgotten. Now there is a hypothesis about degree, that forgotten ideas are unconscious in differing degrees, because as one idea becomes more acceptable to consciousness than it was, the idea next to it is less removed from the threshold of consciousness.

This might be called the hypothesis of *degrees* of repression. Although largely overlooked, it is an important hypothesis, for psychoanalysis is a gradual process, and this implies that one can get to the end of the process only by going through the intermediary parts; this in turn requires the validity of the hypothesis just discussed. But even if the conscious and the unconscious are continuous, they are also basically different, in both structure and function, just as the merging colors of the spectrum are not one color. This hypothesis of degree is important mainly because it implies a mental structure not hinted at in the earlier theory—it implies that the mind, conscious and unconscious together, consists of a warp and weft of ideas that are clustered into networks. In this form the theory implies the hypothesis that a distressing idea which is unconscious is recoverable by free association.

The developed theory. The next step in the development of the theory, however, by introducing interpretation, transforms the theory into psychoanalysis as Freud conceived of it in his maturity and largely as it is understood now. At first, interpretation was used simply to uncover recalcitrant ideas which were in principle accessible through free association (see "Freud's Psycho-analytic Procedure"), but later it was used to bring to light ideas that free association could not uncover (see "On Beginning the Treatment"). This is a radical change, for it constitutes drawing a line between ideas that were once conscious but which have been forgotten (later called preconscious) and ideas which have never been conscious at all and were regarded as being in the unconscious proper. At the beginning of Freud's investigations he found that some complaints could be traced to traumata— unpleasant events which occurred in the patient's consciousness; these traumata had nothing to do with what later became known as unconscious phantasy. Thus, at the

beginning of his work Freud was concerned with preconscious rather than with unconscious material.

Has this any importance, however, for the theory of the unconscious itself as explained above? The dynamic *élan* attributed to forgotten events is the work of the unconscious, not of the preconscious; experiences of events repressed into the preconscious can have some dynamic effect, but such an effect is mild compared to that of the unconscious. So the original structure of the theory remained but was ascribed to another domain, to a deeper layer of the unconscious (Freud, *The Interpretation of Dreams*, Ch. 7). There is, nonetheless, an additional development in the theory of the unconscious at this point because the attempt to interpret the unconscious is not possible without specific theories to this end. The theory of the Oedipus complex, for example, originally involved interpreting to a patient that he hated his father and wanted to murder him in order to possess his mother sexually. Not touching on ideas that had ever been conscious to the patient, it was therefore a theory about the unconscious, linked not so much with free association as with interpretation. Fundamentally, such theories developed as theories not of the preconscious but of the unconscious.

The developed form of Freud's theory of the unconscious may be summarized in the following way: (1) There are networks of ideas—attitudes, thoughts, feelings, objects imagined inside a person, and so on—that he cannot realize he possesses, because of the influence of other such networks, which he also cannot realize he possesses as long as he relies only on free association. (This is ordinarily described as "unconscious" conflict.) (2) These networks and their conflicts (*a*) influence the person's conscious ideas in all situations, reproducing the mutual relationships of the networks, however difficult it may be to recognize them; and (*b*) in particular influence him at different times, so that childhood networks and conflicts influence adult ideas. (3) These networks are related in accordance with a large group of theoretical hypotheses, such as that of the Oedipus complex.

In this summary, (1) might be called the hypothesis of the unconscious, (2*a*) the guise hypothesis and (2*b*) the genetic hypothesis; (3) consists of component theories about specific structures and functions. Together these three hypotheses may be regarded as constituting the theory of the unconscious.

The significance of the earlier history of the idea of the unconscious will now be understandable. In Whyte's detailed survey of Freud's precursors, *The Unconscious Before Freud*, he has shown that some conception or other of the unconscious has been known to man from the beginning of recorded thought. But he makes it clear that the conception was nearly always of a state that exists between conscious events. This is very remote from Freud's theory. Whyte points out, moreover, that only in the twentieth century did a theory of unconscious structure arise. But even this comment does not bring out what is required to discriminate Freud's idea of the unconscious, for a theory of structure might be only of a passive structure. What characterizes Freud's idea is that in it the unconscious is dynamic and rooted in the emotions and that this gives rise to all the richness of conscious life. For such an idea there are scarcely any precursors; Whyte mentions Carus, Schopenhauer, and Nietzsche. The insights shown by these thinkers into the nature of the unconscious was remarkable, but they did not develop them into a system, much less into a scientific theory. Their insights bear to Freud's work the sort of relation that exists between the atomism of the Greek atomists and modern atomic theory.

Although psychoanalysts still hold the theory of the unconscious outlined above, we must consider whether any additional factors amplify the theory significantly and also whether it contains all the features that Freud intended to be included in the theory of the unconscious.

The theory of childhood sexuality, for example, is central to psychoanalysis and widely subscribed to outside psychoanalytic circles, but strictly speaking it is not relevant to the theory of the unconscious. Without this theory, psychoanalysis would be very different, but it would certainly be possible in principle to retain the theory of the unconscious, perhaps combined with some totally different theory. The point can most easily be made plain by inventing a bizarre example. If infantile life were dominated by an overriding ambition to breathe slowly but the impossibility of achieving this proved intolerable, then we might in principle have unconscious functioning with the structure described by the foregoing theory associated with this infantile demand.

What relevance has the theory of tranference, which is fundamental to the later development of psychoanalysis? Interpretation, regarded first as an aid to free association and then as an independent tool, became really operative through the phenomenon of transference. Does this affect the theory of the unconscious? For Freud, it did not, interpretation being simply an instrument to bring about a change in a patient. However, there is an overtone of what might be called an object-relational structure in Freud's view of the unconscious, for he does attribute to the same cause the patient's inability to recall and to yield information to the analyst ("Remembering, Repeating and Working Through"). The patient's inability to yield information to the analyst arises because of his object relationship to the analyst, and Freud's hypothesis here implies that the patient's inability to face his own conflicts has an object-relational basis; although it was W. R. D. Fairbairn, not Freud, who first enunciated this theory (*Psychoanalytic Studies of the Personality*). This later piece of theory does in fact have a bearing on the theory of the structure of the unconscious, but its relevance is complicated. Michael Balint, for example, points out (in "Criticism of Fairbairn's Generalisation About Object Relations") that only through transference do we know what is going on in a patient's mind, but there may be facets that we cannot know about which cannot be revealed by transference. In other words, what we know about a patient is colored by the instrument—and this may not reveal all there is to know. Unless the argument is taken further we cannot know whether the unconscious has solely an object-relational structure as Freud always supposed. The problem of testing and deciding between this and other possibilities is of the utmost difficulty.

There are, in Freud's view, other constituents of the unconscious—for example, libido and (at a further level of abstraction) instincts. That some explanatory entity should be placed there is no surprise but should be disregarded until the clinical structure has been settled.

Defense. Freud's original view was that an idea painful to consciousness is repressed, soon to develop into an unconscious resistance. The later theory of the superego, which is largely an unconscious agent, was the result of an investigation into the nature of the repressing factor (*The Ego and the Id*).

Freud's theory is not entirely consistent, since he developed different aspects at different times and never went into the problem of unifying them. He held that the superego—an unconscious judge and controller—arose from the internalization of the *real* experience of fear of the father. Yet we have seen that the theory of the unconscious, as opposed to the preconscious, was a theory about phantasies that were never conscious in the first place, and it implies that a motive, the distress it causes, and the repressing factors have all been at all times unconscious. This discrepancy could prove fruitful, although it has not been exploited. The two obvious ways out of the contradiction would be either to hold that the superego has unconscious roots and is not based primarily on the real experience of a real father or somehow to work out a theory that an unconscious distress might be kept unconscious by an unconscious agency which had itself been at some time conscious.

Repression. What is the bearing of the unconscious superego upon the theory of the unconscious? For Freud the superego acts as both control and defense; it controls the child's Oedipal desires and defends him from the anxiety caused by castration fears. It was conceived of as operating by means of the mechanism of repression. Let us therefore consider this mechanism. Is repression a fact or a theory about facts? To psychoanalysts it is so familiar as to be accepted as a fact. But the facts are simply that people forget things and that there is an ascertainable motive for forgetting them. The *theory* of repression conjectures a mechanism by which a force is exerted to produce this result. Thus, the fact of repression is hardly in doubt, but there is no knowledge of its mechanism. This is not unreasonable; we do not question the factual certainty of many familiar mechanisms whose workings are nevertheless mysterious, for example, the clutch mechanism of a car. Thus, we may work with a clutch or the fact of repression while only conjecturing the existence of a mechanism that requires investigation.

The next point to consider is the scope of the term. Peter Madison has pointed out that Freud used "repression" to refer both to a repressing force pushing some idea out of consciousness and to defense in general ("Freud's Repression Concept"). This ambiguity can be simply explained: repression was to Freud the paradigm of defense mechanisms, being the first one he studied and therefore the one most familiar to him. It is easily possible, then, that he wrote of "repression" from habit, when with more precision he would have written of "defense" or perhaps of repression as a form of defense. This does not imply that he regarded the other defenses as being actual forms of repression in the narrower sense, and therefore there is no reason whatsoever to suppose that he was confused in his thought, even though there is an ambiguity in his language. However that may be, clearly we should use "defense" as the general term, reserving "repression" for the specific mechanism we have been discussing.

We can now take a further step in investigating the theory of the unconscious. To begin with, the term "unconscious" denoted the contents of what was repressed. Freud's editor, James Strachey, notes that in German the word for "unconscious" is a past participle, not carrying the active sense associated with "conscious" in English. Certainly, in English speaking of "the repressed" rather than of "the unconscious" more readily conveys the meaning required. But, as we have seen, it was not long before it was overtly recognized that the repressing factor was also unconscious. At this point the scope of the term "unconscious" was doubled.

Thus, the theory of repression is an integral part of the theory of the unconscious. This should be stressed, since the theory of the unconscious undergoes a modification as a result of subsequent developments.

POST-FREUDIAN DEVELOPMENTS

Freud himself, even fairly early, recognized the existence of mechanisms of isolation, and undoing, splitting, and projection; we should consider how much any of these alter the theory of the unconscious. The need for such an elaboration has been brought about by Melanie Klein's development of the subject in terms of splitting and projection, which has shown that a structure of the unconscious alternative to the one Freud proposed is possible ("Notes on Schizoid Mechanisms"). Freud's theory included these mechanisms, and we also should see whether it can accommodate the modern modification.

The mechanism of isolation consists in a displacement of affect, but no repression. The idea that would give rise to distress is displaced onto something quite different. It is the relationship between two things, rather than the ideas themselves, that is not fully present to consciousness. But we can hardly speak of a relationship as being repressed.

The phenomenon of splitting indicates this even more clearly: as a fundamental defense, splitting refers not to ideas but to the personality, and then it is rather like the left hand not knowing what the right hand is doing. But there is nothing unconscious about this, in the sense of something's being repressed. In order to keep the split-off components separated, one of them is usually projected onto somebody else. Distressing ideas, then, are perfectly conscious but are ascribed to another person.

This phenomenon suggests an altogether different topological structure of the mind from that suggested by repression. It is as if in Freud's picture the mind is divided horizontally, with the conscious above and the unconscious below, whereas in the phenomenon of splitting the mind is divided by a vertical plane into two segments, both felt to be inside the body unless projection takes place. The two models, however, have something in common—in each case, something is felt to be lost to the personality: either consciousness is deprived of something repressed or the projected part of the personality is lost. Of course, both could occur, but it may also be that splitting

processes are more fundamental, in the sense that repression may be explained as the outcome of a certain kind of splitting.

This is a radical change in theory, yet it does not affect the theory of the unconscious, for the other component hypotheses remain as before. Thus, the new version would say that a motive is split off and projected because of the distress it gives rise to, and in this way it is not accessible to consciousness in the ordinary sense of feeling owned, even though its existence is recognized, and this situation leads to symptoms and inhibitions. Thus, the general outline of the structure remains as before. Nonetheless, new problems arise because whereas repression was explained as resulting from the action of the superego, this action would not explain the phenomenon of splitting, and a new psychology of splitting must be provided (for instance, by Melanie Klein's theory of the paranoid–schizoid position—see *Developments in Psychoanalysis*).

Phases of the theory reconsidered. The foregoing exercise in the method and history of science reveals six phases through which the theory of the unconscious has passed:

The first phase involved the structure of preconscious motivation and preconscious distress, the combination of which constitutes a dynamism producing a neurotic disorder. This was found to be testable.

The second phase brought out an additional hypothesis of degree of repression. It would indeed characterize the first phase but would not be very obviously contained in it. This addition is also testable.

The third phase brought out a distinction between the preconscious and the unconscious; the theory again remained the same, but it was stated in terms not of the preconscious but of the unconscious. The problem of testing becomes much more acute here, because interpretation now plays an independent role and does not simply make conscious preconscious ideas for which there could be independent evidence. Testing here depends on whether such interpretations of unconscious content are in their turn testable. This problem will be discussed later.

In the fourth phase all the constituents of the unconscious were rendered object relational, which is also difficult to test.

In the fifth phase the theory was complicated further by the fact that it was, more or less from the beginning, intended to include ideas of very different levels. So far our discussion has centered on the contents of clinical interpretations, to do with feelings supposed to be actually present in a patient; but metapsychological (that is, explanatory) ideas, whether valid or not, are present in the theory. It would be premature, however, to discuss whether they are testable before we deal with the two decisive problems presented below.

In the sixth phase, the idea of resistance, which had always been included in the theory, became the explicit theory of the superego. The basic idea is defense; it may be divided into (a) the classical idea of repression, and (b) the later idea of splitting, together with projective identification. The problem of testing here is not so acute since the same method of testing used in the third phase of the theory could be applied.

The decisive problems are now the testing of clinical hypotheses and the settling of the question whether the structure of the unconscious is entirely object relational.

The earliest paper on testing clinical hypotheses is an important one, Susan Isaacs' "Criteria for Interpretations." She offered a particular criterion for a false interpretation, although not a general one, and she offered eleven criteria of confirmation, although again no general one. Classic papers were written by Strachey ("The Nature of the Therapeutic Action of Psycho-analysis") and by Freud ("Constructions in Analysis"), but these had to do with the technique of interpretation rather than with the general question of validity. Although very few suggestions have been put forward, a fairly general test was suggested by Henry Ezriel ("Experimentation Within the Psycho-analytic Session"), and a completely general one was suggested by J. O. Wisdom in 1956 ("Psycho-analytic Technology") and worked out, after a valuable contribution by G. Seaborn Jones ("Some Philosophical Implications of Psycho-analysis"), in a subsequent paper by Wisdom ("Testing a Psycho-analytic Interpretation"). There are two main distinctions to be drawn.

Ezriel contended that an interpretation would be confirmed if the response material offered by the patient reproduced the structure of the interpretation, but in a clearer form. The completely general test concerns in addition the prediction of a new defense about to be employed by the patient; for, as Seaborn Jones made clear, it is not sufficient to show merely that an interpretation produced a predictable change. This it might do without being true; it would then be merely what he called "enactive." For an interpretation might produce a predictable change not because it is true but merely because it carries a suggestion effect. Even if the patient's subsequent material bears all the marks of having been suggested by the interpretation, the new defense he uses against the interpretation cannot have been suggested in this way because of its not being referred to in the interpretation; hence, if the patient's defense can be predicted, a suggestion effect is ruled out; hence, the test is not only one of enactivity but also of the truth of the interpretation.

There is almost no literature on the other testing problem—differentiating between an unconscious structure consisting of object relationships and one not so built up. There are two opposing views: Freud always held that the unconscious sought pleasure, that in its deepest layers this aim took precedence, and that in them there was no awareness of objects and therefore no object relationship. Thus, although there was an object-relational constituent in the unconscious, the deepest layers excluded it. But Fairbairn maintained that the unconscious was structured throughout by object relationships, although he produced no fundamental argument to justify his view. Wisdom has pointed out (in "Fairbairn's Contribution on Object-relationship, Splitting and Ego Structure") that the Freudian position can be maintained in the face of any apparent exceptions, just as physicists can always postulate a new form of energy when the principle of the conservation of energy has apparently been violated. Both principles are irrefutable by observation, but they could be refuted if they conflicted with another theory that was testable,

tested, and corroborated (Wisdom, "The Irrefutability of 'Irrefutable' Laws"). The question would then arise whether the clinical theory rooted in Melanie Klein's work, or in Fairbairn's, would turn out to be better tested than the metapsychological theory of Freud. One factor pointing to an affirmative answer is that the former type of theory has wider application because it has been found to be applicable to the therapeutic analysis of children as young as two years old and also to psychotics. A further method of testing the contention is this: it should be possible to settle, from case material alone, the question whether the removal of inhibition against sexual pleasure leads to an improvement of a patient's object relationships, as Freud's theory requires, or whether therapeutic aid that improves the object relationships leads to a lessening of sexual inhibition, as Fairbairn's theory requires. There can be little doubt that the case histories available, including those supplied by Freud, tend to support Fairbairn's view, but the issue has not been closely scrutinized from this angle. It may also be possible to carry out an experimental test to decide between object relationship and primary narcissism (see Wisdom, "What Sort of Ego Has the Infant?").

Looking back over this passage of history we may say that Freud introduced a radically new theory of the unconscious, unanticipated by practically everyone who preceded him, because of two things—the strictly unconscious (as opposed to preconscious) nature of the processes he discussed and the dynamic nature of this unconscious. To this we may add that his theory is testable if the clinical interpretations of unconscious states are testable. Finally, the modifications of the structure of the unconscious that come about through emphasis on splitting rather than repression and emphasis on object relationship rather than the pleasure principle may constitute a vitally important theoretical improvement, though not a revolution against Freud's basic contribution of a dynamic unconscious.

Bibliography

Balint, Michael, "Criticism of Fairbairn's Generalisation About Object Relations." *The British Journal for the Philosophy of Science*, Vol. 7 (1957).

Ezriel, Henry, "Experimentation Within the Psycho-analytic Session." *The British Journal for the Philosophy of Science*, Vol. 7 (1956–1957), 29–48, 342–347. Reprinted in Paul (see below).

Edel, Abraham, "The Concept of the Unconscious: Some Analytic Preliminaries." *Philosophy of Science*, Vol. 31, No. 1 (January 1964), 18–33.

Fairbairn, W. R. D., *Psychoanalytic Studies of the Personality*. London, 1952.

Freud, Sigmund, "Some Points for a Comparative Study of Organic and Hysterical Motor Paralyses" (1893). Translated in Vol. I of *The Standard Edition of the Complete Psychological Works of Sigmund Freud*, 24 vols. James Strachey, general ed. London, 1953–1964.

Freud, Sigmund, *The Interpretation of Dreams* (1900). Translated in *Standard Edition*, Vols. IV and V. See Ch. 7, pp. 610 ff.

Freud, Sigmund, "Freud's Psycho-analytic Procedure" (1904). Translated in *Standard Edition*, Vol. VII. See pp. 247 ff.

Freud, Sigmund, "A Note on the Unconscious in Psycho-analysis" (1912). Translated in *Standard Edition*, Vol. XII. See p. 260.

Freud, Sigmund, "On Beginning the Treatment (Further Recommendations on the Technique of Psycho-analysis I)" (1913). Translated in *Standard Edition*, Vol. XII. See pp. 121 ff.

Freud, Sigmund, "Recollection, Repetition and Working Through (Further Recommendations on the Technique of Psycho-analysis II)" (1914). Translated in *Standard Edition*, Vol. XII. See pp. 145 ff.

Freud, Sigmund, "The Unconscious" (1915). Translated in *Standard Edition*, Vol. XIV. See pp. 166 ff.

Freud, Sigmund, *The Ego and the Id* (1923). Translated in *Standard Edition*, Vol. XIX. See pp. 27 ff.

Freud, Sigmund, *An Autobiographical Study* (1925). Translated in *Standard Edition*, Vol. XX. See pp. 40 ff.

Freud, Sigmund, "Constructions in Analysis" (1937). Translated in *Standard Edition*, Vol. XXIII. Reprinted in Paul (see below).

Freud, Sigmund, and Breuer, Josef, *Studies in Hysteria* (1895). Translated in *Standard Edition*, Vol. II. See pp. 45, 110.

Isaacs, Susan, "Criteria for Interpretations." *The International Journal of Psycho-analysis*, Vol. 20 (1939), 148–160.

Klein, Melanie, "Notes on Schizoid Mechanisms," in Melanie Klein et al., *Developments in Psycho-analysis*. London, 1952.

Madison, Peter, "Freud's Repression Concept." *The International Journal of Psycho-analysis*, Vol. 37 (1956), 75–81.

Paul, Louis, ed., *Psychoanalytic Clinical Interpretation*. New York, 1963.

Seaborn Jones, G., *Some Philosophical Implications of Psychoanalysis* (1961). Unpublished Ph.D. thesis at the University of London.

Strachey, James, "The Nature of Therapeutic Action of Psychoanalysis." *The International Journal of Psycho-analysis*, Vol. 15 (1934), 127–159. Reprinted in Paul, *op. cit.*

Whyte, L. L., *The Unconscious Before Freud*. New York, 1960.

Wisdom, J. O., "Psycho-analytic Technology." *The British Journal for the Philosophy of Science*, Vol. 7 (1956), 13–28. Reprinted in Paul, *op. cit.*

Wisdom, J. O., "Fairbairn's Contribution on Object-relationship, Splitting and Ego Structure." *British Journal of Medical Psychology*, Vol. 36 (1963). See 145 ff.

Wisdom, J. O., "The Irrefutability of 'Irrefutable' Laws." *The British Journal for the Philosophy of Science*, Vol. 13 (1963), 303–306.

Wisdom, J. O., "Testing a Psycho-analytic Interpretation." *Ratio* (1966).

Wisdom, J. O., "What Sort of Ego Has the Infant?," in Emanuel Miller, ed., *Foundations of Child Psychiatry*. Oxford, 1966.

J. O. WISDOM

UNIVERSALS. The word "universal," used as a noun, has belonged to the vocabulary of English-writing philosophers since the sixteenth century, but the concept of universals, and the problems raised by it, has a far longer history. It goes back through the *universalia* of medieval philosophy to Aristotle's τὰ καθόλου and Plato's εἴδη and ἰδέαι. Indeed, Plato may be taken to be the father of this perennial topic of philosophy, for it is in his dialogues that we find the first arguments for universals and the first discussion of the difficulties they raise. Plato believed that the existence of universals was required not only ontologically, to explain the nature of the world which as sentient and reflective beings we experience, but also epistemologically, to explain the nature of our experience of it. He proposed a solution to his problem, but he also recognized the objections to his particular solution. Ever since, except for intervals of neglect, philosophers have been worrying about the nature and status of universals. No account has yet been propounded which has come near to receiving universal acceptance; this reflects not merely disagreement on the answers to be offered but also, and perhaps more importantly, disagreement on exactly what the questions are that we are, or should be, trying to answer.

That in some sense or other there are universals, and that in some sense or other they are abstract objects—that is, objects of thought rather than of sense perception—no philosopher would wish to dispute; the difficulties begin when we try to be more precise. They may be indicated (although not defined) by the abstract nouns which we use when we think about, for example, beauty, justice, courage, and goodness and, again, by the adjectives, verbs, adverbs, and prepositions which we use in talking of individual objects, to refer to their qualities and to the relations between them. In saying of two or more objects that each is a table, or square, or brown, or made of wood we are saying that there is something common to the objects, which may be shared by many others and in virtue of which the objects may be classified into kinds. Not merely is such classification possible, for scientific and other purposes; it is unavoidable: all experience is of things as belonging to kinds, however vague and inarticulate the classification may be. Whatever we see (to take sight as an example) we see as *a something*—that is, as an object of a certain kind, as having certain qualities, and as standing in certain relations to other objects—and although every individual object is unique, in that it is numerically distinct from all others, its features are general, in that they are (or might be) repeated in other objects. Even if there were only one red object in the world, we would know what it would be like for there to be others, and we would be able to recognize another if we were to meet with it. Generality is an essential feature of the objects of experience, recognition of generality is an essential feature of experience itself, and reflection of this generality is shown in the vocabulary of any language, all the words of which (with the exception of proper names) are general. Universals are, by tradition, contrasted with particulars, the general contrasted with the numerically unique, and differing theories of universals are differing accounts of what is involved in this generality and in our experience of it. The leading theories of universals—realism, conceptualism, nominalism, and resemblance theories—can best be explained by an examination of the doctrines of the main exponents. In following that sequence we shall be adhering approximately (although not precisely) to the chronological order in which the rival theories developed, and we shall be historically selective, in that we say almost nothing of the periods in the history of philosophy during which the controversies continued (for example, medieval philosophy) but of which a detailed knowledge is not necessary to a general understanding of the issues involved. The aim here is to present the different views that have been held, not to trace the fortunes of each view throughout the history of the subject.

REALISM

Realist and conceptualist theories of universals are, by long tradition, regarded as opposed because according to realism universals are nonmental, or mind-independent, whereas according to conceptualism they are mental, or mind-dependent. For the realist, universals exist in themselves and would exist even if there were no minds to be aware of them; if the world were exactly what it is now, with the one difference that it contained no minds at all, no consciousness of any kind, the existence of universals would be unaffected. They are *public* somethings with which we are somehow or other acquainted, and a mindless world would lack not universals but only the awareness of them: they would be available for discovery, even if there were nobody to discover them. For the conceptualist, on the other hand, universals are in the mind in a *private* sense, such that if there were no minds, there could be no universals, in the same way as there could be no thoughts or imagery or memories or dreams. As will be seen, whatever may be said for or against realism, pure conceptualism cannot be a satisfactory theory, for it is essentially incomplete; it says something about our consciousness of universals but nothing at all about any basis for this consciousness. Consequently, philosophers who have been conceptualists either have been so because they have been interested only in the epistemological question, in the conceptual structure of human thought and experience, or have combined their conceptualism with another theory designed to answer the ontological question—that is, the question what there is in the world corresponding to our mental concepts or ideas, what our concepts are concepts of. The antithesis between the two theories of realism and conceptualism is not, therefore, as clear-cut as it has often been presented to be.

The two main versions of realism are those of Plato and Aristotle. Plato's came first, and the difficulties it raised, some raised by Plato himself, others added by Aristotle, were what led Aristotle to devise his own quite different, but still realist, account. Plato and Aristotle were both realists in that they accorded to universals an existence independent of minds; where they differed was on the nature of the existence and the status which they believed universals to possess.

Plato. Although it is possible to give, in some detail, a statement of what may be called Plato's theory of universals, and to give it full documentary support by quotations from his writings, we would be mistaken to regard it as a final and fully worked out theory. It was a theory toward which Plato can be seen working his way throughout his philosophical career, not so much by independent arguments as by intertwining strands of thought, all leading in the same general direction. There were a number of facts about the world and our experience of it by which he was impressed and puzzled. His theory evolved as an explanation of them, but he was never satisfied that he had solved his problem. He was his own first critic, and a penetrating one, and to the end of his life he was torn, as is brought out in his dialogue *Parmenides*, between the conviction that his theory was fundamentally correct and the recognition that it posed problems which he found himself unable to solve. It should not be thought, therefore, that he ever produced a final account which he was prepared to rest content with and which needed an Aristotle to find fault with it.

Plato's interest in questions about universals was first aroused by Socrates, by whom he was greatly influenced, whom he introduced as one of the speakers in all his dialogues (with the single exception of *The Laws*), and who in all but the later dialogues appears as the central character actually directing the conversation. Unfortunately, we are presented with difficulties of interpretation, the details of

which we shall not enter into here, because our knowledge of Socrates is derived entirely from descriptions given by other writers, one of whom was Plato. Hence arises the problem of deciding which of the doctrines ascribed to "Socrates" in the Platonic dialogues are those of the actual Socrates and which of them are extensions or even entirely new doctrines developed by Plato himself. In general, it is accepted that the "Socrates" of the early dialogues does represent the views, and even more the methods of philosophical inquiry, of Socrates himself but that as time went on Plato more and more used him as the spokesman of Plato's own views, the transitional stage being marked by such dialogues as *Phaedo* and the *Republic*. We may conclude that while Socrates did not explicitly hold a theory of universals (and we have Aristotle's word for it, in *Metaphysics* 1078b, that Socrates did not hold the view Plato put forward), his philosophical questions were such that Plato held they could not be answered except by such a theory; in other words, Plato, in putting a theory of universals into Socrates' mouth, was not attributing it to Socrates as what he had actually expounded but was maintaining it as the logical consequence of Socrates' own arguments: Socrates stopped short of propounding such a theory himself but was logically committed to it.

Socrates' main interest was in the human virtues, and his aim was to secure a satisfactory definition of the virtue under discussion. His questions were all of the form "What is *X*?," where "*X*" stood for beauty, courage, piety, justice, etc., in one case (*Meno*) even virtue itself. The answers which he received he rejected because they were too narrow or too wide, but more commonly because instead of giving the essential definition of the virtue they gave instances of it or mentioned kinds of it. Thus, it was no answer to the question "What is piety?" to reply that a man is acting piously if he prosecutes a murderer; again, it was no answer to the question "What is virtue?" to reply that the virtue of a man consists in managing a city's affairs capably, that a woman's virtue consists in managing her domestic affairs capably, that there are different virtues for an old man and a young man, for a free man and a slave, etc. Granted that there are many virtues, what is wanted is the one and the same form which they all have and by which they are virtues. The search, then, is for the single and essential form common to all things of the same kind, by virtue of which they are things of the same kind.

The "things" about which Socrates in fact asked his questions were limited because his philosophical interest was limited, but even he did not confine himself to human conduct. He acknowledged, for instance, that health or size or strength must be the same in all its instances, with the consequence that we answer the question "What is health?" only when we have given the essence of health—that is, what is common and peculiar to all instances of health. Plato took this further and maintained (although not without hesitation) that there must be an essence common to all things of a given kind, whatever that kind was. It would apply not only to abstract virtues, such as justice and courage, but also to natural objects, such as trees, and to artifacts, such as tables. An object would not be a table unless it had the same essence (of tablehood) as all other tables; despite the different shapes and sizes that individual tables may possess, there must be a single form or essence, common to them all, which constitutes their being tables and distinguishes them from other objects, such as chairs or beds. Plato summarized his position in the statement "We are in the habit of postulating one single form for each class of particulars to which we give the same name" (*Republic* 596A). And he held it to be true not only of objects designated by nouns (such as "bed" and "table") but also of attributes or qualities indicated by predicates (such as "beautiful" and "greater than"). As there must be a form or essence of bedhood somehow common to all beds, so there must be a form or essence of beauty (or the beautiful) common to all things that are beautiful.

So far Plato had done nothing more than take over the Socratic contrast between the single general, essential form common to a class of particulars and the particulars themselves and extend it more widely than Socrates had done: he found the same contrast not only in the realms of ethics, aesthetics, and mathematics but also in the everyday world of sense experience. But he went on to ask the questions which Socrates had never asked, namely what are we to say about the relationship between the universal form and its particular manifestations, and what are we to say about the nature and existence of the universal itself? His answer was to develop the theory known as the theory of Forms, according to which each universal is a single substance or Form, existing timelessly and independently of any of its particular manifestations and apprehended not by sense but by intellect. His arguments can be distinguished, although not entirely separated, into two general kinds, metaphysical or ontological and epistemological. If knowledge is to be possible at all (and Plato did not doubt either that it was possible or that in certain spheres it was actual), it must be of what is stable and unchanging.

However, the familiar world of ordinary experience does not meet this requirement, for the one constant and striking feature of all objects (and their qualities) in this world is that they are subject to change and decay: both natural objects and artifacts come, or are brought, into being, undergo changes throughout their existence, and sooner or later die or disintegrate and disappear. This is the Heraclitean doctrine of flux, which Plato accepted and which he believed required as its counterpart a nonsensible realm of unchanging stability, without which there could be no knowledge. What can be known must be real, unitary, and unchanging: these are the Forms. Particulars are only semireal, real to the extent that in some way or other, or to some degree or other, they manifest the Forms, unreal to the extent that being material, they lack the perfection of pure Forms and are subject to the laws of material change and decay. Thus, Forms are required, to confer on particulars such reality as they do have, to constitute their being what they are and of what kinds they are. A bed is a bed rather than a table because it somehow manifests the Form Bed. A Form is required not only to explain a particular object's being what it is but also to cause its being what it is; the doctrine is thus not merely a logical but a metaphysical doctrine. Plato emphasized this in the analogy of the sun (*Republic* VI), where he compared the chief Form of all, the Form of the Good, with the sun, which as the light-giving and life-giving agent in the physical world is the prime material cause of natural life as well as of our awareness, through our senses, of the material world.

Another consideration which led Plato to suppose the Forms as transcendent substances was the presence of what he thought to be contradictions in the material world: what is real cannot contain contradictions; therefore the material world cannot be more than an appearance of reality. That a single object should be both beautiful (in one respect) and ugly (in another), or large (in comparison with a second object) and at the same time small (in comparison with a third), was enough, in his view, to show that the Forms were more than immanent. Therefore, not only must there be Forms in order to cause particulars to be what they are, but the Forms must be separate from the particulars because they must be free of the imperfection and defectiveness with which particulars are inevitably infected. The Forms are thus not only independent substances but perfect and ideal patterns, which particulars must fall short of.

This comes out especially in the consideration of mathematical (primarily geometrical) and value concepts, namely those of ethics and aesthetics. For a line to be straight or a figure to be circular, there must be the Forms of Straightness and Circularity. But it is well known that no actual line is ever perfectly straight and no figure is ever perfectly circular; however carefully and precisely drawn, it possesses some curves or kinks that more minute scrutiny could disclose. And what we are thinking about when we study or discuss a geometrical theorem is not the diagram of the circle drawn, freehand or mechanically, on the blackboard but the circle represented by the diagram. We thus have both the diagram of the circle, adequate as a diagram but imperfect as a circle, and the perfect Form of Circularity of which it is a diagram. While this gives rise to the question, which cannot be pursued here, whether Plato distinguished between the Form of Circularity (of which there could not be more than one) and a Perfect Circle (of which, if there could be one, there could be more than one—as required by, for example, a theorem involving two intersecting circles), there is no doubt that he did think a Form not only was the perfect pattern, of which a particular was an imperfect manifestation, but also was what the particular would be if, *per impossibile*, it could be perfect. Thus, to take an aesthetic example, Beauty (or the Beautiful) not only is the pattern which beautiful particulars inadequately manifest but also is itself perfectly beautiful; it is a substance possessing in perfection the essence which its derivative particulars possess only partially or in some degree. As Plato came to realize later (*Parmenides* 131 ff.), and as Aristotle repeated, if a Form stands to its particulars as "one over many," and if the Form is an ideal pattern of which the particulars are imperfect copies, then an infinite regress argument (known as the third-man argument) is generated: for the Form to be predicable of itself as well as of its particulars, it must share a character with them; but then there will be a Form of this character; this second Form will be predicable of itself, requiring a third Form of it, a fourth, and so on ad infinitum.

As was indicated above by the geometrical example,

Plato believed that his theory of Forms accounted for the possibility of knowledge of universal truths, which was the only kind of knowledge strictly meriting the name. When, by working out or following the proof, we learn that a square constructed on the diagonal of a given square has an area equal to double the area of the given square, we have learned a truth which is necessary and universal. It is not something which happens, as a matter of fact, to be true of the squares in our diagram but might turn out not to be true of some other squares; that is, it is not an empirical generalization which subsequent experience might show to be false as a generalization. We have a piece of a priori knowledge, which no possible experience could affect, namely that *if* a square has a given area, and *if* a second square has its sides equal in length to a diagonal of the original square, then the area of the second square *must* be double the area of the first. Our knowledge is not knowledge of our diagram squares, or any others that we care to draw, for, as we have seen, they are not in fact squares. But it is knowledge, and the only thing, therefore, that it can be knowledge of is the Form Square (or the Square).

What defeated Plato in any attempt to give a complete account of his theory was the problem of describing the relation of Forms to particulars. In different places he spoke of the Forms "being in" their particulars, of particulars "participating in" their forms, and of particulars "copying" their forms. Literal interpretation of any of these phrases gives rise to logical difficulties, and to take them metaphorically is to leave the statement of the theory imprecise and the problem unanswered. In Plato's final writings (*Epistle* VII) on the subject there are signs that he was inclined to think that the fault lay with the inadequacy of language to describe what he wanted to describe, but the trouble is deeper than mere paucity of vocabulary. We can form some kind of a picture of his two worlds if we think of the world of Forms as actually existing somewhere, populated by objects like the Standard Meter and the Standard Pound, and we can then think of actual particulars as being imperfect copies of the originals. But that picture, taken literally, is false, because Plato's Forms do not exist in a place or at a time. The mystery of their "existence" becomes impenetrable when we are asked to use the word "exist" in a way that we are incapable of conceiving. In his theory of Forms, with the Forms not immanent but transcendent, the problem of their relation to particulars becomes not almost impossibly difficult to solve but in principle insoluble.

Aristotle. Aristotle, Plato's pupil and successor, is often regarded as the careful scientific-minded thinker, anxious to restrain philosophy within the range of the observable and to avoid the imaginative speculations of Plato. While this picture is in general correct and in particular fits Aristotle's criticisms of Plato's theory of Forms regarded as universals, his own theory of a Form as the object of a definition that describes a thing's essential nature becomes in the end as obscure as Plato's. His criticism that Plato's theory does nothing to provide a scientific explanation of the nature of things applies equally forcibly to his own theory of essences, and natural science, as we know it, began to progress only when, many centuries later, it liberated itself from this aspect of Aristotelianism.

But Aristotle's theory of universals, which is nowhere fully elaborated and has to be pieced together from different passages, is important, both because it offered an alternative to Plato's and because it is more obviously attractive to common sense. His objections to Plato are numerous and detailed but are not all of equal weight. Basically, apart from the infinite regress argument, which he took over from Plato, they come to two: first, that Plato, by making the Forms perfect, separate substances, introduced an unnecessary and unhelpful duplication, and second, that Plato confused the categories of substance and property. Nothing is accounted for by making the Forms perfect patterns of particulars. To attempt to explain the nature of one set of entities by postulating a second and better set does not solve a problem but merely repeats it at a different level: whatever the question was that needed to be answered about particulars, it will need to be answered again about the Forms; mere multiplication answers nothing. Second, Plato was guilty of a logical mistake in treating a Form both as an individual substance (which the "separation" thesis requires) and as a property (which it would have to be to be a universal). Substances are individuals and *have* properties, but they cannot *be* properties, yet Plato's theory treats them as both.

For Aristotle the only true substances were single individual objects, such as Socrates or this table. (It is true that Aristotle introduced a difficulty by treating genus and species also as substances, for they are what it is the aim of science to know, but they are secondary substances, and the knowledge we may gain of them is knowledge *about* primary substances—that is, the individual objects met with in experience.) Universals, therefore, are not substances existing independently of particulars. They exist only as common elements in particulars: the universal *X* is whatever is common to, or shared by, all *x*'s; it is what is predicated of the individual. Individual objects are to be classified into kinds according as they share the same property, and the kinds are to be subdivided into genus and species by the differences between more determinate properties. Thus, all colored objects belong to the genus "color" because they all alike have the property of being colored, whereas red objects and green objects belong to different species of the genus, because the first have the property of being colored red and the second have the property of being colored green. One of the primary tasks of natural science is to divide and classify natural objects by genus and species into the real kinds to which, by nature, they belong.

Aristotle's theory is more economical than Plato's, requiring only one world of being instead of two, the contrast between the two theories being indicated by the labels which they later acquired in medieval scholastic philosophy: Plato's was a theory of *universalia ante rem* (universals independent of particulars), and Aristotle's of *universalia in rebus* (universals in things). And with the possible exception of ideal concepts, such as those of geometry, which Plato had argued had no actual instances, Aristotle's account seems better to fit a fact, or what we take to be a fact, of human experience, namely that a particular really is an instance of its universal. Not only should we say that we get our idea of red, for example, from seeing red objects, such as fire engines or ripe tomatoes, but we should also say (except for philosophical theories of perception) that the object really was red, not that (as with Plato) the tomato tried unsuccessfully to be red but that (with Aristotle) it actually was red. The properties which an object has, and which together constitute its nature, its being an object of that kind, whatever that kind may be (for example, whether it is a horse or a table), are really *in* the object, in some sense of "in." If objects do not and cannot possess *any* of the characteristics that according to experience and the scrutiny of observation they appear to have, then scientific knowledge becomes either altogether impossible or unrelated to the natural world. Aristotle's view avoids the Platonic paradox that nothing in the observable world can *ever* be what it seems to be.

The contrast between the two views comes out again in their accounts of how we apprehend universals. They are agreed both that awareness of universals is implicit in ordinary sense experience (for it is this awareness that conditions our experience as being what it is) and that we are aware of universals not by sense itself but by intellect. Plato could not say that we become aware of them by abstraction from particular instances, because they have separate existence and never are more than defectively instantiated: if our concept of X were only what we could abstract from imperfect instances, we never could apprehend X itself. Therefore there must be some other mode of apprehension, which Plato called ἀνάμνησις (usually translated as "recollection" but less misleadingly interpreted in this context as "recovery"). The human soul has prenatal knowledge of universals and of their mutual relations, and postnatal experience of the ordinary world serves, or may serve, to revive this knowledge in suitable circumstances. Thus, experience does not directly provide us with new apprehensions (of universals) or with new knowledge of necessary truths (connections between universals) but acts as a stimulus to remind us of what we already know but have hitherto in this life forgotten. Plato's argument here, if it is to be regarded as an argument, is a transcendental one (in Kant's sense of the word): our knowledge is a priori, that is, of such a kind that we cannot get it *from* experience, although we do get it *in* experience; therefore it must be innate, that is, knowledge of what we originally knew prior to any experience. As a transcendental argument it could be effective only if it could be shown that there was no other possible way of accounting for our apprehension of universals and our knowledge of universal truths. And Aristotle thought that there was another, less fanciful and less speculative way, derived from actual experiences and memories of previous experiences. Apprehension of a universal, or formation of a concept, is not a sudden once-and-for-all business, given in a single experience, but a gradual process. Sense perception gives rise to memory, and memory conditions subsequent perceptions, so that they are not merely perceptions but recognitions of what is in some degree or other familiar from previous perceptions. Awareness of characteristics thus becomes clearer and more explicit with the growth and variety of experience. By a process of induction, namely intuitive induction, the first primitive awareness of a universal (necessary to any perception) becomes stabilized in the mind, leading ultimately to a clear and articu

late concept of it. Thus, for Aristotle, as for Plato, grasp of universals is by the intellect, but it is by the intellect gradually working on what it is at first dimly and indeterminately conscious of in the data of sense perception. A simple example from arithmetic will illustrate his point. As children we learn to count. We get the idea of 2 from being faced with pairs of objects, and we learn that $2+2=4$ from coming to "see," for instance, that two apples plus two other apples are equal in number to four other apples. But we also come, sooner or later, to "see" that the number 2 characterizes *any* pair of objects, and that $2+2=4$ is a necessary truth, applicable to any two pairs compared with a quartet. We have the power, which becomes actualized in experience, of intuiting clearly the universal in the particular and of intuiting the necessary in the matter of fact; this, for Aristotle, is the beginning of scientific knowledge.

Augustine. Medieval philosophy was not primarily interested in questions about the nature of human knowledge. But its concern with metaphysics, especially in those aspects that carried theological implications, led to a continuation of the dispute between the two versions of realism and later to a nominalist rejection of both. Platonic realism was championed by St. Augustine, for whom divine illumination performed much the same function as Plato's Form of the Good, rendering intelligible by its light the necessity of eternal truths which the human intellect could grasp. Man is above the beasts, not only because he can acquire, by the mind alone, knowledge of eternal truths, but also because even in sensation he judges of material objects by incorporeal standards: in judging a physical object to be beautiful he implies the objective existence of Beauty, both as a universal and as a standard. Again, the intelligible structure of the temporal world, which the reason of man (but not the senses of the beasts) can grasp, is itself nontemporal; for example, the concepts and truths of mathematics, although empirically applicable, are timeless necessities. Ideas as objective essences are exemplars contained "in the divine intelligence." Thus, Plato's theory of Forms enters theology, and the question arises whether Augustine in his theory of ideas supposed that men were in direct contact with the mind of God. It is fairly clear that he did not but much less clear how he could avoid it.

Aquinas. The leading exponent of Aristotelian realism was Thomas Aquinas, who, although professing the greatest reverence for Augustine, departed widely from Augustine's views. Thomas' metaphysics is, like Aristotle's, teleological, maintaining that the nature of things and events is to be explained in terms of the ends which they serve, and he extended Aristotle's contrasts between potentiality and act, between form and matter, and between essence and existence. Essences are universals, which have no being apart from existence but which are intelligible without the supposition of existence. The existence of things does not follow from their essence—otherwise existence could not be, as it clearly is, contingent. Universals are apprehended directly by the mind, but only in the material things the nature of which they comprise; they are not to be found in themselves, although by the processes of abstraction and comparison the mind can approximate to thinking of them in themselves. The chief follower in the Thomist tradition was Duns Scotus, who nevertheless rejected much in Thomas, such as the distinction between essence and existence, and followed Avicenna in differentiating between the "thisness" of an individual object (which distinguishes it from other objects of the same kind) and the nature of an individual object (which distinguishes it from objects of other kinds).

Criticism of realism. Although each of the two versions of realism received vigorous support in the long disputes of medieval philosophy, and although Augustinianism for a time prevailed, Aristotle's version has had the longer-lasting influence, especially on philosophers brought up in the British tradition of empiricism. That things do have common characters and that the characters are objectively real seems hardly deniable, and this is part of what Aristotle's theory asserts. But although it is more hardheaded than Plato's, it does raise its own difficulties, two of which may be mentioned. First, how much does it in fact explain of what it purports to explain? We do not account for two tables' *being* tables better by saying that they have a single characteristic (or set of characteristics) in common than by saying that they are both imitations of a single Form. And if what is to be accounted for is rather our ground for *saying* that they are tables, which is a question not about their being tables but about our justification for believing or claiming to know that they are, then admittedly we are perceptually aware of the characteristics of each, and of their similarity. But is saying that some (or all) of the characteristics of the one table are like (even exactly like) the characteristics of the other what the Aristotelian means to do when he maintains that there is a universal common to them (and any other tables)? This may be doubted, for the Aristotelian asserts that a single universal is present in each of the objects, or that each is an instance of it, all the objects of a given kind sharing in the universal of that kind. But this is metaphorical talk, and to *explain* by metaphor is not to explain at all. As a descriptive statement "These two tables are the same shape" is unobjectionable; as an explanatory statement it is less obviously illuminating. Second, Aristotle's supposition that objects belong to real kinds, which are there for us to discover, ignores the fact that distinctions between kinds or classes are not found but made by us, as was later emphasized by Locke. This difficulty is not fatal to the Aristotelian theory, which could accommodate it by emphasizing different levels of determinacy in a universal or class characteristic, but it leads to the question, pursued by Wittgenstein in the twentieth century, whether it is necessary that any single characteristic at all be common to all members of a single class. If it is not necessary, our recognition of objects as belonging to a certain class does not have to depend on the apprehension of a universal shared by all its members, for it may be that nothing, even in the metaphorical sense, is shared. Aristotle's theory, which prima facie has the merits of being simple and realistic, is perhaps both too simple and not realistic enough.

CONCEPTUALISM

As has already been indicated, conceptualism should not be regarded strictly as a rival theory to realism, even if some of its exponents have mistakenly so regarded it.

Starting from an extreme Aristotelian position, that everything which exists is particular, conceptualism concentrates on the fact that generality is an essential feature of both experience and language, and it seeks to answer the question how mental concepts are formed, how they can be general if the data of experience from which they are formed are particular, and how words are general in their significance. Nominalism carries the process further by maintaining that only words are general. Both theories, even if they answered their own question satisfactorily, would have to face the question what basis in reality there is for the generalization inherent in experience, thought, and language. Some versions ignore this question altogether; others answer it in terms of the similarities and differences to be found between particulars. The essential difference between the theories of conceptualism and nominalism is that while both profess to answer a question about language—how words are general, or how words have meaning—nominalism does it more economically, without interposing concepts between words and what words stand for. The conceptualist says that a word is general or meaningful because in the mind there is a corresponding general concept; he then has to explain what a general concept is. The nominalist thinks that the meaningfulness of a word can be accounted for without postulating a separate mental entity called a concept.

Conceptualism is primarily associated with the three classical British empiricists, Locke, Berkeley, and Hume, all of whom propounded views about what, in the terminology of the time, were called general ideas. They were all empiricists in that they agreed that all ideas, or the elements that ideas are composed of, come from, and can come only from, experience: the mind can work on what is given to it by sense experience but can neither have ideas prior to any experience (a denial of the doctrine of innate ideas and, by implication, of Plato's suggestion of prenatal acquaintance with the Forms) nor create ideas *de novo*. Thus, the essence of empiricism is the Epicurean doctrine, given fresh impetus in the seventeenth century by Pierre Gassendi, that *nihil est in intellectu nisi prius fuerit in sensu* ("Nothing is in the mind which is not first in the senses").

Locke. John Locke was first in the field, with his *Essay on Human Understanding* (1690), a long, rambling, and discursive work composed and revised over many years. Unfortunately, the passages in the *Essay* in which he discussed general ideas, or, as he more commonly and perhaps misleadingly called them, "abstract ideas," are neither so clearly thought out and expressed nor perhaps even so consistent as to save him from varying interpretations. The initial difficulty concerns the word "idea" itself, which is the key word of his philosophy, but which he neither defined nor used so as to escape ambiguity. Sometimes wh... he spoke of ideas in the mind he appears to have meant mental images such as occur in remembering, imagining, and dreaming; in this view thinking is done in images, which are particular in their occurrence and existence but somehow become general in their use. At other times he meant, or at least has been taken to have meant, that abstract ideas are mental entities different from images. At still other times he showed signs of using the word "idea" not as the name for any mental occurrence at all but as shorthand for the meaning of a word. Thus, the idea of red would be not an image of something red but what we mean by the word "red" or what we think an object to be when we think it is red; to have the idea of red is to be able to use the word "red" correctly and to be able to discriminate correctly between those objects that are red and those that are not. Attention here will be paid mainly to the first view, of ideas as images, for it is a conceptualist view; so would be the second, that general ideas are mental occurrences different from images, but this appears to be a view which Berkeley fathered on Locke rather than one which Locke actually held.

According to Locke we form general ideas by a process of abstraction from particular ideas. In two different places he gave what appear to be two different accounts of abstraction. In the *Essay on Human Understanding* (Book III, Ch. 3) he said that a general idea—for example, of man—is formed by leaving out of the particular ideas of various individual men all features that are not common to them all and retaining only what is common to them all. The general idea of animal is arrived at by still further leaving out, "retaining only a body, with life, sense and spontaneous motion, comprehended under the name 'animal.'" If this passage were taken in isolation, regardless of what else Locke said on the matter, there would be something to be said for the Berkeleian interpretation. For Locke appears to have been saying that we start with a number of particular images, each, for example, of a different individual man of our acquaintance, and end with something which is still an image but is now a ghostly general image, characterized not by any of the features that are peculiar to any of the individual men but only by all those that all men share. It was not difficult for Berkeley to ridicule as logically absurd the suggestion of a mental image, all the features of which are (as, in this view, they would be) *determinables*. In his polemic Berkeley did not consider the possibility that Locke *might* have been getting at something different, namely that mental images may be *indeterminate*, so that the logical laws of contradiction and excluded middle do not apply to them; for instance, a mental image of a cloudless night sky is an image of a number of stars but of *no* precise number.

However, Locke's other account of abstraction, which occurs earlier in the *Essay*, seems to be the one he seriously intended. For he came back to it again later in the work than the passage just discussed, and it may even be that in that passage he thought he was still giving the same view as before. In Book II (Ch. 11, Sec. 9) he thus described abstraction:

> The mind makes the particular ideas, received from particular objects, to become general; which is done by considering them as they are in the mind such appearances—separate from all other existences, and the circumstances of real existence. . . . This is called *abstraction*, whereby ideas taken from particular things become general representatives of all of the same kind. . . . Thus, the same colour being observed today in chalk or snow, which the mind yesterday received from milk, it considers that appearance alone, makes it a representative of all of that kind; and having given it the name "whiteness," it by that sound

signifies the same quality wheresoever to be imagined or met with; and thus universals, whether ideas or terms are made.

It should be noted, from the last phrase, that Locke was using the word "universal" in the *subjective* conceptualist way, to indicate a concept or idea, not that of which it is the idea. If there is a problem of *objective* universals raised by a number of things being "all of the same kind" or "the same quality wheresoever met with," Locke showed no sign here of being troubled by it. He was interested only in the question how we form the general ideas which undoubtedly we do have (for without them thought, language, and even experience as we know it would be impossible) when every idea or image which occurs in our consciousness is a particular occurrent. I cannot form an image of whiteness or of white, only of a white something, such as a piece of white chalk or a white snowball. The general idea is not a different idea from the particular idea, somehow extracted from it. It *is* the particular idea regarded in a special way. First, the mind *attends* only to a certain aspect of the idea and ignores the rest; second, it treats the idea in that aspect as representative of everything that is similar *in that aspect*. If "abstraction" is perhaps not the most happily chosen term here, at least Locke's meaning is clear, and he repeated it several times later. A general idea is not one which has a different kind of existence from particulars; all ideas, he said, are particular in their existence. A general idea is a particular idea, used in respect to some aspect as representative of a class, namely the class of things determined by the aspect attended to; in thinking or talking about whiteness the ideas of the piece of white chalk, the snowball, and the glass of milk will all do equally well.

Just how far Locke regarded himself as committed to ideas as images and how far he would have regarded his account as being philosophical rather than psychological (if he could have been induced to accept the distinction) is hard to say. But it is fairly clear that his account is not philosophically satisfactory. He showed himself to be well aware that the real problem is one concerning the applicability and use of general words or terms. But as must have been obvious to him, significant use of words in speech or writing is not in fact paralleled by a corresponding string of introspectable images. Therefore, at best, his claim that a general word is meaningful because it stands for a general idea would have to involve "stand for" in a dispositional sense; that is, a word is meaningful if a corresponding idea *can* be found for it. Even then he would be open to the nominalist criticism that nothing is explained simply by duplicating a general word with a general idea. Furthermore, he stressed that almost all thought is verbal: the use of nonverbal imagery in thinking is restricted to a very narrow and primitive level. And, in fact, in the latter part of the *Essay* he showed signs of interpreting ideas not as pictures corresponding to words but as meanings of words, particularly when he was discussing modes—that is, concepts not necessarily used with existential reference. To have an idea, for example, of murder or of gratitude is to understand and use the words "murder" and "gratitude" in a certain way, and to have a correct idea is to understand and use the words in the same way others do. The question whether A has shown gratitude in his conduct to B is a question not only what A's conduct has been but also whether it sufficiently fits the accepted sense of "gratitude." Finally, Locke extended this to all general ideas and rejected the Aristotelian thesis that apprehending universals is apprehending real kinds, or real principles of classification. In maintaining this he was making a move toward a kind of nominalism, for he was emphasizing the fact that concepts, other than those determined by technical or arbitrary definition, are open-ended. We do not find objects and their features divided by nature or God into real and objectively delimited classes; we observe objects and their features, but the distinction between one class and another is something we ourselves make by criteria of convenience and utility. Similarities and differences are there for us to *observe;* whether the similarities are sufficiently close so that we can place the objects in the same or in different classes is for us to *decide.* A modern example would be the question whether a machine can think, or whether a computer can remember. Such a question, Locke would insist, is to be answered only by seeing what operations the machine performs and then deciding whether they are sufficiently close to what we mean by "thinking" or "remembering" when we talk of our own activities to make it reasonable, rather than misleading, to describe them in these terms.

A consequence of this kind of conceptualism will be that concepts are not permanently fixed, as on a simple realist theory they would be; a concept is liable to development and change, as fresh experience or changes of view show the need or utility of it. For example, a central question of twentieth-century sociology, which concerns not only moral outlooks but also legal decisions and the development of law and penal policy, is the question under what conditions a man is to be held not responsible for his physical actions. But the answer to the question is not to be reached simply by determining whether the physical, psychological, and medical facts of a particular case place it inside or outside the accepted scope of responsibility; it also leads to examining the notion of responsibility itself, which in the slow process of time undergoes modification. Experience being ineluctably conceptual, not only are concepts derived from experience, but concepts shape experience itself, as indeed Aristotle had hinted. If there were nothing else valuable in conceptualism, it would be of importance as a corrective to the naïvete of extreme realism, which suggests that all the material of human experience falls into a scheme of pigeonholes or a fixed mold and that the task of inquiry is simply to find out what the scheme or mold is.

Berkeley. George Berkeley, Locke's immediate successor and fiercest critic, devoted the whole introduction of his main philosophical work, *The Principles of Human Knowledge* (1710), to a violent attack on Locke's theory of abstract ideas, for reasons perhaps not primarily concerned with universals at all. However, it is extremely doubtful whether he had, in fact, either studied Locke carefully enough or interpreted him correctly. Berkeley's own theory of general ideas as particular ideas that become "general by being made to represent or stand for all other particular ideas of the same sort" is expressed in a way which might be a verbatim quotation from Locke himself (cf. Locke, *Essay,* Book III, Ch. 3, Sec. 13: "Ideas are general when they are set up as representatives of many particular things. . . . [They] are all of them particular in their existence . . . their general nature being nothing but the capacity they are put into, by the understanding, of signifying or representing many particulars"). And Hume's enthusiastic comment that Berkeley's view of general ideas as particular ideas *used* generally is "one of the greatest and most valuable discoveries that has been made of late years in the republic of letters" does Hume little credit; his examination of Locke was clearly no more thorough than Berkeley's had been.

If Berkeley had done nothing but propound his account of general ideas, his contribution would have been nil. But, in fact, he did much more. Aware that a central strand in the supposed problem of universals was the fact of language and appreciating the question how sounds made by the human larynx or marks made on paper could be used to convey a *meaning* (this too had been stressed by Locke), he protested against the simple view of *unum nomen unum nominatum,* that every time the same word is used it is accompanied in the mind by the same idea. First, this is empirically false, as anybody could find out by noticing the many different ideas (images) he might have on the different occasions he used the word; for example, "red" might be accompanied sometimes by an image of a red dress, sometimes by an image of a red apple, a red flower, etc., which might in any case all be different shades of red. Furthermore, it is not even true that every time a man uses a word that can be accompanied by an image, it is accompanied by one. The actual occurrence of an image, if not necessary, could not help to explain the meaningfulness of a word. Sometimes Berkeley wrote as if an image were necessary in a dispositional sense; a word is significant if a suitable image *can* be had or produced to correspond to it. Thus, he compared a use of language—for instance, in conversation—to the use of algebraic symbols in a calculation: we can represent a given quantity by the symbol x, and we carry out the calculation without all the time thinking of the quantity represented by x; what matters is that we can, at any time we want to, replace x by the quantity. Similarly, words for the most part, as actually employed, function as cashable counters.

But Berkeley went on to emancipate himself even from this tenuous servitude to ideas as images. He hinted at it when he said that the important thing is the *definition* of a word, not the occurrence or recurrence of an idea: "It is one thing for to keep a name constantly to the same definition, and another to make it stand every where for the same idea: the one is necessary, the other useless and impracticable." But later he went even further and suggested what can be described as an operational theory of meaning. This is nowhere fully developed, chiefly because he abandoned serious philosophical inquiry while still a young man, but unmistakable indications of it persist throughout his writings.

In the *Principles* they appear in two ways, (*a*) the reminder of the diversity of function of language and (*b*) the doctrine of "notions." The tendency among philosophers to try to explain the significance of words in terms of corresponding ideas was due to a simple and entirely false view of language, namely that its sole function was informing, or "the communication of ideas"; this made it easier to think of ideas as pictures translated into words by the speaker and retranslated into pictures by the hearer. (The modern television analogy of visual pictures translated into radio signals by the transmitter and retranslated into visual pictures by the receiving set would not be entirely inept.) But as Berkeley rightly emphasized, to inform is not *the* function of language, only *one* of its functions. It has others, "the raising of some passion, the exciting to or deterring from an action, the putting the mind in some particular disposition"—to which we could add still others, such as asking questions, praying, vowing, swearing, making promises, declaring intentions, and expressing wishes or fears.

It is not entirely clear exactly what Berkeley intended the doctrine of "notions" to be. He acknowledged that his own principles did not allow him to say that we have (or can have) ideas of everything we may significantly talk of, because they did not allow him to say that we have ideas of mind or spirit (ideas being passive and mind or spirit being active); yet a man who uses the words "mind" and "spirit" (to which Berkeley added all words denoting relations) is not uttering meaningless gibberish. Therefore, it must be true of at least some words that we "know or understand what is meant" by them although we can have no corresponding ideas. In these cases we have notions. Notions, as they appear in the *Principles,* do not solve any problem (if one exists) regarding how words that cannot be paralleled by ideas can be significant—they merely occur as a label for the fact that there are such words. They are not the answer but appear to be Berkeley's name for the question. If by "having a notion of *x*" he meant "knowing or understanding the meaning of the word *x*, although not being able to have an idea of *x*," then the question how one can know or understand the meaning of an idealess word is not answered by saying that he has a notion, and there is no reason to think that Berkeley deluded himself into supposing that his doctrine of notions actually gave an *answer* to anything. The *Principles* takes the matter no further than the negative conclusion not only that a word need not be accompanied by an idea but also that some words cannot be. This is the beginning of an admission that the intelligibility of language neither requires nor is illuminated by suppositions about mental imagery. In a much later work, *Alciphron* (1732), Berkeley returned to the topic and showed how (with the examples of force from physics and grace from theology) although frontal questions such as "What is force?" and "What is grace?" could produce no answer, yet these were genuine concepts, because it was true that the use of them (or of the words "force" and "grace") could lead to fruitful results. Or again, "the algebraic mark, which denotes the root of a negative square, hath its use in logistic operations, although it be impossible to form an idea of any such quantity." In allowing that a concept could be fertile even though it could not be cashed, Berkeley was at once breaching the walls of strict empiricism and anticipating

the theory construction of modern science, particularly of modern physics.

Hume. Immediately after Berkeley came David Hume, the third of the great British empiricists and the one who has had the most lasting influence on subsequent developments in the philosophy of that school. He devoted an early section of his *Treatise of Human Nature* (1739) to the subject of abstract ideas (Book I, Part i, Sec. 7), professing to accept Berkeley's doctrine of general ideas and producing arguments to confirm it. But in fact he was not merely repeating Berkeley's views. He took one step backward in maintaining that the use of every general word must be accompanied by a particular mental idea: "'Tis certain that we form the idea of individuals, whenever we use any general term." But he took several steps forward in suggesting how a given idea can represent others of the same kind—that is, how the idea can become general.

Hume's emphasis on the role of the word was even stronger than Berkeley's had been. Whereas Berkeley had supposed that a word becomes general by its relation to a particular but representative idea, Hume put it the other way round, that a particular idea becomes general by being "annexed to a certain term." "All abstract ideas are really nothing but particular ones . . . but, being annexed to general terms, they are able to represent a vast variety." Where Berkeley had contented himself with maintaining that an idea became general by representing all ideas of that kind, Hume offered an account of *how* a particular idea could represent others that were not at the time present to the mind. It did this through custom or habit, by the association of ideas and the association of words. At any given moment a man has only one individual idea before his mind, but because of the resemblances which he has found in his experience, the one individual idea is associated with others of the same kind, which are not actually present to the mind at the time but which would be called up by the stimulus of a suitable experience or a suitable word. Thus, the possession of a general idea or a concept becomes a mental disposition, the readiness, engendered by custom, to have some idea belonging to a given kind, when the appropriate stimulus occurs, and the acquisition of a concept will be the gradual process of (1) learning by experience and habituation to recognize instances and to discriminate between them and instances of a different concept and (2) having the appropriate associations and dispositions set up in one's mind. To have a concept *actually* in mind at any given time is to have in mind an individual idea plus the appropriate associative dispositions.

Hume assigned words a key role in his doctrine of association of ideas, supposing that particular ideas, which resemble one another somewhat but not exactly or in all respects, tend to be associated with one another because each is associated with the *same* general word. The differences between a ripe tomato and a scarlet-painted automobile are more numerous and conspicuous than their similarities, but the idea of the one can readily be associated with that of the other by the fact that the word "red" is used of each, and thus the idea of either could serve as representative of the class of red objects, whatever the variety of objects and the differences between the many shades of red displayed. "A particular idea becomes general by being annex'd to a general term; that is, to a term, which from a customary conjunction has a relation to many other particular ideas, and readily recalls them in the imagination." One could say that according to Hume we learn to think by learning to talk, not the other way round, and that in learning to talk the chief influence is that of custom and association. Here Hume failed, as nominalism also failed, to see that the attempt to account for the generality of an idea in terms of the generality of a word will not do, if taken only as far as he took it. In the sense in which he insisted that every idea is particular, so is every word. Whatever reasons there are for denying the existence of general ideas as distinct from particular ideas will also be reasons for denying the existence of general words as distinct from particular words. Paradoxical though it may seem, the sense in which the word "red" may be said to be general is such that the word "red" cannot occur in any sentences at all, for what occurs in a particular sentence is a *particular* word "red." The fourth word in the sentence "Some automobiles are red" may be very like the first word in the sentence "Red tomatoes are ripe," but they are different individual words, occupying different positions in space (as printed). Even in this case they are not exactly alike (for the first does not, and the second does, start with a capital letter), and other "reds" could be even more unlike—for instance, if they were printed in different fonts of type or were written down by different people.

Consideration of this point would have required Hume to say about a word's being general what he (like Locke and Berkeley) said about an idea's being general, namely that it was based on (or constituted by) the resemblance between particulars. (Difficulties in making out somebody's handwriting stem precisely from its deviating more than usual from the familiar resemblances.) Conceptualism therefore comes down, in the persons of these three authors, on the side of resemblance as being the ontological basis of general ideas. All that actually exists is individual; generalization, or concept formation, is possible only to the extent that individual objects and occurrences, their features, and the relations between them display perceptible resemblances to a greater or lesser extent. But Hume offered, or at least hinted at, a more sophisticated version of resemblance. According to Locke, two objects would resemble each other if they possessed certain features in common—that is, if certain features of the one were identical (in an Aristotelian sense) with certain features of the other. Thus, one object possessing features *abcd* would resemble another possessing features *adef,* but less closely than it resembled one possessing features *acdf.* But Hume saw that this raised difficulties for simple (or unanalyzable) ideas or qualities—for example, that "*blue* and *green* are different simple ideas, but are more resembling than *blue* and *scarlet;* tho' their perfect simplicity excludes all possibility of separation or distinction." They may resemble each other "without having any common circumstance the same." The notion of resemblance as an ultimate relation, without requiring that the respect in which two objects resemble each other should be a quality identical in each, propounded here by Hume, has been taken further in later developments of his theory.

NOMINALISM AND RESEMBLANCE

Nominalist theories. The nominalist view, that only names (or, more generally, words) are universal, "for the things named are every one of them singular and individual" (Hobbes, *Leviathan,* Ch. 4), has had a very long history. It was the subject of much controversy in medieval philosophy, more for the theological heresies it was believed to engender than on grounds of logic, and it was advanced again in the seventeenth century by Thomas Hobbes.

Of the medievalists mention need be made only of two, one early and the other late. Peter Abelard, although fiercely critical of the extreme nominalism of Roscelin de Compiègne, was strongly influenced by it. For Abelard a universal was not a sound (*vox*), as it was for Roscelin, but a word (*sermo*)—that is, a meaningful sound—and it acquired its meaning from its referential use, the reference being mediated by a general idea which is a composite image. Thus, although Abelard was described by his successors as a nominalist, he was only partly and confusedly so; he could as well be called a conceptualist, or even a moderate realist.

William of Ockham, a polemical figure who was pronounced a heretic and excommunicated, produced a number of logical works in which he developed a battery of arguments against realism and supported a form of nominalism. According to him, universals are terms or signs standing for or referring to individual objects and sets of objects, but they cannot themselves exist. For what exists must be individual, and a universal cannot be; the mistake of supposing that it could was the fatal contradiction of Platonic realism. And Aristotelian realism was no better, for it involved its own contradiction, that the identical universal should be present in a number of particulars. Real universals are neither possible nor needed. Rather, universals are predicates or meanings, possessing logical status only, required for thought and communication, not *naming* anything that could possibly exist.

In its extreme form, that there is nothing common to a class of particulars called by the same name other than that they *are* called by the same name, nominalism is so clearly untenable that it may be doubted whether anybody has actually tried to hold it. If all the individuals (objects, qualities, or whatever they were) called by the same name—for example, "table"—had nothing in common but being called by the same name, no reason could be given why just they and no others had that name, and no reason could be given for deciding whether to include an object in or to exclude it from the class. On a realist view certain objects are *called* "tables" because they *are* tables (that is, they partially embody a Platonic Form of tablehood or possess a common Aristotelian feature of tablehood). On an extreme nominalist view they *are* tables only because they are *called* "tables," and no answer at all can be given to the question why certain objects are (or are to be) called "tables" and others not. Perhaps the only extreme nominalist has been Humpty Dumpty. ("'When *I* use a word, it means just what I choose it to mean—neither more nor less.' 'The question is,' said Alice, 'whether you *can* make words mean different things.' 'The question is,' said Humpty Dumpty, 'which is to be master—that's all.'") Moderate nominalism, while retaining the view that only words are universals, saves itself from total subjectivity by basing the use of words on the resemblances between things. Hobbes, for example, in the *Leviathan* (Ch. 4) said: "One universal name is imposed on many things, for their similitude in some quality or other accident." So "table" is a universal word, applicable to any individual objects between which a certain resemblance holds. Objects, their qualities, and their relations are all individual, the only thing that is general being the word which is applicable to objects (or qualities, or relations) of a given class in virtue of the resemblances between them.

Nominalism and a conceptualism such as Hume's here converge, differences being in approach and emphasis rather than in substance. And nominalism must in the end reduce itself to a resemblance theory which, if acceptable, finally renders nominalism unnecessary. Nominalism's only reason for insisting on the universality of the word is its denial of the universality of the thing: things are individuals, and the properties of a thing are individual to it. But the universality of the word depends on resemblances between things; thus, nominalism requires a resemblance theory. However, as was already mentioned in reference to Hume, the nominalist must, to be consistent, go further and recognize that what he says of things, if true of them, must be true of words also, which requires him to make what logicians have called the "type–token" distinction. Any occurrence of the word "red" is individual ("red" as a token), and two occurrences of what would be called the *same* word ("Red" as a type) are occurrences of the same word only in that they resemble each other in the relevant ways. Thus, the universal word "Red" becomes the class of the resembling individual words "red," "*red*," "RED," etc., and once the universality of a word has been analyzed along these lines, the reason for saying that only words are universal is gone, for exactly the same account can be given by the resemblance theory of universality in things. Nominalism was able to present the appearance of being a distinct theory of universals only as long as its exponents and critics alike failed to apply to it the type–token distinction. Once that is applied, words are seen to be on all fours with things, and the question becomes, for words as for things, whether generality can be analyzed simply in terms of resemblances between individuals, as Hume suggested. Nominalism not only *requires* the support of a resemblance theory to explain how a word can have a general use but also, in its only consistent form, *is* a resemblance theory.

Resemblance theories. Whether or not Hume actually held what might be described as the pure-resemblance theory, that is the only form of resemblance theory that is distinctive. The version advanced by Locke, and possibly by Berkeley, too, according to which the degree of resemblance between two objects depends on the extent of qualitative identity between them, collapses into a modified Aristotelian realism. Pure resemblance, although allowing that if two objects resemble each other there must be some respect in which they are similar, would deny that this respect is to be regarded as an identical something common to both; not to deny this would be to reintroduce the Aristotelian universal. Red objects are to be called red simply because they resemble each other in a way in which they do not resemble blue objects, or hard objects, or smooth objects, or spherical objects. Nothing is described by saying that the universal red is what is common to any pair of red objects which is not more accurately and less misleadingly described by saying that both are red—that is, resemble each other in respect of each being red. There is a similarity between the red of the one and the red of the other, and the similarity might be anything from being virtually exact (as in two new red postage stamps of the same denomination) to being only approximate and generic (as in two flags of widely different shades of red, one flag, in addition, being bright and new, the other old and faded). The world is made up of individual things and events, with their individual qualities and relations, and with resemblances in different respects and of differing degrees. Were it not for such resemblances (and contrasting differences), concept formation and language would be impossible; indeed, biological survival would be impossible, too. The resemblance theory is metaphysically the most economical, but it has objections to face, notably two: (1) It does not succeed in dispensing with universals in a traditional sense, such as the Aristotelian, because resemblance itself will have to be such a universal, and if it is, there is no ground for denying others. (2) As two objects which resemble each other must be similar in some respect, the respect must be something common to both.

Although these two objections are frequently reiterated, it is not clear that either has great force, as is shown by H. H. Price's detailed discussion in *Thinking and Experience* (1953). The argument that the resemblance theory requires resemblance itself to be a universal in a sense in which the theory denies that there are any universals has been the more persistent; it is particularly associated with Bertrand Russell (although he was not the first to propound it). But although he advanced it in two books widely separated in time, *Problems of Philosophy* (1912) and *An Inquiry Into Meaning and Truth* (1940), his confidence seems to have diminished. Originally he maintained a realist theory of universals, of a Platonic kind, and held that it could be *proved*, at least in the case of relations, that there must be such universals.

> If we wish to avoid the universals *whiteness* and *triangularity*, we shall choose some particular patch of white or some particular triangle, and say that anything is white or a triangle if it has the right sort of resemblance to our chosen particular. But then the resemblance required will have to be a universal.

That is, we could theoretically dispense with universals of *quality* by analyzing them in terms of *relation*, and ultimately in terms of the relation of resemblance. The latter we cannot dispense with, for if we say that the resemblance between a pair of similar particulars is itself a particular relation, we shall then have to admit a resemblance between that resemblance relation and the resemblance relation holding between another pair of similar particulars; the only way to save ourselves from an infinite regress (of resemblances between resemblances between resemblances . . . between resemblance relations) is to admit that "the relation of resemblance must be a true universal. And having been forced to admit this universal, we find that it is no longer worth while to invent difficult and unplausible theories to avoid the admission of such universals as whiteness and triangularity." In this respect, Russell held, the rationalists were right, as against the empiricists like Hume: the existence of real universals has been proved, at least in the case of the relation of resemblance, and no good reason is left for denying it in the case of other relations and of qualities.

Some years later, in *The Analysis of Mind* (1921), Russell showed more hesitation, when he wrote, "I *think* a logical argument could be produced to show that universals are part of the structure of the world." Finally, in the *Inquiry*, after repeating his original argument, he said, "I conclude, therefore, though with hesitation, that there are universals, and not merely general words."

Price seems to have lost confidence in the validity of Russell's proof even more thoroughly, and far more rapidly. In *Thinking and Representation* (1946) he accepted that resemblance has to be a universal and repeated that the most the resemblance theory would have achieved "would be to reduce all other universals to this one relational universal." He went on: "This is a very notorious difficulty, and perhaps by much repetition it has become a bore. Yet I do not think it has ever been answered." But in *Thinking and Experience* (1953) he thought the difficulty could be answered, and he spent several pages answering it. Admittedly, his first argument is hardly convincing, namely that the opponents of the resemblance theory (such as Russell) are begging the question by assuming the very thing that they have to prove, that there are universals: from the fact that the theory analyzes all other alleged universals in terms of resemblance, and that it is ultimate, it does not follow that resemblance is a universal. We cannot answer the question whether there are *any* universals by replying that even if there are no *other* universals, resemblance must be one. Against Price here, it may be doubted whether Russell's objection is of this question-begging form. The objection, rather, is that the only way of avoiding the admission of resemblance as a universal leads to a vicious infinite regress. Nevertheless, Russell's objection is invalid, as the next stage of Price's answer shows. It is true that the resemblance theory would have to admit different orders or levels of resemblance, resemblances between pairs of particulars, resemblances between these resemblances, and so on ad infinitum. But there is nothing logically vicious or unintelligible about that. The resemblance which we notice between any pair of similar individuals is as individual as they and as the qualities of each; the resemblance which we notice or can find between such a resemblance relation and another resemblance relation holding between another pair of similar individuals is itself individual; the process can be continued as long as patience and imagination hold out. We do not need a real universal of resemblance to stop the regress, simply

because the regress does not need to be stopped. The fallacious assumption at the root of this objection to the resemblance theory is not the question-begging assumption that there are universals but the assumption that unless there are, a *vicious* regress is generated.

The merit of the resemblance theory is that it does not confuse, as the realist theories arguably did, the roles of explanation and description. Why or how tables are tables rather than chairs, and elephants are elephants rather than tigers, is not answered by saying that each is what it is because it instantiates the appropriate universal. The only explaining that has to be done on why a given object is a table is to be done in causal terms. What does have to be explained is something about ourselves, namely how it is that we can (indeed, must) experience in terms of kinds and generality, that we form concepts, and that we develop language for communication. That experience, thought, and language depend on the use of universals, in some sense, is undeniable, and the explanation of this is to be given by a suitably illuminating description of the world we experience. About ourselves the question of universals is a question of explanation. About our world the question of universals is a question of description, and this the resemblance theory seems adequately, and nontendentiously, to provide.

In the twentieth century, philosophers have paid far more attention to actual language and, largely under the influence of Ludwig Wittgenstein, have come to appreciate that even if the notion of there being (in some sense) something common to all instances covered by a single general word is true of some words, it is not true of all, and that even the resemblances within a group of things all called by the same general name may be what Wittgenstein called "family resemblances"—the vague and overlapping likenesses which one sees between the different members of a family. His own example is what "we call 'games.'" He meant "board-games, card-games, ball-games, Olympic games, and so on. What is common to them all? Don't say: 'There *must* be something common, or they would not be called "games"'—but *look and see* whether there is anything common to all" (*Philosophical Investigations*, I, Sec. 66). There is *nothing* common to *all* games, only "similarities, relationships, and a whole series of them at that." The concept of causality, too, has stubbornly resisted the attempts of philosophers to analyze it, as though there were only one *it* to analyze—although the hint that it really requires the Wittgenstein treatment first came from Aristotle himself.

The history of the subject of universals has come a long way from looking for a general entity for which a general word is to be the name (Plato), via looking for recurring identities (Aristotle), selected identities (Locke), and resemblances (Hume), to looking for varying and overlapping resemblances and recognizing that only vain servitude to a theory insists on trying to find what is common to a whole range of overlaps (Wittgenstein). Furthermore, with the development of semantics it has come to be appreciated that not all general words are, even in a stretched sense, "names" at all. They can be significant for their syntactical function, indicating, for instance, condition or conjunction or contrast ("if," "and," "although") or, again, attitudes, outlooks, or degrees of confidence ("perhaps," "probably," "certainly"). The philosophical history of universals has been plagued by the persistent treatment of words as names, which has been made easier by philosophers' taking as their examples only objects and their qualities. But questions about universals are questions about generality, and generality is the essential feature of all words, not just of those that might plausibly be called names.

Bibliography

PLATO AND ARISTOTLE

Plato introduced his theory of Forms into many different dialogues, in particular *Phaedo, Republic,* and *Parmenides;* in the last of these he summarized the trend of his thought in earlier dialogues and subjected it to criticism, which was further developed by Aristotle, as in *Metaphysics* M. Aristotle's own views are briefly indicated in *Posterior Analytics* II, 19. Sir David Ross, in *Plato's Theory of Ideas* (Oxford, 1951), provides a useful account and discussion of the development of Plato's views and Aristotle's criticisms.

MEDIEVAL PHILOSOPHY

Some account of medieval philosophy's treatment of the theme of universals is given in Father Frederick Copleston's *A History of Philosophy,* Vols. II and III (London, 1950). A more detailed discussion of the four key figures in the dispute between realism and nominalism—Augustine, Abelard, Aquinas, and Ockham—is to be found in M. H. Carré's *Realists and Nominalists* (London, 1946). *Selections from Mediaeval Philosophers,* edited by Richard McKeon (London, 1928), contains a few relevant passages. Copleston, in his bibliographies, provides references to editions of the full texts, where available, and to the appropriate volumes of J. P. Migne's *Patrologia Latina.*

SEVENTEENTH- AND EIGHTEENTH-CENTURY PHILOSOPHY

Hobbes's few remarks on universals are to be found in his *Elements of Philosophy,* I, 2, and in *Leviathan,* Ch. 4. Locke scattered comments all over his diffuse and repetitious *Essay on Human Understanding,* but the main entries are II, xi, and III, iii. Berkeley devoted the whole of the introduction to his *Principles of Human Knowledge* to the subject and returned to it, in a rather more sophisticated way, in *Alciphron,* 7.4. Hume dispatched it briskly in his *Treatise of Human Nature,* I, i, 17. Thomas Reid, in his *Essays on the Intellectual Powers of Man,* V, 6, subjected the other philosophers to telling criticism and foreshadowed modern tendencies.

RECENT PHILOSOPHY

In *Studies in Philosophy and Psychology,* Vols. XV–XVII (London, 1930), G. F. Stout reprinted three relevant papers, the last criticizing the resemblance theory and advocating the view of a universal as a "distributive unity" of a class. Bertrand Russell followed his paper "On the Relation of Universals and Particulars," in *PAS* (1911–1912), with *Problems of Philosophy* (London, 1912), which contains two chapters on the subject; it is taken up again in *Analysis of Mind* (London, 1921) and *Inquiry Into Meaning and Truth* (London, 1940). Russell's views are the subject of an article by O. K. Bouwsma in *Philosophical Review* (1943). Other relevant articles are F. P. Ramsey, "Universals," in *Mind* (1925); A. J. Ayer, "On Particulars and Universals," in *PAS* (1933–1934); R. I. Aaron, "Two Senses of the Word Universal," in *Mind* (1939), and "Our Knowledge of Universals," in *Proceedings of the British Academy* (1944); Morris Lazerowitz, "The Existence of Universals," in *Mind* (1946); Nelson Goodman and W. V. Quine, "Steps Towards a Constructive Nominalism," in *Journal of Symbolic Logic,* Vol. 12 (1947); W. V. Quine, "On What There Is,"

in *Review of Metaphysics* (1948–1949); A. N. Prior, in *Mind* (1949); A. C. Lloyd, "On Arguments for Real Universals," in *Analysis* (1951); D. F. Pears, "Universals," in *Philosophical Quarterly* (1950–1951); R. B. Brandt, "The Languages of Realism and Nominalism," in *Philosophy and Phenomenological Research* (1956–1957); Arthur Pap, in *Philosophical Quarterly* (1959–1960); and Renford Bambrough, "Universals and Family Resemblances," in *PAS*, Vol. 61 (1960–1961). The last paper takes as its point of departure the "family resemblance" account of the use of general words given by Ludwig Wittgenstein in *The Blue and Brown Books* (Oxford, 1958), pp. 17–27, and *Philosophical Investigations* (Oxford, 1953), Secs. 65–77. A general survey of the problems connected with universals is undertaken, at a level of no great philosophical difficulty, by R. I. Aaron in *The Theory of Universals* (Oxford, 1952) and, more briefly, by A. D. Woozley in *Theory of Knowledge* (London, 1949). Other books, each containing several chapters on the subject, are Nelson Goodman's *Structure of Appearance* (Cambridge, Mass., 1951), John Holloway's *Language and Intelligence* (London, 1951), and, most detailed of all, H. H. Price's *Thinking and Experience* (London, 1953). Papers by I. M. Bocheński, Alonzo Church, and Nelson Goodman are included in the symposium *The Problem of Universals* (Notre Dame, Ind., 1956).

A. D. WOOZLEY

UTILITARIANISM can most generally be described as the doctrine which states that the rightness or wrongness of actions is determined by the goodness and badness of their consequences. This general definition can be made more precise in various ways, according to which we get various species of utilitarianism.

Act and rule utilitarianism. The first important division is between "act" utilitarianism and "rule" utilitarianism. If, in the above definition, we understand "actions" to mean "particular actions," then we are dealing with the form of utilitarianism called act utilitarianism, according to which we assess the rightness or wrongness of each individual action directly by its consequences. If, on the other hand, we understand "actions" in the above definition to mean "sorts of actions," then we get some sort of rule utilitarianism. The rule utilitarian does not consider the consequences of each particular action but considers the consequences of adopting some general rule, such as "Keep promises." He adopts the rule if the consequences of its general adoption are better than those of the adoption of some alternative rule.

Since, in this context, the word "rule" can be interpreted in two ways, either to mean "possible rule" or "rule actually operating in society," there are actually two species of rule utilitarianism. If we interpret "rule" simply as "possible rule," we get an ethical doctrine strongly resembling that of Kant. It is true that Kant is not normally regarded as a utilitarian, but nevertheless a utilitarian strain can be detected in his thought. If we interpret his categorical imperative, "Act only on that maxim through which you can at the same time will that it should become a universal law," as meaning "Act only on that maxim which you would like to see established as a universal law," and if liking here is determined by the individual's feelings as a benevolent man, then we get a version of utilitarianism which may usefully be called Kantianism. It is true that Kant would object to this appeal to feelings of benevolence and would wish to distinguish sharply between "willing" and "wanting" or "liking." Nevertheless, it is far from clear how Kant's distinction can be defended; and when he elucidates his general principle by means of examples, he does indeed tend to think in terms of the consequences that we should like to see brought about. However, the word "Kantianism" is used here merely as a useful and perhaps not inappropriate label; whether Kant himself would approve of its present application is not an important issue in the present discussion.

If, in our definition of "utilitarianism," we interpret the word "rule" as "actual rule," or "rule conventionally operative in society," we get a form of rule utilitarianism that has been propounded in recent times by Stephen Toulmin, who seems mainly concerned with the justification, and in some cases the reform, of rules of conduct which are actually operative in society.

When we think of the writers with whom the term "utilitarianism" is most naturally associated, namely, Jeremy Bentham, J. S. Mill, and Henry Sidgwick, we must think of utilitarianism primarily as act utilitarianism. However, controversy has recently developed over whether Mill should not rather be interpreted as a rule utilitarian, and there has also been much discussion of the rival claims of act and rule utilitarianism to be viable ethical theories.

R. M. Hare, in his book *Freedom and Reason* (Oxford, 1963), has recently argued that there is no clear distinction between act and rule utilitarianism, since if a certain action is right, it must be the case that any action just like it in relevant respects will also be right. If these respects are then specified in detail, we get a rule of the form "Do actions of this sort." A defender of the distinction between act and rule utilitarianism could reply that since the situations in which actions occur are infinitely variable, and since no two actions have quite the same sorts of consequences, the act utilitarian may not be able to describe the "relevant respects" mentioned above in any less general form than "The action is of the sort that has the best consequences." But if this is so, Hare's principle that if an action is right, then any action which is like it in the relevant respects is also right, does not yield a sufficiently particular form of rule to justify the assimilation of act and rule utilitarianism.

Egoistic and universalistic utilitarianism. Act utilitarianism, unlike rule utilitarianism, lends itself to being interpreted either in an egoistic or in a nonegoistic way. Are the good consequences which must be considered by an agent the consequences to the agent himself (his own happiness, for example), or are they the consequences to all mankind or even to all sentient beings? If we adopt the former alternative, we get egoistic utilitarianism; and if we adopt the latter alternative, we get universalistic utilitarianism. Since what is best for me is unlikely to be what is best for everyone, it is clear that there is not only a theoretical but also a practical incompatibility between egoistic and universalistic utilitarianism. This was not always seen by the early utilitarians, who sometimes seem to have confused the two doctrines. There is, in fact, even a pragmatic inconsistency in egoistic utilitarianism, since an egoist, on his own principles, would be unlikely to wish to be seen in his true colors, and so would have no motive for expressing his ethical doctrine. In this article we shall be concerned with utilitarianism in the universalistic sense.

Hedonistic and ideal utilitarianism. Another distinction, which cuts across that between act and rule utilitarianism, is the distinction between hedonistic and ideal utilitarianism. Utilitarianism has been defined above as the view that the rightness or wrongness of an action depends on the total goodness or badness of its consequences. A hedonistic utilitarian will hold that the goodness or badness of a consequence depends only on its pleasantness or unpleasantness. As Bentham put it, quantity of pleasure being equal, pushpin is as good as poetry. An ideal utilitarian, such as G. E. Moore, will hold that the goodness or badness of a state of consciousness can depend on things other than its pleasantness. According to him, the goodness or badness of a state of consciousness can depend, for example, on various intellectual and aesthetic qualities. In his calculations, the ideal utilitarian will be concerned not only with pleasantness and unpleasantness, but also with such things as knowledge and the contemplation of beautiful objects. He may even hold that some pleasant states of mind can be intrinsically bad, and some unpleasant ones intrinsically good. J. S. Mill took up an intermediate position. He held that although pleasantness was a necessary condition for goodness, the intrinsic goodness of a state of mind could depend on things other than its pleasantness, or, as he put it, there are higher and lower pleasures.

It should be noted that we have assumed that the only things that can be intrinsically good or bad are states of consciousness. Other things can of course be extrinsically good or bad. For example, an earthquake is normally extrinsically bad, that is, it causes a state of affairs that is on the whole intrinsically bad. Moreover, a utilitarian can hold that something which is intrinsically bad, such as the annoyance of remembering that we have forgotten to do something, is extrinsically good, for it is a means to a set of consequences that are on balance intrinsically good. G. E. Moore held that states of affairs other than states of consciousness could be intrinsically good or bad. For an ideal utilitarian, this is a theoretically possible contention, but nevertheless, few ideal utilitarians would find the contention a plausible one, and we shall therefore ignore it in this article.

Normative and descriptive utilitarianism. Utilitarianism may be put forward either as a system of normative ethics, that is, as a proposal about how we *ought* to think about conduct, or it may be put forward as a system of descriptive ethics, that is, an analysis of how we *do* think about conduct. The distinction between normative and descriptive utilitarianism has not always been observed. It is important to bear carefully in mind the distinction between normative and descriptive utilitarianism and to note that objections to descriptive utilitarianism do not necessarily constitute objections to normative utilitarianism.

Historical remarks. Properly speaking, utilitarianism began with Jeremy Bentham (1748–1832), who was a universalistic hedonistic act utilitarian. He put forward his view essentially as normative ethics, but he was unclear about the distinction between normative and factual utterances and may justly be accused of committing what Moore later called the naturalistic fallacy—the fallacy of claiming to deduce ethical principles solely from matters of fact. (David Hume had in effect pointed out this fallacy before Bentham's time.)

Precursors of utilitarianism. Anticipations of Bentham are to be found in the history of ethics. In ancient times Aristippus of Cyrene and Epicurus propounded hedonistic theories. However, their doctrines approximate egoistic rather than universalistic utilitarianism, despite the fact that they were unclear about the difficulty of reconciling the two doctrines and hence tried to have it both ways. The same might be said of Abraham Tucker and William Paley, the more immediate precursors of Bentham, who also injected certain theological conceptions into their systems. The tension between egoistic and universalistic hedonism can also be detected in the eighteenth-century French writer Helvétius, who appears to have influenced Bentham; also, the political philosopher William Godwin should be mentioned. David Hume is often classified as a utilitarian, but he used utility not as a normative or even as a descriptive principle, but as an explanatory one: when asked why we approve of certain traits of character, he would point out that they are traits which either are useful or are immediately agreeable. Both because he used the principle of utility in an explanatory way and because he was primarily concerned with the evaluation of traits of character (virtues and vices and the like) rather than with the question of what actions ought to be done, it is not advisable to regard Hume as a utilitarian.

J. S. Mill. As was mentioned above, there has been some controversy over whether J. S. Mill (1806–1873) ought to be regarded as an act utilitarian or as a rule utilitarian. Mill does not make his position on this issue very clear. Probably he was not very well aware of the distinction, and in any case he would probably have thought it a fairly unimportant one, since he was mainly concerned with the opposition between utilitarianism in general and other systems of ethics which were quite nonutilitarian. Although Bentham had on at least one occasion used the word "utilitarian," it was Mill who introduced it into philosophy. He appropriated it, with some change of meaning, from a passage in the Scottish novelist John Galt's *Annals of the Parish* (Edinburgh, 1821).

Sidgwick. We can with some confidence classify Mill as a normative utilitarian rather than a descriptive one, but the first utilitarian philosopher who was very explicit on this issue was Henry Sidgwick (1838–1900). Sidgwick understood that there is a distinction between normative and factual sentences, although, like G. E. Moore (1873–1958), he thought that ethical principles could be the objects of intellectual intuition. Sidgwick was a universalistic hedonistic utilitarian, but he was also strongly attracted by the claims of egoism. He saw more clearly than earlier writers that there was a theoretical inconsistency in being both an egoistic and a universalistic utilitarian, and he considered the possibility that there might be theological sanctions which would reconcile the two views, if not in theory, then at least in practice.

Later utilitarians. Moore and Hastings Rashdall were ideal universalistic utilitarians, although Moore, with his principle of organic unities, and Rashdall, with his importation into the utilitarian calculations of the moral worth of the actions themselves, introduced considerations which,

if taken seriously, would seem to vitiate the truly utilitarian character of their theories.

A subtle form of rule utilitarianism of the sort we have called Kantianism was propounded in 1936 by R. F. Harrod. Contemporary writers such as Stephen Toulmin, P. H. Nowell-Smith, John Rawls, K. E. M. Baier, and M. G. Singer have propounded views which either are or approximate rule utilitarianism. R. B. Brandt has been sympathetic to rule utilitarianism and has recently defended a rather subtle and complex version of it.

ANALYSIS AND CRITIQUE

Utilitarianism as a descriptive ethics. It is fairly easy to show that both act utilitarianism and rule utilitarianism are inconsistent with usual ideas about ethics, or what can be called the common moral consciousness. For the principles of both systems will in some cases lead us to advocate courses of action which the plain man would regard as wrong. Consider, for example, the case of a secret promise to a dying man. To ease his dying moments, I promise him that I will deliver a hoard of money, which he entrusts to me, to a rich and profligate relative of his. No one else knows either about the promise or the hoard. On utilitarian principles, it would appear that I should not carry out my promise. I can surely put the money to much better use by giving it, say, to a needy hospital. In this way I would do a lot of good and no harm. I do not disappoint the man to whom I made the promise, because he is dead. Nor, by breaking the promise, do I do indirect harm by weakening men's faith in the socially useful institution of promise-making and promise-keeping, for on this occasion no one knows about the promise. Normally, of course, an act utilitarian will keep a promise even when the direct results are not beneficial, because the indirect effects of sowing mistrust are so harmful. This consideration clearly does not apply in the present instance. The plain man, however, would be quite sure that the promise to the dying man should be kept. In this instance, therefore, we have a clear case in which utilitarianism is inconsistent with the way in which, for the most part, people in fact think about morality.

The rule utilitarian, on the other hand, would probably agree with the plain man in the above case, because he would appeal to the utility of the rule of promise-keeping in general, not to the utility of the particular act of promise-keeping. Nevertheless, cases can be brought up which will show the incompatibility of even rule utilitarianism with the common moral consciousness. For example, a riot involving hundreds of deaths may be averted only by punishing some innocent scapegoat and calling it punishment. Given certain empirical assumptions, which may perhaps not in fact be true, but which in a certain sort of society might be true, it is hard to see how a rule utilitarian could object to such a practice of punishing the innocent in these circumstances, and yet most people would regard such a practice as unjust. They would hold that a practice of sometimes punishing the innocent would be wrong, despite the fact that in certain circumstances its consequences would be good or that the consequences of any alternative practice would be bad. In this instance, then, there is a conflict between even the rule utilitarian and the plain man. (This is not, of course, to say that in fact, in the world as it is, the rule utilitarian will be in favor of a practice of punishing the innocent, but it can be shown that in a certain sort of world he would have to be.)

Act utilitarianism as a system of normative ethics. Both act and rule utilitarianism fail, then, as systems of descriptive ethics. But act utilitarianism as a system of normative ethics would seem to have certain advantages over both rule utilitarianism and nonutilitarian, or deontological, systems of ethics (a deontological system of ethics is one which holds that an action can be right or wrong in itself, quite apart from consequences). Moreover, the failure of act utilitarianism as a descriptive system is the source of its interest as a possible normative system: if it had been correct as a descriptive system, then the acceptance of it as a normative system would have left most men's conduct unchanged.

No proof of utilitarianism. A system of normative ethics cannot be proved intellectually. Any such "proof" of utilitarianism as was attempted by Bentham or Mill can be shown to be fallacious. (Mill disclaimed the possibility of proof and spoke more vaguely of "considerations capable of determining the intellect," but he presented an attempted proof nonetheless.) Sidgwick and Moore were clearer on this point and saw that ethical principles cannot be deduced from anything else. They appealed instead to intellectual intuition, but recent developments in epistemology and other fields of philosophy have made the notion of intellectual intuition a disreputable one. The tendency among some recent writers, such as C. L. Stevenson, R. M. Hare, and P. H. Nowell-Smith, has been to regard assertions of ultimate ethical principles and valuations as expressions of feeling or attitude, or as akin to imperatives rather than to statements of fact. In this respect, they develop further the position held much earlier by Hume. Now if we abandon a cognitivist theory about the nature of moral judgments, such as was held by Sidgwick or Moore, and adopt the view that ultimate ethical principles depend only on our attitudes, that is, on what we like or dislike, we must give up the attempt to prove any ethical system, including the act-utilitarian system. We may nevertheless recommend such a system. We may also try to show inconsistencies or emotionally unattractive features of various possible alternative systems.

Appeal to generalized benevolence. In putting forward act utilitarianism as a normative system, we express an attitude of generalized benevolence and appeal to a similar attitude in our audience. (The attitude of generalized benevolence is not the same as altruism. Generalized benevolence is self-regarding, and other-regarding too—I count my happiness neither more nor less than yours.) Of course, we all have in addition other attitudes, self-love, and particular likes and dislikes. As far as self-love is concerned, either this will be compatible with generalized benevolence or it will not. If the former, then self-love does not conflict with act utilitarianism, and if the latter, nevertheless self-love then will be largely canceled out, as among a number of people engaged in discussion.

Arguments against deontological systems. As to particular likes and dislikes, an important case concerns our liking for obeying the rules of some deontological ethics in which we have been raised. However, the following persuasive considerations can be brought up as arguments against the adherent of a deontological system of ethics. It can be urged that although the dictates of a generalized benevolence might quite often coincide with those of an act-utilitarian ethics, there must be cases in which the two would conflict with one another. Would the benevolent and sympathetic persons to whom we conceive ourselves to be appealing be happy about preferring abstract conformity with an ethical rule, such as "Keep promises," to preventing avoidable misery of his fellow creatures?

It will be noticed that the above defense of utilitarianism against deontology is purely persuasive, an appeal to the heart and not to the intellect. It is based on the metaethical view that ultimate ethical principles are expressions of our attitudes and not the findings of some sort of intuition of ethical fact. An intellectualist in metaethics, such as W. D. Ross, could well resist our appeal to feeling by saying that it is possible to *see* that his deontological principles are correct, and that whether we like them or not is beside the point.

Weakness of rule utilitarianism. In defending act utilitarianism, then, we appeal to feelings, namely, those of generalized benevolence. Since people possess other attitudes too, such as loyalty to a code of morals in which they have brought up, the possession of feelings of generalized benevolence is not a sufficient condition of agreement with the act utilitarian. But it is a necessary condition. Now the rule utilitarian also appeals ultimately to feelings of generalized benevolence. Like the deontologist, however, he is open to the charge of preferring conformity with a rule to the prevention of unhappiness. He is indeed more obviously open to such a charge, since he presumably advocates his rule utilitarian principle because he thinks that these rules conduce to human happiness. He is then inconsistent if he prescribes that we should obey a rule (even a generally beneficial rule) in those cases in which he knows that it will *not* be most beneficial to obey it. It will not do to reply that in most cases it is most beneficial to obey the rule. It is still true that in some cases it is not most beneficial to obey the rule, and if we are solely concerned with beneficence, in these cases we ought not to obey the rule. Nor is it relevant that it may be better that everybody should obey the rule than that nobody should. That the rule should always be obeyed and that it should never be obeyed are not the only two possibilities. There is the third possibility that sometimes it should be obeyed and sometimes it should not be obeyed.

Hedonistic act utilitarianism. We shall therefore neglect rule utilitarianism as a system of normative ethics, and consider only act utilitarianism, which will be conveniently put forward in a hedonistic form. The reader will easily be able to adapt most of what is said to cover the case of ideal utilitarianism. Indeed, in many cases the differences between hedonistic and ideal utilitarianism are not usually of much practical importance, since the hedonist will usually agree that the states of mind which the ideal utilitarian regards as intrinsically good, but which he does not, are nevertheless extrinsically good. Bentham would say that Mill's higher pleasures, if not intrinsically better than the lower ones, are usually more "fecund" of further pleasures. This is not to say, however, that there are no cases in which there would not be a significant difference between hedonistic and ideal utilitarianism.

The act-utilitarian principle can now be put in the following form: "The only reason for performing some action *A*, rather than various alternative actions, is that *A* results in more happiness (or more generally, in better consequences) for all mankind (or perhaps all sentient beings) than will any of these alternative actions." Since this principle expresses an attitude of generalized benevolence, we can expect to find a good deal of sympathy for it among the sort of people with whom it would be profitable to carry on a discussion about ethics. It may therefore be possible to obtain wide assent to the principle, provided that we can develop its implications in a clear and consistent manner and that we can show that certain common objections to utilitarianism are not as valid as they are supposed to be. We have already seen that certain objections, based on "the common moral consciousness," fail because they are valid only against descriptive utilitarianism and not against normative utilitarianism.

Determining consequences. Utilitarianism would be an easier doctrine to state if we could assume that we could always tell with certainty what all the consequences of various possible actions would be, and if we could assume that very remote consequences need not be taken into account. In applying the utilitarian principle, we would simply have to envisage two or more sets of consequences extending into the future, and ask ourselves, as sympathetic and benevolent men, which of these we would prefer. There would be no need for any calculation or for any summation of pleasures. We would simply have to compare two or more possible total situations. Sometimes, indeed, the postulate that we need not consider very remote situations will not be necessary. For example, if it be admitted that, on the whole, people are more happy than not, a man and woman who are left alive as sole representatives of the human race after some atomic holocaust could, as utilitarians, decide to have children in the hope that the world would once more be populated indefinitely far into the future. This is because although the generations will extend indefinitely far into the future, there is reason to believe that each generation will be happy rather than unhappy, while if no children are had, there will be no succeeding generations at all, and so no possibility of happiness accruing in the future. In normal cases, however, we do need to assume that remote consequences can be left out of account. Surely, however, this is a plausible assumption, for on the whole, the goodness and badness of very remote consequences are likely to cancel out. In any case, if this assumption cannot be made, also difficulties will arise for many deontological systems (for example, the system of W. D. Ross), which allow beneficence as one principle among others.

Unfortunately, however, we do not know with certainty what the various possible consequences of our actions will be. This uncertainty would not be so bad provided we could assign numerical probabilities to the various consequences. We could then still employ a method similar to that of envisaging total consequences. A very simplified example may make this clear. Suppose that the only relevant consequences are, on the one hand, a 3/5 probability of Smith's being in some state *S*, and on the other hand, if we do an alternative action, a 2/7 probability of Jones's being in some state *T*. We simply envisage 21 people just like Smith in state *S* as against 10 people just like Jones in state *T*. It should be evident how, in theory at least, this method could be extended to more complex cases. However, numerical probabilities can rarely be assigned to possible future events, and the utilitarian is reduced to an intuitive weighting of various consequences with their probabilities. It is impossible to justify such intuitions rationally, and we have here a serious weakness in utilitarianism. It is true that this weakness also extends to prudential decisions, and most people think that they can make prudential decisions with some rationality. But this is not of much help, since in propounding a normative system we are concerned with what we ought to think, not with how we do think. Utilitarianism is therefore badly in need of support from a theory whereby, at least roughly or in principle, numerical probabilities could be assigned to all types of events.

The place of rules in act utilitarianism. Even the act utilitarian cannot always be weighing up consequences. He must often act habitually or in accordance with rough rules of thumb. However, this does not affect the value of the act-utilitarian principle, which is put forward as a criterion of rational choice. When we act habitually we do not exercise a rational choice, and the utilitarian criterion is not operative. It is, of course, operative when we are deciding, on act-utilitarian principles, the habits or rules of thumb to which we should or should not school ourselves. The act utilitarian knows that he would go mad if he deliberated on every trivial issue, and that if he did not go mad he would at least slow up his responses so much that he would miss many opportunities for probably doing good. He may also school himself to act habitually because he may think that if he deliberated in various concrete situations, his reasoning would be distorted by a selfish bias.

APPLICATIONS

Utilitarianism and game theory. The act utilitarian will of course use as some of his premises propositions about how other members of the community are likely to act. For example, if certain individuals are adherents of a deontological morality, their actions will tend to be made predictable and their behavior will constitute valuable information for the act utilitarian when he is planning his own actions. Thus, an act utilitarian who has something important to do with his time may be wise to abstain from voting in an election (assuming that there is no legal compulsion to vote), for he will reflect that most people will in fact go to vote and that elections are very rarely decided by a single vote.

But how should the act utilitarian reason if he lives in a society in which everyone else is an act utilitarian? He needs information about what other people will do, but since they reason as he does, what they will do depends on what they think he will do. There is a circularity in the situation which can be resolved only by the technique of the theory of games.

Moral philosophers have commonly failed to give the correct solution to this sort of question. In the case in which the act utilitarian is asking whether he should do an action *A* or not do it, moral philosophers have commonly envisaged only two possibilities: either everyone does *A* or no one does *A*. They have failed to notice the possibility of what, in the theory of games, is called a mixed strategy. Each act utilitarian can give himself a probability *p* of doing *A*. Thus, in the case of the voting, each act utilitarian might toss pennies or dice in such a way as to give himself a certain probability *p* of voting, so that the best possible proportion of people will turn up to vote and a small proportion will be free to do other things. The calculation of *p* is a simple maximization problem, provided that we know numerical values of the probabilities and numerical values of the various consequences of alternative actions. Of course, this is unlikely to be the case, and the question of a mixed strategy is usually more of theoretical than of practical importance. Moreover, in very many important cases the effect of even a few people acting in a certain way is, in practice, so disastrous that the probability we should give ourselves of acting in this way may be so small that we may as well say, like the rule utilitarians, that we would never do it.

Utilitarianism and praise and blame. Not only do we use moral language to deliberate about what we should do, but we also use moral language to praise people and blame them. Suppose that we use the words "good action" and "bad action" to convey praise and blame, and "right action" and "wrong action" to evaluate what ought to be done. On act-utilitarian principles, then, a right action is one which produces the best consequences. A good action is one which should be praised. Normally we will wish to praise right actions and blame wrong ones, but this is not invariably the case. As Sidgwick has pointed out very clearly, when, as utilitarians, we assess agents and motives as good or bad, the question at issue is not the utility of the actions but the utility of praise or blame of them. Suppose that the only way in which a soldier can save the lives of half a dozen companions is by throwing himself upon a grenade that is about to explode, thus taking upon himself the full impact of the blast and inevitably being killed. The act utilitarian would have to say that the soldier ought to sacrifice himself in this way. Nevertheless, he would not censure the soldier or say that he had acted from a bad motive if he had refrained from this heroic act and his companions had been killed. There is nothing to be gained by censuring someone for lack of extraordinary heroism, and probably much harm in doing so. The act utilitarian should say that the soldier's motive was not a bad one, although his action was as a matter of fact a wrong one.

Consider a case in which an action, normally of trivial import, happens to have very unfortunate consequences. A man with a head cold goes to the office, instead of nursing his illness at home. He is visited by an eminent statesman, who catches the cold and, in consequence, is not quite at his best in carrying out some delicate negotiations. These negotiations just fail by a hairsbreadth, whereas if the statesman had been fully fit they would have succeeded.

In consequence, thousands of people die from starvation, a misfortune which would have been avoided if the negotiations had succeeded. These deaths from starvation would therefore not have occurred if the man with a head cold had not gone to his office in an infectious state. Someone may be tempted to argue as follows: "Surely it is not a very wrong action to go to the office suffering from a head cold. In some cases, where important work has to be done, it may even be praiseworthy. But in this case the action had very bad consequences, and so the utilitarian must say that it is very wrong. There must therefore be something wrong with utilitarianism." The utilitarian must reply that the objector is confusing two things, the rightness or wrongness of an action and the praiseworthiness or blameworthiness of it. The action, he can consistently say, was very *wrong*, but it was not very *bad:* that is, it ought not to be blamed very much, if at all. If we blame it, we are concerned with the utility of discouraging similar actions on the part of other people, and since going to the office with a head cold is not normally productive of very bad consequences, this action, although in fact very wrong, was not a very bad or blameworthy one.

Another reason why utility (or rightness) of an action does not always coincide with utility of praise or blame of it, and hence with its goodness or badness, is that, as Sidgwick pointed out, although universal benevolence, from the act-utilitarian view, is the ultimate standard of right and wrong, it is not necessarily the best or most useful *motive* for action. For example, although family affection may not always act in the same direction as generalized benevolence, it very frequently does so, and is a much more powerful motive than the latter. The act utilitarian may well think it useful to praise an action done from family affection in order to strengthen and encourage this motive, even when in fact the action was not generally beneficial.

Similarly, members of a community may act according to some traditional code of rules and may be likely to become simply amoral if a premature attempt is made to convert them to utilitarianism. A utilitarian may well think, therefore, that he ought to support this traditional nonutilitarian code of morals, if its general tendency is at all beneficent. He may therefore apportion praise and blame among members of this community according to whether their actions are in conformity with this code, and not according to whether they are right or wrong from the utilitarian standpoint. The relations between act utilitarianism and the traditional morality of a community in which an act utilitarian may find himself are very complex, and have been quite thoroughly investigated by Sidgwick.

Bibliography

HISTORY OF UTILITARIANISM

For the history of utilitarianism, see especially H. Sidgwick, *Outlines of the History of Ethics* (London, 1946), with an additional chapter by Alban G. Widgery; Ernest Albee, *A History of English Utilitarianism* (New York, 1902); and Leslie Stephen, *The English Utilitarians* (London, 1900), which contains references to the works of Tucker and Paley. The works of Helvétius are not readily accessible, but a list of various editions can be found in the bibliography of Ian Cumming, *Helvétius, His Life and Place in the History of Educational Thought* (London, 1955).

MAJOR UTILITARIANS

For works by Bentham, see especially his *Fragment on Government and Introduction to the Principles of Morals and Legislation,* Wilfred Harrison, ed. (Oxford, 1948), and his *Deontology,* John Bowring, ed. (London and Edinburgh, 1843). A very scholarly modern work on Bentham is David Baumgardt, *Bentham and the Ethics of Today, With Bentham Manuscripts—Hitherto Unpublished* (Princeton, N.J., 1952). For works by J. S. Mill, see *Utilitarianism, On Liberty, Essay on Bentham, Together With Selected Writings of Jeremy Bentham and John Austin,* edited with an Introduction by Mary Warnock (London, 1962). M. St. J. Packe, *The Life of John Stuart Mill* (London, 1954), gives evidence on p. 53 (footnote) that Bentham used the word "utilitarian" before Mill. An interesting discussion of Mill's ethical principles is given in Karl Britton, "Utilitarianism: the Appeal to a First Principle," in *PAS,* Vol. 60 (1959–1960), 141–154. Britton is also the author of an account of Mill's philosophy, *John Stuart Mill* (London, 1953). A nineteenth-century criticism of utilitarianism is J. Grote, *An Examination of the Utilitarian Philosophy* (Cambridge, 1870). For Sidgwick, see his *Methods of Ethics,* 7th ed. (London, 1907), which is discussed by C. D. Broad in *Five Types of Ethical Theory* (London, 1930). Godwin's moral philosophy is critically expounded by D. H. Monro in his *Godwin's Moral Philosophy* (Oxford, 1953). Ideal utilitarianism may be studied in G. E. Moore, *Principia Ethica* (Cambridge, 1903) and *Ethics* (London, 1912), and in H. Rashdall, *Theory of Good and Evil* (Oxford, 1907). A sympathetic discussion of utilitarianism will be found in A. J. Ayer's essay "The Principle of Utility," in his *Philosophical Essays* (London, 1954).

RULE AND ACT UTILITARIANISM

Many modern writers have espoused views which can be described as rule utilitarianism. See especially Stephen Toulmin, *The Place of Reason in Ethics* (Cambridge, 1951); P. H. Nowell-Smith, *Ethics* (London, 1954); J. Rawls, "Two Concepts of Rules," in *Philosophical Review,* Vol. 64 (1955), 3–32; K. E. M. Baier, *The Moral Point of View* (Ithaca, N.Y., 1958); M. G. Singer, *Generalization in Ethics* (New York, 1961). J. O. Urmson, "The Interpretation of the Philosophy of J. S. Mill," in *Philosophical Quarterly,* Vol. 3 (1953), 33–39, interprets Mill as a rule utilitarian. His view is contested by J. D. Mabbott, "Interpretation of Mill's *Utilitarianism,*" in *Philosophical Quarterly,* Vol. 6 (1956), 115–120. The issue between act and rule utilitarianism is in effect discussed by A. C. Ewing, "What Would Happen If Everyone Acted Like Me?" in *Philosophy,* Vol. 28 (1953), 16–29, and by A. K. Stout, "But Suppose Everybody Did the Same?" in *Australasian Journal of Philosophy,* Vol. 32 (1954), 1–29. J. J. C. Smart, "Extreme and Restricted Utilitarianism," in *Philosophical Quarterly,* Vol. 6 (1956), 344–354, is a defense of act as against rule utilitarianism. The terms "extreme" and "restricted" are used here instead of the more appropriate words "act" and "rule." These last were introduced by R. B. Brandt in his *Ethical Theory* (Englewood Cliffs, N.J., 1959), which contains good disussions of act and rule utilitarianism. Brandt has also developed a complex and subtle form of rule utilitarianism in his paper "In Search of a Credible Form of Rule Utilitarianism," in George Nakhnikian and Héctor-Neri Castañeda, eds., *Morality and the Language of Conduct* (Detroit, 1953). See also H. D. Aiken, "The Levels of Moral Discourse," in *Ethics,* Vol. 62 (1952), 235–248. Rule utilitarianism is criticized by H. J. McCloskey, "An Examination of Restricted Utilitarianism," in *Philosophical Review,* Vol. 66 (1957), 466–485. A Kantian type of rule utilitarianism is presented by R. F. Harrod, "Utilitarianism Revised," in *Mind,* Vol. 45 (1936), 137–156, and J. C. Harsanyi, "Ethics in Terms of Hypothetical Imperatives," in *Mind,* Vol. 67 (1958), 305–316. Jonathan Harrison's article "Utilitarianism, Universalisation and Our Duty to be Just," in *PAS,* Vol. 53 (1952–1953), 105–134, discusses important issues and includes a criticism of Harrod.

NEGATIVE UTILITARIANISM

K. R. Popper, *The Open Society and Its Enemies,* 3d ed., Vol. 1 (London, 1957), Ch. 5, note 6, has put forward some considerations that suggest the possibility of expressing utilitarianism in terms of the prevention of misery rather than in terms of the promotion of happiness, although Popper himself does not seem to be a utilitarian. Such a "negative utilitarianism" has been criticized by R. N. Smart, "Negative Utilitarianism," in *Mind,* Vol. 67 (1958), 542–543.

EXPOSITIONS AND CRITICISMS

An exposition of act utilitarianism as a normative system is given by J. J. C. Smart, *An Outline of a System of Utilitarian Ethics* (Melbourne, 1961). An introductory textbook from an act-utilitarian point of view is C. A. Baylis, *Ethics, the Principles of Wise Choice* (New York, 1958). There are useful chapters on utilitarianism in John Hospers, *Human Conduct* (New York, 1961). The inconsistency of an egoistic utilitarianism is pointed out by B. H. Medlin, "Ultimate Principles and Ethical Egoism," in *Australasian Journal of Philosophy,* Vol. 35 (1957), 111–118. J. Rawls, in his article "Justice as Fairness," in *Philosophical Review,* Vol. 67 (1958), 164–194, holds that one must never act solely to increase the general happiness if in so doing one makes any particular person unhappy. I. M. Crombie, in his article "Social Clockwork and Utilitarian Morality" in D. M. Mackinnon, ed., *Christian Faith and Communist Faith* (London, 1953), suggests that a utilitarian could accuse the deontologist of a sort of idolatrous attitude toward rules. Another valuable point made in this article is that utilitarianism is in a certain way a self-correcting doctrine. See also A. I. Melden, "Two Comments on Utilitarianism," in *Philosophical Review,* Vol. 60 (1951), 508–524; H. W. Schneider, "Obligations and the Pursuit of Happiness," in *Philosophical Review,* Vol. 61 (1952), 312–319; and S. M. Brown, Jr., "Utilitarianism and Moral Obligation," *ibid.,* 299–311, which led to comments by C. A. Baylis and John Ladd, *ibid.,* 320–330. J. O. Urmson, "Saints and Heroes," in A. I. Melden, ed., *Essays in Moral Philosophy* (Seattle, 1958), makes some distinctions which he tentatively suggests may be accommodated more easily by a utilitarian than by a nonutilitarian ethics. A pioneering application of the theory of games to problems of moral philosophy is to be found in R. B. Braithwaite, *Theory of Games as a Tool for the Moral Philosopher* (Cambridge, 1955).

METAETHICAL THEORIES

For the noncognitivist theories of metaethics of C. L. Stevenson, R. M. Hare, and P. H. Nowell-Smith, see C. L. Stevenson, *Ethics and Language* (New Haven, 1944); R. M. Hare, *The Language of Morals* (Oxford, 1952); and P. H. Nowell-Smith, *Ethics* (London, 1954). Hare's sequel, *Freedom and Reason* (Oxford, 1963), contains an interesting chapter on utilitarianism.

J. J. C. SMART

UTOPIAS AND UTOPIANISM. The word "utopia" was coined by Thomas More, who published his famous *Utopia* in 1516. Departing from strict linguistic correctness, More coupled the Greek words for "no" and "place" to invent a name that has since passed into nearly universal currency. By further verbal play the poet laureate of More's *Utopia,* in a few preliminary verses, pointed out the close relation between "utopia" and "eutopia," which means "the good place." Through the succeeding centuries this double aspect has marked utopian literature: it has employed the imaginary to project the ideal.

The words "utopia" and "utopian," however, have been put to many uses besides the one suggested by More's book. Common to all uses is reference to either the imaginary or the ideal or to both. But sometimes the words are used as terms of derision and sometimes with a vagueness that robs them of any genuine usefulness. For example, a proposal that is farfetched or implausible is often condemned as "utopian," whether or not the proposal has any idealistic content. In another, closely related pejorative use, "utopian" designates that which is unacceptably different from the customary or is radical in its demands. The connotation of complete impracticality serves to discredit a threatening idealism. Similarly, daydreams and fantasies—necessitous, frequently bizarre expressions of private ideals—are called "utopian," as if wishful thinking and utopia were synonymous. Even when these words are used neutrally, their coverage is enormously wide. Almost any kind of thoroughgoing idealism—a view of the good life, a statement of fundamental political principles, a plea for major reform—can earn for itself the title "utopian." Furthermore, all literary depictions of imaginary societies are called "utopian," even if they represent some totalitarian or fiendish horror or are primarily futuristic speculations about technical and scientific possibilities that have no important connection to any idealism.

Much historical experience is reflected in this variety of usage. Indeed, the use of these words is often symptomatic of the prevailing attitudes toward social change in general. Nevertheless, a case could be made for reserving "utopia" for speculation, in whatever literary form, concerning ideal societies and ideal ways of life, in which perfection, defined in accordance with common prepossessions and not personal predilections, is aimed at. Perfection is conceived of as harmony, the harmony of each man with himself and with the men around him. The tradition of utopian thought, in this restricted sense, is thus made up of ideas and images of social harmony.

Inspiration of utopianism. The forerunners of the utopian tradition are the fables and myths of the golden age, the Garden of Eden, or some benign state of nature. These inherited stories, although of considerable antiquity, look back to some even more remote time in the dim past when harmony was allegedly the normal condition of life. Remorse or nostalgia is the usual accompaniment of these stories; reality is not what it was, nor can it ever again be what it was, except perhaps through some divine intercession.

An uncontrived harmony characterized the primal felicity. Simple men led simple lives, but because human nature was undeveloped, men were easily made content. If the glories and pleasures of civilization were missing, so were its artificialities and corruptions. Whenever disgust or disenchantment with civilization has become acute, these old stories are retold in order to expose the faults of civilization. But apart from their role in this fundamentally self-conscious method of striking at an existing order, these stories are primarily interesting as repositories of the age-old longings of ordinary humanity. All that the world is not is summed up in short and tantalizing descriptions. Sometime long ago, when men were still in touch with the sources of reality, they lived without domination, irrational inequality, scarcity, brutalizing labor, warfare, and the tortures of conscience; they lived without disharmony of any form. The good life is defined by the absence of these things. Although fondness for an early simplicity may seem regressive, an ignoble attachment to a primitive and subhuman harmony, the impetus for utopianism is to be found here.

The later tradition filled out the picture that is only a sketch in the old myths. More important, the formal utopian tradition transcends the old myths. Whatever

wistfulness for the golden age may be present, there is unanimous agreement that the state of nature cannot be regained. The framework of the good life, the condition of harmony, must be social. It may be more or less civilized, more or less scientific, more or less abundant, more or less hierarchical, more or less free, but it must be organized and institutionally articulated. Throughout the utopian tradition, reality is never defied to the extent of wishing away the very idea of a settled society. In Plato's *Republic*, Socrates can dwell only briefly on the excellence of an amiably anarchic rusticity before his admirer Glaucon forces him to turn his thoughts to the ideal city. This transition can be taken as typical of formal utopianism as a whole.

Varieties of utopianism. Even with a scrupulous adherence to the definition of utopianism as the succession of ideas and images of social harmony, the relevant texts are extremely numerous. The main types of utopias include, first, descriptions of imaginary societies held to be perfect or much closer to perfection than any society in the real world. They are located in the past, present, or future and are contained in treatise, novel, story, or poem with varying degrees of detailed specification and imaginative inventiveness.

The second type of utopia is found in works of political theory in which reflection on the fundamental questions of politics leads the theorist beyond politics to consider the social and cultural presuppositions of the ideal political order and the ends of life which that political order (placed in a certain social and cultural setting) can and should facilitate. Whereas the political theorist comes to the forms and purposes of all institutional life by way of his political concerns and, as it were, incidentally, the utopian writer, with Thomas More as the model, intends from the start a comprehensive view of the ideal society and its way of life, a view in which political forms are not of central importance. Some works of political theory—Plato's *Republic,* for example—so capably discuss nonpolitical matters that they fit into either category.

Those philosophies of history which culminate in a vision of achieved perfection are a third type of utopia. These are the theories of inevitable progress created by men like Condorcet, Hegel, Spencer, and Marx. Hegel and Marx especially would have fought against inclusion in the utopian tradition; they presented themselves as men blessed with unique insight into the nature of reality and its necessary workings carried even to the future, not as men preaching to the world a conception of the ideal. For all that, their writings have been taken by others as utopian. No list of the major sources of utopian literature would be acceptable without them and the other theorists of inevitable progress.

Fourth are those works, sometimes called philosophical anthropologies, in which the writer attempts a definition of what is peculiar to man, of what is genuinely human rather than merely conventional, or of man's potentialities. These discourses are not always consciously utopian; they may be directed to individual reformation or to preparation for the afterlife. Furthermore, the discussion may be carried on without reference to concrete social practices and institutions. That is, they aim to assess the various kinds of human activity, the various pleasures open to men, or the various styles of life made possible by civilization or science. Examples are Schiller's *On the Aesthetic Education of Man,* Herbert Marcuse's *Eros and Civilization,* and Hannah Arendt's *The Human Condition.* But despite the abstract quality of philosophical anthropology, and whatever the intentions of a given writer, it would be unduly constrictive to leave this literature out of account.

In the fifth group are prophecies of profound alteration in man's existence made by religious groups, statements of purpose made by revolutionary groups, and blueprints offered by individual men, sects, and secular associations. Obviously, not all activist and reformist political and religious groups have sought to remake society completely, in conformity with the utopian aim of harmony. Nevertheless, many groups have not been satisfied merely to speculate about the ideal society but have sought to realize it, either by persuasion or violence. Examples are the sixteenth-century Christian millenarian, or chiliastic, sects in Europe or some of the marginal radical figures in the French Revolution, like "Gracchus" Babeuf. And in the nineteenth century, especially in the United States, small bands of eager people, religious or simply high-minded, formed utopian communities on unoccupied land, in isolation from the larger society.

Causes of utopianism. The literature of social harmony is thus extensive and diverse. Some periods and some cultures have been richer in utopianism than others. The question therefore arises as to why men become utopian in their thought or, more rarely, in their action. What causes the desire for change to be absolute, the character of idealism to be extreme and uncompromising? Several answers are found scattered in the history of utopianism; some indicate urgency, others do not.

First, some intellectuals simply need to invent worlds. The construction of a utopia, even if only on paper, is a God-like act and very much resembles the creation of a fictional world by the novelist. A utopia can thus be an effort at mastering the complexity of social phenomena; part of the effort consists of rearranging social phenomena to form a more rational or beautiful pattern. In short, one impulse that sustains utopianism, from Plato to the latest science fiction, is intellectual playfulness.

Another cause is the desire for moral clarity. In the course of carrying one's demands on reality as far as possible, one may achieve a fixed—possibly rigid—position in relation to reality. As a consequence, reality can be constantly put to the test. To the utopian writer improvisation that allows purposes to emerge from the onrush of experience or waits for new means to suggest or impose new ends is nothing more than immersion in reality or a confused and unprepared reception of it. Although the utopian writer may do nothing to improve society, he may still deem it worthwhile to preserve the concept of the ideal. This may be thought desirable even in comparatively decent societies; to insist on the distinction between the acceptable and the ideal can have a chastening influence on those who govern as well as on those who happily go along. The utopian writer promotes dissatisfaction and self-criticism.

Another cause of utopian thought—and one that lacks the quality of detachment present in the two preceding

ones—is the wish to subject society to a total indictment. What is involved here is not a sense that things could be, or can always be, better than they are but that everything, or nearly everything, is intolerable. There is the direct, unappeasable indictment of established institutions, the way of Rousseau in his discourses, William Blake in some of his long poems, Marx and Engels in *The Communist Manifesto,* or D. H. Lawrence in his two books on the unconscious. In works of this sort hatred of reality may be stronger than love of any alternative; the positive utopianism may be only implicit. In indirect indictment the utopianism is explicit; the forms of the ideal society are presented. And because the main aim is to indict, the forms of the ideal society are, at least in large part, the opposite of the forms in existence. The utopian imagination in these instances is constricted by the grave deficiencies of the real world; the urge to replace them by conditions that in no way resemble them or to discredit them intellectually is strong. Utopian writing so motivated may blend into radical satire and produce works like Book IV of Swift's *Gulliver's Travels.* Or it may produce works like William Morris' *News From Nowhere,* which are plainly archaistic and easily expose themselves to the charge of irrelevance. Almost all utopian works contain curiosities and excesses, which can often be explained as compensatory responses to especially terrible features of the real world.

A similar cause of utopian thought is tactical. There are times when it may appear to those bent on reforming society that overstatement is necessary for some degree of success. That is, utopian works need not harbor utopian intentions or even an abstract utopian commitment. Although a writer may lavish great energy on making his utopia plausible and attractive, he may aspire only to contribute to the gradual and partial amelioration of his society. By painting a fair picture of felicity and suggesting that the world is, as presently made up, remote from that felicity, he may encourage an innovating spirit. At the same time, his utopia will give at least guidelines for reform. There may be no real expectation that the utopia will ever fully materialize or, indeed, that pure felicity can be had on any terms. Nevertheless, without that exaggeration, less-than-utopian reform would perhaps be too modest or too slow. Much depends on the persuasiveness of the writer's scheme. For that reason the utopias of reform tend to be less free in their speculation and to depict the completion of certain good tendencies in the real world rather than to overturn it theoretically. Edward Bellamy's *Looking Backward* is an example of this.

The last cause of utopian thought is the most obvious: the conviction that the whole truth about social harmony is known, can be imparted, and should be acted on. There is, of course, a wide variety in the historical situations that call forth such an overweening attitude. But if some radical Protestant groups (like the German Anabaptists of the sixteenth century), some utopian movements of the nineteenth century (like those inspired by the Comte de Saint-Simon, Charles Fourier, and Robert Owen), and the quasi-utopian Marxists are exemplary, there must be a sense of deep, intolerable wrong. There must also be a sense of enormous possibility, of not only righting the wrong but also going beyond to perfection itself, and either an overpowering group- or self-confidence or the conviction that the utopian leaders and their following are the instruments of some higher will or the culmination of some impersonal process. The word "Messianism" perhaps best summarizes this manifestation of the utopian spirit.

Uses of utopianism. Apart from their place in history, of what use are the works of utopianism? The utopian tradition is made up of uninhabited palaces—grand imaginary structures that may amuse the realist if they do not fill him with contempt. In the long series of utopian writings, is there, however, something of enduring value, all question of application aside? There are, in fact, several benefits conferred by utopianism.

As already noted, a cause of utopian writing is playful delight in the act of imagining new kinds of social reality. This delight can be answered by pleasure taken in the results of that playfulness. The standards for judging a utopia from this point of view are primarily aesthetic—plausible novelties in the projected way of life, clever and ingenious details, daring departures from customary practices. The inner coherence of the utopia matters more than any closeness to probability, although naturally too much strain on belief weakens the pleasure. Admiration for the skill of the utopian writer can be mixed with gratitude for being allowed to live another life vicariously. No stimulus to make one's own better need be felt. This may make the utopian enterprise somewhat precious, but it can be a source of idle intellectual satisfaction even to the most conservative temperaments. The utopian works of H. G. Wells are famous for their power to gratify the taste for sampling different worlds, however else they may instruct.

A second use of utopianism is as a record of human aspiration. For the record to be complete, many other kinds of utterance must be consulted, but the long line of utopias supplies a valuable indication. They are peculiarly vivid forms taken by permanent human wants. Read with due allowance for their necessarily eccentric quality, they will shed vivid light on their times. The desperation of a given historical period, together with the limits of its hopefulness, must emerge from a study of its utopian writings. The abundance or paucity of utopian writing is itself an aid to understanding a period.

Third is the contribution of utopian literature to general sociology. The great utopias—Plato's *Republic* and *Laws,* the relevant parts of Aristotle's *Politics,* More's *Utopia,* Campanella's *The City of the Sun,* Morelly's *Code de la nature,* the writings of Saint-Simon and Fourier, H. G. Wells's *A Modern Utopia*—incorporate a great deal of sociological wisdom. Common to these and other utopias is the idea of the integration of social institutions in its most intense version, utopian harmony. To utopian writers no habit or practice seems innocent of significance for the proper maintenance of the utopian society. Utopian writers are therefore constantly pointing out connections between things that appear unrelated. This attentiveness to detail is complemented by a sense of proportion. Part of utopian analysis consists in the attempt to identify the major elements of society and to demonstrate how they act on one another and how each must be adjusted to the others if the best of all possible worlds is to be attained. For all their

care, utopian writers commit a radical abstraction when they create their images of perfection, but this is the price paid by all general sociology, including that which is wholly neutral and descriptive.

The last use of utopianism is moral. Utopian literature is a repository of reflection on human nature. Although not directly concerned to expose frailty, to scrutinize motives, and to astonish with cynical revelations, utopian literature has in it much hard psychological intelligence. Utopian writers disagree among themselves on the malleability of human nature, but rarely is this problem treated lightly. Indeed, it is usually acknowledged as the problem requiring the deepest study and the source of the greatest hesitation. The principal mission of utopianism is to encourage the hope that human nature is malleable beyond the limits assigned by worldly pessimism or theological despair. That the real world, despite its incomprehensible variousness, still does not exhaust the possibilities of human nature is the core of utopianism. The long series of utopian texts enlarge the world by suggesting new character types and new social milieus in which each type could emerge. They also enlarge the world by their claim that the societies of the world ignore, repress, distort, or destroy human potentialities that have not yet been fulfilled. It is true that the concept of harmony rules out some segment of the spectrum of human nature. The essence of antiutopianism is the charge that any imaginable utopia diminishes human nature by not allowing scope to those traits—wildness, excess, perversity, heroism—that threaten harmony and that if the precondition of a harmonious life is the thorough manageability of men, human nature must suffer a terrible diminution. Utopian writers confine their imagination to the realm of the largest happiness, but within that realm, utopians say, much is possible if only the world, or a part of it, could be transformed or would be more permissive. Without subscribing to any set of specific utopian ideas, one can appreciate the efforts of utopian writers to propagate this sentiment.

Bibliography

Buber, Martin, *Paths in Utopia,* translated by R. F. C. Hull. New York, 1950.

Bury, J. B., *The Idea of Progress.* London, 1920.

Cohn, Norman, *The Pursuit of the Millennium.* London, 1957.

Gray, Alexander, *The Socialist Tradition, Moses to Lenin.* London, 1946.

Horsburgh, H. J. N., "The Relevance of the Utopian." *Ethics,* Vol. 67 (1957), 127–138.

Kautsky, Karl, *Die Vorläufer des neueren Sozialismus.* Stuttgart, 1909.

Lovejoy, Arthur O., et al., eds., *A Documentary History of Primitivism.* Baltimore, 1935.

Mannheim, Karl, *Ideologie und Utopie.* Bonn, 1929. Translated by Louis Wirth and Edward Shils as *Ideology and Utopia.* London, 1936.

Mumford, Lewis, *The Transformations of Man.* New York, 1956.

Negley, Glenn, and Patrick, J. Max, eds., *The Quest for Utopia.* New York, 1952.

Noyes, John Humphrey, *History of American Socialisms.* New York, 1961. Originally published in 1870.

Polak, Fred L., *The Image of the Future,* translated by Elsie Boulding, 2 vols. New York and Leiden, 1961.

Popper, Karl, *The Open Society and Its Enemies,* 2 vols. London, 1945.

GEORGE KATEB

V

VACUUM AND VOID. The notions of void and vacuum have from the beginning been attended by a number of conceptual difficulties. In most cosmologies there is a tendency to seek a unity and homogeneity of the primary elements and to avoid discreteness and discontinuity. This tendency led to an early crisis in Greek philosophy, in the monism of Parmenides, which asserted that the first principle of all things must be "the One," without qualities or differentiation and without change or movement. Thus the perceptible, changing world must be illusory. Denial of this conclusion in subsequent natural philosophies involved the introduction of a plurality of real primary elements. Among these philosophies the atomism of Leucippus and Democritus appears to have been an attempt to stay as nearly as possible within the spirit of Parmenides by admitting only two first principles: "Being," which was seen as a multiplicity of material atoms, and "Not-being," which was identified with void space. The atoms corresponded as closely as possible to the "real" in the Parmenidean sense; their only qualities were imperishability and shape, and the existence of void enabled them to move and produce change. Void was utterly without qualities or powers of any kind and, indeed, would almost be said to be "illusory" if this were not to fall back into the Parmenidean impasse. Aristotle discussed the void in his *Physics*, Bk. IV, Chs. 6–9. He began by pointing out that those who hold that the void exists think of it as a kind of empty place, deprived of what it contained when it was full of body, that is, of that which is "heavy" or "light." To disprove the existence of such a void, it is not enough to show that air is a body, for there might be places empty of air as well. The following arguments, Aristotle continued, are put forward by those who believe that void exists: without void there could be no motion, since what is already full cannot contain anything more; compression of bodies and absorption of other bodies implies that some bodies contain void; and finally, void is necessary to separate and distinguish things. But, Aristotle replied, there can be qualitative change in what is full, and there can also be motion if it is rotatory; also, bodies can be compressed and can absorb other bodies by squeezing something else out or by changing qualitatively. More positively, Aristotle had already argued that the place of a body is always understood in terms of the inside limits of its containing body. Thus void cannot be a kind of place, because a body placed in a void could not be said to be in a place and, further, could not be said to move from place to place in a void. In other words, Aristotle denied that a body can have a place unless it is surrounded without interval by other bodies, and he asserted that this by itself is sufficient to rule out the possibility of void. His further, and more empirical, arguments against the void turned on his belief that bodies in a void, if they moved at all, would have to move infinitely fast, but on the other hand, since all unnatural motion (such as the motion of projectiles) requires a mover in continuous contact with the moved, there could be no unnatural motion in a void. Further, compression and rarefaction may be due, not to discrete atoms being more or less loosely packed, but to a continuous matter which is capable of existing in any density. That is to say, "dense" and "rare" may be forms of matter, like "hot" and "cold," which are capable of being present in varying intensities.

Such arguments as these were widely accepted as definitive against the existence of void, or at least against the possibility of a large-scale, continuous void. The Stoics, for example, wholly rejected void within the cosmos as contrary to the natural sympathy of its parts and to the cohesive force of the pervasive *pneuma*, or spirit. Others, however, as reported by Hero of Alexandria in his *Pneumatica* (probably first century A.D.), were prepared to accept discontinuous small vacua dispersed through substances. Hero developed this theory as an attempt to account for the well-known phenomena of pumps and siphons and for the *horror vacui*, which apparently causes attraction of bodies into spaces in order to prevent occurrence of a vacuum. He argued that the material nature of air and the fact that force is needed to produce a vacuum show that continuous vacuum does not exist naturally, but on the other hand, he adopted the atomist, rather than the Aristotelian, theory of density and concluded that expansion increases and compression reduces the small void spaces between the ultimate particles of matter. When a force of rarefaction is withdrawn, the particles come together because their motion is unobstructed in the intervening void, and when a force of compression is withdrawn, the air returns to its original volume by the elasticity of its particles.

Hero's theory acquired some popularity with the revival

of atomism in the early seventeenth century, and its adequacy is discussed, for example, in Galileo's dialogue *Two New Sciences* (1638). It was, however, conclusively overthrown by the inventor of the barometer, Galileo's pupil Evangelista Torricelli, who discovered that the cause of the "suction" of the vacuum, which can support a column of water or mercury in a barometer tube, is the external weight of the atmosphere, and not an internal attractive power. This result suggested similar explanations in terms of external ether pressures for such apparently "attractive" phenomena as cohesion, capillarity, and surface tension, and in general, it made more acceptable the view that mechanical explanations of all physical effects could be found in terms of impacts and pressures rather than attractions and sympathies. Thus the nonmechanical theory of vacuum suction lost its scientific function, and the question of the existence of void became once more primarily a metaphysical question.

Descartes and Leibniz. In the *Principles of Philosophy* (1644), Descartes argued that the nature of body consists solely in extension, and not in hardness or weight or any other quality that can be absent from a body without affecting its nature as body. Since body is thus identified with extension, "it is contrary to reason to say that there is a vacuum or space in which there is absolutely nothing." Vacuum, as we normally understand it, is not absence of all body, but only absence of the body we expect to find; for example, air may have been removed from a vessel by a pump, but what is left is not nothing, but body more subtle than air. Since matter, being extension, is indefinitely divisible, no pump can remove all matter from a space. Cartesian physics was thus committed to the view that space is a plenum. Some of Descartes's successors, however, preferred to rest this view on synthetic, rather than logical, arguments. Leibniz, for example, abandoned the a priori identification of matter and extension when it became clear that matter must have the property of inertia and that the same extensions might have different inertias. But he remained convinced that there is no void, arguing that the perfection of the universe implies that there must be as much matter as possible and also that if there were void, there would be no reason for any exact proportion of matter to void and, hence, that the assumption of void offends against the principle of sufficient reason. It also offends against the principle of continuity, which requires matter to be continuous and indefinitely divisible.

Kant. Kant likewise did not claim that the nonexistence of void is an analytic truth; indeed, he went further than Leibniz in allowing that the "pure understanding" cannot decide the question. He discussed the related problem of atomism versus infinite divisibility as one of the antinomies of the pure reason in the *Critique of Pure Reason,* Bk. II, Ch. II, and concluded that either conception leads to self-contradictions if the world is thought of as a "thing-in-itself." Such contradictions must be avoided by refusing to go beyond the empirical phenomena, in which we may or may not find that there are practical limits to our ability to divide substance. The void, however, is another question. Like atomism, neither the hypothesis of void nor its contrary can ever be proved directly by experience, but unlike atomism neither hypothesis is in itself contradic-

tory, and considerations of pure reason leave the question open. Kant, like his predecessors, pointed out that the hypothesis of void is not necessary to explain the varying density of matter, since density may be a primary property of every point of continuous matter, present in varying intensities like heat. In the continuum theory outlined in his *Metaphysische Anfangsgrunde der Naturwissenschaft,* Kant attempted to give physical arguments against the void in terms of the expansive forces of mutual repulsion, which he ascribed to all parts of matter and which are sufficient at short distances to overcome the attractive force of gravitation.

Post-Kantian philosophy of science has rarely seen the existence or nonexistence of void, as such, as a philosophical problem, but conceptual problems have remained, concerning the nature of the fields of force which pervade otherwise void space and concerning their relation to matter. (These questions, arising from nineteenth-century and twentieth-century physics, are discussed in the articles ACTION AT A DISTANCE AND FIELD THEORY and ETHER. For a further discussion of the history of this problem, see ATOMISM.)

Bibliography

Boas, M., "Hero's 'Pneumatica,' a Study of Its Transmission and Influence." *Isis,* Vol. 40 (1949), 38–48.

Duhem, Pierre, "Roger Bacon et l'horreur du vide," in *Roger Bacon Essays,* A. G. Little, ed. Oxford, 1949. The medieval theory of the vacuum.

Hero of Alexandria, *Pneumatics,* translated by Bennet Woodcroft. London, 1851.

Kant, Immanuel, *Critique of Pure Reason,* translated by Norman Kemp Smith. London, 1958. See especially the "Anticipations of Perception," 1st Division, Bk. II, Ch. II, and "Antinomies," 2d Division, Bk. II, Ch. II.

For additional bibliography, see ACTION AT A DISTANCE AND FIELD THEORY and ETHER.

MARY HESSE

VAGUENESS. To say that a word is vague is to say that there are cases in which there is no definite answer to whether it applies to something. Thus "middle-aged" is vague, for it is not clear whether a person aged 40 or a person aged 59 is middle-aged. Of course there are uncontroversial areas of application and nonapplication. At age 5 or 80 one is clearly not middle-aged, and at age 45 one clearly is. But on either side of the area of clear application there are indefinitely bounded areas of uncertainty. To say that there is no definite answer to the question, Is a person aged 40 middle-aged? is not to say that we have not yet been able to find the answer because of insufficient information. The status of this question is quite different from that of the question, Is Mars inhabited?, where we have a pretty good idea of what information, if obtained, would settle the matter. Our inability to say whether a 40-year-old man is middle-aged is not the result of lack of information about such things as blood pressure and metabolic rate. No additional information would settle the matter, except indirectly by leading us to tighten up the meaning of the word. The indeterminacy is due to an aspect of the meaning of the term rather than to the current state of our knowledge.

The word "vague" is commonly used quite loosely to cover a variety of features of discourse that should be distinguished. We should distinguish vagueness, as just defined, from lack of specificity. If someone says, "We must take steps to meet this emergency," or if an advertisement reads, "It's the hidden quality that spells true value," one might react by saying, "That's a very vague statement." However, the main defect of these statements is lack of specificity rather than vagueness. What causes trouble in these cases is not that it is not clear whether something is to be called a step or a quality. It is rather that the speaker has used the very general terms "step" and "hidden quality" without further qualification, without saying more specifically what kinds of steps or what quality is involved. Of course, the same utterance can in an important way be both vague and nonspecific, as in the advertisement, "Cash loans. Simple requirements." This can be objectionable both because of the failure to be specific as to what the requirements are and because of the vagueness of the term "simple."

Another confusion that has infected many discussions is that between vagueness as a semantic feature of a term, the concept set out above, and vagueness as an undesirable feature of a certain piece of discourse. Vagueness in the first sense is not always undesirable. There are contexts in which we are better off using a term that is vague in a certain respect than we would be using a term that is not vague in this respect. One such context is diplomacy. The American ambassador to the U.S.S.R. may be instructed to say, "My government will strongly oppose any interference in the internal affairs of Hungary." Here the marked vagueness is due to the adverb "strongly." What constitutes strong opposition? Declaring war clearly would be, and simply expressing disapproval in a press conference clearly would not be. Where in between is the line to be drawn? Is pressing for a UN resolution strong opposition? What about an economic embargo or subsidization of anti-Russian elements in Hungary? There is a tactical advantage in the vagueness and lack of specificity of this statement, both in keeping the opposition guessing and in leaving open a wide range of alternatives.

There can also be theoretical advantages to the use of vague terms. In many areas our situation is such that we cannot make maximally precise statements without going far beyond the evidence. Thus we have reason to think that city life imposes more psychological strain on people than country life. In formulating this principle we have used a vague word like "city." Of course we could remove the vagueness in question, which has to do with the minimum number of inhabitants required, by stipulating that any community containing at least 50,000 inhabitants will be called a city. But having done so we can no longer make the statement with any assurance. There is no precise population cutoff point above which there is a marked increase in the psychological strain imposed by the community.

Hence when we use a word which has a certain kind of vagueness, the vagueness may or may not be a liability. Failure to realize this has often led to the assumption that an "ideal" language would contain no vague words.

Kinds of vagueness. Thus far we have focused on examples in which the vagueness stems from the lack of precise boundaries between application and nonapplication along some dimension—age, number of inhabitants, strength of opposition. This kind, which we may call "degree vagueness," furnishes the standard examples in most discussions of the subject, presumably because it is the easiest to discern and analyze; but it is not the only important kind. Another, more complex, source of indeterminacy of application is to be found in the way in which a word may have a number of logically independent conditions of application. A significant example is the word "religion." If we consider clear cases of religions, such as Roman Catholicism and Orthodox Judaism, we find that they exhibit certain striking features, each of which seems to have something to do with making them religious. These include:

(1) Beliefs in supernatural beings (gods).

(2) The demarcation of certain objects as sacred.

(3) Ritual acts focused around sacred objects.

(4) A moral code believed to be sanctioned by the gods.

(5) Characteristic feelings, such as awe and a sense of mystery, which tend to be aroused in the presence of sacred objects and which are associated with the gods.

(6) Prayer and other forms of communication with the gods.

(7) A world view, that is, a general picture of the world as a whole, including a specification of its over-all significance, and a picture of the place of the individual in the world.

(8) The individual's more or less total organization of his life based on the world view.

(9) A social organization bound together by the preceding characteristics.

The existence of a plurality of distinguishable conditions of application does not in itself render a term vague. We can distinguish two conditions of application of the word "square": being a rectangle and having all sides equal. Here there is a definite answer to the question of what combination of these conditions is necessary and what combination is sufficient for the application of the term, the answer being that each of the conditions is necessary but not sufficient and that their combination is sufficient. With "religion" it seems clear that the combination of all the features listed above would be sufficient to guarantee application of the term. But what feature, or combination thereof, is necessary? And is any subset of the features sufficient? There do not seem to be definite answers to these questions. Some people are inclined to take beliefs in supernatural beings as necessary for religion. But the term is applied to systems, such as humanism, Hinayana Buddhism, and Communism, where belief in supernatural beings is lacking, though this application is contested. Again, if we take ritual to be a necessary feature, we are confronted with phenomena like the Quaker movement, where it has dropped out altogether. As for claims that some set of features short of the whole list is sufficient to make something a religion, they all turn out to be controversial. Communism involves an elaborate cultus, sacred objects such as the body of Lenin and the writings of Karl Marx, and a definite world view and an orientation of life based on it. It is not at all clear whether this justifies us in calling it a religion.

In such cases we have a variety of conditions, all of which have something to do with the application of the term, yet are not able to make any sharp discriminations between those combinations of conditions which are, and those which are not, sufficient and/or necessary for application. There will be certain combinations, like the one exemplified by the case of Communism, in which we get uncertainties and disagreements among fluent speakers of the language as to whether the word is applicable. We may call this "combinatory vagueness." (Other examples can be found in the articles EMOTION AND FEELING and MOTIVES AND MOTIVATION.) This kind of vagueness is akin to the phenomenon Ludwig Wittgenstein called "family resemblances" among the things to which a term applies. Using Wittgenstein's terminology, we could say that if one surveys a variety of religions one does not find them all sharing one common essence; one finds rather that they resemble each other in a variety of ways without there being any one resemblance which holds between every pair, just as with the members of a family. Whenever a term exhibits combinatory vagueness there will presumably be a family resemblance between the things to which it more or less clearly applies. Nevertheless the two concepts are not identical. There could be a "family resemblance" term with respect to which there is no indeterminacy of application, though this possibility may never be actually realized.

Another important distinction bisects the one already made. This one has to do not with the source of the indeterminacy but with the kind of question that lacks a determinate answer. So far we have been concerned with the question whether a given term applies to a situation. We may call this "vagueness of application." With many terms we have occasion to raise another question: Granted that the term applies, how many instances of its denotation are there in a given situation? When do we have one such-and-such, as contrasted with two or more? There are situations in which the meaning of a certain term is such that questions of this kind have no determinate answer. We may call this "vagueness of individuation." "Mountain" exhibits vagueness of application because it is not clear just how elevated a land form must be before it can be called a mountain rather than a hill. But there is also an indeterminacy as to what we are to count as one mountain rather than two. How much of a depression must there be between two peaks before they can be said to make up two mountains? Here the vagueness of individuation is one of degree. Combinatory vagueness of individuation is exemplified by "community." Among the features that make for an area's constituting a single community are its integration into a single political order, the accessibility of inhabitants to one another, and its being bounded by relatively uninhabited regions. As long as the conditions are satisfied or not satisfied together, there is no problem. But when we have the second and third without the first, as with Minneapolis and St. Paul, Minnesota, or the third alone, as with the megalopolises growing up around Los Angeles and between San Francisco and San Jose, it is no longer clear what to count as a single community.

The removal of vagueness. Since there are contexts in which it is important to be as precise as possible, it is worth considering the extent to which we can rid our dis-

course of vagueness. Degree vagueness can be removed by quantification. We may redefine "city" to mean "community with at least 50,000 inhabitants" and "cold drink" to mean "drink with a temperature below 45 degrees Fahrenheit." In so doing we will have removed the indeterminacy as to just how many inhabitants a community must have in order to be counted as a city and just how low a temperature a drink must have in order to be counted as a cold drink. But it is by no means the case that we have rendered the terms perfectly precise. "City" is still subject to any vagueness attaching to "community" and "inhabitant." We have already noted vagueness of individuation attaching to the former. "Inhabitant" is markedly subject to combinatory vagueness of application. An inhabitant of a community is one who resides there, but "resides" is subject to vaguenesses both of degree and of combination. Possible discrepancies between legal residence and physical presence give rise to combinatory vagueness. Is a visiting professor at Stanford who is temporarily occupying an apartment in Palo Alto, but who maintains a legal residence in New York City, a resident of Palo Alto or New York City or both during his tenure at Stanford? As for degree problems, consider a man who maintains homes in each of several communities. How much of the year does he have to stay in one of these to be counted an inhabitant? So long as these indeterminacies remain it may be doubtful in a particular instance, even with full information, whether a given community does contain at least 50,000 inhabitants. In the case of "cold drink" we are still subject to any indeterminacies of application attaching to "drink." For example, is a malted milk which is virtually solid to be termed a drink?

Quantification is not required to remove combinatory vagueness—only a simple ruling on what is or is not to count as sufficient and necessary for application of the term. Thus, we may rule that belief in supernatural beings and rituals connected with this belief are sufficient to make something a religion and that each of these features is necessary. But, again, the terms in which these conditions are stated will be more or less vague. Does the spirit of love count as a supernatural being? Is Quaker silence a ritual?

Thus any project of completely ridding our language of vagueness is chimerical. For all practical purposes we must use words to provide more precise definitions of other words, and the task of removing the fresh elements of vagueness which come to light with each new definition seems to be endless. In particular, the device of quantification does not suffice to get rid of all vagueness. One must still use words to specify what it is that is being counted or measured, and these words may be riddled with vagueness. In the social sciences sophisticated mathematical techniques often serve to cover up indeterminacies in the terms used to specify what is being measured. Thus an oral personality may be defined as one who has a certain minimum amount of a need for nurture, who makes a certain minimum number of nonpurposive mouth movements per day, and so on. But we must still ask how we are to determine in a given case whether a person needs to be nurtured or simply to be assisted, and when a mouth movement counts as nonpurposive.

The above considerations do not show that making our

terms more precise is a futile activity. The indeterminacies inherent in "inhabitant" and "community" were not introduced into the term "city" by our tightened definition. On the contrary, they were there all along. They were only brought to light by our success in removing the more obvious indeterminacy concerning the number of inhabitants. Any source of vagueness which can be identified can be removed, and by doing so we render the term more precise. Precision can be increased. It is the ideal of perfect precision that lies at the end of the rainbow.

Semantic implications of vagueness. The pervasive presence of vagueness introduces an extra complexity into any attempt to deal with semantic features of words and sentences. It complicates the job of definition, for even if our definiens is otherwise synonymous with our definiendum, the one may be vague in a way the other is not. A relationship of this sort is what we are seeking when we try to make a term more precise. The hope is that "drink with a temperature below 45 degrees Fahrenheit" has just the same meaning as "cold drink" except that the former lacks an indeterminacy which attaches to the latter. But when we are trying to bring out the actual status of a word rather than to polish it up, what we need ideally is a definiens which matches it in vagueness. In defining "adolescence" as "the period of life between childhood and adulthood" we have a good match. The indeterminacies of the boundaries of adolescence seem to be the same as those which attach to the upper boundary of childhood and the lower boundary of adulthood.

The same problem is involved in trying to decide whether a given statement is analytic, insofar as this question turns on the adequacy of a certain definition. If we want to know whether the statement "if someone lives in a city he lives in a large community" is analytic, we will have to ask whether the vagueness of "city" matches that of "large community." It would be a mistake to suppose that it is in principle possible to determine with precision whether two terms match in respect to vagueness. This would be possible only if there were precise boundaries to areas of indeterminacy of application. This does not seem to be the case, and for good reason. It would be absurd to have the term "city" made just precise enough that its area of indeterminacy of application stretches exactly between 25,000 and 40,000 inhabitants, without going all the way and making a sharp boundary between application and nonapplication, thereby removing this element of vagueness altogether.

Vagueness must also be taken into account in applying criteria of meaningfulness, such as the verifiability criterion. Insofar as a term is vague, the question of what evidence would confirm or disconfirm a statement that predicates it of something does not have a completely precise answer. Thus, we can give no precise answer to the question, What evidence would confirm or disconfirm the thesis that a given society has no religion? For, as we saw earlier, there are certain situations in which it is inherently indeterminate whether what we are dealing with is a religion.

Finally, the fact of vagueness raises problems about the supposedly self-evident "law of excluded middle," which says that every statement is either true or false. Where a vague term is applied in an area of indeterminate application, it is in principle impossible to pronounce the statement either true or false. This problem can be handled by rejecting the law, by denying that in this case we have a statement, or by taking the law to apply only to an "ideal" language.

Bibliography

Alston, William P., *Philosophy of Language.* Englewood Cliffs, N. J., 1964. Ch. 5. A comprehensive account of most of the issues involved.

Black, Max, "Vagueness: An Exercise in Logical Analysis." *Philosophy of Science,* Vol. 4 (1937), 427–455. Reprinted in his *Language and Philosophy.* Ithaca, N.Y., 1949. An important discussion of the Russell article cited below, together with an attempt to explicate vagueness in quantitative terms.

Black, Max, "Reasoning with Loose Concepts." *Dialogue,* Vol. 2 (1963), 1–12. A revision of Black's earlier article with a discussion of the implications of Russell's theory for logic.

Copilowish, Irving M., "Borderline Cases, Vagueness, and Ambiguity." *Philosophy of Science,* Vol. 6 (1937), 181–195. An interesting discussion of Black's first article.

Hempel, Carl G., "Vagueness and Logic." *Philosophy of Science,* Vol. 6 (1939), 163–180. Another interesting critique of Black's article.

Hospers, John, *An Introduction to Philosophical Analysis.* Englewood Cliffs, N.J., 1953. Ch. 1. A competent exposition of Russell's thesis.

Khatchadourian, H., "Vagueness." *Philosophical Quarterly,* Vol. 12 (1962), 138–152. A fresh discussion criticizing Russell's position.

Peirce, C. S., "Vague," in J. M. Baldwin, ed., *Dictionary of Philosophy and Psychology,* 3 vols. New York, 1901–1905. Vol. II, p. 748.

Quine, W. V., *Word and Object.* Cambridge, Mass., 1960. Ch. 4.

Russell, Bertrand, "Vagueness." *Australasian Journal of Philosophy,* Vol. 1 (1923), 84–92. The classical discussion.

Waismann, Friedrich, "Verifiability," in A. G. N. Flew, ed., *Logic and Language,* First Series. Oxford, 1952.

Wittgenstein, Ludwig, *Philosophical Investigations.* Oxford, 1953. Part I, Secs. 65–88. A most influential discussion, which includes a presentation of the notion of "family-resemblances."

WILLIAM P. ALSTON

VAIHINGER, HANS (1852–1933), German philosopher of the "as if." Vaihinger was born in a devout home near Tübingen. Although he developed unorthodox religious views at an early age, he attended the Theological College of the University of Tübingen. Vaihinger wanted to be a man of action, but his extreme nearsightedness forced him into scholarly pursuits. He regarded the contrast between his physical constitution and the way he would like to live as irrational, and his defective vision made him sensitive to other frustrating aspects of existence.

Vaihinger eventually became a professor of philosophy at Halle, but failing vision necessitated his giving up his duties in 1906. He then turned to completing his most important work, *Die Philosophie des Als-Ob* (Berlin, 1911; translated by C. K. Ogden as *The Philosophy of "As If,"* New York, 1924), which had been started in 1876. The volume went through many editions and made the philosophy of fictions well known. Vaihinger also achieved renown as a Kant scholar and founded the journal *Kant-Studien.* He also founded (with Raymund Schmidt) the *Annalen der Philosophie,* a yearbook concerned with the "as if" approach. He was much interested in the theory of evolution and emphasized the biological function of thought. On occasion he expressed himself sharply. For example, when quite young he defined mankind as "a species of monkey suffering from megalomania." This resulted in considerable controversy, and Vaihinger later seemed to regret this definition, although he still found some merit in it.

General point of view. In many ways Vaihinger was attracted to apparent inconsistencies. Although he held theological doctrines to be false in any literal or factual sense, Vaihinger, somewhat like Santayana, found considerable aesthetic and ethical merit in Christian doctrines. Both idealism and materialism interested him, but he found either alone to be unsatisfactory. Indeed, he regarded the problem of the relation of matter to mind as logically insoluble. He was much influenced by Kant and emphasized the importance of categories supplied by the mind in the perception of objects; yet he wanted to modify Kant in a more materialistic and empirical direction.

Vaihinger's urge to absorb elements of apparently conflicting approaches is illustrated by the label he chose for his philosophy: idealistic positivism or positivist idealism. He was impressed by F. A. Lange's *History of Materialism* and respected both Lange's Kantian views and his great knowledge of the natural sciences. But even Lange's Neo-Kantianism needed to be made more empirical and positivistic, in Vaihinger's view. This was to be achieved by recognizing the necessity and utility of acting on the basis of fictions that are known to be false.

Vaihinger praised Schopenhauer's pessimism and irrationalism. Too many philosophers (especially Hegel) had believed that the ideal of philosophy was to furnish a rational explanation for everything. But for Vaihinger both nature and history contain many irrational elements, and he regarded Schopenhauer as one of the few philosophers sincere enough to emphasize that irrationality.

Vaihinger maintained that pessimism gives moral strength, enables one to endure life, and helps to develop a more objective view of the world. He emphasized that in his opinion the difficulties of Germany, and especially its defeat in World War I, were largely attributable to the prevailing optimism of German idealism. He saw a close relation between philosophy and practical politics, arguing that a "rational pessimism" might have prevented the war.

Fictions. The Platonic myths were the first stimuli to Vaihinger's eventual theory of fictions. Later, Kant's antinomies also were influential. Lange had said, "Man *needs* to supplement reality by an ideal world of his own creation"; Vaihinger expanded this view and applied it to science, metaphysics, theology, social ideals, and morality. Fictions are not to be mistaken for true propositions, for fictions are known to be false. They contradict observed reality or are self-contradictory, and so they falsify experience. Something can work *as if* true, even though false and recognized as false.

Vaihinger distinguished his philosophy from any pragmatism which holds that a statement is true if it is useful in practice. In contrast, he argued: "An idea whose theoretical untruth or incorrectness, and therewith its falsity, is admitted, is not for that reason practically valueless and useless; for such an idea, in spite of its theoretical nullity may have great practical importance" (*The Philosophy of*

"As If," p. viii). Nevertheless, he admitted that in practice pragmatism and fictionalism had much in common, especially in their acknowledgement of the significance of heuristic ideals.

Nor can fictionalism be identified with any variety of skepticism. Vaihinger interpreted skepticism as the doubting of some view. Fictionalism does not doubt the correctness of its fictions; it knows them to be wrong. Vaihinger thought that the label "skepticism" was applied to his philosophy because of its views on God and immortality. He suggested that the label "relativism" (in the sense of opposition to absolutism) better fitted his views.

Fictions and hypotheses. Vaihinger distinguished between hypotheses and fictions. Methodologically they are very different, but they are similar in form and hard to separate in practice. According to Vaihinger, a hypothesis is "directed toward reality" and is subject to verification, but fictions are never verifiable, for they are known to be false. In the case of a number of competing hypotheses, the most probable is selected, but in the case of a number of competing fictions, the most expedient is chosen. Vaihinger held that to treat "Man is descended from the lower mammals" as a hypothesis is to say that we believe that if we had lived at the appropriate time, we would have perceived the ancestors of man, that we may still find the remains of those ancestors, and so on. In contrast, Goethe's notion of an animal archetype of which all known animal species are modifications was a fiction. Goethe did not believe the archetype had ever existed; he was saying that all animals could be regarded as if they were modifications of the single type.

Goethe's fiction was of considerable value despite its falsity, since it suggested a new classificatory system and had heuristic value for Darwin's later theory. Hypotheses, then, are constructed with the hope of verification, but "the fiction is a mere auxiliary construct, a circuitous approach, a scaffolding afterwards to be demolished." Thus, what is untenable as a hypothesis, especially if exceptions to it are discovered, may be useful as a fiction. Hypotheses are verified by experience, but fictions are justified by the services they render, by their utility.

Characteristics of fictions. Fictions have four general characteristics: (1) They either deviate from reality or are self-contradictory. (2) They disappear either in the course of history or through logical operations and are used only provisionally. (3) The users of a fiction normally are consciously aware that the fiction lays no claim to being true; frequently in the history of thought, however, the first users of a fiction mistake it for a hypothesis. (4) Fictions are the means to some definite end; fictions lacking that expediency are mere subjective fancies.

The utility of fictions. Vaihinger adopted a basically biological account of the utility of fictions and made lengthy comparisons of psychical and physical processes, holding that the same general notion of utility applies in both cases. He specifically mentioned "ready adaptation to circumstances and environment," the maintenance of a "successful reaction" to external impulses and influences, and "the adoption and acceptance or the repulsion of new elements." A Kantian emphasis also appears in this context. The psyche is not a receptacle into which sense impressions are poured but is, rather, a *"formative force, which independently changes what has been appropriated."* It is also assimilative and constructive. Logical thought, using fictions, "is an active appropriation of the outer world."

Examples of fictions. Vaihinger discussed in great detail specific fictions used in diverse realms of discourse. God and immortality have already been mentioned. It may be a great convenience to act as if the cosmos were orderly and created by an all-powerful and all-good God and as if man were immortal. The virgin birth is another "beautiful, suggestive and useful myth." Vaihinger agreed with Kant that despite the scientific difficulties of the notion, it has practical utility as an excellent symbol of mankind triumphantly resisting evil and raising itself above temptation. In science the atom is a fiction. Both those who defended the literal reality of the atom and the early positivists who rejected its reality on the grounds that atomic theory was internally contradictory were mistaken. The atom is, rather, "a group of contradictory concepts which are necessary in order to deal with reality."

A materialistic notion of the world is false if taken as a hypothesis but is a necessary and useful fiction. Materialism, Vaihinger held, simplifies our notion of the external world and helps to bolster a scientific outlook. Natural scientists carry on their work as if an external material world existed independently of perceiving subjects, and thus science can "proceed on the basis of relations far simpler than those actually presented to a careful observation of reality itself" (*ibid.*, p. 200). The notion of a vital force in biology, while full of difficulties, may have some use as a fiction. Vaihinger regarded such a fiction as "an abbreviation for the sum of all the causes that determine the phenomena of life" (*ibid.*, p. 212). It enables us to express some matters in a simpler way than we otherwise could. To cite one final example, doctrines in social theory, such as the notion of an original social contract, may be helpful. An extremely complicated situation can be grasped by adopting a fiction that deliberately substitutes for "the complete range of causes and facts" a part of that range.

Vaihinger's theory of fictions can be regarded as a denial of the view of W. K. Clifford and others that belief should always be proportionate to the evidence. Intellectually, practically, and morally we need false but expedient fictions to cope with the world. Many traditional philosophic views are mistaken in that they confuse the human need for certain doctrines with the truth of those doctrines; but various forms of skepticism, positivism, and materialism are wrong in assuming that because certain doctrines are false, they should be eliminated.

Theory of mind. According to Vaihinger, all knowledge "is a reduction of the unknown to the known, that is to say a comparison." He held that there are limitations to all thought, although he did not wish to lament them; we cannot leap out of our skins and somehow attain what we cannot attain. These limitations apply not only to man but also to "the highest Mind of all," and they come about because thought originated as a means to an end. The end is to serve the will to live.

The purpose of thought. Vaihinger held that "the test of the correctness of a logical result lies in *practice*, and the purpose of thought must be sought not in the reflection of a so-called objective world, but in rendering possible the calculation of events and of operations upon them" (*ibid.*, p. 5). The purpose of thought is not correspondence with an assumed objective reality; nor is it the theoretical reconstruction of an outer world within consciousness; nor is it the comparison of things and logical constructs. It is pragmatic in the sense that successful logical products enable us to *"calculate events that occur without our intervention."*

Vaihinger maintained that nature proceeds entirely according to "hard and unalterable laws . . . but thought is an adaptable, pliant, and adjustable organic function." Very probably the most elementary physical processes contain certain strivings. In organic beings, those strivings develop into impulses. Man, in his evolutionary development from the animals, has had those impulses transformed into will and action. Thus ideas, judgments, and conclusions act as means of survival.

Senseless problems. Vaihinger put great stress on what he termed the "Law of the Preponderance of the Means over the End." According to this law, the well-adapted means to a specific end everywhere have a tendency to become independent and ends in themselves. Thus the mind sets itself impossible problems that cannot be solved, even by "the highest Mind of all," just because no mind was developed for those purposes. Eventually "emancipated thought" sets for itself senseless problems, among which Vaihinger listed questions about the origin of the world, the formation of matter, the origin of motion, the meaning of the world, and the purpose of life. He gave particular attention to the relation of mind and matter. His philosophy was admittedly inconsistently dualistic; on the one hand it reduced all reality to sensations, and on the other it reduced all reality to matter. But Vaihinger insisted that no logical, rational unification is possible through any philosophy and that the question of the relation of mind to matter is as senseless as that of the purpose of existence.

However, a nonrational solution is possible to the various world-riddles: "in intuition and in experience all this contradiction and distress fades into nothingness." Experience and intuition, Vaihinger said, are "higher than all human reason," and we do not "understand the world when we are pondering over its problems, but when we are doing the world's work." Experience and intuition give us the harmonious unity that reason cannot supply. Philosophers are especially prone to torture themselves with unanswerable questions; the wise man is content if life is successful on the level of practice. Shifts, probably unwarranted, in the meaning of terms like "understand" occur here, but Vaihinger's main point seems to be that there are nonrational solutions to questions which have no rational answers.

Thought and reality. Subjective events alter reality either by adding to it or by subtracting from it. Yet correct practical results are frequently obtained, and in that sense "thought tallies with reality." Hence, both what Vaihinger called logical optimism, the assumption that thought mirrors reality, and logical pessimism, the assumption that thought is always deceptive, need to be avoided. Senseless questions will not be answered in the future by some new philosophic synthesis but, rather, are explained by "looking backwards," by discovering their psychological origin.

Religion. Vaihinger's views on religion illustrate his general reluctance to accept either alternative of some of the traditional philosophic polarities. His early rationalistic, ethical theism later developed into a variety of pantheism. His pantheism then became, during his stay at Tübingen, a kind of Kantian agnosticism and then something close to Schopenhauerian atheism. Vaihinger saw no need to adopt a negative view toward the historical forms of the church and its various dogmas. But even though he regarded many Christian doctrines as fictions of considerable ethical and aesthetic value, doubt entered. For example, although he thought it was a fiction satisfying to many to take the world as if created, or at least regulated, by "a more perfect Higher Spirit," he further insisted that a supplementary fiction was necessary, holding that the "order created by the Higher Divine Spirit had been destroyed by some hostile force."

Vaihinger believed Friedrich Carl Forberg's views on religion were overly neglected. He agreed with Forberg that "theoretical atheism" was harmless and that everyone should have "an attack" of such atheism at least once, in order to find out whether he desired the good for its own sake or merely for some advantage either in this world or in a future world (see ATHEISMUSSTREIT). On the other hand, Vaihinger deplored "practical atheism," understood as the failure to act so as to make the world better. Religion became a mode of behavior rather than the acceptance of certain theoretical views.

Vaihinger held, in agreement with Forberg, that the striving toward the kingdom of God is what matters, not the achieving of it. In fact, it is very likely that the kingdom of God is an actual impossibility. The man who neglects none of his duties to his fellows and helps to further the common good, even though convinced that the world is filled with wickedness and stupidity, practices true religion. Religion is not the belief in the kingdom of God but the attempt to make it come about while recognizing its impossibility. Vaihinger argued that this was the general view of Kant. He believed that this religion not only had warmth and poetry but also "represents in its radical form the highest point to which the human mind, or rather the human heart, is capable of raising itself."

Bibliography

Additional works by Vaihinger are *Hartmann, Dühring und Lange* (Iserlohn, 1876); *Kommentar zu Kants Kritik der reinen Vernunft*, 2 vols. (Leipzig, 1881–1892); *Nietzsche als Philosoph* (Berlin, 1902); and *Die Philosophie in der Staatsprüfung* (Berlin, 1906).

The English translation by C. K. Ogden of *The Philosophy of "As If"* was made from the sixth German edition, specially revised by Vaihinger for the English-speaking philosophical world; it also contains a lengthy and helpful autobiography of Vaihinger that emphasizes the intellectual origins of his views.

See also W. Del Negro, "Hans Vaihinger's philosophisches Werk mit besonderer Berücksichtigung seiner Kantforschung," in *Kant-Studien* (1934), 316–327.

ROLLO HANDY

VAILATI, GIOVANNI (1863–1909), Italian analytical philosopher and historian of science, was born at Crema, Lombardy. He studied engineering and mathematics at the University of Turin, where he later became an assistant to Giuseppe Peano (1892) and Vito Volterra (1895) and lectured on the history of mechanics (1896–1899). In 1899 he resigned his university post to be free for independent work, earning his living by teaching mathematics in high schools. By the end of his life Vailati's ideas were internationally recognized; some of his writings had been translated into English, French, and Polish, and he was personally acquainted with many of the important scholars of his time. However, he was forgotten after his death, and only since the late 1950s has he received renewed attention.

The main feature of Vailati's thought is his methodological and linguistic approach to philosophical problems. Rather than propounding anything resembling a doctrine, Vailati presented concrete examples of how to apply his new methods. He left no complete book, but only some two hundred essays and reviews on a great number of problems in several academic disciplines. The best way to indicate the range of his philosophical interests is, therefore, to report the titles of his most important essays in philosophy. In chronological order, they are "The Importance of Investigating the History of the Sciences" (its bearing on the understanding of scientific method); "Deductive Method as a Tool for Inquiry"; "Questions of Words in the History of Science and Culture" (on semantical problems); "The Difficulties that Impair Any Attempt Rationally to Classify the Sciences"; "The Logical Bearing of Brentano's Classification of Mental Facts"; "The Applicability of the Concepts of Cause and Effect in Historical Sciences"; "The Most Modern Definition of Mathematics" (Russell's); "The Role of Paradoxes in Philosophy"; "The Tropes of Logic" (in which the important point is made that induction cannot be grounded, because if it were grounded, it would become deduction); "The Hunt for Antitheses" (an attack on the philosophical tendency toward unification and a defense of analysis); "The Distinction Between Knowing and Willing"; "The Search for the Impossible" (which contains an assessment of G. E. Moore's *Principia Ethica* and an acceptance of his method); "Pragmatism and Mathematical Logic"; "Toward a Pragmatic Analysis of Philosophical Terminology"; "A Handbook for Liars" (a review of Giuseppe Prezzolini's *The Art of Persuading*); "The Grammar of Algebra" (containing a comparison of the syntax of ordinary language with that of algebra).

Vailati's next important work, "Language as an Obstacle to the Elimination of Illusory Contrasts," is possibly his most concentrated inquiry into the relation between speech and thought and into the influence of speech on thought. Finally should be mentioned the papers Vailati wrote with his pupil, Mario Calderoni—"The Origins and Fundamental Idea of Pragmatism," "Pragmatism and Various Ways to Say Nothing," and "The Arbitrary in the Operation of the Mental Life." To all these articles Vailati brought a sense of humor; independence of judgment; a mind as cautious, matter-of-fact, and candid as one could wish for in a philosopher; complete control of mathematics, symbolic logic, and the history of the subject being examined; and an extremely concentrated style.

Philosophy. For Vailati, philosophy is no superscience that can teach scientists what they should do. It cannot make discoveries; it can only prepare the intellectual climate and furnish some of the necessary tools. It is a neutral enterprise that can receive contributions from people holding different personal beliefs and conceptions. It should avoid the struggle between systems which, "let us hope, will some day end like the reported fight between the two lions who ate one another up leaving only their tails on the ground" (*Scritti,* p. 652). As it has no special field of its own, philosophy should not construct any special language or resort to any jargon but should take into account what is already present in language. When a philosopher wants to ban a problematic term to avoid a related problem, he deludes himself; and when he substitutes for an ordinary-language term a technical term of his own or one drawn from a special science, his policy reminds one of "the advice given to children in jest that one can catch a bird by putting salt on its tail" (*ibid.,* p. 315). The right policy consists in correcting the use of the ordinary term—in using it "technically," if you like, but in a technical use as near as possible to its ordinary use. On the other hand, Vailati denounced as misleading similarity in verbal form or in grammar as contrasted with similarity in thought. He defended the independence of the philosopher with respect to usage as such.

Vailati wrote his most rewarding pages on such subjects as definitions, the difference between statements and other types of sentences, the logic of dispositional expressions versus categorical ones, axioms and postulates, deduction and induction, and the use of experiments. Also of importance are several papers on analytical ethics.

Vailati held that "opinions, whether true or false, are always *facts,* and as such they deserve and require to be made the object of research and verification" (*ibid.,* p. 65). Semantically, this is possible because we can understand and talk about sentences of which it cannot be said that they are either true or false. Indeed, "the question of determining *what we mean* when we propound a given proposition is entirely different from the question of deciding *whether it is true or false*" (*ibid.,* p. 923). On the other hand, mere understanding should not be confounded with scientific method, nor does the study of all that can be significantly said supply us with criteria for assessing truth and falsity. One cannot even begin to deal with the question whether a sentence is true or false before settling the question of what is meant by it. But to decide truth or falsity one must connect present and future experiences in terms of prevision, and propositions and facts in terms of intersubjective verification, both in science and in philosophy. In both ". . . it must be demanded of anybody who advances a thesis that he be capable of indicating the facts which according to him should obtain (or have obtained) if his thesis were true, and also their difference from other facts which according to him would obtain (or have obtained) if it were not true" (*ibid.,* p. 790).

Vailati's "pragmatism." Vailati was a liberal analytical philosopher of the kind that has flourished in England and the United States since World War II. However, he is usu-

ally referred to as the chief Italian "Peircean," or "logical," pragmatist. He was indeed one of the first to read Peirce correctly and to carefully distinguish his thought from James's. But Vailati's thought was too complex and his acquaintance with the history of ideas too thorough, and the concept of pragmatism is itself too manifold, to call him only a pragmatist. Although he stressed the importance of Peirce, he traced Peirce's ideas back to Berkeley and even to Plato's *Theaetetus,* claiming that Socrates was presented in that work as "defending against Protagoras the thesis now supported by Peirce under the name of 'pragmatism'" (*ibid.,* p. 921). If Vailati was impressed by Peirce's criteria for meaning and truth, he was equally impressed by Peano's work in mathematical logic, Mach's principle of the economy of thought, Moore's approach to ethics and Russell's to mathematics, Brentano's classification of mental phenomena, the Leibniz revival (to which Vailati contributed), and James's conception of consciousness.

Vailati did not possess Peirce's speculative power and overwhelming originality, but neither did he share the American's ontological troubles and commitments, and he gave his own researches a more empirical and methodological bent. By "pragmatism" Vailati meant mainly a new freedom of thought, a refusal to subscribe to any given doctrine, a willingness to use new intellectual techniques, and a cooperative attitude toward philosophical problems. He possessed new methods and new ways of thought which were neither positivistic nor idealistic; and he needed a new banner under which to fight his intellectual battle within Italian philosophy, which was then in the process of passing over from nineteenth-century positivism to the neoidealism of Croce and Gentile. Vailati's very individual position within that process helps to account for the long silence about his work, some other reasons being the scattered nature of his publications, the fact that he was in advance of his time, and the intervention of World War I and Italian fascism.

Historical work. As a historian Vailati dealt chiefly with mechanics, logic, and geometry. He made important contributions to the study of post-Aristotelian Greek mechanics, of Galileo's forerunners, of definition in Plato and Euclid, of the influence of mathematics on logic and epistemology, and of Gerolamo Saccheri's work in logic and in non-Euclidean geometry. He gave a remarkable representation (much more than a translation) of Book A of Aristotle's *Metaphysics.* He was particularly interested in the dialectic of continuity and change, in how "the same" problems are faced and solved in different ways in different periods; which, owing to his constant interest in language, meant that he traced the history of the relations between concepts and terms.

Vailati's work as a historian and as an analytical philosopher were closely interwoven; they are two applications of the same attitudes and methods. He saw the difference between theoretical and historical research not so much in their subject matters as in their approach to their subject matters. Philosophers and scientists, he held, should cooperate in historical research and remember that no history is complete unless the social background of ideas is taken into account. In science, past results are not "destroyed" by new ones, for new results make old ones even more important in the very process of superseding them. "Every error shows us a rock to be avoided, while not every discovery shows us a path to be followed" (*ibid.,* p. 65). By his awareness of the importance and his command of the methodology of historical research, Vailati avoided the abstract ahistorical atmosphere and the scientifically biased attitude of many logical positivists.

Logic. Vailati wrote some early papers in symbolic logic, but he was chiefly interested in the function of logic within philosophy. He attacked confusions between logic and psychology and between logic and epistemology.

Correspondence. Vailati's thought cannot be completely evaluated until the hundreds of letters he wrote to Mach, Brentano, Peano, Croce, Volterra, Giovanni Papini, Prezzolini, Giovanni Vacca, and many others, are published. Many concern topics not dealt with in the *Scritti.* These letters constitute one of the last large scientific correspondences of the eighteenth-century kind. They will throw new light on the intellectual history of Europe around 1900 and possibly establish connections hitherto unnoticed or only suspected.

Bibliography

Vailati's manuscripts (some still unpublished) and many of the letters he received are in the Institute for the History of Philosophy of the State University of Milan. The only almost-complete edition of his papers is the *Scritti* (Florence, 1911), which was followed by two anthologies: *Gli strumenti della conoscenza,* edited by Mario Calderoni (Lanciano, 1911), and *Il pragmatismo,* edited by Giovanni Papini (Lanciano, 1911). *Il pragmatismo* includes a completion of Vailati's notes for a book on pragmatism. Some of his best essays were first reprinted in *Il metodo della filosofia,* edited by Ferruccio Rossi-Landi (Bari, 1957), and in *Scritti di metodologia scientifica e di analisi del linguaggio,* edited by M. F. Sciacca (Milan, 1959). Complete collections of the philosophical papers and of the correspondence are in preparation.

The first contemporary scholar to point out Vailati's importance was Eugenio Garin, in 1946; see his *Cronache di filosofia italiana* (Bari, 1955), Ch. 5, Sec. 5. See also Ferruccio Rossi-Landi's introduction to *Il metodo della filosofia;* Rossi-Landi's "Materiale per lo studio di Vailati, in *Rivista critica di storia della filosofia,* Vol. 12 (1957), 468–485 and Vol. 13 (1958), 82–108, with extensive bibliographies and an attempt to classify all of Vailati's papers; and Rossi-Landi's "Some Modern Italian Philosophers," in *The Listener,* Vol. 17 (1957), No. 1450, 59–61 and No. 1451, 97–98. The most complete study is a special issue of the *Rivista critica di storia della filosofia,* Vol. 18 (1963), 273–523, which contains essays by twenty authors.

FERRUCCIO ROSSI-LANDI

VALENTINUS AND VALENTINIANISM.
Valentinus (fl. c. 150) was the founder and first head of one of the leading schools of heretical Christian Gnosticism. Little is known of his life, but he is said to have been educated in Alexandria and, according to Irenaeus, came to Rome under Hyginus (pope 136–140), flourished under Pius (pope 140–154), and continued to the time of Anicetus (pope 155–166). According to Tertullian he was at one time a candidate for the episcopate but was passed over in favor of a "confessor" who had suffered for the faith (Pius?), and in consequence of this rebuff Valentinus broke with the church. Tertullian's other statement that he came to Rome under Eleutherus (pope 175–189) must be erroneous, because Valentinians are already mentioned by Justin Martyr, and Valentinianism

had a long history behind it when Irenaeus wrote his refutation about A.D. 180.

Valentinianism at some point divided into an eastern branch, represented especially by Theodotus, and a western, represented by Heracleon, author of the first commentary on the Fourth Gospel, and by Ptolemy. In some respects the eastern branch appears to have adhered more closely to Valentinus' own teaching, but it is Ptolemy's version of the Valentinian theory that is advanced by Irenaeus as his main target, and it is not altogether easy to determine how much is his and how much goes back to Valentinus. Marcus, a later Valentinian, the success of whose teachings prompted Irenaeus to write his refutation, was addicted to magical practices, but Valentinus himself stood in high repute with the early Church Fathers. For Jerome he ranked with Marcion as the most learned among the heretics, and to Tertullian he was the Platonist among the Gnostics. Hippolytus, in line with his efforts to trace the pedigree of Gnosticism to the Greek philosophical schools, described Valentinus as a Pythagorean and a Platonist.

Sources. Our principal sources of information are still the writings of the early Church Fathers: Irenaeus (especially *Adversus Haereses* I), Hippolytus (*Philosophoumena,* Bk. VI), Clement of Alexandria, Tertullian (*Adversus Valentinianos*), and Epiphanius. Until quite recently our only original materials were some letters and homilies of Valentinus quoted by Clement, the same Father's *Excerpta ex Theodoto,* Ptolemy's "Letter to Flora" preserved by Epiphanius, and the fragments of Heracleon's commentary on John preserved by Origen. The Coptic library from Nag Hammadi, however, includes a number of Valentinian documents, but these have still to be fully evaluated, and in some cases the identity of the author is by no means certain. We are told, for example, that Valentinus wrote a treatise *Peri Triōn Phuseōn,* but the document with this title from Nag Hammadi is reported to show affinities rather with the teachings of Heracleon (cf. Quispel, *The Jung Codex,* p. 57). Irenaeus (*Adversus Haereses* III.11.9) mentions an *evangelium veritatis,* and the occurrence of this phrase at the beginning of another Coptic document prompted its first editors to identify it as the text in question and hence as a lost treatise by Valentinus himself. W. C. van Unnik (*The Jung Codex,* pp. 81 ff.) went further and argued from the absence of features typical of developed Valentinianism that this is an early document, from a period close to Valentinus' break with the church; other scholars, however, have maintained that the developed Valentinian system is in fact presupposed, and the range of New Testament quotations suggests a more advanced stage in the history of the canon than van Unnik's theory would admit. Another document identified as Valentinian is the *Epistle to Rheginus,* or *Treatise on the Resurrection,* but here again questions have been raised. Can we assume identity of authorship for this document and for "The Gospel of Truth"? Or may one or the other or both derive from the Valentinian school without necessarily being the work of Valentinus himself? In the case of "The Gospel of Philip," finally, the latter alternative appears to be correct, since the affinities of this text lie with the *Excerpta ex Theodoto* and the Marcosian theories rather than with other and older versions of the Valentinian system.

The system. Irenaeus' presentation of the theory of Valentinus is complicated, first, by his efforts to take account of deviations, which may represent either the theories of particular leaders of the school or different stages in the development of the theory, and, second, by his introduction of explanatory and illustrative material adduced by the Valentinians in support of their opinions. The main lines, however, are sufficiently clear. At the beginning of all things stands the primal Father Bythos (literally, "abyss"), either alone or in company with the Silence which is his thought. From Bythos and Silence proceed three pairs of aeons (quasi-personal aspects of the Father), which with them form an ogdoad, and from these aeons emanate other aeons, forming a pleroma, or divine realm, of thirty in all. The last of these aeons, and therefore the furthest from the source, is Sophia, who was guilty of a fault (which is variously described) and as a consequence produced a monstrous offspring, called Achamoth, which had to be expelled from the pleroma and was the ultimate origin of the created universe. This aborted offspring set about forming a world in imitation of the pleroma and first of all created the Demiurge in the image of the primal Father. The Demiurge (clearly the God of the Old Testament, as the quotations show) then created heaven and earth and all that is in them, believing in his ignorance that he was himself supreme. In creating man, he first made earthly man, then breathed into him something of his own psychic substance (cf. Genesis 2); finally, unknown to him, a spiritual substance was also mingled with the other elements of humanity. Men accordingly fall into three classes. The spiritual (*pneumatikoi*) are by their very nature destined to salvation, whereas the merely material (*hylikoi*), being "of the earth, earthy," are doomed to be destroyed together with this perishable world. Only the psychic (*psychikoi*) appear to enjoy some measure of free will; at any rate, they are capable of at least a partial salvation but are also exposed to the prospect of a false decision which may condemn them to join the merely material.

Reduced in this manner to its barest outline, the theory appears to be an attempt to account for the evil in the world by postulating a premundane fall—and also a premundane redemption, for Sophia must be restored to her place within the pleroma. Not the least of the difficulties with the theory arises from the fact that the process of redemption appears to be repeated on two or even three different levels: for Sophia herself, for Achamoth, and, finally, for the "spiritual" seed in this world. Similarly, there is an aeon Christ as well as a Jesus in whom the whole pleroma may be said to dwell (cf. Colossians 1:19). Further problems emerge when we attempt to distinguish different versions or different stages of development of the theory and again when we endeavor to investigate the relation between Valentinianism and such other systems as that of the Ophites or that of the Apocryphon of John. It has been held that these are later offshoots from the Valentinian theory, but it appears more probable that they are older versions of Gnosticism, and the question then arises of when and at what stage they were introduced into

Valentinian thought. Did Valentinus attempt, as has been suggested, to Christianize an older pagan gnosis? Or do the documents represent a gradual declension from Christianity? At all events, the Biblical and Christian elements in the system, together with the place accorded to Jesus or the Christ in the scheme of redemption, have sufficed in the eyes of some scholars to vindicate the essential Christianity of Valentinus. Other questions still awaiting investigation are the relative chronology of the documents now at our disposal and the relationship of Valentinianism to contemporary philosophy (for example, that of Numenius) and to such other movements as those represented by Bardesanes and by the Odes of Solomon (which some scholars have held to be Valentinian).

Bibliography

VALENTINIAN TEXTS

Clement of Alexandria, *Excerpta ex Theodoto*, R. P. Casey, ed. London, 1935. F. M. M. Sagnard, ed. Paris, 1948.

Heracleon, *The Fragments of Heracleon*, A. E. Brooke, ed. Cambridge, 1891.

Malinine, M.; Puesch, H. C.; and Quispel, Gilles, eds., *Evangelium Veritatis* ("The Gospel of Truth"). Zurich, 1956. Supplementary volume, Zurich, 1963. Translated, with commentary, by Kendrick Grobel. London and New York, 1960.

Malinine, M., et al., eds., *De Resurrectione*. Zurich and Stuttgart, 1963. The *Epistle to Rheginus*.

Ptolémee, Lettre à Flora, Gilles Quispel, ed. Paris, 1949.

Till, W. C., *Das Evangelium nach Philippos*. Berlin, 1963. Coptic text with German translation. Translated with commentary by R. McL. Wilson as *The Gospel of Philip*. London and New York, 1962.

MODERN WORKS ON VALENTINIANISM

Cross, F. L., ed., *The Jung Codex*. London, 1955. A discussion of the codex; contains three essays originally published in Dutch.

Foerster, W., *Von Valentin zu Heracleon* (Beiheft 7 zur *Zeitschrift für die neutestamentliche Wissenschaft und die Kunde der älteren Kirche*). Giessen, 1928.

Grant, R. M., *Gnosticism and Early Christianity*. New York, 1959.

Jonas, Hans, *The Gnostic Religion*. New York, 1958.

Leisegang, Hans, "Valentinus," in August Pauly and Georg Wissowa, eds., *Realencyclopädie der classischen Altertumswissenschaft*, Second Series, Vol. VII (1948), Cols. 2261 ff.

Sagnard, F. M. M., *La Gnose valentinienne et le témoignage de saint Irénée*. Paris, 1947.

Wilson, R. McL., *The Gnostic Problem*. London, 1958.

R. McL. WILSON

VALLA, LORENZO (1407–1457), Italian humanist, is best known as the man who exposed the Donation of Constantine and thus undermined a leading argument for papal sovereignty in the secular realm. This fact and the reputation for hedonism derived from his youthful work *De Voluptate* ("On Pleasure") have conspired to invest Valla with an air of disrepute that he probably does not deserve. In particular, this reputation does not do justice to Valla's efforts on behalf of a return to the spirit of the Gospel or to his respect for Paul and the early Greek and Latin Church Fathers, in which he clearly anticipates later developments. Nor does it recognize his passion for historical truth and for the defense of plain speaking against what he regarded as metaphysical obscurity and verbalizing. Valla was perhaps the most versatile of the humanists; he initiated a series of attacks upon scholastic logic, theology, and law, in addition to his contributions to historical and textual criticism.

Valla was above all a brilliant philologian and a stanch champion of the new humanities; most of his writing is best understood from this point of view. Valla was born in Rome. He learned Latin and Greek there and perhaps in Florence, and he spent three formative years, from 1431 to 1433, teaching rhetoric at the University of Pavia. Pavia was a lively center of humanists, and it may have been here that Valla heard the discussions of ancient ethics that prompted him to write the earliest of his extant works, the dialogue generally known under the title "On Pleasure" (Valla actually called it "On the True Good"). Several versions of this dialogue appeared, with the speeches variously assigned to different contemporaries of Valla. Contrary to a widespread impression, Valla does not directly endorse Epicurean ethics in the work; he permits speakers to present Stoic and Epicurean ethics and then, in the person of a third speaker, criticizes their views from a Christian standpoint. This third speaker clearly represents the convictions of Valla himself. The Stoic spokesman presents a defense of Stoic *honestas* or virtue, together with a quite un-Stoic complaint against nature, "which has made men so prone to vice." An Epicurean replies, at much greater length, in defense of nature and "utility." Utility is equated with pleasure and described as a mistress among her handmaidens, the virtues, rather than as a harlot among honest matrons. The third speaker criticizes both of his predecessors and argues that the true Christian should disregard the goals of this life and concentrate on the joys that await him in Heaven. However, this speaker accepts without challenge the equating of "the useful" with pleasure; he insists only that the pleasures a Christian should pursue are not those of this world. Thus, despite his rejection of Epicurean morality, Valla's description of heavenly pleasures is more graphic than we are accustomed to expect from a Christian writer. Renaissance *joie de vivre* is allowed to assert itself only in a future life. Does Valla depart radically from earlier Christian doctrine, or does he simply make explicit what would constitute the traditional Christian hope if it were spelled out? Obviously there is room for disagreement here, but there can be no disagreeing with the view of the eminent historian Eugenio Garin that Valla's work on pleasure represents a major Renaissance document.

After sojourns in various Italian cities, Valla entered the service of King Alfonso of Aragon, with whom he remained from 1435 to 1448. During this time in Naples, and probably in connection with Alfonso's quarrels with the pope, Valla wrote his most renowned work—his exposure as a forgery of the supposed Donation of the Emperor Constantine of the Western Empire to Pope Sylvester. Although he was anticipated in this by several earlier writers, among them Nicholas of Cusa, Valla's treatise stands out as a very effective piece of historical criticism and, incidentally, a strong plea for the spiritual purity of the Holy See. In view of the latter it should not appear surprising that Valla was later accepted into the pontifical secretariat and spent the

remaining years of his life in Rome. The genuineness of Valla's respect for historical truth and his scorn for superstition is shown in such statements as this in the treatise on the Donation: "A Christian man who calls himself the son of light and truth ought to be ashamed to utter things that not only are not true but are not even likely."

While with King Alfonso, Valla also wrote a work on free will, *De Libero Arbitrio*, in which he takes issue with Boethius' treatment of free will in the *Consolation of Philosophy*. In his dialogue Valla distinguishes God's foreknowledge, which cannot be said to be the cause of our volitions, from his will. God's accurate prediction that Judas will become a traitor does not excuse Judas. But Valla refuses to deal with the further question of whether God's will, which cannot be denied, takes away human choice. The divine will, he argues, is known neither to men nor to angels; we stand by faith, not by the probability of reasons.

A similar reluctance to engage in argumentative philosophizing appears in the treatise *Dialectic,* an attack upon conventional Aristotelian logic, printed a half-century after Valla's death. Valla here pleads for the elimination of empty subtleties and vain word-juggling. "Let us conduct ourselves more simply and more in line with natural sense and common usage," he says. "Philosophy and dialectic . . . ought not to depart from the most customary manner of speaking." Valla's treatment of the Aristotelian categories is not without interest. The Latin word for entity (*entitas*), for example, is simply a coinage of a participle from the verb "to be" that does not occur in standard Latin and hence ought to be regarded with suspicion. To say that a stone is an entity (*lapis est ens*) amounts to no more than saying that it is a thing (*res*), which is perfectly satisfactory and more clear. Therefore, Aristotle's metaphysics, which deals with "being qua being," is meaningless, suggesting as it does that what "is" is "able not to be." Having protested the positing of mysterious entities, quiddities, and essences and having equated substances with bodies or things, Valla then reduces the remaining nine categories of Aristotle to two: quality and action. Definitions, according to Valla, are explications of all the qualities and actions that are present in a thing. In the course of his exposition, Valla has occasion to challenge the validity of many scholastic distinctions: for example, those between the concrete and the abstract, between matter and form, and so on. Unsatisfactory as Valla's own offerings may be (they are not clearly dedicated to the solution of any specific philosophical problems), nevertheless it must be admitted that a fresh consideration of technical terms was certainly called for at the time and was eventually carried through by later critics.

Valla displays great sensitivity to nuances of meaning in his *Elegantiae Linguae Latinae* ("Elegancies of the Latin Language"), in which he makes careful analyses of the usage of many Latin terms. Critics have observed that Valla's own style was not as elegant as it could have been, but his advice was widely consulted.

Valla was often accused of bad form in his attacks on people and schools of thought, but one must recall that invectives and *ad hominem* attacks were the order of the day. In the Renaissance professional rivalry did not bother to conceal itself under polite or semipolite discussions of issues. Valla defended himself against the charge of malevolence and vindictiveness in a letter to Giovanni Serra, in which he concludes: "I do not censure all authors, but only a few, . . . not all philosophers but some from all sects, not the best but the worst, not impudently but calmly, ready to accept correction should it prove valid."

Bibliography

Valla's works were collected in an edition which was published in Basel (1540). It has been reproduced, along with some treatises and letters missing from the earlier edition, in a recent edition with an introduction by Eugenio Garin (Turin, 1962). The standard biography is still Girolamo Mancini's *Vita di Lorenzo Valla* (Florence, 1891). Valla's treatise on free will is available in English in Ernst Cassirer, Paul Oskar Kristeller, and John H. Randall, Jr., eds., *The Renaissance Philosophy of Man* (Chicago, 1948). *The Treatise of Lorenzo Valla on the Donation of Constantine* has been translated by C. B. Coleman (New Haven, 1922). The treatise on pleasure will be published under the title *De verro bono* by Maristella De Panizza Lorch.

Neal W. Gilbert

VALUE AND VALUATION. The terms "value" and "valuation" and their cognates and compounds are used in a confused and confusing but widespread way in our contemporary culture, not only in economics and philosophy but also and especially in other social sciences and humanities. Their meaning was once relatively clear and their use limited. "Value" meant the worth of a thing, and "valuation" meant an estimate of its worth. The worth in question was mainly economic or quasi-economic, but even when it was not, it was still worth of some sort—not beauty, truth, rightness, or even goodness. The extension of the meaning and use of the terms began in economics, or political economy, as it was then called. "Value" and "valuation" became technical terms central to that branch of economics which was labeled the theory of value. Then German philosophers, especially Rudolf Hermann Lotze, Albrecht Ritschl, and Nietzsche, began to take the notion of value and values in a much broader sense and to give it primary importance in their thinking.

Philosophers from the time of Plato had discussed a variety of questions under such headings as the good, the end, the right, obligation, virtue, moral judgment, aesthetic judgment, the beautiful, truth, and validity. In the nineteenth century the conception was born—or reborn, because it is essentially to be found in Plato—that all these questions belong to the same family, since they are all concerned with value or what ought to be, not with fact or what is, was, or will be. All these questions, it was believed, may not only be grouped under the general headings of value and valuation but are better dealt with and find a more systematic solution if they are thought of as parts of a general theory of value and valuation that includes economics, ethics, aesthetics, jurisprudence, education, and perhaps even logic and epistemology. This conception matured in the 1890s in the writings of Alexius Meinong and Christian von Ehrenfels, two Austrian followers of Franz Brentano. Through them and through others like Max Scheler and Nicolai Hartmann, two twentieth-century German followers of Husserl (himself

influenced by Brentano), the idea of a general theory of value became popular on the Continent and in Latin America. It had some influence in Great Britain, in the works of Bernard Bosanquet, W. R. Sorley, J. M. Mackenzie, John Laird, and J. N. Findlay, but rather less than elsewhere, for, on the whole, British philosophers have held to more traditional terms like "good" and "right." But it received an excited welcome in the United States just before and after World War I. The idea was introduced by Hugo Münsterberg and W. M. Urban, taken up by Ralph Barton Perry, John Dewey, D. H. Parker, D. W. Prall, E. W. Hall, and others, and later refurbished by S. C. Pepper and Paul W. Taylor. This wide-ranging discussion in terms of "value," "values," and "valuation" subsequently spread to psychology, the social sciences, the humanities, and even to ordinary discourse.

Philosophical usages. The uses of "value" and "valuation" are various and conflicting even among philosophers, but they may perhaps be sorted out as follows. (1) "Value" (in the singular) is sometimes used as an abstract noun (a) in a narrower sense to cover only that to which such terms as "good," "desirable," or "worthwhile" are properly applied and (b) in a wider sense to cover, in addition, all kinds of rightness, obligation, virtue, beauty, truth, and holiness. The term can be limited to what might be said to be on the plus side of the zero line; then what is on the minus side (bad, wrong, and so forth) is called disvalue. "Value" is also used like "temperature" to cover the whole range of a scale—plus, minus, or indifferent; what is on the plus side is then called positive value and what is on the minus side, negative value.

In its widest use "value" is the generic noun for all kinds of critical or pro and con predicates, as opposed to descriptive ones, and is contrasted with existence or fact. The theory of value, or axiology, is the general theory of all such predicates, including all the disciplines mentioned above. The classic example in English of this approach is the work of R. B. Perry. In its narrower use, "value" covers only certain kinds of critical predicates and is contrasted with descriptive predicates and even with other critical ones like rightness and obligation. In this case the theory of value, or axiology, is a part of ethics, rather than the other way around. The work of C. I. Lewis is the best example of the narrower approach.

Those who take the wider approach sometimes distinguish "realms of value"; Perry and Taylor, for example, list eight of these: morality, the arts, science, religion, economics, politics, law, and custom or etiquette. Even when "value" is used in the narrower sense, several meanings of the term, or kinds of value, are sometimes distinguished. (The narrower distinctions may also be recognized by those who use value in the wider sense.) These meanings correspond to the senses or uses of "good," which G. H. von Wright prefers to call "forms" or "varieties of goodness." Many classifications of kinds of value, or forms of goodness, have been proposed. Lewis distinguishes (a) utility or usefulness for some purpose; (b) extrinsic or instrumental value, or being good as a means to something desirable or good; (c) inherent value or goodness, such as the aesthetic value of a work of art in producing good experiences by being contemplated or heard; (d) intrinsic value, or being good or desirable either as an end or in itself, which is presupposed by both (*b*) and (*c*); (*e*) contributory value, or the value that an experience or part of an experience contributes to a whole of which it is a part (not a means or an object). A stick of wood may be useful in making a violin, a violin may be extrinsically good by being a means to good music, the music may be inherently good if hearing it is enjoyable, the experience of hearing it may be intrinsically good or valuable if it is enjoyable for its own sake, and it may also be contributively good if it is part of a good evening or week end.

Dewey, however, attacks the distinction between means and ends while stressing the notion of total value or goodness on the whole—goodness when all things are considered. To Lewis' list of kinds of value, some writers, W. D. Ross, for instance, would add moral value, the kind of value or goodness that belongs to a virtuous man, to good motives, or to morally approved traits of character. Von Wright distinguishes instrumental goodness (a good knife), technical goodness (a good driver), utilitarian goodness (good advice), hedonic goodness or pleasantness (a good dinner), and welfare (the good of man). He also mentions moral goodness but argues that it is a subform of utilitarian goodness; Ross would deny this.

(2) "Value" as a more concrete noun—for example, when we speak of "a value" or of "values"—is often used (*a*) to refer to what is valued, judged to have value, thought to be good, or desired. The expressions "his values," "her value system," and "American values" refer to what a man, a woman, and Americans value or think to be good. Such phrases are also used to refer to what people think is right or obligatory and even to whatever they believe to be true. Behind this widespread usage lies the covert assumption that nothing really has objective value, that "value" means being valued and "good" means being thought good. But the term "value" is also used to mean (*b*) what *has* value or *is* valuable, or good, as opposed to what is *regarded* as good or valuable. Then "values" means "things that have value," "things that are good," or "goods" and, for some users, also things that are right, obligatory, beautiful, or even true.

In both usage (*a*) and usage (*b*) it is possible to distinguish different kinds of values, corresponding to the different kinds of value or forms of goodness mentioned above. It is also common to distinguish more or less clearly between material and spiritual values or among economic, moral, aesthetic, cognitive, and religious values.

Some philosophers, especially those influenced by Scheler and Hartmann, think of "value" as a general predicate like "color," which subsumes more specific value predicates analogous to "red" or "yellow." They call these more specific value predicates "values" (*Werte, valeurs*). Just as "a color" does not mean "a thing that has color" but a particular color like red, so "a value" does not mean "a thing that has value" but a particular kind of value, like pleasure value or courage value. These philosophers call a thing that is good "a good" or "a value carrier," not "a value." Since the adjective "valuable" simply means "having value" or "being good" in some sense (or, perhaps better, "having a considerable amount of value"), much of the above will apply to it, *mutatis mutandis*.

(3) "Value" is also used as a verb in such expressions as "to value," "valuating," and "valued." "Valuing" is generally synonymous with "valuation" or "evaluation" when these are used actively to mean the act of evaluating and not passively to mean the result of such an act. But sometimes "valuation" and "evaluation" are used to designate only a certain kind of valuing, namely, one that includes reflection and comparison. In either case "valuation" may be, and is, used in wider or narrower senses corresponding to the wider and narrower uses of "value." For Dewey and Richard M. Hare it covers judgments about what is right, wrong, obligatory, or just, as well as judgments about what is good, bad, desirable, or worthwhile. For Lewis "valuation" covers only the latter use. The expression "value judgment" is also used in both of these ways. Among the writers who distinguish two main kinds of normative discourse, evaluating and prescribing, some, like Taylor, classify judgments of right and wrong as well as judgments of good and bad under evaluations and judgments, using "ought" under prescriptions; others put judgments of right and wrong under prescriptions.

Dewey always distinguishes two senses of "to value." It means either (*a*) to prize, like, esteem, cherish, or hold dear or (*b*) to apprize, appraise, estimate, evaluate, or valuate. In the second sense reflection and comparison are involved; in the first sense they are not. In the first sense, he seems to regard mere desiring or liking as a form of valuing. Others often follow him in this, but some writers limit valuing to acts in which something is not merely desired or liked but judged to be good or to have value. Even Perry, who holds that the statement "X is good" = "X has positive value" = "X is an object of favorable interest," insists that we must distinguish between desiring X and judging X to have value, which would be judging X to be desired.

Thus, words like "value" and "valuation" may be, and are, used in a variety of ways, even when they are used with some care—which is, unfortunately, not often the case both in and out of philosophy. In using the terms, one should choose a clear and systematic scheme and use it consistently. Because of the ambiguity and looseness that the terms often engender, it would seem advisable to use them in their narrower senses or not at all, keeping to more traditional terms like "good" and "right," which are better English, whenever possible.

Philosophical theories. Philosophical theories of value and valuation, whether conceived in the wider or in the narrower manner and whether formulated in the traditional or in the newer "value" vocabulary, have been of two sorts. Normative theories make value judgments or valuations; they tell us what is good or what has value, what is bad, and so on. Metanormative theories analyze value, valuation, and good; they neither make value judgments in this way nor tell us what is good or has value. Instead, they define what goodness and value are and what it means to say that something is good or has value. Sometimes philosophers also offer descriptive generalizations about what is valued or regarded as good in some culture or group of cultures, and explanatory theories about why this is so valued or regarded (Hume, Moritz Schlick, F. C. Sharp, John Ladd). However, this is usually ancillary to their discussions of normative or metanormative questions. In themselves such descriptive and explanatory theories belong to anthropology, psychology, and sociology, not to philosophy. Recently, many analytical philosophers have been maintaining that even normative theories, however important they may be, have no place in philosophy proper, where theories of value and valuation should be limited to metanormative questions.

Normative theories. In the broader conception, a normative theory of value must show, at least in general outline, what is good, bad, better, and best, and also what is right, obligatory, virtuous, and beautiful. In the narrower conception, normative theories of value have usually addressed themselves primarily to the question of what is good in itself or as an end or what has intrinsic value, an approach that Dewey has persistently attacked. They ask not what goodness and intrinsic value are but what the good is, what has value for its own sake, what is to be taken as the end of our pursuit or as the criterion of intrinsic worth.

Some theories have answered that the end or the good is pleasure or enjoyment or, alternatively, that the criterion of intrinsic value is pleasantness or enjoyableness. More accurately, they say that only experiences are intrinsically good, that all experiences which are intrinsically good are pleasant and vice versa, and that they are intrinsically good because and only because they are pleasant. These are the hedonistic theories of value, held by such thinkers as Epicurus, Hume, Bentham, J. S. Mill, Sidgwick, von Ehrenfels, Meinong (at first), and Sharp. There are also quasi-hedonistic theories in which the end or the good is said to be not pleasure but something very similar, such as happiness, satisfaction, or felt "satisfactoriness," to use Lewis' term. Examples are to be found in the writings of Dewey, Lewis, Parker, P. B. Rice, and perhaps Brand Blanshard.

Antihedonistic theories are of two kinds. Some agree that there is, in the final analysis, only one thing that is good or good-making but deny that it is pleasure or any other kind of feeling. Aristotle says it is eudaemonia (excellent activity); Augustine and Aquinas, communion with God; Spinoza, knowledge; F. H. Bradley, self-realization; Nietzsche, power. Others, such as Plato, G. E. Moore, W. D. Ross, Laird, Scheler, Hartmann, and Perry, are more "pluralistic," holding that there are a number of things which are good or good-making in themselves. They differ in their lists but all include two or more of the following: pleasure, knowledge, aesthetic experience, beauty, truth, virtue, harmony, love, friendship, justice, freedom, self-expression. Of course, hedonists and other "monistic" thinkers may also regard such things as intrinsically good but only if and because they are pleasant, self-realizing, or excellent.

Metanormative theories. The scope of metanormative theories may also be inclusive or limited, but both kinds will pose similar questions and offer similar answers. Their questions and answers have been variously stated in the formal or material mode, or the linguistic or nonlinguistic, but they will not be classified here.

One question or group of questions posed by metanormative theories concerns the nature of value and valuation:

what is goodness or value? what is the meaning or use of "good"? what is valuing? what are we doing or saying when we make a value judgment? A subquestion here is what moral value and evaluation are, and how they are distinct from nonmoral value and valuation, if at all. Another question or set of questions has to do with the justification or validity of value judgments and normative theories: can they be justified or established with any certainty by some kind of rational or scientific inquiry? can they be shown to have objective validity in any way? if so, how? what is the logic of reasoning in these matters, if there is one? Here a subquestion is what is the logic of moral justification or reasoning, if there is one, and is it in any way distinctive. Beyond this there is an even more "meta" level of questioning: what is the nature of a metanormative theory, and how can it be defended? This last problem, as well as the subquestions just mentioned, has frequently been discussed in the twentieth century and earlier but will not be considered here.

In reply to the first question or group of questions, some philosophers have held that terms like "value" and "good" stand for properties; that in value judgments we are ascribing these properties to objects or kinds of objects (including activities and experiences), although we may also be taking pro or con attitudes toward them; and that, therefore, value judgments are descriptive or factual in the sense of truly or falsely ascribing properties to things. They are therefore cognitivists or descriptivists in value theory. Of these the naturalists add that the property involved is a natural or empirical one, which can be defined. Aristotle, von Ehrenfels, and Perry claim that value is the relational property of being an object of desire or interest (an interest theory of value); Parker, that it is the satisfaction of desire (another interest theory of value); Lewis and Rice (as well as the early Meinong), that it is the quality of being enjoyed or enjoyable in some way (the affective theory of value). Santayana seems sometimes to hold one of these views, sometimes another, and sometimes to regard value as an indefinable natural quality ascribed to what we desire or enjoy.

Other cognitivists add that value or goodness is a metaphysical property which can neither be observed by or in ordinary experience nor made an object of empirical science. Examples of metaphysical definitions are being truly real (Neoplatonists), being ontologically perfect (Hegelian idealists), or being willed by God (theologians). Still others assert that intrinsic goodness or value is an indefinable nonnatural or nonempirical quality or property different from all other descriptive or factual ones (they even describe it as being nondescriptive or nonfactual). These philosophers are called intuitionists or nonnaturalists (Plato, Sidgwick, Moore, Ross, Laird, Scheler, Hartmann, and perhaps the later Meinong). They all hold that value belongs to objects independently of whether we desire, enjoy, or value them, and even independently of God's attitude toward them—as some metaphysical theorists and naturalists also do. Meinong, Scheler, Hartmann, and Hall contend that value is intuited through the emotions even though it is objective; Sidgwick, Ross, Laird, and others, that it is an object of intellectual intuition.

In recent decades many writers, both analytical philosophers and existentialists, have taken the position that value terms do not stand for properties, natural or nonnatural, and that value judgments are not property-ascribing statements but have some other kind of meaning or function. These writers have therefore been called noncognitivists or antidescriptivists. Their positive theories are varied. Some argue that value judgments are wholly or primarily embodiments or expressions of attitude, emotion, or desire, and/or instruments for evoking similar reactions in others (A. J. Ayer, Bertrand Russell, Charles L. Stevenson). Others maintain that this account of value terms and judgments is inadequate and that value judgments are to be thought of as prescriptions, recommendations, acts of grading, or simply as valuations, not something else (Hare, Taylor, Stephen E. Toulmin, Patrick H. Nowell-Smith, R. W. Sellars, and J. O. Urmson).

Whether value judgments are susceptible to being justified or proved, and, if so, how, depends very considerably on the position taken in answer to the questions regarding the meaning of "good." Some value judgments are derivative—for instance, the conclusion of the following inference:

> What is pleasant is good.
> Knowledge is pleasant.
> Therefore, knowledge is good.

The real question is about the justification of basic or nonderivative value judgments. According to the intuitionist, such judgments cannot be justified by argument, but they do not need to be, since they are intuitively known or self-evident. According to the naturalist, they can be established either by empirical evidence (in Perry's view, by empirical evidence about what is desired) or by the very meaning of the terms involved (analytically or by definition). According to the metaphysical and theological axiologist, they can be established either by metaphysical argument, or by divine revelation, or by definition. Noncognitivists, being of many persuasions, have various views about justification. Some extreme emotivists and existentialists assert or imply that basic value judgments are arbitrary, irrational, and incapable of any justification (Ayer and Jean-Paul Sartre). Others believe that there are intersubjectively valid conventions, like "What is pleasant is good," which warrant our arguing from certain considerations to conclusions about what is good (Toulmin). Still others contend, in different ways, that attitudes, recommendations, commitments, conventions, and, hence, value judgments may be rational or justified, even if they cannot be proved inductively or deductively (Hare, Taylor, J. N. Findlay, and, up to a point, Stevenson).

Bibliography

INTRODUCTIONS

Frondizi, Risieri, *What Is Value?*, translated by Solomon Lipp. La Salle, Ill., 1963. A useful elementary historical and critical work.
Frankena, William K., *Ethics*. Englewood Cliffs, N.J., 1963. Elementary and systematic.
Nowell-Smith, Patrick H., *Ethics*. London, 1954. A recent British systematic and analytical approach.

SYSTEMATIC DISCUSSIONS AND HISTORY

Blanshard, Brand, *Reason and Goodness*. London, 1961. Scholarly and clear.
Laird, John, *The Idea of Value*. Cambridge, 1929. Scholarly and complex.

USAGES OF TERMS

Garnett, A. Campbell, *The Moral Nature of Man*. New York, 1952. Ch. 4 is a useful, clear critique of prevailing semantic confusion.
Lepley, Ray, ed., *Value: A Cooperative Inquiry*. New York, 1949. Both this and the following work illustrate usages, and both contain some good essays by Americans.
Lepley, Ray, ed., *The Language of Value*. New York, 1957.

CONTINENTAL EUROPEAN WORKS

Ehrenfels, Christian von, *System der Werttheorie*, 2 vols. Leipzig, 1897–1898. An early theory of value.
Hartmann, Nicolai, *Ethics*, 3 vols., translated by Stanton Coit. London, 1932. An elaborate example of German intuitionism.
Meinong, Alexius, *Psychologisch-ethische Untersuchungen zur Werttheorie*. Graz, 1894. Another early theory of value and valuation.
Von Wright, Georg H., *The Varieties of Goodness*. London, 1963. One of the latest theories of value.

BRITISH WORKS

Findlay, John N., *Values and Intentions*. London and New York, 1961. A recent value theory influenced by both British and Continental writers.
Hare, Richard M., *The Language of Morals*. Oxford, 1952. An imperativist analysis of value judgments.
Moore, G. E., *Principia Ethica*. Cambridge, 1903. A famous early analytical approach.
Urmson, J. O., "On Grading." *Mind*, Vol. 59 (1950). A later analytical approach.

AMERICAN WORKS

Dewey, John, *Theory of Valuation*. Chicago, 1939. A brief statement of the instrumentalist theory of values.
Lewis, C. I., *An Analysis of Knowledge and Valuation*. La Salle, Ill., 1946. A variation of a pragmatic theory.
Perry, Ralph B., *General Theory of Value*. New York, 1926. A classic work.
Perry, Ralph B., *Realms of Value*. Cambridge, Mass., 1954. Restatement of Perry's value theory; applications to various fields.
Stevenson, Charles L., *Ethics and Language*. New Haven, 1944. An emotive theory.
Taylor, Paul W., *Normative Discourse*. Englewood Cliffs, N.J., 1961. "The first fullscale attempt to use the 'informal logic' approach in general theory of value" (Preface, p. xi).

WILLIAM K. FRANKENA

VALUE JUDGMENTS. See ENDS AND MEANS; HISTORY AND VALUE JUDGMENTS; VALUE AND VALUATION.

VAN HELMONT, JAN BAPTISTA. See HELMONT, JAN BAPTISTA VAN.

VANINI, GIULIO CESARE, was born in Taurisano, in the province of Lecce, Italy, in 1584 or early in 1585. After completing a course of study in law in Naples, he proceeded to Padua to study theology. He entered the order of the Carmelites, and he visited various Italian cities—Venice, Genoa, and perhaps Bologna—and traveled in Germany, England, and France. In 1612, in England, he abjured, but, having aroused suspicion because of his ideas, he moved on again. In 1615, in Lyon, he published his *Amphitheatrum Aeternae Providentiae* (published by the widow of Antoine De Harsy), and in 1616, in Paris, the dialogues, in four books, *De Admirandis Naturae Reginae Deaeque Mortialium Arcanis* (published by Adrian Périer). Both works were given the regular permission of the ecclesiastical authorities but nevertheless aroused suspicions. Vanini then went to Toulouse, where he taught and practiced medicine. In August, 1618, he was arrested by the Inquisition. He was condemned, and then in February, 1619, burned to death after horrible torture.

Vanini's work, which shows repeatedly a kinship with that of Averroës, reflects above all the influence of the writers of the fifteenth and sixteenth centuries, among whom he had a particular predilection for Pietro Pomponazzi, whom he called his master, the prince of the philosophers of his century, and a second Averroës ("in his body Pythagoras would have placed the spirit of Averroës"). Next to Pomponazzi he placed Girolamo Cardano, Julius Caesar Scaliger, and numerous others, whom he drew from freely. His liberal use of other sources, long passages of which he inserted, even verbatim, into his own works, has caused several recent historians to speak of plagiarism and of writings which are "devoid of originality and scientific integrity." In reality, his attitude toward using the writings of others was common in his time; the present-day preoccupation with the citation of sources did not exist (certain Latin writings of Giordano Bruno are a case in point). Furthermore, the writings from which Vanini borrowed generally underwent a marked transformation in his pages.

Intensely critical of all revealed religions (his "atheism" stemmed from this), Vanini believed strongly in the divinity of nature and in the immanence of God in nature, which is eternal and eternally regulated by strict laws ("Natura Dei facultas, imo Deus ipse"). He held that the world is without origin, at least so far as could be established by natural religion. The human spirit is material, the soul mortal. Using arguments and themes taken from Cardano, Vanini stated that there is a natural explanation for all supposedly exceptional and miraculous phenomena in universal determinism; and thus, going back to Pomponazzi, he interpreted rationally all the aspects and forms of religious life.

Despite his frequent declaration that, as a Christian, he would continue to accept on faith even that which reason had disproved, the radical bent of Vanini's criticism escaped no one, and, as the seventeenth century progressed, he became almost a symbol of "atheistic and libertine" thought.

Works by Vanini

Luigi Corvaglia, ed. *Le opere di Giulio Cesare Vanini e le loro fonti,* 2 vols. (Milan, 1933–1934), is a reprint of the original editions with the texts of the "sources" printed alongside to show the "plagiarism." See also Guido Porzio, *Le opere di Giulio Cesare Vanini tradotte per la prima volta in italiano con prefazione del traduttore,* 2 vols. (Lecce, Italy, no date; published 1913), which includes biography, documents, complete bibliography.

Works on Vanini

See F. Fiorentino, "Giulio Cesare Vanini e i suoi biografi," in *Studi e ritratti della rinascenza* (Bari, Italy, 1911); E. Namer, "Nuovi documenti su Vanini," in *Giornale critico della filosofia italiana,* Vol. 13 (1932), 161–198; E. Namer, *Documents sur la vie de Jules-César de Taurisano* (Bari, Italy, no date; published 1965); John Owen, *The Skeptics of the Italian Renaissance* (London, 1893), pp. 345–419; G. Spini, "Vaniniana," in *Rinascimento,* Vol. 1 (1950), 71–90; G. Spini, *Ricerca dei libertini* (Rome, 1950), pp. 117–135.

EUGENIO GARIN
Translated by *Robert M. Connolly*

VARISCO, BERNARDINO (1850–1933), Italian metaphysician, was born at Chiari (Brescia). It was only in the later part of his long life that he developed his philosophy, for he began as a teacher of science and his early outlook was characterized by empiricism and positivism. These views found expression in *Scienza e opinioni* (1901). Thereafter he became interested in the problem of reconciling the scientific and religious ways of understanding the world and moved into metaphysics. In 1906 he was appointed professor of theoretical philosophy at the University of Rome, where he remained until his retirement in 1925. His metaphysic was a philosophy of spirit in the manner of Leibniz and Lotze and won him a considerable reputation in Italy and elsewhere.

The empiricism of Varisco's earlier phase was still apparent in the approach that he employed in constructing his distinctive philosophy. His starting point is the given fact of a plurality of conscious subjects. Each of these has its own private perspective upon the world, and each is also a spontaneous center of activity. In the personal subject, a high level of rationality and self-consciousness has been reached, but this is surrounded by an extensive penumbra of subconsciousness. Varisco thinks of conscious life as shading off imperceptibly into lower levels. Below the level of man's personal existence there is animal life, and it is argued that this in turn shades off into so-called "inanimate" existence. Thus, Varisco arrives at a kind of monadology, or panpsychism. Reality is made up of an infinite number of subjects, although at the level of inanimate nature these subjects are very primitive and have nothing like the self-consciousness of the personal human subject.

Varisco's metaphysic has a dynamic aspect, for these subjects are in constant action and interaction. The variations set up are of two kinds. Some arise from spontaneous activity in the subjects themselves, and in this way Varisco provides for freedom and for what he calls an "alogical" factor in reality. The other kind of variations arises from the mutual interaction of the subjects, and this happens in regular ways, so that the universe has also an ordered, logical character.

The most obscure and presumably the weakest part of Varisco's philosophy is his attempt to move from the plurality of subjects to a unitary reality. His appeal is to the notion of "being," which, implicitly or explicitly, is present in every act of thought whereby a subject grasps an object. Being is identified with the universal subject, with thinking itself in all particular subjects and in the world. In *I massimi problemi,* Varisco says explicitly that the universal subject is a logical conception that falls short of the notion of a personal God, although he believed that teleology and the conservation of value point toward theism. However, in his posthumous *Dall'uomo a Dio* (1939) he completes his pilgrimage from positivism to theism, arguing for a God who limits himself by his creation so that men can cooperate with him in creative activity. Such a view, he believed, supports a religious attitude to life and is especially compatible with Christianity.

Works by Varisco

Scienza e opinioni. Rome, 1901.
La conoscenza. Pavia, 1905.
I massimi problemi. Milan, 1910. Translated by R. C. Lodge as *The Great Problems.* London and New York, 1914.
Conosci te stesso. Milan, 1912. Translated by Guglielmo Salvadori as *Know Thyself.* London and New York, 1915.
Sommario di filosofia. Rome, 1928.
Dall'uomo a Dio. Padua, 1939.

Works on Varisco

Chiapetta, L., *La teodicea di Bernardino Varisco.* Naples, 1938.
De Negri, E., *La metafisica di Bernardino Varisco.* Florence, 1929.
Drago, P. C., *La filosofia di Bernardino Varisco.* Florence, 1944.
Librizzi, C., *Il pensiero di Bernardino Varisco.* Padua, 1942; rev. ed., 1953.

JOHN MACQUARRIE

VARONA Y PERA, ENRIQUE JOSÉ (1849–1933), Cuban philosopher, statesman, and man of letters. Beginning in the mid-1870s, Varona dominated Cuban intellectual life for fifty years. He was a professor of philosophy at the University of Havana, was founding editor of *Revista cubana,* and took an active part in education and politics. A former member of the Spanish Cortes, he became a revolutionary colleague of José Martí, was appointed secretary of public instruction and fine arts after the 1898 revolution, and served as vice-president of Cuba from 1913 to 1917.

Varona, one of the leading Latin American positivists, adapted French positivism and British empiricism to the contemporary sociopolitical and cultural situation of Cuba. Logic, psychology, and ethics were his primary philosophic concerns.

Mill's analysis of induction served as the basis of Varona's work in logic. As a scientific study of the ways in which man thinks and learns, logic assists in providing methodologies for the particular sciences as well as for the educational process. There are three stages in any mental act: the first and third are directed toward the object of experience, the second consists exclusively of mental activity. Unrelated data are obtained from nature; they are then related significantly in terms of ideal constructs, and the resultant schema is again compared with experience through controlled experimentation.

In psychology the root problem is that of human freedom. Varona subordinated the study of psychology to that of physiology and accepted a strictly deterministic position. However, his concern for the political and cultural independence of Cuba demanded an interpretation of man which provided room for freedom. Although man is not free, the development of intelligence provides him with the ability to avoid being an automaton, to understand the nature of causal determination, and thereby to "train and direct it, which is tantamount to overcoming it."

The proper approach to the study of ethics is genetic. Morality is based on the social nature of man, which, in turn, has its roots in the evolutionary biological process. "Man is not sociable because he is moral. . . . Man becomes moral by virtue of being sociable" (*Conferencias filosóficas, tercera serie: Moral.* Havana, 1888, p. 10). Just as the biological organism is dependent upon its natural environment, so the human organism is dependent upon its social environment. Such social dependence constitutes social solidarity. Awareness of this dependence and conscious accommodation of the individual to the social milieu constitutes moral behavior.

Throughout Varona's work and especially in a final book of aphorisms, *Con el eslabón* (Manzanillo, 1927), a subtle, penetrating irony concerning the foibles of human thought and existence was evident.

Bibliography

Varona's collected works are *Obras,* 4 vols. (Havana, 1936–1938). Works on Varona include John H. Hershey, "Enrique José Varona, Cuban Positivist," in *The Humanist,* Vol. 3 (January 1944), 164 ff.; Medardo Vitier, *La filosofia en Cuba* (Mexico City, 1948), Ch. 11; and Humberto Piñera Llera, *Panorama de la filosofia cubana* (Washington, D.C., 1960), Ch. 5.

FRED GILLETTE STURM

VASCONCELOS, JOSÉ (1882–1959), Mexican politician and philosopher, was born in Oaxaca. Vasconcelos was active in the Mexican revolution, directed the reform of Mexican education as secretary of education in the early 1920s, ran unsuccessfully for the presidency in 1929, and subsequently was exiled for a time. He was rector of the National University of Mexico, visiting professor at the University of Chicago, and director of the Biblioteca Nacional de México. The sources of his philosophy were Pythagoras, Plotinus, Schopenhauer, Nietzsche, Whitehead, and especially Bergson. Of Latin American philosophers, Vasconcelos is the most original, venturesome, and impassioned.

He called his philosophy aesthetic monism, scientific realism, and organic logic. The system he developed stressed intuition in addition to scientific experience; the particular, concrete, and heterogeneous; organic wholes; the fluid, living, and psychical; and the methods of art rather than mathematics. The true method of philosophy, Vasconcelos claimed, is to understand the particular phenomenon, not by reducing it to the universal but by relating it to other particulars in an organic whole in which unity is achieved without sacrifice of individuality.

The pervasive term in Vasconcelos' theory of reality is energy, which is unformed in its primordial condition but takes on determinate structures in the three phenomenal orders of the atomic, cellular, and spiritual. The transformation in recent physics of the elementary particle from a rigid body to an "individualized dynamic frequency," Vasconcelos held, emphasizes activity and novelty in the atom, which are reminders of spirit. In the cellular order, internal purposes are introduced. Spirit is eminently creative, but its action follows structures, or a priori methods, of logical inference for intellect, of values or norms for will, and of aesthetic unities for feeling. The early thought of Vasconcelos was pantheistic, finding the creative principle in the self-sufficient pervasive energy of the world. His later thought, after he had returned to the Roman Catholic church, was theistic. It appears that in both periods "spirit," rudimentary or refined, was basic to his view of reality.

In Vasconcelos' aesthetics may be found implications for both reality and the life of spirit. The work of art, an emotionally intuited image, observes principles which, although more lucid in the work itself, have general application in reality. A musical scale is constructed by the musician out of the continuum of natural pitches; its members are discrete tones separated by intervals or jumps. The activity of constructing this scale is analogous to that of intelligence in separating and ordering the objects of sensation; the discontinuity of the tones is similar to that of quantum phenomena in physics. Musical compositions observe three modes of aesthetic unity—melody, harmony, and rhythm—in which the heterogeneous or discontinuous is unified without loss of diversity. A true metaphysics, fortified by modern science, finds the same types of unity in reality, unlike mathematics, which unifies by reduction to homogeneous quantities.

Art, according to Vasconcelos, expresses the transformations of the spirit in the pursuit of value. He distinguished three kinds of art. Apollonian art is formal and intellectual. It can be saved from decay in giganticism or sensuality only by a shift to the Dionysian mode of passionate affirmation of the human will. Dionysian art does not decline; passion either destroys the spirit or saves it by a change to religious ardor. In mystical art, passion is directed from a temporal and human object to an eternal and divine object. Passion need not retreat from fate, as the Greeks thought; as Christianity discovered, it can be fully satisfied in the divine.

A similar conclusion occurs in the ethics of Vasconcelos. A terrestrial ethics, exemplified diversely in empiricism, hedonism, Confucianism, humanism, and socialism, does not take man beyond his animal and human condition. (Apart from this deficiency, a limited socialism stripped of Marxist theory has merit; Vasconcelos was critical of capitalism.) Metaphysical ethics attempts to go further in the name of reason; but the rational universal law of Kant is a discipline appropriate for things and not for spirits. The highest ethics is revelatory; it combines transcendence, emotional illumination, and infinite love. Vasconcelos highly praised the wisdom of Buddhism and of Christianity, but he preferred Christianity because of its affirmation of life.

Bibliography

Principal works by Vasconcelos include *Pitágoras: Una teoría del ritmo* (Havana, 1916); *El monismo estético* (Mexico City, 1918); *Tratado de metafísica* (Mexico City, 1929); *Ética* (Madrid, 1932); *Estética* (Mexico City, 1936); *El realismo científico* (Mexico City, 1943); and *Lógica orgánica* (Mexico City, 1945).

Also see Patrick Romanell, *Making of the Mexican Mind* (Lincoln, Neb., 1952), Ch. 4.

ARTHUR BERNDTSON

VASQUEZ, GABRIEL (1549–1604), Neo-Scholastic theologian, was born at Villascuela del Haro, Spain, and died at Alcalá. Educated in the Jesuit houses of study in Spain, he taught moral philosophy at Ocaña from 1575 to 1577 and theology at Madrid and Alcalá. Eventually he succeeded Francisco Suárez in the chair of theology at Rome, where he taught from 1585 to 1592. His *Commentaria ac Disputationes in Primam Partem S. Thomae* (8 vols., Alcalá, 1598–1615), a lengthy commentary on Part I of Aquinas' *Summa Theologiae*, contains much philosophical speculation. A posthumously published summary of this work, *Disputationes Metaphysicae* (Madrid, 1617), helped to popularize his philosophy.

Vasquez' most influential contribution lies in his distinction between the formal concept in the understanding (a mental entity, or "idea," constituting knowledge, *qualitas ipsa cognitionis*) and the objective concept which is the reality that is known (*res cognita*) through the formal concept (*Commentaria* I, 76, nn. 2–5). Since, in the view of Vasquez, the actual being (*esse*) of the thing that is known is identified with the act whereby it is known (*cognosci*), we may have here one of the sources of idealism in modern philosophy. There is little doubt that Descartes's Jesuit teachers knew the thought of Vasquez, and hence the Cartesian teaching that ideas are direct objects of knowledge may owe a good deal to Vasquez (see the study by Dalbiez). Like Suárez, Vasquez introduced many changes into Thomistic metaphysics. He rejected the view that essence and existence are really distinct, opposed the theory that act is limited by the potency in which it is received, and argued that matter as marked by quantity (*materia signata quantitate*) cannot be the principle that individuates bodily things.

In psychology Vasquez also had teachings that are highly personal. He saw no reason for postulating two intellectual powers in man (agent and possible intellects, in Aquinas) and implied that the one understanding can do the work of both. He regarded man as a composite of soul and body, but he treated these two "parts" almost as if they were two different substances joined together by a peculiar sort of metaphysical semireality which he called a "mode." Here again, we may have a source of Descartes's mind–body problem and of the psychophysical parallelism of post-Cartesianism.

In his long discussion of St. Thomas' proofs for the existence of God, Vasquez again showed a critical attitude toward the thought of Aquinas. In place of the traditional Five Ways of demonstration (which require the acceptance of a metaphysics of causality), Vasquez described a whole new series of arguments of his own. God's existence is demonstrated from the claim that morality requires it (an argument which reappears in Kant) and from various types of "spontaneous assents" based on what one learns from parents, on a survey of the whole of reality (*ex rerum universitate*), and on our knowledge of the divine conservation and governance of the world (*Commentaria* I, 19, nn. 9–12). It is evident that Vasquez' work is one of the reasons that Thomism came to be misunderstood in modern philosophy.

Bibliography

Dalbiez, R., "Les Sources scolastiques de la théorie cartésienne de l'être objectif." *Revue d'histoire de la philosophie,* Vol. 3 (1939), 464–472.

Gilson, Étienne, *Études sur le rôle de la pensée médiévale dans la formation du système cartésien.* Paris, 1930. Pp. 203–207.

Solana, M., *Los grandes escolásticos españoles.* Madrid, 1928. Pp. 109–128.

VERNON J. BOURKE

VAUVENARGUES, LUC DE CLAPIERS, MARQUIS DE (1715–1747), French moralist and epigrammatist, was born at Aix-en-Provence. He early revealed a lofty character that despised egotism and pettiness. Ambitious for glory, he became an army officer at the age of 17, despite a weak physique. He served throughout the Italian campaign of 1734. The later German campaign of 1741, especially the harsh retreat from Prague, ruined his health, forcing him to retire at the age of 26. His hope of a career in diplomacy was dashed by lack of fortune and protection. While vainly waiting at Aix for replies to his petitions for appointment to a post, he contracted a severe case of smallpox which left him disfigured and sickly. His last years were spent in Paris, in unhappy poverty and solitude (despite Voltaire's admiration), but he endured the injustice of men and events with stoic resignation rather than with bitterness. During this period he wrote his *Introduction à la connaissance de l'esprit humain* (Paris, 1746; augmented edition, 1747), which included the supplement "Réflexions et maximes." He also wrote character sketches in the fashion of La Bruyère, although less brilliantly, and *Réflexions sur divers auteurs,* a work of generally sound and objective criticism. He is particularly known for his maxims.

Vauvenargues's life and writings are characterized by their contradictions rather than by their consistency. Weak in health, he had a proud, heroic soul; poverty-stricken, he refused to consider gainful work out of aristocratic prejudice and a dislike for restraint. A lover of peace, he praised war and the martial virtues; opposed to ethical absolutes, he considered greatness of soul and action to be absolute virtues. Extremely unhappy and frustrated in life, his writings are resolutely optimistic; almost without friends, his correspondence reveals a noble ideal of friendship. Inclined to sentiment, he was from youth enamored of Plutarch, Seneca and the Stoic attitudes.

Vauvenargues was a vigorous but not a profound or systematic thinker. He is notable for his incisive insights and formulations, principally in regard to character and moral ideals. He was a deist and not a Christian; but, believing religion necessary to social order, he opposed the propaganda of the *philosophes.* His philosophy, however, was secular in spirit, concerned with the problem of human nature and of what men should be and how they should live. He defended the worth of human nature both against the pessimism of the Christian doctrine of original sin and the corrosive cynicism of La Rochefoucauld. Like other thinkers of his time, he justified the passions. Following Spinoza, he divided the passions into two kinds, according to their motivation: "They have their principle in the love of being [and desire for its] perfection, or in the feeling of its imperfection or withering." However, he warned against submitting to a single dominating passion. In a phrase that calls to mind both Pascal and Niebuhr, Vauvenargues said of man, "The feeling of his imperfection makes his eternal torture." Although he believed that man's need for greatness and importance is laudable, he also maintained that men should respond with charity to the needs of others. Vauvenargues's moments of humanitarianism, however, were devoid of sentimentalism.

Vauvenargues wished to defend the value of self-interest, which is naturally a good, and also to preserve the ethical character of acts. He adopted two main approaches. Before Rousseau did, Vauvenargues distinguished between *amour propre* and *amour de nous-mêmes. Amour de nous-mêmes* allows us to seek happiness outside ourselves: "One is not his own unique object." There is, then, a difference between the satisfaction of *amour propre* and its sacrifice. Against those who held that all acts are motivated by self-interest Vauvenargues maintained that it is absurd to call sacrifice of life, for example, an act of self-interest, for in such an act we consider ourselves as the least part of the whole and lose everything. Still combating La Rochefoucauld, Vauvenargues also argued that the criterion of acts is their effect on others; acts are virtuous if they tend to the good of all, even if they also satisfy self-interest. This definition opened a line of argument that had dangerous consequences in the hands of the materialists: (1) If each man must satisfy his self-interest where he can, men may be considered "fortunately born" or "unfortunately born" but not responsible for their acts. (2) Ethical and political considerations became fused, and eventually, with Rousseau, Fichte, and Hegel, this led to the concept of the "ethical state." How should acts be judged? "Reason deceives us more often than the heart," declared Vauvenargues; like Rousseau, he trusted the "first impulse."

Vauvenargues believed that in regard to happiness, too, each man must follow his fated way; no philosophical formula can guide him. But he did offer one principle: "There is no enjoyment except in proportion as one acts, and our soul possesses itself truly only when it exerts itself completely." To give up action is to fall into nothingness. Existence is a function of becoming. Vauvenargues satirized pitilessly both the indolent and those who engage in aimless agitation. Activity, courage, glory, and ambition summarize his ideal of life and his concept of virtue. Greatness of soul is consistent with evil, as in Catiline; all depends on character and education. The great soul does not care about public esteem; true glory is an intimate feeling, self-satisfying to the point where it may paradoxically disdain action.

Although Vauvenargues was not interested in political philosophy, he did argue against the notion that men are, or may be naturally, politically or socially equal: "Law cannot make men equal in spite of nature." Hierarchy, in all respects, is inevitable.

Vauvenargues frequently espoused contradictory views. Although he developed no important theoretical positions, he occupies a leading rank in the long line of what the French term "moralists," excelling in psychological portraits and the striking but abstract formula of the maxim.

Bibliography

Vauvenargues's works were published in a collected edition as *Oeuvres completes,* in 4 vols. (Paris, 1821); his moral works were published as *Oeuvres morales,* in 3 vols. (Paris, 1874).

For literature on Vauvenargues, see F. Vial, *Une Philosophie et une morale du sentiment: Luc de Clapiers, marquis de Vauvenargues* (Paris, 1938), and G. Lanson, *Le Marquis de Vauvenargues* (Paris, 1930).

L. G. CROCKER

VAZ FERREIRA, CARLOS (1872–1958), Uruguayan educator and philosopher, was born in Montevideo. He became a professor of philosophy and rector at the University of Montevideo and played a prominent part in the theory and administration of primary and secondary education in Uruguay. He wrote voluminously and was a popular lecturer. As a result, he was for several decades a major intellectual force in his country. At various times and in various respects, he was influenced by Spencer, Mill, James, and Bergson, without full commitment to any of them.

Vaz Ferreira was impressed by the fluid complexity of experience, thought, and reality. Words and logical forms impose false precision and system on the contents of thought. The remedy is not a flight from reason but the development of a plastic reason close to experience, life, and instinct, alert to degrees of probability and unwilling to assent beyond the warrant of the question and evidence. The formulation and disposition of metaphysical questions requires the highest degree of caution, but metaphysics is both legitimate and necessary. It is impossible to move far in science without running into metaphysical questions, and it is necessary to cultivate metaphysics in order to understand the symbolic and limited nature of science and to counteract the bad metaphysics that comes into being when metaphysics is neglected. Vaz Ferreira was critical of positive religion but was sympathetic to religion as the emotional apprehension of a possible transcendent being.

The ethics of Vaz Ferreira showed the same skepticism fused with marked human warmth and moral insight. Ethical principles cannot be stated without exceptions or descent into casuistry. Ideals clash and choices are usually between alternatives that contain some evil. An ethically sensitive person therefore is more subject than others to doubt, crisis, and remorse: satisfied conscience is more readily found in those who have a narrow awareness and ready formulas. But an ethically sensitive person may exemplify the perfection of individual morality, in which are combined a feeling for each individual act and a care for all possible results. Vaz Ferreira held that there has been moral progress in the course of history: Ideals have been added from time to time, more persons now share to

some degree in all ideals, and there is greater resistance to evil.

Bibliography

Vaz Ferreira's principal works include *Los problemas de la libertad* ("Problems of Liberty," Montevideo, 1907); *Conocimiento y acción* ("Knowledge and Action," Montevideo, 1908); *Moral para intelectuales* ("Ethics for Intellectuals," Montevideo, 1909); *El pragmatismo* (Montevideo, 1909); *Lógica viva* ("Living Logic," Montevideo, 1910); *Sobre los problemas sociales* ("On Social Problems," Montevideo, 1922); *Fermentario* (Montevideo, 1938).

See also Arturo Ardao, *Introducción a Vaz Ferreira* (Montevideo, 1961).

ARTHUR BERNDTSON

VEBLEN, THORSTEIN BUNDE (1857–1929), American economist and social theorist. Veblen is perhaps best known for his ironic style, a style that was at one with his life. Although he is still thought of abroad as the most influential American social scientist, among social scientists in America his influence has almost vanished. He is virtually unknown to college students, even if a scattered lot of Veblen's concepts—most obviously, "conspicuous consumption"—are unwittingly part of their speech and analyses.

Born on a Wisconsin farm, Veblen developed the most comprehensive and penetrating analysis of American industrial society in the early twentieth century. He emphasized qualitative relationships in the historical process, and his aim was an inclusive theory of social change. However, the largest number of those who have walked in Veblen's footsteps are known for quantitative, essentially unhistorical, often antitheoretical investigations. Where his followers have not deviated from his work in these ways, they have in another: Veblen called for, if he did not usually practice, dispassionate social analysis; many of his most fervent disciples are also quite fervent in their social analyses.

Like his contemporary, Charles S. Peirce, Veblen was a scholar of great intellectual achievement whose academic career was, at best, undistinguished. He took his doctorate in philosophy at Yale, whence he moved to Cornell to study economics. In a year he moved to the new University of Chicago, where he taught, and he also edited the *Journal of Political Economy.* Before long acrimony between Veblen and the administration over his academic and social nonconformity developed to a point where the happiest step for all concerned was for Veblen to leave Chicago. That experience, added to by similar ones at his next teaching post at Stanford, prompted Veblen to write one of his most scathing, if also very useful and sound, books: *The Higher Learning in America: A Memorandum on the Conduct of Universities by Businessmen* (New York, 1918). The original subtitle, abandoned for one reason or another, was "A Study in Total Depravity."

Stanford and Veblen failed to cement relations, and Veblen drifted to the University of Missouri, where he was sheltered by the eminent economist Herbert Davenport. Lectures at the New School for Social Research in New York City, and a brief interlude with the federal government, for which he wrote memoranda connected with World War I, ended Veblen's professional career. The department of economics at Cornell chose to add him to its faculty but that wish was denied by the university administration. Veblen spent his last few years unproductively, in a cabin in the Stanford hills, where he died, embittered against society.

The prime influences on Veblen appear to have been Hume, Darwin, and Marx—although the influence of each was much transmuted by the mind and the circumstances of Veblen. The skepticism of Hume and the evolutionary approach of Darwin combined with the American scene to impel Veblen to launch a barrage of telling criticism (in essays in *The Place of Science in Modern Civilization*, New York, 1919) at what he took to be the metaphysical, teleological, and optimistic qualities of Marxian analysis. But Veblen was not so much a critic as an adaptor of Marx, and his own works may be looked at most usefully in that light.

Darwinian concepts aside, the starting point of Veblen's analysis of society and of social change was fundamentally Marxian. The relationship of tension and change that Marx attributed to the conflict between "the forces of production" and "the mode of production" are present in Veblen's close equivalents, technology and institutions. For both men this relationship deserves and requires investigation within a framework of history (for Marx) or the genetic process (for Veblen).

But if the starting point for Veblen was the same as that of Marx, it was also there that basic similarities ended. For Marx the nineteenth-century assumptions of rationality went unquestioned, but for Veblen those assumptions were high on the list of matters to be investigated. As a consequence Veblen believed that a theory of social change required the integration of social psychology (and the psychology of related matters, such as nationalism and patriotism) with economics, politics, and history. Stemming from this is another difference: For Marx there were "general laws of motion of capitalist society" discoverable by the investigator; for Veblen those general laws had to be so qualified by national and cultural differences that it was not only plausible but also probable that capitalism would work out differently in different nations. Thus the very general quality of the conclusions to be found in *Capital*, when compared with Veblen's differing expectations for capitalism in Great Britain and Germany (in *Imperial Germany and the Industrial Revolution*, New York, 1915) and in the United States (in *The Theory of Business Enterprise*, New York, 1904, and in *Absentee Ownership*, New York, 1923). The point is illustrated by Veblen's findings about Japan and Germany, which (with much prescience) he saw as facing very much the same future despite their very different economic histories. For Veblen the decisive factors for the two nations were those making for extreme nationalism and social irrationality, moving them in much the same direction at much the same speed.

There is a final and striking difference between Marx and Veblen. In addition to his role as a social scientist, Marx was a political activist and propagandist, and his scientific writings were integrally connected with his political aims, concerning which Marx was optimistic.

Veblen was politically aloof, except for a few periods such as his wartime propagandistic activity, and his role was that of Cassandra. Marx saw the class struggle as the means by which the contradictions between the forces and the mode of production would one day necessarily bring about the desired socialist society. Although Veblen would have found that socialist society less repulsive than the capitalist society he analyzed, his mood was gloomy and his vision apocalyptic, as suggested in one of his better-known but by no means unrepresentative observations in *The Instinct of Workmanship* (New York, 1914, p. 25): ". . . history records more frequent and more spectacular instances of the triumph of imbecile institutions over life and culture than of peoples who have saved themselves alive out of a desperately precarious institutional situation, such, for instance, as now faces the people of Christendom."

Veblen's critical energies were spent most persistently in attacking the business system and nationalism, in that order. But he reserved his most savage wit for organized religion, which he considered a special—and the most successful—form of salesmanship (see the appendix to Ch. 11 of *Absentee Ownership*), manned by mental defectives whose business it is "to promise everything and deliver nothing."

Bibliography

Of Veblen's 11 books, his first, *The Theory of the Leisure Class* (New York, 1899), was the most influential and most fundamental.

For the definitive biography of Veblen, see Joseph Dorfman, *Thorstein Veblen and His America* (New York, 1934).

For the most recent account of Veblen as an economist, see Douglas Dowd, *Thorstein Veblen* (New York, 1964). See also David Riesman, *Thorstein Veblen, A Critical Interpretation* (New York, 1953; 2d ed., New York, 1960). Riesman is one of Veblen's severer critics.

DOUGLAS F. DOWD

VECCHIO, GIORGIO DEL. See DEL VECCHIO, GIORGIO.

VEDA. See INDIAN PHILOSOPHY.

VEDANTA. See INDIAN PHILOSOPHY.

VENN, JOHN (1834–1923), British logician, was born at Drypool, Hull, the elder son of the Reverend Henry Venn, a prominent evangelical divine. After early education at Highgate and Islington proprietary schools, he entered Gonville and Caius College, Cambridge, in 1853. On graduating Sixth Wrangler in 1857, he became a fellow and remained on the foundation for 66 years, until his death. During the last 20 years of his residence he was also president of the college. Venn took orders in 1858 and served as a curate in parishes near London before returning to Cambridge as college lecturer in moral sciences in 1862. He married in 1867. In 1869 he was Hulsean lecturer and published thereafter a work entitled *On Some Characteristics of Belief* (London, 1870), but contact with Henry Sidgwick and other Cambridge agnostics, plus the reading of De Morgan, Boole, Austin, and Mill had the effect of transferring his interests from theology almost wholly to logic, and in 1883 he gave up his orders without altogether withdrawing from the church. In the same year he became a fellow of the Royal Society and took the degree of doctor of science.

Venn was among those responsible for the development of the moral sciences tripos at Cambridge and in the course of his teaching published successively the three works by which he is now remembered: *The Logic of Chance* (London, 1866; 3d ed., 1888); *Symbolic Logic* (London, 1881; 2d ed., 1894); and *The Principles of Empirical or Inductive Logic* (London, 1889; 2d ed., 1907). In 1888 he presented his extensive collection of books on logic to the university library and turned in later years to antiquarian pursuits, writing the history of his college and his family and collaborating with his son, J. A. Venn, in the preparation of Part I of *Alumni Cantabrigienses* (4 vols., London, 1922). Venn was an accomplished linguist and throughout most of his long life an active botanist and mountaineer. In addition to designing a simple mechanical contrivance to illustrate his well-known logical diagrams, he is said to have invented a very successful machine for bowling at cricket.

Venn has no strong claim to be regarded as an original thinker. His general position in philosophy was that of an orthodox, though unusually cautious and skeptical, empiricist. Outside the fields of logic and methodology he contributed little of importance, and even within them his role was essentially that of a critic and expositor of ideas first mooted by other men. In that capacity, however, his writings are marked by an acumen, learning, and lucidity which rank them among the best productions of their day. Within its limits, therefore, his reputation is still a high one.

Logic. Venn was a follower of Boole and to a lesser extent of Mill and a defender of both against the criticisms of Jevons on the one hand and of the idealist logicians on the other. His *Symbolic Logic* is an attempt to show not merely that the Boolean algebra "works" but also that it is in the main line of historical tradition and that its supposedly mathematical obscurities are in fact intelligible from a purely logical point of view. Like De Morgan, he is aware of the element of convention in the choice of a logical standpoint and hence of the possibility of alternative versions of the basic propositional forms. He thus contrasts the four Aristotelian (or "predicative") types of proposition with the eight forms of Sir William Hamilton (which reduce on analysis to the five possible relations of inclusion and exclusion between pairs of classes), and compares them both with the fifteen possibilities that arise on his own "existential" view, based on the emptiness or occupancy of the four "compartments" marked out by a pair of terms and their negatives. Unlike some of his predecessors, he sees the difference as one of convenience rather than correctness, and so finds it unnecessary to dispute the merits of the older logic in order to vindicate the claims of the new. A similar tolerance is apparent in his treatment of the vexed issue concerning the "existential import" of propositions, where, after careful discussion, he opts for the presumption that universal propositions do not imply the existence of members in the subject class—a view that the great majority of writers from J. N. Keynes onwards

have since found reason to accept. Less open-minded, perhaps, is his attitude to Jevons' reforms of the Boolean calculus; but he made several improvements of his own, notably in the writing of particular propositions as inequations, and, by the introduction of his diagrammatic methods, he did more than anyone else to render the workings of that calculus intelligible to the nonmathematical mind.

Probability. *The Logic of Chance* is also a work of much value to those embroiled in the mathematical complications of the theory of probability. The rationalistic handling of this subject by earlier writers was not to Venn's taste, and he recognized more clearly than they did the difficulties of relating their a priori computations to the realities of uncertain reasoning in everyday life. Following the suggestions of Leslie Ellis, he therefore identifies the probability of events not with the amount of belief it is rational to have in them but with their statistical frequency of occurrence in the generic class of events to which they belong. He assumes, that is, that the world contains series of resembling events in which individual irregularity in the possession of properties is combined with aggregate regularity "in the long run." The assignment of probability to a type of event is thus a mere matter of ascertaining the relative frequency with which it tends, increasingly, to occur as the series is extended to large numbers; and this is, in principle, not a subjective affair but a perfectly empirical and objective type of inquiry into the properties of a certain kind of group. To define probability in this way is, as Venn realized, to restrict it more narrowly than is usually done. No meaning can properly be attached to the probability of a single event, and the notion becomes equally inapplicable to the large range of judgments expressing partial belief (in theories and the like) which had hitherto been dealt with under this head. There are difficulties, moreover (as he also recognized), in assuming that observed frequencies are a reliable clue to "long-run" or "limiting" frequencies—that it is possible, in effect, on inductive grounds to arrive at such long-run frequencies by means of sample observations, however extended. For such a conclusion can itself be only probable, and that in a sense which Venn does not offer to define. Thus a knowledge of statistical frequency, even if obtainable, would be no sufficient ground for preferring one expectation to another. Probability, as Venn conceives it, is clearly not the guide of life.

Scientific method. The frequency theory of probability has had able defenders since Venn's time and is now less vulnerable to criticism. His version of it remains, however, the classical one, and the majority of later exponents acknowledge their debt to him. By comparison, the scientific methodology set forth in *Empirical Logic* has suffered somewhat from its association with that of Mill, on which it is largely modeled and whose conclusions it largely accepts. Venn differs from Mill chiefly in setting greater store by laws of coexistence than by laws of causal succession. The idea of causation he considers too crude and popular in conception to be of much use in science, and he is accordingly skeptical as to the value of the inductive methods. So far from being a reliable instrument for the discovery of causes, Mill's canons of induction are effective, he thinks, only where the conditions of the problem and its possible solutions have been narrowly circumscribed in advance, and under ordinary circumstances this can seldom be done. Inductive procedures are thus by no means so conclusive as Mill supposed, though we are not therefore justified in assuming, with Jevons, that they can be rationalized by appeal to the calculus of probability. Judgments of probability themselves make use of induction, and the two must therefore be kept, so far as possible, distinct. More generally, the use of formal methods in the classification, ordering, and prediction of natural phenomena can never be more than approximate, owing to the number of simplifying assumptions necessary before it can get under way. Venn's subsidiary discussions of definition, division, hypothesis, measurement, etc., are similarly concerned to stress the difficulties of applying principles to cases and the amount that is taken for granted in doing so. Though less closely acquainted than some other writers with the details of scientific practice, he is also less liable than most to mistake the logic of science for a description of its technique.

Bibliography

Venn has been somewhat neglected by historians of philosophy and no comprehensive study of him exists. For a serviceable brief account, see J. A. Passmore, *A Hundred Years of Philosophy* (London, 1957), pp. 134–136. His views on probability are most fully criticized in J. M. Keynes, *Treatise on Probability* (London, 1921).

P. L. HEATH

VERIFIABILITY PRINCIPLE. The most distinctive doctrine of the logical positivists (see LOGICAL POSITIVISM) was that for any sentence to be cognitively meaningful it must express a statement that is either analytic or empirically verifiable. It was allowed that sentences may have "emotive," "imperative," and other kinds of meaning (for example, "What a lovely present!" or "Bring me a glass of water!") even when they have no cognitive meaning, that is, when they do not express anything that could be true or false, or a possible subject of knowledge. But—leaving aside sentences expressing analytic statements (see LINGUISTIC THEORY OF THE A PRIORI)—for a sentence to have "cognitive," "factual," "descriptive," or "literal" meaning (for example, "The sun is 93 million miles from the earth") it was held that it must express a statement that could, at least in principle, be shown to be true or false, or to some degree probable, by reference to empirical observations. The iconoclasm of the logical positivists was based on this criterion of meaning, for according to the verifiability principle a great many of the sentences of traditional philosophy (for example, "Reality is spiritual," "The moral rightness of an action is a nonempirical property," "Beauty is significant form," "God created the world for the fulfillment of his purpose") must be cognitively meaningless. Hence, like Wittgenstein in the *Tractatus Logico-philosophicus,* they held that most of the statements to be found in traditional philosophy are not false but nonsensical. The verifiability principle, it was maintained, demonstrates the impossibility of metaphysics, and from this it was concluded that empirical science is the only method by which we can have knowledge concerning the world.

The verifiability principle stands historically in a line of direct descent from the empiricism of Hume, J. S. Mill, and Ernst Mach. It has some affinities with pragmatism and operationalism, but it differs from them in some important respects. Pragmatism, as presented by C. S. Peirce, William James, and John Dewey, is the view that the "intellectual purport" of any symbol consists entirely in the practical effects, both on our conduct and on our experiences, that would follow from "acceptance of the symbol." This view, unlike the verifiability principle, makes the meaning of a sentence relative to certain human interests and purposes and to the behavior adopted for the realization of these purposes. Operationalism, as held by P. W. Bridgman and others, is the view that the meaning of a term is simply the set of operations that must be performed in order to apply the term in a given instance. Thus, according to this view, the meaning, or rather *a* meaning, of the term "length" is given by specifying a set of operations to be carried out with a measuring rod. Moritz Schlick and other logical positivists sometimes said that the meaning of a sentence is the method of its verification. But, unlike the advocates of operationalism, they meant by "the method of verification" not an actual procedure but the logical possibility of verification. The verifiability principle had among its immediate antecedents Schlick's *Allgemeine Erkenntnislehre* (Berlin, 1918) and Rudolf Carnap's *Der logische Aufbau der Welt* (Berlin, 1928). It was first formulated explicitly by Friedrich Waismann in his "Logische Analyse des Wahrscheinlichkeitsbegriffs" (1930) and subsequently by Schlick, Carnap, Otto Neurath, Hans Reichenbach, Carl Hempel, A. J. Ayer, and other logical positivists in numerous publications.

PROBLEMS RAISED BY THE PRINCIPLE

The controversial questions concerning the principle are: (1) What is it to be applied to—propositions, statements or sentences? (2) Is it a criterion for determining what the meaning of any particular sentence is, or is it simply a criterion of whether a sentence is meaningful? (3) What is meant by saying that a statement is verifi*able*, or falsifi*able*, even if in practice it has not been, and perhaps cannot be, verified, or falsified? (4) What type of statement directly reports an empirical observation, and how do we ascertain the truth-value of such a statement? (5) Is the principle itself either analytic or empirically verifiable, and if not, in what sense is it meaningful? (6) Is the question that the principle is intended to answer (that is, the question "By what general criterion can the meaning or the meaningfulness of a sentence be determined?") a logically legitimate question?

What is the principle to be applied to? In some of the earlier formulations of the verifiability principle it is presented as a criterion for distinguishing between meaningful and meaningless propositions. However, in an accepted philosophical usage, every proposition is either true or false, and hence a fortiori a proposition cannot be meaningless. To meet this point some of the later exponents of the principle say that a grammatically well-formed indicative sentence, whether it is cognitively meaningful or not, expresses a "statement"; the term "proposition" is retained for what is expressed by a cognitively meaningful sentence—that is, propositions are treated as a subclass of statements. The verifiability principle is then presented as a criterion for distinguishing between meaningful and meaningless statements. This procedure, however, presupposes a usage for "cognitively meaningful sentence," and indeed it is sentences that are normally said to be meaningful or not. Consequently, in still other formulations the principle is presented as applying directly to sentences; the objection to this is that sentences are not normally said to be true or false, and hence they are not said to be verifiable or falsifiable.

In order to meet these difficulties, sentences, statements, and propositions may be distinguished in the following way: A sentence, as we shall understand it, belongs to a particular language, it is meaningful or not, but it is not properly said to be true or false, or to stand in logical relations to other sentences, or to be verifiable or falsifiable. A statement is what is expressed in certain circumstances by an indicative sentence, and the same statement may be expressed by different sentences in the same or in different languages; a statement is properly said to be true or false, it does stand in logical relations to other statements, and it is verifiable or falsifiable. What can or cannot be said of statements applies equally to propositions, except that a proposition cannot be meaningless, that is, it cannot be expressed by a meaningless sentence.

For convenience we shall sometimes speak of sentences as being verifiable or not, and of statements as being meaningful or not. But, more strictly, we shall understand the verifiability principle as claiming that the cognitive meaning or meaningfulness of a *sentence* is to be determined by reference to the verifiability (or falsifiability) of the *statement* expressed by the sentence.

A criterion of meaning or meaningfulness? The earliest presentations of the verifiability principle identified the meaning of a sentence with the logical possibility of verifying the corresponding statement, and apparently, in the last analysis, with the occurrence of certain experiences. This has some initial plausibility in the case of "empirical sentences," that is, sentences containing, apart from nondescriptive expressions, only empirical predicates (for example, "red," "round," "middle C"). An empirical predicate is, by definition, one that stands for a property that can be observed or experienced. Consequently, in the case of such a sentence as "This is red," there is a natural tendency to say that the meaning of the sentence is given by the experience that would verify it. The meaning is understood by anyone who can use the sentence for the purpose of identifying red objects when he sees them and cannot be understood by anyone who cannot identify red objects. It might be argued that a congenitally blind person could be said to understand the sentence "This is red" if he were able to identify red objects in some other way, by touch, for example. But in that case, an early adherent of the verifiability principle might reply, the predicate "red" has, for the person in question, not a visual but a tactual meaning. Our ability to understand empirical predicates, he might say, is plainly restricted by our capacity for sensory discrimination. For example, a person may be able to give a verbal definition of "C♭" as "the note midway

between the notes designated by 'C' and 'C♯'"; but there is an important sense in which he does not know what "C♭" means if he is not able to discriminate quarter tones. It may be fairly objected, however, that this argument rests on the ambiguities of the words "meaning," "stands for," and "designates"; for example, the sense in which a term may be said to have a "tactual meaning" if it designates something tactual is not the sense in which a sentence may have a "cognitive or factual meaning." Moreover, it cannot be correct to identify the meaning of a sentence with the experiences that would verify it, for the characteristics that can be appropriately attributed to an experience cannot be appropriately attributed to the meaning of a sentence, nor conversely—for example, the meaning of a sentence does not occur at a particular time or with a certain intensity, as does an experience. And finally, if the meaning of a sentence were identified with the experiences of a particular person, the verifiability principle would result in a radical form of solipsism.

To meet these objections some other early formulations of the principle identified the meaning of a statement with that of some finite conjunction of statements directly reporting empirical observations. As will appear in more detail later, there are two main replies to this: (1) there are many types of statement whose meaning is not equivalent to that of any finite conjunction of observation statements, and (2) to identify the meaning of one statement with that of another is simply to say that the two statements have the same meaning, and this is not to explain or to give the meaning of the original statement.

For the foregoing reasons, it cannot be held that the verifiability principle is a criterion for determining the *meaning* of any particular sentence. In its later formulations it is presented simply as a criterion for determining whether a sentence is cognitively or factually *meaningful*.

Strong verifiability. In their early formulations Waismann, Schlick, and others held that the cognitive meaning of a sentence is determined completely by the experiences that would verify it conclusively. According to Waismann, for example, in "Logische Analyse des Wahrscheinlichkeitsbegriffs," "Anyone uttering a sentence must know in which conditions he calls the statement true or false; if he is unable to state this, then he does not know what he has said. A statement which cannot be verified conclusively is not verifiable at all; it is just devoid of any meaning." This was sometimes called the requirement of "strong verifiability." It says, in effect, that for any statement S to be cognitively meaningful there must be some finite consistent set of basic observation statements $O_1 \cdots O_n$, such that S entails and is entailed by the conjunction of $O_1 \cdots O_n$. The principal objections to this requirement are: (1) a strictly universal statement, that is, a statement covering an unlimited number of instances (for example, any statement of scientific law), is not logically equivalent to a conjunction of any finite number of observation statements and hence is not conclusively verifiable; (2) any singular statement about a physical object can in principle be the basis of an unlimited number of predictions and hence is not conclusively verifiable; (3) statements about past and future events, and statements about the experiences of other people, are not conclusively verifiable; (4) even if an existential statement (for example, "Red things exist" or "At least one thing is red") is verifiable in the required sense, its denial cannot be verifiable in this sense, for its denial (for example, "Red things do not exist" or "Everything is nonred") is a strictly universal statement. Hence, the requirement of strong verifiability would have the strange consequence that the denial of an existential statement would never be meaningful, and this would involve the rejection of the fundamental logical principle that if a statement S is true, then not-S is false, and that if S is false, then not-S is true; (5) if a statement S is meaningful by the present requirement and N is any meaningless statement, then the molecular statement S *or* N must be meaningful; (6) the present requirement presupposes that observation statements are conclusively verifiable, for unless this is so, no statement at all, not even a statement that is logically equivalent to a finite conjunction of observation statements, will be conclusively verifiable—or cognitively meaningful.

Falsifiability. It was sometimes suggested that conclusive falsifiability rather than conclusive verifiability should be the criterion of a cognitively meaningful statement. The criterion of conclusive falsifiability says, in effect, that a statement S is meaningful if and only if not-S is conclusively verifiable. Consequently, objections analogous to those already considered still apply: (1) existential statements are not conclusively falsifiable, for if S is an existential statement, not-S is a strictly universal statement; (2) even if a universal statement is conclusively falsifiable, its denial is not conclusively falsifiable, since its denial is an existential statement. Hence, the present criterion would have the consequence that the denial of a universal statement would never be meaningful, and again this would involve the rejection of the fundamental principle of logic mentioned before; (3) the present criterion is open to the special objection that a universal statement (for example, "Whatever is pure water boils at 100° C.") would be meaningful, that is, conclusively falsifiable, only if the corresponding negative existential statement (for example, "There is an instance of pure water that does not boil at 100° C.") were assertable, and a fortiori meaningful; but this negative existential statement would be meaningful, that is, conclusively falsifiable, only if the corresponding universal statement were assertable, and a fortiori meaningful. To escape from this circle it would be necessary to have a different and independent criterion of significance for either universal or existential statements; (4) if S is meaningful by the present requirement and N is any meaningless statement, then S *and* N must be meaningful; (5) again, the present requirement presupposes that basic observation statements are conclusively verifiable.

Confirmability. To meet the preceding difficulties the later formulations of the verifiability principle require of a meaningful statement that it should be related to a set of observation statements in such a way that they provide not conclusive verifiability but simply some degree of evidential support for the original statement. This was sometimes called the requirement of "weak verifiability." It says that for any statement S to be cognitively meaningful there must be some set of basic observation statements $O_1 \cdots O_n$ such that S entails $O_1 \cdots O_n$ and that $O_1 \cdots O_n$

confirms, or gives some degree of probability to, S. A formulation of this kind was given by Ayer in the first edition of *Language, Truth and Logic* (1936). He held that a statement is verifiable, and hence meaningful, if one or more observation statements can be deduced from it, perhaps in conjunction with certain additional premises, without being deducible from these other premises alone. The qualification concerning additional premises is introduced to allow, among other things, theoretical statements in science to be verifiable. But this formulation, as Ayer recognizes in the second edition of his book, permits any meaningless statement to be verifiable. For if N is any meaningless statement and O some observation statement, then from N together with the additional premise *if N then O* the observation statement O can be deduced, although O cannot be deduced from the additional premise alone. To meet objections of this kind Ayer introduces a number of conditions; he says (1) ". . . a statement is directly verifiable if it is either itself an observation-statement, or is such that in conjunction with one or more observation-statements it entails at least one observation-statement which is not deducible from these other premises alone," and (2) ". . . a statement is indirectly verifiable if it satisfies the following conditions: first, that in conjunction with certain other premises it entails one or more directly verifiable statements which are not deducible from these other premises alone; and secondly, that these other premises do not include any statement that is not either analytic, or directly verifiable, or capable of being independently established as indirectly verifiable." These conditions are designed *inter alia* to prevent obviously meaningless statements from being verifiable simply by occurring as components of verifiable molecular statements as in the objection to the requirement of strong verifiability (see above), and the objection to the requirement of conclusive falsifiability. The conditions are, however, insufficient for this purpose. As Hempel remarks, according to the present formulation if S is meaningful, then S *and* N will be meaningful, whatever statement N may be. And Church has shown that given any three observation statements O_1, O_2, and O_3, no one of which entails either of the others, and any statement N, it is possible to construct a molecular statement from which it follows that either N or not-N is verifiable. Such a molecular statement is one of the form $(\sim O_1 \cdot O_2) \vee (O_3 \cdot \sim N)$. For $(\sim O_1 \cdot \sim O_2) \vee (O_3 \cdot \sim N)$ together with O_1 entails O_3, and so the molecular statement is directly verifiable; but N together with $(\sim O_1 \cdot O_2) \vee (O_3 \cdot \sim N)$ entails O_2, and therefore N is indirectly verifiable. Alternatively, $(\sim O_1 \cdot O_2) \vee (O_3 \cdot \sim N)$ may by itself entail O_2, and in that case $\sim N$ and O_3 also entail O_2, and therefore $\sim N$ is directly verifiable. Difficulties of the kind raised by Hempel and Church obtain when a component of a molecular statement is superfluous as far as the verifiability of the molecular statement is concerned, that is, when the inclusion or exclusion of the component makes no difference to the verifiable entailments of the molecular statement. To eliminate components of this kind, Brown and Watling have proposed that for a molecular statement to be verifiable, either directly or indirectly, it must contain "only components whose deletion leaves a statement which entails verifiable statements not entailed by the original statement, or does not entail verifiable statements entailed by the original statement." This stipulation is designed to ensure that every component of a verifiable molecular statement either is independently verifiable (that is, "entails verifiable statements not entailed by the original statement") or else contributes to the meaning of the molecular statement in such a way that the molecular statement entails verifiable statements not entailed by any of its components (that is, any of the components alone "does not entail verifiable statements entailed by the original statement"). The intention of these stipulations is to ensure that a meaningless statement cannot occur as a component of a verifiable molecular statement and derive verifiability from the statement in which it occurs.

In two important articles entitled "Testability and Meaning" (1936–1937), Carnap distinguished the *testing* of a sentence from its confirmation; a sentence is "testable" if we know of a particular procedure (for example, the carrying out of certain experiments) that would confirm to some degree either the sentence or its negation. A sentence is "confirmable" if we know what kind of evidence would confirm it, even though we do not know of a particular procedure for obtaining that evidence. Carnap considers four different criteria of significance—complete testability, complete confirmability, degree of testability, and degree of confirmability. All of these exclude metaphysical statements as being meaningless. The fourth criterion is the most liberal and admits into the class of meaningful statements empirical statements of the various kinds that were excluded by the requirement of conclusive verifiability or the requirement of conclusive falsifiability. Each of Carnap's criteria determines a more or less restrictive form of empiricist language, and this, according to his view, is the same thing as a more or less restrictive form of empiricism. Carnap is largely concerned in these articles with giving a technical account of the formal features of such languages. One of the most serious difficulties he encounters is that of giving a satisfactory account of confirmability. His procedure is, in effect, to regard as cognitively meaningful all and only those statements that can be expressed in a formalized empiricist language.

Similarly, Hempel, in his article "Problems and Changes in the Empiricist Criterion of Meaning" (1950), discussed the proposal that a sentence has cognitive meaning if and only if it is translatable into an empiricist language. A formalized language is characterized by enumerating the formation and transformation rules of its syntax and the designation rules for the terms of its basic vocabulary. An empiricist language is one in which the basic vocabulary consists exclusively of empirical terms. As Hempel explains, dispositional terms may be introduced by means of "reduction sentences," and the theoretical constructs of the more advanced sciences (for example, "electrical field," "absolute temperature," "gravitational potential") can be accommodated by allowing the language to include interpreted deductive systems. Hempel claims for his criterion that it avoids many of the difficulties of the earlier formulations of the verifiability principle. The logic of a formalized language may ensure that no universal or existential statement is excluded from significance merely

on account of its universal or existential form and also that for every significant statement its denial is also significant. The vocabulary and syntax of a formalized empiricist language ensures that no meaningless statement will be admitted as significant, even by occurring as a component of a verifiable molecular statement. Nevertheless, leaving purely formal objections aside, the main difficulty of both Carnap's and Hempel's treatment of the verifiability principle is that of giving an adequate characterization of an *empiricist* language. An "empirical term" or an "observation predicate" is one that designates a property that is in principle observable, even though in fact it is never observed by anyone. But if the property has never in fact been observed, how are we to know that it is observable? It may be said that a basic observation statement *"Pa,"* asserting that an object *a* has the observable property *P*, is meaningful only if the experiences that would verify the statement *could* occur. But "could" here cannot mean "factually could," since we can speak meaningfully of occurrences that are factually impossible. Apparently what is meant is that the experiences in question must be logically possible. But then it seems that the only sense that can be given to saying that the *experiences* are logically possible is that the statement *"Pa"* is contingent. However, in *"Pa"* the object *a* is simply named or referred to, and the property *P* ascribed to it—and it seems that every statement of this form must be contingent. Thus, unless a further explanation of the expression "observation predicate" is forthcoming, we have no way of distinguishing between those basic observation statements that are meaningful and those that are not.

Observation statements. Schlick, in an early article entitled "A New Philosophy of Experience," claimed that to understand a proposition we must be able to indicate exactly the particular circumstances that would make it true and those that would make it false. "Circumstances" he defined as facts of experience; and thus it is experience that verifies or falsifies propositions. An obvious objection to this view is that sense experience is essentially private, and hence apparently the cognitive meaning of every statement must be essentially private. Schlick attempted to avoid this objection by distinguishing between the content and form of experience. The content, he said, is private and incommunicable—it can only be lived through. But the form of our experiences, he claimed, is expressible and communicable, and this is all that is required for scientific knowledge. However, Schlick's distinction between content and form cannot save his view from the objection of solipsism; for if the meaning of every descriptive expression is to be found, in the last analysis, in private experience, then this is so not only for qualitative words but also for the relational words that are supposed to describe the form of experience.

Thus, the first problem concerning statements reporting empirical observations is that they should be expressible in such a way that their meaning is not private to any one observer. The logical possibility of verifying a given statement can then be explained without mentioning the experiences of any particular person or indeed the experiences of anyone at all. If basic observation statements can be formulated in the required way, they express logically possible evidence, and hence any statement suitably related to a set of observation statements is verifiable in principle, even though no one is ever in a position to have the relevant experiences, that is, to verify the statement in question.

In order to achieve this result some adherents of the verifiability principle regard certain statements describing physical objects as basic (for example, "This is a black telephone"); others attempt to achieve the same result while still regarding sense-datum or phenomenal statements as basic (for example, "Here now a black patch" or "This seems to be a telephone"). In either case, there is the difficulty of explaining how these statements are related to the experiences that would verify them.

The question whether a statement reporting an empirical observation is conclusively verifiable is, as we have seen, of importance for the criterion of conclusive verifiability and for that of conclusive falsifiability. It has also been thought to be of importance for the criterion of weak verifiability or confirmability, for, it has been said, unless basic statements are certain, or in some sense incorrigible, no other statement can be even probable or confirmable.

Finally, as we noted before, there is also the problem of explaining what is meant by saying that a basic observation statement is verifiable in principle, that is, that certain experiences are logically possible, if in fact the experiences in question never occur. (For a more detailed account of some recent views concerning statements reporting empirical observations see BASIC STATEMENTS.)

Is the principle itself meaningful? It is sometimes objected that the verifiability principle itself, according to the criterion it lays down, must be either analytic or empirically verifiable if it is to be cognitively meaningful. But if it is analytic, then it is tautological and uninformative; at best it only exemplifies a proposed use of the terms "cognitive meaning" and "understanding." And if it is empirically verifiable, then it is a contingent statement about the ordinary use or some technical use of these terms and at best is only confirmable to some degree by the relevant evidence. In either case, it is objected, the principle cannot be the decisive criterion of cognitive meaning that its adherents suppose it to be.

One reply to this objection is that a criterion that determines a certain class of statements cannot have the same logical status as the statements in question. For example, the statement that expresses the principle of causality in effect determines a class of statements, namely, the class of causal statements, but obviously it is not itself a causal statement. Similarly, the verifiability principle, which claims to delimit the class of cognitively meaningful statements, cannot be expected to have the same logical status as the statements it delimits.

In order to understand the status of the verifiability principle, in the form in which it was held by the logical positivists, the following considerations are relevant: (1) They claimed that an essential difference between their empiricism and the earlier empiricism of Hume, Mill, and Mach was that it was based not on any particular psychological assumptions but only on considerations of logic. They may have believed that it is factually impossible for

us to have experiences radically different in kind from those that we now have, but they did not present the verifiability principle as stating or implying this. But then, if the possibility of mystical or religious experiences is allowed, it seems that at least some metaphysical statements are verifiable and therefore meaningful. This conclusion has been accepted by some later adherents of the verifiability principle, but it is evident that the logical positivists wished to present their criterion of meaning in such a way that it would exclude all metaphysical statements from the class of meaningful statements. (2) It might be argued, as Ayer once did, that it is meaningful to say that mystics have unusual experiences, but that nevertheless *we* can have no grounds for supposing that their experiences are relevant to the truth or falsity of any statement of fact, since we have no grounds for thinking that the "object" of such experiences could be described in ordinary empirical terms. The statement "Mystics have experiences that they report by the sentence 'Reality is One'" is empirically verifiable in the ordinary way. But the statement "Reality is One" is not empirically verifiable in the ordinary way. To this, however, the mystic may reply that he can describe in ordinary empirical terms the kind of preparation or discipline he recommends, and if we are not willing to carry out the appropriate procedure we are simply refusing to consider the possibility of verifying mystical statements. The antimetaphysical import of the verifiability principle, he may say, is apparently based on the assumption that we cannot have experiences radically different in kind from those that we now have. (3) Some of the logical positivists (Schlick, the early Ayer) claimed that the verifiability principle is in effect a statement of the sense of "cognitive or factual meaning" and "understanding" that is actually accepted in everyday life. Schlick, for example, said that the verifiability principle is "nothing but a simple statement of the way in which meaning is actually assigned to propositions, both in everyday life and in science. There never has been any other way, and it would be a grave error to suppose that we believe we have discovered a new conception of meaning which is contrary to common opinion and which we want to introduce into philosophy" ("Meaning and Verification"). But, as we have seen, if the verifiability principle is simply a contingent statement about a certain linguistic usage, its logical status cannot justify the degree of confidence that its adherents place in it. (4) Finally, the principle has been regarded as a recommendation or a decision concerning the use of the expression "factually meaningful statement." It has been claimed that this decision prevents radical intellectual confusion and that it promotes clarity in the discussion of many philosophical questions. Carnap and Ayer, among others, have taken this view of the status of the verifiability principle. It should be noted that this does not imply that the principle is regarded as an analytic or necessarily true statement. A principle that expresses a linguistic recommendation is no doubt closely related to a corresponding analytic statement, but the recommendation itself is not tautological and uninformative. A recommendation or a decision has a different logical status; it is not successful by being true or unsuccessful by being false.

More recent criticisms. Following the later work of Wittgenstein it is now widely held among philosophers that to ask whether a sentence is meaningful is simply to ask whether the words that compose the sentence are used according to the rules or practice of a language. Understanding a word, it is said, does not involve "knowing what the word stands for" or "being able to recognize what the word designates"; it involves only the ability to use the word in accordance with certain linguistic rules. Furthermore, the rules governing the correct use of different kinds of words differ enormously, and hence there is not just one way of misusing the words that occur in a sentence and thereby rendering the sentence meaningless. Each of the sentences "I do not exist," "The round square feels depressed," "Nonbeing is infinitely perfect," and "The Absolute enters into but transcends all change" involves a violation of one or more linguistic rules, but of quite different rules. Consequently, it is said, it is not possible to give a general criterion of the meaningfulness of a sentence. The verifiability principle is an attempt to answer the question "Under what conditions is a sentence cognitively or factually meaningful?," but this question, according to the view now widely held, is not one to which it is possible to give an answer that is both general and informative. Two further criticisms are made of the verifiability principle: (1) the principle, it is said, is not at all a criterion of the meaningfulness of a sentence but simply a characterization of an "empirical sentence," (2) the principle confuses the question of whether a sentence is meaningful with the different question of whether the statement it expresses can be known to be true or false. These more recent objections to the verifiability principle occur in most post-Wittgensteinian discussions of the topic of meaning. A useful summary of the arguments is given by J. L. Evans in "On Meaning and Verification."

Truth theory of meaning. It is convenient to begin by examining the second of these two further criticisms. It is concerned with the fact that one component of the verifiability principle is the thesis that the meaning of a statement is given by its truth conditions. This idea, which may be called "the truth theory of meaning," had been employed and stated by philosophers before the discussions of the Vienna circle. It is assumed, for example, by Russell in his theory of descriptions. And Wittgenstein, in the *Tractatus,* said explicitly, "To understand a proposition means to know what is the case if it is true." The formal correctness of this view can be seen from the following definition of the meaning of a statement in terms of its truth conditions. "*Die Sonne scheint* means *that the sun is shining* $=_{Df}$ *Die Sonne scheint* is true if, and only if, the sun is shining"; in general, "S means *that* $p =_{Df} S$ is true if, and only if, p." Nevertheless, it has to be admitted that the truth theory provides no effective clarification of the notion of cognitive or factual meaning. For even if the truth conditions of a statement S can be enumerated exhaustively in terms of a finite conjunction of observation statements $O_1 \cdots O_n$ (and, as we have seen, in very many cases this cannot be done) this entitles us to assert only that S and $O_1 \cdots O_n$ have the same meaning. But this does not clarify what the meaning of S is, or what it is for S to be meaningful. To say simply that two statements have the same

meaning is not to say what either statement means or what it is for either statement to be meaningful. For the kind of clarification that is being sought we now need a different and independent explanation of the meaning of an observation statement. Furthermore, the definition of the meaning of a statement in terms of its truth conditions provides no clarification unless the notion of truth is further explained. The truth of a statement can be defined in terms of its meaning in the following way. "*Die Sonne scheint* is true $=_{Df}$ *Die Sonne scheint* means *that the sun is shining,* and the sun is shining"; in general "S is true $=_{Df}$ S means *that p,* and p.*" But obviously it would be circular to employ this definition of truth in an attempt to clarify the notion of cognitive meaning. The two preceding definitions show, however, that there is a close connection between the notion of cognitive or factual meaning and the notion of truth. And hence, in reply to the second of the two further criticisms of the verifiability principle mentioned above, it may be argued that there must be a close connection between understanding a sentence as expressing a statement of fact and its being possible for one to know whether the statement is true or false.

Meaning and experience. The first of the two further criticisms of the verifiability principle is concerned with the fact that another component of the principle is the thesis that the truth conditions of a statement can be known only by reference to experience. This is the traditional doctrine of empiricism or positivism. The logical positivists (with the exception of Neurath, Carnap, and others, who at one time adopted a "coherence theory" of truth) held this view on the grounds that there are only two ways in which the truth-value of a statement can be ascertained, either a priori or a posteriori. According to their doctrine, if a statement can be known to be true a priori, then it is analytic and tautological and hence not a statement of fact. Therefore, if a statement is a statement of fact, it cannot be known a priori—its truth-value can be ascertained only by reference to experience. The simple dichotomy (either a priori or a posteriori) on which this argument is based has been criticized in more recent philosophy. W. V. Quine, for example, maintains that for the most part the statements that compose the corpus of knowledge have their truth-values determined by linguistic and pragmatic considerations, as well as by the occurrence of certain sensory experiences. He allows, however, that statements "on the periphery" have their truth-values determined by experience. Thus, even in a more qualified version of empiricism the difficulty still remains of making clear what it is to know that a statement is true "by reference to experience."

Nevertheless, the criticism of the verifiability principle now being considered admits that for a sentence to be an "empirical sentence" it must express a statement that is in some sense verifiable, that is, the truth conditions of which can be known by reference to experience. And it may be argued that the grounds on which this is admitted are such that they compel a similar admission for every sentence that can be understood as expressing a statement of fact. It is evident that if a form of language can be used to describe the world—that is, to make statements—its rules cannot be wholly syntactical, that is, of the kind that govern simply the formation and transformation of sentences in the language. For the language to be descriptive it must also have semantic rules, for example, rules that relate the use of its basic predicates to certain states of affairs in the world. Semantic rules may be said to govern directly the use of basic predicates and to govern indirectly, via definitions and other syntactical means, the use of nonbasic predicates. The more detailed analysis of a semantic rule—that is, an account of how such rules function in a language—is a difficult matter which we need not attempt here. For our present purpose it is sufficient to note that it would be a contradiction to say that a language was descriptive but had no semantic rules; similarly, it would be a contradiction for someone to say that he could understand a sentence as expressing a statement although he had not been able to ascertain the semantic rules of the language in which the sentence was expressed. We can now see why many present-day philosophers say that the verifiability principle is simply a characterization of an empirical sentence. If a sentence is used to describe an experienceable state of the world, then the semantic rules governing its predicates relate those predicates, directly or indirectly, to that state of the world. It follows that the sentence expresses a statement that is in principle verifiable. But consider the position of a philosopher who maintains that he uses certain sentences to make statements about the world, although these statements are not verifiable in any sense at all. This position seems to be simply incoherent. If the sentences in question express statements, the use of the predicates that occur in them must be governed by semantic rules; how can these rules be known or explained to anyone else if the states of affairs which the sentences are supposed to describe are not experienceable in any way at all? The philosopher in question may eventually admit that the relevant states of the world are, after all, experienceable—but intuitively or by some other special kind of experience. This, apparently, would be a psychological claim, to the effect that we are capable of types of experience other than those we usually associate with the normal functioning of our sense organs. The onus of proof to show that such experiences are possible plainly rests upon the philosopher in question. But even if such experiences do occur, and are of such a kind that they can be associated, via semantic rules, with the descriptive expressions of a language, this will not provide an exception to the requirement laid down by the verifiability principle—it will, in fact, be simply an extension of that requirement to types of sentences that formerly could not be understood as expressing statements of fact. For a further examination of this question, it would seem that the correct approach would be to give a completely general analysis of "knowing the use of a predicate." Such an analysis cannot be given here, but the following outline may be suggested. In the case of a basic predicate it may be held that (1) an essential part of the use of the predicate is to identify a property, (2) an ability to use the predicate to identify the relevant property does not constitute knowing its use, unless the user also knows what the ability consists in, and (3) the user cannot be said to know this if it is impossible for him to have any kind of experience of the property in question.

Thus, to revert to the first and main criticism of the verifiability principle, it may be admitted that to ask whether a sentence is meaningful is to ask whether the constituent words are used according to the rules of a language. And it may be admitted that the rules governing the use of different kinds of words differ immensely and that there is not just one way in which a sentence can be meaningless. Nevertheless, if the foregoing remarks are correct, a sentence cannot be understood as expressing a statement unless the use of the descriptive expressions that occur in it are governed by semantic rules; and these rules cannot be known or explained to anyone else unless it is possible for the users of the language to have some kind of experience of the states of the world to which the descriptive expressions in question are related. These requirements are, perhaps, all that is essential in the claim made by the verifiability principle in its later formulations.

Bibliography

FORMULATIONS AND FAVORABLE DISCUSSIONS

Ayer, A. J., *Language, Truth and Logic*. London, 1936; 2d ed., 1946.

Ayer, A. J., "The Principle of Verifiability." *Mind*, Vol. 45 (1936).

Ayer, A. J., "Verification and Experience." *PAS*, Vol. 37 (1936–1937). Reprinted in A. J. Ayer, ed., *Logical Positivism*. Glencoe, Ill., 1959.

Ayer, A. J., "Logical Positivism—A Debate" (with F. C. Copleston), in Paul Edwards and Arthur Pap, eds., *A Modern Introduction to Philosophy*. Glencoe, Ill., 1957; 2d ed., rev., New York, 1965.

Brown, R., and Watling, J., "Amending the Verification Principle." *Analysis*, Vol. 11 (1950–1951).

Carnap, Rudolf, "Testability and Meaning." *Philosophy of Science*, Vol. 3 (1936), 419–471, Vol. 4 (1937), 1–40. Reprinted in Herbert Feigl and May Brodbeck, eds., *Readings in the Philosophy of Science*. New York, 1953. Pp. 47–92.

Hempel, C. G., "Problems and Changes in the Empiricist Criterion of Meaning." *Revue internationale de philosophie*, Vol. 4 (1950), 41–63. Reprinted in Leonard Linsky, ed., *Semantics and the Philosophy of Language*. Urbana, Ill., 1952. Also reprinted in Ayer, ed., *Logical Positivism* (see above).

Hempel, C. G., "The Concept of Cognitive Significance: A Reconsideration." *Proceedings of the American Academy of Arts and Sciences*, Vol. 80 (1951), 61–77.

Reichenbach, Hans, "The Verifiability Theory of Meaning." *Proceedings of the American Academy of Arts and Sciences*, Vol. 80 (1951). Reprinted in Feigl and Brodbeck, eds., *Readings in the Philosophy of Science* (see above).

Schlick, Moritz, "A New Philosophy of Experience." *Publications in Philosophy of the College of the Pacific*, No. 1. Stockton, Calif., 1932. Reprinted in *Gesammelte Aufsätze 1926–1936*. Vienna, 1938.

Schlick, Moritz, "Positivismus und Realismus." *Erkenntnis*, Vol. 3 (1932–1933), 1–31. Reprinted in *Gesammelte Aufsätze* and translated in Ayer, ed., *Logical Positivism* (see above).

Schlick, Moritz, "Meaning and Verification." *Philosophical Review*, Vol. 45 (1936), 339–368. Reprinted in *Gesammelte Aufsätze* and in Herbert Feigl and Wilfrid Sellars, eds., *Readings in Philosophical Analysis*. New York, 1949.

Schlick, Moritz, "Form and Content." Three lectures given in London in 1932. Reprinted in *Gesammelte Aufsätze*.

Waismann, Friedrich, "Logische Analyse der Wahrscheinlichkeitsbegriffs." *Erkenntnis*, Vol. 1 (1930–1931).

Whiteley, C. H., "On Meaning and Verifiability." *Analysis* (1938–1939).

Whiteley, C. H., "On Understanding." *Mind*, Vol. 58 (1949).

CRITICISMS

Barnes, W. H. F., "Meaning and Verifiability." *Philosophy*, Vol. 14 (1939).

Berlin, Isaiah, "Verification." *PAS*, Vol. 39 (1938–1939).

Church, Alonzo, review of Ayer's *Language, Truth and Logic*, 2d ed. *Journal of Symbolic Logic*, Vol. 14 (1949).

Copleston, F. C., "A Note on Verification." *Mind*, Vol. 59 (1950). Reprinted, with "A Further Note on Verification," in *Contemporary Philosophy*. London, 1956.

Copleston. F. C., "Logical Positivism—A Debate" (with A. J. Ayer), in Edwards and Pap, eds., *A Modern Introduction to Philosophy* (see above).

Ducasse, C. J., "Verification, Verifiability, and Meaningfulness." *Journal of Philosophy*, Vol. 33 (1936), 230–236.

Evans, J. L., "On Meaning and Verification." *Mind*, Vol. 62 (1953), 1–19.

Ewing, A. C., "Meaninglessness." *Mind*, Vol. 46 (1937), 347–364.

Kneale, W. C., "Verifiability." *PAS*, Supp. Vol. 19 (1945).

Lazerowitz, Morris, "The Principle of Verifiability." *Mind*, Vol. 46 (1937), 372–378.

Lazerowitz, Morris, "Strong and Weak Verification." *Mind*, Vol. 48 (1939) and Vol. 59 (1950). Reprinted in *The Structure of Metaphysics*. London, 1955.

Lazerowitz, Morris, "The Positivistic Use of 'Nonsense.'" *Mind*, Vol. 57 (1946). Reprinted in *The Structure of Metaphysics*.

Lewis, C. I., "Experience and Meaning." *Philosophical Review*, Vol. 43 (1934). Reprinted in Feigl and Sellars, eds., *Readings in Philosophical Analysis* (see above).

O'Connor, D. J., "Some Consequences of Professor Ayer's Verification Principle." *Analysis*, Vol. 10 (1949–1950).

Russell, Bertrand, "On Verification." *PAS*, Vol. 38 (1937–1938).

Russell, Bertrand, *An Inquiry Into Meaning and Truth*. London and New York, 1940.

Stace, W. T., "Metaphysics and Meaning." *Mind*, Vol. 44 (1935), 417–438. Reprinted in Edwards and Pap, eds., *A Modern Introduction to Philosophy* (see above).

Stebbing, L. Susan, "Communication and Verification." *PAS*, Supp. Vol. 13 (1934).

Waismann, Friedrich, "Verifiability." *PAS*, Supp. Vol. 19 (1945), 119–150. Reprinted in A. G. N. Flew, ed., *Logic and Language*, First Series. Oxford, 1951.

Waismann, Friedrich, "Language Strata," in A. G. N. Flew, ed., *Logic and Language*, Second Series. Oxford, 1953.

Warnock, G. J., "Verification and the Use of Language." *Revue internationale de philosophie*, Vol. 5 (1951), 307–322. Reprinted in Edwards and Pap, eds., *A Modern Introduction to Philosophy* (see above).

Wisdom, John, "Metaphysics and Verification." *Mind*, Vol. 47 (1938), 452–498. Reprinted in *Philosophy and Psycho-analysis*. Oxford, 1953.

Wisdom, John, "Note on the New Edition of Professor Ayer's *Language, Truth and Logic*." *Mind*, Vol. 57 (1948). Reprinted in *Philosophy and Psycho-analysis*.

RELATED DISCUSSIONS

Alston, W. P., "Pragmatism and the Verifiability Theory of Meaning." *Philosophical Studies*, Vol. 6 (1955).

Bridgman, P. W., "Operational Analysis." *Philosophy of Science*, Vol. 5 (1938).

Grice, H. P., "Meaning." *Philosophical Review*, Vol. 46 (1957), 377–388.

Heath, A. E., "Communication and Verification." *PAS*, Supp. Vol. 13 (1934).

MacKinnon, D. M., "Verifiability." *PAS*, Supp. Vol. 19 (1945).

Morris, C. W., "The Concept of Meaning in Pragmatism and Logical Positivism," in *Proceedings of the Eighth International Congress of Philosophy* (1934). Prague, 1936.

Nagel, Ernest, "Verifiability, Truth, and Verification." *Journal of Philosophy*, Vol. 31 (1934), 141–148. Reprinted in *Logic Without Metaphysics*. Glencoe, Ill., 1956.

Nelson, E. J., "The Verification Theory of Meaning." *Philosophical Review*, Vol. 43 (1954).

R. W. ASHBY

VICO, GIAMBATTISTA (1668–1744), Italian philosopher of history and social theorist, was born in Naples, the son of a bookseller. Although as a youth he attended a Jesuit college, much of his early study was carried on in solitude in his father's shop. After spending some years at Vatolla as tutor to the nephews of the bishop of Ischia, he returned to his native city in 1695 and was appointed four years later to the chair of rhetoric at the university, a post he held until shortly before his death. The professorship was a minor one, and although its modest stipend gave him security, it offered little more. Throughout his life Vico hoped for better things, and his failure to succeed to the chair of civil law at Naples when it fell vacant in 1723 was a bitter disappointment to him. Nonetheless, the poverty and comparative neglect with which he had to contend throughout his career never discouraged him from the pursuit of his highly original inquiries in the fields of jurisprudence, linguistic scholarship, and history. His first important lecture, *De Nostri Temporis Studiorum Ratione* ("On the Method of the Studies of Our Time"), was printed in 1709, and it was followed almost immediately by a work of considerable significance in the light of the later development of his ideas, *De Antiquissima Italorum Sapientia* ("On the Most Ancient Knowledge of the Italians"). Some years later Vico published his *Diritto universale* (3 vols., Naples, 1720–1722), the subject of which was "the single principle of universal law and its single purpose." In 1725 (the year in which he also wrote his famous autobiography, published in 1728 at Venice in *Raccolta d'opusculi scientifici e filologici*, which was to have been the first volume of a quarterly review) the first edition of his masterpiece, the *Scienza nuova (The New Science)* appeared. Yet Vico was not satisfied with the *Scienza nuova* as it stood, and much of the rest of his life was spent in making extensive alterations and additions to it. As a consequence, the book was largely recast for the second edition (1730), and the third edition (1744) contained still further revisions. The main part of Vico's autobiography, which he composed at the invitation of a Venetion nobleman, describes in fascinating detail the development of his studies and ideas up to the writing of the first version of his chief work. He subsequently expanded the autobiography, giving some account of the modifications introduced into the later editions of the *Scienza nuova*.

Influence of the "Scienza nuova." The *Scienza nuova* has had a curious history. During the eighteenth century it remained largely unread by European thinkers, although it seems that the German writers Johann Hamann and Johann Herder (many of whose ideas interestingly parallel Vico's) may have been acquainted with it. Generally speaking, the theses propounded in the book were too unfamiliar and its overall approach too much out of line with the attitude characteristically adopted by Enlightenment theorists toward problems concerning history and society for its suggestions to find a sympathetic response. It was only in the nineteenth century, when, under the influence of German romanticism, a different intellectual climate prevailed, that Vico's work at last began to arouse genuine interest. In England he was admired and quoted by such writers as Coleridge and Thomas Arnold, and in France he excited the enthusiasm of the historian Jules

Michelet, who spoke of Vico as his master and did much to make his ideas known through translations of passages from his major work. However, recognition of Vico's importance was still slow to develop, and it was not until fairly recent times that his place in the history of European thought came to be at all adequately appreciated. Benedetto Croce and, later, R. G. Collingwood helped focus attention on his work; both were deeply influenced by him, Croce in particular being a devoted, although sometimes unreliable, interpreter of his ideas. Even so, Vico remains to this day a curiously intractable author. His style is often obscure and scholastic, and his pronouncements tend to be dark and suggestive rather than sharp-edged and clear; nor was his mode of presenting and arranging his thoughts conducive to easy understanding. All in all, despite his undoubted genius, it seems unlikely that he will ever be widely read.

Critique of Cartesianism. The best approach to the doctrines Vico advanced in the *Scienza nuova* is through his attitude to Cartesian philosophy. His earliest writings and lectures show clearly the influence of Cartesian ideas. Later, however, he became profoundly critical of Descartes's theory of knowledge and the world, believing that it was too exclusively oriented toward the mathematical and physical sciences, so that other branches of human activity and inquiry, such as art, law, and history, were either totally neglected or else treated as being of no serious consequence. Moreover, Vico argued, the Cartesians misapprehended the nature of the physical sciences themselves, wrongly regarding these as capable of affording us the same kind of certitude that is to be found in the field of geometrical demonstration, the Cartesian paradigm of true knowledge. In pursuance of this claim, Vico adumbrated his own theory of knowledge, the essence of which is contained in the *De Antiquissima Italorum Sapientia.* In that essay Vico singled out for attack three fundamental Cartesian assumptions—the appeal to self-consciousness as a first principle, embodied in Descartes's famous *cogito ergo sum;* the belief that God's existence may be proved a priori; and the reliance upon the method of clear and distinct ideas as a universal criterion of truth.

Underlying all Vico's criticisms was the principle of *verum factum*—"the true (*verum*) and the made (*factum*) are convertible": we can know for certain only that which we ourselves have made or created. Thus, he claimed in the first place that self-awareness of the kind referred to by Descartes in his proof of his own existence occurs only at the level of primitive unreflective consciousness and affords no basis for knowledge in the scientific sense: ". . . the clear and distinct idea of the mind not only cannot be the criterion of other truths, but it cannot be the criterion of that of the mind itself; for while the mind apprehends itself it does not make itself, and because it does not make itself it is ignorant of the form or mode by which it apprehends itself" (*Opere*, Vol. I, p. 136). Likewise, pretended demonstrations of the existence of God are dismissed; all such proofs are said to spring from "impious curiosity" and amount to making oneself "the god of God."

So far as the criterion of clear and distinct ideas is concerned, two things should be recognized. First, many factual propositions may seem clear and indubitable enough, but they may nevertheless subsequently turn out to be false. Second, although propositions of the type exemplified in mathematics unquestionably satisfy the Cartesian criterion of self-evidence, the ground of their certitude is to be sought not in self-evidence but in the fact that mathematical systems are systems which men themselves have constructed. The truths of mathematics are irrefutable because the rules and conventions governing the symbols or concepts used in such systems are created by man and, in the final analysis, are arbitrary. This view, which in outline anticipated an approach that has become widely current only in the present century and was strikingly at variance with the general opinion of his time, led Vico to distinguish (sharply and importantly) between the kind of truth attainable in pure mathematics and that which pertains to discoveries in such experimental sciences as physics. Physics is necessarily "less certain" than mathematics, for in physics we have to do with that which we have not created. Only God can know in the full sense the nature and workings of the universe, since it was he who made it. Material reality can therefore never be transparent to human reason in the manner envisaged by rationalist philosophers. This does not mean, however, that it cannot be known at all in Vico's sense, for in the investigation of the physical world, we are not confined to the role of passive spectators with no active part to play in forming the phenomena to be studied. Rather, through the construction of experiments performed in the light of hypotheses, we to some degree "imitate nature," creating and re-creating the conditions under which natural processes of determinate kinds may be observed to occur. As Vico put it, "The things which are proved in physics are those to which we can perform something similar" (*Opere*, Vol. I, pp. 136–137).

Historical understanding. The theory of knowledge that Vico propounded in explicit opposition to Cartesian epistemology was the starting point from which his revolutionary theory of history and social development evolved. In its final form, the form in which it is to be found in the *Scienza nuova,* this theory implies a further drastic reversal of the Cartesian position. Descartes's own attitude toward the historical studies had been one of barely disguised contempt. When set beside the exact scientific disciplines, whose application to the natural world was producing such startling results, history appeared a poor thing—at best a confused agglomeration of miscellaneous facts, at worst a tissue of fabrications and absurdities. For Vico, however, such depreciation of history was wholly unwarranted. He claimed that not only was it wrong to assume that there exists just one valid method of inquiry to which every branch of study worthy of respect must conform, whatever its specific aims or subject matter, but also that, if comparisons were to be made at all, the historian can, in fact, achieve a more profound knowledge of what lies within his field of investigation than natural scientists can conceivably hope to learn of what lies within theirs. For, however ingenious the techniques for exploring the realm of physical nature may become, that realm remains in the last analysis "external" to man, not of his making. In the case of history, by contrast, the world to be studied and comprehended is the human world. The objects of historical investigation are the results or expressions of human will and contrivance, and as such they are phenomena which the historian, by virtue of his own humanity, is capable of grasping and understanding in a distinctively intimate way. In drawing this line between natural science and the historical or humane disciplines, Vico gave original formulation to a contrast that was later to play a crucial role in the history of thought.

Recognition of the special character of historical understanding was one thing; to provide an acceptable account of how it might be achieved was another. And here again Vico showed himself to be far ahead of his time. He did not wish to maintain, as at first might be supposed, that we should seek to interpret the actions and products of past ages in terms of our own characteristic purposes, interests, and ideas. This would have been to fall into the very trap that had ensnared his predecessors in social and legal theory, including such outstanding figures as Grotius, Pufendorf, and Hobbes. Vico acknowledged a considerable debt to these men, but he nonetheless believed that they had been guilty of certain major errors, errors which would now be attributed to a lack of historical sense or perspective. For in their discussions of the nature and origins of human society and institutions, in their employment of such abstractions as "natural law" and "social contract," they assumed the reality of a fixed and static human nature, unchanging from age to age, and credited men living in remote periods of the past with mental powers and outlooks essentially similar to those exhibited by themselves and their contemporaries. A consequence of this approach was the imposition on historical phenomena of what Vico called pseudo myths, distorting frameworks and schemata which presented a wholly false picture of how men belonging to earlier stages of social growth thought, behaved, and lived.

Rejecting all such misconceptions, Vico maintained that man is a being who can be understood only historically. Therefore, to try to interpret human history in the light of some a priori notion of man's essential nature is to start from the wrong end. It inevitably involves reading back into the hearts and minds of primitive peoples modes of feeling and thinking that are themselves the outcome of a long period of historical development and whose true significance can be appreciated only by tracing their origins and evolution. It was this cardinal point that the great jurists and political theorists of the seventeenth century had failed to recognize, with the result that their controversies concerning such problems as the original construction of civil society had been ultimately barren and artificial. Vico's approach was, by contrast, explicitly genetic—"every theory must start from the point where the matter of which it treats first began to take shape" (*Scienza nuova*, Sec. 314). Moreover, once we emancipate ourselves from the belief that human beings have always looked at themselves and the world in the way in which we do now, once we recognize that the forms of expression and communication natural to us were not shared by men living in less sophisticated times, the task and scope of historical investigation itself takes on an entirely new aspect having profound methodological implications. The materials for reaching a true understanding of the past and of how we

have come to be what we are lie at hand. They are to be found above all in language, together with the myths, fables, and traditions that have been handed down from early times. However, these and kindred sources must be properly interpreted and deciphered; they demand of the historian not only a high degree of critical discernment but also an imaginative capacity for recapturing modes of consciousness utterly different from those with which he is acquainted in his everyday experience.

Language and myth. Language is of especial importance to historical understanding. An enormous number of the terms we use, including the most abstract and theoretical, have their roots in forms of living and experience remote from those to which we are accustomed; an etymological study of their derivation can shed light not only upon the environmental conditions in which the activities of previous generations of men were set but also upon their characteristic responses to those conditions. Further, speech and thought are inextricably bound up with one another. Language is not an artificial medium which men have deliberately constructed to give expression to preexistent ideas but has evolved naturally, the course of its development being inseparable from that of the human mind itself. It follows, Vico maintained, that the forms of language and representation men employ afford invaluable indications of their mental processes and outlooks, and these have, in fact, differed widely over the course of time. Thus, Vico spent much time elaborating the thesis that what today are mere metaphors in our speech had in earlier ages a quite different significance; they represented the terms in which men directly apprehended the world around them and so "made sense" of their experience. Vivid pictorial images and analogies, animistic figures and personifications (such as children use)—these formed the very currency of thought and communication in what Vico called the poetical periods of human history. He insisted, in this connection, that the ability to employ general or abstract words is a relatively sophisticated development, people having in the first instance communicated by means of gestures, pictures, or representative objects, and later by what are termed "imaginative universals" or "poetic characters." What is true of language applies equally to other manifestations of human life and consciousness. If, for instance, we think today of the events described in mythology as being no more than extravagant fictions, or if we are inclined to treat works of poetry or painting as chiefly devised for the pleasure or entertainment they give us, we should take care not to project these present attitudes into the minds of our remote ancestors. There were periods when, far from being regarded as a kind of dispensable embellishment of civilized existence, poetry was, on the contrary, the natural and pervasive mode of human expression. Likewise, the figures of legend and fable represented for the men who created them pregnant imaginative embodiments of truths that related directly to their material circumstances and preoccupations: "Fables," Vico wrote, "are the first histories of the Gentile peoples," and they could be immensely revealing and informative if correctly interpreted.

Cyclical theory of history. One of Vico's most significant insights, which was restated much later in the writings of Herder, Hegel, and Marx, lay in his claim that the various aspects of a society's life at any given stage of its history form a coherent pattern and are intrinsically connected with one another. With a certain type of art or religion go a certain type of economic and political organization, a certain type of law, of manners, of style of thought, and so forth. An interesting example of the type of connection Vico had in mind is the relation he claimed to discern between Athenian legal principles and procedures, on the one hand, and the development of Socratic and post-Socratic philosophical doctrines, on the other (*Scienza nuova*, Secs. 1040–1043). Conceptions of this kind were incorporated within his own "cyclical" theory of historical development, the *corsi e ricorsi* for which he is most often remembered. Human societies pass through determinate stages of growth and decay. There is first a purely "bestial" condition, from which emerges what Vico termed "the age of the gods," when the basic social unit is the patriarchal family. In the age of the gods, order of a kind prevails, the brutal instincts of men being curbed by fear of supernatural powers—the beginnings of religion. The next stage, "the age of the heroes," appears as a consequence of the alliances formed between the fathers of families to meet the challenge provided both by internal dissidence among their own dependents (or *famuli*) and by external attack from "lawless vagrants." Oligarchies are established through these alliances, and society is rigidly divided between patrician rulers and plebeian serfs or slaves. Laws are necessarily cruel and inequitable, and the life and poetry of the heroic age is imbued with ferocious and predatory ideals. This stage is followed by "the age of men," which is engendered not by an abstract reverence for reason and "natural law" but by class conflict; the plebeian class demands and gradually achieves equal rights and a legal system that respects its interests. But the weakening of traditional ties and the questioning of accepted customs and values that results from the establishment of free democratic republics leads inevitably to eventual corruption and dissolution. The end of the cycle comes either through conquest from without or through inner disintegration and a reversion to primitive barbarism, and a new cycle begins.

One example of such a cycle, to which Vico constantly returned and which he characterized as an instance of the "ideal eternal history . . . whose course is run in time by the histories of all nations" (*Scienza nuova*, Sec. 114), is to be found in the history of Roman civilization. Thus, the mythical figure of Romulus is seen as giving symbolic expression to a period when rebellions among the *famuli* against the Vichian "fathers" resulted in the emergence of an essentially feudal society: agrarian clientships were established, and a sharp division, maintained by force, was set between the patrician and plebeian classes. However, in the course of time pressures from below once again forced a change in social and political organization. Rights and privileges, previously reserved for the nobility, were extended to the population as a whole, and a system of "civil sovereignty" was instituted; in contriving such a system, "the Roman people went beyond all others in the world" (*ibid.*, Sec. 1101) and created a truly free "popular commonwealth." Yet the prospects of acquiring personal

wealth and power which the system opened up, together with the spread of destructive skeptical doctrines, led in their turn to discontent and unrest among the people. A period of strong authoritarian rule under the Caesars succeeded in temporarily arresting the process of disintegration, but the forces of unbridled individualism and intellectual corruption (called by Vico the barbarism of reflection) proved in the end to be too powerful, and Rome finally collapsed under the blows of its enemies. Crude as it is in many ways, Vico's account is nonetheless shot through with striking historical insights; he himself was particularly proud of having destroyed the "fiction that the law of the Twelve Tables came to Rome from Greece" by showing the historical impossibility of such a hypothesis, given the conditions and ideas that prevailed in Roman society at the time.

Providence. Vico was throughout his life a devout Catholic, and he habitually spoke of the patterns he believed to be discernible in history as ultimately attributable to the work of "divine Providence." This claim does not at first sight seem to fit easily with his repeated insistence upon man himself as the author and maker of his history. However, whatever difficulties they may otherwise raise, Vico's references to a providential order running through the historical process and shaping it from within may, at least in part, be interpreted as drawing attention to the fact that many of the most striking features of social development appear not to have been the products of human forethought and planning. He pointed out, for example, that institutions which in retrospect are seen to have been of the greatest utility and value often in no way corresponded to the purposes of those whose activities were chiefly instrumental in promoting them, a consideration which later led Hegel to speak of "the cunning of Reason," whereby the petty motives of individuals are used to serve ends that lie beyond the comprehension of the agents concerned. Here, as in so many other respects, Vico anticipated the ideas of subsequent thinkers who, by transforming our view of human history, at the same time helped to transform our conception of human nature itself. The need to see the past in collective or institutional, as well as in purely personal, terms; the conception of the economic and class structure of societies as crucially relevant to the formation of dominant ideologies; the importance of understanding remote periods sympathetically and for their own sakes rather than judging them according to present standards and interests—notions such as these seem familiar enough to contemporary minds. Nevertheless, they have not always been so, and it was in Vico's neglected writings that the first clear intimations of them appeared. For this reason alone, and despite the many absurdities and exaggerations which it also undoubtedly contains, the *Scienza nuova* stands as a landmark in the history of European thought.

Bibliography

Vico's complete works, under the title *Opere complete*, Benedetto Croce, Giovanni Gentile, and Fausto Nicolini, eds., 8 vols. in 11, was published in Bari from 1914 to 1941. Vico's autobiography was translated by T. G. Bergin and M. H. Fisch as *The Autobiography of Giambattista Vico* (Ithaca, N.Y., 1944). *Scienza nuova* was translated from the third edition by T. G. Bergin and M. H. Fisch as *The New Science of Giambattista Vico* (Ithaca, N.Y., 1948).

For literature on Vico, see Robert Flint, *Vico* (London, 1884), which remains a useful and competent introduction to the main lines of Vico's thought. A more arresting discussion is to be found in Benedetto Croce, *La filosofia di Giambattista Vico* (Bari, 1911), translated by R. G. Collingwood as *The Philosophy of Giambattista Vico* (New York, 1913), but Croce is prone to attribute to Vico ideas more characteristic of his own philosophical position than Vico's. More recent studies include A. R. Caponigri, *Time and Idea: The Theory of History in Giambattista Vico* (London, 1953), a curious and rather obscure work; and Isaiah Berlin, "The Philosophical Ideas of Giambattista Vico," an illuminating essay published in *Art and Ideas in Eighteenth Century Italy* (Rome, 1960). The introduction to Bergin and Fisch's translation of Vico's *Autobiography* (see above), also contains an excellent account of Vico's philosophical development.

PATRICK GARDINER

VIENNA CIRCLE, THE. See LOGICAL POSITIVISM.

VISCHER, FRIEDRICH THEODOR (1807–1887), was primarily a poet and philosopher of art but was also engaged in the religious, political, and philosophical issues of his age. As a student of theology at Tübingen, he was already skeptical of the church and its religion. A deep-seated sense of the irrationality of existence made him skeptical of philosophy as well, but in 1830 an intensive study of the philosophy of Hegel impressed him by its reconciliation of existing reality with the ideal. Appointed extraordinary professor of aesthetics and German literature at Tübingen in 1837, he came under the influence of the Hegelian left wing and was soon contributing articles to Arnold Ruge's *Hallische Jahrbücher*. His views on religion were influenced by his friend and colleague D. F. Strauss and in the 1840s by Ludwig Feuerbach, who convinced him that the permanent truth of religion is humanistic and its traditional form self-alienated. But Vischer's politics were liberal rather than revolutionary, and by the mid-1840s he had broken with the extreme Hegelian left because of what seemed to him its dogmatic materialism and the unrealism and demagogy of its social thinking. Yet shortly after he was named full professor in 1844, he was suspended for two years by the Württemberg government because of a characteristically fiery inaugural address in which he denounced the established order in art, religion, and academic life, consigned the art galleries to the flames, and pledged to the established order his "full, undivided enmity" and his "open, hearty hatred."

During his enforced sabbatical, Vischer began his major work, *Aesthetik oder Wissenschaft des Schönen*, which appeared at Reutlingen in six large volumes between 1846 and 1857 (2d ed., Robert Vischer, ed., Munich, 1922–1923). This "science of the beautiful" explicitly presupposed the method and results of Hegelian philosophy, but the influence of Schelling and Solger may have been still more important. For Hegel the progression of increasing adequacy to the Idea proceeded from art to religion to philosophy; Vischer, however, ranked religion the lowest, as the "primitive . . . childhood form of the absolute Spirit" in which the subject is bound through the cult to a fixed and quasi-substantial object which leaves reason in darkness and places imagination under rigid limits. Art was given precedence second only to philosophy and was distinguished much more sharply from religion than in Hegel's system. Although in art consciousness moves in a sensuous medium and not yet in the transparency of pure thought, it is able to circulate freely in this medium and to "find itself in the appearances of the world" (Vol. I, Sec. 5). Its essential object is the beautiful, "the Idea in the form of limited appearance." Although the Idea is not fully present in any existing particular, it is not a mere abstraction but manifests itself in sensuous existence. The beautiful object is the harmonized whole of things in microcosm. As the synthesis of the objectively beautiful in external reality and the subjectively beautiful in imagination, art is the sign of an ultimately reconciled world, despite the loss of a religiously grounded belief in world order and despite the overwhelming everyday experience of a fragmentary and chaotic existence.

Vischer had earlier been able to affirm with Hegel that historical development embodies the Idea and as such is a criterion in art as well as in other areas; but his waning confidence in historical development seems to have been utterly shaken by the disillusioning results of the revolutions of 1848, during which time he served as a frustrated member of the Frankfurt parliament. Even in the first volume of the *Aesthetik*, Vischer denied that the history of art directly reflects the logical development of the Idea of the beautiful, and there is throughout this work a tension between the purely formal "deductions" of the moments of this pure Idea in the numbered paragraphs and the rich discussions of actual works of art in the explications.

Vischer began, however, to repudiate his aesthetic system almost as soon as it was finished and therewith repudiated Hegelian idealism altogether. In his later literary and philosophical works, produced while he was lecturing at polytechnic institutes first in Zurich (1855) and then in Stuttgart (1866), the tension between the ideal and the real was broken. A philosophy that treats of the real world must be grounded in natural science. Meanwhile, there is a hiatus between historical, empirical life and the "dream" of an ideal wholeness. This hiatus constitutes the state of self-alienation, not as a temporary situation to be overcome in history but as the permanent human condition. Art is now seen as a protest against this alienation and as the symbol of a "human soul" which is more an ideal wish than an actual possibility. The tragicomic hero of Vischer's famous novel, *Auch Einer* (Stuttgart, 1878), is a duplex self, an idealist forever thwarted by his actual existence.

Works by Vischer

Kritische Gänge. Vols. I and II, Tübingen, 1844. New series, Vols. I–VI, Stuttgart, 1860–1873. 2d ed., Robert Vischer, ed., 6 vols., Leipzig, Berlin, and Vienna, 1914–1922.

Altes und Neues, 3 vols. Stuttgart, 1881–1882. Includes an autobiography.

Dichterische Werke, Robert Vischer, ed., 5 vols. Leipzig, 1917. Includes *Auch Einer*.

Works on Vischer

Glockner, Hermann, *F. T. Vischers Ästhetik in ihrem Verhältnis zu Hegels Phänomenologie des Geistes*. Leipzig, 1920.

Glockner, Hermann, *F. T. Vischer und das neunzehnte Jahrhundert*. Berlin, 1931.

Oelmüller, W., *F. T. Vischer und das Problem der nachhegel-schen Ästhetik.* Stuttgart, 1959. An excellent modern study of Vischer, with an extensive bibliography.

STEPHEN D. CRITES

VISION. Seeing may be contrasted both with hearing and with feeling by touching. One way in which seeing differs from hearing follows from the truth of our language that we hear an object if and only if we hear a sound which is made by the object. There is no comparable linguistic practice in the case of seeing. This may lead us to think of sight as presenting objects to us directly, hearing only indirectly. One way in which seeing differs from feeling by touching is that if we feel something by touching it, our experience is of feeling it with a particular part of the body. Our visual experience, however, is not of seeing with our eyes. We can imagine a disembodied mind having visual experiences but not having tactile ones. Sight does not require our being part of the material world in the way in which feeling by touching does. One way in which seeing differs from both hearing and feeling by touching is in respect to time. It takes time to hear a tune or to feel the shape of a statue, but one seems to be able to see a landscape instantaneously. Thus, the directness of seeing when contrasted with hearing, its noninvolvement with its object when contrasted with feeling by touching, and its apparent temporal immediacy when contrasted with both hearing and feeling by touching are features that may partly explain the belief that sight is the most excellent of the senses; this is evinced in the use by ancient and modern philosophers of predominantly visual metaphors to describe intellectual apprehension.

Mediate and immediate perception. In vision, as in the other senses, a distinction is commonly drawn between what is immediately perceived and what is perceived only mediately. Examples of a person's mediated perception of something would be his seeing how hot his bath water is, his hearing how fast a train is going, his smelling the ripeness of fruit. To say that his awareness of these things is mediated is not, for example, to deny that the water actually looks hot to him. It is not that he consciously infers the heat of the water from something he can see—its steaminess. It is merely that his being able to see that the water is hot can be explained by reference to the association in his past experience of something that he saw (steaminess) with something that he felt (heat). By virtue of this association and of the steaminess that is visible to him, he can see how hot the water is.

Seeing distance. Berkeley, in *An Essay Towards a New Theory of Vision,* denies that distance is immediately perceived by vision. His argument for this, with which the *Essay* begins, has for its premise a proposition about the sense organ for sight: "Distance being a line directed end-wise to the eye, it projects only one point in the fund of the eye. Which point remains invariably the same, whether the distance be longer or shorter." In other words, the sense organ for sight, an eye, is such that there is nothing in its stimulation which differs systematically with the distance of the object; therefore, nothing could serve as the physiological basis for an immediate awareness by sight of the distance of the object perceived. The inference from this premise about a single eye to the con-

clusion that distance is not immediately perceived by sight is invalid. The sense organ for sight is not one eye but two, and we see with both at once. In looking at something with both eyes there *is* something about the eyes that does differ systematically with the distance of the object.

Berkeley acknowledges both these points in Sections IV and XVI, respectively. In Section XVI he remarks that "when we look at a near object with both eyes, according as it approaches or recedes from us, we alter the disposition of our eyes, by lessening or widening the interval between the pupils." Why does he not allow for the possibility that this alteration in the disposition of our eyes is the physiological basis for immediate visual distance perception? The answer would seem to be that Berkeley has an argument for distance as not being immediately perceived by sight and that this argument is independent of considerations about the functioning of the sense organs for sight. This argument holds (1) that distance is not "properly perceived" by sight and (2) that what is not properly perceived by a sense can be perceived only mediately by that sense. In Section CLVI he writes that "all that is properly perceived by the visive faculty amounts to no more than colours with their variations, and different proportions of light and shade."

In the absence of clearly stated criteria for settling what is properly perceived by any sense, debate about this argument is likely to be inconclusive. Let us suppose, however, that to say that something is properly perceived by a sense is to imply that a person who has not, and has never had, any other sense would yet be able to perceive it by that sense. On this supposition it seems intuitively obvious that the location of an object is not properly perceived by hearing. Directions do not belong in an all-sound world. It is not similarly intuitively obvious that distances do not belong in a world which is only visual. But even if it were, it could still be denied that distance must therefore be perceived mediately by sight. Locations of objects are not perceived mediately by hearing, except in a physiological sense of "mediately" with which we are not concerned. We may not be born with the perceptual capacity to hear a sound as coming from our right or left. Similarly, we may not be born with the perceptual capacity to see an object as being near or far. But our acquiring these perceptual capacities can have an explanation in terms of the interaction, at the physiological level, of the mechanisms subserving different senses. It does not require an explanation in terms of mediation at the level of consciousness.

The Molyneux problem. A related problem was raised by William Molyneux in a letter to Locke, dated March 2, 1693, reproduced in the second edition of Locke's *Essay Concerning Human Understanding:* "Suppose a man born blind, and now adult, and taught by his touch to distinguish between a cube and a sphere. . . . Suppose then the cube and sphere placed on a table, and the blind man made to see; query, whether by his sight, before he touched them, he could now distinguish and tell which is the globe, which the cube?" Molyneux, like Locke and Berkeley, gave a negative answer to this question. As the problem is formulated, it would appear to be an experimental issue, to be settled by investigation of such cases of recovery from early blindness as are reported in works by

M. von Senden and by R. L. Gregory and J. G. Wallace. As an experimental issue, the question is whether such cases "provide evidence of transfer of perceptual information from the tactual sphere to the visual modality" (Gregory and Wallace, *Recovery From Early Blindness*, p. 40); that is, whether they show that a person's acquiring the capacity to tell a cube from a sphere by touch affects the physical basis of vision in such a way that on seeing for the first time, he can tell one from the other by vision, either immediately or in a shorter time than someone without the relevant tactual experience. If it is assumed, as it was by Berkeley, that a person's perceptual capacities can be modified only through conscious learning processes, then the experimental issue will be prejudged in favor of a negative answer.

Primary and secondary qualities. Color, one of the qualities that Berkeley asserted to be properly perceived by sight, was held by Locke to be only a secondary quality (*Essay*, Book II, Ch. 8). The distinction between primary and secondary qualities is part of the representative theory of perception, which states that to perceive some quality of an object is to have an idea of the quality in one's mind. This idea may or may not resemble the quality. Primary qualities do resemble the ideas we have of them; secondary qualities do not but are powers of the object to produce in us the ideas of color, taste, etc., by virtue of the primary qualities. The manner in which qualities, or powers, as they may more appropriately be called in this theory of perception, produce ideas in us is "manifestly by impulse, the only way we can conceive bodies operate in," since it is by impulse that motions are caused in our animal spirits (nerves). This suggests an argument for the view that motion is a primary quality but that color is a secondary one: namely, that while we can understand how a motion can by impulse give rise to a motion, we cannot understand how a color (meaning not a power but a sensible quality) can by impulse give rise to a motion. Locke, however, could not have employed this argument, for he held that we can as little understand how a motion can produce a motion as we can understand how, as he supposed happens in voluntary movement, a motion can be produced by an idea (Book II, Ch. 23, Sec. 28).

Seeing as an achievement. The relevance of studies of the structures, mechanisms, and functionings of animal and human bodies qua percipient to our concept of vision is considered by Gilbert Ryle. In *Dilemmas* his aim is "to show that there is something which is drastically wrong with the whole programme of trying to schedule my seeing a tree either as a physiological or as a psychological end-stage of processes" (Ch. 7). Seeing is not something in which one can be occupied, Ryle believed, as is looking for or looking at something. The verb "see" functions in some respects like the verb "win." Neither stands for bodily or psychological states, or processes. In order to win a race, there must be another runner to beat. Similarly, to see a misprint, there must be a misprint to be seen. It is an achievement. F. N. Sibley comments that the verb "see" is not always or exclusively used in an achievement sense: "To look at or scrutinize an object for a given length of time, one must *throughout that length of time* be seeing it. . . . So here is at least one use of 'see' which is clearly different from the achievement or spotting use." Sibley thinks it questionable whether "see" ever functions as an achievement verb: "Surely it would be hard to find an occasion where someone who had looked for and suddenly seen something would reject the question 'Did you see it for long?' as an absurd one." This question could be sensible and yet "see" still be an achievement verb if "to see' meant the same as "to keep in sight," for keeping something in sight is an achievement. Sibley, however, denies that they mean the same. The difference between "keeping in sight" and "seeing" is like that between keeping the lead and merely being ahead. Keeping something in sight, like keeping the lead, is something that can be done skillfully, carefully, or doggedly; this is not true of simply seeing something.

Seeing as. The verb "see" appears in fact to serve a number of different but related functions. Cases can easily be constructed in which one is in doubt as to whether to say a person sees something, because one of these functions is served but not another. Two of the functions might be called the "in view" and "seeing as" functions. (The former is emphasized by Warnock, the latter by Vesey.) A case in which the former but not the latter is served would be a person's seeing a picture of a tree but not noticing that some of the branches are drawn in the shape of people's heads. Does he see the heads? It is not as if they were hidden from view. But he does not recognize them as heads. If a person sees a bar of soap as a lemon, it seems wrong to say simply that he sees a bar of soap or that he sees a lemon. The first may give the impression that he has recognized the soap as such; the second, that there is a lemon to be seen. What seems reasonable to say is that he sees a bar of soap but sees it as a lemon.

Bibliography

For literature on seeing contrasted with hearing and with feeling by touching, see Hans Jonas, "The Nobility of Sight," in *Philosophy and Phenomenological Research*, Vol. 14, No. 4 (1954), 507–519. See also bibliographies to SOUND and TOUCH.

For the perception of distance by vision, see George Berkeley, *An Essay Towards a New Theory of Vision* (Dublin, 1709); T. K. Abbott, *Sight and Touch: An Attempt to Disprove the Received (or Berkeleian) Theory of Vision* (London, 1864); and D. M. Armstrong, *Berkeley's Theory of Vision* (Melbourne, London, and New York, 1960).

For the Molyneux problem, see John Locke, *An Essay Concerning Human Understanding*, 2d ed. (London, 1694), Book II, Ch. 9, Sec. 8; G. W. Leibniz, *New Essays Concerning Human Understanding* (Chicago, 1916), Book II, Ch. 10; George Berkeley, *An Essay Towards a New Theory of Vision* (Dublin, 1709), Secs. 132–136; M. von Senden, *Space and Sight* (London, 1960); D. O. Hebb, *The Organization of Behavior* (New York and London, 1949), Ch. 2; and R. L. Gregory and J. G. Wallace, *Recovery From Early Blindness* (Cambridge, 1963).

On color, see John Locke, *An Essay Concerning Human Understanding* (London, 1690), Book II, Ch. 8.

For discussions of "see" as an achievement verb, see Gilbert Ryle, *Dilemmas* (Cambridge, 1954), Ch. 7, and F. N. Sibley, "Seeking, Scrutinizing and Seeing," in *Mind*, Vol. 64, No. 256 (1955), 455–478.

Other discussions of sight may be found in G. J. Warnock, "Seeing," in *PAS*, Vol. 55 (1954/1955), 201–218, and G. N. A. Vesey, "Seeing and Seeing As," in *PAS*, Vol. 56 (1955/1956), 109–124.

G. N. A. VESEY

VITALISM is primarily a metaphysical doctrine concerning the nature of living organisms, although it has been generalized, by Bergson for example, into a comprehensive metaphysics applicable to all phenomena. We shall examine vitalism only as a theory of life.

There have been three general answers to the question "What distinguishes living from nonliving things?" The first, and currently most fashionable, answer is "A complex pattern of organization in which each element of the pattern is itself a nonliving entity." In this view, a living organism, and each of its living parts, is exhaustively composed of inanimate parts; and these parts have no relations except those that are also exhibited in inanimate systems. The second answer is "The presence in living systems of emergent properties, contingent upon the organization of inanimate parts but not reducible to them." This answer resembles the first in acknowledging that a living system is exhaustively composed of nonliving parts; it holds, however, that the parts have relations in the living system that are never exhibited in inanimate systems. The third, and least fashionable, answer is "The presence in living systems of a substantial entity that imparts to the system powers possessed by no inanimate body." This is the position of vitalism. It holds, first, that in every living organism there is an entity that is not exhaustively composed of inanimate parts and, second, that the activities characteristic of living organisms are due, in some sense, to the activities of this entity.

The vital entity. The vital entity that animates an organism may, for brevity, be termed its "Life"—a usage that is in fact supported by vitalistic writings. The first thesis of vitalism may be stated as: the Life of an organism is substantial, but it is not—or at least not totally—made up of nonliving substance.

To say that the Life is substantial is to indicate that it has always been conceived more or less closely in accordance with an available doctrine concerning the nature of substance. All vitalists have, for example, held that the Life of an organism is a particular, not a universal; that it is the subject of predicates and not *only* a predicate; and that it is an agent possessing some degree of autonomy with respect to the body it animates. Most, but not all, vitalists have also maintained that Life, or at least an aspect of it, is capable of existence apart from its organism.

Naive vitalism. In addition to regarding Life as a substance, all vitalists have adopted a model that helps to specify the sort of substance it is. It may be helpful at this point to distinguish between naive and critical vitalism. Naive vitalism is embedded in common sense in much the same way as a version of mind–body dualism: everyday speech, common maxims, and habitual metaphors all suggest and support it. This type of vitalism, for example, is simply the most direct and literal interpretation of such expressions as "He lost his life," "a lifeless corpse," "A cat has nine lives," and "Scientists will someday create life in the test tube." When the average man thinks about the nature of life at all, he is likely to be guided by these and similar expressions. Naive vitalism has been and indeed still is the popular doctrine. The model of Life adopted by the naive vitalist is the most familiar one available; Life is regarded as a material substance, usually as a fluid body.

In the most primitive forms of vitalism, the Life is flatly identified with a material fluid, the breath, or the blood.

This view just misses materialism; it is vitalistic only because the fluid is assigned properties unlike those of any other material body, for example, the power of sensation. Slightly less primitive is the view that Life is a fluid like the blood, only invisible and rather more fiery. The doctrine of the spirits as it occurs in Galen and his successors is an example of this sort of vitalism. The process of etherealizing the Life culminates in the view that it is a fluid but one that is assigned no properties other than its power of animating an organism. This is still a prevalent view and was present, for example, in Mary Shelley's *Frankenstein*.

Critical vitalism. Although it has conceptual and historical roots in the material substance models, critical vitalism is far more sophisticated. Its various versions have been elaborated by professional philosophers and biologists; indeed, its two outstanding exponents, Aristotle and the twentieth-century biologist and philosopher Hans Driesch, were professionals in both fields. Aristotle's writings, especially his treatises *On the Soul* and *On the Generation of Animals,* are the standard works of vitalistic doctrine. In them Aristotle established four traditions that, it can be said, virtually determined the course of subsequent critical vitalism: he identifies what has been called here the Life of an organism with its psyche; he locates purposive activity, organic unity, and embryological development as the phenomena that vitalism must take most seriously; he argues that the activities of the part must be understood by reference to the form of the whole and that morphogenesis must be understood by reference to the form of the adult; and finally, he describes the manner of the psyche's influence on its organism as formal, not efficient, causation. In short, critical vitalism after Aristotle takes the soul as the model of the Life and attributes to Life the power of achieving and maintaining organic form.

Nature and history. Vitalism was defined above as a metaphysical doctrine in the sense that it is formulated with a degree of vagueness sufficient to exempt it from empirical refutation. However, this is not to say that vitalism has no implications concerning matters of fact. By means of very plausible arguments, vitalists have derived empirical consequences, some of which have been falsified and some verified. For example, it was argued that since the Life is the blood, a transfusion of blood into a corpse would bring it to life. This experiment failed, but the failure obviously did not refute every version of vitalism or even the doctrine that the Life is the blood. More seriously, Driesch argued that if vitalism is true, then a bit of embryonic tissue that ordinarily develops into a particular organ ought to be capable of developing into other organs. It does happen that some embryonic tissue has this capability. But although Driesch cites such an experiment, he did not actually predict its results. Had they been unfavorable, Driesch would still have had a way to save vitalism. For although he is willing to set limits to the regulative powers of the Life, he gives no antecedent specification of these limits.

In short, vitalism is irrefutable. When this is coupled with the tendency to describe the Life in terms that are among the most problematical in philosophy, it is easy to see that vitalism is subject to the worst aspects of intellectual obscurantism. Its leading exponents, for instance,

William Harvey, Georg Stahl, G. L. L. Buffon, Caspar Wolff, J. F. Blumenbach, Lorenz Oken, and K. E. von Baer, represent no improvement upon Aristotle either in the philosophical elaboration of vitalism or in its application to biological phenomena. The long period from Aristotle to Driesch, on the contrary, was characterized by confused invasions of naive vitalism; by the proliferation of such *ad hoc* entities as life forces, formative impulses, generative fluids, animal heat, and animal electricity; and by the merging of vitalistic thought with other fragments of biological metaphysics, such as the doctrine that living things are arranged along a linear scale corresponding to degrees of perfection (the *scala naturae*), and the archetypal conceptions of organic form. Moreover, vitalism showed a curious tendency to come out on the losing side of biological controversy: after Darwin, it was anti-Darwinian; and it supported the view that organic syntheses could be effected only in a living organism. It also supported the useless and misleading conception of a primordial living substance, the protoplasm, a term and idea that unfortunately still survive.

Hans Driesch. After Bergson, Hans Driesch is the best-known twentieth-century vitalist. (Bergson will not be considered here since his biological views are intelligible only as an application of his more general metaphysics.) Driesch's position may be described as Aristotelianism painstakingly applied to modern findings—some of them the result of his own laboratory researches—in physiology and embryology. He also provides three empirical proofs of vitalism.

Driesch defines vitalism as "the theory of the autonomy of the processes of life." It is doubtful that this rules out any biological theories at all, but it does locate Driesch's major concern. He explicitly distinguishes between vitalism and animism, but he does not define "animism." The term seems to be roughly equivalent to naive vitalism. He also considers vitalistic the view that the parts of an organic system can be understood only by reference to the form of the whole—a view that might preferably be classified as "organismic." But the latter distinction had not been clearly drawn in Driesch's time; he is quite correct in assuming that organismic biology is closer to the vitalistic tradition than, for example, Cartesian mechanism is.

According to Driesch, the Life of an organism is a substantial entity, an entelechy. Driesch employs this term as a mark of respect for Aristotle, although he does not use it with Aristotle's meaning. For Driesch, the entelechy is an autonomous, mindlike, nonspatial entity that exercises control over the course of organic processes; it is not actuality or activity in Aristotle's sense.

Driesch admits that the laws of physics and chemistry apply to organic changes. There is even a sense in which everything that happens in the organism is subject to physicochemical explanation. We may consider, for example, the first division of a fertilized ovum into two blastomeres (daughter cells). Even this relatively simple event can be analyzed as a complex sequence of cooperating chemical syntheses and mechanical movements resulting in, among other things, the duplication of the nucleus, the migration of the daughter nuclei into the opposite sides of the egg, and the formation of a cell membrane between them. Each

step in each sequence is a physicochemical event and could be, at least in principle, described and explained as such. But chemistry and physics cannot explain why the steps occur when and where they do. Thus—and on this point some interpretation is necessary—although each event that constitutes first cleavage is physicochemical, it is subject only to *post hoc* explanation in physicochemical terms. The state of the egg and its environment at time t does not determine what events will begin at later time $t + dt$. But the latter events, after they have occurred, can be exhibited as consequences of events that ended at t. The state of the egg at t determines a range of possibilities; the entelechy influences the course of cleavage, in Driesch's terms, selectively "suspending" and "relaxing the suspension" of these possibilities.

An analogy may shed some light on this doctrine. Suppose that a person's voluntary acts are undetermined, at least at the physicochemical level; that for example, whether or not I clench my fist is not decided by the laws of physics and chemistry. Then the constitution of my body at a given time presents two possibilities, both within my organic capacity: to clench my fist or not. My choice to clench it is analogous to the action of an entelechy. The clenching could not by hypothesis have been predicted on physicochemical grounds, but after its occurrence it can be explained as the outcome of a sequence of physical and chemical events.

Driesch conceives of the laws of nature as placing constraints on the possible activities of a system. For example, the first principle of energetics (thermodynamics) states simply that whatever happens, energy is conserved, but conservation of energy is compatible with any number of actual changes in the system. The entelechy operates in the region of possibilities left open by the operation of laws. Driesch favors a particular metaphor: the entelechy is like an artist who gives form to a material medium, the medium itself both providing possibilities and presenting limitations.

There are, according to Driesch, three "empirical proofs" of vitalism.

(1) In 1888 the German biologist Wilhelm Roux performed the following experiment. Just after the first cleavage of a frog's egg he killed one blastomere with a hot needle. He allowed the other to develop, and it formed a half embryo, resembling a normal embryo that had been cut in two. Roux concluded that the egg is essentially a machine; after cleavage half its parts are in each blastomere.

Driesch performed a similar experiment in 1891 with the eggs of a sea urchin. He separated the blastomeres after first cleavage but found that instead of forming a half embryo, each blastomere developed into a perfect but half-sized larva. This result, Driesch argued, is incompatible with Roux's theory of the successive subdivision of the germ machinery. No machine that could build an organism could possibly build the same organism after it was chopped in two.

Subsequent embryologists have multiplied cases similar to that of Driesch's urchin eggs. Parts of embryos often can generate other than their normal parts. Driesch assigns the term "harmonious equipotential system" to wholes whose parts cooperate in the formation of an organic unity, if the parts themselves also have the potentiality of forming other parts of the unity. The existence of harmonious equipotential systems constitutes the first proof of vitalism.

(2) The formation of a whole sea urchin larva from a single blastomere—one that under ordinary circumstances would form one half of the larva—also provides an illustration of what Driesch calls a "complex equipotential system," that is, a system in which a part, the blastomere, forms a whole, the larva, when it would ordinarily form only a part. The existence of complex equipotential systems provides the second proof.

(3) The third proof is the existence of agency; its paradigm is deliberate human action. The action of an entelechy has been compared to conscious choice, and, indeed, Driesch regards human agency as a special mode of the entelechy's regulation of living processes. But agency characterizes other vital processes as well, especially embryological development. Unfortunately, his definition of agency as "an individual 'answer' to an individual stimulus—founded upon an historical basis" is not made clear.

Vitalism is not a popular theory among biologists, for many reasons apart from its affinity with various lost causes. The successful elucidation of various pieces of biological machinery (for example, the rather successful models of cleavage that at least outline a possible chemical explanation of equipotentiality) have rendered Driesch's first and second proofs rather suspect and, in general, have fostered confidence in the future of nonvitalist theory. There have been numerous philosophical criticisms of vitalism, most of them centering on the rather obvious point that vitalism provides nothing more than pseudoexplanation. The strongest case for vitalism can be summarized as follows. With respect to invulnerability to criticism, vitalism and its most plausible alternatives are in exactly the same position. The various lines of contemporary argument against the possibility of accounting for human agency on an inorganic model lend some support to the vitalist contention that physics and chemistry extend over only some aspects of organic activity.

Bibliography

Agar, W. E., *A Contribution to the Theory of Living Organisms,* 2d ed. Melbourne, 1951.

Aristotle, *The Works of Aristotle Translated Into English,* 11 vols., J. A. Smith and W. D. Ross, eds. Oxford, 1908–1952. See *De Generatione Animalium* (Vol. II) and *De Anima* (Vol. III).

Bergson, Henri, *Creative Evolution,* translated by Arthur Mitchell. New York, 1911.

Driesch, Hans, *The Science and Philosophy of the Organism.* London, 1908.

Driesch, Hans, *The History and Theory of Vitalism.* London, 1914.

Schlick, Moritz, *Philosophy of Nature.* New York, 1949. A classic critique of vitalism.

Schubert-Soldern, Rainer, *Mechanism and Vitalism: Philosophical Aspects of Biology,* translated by C. E. Robin. Notre Dame, Ind., 1962.

Morton O. Beckner

VITORIA, FRANCISCO DE (1492/1493–1546), political and legal philosopher and theologian, was born in Vitoria, capital of the Basque province of Álava, Spain.

While still a boy, he joined the Dominican order in Burgos, and in 1509 or 1510 he was sent to the Collège Saint-Jacques in Paris, where he finished his courses in the humanities and went on to study philosophy and theology. While a student of theology, he directed an edition of the *Secunda Secundae* ("Second Part of the Second Part" of the *Summa*) of St. Thomas Aquinas. The date of his ordination is unknown. From 1516 to 1522 or 1523 he taught theology in the *écoles majeures* of the Collège Saint-Jacques and edited the *Sermones Dominicales* of Peter of Covarrubias, the *Summa Aurea* of St. Antoninus of Florence, and the *Diccionario moral* of Peter Bercherio. He obtained the licentiate and doctorate in theology in 1522. After teaching theology at St. Gregory's monastery in Valladolid from 1523 to 1526, he won by competition the "chair of prime," the most important chair of theology, at the University of Salamanca and held it until his death. Melchior Cano, Mancio, Ledesma, Tudela, Orellana, and Barron, among others, were his disciples. Vitoria helped to formulate the imperial legislation regarding the newly discovered American territories.

With the exception of the prologues to his editions of the works mentioned, Vitoria published nothing during his lifetime. His works include *lecturas* (his class lectures as preserved in the notes taken by his disciples), many of which have been published recently; *relectiones* (extraordinary lectures, which are summaries or popularizations of his ordinary lectures), published for the first time in 1557; and several writings on different topics. Vitoria is famous chiefly for his *relectiones,* the most important of which are *De Potestate Civili, De Potestate Ecclesiae Prior, De Potestate Ecclesiae Posterior, De Potestate Papae et Concilii,* and, particularly, *De Indis* and *De Iure Belli.*

According to Vitoria, political society (*respublica*) is a perfect, self-sufficient society, a moral and juridical person. It is a natural, not a conventional, society. In other words, it is required by nature and has its end set by nature. Actual states are the result of positive human acts, but men are obliged by natural law to live in some form of political society, outside of which no good or full human life is possible. The end of society is twofold: to promote the common good and virtuous life of its citizens and to protect their rights. The proximate origin of political society is the will of families. Authority is an essential property of the state, for without it the organic unity of the citizens and their activity, necessary for the attainment of the common temporal good, would be impossible. Like every natural right, authority derives ultimately from nature's author and resides originally in the body politic. However, since political society is incapable of exercising public authority directly, it must transfer it to one or several rulers. Particular forms of government depend on the will of the citizens. The absolutely best form is monarchy, "for the whole world is most wisely ruled by one Prince and Lord." The reason behind this claim is that monarchy, better than any other form, creates and preserves the necessary unity of social action without unduly curtailing the citizen's freedom; "freedom in monarchy," Vitoria remarked, "is no less than in democracy, wherein discussions and seditions, inimical to liberty, are the unavoidable result of the participation of many in government."

Beyond individual states there is a larger society, the international society constituted by the whole human family. It, too, is natural and necessary, although less strictly so, for the satisfaction of man's needs and the development and perfection of his faculties. International society possesses its own authority, which is immanent in the whole of humankind. From this universal authority derive the laws that establish the rights and correlative duties of the different states. The sum of these laws forms the *ius gentium,* which is partly made up of conclusions drawn from the principles of natural law by natural reason and partly of positive customs and treaties among nations. Vitoria established the chief rights of every nation, whether great or small, as the right to existence; the right to juridical equality; the right to independence (except where a nation is juridically and politically so immature as to be incapable of self-rule, in which case a more civilized nation may temporarily administer it under mandate or keep it in trusteeship); the right to free communication and trade, denial of which by another nation could justify war; and the right—and the duty—of every state to intervene in defense of nations victimized by domestic tyrants or threatened or attacked by stronger nations.

War is licit as a last resort, according to Vitoria, when all other means of persuasion have failed. The cause that justifies a war, whether defensive or offensive, is the violation of a right. An essential condition for the licitness of a war is that the evils resulting from it will not be greater than the good intended. Defensive war can be justly undertaken by any person; offensive war can be launched only by public authority. The ruler waging a just war is invested with power by human society. Just as the state has the power to punish criminals among its citizens, so mankind has the power to punish a nation guilty of injustice. All means necessary for the attainment of victory are permissible in a just war. Once victory is achieved, the conquering nation should exercise its rights over the conquered with moderation and Christian charity.

The thesis that Vitoria was the founder of modern international law has been definitively established by numerous scholars. It was officially acknowledged in 1926, when the Dutch Association of Grotius gave the University of Salamanca a gold medal coined to honor Vitoria as the founder of international law. Also in 1926 the Asociación Francisco de Vitoria was founded in Spain for the purpose of studying and spreading Vitoria's ideas through publications, conferences, and special courses at the University of Salamanca.

Works by Vitoria

Commentarios á la "Secunda Secundae" de Santo Tomás, Vicente Beltrán de Heredia, ed., 5 vols. Salamanca, 1932–1935.
Relectiones Theologicae, edited and translated into Spanish by Luis G. Alonso Getino, 3 vols. Madrid, 1933–1936. There is an English translation and photographic reproduction of the 1696 edition of *Relectiones* in the series Classics of International Law. Washington, 1917.

Works on Vitoria

Beltrán de Heredia, Vicente, *Francisco de Vitoria.* Barcelona, 1939.
Beltrán de Heredia, Vicente, "Vitoria (François de)," in *Dictionnaire de théologie catholique.* Vol. XV, cols. 3117–3133.
Getino, Luis G. Alonso, *El maestro fray Francisco de Vitoria: su vida, su doctrina y su influencia.* Madrid, 1930.
Giacon, Carlo, *La seconda scolastica,* Vol. I, *I grandi commentatori di San Tommaso.* Milan, 1944. Pp. 163–213.
Naszályi, Aemilius, *Doctrina Francisci de Vitoria de Statu.* Rome, 1937.
Scott, James Brown, *The Spanish Origin of International Law,* Vol. I, *Francisco de Vitoria and His Law of Nations.* Oxford, 1934.
Soder, Josef, *Die Idee der Völkergemeinschaft. F. de Vitoria und die philosophischen Grundlagen des Völkerrechts.* Frankfurt am Main and Berlin, 1955.
Solana, Marcial, *Historia de la filosofía española,* 3 vols. Madrid, 1941. Vol. III, pp. 43–91.
Truyol y Serra, Antonio, *Los principios del derecho público en Francisco de Vitoria.* Madrid, 1946.

Felix Alluntis, O.F.M.

VIVES, JUAN LUIS (1492–1540), Spanish humanist, was born in Valencia and died in Bruges. Considerably younger than such scholars as Erasmus, Budé, and Colet, Vives deserves an honorable place among them for his moral seriousness, sincerity of religious belief, promotion of education, and social concern, as manifested in projects for the promotion of peace and the relief of the poor. In many of these respects Vives is approached only by his nearer contemporary, Thomas More; his character emerges very favorably from any comparison with the earlier group. His efforts to secure patronage from the nobility did not blind him to the plight of those more needy than he, nor did he engage in the acrimonious personal quarrels that marred the character of some humanists.

Vives was a fine scholar and an excellent writer. After initial schooling in Spain he went to Paris to attend the university. Here he found still active a school of terminist logicians and physicists whose influence extended, so Vives tells us, to all the higher faculties. The earlier Oxford and Paris developments in logic and physics were being studied by teachers under the influence of the Scottish philosopher and theologian John Major. But the new learning was gaining favor, and there were signs among both students and teachers of dissatisfaction with the nominalist approach. Two of Vives' own teachers, Gaspar Lax and John Dullaert, told him that they were sorry that they had wasted so much time on "useless little questions." The "little questions" concerned such issues as the logical analysis of signification and of inference, as well as the quantification of physical phenomena. The complaint voiced by Vives and by many other humanists concerned not so much the intrinsic value of these discussions as the fact that they were permitted to invade all other fields of learning, often to the exclusion of the proper subject matter. Vives particularly disliked the petty vindictiveness and personal egoism displayed by younger men who delighted in scoring points over older opponents. When Vives returned to the University of Paris after his sojourn at Louvain, he expected to meet with a cool reception because of his book *Adversus Pseudodialecticos* ("Against the Pseudo Dialecticians," 1520), in which he sharply criticized the academic climate at the university. To his surprise, he was warmly received, as he told Erasmus in a letter of 1520, and was assured that terminist quibbling was no longer tolerated in nonlogical discussions.

Vives' criticism of school philosophy was one of the more moderate and informed humanist attacks. He held

Aristotle and the other ancients in high regard but deplored the failure of their followers to observe nature afresh. Vives condemned the undue humility of those who claimed to be only "dwarfs, standing on the shoulders of giants": if we cannot see further than our predecessors, he insists, it is not because we are dwarfs and they giants but because we are lying prostrate on the ground, having given up the search for the truth. Vives insists as strongly as did Lorenzo Valla that philosophical terminology should not be artificial; the usage of such ancient writers as Cicero and Seneca should be taken as models. Philosophers should not depart too far from the speech of the people. Vives admitted, however, that it may occasionally be necessary for philosophers to coin terms of their own as well as to clarify those in ordinary usage.

Vives' own philosophy may be characterized as Augustinian in its general outlines, with eternal salvation and the vision of God overriding lesser concerns. It is in the light of this general orientation that this much discussed "empiricism" must be evaluated. Of all things on earth, it is man's own soul that it most behooves him to know, by means of direct observation. But undue curiosity concerning other things, especially concerning their "inner natures and causes," is out of place and, indeed, impious. To inquire too curiously into the elements, the forms of living beings, or the number, magnitude, disposition, and powers of natural objects is to "tear the seventh veil." Such an attitude is certainly not favorable to purely theoretical scientific inquiry. But Vives' central concern is with man's felicity, and only to the extent that inquiry into nature serves to promote man's felicity is it admissible as part of the curriculum of studies. This curriculum would stress the useful arts, to the analysis of which Vives devoted great attention. In common with humanists in general, Vives stressed the utility of the arts and insisted that they must be systematized or brought into rules and precepts so as to be applicable to the purposes of ordinary life. Inordinate attention to their logical analysis must be curtailed; instead, students are to be constantly reminded of the empirical origins of useful knowledge. In his discussion of method in the arts, Vives explicitly drew on Galen as well as on suggestions in Aristotle.

Neither history nor theology is an art from this standpoint, since neither subject has been reduced to rules. Vives was impatient with the school theology of his time; he found little of value in the controversies between Scotists and Thomists and disliked their fanaticism: "They would accuse each other of heresy if it were not for the mellowing effect of the customs of the school." It has been aptly remarked that Vives' religious thought bears close affinities with northern Pietism as exemplified by the Brethren of the Common Life, the movement that left such an impression on Erasmus. In keeping with this is Vives' obvious sympathy for the common people, a note conspicuously absent from the writings of many other humanists.

On a few points Vives specifically rejected Platonism—for example, in maintaining that God does not require divine Ideas and that we do not have reminiscences of Ideas from our past lives. Vives prefers to explain the insights of Plato's doctrine of reminiscence by means of certain natural relationships between the human mind and

"those first true seeds of knowledge whence all the rest of our knowledge springs," called anticipations by the Stoics. This Stoic doctrine merges easily in Vives' thought, as in that of many of his contemporaries, with an appeal to common sense (*sensus communis*), which here takes on its modern flavor. Common sense furnishes us with an argument for God's existence, there being no people so benighted as to be completely destitute of some knowledge, however dim, of God. Human minds, furthermore, are all informed with the need to worship God, but what form this worship takes is a matter of human persuasion. Here we may trace the influence of Florentine Platonism, with which Vives was quite familiar. Perhaps from the same source is Vives' often repeated assertion that nothing would be more wretched than man if his actions aimed only at earthly ends. He condemns the vices of pleasure (*voluptas*) and pride (*superbia*) as roundly as any other medieval writer. Pride is responsible for the "frenzied craving for knowledge" shown by some men who are anxious to appear distinguished among their fellow men. Only piety, however, can permanently satisfy man and give him rest.

Bibliography

Vives' writings, with the exception of his commentaries on Augustine's *City of God*, were collected by Mayáns y Ciscar, 8 vols. (Valencia, 1782). The biography by Adolfo Bonilla y San Martín, *Luis Vives y la filosofía del renacimiento* (Madrid, 1903), is reliable but not too detailed. See also *Vives: On Education, a translation of the De Tradendis Disciplinis*, translated by Foster Watson (Cambridge, 1913), and Vives' *De Anima et Vita*, M. Sancipriano, ed. (Florence, 1954).

NEAL W. GILBERT

VOID. See VACUUM AND VOID.

VOLITION. For it to be true that a person is moving his hand, it must be true that his hand is in motion. However, the statement "He is moving his hand" does not mean the same as "His hand is in motion." Some philosophers think of a movement (as distinct from a motion) as being really two things causally connected: (1) a mental activity and (2) its effect, a bodily motion. Instances of the mental activity they call acts of volition, or acts of willing.

Descartes. This terminology, however, is neither part of our everyday speech about our activities nor a means of referring to something we can learn, by training in introspection, to detect in ourselves when we perform these activities. It is the expression of a philosophical theory about man's nature, namely, Descartes's theory that a person comprises two distinct substances, soul and body. Gilbert Ryle calls this theory "the dogma of the Ghost in the Machine."

According to the theory, the workings of the body are motions of matter in space. The causes of these motions must then be *either* other motions of matter in space *or*, in the privileged case of human beings, thrusts of another kind. In some way which must forever remain a mystery, mental thrusts, which are not movements of matter in space, can cause muscles to contract. To describe a man as intentionally pulling the trigger is to state that such a mental thrust did cause the contraction of the muscles of his finger. So the language of "volitions" is the language of the para-mechanical theory of the mind. (*The Concept of Mind*, p. 63)

Even Descartes was aware of the disharmony between his doctrine of two distinct substances and the lessons of "ordinary life and conversation" concerning man's nature. In his correspondence with Princess Elizabeth he acknowledged that the plain man's notion is of "one single person who has at once body and consciousness." Descartes tried in vain to find a place for this notion in his conceptual framework by ascribing to us "primitive notions" not only of extension (the essence of body) and of thought (the essence of soul) but also of the union of soul and body. This notion involves the notion of one thing's moving another without contact, a notion which, Descartes held, we misuse by applying it to gravity. That this notion of the union of soul and body was not taken up by Descartes's followers is perhaps understandable in view of his own admission "that the human mind is incapable of distinctly conceiving both the distinction between body and soul and their union, at one and the same time; for that requires our conceiving them as a single thing and simultaneously conceiving them as two things, which is self contradictory."

Malebranche, Leibniz, Spinoza. Descartes's immediate successors retained his distinction between extension and thought but differed in their explanation of the parallelism of mental and bodily events. The occasionalists, Malebranche and others, postulated the intervention of God as the cause of an appropriate bodily event's occurring on the occasion of a mental one, or vice versa. Leibniz achieved the same result by postulating a "pre-established harmony" between that monad which was a man's soul, and the monads that were the reality behind his phenomenal body. Spinoza made soul and body "one and the same thing, conceived now under the attribute of thought, and now under that of extension."

Double-aspect theory. Spinoza held talk of human actions being voluntary to be, in the last analysis, meaningless. This would not seem to be a necessary corollary of a theory in other respects not unlike that of Spinoza, the "double-aspect" theory. This theory was held by G. H. Lewes and others in the second half of the nineteenth century. A linguistic version of the theory, which might be called the "two-languages" theory, is espoused by D. M. Mackay. "We have two different and entirely legitimate languages which we use about human activity," he wrote, a "subject-language" to which belong "words defined from the standpoint of myself as the actor in the situation" and an "object-language" to which belong the words used by an observer describing the situation. Mackay's two-languages theory leaves mysterious the relation of the mental aspect of a voluntary movement to the bodily aspect. In this view "there is no need—indeed it would be fallacious—to look for a causal mechanism by which mental and physical activity could act on one another. Their unity is already a closer (and a more mysterious) one than if they were pictured as separate activities in quasi-mechanical interaction, one of them visible and the other invisible."

Locke and Hume. The point of denying the relation to be causal and the meaning of union (Descartes) or unity (Mackay) in this connection are questions to which an answer may be found by reflection on the controversy as it developed in the writings of the British empiricists Locke and Hume.

Locke held (1) that we get the idea of active power through reflection (introspection) when we perform some voluntary movement, and (2) that we cannot comprehend "how our minds move or stop our bodies by thought." Hume objected to the first proposition and claimed that to see its falsity "we need only consider, that the will being here considered as a cause, has no more a discoverable connection with its effects, than any material cause has with its proper effect." Hume's position is an advance in clarity on that of Locke. Locke did not even hint at what it would be like to comprehend how our minds move our bodies by thought, so it was not clear what he was denying. Hume, however, did say things that suggested what it would be like to discover a connection between the act of will and the bodily motion. If the bodily motion produced by an act of will could "be foreseen without the experience of their constant conjunction," then whatever there might be about the act of will that allowed the bodily motion to be foreseen would constitute "a discoverable connection." Hume, in effect, denied that there was anything about the act of will that allowed the bodily motion to be foreseen.

This way of putting it suggests a reformulation of the question in the following terms: Can an act of will, a volition, be individuated independently of the bodily motion that it is meant to produce? (If it cannot, then there is a connection—an "internal" connection—between them, such that given a specific volition, one can foresee what motion will occur in a body that is functioning normally.) Two possible answers to this question are "No, as a matter of fact" and "No, as a matter of necessity."

Ideomotor theory. The first answer may take the form of the ideomotor theory of voluntary action. This theory is based on the alleged discovery "that every representation of a movement awakens in some degree the actual movement which is its object; and awakens it in a maximum degree whenever it is not kept from so doing by an antagonistic representation present simultaneously to the mind" (William James). The theory holds that having a volition to move a certain part of one's body is simply having an idea either of that movement's occurring or of what it feels like for the movement to be occurring. C. A. Campbell, a contemporary philosopher who holds this theory, goes so far as to deny that a person can will to move his leg if he has forgotten what specific sensations are associated with moving it. There are reasons to believe that the ideomotor theory is, in fact, false. The psychologist C. T. Morgan refers to the supposition that "a memory of a movement must necessarily precede the movement which we desire to make" and comments that "not only is this anticipatory proprioception not necessary, but research has also shown that proprioception alone—or even when combined with a visual image of what the movement should be—is not a sufficient preliminary process to produce 'at will' a movement never before voluntarily initiated."

According to the ideomotor theory, an act of will cannot,

as a matter of fact, be individuated independently of the bodily motion it is meant to produce. But it is a contingent fact that the volition consists in having an idea of the bodily motion in question; it could have been the case that to move my arm I had to have an idea of a movement of some part of my brain or of anything whatever. G. Dawes Hicks gives a reason for believing the connection to be a contingent one and therefore for believing that the character of the act of will might have been different and the outcome the same, or the character might have been the same and the outcome different.

> Seeing that for the realization of a resolve or a purpose the conscious subject is at the mercy of an extraordinarily intricate conjunction of factors lying beyond the range of his inner life . . . the conclusion seems forced upon us that what specifically characterizes volition as a fact of mind must be, to a large extent, at least, independent of the execution which is normally its consequent. The scope of willing, the content of the inner state which we call an act of will, would doubtless be enormously affected if execution habitually happened in a way other than that in which, as a matter of fact, it does happen, but the peculiar characteristic of willing as a state of mind might still be the same as it is now.   ("The Nature of Willing," p. 40)

Hicks does not say why this conclusion should be "forced upon us." The principle of the inference would seem to involve the notion that the conscious subject is dependent on the functioning of his nervous system in precisely the same way that an automobile driver is dependent on the functioning of the steering mechanism of his vehicle: as the driver is at one end of the steering mechanism, so the conscious subject is at one end of the nervous system.

It cannot be denied, of course, that in some sense the conscious subject is dependent on the proper functioning of his nervous system, muscles, and so on. The question is, Can we not recognize this without having to adopt some form of the ideomotor theory?

An alternative approach. If a man who has lost sensation in one arm is asked to put the affected hand over his head while his eyes are closed and is at the same time prevented from doing so by having his hand held down, he will be very surprised on opening his eyes to find that the movement has not taken place. We cannot say that he has moved his hand, because his hand has not moved. But it is not as if he had simply ignored the request. Until he opens his eyes, he is convinced that he has moved his hand. We want to say that he has done something. He did not *try* to move his hand, if one is said to "try" to do something only when one is conscious of having to overcome some obstacle. Evidently to accommodate this case we require some extension of everyday speech about our activities. Let us distinguish between what someone does as a conscious subject and what he does as a person. In the case under discussion the man as a person does nothing, because no motion takes place. What does he do, regarded as a conscious subject? Must the extension of our everyday language be one which suggests that when someone moves his hand, what he does as a conscious subject is something related only externally to the movement? Why should we

not say that the patient in this case moves his hand as a conscious subject but not as a person and leave it at that?

To say this would be to hold that the mental aspect of a voluntary movement necessarily cannot be individuated independently of the bodily movement. If, following Hume, we hold that nothing can be said about an effect from a consideration of the cause alone (prior to experience of their conjunction), then to give this answer would be to deny that the relation between the mental aspect and the bodily aspect is a causal one. What is more, in one interpretation of Descartes's test for distinctness of substances (our being able to understand one clearly and distinctly apart from another), it is to repudiate dualism.

Bibliography

The views referred to in this article are expressed in the following works, listed in order of reference: Gilbert Ryle, *The Concept of Mind* (London and New York, 1949), Ch. 3; René Descartes, *Philosophical Writings*, translated and edited by G. E. M. Anscombe and P. T. Geach (London and New York, 1954), pp. 274–282; Nicolas Malebranche, *Dialogues on Metaphysics and Religion*, translated by M. Ginsberg (London, 1923); G. W. Leibniz, *Discourse on Metaphysics*, translated by P. G. Lucas and L. Grint (Manchester, 1953), Article 33; Benedict Spinoza, *Ethics*, in *Opera Posthuma*, J. Jellis, ed. (Amsterdam, 1677), Part II; G. H. Lewes, *The Physical Basis of Mind* (London, 1877), Problem 3, Chs. 3 and 7; D. M. Mackay, "Brain and Will," in *Listener* (May 16, 1957), 788–789; John Locke, *An Essay Concerning Human Understanding* (London, 1690), Book II, Chs. 21 and 23, Sec. 28; David Hume, *Treatise of Human Nature*, L. A. Selby-Bigge, ed. (Oxford, 1888), pp. 632–633; William James, *Principles of Psychology* (London, 1891), Ch. 26; C. A. Campbell, *On Selfhood and Godhood* (London, 1957), Lecture 8; C. T. Morgan, "Voluntary Control of Movement," in E. G. Boring and others, *Foundations of Psychology* (New York, 1948), p. 50; and G. Dawes Hicks, "The Nature of Willing," in *PAS*, Vol. 13 (1912/1913), 40. Relevant extracts from most of the above works are contained in G. N. A. Vesey, ed., *Body and Mind* (London, 1964).

Recent philosophical work on volition has been much influenced by Wittgenstein's treatment of this and related topics in *The Blue and Brown Books* (Oxford, 1958), especially pp. 150–152, and *Philosophical Investigations* (Oxford, 1953), especially pp. 159–167. Works exhibiting a direct or indirect debt to Wittgenstein include, in addition to Ryle (see above): A. I. Melden, *Free Action* (London and New York, 1961); D. F. Pears, ed., *Freedom and the Will* (London and New York, 1963); B. O'Shaughnessy, "The Limits of the Will," in *Philosophical Review*, Vol. 64, No. 4 (1956), 443–490; and G. N. A. Vesey, "Volition," in *Philosophy*, Vol. 36, No. 138 (1961), 352–365, reprinted in D. F. Gustafson, ed., *Essays in Philosophical Psychology* (New York, 1964).

G. N. A. VESEY

VOLNEY, CONSTANTIN-FRANÇOIS DE CHASSEBOEUF, COMTE DE (1757–1820), French *philosophe* and historian, was born in Anjou. He early showed a scholarly disposition, and at 15 he asked for Hebrew lessons in order to verify translations of the Bible. Inheriting independent wealth, he left for Paris at 17, turned down his father's plea to study law, and, interested in the relation between the moral and the physical aspects of man, chose medicine instead. He also pursued his study of history and languages, and he became involved in the polemics and ideological struggles of the time. In 1783 he gave himself the name Volney and left for Egypt and Syria "to acquire new knowledge and embellish the rest of my life by an aura of respect and esteem." After eight months

in a Coptic monastery, devoted to mastering Arabic, he spent three and a half years traveling on foot throughout Egypt and Syria. The resulting *Voyage en Égypte et Syrie* (1787) is his most enduring production. A remarkable travel book, it differs from those of the romantic travelers (such as Chateaubriand) by its impersonality and its careful, objective account of physical, political, and moral conditions. It was utilized as a guide by Napoleon's armies.

After his return to France, his prestige assured, he was placed in charge of commercial relations with Corsica and, on the outbreak of the Revolution, was elected a representative of the third estate. His revolutionary career was quite distinguished; he defended civil rights and freedoms, attacked the church strongly, and later opposed the excesses of the Jacobins. In 1792 he bought land in Corsica and showed how products of the New World could be successfully transplanted. There he met and became friendly with Napoleon, whose greatness he foresaw. Forced to leave because of unrest in Corsica, he subsequently spent ten months in prison, falsely accused of being a royalist, until he was released after the ninth of Thermidor. Appointed professor of history in the new École Normale, he developed a critical methodology for historical investigation. When that institution was suppressed in 1795, he went to the United States. Well received by Washington, he was happy at first. Adams, however, was unforgiving of Volney's severe criticisms of his political writings, and he felt an animosity toward the French as a result of the XYZ Affair. In addition, a theological quarrel with Joseph Priestley, who was then in America, did not dispose Adams favorably toward visiting philosophers. Accused of being a secret agent, Volney was forced to leave America in 1798, but by then he had traveled all over the country. In 1803 he published *Tableau du climat et du sol des États-Unis d'Amérique*, an objective description famous for its picture of Niagara Falls; in the preface he told of his persecutions.

Back in France, Volney cooperated in Napoleon's coup of the 18th Brumaire and was named senator. However, he frequently opposed Napoleon's dictatorial tendencies, and he also opposed the Concordat of 1801. Napoleon ridiculed him along with his whole group of *idéologues* (including Pierre Cabanis and Comte Antoine Destutt de Tracy), but he later made Volney a count. Volney, however, supported the Restoration and was rewarded with a peerage. Volney was known for his independence and for his ill-tempered, overbearing character.

Works. Volney's most famous work is *Les Ruines, ou Méditations sur les révolutions des empires* (1791), a work conceived in Franklin's study in Paris. Widely read and admired during his lifetime and later, it now seems a shallow piece of rhetoric. It was much read in English, under the title *The Ruins of Empires* (1792). The author contemplates the ruins of Palmyra and wonders how powerful empires, seemingly destined to last forever, succumbed to the universal law of change and destruction. A belated example of "philosophic" polemics, *Les Ruines* promoted deism by a comparative study of religious doctrines and practices, preached tolerance and free inquiry, the unalienable rights of men and peoples, and the right of self-government. Some ethical ideas were sketched, which

Volney developed in *La Loi naturelle*. Thus, man in the state of nature "did not see at his side beings descended from the heavens to inform him of his needs which he owes only to his senses, to instruct him of duties which are born solely of his needs."

Even more interesting as a reflection of moderate views held by *philosophes* at the end of the century is Volney's *La Loi naturelle, ou Catéchisme du citoyen français* (1792). In this work he affirmed a natural law given by God, but this natural law is essentially physical ("the regular and constant order by which God rules the universe"). The moral aspect of natural law is only an extension of the biological requirement for self-preservation and "perfection" on the part of the individual and the species. Consequently, morals could become an exact science. In this work, as in *Les Ruines*, Volney praised the harmony and order of relationships in the universe, declaring that man is no exception to their rule; yet within this impersonal natural law he discerned purpose and final causes, namely, the happiness and perfection of the individual. Physical suffering has a useful natural function, and the advantage of greater sensitivity in man is compensated by the disadvantage of greater suffering. Law is a command (or prohibition) followed by reward or punishment. Moral law depends on general and constant rules of conduct which inhere in the order of things. Moral law is not obvious; rather, it forms "in its developments and consequences, a complex ensemble which requires the knowledge of many facts and all the sagacity of reasoning." The basic principle of natural law is self-preservation, not happiness, which is "an article of luxury." Pleasure and pain are the mechanisms by which natural law works. Men are aware of these laws only in society. Life in society is man's true natural state, since it is necessary for his self-preservation; in what is called the state of nature, man was only a miserable brute. Volney's formulations reveal the infiltration of naturalistic viewpoints into natural law theory. The whole moral dimension of human life is reduced to a basic biological law, and all of morality is based on narrow utilitarian values.

Volney was also the author of works on Biblical chronology (hostile to orthodox interpretations) and on ancient history. He proposed a universal alphabet and the study of culture through language.

Bibliography

Volney's complete works were published as *Oeuvres complètes* in 8 volumes (Paris, 1821) and in 11 volumes (Brussels, 1822).

For literature on Volney, see J. Barni, *Les Moralistes français au XVIIIᵉ siècle* (Paris, 1873); J. Gaulmier, *Volney* (Paris, 1959); and A. Picavet, *Les Idéologues* (Paris, 1891).

L. G. CROCKER

VOLSKI, STANISLAV (1880–1936?), assumed name of Andrei Vladimirovich Sokolov, Russian Marxist journalist and philosopher. Volski studied at Moscow University but was expelled in 1899. He was active in the Bolshevik faction until March 1917, when he broke with Lenin. In 1909 Volski published the only pre-Soviet book-length treatise on Marxist ethical theory, but its "Nietzschean" individualism had little impact on the development of Marxism–Leninism. In the 1920s and 1930s Volski was reduced to the status of literary popularizer and translator. The date and circumstances of his death are still unknown.

According to Volski, class solidarity and discipline are tactically essential to victory in the class struggle, but all binding norms will vanish with the defeat of capitalism. Under socialism individuals will be "freed from the numbing pattern of coercive norms" and from the "idea of duty," the "inevitable companion of bourgeois ·society" (*Filosofiya Borby*, p. 272).

Volski saw societies as weapons that individuals use in their struggle with nature. Typically, in bourgeois societies (based on fixed division of labor), individuals are free to develop only within the narrow confines of their occupational specialties. As a result they are self-alienated, conformist, and myopic. But in socialist society (based on variable division of labor), harmoniously self-determining individuals will grow into unique selfhood as ends in themselves. Their absolute value as persons will not be a formal postulate or imperative, as was claimed by the Russian Kantian Marxists, but rather a goal to be achieved by free struggle and social creativity. In this process "the socialization of methods is accompanied by an individualization of goals" (*ibid.*, p. 300). "Struggle," Volski declared, "is the joy of being," and "socialism is freedom of struggle; everything that increases struggle is good, everything that diminishes it is bad" (*ibid.*, pp. 306, 302).

Assimilating Nietzsche's insight that "enemy" means not "villain," but "opponent," Volski claimed that I should grant full freedom to the individual whose ideal is inimical to mine and that I should strive to make him an "integral personality," working with him to remove external obstacles to our sharp and clear collision. In struggling with me, he enriches me, enlivening my highest values. "Of all those who surround me, . . . the most precious, most essential is he with whom I struggle for life and death." He is both friend and enemy, and we share the "morality of 'friend-enemies'—the morality of the future" (*ibid.*, pp. 310, 311).

Bibliography

Filosofiya Borby: Opyt Postroyeniya Etiki Marksizma ("The Philosophy of Struggle: An Essay in Marxist Ethics"). Moscow, 1909.

Sotsialnaya Revolyutsiya na Zapade i v Rossi ("The Social Revolution in the West and in Russia"). Moscow, 1917.

"Volski," in *Bolshaya Sovetskaya Entsiklopediya* ("Great Soviet Encyclopedia"), 1st ed. Moscow, 1929. Vol. XIII, Cols. 66–67.

GEORGE L. KLINE

VOLTAIRE, FRANÇOIS-MARIE AROUET DE

(1694–1778). Born in Paris of the well-to-do bourgeois Arouet family, Voltaire received an excellent classical education at the Jesuit school of Louis-le-Grand. Thereafter, he abandoned the study of law in favor of literary pursuits. His precocious talents took a satirical bent, which resulted in several banishments from Paris, a brief exile in Holland (1713), and 11 months in the Bastille (1717–1718). He adopted the pen name de Voltaire, was hailed at an early age as the best playwright in France, and was to dominate the French stage for fifty years. An epic poem, *La Henriade*

(1723), celebrated the virtues of Henry IV, France's last tolerant king. A quarrel with the chevalier de Rohan again sent him to the Bastille, from which he was soon released to spend over two years (1726–1729) of exile in England, where he mastered the language and diligently studied English philosophy, literature, and politics. His writings then took a more serious turn. In 1734, after the publication of *Lettres philosophiques*, he was forced to flee Paris again to avoid arrest and spent most of the next 15 years at Cirey in Lorraine, where he studied physics, metaphysics, and history in the company of the learned Mme. du Châtelet. His studies were interrupted for a brief period at court under the protection of Mme. de Pompadour. During these years he was named historiographer of France, and in 1746 he was elected to the French Academy.

After Mme. du Châtelet's death in 1749, Voltaire met a cool reception in Paris and went hopefully, in 1750, to serve as philosopher-poet to Frederick the Great of Prussia. After three years he quarreled with Frederick, and unwelcome in France, he traveled for a year, eventually acquiring property in Switzerland. In 1755 he settled in a Geneva château, which he named Les Délices (it is now the home of the Voltaire Institute and Museum). It was there that he published *Candide* (1759) and the first edition of his *Essai sur les moeurs* (1756). In the year 1759 he acquired an estate at Ferney, just over the border in France, where he was soon to settle for the rest of his extraordinarily active life. The desperate poverty of his tenants and neighbors awakened his conscience to the need for social reform. In 1762 he undertook the defense of the Protestant Jean Calas, who had been tortured, unjustly condemned, and while still protesting his innocence, inhumanly put to death on the rack. The widely publicized defense of Calas was the first of Voltaire's campaigns against religious fanaticism and barbarous judicial procedures. He was now openly hostile to the church because of its alliance with the state and its frequently exercised powers of persecution. Through wise investments Voltaire had acquired vast wealth, and while patriarch of Ferney, he was acclaimed not only France's greatest literary genius but also Europe's greatest champion of humanity. In 1778, in his 84th year, he returned to Paris, where he was hailed by the populace as the defender of Calas and received tremendous ovations. He died in Paris a few months later and was surreptitiously buried outside the city. In 1792 his remains were moved with great pomp to the Pantheon, only to be dispersed at the onset of the Restoration.

Philosophical orientation. Voltaire's philosophical ideas developed to maturity during his exile in England at a time when that country enjoyed a very liberal government. True, Voltaire had previously absorbed the methodical doubt of Descartes, the skepticism of Montaigne, the Epicureanism of the libertine followers of Gassendi, and the critical spirit of his great forebear Pierre Bayle. Nevertheless, it was his contact with English thought that was the decisive factor in the formation of his philosophy. John Morley's statement that Voltaire went to England a poet and returned a philosopher is fundamentally correct. The results of this contact were embodied in his *Letters Concerning the English Nation* (1733) published, with an additional letter of remarks on Pascal's *Pensées*, in the original French as *Lettres philosophiques* (1734). Couched in masterful French prose, this work, often considered one of the most important literary events of the century, was the chief inspiration for the rise of liberal thought on the Continent. It also promoted the French philosophers' acceptance of the empiricism of John Locke and, somewhat reluctantly, of Newton's scientific methods and achievements as opposed to the prevalent Cartesianism.

Moderate in tone but audacious in freedom of expression, the *Lettres philosophiques* present the major themes that were to dominate Voltaire's life and thought, and they therefore serve as an excellent introduction to his philosophy. They were composed as if Voltaire had written them from England in 1728 to acquaint his French friends with England's religious, economic, political, philosophical, and cultural achievements. Voltaire especially praised those aspects of English life that compared favorably with the obsolete French institutions; this work was, as Gustave Lanson remarked, the first bomb hurled against the *ancien régime*. By implication Voltaire condemned the oppressive religious unity in France, the wealth and power of the clergy, the despotism of the king, and the privileges of the nobility; he recommended equal status for merchant and noble, fair distribution of taxes, and free cultivation of the arts and sciences.

Newton. The letters on the sensationalist philosophy of Locke and the scientific findings of Newton were composed in 1732; with the subsequent attack on Pascal they are philosophically the most important passages in the *Lettres*. Newton's principles, which Voltaire discussed further in the *Éléments de la philosophie de Newton* (1738), were to have a profound effect on Voltaire's thought. They encouraged him to beware of theories and hypotheses unsupported by observation and experimentation, and his treatment of Bacon and Newton greatly helped to establish the pre-eminence of empirical philosophy in eighteenth-century French thought. Also, Newton's laws of gravitation inspired in Voltaire an abiding awe of the majesty of the heavens, in comparison with the pettiness of our planet, and an unshakable belief in a supreme intelligence, the Creator of the universe. Shocked by Pascal's recourse to a wager as an argument for God's existence, Voltaire replied that "the heavens declare the glory of God" and that while priests may rely on the catechism to teach children the existence of God, Newton demonstrated it to the satisfaction of philosophers. The earliest expression of Voltaire's mystical sense of cosmic awe occurs in the dedicatory poem of the *Éléments*.

Locke. Locke exerted an even greater influence on Voltaire's philosophy than Newton did. The "Letter on Mr. Locke" was, in fact, the major reason for the official condemnation of the *Lettres philosophiques* and the subsequent order for the author's arrest. This letter reveals Voltaire's great admiration for Locke's epistemological ideas. He praised Locke's advocation of patient analysis of the development and processes of thought, his denial of innate ideas, and his assertion of the necessary limitations of the finite mind in understanding an infinite universe. Voltaire also found support in Locke for his own skepticism concerning the nature of the soul: "A multitude of reasoners [Voltaire was here referring to the theories of certain philosophers and churchmen from Anaxagoras to Malebranche] having written the romance of the soul, a sage at last arose, who gave very modestly its history. Mr. Locke has displayed the human soul in the same manner as an excellent anatomist explains the springs of the human body. He everywhere takes the light of physics for his guide." The most controversial passage, however, was Voltaire's citation of Locke's "sage and modest assertion" that "we shall perhaps never be capable of knowing whether a being, purely material, thinks or not." The implication that God is able to communicate thought to organized matter, that thinking is the function of the brain just as walking is the function of the feet, was to have important repercussions throughout the century.

Pascal. Montaigne, in the turmoil of civil and religious wars, had sought refuge in meditative cultivation of individual man through self-knowledge. Pascal, however, found value in the sufferings of man's terrestrial existence as a painful preparation for the glories of the life to come. Voltaire wished to present a program of social action for the betterment of man's lot on earth, and in the 25th philosophical letter he attacked Pascal as the giant across this path. (The attack also served as a sop to the official censors of the Jesuit order, to which Pascal had been far from kind.) Pascal, who was virtually obsessed with the misery of the human condition, believed that the doctrine of original sin was psychologically the most satisfactory interpretation of human nature that had ever been devised. He explained human existence in terms of divine purpose through the theological doctrines of the Fall and the redemption, predestination, and grace. In Voltaire's mind it was false and dangerous to reduce religion to metaphysics; he argued that Pascal was not a true philosopher, that he had neither an enlightened mind nor a humanitarian heart, and that his views encouraged fanaticism. "Inconceivable" man could be rendered no more conceivable through inconceivable doctrines. Such doctrines can be accepted only as revealed truths, not as reasoned truths. Voltaire's whole career was a devoted effort to emancipate man and reconcile him to his fate:

> I dare take the side of humanity against this sublime misanthropist and affirm that we are neither so wicked nor so unhappy as he thinks. . . . Why try to make us disgusted with life? . . . To look upon the universe as a prison cell and all men as criminals about to be executed is a fanatic's idea. To believe that the world is a land of bliss . . . is the dream of a Sybarite. To think that earth, man, and animals are what they are created to be, is the opinion of the sage.

It is clear that Voltaire admired Pascal's sublime eloquence, shared his view of the pettiness of the world, and accepted his image of finite man hurtling through space between two infinities. He was quite unwilling, however, to accept Pascal's theological deductions. His own feelings of awe before the majesty of the universe were more akin to Fénelon's, from whose *Télémaque* he derived the figure of men as ants crawling, fighting, disputing, on this little atom of mud; in fact, Voltaire developed this theme in two of his own best philosophical tales, *Zadig, ou La Destinée* (1748) and *Micromégas* (1752).

Pascal had had little training either in theology or history, and from Basel, where Voltaire sought refuge in 1734, he wrote a friend that he had been easy on Pascal, especially in his treatment of prophecies and miracles; that not a single one of the prophecies that Pascal referred to can be honestly applied to Christ; and that his discussion of miracles was pure nonsense. But more than 25 years elapsed before Voltaire dared continue the attack.

Voltaire's development and elaboration of the philosophical positions expressed in the *Lettres philosophiques* can be found in heaviest concentration in his philosophical tales, and especially in the many-volumed *Dictionnaire philosophique* published, with additions under various titles, in the decade following the first edition of 1764. In general, Voltaire's metaphysical and religious preoccupations take precedence over his economic and political philosophies, even ethics, the end to which he claimed that all other branches must be referred in the last analysis.

Metaphysics. Having accepted Locke's sensationalist philosophy, Voltaire never abandoned it but also never developed it further. He was content to let Condillac and Diderot attempt to substantiate Locke's theory and to take refuge himself in Locke's insistence on the limits of human understanding. In reply to the question "How can I think?" the ignorant philosopher asks, "Have all the books written in the last two centuries taught me anything about it? . . . I have questioned my reason and asked what reason is: this question has always dumbfounded it."

Nevertheless, in the years following the publication of the "Letter on Mr. Locke" Voltaire was doggedly determined to support Locke's views, even defending, in letters to his Jesuit mentors, God's ability to grant matter the faculty of thought, for, he argued, how could churchmen question God's omnipotence or deny, for that matter, the Thomistic maxim that the intellect contains nothing except what it receives through the senses? Three decades later, in *Le Philosophe ignorant,* his opinion had not changed: "I cannot doubt," he wrote, "that God has not granted sensations, memory, and consequently ideas, to organized matter." Thought is in abeyance during sleep and, presumably, in death. The materiality of the soul is a metaphysical question, whereas its immortality is a matter of faith that can be proved by revelation alone.

Throughout his long life Voltaire consistently maintained his skeptical view of the soul, and he gave this view immortal literary form in the hilarious final chapter of *Micromégas,* in which he ridiculed theories offered by Aristotle, Descartes, Malebranche, and a Thomist theologian. Late in life Voltaire liked to repeat the prayer of the Swiss captain in *Micromégas:* "May God, if there is one, save my soul, if I have one." Yet when La Mettrie and Diderot developed Locke's ideas into a thoroughgoing atheistic materialism, Voltaire resisted with all the power and ability of his intellectual and literary faculties. Like Locke he preferred no explanation to a speculative one. In his opinion all systematizations were both vain and dangerous. He believed that not only the questions "How do we think?" and "How do our arms and feet obey the dictates of our will?" but also the question "What is matter?" were beyond the reach of human reason. To Boswell, who tried in vain to convert him, he wrote in English: "You seem solicitous about that pretty thing called Soul. I do protest you, I know nothing of it; nor whether it is, nor

what it is, nor what it shall be. Young scholars and priests know all that perfectly. For my part, I am but a very ignorant fellow."

Voltaire was always concerned with metaphysical problems, especially the problem of evil, for which he could accept no facile solution. His correspondence shows that he was immediately hostile to the philosophical optimism of Pope and Leibniz. He was acquainted with Leibniz' work as early as 1737, when Frederick the Great sent him Christian Wolff's systematization of the *Theodicy.* He was repelled by the lack of experimental verification for Leibniz' theories of the great chain of being and the monad—"I reduce philosophy to physics," he remarked. He also objected strongly to the purely hypothetical (and theological) explanations for the interaction of mind and matter through a pre-established harmony. The whole *Theodicy,* Voltaire declared, is not worth one of Jean-Antoine Nollet's experiments. And to Frederick he replied, "Metaphysics, in my opinion, is made up of two things, the first what all men of good sense know, the second what they will never know. . . . We are equipped to calculate, weigh, measure, and observe; that is natural philosophy; almost all the rest is chimaera."

However, Voltaire believed that there are limits to human understanding beyond which even science could not pass; this was the main theme of *Micromégas* (1752). Here it is shown that although Maupertuis's verification of Newton's theory of the flattening of the earth at the poles was a remarkable demonstration of man's ability to measure, it in no way helped to solve fundamental metaphysical problems. Men can agree about two or three points that they can understand, but they can only argue to no purpose about two or three thousand that they can never understand.

Although Voltaire's philosophy of common sense was at times too prudent, his skepticism of the experiments made to prove the theory of spontaneous generation has since proved to have been justified. His major error was in refusing, against Buffon, to admit the evidence from fossils that indicated vast geological transformations and supported the theory of transformism. He had scoffed too often at the Biblical story of the Flood to accept evidence which was long used by theologians to support that revelation.

Religion. Voltaire's belief that design and purpose are manifest in nature was the basis of his religion. A consistent and finally a militant theist (he himself used that term in preference to "deist," as he has often been called), he can readily be shown to have accepted at least three of the Thomistic proofs of the existence of God as First Cause, Prime Mover, and the Supreme Intelligence which created the universe with certain ends in view. He summarized his position with the assertion that the existence of a watch proves the existence of a watchmaker. In *Candide* he could ridicule the naive assertion of a theological writer that the nose was fashioned to bear spectacles, but he insisted that it was purposefully designed as the organ of smell. It was left for Diderot and other converts to the theory of evolutionary processes to point out the objections to this argument.

The God of Voltaire, however, did not resemble the God of the Judaeo-Christian tradition. He was a vague impersonal being with no particular concern for the affairs of men. His attributes were beyond human understanding. Voltaire refused to accept all evidence from revelation and rejected the arguments of theologians, even to the point of denying God's providence and seriously questioning his goodness.

The problem of evil. The problem of evil was also a central theme in Voltaire's writings; in his various treatments of it he viewed it from the standpoints of philosophy, religion, and art. The most successful resolutions are in his philosophical tales—*Zadig,* (1748), *Le Monde comme il va* (1748), *Memnon* (1749), and *Candide, ou L'Optimisme* (1759).

In his dictionary article on optimism, "Bien," Voltaire quoted Epicurus, according to Lactantius:

> Either God can remove evil from the world and will not; or being willing to do so, cannot; or he neither can nor will; or he is both able and willing. If he is willing and cannot, he is not omnipotent. If he can but will not, he is not benevolent. If he is neither willing nor able, he is neither omnipotent nor benevolent. If he both wants to and can, whence comes evil over the face of the earth?

Voltaire faced this problem squarely in his poem on the Lisbon earthquake, *Poème sur le désastre de Lisbonne* (1756). The earthquake on All Saints' Day, 1755, had an emotional effect on him the potency of which the modern mind has difficulty conceiving. Although first estimates of the number of casualties were grossly exaggerated, thousands of lives were lost in the tidal wave and in the fires that followed the earthquake, which was all the more disastrous because the churches, with tapers burning, crumbled upon crowds of worshipers. Voltaire's first recorded remarks were directed against the philosophical optimism of Leibniz and Pope, which, he thought, had been proved bankrupt. The theological dogma of original sin and the theory that God had left man free to choose between good and evil in order to test his soul were equally repugnant to him. If the disaster represented God's wrath upon sinners, why was only the city of Lisbon destroyed, why were the innocent punished along with the guilty, and why were casualties greatest in the churches? (The brothels seem to have been spared.) Voltaire wrote his poem at white heat, describing the disaster in his most impassioned verse and reviewing the many unsatisfactory attempts to solve the problem (the skeptical attitude of Pierre Bayle was considered the most acceptable). He ended his first version with the pessimistic admission that there is positive evil in the world and that there is nothing mortals can do about such evils as earthquakes but submit to God's will and adore. Warned by friends of the unacceptability of this ending, he compromised and pretended to be defending the doctrine of original sin against cosmic optimism. He also added a word of hope, ostensibly for the blessings of a future life, and called his poem a sermon.

Philosophical optimism. The ideas expressed in this poem foreshadow Voltaire's undisputed masterpiece, *Candide,* a perfectly composed, witty and devastating attack on philosophical optimism. This doctrine, Voltaire declared, was "a doctrine of despair under a consoling name," be-

cause it accepted evil as a necessary link in the great chain of being, the harmonious whole of this "best of all possible worlds." *Candide* is directed chiefly against Pope's dictum that "whatever is, is right" or that "partial ill is universal good," and the philosophical jargon used by Pangloss is a pastiche of Leibniz' style. Voltaire maintained that the abstract good of the whole could have no meaning for the suffering individual and could be of no consolation to him: "When death crowns the ills of suffering man, what a fine consolation to be eaten by worms!" Such physical evils as earthquakes must be submitted to, but in Voltaire's melioristic philosophy the worst political and religious abuses of his day, the folly of dynastic wars and the cruelties of the Inquisition, could be and had to be eradicated. His solution contains an entirely personal note: "Work without theorizing, for work keeps at bay three great evils: boredom, vice, and need." Only by a frank acceptance of man's fate, with all its limitations, could life be made endurable. A deep concern for humanity and an unmistakable note of optimism underlie the bantering, ironic tone of this account of universal miseries. The seemingly negative portrayal implies a call for positive action and faith in man's eventual ability to improve human conditions.

Providence. In *Zadig,* Voltaire specifically questioned God's providence. The general theme of this Oriental tale is the lack of justice in this world; the good are often punished, and the wicked rewarded. God moves in mysterious ways his wonders to perform, but our limited and not entirely submissive reason is often indignant. Voltaire could not accept the evasive explanation that God's justice is not man's justice, for "how," he asked, "can you expect me to judge otherwise than by my reason or walk otherwise than with my feet?" With the greater freedom of his later years he tackled the problem more directly in his dictionary article "Providence." No amount of prayers in a foreign language will persuade God to cure Sister Fessue's ill sparrow. Here and elsewhere, Voltaire distinguished between a particular and a general providence. He denied the first, for he believed that God created the vast universe according to immutable laws that cannot be altered by the prayers of finite creatures. But God did endow man with reason and feelings of benevolence, which, if properly directed, were all that was needed for man to gain happiness in life. Voltaire's "general providence" would be described today as a benevolent universe.

Religious experience. Submission to God's plan for man and gratitude for his gifts were Voltaire's constant religious attitudes. In addition, he felt a genuine sense of awe and veneration, expressed far too often to be ignored, that could have come only from the personal mystical experience of cosmic grandeur. One such experience, recorded by his secretary, is fictionalized in *Zadig.* Having suffered a number of injustices, Zadig was forced to take flight.

> Zadig directed his course by the stars. . . . He gazed in admiration at those vast globes of light which appear to our eyes as so many little sparks, while the earth, which is in truth nothing but an imperceptible point in nature, appears so great and so noble to our fond imaginations. He looked upon men as they truly are, insects devouring one another on a little atom of

mud. This true picture seemed to annihilate his misfortunes, by showing him the nothingness of his own being and that of Babylon. His soul reached up into infinity and, detached from his senses, contemplated the unchanging order of the universe.

The impelling force of Voltaire's theistic beliefs was derived from an intense cosmic feeling of awe. In "The Coming New Religion of Humanism," Sir Julian Huxley defines religion in terms that most clearly describe what Voltaire thought religion should be:

A religion is an organ of man in society which helps him to cope with the problems of nature and his destiny—his place and role in the universe. It always involves the sense of sacredness or mystery and of participation in a continuing enterprise; it is always concerned with the problems of good and evil and with what transcends the individual self and the immediate and present facts of every day.

Voltaire's entire career bears ample testimony not only to his sense of mystery but to his sense of participation in a continuing enterprise. The year before his death he admitted that there was "something divine" in Pascal's "sublime metaphysics," but he attacked the sublime in Plato and Pascal because they "mistook their visions for truths." "Everything must be reduced to moral philosophy," he declared. Mysticism could offer no escape from that major concern (*Additions aux Remarques sur les Pensées de Pascal*).

Natural religion. Voltaire was religious, but he was not a Christian in any orthodox sense. From the English deists he accepted the idea that Christianity was as old as creation or, in other words, that what is true in Christian teachings is the core of human values that are universally true in all religions. This belief accounts for his admiration of Confucius and his lifelong interest in the Quakers, whose beliefs and practices he deemed most in accord with the primitive Christianity of the Gospels. In his dictionary article "Religion" Voltaire described himself meditating upon the uniformity of light and of the forces of gravity and concluded that moral forces must likewise be uniform. In an imaginary conversation with Christ he found that not a single sacrament of the church was observed in Christ's time. He was willing, finally, to accept Christ as his only master—but only after depicting Christ as a deist or humanist. On the positive side the "Prayer to God" with which he ended his *Traité sur la tolérance* (1763) recognizes the fatherhood of God and the universal brotherhood of man, the *fraternité* of the approaching French Revolution; all men are brothers, Voltaire declared, "from Siam to California." Theological and nationalistic disputes tend only to set them at one another's throats. In the article "Méchant" he summoned men to forget differences of race or religion and bade them "remember their dignity as men," a noteworthy instance of civilization's growing concern for this fundamental humanistic value.

Épître à Uranie, a poem written in 1722, before Voltaire's English exile, was in the main a diatribe against Christian acceptance of the jealous, tyrannical Jehovah of the Old Testament and the inhuman condemnation of all pagans, the virtuous as well as the uninstructed, to eternal punishment. Addressing the benevolent, merciful deity, whom he revered, he declared: "I am not a Christian that I may love thee more." Even the few lines ostensibly devoted to the defense of Christianity express the opinion widely prevalent among intellectuals that all revealed religions were founded on imposture. His final appeal was to the eternal wisdom of the All High, who had engraved natural religion in the hearts of all men and esteemed justice and mercy above sacrifices and burnt offerings. The philosophical sources of this poem were plainly the submerged but still activating libertine ideas of seventeenth-century freethinkers. Voltaire long denied authorship and for fifty years did not dare to include it in editions of his works. After reading Locke, Voltaire could no longer postulate innate ideas to support his view of natural religion, but in the *Poème sur la loi naturelle* (1756) he substituted instincts for innate ideas. The fox does not, until long after birth, seek its prey. Likewise, in man the instinctive senses of equity and benevolence, bases of a morality common to all men, develop gradually but inevitably.

Attack on Christianity. Only at the age of retirement, in the early 1760s, in the relative freedom of his newly acquired estate on the Swiss border did Voltaire launch his serious campaign against Christianity. In his account of the renegade priest Jean Meslier he wrote (1762):

What then are the vain resources of Christians? Their moral principles? These are basically the same in all religions; but cruel dogmas have arisen from them and have preached persecution and dissension. Their miracles? But what peoples have not theirs and what philosophic minds do not despise these fables? Their prophecies? Has not their falsity been demonstrated? Their morals? Are they not often infamous? The establishment of their religion? But did it not begin with fanaticism, was it not fostered by intrigue, and the edifice visibly maintained by force? Its doctrine? But is that not the height of absurdity?

The details of this attack, which became almost the obsession of the last fifteen years of Voltaire's life, were published in scores of miscellaneous pieces and in articles in the *Dictionnaire*. Finally aware that every idea and every reform that he had suggested for the good of humanity met the instant opposition of the established church of his day, Voltaire adopted the motto "Écrasez l'infâme." By *l'infâme* he meant superstition and fanaticism, which led to such repressive measures as the Inquisition. "Those who can make you believe absurdities," he declared, "can make you commit atrocities." The legend that Voltaire was a thoroughgoing atheist is understandable in view of these ideas, but it is not justifiable.

The wit and apparent levity of many of Voltaire's articles and pamphlets long concealed the fact that his criticisms were based on intensive scholarly investigations, to which his library, carefully preserved in Leningrad, gives ample testimony. From the English deists and Conyers Middleton and Hume, Voltaire gleaned his arguments against the miracles; from Anthony Collins, his refutation of the pertinence of Old Testament prophecies. From the German scholar J. A. Fabricius he learned of the apocryphal gospels and pious forgeries of the early church; from the French rationalists, by book or manuscript, he was informed of countless contradictions and inconsistencies in the scriptural record and in the subsequent history of the church. He studied the works of the doctors Grabe, Mill, Cave, and Huet and the endless Biblical commentaries of the Benedictine Dom Calmet. He was also well versed in the works of the Church Fathers, from Origen to Aquinas, and read the most scholarly books on the world's religions. Letters to his intimate friends show his serious purpose. It is evident that he considered the establishment of Christianity a grievous aberration of the human mind, a halt in the progress of humanity.

Ethics. However great the role that metaphysics and religion played in Voltaire's life and works, ethics was always his first concern. His major disagreement with Locke—aside from the question of the "reasonableness" of Christianity—was his firm belief in the existence of universal ethical principles based on natural law. Voltaire believed that the value of positive law depended on the degree to which it represented the just and humane precepts of natural law and that conflicts between men may be resolved in terms of their common human nature. He declared that dogmas disunite, and ethics unite, the human race. Only on this principle could the brotherhood of man be envisaged.

Social ethics. In accord with the thought of his century Voltaire believed that good and evil had no meaning apart from society. He propounded an essentially social ethics, and his major preoccupation was the interest of society, even to the extent of professing socially useful beliefs that he could not personally accept. For instance, he argued that since materialists could not disprove the immortality of the soul and spiritualists could not prove it, social utility weighed the scales in favor of the doctrine of future rewards and punishments. His purpose, he wrote in a letter to d'Alembert (December 6, 1757), was not to prevent his lackeys from attending mass. Moreover, only the threat of ultimate judgment could check the maleficence of an absolute monarch such as Frederick the Great. Forced to abandon his early defense of free will (in "Liberté," *Dictionnaire philosophique*), he expressed to Frederick his regret that truth and social utility could not be harmonized. In general, however, Voltaire preferred utility to his personal beliefs only when they were a matter of opinion and unverifiable.

Voltaire's moral values were also completely humanistic. The happiness of the individual in society was his chief concern. Having endowed man with reason and social instincts, God was, in Voltaire's eyes, beyond good and evil. He liked to describe himself as "a just man, lacking in Grace." His social philosophy is best characterized as melioristic. *Candide* is sufficient proof that he knew full well the miseries that beset mankind (he had experienced many of them himself) but in time reason and enlightenment would prevail—"the less superstition, the less fanaticism: and the less fanaticism, the less unhappiness." For the theological virtues of faith, hope, and charity he substituted faith in man's ability to settle his own problems, hope for a better society, and love of one's fellow men. "Christ never admitted four cardinal and three theologi-

cal virtues: He said, according to truth as old as creation: 'Love God and your neighbor'" ("Moralité," *Dictionnaire philosophique*).

Justice was the underlying principle of Voltaire's intellectual activity and social action; intellectual freedom was its necessary concomitant. "The common sense of the eighteenth century," wrote A. N. Whitehead, ". . . acted on the world like a bath of moral cleansing. Voltaire must have the credit, that he hated injustice, he hated cruelty, he hated senseless repression, and he hated hocus-pocus. Furthermore, when he saw them, he knew them" (*Science and the Modern World*). Voltaire's remark that "if God did not exist, we would have to invent him" is an adaptation of Montesquieu's earlier statement that "if God did not exist, we would have to deify justice."

Whether the idea of justice, foundation of the moral order, is instinctive, as Voltaire wanted to believe, or whether it is acquired through the experience of injustices, as d'Alembert proclaimed, it was the master passion of Voltaire's life as well as the basis of his ethical principles. By common report he celebrated the anniversaries of Henry IV's assassination by François Ravaillac and of the massacre of St. Bartholomew by developing a fever. He could never forget the injustice of his exile to England, the condemnation of his *Lettres philosophiques,* and the repudiation he suffered from the France of Louis XV. His break with Frederick the Great and quarrel with Maupertuis were occasioned by the unjust condemnation of the philosopher Johann Samuel Koenig by the Berlin Academy. Injustices imposed by the tyrannical power of church or state infuriated him. His efforts for reform were long directed against the fanaticism, superstition, and cruelty that characterized the judicial procedures of his day. His attack came to a head with the judicial murder of Jean Calas in 1762. For three long years Voltaire labored tirelessly to establish Calas's innocence and in the end succeeded in having the judgment reversed, the judges condemned, and a royal pension granted to the victim's family.

Judicial reform. In *Voltaire and Beccaria as Reformers of Criminal Law* Marcello Maestro convincingly analyzed the evolution of Voltaire's juridical philosophy—the passage from his basic hatred of intolerance, superstition, and fanaticism, to the actual cases of Calas and Sirven, and, with the appearance of Cesare di Beccaria's *Essay on Crimes and Punishment,* to the conviction that the reform of judicial procedures themselves was essential to the progress of civilization. Montesquieu, appealing to reason and humanity in his *L'Esprit des lois,* had recommended an equitable relation between the punishment and the crime, open and public trials by jury, the abolition of venality in the selection of judges, and caution against the use of civil authority in the punishment of such religious "crimes" as sorcery and blasphemy. Beccaria was the first to write a systematic treatise of enlightened penology. Voltaire immediately sensed its importance and wrote a commentary which, in most of the succeeding editions, was added to the original treatise. It is significant that this was Voltaire's first work to be published in America (Charleston, S.C., 1777), and it helped to promote more humane judicial procedures in the early state constitutions. In Europe many a kingdom and principality adopted the suggested reforms. In her abortive attempt to codify Russian law Catherine the Great declared that these works of Montesquieu and Beccaria were her bedside companions. It matters little that Voltaire did not add much to Beccaria's philosophy. Without Voltaire's fervor, the lucidity of his style, and the widespread audience that his reputation had won for him, the reform of criminal law could hardly have taken Occidental civilization by storm.

Voltaire's discovery of Beccaria and his outrage at the atrocious condemnation to cruel death of the chevalier de la Barre (1766) turned his attention to social reforms during the last years of his career. Judicial injustice was the theme of many of his major works—the *Traité sur la tolérance* (1763); *André Destouches à Siam* (1766), one of his most successful brief satires; the philosophical tale *L'Ingénu, ou l'Élève de la nature* (1767); articles on torture and similar subjects in later editions of the *Dictionnaire philosophique;* and finally, in 1777, only a few months before his death, the *Prix de la justice et de l'humanité.* In this work he began by stating the desirability of preventing crimes, rather than punishing them, and of rewarding virtue. He then proceeded to condemn as a cruel absurdity the death penalty for petty larceny, suggested the advantages to society of forced labor instead of capital punishment, and proposed the establishment of hospitals for the care of children of unwed mothers. He called for caution in the punishment of heresy, sorcery, and sacrilege and in dealing with the crimes of bigamy, adultery, and incest. He did not consider suicide a social menace, and he condemned the usual practice of mutilation of the suicide's body and confiscation of his property. He commended the example of the Romans, who, he declared, were free to live, think, and die as they wished. Above all, judicial procedures should be public and standardized, and a written code publicized; the accused should have benefit of counsel and be tried by a jury of his peers; penalties should not be arbitrary; torture should be abolished; and judgeships should be awarded for merit rather than for a price. In France, Voltaire's suggested reforms were embodied in a number of articles of the Declaration of the Rights of Man of 1789. Article IX specifically declares that men are presumed to be innocent and treated as such until declared guilty.

Historical and political philosophy. Voltaire's philosophy of history was also distinctly ethical and humanistic. For him the object of history was neither the satisfaction of curiosity nor the accumulation of facts but the search for ideals useful in controlling the future. Voltaire's *Charles XII* (1731) was the first work to exemplify the modern approach to history also taken by Montesquieu, Hume, and Gibbon. It was revolutionary in that it treated a contemporary subject, the king of Sweden, and its object was to show that the ambitions of even the most admirable warrior brought nothing but disaster to his nation. Its genuine literary merits, its dramatic interest and lively style, concealed the patient and laborious documentation upon which it was founded.

The *Siècle de Louis XIV* (1751), the history of a century rather than of a king, supported Voltaire's constant theme that the true benefactors of mankind are not its generals but its philosophers, scientists, and poets. It was the result of more than twenty years of careful study of all available

sources, both oral and written. The tremendous advances made in science and the enduring dramatic achievements of the neoclassical school were duly celebrated. If the part played by Louis XIV and his minister Jean Colbert in subsidizing the artists of the age was exaggerated, it was with the carefully veiled intent of satirizing by contrast the repressive measures and lack of consideration of their successors that discouraged the poets and philosophers of Voltaire's day.

Voltaire's most ambitious but less enduring historical work was the *Essai sur les moeurs et l'esprit des nations* (definitive edition, 1769), the first universal history of man. Bossuet had begun his history with the Bible and had explained historical events to the time of Charlemagne as the unfolding of God's will. Voltaire began where Bossuet left off and continued through the Renaissance but with a completely naturalistic approach. He then added his histories of Louis XIV and Louis XV, and in 1765 he wrote a preliminary discourse first published separately as *La Philosophie de l'histoire,* a general view of the peoples and civilizations of antiquity that reached far beyond the Hebrew and Greek origins of Occidental cultures. In this most controversial section of his *Essai,* which is often more philosophical than historical, his instincts were correct, even though the development of archaeology and the social sciences have invalidated many of his conclusions. This work is dominated by Voltaire's conviction that the Hebrew religion had bequeathed superstition, bigotry, and fanaticism to the Christians, whose own religion (according to Bayle) had caused more wars and shed more blood than any other. This was a complete reversal of Bossuet's thought.

Voltaire also wrote a number of formal histories, such as the *Annales de l'empire* (1753) and the *Histoire de l'empire de Russie sous Pierre le Grand* (1759). His *Histoire de l'établissement du Christianisme* (1776), more propaganda than history, is evidence, corroborated by his correspondence, of his reverence for the Augustan age and of his feeling that Christianity had delayed for many centuries the advance of civilization; the Renaissance was truly the rebirth of pagan culture. The philosophers' trust in reason and nature and Voltaire's belief in the idea of progress followed logically from his trust in the worth of reason and nature.

Yet Voltaire also believed that history is an insufficient guide to moral conduct—he once defined history as tricks the living play upon the dead. He emphasized the necessity of recourse to imaginative literature. "The beautiful fables of antiquity," he wrote, "have this great advantage over history, that they present a comprehensible morality: they are lessons in virtue, whereas almost all history is a succession of crimes. . . . History teaches us what human beings are; literature teaches us what they should be" ("Fables," *Dictionnaire philosophique*). The universal moral law that Voltaire thought must be assumed if we are to conceive of man as he ought to be was a logical deduction from his classical persuasion of the oneness of humanity.

Voltaire's economic theories, political philosophy, and recommendations for social reform, expressed in immature form in the *Lettres philosophiques,* were not to receive their full development until after 1759. At that time, as "patriarch" of the newly acquired estates at Ferney, he developed a more active social conscience and interest in the welfare of his tenants. His theory of economics, however, was displayed in *Le Mondain* as early as 1736. In this apparently light and witty poem Voltaire's concern for the full development of arts and letters was combined with current English economic theories to produce an apology for luxury, the growth of commerce, and the wealth of nations. Liberal in its day, the poem was not only a hymn of praise for the civilized life of Paris but also a plea for free enterprise, freedom of trade, and the laissez-faire doctrine of capitalism. The influence of Bernard Mandeville's *Fable of the Bees, or Private Vices, Public Benefits* is both direct and apparent; Voltaire had little sympathy for Fénelon's primitive utopian ideas or the egalitarian, socialistic views that Rousseau was soon to espouse.

Voltaire had adopted from Locke the idea of the inviolability of person and property. Exile in Holland and England had convinced him of the benefits of commerce in promoting the wealth of nations and the well-being of their peoples. The freedom to grow rich was as important to the state as the other freedoms that in later life he was so ardently to propose. The poor, he believed, we always have with us. Otherwise, who would cobble his shoes or plow his fields? More explicitly, in his dictionary article "Luxe" (1764), he declared that luxury was the necessary concomitant of a higher standard of living and human progress. The luxuries of one generation were the common commodities of the next. Excesses could be controlled not by moral exhortations but by reasonable sumptuary laws.

Like most of the philosophers contemporary to him, Voltaire was less concerned with the form of government than with its liberal institutions. With Montesquieu he showed a theoretical preference for democratic rule in a republic but believed it impracticable except in small communities. His main concern was that men should be governed by the law, and only by the law, a fixed and standardized code of laws that left no room for the arbitrary decisions of judges or the interference of rulers. Like Montesquieu, too, he admired the constitutional monarchy of England with its balance of powers, where, borrowing the phrase from Fénelon, "the prince, all-powerful to do good, is restrained from doing evil." More than once, smarting under persecution, he was tempted to flee to England "to enjoy in a free country the greatest blessing I know and man's most cherished right, which is to depend only on laws and not on the whims of men." In France the great diversity of laws and "customs" from province to province gave little hope of reform. "Your common law of Paris," Voltaire wrote in his dictionary article "Lois," "is interpreted differently in twenty-four commentaries: just so many proofs, then, that it is ill conceived. It contradicts one hundred and forty other common laws, all having legal force in the same nation, and all contradicting each other. . . . London was a city for having been burned. If you want good laws, burn your own, then, and make new ones." But such a radical reform, as it turned out, could be brought about only by revolution.

In the final section of one of his most widely disseminated works, *Poème sur la loi naturelle*, Voltaire was con-

cerned chiefly with the relation between church and state. He suggested that it is the duty of the prince to calm religious disputes that disturb the peace of society. The merchant, workman, priest, and soldier are all equally members of the state, and all are equal before the state's universal laws. His poetic appeal was realized in prose in Article I of the Declaration of the Rights of Man, which states, "Men are born, and remain, free and equal before the law," and in Article III, which states, "The principle of all sovereignty resides in the Nation. No body, no individual, can exercise authority which does not emanate expressly therefrom."

In his dictionary article "Lois, civiles et ecclésiastiques" Voltaire is more explicit: "No ecclesiastical law should be of any force until it has received the express sanction of government"; "everything relating to marriages depends solely upon the magistrate"; "all ecclesiastical persons should be under the perfect control of government, because they are subjects of the state"; "magistrates, cultivators, and priests, should alike contribute to the expenses of the state."

Living as he did in a police state, Voltaire was much more concerned with civil rights than with articles of the constitution. Describing the English government in a late article, "Gouvernement," he wrote:

> English legislation has succeeded in restoring to each individual his natural rights, of which nearly all monarchies have deprived him. These rights are: entire freedom of person and property; freedom to speak to the nation in his writings, to be judged in criminal cases by a jury of independent citizens, to be judged according to the precise terms of the law, and to profess peacefully the religion of his choice.

England still served him as a foil for the abuses of the *ancien régime*. Only in his last years, with the advent of the American Revolution and Franklin's presence in France, did he look hopefully across the sea for the birth of a new nation founded on the principles that he had long been advocating.

For France, however, Voltaire did not foresee and certainly did not advocate revolution. Opposed to physical violence and sudden upheavals, he put his trust in the slow but steady progress of civilization. His early efforts were directed toward making man fully conscious of his dignity and toward effecting the social reforms essential to that end. In his old age he became more specifically interested in individual need, and he envisioned an ideal society in which the standard of living would be raised by agricultural improvements and by industries and commerce. He was instrumental in freeing France's remaining serfs and in securing a fairer distribution of taxes. His early contempt for the illiterate "rabble," easy prey to superstition and fanaticism, was tempered by a growing respect for the artisans and tenant farmers of his domain. So in the dialogue *A, B, C* (1768) the advocate of democracy declares: "It is a pleasure for me when my mason, my carpenter, my blacksmith . . . lift themselves above their trade and know more about public interest than the most insolent Turkish commissar."

The specific principles, founded upon a philosophy of reason and humanity, for which Voltaire fought have long since become the heritage of the civilized world.

Works by Voltaire

Oeuvres complètes, L. Moland, ed., 52 vols. Paris, 1877–1885. Standard work for general references.
Voltaire's Correspondence, Theodore Besterman, ed. Geneva, 1953——. Over twenty thousand letters to more than twelve hundred correspondents have been issued in the 102 volumes thus far published; only the index volumes are still to appear.

RECOMMENDED TRANSLATIONS

Philosophical Letters [on the English Nation], translated by Ernest Dilworth. Indianapolis, Ind., 1961.
Candide, Zadig, and Selected Stories, translated by Donald M. Frame. Bloomington, Ind., 1961.
Philosophical Dictionary, 2 vols., translated by Peter Gay. New York, 1963.
Selected Letters, translated by Theodore Besterman. London, 1963.

Works on Voltaire

Aldington, Richard, *Voltaire.* London, 1925. Brief biography, general criticism, more literary than philosophical.
Brailsford, Henry N., *Voltaire.* New York, 1935. Vivid view of Voltaire as reformer.
Cabeen, David C., et al., eds., *A Critical Bibliography of French Literature,* 4 vols. Syracuse, N.Y., 1957–1961. Researchers are referred to Vol. IV, pp. 182–207. Very useful critical estimates, up to 1951.
Gay, Peter, *Voltaire's Politics: The Poet as Realist.* Princeton, N.J., 1959. Scholarly and judicious.
Lanson, Gustave, *Voltaire.* Paris, 1910. Best brief survey.
Maestro, Marcello, *Voltaire and Beccaria as Reformers of Criminal Law.* New York, 1942. Scholarly study of Beccaria's influence on Voltaire.
Morley, John, *Voltaire.* London, 1913. Outdated but still useful.
Pellissier, Georges, *Voltaire philosophe.* Paris, 1908. Excellent general view.
Pomeau, René, *La Religion de Voltaire.* Paris, 1956. Comprehensive and judicious.
Popper-Lynkeus, Josef, *Voltaire, eine Charakteranalyse, in Verbindung mit Studien zur Aesthetik, Moral und Politik,* 2d ed. Vienna, 1925.
Strauss, David Friedrich, *Voltaire: sechs Vorträge.* Leipzig, 1870. Sympathetic view of Voltaire's action in behalf of mankind.
Torrey, Norman L., *Voltaire and the English Deists.* New Haven, 1930; reprinted, Oxford, 1962. Emphasis on the critical deists and Voltaire's Biblical criticism.
Torrey, Norman L., *The Spirit of Voltaire.* New York, 1938; reprinted, Oxford, 1962. A character study.
Waterman, Mina, *Voltaire, Pascal and Human Destiny.* New York, 1942. Brief, scholarly, and to the point.

NORMAN L. TORREY

VOLUNTARISM. The term "voluntarism" (from the Latin *voluntas,* "will") applies to any philosophical theory according to which the will is prior to or superior to the intellect or reason. More generally, voluntaristic theories interpret various aspects of experience and nature in the light of the concept of the will, or as it is called in certain older philosophies, passion, appetite, desire, or *conatus.* Such theories may be psychological, ethical, theological, or metaphysical.

Psychological voluntarism. Voluntaristic theories of psychology represent men primarily as beings who will certain ends and whose reason and intelligence are subordinate to will. The outstanding classical representatives are Thomas Hobbes, David Hume, and Arthur Schopenhauer. Hobbes, for example, thought that all voluntary human behavior is response to desire or aversion, which he brought together under the name "endeavor"; he based his ethical and political theories chiefly on this claim. Hume maintained that reason has no role whatever in the promptings of the will; that "reason is, and ought only to be the slave of the passions, and can never pretend to any other office than to serve and obey them." Schopenhauer, the outstanding voluntarist of them all, believed that the will is the very nature or essence of man and indeed of everything, identifying it with the "thing-in-itself" that underlies all phenomena.

The point of all such theories can best be appreciated by contrasting them with the more familiar theories of rationalism found, for example, in Plato's dialogues or Descartes's *Meditations.* Plato thought that men ideally perceive certain ends or goals by their reason and then direct their wills to the attainment of these ends or goals. This is why he thought no man could knowingly will evil. Thus in the *Symposium* he traced the ascent of the soul toward higher and higher ends, the supposition being that these ends are apprehended first by the senses and then ultimately by the pure or unfettered intelligence, which enlists the will or desire for their pursuit. The corruption of a man was for Plato precisely the dominance of the will, that is, of a man's appetites or desires, this being a deviation from what human nature ideally should be. Descartes, similarly, supposed that the understanding first grasps certain ideas or presents certain ends to the mind and that the will then either assents or withholds its assent, thus following rather than directing the understanding.

Voluntarist theories reject this general picture as the reversal of the truth. Ends and goals, according to these theories, become such only because they are willed; they are not first perceived as ends and then willed. Hume in particular maintained that no sense can be made of the idea, so central to Plato's philosophy, of reason directing the passions, or even of its ever conflicting with them. Reason, he argued, is concerned entirely with demonstrations (deduction) or with the relations of cause and effect (induction). In neither case can it give us ends or goals. Mathematics is used in mechanical arts and the like, but always as a means of attaining something that has nothing to do with reason. The computations of a merchant, for example, can be fallacious, but the ends for which they are undertaken can in no sense be fallacious or irrational. They can only be wise or foolish, that is, such as to promote or to frustrate other ends that are again products of the will. Similarly, Hume thought that no discovery of causal connections in nature can by itself have the least influence on the will. Such discoveries can only be useful or useless in enabling men to choose appropriate means to certain ends, which are in no way derived from reason. "It can never in the least concern us to know," Hume said, "that such objects are causes, and such others effects, if both causes and effects be indifferent to us." Reason therefore can never produce actions or impulses, nor can it oppose them. An impulse to act can be opposed only by a contrary impulse, not by reason. There can, accordingly, be no such thing as a conflict between reason and passion, and the only way in which willed behavior can be "irrational" is for it to be based upon some misconception—for instance, on some erroneous conception of what is a fit means to the attainment of an end which is entirely the product of the will.

The theories of other voluntarists do not differ essentially from Hume's theory, although there are differences of emphasis. All agree that men are moved by their impulses, appetites, passions, or wills and that these are incapable of fallacy or error. There is thus no such thing as a rational or irrational will, although one may will imprudently in relation to other things that one wills. J. G. Fichte expressed this idea when he said that a free being "wills because it wills, and the willing of an object is itself the last ground of such willing."

Ethical voluntarism. It is obvious that the voluntarist conception of human nature contains implications of the highest importance for ethics. If ends or goals are entirely products of the will and the will is neither rational nor irrational, then ends themselves cannot be termed either rational or irrational and it becomes meaningless to ask whether this or that end is really good or bad independently of its being willed. Thomas Hobbes drew precisely this conclusion. To say that something is good, he said, is to say nothing more than that it is an object of one's appetite, and to say that something is bad is only to say that one has an aversion to it. Good and bad are thus purely relative to desires and aversions, which are, of course, sometimes quite different in different men. Wise behavior, on this conception, can be nothing other than prudence, that is, the selection of appropriate means to the attainment of whatever goals one happens to have. Hobbes thought that there is one goal, however, that is fairly common to all men: the goal of self-preservation. His political philosophy thus consisted essentially of formulas by means of which men can preserve themselves in safety and security within a commonwealth.

Essentially the same ideas were defended by Socrates' contemporary, Protagoras, and are reflected in his maxim that "man is the measure of all things." They also find expression in the philosophy of William James and are, in fact, an important aspect of pragmatism in general. James thought that things are good solely by virtue of the fact that they are "demanded," that is, that someone wants them or lays claim to them, and he noted that such a demand might be for "anything under the sun." Considered apart from the demands of sentient beings, nothing in the universe has any worth whatsoever. Hence James concluded that the only proper ethical maxim is to satisfy as many demands as possible, no matter what these happen to be, but at the "least cost," that is, with the minimum of frustration to other demands. It is clear that within the framework of voluntaristic theories like this, no meaning can be attached to asking what is truly worthy of one's desires, unless this question is interpreted to mean "What is in fact satisfying of one's desires?"; nor does it make sense to seek, as did Immanuel Kant, any metaphysical principles of morals. Truth and falsity in ethics are exhausted in questions as to the truth or falsity of various opinions concerning the util-

ity of proposed means to the achievement of ends, that is, to the satisfaction of appetite, desire, and demand. They have no relevance to any questions concerning ends themselves.

Theological voluntarism. Just as the theories thus far described give prominence to the human will over human reason, so certain theological conceptions give prominence to the divine will. Perhaps the most extreme form of theological voluntarism is exemplified in the thinking of St. Peter Damian (1007–1072). He maintained that human reason or "dialectic" is worthless in theological matters, for the simple reason that the very laws of logic are valid only by the concurrence of God's will. God is omnipotent, he said, and can therefore render true even those things which reason declares to be absurd or contradictory. It is thus idle for philosophers to speculate upon what must be true with respect to divine matters, since these depend only on God's will.

A very similar idea has found expression in many and various forms of fideism, according to which the justification of religious faith is found in the very act of faith itself, which is an act of the will, rather than in rational proof. Thus Søren Kierkegaard described purity of heart as the willing of a single thing and emphatically denied that such notions as reason and evidence have any place in the religious life. William James, following suggestions put forth by Blaise Pascal, similarly justified the will to believe, defending the absolute innocence, under certain circumstances, of religious belief entirely in the absence of evidence. Many contemporary religious leaders, pressing the same notion, give prominence to the idea of religious commitment, suggesting that religion is primarily a matter of the will rather than of reason. This is, in fact, traditional in Christian thought, for even the most philosophical and rationalistic theologians, such as St. Anselm of Canterbury, have almost without exception given priority to the act of faith, maintaining that religious belief should precede rather than follow rational understanding. This idea is expressed in the familiar dictum *credo ut intelligam,* which means "I believe, in order that I may understand."

Perhaps no religious thinker has stressed the primacy of God's will in questions of morality more than Søren Kierkegaard, who seems to have held that the divine will is the only and the ultimate moral justification for any act. Strictly understood, this means that an action that might otherwise be deemed heinous is not so, provided it is commanded by God. In the fourteenth century this was quite explicitly maintained by William of Ockham. Ockham said that the divine will, and not human or divine reason, is the ultimate standard of morality, that certain acts are sins solely because they have been forbidden by God, and other acts are meritorious only because they have been commanded by God. He denied that God forbids certain things because they are sins or commands certain things because they are virtues, for it seemed to him that this would be a limitation upon God's will. There can be, he thought, no higher justification for any act than that God wills it, nor any more final condemnation of an act than that God forbids it. The moral law, accordingly, was for Ockham simply a matter of God's free choice, for God's choice cannot be constrained by any moral law, being itself the sole source of that law. This view is frequently echoed in religious literature but usually only rhetorically.

Metaphysical voluntarism. A number of thinkers have believed that the concept of the will is crucial to the understanding of law, ethics, and human behavior generally; a few have suggested that it is crucial to the understanding of reality itself. Such suggestions are found in the philosophies of J. G. Fichte, Henri Bergson, and others, but in no philosophy does it have such central importance as in that of Arthur Schopenhauer. Schopenhauer thought that will is the underlying and ultimate reality and that the whole phenomenal world is only the expression of will. He described living things as the objectifications of their wills and sought to explain not only the behavior but also the very anatomical structures of plants, animals, and men in terms of this hypothesis. The will was described by Schopenhauer as a blind and all-powerful force that is literally the inexhaustible creator of every visible thing. The sexual appetite, which he considered to be fundamentally the same in all living things, was described by him as a blind urge to live and to perpetuate existence without any goal beyond that, and he denied that it had anything whatever to do with reason or intelligence, being in fact more often than not opposed to them. The religious impulse found in all cultures at all times was similarly explained as the response to a blind and irrational will to possess endless existence. In the growth and development of all living things Schopenhauer discerned the unfolding of the will in nature, wherein certain things appear and transform themselves in accordance with a fairly unvarying pattern and in the face of obstacles and impediments, solely in accordance with what is willed in a metaphysical sense but entirely without any rational purpose or goal. On the basis of this voluntarism, he explained ethics in terms of the feelings of self-love, malice, and compassion, all of which are expressions of the will, and he denied—in sharp contrast to Kant—that morality has anything to do with reason or intelligence. He argued that men have free will only in the sense that every man is the free or unfettered expression of a will and that men are therefore not the authors of their own destinies, characters, or behavior. Like other voluntarists, Schopenhauer thus emphasized the irrational factors in human behavior and, in doing so, anticipated much that is now taken for granted in those sophisticated circles that have come under the influence of modern psychological theories.

Bibliography

A good general work on voluntarism that is both historical and critical is Vernon J. Bourke's *Will in Western Thought* (New York, 1964).

Thomas Hobbes's ethical and political theories are developed in his *Leviathan*, of which there are many editions. See also *Body, Man, and Citizen*, a selection from Hobbes's writings edited by Richard S. Peters (New York, 1962).

David Hume's defense of psychological voluntarism is best expressed in his *Treatise of Human Nature*, Book II, Part 3, especially Section 3; the quotations in this article are taken from L. A. Selby-Bigge's edition of that work (Oxford, 1888 and 1955).

For a fairly concise expression of Schopenhauer's voluntarism, see *The Will to Live*, a collection of his essays edited by R. Taylor (New York, 1962).

J. G. Fichte develops the idea of an active power in nature in the first book of his *The Vocation of Man*, R. M. Chisholm, ed. (New York, 1956). The quotation from Fichte comes from his *The Science of Rights*, translated by A. E. Kroeger (Philadelphia, 1869), p. 193.

One of the clearest ancient defenses of a pragmatic basis of laws and institutions is given in Plato's *Protagoras*, where it is ascribed to Protagoras and criticized by Socrates. William James's ethical voluntarism is developed in his essay "The Moral Philosopher and the Moral Life," and the application of his principles to religious belief is given in his "The Will to Believe," both of which are found in nearly all editions of his popular essays.

The theological voluntarism of St. Peter Damian, as well as Ockham's ethical theories, are very well summarized in Frederick Copleston's *History of Philosophy*, Vols. II and III (London, 1950 and 1953). See also Étienne Gilson's *Reason and Revelation in the Middle Ages* (New York, 1950) for a clear account of the opposition between rationalism and fideism. Kierkegaard has eloquently expressed the opposition between reason and religion in many writings, but see particularly his *Purity of Heart*, translated by Douglas V. Steere (New York, 1938).

RICHARD TAYLOR

VYSHESLAVTSEV, BORIS PETROVICH (1877–1954), Russian philosopher and religious thinker. Vysheslavtsev was born in Moscow; he studied at the University of Moscow under the Russian jurist and philosopher P.I. Novgorodtsev and later at the University of Marburg under the Neo-Kantians Hermann Cohen and Paul Natorp. Upon the publication in 1914 of his dissertation, *Etika Fikhte* ("Fichte's Ethics"), he received a doctorate from the University of Moscow and in 1917 was made professor of philosophy at that institution. Expelled from the Soviet Union in 1922, he emigrated first to Berlin, then in 1924 to Paris, where he became a professor at the Orthodox Theological Institute and was associated with Nikolai Berdyaev in affairs of the Russian *émigré* press. Prior to World War II Vysheslavtsev was active in the ecumenical movement. From the time of the German occupation of France until his death he lived in Switzerland.

Vysheslavtsev's lifelong concern with the themes of irrationality and the absolute was already evident in his work on Fichte. He there asserted that beyond the sphere of rationality or "system" lies the irrational sphere, infinite and incapable of being systematized. Through the antinomy of these spheres philosophy arrives at recognition of the Absolute as the infinity which transcends the universe and all oppositions, even the opposition between Georg Cantor's "actual" and "potential" infinities. Because the Absolute underlies every rational construction, it is irrational. It cannot be exhausted by any concept but is "the mysterious limitlessness which is revealed to intuition."

According to Vysheslavtsev, the essence of man's ethical and religious life consists in his relation to the Absolute. He explored this relation in subsequent works, principally *Etika Preobrazhonnovo Erosa* ("The Ethics of Transfigured Eros"), emphasizing the irrational forces in man and interpreting Christian doctrine in the light of the depth psychology of Carl Jung and the French psychoanalyst Charles Baudouin. Vysheslavtsev argued that moral laws cannot guide human conduct successfully, because they are rational rules directed to the conscious will and are defeated by the "irrational antagonism" that stems from man's subconscious. For moral ideals to be significant and effective they must take possession of the subconscious, which they can do only if they are reached through the sublimation of subconscious impulses. Sublimation, operating through the imagination, transforms man's lower impulses into higher ones and turns his inherent, arbitrary freedom into moral freedom that seeks the good. Such sublimation is aided by divine grace and is possible only where the soul turns freely toward the Absolute. Christian ethics is not an ethics of law but "the ethics of sublimation."

In his later years Vysheslavtsev increasingly concerned himself with social problems and wrote a major work on modern industrial culture, *Krizis Industrialnoy Kultury* ("The Crisis of Industrial Culture"), and a trenchant philosophical critique of Soviet Marxism, *Filosofskaya Nishcheta Marksizma* ("The Philosophical Poverty of Marxism").

Works by Vysheslavtsev

Etika Fikhte. Moscow, 1914.
Serdtse v Khristianskoy i Indiyskoy Mistike ("The Heart in Christian and Indian Mysticism"). Paris, 1929.
Etika Preobrazhonnovo Erosa. Paris, 1931.
Filosofskaya Nishcheta Marksizma. Frankfurt am Main, 1952.
Krizis Industrialnoy Kultury. New York, 1953.

Works on Vysheslavtsev

V. V. Zenkovsky, "B. P. Vysheslavtsev, kak Filosof" ("B. P. Vysheslavtsev as Philosopher"). *Novy Zhurnal*, Vol. 15 (1955), 249–261.
V. V. Zenkovsky, *Istoriya Russkoy Filosofii*, 2 vols. Paris, 1948–1950. Translated by G. L. Kline as *A History of Russian Philosophy*, 2 vols. New York and London, 1953.

James P. Scanlan

W

WAHLE, RICHARD (1857–1935), Austrian philosopher and psychologist, was born in Vienna. He was appointed *Privatdozent* in philosophy at the University of Vienna in 1885. A decade later he was called to a professorship in philosophy at the University of Czernowitz, where he taught until 1917. From 1919 to 1933 he again lectured at the University of Vienna. Possessed of originality and an unusually lively style, he published a number of books in the fields of psychology, general philosophy, and ethics.

Wahle is known especially for his relentlessly sharp critique of traditional philosophy, particularly of metaphysics, which he regarded as "one of the most dangerous breeding-places of empty phrases." An absolute, true knowledge, of the sort to which metaphysics aspires, cannot exist. For all knowledge consists in nothing more than that "an image (or idea) is given in dependence on the self"; a reality existing in itself can never be known. Against the traditional philosophical and metaphysical "delusion of knowledge," Wahle set his own positivistic "philosophy of occurrences," according to which the "given" constitutes the sole admissible point of departure for philosophical thought. What are empirically given to us, however, are only freely suspended, surfacelike, passive, powerless "occurrences" (the contents of perception and imagination) that are the effects of unknown "really operative, powerful substantial primitive factors," which remain forever hidden and are in principle unknowable. Wahle's epistemological standpoint, described also as "antisubjectivist product-objectivism" or "agnostic product-realism," lies beyond the antitheses of materialism and spiritualism, realism and idealism (or phenomenalism), objectivism and subjectivism. He regarded all of these positions as false because things are neither essence nor appearance but simply complexes of "occurrences," and the subjective and the objective are identical inasmuch as only neutral "occurrences" are given to us. Thus Wahle's antimetaphysical and skeptical agnosticism leads from illusory knowledge to genuine ignorance, which is the only attainable goal for philosophy.

As a psychologist, Wahle firmly rejected any kind of metaphysics of the soul, as well as faculty psychology and the depth psychology of the unconscious (psychoanalysis). A satisfactory explanation of mental processes, he held, can result only from connecting them with the corresponding physiological prerequisites. There are no independent psychical unities (like the ego), forces, acts, or powers; they appear to exist only because of an inexact style of expression. For example, the ego is neither substance nor force; it is not an independent, simple, active thing at all but only a designation for a certain sphere of occurrences. Similarly, the will is said to be "the reflex action become stable under the accompaniment of images following a concurrence of reflex movements" (*Über den Mechanismus des geistigen Lebens*, p. 371).

Wahle attached special value to obtaining as penetrating an analysis as possible of those mental happenings that proceed essentially in "additive series." In such happenings, besides association, the "constellation" (the state of excitation of the brain at the given moment) is particularly significant. Organic sensations and bodily determinations, as well as the motor system, also play an important part in the processes of thinking, feeling, and willing. Wahle saw in the operations of the brain the antecedents or representatives of conscious processes; to the momentary molecular change of an entire specific brain region corresponds a concrete peculiarity of the given image. The brain, however, is not the "cause" of the mental occurrences or experiences but only the "necessary co-occurrence" of any such occurrence. Both psychopathological phenomena and the origin and formation of character can be understood only physiologically, more particularly from the more or less disturbed (in the case of psychopathology) or undisturbed (in the case of character formation) combined action of a very few elementary brain functions.

Wahle's reflections on the philosophy of culture and history were tinged with skepticism and pessimism, as was his conception of the intellectual capacity and ethical worth of man. Whatever meaning there is in life derives from the existence of love, joy, and pain. Life's highest wisdom is embodied in fulfilling the challenge to be happy with a modesty that is noble, free of illusion, and resigned.

Works by Wahle

Das Ganze der Philosophie und ihr Ende. Vienna and Leipzig, 1894.

Über den Mechanismus des geistigen Lebens. Vienna and Leipzig, 1906.

Josua. Munich, 1912. A second edition was published in 1928.

Die Tragikomödie der Weisheit. Vienna and Leipzig, 1915; 2d ed., 1925.

Entstehung der Charaktere. Munich, 1928.

Grundlagen einer neuen Psychiatrie. Vienna, 1931.

Fröhliches Register der paar philosophischen Wahrheiten ("Cheerful Catalogue of the Few Philosophical Truths"). Vienna and Leipzig, 1934.

Works on Wahle

Flinker, Friedrich, *Die Zerstörung des Ich. Eine kritische Darlegung der Lehre Richard Wahles.* Vienna and Leipzig, 1927.

Hochfeld, Sophus, *Die Philosophie Richard Wahles und Johannes Rehmkes Grundwissenschaft.* Potsdam, 1926.

FRANZ AUSTEDA
Translated by *Albert E. Blumberg*

WALLACE, ALFRED RUSSEL (1823–1913), English naturalist and coformulator with Charles Darwin of the theory of natural selection. Wallace was born at Usk, Monmouthshire. He was largely self-educated, having left school at 14 to serve as a surveyor's assistant with his brother. Like many of his contemporaries he acquired an early taste for the study of nature. But he also read widely and was influenced by the works of Alexander von Humboldt, Thomas Malthus, and Charles Lyell, as Darwin was. In 1844, while teaching school at Leicester, he met the naturalist H. W. Bates (1825–1892), who introduced him to scientific entomology. The two men later embarked on a collecting trip to the Amazon, where Wallace remained for four years examining the tropical flora and fauna.

In 1854, after a brief visit to England, Wallace set out by himself for the Malay Archipelago. He subsequently wrote an account of this trip, *The Malay Archipelago* (London, 1869), which is a fascinating narrative. When he returned in 1862, he had become a convinced evolutionist and was known in scientific circles for his formulation of the theory of natural selection. Another of his scientific contributions was "Wallace's line," a zoogeographical boundary which he drew in 1863 to separate Indian and Australian faunal regions, and which was assumed to pass through the middle of the archipelago.

The rest of Wallace's long life was spent in England, except for a lecture tour of the United States in 1887 and short visits to the Continent. Darwin, Lyell, Huxley, John Tyndall, and Spencer were among his most intimate friends. He wrote extensively on a wide variety of subjects, but biological interests remained central to his outlook and are reflected in such books as *The Geographical Distribution of Animals* (London and New York, 1876), *Darwinism* (London and New York, 1889), *Man's Place in the Universe* (London and New York, 1903), and *The World of Life* (London and New York, 1910).

Wallace first thought of the theory of natural selection in February 1858, when he was ill with a fever at Ternate in the Moluccas. The occasion gave him time to reflect on the mechanism by which species might be altered. He outlined the theory rapidly in a paper, "On the Tendency of Varieties to Depart Indefinitely from the Original Type," and sent it to Darwin, who saw that Wallace had hit upon exactly the theory which he himself had formed and privately written down in 1842. With characteristic generosity he proposed that Wallace's outline should be published

immediately. However, Lyell urged a compromise which resulted in a joint communication from Darwin and Wallace that was read to the Linnaean Society on July 1, 1858. The two men thus received equal credit for the new doctrine, although Darwin was actually the pioneer. The joint communication created no stir at the meeting. However, it was later clearly recognized as a revolutionary document that demolished forever the ancient idea of the fixity of species by formulating a scientific theory of how species change and how their adaptations are secured at each stage of the process.

When Darwin published his famous books, the accord between him and Wallace began to disappear. The view expressed in *The Origin of Species* that evolution required the operation of factors of a Lamarckian as well as of a selective sort was unacceptable to Wallace. For him "natural selection is supreme" and is the sole means of modification, except in the case of man. Hence he became, like August Weissmann, an apostle of Neo-Darwinism. This led him to hold that every phenotypic character of an organism must be useful to that organism in the struggle for life; the principle of utility is of universal application.

With regard to human evolution Wallace differed from Darwin in affirming that man's mental powers, especially "the mathematical, musical and artistic faculties," have not been developed under the law of natural selection. These faculties point to the existence in man of something that he has not derived from his animal progenitors, "something which we may best refer to as being of a spiritual essence." It came into action when man appeared on the evolutionary stage. As he grew older, Wallace put more and more emphasis on the spiritual agency, so that in *The World of Life* it is described as "a Mind not only adequate to direct and regulate all the forces at work in living organisms, but also the more fundamental forces of the whole material universe." For many years Wallace was interested in spiritualism and psychical research. A pamphlet which he published in 1866, *The Scientific Aspect of the Supernatural*, discussed such matters as clairvoyance, apparitions, animal magnetism, and the problem of miracles. It was clear that he took them seriously, and they influenced his general outlook. All this was far removed from anything Darwin was prepared to countenance.

Apart from the theory of natural selection, Wallace's most enduring work was his *Geographical Distribution of Animals*. He also made acute judgments on anthropological matters, such as the evolutionary significance of the human brain and human intelligence. Thus he contended that the brain is a specialized organ which has freed man from the dangers of specialization by vastly increasing his adaptability and that man's intelligence has allowed him to evolve without undergoing major somatic changes. Yet despite Wallace's fertility in producing ideas and his command of a wide array of facts, he never quite succeeded in relating the two. His ideas were not carefully analyzed or tested. At bottom he was a naturalist, with a deep love of nature and an inexhaustible passion for collecting.

Additional Works by Wallace

Contributions to the Theory of Natural Selection. New York, 1871.

My Life: A Record of Events and Opinions. New York, 1905.

Works on Wallace

Eiseley, Loren, *Darwin's Century*. New York, 1958.

George, Wilma Beryl, *Biologist Philosopher: A Study of the Life and Writings of Alfred Russel Wallace*. New York, 1964.

Hogben, L. T., *A. R. Wallace*. London, 1918.

Marchant, J., *A. R. Wallace: Letters and Reminiscences*. London, 1916.

T. A. GOUDGE

WANG SHOU-JEN. See WANG YANG-MING.

WANG YANG-MING (1472–1529), also called Wang Shou-jen, the most important Chinese philosopher from the twelfth century to the present, was a state governor and governmental executive assistant in various departments for some years, but a teacher most of his life. His followers spread all over China. Because of Wang, the School of Mind exercised tremendous influence in China for over 150 years and in Japan for centuries. His impact has been increasingly felt in the twentieth century.

He bitterly attacked Chu Hsi's doctrine of going to things to investigate their principles because he felt that was splitting principle (*li*) and the mind in two and causing the mind to lose its direction, purpose, and concern with moral values. He insisted that principle and the mind are identical. For example, without the principle of filial piety, no one could express filial piety. But the principle must be inherent in the mind, because if it were outside and were in the parents, it would cease to be when the parents die. In this reasoning, Wang was clearly thinking of subjective experience, but he contended that the principles of all things are contained in the mind. Therefore, to investigate things is to investigate the mind. His goal of investigation was not to understand principle through objective study, as was the case with Chu Hsi, but through eliminating selfishness and obscuration to return to the original correctness of the mind.

Thus understanding involves action. "Knowledge is the beginning of action and action the completion of knowledge," Wang argued. No one can really know the road unless he has gone through it. This renowned doctrine of unity of knowledge and action, enunciated in 1509, was original to Wang. No Chinese philosopher before him had advocated it.

In 1521 he enunciated the doctrine of the extension of innate knowledge. By innate knowledge he meant inborn knowledge of the good. Since the mind is principle, if it is free from selfishness and obscuration, it will naturally know what principle is, that is, what should be done. And since knowledge is the same as action, one will naturally extend knowledge by putting principle into practice. The ultimate extension is to "form one body with Heaven, Earth, and all things." The result is the man of humanity (*jen*), who is completely identified with the principle of nature (*t'ien-li*), the highest of all principles.

Bibliography

Works by Wang available in English include *Instructions for Practical Living, and Other Neo-Confucian Writings by Wang Yang-ming*, translated by Wing-tsit Chan (New York, 1963); selections from Wang's writings, translated by Wing-tsit Chan, may be found in Chan's *A Source Book in Chinese Philosophy* (Princeton, N.J., 1963).

For material on Wang, see Carsun Chang, *The Development of Neo-Confucian Thought* (New York, 1962), Vol. II; and Fung Yu-lan, *A History of Chinese Philosophy* (Princeton, N.J., 1953), Vol. II.

WING-TSIT CHAN

WAR. See PEACE, WAR, AND PHILOSOPHY.

WARD, JAMES (1843–1925), English philosopher and psychologist, was born at Hull the son of a merchant, but most of his early life was spent in Liverpool. He was brought up, he records, "in the backwoods of a narrow Congregationalism, uncultured and Calvinistic." At 19 he entered a Congregational college to train for the ministry. With his theological studies he combined courses of private reading for the University of London B.A. and B.Sc. degrees, and after completing these degrees he obtained a scholarship which enabled him to go to Germany in 1869. He spent a year at Berlin and a second year at Göttingen, where he was greatly influenced by the prevailing idealistic philosophies, especially that of Rudolf Hermann Lotze, who combined the interests—scientific, philosophical, and religious—which were dominant throughout Ward's life. On his return to England he accepted the pastorate of a Unitarian chapel at Cambridge, which he resigned a year later. In 1872 he entered Trinity College as a student, was elected fellow in 1875, and was appointed to a lectureship in 1880. In 1897 he was elected to the newly founded chair of logic and mental philosophy, which he held for the rest of his life.

Ward's philosophy was a variant of theistic idealism, distinctive and original chiefly because of his acquaintance with and interest in the natural sciences, especially the biological sciences and the emerging science of psychology. His final philosophical position was developed in the two series of Gifford lectures, *Naturalism and Agnosticism*, delivered at the University of Aberdeen (1896–1898), and *The Realm of Ends*, delivered at the University of St. Andrews (1907–1910). The first series was acclaimed as a powerful polemic against nineteenth-century philosophy of science as preached by Huxley and Spencer. The second series developed positive arguments for theism and teleology based on a panpsychic pluralism similar to that of Leibniz but allowing causal interaction between the monads. These lectures, however, were at most a spirited rearguard action against a type of naturalism already in decline and in defense of a spiritualistic philosophy also in decline.

Ward's place in the history of philosophy rests upon his important contributions to the philosophy of mind: an original analysis of mind and a no less original "genetic" psychology. Both were adumbrated in quite early papers and expanded later in his famous article "Psychology," in the ninth edition of the *Encyclopaedia Britannica*, which by general consent administered the *coup de grâce* to the prevailing associationist psychology as represented by Alexander Bain. The article was further expanded in his magnum opus, *Psychological Principles* (1918).

Ward's analysis of mind. Ward's analysis of mind was a tripartite analysis in two dimensions. In the first dimension three kinds of experiences are distinguished: cognitive, affective, and conative. Although implicit in the writing of

Kant and other Continental philosophers, this analysis was developed most systematically by three British psychologists, Ward, G. F. Stout, and William McDougall. In Ward's system each of these three modes of experience involves a subject (self or ego) actively or passively engaged with certain objects; this is the second dimension of the analysis. In cognition the subject attends to its "presentations"—a term which Ward used in the sense in which Locke used "idea." In feeling pleased or in feeling some other emotion, the subject undergoes distinctive changes of state. In conative experience the subject is in part active again, attending to a distinctive class of presentations—"motor" presentations, or ideas of movement—through which bodily movements are produced. The subject, not being a presentation or object, is not directly known but rather is inferred on the principle that "thinking implies a thinker." By the same ruthless logic Ward held that our feelings, not being presentations, are not directly known but are inferred from their effects upon our thought and behavior. So, too, by this same logic acts of attention are unintrospectible. This analysis is also an account of a causal cycle of events: Cognition determines feeling, which in turn determines conation. Thus, for example, a child's attention is attracted by a visual presentation; if the presentation is pleasant—that is, if it induces pleasure in the subject—attention is then directed to motor presentations which determine bodily movements tending to retain the object in the field of vision. If the sensory presentation is unpleasant, attention is directed to motor presentations which determine aversion of the eyes or other "ostrich-like" avoidance behavior. Such behavior, in the course of development, results in more effective and rational ways of dealing with pleasant and unpleasant presentations.

Ward's genetic psychology. Before the rise of systematic empirical psychology, philosophers had attempted by observation, introspection, and reflection to define the main phases in the development of mind. The general formula was "From the senses to the imagination and from this to the intellect" (quoted from an early writer in *Psychological Principles,* p. 178). The dominant school of thought in the nineteenth century had been that of the associationists, who conceived of the process of the development of mind as consisting in the progressive aggregation of sensations and images, forming complex presentations and trains of thought. In place of this mechanical and atomistic account, Ward proposed one based on a biological model. Presentations, he argued, are not discrete objects but partial modifications in a total presentational continuum, also described by him as a "psychoplasm"—the psychical counterpart of the "bioplasm," which becomes differentiated into the several organs of the various types of organism. In this genetic process as a whole, three main stages or phases are distinguished:

First, within the broad concept of the plasticity of the presentational continuum, three partial processes are distinguished—differentiation, retention, and assimilation—all of which are prior to the transition from sensation to perception and prior to the formation and association of ideas.

Second, there are the several processes of integration, through which sensory presentations become percepts—recognition, localization, and the intuition of things.

At some stage in the process of integration a third stage

of development begins—the emergence, from the primary continuum of sense experience, of a secondary continuum composed of images, and the organization of these images into a "memory thread" and an "ideational tissue." The detailed working out of this genetic theory was carried through with subtlety and considerable erudition which covered much of the growing body of experimental evidence flowing from the psychological laboratories of the Continent.

For convenience of exposition, Ward had introduced at the outset the fictional concept of "the psychological individual"—a single imaginary person in whom the whole process had taken place, as distinct from the series of individuals in whom the process had in fact happened, and each of whom had recapitulated the phases of development which had occurred in his ancestors, before advancing farther. In the final chapters of the *Psychological Principles* Ward eliminated this fiction by adopting the German term *Anlage* for the inherited dispositions or tendencies to develop ancestral characteristics. This concept was central to his philosophical treatment of mental inheritance, and it provided the basis of a rather sketchy account of individual psychology and of the analysis of the concepts of personality, temperament, and character.

Ward's psychology, however, was soon outmoded by the spectacular development of the new psychologies, behaviorism and psychoanalysis, and by the rapid expansion of a scientific psychology based on experimental and biological methods. It was outmoded by the separation of scientific psychology from the philosophy of mind. As a philosophy of mind it was assimilated and transformed into the distinctive system developed by his most outstanding pupil, G. F. Stout, and it was also outmoded by the powerful influence of two successors to his chair, G. E. Moore and Ludwig Wittgenstein.

However, his writings may well be studied again, as a consequence of the revived interest in the phenomenology of experience and reinterpretations of the concept of introspection.

Works by Ward

"Psychology." *Encyclopaedia Britannica,* 9th ed., Cambridge, 1886. Vol. XX, pp. 37–85.

Naturalism and Agnosticism, 2 vols. London and New York, 1899. Gifford lectures.

The Realm of Ends, or Pluralism and Theism. Cambridge and New York, 1911. Gifford lectures.

Psychological Principles. Cambridge, 1918. Contains an expanded version of his *Britannica* article on psychology.

A Study of Kant. Cambridge, 1922.

Essays in Philosophy, W. R. Sorley and G. F. Stout, eds. Cambridge, 1927. A collection of Ward's papers with a biographical memoir by his daughter Olwen Ward Campbell.

Works on Ward

Broad, C. D., "The Local Historical Background of Contemporary Cambridge Philosophy," in C. A. Mace, ed., *British Philosophy in the Mid-century.* London, 1957; 2d ed., New York, 1966.

Hamlyn, D. W., "Bradley, Ward and Stout," in B. B. Wolman, ed., *Historical Roots of Contemporary Psychology.* New York, 1966.

The Monist, James Ward Commemoration Number, Vol. 36, No. 1 (1926). Contains a complete list of his writings as brought up to date by Ward, shortly before his death.

C. A. MACE

WATSON, JOHN BROADUS (1878–1958), American psychologist and founder of behaviorism, was born the son of a prosperous farmer in Greenville, South Carolina. He received an M.A. from Furman (Baptist) College, Greenville, in 1900 and, attracted by philosophy, entered the University of Chicago. Psychology and biology became leading interests and, ineligible for a medical course, he majored in psychology, with philosophy and neurology, receiving the Ph.D. in 1903 with a thesis on neural and behavioral investigations in the rat. As assistant and instructor in psychology at Chicago (1903–1908) he taught orthodox introspective psychology of consciousness but pursued animal behavioral experiments in his own laboratory. In 1908 he became professor of experimental and comparative psychology at Johns Hopkins University.

His first major publication, *Behavior; an Introduction to Comparative Psychology* (1914), immediately established him among the leaders of an objective, experimental, antianthropomorphic science of animal behavior. In the central chapters he explored human behavior by the same methods and for the next two decades pioneered a psychology, behaviorism, which rejected the introspective method together with consciousness, imagery, purpose, and, indeed, mind and studied human behavior by observational and experimental methods in the natural setting and in the laboratory.

Watson set forth a behaviorist program in his textbook *Psychology From the Standpoint of a Behaviorist* (1919), whose later editions (1924, 1929) reported experimental work and elaborated theoretical statements. At Hopkins, Watson established a psychological laboratory in a maternity hospital to study inborn and learned behavior patterns in babies and the process of learning ("conditioning") itself. His university work was interrupted in 1917–1918 by service with the Aviation Section of the U.S. Army, and was abruptly terminated in 1920 when his marriage broke up and he resigned his university post, remarried, and embarked upon a business career in New York. Until he retired in 1946, he was a member of the staff or the board of directors of commercial advertising corporations. Though he continued to write and lectured at the New School for Social Research, New York, his solid research lay behind him and his later writings were restatements of old findings and dogmatic assertions of formerly tentative opinions. An unfortunate example was *The Psychological Care of Infant and Child* (1928), written jointly with his second wife, which rashly ventured from description to prescription and even proscription, advocating a formal, rigid routine with minimal affectionate contact in the upbringing of children from infancy onward. This overreaction against contemporary sentimentality was insecurely based and unpopularly received. It did little for behaviorism and was quickly overtaken by the mother-love school of child psychology. In current behavior theory and therapy the sounder parts of Watson's pedologic work are being retested and restated. From 1946 Watson lived in country retirement, and his death in Connecticut in 1958 was the passing of a figure from psychology's history rather than the loss of a great contemporary.

Watson's behaviorism as a school of human psychology was the radical American wing of a much wider movement away from the introspective study of states of consciousness. Darwin had suggested not only that man, in evolution, was like the animals but also that animals were emotionally and mentally like man. Jacques Loeb's "tropisms," Conway Lloyd Morgan's habit theory, E. L. Thorndike's and H. S. Jennings' "trial and error learning" all proposed less anthropomorphic interpretations of animal behavior. Watson firmly stated that "all behavior, human and animal, is analyzable in terms of stimulus and response, and the only difference between man and animal . . . [is] in the complexity of behavior." He described that complexity in terms of habit formation, integration of habit patterns, and modification of simple stimulus-response reactions by "substitution" of stimuli; later he adopted I. P. Pavlov's terminology of "conditioned reflexes," although his methods resembled, rather, the motor conditioning techniques of V. M. Bechterev. Bechterev's "objective psychology" was anathema to Watson, as was J. R. Angell's "functional psychology," since both retained "mentalistic" concepts. So, for Watson, did later Pavlovian theories of central excitatory/inhibitory states and of temperamental types. Watson denied that "an impulse . . . may be held *in statu quo* . . . or . . . ramble around the nervous system . . . until it can . . . exert its effect." He held that "the nervous system functions in complete arcs"; an incoming impulse exerts immediate effect, apparently delayed response resulting from "implicit activity" of effector organs. He believed thought to be "implicit laryngeal activity"; human superiority, linguistic and intellectual, is attributable to man's complex vocal apparatus; there are no thought images, only "word-movements." Dewey taught Watson philosophy and is surely echoed here, although Alexander Bain had affirmed in *The Senses and the Intellect* (2d ed., London, 1864, p. 346) that "thinking is restrained speaking or acting." In his early works Watson recognized emotions and instincts as inborn patterns of responses which can be conditioned. Emotions are specific patterns of internal bodily adjustments (not "sensations," as in the James–Lange theory); instincts are patterns of outward activity. Later Watson greatly reduced the role in behaviorism of innate patterns, emphasizing that conditioning may begin prenatally. Having reported his famous—then notorious—infant conditioning experiments, he confidently asserted that he could take any healthy infant and, given complete control of the infant's world, could train him to any profession, regardless of heredity.

Thus Watson banished anthropomorphism from animal psychology, only to introduce a restrictive theriomorphism in the study of man; rejecting the soul, he could show only the machine. His work was cleansing and stimulating to psychology but his ultimate extremism alienated support, and current learning theory and behavior therapy owe more to Pavlov's school than directly to Watson. Physiologically his intuitions have not been confirmed. Philosophically the behavioristic approach found favor in operationism and positivism, but Watson's extreme materialistic monism remained sterile.

Works by Watson

Behavior; an Introduction to Comparative Psychology. New York, 1914.

Psychology From the Standpoint of a Behaviorist. Philadelphia, 1919.

Behaviorism. New York, 1924.

Battle of Behaviorism; an Exposition and an Exposure. New York and London, 1928. Written with William McDougall.

The Psychological Care of Infant and Child. New York, 1928. Written with R. A. Watson.

The Ways of Behaviorism. New York, 1928.

"Autobiography," in C. A. Murchison, ed., *A History of Psychology in Autobiography*. Worcester, Mass., 1936. Vol. III, pp. 271–281.

Works on Watson

Bergmann, Gustav, "The Contribution of John Watson." *Psychological Review*, Vol. 63, No. 4 (1956), 256–276.

Woodworth, R. S., "John Broadus Watson." *American Journal of Psychology*, Vol. 72 (1959), 301–310. Obituary.

J. D. Uytman

WATSUJI TETSURŌ (1889–1960), the best philosopher of ethics of modern Japan, known also for his studies of cultural history. He was born in Himeji and died in Tokyo. Watsuji's work can be divided into three categories: his early literary efforts, his philological and historical studies, and his works on an ethical system. Gifted with literary talent, he wrote some short novels and a play while still studying philosophy, but these had no great success. Among his early philosophical essays are those on Nietzsche (Tokyo, 1913) and on Kierkegaard (Tokyo, 1915). His cult of ancient Greece, manifested in *Gūzō saikō* ("The Revivals of the Idols"; Tokyo, 1918), developed into an interest in the cultural history of his own country. His first work on this subject was *Nihon kodai bunka* ("Ancient Japanese Culture"; Tokyo, 1920). Japanese culture and character were to be the subject of his constant study, as was attested by his *Nihon seishin-shi* ("The History of Japanese Spirit"; 2 vols., Tokyo, 1926, 1934). Meanwhile, his other studies, based on philological research, covered the textual questions about Homer, primitive Christianity, early Buddhism, and Confucius. While these works differ in scientific value, they contain many insights and reveal him as more a litterateur than an expert philologist and historian. This is obvious in his well-known *Fūdo* (Tokyo, 1934; translated as *A Climate*, 1961), a work of psychological intuition and deep sensibility rather than a scientific or philosophical study of the conditioning effect of climate on culture.

A turning point in his career was his appointment as assistant professor of ethics at Kyoto University (1925). Out of his lectures at Kyoto grew his *Ningengaku toshite no rinrigaku* ("Ethics as Anthropology"), a treatise of systematic ethics, initiated in 1931. Watsuji's ethic was designed as a Japanese system based upon the essential relationships of man to man, man to family, and man to society. In contrast with the private, individual ethics of the West, his ethic sees man as involved in community and society. *Rinri* (ethics) in Sino-Japanese characters meant for him the principle (*ri*—or li in Chinese) of companionship (*rin*). Furthermore, he introduced the Buddhist dialectic elements (negation of negation) to show how the individual is absorbed into the whole. It is true that in postwar years he rewrote the parts of his ethics concerning the state and the emperor. Yet his achievement was that he systematized—although in Western categories—a traditional ethics which

is a substantial part of the ethos of Japan and also of China. His attitude toward East–West contacts may be surmised from his *Sakoku Nihon no higeki* ("National Seclusion, Japan's Tragedy"; Tokyo, 1951). His two-volume *Nihon rinri shisō-shi* ("History of Japanese Ethical Thought"; Tokyo, 1952) is a major contribution to the subject. Western philosophers who had a great influence upon Watsuji were Husserl and Heidegger.

Bibliography

Japanese primary sources include *Watsuji Tetsurō zenshū* ("The Complete Works of Watsuji Tetsurō"), 20 vols. (Tokyo, 1961–1963), and *Jijoden no kokoromi* ("An Attempt in Autobiography"; Tokyo, 1961).

Watsuji's *Fūdo* has been translated into English as *A Climate* by G. Bownas (Tokyo, 1961). A discussion of his work may be found in G. K. Piovesana, *Recent Japanese Philosophical Thought, 1862–1962* (Tokyo, 1963), pp. 131–145.

Gino K. Piovesana, S.J.

WAYLAND, FRANCIS (1796–1865), American Baptist clergyman, educator, and moral philosopher, one of the central figures in the modification of American collegiate education. As president of Brown University (1827–1855), he introduced proposals to ease the rigidity of the classical curriculum by an approximation of the later elective system. With his mentor, Eliphalet Nott of Union College, Schenectady, N.Y., Wayland approved of the substitution of modern language study for at least some of the required Greek and Latin, encouraged training in science and its practical application, and advocated a more professional faculty employed for longer terms. To some degree his interest in these reforms was the result of his Jeffersonian philosophy of democracy. He was completely in accord with Jefferson's insistence that a republican government can flourish only if the voters are well educated. He argued, too, that native talent was widely diffused and should be given the opportunity to develop through education.

Philosophically, Wayland was a naive realist of the Scottish school of philosophy. His theory of knowledge was basically Lockean sensationalism supported by a faculty psychology. Knowledge is gained by a combination of experience and intuition, leading to inductive generalizations whose certainty he did not question. Ultimately Wayland's epistemology rests upon a theistic assumption, that there is a correspondence between what man finds in the universe and what God put there for man to find. However, Wayland's most important contribution to American philosophic development was moral rather than epistemological. His textbook, *The Elements of Moral Science,* first published in 1835, was very widely used and served as a model for many imitators. In this book Wayland departed from the William Paley form of utilitarian ethics that had been taught in the colleges and introduced an ethical position more dependent upon the deontological position characteristic of Bishop Butler. The Enlightenment emphasis on the rights of man was subordinated to a philosophicoreligious stress upon ethics as a system of duties. The moral quality of an action is declared to reside in its intention rather than in its consequences.

Wayland's moral theory led him to an increasing rejection of the institution of slavery. At first he found intolerable only the thought of being himself a slave owner; later he came to feel that all property in human beings was intolerable. From a mildly antislavery position in 1835, he moved to vigorous abolitionism and support of the Union cause in the Civil War. To at least some of the Southern defenders of slavery, Wayland became the archenemy, particularly because of his insistence that the Scriptures cannot be used to support the institution of slavery. Wayland's exchange of letters with Richard Fuller, a Southern clergyman, published as *Domestic Slavery Considered as a Scriptural Institution* (New York and Boston, 1845), presents the arguments on both sides most effectively.

Bibliography

Wayland's *The Elements of Moral Science* has recently appeared in the John Harvard Library (Cambridge, Mass., 1963) with an extended introduction by the editor, J. L. Blau. Wayland's other major works are *The Elements of Political Economy* (New York, 1837), *Thoughts on the Present Collegiate System in the United States* (Boston, 1842), *The Elements of Intellectual Philosophy* (Boston and New York, 1854). For discussions of Wayland see J. L. Blau, *Men and Movements in American Philosophy* (Englewood Cliffs, N.J., 1952) and Wilson Smith, *Professors and Public Ethics* (Ithaca, N.Y., 1956).

J. L. Blau

WEBER, ALFRED (1868–1958), German sociologist and philosopher of history. Like his older brother Max, Alfred Weber studied law and political economy in preparation for a legal career and later changed to sociology and university teaching. His academic career began in 1899 at the University of Berlin and continued at the University of Prague (1904), where he came into contact with Tomáš Masaryk, then professor of sociology. From 1907 to 1933, Weber held a professorship at Heidelberg; in 1933 he resigned at the rise of the Hitler regime. It was due largely to him that the Heidelberg Institute of Social Sciences became one of the chief centers of sociopolitical research during the Weimar Republic, and under his direction it regained its renown after World War II.

Having established his reputation as an economic sociologist by the publication in 1909 of his work on the location of industry (*Über den Standort der Industrien*), Weber turned to historical and cultural–sociological studies, culminating in his main work, *Kulturgeschichte als Kultursoziologie* (1935). In this work he attempted to discover by sociological analysis the chief structural constituents of the historical process. These constituents he distinguished as the social process, the civilization process, and the culture process; although he distinguished between them, he emphasized their relatedness within the diverse constellations of a given historical continuum. By "social process" Weber understood the reoccurrence of certain societal sequences which, notwithstanding individual variations, reveal sufficient uniformity to provide the basis for a comparative study of different peoples. As an example of such a social process, Weber cited the succession from kinship organization to territorial groupings in diverse sociohistorical entities. The "civilization process" was for him essentially the growth of knowledge concerning the

techniques of controlling natural and material forces. Weber regarded the discovery of these techniques as a continuous and cumulative progress permitting, by virtue of the transferability of such knowledge, an element of homogeneity amid the otherwise heterogeneous sociohistorical circumstances.

Weber's main attention was focused on the "culture process," which he did not regard as transferable. Culture can be understood only by recognizing the historical uniqueness of each case, since culture derives from the creative spontaneity of man, which in turn is the expression of an "immanent transcendence" that is not susceptible to the generalizing methods of science. There can therefore be no causal laws in the domain of culture. To assert their existence seemed to Weber no less mistaken than Herbert Spencer's "wrong-headed social evolutionism" (*Farewell to European History*, p. 49). Like Herder, for whom he had a profound admiration, Weber deplored what he called the Enlightenment's "dogmatic progressivism" as a "dangerous sort of optimism" (*loc. cit.*). The progressivist, evolutionary thesis stemmed, in Weber's opinion, from confusing the culture process with the civilization process, thus misconceiving the nature of culture, for culture does not follow any definite or lineal order of development but occurs sporadically, defying the causal determinism that operates in the realms of science and technology.

Weber's theory of immanent transcendentalism also colored his political views. In place of state socialism (whether of the Bismarckian or the Marxist–Leninist kind), he advocated a "debureaucratized" form of "free socialism," under which man's functional role within the social system would never be that of a mere functionary whose inner sense of right and wrong could be made subservient to reasons of state.

Weber's insistence on viewing the historical world of man as a realm where transcendental but (in contrast to Hegel) immanent determinants are at least as decisive as empirical or material factors reveals not only his fundamental disagreement with the Marxist school of historical determinism but also his most significant point of departure from the sociological methodology of his older brother. Unlike Max Weber, Alfred Weber could not conceive of a meaningful sociological interpretation or explanation of human thought or action which aimed to dispense with a value-oriented perspective.

Alfred Weber may possibly have exaggerated the difference between his methodological approach and that of his brother; it may well be true to say with Arnold Brecht that it is a difference of degree rather than of kind, that Alfred Weber was a latent and partisan relativist and Max Weber an overt and neutral one (*Political Theory*, Princeton, N.J., 1959, p. 278). Be that as it may, Alfred Weber's stress on a specifically historicocultural approach to sociology, no less than his denial of the validity of the naturalistic method in the sphere of human affairs, contributed to the relative lack of understanding of his theories by many contemporary sociologists.

Whatever the ultimate assessment of Alfred Weber as a sociologist, his penetrating insight into the forces that shape human history and his uncompromising adherence to the principle of individual social responsibility place him high in the tradition of thinkers of integrity in scholarship and in action.

Works by Weber

Über den Standort der Industrien. Tübingen, 1909. Translated by C. J. Friedrich as *Theory of the Location of Industries.* Chicago, 1929.
    Gedanken zur deutschen Sendung. Berlin, 1915.
    "Prinzipielles zur Kultursoziologie." *Archiv für Sozialwissenschaft und Sozialpolitik,* Vol. 47 (1920/1921), 1–49. Translated by G. H. Weltner and C. F. Hirschman as *Fundamentals of Culture-Sociology.* New York, 1939.
    Die Not der geistigen Arbeiter. Munich, 1923.
    Deutschland und die europäische Kulturkrise. Berlin, 1924.
    Die Krise des modernen Staatsgedankens in Europa. Stuttgart, 1925.
    Ideen zur Staats- und Kultursoziologie. Karlsruhe, 1927.
    Kulturgeschichte als Kultursoziologie. Leiden, 1935.
    Das Tragische und die Geschichte. Hamburg, 1943.
    Abschied von der bisherigen Geschichte. Hamburg, 1946. Translated by R. F. C. Hull as *Farewell to European History.* New Haven, 1948.
    Der dritte oder der vierte Mensch. Munich, 1953.
    Einführung in die Soziologie. Munich, 1955.

Works on Weber

Barnes, H. E., and Becker, Howard, *Social Thought From Lore to Science,* 2 vols. New York, 1938. Vol. II, Ch. 20.
    Colvin, Milton, "Alfred Weber—The Sociologist as a Humanist." *American Journal of Sociology,* Vol. 65 (1959), 166–168.
    Neumann, Sigmund, "Alfred Weber's Conception of Historico-cultural Sociology," in H. E. Barnes, ed., *An Introduction to the History of Sociology.* Chicago, 1948. Pp. 353–361.
    Salomon, Albert, "The Place of Alfred Weber's *Kultursoziologie* in Social Thought." *Social Research,* Vol. 3 (1936), 494–500.

FREDERICK M. BARNARD

WEBER, MAX (1864–1920), German sociologist, historian, and philosopher, was raised in Berlin. His father was a lawyer and National Liberal parliamentary deputy, his mother a woman of deep humanitarian and religious convictions. The Weber household was a meeting place for academics and liberal politicians. From 1882 to 1886 Weber studied law at the universities of Heidelberg, Berlin, and Göttingen, except for a year of military training. His doctoral dissertation (1889) was on medieval commercial law, and he continued his researches into legal history with a study of Roman agrarian law. In 1890 he was commissioned by the Verein für Sozialpolitik to investigate the social and economic plight of the east German agricultural worker. Between 1894 and 1897 he was professor of economics, first at Freiburg, then at Heidelberg. During the next four years, however, a severe nervous illness forced him into academic retirement and kept him from productive work. His health never recovered sufficiently for him to resume an academic career, and he spent the years preceding World War I mainly at Heidelberg as a private scholar, although he became associate editor of the *Archiv für Sozialwissenschaft und Sozialpolitik* in 1903. During the war he was director of army hospitals at Heidelberg. As a consultant to the German armistice commission at Versailles he helped to draw up the memorandum on German war guilt; he also advised the commission that prepared the first draft of the Weimar consti-tution. Late in the war, Weber had accepted a temporary teaching post at the University of Vienna, and in 1919 he became professor of economics at Munich. He died shortly thereafter.

Sociology, politics, ethics, and economics. Weber was attracted to practical politics as well as to scholarship, and he had a vivid sense of the political and cultural significance of historical and sociological investigations. Nevertheless, he insisted that these two "callings" must be kept apart, for both political and academic reasons. His east German agrarian studies had convinced him that the decline of the *Junkers* as a positive political force made it necessary to foster a professional class of politicians who could direct the German administrative machine. He condemned Bismarck for having failed to cultivate such a class and for thus paving the way for the political dilettantism to which Weber attributed most of the weaknesses of German diplomacy. He also argued that scientific and philosophical inquiries into social phenomena were not capable of settling disputes about ethical and cultural values, commitment to which was a *sine qua non* of worthwhile political activity. Empirical scientific investigation could lead to the discovery of the ultimate motives of human behavior, which would serve as a preliminary to an adequate causal explanation of historical events; it could demonstrate the means necessary to given ends; and it could show otherwise unsuspected by-products of alternative policies. Philosophical analysis could lay bare the conceptual structure of various evaluative systems, place them with respect to other possible ultimate values, and delimit their respective spheres of validity. But such studies could not show that any particular answers to evaluative questions were correct. Weber pointed out that an evaluative choice does not depend merely on technical considerations applied to given ends; it is inherent in the very nature of the criteria used to discuss such questions that dispute about those criteria is both possible and necessary. There would be something incoherent in the idea that such disputes could ever be definitively settled.

Weber argued that the blurring by academic writers of the distinction between fact and value characteristically led to two unwarranted prejudices. First, because of the academic's duty to examine all sides of any question, he was likely to develop a predilection for the middle course, although a compromise "*is not by a hairbreadth more scientifically true* than the most extreme ideals of the parties of the left or right." Second, because the scientific investigator's methods were peculiarly well adapted to discovering the probable results of policies, he was likely to think that a policy's value must also be settled by reference to results. But, Weber argued, policies could be rational, not merely in the sense of adapting means to ends (*zweckrational*), but also in the sense that they consistently and genuinely express the attachment to certain values of an agent who is indifferent to the achievement or non-achievement of further ends (*wertrational*).

Weber denied that any form of social activity could be purely economic. All activities have an economic aspect insofar as they face scarcity of resources and thus involve planning, cooperation, and competition. But economic considerations alone cannot explain the particular direction taken by any social activity or movement; for this, other values have to be taken into consideration. Further, the sociologist's own culturally conditioned values are already involved in the way in which he has isolated an intelligible field of study from the infinite complexity of social life. Hence, there is a certain subjectivity of value at the very foundations of social scientific inquiry, but this need not damage the objectivity of the results of such inquiry.

"Verstehen" and causal explanation. Social phenomena involve the actions of agents who themselves attach a sense (*Sinn*) to what they are doing. Correspondingly, sociology requires an understanding (*Verstehen*) of the sense of what is being studied. Without it, Weber argued, the sociologist would not even be in a position to describe the events he wants to explain. In this respect Weber was squarely in the tradition of Hegel, Wilhelm Dilthey, and Heinrich Rickert, but he developed these philosophical ideas into a methodology and applied it to a vast spectrum of empirical data.

Verstehen is particularly susceptible to the investigator's subjective bias, and the sense of unfamiliar forms of activity is likely to be interpreted by reference to what is familiar, but perhaps only superficially similar. Weber therefore thought that *Verstehen* must be supplemented by what he sometimes seemed to regard as a distinct method of inquiry, causal explanation. He argued that causal explanations in sociology are, as such, completely naturalistic and that the social sciences are distinguished by the addition of *Verstehen*. He did not always see clearly that a method which is to serve as a check on rashly subjective misinterpretations of the sense of an activity must itself be capable of producing more correct interpretations. Nor did he always understand that what he called causal explanation, therefore, must itself already involve the concept of *Verstehen*.

This point can be illustrated by Weber's treatment of authority (*Herrschaft*). As a prelude to a causal treatment, he tried to define authority naturalistically in terms of statistical laws expressing "the probability that a command with a given specific content will be obeyed by a given group of persons." The presence of expressions like "command" and "obeyed" in this definition shows that it already presupposes *Verstehen*. This continues to hold for Weber's further treatment of the various types of legitimation in terms of which he classified authority: the traditional, the rational (bureaucratic), and the charismatic (involving attachment to the person of a powerful individual—Weber regarded charismatic authority as a principal source of social change). Here, as elsewhere in his work, the appeal to statistical laws must be understood as ancillary to the process of arriving at an adequate *Verstehen* and not as belonging to a distinct method of causal inquiry.

The "ideal type." Both *Verstehen* and causal explanation are again involved in Weber's account of the use of "ideal types" in historical and sociological inquiries. Whereas a purely classificatory concept is reached by abstraction from a wide range of phenomena with differing individual characteristics, an ideal type is intended to illuminate what is peculiar to a given cultural phenomenon. Its most char-

acteristic use is in connection with types of rational behavior. The ideal type is a model of what an agent would do if he were to act completely rationally according to the criteria of rationality involved in his behavior's sense. On the one hand, the ideal type facilitates *Verstehen* in that, although not itself a description of reality, it provides a vocabulary and grammar for clear descriptions of reality. On the other hand, although the ideal type is not itself a causal hypothesis, it is an aid to the construction of such hypotheses for the explanation of behavior that deviates from the ideal-typical norm. Weber regarded the three forms of authority (traditional, rational, and charismatic) as well as the theory of the market in economics as ideal types. The most succinct and celebrated application of the concept, as well as of most of his other methodological ideas, is to be found in *The Protestant Ethic and the Spirit of Capitalism.* In this work Weber argued that the development of European capitalism could not be accounted for in purely economic or technological terms but was in large part the result of the ascetic secular morality associated with the twin emphases in Calvinistic theology on predestination and salvation.

Works by Weber

Gesammelte Aufsätze zur Religionssoziologie, 3 vols. Tübingen, 1920–1921. Vol. I, Part 1, translated by Talcott Parsons as *The Protestant Ethic and the Spirit of Capitalism.* London, 1930.

Gesammelte politische Schriften. Munich, 1921.

Gesammelte Aufsätze zur Wissenschaftslehre. Tübingen, 1922.

Wirtschaft und Gesellschaft. Tübingen, 1922. 2d ed., 2 vols. Tübingen, 1925. Part 1 translated by A. M. Henderson and Talcott Parsons as *The Theory of Social and Economic Organization.* Glencoe, Ill., 1947. Vol. II, pp. 735 ff., translated by Don Martindale and Gertrude Neuwirth as *The City.* New York, 1958. Selections (chiefly from Ch. 7) in *Max Weber on Law in Economy and Society,* translated by E. A. Shils and Max Rheinstein. Cambridge, Mass., 1954.

Wirtschaftsgeschichte. Munich and Leipzig, 1923. Translated by F. H. Knight as *General Economic History.* London, 1927.

Gesammelte Aufsätze zur Soziologie und Sozialpolitik. Tübingen, 1924.

From Max Weber: Essays in Sociology, translated by H. H. Gerth and C. Wright Mills. New York, 1946.

Schriften zur theoretischen Soziologie, zur Soziologie der Politik und Verfassung. Frankfurt, 1947.

On the Methodology of the Social Sciences, translated and edited by E. A. Shils and H. A. Finch. Glencoe, Ill., 1949.

Works on Weber

Antoni, Carlo, *Dallo storicismo alla sociologia.* Florence, 1940. Translated by H. V. White as *From History to Sociology.* Detroit, 1959.

Aron, Raymond, *La Sociologie allemande contemporaine.* Paris, 1935. Translated by M. Bottomore and T. Bottomore as *Modern German Sociology.* London, 1957.

Aron, Raymond, *Essai sur la théorie de l'histoire dans l'Allemagne contemporaine.* Paris, 1938.

Bendix, Reinhard, *Max Weber. An Intellectual Portrait.* London, 1960.

Henrich, Dieter, *Die Einheit der Wissenschaftslehre Max Webers.* Tübingen, 1952.

Lennert, Rudolf, *Die Religionstheorie Max Webers.* Stuttgart, 1935.

Mayer, J. P., *Max Weber and German Politics.* London, 1943.

Parsons, Talcott, *The Structure of Social Action.* New York and London, 1937.

Weber, Marianne, *Max Weber. Ein Lebensbild.* Tübingen. 1926.

PETER WINCH

WEIL, SIMONE (1909–1943), French author and mystic, was born in Paris, into a well-to-do family of distinguished intellectuals. During her lifetime she published only articles, dealing mainly with political and social issues, in obscure syndicalist sheets. Her uncompromising dedication to the search for truth and social justice as a way of life made her a significant though much debated personality. She lived a life of stringent deprivation. In spite of ill health she worked in factories, joined the anti-Franco volunteers in Spain, and worked as a farm laborer in the south of France after the 1940 defeat. After 1942 she lived in exile in New York and then in England. Jewish by birth, she wished to partake fully in the suffering of the victims of Nazism, and she allowed herself to die of hunger.

While in her twenties she was trained by Alain (Émile Auguste Chartier) in philosophy and logic. She had a voracious, relentless mind, and her studies included Greek, Latin, Sanskrit, several modern languages, philosophy, Western and Oriental religions, science, mathematics, and literature. Her writings are primarily based on textual comment and syncretic, ahistoric, and controversial interpretations. Her thought is rooted in Platonic and Stoic philosophy reinterpreted in terms of an apparently genuine mystical experience—in 1938 Simone Weil experienced a moment of supernatural revelation and union with Christ. It gave her a mystical sense of vocation as possessor of a truth that she was delegated to transmit.

The bulk of her work, touching on the social, moral, aesthetic, and religious facets of life, was posthumously published. The published works combine fragments, more or less consistently developed and sometimes rather speciously selected, from her notebooks, letters, articles, and memoranda. The three-volume *Cahiers* (two volumes in the English translation) gives the integral but still fragmentary manuscript text from which the first published volumes were drawn.

A systematic interpretation of her work is problematical and, besides, could do her sometimes brilliant, sometimes obscure, paradoxical writing scant justice. Her thought is concentrated in two areas, the social and metaphysical, linked by her special concept of the human person. In a universe ruled by an iron, impersonal necessity, the human being shows an ineradicable expectation of goodness which is the sacred part of the human person. Society, the collective in whatever form, is the "large animal" offering the individual a false transcendency. Modern industrial society uproots but offers no values corresponding to the sacred aspirations of the individual. Not until labor and thought coincide and work is reintegrated into the spiritual edifice of society will the individual regain a sense of freedom, dignity, and community.

Central to Simone Weil's thought is the fundamental human frustration caused by the inherent contradiction between two forces—the rigorous mechanical necessity at work in the universe and the inner expectation of good. Simone Weil developed her metaphysics from this central conflict. She presents a dialectic of divine creation and voluntary personal "decreation" or disindividualization whereby the creature relinquishes the particular and becomes annihilated in divine love through methodical destruction of the self. The destruction of the self is to be attained first by rigorous use of discursive reason pushed to its ultimate limits, at which point there will remain only a wall of unpassable contradictions representing the absurdities of the human condition. The second step is the way of the mystics and involves nondiscursive disciplines—attention, waiting, "transparency," an inner void, and silence followed by certainty. Both methods of approach are apparent in her writing. Her God is impersonal and passive because all-loving. Only through a voluntary withdrawal of God could the act of creation take place. Evil, felt by man as suffering and apprehended by the understanding as the incomprehensible, is the paradoxical lot of the creature because of the nature of the initial act of finite creation by the infinite being.

Works by Weil

For bibliographies see *Selected Essays, 1934–1943*, translated by Richard Rees (Oxford, 1962), pp. 228–229, and Michel Throut, *Essai de bibliographie des écrits de Simone Weil*, Vol. 26, *Archives des lettres modernes* (October 1959, Paris).

The notebooks have been published in French as *Cahiers*, 3 vols. (Paris, 1951, 1953, 1956), and in English translation by Arthur F. Wills as *The Notebooks of Simone Weil*, 2 vols. (London and New York, 1956).

The published selections of her writings include *La Pesanteur et la grâce* (Paris, 1946), translated by Emma Craufurd as *Gravity and Grace* (London, 1952); *L'Enracinement* (Paris, 1949), translated by Arthur F. Wills as *The Need for Roots* (London and New York, 1952); *Attente de Dieu* (Paris, 1950), translated by Emma Craufurd as *Waiting for God* (London and New York, 1951); *La Connaissance surnaturelle* (Paris, 1950); *La Condition ouvrière* (Paris, 1951); *Lettre à un religieux* (Paris, 1951), translated by Arthur F. Wills as *Letter to a Priest* (London and New York, 1953); *Intuitions pré-chrétiennes* (Paris, 1951), parts of which have been selected, edited, and translated by Elisabeth Geissbuhler as *Intimations of Christianity Among the Ancient Greeks* (London and New York, 1957); *La Source grecque* (Paris, 1953); and *Écrits de Londres* (Paris, 1957).

Works on Weil

See J. Cabaud, *Simone Weil* (New York, 1964); G. Kempfer, *La Philosophie mystique de Simone Weil* (Paris, 1960); and I. R. Malan, *L'Enracinement de Simone Weil* (Paris, 1961).

Germaine Brée

WESTERMARCK, EDWARD ALEXANDER (1862–1939), is best known as an anthropologist and sociologist; he is important in philosophy, however, as an exponent of a subjectivist theory of ethics, which he illustrated and supported by a survey of the actual variations in moral ideas. He himself made it clear in *Memories of My Life* that his interest in the sociology of morals arose from a concern with the philosophical question of the status of moral judgments and not vice versa.

Westermarck was born in Helsinki, Finland, of Swedish ancestry and was educated at the University of Helsinki. After 1887 he lived partly in England and partly in Finland, but he also made lengthy visits to Morocco from 1897 on. He was lecturer in sociology at the University of London from 1903 and professor of sociology there from 1907 to 1930; professor of practical philosophy at the University of Helsinki from 1906 to 1918; and professor of philosophy at the Academy of Abo from 1918. Westermarck did not marry, and his life was spent mainly in research, writing, and university teaching. On occasion, however, he joined other Finnish intellectuals in defense of their country's national interests, and he took a leading part in the founding of people's high schools for the Swedish-speaking population of Finland and of the Swedish university at Abo in Finland, of which he became the first rector in 1918.

As an undergraduate Westermarck became (and thereafter remained) an agnostic. The theme of his last book, *Christianity and Morals,* is that the moral influence of Christianity has been, on the whole, bad rather than good. He found German metaphysics distasteful but was attracted by English empiricism, especially that of Mill and Spencer. This interest, together with the aim of using the library of the British Museum, attracted Westermarck to England. Through an interest in evolution he was led to the investigation of the history of marriage, which was to be the subject of his first book. Though much of his later work was based on his own observations and personal knowledge of Morocco, all Westermarck's early anthropological research was carried out in the reading room of the British Museum. On each topic that he studied, he painstakingly collected an enormous volume of data from a wide range of sources. His aim was never merely to amass evidence, however, but to draw general conclusions from it. In *The History of Human Marriage,* for example, he rejected the widely accepted theory of primitive promiscuity or communal marriage, severely criticizing the use of supposed "survivals" as evidence for it and showing that the actual evidence pointed to the extreme antiquity of individual marriage. And throughout this work evolution by natural selection is used as a guiding principle in forming theories and explanations.

Westermarck's second and longest work, *The Origin and Development of the Moral Ideas,* written from 1891 to 1908, is partly philosophical and partly sociological. He began by propounding the subjectivist view of ethics presupposed in the whole plan of the investigation. No ethical principles are objectively valid; moral judgments are based not on the intellect but on emotions; there can be no moral truths. "Consequently the object of scientific ethics cannot be to fix rules for human conduct . . . its task can be none other than to investigate the moral consciousness as a fact." Thus, he discussed the nature and origin of the specifically moral emotions and the analysis of moral concepts, and he carefully examined and attempted to explain the conflicting tendencies to pass moral judgments on overt acts or exclusively on the will.

The bulk of this work treats the moral ideas comparatively and historically in order to confirm this account of the moral consciousness. Westermarck surveyed the varying attitudes and practices of many human societies on such topics as homicide, blood revenge, charity, slavery, truthfulness, altruism, asceticism, regard for the dead, and regard for supernatural beings. This detailed survey showed the continuity between moral and nonmoral retributive emotions and traced the variations in moral ideas to a number of causes.

General conclusions do not readily emerge from this mass of information, but some widely held views are conclusively proved to be false. There is no simple path of moral advance through history; many of the sentiments and rules that we associate with moral refinement are found in primitive peoples, while more barbarous views and practices have sometimes accompanied the advance of civilization. Nevertheless, Westermarck did indicate a few main trends which he expected to continue—the expansion of the altruistic sentiment, the increasing influence on moral judgments of reflection as opposed to sentimental likes and dislikes, and the restricting of religion to the function of supporting ordinary moral rules as opposed to special religious duties.

Ethical Relativity is Westermarck's most exclusively philosophical work. It repeated much from the early chapters of *The Origin and Development of the Moral Ideas,* but it argued more directly for the subjectivist view of ethics and replied to such critics of the earlier work as G. E. Moore, Hastings Rashdall, and William McDougall. Westermarck began by saying that if moral judgments state objective truths, there must be considerations by which their truth can be established, but he showed that typical ethical theories, including hedonism, utilitarianism, evolutionary ethics, rationalism, and the various accounts of a special "moral faculty," are quite unable to defend their basic principles. He recognized that the variability of moral judgments did not in itself disprove objectivism, but he argued that the persistent disagreement even on fundamental principles among the most thoughtful of moral specialists tells strongly against every form of intuitionism. He admitted that our ordinary moral judgments make a claim to objectivity, but he rightly insisted that this does not show that any judgments have objective validity. Our moral judgments result from the "objectivizing" of moral emotions, this being just one example of "a very general tendency to assign objectivity to our subjective experience." This point is of radical importance, for it undermines all attempts to support ethical objectivism by appealing to the meaning of moral terms and incidentally reveals Westermarck's firm grasp of essentials that are often obscured by the current preoccupation with the use of ethical language.

To the argument that the subjectivist theory is fatal to our spiritual convictions and aspirations, Westermarck replied that a scientific theory would not be invalidated even if it were shown to be harmful and that in any case subjectivism, by making people more tolerant and more critically reflective, is likely to do more good than harm. In reply to McDougall he defended his view that there are distinguishable moral emotions, marked off by apparent impartiality.

An important part of *Ethical Relativity* and the earlier work is the analysis of particular moral concepts to show exactly how they are related to emotions. Among other things Westermarck insisted that although the concept of "moral goodness" is based on approval, those of "right," "ought," and "duty" rest not on approval, but on disapproval, of what ought not to be done or ought not to be omitted.

Westermarck admitted that the variability of moral judgments is due largely to differences in knowledge and beliefs, especially religious beliefs, and that insofar as variability can be thus explained, it is not evidence against the objective validity of ethics. However, some variations—in particular, in the breadth of the altruistic sentiment—are due to emotional differences. The gradual extension of morality until it enjoins respect for all mankind and even for animals is due to the expansion of this altruistic sentiment, not to reason or religion. Not only particular moral judgments, but also the broader features of normative theories, are explained by the emotional basis of ethics. This applies not only to various hedonistic views, which are obviously linked to the source of the moral emotions in pleasure and pain, but also to the ethics of Kant, which Westermarck criticized very thoroughly, concluding that "in his alleged dictates of reason the emotional background is transparent throughout" (p. 289).

Westermarck's ethical subjectivism belongs to a persistent, though often unpopular, tradition in philosophy. He himself particularly commended Adam Smith's *Theory of Moral Sentiments*. Westermarck's own chief contributions are his stress on "objectivization," his careful analysis of moral concepts in relation to the emotions, and his moderate and cautious use of the argument from the variability of moral judgments, backed by immense evidence of this variability. His criticism of many contrary views and his defense of his own theory against contemporary critics are also effective, though he did not develop very far the logical and epistemological considerations that tell against the objectivist view of ethics. He formulated his account with considerable care. By making it clear that moral judgments do not report the feelings of the speaker or of anyone else and that moral terms are not necessarily simply expressive of the immediate feelings of the speaker, he protected his view against the stock objections to cruder versions of subjectivism, and he left room for the part played by social demand and custom in the genesis of morality. His formulations are, perhaps, still open to more refined objections, for to give any adequate account of moral concepts is a difficult task. There are also difficulties in his theory of the moral emotions. Nevertheless, some contemporary moral philosophers believe that Westermarck's views on ethics are substantially correct and that he made an important contribution to the development and defense of views of this kind.

Works by Westermarck

The Origin and Development of the Moral Ideas, 2 vols. London and New York, 1906–1908.
The History of Human Marriage, 5th ed., 3 vols. London, 1921.
The Goodness of Gods. London, 1926.
A Short History of Marriage. New York, 1926.
Memories of My Life. London, 1929.
Early Beliefs and Their Social Influence. London, 1932.
Ethical Relativity. London, 1932.
Three Essays on Sex and Marriage. London, 1934.
The Future of Marriage. London, 1936.
Christianity and Morals. London, 1939.

Works on Westermarck

Discussions of Westermarck's philosophical views can be found in Paul Edwards' *The Logic of Moral Discourse* (Glencoe, Ill., 1955), pp. 46–50, 61–64; G. E. Moore's *Philosophical Studies* (London, 1922), pp. 332–336; and L. A. Reid's review of Westermarck's *Ethical Relativity,* in *Mind,* Vol. 42 (1933), 85–94.

J. L. MACKIE

WEYL, (CLAUS HUGO) HERMANN (1885–1955), German-American mathematician, physicist, and philosopher of science. Weyl was born in Elmshorn, Germany, and died in Zurich. He studied at Munich and received his Ph.D. in 1908 from Göttingen, where he was *Privatdozent* from 1910 to 1913. He taught at the Eidgenossische Technische Hochschule in Zurich from 1913 to 1930, lecturing at Princeton in 1928/1929. He taught at Göttingen again from 1930 to 1933 and then returned to Princeton, remaining at the Institute for Advanced Study until 1953, when he became emeritus. He became a naturalized citizen in 1939. In 1925 he received the Lobachevski prize for his research in geometrical theory. Weyl received many honorary degrees and was a member of numerous scientific societies and a civilian member of the Office of Scientific Research and Development in 1944.

Weyl's *Raum, Zeit, Materie* (Berlin, 1918; translated by H. L. Brose from the 4th German edition as *Space-Time-Matter,* London, 1922) is a classic in relativity theory. Weyl also made significant contributions to the formalization of quantum theory (*Gruppentheorie und Quantenmechanik,* Leipzig, 1928; translated by H. P. Robertson as *Theory of Groups and Quantum Mechanics,* London, 1931). Perhaps his most important contribution of philosophical interest in this book was his attempted solution to the problem of a unified field theory in relativity. Such a theory would ultimately express in one general invariant mathematical tensor equation or law the characteristics of gravitational, electric, and magnetic fields, and show the so-called elementary particles (such as electrons or protons) as derivative from that equation. That is, the discontinuous "particles" would be generated and controlled by the continuous unified field. In 1950, in a new preface to *Space-Time-Matter,* Weyl wrote that after his own first attempt at formulating such a theory, "Quite a number of unified field theories have sprung up in the meantime. They are all based on mathematical speculation and, as far as I can see, none has had a conspicuous success." He explained that ". . . a unitary field theory . . . should encompass at least three fields: electromagnetic, gravitational, and electronic. Ultimately the wave fields of other elementary particles will have to be included too, unless quantum physics succeeds in interpreting them all as different quantum states of one particle." (In quantum theory all particles have associated wave fields.) No such theory has as yet been successfully formulated, despite even Einstein's final heroic and desperate attempts along this line.

Weyl also showed the validity in general relativity of a variational principle of least action. He dealt in some detail with the problem of action at a distance by examining and defining more precisely the notion of gravitational waves propagated at a finite speed (the speed of light), as is held in general relativity, in contrast to the older Newtonian theory of an infinite or indefinitely high speed for all gravitational influences. Weyl also espoused a cosmological model in which all observers located on different galaxies anywhere would have equivalent over-all views of the universe.

Weyl's *Das Kontinuum* (Leipzig, 1918) consists, first, of a logical and mathematical analysis of groups and functions and deals with such questions as the axiomatic method (in the manner of Hilbert), the natural numbers (including Richard's antinomy), and the iteration and substitution principles of formal mathematical systems. Second, Weyl analyzed the concept of number in general, in conjunction with the notion of the continuum: the logical foundations of the infinitesimal calculus, with applications to spatial and temporal continua, magnitudes and measures, curves and surfaces. In all of this he explicitly used the ideas of Cantor, Russell, Whitehead, Poincaré, Cauchy, Dedekind, Frege, Zermelo, and Bergson. Throughout, he attempted to distinguish the abstract, idealized, schematized ("objective") mathematical continua of space and time from the intuitive, phenomenal ("subjective") space and time personally and immediately experienced by each individual. Weyl acknowledged a debt to the ideas of Bergson concerning "duration" as given in phenomenal or intuitive time.

Weyl's definitive work in the philosophy of science, *Philosophie der Mathematik und Naturwissenschaft* (Munich, 1927; translated by O. Helmer, revised and augmented, as *Philosophy of Mathematics and Natural Science*, Princeton, 1949), dealt with pure and applied mathematics. In pure mathematics, he discussed mathematical logic and axiomatics, number theory and the continuum, the infinite, and geometry. In the natural sciences, he explained basic questions concerning space, time, and the transcendental world, with special concern for the epistemological problem of subject and object. The transcendental world is, of course, the Kantian idea with Weyl's added notion that this world might be knowable by the physicist. But the question of knowing was precisely the epistemological problem that troubled Weyl, as will be seen below.

In this work Weyl also discussed methodological problems in the theory of measurement and in the formation of scientific concepts and theories. Finally, he attempted to offer a general "physical picture of the world" in the course of analyzing the ideas of matter and causality.

The first German edition of *Philosophy of Mathematics and Natural Science* was written just before the broader philosophical implications of quantum theory had been recognized; hence Weyl added several appendices to the English edition in which he coped with the newer problems. In Appendix C he declared that "whatever the future may bring, the road will not lead back to the old classical scheme." Thus, Weyl had no real hope that a classical mechanical model would ever again be established as the basis of objective reality, and he explicitly emphasized that in quantum theory the relations between subject and object "are more closely tied together than classical physics had recognized." Weyl's notion of the vagueness of the distinction between subject and object in quantum theory has deeper metaphysical implications, of which fact he was clearly aware. How could we know the real world apart from our interactions with it and apart from the consequent indeterminacy in such "knowledge"? What, then, is the physical "object" apart from our subjective knowledge of it?

Weyl's final work was *Symmetry* (Princeton, 1952), published on the eve of his retirement from the institute.

In it Weyl related the precise geometrical concept of symmetry to the vaguer artistic ideas of proportion, harmony, and beauty. In this account he was sensitive to the ideas of Plato and other great Greek classical aestheticians. His illustrated survey ranged from Sumerian art forms through the ancient Greeks and the medievals, and down to contemporary physicists, crystallographers, and biologists, briefly mentioning modern women's fashions.

Bibliography

Other works by Weyl of interest to philosophers of science are: *Die Idee der Riemannschen Fläche* (Leipzig, 1913); *The Classical Groups* (Princeton, 1939); *Algebraic Theory of Numbers* (Princeton, 1940); *Meromorphic Functions and Analytic Curves* (Princeton, 1943); and *The Structure and Representation of Continuous Groups* (Princeton, 1955).

For further works by Weyl and for works on him, see *Biographical Memoirs of the Fellows of the Royal Society*, Vol. 3 (1957), 305–328.

CARLTON W. BERENDA

WHATELY, RICHARD (1787–1863), English logician, fellow of Oriel College, and archbishop of Dublin.

In 1860 Augustus De Morgan said of Whately that "to him is due the title of the restorer of logical study in England." Between 1826, the year Whately's *Elements of Logic* was published, and 1860, George Boole, De Morgan, and John Stuart Mill were writing. It is therefore natural to expect to find adumbrations of their work in Whately, but in his systematic and formal treatment of logic there are remarkably few. Mill did mention that Whately revived the discussion of connotative terms (called attributive by Whately). Whately's section on "the drift of propositions," which is original and perceptive, was ignored until the twentieth century. Yet this is all that was original, and it is to be found only in later editions.

This systematic section was based on Henry Aldrich's cram book, *Artis Logicae Compendium,* published in 1691 and still used at Oxford in Whately's day. The section was conservative. All propositions were considered to be subject–copula–predicate in form. All arguments were held to be reducible to syllogisms and syllogisms to be based on the *dictum de omni et nullo,* for this is the dictum of the first figure, and the other figures reduce to the first (see LOGIC, TRADITIONAL). Modal and hypothetical propositions were squeezed into subject–copula–predicate form. Disjunctives were reduced to hypotheticals and then treated as such.

Why, then, did De Morgan regard Whately as the "restorer of logical study in England"? The book was something of a best seller and the style, roughly Gilbert Ryle vintage 1826, is excellent. But this was not enough.

Whately's achievement was not so much in logic as in moral metalogic; he explained what logicians should have been doing. When he wrote, nearly 250 years after Bacon, no British philosopher had made a convincing reply to the charges leveled against logic from the time of the Renaissance. The case was lost by default, and the status of logic sank so far that it ceased to be something which a philosophical system must make room for, as geometry was, and became something which must accommodate itself to the convenience of the system. Therefore, logic had been continually rewritten to suit current philosophical speculation. The status of logic could not be restored until the subject matter was defined, the rewriting ended, and the charges against it answered.

Logic, said Whately, is "entirely conversant about language," and it is only as reasoning is expressed in language that logic can study it. He was not concerned with whether reasoning can be carried out some other way—by, say, "abstract ideas." This delimitation of the subject for investigation was neutral and did not necessitate subscribing to the nominalism Whately took over from Hobbes.

Once the subject was delimited, the charges against logic could be more effectively answered. Whately granted the common objection, voiced by Locke, that man argued correctly before syllogism was heard of; nevertheless, putting arguments in logical form provides a test of validity. This test applies in all fields. There is no logic peculiar to science or religion. Induction is not a new method of reasoning, as Bacon claimed. Induction means, first, a form of argument; but inductions of this sort are syllogistic. Induction also means generalizing from instances. This is not the province of logic, and logic cannot guarantee the truth of premises so reached. While it is true that in syllogism the conclusion contains nothing that is not in the premises, this does not render it futile, as George Campbell and others had held. "It is peculiarly creditable to Adam Smith and Malthus, that the data from which they drew such important conclusions had been in everyone's hands for centuries" (Whately, *Elements of Logic*, Book IV, Ch. 2, Sec. 4).

By example as well as by argument Whately combated the view that "logic is the Art of bewildering the learned by frivolous subtleties." He illustrated points and drew exercises from discussions in science, sociology, and religion, and thus exhibited logic in use.

Whately's *Elements of Rhetoric* (London, 1828) dealt with the effectiveness of arguments, but it also contains interesting material on such subjects as plausibility and argument from analogy. *Historic Doubts Relative to Napoleon Buonaparte* (London, 1819) is a witty and attractive *reductio ad absurdum* of Hume's short way with miracles. Whately edited and annotated works of William Paley and Bacon, noting the naturalistic fallacy in Paley. He also wrote much on questions of the day relating to Ireland and on religion and economics.

Bibliography

In addition to the works cited in the text, see E. J. Whately, *Life and Correspondence of Richard Whately, D.D.*, 2 vols. (London, 1866).

MARY PRIOR

WHEWELL, WILLIAM (1794–1866), British philosopher and historian of science, was born in Lancaster. He spent the greater part of his life at Trinity College, Cambridge, as an undergraduate, fellow, and tutor, and finally as master of Trinity from 1841 until his death. He twice served as vice chancellor of Cambridge University, and he also taught mineralogy and later (1838–1855) moral philosophy.

Whewell's output was exceptional both in its abundance and in its diversity. Save for a dozen papers on the tides (1833–1850), however, his scientific works were devoted not so much to research as to teaching (*Mechanical Euclid*, Cambridge, 1837) or popularization and to apologetics (*Astronomy and General Physics*, London, 1833; *Plurality of Worlds*, London, 1853). In addition to his scientific writings he published a number of works in moral philosophy (*Elements of Morality, Including Polity*, 2 vols., London, 1845; *Lectures on Systematic Morality*, London, 1846; *Lectures on the History of Moral Philosophy in England*, London, 1852) and pedagogy (*Principles of English University Education*, London, 1837; *Of a Liberal Education*, London, 1845). He also produced editions, with prefaces, notes, and in some instances translations, of works by Newton, Joseph Butler, Hugo Grotius, Plato, and others, as well as sermons, poetry, and occasional or polemical essays.

However, his principal work—in length, scope, and the central position it occupies in his thought—is constituted by the *History of the Inductive Sciences, From the Earliest to the Present Time* (3 vols., London, 1837) and the *Philosophy of the Inductive Sciences, Founded upon Their History* (London, 1840). The former, one of the first general histories of natural science, is erudite yet perfectly readable. The latter, revised and enlarged for its third edition, was published in three parts under separate titles: *History of Scientific Ideas* (2 vols., London, 1858); *Novum Organon Renovatum* (London, 1858); and *On the Philosophy of Discovery* (London, 1860).

According to Whewell, the theory of induction, which had been examined to the point of exhaustion after Bacon formulated it as a program for future science, should be taken up again in view of the fact that the sciences called inductive have been actually established. Notwithstanding the opinions of the "writers of authority" invoked by Mill, the word "induction" can now validly signify only one thing: the method of construction employed in those sciences that all modern thinkers agree to call inductive. And the only means of becoming acquainted with this method is to see it at work in history. (This is the source of the close connection between the two works, the *History* and the *Philosophy*, which matured simultaneously over a period of many years.)

Induction and history. The study of history reveals an inductive process that does not resemble the generalizing argument of the logicians. In the first place, the induction practiced by the scientist is not reasoning that is valid *vi formae* (by virtue of its form). It is quite another way of arriving at truth: a venturesome course taken by the mind, which, as if deciphering a cryptogram, tests or tries out various hypotheses in turn, until by a "happy guess" it hits upon the relevant idea. The question therefore is not under what conditions this procedure is logically correct—it never is—but simply whether its result is sound. Care and rigor assert themselves in the experimental control of the inductive proposition, and not in its elaboration, which allows great freedom to the imagination. It is fruitless to try to set up an "inductive logic" that is symmetrical with deductive logic and that formulates canons analogous to those of the syllogism.

In the second place, scientific induction consists not in

generalizing the observed facts but in colligating them, in binding them together by the intelligible unity of a new conception. Finding this conception requires the initiative of genius. Generalization comes afterward; the decisive discovery is the forging of the idea. Once this idea has taught us how to read experience, it becomes incorporated into experience; and it seems to us that we see it there. Thus, the contribution of the mind to knowledge is ignored: this is the source of the empiricist error. One forgets that the facts have little by little been given form by ideas and that the facts of today (such as the fact that the earth revolves) are the hypotheses of yesterday; our facts are realized theories.

Induction and ideas. Whewell's epistemological analyses have a general philosophical import; indeed, they furnish an indispensable basis for the theory of knowledge. Whewell was one of the first to whom the thought occurred that such a theory could rely validly only on the history of the sciences, examining how this exemplary form of knowledge had developed. Such an examination seemed to him to justify what one might call an inductive rationalism. All knowledge requires an ideal element just as much as an empirical one. By reason of this "fundamental antithesis" Whewell's philosophy at one and the same time is, in contrast with that of the apriorists, a philosophy of induction, and in contrast with that of the empiricists, a philosophy of the idea. Even the experimental sciences rest on certain axioms whose character as necessary truths—acknowledged to the point that one cannot distinctly conceive their negation—can be explained only by the presence in our mind of certain "fundamental ideas." Number, space, time, cause, medium, polarity, affinity, symmetry, resemblance, final cause—new ideas are added to those that precede as one descends the ladder of the sciences. It was this notion that largely inspired Antoine Cournot.

But such a rationalism, stamped with the influence of Kant, is by no means bound up with a deductive idealism. The fundamental ideas are illuminated for us only progressively, in the course of our effort to interpret experience. They *become* elements of the structure of reason; and the principles that they govern pass little by little, as they are better understood, from the status of happy guesses to that of necessary truths which education then makes permanent in the public mind. Through this bold conception of how self-evidence develops, the theory of fundamental ideas is joined with the theory of induction, the idea as category with the idea as hypothesis. Here there would have been a prefiguring of modern theories of the self-construction of the reason had not theological preoccupations led Whewell to locate these "fundamental ideas," from all eternity, in the divine understanding. As a result the apparent invention of these ideas by man is ultimately reduced to a simple discovery.

Although Whewell's authority was recognized, his philosophy was received only with reservation. His theory of fundamental ideas ran counter to the empiricist tradition, and freethinkers regarded the theological setting of the theory as an anachronism. The logicians, for their part, complained that Whewell's theory of induction had altered the sense of the word by wrongly assimilating inductive method to the method of hypothesis and that it had neglected the question of proof. In all these respects Mill was his typical opponent. It is worth remarking, however, that neither he nor the other critics attacked Whewell's most daring and most novel notions, the interesting nature of which seems to have escaped them: the incorporation of ideas into the facts and the development of self-evidence.

Bibliography

In addition to Whewell's works cited in the text, see I. Todhunter, *William Whewell, An Account of His Writings With Selections From His Literary and Scientific Correspondence*, 2 vols. (London, 1878), and Mrs. Stair Douglas, *The Life and Selections From the Correspondence of William Whewell* (London, 1879).

For further information on Whewell's philosophy, see M. R. Stoll, *Whewell's Philosophy of Induction* (Lancaster, 1929); Robert Blanché, *Le Rationalisme de Whewell* (Paris, 1935); C. J. Ducasse, "Whewell's Philosophy of Scientific Discovery," in *Philosophical Review*, Vol. 60 (1951), 56–69 and 213–234; and Silvestro Marcucci, *L'"idealismo" scientifico di William Whewell* (Pisa and Cuneo, 1963).

ROBERT BLANCHÉ
Translated by *Albert E. Blumberg*

WHICHCOTE, BENJAMIN (1609–1683), the guiding spirit of the Cambridge Platonists, was born at Whichcote Hall, Stoke, Shropshire, of "an ancient and honourable family." He was admitted to Emmanuel College, Cambridge, in 1626 and in 1633 was elected a fellow of Emmanuel. Whichcote was renowned as a college tutor for the number and the character of his pupils, who included John Smith and John Worthington, and for the personal attention he paid to them. Ordained deacon and priest in 1636, he was in the same year appointed Sunday afternoon lecturer at Trinity Church in Cambridge, a post he held for nearly twenty years and by virtue of which he exerted considerable influence on the moral and religious life of Cambridge. At a time of violent, dogmatic theological controversy, his sermons were a fervent plea for liberality and toleration. It was his habit to speak from notes; he introduced into pulpit oratory a new, vigorous, colloquial, epigrammatic style in contrast to the traditional formal discourse. Various versions of his Sunday lectures, reconstructed from notes, were published after his death in 1683 and constitute his most substantial work.

In 1643 he temporarily left Cambridge to become rector of North Cadbury in Somerset, where he married. The following year he was invited back to Cambridge to become provost of King's College, the former provost having been ejected by the Puritan Parliament. He accepted only after great hesitation and secured special provision for the support of the former provost. Alone among the newly appointed heads of colleges, he refused to subscribe to the National Covenant, by which he would have sworn to support Calvinist forms of church government and doctrine. He secured a similar exemption for the fellows of his college. In 1650 he was elected vice-chancellor of the university.

His influence at Cambridge was now at its height and aroused considerable alarm among his more orthodox Calvinist colleagues. Especially alarmed was his former tutor at Emmanuel, Anthony Tuckney. In July 1651 Whichcote preached a commencement sermon as vice-chancellor which provoked a lively controversy between Whichcote and Tuckney in the form of letters. Tuckney accused Whichcote of laying too much stress on reason and too little on faith, of being unduly influenced by pagan ideas and by the Dutch Arminians, of being too tolerant of unorthodoxy. In reply Whichcote denied that it is possible to emphasize reason unduly, reason being "the candle of the Lord." Faith not founded on reason was mere superstition. His own ideas, he maintained, derived from meditation rather than from reading; he knew little or nothing, he said, of the Arminians (this is scarcely credible) but was not ashamed of having learned from Plato. As for tolerance, the Christian's duty is to regard with charity the views of other Christians, however mistaken he takes them to be, and to minimize rather than to exaggerate differences. Reason, tolerance, the minimizing of differences—these qualities were characteristic of Whichcote personally and were central to his moral and religious outlook.

With the restoration of Charles II, Whichcote was dismissed as provost of King's College. He complied with the Act of Uniformity and was permitted to preach, finally becoming vicar of St. Lawrence Jewry, London, where he is buried. In London as in Cambridge his sermons, especially those he delivered regularly in the City at the Guildhall, attracted congregations considerable in both quality and numbers. He died as a result of a cold contracted while visiting Ralph Cudworth at Cambridge.

Whichcote wrote nothing. He was essentially a teacher who needed the inspiration of an audience which was physically present. His views have to be extracted from his correspondence, his sermons, and the aphorisms set down in his manuscripts. His leading ethical principle was that actions are good and bad, right and wrong, in their own nature, not because they are commanded or forbidden; the goodness of an action derives from its conformity with the nature of things as apprehended by reason. In his own teaching this principle is invoked against the Calvinist doctrine that moral laws are simply expressions of God's will, but his pupils were able to turn these principles against Hobbes's doctrine that moral laws are expressions of the will of the sovereign. Whichcote initiated the rationalistic tendency in British ethics, which runs through Cudworth, Samuel Clarke, and Richard Price to our own times. But there is nothing dry or formalistic in his rationalism; his emphasis is not on obedience to rules of conduct but on affection and spontaneity. He thought of religion and morality as liberating rather than as imposing rules.

In theology his influence encouraged the development of the characteristically "liberal" point of view, with its emphasis on goodness rather than on creeds. He thought that the Calvinists, in treating as of central importance questions of creeds, government, and ritual, made the same mistake as the high church Anglicans to whom they were so bitterly opposed. These were matters about which men should be left free to differ, choosing whatever forms and formulations help them to live better lives. This was the side of Whichcote's teaching which caught the attention of the third earl of Shaftesbury, who edited a volume of Whichcote's sermons in 1698; historically, it issues in eighteenth-century deism and nineteenth-century liberal theology, as represented, for example, in the work of Matthew Arnold, a great admirer of the Cambridge school.

Bibliography

In 1685 there appeared in London *Select Notions of that Learned and Reverend Divine of the Church of England, Dr. Whichcote,* described as being "faithfully collected from him by a pupil and particular friend of his"; the *Select Sermons* were edited with a preface by the third earl of Shaftesbury in 1698. *Several Discourses,* John Jeffrey, ed., was published in 1701 (London); Jeffrey also edited the first edition of *Moral and Religious Aphorisms,* published in 1703 (Norwich), and a sermon *On the True Nature of Peace in the Kingdom or Church of Christ* (1717). The most useful edition of the discourses is *The Works of the Learned Benjamin Whichcote, D.D.* (Aberdeen, 1751); for the aphorisms see *Moral and Religious Aphorisms,* edited by Samuel Salter (London, 1753), which also includes the correspondence with Tuckney. There is a modern edition of the *Aphorisms* with an introduction by Dean Inge (London, 1930). Ernest Trafford Campagnac, *The Cambridge Platonists* (Oxford, 1901), contains considerable selections from Whichcote.

For works on Whichcote see the bibliography under CAMBRIDGE PLATONISTS. See also Rufus M. Jones, *Spiritual Reformers in the Sixteenth and Seventeenth Centuries* (London, 1914), Ch. 15.

JOHN PASSMORE

WHITEHEAD, ALFRED NORTH (1861–1947), philosopher and mathematician, made one of the outstanding attempts in his generation to produce a comprehensive metaphysical system which would take account of scientific cosmology.

Whitehead was born at Ramsgate on the Isle of Thanet and wrote of his boyhood in a country vicarage on the East Kent coast in the "Autobiographical Notes" (*The Philosophy of Alfred North Whitehead,* pp. 3–14) and, more vividly, in some of the essays in *Essays in Science and Philosophy* (pp. 3–52). The religious (Anglican) background of his home and the experience of companionship with strong characters in a close-knit community made impressions which left their mark on his later philosophy. With these went a Wordsworthian sense of man's continuity with nature. In his education at Sherborne, an ancient public school in Dorset, he was taught the classics and history, less in a detached spirit of scholarship than as exercises in the study of what Michael Oakeshott has called "the practical past"—a living tradition illustrating general ideas and pointing to analogies in contemporary life. This approach to history remained with him and is apparent in his philosophical books, especially *Science and the Modern World* and *Adventures of Ideas.* It is a use of history in the spirit of what Edmund Burke called "philosophic analogy."

Whitehead also learned a good deal of mathematics at Sherborne, and in 1880 he went to Trinity College, Cambridge, with a scholarship in mathematics. In 1884 he was elected to a fellowship at Trinity. Bertrand Russell was his most distinguished pupil, and from 1900 to 1911 they collaborated on the *Principia Mathematica,* which attempted to prove that mathematics could be deduced from premises of formal logic. In his obituary note on Whitehead, Russell wrote that although one or the other would take primary responsibility for writing some parts, every part was always discussed by both of them, the whole work being a complete collaboration. W. V. Quine, in his essay "Whitehead and the Rise of Modern Logic," called *Principia Mathematica* "one of the great intellectual monuments of all time." (The fourth volume, which Whitehead was to have written on the logical foundations of geometry, never appeared.)

Whitehead resigned his lectureship from Cambridge in 1910 and moved to London. He taught at the University of London until 1914, when he became professor of applied mathematics at the Imperial College of Science and Technology. During this period Whitehead did his most intensive work in the philosophy of science.

In 1924, Whitehead accepted an invitation to a chair in philosophy at Harvard University. He was then 63; the transfer gave him the opportunity to develop his philosophy of science into a full-scale metaphysical philosophy.

Whitehead's work is commonly described as falling into the three periods indicated above: the early years in Cambridge up to 1910, when he was collaborating with Russell on the logical foundations of mathematics; the middle years in London up to 1924, when he was writing on the philosophy of science; and the last years in America, when he wrote first and foremost as a metaphysician. This division can, however, be overstressed. The philosophical interests explicit in his later work can be found implicitly in the earlier work, and some of the general assumptions of Whitehead's logical and mathematical work influence the later philosophy. Rather than as a succession of interests, his thought can best be interpreted as a developing unity. This is the approach of Victor Lowe in the essay "The Development of Whitehead's Philosophy" and in his book *Understanding Whitehead*. Wolfe Mays has remarked that the progression of Whitehead's thought can be looked on as a spiral, returning to certain general notions from different standpoints, rather than as a succession of stages.

Logical foundations of mathematics. Whitehead and Russell had been working independently on the logic of mathematics. Russell had become acquainted with the work of Peano in 1900 (Frege's work came to their attention shortly after) and was working on *Principles of Mathematics* (Cambridge, 1903). Since 1891, Whitehead had been working on *A Treatise on Universal Algebra*, for which he was made a fellow of the Royal Society in 1903. In the *Treatise* he developed some ideas of Hermann Grassmann's *Ausdehnungslehre* (theory of extension) of 1844 and 1862, attempting to give a general formal description of addition and multiplication which would hold for all algebras. The *Treatise* was little noticed at the time; it is discussed by Quine in the essay "Whitehead and the Rise of Modern Logic."

In 1906 the Royal Society published Whitehead's memoir *On Mathematical Concepts of the Material World,* in which he put forth an interpretation of concepts formalized in a logico-mathematical scheme as basic notions describing the material world. Whitehead sought to define the concepts of a geometry from which, as a formal system, the theorems of Euclidean geometry can be derived and which can be interpreted by notions of space, time, and matter. At this early stage he was already dissatisfied with the Newtonian scheme of the material world as composed

of atoms each occupying a position in absolute space at an absolute time. In *On Mathematical Concepts of the Material World* the ultimate entities which compose the universe are said to be lines of force. A particle is the field of a line of force at a point; particles are thus defined as elements in a field, and a point as not just having simple location in space but as an element in a linear polyadic relation R, so that $R\,(a, b, c)$ means the points a, b, c are in linear order. This makes the notion of both a point and a particle a vector and not a scalar one.

Whitehead had been impressed as an undergraduate by J. J. Thompson's lecture "The Poynting Flux of Energy in Electrodynamics," describing the transmission of energy with quantitative flow and definite direction (see *Adventures of Ideas,* p. 238); in *The Philosophy of Whitehead* (pp. 235–260) Mays comments on the significance of this notion of the flux of energy for Whitehead's later work, leading to a view of nature as routes of events or occasions inheriting from each other. Lowe says that the developments in physics that interested Whitehead when he wrote the memoir were vector physics, the theories of molecular and submolecular energetic vibration, and the rise of "field" as a basic concept. The influence of all these ideas, generalized in different terminologies, can be seen throughout his work. (For a discussion of the *Principia Mathematica* see LOGIC, HISTORY OF.)

Philosophy of science. The twofold interest in logico-deductive schemes and in empirical interpretations can also be traced throughout Whitehead's work. Indeed, he saw the connection between such schemes and the vague world of our experience as the central problem of philosophy. He sought the connection by describing a logical scheme as a systematic and generalized formulation of relationships crudely observable in experience.

The next link in this line of thought is the development of his method of extensive abstraction. There is an exposition of this in "The Anatomy of Some Scientific Ideas" (*The Organization of Thought,* Ch. 7); it is also discussed in *An Enquiry Concerning the Principles of Natural Knowledge* (Part III). The method of extensive abstraction is a topological device by which such geometrical elements as points are defined, through concepts of "whole and part" and "overlapping," as relations between volumes of a certain shape extending over others of like shape—for example, rectangles, circles, or ellipses—so that a pattern like a nest of Chinese boxes is produced:

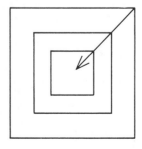

A "point" is not an ideal entity at the center or even an ideal limit of this route of approximation. It is defined as the whole convergent set. Similarly, a straight line can be defined as the direction of a route of overlapping ellipses or oblong rectangles, for example:

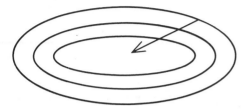

Whitehead looks on this type of definition as having an analogy in a perceived relation. No one can perceive Euclidean points with position and no magnitude or lines with length and no breadth, but volumes extending over other volumes can be perceived. The relations of "extending over" as formulated in the method of extensive abstraction are topological constructs, making precise relations which are also perceptible. This attempt to combine a view of logical schemes as reached from perceived relations with a view of them as theoretical constructs for which interpretations may be sought in experience underlies much of Whitehead's work.

Objects and events. A combination of theoretical construction and alleged derivation from experience also appears in Whitehead's analysis of nature in terms of "events" and "objects" given in the books of his middle period, *The Principles of Natural Knowledge* and *The Concept of Nature.* He claimed continually that the starting point is empirical. Just as in his earlier *On Mathematical Concepts of the Material World* he had attacked the notion of atoms externally related to one another in absolute space and time, so in his later analysis of nature (which he defined as "disclosed in sense experience"), he attacked the ultimacy of the Humean analysis of our experience into distinct impressions of sensation, such as visual sensations of colored patches. He believed that our more deep-seated experience was of something going on with spatiotemporal spread. This "passage" of nature could be divided into "events," so that its constituents are thought of not as enduring atoms but as happenings which can be described as events extending over other events. The writing of this article is a slice of the passage of nature, an event extending over the writing of this sentence, which is an event extending over the writing of this word. Thus, we converge by a route of approximation to what is happening here and now (again, an application of the basic notion of a pattern of volumes and durations extending over one another).

Events display recurrent patterns, the forms and properties of which Whitehead called "objects" and, in the later books, "eternal objects." This is his version of the problem of universals as abstract forms of recurrent recognizable characteristics in the passage of nature. The phrase "eternal objects," along with the interest in Plato shown in his later work, particularly in *Process and Reality,* might suggest that Whitehead took a Platonic realist view of a realm of such abstract entities. This is not so; his view was nearer to the Aristotelian one of *universalia in rebus* or, in his own phrase, "seeking the forms in the facts." His "objects"

are "ingredients" in the process of events; they are "pure potentials" actualizable in an indefinite number of instances. At the same time he was no nominalist; the objects are more than names for observed resemblances. They are properties and relations which are exemplified in recurrences in patterns which can be precisely formulated.

Different types of objects can be distinguished. First, there is a "sense object"; for example, a color like Cambridge blue is perceived as situated in an event. A sense object requires a relation between a "percipient event," the "situation" to which it is referred, and active and passive conditioning events relating the percipient event to the situation. Second, there is the "perceptual object," a determinate association of sense objects in a series of situations strung together in a continuity and perceived as one prolonged event—for instance, that red and black coat. Perceptual objects can be delusive, as in reflections in mirrors or diffractions in water. Third, "physical objects" are those objects whose relations to events condition the appearance of the perceptual objects, as, for instance, the straight stick that appears bent in water. Fourth, "scientific objects" are inferred, nonperceived objects, such as "electrons," that account for the general properties and relations within events that constitute the situations in which physical objects are ingredients. At the stage of science in which Whitehead was writing he instanced electrons as the ultimate scientific objects. He would no doubt have welcomed the further refinements which have occurred since in discoveries of fundamental particles.

Whitehead would also have seen these developments as supporting his distinction between "uniform" and "nonuniform" objects. A uniform object is located in an event throughout a duration and also characterizes any slice of that duration. Perceptual objects are normally uniform; a bar of iron as perceived in any duration however small is still a bar of iron. A nonuniform object needs a minimum time span in order to be expressed at all; he thought a molecule, for instance, cannot exist in a lesser time than that required by the periodicity of its atomic constituents. Whitehead was impressed by the possibility suggested by the physics of his time that the ultimate scientific objects might be nonuniform rather than uniform. The development of quantum theory reinforced this idea. The notion of atomic events, or "occasions," displaying nonuniform objects and forming continuities through their overlapping so that they produce physical and perceptual objects becomes a crucial one in Whitehead's later work. The distinctions and relations between different levels of objects are discussed in *The Principles of Natural Knowledge* (Ch. 7) and, more briefly, in the papers "Time, Space and Material" and "Uniformity and Contingency."

Relativity principle. Objects situated in events form patterns among themselves which are constituents in wider patterns, finally dependent on a uniform pervasive pattern which expresses the uniformity of nature as an ongoing passage of related events with spatiotemporal spread. The attempt to unify notions of space, time, and matter along with his attempt, stemming from *On Mathematical Concepts of the Material World,* to relate these to a set of formal notions underlying a geometry, led Whitehead to have a particular interest in Einstein's general and special theories of relativity. He published his own alternative in *The Principle of Relativity* (1922). He refused to give a crucial role to special facts, notably the velocity of light, and, unlike Einstein, insisted that space must be "homaloidal" (that is, of uniform spread). His reason for this seems to follow from his view of abstraction, which led him to think that a logico-mathematical scheme of notions must be precisely realized in the physical world. Whitehead also believed that the possibility of measurement depended on exact congruence between one region of space and another, independently of physical bodies. Thus, though there are analogies in their conception of relativity, Whitehead's view depends on there being a noncontingent uniformity in spatial relations and is less open to experimental applications.

Whitehead's theory is set forth in his book *The Principle of Relativity* and in his article "Einstein's Theory: An Alternative Suggestion," contributed to *The Times* in 1920 and reprinted in *The Interpretation of Science.* Whitehead's views on relativity have not, however, been taken up by physicists.

Metaphysics. *Science and the Modern World* (given as Lowell lectures at Harvard in 1925) is perhaps the most inspired expression of Whitehead's metaphysical philosophy. It is a book in which lucid and illuminating reflections on the history of science in relation to philosophy are interspersed with technically difficult passages; the book might have been written, as one reviewer remarked, by Dr. Jekyll and Mr. Hyde. But the technical passages are less overlaid with idiosyncratic terminology and a labored attempt at producing a system than is *Process and Reality* (1929). Those who find *Process and Reality* excessively forbidding can gain a very fair impression of the best of the later Whitehead by going from *Science and the Modern World* to his last books, *Adventures of Ideas* and *Modes of Thought.*

In *Modes of Thought* the analysis of nature into events and objects becomes an analysis of nature into "actual occasions," understood as unities which synthesize their relations to other occasions in their own "processes of becoming." Such a unity is called a "concrescence of prehensions," from *concrescere*, "to grow together," the end product being something *concretum*, "concrete," and from *prehendere* "to grasp," suggesting an active relationship but not necessarily a conscious awareness (as is suggested by the word "apprehension").

Instead of events extending over other events Whitehead now spoke of "societies" (also called *nexūs*, the plural of the Latin *nexus*) of actual occasions, which can be structured by subsocieties and which can inherit characteristics from one another in serial order, in which case they are called "enduring objects." "The real actual things that endure [such as stones or animal organisms] are all societies. They are not actual occasions" (*Adventures of Ideas*, p. 262).

This general view of larger units in nature as systems of smaller units with their own inner structure is called "the philosophy of organism." The notion of organism had already been defined in *The Principles of Natural Knowledge* (p. 3) as "the concept of unities functioning and with spatio-temporal extensions," a notion which it is said cannot be expressed in terms of a material distribution at an instant. (The definition of nonuniform objects as needing a time span for their expression may be recalled.) It is suggested that the notion of organism, thus interpreted, could be a unifying one between the physical and biological sciences, physics becoming the study of the smaller and biology of the larger organisms.

Perception. In the earlier books Whitehead had attacked the "bifurcation of nature" as the kind of view of appearance and reality which assigns secondary qualities such as colors to subjective experience and primary qualities to the physical sphere. Instead of this division he wrote about perception as nature ordered in a perspective from the standpoint of an event within nature itself called the percipient event, all perceived qualities being qualities of nature in that perspective.

In *Science and the Modern World* and in *Symbolism* (1927) the view of perception is developed in terms of what it is to be a percipient event. We start from the notion of an actual occasion as a "prehending" entity in active interaction with its whole environment. The primitive mode of perception is not, Whitehead insisted, an apprehension of clear-cut sense data or Humean "impressions of sensation." Rather, it is a vaguer sense of environing realities pressing in upon us. Whitehead called this "perception in the mode of causal efficacy" and thought that it is mediated primarily through kinesthetic organic sensation. "Philosophers," he said, "have disdained the information about the universe obtained through their visceral feelings, and have concentrated on visual feelings" (*Process and Reality*, p. 169 [184]; references to *Process and Reality* give the page of the Cambridge edition, 1929, followed by the page of the New York edition, 1929). This is a causal, not a phenomenalist, view of perception, in which the functioning of the physiological organism (disregarded by Hume) is crucial. Environing events are mediated through the organism, becoming finally transmuted into conscious sensations, which are then projected as sensa qualifying regions of the contemporary world (this is called "symbolic reference" and "perception in the mode of presentational immediacy"). Since there is a time lag between the transmission of influences from the environment and the projection of sensa onto the contemporary world (events which are strictly contemporaneous must in Whitehead's view be causally independent), there is always a chance that perception in the mode of presentational immediacy will not give veridical information about the state of the environment, as when we perceive a yellow patch in the sky which we take to be a star, though the star has long since gone out of existence.

In "the mode of causal efficacy" the qualities of environing events are mediated through organic experiences of the percipient's body. The most difficult aspect in Whitehead's theory is the transmutation of an emotional organic experience into a sensum. He found a link in our use of color words like "red" and "green" to describe certain affective states.

This notion of the sensa as qualifications of affective tone is a paradox for philosophy, though it is fairly obvious to common sense. A red-irritation is prevalent among nerve-racked people and among bulls. The affective tone of perception in a green woodland in spring can only be defined by the delicate shades of the green. (*Adventures of Ideas,* p. 315)

But can an irritation be "red" except by metaphor (waiving the question of whether bulls do have color vision), and does Andrew Marvell's "green thought in a green shade" mean that "green" characterizes the thought or, rather, that there is an overwhelming awareness of green in the environment?

"Process and Reality." Whitehead's comprehensive metaphysical philosophy was presented in "An Essay on Cosmology," in *Process and Reality,* based on the Gifford lectures given at the University of Edinburgh during the 1927/1928 session. Whitehead distinguished cosmology from metaphysics (which he held dealt with the formal character of all facts), maintaining that cosmology described the general characteristics of our "cosmic epoch." That is, it took account of the empirical character of a particular type of world order—in the case of our world order, one characterized by electromagnetic events, dimensions, shapes, and measurability. Laws of nature, Whitehead held, were not part of the ultimate metaphysics of the universe; they could change their character with the rise and fall of different cosmic epochs dominated by different kinds of facts.

Process and Reality is a very difficult book, partly because of its vocabulary and not least when words of ordinary speech, such as "feelings," are used with special meaning. Its manner of presentation is also difficult; the reader is confronted in the second chapter with the "categoreal [*sic*] scheme," comprising a category of the ultimate, 8 categories of existence, and 27 categories of explanation. He may find it advisable to read on and turn back to the scheme in the hope that what is there set out in summary form may become clearer in the light of the further discussions.

Lowe, in *Understanding Whitehead,* gives what is probably the most balanced presentation of Whitehead's work as a whole. Some of its notions are interpreted by analogy with more traditional metaphysical ones in Ivor Leclerc's *Whitehead's Metaphysics,* where comparison starts from the Aristotelian discussion of what it is to be a complete fact. Some aspects of the notions of "actual entities," "eternal objects," and their relations are considered in detail by William A. Christian in *An Interpretation of Whitehead's Metaphysics;* he has a particular interest in Whitehead's doctrine of God and its resemblance to and difference from more traditional views. The main drawback of these otherwise able books is that they seek to elucidate Whitehead's system in its own terms. It is likely that the contribution of *Process and Reality* can be estimated only if philosophers working independently of direct exegesis find that some of its ideas can be developed, perhaps in different terminology, and put to use in particular philosophical problems. It is likely, too, that these will be ways of thinking which take more account of the philosophy of science and vary more from the main tradition of European metaphysics than do these authors. It is a merit in Mays's book *The Philosophy of Whitehead* that it points out that behind *Process and Reality* lies the

influence of Whitehead's early interest in axiomatic systems, as well as in electromagnetic field theories, especially the notion of the flow of energy. The book, however, criticizes Whitehead's realist metaphysical cosmology from the standpoint of a different philosophy of science.

It would be impossible to epitomize *Process and Reality* even in a longer treatment than can be given here. Attention can, however, be called to certain features. There is continuity with lines of thought in the earlier books, but the language becomes more naturally applicable to sentient experience. This is partly due to Whitehead's reading of Bergson, Bradley, and William James, all of whom influenced him in shaping his own particular form of organic pluralism. It is also, however, due to a deliberate onslaught on the notion of "vacuous actuality," existence entirely devoid of subjective experience. Thus, Whitehead's "actual entities," while still linear events, are presented as processes of self-formation with "subjective aim." Actual entities are "epochal" happenings which take a minimal time span to become and which then perish; they are succeeded by others which conform to them and thus secure the continuity which Whitehead held was necessary if we are to have recognition of enduring objects and the expectation of continuing regularities which he believed to be necessary if induction is to be justified. The overlapping of events by other events in a field becomes the "objectification" of an actual entity in other actual entities, whereby the "feelings" and qualities of one entity are transmitted to others.

The notion of objectification is one of the most difficult of all Whitehead's views, and it is doubtful whether any satisfactory elucidation of it has yet been made. He envisaged objectification as more than a response to a stimulus and more than a causal interaction; in some sense it is a genuine re-enactment of the feelings of one actual entity in another, and he maintained that we can experience this transition of feeling. The use of the term "feeling" presents great difficulty. Whitehead used it as a technical term for "the basic generic operation of passing from the objectivity of the data to the subjectivity of the actual entity in question" (*Process and Reality,* p. 55 [65]). This is to maintain that every entity, however lowly, appropriates its responses to the rest of its world in some form of sentient experience, but this does not necessarily involve consciousness. Consciousness he saw as a rare kind of sentience arising within experience; experience does not, as idealists have held, arise within consciousness.

The difficulties in this theory stem partly from Whitehead's insistence that there should not be basically different kinds of entities in the world—organic and inorganic, for instance, or minds and bodies. All entities should display the same general character. He then took certain psychological notions and generalized them (by claiming that consciousness is incidental, not essential) to cover biological and even physical processes.

I find myself as essentially a unity of emotions, enjoyments, hopes, fears, regrets, valuations of alternatives, decisions—all of them subjective reactions to the environment as active in my nature. My unity—which is Descartes' *"I am"*—is my process of shaping this welter of material into a consistent pattern of feelings. The individual enjoyment is what I am in my role of a natural activity, as I shape the activities of the environment into a new creation, which is myself at this moment; and yet, as being myself, it is a continuation of the antecedent world. (*Modes of Thought*, p. 228)

As a description of the kind of concrescence of prehensions I find myself to be, this is persuasive. Extended downward to describe the inner life of molecules, it strains the imagination. The possibility of making this generalization depends, Whitehead said, on our holding that "the energetic activity considered in physics is the emotional intensity entertained in life" (*ibid.*, p. 232). Thus, Whitehead did not concern himself with the issue of freedom versus determinism as a special problem in human action. Insofar as actual entities conform to their environment and immediate past, there is determinism; insofar as any entity modifies its response through its unique subjective element of feeling, there is freedom. So freedom is a "clutch at novelty" that can appear at any point in nature.

Is it, in fact, possible to make the same general categories cover every kind of existent? Whitehead rejected "emergence" views, according to which different levels of existents may display special irreducible properties. (This view also has its difficulties.) Moreover, when Whitehead made the same "categoreal" characteristics apply to all actualities, it is possible that some of the notions which he thus generalized may be of a more abstract type than others with which he connected them; one may suspect, for example, that this is so in the case of energy and emotion. Also, he held that all forms of experience—physiological and psychological and the distinctive kinds of the latter, such as moral, aesthetic, and religious—must all be particular exemplifications of the same basic principles. It is by no means evident that a coherent theory of experience must imply this; there may be reasons why the principles of aesthetics, for example, might differ from those of morality or religion.

Natural theology. Whitehead's interest in religion runs throughout his philosophy and is by no means confined to its later phase, though it is there that he sought to express it in a natural theology. He saw religion as sustaining a sense of the importance of an individual's experience within the social relationships and experience of his life. Beyond this broadly sociological interest, he held that religion was also concerned with permanence amid change. He connected the idea of permanence with the conception of a general ordering of the process of the world which could provide the ground first of "extensive connection," then of all more specific orderings. The ordering of the world, called "the primordial nature of God," has been compared by Mays to a sort of cosmic propositional function, a "form of definiteness" which can then be instantiated by "values" which are actual processes of events. But though Whitehead did indeed speak of the primordial nature of God as a "conceptual prehension" and, as such, "deficient in actuality," the interpretation of it as simply a formal schema omits the point that to Whitehead the notion of "conceptual prehension" includes "appetition," an urge toward the realization of the forms (or eternal objects) so prehended. This drive to realization is said to supply all particular actual entities with their "sub-

jective forms," and God is thus represented as "the principle of concretion" whereby actual processes take their rise. God does not create other actual entities; he provides them with an initial impetus to self-creation. Each actual entity, including God, is a particular outcome of "creativity," which is said to stand for the continual process by which the many elements in the world are synthesized into new unities, each being called a "concrescence," described as a "production of novel togetherness." It is the creative advance into novelty of a pluralistic process. In response to the processes of becoming of the other actual entities of the world, God acquires a "consequent nature," in which they are "objectified" (again this difficult notion of re-enactment) in his own self-formation, which appears to be coterminous with the process of nature.

The difficulties in Whitehead's natural theology are great, not least because he used traditional religious language in ways which may suggest misleading analogies. The most perceptive development of his natural theology is that of Charles Hartshorne, especially in *Philosophers Speak of God* (with William L. Reese, Chicago, 1953) and *The Logic of Perfection* (La Salle, Ill., 1962). Hartshorne states, however, that his own views in natural theology were taking shape before he came in contact with Whitehead's work, which acted as a reinforcement.

Whitehead's influence. It was suggested above that Whitehead's contribution may best appear if other philosophers find seminal ideas in it which they can develop independently. Hartshorne's work in natural theology may be one example; others would be work on concepts on the border between the physical and biological sciences, such as W. E. Agar's *A Contribution to the Theory of the Living Organism* (Melbourne, 1943), J. H. Woodger's *Biological Principles* (London, 1929), and R. S. Lillie's *General Biology and Philosophy of Organism* (Chicago, 1945). Some sociologists have also found support in Whitehead for views of societies as ongoing processes composed of subsocieties with ramified interrelations. H. H. Price has shown interest in the phenomenology of organic rather than visual sensations (see his paper "Touch and Organic Sensation," *PAS*, Vol. 44, 1943–1944, 1–30, especially his treatment of what he calls "bilateral dynamic transactions"). The main influence on contemporary philosophy is no doubt the pioneering logical work of *Principia Mathematica*.

Whitehead received the rare distinction of being awarded the Order of Merit. He had a gift for writing which showed itself at its best in the striking phrase and the vivid metaphor or analogy (some of these have been collected by A. H. Johnson in *The Wit and Wisdom of Alfred North Whitehead*, Boston, 1947). His style is less happy when this very gift of fine writing tempted him to be vaguely grandiose. Hence, rigorous critical interpretation is needed, which is more likely to be rewarding insofar as it leads to more than pure commentary.

Works by Whitehead

A bibliography of Whitehead's works up to 1941, including articles in journals and references to selected reviews of books, was compiled by Victor Lowe and R. C. Baldwin and is in Paul A. Schilpp, ed., *The Philosophy of Alfred North Whitehead* (Evanston, Ill., 1941, 2d ed., New York, 1951). George L. Kline lists

Whitehead's works which have been translated into other languages in William L. Reese and Eugene Freeman, eds., *Process and Divinity; Philosophical Essays Presented to Charles Hartshorne* (La Salle, Ill., 1964), pp. 235–268. A number of essays in this book deal with aspects of Whitehead's work.

Lucien Price's *Dialogues of Alfred North Whitehead* (London, 1961) contains transcripts from memory of some of Whitehead's conversations in his last years. However, the dialogues show the side of Whitehead that came out in conversation with a classical humanist and give little impression of him as a philosopher of science.

Only principal logical and philosophical books and articles are listed below.

A Treatise on Universal Algebra. Cambridge, 1898.

On Mathematical Concepts of the Material World. Philosophical Transactions of the Royal Society of London, Series A (1906). Reprinted in F. S. C. Northrop and Mason W. Gross, eds.; *Alfred North Whitehead: An Anthology.* Cambridge, 1953, pp. 11–82. This book also has extracts from Whitehead's main works and a note on terminology by Gross.

Principia Mathematica, 3 vols. Cambridge, 1910–1913. Written with Bertrand Russell.

An Introduction to Mathematics. London, 1911.

The Organization of Thought. London, 1917. This work, with others presented to the Aristotelian Society between 1916 and 1923, has been reprinted in A. H. Johnson, ed., *Alfred North Whitehead: The Interpretation of Science.* New York, 1961. The chief essays are "Space, Time and Relativity" (1915), "Time, Space and Material" (1919), and "Uniformity and Contingency" (1922); the book also contains other occasional papers on the philosophy of science and some occasional addresses given in Whitehead's last years.

An Enquiry Concerning the Principles of Natural Knowledge. Cambridge, 1919.

The Concept of Nature. Cambridge, 1920.

The Principle of Relativity. Cambridge, 1922.

Science and the Modern World. New York, 1925.

Religion in the Making. New York and Cambridge, 1926.

Symbolism, Its Meaning and Effect. New York, 1927; Cambridge, 1928.

Process and Reality. New York and Cambridge, 1929. Two separate editions.

The Function of Reason. Princeton, N.J., and Oxford, 1929.

The Aims of Education and Other Essays. New York and London, 1929. This includes shorter versions of *The Organization of Thought* and "Space, Time and Relativity," as well as "The Anatomy of Some Scientific Ideas."

Adventures of Ideas. New York and Cambridge, 1933.

Nature and Life. Chicago and Cambridge, 1934. The best general presentation of Whitehead's dissatisfaction with the Newtonian scheme of the material world.

Modes of Thought. New York and Cambridge, 1938.

Essays in Science and Philosophy. New York, 1947.

"Immortality" and "Mathematics and the Good," in Schilpp, *op. cit.* Whitehead's last two lectures.

Works on Whitehead

Cesselin, F., *La Philosophie organique de Whitehead.* Paris, 1950.

Das, Rashvihari, *The Philosophy of Whitehead:* London, 1938.

Christian, William A., *An Interpretation of Whitehead's Metaphysics.* New Haven, 1959.

Emmet, Dorothy M., *Whitehead's Philosophy of Organism.* London, 1932.

Emmet, Dorothy M., *The Nature of Metaphysical Thinking.* London, 1945. Ch. 3 and the Appendix offer a fuller account of Whitehead's theory of perception and its difficulties than does the present article.

Hall, Everett, "Of What Use Are Whitehead's Eternal Objects?" *Journal of Philosophy,* Vol. 27 (1930), 29–41. Presents an interpretation of Whitehead's objects as being abstractions from actual processes.

Johnson, A. H., *Whitehead's Theory of Reality.* Boston, 1952.

Lawrence, Nathaniel, *Whitehead's Philosophical Development.*

Berkeley, 1956. The tendencies toward realism and conceptualism in Whitehead's theory of objects are discussed in this work, which may be consulted generally for the elucidation of Whitehead's philosophy of nature in the middle period.

Leclerc, Ivor, *Whitehead's Metaphysics.* London, 1958.

Lowe, Victor, "The Development of Whitehead's Philosophy," in Schilpp, *op. cit.,* pp. 15–124.

Lowe, Victor, *Understanding Whitehead.* Baltimore, 1962. A discussion of Whitehead's *A Treatise of Universal Algebra* is given in Ch. 6.

Lowe, Victor; Hartshorne, Charles; and Johnson, A. H., *Whitehead and the Modern World.* Boston, 1950.

Mays, Wolfe, *The Philosophy of Whitehead.* London, 1959.

Mays, Wolfe, "On Mathematical Concepts of the Material World' to Whitehead's Philosophy," in Ivor Leclerc, ed., *The Relevance of Whitehead.* London, 1961.

Northrop, F. S. C., "Whitehead's Philosophy of Science," in Schilpp, *op. cit.* Discusses Whitehead's views on relativity.

Palter, R. M., *Whitehead's Philosophy of Science.* Chicago, 1960. Appendix IV gives references to works on Whitehead's views on relativity.

Quine, W. V., "Whitehead and the Rise of Modern Logic," in Schilpp, *op. cit.* Discussion of Whitehead's *A Treatise on Universal Algebra.*

The writers in F. S. C. Northrop, ed., *Philosophical Essays for Alfred North Whitehead* (London and New York, 1936), develop themes suggested by Whitehead's work; so do those in Leclerc, *The Relevance of Whitehead,* a collection of essays to mark the centenary of Whitehead's birth.

There were obituary articles in *Mind,* N.S. Vol. 57 (1948), by Bertrand Russell, "Whitehead and *Principia Mathematica,*" 137–138; C. D. Broad, "A. N. Whitehead 1861–1947," especially 139–148; and Dorothy M. Emmet, "A. N. Whitehead: The Last Phase," 265–274.

Dorothy M. Emmet

WHY. Lack of clarity about the uses of the word "why" is responsible for confusion on a number of philosophical fronts. In this article we shall confine ourselves to two groups of topics where greater attention to the proper and improper behavior of this word might well have avoided the adoption of misguided theories. There is, first, the contrast, or the alleged contrast, between the "how" and the "why" and the view, shared by writers of very different backgrounds, that science can deal only with how-questions. Second, there are certain "ultimate" or "cosmic" questions, such as "Why do we exist?" or, more radically, "Why does the world exist?" or "Why is there something rather than nothing?" Some, like Schopenhauer and Julian Huxley, regard these questions as unanswerable; others, like Gilson and Copleston, believe that they can be answered; but whether these questions can be answered or not, it seems to be widely agreed that they are very "deep." These questions, in the words of the British astrophysicist A. C. B. Lovell, raise problems "which can tear the individual's mind asunder" (*The Individual and the Universe,* New York, 1961, p. 125). Speaking of the question "Why is there something rather than nothing?," Heidegger first remarks that it is "the fundamental question of metaphysics" and later adds that "with this question philosophy began and with this question it will end, provided that it ends in greatness and not in an impotent decline" (*An Introduction to Metaphysics,* p. 20).

HOW AND WHY

The contrast between the how and the why has been insisted on for two rather different reasons. Some writers have done so in the interest of religion or metaphysics. Their position seems to be that while science and empirical research generally are competent to deal with how-questions, the very different and much deeper why-questions are properly the concern of religion or metaphysics or both. Thus, in a widely read book the British psychiatrist David Stafford-Clark insists that the confusion between the how and the why is the "fundamental fallacy" behind "the whole idea that science and religion are really in conflict at all" (*Psychiatry Today*, Harmondsworth, England, 1952, p. 282). Freud in particular is accused of commiting this fallacy in his antireligious writings. Stafford-Clark is not at all opposed to Freudian theory so long as it confines itself to the how of psychological phenomena. Psychoanalysis cannot, however, "begin by itself to answer a single question as to why man is so constructed that they should happen in this way" (*ibid.*, p. 287). Although he repeatedly expresses his own fervent belief in God, Stafford-Clark unfortunately does not tell us how religion answers the question why man is "constructed" the way he is. Perhaps he would answer it along the lines in which Newton answered a similar question about the sun. "Why is there one body in our system qualified to give light and heat to all the rest," Newton wrote in his first letter to Richard Bentley, "I know no reason, but because the author of the system thought it convenient" (*Opera*, London, 1779–1785, Vol. IV, pp. 429 ff.).

Similar views are found in the writings of many professional philosophers. Thus, writing of Newton's work on gravitation, Whitehead observes that "he [Newton] made a magnificent beginning by isolating the stresses indicated by his law of gravitation." But Newton "left no hint, why in the nature of things there should be any stresses at all" (*Modes of Thought*, New York and Cambridge, 1938, pp. 183–184). Similarly, discussing the limitations of science, Gilson declares that "scientists never ask themselves *why* things happen, but *how* they happen. . . . Why anything at all is, or exists, science knows not, precisely because it cannot even ask the question" (*God and Philosophy*, New Haven, 1959, p. 140). For Gilson the two topics mentioned at the beginning of this article appear to merge into one. The why of particular phenomena, he seems to argue, cannot be determined unless we answer the question "why this world, taken together with its laws . . . is or exists" (*ibid.*, p. 72).

Among those who have asserted that science can only deal with how-questions there are some who are not at all friendly to metaphysics or religion. These writers usually add to their remarks that science cannot handle why-questions the comment that no other enterprise fares any better. This "agnostic positivism," as we may call it, goes at least as far back as Hume. We know, he writes, that milk and bread are proper nourishment for men and not for lions or tigers, but we cannot "give the ultimate reason why" this should be so (*An Inquiry Concerning Human Understanding*, Sec. IV, Part I). Hume seems to imply that this unhappy state can never be remedied, regardless of the advances of physiology or any other science. Several writers in the second half of the nineteenth century advanced this position under the slogan "The task of science is to describe phenomena, not to explain them." Ernst Mach, Gustav Kirchhoff, and Joseph Petzoldt were among the best-known figures in central Europe who advocated this view. In England, Karl Pearson, its most influential exponent, conceded that there was no harm in speaking of "scientific explanations" so long as "explanation" is used "in the sense of the descriptive-*how*" (*The Grammar of Science*, Everyman edition, 1937, p. 97). We can indeed "describe how a stone falls to the earth, but not why it does" (*ibid.*, p. 103). "No one knows why two ultimate particles influence each other's motion. Even if gravitation be analyzed and described by the motion of some simpler particle or ether-element, the whole will still be a description, and not an explanation, of motion. Science would still have to content itself with recording the *how*." No matter how far physics may progress, the why will "remain a mystery" (*ibid.*, p. 105).

It is important to disentangle purely verbal from substantive issues in all of this. Insofar as the various writers we have quoted merely wish to assert that causal statements and scientific laws in general are contingent and not logically necessary propositions, little exception could be taken to their remarks. However, they are, or at least they appear to be, saying a great deal more. They all seem to agree that there is a class of meaningful questions, naturally and properly introduced by the word "why" in one of its senses, which cannot be answered by the use of empirical methods. Writers belonging to the first group claim that the answers can be obtained elsewhere. The agnostic positivists maintain that human beings cannot obtain the answers at all.

It is this substantive issue which we shall discuss here, and it is necessary to point out that there are numerous confusions in all views of this kind. To begin with, although this is the least important observation, "how" and "why" do not always have contrasting functions but are in certain situations used to ask the very same questions. Thus, when we know or believe that a phenomenon, A, is the cause of another phenomenon, X, but at the same time are ignorant of the "mechanics" of A's causation of X, we indifferently use "how" and "why." We know, for example, that certain drugs cure certain diseases, but our knowledge is in a medical sense "purely empirical." Here we would be equally prepared to say that we do not know "why" the drug produces the cure and that we do not know "how" it does this. Or, to take a somewhat different case, it is widely believed that cigarette smoking is causally connected with lung cancer. It is also known that sometimes two people smoke the same amount and yet one of them develops lung cancer while the other one does not. In such a case the question naturally arises why cigarette smoking, if it is indeed the cause at all, leads to cancer in one case but not in the other. And we would be just as ready to express our ignorance or puzzlement by saying that we do not know how it is as by saying that we do not know why it is that smoking produced cancer in the first man but not in the second. In all such cases it is clear that science *is* in principle competent to deal with the "why" no less than with the "how," if only because they are used to ask the very same questions.

It is undeniable, however, that in certain contexts "how" and "why" are used to ask different questions. This contrast is most obvious when we deal with intentional, or more generally with "meaningful," human actions. What seems far from obvious, what in fact seems plainly false, is that empirical methods are not in principle adequate to determine the answers to why-questions in these contexts. Let us take as our example the recent theft of the Star of India sapphire and other gems from the Museum of Natural History in New York. We can here certainly distinguish the question why the burglary was committed from the question how it was carried out. The latter question would concern itself with the details of the act—how the thieves got into the building, how they immobilized the alarm system, how they avoided the guards, and so on. The why-question, by contrast, would inquire into the aim or purpose of the theft—were the thieves just out to make a vast amount of money, or were there perhaps some other aims involved, such as proving to rival gangs how skillful they were or showing the incompetence of the police force? Now, the aim or purpose of a human being is surely not in principle undiscoverable, and frequently we know quite well what it is. The person himself usually, though not always, simply knows what his aim is. An orator, for example, who is advocating a certain policy, ostensibly because it is "for the good of the country," may at the same time know perfectly well that his real aim is personal advancement. It used to be said that in such situations a human being knows his own purpose by means of "introspection," where introspection was conceived of as a kind of "inner sense." This way of talking is not inappropriate to situations in which somebody is confused about his own motives, for then special attention to his own feelings, resembling in some ways the effort to discriminate the detailed features of a physical scene, may well be necessary in order to ascertain his "true" aims. Much more commonly, however, a human being simply knows what his aims are, and it would be much better to say that he knows this "without observation" than that he knows it by introspection. In order to find out the purpose of somebody else's action, it is in countless instances sufficient to ask the person a direct question about his aim. Where the agent's veracity is suspect or where a person is the victim of self-deception, it is necessary to resort to more elaborate investigations. In the former type of case one might ask the agent all kinds of other questions (that is, questions not directly about the purpose of his action), one might interview his friends and acquaintances and other witnesses of his conduct, one might tap his telephone and employ assorted bugging devices, and one might perhaps go so far as to question him after the administration of "truth" drugs. In the latter type of case it may not be possible to ascertain the real purpose unless the person undertakes psychiatric treatment. While the practical difficulties in the way of discovering the purpose of an action are no doubt insurmountable in many cases of both these types, empirical procedures are clearly in principle adequate to this task.

We also contrast how- and why-questions when the latter are not inquiries into the purpose of any agent. Here, however, "how" has a different meaning from any previously discussed. In all examples so far considered, how-questions were in one way or another *causal* questions—"How did the thieves carry out their plan of stealing the Star of India?" is a question about the means of achieving a certain goal, and "How is it that smoking produces cancer in one man but not in another?," although

not a question about means, is nevertheless about the processes leading to a certain result. These causal "hows" should be distinguished from what one may call the "how" of "state" or "condition." "How cold does it get in New York in the winter?" "How does the decline in his powers manifest itself?" "How is his pain now—is it any better?" are examples of the "how" of state or condition, and it is how-questions of this kind which we contrast with non-teleological why-questions—"Why does it get so cold in New York in the winter?" "Why did his powers decline so early in life?" "Why is his pain not subsiding?"

It is sometimes maintained or implied, as in the remarks of Stafford-Clark quoted earlier, that why-questions are invariably inquiries about somebody's purpose or end—if not the purpose of a human being, then perhaps that of some supernatural intelligence. This is clearly not the case. There can be no doubt that "why" is often employed simply to ask questions about the cause of a phenomenon. Thus the question "Why are the winters in New York so much colder than in Genoa, although the two places are on the same geographical latitude?" would naturally be understood as a request for information about the cause of this climatic difference, and it is not necessary for the questioner to suppose that there is some kind of plan or purpose behind the climatic difference in order to be using the word "why" properly. In saying this, one is not begging any questions against the theory that natural phenomena like the cold of the winter in New York are the work of a supernatural being: one is merely calling attention to what is and what is not implied in the ordinary employment of "why" in these contexts.

Let us briefly summarize the results obtained so far: in some situations "how" and "why" are naturally employed to ask the very same questions; when we deal with intentional human actions, we naturally use "why" to inquire about the purpose or goal of the agent and "how" to learn about the means used to achieve that goal; finally, how-questions are frequently used to inquire about the state or condition of somebody or something, while why-questions inquire about the cause of that state or condition without necessarily implying that any purpose or plans are involved. In all these cases it appears to be in principle possible to answer why-questions no less than how-questions, and this without the aid of religion or metaphysics.

THE THEOLOGICAL "WHY"

Let us turn now to what we earlier called "cosmic" why-questions. Two such cosmic "whys" need to be distinguished, the first of which, for rather obvious reasons, will be referred to as the theological "why." Here the questioner would be satisfied with a theological answer if he found such an answer convincing in its own right. He may or may not accept it as true, but he would not regard it as irrelevant.

Gilson, whose remarks on the limitations of science were quoted earlier, immediately supplies the answer to the "supreme question" which science "cannot even ask." Why anything at all exists must be answered by saying:

[Each] and every particular existential energy, and each and every particular existing thing depends for its existence upon a pure Act of existence. In order to be the ultimate answer to all existential problems, this supreme cause has to be absolute existence. Being absolute, such a cause is self-sufficient; if it creates, its creative act must be free. Since it creates not only being but order, it must be something which at least eminently contains the only principle of order known to us in experience, namely, thought. (*God and Philosophy,* p. 140)

There is no doubt that many people who ask such questions as "Why does the universe exist?" or "Why are we here?" would also, at least in certain moods, be satisfied with a theological answer, though they would not necessarily accept all the details of Gilson's Thomistic theology. It should be emphasized that one does not have to be a believer in God to be using "why" in this way. The American playwright Edward Albee, for example, recently remarked, "Why we are here is an impenetrable question." Everyone in the world, he went on, "hopes there is a God," and he later added, "I am neither pro-God nor anti-God" (New York *Times,* January 21, 1965). Albee's question "Why are we here?" evidently amounts to asking whether there is a God and, if so, what divine purposes human beings are supposed to serve. He does not definitely accept the theological answer, presumably because he feels unsure of its truth, but he does regard it as very much to the point.

It should be observed in passing that people frequently use the word "why" to express a kind of cosmic complaint or bewilderment. In such cases they are not really asking for an answer, theological or otherwise. This use of "why" is in some respects similar to the theological "why" and may not inappropriately be referred to as the quasi-theological "why." A person who is and regards himself as a decent human being, but who is suffering a great deal, might easily exclaim "Why do I have to suffer so much, when so many scoundrels in the world, who never worked half as hard as I, are having such a lot of fun?" Such a question may well be asked by an unbeliever who is presumably expressing his regret that the workings of the universe are not in harmony with the moral demands of human beings. Even when believers ask questions of this kind, it may be doubted that they are invariably requesting information about the detailed workings of the Divine Mind. In the deeply moving first-act monologue of *Der Rosenkavalier,* the Marschallin reflects on the inevitability of aging and death:

I well remember a girl
Who came fresh from the convent to be
 forced into holy matrimony.
Where is she now?

. . . .

How can it really be,
That I was once the little Resi
And that I will one day become the old
 woman?

How, she exclaims, can something like this be? She is far from doubting the existence of God and proceeds to ask:

Why does the dear Lord do it?

And worse, if he has to do it in this way:

Why does He let me watch it happen
With such clear senses? Why doesn't He
 hide it from me?

The Marschallin obviously does not expect an answer to this question, not, or not merely, because she thinks that the world's metaphysicians and theologians are not quite up to it. She is not, strictly speaking, asking a question but expressing her regret and her feeling of complete helplessness.

However, let us return from the quasi-theological to the theological "why." The difficulties besetting an answer like Gilson's are notorious and need not be reviewed here at length. There are the difficulties, much stressed by recent writers, of saying anything intelligible about a disembodied mind, finite or infinite, and there are further difficulties of talking meaningfully about the creation of the universe. There are the rather different difficulties connected not with the intelligibility of the theological assertions but with the reasoning used to justify them. Schopenhauer referred to all such attempts to reach a final resting place in the series of causes as treating the causal principle like a "hired cab" which one dismisses when one has reached one's destination. Bertrand Russell objects that such writers work with an obscure and objectionable notion of explanation: to explain something, we are not at all required to introduce a "self-sufficient" entity, whatever that may be. Writing specifically in reply to Gilson, Nagel insists that it is perfectly legitimate to inquire into the reasons for the existence of the alleged absolute Being, the pure Act of existence. Those who reject such a question as illegitimate, he writes, are "dogmatically cutting short a discussion when the intellectual current runs against them" (*Sovereign Reason,* Glencoe, Ill., 1954, p. 30). Without wishing to minimize these difficulties, it is important to insist that there is a sense in which the theological why-questions *are* intelligible. The question can be answered for such a person if it can be shown that there is a God. If not, it cannot be answered. Albee and Gilson, for example, do not agree about the truth, or at any rate the logical standing, of the theological assertion, but they agree that it is relevant to *their* cosmic why-question. There is thus a sense in which the questioner here knows what he is looking for.

THE SUPER-ULTIMATE "WHY"

The theological "why" must be distinguished from what we are here going to call the super-ultimate "why." A person who is using "why" in the latter way would regard the theological answer as quite unsatisfactory, not (or not just) because it is meaningless or false but because it does not answer *his* question. It does not go far enough. For granting that there is a God and that human beings were created by God to serve certain of his purposes, our questioner would now ask "Why is there a God of this kind with these purposes and not another God with other purposes?" or, more radically, he would ask "Why was there at some time God rather than nothing?" The Biblical statement "In the beginning God created heaven and earth," Heidegger explicitly remarks, "is not an answer to . . . and cannot even be brought into relation with our question." The believer who stops with God is not pushing his questioning "to the very end" (*An Introduction to Metaphysics*, pp. 6–7). (It is not certain how somebody pressing the super-ultimate why-question would react to the rejoinder of those theologians who maintain that God exists necessarily and that hence the question "Why was there at some time God rather than nothing?" is illegitimate. In all likelihood he would support the view, accepted by the majority of Western philosophers since Hume and Kant, that it makes no sense to talk about anything, natural or supernatural, as existing necessarily.)

There are times when most people would regard these super-ultimate why-questions as just absurd. Stafford-Clark himself speaks with impatience of the "rumination" and the tedious and interminable speculations of obsessional patients. "'Why is the world?' was a question to which one patient could find no answer but from which he could find no relief" (*Psychiatry Today*, p. 112). Yet, at other times, most of us are ready to treat these why-questions as supremely profound, as riddles to which it would be wonderful to have the answer but which, because of our finite intellects, must forever remain unsolved. It is true that certain philosophers, like Schelling and Heidegger, who have frequently been denounced as obscurantists, have laid special emphasis on super-ultimate why-questions; but it would be a total misunderstanding of the situation to suppose that more empirical philosophers, or indeed ordinary people, are not given to asking them or to treating them with great seriousness. It is almost unavoidable that any reasonably intelligent and reflective person who starts wondering about the origin of the human race, or animal life, or the solar system, or our galaxy and other galaxies, or about the lack of justice in the world, the brevity of life, and seeming absolute finality of death, should sooner or later ask "Why this world and not another—why any world?" The scientist Julian Huxley is as far removed in temperament and philosophy from Heidegger as anybody could be. Yet he also speaks of the "basic and universal mystery—the mystery of existence in general . . . why does the world exist?" For Huxley it is science which "confronts us" with this mystery, but science cannot remove it. The only comment we can make is that "we do not know." We must accept the existence of the universe "and our own existence as the one basic mystery" (*Essays of a Humanist*, London, 1964, pp. 107–108). Ludwig Büchner was a materialist and an atheist, and yet he repeatedly spoke of the "inexplicability of the last ground of things." Nor are super-ultimate why-questions confined to those who do not believe in God or who have no metaphysical system. Schopenhauer was supremely confident that his was the true metaphysic, but he nevertheless remarks in the concluding chapter of his main work that his "philosophy does not pretend to explain the existence of the world in its ultimate grounds. . . . After all my explanations," he adds, "one may still ask, for example, whence has sprung this will, the manifestation of which is the world. . . . A perfect understanding of the existence, nature, and origin of the world, extending to its ultimate ground and satisfying all demands, is impossible. So much as to the limits of my philosophy, and indeed of all philosophy" (*The World As Will and Idea,* 3 vols., translated by

R. B. Haldane and J. Kemp, London, 1883, Ch. 50). Similarly, Voltaire, who was a firm and sincere believer in God and who never tired of denouncing atheists as blind and foolish, nevertheless asked, at the end of the article "Why?" in his *Philosophical Dictionary*, "Why is there anything?," without for a moment suggesting that an appeal to God's creation would be a solution. William James, too, although he repeatedly defended supernaturalism, never claimed that it provided an answer to the question "How comes the world to be here at all instead of the nonentity which might be imagined in its place?" Philosophy, in James's opinion, whether it be naturalistic or supernaturalistic, "brings no reasoned solution" to this question, "for from nothing to being there is no logical bridge" (*Some Problems of Philosophy,* New York, 1911, pp. 38–40). "The question of being," he observes later in the same discussion, is "the darkest in all philosophy. All of us are beggars here, and no school can speak disdainfully of another or give itself superior airs" (*ibid.*, p. 46).

Having pointed out how widespread is this tendency to ask and take seriously the super-ultimate why-question, it is necessary to explain why, in the opinion of a number of contemporary philosophers, it must nevertheless be condemned as meaningless. It is the mark of a meaningful question, it would be urged, that not all answers can be ruled out *a priori*; but because of the way in which the super-ultimate why-question has been set up, it is *logically* impossible to obtain an answer. It is quite clear that the questioner will automatically reject any proposed answer as "not going back far enough"—as not answering *his* why. "All explanation," in the words of Peter Koestenbaum, an American disciple and expositor of Heidegger, "occurs within that which is to be explained . . . so the question applies to any possible answer as well" ("The Sense of Subjectivity," p. 54), that is, there *cannot* be an answer. If, however, a question can be put at all, to quote Wittgenstein,

> then it *can* also be answered . . . doubt can only exist where there is a question; a question only where there is an answer, and this only where something *can* be *said*. (*Tractatus Logico-philosophicus*, 6.5 and 6.51)

It must be emphasized that the super-ultimate "why" does *not* express ignorance about the "early" history of the universe. Büchner, for example, had no doubt that matter was eternal and that nothing which could be called "creation" had ever occurred; Voltaire similarly had no doubt that the physical universe was created by God and that God had always existed—yet both of them asked the super-ultimate "why" and regarded it as unanswerable. No doubt, some who have asked super-ultimate why-questions would, unlike Büchner and Voltaire, declare themselves ignorant of the remote history of the universe, but it is not this ignorance that they are expressing by means of the super-ultimate "why."

Those who insist that the super-ultimate why-question is meaningful do not usually deny that it very radically differs from *all* other meaningful why-questions. To mark the difference they occasionally refer to it by such labels as "mystery" or "miracle." Thus Koestenbaum remarks that "questions of this sort do not lead to answers but to a state of mind that appreciates the miracle of existence," they call attention to "the greatest of all mysteries" (*op. cit.,* pp. 54–55). Heidegger writes that the question "is incommensurable with any other" (*An Introduction to Metaphysics,* p. 4) and subsequently observes that "not only what is asked after but also the asking itself is extraordinary" (*ibid.,* p. 10).

Calling the super-ultimate why-question a "mystery" or a "miracle" or "incommensurable" or "extraordinary" does not in any way remove the difficulty: it is just one way of acknowledging that there is one. If it is granted that in all other situations a question makes sense only if an answer to it is logically possible, one wonders why this principle or criterion is not to be applied in the present case. If the defender of the meaningfulness of the super-ultimate why-question admits that in the "ordinary" sense the question is meaningless but that in some other and perhaps deeper sense it is meaningful, one would like to be told what this other and deeper sense is.

The point of the preceding paragraphs is sometimes expressed in a way that is not totally satisfactory. It is maintained that a question does not make sense unless the questioner knows what kind of answer he is looking for. However, while the fact that the questioner knows the "outline" of the answer may be a strong or even conclusive reason for supposing that the question is meaningful, the converse does not hold. One can think of examples in which a question is meaningful although the person asking it did not know what a possible answer would look like. Thus somebody might ask "What is the meaning of life?" without being able to tell us what kind of answer would be relevant and at a later time, after falling in love for the first time, he might exclaim that he now had the answer to his question—that love was the meaning of life. It would be much better to say in such a case that the question, as originally asked, was not clear than to say that it was meaningless. It is not objectionable to condemn a question as meaningless on the ground that the questioner does not know what he is looking for if in the context this is a way of saying that he has ruled out all answers *a priori;* and very probably those who express themselves in this way do not mean to point to some *contingent* incapacity on the part of the questioner but, rather, to a disability consequent upon the logical impossibility of obtaining an answer to the question. It is similar to saying that it is inconceivable that 3 plus 2 should equal 6 when we do not mean to assert a contingent fact about a certain incapacity on the part of human beings but, rather, that "3 plus 2 equals 6" is a self-contradiction.

The conclusion that the super-ultimate why-question is meaningless can also be reached by attending to what has here happened to the word "why." A little reflection shows that in the super-ultimate question "why" has lost any of its ordinary meanings without having been given a new one. Let us see how this works when the question is put in the form "Why does the universe exist?" and when the "universe" is taken to include everything that in fact exists. In *any* of its familiar senses, when we ask of anything, *x,* why it happened or why it is what it is—whether *x* is the collapse of an army, a case of lung cancer, the theft of a jewel, or the stalling of a car—we assume that there is something or some set of conditions, other than *x,* in terms of which it can be explained. We do not know what this other thing is that is suitably related to *x,* but unless it is in principle possible to go beyond *x* and find such another thing, the question does not make any sense. (This has to be slightly modified to be accurate. If we are interested in the "why" of a state of *x* at a certain time, then the answer can certainly refer to an earlier state of *x.* This does not affect the issue here discussed since, in the sense with which we are concerned, reference to an earlier state of *x* is going beyond *x.*) Now, if by "the universe" we mean the totality of things, then our *x* in "Why does the universe exist?" is so all-inclusive that it is *logically* impossible to find anything which could be suitably related to that whose explanation we appear to be seeking. "The sense of the world," wrote Wittgenstein, "must lie outside the world" (*Tractatus Logico-philosophicus,* 6.41), but by definition nothing can be outside the world. Heidegger, who avoids the formulation "Why does the universe exist?" and who instead inquires into the why of *das seiende* (the official translation of this term is "the essent," but Koestenbaum and others quite properly translate it as "things"), nevertheless makes it clear that *das seiende* here "takes in everything, and this means not only everything that is present in the broadest sense but also everything that ever was or will be." "Our question," he writes a little later, presumably without seeing the implications of this admission, "reaches out so far that we can never go further" (*An Introduction to Metaphysics,* p. 2).

For anybody who is not clearly aware of what we may call the logical grammar of "why," it is very easy to move from meaningful why-questions about particular things to the meaningless why-question about the universe. This tendency is aided by the picture that many people have of "the universe" as a kind of huge box which contains all the things "inside it." Voltaire's article "Why?," from which we quoted earlier, is a good example of such an illegitimate transition. Voltaire first asks a number of why-questions about specific phenomena, such as

> Why does one hardly ever do the tenth part good one might do? Why in half Europe do girls pray to God in Latin, which they do not understand? Why in antiquity was there never a theological quarrel, and why were no people ever distinguished by the name of a sect?

He then gets more and more philosophical:

> Why, as we are so miserable, have we imagined that not to be is a great ill, when it is clear that it was not an ill not to be before we were born?

A little later we have what may well be a theological "why":

> Why do we exist?

Finally, as if there had been no shift in the meaning of "why," Voltaire asks:

> Why is there anything?

It should be noted that the argument we have just presented is not in any way based on an empiricist meaning criterion or on any question-begging assumptions in favor of naturalism. Anybody who uses the word "universe" in a more restricted sense, so that it is not antecedently impossible to get to an entity that might be the explanation of the universe, may be asking a meaningful question when *he* asks "Why does the universe exist?" Furthermore, even if "universe" is used in the all-inclusive sense, what we have said does not rule out the possibility that God or various divine beings are part of the universe in this sense. The point has simply been that the word "why" loses its meaning when it becomes logically impossible to go beyond what one is trying to explain. This is a matter on which there need not be any disagreement between atheists and theists or between rationalists and empiricists.

It will be well to bring together the main conclusions of this article:

(1) There is a sense in which "how" and "why" have roughly the same meaning. In this sense science is perfectly competent to deal with the "why."

(2) There are certain senses in which "how" and "why" serve to ask distinct questions, but here too both types of questions can in principle be answered by empirical procedures.

(3) One of the cosmic "whys"—what we have called the theological "why"—is used to ask meaningful questions, at least if certain semantic problems about theological utterances are disregarded. It was pointed out, however, that this does not imply that the theological answers are true or well supported.

(4) Some apparent questions introduced by "why" are really complaints and not questions, and for this reason unanswerable.

(5) What we have called the super-ultimate "why" introduces questions that are devoid of sense, whether they are asked by ordinary people in their reflective moments or by philosophers.

Bibliography

Wittgenstein returned to a discussion of cosmic why-questions in a lecture given in 1930 which was published for the first time under the title "A Lecture on Ethics," in *Philosophical Review* (1965). He makes it clear that although he regards the questions as nonsensical, he "deeply respects" the tendency to ask such questions. The complete text of Voltaire's article "Why?," sometimes called "The Whys," is available in the 6-volume edition of the *Philosophical Dictionary* published in London by J. Hunt and H. L. Hunt in 1824. Views similar to those expressed in the last section of the present article are defended in John Passmore, "Fact and Meaning," in *Thinking and Meaning* (Louvain and Paris, 1963). Jean-Paul Sartre appears to reach similar conclusions in the final section of *Being and Nothingness*, translated by H. E. Barnes (New York, 1956).

Heidegger's fullest discussion of the super-ultimate why-question occurs in Ch. 1 of *Einführung in die Metaphysik* (Tübingen, 1953), translated by Ralph Manheim as *An Introduction to Metaphysics* (New Haven, 1959). Koestenbaum's treatment is contained in his "The Sense of Subjectivity," in *Review of Existential Psychology and Psychiatry*, Vol. 2 (1962), 47–64. Max Scheler discusses the super-ultimate why-question in his essay "Vom Wesen der Philosophie und der moralischen Bedingung des philosophischen Erkennens," in *Gesammelte Werke*, Maria Scheler, ed., Vol. V (Bern, 1954). His position seems to be very similar to that of Heidegger and other existentialists. Scheler concludes that "he who has not, as it were, looked into the abyss of the absolute Nothing will completely overlook the eminently positive content of the realization that there is something rather than nothing" (pp. 93–94).

The only detailed attempt to reply to arguments such as those urged in the present article and to show that the super-ultimate why-question is meaningful, although it is in principle unanswerable, is found in M. K. Munitz, *The Mystery of Existence* (New York, 1965). Clearly theological uses of "why" occur in Ch. 7 of Richard Taylor, *Metaphysics* (New York; 1963) and in F. C. Copleston's remarks in his debate with A. J. Ayer, "Logical Positivism," in Paul Edwards and Arthur Pap, eds., *A Modern Introduction to Philosophy*, 2d ed. (New York, 1965). There are some interesting remarks on what we have here been calling the quasi-theological "why" in Ch. 14 of S. E. Toulmin, *The Place of Reason in Ethics* (Cambridge, 1950).

The general topic of what makes a question meaningful has only very rarely been discussed by philosophers. Rudolf Carnap, in *Der logische Aufbau der Welt*, Part V, Sec. E (Berlin, 1928; 2d ed., Hamburg, 1961), and Moritz Schlick, in "Unanswerable Questions?," in *The Philosopher* (1935), reprinted in his *Gesammelte Aufsätze* (Vienna, 1938), propose empiricistic meaning criteria and conclude that questions which cannot even in principle be answered must be condemned as meaningless. However, as was pointed out in the text, this conclusion does not depend on the adoption of an empiricistic meaning criterion. Thus the phenomenologist Oskar Becker writes that "according to the principle of transcendental idealism a question which is in principle undecidable has no sense—to it there corresponds no possible state of affairs which could supply an answer" ("Beiträge zur phänomenologischen Begründung der Geometrie und ihrer physikalischen Anwendungen," in *Jahrbuch für Philosophie und phänomenologische Forschung*, Vol. 6 (1923), p. 412. There are numerous suggestive remarks in Ch. 20 of Friedrich Waismann's posthumously published *The Principles of Linguistic Philosophy* (London and New York, 1965).

On "how" and "why," in addition to the works quoted in the text, mention should be made of James Martineau, *Modern Materialism* (New York, 1875), where the view is defended that science cannot deal with the "why." Agnostic positivism is defended in E. W. Hobson, *The Domain of Natural Science* (London, 1923). A. J. Ayer in the debate with Copleston supports the position that science can handle why-questions so long as they are intelligible.

When we ask why a person acted in a certain way or why he holds a certain belief, we frequently ask for an explanation in terms of *reasons*. It has been argued by a number of recent writers that such explanations cannot be regarded as a species of causal explanation—at any rate in the sense in which we habitually search for causal explanations in the natural sciences. This topic has not been discussed in the present article since it is treated at some length elsewhere in the Encyclopedia (see HISTORICAL EXPLANATION; PHILOSOPHY OF HISTORY; and REASONS AND CAUSES).

PAUL EDWARDS

WILL. See CHOOSING, DECIDING, AND DOING; DETERMINISM; VOLITION.

WILLIAM OF AUVERGNE or Paris (c. 1180–1249), French theologian and philosopher, was born at Aurillac, taught theology at Paris, and was consecrated bishop of that city by Gregory IX in 1228. His principal work, *Magisterium Divinale*, a collection of treatises—including *On the First Principle* (1228), *On the Soul* (1230), *On the Trinity* (before 1231), and *On the Universe* (1231–1236)— is written in a literary, nontechnical style and includes many philosophical topics. With William of Auxerre, Philip le Grève, and Alexander of Hales he represents the first generation of Paris masters to make a wide use of Aristotelian, Islamic, and Jewish thought in the years immediately preceding the establishment of the friars' schools. William was the first great master of the new age. He used Aristotle and Maimonides in his psychology and cosmogony, but in metaphysics, cosmology, and epistemology he owed much to Plato as transmitted by Augustine. He was familiar with al-Fārābī, Avicenna (whom he criticized), Avicebrón ("the noblest of philosophers"), and Averroës. Cautious in his use of Aristotle when the Philosopher seemed to run counter to Christian doctrine, William distinguished clearly between philosophy and theology and recognized that the former had its own rules and competence.

In metaphysics William was a link in the evolution of the distinction between essence and existence, using Avicenna although aware also of Boethius. *Esse* can either denote the being or essence signified by a definition (such as "rational animal") or bear an existential meaning ("is"). In its latter sense it does not enter into the definition of any being save God, who, strictly speaking, has no definition save existence ("I am who am"). This supplied William with his quasi-Anselmian argument for the existence of God as the necessary principle of all beings save himself. The essence of a being either includes existence or it does not; in other words, it exists either by itself or by the agency of others. If all beings existed in virtue of others, we should have a process to infinity, which William, following Aristotle, could not admit, or a circle of causes, which is no solution to the problem; we are therefore compelled to admit that there is a being existing by itself: God. It has been objected that this leads the mind to God as being, not as God, and it was left to Aquinas to demonstrate the rich actuality of being in God. William, as Gilson remarks, conceived being in a Scotist rather than in a Thomist sense: as something present in all that is, rather than as a constitutive element with innumerable degrees of actuality and richness.

In psychology, although retaining the Aristotelian definition of the soul as the perfective realization of the body, he nevertheless regarded it, as did Plato, as having independent existence. Like Albert the Great after him, William felt that the Platonic conception, so like that of Christian teaching and experience, gave a truer picture of the soul than did the Aristotelian entelechy, which was the final individualization of the human nature rather than the superior governing element in man.

In William's epistemology there was a similar eclecticism. Refusing to regard intellect and will as separate faculties, and holding that the soul itself knows and wills, he would not admit the "agent intellect" of the Muslims, which as a Christian he rejected from another point of view as well. In his view the soul as intellect, with which external beings make contact ever so gently (*exilissime commotus* [*intellectus*]), by means of the senses takes these impressions to itself and forms their "ideas" within itself. Elsewhere, however, he modified this semi-Aristotelian doctrine, speaking of a mirror within the human intellect in which the ideas of things and regulatory moral principles are reflected from the eternal truth, which is God. Corporeal light enables things to impress the senses, thus rousing the intellect to behold the "exemplary"

ideas made visible in the mind by God, who is "intellectual day." Since these ideas are in the soul before it adverts to them, they can be said to be in a sense innate.

Here William stood at the fountainhead of the eclectic Augustinian doctrine of the illumination of the intellect, which passed by way of Alexander of Hales to Bonaventure and Peckham. William rejected the Avicennan doctrine of a necessary and eternal emanation of beings and the sequence of events from the divine understanding. He held that the world was created in or with time and that creatures are absolutely dependent upon the providence and free will of God: indeed, William maintained God's freedom in contrast with Aristotle's necessity of nature to the extent of seeming to minimize secondary causality, whether of nature or human free will; and traces are visible of the methodical use of God's absolute power (*potentia absoluta*) that was to be expounded by Ockham and exploited by his followers.

William of Auvergne, the first thinker to use with courage and insight the rediscovered riches of Aristotle, is an important figure whose influence may appear still more clearly when all his work has been closely scrutinized. He anticipated Albert the Great and Thomas Aquinas in valuing philosophy and treating it as an autonomous science, as well as in his insistence that philosophical argument can be met only by one who is himself trained in philosophy. He was, so far as present knowledge extends, the earliest thinker to present the complex of doctrines later to be known as Augustinian, and his influence is particularly clear in epistemology. Beyond this he foreshadowed the Scotist conception of being and of the divine freedom and even, perhaps, the Ockhamist emphasis on that freedom.

Bibliography

William's complete works are *Opera Omnia*, 2 vols. (Paris, 1674).

Works on William include N. Valois, *Guillaume d'Auvergne* (Paris, 1880); M. Baumgartner, *Die Erkenntnislehre des Wilhelm von Auvergne*, Vol. II in the series Beiträge zur Geschichte der Philosophie des Mittelalters (Münster in Westfalen, 1895); Étienne Gilson, "La Notion d'existence chez Guillaume d'Auvergne," in *Archives d'histoire doctrinale et littéraire du moyen âge*, Vol. 15 (1946), 55–91, and *History of Christian Philosophy in the Middle Ages* (London, 1957), pp. 250–258 and bibliography, pp. 658–661; A. Masnovo, *Da Guglielmo d'Auvergne a san Tommaso d'Aquino*, 2d ed. (Milan, 1945–1946); and F. Ueberweg, *Grundriss der Geschichte der Philosophie*, B. Geyer, ed., 11th ed. (Berlin, 1928), Vol. II, pp. 363–367.

DAVID KNOWLES

WILLIAM OF CHAMPEAUX (c. 1070–c. 1121), Parisian logician and theologian and from 1113 bishop of Châlons-sur-Marne, was a pupil of Manegold of Lautenbach, Anselm of Laon, and Roscelin of Compiègne. He also became a friend of Bernard of Clairvaux. At the turn of the century he taught logic brilliantly in the cathedral school and became archdeacon of Paris. Peter Abelard studied under him and, despite their disagreements, highly esteemed his abilities. William abandoned his chair in 1108 to found a house of Augustinian canons at St. Victor in Paris, but he continued to teach rhetoric and logic publicly. Under his influence the school at St. Victor became the inheritor of the theological aims of the school of Anselm of Laon. William composed theological sentences (*sententiae*) which are almost the earliest manifestation of the desire, experienced in the twelfth century, to produce a systematic theological *summa*. They are characterized, moreover, by the keenness for speculation of one who could manipulate the resources of dialectic. William is therefore important in the history of medieval theological writing.

Only the barest outline of William's logical teaching survives, and much of this is contained in the very critical pages of Abelard's *Historia Calamitatum,* where Abelard describes how he himself forced William to acknowledge defeat and how he deprived William of the support of his followers. William was a logical realist, in his earlier days an ultrarealist. He taught that the universal was a thing (*res*) and was essentially common to all its singulars, being identically, wholly, and simultaneously present in each of them. Individuals of the same species are differentiated not by their essence but only by their accidents, or forms. To this Abelard objected that if the same essence of humanity was totally present in, for example, both Socrates and Plato, Socrates must be Plato. Therefore, so Abelard tells us, William restated the doctrine of the community of universals in the form of the so-called indifference doctrine: the universal is present in its singulars, not essentially but without differentiation. Thus, Peter and Paul share the same (similar but not identical) manhood. In the absence of more informative evidence, William's realism cannot be adequately comprehended, but even if with William medieval realism suffered a major defeat, his personal stimulus to logical and theological studies in the twelfth century cannot be denied.

Bibliography

Abelard, *Historia Calamitatum,* Ch. 2 in J. P Migne, ed., *Patrologia Latina*, Vol. 178. Paris, 1855. Cols. 115–123.

Bertola, E., "Le critiche di Abelardo ad Anselmo di Laon ed a Guglielmo di Champeaux." *Rivista di filosofia neo-scolastica,* Vol. 52 (1960), 495–522.

Lefèvre, G., *Les Variations de Guillaume de Champeaux et la question des universaux.* Lille, 1898.

Lottin, O., *Psychologie et morale aux XIIᵉ et XIIIᵉ siècles,* Vol. V. Gembloux, 1959. Pp. 190–227. An edition of the *Sentences.*

Michaud, E., *Guillaume de Champeaux et les écoles de Paris au XIIᵉ siècle,* 2d ed. Paris, 1867.

DAVID LUSCOMBE

WILLIAM OF CONCHES, the twelfth-century Chartrain philosopher, was born at Conches in Normandy at the end of the eleventh century. He probably studied under Bernard of Chartres, learning at least grammar from him, and began teaching in the early 1120s. About 1140 William, who was perhaps now in Paris, had John of Salisbury as one of his pupils; John found him perpetuating the spirit of Bernard's own teaching. However, opposition from less lettered philosophers led William to return to his native Normandy under the protection of Duke Geoffrey Plantagenet, whose son, the future Henry II of England, he taught. He died sometime after 1154.

William left glosses on Priscian in both an early and a later version, and recent evidence suggests that he may have written glosses on Juvenal. However, his other surviving writings testify above all to a considerable achievement in philosophy and in scientific thought. They include a commentary on the *Consolation of Philosophy* by Boethius which is dependent on older glosses but is animated by an ampler philosophical and physical interest; glosses upon Macrobius; a first version of a commentary upon the Chalcidian version of Plato's *Timaeus;* and a systematic work, the *Philosophia Mundi,* which ranges widely over the topics of God, the universe, and man. William considers the nature of God and his relationship to creation; he also considers the structure and composition of the universe, the elements, the heavens, motion, and geography. Finally, he examines the biology and psychology of man.

These were all youthful writings, completed by the early 1120s. In a second version of his commentary on the *Timaeus,* William abandoned his former assimilation of the Platonic world soul with the Holy Spirit of Christian doctrine. In the later 1140s he continued to modify youthful theses and produced a masterpiece, the *Dragmaticon Philosophiae,* cast in the form of a dialogue with Duke Geoffrey. In this work, which built upon the earlier *Philosophia Mundi,* William developed his physical and astronomical interests and produced the most up-to-date scientific encyclopedia of the mid-twelfth century. Like the *Philosophia Mundi,* it was widely circulated. Some historians consider William to be the author of the *Moralium Dogma Philosophorum,* an influential collection of moralist citations from Scripture, the Church Fathers, and ancient pagan writers.

Much of William's philosophical effort was directed toward ensuring that Christian theology embraced the study of the universe and of man. He saw in Plato's *Timaeus* a doctrine of creation which helped to explain the account given in the book of Genesis. He identified the Platonic archetypal world with the wisdom of God, the Logos of Christian belief. He firmly underlined St. Paul's teaching on the intelligibility of this world (Romans 1.20). The created universe bears the imprint of its creator, and its harmony reveals the fundamental attributes of God—power, wisdom, and goodness. These aspects of God are commonly signified by the names of three divine persons, but William was preoccupied with the creative activity of the Trinity rather than with the intimate relationships of the divine life. Stressing the cosmological function of the Holy Spirit, William presented the third person of the Trinity as the principle of life which animates the world and, in his earlier writings, as identical with the *anima mundi,* or world soul, of Platonic doctrine. Conservative theological opinion was thereby antagonized.

After 1140 William of St.-Thierry, the Cistercian friend of Bernard of Clairvaux, launched an attack against the grammarian of Conches, as he had earlier against Peter Abelard. He criticized William for following Abelard and for transgressing the limits of theological inquiry set by the Fathers of the Church. He accused the Chartrain of Sabellianism and of subordinationism in his cosmological interpretation of the Trinity, and of materialism in making God an immanent regulatory principle of the universe. In the *Dragmaticon* William yielded somewhat to these criticisms, but he was also influenced by new translations of

Greek and Arabic medical writings. His animistic vision of the universe was now tempered by an increased insistence on the power of secondary causes, of nature itself to sustain the universe in cooperation with God. William arrived at a new sense of the autonomous value of nature, and he offered many new perspectives. On the individual human soul and its faculties he joined the medical theories of the newly translated *Pantegni* of 'Alī Ibn al-'Abbas and of the *Isagoge* of Johannitius to the traditional Boethian doctrine. Stimulated by the *Pantegni* as well as by Vergil and Lucretius, he criticized the traditional theory of the four elements as the first principles of things. The Ptolemaic theory of planetary motion appeared in William's *Dragmaticon,* which became a striking witness to the broadening of the contemporary scientific horizon.

Bibliography

Extracts from the *Commentary on Boethius' Consolation of Philosophy* are in J. M. Parent, *La Doctrine de la création dans l'école de Chartres* (Paris and Ottawa, 1938), pp. 122–136, and, edited by C. Jourdain, in *Notices et extraits des manuscrits de la Bibliothèque Impériale,* Vol. 20, Part II (Paris, 1862), pp. 40–82.

Glosses on Macrobius' Commentary on the Dream of Scipio is unedited, but see E. Jeauneau in *Archives d'histoire doctrinale et littéraire du moyen âge,* Vol. 27 (1960), 17–28.

Extracts from *Glosses on Plato's Timaeus* have been edited by V. Cousin, in *Ouvrages inédits d'Abélard* (Paris, 1836), pp. 646–657; by J. M. Parent, *op. cit.,* pp. 137–177; and by T. Schmid, in *Classica et Mediaevalia,* Vol. 10 (1949), 220–266; there is also an edition of Schmid's version forthcoming by E. Jeauneau.

Extracts from *Glosses on Priscian,* edited by E. Jeauneau, are in *Recherches de théologie ancienne et médiévale,* Vol. 27 (1960), 212–247.

Philosophia Mundi may be found in J. P. Migne, ed., *Patrologia Latina,* Vol. 172, Cols. 39–102 (under Honorius Augustodunensis), and in Vol. 90, Cols. 1127–1178 (under Bede).

Dragmaticon Philosophiae, G. Gratarolus, ed., was published under the title of *Dialogus de Substantiis Physicis* (Strasbourg, 1567).

See also *Moralium Dogma Philosophorum,* J. Holmberg, ed. (Uppsala, 1929.)

A study of William is T. Gregory, *Anima mundi. La filosofia di Guglielmo di Conches e la scuola di Chartres* (Florence, 1955).

DAVID LUSCOMBE

WILLIAM OF MOERBEKE

WILLIAM OF MOERBEKE (c. 1215–c. 1286), one of the most competent and influential translators of Greek philosophical texts in the Middle Ages, was born at Moerbeke, near Ghent. He spent a number of years at the papal court in various Italian cities and also lived for some time in Greece and Asia Minor. His translations of Aristotle and other Greek authors began to appear about 1260. At the court of Pope Urban IV (1261–1264) in Orvieto, he made the acquaintance of his fellow Dominican, Thomas Aquinas, then beginning his series of Aristotelian commentaries, who encouraged him in his project of translating Aristotle. For several years before his death William was archbishop of Corinth.

Despite the claims which have sometimes been made about him, William of Moerbeke was not the first to translate the bulk of the Aristotelian corpus directly from Greek into Latin. It is true that in the twelfth century Western scholars had necessarily depended on translations from the Arabic, made in Spain or Sicily, for their knowledge of Aristotle. In the thirteenth century, however, at least partly as a result of the Fourth Crusade, a wider dissemination of Greek scholarship and easier access to Greek manuscripts encouraged Western translators to work directly from Greek originals, and many new translations came into use in the first half of the century. Thus, William's translation of Aristotle's *Metaphysics,* for example, while it may have been the first complete version, was apparently the third Latin translation to be made from the original text. A translation from Greek into Latin (the so-called *Metaphysica Vetus*) was in use at Paris as early as 1210, some time before the appearance of the *Metaphysica Nova,* based on the Arabic version, and a second translation from the Greek (the *Translatio Media*) seems to have been used by Albert the Great as the basis of his commentary. Many other works of Aristotle were similarly available by the middle of the thirteenth century in translations from the Greek as well as from the Arabic. While the extent of his indebtedness to earlier translators has not yet been precisely determined, William is known to have used some of the existing translations from the Greek in his own work.

Considered in themselves, then, William of Moerbeke's translations of Aristotle must be reckoned a less than revolutionary contribution to Aristotelian studies in the medieval West. It is not even known with certainty how far Thomas Aquinas, the outstanding interpreter of Aristotle in the thirteenth century, made use of his colleague's work. Nevertheless, William's translations of Aristotle and of other Greek philosophers, taken as a whole, can be said to have inaugurated a new phase of Aristotelian scholarship in Latin Christendom.

To begin with, William's new translations and revised versions of Aristotle's works gave the West a much more accurate text of "the Philosopher" than it had hitherto possessed. As a translator he was unquestionably superior in most respects to his predecessors. His strict adherence to the letter of the original text has been stigmatized as slavish, but it made his translations an unrivaled instrument of exact philosophical scholarship in his day.

Furthermore, William's translations of various post-Aristotelian authors helped Western scholars to form a clearer picture of the history of Greek philosophy and of the distinctive traits of Aristotle's doctrine. The Arabic versions of Aristotle's works had reached the West in the company of Neoplatonizing commentaries and Neoplatonic writings falsely attributed to Aristotle. Thanks to William's translations of important commentaries by Alexander of Aphrodisias, Simplicius, Themistius, and John Philoponus, and of the *Elementatio Theologica* and other works of the Neoplatonist Proclus, the figure of the historical Aristotle stood out much more clearly than before, and Western thinkers were enabled to distinguish more precisely between the Platonic and Aristotelian approaches to philosophy. William's translation of Proclus was especially important in this connection, showing as it did that the influential *Liber de Causis,* far from being a genuine work of Aristotle, was in fact derived from Proclus' *Elementatio Theologica.*

Through his translation of Proclus William also influenced the development of medieval Neoplatonism. The works which he translated gave a fresh stimulus to the Neoplatonic school formed by Ulrich of Strasbourg and other disciples of Albert the Great and through that school helped to shape the mystical doctrine of Eckhart.

Bibliography

See Martin Grabmann, *Guglielmo di Moerbeke, O.P., il traduttore delle opere di Aristotele* (Rome, 1946).

EUGENE R. FAIRWEATHER

WILLIAM OF OCKHAM (c. 1285–1349), the most influential philosopher of the fourteenth century, apparently was born sometime between 1280 and 1290 at the village of Ockham, in Surrey, near London. Entering the Franciscan order at an early age, he commenced his course of theological study at Oxford in 1309 or 1310, and completed the requirements for the degree of master of theology with the delivery of his lectures on Peter Lombard's *Book of Sentences* in 1318–1319, or, at the latest, 1319–1320. Although an old tradition indicated that he studied under Duns Scotus, it seems unlikely that he did so, since Duns Scotus left Oxford at the beginning of the century and died in 1308. Ockham's writings show intimate familiarity with the teachings of Scotus, but this is explained by the dominant position Scotus had acquired at Oxford, particularly within the Franciscan order.

Ockham's lectures on the *Sentences* made a profound impression on the students of theology at Oxford, but his new way of treating philosophical and theological questions aroused strong opposition by many members of the theological faculty. Normally the completion of his lectures on the *Sentences*, which gave Ockham the status of a *baccalaureus formatus* or *inceptor*, would have been followed by award to him of a teaching chair in theology. The granting of his teaching license was prevented by the chancellor of the university, John Lutterell, who in 1323 went to the papal court at Avignon to present charges against Ockham of having upheld dangerous and heretical doctrines. Because Ockham's academic career was thus interrupted while he was an *inceptor* awaiting award of the teaching license, he came to be known as "the venerable inceptor"—a title later misconstrued as meaning "founder of nominalism" (*inceptor scholae nominalium*).

Ockham was summoned to Avignon in 1324 to answer the charges against him, and he remained there four years, awaiting the outcome. A commission of theologians appointed by Pope John XXII to examine Ockham's writings submitted two lists of suspect doctrines in 1326, but there is no evidence of any final action having been taken on the charges which, in any case, were relatively mild. Despite the lack of a teaching chair, Ockham was extremely active during these years in developing his theological and philosophical positions, writing treatises and commentaries on logic and physics, a variety of treatises on theological questions, and an important series of quodlibetal questions that, presumably, he debated orally at Oxford or at Avignon.

In 1327, while at Avignon, Ockham became involved in the dispute then raging over the question of apostolic poverty, in which the general of the Franciscan order, Michael of Cesena, took a position opposed by the pope. Asked to study the question, Ockham found that a previous pope, Nicholas III, had made a pronouncement that fully supported the position of Cesena and of the majority of the Franciscans. When this controversy reached a critical stage in 1328, and it became evident that John XXII was about to issue an official condemnation of the position held by the Franciscans, Cesena and Ockham, along with two other leaders of the Franciscan opposition, fled from Avignon and sought the protection of Emperor Louis of Bavaria, who had repudiated the authority of the Avignon papacy in connection with the issue of succession to the imperial crown. Immediately after their flight from Avignon, Ockham and his companions were excommunicated by the pope for their refusal to submit to his authority. Under the emperor's protection Ockham took up residence in Munich and devoted his full energies to writing a series of treatises on the issue of papal power and civil sovereignty, in which he held that John XXII had forfeited his right to the papal office by reason of heresy. When John XXII died in 1334, Ockham continued his polemic against the succeeding Avignon popes until 1347, when Louis of Bavaria died and the antipapal position became a lost cause. There is evidence that Ockham at that time sought reconciliation with the papal authority and with the rest of his own order, but the outcome is unknown. It is believed that he died in 1349, a victim of the Black Plague that, in the middle of the fourteenth century, took the lives of most of the intellectual leaders of northern Europe and played a major part in bringing about the cultural decline that lasted for more than a century.

Writings. Ockham's writings fall into two distinct groups associated with the two different periods of his career. All of the political and polemical treatises directed against the Avignon papacy were written during his residence in Munich, between 1333 and 1347. Of these treatises many are solely of historical interest; but the lengthy *Dialogus Inter Magistrum et Discipulum*, written between 1334 and 1338, the *Octo Quaestiones Super Potestate ac Dignitate Papali*, written in 1340, and the *Tractatus de Imperatorum et Pontificum Potestate*, composed around 1347, present Ockham's philosophy of church and state and convey his deep-rooted convictions concerning the religious mission of the church.

The nonpolitical writings that embody Ockham's distinctive contributions to philosophy and theology were probably all written while he was at Oxford and at Avignon, between 1317 and 1328. The earliest of these include the lectures on the *Sentences*, a lengthy exposition of Aristotle's *Physics* extant only in manuscript form, and literal commentaries on Porphyry's *Isagoge* and on Aristotle's *Categoriae, De Interpretatione,* and *De Sophisticis Elenchis;* the first three of the commentaries were published at Bologna in 1496 under the title *Expositio Aurea . . . Super Artem Veterem* ("Golden Exposition . . . of the Ancient Art"). Ockham's most important work on logic, completed before he left Avignon, was a systematic treatise entitled *Summa Logicae*, extant in several printed editions. An incomplete *Summulae in Libros Physicorum* (also given the title *Philosophia Naturalis*) contains an independent treatment of the subjects dealt with in the first four books of Aristotle's *Physics*, and was printed in several editions, beginning in 1495. In manuscript form only there is a work entitled *Quaestiones Super Libros Physicorum*, which was probably one of his later writings; it covers, in the form of disputed questions, most of the topics treated in his earlier literal commentary on the *Physics* but reflects some changes in his views that occurred after the earlier work had been written. Two short compendia of logic, each extant only in a single manuscript version, are believed to be authentic works of Ockham, but they add nothing significant to the doctrines of his *Summa Logicae.*

Of Ockham's theological writings the lectures on the first book of the *Sentences,* known as the *Ordinatio* because Ockham revised and edited them for circulation, are of primary importance. Printed at Lyons in 1495, along with Ockham's lectures on the other three books of the *Sentences,* they are called the *Reportatio* because the text is derived from stenographic versions of the lectures as they were delivered. A modern critical edition of both parts of these lectures on the *Sentences* is very much needed. Of comparable importance for the understanding of Ockham's philosophical and theological doctrines are the quodlibetal questions, printed at Paris in 1487 and again at Strasbourg in 1491 under the title *Quodlibeta Septem.* Three other certainly authentic theological treatises, composed during the Oxford–Avignon period, are the *Tractatus de Corpore Christi* and *Tractatus de Sacramento Altaris,* which have been regularly printed together under the second of these titles, and the *Tractatus de Praedestinatione et de Praescientia Dei et de Futuris Contingentibus,* of which a modern edition, edited by Philotheus Boehner, was published in 1945. The 1495 Lyons edition of Ockham's theological works includes *Centiloquium Theologicum,* whose authenticity has been questioned by many scholars but without decisive evidence. In describing the philosophical doctrines of Ockham, use will be made chiefly of the *Commentary on the Sentences,* the *Summa Logicae,* and the *Quodlibeta Septem.*

CHARACTER OF OCKHAM'S PHILOSOPHY

Ockham's major contributions to the development of late medieval and early modern philosophy were in the areas of epistemology, logic, and metaphysics. His approach to these problems and his concern with them were those of a scholastic theologian, as had been the case with Thomas Aquinas, Duns Scotus, and other leading scholastic thinkers of the thirteenth century. The basic problem of scholastic theology since the beginning of the thirteenth century had been that of finding a means of accommodating the philosophical system of Aristotle within the dogmatic framework of Christian doctrine. To achieve such an accommodation was a philosophical task because no alteration in the articles of the faith could be allowed, and consequently all elimination of contradictions had to be achieved by internal criticism or reinterpretation of the philosophical assumptions and arguments of Aristotle. Aquinas had sought to achieve an essentially external accord between natural philosophy and Christian theology, such as would leave the Aristotelian system internally intact. The Franciscan theologians, from St. Bonaventure to Duns Scotus, had considered this inadequate and had sought to achieve the required integration of philosophy and theology by exploiting the more Platonic elements of

the Aristotelian system, much as the Greek Neoplatonists and the Muslim philosopher Avicenna had done. All of the thirteenth-century syntheses of philosophy and theology involved, in one form or another, the metaphysical and epistemological doctrine of realism—the doctrine that the human intellect discovers in the particulars apprehended by sense experience an intelligible order of abstract essences and necessary relations ontologically prior to particular things and contingent events and that from this order the intellect can demonstrate necessary truths concerning first causes and the being and attributes of God.

Empiricism and nominalism. Ockham's significance, both as a theologian and as a philosopher, lay in his rejection of the metaphysical and epistemological assumptions of medieval realism, and in his reconstruction of the whole fabric of philosophy on the basis of a radical empiricism in which the evidential base of all knowledge is direct experience of individual things and particular events. The counterpart of this epistemological empiricism was the nominalistic analysis of the semantic structure and ontological commitment of cognitive language that Ockham developed in his logical writings. Ockham's empiricism was not phenomenalistic or subjectivistic, and it could be called a realistic empiricism according to a modern usage of "realism"; it presupposed and was based on the principle that the human mind can directly apprehend existent individuals and their sensible qualities, and that it can also directly apprehend its own acts. Insofar as Ockham is called a nominalist, his doctrine is not to be construed as a rejection of any ontological determination of meaning and truth, but rather as an extreme economy of ontological commitment in which abstract or intensional extralinguistic entities are systematically eliminated by a logical analysis of language.

Ockham's razor. The principle of parsimony, whose frequent use by Ockham gained it the name of "Ockham's razor," was employed as a methodological principle of economy in explanation. He invoked it most frequently under such forms as "Plurality is not to be assumed without necessity" and "What can be done with fewer [assumptions] is done in vain with more"; he seems not to have used the formulation "Entities are not to be multiplied without necessity." The principal use made by Ockham of the principle of parsimony was in the elimination of pseudo-explanatory entities, according to a criterion he expresses in the statement that nothing is to be assumed as necessary, in accounting for any fact, unless it is established by evident experience or evident reasoning, or is required by the articles of faith.

Positive theology. As applied by Ockham, the principle of parsimony resulted in an empiricist criterion of evidence that left little room for a natural theology. But since it also reduced physics and cosmology to the status of positive sciences without metaphysical necessity, it left room for a positive theology based on revelation and faith that could no more be refuted than it could be demonstrated by any necessary reasons or observational evidence. Moreover, this positive theology, in which God is conceived as the omnipotent creator of all finite things whose creative and causal action is wholly free and unnecessitated, provided an indirect justification of Ockham's philosophical empiricism, since it demanded a conception of the world of created things as radically contingent in both their existence and their interaction. Ockham made full use of the doctrine of divine omnipotence as an *ad hominem* argument against those who sought to discredit his philosophical doctrine on theological grounds; philosophically, however, the doctrine was equivalent to the principle that whatever is not self-contradictory is possible, and that what is actual, within the range of the logically possible, cannot be established by reason alone but only by experience.

CRITIQUE OF REALISM

Ockham's epistemology and metaphysics were designed to resolve a basic problem that the Scholastics had inherited from the Greek philosophical tradition and that may be summed up in the paradoxical thesis that the objects of thought are universal, whereas everything that exists is singular and individual. Seeking to overcome this gap between the intelligible and the existent, the earlier Scholastics had elaborated various forms of the doctrine called moderate realism, according to which there are common natures in individual existing things, distinct from their individuating principles although not separable except in thought. On the psychological side, these doctrines held that the human intellect abstracts, from the particular presentations of sense experience, an intelligible species, or likeness, by means of which it apprehends the common nature apart from the individuating conditions. The varieties of this moderate realism turned on the answer to the question of whether, in an individual, the common nature is (1) really distinct from the individuating principle or (2) "formally distinct," as Duns Scotus proposed or (3) distinct only according to the mode of consideration although involving some "foundation in the thing" for such distinguishability, as Aquinas held.

Ockham considered all forms of this doctrine of common natures in individual things to be self-contradictory and irrational. If the human nature of Socrates is really distinct from Socrates, then it is not Socrates' nature or essence, for a thing cannot be said to be essentially something that it *really* is not. If the common nature is anything at all, it is either one thing or many things; if one and not many, it is not common but singular, and if not one but many, then each of the many is singular and there is still nothing common.

Criticism of the Scotist view. The answer of Duns Scotus—that the common nature is really identical with, but formally distinct from, the *haecceitas* or individuating differentia that was said to contract the specific nature to singularity—was an attempt to find something intermediate between identity and nonidentity. Ockham argued, against the Scotist thesis, that if the specific nature and the individuating difference are really identical, they cannot be formally distinct; and if they are formally distinct, they cannot be really identical. Scotus had claimed that they are both really identical and formally distinct. Let *a* and *b* represent the individual difference and the specific nature, respectively. Then, since *a* is not formally distinct from *a*,

it follows that if *a* is identical with *b*, then *b* is not formally distinct from *a*. Similarly, since *a* is not formally distinct from *a*, then if *b* is formally distinct from *a*, *b* is not identical with *a*. In these arguments Ockham employs, with great effectiveness, the principle commonly ascribed to Leibniz—that if two things are identical, whatever is true of one is true of the other; and if something is true of one that is not true of the other, they are not identical.

Criticism of the Thomist view. The third answer—that the same thing is singular and universal according to different ways of considering it—is ridiculed by Ockham on the ground that what a thing is in itself can in no way depend on how someone thinks of it. "For with the same ease I could say that a man considered in one way is an ass, considered in another way he is an ox, and considered in a third way he is a she-goat" (*Expositio Super VIII Libros Physicorum*, in Philotheus Boehner, ed., *Ockham: Philosophical Writings*, p. 14). Nor can it be said, as Aquinas appears to say in his *De Ente et Essentia*, that the nature or essence of a thing is in itself neither individual nor universal but is made singular by being received in individuating matter and is made universal by being received into the mind. Anything whatsoever, Ockham insists, is one thing and a singular thing by the very fact that it is a thing, and it is impossible that its unity or singularity is due to something added to it.

Ockham's position. It remains, then, that universality and community are properties only of signs—of language expressions and of the acts of thought expressed by them. The problem of universals therefore is not a metaphysical problem of explaining how abstract common natures are individuated to singular existence, nor is it a psychological problem of explaining how the intellect can abstract from the images of sense experience a common nature inherent in the individuals experienced; for there are no common natures to be individuated or to be abstracted. The problem of individuation is a logical problem of showing how general terms are used in propositions to refer to individuals signified by them; this problem is resolved in terms of the quantifying prefixes and other syncategorematic determinants of the referential use of terms in propositions. As an epistemological problem, the problem of universals is that of explaining how experience of individual existing things can give rise to concepts of universal character and to universally quantified propositions that hold for all objects signified by the subject term. The basis of Ockham's answer to these problems is given in his doctrine of intuitive and abstractive cognition.

INTUITIVE AND ABSTRACTIVE COGNITION

The doctrine of intuitive and abstractive cognition is formulated at the beginning of Ockham's *Commentary on the Sentences* in connection with the question of whether evident knowledge of theological truths can be acquired by man in this life. After distinguishing apprehension from judgment as a distinct act of the intellect, and after showing that every act of judgment presupposes an act of apprehension of what is signified by the terms of the proposition expressing such a judgment, Ockham distinguishes two kinds of intellectual apprehension, intuitive cognition and abstractive cognition.

Intuitive cognition is defined as an act of apprehension in virtue of which the intellect can evidently judge that the apprehended object exists or does not exist, or that it has or does not have some particular quality or other contingent condition; in short, an intuitive cognition is an act of immediate awareness in virtue of which an evident judgment of contingent fact can be made.

Abstractive cognition is defined as any act of cognition in virtue of which it *cannot* be evidently known whether the apprehended object exists or does not exist, and in virtue of which an evident contingent judgment *cannot* be made. That these two ways of apprehending the same objects are possible is clear from experience; while I am observing Socrates sitting down, I can evidently judge that Socrates is seated, but if I leave the room and then form the judgment that Socrates is seated, it is not evident, and may indeed be false.

The important point in this distinction is that intuitive and abstractive cognition do not differ in the objects apprehended, but solely in the fact that intuitive cognition suffices for making an evident contingent judgment concerning the object apprehended, whereas an abstractive cognition does not. Nor is the distinction one between sensation and thought, for however much it may be true that affection of the senses by the external object is a necessary condition for an intuitive cognition of a sensible object, the intuitive cognition is an intellectual act that is presupposed by the act of judgment whose evidence is derived from it. Neither is the distinction one between direct awareness of the object and awareness of something representing the object in its absence; both kinds of apprehension are directly of the object. It is not even logically necessary that the object of an intuitive cognition be present or actually existent, although if, by the power of God, an intuitive cognition of an object were preserved after the object was removed or destroyed, it would then yield the evident judgment that the object was *not* present or that it did *not* exist; for it is self-contradictory, and hence not even within the power of God, for a cognition to yield an evident judgment that an object exists if the object does not exist.

Intuitive cognition of nonexistents. Ockham must admit that an intuitive cognition of a nonexistent object is logically possible because an intuitive cognition, however much it may be caused by the presence of its object, is not identical with its object; hence it is not self-contradictory that it exists without the object's existing. And if we suppose that any effect that can be produced by a created cause can be produced by God without the created cause, this logical possibility could be realized by the power of God. In this way God could, and according to Christian belief did, produce intuitive cognitions of future things and events by which the prophets and saints had evident knowledge of what did not yet exist; and God himself, who apprehends all things intuitively and not abstractively, is aware not only of the things he has created but of all the things he does not choose to create. Thus, an intuitive cognition of a nonexistent object is logically possible, although

it is realizable only by the power of God. Without such divine intervention, however, such cognitions can arise only if the object is present to the knower; and the judgments to which intuitive cognitions can give rise, in the natural course of events, are affirmative judgments of present existence and present fact.

Intuitive cognition of mental states. Ockham does not restrict the objects of intuitive cognition to objects perceptible to the external senses but includes nonsensible actualities that are apprehended introspectively, such as thoughts, volitions, and emotions. Thus the intellect, by reflecting on its own acts, can form evident judgments of the existence of those acts; for example, if I am intuitively aware of Socrates being seated, I can not only judge evidently that Socrates is seated, but I can also give evident assent to the second-order proposition "I evidently know that Socrates is seated." Although Ockham generally holds that the reflexive act is distinct from, and posterior to, the direct act, he speaks as if the evidence of the reflexive act can include that of the direct act.

Derivation of abstractive cognitions. Given an intuitive cognition of some object or event, the intellect thereby acquires an abstractive cognition of the same object or event, which it retains as a *habitus*, or acquired capacity, to conceive the object without any causal concurrence by the object itself; thus, objects that we have experienced intuitively can be apprehended abstractively, the only difference being that the abstractive cognition does not suffice to make evident a contingent judgment concerning the object thought of. If we leave out of account the logically possible case of God's producing an abstractive cognition without a preceding intuitive cognition, the principle holds, according to Ockham, that no abstractive cognition can be had that is not derived from an intuitive cognition of the object or objects conceived. This principle, which corresponds to Hume's thesis that there is no idea which is not derived from one or more impressions, is basic to Ockham's theory of natural knowledge and its source of evidence.

Universality of abstractive cognition. In his earlier formulation of the doctrine of intuitive and abstractive cognition, Ockham supposed that the abstractive cognition immediately derived from an intuitive cognition is a concept only of the singular object of the intuitive cognition. But in his *Quodlibeta* (Quod. I, q. 13) he states that a simple abstractive cognition cannot be a concept peculiar to one singular object to the exclusion of other objects that would, if apprehended intuitively, yield a wholly similar concept. Thus the universality of the concept, in this later theory, is immediately involved in the transition from intuitive to abstractive cognition. The operation is analogous to that of deriving, from a proposition of the form Fa, the open sentence Fx, which becomes a general proposition when the free variable x is bound by a quantifying prefix. In Ockham's terminology, the abstractive cognition has signification but acquires supposition only by formation of a judgment or proposition.

Concepts. The concept, or universal in the mind, is a cognition of objects in virtue of which it cannot be evidently judged that they exist or do not exist. But what sort of reality is such a cognition or concept? One opinion is that the concept is a mental image or species which, because it is a resemblance of the external objects, causes the intellect to become aware of those objects. But Ockham points out, as Hume did later, that such a species could in no way represent to the intellect the objects of which it is a likeness, unless these objects were already known to it—no more, Ockham says, than a statue of Hercules could represent Hercules, or be recognized as his likeness, if the viewer had never seen Hercules.

In his *Commentary on the Sentences* Ockham mentions three theories of the concept as "probable" or tenable. According to the first theory, the concept is not a reality existing in the mind or outside the mind but is the *being conceived* of the external objects, the *esse obiectivum* of the objects—a view that was held by Peter Aureol and had adherents down to the time of Descartes, who in the *Meditations* used this notion of the "objective being" of the concept in proving God's existence from his idea of God. Of the concept thus conceived, Ockham says that its being is its being understood—*eorum esse est eorum cognosci*. A second theory supposes that the concept is a real quality in the soul, used by the intellect for the individuals of which it is a concept, just as a general term in a proposition is used for the individuals of which it is a sign. A third theory, which Ockham finally adopted, is that the concept is merely the act of understanding the individual things of which it is said to be a concept. This theory is preferred on grounds of economy, for inasmuch as any of the theories requires that the intellect apprehend the extramental individuals, this function can be satisfied by the act of understanding without need of any other mental vehicle serving as surrogate for the objects.

Generality of concepts. The question may well be raised of how a concept derived from intuitive apprehension of a single object can constitute an act of understanding a definite set of objects—not any objects whatsoever but just those objects to which the concept is applicable or which, if directly experienced, would elicit that concept. Why should an intuitive cognition of Socrates yield a general concept applicable to just those individuals of which it is true to say "This is a man"? Ockham says that this is because the objects are similar, on which account the abstractive concept elicited by experience of one of the objects is *ipso facto* a concept of all similar objects. The realist might well insist that Ockham, in supposing this similarity in things, is covertly reintroducing the doctrine of common natures; but Ockham replies that similar individuals are similar by reason of what each individual is in itself, and not by reason of anything common. Two things are similar, for example, in being singular things, but this is not because there is one singularity common to the two things. Thus a concept can be a single act of understanding many individuals that are similar, without being an act of understanding anything other than just those individuals themselves. Again the analogy with the open sentence *Fx* is suggested, for if we should ask what things satisfy this function, the answer is that it is any of those things such that *Fx* holds for it. The obvious circularity of this question and answer indicates that any explanation that can be given of the fact that things are conceived in a universal manner by intelligent beings must itself use such universal concepts and thereby must presuppose the fact to be explained.

Concepts as natural signs. In this account Ockham describes concepts as natural signs whose relation to the things conceived is established not by human choice but by the fact that an act of understanding has no content other than the objects understood and arises in the first instance only through direct experience of such objects. Ockham seems to recognize the futility of seeking to account for the possibility of knowledge as such by means of a particular branch of knowledge like physics or psychology; "*natura occulte operatur in universalibus* [nature works in a hidden manner in the case of universals]," he remarks, and is content to leave it at that.

LOGIC AND THEORY OF SCIENCE

Although the human intellect, according to Ockham, can directly apprehend and conceive the individual things that exist independently of our thought, the objects of knowledge (in the sense of *scire*) are propositions, formed within our minds by operations we freely perform by combining concepts derived from intuitive cognitions of things. Only propositions can be true or false, and since knowledge is of the true, its objects are propositions—complexes of signs put together by us. Logic is concerned with these ways of putting concepts together, insofar as these operations affect the truth or falsity of the resultant propositions.

Ockham was skilled in the formal logic developed in the arts faculties of the universities on foundations laid in the twelfth century by Peter Abelard, and represented in the thirteenth century by the treatises of the so-called terminist logicians William of Sherwood and Peter of Spain. The distinctive feature of this logic was its use of the concept of the supposition of terms in formulating the syntactical and semantical properties of cognitive language. In his *Summa Logicae* Ockham systematized the contributions of his predecessors in a reformulation of the whole content of Aristotelian logic on semantical foundations of a purely extensional character. These foundations, exhibited in his analysis of the signification of terms and of the truth conditions of propositions, reveal the ontological basis of his empiricist theory of knowledge and of scientific evidence. Some preliminary distinctions made at the beginning of Ockham's work on logic are important for understanding this analysis.

Logic as a science of language. Logic, as a *scientia sermocinalis*, or science of language, deals with language as a system of signs that can be used in making true or false statements about things signified by those signs. The expressions of spoken and written language are instituted by convention to signify what is naturally signified (or intended) by acts of thought constituting the "inner discourse of the soul." Logic studies the properties of language expressions insofar as they embody the logically essential functions of mental discourse. Medieval logicians distinguished language signs into two basically different types: categorematic signs, which have independent meaning and can function as subjects and predicates of propositions, and syncategorematic signs, which have no independent meaning but exercise various logical functions with respect to the categorematic signs. This important distinction corresponds to that made in modern logic between descriptive signs and logical signs. The categorematic signs, normally called terms, were divided into two distinct and nonoverlapping semantical types: terms of first intention, which signify things that are not language signs, and terms of second intention, which signify language signs or the concepts expressed by them, *as* signs. This distinction corresponds to that now made between the descriptive signs of the object language and the descriptive signs of the metalanguage. In Ockham's view, most of the metaphysical labyrinths in which the thirteenth-century Scholastics became entangled, such as the problem of universals *in re*, arose from the logical mistake of construing terms of second intention as terms of first intention; thus, because the term "man" is predicable of (or inheres in) the singular names "Socrates" and "Plato," they supposed that what is signified by the term "man" is some single reality that inheres in the individuals named by the names "Socrates" and "Plato."

Supposition. "Supposition" is defined by Ockham as the use of a categorematic term, in a proposition, for some thing or things—normally, for the thing or things it signifies. But terms can be used nonsignificatively as names of the concepts they express or as names of the spoken or written words of which they are instances. When used nonsignificatively as the name of the word, they were said to have material supposition; when used nonsignificatively as naming the concept expressed by the word, they were said to be used with simple supposition; but when used significatively for the things signified by them and understood by the concept or act of understanding expressed by them, they were said to be used in personal supposition. The earlier terminist logicians, who were metaphysical realists, had construed simple supposition as the use of a term for the universal nature that they supposed to exist in the individuals denoted by the term in its personal supposition—which is why they called this use simple (or absolute) supposition. But Ockham, who held that universality is a property only of concepts or language signs, rejected this interpretation and construed simple supposition as the use of a term for the concept or mental intention expressed by it.

The ontological foundations of Ockham's logic are exhibited in his analysis of the terms of first intention that Aristotle classified, in his *Categoriae*, as so many different ways of signifying "primary substances"—that is, concrete individuals. The terms Aristotle grouped under the category of substance, as signifying beings qua beings according to what they essentially are, were said by Ockham to be absolute terms, terms that signify nothing other than the individuals for which they can stand when used in propositions with personal supposition. The concrete terms of the so-called categories of accident, which are predicable of substance terms but signify them only as "of such quality," as "so big," or as "in such a place," were called by Ockham connotative terms—terms that refer obliquely to something other than the thing or things for which they

can stand, and imply some contingent factual condition determining the range of objects for which the term can stand. The oblique reference may be to a part or parts of the object directly denotable by the term, to a quality of the object, or to some other thing or things with respect to which the denoted thing stands in some contingent relation—for instance, the term "father" stands for one thing by referring to another thing (a child) and implying that the child was generated by the person who is directly designated by the term "father."

Nominalism. Ockham's nominalism consists in his refusal to construe abstract terms as names of entities distinct from the individual things signified by absolute terms. The realists, while conceding that the concrete forms of connotative terms stand for substances, held that their oblique reference is to entities distinct from these substances but inhering in them—these distinct entities are directly named by the abstract forms of such connotative terms. Thus the term "father," in their view, connotes an entity called fatherhood and implies that it inheres in the thing denoted by the term "father." Similarly the term "large," although predicable of terms signifying substances, was said to connote an entity, distinct from such substances but inhering in them, called quantity or magnitude. Ockham was willing to grant that terms signifying sensible qualities, such as "white," "hot," and "sweet," connote entities that are distinct from substances and are directly signified by the abstract terms "whiteness," "heat," and "sweetness"; hence he admitted as absolute terms the abstract forms of those qualitative predicates. But in all other cases he held that connotative terms, whether concrete or abstract, signify no entities other than those directly signifiable by substance terms or by these absolute quality terms. What the realists had done, in Ockham's view, was to treat facts about substances as entities distinct from those things, as if the fact that a man is six feet tall is an entity distinct from the man but inhering in him, or as if the fact that Socrates has fathered a son is an entity distinct from Socrates and from his son.

From a logical point of view, Ockham's analysis is a restriction of the domain of reference of terms, or of the domain of objects constituting possible values of the variable of quantification, to individual substances and singular (*not* common) sensible qualities. Ontologically, this means that the only things that there are, are individual substances and equally individual qualities. All terms that are not direct names (or absolute signs) of these objects are predicate terms which, although referring to no other objects than these, do so by indicating a contingent fact about such objects.

In thus impoverishing the domain of objects of reference, Ockham enriches the domain of truths to be known about these objects. The frequent charge that Ockham atomized the world by refusing to recognize relations as real entities distinct from substances and qualities fails to take account of the fact that the connotative terms relate the individuals by implying factual conditions by which the objects are tied together in an existential sense—something that cannot be done by treating relations as entities distinct from their relata and, in effect, as just another class of substances. From Ockham's point of view, it was the realists who atomized the world by treating all predicates as absolute names.

In rejecting the thesis that predicates designate entities distinct from the individuals denoted by absolute terms, Ockham rejects the interpretation of the affirmative copula as a sign of the inherence of an abstract entity in the individuals denoted by the subject term. The truth condition of an affirmative categorical proposition, in Ockham's interpretation, is that subject and predicate "stand for the same." Thus, in the proposition "Socrates is an animal," it is not indicated that Socrates has animality or that animality inheres in Socrates, but it is indicated that the individual denoted by the name "Socrates" is an individual for which the term "animal" stands and which it signifies. In universally quantified propositions, the affirmative copula indicates that every individual for which the subject term stands is something for which the predicate term stands; and in particular, or existentially quantified, propositions, the affirmative copula indicates that there is at least one individual signified by the subject term that is also signified by the predicate term.

This analysis of general propositions corresponds closely to the modern formulas $(x)Fx \supset Gx$ and $(\exists x)Fx \cdot Gx$, except that the medieval analysis requires existential import as part of the truth condition of the universal affirmative and does not require existential import as a truth condition of the particular negative. In order for subject and predicate to stand for the same, there must be something they stand for; but it is not required that they stand for something in order that they not stand for the same thing. Ockham skillfully carried out the formal development of truth rules for propositions of more complex forms and for various modalities and used them in formulating inference rules both for syllogistic arguments and for arguments based on truth-functional relations between unanalyzed propositions.

Scientific knowledge. The Aristotelian dictum that science is of the universal was accepted by Ockham in the sense that scientific knowledge is of propositions composed of universal terms, quantified universally for all the individuals signified by the subject term and having the properties of necessity and evidence. Strictly speaking, scientific knowledge is only of demonstrable conclusions evident by reason of indemonstrable, necessary, and evident premises from which they are logically deducible. But Ockham extends the notion of *scientia*, defined as evident grasp of a proposition that is true, to include the indemonstrable premises of demonstrations and also to include evident knowledge of contingent propositions in virtue of intuitive cognition.

Evidence and self-evidence. Since, for Ockham, the universal propositions of scientific demonstrations are formed only from concepts by which things are apprehended abstractively and without evidence of their existence, the question of what kind of evidence such propositions can have is a crucial question for him. This problem reduces to that of the evidence of the indemonstrable premises of the sciences. Aristotle's characterization of such premises as necessary, self-evident (*per se nota*), and primary could not be accepted by Ockham without considerable qualification. First of all, he says that no such propositions are necessary as assertoric categorical propositions, but are necessary only if they are construed as conditionals or as propositions concerning the possible (*de eo quod potest esse*). Second, he distinguishes between two kinds of evidence that such propositions, construed as conditionals or as of the mode of possibility, may have: the proposition may be evident by the meaning of its terms (*per se nota*) or evident by experience (*nota per experientiam*). The first kind of evidence is obtained through the premises of mathematical demonstrations and by those premises of the natural sciences which are analytically evident by the definition of the terms. But in every natural or physical science there are premises that are not *per se nota* but are established by generalization from singular contingent propositions evident by intuitive cognition; such are the premises that state causal laws or correlate dispositional properties with their commensurately universal subject terms.

Induction. What justifies the passage from singular propositions evident by direct experience to universal propositions affirmed for all possible cases? How does evident knowledge that this particular wood is combustible, acquired by direct observation of its burning, allow us to know that any piece of wood, if subjected to fire in the presence of air, will burn? Ockham invokes as justification for such generalized propositions a rule of induction, described as a *medium extrinsecum*, that corresponds to the principle of the uniformity of nature—that all individuals of specifically similar nature (*eiusdem rationis*) act or react in similar manner to similar conditions. He regards this principle as analytically evident from the meaning of "similar nature"; but since it is logically possible, and hence possible by the power of God, that an effect can be produced without its natural cause, the application of this rule of induction in establishing general premises or laws on the basis of experience of particular cases is valid only within the general hypothesis of the common course of nature (*ex suppositione communis cursus naturae*). Consequently, the evidence of such premises of the natural or positive sciences is not absolute but hypothetical. It should be further noted that Ockham, and his contemporaries as well, drew a sharp distinction between what comes to be by nature and what comes to be by the action of voluntary intelligent agents, both man and God. The principle that like causes produce like effects under like conditions is considered valid only on the supposition that no voluntary agencies are involved.

There is a marked analogy between Ockham's view of the evidential status of the premises of the empirical sciences and that of the premises of positive (or revealed) theology. In the one case their evidence is conditional on the hypothesis of a common course of nature, and in the other on the hypothesis of a revealed order of grace freely (and hence not necessarily) provided by God for the salvation of human souls. Neither hypothesis is logically or metaphysically necessary, and each is, in its own domain, used as a methodological principle pragmatically justified by its fruitfulness. What corresponds to Pelagianism in theology is dogmatic Aristotelianism in natural philosophy, and Ockham takes due precautions against both.

METAPHYSICS AND THEOLOGY

Ockham's metaphysics is primarily a critique of the traditional metaphysical doctrines of his scholastic predecessors. Most of these doctrines represent, in Ockham's view, confusions of logical and physical concepts or of ways of signifying things and the things signified. Such is the case with the supposed distinction, in things, between their essence and their existence, and with the distinction between potential and actual being; to say that something exists does not mean that there is something which is of itself nonexistent to which existence is added, and to say that something exists potentially does not mean that "something which is not in the universe, but can exist in the universe, is truly a being" (*Summa Logicae Pars Prima*, 1951, p. 99, ll. 55–58). These are distinctions between two modalities of statements, assertoric and *de possibili*, and not between things denoted by the terms of statements. The old issue of whether "being" is predicated univocally, equivocally, or analogically of substances and accidents, and of God and creatures, is resolved by saying that in the sense in which "being" is equivalent to "something," it is predicated in the same way of everything there is; but if "univocal" is taken as meaning that the term signifies everything according to a single determinate concept, the term "being" is equivocal and has as many meanings as there are kinds of things. The first sense is like saying $(x)(x = x)$; the second, or equivocal use, is indicated if we say *"to be a man* is not *to be white."*

Substance. The term "substance," for Ockham, has the sense of Aristotle's primary substance, or ὑποκείμενον, rather than the sense of intelligible essence, or τὸ τί ἦν εἶναι. Basically, substance is conceived as the individual subject or substratum of qualities, and with regard to corporeal substances Ockham indicates that we are aware of substances *only* as the subject of sensible qualities. Thus he says that "no external corporeal substance can be naturally apprehended in itself, by us, however it may be with respect to the intellect itself or any substance which is of the essence of the knower" (*Commentary on the Sentences* I, d. 3, q. 2), and he adds that "substance is therefore understood in connotative and negative concepts, such as 'being which subsists by itself,' 'being which is not in something else,' 'being which is a subject of all accidents,' etc." (*ibid.*). These remarks suggest that the general terms of the category of substance are not as absolute as Ockham elsewhere supposes, and that the only nonconnotative concept is the transcendental concept "being" or "thing"; on this basis, general names are eliminated in favor of connotative predicates, proper names are eliminated in favor of descriptive phrases, and the whole category of substance is reduced to the referential function expressed in language by the phrase "thing such that . . . ," or by what is equivalent to the bound variable of quantification. Historically, Ockham's conception of substance as the posited (or "supposited") referent of the connotative predicates points toward Locke's "something I know not what" characterization of substance; similarly, Ockham's treatment of sensible qualities as entities distinct from substances (and by the power of God separable, as in the Sacrament of the Altar), along with his contention that

quantitative predicates signify nothing other than substances having parts outside of parts, pointed the way to the seventeenth-century treatment of qualities as secondary and quantitative attributes as primary.

Matter and form. With respect to the notion of cause, Ockham effected a considerable modification of the traditional Aristotelian doctrine. The intrinsic causes, matter and form, were construed physically rather than metaphysically; matter is not, for Ockham, a pure potentiality but is actual in its own right as body having spatially distinguishable parts, its extension being, in the scholastic terminology, the form of corporeity. The concept of form likewise is understood physically in the sense of μορφή rather than of εἶδος, and tends to be understood as shape and structure of the material parts. This is shown in Ockham's rejection of the notion of a form of the whole (*forma totius*) and in his thesis that a whole *is* its parts. Many pages of Ockham's works are devoted to the thesis, defended with an almost ferocious intensity, that quantity is not any entity other than substance (or quality), but *is* substance or sensible qualities as divisible into parts, or as numerable. This doctrine clearly suggests the later view that the primary qualities signified by quantity terms constitute the real essence of substances.

Efficient causes. The tendency toward a more mechanistic theory of natural substances and events is evident in Ockham's treatment of efficient causality. He says that one thing is said to be cause of another if, when it is present, the effect follows, and when it is not present, the effect does not occur. Such a causal relation can be known only by experience, and it is impossible to deduce a priori, from knowledge of one thing, that something else must result from it. This is so on the general epistemological principle that from the cognition of one thing we cannot acquire "first knowledge" of another thing which is really distinct from it but must have intuitive cognition of the latter in itself. Hence the knowledge that one thing is the cause of another, or that something is caused by some other definite thing, is acquired only if we have intuitive cognition of each of the two things and repeated experience of their concomitance or sequence.

Like Hume, Ockham bases our knowledge of causal relations on experience alone and rejects the doctrine that the effect is virtually in its cause and deducible from the essential nature of the cause. But he is not skeptical with regard to the objectivity of causation; his point is that the only evidence we have of causal connections is experience of observed sequences. Although we cannot establish the causal relations between things a priori, and must accept the principle of the uniformity of nature as an act of faith, Ockham's faith in this principle appears to be as firm as his faith in the revealed doctrines of theology. In his *Summulae Physicorum* (II, c. 12) he says: "Leaving out of consideration all free and voluntary agencies, whatever happens by [natural] causes occurs of necessity and inevitably, and nothing of that sort occurs by chance" (1637 ed., p. 14).

Final causes. The Aristotelian doctrine that nature acts for an end is interpreted by Ockham as a pure metaphor. In his *Quodlibeta* (Quod. IV, qq. 1 and 2) he states that it cannot be shown by any self-evident premises or by experience that any effect whatsoever has a final cause, whether distinct from the agent or not distinct from the agent; for that which acts by necessity of nature acts uniformly under like conditions, and it cannot be shown that it does so because of some end desired or aimed at. We speak of natural processes as having ends, not because the agents are really "moved by desire" but simply because natural bodies under similar conditions are observed to act in determinate ways, *as if* aiming at an end. But such language is purely metaphorical.

In applying his strict criteria of evidence to the doctrines of Aristotelian physics and cosmology, Ockham shows that many principles which Aristotle took to be necessary and self-evident are not. The arguments that celestial bodies have no matter and are ingenerable and incorruptible, that there cannot be a plurality of worlds, and that action at a distance is impossible were held by Ockham to be inconclusive and nonevident. Although Ockham was not concerned with establishing a new physics and cosmology to replace that of Aristotle, his critical treatment of Aristotle's arguments and his constant insistence on the possibility of different theories equally capable of accounting for the facts to be explained were influential in creating the intellectual environment in which later fourteenth-century philosophers explored new physical theories and laid some of the foundations for the scientific revolution of the seventeenth century.

Theological knowledge. As a theologian, Ockham was concerned with the question of the cognitive status of theology. The thirteenth-century Scholastics had, for the most part, characterized theology as a science, on the ground that it contains truths which are necessary and "in themselves" evident, even though most of them are not evident to man in his present condition. The question of how we can know that a proposition is evident-in-itself, when it is not evident to us, was answered by saying that a person who does not know geometry may yet be fully assured that a theorem which is an object of belief to him is an object of scientific knowledge to the expert mathematician. Thus, Aquinas said that the articles of faith from which the theologian demonstrates his conclusions are accepted as evident in the light of a higher science (that of God), much as the astronomer accepts the theorems of geometry as premises for his astronomical reasonings but nevertheless demonstrates the conclusions of astronomy in a scientific manner.

Ockham, in a question of his *Commentary on the Sentences* (Prologue, q. 7), examines this and other similar arguments and rejects them as invalid. Every truth evidently known, he says, is either self-evident (*per se nota*), deduced from such, or is evident from intuitive cognition; but the articles of faith are not evidently knowable by man in any of these ways in his present life, for if they were, they would be evident to infidels and pagans, who are not less intelligent than Christians. But this is not the case. Furthermore, it cannot be maintained that theology is a science because it carries out valid processes of deduction of conclusions from the premises accepted on faith, for conclusions cannot be any more evident than the premises from which they are derived.

Impossibility of natural theology. Ockham subjects the *prolegomena fidei*, or propositions about God held to be evidently knowable on natural grounds, to the criteria of evidence and proof that pertain to the natural or philosophical sciences. The issue of whether there is a natural theology as a part of philosophy reduces to the question of whether, from analytic premises evident from the meaning of the terms or from empirical evidence provided by direct experience of the object of theology, such a science is possible. It is conceded by all that man, in his present life, does not have intuitive cognition of God—not, certainly, by getting a degree in theology. But Ockham had argued, with respect to any naturally acquired knowledge, that it is only by intuitive cognition of an object that we can evidently judge that it exists—and the only objects of which we can have simple abstractive concepts are those we have experienced intuitively or those specifically similar to them. From this it follows that we cannot have any simple and proper concept of God nor any direct evidence of his existence. Can we, then, from concepts derived from experience of other things, form a complex concept or description uniquely applicable to God and prove that an object satisfying this nominal definition exists?

Critique of proofs for God's existence. Ockham admits that a descriptive concept of God can be formed from the concept of "being" or "thing" in its univocal (but empty) sense, along with such connotative or negative terms as "nonfinite," "uncaused," and "most perfect." But proving that there exists an object so describable is another matter. The arguments by which his predecessors had attempted to prove God's existence are examined by Ockham with great thoroughness in his *Commentary on the Sentences*, in the *Quodlibeta*, and in the possibly inauthentic *Centiloquium Theologicum*. St. Anselm's so-called Ontological Argument is analyzed (and shown to consist of two different arguments) but is rejected as invalid; and the old arguments from degrees of perfection are disposed of without difficulty.

It is chiefly the causal arguments, in the form used by Duns Scotus, that Ockham takes seriously; and these he examines with extraordinary care because of the way in which Scotus used the concept of infinity in formulating them. Ockham's great logical skill is revealed at its best in his patient and remorseless untangling of the subtleties of the Scotist arguments. Those involving final causality are shown to have no force in themselves, so that the main issues are faced in the arguments from efficient causes. The thesis that there cannot be an infinite regress in the order of efficient causes is rejected as nonevident if the causes are successive in a temporal sense, but Ockham is willing to grant that there cannot be an infinite regress of "conserving causes," since these would have to exist simultaneously. Ockham does, therefore, allow that the existence of at least one conserving cause can be proved if it is granted that there are things whose existence is dependent on conservation by something else; but he immediately points out that we could not prove that there is only one such conserving cause, nor could we prove that the celestial spheres are not sufficient to account for the conservation of the things in the world. Thus the value of this argument for theological purposes is very slight indeed. It is also clear that a natural theology, in the sense involving strictly scientific or evident demonstrations, is completely ruled out by Ockham's basic epistemological principles.

He is willing to concede that it is "probable" that there is one supreme being, that this being is the cause of at least part of the movements and order of the world, and that this being is of an intellectual nature; but since Ockham defines "probable," following Aristotle's *Topics*, as an argument or premise that appears to be true to everyone, to the majority, or to the wisest, all this means is that most people, and the philosophers of old, have believed that there is a deity of this sort.

Positive theology. To conclude, from Ockham's merciless criticism of alleged proofs of theological beliefs, that he was an unbeliever and a religious skeptic would be a mistake—although some have drawn this conclusion. There is much evidence in Ockham's writings of an intense loyalty to the Christian faith and of full commitment to the articles of faith as divinely revealed. What Ockham appears to have found objectionable in the theological work of his contemporaries was their attempt to prove what cannot be proved and their loading of theology with pseudo explanations that merely blunted and obscured the tremendous implications of the fundamental articles of the Christian faith. The omnipotence of God and his absolute freedom are the two articles of Christian belief that Ockham never loses sight of; and in his internal treatment of the content of Christian doctrine, just as in his internal treatment of natural philosophy, Ockham invokes these articles of faith as justification for an empiricist or positivistic position. Just as the hypothesis of the common course of nature is a methodological postulate of physical explanation, so the order of grace as set up in the sacramental system and laws of the church is accepted as a postulate of the Christian life; but just as God is not bound or obligated by the order of nature he has established, so he is not bound or obligated by the order of grace he has established as the "common way" of salvation of souls. Neither order is necessary in itself or a necessary consequence of God's being or essence; the utter contingency of the created world, whose existence and order is a sheer fact without any metaphysical ground of necessity, is for Ockham a consequence of the omnipotence and absolute freedom of God that cannot, and should not, be softened or obscured by attempts to construe it in terms of the metaphysics of pagans and infidels.

ETHICAL AND POLITICAL DOCTRINES

In contrast with most of the thirteenth-century scholastic doctors, Ockham made little attempt to formulate a rational psychology or theory of the human soul. In his *Quodlibeta* (Quod. I, q. 10) he raises the question of whether it can be demonstrated that the intellective soul is a form of the body. Since the Council of Vienne had ruled a few years before that this Thomist doctrine was *de fide* (although the formulation was ambiguous enough to allow some latitude), Ockham was not as critical of it as he might otherwise have been. He points out that a person following natural reason would no doubt suppose that his own acts of understanding and of will, of which he has intuitive cognition, are acts of his substantial being or form; however, he would not suppose this to be an incorruptible form

separable from his body but rather an extended and corruptible form like that of any other material body. If, however, we must understand by "intellective soul" an immaterial and incorruptible form that exists as a whole in the whole body and as a whole in each part, "it cannot be evidently known by reason or experience that such a form exists in us, nor that the understanding proper to such a substance exists in us, nor that such a soul is a form of the body. Whatever the Philosopher thought of this does not now concern me, because it seems that he remains doubtful about it wherever he speaks of it. These three things are only matters of belief" (*ibid.*).

Ockham thought that the Franciscan doctrine of a plurality of forms in the human being is more probable on natural grounds than the doctrine of a single form; indeed, if matter has its own corporeal form (*forma corporeitatis*) as extended substance, the sensitive soul would be a distinct form of organization of this matter; and the intellectual soul, if immortal and incorruptible, might well be in the organic body as a pilot is in his boat. But the only evident knowledge we have of ourselves as minds is the intuitive cognition of our acts of thinking and willing, and the subject of these acts is not apprehended directly as a substance or form. Nor is the faculty psychology elaborated by the earlier Scholastics, with its distinctions of active and passive intellect and of really distinct powers within the soul, evident or necessary. We are aware of the soul only as that which thinks and wills; and since the person who thinks is not other than the person who wills, the terms "intellect" and "will" refer to precisely the same subject, and not to distinct entities or faculties within that subject.

Free will. If it is only by intuitive cognition of our own acts that we are aware of ourselves as intelligent beings, it is only in this way that we are aware of ourselves as voluntary agents free to choose between opposite actions. Ockham defines freedom (*libertas*) as "that power whereby I can do diverse things indifferently and contingently, such that I can cause, or not cause, the same effect, when all conditions other than this power are the same" (Quod. I, q. 16). That the will is free, he says, cannot be demonstratively proved by any reason, "because every reason proving this assumes something equally unknown as is the conclusion, or less known." Yet this freedom can be evidently known by experience, he says, because "a man experiences the fact that however much his reason dictates some action, his will can will, or not will, this act" (*ibid.*).

This liberty of will, for Ockham, is the basis of human dignity and of moral goodness and responsibility, more than the power of thinking—although the two are mutually involved. The seat of morality is in the will itself, Ockham says, "because every act other than the act of will, which is in the power of the will, is only good in such manner that it can be a bad act, because it can be done for an evil end and from an evil intention" (Quod. III, q. 13). Also, every action, other than the act of willing itself, can be performed by reason of natural causes and not freely, and every such action could be caused in us by God alone instead of by our will; consequently, the action in itself is neither virtuous nor vicious, except by denomination from the act of the will. Not even Kant was more concerned to distinguish morality from legality, or the good will from the right action. Ockham had, in Peter Abelard, a medieval precedent for this emphasis.

Free will and God's foreknowledge. Having thus affirmed the total freedom and integrity of the human will, Ockham was faced with the problem of reconciling this with the doctrine of divine foreknowledge of future contingent events, among which the decisions of the human will must be counted. The answer, apparently considered sufficient by Aquinas, that God sees, in one eternal glance, all the decisions of each soul, now and to come, is not sufficient for Ockham. God's intellect is not distinct from his will and his omnipotent causality of all things; hence, says Ockham, "either the determination or production of the created will follows the determination [of the divine will], or it does not. If it does, then the created will acts just as naturally as any natural cause . . . and thus, the divine will being determined, the created will acts accordingly and does not have the power of not acting accordingly, and consequently no act of the created will is to be imputed to it" (*Commentary on the Sentences,* d. 38, q. 1). Ockham considers the problem of how God knows, with certainty and from all eternity, the contingent and free decisions of the human will, an insoluble problem; for both the freedom of the human will and the power of God to know all contingent acts of created beings must be conceded. "It is impossible," he says, "for any [created] intellect, in this life, to explain or evidently know how God knows all future contingent events" (*ibid.*).

Problem of evil. While recognizing the Aristotelian conception of natural good and of virtuous choices in accordance with right reason, Ockham is primarily concerned with the theological norm of moral goodness, which is the will of God expressed in the commandments of both the Old Testament and the New Testament, whereby man is obligated (but not coerced) to love and obey God above all else. Thus, what God wills man to do of man's free will defines the right, and disobedience to God's will defines sin. This provides a solution of the old problem of evil, or of God as cause of the sinful acts of man; for since moral evil is the doing of the opposite of what one is obligated to do, and since God is not obligated to any act, it is impossible for God to sin by his causal concurrence in the production of an act sinfully willed by the creature. But Ockham raises an interesting paradox in this connection by supposing that God might command a man to hate him (or to disobey him). To obey God is to love God, and to love God is to do his will; but if it is God's will that I do not do his will, I do his will if I don't, and don't do it if I do. Hence, this command is impossible for a creature to fulfill; and although there would seem to be no patent self-contradiction in supposing that God could issue such a command, it would seem to be self-contradictory, and hence impossible, for God to will that this command be fulfilled.

God's freedom. Although Ockham recognizes that God has established laws binding the Christian to live in a certain way as a member of the church, participant in its sacraments, and believer in its articles of faith, this fact imposes no obligation on God either to bestow eternal life on the Christian who obeys God's precepts and loves him above all else, or to withhold eternal life from those who do not follow God's laws and love him above all else. "It is not impossible," Ockham says, "that God could ordain that a person who lives according to right reason, and does not believe anything except what is conclusive to him by natural reason, should be worthy of eternal life" (*Commentary on the Sentences* III, q. 8). Similarly, although according to the established order an infused grace is required for a man to be eligible for acceptance by God, Ockham insists that God is not necessitated, by reason of such a created grace given to a man, to confer eternal life on him—"always contingently and freely and mercifully and of his own graciousness he beatifies whomsoever he chooses . . . purely from his kindness he will freely give eternal life to whomsoever he will give it" (*Commentary on the Sentences* I, d. 17, q. 1).

What is distinctive of Ockham's theological point of view is its emphasis on the freedom and spontaneous liberality of God and on the "givenness" of the world that God creates. This stands in sharp contrast to the Muslim characterization of God as the necessary being whose act is equally necessary and therefore determinant of necessity in all that occurs in the created world. Ockham's doctrine of divine omnipotence is not to be understood, as some have done, on the analogy of an oriental potentate issuing arbitrary commands as a pure display of power; rather, it is grounded in the conception of a goodness that is purely spontaneous and unnecessitated, whose gift of existence to creatures and of freedom of choice to man is a perfectly free gift with no strings attached. Ockham's theology of divine liberty and liberality is the complement of his philosophy of radical contingency in the world of existing finite beings and of the underivability of matters of fact from any a priori necessity.

Church and state. Ockham's political and polemical writings on the issue of papal power eloquently convey the thesis that the law of God is the law of liberty and not one of oppression or coercion. The treatise *De Imperatorum et Pontificum Potestate* ("On the Power of Emperors and Popes"), dealing with the papal claim to plenitude of power, makes this very clear. Christ, in instituting the church, did not give Peter a plenitude of power that would give him the right to do everything not explicitly forbidden by divine or natural law; rather, Peter was given a limited and defined sphere of authority and power. Therefore, Ockham argues, the pope has no authority to deprive any human being of his natural rights or of the rights and liberties given to man by God. "As Christ did not come into the world in order to take away from men their goods and rights, so Christ's vicar, who is inferior and in no way equal to him in power, has no authority or power to deprive others of their goods and rights" (*De Imperatorum . . . ,* p. 10, ll. 12–15). Ockham specifies three of these inalienable rights: first, all those rights which non-Christians justly and admittedly enjoyed before the coming of Christ—for any of these rights to be taken from Christians by papal authority would be to make the liberty of Christians less than that of pagans and infidels; second, the disposition of temporal things belongs not to the papal authority but to the laity, according to the words of Christ that the things that are Caesar's should be rendered unto Caesar; third, although the pope is charged with the teaching of God's word, maintenance of divine worship, and provision of such things as are necessary for the Christian in his quest for eternal life, the pope has no power to command or requisition those things which are not necessary to this end, "lest he should turn the law of the Gospels into a law of slavery."

On the important question of who is to be the judge of what is necessary for the legitimate ends of the church, Ockham holds that this cannot be the prerogative of the pope, of those under his command, or of the civil rulers. The ultimate decision should be sought in the Gospel, interpreted not by the clergy alone but by "the discretion and counsel of the wisest men sincerely zealous for justice without respect to persons, if such can be found—whether they be poor or rich, subjects or rulers" (*ibid.*, p. 27, ll. 17–20). This not very practical proposal nevertheless suggests that the membership of the Christian community as private individuals, rather than as officeholders, constitutes the true church. Yet Ockham is not, like Marsilius of Padua, against the principle of the pope as head of the church and vicar of Christ; he only seeks safeguards against abuse of the papal office and illegitimate assumption of tyrannical powers by holders of that office. Legitimate sovereignty, whether papal or civil, is not despotism; the dominion a master has over a slave is not the kind of authority exercised legitimately by a king, pope, or bishop. A pope may turn out to be a heretic and may be deposed—not by the emperor but only by a general council of the church. The imperial power derives from God, not directly but by way of the people who confer upon the emperor his power to legislate; the imperial power is not, as the popes had claimed, derived from the papacy. Ockham's political theory, insofar as it was formulated at all in his polemical writings, was not secularist or anticlerical; it was against absolutism in either church or state and much concerned that the "law of force," which is characteristic of the civil state, should not be adopted by the papal authority, lest the law of God, which is a law of liberty, be corrupted and degraded by temporal ambitions and lust for power.

Works by Ockham

Quodlibeta Septem. Paris, 1487; Strasbourg, 1491.

Summa Totius Logicae. Paris, 1488; Bologna, 1498; Venice, 1508, 1522, 1591; Oxford, 1675. Modern ed. of *Pars Prima* and *Pars IIa et Tertiae Prima*, Philotheus Boehner, ed. St. Bonaventure, N.Y., 1951–1954.

De Sacramento Altaris et De Corpore Christi. Strasbourg, 1491 (with *Quodlibeta*). New ed., with English translation by T. B. Birch, *The De Sacramento Altaris of William of Ockham.* Burlington, Iowa, 1930.

Summulae in Libros Physicorum (or *Philosophia Naturalis*). Bologna, 1494; Venice, 1506; Rome, 1637.

Dialogus Inter Magistrum et Discipulum. Lyons, 1495.

Super Quatuor Libros Sententiarum . . . Quaestiones. Lyons, 1495 (with *Centiloquium Theologicum*).

Expositio Aurea . . . Super Artem Veterem. Bologna, 1496.

The De Imperatorum et Pontificum Potestate of William of Ockham, C. K. Brampton, ed. Oxford, 1927.

Breviloquium de Potestate Papae, L. Baudry, ed. Paris, 1937.

Guillelmi de Ockham Opera Politica. Vol. I, J. G. Sikes, ed., Manchester, 1940; Vol. III, H. S. Offler, ed., Manchester, 1956. Other vols. in preparation.

Tractatus de Praedestinatione et de Praescientia Dei et de Futuris Contingentibus, Philotheus Boehner, ed. St. Bonaventure, N.Y., 1945.

Ockham: Philosophical Writings, Philotheus Boehner, ed. Edinburgh, 1957. Selections with translations.

Expositio in Librum Porphyrii De Praedicabibus, E. A. Moody, ed. St. Bonaventure, N.Y., 1965.

Works on Ockham

Abbagnano, Nicola, *Guglielmo di Ockham.* Lanciano, Italy, 1931.

Baudry, L., *Le Tractatus de Principiis Theologiae attribué à G. d'Occam.* Paris, 1936.

Baudry, L., *Guillaume d'Occam,* Vol. I, *L'Homme et les oeuvres.* Paris, 1950. Contains extensive bibliography of works on Ockham; full information on Ockham's published and unpublished works will be found on pp. 273–294.

Baudry, L., *Lexique philosophique de Guillaume d'Ockham.* Paris, 1958.

Boehner, Philotheus, *Collected Articles on Ockham.* St. Bonaventure, N.Y., 1956.

Federhofer, Franz, *Die Erkenntnislehre des Wilhelm von Ockham.* Munich, 1924.

Gottfried, Martin, *Wilhelm von Ockham.* Berlin, 1949.

Guelluy, Robert, *Philosophie et théologie chez Guillaume d'Ockham.* Louvain and Paris, 1947.

Hochstetter, Erich, *Studien zur Metaphysik und Erkenntnislehre Wilhelms von Ockham.* Berlin, 1927.

Lagarde, Georges de, *La Naissance de l'esprit laïque au déclin du moyen âge,* Vols. IV–VI. Paris, 1942–1946.

Moody, E. A., *The Logic of William of Ockham.* New York and London, 1935.

Moody, E. A., *Truth and Consequence in Medieval Logic.* Amsterdam, 1953.

Moser, Simon, *Grundbegriffe der Naturphilosophie bei Wilhelm von Ockham.* Innsbruck, 1932.

Scholz, Richard, *Wilhelm von Ockham als politischer Denker und sein Breviloquium de Principatu Tyrannico.* Leipzig, 1944.

Shapiro, Herman, *Motion, Time and Place According to William Ockham.* St. Bonaventure, N.Y., 1957.

Vasoli, Cesare, *Guglielmo d'Occam.* Florence, 1953. Contains an extensive bibliography of works on Ockham.

Vignaux, Paul, "Nominalisme" and "Occam," in *Dictionnaire de théologie catholique,* 15 vols. Paris, 1903–1950. Vol. XI, Cols. 733–789 and 864–904.

Vignaux, Paul, *Justification et prédestination au XIVe siècle.* Paris, 1934.

Vignaux, Paul, *Le Nominalisme au XIVe siècle.* Montreal, 1948.

Webering, Damascene, *The Theory of Demonstration According to William Ockham.* St. Bonaventure, N.Y., 1953.

Zuidema, Sytse, *De Philosophie van Occam in Zijn Commentaar op de Sententien,* 2 vols. Hilversum, Netherlands, 1936.

ERNEST A. MOODY

WILLIAM OF SHERWOOD, or Shyreswood (1200/1210–1266/1271), English logician. All that is known for certain of William of Sherwood's life is that in 1252 he was a master at Oxford, that he became treasurer of the cathedral church of Lincoln soon after 1254, that he was rector of Aylesbury and of Attleborough, that he was still living in 1266, and that he was dead in 1271. From references in his works, however, and from the fact that his logic almost certainly had a direct influence on the logical writings of Peter of Spain, Lambert of Auxerre, Albert the Great, and Thomas Aquinas, all of whom were at Paris around the same time, it seems undeniable that he taught logic there from about 1235 to about 1250.

William's impact on his contemporaries went unacknowledged except by Roger Bacon, who, in his *Opus Tertium* (1267), described him as "much wiser than Albert [the

Great]; for in *philosophia communis* no one is greater than he." Bacon's phrase *philosophia communis* must refer to logic; no other kind of work can be definitely attributed to William, and his logical works certainly were influential. They consist of an *Introductiones in Logicam*, a *Syncategoremata*, a *De Insolubilibus* (on paradoxes of self-reference), an *Obligationes* (on rules of argument for formal disputation), and a *Petitiones Contrariorum* (on logical puzzles arising from hidden contrariety in premises). Only the first two were ever published; they are longer and far more important than the last three. A commentary on the *Sentences*, a *Distinctiones Theologicae*, and a *Conciones* (a collection of sermons) have also been attributed to William, though their authenticity is seriously questioned.

The *Introductiones* consists of six treatises, the first four and the last one of which correspond (very broadly) to Aristotle's *De Interpretatione, Categories, Prior Analytics, Topics,* and *Sophistical Refutations,* in that order. The third treatise contains the earliest version of the mnemonic verses for the syllogism "Barbara, Celarent . . . ," and there are other interesting minor innovations in those treatises. The most important novelties are concentrated in the fifth treatise, "Properties of Terms"; it contains the logico-semantical inquiries that gave the terminist logicians their name. William recognizes four properties of terms—*significatio, suppositio, copulatio,* and *appellatio* (see LOGIC, HISTORY OF; SEMANTICS, HISTORY OF). The last three may be very broadly described as syntax-dependent semantical functions of a term's *significatio,* which is its meaning in the broadest sense.

In order to distinguish such medieval contributions from strictly Aristotelian logic, thirteenth-century philosophers spoke of them as *logica moderna.* When William wrote, *logica moderna* was thought of as having two branches, *proprietates terminorum* and *syncategoremata.* In his separate treatise on the latter, William investigates the semantical and logical properties of such syncategorematic words as "every," "except," "only," "is," "not," "if," "or," "necessarily." Both branches may be said to be concerned with the points of connection between syntax and semantics and with the effect those points have on the evaluation of inferences. William's treatment of both is marked by a concern with the philosophical problems to which they give rise.

The ingredients of the *logica moderna* certainly antedate William's writings, but his may very well be the earliest full-scale organization of those elements in the way that became characteristic of medieval logic after his time.

Bibliography

Martin Grabmann has edited *Die Introductiones in logicam des Wilhelm von Shyreswood, Literarhistorische Einleitung und Textausgabe* in *Sitzungsberichte der Bayerischen Akademie der Wissenschaften, Philosophische-historische Abteilung,* Jahrgang 1937, Vol. 10 (Munich, 1937). Norman Kretzmann has translated *William of Sherwood's Introduction to Logic* (Minneapolis, Minn., 1965), and J. Reginald O'Donnell has edited "The Syncategoremata of William of Sherwood" in *Medieval Studies,* Vol. 3 (1941), 46–93.

NORMAN KRETZMANN

WILSON, JOHN COOK (1849–1915), English realistic philosopher and classical scholar. Cook Wilson was born in Nottingham, the son of a Methodist minister. He entered Balliol College, Oxford, in 1868 and studied under T. H. Green and Benjamin Jowett. He was elected a fellow of Oriel College in 1874, having offered mathematics as well as classics at the examination. He visited Göttingen mainly to hear Rudolf Hermann Lotze, who influenced his views on morals, aesthetics, and religion. He was elected Wykeham professor of logic in 1889, a fellow of New College in 1901, and a fellow of the British Academy in 1907.

Cook Wilson's independent mind, somewhat pugnacious temperament, and early desire for literary recognition caused him to spend much of his energies on relatively minor topics. Partly for this reason, the work he published was slight, but after his death a selection of his lectures and papers was edited in two substantial volumes by his friend A. S. L. Farquharson, under the title *Statement and Inference* (1926).

As a teacher Cook Wilson strongly influenced the Oxford realists H. W. B. Joseph, H. A. Prichard, and W. D. Ross, and he was one of those who provoked R. G. Collingwood into indignant reaction. He sympathized with the trend away from the idealism of Green, F. H. Bradley, and Bernard Bosanquet: ". . . from the first I would not commit myself to the most attractive idealism, tho' greatly attracted by it" (*Statement and Inference,* Vol. II, p. 815). Prichard, in the obituary notice "Professor John Cook Wilson" (p. 307), states that "in his early days Cook Wilson accepted the idealism then dominant," and then quotes a lecture of 1880. The passage is not quite conclusive, but it appears that the young Cook Wilson was nearer to idealism than the mature philosopher remembered himself to have been.

Cook Wilson shared with the Cambridge philosopher G. E. Moore a stress on the analysis of questions, a passion for accuracy and lucidity, and a respect for common-sense claims to knowledge; but he was much less flexible than Moore and lacked Moore's ability to concentrate on fundamental issues. His attitude toward ordinary language might be compared with that of J. L. Austin (the term "linguistic analysis" occurs in *Statement and Inference,* Vol. II, p. 759). For Austin, also an Aristotelian scholar, ordinary language was a territory to be explored and mapped. For Cook Wilson, ordinary language, although sometimes suspect, was usually a supporting witness. He opposed ordinary language to "the language of reflection," a language that encourages such fallacies as conceptualism. In this antiprofessional spirit he acutely criticized John Locke's views on simple and complex ideas and on primary and secondary qualities, J. S. Mill on connotation and denotation, Bradley and Bosanquet on judgment, and Bertrand Russell on the class of all classes (Cook Wilson held that there is no such class). He insisted on the importance of a variety of examples, particularly when we are studying usage.

Cook Wilson's main philosophical interests centered on philosophical logic. He regarded psychology, grammar, and metaphysics as nonlogical studies necessary to logic. Logic, he noted, is commonly agreed to deal with inference; inference is a kind of thinking; and thinking includes knowing and nonknowing activities. Knowledge can be occurrent or dispositional. If occurrent, it is to be termed "apprehension." Knowledge is indefinable, and the term "theory of knowledge" should be shunned. The prime example of knowledge, in his view, was given by Euclidean geometry, but we also know the law of causation. We know what it is to believe, opine, and wonder, and we know when we know. We know, noninferentially, that there are other persons. Possibly through religious experience, and in particular the experience of solemn awe, we know that God exists. "We don't want merely inferred friends. Could we possibly be satisfied with an inferred God?"

Cook Wilson studied carefully a state of pseudo knowing to which he gave the name "being under the impression that"—or, as other writers have called it, "taking for granted." This mental state is a possible source of error.

In geometry the main problem is to find the correct construction (on this point Cook Wilson agreed with Kant). In geometrical thinking, as elsewhere (on this point he disagreed with Kant), there is an apprehension of necessary connection, not a necessity of apprehension.

All inference depends, he held, on the existence of necessary connections, and such connections hold between universals. Cook Wilson adopted a moderate realist position concerning universals. He held that the relation of universal to particular is *sui generis*. It is necessary in order that there be any explanation whatever. In particular, the relation explains the meaning of the terms "common" and "same"; it is not the case that these terms explain the relation. More specifically, the universal "triangularity" is "the unity of particular triangularities." However, we cannot properly state that "triangularity is a universal." If we do so, we fall into difficulties of the kind exemplified by Plato's *Parmenides* and by other puzzles about classes and number.

Cook Wilson defined negation in terms of exclusion. He sparred with Lewis Carroll over conditional propositions. He held that a conditional proposition asserts a relation, not between two statements, but between two "forms of statement," or, as he preferred to say, a relation between two problems or questions. He used this account of conditional propositions as one premise in an attempt to demolish non-Euclidean geometries. As he also needed the premises that we know space to be Euclidean and that a figure is indispensable to geometrical reasoning, it is not surprising that mathematicians were unconvinced.

Several of the doctrines noted above will be seen to have influenced, and sometimes anticipated, the thought of later philosophers. Cook Wilson is still well worth reading on negation, meaning, memory, imagination, and other topics.

Works by Cook Wilson

Aristotelian Studies, I. On the Structure of the Seventh Book of the Nicomachean Ethics, Ch. i–x. Oxford, 1879.
On an Evolutionist Theory of Axioms, an Inaugural Lecture. Oxford, 1889.
On the Interpretation of Plato's Timaeus. Critical Studies With Reference to a Recent Edition. London, 1889.

On the Traversing of Geometrical Figures. Oxford, 1905.
Statement and Inference With Other Philosophical Papers, A. S. L. Farquharson, ed., 2 vols. Oxford, 1926. Selections from the manuscripts and other writings, with a portrait, memoir, and selected correspondence. For full bibliography, see *Statement and Inference,* pp. lxvi–lxxii.

Works on Cook Wilson

Collingwood, R. G., *An Autobiography.* Oxford, 1939. Chs. 3–7.
Joseph, H. W. B., "Professor John Cook Wilson, 1849–1915." *Proceedings of the British Academy 1915–1916,* 555–565.
Passmore, J. A., *A Hundred Years of Philosophy.* London, 1957. Ch. 10.
Prichard, H. A., "Professor John Cook Wilson." *Mind,* Vol. 28 (1919), 297–318.
Robinson, Richard, *The Province of Logic: An Interpretation of Certain Parts of Cook Wilson's Statement and Inference.* London, 1931.

EDMUND J. FURLONG

WINCKELMANN, JOHANN JOACHIM (1717–1768), German art historian and founder of scientific archeology, was born at Stendal in Prussia. After early schooling in Stendal and Berlin, he studied theology and classics at Halle and mathematics and medicine at Jena. He held a series of minor positions and then became a librarian at Nöthnitz, near Dresden, where he met many artists and critics who stimulated his interest in the fine arts. Influenced by the papal nuncio in Dresden, Winckelmann became a Catholic; and in 1755, after the publication of his first important work. *Gedanken über die Nachahmung der griechischen Werke in der Malerei und Bildhauerkunst* ("Thoughts on the Imitation of Greek Works in Painting and Sculpture," Dresden and Leipzig, 1754), he went to Rome on a royal subsidy. In Rome he was supported by various high churchmen. In 1758 he visited Naples, Herculaneum, and Pompeii and spent a longer period in Florence. In 1760 he became librarian and surveyor of antiquities to Cardinal Albani and wrote his *Anmerkungen über die Baukunst der Alten* ("Remarks on the Architecture of the Ancients," Leipzig, 1762). In 1763 he was appointed general surveyor of antiquities for Rome and Latium. While general surveyor he published *Abhandlung über die Fähigkeit der Empfindung des Schönen in der Kunst und dem Unterricht in derselben* ("Treatise on the Power of Feeling Beauty and on Teaching It," Dresden, 1764); *Geschichte der Kunst des Alterthums* ("History of Ancient Art," Dresden, 1764); and *Versuch einer Allegorie, besonders für die Kunst* ("An Essay on Allegory, especially for Art," Dresden, 1766). In 1768 Winckelmann was murdered in an inn at Trieste.

Winckelmann was the founder of classical archeology and of art history. He was the first person to consider a work of art not only as an item of contemplative pleasure and imitation or as an object of erudite commentary and psychological characterization, but as a creation of a particular nation and period with its own special geographical, social, and political conditions that expresses the style of the spirit of the milieu as a whole.

Winckelmann's aesthetic theory is found mostly in scattered remarks in his works on ancient art, and his ideas were constantly evolving. They were methodological by-products of his work as a historian systematizing the history of ancient art. For these reasons any reconstruction of Winckelmann's aesthetic doctrines is controversial. These views were nevertheless systematized by his contemporaries, and extended from ancient art to literature both ancient and modern.

Winckelmann was dissatisfied with all received definitions of beauty, and he held that beauty is indefinable—that it is one of the greatest mysteries of nature, and beyond the limits of human understanding. (There is nevertheless an absolute standard of taste. But this cannot be deduced; it must be grasped through a deeper insight into actual works of art.) One general characteristic of beauty is proportion; but to dead proportion must be added living form.

Expression (*Ausdruck*) is a lower stage of beauty. It is a lively imitation of both the soul and the body as passive and active. Pure beauty is reached through the stillness of this feeling of life. The highest stage of beauty arises from the unification of expression and pure beauty in grace. By this unity beauty becomes an appearance of divinity in the representation of a sensible object. The unity of a work of art arises mainly from simplicity (*Einfalt*) and measure (*Mässigung*), or the harmony of opposing traits—for instance, understanding and passion. This process of unification corresponds to the rise from sensible to ideal beauty, or from the imitation of nature to the creation of a higher nature. The observation of nature gives us the means of overcoming spurious standards of beauty and a set of samples to be used by the intellect in creating the higher nature.

Beauty is felt by the senses, but it is understood and created by the intellect (*Verstand*)—which is the faculty of ideas as well as of distinct concepts. The "ideal" (*Das Ideale*), or "spirit" (*Geist*), is the most important and controversial notion in Winckelmann's aesthetics. One kind of ideal is created when an artist combines in one unique whole elements of beauty among different natural objects—for example, by constructing a perfect female figure from separate parts imitating parts of different real women, each of which is the most perfect of its kind. A superior kind of ideal arises when the choice of parts is directed not only by a feeling for proportion, but by a supernatural idea translated into matter—for example, the superhuman perfection of a particular human type or quality such as the combination of attractive manhood and pleasing youthfulness in the Apollo del Belvedere, or of enormous pain in a great soul in the Laocoön. The second kind of ideal is not abstracted from experience, but is derived from an intuition of the beauty of God himself. It is realized through a creative process like that of God creating his own image in man. Ideal beauty of the second kind must show "noble simplicity and quiet greatness" (*edle Einfalt und stille Grösse*). Kant later systematized this double conception in his *Critique of Judgment*.

Because beauty in its highest form is spiritual, it must suggest a deeper ethical meaning. These ethical thoughts are the content of real art. Art makes them intuitively known through allegory. Nature also presents allegories to man; and man himself spoke through images before he spoke in rational language. Painting, sculpture, and poetry all express through allegory invisible things; and thus allegory is the foundation of the unity of the different fine arts.

Simplicity, or unity, gives distinctness (*Deutlichkeit*) to a work of art. Winckelmann held therefore that there is an intuitive, or sensible, distinctness, whereas the then current psychology admitted only intellectual distinctness and allowed only clarity to sensibility. Kant, later, was the first to introduce the concept of intuitive distinctness into the theory of knowledge.

Winckelmann saw in Greek art the standard of ideal beauty. The Greek man was the most spiritually and ethically balanced, and therefore the most physically perfect, because of various climatic, geographical, historical, social, and political conditions. Greek artists could therefore use the most beautiful human specimens as models; and they should be imitated by modern artists. Imitation of nature and imitation of the Greeks is the same thing.

Works by Winckelmann

Monumenti antichi inediti, 2 vols. Rome, 1767.

Werke, 12 vols., Joseph Eiselein, ed. Donaueschingen, 1825–1829.

Werke, W. Rehm and H. Diepolter, eds. Berlin, 1952——. Critical edition.

Kleine Schriften und Briefe, W. Senf, ed. Weimar, 1960.

Works on Winckelmann

Aron, Erich, *Die deutsche Erweckung des Griechentums durch Winckelmann und Herder.* Heidelberg, 1929.

Baumecker, Gottfried, *Winckelmann in seinen Dresdner Schriften.* Berlin, 1933.

Curtius, Ludwig, *Winckelmann und seine Nachfolge.* Vienna, 1941.

Hatfield, H. C., *Winckelmann and His German Critics, 1755–1781.* New York, 1943.

Justi, Carl, *Winckelmann und seine Zeitgenossen,* 3 vols. Leipzig, 1866–1873; 4th ed. Leipzig, 1943.

Rehm, W., *Winckelmann und Lessing.* Berlin, 1941.

Vallentin, Berthold, *Winckelmann.* Berlin, 1931.

Zbinden, W., *Winckelmann.* Bern, 1935.

GIORGIO TONELLI

WINDELBAND, WILHELM (1848–1915), German philosopher and historian of philosophy. Windelband was born in Potsdam and educated at Jena, Berlin, and Göttingen. He taught philosophy at Zurich, Freiburg im Breisgau, Strasbourg, and Heidelberg. He was a disciple of Rudolf Hermann Lotze and Kuno Fischer and was the leader of the so-called southwestern German (or Baden) school of Neo-Kantianism. He is best known for his work in history of philosophy, to which he brought a new mode of exposition—the organization of the subject by problems rather than by chronological sequence of individual thinkers. As a systematic philosopher he is remembered for his attempt to extend the principles of Kantian criticism to the historical sciences, his attempt to liberate philosophy from identification with any specific scientific discipline, and his sympathetic appreciation of late nineteenth-century philosophy of value.

Windelband believed that whereas the various sciences (mathematical, natural, and historical) have specific objects and limit their investigations to determined areas of the total reality, philosophy finds its unique object in the knowledge of reality provided by these various disciplines taken together as a whole. The task of philosophy, he held, was to explicate the a priori bases of science in general. The aim of philosophy was to show not how science is possible but why there are many different kinds of science; the relationships that obtain between these various sciences; and the nature of the relation between the critical intelligence—the knowing, willing, and feeling subject—and consciousness in general.

According to Windelband, both the triumphs and the limitations of contemporary philosophical thought had their origins in Kant's thought. Kant had established the dogma that all knowledge must be of the type provided by the natural sciences. But, Windelband held, if knowledge is limited only to that which can be contained within the categories as set forth in the *Critique of Pure Reason,* then the kinds of activities associated with the will and the emotions—that is to say, the subjects of Kant's second and third critiques—are removed from the province of knowledge. The inadequacies of the Kantian identification of knowledge in general with natural scientific knowledge alone had been demonstrated by the post-Kantian idealists, who sought to construct a theory of knowledge capable of appreciating "the needs of modern culture, and . . . the historical material of ideas" (*History of Philosophy,* p. 569). Idealism failed, however, because it ended by hypostatizing a spiritual sphere which presumably was separate from the world of matter and which operated according to principles utterly different from those which science explicated in general causal laws. Thus, whereas Kantianism had failed to include ethics and aesthetics within the domain of scientific philosophy, idealism failed to provide a place for those aspects of the world revealed by the natural sciences and eternally established as causally determined. It thus appeared to late nineteenth-century thinkers that there were at least two levels of reality, one spiritual and historical, the other material and determined; and it seemed that knowledge itself, far from being one, was at least twofold. On the one hand, it was empirical and discovered laws; on the other hand, it was rational and revealed the essential freedom behind the laws. Such at least had been the contention of Wilhelm Dilthey and the neo-idealists. As long as this division persisted, Windelband held, pessimism, the denial of philosophy, must flourish also.

The way out of the difficulty was to be provided by a fundamental reappraisal in philosophy, a reconsideration of modern thought *ab initio.* For Windelband this meant primarily an attempt to find a way to apply the technique of transcendental deduction to the historical as well as the physical sciences. It also meant liberation from the notion that natural science was the archetype of all knowledge. In an early address, "Was ist Philosophie?" (1882), Windelband distinguished between theoretical judgments (*Urteile*) and critical judgments (*Beurteilungen*). The former expressed the "mutual implicativeness" (*Zusammengehörigkeit*) of two "representational contents" (*Vorstellungsinhalte*); the latter expressed the relation between the judging consciousness (*beurteilenden Bewusstsein*) and the object represented (see *Präludien,* Vol. I, p. 29). Theoretical judgments are judgments of fact and

are always positive; their purpose is to extend the limits of knowledge in a given science. Critical judgments, however, can be either positive or negative, and they express the position assumed by the subject when a given theoretical judgment is endowed with a status as means to some end.

The individual sciences expand the series of theoretical judgments; philosophy examines the relations between the ability of individual consciousness to render judgments and that "consciousness in general" (*Bewusstsein überhaupt*) which is the intuited basis of every critical judgment. Philosophy, then, "has its own proper field and its own problem in those values of universal validity which are the organizing principles for the functions of culture and civilization and for all the particular values of life. But it will describe and explain those values only that it may give an account of their validity; it treats them not as facts but as norms" (*History of Philosophy,* pp. 680–681). The various sciences are concerned with facts, which they organize in different ways according to the ends for which those facts are "constructed." Philosophy, however, is concerned with the processes by which events attain the status of facts for particular sciences.

Critical judgments, then, are rendered in respect not of what is but of what ought to be; in accordance not with laws but with norms. There is a "normative consciousness" (*Normalbewusstsein*) presupposed by philosophy; this "normative consciousness" is *in abstracto* the same as that which, *in concreto,* underlies every scientific, moral, and aesthetic experience. It is not to be thought of as either a metaphysical or a psychological entity. It is, rather, merely the "sum-total of the inter-connections and relations between existents" (*Logic,* p. 59). These relations "are not themselves existents, either as things, as states, or as activities; they can only become 'actual' as the content of the psychical functions of knowing. . . . In itself the realm of the valid is nothing else than the form and order under which that which exists is determined" (*ibid.*). It follows, then, that "this whole is closed to our knowledge; we shall never know more than a few fragments of it, and there is no prospect of our ever being able to patch it together out of the scraps that we can gather" (*ibid.,* p. 65). Therefore, philosophy cannot end in science or in any practical rule of life; it can only point the attention of humanity to the sensed "principles of absolute judgment" which are presupposed in every human confrontation of the world in scientific, moral, and aesthetic experience.

Windelband regarded as baseless every attempt to distinguish between the different disciplines that constitute science on the basis of a presumed essential difference between their objects. The disciplines are distinguished only by their methods, which are in turn functions of the ends or values informing them as instruments of culture. In the address "Geschichte und Naturwissenschaften" (1894), he distinguished between the natural sciences and the historical sciences, and he argued that the natural sciences aim at the construction of general laws and "explain" an event by identifying it as an instance of a general law. Historical sciences, on the other hand, are individualizing; they concentrate on specific events and attempt to determine their specific physiognomy or form. Natural science Windelband termed "nomothetic"; historical science, "idiographic." But, he added, any given object could be studied by both kinds of science. A mental event, if viewed under the aspect of physical causality—as an instance of the working of some general law—was a natural event. That same mental event, described in its individuality and valued for its deviation from the class to which it belonged, became an object of the idiographic sciences. Positivists erred in holding that every event must be viewed nomothetically, just as idealists erred in thinking that certain kinds of events cannot be so viewed. The total picture of the world that consciousness is in principle able to construct can be constructed only through the use of both kinds of investigation. No single event can be deduced from general laws, and no law can be framed out of the contemplation of a single event. "Law and event remain together as the ultimate, incommensurable limits of our representation of the world" (*Präludien*, Vol. II, p. 160).

Works by Windelband

Die Lehre vom Zufall. Berlin, 1870.

Präludien: Aufsätze und Reden zur Einführung in die Philosophie, 2 vols. Freiburg im Breisgau, 1884; 5th ed., Tübingen, 1914.

Lehrbuch der Geschichte der Philosophie. Tübingen, 1892; 14th ed., revised by Heinz Heimsoeth, Tübingen, 1948. Translated by J. H. Tufts as *History of Philosophy.* New York, 1893; 2d ed., New York, 1901.

"Die Prinzipien der Logik," in Wilhelm Windelband and Arnold Ruge, *Enzyklopädie der philosophischen Wissenschaften.* Tübingen, 1912. Translated by B. E. Meyer as *Logic.* London, 1913.

"Geschichtsphilosophie: Eine Kriegsvorlesung, Fragment aus dem Nachlass," Wolfgang Windelband and Bruno Bauch, eds. *Kantstudien, Ergänzungshefte im Auftrag der Kantgesellschaft*, No. 38 (1916), 5–68.

Works on Windelband

Collingwood, R. G., *The Idea of History.* Oxford, 1946. Pp. 165–168.

Gronau, G., "Die Kultur und Wertphilosophie Wilhelm Windelbands," in *Die Philosophie der Gegenwart.* Langensalza, 1922.

Rickert, Heinrich, *Wilhelm Windelband.* Tübingen, 1915.

Rossi, Pietro, *Lo storicismo tedesco contemporaneo.* Turin, 1956. Pp. 149–207.

HAYDEN V. WHITE

WISDOM in its broadest and commonest sense denotes sound and serene judgment regarding the conduct of life. It may be accompanied by a broad range of knowledge, by intellectual acuteness, and by speculative depth, but it is not to be identified with any of these and may appear in their absence. It involves intellectual grasp or insight, but it is concerned not so much with the ascertainment of fact or the elaboration of theories as with the means and ends of practical life.

Wisdom literature. Concern with the art of living long preceded formal science or philosophy in human history. All ancient civilizations seem to have accumulated wisdom literatures, consisting largely of proverbs handed down from father to son as the crystallized results of experience. Perhaps the most ancient known collection of these sayings is the Egyptian "Wisdom of Ptah-hotep," which comes down from about 2500 B.C. The writings of Confucius (sixth century B.C.) and Mencius (fourth century

B.C.), though more sophisticated, are still concerned chiefly with the Tao, the good or normal human life. The early writers of India held views at once more speculative and more disillusioned than those of China; both Buddhists and Hindus found the greatest happiness of man in deliverance from the grinding round of suffering and death and in absorption into Atman or nirvana, where personality and struggle alike disappear. But large parts of the Bhagavad-Gita and the Dhammapada, two classics among the scriptures of India, are devoted to maxims and counsels for the conduct of life.

Of far greater influence in the West has been the wisdom literature of the Hebrew people, which consists of the more philosophical parts of the Old Testament and the Apocrypha. Perhaps the most important of these are the books of Job, Proverbs, and Psalms and the apocryphal book called The Wisdom of Solomon. There is no certain knowledge of who wrote any of them; they are probably the work of many men, extending over centuries. They differ strikingly from the writings of Greek and Chinese moralists in the closeness with which morality is identified with religion. The Hebrew sages were all monotheists who held that God fashioned the world but remained outside it; he had made his will known in the law delivered to Moses. This law set the standard and pattern of goodness for all time; the good man will make it his study and seek to conform his life to it. At the same time these sages reduced the miraculous element in Jewish history; they made no claim to being inspired themselves, and inclining, indeed, to assume that the sole motive of conduct was self-advantage, they offered their prudential maxims as not only conforming to the divine law but also as the product of good sense and sound reason. There is very little evidence that they were affected by Greek thought, though Greek influence must have flowed around them after the conquests of Alexander. It is possible that in their cool and reasonable note, contrasting so sharply with the visionary fervor of the prophets, there is an echo of the reflective thought of Greece.

The Greeks had a wisdom literature of their own which long preceded the appearance of their great philosophers. Hesiod (eighth century B.C.) and Theognis (sixth century B.C.) summed up in poetic form the maxims of traditional morality. Pythagoras (sixth century B.C.), a curious combination of mathematician and religious seer, seems to have found in philosophy the guide of practical life. This view was further developed by the Sophists, who, at a time when libraries and universities were unknown, undertook to instruct young men in the arts, theoretical and practical, that were most likely to lead to success. In their emphasis on success, however, there was something skeptical and cynical; the art of life tended in their teaching to become the sort of craft that enabled one by clever strategy to achieve place and power.

The Greek conception. The first full statement and embodiment of the classic Greek conception of wisdom came with Socrates (c. 470–399 B.C.), who insisted that virtue and knowledge were one, that if men failed to live well, it was through ignorance of what virtue really was. He had no doubt that if men knew what virtue was, they would embody it in their conduct. Thus, he set himself to define the major virtues with precision. His method was to consider particular instances of them and bring to light the features they had in common; this would give the essence and true pattern of the virtue in question. He did not profess to be satisfied with the results of his inquiries, but his acuteness and thoroughness made him the first of the great theoretical moralists, and the courage with which he carried his principles into both life and death gave him a unique place in Western history.

The stress on wisdom was maintained by his disciple Plato. For Plato there are three departments of human nature, which may be described as the appetites, directed to such ends as food and drink; the distinctively human emotions, such as courage and honor; and reason. Of these reason is the most important, for only as impulse and feeling are governed by it will conduct be saved from chaos and excess; indeed, in such government practical wisdom consists. In one respect Aristotle carried the exaltation of reason farther than Plato; in addition to this practical wisdom, he recognized another and purely intellectual virtue, the wisdom that pursues truth for its own sake and without reference to practice. In this pursuit, which can be followed effectively only by the philosopher, lay the highest and happiest life.

It was among the Stoics, however, that guidance by reason was most seriously and widely attempted. In the thought of the Roman emperor Marcus Aurelius (A.D. 121–180), both nature and human nature are determined by causal law, and the wrongs and insults that other men inflict on us are therefore as inevitable as the tides. The wise man will understand this inevitability and not waste his substance in futile indignation or fear. He will conform himself to nature's laws, recognize that passion is a symptom of ignorance, free himself from emotional attachments and resentments, and live as far as he can the life of a "passionless sage." The account given by Marcus Aurelius in his famous journal of his struggle to order his practice and temper by this ideal of austere rationality has made his little book a classic of pagan wisdom.

Modern philosophers. The opinions of modern philosophers on the meaning of wisdom are too various for review here. But it can be noted of these thinkers, as it was of Marcus Aurelius, that their standing as purveyors or exemplars of wisdom bears no fixed relation to their eminence as philosophers. If their chief work lies, as Kant's does, in the theory of knowledge, or as McTaggart's does, in technical metaphysics, it may have no obvious bearing on practical life. Furthermore, by reason of an unhappy temperament, some philosophers of name and influence, such as Rousseau, have been far from notable exemplars of wisdom in either controversy or conduct. On the other hand, there are thinkers who have shown in their writing, and sometimes also in their lives, so large a humanity and good sense that they have been held in especial esteem for their wisdom whether or not they have been of high philosophical rank. Montaigne and Emerson are examples on one level; John Locke, Bishop Butler, John Stuart Mill, and Henry Sidgwick are examples from a more professional level. Among technical thinkers of the first rank, a figure who has left a deep impression for a wisdom serene and disinterested, though a little above the battle, is the famous philosopher of Amsterdam, Benedict Spinoza (1632–1677).

Components of wisdom. Are there any traits uniformly exhibited by the very diverse minds that by general agreement are wise? Two traits appear to stand out—reflectiveness and judgment.

Reflectiveness. By reflectiveness is meant the habit of considering events and beliefs in the light of their grounds and consequences. Conduct prompted merely by impulse or desire is notoriously likely to be misguided, and this holds true of both intellectual and practical conduct. Whether a belief is warranted must be decided by the evidence it rests on and the implications to which it leads, and one can become aware of these only by reflection. Similarly, whether an action is right or wrong depends, at least in part, on the results that it produces in the way of good and evil, and these results can be taken into account only by one who looks before he leaps. Common sense, with its rules and proverbs, no doubt helps, but it is too rough and general a guide to be relied on safely; and the reflective man will have at his command a broader view of grounds and consequences, causes and effects. He will more readily recognize the beliefs of superstition, charlatanism, and bigotry for what they are because he will question the evidence for them and note that when reflectively developed, they conflict with beliefs known to be true. In the same way he will be able to recognize some proposals for action as rash, partisan, or shortsighted because certain consequences have been ascribed to them falsely and others have been ignored. In some activities wisdom consists almost wholly of such foresight. A general, for example, is accounted wise if he can foresee in detail how each of the courses open to him will affect the prospects of victory.

Judgment. There is a wisdom of ends as well as of means, which is here denoted by "judgment." The goal of the general—namely, victory—is laid down for him, but the ordinary man needs the sort of wisdom that can appraise and choose his own ends. The highest wisdom of all, Plato contended, is that required by the statesman, who is called upon to fix both the goals toward which society strives and the complex methods by which it may most effectively move toward them. Unfortunately, at this crucial point where the ends of life are at issue, the sages have differed profoundly. Some, like Epicurus and Mill, have argued for happiness; others, like the Christian saints, for self-sacrificing love; others, like Nietzsche, for power. Many philosophers of the present century have come to hold that this conflict is beyond settlement by reason, on the ground that judgments of good and bad are not expressions of knowledge at all but only of desire and emotion. For these thinkers there is properly no such thing as wisdom regarding intrinsic goods; knowledge is confined to means.

Whatever the future of this view, common opinion is still at one with the main tradition of philosophy; it regards the judgment of values as a field in which wisdom may be pre-eminently displayed. It must admit, however, that this judgment is of a peculiar kind; it seems to be intuitive in the sense that it is not arrived at by argument nor easily defended by it. One may be certain that pleasure is better than pain and yet be at a loss to prove it; the insight seems to be immediate. And where immediate insights differ, as they sometimes do, the difference appears to be ultimate and beyond remedy. Must such wisdom end in dogmatic contradiction and skepticism?

That it need not do so will perhaps be evident from a few further considerations. First, differences about intrinsic goods may be due to mere lack of knowledge on one side or the other. The Puritans who condemned music and drama as worthless could hardly have excluded them if they had known what they were excluding; in these matters wider experience brings an amended judgment. Second, what appears to be intuitive insight may express nothing more than a confirmed habit or prejudice. Where deep-seated feelings are involved, as in matters of sex, race, or religion, the certainty that belongs to clear insight may be confused with the wholly different certainty of mere confidence or emotional conviction. Fortunately, Freud and others have shown that these irrational factors can be tracked down and largely neutralized. Third, man's major goods are rooted in his major needs, and since the basic needs of human nature are everywhere the same, the basic goods are also the same. No philosophy of life that denied value to the satisfactions of food or drink or sex or friendship or knowledge could hope to commend itself in the long run.

It should be pointed out, finally, that the judgment of the wise man may carry a weight out of all proportion to that of anything explicit in his thought or argument. The decisions of a wise judge may be implicitly freighted with experience and reflection, even though neither may be consciously employed in the case before him. Experience, even when forgotten beyond recall, leaves its deposit, and where this is the deposit of long trial and error, of much reflection, and of wide exposure in fact or imagination to the human lot, the judgment based on it may be more significant than any or all of the reasons that the judge could adduce for it. This is why age is credited with wisdom; years supply a means to it whether or not the means is consciously used. Again, the individual may similarly profit from the increasing age of the race; since knowledge is cumulative, he can stand on the shoulders of his predecessors. Whether individual wisdom is on the average increasing is debatable, but clearly the opportunity for it is. As Francis Bacon, a philosopher whose wisdom was of the highest repute, remarked, "We are the true ancients."

Bibliography

For proverbial wisdom see Archer Taylor, *The Proverb* (Cambridge, Mass., 1931), and—old but suggestive—R. C. Trench, *Proverbs and Their Lessons* (London and New York, 1858).

For the problems of determining right and wrong, see any first-rate work on ethics, such as Henry Sidgwick, *The Methods of Ethics,* 7th ed. (Chicago, 1962).

For an analysis of reflection, see, for example, John Dewey, *How We Think* (New York, 1910).

For the place of reason in valuation, see L. T. Hobhouse, *The Rational Good* (New York, 1921), or Brand Blanshard, *Reason and Goodness* (London and New York, 1962).

For some useful popular works see T. E. Jessop, *Reasonable Living* (London, 1948); H. C. King, *Rational Living* (New York, 1912); and A. E. Murphy, *The Uses of Reason* (New York, 1943).

BRAND BLANSHARD

WISDOM, (ARTHUR) JOHN TERENCE DIBBEN, British analytic philosopher, was born in 1904. Wisdom has been closely associated with Ludwig Wittgenstein, whose chair in philosophy at Cambridge he now holds. Wisdom has been professor of philosophy there since 1952. He took his B.A. degree at Cambridge in 1924 and his M.A. there in 1934.

The philosophical problem on which Wisdom has written most is the question of what the nature of philosophy is, and his writings reflect his changing views concerning the proper answer to this question. His writings can be divided into two groups, those through 1934, putting forward one answer to the question, and those from 1936 to the present, consisting of successive attempts to make clear a quite different view of the nature of philosophy, along with applications of this new approach to a number of familiar first-level philosophical problems.

Logical constructions. Wisdom's first book, *Interpretation and Analysis* (1931), compares Jeremy Bentham's notion of a "fiction" with Bertrand Russell's idea of a logical construction—a central notion of British philosophizing in the 1920s and 1930s. According to the theory of logical constructions, to say that a kind of entity X is a logical construction out of entities of kind Y is to say that statements about entities of kind X are translatable into statements about entities of kind Y, the Y's being "more ultimate," "more fundamental," than the X's. (It was often said to be less misleading to say, not "X's are logical constructions," but "'X'" is an incomplete symbol.") Thus, for example, it was said that nations, which are, after all, a kind of "abstraction," are logical constructions out of their nationals, and this meant that statements about, for example, England and France are translatable into statements about Englishmen and Frenchmen. The translation was to be performed not merely by replacement of the words—for "England is a monarchy" does not mean the same as "Englishmen are a monarchy"—but also by changing the predicates, and no doubt the new predicates would be more complicated. Nevertheless, a fact about England is not something "over and above" a fact or set of facts about Englishmen. And other things, too, were said to be logical constructions: propositions were said to be logical constructions out of sentences, people out of mental and bodily events, material objects (including human bodies) out of sense data, and so on. Indeed, Russell and others used the notion very widely; Ockham's razor (according to which "entities must not be multiplied beyond necessity") was given the modern form: supposedly transcendent or abstract entities are everywhere to be regarded as logical constructions out of the more concrete entities given in sense experience. This procedure has the advantage of explicitly blocking a mistaken inference that may arise, for example, from Berkeley's analysis of a material object as a "congeries of ideas" (for "ideas," read "sense data"). Analyzing it in this way suggests, for example, that the apple I hold in my hand is made of sense data and that I would be eating sense data if I ate the apple. But to say that the apple is a *logical* construction out of sense data is only to say that statements about it are translatable into statements about sense data.

G. E. Moore had written (in "A Defense of Common

Sense") that the work of the philosopher was not to find out whether this or that (supposed) matter of fact really was a fact but rather to find the analysis of what we know in knowing the things we do unquestionably know. Thus, I know for certain that I have two hands, but what is the analysis of what I know in knowing this? The followers of Russell and the early Wittgenstein ("logical atomists," as they have been called) saw their task as the analysis of such statements into "atomic statements," which are logically and epistemologically fundamental; they sought to provide translations of statements containing the expression "*X*" into statements which do not contain "*X*," thus justifying the claim that *X*'s are logical constructions.

The first exhaustive treatment of this central notion is to be found in Wisdom's series of five articles entitled "Logical Constructions," which appeared in successive issues of *Mind* from 1931 to 1933. The first three of these essays discuss the relation between sentences in general and the facts expressed by them; the governing idea comes from Wittgenstein's *Tractatus,* where a sentence (on Wisdom's interpretation) is said to be a picture of the fact it expresses. Wisdom tries to bring out precisely what this comes to, in the case not only of such "simple" sentences as "Wisdom killed Al Capone" but also of negations, generalizations, and compound sentences. The fourth and fifth essays are concerned more specifically with logical constructions: How precisely is the analysandum (for example, a statement about sense data) related on the one hand to the fact it pictures and on the other hand to the analysans (a statement about an external object) and the fact it pictures?

In the last of the five essays philosophy is identified with analysis, which is said to provide the required translations. Philosophical propositions are thus verbal (that is, about words), differing only in aim or intention from those of writers of dictionaries: "The philosophical intention is clearer insight into the ultimate structure" of facts, and "philosophic progress does not consist in acquiring knowledge of new facts but in acquiring new knowledge of facts."

The essays "Ostentation" (1933) and "Is Analysis a Useful Method in Philosophy?" (1934) also deal with logical constructions.

The new approach to philosophy. Wittgenstein, who had been away from Cambridge since before World War I, returned there in 1929; his writings from then on show a gradual change in his conception of the nature of philosophy and of language. Wisdom himself returned to Cambridge in 1934 (he had for some years been teaching philosophy at St. Andrews University in Scotland), and his thinking was then strongly influenced by the new view of philosophy being worked out by Wittgenstein. Wisdom's essay "Philosophical Perplexity" (1936) shows that by 1936 a striking change had taken place.

No doubt many within the analytic movement had felt uneasiness about its program, and there had been criticism of the movement from its beginnings, but this was the first appearance in print of an alternative to the earlier reductive account of what philosophers are and ought to be doing. (Wittgenstein's writings of the period were not published until much later, after his death.)

According to the new conception of philosophy (set out briefly in "Philosophical Perplexity" and in greater detail

in "Metaphysics and Verification," 1938), philosophical claims are answers to questions of the forms "What are *X*'s?," "What is it to know that here is an *X*?," "Are there any *X*'s?," "Is there any such thing as knowing that here there is an *X*?," where "*X*" is replaced by some very general term such as "material object," "soul," or "causal connection." Answers to the first pair of questions are of two and only two forms: the reductive (*X*'s are logical constructions out of *Y*'s; knowledge that here is an *X* is really knowledge about *Y*'s), and the transcendentalist (*X*'s are unanalyzable, are ultimate; knowledge that here is an *X* is unique, a special way of knowing appropriate only to *X*'s). A philosopher's answers to the second pair of questions will be connected with his answers to the first pair—for example, a reductionist is less likely to be a skeptic (although some have been both reductionists and skeptics with respect to, say, material objects), whereas a transcendentalist is more likely to fall into skepticism.

In view of their form, answers to the first pair of questions are apt to appear to be strictly definitional (as when one says "Fathers are male parents"), and answers to the second pair may appear to be making straightforward empirical points (as when one says what goes on inside the earth). But the philosopher does neither of these things. A philosophical question arises out of a dissatisfaction with the "categories of being" (in the formal mode, "kinds of statement") implicit in our ordinary way of talking. Reductive answers to the first pair of questions and skeptical answers to the second pair are disguised proposals of alternative categorizations; transcendentalist answers to the first pair of questions and nonskeptical answers to the second pair are disguised proposals that we retain the categorizations already marked in the language. The various answers all bring home to us the likenesses and differences between "categories of being" which are either concealed by or implicit in our ordinary way of talking.

Consider, for example, a certain kind of skepticism about material objects. The skeptic says, "We don't really know that there is cheese on the table" and "It would be well if we prefixed every remark about material things with 'probably.'" Such skepticism draws our attention to a likeness shared by all statements about material objects and to a difference between all such statements on the one hand and statements about sensations on the other. The skeptic forces us to see that if a man makes a statement about a material object—whatever the object, whatever the circumstances—then it always makes sense for us to say "But perhaps he is mistaken"; whereas if he says he is having this or that sensation or sense experience, it would not make sense to say this of him. Ordinary language conceals this, for we ordinarily mark a difference among material-object statements; we say that some are at best probable (such as reports about what is going on inside the earth) and that others (such as reports about what is going on inside our fists) are as certain as any statement about a sensation or experience. Of course the job remains of showing *why* it strikes the skeptic—and us—as important to mark what is pointed to in his claim.

Consider the reductionist view of material objects (see "Metaphysics and Verification"). The reductionist says, "Material objects are logical constructions out of sense data." He draws our attention to a likeness between material-object statements and a certain kind of statement about sense data, a likeness in their mode of verification; if you have already found out that this has, does, and will continue to appear to be (say) a bit of cheese, then there is nothing further to do in the way of finding out whether or not it *is* a bit of cheese. Ordinary language conceals this likeness, for our ordinary use of the words is such that it is simply false to say that "This is a bit of cheese" means the same as "This has, does, and will appear to be a bit of cheese." Or, as it might be put, the reductionist draws our attention to a likeness between the statement "A material-object statement means the same as a certain complex sense-datum statement" and ordinary statements of the form "'*X*' means the same as '*Y*'" that we would unhesitatingly accept as true; and a difference between it and many ordinary statements of the form "'*X*' means the same as '*Y*'" that we would unhesitatingly reject as false.

Whether a philosophical claim is true is not the important question; what we should do with respect to a philosophical question about the nature of *X*'s and our knowledge of *X*'s is to bring out in full all the features of *X*'s which incline one to opt for this or that philosophical answer—thereby bringing out the relevant likenesses and differences between *X*'s (or statements about *X*'s) and other kinds of entities (or kinds of statements). In this way we obtain that illumination of the category of *X*'s which alone can answer the dissatisfaction that was expressed in our philosophical question.

Any account of the nature of a philosophical claim is itself a philosophical claim (for example, an answer to the question "What are philosophical claims?") and is itself to be dealt with in this way. In the essays already mentioned Wisdom also tries to bring out the likenesses and differences between philosophical claims and other kinds of claims which have been stressed by those who supposed that philosophical claims tell us facts about the world and by those who said that these claims are merely verbal.

"Other Minds." The papers mentioned so far are primarily concerned with expounding Wisdom's new view of the nature of philosophy, and the first-level philosophical claims considered there appear for the most part as examples; by contrast, his series of papers entitled "Other Minds" (which appeared in successive issues of *Mind* between 1940 and 1943) is concerned mainly with the first-level questions relating to our knowledge of other minds, and the second-level question on the nature of philosophy is discussed largely in order to shed light on the first-level questions. His aim in these papers is to bring out all the problems which issue in the question "Do we ever know what anyone else is thinking, feeling, experiencing . . . ?" and to give them the sort of treatment he has said a philosophical problem calls for. Roughly, papers I and II bring out the likenesses and differences between statements about other minds and statements about invisible currents flowing through wires; III compares the philosopher's and the plain man's use of "It's at best probable" and "We know by analogy"; IV and V deal with telepathy and extra or extended ways of knowing in general; VI and VII show what considerations rule out the possibility that one should have "direct" knowledge of the

sensations of others—that is, knowledge of the kind one has of one's own sensations (this is done by showing what makes a statement *be* a statement that is not merely about one's own sensations); and VIII deals with the status of the statement "No one has any knowledge at all apart from knowledge as to his own sensations of the moment."

The difference in conception of the nature of philosophy between Wisdom's later work and, for example, the "Logical Constructions" papers has often been discussed. It is therefore worth mentioning that there is also considerable continuity. As previously noted, Wisdom had earlier thought of "the philosophical intention [as] clearer insight into the ultimate structure" of facts; in "Philosophical Perplexity" he still regards it as a search for "illumination of the ultimate structure of facts." He does not, in this paper of 1936 or in any of his later works, regard philosophy as merely the study either of the workings of language for its own sake or of the confusions of ordinary language. The analogy he later drew between philosophy and psychoanalysis has led many people to think he regards philosophy as strictly a kind of therapy. But this has never been his view, and indeed one may regard his successive efforts to characterize the philosophical enterprise as attempts to bring out just what sort of insight and understanding the philosopher does provide (see, for example, "Gods" and "Philosophy, Metaphysics and Psycho-analysis").

Wisdom and Wittgenstein. It is dangerous to talk about the conception of philosophy held by the later Wittgenstein—there are very few remarks on the nature of philosophy in Wittgenstein's posthumously published *Philosophical Investigations,* and those he does make are obscure. Nevertheless, Wittgenstein's manner of dealing with philosophical problems there suggests that Wisdom differs from him at least in his attitude toward philosophy. While Wisdom has always acknowledged his great debt to Wittgenstein, he says of him in "Philosophical Perplexity," "He too much represents [philosophical theories] as merely symptoms of linguistic confusion. I wish to represent them as also symptoms of linguistic penetration." And he reminds us repeatedly that we are not to take his work as representing Wittgenstein's own views.

In sum, Wisdom's view is that the goal of philosophy is an understanding of just what philosophers have at all times sought to understand—"time and space, good and evil, things and persons." In making their case, philosophers have always appealed to linguistic usage—in "The Metamorphosis of Metaphysics" (reprinted in *Paradox and Discovery*) Wisdom brings out the similarity between contemporary linguistic philosophy and older forms of speculative philosophy. But he also reminds us that good philosophy of any age gives us a clearer view not merely of how we may go wrong in our talking and thinking but of how we may go right.

Works by Wisdom

Interpretation and Analysis. London, 1931.
"Logical Constructions." *Mind,* Vols. 40–42 (1931–1933).
Problems of Mind and Matter. Cambridge, 1934. A work of the same period as the "Logical Constructions" papers; it is concerned with perception and with the relation between a man's body and mind in virtue of which it is true to say that that body and mind are his body and mind.

Other Minds. Oxford, 1952. Contains the eight papers that originally appeared in *Mind,* 1940–1943, as well as a symposium contribution entitled "Other Minds" that was originally published in *PAS,* Supp. Vol. 20 (1946) and "The Concept of Mind" and "Metaphysics," the presidential address to the meeting of the Aristotelian Society, November 1950.

Philosophy and Psycho-analysis. Oxford, 1953. Contains "Ostentation," "Is Analysis a Useful Method in Philosophy?," "Philosophical Perplexity," "Metaphysics and Verification," "Gods," "Philosophy, Metaphysics and Psycho-analysis," and other articles and reviews.

Paradox and Discovery. Oxford, 1965. Contains "The Metamorphosis of Metaphysics," "A Feature of Wittgenstein's Technique," "The Logic of God," "Paradox and Discovery," and other short pieces.

Works on Wisdom

Gasking, D. A. T., "The Philosophy of John Wisdom, I and II." *Australasian Journal of Philosophy* (1954).

Passmore, John, *A Hundred Years of Philosophy.* London, 1957. Pp. 367–368, 434–438.

Urmson, J. O., *Philosophical Analysis.* Oxford, 1956. Pp. 76–85, 169–182.

JUDITH JARVIS THOMSON

WITTGENSTEIN, LUDWIG JOSEF JOHANN

(1889–1951), philosopher, was born in Vienna, the youngest of eight children. Ludwig's paternal grandfather, a convert from Judaism to Protestantism, had been a wool merchant in Saxony before moving to Vienna. Ludwig's father, Karl Wittgenstein, had, as a strong-willed boy, rebelled against a classical education, running away to America when he was 17. After two years he returned to Vienna and underwent a brief training in engineering. He went to work as a draftsman, designed and largely directed the construction of a steel-rolling mill, became its manager, in ten years' time was the head of a large steel company, and subsequently organized the first cartel of the Austrian steel industry. Ludwig's mother was the daughter of a Viennese banker. She was a Roman Catholic, and Ludwig was baptized in the Catholic church. Ludwig had four brothers and three sisters; all the children were generously endowed with artistic and intellectual talent. Their mother was devoted to music, and their home became a center of musical life. Johannes Brahms was a frequent visitor and a close friend of the family. One of Ludwig's brothers, Paul, became a distinguished pianist.

Ludwig was educated at home until he was 14. He was an indifferent student, and apparently his greatest interest was in machinery; a sewing machine that he constructed was much admired. His parents decided to send him to a school at Linz, in Upper Austria, that provided preparation in mathematics and the physical sciences rather than a classical education. After three years at Linz, Wittgenstein studied mechanical engineering for two years at the Technische Hochschule at Charlottenburg, in Berlin. He left this school in the spring of 1908 and went to England. In the summer of 1908 he experimented with kites at a kiteflying station in Derbyshire. That fall he registered as a research student of engineering at the University of Manchester. He engaged in aeronautical research for three years and designed a jet-reaction engine and a propeller.

Wittgenstein's interest began to shift to pure mathematics and then to the philosophical foundations of mathe-matics. He chanced upon Bertrand Russell's *Principles of Mathematics* and was greatly excited by it. He decided to give up engineering and to study with Russell at Cambridge. At the beginning of 1912 he was admitted to Trinity College, where he remained for the three terms of 1912 and the first two terms of 1913. Under Russell's supervision he applied himself intensively to logical studies and made astonishing progress. Soon he was engaged in the research that culminated in the logical ideas of the *Tractatus.*

Wittgenstein's most intimate friend during those early years at Cambridge was David Pinsent, a fellow student, to whom he later dedicated the *Tractatus.* When they met in the spring of 1912, Wittgenstein, in addition to studying logic, was doing experiments in the psychological laboratory on rhythm in music. He and Pinsent were united by strong musical interests. They had a repertoire of forty of Schubert's songs, whose melodies Wittgenstein would whistle while Pinsent accompanied him on the piano. Wittgenstein could play the clarinet and had an excellent memory for music and an unusual gift for sight-reading. He retained a deep interest in music throughout his life; in his philosophical writings there are many allusions to the nature of musical understanding.

In 1912, Wittgenstein was doing his first extensive reading in philosophy, and according to Pinsent he expressed "naive surprise" that the philosophers whom he had "worshipped in ignorance" were after all "stupid and dishonest and make disgusting mistakes!" He and Pinsent made holiday junkets to Iceland and Norway, Wittgenstein paying all expenses. Pinsent found Wittgenstein a difficult companion: irritable, nervously sensitive, often depressed. But when he was cheerful he was extremely charming. Sometimes he was depressed by the conviction that his death was near at hand and that he would not have time to perfect his new ideas in logic, sometimes by the thought that perhaps his logical work was of no real value. Even so, his general frame of mind was less morbid than before he had come to Cambridge. For a number of years previously there had hardly been a day, he told Pinsent, in which he had not thought of suicide "as a possibility." Coming to study philosophy with Russell had been his "salvation."

Wittgenstein worked with fierce energy at his logical ideas. In the spring of 1913 he submitted to hypnosis with the hope that in the hypnotic trance he could give clear answers to questions about difficulties in logic. He entertained a plan of going to live in seclusion in Norway for some years, devoting himself to logical problems. The reasons he gave to Pinsent were that he could do better work in the absence of all distractions, but he also said that "he had no right to live in a world" where he constantly felt contempt for other people and irritated them by his nervous temperament. Wittgenstein acted on his plan and lived in Norway from the latter part of 1913 until the outbreak of World War I. He stayed on a farm at Skjolden and later built a hut, where he lived in complete seclusion.

During this period Wittgenstein corresponded with Russell. His letters were warmly affectionate and were full of the excitement of his logical discoveries. However, he expressed the conviction that he and Russell had such different "ideals" that they were not suited for true friendship. Two people can be friends, he said, only if both of them are "pure," so that they can be completely open with one another without causing offense. A relationship founded on "hypocrisy" is intolerable. He and Russell should break off entirely or else limit their communications to their logical work. Both of them have weaknesses, but especially himself: "My life is *full* of the most hateful and petty thoughts and acts (this is *no* exaggeration)." "Perhaps you think it is a waste of time for me to think about myself; but how can I be a logician if I am not yet a man! *Before everything else* I must become pure."

When war broke out Wittgenstein entered the Austrian Army as a volunteer. He served in an artillery group on a vessel on the Vistula and later in an artillery workshop at Cracow. He was ordered to an officers' training school and subsequently served on the eastern front and later with mountain artillery in the southern Tyrol. During these years he continued to work at his book, writing down his philosophical thoughts in notebooks that he carried in his rucksack. He completed the book in August 1918; when he was taken prisoner by the Italians in November, he had the manuscript with him. From his prison camp near Monte Cassino he wrote to Russell, to whom the manuscript was subsequently delivered by diplomatic courier through the offices of a mutual friend, J. M. Keynes.

While serving on the eastern front Wittgenstein bought at a bookshop in Galicia a copy of one of Tolstoy's works on the Gospels, which apparently made a deep impression on him. In the prison camp in Italy he read a standard version of the Gospels, possibly for the first time, and is reported to have been disturbed by much that he found in it and to have questioned its authenticity, perhaps because of the differences from Tolstoy's version.

Wittgenstein was anxious to have his book, *Logisch-philosophische Abhandlung,* published immediately. Shortly after his release from imprisonment and his return to Vienna, in August 1919, he offered it to a publisher. He believed that his book finally solved the problems with which he and Russell had struggled. From Russell's letters, however, he concluded that Russell had not understood his main ideas, and he feared that no one would. He and Russell met in Holland in December 1919 to discuss the book. Russell undertook to write an introduction for it, but the following May, Wittgenstein wrote to Russell that the introduction contained much misunderstanding and he could not let it be printed with his book. Subsequently the publisher with whom he had been negotiating rejected the book. Wittgenstein wrote to Russell, in July 1920, that he would take no further steps to have it published and that Russell could do with it as he wished. The German text was published in 1921 in Wilhelm Ostwald's *Annalen der Naturphilosophie.* The following year it was published in London with a parallel English translation, under the title *Tractatus Logico-philosophicus.* A new and improved English translation was published in 1961.

Most of the notebooks used in the preparation of the *Tractatus* were destroyed on Wittgenstein's order. Three of them, however, from the years 1914–1916, were accidentally preserved and were published in 1961 with a parallel English translation. The notebooks present a vivid picture of the intensity of Wittgenstein's struggles with the problems of the *Tractatus,* and they sometimes help to show what the problems were.

Soon after his return to civilian life Wittgenstein decided to become a schoolteacher. He attended a teacher-training course in order to receive a certificate, and in the fall of 1920 he began teaching classes of children aged nine and ten in the village of Trattenbach in Lower Austria. He was an exacting teacher. He did not get on with his colleagues and was often depressed. When he was transferred to another village he was somewhat happier, for one of the teachers, Rudolf Koder, was a talented pianist. The two of them devoted many afternoons to music, Wittgenstein playing the clarinet or whistling. He remained a schoolteacher until 1926. In 1924 he prepared a dictionary of six to seven thousand words for the use of pupils in the elementary schools of the Austrian villages; this small book was published in 1926.

When his father died, in 1913, Wittgenstein inherited a large fortune. In the summer of the following year he wrote to Ludwig von Ficker, editor of the literary review *Der Brenner,* proposing to send a large sum of money to be distributed among needy Austrian poets and artists. The poets Rainer Maria Rilke and Georg Trakl received sizable gifts of money from this anonymous source. Upon his return to civilian life after the war, Wittgenstein gave his fortune to two of his sisters. Part of the reason for this action was that he did not want to have friends for the sake of his money, but undoubtedly it was largely due to his inclination toward a simple and frugal life.

During his years as a teacher, until Frank Ramsey visited him in 1923, Wittgenstein probably gave no thought to philosophy. Ramsey, a brilliant young mathematician and philosopher at Cambridge, had just completed a review of the *Tractatus* and was eager to discuss the book with its author. He found Wittgenstein living in extreme simplicity in a small village. In explaining his book, to which he was willing to devote several hours a day for a fortnight or more, Wittgenstein would become very excited. He told Ramsey, however, that he would do no further work in philosophy because his mind was "no longer flexible." He believed that no one would understand the *Tractatus* merely by reading it but that some day some person would, independently, think those same thoughts and would derive pleasure from finding their exact expression in Wittgenstein's book.

After his resignation as a schoolteacher in 1926, Wittgenstein inquired at a monastery about the possibility of entering upon monastic life, but he was discouraged by the father superior. In the summer of that year he worked as a gardener's assistant with the monks at Hütteldorf, near Vienna. Meanwhile, one of his sisters had commissioned the architect Paul Engelmann to build a mansion for her in Vienna. Engelmann, a friend of Wittgenstein's, proposed to him that they undertake it jointly. Wittgenstein agreed and actually became the directing mind in the project, which occupied him for two years. The building has been described by G. H. von Wright as "characteristic of its creator. It is free from all decoration and marked by a severe exactitude in measure and proportion. Its beauty is of the same simple and static kind that belongs to the sentences of the *Tractatus.*" During the same period Wittgenstein did some work in sculpture.

Moritz Schlick, a professor in Vienna, had been deeply impressed by the *Tractatus.* He managed to establish contact with Wittgenstein and apparently prevailed upon him to attend one or two meetings of the group founded by Schlick, known as the Vienna circle. Subsequently Schlick and Friedrich Waismann paid visits to Wittgenstein, in which he expounded some ideas that were passed on to other members of the circle.

In January 1929 he returned to Cambridge to devote himself again to philosophy. What produced this renewal of interest is unknown, but it is said that it was provoked by a lecture he heard L. E. J. Brouwer give in Vienna in 1928 on the foundations of mathematics. Wittgenstein found he would be eligible to receive the Ph.D. degree from Cambridge if he submitted a dissertation, whereupon he submitted the *Tractatus*. Russell and G. E. Moore were appointed to give him an oral examination, which they did in June 1929. Moore found the occasion "both pleasant and amusing." Trinity College granted Wittgenstein a research fellowship. At this time he published a short paper, "Some Remarks on Logical Form," which he soon came to think was weak and confused. This paper and the *Tractatus* were the sole philosophical writings of his that were published in his lifetime.

Wittgenstein began to give lectures in January 1930. He remained at Cambridge until the summer of 1936, when he went to live for a year in his hut in Norway and to begin writing the *Philosophical Investigations*. In 1937 he returned to Cambridge and two years later succeeded Moore to the chair of philosophy.

Wittgenstein's lectures made a powerful impression on his auditors. They were given without notes or preparation. Each lecture was new philosophical work. Wittgenstein's ideas did not come easily. He carried on a visible struggle with his thoughts. At times there were long silences, during which his gaze was concentrated, his face intensely alive, and his expression stern, and his hands made arresting movements. His hearers knew that they were in the presence of extreme seriousness, absorption, and force of intellect. When he spoke his words did not come fluently, but they came with force and conviction. His face was remarkably mobile and expressive when he talked. His eyes were often fierce, and his whole personality was commanding. His lectures moved over a wide range of topics and were marked by great richness of illustration and comparison. Wittgenstein attacked philosophical problems energetically, even passionately. Unlike many other philosophers, who really want to retain the problems rather than to solve them, Wittgenstein's desire was to clear them up, to get rid of them. He exclaimed to a friend: "My father was a business man and I am a business man too!" He wanted his philosophical work to be businesslike, to settle things.

When he was not working at philosophy Wittgenstein could sometimes, with a friend, put on a charming mood of mock seriousness in which he said nonsensical things with utmost gravity. These lighthearted moments were, however, comparatively infrequent. Most commonly his thoughts were somber. He was dismayed by the insincerity, vanity, and coldness of the human heart. He was always troubled about his own life and was often close to despair. Human kindness and human concern were for him more important attributes in a person than intellectual power or cultivated taste. He had an acute need for friendship, and his generosity as a friend was striking. At the same time it was not easy to maintain a friendly relationship with him, for he was easily angered and inclined to be censorious, suspicious, and demanding.

In World War II Wittgenstein found it impossible to remain a spectator. He obtained a porter's job at Guy's Hospital in London and worked there from November 1941 to April 1943. He was then transferred to the Royal Victoria Infirmary in Newcastle, where he served as a "lab boy" in the Clinical Research Laboratory until the spring of 1944. He impressed the doctors for whom he worked by the prolonged and concentrated thought he gave to their medical problems. This hard thinking would often result in a new way of looking at the problems. At Newcastle, Wittgenstein devised a simple technique for estimating the area of war wounds that proved of value in determining their treatment.

In 1944 he resumed his lectures at Cambridge. But he became increasingly dissatisfied with his role as a teacher. He feared that his influence was positively harmful. He was disgusted by what he observed of the half understanding of his ideas. "The only seed I am likely to sow is a jargon," he said. He strongly disliked universities and academic life. He felt an increasing need to live alone, perhaps occasionally seeing a friend, and to devote his remaining energies (for several years he had been repeatedly unwell) to finishing the *Investigations*.

In the fall of 1947 he finally resigned his chair. He sought a secluded life, first in the Irish countryside near Dublin, then in an isolated cottage on the west coast of Ireland. He worked hard when his health permitted it. In the summer of 1949 he went to spend three months with a friend in the United States. Upon his return to England, in the fall, he was discovered to have cancer. He wrote that he was not shocked by this news because he had no wish to continue living. During part of 1950 he visited his family in Vienna, then went to Oxford to live with a friend, and afterward made a trip to Norway. In 1951 he moved to the home of his physician in Cambridge. Wittgenstein had expressed an aversion to spending his last days in a hospital, and his doctor had invited him to come to his own home to die. Wittgenstein was deeply grateful for this offer. Knowing that death was imminent, he continued hard at work. The philosophical thoughts that he wrote in his notebooks at this time are of the highest quality.

On April 27 he was taken violently ill. When his doctor informed him that the end had come he said, "Good!" His last words, before he lost consciousness, were "Tell them I've had a wonderful life!" He died on April 29, 1951.

THE "TRACTATUS"

The *Tractatus* is a comprehensive work of extreme originality, yet it is less than eighty pages long. It is arranged as a series of remarks numbered in decimal notation. The following propositions are distinguished by their numbering as the primary theses of the book:

(1) The world is everything that is the case.

(2) What is the case, the fact, is the existence of states of affairs.

(3) A logical picture of facts is a thought.

(4) A thought is a sentence with a sense.

(5) A sentence is a truth-function of elementary sentences.

(6) The general form of a truth-function is $[\bar{p},\bar{\xi},N(\bar{\xi})]$.

(7) Whereof one cannot speak, thereof one must be silent.

Erik Stenius has perceptively remarked that the book has a "musical" structure and that the numbering brings out a "rhythm of emphasis": these seven main propositions are "forte" places in the rhythm.

The picture theory. In a notebook Wittgenstein wrote (*Notebooks*, p. 39): "My *whole* task consists in explaining the nature of sentences." (The German *Satz* will be translated sometimes as "sentence," sometimes as "proposition.") What makes it possible for a combination of words to represent a fact in the world? How is it that by producing a sentence I can *say* something—can *tell* someone that so-and-so is the case?

Wittgenstein's explanation consists in the striking idea that a sentence is a *picture*. He meant that it is *literally* a picture, not merely *like* a picture in certain respects. Apparently this thought first occurred to him during the war, when he saw in a magazine an account of how a motorcar accident was represented in a law court by means of small models (see *Notebooks*, p. 7). So he said: "A proposition is a picture of reality. A proposition is a model of reality as we think it to be" (*Tractatus*, 4.01). The dolls and toy cars could be manipulated so as to depict different ways in which the accident might have taken place. They could be used to construct different propositions about the accident—to put forward different accounts, different models of what took place. Wittgenstein's general conception was that when we put a sentence together we construct a model of reality. "In a proposition a situation is, as it were, put together experimentally" (4.031).

One would not normally think that a sentence printed on a page is a picture. According to the *Tractatus* it really is a picture, in the ordinary sense, of what it represents. Wittgenstein conceived the proof of this to be that although words we have not previously encountered have to be explained to us, when we meet for the first time a sentence that is composed of familiar words, we understand the sentence without *further* explanation. "I understand a sentence without having had its sense explained to me" (4.021). This can appear to one as a remarkable fact. If it is a fact, the only possible explanation would be that a sentence *shows* its sense. It shows how things are if it is true (4.022). This is exactly what a picture does. A sentence composed of old words is able to communicate a new state of affairs by virtue of being a picture of it.

In any picture, according to the *Tractatus*, there has to be a one-to-one correspondence between the elements of a picture and the things in the state of affairs its represents. If one element of a picture stands for a man and another for a cow, then the relationship between the picture elements might show that the man is milking the cow. A picture is a *fact*, namely the fact that the picture elements are related to one another in a definite way. A picture fact shows that the things the picture elements stand for are related in the *same* way as the picture elements.

Since a sentence is held to be a picture, there must be as many elements to be distinguished in it as in the state of affairs it portrays. The two must have the same logical or mathematical multiplicity. Again, this does not *seem* to be true of our ordinary sentences. For Wittgenstein this meant not that it is not true but that our sentences possess a concealed complexity that can be exhibited by analysis.

According to the *Tractatus* a picture must have something *in common* with what it pictures. This common thing is the picture's "form of representation." There are different kinds of pictures, different pictorial notations, different methods of projection. But all pictures must have in common with reality the same logical form in order to be able to picture reality at all, either truly or falsely. This logical form, also called "the form of reality," is defined as the possibility that things in the world are related as are the elements of the picture (2.18, 2.151). Sentences, since they are pictures, have the same form as the reality they depict.

What cannot be said. A picture can depict reality, but it cannot depict its own form of representation. It depicts (represents) its subject from "outside," but it cannot get outside itself to depict its own form of representation. A picture of another form might depict the representational form of a given picture; for instance, a picture in sound might depict the representational form of a picture in color. But in order for the one to represent the form of the other, there must be something that is the same in both. "There must be something identical in a picture and what it depicts, to enable the one to be a picture of the other at all" (2.161). Therefore, *logical* form, the form of reality, which *all* pictures must possess, cannot be depicted by any picture.

This consideration must apply to sentences, too. We make assertions by means of sentences. With a sentence we say something. We say how things are. Things in the world are related in a certain way, and we try to describe that. But we cannot describe how our sentences succeed in representing reality, truly or falsely. We cannot say what the form of representation is that is common to all sentences and that makes them pictures of reality. We cannot say how language represents the world. We cannot state in any sentence the pictorial form of all sentences. "What can be said can only be said by means of a sentence, and so nothing that is necessary for the understanding of *all* sentences can be said" (*Notebooks*, p. 25).

This doctrine implies that in a sense one cannot say what the meaning of a sentence is. With regard to the sentence "*a* is larger than *b*," one can explain to a person what "*a*" and "*b*" each refer to and what "larger" means, but there is not a further explanation to give him, namely what "*a* is larger than *b*" means. We understand the elements of a sentence, and we see how they are combined. But we cannot say what this combination means. Yet we *grasp* its meaning. In some sense we know what it means, because the sentence *shows* its meaning. Anything that can be said can be said clearly, but not everything that is understood can be said. In a letter to Russell, Wittgenstein remarked that his "main contention" was this distinction between what can be said in propositions—i.e., in language—and what cannot be said but can only be shown. This, he said, was "the cardinal problem of philosophy."

The nature of thought. The picture theory of propositions is at the same time an account of the nature of thought. Wittgenstein said: "A thought is a sentence with a sense" (*Tractatus,* 4). This implies that thinking is impossible without language. Since a thought is a sentence and a sentence is a picture, a thought is a picture. The totality of true thoughts would be a true picture of the world.

The view that a thought is a sentence seems to imply that the words of a sentence could be the constituents of a thought. But in a letter written to Russell shortly after the *Tractatus* was completed, Wittgenstein explicitly denied this. A thought consists not of words "but of psychical constituents that have the same sort of relation to reality as words. What those constituents are I don't know." "I don't know *what* the constituents of a thought are but I know *that* it must have such constituents which correspond to the words of Language" (*Notebooks,* pp. 130, 129). It would appear from these remarks that Wittgenstein's view was not that a thought and a sentence with a sense are one and the same thing but that they are two things with corresponding constituents of different natures. Each of these two things is a picture. "Thinking is a kind of language. For a thought too is, of course, a logical picture of a sentence, and therefore it just is a kind of sentence" (*Notebooks,* p. 82).

To say that a state of affairs is conceivable (thinkable) means that we can make a picture of it (*Tractatus,* 3.001). A thought "contains" the possibility of a state of affairs, for the logical form of the thought is the possibility that things in the world are combined in the way the constituents of the thought are combined. Whatever is conceivable is possible. In a spoken or written sentence a thought is "made perceptible to the senses." All thoughts can be stated in sentences; what cannot be stated cannot be thought.

A consequence of these views is that the form of representation of propositions (the form of reality, logical form), which cannot be stated, also cannot be thought. Language *shows* us something we cannot *think.* A function of philosophy is to indicate (*bedeuten*) what cannot be said (or thought) by presenting clearly what can be said. According to the *Tractatus,* therefore, there is a realm of the unthinkable which, far from being a mere wind egg, is the foundation of all language and all thought. In some way we *grasp* this foundation of thought (what we do here cannot really be said); it is mirrored *in* our thoughts, but it cannot be an object of thought.

Obviously the *Tractatus* is a thoroughly metaphysical work; this is not a minor tendency of the book. Yet it was once widely regarded as being antimetaphysical in its outlook. There is some excuse for this interpretation, since at the end of the book Wittgenstein said that the correct philosophical method would be to prove to anyone who wants to say something metaphysical that he has failed to give a meaning to certain signs in his sentences (6.53). But Wittgenstein did not reject the metaphysical; rather, he rejected the possibility of *stating* the metaphysical.

Names and objects. The conception of propositions, and therefore of language, in the *Tractatus* rests on the notion of a *name.* This is defined as a "simple sign" employed in a sentence. A simple sign is not composed of other signs,

as, for example, the phrase "the king of Sweden" is. The word "John" would satisfy this requirement of a simple sign. But a further requirement of a *name* is that it should stand for a simple thing, which is called an "object." According to the *Tractatus* the object for which a name stands *is the meaning* of the name (3.203). It is easy to determine whether a sign is composed of other signs but not whether it stands for something *simple.*

Wittgenstein conceived of objects as *absolutely* simple and not merely as simple relative to some system of notation. "Objects make up the substance of the world. That is why they cannot be composite. . . . Substance is what exists independently of what is the case. . . . Objects are identical with the fixed, the existent. . . . The configuration of objects is the changing, the mutable" (2.021, 2.024, 2.027, 2.0271).

A name is not a picture of the object it stands for, and therefore a name does not *say* anything. A picture in language—i.e., the sentence—can be formed only by a combination of names. This combination pictures a configuration of objects. The combination of names is like a *tableau vivant* (4.0311). (One might think here, for example, of a group of people posed to represent *The Last Supper*). A name is a *substitute* for an object, and a combination of names portrays a configuration of objects—i.e., a state of affairs (*Sachverhalt*).

A reader of the *Tractatus* will be perplexed to know what examples of *names* and of *objects* would be. No examples are given. It is said that names occur only in "elementary" propositions, but there are no examples of the latter notion. Wittgenstein was not able to come to any conclusion about examples. The *Notebooks* show that he was very vexed by this problem. He struggled with the question of whether "points of the visual field" might be simples (see, for example, p. 45). Sometimes he wondered whether any *ordinary* name whatsoever might not be a "genuine" name. And he wondered whether his *watch* might not be a "simple object" (*Notebooks,* pp. 60–61). His final conviction that there are absolutely simple objects was purely a priori. He wrote in his notes:

> It seems that the idea of the *simple* is already to be found contained in that of the complex and in the idea of analysis, and in such a way that we come to this idea quite apart from any examples of simple objects, or of propositions which mention them, and we realize the existence of the simple object—*a priori*—as a logical necessity. (*Notebooks,* p. 60)

The "logical necessity" arises from the requirement that propositions have a *definite* sense. "The demand for simple things *is* the demand for definiteness of sense" (*Notebooks,* p. 63). As it is put in the *Tractatus,* "The requirement that simple signs be possible is the requirement that sense be definite" (3.23). An indefinite sense would be no sense at all. A proposition might be ambiguous, but the ambiguity would be between definite alternatives: either *this* or *that.*

The sentences of everyday language are in perfect logical order. This order rests on the simples—that which is fixed, unchangeable, *hard* (*das Harte: Notebooks,* p. 63).

The simples and their configurations—that is what order *is*. Wittgenstein said: "Our problems are not abstract, but perhaps the most concrete that there are" (*Tractatus*, 5.5563).

Elementary propositions. A combination of genuine names is an elementary proposition. It is not analyzable into other propositions. "It is obvious that the analysis of propositions must bring us to elementary propositions which consist of names in immediate combination" (4.221). An elementary proposition shows (represents) a certain configuration of simple objects.

The picture theory is meant to hold for *all* genuine propositions, not merely for elementary propositions. Wittgenstein said without qualification: "A proposition is a picture of reality" (4.01, 4.021). Elementary and nonelementary propositions are equally pictures: the difference is that in an elementary proposition the pictorial nature is manifest. "It is *evident* that we perceive (*empfinden*) an elementary proposition as the picture of a state of affairs" (*Notebooks*, p. 25). But Wittgenstein admitted that most sentences do not *seem* to be pictures.

> At first sight a sentence—one set out on the printed page, for example—does not seem to be a picture of the reality with which it is concerned. But no more does musical notation at first sight seem to be a picture of music, nor our phonetic notation (letters) to be a picture of our speech. And yet these sign-languages prove to be pictures, even in the ordinary sense, of what they represent. (*Tractatus*, 4.011)

All genuine propositions, according to the *Tractatus*, are analyzable into elementary propositions. This analysis of our ordinary propositions, with their complicated modes of symbolizing—their various "methods of projection"—will make manifest their concealed pictorial nature. In his introduction to the *Tractatus*, written for the first English edition, Russell said:

> Mr. Wittgenstein is concerned with the conditions for a logically perfect language—not that any language is logically perfect, or that we believe ourselves capable, here and now, of constructing a logically perfect language, but that the whole function of language is to have meaning, and it only fulfils this function in proportion as it approaches to the ideal language which we postulate.

That this is an incorrect account of the *Tractatus* is sufficiently shown by Wittgenstein's remark "All the propositions of our everyday language are actually in perfect logical order, just as they are" (5.5563). The analysis achieved by the philosophical logician will not create order where previously there was no order; instead, it will make evident what is already there.

Every genuine proposition has one and only one complete analysis into elementary propositions (3.25). This is so even if every fact consists of infinitely many states of affairs and every state of affairs is composed of infinitely many simple objects (4.2211). The completely analyzed proposition will consist of simple names; the meaning of each simple name will be a simple object; the particular way in which the names are combined in the proposition will *say* that the simple objects in the world are related in the same way. To understand the completely analyzed proposition one need only understand the names—i.e., know what objects they stand for. What their combination means will be immediately evident. Understanding a proposition requires *merely* understanding its constituents (4.024).

As Rush Rhees has remarked, the idea that there are elementary propositions is not an arbitrary assumption. Wittgenstein was trying to solve the question of how language and thought can be related to reality. His basic intuition was that language pictures reality. If this is so, then among the sentences of language there must be some that *show their sense immediately*, which, of course, does not mean that their truth is self-evident. Wittgenstein had no criteria for identifying elementary propositions and could give no general account of their subject matter. But if his intuition was right, then there must be elementary propositions—that is, propositions which show their sense immediately and of which all other propositions are "truth-functions." If this were not so, no sentence could say anything or be understood (Rush Rhees, "The *Tractatus:* Seeds of Some Misunderstandings," pp. 218–219).

Theory of truth-functions. A truth-function of a single proposition p is a proposition whose truth or falsity is uniquely determined by the truth or falsity of p; for example, *not-p* (p is false) is a truth-function of p. A truth-function of two propositions p, q is a proposition whose truth or falsity is uniquely determined by the truth or falsity of p, q; for instance, "p, q are both true" is a truth-function of p, q. According to the *Tractatus* (5) every genuine proposition is a truth-function of elementary propositions. (It is an interesting and difficult question whether this doctrine follows from the picture theory or, on the other hand, is even compatible with it.) If two nonelementary propositions r and s are truth-functions of some of the same elementary propositions, then r and s will be internally related: for instance, one of them may logically follow from the other, or they may be contradictories or contraries of each other. If we see the internal structure of two propositions, we know what logical relations hold between them. We do not need, in addition, a knowledge of logical principles. We can actually do without the formal principles of logic, "for in a suitable notation we can recognize the formal properties of propositions by mere inspection of the propositions themselves" (6.122).

Wittgenstein employed a technique (known as the method of truth tables) for making manifest the truth conditions of a proposition that is a truth-function of other propositions—that is, for exhibiting the relation between the truth or falsity of the latter and the truth or falsity of the former.

There are two limiting cases among the possible groupings of truth conditions of propositions. One case would be when a proposition was true for all truth possibilities of the elementary propositions; this proposition is called a *tautology*. The other would be when a proposition was false for all the truth possibilities; this proposition is called a *contradiction*. Although it is convenient to refer to tautologies and contradictions as "propositions," they are actually degenerate cases, not genuine propositions. They are not pictures of reality. They do not determine reality in any way. They have no truth conditions, since a tautology is *unconditionally* true and a contradiction *unconditionally* false. Wittgenstein compared a genuine proposition, a picture, to "a solid body that restricts the freedom of movement of others." In contrast a tautology (for example, "He is here, or he is not here") "leaves open to reality the whole of logical space." No restriction is imposed on anything. A contradiction (for example, "He is here, and he is not here") "fills the whole of logical space and leaves no point of it for reality" (4.461, 4.462, 4.463).

According to the *Tractatus* the so-called propositions of logic, logical truths, principles of logic are all tautologies. They express no thoughts. They say nothing. We could do without them. But they are not nonsense, for the fact that a certain combination of propositions yields a tautology reveals something about the structures of the constituent propositions. "That the propositions of logic are tautologies *shows* the formal—logical—properties of language, of the world" (6.12).

Necessity. Wittgenstein's picture theory and his explanation of logical truth lead to an interesting doctrine of necessity and also to a denial of any knowledge of the future. Genuine propositions say only how things are, not how things must be. The only necessity there can be is embodied in tautologies (and the equations of mathematics). Neither tautologies nor equations say anything about the world. Therefore, there is no necessity in the world. "Outside of logic everything is accidental" (6.3). One proposition can be inferred from another proposition only if there is an internal, structural connection between them. The existence of one state of affairs cannot be inferred from the existence of another, entirely different, state of affairs (5.135). But that is what an inference to a *future* state of affairs would have to be. Thus Wittgenstein declared that we do not *know* whether the sun will rise tomorrow (6.36311).

Will and action. If we conceive of an act of will (a volition) as one occurrence and the transpiring of what is willed as an entirely different occurrence, it follows from the foregoing doctrines that there can be, at most, a merely accidental correlation between one's will and what happens in the world. I cannot *make* anything happen—not even a movement of my body. "The world is independent of my will" (6.373). In his notes Wittgenstein gave this idea dramatic expression: "I cannot bend the happenings of the world to my will: I am completely powerless" (*Notebooks*, p. 73).

Ethics. According to the picture theory a proposition and its negation are both possible; which one is true is accidental. Wittgenstein drew the conclusion that there can be no propositions of ethics. His thought here was that if anything has value, this fact cannot be accidental: the thing *must* have that value. But everything in the world is accidental. Therefore there is no value in the world. "In the world everything is as it is, and everything happens as it does happen: *in* it no value exists—and if it did, it would have no value" (*Tractatus*, 6.41).

This view is an absolute denial not of the existence of value but of its existence *in the world*. Propositions can state only what is in the world. What belongs to ethics cannot be stated; it is "transcendental" (6.421). The world, and what is in the world, is neither good nor evil. Good and evil exist only in relation to the subject (the ego). But this "subject" to which Wittgenstein referred is also "transcendental." It is not in the world but is a "limit" of the world (5.5632).

The mystical. In the view of the *Tractatus* there are a variety of things that cannot be stated: the form of representation of propositions, the existence of the simple objects that constitute the substance of the world, the existence of a metaphysical subject, of good and evil—these things are all unsayable. Wittgenstein seems to have believed that we have thoughts on these matters only when we view the world as a *limited whole*. This latter experience is what he called "the mystical" (6.45).

Although one cannot *say* anything on these metaphysical topics included in the mystical, this is not because they are absurd but because they lie beyond the reach of language. "Unsayable things do indeed exist" (*Es gibt allerdings Unaussprechliches:* 6.522). This itself is something unsayable. It is one of those sentences of his own of which Wittgenstein declared that although they can produce philosophical insight, they are actually nonsensical and eventually must be "thrown away" (6.54). The final proposition of the book ("Whereof one cannot speak, thereof one must be silent") is not the truism one might take it to be, for it means that there *is* a realm about which one can say nothing.

The "Tractatus" and logical positivism. The *Tractatus* exerted a considerable influence on the so-called Vienna circle of logical positivism. Moritz Schlick, the leader of this movement, declared that the *Tractatus* had brought modern philosophy to a "decisive turning point." It is true that there is some agreement between the predominant views of the Vienna circle and the positions of the *Tractatus*—for example, that all genuine propositions are truth-functions of elementary propositions, that logical truths are tautologies and say nothing, and that philosophy can contain no body of doctrine but is an activity of clarifying thoughts.

But there are fundamental differences. The Vienna circle did not adopt the picture theory of propositions, which is the central idea of the *Tractatus*. A conspicuous doctrine of the circle was that all genuine propositions are reducible to propositions that report "direct perception" or what is "immediately given in experience." This doctrine is not found in the *Tractatus*. A corollary to it is the famous positivist thesis "The meaning of a statement is its method of verification." But the topic of verification is not even brought into the *Tractatus*. The only proposition there that seems to resemble this thesis is the following: "To understand a proposition means to know what is the case if it is true" (4.024). Even here nothing is explicitly said about verification, and a comment immediately following this remark shows that Wittgenstein was not thinking about verification. A proposition, he said, "is understood by anyone who understands its constituents." That is to say, if you understand the words in a sentence, you thereby understand the sentence. There is no mention of a requirement that you must know how to verify what it says.

As previously noted, Wittgenstein was tempted by the suggestion that "points in the visual field" are examples of the simples out of which all meaning is composed. But the final view of the *Tractatus* is that the simples are fixed, immutable things, which exist "independently of what is the case." If so, they cannot be described by propositions and cannot be *given in experience*. The *Tractatus* does not contain, therefore, an empiricist theory of meaning. What it holds is that to understand any sentence one must know the references of the names that compose it; that is all. When you understand a sentence you know how reality is constituted if the sentence is true, regardless of whether you know how to verify what it says. The picture theory is not a verification theory of meaning. It is ironical that the role of *verification* in meaning and understanding receives much attention in Wittgenstein's later philosophy, which obviously is not positivistic, but none at all in the reputedly positivistic *Tractatus*.

Logical positivism and the author of the *Tractatus* were both opposed to metaphysics, but in different ways. For positivism there is nothing at all behind metaphysical propositions except possibly their authors' emotions. "Metaphysicians are musicians without musical ability," said Rudolf Carnap. In the view of the *Tractatus* one may gain insights into the presuppositions and limits of language, thought, and reality. These metaphysical insights cannot be stated in language, but *if* they could be, they would be true insights and not mere muddles or expressions of feeling.

The foregoing sketch of the *Tractatus* has omitted many of its important topics. Wittgenstein wrote in his notes, "My work has extended from the foundations of logic to the nature of the world." In his preface to the *Tractatus* he expressed the opinion that he had obtained the final solution of the problems treated in the book, but he added that one value of his work is that "it shows how little is achieved when these problems are solved."

THE "NEW" PHILOSOPHY

In 1929, Wittgenstein returned to Cambridge, after an absence of more than fifteen years, to resume philosophical research and to lecture. From then until his death he did a huge amount of writing. Among the first works of this period were two large typescript volumes. One, which was composed in the period 1929–1930, has been published under the title *Philosophische Bemerkungen*. The other is a systematic work of nearly 800 typewritten pages written between 1930 and 1932. In both of these volumes Wittgenstein re-examined the problems of the *Tractatus* and revised what he had written there. This led him to questions he had not previously considered. Perhaps it can be said that he found that the logical investigations of the *Tractatus* and its supreme problem of the relation of language to reality had drawn him more and more into questions in the philosophy of psychology. These volumes seem to show that the change from the *Tractatus* to the *Philosophical Investigations* was an intensive but continuous development rather than a sudden revolution.

In 1933–1934, Wittgenstein dictated to his students a set of notes that came to be called the *Blue Book*, and in 1934–1935 he dictated another set, later known as the *Brown Book*. (Although Wittgenstein always wrote in German, the *Blue Book* and the *Brown Book* were dictated in English.) Both circulated widely in typescript, and Wittgenstein's new ideas began to create a stir. The *Blue Book* is clear and lively and is perhaps the beginner's best introduction to Wittgenstein. Nevertheless, it is a comparatively superficial work; Wittgenstein never regarded it as more than a set of class notes. The *Brown Book*, on the other hand, he regarded for a short time as a draft of something that might be published. He worked at a revision but gave it up in 1936, when he began to write the *Philosophical Investigations*. Wittgenstein refrained from publishing the *Investigations* during his lifetime, but his explicit wish was that it be published posthumously, a wish that he probably did not have with respect to any of the rest of the voluminous work he produced between 1929 and 1951.

The *Philosophical Investigations* was published in 1953 in two parts. Part I was written in the period 1936–1945 and Part II between 1947 and 1949. Concurrently with the *Investigations*, Wittgenstein did other writing, which was closely related to the topics of the *Investigations* or even overlapped it. From the years 1937–1944 there are extensive manuscripts on the philosophy of logic and mathematics. *Remarks on the Foundations of Mathematics*, published in 1956, consists of selections, made by the editors, from this material. A quantity of writing in the form of loose notes, probably from the years 1947–1949, is of the same subject matter and quality as the latter part of Part I of the *Investigations*. Wittgenstein's last manuscript notebooks, from the years 1949–1951, treating questions about belief, doubt, knowledge, and certainty, also contain much material that should eventually be published.

"PHILOSOPHICAL INVESTIGATIONS"

Wittgenstein believed that the *Investigations* could be better understood if one saw it against the background of the *Tractatus*. A considerable part of the *Investigations* is an attack, either explicit or implicit, on the earlier work. This development is probably unique in the history of philosophy—a thinker producing, at different periods of his life, two highly original systems of thought, each system the result of many years of intensive labors, each expressed in an elegant and powerful style, each greatly influencing contemporary philosophy, and the second being a criticism and rejection of the first.

Apparently it is possible for a serious student of Wittgenstein to form the impression that "the *Investigations* basically contains an application of the main ideas of the *Tractatus* to several concrete problems, the only difference being the use of language-games instead of the language of the natural sciences which formed the theoretical background of the *Tractatus*." This view is thoroughly mistaken, as will be seen.

The whole of language. It is held in the *Tractatus* that any proposition presupposes the whole of language. "If objects are given, then at the same time we are given *all* objects. If elementary propositions are given, then at the same time *all* elementary propositions are given" (5.524). "If all objects are given, then at the same time all *possible* states of affairs are also given" (2.0124). An elementary proposition is a combination of names, and in order to understand the proposition one must in some sense "know" the objects for which the names stand. In understanding any proposition at all one must know some objects, and therefore, as stated, one must know all objects and all possibilities. Any proposition whatsoever carries with it the whole of "logical space." This view is connected with the idea that there is an *essence* of propositions. The essence of propositions is "the essence of all description, and thus the essence of the world" (5.4711). The essence of propositions is the same as "the universal form of proposition" (*Die allgemeine Satzform*). That there is a universal form of proposition is proved by the fact that all possibilities—i.e., all forms of proposition—"must be *foreseeable*" (*Notebooks*, p. 89; *Tractatus*, 4.5).

The *Investigations* emphatically rejects the idea that each proposition carries with it the whole of language. A sentence does presuppose a "language game," but a language game will be only a small segment of the whole of language. An example of a language game is the following, which appears at the beginning of the *Investigations* (Sec. 2): There are a builder and his helper. The building materials are blocks, pillars, slabs, and beams. The two men have a language consisting of the words "block," "pillar," "slab," "beam." The builder calls out one of the words and the helper brings the building material that he has learned to bring at that call. Wittgenstein called the words and the actions with which they are joined a language game (*Sprachspiel*). He said that it is *complete in itself* and could even be conceived to be the entire language of a tribe. If we think it is incomplete we are only comparing it with our more complex language. In the *Brown Book* there is the analogy of someone's describing chess without mentioning pawns. As a description of chess it is incomplete, yet we can also say that it is a complete description of a simpler game (*Blue and Brown Books*, p. 77). This simpler game does not presuppose chess, nor does the part played, for example, by the word "block" in the game of Sec. 2 imply its use in descriptions or questions.

According to the *Tractatus* every form of proposition can be anticipated because a new form of proposition would represent a new combination of simple objects in logical space. It would be like grouping the pieces on a chessboard in a new way. It would be a different arrangement of what you already have. But in Wittgenstein's later philosophy a new language game would embody a new "form of life," and this would not merely be a rearrangement of what was there before. Suppose the people of a certain tribe use language to describe events that are occurring or have occurred (such as men walking, running, or fighting, or the weather), or that they believe have occurred, but they do not have any *imaginative* use of language. They do not lie, pretend, make supposals, or engage in any imaginative play. Nor does any behavior of pretending occur: the children do not ever, for example, walk on all fours and growl as if they were lions. These people would not understand kidding. If one of us said to them something obviously false and then laughed, they would not know how to take it. (We should remember that among ourselves we differ greatly in our responsiveness to joking and pretense.) What

these people lack is not words but the behavior and reactions that enter into the language games of imagination. Are they capable of *foreseeing* a use of language to convey a play of imagination? They do not even understand it when they encounter it. A new use of language embedded in a new form of life could not be anticipated, any more than could the rise of nonobjective painting.

The essence of language. The *Tractatus* assumes that there is a universal form of language, just as it assumes (6.022) that there is a universal form of number—that which is common to all numbers. The *Investigations* rejects this assumption. There is nothing common to the various forms of language that makes them language. There is not something common to all language games, just as there is not something common to all *games*. We are asked to consider the various kinds of games there are (for example, board games, card games, ball games) and the variety within each kind. If we pick out a feature common to two games we shall find that it is absent from some other place in the spectrum of games. Not all games are amusing, not all involve winning or losing, not all require competition between players, and so on. What makes all of them games, what gives unity to those activities, is not some feature present in all games but a multitude of relationships "overlapping and criss-crossing." Wittgenstein employed the analogy of a family resemblance. One can often see a striking resemblance between several generations of the same family. Studying them at close hand one may find that there is no feature common to all of the family. The eyes or the build or the temperament are not always the same. The family resemblance is due to many features that "overlap and criss-cross." The unity of games is like a family resemblance. This is also the case with sentences, descriptions, and numbers.

> Why do we call something a "number": Well, perhaps because it has a—direct—relationship with several things that have hitherto been called number; and this can be said to give it an indirect relationship to other things we call the same name. And we extend our concept of number as in spinning a thread we twist fibre on fibre. And the strength of the thread does not reside in the fact that some one fibre runs through its whole length, but in the overlapping of the fibres. (Sec. 67)

One of the remarkable features of the *Investigations* is the detail and ingenuity of Wittgenstein's examination of some sample concepts (*reading, deriving, being guided*: Secs. 156–178) in order to bring out the variety of cases that fall under them and to prove that they are not united by an essence. If these concepts do not have an essential nature, then neither do the concepts of *description, proposition,* and *language*. The *Tractatus* was wrong in a most fundamental assumption.

Absolute simples. The *Tractatus* held that the ultimate elements of language are names that designate simple objects. In the *Investigations* it is argued that the words "simple" and "complex" have no *absolute* meaning. It has to be *laid down*, within a particular language game, what is to be taken as simple and what composite. For example, is one's visual image of a tree simple or composite? The question makes no sense until we make some such stipulation as that if one sees merely the trunk, it is simple, but if one sees trunk and branches, it is composite.

> But isn't a chess board, for instance, obviously, and absolutely composite?——You are probably thinking of the composition out of thirty-two white and thirty-two black squares. But could we not also say, for instance, that it was composed of the colours black and white and the schema of squares? And if there are quite different ways of looking at it, do you still want to say that the chessboard is absolutely "composite"? . . . Is the colour of a square on a chessboard simple, or does it consist of pure white and pure yellow? And is white simple, or does it consist of the colours of the rainbow?——Is this length of 2 cm. simple, or does it consist of two parts, each 1 cm. long? But why not of one bit 3 cm. long, and one bit 1 cm. long measured in the opposite direction?   (Sec. 47)

By such examples Wittgenstein tried to show that the ideas of "simple" and "complex" are necessarily relative to a language game. The notion of a simplicity that is not relative but absolute, because all of language is based on it, is a philosophical "super-concept." We have an image but we do not know how to apply it; we do not know what would be an example of an absolute simple.

In the *Tractatus* the existence of simple objects was conceived as following from the requirement that the sense of sentences be *definite*. In the *Investigations* this requirement is regarded as another philosophical illusion. We have imagined an "ideal" of language that will not satisfy actual needs. A sharp boundary has not been drawn between, for example, games and activities that are not games. But why *should* there be one *in general*? Precision and exactness are relative to some particular purpose. The guests are to arrive exactly at one o'clock, but *this* notion of exactness would not employ the instruments and measurements of an observatory. "No *single* ideal of exactness has been laid down; we do not know what we should be supposed to imagine under this head" (Sec. 88). Losing sight of the fact that there are different standards of exactness for different purposes, we have supposed that there is a certain state of complete exactness underneath the surface of our everyday speech and that logical analysis can bring it to light. We have supposed, therefore, that a proposition would have one and only one complete analysis.

In searching for the ideal of perfect exactness we become dissatisfied with ordinary words and sentences. We do not find in actual language the pure and clear-cut structure that we desire. The more closely we examine actual language, the sharper becomes the conflict between it and our philosophical ideal. The latter now begins to seem empty. We do not even understand how it could be realized in actual language. We have been bewitched by a *picture*. Instead of trying to perceive in our language a design too fine to grasp, we need to see more clearly what is really there. We should abandon preconceived ideas and hypotheses and turn to *description,* the purpose of which will be to remove our philosophical perplexities. The substitution of description for analysis, and the new conception that nothing is hidden, is a major change from the *Tractatus.*

Meaning as use. If the picture theory is the central feature of the *Tractatus,* it is important to see how Wittgenstein's new thinking judged that theory. Surprisingly, there is not much explicit discussion of it, and the remarks that do occur are usually enigmatic. But if we take a long view of the new philosophy, there can be no question that it rejects the picture theory. In the later work as well as the earlier, Wittgenstein was concerned with the question, How can a sentence say something; how can language represent reality? The first sentence of the *Blue Book* is "What is the meaning of a word?" and it might equally well have been "What is the meaning of a sentence?" Both philosophical systems are centered on the same question, but the answer given in the second is entirely different. Instead of holding that a sentence has meaning or sense because it is a picture, the *Investigations* says that the meaning of a sentence is its "use" (*Gebrauch*) or "employment" (*Verwendung*) or "application" (*Anwendung*).

Some readers of Wittgenstein have doubted that he spoke of the use of a *sentence,* and others have thought that in any case it is wrong to speak this way. There is no question on the first point. Wittgenstein spoke of the "use" of a sentence in many passages. For example: "But doesn't the fact that sentences have the same sense consist in their having the same *use?*" (*Investigations,* Sec. 20); there are "countless different kinds of use of what we call 'symbols,' 'words,' 'sentences'" (Sec. 23).

The other objection may be important. Some philosophers want to say that a *sentence* cannot have a use. Words have a use; we learn the use of words, not of sentences. We understand sentences without having their sense explained to us, because we understand the use of the words that compose them.

What is espoused here is really the ground of the picture theory of the *Tractatus* (cf. *Tractatus,* 4.021, 4.026, 4.027). In the *Investigations* there is more than one objection to the above argument. Wittgenstein denied that we always understand a sentence, even if it is a grammatically correct sentence whose words we do understand. If someone says, for example, that the sentence "This is here" (saying which, he points to an object in front of him) makes sense to him, "then he should ask himself in what special circumstances this sentence is actually used. There it does make sense" (Sec. 117). "A philosopher says that he understands the sentence 'I am here,' that he means something by it, thinks something—even when he doesn't think at all how, on what occasions, this sentence is used" (Sec. 514). Wittgenstein was saying that these sentences have sense only in special circumstances; in other circumstances we do not understand them—that is, we do not know what to *do* with them.

The view of the *Tractatus* is entirely different. An elementary sentence is a combination of names, and if we know what the names refer to, then we understand the sentence, for it *shows* its sense. "Circumstances" have nothing to do with it. The *Investigations* regards this view as absurd. What does the sentence "I am here" *show?* Certainly it does not show its *use.* What can it mean to say that it shows its sense? A significant sentence is a tool with which a certain job is done. By looking at a sentence you cannot always tell whether it is a tool and, if it is, what job it is used for. The *Investigations* denies the claim that was the basis of the picture theory, namely that "we understand the sense of a propositional sign without its having been explained to us" (*Tractatus*, 4.02).

In holding that (in many cases) the meaning of an expression is its use, Wittgenstein was not declaring that the words "meaning" and "use" are general synonyms. By the "use" of an expression he meant the special circumstances, the "surroundings," in which it is spoken or written. The use of an expression is the *language game* in which it plays a part. Some readers have arrived at the mistaken idea that by the "use" of an expression Wittgenstein meant its *ordinary* or its *correct* use: they have thought that he was an "ordinary-language philosopher." But Wittgenstein studied any use of language, real or imaginary, that may illuminate a philosophical problem. Often he *invented* language games that corresponded to no actual use of language (see, for example, *Blue and Brown Books,* pp. 103–104, 110). The language games are *"objects of comparison* which are meant to throw light on the facts of our language by way not only of similarities, but also of dissimilarities" (*Investigations*, Sec. 130).

The *Tractatus* holds that language is ultimately composed of names, that the meaning of a name is a simple object, and that the sense of a sentence arises from the names that compose it. One name stands for one thing, another for another thing, and the combination pictures a state of affairs (4.0311). Thus, naming is prior to the sense of sentences (although it is also said that a name has meaning only in a sentence: 3.3). A sentence says something because it is composed of names that stand for things. In the *Investigations* two objections are made against this notion of the priority of names. First, the meaning of a word is never the thing, if there is one, that corresponds to the word (Sec. 40). Second, before one can find out what a name stands for one must already have mastered the language game to which the name belongs. In order to learn the name of a color, a direction, a sensation, one must have some grasp of the activities of placing colors in an order, of reading a map, of responding to the words, gestures, and behavior that are expressions of sensation. Merely pointing at something and saying a word achieves nothing. The kind of use the word will have, the special circumstances in which it will be said, must be understood before it can even *be* a name.

One could say that the *Tractatus* conceives of a significant sentence as having the nature of a mechanism. If the parts fit, then the whole thing works: you have a picture of reality. If the parts do not fit, they are like cogwheels that do not mesh. There is, as it were, a clash of meanings. But in the *Investigations* we read: "When a sentence is called senseless, it is not as it were its sense that is senseless" (Sec. 500). If someone said to us, for example, "My head is asleep," we should be perplexed. It would be no help if he said: "You know what it is for an arm or a leg to be asleep. I have the same thing, except that it is my head." Here we do not know what the "same" *is.* It is not that we see that the meaning of "head" is incompatible with the meaning of "asleep." We do not perceive a clash of meanings. But we do not know what behavior and circumstances go with this sentence. It is not

that we see that it *cannot* have a use (because the words do not fit together). The fact is that it does not have a use: we do not know in what circumstances one should say it. "Look at the sentence as an instrument, and at its sense as its employment!" (Sec. 421). Instead of the fundamental notion being the right combination of words and the sense of the sentence being explained in terms of it, it is the other way round: whether the sentence has an "employment" (*Verwendung*) is what is fundamental. This would be our only criterion for whether there is a sense-making combination of parts.

One additional criticism of the picture theory will be noted. Suppose that a sentence were a picture. There would still be a question of how we should apply the picture. If someone showed you a drawing of a cube and told you to bring him one of those things, you might in good faith bring him a triangular prism instead of a cube. More than one way of taking the drawing was possible. It suggests a cube, but it is possible to interpret the drawing differently. A picture represents an old man walking up a steep path leaning on a stick. But could it not also represent him as sliding down the hill in that position? For us it is more natural to take it in the first way, but the explanation of this does not lie in anything intrinsic to the picture. A picture of a green leaf might be understood to be a representation of the color green, or of a specific shade of green, or of leaf shape in general, or of a particular shape of leaf, or of foliage in general, and so on. How a picture is used will determine what it is a picture of. It cannot, therefore, be a fundamental explanation of the sense of sentences to say that they are pictures. Wittgenstein hinted that the picture theory is plausible because we tend to think of portraits that hang on our walls and are, as it were, "idle." If we consider instead an engineer's machine drawing or an elevation with measurements, then the *activity* of using the picture will be seen to be the important thing (Sec. 291).

Logical compulsion. Our discussion may suggest the following view: How a word, sentence, or picture is *interpreted* determines what use is made of it. How a man responds to an order, for example, depends on how he *understands* it, and whether the one who gave the order will be satisfied with that response will depend on what he *meant* by it. If someone understands the algebraic formula determining a numerical series, then he will know what numbers should occur at various places in the expansion of the series. What a person deduces from a proposition will depend entirely on his understanding of the proposition. Wittgenstein once wrote (in a pre-*Tractatus* notebook): "What propositions follow from a proposition must be completely settled before that proposition can have a sense" (*Notebooks,* p. 64). By virtue of grasping the meaning or sense of an expression we know how to employ it: we know when to say it and what action it calls for. Instead of meaning being identical with use, it comes before use, and use is based on it. When you hear a sentence and understand it or give an order and mean it, the action required in responding to the sentence or obeying the order is already, in a queer sense, taken in your mind. In your act of meaning or understanding, "your mind as it were flew ahead and took all the steps" before they were taken physically (*Investigations*, Sec. 188). In taking, or accepting, those physical steps, you would be ratifying what has already transpired in your mind. To do differently would be inconsistent with the previous mental act. Consistency, rationality, requires you to take these steps or draw these conclusions. Understanding carries compulsion with it.

This idea of "logical compulsion" is vigorously attacked in the *Investigations* and in Wittgenstein's writings on the foundations of mathematics. Was Wittgenstein rejecting deductive reasoning and logical necessity? No. He was rejecting this *picture* of logical necessity, namely that when I have understood a proposition and there is a question of what follows from it, I *have* to deduce such-and-such consequences because it was already settled in my understanding of the proposition that it would have those consequences. Wittgenstein's criticism of this imagery creates a continuity between his philosophy of psychology and his philosophy of logic. A part of his criticism could be put as follows: Suppose that two people, *A* and *B*, have received the same instruction in elementary arithmetic. They have been given the same rules and illustrations and have worked through the same examples. Later, when they are required to perform some arithmetical operation, *A* does it right and *B* wrong, although *B* thinks he has done it correctly. We shall say that *A understood* the problem and *B* did not. What does this come to? It could have been that the *sole* difference between them was that *A wrote down* correct numbers and *B* incorrect ones. If this fact is our *criterion* of a difference of understanding, then it is wrong-headed to postulate a difference of understanding to *explain* the fact that *A* and *B* wrote down different answers.

The inclination to insert an act or state of understanding as an intermediary between, for example, hearing an order and executing it is an example of what is called in the *Brown Book* (*Blue and Brown Books*, p. 143) "a general disease of thinking." It consists in always looking for (and "finding") mental states and acts as the sources of our actions. Other examples of this inclination are thinking that one must know where one's pain is before one can point to the place, thinking that we call various shades of red by the name "red" because we see something in common in all of them, thinking that we speak of "looking in our memory for a word" and of "looking in the park for a friend" because we have noticed a similarity between the two cases.

The assumption of mental states to explain our actions comes from a "one-sided diet." If we let our view range over the family of cases of "differences of understanding," we shall discover some in which the only difference between two people who understood a certain proposition differently consists in their having drawn different conclusions from it.

Must we believe, then, that our understanding does not reach beyond the particular training we received and the examples we studied? No. There is a good sense in which it reaches beyond, for we do go on to apply rules in new cases in what we agree is the same way we were taught. Does this agreement have to be explained by the fact that our understanding has penetrated to the essence of the examples? No. This agreement is one of the "extremely general facts of nature" (*Investigations*, pp. 56, 230) that

underlie our concepts. We do handle new cases in the same way. If this strikes us as mysterious, it is a symptom of our confusion. We are trying to imagine that the future steps are taken in the mind, "in a queer sense," before they are taken in reality—as if the mind were a machine that already contained its future movements (*Investigations*, Secs. 193–195).

Wittgenstein was saying that our understanding of a rule is not a state that forces us to apply the rule in a particular way. Someone who has received the ordinary instruction in arithmetic or chess and has applied it normally in the past could go on in the future in a different way but *still be a rational person*. Perhaps he could even give a reasonable defense of his divergence.

If this is true, it makes it seem that there are no *rules*, for a rule forbids some things and requires others. It appears that anything goes, anything can be justified. But then understanding, meaning, language itself all crumble away because they imply rules.

Wittgenstein was not denying, however, that there are rules and that we follow them. He held that the way a rule is applied in particular cases *determines its meaning*. A rule, as it is formulated in a sentence, "hangs in the air" (*Investigations*, Sec. 198). What puts it on the ground, gives it content, is what we say and do in actual cases. And on this there is overwhelming agreement: we nearly always say and do the same. It is this agreement that determines whether a particular action is in accordance with a rule. Rather than to say that we agree *because* we follow rules, it is more perceptive to say that our agreement fixes the meaning of the rules, defines their content. In a sense the content of the rules grows as our practice grows. Instead of thinking of mankind as coerced by the rules of logic and mathematics, we should consider that human practice establishes what the rules are.

Private rules. The idea that the content of a rule can be fixed only by a practice provides a transition to one of the most subtle topics of the *Investigations*, namely the treatment of "private language." The conception that a significant sentence is a picture was replaced in Wittgenstein's thought by the conception that the sense of a sentence is determined by the circumstances in which it is uttered. Swinging a stick is a *strike* and pushing a piece of wood is a *move*—in the circumstances of games. Likewise, saying some words is *making a decision*—in certain circumstances. In one set of circumstances saying a particular sentence would be *asserting* something; in other circumstances saying those same words would be *asking* a question; in still others it would be *repeating* what someone had said.

This is a difficult conception to grasp. We feel a strong inclination to say that the only thing that determines the sense of what someone says is what goes on in his mind as he says it. As Locke put it, "Words, in their primary or immediate signification, stand for nothing but *the ideas in the mind of him that uses them*." Whether some words you uttered expressed a question or an assertion is solely a matter of whether there was a question or an assertion *in your mind*. What the occasion was, what happened before and after, what persons were present—those circumstances are irrelevant to the sense of your words. The only "circumstance" that matters is the mental occurrence at the time of utterance.

Wittgenstein fought hard and resourcefully against this objection. One technique he used was to describe different cases of deciding, asserting, intending, expecting, and so on. The purpose of this was to show that when one utters some words that express, for instance, a decision, one cannot pick out anything that occurred (for example, a thought, an image, some spoken words, a feeling) such that one wants to call *that* the act of deciding.

This technique, although powerful, may provoke the response that the only thing proved is the *intangibility,* the *indescribability,* of the mental phenomenon in question. William James remarked about the *intention of saying a thing* before one has said it: "It is an entirely definite intention, distinct from all other intentions, an absolutely distinct state of consciousness, therefore; and yet how much of it consists of definite sensorial images, either of words or of things? Hardly anything!" This intention has "a nature of its own of the most positive sort, and yet what can we say about it without using words that belong to the later mental facts that replace it? The intention *to-say-so-and-so* is the only name it can receive" (*Principles of Psychology,* New York, 1890, Vol. I, p. 253). Likewise, the decision *to stay an hour longer* cannot be expressed in any other words than those, yet it is a quite definite mental occurrence; one knows it is there!

Wittgenstein opposed this conception not with further description but with an argument. It is the following: If a decision or expectation or sensation were a state or event that was logically independent of circumstances, then no one, not even the subject of the supposed event, could ever determine that it had occurred. First, how would one learn what, for example, deciding is? Since circumstances are supposed to be irrelevant, one could not learn it by observing other people. Apparently one would have to learn what deciding is *from one's own case.* But as Wittgenstein remarked: "If I know it only from my own case, then I know only what *I* call that, not what anyone else does" (*Investigations,* Sec. 347). Thus it would be unverifiable whether two people refer to the same phenomenon by the word "deciding." But worse is to come. One could not even take comfort in the thought "At least I know what *I* call 'deciding.'" You might believe that you have always called the same thing by that name. Yet nothing could determine that this belief was right or wrong. Perhaps the private object constantly changes but you do not notice the change because your memory constantly deceives you (*Investigations,* p. 207)! The idea that you might have a language with logically private rules—i.e., rules that only you could understand because only you could know to what the words refer—is a self-contradictory idea. Following a rule implies *doing the same,* and what "the same" *is* can only be defined by a practice in which more than one person participates.

Wittgenstein's rejection of the intrinsically private, inner object is a consequence of his new conception of meaning. Language requires rules, and following a rule implies a customary way of doing something. It could not be that only once in the history of mankind was a rule followed (Sec. 199). An expression has a meaning only if there is a regular, a uniform, connection between saying the expression and certain circumstances. When we call something *measuring,* for example, a part of the uniformity we require is a constancy in the results of measurement (Sec. 242). A person can be *guided by a signpost* only if there is a regular way of responding to signposts. The meaning of an expression is its *use*—that is to say, the *language game* in which it occurs—that is to say, the uniform relation of the expression to certain *circumstances.* Wittgenstein made explicit the connection between this view of the nature of meaning and his attack on "private" mental contents when he said that following a rule is a *practice* and *therefore* one cannot follow a rule "privately" (Sec. 202).

Works by Wittgenstein

Tractatus Logico-philosophicus. London, 1922. Contains the German text of *Logisch-philosophische Abhandlung,* with English translation on facing pages, and an introduction by Bertrand Russell. Republished with a new translation by D. F. Pears and B. F. McGuinness. London, 1961.

"Some Remarks on Logical Form." *PAS,* Supp. Vol. 9 (1929), 162–171.

Philosophical Investigations, G. E. M. Anscombe, Rush Rhees, and G. H. von Wright, eds., translated by G. E. M. Anscombe. Oxford, 1953. Contains German text of *Philosophische Untersuchungen,* with English translation on facing pages.

Remarks on the Foundations of Mathematics, G. E. M. Anscombe, Rush Rhees, and G. H. von Wright, eds., translated by G. E. M. Anscombe. Oxford, 1956. Parallel German and English texts.

The Blue and Brown Books: Preliminary Studies for the Philosophical Investigations. Oxford, 1958. With a preface by Rush Rhees.

Notebooks 1914–1916, G. E. M. Anscombe and G. H. von Wright, eds., translated by G. E. M. Anscombe. Oxford, 1961. Parallel German and English texts.

Philosophische Bemerkungen. Frankfurt, 1964.

"A Lecture on Ethics." *Philosophical Review,* Vol. 74 (1965). A paper delivered at Cambridge in 1929 or 1930.

Works on Wittgenstein

BIOGRAPHY

Gasking, D. A. T., and Jackson, A. C., "Ludwig Wittgenstein," memorial notice. *Australasian Journal of Philosophy,* Vol. 29 (1951).

Malcolm, Norman, *Ludwig Wittgenstein: A Memoir.* London, 1958.

Russell, Bertrand, "Ludwig Wittgenstein," memorial notice. *Mind,* Vol. 60 (1951).

Ryle, Gilbert, "Ludwig Wittgenstein," memorial notice. *Analysis,* Vol. 12 (1951).

Von Wright, G. H., "Ludwig Wittgenstein: A Biographical Sketch," Malcolm, *op. cit.*

Wisdom, John, "Ludwig Wittgenstein, 1934–1937." *Mind,* Vol. 61 (1952).

"TRACTATUS"

Anscombe, G. E. M., *An Introduction to Wittgenstein's Tractatus.* London, 1959.

Black, Max, *A Companion to Wittgenstein's Tractatus.* Cambridge, 1964.

Colombo, G. C. M., critical introduction and notes to the Italian translation of the *Tractatus.* Milan and Rome, 1954.

Daitz, E., "The Picture Theory of Meaning," in Antony Flew, ed., *Essays in Conceptual Analysis.* London, 1956.

Griffin, James, *Wittgenstein's Logical Atomism.* Oxford, 1964.

Hartnack, Justus, *Wittgenstein og den moderne Filosofi.* Copenhagen, 1960. Translated into German as *Wittgenstein und die moderne Philosophie.* Stuttgart, 1962.

Hintikka, Jaakko, "On Wittgenstein's Solipsism." *Mind,* Vol. 67 (1958).

Keyt, David, "Wittgenstein's Notion of an Object." *Philosophical Quarterly,* Vol. 13 (1963).

Keyt, David, "A New Interpretation of the *Tractatus* Examined." *Philosophical Review,* Vol. 74 (1965).

Maslow, Alexander, *A Study in Wittgenstein's Tractatus.* Berkeley and Los Angeles, 1961.

Pitcher, George, *The Philosophy of Wittgenstein.* Englewood Cliffs, N.J., 1964.

Ramsey, F. P., critical notice of the *Tractatus,* in R. F. Braithwaite, ed., *The Foundations of Mathematics.* London, 1931.

Rhees, Rush, "Miss Anscombe on the *Tractatus.*" *Philosophical Quarterly,* Vol. 10 (1960).

Rhees, Rush, "The *Tractatus:* Seeds of Some Misunderstandings." *Philosophical Review,* Vol. 72 (1963).

Russell, Bertrand, "The Philosophy of Logical Atomism," in *Logic and Knowledge,* R. C. Marsh, ed. London, 1956.

Schlick, Moritz, "The Turning Point in Philosophy," in A. J. Ayer, ed., *Logical Positivism.* Glencoe, Ill., 1959.

Stenius, Eric, *Wittgenstein's Tractatus.* Oxford, 1960.

Wienpahl, Paul D., "Wittgenstein and the Naming Relation." *Inquiry,* Vol. 7 (1964).

"BLUE AND BROWN BOOKS," "INVESTIGATIONS," "REMARKS ON THE FOUNDATIONS OF MATHEMATICS"

Albritton, Rogers, "On Wittgenstein's Use of the Term 'Criterion.'" *Journal of Philosophy,* Vol. 56, No. 22 (1959).

Ayer, A. J., and Rhees, Rush, "Can There Be a Private Language?" *PAS,* Supp. Vol. 28 (1954). Symposium.

Ayer, A. J., "Privacy." *Proceedings of the British Academy,* Vol. 45 (1959).

Bambrough, Renford, "Universals and Family Resemblances." *PAS,* Vol. 61 (1960–1961).

Bouwsma, O. K., "The Blue Book." *Journal of Philosophy,* Vol. 58, No. 6 (1961).

Buck, R. C., "Non-other Minds," in R. J. Butler, ed., *Analytical Philosophy.* Oxford, 1962.

Carney, J. D., "Private Language: The Logic of Wittgenstein's Argument." *Mind,* Vol. 69 (1960).

Cavell, Stanley, "The Availability of Wittgenstein's Later Philosophy." *Philosophical Review,* Vol. 71 (1962).

Chihara, C. S., "Wittgenstein and Logical Compulsion." *Analysis,* Vol. 21 (1961).

Chihara, C. S., "Mathematical Discovery and Concept Formation." *Philosophical Review,* Vol. 72 (1963).

Cook, J. W., "Wittgenstein on Privacy." *Philosophical Review,* Vol. 74 (1965).

Cowan, J. L., "Wittgenstein's Philosophy of Logic." *Philosophical Review,* Vol. 70 (1961).

Dummett, Michael, "Wittgenstein's Philosophy of Mathematics." *Philosophical Review,* Vol. 68 (1959).

Feyerabend, Paul K., "Wittgenstein's *Philosophical Investigations.*" *Philosophical Review,* Vol. 64 (1955).

Fodor, J. A., and Katz, J. J., "The Availability of What We Say." *Philosophical Review,* Vol. 72 (1963).

Gasking, D. A. T., "Avowals," in R. J. Butler, ed., *Analytical Philosophy.* Oxford, 1962.

Hardin, C. L., "Wittgenstein on Private Languages." *Journal of Philosophy,* Vol. 56 (1959).

Hartnack, Justus, *Wittgenstein og den moderne Filosofi,* above.

Kreisel, Georg, "Wittgenstein's *Remarks on the Foundations of Mathematics.*" *British Journal for the Philosophy of Science,* Vol. 9 (1958).

Kreisel, Georg, "Wittgenstein's Theory and Practice of Philosophy." *British Journal for the Philosophy of Science,* Vol. 11 (1960).

Malcolm, Norman, *Dreaming.* New York, 1959.

Malcolm, Norman, *Knowledge and Certainty.* Englewood Cliffs, N.J., 1963. See "Wittgenstein's *Philosophical Investigations*" and "Knowledge of Other Minds."

Malcolm, Norman, "Behaviorism as a Philosophy of Psychology," in T. W. Wann, ed., *Behaviorism and Phenomenology.* Chicago, 1964.

Moore, G. E., "Wittgenstein's Lectures in 1930–1933," in *Philosophical Papers.* New York, 1959.

Nell, E. J., "The Hardness of the Logical 'Must.'" *Analysis,* Vol. 21 (1961).

Pitcher, George, *The Philosophy of Wittgenstein.* Englewood Cliffs, N.J., 1964.

Rhees, Rush, Preface to *The Blue and Brown Books.* Oxford, 1958.

Rhees, Rush, "Wittgenstein's Builders." *PAS,* Vol. 60 (1959–1960).

Rhees, Rush, "Some Developments in Wittgenstein's View of Ethics." *Philosophical Review,* Vol. 74 (1965).

Strawson, P. F., critical notice of *Philosophical Investigations.* *Mind,* Vol. 63 (1954).

Thomson, Judith J., "Private Languages." *American Philosophical Quarterly,* Vol. 1 (1964).

Waismann, Friedrich, "Notes on Talks With Wittgenstein." *Philosophical Review,* Vol. 74 (1965).

Wellman, Carl, "Wittgenstein and the Egocentric Predicament." *Mind,* Vol. 68 (1959).

Wellman, Carl, "Our Criteria for Third-person Psychological Sentences." *Journal of Philosophy,* Vol. 58 (1961).

Wellman, Carl, "Wittgenstein's Conception of a Criterion." *Philosophical Review,* Vol. 71 (1962).

Wisdom, John, *Philosophy and Psychoanalysis.* Oxford, 1953.

Wisdom, John, "A Feature of Wittgenstein's Technique." *PAS,* Supp. Vol. 35 (1961).

Norman Malcolm

WOLFF, CHRISTIAN (1679–1754), German rationalist philosopher of the Enlightenment. Wolff was born in Breslau. Although he studied theology at the University of Jena, his chief interest was mathematics. He received a master's degree from Leipzig and in 1707 was appointed professor of mathematics at Halle. In 1711, on Leibniz' recommendation, he was elected to the Berlin Academy. Wolff's growing reputation and influence aroused the hostility of the Pietists, who in 1723 succeeded in influencing King Frederick William I of Prussia to exile him. He was immediately called to the Calvinist university in Marburg as professor of mathematics and philosophy and, on the accession of Frederick II in 1740, was called back to Halle as professor of law, vice-chancellor of the university, and Geheimrat. In 1743 he became chancellor and in 1745 a baron of the Holy Roman Empire.

Philosophical influences on Wolff. In Breslau, Wolff became acquainted with both Lutheran and Calvinist dogmatic theology. The traditional Aristotelianism of the conservative philosophical milieu there left important traces in his thought. At Jena, Wolff was influenced by Erhard Weigel's use of the "mathematical method" in philosophy, although Weigel died the year Wolff arrived. Wolff also studied Descartes, Malebranche, Pufendorf, and Tschirnhaus and went to Leipzig especially to meet Tschirnhaus. In 1704 Wolff began a correspondence with Leibniz on mathematical and philosophical subjects that lasted until Leibniz' death in 1716. Wolff drew his major metaphysical tenets from Leibniz, but Wolff's interpretation of Leibniz was partially Cartesian. Wolff was also familiar with both Lutheran and Catholic scholastic thought, the former based on Aristotelianism and the latter on Aquinas and Suárez. Protestant and Catholic scholasticism provided him with a basis for his ontology and influenced him on a number of technicalities.

Mathematics. Wolff's first works were on mathematics.

Although he made no original contributions, he did introduce "modern" mathematics into university teaching, and he produced technically refined, comprehensive, and pedagogically excellent textbooks that long dominated the German universities. He was the first to distinguish clearly between pure and applied sciences, and he recommended that both be studied. The goal of mathematics was for him the cultivation of the intellect and the preparation of the mind for the study of all other sciences.

Wolff's philosophical system. In 1709 Wolff began lecturing in philosophy. He was extremely systematic, and his philosophy is the most impressive coherent system produced in the eighteenth century. He opposed the empirical and unsystematic spirit of the school of Thomasius; but he was also dissatisfied with traditional Aristotelian metaphysics, which seemed to him to be only a collection of disconnected notions lacking rigorous systematic order or demonstrated justification. Wolff's own system was to contain nothing that did not strictly follow from self-evident axioms or preceding truths. Like his mathematical model, his system gradually developed its propositions through the synthetic method, by combining a very few simple elements, initially defined, and proceeding from the simple to the complex.

According to Wolff's system, all principles and facts derive from two universal principles, the principle of identity and Leibniz' principle of sufficient reason. The principle of identity is the basis of all knowledge and of all essence and the immediate foundation for all axioms. The principle of sufficient reason is derived by demonstration from the principle of identity and is the basis of all science, of the connection of essences, and of existence. It accounts for the connection of things and of truths by means of reasons and causes. Like the principle of sufficient reason, all other propositions should be deduced from some former one, and every concept defined by previously given concepts.

Wolff defined philosophy as "the science of all possible things insofar as they are possible." By this he meant that philosophy studies essences, and existent things only in respect to their essences, and that it studies what things must be in order to be possible, either as necessary things or as contingent. Wolff held that the existence of finite beings, which he defined as the completion of possibility, was not an object of science, but of history (observation), because existence depends on the free choice of God.

The order of Wolff's system. Wolff expounded his philosophical system first in a series of German works published between 1713 and 1725 and then, in order to reach an international audience, in an incomplete series of Latin works published between 1728 and 1755. The German metaphysics stressed problems of substance and of the world; it was based on the *cogito* and derived the properties of being from those of the human mind. The Latin version showed a greater interest in pure ontology and was more "objective" and closer to the Aristotelian tradition. Therefore, the more subjective German series treated empirical psychology before cosmology, rational psychology, and natural theology. The Latin series covered cosmology before empirical and rational psychology and treated practical philosophy and natural law more exten-

sively. Both series were divided into three major parts: theoretical, experimental (or empirical), and practical philosophy. Theoretical philosophy is a priori or speculative; practical philosophy is partly speculative and partly experimental.

Logic and "ars inveniendi." Wolff's first work in philosophy was his German logic, *Vernünftige Gedanken von den Kräften des menschlichen Verstandes* (Halle, 1713). The discussion, in the scholastic tradition, covered concepts, judgments, and the syllogism. The German logic contained much psychology, but the Latin logic, *Philosophia Rationalis Sive Logica* (Frankfurt and Leipzig, 1728), excluded psychology and connected logic with ontology. Logic for Wolff was the art of demonstration. The sections in his logic on invention and experiment (methodology) are restricted. The discussion of probability is likewise restricted, as Wolff was generally convinced of a broad human capacity to reach truth. Truth is relational and depends on the mutual implication or exclusion of propositions. Wolff restored the dignity of logic from its devaluation by Thomasius, asserting that logic was the condition of science and that "natural" logic was not enough.

Wolff intended to devote a special work to the method of discovery (*ars inveniendi*), to be called *Ars Characteristica Combinatoria*. It was to cover both a priori and a posteriori methods and give heuristic methods for discovering new truths and demonstrating them. This work was to have been the completion of Wolff's entire system, but since it presupposed all subsisting knowledge as systematized in his other works, he never wrote it.

Ontology. Wolff's Latin ontology, *Philosophia Prima Sive Ontologia* (Frankfurt, 1729; critical ed. by J. Ecole, Hildesheim, 1962), was his most important philosophical work. In opposition to Thomasius, Wolff thought the metaphysics of being was of utmost importance. His achievement was to put the principal notions of Aristotelian scholastic ontology into a new "modern" order, greatly developed in detail with every element "mathematically" deduced and set in its established place within the system.

Wolff did for Leibniz' ontology what Cartesian scholasticism and *philosophia novantiqua* had been doing for Descartes's. Wolff connected the modern metaphysical theories of Descartes and Leibniz with scholastic tradition, systematized them, and uncovered their ontological presuppositions and implications.

Cosmology and physics. Wolff claimed to be the first to distinguish between cosmology and physics. Cosmology was the a priori science of every possible material world, that is, of the necessary characteristics of any world. Physics was the empirical study of the contingent characteristics of this world.

In cosmology Wolff rejected Leibniz' doctrine of monads. Material substances are fundamentally different from spiritual substances; they have no power of representation. He agreed with Leibniz that material substances are "metaphysical points" endowed with force. Wolff did not know whether the doctrine of the pre-established harmony of material substances was true. He was a thoroughgoing mechanist, denying both Aristotelian occult qualities and the animism of Thomasius. But the world could not have been created mechanically; only after God set the world in order could it begin to run mechanically. The laws of motion depend on the free decree of God. Wolff accepted Leibniz' conception of body and force and rejected Newton's theory of gravitation. He agreed with Leibniz that the material world as known by man is phenomenal. In physics he recommended that the investigator keep close to observations and experiments and refrain from abstract hypotheses about unknown principles of unobservable events.

Psychology. In empirical psychology Wolff remained closest to Thomasius, but he was more theoretical than Thomasius and lacked Thomasius' interest in individual differences and other factual details. Wolff's psychology was a theory of knowledge and of will, rather than a methodology for acquiring knowledge or a practical help in ethics. He restricted the function of common sense and expanded the function of reason. According to Wolff, empirical psychology studies the powers of the soul as they are discovered by inner sense. He distinguished two general fields of the soul—the cognitive powers and the will (which includes the feelings of pleasure and pain). As with Thomasius, the cognitive powers begin with the "inferior faculty," or sensibility, because knowledge comes only from sensation.

Rational psychology, for Wolff, was the metaphysical study of the soul. He accepted the doctrine of pre-established harmony of soul and body. The soul is an immaterial substance possessing the power of representing the universe and free will. Metaphysically, it is not a *tabula rasa,* because all knowledge originates in its activity. Wolff attempted to prove rationally that the soul is simple and immortal.

Natural theology. Wolff also attempted to demonstrate the existence of God. A priori, he accepted a version of the Ontological Argument based on self-consciousness. A posteriori, he accepted the Cosmological Argument. He claimed that his natural theology was in agreement with revelation but did not attempt to prove rationally anything beyond the existence of God. Wolff agreed with Leibniz that this is the best of all possible worlds, arising from the free and wise choice of God. Protestant thought in the eighteenth century was strongly influenced by Wolff's rationalism.

Teleology and biology. Although Wolff was a rigorous mechanist in cosmology, he also accepted the teleological theories commonly held in Germany and England in his day. He believed that the structure of the world and of the objects in it was aimed at the fulfillment of God's wise ends and that the study of this order was a good method of studying nature. Living bodies were machines, but machines directed toward the fulfillment of God's purposes. His attempt to reconcile mechanism and teleology was probably made to escape the charge of fatalism leveled at him by his opponents.

Ethics and natural law. Wolff's moral philosophy and theory of law were purely rational. He held that good is what increases our perfection and evil is what diminishes it, and that perfection is an objective metaphysical concept. Therefore, he claimed, moral and juridical laws do

not depend on God's will, but on the structure of being. They can be discovered by natural reason independently of Christian revelation.

Wolff held that man is moved to act by the rational representation of perfection and that he has obligations or duties independent of rewards and punishments for carrying them out. Sin arises when sensibility prevails over reason; but sensibility is ruled by free will.

Wolff claimed that politics is based on ethics and tried to establish a balance between the rights of the individual and those of the community. In natural law he was influenced by Grotius and Pufendorf.

Besides this a priori moral philosophy, Wolff presented an a posteriori ethics based on an empirical psychology that described the virtues, passions, and practical customs.

Rationalism. Thomasius and his school had vindicated natural reason in many fields, in opposition to orthodox Lutheranism, but Wolff went far beyond them in founding theology and ethics entirely on natural reason. By "reason" Wolff meant scientific thought rather than common sense. In stressing the value of the speculative philosophical reason and its power to elaborate an extensive system of thought, he extended the human intellect beyond the limits traditionally set for it by the German philosophical schools. This stress on the power of reason led to an emphasis on theory. Going back to the tradition of German Aristotelianism, Wolff emphasized logic and metaphysics against the empiricism of Thomasius' school. Finally, because Wolff conceived of reason as operating mathematically, he constructed a complex deductive system of truths and concentrated on essence, on what is true for all possible things, rather than on existing things.

Wolff did not neglect the role of experience but was less original in empirical studies than in his theoretical work, and his contemporaries and posterity tended to overlook his work in this area. He was thus most influential in his work as an a priori thinker. In the same way, the subjective and psychological aspect of his work, more noticeable in his German than in his Latin works, was forgotten as a result of the interest in his much stronger objective tendencies.

Wolff's importance and influence. Wolff was not an original philosopher; nearly all of his ideas were derived from previous traditions. But as a systematizer his achievement was enormous; and in technical refinement, comprehensiveness, and coherence, his system was the most significant elaborated in Germany up to that time. This system promoted the general diffusion of many important ideas of Leibniz' and first made known in Germany the discoveries of modern science, despite Wolff's denial of the Newtonian theory of gravitation. Finally, Wolff established German philosophical terminology and created a number of new words, such as *Begriff* for "concept."

Wolff's influence on his contemporaries was enormous. Even the revival of the empirical, unsystematic, and psychologizing interests of Thomasius among the "popular philosophers" after the middle of the eighteenth century was accompanied by constant reference to Wolff's doctrines, and his work provided a systematic frame for their lack of system. In fact, Wolff's doctrines were so successful and so widely accepted that they began to appear trivial, and he was thought of as a commonplace philosopher.

However, the work of the new systematic philosophers of the 1770s, like J. H. Lambert (a former Wolffian), J. N. Tetens, and Kant, cannot be considered a revival of Wolffianism. Their thought was too distant from that of Wolff, and Kant and Tetens were consciously opposed to it. Wolff was still highly regarded in Hegel's time, but thereafter his influence declined and almost vanished.

Followers and opponents. Wolff's theories aroused violent reactions. Three waves of attack can be distinguished. The first, as has been seen, was initiated by the Pietists, who were largely followers of Thomasius, though Thomasius himself did not take part in the fight; this attack led to the expulsion of Wolff from Halle in 1723. Wolff was accused of idealism for espousing the doctrine of preestablished harmony; of fatalism and Spinozism for his doctrine of the connection of things and his use of the mathematical method in philosophy; and of making the will completely subservient to reason. (For the second attack, led by A. F. Hoffman and C. A. Crusius, see CRUSIUS, CHRISTIAN AUGUST.)

The final attack on Wolff's doctrines was started by Maupertuis, who had become president of the revived Berlin Academy after Wolff had refused the presidency himself, and was joined by several members of the Academy and some of the pupils of Crusius. Maupertuis advocated French Enlightenment and Newtonian natural philosophy and considered Wolff's detailed and somewhat cumbrous system an offshoot of medieval barbarism. His method of attack was to arrange a series of competitions in which the competitors wrote essays on assigned topics from Wolff's system, topics chosen to bring out the weaknesses of Wolff's positions.

Wolff's influence on his students during his first sojourn in Halle was so great that it partially accounts for the Pietist hostility toward him, but after his return to Halle in 1740 the students were attracted to newer, more modern philosophical teachers.

His real importance lay in his direct influence on the teaching body in German universities. By 1720 some of his pupils, such as L. P. Thümmig and G. B. Bilfinger, were already professors and were ousted with Wolff. But by 1730 Wolff's academic influence was re-established and remained dominant until 1754. Notable among later Wolffians for their independent thought were the literary critic J. C. Gottsched, the aestheticians A. G. Baumgarten and H. F. Meier, and Kant's teacher Martin Knutzen. Others who were significantly influenced by Wolffianism were H. S. Reimarus, J. G. Sulzer, Moses Mendelssohn, and J. H. Lambert. Wolffianism was also accepted by Catholic scholastic philosophers in eighteenth-century Germany.

Wolff's school soon disintegrated after his death under the impact of "popular philosophy" and the revival of Pietist thought. But his influence on eclectic thinkers was considerable and was strong even on such an opponent as Crusius. By the 1740s there were Wolffians in France; later some of his Latin works were reprinted in Italy and Spain and favorably greeted by many Catholic philosophers there.

Additional Works by Wolff

IN GERMAN

Vernünftige Gedanken von Gott, der Welt und der Seele der Menschen. Frankfurt and Leipzig, 1720. Metaphysics.
Vernünftige Gedanken von der Menschen Tun und Lassen. Halle, 1720. Ethics.
Vernünftige Gedanken von dem gesellschaftlichen Leben der Menschen. Halle, 1721. Political science.
Vernünftige Gedanken von den Wirkungen der Natur. Halle, 1723. Physics.
Vernünftige Gedanken von den Absichten der natürlichen Dinge. Frankfurt, 1724. Teleology.
Vernünftige Gedanken von den Teilen der Menschen, Tiere und Pflanzen. Frankfurt, 1725. Biology.
Ausführliche Nachricht von seinen eigenen Schriften. 1726.
Gesammelte kleinere Schriften, 6 vols. Halle, 1736–1740.
Christian Wolffs eigene Lebensbeschreibung, H. Wuttke, ed. Leipzig, 1841. Autobiography.
Briefwechsel zwischen Leibniz und Chr. Wolff, C. I. Gerhardt, ed. Halle, 1860; reprinted, Hildesheim, 1963.

IN LATIN

Ratio Praelectionum Wolfianarum in Mathesin et Philosophiam Universam. Halle, 1718.
Cosmologia Generalis. Frankfurt, 1731.
Psychologia Empirica. Frankfurt, 1732.
Psychologia Rationalis. Frankfurt, 1734.
Theologia Naturalis, 2 vols. Frankfurt, 1736–1737.
Philosophia Practica Universalis, 2 vols. Frankfurt, 1738–1739.
Jus Naturae, 8 vols. Frankfurt, 1740–1748.

Works on Wolff

Arnsperger, W., *Christian Wolffs Verhältniss zu Leibniz.* Heidelberg, 1897.
Campo, Mariano, *Cristiano Wolff e il razionalismo precritico,* 2 vols. Milan, 1939.
Çäsar, J., *Christian Wolff in Marburg.* Marburg, 1879.
École, J., "Cosmologie wolffienne et dynamique leibnitienne." *Les Études philosophiques,* 1964.
École, J., "Un Essai d'explication rationnelle du monde ou la *Cosmologia Generalis* de Christian Wolff." *Giornale di metafisica,* Vol. 6 (1963).
Frauendienst, W., *Christian Wolff als Staatsdenker.* Berlin, 1927.
Gelfert, J., *Der Pflichtbegriff bei Christian Wolff.* Leipzig, 1907.
Hartmann, G. V., *Anleitung zur Historie der Leibniz–Wolffischen Philosophie.* Frankfurt and Leipzig, 1737.
Heilemann, P. A., *Die Gotteslehre des Christian Wolffs.* Leipzig, 1907.
Heimsoeth, Heinz, "Christian Wolffs Ontologie und die Prinzipienforschung Immanuel Kants." *Studien zur Philosophie Immanuel Kants.* Cologne, 1956.
Hoffmann, R., *Die staatsphilosophischen Anschauungen Wolffs.* Leipzig, 1916.
Joesten, Clara, *Christian Wolffs Grundlegung der praktischen Philosophie.* Leipzig, 1931.
Kluge, F. W., *Christian von Wolff, der Philosoph.* Breslau, 1831.
Knüpfer, K., *Grundzüge der Geschichte des Begriffs der Vorstellung von Wolff bis Kant.* Halle, 1911.
Kohlmeyer, E., *Kosmos und Kosmogonie bei Christian Wolff.* Göttingen, 1911.
Levy, Harry, *Die Religionsphilosophie Wolffs.* Würzburg, 1928.
Ludovici, C. G., *Ausführlicher Entwurf einer vollständigen Historie der Wolffischen Philosophie,* 3 vols. Leipzig, 1736–1737.
Ludovici, C. G., *Sammlung und Auszüge der sämtlichen Streitschriften wegen der Wolffischen Philosophie,* 2 vols. Leipzig, 1737–1738.
Ludovici, C. G., *Neueste Merkwürdigkeiten der Leibniz–Wolffischen Weltweisheit.* Frankfurt and Leipzig, 1738.

Philipp, W., *Das Werden der Aufklärung in theologiegeschichtlicher Sicht.* Göttingen, 1957.

Pichler, H., *Ueber Christian Wolffs Ontologie.* Leipzig, 1910.

Piur, Paul, *Studien zur sprachlichen Würdigung Christian Wolffs.* Halle, 1903.

Schöffler, H., *Deutsches Geistesleben zwischen Reformation und Aufklärung.* Frankfurt, 1956.

Tonelli, Giorgio, "Kant, dall'estetica metafisica all'estetica psicoempirica." *Memorie della Accademia delle Scienze di Torino,* Series 3, Vol. 3, Pt. 2 (1955).

Tonelli, Giorgio, "Der Streit über die mathematische Methode in der Philosophie in der ersten Hälfte des 18ten Jahrhunderts." *Archiv für Philosophie,* Vol. 9 (1959).

Tonelli, Giorgio, *Elementi metodologici e metafisici in Kant dal 1745 al 1768.* Turin, 1959.

Tonelli, Giorgio, "La question des bornes de l'entendement humain au XVIII⁰ siècle." *Revue de métaphysique et de morale,* Vol. 66 (1959), 396–427.

Tonelli, Giorgio, "The Law of Continuity in the Eighteenth Century." *Studies on Voltaire and the Eighteenth Century,* Vols. 24–27. 1963.

Utitz, Emil, *Christian Wolff.* Halle, 1929.

Vleeschauwer, H. J. de, "La Genèse de la méthode mathématique de Wolff." *Revue belge de philologie et d'histoire* (1932).

Wundt, Max, *Die deutsche Schulphilosophie im Zeitalter der Aufklärung.* Tübingen, 1945.

Zeller, Eduard, "Wolffs Vertreibung aus Halle," in his *Vorträge und Abhandlungen geschichtlichen Inhalts.* Leipzig, 1865. Vol. I, pp. 108–139.

GIORGIO TONELLI

WOLLASTON, WILLIAM (1660–1724), English moral philosopher, divine, and deist, was born at Coton-Clanford of an old Staffordshire family temporarily in straitened circumstances. Schooled at Lichfield, he entered Sidney Sussex College, Cambridge, in 1674 and received his M.A. in 1681. The following year he became assistant master in Birmingham Grammar School and took holy orders. When, in 1688, he unexpectedly inherited a large fortune, he removed to London and in 1689 married the wealthy heiress of a London merchant. Thereafter, he devoted himself to general learning and moral philosophy. In 1691 he printed privately *On the Design of the Book of Ecclesiastes, or the Unreasonableness of Men's Restless Contention for the Present Enjoyments, Represented in an English Poem* in heroic couplets; a revised edition was published in 1724. *The Religion of Nature Delineated* appeared in 1722; it was so popular that it ran through eight editions by 1750. Queen Caroline is said to have read it three times, and in the Hermitage at Richmond, she placed a bust of Wollaston alongside those of Locke, Newton, and Samuel Clarke. Wollaston died in 1724, a man of wealth and of considerable prestige in intellectual circles.

The religion of nature. In religious speculation Wollaston was fundamentally a rationalist in the line of Clarke. *The Religion of Nature Delineated,* unlike much of the deistical writing of the period, is not a work of polemic but an honest and moderate, if perhaps in some aspects a misguided, effort to determine, without recourse to revelation, what a rational man would consider natural religion to be. Wollaston's thought therefore has affinity with that of Lord Herbert of Cherbury, who attempted to define the common notions of natural religion, as well as with the metaphysics of Clarke. In the *Religion of Nature Delineated,* Wollaston considers the following questions. Is there such a thing as natural religion? If so, what is it? How may a man judge the religions of the world for himself, and how may he enjoy tranquillity of mind in his own religion while tolerating the other religions?

Wollaston concludes that the foundation of religion consists in moral distinctions among the acts of man, whether they be good, evil, or indifferent. Man, by reason of his ability to make such distinctions, is an intelligent and free agent. Truth is the expression of things as they are, and vice constitutes a rejection of the truth; to deny things as they are is virtually to deny the existence of God. To follow nature is to follow God. This does not mean, however, that one should follow exclusively the inclinations of one's individual nature. Since no man is purely rational, each man must consider the nature of others. The great law of religion is for each man not to contradict truth but to treat everything as it really is. Happiness is based on the pleasure–pain thesis, pain being a real evil, pleasure, a real good. Ultimate happiness is the excess of pleasure over pain, and it is the duty of everyone to make himself as happy as possible consonant with the happiness of others. Happiness and truth are thereby inseparably intertwined.

But how does man know what is true? The answer is by reason: "We reason about particulars, or from them; but not by them." Action according to right reason and action according to truth are identical. This is the general law laid down by the author of nature, and this constitutes the religion of nature. The senses are inferior to reason but are to be followed, nevertheless, when not contrary to reason. In instances where certainty concerning the truth is unobtainable, one may act on probability but always under the guidance of reason. The necessity of education by the cultivation of reason is thus demonstrated. Man's desires, his passions, must be submitted to reason. Since man is individual and the principles of reason are universal, the laws of nature forbid the individual to transgress the rights of others. All injustice is wrong and evil, and compassion is one of the highest virtues. Man is to be regarded not only as an individual but also as a social creature, and the purpose of society is the common welfare of all the people. Man-made laws are not infallible but may require alteration from time to time, and no man-made law should contradict a law of nature. Since mutual defense is one of the great ends of society, war against aggression is legitimate and necessary.

Theologically, Wollaston, though basically rationalistic, willingly accepted on a secondary level the theological and the cosmological arguments for the existence of Deity. However, the main argument he advances for the existence of God is the necessity for the First Cause, the one God who is the author of nature, a being of pure reason. God's attributes remain inscrutable to man but must be assumed to be perfect. It follows from God's perfect justice that man is immortal and that the iniquities and evils of this world will be corrected; a particular providence and a future state necessarily exist. And the God of nature, who is the God of reason and the God of justice, is to be worshiped. It is worth noting that it was precisely this type of a priori reasoning about the existence and attributes of Deity that Hume, who was well acquainted with the writings of Wollaston, set out to demolish, especially in the *Dialogues Concerning Natural Religion* (1779).

Wollaston was a man of vast erudition, and his footnotes contain numerous citations not only from the customary ancient Greeks and Romans but also from Hebrew and even Arabic authors. Unlike nearly all the other English deists of the eighteenth century, he was not at all interested in Biblical criticism, internal, textual, or historical. His rationalism is more akin to the thinking of the previous century, the Age of Reason. Perhaps this fact affords the explanation for the attacks on him by two later prominent deists. The young Benjamin Franklin, when in London setting the type for the 1725 edition of *The Religion of Nature Delineated,* refuted Wollaston's advocacy of free will in a little treatise entitled *A Dissertation on Liberty and Necessity, Pleasure and Pain* (1725), a work that he was, however, shortly to repudiate. And Lord Bolingbroke called Wollaston a "whining philosopher," ridiculing his rationalistic "proof" of the existence of angels and other supernatural beings. Nevertheless, there are in Wollaston some evidences of the influence of empirical thinking, presumably that of Locke. Perhaps it was this element of empiricism together with Wollaston's gesture toward the validity of probability under certain circumstances that attracted the early attention of Bishop Butler, who in the *Analogy of Religion* (1736) was to attack rationalism in religion as "that idle and not very innocent employment of forming imaginary models of a world, and schemes of governing it." In 1726, however, Butler, in his *Fifteen Sermons,* had commended Wollaston as "a late author of great and deserved reputation."

Bibliography

See *Life of Wollaston,* prefixed to *The Religion of Nature Delineated,* 6th ed. (London, 1738); R. E. Stedman, "The Ethics of Wollaston," in *The Nineteenth Century and After,* Vol. 118 (1935), 217–225; A. O. Aldridge, "Benjamin Franklin and Philosophical Necessity," in *Modern Language Quarterly,* Vol. 12 (1951), 292–309. See also the general bibliography under DEISM.

ERNEST CAMPBELL MOSSNER

WOODBRIDGE, FREDERICK JAMES EUGENE

(1867–1940), was born in Windsor, Ontario, and attended Amherst College, Union Theological Seminary, and the University of Berlin. He taught philosophy at the University of Minnesota (1894–1902) and Columbia University (1902–1937). At Columbia he also served as dean of the faculty of political science, philosophy, and pure science (1912–1929). Like his colleague John Dewey, he had great influence as a teacher. His influence was less widespread than was Dewey's and was more confined to professional philosophers, but it went deep and is clearly responsible for the revival in the United States of Aristotelian trends of thought. His successor at Columbia University as teacher of the history of philosophy, John H. Randall, Jr., is a notable instance of his influence.

Realism and naturalism. In describing his own philosophical position Woodbridge used the terms realism and naturalism. By realism he meant that life and mind are products that develop, here and there, in the course of the manifold developments in the natural world. Mind, life, consciousness, and soul are activities of certain types of bodies; they never appear apart from those bodies, although mind, once it has emerged in Nature, may come to guide and thus to master some of the occurrences in the world about it. Consciousness is an awareness of some of the things in the environment; it salutes, as it were, those things. Consciousness, far from being the source of the objective world, presupposes its existence. In all this realistic position Woodbridge regarded himself, quite correctly, as reaffirming in modern terms some basic themes of Aristotle's metaphysics.

By naturalism Woodbridge meant much the same thing as he meant by realism. Naturalism, he said, "is an attitude and not a doctrine." Some contemporary writers used the word "Nature" to indicate a norm of perfection which the historical processes in this world seldom bring to fulfillment. Others, especially theologians, used it to connote an inferior mode of being, contrasting it with an allegedly superior spirit or supernature. Woodbridge avoided such implied judgments. He wrote in a hitherto unpublished letter of July 24, 1939:

Let Nature be, as I love to put it, heaven and earth, the sea, and all that in them is, and I do not see how one can here complain of ambiguity; there is no mistaking what is named by the name Nature. So now I have adopted the practice of spelling Nature with a big N to indicate that it is a name given and not a predicate with implications. It is a name for the clearly identified subject-matter of all inquiry, so that now we can ask what Nature *is* and proceed at once to look for answers.

In other writers the word "naturalism" often introduced untested presuppositions and undetected prejudices. Woodbridge took Nature as anything and everything we encounter and want to investigate. He abjured "anticipations of nature" and made no commitments, in advance of careful study and research, as to the "interpretations of nature" which investigation would reveal to be proper and true. Nature is what we find around us, whether we are looking on a top closet shelf, or through telescopic instruments at stellar universes that are distant in both time and space, or at the evidences for ancient cities that long ago disappeared from view. Daily life, technical science, and history alike presuppose Nature; that is, all these kinds of quests for knowledge presuppose simply that there is much to investigate. Naturalism, in Woodbridge's sense of the term, is not a thesis about what kind of world we have; it is a summons to unbiased research.

Woodbridge's writings reflect, in their form as well as in their content, the attitude he called naturalism and realism. He had no interest in producing an intricate tome designed systematically to account for the existence of everything. Rather, he wrote outstanding essays, in each of which he pushed some one line of analysis as far as he then could. His interests are revealed by the titles of his essays: "Substance," "Teleology," "Creation," "Structure," "Evolution," "Behaviour," "Sensations," "Mind," and "Man." In these essays he examined the question of what thing or process or aspect of the world we isolate for inspection when we speak, for example, of "substance" or "teleology." The positions these essays expose are consistent enough, to be sure. But no one is a premise from which others are deduced; rather, each is a fresh inquiry into some facet of Nature. Moreover, Woodbridge maintained that all the possible investigations that might be undertaken still would not exhaust the intricacies of Nature. We may reach some profound conclusions, but we can never properly say concerning any or all of our conclusions that we have discovered the whole truth about Nature.

Time and change. The most influential of Woodbridge's writings are his discussions of time and change (see particularly Ch. 2 of *The Purpose of History*). Woodbridge argues that what happens at any time is not simply or wholly the effect of what has already happened; an event is dependent upon its past as the material upon which activity may be expended, but it is also a new and fresh expenditure of activity upon that material. What occurs is reconstruction, transformation, remaking. What was is thus pushed back into the past, and what becomes takes the place of what was. Time does not move from past through present to future; rather, it moves from the possible to the actual, that is, from one of the potentialities of what formerly was to a single actuality which is brought into existence by an action (whether that action be unconscious chance or conscious choice) upon what was. What comes to us from the past offers us opportunities and often imposes cruel limitations, but it does not make our choices for us. Rather, it allows us to realize our ends insofar as we have understanding of the potentialities it contains. History has no one end; it includes many processes with their many, often incompatible, ends. And human choices, insofar as they are intelligent, may well be effective to some degree. A naturalistic theory of Nature thus issues in a humanistic theory of man.

Works by Woodbridge

The Purpose of History. New York, 1916.
The Realm of Mind. New York, 1926.
The Son of Apollo: Themes of Plato. Boston, 1929.
Nature and Mind. New York, 1937. A volume of essays presented to Woodbridge on his seventieth birthday by students, colleagues, and friends; contains a bibliography of his writings.
An Essay on Nature. New York, 1940.
Aristotle's Vision of Nature, edited with an introduction by J. H. Randall, Jr. New York, 1965.

Works on Woodbridge

Cohen, Morris R., Chapter 17, "Later Philosophy," of *Cambridge History of American Literature.* Cambridge, 1921. Vol. III, pp. 263–264.
Cohen, Morris R., *American Thought.* Glencoe, Ill., 1954. Pp. 315–316.
Costello, Harry T., "The Naturalism of Frederick J. E. Woodbridge," in Y. H. Krikorian, ed., *Naturalism and the Human Spirit.* New York, 1944. Pp. 295–318.
Lamprecht, Sterling P., *Our Philosophical Traditions.* New York, 1955. 486–497.
Randall, John H., Jr., "Dean Woodbridge." *Columbia University Quarterly,* Vol. 32 (December 1940), 324–331.
Randall, John H., Jr., "Introduction" and "The Department of Philosophy," in *A History of the Faculty of Philosophy, Columbia University.* New York, 1957. Pp. 3–57, 102–145.

STERLING P. LAMPRECHT

WOODGER, JOSEPH HENRY, British biologist, was born in 1894 at Great Yarmouth, Norfolk. He was graduated from University College, London, where he studied zool-

ogy, and after war service returned there to teach. The rest of his academic career was associated with the University of London, as reader in biology from 1922 to 1947 and professor of biology from 1947 to 1959. In the term of 1949/1950 he was appointed Tarner lecturer at Trinity College, Cambridge, whose philosophers—C. D. Broad, Bertrand Russell, and Alfred North Whitehead—greatly influenced his early outlook. Later, the influence of the logicians Rudolf Carnap and Alfred Tarski can be seen in his writings, some of which are highly formal studies of the language and principles of biology. The chief work of his early period is *Biological Principles* (1929); the two best-known works of his later period are *The Axiomatic Method in Biology* (1937) and *Biology and Language* (1952).

Underlying the whole of Woodger's activities as a philosopher of science is his concern with a single problem generated by "the contrast between the brilliant skill, ingenuity and care bestowed upon observation and experiment in biology, and the almost complete neglect of caution in regard to the definition and use of the concepts in terms of which its results are expressed." The effect of this has been to arrest the development of the life sciences. Hence, in *Biological Principles* Woodger proposed to examine a number of key concepts that have entered into the chronic controversies and antitheses of biology, such as those between mechanism and vitalism, preformation and epigenesis, teleology and causation, structure and function, organism and environment, and body and mind. He employed the techniques of analysis made familiar by the Cambridge philosophers of the time. These techniques required clarity and precision in the use of ordinary English expressions, but no use of logical symbolism was introduced. Woodger showed that many of the traditional disputes arose either from failure to eliminate metaphysical elements from biological topics or from shortcomings in the biologists' language, which was often sloppy and imprecise. Trouble was also caused by the implicit adoption of theories of knowledge that were not critically evaluated. He objected to phenomenalism, for example, because the arguments used by phenomenalists presupposed the very knowledge that they declared unattainable—knowledge about brains and sense organs as physical objects in the world. In his own alternative to phenomenalism, Woodger contended that the existence of such objects is a hypothesis that "seems unavoidable for anyone who does not believe that when he uses language he is always talking to himself" (*Biology and Language,* p. 69).

In his subsequent work Woodger turned to mathematical logic as a means of reconstructing the language of biology. Here he made some pioneer contributions. *The Axiomatic Method in Biology* utilized the machinery of Whitehead and Russell's *Principia Mathematica* to construct a logical calculus that could be applied to certain nonmetrical concepts of genetics, embryology, and taxonomy. The standard apparatus of logical constants, logical variables, postulates, and theorems was taken over, and to it was added a set of ten undefined "biological constants" together with postulates concerning them. The resulting axiom system permitted the deduction of a number of consequences in the form of precise specifications of such notions as "gametes," "zygotes," "cell hierarchies," "alleles," and so on. A simplified version of this calculus was given in *The Technique of*

Theory Construction (Chicago, 1939), in which a specimen theory that is a fragment of the earlier system was neatly developed.

Biology and Language showed how these matters could be approached from the reverse direction. In a section devoted to the reconstruction of the language of genetics, Woodger did not begin by axiomatizing the set of genetical statements but by recasting observation records in symbolic form and then introducing piecemeal the technical vocabulary needed to move to successively higher levels of theory. This book went beyond classical symbolic logic in its discussion of the language of evolutionary studies, where Woodger developed a special branch of set theory in order to reconcile the gradualness in evolutionary changes with the demand that passage from one taxonomic category to another must take place in one generation.

Logicians have been more appreciative than biologists of Woodger's "experiments" in applied logistic. The abstract formalisms are clear, rigorous, and interesting as logical exercises. Yet although the claims made for them are modest, it might well be argued that it is premature to produce axiomatizations of existing biological knowledge or even that biology is not the sort of science that can be fully reconstructed in axiomatic terms.

Works by Woodger

Biological Principles. London, 1929.
The Axiomatic Method in Biology. London, 1937.
Biology and Language. Cambridge, 1952.

Works on Woodger

Berkeley, E. C., "Conditions Affecting the Application of Symbolic Logic." *Journal of Symbolic Logic*, Vol. 7 (1942), 160–168.

Carnap, Rudolf, *Introduction to Symbolic Logic and Its Application.* New York, 1958. Pp. 213–225.

Goudge, T. A., "Science and Symbolic Logic." *Scripta Mathematica*, Vol. 9 (1943), 69–80.

Gregg, J. R., and Harris, F. T. C., eds., *Form and Strategy in Science: Studies Dedicated to Joseph Henry Woodger on the Occasion of his Seventieth Birthday.* Dordrecht, Netherlands, and Stuttgart, 1964.

T. A. GOUDGE

WOOLSTON, THOMAS (1670–1731), English divine, religious controversialist, freethinker, and deist, was born in Northampton, the son of a successful tradesman. After schooling there and at Daventry, he entered Sidney Sussex College, Cambridge, in 1685, the same college from which the deist William Wollaston had graduated a few years earlier. Woolston received the B.A. in 1689 and the M.A. in 1692. In 1691 he was made fellow of the college and proceeded to take orders, achieving the B.D. in 1699. The study of Origen early led him to an allegorical interpretation of the Scriptures. He was subsequently accused of derangement of the mind and in 1720 was deprived of his fellowship. Two years later he retaliated by printing and dedicating to the master of the college *The Exact Fitness of the Time in Which Christ Was Manifested in the Flesh, Demonstrated by Reason, Against the Objections of the Old Gentiles, and of Modern Unbelievers,* a discourse that he had delivered twenty years earlier as a public exercise both in the chapel of the college and in St. Mary's Church. The theme of this work is expressed in the words "The first Reason, why *the then Greatness of the Roman Empire*

was a fit Circumstance of Time for the Mission of Christ, is, that He might better manifest his Divine Authority and Commission to the civil Powers of the World."

A long series of heterodox religious pamphlets followed which led to unsuccessful prosecution by the government in 1725 and culminated in 1729 with conviction for blasphemy. Woolston was sentenced to a fine of £100, a year's imprisonment, and security for good behavior during life. Failure to meet the fine brought about confinement until his death in January 1731. Samuel Clarke, the rationalistic theologian, had made unsuccessful efforts to get Woolston released. A five-volume edition of Woolston's *Works* was published in 1733.

Woolston's first ironical application of Origen's allegorical method of scriptural interpretation appeared in 1705 under the title of *The Old Apology for the Truth of the Christian Religion Against the Jews and Gentiles Revived.* His anticlerical campaign, particularly directed at those who refused the allegorical way, inspired a number of tracts. *Four Free-Gifts to the Clergy* (1723–1724) accused the "ministers of the letter" of being worshipers of the apocalyptic beast and ministers of Antichrist. *The Moderator Between An Infidel and an Apostate* with its two supplements, all of 1725, continued the attack, the "infidel" being the greatly admired Anthony Collins and the "apostate" being a literal-minded divine. In reality the tracts are defenses of the freethinking Collins and attacks on the clergy who had abandoned the allegorical methods of the Church Fathers.

Another series of tracts from 1727 to 1729 began with *A Discourse On the Miracles of Our Saviour In View of the Present Controversy Between Infidels and Apostates.* Here again Woolston was the disciple of Collins, who had promised to write on the miracles but had never got around to it. In all events, however, Woolston is much more outspoken than Collins would possibly have been. Each of these six tracts, in which he frequently employs the device of an imaginary friend, a learned rabbi, as interlocutor, is ironically dedicated to a different bishop of the Church of England. It is argued that the only evidence for the messiahship of Jesus is found in the Old Testament prophecies, and both prophecy and fulfillment must be interpreted as parables. Many events of Jesus' life (especially the miracles) are patently absurd if given a literal interpretation. Jesus was a spiritual Messiah, healing distempers of the soul, not of the body. Hell, Satan, and the devils are in reality states of mind. Starting with the minor miracles, Woolston deals with 15 in all, concluding with the Resurrection.

If all of Woolston's allegorizing be madness, there is yet method in it. A man of considerable learning, Woolston employs a racy, colloquial, and frequently witty style. For example, the rabbi comments, "I can't read the Story [of the apparitions of Jesus after his death] without smiling, and there are two or three Passages in it that put me in Mind of Robinson Cruso's filling his Pockets with Biskets, when he had neither Coat, Waste-coat, nor Breeches on."

Up to the last Woolston consistently denied that he was an infidel, avowing that he was a believer in the truth of Christianity. His faith in Christianity is perhaps still open to question, but it is certain that he was a deist, whether rationalistic or Christian. He was never a religious fanatic.

Voltaire was much impressed by Woolston's attacks on the miracles and made much use of them.

On all occasions Woolston defended universal and unbounded religious toleration and freedom of thought and of publication. Conversely, he insisted that a hired and established priesthood is the root of all evil, and he vigorously defended such "freethinkers" as the Quakers. Ironically, he was the victim of the authoritarian principles he had dedicated his life to eradicate.

Bibliography

See *Life* of Woolston, prefixed to Vol. I of his *Works,* 5 vols. (London, 1733); *The Life of the Reverend Mr. Thomas Woolston* (London, 1733); Norman L. Torrey, *Voltaire and the English Deists* (New Haven, 1930), Ch. 4. See also the general bibliography under Deism.

ERNEST CAMPBELL MOSSNER

WORLD SOUL. See MACROCOSM AND MICROCOSM; PANPSYCHISM; PANTHEISM.

WRIGHT, CHAUNCEY (1830–1875), American philosopher and mathematician, was born in Northampton, Massachusetts. On the surface, his life was completely uneventful. From 1852 to 1870 he worked as a mathematician for the *Nautical Almanac;* he was twice a lecturer at Harvard College—in psychology in 1870 and in mathematical physics in 1874—and he occasionally tutored private pupils. In 1860 he was elected a fellow of the American Academy of Arts and Sciences, of which he was later secretary. He visited Darwin in England in 1872—the major social event of his life. Between 1864 and 1875 he contributed numerous articles to the *North American Review* and the *Nation.* His longer articles were published posthumously in 1877 under the title *Philosophical Discussions;* his *Letters* appeared in 1878.

Wright was not successful as a lecturer, but he was a splendid tutor, and many interested individuals sought to converse with him. It was through this easy interchange of ideas that men like Charles Sanders Peirce, William James, and Oliver Wendell Holmes, Jr., came to feel the influence of his philosophy. Wright was the mentor of the Metaphysical Club, which met in Cambridge in the early 1870s and included Peirce, James, and Holmes among its members.

Role of scientific concepts. Wright was America's first technically proficient philosopher of science. He constantly criticized Herbert Spencer as being ignorant of the nature of scientific inference. Spencer tried to assemble all the results of scientific investigation and to fit them together into a total picture of the universe. However, Wright claimed, the theoretical concepts and principles of science are not simply summaries of events; rather, they are tools for extending our concrete knowledge of nature. Theoretical concepts, he said, are finders, not merely summaries, of truth.

Some commentators point out that this "working hypothesis" notion of scientific principles is similar to John Dewey's instrumentalism. According to Dewey, all ideas are working hypotheses and all thinking is experimental, scientific thinking being only a limiting case in the sense of having ideal controls. Wright, however, did not formulate an instrumental view of mind in anything like this general sense. All he did was to emphasize the "working hypothesis" nature of scientific concepts; he did not generalize this interpretation into an account of all thinking. To say that Wright "prefigured" Dewey's brand of pragmatism can mean no more than that he provided the logic of scientific inference which later philosophers generalized into a pragmatic view of mind.

Scientific explanation. Wright distinguished two types of scientific explanation. First, an event can be explained by stating the cause of its occurrence even when it is not possible to show that the characteristics of the event are resultants of any combination of characteristics of the cause. Second, in cases like the parallelogram of forces, one can explain not only the occurrence of an event but also its characteristics as resultants of some combination of characteristics of its cause. Wright felt that some events could never be explained in this second sense, and hence he was advocating, in an embryonic way, a doctrine of emergence. He also believed that this distinction would allow a universal determinist, or necessitarian, to account for novelty and newness in the universe. Furthermore, he thought it provided the means for formulating an enlightened materialist doctrine—namely, that all mental events can be explained by physical events in the first sense but not in the second sense.

Evolution. Wright analyzed the logical structure of evolutionary thought in his articles "The Limits of Natural Selection" (1870), "The Genesis of Species" (1871), and "Evolution by Natural Selection" (1872). He called these articles his definition and defense of Darwinism, and Darwin was sufficiently impressed to reprint "The Genesis of Species" and distribute it in England. Since Wright was answering specific questions, his essays have a piecemeal quality, but they are filled with enlightening points. Of particular interest are his comparison of explanation in biology with explanation in geophysics, his analyses of "accident" and "species," and his defense of "every event has a cause" as a presupposition of scientific investigation.

Cosmology. In his cosmological essays Wright condemned the nebular hypothesis and criticized Spencer's defense of it. He referred to the production of systems of worlds as "cosmic weather." He believed that cosmic events, like ordinary weather, show on the whole no development or any discernible tendency whatever. In the stellar world there is a doing and undoing without end. Wright based his nondevelopmental view on what he called the principle of countermovements, "a principle in accordance with which there is no action in nature to which there is not some counter-action" (*Philosophical Discussions,* p. 9). He was, obviously, much impressed with the conservation principles of physics. Beginning with his concept of countermovements, and depending primarily upon the first law of thermodynamics and the conservation of angular momentum, he worked out a technical and elaborate hypothesis about the origin of the sun's heat and the positions and movements of planets.

Other doctrines. Epistemologically, Wright was in the Humean tradition, but unlike many British empiricists he emphasized the empirical verification of beliefs and was indifferent to the origins of belief. Concerning religion, he was an agnostic. James observed that "never in a human head was contemplation more separated from desire." Wright simply had no desires about God one way or another. In moral philosophy he was a utilitarian, defending, in particular, J. S. Mill's views.

The metaphysical topics that most interested Wright were self-consciousness and a priori knowledge. In *Philosophical Discussions* (pp. 199–266), after sketching a naturalistic account of self-consciousness, Wright tried to show that the notion of substance was meaningless. He believed that ultimate reality consisted of "neutral phenomena" and that the distinction between subject and object is only a classification through observation. Wright's position was essentially a neutral monism and was a precursor of William James's notion of pure experience.

Unlike most nineteenth-century philosophers, Wright did not deny the existence of a priori knowledge. Quite to the contrary, he insisted that *all* knowledge, even the perception of qualities as well as relations and abstract concepts, has an a priori element, and this element can be explained experientially (*Letters*, pp. 123–135). This analysis is particularly interesting at the present, since we are currently offered various forms of "factual" or "pragmatic" concepts of a priori knowledge.

Works by Wright

Philosophical Discussions, C. E. Norton, ed. New York, 1877.
Letters, J. B. Thayer, ed. Cambridge, Mass., 1878.
Philosophical Writings. Edward H. Madden, ed. New York, 1958.

Works on Wright

Madden, Edward H., *Chauncey Wright*. New York, 1964.
Madden, Edward H., *Chauncey Wright and the Foundations of Pragmatism*. Seattle, 1963. Contains complete bibliography of articles on Wright.

EDWARD H. MADDEN

WUNDT, WILHELM (1832–1920), German philosopher and psychologist who founded the first psychological laboratory and won world fame as a teacher and scholar. Wundt was born in Neckarau, a suburb of Mannheim. After studying medicine at the universities of Tübingen, Heidelberg, and Berlin, he was a *Privatdozent* from 1857 to 1864 at the Physiological Institute founded by Hermann von Helmholtz in Heidelberg. At the age of 24 he became so severely ill that he was given up by his physicians and remained close to death for several weeks. In this time of crisis he developed his most essential religious and philosophical views, and also his ideas concerning the mental.

In a series of contributions to the theory of sense perception, published between 1858 and 1862, Wundt's interest in psychological problems, an interest derived from his physiological studies, becomes clear. He gave his first psychological lecture in 1862, and in 1863 his *Vorlesungen über die Menschen- und Tier-Seele* (2 vols., Leipzig, 1863, translated by J. G. Creighton and E. B. Titchener as *Lectures on Human and Animal Psychology*, London, 1896). A series of lectures given in 1864 on the fundamentals of physiological psychology was published at Leipzig in 1874 as *Grundzüge der physiologischen Psychologie* (translated

by E. B. Titchener as *Principles of Physiological Psychology*, New York, 1904), his chief work. In the same year Wundt was called to the professorship in inductive philosophy at Zurich. In 1875 he accepted a call to Leipzig, where he founded the world's first experimental laboratory in psychology, the Institut für Experimentelle Psychologie, in 1879. Students from many countries throughout the world became devoted disciples and returned home to found similar institutions.

As a young man in Heidelberg, Wundt was a member of the Baden Stände assembly and the presiding officer of the Heidelberg Society for Workingmen's Education; he was in favor of a patriotic socialism. During the Franco-Prussian War of 1870–1871 he served as an army doctor. As an old man he was rector of Leipzig University (1900) and was overwhelmed with national and international honors and titles. Although in his last years he was practically blind, he did not retire from his teaching position until 1917. A philosophical autobiography was prepared for publication in the year of his death in Grossbothen, near Leipzig.

Philosophy. As a philosopher Wundt was self-taught. He published a system of logic (*Logik*, 2 vols., Stuttgart, 1880–1883; 4th and 5th eds., 3 vols., 1919–1924), a system of ethics (*Ethik*, Stuttgart, 1886; 5th ed., 3 vols., 1923–1924), and a system of philosophy (*System der Philosophie*, Leipzig, 1889; 4th ed., 2 vols., Leipzig, 1919) during the 1880s. He later wrote on historical subjects (*Die Nationen und ihre Philosophie*, 1915; *Leibniz*, 1916). Wundt was a voluntarist and a follower of the German school of idealism; as such he was indebted to Leibniz in particular, and also to Schopenhauer and Hegel. He opposed sensationalism, materialism, and the relativity of values; nevertheless, he drew ideas from contemporary positivism, particularly in his eclectic historicism and his theoretical inclination to a sociological collectivism. This positivist tendency, noticeable until the middle of his career, especially as a kind of defense against metaphysics, was overcome late in his life. Wundt's main concern in logic was exactness in formal derivations; in ethics it was to secure the Leibnizian morality, based on duty, against contemporary utilitarianism and hedonism on the one hand and subjectivism and relativism on the other. Wundt also essentially followed Leibniz in his parallelist treatment of the mind–body problem.

General psychology. If in his philosophy Wundt was primarily an eclectic and historical encyclopedist, he demonstrated his originality in psychology, where he achieved world-wide fame as the real founder of the science and its methodology. However, he was far from wanting to destroy the interconnection between psychology and philosophy. He regarded psychology as the common basis for all scientific and cultural knowledge and the bond uniting all the individual sciences, and therefore as the "science directly preparatory to philosophy."

Nevertheless, Wundt resisted "psychologism" as later formulated and criticized by Edmund Husserl—that is, the reduction of cultural organization and normative evaluations to mere mental processes and the relativization of the timelessly valid to the mere here and now in consciousness.

One of Wundt's main concerns was to investigate conscious processes in their own context by experiment and introspection. He regarded both of these as "exact methods," interrelated in that experimentation created optimal conditions for introspection. Where the experimental method failed, Wundt turned to other "objectively valuable aids," specifically to "those products of cultural communal life which lead one to infer particular mental motives. Outstanding among these are speech, myth, and social custom." Wundt's two main fields of investigation and his two main works, the *Physiologische Psychologie* and his *Völkerpsychologie* ("Folk Psychology," or "Psychology of Nations," 2 vols., Leipzig, 1904; 3d ed., 10 vols., Leipzig, 1911–1920), correspond to this methodological division.

As a follower of Leibniz, Wundt maintained a strict psychophysical parallelism in his basic concepts and rejected any form of theory of reciprocal interaction (causation); however, he limited the mental to the realm of conscious events ("the actual"), in what F. A. Lange referred to as "psychology without soul." Experience should be investigated in its context, "as it is actually given to the subject." In contrast with the natural sciences, the subject matter of psychology is "the content of experience in its immediate nature, unmodified by abstraction and reflection." This claim, which in today's terminology is a strictly phenomenological one, was accompanied by a demand for explanations derived from strict necessity and based on as complete an analysis as possible of the direct, complex findings. Wundt modified the categories of explanation by assuming a unique "psychic causality," which he sought to distinguish from scientific or mechanical causality as including motivation. At this point in his thinking, again following Leibniz, he fought against British and French sensationalism and materialism.

Despite his stress on analytic observation, many notions of Wundt's psychology are transitional to the modern *Ganzheitspsychologie* (psychology of totalities, psychology of wholes) of Felix Krueger and others, among them the "principle of creative resultants or synthesis," which allows perception to transcend a mere addition of stimuli; the "unity of the frame of mind"; and the "value-grade of the total," or feeling and emotion. In his theory of the types of feelings Wundt went beyond the narrow dimensions of pleasure and displeasure, and developed the concept of "total feeling." Although Wundt sought to investigate the elements of conscious processes and their connecting forms, he cannot be counted among the classical sensationalist psychologists because his theory of actuality refers to constantly changing processes rather than to static elements.

Wundt designated the basic mental activity "apperception." Apperception is a unifying function which should be understood as an activity of the will. Feelings are attitudes adopted in apperception toward its individual contents. Thus apperception is simultaneously a descriptive and an explanatory concept. It remained for Krueger, Wundt's pupil and his successor at Leipzig, to remove the limitation to the "pure mental actuality" (structural psychology) and thereby pave the way for the psychology of personality.

Many aspects of Wundt's empirical physiological psychology are still fruitful today. Among them are his principles of mutually enhanced contrasts and of assimilation and dissimilation, for instance, in color and form perception, and his advocacy of "objective" methods of expression and of recording results, especially in language. Another is the principle of heterogony of ends, which states that multiply motivated acts lead to unintended side effects which in turn become motives for new actions.

Social psychology. Wundt believed that his principles of physiological psychology were provable and confirmable in the nonexperimental realm of social, developmental, or cultural psychology, which he called *Völkerpsychologie*. In this field sociological considerations, and particularly the encyclopedic presentation of materials from history and from the other *Geisteswissenschaften* (roughly, "cultural and social sciences," or "humanities"; see GEISTESWISSENSCHAFTEN), became Wundt's main concern, overshadowing actual psychological questions. The "objective products of the collective intellect" in nations—speech, myth (religion), and social custom (law)—that were the original subjects of *Völkerpsychologie* came in practice to include social structures and the arts. In Wundt's analysis, which he applied to an incredible amount of material and which was necessarily modified by later progress in the cultural and social sciences, the principle of the social, prehistoric, collective determination of intellectual development dominated. Concern with the individual and with individual development was neglected for this sociogenetic problem. There is, besides, a methodological gap between phenomenological and experimental psychology and cultural psychology, as was emphasized by Wilhelm Dilthey and Eduard Spranger, wide enough to endanger the unity of psychology.

Despite the outmoded material it contains, Wundt's gigantic lifework still offers a powerful inspiration that has never been totally exhausted, at least partly because, since his time, psychology and the *Geisteswissenschaften* have continued to move farther apart. Felix Krueger said at Wundt's grave, "In him faithfulness to fact was raised to the level of genius." Thoroughness and methodical acuity, combined with universal versatility, created something unique in his work. Wundt has been extolled as the last "polyhistor." Education and esthetics were the only fields to which he made no contribution. E. G. Boring computed his total published output at 53,000 pages—an entire library. The complete list of his works, published by his daughter Eleonore Wundt in 1926, is a hefty brochure. In both philosophy and psychology Wundt's oscillation between idealistic and positivistic tendencies kept him bound to his time and caused a notable lack of consistency. He was a major pioneer of both scientific and cultural psychology, even though he was unable to integrate them. The unity of all sciences through psychology and the development of philosophy out of psychology remain as transient theoretical postulates unrealizable and unrealized by developments since his death.

Additional Works by Wundt

Erlebtes und Erkanntes, Selbstbiographie ("Things Experienced and Perceived, Autobiography"). Stuttgart, 1920.

Wilhelm Wundts Werk, ein Verzeichnis seiner sämtlichen Schriften ("Wilhelm Wundt's Work, A List of His Complete Writings"), Eleonore Wundt, ed. Munich, 1926.

Works on Wundt

Boring, E. G., *A History of Experimental Psychology*, 2d ed. New York, 1950. Pp. 318–347.

Heussner, A., *Einführung in Wilhelm Wundts Philosophie und Psychologie*. Göttingen, 1920.

Hoffmann, Arthur, "Wilhelm Wundt, eine Würdigung." *Beiträge zur Philosophie des deutschen Idealismus*, Vol. 2 (1922).

König, Edmund, *W. Wundt, Seine Philosophie und Psychologie*. Stuttgart, 1901; 3d ed., 1912.

Nef, Willi, *Die Philosophie Wilhelm Wundts*. Leipzig, 1923.

Peters, R. S., ed., *Brett's History of Psychology*. London, 1953. Pp. 479–488.

Petersen, Peter, *Wilhelm Wundt und seine Zeit*. Stuttgart, 1925.

A Wilhelm Wundt Archive, established by his daughter in his house at Grossbothen, was transferred to the Psychological Institute of the University of Leipzig at her death and is administered by the institute.

ALBERT WELLEK
Translated by *Tessa Byck*

WYCLYF, JOHN (c. 1320–1384), scholastic philosopher and ecclesiastical reformer. Born in the north of England, near Richmond, Wyclyf spent most of his adult life in and around Oxford. He served several parishes as priest and held a series of prebends which gave him a modest income. On several occasions he was asked his opinion in matters of government policy toward the papacy, and he appeared once before Parliament. In 1374 Wyclyf was a member of a royal commission of three that met with representatives of the papal Curia at Bruges to attempt to solve the impasse between England and the papacy over England's refusal to pay the Peter's pence. Later he became an adherent of and adviser to the Duke of Lancaster, John of Gaunt, who protected Wyclyf when, under pressure from the English hierarchy, he was charged with heresy. Wyclyf retired, probably on Lancaster's advice, from active public life to his parish at Lutterworth in 1382. In that year he suffered a paralytic stroke but continued his prolific writing until his death, from a second stroke, two years later.

Wyclyf's literary life may be divided into three periods. During the first period, from about 1358 to 1372, he was primarily an academic philosopher, lecturing on logic and metaphysics in orthodox terms. During the second period, from 1372 to 1377 or 1378, he began to apply his realist philosophy to the problems of church and state, an application that resulted in his doctrine of dominion. In the last period, from 1377 or 1378 to 1384, he went much further in his investigation of the basis and structure of the Roman church and came to conclusions quite openly antipapal. During this period papal bulls were aimed against him (1377); he was twice hailed before local bodies on orders from Rome; and many of his conclusions were specifically condemned, although he was not personally disciplined. These same conclusions, in addition to many more, were condemned by the Council of Constance in 1415.

Wyclyf's philosophical presuppositions colored all his thought. The transition from one period of his life to another was barely perceptible and he was able, late in his life, to refer to his earlier expressions with few apologies. In the atmosphere of mid-fourteenth-century Oxford, Wyclyf early had to take a position toward the *universalia post rem* of Ockham's nominalism, then popular and persuasive. He rejected its priority of the particulars over universals in favor of the older Augustinian tradition of *universalia ante rem*. Once he had accepted this position, he followed it to its logical conclusions and constructed a *summa de ente* in 12 books which, while not so systematic as most other *summae* of the thirteenth and fourteenth centuries, nevertheless dealt in great detail with the salient points of dispute between the nominalists, the *doctores moderni*, as he called them, and the protagonists of universal ideas.

The "Summa de Ente." Following his early works on logic, written probably between 1360 and 1365, Wyclyf's *Summa de Ente* occupied him until at least 1370, when his attention was diverted to theology. The *Summa* in its final form consists of two books of six treatises each. The first book treats being in general, the doctrine of universals, and the nature and function of time. These questions are approached from the point of view of man and his cosmos. The second book is pure theology: God's intellection, his knowledge, his will, the Trinity, his ideas and his power to create outside himself. In Wyclyf's grand design the first book is anthropology and the second book is theology. Universals thus may be considered the human parallel of God's ideas. Knowing only the *Timaeus* of Plato's works, Wyclyf adhered to Plato as he knew him from Augustine. His realism was uncompromising. Universals exist *ante rem*, temporally and logically prior to the particular. "The idea is therefore essentially the divine nature and formally the *ratio* according to which God intelligizes [*intelligit*] creatures." These ideas make up the creative mind of God. In a parallel fashion the universal (on man's level) *is* its singular. The singular participates in its universal, which is by nature a projection of an idea in the mind of God. As a creation of God's mind, the singular is incapable of annihilation. For God to allow a singular to be annihilated would be to permit the annihilation of a part of himself— an obvious impossibility.

As he articulated this line of thought, Wyclyf was led to examine the church's doctrine of transubstantiation. He reasoned that the church held that in the Eucharist the substance of bread and wine was annihilated. From about 1379 he attacked the doctrine vehemently on purely logical and philosophical grounds. This position in turn was bitterly attacked by orthodox theologians and later formally anathematized at the Council of Constance. In view of his basic realism Wyclyf could not have done otherwise than he did.

The church. About 1374 Wyclyf had begun a spirited defense of the doctrine of dominion. This concept of the sanctions of power was rooted in Augustine and had recently been propounded by Richard FitzRalph, archbishop of Armagh in Ireland. Dominion or lordship is founded in grace, and he who is without grace has no proper right to exercise dominion. Applied to the religious hierarchy, it would have deprived many of the higher clergy of their power and emoluments.

In 1378 Wyclyf was led, by an incident involving the theory and practice of sanctuary, to examine the nature of the church and the relations of the papacy with the English crown. In the course of the dispute arising from the publication of his views, he came to the clear conclusion that the pope and the cardinalate were unnecessary and that in England the king should control the church, allowing for counsel and advice of theologians in matters of theology.

Wyclyf was a stout defender of the Pauline – Augustinian doctrine of predestination, which he related to and strengthened with his doctrines of universals and necessity. The implications of predestination did not favor a highly organized ecclesiastical organization; if a believer is predestined by God to salvation from all eternity, the church would soon have no reason for existence. Individualism in religious matters could hardly be tolerated by the establishment.

In the last years of his life Wyclyf composed a second *summa,* a *Summa Theologica,* also in 12 books. Not a *summa* in the thirteenth-century style, it was a series of polemical treatises concerned with problems in church or national polity, in defense of his contested opinions. In presentation he remained a Schoolman to the end, but his ideas were disruptive of the establishment, and opposition, at Oxford and in London, was determined and ruthless. The opposition to his efforts at reform is somewhat surprising, in view of his highly pronounced English nationalism; but English clerics were his bitterest opponents. In Wyclyf's view, his thought and action were consistent and consistently rooted in the doctrine of divine ideas, the creative *rationes* by which the universals existed before the particular and were exhibited in the particular, *essentialiter, formaliter, et eternaliter.*

Bibliography

The Wyclif Society published 33 volumes of Wyclyf's works (London, 1883 – 1922) but omitted some important philosophical treatises. See also S. H. Thomson, *Joh. Wyclif Summe de Ente libb. I et II* (Oxford, 1930; reissued Boulder, Colo., 1956), a Latin text with critical introduction; and A. D. Breck, ed., *Joh. Wyclyf De Trinitate* (Boulder, Colo., 1962).

The standard life of Wyclyf is H. B. Workman, *John Wyclif,* 2 vols. (Oxford, 1926). See also K. B. McFarlane, *John Wycliffe and the Beginnings of English Nonconformity* (London, 1952); and J. A. Robson, *John Wyclif and the Oxford Schools* (Cambridge, 1961).

S. HARRISON THOMSON

X

XENOPHANES OF COLOPHON, in Ionia, probably lived from about 570 B.C. until at least the end of the sixth century, although some scholars think he may have lived until the middle of the fifth century. He probably left Colophon when it was captured by the Persians soon after 546 B.C., and thereafter he wandered about the Greek world, especially in Sicily. He wrote a series of poems in various meters from which there survive about 68 lines in elegiacs and over 40 in hexameters. Whether some of the latter came from a separate poem entitled *Peri Physeos* ("On Nature") must remain uncertain, although clearly many lines did deal with physical questions.

Most famous are Xenophanes' satirical attacks on the traditions of the Olympian theology, whose gods he vilified for their immorality. He also made fun of their anthropomorphic character, arguing that animals would make their gods in their own image for no better reasons than men do. More constructively, he argued for a single, motionless, nonanthropomorphic god, "shaking" all things by the power of thought. Later tradition added that his god was spherical, but there is nothing in the fragments to suggest this, and it may represent no more than a projection back from Parmenides, who likened his one being to a sphere. Aristotle says that Xenophanes declared that there was one that was god (or "the One was the god") after concentrating his gaze upon the whole sky. This should probably be taken more literally than has been usual in recent scholarship. Xenophanes' god is motionless in one place (fragment 26) and is probably to be identified with the surrounding sky—and for Xenophanes the sky was probably not even dome-shaped, let alone spherical. Although on this interpretation certain difficulties remain, it is easier than the alternative, according to which the unmoving god is identified with the world itself or the universe, which certainly included change within itself and fairly certainly included locomotion as well. In this case Xenophanes will not properly be classed as a pantheist even if all the physical processes of the world are under the control of his god.

In his physical theories Xenophanes probably held that the whole has no source or origin and so is ungenerated, thus being the first to anticipate the Aristotelian view. But within the whole he certainly supposed that generation and destruction take place. The most likely account is that he supposed earth and water were necessary sources for all living creatures. The observation of fossil remains of fishes in the quarries at Syracuse and elsewhere suggested that there was an alternation of wet and dry ages, but this was a cyclical process within the world and not related to any origin or destruction of the whole. In addition, he went into some detail about the movements of the heavenly bodies, but the surviving accounts are both meager and obscure.

Of greater philosophic interest are his views about knowledge, attested by actual fragments from his poems. In a much discussed fragment (fragment 34) he declared that there is no certain truth about the gods or about anything of which he speaks. For even if the truth were fully said, it would not be known but would be only a matter of seeming. In antiquity some took this statement to mean that no knowledge of any kind is possible, and so Xenophanes was treated as a skeptic. Another view also known in antiquity was that he substituted opinion (or seeming) for knowledge as a source of understanding. This would make him an empiricist. Later writers added to the evidence of fragment 34 the statement that for Xenophanes god *can* know the truth. This has led to a third view, propounded in modern times, that he distinguished two realms of existence. Certain knowledge is possible for men of one realm but not of the other, where only opinion is possible, although god may be able to have knowledge of both. None of these three views seems exactly to fit the words of fragment 34, which states that men can have *no* certain knowledge, only opinion. Nonetheless, the explicit introduction of the contrast between knowledge and opinion is a very important step. The Ionians generally seem only to have attempted to substitute their own knowledge for the false knowledge of others. Xenophanes did believe (fragment 18) that, by searching, men can improve their understanding, but he implies that this will always fall short of knowledge.

The above account is based on the fragments and those statements in the doxographical tradition which may reasonably be supposed to be based on Xenophanes' poems. It ignores the evidence of the section dealing with Xenophanes in the pseudo-Aristotelian treatise *De Melisso Xenophane Gorgia* (*MXG*), and it ignores the associated tradition that Xenophanes was the founder of the Eleatic school. This tradition was known to Aristotle and is referred to in Plato's *Sophist* (242C–D). It may have come from Hippias' schematization of the history of earlier thought, but it is likely to have been developed much further after Aristotle's time. It is fairly certainly the basis of the treatment of Xenophanes in *MXG*, where his doctrines are presented in the language of Parmenides with many of Parmenides' distinctive arguments included. The contrast between the surviving fragments and the arguments in *MXG* makes it unlikely that the latter correctly represents Xenophanes' original statements; it must constitute a mistaken attempt to absorb Xenophanes into the fully developed stream of Eleatic doctrine. The attempt to make Parmenides a direct pupil of Xenophanes should also be rejected. But there were many features in Xenophanes' thoughts as preserved in fragments which did anticipate Parmenides, and to that extent the later tradition was not wholly ill-founded.

Bibliography

Fragments and testimonia in H. Diels and W. Kranz, *Fragmente der Vorsokratiker*, 10th ed. (Berlin, 1961), Vol. I. See also W. Jaeger, *The Theology of the Early Greek Philosophers* (Oxford, 1947), Ch. 3; G. S. Kirk and J. E. Raven, *The Presocratic Philosophers* (Cambridge, 1957), Ch. 5; and W. K. C. Guthrie, *A History of Greek Philosophy* (Cambridge, 1962), Vol. I, Ch. 6.

G. B. KERFERD

XENOPHON (c. 430 B.C.–c. 350 B.C.), Athenian citizen, soldier, gentleman-farmer, historian, and author of many varied and often graceful prose works. When young he knew Socrates, whom he consulted before joining, in 401, the famous expedition to Persia narrated in his masterpiece, the *Anabasis*. Xenophon played a part in leading the defeated remnant back to Greece. Meanwhile, in 399, Socrates had been executed on trumped-up charges. In the subsequent pamphleteering, Xenophon wrote in Socrates' defense. His so-called *Apology of Socrates* is an unconvincing footnote to Plato's; but later he compiled his extensive and valuable *Memorabilia* ("Recollections of Socrates") the work which has given Xenophon, not himself a philosopher, considerable importance to all post-Socratic philosophers. In it Xenophon supplemented his defense of Socrates against specific charges (made in a pamphlet by Polycrates) with a more general description of his character as a man, a friend, and a teacher, strongly emphasizing his beneficial influence on all who knew him and, for illustration, recording many conversations in which Socrates' views or methods were displayed. Xenophon claimed to have heard many of these conversations himself; others were reported to him by friends among the original interlocutors. Some longer sequences of conversations follow up related topics, but individual conversations are never sustained as long as even a short Platonic dialogue. Undeniably, Xenophon's Socrates is less lively in discussion than Plato's and far less impressive in defending his paradoxes. The difference reveals the gulf between Plato and his contemporaries in literary skill and in philosophical understanding. But there is no need to reject Xenophon's testimony, despite persistent attacks by scholars on his honesty. Xenophon's picture of Socrates is his own, drawn from his own and his friends' memories of Socrates, not plagiarized from other "Socratic" writers any more than from Plato; it is authenticated precisely by its failings. Xenophon saw Socrates as a man of enormously strong moral character and a teacher of moral principles revolutionary for their day in their demand for unselfishness and self-control. Xenophon only half understood the philosophical significance of Socrates' views, and for fuller understanding we must turn to Plato; but Xenophon occasionally added important details, and with allowance for Xenophon's limitations an impression of Socrates can be obtained from him which helps us to discern very generally the area in which Plato was presenting his own arguments and no longer those of Socrates.

Xenophon's Socrates demonstrates repeatedly the practical importance of knowledge. He advises young men ambitious to be generals and politicians to acquire knowledge, and draws analogies to show that all skills must be learned; he discusses their respective skills with a painter, a sculptor, a breastplate maker, and even, humorously, with a courtesan. He does not try, as Plato's Socrates did, to question the significance of the craftsmen's knowledge, but only to show that their knowledge can be usefully increased by deeper understanding of the purposes of their various crafts. In turn, he is suspicious of the purely theoretical study of astronomy and geometry beyond their practical uses. Xenophon stresses, nevertheless, that Socrates himself was not ignorant of theoretical science.

Xenophon does not quote in so many words the Socratic paradox "no one errs voluntarily," but he does state that Socrates did not distinguish knowledge from self-control and identified justice and all other virtues with knowledge; knowledge of justice or piety is what produces the just or pious man. Characteristically, however, he repeatedly shows Socrates warning against "weakness of will," and forgets that in the Socratic view, strictly speaking, this could not occur; his admiration of Socrates' own self-control leads him to praise self-control as an independent virtue.

Xenophon occasionally reproduces a Socratic *elenchus*, or interrogation demonstrating an interlocutor's ignorance, and comments that Socrates used this method to stimulate moral improvement in his pupils by inducing them to acquire knowledge. Xenophon shows no grasp of *elenchus* as a philosophical weapon for testing arguments, nor indeed of the Platonic Socrates' insistence that consciousness of one's ignorance may be the best one can achieve. Xenophon's Socrates uses no "irony," but states positive views quite unreservedly. He is interested in definitions and unlike Plato's Socrates confidently provides them; rather surprisingly, he is willing to define "good" and "beautiful" as relative to utility. Perhaps out of many suggestions intended by Socrates to be tentative, or to show the difficulties of definition, Xenophon—in pursuit of certainty—isolated a few solutions as final.

Xenophon at one point described Socrates' method as "leading the discussion back to its basic premise (*hypothesis*)" by establishing, for example, an agreed general definition of the good citizen before assessing a particular citizen's goodness; he tells us that Socrates regarded agreement in discussion as the best guarantee against error. This account of *hypothesis* is much simpler than Plato's in either *Meno* or *Phaedo,* but it is abundantly exemplified in Plato's early dialogues. Xenophon nowhere ascribes to Socrates any theory of Forms, but he quotes a suggestion of Socrates that etymologically "to perform dialectic" means "to arrange things in classes."

Xenophon's entertaining *Symposium* ("Banquet") and *Oeconomicus* ("Household Management") display Socrates taking part in sustained discussions; but here this is a literary device with no biographical intention, and in any case little is attributed to Socrates. Xenophon's idealizing *Cyropaedia* ("Education of Cyrus") shows very slight Socratic influence.

Bibliography

Xenophon's complete works may be found in both Greek and English in the seven-volume Loeb Classical Library edition (London and New York, 1914–1925). The *Memorabilia* in the Loeb edition, translated by E. C. Marchant, appeared in 1923.

For studies on Xenophon's Socrates, see A. Delatte, *Le Troisième Livre des souvenirs socratiques de Xénophon* (Liège and Paris, 1933), and R. Simeterre, *La Théorie socratique de la vertu-science selon les "Mémorables" de Xénophon* (Paris, 1938).

DAVID B. ROBINSON

Y

YAMAGA SOKŌ (1622–1685), Japanese Confucianist of the *kogakuha,* or "school of ancient learning," and codifier of the ethics of the military class, *Bushidō,* the "way of the warrior." Yamaga was born in Aizu, Fukushima Prefecture. At 9 he entered the school of Hayashi Razan in Edo (Tokyo), where he learned the official Chu Hsi doctrine. Interested in military science, he became a master of it. He taught it first at the castle of Lord Asano of Akō (Hyogo Prefecture) and later in Edo, where the novelty of his advocating the use of firearms attracted many followers. In 1666 he wrote *Seikyō yōroku* ("The Essence of Confucianism"), a blunt critique of Chu Hsi's ideas. For this and for his innovations in military science, he incurred the wrath of his two former teachers, Hayashi and the military expert Hōjō Ujinaga, and was exiled from Edo. For the rest of his life he lived under mild confinement at the castle of Lord Asano, instilling into the samurai of Akō the loyalty which was to make 47 of them famous for revenging their lord by slaying the man who had disgraced him and dutifully committing hara-kiri. Their deed and death was immortalized in the drama *Chūshingura.*

In the preface to *Seikyō yōroku,* Yamaga clearly states the program of the "school of ancient learning," adding that the doctrine of Confucius and the ancient sages had been obscured by interpreters and commentators. He dismisses Mencius, Chu Hsi, and Wang Yang-ming easily; he rejects the "great ultimate" (*taikyoku*) of Chu Hsi as a later Buddhist interpolation in Confucianism. The universe, he holds, is explained by the movement of yin and yang, the passive and active elements, and it has no beginning or end. Human nature is neither good nor bad, but ethically neutral. He stresses self-interest, but he urges that common utility take precedence over it.

The term *Bushidō* is a recent one, coined long after his death, but its meaning is clearly traceable to two of his books, *Shidō* and *Bukyō shōgaku.* His "way of the warrior" consists of ethical norms and practical means of fostering in oneself a sense of loyal duty (*gi*) toward one's lord. Mental training is paramount; serenity, sincerity, magnanimity, introspection, and self-restraint are the virtues to be cultivated. Yamaga praised the ancient Chinese sages but he was a strong nationalist who extolled Japan over China.

Bibliography

For Yamaga's works see *Yamaga Sokō zenshū* ("Complete Works of Yamaga Sokō"), Hirose Yutaka, ed., 15 vols. (Tokyo, 1940). For discussion, see Hori Isao, *Yamaga Sokō* (Tokyo, 1963) and W. T. de Bary, Ryusaku Tsunoda, and Donald Keene, eds., *Sources of Japanese Tradition* (New York, 1958), pp. 394–410, which contains selections in translation.

GINO K. PIOVESANA, S.J.

YAMAZAKI ANSAI (1618–1682), Japanese Confucianist notable for his ethical bent and Confucian rationalization of Shintoism. He was raised at Kyoto in a Buddhist monastery; he was so unruly that he was sent to Tosa (now the city of Kōchi) on Shikoku Island, where he came under the influence of Tani Jichū (1598–1649), the originator of the southern branch of the Chu Hsi school of Confucianism in Japan. Having discarded Buddhism, Yamazaki taught Chu Hsi Confucianism in Kyoto and Edo (Tokyo) from 1648. Uncompromising in character, he condescended in 1665 to become the official scholar of Hoshina Masayuki, lord of Aizu (in northeast Japan). At Hoshina's death in 1672 Yamazaki returned to Kyoto and developed his Confucian Shintoism.

Though a stern Confucianist teacher he gathered around him more than six thousand students; among the best were Asami Keisai (1652–1711), Satō Naokata (1650–1719), and Miyake Shōsai (1662–1741). They formed the Kimon or Ansai school. However, Yamazaki's Shintoism held the seed of disharmony; before his death this school split into four. He urged the ethical formula *keinai gigai,* that is, "Devotion within, righteousness without." By "devotion" he meant not simply Confucian self-cultivation but rather a religiously rectified mind related to cosmic reason. By "righteousness" he meant virtue toward others. His maxim, "Learning is knowing and practice," suggests a middle way between overemphasis on mastery of the mind and overemphasis on social virtues.

Yamazaki's Shintoism deserves attention because of its Confucian rationalism and the influence it had in the revival of Shintoist studies in Japan. It is called *Suika Shintō* and elaborates on Confucian cosmogony to explain Japan's mythological creation chronicles. Trying to see a rational core in these legends, he developed the Shinto creed, borrowing from Neo-Confucianism. His best pupils, however, did not follow him in his Shintoist phase; and the *kokugakusha,* the "national learning scholars," did not become the purveyors of a rationalized Shintoism. His most lasting impact was made through his popularization of Confucian ethics and indirect fostering of loyalism toward the emperor. This last trend was exemplified in Asami Keisai, Yamagata Daini, and in the school of Mito historians. Yamazaki is, however, given credit for later loyalist and nationalist trends.

Bibliography

For Japanese sources, see *Yamazaki Ansai zenshū* ("Yamazaki Ansai: Complete Works"), 5 vols. (Nagoya, 1937), and Bitō Masahide, *Nihon hōken shisōshi kenkyū* ("Studies on the History of Feudal Thought in Japan"; Tokyo, 1961), pp. 40–99. An English source is W. T. de Bary, Ryusaku Tsunoda, and Donald Keene, eds., *Sources of Japanese Tradition* (New York, 1958), pp. 363–371.

Gino K. Piovesana, S.J.

YANG CHU was a sophist and philosopher of ancient China who flourished in the first half of the fourth century B.C. His life was shrouded in obscurity, but his influence was so widespread in his time that Mencius compared him and Mo Tzu to floods and wild animals that ravaged the land. Mencius also attacked him for his unwillingness to "pluck a hair from his body to benefit the world." In the Taoist work *Lieh Tzu* one of the chapters attributed to Yang Chu reveals him as an Epicurean who indulged in the pleasures of wine and women. Although these are the images in which Yang Chu has been presented to posterity, he was actually much more than a sensualist and egoist.

According to contemporary sources, Yang Chu was an early Taoist teacher preceding Chuang Tzu. He represented a new philosophical trend toward naturalism as the best means of preserving life in a decadent and turbulent world. The myriad beings, Yang Chu believed, are born with an instinct for survival. Although the highest of all creations, man lacks sharp teeth and claws to protect himself, strong muscles to resist attack, and thick feathers to shield him from the inclemencies of the weather. Thus, he must rely on his intelligence rather than on his strength. Whereas prowess becomes despicable when used in assaulting others, intelligence is a great asset in the struggle for existence.

Yang Chu's main tenet is the completion of man's inner, spiritual nature through self-expression and self-contentment. He did not advocate sheer egoism; rather, he emphasized the fact that self-impairment, symbolized by the plucking of one's hair, will in no way lead to other people's benefit. Although he would not toil for others, neither would he injure them or harm himself in the pursuit of fame, wealth, and rank. These are to be avoided as temptations external to one's nature. On the other hand, there is inherent in man a craving for the pleasures of this world. To seek the gratification of one's desires for such things as fine food and beautiful objects is to yield to one's original nature and in this way to work for its completion.

Although Yang Chu would not have hesitated to seek happiness to his heart's content, he had no yearning for longevity or immortality. One should not unnecessarily shorten one's life, nor should one strive to live beyond one's allotted span of life. In Yang Chu's opinion, to die is just as natural as to live; both are part of the due process of change. Death being unavoidable, it is not to be feared or held in awe, and any ceremony in connection with it is superfluous. It matters not to a dead man whether his body is buried in earth or exposed to the atmosphere, burned to ashes or dumped into water, thrown away in a ditch or dressed in embroidered garments and placed in a stone coffin. What matters is that before death strikes, one should live one's life to the fullest.

To summarize, Yang Chu taught, "If everyone does not harm a single hair, and if everyone does not benefit the world, the world will be well governed of itself." That is, if everyone minds his own business, neither giving nor taking from others, but keeping within his own lot and enjoying what he has, one will not only be happy oneself but also contribute to the welfare of the world.

Works by Yang Chu

Yang Chu's Garden of Pleasure, translated by Anton Forke. London, 1912.
The Book of Lieh Tzu, translated by A. C. Graham. London, 1960. Ch. 7, pp. 135–157.

Works on Yang Chu

Ch'en Tz'u-sheng, *Yang Chu.* Shanghai, 1926. In Chinese.
Fung Yu-lan, *A History of Chinese Philosophy,* translated by Derk Bodde, 2 vols. Princeton, N.J., 1952–1953. Vol. I, pp. 133–143.
Hu Shih, *Chung-kuo Che-hsüeh Shih Ta-kang* ("An Outline of Chinese Philosophy"), 4th ed. Shanghai, 1947. Vol. I, pp. 176–183. In Chinese.

Liu Wu-chi

YOGA has a general and a specific sense. First, it refers to a certain range of methods of contemplation used in the Indian religious tradition, both Hindu and non-Hindu; second, it refers to a recognized school of Hindu metaphysics, allied to particular contemplative techniques within the certain range mentioned above. It is convenient to distinguish these two senses by using respectively the words "yoga" and "Yoga." Literally, *yoga* means "harnessing" or "yoking"—the harnessing or control of one's faculties. It is fairly clear from archaeological evidence from the Indus valley that yogic techniques date from prehistoric times in India. Judging from later evidence, these techniques were associated with a sharp distinction between the eternal element in man, the individual *puruṣa* or soul, and the psychophysical organism. (Buddhism, even if it made use of yoga, put the distinction in a different place; namely, between Nirvana as a permanent state and the impermanent states that make up the individual person.) The object of yoga is to isolate this eternal element and to free it from implication in the material world. Thus, yogic techniques aim at attaining a conscious state in which ordinary mental activities, such as perception and imagination, are suspended.

The techniques used may roughly be divided into physical and mental ones. Both in orthodox and in Buddhist yoga, posture (*āsana*) is important, notably the "lotus posture," which is a variant of the normal Indian mode of sitting. The postures are elaborated into what is virtually a whole system of gymnastics in Yoga. Likewise, Yoga emphasizes control of the breath, a kind of respiratory gymnastics. Physical virtuosity is not regarded as an end in itself, however, and in some traditions—for example, Buddhism—is considerably played down. Physical yoga (known as Haṭha-Yoga in the Yoga system) is a preliminary to mental discipline.

The latter can be illustrated from Buddhist sources. In Buddhism the principal form of discipline (in Pāli, *jhāna;* in Sanskrit, *dhyāna,* or "meditation") is divided into eight or nine stages. In the first four of these, a "device" (*kasiṇa*) is used. The yogin may use a blue flower, a round piece of clay, or other object, on which he concentrates his attention. He contemplates it in abstraction from its surroundings, in such a way that he is no longer aware of the distinction between subject and object, with the aim of isolating it as a mere sense datum. After these stages he goes on to contemplate without the use of such an external aid, but tries to think of reality as consisting solely of empty space, then as pure consciousness, then as nonexistent (he repeats to himself the formula "There is nothing"). Finally, he hopes to reach a region of "neither-perception-nor-nonperception," in which the awareness of being aware of anything is removed. Such mind-emptying techniques are often interpreted as helping to give the contemplator an insight into truth, and it is through the mystical experiences accruing from such techniques that the doctrinal systems believed in by the mystics of various schools are often thought to be verified. Thus, what is "discovered" through yoga is interpreted in a number of ways.

The metaphysical system known as Yoga is meant to underpin and explain the methods of liberation adopted by the yogin. It is one of the six orthodox schools of Hindu philosophy (see INDIAN PHILOSOPHY). The classical exposition is that of Patañjali (c. second century B.C.) in the *Yogasūtras* ("Yoga Aphorisms"), a codification of earlier ideas. Also noteworthy are the *Yogabhāṣya* ("Yoga Commentary") attributed to Vyāsa (fourth century A.D.) and the *Yogavārttika* ("Yoga Exposition") of Vijñānabhikṣu (sixteenth century). But Yoga, as a system, is hardly distinguishable from Sāṃkhya and is an adaptation of the latter in the light of practical considerations. The chief distinction between the two systems is that Yoga introduces the concept of a God (*Īśvara*). However, he has no creative functions but is one among the innumerable souls who happens, unlike all others, never to have been implicated in matter and who can be used beneficially as an object of meditation. Thus, he helps souls to liberation; but this liberation does not involve oneness with God. It consists in isolation (*kaivalya*), a state in which the soul exists eternally without any kind of conscious relation either to matter or to other souls and in which it is exempt from pain.

The other chief difference between Sāṃkhya and Yoga is that the latter stresses contemplative techniques, the former metaphysical knowledge, as the means of liberation. But even this is not a great distinction, since knowledge here, as nearly everywhere in the Indian tradition in this sort of context, means something more existential and intuitive than merely intellectual or theoretical.

The training prescribed in Yoga is divided into eight "stages" (like the Buddhist Middle Path): restraint, discipline, posture, respiration, withdrawal from sense objects, concentration, meditation, and trance. Restraint means moral training; discipline is ascetic and religious—the practice of austerity, meditation on God; posture and respiration comprise the exercises of Haṭha-Yoga; withdrawal from sense objects involves the ability to free oneself from the impact of external stimuli, although an imaginative awareness of phenomena remains; concentration is, in classical Yoga, analogous to the first four stages of Buddhist *jhāna,* save that the examples used are rather different— fire, Viṣṇu, the heart, and so on are employed as the imaginative objects of meditation, and the aim is a kind of penetration into the "real essence" of these entities; meditation is analogous to the second four stages of *jhāna;* and in the last stage one is supposed finally to achieve, through the foregoing techniques, a kind of transcendental knowledge in deep trance. However, the last three stages are hard to differentiate clearly and are sometimes grouped under the same head. The transcendental knowledge attained involves a vivid awareness of the nature of the soul and its essential distinctness from the psychophysical organism. This brings liberation.

There has been some investigation of the physiology of Yoga, and there seems little doubt that a kind of hibernation can be achieved and that the control over lungs, heartbeat and the viscera is, by ordinary standards, remarkable. Some of the more spectacular physical claims, however (such as levitation), are unconfirmed, and some of them are mythological in style. The ascription of magical powers to the yogin is part of the traditional tendency in India to think that austerity and mental discipline can create a force which can even threaten the gods. This in turn both reflects and generates the view that mystical experience is the supreme religious goal, transcending the cult of supernatural beings.

Bibliography

TRANSLATED TEXTS

Jha, Ganganatha, *The Yogadarśana,* 2d ed. Madras, 1934.
Patañjali, *The Yoga System of Patañjali,* translated by J. H. Woods, 2d ed. Harvard Oriental Series. Cambridge, Mass. 1927.

GENERAL ACCOUNTS

Eliade, M., *Yoga, Immortality and Freedom.* London, 1958.
Wood, Ernest, *Yoga.* London, 1959.
Zimmer, H., *Philosophies of India.* New York, 1957.

METAPHYSICS

Dasgupta, S. N., *Yoga Philosophy in Relation to Other Systems of Indian Thought.* Calcutta, 1930.
See also bibliography to INDIAN PHILOSOPHY.

PHYSIOLOGICAL RESEARCH

Koestler, Arthur, *The Lotus and the Robot.* London, 1960.

NINIAN SMART

YUGOSLAV PHILOSOPHY. Three main periods can be distinguished in the history of Yugoslavia and in the development of philosophy there. First, during a prolonged feudal period lasting from the twelfth to the nineteenth centuries, Yugoslav philosophy was predominantly theologically oriented and often created by persons who lived abroad and were part of foreign cultures. During the period of national liberation and the development of a bourgeois society, a period lasting from the beginning of the nineteenth century to the German occupation in 1941, the first philosophical institutions were established, but most professional philosophers were epigones of prevailing foreign philosophical trends. In the present socialist period, the prevailing philosophy is a lively, nondogmatic Marxism which is socially engaged but still retains its intellectual independence and freedom of social criticism.

MEDIEVAL PERIOD

The elements of philosophy were taught in Yugoslav monasteries and church schools from the twelfth century on. Ancient writings were translated, and theological disputations among orthodox Scholastics and various kinds of heretics were carried on. Between the twelfth and the fifteenth centuries a great medieval culture flourished in Serbia. The literature of that period was greatly influenced by Byzantine civilization, but it contains elements of an original philosophy emphasizing the moral value of struggling for freedom and of suffering for noble ends. Although Croatia and Slovenia were occupied by Austrians and Hungarians from the twelfth to the twentieth centuries, each preserved its national and cultural individuality. Catholic theology decisively influenced philosophical thought, and many Croats and Slovenes were educated in Italian, German, and French universities, taking part first in the struggles between Thomism and Scotism and later in those between Aristotelianism and Neoplatonism.

Marko Marulić (Latin, Marulis; Italian, Marulo; 1450–1524), a well-known Croatian moralist and poet, was one of the most erudite humanist theologians of his time. His main works, *Evangelistarium* (1501) and *De Institutione Bene Beateque Vivendi* (1506), were translated into several languages. Some Slovene philosophers took part in the development of humanism at the University of Vienna at the end of the fifteenth century. The most important among them was Matija Hvale (fl. c. 1510), whose *Commentarii in Parvuli Philosophiae Naturalis* (Hagenau, 1513) was the first published work by a Slovene philosopher. In commentaries on scholastic texts in natural philosophy, Hvale attempted to reconcile realism and nominalism and emphasized the importance of the study of ancient authors and the empirical study of nature.

From the fifteenth century to 1804 the Turks occupied Serbia and other parts of eastern Yugoslavia. Extraordinary folk poems from this period express a heroic philosophy of resistance. Ragusa (Dubrovnik), the only free city from the sixteenth to the eighteenth century, became a great cultural center, producing several philosophers who became well known in Italy and France. The most original Yugoslav philosopher at that time was Franja Petrić (Francesco Patrizi, 1529–1597), a violent critic of Aristotle's philosophy who created an original and influential Neoplatonist monistic philosophy of nature, in which light is the generating principle of all things and all knowledge.

The Counter Reformation of the seventeenth and early eighteenth centuries suppressed the further development of Renaissance thought in favor of traditional Scholasticism. Nevertheless, this period produced one of the greatest Yugoslav philosophers and scientists, Rudjer Bošković (Roger Boscovich, 1711–1787). Besides work in physics, mathematics, astronomy, and meteorology, Bošković created an original atomic theory. Atoms are conceived as centers of forces, and attraction between atoms becomes repulsion when the distance between them decreases beyond a certain limit. By this theory, which anticipated fundamental discoveries of modern atomic physics, Bošković explained the general properties of matter and many other physical phenomena. Bošković's theory of knowledge was midway between those of Locke and of Leibniz: mind creates ideas and discovers principles, but it does so under the influence of sensory experience. On the other hand, sensations themselves are the product of both external phenomena and mind.

PERIOD OF NATIONAL LIBERATION

Ideas from the Enlightenment reached western and northern Yugoslavia more in the form of literature than in the form of abstract philosophy. In the second half of the eighteenth century, a number of writers, especially in Croatia, took an anticlerical attitude; fought the primitivism, lack of knowledge, and low moral standards of the people; and advocated the expansion of knowledge and education. The Slovene Franc Karpe (1747–1806) gave philosophical expression to the main principles of the Enlightenment in his *Darstellung der Philosophie . . . als Leitfaden bei der Anleitung zum liberalen Philosophieren* (Vienna, 1802–1803). Karpe criticized Scholasticism, demanded the liberation of reason, and developed a philosophy of nature on the basis of the ideas of Newton, Leibniz, and Bošković.

Serbia and Montenegro. Dositej Obradović (1742–1811) was a young Serbian monk disillusioned by monastic life, the church, and theological dogmatism. He traveled extensively in Europe and Yugoslavia, and through his writings and personal contact he sought to raise the intellectual and moral level of the people, to eliminate ignorance and superstition, to achieve a thorough reform of the church and abolition of the monasteries, and to overcome religious differences for the sake of national unity. After the successful uprising against the Turks in 1804, Obradović opened the first high school in Belgrade (1808) and became minister of education. Obradović's rationalistic, utilitarian philosophy was not original, but it was very influential in Serbia.

The liberation of Serbia and the creation of the first schools that taught philosophy encouraged a number of professional philosophers, But, since they were educated abroad, their works were for some time mere adaptations of German and other philosophers. The strong influence of Kant and Hegel was succeeded by the influence of positivism about 1870. The authentic philosophical thought of this period is found not in the work of the professional teachers of philosophy but instead in poems, folk songs, scientific writings, and, later, in revolutionary political pamphlets. All of these express ideas of national and social liberation.

The most interesting figure in the first half of the nineteenth century was Petar Petrović-Njegoš (1813–1851), prince-bishop of Montenegro, leader of a small and poor people in an incessant struggle against the Turks, and a great poet and thinker. Petrović-Njegoš showed the necessity for human struggle and suffering in his epic religious poem *Luča Microcosma* ("The Ray of the Microcosm," 1845) and made them profoundly meaningful in his other great poem, *Gorski Vijenac* ("The Mountain Wreath," 1847). Difficulties and suffering help to forge the human soul. Without effort and sacrifice nothing really great can be accomplished; even a good song cannot be created without pain. So man should not hesitate to fight against evil and tyranny and to overcome any fear. This heroic philosophy corresponded to the attitudes of Petrović-Njegoš' people in a difficult situation and set forth a moral ideal which enormously influenced their behavior.

Some years later the Serbian Svetozar Marković (1846–1875), in "Realni Pravac u Nauci i Životu" ("The Real Trend in Science and Life," in *Letopis Matice Srpske*, 1871–1872) and other works, developed an activistic anthropological philosophy with a definite program of social change. By this time the ideas of N. G. Chernyshevski and other Russian revolutionary democrats, the materialist philosophies of Ludwig Büchner, Karl Vogt, and Jacob Moleschott, and the evolutionary theories of Darwin and Herbert Spencer had gained considerable ground among Serbian intellectuals. Marković also accepted some of the ideas of Marx and Engels, but he tried to take into account the social and economic backwardness of Serbia as well. He therefore emphasized the role of science and of an educated minority in the historical process. He held that there are objective laws governing social progress but that they depend on the laws of human nature, which can be discovered by an analysis of the history of mankind. Genuine intellectuals help their people to become aware of their sufferings and their real needs and to produce a radical change in their conditions. A social revolution, therefore, presupposes the total intellectual power of the people.

Croatia. In Croatia, which throughout the nineteenth century was still occupied by Austria-Hungary, increasing social conflicts and the penetration of western European liberal ideas led to resistance to feudal clericalism and divisions between young and old, progressives and conservatives, liberals and clericals. At first the central issue was freedom of artistic creation. Later, liberal and progressive forces sought to eliminate the influence of the Catholic clergy in public life and especially in culture. They sought intellectual support either in contemporary materialism and evolutionism or in the anticlerical statements of Max Stirner and Nietzsche.

Zagreb University was founded in 1874. Its first professor of philosophy, Franja Marković (1845–1914), was influenced mainly by Herbart. He wrote a large work on ethics and another on the ethical content of folk proverbs. Duro Arnold (1854–1941), in his *Zadnja Bića* ("The Ultimate Beings," Zagreb, 1893), developed an idealistic system in the tradition of Leibniz, Herbart, and Lotze, but he is better known for his textbooks in logic and psychology, which were used for several decades in Croatian high schools.

Albert Bazala (1877–1947) popularized philosophy, especially through the people's university in Zagreb which he created. He believed that mass education is a revolutionary act which destroys obsolete forms of life. His own voluntaristic activism was expounded in his main work, *Metalogički Korijen Filozofije* ("Metalogical Roots of Philosophy," Zagreb, 1924). Genuine cognition is not based on reason, which operates only with bare abstractions, but on an act of will which leads to a personal, immediate, creative projection of the object.

Vladimir Dvorniković (1881–1956), in *Die beiden Grundtypen des Philosophierens* ("The Two Main Types of Philosophizing," Berlin, 1918) and *Savremena Filozofija* ("Contemporary Philosophy," 2 vols., Zagreb, 1919–1920), tried to reduce all philosophical attitudes to two fundamental types, one formal and static and the other active. These types were based on two general psychological types.

Among other philosophers active at Zagreb University prior to World War II were Marijan Tkalčić (1896–1956), who, in *Pokušaj Odredjenja Filozofije* ("An Attempt at a Determination of Philosophy," Zagreb, 1920), took the experience of crisis as the starting point of philosophy, and Stevan Pataki (1905–1953), who analyzed new trends in the theory of knowledge. Both later became Marxists, Tkalčić writing essays in aesthetics and ethics, and Pataki becoming a leading specialist in pedagogy. Stjepan Zimmerman (born 1884) was the leading neoscholastic Catholic philosopher on the theological faculty at Zagreb.

Slovenia. The Slovene philosopher Jožef Mislej (1761–1840) created a mathematically based philosophical system in the tradition of Leibniz in his *Grundriss einer Totalgrundmathesis* ("Sketch of a Universal Fundamental Mathematics," 2 vols., Vienna, 1818–1830). The most influential trends in Slovenia in the nineteenth and early twentieth centuries, however, were neoscholasticism and positivism; the ideas of the Czech philosopher T. G. Masaryk were later accepted by some social democrats. Between the two world wars France Veber (born 1890) elaborated Alexius Meinong's theory of objects and later published a number of books on science and religion, ethics, the place of man in the world, and other topics, from a predominantly existentialist point of view.

Later Serbian thought. In Serbia at the end of the nineteenth century, the most interesting philosopher was Božidar Knežević (1862–1905), a lonely schoolteacher, philosopher of history, metaphysician, and ethical theorist, who developed a quite original theory of universal evolution. The whole, which is unconscious and general, precedes the part, which is conscious and specific. When the part separates from the whole, there is conflict with the whole and with other parts. From this conflict there arises a new order and proportionality which is only temporary and gives place to a new phase of disintegration. However, in history as a whole, the growth of civilization leads to increasing social justice and the elimination of irrationality in human life. Although Knežević assumed the existence of God as a primary and eternal substance, he held that as human altruism develops, man withdraws from God. Morality and a more moral organization of social life are born out of suffering. It consists in the liberation from all external forces and presupposes the overcoming of ordinary motives for human behavior. Knežević's main work is *Principi Istorije* ("The Principles of History," 2 vols., Belgrade, 1898–1901).

The most original Serbian thinker at the beginning of the twentieth century was Branislav Petronijević (1873–1954), a philosopher of encyclopedic range who also made contributions to geometry and to the special sciences, especially paleontology. In *Prinzipien der Metaphysik* (2 vols., Heidelberg, 1904–1912) Petronijević developed a Leibnizian metaphysical system in which space and time are discrete, being consists of a finite number of individual qualitative units, and matter is the totality of all relatively unconscious units. In his "empiriorationalist" theory of knowledge, Petronijević was more original. In *Prinzipien der Erkenntnislehre* (Berlin, 1900) he tried to establish the possibility of absolute knowledge and argued that even in immediate experience there are simple facts which are logically necessary but which are overlooked by empiricists. Thinking consists of both abstract and concrete concepts; it is not only generalization of experience but also immediate consciousness of reality. There are two fundamental methods of philosophical cognition: empiricosynthetic and speculative–deductive; both can lead to apodictic knowledge.

Dragiša Djurić (1871–1941) tried to reconcile the idealistic positivism of Ernst Laas with historical materialism. Milos Djurić (born 1892) produced many erudite works on ancient philosophy and culture. The religious philosopher Borislav Lorenc (born 1883) developed an activistic idealism. An active group of irrationalist Serbian philosophers attempted to combine the pragmatism of William James and the intuitionism of Henri Bergson with Pan-Slavism and orthodox Christianity.

CONTEMPORARY YUGOSLAV PHILOSOPHY

The socialist revolution in Yugoslavia produced a radical change in the character of philosophical activity. Philosophy was no longer treated as a purely theoretical discipline but as the foundation and critique of all inquiry and social practice. It was thus very attractive to the generation that took active part in the revolution, and the new revolutionary philosophical thought increased the reputation of philosophy among intellectuals generally. The conflict with Stalin in 1948 began a complete break with dogmatism which led to the rediscovery of Marx's humanism and the restoration of the critical role of philosophy in relation to social life as a whole.

Continuity and change. Although many philosophers active in the preceding period did not or could not take part in practical philosophical activity, there is no complete break with prewar Yugoslav philosophy. On the one hand, a few non-Marxist philosophers, some of whom are still active, remained in university departments of philosophy. Notable among these are the late Alma Sodnik at Ljubljana, a positivist historian of philosophy and author of a number of essays on the history of Slovene philosophy; Vladimir Filipović, head of the philosophy department at Zagreb and author of studies in logic and the philosophy of culture somewhat influenced by German phenomenology; Pavao Vuk Pavlović, head of the philosophy department at Skoplje, who developed an irrationalist theory of knowledge in *Spoznaja i Spoznajna Teorija* ("Cognition and the Theory of Knowledge," Zagreb, 1926).

On the other hand, before World War II there was already a tradition of creative Yugoslav Marxist thought which began with Svetozar Marković and came to include the leaders of the Serbian Social Democratic party, Dimitrije Tucović, Dušan Popović, and Sima Marković. Marković was a mathematician and was well acquainted with the results of modern physics. He criticized the idealistic interpretation of modern physics in *Iz Nauke i Filosofije* ("From Science to Philosophy," Belgrade, 1924) and *Princip Kauzaliteta i Moderna Fizika* ("The Principle of Causality and Modern Physics," Belgrade, 1935). After 1920 Marxism was illegal in Yugoslavia, but, after suitable adaptations in terminology and phrasing, a number of original articles on philosophical problems appeared in various leftist journals. Many of the authors of these articles were killed in the war of liberation.

Dušan Nedeljković, professor of philosophy at Skoplje before World War II, criticized contemporary philosophy from the Marxist point of view in *Anti-Bergson* (Skoplje, 1939) and other works. He also published works on Pascal and Bošković and an extensive commentary on Hegel's logic (*Dijalektika*, Belgrade, 1939). After the war he headed the philosophy department at Belgrade until 1954 and published monographs on Leonardo da Vinci, La Mettrie, and pragmatism, as well as many articles on the history of philosophy.

After World War II several new philosophical institutions were created: a new philosophy department at Sarajevo, the department of philosophy in the Institute for Social Studies in Belgrade (with a branch at Zagreb), and an international summer school of philosophy and sociology at Korčula. The Yugoslav Philosophical Association, with societies in the five republics, is active in organizing meetings and symposia. The journal *Filozofija* was founded in 1957, *Savremene Filozofske Teme* ("Contemporary Philosophical Themes") in 1957, and *Praxis* in 1964.

Postwar phases. Three postwar phases can be distinguished. First, there was a period of orthodoxy in the immediate postwar years, when Marxism was identified with dialectical materialism and was treated by many as an ideological system of indubitable truths.

This period was followed by a period of struggle against dogmatism in the 1950s, when a critical attitude toward authorities, an open-minded and creative approach to philosophical problems, and a desire for genuine dialogue with representatives of other philosophical trends developed. However, concrete social and political themes were avoided, and philosophy was still very abstract and insufficiently rooted in Yugoslav social realities.

A third period of increasing trends toward concreteness and practical activism followed. Philosophy is now focused on a critical analysis of the contemporary human condition, particularly on the various forms of alienation in capitalist and socialist societies. Philosophy has increasingly become the critical self-consciousness of Yugoslav society and the reflection of its ultimate humanistic goals.

Divisions. There are still divisions among Yugoslav philosophers. One is between Marxists and non-Marxists, who are influenced mainly by positivism or existentialism. Another is between those Marxists who are mainly engaged in applying and defending the teachings of Marx, Engels, and

Lenin and those who are trying to infuse Marxism with a new spirit and to develop it further, taking into account the achievements of modern science, philosophy, and social practice. Within this last group of Marxists there are also considerable differences. A group centered on the Belgrade philosophy department emphasizes the relevance of scientific results for philosophy and insists that only those philosophical views which are based on objective truth are progressive. It therefore concentrates on modern science, logic, and methodology, and in social philosophy it insists on basing criticism on concrete, reliable knowledge. The other group, centered at Zagreb, advocates the independence of philosophy from the sciences and concentrates on studying the ideas of the young Marx and their roots in Hegel and also on contemporary philosophical anthropology.

The new synthesis. Despite considerable remaining methodological disagreements, a humanism stressing practice and alienation has emerged from the continuous discussion and exchange of views between the Belgrade and Zagreb groups.

The central problem of philosophy is not the abstract relationship of matter and mind but, rather, the place of man in the world: what is and what ought to be, his relation to nature and to other human beings and society as a whole. Classical materialism is not denied but superseded. Material objects exist in themselves, but the objects which we know and deal with are transformed by our practical activity. Practice is therefore the fundamental category of ontology and epistemology: whatever is embraced by a critical ontology is mediated by human physical and intellectual work, and an adequate theory of knowledge presupposes the conception of man as an active, practical being. Perception and cognition are not a mere reflection of the external world but a creative interpretation and transformation of data in the light of language, previous experience, and the practical needs and values of the subject. Knowledge is therefore a historical category and contains subjective, human elements. It is a picture of the world in the perspective of a limited cognitive apparatus and a limited set of goals. However, whenever human practice is repeatedly and intersubjectively successful, this can be explained only on the assumption that in all such cases it was guided by an objective knowledge of the corresponding parts of the world.

There is a real possibility for man to become a free creative being who rationally controls natural and social processes and lives in solidarity with other men in real human community. In the contemporary world man has lost control over the products of his physical and mental activity (the state, political parties, nuclear weapons, religion). He has become enslaved by dull imposed labor and has reduced all the richness of life to an artificial need to possess as many objects as possible and other men to the status of things to be used. Man is alienated: he is not what man could be and ought to be. The supreme value for contemporary Yugoslav philosophy is therefore disalienation, the progressive liberation from all forms of slavery and poverty, both material and spiritual, and the fulfillment of all the potential of the individual.

These principles form the basis of a far-reaching social critique. The role of philosophy is to lay theoretical foundations for a profound revolutionary change in historical reality, not just of the given political or economic system but of all human relations. In this light Yugoslav philosophers try to critically evaluate such contemporary phenomena as the increasing stress on technology and material goods, the existing forms of bureaucracy and democracy, the character of politics (in relation to philosophy, science, and morality), and the meaning and perspectives of socialism.

The method of this activistic philosophy is dialectical. It approaches all phenomena historically and dynamically: the ultimate goal of inquiry is to establish the historical conditions of change. Inquiry should therefore be focused on discovering existing contradictions, with a view to superseding them practically. This philosophy seeks to encompass all dimensions of a phenomenon and to place it in a broad historical context. Such synthesis presupposes previous analysis; at first we simplify objects and draw provisional sharp lines of demarcation; later we re-establish continuity among the different elements of a whole. This philosophy also tends to concreteness; when we use abstract terms, we should bear in mind all the variety of specific cases to which they could be applied. It conceives determinism flexibly. Processes in nature and society are governed by laws, but these laws should be conceived as trends merely. They are relative to a given system of reference and to given initial conditions, both of which can undergo unpredictable change. Man lives in a world in which there is both order and change, and he can therefore behave as a relatively free agent insofar as he becomes aware of external and internal compulsions and is ready to resist them. From this conviction that within certain objective limits man can be free and can create his history, contemporary Yugoslav philosophers are led to a profound optimism and activism.

(See Yugoslav Philosophy in Index for articles on Yugoslav philosophers.)

Bibliography

HISTORIES AND SURVEYS

Atanasijević, Ksenija, *Penseurs yougoslaves*. Belgrade, 1937.

Marković, Franja, "Filozofijski rad Ruđera Boškovića" ("The Philosophical Work of Roger Boscovich"), in *Rad Jugoslavenske Akademije Znanosti i Umjetnosti*, Vols. 87, 88, 90. Published in one vol., Zagreb, 1887–1888. Pp. 543–716.

Marković, Mihailo, "La filosofia jugoslava contemporanea." *Il protagora*, Vol. 2 (1960), 2–43.

Milovanović, Milovan, *Filosofija u Srba* ("Philosophy Among Serbs"). Belgrade, 1904.

Nedeljković, Dušan, *La Philosophie naturelle et relativiste de Rudjer Bošković*. Paris, 1922.

Nedeljković, Dušan, *Aperçus de la philosophie contemporaines en Yougoslavie*. Belgrade, 1934.

ANTHOLOGIES OF CONTEMPORARY THOUGHT

Bošnjak, Branko, and Supek, Rudi, eds., *Humanizam i Socijalizam* ("Humanism and Socialism"), 2 vols. Zagreb, 1963.

Pejović, Danilo, and Petrović, Gajo, eds., *Smisao i Perspektive Sociajalizma* ("The Meaning and the Perspectives of Socialism"). Zagreb, 1965.

Stambolić, Miloš, ed., *Covek Danas* ("Man Today"). Belgrade, 1964.

Marks i Savremenost ("Marx and the Contemporary Age"), 2 vols. Belgrade, 1963–1964.

IMPORTANT CONTEMPORARY WORKS

Bošnjak, Branko, *Povijest Filozofije Kao Nauka* ("The History of Philosophy as a Science"). Zagreb, 1958.

Focht, Ivan, *Istina i Biće Umetnosti* ("The Truth and Being of the Arts"). Sarajevo, 1959.

Kangrga, Milan, *Etički Problem u Karla Marksa* ("The Ethical Problem in Karl Marx"). Zagreb, 1964.

Korać, Veljko, *Marks i Savremena Sociologija* ("Marx and Contemporary Sociology"). Belgrade, 1962.

Krešić, Andrija, *Relacioni Sudovi i Relativnost Spoznaje* ("Relational Propositions and the Relativity of Cognition"). Sarajevo, 1958.

Marković, Mihailo, *Formalizam u Savremenoj Logici* ("Formalism in Contemporary Logic"). Belgrade, 1958.

Marković, Mihailo, *Dijalektička Teorija Značenja* ("The Dialectical Theory of Meaning"). Belgrade, 1961.

Pavićević, Vuko, *Odnos Vrednosti i Stvarnosti u Nemačkoj Idealističkoj Aksiologiji* ("The Relation Between Value and Reality in German Idealistic Axiology"). Belgrade, 1958.

Pavićević, Vuko, *Uvod u Etiku* ("Introduction to Ethics"). Belgrade, 1962.

Pejović, Danilo, *Realni Svijet* ("The Real World"). Belgrade, 1960.

Petrović, Gajo, *Filozofski Pogledi G. V. Plehanova* ("The Philosophical Views of G. V. Plekhanov"). Zagreb, 1955.

Petrović, Gajo, *Filozofija i Marksizam* ("Philosophy and Marxism"). Zagreb, 1965.

Stojanović, Svetozar, *Savremena Meta-etika* ("Contemporary Metaethics"). Belgrade, 1964.

Šešić, Bogdan, *Logika,* 2 vols. Belgrade, 1958–1959.

Vranicki, Predrag, *Historija Marksizma* ("The History of Marxism"). Zagreb, 1961.

MIHAILO MARKOVIĆ

Z

ZABARELLA, JACOPO (1532–1589), was one of the leading Aristotelians of the sixteenth century. Zabarella taught at the University of Padua for 25 years, from 1564 until his death. The fruit of these years of lecturing is contained in his printed works, which include treatises on Aristotelian logic and natural science. His writings in logic, and especially on scientific method, earned Zabarella a reputation as the most outstanding logician of his time; they continued to be read by school philosophers in Germany and Italy for several generations after his death and still command respect as interpretations of Aristotle.

Zabarella proceeds in characteristic scholastic fashion, examining and resolving, independently of each other, a sequence of issues. In the process he canvasses the views of an impressive number of predecessors among the Latins and seems fully conversant with Greek philosophy, including the Greek commentators on Aristotle. The doctrines discussed by Zabarella range, as is usual with scholastic writers, over an immense amount of material, basically that presented by Aristotle in his *Organon* and in the *Libri Naturales*. As a philosopher Zabarella is willing to leave certain arguments to the theologians—for example, whether God could have created prime matter without form. "My advice is to dispute in Aristotelian, not theological, fashion," he remarks. This does not mean, however, that Zabarella was not willing to consider and even to endorse arguments of a strictly philosophical nature presented by theologians; hence, the names of Thomas, Scotus, Gregory of Rimini, and many others frequently occur in his works, along with the appeals to Averroës so frequent among Italian philosophers of his time. Analysis of the arguments advanced by predecessors constitutes one part of Zabarella's presentation (*ratio*); he also appeals to experience (*experientia*), his own or that of most people. Thus, he mentions having climbed the highest hill in the vicinity of Padua, seeing clouds below, and learning when he descended in the evening that it had rained in the valley during the day. But there is no reference to controlled experiment in his writings; in this respect he remained a bookish philosopher, like most university professors of his time.

No one has followed Zabarella carefully through the maze of his discussions in order to secure a clear view of his total thought. The studies we have are partial and will doubtless require revision in the light of increased knowledge of the whole tradition he represents. Nevertheless, some of his conclusions can be definitely stated.

Zabarella regards Aristotle's science as perfect with respect to structure and form, imperfect only with regard to its subject matter. He compares Aristotle's writings on natural science with Euclid's *Elements* and suggests that the philosopher of nature can easily derive theorems of physics from the principles contained in them. Zabarella does not envisage the possibility that Aristotle's approach might be supplemented by mathematics. The fourteenth-century attempts at quantification in physics originating at Paris and Oxford had been transported to Italy by such teachers as Paul of Venice, but Zabarella does not seem aware of these developments. He did not welcome novel hypotheses, preferring, for example, to stand by Aristotle's explanation that the movement of projectiles can be attributed to pushing by the surrounding air (*antiperistasis*). Zabarella rejects the view that the "preceding motion is the cause of the greater velocity of the following motion."

In his discussions of the heavens, Zabarella betrays no concern with the Copernican theory published during his youth. He seems slightly dubious about the epicycles of the astronomers, but in this he was no doubt simply reflecting the doubts of Averroës. Zabarella endorses the view, also derived from Averroës, that the "confused" knowledge of the world supplied by the natural scientist must be made "distinct" by the metaphysician. For example, he concedes that the argument, "Since there is eternal movement, there must be an eternal mover," may be established by the natural scientist, whose bailiwick is the consideration and causal explanation of things in motion. But consideration of immaterial substances in themselves (the "eternal motors") must be left to the metaphysician.

Contemporaries had raised a difficulty in connection with certain mutually canceling actions in nature ("reactions"), which seemed to them to defy the Aristotelian dictum "Nature never does anything in vain." Zabarella points out that such mutual frustration nevertheless does not frustrate nature in general, since all things turn out according to the law of universal nature (*ex lege naturae universalis*).

Another question much discussed in scholastic physics concerned the elements in what we would call chemical compounds (called "mixtures" by the Schoolmen). Do they persist in existence after losing their sensible identity as elements and becoming part of the compound? Various solutions had been proposed to this problem; Zabarella accepts that of Averroës—the same "reality" of the elementary forms of matter is in the elements and in the mixture, but their "formality" is changed.

In Aristotelian metaphysics and philosophy the distinction between matter and form is crucial and difficult, especially in its application to human beings. School philosophers of Zabarella's time exercised a great deal of ingenuity in order to make sense of the Aristotelian doctrine that the soul is the form of the body. There were two main opinions: one, that the soul is a "form giving being" to man; the other, that the soul is merely a "form assisting" in man's operation, much as a sailor presides over the operation of an already formed ship. Zabarella chooses the former interpretation, although not without vacillation.

On another much disputed question, concerning the perception of sense qualities, Zabarella endorses the view of Albertus Magnus that there is no need to postulate an "active sense" (*sensus agens*); certain sensed qualities have it in themselves to multiply their "spiritual" species in the medium, in contrast to such other qualities as heat, which really produce their counterparts in the medium and in the sense of touch.

Zabarella decisively rejects the Averroist thesis of the unity of the intellect, insisting that the intellect is multiplied according to the number of individual men. The intellect is the form of man; since it is not itself "in act," it is able to receive all things spiritually and hence is capable of knowing all things.

Logic. Zabarella's most original contributions lie in his logical works. The nature of logic and its relation to other disciplines were controversial matters even in antiquity, and these controversies were renewed during the Renaissance. Zabarella sides with the Greek commentators on Aristotle in maintaining that logic is not strictly a part of philosophy, but an instrumental discipline furnishing other arts and sciences with tools of inquiry. Two of these tools are order and method. Order is an intellectual habit that teaches us how to dispose suitably the parts of any given discipline so that we can learn it more easily. Method is also an intellectual instrument producing knowledge of the unknown from that which is known, but it permits us to draw syllogistic inferences. The nature of both order and method must be clarified by an analysis of their objectives: ease of learning in the case of order, perfect knowledge (*cognitio*) in the case of method.

These analyses are set forth in Zabarella's treatise *De Methodis* ("On Methods"), in which he challenges two schools of thought prevalent in his time. One, drawn from Neoplatonic commentators on Aristotle, held that there are four methods employed in the arts and sciences: demonstrative, definitive, divisive, and resolutive. The other, advocated by medical men and drawn from Galen, held that there are three orders of teaching any discipline. Zabarella presents a simplified version, reducing the number of orders and methods to two. Contemplative disciplines are transmitted by the compositive order, practical or operative disciplines by the resolutive, which begins with the end to be achieved in any pursuit and reasons backward to an initial step in its direction.

This was traditional Aristotelian doctrine, but Zabarella's elaboration of compositive and resolutive methods was more original. In the natural sciences there are two things to be studied, substances and accidents. Substances can be investigated only by the resolutive method, which begins with sensible effects and "resolves" them into their causes. We know substances when we possess definitions of them, but these definitions, contrary to received opinion, are not "methods." Accidents, on the other hand, can be demonstrated by the demonstrative or compositive method once the principles discovered by the resolutive method are available.

In his work "On the Regress," Zabarella analyzes a special form of demonstration in which "the cause and the effect reciprocate, and the effect is more known to us than the cause." The best example of such a regress is to be found, Zabarella tells us, in Aristotle's *Physics*. We know in a confused way that where there is generation, there is matter, but only demonstration makes it clear to us *why* matter is the cause of generation. We must make use of a "mental examination" which tells us that matter is "that which is apt to receive all forms and privations."

Zabarella reaffirms man's central place in the universe; the operation of the most outstanding part of man is his highest perfection, and this is to be found in contemplation. Man is of a middle nature; he is the most noble animal, created in the image of God, but there is also a sense in which he is ignoble and imperfect, the sense in which we say, "To sin is human" or "After all, he is only a man." Such concern for placing man in nature probably echoes fifteenth-century humanism.

Bibliography

None of Zabarella's works has been translated into English, and this is unfortunate, since he ranks high as an expositor of Aristotle. Furthermore, copies of his *Opera Logica* (published first in Venice, 1578, but many times thereafter) are hard to obtain. The same may be said of his *De Rebus Naturalibus* (Venice, 1590) and his commentaries on the *Physics* and *De Anima*. A modern edition of the *De Methodis* and other logical works would be welcome and would furnish us with one of the most sophisticated expositions of school logic and thinking concerning scientific method to be given during the Renaissance.

For studies on Zabarella, see Ernst Cassirer, *Das Erkenntnisproblem in der Philosophie und Wissenschaft der neueren Zeit* (Berlin, 1906), Vol. I, pp. 134–141; John Herman Randall, Jr., *The School of Padua and the Emergence of Modern Science* (Padua, 1961), pp. 49–63 (gives ample quotations in Latin); N. W. Gilbert, *Renaissance Concepts of Method* (New York, 1960), Ch. 7; and J. J. Glanville, "Zabarella and Poinsot on the Object and Nature of Logic," in R. Houde, ed., *Readings in Logic* (Dubuque, Iowa, 1958).

NEAL W. GILBERT

ZARATHUSTRA. See ZOROASTRIANISM.

ZEN. Zen Buddhism is a form of Mahāyāna Buddhism that is found chiefly in Japan but that in recent times has made an impact on Western countries, notably the United States. There are about nine million adherents of the Zen sects. The term "zen" literally means "meditation," and is derived from the Chinese *ch'ān*, which in turn goes back to the Sanskrit *dhyāna* (in Pāli, *jhāna*). Zen Buddhism stresses a certain kind of spiritual discipline which helps to bring about sudden illumination (in Japanese, *satori*), itself a stage on the way to full enlightenment in the Buddhist sense. Tradition asserts that Zen was introduced into China in 520 by Bodhidharma, who came from south India; but this account may well be apocryphal. Zen writings even ascribe the origin of Zen to the Buddha himself, who—in the legendary account—conveyed the teaching to his disciple Mahākaśyapa. But it was only in the seventh century that the school definitely emerged as a separate Buddhist movement, under the Chinese patriarch Hui-neng (637–713). Introduced into Japan in the twelfth and thirteenth centuries, it represents a synthesis of Indian Buddhist and Chinese (mainly Taoist) ideas. Zen has shaped, and been shaped by, Japanese culture.

The form of Zen is definitely Buddhist, both in its general doctrines—rebirth, the need for the attainment of release, the possibility of the individual's eventual achievement of Buddhahood, as in the Mahāyāna tradition—and in its allegiance to the Buddha himself and to the monastic order (Sangha) instituted by him. At the same time it is recognizably Chinese in spirit. Whereas Indian methods of meditation (*dhyāna*) tend to emphasize the effectiveness of individual effort in control of the mind and the importance of detachment from one's environment, Zen Buddhism emphasizes the spontaneity of illumination and the rapport between the individual and nature (which itself, as it were, acts without effort, spontaneously). These ideas are in line with the teachings of Lao Tzu legendary founder of Taoism, whose quietistic and contemplative attitude went with a theory of the universe as effortlessly governed by the principle which he called the Tao (literally, "way" or "method"). Thus the true sage and Nature are in quiet harmony. Both in art and in life this inspired an aestheticism in which Chinese and Japanese culture have seen nature as replete with spiritual meaning. For Zen Buddhists such secular activities as the practice of archery are capable of being transformed into contemplative disciplines. At the same time, the stress upon religious experience has given Zen an anti-intellectualist slant, and some of the Zen paradoxes must be seen in this light—as designed to break down the tendency to think of the ultimate truth as accessible to merely rational, or even scriptural, inquiry.

Nevertheless, Zen has a kind of metaphysical and scriptural basis, notably in the teachings of the *Lankāvatāra Sūtra* ("Sūtra of the Descent on Lankā," translated into Chinese in the fifth century), which expresses the Yogācāra (idealistic) viewpoint. Yogācāra is a form of absolute idealism, in which pure consciousness, the underlying and embracing principle of things, is identified with the Buddha nature. In stressing the need for contemplative training, the *Sūtra* indicates that it is immediate mystical experience, rather than cerebration, which brings one to ultimate truth and to Buddhahood.

Problems about this thesis are partly responsible for the division between the two main sects within Zen Buddhism, the Rinzai and the Sōtō, introduced into Japan by Eisai (1191) and Dōgen (c. 1225), respectively. The former sect, which is the best-known in the West, chiefly through the writings of D. T. Suzuki (1870–1966), aims at sudden illumination and is more anti-intellectualist. It uses the Yogācāra metaphysics as a starting point, but does not accept an ultimate conceptual distinction between the Absolute and phenomena, or between nirvana and empirical existence. If all discriminations, perceptual and otherwise, are illusory, so likewise is the distinction between the Absolute and phenomena. There is no gap between the spiritual and the secular, and so one should not strive to gain illumination. This is in line with the Taoist concept of "acting through not acting." These claims of the Rinzai school generate paradoxes at two levels—at the theoretical, because the doctrines imply that the doctrinal distinctions are to be transcended; and at the practical, because much effort must go into training adepts in effortlessness. This situation has given rise to unorthodox interpretations of Zen, as typified by "beat" Zen (in California, for instance, as expressed in Jack Kerouac's *The Dharma Bums*), which tends to prize antinomianism and immediate experience, without the prior doctrinal and contemplative training that in Rinzai Zen is considered an essential preliminary.

The Rinzai methods of training fall under two main heads. First, there is the rigorous practice of *za-zen* (literally, "meditation-sitting"), in which the aspirant adopts the usual yogic posture and is given a topic for meditation by the *Rōshi* (spiritual instructor, Zen master). This is often in the form of a *koan* (literally, "public document"), a kind of riddle. For example: We know what the sound of two hands clapping is like, but what is the sound of one hand clapping? These *koans* are designed to break down the conceptualization superimposed on the flow of experience and to bring about intuitive insight. Second, Rinzai Zen uses various secular arts, such as swordsmanship, archery, and the tea ceremony, as means of spiritual training. This reflects the appeal of Zen teachings in medieval Japan, especially to the samurai class, for the removal of the distinction between nirvana and empirical existence means that it is possible to live the illuminated life within the conditions and obligations of one's secular station. This is in accord with the Mahāyāna tendency to open up hope of liberation to laymen, not just to monks.

The contemplative techinques depend closely on the capacity and insight of the *Rōshi*. The respect and obedience toward the master demanded of the aspirant are the institutionalized guarantees that the antinomianism implicit in Zen teachings does not destroy the spiritual discipline aimed at. Strictly, illumination is regarded as a direct transference from the master to his pupil. Thus, traditional Zen cannot be learned on the "do-it-yourself" basis.

The present Western interest in Zen has produced a proliferation of literature on the subject, although on Zen principles there can be no fully adequate exposition save in the context of discipline under the guidance of a Zen master. This interest partly reflects dissatisfaction with the difficulties and divergences of orthodox Western religious doctrines, and Zen appears to offer a pragmatism of religious experience.

Bibliography

For the metaphysical background of Zen, see D. T. Suzuki, *Studies in the Lankāvatāra Sūtra* (London, 1930) and *Essays in Zen Buddhism*, 3 vols. (London, 1927–1934).

The relevant scriptures are found in D. T. Suzuki, *The*

Lankāvatāra Sūtra (London, 1932), and E. Conze, *Buddhist Wisdom Books* (London, 1958).

Heinrich Dumoulin, *A History of Zen Buddhism* (London, 1963), translated by Paul Peachey, is an excellent history.

Popular Western expositions are Alan W. Watts, *The Way of Zen* (New York, 1957); Christmas Humphreys, *Zen, a Way of Life* (London, 1962); and E. Herrigel, *Zen in the Art of Archery* (New York, 1953).

See also R. H. Blyth, *The Zen Teaching of Huang Po on the Transmission of Mind* (London, 1958), and *The Sutra of Wei Lang*, translated by Wong Mou-lam (London, 1947).

On Zen and art, see Nancy W. Ross, ed., *The World of Zen* (New York, 1962), and T. Hasumi, *Zen in Japanese Art* (London, 1962).

NINIAN SMART

ZENO OF CITIUM, the founder of Stoicism, was born in Citium, a small Phoenician-Greek city on Cyprus, about 336 B.C. (the year Alexander became king of Macedonia) and died in Athens about 265 B.C. These dates are a matter of dispute. At the age of 22, he went to Athens, poverty-stricken (some say) as a result of a shipwreck off the Piraeus. Zeno was a Phoenician, but he knew Greek before the shipwreck (if it occurred), and his merchant father had possibly supplied him with writings about Socrates long before Zeno came to Athens. In 300 he started his school, first called the Zenonians, and later called the Stoics because he gave his lectures on the Painted Porch (*Stoa Poikile*) in the marketplace of Athens. The porch was so called because it was where the paintings of Polygnotus were. Epicurus had come to Athens in about 306, celebrating pleasure as the highest good and randomness as the basic condition of the physical universe. Some say that Zeno, in reaction to Epicurus, set up a school defending virtue as the only good and the law of nature or the *logos* as the dominating force in the universe. Personally, he had none of Epicurus' attractive gentleness; he was dark, had a slightly twisted neck, and was severe or even harsh in manner. He ate raw food, drank mostly water, wore a thin cloak, and was apparently oblivious to rain, heat, or painful illness. Three of the many stories Diogenes Laërtius tells strikingly illustrate his philosophy (of which we have only a few fragments).

Once he was chastising a slave for stealing, and when the slave pleaded that it was his destiny to steal, Zeno responded, "Yes, and to be whipped too." His notion of destiny or providence was quite consistent with rewards and punishments.

After someone disapproved of Antisthenes' writings in Zeno's presence, Zeno showed him that author's essay on Sophocles and asked if he thought it had any fine qualities. The critic replied that he did not know. "Then," said Zeno, "are you not ashamed to pick out and mention anything wrong said by Antisthenes, while you suppress his good things without giving them a thought?" This was essentially the response of Zeno and the other Stoics to those who would use the evils in the world as an argument against God or Providence.

The third anecdote is more famous. Zeno was walking on a road, when he tripped and broke his toe. Lying there, he struck the ground and quoted a line from the *Niobe* of Timotheus: "I come of my own accord; why then call me?" He then went home and killed himself (some say he held his breath and died there in the road). This story (quite possibly true) summarizes the Stoic's belief that incidents in nature are the expression of God's will and the instruments of destiny.

For all his severity, Zeno was honored lavishly in life and in death by the city of Athens, which praised not only his temperance and his effect on the young but also the consistency of his life with his teachings.

Because of our fragmentary knowledge of the Early Stoa, it is difficult to distinguish Zeno's contributions from those of his successor Cleanthes and especially from those of Chrysippus, called the second founder of Stoicism, who followed Cleanthes as leader of the Stoa. But the stories about the man are so plentiful that we can trace his development with some precision (though we do not know with how much accuracy). After his arrival in Athens, he read (or reread) Xenophon's *Memorabilia* and admired the calm, rational self-control of Socrates, the philosophical hero of the Greeks. He came under the influence of the Cynic Crates, the ascetic who taught that a wise man, even though a beggar, is a king whose sovereignty lies in his virtue, in his hegemony over his own passions. While associated with Crates it is believed that he wrote his *Politeia* ("Republic"), possibly as an alternative to Plato's book. It was supposed to be a completion of the ideal state which Alexander had failed to complete because of his death. It envisaged a world-wide state, whose citizens were not of Athens or Sidon but of the universe. It was patterned not after local traditions but after universal nature; it had no laws (because there was no crime), no gymnasia for idle activity, no class system, and no hatred; love was the master of this state, and the wise man was no leader here but a simple citizen. Much of this was pure Cynicism, especially the notion of a cosmopolis and the attack on local conventions and laws in favor of natural living.

However, Zeno came to see the difficulties in defending this doctrine (for instance, philosophers were too narrow-minded, contentious, and arbitrary to find the wisdom necessary for ruling such a state). And so he left Crates and turned to Stilpo the Megarian, hoping that the subtle, powerful logic of refutation and defense that the Megarians had developed might help him to build his doctrine on firm foundations. From Stilpo he is said to have learned that the key fault to be avoided was haste in giving assent; and while under his influence he developed not only his formal logic but also his distinctions between degrees of certainty in perceptual knowledge. The lowest degree he represented with an open right hand, fingers extended: here the *phantasia* or mind-picture merely suggests a statement ("That is a tree"). After considering whether it is true, one gives his casual assent (*synkatathesis*) to it—this Zeno represented by partially contracted fingers. When the *phantasia* is clear and the assent is solid, the result of scrupulous attention, one has the *phantasia kataleptike,* or apprehensive mind-picture—this Zeno represented with a clenched fist. Finally, there is *episteme* or science, when all our firmly certain conceptions combine into a system—this Zeno represented by his left hand firmly closed around his right fist. This only the wise man has.

In time Zeno underwent other influences and developed other aspects of his thought. For example, from the Academic Polemo he learned to love poetry as well as the severe arguments of men like Stilpo. But the greatest influence on his metaphysics was Heraclitus of Ephesus. From his studies of Heraclitus, Zeno learned the doctrine of eternal fire, out of which all elements come, the belief in a logos or reason of the universe that gives shape to each thing and harmonizes all things amid perpetual change; and the belief in a deity identical with this logos and also with the eternal fire. Apparently he did not forsake his belief in a cosmopolitan republic but established his belief in it by developing the metaphysics of Heraclitus and the logical inquiries of the Megarians to suit his own purposes.

By the time his school was flourishing (after 300 B.C.), he is said to have coined a word for "duty" (*to kathekon*), which summarized his philosophy by referring to a life according to nature or reason. The wise man, simply because he knows what nature requires, has to do his duty; and in doing it, he is at once virtuous and possessed of spiritual well-being. We do not know if Zeno ever softened his doctrine in the *Politeia* to the effect that all those who were not wise were one's enemies, even if they also were one's closest relatives. But we do know that his writings, with all of their logical and physical insight, were never permanently detached from his desire to make the world a cosmopolis, a universal republic of wise, equal men living according to their rational grasp of nature's laws, in harmony with each other and in tranquillity within themselves.

Bibliography

Arnold, E. Vernon, *Roman Stoicism*. London, 1958. This unaccountably misnamed book—it is as good on Greek as it is on Roman Stoicism—is a rich source of knowledge about the development and mature doctrines of Zeno.

Diogenes Laërtius, *Lives of Eminent Philosophers,* translated by R. D. Hicks. New York, 1925. Volume II, Book 7, "Zeno," is relevant. Diogenes is our main source of knowledge about Zeno and one of our main sources of knowledge about Stoicism as a whole; some of its dates and some other details have been corrected, but it manages to communicate the personality of Zeno and the rigorous doctrines of his school with great power.

PHILIP P. HALLIE

ZENO OF ELEA. In the *Parmenides* (127A–128E), Plato represents Zeno as being "close to forty" when Parmenides was 65 and when Socrates (born 469 B.C.) was a young man. Since there is no reason to think these relative dates are distorted by dramatic license or that Plato was misinformed, and since our other chronological data come from much later sources and are inconsistent among themselves, we have no choice but to assume that, as Plato implies, Zeno was born around 490 B.C. Since he wrote his book as "a young man" (*Parmenides* 128D), it is likely that he produced his paradoxes in the sixties, quite possibly in the early sixties, of the fifth century B.C. Plato speaks of only one book (and so does Simplicius, *In Physica* 139, 5). The attribution to him of more than one book by a late source (Suidas; in Diels and Kranz, 29 A 2) appears to be baseless. Of other facts concerning him, we can be certain only that he was a citizen of Elea, a familiar of Parmenides, and an adherent of his system, defending it against those who ridiculed it (Plato, *Parmenides* 128C, D).

ARGUMENTS AGAINST PLURALITY

There were many arguments against plurality (forty, according to Proclus; in Diels and Kranz, 29 A 15). Two of them contain most of what survives in Zeno's original wording (Frs. 1, 2, and 3; in Diels and Kranz, 29 B 1, 2, 3) and therefore merit the most careful study.

First argument. In the first argument against plurality Zeno undertook to prove that "if [P] there are many [existents]," they must be both [Q] "so small as to have no size" and [R] "so large as to be infinite" (Simplicius, *In Physica* 141, 6–8). His argument had three sections, the proof of [Q], the transition to the proof of [R], and the proof of [R].

Proof of [Q]. The proof of [Q] has been lost. But Simplicius, who must have had its text before him (he proceeds to quote Frs. 1, 2, and 3), reports (*In Physica* 139, 18–19) that Zeno had argued "that nothing has size" on the ground that "each of the many is self-identical and one." Perhaps the further premise on the strength of which Zeno negotiated this curious inference is revealed in Melissus' Fragment 9; it would be good Eleatic doctrine to hold that if a thing is one it can have no parts, or else it would be "many." Zeno's argument in support of [Q] might then have run as follows:

[A1] If there were many things, each of them would have to possess (as minimal conditions for existence) unity and self-identity.
[A2] But nothing can have unity if it has size,
[A3] for whatever has size is divisible into parts,
[A4] and whatever has parts cannot be one.
[A5] Hence, if there were many things, none of them could have size.

Here premise [A1] is impeccable and premise [A3] innocuous. But what of [A4]? Since such predicates as "one" and "many" are semantically incomplete or elliptical, there is no reason whatever why the same logical subject could not be both "one" and "many," provided only the needed complements to the sense were appropriately different; for example, the United States is one (nation) and many (states), an apple is one (apple) and many (parts—halves, quarters, billionths, and so on—of an apple). This truth is so elementary that the reader may wonder if a thinker of Zeno's undoubted powers could have missed it. He might then be reminded that even in Plato's time the logical viability of any conjunction of unity with plurality was disputed by some philosophers (see Plato, *Sophist* 251B, C). There is no good reason to doubt that Zeno, a century earlier, could have fallen into the same semantic trap. His error must have passed undetected, or else it would not have been repeated innocently by Melissus in his Fragment 9.

Transition to the proof of [R]. Zeno next argued that, on the contrary, if there were many existents, each of them would necessarily have some size (greater than zero).

For [a] if it [a sizeless existent] were added to another existent, it would make it [the latter] no larger. For [b] having itself no size, it could contribute nothing by way of size when added. And thus it would follow that [c] the thing added would be nothing. If, indeed (δέ), [d] when [something is] subtracted from another, the latter is not reduced, nor again [is the latter] increased when [the former is] added [to it], it is clear that what is added or subtracted is nothing. (Fr. 2)

The clumsiness of the writing is evident from the parenthetical additions needed to keep the bound variables of the reasoning under control, but this is scarcely surprising in the archaic age of argumentative prose. What of its logic? The major question concerns step [d]. Does Zeno want us to think it a *conclusion* from what precedes? This would be a blunder, since [d] merely restates in a more general form (expanded to cover subtraction as well as addition) the assumption by which the preceding argument would have to be justified; in the version above, no reason was offered for the startling inference from [a] to [c]. But Zeno's text can very well be read with [d] as an assumption (one could even read the connective, δέ, as "because," as von Fritz did in his review of Calogero's *Studi sull'eleatismo*, 105), so that the logical sequence would be as follows:

[d] If an existent did not increase another when added to it, nor yet decrease it when subtracted from it, that existent would be nothing.

[a, b] A sizeless existent would not increase another when added to it [nor yet decrease it when subtracted from it].

[c] Therefore, a sizeless existent would be nothing.

Here it is quite clear that no attempt is being made to prove [d]. This is understandable, since [d] is a premise that everyone (except Eleatic philosophers) would have granted at this time, for it is obviously true of all corporeal existents. And because (outside of Eleatic circles) the conception of *in*corporeal existents had not yet dawned, no one would have felt any good reason for doubting [d]. It might be objected, "Has not Zeno professed to *prove* in the preceding section that existents are sizeless? Would not this entail that they are incorporeal?" This would be true, but irrelevant, since Zeno's tactics are purely dialectical. To prove that his adversaries hold contradictory beliefs Zeno is perfectly justified in picking out different sets of premises to suit his purpose, working with one set that excludes [d] in the proof of [Q] and then beginning all over again in the transition to the proof of [R] with another set of premises, all of which, including [d], his victims would have granted him readily at the start of this debate.

Proof of [R]. Zeno's proof of [R] is as follows:

So if [many] exist, each [existent] must have some size and bulk and some [part of each] must lie beyond (ἀπέχειν) another [part of the same existent]. And the same reasoning holds of the projecting [part]: for this too will have some size and some [part] of it will project. Now to say this once is as good as saying it for ever. For no such [part—that is, no part resulting from this continuing subdivision] will be the last nor will one [part] ever exist not [similarly] related to [that is, projecting from] another. (Fr. 1, first part)

The phrasing here is even clumsier than that of the preceding fragment, so much so that the correct translation has long been missed (for the one given here, see Fränkel, 193 ff. and the Vlastos review of the German version, 195–196). On its simplest construction the reasoning goes as follows: Given any existent, A, it must have size—as Zeno has proved in the transition to the proof of [R], above—and therefore at least two nonoverlapping parts or regions, B and C, must be distinguishable within it. In default of more technical terms in his vocabulary Zeno speaks here of C as "lying beyond" or "stretching out away from" (ἀπέχειν) or again as "sticking out [or projecting] from" or "being ahead of" (προέχειν) B. The same will be true of C; it too will have nonoverlapping parts D and E. This argument can be reiterated ad libitum. Hence, the series of "projecting" parts (C, E, G, · · ·) is unending.

To resume Simplicius' citation (of the apparently intact original text), Zeno concluded: "Thus, if there are many, they must be both small and great: on one hand, [Q] so small as to have no size; on the other, [R] so large as to be infinite" (Fr. 1, concluding part).

Given Simplicius' testimony (*In Physica* 139, 18–19, cited before), we have no choice but to take [Q] here as a carry-over from the proof of [Q] given above. But how is [R] supposed to follow? Zeno must have been proceeding on two assumptions:

(C1) An infinitely divisible existent must contain a complete infinity of parts.

(C2) If each member of an infinitely numerous set has some size (greater than zero), then the aggregate size of the set must be infinite.

But why should he assume (C2)? By the rule of the construction nothing goes into the set (the one consisting of the complements to the projecting parts, that is, B, D, F, · · ·) except parts of existent A, each of them finite (because A is finite; if A were infinite to begin with, the argument to prove it so would be redundant) and ordered in a sequence whose nth term is always smaller than the difference between A and the sum of the preceding $n-1$ terms. In a simple case (probably the very one that Zeno had in mind, given his fondness for "dichotomy"), the nth term is always $A/2^n$. Simple arithmetic, well within Zeno's reach, would have shown him that any partial sum of this sequence ($A/2 + A/4$ or $A/2 + A/4 + A/8$ or · · ·) would be less than A. Assuming then [(C1) above] that the whole sequence would be given as a complete totality, why should he think its sum would be larger than A, and so much so as to be infinitely large? He must have made a further assumption:

(C3) An infinite sequence of terms of decreasing size must have a *smallest* term, ϵ.

On this assumption, A would contain infinitely many parts larger than ϵ (which, like all other parts in the collection, would have a finite size greater than zero). The sum of *this* collection would indeed be infinite: it would have to be at least as large as ϵ times infinity. But (C3) unfortunately entails

(*C*4) An infinite sequence of terms of decreasing size must have a *last* term,

which contradicts the point made in Zeno's text that the sequence has no last member ("for no such [part] will be the last . . ."; Fr. 1, first part).

Is Zeno's error here more shocking than the quite different one he made in the proof of [*Q*] above? Hardly. Thinkers in much later periods, commanding far more advanced analytic tools, have not shrunk from saying point-blank that an infinite sequence *must* have a last ("infinitieth") member; thus, Jakob Bernoulli wrote, "If 10 members are present [in an infinite progression], the 10th necessarily exists, if 100 then necessarily the 100th, . . . if therefore their number is infinite then the infinitieth member must exist" (quoted in Weyl, p. 44). A similar illusion, supervening on the conviction that because every term in the series had some (finite) size, so must this one, would account for his error. Had Zeno formulated these propositions he could scarcely have failed to notice the ensuing clash with the "no last member" clause in his own text. Remaining tacit, the propositions were shielded from critical scrutiny, and the contradiction could pass undetected. Nor did he have, to rouse his suspicions against assumption (*C*2), the conception that the sum of an infinite series could be defined as the limit on which its successive partial sums converge. No one had this conception in antiquity; infinite sequences are not summed by this means in "exhaustion" proofs in Euclid and Archimedes (see Boyer, pp. 34–37, 52–53). In the absence of this conception, (*C*2) could not have seemed nearly as counterintuitive as it seems to us. We know this from the fact that Epicurus endorses (*C*2) without the slightest qualms (*Epistle to Herodotus,* Secs. 56–57; in Diogenes Laërtius, *Vitae Philosophorum,* H. S. Long, ed., 2 vols., Oxford, 1964, Vol. II, p. 521, ll. 3–4 and 7–14), and not only he; it was apparently a widespread assumption in antiquity. (Eudemus *apud* Simplicius *In Physica* 459, 25–26; Sextus, *Pyrrhoneioi Hypotyposeis* 3, 44; Simplicius, *In Physica* 141, 15–16 *et passim;* and *De Caelo* 608, 12–15; 635, 11–26. Cf. Salomo Luria, 106–107.) Indeed, there is good reason to think that Aristotle himself would have approved it, and he even comes close to doing so in *Physics* 187b13–34; he was saved by his ingenious theory of the "potential" infinite, which enabled him to side-step the question "What is the sum of an infinite series?" by denying the "actual" existence of any such series to sum.

Second argument. The second argument against plurality goes as follows:

If [*P*] there are many, it is necessary that [*Q*] they be as many as they are, neither more nor fewer. But if they are as many as they are, they must be finite[ly many].

If [*P*] there are many, [*R*] the existents must be infinite[ly many]. For there are always other [existents] between existents, and again others between these. And thus the existents are infinite[ly many]. (Fr. 3)

The argument for [*Q*], beautiful in its simplicity, is so strong that it is hard to see how anyone could have broken it before the demonstration of transfinite cardinals and superdenumerable sets by Georg Cantor. Otherwise how could the claim that every determinate set is numerable be disproved and the inference from a *definite* totality ("so many as they are") to a *finite* one be invalidated? All one could have done in the circumstances would have been to counter with a *tu quoque* argument—for example, that by the same reasoning one could show that the infinity of the natural integers involves a contradiction. But would Zeno have had to fear such a counterattack? His Eleatic faith that only the One exists would have derived further comfort from the assurance that even that paradigmatic aggregate, the number series, is flawed by contradiction.

The argument for [*R*] makes a new assumption:

(*D*1) Given two existents, there must be at least one between them.

From this it follows that given three existents, there must be at least two more (a fourth between the first and the second, a fifth between the second and the third) and so, generally, if there are *n* existents, there must be at least *n* − 1 more. Is (*D*1) puzzling in view of the fact that the preceding argument allowed for (and, as interpreted, entailed) the distinctness of contiguous existents? Not if we remember Zeno's dialectical method, which picked its premises wherever it found them. Here Zeno may have been thinking of existents that are not only conceptually distinct but also physically separate, counting on his public to grant him that physical separation between any two things is impossible if there is nothing between them to hold them apart. Or, again, he may have been thinking of points on a line, in which case (*D*1) enunciates the mathematical "denseness" of a continuum. In either case he would have all he wanted here—supposed existents whose numerousness can be proved infinite by a simple rule.

Third argument. It is highly probable that a Zenonian original is behind an Eleatic argument which Aristotle reported in *De Generatione et Corruptione* 316a14–34, 325a8–12 and which forms the second half of an argument that Porphyry ascribed to Parmenides but which Alexander and Simplicius held more likely to have been Zeno's (Simplicius, *In Physica* 139, 24–140, 26). The argument is, in substance:

[*E*1] If [*H*₁] an existent were infinitely divisible, no contradiction should arise from the supposition that [*H*₂] it has been divided "exhaustively" (or "through and through," πάντη).

[*E*2] But an exhaustive division would resolve the existent into elements of zero extension. This is impossible, for

[*E*3] no extensive magnitude could consist of extensionless elements.

This argument was a great success in antiquity. Aristotle spoke of it (*De Generatione* 316b34) as the very argument which convinced the atomists that the infinite divisibility of matter was absurd. His own refutation of it (*ibid.*, 316b19 ff.) made no dent on later atomists: Epicurus must have thought the argument perfectly valid, or else he could not have asserted so confidently that if matter were infinitely divisible, being would be reducible to not-being (*Epistle to Herodotus* 56; in Diogenes Laërtius, Vol. II, p. 521, ll. 4–7). Even in modern times some eminent historians of Greek science and mathematics recount the argument as though its reasoning were logically cogent (Tannery, "Le Concept scientifique du continu," 391–392, and *Pour l'Histoire de la science hellène*, pp. 254–255; Heath, *History of Greek Mathematics*, p. 275; Baccou, p. 181). But it is certainly an invalid refutation of hypothesis H_1, that an existent is infinitely divisible. Correctly analyzed, this states no more than that the sequence of divisions to which the existent may be subjected has no lower bound. Thus, it assures us that no matter how many divisions have been performed on it, *a next division may be performed*. But supposition H_2, that the existent has been divided exhaustively, states that the whole sequence of divisions envisaged in H_1 has been completed and a state of affairs has been reached in which *no next division may be performed*. Here we have two entirely distinct hypotheses, and it is by no means clear that the first entails the second. Hypothesis H_2 certainly does not follow from the meaning of H_1, any more than, for example, if one were to assert that (*a*) counting the whole numbers is an endless process, then one could be understood to mean that (*b*) it is possible to have counted them all: one might very well mean to deny (*b*) while asserting (*a*); one might even believe that (*a*) is a good reason for denying (*b*). Therefore, if left unsupported, the claim that H_1 entails H_2 is a sheer *non sequitur*. This is precisely the fault committed by the first premise, [E1], of the argument: it assumes, without the slightest proof, that H_1 entails H_2, for if, as alleged, a contradiction were to result from the supposition that the sequence of divisions has been exhaustively carried out (i.e., that H_2 has been instantiated), this would do absolutely nothing to falsify H_1 unless its logical fortunes were tied by entailment to those of H_2.

It might be noted that this refutation of the argument does *not* assert that H_1 entails the contradictory of H_2. This assertion would raise the more general question whether or not the notion of a completed infinite sequence of this type is logically self-contradictory, which may be held over for the discussion of the next puzzle. Here it need be said only that the argument could be faulted on this further ground if it assumed that the alleged exhaustive division of the existent could be brought about only by a *last* division, which, of course, H_1 positively precludes; a sequence of this ordinal type (which has a first member and whose every subsequent member has a successor) can have no last member. But the argument as stated above (incorporating all that is correctly derivable from the data on this point) does not make this further assumption. (The assumption has been read into it by Tannery, Heath, and Baccou, thereby exposing it to refutation on just that ground by Grünbaum in *Philosophical Problems of Space and Time*, pp. 167–168.)

What of premise [E3]? Its truth would be acknowledged by all ancient thinkers, since they never envisaged the possibility that an extensive magnitude could be constituted of parts except insofar as it could be conceived as resulting from their arithmetical addition—an operation that obviously could not be performed on extensionless points to produce lines, planes, and solids. Hence, the modern mathematical conception of the set-theoretic union of a (superdenumerably infinite) set of points to form a one-dimensional continuum (cf. Grünbaum, *op cit.*, pp. 161 ff.) could scarcely count as a valid objection to the assertion of [E3], although it might well be fatal to certain inferences which otherwise might be drawn from [E3].

ARGUMENTS AGAINST MOTION

Not even one line of the arguments against motion has survived in Zeno's original wording. What we know of them derives almost exclusively from Aristotle's accounts of them in the *Physics*. These accounts have been subject to so many diverse interpretations that it would be quite impossible to expound all of them in this article, to say nothing of assessing their respective merits. The best that can be done here is to offer the most probable construction of their reasoning, referring the reader to two recent studies (Vlastos, "A Note on Zeno's Arrow" and "Zeno's Race Course") for the textual justification.

The Race Course. The argument of the Race Course, to which Aristotle alludes in *Physics* 239b11–13 and 263a4–6, is as follows:

Starting at point S a runner cannot reach the goal, G, except by traversing successive "halves" of the distance, that is, subintervals of SG, each of them $SG/2^n$ (where $n = 1, 2, 3, \cdots$). Thus, if M is the midpoint of SG, he must first traverse SM; if N is the midpoint of MG, he must next traverse MN; and so forth. Let us speak of $SM, MN, NO, \cdots$ as *the Z-intervals* and of traversing any of them as *making a Z-run*. The argument then comes to this:

[F1] To reach G the runner must traverse all Z-intervals (make all the Z-runs).

[F2] It is impossible to traverse infinitely many intervals (make infinitely many Z-runs).

[F3] Therefore, the runner cannot reach G.

But why would Zeno assert [F2]? Probably because he made the following further assumption:

(F4) The completion of an infinite sequence of acts in a finite time interval is logically impossible.

This assumption has enormous plausibility. Even in our own time several distinguished thinkers have argued that it is true (Weyl, p. 42; Black, pp. 95 ff.; Thomson, 5 ff.). Has a good case been made for it? An easy way to do so would be to assume that "completing" the sequence here could be defined only as "performing all the acts in the sequence, *including the last*." If such a definition were mandatory, then, of course, a completed infinite progression such as the Z-sequence (which can have no last member) would be as flat a contradiction as a round square. But "completing" the sequence can be defined, alternatively, as "performing all the acts in the sequence" or "reaching the point when no more acts in the sequence remain to be performed, having omitted none" (see Watling, 39, Owen, 205). Hence, to settle the issue by recourse to the first definition would be to beg the question. Nor, again, would it do to argue that the sequence is uncompletable because *no matter how large a number of acts had been performed,* more of them would still remain to be made (see Black, p. 101). This, too, would beg the question, unless "number" in the italicized phrase were corrected to "finite number," in which case we would get only the tautology that the infinite sequence could not be completed by a finite number of acts.

When the argument for (F4) has been kept clear of both these mistakes, it has so far failed (see Benacerraf, 768 ff.). The most that can be done is to demonstrate a much weaker proposition,

(F5) The completion of an infinite sequence of discrete acts (or states) in a finite time interval is impossible for a *finite state system* (that is, for one which at any given instant is in one of n possible states, where n is finite).

Thus, suppose (1) a system were at any instant in one of two possible states, A and B, the occurrence of one of them immediately preceding the occurrence of the other, and (2) that the system went through infinitely many state alternations between, say, 10:00 and 10:01, A in the first half minute, B in the next quarter of a minute, A again in the next eighth, and so forth. A contradiction would then arise: Given (1), the system would have to be in one of the two states at 10:01. Let this state be A. The occurrence of A would require, as its immediate predecessor, a unique occurrence of B prior to 10:01. But, given (2), this would be impossible: no occurrence of B prior to 10:01 could be A's immediate predecessor, for every such occurrence would be separated from the occurrence of A at 10:01 by infinitely many occurrences of both A and B. This shows that the complete infinite sequence of discrete states hypothesized in (2) is impossible for those physical systems which satisfy (1)—that is, those that are finite state systems. But this, unfortunately, will not cover the Z-runner of Zeno's puzzle, for his progress toward G does not constitute a finite state system: the state of being at G ("the G-state") does not bear the same relation to the state represented by the traversal of some Z-interval (some "Z-state") that any occurrence of A bears to some occurrence of B in (1). In the case of (1) we can always count on an immediate predecessor for any given state. Not so in the Z-runner's case, where (by hypothesis) the G-state has no Z-state as an immediate predecessor. Thus, the demonstration of (F5) would not be of the slightest use for Zeno's purposes. Hence, the *logical* impossibility of the completed Z-runs remains to be proved.

What then of their *physical* impossibility? This no one would dispute. Everyone would concede that no human runner could execute an infinite set of discrete physical motions answering to the Z-runs of the puzzle. But how would this concession advance Zeno's case? Has he done anything to show that such a set of motions *must* be made if the runner is to move from S to G? He has not! Consider how the word "run" has been used in the argument: Its nor-

mal use restricts it to physically individuated motions. Thus, a man who ran from point X to point Y without a break would have made one and only one run; he could not be said to have made even two runs (let alone an infinite number) unless he made a stop or near stop in between. This restriction has been quietly ignored on Zeno's behalf in expounding his argument. We have allowed him a radically different use of the term, according to which *the traversal of any interval we please* by a runner would count as a "run." Let us then write "run_a" for the normal use of the word, "run_b" for its entirely different use in the exposition of Zeno's argument, and consider the consequences: Since we may take SG to be as many (contiguous) intervals as we please, it follows that we may take the single SG run_a to be as many (contiguous) runs_b as we please. Thus, it could be said quite truthfully to be two runs_b (for example, traversals of the SM, MG intervals), or a billion runs_b (traversals of a billion contiguous segments of SG, each of them a billionth of the total length of SG), or $\aleph_0$ runs_b (for example, traversals of all the Z-intervals). Therefore, the fact that the runner has to make infinitely many Z-runs would not begin to justify [F2] if they are only runs_b. This being the case, why should there be any difficulty about making all the Z-runs when all that is needed for this purpose is to make the single run_a from S to G—just as all that is needed to consume $\aleph_0$ parts (parts_b) of an egg is simply to eat an egg?

A possible answer is still left to Zeno, well worth presenting on his behalf so that we may explore the last logical resources of his position without any suggestion that, on the available evidence, he himself was likely to have exploited them in this way. Conceding, as he now must, that he has not proved, and could not prove, that all the Z-runs_a must be made before the runner can reach G, he could point out that it would suffice for his purpose to prove the impossibility of making all of the Z-runs_b (all of which must indeed be made—no Z-interval may be skipped). He could argue for this as follows: Although these Z-runs (the subscript may be dropped now that it has served its purpose) are not physically individuated motions, neither are they arbitrary fictions. Each of them represents a determinate subsegment of the runner's physical motion. Therefore, all of them taken together make up a true description covering the whole of his run from S to G, accounting for every part of it exclusively in terms of Z-runs. How could this be, when (by construction) every Z-run terminates short of G, and hence no Z-run reaches G? How could there be a true description of an event (the run from S to G represented solely in terms of Z-runs) whose occurrence entails the fulfillment of a condition (that of making a run that reaches G), when the description entails the nonfulfillment of that condition (since none of the runs that figure in the description reaches G)?

Here our "Zeno" has fallen back on a new assumption:

(F6) Any point reached by running must have been reached by a unique run that reaches that point (i.e., that terminates at or beyond that point).

Could any assumption be intuitively more compelling? But if we were to grant it, we would have lost the argument. For we could not then hope to get out of the difficulty by retorting that (F6) could easily be shown to be satisfied by some other equally true description of the SG motion (for example, as the one run from S to G). This maneuver would be futile. It would leave us with the paradox that (F6), known to have been fulfilled on this true description of the motion (that is, as the SG run), would be known to have been unfulfilled (not merely not known to have been fulfilled) on another, no less true, description of the very same motion, the one accounting for the whole of it exclusively in terms of Z-runs. To escape this paradox we must reject (F6), explaining that whereas it is a sufficient condition of reaching a point by running—the normal one, the only one we need consider in everyday experience—it is by no means a logically necessary condition: On the Zenonian description of the runner's motion he is in a position to make n Z-runs, where n can be made as large as necessary to cut to less than any preassigned, arbitrarily small interval ϵ the difference between the sum of n Z-intervals and the length of SG. This means that he is in a position to traverse an interval which is *metrically indistinguishable* from SG—a perfectly good way of "reaching" G without having to comply with assumption (F6).

Throughout this discussion we have ignored another of Zeno's tacit assumptions: that an extremely strong physical interpretation is available for the crucial concepts, particularly that of reaching (or being at) a point. Zeno assumes that any position reached by the runner after traversing a finite number of Z-intervals—say, after a trillion of them—would be physically distinguishable from the terminal one at G, as it would also be from infinitely many others intermediate between it and G. The shortest way to refute him would have been to point out that the falsehood of this assumption vitiates the conclusion of his argument. We have forgone this line of refutation in the preceding discussion, and will do so again in the Achilles, in order to show that even if we were to assume that the positions of Zeno's mobiles could be fixed on their physical trajectories with a precision as absolute as that of geometrical points on a linear continuum, Zeno's arguments would still fail. (For Aristotle's alternative construction of Zeno's error in the Race Course, see Vlastos, "Zeno's Race Course," 96–97; for references to some other constructions, see 106, n. 33.)

The Achilles. The argument of the Achilles, to which Aristotle refers in *Physics* 239b15–18, is as follows: As Achilles starts from point S toward point A, the tortoise, already at A, moves ahead. If her speed is r times that of Achilles (where r is a small fraction, say, 1/100), then in the same time, t, that Achilles takes to traverse SA (whose length is s), she will traverse AB (=sr). For the same reason, in the time (now tr) he takes to run through AB, she will traverse BC (=sr²). Thus, we get the unending progressions indicated in the accompanying table.

THE Z-SEQUENCES	THE Z-RUNS			
	RUN 1	RUN 2	RUN 3	· · ·
For Achilles ("the ZA-sequence")	$SA (=s)$	$AB (=sr)$	$BC (=sr^2)$	· · ·
For the tortoise ("the TA-sequence")	$AB (=sr)$	$BC (=sr^2)$	$CD (=sr^3)$	· · ·
The temporal sequence, the same for both	t	tr	tr^2	· · ·

The argument goes as follows:

[G1] Achilles and the tortoise make contemporary Z-runs (that is, such that their nth Z-run begins and ends at the same instant [$n = 1, 2, 3, \cdot \cdot \cdot$]).

[G2] The nth Z-run of the tortoise and the (n + 1)th of Achilles traverse identical Z-intervals.

[G3] Achilles will catch up with the tortoise if and only if a Z-run by Achilles and a Z-run by the tortoise reach the same point at the same instant.

[G4] But, given [G2], at the end of any Z-run the tortoise will be one Z-interval ahead. Therefore, given (G3),

[G5] Achilles will never catch up with her.

However different from the Race Course in design, this puzzle has been built from the same materials: sequences decreasing unendingly in constant ratio, whose members are intervals of space and time. The Z-runs are, as before, runs$_b$ masquerading as runs$_a$. When they are unmasked, [G1] and [G2] remain true by construction, and [G4] is a valid consequence. But does [G5] then follow? Obviously not, unless (G3) were also granted. This ultraplausible premise plays here the same role as did (F6) in the Race Course and may be rejected on the same grounds: Although true enough in ordinary circumstances, it would not be true in the extraordinary ones postulated by Zeno. For there exists a point Q such that the segments SQ and AQ are respectively the limits of the infinite sequence of partial sums of the ZA-series and the ZT-series. If Achilles could make the SQ run, the tortoise would make the AQ run in precisely the same time, and she would be overtaken at Q. By restricting them to Z-runs, Zeno ensures that the SQ and AQ runs will not be made, since neither of them would then make a run which terminates *at Q*. Even so, the infinite sequence of Z-runs would enable each of them to approach Q within any desired standard of approximation, and Achilles would thus have a perfectly good way of catching up with the tortoise without satisfying (G3). (For references to some other interpretations of this puzzle, see Vlastos, "Zeno's Race Course," 106–108 and notes.)

The Arrow. By putting together data drawn from Aristotle's (brutally abbreviated) summary of the Arrow puzzle (*Physics* 239b5–7) and from another source (Diogenes Laërtius, Vol. II, p. 475, ll. 10–11, which is the same as Zeno, Fr. 4, in Diels and Kranz), we get the following argument:

[H1] The arrow could not move in the place in which it is not.

[H2] But neither could it move in the place in which it is.

[H3] For this is "a place equal to itself,"

[H4] and every thing is always at rest when it is "at a place equal to itself."

[H5] But the flying arrow is always at the place in which it is.

[H6] Therefore, it is always at rest.

Premises [H1] and [H2] are from Diogenes Laërtius; [H3] is supplied as a transitional sentence; [H4] is cited verbatim and [*H*5] adapted, with modifications, from Aristotle. (For a defense of this reconstruction, see Vlastos, "A Note on Zeno's Arrow," 3–8.)

Premise [*H*4] is the pivot of the argument. It could mean two quite different things depending on how we read its "when" (see Black, pp. 128 and 144–146; Owen, 216 ff.):

> [*H*4,*i*] Everything is always at rest for any *interval* during which it is "at a place equal to itself."
>
> [*H*4,*ii*] Everything is always at rest for any (durationless) *instant* in which it is "at a place equal to itself."

The second reading offers the simpler explanation of the fact that Zeno thought premise [*H*4] not merely true but so plainly true that he felt no need to argue the point. If we think of the arrow as occupying a given position—being at a place just "equal" to its own dimensions—for a bare instant of zero duration, it will be obvious enough that it cannot be moving just then, for it will have no time in which to move (cf. Black, pp. 133–134). And if the arrow is not moving, must it not be at rest? Even today many persons would be caught off guard by this question and answer unhesitatingly, "Yes."

Fortunately, we have the means for correcting the error—for example, the familiar $v = s/t$ formula: Since a body at rest has zero velocity and covers zero distance, we must have values of zero for both v and s to represent the body's being at rest. But on the hypothesis that the body is resting *for an instant* of zero duration, t would also have to have a value of zero, and we would then get $v = 0/0$, which is absurd, because $0/0$ is a meaningless arithmetical symbol. The only way to have $s/t = 0$ is to assign a value greater than zero to t—that is, to represent the body as being at rest during some temporal interval, however short. Aristotle satisfied himself of the same result without benefit of algebra by means of an analysis of the instant in *Physics*, Book VI, which showed that "neither moving nor resting are possible in the 'now' [Aristotle's term for the instant]" (*Physics* 239b1–2; see also 234a24 ff.).

However, even this would not dissolve the perplexity unless it were pointed out, more explicitly than Aristotle does, that both moving and resting for an instant are not merely false but senseless; the arrow is nonmoving and nonresting for an instant in much the same way that a point is nonstraight and noncurved. For otherwise Aristotle's remark, for all its truth, might simply provoke the question "But if the arrow is not moving for any given instant of its flight *when* and *how* does it manage to move?" The "when?" may be answered curtly by "During some interval containing the given instant." But for the "how?" one must go deeper, exposing the category-mistake that lurks behind the question. Nor can one stop there. One must still explain that while motion *for* (that is, *during*) an instant is senseless, excellent sense can be given to motion *at* an instant by taking "velocity at instant *i*" to mean the *limit* of average velocities during intervals converging to zero and always containing *i* (cf. Black, p. 144). This, needless to say, would take one a long way past Aristotle, let alone Zeno, whose temporal concepts were as far behind Aristotle's as are Aristotle's behind the modern analysis of motion. (For a different reconstruction of the puzzle, using

only the Aristotelian data and the [*H*4,*i*] interpretation of the "when," see H. D. P. Lee, p. 78.)

The Moving Blocks. The Moving Blocks argument, often called the Stadium, appears in Aristotle, *Physics* 239b33–240a17. The reasoning runs as follows:

There are three sets of blocks; since one member of each set will carry the reasoning, we may cut down the machinery to three blocks, *A*, *B*, *C*. Their edges are of equal length, *s*. Block *A* is stationary, and blocks *B* and *C* are moving past *A* in opposite directions at equal speeds. We are then supposed to get a contradiction: *B* will traverse distance *s* both in a given time, *t*, and in half that time, *t*/2, where *t* and *t*/2 are the times that *B*'s leading edge takes to move past *A* and *C*, respectively. "So it follows, he thinks, that half the time equals its double [that *t*/2 = *t*]" (Aristotle, *Physics* 239b35). Aristotle and all our other ancient informants understood this as a (supposed) paradox of relative motion. Although Eudemus thinks it "very silly" and its paralogism "most obvious," neither he nor anyone else in antiquity doubted—on this or any other ground—its Zenonian provenance.

Other interpretations. According to a different interpretation of the Moving Blocks puzzle, popular among modern scholars since first put forward by Paul Tannery (see, for example, Brochard, pp. 7–9; Ross, pp. 81–82; Owen, 208–209; Whitrow, pp. 135–137), blocks *A*, *B*, and *C* would stand for indivisibles and the reasoning would prove that *B*, traversing an atomic quantum of length q_s relatively to *A* in an atomic quantum of time q_t, would traverse length q_s in $q_t/2$ relatively to *C*, thereby dividing a supposed indivisible. Unfortunately, we have nothing to persuade us that there is any historical substance to this conjecture, for there is no hint in any of our sources that any of the quantities in the reasoning were meant to be atomic.

TWO MORE PARADOXES

Against Place. The argument against place, which appears in Aristotle, *Physics* 209a23–25 and 210b22–24, runs as follows:

> [*J*1] Whatever exists is in a place. Therefore,
> [*J*2] place exists. Therefore, given [*J*1] and [*J*2],
> [*J*3] place is in a place, and so on *ad infinitum*.

Premise [*J*1] was so widespread and tenacious an assumption that "*x* is nowhere" was one way of saying "*x* does not exist" (see, for example, Plato, *Phaedo* 70A 2; cf. Aristotle, *Physics* 208a30–31), and Plato could declare: "We [people generally, *not* Platonists] say that it is necessary for whatever exists to be in some place and to occupy some space" (*Timaeus* 52B). Zeno used this premise to discredit [*J*2]. Taking "place" to mean *position* (as in the Arrow), he argued that [*J*1] in conjunction with [*J*2] entails in [*J*3] the semantic absurdity that a position has itself a position in turn. But does [*J*1] entail this nonsense? To show that it does not, Aristotle found it necessary to exploit a fourth-century discovery, that "to be" (there is no separate word for "to exist" in his language), and hence "to be in" has many senses. Along such lines one could refute the supposed entailment, explaining how very special a sort of existent "place" is, how different from those which do "exist in a place." But since this could not be done with the conceptual tools available in Zeno's time, his argument would be unassailable from this quarter, and it is hard to see how else it could have been routed in mid-fifth century.

The Millet Seed. According to the puzzle of the Millet Seed (presented in Aristotle, *Physics* 250a19–21 and in Simplicius, *In Physica* 1108, 18–28), if a bushelful of millet makes a noise when it falls, why should not a single millet seed make a proportionately smaller one and a ten-thousandth part of a millet seed one that much smaller?

Zeno is insinuating that we are fools to believe our ears when they report a house-shaking thud but are deaf to more diminutive agitations. Such a criticism of the senses could scarcely have come except from someone who was prejudiced against them to begin with—as the Eleatics, and only they, are known to have been at the time (see Parmenides, Fr. 7; Melissus, Fr. 8). A more impartial critic would have felt the necessity of giving some reason why audible sounds, when ordered by decreasing size, should have no lower bound. The fact is that they do. Why should that count against them? Why should our insensitivity to subliminal stimuli discredit our sensitivity to those above the limen?

INFLUENCE AND CONTRIBUTIONS

Scholarly opinion on Zeno's influence was dominated during the first half of the twentieth century by a theory put forward in 1885 by the distinguished French historian Paul Tannery, which was incorporated in one form or another into most of the leading histories of Greek mathematics, science, and philosophy of the next sixty or seventy years. Tannery's interpretation included the following theses: (1) Zeno's arguments were not directed against the common-sense belief in plurality and motion. (2) They were aimed against a very special philosophical doctrine which, Tannery claimed, was held at this time by the Pythagoreans—that all objects are made up of elements which were expected to combine somehow the properties of the arithmetical unit, the geometrical point, and the physical atom. Moreover, (3) these Pythagoreans thought that time and motion were similarly discontinuous. (4) Zeno's arguments, understood as onslaughts against (2) or (3) or both, were seen to be "clear, forceful, irrefutable—even those in which nothing but simple paralogisms had been commonly seen" (*Pour l'Histoire de la science hellène*, p. 251). (5) "Zeno's success was complete" (*loc. cit.*). "The theses he had attacked never reappeared after him" (*ibid.*, p. 260). (6) The result was salutary for Greek mathematics, ensuring for it "rigorously precise . . . notions of the point and the instant" (*ibid.*, p. 248). This last contention was given a further twist by another historian of mathematics, H.-G. Zeuthen, who interpreted the unit-point-atoms of Tannery's Pythagoreans as infinitesimals by which, he thought, they had sought to save their doctrine that "all things are numbers" in the face of the discovery of incommensurable magnitudes: by assuming that all continuous magnitudes, physical and geometrical, were composed of "infinitely many infinitely small parts" (Zeuthen, pp. 65–66), the Pythagoreans, according to Zeuthen, could claim that these magnitudes did have a common measure—an infinitely small one—after all.

Zeno and the Pythagoreans. To review the arguments that have been offered for Tannery's theory would be quite impossible in this article. Here, with the utmost brevity, are the reasons why thesis (2) must be considered probably false and this theory's other five theses certainly so:

To accept thesis (1) we would have to set aside the unanimous opinion of antiquity that Zeno was a faithful Eleatic, fully as much so as was Melissus. As such he could not but reject *all* current professions of plurality and motion—starting with those of the man in the street. Nor is there any hint in any of our sources, from Plato to Simplicius, that Zeno's arguments were aimed at any particular philosophical school or had a greater bearing on the views of the Pythagoreans than on those of other people (see Heidel, 21 ff.; Burkert, pp. 264 ff.).

In the case of thesis (2), the only texts that have been (or could be) offered as evidence that a unit-point-atom doctrine was professed by *early* Pythagoreans are of uncertain relevance (it is by no means clear that the units "possessing magnitude" which Aristotle ascribed to Pythagoreans in such passages as *Metaphysics* 1080b16 ff. and 1083b8 ff. are *point-atoms*) and absolutely without chronological specification (there is no indication in these texts that Aristotle had in view there doctrines professed by Pythagoreans more than a hundred years before his own time rather than contemporary ones). Moreover, Aristotle could hardly have thought of early Pythagoreans as maintaining a form of atomism, since whenever he speaks of fifth-century thinkers who "introduce" or teach or uphold "atomic magnitudes," he refers exclusively to the Ionian atomists (*Physics* 187a2–3; *De Caelo* 303a4–6; *De Generatione* 315b26–317a1; *De Anima* 445b18). Finally, the doxographic tradition knows nothing of unit-point-atoms in early Pythagoreanism. On the contrary, it asserts that Ecphantus of Syracuse (late fifth century at the earliest) "was the first to declare that the Pythagorean units were corporeal" (*Aetius* 1, 3, 19; 51, 2 in Diels and Kranz). Fundamental recent studies of early Pythagorean doctrine by Kurt von Fritz ("Pythagoras," pp. 197 ff. and pp. 225 ff.) and Walter Burkert (pp. 30 ff.) find no place for unit-point-atomism, and Burkert argues forcefully against it (pp. 37–38).

Thesis (3), that Pythagoreans held time and motion to be discontinuous, was pure conjecture and most implausible: so abstruse a theory as the quantization of time and motion could not have been seriously entertained until well after the much less daring speculation of the atomic constitution of matter had become thoroughly assimilated by the philosophical imagination—that is, well after Zeno.

Thesis (4) was the main attraction of the theory for Tannery and many others. They hoped to rehabilitate the logical force of Zeno's arguments by showing that their supposed sophisms were in fact acute criticisms of confused and misguided views held by Zeno's own contemporaries. One can understand how the Arrow and the Moving Blocks lent encouragement to this hope, for they were widely believed to be crushing objections to the discontinuity of time, space, and motion. But other Zenonian puzzles do not fit this pattern. Thus, an upholder of discontinuity would reject infinite divisibility on principle. Why then should he swallow it in the Race Course and the Achilles? In Fragment 3 why must he grant that between any two of his number-atoms there must always be a third?

In Fragment 1 would he not be downright stupid to admit that an existent composed of such atoms would be infinitely divisible? And if the argument of this fragment were meant to *rebut* an atomistic conception of reality, how could it have been misunderstood so grotesquely by the Ionian atomists who (if we may judge from Epicurus, discussed in the proof of [R], above), swallowing its fallacy whole, thought it a splendid argument *for* atomism?

Thesis (5) is patently false in view of the mathematical atomism professed by the unnamed opponents of the pseudo-Aristotelian work *De Lineis Insecabilibus* and the atomistic view of space and time to be found in Diodorus Cronus. In each case a Zenonian argument—the Race Course in the first (968a19 ff.), the Arrow in the second (Sextus Empiricus, *Pyrrhoneioi Hypotyposeis* 2, 245, and 3, 71; *Adversus Mathematicos* 10, 86–89)—is put to work for an atomistic view of extensive magnitude which, according to Tannery, Zeno's polemic had exterminated.

On the strength of thesis (6), Helmut Hasse and Heinrich Scholz (in *Die Grundlagenkrisis der griechischen Mathematik*) went so far as to name Zeno "the man of destiny of ancient mathematics in the hour of its gravest crisis" (the discovery of irrational quantities), claiming that his "inexorable critique of the introduction of transfinite processes with infinitesimal elements" (allegedly exemplified in Antiphon's quadrature of the circle and Democritus' fragment on the cone—a generation *after* Zeno) brought Greek science back from "pseudo mathematics" to "the path of scientific rigor." (For a refutation of this fantasy, see van der Waerden, 151 ff.) There is nothing in our sources that states or implies that any development in Greek mathematics (as distinct from philosophical opinions about mathematics) was due to Zeno's influence.

Influence on mathematics. When the Tannery hypothesis and its offshoots have been laid aside, it will not be necessary to go to the other extreme and deny Zeno any influence on the mathematicians. From the Aristotelian data it is clear that Zeno's puzzles had excited great interest: thus, in the *Topics* and *Physics* the Race Course is Aristotle's star example of a tough argument for a false conclusion (*Topics* 160b7–9, 172a8–10, and 179b20–21; *Physics* 223a21–31, 239b10–26, and 263a4 ff.). It is safe to assume that some of the people who worked on the paradoxes were mathematicians and that this sharpened their awareness of the logical traps in and around the concept of infinity. But from just this (which is all we have to go on) we cannot infer that "the subsequent course of Greek geometry was profoundly affected by the arguments of Zeno on motion" (Heath, *History of Greek Mathematics*, p. 272), still less that the mathematicians "realiz[ed] that Zeno's arguments on motion were fatal to infinitesimals" (*loc. cit.*). The first known move in Greek geometry that rigorously excluded infinitesimals, while no less rigorously asserting infinite divisibility, was made by Eudoxus in Euclid's *Elements*, Bk. V, Def. 4. This asserts that when $A > \epsilon$, A has a definite ratio to ϵ if and only if there is an n such that $n \cdot \epsilon > A$—the effect being, obviously, to admit only finite quantities to the theory of proportion and hence to the domain of metrically significant quantities. But this is to all appearances a purely intramathematical development, whose motivation is to perfect the theory of proportion in its application to irrationals and to secure the foun-

dations of "exhaustion" proofs (see Heath, *op. cit.*, pp. 326–329). It postdates Zeno by a century, and none of our sources connects it with him in any way. That Zeno influenced this development, "profoundly" or otherwise, remains a matter of guesswork.

Philosophical influences. We begin to approach firm ground when we turn to Zeno's influence on the philosophers. In discussing the third argument against plurality, whose originator, we admitted above, was probably Zeno, and also in his resolution of the deeper perplexity of the Race Course, Aristotle presents his own theory of the potential infinite as the answer. Since he does not offer any hint of a possible solution along alternative lines, it may well be that Zenonian paradoxes helped convince him that only by the denial of the actual infinite could infinite divisibility be freed from contradiction. Attested more definitely is Zeno's influence on the atomists; it was because "they gave in to the [line of] argument from dichotomy, that they postulated atomic magnitudes" (Aristotle, *Physics* 187a2–3). Although Zeno is not named, Aristotle must be thinking principally of him, since he is the undoubted originator of this line of argument. This, and the fact that two such Zenonian arguments (the proof of [R] in the first argument against plurality and the third argument against plurality, above) are built by Epicurus into the foundations of his theory, suffices to show that Zeno was not taken as merely a spirit of contradiction by great fifth-century thinkers who were not sectaries of Elea. But on others, such as Anaxagoras, he made no dent at all, and even the atomists could have had no use for many of his arguments—for example, the best of his arguments against plurality, Fragment 3: their theory would deny both horns of the dilemma, affirming an actual infinity of atoms (and even of worlds) and giving no quarter to the assumption that between any two atoms there must be a third. His most positive contribution, and his only substantive one to our knowledge, seems to have been made within his own school. The incorporeality of being is never asserted by Parmenides, although his whole system cries out for such a doctrine; this we do find in Melissus: "If being is one [and nothing could be more certain for an Eleatic than that Being *is* one], it cannot have body" (Fr. 9; a statement which it seems we have no choice but to take at face value; for the contrary opinion, see, for example, Booth, "Did Melissus Believe in Incorporeal Being?," 61 ff.). But Zeno's book, written while he was still "a young man," must have preceded that of Melissus. Zeno must therefore be reckoned the first to make this doctrine explicit, as he undoubtedly does, in arguing, according to the reconstruction in the first argument against plurality, above, that whatever has size is divisible into parts and hence cannot be one, since by "size" here he could only have meant three-dimensional extension, and it is impossible to see how he could have denied this to Being without also denying it material bulk.

The service he rendered not to particular schools but to the world is that which made Aristotle name him "the inventor of dialectic." In the Milesians, Xenophanes, and Heraclitus there had been virtually no philosophical argument. This began with Parmenides. But in his poem its free movement is impeded by an alien medium, whose verse-form suits perfectly the seer proclaiming a spiritual vision and very poorly the debater offering to engage all comers in logical combat. At this point Zeno breaks with his master to become the founder of Greek argumentative prose. Comparing his fragments with those of Parmenides, we see marked advances in technique. Fragment 3 is an all-but-perfect piece of logical exposition. The first argument against plurality, for all its unavoidable clumsiness of phrasing and logical syntax, is a remarkable composition, joining three distinct inferential sequences to spring a single dilemma. In these and apparently in all the other arguments, the philosophical paradox is put to work in a radically new way. Heraclitus had used it to signal with Delphic obliqueness new insights which elude direct statement and escape inferential controls (see his Fr. 93). Zeno made it serve a totally different function—that of dramatizing the fact that all-too-familiar beliefs may have implications which are fatal to the credibility of the implicands. In the whole history of philosophy no better device has ever been found for sensitizing us to the possibility that commonplaces may conceal absurdities and hence to the need of re-examining even the best entrenched and most plausible assumptions. That Zeno himself got so few positive results by the use of this method is not surprising; he was hampered by the poverty of his conceptual and semantic tools. His archaic logic gave him no inkling of the role that wholly tacit premises play in determining his seemingly cogent conclusions. And he pursued his work not in the spirit of disinterested inquiry but only to enforce predetermined Parmenidean dogmas, defended but never tested by his arguments. He more than compensated for these and other defects by an uncanny instinct for philosophically important issues and an unsurpassed power to invent philosophically exciting dilemmas.

(See also INFINITY IN MATHEMATICS AND LOGIC.)

Bibliography

Baccou, R., *Histoire de la science grecque de Thales à Socrate.* Paris, 1951.

Benacerraf, Paul, "Tasks, Super-tasks, and the Modern Eleatics." *Journal of Philosophy*, Vol. 59 (1962), 765 ff.

Benardete, José A., *Infinity. An Essay in Metaphysics.* Oxford, 1964.

Bergson, Henri, *Évolution créatrice.* Paris, 1907. Translated by Arthur Mitchell as *Creative Evolution.* New York, 1911.

Black, Max, *Problems of Analysis.* Ithaca, N.Y., 1954.

Booth, N. B., "Zeno's Paradoxes." *Journal of Hellenic Studies*, Vol. 77, No. 2 (1957), 187–201.

Booth, N. B., "Did Melissus Believe in Incorporeal Being?" *American Journal of Philology*, Vol. 79 (1958), 61–65.

Boyer, C. B., *The Concepts of the Calculus.* New York, 1939.

Broad, C. D., "Note on Achilles and the Tortoise." *Mind*, Vol. 22 (1913), 318–319.

Brochard, Victor, *Études de philosophie ancienne et de philosophie moderne.* Paris, 1912.

Burkert, Walter, *Philosophie und Weisheit. Erlanger Beiträge zur Sprach-Kunstwissenschaft,* Vol. X. Nuremberg, 1962.

Burnet, John, *Early Greek Philosophy,* 4th ed. London, 1930.

Calogero, Guido, *Studi sull'eleatismo.* Rome, 1932.

Chappell, V. C., "Time and Zeno's Arrow." *Journal of Philosophy*, Vol. 59 (1962), 197–213.

Chihara, C. S., "On the Possibility of Completing an Infinite Process." *Philosophical Review*, Vol. 74 (1965), 47 ff.

Cornford, F. M., "Mysticism and Science in the Pythagorean Tradition." *Classical Quarterly*, Vol. 16 (1922), 137 ff., and Vol. 17 (1923), 1 ff.

Cornford, F. M., *Plato and Parmenides.* London, 1939. Translation, with introduction and running commentary, of Parmenides' *Way of Truth* and Plato's *Parmenides.*

Diels, Hermann, and Kranz, Walther, *Fragmente der Vorsokratiker,* 6th ed., 3 vols. Berlin, 1952.

Enriques, Federico, and Santillana, Giorgio de, *Histoire de la pensée scientifique,* Vol. II. Paris, 1936.

Fränkel [Fraenkel], Hermann, "Zeno of Elea's Attacks on Plurality." *American Journal of Philology*, Vol. 63 (1942), 1–25, 193–206. Translated into German in *Wege und Formen frühgriechischen Denkens.* Munich, 1955. Pp. 198 ff.

Frege, Gottlob, *Die Grundlagen der Arithmetik.* Breslau, 1884. Translated by J. L. Austin as *The Foundations of Arithmetic.* Oxford, 1950.

Fritz, Kurt von, review of Calogero's *Studi sull'eleatismo. Gnomon,* Vol. 14 (1938), 91 ff.

Fritz, Kurt von, "Pythagoras," in August Pauly, Georg Wissowa, W. Kroll, et al., eds., *Real-Encyclopädie der klassischen Altertumswissenschaft,* Supp. Vol. X. Stuttgart, 1963.

Grünbaum, Adolf, "Relativity and the Atomicity of Becoming." *Review of Metaphysics*, Vol. 4 (1950), 143–186.

Grünbaum, Adolf, "A Consistent Conception of the Extended Linear Continuum as an Aggregate of Unextended Elements." *Philosophy of Science*, Vol. 19 (1952), 288 ff.

Grünbaum, Adolf, "Messrs. Black and Taylor on Temporal Paradoxes." *Analysis*, Vol. 12 (1952), 144 ff.

Grünbaum, Adolf, "Modern Science and Refutation of the Paradoxes of Zeno." *Scientific Monthly*, Vol. 81 (1955), 234–239.

Grünbaum, Adolf, *Philosophical Problems of Space and Time.* New York, 1963.

Grünbaum, Adolf, *Modern Science and Zeno's Paradoxes.* Middletown, Conn., 1967.

Guthrie, W. K. C., *A History of Greek Philosophy,* Vol. I, *The Earlier Presocratics and the Pythagoreans,* Cambridge, 1962; Vol. II, *The Presocratic Tradition From Parmenides to Democritus,* Cambridge, 1965.

Hasse, Helmut, and Scholz, Heinrich, *Die Grundlagenkrisis der griechischen Mathematik.* Berlin, 1928.

Heath, T. L., *A History of Greek Mathematics,* 2 vols. Oxford, 1921. Vol. I.

Heath, T. L., *Mathematics in Aristotle.* Oxford, 1949.

Heidel, W. A., "The Pythagoreans and Greek Mathematics." *American Journal of Philology*, Vol. 61 (1940), 1 ff.

Koyré, Alexandre, *Études d'histoire de la pensée philosophique.* Paris, 1961.

Lee, H. D. P., *Zeno of Elea.* Cambridge, 1936.

Lee, H. N., "Are Zeno's Arguments Based on a Mistake?" *Mind*, Vol. 74 (October 1965), 563–590.

Luria, Salomo, "Die Infinitesimallehre der antiken Atomisten." *Quellen und Studien zur Geschichte der Mathematik,* Vol. 2 (1932–1933), Part B, 106–185.

Mau, Jürgen, *Zum Problem des Infinitesimalen bei den antiken Atomisten.* Berlin, 1957.

Owen, G. E. L., "Zeno and the Mathematicians." *PAS*, Vol. 58 (1957–1958), 199–222.

Raven, J. E., *Pythagoreans and Eleatics.* Cambridge, 1948.

Raven, J. E., "Melissus," "Pre-Parmenidean Pythagoreanism," and "Zeno," in G. S. Kirk and J. E. Raven, *The Presocratic Philosophers.* Cambridge, 1957.

Renouvier, Charles, *Traité de logique générale et de logique formelle,* new ed. Paris, 1912. The first edition appeared in 1854.

Robinson, Richard, *Plato's Earlier Dialectic,* 2d ed. Oxford, 1953.

Ross, W. D., *Aristotle's Physics.* Oxford, 1936.

Russell, Bertrand, *Principles of Mathematics.* London, 1903.

Russell, Bertrand, "Mathematics and the Metaphysicians," in James R. Newman, ed., *The World of Mathematics.* New York, 1956. Vol. II, pp. 1576–1592. The date of Russell's essay is not given.

Russell, Bertrand, *Our Knowledge of the External World.* London, 1914.

Russell, Bertrand, *A History of Western Philosophy.* New York, 1946.

Ryle, Gilbert, *Dilemmas.* Cambridge, 1954.

Solmsen, Friedrich, *Aristotle's System of the Physical World.* Ithaca, N.Y., 1960.

Szabó, Arpad, "The Transformation of Mathematics Into Deductive Science and the Beginnings of Its Foundation on Definitions and Axioms." *Scripta Mathematica,* Vol. 27 (1964), 27 ff. and 113 ff.

Tannery, Paul, "Le Concept scientifique du continu: Zénon d'Élée et Georg Cantor." *Revue philosophique de la France et de l'étranger,* Vol. 20 (1885), 385 ff.

Tannery, Paul, *La Géometrie grecque.* Paris, 1877.

Tannery, Paul, *Pour l'Histoire de la science hellène.* Paris, 1877.

Taylor, Richard, "Mr. Black on Temporal Paradoxes." *Analysis,* Vol. 12 (1952), 38 ff.

Thomson, James, "Tasks and Super-tasks." *Analysis,* Vol. 15 (1954), 1–13.

Untersteiner, Mario, *Zenone.* Florence, 1963.

Vlastos, Gregory, review of Raven's *Pythagoreans and Eleatics. Gnomon,* Vol. 25 (1953), 29 ff.

Vlastos, Gregory, review of Fränkel's *Wege und Formen frühgriechischen Denkens. Gnomon,* Vol. 31 (1959), 193 ff.

Vlastos, Gregory, review of Kirk and Raven's *The Presocratic Philosophers. Philosophical Review,* Vol. 68 (1959), 531 ff.

Vlastos, Gregory, "Zeno," in Walter Kaufmann, ed., *Philosophic Classics.* New York, 1961, Pp. 27 ff.

Vlastos, Gregory, "A Note on Zeno's Arrow." *Phronesis,* Vol. 11 (1966), 3–18.

Vlastos, Gregory, "Zeno's Race Course." *Journal of the History of Philosophy,* Vol. 4 (1966), 95–108. With appendix, "Zeno's Achilles."

Van der Waerden, B. L., "Zenon und die Grundlagenkrise der griechischen Mathematik." *Mathematische Annalen,* Vol. 117, No. 2 (1940), 141 ff.

Watling, James, "The Sum of an Infinite Series." *Analysis,* Vol. 13 (1953), 39 ff.

Weiss, Paul, *Reality.* Princeton, N.J., 1938.

Weyl, Hermann, *Philosophy of Mathematics and Natural Science.* Princeton, N.J., 1949. Originally published in *Handbuch der Philosophie* (Munich and Berlin, 1927) under the title "Philosophie der Mathematik und Naturwissenschaft." Revised and augmented English edition based on a translation by Olaf Helmer.

Whitehead, A. N., *Science and the Modern World.* New York, 1925.

Whitehead, A. N., *Process and Reality.* New York, 1929.

Whitrow, J. G., *The Natural Philosophy of Time.* London, 1961.

Zeller, Eduard, *Die Philosophie der Griechen,* 7th ed., Vol. I, Part I. Leipzig, 1923.

Zeuthen, H.-G., *Geschichte der Mathematik im Altertum und Mittelalter.* Copenhagen, 1896.

GREGORY VLASTOS

ZENO'S PARADOXES.

See INFINITY IN MATHEMATICS AND LOGIC; ZENO OF ELEA.

ZIEGLER, LEOPOLD

ZIEGLER, LEOPOLD (1881–1958), German philosopher of life and religion, was born in Karlsruhe and studied at the Technische Hochschule there, under Arthur Drews, and at the University of Heidelberg. Receiving his doctorate in 1905, Ziegler returned as a *Privatdozent* to Karlsruhe. He later devoted himself entirely to his writing. From 1933 on, he lived in Überlingen.

Like Ludwig Klages and Hermann Keyserling, Ziegler strove to escape from that intellectualism which, he believed, had since Aristotle led Western man to a world view devoid of mystery and value. Like Nietzsche, he viewed the present age as an age of crisis. God is dead, and yet a secular view of the world cannot do justice to what man is. Something in man demands new gods.

The early works of Ziegler were written in the shadow of Eduard von Hartmann, Schopenhauer, and Nietzsche.

Later Johann Jakob Bachofen, Sir James G. Frazer, and C. G. Jung became important influences. Ziegler studied rite and myth to recall modern man to his religious heritage, which had been submerged by intellectualism. Ziegler insisted that we ought to recognize the limitation of intellectualism. The principles of Aristotelian logic have been taken for granted by Western thought, but they are inadequate to the problem of meaning and value. Jakob Boehme, Franz Baader, Nicholas of Cusa, and Hegel suggest an alternative with their dialectic approaches. Ziegler, too, called for a *coincidentia oppositorum,* a reconciliation of the diverse and often seemingly contradictory claims to which we are subject. He conjured up the picture of eternal, universal man in order to recall us to that reality to which myth and rite, religion and philosophy give only inadequate expression.

Bibliography

Zur Metaphysik des Tragischen. Leipzig, 1902.

Der abendländische Rationalismus und der Eros. Jena and Leipzig, 1905.

Florentinische Introduktion. Leipzig, 1912.

Gestaltwandel der Götter, 2 vols. Darmstadt, 1920.

Das heilige Reich der Deutschen, 2 vols. Darmstadt, 1925.

Zwischen Mensch und Wirtschaft. Darmstadt, 1927.

Der europäische Geist. Darmstadt, 1929.

Überlieferung. Leipzig, 1936.

Apollons letzte Epiphanie. Leipzig, 1937.

Vom Tod. Leipzig, 1937.

Menschwerdung, 2 vols. Olten, 1948.

Von Platons Staatheit zum christlichen Staat. Olten, 1948.

Die neue Wissenschaft. Universitas Aeterna. Munich, 1951.

Aus dem Kreis geschnitten. Constance, 1956.

Lehrgespräch vom allgemeinen Menschen. Hamburg, 1956.

There is an autobiography in Raymund Schmidt, ed., *Die Philosophie der Gegenwart in Selbstdarstellungen,* Vol. IV (Leipzig, 1923).

KARSTEN HARRIES

ZIEHEN, THEODOR

ZIEHEN, THEODOR (1862–1950), German psychologist and philosopher, was born in Frankfurt am Main and served as professor of psychiatry at the universities of Jena, Utrecht, Halle, and Berlin. He lived as a private scholar in Wiesbaden from 1912 to 1917, when he returned to teaching as professor of philosophy and psychology at the University of Halle. He retired in 1930.

Ziehen's viewpoint in epistemology is in the broadest sense positivistic. Knowledge must start with that which is experientially given, which Ziehen termed "becomings" (*gignomene*). From this "gignomenal principle" follows the "principle of immanence," according to which there is no such thing as metaphysical knowledge of the transcendental, and therefore it is nonsensical to want to know that which is not given. The first task of philosophy thus consists in seeking the laws of all that is given (the "positivistic" or "nomistic" principle). According to Ziehen, such a "gignomenological" investigation leads to the conclusion that the traditional antithesis between the subjective, mental world of consciousness and the objective, material external world is inadmissible because the given is "psychophysically neutral." We must, however, distinguish two kinds of law-governed relations: The *gignomene* are to be called mental insofar as they are considered with regard to their "parallel components" (the mental, subjective ingredients of experiences, which parallel certain physiological processes); and the *gignomene* are to be understood as physical insofar as attention is fixed on their "reduction ingredients" ("reducts"), which are subject to causal laws.

Thus, Ziehen did not distinguish in the customary manner between material and mental reality; rather, he sought to understand the structure of the given, which he claimed to be the sole reality, in terms of two kinds of regularities—causal laws and parallel laws. Viewed from this "binomistic" standpoint, which assumes a twofold conformance to law in the given, real things appear as possibilities of perception, as potential perceptions, as "virtual reducts" that are both "transgressive" and "intramental." They lie beyond the boundaries of the individual content of consciousness, but they are nevertheless not situated "behind" experience but are immanent in it. Thus, real things represent certain aspects of experience that are determined by the causal type of laws. The processes governed by causal law ("the laws of nature") go along specific paths with a specific velocity; through the parallel laws that direct mental life, the *gignomene* are transformed into individual experiences.

Thus, for Ziehen psychology stood in contrast with the other natural sciences—the causal sciences—as the science of the "parallel component" of the given. Ziehen combated what he considered to be mythologizing faculty psychology, including Wilhelm Wundt's theory of apperception. He advocated a physiologically oriented, analytic, serial, or associationist approach to the subject. To association he added a second factor regulating the course of consciousness—the "constellation." A constellation arises at a given time from the mutual inhibition and stimulation of ideas, and it selects from the many ideas that are associated and, hence, ready for reproduction. In addition to association and constellation, Ziehen assumed three other basic mental functions—synthesis, analysis, and comparison.

Besides the causal laws and the parallel laws, Ziehen assumed a third, more general kind of regularity—conformity to logical laws—common to and set above the two other kinds of laws.

Ziehen also wrote on the philosophy of religion. He identified God with the regularity governing the world. God must be thought of as the essence or embodiment of "regularity in general"; as the totality of logical regularity, of natural laws, and of the laws of mental and spiritual life. It would be an inadmissible anthropomorphism to look beyond the regularities for a personal source of them.

Works by Ziehen

Leitfaden der physiologischen Psychologie. Jena, 1891; 12th ed., 1924.

Erkenntnistheorie auf psychophysiologischer und physikalischer Grundlage. Jena, 1913; 2d ed., published as *Erkenntnistheorie,* 2 parts, 1934–1939.

Die Grundlagen der Psychologie, 2 vols. Leipzig and Berlin, 1915.

Lehrbuch der Logik. Bonn, 1920.

Autobiography in Raymond Schmidt, ed., *Die Philosophie der Gegenwart in Selbstdarstellungen,* Vol. IV. Leipzig, 1923.

Vorlesungen über die Ästhetik, 2 parts. Halle, 1923–1925.

Die Grundlagen der Religionsphilosophie. Leipzig, 1928.

Works on Ziehen

Graewe, H., "Theodor Ziehen zum 90. Geburtstag." *Die Pyramide,* No. 11 (Innsbruck, 1952), 201–202.

Peters, Wilhelm, "Theodor Ziehen zum 70. Geburtstag." *Kant-Studien,* Vol. 37 (1932), 237–240.

Ulrich, Martha, "Der Ziehen'sche Binomismus und sein Verhältnis zur Philosophie der Gegenwart." *Kant-Studien,* Vol. 25 (1921), 366–395.

FRANZ AUSTEDA
Translated by *Albert E. Blumberg*

ZOROASTRIANISM, for more than a thousand years the dominant religion of Persia, is founded on the teachings of the prophet Zarathustra. (Zoroaster is an often used version of his name, and from it the name of the religion is derived; this version reflects ancient Greek transliteration.) Four main stages in the religion's history can be distinguished: the early faith as promulgated by Zarathustra himself; the religion of the Persian Empire under Darius I (who ruled 521–486 B.C.) and his Achaemenid successors; its renewal under the Arsacid (250 B.C.–A.D. 226) and Sassanian (226–641) dynasties; and the late period, when the religion was swamped by Islam but continued as the faith of a minority, some of whom settled in India and are known as Parsis (literally "Persians").

Scriptures. The scriptures are known as the Avesta (or Zend-Avesta) and consist of various hymns, treatises, and poems. They comprise the Yasna, a collection of liturgical writings that contains the important Gāthās (literally "songs"), possibly written by Zarathustra himself; the Yashts, hymns to various divinities; and the Vendidād, which contains prescriptions for rituals of purification and so on. Many of these writings belong to a period when Zoroastrianism had become overlaid by polytheistic elements; some may date from as late as the fourth century, although the majority were composed much earlier. From the fourth century a further and extensive set of writings, which expressed the reformed theology of the Sassanian period, was compiled in the later language of Pahlavi.

Zarathustra and his teaching. There is considerable dispute and uncertainty about the date and place of the prophet's life. Although Greek sources mention dates up to several thousand years B.C., the most plausible theories are that he lived in the tenth or ninth century B.C. or in the sixth or fifth. Although certain evidence points to his having lived in eastern Iran, the language of the Gāthās has been found to belong to northwest Iran. According to the traditions surrounding Zarathustra's life, he converted King Vishtaspa (Hystaspes in Greek transliteration), which proved decisive for the spread of the new religion. Vishtaspa ruled parts of eastern Iran and was the father of Darius the Great, a strong exponent and protector of the faith. These facts lend some support to the hypothesis that Zarathustra lived at the later date and in eastern Iran.

Although traditional accounts of Zarathustra's life are heavily overlaid by legend, it is probable that he was the son of a pagan priest of a pastoral tribe. At the age of thirty or a little later, he had a powerful religious experience, probably of a prophetic nature, analogous to the inaugural visions of such Old Testament prophets as Isaiah. He is reported to have encountered the angel Vohu Manah ("Good Thought"), who took him to the great spirit Ahura-Mazda ("The Wise Lord"), Zarathustra's name for God. Other revelations combined to induce him to preach a purified religion, combating the existing Persian polytheism, which had similarities to the Vedic religion of India. At first he met with considerable opposition, but the conversion of Vishtaspa paved the way for Zarathustra's wide influence, despite the king's later defeat in war and the occupation of his capital. Zarathustra is said to have been killed at the age of 77 during Vishtaspa's defeat, but according to later accounts, he died while performing the fire sacrifice, an important element in the new cultus.

Zarathustra's God had the attributes of a sky god, like the Indian god Varuna. Both were ethical and celestial and were worshiped by the Indo-European Mitanni of the mountainous region to the north of the Mesopotamian plain during the latter part of the second millennium B.C. Zarathustra strongly denounced the cult of the gods of popular religion, equating such beings with evil spirits who seduced men from the worship of the one Spirit. The belief in the malicious opposition to the purified religion that he preached and the incompatibility of Ahura-Mazda's goodness with the creation of evil led Zarathustra to conceive of a cosmic oppostion to God. He mentions Drūj ("The Lie"), an evil force waging war against Ahura-Mazda. From this early concept developed the later Zoroastrian theology of dualism.

Although Zarathustra attacked the existing religion, he also compromised with it. A slight concession to polytheism was involved in the doctrine of the Amesha-Spentas ("Immortal Holy Ones"), such as Dominion and Immortality, which were personified qualities of Ahura-Mazda. It is probable that Zarathustra was making use of certain aspects of the existing mythology and transforming them into attributes and powers of God. He seems to have used the fire sacrifice, a prominent feature of later and modern Zoroastrianism, transforming what had previously been part of the fabric of the polytheistic cultus. Zarathustra's fire sacrifice was also related in origin to the ritual surrounding the figure of Agni (Fire) in ancient Indian religion.

He preached an ethic based on the social life of the husbandman, the good man being one who tends his cattle and tills the soil in a spirit of peace and neighborliness. The good man must also resist worshipers of the *daevas* (gods), who, together with the evil spirit opposed to Ahura-Mazda, threaten the farmer's livelihood. These ideas probably reflected the social conditions of Zarathustra's time and country, when there was a transition from the nomadic to the pastoral life. The *daeva*-worshipers would then represent bands of nomadic raiders, and the new purified religion would be a means of cementing a settled, pastoral fabric of society. One of the Gāthās is a dialogue in which there figures a mysterious being called the Ox Soul, who complains of the bad treatment meted out to cattle upon the earth. The angel Vohu Manah promises that they will be protected by Zarathustra, who prays earnestly to Ahura-Mazda for assistance. These connections between the new religion and a settled cattle-raising

society later became obscured when Zoroastrianism became the religion of the Persian Empire and when they were no longer relevant.

The moral life, however, was not confined to neighborliness and resistance to evil *daeva*-worshipers. It was part of a much wider cosmic struggle, in which the good man participates in the battle of Ahura-Mazda against the evil Angra Mainyu, the chief agent of The Lie (in later language, these were called respectively Ormazd and Ahriman). The battle will consummate in a final judgment, involving the resurrection of the dead and the banishment of the wicked to the regions of punishment. This notion of a general judgment was supplemented by a dramatic picture of the individual's judgment. He must cross to Ahura-Mazda's paradise over the narrow bridge called Chinvat. If his bad deeds outweigh his good ones, he will topple into the dreadful, yawning abyss. Some of this Zoroastrian eschatology came to influence Jewish eschatology, partly through the contact with Persia consequent to the Exile and partly because of the succeeding Persian suzerainty over Israel. Zoroastrianism, therefore, indirectly influenced Christianity.

Development of ritual. When Zoroastrianism came to be the dominant religion of the Persian Empire during the Achaemenid dynasty, there was an increasing trend toward restoring the cult of lesser deities. This was a partial consequence of the adoption of Zoroastrianism as the state cult. Artaxerxes II, for instance, caused images of the goddess Anahita (connected in origin to Ishtar, the Babylonian fertility deity) to be set up in the chief cities of the empire. The cultus came to be administered, in some areas at least, by the priestly class known as the Magi, from which term the word "magic" is derived; the Magi also came to figure in Christian legend about the birth of Christ. This priestly class was probably of Median origin. At first, the Magi had opposed the new faith, but after having adopted it, they began to change its character by importing extensive magical and ritual practices into it. Thus, the later portions of the Avesta contain spells and incantations. Further, the Gāthās were no longer treated simply as expressing Zarathustra's religion and teachings but as having intrinsic magical powers. Their proper repetition could combat the evil powers by which men were beset. However, the full history of the development of Zoroastrianism toward a ritualistic cult has never been fully disentangled, partly because of the intervening changes brought about in the late fourth century B.C. by Alexander's conquest of the Persian Empire and its subsequent division among Greek dynasties. This Hellenistic period, lasting until the Parthian era in the second century B.C. (begun by Mithridates I of the Arsacid dynasty), saw further syncretism, an offshoot of which was Mithraism, the cult of Mithra or Mithras, which later became important in the Roman Empire as a mystery religion.

Development of cosmology. While Zarathustra had stressed the ethical dimension of religion and the Mazdaism, as Zoroastrianism was later called, of the Achaemenid period had emphasized its ritual dimension, the reformed Zoroastrianism established in the Sassanian period displayed a strong interest in the doctrinal dimension of the faith. It is chiefly in this phase of Zoroastrianism that we discover a speculative interest in the workings of the universe. A theory of history was worked out which divided historical time into four eras, each lasting three thousand years. In the first era, God brings into existence the angelic spirits and *fravashis*, which are the eternal prototypes of creatures (and, pre-eminently, of human beings). Since Ahura-Mazda creates by means of thought and since he foresees Angra Mainyu, the latter comes into existence. During the second period, the primeval man, Gayomard, and the primeval Ox (the prototype of the animal realm) exist undisturbed, but at the beginning of the third epoch the Evil Spirit, Angra Mainyu, succeeds in attacking and destroying them. From the seed of these two primeval beings men and animals arise, and there is a mixture of good and evil in the world. The last era begins with Zarathustra's mission; it will culminate in the final divine victory, which will occur partly through the agency of Soshyans, a semidivine savior. The universe will then be restored to an everlasting purified state in which the saved, now immortal, sing the praises of Ahura-Mazda. In this theory of history, the individual's life is linked to the unfolding cosmic drama.

The theory, while assigning the final victory to God, allows the nature and scale of the Evil One's operations to be alarming. Further, if Angra Mainyu arises through the thought of Ahura-Mazda, then evil comes from the Creator. This put the Zoroastrian theologians in a dilemma, and so attempts were made to work out doctrines that would more consistently explain the existence of evil. For instance, the movement known as Zurvanism held that both Ahura-Mazda and Angra Mainyu issued from a first principle, Zurvān (Infinite Time). Zurvān is beyond good and evil; only with the realm of finite time is the contrast between good and evil meaningful. On the other hand, Zurvān, the Supreme Being, dwells in an eternal state, raised beyond the conflicts and contrasts that exist in the temporal world.

Influence and survival. Elements of Zoroastrian teaching and mythology entered into Mithraism and Manichaeanism, and its eschatology had a marked influence on the Judaeo-Christian tradition. However, the Muslim conquest of Persia in the seventh century largely destroyed the religion in its home country. Its survival in India was due to the Zoroastrians who emigrated in order to escape Muslim persecution. This Parsi community, centered chiefly on the west coast in and around Bombay, has maintained the cultus and interprets the faith in a strictly monotheistic sense. Their emphasis on education has given them an influence out of all proportion to their numbers.

Bibliography

Duchesne-Guillemin, J., *Zoroastre*. Paris, 1948.
Ghirshman, R., *Iran*. Baltimore, 1954.
Modi, J. J., *Religious Ceremonies and Customs of the Parsis*, 2d ed. London, 1954.
Zaehner, R. C., *Zurvān: A Zoroastrian Dilemma*. Oxford, 1954.
Zaehner, R. C., *The Dawn and Twilight of Zoroastrianism*. London, 1959.
Zend-Avesta, translated by J. Darmesteter in F. Max Müller, ed., *Sacred Books of the East*. Oxford, 1883.

NINIAN SMART

ZUBIRI, XAVIER, Spanish Christian ontologist, was born in San Sebastián in 1898. He was professor of the history of philosophy in Madrid from 1926 to 1936 and in Barcelona from 1940 to 1942, after an absence abroad during the Spanish Civil War. He then left university teaching to give well-attended "private courses" in Madrid. His influence in Spain has been out of all proportion to the scanty amount of his published work.

Zubiri has been called a Christian existentialist, and indeed that is one aspect of his effort to synthesize neoscholastic theology with certain contemporary philosophies (those of Husserl, Heidegger, and Ortega y Gasset) and with modern science. To achieve this harmonizing of separate disciplines, Zubiri undertook studies in theology, philosophy, and natural science that could well have occupied three scholarly lives. He took a doctorate of theology in Rome and of philosophy in Madrid (where he studied under Ortega) before attending Heidegger's lectures in Freiburg and studying physics, biology, and Oriental languages in various European centers. He has translated into Spanish not only metaphysical works by Heidegger but also texts on quantum theory, atomic science, and mathematical physics generally.

From this extensive study Zubiri concluded that positive science and Catholic philosophy were separate points of view concerning the same reality. The philosopher-theologian cannot dispute, correct, or complete anything in science, but neither does he have to accept the philosophical opinions of scientists. The connection between these two parallel approaches to reality is simply that the sciences always leave us metaphysically hungry and with the feeling that they have not exhausted all the possibilities of knowledge, so they impel us to turn to philosophy. It is only when we come to philosophy in this way that it is really valuable; any philosophy that is undertaken without being forced upon us by scientific study is insipid.

What the sciences must get from philosophy, Zubiri claims, is an idea of nature, a theory of being to delimit their ontological horizons. They cannot themselves build such an idea out of positive facts, although they can criticize and reject unsuitable concepts of nature offered by philosophers. Aristotle provided an idea of nature adequate for the founding of physics, and Scholasticism did the same for modern science: without Duns Scotus and William of Ockham, Galileo's work would have been impossible. Physics is again in crisis, facing problems that cannot be solved by physicists, logicians, or epistemologists but only by ontologists, who can supply a fresh idea of nature within which quantum physics can progress.

In his philosophy of existence, Zubiri accepts the "radical ontological nullity" of man, who is nothing apart from the tasks he has to wrestle with. It is in dealing with his tasks that man comes to be. His nature consists in the mission of being sent out into existence to realize himself as a person. These views Zubiri read into Heidegger and Ortega, but he added a doctrine of "religation." ("Religation" was coined by Zubiri from the Latin *religare*, "to tie," which may also be the root of "religion.") According to this doctrine, we are not simply thrown into existence, as atheistic existentialists say, but are impelled into it by something that we feel all the time as an obligation, a force imposing on us the task of choosing and realizing ourselves. That something is deity, to which we are bound, or tied. Religation, the relation to deity, is the "fundamental root of existence" and the "ontological structure of personality."

Bibliography

Zubiri's works include *Ensayo de una teoría fenomenológica del juicio*, a doctoral thesis on Husserl (Madrid, 1923); *Naturaleza, historia, Dios* (Madrid, 1944); *Sobre la esencia* (Madrid, 1962); and *Cinco lecciones de filosofía* (Madrid, 1963).

For commentary on Zubiri, see Luis Diez del Corral and others, *Homenaje a Xavier Zubiri* (Madrid, 1963), and Julián Marías, "Xavier Zubiri," in *La escuela de Madrid* (Buenos Aires, 1959).

NEIL MCINNES

Index

A

The Encyclopedia contains articles on the following ancient philosophers:
Aenesidemus
Agrippa
Alcmaeon of Croton
Alexander of Aphrodisias
Anaxagoras of Clazomenae
Anaximander
Anaximenes
Antisthenes
Arcesilaus
Archytas of Tarentum
Aristippus of Cyrene
Aristotle
Carneades
Celsus
Chrysippus
Cicero, Marcus Tullius
Cleanthes
Cratylus
Diogenes Laertius
Diogenes of Appollonia
Diogenes of Sinope
Empedocles
Epictetus
Epicurus
Galen
Gorgias of Leontini
Heraclitus
Hippias of Elis
Hippocrates
Homer
Iamblichus
Leucippus and Democritus
Logos
Lucian of Samosata
Lucretius
Mani and Manichaeism
Marcus Aurelius Antonius
Melissus of Samos
Numenius of Apamea
Panaetius of Rhodes
Parmenides
Philo Judaeus
Philolaus of Croton
Plato
Plotinus
Plutarch of Chaeronea
Porphyry
Posidonius
Proclus
Prodicus of Ceos
Protagoras of Abdera
Pyrrho
Pythagoras and Pythagoreanism
Seneca
Sextus Empiricus
Simon Magus
Simplicius
Socrates
Strato and Stratonism
Thales of Miletus
Theophrastus
Thucydides
Timon of Phlius
Xenophanes of Colophon
Xenophon
Zeno of Citium
Zeno of Elea

B

C

D

E

F

Fry, Roger 1–36

Führer durch die Philosophie;
Philosophen lexikon und
philosophisches
Sachwörterbuch
(Sternbeck) 6–185

Fujiwara no Arihira 4–250

Fujiwara Seika 4–251

Full Inquiry into the Subject of
Suicide, A (Moore) 8–44

Funayama Shinichi 4–253

Function (logic) 5–65
continuum problem 2–209
definition 2–322
Frege, G. 4–555

Function (cont.)
recursive function theory 7–89
Russell, B. 7–248 fol.
teleology 8–88, 90

Function, Argument of a:
see Argument of a function

Function, Recursive: see
Recursive function

Functional analysis 3–256

Functional calculus: see
Predicate calculus

Functional characters 4–508

Functional definition 1–314

Functionalism in aesthetics
1–40, 55
Ruskin, John 7–234

Functionalism in Sociology 3–256
Durkheim, É. 2–439
Reich, W. 7–110
sociology of knowledge 7–476

Functionality, Basic theory of
4–508

Functionality, Theory of 4–508

Function of the Orgasm, The
(Reich) 7–105 fol.

Functions (logic) 3–233

Functions, Boolean: see
Boolean functions

Function variables 7–92

Functor-expressions 8–169

Functorial variable 4–442;
5–106

Fundamental functions 5–73

Fundamentals of Concept
Formation in Empirical
Science (Hempel) 3–473

Fundamenta Physices (Regius)
2–38

Fundierung, Axiom der: see
Foundation, Axiom of

Fung Yu-lan 2–95
communism 2–168

Furlong, E. J. 4–137

Furukawa Tetsushi 4–253

Future 6–437; 8–126, 135 fol.

Future contingents, Problem of
5–65
Aristotle 5–1

G

Gabirol, Solomon ben Judah
ibn-: see Ibn-Gabirol,
Solomon ben Judah

Gaius 5–452; 6–256

Galen 3–261
Hippocrates 4–6
logic 4–520; 5–40
pessimism and optimism 6–116
pneuma 6–360

Galenian figure 5–65; 4–520

Galileo Galilei 3–262; 4–227
continuity 2–205
Hobbes, T. 4–35
inertia 5–492
infinity in mathematics and
logic 4–184
Oresme, N. 5–548
philosophy of science,
problems of 6–298
rationalism 7–73
scientific method 7–340, 341
sensationalism 7–416
vacuum and void 8–218

Gallarate Movement 3–267

Gallie, W. B.
historical explanation 4–9
solipsism 7–489

Galluppi, Pasquale 3–267; 4–230
Spaventa, B. 7–517

Galton, Sir Francis
images 4–134
psychology 7–17
racism 7–58

Gandhi 4–4

Garasse, François 3–240

García Máynez, E. 4–398

Gardiner, Patrick 4–9

Gardner, Martin 5–79

Gargantua (Rabelais) 7–57

Garland the Computist 5–254
semantics, history of 7–370

**Garrigou-Lagrange, Réginald
Marie** 3–268

Garve, Christian 3–269

Gasking, Douglas A. T.
causation 2–64
other minds 6–10
questions 7–49

Gassendi, Pierre 3–269, 242
atomism 1–195
common consent arguments
for the existence of God
2–152
existence 3–142
materialism 5–181
Mersenne, M. 5–283
philosophy, historiography
of 6–227
skepticism 7–453
universals 8–199

Gas theory 7–44

Gathas 8–380

Gaunilo 3–273; 5–539

Gauss, Karl Friedrich 4–533

Gautama: see Buddha

Gay, John 3–273

Gay Science, The (Nietzsche)
5–509

Geach, Peter T.
correspondence theory of
truth 2–227
dreams 2–416
existence 3–145
Frege, G. 3–229
metaphor 5–287
performative theory of
truth 6–89

Geach, P. T. (cont.)
propositions, judgments,
sentences, and statements
6–498
thinking 8–102

Gebsattel, V. E. von 6–165

Gedanken und Tatsachen
(Liebman) 5–470

Gedanken und Urtheile über
philosophische, moralische
und politische
Gegenstände . . . (Rabe)
6–179

Gegenstand der Erkenntnis,
Der (Rickert) 7–193

Gehlen, Arnold 3–274; 6–160,
163, 164

Geist 3–275
Hegel, G. W. F. 3–436

Geist der Spekulativen
Philosophie (Tiedmann)
6–277

Geisteswissenschaften 3–275,
305
Carnap, R. 2–28
Dilthey, W. 2–405
historical explanation 4–7
historicism 4–23
Neo-Kantianism 5–473
Spranger, E. 8–1
Wundt, W. 8–350

Gellner, Ernest 4–55; 7–472

Gelugpa 1–419

Gemeinschaft
society 7–472
Tönnies, F. 8–150

General addition theorem 6–470

General ideas 4–120
Hume, D. 4–77
Plato 6–321

General ideas (cont.)
Spinoza, B. 7–536
universals 8–199, 201, 202

General Idea of the Revolution
in the Nineteenth Century
(Proudhon) 6–508

General Introduction to
Psychoanalysis (Freud)
6–513

Generalization, Rule of 5–65;
8–69

Generalization in Ethics
(Singer) 3–132

Generalizations
any and all 1–131
confirmation: qualitative
aspects 2–185 fol.
confirmation, quantitative
aspects 2–188
conventionalism 2–127
Godwin, W. 3–361
induction 4–170
Keynes, J. M. 4–175
laws of science 4–411 fol.
Newtonian mechanics 5–493
number 5–530
philosophy of history 6–248
philosophy of science 6–290
Poincaré, J. H. 6–362
Russell, B. 7–243
see also General propositions;
Induction

Generalizations, Confirmation
of: see Confirmation of
generalizations

Generalizations, Empirical:
see Empirical generaliza-
tions

Generalized benevolence:
see Benevolence,
Generalized

H

I

J

K

L

M

N

Nature (Cont.)
Blake, W. 1–320
Boehme, J. 6–33
Bowne, B. P. 1–357
Bruno, G. 1–407
Butler, J. 1–433
Campanella, T. 2–12
Carneades 2–34
Ch'eng Hao 2–85
Coleridge, S. T. 2–135
creation 2–252
determinism 2–364
Dewey, J. 2–381
Engels, F. 2–390
Enlightenment 2–520
Erigena, J. S. 3–45; 6–32
French philosophy 3–241
Gentile, G. 3–284
Greek philosophy 6–279
Hazlitt, W. 3–429
Hegel, G. W. F. 3–438, 440
Holbach, P. H. T. 4–50
humanism 4–70
Johnson, A. B. 4–287
Kant, I. 7–15
Krause, K. C. F. 4–364
Lamarck, C. de 4–376
Leibniz, G. 7–10
Leopardi, G. 4–437
Lucretius 5–100
Maimonides 5–131
Mill, J. S. 5–321
naturalism 5–448
natural law 5–451 fol.
Nelson, L. 5–465
Neo-Confucianism 2–92 fol.
New England
    transcendentalism 5–480
Oken, L. 5–535
Oman, J. W. 5–537
Palmer, E. 6–21
Pascal, B. 6–52
philosophical anthropology
    6–162
physicotheology 6–300
physis and nomos 6–305
providence 6–510
psychology 7–1
Rousseau, J. J. 7–219 fol.
Samkhya and Yoga 4–156
Schelling, F. W. J. von
    7–308
Schiller, F. 7–313
Schlegel, F. von 7–315
Schopenhauer, A. 7–328
simplicity 7–445
sociology of knowledge
    7–477
Spinoza, B. 6–33; 7–7, 533
Taoism 2–88
Telesio, B. 4–226; 8–92
Tennant, F. R. 8–94
Thoreau, H. D. 8–122
Woodbridge, F. J. E.
    8–345

Nature (Emerson) 1–85
Nature, Philosophical
    Ideas of 5–454
aesthetics 1–24
Anaximander 1–117
Berkeley, G. 1–301
Kant, I. 4–308, 321
Kepler, J. 4–329
Hegel, G. W. F. 3–441
matter 5–213
Schelling, F. W. J. von
    7–306
Swedenborg, E. 8–48
Thomas Aquinas 8–107
Nature, State of
Hobbes, T. 4–40; 6–377
Locke, J. 4–499
natural law 5–452
peace, war, and philosophy
    6–64
Rousseau, J. J. 7–220
social contract 7–465
Nature and Destiny of Man
    (Niebuhr) 5–503
Nature and Principle, School of
    2–85, 92
Nature and Sources of the Law,
    The (Gray) 6–261
Nature, Mind, and Death
    (Ducasse) 2–422
Nature of Existence, The
    (McTaggart) 1–391; 4–116;
    5–230
Nature of Goodness, The
    (Palmer) 6–21
Nature of Historical
    Explanation, The
    (Gardiner) 4–9
Nature of Judgment, The
    (Moore) 5–373
Nature of Life, The
    (Waddington) 6–26
Nature of Thought, The
    (Blanshard) 1–90, 320;
    2–130; 7–127, 128, 410
Nature, Uniformity of: see
    Uniformity of nature,
    Principle of the
Natur und Leben
    (Chamberlain) 2–72
Natyaśastra (Bharata) 4–167
Nauchnye Doklady Vysshei
    Shkoly; Filosofskie Nauki
    (jour.) 6–215
Naumburg, Margaret 6–244
Nausée, La (Sartre) 4–215
Navyanyaya: see New Nyaya
Nazism: see National Socialism
Neapolitan school 4–230
Necessary, Logically: see
    Logically necessary
Necessary and contingent
    statements 5–139
Necessary and sufficient
    conditions 5–60

Necessary and sufficient
    conditions (cont.)
    quantification theory 4–563
    Mill's method of induction
    5–325 fol.
    see also Necessary conditions;
    Sufficient conditions
Necessary being
Avicenna 4–221
Henry of Ghent 3–476
see also Ontological argument
    for the existence of God
Necessary conditions 5–60
causation 2–62
teleology 8–90
Necessary connection
causation 2–58, 62
Hume, D. 3–366; 4–80, 170
laws of science and lawlike
    statements 4–411 fol.
reason 7–84
Necessary propositions 4–481;
    5–139
Necessary statements 2–198
phenomenology 6–149
Necessary truth 5–58
Aristotle 2–199; 5–1
contingent and necessary
    statements 2–198
Hume, D. 4–79
Johnson, A. B. 4–289
knowledge and belief
    4–346
Leibniz, G. W. 2–199;
    3–21; 4–430
linguistic theory of the
    a priori 4–479, 480
logic 4–510; 5–6, 10
Malcolm, N. 5–139
Malebranche, N. 5–142
Mill, J. S. 6–290
Plato 4–349
Whewell, W. 6–290
see also Analytic
    propositions; Logically
    necessary; Logical truth
Necessitas consequentis 5–5
Necessitation 2–59
Necessitation, Rule of 5–7
Necessity
Aristotle 2–198; 8–132
causation 2–58 fol.
contingent and necessary
    statements 2–198
determinism 2–361 fol.
Edwards, J. 2–460
Hume, D. 2–366
Kant, I. 4–318
laws of science and lawlike
    statements 4–411 fol.
Leonardo da Vinci 4–435
Lequier, J. 4–439
Leucippus and Democritus
    4–448
must 5–414

Necessity (cont.)
Nelson, L. 5–466
phenomenology 6–149
Plotinus 6–356
possibility 6–419
Thomas Aquinas 5–294
Wittgenstein, L. 8–333
Necessity (Ananke): see
    Ananke
Necessity, Logical: see
    Logical necessity
Necessity of Atheism, The
    (Shelley) 7–430
Nedeljković, Dušan 8–362
Nederlands Theologisch
    Tijdschrift (jour.) 6–212
Needham, Joseph 2–281
Negate of a set: see
    Complement of a set
Negating antecedent and
    consequent 3–170
Negation 5–458, 69
Aristotle 4–515
correspondence theory of
    truth 2–228
dialectical materialism 2–393
first-order logic 5–20
Hegel, G. W. F. 3–445
logic, traditional 5–44
Mill's methods of induction
    5–325
Moist school 4–524
Parmenides 6–278
Peirce, C. S. 4–547
Petronijević, B. 6–129
Plato 6–278, 328
propositional logic 5–15
Russell, B. A. W. 7–248
semantics 7–349
Stoics 4–519
see also Nothing
Negation, External: see
    External negation
Negation, Internal: see
    Internal negation
Negation of an injunction
    4–522
Negation of the negation
Lenin, V. I. 7–266
Russian philosophy 7–267
Negation of the negation, Law
    of 2–393
Negation symbols 5–16
Negative facts 5–459
Negative feedback mechanisms
    2–281
Negative instance 5–325 fol.
Negative method of agreement
    5–326
Negative names 5–69
Negative propositions 5–72
Negative terms 5–458
Negative theology 5–131
Negative transference 7–106
Negroes 7–60

O

P

The Encyclopedia contains articles on the following philosophers of education:
Comenius, John Amos
Dewey, John
Froebel, Friedrich
Herbart, Johann Friedrich
Locke, John
Pestalozzi, Johann Heinrich
Plato
Rousseau, Jean-Jacques
Spencer, Herbert

The Encyclopedia contains articles on the following philosophers of science and scientists who have contributed to the philosophy of science:
Aristotle
Bacon, Francis
Boltzmann, Ludwig
Braithwaite, Richard Bevan
Bridgman, Percy William
Campbell, Norman Robert
Carnap, Rudolf
Clifford, William Kingdon
Descartes, René
Dingler, Hugo
DuBois-Reymond, Emil
Duhem, Pierre Maurice Marie
Helmholtz, Hermann Ludwig von

Polis 6–371 fol.; 8–8
  see also State

The Encyclopedia contains articles on the following figures frequently classified as pragmatists:
Aliotta, Antonia
Calderoni, Mario
Dewey, John
James, William
Lewis, Clarence Irving
Mead, George Herbert
Nagel, Ernest
Papini, Giovanni
Peirce, Charles Sanders
Quine, Willard Van Orman
Schiller, Ferdinand Canning Scott
Vailati, Giovanni

Q

R

The Encyclopedia contains articles on the following thinkers associated with the Reformation
Althusius, Johannes
Arminius and Arminianism
Calvin, John
Colet, John
Erasmus, Desiderius
Franck, Sebastian
Hus, John
Le Clerc, Jean
Luther, Martin
More, Thomas
Melanchthon, Philipp
Ramus, Peter
Servetus, Michael
Wyclyf, John

S

The Encyclopedia contains
articles on the following
thinkers frequently classified
as skeptics:
Aenesidemus
Agrippa von Nettersheim,
  Henricus Cornelius
Arcesilaus
Bautain, Louis Eugene Marie
Bayle, Pierre
Camus, Albert
Carneades
Charron, Pierre
Cratylus
Descartes, René
Erasmus, Desiderius
Foucher, Simon
Gassendi, Pierre
Glanvill, Joseph
Ghazali, Abu Hamid
  Muhammad
Hamann, Johann Georg
Huet, Pierre-Daniel
Hume, David
Kierkegaard, Søren Aabye
La Mothe Le Vayer,
  François de
Mauthner, Fritz
Mersenne, Marin
Montaigne, Michel Eyquem de
Nicolas of Autrecourt
Pascal, Blaise
Pyrrho
Russell, Bertrand Arthur
  William
Sanches, Francisco
Santayana, George
Schulze, Gottlob Ernst
Sextus Empiricus
Shestov, Leon
Timon of Phlius

T

U

V

W

X

Y

Z